W9-CHB-906

Cultural and Social Anthropology

INTRODUCTORY READINGS IN ETHNOLOGY

Other books by Peter B. Hammond

Yatenga: Technology in the Culture of a West African Kingdom

An Introduction to Cultural and Social Anthropology

Physical Anthropology and Archaeology: Introductory Readings, ed.
(second revised edition forthcoming)

Cultural and Social Anthropology

Introductory Readings in Ethnology

SECOND EDITION

Peter B. Hammond

Macmillan Publishing Co., Inc.
New York
Collier Macmillan Publishers
London

Macmillan Publishing Co., Inc.
866 Third Avenue, New York, New York 10022

Collier-Macmillan Canada, Ltd.

Library of Congress Cataloging in Publication Data

Hammond, Peter B ed.
Cultural and social anthropology.

Includes bibliographies and index.
1. Ethnology—Addresses, essays, lectures.
I. Title.
GN325.H29 1975 301.2 74-4887
ISBN 0-02-349630-4

Designs from the Dover Pictorial Archives selected and edited by Peter B. Hammond.

Printing: 1 2 3 4 5 6 7 8 Year: 5 6 7 8 9 0

Preface

Anthropologists, like other scientists, sometimes differ on the correct way to define, and study, their subject. Those who identify it as human society usually describe themselves as *social* anthropologists. However, the majority, particularly in the United States, find this societal framework too constricting and refer to themselves instead as *cultural* anthropologists. (So far physical anthropologists and archaeologists have held more universally consistent definitions of their respective fields, but they need not be considered here.) As a way of overcoming the imprecise differentiation between two converging perspectives some scholars have begun to refer to their branch of the discipline as *social-cultural anthropology*. The old and respectable term *ethnology* is now often used as well. Both the title I have given this reader and its contents represent my own effort to transcend what I see as an increasingly irrelevant distinction. Both orientations, social and cultural, are clearly valuable and examples of both have been freely mixed in compiling the contents of this book. However, you will see that the selections I have made are neither eclectic nor all-inclusive. To the instructor, the point of view from which they were chosen will be apparent from a glance at the table of contents. To most students my conceptual orientation will become increasingly evident as they read the introductory notes and the articles themselves.

Because increasing internal specialization in cultural and social anthropology has resulted in the proliferation of good articles on a constantly widening variety of important topics, this second edition is much longer than the first. Even so, in preparing it I found far more fine material than I could possibly include. I particularly regret the omission of several articles by Third World anthropologists whose current work is adding a valuably broadened range of perspectives on the study of humankind; they were only left out because of insurmountable problems of translation and copyright. On a somewhat related subject, while you will not find anthropology defined here as the "study of *man*," it will be apparent that I have not successfully overcome the sexist bias still embedded in Standard American English. Please read all general "hes," "hims," and "hises" as and/or "shes," "hers," and "herses." For the rest, as a nonlinguist, I must impatiently await the further evolution of our language.

In reading these selections keep in mind that it is the *concepts*, not the occasional apparent terminological trivia, that count. A good way to check your comprehension of the essential ideas contained in any selection is to ask yourself how you can relate what you are reading to the attainment of a better understanding of yourself and of your own relationship to your own particular society and culture. If you do not easily see the connections, ask your instructor for help. For clarification on unfamiliar terms turn to the glossary at the end of the book.

All of the articles in this edition have been reprinted with the authors' original notes and references intact. As well as serving as a guide to further reading, these provide an idea of how the anthropologist works, how his knowledge of the facts and his awareness of the ideas of others are constantly resynthesized in an ongoing effort to better understand one aspect or another of the most fundamental anthropological question of all: the nature of our species' relationship to society and culture.

In preparing this book my own search for further parts of the answer to this question has been immeasurably aided by the teachings of my students, my colleagues, and the peoples I have worked with in the field in Africa and America. Closer to home, I acknowledge with gratitude the editorial support of Kenneth J. Scott and the help of Ronald C. Harris. Azar Hammond has provided indispensable research assistance and Alexandra Hammond has offered continuous cheer. But most thanks of all go to the scholars whose work gives this volume its value.

My own much smaller part in this book is again dedicated to the memory of Melville J. Herskovits.

Peter B. Hammond

Ouagadougou
Upper Volta, West Africa
1974

Contents

PART SIX
Ideology: Religious and Magical Beliefs and Practices
269

PART SEVEN
The Arts: The Cultural Context of Aesthetic Experience
329

PART EIGHT
Language: The Sociocultural Setting of Linguistic Behavior
385

PART NINE
Method and Theory:
Perspectives on the Collection and Analysis of Ethnographic Data
423

PART ONE
The Secret of Our Survival

Human Reliance upon Society and Culture

The extent of our dependence upon society and our innate capacity to use culture to cope with our survival needs are attributes unique to our species. They are the qualities most important for understanding how and why we differ so much from all the other animals and how and why we so closely resemble all our fellow humans.

We *Homo sapiens* rely on culturally acquired behavior in dealing with nearly all the problems of staying alive. For the rest of the animals this dependence on learning (although almost always present, even in earthworms) is far less important: instinct is their more critical guide. Because all humans share a similar set of biologically determined needs (for food, shelter, sociability, and so on) and because we can only meet these needs by cultural means, all cultures, no matter how seemingly strange, must be fundamentally alike.

This premise that the basic aspects of culture are necessarily universal brings to the study of even the most exotic ways of life of the world's most isolated peoples a good feeling of shared common ground. When an anthropologist goes off to live and study for a year or more with Micronesian fishermen on some sandy South Pacific atoll, with an intrepid band of forest hunters far up the Amazon, or as I have done, with West Africans in the Kingdom of Yatenga and with Native Americans living in remote rural areas scattered throughout the Southeast, it is not the prospect of seeking out evidence of "savage" customs or the titillating lure of witnessing exotic rituals "never before seen by an outsider" that are the forceful attractions. Rather, it is the precious chance to learn something of another group of our fellow humans' special ways of dealing with problems common to us all. For what is learned from the proper study of any people's culture in particular can be applied to increasing our understanding of all cultures in general, including our own.

Living among a people with a radically different way of life can be fascinating, of course, and fun, and a sort of "escape" (it is also often lonely, uncomfortable, unhealthy, occasionally frightening, and sometimes briefly boring). But just as exciting as living within an interestingly unfamiliar culture, and scientifically far more rewarding, is the chance to work in a disciplined way at developing and applying a system for perceiving, recording, and efficiently analyzing the underlying patterns of behavior and the logic of the lifeways of others whose behavior may initially seem unknowably strange.

It is this cautious sorting out of recurrent similarities and the gradual discernment of subsurface sociocultural patterns and processes that can lead to making data-backed, testable generalizations about human behavior that is the scholarly goal central to all work in ethnology, the key to understanding the compelling reasons for our species' reliance upon society and culture for survival.

SECTION I

The Evolution of Our Capacity for Culture

But first this premise of an essential basic sameness uniting all cultures and derived from a common set of biologically based requirements common to *Homo sapiens* has to be fixed firmly in mind. We must understand this unique culture-using capacity that sets us apart from all nonhuman creatures (ant "colonies" and chimpanzee "bands" included). To start, we should take a brief look at our evolution, at how we gradually acquired our special human needs and came increasingly (but slowly, during several million years) to rely on society and culture as a way of meeting them, first just to keep alive, and then ultimately to become—by *cultural* means (and small and comparatively weak as we have always been)—our planet's dominant species, at least so far.

In the following selection, Downs, a cultural ecologist, and Bleibtreu, a physical anthropologist, both specialists in the study of human evolution, put us in our proper place.

Culture: Man's Ecological Niche

James F. Downs
and Hermann K. Bleibtreu

The Problem of Definition

Man must indeed possess some unusual attribute to allow him to survive and prosper in contravention of the general rule that the sole remaining species of a depleted genus must be headed for extinction. Though we have mentioned and will later describe the physical traits of *Homo sapiens,* there is no physical capability to which we can point in explaining our dominance over all other species and our ability to survive in many different earthly (and soon perhaps extra-terrestrial) environments.

In a purely physical sense, man is an extremely

Source: Reprinted with permission of Macmillan Publishing Co., Inc., and the authors, from *Human Variation: An Introduction to Physical Anthropology,* by James F. Downs and Hermann K. Bleibtreu.

generalized creature. Since he is able to take some advantage of most ecological situations, his niche cannot be thought of as a specific place in any food chain. He has no special ability to exploit some unique foodstuff to extract large amounts of energy from plankton or crack seeds with his teeth. How, then, has man survived?

The answer is that man is a special kind of specialist. He is expert in the use of intelligence, the attribute that makes him so adaptable and makes his generalized physical construction an asset instead of a liability. Man's most important physical trait is his brain. And it is *culture*, man's intellectual inheritance, which functions as his own particular ecological niche.

At this point a reader must rightfully ask: "What is culture?" And the answer is far from simple. The concept of culture developed in the late nineteenth and early twentieth centuries, in the infancy of anthropology, and has become a central theme in all branches of the discipline. Yet it has never been defined in a way that is fully satisfactory to all anthropologists. Long and sometimes bitter debates have developed over the proper wording of a definition which it was hoped might have universal acceptance. Today, anthropologists seldom enter into such fruitless exercises, preferring to accept a wide variety of definitions of culture, all sharing a certain basic set of ideas but each one suiting a particular approach to anthropological research.

Such a flexible system of definition is often disturbing to those students who demand simple, clear-cut, and final statements of fact and theory. However, as the student advances in any field of science he will quickly learn that seldom is anything, especially a definition of an operational concept, so static as to preclude alteration, reinterpretation, and development as new insights and information are fed into the scientific system. He will also become grateful for this flexibility, which tends to encourage scientific imagination and ingenuity rather than mere memorization of laws, rules, and definitions laid down by some long-dead authority.

In the absence of a fixed definition of culture, anthropologists can define the concept in ways that suit their particular areas of investigation. For some anthropologists, the idea of culture helps to gain an overall view of the development of the dominant civilizations; for others it structures a comparative study of the internal social practices of different groups; and the concept helps still other scholars to examine the formation of individual personalities and views of reality. Our own operational definition of culture must help us understand our central question: How has man been able to flourish on earth?

For our own purposes, therefore, we can define culture simply as *that element in human behavior which enables man to make the most of his physical capabilities and adapt to different environments without highly specialized biological equipment.* Instead of developing special beaks, wings, or digestive tracts, man has evolved with a brain which, combined with other characteristics, enables him to behave in very special ways. To one degree or another, all animals can respond to their experiences and learn from them. Man, however, is able to do this much better than other animals.

In essence, culture might be described as an absence rather than a presence of certain characteristics. Man is not constrained in his behavior by any large number of instinctive, inherited responses to stimuli. Human infants appear to be born with reflexes for grasping and sucking and a fear response to being dropped and (at a later time) to loud, sudden noises. Human beings also seem to vocalize instinctively—that is, they make sounds, a habit which is singularly nonadaptive to most animals, inasmuch as infantile sounds might attract predators. It is difficult to know whether human beings instinctively seek upright posture and bipedal locomotion, because infants are constantly confronted with adult models to imitate and in most cultures are actively encouraged to walk by their parents and others.

These few instinctive reactions and the general workings of the human physiological mechanisms are not considered to be cultural behavior. Almost all other human activities are more or less cultural in nature. Most of what we do and what we think—even the way in which we perceive experiences and environments—is learned by each new generation of human beings from previous generations.

Within each population there is much individual and eccentric behavior, but even this is usually colored by what one has learned. But simply to say culture is learned behavior is not enough. Animals, as we have stated earlier, learn. The key to culture is that this learned behavior is *transmitted* to the next generation and by them to the next. Another key is that this behavior is shared by a definable group of people who display *common patterns* of activity and perception. Moreover, the behavior which is learned and then taught is not in any sense a collection of random activities. Within each cultural population, behavior is patterned and to a degree consistent. In a sense it is systematic in that major changes in behavior and belief in one area of life will in one way or another affect behavior and belief in other areas.

The Function of Culture in Survival and Development

One important aspect of man's cultural ability is technical. Our brains, coupled with our capable hands, permit us to construct tools, clothing, and shelter, and to manipulate our environment in such ways as building dams, clearing forests, and cooking food. But man's technical achievements are more than the activities of a clever and relatively hairless ape. They rest on his very special ability to organize thoughts, to create symbols, to handle abstract problems, and to transmit these to other human beings. And they also rest on man's unique ability to adjust his relationships with other men by creating behavioral regulations adapted to solve specific problems, both technical and social.

For instance, man is the only animal that places symbolic restrictions on sexual relations with certain other human beings in terms of what we call *kinship*. The terms *mother, father, brother,* and *sister* are not in the final analysis descriptions of natural biological relationships but rather linguistic prescriptions for certain types of behavior expected by English-speaking peoples of certain categories of persons. All humans generally forbid sexual relationships between the persons designated in English as *mothers* and *sons, fathers* and *daughters,* or *brothers* and *sisters.* There are no clear-cut biological reasons why this should be so. In all probability this prohibition (called the incest taboo) functions to force the individual out of the bosom of his or her family and into a wider society to seek a sexual partner. To find such a partner requires the acquisition of social and technical skills upon which survival of the group depends. In order to assure that these things are learned, man has done what no other animal does, created a system of symbols for various kinds of personal relationships—symbols which say in effect that sexual intercourse is forbidden in one direction but is permitted in another.

Similarly, the terms *king, shah, khan, natani, chief,* etc., are arbitrary sound symbols which represent styles or patterns of authority and political organization of human beings in some common endeavor. No such symbolic system exists in a herd of buffalo or pride of lions or troop of gorillas. Social relations exist, but not social symbols. Relationships between individuals in these animal social units are instinctive and unconscious, while those in human groups are the product of voluntary human decisions influenced only indirectly, if at all, by instinct. Because of this, man can change his social institutions to meet the demands of his environment while animals cannot—at least not with the facility and to the degree that such changes can be made by man.

Thus, the newborn animal confronts his environment with a set of inherited abilities and potentials and with minor and rather short-lived assistance from the older generation, which for a brief time may feed, protect, and teach the young. Man, however, is born facing an environment with almost no physical ability to survive. Rather he is cradled in a network of social relationships designed to provide for him an opportunity for survival and learning. What he learns will be the cultural patterns: morals, ethics, and attitudes which allow him to enter into and participate in society, and technical skills needed to do the work assigned to him by society.

Through social relationships and technical abilities, man can extend himself beyond his individual physical limitations. The knowledge and wisdom of men long dead can be transmitted to each succeeding generation and used to its benefit. Tools, clothing, blasting powder, sailing boats, fire, and electricity provide man with actual physical extensions of himself which multiply his strength and broaden his abilities. In order to fly, members of the class *Aves* (birds), as well as extinct flying reptiles and living flying mammals, surrendered their front legs, a process which is irreversible. Man flies through the exercise of his technical ability to make airplanes, rockets, gliders, balloons, or dirigibles. In effect he makes changes in his environment instead of experiencing biological changes.

Man also forms social institutions within which these machines and devices can be produced and maintained. Steel is the product of a special technical system, but the mere knowledge of this system does not insure the production of steel. In addition to technical knowledge, the manufacture of steel requires a society which assigns people various roles important in the manufacture of steel—from puddler to international banker—and institutions which can organize these people into units of production—corporations, unions, governments, customers, etc.

A less complex example of a production-oriented set of cultural patterns is provided by the transition from hunting to agriculture which has occurred hundreds, perhaps thousands, of times in human history. The simple acquisition of agricultural techniques is not enough to bring about this change. Social institutions organized in such a way that some men can devote all their energies to the land, that land may be distributed, and that material goods not produced by the land may be obtained—all must be developed before such a transition can fully take place. In addition, cultural values which support and encourage agricultural activities are necessary.

Culture has another characteristic which is singularly important. Cultural traits can be copied, borrowed, modified, and elaborated upon without altering man's physical characteristics. If an animal species develops a particularly successful adaptive trait it cannot be transmitted to another species. The flying ability of bats was not copied from that of birds; it was produced by a separate line of evolutionary development. Fire, the bow and arrow, writing, monotheism, polygamy, or any other cultural pattern can be imported by one cultural population, following examples provided by other peoples. Such borrowing may take place because the receiving group sees a practical advantage, because they admire the people who introduce the trait, or simply because the new idea tickles their fancy. Nor must the borrowers necessarily use the new trait in the same way or context as it was used originally. This means that expressions of man's cultural potential are variable and the content of any culture (or of all cultures) can change and elaborate at a rate immeasurably faster than that of biological change.

On the other side of the coin, culture practices which become unsuitable in different circumstances can be modified or abandoned without necessarily threatening the existence of human populations. To accomplish the same thing in animal populations, nature must become a wholesale executioner of the "unfit."

Conclusion

Equipped with the potential for culture, our ancestors were able to free themselves from the interminably slow pace of biological adaptation and survive by making cultural adaptations—that is, create their own ecological niche. Man is not specialized for a specific physical environment; rather, he is specialized for the use of culture as a shield between himself and his surroundings—even as a device for altering those surroundings.

It is this fact that argues against the numerous writers who have suggested that culture is equivalent not to an ecological niche, but to a physical adaptation to a niche—analogous to the giraffe's long neck or the porpoise's sleek body-form. If we look at the almost infinite variety of ways that men live, this point of view is difficult to accept. What species of animal has developed wings for one situation, aquatic fins for another, and armored scales for yet another? True adaptations limit the range of situations in which an animal species can survive. Culture extends the physical world of man. Thus, while each cultural variation may function partly as an adaptation to a special environment, culture, taken as a whole, does not.

Rather, the potential to participate in cultural behavior is really the environment into which each new human being is born, and to which the entire species has adapted. Infants without this capacity seldom survive to reproduce, but if even a minimal capacity is present the individual can learn to live in any cultural system. A human's crucial task is to survive not in nature, but in culture. In a sense, man is his own environment.

PART TWO
Technology

The Material Basis of Society and Culture

Our own society is often ambiguously described as "technological," with the implication that in some way, somewhere there could exist a *non*technological society. There could not. No people could survive without some systematic means of combining material equipment (or tools) and techniques to meet their biologically determined and culturally acquired material needs. But obviously all technologies are not alike. They differ tremendously. Specifically *how* they differ is causally related to the form, content, and relative complexity of the other component aspects of a people's culture (their economic, social, and political systems, for example); to the character of their habitat (frozen tundra, tropical rainforest, rocky seacoast); and to their history (centuries of warfare with neighboring groups or millennia of near total cultural isolation).

Determining the essence of these causal connections and—especially for our purposes here—the ways particular patterns of technoenvironmental adaptation foster or interfere with particular forms of sociocultural development are among ethnology's core objectives. Thus technology is properly our first main topic.

But first it should be made clear that everything in every culture, from the Amahuacas' quest of the white-lipped pecary, to Viola Jackson's far-flung kindred, and the marsupial tails that Hageners stick in their wigs (see the selections coming up!), has explainable origins and relevant relations to the integrated totality of which it is always a component part. However, the fact that all aspects of culture exist in potentially understandable and significant relationships to one another does not mean that the fit between them is ever necessarily either neat or permanently set. In fact, most peoples' ways of life are in a loosely synchronized continuous state of fairly rapid flux, ours more than most. Even our fellow humans who are sometimes sloppily described as "still living in the Stone Age" actually have ways of life that are constantly changing, only at a sometimes slower pace.

Further, the assertion that significant functional interrelations link all aspects of culture does not mean that all institutionalized features of human behavior are equally crucial to a society's functioning and to the perpetuation of its culture. Intramural athletics, industrial technology, and Acid Rock are all current aspects of American life, but clearly they are not all equally important to the maintenance of our society or to acquiring an adequate understanding of the processes fundamental to our culture's perpetuation. Of the three, industrial technology is by far the most basic (not that the other activities mentioned are not also worth anthropological attention). It is just that they do not come first. First comes technology. In fact, technology is always a fundamental, first-order aspect of culture. For a people's means of making a living provides the material foundation that sustains the rest of their sociocultural system: their economy; the organization of their social groupings; their politics; their ideology, usually in the form of religion; and their arts. Even their language often reflects their level of technological development and the way of life it supports.

So long as both relative degrees of sociocultural integration and the potential pertinence and often critical causal interrelations of all aspects of culture are remembered (Acid Rock included), some that are less fundamental to human survival can be set aside. And the most basic aspects of culture can be carefully examined one at a time—in an order that logically begins with technology.

The most basic and critical difference between technologies lies in their relative productivity, in their efficiency at securing or harnessing energy to meet human material needs. Take an example we will often return to: all hunter-gatherers, people who do not know how to grow, or *produce*, food and who have not yet learned to domesticate animals, have relatively unproductive, low-energy technologies in comparison with farmers, herdsmen, or peoples with industrially based systems of production.

The hunter-gatherers' reliance on human muscle as a principal power source has an invariably incisive effect on the form and content of the other major aspects of their ways of life. Their population is likely to be small both in size and in density. Unless they have borrowed from technologically more advanced neighbors, they are certain to lack money or markets. The family is usually their most important social unit. They will have no legislature, no courts, no police, no prisons, no armies, and no warfare, although they may sporadically raid their neighbors or fight to defend their hunting territories. They are unlikely to have much formal religious organization, a few part-time ritual specialists at most. Although they will usually have worked out some rudimentary system for counting and record keeping, they will not have developed writing. They will have no cities, no monumental architecture, no symphony orchestras, no class conflicts, no internal political exploitation, almost no problems with pollution or with any of the other accompaniments of the "higher" standard of living that comes with greater technological complexity and productivity. All this is stated neither to put the hunter-gatherers down nor to elevate romantically their rustic way of life. It is used just to illustrate the always causal relationship between technology and the other major aspects of culture. The *less* productive the technology, the *more* deterministic this causative connection is likely to be.

Consideration of the formative role of technology in sociocultural development is best begun with a look at contemporary subsistence patterns that exemplify the major technological "stages" that preceded—in evolutionary sequence—our present-day industrially based patterns for making a living.

SECTION I

Food—The Fundamental Quest

That we need to eat to survive is inescapably evident. The ways people cope with this need can be analytically divided into four categories, four fundamentally different types of subsistence technology: (1) hunting and gathering; (2) horticulture, or primitive farming; (3) herding; and (4) agriculture.

For more than 90 per cent of our history the ancestors of all of us were hunters and gatherers of wild foods. Today those who still follow this most ancient means of making a living have been pushed off into the more inaccessible and/or technologically less readily exploitable parts of the world, deep into tropical forests where heavy rains would carry off the topsoil if the land were cleared for farming, into and around deserts where no outsiders have yet found anything worth drilling or digging for, along a few barren seacoasts where not even the fishing is very good, and, of course, into the more remote parts of the Arctic.

In such regions hunter-gatherers live on. Anthropologists are interested in these now mostly tiny remnant groups for two main reasons: (1) Although such peoples cannot quite be described as still living in the Paleolithic, their contemporary cultures do suggest in a general sense what life was once like for all of us. Incidentally, it apparently was not all bad. Having been killed off or pushed out by now from most of the more comfortable parts of the world, these days the hunter-gatherers' habitats are often rough and life is hard. But even in the undeniably harsh settings in which most are now forced to live, anthropologists who have been working among them report that their lives, though often short, are by no means either nasty or brutish. There is much that is rewarding in their close interdependence and deep feeling of communal responsibility. And where they have enough to get along, they have frequently been observed to be intelligently disinterested in "getting ahead," preferring instead to lie around and enjoy themselves. (This bit of ethnographic evidence has implications for the work ethic that we might well stop to ponder, but we do not have the time!) (2) We find that the study of hunter-gatherers is also valuable because the comparative simplicity of their technology allows us to perceive in unusually sharp relief important causal interrelations between technology and the other aspects of culture. For technological primitivism seems to limit people's options. Their forms of economic, social, and political organization are everywhere strikingly similar. This evidence of parallel causality is something to be taken as scientifically of serious significance (for reasons that will become increasingly apparent as we move along).

Next come the horticulturalists, the simplest of farmers, working the land with hand tools only. Lacking draft animals and plows (and tractors, of course), and often ignorant of any effective alternative means of increasing soil productivity, they must periodically leave their farmlands fallow, to regenerate naturally. Frequently this means that they are required to disrupt their settlements and move on to new areas to clear new land—just one of the sociocultural consequences of this still considerably more productive way of coping with the food quest.

Then, often on land too arid or otherwise unsuitable for farming, we find the herdsmen, living in groups for whom mobility—nomadism and migration—provides an effective means of adjusting to unpredictable, intermittent, and uncontrollable shifts in the availability of pasture and water.

Finally, there are the agriculturalists. They were the first of our kind to have been able to produce an adequate food supply in a single place and thus to have been able to settle down and by a complicated process, closely related to their more efficient means of producing food, to develop social and cultural systems, "civilizations," the complexity of which surpassed anything humankind had ever known, Now we have become so good at farming that most of us are free to do other kinds of work instead. (This is a *really* recently acquired capability, and one that is not yet universal by any means.)

As apparently narrow as its purpose always is, humans' ever-increasing efficiency at the food quest (that we are running low on wheat and that some kids in Milwaukee go to school hungry are *economic* rather than technological problems; see the next Part of the book) has had a fantastic effect on the evolution of nearly all the other aspects of our ways of life as they have developed so far, and as they will develop in a fast-approaching future that threatens catastrophic worldwide famine. That is why we give the food quest so much attention.

Like many former hunter-gatherers, the Amahuaca Indians of Peru have learned primitive farming, or horticulture, only comparatively recently, as a consequence of contact with some of their technologically more advanced neighbors. However, as Carneiro shows, all Amahuaca continue to go out often to track the wild game and to forage for the wild foods they still depend on heavily to meet their subsistence needs.

Several facets of Amahuaca life (their settlement in small, widely scattered extended family groups that move about frequently, and a nonexclusive concept of territoriality) are well suited to their pattern of technoenvironmental adaptation. Authority beyond the level of the kin group is nonexistent. They have no religious leaders. But supernaturalism is of major importance.

Because they are dependent for survival upon often dangerous environmental circumstances they can neither predict nor control in any other way, magic works for the Amahuaca as an integral aspect of their technology, enhancing their sense of prowess as hunters and, they believe, increasing the vulnerability of their prey.

Indian Hunters of the Peruvian Montaña[1]

Robert L. Carneiro

The Amahuaca Indians inhabit the heavily forested region between the Ucayali and upper Juruá and Purús rivers in Eastern Peru. At its greatest extent their territory encompassed perhaps 20,000 square miles (see map in Carneiro 1962:29), but today it has diminished to about a quarter of that size. The population of the Amahuaca, estimated at 6,000 to 9,000 around 1900 (von Hassel 1905:31), is today no more than about 500. Population density, formerly something like one person per two or three square miles, had diminished at the time of field work in 1960–61 to roughly one person for every eight or ten square miles.

Amahuaca settlements are small. About fifteen persons, occupying three or four houses, form the average community. Settlements are located on or near small streams, usually several hours' walking distance apart. Each community is completely autonomous economically as well as politically. Indeed, the same might almost be said of each nuclear or extended family within a community. There are no headmen or shamans, no kin groups larger than the extended family, and very little ceremonialism. All told, Amahuaca social organization is exceedingly simple.

Feuding among Amahuaca communities is very common, and sometimes they fight with their traditional enemies, the Yaminahua. The result is that an Amahuaca settlement is often on the alert against the possibility of attack.

Subsistence is divided almost equally between hunting and horticulture. To be more precise, I would say that about 50 per cent of the food consumed by the Amahuaca is derived from horticulture and 40 per cent from hunting, with the rest coming from fishing and gathering. Although hunting is thus not quite half of subsistence, it nevertheless plays a very important role in determining the small size of Amahuaca local groups, their location, and the frequency with which they are moved, which is about once every year or two.

The habitat of the Amahuaca is an unbroken expanse of tropical rainforest. There are no grasslands anywhere, and even abandoned garden plots revert directly to secondary forest without passing through an intermediate grass stage. The terrain consists of a series of rugged hills and ridges, often rising 200 or 300 feet above the adjacent streams. The heart of the Amahuaca territory is the height of land between the Ucayali and Juruá and Purús river systems. Here the headwater tributaries are born, and as they flow out of this area, are still narrow and shallow. The fish in these streams are small enough in size and few enough in number to make fishing an almost negligible part of subsistence. The primary source of animal protein is hunting, and the forests of the region are well stocked with game.

Meat is an important part of the Amahuaca diet, and no meal is considered really complete without it. A man who is a good provider sees to it that his household never lacks for meat.

Every man is a hunter, and every good hunter enjoys the chase. Such a man may go hunting even when there is still meat at home. Those not so skilled go less often, but because meat is commonly shared among all families in a community no one is without it for long.

The game found in the surrounding forests is abundant and varied. No single species predominates. Being generalized hunters, the Amahuaca seek out and kill most species of mammals in the area. These include monkeys of several kinds, deer, tapir, peccaries (both collared and white-lipped), agoutis, pacas, capybaras, anteaters, armadillos, sloths, porcupines, coatis, and squirrels. Most species of large game birds are hunted, including curassows and par-

Source: From "Hunting and Hunting Magic Among the Amahuaca of the Peruvian Montaña," by Robert L. Carneiro, *Ethnology*, vol. 9 (1970). By permission of the publisher and the author.

[1] Some of the data incorporated into this paper were very kindly provided by Mr. Robert L. Russell of the Summer Institute of Linguistics, who has worked among the Amahuaca for a number of years. However, Mr. Russell is in no way responsible for any errors of fact that may appear here.

tridges. Caimans, lizards, and turtles are also taken.

The only class of animals not eaten by the Amahuaca are carnivores, including jaguars, pumas, ocelots, jaguarundis, tayras, otters, and various types of wolves or wild dogs. A few noncarnivorous animals are also avoided as food, principally giant armadillos, silky anteaters, raccoons, rabbits, opossums, bats, and mice. Other animals not eaten include snakes, vultures and eagles, and a number of smaller birds.

According to Robert L. Russell, who has lived in close contact with the Amahuaca for a number of years, the order of importance of game animals in terms of the weight of meat derived from them is as follows: (1) tapir, (2) howler monkey, (3) spider monkey, (4) deer, (5) collared peccary, (6) paca, (7) cebus monkey, (8) paujil (wattled curassow), (9) guan, (10) pucacunga (bare-faced curassow), and (11) agouti. As far as taste is concerned, the two kinds of game most favored by the Amahuaca are tapir and spider monkey. Despite such dietary preferences, however, it is difficult to predict what a day's hunt will bring. For example, on one occasion two brothers living in adjacent houses shot two tapirs in three days but went several weeks before killing another one.

The hunting technology of the Amahuaca is very simple. The bow and arrow constitutes their principal weapon, and almost their only one. Spears and blowguns are lacking, as are snares, nooses, pitfalls, deadfalls, and any kind of hunting traps or nets. Except on rare occasions when a number of men may co-operate in attacking a passing herd of white-lipped peccaries, there is no collective hunting.

The bow and arrow is the inseparable companion of every Amahuaca man. Not only is it the means of obtaining much of his food, but it is also his principal weapon of attack or defense in a frequently hostile environment. Rarely does a man so much as leave his house without taking his bow and arrows with him. And in the hands of an Amahuaca, trained from childhood in its use, the bow and arrow becomes a very effective weapon.

The stave of an Amahuaca bow is made from the wood of the *pihuayo* or peach palm (*Guilielma speciosa*). This is the strongest and most resilient of the palms in the region, and probably equal or superior to any bow wood available in Amazonia.[2] The average length of Amahuaca bows is between 6 and 6½ feet, but occasionally they are up to a foot longer.

The bowstring is made from the inner bark fibers of the *setico* tree (*Cecropia leucocoma*), twined by the hunter on his thigh.[3] In total length a bowstring may be 15 feet or more, the extra length being wrapped around the upper limb of the bow to use as a spare in case the bowstring should break. The Amahuaca always keep their bows strung, ready to use. The resiliency of *pihuayo* wood is such that it loses little of its "cast" even when kept under continuous tension for a long time.

Some men wrap a thin strip of smooth, flattish bark from a vine around the bowstave in order to protect the bow hand from the fine slivers which, with repeated flexing, sometimes separate from the bow.

Arrows are somewhat over 5 feet in length. The shaft of the arrow is made from the long straight flower stem of the cane *Gynerium saggitatum*.[4] Into the soft pithy center of this cane is driven a foreshaft of hard wood, usually *pihuayo*. The most common type of point attached to this foreshaft is made from bamboo. It is lanceolate in shape and some 12 to 15 inches long. As these arrow points are dulled or broken in use, they are resharpened, and an old point may have been trimmed down until it is no longer than 5 or 6 inches. While designed especially for use against large game, such as tapir, deer, and peccaries, bamboo points are commonly used against game of any size.

Bamboo, which has a thin siliceous layer on the outside, takes a fine cutting edge and a very sharp point. Thus an arrow with such a point

[2] In the ethnographic literature for the Montaña one often finds the statement that bows are made of "chonta" palm. This term is a rather indefinite one. It is sometimes applied to *Guilielma speciosa*, but also to palms of the genus *Bactris*, and, by popular writers, to almost any palm.

[3] *Cecropia* bast fiber, which is very strong, appears to be the favorite material for the manufacture of bowstrings among Amazonian tribes generally.

[4] This type of cane grows wild in the low marshy areas bordering the Urubamba River, but not in the hilly regions where the Amahuaca live. However, the Amahuaca plant *Gynerium* in their gardens, or in special plots, especially for the arrow cane. When the cane flowers, the long straight flower stems are removed and stored in barkcloth cylinders suspended from the roof of the house until needed.

has great penetrating power.[5] Sometimes, however, the sides of a bamboo point are not left smooth, but are notched to make it more difficult for an animal to shake itself free of the arrow.

A less common type of arrow point consists of a somewhat longer *pihuayo* wood foreshaft, self-barbed, and sharpened to a point. A sliver of monkey bone, sharpened at each end, may sometimes be attached at an angle to the tip of the foreshaft. Arrows of these two types are designed for use against smaller game—monkeys, birds, rodents, etc. Blunt-headed wooden arrow points are occasionally made for shooting birds. Their advantage is that they do less damage to the bird's plumage, and are not so likely to stick in the trees.

The Amahuaca do not poison their arrows. They do, however, apply a thin layer of an orange-colored resin—apparently a form of copal—to their bamboo points. Although the Amahuaca believe that this resin will cause a wounded animal to die faster, it seems in fact to be more of an irritant than an actual poison.

Arrow feathers are attached only at their ends,[6] and are applied with a slight spiral so that the arrow rotates in flight, thus increasing its stability.

A hunter draws his bow to a point well behind his ear, and at full draw the average bow pulls 60 to 75 pounds. This relatively heavy bow weight, combined with a sharp, tapering bamboo blade, can send an arrow entirely through an animal.

Hunting is a year-round activity. During the dry season, when a man spends a good deal of time clearing and planting his garden plot, he hunts less frequently, but during the rainy season, when no such chores occupy his time, he goes hunting about every second or third day. Some men prefer to hunt alone, but two men, especially brothers or a father and son, may often hunt together. Generally, though, no more than three men comprise a hunting party, since more than this are said to frighten the game. Rarely, a man may go into the forest with his wife, spending the day hunting while she collects fruits, nuts, or other forest products.

Hunters leave early in the morning, often before six o'clock, to take full advantage of the daylight hours. If he sees little game, a man may spend the entire day looking, returning home around dusk. Even if successful, a hunter may stay out a good part of the day, killing as much game as he can before returning. Some men go hunting without breakfast and take no food with them, feeling that the added incentive of hunger will help them make an early kill. Others, however, take a little food with them in a small carrying basket, or perhaps wrapped in a leaf.

Sometimes a man may set out to hunt a particular kind of game, especially tapir or spider monkey, because these are the animals whose flesh is most prized. Tapirs may also be hunted for their fat, which is mixed with achiote (*Bixa orellana*) for body painting during feasts. Similarly, a man may hunt agoutis or pacas expressly for their chisel-like incisors. In such instances, the hunter heads toward an area of the forest where he has reason to think these animals are most likely to be found. When hoping to kill a tapir, for example, an Amahuaca often heads for the Curiuja River, an area where there is less hunting and therefore more game of every sort. On a relatively long trip like this a hunter may spend the night in the forest and return home the next day. He does not encumber himself by taking along his hammock, but, when night overtakes him, makes himself a sleeping mat out of palm leaves and erects a simple shelter.

The Amahuaca do not have defined territories, and a man may hunt in any area of the forest, even if it is close to another settlement, without asking permission and without being considered guilty of trespass. Because Amahuaca communities are so small, so widely scattered, and so frequently moved, there is little reason for them to demarcate a territory precisely, or to try to keep others from hunting in it.

5 Even when propelled by only the force of gravity an arrow can penetrate deeply. One Amahuaca was said to have been killed when his own arrow, falling out of a tree as he attempted to retrieve it, pierced his neck and entered his chest cavity. Two other men whom I knew each bore a couple of scars on their bodies where they had been wounded by their own arrows in the same manner.

6 This is the so-called "bridge feathering," typical of the tribes of the Ucayali basin. Some Amahuaca had arrows showing "Peruvian cemented feathering," in which the feathers are secured in place by being wrapped along their entire length with cotton thread, and then cemented with beeswax. The Amahuaca appear to have learned this type of feathering from the Yaminahua to the east.

When a hunter sets out, he usually avoids an area recently hunted by someone else, since the game there may have been shot or driven away. A network of hunting trails fans out from each settlement, and hunters follow these trails, at least at first. Often the hunter makes a circuit, leaving by one trail and returning by another, thus seeing more of the forest and increasing his chances of finding game.

After following a trail or a stream bed for awhile, a hunter may then cut across to another trail or stream. He is always on the alert, listening for animals, watching for movements of the undergrowth or of branches which may reveal their presence. If he hears the cry or the movement of an animal, he hurries toward it, yet moving carefully and taking advantage of the natural cover in order to conceal his presence. Whenever possible, he stays downwind of the animal.

Disguises are never worn in hunting, but a man may occasionally make some attempts at camouflage by sprinkling or smearing himself with the juice of the huito fruit (*Genipa americana*). When exposed to the air for an hour or two, the juice of this fruit turns black, and the mottled pattern formed on his body renders him less conspicuous. To cover up his scent a hunter often rubs aromatic leaves, such as vanilla, over his body, or places these leaves under his belt.

Although an Amahuaca is a good marksman with bow and arrow, what makes him an outstanding hunter is not so much his archery as his skill in tracking game and in working in close enough for a good shot. Every significant detail of the life habits of game animals is part of an Amahuaca hunter's knowledge. He knows the sound of their cries, what food they eat, and what their excrement looks like. He can detect the presence of peccaries or howler monkeys by their sharp scent, and can identify spider monkeys by the characteristic noise they make while eating fruit in the trees. From the tooth marks on a fruit he can tell what animal had been feeding on it, and approximately when it left.

If a hunter comes upon the trail of an animal, and it is fresh enough, he will follow it. The freshness of a set of tracks is gauged not only by how wet it is but also by the amount of dust and debris that has accumulated on it. On soft ground a man can tell not only what animal's tracks he is seeing, but also how large it was, how fast it was moving, and how long ago it went by.

The tracks of virtually every game animal are readily distinguished. During one hunting trip on which I accompanied two hunters I had pointed out to me the tracks of an armadillo, a raccoon, a deer, an agouti, a collared peccary, a paca, a giant armadillo, an otter, a tapir, a caiman, and an oriole.

If animal tracks are old, or if the ground is hard and the tracks are not readily visible, a hunter may still be able to detect the recent presence of game. He scans the forest floor for bits of fruit or fresh excrement, and studies the displacement of leaves and twigs. From the amount of exudation on a broken twig, for example, a hunter can judge how long ago an animal passed by.

When a hunter hears an animal, he attempts to fix its location more precisely by imitating its cry and trying to get it to respond.[7] Monkeys may reply by chattering, and a tapir by giving its shrill whistle. A deer may paw the ground. In any case, the animal's response enables the hunter to ascertain its position more exactly and thus to approach closer. The hunter may even succeed in drawing a curious animal close to him. For example, should a hunter chance upon some young, such as a fawn or a baby peccary, he will seize it, knowing that its plaintive cry is likely to bring the mother within arrow range.

The whole purpose of tracking and mimicry is to allow the hunter to approach as near as possible before shooting. Long distance shots are avoided, not only because marksmanship decreases with distance, but also because the intervening foliage can easily deflect an arrow. Generally, a hunter tries to close to within 40 feet or less before shooting. When he finally looses an arrow, he aims for a vital spot if he can, often just behind the rib cage. A bamboo point has such a long cutting edge that it may sever many blood vessels and cause considerable bleeding. If wounded by a well-placed arrow, an animal may be unable to travel far before collapsing. Barbed arrows do less cutting, but, lodging in the animal more securely, they help slow it down by rubbing or catching against the brush as it attempts to flee.

[7] Once, when I asked a man to demonstrate the art of imitating animal cries, he proceeded to imitate no fewer than 35 different animals, one after another.

If two or three men are hunting together, they generally separate when they hear an animal and attempt to close in on it from opposite sides. The first one to shoot an arrow at the animal may be allowed to finish it off. But if it appears likely that the animal is about to escape, his companions shoot too.

As mentioned earlier, the only occasion when a number of men co-operate in hunting is when a herd of white-lipped peccaries is detected near the settlement. Unlike collared peccaries, which travel singly or in pairs, white-lipped peccaries travel in herds of up to 100. A group of hunters may be able to kill as many as ten peccaries before the rest take flight. A lone hunter coming upon a herd of feeding peccaries from the downwind side, approaches them stealthily and attempts to kill one or two before the others discover his presence. Once alerted, the peccaries either flee or charge. Because of their sharp tusks and their compact ranks, their charge is dangerous, and a hunter caught in their path can save himself only by climbing a tree.

The Amahuaca have dogs, and these are an important asset in hunting.[8] By catching the scent of animals and following their spoor, dogs enable the hunter to locate more game than he could by himself. Dogs are also very helpful in locating animals living in burrows or hollow tree trunks. Besides finding game, dogs also help in killing it by bringing it to bay, or by so annoying an animal that it stops to bite or snarl at his pursuers, thus allowing the hunter to catch up with it.

The Amahuaca erect hunting blinds at places where animals come to drink, or where the ripe fruit of a tree are falling, or some other place which game is likely to frequent. Blinds are sometimes also built near garden plots if agoutis or deer or other predators have been eating the crops. They are made by inserting the butt ends of four or more palm leaves into the ground, and drawing together and tying the upper ends. Here and there the leaflets are separated to provide peepholes. A blind is about 5 feet in diameter and tall enough to allow a man to stand inside.

Sometimes a man builds a blind in the trees to hunt monkeys, such as red howlers, which frequent the higher branches and are not easily seen from the ground. Or a hunter may simply climb a tree to a vantage point above a passing troop of monkeys and shoot down on them. In this way he may manage to shoot two or three monkeys before the rest realize what is happening. Tree climbing is usually done by means of a climbing ring made by coiling a length of thin vine. The ring thus formed is placed around the insteps, and permits the climber to brace his feet against opposite sides of a small tree, as he reaches up to take a firm handhold. Once he has his new hold, he then pulls his feet up behind him.

A few other hunting techniques used by the Amahuaca may be mentioned. In hunting tapirs, use is sometimes made of a palm-wood sword up to four feet long with sharp edges tapering to a fine point. A cornered tapir is stabbed with such a sword.

Clubbing is the usual way to kill an armadillo, since its carapace is hard enough to ward off an arrow. Clubs may also be used against white-lipped peccaries, caimans, and agoutis.

Burrowing animals like armadillos or agoutis may be lured out of their holes with cries, or smoked out with dry palm leaves which have been ignited. If this fails, one end of the burrow may be stopped up and the animal dug out.

To bring back the game he has killed a hunter accommodates it in a palmleaf basket which he braids on the spot and carries on his back by means of a tumpline. Smaller game, like monkeys, is brought back whole, but larger game may be cut up for easier carrying. The two feet on each side of a deer may be tied together, the hunter's arms inserted through the loops thus formed, and the animal carried home like a knapsack.

Tapirs, which may weigh as much as 500 or 600 pounds, are naturally too large to bring back in one trip. A hunter will cut up a tapir, remove the viscera and other internal organs, and carry these and as much of the meat as he can back to the house. The parts of the animal left behind to be retrieved the next day must be carefully protected from scavengers. Leaves are usually placed over them, weighted down with sticks, and then covered with dirt. This

[8] The dog may well be post-Columbian among the Amahuaca, as it seems to be among most Amazonian tribes. There is little direct evidence for this, but the Amahuaca do call the dog *indo*, the same term they use for jaguar.

prevents jaguars and other carnivores from catching the scent.[9]

That evening, when he is back at the settlement, or early next morning, the hunter hoots in a conventional way to inform the rest of the men that he has shot a tapir and is going to retrieve it. This is an invitation to others to come along, and those who accompany him are allowed to keep the portions of the carcass they bring back. When the men go out to retrieve a tapir, their womenfolk spend a good part of the day gathering firewood and making a babracot on which to roast the meat.

A lone hunter, returning from the forest, may appear at his house sad-eyed and empty-handed, as if he had had no luck. But this is often a deception, and a carrying basket full of meat may at that moment be sitting by the trail just outside the clearing. When the hunter finally tells his wife about it, she goes to fetch it. It is considered impolite to ask a hunter who has just returned from the forest what success he has had, for if he has caught nothing, he is embarrassed, and the Amahuaca never embarrass one another.

Large game, even if brought back by the hunter unaided, is often shared with other families. Smaller game, however, is consumed by the hunter's family alone. A tapir may provide meat enough for a week, even if shared. To preserve it that long the meat is roasted over a slow fire until thoroughly dry.

There are no rules for the distribution of game. No specific portion of the animal is reserved for the hunter or for particular kinsmen.

Hunting Magic

It has often been observed that supernaturalism tends to surround those activities which are either uncertain or hazardous or both, while, conversely, little or no supernaturalism accompanies those spheres of life where security and predictability prevail.[10] The Amahuaca certainly bear out this generalization. Almost no supernaturalism is connected with horticulture, which yields very abundantly and reliably. On the other hand, hunting, whose outcome is never certain, and often involves an element of personal danger, is attended by considerable supernaturalism.

Not all aspects of Amahuaca hunting are, however, permeated with magical practices. For example, propitiation of the spirits of game animals, so prominent a feature in hunting among North American Indians, does not occur among the Amahuaca. Only a few game animals are thought to have spirits, and these are never propitiated, either before or after the animals are killed.[11] Nor is any attempt made to secure the assistance of animal spirits in hunting.

The Amahuaca do not have totem animals, and do not prohibit the killing of any animal, whether it is eaten or not. It is true that certain animals—especially carnivorous ones—are not eaten, but the failure to eat such animals appears to derive from a general repugnance to their eating habits rather than from an explicit religious prohibition.[12] Vultures, for example, are considered unfit to eat "because they eat rotten things."

Also absent from Amahuaca hunting magic are rituals designed to make animals increase in numbers. The depletion of game in an area is recognized as being the result of overhunting, and the only remedy sought is the purely rational one of moving the settlement to another part of the forest.

Amahuaca supernaturalism, as it relates to hunting, can best be summarized by saying that it is positive rather than negative. There is little or nothing that a hunter must not do to have success in hunting, but there are many things he can and does do. Positive kinds of hunting magic vary considerably. Some of it acts on the hunter himself, or on his weapons, helping him to find game sooner, to see more of it, or to make his arrow fly truer. Other hunting magic

9 If an animal is killed early in the hunt its carcass may be placed in a stream to retard spoilage until the hunter is ready to return and retrieve it.

10 ". . . supernaturalism varies inversely with the extent and effectiveness of naturalistic control. In activities where man has little actual control, or where chance and circumstances play a prominent part . . . recourse to supernaturalism is great. In activities where man's control is extensive and effective . . . resort to supernaturalism will tend to be meager and perhaps only perfunctory" (White 1959:272). See also Linton (1936:429-431), Malinowski (1954:30-31), and Oberg (1940:151).

11 For an account of Amahuaca spirit beliefs see Carneiro (1964).

12 A number of Amazonian tribes do not eat deer because they believe it to be the ultimate repository of human souls. The Amahuaca have no such belief.

acts on the game, making animals "tamer" so they can be seen and shot more readily. Some of these practices may now be examined.

Smearing blood from an animal on the bowstring or bowstave is thought to make the bow more effective against other animals of that species. This is done especially with a new bow, or with blood from the first animal of that species killed with the bow. Arrows as well as bows may be magically treated. A man may run the further end of his arrow through the body of an animal several times, smearing it with blood and thus making it shoot straighter.[13] Some hunters say that the blood of certain animals—a small lizard, for example—is particularly effective in this respect.

The blood of an animal may also be applied to the hunter's own body. It is common for a boy who is beginning to hunt to have the blood of a tapir rubbed over his body so he will turn out to be a successful hunter. Some informants reported that the blood of the tapir, peccary, agouti and spider monkey was occasionally drunk for better luck in hunting these animals.[14]

Plants of various sorts also figure in hunting magic. Certain kinds of leaves are often wrapped around the bowstave or tucked under a hunter's belt for luck. Herbal infusions are also employed. Most common among these is *kumba ra'o* (called *chiricsanago* in Peruvian jungle Spanish), which appears to come from a species of *Rauwolfia*. The roots of the plant are scraped into water, which is then heated almost to boiling. After drinking this potion a man becomes dizzy and his body feels cold, "as if it had rained on you," one informant said. After taking it, one's aim improves and game animals become "tame," allowing themselves to be easily killed. Various kinds of *kumba ra'o* are specific for particular species of animal.

Another class of plants used in hunting magic are called *sako* in Amahuaca and *piripiri* in jungle Spanish. Most of these appear to be sedges of the genus *Cyperus*. The leaves are crushed in water and smeared on the arms and wrists. Or the infusion may be boiled and applied to the body. As with *kumba ra'o,* there are *piripiri* plants specific to various game animals. *Piripiri* is said to enable a man to see a lot of game.

Still another type of hunting magic involves drinking the excrement of the boa constrictor. Picking at certain scales on the tail markings of the boa is also thought to be magically effective. In addition, an infusion made by boiling hawk's talons may be smeared on the hands and wrists of a boy or young man to make him a better hunter. The talons themselves may be scraped along the back of the hands until blood is drawn, "so that no spider monkey will escape."

Strips of inner bark from a tree with a very caustic sap are occasionally tied around a boy's wrists or forearms, burning a ring around the arm which remains as a permanent scar. This is done so that, again, "no animal will escape." During one hunting trip I observed a man crush the leaves of a certain plant in his upraised hands and allow the caustic juice to trickle down the inside of his arms to the biceps. This, he said, would bring him luck in hunting spider monkeys.

Stronger forms of magic are sometimes resorted to, especially if a hunter has had several unsuccessful hunting trips in succession. He may cut a wasps' nest from a tree and stand holding it, allowing himself to be stung by the wasps. If the pain becomes unbearable, he runs through the forest, still carrying the nest, so that fewer wasps will sting him. For the next two or three days he may be very ill and badly swollen from the effect of the stings, but he is sure to emerge from the ordeal a better hunter.[15]

But the strongest hunting magic of all is for a man to inoculate himself with the very toxic

[13] One Amahuaca, on the island of Chumichinía in the Ucayali River, told me that if a man had sexual relations before going hunting his arrow would miss its mark. This belief, however, seems to have been derived from the neighboring Conibo or Campa, and is absent among the Amahuaca on the upper Inuya. There, a man may have sexual relations with his wife even while he is out hunting with her in the forest. Moreover, the behavior of women who remain at home while their husbands are out hunting is in no way restricted.

[14] The Amahuaca sometimes drink human blood, too, but not as part of hunting magic. It is usually done by the close female relative of a man who has been wounded by an animal or an arrow. The blood may be drunk directly from the wound, or collected in a small bowl and drunk from this. The practice is considered therapeutic for the injured man.

[15] I have also seen a hunter allow himself to be stung by ants he encountered on the trail in the forest, for the same purpose.

secretion of a small frog which the Amahuaca call *kambó*.[16] This secretion is scraped off the back of the frog with a stick. Then, taking a live brand, a man burns himself in several places on the arms or chest, and rubs this secretion into the burns. Within a short time he becomes violently ill, suffering uncontrollable vomiting and diarrhea. For the next three days, while under the influence of the toxin, he has vivid hallucinations which are regarded as supernatural experiences.[17] When he finally recovers, he is convinced that his hunting is bound to improve.

Even dogs are treated magically. To enable a dog to find land turtles, an infusion from a certain *piripiri* plant may be given to it to drink or put into its nose or eyes. The owner of a dog which is no longer hunting well attempts to sharpen its scent by putting tapir dung, pepper juice, or a paste of ants' nest up the dog's nostrils. A poor hunting dog may even have its tail docked, to see if this will help.

Summary

Although the Amahuaca have practiced horticulture for centuries, they continue to rely heavily on hunting in their subsistence. The dense forest in which they live provides game in variety and abundance. Highly skilled in the use of the bow and arrow and in tracking and stalking animals, the Amahuaca are very proficient hunters. But not content with their physical skill alone, they attempt to improve their hunting by magical means. The effect of this magic, as the hunter sees it, is, on the one hand, to enhance his own ability and, on the other, to increase the susceptibility of the game.

REFERENCES CITED

Anonymous, 1965, "Lethal Kokoi Venom Related to Hormones," *MD* 9, 112.

Carneiro, R. L., 1962, "The Amahuaca Indians of Eastern Peru, *Explorers Journal* 40, iv, 26–37.

——— 1964, "The Amahuaca and the Spirit World," *Ethnology* 3, 6–11.

Hassel, Jorge M. von, 1905, "Las tribus salvajes de la region amazónica del Perú," *Boletín de la Sociedad Geográfica de Lima* 17, 27–73.

Linton, R., 1936, *The Study of Man.* New York.

Malinowski, B., 1954, *Magic, Science and Religion and Other Essays*, Doubleday, Garden City, N.Y.

Oberg, K., 1940, The Social Economy of the Tlingit Indians. Ph.D. dissertation, University of Chicago.

Wassén, S. H., 1935, "Notes on Southern Groups of Chocó Indians in Colombia," *Etnologiska Studier* 1, 35–182.

——— 1955–56, "On Dendrobates-Frog-Poison Material Among Emperá (Chocó)-Speaking Indians in Western Caldas, Colombia," *Etnografiska Museet Årstryck*, 73–94.

White, L. A., 1959, *The Evolution of Culture*, New York.

[16] I was not able to identify this frog, but it may be related to the *kokoi* frog, *Phyllobates bicolor* (or *Dendrobates tinctorius*) of Colombia, whose secretion is used by the Chocó Indians to poison their blowgun darts (Wassén 1935:99–100; 1955–56:78–81). *Kokoi* poison has recently been discovered to be the most toxic natural substance known (Anonymous 1965:112).

[17] The Amahuaca also drink *ayahuasca* (*Banisteriopsis caapi*) to induce spirit visions, but do not do so to assist them in hunting.

Whatever the specifics of their habitat and history, the ways of life of peoples with a pastoral, nomadic technology are usually assumed to be marked by certain fundamental similarities—in aspects of economic, social, and political organization—that are generally explained as responses to this widespread pattern of technoenvironmental adaptation, an adjustment well suited to the often changing conditions typical of the fragile habitat of most pastoral nomadic peoples.

Here Salzman details the subsistence technology of the Shah Nawazi Baluch of Iran and relates it to the other aspects of their culture in an ethnographic case that tests some of the prevailing theoretical generalizations concerning the sociocultural consequences of pastoral nomadism.

Movement and Resource Extraction Among Pastoral Nomads: The Case of the Shah Nawazi Baluch

Philip Carl Salzman

In discussions of particular kinds of adaptations, such as pastoral nomadism, there is a tendency to rely on ideal types as the basis of conceptualization. These ideal types make classification easy, but they oversimplify in three ways: First, too few criteria are taken into account in the conceptualization. Second, these criteria are assumed to vary together, rather than independently of one another. Third, variation is thought of in terms of discrete breaks and radical differences, rather than gradual curves and subtle shadings. Thus, as is too often the case, the price of simplicity is inaccuracy. And this inaccuracy resulting from ideal typical conceptualization is frequent in attempts to generalize about particular kinds of adaptation. (e.g. Cohen 1968) For conceptual purposes, the solution is that discussions should be framed in terms of dimensions and the ranges of variation on those dimensions. (Salzman 1967: 118–119) For the statement of substantive generalizations, complexities cannot be avoided, and must of course be themselves subjects of discussion.

The purpose of this essay is to present several general statements, both conceptual and substantive, about movement and resource extraction among pastoral nomads. These general points will be illustrated by ethnographic data from the Shah Nawazi Baluch[1] and further documented by limited reference to the literature. Introductory comments on the Shah Nawazi will be presented, and then the general statements, each followed by relevant ethnographic material.

The Shah Nawazi Baluch are located in the northern highland region, the Sarhad, of Iranian Baluchistan. The several thousand souls of the tribe are unevenly distributed throughout the east central Sarhad plateau, the Morpish mountains bordering the plateau to the east, and the Mashkel drainage basin to the east of the mountains, a total area of approximately 10,000 square kilometers. The climate ranges in different parts of this territory from subtropical steppe to subtropical desert, with cold to mild winters and hot summers. Annual precipitation ranges up to 150 mm. (approximately 6 inches), and usually falls in the winter. Natural vegetation ranges from spare distribution of grass and herbaceous plants to the absence of natural vegetation.

The Shah Nawazi, traditionally known as the Yarahmadzai, are tribally organized through the use of a patrilineal idiom, all members being patrilineal descendants of the founding ancestor of the tribe. There is a chiefly lineage which provides the tribal Sardar. Local communities, between 20 and 100 souls each, are identified with shallow patrilineages, although members of other lineages are often present. The headman of each local community comes from the dominant lineage of that community. Preferential bilateral endogamy results in local social integration having a bilateral nature.

The economy of the Shah Nawazi is a multiresource one; that is, it depends upon the exploitation of a number of different kinds of resources. *The economies of most peoples are not based upon a single resource, but rather upon multiple resources: this is just as true of so-called pastoral nomads. Furthermore, the extraction of one kind of resource within an adaptation often depends upon or is facilitated by products drawn from other resources as part of the adaptation.*

Prior to pacification by the Iranian Government in 1928–35, the Shah Nawazi extracted products from three major and two minor resources: The major resources were herds of goats and sheep (in a 2 to 1 ratio) and camels, date palm groves, and trade caravans and Persian-speaking peasants tapped through predatory

Source: From Philip Carl Salzman, "Movement and Resource Extraction Among Pastoral Nomads: The Case of the Shah Nawazi Baluch," *Anthropological Quarterly*, Vol. 44 (1971), pp. 185–197. Used by permission of the publisher and the author.

[1] Ethnographic field research was carried on in 1967–68 as part of the author's dissertation research. The field trip was financed by a grant from the National Science Foundation.

raiding. The minor resources were grain agriculture and hunting and gathering.

From the animals were drawn foodstuffs, including milk, which was consumed in various states of sweet and sour, pure and mixed with water, and processed into clarified butter and dried solids; meat; and also raw materials for crafts, such as hair and wool for various types of grain, camel and saddle bags, rugs, and tent material, and skins for water and milk bags. Camels in addition provided transport for both people and goods.

Dates were eaten plain and as crushed pulp mixed with clarified butter. In addition to dates, the palms provided raw materials for making rope and mats.

From raiding came foodstuffs (both animal and vegetable), valuables (including jewelry and carpets), and captives for slavery.

Hunting and gathering made available foodstuffs, including meat from game such as gazelle, rabbit, and birds, and vegetables such as wild onions, nuts from wild pistachio groves on the southern border of the tribal territory, and salt from local deposits.

Small-scale irrigation cultivation, primarily by slaves and a serf-like subject population, provided a limited amount of grain.

While most of this production was for local consumption, some, especially animals and animal products and probably the proceeds of raiding, was used for acquisition of grain, cloth, and perhaps craft goods through exchange in the Persian territory of Sistan, to the north of Baluchistan.

Since pacification curtailed raiding, other sources of income were sought. By the 1960s, there was considerable migrant labor, both within Baluchistan on Government projects and outside of Baluchistan in Iran, Pakistan, and the Arab states of the Persian Gulf, and an expansion of agriculture, primarily through an increase of irrigation facilities. Pastoralism of goats, sheep and camels, and date palm cultivation have continued as major forms of extraction. With the prohibition of firearms and the increased although still quite limited availability of vegetables through expanded cultivation, hunting and gathering have declined somewhat, but continue to be a significant but minor method of extraction. Exchange within the area has become possible with the Government-stimulated development of administrative towns and consequent establishment of markets.

The variety of resources and of methods used to extract products has its basis in demands related to both quantity and variety. The area is a harsh and difficult one, and sources of both foodstuffs and craft materials are scarce and resources difficult to extract. Success in the different forms of resources extraction described above is furthermore subject to varying environmental pressure through time. For example, droughts are common, as is disease, and both have devastating effects upon herds In the early 1960s, a severe drought all but wiped out tribal herds, and by the late 1960s the numbers of sheep and goats per tent averaged between 10 and 15, hardly enough for supplementary use and certainly too limited for primary subsistence use.

In the past raiding was (and currently migrant labor is) important in bridging the gap between local resources and subsistence needs, but date and grain cultivation and hunting and gathering provide a necessary supplement. The various resources provide foodstuffs of different types, but even so the diet, consisting primarily of bread, milk and milk products, dates, salt (and purchased tea), and a few seasonally available greens, with an occasional addition of meat, is a monotonous and limited one. The variety obtained through the exploitation of the various resources is not great, and further restriction would meet with objections and perhaps increased health difficulties.

The facilitation of one type of resource extraction by another is seen in the use of products from one kind of resource in the exploitation of another type of resource. The pastoral sector is supported by others in several respects: Food for animals is often a product of human labor in other sectors rather than derived exclusively from grazing. This is especially true during the winter, when pasturage is extremely sparse. Pregnant camels, and often young or weak camels, are fed roots of undomesticated plants which have been dug out by the herdsmen for this purpose. Kids and lambs are fed on a variety of domesticated products, including dates, date pits, grain, and chaff. Date pits are saved and processed by cracking and soaking before being fed to the animals. The cracking of the pits by a stone-on-stone method results in the most characteristic domestic sound of the winter season, just as the churning of butter in skins provides the most characteristic domestic sound of the springtime. The palm horticulture sector also provides the raw materials used in making ropes necessary for animal-pen fence webbing, for the securing of goods in animal-based transport, and for tent supports and accessories. (The latter two functions can be considered part of the pastoral sector, for the movement entailed requires such supporting equipment.)

Moreover, the use of the date palm groves depends upon animal transport of people and goods to and from the groves, and of the various products extracted, carried in bags made from animal wool and hair, away from the groves. Not only is date horticulture supported by animal transport, but so, too, are gathering and grain cultivation: In the former case, the collection and transport of salt and of wood for fires depends upon the availability of animals. In the latter case, the animals provide manure fertilizer for the fields. Herding camps and their herds move onto the fields immediately after the grain harvest, breaking their tight formation and spreading their tents over the land for the only occasion during the yearly cycle in order that the animals' droppings will be distributed over the fields.

In sum, it can be seen that in the multi-resource economy of the Shah Nawazi, various types of resources are exploited, and these different types supplement each other in adding to the total quality of products available for consumption and exchange, and complement one another in providing variety. In addition, there is often a meshing of the different resources, in that the products of one or more are useful in extracting products from the other resources.

Many well known "pastoral" societies exhibit a similar pattern. Capot-Rey gives several cases of multi-resource economy from North Africa. "In the central Sahara, it is enough for rain to cause the *taouit* . . . to flower and bear, for the upper part of the Ahaggar to be invaded by whole families, both nomads and settlers, anxious to harvest the seeds." (Capot-Rey 1962:303) In Mauritania, pastoralists own substantial date palms or accord them protection. "In these circumstances, the return to the oasis for the date harvest becomes a major event interrupting the pastoral migrations. . . ." (Capot-Rey 1962: 304) And "throughout northern Libya, the nomads have fields in the *oudianes* and palms and olive trees near the villages." (Capot-Rey 1962: 306) The Nuer depend upon horticulture and fishing as heavily as upon their beloved cattle for food (Evans-Pritchard 1940), and the Karimojong depend upon horticulture as much as upon their herds (Dyson-Hudson 1966). The Basseri of the Zagros hunt and gather, and cultivate grain, albeit not enthusiastically (Barth 1961). To the extent that such modes of extraction are recent developments, they are most likely replacements for other kinds of exploitation, such as extortion and predatory raiding, now impracticable as a result of encapsulation by nation-states bent upon pacification.

There are, however, certain pastoral groups which seem to depend almost exclusively upon exploitation of their herds. Such "pure pastoralists" might include the pastoral Masai and Bedawib Beja, among others (Jacobs 1965), and perhaps the Lapps. But such a uni-resource adaptation, even if a number of ethnographic cases can be found, is the rare exception, rather than the rule, and should not be taken as representative of pastoral peoples in general.

In discussing whether one or another resource or a particular combination of resources is extracted, one can avoid discussing nomadism, which is not *logically* entailed in the extraction of any particular kind of resource. The question about the part of nomadism in any adaptation is an empirical one: what role does nomadism play in the extraction of various resources? Consequently, *nomadism and resource extraction must be kept conceptually distinct, so that they can be related empirically*. Nomadism is a kind of movement: the movement of the family or group residence in the course of the yearly round. Pastoralism, hunting and gathering, agriculture, and commercialism are the extraction of goods from certain kinds of resources: domesticated animals, undomesticated animals and plants, domesticated plants, and markets, respectively. Nomadism could logically be associated with the extraction of any of these or with various combinations, but may or may not be thus associated empirically. Therefore, to say "pastoral" does not necessarily entail "nomadic," and to say "nomadic" does not necessarily entail "pastoral." This point can be illustrated with an examination of Shah Nawazi nomadism, which is not linked exclusively with the extraction of a particular kind of resource, but is rather associated with the extraction of different kinds of resources at different phases in the yearly cycle.

In the winter (December, January, February), the tribesmen live with their animals in herding camps consisting of clusters of from five to twenty black goat-hair tents on the Sarhad plateau. The camps are located in their customary winter areas and do not move, because the uniform lack of pasturage throughout the territory consequent upon the summer drought followed by the winter freeze provides no pastoral purpose for relocation. The primary pastoral activity is protecting the animal from cold, by housing the sheep and goats in the tents, building shelters for the kids and lambs, and providing blanket-cloaks for the camels; and from starvation, by providing food for the weaker animals. Spring (March, April, May) is the richest time, for both animals and men, because the warm weather following the winter rains (up to 6 inches) brings up new green shoots for the first time in nine months, and there is pasturage for the animals and milk for the young animals and the tribesmen. This is also the time of much movement, because the presence of pasturage is not uniform throughout the tribal territory, but varies from place to place, from week to week, and from year to year. As many as ten migrations, some quite short, others of many miles, are not unusual for a camping group during this period (Salzman 1970). Because of unpredictable micro-environmental variations, the timing, direction, and distance of any given migration is not known before-hand; each migration is an *ad hoc* tactical adjustment based primarily upon needs of the animals and the perceived circumstances of the environment. The overall pattern is a complex one of changes of direction and criss-crossing of migration paths, with each camping group following its own unique pattern according to its own lights, a pattern predicated upon an "open pasture" land tenure policy throughout the tribe.

Pastoral migration slacks off during the first part of summer (June, July), for most of the tribesmen have some part in the grain harvest. But late summer and early autumn (August, September, October) is the period of *hamin*, the date harvest, and this necessitates another migration, one which in terms of time (8 days) and distance (approximately 100 miles) is the major migration of the yearly cycle. The tribesmen leave the Sarhad plateau (5500 feet), travel through the Morpish mountain range, and descend to the Hamun-i Mashkel drainage basin (1500 feet). It is here that the date palm groves are located, because of the warm climate and availability of water (5 feet under the surface). Most noteworthy for our purposes is that this migration is in no respect made for pastoral purposes. The herds and flocks, in fact, are left behind on the Sarhad plateau under the supervision of shepherds. There is no pasturage in the Hamun area and the animals would have a difficult time surviving. Likewise the tents and much other household paraphernalia are left on the Sarhad, the tribesmen living in mud-brick huts in the date groves. This migration, then, is not a pastoral one, but rather a migration to take the tribesmen from the area of pastoral enterprise, the Sarhad, to the area of date cultivation, the Mashkel basin.

This migration can perhaps be best labeled "trans-resource," for its purpose is to move from one kind of resource to another.[2] Such a "trans-resource" migration is necessary for the Shah Nawazi, because two of their major resources are spatially separated in areas which are useful exclusively for the resources found there and of no use for the other type of resource. Without the "trans-resource" migration the tribesmen would be hard put to have the multi-resource adaptation and economy that they presently enjoy. (See also the examples from Africa mentioned above.) This case of the "trans-resource" migration is useful for our purpose in that it clearly illustrates the distinction between nomadism, as manifested in such migrations, and any particular mode of resource extraction, such as pastoralism. The clear behavioral separation between nomadism and pastoralism in the Shah Nawazi case emphasizes the need for a conceptual distinction between nomadism and resource extraction in the examination of other nomadic groups, whether or not such a clear behavioral separation is evident.

It is not necessary, of course, to range very far in the ethnographic literature to find cases with various combinations of nomadism and resource extraction. The most obvious case would be nomadic hunters and gatherers (Lee and DeVore 1968), the presence of whom in the Sahara led Briggs (1960) to implicitly distinguish between nomadism and resource extraction. Sedentary pastoralism, in both "mixed farming" and "ranching," is another important alternative combination. Less well known, and virtually absent from the literature, is nomadism and

[2] I have elsewhere (Salzman 1969) called this a "multi-resource migration," but this phrase is better used in a different fashion, as is indicated below.

market exchange, as in migrant laborers and migrant tradesmen (Srivastava 1958).

The use of the conceptual distinction suggested here is a first and necessary step in analysing the impact of nomadism *per se*, in its different variations, on social organization and culture, and the impact of the various forms and combinations of resource extraction *per se* on social life. In this respect, comparisons of nomadic hunters, pastoralists, and laborers, for example, might be more illuminating than comparisons between pastoral nomads.

The spring migrations of the Shah Nawazi were primarily for pastoral purposes. This "primarily" is a necessary qualification, for *whatever the primary purpose of a migration, various other considerations are taken into account and influence the timing, direction and length of the move.* A migration made primarily for pastoral purposes, in order to relocate the animals near pasturage, water or herding personnel, will be influenced in its attributes by other factors, including access to other kinds of resources and the pressure of social forces. This phenomenon is in part a consequence of the multi-resource adaptation and economy, within which the needs and demands of one kind of resource extraction are considered in the context of the needs and demands of other forms of resource extraction. It is also partly a consequence of other, non-economic factors—social, religious, health, political—that impinge upon peoples' daily lives.

One of the major factors influencing the migrations of the Ja'far Dadolzai camping group in the spring of 1968 was the interest that various members of the camp had in the *qanat*-irrigated[3] grain cultivation at Shagbond, two miles to the east of the camp's winter camping area at Pusht-i Kamal. Some members of the group owned land[4] and were cultivating grain there; others were working as hired laborers on the fields and "on the water" there. Other members of the camp had interests in the grain cultivation elsewhere, or had no interests in cultivation.

Those with labor to perform at the area(s) of the cultivation had to move from their residences in the camp to those areas and back, and consequently desired to minimize the distance between the camp and their areas of cultivation. These same men also had animals, and were concerned that the animals have access to good pasturage, and so they had to weigh and balance the conflicting demands of these two forms of resource extraction and come to some reasonable compromise. At the same time, other men in the camp with only pastoral interests were trying to maximize satisfaction of the needs of their animals. The result, given the micro-variations in the unpredictable environment, was a continuing debate and dialogue within the camp about the timing and direction of migration and the desired location of future sites. Decisions about specific migrations were attempted syntheses of the differing interests of the camp members and of the different demands of the various modes of resource extraction (Salzman 1970).

Likewise, other, non-economic, factors intruded in the decisions about the "primarily" pastoral migrations. At the beginning of the season, people were anxious to move from their winter site, partly to acknowledge symbolically that the season of plenty was at hand, partly to "get moving" after the torpor of the winter season, and partly to leave behind the collected refuse, animal and other, of the extended winter camping period. Later, the local water supply was not sufficient and the women had to travel too far for the domestic supply. They were quite vocal in their desire to move closer to a water source, and their demand was heeded without great delay. Another example is the desire of a camp elder's wife to reside with her family in another part of the tribal territory, and that elder's arguments, couched mainly in a pastoral idiom, for migration to that area.

The presence in a given location of other groups with whom there are cordial or hostile relations can influence, other things being equal, the decision to camp in that location. Finally, the presence or absence of men or women camp members influences the timing of migration, for labor demands as well as courtesy recommends the participation of as many household members as possible in migration. Certain migrations were put off for several days while the return of camp members was awaited.

In sum, even when migrations are seen as

[3] The *qanat* is an underground irrigation tunnel which taps the water table, and is the traditional method of irrigation in Iran. Wulff (1966:251–255). Two diesel engine pumps were established in Shah Nawazi tribal territory in the 1960s.

[4] It is actually the irrigation water that was owned, with rights over the land being established by use.

primarily for one purpose, many factors are taken into account and influence the final decisions about timing and distance of migration and location of site. In certain cases, the larger general purposes of migration might be for the exploration of more than one kind of resource, and such a migration might be called "multi-resource" migration. The closest example of this among the Shah Nawazi is the move of the camps onto the agricultural fields, where the animals graze on the stubble and leave their droppings to fertilize the land. In this case, the relocation was clearly for the benefit of both the animals and the fields, for both pastoral and agricultural purposes. Such "multi-resource" migration is perhaps more usual than is apparent from the literature on nomadism.

The description of nomadism among the Shah Nawazi has emphasized migration, but the importance of movement is not limited to migration. *The movement which is a part of the adaptation of a nomadic group includes not only migration, but also less socially encompassing moves,* such as the trip, a move entailing an overnight stay but not a relocation of residence. These moves, although not as spectacular as migration, are nonetheless essential to the maintenance of the adaptation. Two of the major kinds of trips among the Shah Nawazi are integral to their multi-resource adaptation: in both cases, the trips, taking place during the spring, are from the pastorally oriented herding camps to the location of cultivation.

The first type of trip is from the camp, during this period out in the pastures with the animals, to the areas of grain cultivation. Individuals with interests, either through ownership or through wage labor, in grain cultivation must perform agricultural tasks or else oversee the irrigation. In the latter case, periods up to 24 hours must be spent "on the water" in order to see that the crops are properly irrigated. As both the pastoral and grain resources are on the Sarhad, and the location of pasturage differs from time to time and year to year, the distances from the camps to the areas of cultivation vary considerably. In some cases, one day journeys satisfy the requirements; in other cases, long distances must be covered and overnight stays are necessitated. During portions of the spring of 1968, members of the Ja'far camping group with agricultural interests at Shagbone had to travel 30 miles each way and spent one or more nights at the area of cultivation.

The second type of trip is from the herding camps on the Sarhad to the date groves at Mashkel. If the date palms are to bear a substantial load of dates, the palms must be pollinated by human labor. For this purpose, a body of men from each camp left the Sarhad, made the 8 day move to Mashkel, and remained there for a number of weeks performing this task. In the meantime, the herding camps, with a skeleton crew of adult males, continued on their "pastoral" migrations on the Sarhad. Other kinds of trips can be cited, such as those entailed by raiding in prepacification days and those presently entailed in migrant labor.

While the trips among the Shah Nawazi are "trans-resource" moves, trips play a crucial part in the pastoralism of many other peoples. Quite often, the herds are sent separately into cattle or camel camps with young men or adult men to look after them. The mobility of herds with lightly equipped shepherds is greater than that of domestic establishments, and the herds can be sent distances to make use of pastures unavailable if they were tied to the residences. Karimojong cattle camps (Dyson-Hudson 1966), Somali camel camps (Lewis 1961) and Kababish camel camps (Asad 1970) all operate independently of domestic camps, for at least certain periods of the year, and the trips entailed in these operations are distinct from migrations of the domestic establishments.

Such trips depend, to an extent, upon the same kinds of material support, such as transportation of people and goods, that are necessary for migration. But they must be considered as important as migration for the adaptation, which would not be possible without them. In most cases, these trips are predicated upon and reflect a division of labor within the household, or between households, and thus underlie the need for a number of workers, usually sons, within each domestic group or else extra-household economic alliances to provide the necessary personnel.

To return to the initial point, it is clear that ideal-typical conceptualization of pastoral nomadism, as represented in such distinctions as "pure nomad," "semi-nomad," and "transhumant" so distorts through oversimplification and misrepresentation as to be less than useful. The appropriate questions to be asked about "pastoral nomads" deal with logically independent dimensions which vary in degree along each continuum. Our task, of course, is to relate empirically, rather than on an *a priori* "logical" basis, the various positions on the different dimensions. Before we can attempt this, it is necessary to establish the positions of different peoples on the different dimensions, by asking to what extent each engages in the exploitation of non-pastoral resources, and by asking what part nomadism plays in the adaptation.

REFERENCES CITED

Asad, Talal
1970—The Kababish Arabs. London: Hurst.
Barth, Frederik
1961—Nomads of south Persia. New York: Humanities.
Briggs, L. Cabot
1960—Tribes of the Sahara. Cambridge: Harvard University Press.
Capot-Rey, R.
1962—The present state of nomadism in the Sahara. *In* The problems of the arid zone. Paris: UNESCO.
Cohen, Yehudi A.
1968—Culture as adaptation. *In* Man in adaptation: the cultural present. Yehudi A. Cohen, ed., Chicago: Aldine Pub. Co.
Dyson-Hudson, Neville
1966—Karimojong politics. Oxford: Clarendon Press.
Evans-Pritchard, E. E.
1940—The Nuer. Oxford: Clarendon Press.
Jacobs, Alan H.
1965—African pastoralists: some general remarks. Anthropological Quarterly 38:144–154.
Lee, Robert and Irven De Vore, eds.
1968—Man the hunter. Chicago: Aldine Pub. Co.
Lewis, I. M.
1961—A pastoral democracy. London: Oxford University Press.
Salzman, Philip C.
1967—Political organization among nomadic peoples. Proceedings of the American Philosophical Society 111:115–131.
1969—Multi-resource nomadism in Iranian Baluchistan. Presented at the annual meeting of the American Anthropological Association, New Orleans.
1970—Movement and adaptation among the Yarahmadzai Baluch. Manuscript.
Srivastava, Ram
1958—The Bhotia nomads and their Indo-Tibetan trade. Journal of the University of Saugar 7:1–22.
Wulff, Hans E.
1966—The traditional crafts of Persia. Cambridge: M.I.T. Press.

"Per man hour of energy expended," agriculture is almost always more productive than horticulture or herding because the techniques involved—irrigation, the use of fertilizers, often the plow and draft animals—greatly increase the land's potential yield.

Employing a complex system of terracing and erosion control, composting and crop rotation, fields close to the household of the Kofyar hill farmers of Nigeria are worked intensively almost all year round. In fields farther away, shifting cultivation is the more important means of achieving soil regeneration. Netting's description of these West African farmers' adaptation to their environment, in a study of Kofyar cultural ecology from which this selection is taken, links their high population density and a land-holding system that stresses individual proprietorship to a pattern of sociopolitical organization that renders widespread political integration unnecessary. Kofyar religious practices are similarly localized.

But recently these traditionally autonomous hill farmers have begun to grow crops for cash, a shift that seems certain to affect their centuries-old autonomy.

Intensive Agriculture in the Kofyar Hills

Robert McC. Netting

Kofyar agriculture is based on the intensive cultivation of a clearly defined land area adjoining or encircling the residence of the farmer. The Kofyar refer to this plot as *mar koepang,* and I have used the literal translation "homestead field" throughout. Intensive agriculture is a system by which soil fertility is continuously maintained or restored, allowing successive food crops to be produced with little or no intervening fallow period. This may take place naturally as a result of the periodic deposit of nutrient elements by water or wind or through human intervention. Intensive agriculture differs from shifting or swidden cultivation "in which impermanent clearings are cropped for shorter periods in years than they are fallowed" (Conklin 1961:27).[1] The shifting pattern is by far the more usual in Africa, and some of its variations have been described among the Bemba (Richards 1939), the Zande (De Schlippe 1956), and the Tiv (Bohannan 1954). Allan (1965) has provided a detailed survey of several systems in East and Central Africa. The Kofyar also practice a type of shifting cultivation in bush fields, *margoon,* which must be regularly fallowed, but their primary dependence for staple food crops is on the intensively worked homestead farm.

I suspect that the combination of intensive and extensive or shifting cultivation is a very widespread practice, providing as it does for adjustment to differing soil conditions, plant requirements, and needs for the care and protection of the growing crop. With a variety of crops and field types, the farmer is also protected against total loss due to unpredictable climatic fluctuations. Examples of the combination of cultivation systems include the "house" and "far" farms of the Nuba (Nadel 1947:16), the intensively cultivated *lai lo* and the *zo lo* swidden fields of the Chin (Lehman 1963:54), and the valley gardens and mountain swiddens of the Kapauku (Pospisil 1963:87ff.). The infield-outfield arrangements found in northern Europe may be a continuation of a similar pattern already present in the Neolithic period (Evans 1956:229).

Agricultural Technology

The farming implements of the Kofyar are few and simple. The major tool is a typical Sudanic hoe (*can*) with a spade-shaped iron blade set with a tang into a short crooked wooden handle. Hoes are locally forged and were formerly items of considerable value. The iron was smelted by the Sura on the high plateau in furnaces whose remains still exist. The hoe blade is about one foot in length and longer than it is wide. The cultivator holds the hoe handle in both hands and swings his body from the hips, driving the blade into the soil in front of him and pulling it toward him. By changing the angle of entry it is possible to dig a deep furrow or merely skim off the topsoil, and this latter technique is especially useful in manipulating thin, rocky soil and building ridges. Earth can be lifted and accurately dumped by a slight motion of the wrists. Smaller Hausa-type hoes are sometimes used for weeding on the plain. The only other tools of importance are the ax (*sep*) with a long, narrow, iron blade inserted in a heavy knobbed wood handle, and a small, curved, iron-bladed sickle used for reaping small grain and cutting forage grass.

Source: From Robert McC. Netting, *Hill Farmers of Nigeria* (Seattle: University of Washington Press, 1968). Used by permission of the publisher and the author.

[1] The distinction between intensive and shifting agriculture applies only to the usual duration of cultivation of particular fields and does not necessarily refer to the amount of labor expended or the permanency of settlement in an area. The same contrast has been made by Hatt between semi-agriculturalists and full agriculturalists without the plow (Curwen and Hatt 1953:246) and by Goldschmidt (1959:193) between horticulturalists and agriculturalists. I have consistently referred to Kofyar intensive agriculture as farming rather than gardening because of its emphasis on cereals rather than root crops or vegetables (cf. Barrau 1958:79).

Most cutting of millet and sorghum heads is done with old knife or spear blades. A digging stick is used only to harvest sweet potatoes.

Food-processing equipment consists of tree-trunk mortars and log pestles (*shing*), woven winnowing trays (*koetut*), and grinding stones (*fin*), along with a wide variety of wooden bowls, clay pots, and coiled baskets. Food is stored in jars, cylindrical mud-walled granaries both outside and inside huts, baskets, and calabashes. A heavy wooden drying stage for storing harvested grain is a fixture in most homestead courtyards and provides a shady shelter for many household activities. With the exception of some pots, these items are undecorated and purely utilitarian. They differ only in detail from the tool kit of neighboring peoples and indeed of Sudanic agriculturalists in general.

Intensive agriculture is only possible when techniques are available for the conservation and periodic enrichment of the soil. In hill areas especially, erosion can quickly strip the slopes of soil once the natural tree growth and grass have been removed. Perhaps the most impressive feature of the Kofyar countryside is the way in which systems of terraces (*pang*) have been built up the hills to stabilize the soil and provide a series of stepped, level benches suitable for farming. Retaining walls (*fukoepang*) of rough stone laid without mortar and rising one to six feet anchor the terraces. Smaller walls are used in the bush fields, while high walls are erected close to the homestead to provide wider unobstructed areas for intensive farming. Terraces are almost always at right angles to the slope, and they vary in height and distance apart according to the existing contour. The building of walls serves not only to create surfaces that resist washing but also to secure a greater depth of soil and usefully consolidate the stones that litter the slopes. Oil palm trees planted on the edges of terraces further stabilize the earth.

To questions about the age of terraces, most Kofyar say only that they have been there since before anyone can remember and that no one knows the names of the builders. Stone wall building is still practiced when terraces must be repaired or corrals built, and a few old men once personally engaged in major terracing around their own homesteads. The method was to build up a stone wall leaning slightly in from the vertical toward the hill slope. After the wall had risen a foot or two, earth was hoed down from the slope above to fill in the space behind it. If a higher wall was required, the process could be repeated. The work seems usually to have been done by the owner of the farm and his household with occasional help from near neighbors. Terraces were built or improved, bit by bit, over a period of years. Large groups of people worked together only on one-day repair parties.

Terracing alone is not the final solution to problems of conservation and water control. Since all of the Kofyar rainfall of forty to sixty inches comes within six months and some storms may deposit up to two inches a day for several consecutive days, runoff and potential erosion are a danger even to level land surfaces. Many crops will not flourish if they remain submerged for any length of time, yet they may also require substantial moisture in the soil to tide them over from the last rains in early October until harvest time in December. A characteristic African solution to the problem of keeping crops above the standing water resulting from heavy rains is to create ridges or mounds. This has the added advantage in areas of thin soil as the Kofyar hills of concentrating top soil in ridges around the roots of the growing crops. By shaping the eight-to sixteen-inch-high ridges (*sagan*) into closed rectangles from four to six feet long, and two to four feet wide, the Kofyar create both high ground for planting and a series of enclosed hollows (*ciil*) which trap water. The system, called basin listing or tie ridging by agronomists, is used on top of hill terraces and on intensively farmed plains fields. A very similar practice has been noted among the Nuba by Nadel (1947:16). Its utility is demonstrated after a rain when fields appear checkered with pools, divided from each other by earth ridges. The growing plants on the ridges are not inundated, and water is allowed to sink gradually into the soil both to furnish future moisture and to prevent destructive runoff. Hill streams clear quickly after a rain since they contain little silt. Their beds are U-shaped, often six to eight feet below banks that are perpendicular and uneroded. Gullying is very rare in the cultivated areas of Kofyar. That erosion would take place if unchecked is seen in bush paths descending hills, which frequently form watercourses in the wet season and are scoured down to the bare rock.

Ridging may be adapted to varying topographic conditions and the differing needs of food crops. At the foot of a hill that may be terraced and basin-listed in the usual way, the slope becomes increasingly gentle, and water may have a tendency to collect. Such an area, termed *jagat* by the Kofyar, is sodden or marshy, and the problem is one of drainage rather than retention of moisture. To farm such land, ridges are built parallel to the contour of the slope. The ridges are not continuous, and regularly spaced gaps are left which form ditches leading down the hill. The ditch floor is lower than the depressions between the parallel ridges, so that water does not stand. The drainage ditches are spaced closely enough together so that no single one will carry a large volume of water and thus deepen its channel. The height of the ridges depends largely on the dampness of the spot, and where a heavy volume of water is expected, ridges are shortened and built up until they become mounds as high as two and a half feet. Some areas at the foot of the hills are as level as table tops and must cope with a great deal of rain and ground water in the first part of the wet season and a growing scarcity of water toward the end. Farmers of Dimmuk and adjoining Kwalla, where this problem is acute, raise two- to three-foot earth ridges around their homestead fields and plant the staple sorghum (guinea corn), millet, and beans on large mounds or hummocks that keep the roots clear of water when young but allow them to tap the stored ground moisture as they mature.

Some crops require little moisture and can survive on relatively infertile land. Acha, or hungry rice (*Digitaria exilis*), is a very small grain whose seed head resembles that of its relative, the common crab grass. It is sown broadcast rather than being planted only on ridges. Small ridges three to four inches high are made parallel to the direction of the slope, and there are no cross ridges along the edges of the terraces. If basins were made, the acha which grew in the standing water would not do well. Consequently, every effort is made to keep water from being confined. That soil nutrients are thereby lost to runoff is known to the Kofyar. Their usual explanation for exhausted or leached white (*piya*) soil is that *am mang*, "the water took it." But they also realize that acha grows on land that would not support other crops and is well adapted to bush fallowing where long continued production is not expected.

On swampy plots a farmer has the option of employing the ridge and ditch system described above or attempting to retain all rain water and use the resulting paddy for growing wet rice. On the plain at the mouths of narrow, steep-sided valleys cutting back into the hills, Kofyar farmers heap up high continuous ridges around their rice plots. They depend on conserving rainfall that does not sink readily into damp impervious ground rather than irrigating with impoundments and ditches. Some cultivators combine the two systems, growing standard food crops in drained patches and using the ditch bottoms for rice. Road repairs in the Kofyar area must be delayed until after the rice harvest because the ditches on either side of the roads are planted in rice.

The example of practical engineering in the building of terraces and the adaptation of different ridging techniques to varying conditions is striking. One expert, after describing the more modest terraces and ridges of the neighboring Angas people, called them a "perfect demonstration of theoretical anti-erosion measures carried out on a wide and successful scale over a period of centuries" (Fairbairn 1943:190). Professional agriculturalists have told me that the traditional methods of soil conservation practiced by the Kofyar could not be improved upon. It is obvious, however, that such extensive efforts at erosion control and water conservation would be economically feasible only if the land so treated could produce heavily and on a sustained basis. The Kofyar area lacks alluvial plains or any other source of natural soil regeneration. The deficiency is supplied by regular application of organic material. The staple cereals of early millet (*maar*) and sorghum (*swa*) are grown together with cowpeas (*oeroem*) in the homestead farm. All three are interplanted every year on the same plot. Average hill land can support only a year or two of sorghum alone before yields decline markedly. Yet high production has been maintained for generations on the same homestead farms without soil exhaustion. Fertility is sustained at high level by annual applications of compost and animal dung.

In every area where stone is available the Kofyar build sturdy circular enclosures from ten to fifteen feet in diameter and up to eight feet deep. Within such corrals (*bit*), which are a fixture of every homestead, goats are staked out each day for the entire length of the growing season. Food for the animals in the form of grass and leafy branches is brought every day by the household members. The forage is always more than the goats can eat. It builds up in layers mixed with goat dung and urine from

April, when the crops sprout, through the December harvest. At night, the goats are penned in a hut where dung also collects, so that for nine months of the year every available bit of manure is retained.

When the corral is emptied just before the rains, a substantial quantity of fertilizer (*zuk*) can be returned to the land. In one case the compost from a filled corral 15 feet 8 inches in diameter and 7 feet 7 inches deep, with a capacity of 1,452 cubic feet, was distributed in 388 basket loads over .4 acre. Even the small corral of a relatively poor household may yield more than 400 cubic feet of compost. Added to this is the manure from the goat hut and from other buildings housing sheep or horses which graze outside the village during the day. Large walled corrals are also built for cows, but they are not stall-fed, and their dung simply washes out through a drain onto nearby fields. People in plains villages where building stone is lacking make low enclosures of logs around pits where goats are tied. Yet the hill dwellers seem generally to collect greater quantities of compost, perhaps because unfarmed slopes around the villages provide an accessible source of fodder. One of the major reasons given for the borrowing of livestock is that this provides manure for fertilizer. Individuals also customarily defecate on the homestead field at some distance from their huts. In Latok where the land is overworked and organic material is at a premium, round stone enclosures (*dann es*) are built for the collection of nightsoil.

With their knowledge of the value of fertilization, the Kofyar have readily adapted to a symbiotic relationship with Fulani herders. These pastoral nomads have only recently appeared in the area, which previously was barred to them by tsetse fly infestation (Stenning 1957). The Fulani are paid in cash and given free labor in carrying loads and erecting shelter in exchange for camping with their cattle on bush fields. This allows plots that were formerly farmed by shifting cultivation to come into intensive use. The Kofyar's acceptance and indeed competition for the benefits of manuring contrasts with the active hostility of the Birom, a tribe on the high plateau, whose people contended that animal dung was injurious to crops (Perham 1946:197–98).

Fertilization is not confined to the use of the dung-cum-decayed-vegetation compost. When bush fields are being prepared for groundnut cultivation, the first step is the pulling of all grass and brush. This material is given a few days to dry before the field is hoed. Piles of brush are placed here and there on the newly made ridges and fired to provide beds of ashes for the planting. Every bit of wood ash from cooking fires in the homestead is also saved in small huts built for the purpose. Baskets of powdery gray ash are taken to the fields by women when groundnuts are one to two months old and a handful is sprinkled on each plant. The same treatment is given to sweet potatoes. Small seedbeds for the sprouting of eleusine are prepared on spots where corn stalks and other agricultural refuse has been burned. The seeds may be mixed with goat dung before being stirred into the soil. Remaining stalks and leaves of plants such as maize, groundnuts, and early millet are carefully returned to the soil after harvest. In acha fields, grass and weeds are not burned but rather uprooted and buried under the small ridge. The Kofyar say that acha benefits from decomposing vegetation rather than ash. They are also aware that acha grown in rich soil or manured land would not do well. Evidently the plant is adapted to rather poor soils, and when it is given extra nutriment it grows too quickly and its weak stalk cannot support the seed head.

In bush fields where only wood ash and turned-under vegetation are used, the productive period of a field is lengthened by crop rotation. This is usually an alternation between groundnuts and acha. Hill practice is to begin with a light sowing of acha the year in which the land is first cleared, followed by a full sowing of acha the next year, and groundnuts alternating with acha from then on. Since groundnuts are harvested early, some farmers may follow them with late millet transplanted from seedbeds (*sunggul*) and thus secure two crops from a field in a single year. People are aware that a field where acha is repeatedly planted is more quickly exhausted (*bes piya*) than one where the leguminous nitrogen-fixing groundnut is cultivated in rotation with other crops. Bush fields in the hills may be used for six to nine years, depending on the length of the preceding fallow period, but the greater pressure on plains land near villages means that fallows are shortened from more than fifteen years to less than ten. Plains fields are said to produce well for only four years at a time. Sorghum may be planted once or twice at the beginning of a cropping cycle, but its greater demands on the soil restrict its use in bush field rotation schemes.

The Farming Calendar: Crops and Techniques

Kofyar calendrical notions are of an approximate nature, and the most frequently mentioned periods of time are the four seasons. The early rains, called *lok,* extend from late March through June and are followed by the later rains, *pas,* from July through September. *Waap* refers to the October to mid-December dry season when the harmattan begins to blow, and the hot, dry period of late December to March, which extends up to the coming of rain, is known as *lugun.* Names exist for the lunar months, but they are little used, and even those older men charged with scheduling ceremonies that fall in a certain moon occasionally make mistakes concerning them.[2]

The Kofyar farming year begins its annual cycle in March (see Fig. 1). Four and a half or five months have already passed with very little precipitation, and the first stirring of the soft, rain-bearing south winds has been felt. It is time to clean rubbish from the homestead fields and prepare them for planting. Every household must empty its corral, spreading the compost on the old homestead field and on any extensions of it that are being brought into intensive cultivation. This may be followed by a preliminary working (*pyan*) of the field in which the soil is merely turned over with a hoe or small ridges are made. Though it is well known that this early hoeing encourages quick growth, it is often bypassed on hill farms. There the compost remains in piles until the first cultivation mixes it with the soil. Farmers in the Latok area customarily burn field rubbish in heaps so that the resulting mounds of ash may be used as seedbeds for eleusine. There is usually very little refuse remaining in homestead fields by the end of the dry season. Crop plants are grown so thickly and cultivated so carefully that practically no weed growth can take hold. Sorghum stalks are collected and stacked for use as cooking fuel. With the coming of the dry season, the remaining green plants wither, and there is not enough moisture to allow new growth to get started. Consequently, the farm around the compound is so barren as to constitute an effective firebreak when the long bush grass is being burned.

Planting in the Kofyar area is not geared to any signs in the heavens or the wild vegetation, but to the single fact of rain. The first shower at the close of the dry months sends women out with seeds of pumpkins and other cucurbits for planting in scattered hills ten or twelve feet apart. As their name, *tokmang,* "the bringer of sauce," implies, pumpkins are valued for their quick-sprouting leaves which make a favorite sauce for the staple cereal porridge. (For English names of crops, botanical designations, Kofyar and Hausa names, see Table 1.) If the rain has been a heavy one, early millet, sorghum, and maize may also be planted. A soaking rain is required to sprout these crops, and they may be planted whenever it comes, whether before the middle of March or well into April.

Planting is done with a hoe handle. Its point is used to open a shallow hole, seeds are drib-

[2] Various Kofyar informants gave either twelve or thirteen names for the lunar months in one year. The names relate to the important activities pursued at that time, and there was general agreements as to the order of the months. The year begins with the first rains, which herald the start of farming.

Month	*Kofyar name*	*Activity*
	fungfung	Preparing homestead field, possibly planting
March		*maap* celebrated
	voevigir	Drinking the sweet juice of locust bean pods
April	*wuplayi*	Big rains, planting
May	*ɓangɓalang*	First heavy work of hoeing the homestead farm
June	*ɓiyel*	Planting cowpeas
July	*kelele*	Harvesting and drying early millet
August	*moeka*	Hungry time, look for small yams
September	*fwap*	Heavy rains
October	*saa*	Dancing *gala,* transplanting late millet
November	*tarshit*	Moon of cutting roofing grass, paying bride price
December	*kwakwa*	Dancing *kwakwa* on the plains, harvesting acha
January	*tardiip*	Moon of harvest
February	*canyang*	Cutting guinea corn stalks

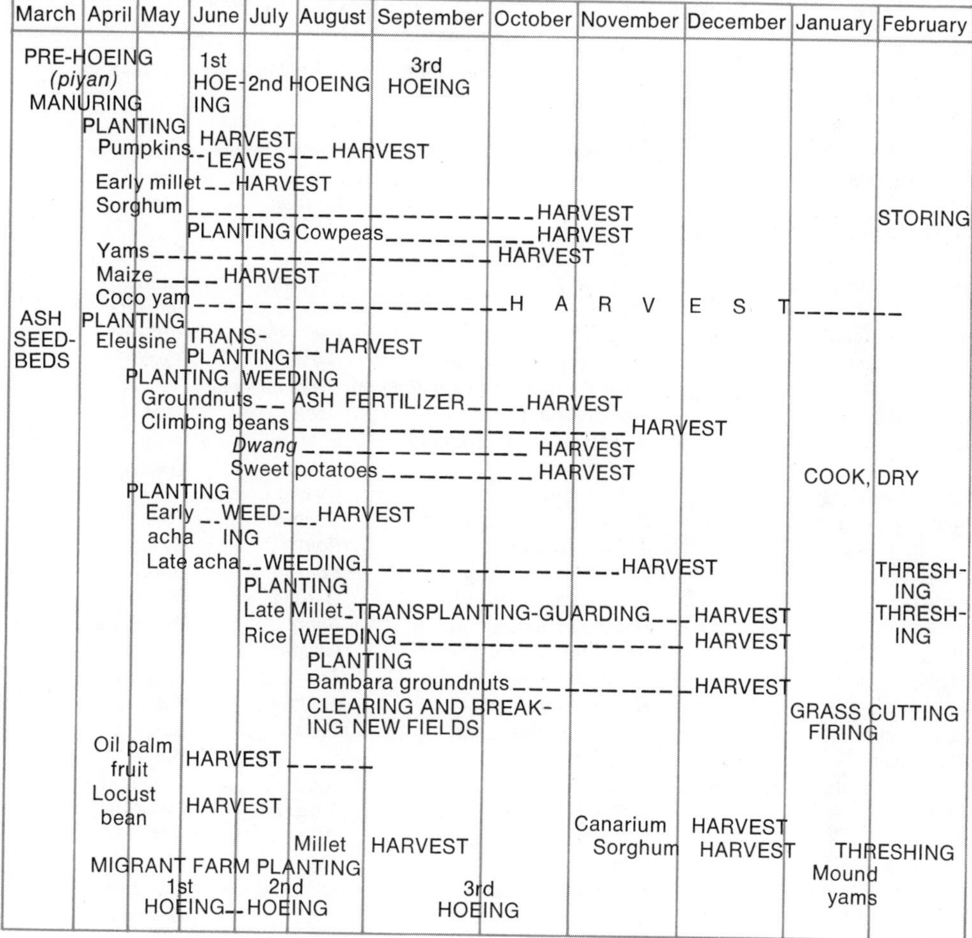

Figure 1. Farming calendar.

bled in from the left hand, and the hole is covered with an outward push of the hoe handle, all in a series of rapid motions. Small hills are hurriedly hoed up to receive the millet seeds. These may be in the middle of the previous year's rectangular ridge or, where mounds are used, in the place where a bite has been hoed from the side of the old mound to start a new adjoining heap. Ten to fifteen millet grains are put into each hill. This allows for transplanting if some seeds fail to germinate or are burned out as shoots. Only about half of the entire homestead field is seeded with millet. The rest may be filled with transplanted shoots. Enough seed is always saved so that another planting is possible if the first fails through lack of rain. Sorghum, which grows more slowly than millet, is planted in small holes scratched on the sides of old ridges. Six to ten seeds are dropped at a time in holes two to three feet apart.

Maize seeds are sprouted in water for two days before planting. Where maize is a staple, it is planted two grains to a hole about two feet apart. More usually it is a secondary crop, planted sparsely here and there about the field. At about the same time, the tiny seeds of eleusine are mixed with goat dung and stirred into the ashes of the seedbed mounds. Yams, like eleusine, are a minor crop in the hills and traditional plains villages. Yam ridges may be made shortly after the first planting, and they usually border the manured portion of the homestead field. About six inches of topsoil is taken from a rectangular area perhaps eight by five feet and piled into a surrounding ridge one and a half to two feet high. Yams are not

Table 1. *Domesticated Plant Names**

English Names	Botanical Designations	Kofyar	Hausa
Sorghum, guinea corn, kaffir corn	*Sorghum vulgare*	*Swa*	*Dawa*
Early millet, bulrush millet	*Pennisetum typhoideum*	*Maar*	*Gero*
Late millet, pearl millet (?)	*Pennisetum spicatum*	*Kas*	*Dauro*
Maize, corn	*Zea mays*	*Swapas*	*Masara*
Acha, acha grass, fonio, hungry rice	*Digitaria exilis*	*Goezuk*	*Acha*
Eleusine, finger millet	*Eleusine corocana*	*Koetung*	*Tamba*
Rice	*Oryza sativa*	*Kapa*	*Shinkafa*
Sesame, beniseed	*Sesamum indicum*	*Lem, koedul*	*Ridi*
Coco yam, taro	*Colocasia esculentum* (Also *Xanthosoma sagittifolium*)	*Gwan* / *Gwan nassara*	*Gwaza*
Sweet potato	*Ipomoea batatas*	*Doeku*	*Dankali*
Yam	*Dioscorea alata, rotundata*	*Shim*	*Doya*
Rizga	*Coleus dazo*	*Vuu*	*Risga*
Hausa potato	*Coleus dysentericus*	*Dwang*	*Tumuku*
Potato yam, bulbil-bearing yam	*Dioscorea bulbifera*	*Doetwon*	*Doyar bisa*
Groundnut, peanut	*Arachis hypogea*	*Kom*	*Gyada*
Bambara groundnut	*Voandzeia subterranea*	*Komzugut*	*Gurjiya*
Cowpea	*Vigna unguiculata* (?)	*Oeroem*	*Wake*
Lima bean	*Phaseolus lunatus*	*Bala*	*Wake, waken ankwai*
String bean	*Phaseolus vulgaris*	*Chagar*	
Pumpkin	*Cucurbita pepo* (?)	*Tokmang*	*Kabewa*
Okra, gumbo	*Hibiscus esculentus*	*Tokla*	*Kubewa*
Red pepper	*Capsicum frutescens*	*Shita*	*Barkono*
Bitter tomato	*Solanum incanum*	*Kul*	*Gauta*
Gourd, Calabash, bottle gourd	*Lagenaria vulgaris*	*Jang*	*Duma, kwarya*
Oil palm	*Elaeis guineensis*	*Mwor bang*	*Kwakwa*
Canarium	*Canarium schweinfurthii*	*Paat*	*Itile*
Locust bean	*Parkia filicoidea*	*Mes*	*Dorowa*
Mango	*Mangifera indica*	*Mangoro*	*Mangoro*
Pawpaw	*Carica papaya*	*Viyap*	*Gwanda*

* For plant names and botanical designations, I am dependent largely on Dalziel (1937). Uncertain attributions are question marked. H. L. Li identified specimen seeds of *Phaseolus lunatus*.

manured, and their plot is usually changed from year to year. The potato yam called *doetwon,* which has edible bodies both under the soil and on climbing vines, is planted on similar ridges that may even be slightly higher and are manured on top. Yams and *doetwon* are both provided with cut tree branches to climb. Coco yams may be planted in conical heaps about two feet high. These are usually a more important source of food than true yams. Each heap is capped with straw and dead grass, both for their fertilizing effect and as a protection against the mound being washed away by heavy rains.

The first hoeing (*ar,* "to bite") takes place from six weeks to two months after planting, when the shoots are eight to twelve inches high. At this time, millet may be thinned and transplanted evenly over the field. The hoe digs six to nine inches deep, turning over the soil, burying the weeds, hilling the infant millet plants, and banking the edges of the terraces. No ridges are built at this time. Along the stony borders of the terraces, eleusine may be transplanted because it can flourish without much depth of soil. The initial hoeing is even more thorough in those villages where maize and coco yams replace millet and sorghum as homestead crops. There the land is dug (*fus,* "to stab") to a depth of one and a half feet, with workers advancing in a line. The coco yams that have remained in the ground from the last season are separated from their clumps, their new leaves cut off, and the corms placed about six inches apart and six to eight inches below the surface. The hoer passes earth between his legs and occasionally turns to plant the coco yams in the earth that piles up behind him. Extra coco yams are piled to one side, a few for eating but most of them sprouted and no longer of any use. Maize plants are carefully skirted or occasionally moved a few feet to a better location. Cucurbits and okra are also noted and preserved in place. It is at this time that climbing lima and string beans are planted on the ridges bounding the field or on terrace edges. The bean vines form an attractive fence bordering the path as they climb the branching tree limbs that are later put in place as supports.

Groundnut planting may begin as soon as the homestead farm has been completed, and work goes on from mid-May into June. The crop requires strong sunlight and seems to thrive in thin soil. Stony unshaded bush land that appears exhausted can still produce sizable crops of groundnuts. Excessive dampness in the soil causes the groundnuts to rot before they are ripe. Unmanured areas near the homesteads may be planted in groundnuts first before the larger bush fields one-half mile or more from the villages are farmed. Where there is sufficient soil, ridges are thrown up averaging one foot in height and one to two feet in width. The basin listing rectangles are about five feet across from the midpoint of one ridge to the midpoint of the parallel one, and six to eight feet long. The long sides of the rectangles are parallel to the slope of the hill and at right angles to the edges of the terraces. As the field is hoed, old ridges are divided in half, part of the earth being pulled to the left and part to the right. The new ridges are thus midway between those of the preceding year. They are formed of the tops of old ridges combined with the topsoil washed into the basin. All grass is turned under in this process, so that almost no greenery is visible after hoeing. The short-bladed Sudanic hoe, which can be used almost parallel to the surface of the ground, is an efficient tool for lifting off the topsoil and concentrating it on ridges.

Once the ridges have been completed, seeds are planted by dropping them two at a time from the left hand into small holes opened and covered by the right hand with a single continuous motion. Holes are made on alternate sides of the ridge top nine to twelve inches apart. All seeds have previously been shelled and inspected, and any shrunken or moldy kernels removed. In some areas acha may be sown in the basins surrounded by groundnut ridges. Even before groundnuts are planted, an early variety of acha called *napiya* will be put in on different bush fields. Since this type grows in poor soil and is ready for harvest by August or September, it is particularly valued by plains villages. Acha tides over the family for several months until the sorghum is ripe.

In intervals between work on groundnuts in June, minor root crops are often planted. Each woman and child old enough to hoe may have a sweet potato plot consisting of ridges or mounds up to two feet high. These are planted with vine cuttings from tubers that were never dug the preceding year. Pieces of vine are pushed into the soil on the top and sides of the ridge, where they take root. Smaller ridges about the same size as those used for groundnuts are made for a little plant called *vuu,* which has reddish-skinned roots about the size and shape of wrinkled fingers. *Vuu,* like sweet potatoes, does best in a sunny location and is fertilized only with ashes. Broad flat ridges separated by shallow channels hold *dwang,* a black-skinned oval tuber looking and tasting like a very small Irish potato. *Dwang* requires manure or the natural richness of bottom land near a stream.

Among the major homestead crops, are a number of kitchen garden varieties grown principally for seasoning. Most hill households grow enough capsicum red peppers for their own use, with perhaps a small surplus for trade. The same is true of the *kul,* a bitter tomatolike vegetable which gives a viscous quality to sauce. The black seeds of a hibiscus called *gogor,* coming from bright red capsules, are familiar on the plains and are also used for sauce. Leaves, fruit, and seeds of the cucurbits are all eaten, and the okra pod is used both fresh and dried. A small gourdlike plant called *ser* is grown for its seeds, which are collected after the pulp has rotted away in an underground pit. Sesame (called beniseed in Nigeria)—red, white, and black—is a popular seasoning for meat and porridge, and it is frequently interplanted with sorghum. Most homestead farms have a few plants of tall, woody cotton whose fiber is spun by both men and women of the household.

Early millet grows at an astonishing rate, beginning to head toward the end of the second month, with the tallest stalks already ten feet high. With proper rainfall, the bulrushlike heads may be fifteen to twenty-four inches long by early July and ready for reaping. Stalks are pushed over with the foot, and the seed head is severed by being pressed against a knife held in the hand. The millet is collected in a courtyard or on a flat rocky outcropping with a circular stone wall and there dried. It is at this time that the seed for the following year is selected and bound in special bundles. Seed heads of outstanding fullness and uniformity are similarly put aside at the time of maize and sorghum harvests.

In those parts of the Kofyar hills where the late acha is a staple crop, work begins on the bush fields during the latter half of June. The farmers first pull the grass and weeds that have grown on the terraces and in the cracks of the stone walls. The uprooted vegetation is laid in a row between two old ridges and buried under a light cover of earth to form the basis of a new ridge. The low ridges for acha all run in the same direction with no cross-ridging. On an unterraced field the continuous ridges run across the slope. This form of hoeing is called *tal,* and the actual sowing, *fu,* is done broadcast by men. The tiny acha seed is mixed with condiment seeds such as *gogor* or *koedul* and then scattered with wide sweeping motions of the hand. Sometimes the seed is thrown sharply at the sides of a calabash so that it rebounds in various directions onto the field. Following the sowers come women with leafy branches or palm fronds sweeping (*bwur*) the earth haphazardly to cover the seed and hide it from birds. People hope for a rain shortly after planting so that the acha will rapidly sprout and take root.

The second major hoeing (*fus yit*) of the homestead farm may begin in July, but it is sometimes put off until August. The millet stalks and weeds are buried under ridges running at right angles to the edges of the terraces. Transverse ridges are also made to support the growing sorghum and form the rectangular basin which conserves moisture and halts runoff. At the same time cowpeas are planted, and they soon form a dense ground cover.

When new bush fields must be opened in the hills, the heavy work of clearing takes place in late July. Most of the second-growth trees are felled with axes except for an occasional one left to give shade to field guards and workers. Trees are cut off about three feet above the ground, or, if they are very large, the farmer merely climbs them and lops off branches. Felled timber and brush are piled along the edges of terraces to keep the newly uncovered soil from washing away. The soil is rapidly turned over but not ridged, and lightly sown in acha. A significant crop is not expected the first year, which is called *sak gagar,* "farming the fallow." During the next dry season the brush is burned, leaving ash for later working into the soil. The second year, *tal tuk,* should see the field in normal production.

By mid-July the first maize is ready for eating. Maize is hoed twice, the second time in late June. Some is eaten fresh as roasting ears, but most of the crop is allowed to dry and harden in the field. Husked ears are either put by in baskets for immediate use or braided into bundles and hung from house rafters.

On the plains, rice must be planted in late July in paddies, ditches, and flood plains. The hill people from Bong village northward plant their late millet in seedbeds at the same time. The ground is merely turned over, and no ridges are made, but in a particularly wet patch depressions may be hollowed out here and there to collect excess water. The third hoeing (*tanggon*) of the homestead farm comes in September, when the sorghum is already beginning to form seed. It is not as arduous as previous cultivations, seldom requiring more than eight days of work, and its completion marks the end of the heavy work of the agricultural year for many Kofyar.

The last crop to go into the ground is the Bambara groundnuts, which are planted in rectangular ridges during August. Weeding goes on in August and September, with a small hoe used for groundnuts, and coco yams and acha fields weeded by hand. Late millet grown to eight to twelve inches by October is ready for transplanting. New rectangular ridges are made for this purpose even in fields where groundnut ridges already exist. The seedlings are stuck into the ridge on either side and down the center, forming three rows. Each plant is placed at an angle approaching the horizontal because it is said that the leaves of seedlings pointing straight up would quickly wither in the hot sun.

The early varieties of acha and eleusine are mature by August or September. Acha is reaped with a short curved sickle and rubbed between the hands to separate the seeds from the stems. It is threshed in the field rather than being initially stored on the stalk as are most grains. Groundnuts can be pulled in October. The plants are loosened from the soil by a hoe driven in under them. In a shady corner of the field the nuts are plucked from the roots and then carried in baskets to flat rocks where they are dried for storage. The groundnut stems are redistributed around the field to be turned under at the next hoeing. Harvest begins in earnest during November, with the heads of sorghum being cut and brought back in bundles to the homestead drying rack (*par*). Cowpeas are collected at approximately the same time. Root crops are ready, and people begin to eat coco yams, sweet potatoes, *dwang vuu,* yams, and cassava. Most of these are left in the ground, which is by now quite dry, and gathered from day to day according to need. Sweet potatoes are dug first with a stick, getting the tubers near the surface that might otherwise be dug out by goats. Later in the season the entire mound may be destroyed with a hoe to get at all the remaining potatoes. Sweet potatoes do not keep well in the ground, so effective storage for wet season use is only possible by slicing and sun-drying the tubers (cf. Johnston 1958:119). Coco yams are uncovered with a hoe. String beans are picked (*te*) and eaten while still green in August and September, but the larger reddish bean is allowed to dry on the vine before being gathered in December.

Late acha ripens in the latter part of November and is reaped with its associated sesame. The late acha is bundled into headloads and returned to the homestead for drying. Rice is reaped in a similar manner during December. Late millet in bush fields must be guarded from monkeys during its last months. Harvesting of late millet begins in December and may extend until after the first of the year. The seed heads and about twelve inches of stalk are cut off, using an old knife blade, and when a handful is collected it is bound into a sheaf and tossed aside. When the field has been finished, the sheaves are gathered, and thirty-five to forty-five are tied together to make a headload. The late millet is stacked next to the acha on the drying rack, where it remains until shortly before the first rains.

The final activities of the agricultural year are those connected with threshing and storage of cereal grains in February. Early millet and sorghum are usually kept in the seed head and pounded in a wooden mortar just before use. Millet is put away as soon as it is dry, and sorghum is divided and repacked in February. Both are stored in living huts on wooden racks with fires below so that the smoke can help prevent pest damage, or in domed mud granaries. When large amounts of grain are available for sale, it is threshed by being beaten with heavy posts in a cleared courtyard and then winnowed. Late millet is threshed all at one time by being pounded (*tu*) in mortars. The grain is then winnowed and poured into large potlike mud granaries inside houses. The small seeds of acha are loosened from their stems by being rubbed vigorously against a rough stone or a section of hollowed-out log and are then stored in open baskets. Beans are treaded (*dal*) on the homestead floor to separate them from their dried pods. Sesame is beaten (*bwop*) with a stick on a level rocky outcropping and the seed swept up with brooms.

Tree crops are significant both to the diet and to the exchange economy of the Kofyar, but their care does not demand periods of continuous labor. Small fruit trees may be protected from goats, and oil palms are occasionally planted, but most economic trees are self-seeded. A prime marker of Kofyar village settlement is the oil palm that grows on homestead farms. The Kofyar prune dead fronds annually and promote tree growth by cultivating around the base of trees. Oil palms are abundant in hill villages such as Bong, where the water supply is good, and where deep soil exists in stream valleys. The trees are somewhat less abundant on the plains. Palm fruit is harvested as it ripens during the wet season by young men who climb the trees and cut off the bunches with axes. The fruit is mashed and the pulp boiled to recover the yellow-orange oil used in cooking. The palm kernels are dried, cracked, and eaten as nuts. Individual producers sell oil in bottles and four-gallon tins at plains markets. Tapping of oil palms for palm wine is a recent innovation practiced only by immigrant Ibos.

The purple olivelike fruit of large canarium trees is knocked down with long sticks during the period of November to January. It is both cooked for eating and processed into a clear golden oil that is in demand in the market. The pods of the locust bean tree mature between May and August, and brown cakes made from the seeds are sold as condiments. A few mango trees, and pawpaws, or papayas are found near the entrance to most homesteads. Mangoes have been introduced into the area and are most prevalent on the plains, where they are appreciated both for their fruit and for the deep shade they provide. Within most villages, almost the only tree growth apparent is of the above-mentioned economic species, with an occasional *Ficus* used for poles and for goat forage during the dry season. Kofyar livelihood does not depend on their orchards, and the number of economic trees varies considerably on different homesteads. But oil and fruit are highly valued both for food and exchange, and a major reason people give for remaining on ancestral land is often the presence there of tree crops.

The Ecological Balance and Its Conscious Maintenance

The preceding agricultural calendar and survey of farming techniques may give the impression that the Kofyar possess a bewildering multiplicity of crops and grow all of them extensively. It is true that the entire list of food plants is familiar to the Kofyar, but only a few of them are basic staples of the diet. Exactly what is grown and the relative proportions of the various crops are determined by the striking of an ecological balance. Given factors of rainfall, climate, topography, and soil conditions must be related to human capabilities in terms of agricultural techniques, organization of labor, physical needs, and practical knowledge. The basic Kofyar methods of terracing and ridging, manuring, and crop rotation give them a remarkable degree of control over their environment. Yet, in their territory the Kofyar must cope with differences of altitude of up to fifteen hundred feet, terrain that varies from dead level to vertical, water scarcities and surpluses, and soil that may be deep in humus, stony, volcanic, or sandy. Because of historical conditions that made physical expansion dangerous, the Kofyar could not confine themselves to a particular advantageous type of environment. Instead, they adapted themselves to the multiple variations of their limited habitat. It is this series of modifications, of delicate adjustments to varying environments, which most clearly attests to Kofyar agricultural skill.

Bong village, in which I lived during much of my field work, was atypical in its homestead crops. The standard intensive complex on the plains and in many of the Kofyar hill villages is made up of interplanted early millet, sorghum, and cowpeas with pumpkin, okra, *ser* gourds, *gogor* and a few maize plants.[3] Bong homestead farms feature maize and coco yams with pumpkins and climbing beans. Less than half a mile east of Bong, the satellite hamlet of Koepal follows the standard pattern. Coco yams are a subsidiary crop planted in a separate plot. The village of Zugal, three miles north of Bong, also has the standard homestead complex but lacks early millet. When I asked the reason for these variations, answers were invariably in terms of productive efficiency rather than custom or preference for certain foods. Bong people said that they avoided early millet and sorghum because these did not yield well in their village. To further questions, they replied that their special crops were necessitated by the shadiness or windiness of their location. Though I did not at first understand these explanations, they became clear as the agricultural year progressed.

Bong is perched on the edge of a steep valley running north and south and terminating just below the village. The conical volcanic core, Moelaar or Bong Peak, rises on this scarp to a height of 3,400 feet and is the pinnacle of the surrounding country. The rain-bearing winds sweep toward the plateau almost invariably from the southwest. They come up the stream valley from the south and encounter the steep slope leading to Bong. In rising quickly the warm air currents are cooled and precipitation forms. This orographic phenomenon is visible many mornings during the wet season, when Bong is blanketed in fog settling on it from the direction of the peak. The neighboring villages are not so high, and thus they do not have the same incidence of fog. Both the Kofyar themselves and outside observers (Findlay 1945) remark on the cold and damp of Bong. My own crude rainfall collection figures give Bong approximately 27 inches for the 80 days beginning June 1, while Kwa, on the plains, had 18.24 inches. Coco yams are frequently planted in swamps or along stream margins, but the extra precipitation in Bong allows them to thrive in ordinary fields. According to Johnston (1958: 116), coco yams do best in moist, well-matured soil and shady mountain glades, an environment identical to that of Bong.

The rain and heavy dew in Bong are also favorable for the growth of oil palms, and since these valuable trees are carefully tended wher-

[3] This association parallels almost exactly the crops grown on manured compound gardens by a number of groups in northern Ghana (Allan 1965:242–43).

ever they take root, the homestead farms are often well shaded. The amount of moisture and the reduction of direct sun by fog and shade are both injurious to sorghum. Maize, on the contrary, is benefited by increased moisture (Johnston 1958:66). That this is actually the reason for the change in basic crops is proved within Bong village itself. Those homesteads on the high ground to the southwest boast the best coco yams, and the people credit them directly to the moisture in the air around the peak. On the northeast slopes of the village, which are considerably lower and face away from the wind, the land is noticeably dryer and more open. Coco yams and maize are still grown, but a portion of each homestead field is devoted to sorghum. If larger cereals are planted in the bush, it is sorghum that is planted north and east of the village and maize on the west. This is due not only to quantitative differences in sunlight and precipitation but the ravages of a strong south wind (*foefong*) that may blow in September. Exposed sorghum would be flattened before it ripened, while the earlier-maturing maize would already have been harvested. All these factors are taken into conscious account by the farmers.

Sometimes the adaptation to local conditions necessary may result in extra labor. The transplanting of the smaller late millet into extensive ridged fields is recognized as being more arduous than the growing of early millet in the homestead farm. As one goes higher into the hills, early millet ceases to be important, and on the high plateau only the later variety is cultivated. I am not sure of the exact reason for this, but it may have to do with the increased precipitation on the plateau. The late millet requires a moister climate than the early three-month variety and is not found north of Zaria (Irvine 1953:107). Bong farmers claim that early millet turns black instead of ripening properly in their village. This may indeed be the case, because if the weather is wet or even misty the seeds may be attacked by molds that spoil the yield and quality (Irvine 1953:108). I have also heard complaints of birds harming early millet, and it may be that the Bong palms shelter a larger than average population of the particularly destructive finches. Whatever the predisposing factor is, it evidently becomes effective part way through the Kofyar hills. Latok, Kofyar, and Lardang plant only the early millet. The hamlets of Koepal and Kook and the village of Bogalong on a southeast-northwest line plant both. North of this line, in Bong, Zugal, Kwa-Bul, and Koeper, only the late millet grows.

Though crops differ in response to environmental demands, it is possible to substitute one for the other to fulfill the same dietary need. The two kinds of millet are equally useful in making beer. The ground cowpeas, which cannot grow under the thick leaves of Bong coco yams, are replaced by a twining bean that climbs tree-branch arbors to its place in the sun. Not enough maize can be grown in Bong to match the general level of sorghum production. But consumption of cereals is maintained by the planting of acha on the bush fields that Bong has in comparative abundance. The yam does best under the fertile, hot conditions of the lowlands south of Kofyar, and the migrant farmers there eat it in quantity. The poorer soils and the heavier rainfall of the hills seem better suited to the cultivation of sweet potatoes and coco yams. Special household needs may also enter into the determination of what crops to grow. It was said of a Kwa man who put a sizable manured field into eleusine, "He has many small children." Eleusine is used to make a thick nourishing gruel (*waar*) which is valued as a food for infants and youngsters.

The hill Kofyar differ from many African farmers in that they have no period of the year when food is in very short supply. There is no annual "hungry time" (cf. Richards 1939; Haswell 1953:9) in the hills, and older inhabitants can remember no time of scarcity that approached the severity of famine. This is due not only to the farming techniques but also to the variety of crops and the staggered times of maturation. Figure 2 shows the layout of a Bong intensive homestead farm and village fallow, and it gives some indication of the relative area assigned to each crop.

Crops are planted at various times from late March to August. In any one year certain crops may fail, but others will almost surely survive. Bong's 1961 groundnut harvest was poor because of erratic rainfall, but the late acha planted a month later gave a bountiful crop. It is also possible that early millet may do very well, while the late maturing sorghum in the same field will be disappointing. During the wet period of July through October, when the new crops of major staples are not yet ripe and old supplies are being exhausted, the Kofyar garner their early millet and groundnuts along

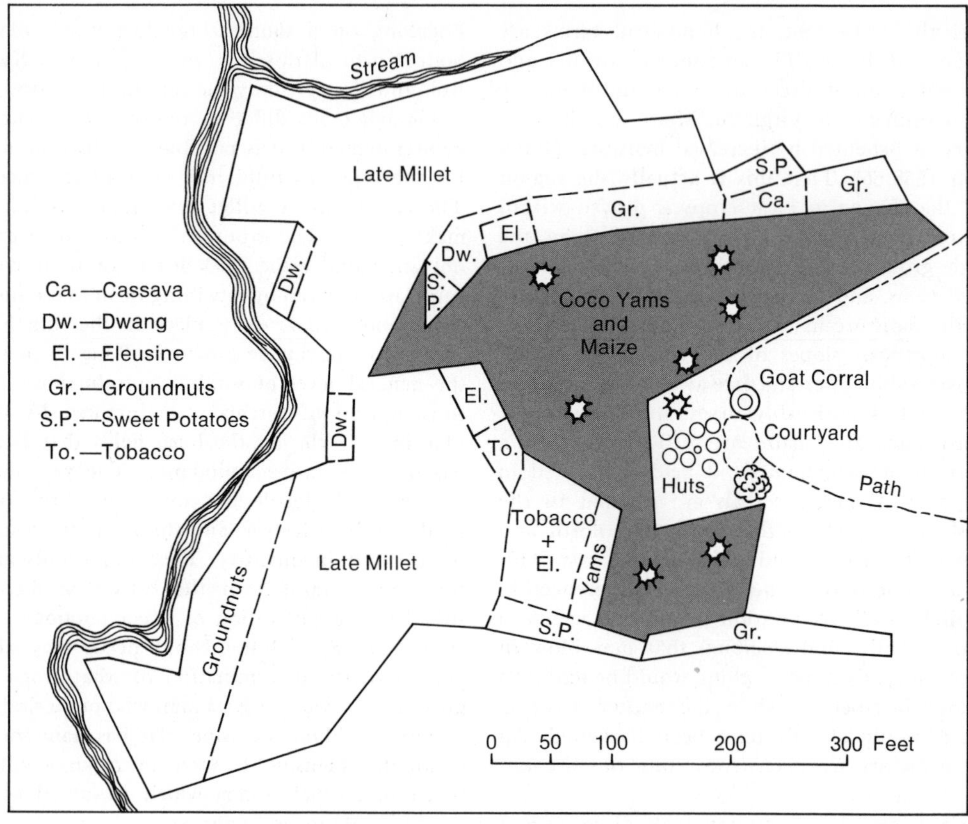

Figure 2. Homestead and village bush field of Dalung, Bong.

with small harvests of maize, string beans, and acha. These are the "hunger breakers" that tide them over. The very early acha (*natagal*) is grown solely for this purpose in the Kwa area. Even with a periodic plague of locusts eating every green thing, such root crops as coco yams and sweet potatoes are not destroyed. It is true that in the past the plains villages sometimes ran low on food and were forced to beg or extort supplies from their hill neighbors. This was due both to the limited land available for bush fields on the plains and to the less dependable rainfall there. Now, with the opening of Namu vacant lands, plains dwellers can easily fill their needs.

The suitability of soil types and conditions for different crops is accurately judged by the Kofyar farmer. Sorghum should have brown soil whose color indicates a fair content of humus. Groundnuts will grow either on red volcanic or light-colored leached soils, doing best when there is not too much organic matter in the field. Kofyar farmers classify soils by color, texture, and moisture content. Dark brown or black earth (*yilchip*) is preferred for the demanding crops: sorghum, yams, and coco yams, but most homestead fields would be classed as *baan,* light reddish brown. Red volcanic soil (*jing*), often occurring with black pitted cinders in old lava flows, is considered inferior. It will grow sorghum, but it is less satisfactory for millet. It is also more difficult to work, clinging in a gluey mass to the hoe when wet. Waterlogged soils such as the swampy *jagat* and the alternately muddy and hard, cracked *jak* are used for moisture-loving rice and coco yams. Soils that are leached of organic matter are characterized as *yilpiya,* white land, or *es,* sand. No farming at all is attempted on seriously degraded plots or on areas of hard, lateritic material (*sang*) and earth used for building purposes (*wanju*).

As fertility declines, the Kofyar change crops to suit it. When a Bong homestead is deserted, the field may still be kept in coco yams for several years though no manure is applied. When production falls off, it is switched to the groundnut-acha or the late millet-acha rotation.

Migrant bush farmers start with sesame on the deep, reddish brown virgin soil of Namu. Yams are planted next, but they grow best on fresh soil, so a new field is cleared for them annually. They are followed by the millet-sorghum-cowpea complex, which may be maintained for seven or eight years. By this time the soil has been visibly depleted, becoming lighter in color and increasingly granular in texture. A sandy field of this type can then support groundnuts or cotton for three or four years before being fallowed.

Wild plants are also indicators of soil fertility. The common wild grass (*togos*) used for thatching grows only three or four feet high on fallowed land that has not yet recovered its fertility. If the grass reaches six feet or more in one season the field is ready for another cropping cycle. The Kofyar say the land is *wam,* that is, "rotten," like decomposing organic material. Grass pulled from such a field will come up with earth tangled in its roots This shows that the soil is soft and crumbly, in good condition for farming. The failure of tree growth to return to fallowed land is a sign that it has been overworked and will regain its fertility only very slowly.

Of the twenty-four cultivated plants that according to Murdock (1959:68) were domesticated in the Western Sudan, the Kofyar utilize fifteen, which include almost all of their major food crops. Most of the Kofyar staple crops are grown in a number of varieties whose special characteristics are known and utilized. Acha may be of the early *natagal* or the late *napiya* and *koechip* types, which are planted and ripen at successively later periods. The first two varieties do best on poorer, well-sunned fields; the latter gives heavier yields. Subvarieties are classified according to color and taste. Among six varieties of sorghum, *swa kong* thrives in the hills where water is plentiful, while the red *swa bang* likes volcanic soil. Different varieties may be used on home and migrant bush farms. For instance, the Namu bush millet ripens in close to four months rather than three, so that work on it can be fitted into the slack times when stages of the home farming operation have been completed. Small early millets such as *carkum* and *cong* are used for pap, while the larger types are reserved for beer.

The Kofyar are quick to adopt new strains that have some readily perceptible advantage. Bong grows a fine yellow ear of maize that came from the Fulani (and may be of recent European origin). Though this acquisition supposedly took place only around 1950, no samples remain of the maize formerly grown. The old variety, according to informants, was bigger but not so tasty or uniform. The same process of adoption is now taking place with a type of groundnut (*kom nasava,* "the groundnut of the white man"), which has a thinner hull and a larger seed than those formerly grown. A number of people spontaneously requested tomato seeds from my garden, though the plant was formerly unknown in the area. Other crops, notably yams and cotton, have been expanded to meet market demands. It is said by the people of Bong that long ago they did not have the groundnut, and that late millet came from the north less than one hundred years ago. Sweet potato cultivation has increased within the memory of living informants. A 1958 agricultural report noted "a marked increase in the past four years in the planting of swamp rice" near Dimmuk and Kwa. The Kofyar farmers who sow rice broadcast and erect sizable earth bunds to retain water have planted the crop only for the last ten or fifteen years.

Beliefs held by Kofyar seek to account for the planting of various varieties. In Kofyar village it is thought that early and late millet are "not friends" and cannot be cultivated together. It is pointed out that the few villages where both types are grown often have inferior early millet harvests. In Bogalong late millet must be threshed outside the village before it comes into the presence of the early homestead crop. Twelve named varieties of acha exist in Bong, and different ones are said to "like" (*dem*) different farmers. It may be that a man grows a different one than his father because he did not get good yields from the former strain

Field Types

Though the observer is most impressed by the permanent cultivation of the Kofyar homestead farms, there are also several other field types that give flexibility to the agricultural system. These form a complete spectrum from plots that grow a single crop and are then abandoned to semipermanent fields that remain in almost continuous production of small grains and peanuts. Kofyar bush fallows differ in several ways from the shifting or swidden cultivation in areas of dense tropical rainfall. The large, dense plant associations which both protect the earth and continually return nutrients to the soil (Geertz 1963:24) are not needed, and Kofyar may sow entire savanna fields in single crops. The soil-conserving function of native trees and grasses is taken over by permanent terraces and ridging. The initial burning of tree growth in a fallowed area seems less important in maintaining fertility than the combination of relatively less demanding crops, regular rotation, careful turning under of organic material, and, in the case of groundnuts, fertilizing with household ash The efficacy of these techniques is seen in the six- to nine-year productive span of hill fields as distinguished from the one to three years during which rain forest swiddens can give significant yields. The Kofyar do not complain of significant invasions by weeds, but they do attempt to group bush fields together as a partial defense against wild animals. Their preferred fallow periods are fifteen to twenty years, but there are some overworked hill slopes that will not regenerate bush and tree growth within this time. The Kofyar might be said to practice shifting cultivation intensively, a type of land use that Allan calls "recurrent cultivation" (1965:33).

Fields farmed by the Kofyar system of shifting cultivation are of three types, depending on their location and use. I have called them village, bush, and migrant bush fields, though the Kofyar themselves do not make these distinctions. Village fields are those contiguous to the manured homestead farms and lying within the settled area. They may have been intensively cultivated in the past as a homestead site, but with the death or moving away of the occupants, they revert to a rotation of acha, late millet, and groundnuts or assorted tubers and are fallowed irregularly. Parts of such small fields may be manured again if the owner expands his present intensive farm or a new homestead is built there. These conveniently situated plots may be cultivated for longer periods than they are rested, but the more demanding crops (sorghum, early millet) are never planted on them, and yields appear to be low.

The extent of village farms depends on the type of farming and on the pressure of population within the settlement. In Bong, where homestead farms are small, there are not enough households to occupy all the available sites in the village. Most families have approximately an acre devoted to minor grains, tubers, and occasionally tobacco or eleusine, all within the settled area. Kofyar, with the more typical large homestead farms, has correspondingly smaller village fallowed plots. On the plains in Kwa and Dimmuk, homesteads are crowded so close together that virtually no land remains for subsidiary crops.

Bush farms in both hill and plains areas are those lying outside the settled perimeter of the village but seldom more than thirty minutes' to an hour's walk away. They are terraced where necessary, but the walls are often lower and the benches narrower than those inside the village. They are never manured (except when Fulani herders can be persuaded to camp on them), and they must be fallowed to restore fertility. No one spends the night in nearby bush fields, and the only type of structure there is a rough shelter for those who guard the ripening grain from animal pests.

Migrant bush farms require a journey of from several hours to a day. For the most part they occupy vacant plain land south of the Kofyar country. Their distance from the homesteads of the owners prevents commuting and makes necessary the building of a self-contained bush residence. Since migrant bush fields are located on virgin or fully regenerated plots, they can support several years of heavy homestead crops (sorghum, early millet, cowpeas), as well as yams, without fertilization. Unlike the homestead and local bush fields, they are geared largely to producing a surplus that can be sold for cash.

REFERENCES CITED

Allan, W., 1965, *The African Husbandsman*, Oliver and Boyd, Edinburgh.

Barrau, J., 1958, *Subsistence Agriculture in Melanesia*, Bishop Museum Bulletin 219, Honolulu.

Bohannan, P., 1954, *Tiv Farm and Settlement*, Colonial Research Studies, 15, Colonial Office, London.

Conklin, H., 1957, *Hanunoo Agriculture, FAO Forestry Development Paper* No. 12, Food and Agriculture Organization of the United Nations, Rome.

Curwen, E. C., and G. Hatt, 1953, *Plough and Pasture*, Schuman, New York.

Dalziel, J., 1937, *The Useful Plants of West Tropical Africa*, Crown Agents for the Colonies, London.

De Schlippe, P., 1956, *Shifting Cultivation in Africa,* Routledge and Kegan Paul, London.
Evans, E., 1956, "The Ecology of Peasant Life in Western Europe," in W. Thomas (ed.), *Man's Role in Changing the Face of the Earth,* pp. 217–239, Chicago U.P., Chicago.
Fairbairn, W., 1943, "Forestry in Plateau Province," *Farm and Forest* 4:182–192.
Findlay, R., 1945, "The Dimmuk and Their Neighbors," *Farm and Forest* 6:138–142.
Geertz, C., 1963, *Agricultural Involution,* California U.P., Berkeley.
Goldschmidt, W., 1959, *Man's Way,* Holt, New York.
Haswell, M., 1953, *Economics of Agriculture in a Savannah Village,* Colonial Research Studies No. 8, Colonial Office, London.
Irvine, F., 1953, *A Textbook of West African Agriculture,* Oxford U.P., London.
Johnstone, B., 1958, *The Staple Food Economies of West Tropical Africa,* Food Research Institute, Stanford.
Lehman, F., 1963, *The Structure of Chin Society,* Illinois Studies in Anthropolgy No. 3, Illinois U.P., Urbana.
Nadel, S., 1947, *The Nuba,* Oxford U.P., London.
Perham, M., 1946, *The Economics of a Tropical Dependency,* Faber and Faber, London.
Pospisil, L., 1963, *Kapauku Papuan Economy,* Yale University Publications in Anthropology, No. 67.
Richards, A., 1939, *Land, Labour, and Diet in Northern Rhodesia,* International African Institute, London.

SECTION II

Technological Change

Evidence of the causal role of technological change in precipitating particular patterns of sociocultural development has led to the suggestion that the circumstances necessary for the successful achievement of industrialization might cause the cultures of all industrializing societies—despite noisy political protestations to the contrary—gradually to grow more and more alike, to *converge*, becoming increasingly similar in the organization of their economies and in the structure of their social groupings (familiar example: the shrinking size of the family household that seems nearly everywhere to accompany industrialization). Many also see growing structural similarities in the political organization of all industrializing states.

It appears that the aspects of culture are so interrelated and that technology is so fundamental to that interrelationship that technological change can never occur without having such powerful effects that those unprepared are often left deeply disoriented, especially when such changes happen fast, as they usually do these days. No more millennia of comfortably slow adjustment to the results of the invention of the wheel, not even the hundred years or so we had to become accustomed to electricity. The nuclear-powered postindustrial age is upon us, we hear, and most of those who are thinking ahead assume that our ways of living will be radically transformed by a time as close as the twenty-first century. "Transformed," but how? What should we be doing to get ready? Well, for a start, we might try to acquire some practical insights by pondering the cataclysmic effects that rapid, often forced, technological change has had upon some of our Third World brothers and sisters whose technological "backwardness" we have been trying assiduously to reverse. As many a little older and slightly wiser Peace Corps returnee will affirm, not all of the cultural consequences of technological modernization in "underdeveloped" areas have been either anticipated or happy. Some might have been avoided, most others were probably inevitable —trying to figure out which is a tricky, intriguing, and critical anthropological question.

Here Sharp offers us a case in point: of how a presumably well-meant try to help a group of "backward" Australians to improve themselves materially by passing out some shiny new steel axes threw their entire culture out of whack. One small, blundering effort at technological innovation had consequences that, in microcosm, were almost as wastefully tragic as our efforts to modernize (on our terms) the traditional technologies of our own aborigines, the Native Americans.

Two things to watch for in reading this poignant, now classic account are (1) evidence that technological change cannot occur in a cultural vacuum and (2) a compelling illustration of the costs of trying to give technical assistance to the people of another culture without first getting to know them and to understand the causal connections that link logically the many aspects of their traditional way of life.

Technological Innovation and Culture Change: An Australian Case

Lauriston Sharp

I

Like other Australian aboriginals, the Yir Yoront group which lives at the mouth of the Coleman River on the west coast of Cape York Peninsula originally had no knowledge of metals. Technologically their culture was of the old stone age or paleolithic type. They supported themselves by hunting and fishing, and obtained vegetables and other materials from the bush by simple gathering techniques. Their only domesticated animal was the dog; they had no cultivated plants of any kind. Unlike some other aboriginal groups, however, the Yir Yoront did have polished stone axes hafted in short handles which were most important in their economy.

Towards the end of the 19th century metal tools and other European artifacts began to filter into the Yir Yoront territory. The flow increased with the gradual expansion of the white frontier outward from southern and eastern Queensland. Of all the items of western technology thus made available, the hatchet, or short handled steel axe, was the most acceptable to and the most highly valued by all aboriginals.

In the mid 1930's an American anthropologist lived alone in the bush among the Yir Yoront for 13 months without seeing another white man. The Yir Yoront were thus still relatively isolated and continued to live an essentially independent economic existence, supporting themselves entirely by means of their old stone age techniques. Yet their polished stone axes were disappearing fast and being replaced by steel axes which came to them in considerable numbers, directly or indirectly, from various European sources to the south.

What changes in the life of the Yir Yoront still living under aboriginal conditions in the Australian bush could be expected as a result of their increasing possession and use of the steel axe?

II. The Course of Events

Events leading up to the introduction of the steel axe among the Yir Yoront begin with the advent of the second known group of Europeans to reach the shores of the Australian continent. In 1623 a Dutch expedition landed on the coast where the Yir Yoront now live.[1] In 1935 the Yir Yoront were still using the few cultural items recorded in the Dutch log for the aboriginals they encountered. To this cultural inventory the Dutch added beads and pieces of iron which they offered in an effort to attract the frightened "Indians." Among these natives metal and beads have disappeared, together with any memory of this first encounter with whites.

The next recorded contact in this area was in 1864. Here there is more positive assurance that the natives concerned were the immediate ancestors of the Yir Yoront community. These aboriginals had the temerity to attack a party of cattle men who were driving a small herd from

Source: From Lauriston Sharp, "Steel Axes for Stone-Age Australians," *Human Organization*, Vol. 2 (1952), pp. 17–22.

[1] An account of this expedition from Amboina is given in R. Logan Jack, *Northmost Australia* (2 vols.), London, 1921, Vol. 1, 18–57.

southern Queensland through the length of the then unknown Cape York Peninsula to a newly established government station at the northern tip.[2] Known as the "Battle of the Mitchell River," this was one of the rare instances in which Australian aboriginals stood up to European gunfire for any length of time. A diary kept by the cattle men records that: ". . . 10 carbines poured volley after volley into them from all directions, killing and wounding with every shot with very little return, nearly all their spears having already been expended. . . . About 30 being killed, the leader thought it prudent to hold his hand, and let the rest escape. Many more must have been wounded and probably drowned, for 59 rounds were counted as discharged." The European party was in the Yir Yoront area for three days; they then disappeared over the horizon to the north and never returned. In the almost three-year long anthropological investigation conducted some 70 years later—in all the material of hundreds of free association interviews, in texts of hundreds of dreams and myths, in genealogies, and eventually in hundreds of answers to direct and indirect questioning on just this particular matter—there was nothing that could be interpreted as a reference to this shocking contact with Europeans.

The aboriginal accounts of their first remembered contact with whites begin in about 1900 with references to persons known to have had sporadic but lethal encounters with them. From that time on whites continued to remain on the southern periphery of Yir Yoront territory. With the establishment of cattle stations (ranches) to the south, cattle men made occasional excursions among the "wild black-fellows" in order to inspect the country and abduct natives to be trained as cattle boys and "house girls." At least one such expedition reached the Coleman River where a number of Yir Yoront men and women were shot for no apparent reason.

About this time the government was persuaded to sponsor the establishment of three mission stations along the 700-mile western coast of the Peninsula in an attempt to help regulate the treatment of natives. To further this purpose a strip of coastal territory was set aside as an aboriginal reserve and closed to further white settlement.

In 1915, an Anglican mission station was established near the mouth of the Mitchell River, about a three-day march from the heart of the Yir Yoront country. Some Yir Yoront refused to have anything to do with the mission, others visited it occasionally, while only a few eventually settled more or less permanently in one of the three "villages" established at the mission.

Thus the majority of the Yir Yoront continued to live their old self-supporting life in the bush, protected until 1942 by the government reserve and the intervening mission from the cruder realities of the encroaching new order from the south. To the east was poor, uninhabited country. To the north were other bush tribes extending on along the coast to the distant Archer River Presbyterian mission with which the Yir Yoront had no contact. Westward was the shallow Gulf of Carpentaria on which the natives saw only a mission lugger making its infrequent dry season trips to the Mitchell River. In this protected environment for over a generation the Yir Yoront were able to recuperate from shocks received at the hands of civilized society. During the 1930's their raiding and fighting, their trading and stealing of women, their evisceration and two- or three-year care of their dead, and their totemic ceremonies continued, apparently uninhibited by western influence. In 1931 they killed a European who wandered into their territory from the east, but the investigating police never approached the group whose members were responsible for the act.

As a direct result of the work of the Mitchell River mission, all Yir Yoront received a great many more western artifacts of all kinds than ever before. As part of their plan for raising native living standards, the missionaries made it possible for aboriginals living at the mission to earn some western goods, many of which were then given or traded to natives still living under bush conditions; they also handed out certain useful articles gratis to both mission and bush aboriginals. They prevented guns, liquor, and damaging narcotics, as well as decimating diseases, from reaching the tribes of this area, while encouraging the introduction of goods they considered "improving." As has been noted, no item of western technology available, with the possible exception of trade tobacco, was in

[2] R. Logan Jack, *op. cit.*, pp. 298–335.

greater demand among all groups of aboriginals than the short handled steel axe. The mission always kept a good supply of the axes in stock; at Christmas parties or other mission festivals they were given away to mission or visiting aboriginals indiscriminately and in considerable numbers. In addition, some steel axes as well as other European goods were still traded in to the Yir Yoront by natives in contact with cattle stations in the south. Indeed, steel axes had probably come to the Yir Yoront through established lines of aboriginal trade long before any regular contact with whites had occurred.

III. Relevant Factors

If we concentrate our attention on Yir Yoront behavior centering about the original stone axe (rather than on the axe—the object—itself) as a cultural trait or item of cultural equipment, we should get some conception of the role this implement played in aboriginal culture. This, in turn, should enable us to foresee with considerable accuracy some of the results stemming from the displacement of the stone axe by the steel axe.

The production of a stone axe required a number of simple technological skills. With the various details of the axe well in mind, adult men could set about producing it (a task not considered appropriate for women or children). First of all a man had to know the location and properties of several natural resources found in his immediate environment: pliable wood for a handle, which could be doubled or bent over the axe head and bound tightly; bark, which could be rolled into cord for the binding; and gum, to fix the stone head in the haft. These materials had to be correctly gathered, stored, prepared, cut to size and applied or manipulated. They were in plentiful supply, and could be taken from anyone's property without special permission. Postponing consideration of the stone head, the axe could be made by any normal man who had a simple knowledge of nature and of the technological skills involved, together with fire (for heating the gum), and a few simple cutting tools—perhaps the sharp shells of plentiful bivalves.

The use of the stone axe as a piece of capital equipment used in producing other goods indicates its very great importance to the subsistence economy of the aboriginal. Anyone—man, woman, or child—could use the axe; indeed it was used primarily by women, for their's was the task of obtaining sufficient wood to keep the family campfire burning all day, for cooking or other purposes, and all night against mosquitoes and cold (for in July, winter temperature might drop below 40 degrees). In a normal lifetime a woman would use the axe to cut or knock down literally tons of firewood. The axe was also used to make other tools or weapons, and a variety of material equipment required by the aboriginal in his daily life. The stone axe was essential in the construction of the wet season domed huts which keep out some rain and some insects; of platforms which provide dry storage; of shelters which give shade in the dry summer when days are bright and hot. In hunting and fishing and in gathering vegetable or animal food the axe was also a necessary tool, and in this tropical culture, where preservatives or other means of storage are lacking, the natives spend more time obtaining food than in any other occupation—except sleeping. In only two instances was the use of the stone axe strictly limited to adult men: for gathering wild honey, the most prized food known to the Yir Yoront; and for making the secret paraphernalia for ceremonies. From this brief listing of some of the activities involving the use of the axe, it is easy to understand why there was at least one stone axe in every camp, in every hunting or fighting party, and in every group out on a "walk-about" in the bush.

The stone axe was also prominent in interpersonal relations. Yir Yoront men were dependent upon interpersonal relations for their stone axe heads, since the flat, geologically-recent, alluvial country over which they range provides no suitable stone for this purpose. The stone they used came from quarries 400 miles to the south, reaching the Yir Yoront through long lines of male trading partners. Some of these chains terminated with the Yir Yoront men, others extended on farther north to other groups, using Yir Yoront men as links. Almost every older adult man had one or more regular trading partners, some to the north and some to the south. He provided his partner or partners in the south with surplus spears, particularly fighting spears tipped with the barbed spines of sting ray which snap into viscious fragments when they penetrate human flesh. For a dozen such spears, some of which he may have obtained from a partner to the north, he would receive one stone axe head. Studies have shown that the sting ray barb spears increased in value as they move south and farther from the sea. One hundred and fifty miles south of Yir Yoront one such spear may be exchanged for one stone axe head. Although actual investigations could not be made, it was presumed that farther south, nearer the quarries, one sting ray barb spear would bring several stone axe heads. Apparently people who acted as links in the middle of the chain and who made neither spears nor axe heads would receive a certain number of each as a middleman's profit.

Thus trading relations, which may extend the individual's personal relationships beyond that of his own group, were associated with spears and axes, two of the most important items in a man's equipment. Finally, most of the exchanges took place during the dry season, at the time of the great aboriginal celebrations centering about initiation rites or other totemic ceremonials which attracted hundreds and were the occasion for much exciting activity in addition to trading.

Returning to the Yir Yoront, we find that adult men kept their axes in camp with their other equipment, or carried them when travelling. Thus a woman or child who wanted to use an axe—as might frequently happen during the day—had to get one from a man, use it promptly, and return it in good condition. While a man might speak of "my axe," a woman or child could not.

This necessary and constant borrowing of axes from older men by women and children was in accordance with regular patterns of kinship behavior. A woman would expect to use her husband's axe unless he himself was using it; if unmarried, or if her husband was absent, a woman would go first to her older brother or to her father. Only in extraordinary circumstances would she seek a stone axe from other male kin. A girl, a boy, or a young man would look to a father or an older brother to provide an axe for their use. Older men, too, would follow similar rules if they had to borrow an axe.

It will be noted that all of these social relationships in which the stone axe had a place are pair relationships and that the use of the axe helped to define and maintain their character and the roles of the two individual participants. Every active relationship among the Yir Yoront involved a definite and accepted status of superordination or subordination. A person could have no dealings with another on exactly equal terms. The nearest approach to equality was between brothers, although the older was always superordinate to the younger. Since the exchange of goods in a trading relationship involved a mutual reciprocity, trading partners usually stood in a brotherly type of relationship, although one was always classified as older than the other and would have some advantage in case of dispute It can be seen that repeated and widespread conduct centering around the use of the axe helped to generalize and standardize these sex, age, and kinship roles both in their normal benevolent and exceptional malevolent aspects.

The status of any individual Yir Yoront was determined not only by sex, age, and extended kin relationships, but also by membership in one of two dozen patrilineal totemic clans into which the entire community was divided.[3] Each clan had literally hundreds of totems, from one or two of which the clan derived its name, and the clan members their personal names. These totems included natural species or phenomena such as the sun, stars. and daybreak, as well as cultural "species": imagined ghosts, rainbow serpents, heroic ancestors; such eternal cultural verities as fires, spears, huts; and such human activities, conditions, or attributes as eating, vomiting, swimming, fighting, babies and corpses, milk and blood, lips and loins. While individual members of such totemic classes or species might disappear or be destroyed, the class itself was obviously ever-present and indestructible. The totems, therefore, lent permanence and stability to the clans, to the groupings of human individuals who generation after generation were each associated with a set of totems which distinguished one clan from another.

The stone axe was one of the most important of the many totems of the Sunlit Cloud Iguana

[3] The best, although highly concentrated, summaries of totemism among the Yir Yoront and the other tribes of north Queensland will be found in R. Lauriston Sharp, "Tribes and Totemism in Northeast Australia," *Oceania*, Vol. 8, 1939, pp. 254–275 and 439–461 (especially pp. 268–275) ; also "Notes on Northeast Australian Totemism," in *Papers of the Peabody Museum of American Archaeology and Ethnology*, Vol. 20, *Studies in the Anthropology of Oceania and Asia*, Cambridge, 1943, pp. 66–71.

clan. The names of many members of this clan referred to the axe itself, to activities in which the axe played a vital part, or to the clan's mythical ancestors with whom the axe was prominently associated. When it was necessary to represent the stone axe in totemic ceremonies, only men of this clan exhibited it or pantomimed its use. In secular life, the axe could be made by any man and used by all; but in the sacred realm of the totems it belonged exclusively to the Sunlit Cloud Iguana people.

Supporting those aspects of cultural behavior which we have called technology and conduct, is a third area of culture which includes ideas, sentiments, and values. These are most difficult to deal with, for they are latent and covert, and even unconscious, and must be deduced from overt actions and language or other communicating behavior. In this aspect of the culture lies the significance of the stone axe to the Yir Yoront and to their cultural way of life.

The stone axe was an important symbol of masculinity among the Yir Yoront (just as pants or pipes are to us). By a complicated set of ideas the axe was defined as "belonging" to males, and everyone in the society (except untrained infants) accepted these ideas. Similarly spears, spear throwers, and fire-making sticks were owned only by men and were also symbols of masculinity. But the masculine values represented by the stone axe were constantly being impressed on all members of society by the fact that females borrowed axes but not other masculine artifacts. Thus the axe stood for an important theme of Yir Yoront culture: the superiority and rightful dominance of the male, and the greater value of his concerns and of all things associated with him. As the axe also had to be borrowed by the younger people it represented the prestige of age, another important theme running through Yir Yoront behavior.

To understand the Yir Yoront culture it is necessary to be aware of a system of ideas which may be called their totemic ideology. A fundamental belief of the aboriginal divided time into two great epochs: (1) a distant and sacred period at the beginning of the world when the earth was peopled by mildly marvelous ancestral beings or culture heroes who are in a special sense the forebears of the clans; and (2) a period when the old was succeeded by a new order which includes the present. Originally there was no anticipation of another era supplanting the present. The future would simply be an eternal continuation and reproduction of the present which itself had remained unchanged since the epochal revolution of ancestral times.

The important thing to note is that the aboriginal believed that the present world, as a natural and cultural environment, was and should be simply a detailed reproduction of the world of the ancestors. He believed that the entire universe "is now as it was in the beginning" when it was established and left by the ancestors. The ordinary cultural life of the ancestors became the daily life of the Yir Yoront camps, and the extraordinary life of the ancestors remained extant in the recurring symbolic pantomimes and paraphernalia found only in the most sacred atmosphere of the totemic rites.

Such beliefs, accordingly, opened the way for ideas of what *should be* (because it supposedly *was*) to influence or help determine what actually *is*. A man called Dog-chases-iguana-up-a-tree-and-barks-at-him-all-night had that and other names because he believed his ancestral alter ego had also had them; he was a member of the Sunlit Cloud Iguana clan because his ancestor was; he was associated with particular countries and totems of this same ancestor; during an initiation he played the role of a dog and symbolically attacked and killed certain members of other clans because his ancestor (conveniently either anthropomorphic or kynomorphic) really did the same to the ancestral alter egos of these men; and he would avoid his mother-in-law, joke with a mother's distant brother, and make spears in a certain way because his and other people's ancestors did these things. His behavior in these specific ways was outlined, and to that extent determined for him, by a set of ideas concerning the past and the relation of the present to the past.

But when we are informed that Dog-chases-etc. had two wives from the Spear Black Duck clan and one from the Native Companion clan, one of them being blind, that he had four children with such and such names, that he had a broken wrist and was left handed, all because his ancestor had exactly these same attributes, then we know (though he apparently didn't) that the present has influenced the past, that the mythical world has been somewhat adjusted to meet the exigencies and accidents of the inescapably real present.

There was thus in Yir Yoront ideology a nice balance in which the mythical was adjusted in part to the real world, the real world in part to the ideal pre-existing mythical world, the adjustments occurring to maintain a fundamental tenet of native faith that the present must be a mirror of the past. Thus the stone axe in all its aspects, uses, and associations was integrated into the context of Yir Yoront technology and conduct because a myth, a set of ideas, had put it there.

IV. The Outcome

The introduction of the steel axe indiscriminately and in large numbers into the Yir Yoront technology occurred simultaneously with many other changes. It is therefore impossible to separate all the results of this single innovation. Nevertheless, a number of specific effects of the change from stone to steel axes may be noted, and the steel axe may be used as an epitome of the increasing quantity of European goods and implements received by the aboriginals and of their general influence on the native culture. The use of the steel axe to illustrate such influences would seem to be justified. It was one of the first European artifacts to be adopted for regular use by the Yir Yoront, and whether made of stone or steel, the axe was clearly one of the most important items of cultural equipment they possessed.

The shift from stone to steel axes provided no major technological difficulties. While the aboriginals themselves could not manufacture steel axe heads, a steady supply from outside continued; broken wooden handles could easily be replaced from bush timbers with aboriginal tools. Among the Yir Yoront the new axe was never used to the extent it was on mission or cattle stations (for carpentry work, pounding tent pegs, as a hammer, and so on); indeed, it had so few more uses than the stone axe that its practical effect on the native standard of living was negligible. It did some jobs better, and could be used longer without breakage. These factors were sufficient to make it of value to the native. The white man believed that a shift from steel to stone axe on his part would be a definite regression. He was convinced that his axe was much more efficient, that its use would save time, and that it therefore represented technical "progress" towards goals which he had set up for the native. But this assumption was hardly born out in aboriginal practice. Any leisure time the Yir Yoront might gain by using steel axes or other western tools was not invested in "improving the conditions of life," nor, certainly, in developing aesthetic activities, but in sleep—an art they had mastered thoroughly.

Previously, a man in need of an axe would acquire a stone axe head through regular trading partners from whom he knew what to expect, and was then dependent solely upon a known and adequate natural environment, and his own skills or easily acquired techniques. A man wanting a steel axe, however, was in no such self-reliant position. If he attended a mission festival when steel axes were handed out as gifts, he might receive one either by chance or by happening to impress upon the mission staff that he was one of the "better" bush aboriginals (the missionaries definition of "better" being quite different from that of his bush fellows). Or, again almost by pure chance, he might get some brief job in connection with the mission which would enable him to earn a steel axe. In either case, for older men a preference for the steel axe helped change the situation from one of self-reliance to one of dependence, and a shift in behavior from well-structured or defined situations in technology or conduct to ill-defined situations in conduct alone. Among the men, the older ones whose earlier experience or knowledge of the white man's harshness made them suspicious were particularly careful to avoid having relations with the mission, and thus excluded themselves from acquiring steel axes from that source.

In other aspects of conduct or social relations, the steel axe was even more significantly at the root of psychological stress among the Yir Yoront. This was the result of new factors which the missionary considered beneficial: the simple numerical increase in axes per capita as a result of mission distribution, and distribution directly to younger men, women, and even children. By winning the favor of the mission staff, a woman might be given a steel axe which was clearly intended to be hers, thus creating a situation quite different from the previous custom which necessitated her borrowing an axe from a male relative. As a result a woman would refer to the axe as "mine," a possessive form she was never able to use of the stone axe. In the same fashion, young men or even boys also obtained steel axes directly from the mission, with the result that older men no longer had a complete monopoly of all the axes in the bush community. All this led to a revolutionary confusion of sex, age, and kinship roles, with a major gain in independence and loss of subordination on the part of those who now owned steel axes when they had previously been unable to possess stone axes.

The trading partner relationship was also affected by the new situation. A Yir Yoront might have a trading partner in a tribe to the south whom he defined as a younger brother and over whom he would therefore have some authority. But if the partner were in contact with the mission or had other access to steel axes, his subordination obviously decreased. Among other things, this took some of the excitement away from the dry season fiesta-like tribal gatherings centering around initiations. These had traditionally been the climactic annual occasions for exchanges between trading partners, when a man might seek to acquire a whole year's supply of stone axe heads. Now he might find himself prostituting his wife to almost total strangers in return for steel axes or other white man's goods. With trading partnerships weakened, there was less reason to attend the ceremonies, and less fun for those who did.

Not only did an increase in steel axes and their distribution to women change the character of the relations between individuals (the paired relationships that have been noted), but a previously rare type of relationship was created in the Yir Yoront's conduct towards whites. In the aboriginal society there were few occasions outside of the immediate family when an individual would initiate action to several other people at once. In any average group, in accordance with the kinship system, while a person might be superordinate to several people to whom he could suggest or command action, he was also subordinate to several others with whom such behavior would be tabu. There was thus no overall chieftainship or authoritarian leadership of any kind. Such complicated operations as grass-burning animal drives or totemic ceremonies could be carried out smoothly because each person was aware of his role.

On both mission and cattle stations, however, the whites imposed their conception of leadership roles upon the aboriginals, consisting of one person in a controlling relationship with a subordinate group. Aboriginals called together to receive gifts, including axes, at a mission Christmas party found themselves facing one or two whites who sought to control their behavior for the occasion, who disregarded the age, sex, and kinship variables of which the aboriginals were so conscious, and who considered them all at one subordinate level. The white also sought to impose similar patterns on work parties. (However, if he placed an aboriginal in charge of a mixed group of post-hole diggers, for example, half of the group, those subordinate to the "boss," would work while the other half, who were superordinate to him, would sleep.) For the aboriginal, the steel axe and other European goods came to symbolize this new and uncomfortable form of social organization, the leader-group relationship.

The most disturbing effects of the steel axe, operating in conjunction with other elements also being introduced from the white man's several sub-cultures, developed in the realm of traditional ideas, sentiments, and values. These were undermined at a rapidly mounting rate, with no new conceptions being defined to replace them. The result was the erection of a mental and moral void which foreshadowed the collapse and destruction of all Yir Yoront culture, if not, indeed, the extinction of the biological group itself.

From what has been said it should be clear how changes in overt behavior, in technology and conduct, weakened the values inherent in a reliance on nature, in the prestige of masculinity and of age, and in the various kinship relations. A scene was set in which a wife, or a young son whose initiation may not yet have been completed, need no longer defer to the husband or father who, in turn, became confused and insecure as he was forced to borrow a steel axe from them. For the woman and boy the steel axe helped establish a new degree of freedom which they accepted readily as an escape from the unconscious stress of the old patterns—but they, too, were left confused and insecure. Ownership became less well defined with the result that stealing and trespassing were introduced into technology and conduct. Some of the excitement surrounding the great ceremonies evaporated and they lost their previous gaiety and interest. Indeed, life itself became less interesting, although this did not lead the Yir Yoront to discover suicide, a concept foreign to them.

The whole process may be most specifically illustrated in terms of totemic system, which also illustrates the significant role played by a system of ideas, in this case a totemic ideology, in the breakdown of a culture.

In the first place, under pre-European

aboriginal conditions where the native culture has become adjusted to a relatively stable environment, few, if any, unheard of or catastrophic crises can occur. It is clear, therefore, that the totemic system serves very effectively in inhibiting radical cultural changes. The closed system of totemic ideas, explaining and categorizing a well-known universe as it was fixed at the beginning of time, presents a considerable obstacle to the adoption of new or the dropping of old culture traits. The obstacle is not insurmountable and the system allows for the minor variations which occur in the norms of daily life. But the inception of major changes cannot easily take place.

Among the bush Yir Yoront the only means of water transport is a light wood log to which they cling in their constant swimming of rivers, salt creeks, and tidal inlets. These natives know that tribes 45 miles further north have a bark canoe. They know these northern tribes can thus fish from midstream or out at sea, instead of clinging to the river banks and beaches, that they can cross coastal waters infested with crocodiles, sharks, sting rays, and Portuguese men-of-war without danger. They know the materials of which the canoe is made exist in their own environment. But they also know, as they say, that they do not have canoes because their own mythical ancestors did not have them. They assume that the canoe was part of the ancestral universe of the northern tribes. For them, then, the adoption of the canoe would not be simply a matter of learning a number of new behavioral skills for its manufacture and use. The adoption would require a much more difficult procedure; the acceptance by the entire society of a myth, either locally developed or borrowed, to explain the presence of the canoe, to associate it with some one or more of the several hundred mythical ancestors (and how decide which?), and thus establish it as an accepted totem of one of the clans ready to be used by the whole community. The Yir Yoront have not made this adjustment, and in this case we can only say that for the time being at least, ideas have won out over very real pressures for technological change. In the elaborateness and explicitness of the totemic ideologies we seem to have one explanation for the notorious stability of Australian cultures under aboriginal conditions, an explanation which gives due weight to the importance of ideas in determining human behavior.

At a later stage of the contact situation, as has been indicated, phenomena unaccounted for by the totemic ideological system begin to appear with regularity and frequency and remain within the range of native experience. Accordingly, they cannot be ignored (as the "Battle of the Mitchell" was apparently ignored), and there is an attempt to assimilate them and account for them along the lines of principles inherent in the ideology. The bush Yir Yoront of the mid-thirties represent this stage of the acculturation process. Still trying to maintain their aboriginal definition of the situation, they accept European artifacts and behavior patterns, but fit them into their totemic system, assigning them to various clans on a par with original totems. There is an attempt to have the myth-making process keep up with these cultural changes so that the idea system can continue to support the rest of the culture. But analysis of overt behavior, of dreams, and of some of the new myths indicates that this arrangement is not entirely satisfactory, that the native clings to his totemic system with intellectual loyalty (lacking any substitute ideology), but that associated sentiments and values are weakened. His attitudes towards his own and towards European culture are found to be highly ambivalent.

All ghosts are totems of the Head-to-the-East Corpse clan, are thought of as white, and are of course closely associated with death. The white man, too, is closely associated with death, and he and all things pertaining to him are naturally assigned to the Corpse clan as totems. The steel axe, as a totem, was thus associated with the Corpse clan. But as an "axe," clearly linked with the stone axe, it is a totem of the Sunlit Cloud Iguana clan. Moreover, the steel axe, like most European goods, has no distinctive origin myth, nor are mythical ancestors associated with it. Can anyone, sitting in the shade of a *ti* tree one afternoon, create a myth to resolve this confusion? No one has, and the horrid suspicion arises as to the authenticity of the origin myths, which failed to take into account this vast new universe of the white man. The steel axe, shifting hopelessly between one clan and the other, is not only replacing the stone axe physically, but is hacking at the supports of the entire cultural system.

The aboriginals to the south of the Yir Yoront have clearly passed beyond this stage. They are engulfed by European culture, either by the mission or cattle station sub-cultures or, for some natives, by a baffling, paradoxical combination of both incongruent varieties. The totemic ideology can no longer support the inrushing mass of foreign culture traits, and the myth-making process in its native form breaks down completely. Both intellectually and emotionally a saturation point is reached so that the myriad new traits which can neither be ignored nor any longer assimilated simply force the aboriginal to abandon his totemic system. With the collapse of this system of ideas, which is so closely related to so many other aspects of the native culture, there follows an appallingly sudden and complete cultural disintegration, and a demoralization of the individual such as has seldom been recorded elsewhere. Without the support of a system of ideas well devised to provide cultural stability in a stable environment, but admittedly too rigid for the new realities pressing in from outside, native behavior and native sentiments and values are simply dead. Apathy reigns. The aboriginal has passed beyond the realm of any outsider who might wish to do him well or ill.

Returning from the broken natives huddled on cattle stations or on the fringes of frontier towns to the ambivalent but still lively aboriginals settled on the Mitchell River mission, we note one further devious result of the introduction of European artifacts. During a wet season stay at the mission, the anthropologist discovered that his supply of tooth paste was being depleted at an alarming rate. Investigation showed that it was being taken by old men for use in a new tooth paste cult. Old materials of magic having failed, new materials were being tried out in a malevolent magic directed towards the mission staff and some of the younger aboriginal men. Old males, largely ignored by the missionaries, were seeking to regain some of their lost power and prestige. This mild aggression proved hardly effective, but perhaps only because confidence in any kind of magic on the mission was by this time at a low ebb.

For the Yir Yoront still in the bush, a time could be predicted when personal deprivation and frustration in a confused culture would produce an overload of anxiety. The mythical past of the totemic ancestors would disappear as a guarantee of a present of which the future was supposed to be a stable continuation. Without the past, the present could be meaningless and the future unstructured and uncertain. Insecurities would be inevitable. Reaction to this stress might be some form of symbolic aggression, or withdrawal and apathy, or some more realistic approach.

PART THREE
Economic Organization

Production, Distribution, Consumption—and "Development"

Technology and economic organization—separate aspects of culture—are too often confused. Technology refers to the tools and techniques people use to modify natural resources to meet human needs. Economic organization pertains to the processes by which these tools, techniques, and resources are organized.

Spear throwing is part of the Amahuaca hunter's technology. But who made the spear; how the hunter acquired it; the limits on his rights to use it, to lend it, give it away or trade it, and on what terms; how its value is determined, measured, and calculated—all these are *economic*, not technological questions. The same distinctions can be made between the camel-herding methods of the Shah Nawazi and the way they manage the exchange of their livestock for other goods; or between Kofyar irrigation techniques and how they allocate land, organize farm work, and distribute the harvest; all of the latter are economic issues. Getting this difference straight is essential to dealing clearly with a major theoretical question in cultural and social anthropology, and in the "real world" as well. That question centers on the extent to which technology and economic organization can vary independently of one another. For instance, to what degree does the pattern of technoenvironmental adaptation of Amahuaca hunters either determine or set sharp limits upon the range of variation possible in the form of their economic organization? Is it evidence of a significant causal connection or just accidental that they have no labor for wages, no markets, and no money? How necessarily alike are the economic systems of *all* hunting and gathering peoples? In what ways do the economic systems of all pastoral nomads resemble one another? Those of all primitive farmers? Do the similarities result from chance or necessity? To return to a question closer to home: given the similarity of the industrial technologies of the United States and the Soviet Union, how fundamentally dissimilar can their economic systems remain? Are they growing more different or more alike? Are the economic systems of all industrializing nations inevitably coming to resemble one another more and more closely? If so, is a causal link between technology and economic organization the reason? Or can the resemblances be explained by borrowing? What surprises will the Chinese have for us as they continue to industrialize? Can the subsistence technologies of such comparatively underdeveloped areas as the Upper Volta, West Irian, Haiti, Cambodia, Paraguay, and Appalachia be radically altered without changing the traditional economic order in these diverse corners of the Third World?

Learning what we need to know to answer these questions is a task of more than academic interest. With such understanding we can more clearly foresee the outlines of tomorrow's global society and culture. With luck we may perceive—in time to take preventative action—that certain necessary changes in obsolete economic forms would so threaten the privilege of those presently in power that they might prefer to risk atomic holocaust rather than relinquish their favored status. At that "point in time," presumably, the urgency of all anthropological inquiry would be replaced by the survivors' search for nonradioactive cave space.

In any event, the question of the role of economic organization in society and culture deserves thoughtful examination. Until about fifteen years ago the successful cross-cultural analysis of economic systems was handicapped by the lack of a theory sufficiently sophisticated to transcend considerations of market capitalism—an economic set-up familiar to us, but by no means universal. Puzzled anthropologists have since hotly disagreed on what to do when they encountered cultures lacking either money or markets, or *with* money and markets that seemed to function in ways that contradicted coveted concepts of economic "rationality" and left the work of demand-curve drafters in disarray.

It became necessary to revamp our culture-bound theory so that we could cope better with the growing ethnographic evidence that "economic man" is a more versatile, less narrow-minded fellow than we had assumed.

SECTION I

Allocating the Means of Production

So far in economic anthropology, systems of distribution or exchange have received most of the attention. The equally basic issue of production organization has been slighted. Here the central question is who controls (and how) the raw materials (land, wildlife, water), the capital equipment (digging sticks, spear throwers, power plants), and the labor that must be combined to *produce* goods and services. It is a question that has not yet been well enough answered.

A reality-based theory in economic anthropology must be derived from a sound cross-cultural sampling of the varying ways people organize materials and labor to meet both universal human needs and those that are the result of a particular pattern of cultural conditioning. Part of the reason we have not progressed faster is because of our preoccupation with the market. We tend to assume that it is always within the market that almost *anything* —land, labor, even love—can be acquired for a price. Of course, that is not actually how it works, even for us. Most really big deals seem to be made outside the market, at least these days. And the market plays little, if any, part in the organization of basic production in many of the nonindustrialized societies most economic anthropologists have studied.

Our own concepts of ownership, both private and public, have repeatedly proved inadequate to analyze the ways in which others allocate rights of access to productive goods. Probably the most fundamentally troublesome misunderstanding, one that helps explain the long, sordid history of the expropriation of native peoples' lands (example: the Dutch "purchase" of Manhattan island for twenty-four dollars), derives from the special ideas about ownership of the means of production that set us apart from most nonindustrialized peoples. Among them, almost universally, the allocation of productive goods is structured on the basis of relationships in which ties of kinship and community are foremost.

The Bohannans describe how a West African people with whom they lived and worked for years dealt with the problem of determining rights to use the land, an always primary productive good and one that for most of human history has been regulated by family organization (always mediated, of course, by need); just as it still is among the Tiv.

Land Rights Among the Tiv

Paul and Laura Bohannan

Ideas about space reflected in English and related languages are so specialized—so refined to fit specific institutional situations—that it is difficult to understand other cultural perceptions of social ecology (Hall 1963; 1966). The concepts of "ownership" and "property" are highly specialized and are dependent on specific technological, social, and legal institutions which are by no means universal. Nevertheless, a large number of writers dealing with "land tenure" have assumed the English and American specifics and then tried to understand the general and the exotic in terms of them. Needless to say, it has not worked well.

The literature on land tenure is one of the largest—and one of the poorest—in all of social and legal science. Its poor quality is comparable only to that of the late nineteenth-century writings on "primitive religion," with the difference that "land tenure" had no Tylors, Robertson-Smiths, or Durkheims. Lévi-Strauss (1963) recently claimed that "totemism" could be understood in terms of nineteenth-century Western needs and philosophies, but scarcely in folk terms or in terms of twentieth-century social and cultural theory. In analogy, we claim here that "property" and "land tenure" and "ownership" studies in the ethnographic literature can be explained in terms of Western legal philosophy and economic history from the waning of the Middle Ages until about World War II. Only if we first consider Western history a specific example of a generalized phenomenon can we bring into focus the problems and data of essentially different systems of arrangement of society in terrestrial space, and exotic economic, political, and mythopoeic arrangements for linking men and space together.

Land Tenure

What is it, then, that Westerners mean by "land tenure"? What do we mean by "land," and what by "tenure"?

Every people must have some view of the physical milieu—the "folk geography" of the world and their part of it. Westerners divide the earth's surface by use of an imaginary grid, itself subject to manipulations and redefinitions. We then plot the grid on paper or on a sphere, and correlate the physical features of the land and sea with this grid. We have developed instruments for locating ourselves on the earth's surface in relation to the positions of the stars. There are precise rules for symbolizing the information from the instruments. We have perfected a system of measurement which allows us to repeat precisely operations carried out in the past; thus we have been able to locate and measure pieces of the earth's surface and to record our computations on gridded maps. These measured pieces become, for some purposes at least, identifiable "things."

Land, whatever else it may be, is for Westerners a measurable entity divisible into thing-like "parcels" by means of mathematical and technical processes of surveying and cartography. This complex notion of "land," with its accompanying technology, is an essential of present-day Western land tenure, as well as of the Western market-oriented economy.

The ideas of "tenure" in our own system are even more tangled. First of all, "tenure" assumes a conception of "land" of the sort we have already described. Only if it is divisible and the divisions stable and measurable can "land" be "held." Only if land is cut up into definable units can it enter the market or, as the jurist sees the same phenomenon, be subject to contract. Contract and a land market constitute specific types of relationships between men and land.

However, holding a piece of "real property" is more than a mere relationship between a man and a thing-like piece of land. As the best jurisprudential opinion has long told us, it is a relationship among persons. "Tenure" has to do with rights *in* land *against* or *with* other persons. Thus, in addition to the man-land unit, usually called a "property system" by Westerners, we have a man-man unit, which is part of the social

Source: From Paul and Laura Bohannan, *Tiv Economy* (Evanston, Ill.: Northwestern University Press, 1968). Used by permission of the publisher and the authors.

system in general and of the legal system in particular.

When Westerners discuss land in terms of the social or legal system, they do so in terms of "rights." "Rights" are attributes of persons against other persons. But in European languages, with the particular notions of land they reflect, "rights in land" can become attributes *of the land.* This "land right" links a person and a piece of land.

The equation of rights of people with rights in land, making one the obverse of the other, does not occur in most African societies. Therefore, when we turn from the Western to the Tiv situation, we must ask how we can classify Tiv attitudes toward "land" and Tiv versions of "tenure."

This matter can best be examined by generalizing the factors we have found so they can guide our work in exotic cultures. The three factors are: a concept of geography, a model of correlating man with his physical environment, and a social system with a spatial dimension. These factors can be restated as axioms: (1) A people has a representation of the country in which it lives; that representation can be analyzed in analogy to the Western map. (2) Members of any society have a set of concepts for speaking about and dealing with the relationships between themselves and the earth they exploit. (3) The spatial aspect of any social organization has some overt expression in word and deed. The study of land in society is the way in which any people associates map, property, and spatial relationships.

Land Maps

It is, we believe, a fact that no African societies used indigenously an astrally based map such as our own, although a few peoples elsewhere, notably the Polynesians, did do so. Astral maps are, of course, seafarers' maps. A few African peoples did divide up the earth's surface into pieces by using terrestrial landmarks. The Kikuyu (Sluiter 1960) and the Haya (P. Reining: personal communication) are notable examples. In both cases, some form of land transfer similar to "sale" did exist under limited conditions; in at least the Kikuyu case, however, land "tenure" was regarded as part of the kinship system.

Other African societies have "tenure" relationship to land of a sort very different from "ownership" or "contract." Two of probably many types can be distinguished here. The first is represented by rain shrines among the Tonga (Colson 1954) or saints' graves among the Cyrenaican Bedouin Arabs (Evans-Pritchard 1949). Rather than pieces of land with boundaries, there are points on the land, marked by shrines, that form the center of activity of a social group; the "map" is a juxtaposition of geographical points intruded into the social system by a religious idiom.

In the second type of "non-property" system, of which the Tiv are an example, the social organization is conceived in terms of pure space, and is only incidentally linked with the physical environment for comparatively short periods of time by activities such as farming. Tiv see geography in the same terms in which they see social organization. As we have noted, the idiom of descent and genealogy provides not only the basis for lineage grouping, but also for territorial grouping.

This "genealogical map" of Tivland moves about the surface of the earth in sensitive response to the demands of individual farmers as those demands change from year to year. Association of the genealogical map with specific pieces of ground is of brief duration only; a man or woman has what we have called "farm tenure," i.e., precise rights to a farm during the time it is in cultivation. But once the farm returns to fallow, the specific rights lapse. However, a man always has rights in the "genealogical map" of his agnatic lineage, wherever that lineage may happen to be on the terrain. These rights, which are part of his birthright, can never lapse. A mathematician has suggested that whereas the Western map, based on surveys, resembles geometry, the Tiv notion resembles topology—"geometry on a rubber sheet." The Western map must be rigid and precise if the principle of contract is to work; the Tiv map must constantly change if the principle of kinship grouping is to work.

Instead of seeing maps in terms of man-thing units such as property, Tiv axiomize the spatial aspect of their social groups. This "social map" leaves them free to question the ways in which social groups or individuals are attached to exploitational rights in the earth. This is the exact opposite of Westerners, who axiomize their maps in terms of their property norms and values and see the social system which results as fundamentally a series of contracts and hence open to change and to question. In short, Westerners can question the social group more easily than a concept of property, while Tiv can question their property-like concepts more easily than their social groups.

Land Rights

Within the minimal *tar* every piece of cultivated ground, from the largest yam field to the most insignificant patch of cassava, can be referred to by somebody as "mine." Such a statement does not imply "ownership" of the land, but rather the "farm tenure" which gives that person some rights in the crops then growing on that farm. Such rights can be defined closely.

If the investigator is standing beside a farm in a minimal *tar*, A, and asks a man of a different minimal *tar*, B, "Whose farm is this?" he will be told, "It is the farm of minimal *tar* A," giving the patronymic. One is not likely to be successful in getting a more precise reply. If, however, one is standing beside the same farm in minimal *tar* A and asks a man of the segment associated with minimal *tar* A, "Whose farm is this?" the first reply will probably be, "It is ours." If the investigator asks which compound head the farm belongs to, the name will be given; the name of the woman who works the land and who will harvest and sell the crops or the name of her husband may be volunteered.

Again, if the ethnographer asks a woman whom he finds weeding a farm, "Whose farm is this?" she will say, "It is mine." In order to get further information one must ask, "Whose wife are you?" If, however, one asks this woman's husband, "Whose farm is this?" he will say, "It is mine." In order to get any further information one must ask, "For which wife did you hoe it?" or, "Who is your compound head?" If one further asks the compound head whose farm it is, he will reply, "It is mine." To get more precise information one must ask, "For which woman did you hoe it?" or "Which of your youngsters hoed his wife a farm here?"

In these answers are found the cluster of rights in a particular farm. A woman has rights in the farm: she owns and controls most of the produce which is grown on it; she has corresponding obligations to feed her husband and her children from the produce of her farm. Her husband also has his rights in the farm: he made it for his wife with the help of some of his kinsmen; millet or beniseed grown on it during its cultivation cycle belongs to him; he will eat from it and pay his tax from it. The compound head has other rights in the farm: he allotted it to the husband for him to make his wife a farm there; he has a right to a small portion of the crop for purposes of hospitality and ritual if he needs it; he has the final word in determining the size of the farm. That farm is the symbol of the compound head's good faith in fulfilling the needs of his subordinates.

The map of Figure 1 shows the farms of most of the people of a large compound in MbaGor. It is meant to bring out the different portions claimed by different women, the juxtaposition of farms of the various women making up a basic labor group of attached wives or daughters-in-law, the larger portions claimed by the husbands of the women, and the whole claimed by the compound head.

Besides these rights in specific pieces of cultivated land, Tiv also claim rights to *sufficient* land. (1) Every wife or widow of a compound member has a right to a farm from which to feed herself and her dependents. (2) Every adult male who lives in the compound has a right to a farm sufficient to feed himself and his dependents. (3) Every compound head has a right to sufficient land to feed himself and all the members of his compound, including the rights of sufficient fallow land to allow for revitalization of exhausted soil.

Sanctions

Both sets of rights—to specific farms and to sufficient land—have easily recognized sanctions. Rights to specific farms are protected by ritual sanctions. Tiv erect magical emblems called *akombo* to protect farms against interlopers, thieves, and witches. This emblem consists of a bundle of sticks or a braided palm frond, a stone or a potsherd, placed on the ground or hung on a pole at the "top" of a field. The *akombo* are said to inflict disease or misfortune on anyone who meddles with the farm. The right to erect this magical emblem on a specific field is part of the basic cluster of rights in the field: a woman can erect an *akombo* on her own field; and her husband or the compound head can erect an *akombo* on this field. A woman may ask her husband to erect one on her farm, though more often he simply does it. A man can ask his compound head to erect an *akombo* on his farm; the compound head would not do so without being asked. No

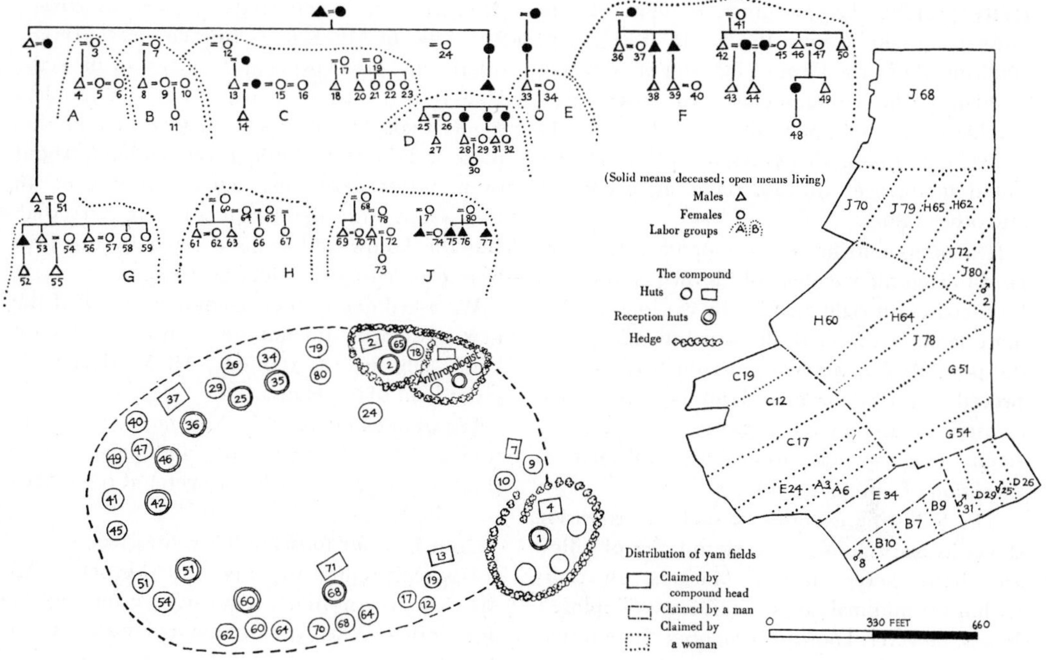

Figure 1. Kyagba's compound in MbaGor.

one else dares do so (unless he is paid by one of these three) lest the *akombo* attack the person who put it up.

In southern areas an *akombo* is usually found on any piece of cultivated ground, although some men do not erect them until late in the season. Except for *akombo* hung on economically valuable trees, they are rarely found on uncultivated ground. Fallow is not in need of *akombo* protection, although in some boundary disputes the emblems are brought into play.

Although an *akombo* would seize (*kor*) any person within the compound who took food he was not entitled to, it serves primarily as a protection against outsiders. Within the compound, moral sanctions of family (including co-wives) and co-residence are usually sufficient protection of one's rights to specific land.

Rights to sufficient land also have obvious sanctions and reciprocal obligations. A woman has a right to a farm sufficient to feed herself and her children. If she doesn't get it, she leaves. Her husband must either make her a farm or lose his wife and bridewealth. If a man is too ill to make his wife's farm, his brothers or age-mates hoe for her. Every adult male in the compound, then, must have a right to land on which to make farms for his wives.

An agnatic member of the lineage associated with the minimal *tar* has rights to sufficient land within that minimal *tar* because of his agnation. A man who is not an agnatic lineage member is given such rights for the period of his residence. If a compound head does not provide fields—and provide them willingly, with no fussing, nagging, or fighting—an aggrieved agnate follows one of two courses: he either moves out and builds a compound for himself, after which he can claim a part of "his father's fallow" and have the claim settled by the elders of the minimal segment; or he moves his family to his mother's people, where he is given fields. A non-agnate simply leaves. The sanction is the same as in the case of a wife: physical separation. The fear of "sitting alone" is acute among the Tiv. A man who wrangles with his sons and brothers soon finds himself "sitting alone," without labor, unable to work his fields. A bad temper or a surly, stingy nature "spoils the compound."

The right of every compound head to sufficient land to feed his dependents is of a basically different kind: a "right against the world." Generally speaking, the only sanction among Tiv to enforce a right against the world is self-help, traditionally in the form of fighting or "fighting by night" (the Tiv euphemism for witchcraft). Self-help calls into play all sorts of subsidiary rights and duties, the sanctions of which are found in lineage, kinship, religious, economic, and other values.

If a compound head does not have sufficient land to feed the members of his own compound, he exercises his right against the world and takes more land. His right to do so is limited only by the possibility of his being driven from it. The procedure for taking more land, however, is circumscribed. Except for migration— a very different matter—it is always accomplished by extension of "present holdings."

The following example of such an extension shows its main points. The boundaries of fallow are almost never marked. Markers, especially within the minimal *tar*, are universally deplored. It was, however, known throughout the minimal lineage that Andza had rights to land next to Ikpaor, Doga, and Iyorver (see Table 1). Andza, Doga, and Iyorver had a common father's father's father, but their agnatic link with Ikpaor was still another generation removed. When the time came for Andza to farm fallow he had used several years previously, he therefore extended his former holdings toward Ikpaor, not toward his closer agnates, Doga and Iyorver. In areas of land shortage Tiv say, "Would you cause hunger in the compound of your mother's son (*wanngo*, 'a close relative') if you can get land from your father's son (*wanter*, 'a more distant relative')?"

This pattern was vividly apparent when a group of Hausa established a village at a market site within the area of MbaDuku. The presence of resident Hausa is the mark of a big market. Most MbaDuku favored a Hausa settlement. After considerable negotiation, a site was selected in the *tar* of MbaKov (a lineage of MbaDuku/MbaIkaa.) MbaKov people agreed to have the Hausa on this site, but they foresaw a problem sooner than did the others. At this site a market place and the Hausa village were laid out. About twenty acres were taken out of cultivation. No food crops were destroyed; all were harvested. But the fallow and fields covered by this area were claimed by six different compounds.

We asked one of these compound heads if the new settlement did not run him short of farm land. "Oh, no," he replied. "All MbaDuku has given land to the Hausa."

We didn't understand. "You *saw* us," he continued. "All MbaDuku met and decided that this was the place for the market and the village to be built."

"But it's *your* food land!" we insisted.

His reply stated the Tiv view precisely: "All MbaKov [the minimal segment] are the sons of one mother. When you need more land you go to your brother and you say, 'My brother, give me land on which to make a farm for my wife so that she may eat.' The brother says, 'Of course' (*Ka sha mi*), and if he in turn is short of land he goes to the brother at his back [i.e., the person who bounds his land but who is more distantly related than the first man, to whom he gave land] and says, 'My brother, will you give me land so that I may hoe a farm for my wife, so that she and her children may eat?' He says, 'Of course,' so the man hoes the farm. That man then goes to his brother in MbaAji [the companion minimal segment] and says, 'My brother [using the same term, *wanngo*], will you give me land . . .' " and so on.

Discussing this later we received a fuller explanation. Our informant drew a diagram on the ground. First, he said that MbaKov land looks

Table 1. *Lineage Relations in a Land Dispute*

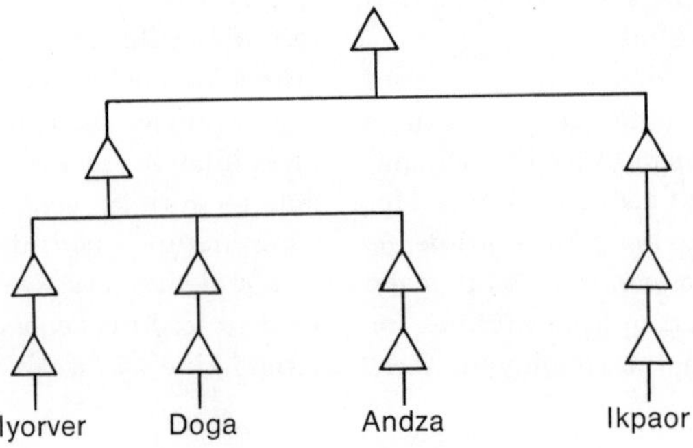

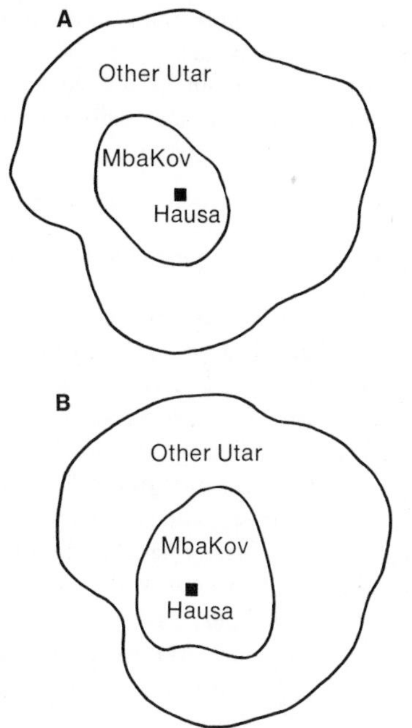

Figure 2. Sketch of land adjustment for a Hausa market.

like this (a circle), and it is surrounded by other *utar* (which he named; see the larger concentric circle of Figure 2). Then he explained again the process of extending holdings at the expense of the genealogically most distant kinsmen whose land adjoins your own. As he went on he changed the diagram until it had the appearance of that shown in Figure 2. "You see," he ended, "all MbaDuku—all Kunav [for the concentric circle surrounding MbaKov could represent either]—are giving land to the Hausa!"

While the Hausa community was being laid out, the men who were being dispossessed from part of their farms shouted and argued foot by foot. They were opposed by the government chief and a few of the more vocal elders; the Hausa very wisely stayed out of the dispute. On the surface one might have assumed that the chief had a right to move his people off a given piece of land or that he had some sort of superior right in it. No Tiv, including this chief, saw it that way. By shouting over this specific piece of land the farmers were impressing on all comers their rights to sufficient land. When the time came for them to take more land, they wanted their case to be remembered. The shouting and argumentation were, in a way, a mnemonic formality.

Rights of women always depend on residence and marriage. A woman has rights in her farms in the *tar* of her husband as long as she is resident there. She has a right to sufficient land in her husband's minimal *tar* as long as she is married to him (or her levir), whether the right is exercised or not. Women have no land rights in their natural *utar,* and few live there once they have married. If one does, she works on "the farms of her mother." Her brothers may hoe her a very small farm for a year or two, but she is still said to be "tending" the farm of her mother. No one has an obligation to her; such an obligation to an unmarried woman is incumbent only on sons and brothers.

Rights of men depend on agnation or matrilateral kinship and residence. A man has rights to sufficient land, as well as to specific cultivated land, in the *tar* of his agnatic minimal segment. Although these rights can be exercised only while he is resident in this *tar,* they never lapse. Rights of agnates can be revoked only by ritual exclusion from the agnatic lineage. This was formerly possible if a man changed lineages when the children of complementary exchange marriages were equalized (Akiga 1939:118–20), or if he were sold into slavery for his crimes. Today both these possibilities are prohibited by law. If a man is accepted as a resident by a non-agnatic kinsman or friend, he is given land. His rights lapse when he leaves that *tar.*

The right of an agnate to a specific piece of land within the minimal *tar* is often in question, but in the several score of land disputes we saw from 1949 to 1953, the right of an agnate to sufficient land was never questioned. No informants could discuss, even hypothetically, a situation in which an agnate was refused land in his minimal *tar.* None got beyond the platitude, "You can never refuse your father's son." To do so would be an act canceling agnation.

Thus land rights are a part of the birthright of every man; they are an aspect of his social and political status. To be without land is to be without kin. But a man has specific land only when he is in residence. On his return after an absence, he settles among his full brothers, beside his half-brothers. This agnatic birthright carries with it rights to land intermixed with, but disinct from, that of a man's full brothers. Their land is intermixed with, but distinct from, that of their half-brothers. The land of the entire group is intermixed with, but distinct from, that of other men of the compound. Land rights are a spatial aspect of agnatic filiation.

Land rights are simple among Tiv; they are, in fact, so simple that the anthropologist must state some of the things which they are *not* in order to avoid being misunderstood.

"Communal Tenure"

Tiv land tenure is *not* communal tenure. It is a matter of regret that this concept, which Malinowski (1935 1:319) called "the undying fallacy of anthropological work," has refused to die. In a fully developed, contractually oriented society like our own, communal ownership can and does exist. That is to say, the commune, whatever its nature, is regarded as a jural person—a corporation aggregate capable of legally owning property. The difficulty arises when this legal fiction is applied to African land systems. "Communal tenure" is an illusion that results from viewing the systematic exploitation by kinship groups of their environment through the distorting lens of Western market-oriented and contract-dominated institutions of property and ownership. Sir Henry Maine pointed out long since that in a community based on kinship, land is an aspect of the group, but *not* the basis for grouping.

Rights are attributes of persons. "Titles" are attributes of land. Tiv rights of persons in specific farms and to sufficient land are all individual rights. Tiv do not recognize any concept of "title." No matter how many other persons have another right to a piece of land in which X has a right, X's individual right still remains. A woman, her husband, and their compound head each has an individual right in a given farm. No one else has those particular rights. To change the frame of reference from the people to the farm by saying that the farm is the "community" property of some members of the compound is to distort the Tiv view so greatly as to make comparative study banal.

Tiv always use a *person's* frame of reference. They never use the *land* frame of reference with its insistence on some concept of "ownership." There are several references in this report to "our field" and "our fallow." This meaning of "our" is analogous to the commonly heard "our wife." "Our wife" means a woman who is the wife of a man with whom the speaker is identified, usually by lineage membership. It certainly does not indicate polyandry. Equally, "our farm" means one to which one or several individuals with whom I am associated can claim rights. It does not indicate "communal ownership" or even collective rights.

Inheritance, Rental, and Sale

Land rights can be acquired in two ways: by status and by gift. "Inheritance" cannot give one greater rights than one already has. To make this point completely clear, we shall discuss inheritance briefly. Tiv do not have a word in their language which corresponds to the English word "inherit." Both Tiv dictionaries define *dyako* as "heritage"; nevertheless, it has this meaning only by extension. While a man is alive his *dyako* is his property: wives, spears, reception hut, clothing, crops, and livestock. When he dies, his heir is said to "eat" (*ya*) the *dyako*. One may also "eat the *dyako* of so-and-so" before the death of the owner. This sentence refers to major gifts from one's elders, and was said of gifts we made from our belongings before leaving the field. Basically, *dyako* means "personal property." It includes seed yams, but not land or farms.

To succeed a man to a status or position is to "sit on his head." This phrase is also used when a man's son, younger brother, or recognized agent deputizes for him. A new compound head either "sits on the head" of his deceased predecessor, or, most commonly, is said to "eat the compound" of his predecessor.

Land is relevant in the context of splitting a compound or splitting the field . . . but not in the succession to the status of compound head or inheritance of *dyako*. The Tiv state two "rules" which sound enough like "inheritance laws" that they should be examined carefully: (1) At the time the fields are "split" a man has a right to that portion of his father's land which was farmed by his mother, and (2) if full brothers split their land, they say it is split on the basis of what has been farmed by their respective wives.

We were discussing inheritance with a son of a polygynist who had three sets of sons. The young man assured us that each set of sons would take the land of their mother; he pointed out the actual yam fields of these women as the indication of where each group of sons would farm. We asked, "What will happen if your group gets larger than that of your half-brother? What if you become twenty, but they become only ten?" His immediate reply was "He will give me land; we would not split the field." But we asked what would happen if the half-brothers too were short of land; would he still get land from them? "That would spoil the compound," he said seriously. "I would get it from my father's son" (i.e., from a still more distant agnate).

What Tiv are in fact saying is that they take their position in the lineage and the rights that go with it from their fathers, and that their separate mothers account for the internal structure of the group. Although they see the lineage in spatial terms, they do not see any correlation between genealogy and specific farms. They see the genealogy as evidence of rights to sufficient land.

These concepts do not pretend to allow for equal sharing of farms among all of a man's sons and brothers. rather they allow for every man's right to land, in view of his genealogical position. Indeed given the migration patterns of the Tiv . . ., it would be impossible for a man actually to use the ground that his mother farmed. He does, however, "inherit" his position in the system through her and through his father.

A Tiv may be given temporary rights to reside and farm in areas where he has no agnatic rights to the land. He pays no one for this land; his kinsmen say that they "gave him a farm." However, his rights lapse when he leaves. In a few exceptional cases a farm is "given" for the length of a rotation cycle to non-residents. In the land-hungry areas of southern Tivland, a compound head who finds himself with many absent dependents—hence a nominal right to more land than he can use without making his fields too big to work (thereby leading to envy and witchcraft)—grants the right to make a farm to a man living in a neighboring minimal *tar*, and filiated to the lineage of the neighboring *tar*.

In MbaGor, Tsavkor found himself "sitting alone" because people were convinced that he had perpetrated a particularly heinous piece of witchcraft. He knew that if his farms lay fallow for more than the minimal time for bare recovery, he would lose them through occupation by his neighboring agnates. His problem, then, was to keep enough land in legitimate use to be able to retain it against the day when his people returned to him or to his successor. He solved his problem by giving land to four different individuals who were living in the companion minimal lineage, MbaWandia. Two of these men were his matrilateral kinsmen. The third recipient was a daughter's son of MbaWandia, whose position there was weak and who was not a strong enough personality to gain as much land from his host as he thought he needed. The fourth was an agnatic member of MbaWandia: a quiet, meek man who was the younger full brother of one of Tsavkor's most cherished adversaries.

These men hoed farms for their wives on Tsavkor's land. The trilogy of rights to these farms shows some important differences from the ordinary. Tsavkor had no right to any of the produce, and certainly he received no rent in money. He had no obligation to see that a non-resident farmer of his fields had *sufficient* land. The non-resident farmer had no obligation to take part in any land action brought by or against Tsavkor, although his interest might lead him to do so. The rights of the non-resident farmer are temporary, almost never exceeding a single crop rotation.

To call such persons "tenants" seems a marginal usage of the term. No question of residence is involved, no question of rent—even in kind or as token—enters into the matter. It is solely a device on the part of the "giver" to maintain his rights in a specific farm against the rights of his agnates to sufficient land.

Tiv are unequivocal (once you have made them understand the question) in saying that they cannot and do not rent or sell land. There is no word in Tiv which even remotely approximates the English word "rental," nor is there a word that can be used in respect to land that might be translated as "pledge" or "mortgage." Tiv of Kunav and Shangev are not unfamiliar with the idea of rental, however. They knew the Hausa colony in Obudu paid a small annual ground rent which went into the Native Treasury of the Obudu District. Tiv consider this procedure immoral. To them it smacks of taking money for hospitality, thereby nullifying the hospitality. One Tiv summed it up by saying, "Isn't a guest a guest?"

The Hausa settlers in MbaDuku certainly paid no land rent; they said so themselves, the Tiv all said so, and we believe that we obtained enough information on the money that changed hands among them to be sure that nothing even resembling a rental for the village site was ever considered. They did pay for labor performed and for building materials, but they did not pay for the land on which they lived or had their garden plots.

Whenever we asked too insistently about

rentals, Tiv always asked, "Are *you* paying anything for permission to live here?" and we had to admit that we were not.

Though no cases were found in 1950 of land being farmed for money or produce rent, we were told that about three years before our study one Iyon man had offered the Uge £6 for the right to farm a complete crop cycle in their country. The particular people whom he approached agreed to the arrangement, but the elders of the Uge refused to give their permission, so nothing had ever come of it.

When we returned to MbaDuku in 1952, we discovered one case in which a man of MbaGor had accepted *3s.* from a man of MbaWandia for permission to clear some swamp land and plant rice. The MbaGor man said it was for one year only, and his swamp land would be cleared for him.

We also found an account in old administrative files about an occasion on which Gav (companion lineage to Kunav) encroached on Ogoja Division tribes: they were fined heavily but were allowed to retain the farms they had planted. As soon as the people and administration of Ogoja Division discovered that the Tiv thought this an excellent bargain, they no longer allowed Tiv to retain the farms.

All Tiv deny that they sell land. When pressed they are likely to ask, "What would we sell?" To Tiv, such an answer is sufficient. Land is, for them, a unique category. Nothing is exchangeable for it. Tiv could not exchange land for wealth to use as bridewealth as do the Jaba Kwoi (Cole 1949) because land and such wealth (or women themselves) have, in the Tiv view, nothing in common to make them exchangeable. On the other hand, they do not exchange land for other land (Cole 1949 cites such cases among the Kagoro; Jones 1949 mentions it as an Ibo practice) because land is associated with a segment in a lineage system, and hence with agnation.

There is one other, and even more important, reason why Tiv cannot sell land. We have seen that rights to land follow residence rights and are of two kinds: permanent rights to land and temporary rights to farms. No one can *buy* rights to land in a *tar* in which he is living; he has a right to sufficient land already. No one can *buy* land in a *tar* in which he is not living, because he is not living there. No one can buy a farm because it is a part of his living arrangements.

If land runs short in one's own *tar*, one takes land from an adjoining *tar*. All Tiv see the *tar* as expanding with the synchronous processes of passage of time and increase of population (proved to Tiv satisfaction by reference to lineage genealogies). This has led to the doctrine, *not* of transfer of land, but of movement of people and social groups, as the next chapter will show.

Summary

The task of this article has been to examine the ways in which "land" and territoriality are institutionalized by the Tiv in the absence of market allocation. In carrying out that task we saw that the relationship between people and things, which in English is translatable into a set of "ownership" ideas, backed by "property" law and deep regard for the property of others, is seen as a social relationship by Tiv. Such a task is one of the most difficult that anthropology presents: understanding phenomena as they are manifested in the absence of simplifying ideas. Yet only by so doing can we see the significance of the simplifying idea as well as the need for it.

REFERENCES CITED

Bohannan, Paul and Laura, 1968, *Tio Economy* (Evanston, Ill.: Northwestern University Press, Chapter 7).

Cole, C., *Report on Land Tenure, Zaria Province,* Government Printer, Kaduna.

Colson, E., 1954, "Ancestral Spirits and Social Structure Among Plateau Tonga," *International Archives of Ethnography,* XLVII, 21–68.

Evans-Pritchard, E., 1949, *The Sanusi of Cyrenaica,* Clarendon Press, Oxford.

Hall, E., 1963, "A System for the Notation of Proxemic Behavior," *American Anthropologist,* LXV, 1003–26.

Jones, G., 1949, "Ibo Land Tenure," *Africa,* XIX.

Lévi-Strauss, C., 1963, *Totemism,* Beacon Press, Boston.

Malinowski, B., 1935, *Coral Gardens and Their Magic,* 2 Vols., Allen and Unwin, London.

Sluiter, G., 1960, *Kikuyu Concepts of Land and Kin,* Master's Thesis, University of Chicago.

In most cultures the organization of work is markedly different from our own individualistically oriented model in which working for oneself is idealized even among union laborers on the assembly line, and the concept of work organized for the collective good is still a little suspect. In most nonindustrialized societies, as in this illustration from Ethiopia, work is organized on the basis of either kinship or communal interest.

Only in stratified societies, where wealth and power are differentially allocated, can some compel others to do their work for them, either through coercion—by enslavement, serfdom, or some other form of involuntary servitude—or through the labor market, where cash wages and the necessity of meeting subsistence needs through cash purchases function to organize work by imposing monetary measures on demand and supply. Here, in an excerpt from a much longer account of his fieldwork in Ethiopia, Stauder describes a far older, still widespread system.

Majangir Work Organization

Jack R. Stauder

All Majangir are organized by households or "domestic groups." (For a discussion of the "domestic group" as a general concept, see Fortes: 1958.) The Majang domestic group is a distinct economic unit. The modal form of this group is the nuclear family. But many of Majang domestic groups do not include complete nuclear families and many others include persons extra to the nuclear family. The actual composition of domestic groups is best described numerically. But before looking at the forms taken by the Majang domestic group, it is necessary first to describe the general conditions which govern its formation. These conditions have to do with the production and distribution of food and other necessities.

Virtually every Majang belongs to a domestic group, because a pooling of labor and skills is necessary if one is to obtain a normal livelihood by Majang standards. The necessity for collaboration in subsistence activities is essentially a function of the sexual division of labor as conceived and practised by Majangir. Males and females must depend on each other, for each sex is trained in certain skills the other sex is not. In addition, many tasks not requiring special skills are nevertheless conventionally assigned to one sex or the other as its particular responsibility.

The conventions of the sexual division of labor are in most cases not rigidly maintained. When necessary, a man or woman will often do some unskilled task normally and normatively done by the opposite sex. A person who breaks this convention is not usually embarrassed, but may often resent the necessity. Members of each sex expect members of the other to do certain jobs as their side of the general partnership between sexes, and reinforcing this partnership are the jobs which in fact only one sex is able by training to do well. In Table 1 are summarized the important aspects of the sexual division of labor.

A domestic group is formed when a man, or several men, undertake the male tasks listed in Table 1 for the sake of a woman, or several women, who in return undertake the female tasks for the sake of the male partner(s). The partners in this group pool their labor and skills, and the resulting products of their joint effort are pooled also. The benefits of their undertaking are shared by both male and female partners, and also by any of their dependants not able to contribute labor to the partnership. The partners and their dependants constitute a domestic group. All Majangir are divided into these small groups, with very little overlap of membership. . . .

Although Table 1 presents the essential responsibilities of the male and female members

Source: Reprinted from *The Majangir* by Jack R. Stauder by permission of Cambridge University Press and the author.

Table 1. *Sexual Division of Labor*

Male Tasks	*Female Tasks*
Clear fields, slash, chop, burn	Cultivate fields, plant, weed, guard from pests, harvest
Hunt, trap and fish	Gather wild greens and mushrooms
Make hives, gather honey, brew honeywine	Pound grain to flour
Sell honey, buy trade goods	Cook meals requiring boiling or steaming
Build huts	Prepare and brew grain beer
Fight and defend against dangerous enemies, animal and human	Brew *kari* (coffee leaves)
	Fetch water from stream or spring
Fashion wood and iron implements	Care for small children
Weave basketry	Make pots

of a domestic group, an adequate description requires an outline of how the group is seen to operate as such, in specific activities.

Fields and Crops. The domestic group is a crop-producing unit. The men of the group are responsible for clearing the yearly set of fields . . ., and the women of the group are responsible for most of the subsequent care of the fields, though men and children may help. Especially in the production of grains, the most important kind of crop, male and female responsibilities are complementary, and every grain field must be a joint enterprise of at least two persons, one of each sex. But less important kinds of crops are also usually produced as a joint enterprise.

All the working members of a domestic group normally cooperate to clear and care for a single set of fields (*gedi, bori, kate, nyumwe* . . .). A group containing several males and females may, however, in addition to this set, make separate fields—usually slash—mulch sorghum fields (*kate*) or sesame fields (*nyumwe*). In these cases, a male/female pair within a domestic group takes responsibility for a separate field. Such pairing off within the domestic group is inconsequential, however, for the harvested crops of the separate fields are pooled, together with what other crops have been produced in the same fields by the entire group. Also, assistance, when needed, is freely asked for and given within a domestic group regardless of separate field responsibilities. This is not normal between different domestic groups.

Neighborhood or community working parties are often gathered to do the heavier agricultural tasks. A domestic group provides drink to attract and compensate the people who come to help. Any member of the domestic group may provide the ingredients for the drink—if grain beer, it is usually made from the group's pooled resources—and any member may provide the labour to make the drink. Who contributes what to the drink does not determine rights of ownership. The subsequent produce of the field belongs to the entire domestic group, and is pooled with their other stores.

Wild Products. The domestic group is a food-pooling unit. Its members do not necessarily cooperate in every productive activity—though males and females cooperate in producing grain crops—but what food its members do produce singly or collectively they largely produce for their domestic group, not for themselves as individuals. The members of the group pool the fruits of their production. This is true of crops and also of wild products such as meat, fish, greens and mushrooms.

Only women should gather and cook wild (or

domestic) greens and mushrooms. In this case, men would be embarrassed to be seen, by women, cooking or gathering these items, though men will sometimes do so secretly for themselves when their female partners have neglected them. It is the responsibility of the women of the domestic group to gather and cook greens and mushrooms and to distribute the dish to all the members of their group to eat.

On the other hand, women never hunt or trap or skin game, and they rarely fish. But it is the responsibility of a man, when he obtains some game or fish, and after having perhaps eaten certain portions of it, to bring the remainder home to present to the women (or woman) of his domestic group. The women then cook it and distribute it to all the members of the group to eat, including to the man who provided it.

Food Stores and Meals. Majang eating habits are irregular. During the day individuals eat whatever food comes to hand, whenever it is offered, or cook food for themselves if they are hungry. The staple food stores of a person's domestic group are normally always freely available to him, without his having to ask, at his home. The pooled grain crop of all the harvested fields of a domestic group is kept in one of the group's huts, or perhaps in two or three if the harvest was large. While fresh, maize may be taken directly from the field, and root crops are always pulled from the ground as wanted. Normally, a person takes freely what food he (she) wants to cook and eat himself from the crops jointly owned by all the members of his group. In a small minority of cases . . ., the crops are divided after harvest and some members of the group will be restricted from taking freely from one portion or another.

Except in these few instances, and except in times of scarcity when senior members of the group exercise a sort of rationing to conserve food stores, all members can and do help themselves to the uncooked food of their domestic unit, without asking permission. This right, together with the pooling of labor and produce, is the most distinctive feature of domestic group membership, for normally one would never take the food of another domestic group without asking and receiving permission; or, more typically, being invited to take.

Except for smaller children, every Majang is then able when at home to take freely raw food and cook a meal for himself (herself). All starch staples and some relishes may be cooked by toasting on a shard, baking in embers or roasting beside a fire—techniques at which Majangir, of whichever sex and any age over six, are all adept. Most day-time meals are cooked in this way, by individuals for themselves.

However, the women of a domestic group are responsible for cooking, not all meals, but certain kinds of meals, for the consumption of the entire group. These meals may be simple boiled foods, though men sometimes also boil food for themselves. But preferably women should cook for men the favourite staple meals of the Majangir, either a stiff grain porridge (*kyu*) or a sweet grain cake (*shoe*). These dishes require special sex-linked skills to prepare, including the hard labour of reducing the grain to flour or paste. Consequently, men depend entirely on women to provide them with these foods. Men also depend on females to prepare the most available kinds of relish, sesame paste and boiled greens.

The facts are summarized in Table 2.

The important considerations are these: (1) a good meal, to Majangir, should include a relish (*malan*) as well as a staple, and the best staples are grain cooked as porridge (*kyu*) or cake (*shoe*); (2) a good life, to Majangir, should include frequent good meals; (3) good meals can be prepared only by females.

These considerations explain the importance of the women's responsibility to prepare some meals for their domestic groups. The domestic partnership is often summarized by men: *Pura aguto jati, le ko keje kyu,* "I make fields for a woman, so she will make porridge." Ideally women should make for their group one meal a day, usually for the evening. In actual practice, a man is usually satisfied to receive a meal about every other night from the women of his group. For other meals, he depends on his own cooking.

Drink. Only males provide honeywine, for only they practise apiculture. Only females provide grain beer, for its preparation requires their sex-linked skills. Neither drink is brewed for consumption only within the domestic group; drink is made to be offered especially to persons outside the group. But often drink is brewed for working parties to help make fields, huts, etc., which will belong to the domestic group as a whole. In these cases, as I have said, any member of the domestic group may make the drink or provide its ingredients; the group as a whole benefits. When a working party is

Table 2. *Methods of Preparing Different Foods, by Sex*

		Cooked by Women Only	*Cooked by Men or Women*	
		Pounding, or Grinding, plus Boiling or Steaming (keji)	*Boiling Only* (keji)	*Roasting on Spit* (medee); *Baking in Embers* (tuje); *or Toasting on Shard* (waye), etc.
Starch staples	Dry maize, sorghum	× (*kyu*)	×	×
	Sweet maize, sorghum	× (*shoe*)	×	×
	Tubers and pumpkins		×	×
Relishes (*malan*)	Greens and mushrooms		×*	
	Sesame, pumpkin seeds	×		×
	Meat and fish		×	×

Women cook for entire group domestic group (first two columns)

Individuals, men or women, cook for themselves (last two columns)

*Ideally done only by women.

necessary, every member of the domestic group is obliged to contribute whatever he or she can at the time to make drink for the party. Failure to fulfill such obligations leads in course to sharp dissension and perhaps to dissolution of the group. . . .

Trade Goods. Men personally own the honey their hives produce. If a man's domestic group needs his honey for a drinking party then he should use it for this. But if it is not needed for this purpose, then according to Majangir a man is theoretically free to sell the honey and buy whatever he wants for his personal use or to give to whomever he wants. In practice, of course, such freedom is constricted by actual social relations. Also, men are expected to provide their domestic units with such items as machetes, axes, bullets, salt, and in times of famine purchased food: any item related to the unit's subsistence needs.

Home-made Tools and Utensils. Men should provide the females of their domestic group with any home-made items that are necessary to the subsistence of the group, but which women cannot make well for themselves. These include baskets, wooden mortar and pestle for pounding grain, handles for iron tools, etc. Women, however, are responsible for making their own pottery.

Shelter. Men construct all the huts for their domestic unit, except for occasional, very flimsy shelters put up by women or children, usually for field-watching.

Water. The females of a domestic group should provide for all its members' cooking and drinking needs. This task requires several trips a day to stream or spring.

Certain items such as tobacco, beads, cloth, cosmetics, pipes, leather, etc., are not produced or pooled or distributed on the basis of domestic group affiliations. Persons belonging to the same domestic group cannot borrow or take these items from each other without asking for them (as they can do food, tools, etc.). Rather, they must ask each other to lend or give them these things, just as they would ask members of other domestic groups. These items are noticeably further removed from subsistence in its narrower sense—the means for staying alive—than the items which are shared freely within the domestic group. The essential function of the domestic group among the Majangir is simply to provide a livelihood for its members by the means described.

The domestic group jointly owns and uses an "estate": a collection of property including fields, huts, tools and stores of foods. The Majang domestic group may be called a "corporate" group, but unlike groups normally called "corporate," it does not have a continuous existence independent of that of its members. No doubt this fact is related to the nature of its property, its estate, which in the Majang economy has no permanent value. Its fields and food stores must be renewed every year, even every season, if a domestic group is to continue. Labor, not property, is the crucial factor. Some domestic groups have very short lives. If partners fail in their obligations to each other, or if for any other reason they should not want to continue in partnership, their domestic unit easily breaks up and the persons in it find others with whom to join. . . .

The domestic group which continues over a long period of time is usually based on nuclear family ties. But the developmental cycle of a family establishes its own limits to the lifetime of a domestic group composed of a nuclear family. As a corporate unit having no permanent estate, but depending on its members' labor, the domestic group must rely for its coherence over time on the constant inter-relationship of its members, organized to renew periodically the estate. But the existence of the domestic group is then subject to the breakdown of these working relationships, a breakdown which can be brought about not only by its members' diverse wills and at their convenience, but also by inevitable or accidental developments in its members' lives.

SECTION II

Distributing Goods and Services

Once produced, there has to be a system for distributing goods and services. The requirement is universal; the organization of such systems varies. For separation and analysis three distinctive ways of organizing distribution can be identified. First is *reciprocity*, in which goods of approximately equivalent value are exchanged between individuals and groups of roughly equal status, and in which assurance that each participant will meet his part of the bargain to reciprocate is principally controlled by social pressure and the fear of losing valued trading partners. For example, in our society gift exchange is usually reciprocal; if not, it rarely continues. Second, there is *redistribution*, in which goods and services move toward an allocative center and out again. (Taxes collected in money and returned in services provide a familiar example.) However, with redistribution, all participants in the exchange relationship are not necessarily of equal status, and coercion is often involved. Because of this an equivalent "return" is less assured. (See your friendly local Commissioner of Public Works.) Third is *market* exchange.

In many societies all three processes operate, as they do in our own. But usually one provides the dominant mode, the main means by which most goods and services are moved. For us the market has been the principal place and money purchase the major process of exchange. But redistribution is coming up fast. Reciprocity, in every form from campaign contributions to wedding presents, is in the still distant place of third importance.

These exchange models are idealized. They are used here simply to provide a coherent set of organizational categories to check, for descriptive accuracy and analytical usefulness, against the ethnographic evidence.

India has a culture in which still important bonds of kinship are constantly reinforced by the reciprocal exchange of goods and services among family members. India also has a highly stratified society in which wealth is distributed with alarming inequality. Highly concentrated in the bank accounts of box holders at the Bombay Polo Grounds, it is nearly nonexistent among the thousands of beggars who sleep in Calcutta's streets.

Neale describes reciprocity and redistribution as they operate in India's country villages, where the persistence of such processes points up the limitations of market-based explanations of economic exchange.

Reciprocity and Redistribution in Rural India

Walter C. Neale

The discipline of economic history has to deal with many areas and many periods in which productive and distributive activities do not depend on buying and selling or the concept of economic efficiency. The economic activities of such nonmarket societies can present themselves in bewildering complexity unless we possess some broad exploratory approach as an alternative to the market theorem. In the case of the Indian village the need for such nonmarket alternatives has been recognized by a succession of students, but a satisfactory solution requires positive patterns of a nonmarket type. This article will show how some of the intractable aspects of the village economy yield to the concepts of reciprocity and redistribution.

The Indian village has been described as precapitalistic, as having a barter economy, a subsistence economy, or as being communistic or collectivistic. However, "precapitalistic" tells us only that it is not capitalistic, and implies a sequence with teleological overtones. A "barter economy" refers to the absence of money, and is, as we shall see, misleading. A "subsistence economy" means only that the main occupation is agriculture, and usually implies poverty. As for "communistic," the term is vague. It is not used in the sense of modern variants of Marxism, but refers to a state of affairs in which both none and all are owners. While the term "collectivistic" recognizes this difficulty by implying that public property requires some definite organization in order to function, it still does not tell us much about specific economic operations. In any case no explanations or descriptions starting from such concepts can develop a set of formal principles showing how the production of goods is organized and how the goods are distributed. All these terms serve merely to stress the absence of certain market institutions in the village system, and while the denial of the existence of the market is correct, no frame of reference for positive description or analysis is offered by them.

The problem of describing the Indian village economy was attacked chiefly by a succession of British administrators of India who had practical purposes in mind, and then by Sir Henry Maine.

From the beginning of the nineteenth century the village community and its economic structure has been a subject of serious consideration. In 1819 Holt Mackenzie, a revenue officer of the East India Company's Bengal administration, submitted a minute on the various forms of land tenure to be found in the newly acquired districts to the northwest of Bengal. His analysis was inspired by the practical desire for a simple, sure, and yet just way of assessing and collecting revenue. The administrators were faced with the task of raising the revenue and had to work out the technical means to that end. In order to develop an effective revenue system they had to place responsibility for payment on particular persons or groups, and a knowledge of the village structure was necessary in order to decide who these persons or groups should be.

There were two considerations. First, the Company had but few officers to administer a very large territory. Responsibility had to be placed where assessment and collection required the least direct supervision and framed in such a way that enforcement would be easy, if not automatic. This consideration reinforced a natural bent to model India after the system existing in the English countryside. Second, equity required that those who enjoyed rights in the land and its produce should be protected in those rights. Further, it required that those who were made responsible for payment of the revenue should have a chance to profit from their responsibilities so long as they did not do so at the expense of the customary privileges of those placed under them in the revenue hierarchy. This second consideration reinforced the tendency to regard Indian rural areas as counterparts to the hierarchical system in the English countryside, where it could be fairly said that the squirearchy did protect its tenants while profiting from their own position. In order to

Source: Reprinted with permission of Macmillan Publishing Co., Inc., from *Trade and Markets in the Early Empires,* by Polanyi, Arensberg, and Pearson (eds.).

accomplish these aims the officers of the Company had to be certain that they knew who controlled the produce of the village, and thus would be able to meet the demands of the revenue administration, and they also had to know what rights and obligations attached to other members of the community.

The scope of the problem was but slowly realized. In the latter part of the eighteenth and the first decade of the nineteenth century the Company had simply contracted with local personages of power, or revenue farmers, but unrest and dissatisfaction soon showed that stability of the revenue and economy of administration could only be achieved in the long run if the officers of the Company understood the true relationships obtaining among the native villagers. It was for these reasons that Holt Mackenzie set forth the traditional rights and duties of those living on the land in north western Provinces.

In addition to the considerations governing the administration of the revenue, the British were faced with a policy decision of how to divide between the Company and other claimants the economic return attributable to land. Until this matter of principle was settled, a permanent system could not be devised. The problem was phrased in terms of ownership. It was accepted as axiomatic that some person or group of persons "owned" the land, and, equally, that whoever owned the land had a right to the economic rent, or, as it was then called, the "net assets" resulting from the productivity of the land. Thus a decision on a matter of policy—how high the land revenue assessment should be—came largely to rest on the answer to a question of law; whether the ruler and his heirs, the Company, or certain private persons or groups of persons owned the land.

The decision did not, however, rest on the legal question alone. It was no less important to keep consistently to some practical ideal of rural organization. A persistent aim of the British was to create a native landed gentry. That the Company's servants thought in terms of the English system of landlord, farmer, and agricultural laborer is shown by the Permanent Settlement of Bengal. The Permanent Settlement was a fixing in perpetuity of the amount of land revenue due from those whom the British recognized as owners. The belief was that these owners would use the profits of their privileged position to develop the countryside and bring prosperity to agriculture.

The ideas which the British brought to India were out of tune with the actual relationships of Indian cultivators and artisans. The British found themselves committing one error after another and thereby compounding their difficulties in administering a foreign land. Instead of finding landlords and tenants operating through a system of prices, bargaining, and contracts, the British found a maze of caste and custom regulating inter-family relationships. Where the British expected to find an owner they found a profusion of overlapping claims.

These questions came to the attention of scholars with the publication of Sir Henry Maine's work.[1] His original interest lay in the history of Roman legal institutions. In examining the laws and customs of ancient Hindu society he wanted at first merely to illustrate the structure of early Roman law. He found support for his interpretation of Roman law as primarily interfamilial by analogy with Hindu law and custom, and argued that the Hindu village was the prototype of the family system of ancient Rome and early Europe. Reaching out from Roman law to Hindu law, Maine found his interests leading him into a comparative jurisprudence encompassing not only Roman and Hindu law, but also early Germanic law and the Brehon Code of ancient Ireland.

As Maine's interests spread over a wider geographical area, so also did they spread over a wider area of social thought. From an interest in the development of Western personal and property law the pursuit of origins brought him insights into the structure of the Eastern village community. The invaluable contribution to economic history came with his proof that the Indian village economy did not center on the market; that in fact some new frame of reference was needed in which to discuss its characteristics. Maine himself made the fundamental differentiation between status society and contract society—a distinction which proved extraordinarily fruitful, yet still failed to indicate the

[1] Sir Henry Sumner Maine, *Ancient Law* (New York, 1906), especially chapters I, V, and VIII; *Village Communities in the East and West* (London, 1861); *Dissertations on Early Law and Custom* (New York, 1886) especially chapters I through IV.

variety of institutions of a status nature or to spell out the formal arrangements that status economies may use.

Maine recognized that the Hindu village was a closed unit with rights and obligations of its own. It was made up of extended or joint family groups and castes whose legal and economic relationships were interfamilial rather than interpersonal. Our conception of property rights, and consequently of alienability, sale, and market relationships was not applicable to a system organized on principles of a religio-legal nature.

The Hindu village as pictured by Maine has since been criticized as inaccurate in detail,[2] but the general direction of his argument is not open to question. The importance of his discoveries lay in their emphasis upon the corporate unity of the village economy, upon its system of collective responsibility, and above all on status as a rationale of motivation, and as the principle on which the village economy was organized and integrated. The problem of the structure of the village community thus centered on the question of how precisely status was used to organize its economy.

While the range of interests encompassed by the work of Sir Henry Maine and the work of British administrators extended from practical questions of establishing responsibility for the payment of revenue to comparative jurisprudence, they never engaged in a formal analysis of the principles of economic integration of the village economy. Maine and his successors were interested in law and rights, while the administrators did not feel called upon to move beyond solutions to their immediate concern with finding a workable system for collecting the revenue and dividing the return from land between the ruler and the ruled. Once the impact of British administration itself had altered original native conditions the problems of administration were so deeply affected by past British actions that an analysis of the "native state of affairs" must have appeared to the practical administrator as of academic interest only.

The intention of this paper is to show that the structure of the village economy and the nature of land revenue can be far better explained by the concepts of reciprocity and redistribution than they can by the more usual terms of economic theory or by the vaguer terms of pre-capitalistic, barter, or subsistence economy.

Reciprocity means that members of one group act towards members of another group as members of that group or a third or fourth group act toward them. There is no implication of equality, justice, or the golden rule. Rather, reciprocity implies only that there is a two-way or round-the-circle flow of goods as exemplified in the Melanesian Kula ring or the Trobriand Islanders' fish and yams transfer between coastal and inland villages. The groups are mutually self-supporting in regard to the articles involved in the reciprocative relationship.

Redistribution means that the produce of the group is brought together, either physically or by appropriation, and then parcelled out again among the members. Again there is no implication of equality of treatment, fair shares, or payment for value. The social pattern is characterized by centricity—peripheral points all connected with the central point.

The symmetrical patterns of reciprocative relationships may merge with the centralized pattern of redistributive relationships, as with the Trobriand Islanders, where the king is the redistributive center of a large number of reciprocative relationships with the brothers of his many wives.

In putting these concepts to use in the patterning of empirical economies it must be understood that reciprocity and redistribution do not provide classifications for economies as a whole, for both kinds of relationships may be found in the same economy, either in regard to different goods or in regard to different groups of people. The different relationships of the various groups can be patterned on one or the other, or sometimes both principles. The strength of these concepts lies in their ability to reduce complex relationships to simple patterns. As shall appear, the maze of relationships in the Indian village economy can be set out in terms of reciprocity and redistribution applied to the groups that make up the village as well as to the main goods and services.

Two focal points in the workings of the village economy have so far resisted analysis. The one

[2] See B. H. Baden-Powell, *The Origin and Growth of Village Communities in India* (London, 1899), especially in regard to geographical variations in the village hierarchy, and the impossibility of establishing an original or "pure" village type.

concerns the economic structure of the village; the other refers to the nature of land revenue, its source and its position in the village economy.

The Village Economy

The three main bodies of Indian social organization were the *joint family,* made up of related members, numbering up to a hundred or more; the *village,* essentially a grouping of such families; and the *castes.* The family generally was a self-sufficient unit under the direction of its head or its senior members. Where special skills or certain specific services were required, it could call on the village artisans, servants, or priests. The basic political and social unit was the village. Within its confines almost all economic needs were satisfied. The caste system was much wider than the village and its lines cut across village lines. It was founded upon religious sanction. Over these basic units ebbed and flowed the surf of political life. Sometimes it was the life of empires such as the Gupta and Mughal Empires. More often it was organized in petty kingdoms varying in size from the area of a New England township to a very few square miles.

In eighteenth-century Oudh[3] we find a society in which the cultivators are "independent of each other, but connected through village heads, and the villages also independent among themselves, but joined in allegiance to a common Raja; the basis of the whole society being the grain heap, in which each constituent rank had its definite interest." [4] The village did not hold its lands in common but it did have common officials and servants: watchman, headman, clerk, blacksmith, carpenter, herdsman, washerman, barber, priest, and potter. These officials and servants received their remuneration in a share of the cultivators' grain heaps.

Production of food, the main material item in Indian life, was the business of the joint agricultural family. The officials and servants saw to their jobs, doing the appropriate work as and where it was needed. Throughout the year there was no exchange or payment for services rendered. The herdsman watched the cows and the blacksmith made the implements and repaired any ploughs that broke. Each activity was carried on according to the custom and tradition of the village and within the joint family according to its traditions, station in life, and the judgment of its head.

At harvest time the means of subsistence for the rest of the year were distributed. The system of allotting shares in the gross produce of the village was highly complex, yet it did not require any previous knowledge of total gross produce to be divided among the members of the community. While the exact arrangements in the division and distribution of the produce varied from place to place, we may take as a typical example the system recorded by W. C. Bennett.[5]

Distribution in Gonda took place in three stages: From the standing crop; from the undivided grain heap of each cultivator; and from the heaps after the cultivator had contributed to the Raja's heap.

From the standing crop of each cultivator the watchman, the blacksmith, the carpenter, the herdsman, the priest,, and often the cultivator himself cut a twentieth of a *bigha.*[6] Next, the crop was harvested and threshed by the whole community, the grain from the fields of each cultivator being heaped in a separate pile on the community threshing floor. The "slave-ploughman" [7] took a share varying from a fifth to a seventh of the heap of the cultivating family to which he was attached. To this share he added a *panseri.*[8] From each pile each person who had cut or threshed the crop (and this meant everyone) took a sixteenth of the rice and the "fattest sheaf in thirty" of the other crops. Then the carpenter, blacksmith, barber, washerman, and watchman each took twelve *panseris* of threshed grain from each cultivator for each four-bullock plough he owned, and six *panseris* for each two-bullock plough. When these shares had been passed out the grain heaps were divided in half, the cultivator retaining one half and the other going to the Raja, subject however ·to

3 Now part of Uttar Pradesh, in north-central India.

4 W. C. Bennet, *Final Settlement Report on District Gonda* (Allahabad, 1878), pp. 48–9.

5 *Op. cit.*, pp. 4–8.

6 A *bigha* is a measure of land which varied from place to place, from a quarter of an acre in Bengal to two-thirds of an acre in U.P., with other variants both elsewhere and within these provinces. The right to the standing crop was called *biswa.*

7 Apparently a typical "debt-slave."

8 One twenty-second of a *maund* of eighty-two pounds.

further distributions One *sir*[9] in every *maund* of the Raja's heap was returned to the cultivator, another *sir* was given to the scribe, a "double handful" to the priest, and a tenth of the remainder was given to the village headman. From the cultivator's remaining heap the blacksmith and carpenter each received three more *panseris,* the herdsman one more, and a *sir* or two went to the scribe.

The matter is certainly intricate. Given all the data it would still be possible, of course, to compute the fraction of the total going to any cultivator or servant or to the Raja, but it is not possible to express it in any formula shorter than several pages in length and utterly unmanageable in practice. The proportions vary with the number, size, and distribution of cultivators' holdings, the number, size and distribution of ploughs, the number of bullocks, the number and distribution of slave ploughmen, as well as the amount of gross produce. Not only do the deductions depend upon variations among these factors but some of the deductions are stated in proportional and some in absolute terms. Besides the inordinate length and cumbersomeness of the formula, there is the fact that the fraction could still not be converted into actual figures since the total was unknown. But again, here lies the true strength of the system employed.

Despite the numerous factors involved and the unknown total, the system was not confusing to the participants. It was simple to operate precisely because no aggregate data were required. The operational device took care of the problem, and the device is described by the phrases used, such as: "One *sir* in every *maund,*" "one seventh of the heap." Each step in the distribution was carried out separately. If the slave-ploughman was to get a seventh of the heap, six measures were ladled out to the cultivator, and a seventh to the slave until the heap disappeared. With each proportional division the same process was followed, so that at no point was it necessary to know how much grain there was in the heap. The only accurate measures needed were a container for a *panseri* of grain and one for a *sir* of grain.[10] Any measure could be used for the other sharing processes, for all they did was to dispose of the heap, so many measures to this pile, so many to that. By such a simple device a great many claimants were served in a great many different ways without need for accounting. Furthermore, honesty was assured because the distribution was public, taking place under the eyes of the villagers and of the Raja or his representative.

There were built-in devices which assured each villager a minimum income, and which also tended to equalize the incomes of all the villagers. The fixed quantities going to the village servants gave them a basic minimum even if the harvest was so small that their proportional shares would not support them. When the cultivator "pre-harvested" a twentieth of a *bigha* of his own land the proportion of the revenue the small-holder was expected to carry was reduced in the same way that the personal exemption reduces the relative burden of the income tax on the man with a small income. The contribution of a sixteenth of the rice heap and a thirtieth of other crops to the common heap and then dividing the heap equally among all the villagers also tended to equalize incomes since the wealthier contributed more than the poor, while each shared equally.

There was scant regard for economic rationality in the distribution. Some rough approximation to work rendered is indicated in the carpenters' and blacksmiths' shares based upon number and size of ploughs, which were also related to the area protected by the watchmen, but this cannot be said of basing the washerman's and barber's shares on the same criteria. The only approach to payment based on service was that to the herdsman per bullock cared for.

Each villager participated in the division of the grain heap. There was no bargaining, and no payment for specific services rendered. There was no accounting, yet each contributor to the life of the village had a claim on its produce, and the whole produce was easily and successfully divided among the villagers. It was a redistributive system.[11]

[9] A fortieth of a *maund.*

[10] In addition, the exact size of a *panseri,* or *seer* varied from village to village, and for that matter still does.

[11] It may be of interest to mention that distributions in kind at the time of harvest are still widespread in India. In the Deccan they are known as "*balvta*" payments; in the Punjab as payments to "*kamins.*" These are still customary rather than bargained shares, but the figures this writer has seen for individual holdings indicate that such payments are now a small proportion of artisans' and servants' income.

Below and above the village level the redistributive pattern continued to prevail. Below, the share remaining to the cultivator's joint family was managed by the head of the family and parcelled out to the members of the family. The handling of the family's share was a matter of administration on a small scale, the principle being redistributive, for the grain was held in common and its consumption was regulated by handing out from the family store.

Above the village level there might be only one or there might be a multiplicity of political authorities, depending on the size of the kingdom and the degree of central control which the king was able to exercise. Whether any economic function was or was not performed by the authorities, the division of the grain heap at the village level was the foundation upon which political authority rested. As the size of the kingdom grew the number of intermediate authorities multiplied, although strong kings attempted to eliminate some of them. The ruler's share was distributed among the competing levels of the military and political bureaucracy according to their relative strengths. In a large kingdom with a moderately powerful center, such as the Mughal Empire was at times, there was a hierarchy of redistributive centers with the village grain heap at the bottom and the king's storehouses at the top. In between, the local powers and provincial governors maintained their own storehouses, retaining a share and passing on the remainder to the level above. In regard to grain, the whole political and social structure was founded on redistribution.

Intertwined with the redistributive system of family-village-kingdom was the caste system through which crafts and their services were organized. No contract, no bargaining will account for its structure. It was founded on reciprocity. Every member of each caste contributed his services and skills to the support of every member of the other castes. Its sanction was religious, while its function was largely economic. Rather than a simple dual symmetry, a multiple symmetry underlay the caste system: a large number of groups were sharing out their services among each other although they acted independently. Each caste was economically entirely dependent upon the performance of their duties by the other groups. The members of the society could survive only if each caste did its job for the others, yet each caste remained a "self-governing community" and "set up its own standards of life and conduct."[12] Territorially the castes cut across village and political boundaries and functioned whatever course political life was taking.

Briefly, it can be said that relationships were reciprocative in regard to services, and redistributive in regard to agricultural produce.

But the reciprocative caste system as a whole was itself an element within the redistributive system of the village. The functions of priest, watchman, barber and carpenter were caste functions and it was by virtue of each member of each caste within the village fulfilling his or her religiously sanctioned duties that the grain heap was there to be divided at harvest time. Cultivator-artisan relations might therefore be said to be both reciprocative and redistributive. The artisan was supplying the cultivator with his skills, and the cultivator in turn, and regardless of the specific services the artisan had performed for him, supplied the artisan with agricultural products. At the same time the artisan and the cultivator jointly contributed to the production of a village grain heap which was in turn redistributed to all the residents of the village.

This analysis of the pre-British Indian village shows that formal principles are available to us which are capable of describing a non-market economy. There is no reason why such an economy should be described with negative references or irrelevant ones. An economy is not analyzed by placing it before capitalism in an evolutionary sequence; nor by the mere statement that money is not used. Barter, as a classification, is, if anything, inaccurate, for neither interfamily nor intercaste bargaining was practiced. While there is no disputing the poverty of the Indian villager, the system under which he worked did not depend on the fact that he was at a subsistence level. The same principles were as applicable to the well-to-do village as to the poorer ones, and as applicable to the wealthy rulers as to the peasant cultivators. To call the village economy communistic puts the problem in the wrong light, for our present-day concepts

12 L. S. S. O'Malley, *Modern India and the West* (London, New York, 1941), p. 5.

of ownership are here inapplicable. Things were not held in common in the Indian village. Rather, different families as well as other groups had different kinds of rights.

To say that the services in the village economy were patterned out by reciprocity and the grain by redistribution still leaves open for detailed description the particular procedures used and shares received by the participants. However, it does acquaint us with the structure of the manifold village activities so that we perceive how it came about that these activities were made to mesh. More than that, we may also, within reasonable limits, compare the organization of the Indian village economy with the organization of other economies—group by group, product by product and service by service.

The Nature of Land Revenue

The concepts of reciprocity and redistribution will also help to clarify the old problem of where and how land revenue fitted into the structure of the Indian economy. This was, and is, a problem of great practical importance, for the British Raj drew its resources from the land revenue, and today the Indian states still depend upon the same revenue for their development programs. Both ease of, and justice in, administration of the revenue depended upon an accurate appraisal of the nature and function of land revenue.

The question whether to regard land revenue as a rent or as a tax exercised the minds of British administrators for a century.[13] When the East India Company began to govern India in the last half of the eighteenth century land revenue was the major source of revenue for the native rulers. The Company perforce adopted their fiscal system, and set out to rationalize it. Having succeeded to the political position of the native rulers, the Company had also succeeded to their rights to land revenue. It naturally wished to determine the origin, source, and nature of land revenue so as to adjust the assessment and collection of the revenue correctly.

The officers of the East India Company, thinking in European terms, saw only two possibilities, and took the view that their administration of the revenue must depend upon the answer. Land revenue was either a tax on land or it was the rent of the land. If land revenue were in the nature of a tax, then it should be administered according to the canons of taxation, which required that the tax should be as low as possible after allowing for legitimate expenses of government. Any surplus from the land over the costs of management, cultivation, and taxation would then be the property of the owner of the land and should go to him. Assessment of the revenue would then present the problem of an equitable allotment of the gross revenue burden among the owners who were made responsible for payment of the revenue. On the other hand, if land revenue were the rent of the land, then there would be no limit to what the government could claim other than what the traffic would bear. As the owner of the land, the government could claim any surplus over the costs of production, and the rent of land would be a legitimate source of profit to the East India Company. Assessment would in principle be a problem of competitive renting of land holdings, and the government would not have to worry about the equity of each assessment.

While this was the underlying issue of principle in the discussion, three other considerations weighed heavily with the British. Until 1790 the first two of these had shaped policy. One was the absence of a staff of trustworthy civil servants. The other was the great need for revenue.

The absence of a staff made it impossible to attempt a just settlement of the revenue in individual cases, so that the Company had to settle for a rough and ready system requiring neither knowledge nor honesty on the part of those responsible for seeing that the revenue flowed into the Company's coffers.

The great need for revenue meant that the Company felt it had to charge as much as the traffic would bear, no matter what principle was applicable to the revenue. This amounted

[13] By the last quarter of the nineteenth century the problem had become, so far as the British officials were concerned, academic. The methods of assessing and collecting the revenue had been established and no new insight into the original state of affairs would have induced the British to alter their procedures. When Baden-Powell (*op. cit.*), writing in the 1890's, mentioned the history of the dispute over the nature of land revenue, but insisted most strongly that it was a matter of no importance because it was by then clear that land revenue was *de facto* and *de jure* a prior charge on the land, its produce being "hypothecated" to the land revenue by virtue of British legislation.

to the view that the legitimate expenses of government would absorb the whole of the economic rent, and more if that were possible.

Both considerations were met by the system adopted in the early years: the right to collect the revenue was sold by auction, the native tax-farmer being allowed a ten percent allowance for his labor and, in practice, whatever else he could extract from the cultivator. Thus the Company achieved a maximum extraction rate[14] and needed few administrators. However, the system could be justified neither on grounds of equity nor on those of efficiency, and certainly led to widespread dissatisfaction and disaffection.

The third consideration to modify a Company policy based on the solution to the rent *v.* revenue controversy was the belief that a stable landowning class could be created to govern the country-side; that this class would build up the agricultural and natural resources of the area; and that the stability and prosperity so achieved would lead to large trading profits for the Company. This meant taking a long view, anticipating ample future gains at the price of a somewhat reduced tax revenue for the present. It was this consideration, combined with the simplicity of the arrangement and the guarantee of a minimum revenue, that led to the introduction of "permanent settlement" in 1790. Permanent settlement meant that the revenue assessment was fixed in perpetuity, the landowner retaining any future increase of income accruing to the land so long as he paid the assessment.

The policy of permanent settlement was dropped after 1795, but until the late 1860's it was constantly upheld by a sizeable number of Company officials and, later, government officials. Temporary settlements, in which the revenue was fixed for periods up to thirty years, were made in the areas west of Bengal as they came under Company government, and the question whether land revenue was a rent or a tax came to the fore.

The specific issue of fact on which the debate over the nature of land revenue turned was whether the Emperor at Delhi was or was not the owner of the land at the time the Company succeeded to his powers. Such a question of absolute property, being one which can only be asked in a market economy, was in the nature of things insoluble. In dividing the grain heap between the Raja, the cultivators, and the artisans there was no need to differentiate between rent and tax—one only needed to know the operational devices by which the Raja's share was determined. Nevertheless, the debate continued for years. In practice, victory went to those who supported the view that land revenue was a tax. Certainly the permanent assessment of Bengal implied that answer, as did the progressive reductions in the share of rents taken as revenue in the districts to the northwest of Bengal.

Did choosing "tax" instead of "rent" make a difference? It is doubtful whether it did. Whatever it deemed to be the correct position, the Company had good reason to reduce the burden of revenue so as to keep the population moderately happy. What did make a difference was the attitude that prompted the question to be put in terms of rent *v.* tax.

The alternative of rent *v.* tax stemmed from a deep misunderstanding of the nature of the land revenue. The British administrators were treating land revenue as if it were part and parcel of a market system. Once that assumption is made land revenue must be either rent or tax. If it is rent, land revenue is a return to the inherent productive capacity of the soil and must be measured by the difference between the value of the product and the costs of production, for rent implies that the market evaluates the contribution of land to the productive process. But while in an abstract sense there is always a rent for land because land contributes to the productive process, it is impossible to determine its amount unless there is a market on which people express their judgment of that contribution by offering to pay for its use. They do so by paying a rent. When it became apparent to the British administrators that there was no market for the use of land they made efforts to calculate the amount of rent which would be paid if there were such a market. This is called "imputing economic rent." The effort of course proved unavailing. How can the value of a product be computed when so much of it is consumed by the producer and never reaches the market? What meaning can be attached to computations based on prices that vary widely within an area? How can one compute costs

14 There is evidence that optimistic tax farmers actually overrated their capacity to collect, and that the revenue may have exceeded the maximum the Company should legitimately have expected.

when virtually all the costs are implicit and there is no such thing as a standard wage for agricultural labor? Economic rent is a quantity that requires a market system, and could not therefore have meaning in the context of the Indian village economy.

A decision to regard land revenue as a tax also implied a market. Since government services must employ economic resources and since it may be impossible or undesirable to sell these services on a market, the government must extract a sum from the current income stream, either directly by a tax on payments made, or indirectly on values created by the market. These taxes are generally levied on income, on property, or on transactions. Taxes on income and property are levied as proportions of the value which is arrived at by the "bid and ask" process of the market. Taxes on transactions are either a proportion of the price at which the goods change hands or a flat rate depending on the quantity of goods which change hands. While it is true that the government can raise money by a charge on transactions that are free of market elements, such as a poll-tax, or upon the mere existence of an item, such as "windows in walls," it is generally true that the British had market values and market transfers in mind when they considered taxes.

That the market was implicit in the concept of a tax is shown by the first attempts at assessing the land revenue. Assiduous efforts were made to compute the "net assets" of estate in land. These were to be computed by deducting from the gross value of the produce the costs of production including wages of labor and profits on capital. Now, the remainder, the net assets, is by definition economic rent. For the reasons outlined above the attempts to compute net assets were never successful. Eventually the British administration fell back on going by rule of thumb, and simply tried to find out how much the owner responsible for the payment of land revenue was collecting from his tenants, and then charging him with part of the rent.

That land revenue was not a straightforward tax was further illustrated by the problems associated with the various proposed methods of levying it. The main proposals were that land revenue be regarded as a share in the gross produce of the land, either in kind or in money value; a money share in the net produce of the land (i.e., the economic rent); or, finally, a money share in the rents actually collected by the proprietor.[15] All three met difficulties in administration and in a just application of the principle invoked.

A share in kind is difficult to collect, and for a modern government there is the added problem of converting the produce into money. These were not problems for the earlier rulers. In the first place, the taking of a share in kind fitted neatly into the common village harvest and distribution. Secondly, it was evidence of the prerogatives and power of the ruler. Thirdly, the ruler did not need or wish to convert his share into money until well into the Mughal period. The British, on the other hand, did not desire to fit into the village distribution in the personal way in which the Raja did, and furthermore were simultaneously engaged in market trading activities and did not want a share in kind. Eventually as the concepts of British law and the produce of British industry entered the village, the redistributive system lost much of its relevance. The share of the grain heap, whether in kind or in money, did not accurately reflect ability to pay, and the British did not wish to be affected by the fluctuations in income which such a sharing system involved. If the share of gross produce were to be taken in money there would be the trouble of estimating the produce and arriving at a price for conversion into money values, in the absence of a market.

A tax based on economic rent could only prove impossible to assess. It is noteworthy that after nine years of effort in the north western Provinces, the Company's officers observed that it might take another half century to compute the economic rents for the rest of the province.

Land revenue based on the rents actually paid, which was the compromise the British finally adopted, was obviously inequitable. In addition, its computation was so burdensome that the assessments were revised only every thirty years. At best, the rents reflected values as of the time the leases were made, but as a rule

[15] By the nineteenth century something which we might as well call rents were paid. They grew out of the Mughal conversions of revenue shares into money payments in some districts, but mostly out of the legal concepts imposed by the British. The amounts paid and here called rents were a mixture of traditional payments of various sorts and of the market forces introduced by the British.

the actual amounts charged in rent were affected by caste, local custom, and to no small degree, by favoritism. Unless these extraneous considerations were eliminated, the actual rents would not reflect the ability of the various holdings to pay revenue A complex set of rules therefore came into being to guide the officers in their attempts to adjust the recorded rents. These rules boiled down to a general rule that the officer assessing the revenue should try to adjust recorded rents to the rents at which a genuinely competitive market would arrive. However, a tax on economic rent or actual rents paid is not the same as an income tax, and the British system has been criticized on the grounds that taxes on rent are not taxes on ability to pay, nor can it be shown that they are equitable according to any other generally accepted standard.

The fact of the matter is that land revenue cannot be levied in such a way as to satisfy the canons of taxation as understood in the modern world. It is not a tax on values created by the market nor is it a tax on transactions. The incidence of a tax should be foreseeable if it is to be just. Yet the incidence of land revenue is not foreseeable. Even under the original native system the revenue share of the Raja lacked this characteristic. One could alter the shares in the grain heap so as to give certain participants more, but the ultimate effect of merely changing the Raja's share was anything but obvious. Consequently the efforts to adapt the native system to British conceptions of taxation was fraught with difficulties.

These perpetual difficulties which beset the British had their roots in their misconception that land revenue was a tax like any other tax commonly levied where a market system obtains. The picture of the village economy as presented in the preceding section shows the correct answer to be that land revenue formed part of a nonmarket system. Taxes are affected by, and in turn affect, the working of the price mechanism, but land revenue under the Mughals and before left unaffected the cultivator's choice of crops, his methods of cultivation, and his reciprocative and redistributive relationships with the village artisans. The cultivator's decisions were made prior to and independently of the assessment of land revenue. The solution was, then, that land revenue was the ruler's share in the produce of the land under a redistributive system. It is not a phenomenon of the market order and cannot be translated into market terms. To ask whether land revenue was a rent or a tax was to misconstrue the economic organization of pre-British India. It falsely assumed that the use of market terminology would prove revealing; actually employment of such terminology clouded the issue. To understand the nature of land revenue one must understand the original native system: here the patterning of the economy in terms of reciprocity and redistribution can alone provide a clear picture.

Sir Henry Maine first presented to Western scholars a picture of the village economy. He characterized it as a "status" as opposed to a "contract" economy. While there can be nothing but admiration for this seminal insight, it left unanswered the question of the principles upon which some seemingly intractable problems of status economies rested. Yet once a pattern of these status relationships is drawn, the concepts of reciprocity and redistribution reveal the comparatively simple devices for distributing services and their products.

These concepts also throw light on the underlying difficulties which have dogged the efforts of modern administrations to adopt and adapt the devices of a redistributive economy to the market system. The land revenue which was the Raja's share in the village grain heap became the foundation stone of British fiscal resources in India, and is still today a major source of government revenue. Even in our time no generally satisfactory system for assessing and collecting this tax has been found.

A scheme for patterning nonmarket economic activities such as is suggested here is needed, if we are to understand institutions and devices which have their origin in nonmarket economies.

Even in societies where its presence is dramatically evident, especially when the local marketplace is "colorful," market exchange is often peripheral to the processes by which most goods and services are distributed. For example, many farming peoples take only their comparatively small surpluses to market, after they have set aside enough of what they have produced to meet most of their subsistence needs. They engage in market exchange for money profit to acquire cash to pay their taxes, to buy a few necessities they do not make for themselves, and to purchase an occasional luxury item of foreign make. Under these circumstances the marketplace, although often vividly present, is not the location and money purchase is not the process through which most goods are distributed within the society.

Peasant markets represent a sort of intermediate stage between those technologically simpler societies in which reciprocity and redistribution are the main distributive processes and advanced agricultural and industrial societies in which market exchange has taken over as the major mover of most goods.

In Ortiz's description, the Colombian rural market appears to fall into this developmentally transitional category, and her analysis has critical implications for appraising the entire question of market versus nonmarket economies as it has developed so far.

Colombian Rural Market Organization

Sutti Ortiz

Detailed studies of market places are of theoretical importance, for they can teach us a great deal about patterns of production and consumption, and about the nature of business transactions. Just as important is the study of market place networks, how they spread over a given territory and how they are structured. Skinner's (1964–5) careful study of Chinese markets, and similar studies in Guatemala (Guatemala 1947) and Mexico (Malinowski & Fuente 1957; Foster 1948), are excellent examples of how the inter-linking of markets affects the flow of goods and social relations within the area served.

A comparative study of some African market networks has led Bohannan and Dalton to propose (1962: 25) that the market *place* is characteristic of economies in which the market *principle* is peripheral, and that the more pervasive the market *principle* is, the less is the economic importance of the market *place*. This paradox (which is illusory if one remembers to distinguish clearly between market place and market principle) summarizes neatly the African cases discussed in Bohannan and Dalton's book, but it does not hold true for the Colombian marketing structure. The Yoruba markets may well be places where peasant women earn small amounts of money, but in rural Colombia the market place is neither where peasant women earn pin money nor where cash crops are sold; it is the place where middlemen sell their import goods to part-subsistence peasant farmers.

From a discussion of the distribution of market places in Colombia it will become evident that the existing market models cannot be applied usually. Furthermore, many of the conclusions so far derived are erroneous because they have only taken into account those sectors of the marketing organisation which resemble an "ideal type" of what a peasant market should be, and have failed to consider geographical spread and regional limitations.

Bohannan and Dalton's proposal assumes a correlation between the degree of integration to a market economy and the nature of the place where transactions take place. Sahlins (1965), furthermore, assumes that the higher the degree of integration—in his model, the greater the value of external trade—the greater the disruption of the existing distributing mechanism. The material I discuss here shows that this is not necessarily the case. The maintenance of traditional distributing mechanisms is in some cases the result of a closer integration of the peasant sector into the national economy; the correlation may thus be an inverse one.

The market place organization examined here is only one of the channels through which the peasant sector is linked to other sectors of the Colombian economy. The other important trading channel is that of the chains of shop-

Source: From Sutti Ortiz, "Colombian Rural Market Organization: An Exploratory Model," *Man,* Vol. 2 (1967), pp. 393–412. Used by permission of the author and the Royal Anthropological Society of Great Britain and Ireland.

I am grateful to my colleagues in the Department of Anthropology, London School of Economics and Political Science, and especially to Professor Raymond Firth, for criticisms of the draft of this article.

keepers and to a lesser extent of itinerant traders. These trading channels, though not totally independent of each other, are in many ways distinct and contrasting in the type of trading relations they bear. The main contrast is that on the whole market trade is more impersonal than shop trade. Each type of relationship has its advantages and disadvantages, but what concerns us here is that each channel links, in a different way, the producer to the distributors and the consumers. Hence the nature of the economic integration of the peasant to other sectors of the economy will depend on the extent to which he depends on shop traders or market traders for exchange.

Traders are and must remain in a position of power in order to profit from a transaction. They monopolize information in order to retain a privileged bargaining position. Though the trader may not actually have greater power than the buyer, he is nevertheless in a position to create belief about his power and thus to improve his bargaining position. An outside market trader is in a better position to monopolize useful information, to create belief about his power and to specialize in those goods which have high buying preference. He can thus try to assure his bargaining position, although the impersonality of the trading relationship also helps the buyer to bargain freely and hence challenge the power of the market trader. This type of relationship always strives towards a balance of power but never achieves it.

It is because trading relations with shopkeepers are more personal in nature that fringe benefits are forthcoming (i.e. credit, special orders and personal services). These benefits are of course important to the producer, but one must not overlook the crucial point which weakens the bargaining power of the buyer in this type of trading relationship. In a personal trading relationship the buyer cannot entirely withdraw from a transaction because this would threaten the maintenance of the relationship and thereby affect the fringe benefits which are still pending from previous exchanges. A Colombian Indian is expected to bargain, but if he walks out of the shop a stream of insults will follow him and this will be counted against future requests.

Transaction cannot, therefore, be classed simply as balanced reciprocity nor as negative reciprocity (Sahlins 1965: 147–9). Participants have conflicting interests; each wants to maximize utility, but because utility is not expressed purely in the price terms of the transaction the expectations of subsequent exchanges will temper overt bargaining and affect prices in transactions. The buyer cannot easily withdraw since the effective preference is not the only determinant of price or of the possibility of transaction.

In this article I shall not discuss every aspect of the integration of the peasant sector to the Colombian economy; I shall discuss mainly the market place organization, and refer to other channels only where relevant. I must stress here that no hypothesis or model should refer to the degree of integration without explicitly stating the relative importance of the various channels of integration; this is my main criticism of Bohannan and Dalton's correlation as well as of Sahlins's model.

Since I cannot hope here to outline a model of the market place network for the whole of Colombia, I analyze the detailed information gathered in two municipalities[1] (see map) and more general information for the surrounding regions.[2] I hope that this will help to delineate propositions which can then be tested on a wider

1 The administrative unit immediately below the national level is the department. There is no intermediate administrative unit between the department and the municipality. Municipalities are almost totally dependent on the department and resemble the "counties" or "townships" of the United States. They are formed around a town which must have a population of at least 500 inhabitants. Some municipalities are also responsible for the administration of large rural areas as are the two I discuss in detail, while others in more densely populated districts may consist of a city and the immediately surrounding area alone. I have used the term "municipal township" to refer to a town which is also the administrative center of a municipality.

2 Information on market behavior was collected during one year (1960–1961) of field research in San Andrés (municipality of Inzá, Cauca); I was then able to record weekly information for the Inzá and San Andrés markets and occasional information for the Belalcazar market. Additional knowledge on market organization was gained through short visits to other districts of the Departments of Cauca, Huila and Cundinamarca. Miss Osborn was able to contribute some general information for the rural areas of the Department of Nariño. The writings of Fals Borda (1955), Sayres (1956) and Reichel-Dolmatoff (1961) have yielded useful comparative information.

scale. While stressing the contrast between an economy of strongly peasant character and a marketing system which has its foundations in the commercial centers, I shall raise three main questions:

1. Can a market organization of this type successfully integrate the peasant into national life?
2. Is an important market place organization well adapted to the needs of the peasant farmer?
3. Can this system stimulate economic activity and bring about innovation?

I will concentrate on a description of market places, but will mention other trading channels whenever necessary. Ambulant traders are only important in areas with no market places and no settlements. The commercial activities of shops located in settlements—which are, in fact, more important than the ambulant traders—will be compared with those of market sellers. As with ambulant traders and market vendors, shopkeepers use the same supply sources and often sell in the market square.[3]

Rural Colombian Market Places

Colombia is a country with large, modern industrial cities; nevertheless 50 per cent of its population is rural and makes a living from small-scale farming. Scattered over a large mountainous territory, the peasants are not always close to important rural centers. In fact, in some areas of Colombia (e.g. parts of the Departments of Nariño, Cauca, Huila, Caldas, Boyacá, Santander and Tolima) one-third of the farming population resides in so-called remote areas, sometimes linked by dirt roads but more often than not only by difficult mountain paths. Most of these farmers do not even live in settlements, but at a considerable distance from each other and from political and commercial centers. Although they represent an important productive sector, they are removed from the main stream of commercial activities, hardly affected and rarely protected by the national government. Rural government is not very effective. A farmer pays his taxes and informs the police or the local government official of any serious criminal offense. He may also ask for help to collect debts or punish a thief, but only when informal methods have failed. He knows the authorities to be relatively powerless and therefore he often by-passes them.

The distribution pattern of market places in Colombia is not very dense nor does it serve to distribute local products in such a way as to inter-link rural areas with each other. Markets in Colombia function mainly to distribute to rural areas industrial products as well as those products (maize, potatoes, unrefined sugar, etc.) which are produced in regions surrounding the main commercial centers and are handled by important middlemen residing in the same big commercial centers. The market vendors in rural Colombia sell those goods which the peasant needs and cannot produce in sufficient quantities, if at all.

For example, in the Inzá market, a municipal market of secondary importance, most of the food and manufactured goods sold in the square are brought in by middlemen from urban suppliers. On an active market day during the 1960 harvest season about £57 worth of foodstuffs was sold on the market square. Of this, £39 worth was brought by middlemen who purchased their supplies from traders in urban centers (maize, raw sugar and potatoes) ; £12 worth of potatoes was brought by producers who live in surrounding regions; and only £6 worth of miscellaneous foodstuffs was brought by local peasant farmers. Animals raised in the areas and butchered by local middlemen brought about £74. Manufactured goods brought from urban centers by professional traders on this particular day amounted to at least £158. On other days peasant producers may be very few indeed. Coffee, the main cash crop of the area, is not sold on the square.

There is a limited number of market places throughout the country, most of which are concentrated around the urban clusters of the central Andean area. But even in this relatively densely populated area, markets are restricted on the whole to municipal townships or im-

[3] Bohannan and Dalton (1964:7) have pointed out how important it is to take into account other distribution chains, as market places may be outlets for only a limited type of product. They should also have stressed that a market place network may not necessarily serve a vast area; the commercial scope of this network of distribution may be quite limited and affect the function of the market place as a focus for transactions.

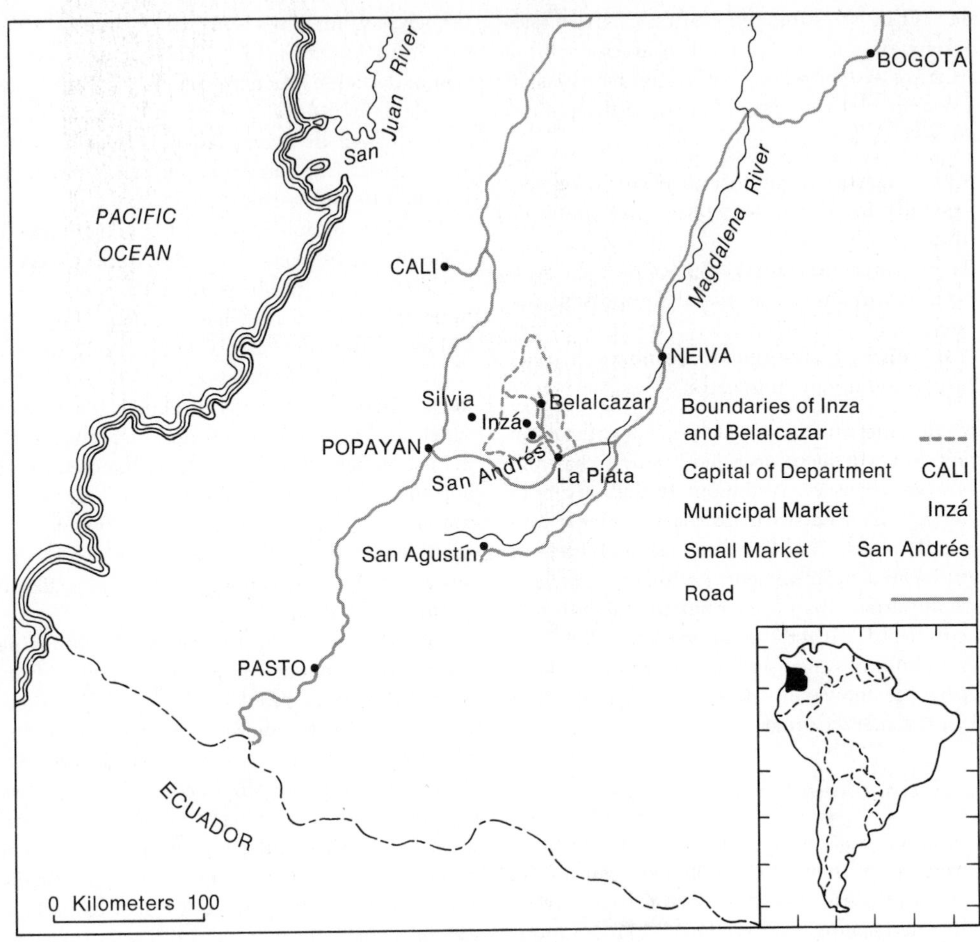

Map of south-western Colombia.

portant cities, and even then there are many municipal townships lacking a market place. Such municipal markets are stocked directly from the commercial centers, and there is little inter-market trade. Inter-regional commercial movement occurs only within the area serviced by a municipal market. A market seller from a municipal market may attend a secondary rural market. To facilitate the presentation of the data I have classified rural market places into (1) small rural markets, (2) municipal markets.

Small Rural Markets. These are very rare. Only a few communities can sustain such markets for a long period. In fact, some of the so-called weekly markets are so small that you may pass them without noticing them; two vendors and an occasional buyer do not make a market place, and I exclude them from this discussion. Markets can attract people only if enough traders with a large array of goods attend regularly. Usually these traders go to municipal markets, where they can be sure of a large enough resident population ready at hand.

Small rural markets are often held at transfer points, where the trader has to unload and carry the merchandise himself or hire horses for the last lap of his trip. It is at this point that the middlemen stop, unload their wares, and organize a weekly market. If this transfer point is too far from a population nucleus the markets specialize in wholesale trade and the buyers later resell their wares at more distant market places. Usually such wholesale centers disband when a new section of the road is built unless they can attract a considerable number of small buyers. In the municipality of Inzá there is one transfer point wholesale market, and on the road leading away from the municipality there is another wholesale-retail transfer point market place which is active enough almost to rank as a municipal market.

San Andrés is the only other market which is well enough known and attended by a sufficient number of people to warrant the title of small market. Once a week twenty to thirty non-resident adults gather on the village green, examining with curiosity the wares neatly displayed by the three or four ambulant traders. The weekly calf is slaughtered at dawn, and shortly afterwards residents of San Andrés stand hopefully at the edge of the paths that lead up the mountain slopes, waiting for the Indians to bring in small supplies of cassava, beans, onions, arracacha and plantains. I do not exaggerate when I say that the food brought to the market is grabbed from the bags by anxious housewives, even before the Indian manages to release his load. Though I sympathize with the complaints of my Indian friends about this, I must admit that unless the buyers acted quickly they would lose the only chance of getting, say, a few onions to spice their food.

The Indian's resistance to selling on the San Andrés square can be accounted for if we examine economic relations within the Indian peasant sector. I shall only say here that not to sell is a rational move, and that in fact the income derived does not warrant the advantages and security Indians have thereby to forego (Ortiz 1963; in press).

Why then is there a weekly market? San Andrés is a very small settlement (about twenty-five families); but at least it is big enough to be called a settlement, and it is possibly the largest (apart from the municipal administrative center) within an area of 624 sq. km. More important still, once a week Indians living in a nearby reservation[4] come down to the settlement to attend the reservation council meeting and to see their friends. Hence the trader has a congregation of possible buyers to warrant his trip. A reservation near a settlement of wealthier peasants and close to road transport is likely to have a market. Out of the nineteen reservations in the municipalities of Inzá and Páez only two hold weekly markets, and these are the only reservations close to such richer settlements and with roads linking them to municipal townships.

Indians bring food for sale at the San Andrés market only when they desperately need some cash; they never sell their cash crops in the square. The San Andrés market has not developed as an institution for intra- or inter-community exchanges. The total foodstuffs sold at the market in the month of April 1961 (selected because it is the month when Indians are short of cash and have food to sell) was: 7 stems of plantains; 1 large sack of spring onions; 15 lb. of beans; 50 ears of fresh maize; 25 lb. of dried maize; 1 bushel of peaches; 24 cabbages. The total amount of food sold in thirty-five market days during a period of one year in 1960–61 was: 47 stems of plantains; 110 lb. of maize; 140 lb. of potatoes; 250 tubers of cassava; 140 lb. of beans; 120 ears of fresh maize; 1 bushel of peaches; 2 bushels of oranges; 230 tubers of arracacha; 25 lb. of garlic; 90 cabbages; 8 marrows; 6 lb. of unrefined sugar; 36 cucumbers; unspecified amounts of eggs and green onions. This amount of food has to be evaluated in terms of the two hundred Indian part-subsistence farmers who shop there irregularly and of the twenty-five non-Indian resident farmers of San Andrés, most of whom do not plant subsistence crops.

The main activity on the square is not the sale of food, but rather of imported manufactured goods, of meat (a weekly calf), and of imported food to resident whites and Indians (some of whom have to travel considerable distances). During the harvest season there is enough money and movement to encourage subsidiary activities such as the sale of bread and cooked food.

A trader seldom hopes to sell more than £2 worth of merchandise and I often registered totals of 4s. for a day's trade. During the harvest month when all peasants have money, the manufactured goods sold on a market day might amount to at most £15. The annual sales of this type do not match the amount sold annually by the local shops; the annual receipts of the latter can be conservatively estimated at £815, while the gross income of the market place traders does not surpass £300, and is more probably nearer to £220. (This figure does not include the sale of

[4] Reservations are semi-autonomous political communities within a municipal territory. They are inhabited exclusively by descendants of an Indian community, which during the colonial period received from the Spanish Crown rights to settle and cultivate a given territory. Indians do not have to reside within the reservation if they do not wish to.

meat.) It is true, however, that the six shops around the settlement specialised in different types of goods; most of their stock is made up of salt, potatoes, raw sugar, soft and alcoholic drinks, and a variety of small food items as well as hardware.

Municipal Markets. These are usually held on Saturdays; thus buyers and sellers cannot attend markets located in different municipalities in any one week, although there are exceptions to this rule particularly in municipalities located close to important commercial centers, where markets are held several times a week.

On the appointed day, local producers, ambulant traders and other middlemen begin to fill the municipal town's square where they set up stalls or display their goods on the ground. A market tax has to be paid according to the market space used by the trader. Most markets close at midday and there are seldom any special buildings; thus they cannot be held during rainy days. There is no special market organization and no records are kept of market transactions. The municipal authorities assume the responsibility for keeping the peace, cleaning the market square and collecting the tax.

Without the help of official records it is almost impossible to estimate the volume of trade on the square. Trade is too active to make complete, detailed observation possible, and traders are too suspicious of outsiders to give out information. Scissors, needles, miniscule amounts of medicines surrounded by an assortment of ribbons and tools cover the blankets which a trader stretches on the ground and which he semi-circles with shining stacks of aluminum kettles. Next in line a screaming voice announces the prices of colorful cottons displayed against a wall, and a local craftsman stands quietly hoping that a client will come and ask for any one of his home-made wares. Sellers always look for the company of others offering similar goods, and thus the market assumes a very neat and simple organization which makes comparative shopping very easy. If the municipal town is large there are enough resident craftsmen and a big enough demand to encourage local peasants to manufacture household or agricultural wares for sale on the square. Pottery vessels, bags, cordage, candles, would be included in a very important municipal market. But Inzá—the municipality I am using here as an illustration—with an administrative center of about 500 inhabitants, manages to assemble only about twenty ambulant traders with wares manufactured in cities, a number of middlemen well stocked with food staples, a very small group of local producers selling maize or vegetables, and one or two local craftsmen. No wholesale trade is allowed to take place in the square during market hours. It is in these municipal towns that market receipts may often surpass receipts of local stores. Annual estimates for Inzá market place sales are as follows:[5]

Foodstuffs	£3,000
Manufactured goods	£3,400

while store receipts could not amount to more than £3,700. Thus, the commercial importance and specific nature of trade varies with size of the market town and probably with population density in the surrounding area as well.

But the nature of market places does not relate simply to the size of town. In very small settlements, like San Andrés, the backbone of the market is formed by the meat seller and the ambulant trader. In larger centers, like Inzá, the market is the place where most of the retail transactions take place. But in the still bigger rural population centers it is food sellers and local artisans who give the market place its busy appearance; however, in these centers local shops are well stocked with manufactured goods and may sell more than the market traders. In the bigger cities markets are large and active but lack the peasant character of some rural markets.

It is therefore the demographic as well as the social and economic character of an area which determines the nature of the market place. In Colombia, a town with less than two thousand people cannot absorb the food production of its dependent peasant population, and the market will be supplied by those few producers who live close to the main square. Furthermore, a municipality with a large Indian reservation will have a central market offering a very distinct array of goods, not at all comparable to other market places.

The territory served by a market place depends on its commercial success. A market like Inzá manages to attract regularly only those

[5] The amounts listed are approximations based on estimates as no statistical information is available and no records are kept by authorities or by traders. Hardware sales are greater than food sales and the amount stated can only be a rough estimate as not all traders were willing to supply information.

peasants who live no more than 10–15 km. away. Availability of transport will affect the size of the market community, but as bus fares are usually too high for most peasants, roads only directly affect the attendance of traders.

What is important to note, and is very often forgotten, is that market networks may spread far and wide, and serve peasants who live in remote areas, but that not every neighborhood is covered. Thus, there are many peasants whose trading activities remain outside the market place centers. Colombia provides clear examples of this situation due to its very sparse rural population, but these are not altogether different from examples of networks described for other countries in the literature.

There is little or no trade movement between municipal markets. Each one of them is in direct commercial contact with one or perhaps two city markets. It is in these big cities that middlemen buy wares to sell at the municipal markets, and also where they sell the cash crops they have purchased. The marketers of Inzá use the cities of Popayán and Neiva (both with over 3,000 inhabitants) as supply centers as well as outlets for coffee. During the harvest middlemen travel to Neiva because it is a better outlet for cash crops (it has a direct rail connexion to Bogotá), while the rest of the year they go to Popayán where they find cheap potatoes and good unrefined sugar (both local products) to bring back to Inzá.

The Development of Peasant-like Markets

Specialization has been said usually to occur when there is a high enough population density, but in Colombia specialization is the result of striking climatic variations within very short distances. Some of the peasant families I studied were primarily coffee producers while others, who still lived close enough to be included in my sample, could only grow potatoes. Though ecology favors agricultural specialization within a region, dense market networks were not developed as a result of this specialization.

Certainly trade channels existed in precolonial times and were maintained after the coming of the Spaniards. Tribute payments, required of the Indians in the form of European crops such as wheat, led to the production of crops for export at the expense of the production of subsistence crops. Thus, channels for agricultural exports were established and became part of the socio-political linkage of rural areas to the new centers of power. Economic relations within the community adapted themselves to the development of external trade which continued even after the abolition of tribute payments, being then for the purchase of new tools and goods. Hence specialization and export of agricultural products occurred in Colombia as a result of ecological factors and colonial policy.

But specialization did not encourage the development of peasant market networks in Colombia as it did in Peru, Ecuador, Mexico and Guatemala. The development of peasant markets requires, I believe, a high population density or the proximity of an urban demand sector,[6] as a comparison with the other countries mentioned would suggest. Guatemala and Mexico were more densely populated than Colombia, and though the over-all density for Peru and Ecuador during the colonial and early republican period was probably similar to or lower than that of Colombia (Safford 1966) at least these two countries had the advantage of mining communities which offered the commercial world a ready market for their products.[7] In Colombia peasant markets developed only around the main urban centers, where the existence of demand and the density of the neighboring rural population were high enough to warrant the development of more or less adequate transport services (around Bogotá, Tunja, Antioquia, El Socorro, Cauca Valley).

Although Colombia lacked an extensive peasant market network, trade did flourish in spite of costly and difficult transport (about five

[6] This is similar to Port Moresby (Belshaw 1952) which developed a market of local peasant producers who supplied a town of 12,000 to 15,000 inhabitants.

[7] In the early nineteenth century Colombia and Peru had similar populations of about 600,000 to 700,000 (Kubler 1946; Lannoy & Perez 1961) and probably a similar density, that is of 1–2 per sq. km. But Peru's population was probably concentrated earlier around very important mines. It was in the twentieth century that Colombia's population began to increase; in the early part of the century it was 3–4 per sq. km. and at present it reaches an overall average of 11 per sq. km. Peru's present-day density is not much above 8 per sq. km.

times higher than in the U.S.A.) ; there are accounts of traders from Bogotá and Tunja who sent their cotton goods up to 300 miles away. The development of an indigenous urban-based trade was helped by the isolation of the Andean area from any of the entry ports which thereby protected traders there from foreign competitors. Hence trading skill and rural demand were sufficient to encourage a home industry and urban-base trading, but population density was probably too low in the rural areas to encourage peasant industries and peasant markets.

There is a further reason which explains the limited growth of the already existing rural market places. I have already pointed out that peasants do not like to sell subsistence crops on the market place in spite of the fact that there is a demand, limited though it may be. The Indians explain their refusal with reminders of the criticism which a member of the community undergoes when he is seen to be selling at the market place too often; he is said to be greedy and irresponsible and as a sanction, co-operation is withdrawn, labor exchanges are stopped and food is not sold or loaned to him when he needs it. This rule against sale is part of another rule which specifies a lower rate of exchange for foodstuffs traded amongst community members (Ortiz 1963; in press) . When in need of food an Indian may purchase cheaply or borrow from a friend, kinsman or neighbor with whom ties of reciprocity already exist. It is because of this that surpluses must be retained; selling on the square or in the open market is tantamount to refusing to sell at this lower rate. Non-Indians are of course included in these circles of exchange and in this way the local population is supplied with food. This system of distribution acts as an insurance mechanism for a peasantry which has lower revenue than the rest of the peasantry and limited access to credit and loans. Once subsistence is assured, then it is easier to face the risks of cash crop development (coffee in this area) . This limits the possible development of food crop production, which is in any case unlikely to be warranted by local demand. In fact, peasants around the city of La Plata (2,416 inhabitants and a rural density of about 12 inhabitants per sq. km.) complained that the local market could not always absorb their production and one of them tried unsuccessfully to use San Andrés as an outlet for his cassava harvest, though it meant a bus trip of four hours. Extensive food production has to be channelled to large urban centers through the existing import-export trade channel. The Indians' refusal to participate in markets by selling their local products suggests why the San Andrés, Belalcazar and Inzá markets have never developed a peasant trading section similar to those found in Guatemala, Ecuador and Peru. The interpretation given for the area studied may not, of course, apply to the rest of Colombia, and further regional studies should be made before formulating a nation-wide generalisation. The only rural markets (of those visited) where trade was also geared to local redistribution were those of Sylvia (an Indian potato growing area of similar density but with a township of 2,754 inhabitants) and San Agustín, a peasant area also of similar density and a township of 2,500 inhabitants.[8]

The above analysis of economic relations does not fit the model suggested by Sahlins (1965: 179–86) . He assumes that an external trade in subsistence products in return for prestige items and tools of production implies an internal ban on sharing them or a corresponding requirement of a *quid pro quo* in intra-community dealings resulting in a disruption of the ordinary distributive mechanism. His disregard of possible insurance mechanisms leads him to oversimplify the model. Even in those potato growing areas within the region of Colombia which I am discussing here (potatoes being the main cold country staple) , export of this cash crop does not lead to disruption of the internal distributive systems which operate at lower rates of exchange.

8 Port Moresby affords another interesting comparison. Belshaw (1952) remarks that prices are customary; however, traders try to exploit the supply and demand ratio to the indignation of the buyer who considers the practice of selling food at a maximum profit to be unethical. Traders in this case are selling to a native sector of limited resources. It is also worth noting that Port Moresby had a population of about 12,000 to 15,000 when Belshaw studied it and that other market areas discussed such as Pátzcuaro (Foster 1948) are supplying towns of 1,000 to 9,000 inhabitants or like Guatemala (Inst. Indigenista Nacional 1947) which has a population density of over 31 per sq. km. Neale and Singh's (1965) study of Indian markets indicates that there the fertility of the area and historical chance as well as topographical accidents are more important in determining location and importance of markets than are road connections or competition.

Internal distributive mechanisms are more likely to be disturbed by the intrusion of merchants with capital than by the need to export. Guatemala is a case in point; indigo was a flourishing export in the eighteenth century and Spanish merchants, attracted by the trading possibilities and with sufficient capital to exploit them, promoted a very lucrative commerce. By extending credit and channelling commerce through government officials and Indian officers in distant provinces, traders found an easy outlet for their manufactured products (Floyd 1966) and managed to control exchanges.

Import Market Place Organization and the Imbalanced Integration of Peasant Sectors

Mintz (1959: 20) has suggested that market mechanisms articulate different segments of a single society—classes, castes, occupational groups and the like—through the set of transactions which maintains production and distribution. He contrasts market place organizations like those described by Polanyi *et al.* (1957), which are subject to custom, ritual, hereditary assignment of position, fixed price regulation, with the peasant market place organizations of Haiti, Jamaica, Guatemala and Mexico, which are free of the above-mentioned constraints. In the second case the flow of goods, services and sellers is relatively free, while in the first case the flow is limited and fixed in such a way that the channels of articulation cannot change quickly.

Here I discuss yet another type of articulation. This market place organization unlike the African and medieval European organizations, is not embedded in the social, political and religious framework. The flow of goods and services is relatively free, but yet there are socio-economic constraints which define and limit the articulation of the peasantry.

In the first place, the chain of market places is organized around the import of goods and as has been mentioned, little horizontal trading is carried out and export trade is forbidden by local authorities. The market thus links the peasants to outside sellers and not to other peasant producers except in so far as they come together on the market square; even then those who meet are the ones who live in the area near the market town. Friends and neighbors will meet and in this way keep in touch with each other; the practice of exchanging drinks with kinsmen and friends maintains a flow of reciprocity. But transactions do not bring a peasant into close association with other peasants.[9]

Market sales are for cash and no credit is extended except in very unusual circumstances and by very few individuals. Sellers belong to a different social environment, class and income group from buyers. The transaction and the bargaining relation stresses the existing social distance rather than diminishing it. There is only one common element in the relationship: that the preference to sell the product overlaps with the peasant's preference to buy it. No information is given as this would affect the power balance necessary for a successful sale, and no close friendship is established as this would affect the concessions that the seller is willing to make (except when buyer and seller are already friends or co-parents). I do not imply that there are absolutely no small middlemen whose operations rest on strong personal ties with a number of clients. In the San Andrés markets there was one such middleman who was a local resident. In Inzá out of an average of twenty middlemen there were three who stayed in the town for a few months. These men operated on

[9] The number of food producers in Inzá who sell on the market square depends on weather conditions as well as on demands made by seasonal crops. During the period August-November there is little food available for consumption or sale, and as a result one can seldom see more than nine food producers selling at the market. December and January are the coffee harvest months and people need to buy extra food for their laborers or to supplement their dwindling resources; food producers selling at the market increase in number to about fifteen but their own involvement in coffee harvesting keeps the number of sellers below that. After the coffee harvest and until the lean month of August producers have both the time and the clientele to warrant a trip with supplies to Inzá; twenty-eight to thirty-five producers can be seen on the square selling a variety of fruits and vegetables. Potato producers from the other side of the mountains sometimes come to sell at Inzá where they can get a higher price, but mountain paths are treacherous and seldom did I see more than two and never more than four.

The number of ambulant traders in the area studied is very small; I only know of two who supply ten Indian reservations with imports. Furthermore only three times during the year of my field work did I see an ambulant trader come to San Andrés. But this pattern can vary from area to area, of course.

a small enough margin to encourage them to develop a steady clientele of people who would sell coffee in exchange for goods, or who would allow them to act as brokers in the sale of a cow or horse. One can thus say that the import character of the market place facilitates the contact of commercial centers with peasants but not necessarily the other way round.

Restrictions on the sale of wholesale goods on market squares exclude peasant markets as channels for the export of staples. By limiting the channels of contact as well as the center of contact, and by stressing the impersonality of market transactions, the import-type of market organization gives a dual character to the Colombian economy. On the one hand we have universalistic, impersonal economic relations, while on the other hand we have particularistic and personal economic relations. The import market organization stresses the difference and acts to impede a better integration of the two systems. This is not the same as Boeke's (1953) differentiation of economies into two sectors; in fact, I want to indicate that this differentiation is more apparent than real, and that impersonal economic relations are also part and parcel of the peasant sector.

Mintz (1959: 22) suggests that an insistence, based on custom and law, that certain products should not be sold on the market place limits the growth of certain intermediaries and affects the market as a mechanism of social articulation. I would like to add that in many cases these limitations are the result of the particular character of the market. The Indians object to the sale of food in the market because of the impersonality of the organization, and authorities forbid wholesalers because of shortage of locally grown food supplies. The duality of the economy fosters a differential valuation of goods (which certainly existed during the colonial period between tribal groups and Spaniards), and maintains a marketing system whose existence rests on this differentiation.

Later on it will be shown that this import system has a built-in mechanism which limits its expansion potential and threatens the effectiveness of municipal organization. If we also add that it only manages to serve about a quarter of the peasant population concentrated around bigger provincial urban centers, it will be obvious why it is not a successful means of articulating the peasant sector to Colombian national life.

The Import Market Place Organization and the Needs of the Peasant Sector

The import character of the Colombian market place organization as well as the limited number of middlemen who are responsible for the distribution of manufactured goods and imported staples, give the purchaser the obvious advantage of a lower price than he would have to pay if goods had to pass through innumerable retailers and wholesalers. Furthermore, frequent travel by local traders to main commercial centers does encourage the introduction of new techniques which would otherwise have taken longer to reach distant rural areas. However, in spite of these advantages, this type of market place organization fails to perform what should be the main function of a distributive system: to reallocate available resources so as to realize their productive potential and to stimulate productive growth. A peasant-like market place organization would have performed this function by:

1. Increasing the liquidity of food crops. Small amounts of food could be exchanged for tool replacements or seed purchases at the moment when they are needed without forcing the peasant to incur high interest (hidden interest) credit purchases.
2. Reducing the loss of capital incurred when crops are stored (Belshaw 1965).
3. Stimulating the creation of a class of craftsmen, thus increasing the possible avenues open to peasants for capital accumulation.
4. Stimulating the formation of a local entrepreneurial class. Traders may start with little capital and amass a considerable trading potential, as can be seen from the Javanese and Haitian examples.

These are only some of the factors which make peasant markets well adapted to low income part-subsistence economies. The fact that Colombia has developed the market structure it has means that, at least to a certain extent, there was a suitable response to existing economic conditions. I have after all explained that for the area of Inzá, sales in the market place were avoided.

It does not necessarily follow that the Colombian distributive mechanism is best suited to the remote rural areas. The present system had its roots in the urban centers; as I said earlier, once it reached the more distant and poorer municipalities local peasants could no longer compete with a trading sector with higher capital, knowledge and experience. However, it would be pointless to labor the argument that the marketing system fails because it does not increase the liquidity of assets or perform a storage function, for this failure can be attributed to the conscious refusal of Indians to sell their products on the market square. It is more profitable to analyze the failures of the system in those spheres where people attempt to make it function successfully.

The Limited Trading Potential of Import Market Networks

Middlemen take their wares to a market place for the simple reason that there is an available clientele; if the attendance increases, their income from sales will also rise. The popularity of the market depends on the opportunities it offers to the clientele and on the number of inhabitants who reside within 20 km. of the market square. For example, the area around Bogotá, the savannah of Bogotá as it is called, has a much higher population than remote municipalities like Inzá and therefore the latter area will have a lower limit of possible market participation than the Bogotá area. Geographical location, road connection and local entrepreneurial potential will affect the attractiveness of the display of wares. Belalcazar, a town close to Inzá, attracts many more traders who, thanks to relatively good road connections with La Plata and Neiva, find it easier to bring a larger and more varied selection of merchandise than those who have to make the more arduous trip to Inzá.

There are also a number of other factors which affect market attendance. As is obvious from the description of activities at the market place, it is not just trading opportunities which attract potential customers to the square. The San Andrés Indians come down to the little hamlet on market days because the reservation council meets there; peasants often go to Inzá because there is some official business to attend to. The attendance of farmers who reside outside the market town is the *raison d'être* for holding a market in a small town. Services offered by government or other agencies located in towns will attract the necessary clientele which in turn will attract more traders, and make a competitive and active trading center out of the local market place.

Probably most municipal townships at one time or other hold, or attempt to organize, regular markets (the meat stalls of most hamlets show such incipient attempts). To go to market on Saturday and to church on Sunday is an almost universal pattern throughout Colombia, and one aspired to by both colonial and republican administrators. But if local government fails to provide extra incentives the population of a municipality will attend instead that market which is closest to their residence or offers the best trading possibilities.

There are some obvious administrative consequences of the fact that local residents may not keep in touch with their own municipal township. In the first place it makes it very difficult and expensive to administer the area. Local government lacks the resources and personnel to administer its territory efficiently, hence some local governmental functions, as for example social control and organization of local improvement projects, depend partly on having the local population visit the municipal township rather than on having to hire officials to keep in touch with a widely scattered rural population.

Municipal revenue in the distant rural municipalities depends to a large extent on market tax and fines. Land tax revenue is low, and unless they can collect other taxes such as market tax, municipalities lack sufficient funds and as a result have to depend on subsidies from the departmental level—a problem which has been discussed by numerous Colombian specialists (Gaitin 1964). Municipal townships with poorly attended markets often increase the basic rate of their market tax and levy petty fines, in order to offset revenue loss due to the low participation of tradesmen. The consequences of this policy are detrimental to the commercial success of the town. To be fined 4s. for having tied one's horse to the wrong tree amounts to the loss of a day's work and a decrease in trading revenue. Inhabitants become increasingly irritated, arguments break out on every market day, tensions grow and municipal governments topple. These apparently trivial upsets should not be underestimated, for they may seriously affect the annual pattern of investment of those traders short of capital resources.

Hence, the growth and development of a market place rests initially on the strength of local government and, in turn, once the market is itself active enough to attract the public it will help to strengthen the political structure.

Rural markets, of course, compete with each

other. I have already mentioned the competition and relative success of the Belalcazar market at the expense of the neighboring Inzá market. Farmers will choose, given the opportunity, the more active neighboring commercial center, and thus reduce the effectiveness of their own municipal government by failing to keep in touch with it or make use of the market in their own township. When in competition with each other, more active markets will kill off other less important neighboring markets. This phenomenon has not only been observed in the municipalities I studied but also in areas closer to Bogotá (Fals Borda 1955). I suspect that the type of market-place organization which I have called "import" is much more likely to limit its operations to a few centers with fast turn-over than to expand throughout the countryside. Traders depend on motorized transport which is not available throughout rural areas. To adapt their activities to other transport would be difficult and costly. A market organization with a peasant base would probably cover a wider territory, because the number of local small traders would be large and could more easily cope with transport difficulties. It could be argued that, since the function of import marketing channels is to increase the revenue of the middlemen, a few better attended markets are, from the point of view of trading, less costly and just as successful. Such an argument totally disregards the fact that there are practical limitations to the number of people who attend a market place. I have suggested that attendance can be expected only from within a 20 km. radius except in cases where road transport is well developed—a point which will be discussed below. Farmers living further away make their purchases instead at local shops. Hence the import nature of the marketing organization, coupled with competitive relations between trading centers, instead of encouraging the development of the market place network furthers the proliferation of satellite trading stores. This is what has happened in distant rural areas where every settlement has just about as many trading shops as there are residents with sufficient capital to open one.[10] I do not intend to explain the existence or number of trading shops on this basis; I only want to point out that this is another problem which should be discussed with reference to trading networks. The main San Andrés buyers lost £74 annually of their assets in the purchase of potatoes, salt and sugar alone, due to differences in prices between the San Andrés store and the Inzá market.

In the municipality of Inzá, markets do not service with regularity more than 2,000 to 3,000 inhabitants out of a total municipality population of 11,398, and seldom more than 250 nonresidents attend markets at any one time. The proportion for the municipality of Belalczar is similar. It is only in the more densely populated municipalities of the department, with large urban centers, that municipal markets will be buying centers for a larger proportion of the population. In fact, the Inzá figure is representative of most rural municipalities, and it tells us that only about a quarter of the farming population can normally hope to trade on a market square frequently enough to take advantage of lower prices and more varied merchandise. The rest have to depend on local shopkeepers and, to a lesser extent, on ambulant traders.

Import Market Organization and the Intra-regional Movements of Goods

The disappearance of markets could easily have been avoided had the market centers been so timed as to follow each other throughout the week in order to facilitate the movement of traders from one to the other. This frequently happens in many peasant societies, as has been reported in great detail for Mexico, Guatemala, China, etc. There is no obvious commercial reason why the inter-linking of markets into regional rings should not have occurred; in fact, it would have given greater scope to the activities of traders who now find relatively unrewarding the task of moving merchandise from one settlement to another in search of clients. There were very few ambulant traders in the area I studied; it was an activity resorted to when trading ventures were bad and when the trader had no land to fall back on. I knew of only two traders who occasionally visited the neighborhood on their

[10] There is about one shop per 130 inhabitants in rural districts similar to the one discussed; while in Medellín, a big commercial center, there is about one shop per 30 inhabitants, probably with a higher volume of trade.

way to Indian reservations further north. On the other hand secondary markets within a municipality, except in the department of Nariño, are held during the week so as not to interfere with the Saturday market at the municipal township.

Market traders are mostly outsiders who would undoubtedly profit from the existence of market rings, but to them their absence is not so critical because they can just as easily attend daily city markets in other regions. Pressure from interested local traders and craftsmen could have led to the formation of a regional market place system. The majority of the important market traders is not sufficiently interested in this development to take any action. I would also argue that the existing market organization has discouraged the formation of any group of local market traders and craftsmen which could have taken such action.

The factors preventing a more rational coordination of the distributive mechanism are not purely economic but have also to be explained by analyzing the political sub-system. Traders have primarily economic goals, but they are also influenced by political considerations. Power can easily be transferred by them from one area of activities to another; that is, their liquid assets can be translated into a political following. The nature of the political organization will thus help us to explain the competitive relations between politcal centers which are also market centers. To understand these competitive relations we must not conceive of polity and economy as two separate structures only barely influencing each other, but as integrated structures.

Municipalities are the basic units for local government. For the most part these administrative units have been demarcated around towns of 500 inhabitants or more. Since the population is not concentrated in towns, the size of the municipal capital does not, strictly speaking, reflect the population density in the rest of its territory. In some cases municipal territories are large and mountainous like Inzá with 760 sq. km., while others like Tensa (Boyacá) comprise only 24 sq. km. If new urban centers develop in an existing municipality, residents will petition for the creation of a new political unit. Thus municipalities are constantly being created (from 1938 to 1951 nineteen new municipalities were added to the 828 then in existence). Their new status gives the local residents more financial support, greater educational facilities and the probability of new roads to connect them to larger urban centers. Thus municipal units develop due to separatist forces within old municipalities. The struggle for independence from a parent unit is an involved and drawn out one. Every growing township harbors such aspirations, often encouraged by participation in different political parties. In Inzá the rivalry over market participation effectively blocked the organization of bus services for market transport between Belalcazar and Inzá. It is a matter of choice whether resources are to be used to concentrate power in one area or whether they are to be used to facilitate the linking of areas and thus possibly dilute the existing effective political power.

Resident traders strive to be politically influential in their municipalities either because they have political aspirations or because their trading activities will benefit from any political connections. If they reside in a town which is not a municipal township they will probably support any separatist movement, for they will benefit from the new roads and other administrative improvements which will result when the town is made into a separate municipal unit. Traders' activities are concerned mostly with import of goods and export of cash crops; motorized transport to cities is more important to them than to a small trader, and the latter would benefit more from the proliferation of markets organized so that they follow each other through the week.

The Import Market Network and the Local Potential

"We note next that specialization and trade also requires that market places should be organized. Lack of markets is one sign of the primitive community" (Lewis 1963: 76). Though the above quotation requires a qualification in view of the Colombian example, it cogently states an important point: local specialists require an accessible outlet, for example, a nearby market place, for their small outputs.[11] Without easy access to the buyer, local craftsmen or small local industries are unlikely to develop. Local stores

[11] For a detailed discussion on the role of small middlemen and the function of apparently inefficient marketing systems see Bauer & Yamey (1954). Many of the points discussed here have been treated at greater length and in a slightly different context in the article here cited.

do not stock such craftsmen's products. The cost of handling merchandise of limited demand would make the price prohibitive and non-competitive with longer lasting industrial products. At Inzá, clay pots could be purchased from a potter who travelled 10 km. to attend the market. She was the only manufacturer who regularly offered her wares for sale; the other producer sometimes brought a variety of goods; a chair, a mattress and cords as well as pots, at irregular intervals. At other bigger rural market places like Sylvia and San Agustín, the number of craft producers and the variety of crafts produced for sale was greater. These two towns each have a population of about 2,500, which accounts for the difference, though population density in surrounding areas is similar to that of Inzá. But the question here is whether or not the existing marketing organization makes the best possible use of local productive potential. Not every participant can become a craftsman, partly because he requires knowledge, ability and easy access to necessary resources (clay, wood, etc.) in order to make production profitable. A readily available outlet for his production is also essential. The larger the area serviced by a market place the greater the chance that craftsmen will live within the area and that local goods will be sold on the square. Pottery, storage bags, cordage and wooden utensils made locally are much cheaper than similar items imported from distant urban centers, as well as having special uses.

There are two ways to increase the marketing area: by inter-linking markets or by organizing motor transport, a point which Belshaw stresses as an important factor in economic development. Transport requires roads, and in a country like Colombia construction of added mileage is expensive. So far Colombia's 36,890 km. of roads (1,459 km. in the Department of Cauca and 20 km. in Inzá in 1960) only link the municipal capitals with important urban centers and cross some of the rural territories. If transport on these roads were geared to rural needs, marketing activities would be encouraged; but so far the entrepreneurs investing in trucks find it more profitable to cater for the needs of city traders and to transport stock for stores or export crops than to organize schedules to suit the needs of the small peasant producers, craftsmen and market attendants. The latest bus service instituted in the Inzá municipality was a regular Saturday morning service on 11 km. of its only road, for those who wanted to attend the market. Thus, while the import-export market trader can usually be assured of motor access to and from the market, the small peasant producer cannot. Only a municipal government pressed by the local population will demand that bus services be provided to local citizens. Hence the first ones to be served will be the import-export trader and the producers and purchasers who live within the municipal boundaries of the market place and close enough to a road. Uneven transport introduces certain frictions in the marketing organization which favor not only certain types of trade but also certain types of resident.

Marginality in market participation has so far been related to distance and transport difficulties. It may also be the result of the participants' tenuous relations with traders and with those individuals who may affect trading relations. Important middlemen and buyers may equally be affected by minimal linkage with the municipality because they have to compete with traders and buyers who are in multiplex relations with local authorities and local distributors. In Inzá, for example, traders who came irregularly and had no reciprocal social or economic ties with high officials were at the mercy of the municipal mayor who charged them a disproportionately high tax.

Municipal authorities are supposed to help citizens collect their bad debts (cf. Dewey 1962). The debtor will be called to the mayor's office or the police be sent to search for him, he will be given a stern warning, fined or eventually sent to jail. The more ineffective the administration of the municipality, the more unlikely its success in this function. The greater the tension between non-resident traders and government, the less likely that municipal authorities will take the trouble to co-operate in difficult cases, and in turn the stricter will be the terms for credit. Credit is very important for small Colombian farmers because of the cyclical nature of income and expenditure; without it, it is very difficult if not impossible for a farmer to expand his cash crop activities. Social sanctions to enforce payment are not always possible when the population is so dispersed and traders do not reside locally.

The Role of the Import-Export Market Network in Economic Development

Undoubtedly, one of the functions of competition in trading is to stimulate the introduction of new, useful products and to lower prices by cutting down the number of middlemen and by selecting those with greater commercial sense. Certainly competition may modernize trading networks, but it does not make an innovator out of a trader. In rural Colombia it must be remembered that traders are cultivators and cattle breeders as well.

An efficient import organization will favor the development of small-scale manufacturing or processing industries. Owners of small seasonal shops can organize small processing industries based on technical ideas introduced from urban centers and with machinery bought at competitive prices. The export channels, if efficient, can handle the distribution of small firms' output. This has not been the case in rural Colombia in areas far from urban centers. There are many reasons for this serious failure. Traders and residents of market towns are usually too busily employed in lucrative farming or commercial activities to spend time in activities which involve a number of unknowns. Such persons are likely to introduce innovations which cut labor input and allow expansion and diversification of interests. In the area studied there has been a sudden growth of sugar processing, with improved motorized sugar mills replacing the old wooden ones or more recent animal-powered metal mills. However, it seems unlikely that expansion will continue because, although import facilities eased the introduction of machinery, the export of *panela* (raw sugar cubes) to urban centers has to compete with the cheaper industrial product. As long as it can obtain cheap sugar cane from Indians planting in small lots or selling to pay debts, the industry will continue to expand because the *panela* is of higher quality; but the urban supply sector has its limitations. Lewis's (1963: 77) suggestion that efficient and cheap marketing agencies overcome the disadvantages of small firms is true as long as they are orientated towards the goals of the firms. A peasant market network would have been more efficient because it would have distributed the product where urban competition is lowest. The organizing locus of the existing marketing chain in Colombia is situated in commercial centers and geared to their needs. As Lewis suggests, if the small firm were surrounded by agencies—private, co-operative or statutory—which took over all functions that have to be performed on a large scale, small firms would be more likely to succeed.

The local prestige of traders is greatly enhanced if they are the only links that rural areas have with political and commercial centers. Trading is an attractive occupation; to dabble in trade has become "the thing to do" for the local elite of agriculturalists, even if they do not make much of a profit. However, a multiplicity of traders brings all sorts of problems. It does not really increase competitive efficiency; instead it raises the prices of imported goods and lowers the purchasing power of the local population. It also means a wastage of local savings, for the profits are not worth mentioning and the prestige of traders discourages individuals from becoming true entrepreneurs.

The local trader-entrepreneur is in close contact with the rural population and is therefore aware of local problems. He is in a relationship of superiority to them, which he must maintain in order to bargain successfully. His activities are always surrounded by secrecy and the information he passes on is, very understandably, received with a great deal of mistrust. Traders are the source of information on prices outside the region and on government regulations concerning purchasing of cash crops as well as on possible terms of credit from banks or government credit agencies. Their success as traders depends, in such a highly competitive system, on their giving either wrong or incomplete information. Sometimes this is done to discourage others from using the same profitable sources or to show off as accomplished bargainers. They cannot therefore inspire enough confidence to be successful innovators unless they themselves organize the enterprise.

Contact with larger centers will teach the trader marketing techniques. But any thorough modernization through marketing arrangements will be limited because it also requires the breaking down of farming self-sufficiency or part self-sufficiency. This is impossible within the present level of capital available to the producer and the high level of risk in most cash crop activities. Government interference is necessary. In a country like Colombia, with strong regional differences, government participation in regulating economic activities cannot be left to central agencies but must be carried out locally. Local agencies administering centrally co-ordinated programs could be the best solution, but regional conditions sometimes require different kinds of arrangements. Local co-ordination must be achieved and a strong and efficient local government could be successful in accomplishing it. The question that remains is one to be answered by those with experience of strong local government organization. That is, would it be likely that a strong local government would hinder rather than encourage reform?

Conclusion

In this article I have shown that Dalton and Bohannan's model cannot be universally applied. The market place in Colombia is not the place where most exchanges take place, at least in the more remote rural areas. The importance of the market place is to be seen in municipal townships, while again in the main cities it is in the shops that most transactions take place.

The Colombian market organization has served to illustrate the point that the origin of a particular marketing system depends on population density and on the economic structure of a particular region. In Colombia, once the locus of the marketing system was established in the bigger commercial centers a new type of organization did not evolve. The import channel thus established had a feed-back effect on the economic structure of distant rural areas; this was manifested by the maintenance of traditional patterns of exchange—contrary to what Sahlins predicted, and the dual character of the Colombian rural economy.

Models, in this case representing economic relations, are useful devices which, by simplifying reality, help to suggest propositions. I have outlined an exploratory model of the Colombian market place organization in the hope that it will encourage further research in other areas of Colombia as well as suggest propositions about the operation of this type of market place system. The model is based on limited empirical research, and confirmation with data from other areas of Colombia is now required.

Several striking characteristics of the import type market organization have come to light which, even if found not to be true for all areas of Colombia, certainly apply to the areas studied. Here, rural markets serve only one quarter of the rural population and poorly integrate this farming sector to the national economy. Transactions are impersonal and the existing market organization bolsters the power of the important middlemen. The consequences which can be foreseen and at least partly confirmed are several. In the first place, competition does not lead to further expansion; instead, in some cases it leads to the closure of market places. Secondly, competition and imperfections of the market are responsible for the formation of coalitions, which in the case examined have resulted in the exclusion of food in large quantities from the market place. Thirdly, the existing import market place organization bolsters the position of the large middlemen, and the expansion of the sector of small middlemen and craftsmen is inhibited. The latter group would have better served the needs of the small producer and would have been a better source of reliable and relevant information to the farmer.

Market place systems have often been analyzed with information gathered at the main market centers. The data in this article give us instead a detailed account of market places which are relatively small and distantly located. And the conclusions derived from it are quite different from the conclusions suggested in other studies. I have cited the work of Bauer and Yamey (1954) in outlining the functions of peasant markets. My material backs their findings, namely, that a peasant economy is better served by apparently inefficient peasant markets than by the import type markets described here.

REFERENCES

Bauer, P. T. & B. S. Yamey 1954. The economics of marketing reform. *J. polit. Econ.* 62:210–35.

Belshaw, C. 1952. Port Moresby canoe traders. *Oceania* 23:26–39.

Boeke, J. H. 1953. *Economics and economic policy of dual societies.* New York: Institute of Pacific Relations.

Bohannan, P. & G. Dalton 1962. *Markets in Africa.* Evanston: Northwestern Univ. Press.

Dewey, A. 1962. Trade and social control in Java. *J. R. anthrop. Inst.* 92:177–91.

Fals Borda, O. 1955. *Peasant society in the Colombian Andes: a sociological study of Saucio.* Gainesville: Univ. of Florida Press.

Floyd, T. S. 1966. The indigo merchant: promoter of Central American economic development 1750–1808. *Business Hist. Rev.* 39:466–89.

Foster, G. M. 1948. The folk economy of rural Mexico with special reference to marketing. *J. Marketing* 13:53–62.

Gaitan, G. 1964. *El municipio colombiano.* Bogotá: Imprenta Departamental Antonio Nariño.

Guatemala, Inst. Indigenista Nacional. 1947. Mercados regionales guatemaltecos. *Bol. Inst. indig. nac. Guat.* 2:148:68.

Kubler, G. 1947. The Quechua in the colonial world. In *Handbook of South American Indians* (ed.) J. Steward. Washington D.C.: Smithsonian Institute.

Lannoy, J. L. and G. Peréz 1961. *Estructuras demográficas sociales de Colombia.* Bogotá: Centro de Investigaciones Sociales de FERES.

Lewis, W. A. 1963. *Theories of economic growth.* London: Unwin.

Malinowski, B. & J. De la Fuente 1957. *La economia de un sistema de mercados en México.* (Acta anthrop. Méx. I). México: Escuela Nacional de Antropología y Historia.

Mintz, S. 1959. Internal market systems as a mechanism of social articulation. In *Intermediate societies, social mobility and communication* (ed.) V. F. Ray (Proc. am. ethnol. Soc. 1959). Seattle: Univ. Washington Press.

Neale, W., H. Singh & S. P. Singh 1965. Kurali market: a report on the economic geography of marketing in northern Punjab. *Econ. Dev. cult. change* 13:129–69.

Ortiz, S. 1963. The Economic Organization of a Paez Indian community. Thesis, University of London.

——— In press. The structure of decision-making with special reference to Indians of Colombia). Paper presented to the Conference of the Association of Social Anthropologists, Oxford, 1963.

Polanyi, K., C. M. Arensberg & H. W. Pearson 1957. *Trade and market in the early empires.* Glencoe, Ill.: Free Press.

Reichel-Dolmatoff, Gerardo & Alicia. 1961. *The people of Aritama.* London: Routledge & Kegan Paul.

Safford, F. 1966. Foreign and national enterprise in nineteenth century Colombia. *Business Hist. Rev.* 39: 503–27.

Sahlins, M. 1965. On the sociology of primitive exchange. In *The relevance of models in social anthropology,* (ed.) M. Banton. (Ass. social Anthrop. monogr. I). London: Tavistock Publications.

Sayres, W. C. 1956. Indians and the market: a Colombian community. *Am. J. Econ. Sociol.* 16:1–10.

Skinner, G. W. 1964–65. Marketing and social structure in rural China. *J. Asian Stud.* 24:3–45, 195–229, 363–401.

SECTION III

Economic Change and "Development"

You hardly need to turn to a textbook for evidence that economic change is almost invariably hooked up causally to most of the other major aspects of culture. It rarely occurs unaccompanied by technological innovation. It never takes place on a significant scale without shaking up the prevailing social system. In the sense that control over productive goods and the wealth they produce is coterminous with political control, little ever happens in the way of important economic change without causing political repercussions. Ideology is always a strong part of the picture, too, as is obvious in any discussion of economic change that is "good" and to be encouraged versus that which is "bad" and to be suppressed. Supportive examples extend from the now long-stagnant, fire-gutted riot corridors of almost any American "inner city," to the even more badly charred rice paddies of Indochina, the sere battlefields of the Middle East, and the burnt remains of insurgents' encampments in southern Africa and Latin America.

The issue is thus one of more than ivory tower ethnological interest. Looking around, the scene on nearly every side suggests that a better understanding of the cultural causes and consequences of economic change—especially of that once hallowed, but now suspect kind of change called development—is a necessity that has already affected all of us still living, and millions who have just recently died.

How is development to be accomplished so that it is truly responsive to the pressing material needs of Third World peoples? There are two ideologically opposite answers: (1) by the gradual readjustment of existing sociocultural institutions; (2) by radical structural transformation of all sociocultural institutions whose dependence on maintenance of the established order compels them to oppose any fundamental economic change that might threaten their privileged position.

An economist long familiar with the theoretical aspects of economic anthropology, Frank has also been a front-line participant observer in the struggle for economic change in Latin America. Here he suggests the proper analysis of some hard facts.

The Development of Underdevelopment in Latin America

Andre Gunder Frank

We cannot hope to formulate adequate development theory and policy for the majority of the world's population who suffer from underdevelopment without first learning how their past economic and social history gave rise to their present underdevelopment. Yet most historians study only the developed metropolitan countries and pay scant attention to the colonial and underdeveloped lands. For this reason most of our theoretical categories and guides to development policy have been distilled exclusively from the historical experience of the European and North American advanced capitalist nations.

Since the historical experience of the colonial and underdeveloped countries has demonstrably been quite different, available theory therefore fails to reflect the past of the underdeveloped part of the world entirely, and reflects the past of the world as a whole only in part. More important, our ignorance of the underdeveloped countries' history leads us to assume that their past and indeed their present resembles earlier stages of the history of the now developed countries. This ignorance and this assumption lead us into serious misconceptions about contemporary underdevelopment and development. Further, most studies of development and underdevelopment fail to take account of the economic and other relations between the metropolis and its economic colonies throughout the history of the world wide expansion and development of the mercantilist and capitalist system. Consequently, most of our theory fails to explain the structure and development of the capitalist system as a whole and to account for its simultaneous generation of underdevelopment in some of its parts and of economic development in others.

It is generally held that economic development occurs in a succession of capitalist stages and that today's underdeveloped countries are still in a stage, sometimes depicted as an original stage, of history through which the now developed countries passed long ago. Yet even a modest acquaintance with history shows that underdevelopment is not original or traditional and that neither the past nor the present of the underdeveloped countries resembles in any important respect the past of the now developed countries. The now developed countries were never *under*developed, though they may have been *un*developed. It is also widely believed that the contemporary underdevelopment of a country can be understood as the product or reflection solely of its own economic, political, social, and cultural characteristics or structure. Yet historical research demonstrates that contemporary underdevelopment is in large part the historical product of past and continuing economic and other relations between the satellite underdeveloped and the now developed metropolitan countries. Furthermore, these relations are an essential part of the structure and development of the capitalist system on a world scale as a whole. A related and also largely erroneous view is that the development of these underdeveloped countries, and within them of their most underdeveloped domestic areas, must and will be generated or stimulated by diffusing capital, institutions, values, etc. to them from the international and national capitalist metropoles. Historical perspective based on the underdeveloped countries' past experience suggests that on the contrary, economic development in the underdeveloped countries can now occur only independently of most of these relations of diffusion.

Evident inequalities of income and differences in culture have led many observers to see "dual" societies and economies in the underdeveloped countries. Each of the two parts is supposed to have a history of its own, a structure, and a contemporary dynamic largely independent of the other. Supposedly only one part of the economy and society has been importantly affected by intimate economic relations with the "outside" capitalist world; and that part, it is held, became modern, capitalist, and relatively developed precisely because of this contact. The other part is widely regarded as variously isolated, subsistence-based, feudal, or pre-capitalist, and therefore more underdeveloped.

I believe on the contrary that the entire "dual" society thesis is false and that the policy recommendations to which it leads will, if acted upon, serve only to intensify and perpetuate the very conditions of underdevelopment they are supposedly designed to remedy.

A mounting body of evidence suggests, and I am confident that future historical research will confirm, that the expansion of the capitalist system over the past centuries effectively and entirely penetrated even the apparently most isolated sectors of the underdeveloped world. Therefore the economic, political, social, and cultural institutions and relations we now observe there are the products of the historical development of the capitalist system no less than are the seemingly more modern or capitalist features of the national metropoles of these underdeveloped countries. Analogous to the relations between development and underdevelopment on the international level, the contemporary underdeveloped institutions of the so-called backward or feudal domestic areas of an underdeveloped country are no less the product of the single historical process of capitalist development than are the so-called capitalist institutions of the supposedly more progressive areas. I should like to sketch the kinds of evidence which support this thesis and at the same time indicate lines along which further study and research could fruitfully proceed.

The Secretary General of the Latin American Center for Research in the Social Sciences writes in that Center's journal: "The privileged position of the city has its origin in the colonial period. It was founded by the Conqueror to serve the same ends that it still serves today; to incorporate the indigenous population into the economy brought and developed by that Conqueror and his descendants. The regional city was an instrument of conquest and is still today an instrument of domination." [1] The Instituto Nacional Indigenista (National Indian Institute) of Mexico confirms this observation when it notes that "the mestizo population, in fact, always lives in a city, a center of an intercultural region, which acts as the metropolis of a zone of indigenous population and which maintains with the underdeveloped communities an intimate relation which links the center with the satellite communities." [2] The Institute goes on to point out that "between the mestizos who live in the nuclear city of the region and the Indians who live in the peasant hinterland there is in reality a closer economic and social interdependence than might at first glance appear" and that the provincial metropoles "by being centers of intercourse are also centers of exploitation." [3]

Thus these metropolis-satellite relations are not limited to the imperial or international level but penetrate and structure the very economic, political, and social life of the Latin American colonies and countries. Just as the colonial and national capital and its export sector become the satellite of the Iberian (and later of other) metropoles of the world economic system, this satellite immediately becomes a colonial and then a national metropolis with respect to the productive sectors and population of the interior. Furthermore, the provincial capitals, which thus are themselves satellites of the national metropolis—and through the latter of the world metropolis—are in turn provincial centers around which their own local satellites orbit. Thus, a whole chain of constellations of metropoles and satellites relates all parts of the whole system from its metropolitan center in Europe or the United States to the farthest outpost in the Latin American countryside.

When we examine this metropolis-satellite structure, we find that each of the satellites, including now underdeveloped Spain and Portugal, serves as an instrument to suck capital or economic surplus out of its own satellites and to channel part of this surplus to the world metropolis of which all are satellites. Moreover, each national and local metropolis serves to impose and maintain the monopolistic structure and exploitative relationship of this system (as the Instituto Nacional Indigenista of Mexico calls it) as long as it serves the interests of the metropoles which take advantage of this global, national, and local structure to promote their own development and the enrichment of their ruling classes.

These are the principal and still surviving

[1] *América Latina,* Año 6, No. 4 (October-December 1963), p. 8.
[2] Instituto Nacional Indigenista, *Los centros coordinadores indigenistas* (Mexico, 1962), p. 34.
[3] *Ibid.*, pp. 33–34, 88.

structural characteristics which were implanted in Latin America by the Conquest. Beyond examining the establishment of this colonial structure in its historical context, the proposed approach calls for study of the development—and underdevelopment—of these metropoles and satellites of Latin America throughout the following and still continuing historical process. In this way we can understand why there were and still are tendencies in the Latin American and world capitalist structure which seem to lead to the development of the metropolis and the underdevelopment of the satellite and why, particularly, the satellized national, regional, and local metropoles in Latin America find that their economic development is at best a limited or underdeveloped development.

That present underdevelopment of Latin America is the result of its centuries-long participation in the process of world capitalist development, I believe I have shown in my case studies of the economic and social histories of Chile and Brazil.[4] My study of Chilean history suggests that the Conquest not only incorporated this country fully into the expansion and development of the world mercantile and later industrial capitalist system but that it also introduced the monopolistic metropolis-satellite structure and development of capitalism into the Chilean domestic economy and society itself. This structure then penetrated and permeated all of Chile very quickly. Since that time and in the course of world and Chilean history during the epochs of colonialism, free trade, imperialism, and the present, Chile has become increasingly marked by the economic, social, and political structure of satellite underdevelopment. This development of underdevelopment continues today, both in Chile's still increasing satellization by the world metropolis and through the ever more acute polarization of Chile's domestic economy.

The history of Brazil is perhaps the clearest case of both national and regional development of underdevelopment. The expansion of the world economy since the beginning of the sixteenth century successively converted the Northeast, the Minas Gerais interior, the North, and the Center-South (Rio de Janeiro, São Paulo, and Paraná) into export economies and incorporated them into the structure and development of the world capitalist system. Each of these regions experienced what may have appeared as economic development during the period of its golden age. But it was a satellite development which was neither self-generating nor self-perpetuating. As the market or the productivity of the first three regions declined, foreign and domestic economic interest in them waned and they were left to develop the underdevelopment they live today. In the fourth region, the coffee economy experienced a similar though not yet quite as serious fate (though the development of a synthetic coffee substitute promises to deal it a mortal blow in the not too distant future). All of this historical evidence contradicts the generally accepted theses that Latin America suffers from a dual society or from the survival of feudal institutions and that these are important obstacles to its economic development.

During the First World War, however, and even more during the Great Depression and the Second World War, São Paulo began to build up an industrial establishment which is the largest in Latin America today. The question arises whether this industrial development did or can break Brazil out of the cycle of satellite development and underdevelopment which has characterized its other regions and national history within the capitalist system so far. I believe that the answer is no. Domestically the evidence so far is fairly clear. The development of industry in São Paulo has not brought greater riches to the other regions of Brazil. Instead, it has converted them into internal colonial satellites, decapitalized them further, and consolidated or even deepened their underdevelopment. There is little evidence to suggest that this process is likely to be reversed in the foreseeable future except insofar as the provincial poor migrate and become the poor of the metropolitan cities. Externally, the evidence is that although the initial development of São Paulo's industry was relatively autonomous it is being increasingly satellized by the world capitalist metropolis and its future development possibilities are in-

[4] "Capitalist Development of Underdevelopment in Chile" and "Capitalist Development of Underdevelopment in Brazil" and *Capitalism and Underdevelopment in Latin America* (New York & London: Monthly Review Press, 1967 and 1969).

creasingly restricted.[5] This development, my studies lead me to believe, also appears destined to limited or underdeveloped development as long as it takes place in the present economic, political, and social framework.

We must conclude, in short, that underdevelopment is not due to the survival of archaic institutions and the existence of capital shortage in regions that have remained isolated from the stream of world history. On the contrary, underdevelopment was and still is generated by the very same historical process which also generated economic development: the development of capitalism itself. This view, I am glad to say, is gaining adherents among students of Latin America and is proving its worth in shedding new light on the problems of the area and in affording a better perspective for the formulation of theory and policy.[6]

The same historical and structural approach can also lead to better development theory and policy by generating a series of hypotheses about development and underdevelopment such as those I am testing in my current research. The hypotheses are derived from the empirical observation and theoretical assumption that within this world-embracing metropolis-satellite structure the metropoles tend to develop and the satellites to underdevelop. The first hypothesis has already been mentioned above: that in contrast to the development of the world metropolis which is no one's satellite, the development of the national and other subordinate metropoles is limited by their satellite status. It is perhaps more difficult to test this hypothesis than the following ones because part of its confirmation depends on the test of the other hypotheses. Nonetheless, this hypothesis appears to be generally confirmed by the non-autonomous and unsatisfactory economic and especially industrial development of Latin America's national metropoles, as documented in the studies already cited. The most important and at the same time most confirmatory examples are the metropolitan regions of Buenos Aires and São Paulo whose growth only began in the nineteenth century, was therefore largely untrammeled by any colonial heritage, but was and remains a satellite development largely dependent on the outside metropolis, first of Britain and then of the United States.

A second hypothesis is that the satellites experience their greatest economic development and especially their most classically capitalist industrial development if and when their ties to their metropolis are weakest. This hypothesis is almost diametrically opposed to the generally accepted thesis that development in the underdeveloped countries follows from the greatest degree of contact with and diffusion from the metropolitan developed countries. This hypothesis seems to be confirmed by two kinds of relative isolation that Latin America has experienced in the course of its history. One is the temporary isolation caused by the crises of war or depression in the world metropolis. Apart from minor ones, five periods of such major crises stand out and are seen to confirm the hypothesis. These are: the European (and especially Spanish) depression of the seventeenth century, the Napoleonic Wars, the First World War, the Depression of the 1930's and the Second World War. It is clearly established and generally recognized that the most important recent industrial development—especially of Argentina, Brazil, and Mexico, but also of other countries such as Chile—has taken place precisely during the periods of the two world wars and the intervening Depression. Thanks to the consequent loosening of trade and investment ties during these periods, the satellites initiated marked autonomous industrialization and growth. Historical research demonstrates that the same thing happened in Latin America during Europe's seventeenth-century depression. Manufacturing grew in the Latin American countries, and several, such as Chile, became exporters of manufactured goods. The Napoleonic Wars gave rise to independence move-

5 Also see, "The Growth and Decline of Import Substitution," *Economic Bulletin for Latin America*, IX, No. 1 (March 1964); and Celso Furtado, *Dialectica do Desenvolvimiento* (Rio de Janeiro: Fundo de Cultura, 1964).

6 Others who use a similar approach, though their ideologies do not permit them to derive the logically following conclusions, are Aníbal Pinto, *Chile: Un caso de desarrollo frustrado* (Santiago: Editorial Universitaria, 1957); Celso Furatado, A *formaçao económica do Brasil* (Rio de Janeiro: Fundo de Cultura, 1959) which was recently translated into English and published as *The Economic Growth of Brazil* by the University of California Press; and Caio Prado Junior, *Historia Económica do Brasil* (7th ed., São Paulo: Editora Brasiliense, 1962).

ments in Latin America, and these should perhaps also be interpreted as in part confirming the development hypothesis.

The other kind of isolation which tends to confirm the second hypothesis is the geographic and economic isolation of regions which at one time were relatively weakly tied to and poorly integrated into the mercantilist and capitalist system. My preliminary research suggests that in Latin America it was these regions which initiated and experienced the most promising self-generating economic development of the classical industrial capitalist type. The most important regional cases probably are Tucumán and Asunción, as well as other cities, such as Mendoza and Rosario, in the interior of Argentina and Paraguay during the end of the eighteenth and the beginning of the nineteenth centuries. Seventeenth- and eighteenth-century São Paulo, long before coffee was grown there, is another example. Perhaps Antioquia in Colombia and Puebla and Querétaro in Mexico are other examples. In its own way, Chile was also an example since before the sea route around the Horn was opened this country was relatively isolated at the end of a long voyage from Europe via Panama. All of these regions became manufacturing centers and even exporters, usually of textiles, during the periods preceding their effective incorporation as satellites into the colonial, national, and world capitalist system.

Internationally, of course, the classic case of industrialization through non-participation as a satellite in the capitalist world system is obviously that of Japan after the Meiji Restoration. Why, one may ask, was resource-poor but unsatellized Japan able to industrialize so quickly at the end of the century while resource-rich Latin American countries and Russia were not able to do so and the latter was easily beaten by Japan in the War of 1904 after the same forty years of development efforts? The second hypothesis suggests that the fundamental reason is that Japan was not satellized either during the Tokugawa or the Meiji period and therefore did not have its development structurally limited as did the countries which were so satellized.

A corollary of the second hypothesis is that when the metropolis recovers from its crisis and re-establishes the trade and investment ties which fully re-incorporate the satellites into the system, or when the metropolis expands to incorporate previously isolated regions into the worldwide system, the previous development and industrialization of these regions is choked off or channeled into directions which are not self-perpetuating and promising. This happened after each of the five crises cited above. The renewed expansion of trade and the spread of economic liberalism in the eighteenth and nineteenth centuries choked off and reversed the manufacturing development which Latin America had experienced during the seventeenth century and in some places at the beginning of the nineteenth. After the First World War, the new national industry of Brazil suffered serious consequences from American economic invasion. The increase in the growth rate of Gross National Product and particularly of industrialization throughout Latin America was again reversed and industry became increasingly satellized after the Second World War and especially after the post-Korean War recovery and expansion of the metropolis. Far from having become more developed since then, industrial sectors of Brazil and most conspicuously of Argentina have become structurally more and more underdeveloped and less and less able to generate continued industrialization and/or sustain development of the economy. This process, from which India also suffers, is reflected in a whole gamut of balance-of-payments, inflationary, and other economic and political difficulties, and promises to yield to no solution short of far-reaching structural change.

Our hypothesis suggests that fundamentally the same process occurred even more dramatically with the incorporation into the system of previously unsatellized regions. The expansion of Buenos Aires as a satellite of Great Britain and the introduction of free trade in the interest of the ruling groups of both metropoles destroyed the manufacturing and much of the remainder of the economic base of the previously relatively prosperous interior almost entirely. Manufacturing was destroyed by foreign competition, lands were taken and concentrated into latifundia by the rapaciously growing export economy, intra-regional distribution of income became much more unequal, and the previously developing regions became simple satellites of Buenos Aires and through it of London. The provincial centers did not yield to satellization without a struggle. This metropolis-satellite conflict was much of the cause of the long political and armed struggle between the Unitarists in Buenos Aires and the Federalists in the provinces, and it may be said to have been the sole important cause of the War of the Triple Alliance in which Buenos Aires, Montevideo, and Rio de Janeiro, encouraged and helped by London, destroyed not only the autonomously developing economy of Paraguay but killed off nearly all of its population unwilling to give in. Though this is no doubt the most spectacular example which tends to confirm the hypothesis, I believe that historical research on the satellization of previously relatively independent yeoman-farming and incipient manufacturing regions such as the Caribbean islands will confirm it further.[7] These regions did not have a chance against the forces of expanding and developing capitalism, and their own development had to be sacrificed to that of others. The economy and industry of Argentina, Brazil, and other countries which have experienced the effects of metropolitan recovery since the Second World War are today suffering much the same fate, if fortunately still in lesser degree.

A third major hypothesis derived from the metropolis-satellite structure is that the regions which are the most underdeveloped and feudal-seeming today are the ones which had the closest ties to the metropolis in the past. They are the regions which were the greatest exporters of primary products to and the biggest sources of capital for the world metropolis and were abandoned by the metropolis when for one reason or another business fell off. This hypothesis also contradicts the generally held thesis that the source of a region's underdevelopment is its isolation and its pre-capitalist institutions.

This hypothesis seems to be amply confirmed by the former super-satellite development and present ultra-underdevelopment of the once sugar-exporting West Indies, Northeastern Brazil, the ex-mining districts of Minas Gerais in Brazil, highland Peru, and Bolivia, and the central Mexican states of Guanajuato, Zacatecas, and others whose names were made world famous centuries ago by their silver. There surely are no major regions in Latin America which are today more cursed by underdevelopment and poverty; yet all of these regions, like Bengal in India, once provided the life blood of mercantile and industrial capitalist development—in the metropolis. These regions' participation in the development of the world capitalist system gave them, already in their golden age, the typical structure of underdevelopment of a capitalist export economy. When the market for their sugar or the wealth of their mines disappeared and the metropolis abandoned them to their own devices, the already existing economic, political, and social structure of these regions prohibited autonomous generation of economic development and left them no alternative but to turn in upon themselves and to degenerate into the ultra-underdevelopment we find there today.

These considerations suggest two further and related hypotheses. One is that the latifundium, irrespective of whether it appears today as a plantation or a hacienda, was typically born as a commercial enterprise which created for itself the institutions which permitted it to respond to increased demand in the world or national market by expanding the amount of its land, capital, and labor and to increase the supply of its products. The fifth hypothesis is that the latifundia which appear isolated, subsistence-based, and semi-feudal today saw the demand for their products or their productive capacity decline and that they are to be found principally in the above-named former agricultural and mining export regions whose economic activity declined in general. These two hypotheses run counter to the notions of most people, and even to the opinions of some historians and other students of the subject, according to whom the historical roots and socioeconomic causes of Latin American latifundia and agrarian institutions are to be found in the transfer of feudal institutions from Europe and/or in economic depression.

The evidence to test these hypotheses is not open to easy general inspection and requires detailed analyses of many cases. Nonetheless, some important confirming evidence is available. The growth of the latifundium in nineteenth-century Argentina and Cuba is a clear case in support of the fourth hypothesis and can in no way be attributed to the transfer of feudal institutions during colonial times. The same is evidently the case of the post-revolutionary and contemporary resurgence of latifundia, particularly in the north of Mexico, which produce

[7] See for instance Ramiro Guerra y Sánchez, *Azúcar y Población en las Antillas,* 2nd ed. (Havana 1942), also published as *Sugar and Society in the Caribbean* (New Haven: Yale University Press, 1964).

for the American market, and of similar ones on the coast of Peru and the new coffee regions of Brazil. The conversion of previously yeoman-farming Caribbean islands, such as Barbados, into sugar-exporting economies at various times between the seventeenth and twentieth centuries and the resulting rise of the latifundia in these islands would seem to confirm the fourth hypothesis as well. In Chile, the rise of the latifundium and the creation of the institutions of servitude which later came to be called feudal occurred in the eighteenth century and have been conclusively shown to be the result of and response to the opening of a market for Chilean wheat in Lima.[8] Even the growth and consolidation of the latifundium in seventeenth-century Mexico—which most expert students have attributed to a depression of the economy caused by the decline of mining and a shortage of Indian labor and to a consequent turning in upon itself and ruralization of the economy—occurred at a time when urban population and demand were growing, food shortages were acute, food prices skyrocketing, and the profitability of other economic activities such as mining and foreign trade declining.[9] All of these and other factors rendered hacienda agriculture more profitable. Thus, even this case would seem to confirm the hypothesis that the growth of the latifundium and its feudal-seeming conditions of servitude in Latin America has always been and is still the commercial response to increased demand and that it does not represent the transfer or survival of alien institutions that have remained beyond the reach of capitalist development. The emergence of latifundia, which today really are more or less (though not entirely) isolated, might then be attributed to the causes advanced in the fifth hypothesis—i.e., the decline of previously profitable agricultural enterprises whose capital was, and whose currently produced economic surplus still is, transferred elsewhere by owners and merchants who frequently are the same persons or families. Testing this hypothesis requires still more detailed analysis, some of which I have undertaken in a study on Brazilian agriculture.[10]

All of these hypotheses and studies suggest that the global extension and unity of the capitalist system, its monopoly structure and uneven development throughout its history, and the resulting persistence of commercial rather than industrial capitalism in the underdeveloped world (including its most industrially advanced countries) deserve much more attention in the study of economic development and cultural change than they have hitherto received. Though science and truth know no national boundaries, it is probably new generations of scientists from the underdeveloped countries themselves who most need to, and best can, devote the necessary attention to these problems and clarify the process of underdevelopment and development. It is their people who in the last analysis face the task of changing this no longer acceptable process and eliminating this miserable reality.

They will not be able to accomplish these goals by importing sterile stereotypes from the metropolis which do not correspond to their satellite economic reality and do not respond to their liberating political needs. To change their reality they must understand it. For this reason, I hope that better confirmation of these hypotheses and further pursuit of the proposed historical, holistic, and structural approach may help the peoples of the underdeveloped countries to understand the causes and eliminate the reality of their development of underdevelopment and their underdevelopment of development.

[8] Mario Góngora, *Origen de los "inquilinos" de Chile central* (Santiago: Editorial Universitaria, 1960); Jean Borde and Mario Góngora, *Evolución de la propiedad rural en el Valle del Puango* (Santiago: Instituto de Sociología de la Universidad de Chile); Sergio Sepúlveda, *El trigo chileno en el mercado mundial* (Santiago: Editorial Universitaria, 1959).

[9] Woodrow Borah makes depression the centerpiece of his explanation in "New Spain's Century of Depression," *Ibero-Americana*, No. 35 (Berkeley, 1951). François Chevalier speaks of turning in upon itself in the most authoritative study of the subject, "La formación de los grandes latifundios en México," *Problemas Agrícolas e Industriales de México*, VIII, No. 1, 1956 (translated from the original French and recently published by the University of California Press). The data which provide the basis for my contrary interpretation are supplied by these authors themselves. This problem is discussed in my "¿Con qué modo de producción convierte la gallina maíz en huevos de oro?" which is reprinted as Chapter 15 in my book *Latin America: Underdevelopment or Revolution;* and it is further analyzed in a study of Mexican agriculture under preparation by the author.

[10] "Capitalism and the Myth of Feudalism in Brazilian Agriculture," in *Capitalism and Underdevelopment in Latin America.*

PART FOUR
Social Organization

The Forms and Functions of Human Groups

In its greatly varied forms, based on kinship and community, association, class, caste, sex, and ethnicity, social organization has probably received more of anthropologists' concentrated attention than any other aspect of culture. Social groups based on kinship have been studied most of all; probably for two main reasons.

The family is the oldest of all social groups. First organized, at least in its nuclear form (parents and children) by our socially inclined prehuman ancestors, it persists as the group of primary significance in structuring the life experience of the individual and the organization of the community. Still for most, and once for all, people, kin groups have provided the main basis for economic cooperation, social action, education, and maintenance of social order.

Many societies have long since evolved other means of coping with these universal human problems through extrafamilial organizations that transcend or even replace the kin group: economic and social systems, schools, associations of all sorts, and even international organizations. Yet the historical development of all these institutions can be traced back to the human family, and to the rules and regulations that originated there out of our ancient dependence for survival upon orderly social life. In this sense the study of kinship organization is always the logical first step in the study of social groups.

A second, initially more pragmatic, reason why kinship studies have been of such interest is that many of the first anthropologists were employed by European and American colonial administrations that early became aware that kinship organization was a major force in structuring the lives of "the natives" and was thus important to understand in order to control the aboriginal peoples they sought to exploit economically.

Today, for mostly different reasons (although many now wiser "natives" are still understandably wary), keen anthropological interest in kinship organization continues. Partly, perhaps, because of the head start the field received, it is methodologically and theoretically far more advanced than many other branches of ethnological inquiry. Several generations of brilliant scholars have rendered kinship amenable to study with a degree of objectivity and often mathematical precision that is still hard to find in the study of other aspects of social organization.

The study of associations, especially secret societies, was also perceived early as another obvious key to understanding and thus controlling the societies of subject peoples. For such associations are frequently a major adjunct or alternative to kinship in the regulation of social relationships. This old line of anthropological interest grows increasingly relevant as association overtakes kinship as a basis for group affiliation in many parts of the world.

An aspect of social organization that has not yet received adequate attention from anthropologists (who really ought to know better) is systems of social, ethnic, and sexual differentiation and stratification. Such systems are usually marked by the organization of society into a series of hierarchically ranked groups, set above or below one another on the basis of differences in class, caste, sex, or ethnic status. This sort of stratification seems to emerge only in societies with a level of technoeconomic development sufficiently productive to make materially possible the ordering of groups in terms of relative differences in wealth and power. Many of the technologically least developed societies that were, as a consequence, most vulnerable to colonial conquest lacked such systems. Others only began to develop them as their subjugation under colonial domination fostered the subsidization of at least a small aboriginal elite through whom the colonialists could rule indirectly, and thus less obtrusively.

Three systems of social differentiation and stratification, based on class, sex, or ethnic category, are available for anthropological study within our own culture. But so far anthropologists have been reluctant to work so close to home. (Indeed, for some, study in mostly remote settings has been a principal means of keeping their professional identity distinct from that of sociologists.) Where anthropologists have turned to the study of their own society, whether to stratification or to any other aspect of social organization, their attention has most often been directed to ethnographic investigation of the poor, especially the nonwhite poor. Although such inquiry has usually been motivated by genuine and appropriate compassion for the disadvantaged, the results are almost always incomplete, because a *part*, especially a vulnerably dependent part, of any social system, cannot be adequately studied without giving the total social system equally close scrutiny. Neither anthropologists nor other scholars can study blacks locked into urban ghettos or Native Americans locked out in rural slum reservations without studying also the larger, more powerful, and mostly white middle class whose behavior, especially in defense of its privileged position, is crucial to figuring out how the "system" works that keeps each group in its culturally defined "proper" place.

From the beginning the development of our capacity to use culture and to live in society has been marked by an ongoing evolution of social groups in the direction of increasingly diverse, complex, and overlapping forms. An example of this is the recent movement of families from small-scale, comparatively homogeneous rural farm communities to heterogeneous urban centers and to those sprawling, diffusely organized new social entities called suburbs, the latest but certainly not the last change in the unfolding of new forms of social grouping responsive to the evolving needs of our constantly changing society and culture.

Despite the revolutionary nature of many of these recent configurations, kinship plays a persistently important role in new forms of social organization nearly everywhere, from ascribing union membership in West Africa to determining ethnic group affiliation in the United States.

SECTION I
Kinship

By now the central role of kinship studies in ethnology requires no further reiteration. Instead, we should briefly identify some of the major categories of kinship organization. First comes marriage and the formation of domestic groups, two universal institutions that vary tremendously in specifics of form. There is a great deal of literature in anthropology on marriage, particularly on marriage rules: on who can and cannot marry whom, and on the reasons why. Anthropologists understand less about the processes by which marriages are terminated, beyond stating the obvious—by death, separation, or divorce.

Analysis of domestic group composition also needs more work. Part of the problem of studying households is that they are never neat. So much of what happens within them spills over into economics, psychology, and other fields. Also, domestic groups are particularly fluid, constantly acquiring new members by birth and by marriage and losing others as they grow up and move off, grow old and die.

The study of descent systems, of how people reckon their relationships, both *consanguineously* (by "blood") and *affinally* (by marriage), and of the ways each system structures the assignment of rights to property and to the assumption of economic, social, political, and religious positions, is a complex field, methodologically so far ahead of others that the abstract analytic elegance with which some anthropologists render their findings occasionally makes it difficult to remember that their subject is people. How people behave in some of the most important relationships in their lives, usually following their culture's rules, but often bending them and sometimes necessarily breaking them, reflects an adaptive flexibility seemingly belied by the rigid precision of some scholars' kinship charts.

As the institution through which family groups are formed and extended, marriage is almost universal. Yet a cross-culturally accurate way of defining what marriage entails, identification of its universal attributes, has proved elusive. This is because the components of marriage—the culturally prescribed social, economic, emotional, and sexual role responsibilities of marriage partners—are greatly varied. In fact, they seem to be growing ever more so, through the advent of "open marriage" and the increasing establishment of alliances based on friendship, trust, and an announced willingness to share, to relate sexually, and to bear and raise children, without any of the traditional parental, legal, or religious sanctions and with decreasing concern for conventional familial role playing.

Culturally approved means of dissolving marriage are also undergoing rapid change. Divorce is increasing in some places, dropping off sharply elsewhere, and being ignored by many as an unnecessary or irrelevant procedure for ending alliances that do not provide the satisfaction necessary to keep them going.

From a far-off Alaskan people, Burch offers a fresh perspective on relationships that for many of us are too close to be perceived with the objectivity necessary to evaluate their full cultural significance.

Marriage and Divorce Among North Alaskan Eskimos

Ernest S. Burch, Jr.

Introduction

"Do the Eskimos *really* trade wives?" This is a question that seems invariably to greet travelers returning from the Far North. Obviously, the American public is generally aware of the custom and is fascinated by it. Unfortunately, the practice has been exploited by the movies and the popular press more for its dramatic effect than for its educational value. More seriously, even the professional anthropological literature contains more fiction than fact when dealing with Eskimo "wife-trading." Consequently, social scientists as well as laymen tend to be grossly misinformed on the subject.

Recent research, however, has provided new information on numerous aspects of Eskimo* social life. Specialists have also been re-evaluating the earlier material, and are now in a position to correct some of the errors present in the literature. Far from being the casual and promiscuous affair that it is generally pictured to have been, "wife-trading" was a very serious matter to the Eskimo. We now know that it was an integral part of their system of marriage, which also included polygamous as well as monogamous forms of union. Both "wife-trading" and polygamy, once thought to be manifestations of "anarchy," turn out to have been components of a complex but well-ordered system. In addition, it has been learned that the marriage system meshed with the other aspects of Eskimo kinship in an entirely consistent pattern. Many questions about Eskimo kinship (including marriage) remain unanswered, but the outlines of the system are now fairly clear.

The purpose of this paper is to present a general description of Eskimo marriage and divorce as we have now come to understand it, but it has been necessary to impose certain restrictions on the scope of the discussion. The first of these is with regard to the geographic area covered. The Eskimos formerly occupied a vast portion of northern North America, extending from the eastern tip of Siberia clear across the top of the continent to the east coast of Greenland. The people inhabiting this huge area were by no means as homogeneous as they are generally assumed to have been, and there were many regional variations in all aspects of social life. That such differences occurred in the realm of kinship specifically has been made quite clear by

Source: "Marriage and Divorce Among the North Alaskan Eskimos" by Ernest S. Burch, Jr., from the book *Divorce and After* by Paul Bohannan, copyright © 1970 by Paul Bohannan. Reprinted by permission of Doubleday & Company, Inc., and the author.

* Eskimos resident in Alaska are American citizens. However, when the word American is used in this essay, it should be understood to mean "middle-class American of whatever race, color, or national origin." The point is to separate the Eskimo traditional and present-day usages from those that the readers of this book are accustomed to, and any other way of saying it eventually becomes stilted as the reader proceeds.

the best of the recent (and relevant) studies.[1] There do seem to be some common threads running through at least the marital customs of many Eskimo groups, but it will be difficult to know what they are with any precision until more of the research now in progress has been published. Tenable generalizations on the subject may be forthcoming in the near future, but it would be premature to attempt them at this time. Consequently, in an effort to keep the presentation on as firm ground as possible, the discussion will be limited to the group that has been more thoroughly studied[2] than any of the others. This group, the "North Alaskan Eskimos," inhabits the northern portion of Alaska between (roughly) Bering Strait and the Canadian border.

A second limitation on the scope of the essay is based on the difference between the "traditional," and the "modern" or contemporary periods in North Alaska. While the North Alaskan Eskimos were by no means isolated from other peoples prior to the arrival of Europeans, they did operate in terms of what is properly regarded as an indigenous system of behavior. Around the middle of the nineteenth century, however, whaling ships began to arrive in the area in substantial numbers. The whalers were followed by traders, missionaries, government representatives, and various others, and the native ways of doing things began to undergo numerous changes as a result of this contact. The process was greatly accelerated when the United States Government established schools and government-directed reindeer herds in the area around the turn of the century. Since the agents of change have been largely American, the changes which have occurred have generally been toward the American way of doing things, and away from the traditional Eskimo one. Since the purpose of this paper is to describe a system that is quite different from our own, my concern will be solely with the former Eskimo ways of doing things rather than with the current ones, which approximate ours in many respects.

Eskimo Marriage

For purposes of scientific analysis, a "marital" relationship can be defined usefully as any relationship in which sexual intercourse is an integral component. In our society, sexual intercourse is institutionalized *only* between husband and wife. Sexual relations between other categories of individuals do in fact occur, however, even though generally considered morally wrong. In other words, from a scientific point of view, only one of the several forms of marriage which *actually* occur in our society is of the single type *ideally* permitted. This monogamous approach of "one man–one woman" is by no means universal in human affairs, however, and numerous peoples around the world permit or even highly value marital ties of various other kinds. Eskimo societies were of the latter type, with the result that the Eskimo marriage system was more complicated than our own.

The basic building block of the North Alaskan Eskimo marriage system, the *ui-nuliaq* relationship, is illustrated in Figure 1.[3] This relationship obtained between a man and a woman who lived together and who had socially approved sexual relations. Superficially, this relationship appears identical to our own husband-wife relationship. As will become apparent later on, however, the two relationships differ in quite significant respects. In addition, where the American husband-wife relationship comprises virtually all there is to marriage in our society, at least ideally, the *ui-nuliaq* relationship was merely the keystone of a more extensive system. (In order to keep the two clearly distinguished from one another, I will use the Eskimo words when referring

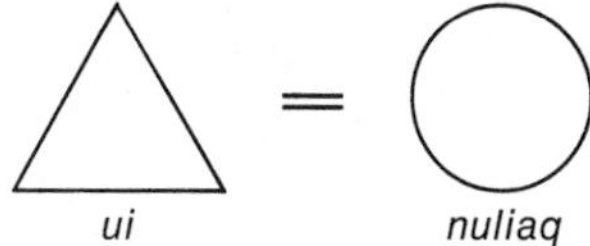

Figure 1. Simple residential marriage.

[1] (Befu, 1964; Ben-Dor, 1966; Damas, 1963, 1964; Gradburn, 1964; Guemple, 1965, 1966; Heinrich, 1960, 1963; Hughes, 1958, 1960; and Lantis, 1946, 1960.)

[2] The studies most relevant to this paper are the following, only a portion of the total literature on North Alaska: Burch, 1966; Gubser, 1965; Heinrich, 1955a, 1955b, 1960, 1963; Pospisil, 1964; Pospisil and Laughlin, 1963; and Spencer, 1959. For a general description of the life of the people living in the northern portion of this region, see Chance, 1966.

[3] In this and subsequent diagrams, a triangle indicates a male and a circle a female. An equal sign indicates a marital tie. These symbols are in common use among anthropologists.

to their system, and the English terms when referring to ours. Other Eskimo relationships that ideally have no counterparts in our system will be referred to alternately by English and Eskimo terms.)

The establishment of the *ui-nuliaq* relationship depended on two factors, those of coresidence and socially approved sexual intercourse. In other words, all that was required for this kind of marriage was for a man and woman to live together in the same house (which was usually shared with other relatives) and have sexual intercourse. Once these two conditions had been met even for a brief period, the relationship was considered established. The Eskimos did not have any marriage ceremony and in fact, there seems to have been no ritual whatsoever associated with the founding of the *ui-nuliaq* relationship. Not only is this total lack of ceremonial embellishment unusual from a cross-cultural perspective, it was in distinct contrast to other aspects of Eskimo life. Taboos, rituals, and ceremonies of various kinds were associated with almost every daily activity and, to me, their absence here is indicative of the rather unimportant place that the *ui-nuliaq* relationship had in the ideal[4] Eskimo scheme of things.

The primary elaboration on the *ui-nuliaq* theme is illustrated in Figure 2, which represents the polygynous[5] residential marriage situation. Here we have a single man living together with two women, and having socially approved sexual relations with both of them. The *nuliaqpak* is the *nuliaq* the man acquired first, and the *nukarak* is the one he married second (regardless of the relative ages of the two women). His relationship with each followed the basic *ui-nuliaq* pattern almost completely, at least ideally. Having the two women living together, however, resulted in the existence of still another relationship within the general marital context, namely that of "co-wives," or the *aipaq-aipaq* relationship (an analysis of which is outside the scope of this paper).

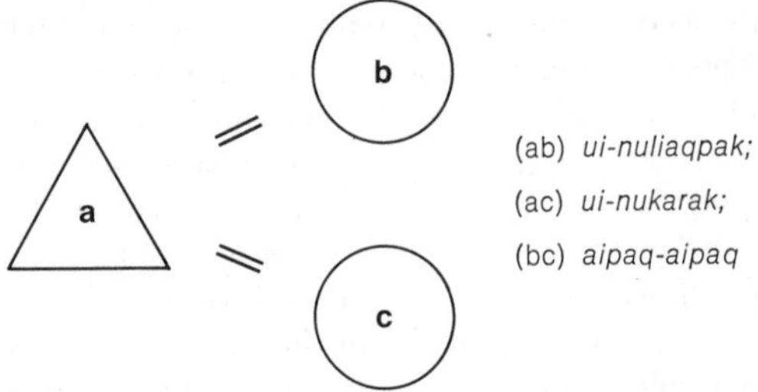

Figure 2. Polygynous residential marriage.

We have no exact figure on the frequency of polygynous unions in the traditional society, but there were, of course, strict demographic limitations on the possibilities. If men and women were roughly equal in number in the society,[6] either the number of polygynous unions was very low, or many men had to go unmarried. Since we know that virtually every man in the society did get married, and spent most of his adult life that way, we must conclude that polygynous marriages were fairly uncommon. They were highly acceptable, however, and numerous cases have been attested. Rather than being commonplace, they seem to have been more on the order of a luxury: something to be achieved when a man was rich enough to support more than one wife. Generally, polygynous unions involved only two women, but there are cases on record of especially wealthy men in the larger villages having three wives. One man at Point Hope was said to have had five at the time of his death.

The other primary elaboration on the *ui-nuliaq* theme, namely, the polyandrous union, is illustrated in Figure 3. In this case, there were two men involved, both of whom had approved

[4] *Actually,* of course, the relationship was a crucial one for the society from a number of points of view.

[5] In everyday American speech, we are accustomed to using the term "polygamy" to refer to the situation of a man having two or more wives. Technically, however, such a situation is known as "polygyny." Its counterpart, where one woman has two husbands, is called "polyandry." Both polygyny and polyandry are included under the rubric "polygamy," which means simply "plural marriage" of any kind.

[6] It has sometimes been claimed that baby girls were frequently put to death at birth in the traditional society. This situation would have resulted in more men than women, a further limitation on the possibilities for polygyny. The *actual frequency* of infanticide of any kind has been questioned (Burch, 1966), however, at least insofar as the North Alaskan Eskimos are concerned. On the other hand, it has been suggested that the hazards of hunting would have resulted in a higher death rate for men than for women. This would have increased the opportunities for polygyny. While this seems a reasonable proposition, it is one that has yet to be examined with sufficient thoroughness to permit definite statements on the subject one way or the other. Consequently, we must assume that males and females were roughly equal in number in the society until it is demonstrated to have been otherwise.

sexual relations with one woman within the coresidential context. The woman was the *nuliaq* of both men. The man whom she married first was her *uikpak,* and the one she married second was her *nukarak.* The relationship between the two men was that of *nuliaqan-nuliaqan,* or "co-husbands."

The frequency of polyandrous unions in the traditional society cannot be determined with precision, but it is certain that they were extremely rare, much more so than their polygynous counterparts. Actual cases have been documented, however, and it is clear that the system had a place for such marriages if people wished to get involved in them. It seems that the scarcity of polyandrous marriages was a function of the strains that were inherent in them. On the one hand, problems resulted from the competition of the two men for the sexual relations with the one woman. On the other hand, they stemmed from the tremendous economic burden placed on one woman having to do all the butchering, sewing, and other work that being married to two hunters would entail. These tasks would of course be in addition to the duties of childbearing and child rearing that would devolve upon her. When people did align themselves in a polyandrous marriage, it usually did not last long as a result of these factors. The Eskimo themselves were aware of the problems involved, and most of them simply avoided getting into such situations.

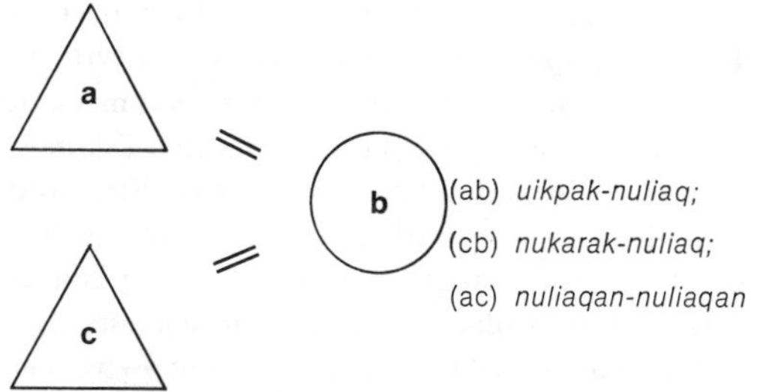

Figure 3. Polyandrous residential marriage.

The final form of institutionalized marriage among the North Alaskan Eskimos was the celebrated "wife-exchange" situation.[7] This arrangement, illustrated in Figure 4, involved *two ui-nuliaq* pairs becoming associated with each other, the participants engaging in sexual relations with each other's spouse.

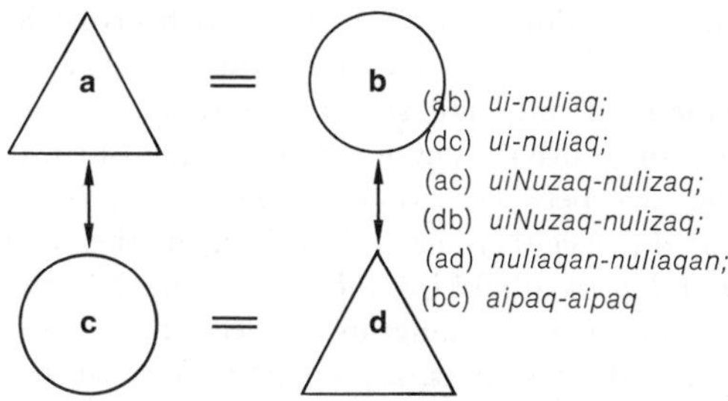

Figure 4. Comarriage.

This is different from any of the other forms of marriage in that here the individuals involved did not reside together on a permanent basis, but merely exchanged sexual partners for brief periods. The relationships established through the sexual exchange were binding outside of the scope of the exchange itself however. Because of its intimate connection with the other forms of marriage, and its general importance in Eskimo life, I shall refer to this custom as "comarriage." The other labels of "wife-trading" and "wife-exchange" have connotations which are misleading in a number of respects.

It is important to remember that while sexual relations were repeated often in most (but not all) comarriages, intercourse was really nothing more than the validating act of the union. Significantly, it had to take place only on one occasion for the relationships to be established for the lifetimes of the participants. Thus, if two couples agreed to unite in comarriage, all that was required was that each man spend a single night with the other man's wife. After that, even if the exchange was never repeated, the participants were considered to be cospouses.

In a comarriage, the relationships that were considered to be the most important were those between the two men, on the one hand, and the two women, on the other. For the co-wives (*aipaq*) and cohusbands (*nuliaqan*), comarriage meant strong bonds of friendship, mutual aid,

[7] The field research which formed the basis for the "breakthrough" in our understanding of this custom was conducted by Albert Heinrich (1955a, 1955b, 1960, 1963). Heinrich's work was followed by a study in which Guemple (1961) reviewed the entire literature, both published and unpublished, dealing with exchange practices. Subsequent field research of my own has confirmed the general conclusions reached by Heinrich and Guemple, and has started to fill in the details.

and protection. The tie between each man and the other's *nuliaq* was institutionalized as a superficial one, and sex was of secondary importance once the union had been established. If the ties between cospouses (*uiNuzaq-nulizaq*) did in fact become stronger than the two *ui-nuliaq* relationships, the participants had the option of exchanging on a permanent basis rather than a temporary one. In any case, the cospouse relationship was the weakest of the four. Both popular and scientific writers have consistently failed to appreciate this fact.

One of the obvious implications of the terms "wife-exchange" and "wife-trading" is that it was the *nuliaq* alone who was traded.[8] This implication is incorrect, for the *ui* was exchanged just as surely as was the *nuliaq,* if not more so. Just how the exchange was effected depended on the circumstances, but, whenever possible, the wives stayed home and the husbands traded places for the night, returning home during the day. Most often, however, comarriages were established between couples who normally reside in different villages. Under such conditions, the principals might exchange sex partners whenever they happened to come together in the same place. This might occur fairly frequently if the home villages were not too far apart, but otherwise might take place only once a year or so, or perhaps even less. In some cases, they only took place once, even though the bonds thus established were permanent.

The term "wife-exchange" implies that the decision about establishing an exchange was taken solely at the discretion of the husband, but here again the popular conception is incorrect. As Heinrich has so clearly demonstrated, and as my own research has confirmed, the *ui* had absolutely no right to order his *nuliaq* around in such matters. On the contrary, the women had just as much to say about whether or not an exchange union would be established as did the men. Moreover, the women as well as the men could take the initiative in getting one started. In any case, the matter of "trading" never entered the situation.

There is little doubt that comarriage was institutionalized to a high degree among the traditional North Alaskan Eskimos. Statistics are lacking, but there is reason to believe that it was very widespread. Indeed, the majority of the adult population of the society may well have been involved in comarriage situations. Unfortunately, the extreme disfavor with which the practice was viewed by the American teachers and missionaries in the region was quickly and thoroughly impressed upon the Eskimos, with the result that nowadays it is extremely difficult to get information about it. Nonetheless, the following considerations have been established with sufficient thoroughness as to be considered facts: (1) comarriage was an integral part of the more general marriage system; (2) it involved behavioral patterns that were highly institutionalized; and (3) promiscuity had virtually nothing to do with it.

It has sometimes been alleged that part of Eskimo hospitality involved loaning a wife to a visiting male guest, and much has been made of this in the popular literature on the Eskimos. Since the distinction between "wife-trading" and "wife-lending" is a rather fine one, I would like to clarify the matter at this point. To put it briefly, the available information suggests that "wife-lending," in the sense of letting a stranger have sexual relations with one's wife, was totally non-existent among the North Alaskan Eskimos. It is well known, for example, that in the traditional society, complete strangers were invariably killed on sight[9] unless one of the following conditions was met: (1) the strangers were numerous enough to be able to protect themselves; (2) the strangers had relatives in the area to serve as their guarantors and protectors; or (3) the strangers were encountered on certain special occasions, such as a Messenger Feast (cf. Spencer, 1959:210ff.) or a summer trading festival when hostility of this sort was temporarily put aside. Strangers were despised and feared, and it is rather difficult to reconcile this thoroughly documented fact with the alleged practice of sexual hospitality. If a visitor had any sexual relations with a host's wife, one may be sure that the individuals were well known to each other, and that they were merely continuing a previously established relationship.

It seems that it was the American whalers and traders who in fact instituted something that might be called "wife-lending" in North Alaska. These strangers to the region took advantage

8 Heinrich, 1955a:134ff.

9 The North Alaskans were apparently more extreme in their treatment of strangers than were other Eskimo groups.

of the peculiarities of the Eskimo marriage system on the one hand, and of their own wealth and power relative to that of the Eskimos on the other. In the former case, the white men pretended that they were getting into some sort of institutionalized marriage arrangement with the Eskimos, then refused to abide by the appropriate Eskimo rules of behavior. In the latter situation, the white men sometimes took Eskimo women by force, knowing that the Eskimos would not dare retaliate. In other cases (probably most frequently), the Eskimos themselves agreed on such sexual liaisons in the hope of getting some trade goods or whisky, more or less on the order of prostitution. In any case, such affairs were not native to the Eskimo way of life, but a consequence of the social breakdown which followed the arrival of rich and powerful outsiders.

Returning now to the institutionalized Eskimo marriage system, one can see that the several forms of marriage fit together rather neatly. A comparison of Figures 1 through 4 will reveal that the keystone of the system, the *ui-nuliaq* relationship, was common to all the marital arrangements. The other forms of marriage can be most easily understood simply as elaborations of this basic theme. Sexual intercourse was the common feature running through all the marriage forms, and residence was the variable. In the case of the *ui-nuliaq* type of marriage, there were two people involved, and they lived together and apart from any other spouses. In the plural forms of residential marriage, there were simply two or more members of the one sex or the other living with a single member of the opposite sex. Finally, in comarriage, the cospouses simply did not live together on a regular basis. The two additional relationships, those of cohusbands and co-wives, served to relate any members of the same sex who happened to be involved in *any* of the plural forms of marriage.

It is interesting to note that the various forms of marriage do not seem to have been mutually exclusive. An *ui-nuliaq* marriage, of course, was not only compatible with but was a prerequisite for each of the other alternatives. It is not certain, however, just how either of the plural forms of residential marriage co-ordinated with comarriage. Thus, if a man had two *nuliaqs*, just how would an exchange have been effected with another marital unit having only one man and one woman? Or how did two polygynous (or polyandrous) units establish an exchange union with each other, if they could do so at all? One can readily see that if all the logical combinations of the various basic forms of marriage could have been participated in at the same time by the same people, the real-life situations must have been quite complex. Unfortunately, the answers to the above and related questions are as yet unanswerable, although educated guesses could perhaps be made. Since all the forms of plural marriage are now either carried on in secret or are no longer practiced in North Alaska, they may remain unanswered forever. About the only thing that appears definite at this point is that a single couple could be associated through comarriage with more than one other couple at the same time.

It is instructive to consider the implications of the various forms of Eskimo marriage on subsequent generations. In the gross sense, all the offspring of *any* kind of marital arrangement were considered to be siblings to one another. Finer distinctions[10] were made as to "full," "half," "step-" and "co-" siblings, but the children were nonetheless considered to be brothers or sisters of one sort or another. This fact is significant, for in the Eskimo scheme of things, sibling relationships were extremely important, much more so than they are in the contemporary United States. Eskimo siblings were morally bound to co-operate in almost all the major activities of life, an obligation that held regardless of the form of marriage that produced or connected them.

The marital ties made at one generation level, which resulted in sibling connections at the second-generation level, produced cousin relationships at the third, and so on. The ties of kinship, once established, continued downward through the generations regardless of the form of marriage that was involved initially.[11] The same obligations and activities that were ap-

[10] As is true of most aspects of kinship, the Eskimos divided siblings along different lines than we do, a matter which cannot be more fully explored here.

[11] After a time, almost everyone in an Eskimo village could become related through this process if carried on over even a few generations. There were, however, various social mechanisms for getting around this problem when necessary. In addition, certain factors operated to counteract this unifying tendency, so that actual situations were generally less complicated in this respect than one might be led to suspect.

propriate to the descendants of a simple residential marriage also held for the descendants of all the plural-marriage forms. The descendants of *any* sort of marital connection were ideally forbidden to marry one another as a result of the incest restrictions placed on relatives. This fact lends considerable support to the conclusion that each of the several forms of Eskimo marriage was really a form of marriage and not something else, for they all resulted in what was regarded as true kinship for the descendants.

Eskimo Divorce

The most fruitful application of the concept of "divorce" to the Eskimo situation is clearly in connection with the *ui-nuliaq* relationship since it was the keystone of the entire system. In this case what is said applies equally to the polygynous and polyandrous situations except that only one man and one woman were normally involved in each instance of divorce. (There was no rule preventing a person from divorcing two spouses simultaneously; however, it just does not seem to have happened very often.) There is also a practical reason for excluding the cospouse relationship from this discussion, namely, a lack of relevant data. Whether or not anything which might be usefully labeled "divorce" ever occurred in connection with comarriage has not yet been determined as far as I know.

For all practical purposes, Eskimo divorce consisted in the breaking of the residence tie, and the termination of sexual relations invariably followed. Like marriage, divorce was accomplished without ceremony. All that was involved was one or the other spouse leaving the other, or else making the other one go, depending on the circumstances.[12]

If they were living with the *ui's* relatives and the *nuliaq* wished to leave, she could simply walk out on him. Ideally, at least, he could do nothing to stop her. Likewise if they were living with his relatives and the *ui* wished his *nuliaq* to leave, he had only to wait until she was out of the house, then scatter all her belongings outside the door. When she returned, the hint would be obvious. If they were living with the *nuliaq's* relatives, similar procedures in reverse would be followed. Ideally, either spouse could take the initiative in breaking off the residence tie, although in fact husbands had a bit more control over such situations than did wives simply by virtue of their superior physical strength. If a wife was really determined, however, the husband could not stop her from leaving him, regardless of how he felt about the situation.[13] If both the *ui* and *nuliaq* were agreed on a separation, an immediate result was assured.

One significant feature of Eskimo divorce was that the breaking of the residence tie did not terminate the marital relationship. Once such a relationship had been established, it held for the lifetimes of its members, regardless of whether or not either sexual relations or coresidence were continued. What divorce did was to *deactivate* the relationship. In other words, when the residence tie was broken, the relationship was generally ignored in the course of daily life even though it was still there in theory. In the United States we sometimes have inactive relationships with relatives outside our immediate family, such as cousins, especially second cousins. We may know who our cousins are, and perhaps where they live, but we may never have any contact with them directly, even though the relationship is still there. If the members of such a relationship ever have occasion to activate it, it is a simple matter for them to do so.

In Eskimo divorce, the individuals either avoided each other altogether, or they acted as *ui* and *nuliaq*. There was nothing on the order of the "exspouse" relationship that so frequently occurs in our society, and even divorced Eskimo spouses thought of and referred to each other as *ui* and *nuliaq*. Indeed, it not infrequently happened that divorced spouses got back together again. Since the relationship had never been dissolved in the first place, re-establishment of the residence tie simply meant the reactivation of an already existing relationship. In America, if a husband and wife get divorced and then decide to get back together again, they would ideally have to go through the entire marriage procedure again, although actually they sometimes do not.

On the basis of the above considerations, it may be argued that the Eskimos did not have an institution which can appropriately be called "divorce." Indeed, Eskimo "divorce" was more

12 Heinrich, 1955a:170.

13 This greatly minimized the possibility of a wife being "exchanged" or "loaned" by her *ui* to another man. If she did not approve, she could divorce her husband on the spot.

like our separation than our "divorce." Properly speaking, of course, the American institution is a legal proceeding, nothing more and nothing less. In that sense it is correct to say that the Eskimos did not have "divorce." But, when you disregard the technicalities and look at situations, the two systems are not so different. The basic point is whether or not two spouses stay together or separate. It has been shown by Goode (1956:186, 187), for example, that the greatest emotional disturbance in the American situation comes at the time of physical separation, not at the time of the legal action. Hunt (1966:5) echoes Goode's conclusion, saying that "an emotionally genuine separation constitutes the death of a marriage, and divorce is merely its burial." On the other hand, the legal proceeding by no means necessarily terminates interaction between spouses. Indeed, Hunt[14] goes so far as to say that "divorce, though it cancels the partnership of man and wife, *never* severs their relationship entirely" [italics mine]. In short, in America, the legal matter of divorce has relatively little effect on the *de facto* aspects of the overall situation. It seems to be more of a symbol than anything else. Consequently, while the Eskimos did not have divorce in the technical sense of that term, I feel justified in maintaining that situations occur(red) in both societies, which are usefully compared under the rubric of "divorce."

It is of course impossible to know with certainty the extent of divorce among the traditional North Alaskan Eskimos, but there is reason to believe that the divorce rate (in the Eskimo sense) approached 100 per cent. That is, virtually everyone broke the residence tie with their spouse at least once, and many did so several times. What is not clear is the extent to which the initial tie was later reactivated as opposed to the frequency with which totally new spouses were acquired. Even here, however, the rate seems to have been fairly high, especially in the first years of married life.

The conditions which resulted in divorce among the Eskimos varied, of course, but some factors were clearly more significant than others. The most frequently cited source of strain in the *ui-nuliaq* relationship was infidelity on the part of one or both spouses. "Infidelity," in this case, means sexual relations outside the scope of the marriage system. Those involved in plural marriage were institutionalized, and hence did not constitute infidelity. Infidelity alone, however, did not necessarily result in divorce (although it might), but it certainly placed a strain on the *ui-nuliaq* relationships involved.

Another serious source of strain was the failure on the part of one or the other spouses to meet his or her economic obligations. In the traditional society, the family was economically self-sufficient to a high degree. It was the major locus of production, and both spouses were involved to an equal extent. The division of labor along sex lines was so complete, however, that there was virtually no overlap in the activities of the two. Consequently, when either shirked his or her responsibilities, the whole family suffered. In a society where life hovered around the subsistence level a good bit of the time, there were rather strict limits on the extent to which laziness and/or incompetence in economic pursuits could be tolerated. If a person was working hard, and his (or her) spouse was either unwilling or unable to carry her (or his) proper share of the load, it was only a matter of time before the strains in the relationship would become intolerable.

Disputes over child rearing also seem to have been a significant source of strain, although for different reasons than are usually involved in our society. When an American husband and wife argue about how to raise children, they are generally disagreeing on one of the two following points: (1) how to handle a specific incident; or (2) a general aspect of the upbringing of *all* their children. For the Eskimos on the other hand, the methods involved were pretty much agreed on, and followed traditional lines. The problems resulted from the apparently widespread tendency for a parent to strongly favor one child, who was usually *not* favored by the other parent. The favored child was exempt from normal rules of behavior as far as the favoring parent was concerned, but not from the viewpoint of the non-favoring parent. Consequently, when one parent scolded his or her spouse's favorite child, regardless of the reason, the other parent would become extremely incensed, and a quarrel would result. The depth of the emotions which could be generated in such situations was considerable.

[14] Hunt, 1966:203.

The above seem to have been the major sources of strain in the *ui-nuliaq* relationship, but they were by no means the only ones. Other sources included personality clashes, with all that they entailed, in-law trouble, jealousy, barrenness, and minor irritations of all kinds. Significantly, the *ui-nuliaq* relationship was not expected to contain any serious strains. Indeed, some things we would scarcely regard as justification for an argument were sufficient grounds for an Eskimo divorce. If friction developed between spouses, separation was an acceptable alternative at all times. Divorces also resulted from factors other than strains within a marital union, however. For example, a person might leave a spouse to go live with someone else who seemed more desirable even though the first one was generally quite acceptable. Divorce could be instituted on purely individual initiative, and justification for such action did not have to be made to anyone. Irresponsibility in such matters was not encouraged, however, and a person who evidenced extreme instability in marital associations would eventually have a difficult time obtaining a spouse.

One of the more interesting things about Eskimo divorce is the consequences that remarriage had for the various individuals involved. A hypothetical remarriage situation is illustrated in Figure 5, in which two couples who were divorced then married each other's spouses. It should be noted that remarriage rarely followed this particular pattern because two divorced couples were not likely to remarry on a parallel basis such as this one. More often, an *ui* would marry someone that had no or only distant connections with the person that his *nuliaq* married. The resulting types of relationships would be the same regardless of the number of individuals involved, however, hence the utility of the diagram.

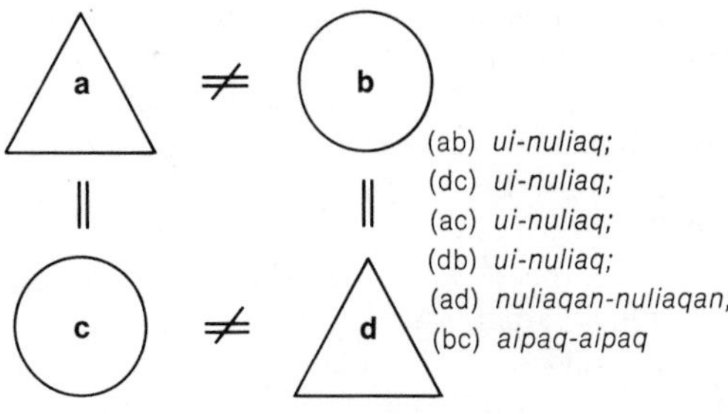

Figure 5. Divorce and remarriage.

Since the *ui-nuliaq* relationship, once established, held for the lifetimes of its members, the original link between the two marital couples in Figure 5 is not broken by divorce; it is merely deactivated. Since everyone in the diagram got remarried, however, two new *ui-nuliaq* pairs were created in addition to, not in replacement of, the original pair. The interesting thing is the relationships that resulted for the two men and the two women involved. As Figure 4 indicates, the women stood in the relationship of co-wives (*aipaq-aipaq*) and the two men were cohusbands (*nuliaqan-nuliaqan*). A comparison to Figures 4 and 5 will indicate that divorce and remarriage was almost identical in its formal aspects with the highly institutionalized comarriage situation. The only difference is that the relationship between cospouses (*uiNuzaq-nulizaq*) was not established in the case of divorce and remarriage, being replaced there by the residential marital relationship of *ui-nuliaq*. The similarity that Eskimo divorce and remarriage had with the basic forms of plural marriage has prompted Heinrich (1963) to label it "marriage in lesser degree," rather than as divorce.

Divorce, with the virtually universal remarriage, was for all practical purposes an integral part of the Eskimo marriage system because it resulted in the establishment of the same set of relationships as did marriage itself. Consequently, the four relationships in the system can be defined as follows: (1) the *ui-nuliaq* relationship existed between any man and woman who had *ever* had socially approved sexual relations while living together; (2) the cospouse relationship (*uiNuzaq-nulizaq*) relationship obtained between any man and woman who had had socially approved sexual relations with each other while *not* living together; (3) the cohusband (*nuliaqan-nuliaqan*) relationship held between two men who had had socially approved sexual intercourse with the same woman; (4) the co-wife (*aipaq-aipaq*) relationship obtained between two women who had had socially approved intercourse with the same man. The "had had" feature is an essential component of the above definitions because in no case did the defining criteria have to be maintained for a very long time. Likewise, a considerable length of time could elapse between the establishment of one relationship and the setting up of another. Thus, a man could enter into an *ui-nuliaq* relationship with a woman, divorce her, and marry another woman twenty years later, and the two women would still be in the co-wife relationship.

The above consequences of divorce and remarriage were of considerable importance in the traditional society. If a man and the new husband of his divorced wife had anything to do with each other at all, they were expected to behave in terms of the same highly structured relationship that obtained between the two men in an exchange-marriage arrangement. This meant that they were under obligations of mutual friendship and support. A similar situation held for the women. In short, they had the choice of avoiding each other altogether, or of getting along on very good terms indeed. The jealousy and mutual antagonism which might be expected in such situations were considered inappropriate. They did in fact occur sometimes, of course, but were considered wrong by the other members of the society. In any case, the ideal alternatives were clearly defined, as were the resulting behavior patterns once a choice had been made.

The effect that Eskimo divorce had on the children is not clear at our present state of knowledge, but was probably minimal in its negative aspects. The results varied considerably depending on the situation. If a single, very young child was involved, it was generally adopted by another family, usually relatives of one of the parents. Since the Eskimos had a well-established, highly institutionalized, and generally very satisfactory system of adoption (which cannot be gone into here), such a procedure was not upsetting to anyone. The child would not lose his ties with his real parents when taken in by someone else, it would merely gain some additional ones. When more and/or older children were involved, they usually stayed with the mother. Even while fairly young, however, Eskimo children were permitted to exercise a fair amount of individual discretion as to the person with whom they wished to live. Adolescents could pretty much make up their own minds on the subject. As was the case for marriage proper, divorce and remarriage results in the establishment of sibling ties for all the children of all the participants; hence there were no problems in this area either.

Property rarely caused any difficulties in Eskimo divorce because, on the whole, goods were individually owned, with fairly little overlap between the sexes. Consequently, when a divorce was effected, each person simply kept his or her own belongings. If there was any trouble at all, it usually occurred in situations where a man had been living with his wife's relatives and had helped them in some major construction effort, such as building the house in which they were living, which would entitle him to part ownership in it. Here, of course, the problem was not between the *ui* and *nuliaq*, but between the man and his *nuliaq's* relatives.[15] Its resolution depended on a number of situational factors that need not be considered here.

Discussion

It is revealing, in the analysis of divorce, to consider what the marital relationship would be like if it were functioning normally. It is also instructive in the attempt to understand any institution in one society to contrast it with the appropriate one in another. The traditional North Alaskan Eskimo *ui-nuliaq* relationship and its contemporary American counterpart, for example, differed in a number of ways. For the remainder of the paper, therefore, I am going to compare the two systems and outline their similarities and differences as I see them with respect to both marital relationships and the divorce situation. Although my primary concern here is with the Eskimos, it will sometimes be necessary to discuss our own system in some detail to bring out the contrast between the two.

One distinctive feature of the *ui-nuliaq* relationship is its similarity to what we call a "contract" relationship. Such a relationship is known in professional jargon as a "functionally specific" one. As defined by Levy,[16] this means that the various "activities or rights and obligations or

[15] This raises the question of where the *relatives* of the spouses fit into the divorce situation. This question, which is not often dealt with, would probably be a most interesting one to consider, especially in any sort of cross-cultural analysis of marriage, divorce, and their implications.

[16] Levy, 1952:256.

performances that [were] covered by the relationship [were] precisely defined and delimited." If someone had asked a traditional Eskimo couple to list what was supposed to be involved in their relationship, they probably could have answered quickly and precisely, and then stop, having listed everything they thought relevant. If the same question were put to a contemporary American couple, however, they would probably have some difficulty in answering. They could perhaps name a few especially important things in relatively short order, but beyond that they would likely be overwhelmed by the number and variety of considerations involved.

It should be recognized, however, that the *ui-nuliaq* relationship was not functionally specific to the extent that is the case with a true contract relationship, in which both definition *and* delimitation are quite precise. In the *ui-nuliaq* case most of the considerations were relatively precisely defined, but the relationship was not precisely *delimited* to the extent that an Eskimo could state exactly where his duties vis-à-vis his spouse ended and where they began. The data suggest, however, that in both respects the Eskimos went far beyond our own husband-wife relationship, and I strongly suspect that they were relatively extreme from the viewpoint of marital relationships in any society in the world.

Of the various orientations involved in the *ui-nuliaq* relationship, sexual relations were obviously important, but the relationship was economically oriented to a degree that must be unusual for relationships in the marital category.[17] That is to say, the production of goods and services occupied an especially important place among all the activities involved in *ui-nuliaq* interaction from the Eskimos' own point of view. The *ui* was primarily a hunter, and most activities revolved around the chase, and the manufacture and maintenance of hunting and household implements. He was also primarily responsible for the education of his sons. The *nuliaq,* on the other hand, was responsible for the skinning and butchering of the game that her husband killed. She also had to make and maintain the family clothing, store and prepare the food, look after the small children, and educate her daughters. The duties of the spouses overlapped very little. Beyond these predominantly economically oriented activities and sexual intercourse, there was little involved in the relationship, at least ideally.

With respect to the contemporary American situation, however, the same assertions could not be made, at least with reference to the ideals of married life. While it is clear that economic considerations are very important in the relationship between husband and wife, I think it fair to say that a marriage in which they are emphasized to the same extent as was ideally the case among the Eskimos would be regarded by most Americans as one which is headed for disaster. Indeed, I would not be surprised if the American husband-wife relationship was found to be one of the most diffusely oriented marital relationships of any in the world, certainly at the opposite end of the continuum from its Eskimo counterpart.

So far, of course, I have been talking about the ideal situation with respect to the substantive definition of the relationships. Actually, however, many Eskimo marriages were relatively functionally diffuse, while many American marriages are relatively functionally specific. The interesting thing about the North Alaskan situation is that to the extent that the individuals involved in a particular *ui-nuliaq* relationship were living under favorable economic circumstances, the greater the extent to which their relationship was likely to approach the ideal of functional specificity. Couples who were living in isolated camps of perhaps one or two families were generally involved in very diffuse relationships, but the larger the settlement in which the same couples might live, the less that *ui* and *nuliaq* would have to do with each other outside of sexually and economically oriented activities. In some of the larger maritime villages, *ui* and *nuliaq* might only see one another at sporadic intervals (see below).

There was very little communication between an *ui* and his *nuliaq,* and little was expected. Furthermore, as one might suppose in a functionally specific relationship of this sort, the communication that did take place dealt largely with the practical problems of the day, and

[17] I do not mean to imply by this remark that economic functions alone were served by this relationship. On the contrary, numerous others, many of them crucial for the operation of the society, were also fulfilled through the operation of the *ui-nuliaq* relationship, but on the whole they seem either to have been unrecognized or were simply considered relatively unimportant by the Eskimos themselves.

little else. Indeed, as was mentioned above, Eskimo husbands and wives were not often in one another's company.[18] The men spent their time hunting or visiting with other men, while women were either working in the house, or visiting with other women. In the larger villages and elsewhere whenever conditions permitted, the men generally spent most of their waking hours in a special building known as a *kazgi*,[19] and even ate their meals there, completely separated from their wives and young children.

In the contemporary United States, however, the situation is quite the opposite, at least ideally. Husbands and wives are expected to share experiences, ideas, secrets, and so forth, and to spend a major portion of their free time in one another's company. Not only is communication between husband and wife supposed to be frequent and informative, it is expected to be of an emotionally satisfying kind that theoretically cannot be found outside of marriage. Actually, of course, many husbands and wives interact more along the lines of their Eskimo counterparts than according to the American ideal, but, when they do, it is a sign of breakdown in the relationship. To the Eskimos, lack of communication between spouses was not only the normal state of affairs, it was regarded as the "right" one. An interesting point made by Dr. Jessie Bernard is that the requirements of the American custom greatly increase the opportunities for communication at *cross-purposes*. The result is that one of the most highly institutionalized aspects of the husband-wife relationship is also one of the primary loci of strain in that relationship. The Eskimos, by minimizing communication of any kind, were able to avoid this particular problem.

Another important difference between the Eskimo and American system is in the intensity of the emotional involvement in the marital situation. It is well known, of course, that love is considered the keystone of American marriage, and a vast folklore and literature has grown up to tell us why this must be so. Not only are American couples expected to be in love with each other, they are expected to demonstrate that affection in a variety of ways, both publicly and privately. The *ui-nuliaq* relationship, however, was much less intense than its American counterpart. Cases of romantic unions did in fact occur, but they do not seem to have been overly common. In any case, love certainly was not institutionalized as a component of the relationship. One was expected to feel affection for a spouse, but not necessarily a great deal of it. And, regardless of one's actual feelings, the demonstration of affection for one's spouse in public was regarded as being improper. It was probably minimal (although present) even in private.

Perhaps the most significant contrast of all between the two systems is in the relative strength of the appropriate relationships. In the Eskimo case, the *ui-nuliaq* relationship was ideally a very weak one (although strong ones did sometimes occur in fact). In other words, if one had to choose between the obligations to one's spouse and those to almost any kind of "blood" relative, one was expected to choose in favor of the latter in virtually every case. In America, however, there are rather few obligations and commitments that take precedence over those between husband and wife. The general obligations to "God and country" are perhaps the only ones that unequivocally come before those to one's spouse, at least ideally. Even here, provision is made for the spouse wherever possible (such as when married men are deferred from the draft). Actually, of course, it often happens that individuals choose in favor of their job, their golf partners, their parents, their bridge club, or whatever, over their spouse. Doing so constitutes a breakdown of the marriage, however. Continued deferment of one's obligations to one's spouse in favor of those to virtually anything *but* "God and country" will frequently lead to severe strains in the relations between husband and wife, and perhaps to separation and divorce.

It is sometimes argued that the rising divorce rate in the United States is a sign that the husband-wife relationship is rapidly losing its former strength. One implication of such a conclusion for the present discussion would be that the American marital relationship is becoming

[18] The North Alaskan Eskimos seem to have been more extreme in this respect than their relatives to the east in Canada and Greenland. This is possibly a consequence of the fact that subsistence conditions were generally more favorable in Alaska than they were to the east, hence this particular ideal would have been more easily attained there.

[19] Spencer, 1959:182ff.

more like the traditional Eskimo one, at least in this particular respect. I think that such a conclusion is unwarranted, however. I suspect that a thorough examination of the *actual* reasons behind the divorces in the United States, without any regard for what is said in court, would reveal that, on the contrary, the husband-wife relationship is even stronger than it was in former decades. What is happening, I suggest, is that since divorces are becoming progressively easier to come by, people are beginning to demand that their spouses live up to the ideals of the relationship to a higher degree *in fact* than was formerly the case, or forfeit the relationship altogether. Easy divorce in both the Eskimo and American systems provides a means by which a person can hold a spouse effectively responsible for his or her behavior. The difference lies in the kinds of behavior which are expected in the first place.

It is clear that the *ui-nuliaq* and husband-wife relationships, however similar they might appear in a diagram, occupied vastly different niches in quite different systems. It is not surprising, therefore, that divorce should have different causes and consequences in each. If it were possible to measure such things with any precision, I am sure that we would find that the *ui-nuliaq* relationship was generally subjected to fewer, and usually weaker, strains than is the case for its American counterpart. This, despite the fact that divorce was probably much more frequent among the Eskimos than in the contemporary United States. The major difference, however, lies in the fact that in America there is an overwhelming obligation to contain any and all strains which might be generated in such a relationship, whereas the Eskimos felt very little responsibility of this sort. No wonder, then, that in America[20] the divorce of mature, stable individuals is preceded by varying amounts of anguish, soul searching, sleepless nights, and so forth. It is an unhappy event for the people involved, and usually for their relatives and close friends as well. Indeed, the more one has accepted the values of our society, the more extreme the emotional strain of a divorce is likely to be. This does not mean that even the most stable person will not get divorced under the right conditions, but when he does, it is usually an extremely painful experience.

To the Eskimos, however, divorce was hardly a catastrophe. As far as economic considerations were concerned, the separated spouses could turn to relatives for temporary support. Since they usually remarried within a relatively short time,[21] divorce generally caused few difficulties in the economic sphere. Furthermore, in the case of famine or any other crisis, the full obligations of mutual support were incumbent on the individuals involved regardless of how antagonistic they might be at the time. Unfortunately, we do not know with any certainty what the psychological consequences of divorce were in the traditional period. We do know, however, that the individuals involved in a divorce situation were often extremely aroused, usually in the form of anger. The psychological impact was probably very superficial in nature, however, certainly much less than what it seems to be in the contemporary United States. For the Eskimos, a rift with one's parents or siblings was an infinitely more traumatic experience than was a break with one's spouse.[22]

There is also a distinct difference between the two societies with regard to the extent to which the postdivorce situation is structured. That is, they differ with respect to the extent to which behavioral guidelines for divorcees are institutionalized. When an American couple gets divorced, for example, their obligations to one another, usually with reference to the children (if any), property, and economic support, are generally fairly carefully defined in the courts. Outside of these few, albeit important considerations, however, the divorce situation seems

[20] My remarks on the postdivorce situation in the United States are based largely on Goode's study *After Divorce* (Free Press, 1956), and Hunt's *The World of the Formerly Married* (McGraw, 1967). The discussion is most applicable to the middle and upper levels of United States society, and less so at the lower levels.

[21] Precise data are lacking but the "between-marriage" period for the traditional North Alaskan Eskimos was probably measured in terms of days, weeks, or months, but rarely, if ever, in years. This is in sharp contrast with our own system.

[22] This brings up an important point which should not be overlooked, namely, that the Eskimos did have other, non-marital relationships which were very strong indeed. Among the Eskimos, parent-child, sibling, and cousin relationships *at least* were all much stronger than are the comparable relationships in our own society.

to be almost totally unstructured. The individuals involved have to improvise their own rules of behavior. Indeed, it is just this lack of definition which Goode[23] cites as the major cause of the high remarriage rate among divorced Americans. The situation is so poorly defined, he argues, that most people find it very uncomfortable to stay in it, and they seek the only acceptable way out, namely, remarriage.[24]

Divorced Eskimos, however, were in no such position. On the whole, they were expected to avoid each other, but even when confronting each other face to face they knew how they were supposed to act. They could follow socially approved alternatives which they knew in advance, and they did not have to make things up as they went along. There was considerable pressure on Eskimos to remarry, but in their case the pressure stemmed from the need to have an economic partner of the opposite sex. Lack of social definition of their status in life was never a factor.

Another difference between Eskimos and Americans is the position of the children in a divorce situation. For the Eskimos divorce was not only clearly defined with respect to any children involved, it was fully integrated with the kinship system in general. Eskimos generally had several sets of siblings, a full biological set, possibly a set or two of half-siblings, and probably one or more sets of exchange siblings. Likewise, an Eskimo was liable to have more than one set of parents, a full biological pair, perhaps an adoptive pair, and possibly one or more step-parents. Since the notion of multiple sets of siblings and parents was a feature of Eskimo kinship at its *best*, it is unlikely that the new relationships created through divorce and remarriage caused any serious problems.

In America, however, it is generally agreed that divorce produces trauma of varying degrees of severity for the children involved. Even if the degree of psychological and emotional impact of divorce on the children is not known with precision, it is clearly negative. The picture of estranged parents staying together "for the children's sake," long after their own relationship has failed, is a familiar one to all of us. The argument that the strains resulting from two such people living together might be even harder on the children than a divorce would be is beside the point, regardless of what truth it might contain in a given case.

Interestingly enough, when an American couple gets divorced especially if there are children, the resulting situation is in some respects not unlike the one described for the Eskimos. Goode[25] and Hunt[26] have both found that divorce by no means necessarily breaks the bond between husband and wife in our society, and that often the behavior of a divorced person continues to be shaped by the attitudes of the former spouse for some time. As a minimum, certain economic obligations tie the two ex-spouses together, and if there are children involved, it is very difficult for them to avoid seeing each other on occasion. In America, the illusion is that divorce terminates interaction between spouses altogether, while in fact it is rarely the complete break we tend to think it is. In the Eskimo case, the illusion was that the divorce situation meant a continued active relationship, while in fact interaction between spouses was either greatly reduced or ceased completely.

A similar situation obtains for the other relationships involved. Say, for example, that American children of a first marriage go with the mother, as is normally the case. When she remarries, which she is likely to do, these children suddenly find themselves with two fathers, a "real" one and a "step" one. Now, if the mother has children by her second husband, they become half-siblings to the children she had by her first. If the second husband had children of his own by a previous marriage, the situation is even more complex, but rather similar to the *standard* Eskimo situation.

Likewise, if the first husband remarries and

[23] Goode, 1956:207, 216.

[24] Hunt's (1966) more recent account of the postmarital situation indicates that the patterns which are now beginning to develop to guide behavior during this period are overwhelmingly oriented to getting people over the trauma of their divorce, and to the location and recruitment of new spouses. In other words, the "formerly married" state remains highly unsatisfactory to most people involved in it even though some sort of structure is beginning to evolve. This suggests that it is not lack of definition that is the key to remarriage. On the contrary, I see it as another affirmation of the great strength which marriage has in our society.

[25] Goode, 156:306.

[26] Hunt, 1966:Chapter 7.

has children by his second wife, then those children are half-siblings to those he had by his first wife, and so on. To the American mind this is an extremely complicated situation, and probably a highly ambiguous one.[27] What are the relationships of the several sets of half- and step- and full-siblings to be like? How are the two husbands supposed to behave toward each other when they meet (which may be unavoidable at times)? How are the two women supposed to act toward each other? The Eskimos would have had a set of ready answers for questions like these because such situations were not only commonplace in their society even without divorce, they were highly institutionalized. Many Americans are now in situations similar to the hypothetical ones outlined above, yet they have no standards of behavior to guide them.

Superficially, at least, the traditional North Alaskan Eskimos and the contemporary Americans are rather similar with respect to the *de facto* consequences of divorce, no matter how different the two systems might be ideally. The most obvious difference is that for the Eskimos the postdivorce situation was clearly defined and institutionalized for *all* parties, whereas in the United States it is not. It is clear, however, that due to radically different conceptions of what marriage is supposed to be like in the first place, divorce has quite a different type of impact on the individuals involved. Goode (1956:216) argues that life goes on, and that the wounds of an American divorce heal in time, as do those of a loved one's death and other life crises. There, however, lies the rub, for a wound always leaves a scar. For the Eskimos there was no wound, hence no scar. For them it was not a matter of "life going forward" in spite of it all, for there was no crisis to be overcome; life merely went on pretty much as usual, with perhaps a few temporary complications.

In conclusion, it seems apparent that divorce can never be understood except in relation to the whole of which it is a part. More specifically, divorce is non-existent apart from marriage, and neither can be understood without a consideration of their positions in the society as a whole. Eskimo society was set up in such a way that divorce was neither greatly upsetting to the principals involved nor disruptive of the community at large. Emotional and social stability depended on the operation of other relationships which, to them, were more important. This does not mean, as has sometimes been claimed, that the Eskimos were totally lacking in moral standards. On the contrary, they had very definite values—values which were strongly held. They were simply different than ours. In the final analysis, the problem seems to be largely one of emphasis. The degree to which a particular marital relationship is emphasized in a society is of crucial importance in this respect and must be taken into consideration in any analysis of divorce.

27 Even though the postmarriage situation is becoming increasingly structured in the United States with respect to husband-wife interaction, I have yet to hear of any satisfactory developments along these lines as far as children are concerned.

The domestic group formed at marriage usually is soon added to, with the birth of children or the incorporation of unmarried siblings, parents, in-laws, and other relatives. Often nonkinsmen join the household as well. Whatever the specifics of its membership, the social, economic, and emotional functions of the domestic group are typically of formative importance in the life of the individual and the organization of his community.

Every society has culturally prescribed rules for the proper organization of the domestic group. Who must be included or excluded is defined with precision. The location of the household, near the husband's parents, close to those of the wife, or separate from both, to cite only three of several alternative residence rules, is almost always firmly set. The rights and obligations of all members are invariably culturally prescribed, with sanctions specified for those whose failure to follow the rules is seen as a threat to societal stability and to whatever moral order prevails.

The organization of the household of the Jívaro Indians of the Ecuadorian Amazon described in detail by Harner illustrates the complex sociocultural functions that make the domestic group a critical subject of ethnological inquiry.

"The Jívaro Household"

Michael J. Harner

The Household, Child-rearing, and Kin

Most Jívaro households are very close-knit economic and social units, in contrast to the neighborhood and tribal society as a whole. Each house, averaging about nine occupants, is usually isolated a half-mile or more from the next; but sometimes two, or rarely three, houses may be located within three hundred yards of one another. Adjacent houses, when they occur, invariably belong to close relatives, usually one being that of a middle-aged man and the other(s) of his son(s)-in-law. Even such limited concentrations are not very permanent, due to such factors as quarreling between the neighboring relatives or the gradual depletion of the local wild game supply.

A household tends to have a typical composition of: one man, two wives, and seven children; or a man, one wife, and three children. Often another relative, such as the widowed mother or an unmarried brother of the head of the household, also resides in the dwelling. Upon marriage of a daughter the house's population is augmented by the son-in-law (*awe*), who will tend to remain until the birth of his wife's first child. Thereafter, according to the norm, the son-in-law and his family dwell in a new house nearby.

Sometimes matrilocal residence is avoided altogether when the suitor substitutes the gift of a shotgun to his father-in-law, instead of performing the more common bride-service. This substitution of bride-price for bride-service tends to occur in cases where the suitor feels that a period of matrilocal residence would be a liability, rather than an asset to him, e.g., when his bride's family lives in a neighborhood containing a number of enemies of the suitor's family or when he is already married and must take his bride home with him.

The man is formally head of the household and also informally seems generally to dominate his family. He is responsible for protecting his wife (wives) and children, for hunting and fishing, for clearing the forest for garden plots, and for cutting and bringing in fire logs. He also does some very limited garden chores and weaves the family's homemade garments. His wife (wives) is responsible for the overwhelming majority of the agricultural tasks, as well as for cooking and beer preparation, pottery making, and tending the children, chickens, and pigs, if any. When a son-in-law is resident in the household or living nearby, he helps his father-in-law at his various tasks, and also contributes game and firewood to his father-in-law's household. The son-in-law's wife also often helps her mother, even when resident in another neighboring house. A man and his son(s)-in-law normally consider themselves mutually obligated to defend each other's households from enemies.

Men strongly prefer to have two or more wives. The subsistence productivity of the household closely correlates with the number of wives possessed by a man, because the women are responsible for most of the agricultural production. Thus, a satisfactory household production of food and the important manioc beer is dependent upon polygyny.

The most common number of wives for a man to have is two, one, or three, in that order. The emphasis on polygyny, in part, reflects the fact that the ratio of adult females to adult males is approximately 2:1, largely as a consequence of the attrition of the adult male population through killing. The demand for wives nevertheless exceeds the supply, as evidence by the common practice of "reserving" a prepuberty girl as a future wife by giving gifts of featherwork and trade goods to her parents. Not infrequently, her future husband then takes her home with him to raise her in his house prior to the actual consummation of the marriage. The extreme nature of the demand for wives is illustrated by the fact that men sometimes get a pregnant woman and her husband to agree to "reserve" the unborn child for him if it should be female. Needless to say, these practices result in marriages in which the husband is often substantially older.

An unmarried girl of post-puberty age is normally courted and involved in the decision to become a wife. The suitor, after he informally ascertains her willingness, sends a close male kinsman of his own generation to act as a go-between to sound out the girl's father who, in turn, consults with the girl and her mother. If the go-between reports back to the suitor that there is no opposition, then the latter goes late one afternoon to the house of the girl and her parents, and sleeps that night in the men's end of the house. Before dawn, he leaves the house with a blowgun and goes hunting, attempting to kill a large number of birds and monkeys in order to impress the girl's parents with his competence. When he returns, he offers the game to the girl to cook and he awaits her final decision. If she has decided to marry him, she will squat down beside the suitor when she serves the cooked food and join him in eating it. From that moment on, they are considered husband and wife and will sleep together that night.

The importance of wives in producing food and beer goes far beyond the subsistence requirements of the household itself. Plural wives assure a surplus production which will make possible adequate entertainment of visitors from other households. The Jívaro place a high value on drinking beer and eating (perhaps in that order), so that one's status in a neighborhood is greatly affected by one's generosity with beer and food. No one can expect to have many friends unless he is a good host; and he cannot easily meet the requirements of good hospitality without plural wives as a labor force.

A man also prefers to have plural wives so that one will be available to accompany him when he goes hunting while the other(s) tends the household and garden. The wife who goes with him not only handles the dog and acts as the intermediary with Nuŋuí, but also assists him by carrying a machete and a basket of manioc and other provisions. Usually the preferred companion for such hunting trips is the youngest wife, who is least likely to be encumbered with children and therefore most willing to go. The wife often looks forward to hunting trips as an opportunity to have sexual intercourse in privacy, away from the rest of the household. Having sexual relations on the hunt is, however, viewed as dangerous by the man, it being believed that after intercourse he is particularly susceptible to being bitten by a poisonous snake. Nevertheless, men often engage in sexual activity when they take their wives hunting.

Men also claim that they would rather go hunting than to engage in sexual relations with the possible consequence of pregnancy, since babies interfere with the mobility of their wives to accompany them in hunting. Therefore, men usually state that they are reluctant to engage in sexual intercourse more often than about once every six to eight days. Field observations, of course, were difficult to make on this point, but my impression is that these particular statements were not too inconsistent with their behavior. Men also believe that having more than one wife decreases, rather than increases, the likelihood of reproduction. The reasoning is that a second wife permits a man to spend more time hunting and thus reduces the frequency of his acts of sexual intercourse. The arduous, mountainous travel required in hunting may also, in itself, divert potential sexual energies.

While many young wives seem to prefer the childless situation which makes it easy for them to go hunting with their husbands, an attempt at contraception is usually only made by single lovers. The attempt essentially employs sympathetic magic rather than herbs and only is believed to work if the male partner is a shaman. The girl brings him a raw chicken egg, he blows on it, and she swallows the egg while he holds her head underwater in a stream. This act is specific only to the young man, and is believed to prevent the girl forever from being impregnated by him. The Datura plant is occasionally used as an abortive by unmarried women.

Women often do want children and, if no conception takes place after a long period of time, may resort to an antisterility remedy, which consists of the pulverized leg bone of a fox, which is mixed with manioc beer and drunk. Both men and women say that the preferred first child is a boy, which is justified on the basis that the father needs, and would enjoy having, a son to go hunting with him. Ideally, the birth of a son should be followed by that of a daughter. There is no clear-cut prejudice against offspring of one sex as against the other.

The Jívaro are aware of the relationship between insemination and pregnancy, and predict that a fully mature woman can give birth to a baby when the *naitka* tree (botanical identification unknown) has flowered three times after her marriage. The *naitka* flowers twice a year, so their estimate is a year and a half. If the bride is just barely past puberty, they estimate that a longer period, five *naitka*, or two and a half years, is required.

Since premarital sexual relations are common, the birth of a child in a shorter period after marriage is not a cause for surprise. After the birth of the first baby, a three *naitka* minimum is estimated for the next.

It is recognized that pregnant women have strange food cravings and may practice geophagy, something never done by anyone else in the society. They may eat, in small amounts, unfired pottery clay or the brown earth from tubular, above-ground anthills. When birth is expected within five days or so, the woman's diet is restricted to exclude the meat of certain wild birds.

Preparation for the birth primarily consists of placing two stout forked sticks, supporting a crossbar about two and a half feet above the ground, in the expectant mother's garden. At the time of birth, a clean banana leaf is placed under the crossbar, and the mother squats on it with her arms hanging over the bar. Two persons assist her, ideally her husband and her mother. One holds her arms down over the crossbar and the other gets behind her and helps to work the baby down and out to fall on the banana leaf. If it is raining, the birth takes place in the house, but the garden is otherwise preferred by the mother for privacy, because she is "embarrassed."

No couvade is observed by the new father. Rather, he can go forth daily to hunt game and, if he has no other wife, he takes on the responsibility of fetching water, digging up the manioc in the garden, washing it in the stream, and carrying it into the house. There it is cooked by his recuperating wife, who is not supposed to undertake other household or garden tasks for about two weeks. If she should fail to rest adequately for such a period, it is believed that she will be bedridden for a long time, due to becoming sick from "handling cold water," such as when washing the manioc. In order to protect the health of the baby, both parents observe certain dietary restrictions, such as avoiding eating any birds that forage close to the ground, or consuming the entrails of any animal. It is also believed that if either parent engages in extramarital sexual relations during the child's infancy, the infant will die, vomiting.

When the baby is a few days old, it is given a mild hallucinogenic drug, *tsentsemä* (botanically unidentified). The uncooked leaf of this plant, which can be used by persons of all ages, is masticated and fed to the infant, whether male or female. The purpose of the administration of this hallucinogen is to help the baby possibly to see *arutam*, and thus get supernatural power to help its survival. If the baby becomes sick, the drug may be given again.

The child is given a name within a few days after being born. In some families, the father names both sons and daughters; but in others, the father may give the boys their names and the mother may bestow the names on the girls. If the father's father or the mother's mother are still alive, they may be asked to name the child of their own sex. In any event, ideally the child should be named for a deceased relative of the parental or grandparental generation on either side of the family who, if male, was respected for killing and working hard and, if female, respected for working hard. The names are often those of animals, especially birds, while many others have no meaning other than as names. Within a few days of naming, both the male and female infants have their ears pierced.

Infanticide is regularly practiced only in the case of deformed children. It is accomplished by crushing the infant with a foot. Sometimes unmarried girls kill their "illegitimate" babies immediately upon birth if they have no expectation of marrying the father. Infanticide of undeformed babies by married women seems to be unheard of. Birth of twins is never a reason for infanticide.

After the first two weeks or so, the new mother returns to the garden. The work there is arduous, involving much squatting and stooping in connection with harvesting manioc and, especially, weeding. As a result, she normally leaves the infant at home in a small hammock by her bed. Since the garden work takes many hours of her day, the baby often becomes hungry and cries a great deal without getting attention. If there is a daughter approximately four years of age or more in the household, the baby's mother will ask her to tend it. When the infant cries considerably, the baby-tender will pick it up and sing to it. Not surprisingly, the typical lullaby among the Jívaro is not sung by the mother, but by a female child, and the words of it are addressed to the mother to come back from the garden to nurse the infant:

Dear mother, dear mother
Come soon, come soon.
The baby is crying,
The baby is crying.
For lack of your milk,
It will die.
For lack of your milk,
It will die.
Dear mother, come quickly,
Dear mother, come quickly,
The little monkey is singing,
The little monkey is singing.

Often the mother does not return for several hours, and the baby-tender often attempts to satisfy the infant's hunger by chewing up boiled manioc and spitting it into the baby's mouth. Any other mothers in the household who may be lactating do not offer to feed the baby, and wet-nursing is unknown. If a mother finds herself unable to provide the baby with enough milk, she feeds it masticated manioc or a bit of beer.

When the baby begins teething it will also be fed steamed hearts of palm with a consistency softer than that of boiled noodles. Small bits of chewed meat are provided soon thereafter.

The birth of a new baby normally does not entail the weaning of the earlier one, and it is a common sight to see an infant and a four- or five-year-old being fed by the mother, with one at each breast. Puppies are highly valued and cared for by the women, and one may likewise be seen being breast-fed simultaneously by a woman along with her own infant. Weaning is not emphasized and may not take place until the child is six or seven years old. The mother may accomplish this by putting a mildly hot pepper on her nipples. If that has little effect, she has recourse to a hotter variety.

The infant is wrapped loosely in a piece of cloth, which is taken off and used, with water, to wipe the child clean of excrement. The cloth is then washed and dried over a fire for reuse. A baby's excessive crying may be interpreted as evidence that it is "very hot," i.e., has a fever, and the mother may bathe it in lukewarm water to cool the child sufficiently so that it will fall asleep. Sometimes a mother, on being awakened by a baby's crying, will scold and strike it in anger.

To teach the child to walk, the father lashes a stave railing around the three open sides of the mother's bed to create a simple "crib" which the child can grasp for support.

The attitude toward toilet training is quite relaxed. When a toddler starts to defecate or urinate in the house, it is taken outside; but it is not castigated verbally or otherwise. The mother simply digs up the soiled portion of the dirt floor and throws it out. The simplicity of this solution, together with the fact that adults themselves may urinate on the floor at night to avoid exposing themselves to possible attackers ouside the house, helps one understand their attitude. Later, the child is simply told to go outside, but if it fails to do so, there is no condemnatory admonition. Finally, however, if the child is still failing to go out of the house by the time it is about five years old, then the mother will speak her disapproval. As a last resort, she may spank the child lightly with a vine.

Children are encouraged to wash their hands and to bathe. They are told that if they do not wash their hands before eating, their growth will be delayed and stunted. Girls are told, in addition, that they must wash their hands before preparing beer or else the product will not be satisfactory. It is believed that if children are not taught to bathe at an early age, they will be afraid of cold water and their parents will find it necessary to drag them to the stream. Getting the child used to bathing is also seen as connected with teaching it, in the process, to swim well, a skill which is considered essential to survival because of the frequent necessity of crossing streams and rivers which are often dangerously swollen and rapid.

Children tend to be discouraged from playing, since it is felt that such behavior leads to a disinclination to work. Jesting or joking by children is similarly frowned upon, because it is believed to lead to lying in adult life. Nonetheless, children do often try to play until halted by their parents, who are likely to stop them more rapidly if children of both sexes are playing together. If a particular older child, who is visiting, has a reputation for playing and jesting, parents may tell their own offspring not to play with the visitor.

At this point, it seems appropriate to point out that one of the more significant features of Jívaro socialization may be the relative isolation of children from peers outside their own polygynous nuclear family, due to the extreme dispersion of households in the forest. This isolation seems likely to be conducive to a sense of alienation from the rest of the tribe, particularly when coupled with the traditional early morning lectures which fathers give to "make them be careful" in dealing with others beyond the household and which emphasize the deceitful and treacherous characteristics of other tribesmen. Adding to the child's sense of insecurity vis-à-vis the rest of the population is the frequent attribution of illness within the household to the bewitching activities of hostile shamans. Finally, the dispersion of the population in small households over a large area results in a very poor communication system in which fourth- or fifth-hand information usually arrives garbled and exaggerated through repetition, the erroneous rumors giving rise to misunderstanding, suspicion, and hostility.

Children frequently steal portions of cooked meat from one another and wrestle over them, which reflects the fact that meat is not always abundant in the household, depending on the father's hunting success and his immediate commitment to some other task, such as clearing trees. There is also a reluctance to give a small child more than a single piece of meat, for it is believed that varying the portion may cause it to cry when it doesn't get as much as it did on a previous occasion.

While stealing and wrestling over meat is disapproved of and, if repeated, may be punished by the father by spanking with a nettle, wrestling for its own sake between boys is approved and encouraged, although the father may advise them not to hurt one another. Sometimes nettle spanking may be used to stop children from playing, or the father may find it sufficient simply to threaten to bring a nettle. A child who regularly grabs things that he might damage, such as pottery bowls, may have his hands beaten with a nettle. In general, however, there is little in the Jívaro house that a child can damage, since pottery not in use is stored on high bamboo shelves, and personal effects are suspended in baskets out of their reach. As a result, discipline with regard to safeguarding property is not emphasized.

If a child is extraordinarily bad, and, despite nettle spanking, continues breaking pottery vessels, taking meat without asking permission, and stealing peanuts from storage baskets above the rafters, the parents may undertake the harshest punishment they ever use on children. This consists of dropping a large quantity of hot peppers into a small fire and forcing the child to remain over the fire under a large cloth until he becomes unconscious. When he recovers, he may be admonished that if he again misbehaves, he will have all his hair burned off. However, this threat apparently is never carried out.

A much more subtle method of disciplining children consists of administering the juice of the *maikua* (*Datura arborea*) plant to them. This action is usually taken when a child is disrespectful of his father and calls into question his knowledge and authority. As one informant put it, "Only some sons obey their fathers. Some say, 'The old man is very old—he doesn't know what he is talking about.' It was like this in the oldtime, too." The administration of this particularly strong hallucinogenic extract is designed to put him into a trance state to see the supernatural world. It is believed that there he will discover that many of the claims the father has been making about the nature of reality are true and he will be less disrespectful. In addition, the hallucinogenic experience may put him in contact with an *arutam* . . . , and this also is seen as a possible bonus for the development of his character. This is a culture where a parent may threaten to give a child a hallucinogenic drug if it misbehaves.

The use of hallucinogens in child-rearing is by no means restricted to disciplinary problems. As has been noted earlier, the relatively mild *tsentsemä* is given to a new-born infant. If the child is female, *tsentsemä* is again administered, with a little tobacco water, when she is between about two and eight years old. Her parents hope she may acquire *arutam* soul power and thus be able, when she grows older, to work hard and have success in reproducing children, raising crops, chickens, and pigs. She is administered the drug within the context of a four-day feast and dance, *uči auk* ("child swallowing"), in which approximately half a dozen such girls participate together. Prior to the event the girls observe dietary restrictions for about a week, not eating the meat of any mammals or birds. The ceremonies take place in and near the house of the host, a father of one of the girls. On the first day the girls dance until midafternoon. Then they are given *tsentsemä* and are taken at nightfall to palm thatch lean-to's in the adjacent forest, where they will lie down to have visions and dreams of bountiful crops, chickens, and pigs. Meanwhile, the adults dance and drink in the house until dawn. The same procedure is repeated for three additional nights.

The most important use of hallucinogens in child-rearing, from the Jívaro point of view, is to assist a boy in seeing an *arutam* at a sacred waterfall, since his life is believed to depend upon it. . . . Of all a boy's childhood experiences, nothing is considered to compare in importance with the experience. The power deriving from the acquired *arutam* soul is seen in Jívaro terms as an enculturating and socializing device, since its force is believed to promote almost all the value aspects of character, including honesty, inclination to work, and intelligence; as well as to increase the actual knowledge of the child.

Training in work and skills conforms to the adult sexual division of labor. A girl from about the age of four to six is not expected to do much more than care for the baby, if any, while the mother is working in the garden or preparing beer in the house. She is instructed, among other things, to keep the infant from eating dirt and from being bitten by ants, and to rock it in its hammock. She is also supposed to sweep the house floor at least daily and throw out the accumulation of refuse. If there is no infant, this will probably be her only duty.

A girl approximately six years or older may have not only the above tasks, but also directly assists her mother in garden work of all kinds, including planting, weeding, and harvesting. When her mother is making pottery, she imitates her by making and firing miniature vessels and also may form and fire miniature dogs. No dolls in human form are produced, however. A boy who may be tempted to work with clay is discouraged by his father, who advises him not to touch it or else the boy's penis will one day stay soft and limp like a coil of clay.

A boy, when about four, begins to learn the art of blowgun hunting. His father gives him a small hollow reed less than a foot long and makes little darts. The child, who at that age tags along after his mother to the garden, uses it to shoot at butterflies. When he is about six, his father presents him with a real minature blowgun and a dart quiver. Then, while his mother works in the garden, he wanders about, shooting at the hummingbirds coming to feed at the flowers of the manioc plants. Those that he kills, he brings to her to cook, which she does gravely. He is not allowed to eat them himself, it being believed that he cannot kill again if he does so. By approximately nine years of age, his skill normally has advanced to the stage that he is killing larger birds lurking in the trees around the garden. His father then takes him hunting and gives him his first formal instruction in killing game, and has him assist by carrying it home. In the house, the father encourages the development of other male skills by showing approval when the son attempts to make miniature baskets or model houses and rafts.

Post-puberty boys perform most of the tasks of their fathers, including participation in the defense of the house and in attacks on enemies. A son may accompany his father on a raid as early as the age of six; but it is more common for this to happen when he is nine or older.

When a boy reaches the age of about sixteen, he formally undertakes to establish his adult status by going into the forest, killing a tree sloth, and making a *tsantsa* of its head. . . . Then two *tsantsa* feasts of celebration are given by the father or other older male relative in which all the ritual precautions of the human head *tsantsa* celebration are observed, although the feasting is not as lavish.

With the second feast, the transition of the head-taker into adult life is implicitly recognized, and he is now entitled to wear the *etsemat,* the basic headpiece of Jívaro men, consisting of a long cotton band with a red and yellow toucan feather tassel. The donning of this headband has significant overtones since it is used by men not only to keep their hair in place but also in war to hang a human head from the shoulder. He may also now carve a round stool for himself, although he usually does not do this until, or unless, he has participated in a regular killing expedition. Finally, the giving of the feasts means that he is entitled to get married, but he probably will not actually do this until he is about twenty-one to twenty-three years old.

A somewhat analogous pair of feasts is given as puberty celebrations for a girl. Both feasts are sponsored by the girl's father, the first being a minor affair of two days' length; the second being given about half a year later, after her family has been able to accumulate enough chickens and pigs to feed a large number of guests for six or seven days. The supernatural aspect of this "coming out" celebration centers around the girl drinking water mixed with crushed green tobacco leaves in order to enter the supernatural world while sleeping in a nearby lean-to and to have dreams that will augur success in raising garden crops and domesticated animals. The feasts are known as *nua tsaŋu* (woman tobacco) or *kasakü*.

Polygyny is preferred in the sororal form because sisters are reputed to get along better with one another. A man normally hopes that his father-in-law (*iči*) eventually will give him all the latter's daughters as wives. Accordingly, the son-in-law's conscientious post-marital bride-service is usually performed to keep his wife's father favorably impressed, so that he will provide such additional brides. Thus men occasionally may obtain several sisters as wives. In such cases, the man is assured of an outstanding production of beer and food and, presumably, a relatively tranquil polygynous family.

Wives who are sisters usually work out a hierarchial relationship, with the eldest (characteristically the first bride) assuming direction of activities within the house. The second wife, likewise, somewhat dominates the third, and so on. Still each wife has her own section of the garden which she exclusively works, her own cook-fire, bed, and pottery vessels. Not uncommonly, when a man marries a widow who has an unmarried daughter, the daughter will eventually, and casually, become his second wife. In such cases of stepdaughter marriage, the mother tends to retain a relatively dominant position over her daughter. The situation is usually more individualistic in the case of wives who are not sisters or mothers and daughters. These tend to be too antagonistic to submit to a consistent dominant-subordinate relationship in household activities.

The most difficult situation tends to occur when a husband brings home a new wife who is not a sister of his pre-existing wife (wives). Since he is already married, he cannot practice temporary matrilocality at the house of his new wife's parents, and thus he must introduce her into a household where the other adult female(s) will tend to be antagonistic. Usually the husband attempts to bring the bride in unannounced so as to take his other wife (wives) by surprise, and tries to act as though the new wife is just a routine addition to the household. Reportedly, however, it is common for an irate pre-existing wife to unleash a temper tantrum, throwing pottery vessels and other handy artifacts at the husband. She may also soon be engaging in quarrels and hair-pullings with the new addition, but normally life in the dwelling gradually settles down, particularly after the new wife has a baby.

The only kinswoman with whom marriage is formally sanctioned is a cross-cousin (*wa͡be*) from either parent's side of the family. A man does have the alternative of finding a marriage partner outside of his kindred, but this normally requires him to move out of his home neighborhood (because of the practice of temporary matrilocality) and consequently to live among strangers who may be intent on killing him for some earlier wrong by one of his kinsmen or simply because he took one of their own preferred potential mates. Slightly over half of actual marriages are with cross-cousins.

With the normatively unrestricted practice of polygyny creating a high demand for unattached women throughout interior Jívaro society, the preference for cross-cousin marriage promotes conflict in the nuclear family when brothers become old enough to marry, for they all share the same few preferred mates. Not surprisingly, many of the disputes among kinsmen thus arise between brothers over the question of wife acquisition, and the practice of matrilocal residence tends to isolate the brothers from one another. In fact, the norm is for a man to side with his *iči* (father-in-law and father of cross-cousins) and *sai* (wife's brother and male cross-cousins) in disputes against his own consanguineal relatives. The potential reward of obtaining more daughters as wives from his father-in-law often acts as an additional, but unspoken, inducement for a man to take the side of his in-laws in a quarrel.

By the time a man is ready to seek a female cross-cousin (*wabe*), her father may be dead, and he thus commonly must instead ask her brother (his *sai*) for her. Since there is a scarcity of marriageable women, it is common for her brother to demand reciprocity as part of the agreement, i.e., an exchange of sisters for marriage. Such an arrangement has the advantage of entailing none of the bride-service obligations which would be due the bride's father if he were alive, and of not requiring the normal temporary matrilocal residence at the bride's father's house, which may be in a "dangerous" neighborhood for the groom. As a by-product, the sister exchange also can cement friendly relations between cross-cousins of the same generation, as may be seen in the following case described by one informant:

> Tukupï and Ašaŋä are male cross-cousins [*sai*]. Tukupï had an unmarried sister, Nampirä. Ašaŋä asked Tukupï for her (the father of Tukupï and Nampirä was dead). Tukupï gave her to Ašaŋä, and Ašaŋä and Nampirä became husband and wife. But then Ašaŋä did not want to give *his own* sister to Tukupï. Also Ašaŋä frequently beat Nampirä when he got drunk.
>
> So Tukupï went to the house of Ašaŋä. He said, "Why do you beat my sister? If you want to hit my sister, then hit me."
>
> They began to fight (wrestling and hitting each other with pieces of wood). Then Tukupï left. Thereafter, whenever they met, they fought. Finally, Ašaŋä gave his sister to Tukupï. Thereafter, when Ašaŋä beat Tukupï's sister, Tukupï beat Ašaŋä's sister.
>
> Tukupï said, "Before, when you beat my sister, I went to fight you. But now that you have given me your sister, I will beat her instead."
>
> So now everything is friendly between Tukupï and Ašaŋä.

Joking relationships are restricted to cross-cousins, with emphasis on humor between cross-cousins of the opposite sex, who frequently banter flirtatiously with each other. The jokes are often explicit sexual challenges, even between persons married to others and, when engaged in by elderly cross-cousins, are often the occasion for general mirth in the household. The Jívaro explain that they cannot joke with other relatives because of their "respect" for them. The highest degree of such respect is shown by a man to his mother-in-law, from whom he averts his eyes when speaking with her. For a man to look directly into the eyes of a woman, even in conversation, is considered flirtatious behavior, and for him to look into the eyes of another man is considered a hostile act.

Beyond the polygynous nuclear family, the basic Jívaro kin group is a personal bilateral kindred with a slight patrilineal tendency. The personal bilateral kindred, however, should not even be referred to as a "group," for as Murdock has noted, a person shares an identical kindred only with his siblings and even then only before marriage. Since each person has a different kindred, his personal kin rights and obligations can coincide only with those of siblings of the same sex. Classification of kinsmen is by degrees of distance from one's self (*ego*), rather than in terms of membership or non-membership in some sort of corporate unit, as is commonly found in unilineal descent societies. The Jívaro thus possess the most insecure of the basic types of kinship systems, and lack clearly defined descent groups which can protect their members from outside enemies and which can settle disputes among relatives.

The Jívaro version of the kindred seems even more insecure than most for the individual, for in disputes any serious reckoning of kinship is a source of considerable confusion, involving disagreements over degree of relatedness, even in the case of a single person. In any serious discussion of kin obligations among the Jívaro, all single-word, or elementary, kin terms of reference have added to them the modifier "true" (*nekás*) or "branch" (*kaná*) to pin down degrees of relationship (see Table 1 and Figure 1 for the elementary kinship terms). In the case of any specific relative, these modifying terms can often be substituted for one another, depending upon the degree of closeness of relationship which the speaker wishes to recognize in a given situation. The only kin always defined as "true" relatives are a person's biological grandparents, parents, siblings, children, cross-cousins, and fathers of his cross-cousins. The only relatives who are always assigned to the "branch" category are affinal kin who, prior to marrying, were not considered by *ego* to be relatives of any degree. Since definition of degree of kinship is thus commonly manipulated at will, a person is often uncertain as to how his relatives will define their obligations and rights in any given dispute. The use of these "true" and "branch" modifiers almost doubles the varieties of relationship distinguished, so that many of the relatives in the kindred are unlikely to be defined as precisely the same, even by two siblings, in any particular crisis.

The utilization of these "true" and "branch" modifiers may be somewhat clarified by a few examples. According to the kinship rules, *ego* is expected to side with a true relative in a dispute with a branch relative of the same elementary category. However, *ego* must often decide at the time which of the two disputants is the "true" one and therefore deserving of his aid. No mat-

Table 1. *Kinship: Elementary Terms of Reference and Terms of Address*

Key to abbreviations

Br	brother	Gs	grandson
Da	daughter	Hu	husband
Fa	father	Mo	mother
Gc	grandchild	Si	sister
Gd	granddaughter	So	son
Gp	grandparent	Wi	wife

The abbreviations also represent the possessive form; thus, MoBrDaSo is mother's brother's daughter's son.

O	a formerly more common term
N	a recently innovated term
A	a term recently borrowed from the Achuara

Male Speaking; Terms of Address in Parentheses

FaFa, MoFa *apači* also GpBr (*apači* O; *apáčiru* O)

FaMo, MoMo *nukuči* also GpSi (*nukučí* O; *nukučiči* N)

Fa, FaBr, MoSiHu *apa* (*apawa*; *apačï*; *apawači*; *apa* N A)

Mo, MoSi, MoBrWi, FaSi, FaBrWi *nuku* (*nukuači*; *nukúa*); if *ego* marries a daughter of MoBrWi, FaSi, or FaBrWi, *tsatsa* (*nukúa*) is substituted for *nuku* with regard to the bride's mother.

FaSiHu, MoBr, WiFa *iči* (*iči*)

Br, FaBrSo, FaSiDaHu, MoSiSo, MoBrDaHu *yači* *yatsuči*—younger to older brother, *umpá*—older to younger)

Si, FaBrDa, FaSiSoWi, MoSiDa, MoBrSoWi *umaí* (*makú*; *umači* N; *umaimi* O; *umaímiči* O; *umáčiru*)

SiHu, FaSiSo, FaBrDaHu, MoBrSo, MoSiDaHu, WiBr *sai* (*saikma*)

BrWi, FaSiDa, FaBrSoWi, MoBrDa, MoSiSoWi *wahe* (*umači*)

So, BrSo, FaBrSoSo, FaSiDaSo, FaBrDaDaHu, FaSiSoDaHu, MoSiSoSo, MoBrDaSo, SiDaHu, MoSiDaDaHu, MoBrSoDaHu *uči* (*umpá*; *suki* O; *aišmaŋči* O; *aišmaŋá* O; *aišmaŋru* O)

Da, BrDa, FaBrSoDa, FaSiDaDa, FaBrDaSoWi, FaSiSoSoWi, MoSiSoDa, MoBrDaDa, SiSoWi, MoSiDaSoWi, MoSiSoDa, MoBrDaDa, SiSoWi, MoSiDaSoWi, MoBrSoSoWi *nawanta* (*makú*; *makuči*)

DaHu, BrDaHu, SiSo, FaBrDaSo, FaSiSoSo, FaBrSoDaHu, FaSiDaDaHu, MoSiDaSo, MoBrSoSo, MoSiSoDaHu, MoBrDaDaHu *awe* (*aweči*; *awetá*)

SoWi, BrSoWi, SiDa, aBrDaDa, FaSiSoDa, FaBrSoSoWi, FaSiDaSoWi, MoSiDaDa, MoBrSoDa, MoSiSoSoWi, MoBrDaSoWi *awe* (*aweči*; *awetá*)

Gs, Gd, Gc *tiraŋi* (*tiraŋi*; *tiraŋči*)

Wi *ekentu*; *nua* (*ekenturu* O). First wife: *tarimta*. Second wife: *učíč nua*. Third wife: *yamaí nuatčmu*.

Female speaking; Terms of Address in Parentheses

Terms are the same as for male speaking, except for the following:

Br, FaBrSo, FaSiDaHu, MoSiSo, MoBrDaHu *umaí* (*umači* N; *umaimi* O; *umaímiči* O; *umáčiru*)

Si, FaBrDa, FaSiSoWi, MoSiDa, MoBrSoWi *kai* (*kaičiru*, *kaiči*—younger to older sister; *makú*—older to younger)

SiHu, FaSiSo, FaBrDaHu, MoBrSo, MoSiDaHu *wahe* (*umači*)

BrWi, FaSiDa, FaBrSoWi, MoBrDa, MoSiSoWi *yua* (*yuači*; *yuamči*; *yuačiru*)

So, BrSo, FaBrSoSo, FaSiDaSo, MoSiSoSo, MoBrDaSo, SiSo, FaBrDaSo, FaSiSoSo, MoSiDaSo, MoBrSoSo *uči* (*aešmaŋá*; *áešmaŋru*)

Da Hu, BrDaHu, FaBrSoDaHu, FaSiDaDaHu, MoSiSoDaHu, MoBrDaDaHu, FaBrDaDaHu, FaSiSoDaHu, SiDaHu, MoSiDaDaHu, MoBrSoDaHu *awe* N (*aweči* N; *awetá* N; *antepá* O) *Awe* has replaced *antepä*, the male-speaking term of reference being adopted.

Da, BrDa, FaBrSoDa, FaSiDaDa, MoSiSoDa, MoBrDaDa, BrSoWi, SiDa, FaBrDaDa, FaSiSoDa, FaBrSoSoWi, FaSiDaSoWi, MoSiDaDa, MoBrSoDa, MoSiSoSoWi, MoBrDaSoWi *nawanta* (*makú*; *makuči*)

SoWi, SiSoWi, FaBrDaSoWi, FaSiSoSoWi, MoSiDaSoWi, MoBrSoSoWi *nahatï* O (*naháturu* O; *makú*; *aweči* N; *awetá* N) *Nahatï* is beginning to be replaced by *awe*, the male-speaking term of reference being adopted.

Hu *aeš* (*áeširu*)

Co-wives are normally referred to by the *kai* term.

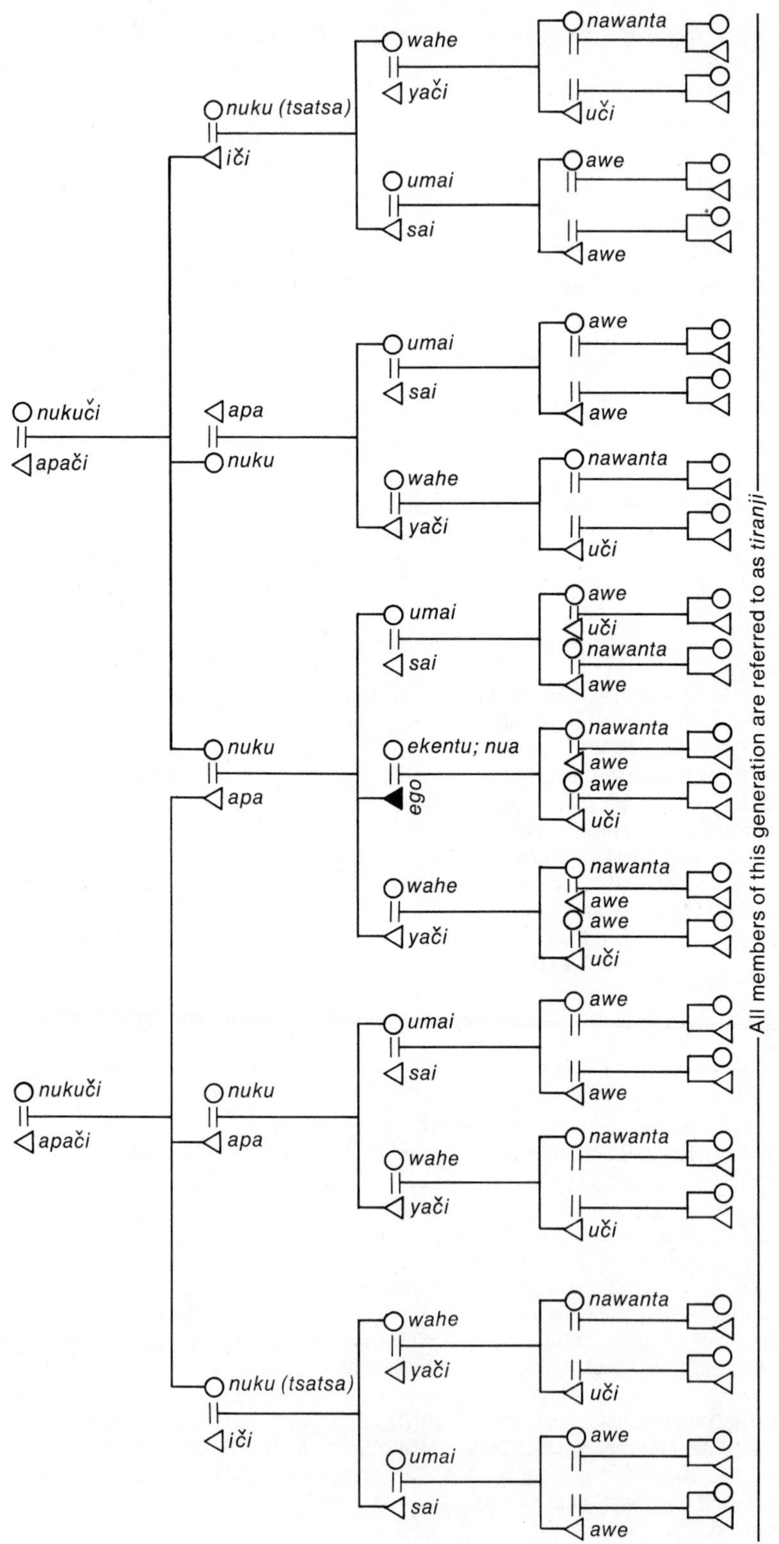

Figure 1. Kinship chart. Elementary terms of reference (male speaking).

ter whose side *ego* decides to join, the abandoned party may be expected to accuse him of not living up to his kinship obligations. If *ego* does not join either party in the dispute, then both tend to level that accusation at him.

Similarly, another relative may manipulate the terminology when *ego* requests help from him. *Ego* may request aid from a parallel cousin, for example, saying, "You are my true 'brother' (*nekás yaci*) and therefore you must help me in my dispute against this man who is only your branch 'brother-in-law' (*kaná sai*)." If the parallel cousin does not wish to accede to the request, he replies, "I wish I could help you, but you are mistaken. You are really my branch 'brother' (*kaná yaci*), not my true 'brother,' and since this enemy of yours is really my true 'brother-in-law' (*nekás sai*) it would not be right."

Although often a source of frustration and confusion, this manipulation of defined degree of relationship can serve to save a man's life. When he visits a strange house, the host may subject him to an interrogation regarding the names of his relatives and their degree of relationship to the visitor, pretending a purely friendly interest in the subject. Usually, however, the host really wants to determine whether his visitor is a close relative of any of his enemies. In answering his interrogator, the visitor carefully puts into the "branch" category as many of his relatives as possible, particularly those whom he thinks may be enemies of the host. At the same time, he promotes to the "true" category those of his relatives whom he knows are friendly to the interrogator or the interrogator's relatives. A good memory of kin relationships of both enemies and friends is, of course, essential to this sometimes adroit manipulation of the "true-branch" definitions.

Failure to manipulate kin classification successfully can result in the visitor's food or beer being poisoned or in his being ambushed by the host after he leaves the house. It is not surprising, therefore, that fathers often spend an hour or more before dawn lecturing their sons on the degree of relationship between a variety of enemies and friends in their own and other neighborhoods. Such lectures also include advice on how to avoid dangerous entanglements, how to get along well with kinsmen, and how to survive in general, as illustrated by this excerpt from such a morning monologue:

Listen, son, when you grow up, do not enter the house of Ampušä, who is my enemy. When I die, when my daughter is grown, she can marry whom she wants. If her husband is from a distant neighborhood, don't go to visit her. Afterwards, when you have married and I am dead, if you have a daughter, I know that one day the son of my enemy will make peace with you. But don't give him your daughter, or he will kill you. When I die, you have to give your sister to your true [*nekás*] *sai*. Thus you will live in peace and there will be no fighting or anything. If you give her to another man, then when you drink beer and get drunk, that man, although he is married to your sister, can speak to my enemy to plot your death. Thus are they accustomed to kill.

Then when your daughter is married, never speak harshly to your *awe* [son-in-law] or get mad at him or he will leave your daughter and become your enemy. When one never gets angry with his *awe*, and lives peacefully, the *awe* divides his game, and also his chickens and pigs, with you. Sometimes, when we get old, we cannot build a house. But if we have an *awe*, he will help build it.

Never beat your wife or get drunk. If some other man sees this happen and talks about it, it will be a shame. If you live well and give your daughter to an *awe*, then the father or brother of this *awe* may come to visit in order to see how you live. If you don't live well together, then the father of this *awe* will say, "This man is bad."

Also you must tell your daughter, "Obey your husband, supply good food, and do not commit adultery with other men. Otherwise he will surely beat you. And if the family of your husband comes to visit, you have to get up immediately and serve beer and food to the guests. If you don't, then they and many other people will say that you don't get up, even though your husband asks you to do so, and this is bad."

When you are living well, thus, with all your *sai* and *yači*, if someone comes and kills your *sai*, you have to avenge him. First of all, you have to bathe in the sacred waterfall, see *arutam*, and then you can kill. If you have not encountered *arutam*, you must not go kill, because you will die. When they kill someone in your family first, then you have to go and kill one of them. You can win by explaining that they killed first and that you are simply avenging his death. In this way, you can win. Also send the message, "If you kill me, my family will kill you." Then they also will say, "Yes, it is true. We cannot continue living and fighting. Let us calm down a bit. Since we are the same people, let us live peacefully. I want to stay in my house. I want to eat well." When they speak thusly, the feuding will end.

Learn to work. Let us work together. Since we have lots of beer, let us work together. Then when

I die, you will know how to work. When we kill a pig, let us eat well, because when we die, it is all finished. So let us work well and eat well while we live. When we work, we work until midafternoon. When you are young, you want to work all day. But I tell you, "Enough, enough. It is very late. We have to return to the house and you have to bathe. Then let us eat well."

When I die, how is it going to be with you? Sometimes when another man drinks beer, he gets angry. But this is bad. You must not do this. When you are drinking, take a nap and then you can get up and drink some more. Dance. Never speak harshly, because some men thus start fighting with their *yači*, Don't do this or otherwise when you travel elsewhere the people will know and speak to one another about it. So don't do this, because then this will be a great shame.

There are four main ways of tracing genealogical descent: (1) through the father's side, *patrilineally*—ancestry is reckoned through the male line, and for most social purposes the biological tie to the family of the mother is given less attention; (2) through the mother's side, *matrilineally*—descent is traced through the female line, and affiliation with the father's kin group is given less importance; (3) through both lines, *double descent*—a person's genealogical relationship to the descent group of each parent is recognized and attributed approximately equal significance; (4) through both sides (but not very far), *bilateral descent*—the system followed in our own society. Relationship to some but not all of the kinsmen of each of our parents is recognized. Because the particular relatives grouped by this system, called a kindred, is different for every person, except full brothers and sisters, such a group is rarely able to take the sort of sustained supportive action possible for unilineal descent groups, either matrilineal or patrilineal.

Despite the structural impediments to its acting as a permanently organized group, the kindred Stack describes here is clearly a descent group that can be adaptively mobilized to supplement or replace other sources of social, economic, and emotional support.

The Kindred of Viola Jackson[1]

Carol B. Stack

Introduction

Concepts can become so widely accepted and seem so obvious that they block the way to further understanding. Descriptions of black American domestic life (Frazier 1939; Drake and Cayton 1945; Abrahams 1964; Moynihan 1965; Rainwater 1966a) are almost always couched in terms of the nuclear family and in terms of the fashionable notion of a matrifocal complex. But in many societies the nuclear family is not always a unit of domestic cooperation, and the "universal functions" of family life can be provided by other social units (Spiro 1954; Gough 1959; Levy and Fallers 1959; Reiss 1965). And matrifocal thinking, while it may bring out the importance of women in family life, fails to account for the great variety of domestic strategies one can find on the scene in urban black America. The following study suggests that if we shed concepts such as matrifocality we can see that black Americans have evolved a repertoire of domestic units that serve as flexible adaptive strategies for coping with the everyday human demands of ghetto life.

Source: Reprinted with permission of Macmillan Publishing Co., Inc., from *Afro-American Anthropology* edited by Norman E. Whitten, Jr., and John F. Szwed. Copyright © 1970 by The Free Press, a Division of Macmillan Publishing Co., Inc., and used by permission of the author.

[1] The author would like to thank Professors E. Bruner, D. Shimkin, F. K. Lehman, D. Plath, and O. Lewis, and Mr. W. Ringle, for their interest in this work and helpful comments.

In the fall of 1966 I began to investigate black family organization in midwestern cities. I concentrated upon one domestic family unit—the household of Viola and Leo Jackson—and their network of kinsmen, which proved to number over 100 persons.[2] My immediate aim was to discover when and why each of these people had changed residence, and what kind of domestic unit they joined during the half-century since they had begun moving north from Arkansas.

The data show that during the process of migration and the adjustment of individuals to urban living, clusters of kin align together for various domestic purposes. It soon became clear that matrifocal thinking provided little insight into the organization of domestic units of co-operation, for example, those groups of kin and non-kin which carry out domestic functions but do not always reside together (Bender 1967). In certain situations such as the death or desertion of a parent, the loss of a job, or in the process of migration it was found that an individual almost always changed residence. But matrifocality proved to be a poor predictor of the kind of domestic unit the individual might subsequently enter. Among Mrs. Jackson's kin one can find various assortments of adults and children cooperating in domestic units: children living with relatives other than their parents, and also clusters of kin (often involving the father) who do not reside together but who provide some of the domestic functions for a mother-and-child unit in another location. Not only does matrifocal thinking fail here, but also little or nothing in the current writing on black American family life helps deal with questions such as the following that arise when we examine Mrs. Jackson's kin: Which relatives can a person expect will help him? Which relatives will care for parentless or abandoned children? And who will look after the ill and elderly? I will discuss these questions, and the challenge that Mrs. Jackson's kin and their lifeways put to our powers of explanation. First, however, I will deal briefly with the nature of matrifocal thinking.

The Matrifocal Complex

Matrifocality has become a popular replacement for the discarded nineteenth-century concept of matriarchy. Some would argue that matrifocality is more sophisticated, but I suggest that it is no more useful than matriarchy for characterizing urban Negro households.

When the rules for reckoning kinship are not explicit, then it is difficult to determine the basis upon which households are formed. As so, as M. G. Smith (1962b:7) has pointed out, by necessity the anthropologist then must rely on data on household composition. It is in this context that the term "matrifocality" is most widely used. However, it also has been used to refer to at least three units of information: (1) the composition of a household, (2) the type of kinship bond linking its members, and (3) the relationship between males and females in the household. In fact, matrifocality tells us little about the actual composition of the household, and the relational link upon which the household is formed. Schneider (1961) points out that in the past the terms "matrilocal marriage" and "matriliny" were used interchangeably (see Bachofen 1861) and that the matriarchal complex referred to a household which did not include the husband or father. Both González (1965) and Smith (1962b) use matrifocality to refer to the composition of households. These and similar formulations ignore the developmental history of domestic groups (Goody 1958). In addition, they supply no information on the age and circumstances in which individuals join households, the alternatives open to them, the relational links they have with other members, or who the members are. *Matrifocality is not a residence rule, and in particular, it is not a rule for post-marital residence.* Residence, one of the dynamics of social organization, can be understood only if the basis for the active formation of households is known.

A further complication is that notions such as matrifocality, maternal family (C. King 1945), and matriarchy inadvertently are associated with unilineal descent. It was Bachofen's contention (1861) that matriliny (descent through women) and matriarchy (rule by women) were but two aspects of the same institution (Schneider 1961; Lowie 1947). This claim had to be discarded when observers failed to find any generalized authority of women over men in matrilineal societies. This controversy is well known. What is less widely appreciated is that there is a close parallel between matriarchal and matrifocal thinking, in that both imply descent through

[2] Names throughout the paper are pseudonyms.

women. For example, M. G. Smith (1962b) defines Caribbean matrifocal households as ones which are composed of blood-related women plus all their unmarried children. González (1965:1542) defines consanguineal households in terms of the type of kinship bond linking adult men and women in the households such that no two members are bound together in an affinal relationship. She suggests that consanguineal households may also be matrifocal (1965:1548) and that there is evidence that consanguinal households exist among lower class Negro American groups (DuBois 1908; Frazier 1939; C. King 1945). The tentative classification that emerges from studies of black American households as consanguineal or as both consanguineal and matrifocal is confusing. In this confusion the use of the notion of matrifocality roughly coincides with Schneider's (1961 : 3) definition of matrilineal descent units in which he states that the "individual's initial relationship is to his mother and through her to other kinsmen, both male and female, but continuing only through females." *Matrifocality is not necessarily a correlate of matrilineal descent, nor does it imply a structure for linking families in the same community.*

The term "matrifocality" may have value as an indication of the woman's role within the domestic group, but it tells us little about authority, decision-making, and male-female relationships within the household, among extended kin, and in the community. Used in this context to refer to a dominant female role, and as a designate of residence classification, reference to the matrifocal household may lead to confusion between residence and role behavior. Analysis of role relationships and interactional patterns which is limited to their classification as matrifocal is at best uninteresting. The role organization of urban Negro households exists in a dynamic system which can be illustrated by the life histories of individuals in households as they adapt to the urban environment. This adaptation comes out dramatically when one examine's Viola Jackson's kin and their many ways of forming a domestic unit.

Frequently, discussions of matrifocality and consanguineal households ignore crucial aspects of family organization. Some of the matrifocal thinkers seem to assume that children derive nothing of sociological importance from their father, that households are equivalent to the nuclear family, and that resident husband-fathers are marginal members of their own homes (M. G. Smith 1957b). A look at Viola Jackson's kindred raises doubts about many of these assumptions.

Urban Family Organization

Clusters of Kin. The past fifty years have witnessed a massive migration of rural, southern blacks to urban centers in the United States. The kindred of Viola Jackson are a part of this movement. Ninety-six of them left the South between 1916 and 1967. Some of them first moved from rural Arkansas to live and work harvesting fruit in areas around Grand Rapids and Benton Harbor, Michigan, and Racine, Wisconsin; eventually they settled in the urban North. Two major patterns emerge from their life histories: (1) relatives tend to cluster in the same areas during similar periods: and (2) the most frequent and consistent alignment and cooperation appears to occur between siblings.

During the process of moving, Viola Jackson's kin maintained communication with relatives in the South. They frequently moved back to the South for short periods, or from Chicago and other midwestern cities to fruit harvesting areas on a seasonal basis. Therefore it is difficult to separate the data in terms of phases such as "migration" and subsequent "urban adaptation." During some seasons bus loads of rural blacks were brought to the North to harvest fruit. Many families worked their way back South only to repeat the process in order to avoid the poverty and unemployment there. This circulatory migration mainly involved the younger families and individuals.

Frequently, migrant workers follow their relatives and large urban neighborhoods reflect the geographical boundaries of the hinterland. Once these facts are established it is important to find out who made the original move, his age at the time of the move, which relatives joined one another to form households, and the context of each move.

Between 1916 and 1967 Mrs. Jackson's kin lived in five states, and groups of 10 to 15 individuals tended to cluster in the same areas during the same time periods. An example of this can be seen in Table 2, which shows where Viola's mother and siblings were living during that time period.

The basis for the active formation of households during migration and urban settlement can only be understood if material developing out of life histories is related to the realities of kinship and non-kinship factors. During this period of migratory wage labor in the young adult's life, the data show that the strongest alignment is of cooperation and mutual aid among siblings of both sexes (after the age of thirteen). Siblings left the South together, or shortly followed one another, for seasonal jobs. They often lived together in the North with their dependents and spouses, or lived near one another, providing mutual aid such as cooking and child care.

Domestic Arrangements

Case 1. In 1945 *C* left her husband and daughter in the South with his parents and moved to Racine, Wisconsin, to harvest fruit. At the same time *C*'s brother's wife died leaving him, *J*, with two young sons. *J* decided to move north and join *C* in Racine. He and his two sons took a bus to Racine where he got a job in a catsup factory. The company furnished trailers which *C* and *J* placed next to each other. *C* cooked for *J* and his two sons and cared for the children. They were cooperating as a single domestic unit. This situation continued for about a year and a half and then they all returned to the South.

Case 2. By 1946 Viola and Leo had four children and Leo was picking cotton. They were anxious to leave the South in order to find better wages and living conditions. Viola, Leo, and their children joined a bus load of people and moved to join Viola's brother, *L*, in Benton Harbor, Michigan. In Benton Harbor all the adults and the older children worked harvesting fruit. At the same time Leo's twin brother and Viola's brother, *J*, and his two sons moved to Benton Harbor. Leo's twin brother moved into Viola's and Leo's household. *J* and his sons

Table 1. *Residence and Kin Clusters*

Area and Time Period	*Ego's Mother (Magnolia)*	*Ego (Viola)*	*B*	*Z*	*Z*	*Z*	*B*
Arkansas 1916–1917	X	X	X				
Arkansas 1928–1944	X	X		X	X	X	X
Blythe, Calif. 1927–1928	X	X	X				
Grand Rapids, Mich. 1944–1946			X		X		
Racine, Wisc. 1947–1948		X		X			X
Benton Harbor, Mich. 1946–1948		X	X	X			X
Decatur, Ark. 1948–1952	X	X			X		X
Chicago, Ill. 1950–1953				X			
Champaign, Ill. 1952–1954	X	X	X				
Gary, Ind. 1954–1955			X				
Champaign, Ill. 1955–1967	X	X	X		X	X	X
Chicago Heights, Ill. 1959–1967				X			
Chicago, Ill. 1965–1967			X				

moved into the household of *J's* brother, *L*, and *L's* wife.

Case 3. In 1948 *C* decided to move north again. This time she took her daughter with her. She moved to Benton Harbor where Viola and her family, their two brothers, *L* and *J*, and Leo's twin brother were all living. *C* and *J* and their children began cooperating as a single domestic unit as they had in Racine.

The pattern described above of cooperation and mutual aid among siblings becomes even more apparent as these individuals move to urban areas. Sibling alignment in the urban context will be discussed in the next section.

Sibling Alignment and Kin Co-operation in Urban Areas

Understanding residence and family organization for people whose economic situation is constantly changing, and who therefore frequently change households, is not easy. Aside from the common observations of household composition based upon where people sleep, there are many other important patterns to be observed, such as which situations lead to a change in residence, which adults share households, and with which adult relatives are children frequently living.

One pattern, a continuation of a pattern formed during the early stages of migratory labor, is the cooperative alignment of siblings. By the time the majority of Viola Jackson's relatives had established permanent residence and jobs in the North there were numerous examples of siblings forming co-residential and/or domestic units of cooperation. These sibling-based units, apparently motivated by situations such as death, sickness, desertion, abandonment, and unemployment, most often focused around the need for child-care arrangements. Here are two examples:

1. Sister/Brother. In 1956 Viola and Leo were living in Champaign, Illinois. Viola's brother, *J*, took the train from the South to visit them. After the visit he decided to move to Champaign with his two sons and look for work. *J* rented a house near Viola's and got a construction job. When he brought his sons to Champaign, Viola cooked for them and cared for them during the day.

2. Sister/Sister. In 1959 Viola's sister, *E*, was suffering from a nervous breakdown. *E's* husband took their four youngest children to his mother in Arkansas. *E's* sister, *C*, was living in Chicago and she cared for *E's* oldest daughter. After *E's* husband deserted her, *E's* twin sister, *M*, moved into *E's* house. The household was composed of *E*, her oldest daughter who had been in Chicago, *M*, and *M's* two youngest daughters.

These alignments may be largely attributed to adaptation to urban socio-economic conditions. One such urban pattern is a minimum of emphasis on the inheritance of property. For obvious social and economic reasons, poor and highly mobile urban apartment dwellers do not develop strong ties to a homestead or a particular piece of land, even though they may express strong regional and even neighborhood loyalty or identification. This contrasts with the rural South and with Young's and Willmott's (1957) observations that apartments in Bethnal Green were kept in the family. The high frequency of moving from one apartment to another in economically depressed urban areas is related to the degree of overcrowding, the shortage of apartments, urban renewal, and the changing employment situation. Another situation causing these alignments to form is the arrival of a new migrant to the urban area wherein he lives with siblings. With time, if he successfully establishes himself in a job in the urban area he may move out of his sibling's household.

Sibling Alignment and Kin Co-operation in Urban Areas

It has already been pointed out that migration, unemployment, sickness, and desertion by necessity often lead to a change in residence. Most often these changes are closely related to the need for child-care arrangements. The choices and expectations involved in placing children in a relative's home largely focus around which adult female relatives are available. In selecting the specific relative, the following criteria are considered: the geographical locations of these adult female relatives; their source of financial support, their age, their marital status, the composition of their household, and the ability of the people making the decision to get along with these females. At the same time, due to the flexibility and mobility of urban individuals, decisions frequently center around the relational link the child has with female members of a particular household. This means that the distance and location of a household, for example, are not a great deterrent, and that in fact the economic, distance, and other decisions are made after the kin criteria are met.

Children in the extended kin network of Viola Jackson frequently live with relatives other than their biological parents. The child-female links which most often are the basis of new or expanded households are clearly those links with close adult females such as the child's mother, mother's mother, mother's sister, mother's brother's wife, father's mother, father's sister, father's brother's wife.

Some examples are given at the bottom of this page.

These examples do indeed indicate the important role of the black female. But the difference between matrifocal thinking and thinking about household composition in terms of where children live is that the latter can bring to light the dynamics of household formation, and the criteria, rules, and decisions that the process entails.

The summaries of the social context in which children changed households indicate which adult female relatives are frequently called upon for service. The alignment and cooperation between siblings, such as mother's sister and father's sister, has already been noted. This has been underestimated by workers who select the grandmother household (especially mother's mother) as the only significant domestic unit. It must be noted that the crucial role which paternal as well as maternal grandmothers assume in socialization is a frequent, but definitely not a unique, alternative.

Since social scientists have stressed the existence of female-centered, woman-headed, matrifocal black families, it is of particular interest to look at the formation of grandmother households in Viola's kin. Here is a summary of the households in which Viola's mother, Magnolia, has lived.

When a grandmother household is characterized as matrifocal we get little insight into the dynamics of its formation. At best, it suggests a mother hen who gathers her chicks about her. After age sixty, Magnolia's residence was determined by her children, who decided to bring her to the urban North to care for her. Her move North was prompted by her children's concern for her health and well-being.

We find that Magnolia has frequently shared households with her children and grandchildren. In fact, she has consistently moved to join her daughter's households to be cared for, or to care for her grand-children. Instead of simply gathering her flock, each move and new household in which Magnolia lived after age sixty was formed on a different basis.

By the time Magnolia was elderly she was living in the urban North in a grandmother household caring for her grandchildren. This was the result of the illness and subsequent death of one of her daughters. At this time a house was rented and maintained for Magnolia

Relational Link	*Domestic Unit*
Mother	Viola's brother married his first wife when he was sixteen. When *she* left him, she kept her daughter.
Mother's mother	Viola's sister, *M*, never was able to care for her children. In between husbands, her mother kept her two oldest children, and after *M's* death, her mother kept all three of the children. Her brother offered to keep the oldest girl.
Mother's mother	Viola's daughter (age 20) was living at home and gave birth to a son. The daughter and her son remained in the Jackson household. The daughter expressed the desire to set up a separate household.
Mother's sister	*M* moved to Chicago into her sister's household. The household consisted of the two sisters and four of their children.
Father's mother	Viola's sister, *E*, had four daughters and one son. When *E* was suffering from a nervous breakdown her husband took three daughters and his son to live with his mother in Arkansas. After his wife's death he also took the oldest daughter to his mother's household in Arkansas.
Father's mother	When Viola's younger sister, *C*, left her husband in order to harvest fruit in Wisconsin she left her two daughters with his mother in Arkansas.
Father's sister	When Viola's brother's wife died, he decided to raise his two sons himself. He kept the two boys and never remarried. His residence has consistently been close to one or another of his sisters who have fed and cared for his two sons.

Magnolia

Age	Context of Domestic Unit or Household
60	In 1958 Magnolia's second husband died and she was left alone with her daughter's (*M*) two oldest children. Viola sent her two oldest sons to care for Magnolia and the two children.
62	In 1960 Magnolia moved to Champaign and joined the household of her twin daughters, *E* and *M*, bringing *M's* children with her.
65	After *E's* death, Magnolia and her daughter moved to Danville, Illinois, with *M's* two children, who Magnolia raised in the South, and *M's* two youngest children.
67	After *M's* death, Magnolia joined her daughter Viola's household for a short time.
67	Soon afterward, Viola and her husband rented a nearby house for Magnolia and the four grandchildren. Magnolia is on welfare, cares for the four children, and constantly receives help from the Jacksons and from her children living in Chicago.

and the four grandchildren by Viola and her husband, Leo. The rented house was one block from Viola's home and the two households functioned primarily as a single domestic unit of cooperation. The cluster of relatives consisted of four generations: Magnolia, the four grandchildren, Viola and Leo Jackson, ten of their children, and their grandchild, the son of Viola Jackson's oldest daughter.

This four-generational kin cluster is not a co-residential unit, but a domestic unit of cooperation. The main source of financial support consisted of Leo's seasonal construction work, welfare payments to both Magnolia and Viola's daughter (for her son), and the part-time jobs of some of the teenage children. These individuals used Viola's house as home base where they shared the evening meal, cared for all the small children, and exchanged special skills and services. Frequently, Viola's brother (whose wife had died) ate with the group and participated in the exchange of money, food, care for the sick, and household duties. The exchange of clothes, appliances, and services in crisis situations extended beyond this kin cluster to relatives in Chicago and St. Louis. This group is an example of an urban kinship-based domestic unit which formed to handle the basic family functions.

Concluding Remarks

The examples from the preceding sections support the suggestion that domestic functions are carried out for urban blacks by clusters of kin who may or may not reside together. Individuals who are members of households and domestic units of cooperation align to provide the basic functions often attributed to nuclear family units. The flexibility of the blacks' adaptation to the daily social and economic problems of urban living is evidenced in these kinship-based units which form to handle the daily demands of urban life. In particular, new or expanded households and/or domestic units are created to care for children. The basis of these cooperative units is co-generational sibling alignment, the domestic cooperation of close adult females, and the exchange of goods and services between the male and female relatives of these females. To conclude, it is suggested that these households and domestic units provide the assurance that all the children will be cared for.

REFERENCES CITED

Abrahams, R., 1964, *Deep Down in the Jungle,* Folklore Associates, Hatboro, Pa.

Bachoffen, J., 1861, *Das Mutterecht,* Benno Schwabe, Basel.

Bender, D. 1967, "A Refinement of the Concept of Household: Families, Co-residence, and Domestic Functions," *American Anthropologist* 69:493–504.

Drake, St. C., and H. Cayton, 1945, *Black Metropolis,* Harcourt, Brace, New York.

Du Bois, W., 1908, *The Negro Family,* Atlanta U.P., Atlanta.

Frazier, E. F., *The Negro Family in the United States,* Chicago U.P., Chicago.

González, N., 1965, "The Consanguineal Household and Matrifocality," *American Anthropologist* 67:1541–49.

Goody, J., 1958, (ed.), *The Developmental Cycle in Domestic Groups,* Cambridge U.P., London.

Gough, K., 1959, "The Nayars and the Definition of Marriage," *Journal of the Royal Anthropological Institute* 89:23–34.

King, C., 1945, "The Negro Maternal Family: A Product of an Economic and Cultural System," *Social Forces* 24:100–04.

Levy, M., and L. Fallers, 1959, "The Family: Some Comparative Considerations," *American Anthropologist* 61:647–51.

Lowie, R., 1947, *Primitive Society,* Boni and Liveright, New York.

Moynihan, 1965, *The Negro Family,* Government Printing Office, Washington, D.C.

Rainwater, L., 1966, "Crucible of Identity: The Negro Lower-Class Family," *Daedulus* 95 (2) :172–216.

Reise, I., 1965, "The Universality of the Family: A Conceptual Analysis," *Journal of Marriage and the Family* 27:443–53.

Schneider, D., and K. Gough, 1961, (eds.), *Matrilineal Kinship,* California U.P., Berkeley.

Smith, M., 1957, "Introduction," in E. Clarke (ed.), *My Mother Who Fathered Me,* Allen and Unwin, London.

——— 1962, *West Indian Family Structure,* Washington U.P., Seattle.

Spiro, M., 1954, "Is the Family Universal?" *American Anthropologist* 56:839–46.

SECTION II
Associations

Associations can be secret. They can be voluntary and they can be ascribed on the basis of sex or age. They often cut across kinship ties to provide the individual with a useful alternative basis for group affiliation. When you cannot get along with your parents or your husband (or his parents), often you can get away from them all by joining a club. For the community, associations provide a significant basis for economic mobilization (consumer boycotts, the National Association of Manufacturers), for social action (pollution control, planned parenthood), and for influencing the political system (Students for a Democratic Society, Young Americans for Freedom).

A radical change is occurring in the social organization of most industrializing societies. Associations are increasingly replacing kin groups as many peoples' most important source of group affiliation. Anderson traces the historical development of this manifestation of revolutionary change in the organization of our social lives.

Voluntary Associations in History

Robert T. Anderson

Where societies today are experiencing rapid social change, formal voluntary associations typically are found. Yet associations have also been prominent in the past, not only in pre-industrial nations, such as those of Rome and medieval Europe, but equally in societies which were less complex politically and economically, including tribes on the American plains and communities in Oceania, parts of Africa, or along the Pacific coast of native North America. There is much we still need to know about voluntary associations. Even so, enough has been

Source: Reproduced by permission of the American Anthropological Association from *The American Anthropologist,* Vol. 73, No. 1 (1971) and the author.

done, particularly in the last couple of decades, to allow some preliminary assessment of the place they have in the evolution of society.[1]

Paleolithic-Mesolithic Bands

The history of formal common interest associations during the first million years or so of human existence lends itself to brief statement: there were virtually none.[2] We can say this with confidence, even though the evidence is what a court of law would term circumstantial. Because they normally lived in small bands scattered thinly across forests and plains, paleolithic and mesolithic men would not normally have formed groups on the basis of common interest rather than of territory or kinship.[3] Their needs could have been totally met as societies of small bands of related families roving circumscribed territories.

What we know of living hunters and foragers of a mesolithic sort confirms this assumption. Walter Goldschmidt, in dealing with the issue, points out that in a few instances a kind of religious sodality may have cut across band and family ties, as in the totemic groups of some Australian aborigines today. Such groups are rare (1959:155–156). It is true that where they do occur, they may constitute an important part of the social system. In the example of the native Australians, totemic group members have fundamental responsibilities in a complex of rituals believed necessary for the cyclical replenishment of game and plants.

Totem groups also lubricate inter-tribal communication, since membership requires movement for ritual purposes (Elkin 1964:151–158). But normally among living nomadic hunters, social activities are individual, family, or band matters.

Although rare, the common interest associations of hunting nomads invariably unite individuals in terms of religious beliefs.

That tie to religion provides an additional clue to the early history of sodalities. Inferences concerning the origins of religion become, by extension, inferences concerning the early history of common-interest associations, and lead to a somewhat more refined reconstruction.

The expected tie to religion makes it extremely unlikely that sodalities existed in the lower paleolithic, when man apparently had not yet developed any kind of religious habits, or in the middle paleolithic, when the earliest glimmerings of religion took shape, in the archaeological record, as purposeful, but still crude burial customs. Not until well into the upper paleolithic of western Europe, when men first practiced art and used caves for rituals of uncertain nature, probably no earlier than 25000 B.C., only then is it at all likely that the first primitive sodalities flickered into life. That possibility increases with the mesolithic, though even then, common interest groups must have been rare, as Goldschmidt has argued.

The description Harold E. Driver gives of the Indians of North America reinforces this conclusion. He documents the absence of any kind of common interest grouping among most Arctic, Sub-Arctic, Plateau, Great Basin, and Northeast Mexican peoples (1961:406). More, the unusual cases which do occur among these hunting and gathering societies are invariably in places closest to other areas from which such practices might have been borrowed. At least in part, the rare occurrences among living mesolithic societies seem the result of diffusion from more advanced neighbors.

Not all mesolithic societies have been nomadic. In a few favored places, natural food resources have been rich enough and localized enough to allow permanent villages, a form of settlement otherwise possible only with plant husbandry. In prehistoric Denmark, for example, the Ertebølle people were able to settle this way because they could exploit a bountiful resource of fish and crustaceans. From the shell mounds they piled up over generations of sed-

[1] This paper was prepared for the seminar session on "Volunteer Action Theory and Research: Steps Toward Synthesis," as organized by David Horton Smith for the 65th Annual Meeting of the American Sociological Association in Washington, D.C., August 31–September 3, 1970.

[2] For a summary of earlier speculation on the history of voluntary associations, see Lowie 1948:309–312. For a brief statement on the principles of evolutionary reconstruction, see Service 1962:3–10, or Service 1963:xvi–xx.

[3] For comparative analysis, a very broad definition of voluntary association is required. In this essay, the terms voluntary associations and its synonyms, including the term sodality, are taken to refer to formally constituted groups bound primarily by ties of shared interest rather than kinship or coresidence (see Lowie 1948:14; Sills 1968:362–363; Anderson 1964:175–176).

entary life, however, the archaeologist finds no clue as to the presence or absence of sodalities.

We do have information about the social organization of recent and contemporary mesolithic villages. Indians of the Northwest Pacific Coast, for example, established permanent settlements on the basis of enormous salmon runs, and the Central Californian Indians lived in hamlets supported by a variety of wild foods, including a plentitude of acorns. These Indians, we know, had what Driver refers to as "relatively important sodalities" (Driver 1961: 407–413).

Mischa Titiev indicates something of the importance these associations could have in a succinct statement about one of the Northwest Coast tribes. "During the summer season," he writes, "the social organization of the Kwakiutl was based on ties of descent that sorted the people into clans. In the winter months, however, there prevailed an entirely different grouping, which depended on membership in secret societies. Individuals from each clan had a number of these societies from which to choose . . ." (1963:465–466). It appears, in sum, that circumstances at times allowed advanced hunting and gathering peoples to settle in villages. Such early, pre-agricultural villages probably organized some ritual activities as common interest enterprises. Such sodalities would expectedly have been important in social functions and rich in cultural associations.

Neolithic Villages

Villages, and with them sodalities, are unusual among mesolithic peoples. Villages are customary among cultivators. And when such villages are not integrated into complex political and economic systems, they seem characteristically to sponsor the elaboration of sodalities. Certainly, horticultural villagers in native North America, Oceania, and Africa evolved fascinating varieties of common interest associations. It seems reasonable to conclude that prehistoric horticultural villagers often did the same. If that is so, the emergence and spread of the neolithic may be taken as a rough chronicle of the first widespread elaboration and diffusion of common interest associations. For those who like their dates in years, even when they are very inexact, this would yield a beginning date of between 7000 B.C. and 8000 B.C., when a few agricultural communities first appeared in the Middle East, a date when associations still were not common. (Rare, early mesolithic villages could not have been more than a few thousand years earlier than this. Ertebølle is much later.)

These rough calculations would place the widespread growth and diffusion of early sodalities in the millennia after 7000 B.C., when the neolithic diffused from centers in the Middle East, Southeast Asia and Nuclear America to major parts of the inhabited earth. In the process, older mesolithic societies were eradicated, absorbed or displaced, until they remained only as a diminished minority in marginal areas. The process has had no clear end. It lasted into our era. Neolithic settlers were still moving onto uninhabited islands in Oceania as recently as circa A.D. 1000, when the Maori moved to New Zealand. Even within the last century, cultivators have pushed into residual mesolithic enclaves in many places, including South Africa, for example, where the Bushmen have been driven off all but the forbidding Kalahari Desert by neighboring Bantu peoples. In the same decades, of course, both mesolithic and neolithic societies have been threatened, transformed, or destroyed by urban-industrial intrusions, so the situation now is quite complex. What is clear, is that villages, and presumably sodalities, became widespread phenomena.

Long ago, Robert H. Lowie drew attention to the importance of associations where they occur. "Sex moieties, divisions on the basis of matrimonial status, social clubs, secret fraternities, all criss-cross the bonds of the family and sib, creating new units of incalculable significance for the individual's social existence (1947:296). Lowie really meant it when he described their significance as incalculable. He could find no common characteristics beyond the fact that they all excluded non-members (1947:336). For a generation anthropologists shared this point of view. Research, as a result, was limited largely to acquiring more descriptions of specific cases, and to attempting cautious historical reconstructions of a very limited sort.

Lowie himself provided a thorough description of Crow sodalities (1935). He also compared the associations of numerous Indian tribes of the Plains to hypothesize that in that part of the world, age societies were a local and late development out of simpler antecedents (1947:334). Others contributed studies of associations in other parts of the world, so that when Lowie wrote a new book on social organization a quarter of a century after his first one, he could draw on a much enlarged reservoir of descriptive reports. Yet even then, he could find no satisfactory way to generalize about the place of associations in social organization. "Since sodalities represent a congeries of diverse associations set off by negative rather than positive criteria, they defy logical classification," he concluded (1948:295).

Following the work of Lowie and the stimulus he gave to such studies, the effort to comprehend the character of associations has turned for some to an evolutionary perspective which stresses the role of common interest associations in societies at a certain stage of development. Elman Service, working in terms of a progressive sequence of band, tribe, chiefdom, primitive state, and archaic civilization, observes that sodalities have been reported for some bands, although it is rare, that they occur commonly at the tribal level, and that above that level they are found in increasing variety. Above all, however, he sees sodalities as most significant at tribal level, because at that stage they are more numerous, larger and more socially significant than among bands, where they are rare, yet they are not supplemented by other integrative institutions as in chiefdoms and states. Particularly in achieving some degree of pan-tribal solidarity, they may perform essential institutional functions (1963:XXI–XXIII).

Walter Goldschmidt, who also works in terms of an evolutionary model, was perhaps the first to insist that sodalities became increasingly important in that "middle range" of societies which more or less corresponds to the tribal level or the Neolithic Era. Having particularly in mind the surviving examples of societies in Melanesia, Africa, and North America, but referring as well to the non-cultivating villagers of Central California and the Northwest Pacific Coast, his attempt to generalize shows we have not gotten much beyond the work of Lowie in our comprehension of the role of sodalities in such communities.

> There is always a magico-religious aspect to such groups. They are characterized by ritual induction or initiations, by secret rites and ceremonies, and by a system of mythological justification. Often they also have a power function, uniting the senior men, the adults, or some especially selected group as against the women and children or all outsiders. Occasionally there are countervailing women's organizations [Goldschmidt 1959:156].

The secret societies which occur in some communities have particularly intrigued many investigators, even though E. D. Chapple and C. S. Coon years ago argued that categorizing associations as secret was of little value. They argued that secrecy, defined as "the enforced isolation of the members of an institution during some or all periods of their interaction as members of the system," occurs to some extent in every institution, and is therefore not "diagnostic of associations." Families and nations also have secrets (1942:442–443). Even so, sodalities in some social systems, and particularly in many of those of West Africa, Melanesia, and North America, do stand out for the extremes to which they emphasize, formalize, and build upon secrecy in carrying out their activities.

Kenneth Little, in a survey of West African examples, finds secret societies highly effective as guardians of tradition. Through them, the larger society may educate its young, train its warriors, regulate sexual conduct, perform religious rituals, and supervise political and economic affairs. Such associations may also provide important social services, including medical treatment, entertainment and recreation (1949). Discussing the highly secretive Poro society as it occurs among the Kpelle of Liberia, James L. Gibbs, Jr., particularly noted political functions. He describes judicial activities, for example. The fraternity could punish tribesmen for incest, arson or other delict. Further, the group assumes administrative prerogatives. "Several bits of field data confirm the view," he concludes, "that political power and Poro power tend to be lodged in the hands of the same individuals, and it is not unlikely that chiefs utilize Poro mechanisms to underscore their political decisions. By 'putting the country under Poro oath' all of the men of a given area can, under penalty of Poro sanctions, be required to carry out a specific action or abstain from one . . ." (1965:219–221).

The fact that other institutions normally maintain secrecy about some of their activities, and the fact that non-secret associations may duplicate, in a general way, any of the functions achieved by a secret organization, does not diminish the significance secrecy has when it is explicitly built upon to turn sodalities into effective social agencies. However diverse in their particular functions, such associations share a distinguishing characteristic. "As a rule secrecy is employed for more effective control over non-members and the uninitiated or for more stringent maintenance of the internal solidarity of the group of individuals who have discovered or built up common interests" (Miller 1934:621). To this extent, at least, a cross-cultural category of secret societies has value for comparative analysis.

In a similar way, age-sets (associations which generally group individuals by sex as well as by age) constitute a category with particular potentialities in social organization. In many African societies especially, age-sets have been found to have social and political functions which cross-cut or complement the generally more pervasive functions of lineage and clan. Among the Nandi (Huntingford 1960) and the Nuer (Evans-Pritchard 1940), for example, men separated by lineage loyalties are united by age-set sentiments and commitments, an arrangement which tends to reduce factionalism in the tribe. Among the Nyakyusa, Monica Wilson found that age superseded kinship as the most important organizational principle. A new local community there is established when land is allocated to a group of young men and their wives. Since the villagers are diverse in their kin relationships, the initial bond of solidarity is membership in a single age grouping. In this way, age-mates create something sufficiently unique to merit the special term, age-villages (1963).

Sodalities in the "middle range" of societal evolution, in short, have important social and cultural functions. Efforts to generalize about them, however, have not yet yielded very impressive results. We have not yet cracked the nut on which Lowie worked. The best we can do is to characterize them broadly and note regularities limited to particular parts of the world or to particular associational mechanisms such as secrecy or age alignment. Lowie did as much, half a century ago.

Preindustrial States

The next period in the history of associations is one in which the place of the institution in social behavior was important, to be sure, yet very different from what it had been. The centuries around 3000 B.C. may be taken to approximate inauguration of this new phase. In Mesopotamia and Egypt at that time, the first bronze age cities were built. In subsequent millennia, early towns emerged in India, China, Mesoamerica, and Africa. With the passage of time, cities, nations, and empires appeared in various parts of the world. While some were growing to moments of greatness, others declined to extinction or had not yet begun their historic venture. With time, too, technological and political complexity progressed, so that early towns seem small and simple in later comparison.

The history of early cities and states is an historical maze. Yet many analysts encapsulate it as a single unit for socio-cultural study, the period or the category of preindustrial cities or states (Sjoberg 1960). Among anthropologists, in spite of its ambiguities, the contrast of preindustrial with industrial, of traditional with modern, has been a widely accepted strategem of analysis (Foster 1953a:163).

As we have seen, very few regularities have been defined for associations in societies of a neolithic sort. Nearly none are proposed for those of the preindustrial urban world. We get merely descriptions: the *collegium* or *sodalitas* of Rome, (Brinton 1930), the merchant association of Greece and Egypt or the guild of the Middle Ages in Europe (Nicoló 1932). And even these provide only a distorted picture, since they usually say nothing of those great orphans of history, the peasantry and the proletariat. Where records survive, they generally are silent about sodalities in the higher classes. Only rarely do they give evidence that associations existed among plebeians and rustics.

What we do know of associations in preindustrial states is not quite what unexamined assumptions about steady evolutionary progress might lead one to expect (Banton 1968:358; Goldschmidt 1959:156–157). Even though voluntary associations were prominent in the neolithic, and even though they have become prominent in recent, post-industrial societies, they were often restricted or absent in major parts of stratified, urban societies of the preindustrial sort. Put differently, between the crests of association development in neolithic communities and modern industrial nations lies a trough of quiescence, when the importance of associations was comparatively reduced.

Paucity of the historical record allows one only

to illustrate rather than systematically to sample the place of associations in traditional nations. We may note that in China, merchants formed guilds. But the highest and lowest classes seem largely devoid of sodalities until nineteenth century political chaos and incipient modernization led villagers to form shared interest associations on a scale unknown to them before.[4] Ancient Rome had more association activity than most preindustrial states. In addition to merchant guilds, many Romans belonged to the congregations of religious cults or to club-like groups. Peasants may have remained largely untouched by such movements, however. In traditional Europe, guilds epitomized the potentialities of common interest groups. Clubs did appear, but they were late, and matured as concomitants of emergent industrialization involving mainly the upper and middle classes. Peasants rarely formed voluntary associations of any kind (Anderson 1970: *passim;* Boak 1932; Brinton 1930:574; Lowie 1948:295, 307, 312–313; Nicoló 1932:206; Sjoberg 1960:187–196).

From such a sampling of the historical record, we illustrate a tentative generalization: in traditional civilizations from ancient Ur to recent Europe and China, sodalities were confined mainly to the merchant class. Peasants and the elite generally organized solely in terms of territory and kinship.

Perhaps because sodalities were prominent in Rome, which greatly influences our thinking about classic society; perhaps because merchant guilds, which greatly influence our thinking about the Middle Ages, seem typically to have enlivened European city life with their activities; and perhaps merely because the record so neglects peasant villages where sodalities were rare, one of the most intriguing questions about the history of voluntary associations is itself generally neglected. Why did the elaborate associational traditions of the neolithic decline so thoroughly?

With the growth of states, sodalities in villages seem typically to have become extinct or not to have developed (Hamer 1967:89–91). As foci of political power, including a degree of pan-tribal influence, their very success in the neolithic no doubt doomed them. The state imposed its own authority in their place. Other institutions took up surviving functions. The state itself regulated part of village life. Various kinds of family and village structures organized the rest (Wolf 1966: 60–95; Foster 1965:301–302). In some areas, loose associations met special needs, as in formalized but usually impermanent or semipermanent harvesting associations found in many parts of the world. But peasants typically restricted their associational commitments to mutual aid. "There must be a limit," Wolf argues, in making such observations, "to the degree to which one's own resources can become committed to those of a neighbor, lest one be dragged down by his potential failure" (1966: 80).

Consistent with his own observations, the mutual-aid clubs, parent-burial associations, sugar-making groups, irrigation societies, and crop-watching societies which Wolf refers to for Chinese villages must be regarded as exceptional rather than typical (Wolf 1966:83; see note 4). They were probably the product in China, for the most part, of deterioration of the state apparatus, a partial return, in other words, toward a more pristine condition, even though the form such sodalities took may have reflected early industrial influence. In a similar way, the prominence of formal voluntary associations in colonial Bali (Geertz 1959) was associated with freedom from heavy-handed state control. The island, in its remoteness, was a buffer against

4 As concerns the upper class, Cheng Ch'eng-K'un stresses the extent to which the large family, more typical of the gentry than of the peasantry, "was self-contained, self-disciplined, self-perpetuating, and self-sufficient. It fulfilled almost all the functions of an organized society . . ." (Cheng 1953:85). With families of this sort, the gentry had little need to establish sodalities. This assumption is borne out in accounts of gentry life, which are notable for not attaching importance to associations (see Yee 1963; Fei 1953).

As concerns the peasantry, Daniel H. Kulp II describes several kinds of sodality found in South Chinese villages (Kulp 1953:119–122). Only the Parent Burial Association is said by him to be old, however, and antiquity otherwise is not indicated. It is notable that twentieth century traditional villages in both the south and the north have been described, in at least four instances, with no indication that voluntary associations were present or more than a rather insignificant part of the social structure (Fei 1946; Hsu 1949; Osgood 1963; Yang 1945).

For a description of merchant associations see Morse 1966. For a view less polemic than mine of voluntary associations in China, see Freedman 1958:82-s; note also, Gamble 1963:33–42.

total erosion of the neolithic condition. Certainly, however, where the state permits, where circumstances require, and where traditions encourage, sodality formation may take place among peasants (Hamer 1967–89–91). Villages in Spain and Latin America provide a cogent example, since they support religious brotherhoods of greater or lesser social significance (Foster 1953b). Many though not all villages in Tokugawa Japan had sodalities in the form of age grades, shrine associations and cooperative groups (Befu 1965:30; Norbeck 1962:74–75). Other examples could be cited.

The failure of sodalities normally to materialize within the ruling class is equally as impressive as their failure importantly to survive or emerge in peasant villages. The reduced size of the elite population is undoubtedly the critical feature here as with simple bands of hunters. The ruling class in an agrarian nation is normally small enough to constitute a face-to-face society. Aristocrats typically coagulate into lineages, while the personal contacts of such individuals and their kinsmen provide all the necessary larger networks of social interaction. Sodalities would be superfluous. Where common interest does appear as a basis for union, it takes place as loose, more or less ephemeral groupings. The entourage of Eleanor of Aquitaine was no more, really, than a peripatetic cluster of courtiers (Kelly 1950:198–212, *passim*).

Preindustrial merchants seem led toward the creation of sodalities just as firmly as others seem led away from them (Sjoberg 1960:188–189). Their population size was not necessarily great (Sjoberg 1960:36–37). Mere density of population did not lead to their growth. Nor did they appear merely because kinship ties were too inchoate. In Europe, family ties often were weak (Lopez 1952:268, 295–296). But in parts of Africa, guilds have replaced well-developed lineage structures among urban craftsmen (Lloyd 1953). Guilds seem, above all, a response to the need for those with a shared interest in a craft or occupation to unite for economic and political power (Sjoberg 1960:190). Certainly the need for power was important in the growth of guilds in medieval Europe. While aristocrats controlled government in larger ways, merchant sodalities claimed smaller realms of commerce, small sovereignties within towns. Often they claimed the towns themselves, in which cases guild organization became town government (Carus-Wilson 1952:368–369, 373–374, 383–386; Jones 1952:510–518; Lopez 1952:295; Mumford 1961:269–273; Painter 1951:79–84; Pirenne 1956:133–134). In other parts of the world, too, merchant guilds seem more than all else a response to the need for power (Morse 1966:2–3; Miner 1965:53–60). Only through a heightened degree of self-government could merchants maintain the freedom of movement and of industry which was essential to their success, and guilds gave them that self-government (Painter 1951:71–73).

Preindustrial states, in brief, typically supported a considerable elaboration of associations within the merchant community. But among aristocrats and peasants the institution was rare. Merchants and artisans comprised only a small part of the state as a whole. Perhaps 90 per cent of the total population of such nations had no personal involvement in voluntary associations of any kind.

Industrial Nations

Modern urban-industrial growth is a worldwide phenomenon, although it first took shape in Europe and North America. Where it took place in the West, it was correlated with a new, wider development of voluntary associations (Rose 1958 *passim*). As permitted by the government—and often the government outlawed or limited them (Rose 1958 *passim*)—associations proliferated at all levels of society. The new working class joined or imitated older artisans in establishing unions. The expanded elite, its rank swelled by industrialists and businessmen, founded clubs and action groups. Cooperative associations and other sodalities spread into villages. New involvement in urban-industrial society seemed to bring with it a new need to create institutions on an intermediate level, larger than the family, yet smaller than the state (Sills 1968:373–374). A new phase in the history of voluntary associations was inaugurated.

As a prominent feature of transformed voluntary associations, their mode of operation changed. Subsequent to the evolution of democratic and bureaucratic techniques in government, and related to it, sodalities have shifted to electoral and bureaucratic norms and procedures. This new quality of associations may be characterized as rational-legal (Anderson 1965:9–12). A rational-legal association possesses written statues clearly defining the membership, participant obligations, leadership roles, and conditions of convocation. It normally possesses a legally recogized corporate identity. It is rational in the sense that as a body it is geared to efficiency in making decisions and taking action, particularly as leaders are, in principle at least, impartially chosen by election of the most qualified to take office. It is legal in the sense that compliance in decisions and actions is sanctioned by the impersonal force of law. In all these ways, a rational-legal association represents a new kind of sodality. As the industrial revolution spread throughout the world to towns and cities as well as into rural communities in urban hinterlands, new social forms spread too, including the new type of voluntary association. Rational-legal associations are now found in every part of the globe, especially in cities, but also in many rural areas (e.g., Sills 1959; Norbeck 1961:312).

What place do rational-legal associations occupy in the scheme of things? David L. Sills has pointed out how difficult it is to decide in any complete way what the social and individual benefits of voluntary associations may be (Sills 1968:372–376). Here as elsewhere, we fall very much short of our target as we look for regularities. Yet, a few can be identified. They concern the capacity associations have to facilitate the transition of individuals and societies to participation in the modern world. (See Smith 1966.)

It should be stressed immediately that rational-legal associations may be established in a traditional community in advance of substantive incorporation of that community into the new international milieu. When that occurs, whether it is in cities or in villages, the new type of association apparently does not introduce significant change in the social organization of the adopters (Anderson and Anderson 1962: 161). Quite the contrary, the intrusive sodalities seem to adapt to traditional norms. To do this the association typically retains its formal structure based on written statutes, but functions informally in terms of traditional modes of interaction. This was true, for example, of some voluntary associations established as recently as the early 1960's in Hyderabad, a city in India which has only since then wrenched substantially away from pre-industrial anachronisms (Anderson 1964:180). It seems equally true of rational-legal associations established in Sicily in the last couple of decades (Levi 1958:180–187; LaPalombara 1957:42).

It appears that modern associations not only do not in themselves introduce rational-legal modes of interaction to a traditional society, they may actually enhance the integrity of traditional social institutions. In numerous parts of Europe, voluntary associations are found to reinforce social stratification at the village level by restricting membership to individuals from a given stratum. Where this occurs, the practice symbolizes in a new way the persistence of customary strata. It also enhances the capacity of a socio-economic stratum to function as a representative, action-taking body within the community (Anderson and Anderson 1965:287–289). Far from modernizing traditional communities, rational-legal associations by themselves seem to actually enhance the capacity of old communities to persist structurally secure.

Something similar may be said for cities. Voluntary associations may play a special role for migrants. Often they allow villagers to recreate in a distant, urban milieu something of the traditional society they were accustomed to. Tribal associations in west Africa may function this way. Speaking of urbanization in that part of the world, Kenneth Little notes that ". . . of all the societies organized by migrants, voluntary associations of fellow tribesmen are often the most common." He goes on to give an example. "Ibos in Lagos at the present day belong to 'meetings' which correspond roughly with the basic social units at home—village, village group, and clan" (1968:26). Migrants transplant, in this way, traditional institutions to foreign soil. While Claude Meillassoux finds the village association only very loosely organized in Bamako, a town in Mali, he does argue that such a group ". . . is the prolongation into the city of village life and loyalties. . ." (Meillassoux 1969:78). The process is undoubtedly worldwide. Peasant Ukrainians who had migrated to towns and cities in France, for example, transplanted village customs as the activities of multipurpose associations in the host country (Anderson and Anderson 1962:162, 167–168). Michael Kenny found twentieth century Spaniards in Mexico City organized into formal voluntary associations which apparently help expatriates maintain their "ethnic identity" (1962:174).

Michael Banton and David L. Sills each have stressed the social integrative functions of urban associations (Banton 1968:361; Sills 1968:373). Banton in particular found in Freetown, Sierra Leone, that such groups meet a need for social control. By rewarding approved behavior and withholding approval or punishing that which is not approved, they dampen immorality, delinquency, and crime (1957). An important function of voluntary associations in cities, in fine, is their capacity at times to maintain a stable base for traditionalists resident in a non-traditional milieu.

Where fundamental economic and demographic changes are occurring, on the other hand, the new modernity apparently gains momentum with the help of rational-legal associations. Sometimes, the new associations seem founded to meet needs not obviously the responsibility of any older organization. Chapple and Coon see this as a dominant characteristic. "It must be remembered that, whatever the other characteristics of an association, it is always formed at the point of tangency of several institutions, or of subsystems within an institution" (1942:418). A parent-teacher association, to illustrate, joins individuals from the family with others from the school, each otherwise members of separate groups. In a comparable way, the Alaska Native Brotherhood may be said to unite clans and tribes in a new union in North America (Drucker 1958:73–74, 103–107), and the Kenya African Union welded divergent tribes together in colonial East Africa (Leakey 1952:93).

Although some associations do form on the tangents of established groupings, other bases for organization also occur. Under urban influence, the association may unite in ways not obviously related to older alignments. Edward Norbeck notes the growth of common interest groups in Japan to organize activities in villages in which real and fictive kinship had atrophied (1962:81). In Bamako, some associations group "on the sole basis of Western values: money, education, and status seeking." The older family class and tribal ties of Mali are ignored (Meillassoux 1968:145).

Often associations are neither tangential to other groups nor independent of them, but rather, reorganize or duplicate old institutions to give them a new rational-legal structure. In this way, traditional institutions remain viable in a changed society. The process may take the form of a reorganization of the old groups. S. D. Gamble reports that in eleven Chinese communities before 1933, the trend was for cooperative groups to evolve "from the informal to the formal and from the customary to the legal basis" (1963:33–42). In India, the modern success of the Ramakrishna Monastery is correlated with its formal reorganization as a rational-legal association consciously patterned on western models. The old monastic structure was submerged in the new (Gambhirananda 1957). Some castes have done the same, coopting hereditary leaders into the new structure by electing them to newly defined offices.

In many places, a traditionally organized group persists alongside of a new rational legal association with substantially the same membership. Many castes retain a traditional structure, but add to it a new caste association, its officers sometimes vying with the hereditary leadership, sometimes cooperating with it (Anderson 1963). In France, the capacity of the family to survive is enhanced by the effectiveness of family associations which supplement but certainly do not replace the traditional entities (Anderson and Anderson 1965:213–216). Tribes in East Africa organize for contemporary purposes in a similar way (Beidelman 1970; also, Banton 1956); so have secret societies in West Africa (Ruel 1964). According to Edward Norbeck, age grades in Japan have become youth associations in recent years (1953:376, 382). Kenneth Little reports that some clans in West Africa remain meaningful for migrants as modern clan associations are established in towns and cities. In the city, "A person can no longer go to a fellow clansman in the expectation of receiving help automatically in the way it was given in the past," Little observes. "The urban version of a clan, therefore, has a new hierarchy of officers and a new set of duties and privileges which are limited to registered members (1965:31–32). The establishment of rational-legal associations in cases like these apparently provides the means of adapting for modern success groups otherwise held together by traditional loyalties and obligations. It is a recurrent phenomenon which merits further study.

Part of the versatility of voluntary associations in urban-industrial circumstances is the training function they have for individuals not yet accustomed to modern role playing. It seems particularly true for individuals of tribal or peasant background. The Alaska Native Brotherhood socialized Indians to techniques necessary for success under American rule (Drucker 1958: 17–18). Philip Drucker notes that "There seems to have been a deliberate attempt to create a large number of offices in order to give as many people as possible the opportunity of getting experience in the business of the organization" (1958:23–24; see Banton 1956:366). Similarly in parts of Africa, participation in voluntary associations trains individuals in skills they can apply more widely in city life (Hamer 1967: 84–86; Little 1965:103–117). In some cases, the capacity of the association to train may be enhanced as it merges traditional with modern activities (Anderson 1966:339). As Kenneth Little has observed, ". . . by continuing such familiar norms as kinship, the provision of proper burial rites, etc., the associations make the inovations seem less strange. They build for the migrant a cultural bridge and in so doing they convey him from one kind of social universe to another" (Little 1965:87).

The educational potentiality of voluntary associations must not be exaggerated, however. In some cases, participation seems to follow rather than precede socialization of the individual to new norms. Perhaps in most cases, education only extends a process already underway, so that it constitutes a secondary, but not a primary training ground. Participation in Rotating Credit Associations in India, it has been argued, build on either traditional or modern norms, and fail therefore to teach villagers and urban migrants how to participate in commercial encounters, since traditional individuals unite in terms of older, non-commercial sanctions (Anderson 1966:339). The social clubs of Bamaka, to give another example, seem capable of polishing an individual's fluency in French and his effectiveness in urban activities. But recruitment requires a high degree of polish and effectiveness in the first place, so that the training function is additive rather than fundamental (Meillassoux 1968:138–139). Many nineteenth century Danish peasants got their first real lessons in modern involvement from joining a cooperative society. Yet it is notable that the leaders of cooperative associations typically were already transformed as individuals through earlier education in folk high schools, through participation in religious revivals and through involvement in political democracy (Rørdam 1965:155). Associations, in short, may provide the primary educational experience for some individuals, but for a population as a whole they apparently require reinforcement from other institutions.

In urban-industrial nations, voluntary associations acquire new, highly important functions. They contribute to the stability of modern societies by providing social units intermediate between the individual and the community. They seem especially effective as institutions supportive of social change. Yet voluntary associations are vehicles of change, not motors of change. They function to adapt the social structure for modern requirements. They function to adapt individuals for modern participation. But they do not create a new social structure in a traditional society, and they do not socialize an individual when circumstances more broadly are not favorable. "Voluntary associations, therefore, seem like bubbles rising and disappearing on the surface of boiling water. It is from deeper sources that the people who stir them find their motivation, and it is at more significant levels that we must try to explain a society. . ." (Meillassoux 1968:147).

REFERENCES CITED

Anderson, Robert T.

1963 Preliminary report on the associational redefinition of castes in Hyderabad-Secunderabad. Kroeber Anthropological Society Papers, No. 29.

1964 Voluntary associations in Hyderabad. Anthropological Quarterly 37(4).

1966 Rotating credit associations in India. Economic Development and Cultural Change 14(3).

1970 Traditional Europe (tenth to eighteenth centuries): a study in anthropology and history. Belmont, California: Wadsworth Publishing Co.

Anderson, Robert T., and Barbara Gallatin Anderson

1962 Voluntary associations among Ukrainians in France. Anthropological Quarterly 35(4).

1965 Bus stop for Paris: the transformation of a French village. New York: Doubleday.

Banton, Michael

1956 Adaptation integration in the social system of Temne immigrants in Freetown. Africa 26(4).

1957 West African city: a study of tribal life in Freetown. London: Oxford University Press.

1968 Voluntary associations. I. anthropological aspects. International Encyclopedia of the Social Sciences, Vol. 16. New York: Macmillan and Free Press.

Befu, Harumi

1965 Village autonomy and articulation with the state: the case of Tokugawa Japan. Journal of Asian Studies 25(1).

Beidelman, Thomas O.

1970 Umwano and Ukaguru students' association: two tribalistic movements in a Tanganyika chiefdom. *In* Black Africa: its peoples and their cultures today. John Middleton, ed. New York: Macmillan.

Boak, A. E. R.

1932 Late Roman and Byzantine guilds. Encyclopedia of the Social Sciences, Vol. 7. London: Macmillan.

Brinton, Crane

1930 Clubs. Encyclopedia of the Social Sciences, Vol. 3. London: Macmillan.

Carus-Wilson, Eleanora

1952 The woolen industry. The Cambridge Economic History of Europe, Vol. 2. Cambridge: Cambridge University Press.

Chapple, Eliot Dismore and Carleton Stevens Coon

1942 Principles of anthropology. New York: Henry Holt and Co.

Cheng Ch'eng-K'un

1953 Familism the foundation of Chinese social organization. Societies Around the World, Vol. 2. Irwin T. Sanders, et al., eds. New York: Dryden Press. (First published, 1944.)

Driver, Harold E.

1961 Indians of North America. Chicago & London: University of Chicago Press.

Drucker, Philip

1958 The native brotherhoods: modern intertribal organizations on the North-west Coast. Bulletin 1968. Smithsonian Institution. Bureau of American Ethnology. Washington, D.C.: Government Printing Office.

Elkin, A. P.

1964 The Australian aborigines. Garden City, New York: Doubleday and Co. (Originally published, 1938.)

Evans-Pritchard, E. E.

1940 The Nuer. A description of the modes of livelihood and political institutions of a Nilotic people. Oxford: Clarendon Press.

Fei Hsiao-T'ung

1946 Peasant life in China: a field study of country life in the Yangtze Valley. New York: Oxford University Press.

1953 China's gentry: essays on rural-urban relations. Chicago & London: University of Chicago Press.

Foster, George M.

1953a Cofradia and compadrazgo in Spain and Spanish America. South-western Journal of Anthropology 9(1).

1953b What is folk culture? American Anthropologist 55(2).

1965 Peasant society and the image of the limited good. American Anthropologist 67(2).

Freedman, Maurice

1958 Lineage organization in south-eastern China. London School of Economics Monographs on Social Anthropology, No. 18. London: Athlone Press.

Gambhirananda, Swami

1957 History of the Ramakrishna math and mission. Calcutta: Advaita Ashrama.

Gamble, S. D.

1963 North China villages: social, political and economic activities before 1933. Berkeley. University of California Press.

Geertz, Clifford

1959 Form and variation in Balinese village structure. American Anthropologist 61(6).

Gibbs, James L., Jr.

1965 The Kpelle of Liberia. Peoples of Africa. James L. Gibbs, Jr., ed. New York: Holt, Rinehart and Winston, Inc.

Goldschmidt, Walter
1959 Man's way: a preface to the understanding of human society. New York: Henry Holt and Co.

Hamer, John H.
1967 Voluntary associations as structures of change among the Sidamo of southwestern Ethiopia. Anthropological Quarterly 40(2).

Hsu, Francis L. K.
1949 Under the ancestors' shadow: Chinese culture and personality. London: Routledge and Kegan Paul.

Huntingford, G. W. B.
1960 Nandi age-sets. Cultures and societies of Africa. Simon and Phoebe Ottenberg, eds. New York: Random House. (First published, 1953.)

Jones, Gwilym Peredur
1952 Building in stone in medieval Western Europe. The Cambridge Economic History of Europe. Vol. II. Cambridge: Cambridge University Press.

Kelly, Amy
1950 Eleanor of Aquitaine and the four kings. New York: Random House.

Kenny, Michael
1962 Twentieth century Spain expatriates in Mexico: an urban sub-culture. Anthropological Quarterly 35(4).

Kulp, Daniel H., II
1953 Village associations. *In* Societies around the world, Vol. 2. Irwin T. Sanders, et al., eds., New York: Dryden Press. (First published, 1925.)

LaPalombara, Joseph
1957 The Italian labor movement: problems and prospects. Ithaca: Cornell University Press.

Leakey, L. S. B.
1952 Mau Mau and the Kikuyu. London: Methuen and Company.

Levi, Carol
1958 Words are stones. Impressions of Sicily. Angus Davidson, trans. New York: Farrar, Straus and Cudahy.

Little, Kenneth
1949 The role of the secret society in cultural specialization. American Anthropologist 51(2).
1965 West African urbanization: a study of voluntary associations in social change. London: Cambridge University Press.

Lloyd, Peter C.
1953 Craft organizations in Yoruba towns. Africa 23(1).

Lopez, Robert B.
1952 The trade of medieval Europe: the south. The Cambridge economic history of Europe, Vol. II. Cambridge: Cambridge University Press.

Lowie, Robert H.
1935 The Crow Indians. New York: Farrar and Rinehart, Inc.
1947 Primitive society. New York: Liveright Publishing Corporation. (First published, 1920.)
1948 Social organization. New York: Rinehart and Co.

Meillassoux, Claude
1969 Urbanization of an African community: voluntary associations in Bamako. Seattle and London: University of Washington Press.

Miller, Nathan
1934 Secret societies. Encyclopedia of the Social Sciences, Vol. 13. London: Macmillan.

Miner, Horace
1965 The primitive city of Timbuctoo. Rev. ed. New York: Doubleday. (First published, 1953.)

Morse, Hosea Ballou
1966 The gilds of China, with an account of the gild merchant or Co-Hong of Canton. Taipei: Ch'eng-Wen Publishing Co. (First published, 1909.)

Mumford, Lewis
1961 The city in history: its origins, its transformation, and its prospects. New York: Harcourt, Brace and World.

Nicoló, Mariano San
1932 Guilds in antiquity. Encyclopedia of the Social Sciences, Vol. 7. London: Macmillan.

Norbeck, Edward

1961 Cultural change and continuity in northeastern Japan. American Anthropologist 63(2) part 1.

1962 Common-interest associations in rural Japan. *In* Japanese culture: its development and characteristics. Robert J. Smith and Richard K. Beardsley, eds. Viking Fund Publications in Anthropology, No. 34.

Osgood, Cornelius

1963 Village life in old China: a community study of Kao Yao Yünnan. New York: Ronald Press.

Painter, Sidney

1951 Mediaeval society. Ithaca, New York: Cornell University Press.

Pirenne, Henri

1956 Medieval cities: their origins and the revival of trade. Tr. F. D. Halsey. Anchor Books. New York: Doubleday. (First published, 1925.)

Rose, Arnold M.

1958 The institutions of advanced societies. Minneapolis: University of Minnesota Press.

Ruel, M. J.

1964 The modern adaptation of associations among the Banyang of the West Cameroon. Southwestern Journal of Anthropology 20(1).

Rørdam, Thomas

1965 The Danish folk high schools. Sigurd Mammen, trans. Danish Information Handbooks. Copenhagen: Det Danske Selskab.

Service, Elman R.

1962 Primitive social organization: an evolutionary perspective. Studies in anthropology. New York: Random House.

1963 Profiles in ethnology. New York: Harper and Row.

Sills, David L.

1959 Voluntary associations: instruments and objects of change. Human Organization 18(1).

1968 Voluntary associations. II. Sociological aspects. International Encyclopedia of the Social Sciences, Vol. 16. New York: Macmillan and Free Press.

Sjoberg, Gideon

1960 The preindustrial city, past and present. Glencoe, Illinois: The Free Press.

Smith, David Horton

1966 The importance of formal voluntary organizations for society. Sociology and Social Research 50(4).

Titiev, Mischa

1963 The science of man, Rev. ed. New York: Holt, Rinehart and Winston.

Wilson, Monica

1963 Good company. A study of Nyakyusa age-villages. Boston: Beacon Press. (First published, 1951.)

Wolf, Eric R.

1966 Peasants. Foundations of Modern Anthropology Series. Englewood Cliffs, New Jersey: Prentice-Hall.

Yang, Martin C.

A Chinese village: Taitou, Shantung Province. New York: Columbia University Press.

Yee, Chiang

1963 A Chinese childhood. New York: W. W. Norton and Co.

SECTION III

Social, Ethnic, and Sexual Differentiation and Stratification

In many larger-scale societies a third major principle serves as the basis for organizing social groups: differences in caste status, class position, ethnic identity, or sex. Groups formed as the result of such differences are always ranked hierarchically, with some in a superior position, enjoying greater wealth, easier access to political power, higher prestige, and generally more favorable life chances—better health and longer life, greater material comfort, and superior opportunities to develop their potential.

Descending from the privileged few at the top, those groups progressively further down in the hierarchy are impeded by increasingly difficult obstacles to sharing equally in whatever benefits their society has to offer. Their group economic position is inferior, their social status is lower, and their chances of exercising political power are not as good. They always have lower prestige, and often, as in the caste system, their subordinate position in the hierarchy is reinforced by beliefs that assert their innate (even deserved) inferiority, their ritual uncleanliness, and the religious rightness of their remaining in their properly inferior place.

Berreman, who has studied them in both India and Alabama, looks critically at the ways systems of social, ethnic, and sexual differentiation and stratification work among ourselves and elsewhere, to the cultural and social detriment of us all.

ıvidious Distinctions

Gerald D. Berreman

stratified when its mem- ... ıto categories which are dif- ... erful, esteemed, and rewarded. ... s of collective social ranking vary wı ... the ideologies which support them, in the ıistinctiveness, number, and size of the ranked categories, in the criteria by which inclusion in the categories is conferred and changed, in the symbols by which such inclusion is displayed and recognized, in the degree to which there is consensus upon or even awareness of the ranking system, its rationale, and the particular ranks assigned, in the rigidity of rank, in the disparity in rewards of rank, and in the mechanisms employed to maintain or change the system.

For purposes of study, such systems have been analyzed variously depending upon the interests and motives of the analyst. One of the most frequently used bases for categorizing and comparing them has been whether people are accorded their statuses and privileges as a result of characteristics which are regarded as individually acquired, or as a result of characteristics which are regarded as innate and therefore shared by those of common birth. This dichotomy is often further simplified by application of the terms "achieved" versus "ascribed" status. Actually, what is meant is *non*-birth-ascribed status versus birth-ascribed status. The former is usually described as class stratification, referring to shared statuses identified by such features as income, education, and occupation, while the latter is frequently termed caste or racial stratification or, more recently, ethnic stratification, referring to statuses defined by shared ancestry or attributes of birth.

Regardless of its characteristics in a particular society, stratification has been described as being based upon three primary dimensions: class, status, and power, which are expressed respectively as wealth, prestige, and the ability to control the lives of people (oneself and others).[1] These dimensions can be brought readily to mind by thinking of the relative advantages and disadvantages which accrue in Western class systems to persons who occupy such occupational statuses as judge, garbage man, stenographer, airline pilot, factory worker, priest, farmer, agricultural laborer, physician, nurse, big businessman, beggar, etc. The distinction between class and birth-ascribed stratification can be made clear if one imagines that he encounters two Americans, for example, in each of the above-mentioned occupations, one of whom is white and one of whom is black. This quite literally changes the complexion of the matter. A similar contrast could be drawn if, in India, one were Brahmin and one untouchable; if in Japan one were Burakumin and one were not; if in Europe one were Jew and one were Gentile; or if, in almost any society, one were a man and one a woman. Obviously something significant has been added to the picture of stratification in these examples which is entirely missing in the first instance—something over which the individual generally has no control, which is determined at birth, which cannot be changed, which is shared by all those of like birth, which is crucial to social identity, and which vitally affects one's opportunities, rewards, and social roles. The new element is race (color), caste, ethnicity (religion, language, national origin), or sex. The differences in opportunities and behavior accorded people as a result of these criteria are described by such pejorative terms as racism, casteism, communalism (including especially ethnic and religious discrimination), and sexism. To be sure, the distinctions are manifest in class, status, and power, but they are of a different order than those considered in the first examples: they are distinctions independent of occupation, income, or other individually acquired characteristics. While the list includes a variety of criteria for birth-ascription and rank with somewhat different implications for those to whom they are applied, they share the crucial facts that: 1. the identity is regarded as being a consequence of birth or ancestry and hence immutable; 2. the

Source: From *Race,* Vol. XIII, No. 4 (April 1972), published for the Institute of Race Relations, London, by the Oxford University Press. © Institute of Race Relations, 1972. Used by permission of the publisher and the author.

1 Max Weber, *From Max Weber: Essays in Sociology,* H. H. Gerth and C. W. Mills trans. and ed. (New York, Oxford University Press, 1946); W. G. Runciman, "Class, Status and Power?" in *Social Stratification,* J. A. Jackson, ed. (London, Cambridge University Press, 1968), pp. 25–61.

identity confers upon its possessor a degree of societally defined and affirmed worth which is regarded as intrinsic to the individual; 3. this inherent worth is evaluated relative to that of all others in the society—those of different birth are inherently unequal and are accordingly adjudged superior or inferior, while those regarded as being of similar birth are innately equal. The crucial fact about birth-ascription for the individual and for society lies not so much in the source of status (birth), as in the fact that it cannot be repudiated, relinquished, or altered. Everyone is sentenced for life to a social cell shared by others of like birth, separated from and ranked relative to all other social cells. Despite cultural differences, therefore, birth-ascribed stratification has common characteristics of structure, function, and meaning, and has common consequences in the lives of those who experience it and in the social histories of the societies which harbor it.

The specific question motivating the present discussion is this: is social ranking by race absolutely distinctive, not significantly distinctive at all, or is race one criterion among others upon which significantly similar systems of social ranking may be based? While identifying the last of these as "correct" from my perspective, I shall insist that the answer depends entirely upon what one means by "race," and by "distinctive," and what one wishes to accomplish by the inquiry. No satisfactory answer can be expected without comparative, cross-cultural analysis encompassing a number of systems of social differentiation, social separation, and social ranking, based on a variety of criteria, embedded in a variety of cultural *milieux,* analyzed by reference to various models of social organization, and tested against accounts of actual social experience. The attempt to do this leads to a number of issues central and tangential to the study of stratification and race, some of which have been overlooked or given short shrift in the scholarly literature, while others are well-discussed in particular disciplinary, regional, or historical specialities without necessarily being familiar to students of other academic domains to whose work and thought they are nevertheless relevant.

There is not space here to present ethnographic and historical documentation for particular instances of birth-ascribed stratification. I have done so briefly in another paper, citing five societies on which there is fortunately excellent published material vividly exemplifying the kinds of social systems I refer to in this paper, and their implications for those who comprise them: Ruanda, India, Swat, Japan, and the United States. I recommend those accounts to the reader.[2]

[2] See for Ruanda: Jacques J. Maquet, *The Premise of Inequality in Ruanda* (London, Oxford University Press, 1961); for India: F. G. Bailey, "Closed Social Stratification in India," *European Journal of Sociology* (Vol. IV, 1963); Gerald D. Berreman, "Caste: The Concept," in *International Encyclopedia of the Social Sciences,* D. Sills, ed. (New York, Macmillan and The Free Press, 1968), Vol. II, pp. 333–9; André Béteille, *Castes Old and New* (Bombay, Asia Publishing House, 1969); Louis Dumont, *Homo Hierarchicus* (London, Weidenfeld and Nicolson, 1970); J. H. Hutton, *Caste in India, Its Nature, Functions and Origins* (London, Cambridge University Press, 1946); Adrian C. Mayer, "Caste: The Indian Caste System," in D. Sills, ed., op. cit. 339–44; M. N. Srinivas, *Caste in Modern India and Other Essays* (Bombay, Asia Publishing House, 1962), and *Social Change in Modern India* (Berkeley, University of California Press, 1966); for Swat: Fredrik Barth, "The System of Social Stratification in Swat, North Pakistan," in *Aspects of Caste in South India, Ceylon and North-West Pakistan,* E. Leach, ed. (London, Cambridge University Press, 1960), pp. 113–48; for Japan: George DeVos and Hiroshi Wagatsuma, eds., *Japan's Invisible Race: Caste in Culture and Personality* (Berkeley, University of California Press, 1966); Shigeaki Ninomiya, "An Inquiry Concerning the Origin, Development and Present Situation of the *Eta* in Relation to the History of Social Classes in Japan," *The Transactions of the Asiatic Society of Japan* (Second series, Vol. 10, 1933); cf. Herbert Passin, "Untouchability in the Far East," *Monumenta Nipponica* (Vol. 2, No. 3, 1955); for the United States: Allison Davis, B. B. Gardner, and M. R. Gardner, *Deep South: A Social Anthropological Study of Caste and Class* (Chicago, The University of Chicago Press, 1941); John Dollard, *Caste and Class in a Southern Town* (Garden City, New York, Doubleday, 1957); Gunnar Myrdal, *An American Dilemma: The Negro Problem in Modern Democracy* (New York, Harper, 1944); Alphonso Pinkney, *Black Americans* (Englewood Cliffs, New Jersey, Prentice-Hall, 1969); Peter I. Rose, ed. *Americans from Africa,* Vol. I: *Slavery and Its Aftermath* and Vol. II: *Old Memories, New Moods* (New York, Atherton Press, 1970). See also contrasts with South Africa: Pierre van den Berghe, *South Africa, a Study in Conflict* (Berkeley, University of California Press, 1967); Latin America: Marvin Harris, *Patterns of Race in the Americas* (New York, Walker, 1964); Julian Pitt-Rivers, "Race, Color and Class in Central America and the Andes," *Daedalus* (Spring, 1967); the Caribbean: M. G. Smith, *The Plural Society in the British West Indies* (Berkeley, University of California Press, 1965). G. D. Berreman, *Caste in the Modern World* (New York, General Learning Press, forthcoming).

Models for Analysis

In the course of scholarly debate concerning the nature and comparability of systems of collective social ranking, a number of models and concepts have been suggested, implied, or utilized. A framework can be provided for the present discussion by identifying some of these and analyzing whether and to what extent each is relevant and applicable to all or some systems of birth-ascribed social separation and inequality, with special attention to the five societies cited above.

STRATIFICATION. By definition, stratification is a common feature of systems of shared social inequality—or ranked social categories—whether birth-ascribed or not. Where membership in those categories is birth-ascribed, the ranking is based on traditional definitions of innate social equivalence and difference linked to a concept of differential intrinsic worth, rationalized by a myth of the origin, effect, and legitimacy of the system, perpetuated by differential power wielded by the high and the low, expressed in differential behavior required and differential rewards accorded them, and experienced by them as differential access to goods, services, livelihood, respect, self-determination, peace of mind, pleasure, and other valued things including nourishment, shelter, health, independence, justice, security, and long life.

Louis Dumont, in *Homo Hierarchicus,* maintains that the entire sociological notion of stratification is misleading when applied to South Asia, for it is of European origin, alien and inapplicable to India. He holds that the term implies an equalitarian ideology wherein hierarchy is resented or denied, and that it therefore obscures the true nature of India's hierarchical society, based as it is on religious and ideological premises peculiar to Hinduism which justify it and result in its endorsement by all segments of Indian society. Stratification, he maintains, is thus a "sociocentric" concept which cannot cope with the unique phenomenon of Indian caste.[3] My response to this is twofold: first, the caste hierarchy based on the purity-pollution opposition as Dumont insists, is well within any reasonable definition of stratification, for the latter refers to social structure and social relations rather than to their ideological bases; and second, Dumont's description of the functioning of, and ideological basis for, the caste hierarchy is idealized and similar to the one commonly purveyed by high caste beneficiaries of the system. Few low caste people would recognize it or endorse it. Yet their beliefs and understandings are as relevant as those of their social superiors to an understanding of the system. The low caste people with whom I have worked would find Dumont's characterization of "stratification" closer to their experience than his characterization of "hierarchy."[4]

Use of the stratification model focuses attention upon the ranking of two or more categories of people within a society, and upon the criteria and consequences of that ranking. Often, but not inevitably, those who use this concept place primary emphasis upon shared values and consensus, rather than power and conflict, as the bases for social ranking and its persistence. This emphasis is misleading, at best, when applied to systems of birth-ascribed ranking, as I shall show. It is obvious, however, that while many systems of stratification are not birth-ascribed, all systems of birth-ascribed ranking are systems of social stratification, and any theory of social stratification must encompass them.

ETHNIC STRATIFICATION. Probably the most recent, neutral, and non-specific term for ascriptive ranking is "ethnic stratification." "An ethnic group consists of people who conceive of themselves as being alike by virtue of common ancestry, real or fictitious, and are so regarded by others,"[5] or it comprises "a distinct category of the population in a larger society whose culture is usually different from its own [and whose] members . . . are, or feel themselves, or are thought to be, bound together by common ties of race or nationality or culture."[6] Undoubtedly the systems under discussion fit these criteria. Use of the adjective "ethnic" to modify "stratification" places emphasis upon the mode of recruitment, encompassing a wide variety of bases

[3] Dumont, op. cit.

[4] Gerald D. Berreman, "A Brahmanical View of Caste: Louis Dumont's *Homo Hierarchicus," Contributions to Indian Sociology* (New Series, No. V, 1972).

[5] Tamotsu Shibutani and Kian M. Kwan, *Ethnic Stratification: A Comparative Approach* (New York, Macmillan, 1965), p. 572.

[6] H. S. Morris, "Ethnic Groups," in D. Sills, ed., op. cit., Vol. 5, p. 167.

for ascription, all of which are determined at birth and derive from putative common genetic makeup, common ancestry, or common early socialization and are therefore regarded as immutable. This commonality is held responsible for such characteristics as shared appearance, intelligence, personality, morality, capability, purity, honor, custom, speech, religion, and so forth. Usually it is held responsible for several of these. The ranked evaluation of these characteristics, together with the belief that they occur differentially from group to group and more or less uniformly within each group serves as the basis for ranking ethnic groups relative to one another.

Van den Berghe has held that "ethnic" should be distinguished from "race" or "caste" in that the former implies real, important, and often valued social and cultural differences (language, values, social organization), while the latter are artificial and invidious distinctions reflecting irrelevant (and sometimes non-existent) differences in physiognomy, or artificial differences in social role.[7] This is a useful point. In the recent sociological literature, however, "ethnic" has increasingly been used to refer to *all* social distinctions based on birth or ancestry, be they associated with race, language, or anything else. This is the usage adopted here. Moreover, as I shall elaborate in discussing pluralism below, race and caste entail the kinds of cultural distinctions cited by van den Berghe as diagnostic of ethnic diversity, for the social separation implied by those systems ensures social and cultural diversity. For example, van den Berghe's assertion that "notwithstanding all the African mystique, Afro-Americans are in fact culturally Anglo-American,"[8] has been countered by ample evidence that the African origin, social separation, and collective oppression of blacks in America *has* resulted in an identifiable Afro-American culture.[9]

All systems of ethnic stratification are thus based on ancestry, approximating a theory of birth-ascription, and if the definitions set forth by advocates of this term are accepted, most systems of birth-ascribed stratification can properly be designated ethnic stratification. Perhaps the only recurrent exception is sexual stratification, wherein inherent, birth-ascribed, and biologically determined characteristics which are *independent* of ancestry are the basis for institutionalized inequality. This instance, exceptional in several respects, will be discussed separately below, and hence will not be alluded to repeatedly in intervening discussions although most of what is said applies to it also.

CASTE. A widely applied and frequently contested model for systems of birth-ascribed rank is that of "caste," deriving from the example of Hindu India where the *jati* (almost literally "common ancestry") is the type-case. *Jati* in India refers to interdependent, hierarchically ranked, birth-ascribed groups. The ranking is manifest in public esteem accorded the members of the various groups, in the rewards available to them, in the power they wield, and in the nature and mode of their interaction with others. *Jatis* are regionally specific and culturally distinct, each is usually associated with a traditional occupation and they are usually (but not always) endogamous. They are grouped into more inclusive, pan-Indian ranked categories called *varna* which are frequently confused with the constituent *jatis* by those using the term "caste." The rationale which justifies the system is both religious and philosophical, relying upon the idea of ritual purity and pollution to explain group rank, and upon the notions of right conduct (*dharma*), just deserts (*karma*), and rebirth to explain the individual's fate within the system. As an explanation of caste inequalities this rationale is advocated by those whom the system benefits, but is widely doubted, differently interpreted, or regarded as inappropriately applied by those whom the system oppresses.

Many students of stratification believe that the term "caste" conveys an impression of consensus and tranquillity that does not obtain in systems of rigid social stratification outside of India. That notion, however, is no more applicable to, or derivable from, Indian caste than any other instance of birth-ascribed stratification.[10]

[7] Pierre van den Berghe, "The Benign Quota: Panacea or Pandora's Box," *The American Sociologist* (Vol. 6, Supplementary Issue, June 1971).

[8] Ibid., p. 43.

[9] Cf. Robert Blauner, "Black Culture: Myth or Reality?" in Rose, *Old Memories, New Moods*, pp. 417–43.

[10] Gerald D. Berreman, "Caste in India and the United States," *The American Journal of Sociology* (Vol. LXVI, September, 1960); cf. Berreman, "A Brahmanical View of Caste . . .;" op. cit.

If one concedes that caste can be defined cross-culturally (i.e., beyond Hindu India), then the systems under discussion here are describable as caste systems. That is, if one agrees that a caste system is one in which a society is made up of birth-ascribed groups which are hierarchically ordered, interdependent, and culturally distinct, and wherein the hierarchy entails differential evaluation, rewards, and association, then whether one uses the term "caste," or prefers "ethnic stratification," or some other term is simply a matter of lexical preference. If one requires of a caste system that it be based on consensus as to its rationale, its legitimacy, and the legitimacy of the relative rank of its constituent groups, then none of the examples mentioned here is a caste system. If one requires social tranquillity as a characteristic, then too, none of these is a caste system. If one allows that a caste system is held together by power and the ability of people within it to predict fairly accurately one another's behavior while disagreeing on almost anything or everything else, then all of these systems will qualify. If one requires a specifically Hindu rationale of purity and pollution and/or endogamy and/or strict and universal occupational specialization, then one restricts caste to India and to only certain regions and groups within India at that. If one requires for castes, as some do, a tightly organized corporate structure, then too one would exclude even in India some *jatis* and other groups commonly called "castes." (This, however, does seem to me to be the structural criterion which comes closest to differentiating Indian *jati* from other systems of birth-ascribed stratification such as that of the United States. Corporateness evidently emerges as a response to oppression and as a mechanism for emancipation even where it has been previously minimal, e.g., in Japan, Ruanda, and the United States. Thus, the corporateness of Indian *jatis* may represent a late stage of development in caste systems rather than a fundamental difference in the Indian system.)

Jati in Hindu India and the equivalent but non-Hindu *quom* organization in Swat and Muslim India, are each unique, yet both share the criteria by which I have defined caste, as do the tri-partite system of Ruanda and the essentially dual systems of Japan and the United States, and all share in addition (and in consequence, I believe) a wide variety of social and personal concomitants. Caste is a useful and widely used term because it is concise, well-known, and in fact (as contrasted to phantasy), the structural, functional, and existential analogy to Indian caste is valid for many other systems.

RACE. Systems of "racial" stratification are those in which birth-ascribed status is associated with alleged physical differences among social categories, which are culturally defined as present and important. Often these differences are more imagined than real, sometimes they are entirely fictional and always a few physical traits are singled out for attention while most, including some which might differently divide the society if they were attended to, are ignored. Yet systems so described share the principle that ranking is based on putatively inborn, ancestrally derived, and significant physical characteristics.

Those who use this model for analysis generally base it upon the negative importance attached by Europeans to the darker skin color of those they have colonized, exterminated, or enslaved. A good many have argued that racially stratified societies are *sui generis*; that they are unique and hence not comparable to societies stratified on any other basis.[11] There is often a mystical quality to these arguments, as though race were an exalted, uniquely "real," valid, and important criterion for birth ascription, rendering it incomparable to other criteria. An element of inadvertent racism has in such instances infected the very study of race and stratification. In fact, as is by now widely recognized, there is no society in the world which ranks people on the basis of biological race, i.e., on the basis of anything a competent geneticist would call "race," which means on the basis of distinctive shared genetic makeup derived from a common gene pool. "Race," as a basis for social rank, is always a *socially* defined phenomenon which at most only very imperfectly corresponds to genetically transmitted traits and then, of course, only to phenotypes rather than genotypes. Racists regard and treat people as alike or different because of their group membership defined in terms of socially significant ancestry, not because of their genetic makeup. It could not be otherwise, for

[11] Oliver C. Cox, "Race and Caste: A Distinction," *The American Journal of Sociology* (Vol. L, March, 1945); cf. Oliver C. Cox, *Caste, Class and Race* (Garden City, New York, Doubleday, 1948).

people are rarely geneticists, yet they are frequently racists.

To state this point would seem to be superfluous if it were not for the fact that it is continually ignored or contested by some influential scholars and politicians as well as the lay racists who abound in many societies. To cite but one well-known recent example, Arthur Jensen, in his article on intelligence and scholastic achievement, maintains that there is a genetic difference in learning ability between blacks and whites in the United States.[12] Nowhere, however, does he offer evidence of how or to what extent his "Negro" and "White" populations are genetically distinct. All of those, and only those, defined in the conventional wisdom of American folk culture to be "Negro" are included by Jensen, regardless of their genetic makeup, in the category whose members he claims are biologically handicapped in learning ability. Thus, large numbers of people are tabulated as "Negroes," a majority of whose ancestors were "white," and virtually all of Jensen's "Negroes" have significant but highly variable percentages of "white" ancestry. Although, also as a result of social definition, the "whites" do not have known "Negro" ancestry, the presumed genetic homogeneity of the "whites" is as undemonstrated and unexplored as that of the "Negroes." In short, there was no attempt to identify the genetic makeup or homogeneity of either group, the genetic distinctiveness of the two groups, or whether or how genetic makeup is associated with learning ability, or how learning ability is transmitted. This kind of reasoning is familiar and expectable in American racism but not in a supposedly scientific treatise—a treatise whose author berates those who deplore his pseudoscience as themselves unscientific for failing to seriously consider his "evidence." The fallacy in Jensen's case is that he has selected for investigation two socially defined groupings in American society which are commonly regarded as innately different in social worth and which as a result are accorded widely and crucially divergent opportunities and life experiences. Upon finding that they perform differentially in the context of school and test performance, he attributes that fact to assumed but undemonstrated and uninvestigated biological differences. Thus, socially defined populations perform differently on socially defined tasks with socially acquired skills, and this is attributed by Jensen to biology. There are other defects in Jensen's research, but none more fundamental than this.[13] One is reminded of E. A. Ross's succinct assessment of over fifty years ago, that "race" is the cheap explanation tyros offer for any collective trait that they are too stupid or too lazy to trace to its origin in the physical environment, the social environment, or historical conditions."[14]

The point to be made here is that systems of "racial" stratification are social phenomena based on social rather than biological facts. To be sure, certain conspicuous characteristics which are genetically determined or influenced (skin color, hair form, facial conformation, stature, etc.) are widely used as convenient indicators by which ancestry and hence "racial" identity is recognized. This is the "color bar" which exists in many societies. But such indicators are never sufficient in themselves to indicate group membership and in some instances are wholly unreliable, for it is parentage rather than appearance or genetics which is the basis for these distinctions. One who does not display the overt characteristics of his "racial" group is still accorded its status if his relationship to the group is known or can be discovered. The specific rules for ascertaining racial identity differ from society to society. In America, if a person is known to have had a sociologically black ancestor, he is black regardless of how many of his ancestors were sociologically white (and even though he looks and acts white). In South Africa, most American blacks would be regarded as "colored" rather than "black." Traditionally, in a mixed marriage, one is a Jew only if one's mother is a Jew. In contemporary India, an Anglo-Indian has a male European ancestor in the paternal line; female and maternal European ancestry are irrelevant. In racially stratified societies, phenotypical traits are thus never more than clues to a person's social identity.

As Shibutani and Kwan have noted, "a color line is something existing in the presuppositions

[12] Arthur R. Jensen, "How Much Can We Boost I.Q. and Scholastic Achievement?" *Harvard Educational Review* (Vol. 39, No. 1, Winter, 1969).

[13] See the various articles comprising the "Discussion" of Jensen's article in *Harvard Educational Review* (Vol. 39, No. 2, Spring, 1969).

[14] E. A. Ross, *Social Psychology* (New York, Macmillan, 1914), p. 3.

of men," [15] ". . . what is decisive about race relations is not that people are genetically different but that they approach one another with dissimilar perspectives." [16] Van den Berghe makes a similar point: "Race, of course, has no intrinsic significance, except to a racist. To a social scientist, race acquires meaning only through its social definition in a given society." [17]

This is illustrated by the title of DeVos and Wagatsuma's book, *Japan's Invisible Race*, dealing with the hereditarily stigmatized and oppressed Burakumin. The Japanese believe that these people are physically and morally distinct, and their segregation and oppression are explained on that basis when in fact they are not so at all. Instead they are recognizable only by family (ancestry), name, occupation, place of residence, life style, etc. The Burakumin thus comprise a "race" in the sociological sense of Western racism, but an "invisible" (i.e., not genetic or phenotypic) one. The authors subtitled the book, *Caste in Culture and Personality*, shifting the analogy from that of race (in the West) to that of caste (in India). The book could as well have been entitled: *Caste in Japan: Racial Stratification in Culture and Personality*.

The Japanese example brings up a point which needs to be made about the alleged uniqueness of "racial" stratification. *All* systems of birth-ascribed stratification seem to include a belief that the social distinctions are reflected in biological (i.e., "racial") differences. That is, caste and other ethnic differences are said to be revealed in physical makeup or appearance. Associated with these supposed natural and unalterable inherited physical characteristics are equally immutable traits of character, morality, intelligence, personality, and purity. This is the case in Japan, where no actual physical differences can be detected; it is true in India and Swat where physical stereotypes about castes abound but actual differences are minimal; it is true in Ruanda where the ranked groups all are black but are said to differ in stature and physiognomy as well as in culture; it is true in the United States where the physical differences are commonly and erroneously thought to be absolute. Cultural factors have to be relied upon in addition to whatever biological ones may be present, in order to make the important discriminations upon which ranked social interaction depends, and even then mistakes are frequently made. Throughout the world, people who look distinctive are likely to be regarded as socially different; people who are regarded as socially different are likely to be thought to look distinctive. They are also likely to be required to dress and act distinctively.

I suggest that, just as societies frequently dramatize the social differences among kin groups (e.g., sibs, clans, phratries) by giving to them totemic names and attributing to them characteristics of animals or plants, thereby identifying the social differences with biological species differences,[18] so also, societies with birth-ascribed status hierarchies dramatize and legitimize *these* crucial social differences by attributing to them innate biological, hence "racial," differences. As a result, the concept of miscegenation arises, based on an ideology of innate difference contradicted by a persistent and recurrent perception of similarity by people of opposite sex across social boundaries.[19]

Thus, caste organization and ethnic stratification include racism; racial stratification is congruent with caste and ethnic stratification. Their ultimate coalescence is in the imputation of biological differences to explain and justify birth-ascribed social inequality. In this regard, sexual stratification can be seen to be a phenomenon of the same order.

This universality of racism in birth-ascribed stratification can be understood in the fact that physical traits not only dramatize social differentiation, but can also explain and justify it. The effect of such explanation is to make social inequality appear to be a natural necessity rather than a human choice and hence an artificial imposition. Social distinctions are man-made and learned; what man makes and learns he can unmake and unlearn. What God or biology has ordained is beyond man's control. The former may be defined as artificial, unjust, untenable, and remediable; the latter as inevitable or div-

15 Shibutani and Kwan, op. cit., p. 37.

16 Ibid., p. 110.

17 Pierre van den Berghe, *Race and Racism* (New York, Wiley, 1967), p. 21.

18 Claude Lévi-Strauss, "The Bear and the Barber," *Journal of the Royal Anthropological Institute* (Vol. 93, Part 1, 1963).

19 Winthrop D. Jordan, *White Over Black* (Baltimore, Penguin Books, 1969), pp. 137–8.

inely sanctioned. This is important because birth-ascribed stratification is widely or universally resented by those whom it oppresses (at least as it affects them), and advocated by those it rewards. Both categories share the human capability of empathy, and it inspires envy and resentment in the one and fear or guilt in the other. Racism—the self-righteous rationalization in terms of biology—is a desperate and perhaps ultimately futile attempt to counteract those subversive emotions.

In sum, "race," as commonly used by social scientists, emphasizes common physical characteristics (as does "sex"); "caste" emphasizes common rank, occupational specialization, endogamy, and corporate organization; "ethnic stratification" emphasizes cultural distinctiveness. These are real differences in meaning, but the degree of empirical overlap in systems so described, and the commonalities in the existential worlds of those who live within them are so great as to render the distinctions among them largely arbitrary, and irrelevant, for many purposes. Individual cases differ, but as types of social stratification, they are similar. With equal facility and comparable effect, they utilize as evidence of social identity anything which is passed on within the group: skin color, hair form, stature, physiognomy, language, dress, occupation, place of residence, genealogy, behavior patterns, religion. None is wholly reliable, all are difficult to dissimulate. In any case, strong sanctions can be brought to bear to minimize the temptation to "pass" among those who might be capable and tempted. As the case of India suggests and Japan confirms, social criteria can be as rigid as physical ones.

"RACE" VERSUS "CASTE." Considerable controversy has surrounded the terms "race" and "caste" when applied outside of the contexts in which they originated and to which they have been most widely applied: Western colonialism and Hindu India, respectively. This is understandable because there are important peculiarities in each of these situations, and to extend the terms beyond them requires that those peculiarities be subordinated to significant similarities. Systems of birth-ascribed inequality are sufficiently similar, however, to invite comparative study, and some general term is needed to refer to them. "Caste" has seemed to me more useful than "race," because it refers to social rather than allegedly biological distinctions, and it is the social distinctions which are universal in such systems. If it were a catchier term, "ethnic stratification" might replace both in the social scientific literature. Unfortunately it is not, so we must probably await a better term or tolerate continuing terminological dispute and confusion. In any case, it is the nature of birth-ascribed stratification—the ideas, behaviors, and experiences, which comprise it, the effects it has on persons and societies and, quite frankly, the means by which it may be eliminated—in which I am interested. The words applied to it are of little importance. When I try to explain American race relations to Indians, I describe and analyze America as a caste stratified society, with attention to the similarities and differences in comparison with India. If I am trying to explain Indian caste stratification to Americans, I describe and analyze India as a racist society, with attention to the similarities and differences in comparison to the United States. I do this as a matter of translation from the social idiom of one society to the other. It is the most economic, vivid, and accurate way I know to convey these phenomena to people whose experience is limited to one system or the other. I do not think Indian caste *is* American race, or vice versa, but neither do I think that race stratification in America *is* race stratification in South Africa, or that caste in India *is* caste in Swat, or that caste in the Punjab *is* caste in Kerala. Neither do I think racial stratification and racism are the same for blacks, Chicanos, and whites in America, or that caste stratification and racism are the same for sweepers, blacksmiths, and Rajputs in Hindu India. There are features in all of these which are the same in important ways, and by focusing on these I think we can understand and explain and predict the experience of people in these diverse situations better than if we regard each of them as unique in every way.

Objections to the cross-cultural comparison of race and caste depend either on an insistence that the two would have to be wholly identical to justify such comparison, or more commonly, on misconceptions about one or both of the systems being compared. It is worthwhile to identify and comment upon some of these objections.

1. The most prevalent objection among experts on Western social stratification is that caste status is accepted and endorsed by those in the system whereas racial stratification is objected to and striven against by those it oppresses. Thus Cox asserts that "while the caste system may be

thought of as a social order in stable equilibrium, the domination of one race by another is always an unstable situation. . . . The instability of the situation produces what are known as race problems, phenomena unknown to the caste system." I have contended with this claim in some detail elsewhere.[20] Suffice it to say here that anyone who has known low caste people in India can affirm that this particular contrast is imaginary, as can anyone who knows the history of religious conversion, social reform, and social mobility striving in India, who has followed the reports of the Commissioner of Scheduled Castes and Tribes, or who simply reads the news releases from India today.

2. It is often argued that caste in India is unique and noncomparable because of the elaborate religio-philosophical rationale which underlies it, and that racial stratification is unique because it is based on color.[21] As I have pointed out, these contentions are questionable on empirical grounds. Few would deny, for example, that caste exists in Swat as well as India, and that it exists in Mysore, India, among both the Lingayats and the Hindus, yet the rationale is very different in each of these cases. On the other hand, few would deny that color consciousness is an important part of the ideology and metaphor of caste in India.

But on another level, these arguments are not necessarily relevant to the issue of comparison. That phenomena are in some respects different does not make them incomparable. They may still be similar in crucial respects. Everything is, after all, unique, but there can be no science of the unique. The claim for comparability can be refuted by showing that the facts are in error, or that the interpretations of their significance are fallacious, not by citing differences extraneous to the argument being made. Moreover, comparability (or incomparability) for one purpose or in one context does not imply comparability (or incomparability) for another purpose or in another context. The test must be whether or not and how well explanation can be derived from a particular comparison.

If one knows that a society is characterized by birth-ascribed stratification, he can predict a great deal about the experiences and attitudes of people at different levels within it, about the social, political, and economic behavior they are likely to engage in under various circumstances, and about the nature and consequences of social conflict.[22] This, to my mind, justifies the comparison.

3. A number of specific characteristics of caste in India or race in the West have been cited as bases for non-comparability with other systems of birth-ascribed stratification. (a) *Endogamy* has been cited as essential to caste. However, what is crucial and universal in a caste system is not endogamy, but birth-ascribed membership in a ranked category or group. Endogamy is the most common method for achieving this in India and elsewhere, but a firm patrilineal or matrilineal rule of status assignment will do as well, and so will a rule which assigns to an individual the caste of his higher status parent or of his lower status parent, or one which designates that an individual whose parents are of castes A and B will be of caste C. All of these rules of birth-ascription occur in South Asian castes.[23]

(b) *Occupational distinctiveness* has been cited as essential to caste. This is indeed an almost inevitable concomitant of social separation, stratification, and interdependence, be it birth-ascribed or not. But again, it is not universal among castes even in India, nor is it lacking in racial and sexual stratification. Some have maintained that caste, without a conspicuous racial basis, cannot exist in a complex society simply because the anonymity of such a society would make dissimulation and passing too easy to sustain a caste system where no physical indicators

[20] Cox, *Caste, Class and Race,* p. 433, cf. Berreman, "Caste in India and the United States," op. cit.; Berreman, "A Brahmanical View of Caste . . . ," op. cit.: Gerald D. Berreman, "Caste, Racism and 'Stratification,'" *Contributions to Indian Sociology* (No. VI, December 1962); Martin Orans, "Caste and Race Conflict in Cross-Cultural Perspective," in *Race, Change and Urban Society,* P. Orleans and W. R. Ellis, eds., comprising *Urban Affairs Annual Reviews* (Vol. 5, 1971).

[21] Dumont, op. cit., Cox, *Caste, Class and Race.*

[22] Berreman, "Caste in India and the United States," op. cit., Gerald D. Berreman, "Caste in Cross-Cultural Perspective: Organizational Components" comprising Chapter 14, "Structure and Function of Caste Systems," and Chapter 15, "Concomitants of Caste Organization," in *Japan's Invisible Race,* DeVos and Wagatsuma, eds., op. cit.; Gerald D. Berreman, "Stratification, Pluralism and Interaction: A Comparative Analysis of Caste," in *Caste and Race: Comparative Approaches,* A. de Reuck and J. Knight, eds., (London, J. and A. Churchill, 1967); Orans, op. cit.

[23] Cf. Berreman, "Caste in Cross-Cultural Perspective . . . ," op. cit., pp. 279–81.

of identity existed.[24] It is probably true that in the anonymity and mobility of contemporary urban life, rigid ethnic stratification is increasingly difficult to maintain when the indicators of identity are learned, for learned characteristics can be unlearned, suppressed, or learned by those to whom they are inappropriate. To manipulate these indicators is often difficult, as the persistence of the Burakumin of Japan makes clear, because the identifying characteristics may be learned very early (language, gesture), and may be enforced from without as well as from within (dress, deference, occupation), but it is possible, as instances of passing make clear.[25] The more personal relationships of traditional, small-scale societies, together with their formal and informal barriers and sanctions against casual or promiscuous interaction militate against the learning or expression of inappropriate status characteristics and conspicuous indicators of status are largely unnecessary. Reliable, immutable, and conspicuous indicators of identity are thus more important to systems of birth-ascribed stratification in the anonymity and mobility of the city than in the village, but the internal pressures of ethnic pride combined with the external pressures of ethnic discrimination and the vested interests which sustain it make such systems possible in even the most unlikely-seeming circumstances.

(c) Some have argued that the corporate structure of many Indian castes renders them incomparable to most instances of ethnic stratification, a point which I have discussed above . . . and will therefore not repeat.

(d) The comparison between black-white stratification in America and Indian caste is occasionally contested on grounds that the former is a *dichotomy* while the latter is a *complex hierarchy*. This is a real difference between the two, but it does not make them incomparable. It is a difference in numbers of groups, not in race versus caste. For one thing, there are other racial or caste-like groups in American society: Native Americans, Chicanos, Puerto Ricans, Asians, etc. In India, on the other hand, most interaction is not caste specific so much as it is specific to categories of castes (categories such as "untouchables," "twice-born," the *varnas*, etc.), thereby simplifying the interactional situation greatly. For example, the *Khas-Dom* (twice-born versus untouchable) dichotomy in the mountain area of my research[26] and the Brahmin-non-Brahmin dichotomy in South India are quite comparable to the situation described as the color-bar elsewhere. One probable difference between dichotomous and multiple hierarchies may be that in the former the oppressed characteristically oppose the system as such. To rise within it would be to displace the privileged—to reverse the hierarchy—and that is impracticable. To overthrow the system is to erase their oppression and vice versa. They have nothing to lose but their inferiority. In multiple hierarchies, objection may more characteristically be made not to the system, but to the place of one's own group within it, the reason being that to overthrow the system is not feasible for any one of the many groups within it, each of which is relatively small, weak, and in competition with others. Moreover, successful overthrow would result not only in equality with elites, but equality with erstwhile inferiors. Therefore, it is regarded as more practicable and more rewarding to attempt to rise within the system than to eliminate the system itself. These remarks apply to systems of birth-ascribed stratification regardless of the criteria used.

(e) Finally, it is sometimes held that racial stratification is an outgrowth of Western colonialism, and hence India can be regarded as an example thereof only in the relationship of Indians to the British, not in the relationship among indigenous castes. I would maintain that caste in India is in fact a product of colonialism and that its present manifestations are closely analogous to the "internal colonialism" which Blauner, among others, has described for the United States (see below).[27] In India this is an instance of what has recently been termed "fourth-world" colonialism, i.e., exploitation inflicted by "third-world" (non-Western) people on their internal minorities, analogous to that they have often experienced themselves at the hands

[24] F. G . Bailey, "Closed Social Stratification in India," op. cit., p. 113.

[25] Cf., George DeVos and Hiroshi Wagatsuma, "Group Solidarity and Individual Mobility" in *Japan's Invisible Race,* pp. 245–8; Harold R. Isaacs, *India's Ex-Untouchables* (New York, John Day Company, 1965), pp. 143–9 et passim.

[26] Gerald D. Berreman, *Hindus of the Himalayas: Ethnography and Change* (Berkeley, University of California Press, 1972), pp. 200 ff.

[27] Robert Blauner, "Internal Colonialism and Ghetto Revolt," *Social Problems* (Vol. 16, No. 4, Spring, 1969); Robert Blauner, *Racial Oppression in America* (New York, Harper and Row, 1972).

of "first-" and "second-world" colonialists (Western non-communist and communist nations, respectively).

In short, the further one probes into the nature and dynamics of race and caste, and into the experience of those who live them, the more it becomes apparent that they are similar, comparable, phenomena.

COLONIALISM. The concept of colonialism has gained popularity in recent years for the analysis of racism and racial stratification in the West.[28] It therefore merits further discussion. This model focuses on the history of Western expansion and the exploitation of alien peoples, emphasizing notions of the superiority of the dominant, Western, white society whose members arrogated privilege to themselves through the exercise of power (usually technological, often military) to dominate, control, exploit, and oppress others. Racism has been an integral aspect of this process, for there usually have been differences in color between the colonizer and the colonized which were used to account for the alleged inferiority in ability, character, and mentality which in turn were used to justify colonial domination. Colonialism has been most often described as the result of overseas conquest, in which case the colonizing group has usually comprised a numerical minority. Less often colonialism has included conquest or expansion across national boundaries overland, but the results are the same, if the romance is less. These phenomena have recently come to be termed "external colonialism," in contrast to "internal colonialism" which refers to similar domination and exploitation, within a nation, of an indigenous, over-run, or imported minority. This distinction directs attention to the *locus* of colonial domination whereas the distinction between third-world and fourth-world colonies cited above, directs attention to the *sources* of that domination.

While it has not been much easier to gain acceptance of the colonial model for analysis of American race relations than it has been to gain acceptance of the caste model, it is clear that here again, the problem is semantic rather than substantive. Some of those who argue persuasively the cross-cultural and multi-situational applicability of the colonial model, deny such applicability for the caste model and in so doing use precisely the logic and data they deplore and regard as faulty when their intellectual adversaries deny applicability of "colonialism" outside of the classical overseas context.[29]

Colonialism, external and internal, is a process which has occurred repeatedly, in many contexts, with many specific manifestations and many common results. It long antedates the recent period of European and American expansion. Caste stratification, racial stratification, ethnic stratification, and "pluralism" have been its recurrent products.[30] The point can be made with specific reference to caste in India. Rather than regarding colonialism as an antecedent condition which excludes traditional India from the category of racially or ethnically stratified societies, it can well be used as a basis for assigning India historical priority among such societies, in the contemporary world. That is, traditional India may represent the most fully evolved and complex post-colonial society in the world. It is easy to obtain explanations of caste from informants or books in India which refer directly to the presumed early domination of primitive indigenes by advanced invaders. There is little doubt that the present caste system had its origins some 3,000 to 3,500 years ago in a socio-cultural confrontation that was essentially colonial. Low status was imposed on technologically disadvantaged indigenes by more sophisticated, militarily and administratively superior peoples who encroached or invaded from the north and west, arrogating to themselves high rank, privileges, and land. The large number of local and ethnic-

28 Cf., Blauner, "Internal Colonialism . . . ," op. cit.; Stokely Carmichael and Charles Hamilton, *Black Power* (New York, Random House, 1967); Frantz Fanon, *The Wretched of the Earth* (New York, Grove Press, 1966); O. Mannoni, *Prospero and Caliban: The Psychology of Colonization* (New York, Praeger, 1956); Albert Memmi, *The Colonizer and the Colonized* (Boston, Beacon Press, 1967).

29 Cf. Blauner, "Internal Colonialism . . . ," pp. 395–6.

30 Gerald D. Berreman, "Caste as Social Process," *Southwestern Journal of Anthropology* (Vol. 23, No. 4, Winter, 1967); Blauner, *Racial Oppression in America*; S. F. Nadel, "Caste and Government in Primitive Society," *Journal of the Anthropological Society of Bombay* (Vol. 8, 1954); J. S. Furnivall, *Colonial Policy and Practice: A Comparative Study of Burma and Netherlands India* (London, Cambridge University Press, 1948) ; M. G. Smith, *The Plural Society in the British West Indies* (Berkeley, University of California Press, 1965); James B. Watson, "Caste as a Form of Acculturation," *Southwestern Journal of Anthropology* (Vol. 19, No. 4, Winter 1963).

ally distinct groups on the sub-continent were fitted into a scheme of social hierarchy which was brought in or superimposed by the high status outsiders, culminating in the caste system we know today.[31] Social separation and social hierarchy based on ancestry became the essence of the system; colonial relations were its genesis. Even today, most tribal people—those who are geographically and economically marginal and culturally distinct—are incorporated into Hindu society, if at all, at the bottom of the hierarchy (except in those rare instances where they have maintained control over land or other important sources of income and power).

If one were to speculate on the course of evolution which ethnic stratification might take in the United States in the context of internal colonialism, of rigid separation, hierarchy, and discrimination which are part of it, and the demands for ethnic autonomy which arise in response to it, one possibility would be a caste system similar to, though less complex than that of India. The historical circumstances may be rather similar despite the separation of many hundreds of years, many thousands of miles and a chasm of cultural difference. Actually, development of the degree of social separation common in India seems at this point unlikely given the mass communications and mass education in the United States, its relative prosperity, and the rather widespread (but far from universal) commitment to at least the trappings of social equality. But surely if anything is to be learned from history and from comparison, the case of the Indian subcontinent should be of major interest to students of American race and ethnic relations, social stratification, and internal colonialism.

In sum, colonialism is as inextricable from caste and race as caste and race are from one another. There may be instances of colonialism where birth-ascription is or becomes irrelevant, but every instance of caste, race, and ethnic stratification includes, and relies for its perpetuation upon, the kind of ethnic domination and exploitation that defines colonialism.

Class. Closely associated with each of the models discussed here is that of social class. Class is a matter of acquired status rather than of birth-ascription, and is in this respect distinct from race, caste, and ethnic stratification, with different social consequences. In a class system, one is ranked in accord with his behavior and attributes in accord with his rank. In a class system, individual mobility is legitimate, albeit often difficult, while in ascribed stratification it is explicitly forbidden. Systems of acquired rank—class systems—prescribe the means to social mobility; systems of ascribed rank proscribe them. As a consequence, a class system is a continuum; there are individuals who are intergrades, there are individuals in the process of movement, there are individuals who have experienced more than one rank. Miscegenation is not an issue because there are no ancestrally distinct groups to be inappropriately mixed. A birth-ascribed system is comprised of discrete ranks on the pattern of echelon organization, without legitimate mobility, without intergrades; the strata are named, publicly recognized, clearly bounded. Miscegenation is therefore a social issue. In a system of acquired ranks, the strata may be indistinct, imperfectly known, or even unknown to those within the system. In fact, there is considerable debate among students of stratification as to whether or not awareness of class is essential to a definition of class. Some hold that social classes are properly defined by social analysts who use such criteria as income to designate categories which may be entirely unrecognized by those in the society.

In a class system individuals regard themselves as potentially able to change status legitimately within the system through fortune, misfortune, or individual and family efforts. In a birth-ascribed system, individuals know that legitimate status change is impossible—that only dissimulation, revolution, or an improbable change in publicly accorded social identity can alter one's rank and hence life-chances.

Despite these differences, class is in no way incompatible with birth-ascribed systems. In fact, in so far as it is a term for categories of people ranked by income, occupation, education, and life style, it co-occurs with them. Low castes, despised races, ethnic minorities, and colonized people comprise economically and occupationally depressed, exploited classes who are politically and socially oppressed; high castes, exalted races privileged ethnic groups, and colonizers comprise economically and occupationally privileged, power-wielding, elite classes who live off

[31] Cf. Irawati Karve, *Hindu Society: An Interpretation* (Poona, Deccan College Postgraduate and Research Institute, 1961).

the labor of others. In this respect, class differences pervade and reinforce systems of birth-ascribed stratification. Furthermore, it is not unusual to find significant class differentials within a caste, racial, or ethnic group or within a colonized or colonial group.[32] That is, class, in the conventional sense often occurs conspicuously within such groups, and may also bridge their boundaries without obscuring them. But it is not possible to analyze birth-ascribed stratification solely in terms of class, for no amount of class mobility will exempt a person from the crucial implications of his birth in such systems.

Those who have sought to identify the positions of European immigrants to America such as the Poles, Italians, and Irish, with the position of blacks, Native Americans, Chicanos, and Asians have failed to discern the essential fact that racism is the basis of American caste, and that it bestows upon those who experience it a unique social, political, and economic stigma which is not bestowed by class or national origin. Second generation white Europeans can meet all of the criteria for acceptance into the American white race-caste for they are regarded as being only culturally different. A fifteenth generation American black, or a fifteen-hundredth generation American Indian cannot, for their differences are regarded as innate, immutable, and crucial. Equalitarianism has produced no "American dilemma" among racists, as Myrdal believed, simply because it is an equality for whites only, and its extension to other groups has moved slowly, painfully, and with vehement opposition, even where it has moved at all.

Systems of collective social rank, whether ascribed or acquired, are systems for retaining privilege among the powerful and power among the privileged, reserving and maintaining vulnerability, oppression, and want for those upon whom it can be imposed with minimal risk while retaining their services and their deference. In this way they are similar. In the principles of recruitment and organization by which that similarity is effected and in the individuals' prospects for mobility they differ, and those differences have important consequences for individual life experience and social processes in the societies which harbor them.

PLURALISM. Pluralism is a model which has been applied to socially and culturally diverse societies since the writings of Furnivall on South-East Asia.[33] Cultural pluralism obtains when "two or more different cultural traditions characterize the population of a given society"; it is "a special form of differentiation based on institutional divergences."[34] Systems of birth-ascribed stratification are inevitably systems of social and cultural pluralism because they are accompanied by social separation. In a caste system, "Because intensive and status-equal interaction is limited to the caste, a common and distinctive caste culture is assured. This is a function of the quality and density of communication within the group, for culture is learned, shared and transmitted."[35] The same is true for any system of racial or ethnic stratification. M. G. Smith has noted, "it is perfectly clear that in any social system based on intense cleavages and discontinuity between differentiated segments the community of values or social relations between these sections will be correspondingly low. This is precisely the structural condition of the plural society."[36] And I have noted elsewhere that,

> . . . castes are discrete social and cultural entities. . . . They are maintained by defining and maintaining boundaries between castes; they are threatened when boundaries are compromised. Even when interaction between castes is maximal and cultural differences are minimal, the ideal of mutual isolation and distinctiveness is maintained and advertised among those who value the system. Similarly, even when mobility within, or subversion of the system is rampant, a myth of stability is stolidly maintained among those who benefit from the system.[37]

Mutual isolation of social groups inevitably leads to group-specific institutions (an important cri-

32 Davis, Gardner, and Gardner, op. cit.; St. Clair Drake and Horace R. Cayton, *Black Metropolis* (New York, Harcourt, Brace, 1945); Dollard, op. cit.; Marina Wikramanayake, "Caste and Class Among Free Afro-Americans in Ante-bellum South Carolina," paper delivered before the 70th Annual Meeting of the American Anthropological Association (New York, November 1971).

33 Furnivall, op. cit.; cf. Malcolm Cross, ed., *Special Issue on Race and Pluralism, Race* (Vol. XII, No. 4, April 1971).

34 M. G. Smith, op. cit., pp. 14, 83.

35 Berreman "Stratification, Pluralism and Interaction . . . ," op. cit., p. 51.

36 M. G. Smith, op. cit., p. xi.

37 Berreman, "Stratification, Pluralism and Interaction . . . ," op. cit., p. 55.

terion for pluralism according to Furnivall), because members are excluded from participation in the institutions of other groups.

Caste, race, and ethnic stratification, like all plural systems therefore, are systems of social separation and cultural heterogeneity, maintained by common or over-riding economic and political institutions rather than by agreement or consensus regarding the stratification system and its rationale.[38] This does not deny consensus, it only defines its nature:

> In caste systems, as in all plural systems, highly differentiated groups get along together despite widely differing subjective definitions of the situation because they agree on the objective facts of what is happening and what is likely to happen—on who has the power, and how, under what circumstances, and for what purposes it is likely to be exercised. They cease to get along when *this* crucial agreement changes or is challenged.[39]

The constituent social elements of plural societies need not be birth-ascribed, and they need not be (and sometimes are not) ranked relative to one another, although by Furnivall's definition, one element must be dominant. In fact, unranked pluralism is the goal many ethnic minorities choose over either stratification or assimilation. But a system of birth-ascribed stratification is always culturally, socially and hence institutionally heterogeneous, and thus pluralistic.

HIERARCHY AS SYMBOLIC INTERACTION. I have elsewhere described the universality among social hierarchies of patterns of interaction which symbolize superiority and inferiority.[40] Social hierarchy, after all, exists only in the experiences, behaviors, and beliefs of those who comprise it. Interpersonal interaction becomes the vehicle for expression of hierarchy: for asserting, testing, validating, or rejecting claims to status. Almost every interaction between members of ranked groups expresses rank claimed, perceived, or accorded. When the hierarchy is birth-ascribed, the membership of its component groups is ideally stable, well-known, and easily recognizable. In such systems people are perceived by those outside of their groups almost wholly in terms of their group identity rather than as individuals. They are regarded as sharing the characteristics which are conventionally attributed to the group and they share the obligations, responsibilities, privileges, and disabilities of their group. In intergroup relations, therefore, one individual is substitutable for another in his group, for all are alike and interchangeable. This is the setting for prejudice, discrimination, bigotry, chauvinism, and is an ideal situation for scapegoating. These attitudes and their behavioral consequences are designated and deplored by such terms as racism, casteism, communalism (referring to ethnic chauvinism of various sorts), and recently, sexism. They are characterized by domination, deprivation, oppression, exploitation, and denigration directed downward; obedience, acquiescence, service, deference, and honor demanded from above. They result in envy, resentment, dissimulation, and resistance arising from below, balanced from above by fear, guilt, and that combination of arrogant self-righteousness and rationalization which is found in all such systems. Maya Angelou has aptly characterized the result in American race relations as "the humorless puzzle of inequality and hate"; "the question of worth and values, of aggressive inferiority and aggressive arrogance"[41] which confronts and exacts its toll not only from black Americans, but from the denizens of all those jungles of inherited inequality I call caste systems. It is this quality of interpersonal relations rather than any particular event or structural feature which struck me most vividly, forcefully, and surprisingly as similar in Alabama and India when I first experienced them for over a year each within a period of five years.[42] For me, this is the hallmark of oppressive, birth-ascribed stratification.

A specifically interactional definition of caste systems applies equally to all systems of birth-ascribed stratification: *"a system of birth-ascribed groups each of which comprises for its members the maximum limit of status-equal interaction, and between all of which interaction is consistently hierarchical."*[43] The cultural symbols of

[38] Cf. Furnivall, op. cit.

[39] Berreman, "Stratification, Pluralism and Interaction . . . ," op. cit., p. 55.

[40] Ibid., cf. McKim Marriott, "Interactional and Attributional Theories of Caste Ranking," *Man in India* (Vol. 39, 1959).

[41] Maya Angelou, *I Know Why the Caged Birds Sings* (New York, Bantam Books, 1971), p. 168.

[42] Cf. Berreman, "Caste in India and the United States," op. cit.

[43] Berreman, "Stratification, Pluralism and Interaction . . . ," op. cit., p. 51.

hierarchical interaction vary; the presence and importance of such symbols is universal and essential to racism, casteism, and their homologues.

HIERARCHY AS IDEOLOGY. Dumont has emphasized the point that Indian caste is unique in that it is based on an ideology of hierarchy defined in terms of ritual purity and pollution.[44] He regards other systems of hierarchical social separation as non-comparable because of the inevitable differences in the ideologies supporting them. In the comparative framework which I advocate, I maintain simply that the Hindu rationale is one of several ideologies (cf. those of Islamic Swat, of the South Indian Lingayats to whom purity is irrelevant, of Ruanda, of Japan, and the United States) which can and do underlie and justify systems of birth-ascribed social hierarchy. Each is unique to the culture in which it occurs; each is associated with remarkably similar social structures, social processes, and individual experiences. I believe that anyone who has experienced daily life in rural India and the rural American South, for example, will confirm the fact that there is something remarkably similar in the systems of social relations and attitudes. I believe that anyone who has experienced daily life in an urban slum, a public market, or a factory in India and the United States would come to the same conclusion. That similarity is generated by birth-ascribed stratification and it is not concealed by differential ideologies.[45]

Contrary to another of Dumont's assumptions (shared with Cox), there is nothing incompatible between an ideology which underwrites a hierarchy of groups and a notion of equality within each group. This combination, in fact, is found not only in the United States where it accounts for the above-mentioned absence of a real "American dilemma" in race relations, but also in each of the other systems described here. Members of each ranked group are *inherently unequal* to those of each other group and are by birth *potentially equal* to those of their own group. More importantly, the existence of an ideology of hierarchy does not mean that this ideology is conceived and interpreted identically by all within the system it is presumed to justify or even that it is shared by them. Acquiescence must not be mistaken for concurrence. Dumont's assumption to the contrary is the most glaring weakness in his analysis of Indian caste.[46]

SEXUAL STRATIFICATION. Finally, in my discussion of models for analysis, I turn to the controversial and sociologically puzzling matter of sex as a basis for social separation and inequality. The special problems which the sexual criterion poses for the student of stratification are both academic and substantive. The academic problems derive from the history of the study of stratification. Although the role of women in various non-Western societies has been discussed by anthropologists (including prominently Margaret Mead), and the position of women in European societies has been discussed by some social historians, the sexual dichotomy rarely appears in sociological works on stratification. That this criterion has been largely ignored or dismissed by stratification theorists is attributable to several factors not the least of which is no doubt that members of the privileged sex have authored most of the work and to them such ranking has not been a problem and hence has not been apparent. Also, their culturally derived biases have been such that this kind of ranking was taken for granted as a manifestation of biological differences. "Many people who are very hip to the implications of the racial caste system . . . don't seem to be able to see the sexual caste system and if the question is raised they respond with: 'that's the way it's supposed to be. There are biological differences.' Or with other statements which recall a white segregationist confronted with integration."[47] The biological rationale—what Millet refers to as the "view of sex as a caste structure ratified by nature"[48]—recalls also the justification offered for *all* birth-ascribed dominance–exploitation relationships be they caste in India, Burakumin status in Japan, sexual roles, or any other. In each instance the plea is

44 Dumont, op. cit.

45 Cf. Berreman, "Caste in India and the United States," op. cit.; Berreman, "Caste in Cross-Cultural Perspective . . . ," op. cit.; Gerald D. Berreman, "Social Categories and Social Interaction in Urban India," *American Anthropologist* (Vol. 74, No. 3).

46 Cf. Berreman, "A Brahmanical View of Caste . . . ," op. cit.

47 Kate Millet, *Sexual Politics* (New York, Avon Books, 1971), p. 19.

48 Casey Hayden and Mary King, "Sex and Caste," *Liberation* (April, 1966), p. 35; cf. Millet, op. cit.

that they are uniquely *real*, significant, unavoidable, and natural differences, and therefore they must be acted upon. Thus, in an interview about their new book, *The Imperial Animal,* which is said to claim that males have dominated human history because "the business of politics . . . is a business that requires skills and attitudes that are peculiarly male," anthropologists Robin Fox and Lionel Tiger were reported to have vehemently denied that their theory about the reasons for women's roles might be a sexist theory. " 'These are the facts, don't accuse us of making up the species,' Tiger said." And again, " 'Because this is a racist country, people relate sexism to racism.' But these two reactions are actually different because while there are no important biological differences between races, there are very important differences between the sexes." [49] Whether the differences are real or not (and who would deny that males and females differ in important ways?), the sociological and humanistic question is whether the differences require or justify differential opportunities, privileges, responsibilities, and rewards or, put negatively, domination and exploitation.

Birth-ascribed stratification, be it sexual, racial, or otherwise, is always accompanied by explanations, occasionally ingenious but usually mundane and often ludicrous, as to why putative natural differences do require and justify social differences. Those explanations are widely doubted by those whose domination they are supposed to explain, and this includes increasing numbers of women.

The substantive issues which becloud the topic of sexual stratification have to do with the mode of recruitment, the socialization, membership, and structural arrangements of sexually ranked categories. First, there is the fact that while sex is determined at birth, it is not contingent upon ancestry, endogamy, or any other arrangement of marriage or family, and is not predictable. It is the only recurrent basis for birth-ascribed stratification that can be defensibly attributed solely to undeniably physical characteristics. Even here there are individual or categorical exceptions made for transvestites, hermaphrodites, homosexuals, etc., in some societies as in the case of *hijaras* in India.[50] The significance (as contrasted to the fact) of the diagnostic physical traits—of sexual differences—is, however, largely socially defined, so that their cultural expressions vary widely over time and space. Second, as a concomitant to the mode of recruitment, males and females have no distinct ethnic or regional histories. It must not be overlooked, however, that they do have distinct social histories in every society. Third the universal co-residence of males and females within the household precludes the existence of lifelong separate male and female societies as such, and usually assures a degree of mutual early socialization. But note that it does not preclude distinct male and female social institutions, distinct patterns of social interaction within and between these categories, or distinguishable male and female subcultures (in fact the latter are universal) including, for example, distinct male and female dialects.

Partly as a consequence of these factors, the nature and quality of segregation of the sexes has not been defined by sociologists as comparable to that of the other ascriptive social categories discussed here. Nevertheless, most of the characteristics of birth-ascribed separation and stratification (racial, caste, ethnic, colonial, class, and pluralistic characteristics), and virtually all of the psychological and social consequences of inborn, lifelong superiority–inferiority relations are to be found in the relationship of males and females in most societies. These stem from similar factors in early socialization and from stereotypes and prejudices enacted and enforced in differential roles and opportunity structures, rationalized by ideologies of differential intrinsic capabilities and worth, sustained and defended through the combination of power and vested interest that is common to all birth-ascribed inequality. I have elsewhere contrasted some of the consequences of these assumptions and behaviors in the United States and India as reflected in the political participation of women in the two nations although

[49] Fran Hawthorne, "Female Roles Examined by Rutgers Professors," *Daily Californian* (Berkeley, 6 October, 1971), p. 5. See also Millett, op. cit., p. 57, for a summary of the common psychological traits and adaptational mechanisms attributed to blacks and women in American society as reported in three recent sociological accounts.

[50] Cf. G. Morris Carstairs, *The Twice-Born* (Bloomington, Indiana University Press, 1958), pp. 59–62 *et passim*; Morris E. Opler, "The Hijarā (Hermaphrodites) of India and Indian National Character: A Rejoinder," *American Anthropologist* (Vol. 62, No. 3, June, 1960).

this is dwarfed by Millett's more recent work on male domination, its sources, and manifestations in the West.[51]

If we agree with van den Berghe that "race can be treated as a special case of invidious status differentiation or a special criterion of stratification," [52] I think we are bound to agree that sex is another.

Consequences of Inherited Inequality

Assuming that there are significant structural and interactional similarities among systems of birth-ascribed stratification, the question can still be legitimately asked, "so what?" Is this merely a more or less interesting observation—even a truism—or does it have some theoretical or practical significance? My answer would be that it has both, for such systems have common and predictable consequences in the individual lives of those who live them and in the cumulative events which comprise the ongoing histories of the societies which harbor them.

> Caste systems are living environments to those who comprise them. Yet there is a tendency among those who study and analyse them to intellectualize caste, and in the process to squeeze the life out of it. Caste is people, and especially people interacting in characteristic ways and thinking in characteristic ways. Thus, in addition to being a structure, a caste system is a set of human relationships and it is a state of mind.[53]

Their "human implications" are justification enough for studying and comparing systems of birth-ascribed stratification. There are neither the data nor the space to discuss their implications fully here, but I will suggest the nature of the evidence briefly, identifying psychological and social consequences. I am well aware that many features of such systems are found in all sharply stratified societies. Some are characteristic of all relationships of superordination and subordination, of poverty and affluence, of differential power. Others are found in all societies made up of distinct sub-groups whether stratified or not. It is the unique combination of characteristics in the context of the ideal of utter rigidity and unmitigable inequality which makes systems of stratification by race, caste, ethnicity, and sex distinctive in their impact on people, individually and collectively.

Beliefs and attitudes associated with rigid stratification can be suggested by such terms as paternalism and dependence, *noblesse oblige*, arrogance, envy, resentment, hatred, prejudice, rationalization, emulation, self-doubt, and self-hatred. Those who are oppressed often respond to such stratification by attempting to escape either the circumstances or the consequences of the system. The realities of power and dependence make more usual an accommodation to oppression which, however, is likely to be less passive than is often supposed, and is likely to be unequivocally revealed when the slightest change in the perceived distribution of power occurs. Those who are privileged in the system seek to sustain and justify it, devoting much of their physical effort to the former and much of their psychic and verbal effort to the latter. When these systems are birth-ascribed, all of these features are exacerbated.

Kardiner and Ovesey conclude their classic, and by now outdated, study of American Negro personality, *Mark of Oppression*, with the statement: "The psycho-social expressions of the Negro personality that we have described are the *integrated* end products of the process of oppression." [54] Although it is appropriate to question their characterization of that personality in the light of subsequent events and research, there is no doubt that such oppression has recurrent psychological consequences for both the oppressor and the oppressed, as Robert Coles has demonstrated in *Children of Crisis* and subsequent works.[55]

Oppression does not befall everyone in a system of birth-ascribed inequality. Most notably, it does not befall those with power. What does befall all is the imposition by birth of unalterable membership in ranked, socially isolated, but interacting groups with rigidly defined and con-

[51] Gerald D. Berreman, "Women's Roles and Politics: India and the United States," in *Readings in General Sociology,* R. W. O'Brien, C. Schrag, and W. T. Martin, eds. (4th Edition, Boston, Houghton Mifflin Co., 1969). First published, 1966. Cf. Millett, op. cit.

[52] van den Berghe, *Race and Racism,* op. cit., p. 22.

[53] Berreman, "Stratification, Pluralism and Interaction . . . ," op. cit., p. 58.

[54] Abram Kardiner and Lionel Ovesey, *Mark of Oppression* (Cleveland, The World Publishing Co., 1962), p. 387.

[55] Robert Coles, *Children of Crisis* (Boston, Atlantic–Little, Brown, 1964); with Jon Erikson, *The Middle Americans* (Boston, Little, Brown, 1971).

spicuously different experiences, opportunities, public esteem and, inevitably, self-esteem. The black in America and in South Africa, the Burakumin of Japan, the Harijan of India, the barber or washerman of Swat, the Hutu or Twa of Ruanda, have all faced similar conditions as individuals and they have responded to them in similar ways. The same can be said for the privileged and dominant groups in each of these societies, for while painful consequences of subordination are readily apparent, the consequences of superordination are equally real and important. Thus, ethnic stratification leaves its characteristic and indelible imprint on all who experience it.

The consequences of such stratification include many of the attitudes and responses vividly described in literature on black-white relations in the United States. Immediately to mind come accounts of the black experience, such as James Baldwin's *Notes of a Native Son, Nobody Knows My Name,* and *Go Tell It On the Mountain;* Claude Brown's *Manchild in the Promised Land*; Eldridge Cleaver's *Soul on Ice*; Ralph Ellison's *Invisible Man*; Richard Wright's *Native Son* and *Black Boy*; and Malcolm X's *The Autobiography of Malcolm X.* Outstanding among those dealing with the white experience in relation to blacks are W. J. Cash's *The Mind of the South*; Lillian Smith's *Killers of the Dream* and *Strange Fruit.* The psychiatrist Robert Coles has provided insights into both sides of the American caste barrier in his works cited above.

Corresponding literature on other caste-like systems include, for India, Mulk Raj Anand's *Untouchable*; Hazari's *An Indian Outcaste: The Autobiography of an Untouchable*; Harold Isaac's *India's Ex-Untouchables*; and from the British side, E. M. Forster's *Passage to India*; and in Burma, George Orwell's *Burmese Days.* On Japan, we can refer to the contributors to DeVos and Wagatsuma's *Japan's Invisible Race,* and, cited therein, Ninomiya's "An Inquiry Concerning the Origin, Development and Present Situation of the *Eta* . . . ," and Shimazaki Tōson's *Hakai (Breach of Commandment).* Works on South Africa include Alan Paton's *Cry the Beloved Country* and *Too Late the Phalarope*; Albert Luthuli's *Let My People Go*; and van den Berghe's *Caneville* and *South Africa: A Study in Conflict.* Telling analyses of colonial situations include Franz Fanon's *Wretched of the Earth,* and Albert Memmi's *The Colonizer and the Colonized,* both deriving from Algeria; O. Mannoni's *Prospero and Caliban,* from Madagascar; J. C. Heinrich, *The Psychology of a Suppressed People,* on India. This listing does not do justice to the relevant literature, but is suggestive of it.

Research on the psychological consequences of racism in the United States is well-known and voluminous, though restricted almost exclusively to black-white relations. Although this literature has followed many blind leads and has been distorted by many subtle (and some not-so-subtle) biases, stereotypes, and prejudices, it nevertheless suggests that the public and self-disparagement or aggrandizement and the differential opportunities which go with birth-ascribed status, low and high, result in characteristic psychological problems and resort to characteristic psychological mechanisms.[56] Comparable literature on non-Western societies is scanty but increasing.[57]

The consequences of birth-ascribed stratification are self-fulfilling and self-perpetuating, for although low status groups do not adopt views of themselves or their statuses which are consistent with the views held by their superiors, they are continually acting them out and cannot avoid internalizing some of them and the self-doubts they engender, just as high status groups internalize their superiority and self-righteousness. The oppression of others by the latter serves to justify and bolster their superiority complex and to rationalize for them the deprivation and exploitation of those they denigrate. "Once you denigrate someone in that way," say Kardiner and Ovesey, "the sense of guilt makes it imperative to degrade the subject further to justify the whole procedure." [58] Gallagher notes that in the southern United States,

56 Berreman, "Stratification, Pluralism and Interaction . . . ," op. cit., Cf. Thomas F. Pettigrew, *A Profile of the Negro American* (Princeton, D. Van Nostrand, 1964); Stanley M. Elkins, *Slavery* (Chicago, University of Chicago Press, 1959); Mina Davis Caulfield, "Slavery and the Origins of Black Culture: Elkins Revisited," in *Americans From Africa: Slavery and Its Aftermath,* P. I. Rose, ed., J. H. Rohrer and M. S. Edmonson, *The Eighth Generation Grows Up* (New York, Harper and Row, 1960).

57 Santokh S. Anant, "Child Training and Caste Personality: The Need for Further Research," *Race* (Vol. VIII, No. 4, 1967); Santokh S. Anant, *Inter-Caste Attitudes* (provisional title), (Delhi, Vikas Publications, 1972); K. K. Singh, *Patterns of Caste Tension* (Bombay, Asia Publishing House, 1967); DeVos and Wagatsuma, op. cit.

58 Kardiner and Ovesey, op. cit., p. 379.

> By the attitudes of mingled fear, hostility, deprecation, discrimination, amused patronage, friendly domination, and rigid authoritarianism, the white caste generates opposite and complementary attitudes in the Negro caste. It is a touch of consummate irony that the dominant group should then argue that the characteristics which exhibit themselves in the submerged group are "natural" or "racial."[59]

The products of oppression are thus used to justify oppression.

CHANGE AND EMANCIPATION. The self-reinforcing degradation described above combines with greed and fear of status-loss or revolt to comprise a dynamic of oppression which, in birth-ascribed stratification, probably accounts for the widespread occurrence of pariah status or untouchability. Elites characteristically justify oppression by compounding it; they enhance their own rewards by denying them ever more stringently to social inferiors, and they strive to protect themselves from challenges to status and privilege from below by rigidifying the status boundaries, reinforcing the sanctions which enforce them, and increasing the monopoly on power which makes the sanctions effective. This assures increasing social separation and hierarchical distance between groups until such time as it generates rebellion, reform, or disintegration.

The fact that social order prevails most of the time in any given instance of inherited inequality does not mean that all of those in the system accept it or their places within it willingly, nor does it mean that the system is either stable or static. It most often means that power is held and exercised effectively by those in superordinate statuses, for the time being. Such systems are based on conformity more than consensus, and are maintained by sanctions more than agreement. Nevertheless, change is inherent, resistance and mobility-striving are universal, and effective challenges to such systems are probably ultimately inevitable because the response they elicit from those they oppress is subversive. The possibility of acting out the subversion depends largely upon the balance of power among the stratified groups and the definitions of the situation their members hold. The processes of change and patterns of conflict which lead to them are major areas of commonality in such systems.[60]

The history of every caste system, of every racially stratified system, of every instance of birth-ascribed oppression is a history of striving, conflict, and occasional revolt. That this is not generally acknowledged is largely a result of the fact that most of these actions occur in the context of overwhelming power and uncompromising enforcement by the hereditary elites and are therefore expressed in the form of day-to-day resentment and resistance handled so subtly and occurring so routinely that it goes unremarked.[61] Even conspicuous manifestations are likely to be quickly and brutally put down, confined to a particular locality or group, and knowledge of their occurrence suppressed by those against whom they have been directed. These phenomena often can only be discovered by consulting and winning the confidence of members of oppressed groups, and this is rarely done.

Only the most spectacular instances of resistance, and the few successful ones are likely to be well-known. Immediately to mind come such martyrs to the cause of emancipation of oppressed peoples as the Thracian slave Spartacus, who led a rebellion against Rome; the American slave rebellion leaders Gabriel and Nat Turner; the white abolitionist John Brown; and the contemporary leaders of black emancipation in America, Martin Luther King, Medgar Evers, and others (too many of them martyred) among their fellow leaders and supporters, black and white. No doubt there are many more, most of them unknown and unsung, in the history of all groups whose members society condemns by birth to oppression. In the folk history of every such group, and in the memory of every member, are instances of courageous or foolhardy people who have challenged or outwitted their oppressors, often at the cost of their own foreseeable and inevitable destruction.

Better-known and better-documented than the individuals who led and sometimes died for them, are the emancipation movements which

[59] B. G. Gallagher, *American Caste and the Negro College* (New York, Columbia University Press, 1938), p. 109.

[60] Berreman, "Caste as Social Process," op. cit.

[61] Raymond Bauer and Alice Bauer, "Day to Day Resistance to Slavery," *Journal of Negro History* (Vol. 27, October 1942); Douglas Scott, "The Negro and the Enlisted Man: An Analogy," *Harpers* (October 1962), pp. 20–1; cf. Berreman, "Caste in India and the United States," op. cit.

have occurred in most such societies—movements such as those for black power and black separatism in the United States, anti-casteism and anti-untouchability in India, Hutu emancipation in Rwanda and Burundi, Burakumin emancipation in Japan, and anti-apartheid in South Africa. All have depended primarily upon concerted efforts to apply political, economic, or military power to achieve their ends. They have comprised direct challenges to the systems. Most have followed after the failure of attempts less militant, less likely to succeed, and hence less threatening to social elites—attempts towards assimilation or mobility within the systems such as those of status emulation.

The movements among black Americans (and more recently among other ethnically stratified groups in America such as Chicanos and Native Americans, and among women), are too well-known and well-documented to require enumeration here.[62] Anyone who reads the American press and especially the black and left press, cannot avoid being aware of the main currents in this area.

Emancipation movements outside of the West are less known to European and American readers, but they are more numerous than can be indicated here albeit quite poorly documented. Any list would have to include the following obvious examples:

India: Escape from the consequences of caste stratification has been a primary appeal of every religion and social reform movement to gain adherents in India from the beginnings of Jainism and Buddhism in the sixth century B.C., through Islam which became a significant religion in India from the eleventh century A.D.; Sikhism from the early sixteenth century; Christianity, dating from the 'Syrian Christians' of the first or sixth century A.D. in Kerala, followed in the sixteenth century by converts of Portuguese and French Catholic missionaries and in the nineteenth century by Anglican and Protestant converts; various Hindu reform movements including the Brahmo Samaj and Arya Samaj of the early and late nineteenth century, respectively; the post-Independence resurgence of "neo"-Buddhism among low castes as an explicitly anti-caste phenomenon under Dr. B. R. Ambedkar, the revered leader of Indian untouchables for many decades and founder of the Scheduled Castes Federation and its successor in the later 1950s, the All-India Republican Party.

Regional movements have been many, among the best-known of which are the Maharashtrian anti-Brahmin movement under the leadership of Jotirao Phule in the 1870s, a largely middle-caste Maratha movement, and in the same area an emancipation movement among untouchable Mahars which matured into the above-mentioned Scheduled Caste Federation under Ambedkar.[63]

Innumerable local and regional movements, primarily in urban centers, have arisen whose aim has been to emancipate the members of a caste or cluster of castes, to force public recognition of higher status for a caste, or to ameliorate their caste-based disabilities through solidarity and political action.[64] There can be

62 Cf. Carmichael and Hamilton, op. cit.; Eldridge Cleaver, *Soul on Ice* (New York, Dell Publishing Co., 1968); E. U. Essien-Udom, *Black Nationalism* (New York, Dell Publishing Co., 1962); Lewis M. Killian, *The Impossible Revolution? Black Power and The American Dream* (New York, Random House, 1968); Martin Luther King, *Stride Toward Freedom* (New York, Harper Brothers, 1958); C. Eric Lincoln, *The Black Muslims in America* (Boston, Beacon Press, 1962); Louis E. Lomax, *The Negro Revolt* (New York, New American Library, 1962); Raymond J. Murphy and Howard Elinson, *Problems and Prospects of the Negro Movement* (Belmont, California, Wadsworth, 1966); Pinkney, op. cit.; Rose, op. cit.; Charles E. Silberman, *Crisis in Black and White* (New York, Random House, 1964); Stan Steiner, *The New Indians* (New York, Harper and Row, 1968); Stan Steiner, *La Raza: The Mexican Americans* (New York, Harper and Row, 1970); Howard Zinn, *S.N.C.C., The New Abolitionists* (Boston, Beacon Press, 1964).

63 Charles H. Heimsath, *Indian Nationalism and Hindu Social Reform* (Princeton, Princeton University Press, 1964); Owen M. Lynch, *The Politics of Untouchability* (New York, Columbia University Press, 1969); Gail Omvedt, "Jotirao Phule and the Ideology of Social Revolution in India" (Dept. of Sociology, University of California, Berkeley, 1971), mimeographed paper; cf. B. R. Ambedkar, *The Untouchables: Who Were They and Why They Became Untouchables* (New Delhi, Amrit Book Co., 1948); B. R. Ambedkar, *What Congress and Gandhi Have Done to the Untouchables* (Bombay, Thacker and Co., 1946); B. R. Ambedkar, *Annihilation of Caste* (Bombay, Bharat Bhusan Press, 1945).

64 Orans, op. cit.; Martin Orans, *The Santal: A Tribe in Search of a Great Tradition* (Detroit, Wayne State University Press, 1965); Lloyd I. Rudolph and Susan H. Rudolph, "The Political Role of India's Caste Associations," *Pacific Affairs* (Vol. 33, 1960); James Silverberg, ed., *Social Mobility in the Caste System in India*, Supplement III: *Comparative Studies in Society and History* (The Hague, Mouton, 1968).

little doubt that contemporary revolutionary parties and movements in India depend to a significant extent on their appeal to oppressed castes whose members see them as vehicles to emancipation.

In addition to these sophisticated efforts at emancipation, upward mobility movements among low castes are endemic to all regions of India, and have evidently been so throughout its history. These movements entail a claim to high status that has not been recognized. They co-ordinate and enforce among the members of a caste emulation of the behaviors and attributes of high castes in the hope that this will result in public recognition of the claim. This process has been termed "Sanskritization," in recognition of the fact that the behaviors adopted are often those prescribed for high castes in the sacred Sanskrit literature.[65] Emulation alone, however, no matter how successfully done, is not enough to confer status, for status in a caste system is not based on behavior but on birth. To change the societal definition of a caste's status requires a concerted, sustained, and powerful group effort, and it is most often unsuccessful.

In addition, as Harold Isaacs has documented in *India's Ex-Untouchables,* individuals occasionally escape the consequences of their caste status into rewarding caste-free occupations in cities, often as a result of education and sometimes by the successful concealment of their caste identities (passing). In rural areas, some people emigrate to cities to escape the disabilities of their caste status; some cluster together in low-caste communities to avoid daily contact with, and humiliation by, their caste superiors; a few are able to acquire a degree of exemption at the cost of conventional family life through adoption of non-priestly religious roles or resort to various socially deviant identities.[66]

Japan. Publicly recognized emancipation movements among the Burakumin of Japan have been many, militant, and frequently violent following the official Edict of Emancipation of 1871. They have been so well documented and conveniently summarized by Totten and Wagatsuma that to repeat the information would be superfluous. Wagatsuma has carried the chronology of political militance through the post-World War II period, and has also documented non-political, religious, and educational approaches to amelioration of Burakumin oppression.[67] The similarities to emancipation efforts in India and the United States are little short of uncanny. The occurrence and problems of "passing" among Burakumin, and the limited rewards to be acquired through educational, occupational, and residential mobility are closely parallel to those reported for India and the United States.[68]

Ruanda. In Ruanda and nearby Urundi, the dominant Tutsi seemed until fifteen years ago to be in firm control, with the subordinate Hutu and Twa relegated to dependent economic and political roles.[69] But this proves to have been a false calm. In 1957, while Ruanda was still part of the Belgian trust territory of Ruanda-Urundi, the Hutu issued the Bahutu Manifesto which initiated an emancipation movement. Opposing political parties then arose, advocating Hutu emancipation on the one hand and Tutsi supremacy on the other. The brutality of the latter unleashed a successful Hutu revolution in 1959, in which most of the Tutsi were driven from the country. The resultant Hutu government was confirmed when the emancipation party won overwhelmingly in a plebiscite in 1961. That party was in power when Ruanda became independent Rwanda in 1962, and has remained so despite frequent incursions by Tutsi from across the Rwanda borders. In the adjacent kingdom of Burundi (formerly Urundi and part of the same trust territory), the Hutu emancipation movement was suppressed by the Tutsi-dominated government after independence in 1962, and inter-caste tension thereafter increased. When the Hutu won a majority of governmental seats in the election of 1965, the king refused to

[65] M. N. Srinivas, *Caste in Modern India and Other Essays* (Bombay, Asia Publishing House, 1962), pp. 42–62; M. N. Srinivas, *Social Change in Modern India* (Berkeley, University of California Press, 1966), pp. 1–45.

[66] Cf. Berreman, *Hindus of the Himalayas*, Epilogue, "Sirkanda Ten Years Later."

[67] George O. Totten and Hiroshi Wagatsuma, "Emancipation: Growth and Transformation of a Political Movement," in DeVos and Wagatsuma, op. cit., pp. 33–67; Hiroshi Wagatsuma, "Postwar Political Militance," and "Non-Political Approaches: The Influences of Religion and Education," in DeVos and Wagatsuma, op. cit., pp. 68–109.

[68] George DeVos and Hiroshi Wagatsuma, "Group Solidarity and Individual Mobility," in DeVos and Wagatsuma, op. cit., pp. 245–56.

[69] Maquet, op. cit.

name the majority government. This led to an unsuccessful Hutu coup, put down by the army, after which most of the Hutu leadership was shot. These Hutu emancipation efforts were perhaps a surprise to the Tutsi overlords, but they came as no surprise to any serious student of birth-ascribed oppression, for such systems are always fraught with tension and resentment which await only a belief in the possibility of success for drastic change to be attempted from below.

Henry Adams characterized the slave society of Virginia in 1800 as "ill at ease." [70] This seems to be the chronic state of societies so organized—the privileged cannot relax their vigilance against the rebellious resentment of the deprived. That such rigid, oppressive systems do function and persist is a credit not to the consensus they engender any more than to the justice or rationality of the systems. Rather, it is a tribute to the effectiveness of the monopoly on power which the privileged are able to maintain. When in such systems deprived people get the vote, get jobs, get money, get legal redress, get guns, get powerful allies, get public support for their aspirations, they perceive a change in the power situation and an enhancement of the likelihood of successful change in their situation, and they are likely to attempt to break out of their oppressed status. These conditions do not generate the desire for change, for that is intrinsic; they merely make it seem worthwhile to attempt the change. Sometimes the triggering factor is not that the deprived believe conditions have changed so that success is more likely, but rather that conditions have led them to define the risk and consequences of failure (even its virtual certainty) as acceptable. Resultant changes are often drastic and traumatic of achievement, but they are sought by the oppressed and by enlightened people of all statuses precisely because of the heavy individual and societal costs of maintaining inherited inequality and because of its inherent inhumanity.

An important difference between the dynamics of inherited stratification and acquired stratification results from the fact that in the latter, power and privilege accompany achievable status, emulation is at least potentially effective, and mobility and assimilation are realistic goals. Therefore energies of status resentment may rationally be channelled toward mobility. Most immigrant groups in the United States, for example, have found this out as they have merged with the larger society after one or two generations of socialization. But in a system where inherited, unalterable group identity is the basis for rewards, emulation alone cannot achieve upward mobility, and assimilation is impossible so long as the system exists (in fact, prevention of assimilation is one of its main functions). Only efforts to destroy, alter, or circumvent the system make sense. In the United States, blacks, Chicanos, and Native Americans have found this out. Only in response to changes in the distribution of power is such inherited status likely to be re-evaluated and the distribution of rewards altered.

Conclusion

"Race" as the term is used in America, Europe, and South Africa, is not qualitatively different in its implications for human social life from caste, *varna*, or *jati* as applied in India, *quom* in Swat and Muslim India, the "invisible race" of Japan, the ethnic stratification of Rwanda and Burundi. Racism and casteism are indistinguishable in the annals of man's inhumanity to man, and sexism is closely allied to them as man's inhumanity to woman. All are invidious distinctions imposed unalterably at birth upon whole categories of people to justify the unequal social distribution of power, livelihood, security, privilege, esteem, freedom—in short, life chances. Where distinctions of this type are employed, they affect people and the events which people generate in surprisingly similar ways despite the different historical and cultural conditions in which they occur.

If I were asked, "What practical inference, if any, is to be drawn from the comparative study of inherited inequality—of ascriptive social ranking?" I would say it is this: There is no way to reform such institutions; the only solution is their dissolution. As Kardiner and Ovesey said long ago "*there is only one way that the products of oppression can be dissolved, and that is to stop the oppression.*" [71] To stop the oppression, one must eliminate the structure of inherited stratification upon which it rests. Generations of Burakumin, Hutu, blacks, untouchables, and

[70] Henry Adams, *The United States in 1800* (Ithaca, New York, Cornell University Press, 1961), p. 98.
[71] Kardiner and Ovesey, op. cit., p. 387.

their sympathizers have tried reform without notable success. Effective change has come only when the systems have been challenged directly.

The boiling discontent of birth-ascribed deprivation cannot be contained by pressing down the lid of oppression or by introducing token flexibility, or by preaching brotherly love. The only hope lies in restructuring society and redistributing its rewards so as to end the inequality. Such behavioral change must come first. From it may follow attitudinal changes as meaningful, status-equal interaction undermines racist, casteist, communalist, and sexist beliefs and attitudes, but oppressed people everywhere have made it clear that it is the end of oppression, not brotherly love, which they seek most urgently. To await the latter before achieving the former is futility; to achieve the former first does not guarantee achievement of the latter, but it increases the chances and makes life liveable. In any case, the unranked pluralism which many minorities seek requires only equality, not love.

To those who fear this course on the grounds that it will be traumatic and dangerous, I would say that it is less so than the futile attempt to prevent change. Philip Mason spoke for all systems of inborn inequality when he called the Spartan oppression of the Helots in ancient Greece a trap from which there was no escape.

> It was the Helots who released the Spartans from such ignoble occupations as trade and agriculture. . . . But it was the Helots who made it necessary to live in an armed camp, constantly on the alert against revolt. . . . They had a wolf by the ears; they dared not let go. And it was of their own making; they had decided—at some stage and by what process one can only guess—that the Helots would remain separate and without rights forever.[72]

That way, I believe, lies ultimate disaster for any society. A thread of hope lies in the possibility that people can learn from comparison of the realities of inherited inequality across space, time, and culture, and can act to preclude the disaster that has befallen others by eliminating the system which guarantees it. It is a very thin thread.

72 Philip Mason, *Patterns of Dominance* (London, Oxford University Press for the Institute of Race Relations, 1970), p. 75.

PART FIVE

Political Organization

Authority, Law, Diplomacy—and Armed Aggression

Every political organization can be analytically separated into two basic components: a system for maintaining internal order and a means of regulating external relations. In very small-scale societies both of these functions are taken care of within the context of the kinship system. Authority based on seniority within the kin group and recognition of a particular member's special leadership ability (in hunting, in finding the right words to sum up both sides' positions in a dispute and to develop consensus on its proper settlement) are often all there is to allocating decision-making authority. And most of the time the exercise of even such limited leadership as this may not be necessary. Cultural homogeneity, custom, continuous face-to-face interaction, pressure for conformity, fear of ridicule, avoidance of the dangerously divisive effect of conflict, and the threat of supernatural punishment all combine to assure that day-to-day life can go on without calling upon any of the local "leaders" for direction. The need for leadership occurs only during periods of crisis and lasts only until they are past. The initiative and direction required to organize a group hunt, to intervene in a quarrel, to lead a raid, or to mobilize the group for defense, is inevitably transitory. Because their authority is not continuingly necessary, there is no way such intermittent leaders can ever consolidate and perpetuate their temporary power.

Usually the considerable increases in population size and in socioeconomic complexity that come with the higher level of productivity made possible by farming or herding are the conditions necessary to foster the emergence of political organization as a structurally separate system, increasingly independent of kinship. With technological growth and greater diversification of economic and social roles, more trade, the possibility of differential accumulation of wealth, the proliferation of special interest groups (landlords and peasants, artisans and tradesmen, the poor and the rich), the political picture changes radically. The administration of society, by legislation, coercive law enforcement, diplomacy, and organized warfare becomes the full-time tasks of leaders who collectively comprise a system that is no longer based on kinship and has become a government.

The development of political anthropology has been influenced by political science in much the same way that economic anthropology has been affected by economics. Translation of the method and theory of political science into anthropologically usable terms requires that the culture-bound perspectives of scholars mostly familiar with Euroamerican political structures be replaced with a model that takes into account the far wider range of variation observable both among contemporary non-Western peoples and from a look at the evolutionary development of the political system from the prototype of the semiautonomous family band to such multinational entities as the United Nations.

As well as being culture-bound, political science has also been nonscientifically normative: too ready to apply ethnocentric judgments about good and bad political forms to the systems of all peoples, including many whose cultural goals are entirely different from our own. As a result, for many the first step in political anthropology entails *unlearning*, letting go of the notion that those familiar political forms we have been conditioned to regard as superior are not necessarily "good" for everyone; in fact, they may often be seriously maladaptive.

This assertion is certainly not intended to suggest granting empty-minded acceptance and equal credit to every people's form of government. It is made only to advocate more objective criteria for making cross-cultural political judgments. A look at authority systems in evolutionary perspective provides a point of view that is probably as free of ideological bias as any we can hope to attain.

SECTION I

Authority Systems

Three basic structural types can be identified by looking at the varied forms political organization takes among the peoples of the world. The oldest and simplest is the family *band*, a group whose members live together more or less continuously, are generally all bound together by ties of kinship and common interest, and whose limited rights to exercise authority over one another are based primarily on kinship. Reliance on customary precedents, the development of consensus, and fear of the withdrawal of cooperation, rather than imposed authority or coercion, is the principal mode of political expression.

Second, and at a slightly higher level of sociocultural complexity, are *noncentralized political systems* in which authority often transcends the basis of kinship. That is, some individuals or groups occasionally have the right to make decisions affecting the actions or the status of others who are not kinsmen or to whom they are only remotely related. Or groups may be bound together by ritual ties and their cooperative interaction assured by the threat of imposing supernatural sanctions. Social order can be maintained and mobilization may be possible in groups of considerable size even though they lack the apparatus of "government."

Third are *centralized authority systems.* Their presence is apparent in those societies in which responsibility for managing most facets of community life no longer rests with the family elders, but is legitimately held by a group that specializes in administration more or less full time. In the early stages of political centralization, kinship usually continues to play a significant role. To take the most familiar example, often a ruler is the eldest responsible member of a kin group that holds a traditionally sanctioned right to exercise force, as necessary, in order to govern. When the ruler dies, his power is inherited by his eldest offspring.

Many Native Americans who first came into contact and conflict with the colonialist invaders of their territories were organized at the simplest of these three levels of political organization: into bands. As a system the band works well so long as neighboring peoples are similarly organized. But because of its smallness, the limited coercive powers of its leaders, and the consequent difficulty of mobilizing and maintaining a large fighting force, as a type of political organization the band renders its members particularly vulnerable to conquest by enemies whose more centralized authority systems enable them to muster the winning military strength and to administer their conquests in a way that band organization does not allow.

In his description of the band organization of the Apache, Basehart, an expert on the Indians of the U.S. Southwest, illustrates the particular adaptive value of this political form to nomadic hunter-gatherers, peoples whose level of technoenvironmental adaptation is recurrently associated with this comparatively simple level of political development.

Band Organization of the Mescalero Apache*

Harry W. Basehart

Introduction

The problem examined in this paper constitutes a kind of paradox: how is it that in a society with a markedly egalitarian ideology, where the right of the individual to make and carry out his own decisions has unchallenged priority, the role of the leader is the crucial feature in the constitution of political units? To place the paradox in perspective, it should be noted that the leader lacks coercive authority and plays no key role in economic redistribution. The characteristics of the small groups centering on leaders among the Mescalero Apache of the mid-19th century, and of leadership as it pertains to these groups, are the central themes which will be explored in attempting to resolve the paradox.

From a more general perspective, the study is concerned with the analysis of one of the structurally significant levels of social integration—the political dimension—in this society of equestrian hunters, gatherers, and predators. Groups comprising leaders and their followers, which I have chosen to term "bands" for simplicity of reference, were the major units with political functions among Mescalero. Decisions with respect to a variety of problems—economic, political, solidary, and ritual—were effected in the context of the band. The political complexion of these units was colored by processes initiated in the course of adaptation to internal and external problems; the latter involved relationships among similar units and links with the larger, non-Mescalero, political field. The band leader was particularly important in connection with these problems; his role can be thought of as a homeostatic mechanism regulating (or failing to regulate) these varied political pressures.

Although political integration was a function of the segmental band organization, the maximal level of social integration was represented by the predominantly economically-oriented resource holding corporation. Comprising all those recognized as Mescalero, the corporation was not a corporate group; nevertheless, it was characterized by perpetuity and by a single jural personality (Basehart 1967).

Fundamentally, the Mescalero social system was predicated upon kinship: cognatic consanguineal bonds and affinal ties were the essential anchoring points for the extensive network of social relations. The kinship dimension is treated only incidentally in this paper, since primary emphasis is placed on the organization and operation of political units. Membership in these units was not determined exclusively by kinship criteria; neither genealogically demonstrated

Source: From Harry W. Basehart, "Mescalero Apache Band Organization," *Southwestern Journal of Anthropology,* Vol. 26 (1970), pp. 87–106. Used by permission of the publisher and the author.

* Research among the Mescalero Apache was supported by the Apache tribe of the Mescalero reservation in connection with their land claims and by National Institute of Mental Health Grant M-3088. L. Bryce Boyer, M.D., and the author were co-principal investigators for the latter project. A brief version of this paper was presented at the Apache Symposium organized by Keith Basso for the annual meeting of the American Anthropological Association in New Orleans, La., November 1969. I wish to thank Stanley Newman and L. Bryce Boyer for comments on the preliminary draft of the article.

connection nor stipulated kinship were requisites for affiliation with any particular band.

This examination of Mescalero band organization and leadership is an exercise in historical reconstruction. Typically, an enterprise of this kind is hazardous and, hence, I have used historical resources, particularly those concerning the relations between agents of the United States government and Mescalero during the latter part of the 19th century, in an effort to supplement and document materials secured through field research. The emphasis of the study is on a systematic synchronic description of one aspect of social structure, although I have attempted to place this description in an historical context wherever possible. Finally, there is the question of the extent to which the analysis is informed by the point of view of the Mescalero actors who have provided the basic information. In my judgment, the fit between informants' constructs and the synthetic and analytic statements in the following discussion is reasonably good; there is not isomorphism, but there is congruence.

Background

In 1848, when the United States assumed sovereignty over New Mexico, the Mescalero Apache utilized an extensive territory east of the Rio Grande in southern New Mexico, western Texas, and northern Mexico. Their subsistence, based upon hunting, gathering, and predation, required a high degree of mobility to exploit the variable resources of different ecological zones. Equality of rights of access to the animal and plant resources assured to all Mescalero by virtue of membership in what I have termed the "resource holding corporation" (Basehart 1967), together with the plunder secured through raiding, provided a margin of subsistence security. The degree of dependence upon a particular economic activity was not only a function of the productivity of natural resources in relation to technology, but of the wider political field in which Mescalero were involved, particularly by virtue of predation. During some portions of the 18th century, e.g., the booty acquired by raiding the Spanish frontier settlements formed a major contribution to the Indian economy, but at other times punitive expeditions and peace treaties necessitated recourse to non-predatory modes of adaptation (cf., e.g., Thomas 1932:10–11; Thomas 1941: 125–129).

As heir to the Mexican territories of the Southwest, the United States succeeded as well to the series of problems associated with the Apache presence in the region. The opposition and conflict which had marked the relations of the Mescalero and previous foreign powers continued during the American regime until the reservation confinement of the tribe in 1873.

Historical documents for the period of U.S. control suggest that military and civil authorities were potent agents of change for the Mescalero, but it is not evident that the political forms remarked by informants and sketched in early reports were altered radically. It is true, of course, that the establishment of Fort Stanton, New Mexico, in the heart of the northern mountains in 1855 resulted in the concentration of a portion of the tribe in the vicinity of the fort. Officials recognized a "principal chief" through whom communications were channeled, and regarded this spokesman as the leader of a "peace" party. But those army officers who acquired even limited familiarity with the Indians realized that the office of principal chief was an imposed legal fiction. The effective political units continued to be small groups centering on leaders, as the repeated references to the names of various "captains" in the documents suggests.

The concentration of groups near Fort Stanton was important in underlining for outside observers the extent to which Mescalero subsistence depended upon mobility. Fort commanders not only proscribed raiding, but for a time attempted to confine Indian movements to the narrow limits defined by an agreement made at Dog Canyon in 1855 (Pee 1855). The application of the policy quickly led to destitution and starvation for the Indians; to cite only a few reports in illustration, Captain Van Horne in 1856 noted that "the people are miserably poor and very badly clad. They avidly devour a dead mule and eat up the leavings of dogs" (Van Horne 1856), while Lt. Col. Reeve in 1858 remarked on the destitute condition of the Mescaleros who were then receiving small rations of corn and beef (Reeve 1858a).

In assessing the impact of American power on Mescalero social organization it is important to bear in mind that the Apache faced similar pressures over a lengthy period of time. Spanish policy for the control of the northern frontier had involved military expeditions, defensive bastions, and attempts to settle the Indians through the provision of rations, the introduction of farming, and the construction of special communities in the vicinity of presidios. Conflict with the Comanche also assumed increasing importance by the latter portion of the 18th century; Cordero (Matson and Schroeder 1957:354) claimed that by 1796 the group he referred to as "Mescalero" had been reduced to a small number of families as a result of the Comanche struggle. It is reasonable to suggest, then, that the features of political organization to be discussed below do not represent adaptation to a novel repertoire of problems. At a minimum, the form of Mescalero political units could not be inconsistent with the requirements of the continual emergency war footing engendered by the features of the wider political field in which the tribe was enmeshed.

Mescalero Band Organization

The maximal level of integration among Mescalero, as I have pointed out elsewhere (Basehart 1967:277), did not comprehend a political nexus; there was no tribal chief, no council of leaders, and no devices for decision making which could implicate the tribe as a whole. It might be argued that all Mescalero acknowledged at least one general norm—the right of freedom of access to resources—and that tribesmen therefore were bound together under a common rule of law, but there was no superordinate authority empowered to administer this "law," as there was no single office for dealing with pressing questions of offense and defense. Bands did act in concert on particular occasions, but there is little evidence to support the assertion of Major Carleton's informant in 1853 that: "When they are engaged in war, or upon any other enterprise of importance, these bands become united . . . [and] choose a head-man to direct affairs for the time being" (Carleton 1855: 315). Indeed, this view is contradicted by the statements of two "captains or chiefs" (Palanco and Santos) who visited Lt. Col. Miles at Ft. Fillmore in 1854: ". . . they replied, their nation was broken up into bands, there was no head captain or chief, but each acted independently and as he thought proper" (Miles 1854).

While the tribe was not a political entity, the wider integration of the resource holding corporation had a significant implication for political behavior in that decisions by bands in relation to public goals did not lead to conflict over subsistence. Thus, one potential source of tension among these units was minimized and the principle of mobility was maximized.

With this background it is possible to turn to a more detailed examination of salient features of the band. The following topics will be discussed: number of bands; band size; territoriality; membership composition; production and distribution; inter-band relations; and offense and defense.

Numbers of Bands and Band Size. Despite many limitations, documentary sources provide the most definitive evidence as to the number and size of Mescalero bands during the early period of American contact. Informants' statements with respect to pre-reservation group size were clouded by their conviction that there were very large numbers of Mescalero at that time and by the viewpoint exemplified by one very old man's comment that "there never was any reason to count the number of tipis."

I have examined historical materials (primarily letters from military officers and Indian agents) for references to leaders during the years 1849 through 1861. For purposes of discussion, the names of "chiefs and captains" were grouped into two time periods: (1) from 1849 to 1854, when American officials sought to deal with an undifferentiated Apache entity and no treaties signed exclusively by Mescaleros appear in the records; (2) from 1855 to 1861, a period marked initially and finally by treaties involving only Mescalero leaders. The names of 19 different leaders were recorded between 1849–1854 for an area ranging from Manzano and Anton Chico, New Mexico, on the north to Presidio del Norte, in Texas, on the south. The most extensive lists for this time period were provided by Carleton's 1853 diary with 7 names (Carleton 1855:315), and by a letter from Lt. Col. Miles at Ft. Fillmore which noted the names of 9 band leaders (Miles 1854). The number of names increased markedly for the 7-year period 1855–1861, with references to 31 leaders; 5 of these were reported to have died or been killed by 1857. The largest registers of names are those of the 1855 Fort Thorn treaty, where 16 signatures appear, and a treaty revision of 1861 with 14 names (Roberts 1861). Sixteen names appear also in the minutes of a talk between Lt. Col. Miles and leaders at Dog Canyon (Pee 1855). To summarize, historical reports indicate that United States authorities recognized as many as 26 leaders at a given time among Mescalero during the years 1855–1861.

It is possible that the estimation of the number of bands by the enumeration of leaders' names exaggerates the segmented character of Mescalero political organization. But I do not think so. Some names mentioned in the documents may be those of fledgling leaders who may not have been able to maintain their positions over time but, as later materials will suggest, this is an expectable feature of the political process. Further, the available documents do not provide comprehensive coverage for the southern part of the Mescalero range; for example, the names of only six leaders who favored the territory beginning with the southern portion of the Guadalupe mountains were noted. Since there is no evidence indicating that groups in this region differed from those in the north who were better known to American officials, it is not likely that estimates based upon historical data are inflated.

Historical materials provide only a few references pertinent to the question of band size. The most significant general account is that of Carleton's informant, based upon 8 months residence as a Mescalero captive. He reported the strength of 7 bands in terms of "fighting men" as follows: 40; 9; 19; 20; 15; 13; 19. In addition, two chiefs in the Sacramento mountains were said to have 50 warriors (Carleton 1855:315). Information complementing Carleton's record is sparse. Venancio and Mateo visited Apache Agency in 1859 with 15 men and boys and 45 women and children (Steck 1859b), and Manuelito was said to have "about" 30 warriors when attacked by Capt. Graydon in 1862 (Carson 1862). An anonymous memorandum of 1857 includes figures juxtaposed to four leaders' names; presumably, these refer to group size. The figures are: 120, 140, 150, 160. Other indications of band size are provided by estimates of the number of "lodges": Cigarito's camp in 1849 had 25 lodges (Whiting 1938:276); "José Cito" was said to head about 20 lodges in 1851 (although Carleton credited him with but 9 warriors in 1853); late in 1869 Lt. Cushing destroyed a Mescalero rancheria consisting of "40 to 50 wigwams," and another of "about 25 wigwams" (Hennisee 1870).

I have used these and similar sources (Basehart 1967:282) to offer "an informed guess as to band size . . . [estimating] that numbers ranged from about 45 to 300 men, women, and children. The majority of bands at this time [in the 1850s] were intermediate in size, with a population of about 90 to 100 persons."

Informants' accounts corroborate the documentary materials in a general way. A few older Mescalero were familiar with the names of pre-Fort Stanton leaders such as Cadete, but the majority of references were to chiefs of the early reservation period—Natsile, San Juan, Roman, Tobacco. In addition, a number of less widely known men were designated as leaders by different informants and as "prominent men," but not leaders, by others. If these two categories are considered together, the number of leaders would approximate that reported for the 1850s. Further, groups with prominent men as their focus were small in size, suggesting a range of variation in band size consistent with the available evidence from the historical records.

TERRITORIALITY. The spatial aspect of Mescalero band organization needs careful statement if an adequate description is to be achieved. It is important to emphasize that bands were not local groups; they were not resource holding units, and exercised no control over a specific portion of land. At the same time, as I have noted (Basehart 1967:286), Mescalero recognized large named geographical regions which certain bands tended to frequent and within which particular leaders and their groups had favored camping places. But the exercise of these preferences was always subject to the subsistence pressures which were the critical determinant of Mescalero location at a particular time.

American officials were primarily interested in classifying the Indians as peaceful or hostile, but they also tended to seek information linking leaders with particular territories. For example, in 1854 Lt. Col. Miles wrote that two chiefs of bands ranging west of the Sacramento mountains to Manzano had reported on the localities occupied by 7 other groups. A hostile leader, Santa Ana, ranged from the Sacramentos to Guadalupes; 3 bands were east of the Sacramentos; and 3 others were located south of these latter (Miles 1854). The geographical references are highly general, but even so the statement tends to overformalize the bonds between leader and territory. When the names and locations of leaders recorded during the early portion of U.S. control are plotted on maps, the historical documents lend support to the emphasis placed here on band mobility. Leaders' names are duplicated in varied locales extending from Agua Nueva in Mexico in the south to the White mountains and as far north as Anton Chico, New Mexico.[1]

The polarization of Mescalero into northern and southern divisions delineated by Agent Steck receives only slight support from ethnographic and historical sources. Steck considered that the northern portion of the tribe constituted the "peace party" and asserted that "at least 3/4 of the robberies committed by Mescaleros have been committed by Agua Nuevo Apaches . . ." (Steck 1856). These Apaches, he wrote, "belong to the dept. of Texas, live in the southern portion of the Guadalupe and in the Limpia Mts. from there into the mts between the City of Chihuihui and the Rio Grande . . ." (Steck 1857b). Nevertheless, "southern" leaders also frequented the Sacramentos (Steck 1859a) and northerners appeared in the southern Guadalupes and elsewhere in the south. The patterns of movement of leaders and their groups reported by informants covered a geographical range from north to south; in the course of time most leaders visited the "network foci" and sacred places located in both northern and southern reaches of Mescalero territory (Basehart 1960:106–110; 1967:279–281, 284). When the Mescalero as a whole are considered, group movements were conditioned by environmental factors, including climate and seasonal developments affecting plant and animal life, so that there was a tendency for people living in the north to shift gradually southward with the approach of winter. Similarly, southern groups were likely to move to the northern mountains during the summer. These general patterns should not be overformalized, however; there were many exceptions and decisions about actual group movements at any particular time depended upon the assessment of the relative importance of multiple variables.

In summary, then, Mescalero statements exalting their one-time freedom to roam as they pleased appear something more than nostalgic constructs developed to counter the boundedness of contemporary reservation life. Leaders and their groups did manifest long term preferences for particular localities, other factors being equal. I do not know that groups with favorite spots in the same general area considered themselves as sharing a larger territorial communion, although these regions were recognized by Mescalero names. Commitment, ideologically and in terms of resource utilization, was to mobility as opposed to geographical entrenchment.

Band Membership. Band composition, like band size, was variable, subject to fluctuation over time, and determined primarily by the character of the leader. Kinsmen of the leader comprised the nucleus of the unit and ordinarily were, as well, its persisting feature. However, kinship was not a defining attribute for recruitment to the band; a close relative of the leader could choose to affiliate with another group, and even small bands were not composed exclusively of kinsmen. The constitution of the band was influenced by the options open to its members, who were free to align themselves with another group, or with no group at all, as they chose. A specific band might persist over time, but it need not do so. As bands grew, lost members, disappeared, and new groups developed there was a continual but gradual redistribution of the population. In this state of flux the fixed reference point was provided by the leader, for whatever the fortunes of a particular group, the system of leaders and followers was the perduring feature of the political scheme among Mescalero.

Detailed information on band composition during the 1850s could hardly be expected, but it is possible to reconstruct the general features of one leader's group for a later period on the basis of informants' accounts. In the 1880s this band occupied a relatively remote area of the reservation some 35 miles from Agency headquarters, and members had little contact with government officials.

At various times the band included three different groups whose members were unrelated or linked by genealogical ties so remote that kinship was not considered a binding element for the group as a whole. Two of the groups occupied camp sites situated about a mile apart; the third group was less strongly attached and might camp in the area for several years, move to another part of the reservation, and return once more to the band.

The leader's camp, referred to as the Lower group, was composed of a small cluster of con-

[1] The mobility of Mescalero leaders and their groups is evidenced by the migratory patterns described briefly in previous reports (Basehart 1967:279–281; Basehart 1960:106–110).

sanguineal and affinal kinsmen including the leader and his wife; the latter's mother; 2 sons, one of whom was married but had no children; and 2 married daughters with their husbands, children, and the mother of one of the husbands.

The camp of the Upper group was of more heterogeneous composition. In the kinship nucleus of the elder and his wife were 2 married sons and their children; the brother of one of the daughters-in-law, his wife, wife's mother, and wife's sister; 2 married daughters and their husbands; and one unmarried daughter. In the same camp, but unrelated to the elder, were 2 brothers, their wives, and children.

Information with respect to the membership of the third group associated with this leader is muddled as well as deficient. Most informants considered that the elder was a prominent man who had attracted a few people other than kinsmen to himself, but they were unable to specify the composition of the group. Others linked the elder with another man who, with his brother, had achieved some renown through raiding. The two elders were said to be married to sisters, with the combined families roaming in the Staked Plains region. The data are frequently contradictory but it seems clear that the elder, his family, and allies did camp for extended periods in the remote corner of the reservation favored by the band under discussion.

The variation in informants' statements with respect to the composition of this band may be taken as representative of the flexibility of bands in general. Thus, two brothers who were kinsmen of an in-married female of the Upper band segment lived in the area for a time; both were suspected of witchcraft and moved elsewhere. The taint of witchcraft remained with the group, however, and was the basis for strained relationships between the segments. Eventually a quarrel developed during a drinking party, the leader was killed and the band dissolved.

The extent to which similar events led to band fission or breakdown in earlier days is difficult to determine. Fights accompanying drinking are reported in ethnographic and historical accounts, but the effect on group organization is unclear. Vengeance was likely to follow immediately after an act of violence, but if the guilty party escaped and remained away from the band for a year or so, he could regain membership in his original group. The minimal role of ascription in defining band membership made it easy for individuals and larger units to become followers of another leader, and it might be expected that this option would be elected when friction became evident. The instance of band dissolution remarked above occurred in late reservation days when band mobility was restricted and pressures for a sedentary mode of life had become effective. Thus, tensions which might have been contained by the flexible band organization apparently became explosive when constrained in a bounded field of social relations.

The inclusion of both married sons and daughters in the membership of Upper and Lower segments of the band may appear to conflict with Mescalero norms stressing matrilocal residence after marriage, the strong bonds between mother and daughter, the perception of the son-in-law as an economic asset, and the great importance attached to respect in defining relations between an in-marrying male and his affines. However, it is not evident that the presence of married offspring of both sexes represents a departure from earlier custom. Informants did emphasize that a young married couple should reside initially in the wife's mother's camp, but they placed equal stress on the prerogative of the couple to decide for themselves their later residential arrangements. If the son-in-law was a good husband and provider, the girl's parents preferred that the couple continue residence with them, but it does not seem that they had a jural right to demand conformity to their desires. Matrilocal residence may have been statistically predominant, but exceptions would not violate expressed norms. Further, political factors possibly exerted pressure for the retention of married sons and daughters in the core kinship clusters of leaders and elders. Documents from the 1850s and later years occasionally report sons succeeding fathers as "chiefs," and imply that the former had been active members of their fathers' groups. This pattern, of course, would be consistent with the organization of the Upper and Lower segments of the group which has been described as illustrating the principles of Mescalero band composition.

Production and Distribution. The majority of productive activities were carried out in the context of the band, although the extent to which the group constituted a single foraging unit depended upon its size. In addition, larger groups were considered advantageous for certain tasks such as bison hunting, so that several bands or segments of them might unite for hunting on the plains. In general, hunting and gathering activities were organized informally, with participation in a particular activity open to all members of the band but required of none.[2] For a band of average size—perhaps 100 persons—foraging parties of men and women at any given time were likely to include only a portion of the group's membership. Hunting or collecting by solitary individuals was condemned as representing stinginess; this was particularly true for hunting, since every member of the hunting party was entitled to share the meat and other products of animals killed. According to informants, the male membership of a band did not form a distinctive unit for raiding. Any warrior, in theory, could propose a raid, drawing upon volunteers from his own band as well as others who became acquainted with the plan and were enticed by the prospect of booty.

Subsistence activities, then, centered about the band, although cooperative task groups were rarely composed of all the able-bodied members of the unit. Nevertheless, from another perspective, the band can be considered as a unitary productive group, since the membership of various task groups fluctuated over brief periods of time. Individuals who hunted or collected together on one occasion were likely to associate with others at another time, whether for the same or different tasks. The shifting alliances of kinsmen and neighbors in productive activities resulted in an intricate cooperative network of a flexible character focusing on the band but capable of extension beyond it to adapt to exigencies of the subsistence quest.

Patterns of reciprocity insured the circulation of subsistence products throughout the band. Successful hunters, upon their return to camp, could expect to receive visits from relatives, friends, and neighbors; the visitors were considered entitled to gifts of meat and could not be turned away empty-handed. Thus, in addition to the sharing of game among members of the hunting party, further distribution brought the majority of the family units in the camp into the exchange system. Livestock secured as booty in raids were eventually slaughtered (except for horses) and the meat distributed in the same way as for game.[3] If a number of horses were captured, they were divided among members of the raiding party; warriors with excess horses might present one to in-laws or other kinsmen, or to an elderly man or woman without transportation. Wild plant foods likewise were widely disseminated by means of transactions initiated by visits after women returned from gathering expeditions. It is worth noting, incidentally, that the more reliable subsistence pursuit of gathering was not characterized by the sharing of the collected products among the women of the task group, in contrast to the obligatory distribution of meat among those participating in a hunt. Game and wild plant foods in excess of immediate needs were preserved and stored for future use by individual family units.

Although the band was a focus for production and distribution, it was not a wholly independent economic entity. Not only might members of other bands be included in particular task groups and visitors share in the distribution of foodstuffs, but the band ultimately was dependent upon freedom of access to the varied resources available in the total tribal territory.

INTER-BAND RELATIONS. Mescalero bands were autonomous and equivalent political units despite the considerable variation in the number of members comprising the groups. The bands constituted a segmentary organization in that structurally similar units were replicated throughout Mescalero territory. In a very broad sense bands also may be thought of as segmentally opposed, if it is remembered that groups were open rather than closed and that, over time, groups were continually forming and reforming. Bands competed with one another for members and opposed one another in attempting to maintain their identity.

Intergroup relationships were not characterized by conflict. Common membership in the resource holding corporation eliminated a potential major source of conflict over access to subsistence resources. Bands, further, were not

[2] The extent to which captives were utilized for production aside from labor within the camp is not clear. Whiting (1938:277–278) reported of Cigarito's camp in 1849: "Each lodge also has a Mexican slave, a boy or girl stolen in infancy and brought up by the blows of the women to very severe labor. Literally do the Mexican race thus become hewers of wood and drawers of water, bondsmen to the Indian." However, some captives became fully assimilated to Mescalero life ways, and assumed customary male or female roles.

[3] Steck, in 1857, estimated that ½ of the subsistence of non-rationed Apache bands was derived from stealing (Steck 1857a).

vengeance units; no band member was required to "take up the fight" for an injured party simply because of shared group membership. Informants recalled numerous instances of intragroup violence, but only one example of conflict between bands was reported. In this case, both groups were reputed to be quarrelsome and "tough"; there was mutual dislike between the leaders. Eventually the bands engaged in an open fight during a ceremonial in the Guadalupe mountains, several persons were killed, and one group left Mescalero country to live among the Jicarilla for a number of years.

The character of intergroup relations also was influenced by a widely ramified network of consanguineal and affinal ties. As noted earlier, band membership was not defined exclusively by kinship and, while the group was not exogamous, cognatic kin restrictions channeled the majority of marriages outside the band. It is unlikely that every Mescalero leader's group could claim to have kinsmen in every other group, but kinship links were very extensive.[4]

Opportunities for social interaction, in addition to encounters in the course of the subsistence quest, were furthered by the presence of network foci and by ceremonies, especially the puberty ritual for girls, which attracted large numbers of visitors.

Finally, the flexibility of band membership contributed to solidary ties among these units. Individuals could and frequently did shift their band affiliations for a number of reasons: to escape conflict or vengeance; when in mourning; in fear of witchcraft; to attach themselves to a particularly successful leader. These shifting allegiances aligned persons in different oppositions at various times, restricted the development of exclusive solidarities, and reduced the possibility of intergroup conflict.

OFFENSE AND DEFENSE. Informants conceived of the band as the major locus for personal security and cited its role in defense as the most important function performed by the unit. The mountains, although offering some protection, were not a secure haven, while the plains were even more hazardous. Mescalero thought of themselves as constantly exposed to enemy attack; thus, camp sites commonly were selected for their defensive potential rather than for convenience. The disposition of lodges in the camp reflected Mescalero conceptions of tactical advantages in different ecological zones: in the mountains lodges tended to be scattered, while they were grouped together more closely on the plains.

The band acted as a unit for defense rather than offense. The hit-and-run raid was the characteristic offensive tactic; as noted above, members of a raiding party might be drawn from a single band or from several groups. Offensive and defensive tactics were opportunistic. If a raiding objective was strongly defended the warriors sought another target, and a camp usually would be actively defended only when the attacking force was weak. The major advantage of the band for defense was that it provided sufficient manpower for guarding the camp and for engaging in delaying action in the event of an attack, while the group was small enough to permit rapid escape when necessary.

Although Mescalero generally avoided large scale confrontations with an enemy, historical sources and informants' accounts indicate the possibility of concerted action on occasion. In engagements with United States army units in 1855, according to Steck, the military strength of northern groups was greatly augmented by "Mescaleros belonging to the state of Texas and Chihuihui [who] were fighting and acting with them" (Steck 1856). Lt. Lazelle's account of his pursuit of raiders who stole stock from San Elizario offers another example of Mescalero ability to bring together larger forces under propitious circumstances. Lazelle, with 30 men, followed the trail of the raiding party for several days and eventually encountered 30 armed warriors in the Dog Canyon area of the Sacramentos. The troops advanced to the raiders' camp—the lodges were temporary structures of boughs and leaves, and women and children were absent—but did not attack because their position was unfavorable. When Lazelle and his command engaged the Indians on the following day, the latter's force had been reinforced and numbered 50 to 60 warriors. The American troops suffered casualties in the skirmish that followed and were forced to retreat (Lazelle 1895). Two Mescalero leaders and their people were charged with re-

4 Kin ties between bands were noted occasionally in the historical records; as one example "Binanchio," the leader of a group whose activities tended to center on the southern portion of the Mescalero area, was married to the daughter of Manco, one of the leaders at Fort Stanton (Reeve 1858b).

sponsibility for the fight in informants' reports to Steck (Steck 1859b). At the same time it should be emphasized that there was no organization for regularly assuring collective action by a number of bands under a single "headman" for warfare or other "enterprises of importance," as Carleton's guide had maintained (Carleton 1855:315).

Documentary materials affirm informants' perceptions of their situation as one requiring constant vigilance in the face of persistent danger of enemy attack. Lax security could lead to disaster, as when Lt. Cushing's forces surprised a rancheria of 40 to 50 lodges late in 1869 in the southern Guadalupes. The Indians fought a delaying action which permitted residents of the camp to escape, but a number of warriors were killed and a large store of provisions and equipment abandoned (Cushing 1870).

Leaders and Leadership

Mescalero leaders were men of influence rather than wielders of power. To state this is not to imply that leaders were ineffective; on the contrary, they were the embodiment as well as the symbol of Mescalero polity. In discussions of decision making the counterpoise of the rugged individualism of the ordinary Mescalero was the model of the "good thinking man"—the leader. In the metaphor of one informant, "Only the leader has a swivel in his neck, so he can turn; the others have a stiff neck, so he guides them, commands them." In fact, the leader did not command; he could not order his followers to take any specific course of action; however reasonable. He could exhort and persuade, and his effectiveness was in large measure a function of his ability to "preach to the people," as Mescalero say. "Good thinking" and "good talking" were inseparably linked attributes of the leader. Other qualities, such as renown as a warrior, were decidedly secondary in importance. An inarticulate man, however great his knowledge and experience, would be unable to assume the role of leader. But in spite of the emphasis placed on verbal facility as a prerequisite for leadership, the Mescalero leader was not described as gregarious. He was expected to offer food and drink to his followers after the customary morning discussion of problems, as he was expected to be generous and aware of the needs of his people. I have the impression (though the evidence, admittedly, is slight) that leaders tended to maintain a degree of social distance from ordinary members of their bands, preserving a demeanor of dignity and, perhaps, aloofness.[5]

Reciprocal respect governed the relationships between leaders and members of their bands. Respect was the major prestation extended to the leader, and in return he was expected to have respect for his people; failure to conform to this expectation could result in the dissolution of the band. According to some informants a leader might occasionally be offered gifts of subsistence products or other items, but these were neither presented regularly nor in large amounts. The leader, then, did not serve as a focus for the collection and redistribution of subsistence or other products.

There was not a one-for-one correspondence between leadership and prowess in warfare and raiding. Some mid-19th century leaders were noted as raiders, but others were not. Informants disagreed as to whether leaders ought to accompany raiding parties, but achievement in this domain was not considered an essential quality for a leader. Whether, as some Mescalero claimed, leaders essentially were peaceful men who discouraged raids is doubtful; probably these statements reflect the altered role of leaders in the reservation period.

Leadership was not linked to the possession of supernatural power, even though it is likely that leaders, like other Mescalero, had access to some source of power. The role of seer, in particular, was considered distinct from that of leader, and accounts of the acquisition of supernatural blessings do not feature leaders as recipients.

Consistent with the emphasis on wisdom and experience as attributes of leadership, informants considered that full adult status was a prerequisite for assumption of the leader's role. A youth in his 20s who had for years participated in raids might arouse sufficient support to form and lead a raiding party, but his authority was

[5] Leaders did not wear distinctive regalia, although historical records note that a few had adopted hats and other articles of Spanish clothing. The leader's lodge, usually a commodious tipi, was situated in the center of the camp; in 1849 Whiting noted that the only tipi in Cigarito's Davis mountain camp was that of the leader (Whiting 1938:276).

limited to that specific task. Experience, ordinarily gained through maturity, constituted the most heavily weighted criterion for the leadership of various task groups. The historical materials rarely specify the ages of leaders, but it is a reasonable inference that in most cases American agents dealt with mature men. Several chiefs were elderly men: Cigarito, in 1849, was an "old and portly man" (Whiting 1938:270); Barranquito was reported to be a "feeble old man" (Miles 1855); Pluma was listed as the "old chief" in a document of 1857 (Anonymous 1857). At the same time, some leaders must have been considerably younger: Whiting estimated that Gomez was 30 or 35 years old; Barranquito died in 1856 and was succeeded by his son, Cadete (Van Horne 1956) ; by 1857 Jose Pino had succeeded his father, Pluma, as leader, although the latter was still alive (Anonymous 1857).

Equality of access to resources and reciprocal gift-giving limited the development of differences in wealth among members of a band but did not prevent some individuals from acquiring a greater store of valued items, especially horses. The leader, however, was not a wealthy man; the demands upon his generosity were too great to permit accumulation. Through diligent industry the leader was expected to be able to procure goods sufficient for the requirements of hospitality. By example and by exhortation he sought to insure that his less fortunate followers received at least a minimal share in whatever good fortune the band might have.

Mescalero offer a clear conceptual distinction between individuals categorized as "chiefs" and others whom they class as "prominent men," but not leaders or chiefs. Earlier, I referred to the latter as "elders," and the term is not altogether inapt since longevity was valued and the long-lived person was accorded special recognition. The incumbents of a variety of roles (some of which were open to women as well as men) might be considered prominent—for example, warriors, seers, hunters, and shamans. However, I am concerned primarily with those persons whom Mescalero regard as filling a leadership role, in addition to whatever other roles they may have occupied. There was considerable disagreement among informants as to the proper classification of "elders" (i.e., "prominent men"); some considered them to be leaders—albeit with a small number of followers —while others regarded them as equivalent to family heads within the band. The conceptual distinction between prominent men and leaders evoked greater informant consistency than did judgments about the position of particular individuals, which appear to reflect the reference group orientations of the informants. It is possible that the dichotomy attained importance after the 1850s, as American officials attempted to impose a "head chief" upon the Mescalero. As noted earlier, group size varied considerably in the 1850s, but it is not evident that the leaders of smaller groups were subordinate to chiefs with larger followings. In general, then, it seems probable that the category of prominent man, with the connotation of relatively permanent subordination to a leader, was a development of the reservation situation. And the uncertainty manifested by Mescalero as to who was or was not a leader again suggests that the partitioning of the role of leader had greater conceptual than practical significance.

Thus far I have examined leadership in terms of various qualities which have relevance for the role of leader. Now, I propose to review aspects of leadership which depict the leader as a man of action in relation to internal and external problems of the band. I will discuss, first, his role in decision making and affect management within the band and, second, his relation to outsiders as representative of the band.

A critical feature of leadership emerged in the process of decision making, where the mettle of the leader was constantly tested. The leader exercised no power, but his contribution as catalyst in the development of decisions was of major importance. Typically, members of the band gathered at the leader's lodge in the early morning and the leader initiated a discussion of current problems. An exchange of views followed, with the leader proffering a suggested solution for the question at issue. Often the leader's proposal was accepted without debate; if opposition developed, a compromise might be attempted. When consensus could not be reached, the gathering simply dissolved. The leader's judgment and skill in persuasion was severely tested under these conditions, as failure to assess adequately the disposition of his followers could result in the fragmentation of the band. Particularly in large bands, the leader's conception of a program adaptive to public goals might conflict with the interests of segments of the group, so that it would be necessary for the former to weigh the importance of a proposed course of action for the group as a whole against the possibility of loss of members.

In addition to the group perspective which the leader brought to bear on his program formulations, he had the advantage of greater access to information and, probably, a more profound understanding of the range of alternatives open to the band. Visitors, including his peers, sought the lodge of the leader and provided reports on current conditions in other parts of Mescalero territory. Although a leader probably had no more detailed knowledge of ecology than other members of the band, his assessment of the multiple variables involved in decisions with respect to major subsistence movements often reflected his "good thinking." An illustration is provided by informants' accounts of the selection of a site for a permanent reservation settlement when the tribe was removed from Fort Stanton. Several leaders proposed different locations, but neglected to consider one or another ecological factor. The "good thinking" leader—variously identified by different informants—argued for the advantages of the modern Agency area, pointing to the abundance of game, firewood, and water for irrigation.

A successful leader needed to be aware of tensions within the band, which could pose problems requiring the utmost in resourcefulness. On some occasions he served as a mediator in disputes, but more than a modicum of delicacy and skill was essential since an inept move by the leader could result in accusations of meddling or favoritism. At the same time the leader's attempts to reduce tension were buttressed by his reputation for "good talk," or "preaching." Mescalero evidence a strong distaste for people who "talk too much" and are wary of gossip, which may lead to charges and counter-charges of witchcraft. In a solidary group, this "bad talk" was countered by the "good talk" of the leader, emphasizing the major values crucial to community solidarity. The leader was the exemplar of the moral order, stressing by behavior and word the values of sharing, generosity (especially to the poor and solitary aged), industriousness, cooperation, and vigilance. It is not an exaggeration, I think, to view this expressive aspect of leadership as the critical bonding element in group solidarity. The post of leader was the major fixed point in the flux of the social landscape, apart from kinship; most Mescalero sought to orient themselves by this persisting symbol of sociability. Strong commitment to leaders was the rule rather than the exception. As one informant remarked: "There's no guidance without the leaders and that guidance they have to have."

In external relationships the leader represented his band vis-à-vis like units and in relation to foreigners. This aspect of the leader's role became increasingly significant during the period of Anglo-American contact, to judge by the historical records, although it had been important earlier, as well. By the 1850s some leaders had become skilled in using their representative role to create images designed to win approval and support from foreigners. Consider the plight of Barranquito, as reported by Lt. Col. Miles in 1855:

> Belanquito [spelling uncertain] has professed entire ignorance of everything tending to rascality in his nation. He says he would be the last to hear of it, and is in daily apprehension of being killed by other bands. His own whipped him this day week. He of course must lie to screen his men, for he sent Indians in when Haywards horse was stolen to inform me that a man of Francisco's party had taken it. He is a poor feeble old man, with no authority or consideration, troublesome, *and in the way*. . . .

The details provided by Barranquito are dubious, but they constitute a well-designed instance of impression management. To arouse compassion the leader displayed his weakness; he emphasized his lack of power as a prelude to a disclaimer of responsibility for the actions of his band. But, despite the dubiety of the particulars of this account, the statements form an impeccable record of the realities of power in the Mescalero band. Historical sources provide numerous instances of leaders acting in representative roles in relation to American officials and, as well, to one another.

The multiple expectations linked with leadership militated against the development of hereditary principles of succession. Nevertheless, a son, brother, or other relative closely associated with a leader occupied a strategic position in that he could familiarize himself with the problems of the post. As noted earlier, sons of two leaders succeeded their fathers in the 1850s, while at least one uncle of Cadete was a leader (Anonymous 1857). Mescalero did not always find the preferred qualities in their leaders, and recognized that more than one style of leadership was possible. There were limits to permissible variation in role performance, however; a leader who exceeded these limits was faced with the ultimate sanction of desertion. His followers simply left the camp and aligned themselves with other groups. As an example, an informant cited the case of a man who lost his position as "chief" when it was discovered that he was dishonest, unreliable, and a liar. I could not determine the frequency of failed leaders from available data, but informants appear to believe that the conjunction of qualities necessary for effective leadership was relatively uncommon.

In this discussion of leadership I have depended largely upon ethnographic data secured from Mescalero informants whose experiences at best date to the Fort Stanton period preceding the establishment of the present-day reservation. It is reasonable to ask whether informants' reports may not represent changes in leadership patterns fostered by the conditions of reservation control. Is the leader whose expressive function embodied band solidarity, the "good thinking" man, the product of recent social change? A number of lines of evidence, including historical data, could be pursued in attempting to answer this question. However, I will limit myself to two points: (1) there was some continuity of leadership from pre- to post-reservation periods, so that characterizations of early post-reservation leaders need not be caricatures of earlier leaders; (2) the problems confronting Mescalero in the course of Anglo-American contact were different in degree rather than kind from those faced during the Mexican and Spanish periods. There is no clear evidence that a different type of leadership was immediately required by United States control which, in any event, was not completely effective until about 1880.

Conclusion

Mescalero social organization has been depicted in terms of two levels of integration: on the one hand, the tribal resource holding corporation and, on the other, the small band centered on the leader.[6] At the maximal level of integration the resource holding corporation linked tribal members through their shared right to exploit a territory common to all. The character of the integration provided by the multifunctional band is perhaps more obvious, in part because anthropologists commonly have examined this process by reference to the political variable, and the band is the effective political unit among Mescalero. At this point I wish to explore briefly the problem of the adaptive-integrative significance of the band and of leadership with particular reference to the variables of mobility and flexibility.

Mescalero subsistence required access to a range of resources which varied geographically, seasonally, and over time. The exploitation of these resources necessitated traversing an extensive territory, as well as lesser movements when animal and plant foods were discovered. With the availability of horses, rapid movement of large groups would have been possible, but in practice subsistence moves were gradual, with members of the band seeking to maximize whatever windfalls they might encounter on their route. In good years the combined resources accessible to Mescalero might have supported aggregations larger than bands for extended periods, but small groups were just as effective under these optimal conditions. When food sources were scarce, bands scattered over the territory provided for maximal utilization, while minimizing problems of distribution and consumption. Further, as noted earlier, the common defensive tactic was based upon the mobility assured by groups of small size.

The external pressures which placed Mescalero on a constant emergency footing contributed to the continued importance of flexibility for their social organization. The open character of band membership permitted the redistribution of personnel in the event of losses in warfare and raiding. In competition among bands there was selection for the efficient leader; the ineffective chief was deserted by his followers and his group failed to persist as an independent entity. Flexibility applied to interband relationships also, as both alliance and disjunction were feasible when situationally warranted. Relations among groups were not defined in pyramidal

[6] In addition, I recognize a third level of integration of the Mescalero social system: the domestic level. However, problems of kinship and family organization related to this level of integration have not been explored in this paper.

fashion, however, and there was no genealogical or other specified form to order the massing of segments. At the political level the autonomy of the band paralleled the individual's right to independent decision.

In the context of mobility and flexibility the role of the leader acquires added significance. For all that he was but first among equals, he was the firm reference point in a system lacking fixed membership groups above the level of domestic units. The institution of leadership preserved the options of the individual at the same time that it fostered the processes that maintained a structure of autonomous political segments. It is appropriate that, for Mescalero, the leader rather than a territorial locus was the prime symbol of the band. Whereas the widest integration of Mescalero society was achieved through the resource holding corporation in which each individual was a shareholder, the band was the essential intermediate unit, mediating between the shareholder and the maximal extension of solidarity represented by the corporation.

BIBLIOGRAPHY

Anonymous

1857 Names of some of the Principal Mezcalero Apaches who have been in at Fort Stanton. March 25, 1857. (Probably a draft memorandum).

Basehart, Harry W.

1960 *Mescalero Apache Subsistence Patterns and Socio-Political Organization.* The University of New Mexico Mescalero-Chiricahua Land Claims Project (mimeograph).

1967 The Resource Holding Corporation Among the Mescalero Apache. *Southwestern Journal of Anthropology* 23:277-291.

Carleton, James Henry

1855 Diary of an Excursion to the Ruins of Abo, Quarra and Gran Quivira, in New Mexico, under the Command of Major James Henry Carleton, U.S.A. *Ninth Annual Report of the Smithsonian Institution,* Washington, D.C.

Carson, Col. C.

1862 Carson, Col. C., Fort Stanton, New Mexico. October 30, 1862. Unpublished letter to Lt. B. C. Cutler. The National Archives, Record Group No. 98, Washington.

Cushing, Lt. H. B.

1870 Cushing, Lt. H. B., Fort Stanton, New Mexico, January 8, 1870. Unpublished report to post adjutant. The National Archives, Record Group No. 98, Washington.

Hennisee, Lt. A. G.

1870 Hennisee, Lt. A. G., Fort Stanton, New Mexico. January 31, 1870. Unpublished letter to Major William Clinton. The National Archives, Record Group No. 75, Washington.

Lazelle, Lt. H. M.

1859 Lazelle, Lt. H. M., Fort Bliss, Texas. February 18, 1859. Unpublished letter to Lt. William Jackson. The National Archives, Record Group No. 98, Washington.

Matson, Daniel S., and Albert H. Schroeder

1957 Cordero's Description of the Apache—1796. *New Mexico Historical Review* 32:335–356.

Miles, Lt. Col. D. J.

1854 Miles, Lt. Col. D. J., Fort Fillmore, New Mexico. September 18, 1854. Unpublished letter to W. A. Nichols. The National Archives, Record Group No. 98, Washington.

1855 Miles, Lt. Col. D. J., Fort Fillmore, New Mexico, August 12, 1855. Unpublished letter to Dr. M. Steck. Steck Papers, University of New Mexico Library, Albuquerque.

Pee, P. E., Lt.

1855 Minutes of a "Talk" held at Dog Canyon on the third of April, 1855. National Archives, Record Group No. 75, Washington.

Reeve, Lt. Col. G. V. D.

1858a Reeve, Lt. Col. G. V. D., Fort Stanton, New Mexico. January 6, 1858. Unpublished letter to Major W. A. Nichols. The National Archives, Record Group No. 98, Washington.

1858b Reeve, Lt. Col. G. V. D., Fort Stanton, New Mexico. July 15, 1858. Unpublished letter to Major W. A. Nichols. The National Archives, Record Group No. 98, Washington.

Roberts, Col. B. S.

1861 Roberts, Col. B. S., Fort Stanton, New Mexico. May 24, 1861. Unpublished letter to Col. J. L. Collins. The National Archives, Record Group No. 75, Washington.

Steck, M.
1856 Steck, M., Fort Stanton, New Mexico. November 17, 1856. Unpublished letter to Governor Meriwether. Steck Papers, University of New Mexico Library, Albuquerque.
1857a *Annual Report of Commissioner of Indian Affairs.* Attached report No. 123.
1857b Steck, M., Apache Agency, New Mexico. June 8, 1857. Unpublished letter to Col. J. L. Collins. Steck Papers, University of New Mexico, Albuquerque.
1859a Steck, M., Apache Agency, New Mexico. February 11, 1859. Unpublished letter to Col. James L. Collins. The National Archives, Record Group No. 75, Washington.
1859b Steck, M., Apache Agency, New Mexico. February 27, 1859. Unpublished letter to Col. James L. Collins. Steck Papers, University of New Mexico Library, Albuquerque.
Stevenson, Capt. O. L.
1861 Stevenson, Capt. O. L., Fort Stanton, New Mexico. February 13, 1861. Unpublished letter to Capt. D. H. Marcy (?).
Thomas, A. B.
1932 *Forgotten Frontiers: A Study of the Spanish-Indian Policy of Don Juan Bautista de Anza, Governor of New Mexico, 1777–1787.* Norman: University of Oklahoma Press.
1941 *Teodoro de Croix and the Northern Frontier of New Spain, 1776–1783.* Norman: University of Oklahoma Press.
Van Horne, Major J.
1856 Van Horne, Major J., Fort Stanton, New Mexico. July 1, 1856. Unpublished letter to M. Steck. Steck Papers, University of New Mexico Library, Albuquerque.
Whiting, William Henry Chase
1938 "Journal of William Henry Chase Whiting, 1849" in *Exploring Southwest Trails, 1846–1854,* by Philip St. George Cooke, William Henry Chase Whiting, Francois Xavier Aubry, (ed. by Ralph B. Bieber.) The Arthur H. Clark Co., Glendale, California.

Noncentralized political systems characteristically provide a means of regulating conflict, administering internal affairs, and coping with external political relations among populations considerably larger than those of the band. Because of the semiautonomy of the extended kin group as a productive unit, most intervening action is still taken by elder kinsmen—in consultation, when necessary, with the senior members of neighboring groups with whom they are allied through marriage.

Consequently, differences between those most likely to come into contact—that is, those closest by—can often be settled in accordance with the rules that guide interaction, and usually prescribe cooperation, among groups united through marriage alliances. When this procedure occasionally proves unworkable, settlement is often achieved through appeal to the intervention of some "nonpolitical" person, usually a religious figure, whose ritual powers enable him to compel a settlement by threatening to evoke supernatural punishment upon any who fail to cooperate in reaching an accord.

Beyond the spread-out network of ties based on common blood or established through marriage the chances are that contact and the possibility of conflict will occur only intermittently. As a result permanent centralization of authority beyond the kin group is unnecessary even where the population is quite large and many of its members are not related.

This is the case with the El Shabana of Iraq. Fernea's description suggests how such noncentralized forms of political organization contain the structural elements necessary to evolve into the systems of fully centralized government, still deriving their structure from the kinship system, that have been a marked feature of the political history of much of the Middle East.

Segmentation of Authority Among the El Shabana of Iraq

Robert A. Fernea

Tribesmen in the Daghara area proudly claim descent from the great Bedouin tribes of the Arabian Peninsula and the Syrian Desert. The El Shabana tribesmen assert that they came originally from the Nejd during the eighteenth century, and are ultimately related to the Shammar. If this is correct, the tribal system of the El Shabana is partly the result of transformations that have occurred as the ancestors of the present-day tribesmen switched from the pastoral nomadism of desert life to a more sedentary existence in the Euphrates basin. The importance of this change should not be exaggerated, however. For the borders between Iraq and the rest of the Arabian Near East have never been effectively closed, and the settled tribesmen along the southern Euphrates have had continued opportunity for interaction with nomadic Bedouin. Although the settled tribesman sometimes appears to look down on the Bedu nomad of today, he takes pride in being able to demonstrate certain traditional characteristics of the desert Bedouin.

Pride in ancestry, emphasis on generous hospitality, recognition of the duty to revenge kinsmen wronged in feud, and belief in the values of warriorhood—these and other features are widely shared by both settled and nomadic Arabs from the deserts of Saudi Arabia, Syria, and southern Iraq. Therefore, although it is not the purpose of this discussion to trace the differences and similarities between traditional Bedouin culture and the culture of the Daghara Arabs, it should be remembered that close, persistent relations existed historically between these two groups and continue to exist at the present time.

In the last thirty years the introduction of effective local administration by a national government has brought many changes in the Daghara area, including pacification, taxation, land registration, and control over the large waterways. Formal classroom education and medical facilities have been introduced. Possibly a course has been established which will result in the ultimate dissolution of the tribe as a social system. But the tribe remains an organization of importance in the current affairs of this region and cannot yet be totally regarded as of merely historical interest.

The tribal system of the El Shabana may be defined either as a cultural ideal or as an imperfectly realized sociological reality: there is no absolute correspondence between the two possible statements although they are importantly related. As a cultural ideal, the tribal system is of considerable importance to the tribesman. Utilizing the idiom of kinship in some instances or the proper names of tribal groups in others, a man identifies himself and other tribesmen as if the cultural model absolutely prevailed. By so doing he helps perpetuate a system which originated in other than the present circumstances. Only by understanding the tribal system as part of the felt and conscious cultural equipment of the tribesman can we accept and understand the present apparent contradiction between the tribal cultural model and the equally real atribal economic and political relationships.

The contradictions may be partly explained by assuming that certain values and convictions rather than economic and political "realities" reinforce the cultural ideal. In Islamic culture as a whole, the pervasive and dominating belief is that earthly differences between men which place one above the other in an economic or political hierarchy are absolutely unimportant when compared with the differences between man and God. For men in submission to God are equally His servants and the God of Islam sanctions no status differences between men.[1] This is not to suggest that Daghara tribesmen believe God has ordained the cultural ideal of

Source: Reprinted by permission of the publishers and the author from *Shaykh and Effendi: Changing Patterns of Authority Among the El Shabana of Southern Iraq*, by Robert A. Fernea, Cambridge, Mass.: Harvard University Press, Copyright, 1970, by the President and Fellows of Harvard College.

[1] Some years ago an issue of a popular magazine featured a cartoon showing a Cadillac in the desert and two men, presumably the driver and the owner, praying in the sand beside it. Qua cartoon, the drawing was in poor taste. However, it presented a scene frequently seen in the Near East—an apparent paradox no less significant today than in the past.

the tribal social system, but only that considerable congruity exists between a man's view of other men according to the tenets of Islam and a man's conception of himself and other men in the perspective of the cultural vision of the tribal system. The "real world" of superordinate and subordinate human relations and the "ideal world" of equality before God seem nowhere to have achieved better mutual accommodation than in the predominantly Islamic states of the world.

The cultural ideal, derived from information provided by numerous informants, may be explained by utilizing the descriptive category of "segmentary lineage systems," originally specified by Evans-Pritchard and Fortes and others in *African Political Systems*,[2] and later elaborated in such studies as *Tribes Without Rulers*, edited by John Middleton and David Tait.[3] In order to present the cultural ideal, and as a point of departure for the remainder of the discussion, the concept of segmentary lineage systems appears to be useful. After utilizing this concept, however, we shall begin to see how, in terms of interpersonal relations, the social organization of the El Shabana is not a functioning segmentary system.

Middleton and Tait expand the typology suggested by Evans-Pritchard and Fortes, noting two basic features of segmentary systems:

> The term "segmentary" has been used in reference to several types of social systems, but the essential features are the "nesting" attribute of segmentary series and the characteristic of being in a state of segmentation and complementary opposition. The series may be one of lineages, smaller ones nesting inside and composing larger ones, which in turn compose still larger ones, and so on; or it may be one of the territorial groups (hamlets, villages, sections, tribes, nations) or of others. Subtraction or change in size of segments leads to a re-organization, although not necessarily a re-structuring, of the total system. Analysis of the process involved in this reorganization within an unchanging total structure has led to the use of the term to refer to the second characteristic. This is the process of continual segmentation of the structure.[4]

By "continual segmentation of the structure" the authors refer to the process whereby new segments of the same order within the structure separate (or merge) in response to factors such as population pressure or subsistence requirements. The process of merging or uniting is such that the parts of the segmentary system remain formally equal, whether or not the population or wealth of the segments remains equal. The cultural model may prevail whether or not the society's resources are sufficient to fill all the parts of the theoretical structure.

When, however, factors in the natural or social environment are such as to result in an inequitable distribution of economic wealth or political power between the ideally equal segments of the social systems, the latter clearly may cease to function as described above. Once a subsection within such a system has a monopoly of power, the checks and balances of complementary opposition are clearly at an end and the tribal system becomes centrally rather than segmentarily ordered for most political and economic purposes. This is very close to being the case among the Arabs of Daghara.

The Arab Bureau in 1918 estimated that the El Shabana had a population of 900 adult men.[5] Modern government censuses include El Shabana tribesmen, but population figures are no longer broken down into tribal groups. The El Shabana population also varies with the seasons; sometimes tribesmen return to the settlements only during important festivals; in other instances they may work in cities during the summer and return to live with their fellow tribesmen during the cold months. Conditions made it impossible for me to carry out a formal census; however, the informal guess of local residents is that the present population of the El Shabana is from 450 to 600 adult males. Tables 3 and 4 are based on a household survey conducted in 1958 among the El Shabana tribesmen living close to Daghara village.

The El Shabana are only one of 12 tribes or ashiras belonging to the El Aqra, a loose tribal confederation or *sillif*. In 1919 the El Aqra was estimated to include 5050 adult males. Using the same kind of informed guesses, I conclude that the El Aqra today numbers between 2500 and 3000 men. In any case, the twelve ashiras of the

[2] M. Fortes and E. E. Evans-Pritchard, eds., *African Political Systems* (London, 1950).
[3] John Middleton and David Tait, eds., *Tribes Without Rulers* (London, 158).
[4] *Ibid.*, p. 7.
[5] Great Britain, Arab Bureau, *Arab Tribes of the Baghdad Wilayat 1918*, (Calcutta, 1919), p. 2.

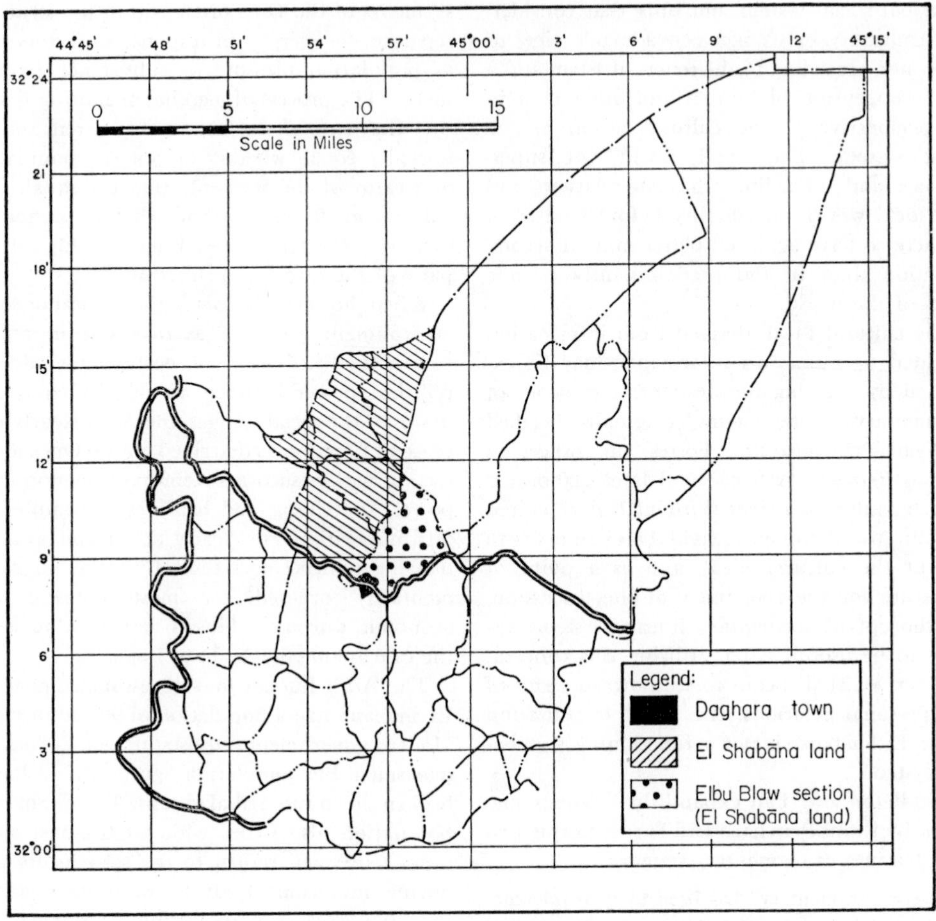

Map 1. Daghara district

El Aqra sillif constitute only a part of the tribal population of this region of southern Iraq.[6]

Ideally and traditionally, the sillif should control a single dira or domain of contiguous land in one region. Before 1918 this was the case. The El Shabana, living on approximately thirteen square miles of land with hamlets of tribesmen scattered over the area, formed part of a larger territory unit controlled by the El Aqra sillif.

The Agrah group lies along the Daghghara from its mouth to about five miles below Daghghara village, from the Shatt el Hillah. It continues along the left bank of the Shatt el Hillah from the mouth of the Daghghara up to and including the Dahayah Canal, some 10 miles below Diwaniyah, and on the right bank of the Shatt el Hillah from below the Bazil canal to opposite the Dahaya, with the Albu Muhammid (Khazʿayl) scattered among them.[7]

Today, as Map 2 (drawn by the local irrigation engineer) shows, El Aqra tribesmen continue to occupy lands near the mouth of the Daghara canal. However, other individuals and small

[6] The Middle Euphrates valley, once dominated by the El Khazaʿil confederation whose dominion was broken by Midhat Pasha, is now the scene of numerous tribal groupings, some larger than the El Aqra, others much smaller. While the description which follows rests almost entirely on familiarity with one tribe, casual contacts and conversation with other observers lead to the conclusion that the qualitative aspects of the description generally pertain to the tribes of the Hilla-Diwaniya area, but only in a much more limited degree to other regions of southern Iraq.

[7] Great Britain, Arab Bureau, *Arab Tribes,* p. 2.

Table 1. *Type of marriage within two fakhds of the Elbu Ubayd a shabba of the El Shabana*

	Elbu Najim	*% of Total*	*Elbu Muhammad*	*% of Total*
(Plural marriages[a]	2	4.6	10	13.1)
Parallel cousin marriages	11	25.0	21	28.0
Intra-fakhd marriages[b]	11	25.0	11	14.0
Intra-shabba marriages	2	4.9	2	02.6
Intra-ashira marriages	6	14.5	18	24.0
Intra-sillif marriages	1	02.4	5	07.0
Marriages with Sada	3	06.9	2	02.6
Marriages with servants			1	01.4
Marriages with mother's relative (mother not parallel cousin)			1	01.4
Marriages with foreigners	9	21.3	9	11.0
Origin of marriage unknown			6	08.0
Total number of marriages	43	100	76	100

Data based on genealogies complete to a depth of four generations.
[a] Each category is exclusive, with the exception of plural marriage. For example, a parallel cousin marriage is not counted as an intra-fakhd marriage. Plural marriages are counted in the appropriate categories.
[b] Intra-fakhd marriage is usually defined as "male ego marries FaFaBrSon's daughter."

groups have now moved in, presumably after purchasing land in the area. Gertrude Bell, writing in 1918 as secretary of the Arab Bureau, noted that the El Aqra seemed to be split into two factions. The movement of several ashiras out of the Daghara area is associated with this split.[8] Today some ashiras of the El Aqra live some forty miles away from the El Shabana in Shamiyya, the rice-growing district of Diwaniyya province. The ashiras of the El Aqra sillif still living in the vicinity of the El Shabana may be noted on Map 1. Thus this tribal organization no longer controls, according to traditional ideals, one dira or contiguous area of land.

The gradual break-up of land control is also evident at the ashira level. Presently tribesmen from eleven subsections or *shabbas* are identified as occupying El Shabana territory, while members of two or perhaps three others have scattered. Among the shabbas, great inequality in population size is found, partly because the land belonging to some groups is productive while in other instances it is so poor that tribesmen have been forced to find employment elsewhere.

The regional terms for the lineage-based segments among the tribal people of Daghara are as follows, beginning with the smaller groupings and ending with the most inclusive grouping. Segments are listed in order of their "nesting."

primary section[9]	*fakhd*
secondary section	*shabba*
tertiary section	*ashira*
quarternary section	*sillif*

Among the El Shabana, a shabba may contain two or three fakhds. Structurally, each of the segments "opposes" the other segments of the same level which share its "nest." Informants stress equality of status among comparable tribal subsections; no segment is superior to other segments at the same structural level. Smaller segments may cooperate as part of the same ashira for limited purposes. On other occasions shabbas may even resort to physical violence against each other.

The lineage system is based on aggregates of agnatic kinsmen defined according to descent from a common paternal ancestor. Patrilineality is of overwhelming importance in this society; the tribesman's position within the formal organization of the tribe as well as his more general reputation and social standing in the community at large depend on his paternal ancestry. The fact that marriages are preferentially contracted within the descent group in no

[8] *Ibid.*, p. 3.
[9] A still smaller segment, the *hamula,* will be discussed later.

Tribal Segment	Approx. No. of Adult Males	Kinship
1. sillif (El Aqra)	5000	1. No traceable kinship except by recent marriages. The belief exists of common descent from the Shammar, a great tribal division with both sedentary and nomadic sections.
2. ashira (including El Shabana, El Amaysh, El Zillazla, Elbu Zayyat, El Amr, El Nayil, El Hillalat, El Murad, etc.)	500–900	2. Descent from a common ancestor or from the ancestor who first became associated with the given ashira. Only experts can provide a complete line of patrilineal descent.
3. shabba (within the El Shabana, these include the Elbu Ubayd, El Jamiʿyyin, Elbu Khazʿal, El Shidayda, El Mujarilin, El Hakam, El Khalat, Elbu Salih, Elbu Jurayd, El Ghrush, El Shawahin, etc.)	20–50	3. Descent from a common ancestor. Usually a complete patra-genealogy can be provided but with a sharp decline in knowledge of collaterals above the fifth generation.
4. fakhd (within Elbu Ubayd shabba: Elbu Najim, Elbu Muhammad.)	10–30	4. A group of not more than five nor less than three generations depth. Collaterality usually completely known except for cognates resulting from occasional "foreign" or exogamous marriages.
5. hamula	See discussion below	
6. bayt		

way modifies the unilineality of the kinship system upon which tribal organization is based.[10]

The following chart of the tribal system outlines the actual kinship groupings within each segment:

The two additional segmentary divisions, the *hamula* and the *bayt,* are of a still lower, less inclusive order than the fakhd. The hamula was given as a division of the fakhd. Yet persistent questioning revealed only one instance of the hamula among the fakhds of the El Shabana: this term was used to distinguish the shaykh's father, his sons, and the shaykh's sons from the rest of their lineage group. This lineage, to be discussed further, is one instance in which the realities of this system depart from the characteristics of a model segmentary system.

The term bayt ideally refers to a living man and his descendants. Normally this would include a father and his sons (including married sons and their young siblings) who live together. However, married sons frequently do *not* live with their fathers. In such cases, the individual households were also called bayts. Any fakhd is composed of numerous bayts, but the use of the term varied between reference to the "ideal" father-sons grouping and to actual households (see Table 3).

In the idiom of kinship, ego refers to the members of his shabba as *awlad ammi,* that is, "my father's brother's sons." The usage is classificatory as the group may include men whose agnatic tie is a common ancestor four or five generations distant. Several collateral lines of descent are thus often joined in a shabba. Of course, affines usually also enjoy bonds of cognatic relationship because of the preferred practice of endogamous marriage.

Where segmentation into fakhds has occurred within a given shabba, a man may also refer to the members of his fakhd as awlad ammi. The agnatic ties between the men of any one fakhd obviously will be closer than the ties they share with the members of the other fakhds of the shabba, but the terms of reference do not commonly take the distinction into account.

The residence pattern of these parallel lineal and tribal systems may be expressed in the following diagram:

[10] See Raphael Patai, "The Structure of Endogamous Unilineal Descent Groups," *Southwest Journal of Anthropology,* 21, no. 4 (1965), 325–349.

bayt	same house
hamula	same area within hamlet
fakhd	same hamlet
shabba	same or nearby hamlets
ashira	contiguous land and neighboring hamlets
sillif	the same area but not perfectly contiguous land-holdings — may have been one dira historically

Residence is patrilocal; men state that it is good for brothers to live together in the same household with their father.[11] However, men frequently establish independent households when their father dies, and for various reasons (specific quarrels were frequently cited) may leave the parental home before the father's death. It is said that brothers are more likely to continue to live together if they are uterine siblings; this deserves fuller investigation, for there is some indication that uterine brothers may also most frequently register land jointly or avoid formally dividing their patrimony.

A single residence may include a courtyard, sleeping and reception rooms, as well as animal shelters and other detached structures; all buildings are contained within a single area surrounded by a wall. The local definition of a single "household" is not based upon simply living in a single compound. Rather, several men may live in a single compound but a man is considered to have a separate household if he manages his financial affairs independently of his kinsmen. In collecting the census data (see Table 3) the local social definition of a single household was adopted, so that if two brothers and wives and children lived in the same compound but the brothers did not pool their resources, the men, with their dependents, were listed as individual households. Evidence indicated that separating finances was the first step toward the establishment of individual residence, and that the separation of joint families was frequently desired but impossible because of the high cost involved in building new dwellings.

The shabba is the tribal segment most frequently identified with a hamlet. When one asks to whom a cluster of houses belongs, the proper shabba name is the most common response. In some instances shabbas have not divided into fakhds, but where such segmentation has occurred, lack of suitable land may make physical separation impossible and the members of the fakhds are often obliged to continue to reside in the same hamlets. If the fakhds separate as a result of some serious quarrel and a desirable location for a new hamlet is available within the landholdings of the shabba, then it is probable that a new hamlet will be established.

Thus residence is also patterned, generally in accord with the kinship and tribal systems. Traditionally, the closer the kinship between two men through a common ancestor, the greater the likelihood that they will be living in the same vicinity. If men lack any traceable kin ties it is unlikely they will be living in the same tribal hamlet. The shabba which is unsegmented or which may include as many as three fakhds is the largest (most inclusive) tribal grouping in which men are likely to live in the same hamlet, cultivating adjacent plots of land and in some cases owning land jointly (this will be discussed further below, but see Map 3). However, all segments of the El Shabana ashira hold land in a common territory.

Let us compare this system for a moment with that of the Nuer of the Sudan, the classic example of the model segmentary system. Evans-

[11] There were a few instances noted where a man lived with his wife's father. This arrangement (called gaʿadi) was agreed upon before marriage. Informants said fathers attempted to make this part of the marriage settlement when they lacked male descendants and wanted a son-in-law to look after them in old age. In return, a bridegroom accepting such an arrangement would have to pay little bride price and was the major, if not the only, inheritor of the wife's father's estate. Most tribesmen viewed such an arrangement with humorous contempt.

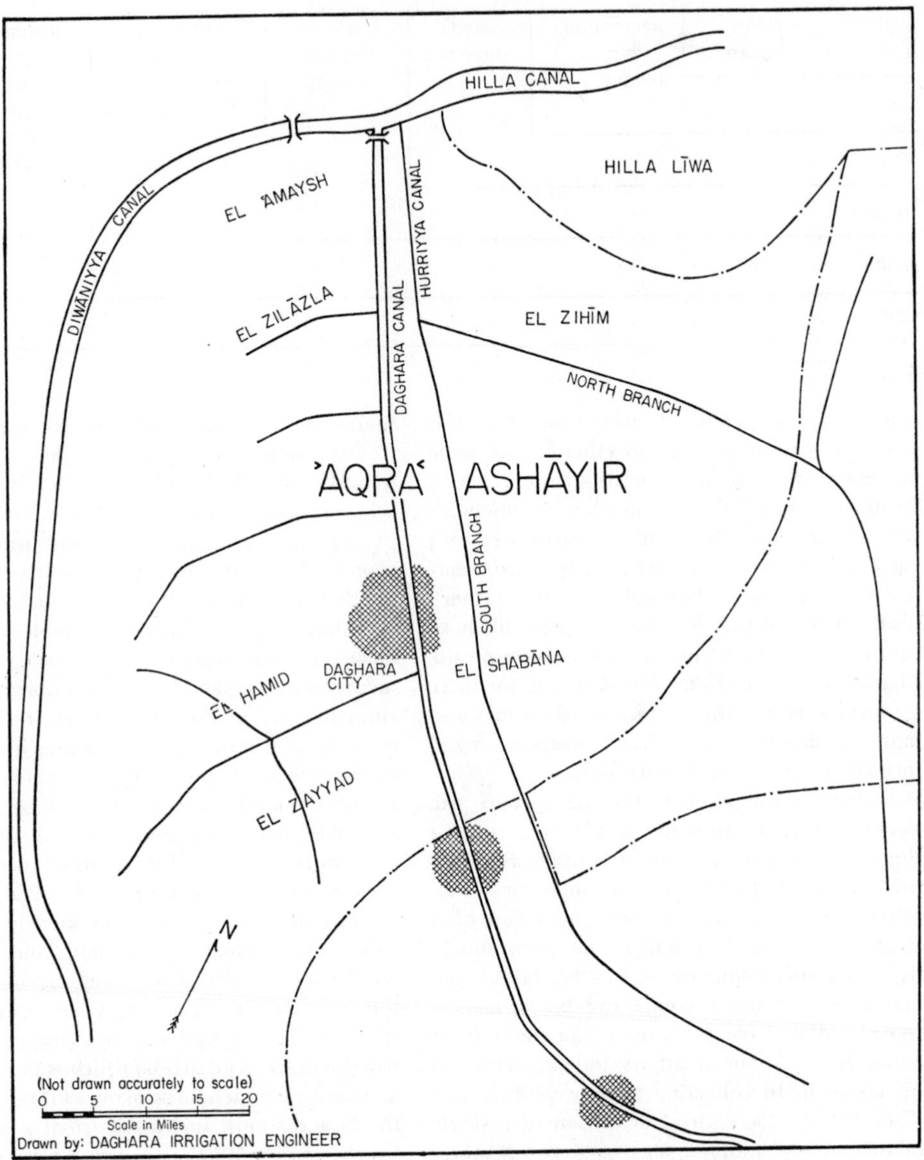

Map 2. Sketch of Daghara area showing positions of ashāyir of El ʾAqraʿ sillif

Pritchard states that "Nuer lineages are not corporate localized communities," though certain lineages have special associations with certain localities. Local communities become a network of kinship ties, in spite of the fact that different lineages reside together within them, because of rules of exogamy applying to the lineage groups.[12] Such is obviously not the case

12 The pastoral adaptation of the cattle-owning Nuer also may result in frequent contacts between members of relatively exclusive segments. However, the fact that the El Shabana tribesmen are cultivators living together according to membership in exclusive segments does not mean the opportunity for casual contacts with tribesmen other than members of their own fakhd or shabba is lacking. Tribesmen go to Daghara village frequently and have contact with a wide range of persons on such occasions. In addition to the more formal gatherings of tribal members, my impression is that there is no lack of opportunity for intra- and even inter-ashira contacts between tribesmen.

Table 2. *Type of marriage within the El Shabana tribal settlement in Daghara village*

		% of Total
(Plural marriages[a]	9	10.0)
Parallel cousin marriages	37	43.0
Intra-fakhd marriages	7	08.1
Intra-shabba marriages	11	12.8
Intra-ashira marriages	8	09.3
Intra-sillif marriages	3	03.5
Marriages with Sada	3	03.5
Marriages with mother's relative (mother not parallel cousin)	1	01.2
Marriages with foreigners	16	18.6
Total number of marriages	86	100

Data based on a census of the 77 households in the settlement.
[a] These marriages are included in the appropriate categories below.

with the El Shabana where the lineage-based hamlet tends to be endogamous and contiguous with a tribal division.

Quite obviously the closer the kinship tie and the closer men live to each other, the more interests they have in common, and the more frequent the contacts between them. The range of common interests shared by the members of tribal groupings is most inclusive within the fakhd, and common interests are fewest between individuals who are related only by sillif membership. Structurally the reasons for this are clear: the interests which men have in common through kinship are of the same order as the common interests of members of the same tribal segments. Furthermore, the lineage-based tribal segments follow a pattern of territorial localization exactly paralleling social segmentation; each segment literally, as well as figuratively, "nests" within the other. Finally, the preference for and percentage of endogamous marriages is most intense at the "center" of the parallel systems of tribe and kinship, as may be seen in Tables 1 and 2.

Conflicts occur between fakhds of the same shabba, between shabbas of the same ashira, and between ashiras of the same sillif. The "higher" the segmental level at which conflict occurs, the less intense the social sanctions which can resolve the dispute or prevent its developing into a long-lasting feud.

I will show how differences in landholding (in particular) may make segmental equality at each level less than a social reality. Finally, I will turn to the ties which bind this somewhat segmental organization together. The evidence to support the contentions thus far presented must emerge slowly as I proceed with the discussion. The next paragraphs will provide an outline of some of the functions and activities at each level of segmentation in this tribal organization.

Tribal Sections

The Sillif. Members of the El Aqra sillif claim historic relationship with the Shammar. Yet for all practical purposes the sillif itself is the most inclusive tribal grouping with which individual tribesmen identify themselves. The sillif includes groups of members living far apart, and while it is concentrated in one general area, it does not hold land as a unit. Under such conditions, it is not surprising that the nature of the intrasillif relationship varies considerably from group to group.

The only institution which is identified with the entire sillif as well as with some section of it is the mudhif or guest-house of the sillif leader or ra'is. Such a mudhif is also an ashira center, just as the sillif leader (the ra'is) is also shaykh of an ashira. The building takes on an inter-ashira character on those occasions when a sillif-wide feast is held or an inter-ashira dispute is arbitrated.

Table 3. *Composition of households within the El Shabana tribal settlement*[a]

Total number of households	77
Total number of persons in households	399
Largest household (no. of persons)	11
Smallest household (no. of persons)	2
Average size of household (no. of persons)	5.1
Persons in household other than nuclear family	
Husband's mother	13
Husband's father	1
Wife's mother	2
Wife's father	0
Husband's sister (unmarried, widow or divorced)	10
Wife's sister (unmarried, widow or divorced)	1
Husband's brother (unmarried)	1
Married sons and wives	11
Married daughter (husband absent)	1
Daughter-in-law (husband absent)	1
Husband's sister's son	1
Sister of brother's wife	1
Total persons in households other than nuclear family	43

Data based on census of the 77 households in the settlement.
[a] "Household" is defined as those persons dependent on a single adult male, or in which adult males share expenses.

Traditionally, the mudhif of the ra'is or sillif leader is built with the help of the entire sillif; in practice, this help is by no means universal and whether or not such help is forthcoming depends on the warmth of the relationship between the ra'is and wealthy and influential men in the other ashiras.[13] It is in the mudhif that ashiras, on specific occasions, publicly acknowledge sillif membership. Tribesmen claim that when the ra'is of the El Aqra, Haji Atiyah, died in 1950, all adult males of the El Aqra visited the Haji's mudhif during the thirty days of mourning (*fatiha*) following his death. In general, when the shaykh of any ashira dies, or when an important marriage takes place, the shaykhs of the other ashiras of the sillif customarily travel to the mudhif of the leader involved. During the days of feasting associated with the 'Id el Fitr and the 'Id el Adha, leaders of some of the component ashiras usually visit the mudhif of their sillif leader. Such visits imply a formal declaration of membership in the sillif and an avowal of loyalty to the sillif leader.

The expense of a sillif-wide feast is borne first of all by the host ashira, but privately contributions are offered by and accepted from other wealthy men in the sillif. Unless other members of the sillif shared the cost, such feasts would be a real financial burden to the host ashira, for a large meal is served to all those present on the day of a marriage, on each day of the religious feast, and on each of the thirty days of mourning following the death of a shaykh.

In 1957 Haji Mujid Atiyah El Sha'lan, the present shaykh of the El Shabana tribe who is also leader of the El Aqra sillif, traveled five hours by car and by boat to attend the fatiha for one of the shaykhs of an El Aqra ashira. The fatiha was held in the mudhif of the deceased. Over a thousand men were present, not only from El Aqra but from tribes of neighboring sillifs. Thirty sheep had been killed to feed the guests, and 400 kilos of rice and 500 of barley were consumed on this one day. Attendance was not, of course, so heavy on each of the thirty days; this was a special day, for Haji Mujid, the rais of the sillif, had come. But feasts on 'Ids and at marriages may involve at least ten sheep and a proportionate amount of rice.

The institution of the *hosa,* a kind of group

13 The mudhif of Haji Mujid El Sh'alan is estimated to have cost more than $2500; the shaykh stated that not more than a tenth of this cost was contributed from ashiras other than the El Shabana.

rally, is a tangible expression of group membership within the sillif. The hosa is performed as part of any general gathering, and when more than one ashira participated in the celebration of a feast, hosas were always a conspicuous part of the day's activities.

In the past, the hosa was an expression of group solidarity before going to war or setting out on raiding parties, and today continues to be somewhat like a pep rally. Although it involves rhythmic group movement, the hosa is not principally a dance. Before or after the meal on the feast-day, tribesmen from the same ashira gather together outside the mudhif (if it is only an ashira-wide feast, the men from the same shabba gather together). A tribesman known for his talent in the hosa begins by chanting a verse to which the other tribesmen add a refrain or chorus. At the end of the chorus, the versifier chants another stanza which is again followed by the chorus. Other tribesmen in the meantime have composed verses and will break in with their own offerings. The verse leader stands slightly in front of the crowd of men who circle during the chorus, moving together, holding rifles high above their heads, and firing them into the air from time to time. The sound and sight of dozens, sometimes hundreds of men chanting and moving together in the hot sun and firing rifles is a spectacle not soon forgotten. Hosa chants are usually rhymed couplets praising the courage, the wisdom, the honor of the rais or shaykh, or describing past glories and feats of arms of the tribal group. Tribal leaders did not take part in the hosas themselves but stood watching in modesty, inside the mudhif.

The common interests of sillif membership rest in the traditions of peaceful relations between member ashiras and of mutual aid in common defense. Within the sillif, an alternative to self-help is always present in the opportunity to negotiate peacefully, abetted by other parties in the sillif who are not directly involved. For the sillif constitutes the maximal indigenous jural community in the system. This is its major formal function at the present time. The shared belief is that members of the same sillif should be at peace, and within the sillif precedents have been set and social customs exist by means of which feuds may be settled and fighting ended. The general agreement that unresolved conflicts within the sillif are improper does not suffice to end such disputes in a short period of time; in fact it is possible that some quarrels within a sillif may never be fully resolved. Such consensus does, however, create an atmosphere of expectation, places subtle pressure on contestants to negotiate settlement, and provides a large number of interested third parties who are willing to contribute their time and energy toward the resolution of enmities.

Arab tribesmen have been justly recognized for their prodigious ability to remember lengthy genealogies. They deserve equal attention for their development of an elaborate and detailed oral customary law. For example, within the sillif an unwritten traditional rate of compensation has been established for all recognized offenses occurring between ashiras. In the case of homicide, one ashira is required to give three women as *fasl* (blood-payment) to the ashira of the murdered man (ultimately such compensation usually goes to the kinsmen of the deceased). If, for various reasons, women are not provided, equivalent payments in guns or money must be made.

To understand something of the mechanisms and procedures of sillif adjudication, let us examine one case:

> A man from the Elbu Nahud fakhd of the Elbu Nayil ashira met a friend of his from the Elbu Zayyat ashira on the road near Daghara village. (Both ashiras are from the El Agra sillif.) The man from the Elbu Nayil had a gun. Somehow an argument developed centering around the gun. The man from Elbu Zayyat grabbed the gun and killed the man from the Elbu Nayil. Two months later the man who did the killing had been caught and jailed by the government. However, the dead man's gun had not been returned to Elbu Nayil, nor had there been any fasl settlement. The Elbu Nayil shaykh insisted his group would not consider beginning negotiations until the gun was returned. He said the return of the gun was an entirely different issue from the fasl. Haji Kadim, from the family of the man now in jail, claims the gun cannot be found and that it was probably thrown into the canal.

This interchange took place in 1958 in the mudhif of Haji Mujid, rais of the El Aqra sillif. Discussions normally take place on neutral ground, and the mudhif of the sillif leader is commonly selected as the site, if the leader is not a partner to the dispute. Intermediaries—friends of one or both of the groups involved—prepare the way for face-to-face meetings between those most directly involved in the dispute.

> I asked Kamal afterward why the groups had come here to the mudhif of the leader of the El Shabana

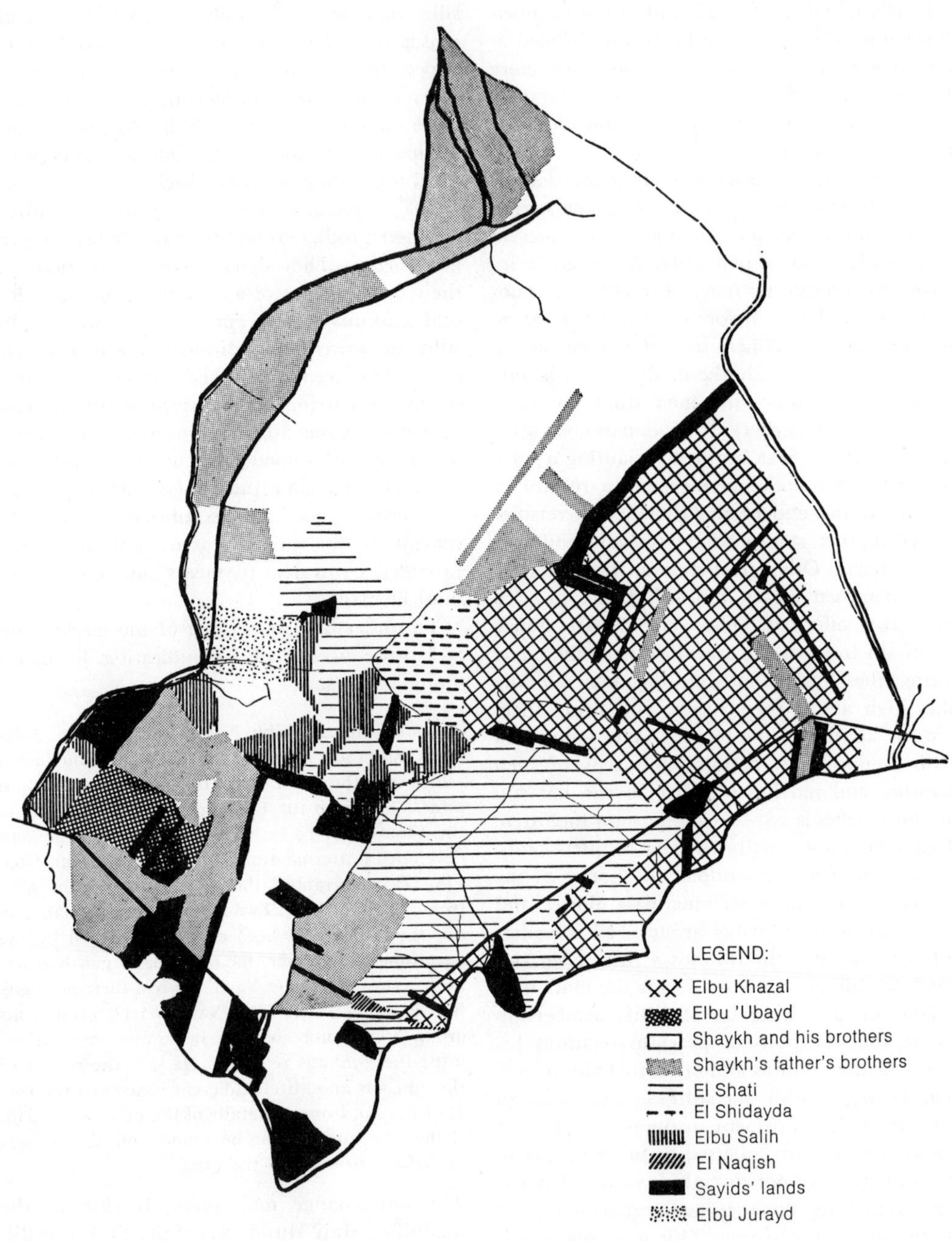

Map 3. Land occupied by shabbas of the El Shabāna: Elbu Blaw section.

ashira and Kamal replied it was because the shaykh of the El Shabana is also the rais of the entire sillif. When I asked why so many people were participating in the discussion who were apparently not from either contesting group, Kamal replied that they were asked to come by both sides as "witnesses" (*shahud*, sing. *shahid*). These witnesses appeared to do most of the talking, insisting on certain procedures necessary for the settlement of the problem. Kamal said that those witnesses who are not from the two ashiras directly involved, are from other ashiras who in the past stood with one or the other of the contesting ashiras in fights with other groups.

After the preliminary condition of the return of the gun was met, discussions began about the fasl which would be paid to the murdered man's group. This case had not been settled by March, 1958, and it would have been surprising if the murdered man's group had been willing to discuss fasl so soon. Yet the pressure is there from the rest of the sillif, and particularly from the leaders, at least to begin discussions. Until fasl is accepted, however, the way is open for a feud to develop; if no settlement has been reached nothing within tribal custom forbids the murdered man's family from taking the life of a member of the offending group. Usually a revenge killing has as its victim a son or brother of the murderer, although in one case a killer's father's brother's son was slain in revenge. In the past like incidents apparently grew to such proportions that two whole ashiras became mortal enemies. Once the *qadma*, or down payment of the fasl, is accepted, however, blood revenge becomes socially censurable.[14]

Besides constituting a jural community within which shared expectations and customs exist concerning the arbitration of inter-ashira disputes, the sillif also has a range of standing agreements with neighboring but unrelated tribal groups. If a killing takes place between the El Aqra sillif and sillif X, past agreements are remembered and used as a basis for settlement of the new problem. In contrast to intra-sillif disputes, disputes between two sillif cannot be brought to the point of arbitration unless the parties involved wish to arbitrate, to avoid further trouble. Since 1918, however, the local representatives of the central government have frequently put considerable pressure on responsible tribesmen to see that discussion gets under way.

The entire sillif of El Aqra, with its twelve ashiras and total membership of more than 5000 men, appears rarely to have fought as a single group. Instead, certain ashiras traditionally came to each other's aid. In the last quarter of the nineteenth century, those ashiras located around the mouth of the Daghara Canal joined forces to protect their water suply and their relatively contiguous holdings of land from the tribes of Afaq, further down the Daghara waterway. The common bond of sillif membership is permissive, but not compulsive, with respect to mutual aid. Gertrude Bell in 1919 noted that there was a long-standing division in the El Aqra sillif between certain ashiras.[15] In 1930, Haji Atiyah El Sha'lan, leader of the El Aqra sillif and shaykh of the El Shabana (father of the present shaykh), led the tribes of the Middle Euphrates in revolt against the authority of the central government. But even on this occasion only certain ashiras of the sillif joined in the fighting with the El Shabana. Thus it appears that in intra-sillif relationships the cultural ideal of equality between the structurally equal tribal segments is most nearly realized. While, in the case of the El Aqra sillif, the ashira of the sillif leader, the El Shabana, is stronger than any other ashira in the sillif, any several ashiras combined are equally as strong. Thus persuasion rather than coercion appears to have been the most important factor in determining the course of inter-sillif relationships.

The Ashira. Interaction between members of the same ashira is much more frequent than among men sharing only affiliation with the same sillif. Traditionally tribesmen of the same ashira gather at the mudhif of their shaykh on each of the major religious feasts of the Islamic year. Since the mudhif of Haji Mujid Sha'lan, the present shaykh, is located near Daghara village, tribesmen frequently stop there en route to or from their homes. Tribesmen may eat a meal at

[14] Revolutionary political change in Iraq has not put an end to such activities. In May 1966 the rais of the El Aqra was obliged to make an arduous journey to the Shamiyya region in order to arbitrate a dispute between two ashiras of the sillif who moved there around 1919. The problem in this case involved the abduction of a young woman by a youth from another ashira. The couple had disappeared for several years but had recently been discovered in Iran by the girl's father, who killed them both. The boy's family demanded fasl, though by tradition her father was within his rights. The issue has not been resolved.

[15] Great Britain, Arab Bureau, *Arab Tribes of the Baghdad Wilayat*, pp. 2–3.

the mudhif, spend the night, or simply pause to visit for a few minutes with whomever may be present. The mudhif is in this sense a common social center shared by all members of the same ashira. A man who is the guest of the shaykh in the tribal mudhif is also considered a guest of all tribesmen in the given ashira.

The cost of building a mudhif is borne primarily by the shaykh, but contributions of labor, food to feed the specialists who direct its construction, and money, are made by members of the ashira.[16] Similarly, the various segments of the ashira contribute sheep, chickens, and grain to the ashira-wide feasts which occur several times a year. A large section of land is set aside to supply the mudhif with food. While this land is now registered in the name of the shaykh, and while it is doubtful that all the produce from that land is necessary to supply food consumed by guests and tribesmen in the mudhif, this tradition of "mudhif land" is sometimes mentioned to justify (in part) the much larger holdings of the shaykh.

The mudhif is, then, the most important focus of ashira activities. Until the area was pacified, the mudhif was the center where members of the same ashira gathered before going into battle, where, in fact, political issues important to the whole ashira were discussed. As Shakir M. Salim notes, the mudhif serves as a "social center, political conference chamber, and a court of justice" [17] for the group associated with it. A man's reputation with his fellow tribesmen is witnessed in the mudhif by the behavior of those present when he enters. If it may be said of a man "They rise for him in the mudhif," *yqumun ila bil mudhif,* this is indicative of relative high prestige.

Less than ten years ago no El Shabana tribesman would sit in the village coffee shops; his coffee-drinking was limited entirely to the mudhif of the shaykh or to other smaller tribal mudhifs. Today the mudhif is less used than before as a meeting place by members of the ashira. Nevertheless, on the great feasts ʿId el Fitr and ʿId el Adha) the mudhif of Haji Mujid, shaykh of the El Shabana, may still be visited by nearly a thousand tribesmen in one day. As a common meeting ground for members of the ashira, its importance cannot be underestimated and the reported decline in mudhif attendance might well be considered indicative of the waning importance of ashira membership to the tribesmen.

When hosas are performed at ashira-wide feasts, performing groups again express segmental solidarity within the unifying larger group. Hosas begin with the participation of the largest exclusive groups present; in the sillif feast all present members of a given ashira act as a single group. In an ashira-wide gathering, individuals participate in hosas with the other members of their shabba who are present. One group opens the hosa and other groups begin performances of their own. Then the hosa assumes a new variation: the groups of men, chanting and firing guns into the air, run toward each other, stopping when they meet, circling back and coming forward again to repeat the pattern. An element of competition and mock combat may be seen in such activity, as each group vies to produce the finest and most moving verses and generally to make the best showing. Tempers run high and occasionally scuffles occur. In the past, all of this took place on horseback, perhaps providing an even greater similitude to battle and an opportunity for demonstration of skill.

The occasions when the hosa is performed appear charged with emotion and conviction. Whether they occur on the level of sillif organization, in ashira, or even shabba groupings, they constitute an activity which is organized on the basis of the tribal sections present at a given gathering. In a sense, these occasions are an expression of the latent opposition between segments at the same level of tribal organization, and indicate some depth of emotional commitment to membership in the particular tribal groupings involved.

The ashira is also a jural community; but different from the jural community of the sillif, for it is one within which the shaykh (whose authority will be a subject for discussion in the following chapter) could force disputing parties to come to terms. If necessary, informants say, the shaykh could send armed men to bring disputants to the mudhif to discuss the problem and arrange for a customary settlement. Individual crimes which conspicuously violated the

16 See the photograph of a mudhif under construction (Fig. 5). This one is smaller than the one of the shaykh; it was being constructed by a fakhd.

17 Salim, *Marsh Dwellers of the Euphrates Delta,* pp. 72–82.

Table 4. *Occupations of men living within the El Shabana tribal settlement*

Occupation		Number
Large landowner		3
Medium landowner		6
Small landowner		8
Fallah		7
Fallah and sheep herder		1
Local sheep trader		7
Sheep exporter		3
Small grain wholesaler		2
Traveling produce salesman		2
Buffalo milk producer and retailer		1
Employed by shaykh		7
personal guard	3	
servant	1	
coffee server in mudhif	2	
descendant of Negro slave	1	
Government guard		2
Porter		2
Taxi-driver		2
Worker in mud (this is defined as any man who may do building with mud, repair streets, and do other common labor)		7
Street cleaner		3
Weaver		2
general weaver	1	
weaver of abbayas	1	
Tailor		3
general tailor	2	
tailor of abbayas	1	
Jeweler		1
Ironsmith		1
Sweetcake seller		1
Mumin (religious specialists)		3
Students (in school or college away from village)		3
Local charity cases		4
support by son in army	1	
blind (support by community)	1	
blind (relative of shaykh and supported by him)	1	
part charity case, part worker in mud	1	
Working away from settlement		4
works in Basra	1	
works in Hilla	1	
works in Karbala	1	
cloth merchant in Shamiyya	1	
TOTAL		85

Data based on a census of the 77 households in the settlement.

moral code of all tribesmen—such as rape or thievery—might result in physical punishment as decreed by the shaykh and the *ajawid* (or elders) of the tribe, or in banishment of the defendant and the kinsmen who supported him. In one such case, a whole fakhd is reported to have moved elsewhere after one of the men of that group had been accused of stealing.

The mudhif of the shaykh of an ashira is the center of jural activities. Disputes which arise between members of two shabbas are argued before the shaykh and the ajawid. No matter how strong the feelings between contesting parties, they must, in the mudhif, sit quietly and behave with dignity. The mudhif of the shaykh even has some sacred character in that it is a place for swearing strong oaths of vengeance or of peace.

The Shabba and the Fakhd. Among members of the same shabba, interaction is much more frequent than among men sharing membership only in the sillif or the ashira at a structurally "higher" level of tribal organization. The small mudhifs typically found in shabba hamlets are meeting places where the men gather informally in the evenings, or for most of the day when no work needs to be done. Several mudhifs may be found in the same hamlet, depending on the wealth of the members. These mudhifs are commonly supported and built by a minimal lineage group: in one instance three brothers and two grown sons of a deceased fourth brother took turns in supplying coffee and food for any guest, the responsibility returning to the same man every fifth week.

The fact that notably less formality is observed in behavior within the small shabba mudhifs may be related to the relative absence of differential rank between members of the same shabba (or fakhd). Except for the respect paid by young men to their elders (typical of all sectors of Arab society), in the shabba mudhifs no special deference is shown to any particular man, as it is in the shaykh's mudhif, reflecting the lack of institutionalized leadership at this level of tribal organization. While for each shabba a man is recognized as *surkal*, members of given shabbas consistently stated that surkals never settled conflicts themselves—in fact, questions about the surkal were met with humorous remarks, and it was clear that the title carried little prestige.[18]

On the jural level, shabbas, which were sometimes subdivided into fakhds and at other times in other cases undivided, were said to be responsible for a standard contribution to fasl or blood payment when one was required from the whole ashira. One shabba, larger than the others, was said to pay one and one-half times more than the others because of its greater size. When a member of one shabba committed an offense against a man from another shabba, the latter group was spoken of as requiring compensation from the former, regardless of whether either or both groups were internally divided into fakhds. Informants reported that one fakhd could require compensation from or exact vengeance against a second fakhd within the same shabba.

The shabba, as a named segment of the ashira, may have originated through the landholding function of a lineage group. All other terms designating parts of the tribal organization (sillif, ashira, fakhd, and hamula) have Arabic roots relating to parts of the body or blood relationship.[19] But the term *shabba* stems from a root from which words like "area" or "district" may be derived. Although "shabba" is not used by nomadic tribesmen in the area, the term has become so accepted among settled tribesmen that a man from the El Shabana was obviously surprised when speaking with a Bedu (at my instigation) to find that the Bedu had no such grouping. Among the settled tribesmen, the use of the term to designate a social grouping is so firmly established that tribesmen refer to men as belonging to such-and-such a shabba even when the men no longer own land among the El Shabana and the membership of that shabba is scattered. At the same time, the less abstract application of the term is still found in situations where, for example, the sons of male siblings of Abdullah have a serious disagreement with the sons of the male siblings of Hassan. One group becomes then the Elbu Abdullah and the other, the Elbu Hassan: neither retains the original name of their common ancestor, Jawad. Regardless of the difficulty which caused the split, both groups continue to occupy the same section of

[18] There is another group of men commonly referred to as "surkal" in southern Iraq. These men are overseers of the farming activities of fellahin employed by large landowners. The shaykh of the El Shabana employed such men; the difference between them and the surkals of the shabbas of the ashira was carefully explained, however. The latter appear to have come into existence as first the Turkish and then the British administrators required a class of persons with whom they could deal within the tribe other than the shaykh. However, surkals as overseers seem never to have been of much importance in the Daghara region, as contrasted with areas further south. See Jewaideh, "Midhat Pasha and the Land System of Lower Iraq," pp. 130–133.

[19] *Sillif* means "those who have come before," "ancestors," "forefathers"; *ashira* means "clan," "kinsfolk," from a root meaning "pregnant"; *fakhd* means "thigh"; and *hamula* "to bear," as in pregnancy.

land and neither can move without losing its land rights. Thus the term Elbu Jawad, the name of a fakhd which occupied a "shabba of land and water," becomes a term which also names a larger-than-fakhd grouping; the original term is retained and Elbu Jawad thus refers to the two fakhds, the Elbu Abdullah and the Elbu Hassan, as well as to the section of land they jointly occupy.

The shabbas of the El Shabana were not all established at the same time. Informants report that groups of men would agree to fight beside the El Shabana and share fasl with them and would be assigned land to cultivate after the fighting had ended. Thus a shabba may, in a sense, have been the unit of tribal adoption, so linked was land use to this process.[20]

The Sada: Blessed are the peacemakers, for they shall be called the sons of God. The Sada, though small in numbers, are an important part of the El Shabana. Strictly speaking, they are an independent group who live with the tribe and constitute perhaps 20 percent of the tribal population. Sada are men and women who claim descent from the Prophet Muhammid, and carry the honorific title "Sayid" before their proper names. Some religious specialists come from their ranks, but the majority of Sada take part in the same subsistence activities as the ordinary farmer-tribesmen.

The Sada associated with the El Shabana are members of two "tribes," that is, they classify themselves into two named groups. However, the named segments of these two groups do not occupy contiguous areas of land, as is true of the secular tribe. Rather, small numbers of Sada live on land within the shabba areas; this land has been given to the Sada by each shabba of the El Shabana. Thus one Sayid and his sons may live with one shabba and another minimal lineage group with another shabba. Sometimes the Sada live in the hamlet of the shabba whose land they have been given; at other times, groups of Sada live in small hamlets of their own. Direct questioning about why a Sayid was given land reveals only that it is considered a religious duty. In some areas of southern Iraq (which is almost entirely occupied by members of the Shiʿa sect of Islam), a few large landholders today provide land which Sada may cultivate without paying rent. By providing land for Sada, a Moslem upholds charity, one of the five pillars of Islam. Most tribal families have Sada neighbors to whom they traditionally give gifts of food on the great Islamic feasts, and many pious Moslems donate their services to the Sada occasionally or provide goods at specially low prices for them.[21]

In return for being an object of good works among the tribesmen, a man claiming the descent and privileges of a Sayid is expected to lead an exemplary life, which incidentally may contribute to the unity of the whole ashira and minimize the conflicts between ashira segments. All good Moslems ought to be at peace with all but non-Moslems; Sada are never supposed to participate actively in fighting. Thus in the days of feuding between shabbas, the Sada associated with each shabba theoretically remained free of active fighting and did not become involved in blood feuds. In view of this, it is not surprising that both by tradition and practice, Sada take an active part in peacemaking.[22]

Sada do not appear to be particularly prominent as *muhakkim* (judges) between disputing factions. Rather they are prominent as emissaries between alienated groups. Since a Sayid living with shabba X frequently has a brother or cousin living with shabba Y, when these two groups become embroiled in controversy no more convenient channel of communication is available than the Sada, who may formally or informally find out what is the feeling in the opposing group, and provide information necessary for negotiation between the feuding groups before formal face-to-face adjudication ever begins.[23]

When the shaykh wants the support of the entire ashira, for fighting or for some other corporate enterprise such as building a mudhif or

20 See Chapter VII. (Not reprinted here.—*ed.*)

21 For example, I knew several men who regularly plowed for certain Sada without charging for it in any way; one young girl always sewed for the women of a Sayid's family without accepting payment for her work.

22 Another example of how Sada fulfill more closely the ideal cultural patterns is their attitude toward marriage. While it is said that tribesmen *should not* allow their women to marry outside their own lineage group, informants claim that Sada *never* give their women to non-Sada. Sada men can marry non-Sada women, however, and thus often have affinal ties with the group with whom they live.

23 Compare in this regard Laura Nader, "Choices and Legal Procedure, Shiʿa Moslem and Mexican Zapotec," *American Anthropologist,* 67 (1965), 394–399.

giving a large feast, his first action is to call in Sada with whom he has had close relations (for example those to whom he has given land or goods in the past) and insure their support for his project. The Sada then accompany a son of the shaykh or some other *wakil* (representative) to the hamlets of the various segments, assuring the tribal group of the justice and goodness of the shaykh's cause, and reminding them of the advantages of being part of the El Shabana.

Sada, then, by virtue of their quasi-sacred position, their abstention from fighting, plus their residence with all the segments of the ashira, contribute importantly to the restoration of unity among substantial groups and help in the formation of a general consensus of opinion on issues involving the entire tribe.

Land Holding. Historically the tribe in southern Iraq has been a landholding unit, the proprietary interests of its members presumably becoming ever more localized as their subsistence pattern became increasingly agricultural. Contiguous and common land-holding has played an important, even fundamental, part in maintaining the institutions of tribal life in this region.

As may be seen on Map 2, the El Shabana today occupy a continuous area of land. No clear evidence suggests that land was ever considered the corporate property of an ashira. Rather, informants say, segments of the ashira always claimed certain sections of land, and within the segments individual men and their sons claimed the right to farm certain fields. Dowson reports that in general shaykhs assigned landholdings to their tribesmen.[24] However, El Shabana informants insisted that when the El Shabana took over their land from the El Khazaʿil they had enough land so that there was no controversy about who was to take what holding. Clearly, the shaykh did not, in such circumstances, have to assign a piece of land to each warrior but rather may have been called upon to resolve disputes over choice locations. But during the eighty years the El Shabana has occupied this land the relative amounts held by each shabba have changed through fighting between shabbas within the ashira, and later, through purchases of land.

Today certain members of the same shabbas and, in greater degree, of the same fakhds, are frequently joint owners of small plots of land, and, insofar as this is true, land ownership is one of the common interests and ties between kinsmen. Joint ownership also helps retard the division of land into plots too small to be farmed or without access to irrigation water. On the other hand, a tribesman always stated that if it were possible, he would *prefer* to own land individually, even though owning land with one's brothers and cousins was spoken of positively. If land could be acquired easily, lawfully or otherwise, it is likely that more men would own land individually. Under present conditions, however, additional land cannot be acquired except through the expenditure of money which the average tribesman does not have. Some tribesmen have sold land to the shaykh or his relatives (the only tribesmen with investment capital), but many individual tribesmen also have retained some property, for owning even a very small amount of land confers considerable prestige whereas to be landless is to forever join the lowly ranks of the fallahin.

Map 4 illustrates the type and amount of joint land registration in the Elbu Blaw district of El Shabana land holdings. Within the total of 505 registered plots of land, a single man may be registered several times as an individual or joint owner. The land belonging to the shaykh's shabba is for the most part owned jointly by him and his close agnatic relatives, the largest amount being held by the shaykh and his two uterine brothers. Excepting them, approximately equal amounts of land appear to be registered as (a) owned by individual men; (b) owned jointly by brothers; and (c) held by brothers and patri-cousins together. Proportionately the smallest amount of land is registered in the names of *all* the men belonging to a fakhd or shabba. What accounts for the different types of registrations?

One answer is suggested by comparing genealogies with registrations. At least three generations of men have worked the land in the eighty years of its occupation by the El Shabana. When the land registration took place in the nineteen-forties, some members of the second generation still survived, but in most cases these survivors had outlived their siblings and many of their collateral relatives. Generally these surviving men appear to have registered their holdings as individuals; thus old men or men without male siblings are most likely to have landholdings independent of others.

24 See quotation, page 31, Chapter II. (Not reprinted here.—*ed.*)

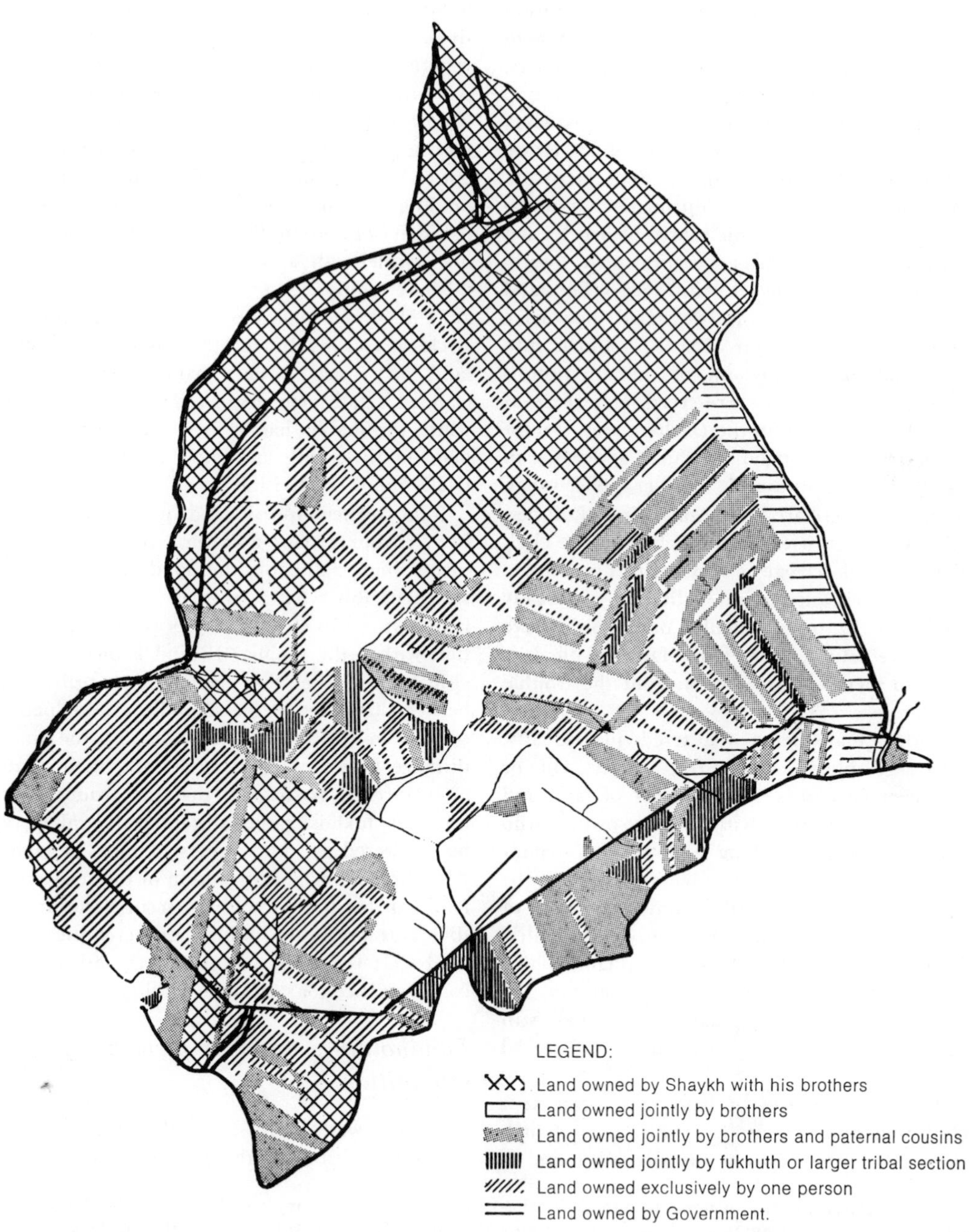

Map 4. Types of land ownership among tribesmen: Elbu Blaw section of El Shabāna land.

While second-generation men could have jointly registered land with third-generation men, out of the 505 registrations only ten were shared between father's son and father's brothers. The only other instances in which such a group of kinsmen were registered together was when land was registered in the name of an entire fakhd or shabba (see Map 4). Sons take considerable care to see that uncles do not usurp their inheritance, a classic source of bad feeling and disputation. Third-generation men (brothers and cousins), faced with registering land which brothers had jointly farmed, may have discovered that division of these holdings into individual pieces was out of the question if water access was to be preserved. If a piece of land is to be farmed in the Daghara area, it must connect with a distributary canal, and while in theory one can always dig another feeder canal, in practice there are limitations. First of all permission to pass a canal through someone else's already small acreage is very difficult to obtain. And in a majority of cases division of already small plots into still smaller ones would have made the returns from grain farming on each piece so small as hardly to warrant the trouble of planting.

Rather than being registered individually, these small plots were registered jointly. One or two men farm these small pieces of land and then divide the crop with other co-owners who may have been working elsewhere as tenant farmers. While the share each receives may be miniscule, each can still claim ownership of land. Individuals who derive only the smallest fraction of their livelihood from land which they own, and who live and work most of the year far from the El Shabana holdings, still maintain a dwelling in their hamlet and regard it as home.[25]

Thus many pieces of land have been kept cultivated under joint ownership even though they could not possibly support all those to whom the land belonged. Since the El Shabana holdings have, in the past twenty years, progressively deteriorated through salination and waterlogging, income has accordingly decreased. An estimated third to a half of El Shabana land is now useless for cultivation,[26] and only a small percentage of El Shabana tribesmen earn their entire living from farming their land. But joint holdings are not often abandoned until the land has deteriorated to the point where not even one farmer can support himself and his immediate family.

Land owned by groups extending beyond the circle of cousins and brothers is usually either land on which a date palm garden exists, claimed by all members of a shabba, or land on which the shabba hamlet is located. Date palms demand little care and their produce is practically infinitely divisible.

Joint ownership of land undoubtedly has been encouraged by a cultural tradition which places high value on the solidarity of lineal kinsmen. But what is the effect of registering land ownership upon the process of segmentation within the shabba? If land is owned individually in the first generation, registered between brothers in the second, between patricousins in the third, and so on, by the time distance between living adults and their common ancestor is so great that the group splits into two fakhds, rather distant collaterals may be registered as joint owners of plots of land. Also the territorial distribution of the registered land can hardly follow the descent pattern; individuals may inherit jointly registered pieces of land scattered from one end to the other of a common ancestor's original holding.

Landholdings and Complementary Opposition

Land and water rights are both permissive and restrictive factors in the internal organization

25 The pattern of land ownership among the shaykh's lineage is an example of how land may be owned where there is a large amount held by a small group of kinsmen. The largest holdings of the shaykh's lineage are registered in the name of the shaykh and his two uterine brothers. The second largest holdings of the shaykh's lineage are jointly registered in the name of the nine sons of the shaykh's father. In fact, only the uterine brothers farm their lands as one unit; the other holdings are farmed by individuals who each take a section of the jointly registered land. This example is instructive; enough land was available for each sibling to register land in his own name, and this land would have been sufficient to provide subsistence for each sibling. Yet this was not done. The shaykh's shabba had established extensive claims to land before the registration, and, as I have noted, has been able to increase these holdings by utilizing the economic surplus which only this group within the ashira has enjoyed in recent years.

26 An independent survey of the region puts half the fertile land out of production as of 1958. Currently the percentage is said to be much higher.

of the ashira, and affect the relative position of the segments. To understand the relationship between landholdings and a segmentary social system, let me propose a hypothetical history:

> Several fakhds together establish control over an area of land. Each fakhd begins to cultivate its own section of land. In the beginning there is enough land so that the initial fakhds "adopt" other small lineage groups in order to bolster their strength. This, of course, increases the ability of the ashira membership to enlarge its total land area, should there be resistance from nearby groups. Eventually the other tribal groups in the area surrounding the ashira in question may finally succeed in firmly establishing their own land rights and successfully prevent further encroachment. When, by chance, the number of men in one fakhd becomes greater than another, the larger fakhd may attempt to expand its landholdings at the expense of neighboring fakhds.[27]
>
> However, neighboring fakhds, now constituting another shabba or shabbas, might combine to prevent this encroachment on their territory; structurally, we might say this illustrates the process of complementary opposition between segments at equal levels of organization.

This hypothetical history cannot be proved to *exactly* fit the course of events among any group of tribal cultivators near Daghara. But it is true that in the past frequent "revolutions" took place within the ashira; "revolutions" in which one shabba would rise up and take land from others. El Shabana tribesmen recall that three different shabbas have held the largest section of land at various times in the eighty years of control of El Shabana's present land area. The shaykh of the El Shabana in each case came from the lineage group which controlled the largest area of land. (Today, of course, landholding is fixed through registration.)

The end product of the process we have been describing is graphically illustrated in Maps 2, 3 and 4, which show one of the five contiguous sections of land owned by men of the El Shabana. The Elbu Blaw section was selected for illustrative purposes not because it was necessarily representative, but because it contained the largest number of landholding divisions (505 separate registrations.)

Map 3 first of all provides an illustration of the correspondence already mentioned between tribal groupings and land: the complete holdings of the Elbu Khazal shabba are seen to lie within a common boundary. The Elbu Ubayd lands similarly lie within a common boundary. Only part of the land belonging to the Elbu Salih is shown on this map—the rest of their holdings fall in the adjacent district, to the west. The fragmentary holdings of the El Naqish shabba represent the remaining land belonging to a group which left the area after 1900 during failure of water on the Daghara canal. The Elbu Qlawa similarly have lost most of their land; what is left is badly situated in relation to the canal system, and nearly all members of this group live and work away from the El Shabana area. It is thus apparent that some shabbas of the El Shabana are in a far superior position to others.

Today one shabba, El Jamiʿyyin, that of the shaykh, owns the greatest percentage of tribal lands, five to six times more land than any other shabba within the ashira. This is far more land than is necessary to support the ashira mudhif or to fulfill the responsibilities attached to the position of the shaykh. He and his close agnatic kinsmen are economically in a position far superior to any other tribesmen. In the past, shaykhs of sedentary ashiras may have customarily held more land than their fellow tribesmen; today men loyal to the shaykh continue to justify his disproportionately large holding by saying that it is necessary to support the mudhif —in other words, to permit him to extend the customary lavish hospitality characteristic of such establishments. Yet it is obvious that, at least under present conditions, being a shaykh offers the possibility of securing more land, and owning more land is characteristic of men who are shaykhs. Upon the death of Shaykh Haji Atiyah, his son Mujid, the present shaykh, was able to successfully claim much more land than his brothers because Mujid was recognized as shaykh by the government. However, that land was already in the possession of Mujid's group, and under present conditions it is unlikely that the land would have been given to some other man whom the tribesmen might have wanted to be shaykh.

Shaykh Mujid's father and kinsmen claimed

[27] At the same time, we might suppose that as a given fakhd further segmented, its size increased. As land around it was occupied, the two segments did not move far apart, but continued to cultivate contiguous lands. At this point we might expect that the term "shabba" came to refer to a social grouping of men, i.e., two fakhds as discussed above.

lands belonging to other lineage groups within the El Shabana who deserted their fields at the time of drought around 1900. These other groups did return but were never able to regain full occupancy of their previously held lands. The interference of outside powers since the advent of British control has prevented segments of the El Shabana from combining to strip the shaykh and his kinsmen of their holdings, if, indeed, such a course of events would have occurred.

The relationship between landholding and tribal segments within the ashira may be further understood by looking at the El Shatti group's holding on Map 3. This single holding is as large as the contemporary landholdings of several other shabbas combined. Tribal informants mentioned the El Shatti as a shabba. Other informants (including men from the shaykh's family) never mentioned a shabba called El Shatti, but said that El Shatti was part of the shaykh's shabba, the El Jamiʿyyin. In terms of descent, the group of men called El Shatti are as closely related to the shaykh and his brothers as are many kinsmen within the same fakhd.

Shatti (the man for whom the group is named) was the only son of the present shaykh's father's father's only brother. Shatti had five sons who, in the 1940's, registered their land jointly. Of these five sons, three are now dead, but their sons, the two living original sons, and *their* sons, now constitute a group of eleven men, the El Shatti. The eldest sons of the shaykh persistently referred to the El Shatti as a fakhd of the shaykh's shabba: other tribesmen did not mention the El Shatti's agnatic tie with the shaykh, but said that the El Shatti constituted a shabba with one fakhd. Further, in outlining the named sections of the El Shabana, many tribesmen list the El Shatti, a shallow descent group, as equal to other shabbas, or groups of much deeper descent.

Thus it appears that the acquisition of an exceptionally large amount of property by one kin group is of primary importance in establishing its equivalence to groups of a very different structural order. This is yet another example of the confounding of the segmentary system and at the same time the tribesmen's persistent efforts to fit unequal tribal groups into their idealized conceptions of the tribal system.

The shaykh's segment provides other clues to the nature of the relationship between landholdings and tribal organization, for the El Shatti example is not the only way in which the shaykh's group constitutes an exception to the model segmentary system. The El Jamiʿyyin, the named group to which the shaykh and his agnates belong, was sometimes referred to by tribesmen as a shabba and at other times was called a fakhd. When tribesmen included the El Jamiʿyyin in listing shabbas of the El Shabana, they would be asked, "then to what fakhd of the shabba El Jamiʿyyin do the shaykh and his brothers belong?" Frequently, after a pause, the tribesmen would say, "he and his brothers belong to the hamula el Shaʿlan." This is the instance in which the hamula was mentioned—a group ideally at a lower "nesting" level of organization than the fakhd. What is the explanation of its presence within the shaykh's lineage group? The father of the present shaykh and the father's brothers constituted a faction which fought other men within the tribe and within the shaykh's own lineage group to secure the shaykhship. The father and his brothers became known by the name of their father, Shaʿlan. The success of this struggle and the permanence of the resulting split within the shaykh's descent group presumably led to social recognition of the faction as a single unit. As the maps of landholdings illustrate, it is this group, the shaykh and his paternal uncles, which holds by far the largest amount of land in the Elbu Blaw section. No hamula division was mentioned for other fakhds; it may be that no issue leading to a development of factions was sufficiently strong to overcome the several ties between members of such groups.

Both the example of the El Shatti "shabba" [28] and the two-generation "hamula" distinction within the El Jamiʿyyin, constitute phenomena not consistent with the model segmentary system. In both instances shallow lineage groups have been made conspicuous through acquisition of large amounts of land. By their large landholdings the El Shatti are economically much better off than the average tribesman and the

[28] It should be added that conceivably tribesmen were using the term "shabba" relative to the El Shatti in the geographic, rather than social, sense of the term. However, since they were mentioned with shabbas when the term was clearly being used to mean social groups, I believe my interpretation is correct.

shaykh's uncles and brothers are the wealthiest group of agnates in the El Shabana ashira. This is not lineage segmentation according to the classic model, but rather economic stratification according to land-based wealth. The land reform act, passed after the July, 1958 revolution in Iraq, required that the shaykh dispose of all but a thousand mesharas of his land. This meant that over half of his holdings must be redistributed. It was conceivable, but not likely, that redistribution might have a salutary effect on tribal organization by permitting other El Shabana segments to recover lost land, and thus permit more than the present fifteen percent of tribesmen to make a living exclusively from farming their own holdings.[29]

The segmentary model, which still seems to be part of the tribesmen's conception of their organization, may possibly have "fitted" the presedentary social system of the Daghara Arab, presumably in the sense that inequities would have been more readily adjusted under the more flexible conditions of nomadic life. Even after the El Shabana settled, a somewhat more segmentary system might have prevailed before the area was pacified, the shaykh recognized by the government, and landholdings within the tribal dira fixed by registration. For convenience, the divisions within the El Shabana ashira will continue to be referred to as "segments," but it is obvious that since the lineage system does not altogether correspond with the named groupings within the ashira, the segments which tribesmen may name as similar to one another are structurally not always at the same level. In reality, then, the structurally "equal" segments of this system have, under contemporary conditions, been deprived of the capacity to stand in balanced complementary opposition to one another.

[29] This was not, in fact, the case. The shaykh divided among the members of his immediate family the land he owned in excess of 1000 mesharas. On an overall basis, the redistribution of land owned by the other, much larger landowners in the region, far from being of either economic or social benefit, has actually contributed to a drastic decline in land under production—some say over one third less land is being farmed now than before the revolution. It is said that farmers abandoned their newly acquired land after the first season or two. There are a number of reasons for this. One is that no one provided seed or organized canal work, as the shaykh or his overseers had previously done. Another reason mentioned was that the rules of agrarian reform called for total cultivation of the plots of 40 meshara each, rather than allowing half to remain fallow. This, it was said, caused the land to become exhausted in a short time. It also meant that there was little or no place for grazing livestock—a major source of income, as we have seen.

Centralized authority systems are easier for us to understand because they more closely resemble our own form of political organization. Family ties have obviously not yet become entirely irrelevant in structuring the allocation of authority in societies like ours. Nepotism is not quite dead, and a few family dynasties still wield considerable political clout. But most authority for making decisions that affect domestic and foreign affairs has long since passed into the hands of people and groups whose right to power is ascribed on the basis of criteria other than kinship.

This has happened because of the growth and diversity of our population. So many of us move around so much. We are so frequently in contact with others with whom we share no ties of kinship, community, or common interest, that we could rarely, if ever, find a common senior kinsman whose right to regulate our relations with others would be commonly recognized.

Government has emerged among us as a structure and a process that has almost entirely replaced the kin group in adjusting the relationships that tie our society together and bind it also to an international network of alliances. But this development is relatively recent in history. It first occurred largely as a consequence of the need for new forms of governance that nearly everywhere followed the development of advanced farming. Much can be learned about the early evolution of political forms now familiar to us by examining the forces affecting state formation in parts of the world where the process is still going on—as in this case from Uganda that Kottak describes.

Ecological Variables in the Origin and Evolution of African States: The Buganda Example

*Conrad P. Kottak**

Anthropologists have been interested in African societies and cultures for several decades. Few will dispute the contributions which British social anthropologists and others have made to the understanding of African institutions, especially in the domains of kinship and marriage, political organization, and most recently in urban studies. Many of these studies, however, have been avowedly synchronic; they are intended as descriptions of societies at a single time level. Even in those cases where the anthropologist has been privileged to conduct research within the same society over an extended period of time, the problems of social and cultural change which he documents generally involve modifications of "traditional" institutions and behavior in the context of colonialism, postcolonialism, and world capitalism. While such studies are extremely important, the processes they describe do not exhaust the limits of the study of change in African society.

A surge of interest in precolonial African history has arisen rapidly with the end of colonialism. In the United States, under the guidance of Professor Vansina and others and with the inspiration of certain British historians, the study of African history has become a recognized specialty in many American universities, and one which seems to be in great demand. Anthropologists, too, have grown more interested in the African past. Given their long established acquaintance with Africa and the fact that anthropology includes, by virtue of anthropological archaeology, an historical dimension, it seems likely that more and more anthropologists will begin to orient their research interests towards the interpretation of African history. Africa is a most appropriate laboratory for the study of sociocultural process, for the societies of precolonial Africa exhibit a rich diversity in terms of complexity and range of adaptation to a variety of environments. Some of the world's most complex and tightly organized preindustrial civilizations, including Buganda, the subject of this paper, grew up on the African continent, while at the other end of the cultural evolutionary continuum, there are few societies less complex in technology and social organization than the Bushmen of the Kalahari Desert. In addition, the fact that sources of information about African history are rich when compared to other nonliterate areas also facilitates the study of long-term change. We have at our disposal accounts written by Arab and European merchants, scholars, travellers, explorers and missionaries. Furthermore, in the absence of writing in most African societies, the elites and sometimes the masses have developed an elaborate oral tradition, one of the major concerns of which is tracing genealogy. However, it is also true that many of the major problems for the cultural anthropologist interested in the precolonial African past, including many in this paper, will be resolved only through field work by anthropological archaeologists. With this caveat issued, the reader will understand why this paper must be suggestive and speculative in intent. This is not to say that it may not be right.

The contributions which the historian and the anthropologist can make to the understanding of African history are complementary, but of course there are differences in approach. Given their characteristic concern with institutions and with

Source: Reprinted from *Comparative Studies in Society and History*, Vol. 14, No. 3 (June 1972), pp. 351–379, by permission of Cambridge University Press and the author.

* I wish to thank Elliott P. Skinner and Nan Pendrell for their helpful comments on an earlier version of this paper.

forms of social structure, it is probable that anthropologists will concentrate more on the elucidation of changes in form of African societies than on the reconstruction, in the manner of Vansina and other adherents of historical inquiry through oral tradition, of individual events. The present paper, representing an inquiry into the origin and evolution of political organization in the Interlacustrine area (Great Lakes region) of East Africa, is intended as this kind of anthropological contribution. In it I attempt to employ in the analysis of East African state developments some forms of interpretation of sociocultural phenomena recently elaborated by American anthropologists. Since these forms of interpretation have proved fruitful in understanding developments in other parts of the world, it seems likely that they may be useful in explaining East African developments. The approach which will be adopted in this paper owes a great deal to Julian Steward's (1955) multilinear evolutionary, Marvin Harris's (1968) cultural materialist and Sahlin's and Service's (1960) specific evolutionary approaches. It attempts to isolate the most decisive factors, ecological and economic, which not only permitted a specific African state system to develop, but also, in a general sense, dictated the form of that development. In a larger sense the results of this study of political and socioeconomic evolution in Buganda should strongly suggest that some prevalent ideas about how African states and stratified systems have come into being will have to be reexamined.

In particular, conquest theories of state origins so often invoked to "explain" state and stratified systems in East Africa will have to be reconsidered. There has been a regrettable tendency, developed during the colonial period (cf. Sanders, 1969), to assume that wherever sophisticated political developments have occurred in East Africa, they could not possibly have developed internally. They must either have been borrowed from some "superior" group or been imposed by conquerors of some sort. Whether Nilotes or "Nilo-Hamites" conquering Bantu, or Cushites or Hamites conquering some indigenous population, the resulting picture has been the same—a dominant ruling class or caste of ultimately foreign origin, which somehow managed to form a state out of something that was not a state before.[1] I could find no evidence that conquest of a native population by outsiders played a decisive role, if indeed any, in the origin of the state in Buganda. Perhaps scholars have assumed, having witnessed so many examples of European conquest and colonialism in non-European areas, that this is the only, or the principal, way in which a societal form can be changed.

One of the crucial points of this paper has been made by Julian Steward (1955)—even if the state had been borrowed or imposed, one would still need to demonstrate the conditions which made such borrowing or imposition possible. Why, if outsiders could impose a central administration, could not insiders have done the same thing? Even if the "concept" or the "idea" of the state has diffused, how does one explain why one society exposed to this idea adopted centralized control while another rejected it? I suggest that answers to these questions lie in a detailed examination of technico-environmental niches exploited by societies, and those other, supralocal, niches in which they may, usually through trade, be involved. Thus, I address myself to two questions: (1) what kinds of relationships between men (their techniques, their ways of organizing groups, their ideas) and their environment (physical, biotal, and social) have favored or hindered state developments; and (2) how have internal developments in human populations been affected historically by their relationship to other human societies (outsiders)?

This paper will be divided into two parts. In the first, I examine the political organization and socioeconomic structure of Buganda as it has been reported by European travellers in the middle of the nineteenth century and by anthropologists who subsequently have described Buganda. In the second, I attempt to suggest how and why Buganda developed into a state from something which was less than a state. Finally, economic foundations of the Ganda state are compared to those of other African societies and the interacting ecological variables which produced state organization in Buganda are considered in the light of explanations of state origins which have been developed from consideration of other societies.

[1] Assumptions of conquest in the origin of East African states are included in several selections in *Problems in African History,* an anthology edited by Collins (1968). See, for example, Crazzolara (1950, in Collins, 1968, p. 148); Huntingford (1963, in Collins, 1968); and Wright (1953, in Collins, 1968).

I. Buganda: A Synchronic View

ENVIRONMENTAL SETTING. The former kingdom of Buganda, now part of the independent nation of Uganda, lies on a plateau with an average elevation of 4,000 feet between Lake Victoria and the western Rift. Much of Buganda consists of low, flat-topped hills separated by swampy valleys. The most productive soil in Buganda is known as *murram.* It is part of the Bukalsa Cantena, a pattern of soils which stretches in four bands from hill top to valley floor. The *murram* is the red earth found just below the hill summits and extending to the edge of the swamp. Grazing land for livestock—cattle, sheep, and goats—is found on the hill top. Cultivation of agricultural products sometimes extends down to the soil on the edge of the swamps (M. Fallers, 1960, p. 33).

These soils can support heavy cultivation in areas where the temperature and rainfall pattern are favorable. Since temperature varies little in Buganda, with no mean annual temperature below 65° F., rainfall is the crucial variable. Rainfall is bimodal, i.e., there are two rainy seasons, each followed by a dry season. Generally, however, there is rain in every month. There are two zones of moderate to heavy rainfall in the northwest and southeast of Uganda. These zones are separated by a drier belt, broad in the northeast and southwest and narrowing in the center. The moderate zones experience a minimum-maximum range of 40″ to 65″ or 70″ in nine years out of ten. The drier belt expects a range of 25″ to 33″ as minima, and 40″ to 48″ as maxima in a similar period (Fallers, 1960, p. 33). The vegetation of the first zone is elephant grass or long grass, while short grass grows in the moderate rainfall zones. Generally speaking, there is the greatest population density and most extensive cultivation of varieties of bananas and plantains in the areas of the heaviest rainfall. Population densities range from 200 to 1,000 persons per square mile in these areas (McMaster 1963). There is extensive local variation in rainfall throughout the area, however. Variables such as its distribution between the two seasons and the pattern in which the rain falls are currently being studied. All should have significant micro-ecological implications.

In the vicinity of Lake Victoria there is a more even spread of rainfall, so that even the theoretically dry seasons which follow the solstices are hardly ever completely dry. In northern Uganda there is a tendency towards convergence of the rainy seasons, producing a definite winter drought. Thus, although the total annual precipitation is higher than or as high in some of the northern areas as in the south, where Buganda lies, its agricultural effectiveness is greatest in the narrowly equatorial regions of Buganda. The crucial factor determining agricultural potential in this region is not the amount of rainfall, but its distribution throughout the year.

The most productive and secure agricultural areas in Uganda are the western slopes of Mount Elgon (where population density among the Bagisu runs as high as 1,000 per square mile), a more extensive area to the north of Lake Victoria which comprises the southerly parts of Buganda and Busoga, and finally, in order of superiority, come areas of Toro, Bunyoro, and the West Nile districts in the west and northwest of Uganda (Wrigley, 1957, pp. 2–3).

M. Fallers (1960) states that at the time of Speke's arrival in Buganda in 1862, it was perhaps the largest and most powerful of the states in the Great Lakes area. It extended from the ruler's court on the northwestern shore of Lake Victoria to the East, exacting tribute from southern Busoga; across the lake to control, partially at least, the Sese Islands; to the north to the borders of powerful Bunyoro; and to the south through Buddu. A different opinion is offered by Wrigley (1957, p. 4) who states that Buganda, while smaller in area than Bunyoro, was the more tightly knit of the two kingdoms. There is no doubt that Buganda had the larger population. There are now more than one million Ganda (Southwold. 1965, p. 85) while the Nyoro population is only 110,000 (Beattie, 1960, p. 1). Most of the surrounding tribes, even Bunyoro on occasion, had paid tribute to the Ganda kings by 1862.

It has been stated above that the critical factor in determining agricultural potential in the Interlacustrine area is not the amount, but the distribution of annual rainfall. Because there was rain throughout the year, a kind of permanent cultivation which relied on a perennial crop, the banana, was possible in Buganda, but not in Bunyoro. The climate of Buganda fulfills the requirements for successful banana or plantain cultivation: a tropical climate in which the temperature never falls below 50° F. nor rises about 105° F., and a fairly even rainfall, with no marked dry seasons, throughout the year.

Banana trees have the advantage of bearing all year round in contrast to those annual crops which are cultivated as staples in Bunyoro and as supplements to the banana diet in Buganda. The grain staples must be planted in the rainy and harvested in the dry season. Not only can bananas be harvested around the year, they also yield for a considerable period of time. They are perennials rather than annuals. Bananas have been raised on the same soil in Buganda for as long as forty years with little or no decrease in yields. Because they yield throughout the year and are perennials, Wrigley (1957, p. 71) contends that bananas are characterized by a greater certainty and a lower labor cost than almost any other plant. He argues that food production in Buganda based on banana cultivation, was so certain and so easy, in fact, that it could be relegated to the background of life and be left entirely to women (Wrigley, 1957, p. 71).

The factors noted above combine to suggest that the exploitation of the plantain as the principal vegetable staple is eminently compatible with a social system in which a great deal of labor can be marshalled from the local community and put to work for a higher level authority. Subsistence does not suffer if men are withdrawn to take part in public works, warfare, or other activities either for themselves, for fulfilling social obligations, or for rendering service to a political authority higher than the local community.

Yet, despite the fact that the banana is a highly productive staple per unit of land and unit of labor invested, the plantain diet must be supplemented with other foods. The caloric value of the banana is inferior per unit weight to that of wheat, rice, millet, maize, and the major grain staples of the world and to manioc or cassava flour, derived from a major root staple in Africa and elsewhere. The plantain yields 128 calories per 100 grams, about one-third as many as cassava flour, rice, wheat, maize, and other grains (Latham, 1965, pp. 249–50). This is primarily a result of the fact that the composition of the banana is about 80% water, 19% sugar, and 1% starch (when ripe) (Von Loeseche, 1950, pp. 12, 23, 143–4). While slightly richer in protein than fresh manioc, the plantain is still an inferior source of this nutrient when compared to other world staples (0.7 grams per 100 for fresh manioc, 1.0 for the banana, 8.0 for rice) (Latham, 1965, pp. 249–50). In order to supply minimum daily requirements of 55 grams of protein and 2,500 calories, one would have to consume 5.5 kilograms of bananas (for the protein) or 2 kilograms for the calories alone. Such intake requirements would probably tax even the stomach trained from infancy to maximize banana consumption. While the banana can be a very important staple, it cannot supply the minimum daily requirements of essential nutritive elements.[2] Other sources have to be exploited for subsistence, and, as will be shown below, this fact had profound implications for the development of an interregional network of exchange and redistribution and the emergence of a state in Buganda.

Some have argued that the banana is too much the staple of Buganda. The traditional Baganda are said to have grown little of any other food crop. Today, an estimated 29.1% of acreage under cultivation in Buganda is devoted to bananas. This percentage must have been higher in the past, since cash crops, principally cotton and coffee, account for 40% of the crop acreage today. Sweet potatoes, another traditional staple for the Baganda, account for only 6.1% of agricultural land under cultivation. They constitute for the peasantry the second major source of food (Mukwaya, 1953, p. 4).

FOOD SHORTAGE AND STORAGE. There is little indication that famine was salient as a negative check on population growth in Buganda. While M. Fallers (1960) states that droughts are frequent and serious in Buganda, arguing that the Ganda would be short of food in a drought should the annuals fail and bananas become scarce, she does not document the frequency of droughts and their effects on banana production and subsistence in general. Sir Harry Johnston (1902) contends that although drought may be hard felt in Buganda, it comes on few occasions.

[2] The deficiency of the plantain in supplying nutritive elements when compared to the major staples of the world extends from calories and proteins to vitamins and essential minerals. Only in vitamin A does the banana have an advantage over the grains. It is a fair source of calcium and iron, and rich in magnesium, sodium, cobalt, and potassium, and to a lesser extent in phosphorus (Von Loeseche, 1950, pp. 12, 23, 143–4; Latham, 1965, pp. 249–50). As noted in the text, however, a balanced diet requires more than these minerals.

Wrigley (1964, p. 18) concurs that failure of the Ganda food supply was rare.

Fallers also points out that there is little provision for the processing and storage of food in Buganda, and this is certainly true when one compares Buganda to societies with annual grain crops and granaries, or to the storage facilities of industrialized economies. However, Roscoe (1911) has argued that no storage is needed, since the occasional shortages of rain never cause famine in Buganda. In contrast to grain crops, one does not need to store the banana, since a banana grove can provide fruit continuously throughout the year and since bananas can be plucked off the plant whenever they are needed (Southwold, 1965, p. 109). In this respect, the banana is similar to root crops, which can be left in the ground to be dug or pulled up when needed.

There are no insurmountable problems involved in transporting and marketing plantains, though they are bulky and heavy. They can be picked green and will continue to ripen off the tree. It is also known that even ripe bananas may be dried, and dried bananas were traded in Buganda.

The protein needs of the Ganda, which the banana could not supply, were met by hunting, fishing, and livestock. Sheep, goats, cattle, fowl, and buffalo were kept and eaten. Protein was also obtained by eating termites or white ants, locusts, and the kungu fly or gnat. Small game, including the antelope, was hunted. Fishing was extremely important in the areas of Buganda nearest the lakes, and the allocation of this fish through a redistributive hierarchy seems to have been one important way of keeping peripheral areas under the control of the central administration. Near the lakes and rivers, fish are said to have provided a relatively stable supply of protein. Fish are reported to have constituted one of the most significant items of the peasant diet, and chiefs are said to have eaten fish at least once a week (Roscoe, 1911, p. 439).

As a contrast to the Ganda, one may note that the traditional staple of the Nyoro, their northern neighbors was eleusine millet, also known as small millet or *bulo*. This annual is superoir to the plantain in caloric, protein, and vitamin value, but lacks the permanency and high yield per unit of labor. In addition, because its nutrient composition was much better, it could be more of a staple (although other crops were also cultivated in Bunyoro) (Roscoe, 1911, p. 203; Beattie, 1960, p. 2). There was less need for the Nyoro to seek alternative sources of essential nutrients.

It is likely that the need for coordination of different ecological adaptations within a single unit was reduced in Bunyoro when compared to Buganda, and that this important function, which, as I discuss in greater detail below, acted to centralize and maintain a territorial administrative system in Buganda was less developed in Bunyoro. This may be one reason for the eventual dominant position of the Ganda state in the Interlacustrine region.

Division of Labor by Sex. Owing to the differences in the basic economies of Buganda and Bunyoro, that of an agricultural nation relying on the cultivation of perennial bananas on permanent plots as the principal staple as opposed to a society which mixed cattle pastoralism with the cultivation of millet and other annual crops, there was an important variation between the two kingdoms in the sex-based division of labor which provided a major foundation for the more tightly knit state system in Buganda. One of the distinguishing attributes of all states is specialization in economic roles so that parts of the population are not engaged in subsistence activities. Where such specialization is mentioned in the context of the state, we usually think of craft, administrative or religious specialists. In the case of Buganda, however, there was an even more obvious specialization; it was based on sex. There seem to be few societies with plant cultivation as a subsistence base in which men are freed so completely from agricultural tasks. It is possible to conceive of societies in which this freedom from agricultural labor would be expressed solely in terms of greater leisure time for the males. But leisure time for the masses is not a common correlate of archaic or nonindustrial states. Male labor formed the defensive and offensive subsystem of the Ganda state. In addition male labor was diverted to craft production, fishing, canoe manufacture, and public works and transportation projects.

In subsistence cultivation in Buganda, women were the main producers. A group of wives and female agnates formed the production-distribution nexus of the Ganda household. Males supplied the labor force for and distributed goods and services of the household to the hierarchical levels above the peasant holding. In Bunyoro, the less certain subsistence base of eleusine millet and other annuals required a greater expenditure of masculine labor in clearing new land and in other aspects of production. A strong pastoral element in the Nyoro economy also emphasized the productive labor of males. The Nyoro male had less time to spend in the service of chiefs and kings. Greater agricultural uncertainty prevented the flow of resources in Bunyoro from being as regular as it was in Buganda.

SETTLEMENT PATTERNS AND POPULATION DENSITY. There were significant differences in the settlements inhabited by peasants, chiefs, and king (Kabaka). In early times the Ganda settlement patterns appears to have been one of groups of households strung out along hillsides. For convenience, such a group will be called a village. Villages were separated from their neighbors by belts of swamps and forests. Such communities were organized by kinship and descent. As population grew, lineages split and dispersed. By at least the seventeenth century, many clans acknowledged the supremacy of the Kabaka. It has been asserted that in the course of political evolution, the Ganda village changed from a settlement of relative equals, based on the principle of the corporate lineage with a hereditary headman to a colony of serfs living under a feudal lord (Wrigley, 1957, pp. 71–2). The Baganda apparently have never lived in closely clustered groups of dwellings, but in family households (*byalo*).

The village in which a Ganda subchief lived did not differ in kind from ordinary peasant villages. It included perhaps a few more people or slightly more substantial dwellings, but the difference was not marked. Mair contends that the smallest Ganda chieftainship had control over 20 to 30 men or households (1934, p. 161). I suspect that she is speaking here of a *kyalo*, or village. The settlements of important chiefs and kings followed the topography in roughly the same manner as those of the peasantry. All settlements were located on hills. The higher chiefs perhaps had hundreds of wives and large personal estates which they obtained from the Kabaka (Roscoe, 1911, p. 13). In their settlements, in addition to their wives, lived a male retinue consisting of kinsmen, bodyguards, musicians, artisans, and other dependents of the high chiefs (Wrigley, 1964, p. 21). Every wife of the chief, or even of the Kabaka, including the principal wife, maintained her plantain garden near the group of houses (Mair, 1934, p. 95; Roscoe, 1911, p. 200). Roscoe indicates that there might have been as many as 1,000 persons living in a chief's group of dwellings (1911, p. 336). He is referring, probably, to the county chief.

Population estimates for Kampala, the capital of Buganda, at the time of Kabaka Mutesa, in 1862, run as high as 77,000 (Fallers, 1960, p. 22). Wrigley thinks that Kampala was probably the largest agglomeration of population in interior Africa, and that it had certain urban characteristics by the time Mutesa had ascended the throne (Wrigley, 1957, p. 73). Kampala, the capital, was the heart of the Ganda state and the center of the redistributive network that encompassed it.

The king's wives always had large estates at the capital for the cultivation of plantains (Roscoe, 1911, p. 200), although the royal court certainly did not rely solely on banana cultivation at the capital for its food. By the time of Speke's visit in 1862, chiefs were required to spend most of their time at the capital. There were also work parties of peasants there on a constant basis, to construct and repair the royal buildings and to engage in other royally inspired public works projects, including the construction and maintenance of a road system. In addition, there were specialists serving the king and his court. A lively trade and market activity existed in Kampala in 1862. In Bunyoro all political centers are on a much smaller scale, and there is no site which can be compared with Kampala. When estimating the size of the king's (Kabarega's) court in Bunyoro, Johnston (1902) mentions 1,000 to 3,000 wives and concubines of the king and 2,000 of what he calls prostitutes. On the other hand, the court of Mutesa, who ruled in Buganda contemporaneously with Kabarega, is said to have included 18,000 royal wives and maiden servants, all of them residents of the capital (Kagwa, 1934, p. 55).

THE POLITICAL HIERARCHY AND LAND TENURE. In the Buganda of 1862, political authority and land rights were coterminous. This may be inferred from the common expression that the chief does not rule land, but rules the people. By the time of Mutesa, the king and the chief undoubtedly did rule both land and people. Rights to land, formerly allocated on the basis of membership in a patrilineal descent group, were more and more allocated on a nonkin basis (Southwold, 1965, p. 96).

At the head of the Ganda state was the Kabaka, or king. Equal to the Kabaka in rank, but not in power, were his mother, the Namasole, and the Queen or Lubuga—the royal counterpart of the Kabaka, though she was not his wife. She was a half-sister chosen for this ritual position by the Kabaka upon his succession to the throne. The Kimbugwe was the next official in the rank order. He was appointed by the Kabaka to take charge of the national temple and the royal fetish. The Katikiro (prime minister) shared equal rank with the Kimbugwe, but he wielded a great deal more power. At times his position is said to have been virtually on a par with that of the Kabaka (Mair, 1934, p. 181).

Responsible to the prime minister were the chiefs of the counties or *ssazas*, of which there were ten by 1862. Each county was divided into a number of subcounties ruled by lesser chiefs called Bakungu, who were responsible to the county chiefs. These subcounties were in turn divided into parishes, governed by Batongole and responsible to the Bakungu. With the exception of two of the subcounty chiefs whose positions were hereditary, all the occupants of positions in the political hierarchy were appointed by each new Kabaka as he assumed office (Mair, 1934, p. 160).

Parallel to the political hierarchy, but of subsidiary importance, was the pyramidal structure of clan authority. Clans were nominally exogamous, patrilineal, and each had a major and minor totem. The Bataka were the clan chiefs who controlled the clan lands. Their positions were hereditary and inalienable, but the Kabaka had to confirm all major clan appointments and also exercised his power to appoint territorial chiefs over the land surrounding the clan estate. Clans were subdivided into subclans (*siga*), lineages (*mutuba*), and sublineages (*lunyiri*). Each clan, subclan, and lineage had estates on which its members were buried. The most important estate, which was considered to be the original site of the clan lands, was under the control of the clan head.

As noted above, rights in land closely followed the structure of political authority. Four main types of control over land were important in Buganda in 1862. These were (1) clan rights, known as Obutaka; (2) the rights of the king and his chiefs, known as Obutongole; (3) the rights of an individual acquired by inheritance, i.e., land rights given in perpetuity by another person, usually the Kabaka; and finally (4) peasant rights of occupation, known as Ehibanja. It will be helpful to examine each of these four types in detail.

(1) Clan rights. There were forty-eight clans in Buganda traditionally, as compared to approximately 150 in Bunyoro. At least five of them claimed to have been in Buganda prior to the advent of *Kintu*, the "first Kabaka." Others are believed to have come in with one of the "invading dynasties," while another group of clans had sought and obtained land and protection from particular kings in the past. Still others originated as individuals were awarded land by the Kabaka on which they founded their own clans. Finally there was a group of clan lands in conquered territories. Hills and villages throughout Buganda were claimed by clans as their traditional lands. These were the burial sites of senior ancestors, clan and lineage heads. No such claim covers one continuous territory or a large number of adjacent villages today. The greatest concentration of claims is located near past residences of the particular kings who had allocated lands to particular clans (Mukwaya, 1953, pp. 7–8). By the beginning of the eighteenth century, in only a few of these villages did clansmen constitute a majority of residents. Most villagers were nonrelatives, attached to the senior clansmen, treating him as their chief. The village functioned on a nonkin basis (cf. Southwold, 1965, p. 96).

No longer were patrilineal clans the principal structural units in Ganda society; no longer did they provide the framework for everyday social relations. Baganda, by 1862, lived their lives within the context of a political state system. They were members of a territorial unit, an integral part of a centralized political hierarchy. The political authority of the king maintained a wide area for the free personal mobility of his subjects. Yet the preexisting structure, based on descent, was utilized by and incorporated into the growing state. A system of transferable chiefs became possible. The king appointed the more capable of the clan leaders, who would take their kinsmen along with them as they moved to the districts which had been allocated to them. The efficacy of descent as an organizational device remained greatest in those areas which were farthest removed from the capital, as the estates of the king and the royal relatives were closest to the capital, and the grants to chiefs and palace officials were usually made in this nearby area. In the outlying provinces, the clan heads combined kinship functions with rights and duties derived from their positions in the political hierarchy. On the other hand, Fallers (1964, p. 76) indicates that close to the capital, the heads of the traditional Buganda clans, presiding as political chiefs over villages whose populations were composed primarily of nonkinsmen, remained a check on the king's power.

(2) The rights of king and chiefs. The king controlled some of the richest villages and had a greater number of estates spread throughout Buganda than any other individual. Each palace official was in charge of a number of estates which belonged to the Kabaka. Each chief had, in his county or subcounty, a number of personal estates, with subsidiary chiefs who he appointed for each one (Mukwaya, 1963, pp. 10–11). The king's relatives each had different villages in different parts of the country, as did his prime minister, the Keeper of the Fetish, and military officials. The essential features of these rights are the following: (a) they covered certain estates attached to particular offices, and one's usufructuary rights terminated with the death of the holder of the office, or through his promotion or demotion, which were common occurrences in Buganda; (b) the estates of the king's relatives and those of the more important chiefs were not subject to the normal procedures of tax and tribute collection. Presents to the king were substituted. Since 1840, when King Suna made the reform, each captain of a band of warriors was granted a number of villages to be controlled directly by him or his assistants. Here his warriors settled. Some of these estates were located on the fringes of the kingdom and, among other functions, apparently served as frontier outposts from which neighboring groups were absorbed into the state (Mukwaya, 1953, pp. 12–13).

(3) Individual hereditary rights. These were other minor claims to land control which carried no associated political duties. These claims were based either on long occupation of one particular holding which was recognized by the Kabaka, and in this sense were similar to lineage lands, or they were based on an original grant of one holding or one small estate to an individual chief or peasant by the Kabaka himself. These holdings were small and carried no political rights or duties. They were permanent in the sense that occupancy was for life and could be passed on to heirs. The owners were free of the labor obligations due to chiefs from peasants, but they could be summoned for other political or military duties (Mukwaya, 1953, pp. 11–13).

(4) Peasant rights of occupation. Every individual had the right to the occupation and use of land, although the number of people who had unimpaired access to control of land was limited by the factors noted above. The peasant's rights could be allocated on a kin basis if he lived on the land of his clan or lineage, or alternatively on a nonkin basis, as the subject of some chief in the political hierarchy. His position was generally similar regardless of the method by which he derived his rights to soil utilization. His security of tenure was apparently slightly greater if he lived on a kinsman's land. This factor sometimes gave rise to wholesale migrations of peasants as people followed a successful clansman in a progression from bigger to bigger chieftainships (Mukwaya, 1953, pp. 13–14). Other writers have mentioned the tendency of Ganda peasants to follow any popular chief. The compendium of peasant rights in 1862 was more or less as it is today: grazing rights, water rights, rights to trees and firewood, the right to remain in possession and to transmit to heirs contingent on their appropriate social and political behavior. In return, the peasant gave tribute to his chief or the head of his clan, and a part of this was ultimately passed on to the king.

II. Buganda: A Diachronic View

What variables were responsible for the emergence of the Ganda state? Anthropologists, especially anthropological archaeologists, who have investigated the origins and evolution of states in many parts of the world have generally attributed causal roles to ecological variables. Similarly, my interpretation of sociocultural evolution in Buganda postulates certain interacting ecological variables as responsible for the evolution of state organization in Buganda. These variables involve, on the one hand, a local human ecosystem, called Buganda, consisting of a human population and its sociocultural means of adaptation to a variety of microenvironmental niches located within the boundaries of the Ganda polity, and on the other, a regional or supralocal ecosystem formed by intersocietal relations within the Interlacustrine area and beyond. Consideration of this wider ecosystem is essential, for one cannot understand Buganda's evolution without considering its relations with Bunyoro; nor can one fathom the evolution of either if one ignores trade routes with the East African coast, the Sudan, and other, less certainly known areas. The local ecosystem in the area now inhabited by Buganda is first examined, to be followed by a discussion of the wider ecosystem formed through exchange systems within the region.

PRE-AGRICULTURAL ADAPTATIONS IN THE LAKES REGION. Archaeological evidence for the Interlacustrine area has been sparse and inconclusive. Perhaps around 7,000 years ago the Magosian of eastern and southern Africa was succeeded by regional variants of the Wilton and Nachikufan cultures. The Wilton is generally found in drier, open country, while the Nachikufan is found in the savannah and woodlands of Zambia and in parts of Tanzania (Cole, 1963, p. 45). The Wilton culture of East Africa has been divided into three phases, partly contemporaneous with one another and distinguished on the basis of the different locations of the sites involved. Wilton "A" people lived in the open; Wilton "B" people inhabited rock shelters, while Wilton "C" people lived on the shores of lakes.[3] The culture which concerns us most directly is Wilton "C." It is found with huge shellfish middens beside the lakes of East and Central Africa, as well as on the sea coast of South Africa (Cole, 1963, p. 46). Skeletons associated with shell mounds have been found near Kanam on the Kavirondo Gulf of Lake Victoria. The skulls are similar to those of the Bushmen, who Cole (1963, p. 46) thinks may be descended from this type of people. Similar lake dwellers were responsible for the Ishango culture, reported by Heinzelin.

The Wilton and similar Lakes' sites are the remains of populations who must have relied for subsistence on hunting, fishing, and collecting of flora and shell fauna. In the Interlacustrine region these cultural adaptations were eventually replaced by populations whose ecological niches included plant, specifically banana, cultivation, and an iron-age technology.

An iron-age technology and cultivation of the banana are long established in Buganda. Recent Carbon 14 dates from the Great Lakes region of Africa suggest that food producing populations, wielding an iron-age tool kit and manufacturing dimple-based pottery in the Lakes region and channeled or grooved pottery in Zambia, expanded rapidly in East Africa between the first and the fifth centuries A.D. It is probable that these populations were proto-Bantu in the early stages of an adaptive radiation which ultimately would accomplish the settlement of most of Central and Southern Africa.

BANANAS, IRON AND AFRICAN HISTORY. To either and/or to both iron and the banana several scholars have attributed major roles in African history. (Murdock 1959) stresses the importance of the banana and other Southeast Asian food crops in the expansion of the Bantu from what he, following Greenberg (1963), regards as an ancestral homeland in plateau Nigeria and the adjacent Cameroons, to occupy most of the land area of Central and Southern Africa. For Murdock the reception by the proto-Bantu of Malaysian food plants, transmitted from the Ethiopian lowlands across the forest region below the southern Sudan, triggered Bantu expansion, as it allowed the proto-Bantu to enter and colonize the equatorial forest for the first time with appropriate tropical forest plants. Greenberg and Murdock agree that the proto-Bantu differentiation, and therefore expansion, has taken place within the past 3,000 to 2,000 years. For these scholars, presumably the plaintain would have entered the Lakes region as early Bantu, having radiated in the tropical forest, penetrated the East African uplands through the Nile-Congo divide and colonized, with the banana, the Great Lakes region from the northwest (cf. McMaster, 1963, for a similar view).

For others, iron spears and an iron-age technology were responsible for Bantu expansion, radiation in the tropical forest and, following this, the eventual occupation of the Lakes area, again through the Nile–Congo divide and from the northwest. Still other views bring iron-working techniques to the Interlacustrine Bantu from the north, but not necessarily with the proto-Bantu. For some, techniques of iron-smelting reached the Lakes from Meroë by diffusion. This hypothesis is suspect in view of the improbability that the proto-Bantu, lacking an iron-age technology, could have penetrated the forest and therefore have been in the Lakes region to receive this diffused knowledge. It seems likely, especially in view of the work of Guthrie, Oliver, and Hiernaux, to be discussed below, that the proto-Bantu did wield an iron-age technology by the time they settled around Lake Victoria.

The banana seems to have been more decisive than iron in the actual colonization of the Lakes region by the proto-Interlacustrine Bantu. Guthrie's (1962 and elsewhere) linguistic work on the Bantu problem has recently received support from anthropobiological studies by Hiernaux (1968). As Oliver (1966) points out,

[3] I make no assumption that these three types, if indeed contemporaneous, represent distinct social units. It is possible that the different sites may have been associated with seasonally or functionally differentiated activities rather than with different societies or cultures.

Guthrie's hypotheses about the site of proto-Bantu population explosion can be viewed not as contradictory to but as compatible with Greenberg's. Greenberg located the proto-Bantu homeland in Nigeria and the Cameroons, just north of the tropical forest. For Guthrie, on the other hand, the site of proto-Bantu expansion lay in the light woodland zone to the south of the tropical forest. Guthrie postulates that a small group of proto-Bantu penetrated the forest, following rivers in canoes, and eventually emerged in the southern woodland zone. Here, with an iron-age technology they rapidly radiated along an elliptical area both east and west of a center in the Luba–Katanga region.

Oliver (1966) and Hiernaux (1968) agree with this interpretation on the basis of a series of Carbon 14 dates within this elliptical area, suggesting a rapid expansion of iron-age channeled or grooved and dimple-based pottery-making traditions in the four centuries A.D. Furthermore, Oliver suggests that as the proto-Bantu expanded through this elliptical area south of the forest they eventually established contact with Indonesian mariners on the East African coast. We know that Madagascar was being colonized in the first four centuries A.D. (Verin, Kottak, and Gorlin, 1971). It was from the Indonesians on the East African coast that the proto-Bantu received the Southeast Asian food crops, including the banana. Posnansky (1964) suggests that the banana-cultivating Interlacustrine Bantu eventually reached the region of Buganda along a route from the Mozambique Coast via the mouth of the Zambezi River and through the Great Lakes. Oliver (1963) thinks that the Interlacustrine Bantu reached their present homeland from the south in the second half of the first millenium A.D. Population increase in the Lakes area then produced emigrations which, moving through the forest, eventually gave rise to the equatorial Bantu and a reoccupation of the original homeland on the northern fringe of the forest by some of the Bantu speakers found there today.

There is considerable agreement that the banana has been cultivated in the Buganda region for between 1,500 and 2,000 years. McMaster (1963) argues for 1,500 years, but no longer, on the basis of the complexity of banana cultivation techniques among the Ganda and other Interlacustrine Bantu. Posnansky (1964), on the basis of botanical evidence, suggests as long as 2,000 years. A date of 1,500 years ago seems reasonable to me for the transition in the region which was to become Buganda from an economy based solely on fishing, hunting, and collecting to one which combined the cultivation of bananas with these extractive strategies. What were the probable implications of this change in subsistence strategy for the local and ultimately for the regional ecosystem?

THE EMERGENCE OF RANKING. Changes in subsistence strategies of parallel magnitude have occurred in other parts of the world. Consideration of some of these may shed light on the early stages of Ganda society, as Bantu populations settled on the northern shores of Lake Victoria. In an article dealing with possible causes of the evolution of the state, Morton Fried (1959) has considered changes of social forms from egalitarian to ranked which have followed a shift in subsistence strategy from nonsedentary societies to permanent cultivation.[4] Fried uses the terms "egalitarian" and "ranked" in the context of a series of evolutionary types or "levels of sociocultural integration." Empirical societies approximate one or another of three broadly different ideal sociopolitical types, called by Fried "egalitarian," "rank," and "stratified." The "state" comes into being to maintain the order of the stratified society, and, in this sense, might be considered a fourth type, though Fried has been able to find few stratified societies which are not also states.

Fried defines an egalitarian society as one in which there are as many positions of prestige in any given sex–age category as there are persons capable of filling them. The rank society, on the other hand, has fewer positions of valued status than individuals capable of handling them. Most rank societies have a fixed number of such positions. While the rank society operates on the principal of differential status for members with similar abilities, these statuses are, however, devoid of privileged economic or political power. These are the societies of the "big men," distinguished not by their hoarding of wealth and power, but by their generosity (cf. Sahlins, 1963).

A shift from egalitarian to rank-organized society was probably the result of the introduction of banana cultivation into the local ecosys-

[4] Fried dealt specifically with the shift from shifting (slash and burn) cultivation to hydroagriculture and sedentary life as causative in the transition from egalitarian to rank and stratified forms of society. Fried's 1959 article has subsequently elaborated into a book *The Evolution of Political Society,* 1967.

tem in Buganda. Land itself would not have been a strategic resource to the groups of hunters-fishers-collectors who have been postulated as inhabiting the northwest shores of Lake Victoria before the advent of the agricultural Bantu. With the introduction of the plantain, there is a subsistence shift, as in hydroagriculture, to plots which will remain under permanent cultivation for decades, perhaps even for generations. If access to land were made the specific prerogative of small-scale kin groups, Bantu or otherwise, ranking probably would emerge. Once established as the principal subsistence crop, plantains were capable of producing a large and reliable caloric yield per unit of land, and per unit of labor, given the technology and the environmental setting. It would certainly have been a more productive adaptation than the hunting-collecting-fishing which preceded it in the same area, for hunting, fishing, and shell collecting activities could continue alongside of banana cultivation with its low labor requirements. Population increase would be rapid at first, and segmentation of unilineal descent groups would ensue. By this time, there would certainly be a well developed rank-organized society, with kin heads serving as foci of institutionalized generosity and incipient loci of redistribution of strategic resources.

Fried sees the shift from slash-and-burn cultivation to hydroagriculture as a mechanism which may have brought about not only the emergence of ranking, but also of stratification. Indeed, in his view, a society may pass directly from egalitarian to stratified. According to Fried the major difference between the ranked and the stratified society lies in the fact that in the latter certain privileged members of a given age-sex category have unimpeded access to strategic resources and power, while others in that category do not (Fried, 1959, p. 771). Features which accompany stratification include a formal statement of legal principles, machinery of adjudication, and a formally constituted police authority. Fried agrees with Morgan, Maine, and Engels that in the stratified society, prime authority has shifted from kinship to territorial means. Other corollary features of the stratified order are payment of dues, rent, and taxes in labor or in kind; exploitation, as in drudge slavery or involved divisions of labor and intricate class systems; and the emergence of communities composed of kin parts or nonkin parts which, as wholes, operate on the basis of nonkin mechanisms.

Did the shift to permanent cultivation which the banana made possible in Buganda lead directly to stratification or merely to ranking? I choose to speculate that only ranking emerged. A direct transition to stratified organization seems unlikely unless there is some kind of limitation to further population expansion. In the absence of such a limitation, which could be either physical or intergroup, population growth would be expressed in social structure through fissioning of equivalent segments, as individuals and minimal segments break off from their localized descent groups to settle new areas and to form apical points for sublineages, lineages, and eventually clans of their own. There probably were no such limits to segmentary expansion of this sort in the Interlacustrine area at the time at which the banana was introduced. The Baganda would have been free to expand with their iron-age technology and their plantains through the forests until further expansion was blocked by other groups or until they reached the natural limits of the banana niche.

THE ORIGINS OF THE STRATIFIED SOCIETY IN BUGANDA. Some of these segments of unilineal descent groups were eventually forced further and further from the lake shores and were thereby in danger of relinquishing a diversified diet based on fish, a necessary source of protein, as well as plantains. It would have been advantageous for people farther from the lake to maintain their ties with kinsmen closer to its shores. The foci of redistribution within the descent group structure could now function not only to redistribute surpluses, products and people, but also to move resources from one ecological niche to another. Ranking of some of the clans or descent groups over others would be a probable result of differential population increase among clans produced by variable productivity of microenvironments within Buganda. There are several indications that in prestate Buganda the Kabaka's clan[5] was of equivalent rank to other

[5] It had become the custom at least by the nineteenth century for each Kabaka to take his mother's rather than his father's clan affiliation. There was therefore no royal clan recognized in Buganda. The opportunity of the commoner clans to provide wives to the reigning king and the custom that the king belonged to his mother's clan offered the possibility to the commoner clans that the next Kabaka might be a fellow clan member. This has been stressed as one of the ways of making political sovereignty more palatable to the Ganda.

Ganda clans. ". . . Baganda believe, and there is no *a priori* reason to doubt them, that over the centuries the Kabaka moved from a position of *primus inter pares* among heads of patrilineal descent groups to that of a despotic monarch who could remove areas from descent group control and put in charge of them personal appointees of his own choosing" (Fallers, 1964, p. 76). The larger clans not only would have had more members and hence more support in the case of interclan feud, they also would have been sending off migrants and therefore occupying a wider environmental spectrum than smaller descent groups. The key statuses in the redistributive network could gradually have gained differential access to strategic resources, by virtue of the sheer volume of the goods and supporters which they controlled. This is a possible explanation for the emergence of stratification in Buganda. Like the additional hypotheses which will be offered below, it can serve only as a plausible explanation in the absence of archaeological tests.

A second hypothesis which, in combination with the first, may explain the emergence of social stratification in Buganda involves the postulation of a developing supralocal or intersocietal exchange network. The volume and the diversity of trade products may reach a point at which the traditional foci of collection and redistribution are no longer capable of handling the trade volume. At this point, a special purpose subsystem may develop in the society to coordinate the provision and movement of products from one ecological zone to another and across political boundaries of societies. At some point in Ganda history trade links were established between a pastoral population in the short grass zone to the north and west of the Ganda forest and the Ganda themselves. As will be seen below, officials of the Ganda state were controlling this trade by the eighteenth century.

The identity of these pastoral groups is unknown. Sir Harry Johnston (1902) postulated that, in the mid-fourteenth century, the western coastlands of Lake Victoria were loosely held appendages of two or three Hima or pastoralist kingdoms encompassing Toro, Ankole, and Karagwe. Johnston states that, perhaps for reasons of health, the Hima made no attempt to occupy the richly forested counties of Kiagwe, Buganda, Budda, and Kiziba. Since all of the latter are areas of plantain cultivation, it would seem that the absence of suitable grazing land for large herds of cattle in these areas, rather than poor health conditions, would better explain the absence of the Hima from the banana zones. The Lake country, according to Johnston's reconstruction, served as the hunting ground of the Hima for agricultural slaves. From the Lake counties the pastoralists also obtained coffee berries and barkcloth for clothing (Johnston, 1902, pp. 678–9). One may question Johnston's reconstruction on the following basis: it seems unlikely that pastoralists would have been able to subjugate a forested agricultural zone. On the one hand, certain resources strategic to pastoralism are lacking in the high rainfall zone. On the other, it is hard to see how certain limitations within "Hima" technology (e.g., no horses, the handicaps of traveling through a swampy area) could have effectively threatened the peasantry near the Lake, but the presence of a pastoral population just outside the banana zone could certainly have stimulated the development by the Ganda of a defensive pose. It seems more profitable to suggest that both societies benefited from a trade relationship, although there is no way of knowing how and by whom this trade was mediated.

Interregional trade was certainly of importance by the eighteenth century. Singo, located between Buganda and Bunyoro, which eventually becomes a district of Buganda, is said to have derived its wealth from trade in iron, hoes, salt, and cattle, primarily between Bunyoro and Buganda (Wainwright, 1954, p. 114, and Kagwa, 1934, p. 162). Kiagwe, also incorporated into expanding Buganda, and located to the east, between Buganda and Busoga, is said to have derived its riches, part of which were passed on to the Buganda population, from good gardens, the manufacture of musical instruments, hunting in the large forests and the provision of ivory, trade in a plentiful and highly valued variety of coffee, and from its outlets for food supplies in "numerous markets along the lake shore," which were attended by peoples from the islands and from Busoga (Roscoe, 1911, pp. 248–50, Kagwa, 1934, pp. 162–3).

Other divisions of the Ganda state also specialized in the provision of definite products. In an area of diversified ecological niches, such as the Interlacustrine area, indigenous trade networks and the regulation of inter-regional exchange was definitely a function of the Ganda state of the eighteenth and the nineteenth centuries. I am here suggesting that this economic system took time to develop, as did a sociopolitical system to oversee it. This exchange network, in turn, may ultimately have provided incentives for cooperative activities in the form of construction and maintenance of roads, fleets of canoes, bridges, etc., and may thus have further strengthened the trend towards stratification. By the eighteenth century, the characterization of these activities as "cooperative" would be misleading. Public works projects involving transportation and communication were unavoidable for the peasant members of the Ganda population.

THE EVOLUTION OF THE STATE IN BUGANDA. I shift now from consideration of the reasons for the emergence of stratification in Buganda to the causes of the evolution of the state. Fried regards the state as a device whose principal functions include maintaining general order and supporting the order of stratification (Fried, 1959, p. 727). The major concerns of its rulers are defense of the idea of hierarchy, property relations, and the power of law. In implementing these primary functions, a number of secondary functions come into play. Fried suggests that there are few if any societies which are stratified but which lack state organization. This suggests that once stratification is present, the state develops very quickly. Most of the theories which have been offered for the origin of states in East Africa involve the notion of conquest. Generally, pastoral populations have been seen as conquering agricultural populations and, in doing so, erecting a stratified state with themselves as rulers.

It seems likely that the presence of pastoralists in the short grass zones to the north and west of Buganda was a variable involved in the evolution of the state in Buganda, but not through conquest. The appearance of pastoralists and large herds of cattle in these short grass zones stimulated state development in Buganda in two ways: (1) by adding cattle to the interregional exchange network; and (2) by producing a defensive pose on the part of the Ganda.

Migrations of Nilotic Lwoo-speaking pastoralists seem to have reached Bunyoro by the late fifteenth and early sixteenth centuries (Collins, 1968, p. 118). During the sixteenth century they expanded within the short grass zone. E. C. Lanning (1953) has excavated giant earthworks in the short grass country to the west of Buganda, interpreting them as either cattle kraals or fortified camps of a pastoral population which occupied this region between 400 and 600 years ago. It is not known if these earthworks were the products of Lwoo-speaking Nilotes or a prior population recalled as Bachwezi in Nyoro oral tradition, whom the Lwoo-speaking Nilotes, or Bito, as Nyoro call them, are supposed to have driven to the south.

Johnston's (1902) speculative reconstruction of Hima pastoralist kingdoms in the fourteenth century has been noted above. Oliver (1963, p. 182) equates the Ganda kingdom ruled by Kabaka Kintu's son Chwa with the Chwezi dynasty of Bunyoro. He envisions a single, feudal-like political unit dominated by Hima pastoralists under kings of the Chwezi clan, which lasted for a short time, and was ultimately overthrown by Lwoo or Bito invaders from the North. After the gradual Lwoo infiltration had culminated in the defection of the Chwezi overlords, there was a division of the kingdom, in which subdynasties of the Bito family were planted out as tributary rulers of the central provinces of the former Chwezi kingdom. Among these provinces was the nucleus of modern Buganda, which was allocated to Kato Kimera, said to have been the twin brother of Rukidi (the first Bito monarch of Bunyoro). In Buganda tradition, Kabaka Kimera is regarded as Kabaka Chwa's grandson (Oliver, 1963, p. 182).

It would seem that conquest is so firmly established as an "explanation" for East African state structures that it has deflected attention from the more vital problem of determining the mechanisms and processes of state development. If there was a Bachwezi empire, one must attempt to explain how it got there. One must further explain why there is no physiological or linguistic evidence for Hima influence in Buganda, if he is to accept the common assumption that the Chwezi were Hima. Confronting these problems, Wrigley (1958) has offered a view which dissents from the Chwezi-Hima hypothesis. Dismissing the Chwezi as phantoms of mythology, Wrigley conjectures that there was once in this area a large loose-jointed Bantu kingdom of the same general type as those of the Congo, Lunda, and Monomotapa. This empire broke down many centuries ago, leaving its central area to be occupied by small groups of herding folk. Later on, but not before 1500, there arose in the North, under Lwoo leadership, a new expansionist power which owed its successes mainly to the possession of the best supplies of iron, located presumably in Bunyoro and strategic in the production of arrows and spears. The quasi-feudal Hima and Tutsi states, e.g., Banyankole, Rwanda, Burundi, developed largely in response to the necessities of defense against these marauders.

Wrigley's suggestion of cooperation induced by defensive considerations as an alternative to conquest in explaining the origin of major East African states is valuable, but does not tell the whole story. Other variables are necessary to explain the development of states in East Africa. In the case of Buganda, there are several variables involving the local ecosystem. There are others involving an interregional exchange system, a supralocal ecosystem. These variables interacted to produce stratification and the state in Buganda. Within the local ecosystem, I have stressed the role of the banana. I have pointed out that the banana makes permanent cultivation possible and that it enables male labor to be diverted from subsistence to other kinds of activities. I have also argued that the nutritional attributes of the banana make it an incomplete staple and necessitate the exploitation of other foods. I have stated that this was important in the development of an exchange system linking different components of the Ganda population as they occupied environments away from the lake, with its rich sources of protein in fish. The expanding exchange system ultimately came to extend to non-Ganda populations, and this network came under the control of the Ganda polity.

Since we know that there were migrations of Nilotes into the short grass region of Uganda during the sixteenth century, it is appropriate to consider their contribution to the development of the state in Buganda. It is my contention that Buganda adopted a defensive pose against the Nilotic intruders and the northern state of Bunyoro to protect the emerging exchange network. Once the defensive pose had been adopted, the subsistence base of the Ganda and their geographical placement with reference to routes of trade and exchange favored their ultimate advancement over other populations of the Interlacustrine region. Most vital, the male population of Buganda could be mobilized into a military subsystem. At first this military subsystem served the purpose of defense. Ultimately it proved to be viable as an offensive mechanism which progressively extended the boundaries of Buganda at the expense of neighboring populations during the eighteenth and the nineteenth centuries. If the Lwoo-speaking invaders ever ruled Buganda, as they appear to have ruled Bunyoro and as oral traditions seem to suggest (Beattie, 1960, p. 16), such rule was only tenuous and ephemeral. Since Buganda could not support significant herds of Bito cattle, if a Bito subdynasty was ever established there, it must have weakened gradually until it was ultimately absorbed by Bantu Ganda. Eventually Buganda cut off relations with the Bito capital in Bunyoro and continued its own development, aided by its subsistence base and its more favorable position with respect to trade routes from the Coast. From this time onward, Buganda assumed the offensive.

THE DEVELOPMENT OF BUGANDA AS REFLECTED IN ROYAL GENEALOGIES. It is difficult to reconstruct the history of Buganda in more than general terms, but one can see a clear picture emerging at least by the seventeenth century as a stratified society becomes a mature state. This picture is one of increased political power, authority, and force at the disposal of the centralized hierarchy, headed by a sovereign gradually devoided of military and ritual functions, and assuming a solely secular and political character. During the late seventeenth and eighteenth centuries, incessant conflicts between rival clans and princes may have reinforced and stimulated the power of the king. During this period the boundaries of Buganda were constantly enlarged; the fiscal network reached farther and farther from the locus of redistribution at the capital. The control over the army and its booty in the form of cattle, women, and slaves was the basis of the king's power over the chief and of the chief's power over the peasant. The booty which reached the Kabaka was of significant proportions from the mid-eighteenth century onwards. For a time Buganda was able to control, in large measure, the export trade from a wide region extending to the north-west, north, and east of the kingdom itself.

By examining the legendary accounts of the reigns of the traditional kings of Buganda, one observes significant changes and the point at which the emergence of the state probably took place.

The use of traditional sources: genealogy and native history requires a brief defense. All social anthropologists know that myth and genealogy serve as a charter which validates the social structure of the people who develop them. However, this truism should not blind us to the fact, as Vansina (1965) has stressed, that there may often be historical truth involved in oral traditions and genealogies. It will be assumed in the following analysis that the student of history should make use of all information at his disposal in his attempt to reconstruct the past. He is aided in his interpretation of elements of myth and genealogy by comparative ethnology and archaeology. The laws and regularities which have been formulated from the study of better documented historical sequences enable him in many instances to make a judgment about the likelihood of a particular reported sequence of events.

This dynastic history is recounted in Sir Apolo Kagwa's book, *Customs of Baganda* (1934). The significant variables which Kagwa includes are the numbers of the king's wives and concubines and his court officials. Until the time of the sixteenth Kabaka, Katerega, no king had more than nine wives or ten officials at his court. With Katerega, however, who is associated in oral tradition with an increased emphasis on military operations and raiding, there is a change of scale in the status of the Kabaka in Ganda society. The number of wives of the king, including reserve wives, and maiden servants increases to 309.[6] Developed stratification seems very likely at this point. This reign comes near the beginning of the eighteenth century. Katerega is said to have loved warriors, and to have rewarded two warriors with office and land for their clans to hold in perpetuity, as a result of their bravery in warfare.

Between Katerega and the twenty-first king, Ndaula, the maximum number of wives is 200. With Ndaula, there is another leap, this time to 508. Ndaula is said to have been the first Kabaka to separate church and state. He is reputed to have allocated his priestly duties to one of his sons, whose descendants thereafter succeeded to the office with each new Kabaka. At this point the stratification system is well enough established so that an ideology of divine association is no longer necessary to support the Kabaka's authority. The separation of the office of priest from that of king may also indicate that the Kabaka had other duties more pressing than ritual, or that he was perhaps away from the capital for significant periods of time.

A single exception to the general trend towards an increase in central authority is the twenty-second Kabaka, who was noteworthy only for his lack of control of power, force, and authority. It is said that he tried to destroy his sister, who, on learning of the plot, decided to escape into Bunyoro with her other siblings. The sister was ultimately able to kill the king. Kagwa indicates that this Kabaka is remembered as an especially cruel one, that he was given no tomb, and that he was especially despised because of the fact that he had ordered oak trees to be dug up, "no matter how deep their roots were" (Kagwa, 1934, p. 32). Apparently the status of absolute monarch did not yet exist in Buganda. The twenty-fourth Kabaka is reported to have ravaged Busoga and to have dismissed several chiefs and replaced them with war heroes (Kagwa, 1934, p. 33). He had 510 wives. The twenty-eighth king is reputed to have captured the districts of Kiziba and Buddu. Kiziba is said to have paid an annual tribute of cowry shells and trade goods which entered that province from the south. Buddu, which the Kabaka captured from Bunyoro, was a large and important district and one of the most wealthy (Roscoe, 1911, p. 234). All of the traders who later came into Buganda from the Coast followed a route around the Lake, through Buddu.

The twenty-eighth king is reported to have had 600 wives and 15 officials at his court. A really dramatic expansion in scale comes with the advent of the twenty-ninth Kabaka, Semakokiro, who had 8,500 wives and 32 court officials (Kagwa, 1934, pp. 39–40). He is said to have pushed Buganda's border westward. The significant event of his reign was the introduction of cotton goods to Buganda. Furthermore, ivory huntsmen are said to have become a professional group during his administration. The slave and ivory trade had at last reached Buganda and had plummeted this stratified society into state formation. The success of Buganda's military operations in surrounding groups, which may be read in the sovereign's female entorage, 8,500 of them, is dramatic. Bunyoro, situated to the northwest, was less favorably disposed and suffered in comparison to Buganda as a consequence. The introduction of these trade goods is the most attractive explanation for Buganda's advance. The developed Ganda state owed its existence to reinforcement of the traditional stratified system through inclusion within an externally oriented trade network and to the introduction of a foreign currency. The office which in the ranked society had been associated with ceremonial generosity, and in the stratified society with re-

6 All figures below include reserve wives, concubines, and maiden servants in addition to official wives.

distribution of surpluses and of good and services from different ecological niches, had become a status, linked with other roughly similar statuses into a superordinate group, controlling access to trade goods and other strategic resources.

The immediate source of cotton and cowry shells lay to the south of the Lake (Roscoe, 1911, p. 225). It is claimed that Semakokiro brought a man from Singo to act as blacksmith to make axes for building a large fleet of canoes. These canoes were to become the principal means of commerce with the countries to the south of Lake Victoria, and the principal means of connecting the main road from the East Coast to the capital of Buganda. Roscoe suggests that it was through canoes that Buganda's influence was so widely extended. A group of specialists in the manufacture of large canoes gradually developed to provide canoes to accommodate Stanley's estimate of from 16,000 to 20,000 men in what he calls the Ganda navy (Fallers, 1960, p. 43). Semakokiro is reputed to have moved his capital repeatedly, to have ruled for many years, and to have adopted the practice of burning the princes —potential rivals to his throne. The sovereign's unimpeded access to strategic resources is jealously guarded at this point.

During the reign of the successor, Kamanya, constant rebellions and disturbances are reported. The king is said to have had many of his sons killed and to have put to death many chiefs and commoners. He is said to have offended the gods by having canoes carried overland to the Nile River (Roscoe, 1911, p. 226). He further extended the western border of Buganda and is reported to have had 11,000 wives and 44 court officials.

His successor, a surviving son, Suna II, reputedly had 20,000 wives and maiden servants and 45 officials around his court. He began his rule in 1810. It was during his reign, in 1844, that Arab traders were actually admitted into Buganda. With them came firearms and gunpowder which were exchanged for ivory and slaves. A massive slaughtering of his subjects is said to have gone on during Suna's reign. The king is supposed to have spent a good deal of his time hunting, probably with a rifle. A successful campaign against Busoga was waged during this reign; other new territories were added, and Buganda's borders were strengthened through the perfection of an army organization which, when fully mobilized, is said to have been able to produce 50,000 warriors. The traditional accounts also make Suna II responsible for improving sanitation standards in the capital (Kagwa, 1934, p. 227).

The reigns of Kabakas Suna II and Mutesa, his successor, represent the climax of state development in Buganda. Mutesa's reign may be considered to be a culmination of the Ganda state. Some of its major accomplishments will be mentioned. He reinforced the traditional military authority by the creation of a standing army and the allocation of estates to warriors as a regular reward in lieu of pay in money or kind. Access to cotton and calico cloth was given to the chiefs. Trade was extended to the Island Karagwe and further south. Through the numerous guns which had entered Buganda, the armies of the king were able to reduce the surrounding tribes to a more permanent subordination than previously. The whole of the Busoga, Koki, and Kiziba districts to the south were added to Buganda.

British intervention and the establishment of missionary posts in Buganda resulted in conflicts and changes which shook the foundations of the Kabaka's authority. Mwanga, Mutesa's successor, was plagued by factional disputes. In contrast to his father's 18,000 wives and maiden servants, Mwanga had only 1,500. The number of court officials declined from 64 under Mutesa to 22 during Mwanga's reign. This is fewer than any reign since the time of the first introduction of cotton cloth into Buganda. It is beyond the limits of this paper to examine the changes which took place during the later years of Mutesa's reign and considerably undermined the traditional state system under him and his son Mwanga.

III. The Relevance of Buganda to the Understanding of the Evolution of States in Africa and in General

While in the title of this paper I have alluded to "the origin and evolution of the state," I have not been concerned with specifying the causal variables involved in the evolution of all states, because I believe that there are several different paths to statehood. I have suggested, however, that examination of variables involving local and regional ecosystems of specific societies will be most revealing in explaining why they developed the way they did. In the reasons for its development, Buganda offers contrasts with states elsewhere in Africa and in other parts of the world. A brief examination of state developments in other parts of Africa will help place Buganda in a wider, comparative perspective.

When compared with Buganda, the local ecosystems of the states of the Western Sudan seem deficient. Permanent cultivation is usually not characteristic. Yet urban centers have arisen in the western Sudan as seats of a governmental decision-making apparatus with authority over urban and outlying populations. The foundations of these states lie in the regional ecosystem. States whose authority radiated from such centers actually have arisen by overseeing the movement of strategic resources from one region to another. In the process of transshipment modifications of some goods by craftsmen took place, and some goods were withdrawn, rather than shipped on, in order to underwrite the subsistence and culturally derived needs of the personnel residing in the centers in question.

Irrigation, to which Wittfogel and others have attributed a causative role in the evolution of the state, was not important in the evolution of sub-Saharan African states with the possible exception of Meroë, obviously of ancient Egypt and of highland Madagascar. Mediation of exchange of products from different ecological zones has been the foundation of most African states. In post-European contact states, superior arms have also contributed to the formation of states, conferring the possibility of enforcing and making binding decisions made by state personnel. Good examples are the West African states of Dahomey and Ashanti, where slaves and African products were exchanged for guns, which allowed the predatory expansion of Dahomey and Ashanti, and also for luxury goods to underwrite the living standards of the resource controllers, the state personnel.

Finally, certain African states seem to have arisen as tribal populations adopted defensive poses induced by external threats posed by both states and by tribal societies organized for predatory expansion (cf. Sahlins, 1961).

A set of interacting variables has been adduced as causative in the evolution of social stratification and the state in Buganda. No one of these variables could have produced the state alone, but in combination they gave rise to socioeconomic differentiation of the Ganda population and the development of an administrative subsystem the special purpose of which was to allocate and reallocate land, people, and products. Another special purpose subsystem developed for defensive, and ultimately assumed offensive, functions. Finally, both subsystems interacted to maintain themselves, as Fried says in his definition of the state, to strengthen and to maintain general order and the order of stratification.

The variables responsible for the evolution of the Ganda state may be briefly summarized. Unlike the majority of African societies, the subsistence economy of the Ganda rested on permanent cultivation rather than shifting cultivation or pastoralism. The same land could be used from year to year; settlements could be permanent, and large population size and density could be supported. The heartland and birthplace of Buganda lay in a fertile ecological zone of elephant grass extending to a radius of about fifty miles around the capital, Kampala (Southwold, 1965, p. 86). This banana grove zone was located between the shore of Lake Victoria, where fishing was a vital part of subsistence, and a short grass zone suitable to cattle herding. Population increase led to descent group segmentation and eventually gave rise to redistributive foci which linked the people and products of different microenvironments. Competition from neighboring states and tribal societies organized for predatory expansion (Bunyoro and Lwoo speakers) placed a selective premium on the adoption by Buganda of a defensive pose. The banana economy enabled men to be removed from subsistence tasks and their labor to be utilized by the defensive subsystem. The military apparatus developed out of the need for defense eventually became a fully developed special purpose subsystem oriented towards offensive activities. It allowed expansion, the incorporation of new ecological zones and the control by the Ganda state of products originating in such zones. The resources of these zones gave new support to the Ganda state, particularly as areas where iron ore, essential to the manufacture of spears and arrows, were controlled. The exchange network controlled by the Ganda state in the mid-nineteenth century involved the movement of goods originating in Bunyoro to the north, and through the southern provinces, a link up with Islamic traders from the East African Coast. In no other state in the Interlacustrine region were all these variables present. This is the explanation for Buganda's superordinate position in the Lakes region in the nineteenth century.

Finally, what is the relevance of Buganda to the development of states in general? Morton Fried had drawn a distinction between "pristine" and "secondary" states.

It seems likely that the only truly pristine states, those whose origin was *sui generis*, out of local conditions and not in response to pressures emanating from an already highly organized but separate political entity—are those which arose in the great river valleys of Asia and Africa and the one or two comparable developments in the western hemisphere. Elsewhere the development of the state seems to have been "secondary" and to have depended on pressures, direct, or indirect, from existing states. Where such pressures exist, the process of development is accelerated, condensed and often warped, so that a study of contemporary state formation is a murky mirror in which to discern the stages in the development of the pristine state (Fried, 1959, p. 713).

I find it hard to say whether Buganda should be regarded as a pristine or a secondary state. This paper illustrates for one specific evolutionary sequence what I think has been generally true of state systems throughout the world, even those which Fried would call pristine—no population develops a state entirely by itself. There have been trade contacts between most of the major states of the Old World, and interregional exchange certainly played a role in Mesoamerican and perhaps Peruvian developments. A view which focuses attention on processes of socioeconomic evolution rather than on the source of diffused "innovations" makes the distinction between pristine and secondary states a false one.

BIBLIOGRAPHY

Beattie, John (1960), *Bunyoro: An African Kingdom*. New York: Henry Holt.

Cole, Sonia (1963), "The Stone Age of East Africa," in Roland Oliver and Gervase Mathew (eds.), *History of East Africa*. Oxford: Clarendon Press.

Collins, Robert O. (ed.) (1968), *Problems in African History*. Englewood Cliffs: Prentice-Hall.

Davidson, Basil (1959), *The Lost Cities of Africa*. Boston: Little, Brown and Co.

Engels, Frederick (1963), *The Origin of the Family, Private Property, and the State*. New York: International Publishers, New World Paperbacks. Various other editions.

Fallers, L. A. (1964a), assisted by F. K. Kamoga and S. B. K. Musoke. "Social Stratification in Traditional Buganda," in L. A. Fallers (ed.), *The King's Men*. London: Oxford University Press, pp. 64–116.

——— (ed.) (1964b), *The King's Men: Leadership and Status in Buganda on the Eve of Independence*. London: Oxford University Press.

Fallers, Margaret Chave (1960), *The Eastern Lacustrine Bantu: Ganda, Soga*. London: International African Institute.

Fried, Morton H. (1959), "On the Evolution of Social Stratification and the State," in Stanley Diamond (ed.) *Culture in History*. New York: Columbia University Press.

——— (1967), *The Evolution of Political Society*. New York: Random House.

Greenberg, Joseph (1963), *Languages of Africa*. The Hague.

Guthrie, Malcolm (1962), "Some Developments in the Prehistory of the Bantu Languages." *Journal of African History,* 3:2, pp. 273–82.

Harris, Marvin (1968), *The Rise of Anthropological Theory*. New York: Crowell.

Hiernaux, Jean (1968), "Bantu Expansion: The Evidence from Physical Anthropology Confronted with Linguistic and Archaeological Evidence." *Journal of African History,* 9:4, pp. 505–15.

Huntingford, G. W. B. (1963), "The Peopling of the Interior of East Africa by Its Modern Inhabitants," in Roland Oliver and Gervase Mathew (eds.), *History of East Africa*. Oxford: Clarendon Press.

Johnston, Harry (1902), *The Uganda Protectorate*. New York: Dodd, Mead and Co.

Kagwa, Apolo (1934), *The Customs of the Baganda*. New York: Columbia University Press.

Lanning, E. C. (1953) , "Ancient Earthworks in Western Uganda." *Uganda Journal,* 17:1.

Latham, Michael (1965), *Human Nutrition in Tropical Africa*. Rome: Food and Agricultural Organization of the United Nations.

Maine, H. S. (1954), *Ancient Law*. London: Dent. Various other editions.

Mair, Lucy P. (1934), *An African People in the Twentieth Century*. London: Routledge.

McMaster, D. N. (1963), "Speculations on the Coming of the Banana to Buganda." *Uganda Journal,* 27:2.

Morgan, L. H. (1877), *Ancient Society*. New York: Henry Holt and Co.

Mukwaya, A. B. (1953), *Land Tenure in Buganda: Present Day Tendencies*. Nairobi: The Eagle Press.

Murdock, George Peter (1959), *Africa: Its Peoples and Their Culture History*. New York: McGraw-Hill.

Oliver, Roland (1963), "Discernible Developments in the Interior: *c.* 1500–1840," in Roland Oliver and Gervase Mathew (eds.), *History of East Africa.* Oxford: Clarendon Press.

——— (1966), "The Problem of the Bantu Expansion." *Journal of African History,* 7:3, pp. 361–76.

Oppenheimer, Franz (1926), *The State.* New York. Various other editions.

Posnansky, Merrick (1964), "Bantu Genesis." *Uganda Journal,* 25:1, pp. 86–92.

Roscoe, John (1911), *The Baganda.* London: Macmillan.

Sahlins, Marshall D. (1961), "The Segmentary Lineage: An Organization of Predatory Expansion." *American Anthropologist,* 63:2, pp. 332–45.

——— (1963), "Poor Man, Rich Man, Big Man, Chief: Political Types in Melanesia and Polynesia." *Comparative Studies in Society and History,* 5:3, pp. 285–303.

Sahlins, Marshall D., and Elman R. Service (1960), *Evolution and Culture.* Ann Arbor: University cf Michigan Press.

Sanders, Edith (1969), "The Hamitic Hypothesis, Its Origin and Functions in Time Perspective." *Journal of African History,* 10:4, pp. 521–31.

Service, Elman R. (1962), *Primitive Social Organization: An Evolutionary Perspective.* New York: Random House.

Southwold, Martin (1965), "The Ganda of Uganda," in James L. Gibbs (ed.), *Peoples of Africa.* New York: Holt, Rinehart and Winston, Inc., pp. 81–118.

Speke, John H. (1908), *Journey of the Discovery of the Source of the Nile.* London: Dent.

Steward, Julian H. (1955), *Theory of Culture Change.* Urbana: University of Illinois Press.

Vansina, Jean (1965), *Oral Tradition: A Study in Historical Methodology* (translated from the French by H. M. Wright). Chicago: Aldine.

Verin, Pierre, Conrad P. Kottak and Peter Gorlin (1971), "The Glottochronology of Malagasy Speech Communities." *Oceanic Linguistics,* 8:1, pp. 26–83.

Von Loeseche, Harry W. (1950), *Bananas.* New York: Interscience Publishers.

Wainwright, G. A. (1954), "The Diffusion of *-uma* as a Name for Iron." *Uganda Journal.* 18:2 (September).

Wrigley, C. C. (1957), *Buganda: An Outline Economic History. Economic History Review.* Series 2, 10.

——— (1958), "Some Thoughts on the Bachwezi." *Uganda Journal,* 22:1.

——— (1964), "The Changing Economic Structure of Buganda," in L. A. Fallers (ed.), *The King's Men.* London: Oxford University Press, pp. 16–63.

SECTION II

Law, Diplomacy, and Warfare

Enacting and enforcing laws, organizing diplomacy, and mobilizing for armed aggression all occur within the context of one or another of the kinds of political organization just described. But the processes entailed in these universally important political activities are distinctive enough to warrant separate attention.

Although the development of laws and of systems for assuring compliance with them can probably be safely described as an aspect of every political system, the legal process becomes increasingly separable from kinship organization as the overall complexity of a society increases. In the band, custom, consensus, and common recognition of the compelling need to avoid societal disruption take care of most of the issues that in larger-scale societies are dealt with by increasingly intricate legislative and judicial means.

The same is true of diplomacy and armed aggression as alternative means of regulating external relations. In societies organized on a very small scale, diplomacy may be no more than a part of the code of etiquette that guides conduct between in-laws. For bands in a single area are usually connected by a network of reciprocal alliances established through marriage. And warfare, as anything like what we know it to be, just cannot exist. Compared to ourselves, force is rarely used either internally or externally as a way of settling differences. Disputants who do come to blows usually do so without involving others. Feuding between groups occurs, of course, and so does raiding, but on nothing like the sustained and bloody scale familiar in more "advanced" societies. This is not necessarily because our technologically less developed contemporaries are naturally less aggressive. The material conditions of their lives simply make massive militarism politically impossible.

Somewhat surprisingly, the study of warfare is a fairly new field in ethnology. In contrast, as Koch demonstrates, the legal systems of non-Western peoples have been a major focus of anthropological interest from the discipline's earliest days.

Law and Anthropology

Klaus-Friedrich Koch

Almost two decades ago Riesman (1951) published an article in which he criticized the lawyer for his ethnocentric view of law and invited the anthropologist to study the organization and functions of American legal institutions and the activities of lawyers. Very few anthropologists have done so. In fact, few anthropologists have made the general study of law their special area of research. In this country, there are perhaps a dozen or two. However, the field is now beginning to attract more people. As a look at the tables of contents and the indexes of ethnographic monographs published in recent years will show, most anthropologists still neglect to report on the law of the people they have studied —yet rarely fail to have chapters on social organization, economy, religion, and the remaining traditional categories with which we "domainize" the culture of a society. Legal scholars, on the other hand, often in cooperation with sociologists and political scientists, have increasingly turned to the kind of research which Schubert (1968) has called, "behavioral jurisprudence." Outside the United States, this interdisciplinary focus in the study of law and society has been very productive in Scandinavia (see Blegvad 1966).

I propose to outline some of the areas of research in the anthropology of law and to discuss our methodology. You will notice that communication between lawyers and anthropologists is, at times, difficult because of a certain lack of lexical competence on the part of the anthropologist in talking about the "lawyer's law" on the one hand, and the lawyer's unfamiliarity with anthropological concepts on the other. Today, certainly, few anthropologists accept Lowie's view (1927:51): "What to an anthropologist is naturally the most important thing is the relationship of anthropology and law, to wit, how his own discipline may benefit from a neighboring branch of knowledge."

Perhaps it is wise to eliminate from discussion one question that has proven to be a very unprofitable ground for debate, although it might appear to some to be central to any talk about law. (If so, I should like to disqualify myself for such debate.) The question is: "What is law?" It is true, when I say I do research on the law of a people, I should know what it is that I study. But for me this requires only a very rough delineation of a particular focus on some fields of social relations and the ideology connected therewith. If this were not so, it might indeed be awkward to speak of the law of an illiterate tribe where no courts, lawyers and police exist. Definitional discussions have usually proven to be very sterile exercises, especially if they are pursued with minimal reference to empirical data and do not result in a categorization of variables and a conceptualization of pertinent research strategies. No one has ever disputed the universal existence of something we call economy. Australian aborigines knowing no metal or pottery and living solely on edibles gained in exploitative hunting and gathering have economy in spite of their primitive technological inventory and their simple system of transfer of goods and services. If economy has to do with "how people make a living," law—for me—has to do with "how people make living a relatively ordered social existence." And if one can have an economy without a decimal system of accounting, without money, and without banks, I suppose one can have, or even must have, law without codices and courts. As soon as we begin to be curious about the *ways* in which people attempt to settle disputes, resolve conflicts, and control violence, these traits of our own legal system (courts, codes) become examples, not standards, of cultural experimentation in the legal domain. I am content to state that law is a polysemic *concept* whose diverse cognitive aspects permit its use as a labeling category in manifold ways. The heuristics of scientific inquiry demand selectivity and emphases as required by the purpose and aim of our investigation. The anthropological study of law concerns the description and analysis of processes and institutions by which people manage to maintain what has been termed a "practical

Source: Reprinted from *Law and Society Review,* Vol. 4, 1969, pp. 11–27. Used by permission of the publisher and the author.

equilibrium," mitigate frictions that are bound to arise, and resolve conflicts that issue from unmitigated friction.

One more introductory remark: There seem to be two major schools of thought in the science of society. One views a social system essentially as a stable network of ordered social relations integrated by a commonly accepted value system. Dahrendorf (1959) has labeled this view, "integration theory." The other view, "coercion theory," in Dahrendorf's terminology, assumes that every society is constantly in a process of change and displays ubiquitous dissensus and conflict, which must be channelled and controlled by coercion facilitated by an inherently differential distribution of power. Obviously, these different conceptual models of society result in, even require, different methodological approaches. The first will tend to view conflict as somewhat deviant behavior; the second as normal and inherent in the structural arrangements of social relations. Whatever the epistemological background of the two conceptualizations of society may be, either one is useful for the explication of certain aspects of its organization. In my own research I find it useful to elucidate the structure of social relations through an analysis of conflict. In other words: I attempt to find out something about integration, consensus, and stability by looking at events which reflect competition for valued goods and positions, dissensus over norms, and conflicts of interest. In short, I try to understand the culture of a society by investigating where it doesn't work out, so to speak. A look at American society in 1969 might immediately indicate some strategic advantages of this methodological orientation.

Development Before 1954

Let me now give a very brief review of the development of the anthropology of law. In the history of ideas, as in any history, dates and names are used to divide history into periods marked by events which we assume changed the course and manner of thought about nature and culture. In the nineteenth century, inspired by the work of the economist and demographer Malthus, biologists (especially Darwin) and social scientists (especially Spencer) developed theories of evolutionary processes that crucially altered traditional modes of thinking about the origins and evolution of culture.[1] Anthropologists in the last quarter of the nineteenth century and in the early decades of this one were busy searching libraries for data with which to illustrate the development of cultural institutions. The development itself was seen as a more or less fixed sequence of intellectual, technological, and moral accomplishments—a model that did much to delay the development of a science of culture which requires that explications be made in reference to a model, itself derived from an analysis of the data to be explained. Legal scholars like Post and Kohler used ethnographic records to compile inventories of law codes for primitive societies which were then fitted into some sort of evolutionary scheme. Their frame of inquiry was their own legal systems and much of their labor was spent on a cataloguing of rules. The social context of legal activity was lost, and the conditions under which conflicts arose were rarely retrieved. Considering the adverse circumstances under which the data were collected, one arrives at the sad but realistic judgment that most of their work has not produced any insights into legal ideology, or the processes of dispute settlement that are of value either to comparative jurisprudence or to anthropology. A notable exception to be mentioned is certain ideas in Maine's *Ancient Law.* Devoid of its universalistic premise, Maine's theory concerning the legal implications of the sociology of status relationships indicated exactly those relationships that critically, though not exclusively, structure the sociolegal domain in most societies commonly studied by anthropologists.[2]

Anthropologists, however, didn't do much better. The legal scholar Ehrlich (1936) had early demonstrated that law cannot be studied as something apart from the social context in

[1] For an extensive recent discussion on the development and interrelationships of biological and sociocultural theories of evolution, see Harris (1968: chs. 4–7).

[2] Compare Gluckman's appreciative comments in his *Ideas of Barotse Jurisprudence* (1965: XVI and throughout) and Redfield's (1950) discussion of Maine. Concerning the evolutionary significance of the "Mainean shift" from status to contract, Hoebel (1954:329) explained that the most decisive shift in the development of law has been a procedural adaptation by which "privilege-rights and responsibility for the maintenance of the legal norms are transferred from the individual and his kinship group to the agents of the body politic as a social entity."

which it is operative. He argued convincingly for the necessity of relating form and content of law to social organization.[3] Anthropologists, however, continued to neglect this contextual focus, and their descriptions remained inaccurate because of uncritical categorizations set in terms of western jurisprudence. Moreover, much energy was wasted on questions such as, "Is law universal?" or, "Do all societies have law?" Today we find such questions not only uninteresting, but truly unproblematic as well. That is, they do not direct our attention to problems we wish to explain.

The reorientation of anthropological inquiry from historical ethnology to a functionalistic analysis of social relations in their cultural context became dramatically evident in the work of Malinowski, four decades ago. While Malinowski's only empirical study of law, *Crime and Custom in Savage Society* (1926), represents a grossly inadequate account of assorted observations made among the Trobriand Islanders, his theoretical contributions to the study of law were important in their programmatic compass.[4] Empirical long-term field studies were now recognized as the conditio sine qua non of anthropological research. Among the first ethnographically useful studies on law were those by Barton (1919) on Ifugao Law, Kroeber (1925) on the law of the Yurok Indians, and Gutmann (1926) on the law of the Chagga.

A really significant advance in legal anthropology was made with the work of Hoebel among the Indians of the Great Plains. His *Political Organization and the Law-Ways of the Commanche Indians* (1940) and *The Cheyenne Way* written with Llewellyn (1941) represent the first successful attempts to study law in relation to the ethos and organization of society. The importance of the latter work lies in a rigorous application of the case method. In fact, this approach has proven to be the most effective heuristic device in legal anthropology, and no study of value has subsequently been done in this field that is not based on cases. In 1954, Hoebel published his *The Law of Primitive Man.* While it gives a useful survey of the range of legal institutions and procedures encountered among illiterate peoples, its attempt to analyze total legal systems in terms of Hohfeld's scheme, reformulated along lines suggested by Radin (1938), is largely unsuccessful. The final chapter of the book, incidentally, is the last attempt—for the time being—of a noted anthropologist to establish a relative chronology for the development of legal institutions.

Development After 1954

After 1954 a small number of excellent studies in the anthropology of law have appeared: Gluckman's work (1955) on Barotse courts in Zambia, Bohannan's study (1957) of the Tiv in Nigeria, Pospisil's study (1958) of law among the Kapauku in New Guinea, and Gulliver's book (1963) on the Arusha in Tanzania. Each of these authors makes at least one significant contribution: Gluckman showed the advantages of comparative study for elucidating principles both of Western legal systems and of tribal societies, and he presented one of the finest expositions of judicial reasoning in its social context.[5] Bohannan warned us of the difficulty and often the impossibility of applying our concepts to an analysis of law in non-Western societies. Pospisil reminded us that law exists on different, often hierarchically ordered, levels in society, each level comprising groups of the same type and the same degree of inclusiveness.[6] Gulliver demonstrated that an understanding of

[3] For a recent appraisal of Ehrlich's work, see Littlefield (1967).

[4] This is essentially evident in Malinowski's last-written treatise on the subject (1942). For critical discussions of Malinowski's work on law see Hoebel (1954:177–210) and Schapera (1957). Incidentally, the often mentioned book of Hogbin, *Law and Order in Polynesia* (1934), written while the author worked with Malinowski at London University, presents very sketchy ethnography with a few fragmentary cases interspersed in the account, and the analysis is confined to statements paraphrasing Malinowski's ideas.

[5] Gluckman's study has received wide and varied critical recognition. Chapter ix of the second edition (1967) discusses the major reviews of the first edition in great detail.

[6] This recognition is, of course, not new, and it is shared with legal scholars. Both von Gierke and Ehrlich wrote about these phenomena. And in the work of Gray, whose writings did much to eliminate rigid fundamentalist legal dogmatism from jurisprudence, we find statements that appear contemporaneous with those of our own day. For example: "If any organized body of men has persons or bodies appointed to decide questions, then that body has judges or courts, and if those judges or courts in their determination follow general rules, then the body has Law and the members of the body may have rights under that Law" (1921:109).

certain legal processes requires not only the knowledge of the sociocultural context of dispute settlement, but equally so a knowledge of past conflicts between parties concerned in any particular case.

Principally, the anthropological study of law proceeds on the following premises:

1. The law of a people, or the legal system of a society, must be investigated in the context of its political, economic, and religious systems, as well as within the social structure of interpersonal and intergroup relations.
2. Law can best be studied through an analysis of the procedures that deal with the resolution of disputes, or—in a broader perspective —with the management of conflict.
3. Procedures, in turn, will become apparent if research is focused on the trouble case as the unit of description, analysis, and comparison.
4. In order to render a valid report on the law of a people, two separate but related tasks have to be worked out. One is to ascertain the cognitive categories by which the people whose legal system is to be studied structure *their* ideas of wrongs and *their* ideas of forms and procedures of redress to be taken. The other task requires a translation of these categories into our medium of communication. This is an exceedingly difficult job, for it demands both that the essential features of the native system not be distorted *and* that they be cast into a scientific terminology which makes cross-cultural comparisons possible.

The range of problems in the field of law investigated by anthropologists is, of course, rather extensive. They include the following:

1. What are the types of adjudicating or mediating agents operating in society?
2. What is the basis of their authority to exercise these roles in dispute settlement?
3. Which disputes are amenable under specific conditions to negotiated compromise settlements and which require adjudication?
4. Which procedures are taken for each type of dispute under given conditions? (This question implies inquiries into such aspects as apprehension of the accused, locale, evidence, etc.)
5. How are juridical decisions enforced?
6. What exosystemic functions and effects attach to legal processes? (This includes inquiries into the network of social, psychological, economic and political relationships between the parties, their representatives or supporters, and the authorities.)[7]
7. How does law change?

Given this methodology and these problems, comparative anthropological research seeks to establish the existence of patterned correlations between specific factors indicated by the questions listed. These correlations may concern legal aspects only, or they may concern the cooccurrence of particular legal institutions and particular social-structural, economic, religious, and political systems or aspects thereof. Occasionally discovered correlations lead to the formulation of a hypothesis that has predictive value. (Compare Nader, 1965 and Whiting, 1965.)

My own research (1967) among the Jalé people in the interior of New Guinea resulted in an examination of the sociological and psychological factors that are correlated with the absence of any third-party adjudication. Following the cross-cultural approach, I extracted sufficient information from research done in other societies to causally link the absence of third-party adjudication to a prevalence of violence (including intrasocietal warfare) in processes of conflict management. Furthermore, both features were shown to be correlated with (a) the existence of multiple independent political units on the community level, (b) the presence of power groups composed of coresident members of patrilineages, (c) the absence of crosscutting group affiliations, and (d) certain specific processes of socialization.

Anthropology's Contribution to Law

What are the potential practical contributions of anthropology to jurisprudence? There are three general areas in which I anticipate anthropological research to be useful. The first concerns the law of newly independent nations; the second, aspects of law in our own society; and the third, problems in international law.

[7] For an analysis of the effect of legal activities on leadership and social control in a society without formal political offices and the sanctioned use of physical coercion, see Frake (1963).

LAW IN NEWLY INDEPENDENT NATIONS. A recent report (Salacuse, 1968) estimated that African nations after independence have enacted "nearly a quarter of a million pages of legislation" despite efforts to "nationalize" much of the colonial law. Obviously, the problem of granting validity to multiple unwritten customary legal systems (plus variants of Islamic law in some of the East and West African nations) required more knowledge of the workings of these diverse systems than lawyers trained at French and British law schools could mobilize. Sometimes an assumption such as, "A uniform law was necessary . . . for the effective administration of justice" (Salacuse: 40) precluded *eo ipso* uniformly beneficial legislation. On the other hand, any special provisions for particular ethnic groups could easily be interpreted as discriminatory. Other major problems concerned the need for laws that could protect and foster the development of social services and a modern economy.[8] Whether the Ethiopian legal experiment serves this purpose is questionable. In Ethiopia, a country without a colonial legal heritage, the Emperor commissioned a Frenchman to write the civil code, an Englishman to write the criminal procedure code, and a Swiss lawyer to write the penal code. The premises upon which the French draftsman of the Ethiopian civil code proceeded with his research boded failure for the whole project. Its author wrote:

> Vouloir établir un Code sur la base des coutumes m'a paru . . . illusoire. Les coutumes éthiopiennes n'existent, en effet, qu'au sein de communautés de village ou de tribu, sociétés fermées, *dans lesquelles la notion de droit n'a pas sa place;* elles n'ont pas le caractère de coutumes juridiques. L'essentiel n'est pas dans le procès de donner à chacun son dû [suum cuique tribuere] comme veut le droit; l'essentiel est de maintenir les bons rapports, la cohésion et l'harmonie dans la communauté. [David, 1963:161–162; emphasis added][9]

After my discussion in the first part of this paper, any comment on this nonsense seems superfluous.

Anthropological studies would certainly be useful to assess the needs for and advantages of plural legal systems and to evaluate the effects, desirable or undesirable, of enforcing national legal codes on the "village level," especially with regard to issues involving land tenure and kinship relations, including customary patterns of succession, inheritance, marriage, and divorce.[10] To my knowledge, few anthropologists have been asked to serve as consultants, but Schapera (1938) has done an excellent job in such a capacity.[11]

What may happen if legalistic doctrine dominates in colonial legislation is illustrated by regulations enacted in the British colony of the Gilbert and Ellis Islands in the South Pacific. Regulation No. 27, 2 reads as follows:

> Persons going to latrines shall not tear leaves from coconut trees which do not belong to them for latrine purposes. Fine, 2 s.

Regulation No. 27, 5 stipulates:

> It is prohibited to defecate or urinate above high water mark on any beach between villages. Persons forced by nature to defecate in the bush must cover the feces with not less than six inches of soil. Fine, 1 s. to 2 s.

[8] For other studies in the field of law in developing societies, see Afrika Instituut (1956) which has extensive bibliographies; Kuper and Kuper (1965); Anderson (1968); and Lundsgaarde (1968). (Lawyers and legal draftsmen are becoming more aware of the relevance of a thorough knowledge of customary law as a prerequisite to "legal engineering" projects undertaken in developing nations. Indications of such a trend are noted in a collection of essays edited by Hutchison [1968].)

[9] Translated [by author] as follows:

> To wish to establish a code on the basis of customs seemed to me . . . illusory. In fact, Ethiopian customs exist merely in the midst of village or tribal communities, closed societies in which the notion of law has no place; they don't have the character of jural customs. The essential is not in the process of giving everybody his due [*suum cuique tribuere*] as the law demands; the essential is to maintain good relations, cohesion, and harmony in the community.

[10] For a useful discussion concerning the problem of legal pluralism and a unified national law, see Jaspan (1965).

[11] I might add here that historical jurisprudence could provide some comparative information if the records on the introduction of Roman law into early German legal systems, for example, are sufficiently detailed, but this remains to be researched.

One wonders, indeed, how these regulations were enforced, how evidence was secured and produced before the Crown's magistrates. Did, for example, the exact amount to be paid by a careless person whom nature drove into the bush depend on the measured difference in thickness of soil cover required by law and that actually supplied?

In another British colony in the Pacific, in Fiji (where I did field work in the summer of 1968), a dual legal system has been in force since annexation in 1874: one for the Fijians, the other for all the other residents in the colony: Europeans, Chinese, Polynesians, and the Indians who began to outnumber the native Fijians by 1945). The purpose of special courts and the regulations was, to quote from the record of a Fiji Legislative Council debate in 1944,

> to enable people living in remote villages to settle their differences according to their way of life, judged by men who undoubtedly make mistakes in procedure, but who know the people and to a very great extent give them satisfaction. . . . It is more satisfactory for a native litigant to go to a Fijian magistrate nearby whom he knows and lay his complaint than to go miles to a government station where he might have to wait hours for the District Officer and in the end perhaps be misunderstood. [Knox-Mawer, 1961:646–647]

Yet, in 1968, with independence to come in the near future, these provisions were repealed. The reasons for this change given to me by government officials and members of the judiciary were manifold. There was some discussion about the need for a uniform legal system with the onset of independence, some talk about special courts degrading the Fijians to second-class citizens, and pronouncements such as are reflected in the following quote from Legislative Council Paper No. 13 (1959): "There seems to be no good reason why the archaic system of peripatetic courts should be maintained in the age of the motorbus" (Knox-Mawer: 647). To my knowledge, no provision was made, no funds were set aside, to study the effect of this change on the "administration of justice" in general. Given the nature of transport facilities, what will happen, for example, in an interpersonal conflict where the parties are villagers who may have to travel many hours on foot to get to the nearest bus stop?

There is another item from Fiji that any legal anthropologist would find interesting and worth a detailed study: A clerk in the Supreme Court at Suva, who is an Indian of high status, settles more than half of all civil cases involving Indians before the complaint is ever put on paper. The man does this work on the corridors of the court building, in his office, and if invited, in the homes of the disputants. The estimate was made by a judge at the Supreme Court, who also expressed approval and admiration of the clerk's activity. A study of the informal techniques used by this clerk would, for example, result in the recognition of some features that are greatly adaptive to the specific requirements of procedures for the settlement of disputes among members of the Indian communities.

LAW IN CONTEMPORARY SOCIETY. As I have said, very few anthropologists have studied aspects of American law, although it is often a matter of useless definition to categorize a study as being sociological or anthropological. Skolnick's recent book, *Justice Without Trial* (1967) certainly qualifies as a well-conceived and well-executed ethnographic study of law enforcement agencies and the behavior of their officers, especially because it contains a great amount of data gathered by "participant observation," rather than data exclusively compiled from interviews, questionnaires, census charts, and records. An anthropological orientation toward issues in American law is also seen in the work of Professor Herma Kay of Berkeley Law School. Focusing on the kinship systems of American society, Kay (1965) examined court decisions on the legitimation of children born illegitimate and discovered that the California courts have developed a legal concept of the family that is derived from empirical reality and is "based upon the common residence pattern of father, mother, and child and upon the actual performance of the roles of parent and child within this setting between persons not biologically related." As this concept implies a definition of the family that is by no means in accordance with the commonly held and culturally approved ideology, a gradual convergence toward the legally sanctioned domestic arrangements is predicted.

Bohannan, an anthropologist, has reviewed the sociocultural consequences of divorce adjudication (1967). He noted that the form and manner of divorce in American society makes no satisfactory provision for the existence of the "ex-family," and that the legal termination of a marriage often signifies the serious failure of our legal system to provide formal means for reconciliation of marital conflicts. In many societies these means are an integral part of the general jural relationships created by the connubium and the formation of the conjugal household.

If these studies indicate something of importance, it appears to be this: perhaps more than ever before, in his efforts to adapt his principles and codes to changing sociocultural conditions, the lawyer cannot be content with retrospectively mining statutory and case law and adhering to the doctrine of *stare decisis*. Instead, if the expression "good law" means anything, legislator, judge, and legal scholar will have to look ahead and anticipate the needs of the future by recognizing the trends of social (and technological) change. It seems obvious that the cooperation of the social scientist would help the lawyer make the law an effective instrument of deliberate and guided change. Within the technological field, Ralph Nader's efforts have shown the potential benefits of an "activated law," which does not depend on reasoned argumentation alone, but demands empirical research.[12]

As regards criminal law, Swett's article analyzes cultural biases in the American legal system as they are reflected by police behavior and in adjudication in the criminal courts.

In respect to these and similar problems, anthropologists could provide the legal profession with useful data derived from an analysis of empirical situations. Moreover, the day may come when expert testimony will include that of the sociologist and anthropologist in addition to that of the technician and psychologist. Precedents exist: Anthropologists have, on occasion, served as expert witnesses in cases involving Indians. On a larger scale anthropology might find some practical application in suggesting guidelines for legislative and administrative policies in areas where current provisions are inadequate to deal with new problems brought about by rapid sociocultural change. However, few anthropologists have so far been trained to competently study "complex societies" or have applied their skills in the field of "urban anthropology."[13]

INTERNATIONAL LAW. Finally and briefly, there is the problematic nature of international law. It appears that legal scholars and political scientists concerned with the formulation and effective application of internationally binding rules have drawn predominantly from national legal ideologies of European tradition. Any analogous constructs, however, would presuppose global and administrative systems like those of modern states. In many ways, the problems of a global legal system resemble those encountered by the newly independent nations trying to agglomerate a diversity of legal systems into a synthetic whole—only the dimensions are much greater and even more complicated (Luard, 1968: ch. 10). Again the comparative perspective of the anthropologist might aid at least in gaining a more accurate conceptualization of these problems. Some insights into practicable systems might, indeed, be gained from a more comprehensive knowledge of plural legal systems that operate under different premises, fulfill different purposes, and employ different procedures. With due recognition of all dimensional discrepancies, is it not so that tribal societies without an integrative political superstructure represent a microcosm of the international scene?[14] If anthropology cannot provide the answers, it may at least suggest the directions in which to look for the appropriate questions.

[12] The question of which regulatory powers should be given to administrative agencies and which are best left to the courts is another issue to which empirical research may be applied.

[13] For a recent collection of pertinent articles see Banton (1966).

[14] As Hoebel (1954:331) put it, "International law, so-called, is but primitive law on the world level." This recognition is also evident in the work of political scientists. Compare with, for example, Masters (1964) and Barkun (1968). It should be noted, however, that Barkun's book (and other contributions from political science) contain numerous factual errors which, expressed as categorical generalizations about "primitive societies," apparently derive from untutored reading of the ethnographic literature. Furthermore, the usefulness of such abstract systematics as presented by Barkum (1968: ch. 8) will have to be assessed by application in comparative empirical research.

REFERENCES

Afrika Institut (1956) The Future of Customary Law in Africa. Leiden: Universitaire Pers Leiden.

Anderson, J. N. D. (1968) [ed.] Family Law in Asia and Africa. New York: Praeger.

Banton, M. (1966) [ed.] The Social Anthropology of Complex Societies. New York: Praeger.

Barkun, M. (1968) Law Without Sanctions: Order in Primitive Societies and the World Community. New Haven: Yale Univ. Press.

Barton, R. F. (1919) "Ifugao law." Univ. of California Publications in Amer. Archaeology and Ethnology 15, 1:1–186.

Blegvad, B. M. P. (1966) [ed.] "Contributions to the sociology of law." Acta Sociologica 10, 1–2 (Special Publication).

Bohannan, P. (1957) Justice and Judgment Among the Tiv. London: Oxford Univ. Press.

——— and K. Huckleberry (1967) "Institutions of divorce, family and the law." Law & Society Rev. 1 (June): 81–102.

Dahrendorf, R. (1959) Class and Class Conflict in Industrial Society. Stanford: Stanford Univ. Press.

David, R. (1963) "The Reconstruction of Civil Code in the African States." [In French] Annales Africaines, (1962) 1:160–170.

Ehrlich, E. (1936) Fundamental Principles of the Sociology of Law. Cambridge, Mass.: Harvard Univ. Press. [Original (1913) in German.]

Frake, C. O. (1963) "Litigation in Lipay: a study in Subanum law," in Proceedings of the Ninth Pacific Science Congress 3:217–222.

Gluckman, M. (1967) The Judicial Process Among the Barotse. Second Edition. Manchester: Manchester Univ. Press.

——— (1965) The Ideas of Barotse Jurisprudence. New Haven: Yale Univ. Press.

Gray, J. C. (1921) The Nature and Sources of the Law. New York: Columbia Univ. Press.

Gulliver, P. H. (1963) Social Control in an African Society: A Study of the Arusha, Agricultural Masai of Northern Tanganyika. Boston: Boston Univ. Press.

Gutmann, B. (1926) The Law of the Chagga. Abhandlungen der Sachsischen Statlichen Forschunginstitute, Forschungsinstitut fur Psychologie, Nr. 7. [In German.]

Harris, M. (1968) The Rise of Anthropological Theory: A History of Theories of Culture. New York: T. Y. Crowell.

Hoebel, E. A. (1954) The Law of Primitive Man: A Study in Comparative Legal Dynamics. Cambridge, Mass.: Harvard Univ. Press.

——— (1940) "The political organization and law-ways of the Comanche Indians." Amer. Anthropological Assn. Memoir 54, Santa Fe Laboratory of Anthropology 4.

Hogbin, H. I. (1934) Law and Order in Polynesia: A Study of Primitive Legal Institutions. London: Christophers.

Hutchison, T. W. (1968) [ed.] Africa and Law: Developing Legal Systems in African Commonwealth Nations. Madison: Univ. of Wisconsin Press.

Jaspan, M. A. (1965) "In quest of new law: the perplexity of legal syncretism in Indonesia." Comparative Studies in Society and History 7, 3:252–266.

Kay, H. H. (1965) "The family and kinship system of illegitimate children in California law." Amer. Anthropologist 67, 6 (Part II): 57–81.

Knox-Mawer, R. (1961) "Native courts and customs in Fiji." International and Comparative Law Q. 10 (July): 642–647.

Koch, K. F. (1967) "Conflict and its management among the Jalé people of West New Guinea." Ph.D. dissertation. Berkeley: Univ. of California.

Kroeber, A. L. (1926) "Law of the Yurok Indians," in Proceedings of the Twenty-Second International Congress of Americanists, Third Session: 511–516.

——— (1925) "The Yurok law and custom," In Handbook of the Indians of California, Bureau of American Ethnology Bulletin 78. Washington, D.C.: Smithsonian Institution.

Kuper, H., and L. Kuper (1965) [eds.] African Law: Adaptation and Development. Berkeley: Univ. of California Press.

Littlefield, N. O. (1967) "Eugen Ehrlich's fundamental principles of the sociology of law." Maine Law Rev. 19, 1.

Llewellyn, K. N. and E. A. Hoebel (1941) The Cheyenne Way: Conflict and Case Law in Primitive Jurisprudence. Norman: Univ. of Oklahoma Press.

Lowie, R. H. (1927) "Anthropology and law," in W. F. Ogburn and H. Goldenweiser (eds.) The Social Sciences and Their Interrelations. Boston: Houghton-Mifflin.

Luard, E. (1968) Conflict and Peace in the Modern International System. Boston: Little-Brown.

Lundsgaarde, H. P. (1968) "Some transformations in Gilbertese law: 1892–1966." J. of Pacific History 3:117–130.

Maine, H. S. (1963) Ancient Law: Its Connection with the Early History of Society and Its Relation to Modern Ideas. Boston: Beacon Press.

Malinowski, B. (1942) "A new instrument for the interpretation of law—especially primitive." Yale Law J. 51, 8:1237–1254.

——— (1926) Crime and Custom in Savage Society. London: Kegan, Paul, Trench, Trubner.

Masters, R. D. (1964) "World politics as a primitive political system." World Politics 16, 4:595–619.

Nader, L. (1965) "Choices of legal procedure: Shia Moslem and Mexican Zapotec." Amer. Anthropologist 67 (April): 394–399.

Pospisil, L. (1958) "Kapauku Papuans and Their Law." Publications in Anthropology 54. New Haven: Yale Univ.

Radin, M. (1938) "A restatement of Hohfeld." Harvard Law Rev. 51, 7:1141–1164.

Redfield, R. (1950) "Maine's Ancient Law in the light of primitive societies." Western Political Q. 3: 574–589.

Riesman, D. (1951) "Toward an anthropological science of law and the legal profession." Amer. J. of Sociology 57, 2:121–135.

Salacuse, J. W. (1968) "Brightening the revolution: developments in African law." Africa Report (March): 39–45.

Schapera, I. (1957) "Malinowski's theories of law," in R. Firth (ed.) Man and Culture: An Evaluation of the work of Bronislaw Malinowski. London: Routledge & Kegan Paul.

——— (1938) A Handbook of Tswana Law and Custom. Published for International Institute of African Language and Culture. London: Oxford Univ. Press.

Schubert, G. (1968) "Behavioral jurisprudence." Law & Society Rev. 2 (May): 407–428.

Skolnick, J. H. (1966) Justice Without Trial. New York: John Wiley.

Swett, D. H. (1969) "Cultural bias in the American legal system." Law & Society Rev. 4:79–110.

Whiting, B. B. (1965) "Sex identity conflict and physical violence." Amer. Anthropologist 67, 6 (Part II): 123–140.

APPENDIX

The references listed below will direct the reader to a few selected studies in the anthropology of law. Most of these I have personally found useful for introductory courses, in addition to the works listed in the text of this paper. For additional titles, see Laura Nader, Klaus F. Koch and Bruce Cox (1966) "The Ethnography of Law: A Bibliographic Survey," *Current Anthropology* 7:267–294. This is the most comprehensive annotated bibliography of anthropological studies available (about 700 entries). It contains an introductory section that explains the selection and organization of the material and includes references to other specialized bibliographies. For books and articles published during and after 1965, consult the sections entitled "Traditional Legal Framework and Moral Codes," "War," "Problems of Administration of Law," "Modern Judicial Processes," and pertinent index entries in the *International Bibliography of the Social Sciences—Anthropology* (volumes XII and the following).

Compendious reviews of the development, scope, and aims of the anthropology of law are provided in the following articles:

Nader, L. (1965) "The anthropological study of law." Amer. Anthropologist 67, 6 (Part II): 3–32.

Pospisil, L. (1968) "Law and order," pp. 201–222 in J. A. Clifton (ed.) Introduction to Cultural Anthropology. Boston: Houghton-Mifflin.

Important recent discussions of methodological issues are found in the following:

Epstein, A. L. (1967) "The case method in the field of law," pp. 205–230 in A. L. Epstein (ed.) The Craft of Social Anthropology. London: Tavistock.

This is one of the best reviews of the principal method used in the ethnographic study of law and conflict. It presents both a survey of relevant studies in this field and a critical appraisal of the research techniques used.

Gluckman, M. (1965) "Introduction: the process of tribal law," pp. 1–26 in The Ideas of Barotse Jurisprudence. New Haven: Yale Univ. Press.

This chapter is mainly a discussion of judicial principles and legal procedures in certain types of societies in which social relations are principally structured by status relationships.

LeVine, R. A. (1961) "Anthropology and the study of conflict: introduction." J. of Conflict Resolution 5:3–15.

This article presents a concise conceptual statement about structural levels of conflict, conflict-indicating culture patterns, attitudinal concomitants of conflict, sources of social conflict, functional value of conflict, and patterns of conflict control and resolution.

Nadel, S. F. (1956) "Reason and unreason in African law." Africa 26, 2:160–173.

In this review of J. N. D. Anderson's *Islamic Law in Africa* (1954), Max Gluckman's *The Judicial Process* (1955), and P. P. Howell's *A Manual of Nuer Law* (1954), the author deals mainly with problematic concepts used in these studies.

The following studies emphasize the politics of conflict management:

Beattie, J. H. M. (1957) "Informal judicial activity in Bunyoro." J. of African Administration 9, 4:188–195.

Provides case data to show how informal tribunals operating outside the official court system function to preserve social solidarity and community cooperation.

Glasse, R. M. (1959) "Revenge and redress among the Huli." Mankind 5:273–289.

Presents a detailed description of an institutionalized system of revenge and redress in New Guinea which periodically restructures alliances between groups. The data are important for any discussion of social control in societies without a centralized political power structure.

Kopytoff, I. (1961) "Extension of conflict as a method of conflict resolution among the Suku of the Kongo." J. of Conflict Resolution 5, 1:61–69.

This paper examines specific political implications of conflict management and presents a methodological discussion of "culture" and "social structure" as explanatory concepts.

Van Velsen, J. (1964) The Politics of Kinship: A Study in Social Manipulation Among the Lakeside Touga of Nyasaland. Manchester: Manchester Univ. Press.

An elaborate analysis of the working of a highly flexible political structure in conflict situations illustrated by a number of well-documented cases.

Psychological approaches are used, for example, in these studies:

Gibbs, J. L. (1963) "The Kpelle Moot: a therapeutic model of the informal settlement of disputes." Africa 33, 1:1–11.

This study concerns the integrative function of informal litigation and argues for the necessity of a conjunct analysis of formal and informal processes of conflict resolution. It also demonstrates the usefulness of complementing a structural and procedural analysis of dispute settlement with a psychological one.

LeVine, R. A. (1962) "Witchcraft and co-wife proximity in southwestern Kenya." Ethnology 1, 1:39–45.

An examination of cross-cultural evidence on the basis of a psychodynamic theory showing that the structure of domestic groups may determine the nature and volume of hostile interaction.

Whiting, B. B. (1965) "Sex identity conflict and physical violence: a comparative study." Amer. Anthropologist 67, 6 (Part II): 123–140.

Based on material from six cultures, this study offers four hypotheses relating socialization practices to specific patterns of conflict behavior.

Other comparative studies on law include the following:

Nader, L. (1965) "Choices of legal procedure: Shia Moslem and Mexican Zapotec." Amer. Anthropologist 67 (April): 394–399.

This article suggests a hypothesis linking a dual village organization with the absence of community court or council systems of settling conflict.

Roberts, J. M. (1965) "Oaths, automatic ordeals, and power." Amer. Anthropologist 67, 6 (Part II): 186–212.

Using statistical techniques for the analysis of cross-cultural data the author concludes that oaths and automatic ordeals function to maintain law and order in societies with weak authority and power deficits.

Long in the past most societies were surrounded by neighboring peoples who lived at approximately equivalent levels of technoenvironmental development. Both friendly and hostile neighboring groups were generally of approximately equivalent strength. With sides more or less evenly matched, when diplomacy failed it was at least likely to be a fair fight. Now nearly everywhere such times are gone.

Small-scale societies find themselves up against far more powerful adversaries. Only a few diehard colonial regimes are still fighting to "pacify" ungratefully rebellious native populations, as in Angola, Mozambique, and Guiné-Bissau. But the central governments of nations on almost every continent are struggling against small separatist ethnic minorities: in Brazil and Colombia, Cambodia and Vietnam, in Ethiopia and Chad, India and Japan, and of course, the United States.

The diverse peoples of the enormous island of New Guinea face Indonesian patrols in West Irian and in the east the growing interference of the new government of Papua-New Guinea. As Vayda illustrates, traditional processes of diplomacy and warfare persist in New Guinea as well, in forms that underscore the universal relationship between patterns of technoenvironmental adaptation and intergroup tension.

War and Peace in New Guinea[1]

Andrew P. Vayda

This paper is a sequel to an earlier one showing that fighting for revenge, as illustrated by materials on the Maoris of New Zealand, can be part of a multiphase process including also a phase of attempted territorial conquests and serving to regulate the territorial expansion and dispersion of populations (Vayda, 1970). The present paper provides materials for exploring interpretations that are possible when fighting for revenge and various other practices characteristic of some phases of the total process are found among populations which, unlike the Maoris in pre-European times, are not manifestly expanding. The data used here are derived almost wholly from field work among the Maring people of the Bismarck Mountains of eastern New Guinea, but the kind of interpretation to be offered should be applicable also, as will be suggested in a concluding section, to the study of warfare and ecological processes among other populations of primitive farmers and warriors.

The Maring Region and People

The Maring region is used here as the designation for a rugged forested area of about 190 square miles within which live some 7,000 people sharing certain cultural characteristics and speaking the Maring language, which has been classified as belonging to the Central Family in the Eastern New Guinea Highlands stock (Wurm and Laycock, 1961; Bunn and Scott, 1963). Cutting across the region is the Bismarck Range, flanked by the Simbai River to the north and the Jimi River to the south. About 2,000 of the Marings live in the Simbai Valley and the rest are in the Jimi Valley. Subsistence activities throughout the region are the traditional ones of slash-and-burn farming of tuberous staples and other crops, pig husbandry, pandanus tree cultivation, and some gathering of wild plant foods and hunting of feral pigs, small marsupials, and birds.

Source: From Andrew P. Vayda, "Phases of the Process of War and Peace Among the Marings of New Guinea," *Oceania,* Vol. XLII, No. 1 (September 1971), pp. 1–23. Used by permission of the publisher and the author.

[1] This paper was presented at the seventieth Annual Meeting of the American Anthropological Association in New York City in 1971. I thank William C Clarke, Mark D. Dornstreich, Paula Brown Glick, Mervyn Meggitt, Roy A. Rappaport, and Cherry Lowman Vayda for reading a draft and commenting on it. The map was prepared by William C. Clarke and Ian Heyward, who used a base map drawn by Ian Hughes. Another version of the paper is planned as a chapter in a book tentatively entitled *War, Peace, and the Structure of Adaptive Response Processes* that I am writing on war and peace as an ecological process.

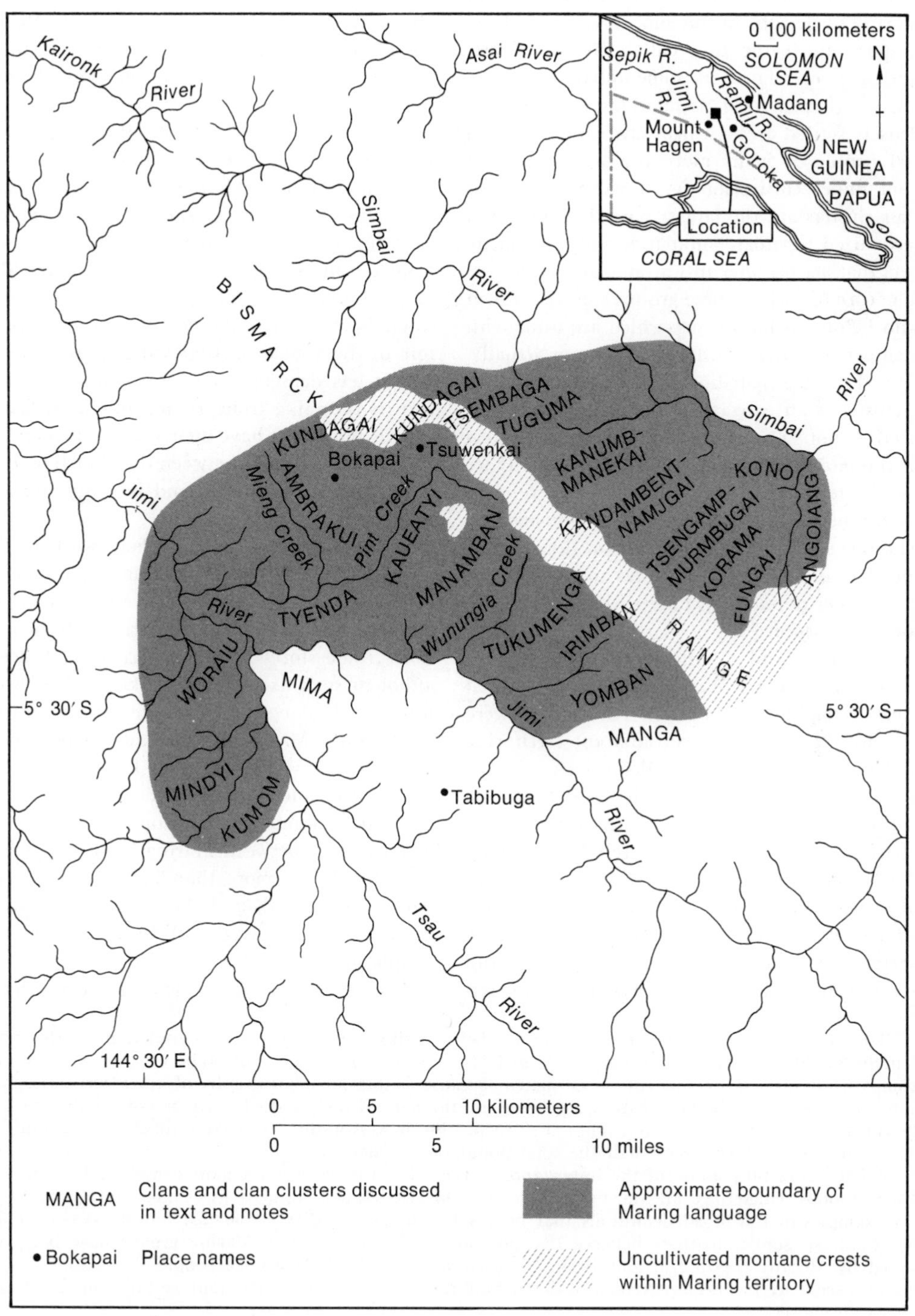
Kaironk
River
Asai River
Simbai
River
BISMARCK
RANGE
Sepik R.
0 100 kilometers
SOLOMON SEA
N
Jimi R.
Ramu R.
Madang
Mount Hagen
Goroka
NEW GUINEA
PAPUA
Location
CORAL SEA
River
Simbai
KUNDAGAI
KUNDAGAI
TSEMBAGA
TUGUMA
Tsuwenkai
Bokapai
KANUMB-MANEKAI
KANDAMBENT-NAMJGAI
KONO
ANGOIANG
TSENGAMP-MURMBUGAI
KORAMA
FUNGAI
Jimi
Mieng Creek
AMBRAKUI
Pint Creek
KAUEATYI
MANAMBAN
Wunungia Creek
River
TYENDA
TUKUMENGA
IRIMBAN
YOMBAN
WORAIU
MIMA
Jimi
MANGA
5° 30′ S
5° 30′ S
MINDYI
KUMOM
Tabibuga
River
Tsau
River
144° 30′ E
0 5 10 kilometers
0 5 10 miles
MANGA Clans and clan clusters discussed in text and notes
• Bokapai Place names
Approximate boundary of Maring language
Uncultivated montane crests within Maring territory

Population is unevenly distributed, becoming less dense where the Simbai and Jimi Rivers reach lower altitudes—at the eastern end of Maring settlement in the Simbai Valley and the western end in the Jimi Valley. Gross contrasts in density correlate with some differences in the organization of local populations. In the more densely settled areas, which have either close to 100 people or many more per square mile of land under cultivation or in secondary forest, clan clusters are the largest named groups with recognized territory boundaries and with members that act together in war and in ceremonies. The core of each of these groups consists of men who belong to local clans, which are units with members putatively, although often not actually, related through patrilineal descent. Each clan in a cluster is an exogamous unit, but the cluster itself is not. There are about a dozen clusters in the more densely settled Maring areas. If we use the term clan cluster population to refer to all the people, whether agnates or non-agnates, who live and garden continually on the lands of the clans of a cluster, we can say that the size of clan cluster populations ranges from some 200 to some 850 people.[2]

The same kind of integration of clans into clusters is absent from the less densely settled areas. Sometimes in warfare here, there were alliances of clans that had adjacent territories, and it is possible to devise definitions whereby any allied clans may be regarded as constituting a clan cluster.[3] However, it needs to be emphasized that these alliances rarely last for more than a generation, and, even while they are still in force, the allied clans do not necessarily have all friends and enemies in common, and they perform separately (and sometimes as hosts and guests rather than as co-hosts) the main ceremonies of the long sequence of rituals that follow warfare.[4] For purposes of the present article, it makes sense to refer to allied clans simply as allied clans and to reserve the clan cluster designation for the more highly integrated named multi-clan groups of the more densely settled Maring areas.

A further contrast between these areas and the lower-density ones lies in the shape and location of group territories. In the former areas most clusters, and many clans within them, occupy territories that extend in irregular bands, from the mossy forests by the crest of the Bismarck Range at an altitude of 6,000–7,000 feet to lands at about 2,000 feet at or near the bottom of the Simbai or Jimi Valleys.[5] Some clans in the less densely settled areas also have territories dropping from the top of the Bismarck Range, but others have their lands only on small mountains and spurs between the Simbai or Jimi River and its tributaries and in basins formed by these tributaries.

At the time of our initial field work in the Maring region in 1962,[6] the Maring people in general, and especially those in the Simbai Valley, had had hardly any impact yet from missions, trade stores, or labor recruiters. Indeed, although steel axes and bush knives had been introduced along native trade routes in the 1940's, some Maring groups had not been contacted by any white men until four years before our arrival, and had not been brought under Australian administrative control until 1960. The last wars between Maring local groups had been fought no more than half a dozen years before our arrival, and the enmities persisting from these wars were still strong among the people in 1962.

The nature of these wars, as reconstructed

[2] The imprecision in my statement of the number and size of the clan cluster populations in the more densely settled parts of the Maring area is mainly a result of my being uncertain whether some of the groups whose densities could not be estimated (because usable air photographs of their territories had not been made) are to be regarded as being in the more densely settled parts or not. As discussed in Lowman-Vayda (1968:202–203 and footnote 4 on p. 240), it was possible to make estimates of densities in the territories in which almost half the total population resides.

[3] Before being fully aware of the importance of the differences between the more densely and less densely settled groups. I described all Marings as belonging to clan cluster populations (Vayda and Cook, 1964). For examples of the broad definitions that permit this usage, see Clarke, 1968:53; Lowman-Vayda, 1968: 205. Contrasts similar to those between the more and less densely settled Maring groups have been observed by Meggitt (1957*b*:37ff. and 1965:272) between the Ipili and Mae Enga peoples.

[4] This sequence has been described in detail by Rappaport (1967) from the vantage point of the Tsembaga clan cluster.

[5] Similar distributions of territories have been reported both from other parts of the world and from elsewhere in New Guinea (Brookfield and Brown, 1963:170.)

[6] Conducted by R. and A. Rappaport, C. Lowman-Vayda and myself under a National Science Foundation grant (No. G23173).

from informants' accounts, will be indicated in succeeding sections as part of the description of the multi-phase process operating among the Marings.

Antecedents of Fighting

In considering the Maring process, we need not dwell at great length on the peaceful phase immediately preceding the outbreak of fighting. I have suggested elsewhere that a corresponding phase among other peoples—for example, the Maoris (Vayda, 1970:564–66)—involved increase in the pressure exerted by a group upon its existing territory so that the members were stimulated to commit offenses against other groups and to commit more and more of them, or more and more severe ones, as population pressure increased. The provocations to warfare were cumulative. By contrast, although the provocations in the Maring case were offenses similar to those characteristic of the pre-war phase among the Maoris, the available evidence gives no indication that the offenses had a cumulative effect in provoking war or that their commission correlated with the pressure of particular Maring groups upon their land.

Let us note at this point what the offenses provoking war were. Informants were able to specify the proximate causes of 39 Maring wars for me, and in almost every case some offense by the members of one group against the members of another was involved. Murder or attempted murder was the most common, and occurred in 22 of the cases. Other offenses mentioned included poaching, theft of crops, and territorial encroachment; sorcery or sorcery accusations; abducting women or receiving women who had eloped; rape; and insults.[7] Sometimes these led directly to war and sometimes to homicide first.

It is possible to argue on *a priori* grounds that almost all of those offenses, along with the provocations to commit them, should have increased, among the Marings as among other peoples, with population pressure, which entails a heightening of tensions and of competition over resources. However, it is also possible that the Marings needed less of an accumulation of grievances to incite them to war than did such other peoples as the Maoris. This would be consistent with the fact that among the Marings the account kept of all offenses that one's group made against others and that others made against the group was not as strict as among the Maoris.[8]

More significantly, it would also be consistent with the fact that for each Maring group there were recurrent periods of years when warfare was ritually proscribed. That is to say, if the Marings tended not to undertake wars while the ritual proscriptions were in force, then perhaps they could fight on the basis of fewer provocations than did the Maoris and still not fight so frequently as to jeopardize their survival.[9] The proscriptions became effective after wars and applied to members of the groups that had been the main belligerents and were able to maintain themselves on their own territories. When warfare ended, the men of these groups performed certain rituals. These involved thanking the ancestor spirits for their assistance in the fight, sacrificing for them whatever mature and adolescent pigs were on hand, and promising them many more pigs, commensurate with the help received, to be sacrificed when the group had a herd large enough for holding a festival—something of the order of 170 pigs for a festival hosted by about 200 people.[10] Until the festival,

[7] The cases of territorial encroachment are referred to in a later section.

[8] On the Maori practice in this regard, see Vayda, 1960:45.

[9] This is a view presented in detail by Rappaport in his book (1967) on Maring ritual and ecology; he also notes (p. 152, note) that there have been violations of the ritual proscriptions. Three cases of what may have been violations are known to me: the Kauwatyi raid on the Tyenda in 1955, the fighting initiated by the Manamban against the Kauwatyi in 1956, and the Tukumenga attack on the Manamban in 1956. Details of these hostilities are given later in this paper.

[10] The figures are based on the pigs and people involved in the festival held by the Tsembaga clan cluster population in 1962–63, as described by Rappaport (1967). Groups smaller than the Tsembaga and with smaller territories held festivals with considerably fewer pigs, while larger groups are said to have held festivals with several hundred pigs. Elsewhere (Vayda, in press) I have made the following observations: ". . . the people tend to hold the festivals when they can afford to—when they have had good fortune for a number of years and when, accordingly, pigs may have become 'too much of a good thing' for them. Indeed, there is evidence that when pig herds become large they also become burdensome and cause people to agitate for pig festivals, for expanding pig populations increasingly compete with human

warfare was not to be undertaken because, in the Maring view, there would be no help forthcoming from either spirits or allies until they received their just rewards. The periods required for raising herds considered sufficiently large thus corresponded as a rule to periods of nonaggression. Moreover, these periods, which lasted usually some 10 years, tended to be marked not only by an absence of open fighting between groups but also by an absence of provocations or offenses between them. This is because, as will be discussed later, the use of land in places where there was likelihood of contact with members of other groups tended to be avoided by people as long as they could not feel secure in having the support of their ancestor spirits when potentially hostile outsiders or their potentially malefic magic were encountered. In other words, until the spirits were appeased with pig sacrifices, intergroup offenses were unlikely simply because intergroup encounters were avoided. Obversely, as soon as the outstanding obligations to spirits and allies had been met, people were more readily disposed to repair to the borderlands of their territories so that encounters with members of other groups and, concomitantly, disputes with them were likely to take place. Informants gave accounts of wars that broke out within two or three months or even within weeks after the termination of a pig festival.[11]

There is, moreover, no evidence that provocations to war and then warfare itself ensued less quickly after pig festivals among the Maring groups exerting least pressure upon their land. Some of the smallest Simbai Valley clan populations, living at the edge of a vast expanse of unoccupied forest extending eastwards along the Bismarck Range, fought as often as did some of the large clan cluster populations of the central Maring area, where there are not only higher population densities but also such other indicators of greater pressure upon resources as shorter fallow periods for garden plots, more painstaking harvests from the gardens, and, as a result of more intensive land use in a few places, some tracts of permanent grassland and degraded secondary forest, both of which are rare in the low-density territories.[12] Most Maring groups seem to have averaged one or two wars per generation, and it is in the wars themselves and their aftermaths and not in the antecedents of fighting that we must look for mechanisms operating in response to demographic factors.

Two Phases of War: Nothing Fights and True Fights

All Maring groups sometimes took part in engagements that they called small fights or nothing fights. In these, the warriors repaired each morning from their homes to prearranged fight grounds at the borders of the lands of the two main belligerent groups. The opposing forces took up positions close enough to each other to be within the range of arrows. Thick wooden shields, as tall as the men and about two feet six inches wide, afforded protection in combat.[13] With the bottoms of the shields resting on the ground, warriors darted out from behind them to shoot their arrows. Some men also emerged temporarily from cover in order to taunt their foes and display bravery by drawing

---

beings for garden food, and their care calls for larger and larger outlays of energy by the pig-keepers" (cf. Rappaport, 1967:153–65; and Vayda, Leeds and Smith, 1961). One Simbai valley group, the Kanumb-Manekai, with a resident population of 91, was beginning its festival in March, 1963, and informants from the group told me that they had originally planned to wait for the return of some of their young men from coastal employment before holding their festival, but then had had to decide to go ahead without them—because there were "too many pigs destroying gardens." When I made a census of Kanumb-Manekai pigs in June, 1963, prior to the wholesale killing of pigs in the festival, I found 62 adult pigs (23 males and 39 females) and 26 piglets.

11 The most recent war in which a main belligerent was the Tsembaga clan cluster studied by Rappaport (1967:218) began within three months of the end of a Tsembaga pig festival. In the case of the last war between the Yomban and Manga clusters of the Jimi Valley, the first provocation to fight was made while the Yomban were still engaged in their pig festival. Their old enemies, the Manga, shouted at them, "You're not men—you're women. We killed some of you, but you didn't kill us. So what are you making a festival for?" The incensed Yomban concluded their festival and then quickly repaired to Manga territory, where they killed one man and four women in a garden by first spearing them and cutting them up with axes. The war was on.

12 This comparison is based on Clarke, 1966:348–52. Further discussion of differential pressure on the land is presented below.

13 For descriptions of Maring shields and their use, see Lowman-Vayda, in preparation.

enemy fire. At the end of each day's fighting, the men returned home. Although these small bow-and-arrows fights sometimes continued for days and even weeks, deaths or serious injuries were rare. Indeed, Rappaport (1967: 121–23), in his discussion of the fights as described to him by warriors of the Tsembaga cluster, suggested that rather than serious battles they were, among other things, settings for attempts at conflict resolution by non-violent means. They brought the antagonists, as he noted, "within the range of each other's voices while keeping them out of the range of each other's deadlier weapons." Sometimes the voices at the fight ground uttered insults, but there also were times when moderation was counseled (especially by men who came as allies of one belligerent group but also had ties with the other) and when settlements of disputes were negotiated so as to obviate escalation of the fighting to a more deadly phase.

When there was escalation, the Maring pattern was for it to be to a phase involving what informants called true fights—fights in which not only bows and arrows and throwing spears but also axes and jabbing spears, the weapons of close combat, were used. While the small fights were still going on, advocates of escalation as well as the Maring equivalents of doves were speaking out. Whether the hawks would prevail depended upon a variety of factors—for example, the fighting strength of the enemy as displayed in the nothing fight, the casualties if any, and the nature of previous relations between the antagonists. Sometimes a group chose to escalate a fight in order to attempt to even the score with the enemy in killings, while at other times a group abandoned a fight because it had already suffered too many deaths.[14] It is possible that the enemy's show of force in the nothing fight was sometimes sufficient to induce a group to flee without submitting to any further test of arms; accounts that Rappaport (1967: 124) received from some Tsembaga informants suggest this. The nothing fights may be said to have had what some authors would describe as an epideictic aspect (Rappaport, 1967: 195; Wynne-Edwards, 1962: 16–17). And, as in the case of other epideictic phenomena, what the fights disclosed to the participants about the size of their rivals' groups could lead to behavior changing the size or dispersion of the groups involved.

If a consensus in favor of escalation to a phase of true fights did develop on both sides, the antagonists, after shouting to each other that the time had come for more serious warfare, withdrew to make elaborate ritual preparations for it for at least two days.[15] When they returned to the fight ground, they took up positions in formations several ranks deep. While men in the opposing front ranks fought duels with one another from behind their huge shields, they were provided with cover by bowmen who were in the ranks further to the rear and who shot at any enemy warrior exposing himself. Front positions were exchanged for rear ones from time to time in the course of battle, and sometimes individual men temporarily withdrew from combat in order to catch their breath. Most fatalities in these true fights seem to have occurred when an enemy arrow or throwing spear brought down a man in the front ranks so that he could be finished off with axes in a quick charge from the enemy front line. Because of the protection that the shields afforded and because the fighting was from static positions rather than involving any appreciable tactical movements, the warfare could proceed for weeks and even months without heavy casualties. Each morning when there was to be fighting, the able-bodied men who were the warriors assembled near their hamlets and went *en masse* to the fightground for their day's combat, while the women remained behind to attend to routine gardening and domestic tasks. The men themselves did not fight daily. When it rained both sides stayed in their houses, and, by mutual agreement, all combatants sometimes took a day off to re-paint their shields, to attend to rituals in connection with casualties, or simply to rest. There could even be intervals of as long as three weeks during which active hostilities were suspended and the men worked at making new gardens.

It must be emphasized that these truces had to be agreed to by both sides. If only one side absented itself from the fight ground, this was in effect a signal to the other side to consider escalating to another kind of military action: what is to be described below as routing. Although

[14] There are illustrations of both kinds of decisions in informants' accounts of warfare—for example, fights between the Irimban and Yomban clusters and between the Manamban and Tukumenga clusters.

[15] A description of these preparations is given in Rappaport, 1967:125–38.

this was an action that characteristically lasted but a few hours at the most, it can be usefully discussed as a separate phase in the process of war and peace. Before turning to it, however, we must consider what role allies could have in bringing about routs and what alternative there could be to nothing fights and true fights as the phases of hostilities antecedent to routing.

Allies

The prelude to a group's being routed could be a reverse at the fight ground, and this could, as Rappaport (1967: 139) noted in his account of the last war between the Tsembaga and Kundagai clusters in the Simbai Valley, come about through the failure of allies to appear in force. It should be understood that a Maring war characteristically had two groups as the main belligerents and that allies were men belonging to other groups and participating in the fighting because of individual ties between them and the members of the two main belligerent groups. The longer that fight-ground hostilities dragged on, the more difficult it became for the main belligerents to maintain the support of allies, who, naturally enough, had their own affairs to attend to. In the case of the Tsembaga, the greatest number of their allies belonged to the neighboring Tuguma cluster, and it was on the day when the Tuguma did not come to the fight ground that the Kundagai, still supported by their own allies and aware of their numerical advantage, mounted a charge in which the Tsembaga suffered heavy casualties. The routing of the Tsembaga ensued.

There also were times when a group learned in advance that needed allies were withdrawing their support. Instead of fighting and dying in a lost cause, the group fled to refuge immediately and its adversaries were left with houses and gardens to destroy but no people to slaughter. The Kanumb group is said to have fled in this manner in its last war with the Tuguma cluster (Rappaport, 1967: 139).

In view of the importance of allies for success, it must be understood that whether their support in sufficient numbers and for long enough time would be forthcoming was not a capricious matter. Those from whom help might come were non-agnatic kinsmen living elsewhere and also other men recruited by such non-agnatic kinsmen. Of the two main belligerent groups in a war, the larger one would thus be likely to have its numerical advantage magnified by having more allies. Being larger, it would as a rule have formed more numerous ties with other groups through marriage. Also, other things being constant, the group that was doing a better job of using its land and growing crops and pigs on it would have an advantage for receiving support, for it would have been better able to make prestations of pigs and other valuables so as both to maintain the allegiance of existing kinsmen in other groups and to create new ties through new marriages.

It needs to be emphasized that merely having kinsmen in other groups was not sufficient to ensure their support. If relations with them had not been kept active through prestations of goods and through services such as helping the kinsmen in their own wars and acting as intermediaries for them in trading goods over long distances, the kinsmen were not likely to be quick to give military assistance. Indeed, a number of Marings that we met had refused to give such assistance to affines who they felt had slighted them. Moreover, it should be noted that the principle of helping kinsmen often left latitude as to where aid should be rendered at a particular time, for one was apt to have kinsmen engaged in different wars simultaneously or in a single war on opposing sides. Under such circumstances calculations of self-interest were a factor in decisions about aid. Thus one redoubtable warrior from the Fungai clan initially helped his affines in the Murmbugai clan, but when he felt himself to have been insufficiently requited for his efforts he switched to the side of the Murmbugai's enemies, the Korama, a clan that also contained some of his kinsmen.

The Kauwatyi cluster of the Jimi Valley, never routed from its territory and with some 850 in the cluster population, is an example of a large, aggressive, successful, and centrally-located group whose side it was advantageous to be on. The Kauwatyi got even more help than they wanted or needed from their many kinsmen in almost all groups on both sides of the Bismarck Range. According to Kauwatyi informants, the superfluous allies were tolerated at the nothing fights and duly rewarded with pork on subsequent ceremonial occasions, but were not asked to join in the more deadly fighting in which any deaths suffered by allies would have had to be recompensed profusely—with brides among the prestations—by the Kauwatyi themselves. No doubt it was an advantage to the Kauwatyi not to have these allies helping the enemy, even if their direct aid could be dispensed with.

The last war that the Kauwatyi fought was against the Manamban cluster in 1956, and it was a war in which the Kauwatyi did seek allies—but they were allies from a specific group, recruited for a specific tactical operation. Some of the antecedents and consequences of the involvement of these allies, men from the Tukumenga cluster, in the war are worth recounting here, for they nicely illustrate the kinds of hardheaded strategic considerations that could be operative in decisions about launching attacks and becoming allies. Initially, while the Kauwatyi-Manamban war was going on, most of the Kauwatyi Tukumenga allies were involved in hostilities elsewhere. Tukumenga territory is bordered on the west by the territory of the Manamban and on the east by that of the Yomban, and one or the other of these clusters has been the enemy in all but one of the six recent wars in which the Tukumenga have been one of the main belligerents.[16] At the beginning of 1956 the Tukumenga were not themselves the main belligerents in any war, although large numbers of Tukumenga men were helping the Manga cluster, a non-Maring group, in fight-ground battle against the group that had been their own enemy in their last war: the Yomban.[17] Since the Yomban cluster, of more than 700 people, was about twice the size of the Manga, the substantial help received by the Manga from the Tukumenga was no doubt of critical importance to the Manga cause. When hostilities broke out between the Kauwatyi and the Tukumenga's other traditional enemy, the Manamban, the war was already on between the Yomban and the Manga and it was to the Manga that the Tukumenga men continued to give their help. Each morning they went by a track near the Jimi River, far from the Yomban settlements, to the Manga-Yomban fight ground and, after a day of combat, they returned home each evening the same way. This had been going on for many weeks when in late April or early May two of the Kauwatyi leaders came secretly to the Tukumenga houses (but not to those where men with Manamban affines might betray the plans) and asked for help in a concerted attack upon the Manamban to take place on the following morning. Part of the proposal was that after defeating and routing the Manamban the Kauwatyi and Tukumenga would attempt to take over the Manamban territory, with the new boundary between the two victorious groups to consist of Wunungia Creek in the center. The Tukumenga agreed to the plan; the Yomban-Manga war had been dragging on to no effect, whereas here there was a prospect of a quick and advantageous victory. The Kauwatyi leaders returned to their homes, while the Tukumenga warriors collected their weapons, performed certain pre-fight rituals,[18] and then made their way to the forests high above their settlements. Here they arranged their shields to form makeshift houses, made fires in the middle of these, and then slept. At dawn they moved along the top of the Bismarck Range and then descended to the Kauwatyi-Manamban fight ground so as to come upon the enemy's rear and take him by surprise. The Manamban were easily routed. After joining in the work of destroying the houses and gardens, the Tukumenga went with the Kauwatyi to the houses of the latter and then returned towards the evening to their own houses via the tracks down near the river. On their way back, they could see to the east the smoke and fire which were issuing from the settlements of the Manga: the Yomban had taken advantage of the one-day absence of the Tukumenga. They had mounted a charge which took the lives of five Manga warriors and had followed this up with the routing of the Manga and setting fire to their houses.

16 The exception consisted of a war in which the Tukumenga stayed on the north bank of the wide and deep Jimi River and their adversaries, the Mima, stayed on the south bank. Actual fighting was limited to shooting arrows across the water. After more than a month of this, and with nobody killed, some Tukumenga said: "It is no good to fight distant enemies. Our bellies are still angry; so let us kill some people nearby." They found two Manamban men doing garden work and killed them. The Tukumenga then abandoned the war against the Mima and fought the Manamban (cf. Vayda, 1967:134).

17 The Yomban are the easternmost Maring group in the Jimi Valley. The Manga are the next group to the east and are Narak-speakers but have customs in warfare hardly different from those of their Maring neighbors (see Cook, 1967). Adopting the terminology favored by some anthropologists (e.g. Salisbury, 1963:257–58), we could say that the Yomban and the Manga belonged to a single "league."

18 Including those described in Rappaport, 1967:152, footnote 9, citing accounts that I obtained in 1966 from Tukumenga participants in the fighting.

An Alternative Phase: Raids

The Tukumenga and Manamban cluster each comprised some 600 people, and the size of the Kauwatyi and Yomban was, as previously noted, even greater. Only one other Maring group, the Kundagai of the western part of the Maring region in the Jimi Valley, approached these four clusters in size. In the case of the much smaller groups of the less densely settled Maring areas, warfare could be conducted essentially in the manner already described, although, obviously, on a much smaller scale. However, among these groups another mode of fighting, employed only rarely among the large clusters, also seems to have been common and to have constituted an alternative to nothing fights and true fights as antecedents of routing. This was raiding and consisted usually of stealing in the night to the houses where the men of an enemy clan slept—the 30 or so men in a clan would have their sleeping quarters distributed among perhaps four or five houses. At dawn the raiders made fast the doors of as many of these as possible and then shot their arrows and poked their long spears through the leaf-thatched walls. If the men inside succeeded in undoing the doors, they were picked off by raiders waiting behind the fences. With a numerical advantage on the side of the raiders, these tactics could annihilate the manpower of an enemy clan. This is what may have happened to the Woraiu, a now extinct Maring group that had been living on the south side of the Jimi River, where it was attacked by an alliance of the Mindyi and Kumom clans. However, in the accounts that I received from informants in the low-density Maring areas in the eastern Simbai Valley rather than in the Jimi, the raiding force never seems to have been large enough to take care of all of the enemy men's houses. The raiders in all cases, after killing a few, were forced to retreat because of counter-attacks by warriors from houses other than those raided.

These eastern Simbai accounts underscore that this mode of fighting could as a rule be effective only when the enemy group attacked was small. Otherwise the position of raiders deep in enemy territory could be extremely perilous, for warriors might rise up against them from all sides before they could make good their retreat. In the light of these considerations, it is not surprising that raiding should have been uncommon among the large populations. Indeed, I was told of only one clear case in which the fighting force of such a population attacked the enemy in his settlements without previously having tested him in fight-ground battle, and it is significant that the attack was made by the Kauwatyi, the largest of the Maring populations, against the Tyenda, a group less than half its size. The Kauwatyi men had gone during the night to Tyenda territory and, at dawn, appeared *en masse* and fully armed at the Tyenda settlements. The Tyenda just ran while the Kauwatyi wrought death and destruction. This attack took place in 1955. The Kauwatyi suffered no fatalities and the Tyenda, a group of about 300, lost 23. It is hardly likely that a similar attack by the Tyenda against the Kauwatyi swarm would have been successful.

Routs and Their Aftermath

The phase designated here as routing consisted, as already suggested, of going to the enemy settlements, burning the houses there, killing indiscriminately any men, women, or children found in the settlements, and, after having put the survivors to flight, destroying gardens, fences, and pandanus groves, and defiling the burial places. These proceedings sometimes took place immediately after the enemy warriors had broken ranks and fled in response to a charge at the fight ground. That is to say, the fleeing warriors would rush to their hamlets, gather their women and children, and then flee to seek refuge, while the routers wreaked as much death and destruction as they could. This is what happened in the war in which the Kauwatyi and Tukumenga jointly routed the Manamban. At other times the routing did not take place until the day after losses at the fight ground; the side that had suffered them would fail to appear and its antagonists would thereupon proceed to the settlements to burn and to kill. A Yomban-Tukumenga fight had this outcome.

Routing was not an inevitable consequence of the true wars of the Marings. It was possible, before events moved into the routing phase, for both sides to opt for an armistice whereby there could be no warfare between them until after a massive pig festival such as was referred to earlier. Rappaport (1967: 143) suggested that armistice was the more likely course when the number of killings between the antagonists was equal or when both agreed that, regardless of any disparities in the homicide score, the pressure of subsistence tasks made it impractical to continue hostilities. This may well be. However, on the basis of information about warfare involving either the Tsembaga or Tuguma cluster, Rappaport (1967: 142) has made the further suggestion that true wars ended most frequently with armistice. This suggestion is not in accord with the accounts that informants gave me concerning the termination of 29 such wars. Nineteen of these ended with the routing of people and the destruction of their houses and gardens. The important point is that the phase of true wars, like that of nothing fights, was one from which there could be either a return to peace or else escalation leading to further testing of the antagonists. That this was testing of the belligerents' capacity not only to defend themselves but also to defend and use land can be seen in the aftermath of routs.

The routs themselves did not necessarily have a decisive effect on these capacities. The Woraiu, as noted in the preceding section, may have had their manpower effectively destroyed when they were raided by the Mindyi and Kumom, but such annihilation of the fighting force of a group cannot have been common. The Marings, unlike such other peoples as the Maoris, did not customarily pursue an enemy beyond his settlement. To have done so would have been, according to informants, inviting death; so, as already indicated, the victors stayed behind and burned houses, ravaged gardens, and performed other destructive acts. The two Maring wars in which informants belonging to defeated groups claimed to have suffered the heaviest losses were the ones fought against the Kauwatyi by the Tyenda and the Manamban in the mid-1950's. When some 300 Tyenda were routed following the Kauwatyi's surprise raid, 14 Tyenda men, six women, and three children were killed. The 600 Manamban lost only eight men and three women in the course of being routed by the combined forces of the Kauwatyi and Tukumenga (although there had been 20 other Manamban deaths at the fight ground previously). If these figures indicate the heaviest mortality suffered in Maring wars, it may be questioned whether routs in general were effective in decisively altering the capacity of groups to defend and use land.

Let us consider, then, the testing of the antagonists in the aftermath of routs. First of all, during the period or phase which may be described as that of refuging by the routed group. The first opportunity that such a group had to show its mettle in this period was in the selection of a place of refuge. I have accounts of 21 routs. In seven of these the groups did not even leave their own territory and took refuge in portions of it at some distance from the borderlands where the enemies had engaged them. Among the 14 other cases the members of some routed groups fled across the Bismarck Range or the major rivers, but there were others where they remained closer and, indeed, sometimes continued to maintain a claim to their territory by going to it for food.

In the case of groups taking refuge outside of their own territories, a major test versus the enemies lay in making the return. Rappaport's discussion of routs suggested that defeated groups often failed to do this (Rappaport, 1967: 145). However, in 13 of my 14 cases the routed groups did, indeed, return; the one exception involved the Woraiu, who, as noted earlier, may have had their manpower effectively destroyed when they were raided by the Mindyi and Kumom. Unfortunately, the interpretation of these data is made difficult by the fact that the routed groups in seven of the cases referred to made their returns after the Australian administration had established its presence. It may be—as indeed Rappaport (1967: 145) suggested it was—that some of the groups, especially after having fragmented for the sake of obtaining refuge in one or another of the places where there were kinsmen or friends of individuals, would not have reconstituted themselves and repossessed their territories if not for the security and protection that the Australian presence afforded. There is, unfortunately, no evidence on which firm conclusions about this may be based. It seems likely, however, that Australian intervention did enable some groups to return to their territories more quickly and to rebuild their settlements in closer proximity to those of their enemies than would have been the case otherwise. This was most notably so in the case of the Manga. After being routed by the Yomban in 1956, they fled across the Jimi to friends and kinsmen living around a place called Tabibuga. From there, word of the Manga defeat was carried south across the Wahgi-Sepik divide to Minj, the Government sub-district headquarters. The Assistant District Officer there had visited the Yomban-Manga area previously with armed patrols—in 1953 and 1955. When an aerial survey confirmed the destruction of the Manga settlements, a new patrol was organized and marched along the tracks to the area some time in May, less than a month after the routing of the Manga. The Manga themselves were first taken back to their land by the patrol, which then proceeded to move against the Yomban. The ambushes that Yomban warriors armed with axes had prepared were unsuccessful, but they nevertheless continued to shower arrows upon the patrol and finally fled only after six of their number had been shot dead by police. This intervention, however, was quickly followed by what was to have a more continuous impact. A Patrol Post was established at Tabibuga with an Australian in charge and a complement of armed native police to extend *Pax Australiensis* into the Jimi Valley. Tabibuga is but a couple of hours' walk from the Manga settlements, so the people now had the security to devote themselves to rebuilding their houses on their former sites and to using their lands once more.[19]

Members of some other groups, perhaps partly because of their greater distance from Tabibuga, were more hesitant about leaving their refuges, but eventually all the Jimi Valley groups, with varying degrees of help and supervision from Tabibuga, were repatriated. From July through to October of 1956 there were monthly visits to the disturbed areas by Australian officials. Among the instructions given to the people were that they were to rebuild their houses and gardens, to report any raids to the patrol officer, and to keep their own noses clean unless they wished to be very severely dealt with. Weapons also were collected and burned publicly. By early October the officer, Barry Griffin, stated that all the recently routed Maring groups of the Jimi Valley—the Ambrakui, the Manamban, and the Tyenda—had, like the Manga, been restored to their lands.

Actually the statement, at least in October, 1956, could not be made accurately without qualifications that are suggestive as to what might have been the aftermath in the absence of intervention. While all the groups had been restored to some degree, there were, it must be noted, variations. Thus the Ambrakui, who had been routed some time around 1954 as a result of fighting that began with land encroachments by the Kundagai,[20] had taken refuge on the south side of the Jimi River, mainly on the lands of the Mima cluster, which included numerous affines and friends. From Mima territory, some of them accompanied a patrol led by Griffin at the end of September, 1956, to their abandoned territory north of the river. He instructed them to re-settle there and left a few police in the general area to help in the work. He also held discussions with both Kundagai and Ambrakui about their lands and then affirmed boundaries which, according to what I was told by Ambrakui informants in 1963, corresponded to the ancestral ones between the lands of the two groups. However, when he revisited the territory in June of 1957 he saw that the resettlement, averred in October of the previous year, was still far from complete: the men had, in effect, simply been visiting their old lands, while the women, children, and pigs had, for the most part, not even been doing that; they had remained in their Mima refuges. New gardens had not been made in the old lands. Only with increased police supervision and with further warnings to the Kundagai was the full return finally effected later in 1957. Less than five years later there were new land encroachments by the Kundagai. In response to the complaints of the Ambrakui, the patrol officer (a successor of Griffin) sent police to destroy Kundagai plantings on Ambrakui land and to arrest the offenders and bring them to Tabibuga. These incidents show that the 250 Ambrakui, one of the smallest of the Maring cluster populations, still had in the Kundagai a powerful enemy that was ready to act aggressively unless stopped by superior force. Any Ambrakui skittishness about being repatriated is perhaps not surprising.

In contrast, members of the large and powerful Manamban cluster, after having fled for

[19] My account of the routing of the Manga is based upon information from Yomban informants and written résumés of the official patrol reports. The latter were kindly supplied in 1963 by Mr. J. K. McCarthy, then Director of the Department of Native Affairs, Territory of Papua and New Guinea. Other reports of government contacts with Maring groups, including those on which the next four paragraphs are based, were kindly made available by the Simbai and Tabibuga Patrol Officers in 1963 and 1966. Published accounts of the patrol post at Tabibuga and some of the work done from there include Attenborough, 1960: Chapter 5, and Souter, 1964:235.

[20] See below.

refuge to at least 10 different groups on both sides of the Bismarck Range, began drifting back to their own territory within a week or two of having been routed by the Kauwatyi and Tukumenga in late April or early May of 1956. When the patrol from the sub-district headquarters at Minj arrived to confront the Yomban, some Manamban were already back on their land and a delegation of them went to Yomban territory to meet with the Australian officer. A Government patrol that included Manamban territory in its itinerary in July, 1956, reported that the Manambans had not yet returned but that a fair gathering of them assembled. According to the head count made there were 239 people. This constitutes about 40%. When Griffin arrived 16 days later to make a census, he saw 305 people and recorded their names. The return of the remainder proceeded smoothly thereafter.

The third people, the Tyenda, seemed to have been intermediate in their readiness to be repatriated—less timid than the Ambrakui, less bold than the Manamban. Not a large group, they nevertheless had had support even in refuge from numerous allies among the powerful Kundagai and Manamban. The former was the group that most of the Tyenda had been refuging with following their rout at the hands of the Kauwatyi in 1955, and they had continued to go to their own lands for food. Indeed, on one occasion they had killed four Kauwatyi men pursuing a pig deep into Tyenda territory, and the Kauwatyi were thereafter afraid to go far beyond the old boundary between the two groups. As for the Manamban, their support had been demonstrated by the response to a Tyenda kinsman's pleas for revenge against the Kauwatyi who had killed his children and brothers; the Manamban had gone *en masse* to challenge their old enemies by killing a Kauwatyi man. This had led to the Kauwatyi-Manamban war ending with the Manamban rout in 1956. The enmity between the Kauwatyi and the Manamban had been of long standing, but this very fact points up a difference between the position of the Tyenda and that of the Ambrakui, for the latter had no strong group to which they could turn to make common cause against the foe that had routed them. It is consistent with this that when the Ambrakui were still remaining close to their Mima refuge in June, 1957, the Tyenda were found by Griffin to be going ahead well with resettlement and to have prepared extensive new gardens in their territory. On the basis of the variations in the tempo of resettlement even with Government support, it may be supposed that, in its absence, the Ambrakui would not have returned but the Manamban would have, and so perhaps, at least to a part of their land, would have the Tyenda.

Groups failing to return would, in effect, be leaving their territories for others eventually to annex. This would mark the end of a cycle of testing of the capacity to defend and use the land. New multi-phase cycles could then begin with fresh outbreaks of hostilities and with new sets of contending groups.

If, however, routed groups did return, the cycle of testing did not end with repatriation. What happened to groups and their lands after warfare in which no group had been permanently routed? This is the question with which we must now deal.

Two Kinds of Peace: With and Without Land Redistribution

Usually the defeated groups, whether they had been routed or not, made new settlements further than their old ones from the borders with the enemies who had beaten them. In the Maring view, the rationale for this course of action was not only to avoid the enemies but also to avoid their malefic magic, thought to infest the borderlands where the fighting had taken place. The worse the defeat had been, the more the enemy and his magic were to be feared, and, in extreme cases, new settlements of a group were made deep within the forests that had previously been used for hunting rather than for gardens or long-term residence.[21] At times the new settlements were made not even in the group's own territory, although that continued to be used for making gardens and for other economic activities. Houses were constructed on the land of a neighboring group that was friendly. This constitutes in effect the same pat-

21 The Manamban and the Manga in the Jimi Valley and the Kono and the Angoiang in the Simbai Valley have done this. After the officer and his police had demonstrated the power of their magic by shooting six Yomban dead, some of the Yomban went to hunting grounds north of the crest of the Bismarck Range and made settlements there.

tern of settlement and land use as operated among the Tyenda while they were refuging with the Kundagai. The pattern is noted here again because it was put into effect by some groups like the Tsembaga (see Rappaport, 1967: 145) and the Murmbugai of the Simbai Valley not when in their original places of refuge after having been routed but rather when they had returned from those places to use their own territories even if not to live on them. The Murmbugai were still following this pattern in 1963, some seven or eight years after they had been defeated by the Kandambent-Namigai group. This was not the first time that the Murmbugai had done this. The Korama clan had destroyed their houses in an earlier war, and they had made new ones on the Tsengamp clan territory, whence they issued forth in due time to destroy the Korama settlements.

Some defeated groups succeeded in rehabilitating themselves fully. The gardens that they made on their lands grew well, their pig herds increased, their allies stood by them, and they accumulated the wherewithal to make the appropriate sacrifices to appease the ancestor spirits. The members of such groups eventually felt strong enough and secure enough to stand up to the old enemies and their magic and, some 10 years after the warfare, they would return to the borderlands, utter spells to chase the enemy spirits and the corruption caused by them back to enemy territory, and then would plant new boundary stakes where the old ones had been.[22] This last action signified that the *status quo ante bellum* was to be restored as far as territories were concerned—that there was to be peace without land redistribution. The stake-planting would be followed by a pig festival in which, as previously noted, the outstanding obligations to allies and ancestor spirits would be met and their help in future encounters with enemies would thus, most beneficially for morale, be secured.

But not all defeated groups that gained subsistence from their own lands after warfare had their confidence—and the grounds for confidence—restored to this same high degree. For some groups, perhaps with the loss of men and destruction of resources suffered in warfare compounded by post-bellum adversities such as diseases affecting themselves or their pigs, the borderlands where the enemy, his spirits, and his magic were thought to lurk continued to be places of fearsome peril. If a group did not rehabilitate itself sufficiently to be able to assert itself at its old boundaries by planting stakes there, it might simply leave some territory to be annexed by enemies. Informants stated this as a possibility but were unable to cite any recent examples.[23] They did, however, refer to certain dispositions by the Tyenda as an example of an alternative that groups not strong enough to confront their old enemies at the borderlands might have recourse to. The dispositions occurred after the last defeat of the Tyenda at the hands of the Kauwatyi and consisted of giving to the Kundagai groups of Bokapai and Tsuwenkai about 1.8 square miles in the higher altitudes in the northern part of Tyenda territory. This land, running as a band from the crest of the Bismarck Range down to the Pint River and, in its lower reaches which are best suited for gardens, bordering Kundagai territory on the west and Kauwatyi territory on the east, comprised about 30–40% of the total territory of the Tyenda. By giving the land to their Kundagai friends, including those who had provided them with refuge after their rout by the Kauwatyi, the Tyenda were requiting help in the past, making future help from them more likely, and, perhaps most importantly, arranging to have friends at the boundary between the land that the Tyenda were relinquishing and the land to which they were holding on. It must be added that in this last regard the Tyenda were not completely successful, for the Kauwatyi quickly appropriated for their own agricultural use some of the ground in question before the Kundagai had a chance to occupy it. As a result the Kundagai, kept by the *Pax Australiensis* from seeking redress through the traditional recourse to arms, were planning to bring the Kauwatyi before the Government courts over the matter. These effects can be argued also to have been advantageous for the Tyenda insofar as they were diverting the hostility and aggressions of the Kauwatyi from the Tyenda themselves. In any event, a more densely settled group—whether the Kundagai or the Kauwatyi—was getting land from the Tyenda, which had relatively low population

22 Rappaport (1967:166 ff.) gives details of the stake-planting ceremonies.

23 An example not from a recent war but rather from the early years of this century is discussed by Rappaport (1967:171).

density before bestowing the northern territory upon the Kundagai.[24] The example suggests that there may have been a variety of ways in which land redistribution following routing and refuging took place and that some of these ways may themselves have been multi-phase processes. The fact that in our exposition here we have distinguished not multiple post-refuging phases involving land redistribution but rather only a single phase designated as peace with land redistribution may well constitute an oversimplification of processes that actually took place in the past. If, however, this should be the case, it must be said that the oversimplification is unavoidable, since the post-refuging redistribution processes have hardly been operating recently, and details about them are, accordingly, hard to come by.

By regarding peace without land redistribution and peace with it as alternative phases antecedent to new rounds of fighting, we may be guilty of further oversimplification. Some hazy accounts of events that took place long ago suggest that redistribution could be a slow postbellum process involving groups that had appeared initially not to have relinquished any of their lands. An example of such an account concerns an original autonomous group—either clan or clan cluster—called the Kombepe. Towards the end of the last century, before any of our informants had been born, these people had their own discrete territory in the low altitudes between the Mieng and Pint Creeks, were neighbors of the Kundagai and the Ambrakui, and had a number of affines in both. When a dispute arose between some Kundagai and Kombepe, the Kundagai took their affines among the Kombepe home to their settlements for safety and then made an attack upon the remaining Kombepe. Of these the ones surviving went as a group to live with the Ambrakui and now constitute a clan of that cluster. In other words, the Kombepe split into two groups and ceased to exist as a single autonomous group. They did not, however, thereby cease to maintain their rights to their ancestral ground. Some of this continued as the land of the Kombepe staying with the Kundagai and the rest of it as the land of the Kombepe affiliated with the Ambrakui. But the two groups of Kombepe made grants of usufruct to their respective hosts. In the case of the Kundagai Kombepe, their failure to have many descendants resulted in the eventual complete absorption of themselves and their lands by the Kundagai. Informants were unable to provide any details of the process.

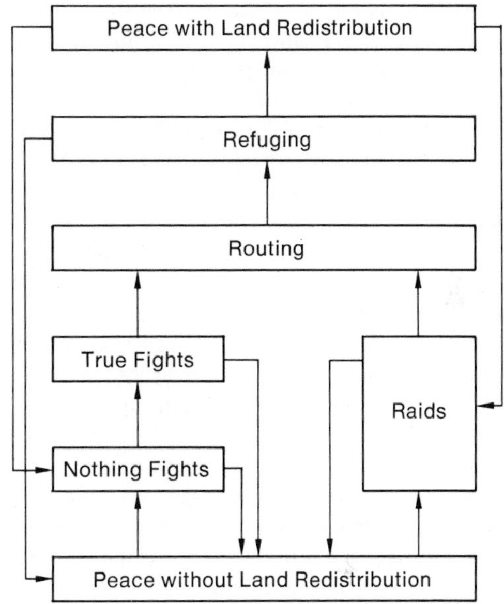

Phases of the process of war and peace among the Marings.

But regardless of possible, even if largely unknown, complexities in post-bellum redistribution, the fact remains that most groups in recent decades have held on to their own lands after warfare.

Discussion: Population Pressure and the Persistence of Systemic Processes

Why did the cycle of phases in recent times so often end before escalation to territorial conquests? A possible answer is that population decline has left each group with numbers which, on the one hand, could be sustained adequately on its existing land and, on the other, were insufficient for effective exploitation of additional areas. Although detailed demographic and

[24] Here, as before, I am defining as more densely settled those groups that have either close to 100 people or many more per square mile of land under cultivation or in secondary forest. Tyenda density prior to the land transfers was only about 60 people per square mile of such land.

ecological data for substantiation of this possibility are lacking, various observations in accord with it may be made. Thus, we do have evidence that, at the time of our field work, the Maring population as a whole had been declining for some years, apparently mainly because many people had not yet developed resistance to diseases introduced by Europeans. A dysentery epidemic carried off at least 20% of some groups in the late 1930's or early 1940's, and in more recent years, the average rate of decline has been about 1% annually. This is a preliminary estimate from census data now being subjected to detailed analysis by Georgeda Buchbinder.

There can of course have been population decline without its having been of such magnitude and generality as to have eliminated any appreciable pressure to which the territories of particular groups may have previously been subjected. The fact is, however, that when we were doing our field work in the 1960's we could find no clear evidence of such pressure anywhere in the Maring region except in Kauwatyi and Kundagai territory, where there were tracts of permanent grassland and degraded secondary forest. Apart from this, the indicators of pressure and concomitant environmental deterioration such as are to be found in more intensively exploited parts of the highlands were absent—no sediment-laden streams and no rill wash or sheet erosion except on trails, bare clay houseyards, and occasional landslides (compare Street, 1969: 105, on the Chimbu region, with Street, n.d.: 4–5, on the Maring region).

An absence of pressure is suggested also by the amount of land which is in primary forest (P.F. for short).[25] Air photographs of territories of groups containing 3,240 people, almost half the total Maring population, are available (see footnote 2); these territories constitute an area of 55 square miles, of which 40% is P.F. Overall population density per square mile of P.F. in this area is 150, and only one group, with 800 people per square mile of such forest, seems to have less than it needs. No other groups have more than 245 people per square mile of P.F. The groups with ample P.F. could subsist from new gardens made in some of it when they were compelled by warfare or other circumstances to abandon their garden sites and settlements in secondary forest tracts.[26]

Significantly, the group with the proportionately least amount of P.F. is the Kauwatyi. According to informants from the group, they have imposed upon themselves a taboo whereby no gardens may be made in the little more than a square mile they have of P.F. It must be noted that such forest is an important resource area in its own right for game, firewood, building materials, and various wild food plants.[27] The Kauwatyi, like other groups, had to keep some land in P.F. in order to have access to these resources. The unavailability of Kauwatyi land for what might be called "internal pioneering"—a group's conversion of P.F. within its own territories into garden land—may have been an important factor promoting the land encroachments and aggressions by these people against their neighbours.[28] Only one other group in recent times committed land encroachments that led to warfare. This was the Kundagai of Bokapai, who, in the mid-1950's, fought the Ambrakui after having begun to make gardens on their land. The Kundagai are not among the groups whose land in P.F. can be estimated from the available air photographs, but local informants told me that they were short of such land. It is noteworthy that they are the one large group which, as suggested earlier, might have succeeded in permanently displacing another and taking over its territory if the administration had not intervened.

[25] It should be noted that with regard to P.F. used as hunting grounds there was not always clear definition of what was within a group's territorial boundaries and what was not. I plan to devote another article to a consideration of the significance of the varying nature of rights to hunting grounds. Here, for the purpose of calculating the size of group territories and the extent of P.F. within them, I have followed two arbitrary rules: (1) to regard as being within a group's territory all the forest which the members of only that group described as being theirs; and (2) to regard as not belonging to any group those portions of the forest to which members of more than one autonomous group claimed rights.

[26] Some of the groups that were converting portions of their P.F. into farmed land after warfare are specified in footnote 21. A constraint that should be noted here is that almost all groups had some P.F. located on land too high (and therefore too cold or too often covered by clouds) for effective cultivation of root crops by Maring techniques.

[27] P.F. resources utilized by the Marings are included in the lists provided in Clarke, 1968: Appendices A and C, and Rappaport, 1967: Appendix 8.

[28] This was first suggested to me by C. Lowman-Vayda.

What is important in the present context is not so much the indication of pressures for the Kauwatyi and the Kundagai but rather the absence of it for the other groups. Does this mean, however, that these latter groups were not suffering from pressure which might be conducive to conquest? The answer must be not necessarily; as I have argued elsewhere (Vayda, 1961: 353–54), it is unjustified to assume that a group will take land from neighbors only when the source of pressure is its having numbers as great as or possibly even greater than its existing territory can support under a given system of land use. Food supplies diminishing slowly as the size of a group increases might, for example, predispose members to territorial conquests long before they attain numbers equivalent to the maximum which their original territory can carry and long before there is readily visible environmental deterioration (cf. Birdsell, 1957: 54; Vayda, 1970: 564–65). Unfortunately we do not have the data that might indicate how far such a process of diminution of food supplies had gone, if it was operating at all, among particular groups at particular times. And while Rappaport (1967: 87–96 and Appendix 10) has made some calculations of the carrying capacity of Tsembaga territory and has tentatively concluded that Tsembaga numbers were well below capacity, we have no adequate basis for making reliable estimates of just how much below the carrying capacities of their territories were the sizes of various groups at different times and in different parts of the Maring region. Such estimates would have to be based on ecological investigations more lengthy and comprehensive than those which have been made throughout the Maring region or throughout any other region where there has been primitive warfare in recent times (see Street, 1969). In short, we cannot argue categorically that absence of population pressure explains the non-escalation to territorial conquests in recent Maring warfare.

Nevertheless, even if there were significant pressure of which we are not aware, it is clear enough that there was nothing comparable in magnitude to the pressure associated with territorial conquests among such people as the Central Enga, whose region is much more densely settled and intensively exploited.[29] As noted by Meggitt (1957*a*: 135–36; 1965: 82, 218; n.d.: 31), when population increase was adding to the pressure on the resources of centrally located Enga clans, there was no unoccupied arable land for their extra members to use and the conquests of the territories of other clans had to be attempted. Enga warfare regularly featured the destruction of weaker clans and resulted in a continual redistribution of arable land between groups.

Such contrasts to the Maring situation make it reasonable to hypothesize that there are certain thresholds of pressure that groups such as those of the Maring and Enga regions must reach before they undertake territorial conquests and, further, that Enga and other highlanders[30] were attaining these thresholds in recent times while Maring groups, with the possible exception of the Kauwatyi and Kundagai, were not. In the absence of more precise quantitative data, we can regard this only as a working hypothesis—which, it would be hoped, would lead to further field investigations. However, certain questions raised by the hypothesis are appropriate for consideration here. These relate to the persistence of systemic processes.

Recent Maring warfare as I have described it here and early nineteenth century Maori warfare (Vayda, 1970) were similar in having features that could be interpreted as no longer doing something they had formerly done, i.e., as no longer leading to territorial conquests as an adaptive means of reducing disparities between groups in their man/resource ratios. Does this mean, then, that the conclusion reached about the Maoris after their adoption of muskets must apply also to the Marings; namely, that their traditional system had been disrupted and that the persistence of fighting among them was a case of non-adaptive cultural lag? The answer is no, for, as suggested by the hypothesis just discussed, recent Maring warfare may have been

[29] Population density of the 55,000 Central Enga "averages about 110 to 120 per square mile" and some Enga groups have densities of over 300 people per square mile (Meggitt, 1962:158 and n.d.:2). Density in the Maring region as a whole averages less than 50 per square mile, and no Maring group has a density exceeding an average of 85 per square mile of a group's total territory. For contrasts in intensity of land use between Maring areas and a location in the Tairora-speaking region of the eastern part of the highlands, see Clarke, 1966. See also Brookfield's table (1962:244–45) presenting data on 25 highland localities.

[30] For example, the Chimbu as described by Brookfield and Brown (1963:79) and by Vial (1942, especially p. 8).

operating in a manner which was both appropriate to the prevailing demographic and ecological conditions and also in keeping with the traditional functioning of the larger system of population dispersion and land redistribution in which Maring fighting, routing, refuging, and returning from refuge were components. In other words, even if territorial conquests had been only an infrequent rather than a regular aftermath of Maring warfare for a considerable time, the warfare remained the kind that could, through an already institutionalized systemic process, lead again to the adjustment of man/resource ratios whenever demographic and ecological conditions changed sufficiently to make it appropriate for this to happen.[31] Moreover, significant change in the conditions was a continuing possibility in the Maring region: new crops or new diseases could be introduced; the size of a population could be swelled by the arrival of refugees from elsewhere (cf. Watson, 1970); the demography of particular local groups could be drastically altered as, in the course of shifting their garden sites and residences in accordance with the requirements of swidden agriculture, they unwittingly moved either into a malarial zone or out of it. The adaptiveness of the institutionalization and persistence of a multi-phase process of war and peace with regulated escalations from phase to phase may be argued to derive from this changeability in demographic and ecological conditions.

I suspect that similar changeability obtained in both New Guinea and the rest of the world in places from which we have reports of modes of hostilities similar to recent Maring warfare. Conclusions from such reports to the effect that the warfare of the people studied—for example, the Dani and Jalé of West Irian (Heider, 1967: 838; Koch, 1970*a* and 1970*b*: 43 ff.) or the headhunters of north-east India (Fürer-Haimendorf, 1968: 28)—was unrelated to the adjustment of man/resource ratios need to be re-examined in light of the possibility suggested here.[32] In other words, just as about the Marings, it needs to be asked also about these other peoples whether their reported warfare might not have constituted only the first phases of a systemic process that would regularly escalate to territorial conquests and adjustments under some recurrent conditions, even if not under the conditions that obtained at the time of the hostilities which the ethnographers have described.

[31] When, if ever, such conditions obtained throughout the Maring region is problematic. Stanhope (1970: 38) has tentatively suggested that malaria and the limitations on food production imposed by the steep slope of the land have made Maring areas in the Simbai Valley a part of an ever-dying periphery into which populations spilled over from ever-expanding centers in the highlands. What Stanhope calls his model does not, however, rule out major population pressures in the past in the Simbai areas, for it does not specify either the time of arrival of malaria or the extent to which populations spilling over from the centers moved into the periphery by means of expansive warfare.

[32] While I have made no careful study of the data on warfare in these other regions, I can refer to some specific information which is in accord with the suggested possibility. Thus, in the case of the headhunters in north-east India, it is known that there were times when their warfare did lead to the taking of land (Shakespear, 1912:3–8; Soppitt, 1885:19–20). In the case of the Dugum Dani, Heider (1970: Chapter 3) found that, between his first period of field work in the early 1960's when he observed the ritualistic warfare depicted in the well-known film *Dead Birds* and his return visit in 1968, warfare had escalated to a secular phase which could lead to territorial conquests and which the Dani ethnographers had not previously known to be the kind of recurrent phase described by Heider in his latest work. Unfortunately, the data on Dugum Dani demographic and ecological conditions are inadequate for any rigorous testing of hypotheses about the role of warfare in adjusting man/resource ratios.

BIBLIOGRAPHY

Attenborough, D. (1960): *Quest in Paradise,* London.

Birdsell, J. B. (1957): "Some Population Problems Involving Pleistocene Man," *Cold Spring Harbor Symposia on Quantitative Biology,* Vol. 22, pp. 47–68.

Brookfield, H. C. (1962): "Local Study and Comparative Method: An Example from Central New Guinea," *Association of American Geographers, Annals,* Vol. 52, pp. 242–54.

Brookfield, H. C., and Brown, P. (1963): *Struggle for Land,* Melbourne.

Bunn, G., and Scott, G. (1962): *Languages of the Mount Hagen Sub-district,* Ukarumpa, Eastern Highlands, Territory of New Guinea: The Summer Institute of Linguistics.

Clarke, W. C. (1966): "From Extensive to Intensive Shifting Cultivation: A Succession from New Guinea," *Ethnology,* Vol. 5, pp. 347–59.

Clarke, W. C. (1968): *The Ndwimba Basin, Bismarck Mountains, New Guinea: Place and People,* unpublished Ph.D. dissertation in geography, University of California, Berkeley. (To be published as *Place and People: An Ecology of a New Guinean Community,* Berkeley.)

Cook, E. A. (1967): *Manga Social Organization,* unpublished Ph.D. dissertation in anthropology, Yale University, New Haven.

Fürer-Haimendorf, C. von (1968): "Violence: Can We Break the Habit?" (review of *War: The Anthropology of Armed Conflict and Aggression,* edited by M. Fried *et al.*), *Saturday Review,* June 1, pp. 27–29.

Heider, K. G. (1967): "Speculative Functionalism: Archaic Elements in New Guinea Dani Culture," *Anthropos,* Vol. 62, pp. 833–40.

Heider, K. G. (1970): *The Dugum Dani,* Viking Fund Publications in Anthropology No. 49, New York.

Koch, K.-F. (1970*a*): "Cannibalistic Revenge in Jalé Warfare," *Natural History,* February, pp. 40–51.

Koch, K.-F. (1970*b*): "Warfare and Anthropophagy in Jalé Society," *Bijdragen tot de Taal-, Land- en Volkenkunde, Anthropologica,* Vol. 12, pp. 37–58.

Lowman-Vayda, C. (1968): "Maring Big Men," *Anthropological Forum,* Vol. 2, pp. 199–243.

Lowman-Vayda, C.: *Art and War in a New Guinea Society* (in preparation, to be published by the Museum of Primitive Art, New York).

Meggitt, M. J. (1957*a*): "Enga Political Organization: A Preliminary Description," *Mankind,* Vol. 5, pp. 133–37.

Meggitt, M. J. (1957*b*): "The Ipili of the Porgera Valley, Western Highlands District, Territory of New Guinea," *Oceania,* Vol. 28, pp. 31–55.

Meggitt, M. J. (1962): "Growth and Decline of Agnatic Descent Groups Among the Mae Enga of the New Guinea Highlands," *Ethnology,* Vol. 1, pp. 158–65.

Meggitt, M. J. (1965): *The Lineage System of the Mae-Enga of New Guinea,* Edinburgh.

Meggitt, M. J. (n.d.): "Pigs Are Our Hearts!: The Te Exchange Cycle Among the Mae Enga of New Guinea," paper for publication in a symposium, ed. A. Strathern, concerning systems of exchange in the New Guinea highlands.

Rappaport, R. A. (1967): *Pigs for the Ancestors,* New Haven.

Salisbury, R. F. (1963): "Ceremonial Economics and Political Equilibrium," *VI*[e] *Congrès International des Sciences Anthropologiques et Ethnologiques, II. Ethnologie,* Vol. 1, Paris: Musée de l'Homme.

Shakespear, J. (1912): *The Lushei-Kuki Clans,* London.

Soppitt, C. A. (1885): *A Short Account of the Kachcha Nâga (Empêo) Tribe in the North Cachar Hills,* Shillong.

Souter, G. (1964): *New Guinea: The Last Unknown,* Sydney.

Stanhope, J. M. (1970): "Patterns of Fertility and Mortality in Rural New Guinea," *People and Planning in Papua and New Guinea,* ed. M. W. Ward, New Guinea Research Bulletin No. 34, Canberra.

Street, J. M. (1969): "An Evaluation of the Concept of Carrying Capacity," *Professional Geographer,* Vol. 21, pp. 104–107.

Street, J. M. (n.d.): "Soil Conservation by Shifting Cultivators in the Bismarck Mountains of New Guinea," unpublished paper.

Vayda, A. P. (1960): *Maori Warfare,* Polynesian Society Maori Monographs No. 2, Wellington.

Vayda, A. P. (1961): "Expansion and Warfare Among Swidden Agriculturalists," *American Anthropologist,* Vol. 63, pp. 346–58.

Vayda, A. P. (1967): "Research on the Functions of Primitive War," *Peace Research Society (International), Papers,* Vol. 7, pp. 133–38.

Vayda, A. P. (1970): "Maoris and Muskets in New Zealand: Disruption of a War System," *Political Science Quarterly,* Vol. 85, pp. 560–84.

Vayda, A. P.: "Pig Complex," *Encyclopaedia of Papua and New Guinea,* Melbourne (in press).

Vayda, A. P., and Cook, E. A. (1964): "Structural Variability in the Bismarck Mountain Cultures of New Guinea: A Preliminary Report," *New York Academy of Sciences, Transactions,* Vol. 26, pp. 798–803.

Vayda, A. P., Leeds, A., and Smith, D. B. (1961). "The Place of Pigs in Melanesian Subsistence," *Proceedings of the 1961 Annual Spring Meeting of the American Ethnological Society,* ed. V. E. Garfield, Seattle.

Vial, L. G. (1942): "They Fight for Fun," *Walkabout,* Vol. 9, No. 1, pp. 5–9.

Watson, J. B. (1970): "Society as Organized Flow: The Tairora Case," *Southwestern Journal of Anthropology,* Vol. 26, pp. 107–24.

Wurm, S. A., and Laycock, D. C. (1961): "The Question of Language and Dialect in New Guinea," *Oceania,* Vol. 32, pp. 128–43.

Wynne-Edwards, V. C. (1962): *Animal Dispersion in Relation to Social Behaviour.* Edinburgh.

PART SIX
Ideology

Religious and Magical Beliefs and Practices

Ideology, some system of beliefs explaining human origins, defining our place in the cosmos, providing a guide to our relations with others, and accompanied always by a system of observances, is a universal aspect of culture. Although most ideological systems are based on metaphysical premises and entail belief in one or more sources of supernatural power—gods, spirits, angels, devils, and so on—supernaturalism is *not* an essential component of ideology. For many, nonreligious, scientifically or philosophically derived beliefs provide with equal adequacy the explanations every people require to give meaning to their existence, to guide and to justify their actions. The beliefs of the atheistic humanist, the nihilist, and the agnostic are often just as strongly held and provide sources of emotional comfort and security similar to those derived from religious conviction. We all know some individuals, and some of us know whole groups of people, who are explicitly nonreligious. But none of us knows anyone without an ideology.

Whether it is based on or includes belief in the supernatural, every ideology is comprised of two major components: (1) a system of beliefs; and (2) a system of observances based on these beliefs that function to reinforce them. The Moslem pilgrim to Mecca observes a ritual that he believes was prescribed by his deity. In doing so his faith is deepened. The Orthodox Jew avoids pork in observation of a dietary law he regards as divinely dictated. Each repetition of this ritual abstinence is a reminder of the belief that prescribes it. The Christian who gathers with others to worship at daybreak on Easter acts in accordance with the belief that Jesus rose from the dead and was carried bodily up to heaven. Participation in ceremonial re-enactment of the Resurrection reportedly leaves the true believer "spiritually renewed." The belief system provides the guides both to such ritual actions as these and to everyday living. Following the religiously prescribed path offers believers both a sense of ideological righteousness and of increased security in relation to the supernatural powers—religious or magical (or both)—that they believe affect their lives.

Because most of the peoples of the world still adhere to supernaturally based beliefs, religion and magic have so far received more attention from anthropologists than other ideological forms. Consequently we know more about these two subjects than we do about nonsupernatural systems of belief and practice. So far ethics and values have rarely been separately examined, for example. Instead, they have been studied (perhaps properly) as aspects of essentially economic, social, or political philosophies. Their place in anthropological inquiry is not yet as well defined as it needs to be.

But about religion and magic quite a lot has been learned. In fact, "primitive religion," a title that may initially evoke visions of thundering drums, mumbled incantations, satanic shrieks, and sweaty bodies writhing in fertility rites, is an old subject in ethnology. With proper study this understandable fascination with the possibility of vicariously observing heathenish practices gives way to an appreciation of other people's beliefs and observances as logical projections of their culturally determined life experience.

The observances that accompany ideology always vary in accordance with the beliefs themselves. They may take such diverse forms as prayer, sacrifice (a quarter in the collection plate, abstinence from alcohol, a severed human head), withdrawal from the world, celibacy, promiscuity, elaborate liturgy, stark ceremonial simplicity, mutilation, and even self-destruction. Regardless of their specific composition, such observances usually offer the believer a means of establishing and maintaining a secure relationship with what he considers to be the supernatural sources of his support. When such actions fail to bring the result desired, an explanation is always available: the greater wisdom of the deity, the unworthiness of the supplicant, or the maliciousness of an intervening spirit.

In short, some system of beliefs and observances providing people with a reason for being and a rationale for action is the universal. The specifics of creed and ceremony are the variables.

SECTION I

Religious Controls and Religious Change

A major function of every system of beliefs and observances is to offer its adherents a sense that they comprehend the forces that affect their lives and that by properly applying this understanding they can control in some measure the effect of such forces. No matter how apparently selfless, every form of worship aims at control. Its purpose is to achieve change, usually to improve the status of the worshiper, of someone else, of some group, or of the world, by supernatural means—alleviating suffering, enhancing the believer's chances of heavenly reward, or sending an adversary to hell.

In technologically advanced societies such as our own, efforts at control through supplication are often low-key and sometimes seem lacking in a sense of urgency or even conviction. Perhaps this is because we now have so many alternative means of trying to acquire control over the forces that affect us. Many of these alternative techniques are explicitly scientific and nonsupernatural. It has been observed that it is only when these means seem to fail that many turn with fervor to magicoreligious ways of seeking help.

In our society this switch from reliance upon supernaturalism to science as a source of control has occurred slowly, through long centuries of comparatively gradual ideological adaptation to ongoing social and cultural changes. Schisms have occurred, of course. Wars have been fought, at least partially, over ideological differences. But whether orderly or full of conflict, the process has been comparatively slow; slow enough, for example, to enable two of the great religions of the Middle East, Judaism and Christianity, to adjust their original theological tenets so that millions still find them useful guides to modern living.

Ideological accommodation becomes more difficult as the rate of cultural change speeds up. Beliefs and practices thought to have been divinely inspired (and usually conveyed to humankind through the intermediary of a prophet) usually define forms of traditional cultural behavior as being religiously right and condemn new and alternative forms as religiously wrong. Often new forms are pronounced sinful and those who adopt them risk supernatural punishment.

When quickly changing cultural circumstances render past patterns of behavior maladaptive, the devout are caught in a bind. Abandoning old ways and following what is new in patterns of economic, social, and political behavior may enhance their survival chances in this life. But, according to their beliefs, such changes may imperil their immortal souls and dim their prospects for a joyous hereafter. The conflict between ideology and the exigencies of action in a changing world is painful. Part of the pain often comes from a sense of losing control.

Whatever the level of efficiency and sophistication of a particular people's pattern of technoenvironmental adaptation, they are all—*we* are all—dependent for survival upon the action of natural forces (climatic, geological, topographical, and demographic) over which we are powerless. Natural laws can never be altered. All we can do is try to understand them and adjust our behavior accordingly.

Most people tend not to accept this distinction and strive persistently for mastery over the forces of nature that so radically affect their well-being. Whenever most natural phenomena and most cause-and-effect relationships are explained in magical and religious terms people logically seek magicoreligious means of controlling them. Frequently they do so through participation in rituals similar in their intended function to those of the Tsembaga of New Guinea described by Rappaport. His account both suggests the unperceived adaptive value of such ritual observances and underscores the widespread interplay between dependence upon the forces of nature and human efforts at control through ritual action.

Ritual Regulation of Environmental Relations Among the Tsembaga[1]

Roy A. Rappaport

Most functional studies of religious behavior in anthropology have as an analytic goal the elucidation of events, processes, or relationships occurring within a social unit of some sort. The social unit is not always well defined, but in some cases it appears to be a church, that is, a group of people who entertain similar beliefs about the universe, or a congregation, a group of people who participate together in the performance of religious rituals. There have been exceptions. Thus Vayda, Leeds, and Smith (1961) and O. K. Moore (1957) have clearly perceived that the functions of religious ritual are not necessarily confined within the boundaries of a congregation or even a church. By and large, however, I believe that the following statement by Homans (1941: 172) represents fairly the dominant line of anthropological thought concerning the functions of religious ritual:

> Ritual actions do not produce a practical result on the external world–that is one of the reasons why we call them ritual. But to make this statement is not to say that ritual has no function. Its function is not related to the world external to the society but to the internal constitution of the society. It gives the members of the society confidence, it dispels their anxieties, it disciplines their social organization.

No argument will be raised here against the sociological and psychological functions imputed by Homans, and many others before him, to ritual. They seem to me to be plausible. Nevertheless, in some cases at least, ritual does produce, in Homans' terms, "a practical result on the world" external not only to the social unit composed of those who participate together in ritual performances but also to the larger unit composed of those who entertain similar beliefs concerning the universe. The material pre-

Source: From Roy A. Rappaport, "Ritual Regulation of Environmental Relations Among a New Guinea People," *Ethnology,* Vol. 6 (1967), pp. 17–30. Used by permission of the publisher and the author.

1 The field work upon which this paper is based was supported by a grant from the National Science Foundation, under which Professor A. P. Vayda was principal investigator. Personal support was received by the author from the National Institutes of Health. Earlier versions of this paper were presented at the 1964 annual meeting of the American Anthropological Association in Detroit, and before a Columbia University seminar on Ecological Systems and Cultural Evolution. I have received valuable suggestions from Alexander Alland, Jacques Barrau, William Clarke, Paul Collins, C. Glen King, Marvin Harris, Margaret Mead, M. J., Meggitt, Ann Rappaport, John Street, Marjorie Whiting, Cherry Vayda, A. P. Vayda and many others, but I take full responsibility for the analysis presented herewith.

sented here will show that the ritual cycles of the Tsembaga, and of other local territorial groups of Maring speakers living in the New Guinea interior, play an important part in regulating the relationships of these groups with both the nonhuman components of their immediate environments and the human components of their less immediate environments, that is, with other similar territorial groups. To be more specific, this regulation helps to maintain the biotic communities existing within their territories, redistributes land among people and people over land, and limits the frequency of fighting. In the absence of authoritative political statuses or offices, the ritual cycle likewise provides a means for mobilizing allies when warfare may be undertaken. It also provides a mechanism for redistributing local pig surpluses in the form of pork throughout a large regional population while helping to assure the local population of a supply of pork when its members are most in need of high quality protein.

Religious ritual may be defined, for the purposes of this paper, as the prescribed performance of conventionalized acts manifestly directed toward the involvement of nonempirical or supernatural agencies in the affairs of the actors. While this definition relies upon the formal characteristics of the performances and upon the motives for undertaking them, attention will be focused upon the empirical effects of ritual performances and sequences of ritual performances. The religious rituals to be discussed are regarded as neither more nor less than part of the behavioral repertoire employed by an aggregate of organisms in adjusting to its environment.

The data upon which this paper is based were collected during fourteen months of field work among the Tsembaga, one of about twenty local groups of Maring speakers living in the Simbai and Jimi Valleys of the Bismarck Range in the Territory of New Guinea. The size of Maring local groups varies from a little over 100 to 900. The Tsembaga, who in 1963 numbered 204 persons, are located on the south wall of the Simbai Valley. The country in which they live differs from the true highlands in being lower, generally more rugged, and more heavily forested. Tsembaga territory rises, within a total surface area of 3.2 square miles, from an elevation of 2,200 feet at the Simbai river to 7,200 feet at the ridge crest. Gardens are cut in the secondary forests up to between 5,000 and 5,400 feet, above which the area remains in primary forest. Rainfall reaches 150 inches per year.

The Tsembaga have come into contact with the outside world only recently; the first government patrol to penetrate their territory arrived in 1954. They were considered uncontrolled by the Australian government until 1962, and they remain unmissionized to this day.

The 204 Tsembaga are distributed among five putatively patrilineal clans, which are, in turn, organized into more inclusive groupings on two hierarchical levels below that of the total local group.[2] Internal political structure is highly egalitarian. There are no hereditary or elected chiefs, nor are there even "big men" who can regularly coerce or command the support of their clansmen or co-residents in economic or forceful enterprises.

It is convenient to regard the Tsembaga as a population in the ecological sense, that is, as one of the components of a system of trophic exchanges taking place within a bounded area. Tsembaga territory and the biotic community existing upon it may be conveniently viewed as an ecosystem. While it would be permissible arbitrarily to designate the Tsembaga as a population and their territory with its biota as an ecosystem, there are also nonarbitrary reasons for doing so. An ecosystem is a system of material exchanges, and the Tsembaga maintain against other human groups exclusive access to the resources within their territorial borders. Conversely, it is from this territory alone that the Tsembaga ordinarily derive all of their foodstuffs and most of the other materials they require for survival. Less anthropocentrically, it may be justified to regard Tsembaga territory with its biota as an ecosystem in view of the rather localized nature of cyclical material exchanges in tropical rainforests.

As they are involved with the nonhuman biotic community within their territory in a set of trophic exchanges, so do they participate in other material relationships with other human groups external to their territory. Genetic materials are exchanged with other groups, and certain crucial items, such as stone axes, were in the past obtained from outside. Furthermore, in

2 The social organization of the Tsembaga will be described in detail elsewhere.

the area occupied by the Maring speakers, more than one local group is usually involved in any process, either peaceful or warlike, through which people are redistributed over land and land redistributed among people.

The concept of the ecosystem, though it provides a convenient frame for the analysis of interspecific trophic exchanges taking place within limited geographical areas, does not comfortably accommodate intraspecific exchanges taking place over wider geographic areas. Some sort of geographic population model would be more useful for the analysis of the relationship of the local ecological population to the larger regional population of which it is a part, but we lack even a set of appropriate terms for such a model. Suffice it here to note that the relations of the Tsembaga to the total of other local human populations in their vicinity are similar to the relations of local aggregates of other animals to the totality of their species occupying broader and more or less continuous regions. This larger, more inclusive aggregate may resemble what geneticists mean by the term population, that is, an aggregate of interbreeding organisms persisting through an indefinite number of generations and either living or capable of living in isolation from similar aggregates of the same species. This is the unit which survives through long periods of time while its local ecological (*sensu stricto*) subunits, the units more or less independently involved in interspecific trophic exchanges such as the Tsembaga, are ephemeral.

Since it has been asserted that the ritual cycles of the Tsembaga regulate relationships within what may be regarded as a complex system, it is necessary, before proceeding to the ritual cycle itself, to describe briefly, and where possible in quantitative terms, some aspects of the place of the Tsembaga in this system.

The Tsembaga are bush-fallowing horticulturalists. Staples include a range of root crops, taro (*Colocasia*) and sweet potatoes being most important, yams and manioc less so. In addition, a great variety of greens are raised, some of which are rich in protein. Sugar cane and some tree crops, particularly *Pandanus conoideus*, are also important.

All gardens are mixed, many of them containing all of the major root crops and many greens. Two named garden types are, however, distinguished by the crops which predominate in them. "Taro-yam gardens" were found to produce, on the basis of daily harvest records kept on entire gardens for close to one year, about 5,300,000 calories[3] per acre during their harvesting lives of 18 to 24 months; 85 per cent of their yield is harvested between 24 and 76 weeks after planting. "Sugar-sweet potato gardens" produce about 4,600,000 calories per acre during their harvesting lives, 91 per cent being taken between 24 and 76 weeks after planting. I estimated that approximately 310,000 calories per acre is expended on cutting, fencing, planting, maintaining, harvesting, and walking to and from taro-yam gardens. Sugar-sweet potato gardens required an expenditure of approximately 290,000 calories per acre.[4] These energy ratios, approximately 17:1 on taro-yam gardens and 16:1 on sugar-sweet potato gardens, compare favorably with figures reported for swidden cultivation in other regions.[5]

Intake is high in comparison with the reported dietaries of other New Guinea populations. On the basis of daily consumption records kept for ten months on four households numbering in total sixteen persons, I estimated the average daily intake of adult males to be approximately 2,600 calories, and that of adult females to be around 2,200 calories. It may be mentioned here that the Tsembaga are small

[3] Because the length of time in the field precluded the possibility of maintaining harvest records on single gardens from planting through abandonment, figures were based, in the case of both "taro-yam" and "sugar-sweet potato" gardens, on three separate gardens planted in successive years. Conversions from the gross weight to the caloric value of yields were made by reference to the literature. The sources used are listed in Rappaport (1966:Appendix VIII).

[4] Rough time and motion studies of each of the tasks involved in making, maintaining, harvesting, and walking to and from gardens were undertaken. Conversion to energy expenditure values was accomplished by reference to energy expenditure tables prepared by Hipsley and Kirk (1965:43) on the basis of gas exchange measurements made during the performance of garden tasks by the Chimbu people of the New Guinea highlands.

[5] Marvin Harris, in an unpublished paper, estimates the ratio of energy return to energy input ratio on Dyak (Borneo) rice swiddens at 10:1. His estimates of energy ratios on Tepotzlan (Meso-America) swiddens range from 13:1 on poor land to 29:1 on the best land.

and short statured. Adult males average 101 pounds in weight and approximately 58.5 inches in height; the corresponding averages for adult females are 85 pounds and 54.5 inches.[6]

Although 99 per cent by weight of the food consumed is vegetable, the protein intake is high by New Guinea standards. The daily protein consumption of adult males from vegetable sources was estimated to be between 43 and 55 grams, of adult females 36 to 48 grams. Even with an adjustment for vegetable sources, these values are slightly in excess of the recently published WHO/FAO daily requirements (Food and Agriculture Organization of the United Nations 1964). The same is true of the younger age categories, although soft and discolored hair, a symptom of protein deficiency, was noted in a few children. The WHO/FAO protein requirements do not include a large "margin for safety" or allowance for stress; and, although no clinical assessments were undertaken, it may be suggested that the Tsembaga achieve nitrogen balance at a low level. In other words, their protein intake is probably marginal.

Measurements of all gardens made during 1962 and of some gardens made during 1963 indicate that, to support the human population, between .15 and .19 acres are put into cultivation per capita per year. Fallows range from 8 to 45 years. The area in secondary forest comprises approximately 1,000 acres, only 30 to 50 of which are in cultivation at any time. Assuming calories to be the limiting factor, and assuming an unchanging population structure, the territory could support—with no reduction in lengths of fallow and without cutting into the virgin forest from which the Tsembaga extract many important items—between 290 and 397 people if the pig population remained minimal. The size of the pig herd, however, fluctuates widely. Taking Maring pig husbandry procedures into consideration, I have estimated the human carrying capacity of the Tsembaga territory at between 270 and 320 people.

Because the timing of the ritual cycle is bound up with the demography of the pig herd, the place of the pig in Tsembaga adaptation must be examined.

First, being omnivorous, pigs keep residential areas free of garbage and human feces. Second, limited numbers of pigs rooting in secondary growth may help to hasten the development of that growth. The Tsembaga usually permit pigs to enter their gardens one and a half to two years after planting, by which time second-growth trees are well established there. The Tsembaga practice selective weeding; from the time the garden is planted, herbaceous species are removed, but tree species are allowed to remain. By the time cropping is discontinued and the pigs are let in, some of the trees in the garden are already ten to fifteen feet tall. These well-established trees are relatively impervious to damage by the pigs, which, in rooting for seeds and remaining tubers, eliminate many seeds and seedlings that, if allowed to develop, would provide some competition for the established trees. Moreover, in some Maring-speaking areas swiddens are planted twice, although this is not the case with the Tsembaga. After the first crop is almost exhausted, pigs are penned in the garden, where their rooting eliminates weeds and softens the ground, making the task of planting for a second time easier. The pigs, in other words, are used as cultivating machines.

Small numbers of pigs are easy to keep. They run free during the day and return home at night to receive their ration of garbage and substandard tubers, particularly sweet potatoes. Supplying the latter requires little extra work, for the substandard tubers are taken from the ground in the course of harvesting the daily ration for humans. Daily consumption records kept over a period of some months show that the ration of tubers received by the pigs approximates in weight that consumed by adult humans, i.e., a little less than three pounds per day per pig.

If the pig herd grows large, however, the substandard tubers incidentally obtained in the course of harvesting for human needs become insufficient, and it becomes necessary to harvest especially for pigs. In other words, people must work for the pigs and perhaps even supply them with food fit for human consumption. Thus, as Vayda, Leeds, and Smith (1961: 71) have pointed out, there can be too many pigs for a given community.

This also holds true of the sanitary and cultivating services rendered by pigs. A small number of pigs is sufficient to keep residential areas clean, to suppress superfluous seedlings in aban-

[6] Heights may be inaccurate. Many men wear their hair in large coiffures hardened with pandanus grease, and it was necessary in some instances to estimate the location of the top of the skull.

doned gardens, and to soften the soil in gardens scheduled for second plantings. A larger herd, on the other hand, may be troublesome; the larger the number of pigs, the greater the possibility of their invasion of producing gardens, with concomitant damage not only to crops and young secondary growth but also to the relations between the pig owners and garden owners.

All male pigs are castrated at approximately three months of age, for boars, people say, are dangerous and do not grow as large as barrows. Pregnancies, therefore, are always the result of unions of domestic sows with feral males. Fecundity is thus only a fraction of its potential. During one twelve-month period only fourteen litters resulted out of a potential 99 or more pregnancies. Farrowing generally takes place in the forest, and mortality of the young is high. Only 32 of the offspring of the above-mentioned fourteen pregnancies were alive six months after birth. This number is barely sufficient to replace the number of adult animals which would have died or been killed during most years without pig festivals.

The Tsembaga almost never kill domestic pigs outside of ritual contexts. In ordinary times, when there is no pig festival in progress, these rituals are almost always associated with misfortunes or emergencies, notably warfare, illness, injury, or death. Rules state not only the contexts in which pigs are to be ritually slaughtered, but also who may partake of the flesh of the sacrificial animals. During warfare it is only the men participating in the fighting who eat the pork. In cases of illness or injury, it is only the victim and certain near relatives, particularly his co-resident agnates and spouses, who do so.

It is reasonable to assume that misfortune and emergency are likely to induce in the organisms experiencing them a complex of physiological changes known collectively as "stress." Physiological stress reactions occur not only in organisms which are infected with disease or traumatized, but also in those experiencing rage or fear (Houssay *et al.* 1955: 1096), or even prolonged anxiety (National Research Council 1963: 53). One important aspect of stress is the increased catabolization of protein (Houssay *et al.* 1955: 451; National Research Council 1963: 49), with a net loss of nitrogen from the tissues (Houssay *et al.* 1955: 450). This is a serious matter for organisms with a marginal protein intake. Antibody production is low (Berg 1948: 311), healing is slow (Large and Johnston 1948: 352), and a variety of symptoms of a serious nature are likely to develop (Lund and Levenson 1948: 349; Zintel 1964: 1043). The status of a protein-depleted animal, however, may be significantly improved in a relatively short period of time by the intake of high quality protein, and high protein diets are therefore routinely prescribed for surgical patients and those suffering from infectious diseases (Burton 1959: 231; Lund and Levenson 1948: 350; Elman 1951: 85ff; Zintel 1964: 1043ff).

It is precisely when they are undergoing physiological stress that the Tsembaga kill and consume their pigs, and it should be noted that they limit the consumption to those likely to be experiencing stress most profoundly. The Tsembaga, of course, know nothing of physiological stress. Native theories of the etiology and treatment of disease and injury implicate various categories of spirits to whom sacrifices must be made. Nevertheless, the behavior which is appropriate in terms of native understandings is also appropriate to the actual situation confronting the actors.

We may now outline in the barest of terms the Tsembaga ritual cycle. Space does not permit a description of its ideological correlates. It must suffice to note that Tsembaga do not necessarily perceive all of the empirical effects which the anthropologist sees to flow from their ritual behavior. Such empirical consequences as they may perceive, moreover, are not central to their rationalizations of the performances. The Tsembaga say that they perform the rituals in order to rearrange their relationships with the supernatural world. We may only reiterate here that behavior undertaken in reference to their "cognized environment"—an environment which includes as very important elements the spirits of ancestors—seems appropriate in their "operational environment," the material environment specified by the anthropologist through operations of observation, including measurement.

Since the rituals are arranged in a cycle, description may commence at any point. The operation of the cycle becomes clearest if we begin with the rituals performed during warfare. Opponents in all cases occupy adjacent territories, in almost all cases on the same valley wall. After hostilities have broken out, each side performs certain rituals which place the opposing side in the formal category of "enemy." A number of taboos prevail while hostilities continue. These include prohibitions on sexual intercourse and on the ingestion of certain things—food prepared by women, food grown on the lower portion of the territory, marsupials, eels, and, while actually on the fighting ground, any liquid whatsoever.

One ritual practice associated with fighting which may have some physiological consequences deserves mention. Immediately before proceeding to the fighting ground, the warriors eat heavily salted pig fat. The ingestion of salt, coupled with the taboo on drinking, has the effect of shortening the fighting day, particularly since the Maring prefer to fight only on bright sunny days. When everyone gets unbearably thirsty, according to informants, fighting is broken off.

There may formerly have been other effects if the native salt contained sodium (the production of salt was discontinued some years previous to the field work, and no samples were obtained). The Maring diet seems to be deficient in sodium. The ingestion of large amounts of sodium just prior to fighting would have permitted the warriors to sweat normally without a lowering of blood volume and consequent weakness during the course of the fighting. The pork belly ingested with the salt would have provided them with a new burst of energy two hours or so after the commencement of the engagement. After fighting was finished for the day, lean pork was consumed, offsetting, at least to some extent, the nitrogen loss associated with the stressful fighting (personal communications from F. Dunn, W. MacFarlane, and J. Sabine, 1965).

Fighting could continue sporadically for weeks. Occasionally it terminated in the rout of one of the antagonistic groups, whose survivors would take refuge with kinsmen elsewhere. In such instances, the victors would lay waste their opponents' groves and gardens, slaughter their pigs, and burn their houses. They would not, however, immediately annex the territory of the vanquished. The Maring say that they never take over the territory of an enemy for, even if it has been abandoned, the spirits of their ancestors remain to guard it against interlopers. Most fights, however, terminated in truces between the antagonists.

With the termination of hostilities a group which has not been driven off its territory performs a ritual called "planting the *rumbim*." Every man puts his hand on the ritual plant, *rumbim* (*Cordyline fruticosa* (L.), A. Chev; C. *terminalis*, Kunth), as it is planted in the ground. The ancestors are addressed, in effect, as follows:

> We thank you for helping us in the fight and permitting us to remain on our territory. We place our souls in this *rumbim* as we plant it on our ground. We ask you to care for this *rumbim*. We will kill pigs for you now, but they are few. In the future, when we have many pigs, we shall again give you pork and uproot the *rumbim* and stage a *kaiko* (pig festival). But until there are sufficient pigs to repay you the *rumbim* will remain in the ground.

This ritual is accompanied by the wholesale slaughter of pigs. Only juveniles remain alive. All adult and adolescent animals are killed, cooked, and dedicated to the ancestors. Some are consumed by the local group, but most are distributed to allies who assisted in the fight.

Some of the taboos which the group suffered during the time of fighting are abrogated by this ritual. Sexual intercourse is now permitted, liquids may be taken at any time, and food from any part of the territory may be eaten. But the group is still in debt to its allies and ancestors. People say it is still the time of the *bamp ku*, or "fighting stones," which are actual objects used in the rituals associated with warfare. Although the fighting ceases when *rumbim* is planted, the concomitant obligations, debts to allies and ancestors, remain outstanding; and the fighting stones may not be put away until these obligations are fulfilled. The time of the fighting stones is a time of debt and danger which lasts until the *rumbim* is uprooted and a pig festival (*kaiko*) is staged.

Certain taboos persist during the time of the fighting stones. Marsupials, regarded as the pigs of the ancestors of the high ground, may not be trapped until the debt to their masters has been repaid. Eels, the "pigs of the ancestors of the low ground," may neither be caught nor consumed. Prohibitions on all intercourse with the enemy come into force. One may not touch, talk to, or even look at a member of the enemy group, nor set foot on enemy ground. Even more important, a group may not attack another group while its ritual plant remains in the ground, for it has not yet fully rewarded its ancestors and allies for their assistance in the last fight. Until the debts to them have been paid, further assistance from them will not be forthcoming. A kind of "truce of god" thus prevails until the *rumbim* is uprooted and a *kaiko* completed.

To uproot the *rumbim* requires sufficient pigs. How many pigs are sufficient, and how long does it take to acquire them? The Tsembaga say that, if a place is "good," this can take as little as five years; but if a place is "bad," it may require ten years or longer. A bad place is one in which misfortunes are frequent and where, therefore, ritual demands for the killing of pigs arise frequently. A good place is one where such demands are infrequent. In a good place, the increase of the pig herd exceeds the ongoing ritual demands, and the herd grows rapidly. Sooner or later the substandard tubers incidentally obtained while harvesting become insufficient to feed the herd, and additional acreage must be put into production specifically for the pigs.

The work involved in caring for a large pig herd can be extremely burdensome. The Tsembaga herd just prior to the pig festival of 1962–63, when it numbered 169 animals, was receiving 54 per cent of all of the sweet potatoes and 82 per cent of all of the manioc harvested. These comprised 35.9 per cent by weight of all root crops harvested. This figure is consistent with the difference between the amount of land under cultivation just previous to the pig festival, when the herd was at maximum size, and that immediately afterwards, when the pig herd was at minimum size. The former was 36.1 per cent in excess of the latter.

I have estimated, on the basis of acreage yield and energy expenditure figures, that about 45,000 calories per year are expended in caring for one pig 120–150 pounds in size. It is upon women that most of the burden of pig keeping falls. If, from a woman's daily intake of about 2,200 calories, 950 calories are allowed for basal metabolism, a woman has only 1,250 calories a day available for all her activities, which include gardening for her family, child care, and cooking, as well as tending pigs. It is clear that no woman can feed many pigs; only a few had as many as four in their care at the commencement of the festival; and it is not surprising that agitation to uproot the *rumbim* and stage the *kaiko* starts with the wives of the owners of large numbers of pigs.

A large herd is not only burdensome as far as energy expenditure is concerned; it becomes increasingly a nuisance as it expands. The more numerous pigs become, the more frequently are gardens invaded by them. Such events result in serious disturbances of local tranquility. The garden owner often shoots, or attempts to shoot, the offending pig; and the pig owner commonly retorts by shooting, or attempting to shoot, either the garden owner, his wife, or one of his pigs. As more and more such events occur, the settlement, nucleated when the herd was small, disperses as people try to put as much distance as possible between their pigs and other people's gardens and between their gardens and other people's pigs. Occasionally this reaches its logical conclusion, and people begin to leave the territory, taking up residence with kinsmen in other local populations.

The number of pigs sufficient to become intolerable to the Tsembaga was below the capacity of the territory to carry pigs. I have estimated that, if the size and structure of the human population remained constant at the 1962–1963 level, a pig population of 140 to 240 animals averaging 100 to 150 pounds in size could be maintained perpetually by the Tsembaga without necessarily inducing environmental degradation. Since the size of the herd fluctuates, even higher cyclical maxima could be achieved. The level of toleration, however, is likely always to be below the carrying capacity, since the destructive capacity of the pigs is dependent upon the population density of both people and pigs, rather than upon population size. The denser the human population, the fewer pigs will be required to disrupt social life. If the carrying capacity is exceeded, it is likely to be exceeded by people and not by pigs.

The *kaiko* or pig festival, which commences with the planting of stakes at the boundary and the uprooting of the *rumbim*, is thus triggered by either the additional work attendant upon feeding pigs or the destructive capacity of the pigs themselves. It may be said, then, that there are sufficient pigs to stage the *kaiko* when the relationship of pigs to people changes from one of mutualism to one of parasitism or competition.

A short time prior to the uprooting of the *rumbim*, stakes are planted at the boundary. If the enemy has continued to occupy its territory, the stakes are planted at the boundary which existed before the fight. If, on the other hand, the enemy has abandoned its territory, the victors may plant their stakes at a new boundary which encompasses areas previously occupied by the enemy. The Maring say, to be sure, that they never take land belonging to an enemy, but this land is regarded as vacant, since no *rumbim* was planted on it after the last fight. We may state here a rule of land redistribution in terms of the ritual cycle: *If one of a pair of antagonistic groups is able to uproot its rumbim before its opponents can plant their rumbim, it may occupy the latter's territory.*

Not only have the vanquished abandoned their territory; it is assumed that it has also been abandoned by their ancestors as well. The surviving members of the erstwhile enemy group have by this time resided with other groups for a number of years, and most if not all of them have already had occasion to sacrifice pigs to their ancestors at their new residences. In so doing they have invited these spirits to settle at the new locations of the living, where they will in the future receive sacrifices. Ancestors of vanquished groups thus relinquish their guardianship over the territory, making it available to victorious groups. Meanwhile, the *de facto* membership of the living in the groups with which they have taken refuge is converted eventually into *de jure* membership. Sooner or later the groups with which they have taken up residence will have occasion to plant *rumbim*, and the refugees, as co-residents, will participate, thus ritually validating their connection to the new territory and the new group. A rule of population redistribution may thus be stated in terms of ritual cycles: *A man becomes a member of a territorial group by participating with it in the planting of rumbim.*

The uprooting of the *rumbim* follows shortly after the planting of stakes at the boundary. On this particular occasion the Tsembaga killed 32 pigs out of their herd of 169. Much of the pork was distributed to allies and affines outside of the local group.

The taboo on trapping marsupials was also terminated at this time. Information is lacking concerning the population dynamics of the local marsupials, but it may well be that the taboo which had prevailed since the last fight—that against taking them in traps—had conserved a fauna which might otherwise have become extinct.

The *kaiko* continues for about a year, during which period friendly groups are entertained from time to time. The guests receive presents of vegetable foods, and the hosts and male guests dance together throughout the night.

These events may be regarded as analogous to aspects of the social behavior of many nonhuman animals. First of all, they include massed epigamic, or courtship, displays (Wynne-Edwards 1962: 17). Young women are presented with samples of the eligible males of local groups with which they may not otherwise have had the opportunity to become familiar. The context, moreover, permits the young women to discriminate amongst this sample in terms of both endurance (signaled by how vigorously and how long a man dances) and wealth (signaled by the richness of a man's shell and feather finery).

More importantly, the massed dancing at these events may be regarded as epideictic display, communicating to the participants information concerning the size or density of the group (Wynne-Edwards 1962: 16). In many species such displays take place as a prelude to actions which adjust group size or density, and such is the case among the Maring. The massed dancing of the visitors at a *kaiko* entertainment communicates to the hosts, while the *rumbim* truce is still in force, information concerning the amount of support they may expect from the visitors in the bellicose enterprises that they are likely to embark upon soon after the termination of the pig festival.

Among the Maring there are no chiefs or other political authorities capable of commanding the support of a body of followers, and the decision to assist another group in warfare rests with each individual male. Allies are not recruited by appealing for help to other local groups as such. Rather, each member of the groups primarily involved in the hostilities appeal to his cognatic and affinal kinsmen in other local groups. These men, in turn, urge other of their co-residents and kinsmen to "help them fight." The channels through which invitations to dance are extended are precisely those through which appeals for military support are issued. The invitations go not from group to group, but from kinsman to kinsman, the recipients of invitations urging their co-residents to "help them dance."

Invitations to dance do more than exercise the channels through which allies are recruited; they provide a means for judging their effectiveness. Dancing and fighting are regarded as in some sense equivalent. This equivalence is expressed in the similarity of some pre-fight and pre-dance rituals, and the Maring say that those who come to dance come to fight. The size of a visiting dancing contingent is consequently taken as a measure of the size of the contingent of warriors whose assistance may be expected in the next round of warfare.

In the morning the dancing ground turns into a trading ground. The items most frequently exchanged include axes, bird plumes, shell ornaments, an occasional baby pig, and, in former times, native salt. The *kaiko* thus facilitates trade by providing a market-like setting in which large numbers of traders can assemble. It likewise facilitates the movement of two critical items, salt and axes, by creating a demand for the bird plumes which may be exchanged for them.

The *kaiko* concludes with major pig sacrifices. On this particular occasion the Tsembaga butchered 105 adult and adolescent pigs, leaving only 60 juveniles and neonates alive. The survival of an additional fifteen adolescents and adults was only temporary, for they were scheduled as imminent victims. The pork yielded by the Tsembaga slaughter was estimated to weigh between 7,000 and 8,500 pounds, of which between 4,500 and 6,000 pounds were distributed to members of other local groups in 163 separate presentations. An estimated 2,000 to 3,000 people in seventeen local groups were the beneficiaries of the redistribution. The presentations, it should be mentioned, were not confined to pork. Sixteen Tsembaga men presented bridewealth or child-wealth, consisting largely of axes and shells, to their affines at this time.

The *kaiko* terminates on the day of the pig slaughter with the public presentation of salted pig belly to allies of the last fight. Presentations are made through the window in a high ceremonial fence built especially for the occasion at one end of the dance ground. The name of each honored man is announced to the assembled multitude as he charges to the window to receive his hero's portion. The fence is then ritually torn down, and the fighting stones are put away. The pig festival and the ritual cycle have been completed, demonstrating, it may be suggested, the ecological and economic competence of the local population. The local population would now be free, if it were not for the presence of the government, to attack its enemy again, secure in the knowledge that the assistance of allies and ancestors would be forthcoming because they have received pork and the obligations to them have been fulfilled.

Usually fighting did break out again very soon after the completion of the ritual cycle. If peace still prevailed when the ceremonial fence had rotted completely—a process said to take about three years, a little longer than the length of time required to raise a pig to maximum size—*rumbim* was planted as if there had been a fight, and all adult and adolescent pigs were killed. When the pig herd was large enough so that the *rumbim* could be uprooted, peace could be made with former enemies if they were also able to dig out their *rumbim*. To put this in formal terms: *If a pair of antagonistic groups proceeds through two ritual cycles without resumption of hostilities their enmity may be terminated.*

The relations of the Tsembaga with their environment have been analyzed as a complex system composed of two subsystems. What may be called the "local subsystem" has been derived from the relations of the Tsembaga with the nonhuman components of their immediate or territorial environment. It corresponds to the ecosystem in which the Tsembaga participate. A second subsystem, one which corresponds to the larger regional population of which the Tsembaga are one of the constituent units and which may be designated as the "regional subsystem," has been derived from the relations of the Tsembaga with neighboring local populations similar to themselves.

It has been argued that rituals, arranged in repetitive sequences, regulate relations both within each of the subsystems and within the larger complex system as a whole. The timing of the ritual cycle is largely dependent upon changes in the states of the components of the local subsystem. But the *kaiko*, which is the culmination of the ritual cycle, does more than reverse changes which have taken place within the local subsystem. Its occurrence also affects relations among the components of the regional subsystem. During its performance, obligations to other local populations are fulfilled, support for future military enterprises is rallied, and land from which enemies have earlier been driven is occupied. Its completion, furthermore, permits the local population to initiate warfare again. Conversely, warfare is terminated by rituals which preclude the reinitiation of warfare until the state of the local subsystem is again such that a *kaiko* may be staged and completed. Ritual among the Tsembaga and other Maring, in short, operates as both transducer, "translating" changes in the state of one subsystem into information which can effect changes in a second subsystem, and homeostat, maintaining a number of variables which in sum comprise the total system within ranges of viability. To repeat an earlier assertion, the operation of ritual among the Tsembaga and other Maring helps to maintain an undegraded environment, limits fighting to frequencies which do not endanger the existence of the regional population, adjusts man-land ratios, facilitates trade, distributes local surpluses of pig throughout the regional population in the form of pork, and assures people of high quality protein when they are most in need of it.

Religious rituals and the supernatural orders toward which they are directed cannot be assumed *a priori* to be mere epiphenomena. Ritual may, and doubtless frequently does, do nothing more than validate and intensify the relationships which integrate the social unit, or symbolize the relationships which bind the social unit to its environment. But the interpretation of such presumably *sapiens*-specific phenomena as religious ritual within a framework which will also accommodate the behavior of other species shows, I think, that religious ritual may do much more than symbolize, validate, and intensify relationships. Indeed, it would not be improper to refer to the Tsembaga and the other entities with which they share their territory as a "ritually regulated ecosystem," and to the Tsembaga and their human neighbors as a "ritually regulated population."

BIBLIOGRAPHY

Berg, C. 1948. Protein Deficiency and Its Relation to Nutritional Anemia, Hypoproteinemia, Nutritional Edema, and Resistance to Infection. Protein and Amino Acids in Nutrition, ed. M. Sahyun, pp. 290–317. New York.

Burton, B. T., ed. 1959. The Heinz Handbook of Nutrition. New York.

Elman, R. 1961. Surgical Care. New York.

Food and Agriculture Organization of the United Nations. 1964. Protein: At the Heart of the World Food Problem. World Food Problems 5. Rome.

Hipsley, E., and N. Kirk. 1965. Studies of the Dietary Intake and Energy Expenditure of New Guineans. South Pacific Commission, Technical Paper 147. Noumea.

Homans, G. C. 1941. Anxiety and Ritual: The Theories of Malinowski and Radcliffe-Brown. American Anthropologist 43:164–172.

Houssay, B. A., *et al.* 1955. Human Physiology. 2nd edit. New York.

Large, A., and C. G. Johnston. 1948. Proteins as Related to Burns. Proteins and Amino Acids in Nutrition, ed. M. Sahyun, pp. 386–396. New York.

Lund, C. G., and S. M. Levenson. 1948. Protein Nutrition in Surgical Patients. Proteins and Amino Acids in Nutrition, ed. M. Sahyun, pp. 349–363. New York.

Moore, O. K. 1957. Divination—a New Perspective. American Anthropologist 59: 69–74.

National Research Council. 1963. Evaluation of Protein Quality. National Academy of Sciences—National Research Council Publication 1100. Washington.

Rappaport, R. A. 1966. Ritual in the Ecology of a New Guinea People. Unpublished doctoral dissertation, Columbia University.

Vayda, A. P., A. Leeds, and D. B. Smith. 1961. The Place of Pigs in Melanesian Subsistence. Proceedings of the 1961 Annual Spring Meeting of the American Ethnological Society, ed. V. E. Garfield, pp. 67–77. Seattle.

Wayne-Edwards, V. C. 1962. Animal Dispersion in Relation to Social Behaviour. Edinburgh and London.

Zintel, Harold A. 1964. Nutrition in the Care of the Surgical Patient. Modern Nutrition in Health and Disease, ed. M. G. Wohl and R. S. Goodhart, pp. 1043–1064. Third edit. Philadelphia.

Every people is as dependent for survival upon society as it is upon nature. For most, dependence upon the kin group is strongest. And for many this dependence is projected into a view of the afterlife that is structured in a way strikingly similar to that of the prevailing social order. Gods and other potent beings are believed to possess on a more grandiose scale powers much like parents' powerful relationship to their children: creating them, nurturing them, and looking out for their well-being—at least so long as they obey parental rules.

Ancestor worship is the most concrete instance of this widespread tendency to perceive the supernatural as organized similarly to society. The authoritative roles of senior members of the family are believed to be retained and strengthened after death. As ancestral spirits they watch over their descendants, protecting and helping those who follow the approved codes of conduct and threatening to punish—with disease, death, crop failure, bad luck in love—those who stray from the path of right action first set out by the ancestors. Although no longer living, they continue to play an important role in family affairs. And they can critically affect their descendants' destinies.

Kopytoff explores this phenomenon in Africa, where ancestor worship almost invariably reflects the importance of strong family ties as a major source of personal security and community stability.

Ancestors as Elders in Africa[1]

Igor Kopytoff

Ancestor cults and ancestor worship loom large in the anthropological image of sub-Saharan Africa and few would disagree with Fortes that "comparatively viewed, African ancestor worship has a remarkably uniform structural framework" (Fortes, 1965:122). The general pattern may be quickly summarized. Ancestors are vested with mystical powers and authority. They retain a functional role in the world of the living, specifically in the life of their living kinsmen; indeed, African kin-groups are often described as communities of both the living and the dead. The relation of the ancestors to their living kinsmen has been described as ambivalent, as both punitive and benevolent and sometimes even as capricious. In general, ancestral benevolence is assured through propitiation and sacrifice; neglect is believed to bring about punishment. Ancestors are intimately involved with the welfare of their kin-group but they are not linked in the same way to every member of that group. The linkage is structured through the elders of the kin-group, and the elders' authority is related to their close link to the ancestors. In some sense the elders are the representatives of the ancestors and the mediators between them and the kingroup.

Fortes has extended our theoretical understanding of African ancestor worship more recently by further clarifying some of its structural features (1965). Amplifying Gluckman's (1937) distinction between ancestor cults and the cults of the dead, Fortes brings out the importance of the "structural matrix of [African] ancestor worship," noting *inter alia* the relative lack of elaboration and indeed interest among the Africans in the cosmography of the afterworld in which the ancestors reside. The African emphasis is clearly not on how the dead live but on the manner in which they affect the living. Different ancestors are recognized as relevant to different structural contexts (as, for example, in groups of different genealogical levels) ; not all but only certain dead with particular structural positions are worshipped as ancestors; and the behavior of ancestors reflects not their individual personalities but rather a particular legal status in the political-jural domain.

In this paper I shall describe some activities and relationships among the Suku of southwestern Congo (Kinshasa). It will be apparent that the description conforms to the generalized pattern of African ancestor cults and is congruent with Fortes's analysis. But, I shall show that there are difficulties in characterizing the Suku complex as an "ancestor cult" and shall bring in additional data on Suku lineage structure. I shall then contend that Fortes's analysis, while

Source: Igor Kopytoff, "Ancestors as Elders in Africa," *Africa,* Vol. 41 (1971), pp. 129–141. Used by permission of the publisher and the author.

[1] The first version of this paper was delivered at the 67th Annual Meeting of the American Anthropological Association, 21–4 November 1968, at Seattle, Washington, under the title: "African Ancestor Cults Without Ancestors?"

pointing in the right direction, does not go far enough because it does take the final step of shedding the ethnocentric connotations of the very term "ancestor"—connotations that have a bearing on theory. I shall also try to show that by viewing what have been called African ancestor cults as part of the eldership complex, we can account more simply for many of Fortes's generalizations and at the same time make redundant some of the problems he raises.

The fundamental social and jural group among the Suku is the corporate matrilineage, generally consisting of some thirty-five to forty persons. Married couples live virilocally, and males live patrilocally at least until their father's death and often beyond. The membership of a matrilineage is dispersed over several villages but within an area that is not too large to preclude easy communication, consultations, and joint action in important matters. The matrilineage is a corporate unit in economic, political, jural, and religious respects. Each matrilineage is centred in a particular village which bears its name and is its administrative and ritual headquarters, containing the formal lineage head (the oldest male member) and, usually, several other older members (Kopytoff, 1964, 1965).

The dead members of the lineage, as a collectivity, are appealed to in times of crisis (such as a serious sickness or a series of misfortunes) and, more regularly, on such occasions as the marriages of women of the lineage, the breaking of sexual taboos affecting these women, the coming-out ceremony for infants, and, yearly, before the large communal hunts of the dry season. The general pattern is as follows: the head of the lineage and two or three older men of his generation go at night to the grave—any grave —of a deceased member of the lineage who was older than any of them. The Suku have no special burying places and graves are dug at random in the bush outside the lineage center or near crossroads; the graves are not maintained and they eventually return to bush, so that the site of a particular grave is usually forgotten in time. The location of recent graves is of course remembered, and the lineage head and the older men usually go to the grave of the last deceased man who was older than they. The other appropriate place to address the dead is at the crossing of paths.

At the grave or at the crossroads, the old men "feed" the dead certain foods considered to be their favorite: particular kinds of forest mushroom and wild roots, palm wine, and sometimes even manioc, the Suku staple. A small hole is dug in the ground and the food is put into it. Communication with the dead takes the form of a conversational monologue, patterned but not stereotyped, and devoid of repetitive formulae. One speaks the way one speaks to living people: "You, [such and such], your junior is ill. We do not know why, we do not know who is responsible. If it is you, if you are angry, we ask your forgiveness. If we have done wrong, pardon us. Do not let him die. Other lineages are prospering and our people are dying. Why are you doing this? Why do you not look after us properly?" The words typically combine complaints, scolding, sometimes even anger, and at the same time appeals for forgiveness.

At the coming-out ceremonies for infants and at marriages, the dead members of the lineage are informed of the event; pleas are made for their approval and their efforts in insuring the success of the newborn or of the marriage and the children that will be born to it. Before the large communal hunts of the dry season, the dead members are asked to extend good luck to the enterprise. They are told that the people are hungry for meat, they are reprimanded for not granting enough meat, and they are shamed their own people should be eating less well than other lineages. Finally, dead members of the lineage are always referred to publicly by the living elders on all ceremonial occasions involving the lineage as a unit.

These activities clearly fit the general pattern of African "ancestor cults." The ancestors are seen as retaining their role in the affairs of their kin-group and only of their kin-group. They are propitiated with "sacrifices." They are seen as dispensing both favours and misfortune; they are often accused of being capricious and of failing in their responsibilities, but, at the same time, their actions are related to possible lapses on the part of the living and are seen as legitimately punitive. The features of the "cult" emphasize the nature of the social relationship while details of the life of ancestors in the other world are de-emphasized and are, indeed, of little interest to the Suku. It is primarily the jural context that dominates the relationship with the ancestors and not the personal characteristics they may have had when they were alive.

There is, however, one immediate problem

that arises in calling this an "ancestor cult": the Suku have no term that can be translated as "ancestor." These dead members of the lineage are referred to as *bambuta*. Literally, *bambuta* means the "big ones," the "old ones," those who have attained maturity, those older than oneself; collectively, the term refers to the ruling elders of a lineage. A *mbuta* (singular) is literally anyone who is older than ego. The meaning is comparative. Eldership is not an absolute state of being old; being a *mbuta* is always relative to someone who is younger. Within the lineage, a *mbuta* is any older adult, older siblings as well as those of the generations above. My *bambuta* collectively are all the members of the lineage who are older than I, whether they are alive or dead. In jural contexts, where authority is vested overwhelmingly in the males, the term is effectively narrowed to all my male seniors. The lineage is thus divided into two named groups: those above me who are my *bambuta,* and those below me—my *baleke*—to whom I am an elder. By contrast, no semantic distinction is made within the lineage between those who are alive and those who are dead.

An elder—any elder—represents to a junior the entire legal and mystical authority of the lineage. The very fact of eldership confers upon a person mystical powers over the junior. He can curse his junior in the name of the lineage, thereby removing from him the mystical protection of the lineage. The curse can be formal and public, but it can also be secret and even unconscious. To use a contemporary metaphor, a Suku is under the "umbrella" of the power of his lineage; removal of this protection exposes him to the outside world, and the world is a dangerous place to be in when one is not attached to a kin-group. As the Suku phrase it, a curse "opens the road to misfortune"; though it does not actively cause misfortune. An elder's curse, always implicitly made in the name of the lineage, can only be removed by an older elder—one to whom the previous elder is a junior.

Lineage authority and the representation of the lineage to the outside world are organized on a continuum of age, that is, of relative eldership. Within this formal continuum based purely on relative age, there is also the principle of generational solidarity. Lineage members of the same generation are closer to each other and tend toward greater though never actual equality. Thus, the inequality of power and authority is most pronounced between generations. It is most presumptuous for the junior generation to question, under normal circumstances, the decisions of the senior generation and the ways in which they have been arrived at. It is the generation above me that represents to me the full authority of the lineage; generational solidarity as well as inter-generational distance means that, unless I have knowledge to the contrary, I must assume that the decision of one senior represents the decision of all seniors. This generational structure also expresses a continuum of authority. If I am middle-aged, the decision by elders of the generation above me carries for me the authority of all the senior generations above me. To a junior in the generation below me, my decision similarly carries the authority of my generation together with all the generations senior to it. To the junior, then, lineage authority is most directly embodied in the generation immediately above him, and it is presumptuous for him to go over their heads, so to speak, to yet more senior generations. Conversely, the authority of eldership is most directly exercised upon those of the generation immediately below, as they in turn properly exercise it over the generation below them. Exercising authority over the second lower generation, over the heads of the intervening one, is somewhat inappropriate. This results in muting the outward expression of authority between the alternating generations of a lineage, a pattern congruent with the relaxed etiquette between alternating generations.

In any context, the lineage is fully and legally represented by the oldest adult member of the lineage who is present. Let me give a few examples. In common with many Central African peoples, the name of the lineage is formally carried by the head of that lineage. Thus, the head of the lineage Kusu is addressed as Kusu. But this general rule expresses a more complex structure. The identification of the lineages name with the person extends to the entire membership of the lineage; it is the lineage as a whole, *qua* corporate group, that holds the title. Cunnison (1951), writing on the Luapula peoples, has analysed this particular usage in which a person discussing his lineage and its history in the past, will refer to it by the pronoun "I." A similar usage exists among the Suku. The oldest lineage member who is present in any situation can refer to himself by the name of his lineage, and is so addressed by others. For example, an infant who is a member of the royal lineage is addressed as *Mini Kongo,* the title of the Suku king, as long as no other older member of the royal lineage is present. The moment an older member arrives on the scene, the title is shifted to him. A young man of Kusu lineage will refer to himself as Kusu and, a moment later, after an older lineage mate has arrived, he will refer to him as Kusu and will cease applying the title to himself. Ultimately, of course, if all the members of the lineage are present, the title Kusu devolves upon the oldest male member of the lineage who is also its formal head.

The continuum of eldership in representing the lineage has a jural significance in interlineage relations. Let me illustrate with an extreme example. A young man became angry with his elders and, without consulting anyone, sold to another lineage a hunting area belonging to his own. The transaction was fully legal, since he was a legitimate spokesman for his lineage in the context in which the transaction took place. His own lineage was, of course, incensed by the action; in the old days he might have been sold or even killed. But the significant point here is that the legality of the transaction was not questioned.

In short, to those on the outside, a lineage is represented by the oldest member present. Within the lineage, the lineage is represented to any one member by any older member present and, collectively, by all older members living and dead. The principle of eldership operating within the lineage corresponds, in its external relations, to its "chieftainship" (*kimfumu*). Lineage "chieftainship" is also a relative, not an absolute matter; for the outside world, it is carried by the oldest member present. Thus, the Suku say that "everyone is a chief"—just as everyone is an elder.

Let us consider now some additional features of the ritual preceding the collective hunt of the dry season. Before the hunting season begins every Suku secures hunting luck by obtaining reassurance that the lineage wishes him well, that he continues to be under its protection. This reassurance can in principle be obtained verbally from any elder; more appropriately, it is obtained from anyone in the generation above. Young men go to the middle-aged and the middle-aged go to the old. There is a pattern in asking for luck: one beseeches, one complains, one reproves, one asks forgiveness. On his part, the older man signifies his goodwill by giving the junior some *pemba* (white clay); he also uses the occasion to remind the young man of his obligations to the old, to scold him lightly for his past misdemeanours, and to ask his forgiveness for past misfortunes. The manner of addressing the living elder is the same as the one used in addressing the dead. The Suku regard the two activities as being not merely analogous but identical, and the differences between them as incidental and contextual. Everyone goes to his elder. If I am young, I go to my elders who happen to be alive. The old people go to their elders; but since these are dead, they are to be found at the grave or at the crossroads at night. Given the continuum of eldership, the use of any grave, as long as the dead is older than the petitioner, is understandable. Also understandable in this context is the neglect of older graves. In the light of the structure of eldership, this neglect does not represent a "weak" ancestor cult nor does it indicate shallowness of lineage structure.

If there be a "cult" here, it is a cult of *bambuta,* of elders living and dead. Every junior owes *buzitu* ("honor," "respect") to his seniors, be they "elders" or "ancestors" in Western terminology. A single set of principles regulates the relationship between senior and junior; a person deals with a single category of *bambuta* and the line dividing the living from the dead does not affect the structure of the relationship. Where the line is relevant is in the method of approaching the elder. The dead must of necessity be approached differently from the living; interaction with them necessarily appears one sided and conversations with them necessarily become monologues. Also, interaction with them is necessarily less frequent and when it occurs, it is formal—but no less formal than is the interaction with living elders on ceremonial occasions. The offer of palm wine is normal at all formal occasions when a junior approaches a senior; but dead elders, in their capacity of the dead, also have their preferred foods—the special forest mushroom and roots. Thus, it is the special methods of approach, inevitably characterizing dealings with the dead as opposed to the living, that give these dealings the special cast that makes us, as anthropologists and outsiders, call it a "cult." The dead *qua* dead also know more and see things that living elders do not; they are, therefore, more powerful and can sometimes be more helpful. Also, though the reasons for action by any elder are often obscure to the juniors, actions by dead elders are particularly obscure since no explanations from them are ever possible. In short, there is a difference in the manner in which the dead are approached, in contrast to the living. But the difference is related to their different physical states, even while they remain in the same structural positions *vis-à-vis* their juniors.

The Suku pattern described above is congruent with most ethnographic descriptions of African "ancestral cults" and of the role of elders. Where the Suku case may appear distinctive is in the accompaying linguistic and semantic pattern of encompassing under the single term *mbuta* the continuum of eldership while neglecting the line between the living and the dead. But the Suku are far from unique in this. Comparative linguistic evidence suggests that the merger or a very close semantic association of "ancestors" with "elders" is widespread in Africa, particularly in Bantu Africa.[2]

The accompanying table shows the distribution of the radicals used in several Bantu languages to form terms that have been translated as "elders" *and* "ancestors." It can be seen that a situation similar to that of the Suku, with their single "ancestor/elder" term, is also found in Ovambo, Lele, Songye, Nkundo, Bobangi, Ila, Lamba, Yao, Bondei, Bantu-Tiriki, and Zulu. Separate terms that are, nevertheless, very similar and derivative from the same radical, are found among the Kongo, Ntomba, Yao, Ankole, and Karanga. It will also be noted that when terms for "ancestor" and "elder" are reported to be different, or when alternative terms exist, the separate terms, nevertheless, derive from the same radicals that have occurred in the preceding cases. Finally, there is an occasional pattern for a single term to stand for "grandfather/ancestor."

Three common Bantu radicals stand out in the table: *-kulu, -kale*, and *-koko.*

The semantic core of *-kulu* (*-kuru, -kolo, -koro, -guru*) is "to grow, to become big" and its usual semantic field in Bantu languages includes "to grow up, to mature, to become adult, to become old, to be important" (with their respective adjective and noun forms). In many languages there is a semantic drift towards "older" (comparative) and "elder" (noun). In some languages, there is a further drift towards "the old ones," used in the English sense of "ancestors." (The direction of the semantic drift is from "elder" alone to the combined "elder/ancestor.") Thus, an appropriate translation of the core meaning of *-kulu* would be the French *grand* (with its associated verb *grandir*), and "elders/ancestors" formed from this radical would be rendered as *les grands* (a term that French-speaking Africans in fact sometimes use with striking semantic appropriateness: *les grands*, after all, can be alive as well as dead).[3]

By contrast with *-kulu, -koko* appears to be a semantically primary term and the pattern of its semantic drift is in the opposite direction: it stands for "ancestor" alone or "ancestor/grandparent" or "ancestor/grandparent/elder." The semantic core is perhaps best rendered as "forefather."

The third radical *-kale* is a common Bantu term for "long ago," "in the old days," "aged (in time)," "ancient," "antecedent in time," etc. (like *-kulu*, it is among Meinhof's Ur-Bantu forms). An appropriate rendering of the core

[2] Monica Wilson speaks of Nyakyusa "senior kinsmen, living and dead" having a "mystical power over their juniors" and of the "cult of senior relatives" which she parenthetically equates with "ancestor cults" (1957:3, 4, 226). But this is exceptional in ethnographic reporting. The overwhelming pattern in ethnographies is to treat "elders" separately from "ancestors" and this may influence linguistic reporting as well. In my combing of the ethnographic literature for the terms for "ancestors" and "elders," an unexpected discovery was the extent to which ethnographies often discuss "ancestral cults" and the position of elders without giving native terms for one or the other and especially for both at the same time. One is tempted to see this as reflecting the hold that these terms have on us as designating necessarily separate categories. We all know, before even getting to the field, that Africans have elders (that is, "social structure") and ancestors (that is, "religion"). A combing of dictionaries is somewhat more rewarding, constrained as they are by the existing semantics. These are, of course, most revealing when one can get a full range of English terms for the single African word.

[3] Interestingly, the English *old* parallels, etymologically, the semantics of the Bantu *kulu:* Old English *oud,* Frisian *alt,* Old Norse *ala* (to rear, to grow up), and Latin *alere* (to begin, to grow) and *adultus.* With *kulu,* of course, we are dealing with a term whose *present* core meaning is "to grow, etc." and which repeatedly drifts in many languages (but not in all) towards "elder" and among some of these towards "ancestor." Hence the applicability of the term "semantic drift," by analogy to Edward Sapir's "linguistic drift" indicating parallel grammatical changes occurring in languages of the same stock after they had separated (Sapir, 1921/1949:171ff.).

Table 1. *The Use of Common Radicals in Forming Terms for "Elders" and "Ancestors" in Selected Bantu Languages*

	Radicals Used				
	-kale	*-kulu*	*-koko*	*-ka(ka)*	*other*
Ovambo		eld/anc			
Kongo		eld, anc			eld (*-uta*)
Suku					eld/anc (*-uta*)
Lele					eld/anc (*-ota*)
Songye	eld	eld/anc			
Nkundo			anc/gp/eld	anc	eld (*-gambi*)
Ntomba			anc, eld	anc/gp	eld (*-gambi*)
Ngala	eld	eld	anc/gp		
Bobangi			anc/gp/eld		
Ila	eld/anc			gp	eld (*-alu*)
Lamba	anc	eld/anc			
Yao	eld/anc	eld, anc			anc/eld (*-kolo*)
Ankole	eld	eld, anc/gp			
Bondei		eld			anc/eld (*-dala*)
Tiriki		eld			anc/gp/eld (*-guga*)
Karanga		eld, anc			
Zulu		eld/anc	anc/gp		eld (*-guga, -dala*)

Note: Ancestors: "anc"; Elders: "eld"; grandfather or grandparent "gp." An oblique stroke means that a single African term combines the two or three English terms (e.g. "eld/anc" indicates that one term means both "elder" and "ancestor"). A comma means that the two terms are constructed from the same radical (e.g., in Karanga, *makuru*, "elders," and *vakuru*, "ancestors").

meaning is "ancient" in its primary reference to the time scale, to "dating back, originating in the past," and in its secondary reference to "old" (when it indicates the *state* of a subject as derived from its position on a time scale). The French noun *les anciens* (unless one chooses the awkward "antecedent") seems to translate the core meaning with its extensions (and French-speaking Africans do sometimes use this term). The semantic drift of *-kale* is sometimes towards "elder" only, sometimes towards "ancestor" only, and sometimes towards the combined "ancestor/elder" (*les anciens* can appropriately refer to the living *or* the dead *or* both).

The other less common radicals that occur in the formation of what we translate as "elders" and/or "ancestors" are *-dala* ("old" or "far in time") and *-alu* (which may or may not be related to *-kale*) ; *-ka* or *-kaka,* used for "grandparent" or "grandparent/ancestor" ("forefather"?) ; and *-uta/-ota* (as in Suku *mbuta*) whose core meaning is "to beget/bear."

Thus, there are, in Bantu Africa at least, three principal ways in which the associated ideas of "eldership" and "ancestorship" are expressed. One is by semantic drift from "to grow big," elders or elders/ancestors being *les grands.* The second is by semantic drift from "ancient," so that elders or ancestors or elders/ancestors are rendered as *les anciens.* The third is by the use of a prime term for "ancestor" that may, by semantic drift, also cover ancestor/grandparent and even ancestor/grandparent/elder.

The semantic association between "ancestor" and "elder" is not restricted to Bantu languages. In Igbo, *ńnà* is used both for elder male relative and ancestor. In Mossi, the radical *kud-* occurs in "elder," "ancestor," and "ancient times." In Sango, *-kota* is used for elder relative, elder, ancestor, and dignitary. In Mangbetu, *-koko* occurs in "ancestor" and "to grow." Among the Mandinka, the radical *ke* defines a cluster of age, authority, eldership, and ancestorship.[4] In Kanuri, *kur-* occurs in terms having to do with "old times," and authority.[5]

We can speak, then, of the presence in many

[4] Personal communication from Dr. Peter M. Weil.

[5] Homburger (1941:250–1) considers Bantu *-kulu* to be related to such forms as Zande *kuru,* Mossi *kud-re,* Mande *koro,* and Kanuri *kure.* Their semantic cores are identical ("big/old/grown") and they show similar semantic drifts towards "important," "elders," and "ancestors." With the possible exception of Kanuri, these languages are, of course, related.

African cultures of a semantic association of growth, age, maturity, ancientness, eldership, ancestorship, and authority. This cluster conditions the semantic drift of terms along an "adult-elder-ancestor" dimension. Consequently, we find within this semantic cluster a general category best rendered by the French *les grands/anciens* and that we shall refer to in English by the term "elder/ancestor." But the further distinction within this category between the living ("elders") and the dead ("ancestors") is one that is not always made in African languages. Insistence on the conceptual primacy of this division between the living and the dead is, I submit, an ethnocentric distortion of the African world view, a distortion that prevents our understanding of what we have persisted in calling "ancestor cults" and "ancestor worship."

The Western ethnocentric conviction that "ancestors" must be separated from living "elders" conditions the cognitive set with which we approach African data and theorize about them. Not only is our term "ancestor"—meaning an ascendant who is dead—denotatively ethnocentric but it is also connotatively so. Western cultural tradition (which includes ghosts) accepts that the dead can be endowed with extraordinary powers. The dead belong to what we call the "supernatural world." A Western anthropologist, working in an African society, finds it easy to accept without much further questioning that the dead, including the "ancestors," should be believed capable of extraordinary doings, that they should "mystically" confer benefits, that they should visit sickness upon the living, that they should have "supernatural" powers. Such beliefs about the dead are culturally acceptable to us, and it is appropriate that such dead should have a "cult." But living people in our cultural conceptions do not have such "mystical" powers merely because they happen to be older. If they are said by Africans to have such powers, these must be "derived" from elsewhere; and the ancestors, being dead, are seen as an appropriate source.[6]

Our interpretations have had two opposing emphases. In the ethnographies, dealing descriptively with African beliefs, it has generally been held that Africans see the powers of the elders as derivative from the power of the ancestors. By contrast, on the theoretical level (where our cultural assumptions come to the fore and where ancestors cannot "exist" except as a symbol and an abstraction), the directionality of the explanation is exactly reversed; the powers with which ancestors are endowed become a "projection" of the palpable powers of living elders. This latter interpretation is the gist of Fortes's (1965) formulation. But what, then, of the mystical powers that elders hold directly and on their own, as among the Suku? Are they in turn to be seen as re-projections from the ancestors? When we see the powers over the juniors of both living elders and ancestors as derivative from eldership *per se*, both the above interpretations of the "sources" of power come to be beside the point. The problems they attempt to solve arise in the first place from an ethnocentric categorization of the ethnographic data.

The reformulation of the problem around the broader category of "eldership" carried other semantic implications for anthropological terminology (and consequently for the theory built on this terminology). We talk of ancestor "cults" and even of ancestor "worship." In their modern meanings[7] these English words are culturally appropriate in describing dealings with the dead and the supernatural. By contrast, we would hesitate to apply the terms "cult" and "worship" to relations with the living. Yet, if the Suku and others "worship" their dead elders, then they also "worship" their living elders. If they have a "cult" of dead elders, the same "cult" applies to the living. Obversely, if the living elders are only "respected," then so are the "ancestors," and no more than that.

These points are very well illustrated by Kenyatta (1938:265–8), with his inside view of Kikuyu culture, when he discusses "ancestors."

[6] To introduce a personal note, I had no difficulty in the field in accepting the idea that the dead "ancestors" should have "supernatural" powers. But I must have driven my informants to distraction by insisting on pursuing the question of the "why" and the "where from" of the powers of the living elders. It took a kind of methodological (and cultural) leap of faith to accept as a terminal ethnographic datum that if the dead can appropriately do supernatural things, why not also the living?

[7] The English word "worship" carried, to be sure, a less religious connotation in Old English, referring merely to "dignity," "honour," and "worthiness"—appropriate to one aspect of the African relationship with both elders and ancestors, but still missing its associated aspect of familiarity that, when necessary, allows scolding.

"In this account, I shall not use that term [worship], because from practical experience I do not believe that the Kikuyu worship their ancestors. . . . I shall therefore use the term 'communion with ancestors.'" Kenyatta's European analogy is revealing: "There appears to be such communion with ancestors when a European family, on special occasions, has an empty chair, the seat of a dead member, at table during a meal. This custom might be closely equated with Gikuyu behavior in this respect." "The words 'prayer' and 'worship,' *gothaithaiya, goikia-mokoigoro,* are never used in dealing with the ancestors' spirits. These words are reserved for solemn rituals and sacrifices directed to the power of the unseen." As to the question of what is so often called "sacrifice": "The gifts which an elder gives to the ancestors' spirits, as when a sheep is sacrificed to them, and which perhaps seem to an outsider to be prayers directed to the ancestors, are nothing but the tributes symbolizing the gifts which the departed elders would have received had they been alive, and which the living elders now receive."

By using terms such as "cult," "worship," and "sacrifice," we introduce semantic paradoxes which we then feel compelled to explain. Thus, in the International African Institute's Salisbury seminar (Fortes and Dieterlen, 1965:18), "the view that ancestors are generally represented as punitive in character was discussed at length." The need to understand why an object of "worship" should be "punitive" arises from the semantics of the terms used. We are told in the report on the seminar that "Professor Mitchell concluded that ancestors seemed to be normally ambivalent, inflicting punishment to demonstrate the legitimate authority and exercising benevolence when appealed to. He linked this up with some remarks of Dr. Turner, who gave instances of ancestor worship being significant in group rituals of solidarity and expiation aimed at restoring amity within a community. Such rituals, Professor Mitchell suggested, would be directed towards the ancestors in their benevolent aspect, whereas in the case of misfortune the punitive aspect would be invoked in order to provide an interpretation." Such theoretical involution is unnecessary. The attitude to elders (dead or alive) is normally ambivalent; they both punish and exercise benevolence, and they necessarily participate in restoring amity within the lineage. Mitchell's complex theoretical interpretation ignores what almost every ethnography and every general descriptive statement on African ancestor "cults" have always stressed: that African lineages are communities of both the living and the dead. Gluckman and Fortes rightly stress that "ancestor cults" are not the same thing as the cults of the dead. But this irrelevance of the "deadness" of ancestors has implications for the very idiom in which theoretical problems are cast.

Once we recognize that African "ancestors" are above all elders and to be understood in terms of the same category as living elders, we shall stop pursuing a multitude of problems of our own creation. There is nothing startling that the attitude to elders wielding authority should be ambivalent. Fortes (1965:133) makes the important point that what matters in ancestors is their jural status, that (speaking of the Tallensi) "the personality and character, the virtues or vices, success or failures, popularity or unpopularity, of a person during his lifetime make no difference to his attainment of ancestorhood." But, we should add, neither do these variations make a difference in the authority invested in eldership; what matters in *formal* relations is the formal status, in dead elders as well as those alive. "It is not the whole man, but only his jural status as the parent or parental personage, (in matrilineal systems) vested with authority and responsibility, that is transmuted into ancestorhood" (ibid.). But from the point of view proposed here, what occurs is not a "transmutation" but a *retention* of status by the now dead elder. The status, that is, remains unaffected by death, while one's purely personal and idiosyncratic relationship with the elder is necessarily changed. Similarly, when Fortes states: "Ancestor worship is a representation or extension of the authority component in the jural relations of successive generations," we can restate this more simply and, I would claim, more realistically and more in keeping with African conceptions as follows: "Elders, after they die, maintain their role in the jural relations of successive generations." In Fortes's theory, people are believed to "acquire," upon death, the power to intervene in the life of their juniors. I would claim that they "continue" to have that power.

Such rephrasing simplifies the interpretation of ethnographic data. Thus, in Fortes's formulation, the son begins "officiating" in the "cult" only upon his father's death because he now becomes a jural adult (Fortes, 1965:130–2). This succession means "ousting a predecessor," and "sacrifice" to the ancestors may be a psychologically reassuring mode of ritual reparation; the ancestor cult becomes a psychological "refuge" (Fortes, 1965:140–1, 1945:9). Without questioning the psychological dynamics specific to the Tallensi, one may suggest another formulation that would seem to be more appropriate for dealing with the general phenomenon of "sacrifice" in African "ancestor cults," since these guilt feelings and their relief cannot be shown to exist in all of these societies. We see among the Tallensi a continuum of intergenerational eldership. The power of the kin-group is represented to me (a Tale) by my father, as his father represents it to him. My father "worships" (respects) and "sacrifices" (gives tribute) to his dead father, as I respect and give tribute to him. When my father dies, my relationship with him continues (Fortes, 1959:48ff.). The chain of relationships over the generations remains unaltered, though the method of interaction with my father becomes necessarily different when he is dead. If we express this difference by speaking of "worship" and "sacrifice," in contrast to "respect" and "gift or tribute," it is because we, as Westerners, find such terms more appropriate to express dealings with the dead. And, further, "sacrifice," "expiation," and "guilt" is a comfortable semantic cluster for us. But there is surely a danger here of transmuting the semantic biases of the observer's culture into problems of the ethnology of the observed.

By treating the phrase "ancestor cults" as a rather misleading way of referring to an aspect of the relationship with elders in general, a matter that Fortes sees as a puzzle can be re-examined in a new light. The puzzle is in the fact that the Tiv and the Nuer, with genealogically based social systems not unlike those of the Tallensi, lack "ancestor worship" (Fortes, 1965:140). There is indeed a puzzle if one insists upon seeing the ancestor cult as a *symbolic projection* of the social system. In the view presented here, on the other hand, the ancestor cult is an integral *part* of the system of relationship with elders. The relationship with dead elders (that is, "ancestors") is seen as being on the same symbolic plane as that with living elders and not as secondary to it or derivative from it. From this point of view the over-all structural similarities among Tallensi, Tiv, and Nuer should not be expected to result in similar ancestor cults. Other facts would seem to be more relevant to the relationship with ancestors *qua* dead elders: the meaning and structure of eldership, the nature of the authority attributed to it, and the beliefs about the effect of death upon the elder's role.

For the Tiv, the question to be asked is, what is there in the Tiv relationship with elders that makes for relative indifference to dead elders? Pervasive Tiv egalitarianism de-emphasizes the authority of eldership and indeed exacerbates the authority problems that inhere in such segmentary systems (Bohannan, 1953:31ff.). Neither genealogical position nor age confer, of themselves, special powers on the living, while the dead are believed to have no effect on the living (ibid:83). In short, Tiv elders *qua* elders have little influence on the lives of their juniors, be the elders alive or dead. Their formal authority here is minimal and genealogically shallow. Though a relationship with the dead is not entirely lacking (Bohannan, 1969:i:35ff., and 43), it is confined to one's parents. As to the Nuer, here also elders do not carry authority and power simply by virtue of their eldership (Evans-Pritchard, 1940:179–80). The elders' passage into the other world does not change their situation in this respect.

Though "ancestor cults" should not be equated with cults of the dead, beliefs about the dead are nevertheless relevant, as illustrated by the Songye who may also be said to lack an "ancestor cult," but for rather different reasons. Here, living elders have authority; once they die, however, the relationship with them as dead elders does not last because they become reincarnated in their grandchildren.[8]

To conclude,[9] the selection by anthropologists of the phrases "ancestor cult" and "ancestor worship," in dealing with African cultures, is semantically inappropriate, analytically misleading, and theoretically unproductive. Fortes has rightly emphasized that the essential features of these activities are to be found not so much in

[8]Personal communication from Dr. Alan P. Merriam.

[9]In this paper, I have discussed only the elders/ancestors of the descent group itself, and I have made no refernce to the "extra-descent group ancestor cults" discussed by McKnight (1967). Briefly summarized, McKnight's point is that the "extra-descent group ancestors" (that is, paternal ancestors in the matrilineal systems, and maternal ones in the patrilineal) are not benevolent as they should be in terms of Radcliffe-

the fact that the people concerned are dead as in the structural matrix in which they are placed. But he does not go far enough. By retaining the term "ancestor" (rather than use, say, "dead elders"), he continues to give undue weight in his interpretations to the fact that the persons are dead. The term "ancestor" sets up a dichotomy where there is a continuum. By conceptually separating living elders from ancestors, we unconsciously introduce Western connotations to the phenomena thus labelled and find ourselves having to deal with paradoxes of our own creation and with complex solutions to them. It is striking that African "ancestors" are more mundane and less mystical than the dead who are objects of "worship" should be in Western eyes. African elders, on the other hand, look more mystical to us than we are willing to allow the living to be. Similarly, Africans treat their living elders more "worshipfully" than the English term "respect" conveys, and they treat the ancestors with less "respect" and more contentiousness than the term "worship" should allow.

These are all paradoxes that stem from the difficulty of our vocabulary to accommodate to the fact that African living elders and dead ancestors are more similar to each other than the Western living and dead can be, that an elder's social role does not radically change when he crosses the line dividing the living from the dead, and that African "ancestorship" is but an aspect of the broader phenomenon of "eldership." The intial theoretical problem here is not so much that of uncovering deep psychological and symbolic processes as it is of probing African cultural categories and of finding adequate translations of these into the Western language used for theorizing. The terminological recasting that is proposed here (with a consequent recasting of the cognitive categories of the theorist) suggests that our understanding of variations in what we have called "ancestor cults" must begin with the analysis of eldership in particular African societies. Finally, these redefinitions also resolve the puzzle of finding "ancestor cults" to be, on the one hand, so very characteristic of Africa as a culture area and, on the other, to be inexplicably and erratically absent here and there within the area. No such problem arises when we realize that the cultural trait to be examined is not "ancestorship" but the more widely distributed African recognition of "eldership."

Brown's theory of extension of sentiments. McKnight shows that the relations with the kin-group of the "residual parent" need not duplicate the sentiments of the relationship with that parent. Thus, in a patrilineal society, one can be on the warmest of terms with one's mother and her brother and still have strained and even hostile relations with their kin-group as a corporate entity and with other relatives in it. And it is these latter relations that condition the relations with the "extra-descent group ancestors." McKnight's mode of analysis is consistent with the one used here. I would merely use the term "relationship with the dead elders of the extra-descent group" instead of "extra-descent group ancestor cults."

BIBLIOGRAPHY

Bohannan, Laura and Paul. 1953. *The Tiv of Central Nigeria*. London.

——— 1969. *A Source Notebook on Tiv Religion* (*v. 1: Cosmos, Soma, Psyche and Disease*). New Haven, Conn.

Cunnison, Ian. 1951. *History of the Luapula,* Rhodes–Livingstone Papers, 21.

Evans-Pritchard, E. 1940. *The Nuer*. Oxford.

Fortes, Meyer. 1945. *The Dynamics of Clanship Among the Tallensi*. London.

——— 1959. *Oedipus and Job in West African Religion*. Cambridge.

——— 1965. "Some Reflections on Ancestor Worship," in *African Systems of Thought,* ed. M. Fortes and G. Dieterlen. London.

——— and Dieterlen, G. (eds.). 1965. *African Systems of Thought*. London.

Gluckman, M. 1937. "Mortuary Customs and the Belief in Survival After Death Among the South-Eastern Bantu," *Bantu Studies,* xi.

Homburger, L. 1941. *Les Langues négro-africaines et les peuples qui les parlent*. Paris.

Kenyatta, Jomo. 1938. *Facing Mount Kenya: The Tribal Life of the Gikuyu*. London.

Kopytoff, Igor. 1964. "Family and Lineage among the Suku of the Congo," in *The Family Estate in Africa,* ed. Robert F. Gray and P. H. Gulliver. London.

——— 1965. "The Suku of Southwestern Congo," in *Peoples of Africa,* ed. James L. Gibbs, Jr. New York.

McKnight, J. D. 1967. "Extra-Descent Group Ancestor Cults in African Societies," *Africa,* xxxvii. 1–21.
Sapir, Edward. 1921. *Language.* New York (reprinted 1949).
Wilson, Monica. 1957. *Rituals of Kinship Among the Nyakyusa.* London.

For the terms for "ancestors" and "elders" in the African languages mentioned, I have used the following sources: Mary Douglas, *The Lele of the Kasai, London,* 1963; Walter Sangree, *Age, Prayer, and Politics in Tiriki, Kenya,* London, 1966; and the dictionaries of the respective languages by the following: C. W. R. Tobias and B. H. C. Turvey 1954 (Ovambo/Kwanyama), W. Holman Bentley 1887 (Kongo), R. P. A. Semain 1923 (Songye), G. Hulstaert 1952 (Nkundo/Lomongo), M. Guthrie 1935 (Ngala), M. Mamet 1955 (Ntomba), J. Whitehead 1899 (Bobangi), Edwin W. Smith 1907 and J. Torrend 1931 (Ila), C. M. Doke 1933 and 1963 (Lamba), G. M. Sanderson 1954 (Yao), C. Taylor 1959 (Ankole), Herbert W. Woodward 1882 (Bondei), C. S. Louw 1915 (Karanga), D. McJ. Malcolm 1966 and C. M. Doke and B. W. Vilakazi 1958 (Zulu), R. P. Alexandre 1953 (Mossi), B. F. and W. E. Welmers 1968 (Igbo), Charles A. Taber 1965 (Sango), A. Vekens 1928 (Mangbetu).

Whenever human destiny is believed to be determined by the operation of supernatural forces, people logically turn to the supernatural when things go wrong. Some seek only solace. But in time of deep crisis many turn to religion with the aim of altering the course of their lives. During the last centuries of colonialist expansion many aboriginal peoples have seen their traditional cultures threatened with obliteration by outsiders. Often the victims have explained the overwhelming technological superiority of their invaders as resulting from the conquerors' more efficient means of controlling the supernatural.

Traditional religious beliefs and rituals have suddenly been found to be discouragingly ineffective in coping with the puzzling demands of pale foreigners whose impressive wealth —kerosene lamps, jeeps with four-wheel drive, transistor radios, and tinned fish—is all, apparently, in miraculously unlimited supply. Suddenly overtaken by such unexplainable events, aboriginal peoples often try radical religious change as a means of finding some explanation for their plight and some means of relieving the sense of powerlessness and demoralization that always grips those who conclude that their old ways are no longer workable.

Under the guidance of messianic leaders, religious movements such as the one described here by Burridge have occurred on every continent at one time or another as native peoples have found their views of the world and of how to survive in it profoundly altered by unanticipated, rapid, and frighteningly frustrating contact with technologically powerful outsiders.

New Heaven, New Earth: Millenarianism in Polynesia

Kenelm Burridge

Opening the Problem

To dream a dream and make it come true; to realize the shape of what can be seen only in the mind's eye; to feel compelled to bring about the seemingly impossible—-these are the prerogatives of man. James Naylor was ploughing his fields when, in a blinding and timeless moment, he knew why he had been born. Like Saint Paul, who never wavered in his adherence to a truth

Source: Reprinted by permission of Schocken Books Inc. from *New Heaven New Earth* by Kenelm Burridge. Copyright © 1969 by Basil Blackwell, and by permission of the author.

revealed to him in a vision, James Naylor, despite the cruelties of parliament and a bigoted religious orthodoxy, remained steadfast in what his vision had revealed to him. Driven by her voices, a French peasant girl put new life into a dispirited army and routed the alien invader. She was burned at the stake as a heretic and witch; she was also canonized Saint Joan. Ann Lee claimed to be the new Christ; Joseph Smith had a vision of heavenly bliss to be realized in an earthly community life; and thousands of miles and moments away a Maori, a Papuan, an African, an Indian—each is impelled to tell his good news of a new way of life. Whether as fool, fraud, saint, respectable bourgeois, farmer or tycoon, the pain of the millennium belongs only to man. It is why he is man, why, when the time comes, he has to make a new man.

Some fifty years ago Haddon wrote:[1]

> An awakening of religious activity is a frequent characteristic of periods of social unrest. The weakening or disruption of the old social order may stimulate new and often bizarre ideals, and these may give rise to religious movements that strive to sanction social and political aspirations. Communities that feel themselves oppressed anticipate the emergence of a hero who will restore their prosperity and prestige. And when the people are imbued with religious fervour the expected hero will be regarded as a Messiah. Phenomena of this kind are well known in history, and are not unknown at the present day among peoples in all stages of civilization.

A forceful and succinct enough statement. In the space of a paragraph Haddon describes the kind of activity we are setting out to examine. It is worthwhile going over it to make sure we know what we mean by some of the words Haddon uses.

Religion and Redemption. What we mean by "religious activity" is clearly of key importance. Writing at the time he did Haddon may have had in mind Tylor's minimal definition of religion: "the belief in spiritual beings."[2] Or, since it is more usual and puts more generally much the same point as Tylor made more specifically, it may be that Haddon thought of "religious activity" as essentially defined by a belief in the supernatural. But neither of these definitions is of much sociological value as they stand. For though we can observe rites and rituals and infer their symbolic references with some accuracy, the problem of belief begs the question, we cannot know what a spiritual being is without further qualification, and it is too often tempting to define a belief in the supernatural in terms that would scarcely apply to anybody anywhere.[3] We need a broader view, one that subsumes the variety of activities that may be religious.

Meditating on the infinite may be a religious activity, so may writing a check, eating corpses, copulating, listening to a thumping sermon on hell fire, examining one's conscience, painting a picture, growing a beard, licking leprous sores, tying the body into knots, a dogged faith in human rationality—there is no human activity which cannot assume religious significance. When it does so it has overriding importance. It points to that which permeates and informs a whole way of life, and, more crucially, it indicates sources or principles of power which are regarded as particularly creative or destructive.[4] Indeed, all religions are basically concerned with power. They are concerned with the discovery, identification, moral relevance and ordering of different kinds of power whether these manifest themselves as thunder, or lightning, atomic fission, untrammelled desire, arrogance, impulse, apparitions, visions, or persuasive words. Within these terms a spiritual being, whether thought of as a deity or ghost or human being or angel or goblin or fairy, becomes a named and identified source or principle of power with particular and often measurable at-

[1] *Chinnery and Haddon,* p. 455.

[2] *Tylor,* p. 424.

[3] If a "spiritual being" is expressly not human, it still must involve questions as to mass, visibility, and attributes of biolocation. Not to "believe in" phenomena such as trances, stigmata, possession, levitation, walking on hot coals without being burned, or skewering the cheeks without leaving a wound—which are all above or beyond the natural, not found in nature—is surely equivalent to being a "flat-earther."

[4] When we say of a man that "art is his religion" we mean that he gives overriding importance to art, that he is particularly concerned with nurturing and developing his sources of inspiration, and guarding himself against those influences which might endanger his inspiration, betray his integrity as an artist, or nullify his ideas on what Art should be or do. The same applies to those of whom we might say "science is his religion," or "socialism is his religion," or "anthropology is his religion."

tributes and ranges of power.[5] And all that is meant by a belief in the supernatural is the belief that there do exist kinds of power whose manifestations and effects are observable, but whose natures are not yet fully comprehended.

Religions, let us say, are concerned with the systematic ordering of different kinds of power, particularly those seen as significantly beneficial or dangerous. This entails a specific framework of rules. But because a religion is concerned with the truth of things, and reaches out to discover and identify those sorts of power which, though sensed and affective, are currently not wholly comprehended, its rules about the use and control of different kinds of powers are grounded in an interplay between experience, working assumptions, and those more rooted assumptions we call faith. As experience widens and deepens, some of the rules and assumptions will be qualified, and others abandoned altogether—a developmental process in which received truths or assumptions give way to new truths, and in which the new truths become in their turn the received assumptions of future generations. These assumptions are community truths, truths which command a consensus. From them are derived the sets of moral imperatives, obligations, and rules of conduct to which men, because they live in community, subject themselves. Yet though man governs his condition with explicit and articulate rules of this kind, they are rarely interconsistent. Concrete situations often involve selecting one rule at the expense of another, and individuals, whether selfishly or otherwise motivated, accord differing priorities to some obligations at the expense of others. And here too we touch on the essence of religious activity. For, given a context determined by current assumptions about power, the process whereby individuals attempt to discharge their obligations in relation to the moral imperatives of the community is no less than a "redemptive process."

From the pen of a social scientist, "redemptive process" seems a curious phrase. But it is useful. The human condition appears as one of general indebtedness: a feature which we acknowledge in variations of the aphorism "paying our debt to society." For whether the capacities of a human being are given him by God and/or a particular combination of genes, his potential can only be realized after a long process of feeding, nurturing, teaching and training by parents and others. Society, moreover, prescribes the attitudes and activities by which its members can pay back or redeem the debt incurred in being nurtured, made morally aware, and enabled to exert and realize their potential. While these prescribed activities may be thought of as "redemptive media," the media through which the debt is repaid or redeemed, the process of engaging in the activities—activities which are ordered in terms of particular kinds of obligations—is, in our idiom, the redemptive process, a process which leads on to redemption itself. But this, the payment of the debt in full, can only be realized when a human being becomes in himself completely unobliged, without any obligation whatsoever—a free-mover in heaven, enjoying nirvana, or joined with the ancestors. For since existence in community, a moral order, necessarily entails existence within a network of obligations, redemption itself can only be realized at or after that appropriate death which brings to an end an appropriate mode of discharging one's obligations.

We may now move towards a working definition of religion and religious activity. Let us say that they refer to

> The redemptive process indicated by the activities, moral rules, and assumptions about power which, pertinent to the moral order and taken on faith, not only enable a people to perceive the truth of things, but guarantee that they are indeed perceiving the truth of things.[6]

This definition has several advantages. Instead of tucking religion into an obscure and even almost irrelevant compartment of social life, we give it the overriding importance it actually seems to have. For not only are religions concerned with the truth about power, but the reverse also holds: a concern with the truth about power is a religious activity. Operationally, this concern is expressed in maintaining or challenging the rules which govern the use and control of power. And these rules assume the form of a set of moral discriminations which, in constricting animal man, also provide him with opportunities for realizing his moral nature and potential. The definition implies, and therefore leads us to expect—despite the conservatism of

5 This holds even though it might be said that a "spiritual being" is but the rationalized projection of some internal impulse.

6 Cf. *Lienhardt,* pp. 327–9; *Yinger,* pp. 9, 71–2; *Vernon,* pp. 46–57; *Horton.*

particular religious orthodoxies—that religious activities will change when the assumptions about the nature of power, and hence the rules which govern its use and control, can no longer guarantee the truth of things.

The use of this definition spares us unnecessary wrangling with distinctions between religion and magic. We are not led into the impasse of calling the religions of other peoples bundles of superstitions. We are insulated from the prejudgements contained in the dichotomies rational/irrational and secular/religious. If a general rationality and order among human beings and their affairs are not assumed from the start, sociological analysis must founder. The label "irrational" tends to become a portmanteau of ethnocentric prejudices, for faith is faith whether thought of as religious or secular. More positively, with this definition we can identify activities and movements of generally millenarian type where the words "God," "deity," or "spiritual being" or their synonyms in other languages are not in evidence. Because politics, too, are concerned with power, it becomes clear and explicit that no religious movement lacks a political ideology. And, accepting the political significance, we are forced to look at the ways in which wealth is distributed, and we must take account of what powers are dependent on various kinds of wealth.

If it is not to become overly ethnocentric, anthropology or comparative sociology must, initially, use broad concepts capable of containing the varied arrangements offered by different cultures. The "redemptive process" is just such a concept. Not necessarily hedged with mystery, it is something we can observe, ask about, talk about. The rules which govern the use of power can be determined. Both emerge from the ways in which individuals discharge or evade their obligations, what they do to counter or meet the consequences of evasion, how they cope with a pledge redeemed, what they say the consequences will or might be. We can, too, identify preliminary or temporary states of redemption.[7] Finally, we can accept provisionally the crude formula, Salvation = Redemption = Unobligedness, or release from all obligations. For, by examining the kinds of redemption or releases from obligation that are offered by particular kinds of millenarian activity, we might be able to see more accurately what assumptions and rules are currently not revealing the truth of things, what kinds of redemptive process would be more in tune with an actual or desired distribution of power.

New Ideals. It will be clear from what has been said above that "periods of social unrest" and the "weakening or disruption of the old social order" refer to situations where the relevant assumptions about power are weakening and no longer enable individuals to perceive the truth of things. They cannot project a satisfactory redemptive process. Hence the "new and often bizarre ideals." These may be seen as attempts to reformulate assumptions about power so that they may account for the widening experiences of everyday life and provide the basis for a new mode of redemption. New ideals, new assumptions certainly. But whether or not they are bizarre is entirely subjective. No one, it may be assumed, does seriously what he himself thinks is bizarre. Just as other kinds of seeming strange and esoteric activities in foreign cultures have yielded their mystery to investigation, so again and again the apparently bizarre in millenarian movements has been shown to be unexceptionable in the circumstances, given the premises. The hypothesis that millenary activities predicate a new culture or social order coming into being—which is what Haddon implies when he speaks of these movements as sanctioning "social and political aspirations"—is a fair one. Certainly it is more scientific to regard these activities as new-cultures-in-the-making, or as attempts to make a new kind of society or moral community, rather than as oddities, diseases in the body social, or troublesome nuisances to efficient administration—though of course they may be all these as well.

Finally, of course, a millenarian movement is a new religion in the making. New assumptions are being ordered into what may become a new orthodoxy.

Oppression. Haddon wrote in the heyday of British Imperial and colonial power. Despite the purposeful widening of the problem in the last sentence—which is often left out when authors quote him—it is fair to say that most anthropologists have understood by "oppressed" simply the

[7] See, for example, *Burridge* (5), pp. 226–9, where a New Guinea people, after a series of reciprocal exchanges or discharges of obligation, attain to a state known as *mngwotngwotiki,* a word which connotes a particular field of relations in which the individuals concerned are temporarily unobliged to each other.

effects of the machinery of colonial expansion and government. The vast bulk of anthropological evidence has been drawn from the colonial situation: the effects of the activities of missionaries, traders, settlers, commercial enterprises and administrative bodies upon subject peoples; the whole business of a sophisticated, often greedy and highly technological civilization imposing its rules and conventions and experience upon those who, hitherto, had led a relatively simple life in small communities based upon hunting, fishing, agriculture and handicrafts. Such evidence may well give a distorted impression, and it is useful to bear in mind that "oppression" does not necessarily come from outside a particular cultural boundary. A people or group may oppress themselves and may only afterwards direct their frustrations at outsiders.[8] Hence perhaps Haddon's telling phrase: "Communities that *feel* (my italics) themselves oppressed. . . ." Further, it should not be thought that the word "oppressed" could refer to anything more than what we have identified already: traditional assumptions weakening, a moral order decaying, a positive and active if not always apparently sober will to participate in wider or different categories of understanding whether these are phrased in economic or political or more mystical terms. "Feeling themselves oppressed" by current assumptions about power, participants in millenarian activities set themselves the task of reformulating their assumptions so as to create, or account for and explain, a new or changing material and moral environment within which a more satisfactory form of redemption will be obtained.

HEROES. The "emergence of a hero" touches the well-springs of an abundant literature. We can afford to be brief. If he is to be accepted as such, a hero or prophet or messiah must make his presence known to the community that is expecting him; and in order to be recognized and enabled to communicate with his followers he must conform in some way to the popular image of a hero or prophet or messiah. Since existing authorities are quick to scent a challenge, it is only prudent to gain the support of respected leaders of the community without appearing as a rival to them; and this an emerging hero can only do if what he has to say expresses and articulates just those questions which the community feels disturbed and anxious about. Further, he should provide clear and acceptable answers or solutions to the questions being asked. Is acceptance really dependent on Haddon's rather vague "religious fervor"? Perhaps. But even if observers of the scene were competent to analyze effectively the hysteria and similar emotional disturbances which accompany many a millenarian movement, within the terms of our view of religion we can see that many other more accessible and as relevant features enter into the developing situation: differences in economic and political circumstances; variations in capacities and opportunities as between millenarian groups and others; impasses of communication and understanding.

Nonetheless, providing that we understand by "religious fervor" not simply an emotional exhibition, but a state-of-being having sociological relevance, it is an important phrase. New assumptions which predicate the creation of a new man, a new culture, society or condition of being are being wrought. And these relate directly to "prosperity and prestige"—though not necessarily to a restoration of traditional kinds of prosperity and prestige. The new assumptions tend to meet in the hero and his (divine) revelation, and almost always refer to a "prosperity and prestige" that are consistent with, and even define, the new conditions of being, the new man. As we shall see, an adequate or more satisfactory way of gaining prestige, of defining the criteria by which the content of manhood is to be measured, stands at the very heart of a millenarian or messianic movement. And these criteria relate on the one hand to gaining or retaining self-respect, status, and that integrity which is implied in the approved retention of a particular status; and on the other hand to an acknowledged process whereby redemption may be won.

Logically, a messianic movement is one that requires a messiah. And so accustomed are we to a "movement" having a leader or hero or prophet that we tend to forget that some millenarian activities may take place without one. There must have been many episodes or occurrences in history, as there certainly have been in Oceania in recent times,[9] which, lacking one who could be identified as a leader, still evoke

8 Below, pp. 92–4 [of *New Heaven New Earth*].
9 See *Burridge* (3), pp. 1–4.

new assumptions and are otherwise of the same genre as those more coherently organized activities in which some kind of hero or prophet or messiah has been identified. In such cases, one may say, the new assumptions are implicit rather than explicit. The messiah or hero or prophet is but an emerging idea, unrealized as yet in the flesh.

PROPHETS. There is no need to say much about the words "messiah," "hero," "prophet," "chiliastic," "millenarian," "messianic," "cult," "movement," "activities." To think that each term refers to a distinct person or situation obscures rather than clarifies, closes rather than opens the sociological problem. Only when the activities have been made to yield to a general conceptual framework may we go on to distinguish different types. Thus although outside the Judaeo-Christian-Islamic traditions there can in the strict sense be no prophets, messiahs or messianic traditions or expectations—though there may well be traditions of a messianic type, and many whom we could say were heroes—we shall use the word prophet to refer to the leader, prime mover, star or central personality in the kinds of activities we are discussing. Chiliastic, millenarian and messianic will be regarded as synonymous terms; and whether the activities constitute a cult or a movement the reader may decide for himself.[10] Such usage does not prejudge any useful distinctions there might be between these terms, but it does avoid argument as to whether a person was really a hero or messiah or false or true prophet before we are in a position to make the argument worthwhile. Being ourselves the children of a long-established tradition of messianic expectations there are advantages in using familiar terms, opportunities only for confusion in adding to the plethora of nomenclatures invented over recent years.[11]

On the other hand, temptations to seize on similarities at the expense of differences should be resisted. As we shall see, there are pertinent differences between one kind of millenarian activity and another. There are also different kinds of prophet—a half-crazed woman obsessed with her visions, for example, or a sickly lad who dreams a dream upon which others act, but who himself is heard of no more; a shrewd man of stature with organizing ability; a visionary or seer given to trances; or a saintly man misled by his own piety. Further, at least in the preliminary stages before a movement has cohered, there may be no prophet at all—just a series of apparently impulsive activities accompanied by inchoate ideas, feelings and emotions. Only when the inchoate ideas have begun to cohere into new assumptions may a prophet emerge to articulate them, show them forth, make them explicit. This is the revelation which, thought of as divinely inspired, provides the basis for a new departure, a new mode of redemption.

Every millenarian movement for which we have evidence comes to us as a story, as a narration of historical or quasihistorical events. Often, too, we find either *ad hoc* or systematic attempts to relate the events of the story to events and features of social relationship which lie outside the confines of the story itself. This, in essence, is what is meant by "extracting the sociology from the history." The issue is how satisfactorily, completely and systematically it may best be done. What we have attempted in developing each brief excursus above in terms of the content of others is a movement towards defining particular kinds of social relations in terms of the content of other kinds of social relations. We have rejected religion as simply a belief in spiritual beings; oppression as necessarily connoting the colonial situation; the prophet as a particular personality type. Instead, we have tried to make some interrelated statements about millenarian activities which can be filled out with empirical fieldwork material.

To summarize:

(a) We are discussing assumptions about power which, whether or not investigator or people concerned think of them as pertaining to spiritual beings, predicate or entail a particular redemptive process.
(b) While the redemptive process is discoverable in discharges and evasions of obligation, redemption itself refers to complete release from obligation and is roughly equivalent to salvation.
(c) The redemptive process, and so redemption,

10 While "activity" is a general descriptive term, one may suggest that a cult, concerned with a particular source of power, is already organized, firm and static, whereas a movement seeks to impose its ideas and present organization upon a wider field.

11 Below, pp. 102–3 [of *New Heaven New Earth*].

bears significantly on the politico-economic process, particularly the prestige system.

(d) A prestige system is based upon particular measurements of manhood which relate to gaining or retaining self-respect and integrity, and which refer back to the politico-economic process, the redemptive process, and assumptions about power.

Accepting these points as a baseline, millenarian movements involve the adoption of new assumptions, a new redemptive process, a new politico-economic framework, a new mode of measuring the man, a new integrity, a new community: in short, a new man. A precondition of this regeneration is a dissatisfaction with the current system. But if we describe this precondition as "feeling oppressed," the "oppression" does not necessarily derive from an external political control: it may be rooted in internal dissatisfactions with present assumptions, rules and modes of redemption. Either way, we are interested in the patterns described when faith belies experience, when given assumptions about power no longer reveal the truth of things, when the redemptive process must change to accord with the new assumptions born of new experience. When, as may happen, the new assumptions and rules are implicit and unorganized, millenarian activities may take place without a prophet being identifiable. A prophet is he or she who organizes the new assumptions and articulates them; who is listened to and found acceptable; whose revelation is accorded authority for however brief a period. But a prophet cannot identify himself in terms of the community as it is: he identifies himself in an image of what might or should be. When the prophet is missing we are like a detective investigating a murder without a motive, or a playwright whose characters are looking for a protagonist. Nevertheless, if we know something about the circumstances and their general pattern, we can make calculated guesses as to what might have been.

Sometimes the evidence at our disposal is thin. But this does not matter so long as our conceptual framework seems adequate to the information we have, and so long as it helps us to identify what we are looking for. Given these features, the framework itself may allow us to fill in some of the gaps.

Polynesian Illustrations

We now look at examples of the kinds of historical events we are trying to render sociologically intelligible. Most of them are taken from Oceania. This is not only because the bulk of the anthropological material comes from Oceania, but because the activities there make a variety of points relatively succinctly and enable us to tease out the detail most economically. The first group of three examples is concerned with Polynesians.

THE HAUHAU MOVEMENT, 1862.[12] The *Hauhau* movement of the Maori people of New Zealand arose directly from a prior movement known as the "King movement," which was a purely political or administrative accommodation. Having become aware that white settlers were not temporary guests, but were taking or buying their hereditary lands and had come to stay, some of the Maori tribes between Taranaki and Waikato in the North Island confederated together under an elderly chief who took the title of King Potatau I. Not all the Maori in the area fully acknowledged the paramountcy of Potatau I, but he served as a rallying point and spokesman in disputes with white settlers and the not always scrupulous land agents of the colonial administration.[13] In any event King Potatau, a vacillating man whose title did not match his ability, could exert little authority. There were troubles, accidental deaths and murders, and consequent reprisals. And the punitive expeditions sent into the area by the European administration led to more reprisals by the Maori.

All these activities came to a head in the *Hauhau* or *Paimarire*[14] movement. The founder of the movement was Te Ua (full name, Te Ua Horopapera Haumene), a man who in his youth had fought against white settlers, afterwards becoming a Christian and taking instruction from Christian missionaries. He was thought to be a lunatic, well known as subject to fits and trances. One day towards the end of 1862 or the begin-

12 Main sources are *Cowan; Babbage; Harrop; Greenwood; Winks.*

13 All Maori tradition was against a paramountcy that had not been directly earned through feasts, gift giving, and war. A Chief had to command rather than beg for respect and obedience.

14 *Pai Marire* means "Good and Peaceful."

ning of 1863, Te Ua announced that the angel Gabriel had appeared to him in a vision. As a "redemption for his people, who had become forgetful, desolate and in doubt," [15] Te Ua said, he would sacrifice his own son. Succeeding only in injuring the boy, Te Ua had another vision of the angel Gabriel and was instructed to take his son to a stream and bathe his wounds. A miraculous cure was reported, local Maori began to give Te Ua more serious attention. Now Te Ua, whose favorite work during his Christian period had been the Book of Revelations, announced that the angel Gabriel had revealed a new religion to him: the *Pai-marire*. The religion of England was false, said Te Ua. No notice should be taken of the Christian sabbath. Men and women should live promiscuously, so as to have children "as the sands." The priests of this new religion would have superhuman powers. Uttering the word "*Hau!*" would bring victory against the whites and recruit legions of angels who were waiting to help the Maori drive the Europeans into the sea. When the Europeans had gone, men from Heaven would teach the Maori all the arts and science of Europeans. By means of the spells, prayers and rituals which the angel Gabriel had revealed, Te Ua's followers would gain the gift of tongues and other miraculous powers. The priests would be able to teach English to adherents in one lesson.[16]

The central feature of *Pai-marire* ritual was a mast which had been salvaged from the *Lord Worsley*, a ship which had run ashore near Cape Egmont only a short while previously, and in the "salvage" of whose cargo Te Ua had been involved. Crossed with a yard, rigged with stays and halliards and adorned with flags and pendants inscribed respectively with a St. George's cross, a St. Andrew's cross or cruciform, and the symbol Ð,[17] the mast, set up in the village by the *marae* or traditional meeting place and burial ground, was known as a *niu*.[18] The rites themselves consisted of Te Ua or a leading disciple standing at the foot of the *niu* or mast inside a set of railings painted red, the followers circling around the pole, chanting hymns which Te Ua had taught them. The angels of the wind, Te Ua said, would visit the faithful during the rites. And to make it easier for the angels to descend, ropes' ends dangled from the yards, participants holding them as they circled the mast as though in maypole dance. Engaging in the rites, Te Ua said, would make the participants invulnerable to the bullets of the white man. In battle, soldiers of the *Pai-marire* should raise the right hand, palm outward and fingertips to wrist in the vertical plane parallel to the body, and shout "*Pai-marire-hau! hau!*"

The Maori word *hau*, uttered staccato as a bark, may refer to the wind, to breath, or the life principle. Reduplicated, and used as a verb, it has the meaning "Strike! Attack!" [19] To the call "*Poriri-hoia!* Fall-in, Soldiers!" the congregation would gather round the pole or *niu*, take up a military order, and proceed round the pole. The chants were repetitive, many being pidgin renderings of European phrases. Thus

> *To Mai Niu Kororia, mai merire!*
> *To rire, rire!*
>
> My Glorious Niu, have mercy on me!
> Have mercy, mercy! [20]

[15] *Winks*, p. 214. Quoting a document by the hand of Te Ua, captured by an English soldier, and published and translated in the *Taranaki Herald* on May 27th, 1865.

[16] *Harrop*, p. 217.

[17] In *Babbage* (p. 30) it is represented that this symbol is a bow and arrow, and, since the Maori did not use bows and arrows, the symbol, it is said, shows how European elements are mixed in with the traditional Maori culture. But though there is evidence that Maori knew about bows and arrows, and might have thought of this symbol as a bow and arrow, those conversant with Polynesian art styles and symbolism will know that an oft-repeated motif, especially among the Maori, was that of a tongue protruding from the mouth of a divinity, thus:

To the present writer it seems much more likely that the symbol Ð is a diagrammatic representation of the protruding tongue, the meanings of which cluster round the themes of generative, competent and defiant power (Cf. *Langewis*). *Harrop*, p. 160, shows the flag of the Maori King with a cruciform and three stars.

[18] *Niu* in traditional Maori culture were sticks or poles used in divination rituals.

[19] The Maori word *hau* is exceedingly complex. Generally speaking it carries the idea of power being exerted. Reduplicated and used as a noun (*hauhau*) it is the bludgeon used for killing birds. See *Williams, H. W.; Cowan*, pp. 6–7; *Winks*, pp. 200–2; *Tregear*.

[20] *Cowan*, p. 10.

would be repeated several times, the words *mai-merire* being thought to be Maori renderings of the Latin *miserere mei*.[21] One of the *Pai-marire* prayers translates in abbreviated form as follows:

By belief in the Ruler, all men shall be saved in the day of the passing over and the pouring out of blood, lest they should be touched by the destroyer, the enemy, the Governor, and his soldiers. This is my earnest striving to you. O Ruler, that the heart of the Governor should be drawn forth by you that it may be withered up in the sun, not to see any brightness because he is the Bad Devil in the world, and destroyer of men.[22]

The "Governor," of course, refers to the head of the white colonial administration.

The *Pai-marire* or *Hauhau* movement first came to the notice of the colonial government in a battle. A captain Lloyd with a company of soldiers penetrated into the country where Te Ua was influential, and, posting his sentries without due care, the captain and his men were ambushed by a party of Maori charging down on them from the bush and shouting *"Pai-marire-hau! hau!"* Taken by surprise, the soldiers were routed, leaving many dead and wounded behind them. These last the Hauhaus de-capitated, smoking the heads in traditional man-ner and then exhibiting them around the neighborhood. With this initial victory the movement spread fast. Tall *niu* poles were erected in village after village. Te Ua instructed disciples and lieutenants in the prayers, rites and incantations of the movement. There were further acts of savagery. A lone missionary, a man who had lived amongst the Maori for most of his working life, and who had hitherto been apparently well loved by them, was crucified, his eyes being swallowed whole as a symbol of the treatment to be meted out to Queen and Parlia-ment.[23] Further miraculous powers were at-tributed to Te Ua. It was said, for example, that through his own spirit familiar—in Polynesian tradition sorcerers were believed to have spirit familiars from whom they obtained information and instructions not available to ordinary men —which appeared to him in the guise of an owl, he was forewarned of, and thus escaped, a punitive expedition which had been sent out to capture him. Such incidents, whether or not they actually occurred, were thought or believed to have occurred, had wide currency, and confirmed the popular belief in Te Ua's great personal *mana* or powers and qualities of leadership and command. He was successfully doing what he said he could do.

In the face of organized European soldiery, however, a millitant movement such as the *Pai-marire* could not last for long. In 1886 Te Ua surrendered to General Chute and pleaded for clemency both for himself and his followers. This clemency was granted and honored.

That the overt and efficient impetus of the movement was based in economic conditions is hardly to be doubted. One of the chiefs of Opotoki informed Bishop Williams of his con-version to *Pai-marire* with the words:

Bishop, many years ago we received the faith from you. Now we return it to you, for there has been found a new and precious thing by which *we shall keep our land*.[24]

Again, as one Hauhau adherent harangued a group of villagers:

These men, these missionaries, were always telling us, "Lay up for yourselves treasure in heaven." And so, while we were looking up to heaven, *our land was snatched away* from beneath our feet.[25]

Land and who should use it for what was a real and concrete problem. For while the Maori sys-tem of subsistence agriculture required large parcels of land which could be allowed to re-turn to forest, lie fallow, and then support the growth of the numerous wild stuffs which the Maori also harvested, the Europeans required relatively small areas of permanently cultivated lands, and vast areas of grassland on which they could rear sheep. The conversion of forest and scrub into permanent grassland affected the Maori most. They had no sheep and were not interested in rearing them even if they could get hold of them. They were deprived of im-portant foodstuffs, edible wild flora and fauna. They were unable to get sufficient access to tradi-tional industrial material resources such as wood and fibrous plants.

21 Idem.
22 *Harrop*, p. 244.
23 *Harrop*, p. 247.
24 *Cowan*, p. 492 (my italics).
25 *Harrop*, p. 280 (my italics).

Keeping in mind the positively expressed objectives of learning English and all the arts and sciences of Europeans, which activities represent new assumptions about power, new ways of expressing obligations, new redemptive media, it is still worthwhile pursuing the issue of land. For this was more than a valuable economic resource. Traditional Maori sentiments of attachment to particular parcels of land, on account of their association with the ancestors, social groupings and deities, joined the living with the glories and values of the past. Through the industrious and efficient exploitation and conservation of land and its resources a man gained prosperity and prestige, made himself worthy of the ancestors, commanded respect from his fellows. Further, intimately related to gaining and losing lands were the capacities to fight and wage war successfully. These features were of prime importance in the accumulation of *mana*: that power of command over resources and other people which contained the essence of Maori integrity.[26] Thus, while the loss of their lands put Maori integrity squarely in question, the *Pai-marire* not only brought together the relevances of land and war, but, in rescuing these traditional criteria of integrity for the future, also pointed to new ways in which a new and larger integrity, a more embracing redemption, might be won.

The King movement reveals the Maori as beginning to adopt the political symbols, forms, and presumably part at least of the categories of understanding of the wider and more powerful community. But this political response could not but fail. The balance of powers was too one-sided. There is little evidence of any real consensus as between Pakeha (whites) and Maori. And even if there was it would be naïve to think that the differences in power deployed by either side would not have been exploited. Nevertheless, it might well be asked whether, without the experience of the political failure of the King movement behind them, any Maori would have rallied to Te Ua and his *Pai-marire* movement. We can hazard a guess, but we cannot know. On the other hand, we can say that since the *Pai-marire* overleaped and transcended the political objectives of the "King movement," the latter may have been a necessary educative preliminary. Moreover, we do know that the religious content of the *Pai-marire*—those new assumptions about power the effects of which, Te Ua asserted, would more than counter-balance the differences in powers wielded by Pakeha and Maori—survived the apparent political failures of the King and *Pai-marire* movements to be realized in a quasi-political form later on. For after the Hauhas had been broken up, Te Kooti, once a *Pai-marire* convert who had been captured by government forces and deported, returned to his native village after peace had been established. And there he founded what was to become a dissident but syncretic religious sect known as the *Ringatau*.[27] Welding together selected Christian and Maori elements, the *Ringatau*, whose core is composed of the descendants of the followers of Te Kooti, survives today.

Given this continuum between the King movement, the *Pai-marire*, and the *Ringatau*, the "success" or "failure" of the *Pai-marire* can only be very narrowly judged by reference to the hopeless war, the mast and its ropes' ends, Te Ua begging for clemency, or an angel slithering down a rope to make a warrior invulnerable to bullets. Rather should it be judged by the *Ringatau* on the one hand, and current conditions and assumptions in the Waikato and Taranaki areas on the other. For these conditions of being, despite what particular individuals at the relevant times might have thought they could forsee, want, or bring about, are what in fact the *Pai-marire* movement helped in an important way to effect. Whether we conceive of the time perspective as spread over a period of weeks, years or generations, we ought to think of a millenarian movement as having (possible) political antecedents and sectarian consequences. It suggests, at the last, that we should look for antecedents and consequences, sectarian or otherwise. By looking at the sequence of events objectively we may gain some understanding of what at first sight seems silly, ill-considered, and even unrelated.

[26] The ability to fight and wage war successfully was intimately related to virility, sexual prowess and generative powers. Genital powers, command over others, fruitful exploitation of land resources, and the ability to fight well with courage and cunning, together spelled out the requirements of integrity.

On *mana* see *Gudgeon; Hogbin; Williamson* (2); *Capell; Firth* (3), among many other more imaginative but perhaps less reliable analyses.

[27] See *Greenwood.*

THE SIOVILI OR "JOE GIMLET" CULT.[28] The activities known as the *Siovili* or Joe Gimlet cult —*Sio* is anglicized to "Joe," and a *vili* is a drill or gimlet—took place in Samoa in the 'thirties and 'forties of the last century. Like other Polynesians, the Samoans were a proud and aristocratic people. They were disdainful of the first Europeans of their acquaintance, thinking them inferior, unhealthy and smelly. Still, after a few years they began to covet the varieties of artifacts which Europeans had. And they connected the possession of these goods not much with the abilities and capacities of Europeans themselves as with their forms of belief, their assumptions about power. If by believing in entities called "God" and "Jesus Christ" and following a series of prescribed rituals these lesser folk could have all these goods, what was to prevent Samoans gaining the same kind of access? It was in this kind of ambience of eager and covetous expectation that Siovili, nicknamed Joe Gimlet, was to find his metier.

Siovili was a native-born Samoan, an early convert to Christianity who always thought of himself as a Christian. He had traveled widely in European ships, visiting Australia among other places. Of particular importance is the fact that one of his voyages had taken him to Tahiti where he had been closely associated with the *Mamaia* movement. This, taking place in 1827, was essentially a politically based schism between two parties of Tahitian Christians. Nevertheless, in the course of the dispute activities of millenarian type took place, and Siovili, a man who was in any case subject to trances, visions, and traditional forms of spirit possession, was much impressed.

When, soon after his Tahitian experience, Siovili returned to Samoa, he had a number of visions which, in revealing a variety of rites and practices, also held out the promise of an abundance of European goods. He attracted a number of followers, who also believed themselves to be Christians. "Don't speak to me," said a Siovili adherent to a Samoan Christian teacher who had been warning him of the dangers of eternal damnation, "I have got a foreign religion as well as you, and mine is as good as yours. Attend to your own soul, I am attending to mine." [29] So far as one may speak of "worship" in this context, Jehovah and Jesus Christ were worshipped by Siovili and his adherents; Jehovah and Jesus Christ were thought to be speaking through Siovili. Access to European goods seems to have been thought to go with the fact of being a Christian. But we cannot without some distortion say that Samoans became Christians in order to obtain European goods—though of course it is possible that some did. Many Samoans who wanted European goods did not become Christians.

One of Siovili's followers was an old woman, herself subject to trances and spirit possession.[30] And she, believing herself to have become possessed by Jesus Christ, announced that Christ was about to return to earth, and that the dead would rise from their graves. Growing crops, she went on, should be plucked from the ground and thrown away; cemeteries should be weeded and tidied. Then Jesus would come walking across the sea, destroy everything, and call down an abundance of food, crops and manufactured goods from the sky. The people of the woman's neighborhood, most of whom seem to have been Christians, did as they were bid, assembling on the beach to await the coming of the Lord. The first day passed. . . . "Tomorrow," said the old lady encouragingly, "Tomorrow He will come." The second day passed. . . . "Christ wishes us to wait three days," said the old lady. The third day came and went. After the fourth day the expectant community returned to their gardens to rescue what they could of their crops. Nonetheless, Siovili's followers retained their integrity as a group, and survived as such in Samoa for a couple of decades or more. They would gather together in lonely bush places to pray, particularly in a dark hut where lay the tattered remnants of a bible which *Siovili* claimed he had been able to read. No less than the manufactured goods of Europeans the capacity of white folk to read and write and so communicate with each other over distances impressed them greatly.[31]

A hymn sung by followers of Siovili translates as follows:

Dash did the ship of the two sailors through the waves,
Necklaces, O Necklaces!

28 See *Freeman.*

29 *Freeman,* p. 191.

30 As a woman, of course, she was in an underprivileged position. Cf. *Lewis.*

31 Compare the *Pai-marire,* above, p. 298.

They two arrived at the country of Britain,
Necklaces, O Necklaces!
A Great Lord is the King of the Skies,
Necklaces, O Necklaces!
Cry to be sent, cry to be sent,
Necklaces, O Necklaces!
Siovili sailed with the ship dashing through the waves,
Necklaces, O Necklaces!
And the living water is come to Eva [in Samoa],
Necklaces, O Necklaces!
Dash did the ship of the two sailors through the waves,
Necklaces, O Necklaces!
And they two arrived at Botany Bay,
Necklaces, O Necklaces!
The Governor is a great King,
Necklaces, O Necklaces!
Dash did the ship of the two sailors through the waves,
Necklaces, O Necklaces!
The two reached the Land of Compassion,
Necklaces, O Necklaces!
A Great Lord is King Jehovah,
Necklaces, O Necklaces! [32]

The hymn, which reveals both Christian and traditional Samoan elements, and which reflects the personal experiences of Siovili himself in the greater community, was sung in the manner of the traditional dancing songs. The chorus "Necklaces, O Necklaces!" refers to the strings of blue beads which the first Europeans brought to Samoa, and which became the symbol of the white man's goods. In the *Pai-marire* case, it will be remembered, the Governor was an object of malediction. Here the Governor is praised. Looking at these features more closely we can perhaps appreciate that whilst many Maori were literate and had enjoyed a reasonable access to European goods by the sale of their lands, they could not stem the flood of white settlers, their objections to whom they personalized in the Governor. In the Samoan case, where there was no settler problem, the economic component of the activities centered around access to a different kind of scarce commodity, European manufactured goods. The Governor, a remote but powerful representative of the whites, is praised and implicitly prayed to give of his bounty as a Samoan chief would be expected to do.[33] In both cases, however, the significance of the economic components is defined by their relation to prestige and integrity, not simply by virtue of scarcity or becoming scarcer.

Samoans, like other Polynesians, found prestige in *mana*—command over others—a feature which went together with a series of graduated titles. These could be earned, or retained when inherited, by a judicious and efficient use of resources in order to provide feasts and participate in exchanges of treasure articles such as fine mats and *tapa* cloth. To give the kinds of feasts which would add to his *mana* and qualify him for higher titles, to increase his turnover of exchanges of treasure articles in relation to others—which also added to *mana* and was a necessary qualification for gaining higher titles —a man had to be able to command the goodwill, co-operation and labor of others. And this he could only do, first, by demonstrating his industry, skill, efficiency and organizational powers in the basic subsistence activities, fishing and horticulture; and second, by conforming to the image of the good man—roughly, cunning, effectiveness and generosity unalloyed by greed and selfishness. Though of course the possession or lack of a variety of other attributes and qualities might add to, or detract from, these basic requirements, the latter were quite definitive. But the differential between those of otherwise apparently equal merit—for almost all in a community were more or less equally competent at fishing and farming, only the inherently lazy or mentally deficient or obstinately non-conformist being markedly inferior in productive capacity—was to be found in the rates of turnover of exchanges of treasure articles. The man with a relatively high or increasing rate of turnover attracted followers and dependents. The man with a relatively low or decreasing rate of turnover found it difficult to retain such followers and dependents as he might have had. Herein lay the value and significance of European goods: they could be exchanged. Having scarcity value as well as reflecting the initiative and ability of one who could obtain them, the passage of European goods in an exchange could make all the difference in a generalized situation of competition for *mana* and titles. Even today village Samoans pursue European goods, chiefly tinned fish, not for purposes of consumption but to pass on to others in exchange. Samoans are thus involved in a credit system in which the

32 *Freeman*, p. 188. There is no indication who the "two sailors" were.
33 There was no "Governor" in Samoa at the time.

more able gain the confidence of others. The capacity to gain such confidence indicates the meaning of *mana,* and the possession of *mana* is acknowledged in titles.

The activities associated with Siovili do not amount to much. Politically insignificant, they were simply a scatter of episodes which troubled no administration though they possibly amused the few resident Europeans. Nevertheless, they can be analyzed within the terms suggested. And these identify the activities as millenarian in nature. Encountering a different kind of power, and different assumptions about power—those of Europeans—some Samoans attempted to come to terms with them. At the time politically oppressed by no one in particular, but coveting European goods, some Samoans yet felt themselves oppressed or frustrated by their inability to obtain a sufficiency of European goods. This prevented them from gaining those heights of prestige and integrity which the possession of European goods would have given them the opportunity to attain. Or, to put it another way, they had to be content with less than the best. Conceiving a higher, finer or more difficult or worthwhile mode of redemption, they had to be content with a lower, grosser and less satisfying one. With assumptions about power—particularly those whose realization could add to *mana* and so to an overall integrity—in question, a well-traveled prophet, experienced in the ways of white men and their powers, not only expressed current doubts but attempted to resolve them by articulating acceptable answers: "Take over European assumptions about power if you want their kinds of powers."

As in the *Pai-marire,* the "success" or "failure" of the activities sparked off by Siovili should not be judged against the disappointment of those who waited in vain for Christ to come over the sea, nor by the continuing normal weather conditions which failed to shower goods from the sky. These are things which we who know so much better can afford to chuckle about. Rather should we note the sustained interest of Siovili's followers in attempting to realize the new assumptions which had been brought into their cognizance, the attention they paid to the techniques of the new powers they had encountered —writing in particular—and the conditions obtaining in the region when Siovili himself was but a memory or almost forgotten. Siovili and his followers put to the test an hypothesis about power, and in the action something was learned about the truth.

A Cook Islands Movement. Both the *Pai-marire* and *Siovili* activities, which occurred over a century ago, show us small groups of people attempting to grasp at viable assumptions about the conditions of being in an environment in which power, and the allocation of particular kinds of power, were changing or had changed. Much nearer our own time, but with the same kind of relevance, is a movement which is reported as having taken place in the Cook Islands in 1947.[34] In this case the prophet was an old lady with a reputation for powers of spirit possession. She had made a journey to Rarotonga, and whilst there two spirits had appeared to her in a dream. They told her to return home and prepare the people to receive a shipload of European goods which would come to her island in a spirit ship. Accordingly, the old lady returned to her native village, called a meeting, and was soon possessed by the spirit of her elder brother. The latter spoke through her to the assembled villagers, instructing them to make a sacred place or *marae*. When the *marae* was complete the spirit ship would come to the island laden with bully beef—at the time the most desired and scarcest imported food. Though the site indicated by the spirit as proper for the *marae* was about two miles inland, since the ship was to be a spirit ship this was no obstacle.

At some expense in voluntary labor and sweat, therefore, the *marae* was built, and the community waited as the appointed day for the ship to arrive drew nigh. At the last moment, however, the prophet insisted that her followers should receive a form of baptism—a mark on the forehead made with red clay and water in the name of Satan. One man refused this baptism. He asserted that he had already been baptized in Christ. At this the old lady exclaimed that now all their efforts would probably be in vain. Still, she would ask the gods to be merciful and send the ship notwithstanding. . . .

After three days of waiting for the ship at the *marae* the company disbanded, blaming the single recalcitrant for the failure of the ship to arrive.

Though this Cook Islands movement bears most of the hallmarks of a typical Melanesian

[34] See *Crocombe.*

"cargo" movement, if we remember the old woman of the *Siovili* activities,[35] the role of the *marae* in the *Pai-marire,*[36] and know something about traditional forms of spirit possession in Polynesia,[37] we can appreciate that the cultural idiom is Polynesian rather than Melanesian. It is also worth bearing in mind that the Cook Islanders were converted to Christianity in the 1820s and 1830s—five or six generations of Christians. While there is little doubt that, in common with other administrations, the administration of the Cook Islands might be improved, no one could within reason call it oppressive. Yet life tends to be dull, few ships call, the islands are isolated, aside from the mainstream of civilized and moneyed life. The inhabitants live within the confines of a simple subsistence economy based on horticulture and fishing. There are a few trading concerns which sell sundry supplies and provisions and bring a little money into the islands through the export of copra and dried sea foods. The administration itself brings money into the islands, and migrants to New Zealand send some of their wages home to their relatives. Still, some Cook Islanders, who perhaps were unable to make money for themselves, coveted the goods that only money can buy. As was the case with Siovili and his followers, the Cook Islanders in question may be taken to have conceived a different or more satisfying form of redemption. Either, with goods coming freely across the sea, they would have been discharged from all obligations of a material kind; or, given such access to goods, they would have been able to discharge their personal obligations to each other in terms of assumptions which included the power to gain free access to the goods. And with the help of a traveled old lady they attempted to realize the assumptions she had articulated to them. She it was who seemed to bring the improbable into the field of the possible.

How difficult was it for the old lady to do this?

Not all millenarian movements evidence the spirituality some might prefer as the basis of religious activity. If true faith springs only from syntheses of spiritual and pragmatic experience, we welcome the confident assurance that life would be just as we wanted it to be if we but filled in the coupon. Though for many Europeans of an idealist or romantic turn of mind the Polynesian Islands seem a paradise where no one need worry about money, for some Polynesians it is perhaps this very lack of money that contributes towards envisaging a millennium where there is an abundance of those things that only money can buy.

[35] Above, p. 302.
[36] Above, p. 299.
[37] See *Ellis; Best; Williamson* (1) and (2); *Firth* (4); *Guiart* (3).

REFERENCES CITED

Babbage, S., 1937, *Hauhauism,* New Zealand.

Best, E., 1924, *Maori Religion and Mythology,* Wellington, New Zealand.

Burridge, K., 1960, *Mambu: A Melanesian Millenium,* London.

——— 1965, "Tangu, Northern Madang District," in P. Lawrence and M. Meggitt (eds.), *Gods, Ghosts, and Men in Melanesia,* O.U.P., Melbourne, pp. 224–49.

Capell, A., 1939, "The Word 'mana': A Linguistic Study," *Oceania* IX:89–126.

Chinnery, E. and A. Haddon, 1917, "Five New Religious Cults in British New Guinea," *The Hibbert Journal,* XV, No. 3, pp. 448–63.

Crocombe, R., 1961, "A Modern Polynesian Cargo Cult," *Man,* 28.

Ellis, W., 1929, *Polynesian Researches,* 2 volumes, London.

Firth, R. 1940, *The Work of the Gods in Tikopia,* London.

Freeman, J., 1959, "The Joe Gimlet or Siovili Cult," in J. Freeman and W. Geddes (eds.), *Anthropology in the South Seas,* New Plymouth, New Zealand, pp. 185–99.

Greenwood, W., 1942, "The Upraised Hand," *Journal of the Polynesian Society,* Volume 51, pp. 1–81.

Gudgeon, W., 1905, "Mana Tangata," *Journal of the Polynesian Society,* Volume 14, No. 6, pp. 81–90.

Guiart, J., 1962, *Les Religions de L'Oceanie,* Paris.

Harrop, A., 1937, *England and the Maori Wars,* London.

Hogbin, I., 1936, "Mana," *Oceania,* Volume 6, No. 3, pp. 241–74.

Langewis, L., 1956, "Lamak and Malat in Bali," *Royal Tropical Institute,* No. CXIX, pp. 37–45.

Lewis, I. 1966, "Spirit Posession and Deprivation Cults," *Man,* Volume I, No. 3, pp. 307–29.
Lienhardt, R., 1956, "Religion," in H. Shapiro (ed.), *Man, Culture, and Society,* New York, pp. 310–29.
Tregear, E., 1904, "The Pai-Marire word *Hau", Journal of the Polynesian Society,* Volume 13, p. 193.
Tylor, E., 1891, *Primitive Culture,* 2 volumes, London.
Vernon, G., 1962, *Sociology of Religion,* McGraw-Hill, New York.
Winks, R., 1953, "The Docrine of Hauhauism," *Journal of the Polynesian Society,* Volume 62, No. 3, pp. 199–237.
Williams, H. 1917, *A Dictionary of the Maori Language,* Wellington, New Zealand.
Yinger, M., 1957, *Religion, Society and the Individual,* Macmillan, New York.

SECTION II

Magical Controls— Witchcraft, Divination, and Curing

Belaboring the analytic distinctions between religion and magic is not a very invigorating intellectual exercise. The standard distinction made is that religion entails the belief in supernatural beings and that religious observances are essentially supplicative. The deity is *asked* for aid. But aid is not certain to follow; God will decide and do what is best. Magic is characterized by the greater prominence of belief in supernatural powers that may be embodied in particular objects, actions, or events—a lucky charm, avoiding walking under a ladder, a black cat crossing one's path. Magical observances are thus *manipulative.* If carefully followed, the magical formula automatically gets results. Witchcraft, divination, and curing are the three forms most often taken by those who try to control events by magical means.

When efforts at magical control are unsuccessful, it is usually assumed that an error has been made, a formula not properly followed: an essential ingredient was left out of a potion, the wording of an incantation was incorrect, or the stars were not in proper position. So long as stress persists and there is no available alternative for dealing with it, failure to achieve relief by magical means rarely results in a loss of faith. On the contrary. Next time efforts to get it right are likely to be doubled.

Considering the widespread belief that most important things that affect human life are caused by the supernatural, it is not surprising that times of tension and crisis are often accompanied by an increase in witchcraft accusations, spirit possession, and reports of other forms of supernatural power at work. Otherwise unexplainable misfortune is frequently assumed to emanate from some malevolent person's manipulation of the forces of evil. Often this assumption is, in a sense, correct. Those jealous of the apparent good luck of others, frustrated by their own hard times, or eager to avenge some wrong, do frequently turn to witchcraft as a means of venting their hostility, of covertly getting even without getting caught.

Belief in the supernatural source of power of those who practice witchcraft and can induce spirit possession is unnecessary to understand why their methods are so frequently effective. Reliance on witchcraft and belief in spirit possession, as Lewis indicates, set reactions in motion that often have a dramatic psychological and social impact—particularly upon those who are already deprived, frustrated, and discontented.

A Structural Approach to Witchcraft and Spirit Possession

I. M. Lewis

Introduction

It has long been recognized that unsolicited possession by malevolent, capricious spirits may serve as an explanation of illness and affliction in much the same fashion as witchcraft and sorcery. But, whereas a substantial body of anthropological research amply demonstrates how accusations of witchcraft reflect social tensions, recognition that a corresponding nexus also exists in the case of possession by such spirits is still something of a novelty. After certain necessary preliminaries, this paper illustrates by way of a few selected ethnographic examples how what I shall call "peripheral" spirit-possession does relate to situations of stress and conflict. It then ventures into a wider discussion of the possible structural correlates of witchcraft on the one hand, and of spirit-possession on the other.

I shall argue that the most significant distinction between these two phenomena is not the obvious cultural one, but the manner in which they operate and are utilized. The victim of affliction who attributes his difficulties to witchcraft is employing a direct strategy which assigns responsibility for his troubles to a rival or enemy. On the other hand, the victim who interprets his affliction in terms of possession by malevolent spirits utilizes an oblique strategy in which immediate responsibility is pinned, not on his fellow-men, but upon mysterious forces outside society.[1] Here it is only indirectly that pressure is brought to bear by the victim on the real targets that he seeks to influence. It is in the reaction of other members of his society to an affliction, for which the victim is not himself accountable, that a measure of redress is achieved. From the standpoint of the victim of affliction, the effect may be broadly similar inasmuch as in both strategies he becomes the center of attention and succour. But the fact that the means of achieving this end differ in the two cases, and have different effects on other members of society, suggests that one strategy might be more appropriate to a given set of social circumstances than the other. This suggests that there should in fact be distinct social correlates of each strategy; and, as I hope to show, I think that this is to a certain extent empirically true.

Let me first explain, however, what I mean by the expression "peripheral possession." I have in mind two aspects of peripherality. First, the spirits with which we are here concerned are themselves peripheral in the sense that they are not morally charged powers held to be responsible for upholding public morality by rewarding meritorious acts and punishing sins. On the contrary, they have no direct moral responsibility and are quite separate from other spirits which may be invoked as the guardians of customary morality. Thus they stand apart from the central morality cults of the societies in which they cause such wanton affliction, and, indeed, are regularly believed to be of foreign origin and provenance. Sometimes they are conceived of as the spirits of hostile neighboring peoples and, perhaps equally frequently, as mischievous nature spirits totally outside society and culture.

Second, contrary to the arbitrary and capricious qualities with which they are credited, these spirits are in fact often mobilized in particular social contexts which can be charted and specified with at least as much clarity and predictability as in the case of witchcraft accusations. One of the most obvious and widespread of these is the marked predilection which such spirits regularly show for women in general, and, on a more restricted front, for certain depressed and despised categories of men, as well as individuals of either sex in circumstances of unusually severe social disability (cf. Lewis, 1966; Wilson, 1967).

Since, however, particularly when they belong

Source: From I. M. Lewis, "A Structural Approach to Witchcraft and Spirit Possession," *Witchcraft Confessions and Accusations,* edited by Mary Douglas (London: Associated Book Publishers Ltd., 1970). Used by permission of the publisher, and the author.

[1] I recognize, of course, that the use of external "witches" as scapegoats corresponds closely, in its effects, to this oblique use of spirit-possession. As I argue later in the paper, the line between what is usually called "spirit-possession" and what is usually called "witchcraft" is by no means absolute.

to low-status or low-caste groups, men may also be involved, the high incidence of possession in women cannot very plausibly be ascribed to any inherent biological predisposition on their part. On the contrary, the facts here point to a common denominator of deprivation, frustration, and discontent. This conclusion is moreover fully supported by an examination of the treatment or response given to the victims of these spirit maladies. What clearly emerges is the special consideration, privileges, and unusually exalted status accorded to women who in other circumstances are treated as legal minors, or to men in subordinate positions who are normally subject to strong discrimination.

For those who fall in such "peripheral" social categories, as well as for abnormally hard-pressed and precariously placed individuals, such possession has much to offer as a response to affliction where its treatment leads to the enhancement, even if only temporarily, of position and status. To demonstrate this function of peripheral possession is not, of course, to offer a total explanation of the existence of the phenomenon. Nor does it rule out the possibility that other functions may also be served concurrently, or separately, by what some writers have called the possession syndrome.

Typical Examples of Peripheral Possession

These points can best be documented by reference to a few ethnographic examples. Consider, first, the BaVenda of Southern Africa as described by Stayt (1931). Among the BaVenda there is a central morality cult of patrilineal and matrilateral ancestors. However, Stayt also records that from 1914 onwards there has been an upsurge of new, non-ancestral spirits which are identified as having come from neighboring Shona tribes. These invasive powers (*tshilombo*) which possess women, causing them to speak in Chi-Karanga, or in a mixture of that language and Venda, provide a clear example of what I mean by peripheral spirits. They are above all mischievous, causing illness, and usually live in the crevices of trees where they make weird, unnatural noises (Stayt, 1931, p. 302). Their presence in sick married women whom they regularly torment is diagnosed by doctors (*nganga*). Following diagnosis, the husband quickly summons help, especially from his wife's kin, and calls in the services of a drummer who knows the spirit-dance beat (*molombo*) and of a rattle-diviner (a female shaman). The patient, who is plied with medicines, eventually responds to the music and dances wildly until she falls on the ground. After repeated periods of dancing and resting, the spirit eventually reveals itself by a deep bull-like grunt from the patient who is now questioned by the rattle-diviner shaman. The spirit usually replies in some such terms as follows: "I am so and so, and I entered you when I was walking in a certain place; you did not treat me well; I want a present, some clothes or ornaments." She may, adds Stayt, even demand such symbols of male authority as a spear or axe of her ancestors, or a tail-whisk or kerrie stick, as well as the brightly colored clothes favored by the spirits. All the objects demanded are readily promised by the husband and relations of the afflicted woman. Her husband also provides a goat for his wife to feast on, and pays for the diviner's services. All these gifts are offered indirectly to the woman through her invasive familiar, who is exhorted to take them and permit the patient to recover.

Such relief, however, is only temporary. Following her first possession, a married woman regularly succumbs at times of difficulty and distress to further attacks of possession and, when seized by the spirit, dons her special clothes and dances the *molombo* beat. She is in fact now a novitiate member of a coterie of recurrently possessed women and may in time graduate to the position of female rattle-diviner, or shaman, who is a mistress of spirits. Whenever she is possessed, her husband and relatives must treat her with respect and consideration, saluting her "as if she were a chief." Her husband, in turn, is addressed as "grandchild." And, of course, each new attack of possession involves further outlays of gifts and food by the husband. It is therefore perhaps not surprising to learn that, after the departure of the spirit following such an attack, the woman often becomes very fat (Stayt, 1931, p. 305)!

It is obvious that what is involved here, if not a mystically couched feminist movement, is a culturally accepted procedure whereby downtrodden wives in this male-dominated society press their claims for attention and regard from their menfolk. Individual cases of possession are responses to situations of stress or discontent where more direct methods of ventilating grievances are blocked or not available. The formal ideology of male dominance is maintained in this society where divorce is rare and allowed only in very special circumstances (see below).

This aspect of the situation emerges clearly in a case cited by Stayt (pp. 306–307). Here the victim was not a married woman, but a girl betrothed against her will to a man she did not like, such arranged marriages being the norm. In this instance, after being taken unwillingly to her betrothed's village, she bolted home. There her father beat her soundly and she ran off into the bush and disappeared completely for six days. After this she returned looking very ill and complaining bitterly. Her father sent for a doctor who diagnosed that the reluctant bride was possessed by a spirit. That night the girl rose and commanded her father to follow her. He protested but, since she spoke in a strange Chi-Karanga spirit-voice, he was afraid of her and obeyed. It is hardly necessary to follow this account further here, except to say that this was the beginning of this girl's career as a mistress of spirits. By the time Stayt arrived, he found that this woman had become one of the most famous rattle-diviners and shamans in Vendaland.

I do not need to labor the point I am making about the use made by women of these spirits, but I want now to refer briefly to the Gurage of Ethiopia to show how the locus of spirit-possession may be widened to include men in subordinate social categories. The Gurage have a main morality cult centering on a male God (*waka*) who is worshipped by men as the upholder of social values and general morality. This cult does not involve possession. They also have, however, a cult centering on a female deity (*damwamwit*) who is worshipped by and possesses all free-born women and all men of the despised Fuga carpenter class. Participation by women or Fuga men in the calendrical rites addressed to this spirit, or possession by her in times of particular distress or affliction, enables both to behave and to be treated as though they were noble Gurage males (Shack, 1966). Again, despite its at least initial association with illness and its continuing connection with distress and discontent, the advantages of possession are obvious. And in the case of the Fuga, possession-involvement in the cult evidently represents a sort of mystical neutralization of revolutionary tendencies, much in the same manner as Luc de Heusch has suggested applies with Hutu participation in the *kubandwa* possession-cult in Rwanda (de Heusch, 1966, pp. 158ff.).

A similar content seems to have been present in the nineteenth-century Fijian water-baby cult, which presaged the later cargo cults of the region and which, in its nomenclature at least, is also in some respects a precursor of our contemporary "flower people." Here young people and minor chiefs excluded from high positions in the traditional power structure rallied together to join the water-baby cult, being possessed by forest- and water-sprites, and taking new personal names—usually those of flowers (Worsley, 1957, pp. 26–27).

As a final illustration I refer to M. E. Opler's richly documented analysis of spirit-possession in Northern India (Opler, 1958). Here, in Uttar Pradesh, disaffiliated malevolent spirits, or ghosts, haunt the weak and vulnerable and those whose social circumstances are precarious. Thus the young married woman "beset by homesickness, fearful that she may not be able to present sons to her husband and his family, may label her woes a form of ghost possession." And, "if she has been ignored and subordinated, the spirit possession may take an even more dramatic and strident form as a compensation for the obscurity under which she has labored" (Opler, op. cit., p. 565). Equally, people of low caste express their aggression towards the higher castes to which they are subordinated through possessing spirits which allow them to insult and castigate their superiors. Those of high caste, in turn, tend to be "persecuted by large, dark, low-caste spirits." And, most interestingly, in the troubled period following Partition, "the ghosts of deceased Muslims were exceedingly active in persecuting Hindus" (Opler, op. cit., p. 566).

Peripheral Possession and Witchcraft

These examples show clearly how the incidence of possession by peripheral spirits relates to social tensions, particularly between subordinate and superior. The parallel with witchcraft and sorcery accusations is obvious. It remains to explore the distinctions that were noted earlier between these phenomena as, respectively, oblique and direct redressive mystical strategies. Perhaps before we attempt this, however, we should dispose of the prior question: If spirit-possession and witchcraft (or sorcery) both reflect tensions, albeit in different ways, are they mutually exclusive? For those who approach the question from the cosmological angle, the answer usually given is: Yes. Thus, in his paper

Table 1. *Social Contexts of Peripheral Possession and Witchcraft*

People	*Context of Primary Peripheral Spirit-Affliction*	*Context of Witchcraft (and/or Sorcery)*
Akamba	domestic domain: women versus men	generalized enmity, including that between co-wives
BaThonga	ditto	ditto
Lenje	ditto	ditto
Taita	ditto	ditto
BaVenda	ditto	ditto
Zulu	ditto	ditto
Valley Tonga	ditto	ditto
Luo	ditto	ditto
Lugbara	?	ditto
Banyoro	ditto	ditto
Gurage	ditto, and subordinate Fuga contra free-born Gurage men	?

on Nuba shamanism, Nadel says: "The Nyima have no witchcraft. Shamanism absorbs all that is unpredictable and morally indeterminate and saves the conception of an ordered universe from self-contradiction" (Nadel, 1964, p. 34). Likewise, many would tend to argue that people who suppose that spirits can injure them out of pure malevolence do not require the idea of a witch to fill a gap in their picture of the universe.

The facts are, however, quite the contrary. In many cultures, witchcraft and malevolent spirit-possession of the kind discussed here both occur. This is so for a start among the Venda; and equally among the Kamba, BaThonga, Lenje, Zulu, Pondo, Valley Tonga, Luo, Lugbara, Banyoro, and Taita—to cite merely a few scattered African examples on which data are readily available. Indeed, the very common association of witchcraft with spirit-familiars—often of opposite sex to the person possessed—is a rather obvious indication of the impossibility of regarding these mystical forces as mutually exclusive in any given society or culture. Nor, of course, is it necessary to look very far afield for striking examples of the coexistence of witchcraft and spirit-possession. Our own sixteenth- and seventeenth-century Christian culture is abundantly rich in instances of witches whose malign power was intimately connected with invasive incubi and succubi.

Thus, evidently, in many cultures these two forces coexist and sometimes even blend into a hybrid entity. This evidence provides us with an excellent opportunity for testing our initial deduction that, since they represent different strategies of attack, spirit-possession and witchcraft should have distinct social correlates, or occur in contrasting social situations. Table 1, which summarizes the evidence from some of the peoples I have referred to, seems to indicate that this is the case. In the examples listed, involuntary seizure by capricious peripheral spirits appears to be primarily restricted to the domestic domain, where it is used by female dependants against their menfolk; and sometimes, as with the Gurage, it is also applied by male subordinates to bring pressure to bear upon their superiors. Witchcraft and sorcery accusations, by contrast, seem to operate in a wider sphere of interaction and to be utilized in general contexts of hostility, particularly between equals, or between superior and subordinate. Where, moreover, witchcraft accusations are leveled by an inferior against a superior (as in the case of the unpopular Lugbara elder), the intention is to cast the superior down from his pedestal and to assert equality. More specifically, in the polygynous family nexus: rivalry between co-wives characteristically takes the form of accusations of witchcraft (or sorcery); in conflict between husband and wife, the latter tends to resort to spirit-possession, while the former may accuse his wife of witchcraft.

I do not claim that these distinctions are absolute, but I think that the evidence indicates trends in these two directions. This suggests that the oblique spirit-possession strategy attempts to redress a situation of adversity by making claims for attention and demonstrations of regard from a superior in a relationship of inequality without completely challenging that relationship. It expresses insubordination, but not generally to the point where it is desired to sever the relationship or subvert it entirely. It ventilates aggression and frustration within the *status quo*. Witchcraft and sorcery accusations, on the contrary, representing as they do a much more direct line of attack, express hostility between equal rivals, or between superior and subordinate (here paralleling the operation of spirit-possession in the reverse direction), and often seek to sunder an unbearably tense relationship (cf. Marwick, 1965, pp. 171–191). Thus, where they occur together in the same culture as alternative strategies, generally peripheral spirit-possession offers a milder, less revolutionary line of attack, a conflict strategy which is less disruptive in its effects.

Consistent with these distinctions, possession-afflictions in wives do not normally seem to provide immediate grounds for divorce by the husband, whereas accusations of witchcraft directed against a wife may be used to this effect. Thus, for example, among the Venda, where in Stayt's time at least divorce was rare and not readily obtained, one of the special circumstances in which a wife could be divorced was precisely when she had been designated a witch (Stayt, 1931, p. 152). Again among the Venda, some indication of the relative strengths and severity of the two lines of attack is provided by the fact that, if peripheral spirit-possession actually led to a possessed woman's death, her husband would accuse his wife's mother of being a witch and would demand and receive compensation for the killing (Stayt, op. cit., p. 305).

Finally, at the cosmological level also, I think that we can detect the same regular contrasts between the severity and relative heinousness of the two types of power. Witchcraft and sorcery are regularly identified with incest and subversion, or even inversion of all commonly accepted moral values. In the popular folk view they represent the negation of morality and of normal social relations. The peripheral spirits with which we are concerned here, however, although also evil, are often not painted quite so black. Above all, they are capricious and mischievous, striking without any cause that can be directly referred to social relations or moral assumptions. In fact they seem to epitomize amorality rather than immorality: they stand totally outside society and inhabit a world apart from that of men, yet one that in many ways is modeled on that of men. Typically, they range free in nature and are not subject to human constraints. Characteristically, they roam wild in the bush, are disaffiliated, inhuman, and come from outside any given culture in which they figure as sources of tribulation. All this seems consistent with the distinctions noted previously between these two types of mystical attack.

Possession and Witchcraft Divination

So far I have been arguing that where spirit-possession and witchcraft both occur in the same culture they tend to function in different social contexts and to have different social effects, although I admit that the differences may be only of degree. However, in many societies the situation is in reality more complex than this, since the two phenomena frequently merge or coalesce into a hybrid force, at least in some contexts.

Thus for example among the Lugbara (Middleton, 1969) there are two separate classes of diviner: the first, who are exclusively men and whom Middleton calls oracles, divine sickness caused by the ancestors in punishment of sins. The second, exclusively women, or homosexual males, divine in cases of sickness ascribed to witchcraft or sorcery. These latter female diviners, unlike their male counterparts, are inspired through possession by peripheral spirits. From Middleton's earlier published data it is

Table 2. *Peripheral Possession Linked with Divination and Witchcraft*

People	*Context of Primary Phase*	*Context of Secondary Phase*
Luo	conjugal and domestic	anti-witchcraft divination; diviners suspected of witchcraft
Banyoro	ditto	ditto
Lenje	ditto	ditto

not clear to me whether spirit-possession also operates in the conjugal context discussed earlier in this paper, but it is surely highly significant that here we find spirit-possessed women enlisted as diviners in cases of witchcraft and sorcery which often arise in situations of lineage fission and lead to the dissolution of the authority of established leaders (Middleton, 1960). Among the Lugbara, such spiritually inspired divination is reported to be a recent innovation. This suggests that it may perhaps be interpreted as a kind of spiritual suffragette movement having the effect of opening up new and highly significant avenues of social advancement for women.[2]

Whether or not this is a valid interpretation, here we see spirits enlisted in the fight against witches: whether diviners are also sometimes suspected of being themselves witches or sorcerers is not clear at the moment. However, in a number of other cases (Table 2) this association is definitely present. In Bunyoro, for instance, where it is evident from some of Beattie's case-material (1961, p. 24) that peripheral spirit-possession may function as a restitutive mechanism in the conjugal situation, the same type of possession is also involved in one kind of sorcery and in divination (Beattie, 1963, pp. 44–54). Here "professional sorcerers" who sell their services to the public are also spirit-inspired diviners; and sorcery can be employed either through the use of malevolently powerful *mahembe* horns, or through medicines and techniques supplied by mediums possessed by peripheral spirits of foreign origin.[3] The latter spirits, called *mbandwa,* include the Cwezi "hero-gods" associated with the former legendary rulers of Bunyoro.

Again, among the Luo of Kenya, where a well-defined peripheral spirit-possession cult connected with women has been clearly described by Michael Whisson (1964), diviners may also be inspired by such spirits both to cure and to cause disease. In this case married women regularly succumb to possession-afflictions to bring pressure on their husbands, and in due course graduate to become spirit-possessed diviners. Those who thus come to control these spirits, however, may also use them in witchcraft against others. Much the same appears to be true in the case of the Lenje described by Earthy (1933, pp. 196ff.), where wives are armed by spirit-possession against their husbands and may also graduate in time to become mistresses of spirits operating both as diviners and as sorcerers (or witches). Male diviners, in contrast, operate in the context of the ancestor cult.

In dealing with this and other similar material it seems to me useful to distinguish between what might be called a "primary" and a "secondary" phase in the onset and socialization of possession. In the primary stage, women use "involuntary" and uncontrolled possession in the domestic domain as a recurrent means of coping with the stresses and difficulties of matrimony, for which (with true female logic) they hold their husbands responsible. These are alleviated by gifts and special gestures of conciliation from the husbands. In the secondary phase, such women have graduated through membership of a regular possession coterie or cult group to become controllers of spirits. They now function as diviners, thus assuming an active role which readily leads them to be accused of being witches or sorcerers. The factors that lead them into the second phase may relate to radical changes in their domestic situation (e.g. divorce or bereavement), or to different stages in the developmental cycle of the family. In any event, I suggest that the hostile reactions that primary-phase possession undoubtedly evokes on the part of men come to focus mainly on the secondary phase, in which possessed women, controlling

2 Although very little is generally known of the history of peripheral possession cults in tribal societies, most observers of these cults, at least in Africa, report that they have arisen within this century. Since, almost invariably, they predominantly involve women and clearly operate to some extent as women's protest movements, it seems probable that they reflect changing aspirations and attitudes towards their traditional status on the part of women. Thus, as the character of the spirits themselves suggests, they seem to be responses to social change, and, perhaps, often direct reactions to the diffusion of modern views on the enfranchisement of women. Certainly, contrary to Wilson's unconvincing assertions concerning the alleged complete socialization of women in traditional roles (Wilson, 1967), in many cases there is direct evidence of spirit-possessed women seeking to assume male roles which they specifically covet, and their exclusion from which they explicitly resent. For particularly clear evidence of this, see Harris (1957).

3 The fact that Banyoro diviners are often inspired by peripheral spirits associated with witchcraft, and are frequently women, seems to me to go far to explain why it is that divination is connected with the left-hand—an ethnographic "puzzle" that Dr. Rodney Needham has recently sought to explore by means of an elaborate excursion into symbolic analysis (Needham, 1967).

their spirits, assume authoritarian roles which more directly threaten, or challenge, male authority. Hence the assumption that such diviners may be sorcerers (or witches). Hence also the equation, controlled spirit-possession = divination-sorcery (or witchcraft).

Conclusions: Strategies of Mystical Attack

So far we have been concerned with possession by peripheral spirits as a response to tension experienced in different social contexts and its institutionalization in divination by women who are liable to be concurrently suspected of being witches. In other cultures a further pattern of association between witchcraft and possession is evident.

Among the Pondo of South Africa, for example, witchcraft is quite unambiguously connected with possession by evil peripheral spirits. Witches are generally women and are inspired by obscene familiars—the *tokoloshe,* with their grotesquely large penises, and through whose malign power they can illegitimately destroy life and property (Hunter, 1936, pp. 275–320). The concept of witchcraft here is very close to that held in Europe between the fifteenth and seventeenth centuries, with witches inspired by possessing incubi. As in European witchcraft, among the Pondo the possession of such familiars is taken as proof of witchcraft. Here, however, it seems that no distinction is made between "primary" possession in the conjugal sphere and witchcraft at large; that is, there is no specialized female possession which can be distinguished from witchcraft and used against husbands in the marital context. Yet women also figure significantly as diviners, fighting witchcraft; but in this case they are possessed not by peripheral spirits (= witchcraft), but by the ancestors. Thus an unambiguous conceptual distinction is made between those spirits that animate witchcraft and those that inspire anti-witchcraft diviners, although both roles are generally held by women. Antisocial malevolence is ascribed to the invasive peripheral spirits which possess witches; diviners owe their power to the ancestors who uphold customary morality. These female diviners thus act as auxiliary functionaries in the Pondo main morality cult of ancestors.

This clear-cut polarity between the sources of witchcraft and the afflictions ascribed to its influence on the one hand, and of ancestor-inspired diviners on the other, is fairly closely paralleled among the Gusii (LeVine, 1963). Much the same applies in Christian Ethiopia (Levine, 1965, pp. 68ff.), and in those Philippine communities recently described by Lieban (1967) where sorcerers are inspired by malign peripheral spirits, and diviners and healers by good spirits which are part of the main morality cult; in this case the cult is that of Latin Christianity, and it has not only morphological resemblances but also direct historical links with the older European tradition. The essays by Brown (pp. 17–45) and Cohn (pp. 3–16) in this volume discuss European witchcraft in detail.* Here I would only reiterate that, in its developed form, European witchcraft involved possession by devils, while power to treat the bewitched and to cast forth their satanic spirits lay with clerical exorcists who were inspired by Christ and the Holy Ghost. In practice, this ideologically rigid polarity was sometimes transcended in those not uncommon cases where exorcising priests themselves fell a prey to the devils they sought to exorcise.

There are thus at least two patterns of connection between witchcraft (or sorcery) and spirit-possession. In the first, possession by peripheral spirits is the source both of witchcraft and of anti-witchcraft divination, of affliction and its remedy. In the second, peripheral spirits animate only witchcraft; divination is inspired by powers which directly uphold social morality. From the material discussed in this paper it seems that, where peripheral possession has an unsolicited, uncontrolled, primary phase (as in the domestic situation), its controlled use in divination automatically associates the latter with witchcraft. Since it can be applied for good (divination) as well as for evil purposes (sorcery) there is no need to enlist the main morality powers as alternative sources of divinatory and curative inspiration. Where, however, the possessed person is not regarded as the helpless victim of the spirits but is believed to have solicited their support, and only a controlled nexus between possession and peripheral spirits is posited, it becomes necessary to enlist the main morality powers in divination and healing. In the first case, peripheral possession-afflictions are ultimately dealt with by taming and domesticating the spirit, by bringing it under control.

* Not reprinted here.—*ed.*

When this happens, those who can control spirits and treat the afflicted are automatically suspected of being witches. In the second case, evil peripheral spirit-possession is treated by the exorcism of the afflicting spirit, by casting it out, not by taming it; and this requires the enlistment of superior mystical forces.

I do not claim that these conclusions by any means exhaust the problems discussed in this paper. Nor do I maintain that in all circumstances an unequivocal distinction can be made between the operation of peripheral possession and the operation of witchcraft where these two phenomena coexist separately in the same society. But I do suggest that it would be useful to examine other data from the point of view I have put forward here. This approach has at least the merit of shedding some new light on phenomena which are customarily treated as existing in water-tight compartments, subjected to very different styles of analysis, and even mistakenly regarded as being mutually incompatible.

Indeed, in order to understand the strategy employed by the victim of affliction in seeking an advantageous outlet for his distress, either through the medium of spirit-possession or by accusing one of his fellows of bewitching him, it may sometimes be more illuminating to discard the culturally grounded expressions "spirit-possession" and "witchcraft" altogether and think rather in terms of oblique and direct mystical attack. It may seem strange to speak of the action of the accuser, rather than of the accused, as mystical attack. But it is after all the accuser, and not the accused witch, who sets the whole process in motion; and it is certainly the "witch" against whom public opinion is mobilized, and who is ultimately the victim of social action. If we adopt this point of view, it is obvious that witchcraft is not the only mode of direct mystical attack: cursing also belongs here. Thus the ambivalent aspects of the Lugbara elder's role as legitimate invoker of the ancestors' curse and as a suspected witch fall into place, and it becomes easier to understand other cases of "witchcraft" used legitimately, or in a socially accepted fashion.

REFERENCES

Beattie, J. 1961. Group Aspects of the Nyoro Spirit Mediumship Cult. *Human Problems in British Central Africa (Rhodes-Livingstone Institute Journal)* 30:11–38.

——— 1963. Witchcraft and Sorcery in Bunyoro. Pp. 32–54 in J. Middleton & E. H. Winter (eds.), *Witchcraft and Sorcery in East Africa.* London: Routledge & Kegan Paul.

Colson, E. 1969. Spirit Possession Among the Tonga of Zambia. In J. Beattie & J. Middleton (eds.), *Spirit Mediumship and Society in Africa.* London: Routledge & Kegan Paul.

Earthy, E. 1933. *Valenge Women.* London: Oxford University Press.

Gluckman, M. 1954. *Rituals of Rebellion in South-East Africa.* Manchester: Manchester University Press.

Harris, C. 1957. Possession Hysteria in a Kenyan Tribe. *American Anthropologist* 59 (6):1046–1066.

Heusch, L. de. 1966. *Le Rwanda et la Civilisation interlacustre.* Bruxelles: Institut de Sociologie de l'Université libre.

Hunter, M. 1936. *Reaction to Conquest.* London: Oxford University Press.

Junod, H. A. 1922. *The Life of a South African Tribe.* New York.

Levine, D. N. 1965. *Wax and Gold: Tradition and Innovation in Ethiopian Culture.* Chicago: Chicago University Press.

LeVine, R. 1963. Witchcraft and Sorcery in a Gusii Community. In J. Middleton & E. H. Winter (eds.), *Witchcraft and Sorcery in East Africa.* London: Routledge & Kegan Paul.

Lewis, I. M. 1966. Spirit Possession and Deprivation Cults. *Man* (n.s.) 1:307–329.

Lieban, R. 1967. *Cebuano Sorcery.* Berkeley–Los Angeles: University of California Press.

Lindblom, G. 1920. *The Akamba in British East Africa.* Uppsala.

Marwick, M. 1965. Some Problems in the Sociology of Sorcery and Witchcraft. In M. Fortes & G. Dieterlen (eds.), *African Systems of Thought.* London: Oxford University Press (for the International African Institute).

Middleton, J. 1960. *Lugbara Religion.* London: Oxford University Press (for the International African Institute).

——— 1969. Oracles and Divination Among the Lugbara. In M. Douglas & P. Kaberry (eds.), *Man in Africa.* London: Tavistock Publications.

Nadel, S. F. 1946. A Study of Shamanism in the Nuba Hills. *Journal of the Royal Anthropological Institute* 76:25–37.

Needham, R. 1967. Right and Left in Nyoro Symbolic Classification. *Africa* 37 (4):425–452.

Opler, M. E. 1958. Spirit Possession in a Rural Area of Northern India. In W. A. Lessa & E. Z. Vogt (eds.), *Reader in Comparative Religion*. New York: Row, Peterson.

Shack, W. 1966. *The Gurage*. London: Oxford University Press.

Stayt, H. 1931. *The BaVenda*. London: Oxford University Press.

Whisson, M. G. 1964. Some Aspects of Functional Disorders Among the Kenya Luo. In A. Kiev (ed.), *Magic, Faith and Healing*. New York: Free Press of Glencoe.

Wilson, P. J. 1967. Status Ambiguity and Spirit Possession. *Man* (n.s.) 2 (3):366–378.

Worsley, P. 1957. *The Trumpet Shall Sound: A Study of "Cargo" Cults in Melanesia*. London: MacGibbon & Kee.

Where alternative medical explanations are unavailable, falling ill is usually attributed to supernatural causation. In the absence of science, reliance on magic and religion serves again as the apparently best way of trying to control events that affect human life.

Curing is often a major part of the religious specialists' work. Their effectiveness as healers supports their claims to closeness to the powers of the supernatural, strengthens their status, and reinforces their social power. Once more it is unnecessary to accept the premise of a special relation to the supernatural to comprehend the curers' effectiveness. For again compelling social and psychological forces are used to help the afflicted.

In the magicoreligious treatment of mental illness, the techniques of showing sympathy with the patient's real suffering, encouraging the re-examination of past traumatic experiences, and assuring continued concerned attention are strikingly similar to the basic methods of contemporary psychotherapy. The converse is also true.

In addition to recognizing that "medicine men" often use herbs and roots of proved medical efficacy, Edgerton's account of a Hehe psychotherapist at work suggests that we must also acknowledge that the therapeutic techniques of modern psychiatrists are frequently similar to those used by so-called witchdoctors—not by coincidence, but because they get results.

A Traditional African Psychiatrist

Robert B. Edgerton

Interest in non-Western psychiatry in the past decade has produced a substantial literature, much of it relating to Africa. Nevertheless, the coverage of African societies has only begun, and the preliminary findings that we now possess may be one-sided. Thus, despite the sometimes positive evaluations of such men as Prince (1964). Collis (1966) and Lambo (1964) in Nigeria, and Gelfand (1964) and Loudon (1960) in Southeast Africa, many writers continue to feel that traditional African psychiatric practices have little instructive value for Western psychiatry. Others have been even more critical, believing that the magical practices of African healers are inimical to science. For example, Margetts (1965:115) writes that native healers "can do little good in a mental health programme and may do harm. They have no rational place in the modern technological world . . ."; however, he adds that analyses should be made of their folk medicines.

Before any considered opinion on the nature of traditional African medicine or "psychiatry" can be reached, we not only need more research

Source: From Robert B. Edgerton, "A Traditional African Psychiatrist," *Southwestern Journal of Anthropology,* Vol. 27 (1971), pp. 259–276. Used by permission of the publisher and the author.

from additional areas of Africa, but research which adopts additional perspectives. The following report is offered because its practitioner, a Hehe of Tanzania, is a specialist in psychiatry, and his beliefs and practices, particularly as they emphasize botanical and pharmacological empiricism, complement our knowledge of African ethnopsychiatry as it is practiced in other parts of Africa.[1]

The Hehe

The Hehe are a Bantu-speaking people located in the Southern Highlands Region of Tanzania, formerly Tanganyika. Their territory stretches from the Great Ruaha River on the north and west to the escarpment of the Kilombero Valley on the south and east. Most of this area is high rolling woodland or grassland, but some Hehe occupy arid lowland savanna areas and others live at higher elevations in mountain rain forest. The Hehe were a congeries of small chieftancies until they were united by the aggressive military and diplomatic actions of Muyugumba and his son, Mkwawa. By extending Hehe hegemony over much of southcentral Tanganyika, these men established the Hehe as a kingdom of considerable military and political power. After early victories over the Germans, Mkwawa was defeated and killed in 1894. The Germans restored the independence of territories conquered by the Hehe and confined the Hehe state to its present boundaries.

The Hehe, who now number over 200,000, live in dispersed homesteads which are organized into neighborhoods. A homestead is typically occupied by a man, his wife or wives, and their children. It is surrounded by its fields of maize, millet, beans, cassava, and squash and by small numbers of cattle, sheep, and goats. Each Hehe neighborhood is bound together by ties of kinship and friendship, by ceremonial activities, and by cooperative work parties. In addition to the strong ties of kinship, the Hehe recognize a hierarchy of lesser and greater chiefs who possess considerable traditional authority and have obligations to the British administration.[2]

When the Hehe fall ill, as they often do, they may attribute their misfortune to any of several sources: to natural phenomena such as worry, impure water, or faulty inheritance, to witchcraft, or to legitimate retribution for the violation of Hehe norms. If the source of illness is seen as natural, a Hehe may seek help from a European-trained physician or medical helper in a nearby town. But even for "natural" illnesses, the patient is likely also to seek out a traditional doctor—an *mbombwe*—and where the source of illness is other than natural, he is certain to do so. There are many such doctors (the Swahili term is *mganga*) throughout Hehe territory, and their advice is continually sought. Some, of course, are more highly regarded than others. The best known native doctor in the Iringa area was a man whom I shall name Abedi. Unlike most traditional Hehe doctors who attempt to treat any disorder, Abedi is a specialist in mental disorders—he is a Hehe psychiatrist.

Abedi's Training

Abedi was the headman (*jumbe*) of an area near Iringa until early in the 1950's when he encountered some sort of difficulty with the British administration. Accused of malfeasance, he left the post in 1955 and turned to full-time practice as an *mbombwe*. Abedi was born around 1910 to a man who had been a renowned *mbombwe,* a doctor to the King, Mkwawa, himself. Thus Abedi's father had access to the traditional medicine not only of the royal clan and court of the Hehe, but also from those neighboring tribes whom the Hehe conquered. Abedi's mother was also an *mbombwe,* who, like Abedi, was known as a specialist (her specialty was female disorders).

Abedi's formal training as an *mbombwe* did not begin until he was an adult, by which time his father was quite elderly. Abedi learned primarily from his father, but also studied with his mother who gave him intensive instruction in botany. Much of his training was highly practical, giving attention to the method of diagnosis and treatment, observation of symptoms, collec-

1 This paper is based upon research carried out as a part of the "Culture and Ecology in East Africa" project, sponsored by the University of California, Los Angeles, under the direction of Walter Goldschmidt. The research was supported by the National Science Foundation and by Research Grant No. M-4097 from the National Institute of Mental Health. Support was also received from the California State Department of Mental Hygiene and the Mental Retardation Program, NPI, UCLA.

2 For additional information concerning the Hehe, see Brown and Hutt (1935), Nigmann (1908) and Winans (1965). All descriptions in this paper apply to the period prior to independence.

tion of plants and roots, knowledge of inherited disorders, etc. But an equal emphasis was placed upon the supernatural. Abedi inherited his father's *lyang'ombe,* a small metal object that appeared to be an old European belt buckle. Through prayer, the *lyang'ombe* could be imbued with God's power to cure. Abedi learned to pray to God (*Nguluvi*), to practice divination, to discover the cause of witchcraft, to defend against witchcraft, and to employ magic. His father also gave him protection against the malevolence of witches, who might be angered because he cured those whom they had sickened, by rubbing a secret medicine (*gondola*) into a series of cuts (*nyagi*). These cuts are located on the thumb of the right hand, the third joint of the small finger of the left hand, the wrist, elbow, both temples, forehead, hairline, sternum, chest, neck, nipples, ribs, spine, ankles, knees, and toes. Abedi must reinforce this protection from time to time by reopening the cuts and adding fresh *gondola.* Abedi has also purchased magical knowledge and herbal medications from other traditional doctors over a large area of southern Tanzania.

Abedi's specialization in mental illnesses began during his apprenticeship when he first hallucinated ("hearing voices of people I could not see") and ran in terror to hide in the bush. He was discovered and returned to his father's care, but lay ("completely out of my senses") for two weeks before being cured. The cause was diagnosed as witchcraft and since the cure, Abedi has never been sick again. This experience initiated Abedi's interest in mental illness, and the subsequent mental disorders of his sister and his wife reinforced it. At different times, both women became violently psychotic, but Abedi quickly cured them both. These two cures not only heightened Abedi's interest in psychiatric phenomena, but they led to his reputation as a skillful psychiatrist.

Diagnosis, Etiology, and Prognosis

Although, as we shall see later, Abedi sometimes makes home visits, almost all of his patients came to him in what we might call his "office." The office is a small house, 10 by 20 feet, flimsy and poorly thatched, unlike ordinary Hehe houses, which are massive and solid structures. It has the look of a temporary building, but Abedi has been practicing medicine in it for eight years. The inside of his "office" is remarkably cluttered, with large pots, baskets, and gourds in every corner and hanging from the walls. These containers are filled with the roots and leaves from which Abedi mixes his medicines on a small table in one corner of the office. In his small office he stores, sorts, grinds, and boils his medications before packaging them in a variety of bottles, leaves, horns, small gourds, and leather pouches.

Seeking treatment from Abedi in his office often requires interrupting him in the course of preparing his medications, but he always greets a patient warmly as he asks him (and the usual family members or kinsmen who attend him) to be seated by the fireplace before he begins his diagnostic routine.

In proceeding with his diagnosis, Abedi must keep in mind his nosology of disorders (the catalogue of illness categories that he knows), the signs and symptoms, and the patient's biography —including past illnesses and, especially, antagonists who might want to bewitch him. In short, Abedi is concerned with the entire social context of the patient and his illness—a context which Abedi enters and typically alters—for while successful treatment pleases some, it may displease others (Winans and Edgerton 1964).

In a general way, Abedi recognizes a great variety of illnesses such as impotence, venereal infections, infertility, stomach and bowel ailments, respiratory disorders (including pneumonia and asthma), orthopedic malfunctions, and fevers. He also recognizes more specific diseases such as tracoma, tetanus, malaria, and smallpox. While he may choose to treat all such disorders with specific medications he has developed for that purpose, it is only when the disorders are "mental" (when the locus of disorder, in his perspective, is in the mind) that his diagnosis categories achieve any prognostic differentiation. Indeed, his categories of mental illness are defined by criteria that are based far less upon symptoms than they are upon etiology and prognosis.

Hehe men and women who live in the area near Abedi typically described mental illness in behavioral terms, perceiving its onset as sudden, with aggressive behavior that can result in human injury, but rapidly "cooling" to a fearful and stuporous retreat from human interaction (Edgerton 1966). They made no distinctions among psychotics. Abedi's views of mental illness were more complex. He recognized two symptoms as being indicators of excessive worry:

headache and stomach pain. He felt that both responded well to removal of the source of worry and to his herbal medications. For extreme cases, he recommended that the patient move away from his neighborhood for a prolonged vacation with kinsmen. He denied, however, that worry was a common cause of psychotic conditions. He also recognized epilepsy by its *grand mal* seizures, and mental retardation by the fact that intellectual ability was deficient from birth. Mental retardation he deemed untreatable, but he felt that epilepsy, which he said was an inherited condition, was curable by medication if treatment were begun in the first few days after the initial seizure.

Among psychotic conditions, he recognized five: *litego, mbepo, lisaliko, kuhavila* and *erishitani*. *Litego* is marked by depression and guilt, by fever and headache, and sometimes by unusual or bizarre behavior. It never produces thought disturbances. Because it is caused by moral retributive magic brought on by wrongdoing, it cannot be treated medically (or the *mbombwe,* too, would be sickened by the moral magic). Instead it requires confession, apology, and the payment of compensation. Without such restitution, *litego* can be fatal (Winans and Edgerton 1964).

Mbepo is marked by disturbances of behavior (running wildly, destroying property, and assaulting people) as well as by thought disturbances (inability to concentrate, hallucinations, visions, and a loss of touch with reality). It is a product of evil—in this case, witchcraft—and hence it can be cured without wrongdoing by a skilled and protected *mbombwe* (the protection is essential lest the thwarted witch turn his evil upon the doctor).

Lisaliko is indistinguishable from *mbepo* in its symptoms but its causes are natural, not supernatural. These causes include faulty inheritance, febrile illness, poisoning, and, very rarely, excessive worry. It is curable if treated early.

Kuhavila is a particularly violent sort of psychosis, even more so than *mbepo*. Persons afflicted with *kuhavila* actually kill others, and abuse them violently if unable to kill them. They also have prolonged fevers, go naked, eat feces, and run about without apparent purpose except to attack others. The disorder is caused by a specific sort of magic, which can only be acquired by a woman who has intercourse with her father. Such women must continue the incestuous relationship to maintain their power, but their male offspring may inherit the power without continuing the incestuous relationship. This form of psychosis is easily cured by a native doctor who possesses the appropriate magic to "see" the witch and establish protective magic, as well as the requisite medications.

Erishitani is produced only by Muslims who direct "devils" (*erishitani*) to enter the body of their victim, and "like the wind, squeeze out a person's blood, leaving him mad." The symptoms are an affectlessness and mental vacuity—literally, an emptiness. It can only be cured successfully by other Muslims; Abedi attempted two such cures and failed both times.

In his diagnostic search for symptoms, Abedi never touches the patient. He observes carefully, although usually unobtrusively, and he carefully questions the patient and any available kinsmen or friends. The questioning is often lengthy, involving what appears to the patient (or kinsmen) to be nothing more than an exchange of pleasantries and a concern for mutual acquaintances. In reality, it appeared that Abedi was probing carefully for an understanding of the social context of the illness. Who might be an enemy? What is the patient fearful about? Has he had a similar problem before? Do such illnesses run in his family?

Following the period of informal conversation, Abedi initiates his formal divinatory procedures. He begins by praying to *Nguluvi* to give him the power to see the cause of the sickness and to understand what ought to be done. He then takes out his *lyang'ombe,* kisses it to imbue it with God's power, and begins to divine by means of his *bao*. The *bao* is a paddle-shaped board about 8 inches long and 3 inches wide, with a groove in which a small wooden cylinder is rubbed running diagonally along its upper surface. Abedi places the board on the ground, puts the *lyang'ombe* on its narrow end, and holds both objects down with his foot. He then sprinkles water on the groove and begins rubbing the wooden cylinder in it. As he manipulates the *bao,* he chants in a low liturgical voice interrupted from time to time by a question he addresses to the *bao*. As the water in the groove dries up, the counter moves less easily and at some point it will stick. This is taken as an affirmative answer to the last question addressed to the *bao*. As long the counter moves freely, the answers to questions addressed to it are usually taken to be negative. In any case of illness, Abedi asks five preliminary questions: Did the patient commit adultery? Did he steal? Did he borrow money and refuse to repay it? Did he quarrel with someone? Did he actually have a fight with someone? In some instances, the answer to all the questions is negative. This indicates that the patient has become ill for no good reason and hence the cause is natural. Or, it means that effective counter magic must be made against the evil person who has performed magic or witchcraft against the patient without cause. This Abedi determines by further questions. He then asks specific questions about his ability to cure the patient, alternating "yes" and "no" questions until the *bao* answers. Finally he asks about the effectiveness of various medicines until the *bao* selects for him the medicine favored by God.

Throughout the investigations and supplications Abedi takes great care, for both he and his patient realize that the treatment of illness is dangerous, involving as it does not merely natural phenomena but such critical matters as moral magic, witchcraft, spirits, and the like. All realize that a faulty diagnosis endangers the doctor as well as the patient.

Treatment

Although Abedi's treatment routine varies somewhat depending upon the diagnosis he reaches, for almost all of the "mental illnesses" that he recognizes (*mbepo, lisaliko,* etc.), his treatment follows a prescribed course. First, the patient must be made tractable. Only a few patients are quiet enough that Abedi will begin their treatment without subjecting them to some degree of restraint. Most patients are agitated and difficult to manage, and they are either tied sitting to the center post of Abedi's office or, if treated at home, they are shackled to a bed. Next, all patients are purged. For this purpose Abedi maintains a ready supply of purgatives and emetics. The emetic is administered first; if the patient will not cooperate by swallowing the medication, a liquid preparation, his nose is held until he is compelled to swallow. If vomiting should not quickly ensue, Abedi assists by tickling the patient's throat with a feather. As soon as vomiting has taken place, a purgative is given with almost universal success within a few hours. Once purged, the patient is allowed to rest but is usually permitted only water until Abedi's specific medications have been prepared and administered.

As we have seen, Abedi's *bao* has already identified the appropriate medications, but it may take Abedi several hours, or even overnight, to prepare the prescriptions. In some cases, the necessary ingredients have already been collected, ground into powder, and stored, but in other instances Abedi must sort out the correct mixture of leaves, roots, patent medicines, and other substances before mixing them. Occasionally, he must actually go out to collect the ingredients. Some medications cannot even be selected until Abedi has gone to a crossroad (a place where village footpaths intersect or, ideally, trisect), stood naked at midnight, and used his magical powers to "see" the correct medicine (the *bao* is not involved in this form of divination). Sometimes the medication must be mixed at the crossroad as well, and in rare circumstances, the patient must ingest the medicine at the same crossing. Where selection of a medication has proven particularly difficult, and where the cause of the psychosis has been diagnosed as witchcraft, the patient himself may be made to act as an oracle in the selection of his own medication. This is done by burning a mass of *Cannabis sativa,* covering the patient with a blanket, and forcing him to inhale the smoke for a period of an hour or more. The patient identifies the person who has bewitched him, and by answering Abedi's questions with "yes" or "no," selects an effective medicine.

Once assured that the medication of choice is known and available, Abedi "cooks" it by boiling the powdered ingredients over a fire in full view of the patient and his kinsmen. Most of the resulting medications are taken as liquids, usually drunk in a glass of tea. A few medications are rubbed on the skin as ointment, others are rubbed into shallow linear incisions, and a few are inhaled. Before the medicine is actually given, Abedi offers a brief *sotto voce* prayer for the success of the medicine and spits once or three times upon the patient's head as a blessing for good luck. Doses of medicine are repeated at varying intervals until a cure is effected. Abedi accepts no payment for his treatment (except a small retainer for house calls) until such time as the patient has recovered.

An Illustrative Case

The following case is one which I was able to follow closely from its inception to its remission. A 17-year-old boy, related to a Hehe man whom I knew, was stricken with a high fever. When his fever continued for six days, his parents took him to a nearby hospital for European medical care. Once in the hospital, he lay in a coma for the better part of six days, occasionally returning to consciousness with violent efforts to escape his bed and flee. He became so violent in his delirium that he was tied to his bed, but it was not until his struggles tipped the bed over that he would lie quietly. No sedatives calmed him and no diagnosis was made, although malaria was suspected. At no time was he able to speak coherently, although he did mutter to himself.

His parents complained that he was receiving inadequate care (the European medical officer was on leave) and that his condition had not improved. They took him home where he continued to be delirious. When he showed no improvement and refused food by the seventh day of treatment, his parents and his uncle asked me if I would take them to see Abedi, who was some 45 minutes away by automobile. This we did immediately. Abedi could have had no warning that we were coming, and it is difficult to believe that he knew anything about so distant a family and their sick child. After customary greetings, the sick boy's uncle said, "I want to ask you about a sick person." Abedi sat down with his *bao* and after a few minutes he announced that the person was male, about 18 years old. The uncle was suitably impressed and asked Abedi to undertake treatment. Abedi asked to see the patient, but was told that the boy could not be moved. Abedi accepted this necessity and began at once his prayer to *Nguluvi* to give him the power to see and to cure. After praying in his monotonous manner for four minutes, he began to divine, sliding the piece of wood along his *bao* while asking the routine questions.

After five minutes of divination, Abedi found an answer: the boy had been bewitched by someone in a mountainous area several miles from his home. The witch's identity could not be seen, but it was known that the boy's illness was *mbepo,* caused by eating a "medicine" which was lodged in his chest making breathing difficult, disorienting his mind, and threatening his life. When he heard this, the uncle asked that Abedi go and treat the boy without delay. Abedi said that he had made plans to be elsewhere and such a trip would be most inconvenient. The uncle then threw one shilling (14 cents) at Abedi's feet. He picked it up, committing himself to walk over 25 miles round trip.

Once this matter was settled, Abedi again consulted his *bao,* asking which of his medicines would cure the boy. The *bao* chose first the usual emetic and purgative, next, a "tranquilizer" called *ngambe* ("to cool his heart and stop his wildness"), and then another to counteract the evil "medicine." Each medication was already available in Abedi's containers so he poured out the correct amounts, perfunctorily tasting each with his tongue ("to prove that it is not a poison") before wrapping each separately in a corn husk and tying it with bark. Before leaving, Abedi again consulted his *bao,* this time to determine the order in which the medications should be given. The answers were given quickly and the order was the standard one used with most patients.

I then offered to take everyone to see the sick boy. Abedi probably knew that I would do so on this occasion, but he must also have known that I could not be counted upon to do so on subsequent days. When we arrived, the boy lay bound to a bed. Seven days without food had left him emaciated. He stared at me, the only non-African, but did not speak. He had a massive facial tic and there was a marked tremor of his extremeties. Abedi approached him without any ceremony and attempted to force the emetic past his lips. The boy struggled and moaned and it was only with assistance and by holding the boy's nose that Abedi compelled him to swallow. The purgative followed without delay. Abedi then unwrapped his second medication —the "tranquilizer"—and mixed it with water, creating a cup full of a foul-smelling, rather slimy, green liquid. Filling his mouth with this preparation, Abedi spat three times on the boy's head. Briefly reciting his prayer for healing, Abedi rubbed the remainder of the medication on the boy's head, pulling three hairs as he did so. To these three hairs he added the green paste that he next scraped off the boy's head, tying them together in a rag that was tied to the patient's wrist. Later, the same medication would be given internally, but first the patient must vomit.

While waiting for the emetic to take effect, Abedi unwrapped his third medicine, a powder to provide protection against witchcraft. It was rubbed into the boy's nostrils; it too he would later take by mouth. Although Abedi said that the emetic usually takes effect in ten minutes, this time nothing happened. Abedi and the assembled kin agreed that the boy's seven day fast was the reason for the delay. Abedi instructed everyone to wait, deciding not to tickle his throat with a feather, or to administer more of the emetic. Everyone waited quietly, sometimes leaving the room to talk in the courtyard. After two hours, the boy vomited, and all gathered around to examine the two long yellow strands of vomitus carefully. All agreed that the vomitus was unique—not mucous, not worms, nor any normal contents of the stomach. They agreed that it must be as Abedi said: the boy had vomited the "medicine" that was the source of his illness.

Abedi next gave the second and third medication by mouth, saying that the patient would sleep and that he need not be tied any longer—"his heart has been cooled." At this point, Abedi left to walk back to his office where he would see other patients. The boy slept all afternoon, awakening at about six o'clock to ask for food. He ate, to the joy of everyone, then slept quietly all night. Abedi returned each morning to see his patient and to repeat applications of the second and third medications. For two more days the boy slept and ate without speaking. On the fourth day of treatment he spoke rationally. By the eighth day he was able to leave the bed for short periods. After 15 days Abedi pronounced him cured, and the boy did indeed appear to be normal.

Abedi said, following the cure, that the original diagnosis had been incorrect (Edgerton 1969). The boy suffered from *kuhavila,* not *mbepo,* because there is no fever with *mbepo.* When asked how the *bao* could be wrong he said, "It happens sometimes." He explained further that he could have cured the boy in one day had he seen him on the initial day of illness, but that once the "medicine" had time to take effect the recovery was always protracted. The parents were said to have paid Abedi 100 shillings for his services, but I do not know how the fee was settled upon or whether it was paid in several installments.

Discussion

The foregoing case is intended to illustrate some of the typical features of Abedi's therapeutic routine, but it is also directed to the point that his therapy for "mental" illness is often, perhaps even usually, rewarded by the remission of symptoms. There are obvious reasons why this pattern of apparent remission should not be construed as a "cure." For one thing, the symptoms presented by Abedi's patients are so diverse as to challenge the therapeutic arsenal of any doctor, African or Western. What is more, while my four week study of his practice revealed striking success in the remission of symptoms, it would be naive to suppose that failures could not have been hidden from me had Abedi chosen to do so. Finally we have no way of knowing how often the symptoms would have vanished under differing treatment or with no treatment at all. We do know, however, that rapid and seemingly complete recovery from apparently psychotic conditions has been reported from several parts of Africa.[3] Any discussion of the efficacy of Abedi's treatment must await properly designed research of the sort begun in West Africa by Collis (1966). The purpose of this discussion is to compare Abedi's treatment routine with principles of treatment reported from other parts of Africa and to ask why his therapeutic practices have taken their particular form.

Analysts of "primitive medicine" from Ackernecht (1943) to Frank (1961) have emphasized the role of suggestion in treatment. Recently, Kiev (1964) concluded that two universals of non-Western psychiatry were suggestion and confession. Others have expanded this list to include faith, catharsis, group support, and suggestion (Kennedy MS). Let us examine the role of each of these in Abedi's psychiatric practice.

FAITH. By faith I mean the generalized expectation on the part of the patient that treatment of the sort offered by the traditional doctor *can* be effective. These expectations are difficult to determine and research reports regarding them are generally superficial. The Hehe data are also superficial, although here at least some quantification and comparison is possible. For example, 36 of 123 Hehe respondents in a neighborhood near Abedi's office said that psychotic patients could be cured, 12 said that they could not, and 75 were unsure. This degree of expressed faith was much greater than that shown by the Pokot of Kenya or the Sebei of Uganda, but less than that indicated by the Kamba of Kenya (Edgerton 1966:416). We can probably conclude that while the Hehe have some faith in psychiatric treatment they also maintain ample skepticism. Turning now to Abedi, who is cer-

[3] For a review of bibliographic sources relating to this question see Collis (1966:25).

tainly the most highly regarded doctor in this area, we see that even where his ability is concerned, a degree of what might be considered skepticism remains. For example, in the case presented earlier of serious and prolonged illness, the boy's parents were in no hurry to see a native doctor and while they had heard of Abedi's reputation, they had no blind faith in his ability. They, as did others, began their contact with Abedi by testing him—could he identify the sick boy and his illness? And all patients withhold payment until a cure has taken place (a practice which is as unusual in Africa as in the West). Thus while Hehe patients approach Abedi with some faith in his reputation as a doctor, most enter treatment with an attitude that combines hope and doubt. For his part, Abedi does nothing to foster or require a testimonial of faith before treatment begins. Instead he is content to rely upon his treatment itself.

CATHARSIS. For the Hehe, as for other African peoples, catharsis through confession is a commonplace. In childbirth, as in many forms of illness, both Hehe patient and spouse or other kinsmen must confess and apologize for wrongful thoughts or acts before birth or recovery can take place (Winans and Edgerton 1964). Nevertheless, Abedi makes virtually no use of catharsis in his practice. He never asks a patient or kinsman to act out any hidden desire and only very infrequently do his questions to the *bao* elicit any sort of confession from a patient. Asked about this anomaly, Abedi said, "Talking cures nothing. Medicines cure."

GROUP SUPPORT. There are reports from several African societies that point to the importance of group support in the treatment of mental illness. In West Africa, for example, group support may be supplied by religious cults (Prince 1964), secret societies (Dawson 1964), or by elaborate "discharge ceremonies that ritualize the patient's cleansing of illness, death, and rebirth into a new life" (Prince 1964). Elsewhere, the patient may receive support by moving from one area and social network to another. Among the Ndembu of Northern Rhodesia, the patient's kinsmen may join with hostile persons in what amounts to group therapy, complete with catharsis and social reintegration (Turner 1964).

While Abedi permits kinsmen of his patients to be present throughout his diagnosis and treatment he does nothing to solicit group support. As with his disavowal of confession, this neglect of group concern is remarkable, for just such group support is a regular feature of childbirth and the recovery from many illnesses. As with catharsis, other Hehe doctors I knew did require that their patients undergo treatment within a larger social nexus.

SUGGESTION. Research on African psychiatric practice has emphasized the role that suggestion plays in treatment. For example, Prince (1964: 110), writing about the Yoruba, refers to a "continuous barrage of suggestions at all levels from the most intellectual to the most concrete and primitive." Others have attributed whatever success the African therapies may have entirely to suggestion, noting that Africans are highly suggestible.[4] There can be no doubt that suggestion plays an important part in Abedi's practice, and yet Abedi makes little or no use of a variety of practices widely employed in Africa to heighten suggestibility or to implant specific ideas. For example, Abedi never alters his own personality to indicate special powers, nor does he claim direct communication with supernatural powers through dissociation or possession. Neither does he employ special effects through legerdemain or ventriloquism. He makes no attempt at indirect communication by means of allegory, simile, traditional or sacramental stories. He never gives commands, nor does he attempt to change his patient's consciousness through hypnosis, drumming, or dancing to exhaustion (cf. Whisson 1964). What is more, he utilizes none of the many versions by body contact common in Africa such as rubbing, sucking, bathing, or such stressful ones as whipping, burning, or steaming.

Kennedy (MS) and others have noted the significance of dramatic rituals and powerful symbolism in psychiatric practice in Africa and throughout the non-Western world. For example, Gelfand (1964) notes the flamboyant regalia of Shona "medicine men"; the Yoruba, Luo, and Ndembu all enact potent rituals in the service of therapy. However, Abedi's use of ritual is minimal, being confined almost entirely to a few ritual acts on the first day of treatment. Others have noted that non-Western psychiatrists rely upon settings so suffused by religious

[4] For example, see Collis (1966), Laubscher (1937) and Turner (1964:232).

or magical symbolism that they are set apart from the ordinary world (Kennedy MS). Again, nothing could be more prosaic than the settings in which Abedi works.

Abedi's principal uses of suggestion lie in his appeals for supernatural guidance or power and in his utilization of potent medications. Although Abedi's frequent prayers for divine assistance are understated and humble, they nonetheless must serve to impress patients, as must also the divine and magical power that resides in his *lyang'ombe*. And, of course, the *bao* is an impressive divinatory device, especially when it reveals information about the patient that would seem to be inaccessible to Abedi by normal means. It is possible that Abedi maintains an "intelligence system" in the form of boys who inform him of matters relevant to actual or prospective patients, but I saw no evidence that he did so. Abedi's knowledge of magic and his occasional visits to crossroads and the like must also contribute to the supernatural aura that he is able to establish.

Probably of equal importance, however, is the placebo effect of Abedi's medications. Several of his preparations contain copper sulphate which has the impressive property of turning from blue-green to white when heated. The patients whom I watched during their first exposure to this transformation were visibly startled. Similarly, his infrequent but copious use of *Cannabis sativa* may produce impressive psychological changes, and the reliable effects of his standard emetics and purgatives must alike create in a patient a sense of the dramatic power of Abedi's medications. The resulting alteration of psychological and bodily states should produce a heightening of suggestibility. Such effects from the use of herbal remedies by African doctors have been widely noted.[5] However, in recognizing the prominent place of suggestion in Abedi's use of drugs, we should not overlook the possibility that some of his medications possess specific psychopharmacological action that may have value in the treatment of mental illness (Gelfand 1964).

Abedi as Pharmacologist

Abedi's pharmacopoeia is extensive. In addition to emetics, purgatives, and his specific preparations for mental illness or epilepsy, he keeps on hand many drugs for gastro-intestinal disorders, as well as a variety of aphrodisiacs for men, and, for women, various drugs specific for infertility, miscarriage, menorrhagia, and the like. Most of the botanical knowledge that underlies his drugs was inherited from his father and mother, but some knowledge was purchased and some preparations were purchased ready-made (e.g., copper sulphate). I collected seven preparations said to be specific for mental illness or epilepsy. Of these, several were described by Abedi as (and were seen by me to have the apparent effect of) soporifics or tranquilizers. Of these, the most potent was called *mwini*.

Following this lead, the botanist, Mildred Mathias, and the pharmacologist, Dermot Taylor, visited Abedi. Concentrating their collection upon plants that might affect the central nervous system, they went with Abedi while he collected the plants essential to his medications for mental illness and epilepsy. They traveled throughout the Southern Highlands Province, finding medicinal plants in all of the micro-habitats in that diverse area. In all, 37 species of plants were collected, representing 35 genera in 26 plant families. Some individual medications contained as many as 11 species of plants (Mathias 1965: 87–88).

Abedi's empirical knowledge of the botany of Hehe territory was considerable, and so was his pharmacological skill in preparing and administering these medications. For example, several of these plants contain violent emetics and purgatives which can produce death in overdose (Mathias 1965:87). Yet, of over 120 Hehe questioned, none had heard of so much as an accusation that Abedi's medications had ever killed a patient. Recall, too, that Abedi refused to increase the standard dosage of his emetics and purgatives when they did not have an immediate effect upon the boy in the previous case. In the mixing of each medication, Abedi takes care to prepare and measure each ingredient, and he does so with the secular manner of a pharmacist, not that of a magician. Yet his preparations are not confined to the leaves and roots of plants with at least potential psychopharmacological effect. He often adds to his medicine such magical substances as the aforementioned copper sulphate, powdered rock from the sea coast, corn flour, the blood of a black cock, and the urine or

[5] For example, see Collis (1966), Gelfand (1964), Kiev (1964) and Prince (1964).

powdered bones of a sheep. Abedi insists that these latter substances are as essential to certain of his medications as the plant components. In this sense, he is not without full commitment to the Hehe world of supernatural belief. But other medications contain only leaves and roots. For these, no magic in preparation, content, or administration is employed. Abedi's pharmacopoeia has its supernatural elements, but they are relatively few, and may be relatively unimportant.

Neither is there evidence that he regularly employs his medications in the manner of a charlatan. To be sure, we can point to the fact that he feels the need for copper sulphate, which he says that he regards as just another vital ingredient, and that he sometimes uses *Cannabis sativa* to evoke witchcraft accusations from his patients. But unlike doctors among the Yoruba, he does not use hallucinogenics to worsen a patient's condition simply in order to achieve a spectacular treatment success by withdrawing the toxin (Prince 1964:118). Nor does he employ *Datura* to evoke confessions of witchcraft or to induce psychosis, although he knows of its properties, is aware that it grows in many accessible places, and knows that other "medicine men" in Tanzania, including those among the nearby Mtumbi, use it for those purposes (Linehardt 1968:75–76). He said, "*Datura* can cause madness but it cannot cure it." I agree with Lienhardt (1968:74) that the medications used or sold by many a *mganga* in Tanzania are known to be useless by the so-called doctor himself. Abedi stands apart from fraud. He believes in the efficacy of his medications.

Demonstrating that Abedi is a serious empiricist about his medications is one thing; demonstrating that the medicines have any specific effect upon the central nervous system is quite another. The final word here must await complete pharmacological analysis, of course, but we might note that Abedi's treatment regime follows that of the Yoruba of Nigeria—emetics and purgatives followed by a drug that seems to induce sleep and tranquility. For the Yoruba, this drug is *Rauwolfia,* the source of reserpine (Prince 1964: Hordern 1968). Abedi's "tranquilizing" drugs, especially the one he calls *mwini,* were observed to induce both sleep and, following sleep, tranquility. These effects may be a product of verbal suggestion, but if this is so, then the suggestion must be very subtle, for I have witnessed the use of this drug on ten occasions, and on none of these occasions could I detect any verbal suggestion that would lead to sleep or tranquility. My Hehe-speaking interpreter also failed to discover any such cues. On the other hand, this drug (and others he employs) *could* have soporific or tranquilizing effects since Abedi's pharmacopoeia included 19 alkaloid-producing plant families.

Although the pharmacological analysis of *mwini* has proven difficult in research with laboratory animals, psychopharmacological activity (some of it soporific) has been noted. The drug had a quietening effect upon mice, reducing their activity noticeably. It also doubled the barbiturate sleeping time (modern tranquilizers will increase it six or seven times). Because of difficulties in acquiring sufficient quantities of the plant and in developing techniques for the assay of this plant material, a more active fraction from the plant could not be obtained. The plant involved was *Limosella major* Diels, a member of the Scrophulariaceae. The family has not been noted for its medicinal properties.[6]

Conclusion

In his practice as a traditional African psychiatrist, Abedi not only must, but does, live within the belief systems of his culture, and these beliefs center around the etiological and prognostic significance of magic and witchcraft. Abedi diagnoses and treats mental disorders within the constraints posed by this supernatural system, constraints that emphasize his vulnerability to danger in equal measure to that of his patients. He believes in supernatural causes of illness, and he excels in discovering and in thwarting such causes. At the same time, however, he recognizes natural causes of illness and he seeks medication that will cure, not merely impress. He has stated this conviction, and his actions have given his convictions legitimacy. Only extensive botanical and pharmacological research can determine to what extent he has succeeded in locating medications whose suc-

[6] My thanks are due Dr. Dermot Taylor, Department of Pharmacology, UCLA, for the information concerning the psychopharmacology of *mwini*. I am also indebted to Dr. Mildred Mathias, Director, Botanical Gardens-Herbarium, UCLA, for identifying the plant and for additional information concerning it.

cesses are due to specific action and not to the placebo effect. If future analyses should show that the medications have specific actions upon the central nervous system, it would be an error to conclude that such action is a fortuitous product of the more or less random collection of leaves and roots. Abedi, and other Hehe doctors before him, have believed not only in supernatural causation and treatment of illness, but also in herbal remedies.

For example, Mkwawa, the King, and members of his court, were highly pragmatic men who displayed a keen interest in innovation. Their empiricism was especially notable in regard to botany. Mkwawa imported several plants to his kingdom from other parts of East Africa, seeking not only better medicinal plants but better food sources and even superior shade trees. He also experimented with cross-breeding cattle. At the same time, Mkwawa and his court retained their traditional beliefs in witchcraft, divination, and the like. Abedi's father, as physician to Mkwawa, was a member of this elite, among whom traditional belief in supernatural causation coexisted with an intense pragmatic interest in natural cause and effect.[7] Years of empirical effort have yielded Abedi's pharmacopoeia and his knowledge of it. It would be surprising indeed if his medications did not possess some specific pharmacological effectiveness.

In comparison to traditional doctors in other parts of Africa, as well as among the Hehe, Abedi is notable for his secular approach to medicine. He does not reject the supernatural beliefs or practices of his culture. On the contrary, he excels in their use. But he does attempt to go beyond them by formulating principles of natural causation and by empirically discovering chemical cures. In this sense, he has transcended his culture, and such transcendance is an achievement for any man. Yet, whether Abedi's success in treating mental illness has anything to do with the pharmacological action of his drugs or not, he possesses the essential attitude of a scientist—a belief in natural causes and effects, and an empirical method of seeking out causal relationships. His story is worth recording simply because he has made the effort to find useful drugs, to continue the beginnings of science within a pre-scientific system of medicine.

There is nothing necessarily contradictory about Abedi's continuing commitment to a world of supernatural cause and effect. As Koestler (1963) has pointed out, such beliefs were very much a part of the lives of Kepler, Galileo, Newton, and others who nevertheless brought about scientific revolution. Abedi is no Newton either in intent or accomplishment, but neither is he simply a magician-herbalist. He believes that supernatural practices are necessary but not sufficient for a cure. Only medicines are sufficient, and he is devoted to the discovery of more effective chemical agents. Abedi's own words best reflect this quest: "I became a doctor to cure people. Medicines cure, nothing else works. I have some very strong medicines, but I always hope to find better ones. I would like to be able to travel to a place where roots stronger than those around here grow. My medicines cure some things. If I had stronger roots I could cure more." Abedi undoubtedly undervalues the importance of suggestion in his practice of psychiatry, just as he no doubt overvalues the efficacy of his medications. His commitment to empiricism is botanical, not psychological.

Abedi is not the first of his kind in pre-scientific societies: curare, quinine, digitalis, atropine, reserpine, and many other valuable drugs attest to that. The dominant presence of a scientific ethos does not exclude magical practices in modern Western psychiatry. This we realize all too well.[8] We should remind ourselves that the dominance of a supernatural ethos in non-Western psychiatry does not exclude the presence of beliefs and practices that are of significance for science.

[7] See Collis (1966), Gelfand (1964) and Mathias (1965).

[8] The literature on this subject is vast, but for some useful introductory views, see Ackernecht (1959), Honigfeld (1964), and Alexander and Selesnick (1966).

BIBLIOGRAPHY

Ackernecht, Erwin

1943 Psychopathology, Primitive Medicine and Primitive Culture. *Bulletin of the History of Medicine* 14:30–67.

1959 *A Short History of Psychiatry*. New York: Hafner.

Alexander, Franz and Sheldon T. Selesnick
1966 *The History of Psychiatry. An Evaluation of Psychiatric Thought and Practice from Prehistoric Times to the Present.* New York: Harper and Row.
Brown, G. G. and A. McD. Hutt
1935 *Anthropology in Action.* London: Oxford Press.
Collis, Robert J. M.
1966 Physical Health and Psychiatric Disorder in Nigeria. *Transactions of the American Philosophical Society* 56:5–45.
Dawson, John
1964 "Urbanization and Mental Health in a West African Community," in *Magic, Faith, and Healing* (ed. by Ari Kiev), pp. 305–342. New York: The Free Press of Glencoe.
Edgerton, Robert B.
1966 Conceptions of Psychosis in Four East African Societies. *American Anthropologist* 68:408–425.
1969 "On the 'Recognition' of Mental Illness," in *Changing Perspectives in Mental Illness* (ed. by Stanley C. Plog and Robert B. Edgerton), pp. 49–70. New York: Holt, Rinehart and Winston.
Frank, Jerome
1961 *Persuasion and Healing.* Baltimore: Johns Hopkins Press.
Gelfand, Michael
1964 "Psychiatric Disorder as Recognized by the Shona," in *Magic, Faith, and Healing* (ed. by Ari Kiev), pp. 156–173. New York: The Free Press of Glencoe.
Honigfeld, Gilbert
1964 Non-specific Factors in Treatment. *Diseases of the Nervous System* 25:145–156, 225–239.
Hordern, Anthony
1968 "Psychopharmacology: Some Historical Considerations," in *Psychopharmacology: Dimensions and Perspectives* (ed. by C. R. B. Joyce), pp. 95–148. London: Tavistock.
Kennedy, John G.
MS "Cultural Psychiatry," in *Handbook of Social and Cultural Anthropology* (ed. by J. J. Honigmann). Chicago: Rand-McNally (in press).
Kiev, Ari (ed.)
1964 *Magic, Faith, and Healing.* New York: The Free Press of Glencoe.
Koestler, Arthur
1963 *The Sleepwalkers. A History of Man's Changing Vision of the Universe.* New York: Grosset and Dunlap.
Lambo, T. Adeoye
1964 "Patterns of Psychiatric Care in Developing African Countries," in *Magic, Faith, and Healing* (ed. by Ari Kiev), pp. 443–453. New York: The Free Press of Glencoe.
Laubscher, B. J. F.
1937 *Sex, Custom and Psychopathology. A Study of South African Pagan Natives.* London: Routledge and Kegan Paul.
Lienhardt, Peter (ed. and translator)
1968 *The Medicine Man. Swifa ya Ngurumali.* Oxford: The Clarendon Press.
Loudon, J. B.
1960 "Psychogenic Disorder and Social Conflict Among the Zulu," in *Culture and Mental Health* (ed. by Marvin Opler), pp. 351–369. New York: Macmillan.
Margetts, Edward L.
1965 Traditional Yoruba Healers in Nigeria. *Man* 65:115–118.
Mathias, Mildred E.
1965 "Medicinal Plant Hunting in Tanzania," in *Ecology and Economic Development in Tropical Africa* (ed. by David Brokensha), pp. 83–92. Berkeley: Institute of International Studies, University of California.
Nigmann, E.
1908 *Die Wahehe.* Berlin: Ernst Siegfried Mittler und Sohn.
Prince, Raymond
1964 "Indigenous Yoruba Psychiatry," in *Magic, Faith, and Healing* (ed. by Ari Kiev), pp. 84–120. New York: The Free Press of Glencoe.
Turner, Victor
1964 "An Ndembu Doctor in Practice," in *Magic, Faith, and Healing* (ed. by Ari Kiev), pp. 230–263. New York: The Free Press of Glencoe.

Whisson, Michael G.
1964 "Some Aspects of Functional Disorders Among the Kenya Luo," in *Magic, Faith, and Healing* (ed. by Ari Kiev), pp. 283–304. New York: The Free Press of Glencoe.
Winans, Edgar V.
1965 The Political Context of Economic Adaptation in the Southern Highlands of Tanzania. *American Anthropologist* 67:435–441.
Winans, Edgar V. and Robert B. Edgerton
1964 Hehe Magical Justice. *American Anthropologist* 66:745–764.

PART SEVEN

The Arts

The Cultural Context of Aesthetic Experience

Of all the universal aspects of culture, perhaps art has been the least well studied by anthropologists. Certainly they have worked at it. The descriptive literature on "primitive art" is extensive. But so far the theoretical payoff has been disappointingly thin. Even so, a number of general assertions about the interrelations between culture and aesthetic expression can confidently be made.

First and most evident is the fact that art in most cultures is rarely a thing apart. Rather, it is an integral aspect of nearly every major form of cultural behavior from technology to ideology. Take some examples. Tools and weapons are invariably fashioned to be not only efficient, but also aesthetically pleasing in shape, color, and finish. Criteria of efficiency, technical virtuosity, and beauty are so generally linked that the distinction between fine craftsmanship and artistry is frequently arbitrary. Function and aesthetic effect are totally intermingled—in the curving line of a well-turned bow, the sweeping span of an outrigger, or the contours of an Eames chair. Not that this balance is always maintained. Other cultural factors, considerations of social position or economic interest may intrude, requiring "embellishments" that impair function, as they do in many soon obsolete overstyled appliances, in some architecture, and in automobiles so designed that they can be easily entered only by the agile young and a few middle-aged contortionists.

But, of course, the more fundamental relationship between art and technology concerns the ways differing levels of technological adaptation affect the kind of materials and the amount of time available to artists. The hunter-gatherer's palette is largely limited to a few pigments easily obtainable in nature—charcoal, ochre, clay, blood, and the juice of berries. The petrochemical industry offers the artist in our society a far wider range of colors, textures, and consistencies to work with. The artist in a hunting and gathering society is by necessity only a part-time artist. In societies with a more abundant material base, work in the arts becomes for many a full-time specialty.

The relationship to economics can be just as close. Artistic expression is often tightly constrained by economic considerations. In our society, for example, although few artists starve, most monetary support for aesthetic expression goes into such commercial forms as advertising, TV, and money-making movies. And even the "fine arts" are heavily affected by market considerations: scarcity, for instance, invariably determines that an "original" will be far more highly valued than an indistinguishable reproduction.

Artistic expression is associated with nearly all social occasions of consequence. In fact, the importance of an event is often reflected in the extent of the participants' attention to self-decoration, to the embellishment of the setting, and to acting in accordance with whatever patterns of social behavior are currently aesthetically "in."

That art and politics are also closely related is manifested in everything from the always special adornment and ceremonial accoutrements of political leaders, the pageantry and highly stylized oratory invariably associated with major political occasions, and the lengthy and elaborate myths and legends that legitimize and exalt the status of people, places, and events associated with a particular political system.

The relation of art to ideology is clearest of all. Many, perhaps most, of the forms of aesthetic expression of non-Western peoples—especially in sculpture, music, and dance—have always been tied closely to religious rituals. Such disparate graphic and plastic forms as Florentine cathedral ceilings and West African masks function to embellish religious objects and to communicate and reinforce the beliefs that inspired their creation. Those beings so beautifully portrayed in oils high above the cathedral floor are part of the depiction of events central to the worshipper's system of beliefs. Similarly, West African dancers' masks are often believed to embody the power of important deities in the people's pantheon.

Socially isolated, alienated artists—especially those working in whatever forms are culturally defined as avant garde and whose work may often be incomprehensible to most of their potential public—are apparently the product of a set of sociocultural circumstances peculiar to a few societies like our own. Among us the always tenuous balance between innovative personal expression and adherence to culturally approved canons of what constitutes art seems to be especially fragile. And the comparatively exotic notion that art can or ought to exist for art's sake alone is widely held. In smaller-scale, more homogeneous societies the vision of the artist and all others is far more likely to be similar. Art may be abstract, but it is expressed in a symbolic idiom—the highly styled scrollwork of Bush Negro wood carvers in Surinam, the design motifs of Navajo blanket makers, or the intricate gestural language used by Javanese puppeteers—that the artist's audience can easily understand.

Given the almost universally close functional interrelationship between art and the other aspects of culture, and the heavy evidence that the artist's job usually entails more than creating a thing of beauty, the study of artistry provides a splendid context for studying the dynamics of human creativity. How does the artist cope with the central paradox of his task: combining technical virtuosity and attention to tradition in creating something that is aesthetically new? Understanding how these apparently conflicting expectations are reconciled by the artist is central to developing a clearer picture of both the role of the artist in society and the place of art in anthropology.

SECTION I
Tangible Forms and Cultural Functions

To the observer from another culture, graphic and plastic forms of aesthetic expression are most easily perceived as "art." They are also easiest to extricate analytically and physically from their sociocultural context. In fact, European and American museums are full of some of the finest examples of the work of "non-Western" artists. Much of it was taken as plunder, carried off or sent on command as tribute to such distant annexes of colonial power as the British Museum, the Royal Museum of the Belgian Congo, and the Smithsonian Institution. Equally fine pieces continue to move in quantity through the showrooms of commercial galleries and into the hands of collector-investors.

But much of the best has been lost forever; for several reasons. Much art was originally created—especially masks and other kinds of sculpture—to serve as a ritual accessory to religious ceremonies that are no longer observed. As traditional ideologies have changed or been abandoned, artists' fidelity to traditional forms and their patrons' insistence upon technical mastery are no longer sanctioned by fear of supernatural punishment. Elsewhere, in New Guinea, for example, some works of art are regularly discarded once their ritual functions are fulfilled. Further, many of the materials used by non-Western artists are soft and fairly perishable. Exposure to heat, humidity, and termites has taken a destructive toll. And many works of non-Western art were smashed up and burned by early missionaries who correctly recognized them as the symbols of belief they were determined to destroy.

Despite the formidable losses suffered as a consequence of these combined forces, much of great value remains—enough that the term *value* must be used with care. "Anthropologically" value refers to the aesthetic worth and scholarly importance of what remains and what is still being produced by non-Western artists, mostly in a traditional genre, but increasingly in new forms, some of which have been too readily dismissed as mere "airport art," and—more crassly—*value* refers to the market worth of "primitive art" as it becomes scarce.

As new motives, differing demands, and changing techniques are presently transforming the work of many non-Western artists, the opportunity to learn, as d'Azevedo has done, from those still at work in traditional ways becomes increasingly precious.

Gola Mask Makers[1]

Warren L. d'Azevedo

This paper is concerned with the role and status of certain woodcarvers among the Gola and some adjacent peoples of western Liberia. These craftsmen perform a unique service which highlights the function of a particular kind of personality and creative ability in the tribal societies of the region. They are the makers of the supreme objects of aesthetic appreciation and ritual deference, yet woodcarvers are persons of ambivalent social character who are seldom eligible for a titled position among the custodians of tradition and sacred institutions. In the following pages I will describe a situation in which the virtuoso craftsman emerges as the creative artist at odds with his society, while at the same time being accommodated by a symbolic and traditionally validated role which orients his talent to a prime social task.

The material upon which this discussion is based was collected among the Gola, Vai, and De chiefdoms of the coastal section of western Liberia. These people constitute a segment of what has been termed the "Poro cluster" of tribes whose distribution and relatively common cultural features have been described elsewhere [d'Azevedo, 1962 (1) and (2)]. Briefly, however, it may be pointed out that the Poro-type pantribal and intertribal male association has its most intensive distribution among the Mande-speaking and Mel-speaking[2] peoples of northwestern Liberia and southern Sierra Leone. Closely connected with Poro is the Sande (or Bundu) female associations which are localized as lodges among the women of specific chiefdoms. They are also spread throughout the region and have a wider distribution than Poro. The tribes of this cluster are divided into numerous petty chiefdoms traditionally controlled by the landowning patrilineages of the founders of each unit. The economy is based upon intensive slash-and-burn agriculture with supplementary hunting and fishing. Warfare, trade, population mobility, and periodic confederacies have characterized relations among groups for centuries.

The Myth

The greatest public dramas of life are played out in the cycle of ceremonies connected with the recruitment and maintenance of membership in the all-powerful and universal male and female secret associations.[3] The major theme of these dramas is the unresolved rivalry between the sexes and the unrelenting struggle of the ancestors—together with their ancient tutelaries among the nature spirits—to ensure the integrity and continuity of the community. The actors are the uninitiated youth, all the adult men of Poro, all the adult women of Sande, the sacred

Source: From *Primitive Art and Society* by Anthony Forge, published by Oxford University Press. Reprinted by permission of the publisher and the author, Warren L. d'Azevedo.

1 The field research which made these observations possible was supported by grants from the Ford Foundation in 1956–7, and from the Social Science Research Council in 1966.

The author wishes to acknowledge a debt of gratitude to Professor Raymond Firth for early encouragement and the example of his own work, as well as for the opportunity to present and discuss these materials during the intensive conference on Primitive Art and Society which he chaired at the Wenner-Gren Foundation Symposium in 1967. Thanks are also due to Anthony Forge, Robert Goldwater, and Douglas Newton who shared in the tasks of organizing the conference.

2 Recent discussions by linguists have indicated the necessity for extensive revision of earlier classifications of these languages. Among these are Welmers, 1958, and Dalby, 1965.

3 In the literature on this region, these associations are often referred to as "secret societies." Initiation and life-long membership in one or other of the mutually exclusive organizations is compulsory for all citizens. They are "secret" in the sense that non-members are rigorously denied knowledge of rites and lore, and that "secrecy" is a core value inculcated in the members. Each of the tribes of the Poro cluster of peoples in this region have their own names for these associations. "Sande" and "Bundu" have a wide distribution as terms for the female association. However, though Poro is a general term for the male association where it occurs, there are special local terms as well. The Gola refer to it as *Bõ*, or *Bõ Poro*.

elders representing the ancestors, and the masked impersonators of the nature spirits who are allied with the founders of the country.

The plot which ties the cycle together is simple and is derived from myth which explains the origin of crucial institutions. In the beginning, it is said, there was Sande. Women were the custodians of all ritual and the spiritual powers necessary for defending sacred tradition in the interests of the ancestors. The initiation and training of females for their roles as wives and mothers was a central task in which the entire community participated. The generations spring from the wombs of women, and it is the secret knowledge of women which ensures the fertility of families, of the land, and of all nature. For this reason, women have always been more diligent than men in the tending of ancestral graves and in the guarding of the shrines of spirits who protect the land.

The primacy of Sande in general myth among the Gola is attributed to the conditions attending their origin as a people. It is believed that all "real" Gola of the extended territory which they occupy today may trace their descent patrilineally (or ambipatrilineally) to the ancient lineages of chiefdoms in an interior homeland region known as Kongba. Thus, the founding ancestors of these legendary units constitute the original ancestors of all the Gola, though local genealogies seldom include them except to name the migrant ancestors who is claimed to be the link to Kongba. The original lineages and chiefdoms emerged under a charter between the founders of Kongba and the autochthonous nature spirits whose land they occupied. The particular class of spirits to whom the founders were obligated for patronage were those who resided under the waters—the "water people." These spirits helped the ancient Gola to drive away monsters from the territory, and guaranteed the fertility of the land. In return they required an exchange of women in marriages that would validate a co-operative alliance between the human and spirit communities.

Thus the spiritual male and female spouses of the founders became the ancestral tutelaries whose descendants formed similar alliances with complementary human descent groups in each succeeding generation.[4] Moreover, in each generation there were to be certain human beings assigned to the special role of regulating commerce between human beings and the water spirits. These persons were designated by titles which passed down through specific core lineages of those founders who originally held such positions. The first *Mazo* was, therefore, the woman chosen among the founding families to carry out this task. The title became a property of her patrilineage, while one of her elder male lineage mates was given the title of *Mama fuu'ɔ* to serve as her sponsor in sacred office. The *Mazo* and her "brother" were responsible for the organization and control of all women of the legendary Gola chiefdoms in order to inculcate in them the crucial tradition of alliance with the nature spirits, their sacred role as potential wives and procreators in two worlds, and their special responsibilities with regard to the propitiation of two classes of ancestors. This is how, it is said, Sande came into being.

In Sande ritual, the *Zogbe* is the masked impersonation of the male water spirit of a lineage —parallel to that of the *Mazo's* core lineage— in the spirit community.[5] During sessions of Sande, or at any time when his services are required, he asserts the ancient rights of his "people" by venturing into the human community in visible form to officiate and to ensure the continuity of the charter. The women of Sande are referred to as his "wives," and human males are not to interfere with any of the demands that might be made upon their own wives or their female relatives while Sande is in session. In a populous chiefdom there may be many *Zogbea* visiting from the other world, each presiding over a band of women assigned by the local *Mazo*. During the session, women are said to "control the country." Their normal activities are curtailed by rigorous involvement in the complex rites and numerous tasks of "cleansing the land," training initiates, and tending ancestral shrines. Men complain that their own interests are being neglected, but the powers of Sande are great and its work must be carried out for the good of all.

4 Theoretically, the lineages of water spirits derived from the original charter alliance constitute relatives of the local human descent group "on the *jina* side." This community of water spirits stands in the same relationship to the local human community as do the individual tutelaries (*neme*) who engage in private alliances with human beings.

5 The impersonation is carried out by a high ranking woman of Sande.

In brief outline, these are the essential features of Sande as they are expressed in general myth. The myths of the founding of new chiefdoms in the expanded territory of the Gola are local restatements of the grand design, and ritual is an enactment of modified commitments to the ancient charter. The founding ancestor is directed by a diviner to make a pact with the local nature spirits. This pact invariably involves a "friendship" with a woman of the spirit world, and the assignment of one of the founder's female relatives to a similar alliance with a male relative of his spirit spouse. Just as the founder is frequently given a vague genealogical connection with the lineages of Kongba, the local nature spirits with whom the pact is made are thought to have kinsmen among those of their kind who were allied with the original Gola. Local Sande lodges are led by a succession of women who inherit the title from a core lineage of the founder, often the same lineage from which kings and other officials are selected. Therefore emphasis is placed upon sacred obligations to local ancestors and nature spirits, but always with reference to the stipulations of the grand charter, the sacred lore of Gola origin.

In the ancient days of peace and perfect social order—long before the Gola began to migrate from Kongba—it is said that Sande was the single and all-powerful sacred institution. Though men ruled, women controlled all communal intercourse with the ancestors and their spirit guardians, and men submitted to female domination in ritual matters. It is even suggested, in some versions of this lore, that Gola men had not learned about circumcision in those distant days. But there came a time of terrible wars in which enemies attacked and tried to destroy the country. When the men of the Gola chiefdoms attempted to organize themselves for defence, the women resisted because it interfered with the activities of Sande. In their view, Sande, alone, with its powerful spiritual guardians would be sufficient to protect the land and its people. But the attacks continued and the situation became desperate. Furthermore, men learned that women cannot be trusted with the secrets of war; for though they jealously kept the secrets of Sande from men, they would speak out the plans of men to their enemies. This is how the ancient Gola men learned what every man knows today. A man cannot trust his wife unless she is from his own family, for a woman is loyal only to her own kin and to Sande. A woman can betray her husband's family and chiefdom.

Thus women and war brought about Poro.[6] With war came disaster, and women could not understand it or cope with it. As a consequence, it was necessary for men to find a special instrument of power of their own. They searched the forests of the interior until they discovered an awful being, much like the monsters which had once roamed the land and had been driven out by the ancestors and their spirit allies. The being was captured, and certain brave men were assigned the task of subduing and tending it. They and certain qualified descendants of their lineages came to be known as the *Dazoa* of Poro, the highest and most sacred officials of the men's secret organization. The strange being they had captured became the Great Spirit of Poro whose aspect was so frightful that women could not look upon it, and even the *Zogbea* were reluctant to test its power. Armed with their new spirit, the men were able to subdue the women. Boys began to be taken from the care of their mothers at an early age in order to prepare them for the rigors of manhood. They were removed from all female company to teach them obedience to their elders, secret signs by which they would recognize their fellows, endurance of all kinds of hardship, self-reliance, the arts of war, as well as co-operation and absolute loyalty to the Poro. Women and strangers were told that the boys had been "eaten" by the Poro Spirit which would eventually give birth to them in a new adult form. Circumcision was explained as part of the process of being reborn. The Poro Spirit removed all that was "childish and useless" in order to produce men. During the Poro session the Great Spirit was never seen by outsiders. It remained in the seclusion of the secret forest grove of Poro guarded by a *Dazo* and the leading men. But its terrible voice could be heard admonishing the boys and raging to be set free among the uninitiated of the community.

When the Poro became strong, the women beseeched the men to remove their Great Spirit and allow things to be as they were. But the men refused. They did, however, agree to an arrangement. The *Mazoa* of Sande and the new *Dazoa*

[6] This statement is the most common response of elders who are asked about the origin of Gola Poro.

of Poro decided that each association would take its turn of control over the country. The Poro would have four years to carry out its tasks, and the Sande three years. At the end of its session the presiding association would remove its spiritual powers from its grove to allow for the entrance of the other. Since that time, the number four has been the sign of men, and the number three the sign for women.

The Enactment

In all the extended chiefdoms of the Gola, the endless rotation of Sande and Poro sessions are co-ordinated by the *Dazoa* who are responsible for various sections of territory inhabited by Gola. The Poro sessions do not begin until all the chiefdoms have completed the sessions of Sande and there has been a year or more of interval "so that the country can rest." Then the *Dazoa* secretly confer and send word among the groves of the chiefdoms that Poro is about to claim the country. Just as in the ancient days of origin, the Poro Spirit is led stealthily into the chiefdom and confined in the local Poro grove. Word spreads that it has been brought from the deep interior forests and that it is wild and hungry after its long absence. Young boys and uninitiated men begin to disappear, causing consternation to mothers and quiet satisfaction to fathers.

When all is in readiness, a *Dazo* appears in each of the chiefdoms and announces that the time has come for men to assume leadership again. At the sacred towns of the groves he heads a procession of all the men of Poro to the Sande enclosure where the *Mazo* and the leading women of Sande are waiting. The *Dazo* requests that she turn over her power and send the *Zogbe* protectors back to the forests and rivers whence they came. He informs her that the Great Spirit of the men is already in the Poro grove and that it has begun to gather boys for training. The *Mazo* confers with her attendants and reluctantly agrees. At that moment the Poro Spirit is heard singing in the grove. It sings of its great hunger, and begs that uninitiated boys be brought to it for food.

During the following weeks all the boys of appropriate age disappear from the villages of the chiefdom, and uninitiated men are ambushed on the roads and will not be seen again until the end of the session. It is explained to the women that though they have been eaten by the Poro Spirit, they will be born again from its stomach in a new, clean, and manly form. It is a time when women weep for their lost sons and men smile wisely because of the return of masculine principles to the world. There is much rejoicing among men, and emblems of male supremacy and strength appear at all feasts and public ceremony. Foremost among these are the masked figures, the "dancing images," which represent spirits controlled by the various subgroups of local Poro. One of these figures is known as *Gbetu* whose magnificent helmet mask and awesome acrobatic feats create an atmosphere of intense excitement at feasts and other ceremonies.[7]

However, these masked figures do not have the same ritual importance as the visible *Zogbe* of Sande or the invisible Great Spirit of Poro. They are the "entertainers" or "mummers" of Poro and represent minor spirits who have been brought to enhance the ceremonies of men. They are handled by their attendants as scarcely tamed animals who must be whipped, cajoled, and contained. This is a symbolic projection of the role of the great Poro Spirit which must be rigorously controlled by the men of Poro to restrain it from doing harm to the community.

At the end of the four-year Poro session, it is announced that the Great Spirit is about to give birth to newly adult males.[8] A mass mourning ceremony takes place as a wake for the boys who had "died" four years before. The ceremony concludes with the entrance of the initiates into town, their bodies rubbed with clay, and their faces and movements those of dazed strangers. They do not recognize their mothers or other female relatives. They must be encouraged by gifts and endearments to speak or to look at human beings. This condition lasts for days until they are ritually "washed" by the elders of Poro. They are dressed in all the finery their families can afford and are placed on display in the

[7] The *Gbetu* represents a mountain spirit and was used as a "messenger" of Poro and local rulers in the past. It is one of five or six subsidiary spirits of Poro each "owned" by small co-operative groups of local members.

[8] Though the Gola have held to the traditional length of "bush school" sessions more tenaciously than most neighboring peoples, initiates are released earlier in some of the chiefdoms near the coast where Liberian government influence has been greater.

center of the town. Their first act is to demand food, but they show their new independence and male vigor by wringing the necks of chickens brought to them as gifts. They address their female relatives authoritatively and maintain an attitude of aloof contempt for all commonplace human emotions. The final ceremony is marked by their public performance of the skills they have learned during the Poro session. There are exhibits of dancing, musicianship, and crafts after which they return to their homes accompanied by proud parents.

Within a short time the women of Sande will have laid the plans for reinstatement of their own session. At last they approach the chief and elders of the chiefdom with the request that the *Dazo* return and remove the Great Poro Spirit from the country. When the time is finally agreed upon, the *Dazo* is called to conduct the ceremony of transition. His demeanor is one of great reluctance and annoyance. Why has he been disturbed? In what way have the women shown that they have earned the right to take over the country? Each day he dances in the central clearing of the town surrounded by his musicians and the men of Poro. He continues to deny the solicitations of the *Mazo*. At last he relents, and a time is specified for the removal of the Poro Spirit. The women are ordered into their houses along with all the uninitiated, and the shutters and doors are closed. The Great Spirit can be heard singing sadly as it is led by the men from their grove and through the town. At moments it rebels and howls in anguish. It must be dragged forcibly, and its teeth leave long grooves in the dirt of the paths. At last it is gone, and the sound of guns being fired indicates that the men have succeeded in driving it away in the company of its keeper, the *Dazo*.

The *Mazo* is summoned from her house to meet with the elders of Poro in the center of the town. They hand her the emblem of power of the secret societies. The moment this transaction takes place, she and her attendants shriek with joy and call the women to take over the country. The men flee into the houses as the *Zogbea* and their singing women attendants stream from the sacred Sande grove and from the various houses of the town. The *Zogbea* rush here and there, waving their spears at tardy men, and the women cry warning that the country will now return to proper leadership. The entire day is spent exacting fines from chiefs and other important men for the "crimes" that have been committed during the rule of men. They admonish children and remind them of their duties. Towards evening the men dare to move about more freely. They are invited by the women to take part in a joyous festival during the night, but are warned to remain respectful and humble before the *Zogbea*, "our new husbands who have come to rule the land."

This cycle of male and female secret society activity is part of the rhythmic chronology of tribal life and may be said to mark the decades of passing time while the agricultural cycle marks the years. Individuals frequently determine their ages by the number of farms since their birth as well as by the name of the secret society session in which they were initiated. The institutionalization of male and female principles in two compulsory organizations, each with its own structure of administration and its own secret body of knowledge, has a profoundly pervasive influence throughout every aspect of culture. It qualifies all interpersonal relationships by its rigorous codification of male and female roles and by its pressure to conformity with traditional concepts of ideal social order involving absolute obedience to authority as represented by the hierarchies of age, lineage status, and official position. The notion of "secrecy" is a paramount value in this system—secrecy between men and women, secrecy between the aged and the young, and secrecy between the initiated and uninitiated.

The most common expression of this mutual exclusiveness of spheres of knowledge is the continual reference to "women's business," "men's business," or "society business." Men will disclaim any knowledge of the content of Sande ritual or training, and women adamantly deny any curiosity concerning the mysteries of Poro. Children must never inquire into these matters, and non-initiates are warned that banishment or worse will befall anyone whose eyes, ears, and minds are not closed to all mysteries which lie behind the public performances of the secret associations.

In this context, the mutual exclusiveness of activities and information creates the necessity for intermediaries between Poro and Sande. These roles are performed by certain of the elder women and men who carry sacred titles in the local organizations. All such persons are assigned the general title of *zo*. Thus, the *Mazo* and the *Dazo* are the titled heads of the Sande and Poro respectively. The *Mazo* is aided by three or four elder women attendants who are also *zonya* (plural), and there are a number of colleagues and assistants of the *Dazo* in each Poro lodge. All such persons are *zonya*, and their specific titles are conferred by Poro and Sande in accordance with criteria of age, service, personality attributes, and required lineage status. The formal title of *zo* may also be conferred on certain other respected elders who are masters of crucial knowledge and skills that have benefited the entire community. Such persons may be respected herbalists, diviners, bone healers, snakebite curers, or special craftsmen. Elder blacksmiths who have been permanent residents of the community and who are members of high ranking lineages are invariably *zonya*. The term *zo* is also used informally as a reference to any admired and proficient individual in the same sense as we speak of someone as a "master" or "expert," but this is quite distinct from the use of the title for the traditional offices.

The leading official *zonya* are said to be beyond the age which restricts their involvement to one or other of the secret associations. Their age and experience are considered to have removed them from the petty rivalries of local lineage segments, from the temptations and irresponsibilities of younger persons, or from the passions and immediate concerns of sexuality and procreation. They are the "grandparents" of the people and are about to join the ancestors. The *Mazo* and her attendants are women who know all matters pertaining to Sande and who have also learned the major secrets of Poro from their counterparts in the male organization. The *Dazo* and his aides are also informed of the mysteries of Sande. It is through the agency of these elders that the continuity and mutual cooperation of the sacred institutions is maintained through each generation. The average person views this commerce between the closely guarded provinces of male and female authority with awe, and a high degree of charisma is associated with the roles of those who move freely in this regard.

This charisma is shared to some degree by the *zo* specialists who perform necessary services for both Poro and Sande which require knowledge of sacred procedures. The blacksmith is a prime example of such a role in that he is not only master of the resources and techniques of metallurgy which provide the implements of agriculture and warfare, but he is the secret maker of certain emblems of sacred office as well as of the tools of circumcision and scarification for both associations. In this position he commands information about the most secret rituals. To some extent other *zo* specialists perform duties which might take them, under certain carefully arranged conditions, into the groves of the society of the opposite sex. It is this peculiar aspect of their roles which is a basic feature of official *zo*-ship.

Mask Makers and the Personal Myth

Among the specialists who perform crucial services for both Poro and Sande, the position of the master woodcarver is unique. Despite the fact that the woodcarver is the creator of the masks which represent the most powerful supernatural guardians of the secret societies, I know of no instance where the formal title of *zo* has been assigned to a woodcarver during the period of his most productive activity as a craftsman. The product of the woodcarver's art is central to the public drama of Sande. He participates intimately in the affairs of the woman's organization to a degree allowed to no other man excepting the eldest sacred officials. His involvement in the secret stagecraft and technology of ritual is every bit as important as that of the blacksmith. Yet the carver, regardless of the excellence of his work, appears to be excluded from the company of the *zonya*.

As these matters are subject to the most extreme secrecy and sanction, it is rarely possible for the investigator to inquire directly about them. I spent more than a year among the Gola and other neighboring peoples before I encountered woodcarvers who would reveal that they were producers of masks, and it was much longer before I was able to discuss these materials with them or with any other person. Fear of exposure is intense, for heavy fines and disgrace can follow the discovery that an individual has converted sacred objects to the external market or has revealed the conditions of their production.

I found, however, that woodcarvers were quite willing to discuss any aspect of their craft and to produce examples of it for non-traditional purposes as long as they could be assured of being undetected by those members of their own culture who would bring them to account. This was not true of any of the official *zonya* whose circumspection and limited tolerance with regard to questions concerning Sande and Poro is a standard response. It seemed to me, therefore, that woodcarvers represented something quite unusual among those persons who were involved by skill and knowledge in the preparation of the impressive effects and illusions of public ritual. It appeared that they were less moved by the social value of their role than by subjective concerns such as recognition for the masterpieces for which they cannot receive direct public acclaim. These early impressions proved to be well-founded, and subsequent observation has confirmed my view that the woodcarver in this area represents, in personal orientation as well as social status, many of the characteristics which are associated with our own concept of the artist.

Vocational specialization is not highly developed among the coastal groups of western Liberia. There are few full-time specialists of any kind, and these invariably supplement their incomes by farming or periodic shifts to alternative pursuits. The professional *zonya* are relieved of direct subsistence tasks due to their age and hereditary status within the large and relatively wealthy lineages of the founders of a chiefdom. Political offices are also hereditary and provide, at least for major chiefs, the emoluments and services which make a full-time political vocation possible. Among craftsmen, it is only the local official blacksmith who can be said to be a full-time professional supported by the local community. His position is also an hereditary one, and the nature of his craft is such that there is a continuous demand for his products locally, and a traditional assignment of community labor to assist him in farming and other subsistence activities.

Professionalism, aside from the above vocations, is achieved only by those who appeal to a wider area of demand than that of the local community, or by those who are supported as clients of wealthy patrons. Thus, itinerancy and patronage are requirements of any full-time specialization which does not carry the traditional credentials of local sponsorship. Highly skilled singers, dancers, musicians, and craftsmen may make their services available throughout a region and are frequently solicited from distant chiefdoms of other tribes. In the past they were part of the heterogeneous retinues of great chiefs, and were often the instruments of competition for prestige among powerful rulers. In more recent times there has been some replacement of these traditional supports of specialization by new external spheres of demand created by foreigners and by national government interest in tribal culture.

With the exception of the locally sponsored *zonya,* an aura of mixed distrust and admiration surrounds the full-time specialist of any kind. As persons of exceptional ability, they are no longer fully dependent upon sponsorship or approval from their own families, or from the community of their origin. They are likely to shift their loyalties in accordance with the fortunes of patronage. Every local group of any prominence has its own roster of talented amateur craftsmen and performers who contribute to the on-going economic, recreational, and ceremonial needs of the community. The community can also rely to some extent on its own healers and diviners who are permanent residents engaged in part-time practice. But few people can avail themselves of the services of the famous specialist whose name has spread far and wide, who has become associated with legends of remarkable successes, and who is sought after by the wealthy and the great. Their talent seems to be derived from special powers that others lack, and their individualism and apparent freedom of choice is attributed to the kind of "luck" that comes from commerce with private supernatural agencies.

Almost without exception, renowned specialists are believed to be sponsored by one of a variety of possible tutelaries among the classes of *jina* who are thought to engage in "friendships" with certain human beings. Such tutelaries are called *neme* among the Gola, a term which means literally "the thing belonging to one," but they are also spoken of as "friends." All great and successful persons are suspected of having a spiritual liaison of this sort. The *neme* relationship is both feared and envied. Since it is often kept secret, there is no way for the average person to be certain that it exists except by careful observation of the behavior and fortunes of those suspected. Among the venerable *zonya* there are those who are known to be sponsored by a powerful *jina*. Yet they have the gratitude and trust of the community because their private spiritual guardian has been inherited by them from among the totemic spirits who have been associated with their ancestors since time immemorial. Though the *zo* may not always speak freely of this spiritual connection, the fact of its existence and, usually, the conditions of its consummation are matters of public tradition.[9]

There are, on the other hand, many free-roving *jina* who seek mutually rewarding friendships with human beings. Such friendships may be established before a person is born, or they may come later in life as a result of a dream or a waking encounter. There are good and bad *jina* just as there are good and bad human beings. An evil or ambitious person may become the ready instrument of an evil spirit. Most persons claim that they have, at one time or another, rejected the advances of *jina* who approach them with seductive promises of love and luck. The rejection must be emphatic, for once a pact is made the *jina* has complete power over one and will wreck vengeance if it is broken. A good human being may make a private pact with a free-roving *jina*, but such pacts are usually made early in life, or even by the human soul before a person's birth. Sudden and unexpected success at the expense of others is always attributed to either sorcery or to a newly established pact with an evil *jina*, whereas consistent excellence in a line of work is usually attributed to a benign and lifelong spiritual friendship. From the point of view of the average person, however, any such phenomena are considered precariously unpredictable and fraught with danger for the community.

In this context, a clear distinction must be made between the notions of communal and private spiritual guardianship. As pointed out above, the spiritual sponsorship of the honored *zonya* is derived from the totemic tutelaries of the ancestors of the high-status descent groups of the community. These are closely connected with the supernatural beings who are represented in Sande ritual. The ancestors acting through their living agents, the sacred elders, demonstrate the essence of the myth which unites the community with its ancient protectors among the autochthonous nature spirits of the locality. It is under these conditions that the *neme* concept is expressed on the level of communal tradition and organization. At the same time, there are numerous opportunities for the private pursuit of fortune through the auspices of human or supernatural patrons. The use of personal sources of power or luck is considered to be the most direct means to advantage. It does not require the arduous courting of public favor, the obsequious obedience to one's elders, or the ascribed virtues of wealthy family or high lineage rank. But the risks to self and family are great, for the powerful controls exerted by the sacred institutions are neither effective nor enforceable under these conditions.

The personality characteristics often associated with renowned independent specialists are conceit and lack of humility before superiors. These are traits which are said to accompany the aggressive assurance which comes from having a strong private tutelary. It is much the same behavior which one might expect from a person who is backed by a powerful human patron who protects him from the indignation of others and encourages his wilfulness as a reflection of the patron's own prestige. Great chiefs of the past were surrounded by "followers" or clients, many of whom were from foreign chiefdoms and not connected by ties of kinship to the local community. These were warriors, diviners, entertainers, and craftsmen of all sorts who had become attached to the ruler's household. The favoritism afforded them was frequently the source of friction within the chiefdom, for they were partially insulated from the sanction of local kinship groups or secret associations. Such persons were sometimes referred to as the "spoiled children of the king" whose fate depended entirely upon the fortunes of the chiefdom and the whims of the royal household.

In the case of individuals thought to have private supernatural sponsorship, the traits of pride and arrogance might be even more pronounced and less susceptible of regulation. This was particularly true of highly skilled persons whose products or services were so superior to those of others that they were in constant de-

9 The term *jina* has had wide currency throughout West Africa and is similar to the Arabic and Latin terms for tutelaries or the residing spirits of a place. Among the Gola, the term refers to all classes of nature spirits, exclusive of ancestral spirits. These are spirits of the waters, mountains, forests, animals, etc. The most common and powerful in forming *neme* relationships are the spirits of the water (*yun kuwi*) who are believed to have some vague totemic connection with the most ancient ancestors and the heroic founders of chiefdoms. A person's *neme* is usually of the opposite sex and the relationship is ordinarily depicted as an amorous one. For a more detailed discussion of these phenomena in the context of social organization, see d'Azevedo, 1973.

mand despite their strange behavior. Not all specialists were in this category, for many disclaimed any supernatural guidance. But others, among whom were usually the most famous, tended to proclaim and dramatize their spiritual resources. Some who presented themselves in this light commanded the respect due only to the official *zonya.* It might be said of such a person that "he is a true *zo* for his work," which is a high form of praise, but also indicates that he is a *zo* without portfolio, so to speak. One might also hear the expressions "he is a *zo* before his time," or, "he has crowned himself *zo,*" suggesting awareness of the ambition and striving for recognition that is frequently a component of the personality of the talented and popular person.

Though these characteristics were in the past, and are today associated with all specialists whose excellence appears to be derived from private connection with supernatural agents, they are said to be especially evident among those whose skills are demonstrated in public display, and who exhibit themselves or their works at festivals and ceremonies. Famous singers, dancers, musicians, story tellers, and masters of legerdemain are commissioned to participate in these events, and many others come unsolicited to collect gifts. Much of the quality of any great gathering, whether it be a funeral feast, a celebration for a dignitary, or the festivity surrounding ritual, is provided by the excitement of competition for public recognition among these performers. Great female singers, in particular, are centers of attention. Many of them are already legend because of their important lovers, their endurance and creativity as leaders of songs, their beauty, and the personal myth of supernatural inspiration which they help to perpetuate. Such women often claim to have a *jina* lover who trains their voice and brings them songs. The *jina* is not jealous of human husbands or lovers, but is a ruthless taskmaster of their talent and success. Singers are often childless and they will state that barrenness is a condition imposed by their *neme.*

A similar aura of private sacrifice and supernatural liaison surrounds other exceptional performers and artisans whose fame has spread far and who seem to have found alternatives to the limited avenues of advancement in the local community. They are most often young or in the prime of life. They flaunt their unusual deportment and supernatural connections in ways that would be unacceptable from the average person. Yet they may be persons of low birth, disreputable and untrustworthy in all else, and quite unlikely candidates for *zo*-ship even in old age.

The master woodcarver has a special place in this category of persons. As maker of the prime ritual objects of Poro and especially Sande, his craft and his activities are under continual scrutiny. Without his expert services, the required perfection and impressiveness of the masks which represent the spiritual power of the secret societies would not be achieved. Among the Gola, Vai, and De, of the coastal Liberian section of Poro tribes, these masks constitute not only the epitome of the woodcarver's art, but are a major focus of aesthetic and ritual values. Unlike some of the more populous tribes of the interior, where guild specialization and numerous secret associations in addition to Poro and Sande create conditions for a greater variety and productiveness in woodcarving forms, the coastal tribes concentrate on a few basic types of masks and figurines.[10]

Not all men known as woodcarvers produce masks for the secret societies. Woodcarving, like other skills, is generalized in so far as many young men carve combs, dolls, toys, swagger sticks, and utensils as part of their training in Poro as well as for gifts and petty trade. But the term *yun hema ku* (one who carves wood) is usually applied to a man for whom this activity is a recognized vocation and who is at least suspected of having carved objects of ritual importance. He is also a man whose skill is considered to be extraordinary and who is believed to be inspired by a tutelary. Among woodcarvers themselves there is considerable difference of opinion as to whether supernatural guidance is a necessary factor in superior workmanship and success. Those who claim to receive their "ideas" directly through a "dream" which comes as a gift of a *jina* friend are emphatic in claiming ascendancy to such work, and state that they are able to recognize the work of "dreamers" as against those who do not dream.

[10] The highly developed tradition of mask production in relation to Poro and other associations of peoples in eastern Liberia are described in Harley, 1941, and Harley and Schwab, 1947 and Harley, 1950.

When confronted by the fact that a certain carver whom they have praised denies supernatural aid, these men will take the position that the denial is a subterfuge. On the other hand, some carvers who seem honestly to deny any consciousness of supernatural guidance will admit the possibility that they are given such aid without their knowledge. They are also prone to admire the dramatic stance of those excellent carvers who claim to be "dreamers," and who attribute each new work to the productive exchange of the *neme* relationship.

Once the woodcarver has participated in the production of Sande or Poro masks that actually appear in public, he has become a peculiar individual of a type for which there is no counterpart in the culture. The objects he produces are not to be thought of as having been made by human hands but are, rather, the visible form of a supernatural being. The more remarkable his execution of the mask, the greater is the reinforcement of the desired public illusion, and the greater is his surreptitiously acknowledged fame. No one is ever to allude to a mask as having been made, or to refer to this aspect of the woodcarver's craft. Children are severely punished for even inquiring about such things, and adults may be fined heavily for an inadvertent slip in public. I found that most very young people claimed never to have considered the possibility of local human workmanship being involved in the production of these masks, and adults who claimed to have wondered about it in their youth say that they had concluded that all such things had been made long ago and were passed down by the ancestors.

Those few who will discuss these matters freely describe their youthful discovery that such objects were made by living men as having evoked in them the most intense anxiety. It seemed unbelievable that ordinary men could have made such marvellous things, and they claim never to quite get over this feeling. For this reason it is still a very shocking experience for rural villagers or their children to come across one of these masks in the shop of an urban trader. Fear and indignation are followed by attempts to track down the source of the illicit object and to punish the betrayer of the secrets. I have noticed in such situations that people do not always recognize the work they see as authentic, but think of it as a possible copy made by an unscrupulous Mandingo or other foreign craftsman. This response is, I think, genuine, for few people in the more traditional sections of the interior see these masks apart from their public presentation in ritual, and tend to perceive them quite differently when these conditions are not operative. A striking exception to this is the response of woodcarvers themselves. They make immediate judgments about masks as masks, as products of degrees of skill, and as representative of the styles of particular carvers. Very few other members of the culture make objective judgments of this kind. Discussions concerning the quality of a piece of workmanship rarely occur except on those occasions when certain leading persons in either Poro or Sande prepare to commission a carver to copy an old mask or to create a new one.

A degree of choice is exercised in the selection of a carver, but the choice is limited by the scarcity of carvers and by the vast difference in cost between the work of an ordinary craftsman and that of the rare master carver. The importance of a particular mask does not, however, depend entirely upon the quality of workmanship. Each of the spirit impersonations has its own name and a distinct "personality" expressed in its dancing, its public mannerisms, and through the legends of its peculiar powers. Thus certain masks which are seen in ritual may be, from the master carver's point of view, very poor workmanship; yet the respect and admiration afforded it by the public and by its ritual followers may be great. On the other hand, the appearance of a magnificently executed mask will invariably elicit expressions of awe and delight from a crowd. The aesthetic values awakened by technical proficiency and creative innovation are an enhancement of the fundamental traditional values associated with these ritual objects, but are not crucial to their effectiveness. The artistic component is, therefore, optional and the role of the exceptional carver is considerably influenced by the fact that he controls a skill whose rare products are highly desirable but not essential. The work of a less skilled craftsman might be solicited for practical reasons.

In order to understand the special value which is attached to products of exceptional talent, it is necessary to know the conditions under which the woodcarver learns his craft and at what point certain carvers become producers of secret society masks. Formal associations of specialists do not exist among the Gola, Vai, or De. Excepting for the blacksmith and the official *zonya,* few vocations are hereditary. Becoming a specialist, therefore, is individualistic in orientation and involves factors of personal inclination, self-appointment, and opportunity. Most professional woodcarvers with whom I have worked attribute their choice of a vocation to the force of their own incentives in the face of obstacles created by their families. They claim that any special talent is looked upon with jealousy by others and as a potential threat to the family in its efforts to develop loyal and dependable members. Intensive devotion to one activity—particularly where it seems to be accompanied by unusual personality traits—is discouraged by adults. The development of varied skills during the sessions of Sande or Poro training is encouraged, however, for this occurs in the context of a program directed by adults.

The attitude which woodcarvers attribute to the community with regard to themselves is confirmed by my own observations. Woodcarvers, like professional singers, dancers, and musicians, are generally looked upon as irresponsible and untrustworthy people. If they achieve a degree of success, it is said that their independence and self-concern removes them from the control of family or local group, and provides them with alternatives through new attachments and patronage. They are said to yearn for admiration and are always to be found where there are crowds. They squander their resources foolishly and are impoverished in their old age. But most important of all is the danger which everyone knows to surround such work if it becomes the major preoccupation of an individual.

One woodcarver recounted how his mother begged him to give up his work because of its threat to the fertility of the women of the family. Another told how his father had angrily destroyed the tools he had made for himself as a child in imitation of those he had seen in the kit of an adult carver. Others spoke of having run away to a more tolerant relative, or placing themselves under secret apprenticeship to a local or itinerant carver. Such men, whether great or lesser craftsmen, distinguish themselves in retrospect from the other children they knew in youth who may have learned to carve for enjoyment, but who never persevered. They speak of having been driven by an urge to carve that they could not control. This is true even of those who do not admit to an active *neme* relationship. Another common feature of this early experience is a sense of having been different from others in curiosity and ambition. Each claims to have been inordinately ambitious and determined to prove himself superior. This was accompanied by a prying curiosity about things inappropriate to his age, and resulted in rejection or punishment.

The Creation of a Deity

Among the things which every woodcarver mentions as one of the great wonders of youth were the *Zogbea* spirits of Sande and the masked images of Poro. One Gola carver said that he had surmised as a child of seven or eight that the head-dresses of these figures had been carved by living men and that, in one case at least, he had guessed that a particular local carver had been the creator because of a similarity between the designs he had placed on a drum and those on a *Zogbe*. When he mentioned this to other children, his parents heard of it and he was severely whipped. He describes his interest in the masked figures of the secret associations as an obsession, and says that he often dreamed of them or saw himself carving them from blocks of wood. He once swore a number of boys his own age to secrecy and took them to his hidden workplace in the forest. There he showed them the crude Sande *Zogbe* and Poro *Gbetu* that he had carved. He remembers the thrill of experiencing their shocked admiration at his audacity and skill. When this escapade was discovered, his punishment was so severe that he does not speak of it, but merely says that his family wanted to destroy him. They finally sent him away to an older brother in a distant village, a silversmith.

In that village he met an adult carver who made ornate utensils and ornamental objects for trade, but who would not reveal himself as a maker of masks. He took to tracking the man into the bush and soon found where he did his secret work. He spied on him for days as he completed a *Zogbe* mask, an experience he recalls as the greatest and most moving of his life. When it was almost finished, he walked boldly into the clearing. The man sprang up with his cutlass and threatened the boy with death for spying and intruding. But the latter felt such great joy that he had no fear. "I only said to that man, I am here, I can do what you are doing, I want you to show me what you know." The carver eventually took him into training, his first formal instruction.

Shortly after this event he began to have overwhelmingly vivid dreams. Once a woman's voice spoke to him. She offered love and "great ideas." She began to come to him frequently and brought "patterns" which she would draw on the sand before him to guide his work. His first *Zogbe,* sponsored by his teacher and inspired by his *neme,* was so successful that the older carver presented it as his own work to the first group of Sande women who commissioned him for a mask. It was not until much later, however, that his name became known to a few people in the secret associations so that he was approached independently. More than ten years after these experiences (when I had first known him) he was sought after among Gola, De, Vai, and Kpele chiefdoms. He was never able to catch up with the demand for his work. He complained of the exhaustion it brought him and he frequently disappeared for months to do farming or wage labor in order to recover his interest. During these periods he says that his *jina* avoids him, as though she too is resting.

Though differing in detail and intensity, the experience of other master carvers is similar. Some do not claim *neme,* and some are not so driven to direct confrontation with the norms of their society, but the theme of misunderstanding and the lonely pursuit of a beloved craft is consistently expressed. Another theme which appears in the discourse of adult carvers and their admirers is that of the man who lives daringly, who has surmounted obstacles, and who has intruded into realms which even the elders fear. It is essentially the theme of the precocious child who is ridiculed, defies his elders, masters their knowledge, and then produces something of his own which all must acclaim. The woodcarver may see himself, and is often seen by others, as the omnipotent free agent whose vision is indispensable to the very society which holds him in distrust and contempt. All these factors contribute to the charisma of the master woodcarver, and to the romanticism associated with his role.

The primary source of the woodcarver's unique status among craftsmen and performers is the special connection which they have, as men, with the female secret association. It is in this capacity that they enter into an intimacy with sacred female mysteries that is given to no other men excepting the highest ranking elders of Poro. The elders are considered to be free of the temptations of youth and wise enough to bear the great burden of public trust. The woodcarver, however, is neither an elder nor a *zo.* He is seldom a substantial citizen and in many other respects might be looked down upon by the community. Yet it is this same craftsman who may participate in a highly ritualized and sexualized commerce with the leading women of Sande.

The organization of any local Sande lodge is maintained under the authority of the *Mazo* and her elder *zo* assistants. The initiated women of the community are ranked into three "degrees" in accordance with their age, lineage status, and dutiful service to Sande. The women of the "third degree" are usually of middle age and constitute a body of the leading matrons of the community. It is from this group that the impersonators of the *Zogbe* are chosen. For this role a woman must be a great dancer, show exceptional endurance and forceful personality, and be beyond reproach in performance of Sande tasks. It is also required that she be a member of one of the lineages from which *Mazoa* are recruited, for the rigors of the *Zogbe* impersonation are considered to be an essential and final part of the training for a *Mazo.*

In each Sande grove the number of *Zogbe* groups depends upon the size of the local membership. A *Zogbe* presides over a group of from ten to fifteen followers of second degree status, and is attended by a few assistants of the third degree. The leader of the group, who is also the impersonator of the *Zogbe,* is responsible for the care of the mask and costume of the image. Many of the *Zogbea* of a given local lodge are ancient and have appeared for generations in each Sande session. Upon the death or the upgrading of the leader of a group, a new leader and impersonator must be chosen. This must be someone not only with the necessary status qualifications, but one who has learned the style of behavior or the "personality" of the *Zogbe* she is to impersonate. Masks and costumes must be renewed frequently, for the life of a mask in active service is seldom as long as twenty years. And should the female membership of the community increase, it may be necessary to "bring out" new *Zogbea.*

Towards the end of the four-year Poro session, the leading women of Sande secretly begin making preparations for the Sande session to follow. The preliminary preparations involve the repairing and renewal of ritual paraphernalia. The women of each group meet and discuss the problem of commissioning a carver and acquiring the necessary funds. Secret inquiries are made through elder male relatives, and negotiations are cautiously begun. In some instances carvers who have been solicited previously are approached to repair their own work, or to copy a piece. But in the "bringing out" of a new *Zogbe* it is often thought most desirable to find a carver whose work has attracted attention in other chiefdoms and whose fame has spread through the groves of Sande. This is very expensive, for the group is competing with many others for the services of a carver. Only very determined and well-to-do groups of Sande women can afford to make such arrangements. But it is under these circumstances that the greatest excitement is generated and the prestige of a *Zogbe* group is enhanced. It also provides the conditions for the classic relationship between the women and the creator of the sacred image.

Great carvers are commissioned by Sande in one of two ways. If a carver is known by a member of the group, through kinship or other connections, he might be approached directly. Where possible this is the procedure used because it means that the Sande group can deal with the carver independently and it ensures an element of surprise and mystery in the first appearance of the mask. On the other hand, it places the major burden of expense, as well as the control of the arduous encounter with the carver on the women themselves. Therefore, another procedure is more frequently employed whereby the women commission a carver through the good offices of an elder of Poro or the ruler of the chiefdom. Such a man can summon the carver and provide him with the hospitality that may encourage him to accept the commission.

The contact between the women and the carver follows a pattern that obtains to some degree in all relations between skilled specialists and their patrons. But the classic arrangement between woodcarvers and their female patrons is uniquely elaborate and intense. When a carver is approached secretly by the emissary of a Sande group, he is brought "encouragements" in the form of token gifts of money and cooked food. It is said that in the past some carvers were given large sums of money or the equivalent at this point, and presented with a slave. There are also legends of Sande groups studying the amorous habits of a carver and contriving his capitulation to their terms by assigning one of their members to the task of captivating him prior to negotiations. Carvers claim that women make strong medicines in order to control the proceedings. The situation is spoken of as one of "war" in which a man must defend himself against the wiles of women.

In his first dealings with the women the carver impresses them with the importance of his own role. He appears distracted by overwork and reluctant to take a new assignment. He claims to have an enormous thirst for strong drink, to be very hungry, to be in need of cohabitation with a virgin. He keeps them waiting for appointments and may even disappear for a day or two. He attempts to embarrass and subdue them by alluding to the secrets of Sande he has learned in his work. He wittily inquires why it is that they must come to a man such as himself for so important a task, or he berates them for trying to seduce and cheat him. The women, in turn, continue to bring him small gifts and promise to "satisfy" him if he will do the work. They offer to cohabit with him or to find him the love he wants. All of this is carried out in an atmosphere of intense enjoyment. At the same time the women will appear to be angered by the unruly and disreputable person they have been forced to deal with and, at certain points in the negotiations, may make veiled threats of supernatural sanction.

If the negotiations are concluded favorably, certain terms will have been agreed upon which will guide the relations until the completion of the project. The woodcarver often requires total support during the period of his commission. As the work may take from one to two weeks, during which time he must remain almost continually in the seclusion of the forest workplace, he demands to be fed, entertained, and dealt with in accordance with the personal code which supports his inspiration. Some carvers, particularly those with strong tutelaries, require that the women who visit them in the forest humble themselves by complete nudity. Others may demand that "wives" be brought to them whenever they declare a need for sexual gratification. Still others prefer to work in total privacy, claiming that this is the condition prescribed by their tutelaries. Food and other necessities are brought to a separate place in the forest and left for the carver to take them when he pleases.

The women, for their part, will attempt to direct the work of the carver by insisting upon particular stylistic elements, and lecturing him on the character and powers of the *Zogbe* whose image he is creating. The attempted influence upon the carver may include direction as to the use of certain standard motifs such as deer horns, fish or snake scales, neck wrinkles, hair plaiting, or even the desired facial expression of the deity. A highly individualistic carver will invariably resist such advice, or will accommodate only those suggestions which fit into his subjective plan. Woodcarvers have been known to destroy their unfinished work in a rage because of continued criticism as the work progresses. This is always the cause of scandal, and every effort is made to avoid a break with the carver. Some woodcarvers are more tractable and will accept advice or close supervision with the idea of producing a mask which is exactly what the women have themselves envisaged. But master woodcarvers who are "dreamers" speak of such men as "slaves of the knife" who get their ideas from others and who lower the standards which in former times surrounded the woodcarver with glory.

The struggle between the carver and the Sande group may continue throughout the process of production and even for a long while after. When the mask is completed the carver gives it a name, the name of a woman he has known, or a name given by his tutelary. But the Sande women have already selected a male name for their spiritual "husband," and the carver will insist upon a special fee from them for the right to use another name. He will also instruct the women concerning the care of the mask and inform them of the rules which govern its "life." These rules involve strong prescriptions with regard to the storage of the mask, the maintenance of its surface texture, and certain restrictions that may limit its public appearance or necessitate sacrifices to the carver's tutelary. In this sense, the carver affirms his symbolic ownership of the mask. He tells the women that he has the power to destroy his work at any time if it is treated with disrespect (that is, if the rules are not followed).

This threat of the carver is an effective one, for there are many tales of *Zogbe* masks cracking or bursting into pieces with a loud report before the horrified eyes of the spectators. An occurrence of this kind is considered to be a disaster of such terrible proportions that the sponsoring group of the *Zogbe* may be banished while angry spirits are propitiated. The destruction or "shaming" of a *Zogbe* can be caused by a rival *zo,* or by sorcery. But such an event is frequently attributed to a displeased carver. The source of his displeasure is usually the failure of the commissioning group to complete final payment for his work, or their failure to show him the respect he feels is due him. For this reason, every effort is made to satisfy a carver and to conclude all arrangements with him amicably.

But the peculiar relationship between the carver and the new owners of the mask is never fully terminated. He enjoys special privileges with the group. They refer to one another jokingly as "lovers" and he, theoretically at least, can expect sexual favors from them. The relationship is carried on with the air of a clandestine affair, with the woodcarver in the unique position of a male sharing secret knowledge and illicit intimacies with important women of Sande. Whenever he is present during the public appearance of his mask, the *Zogbe* and its followers must acknowledge him in the crowd by secret signs of deference. The women bring him food, arrange liaisons for him, and praise him by innuendo in their songs.

A productive woodcarver will have helped to create *Zogbea* for Sande lodges in many chiefdoms. During the years of the Sande session he may visit various villages to see his work and to receive the homage due to him from the women. He is among the few men who can move about freely and confidently during this period, for he is protected from many of the sanctions of Sande by his compromising knowledge of its ritual. Woodcarvers speak nostalgically of the pleasure they receive from watching their masks perform as fully appointed *Zogbe.* They mingle with the crowds, listen for comments, and watch for every spontaneous effect of their work. They are critical of the leading woman who impersonates the spirit, particularly if her performance is not equal to the intended characterization, and word will be sent to her through her followers. No other man could think of such direct intrusion into Sande matters excepting the most honored *zo* of local Poro.

One carver explained to me that the sensation of watching his masks "come to life" was one of intense and mysterious fulfilment.

I see the thing I have made coming out of the women's bush. It is now a proud man *jina* with plenty of women running after him. It is not possible to see anything more wonderful in this world. His face is shining, he looks this way and that, and all the people wonder about this beautiful and terrible thing. To me, it is like what I see when I am dreaming. I say to myself, this is what my *neme* has brought into my mind. I say, I have made this. How can a man make such a thing? It is a fearful thing I can do. No other man can do it unless he has the right knowledge. No woman can do it. I feel that I have borne children.

This identification of the created object as an offspring is not uncommon among woodcarvers who have a tutelary. They speak of the exhaustion which follows the completion of each mask and how continued production is impossible without periods of rest and distracting activity. The "dream" which provides the inspiration for a specific work is often referred to as the "gift" of a loving *neme,* and the completed work as the child of the union.

In the setting of his society, the master woodcarver is an individual whose role is imbued with the kind of romance and grudging admiration reserved for the brilliant and useful deviant in many other societies. The most significant aspect of his role is the freedom it affords him with regard to the traditionally hostile and mutually exclusive camps of male and female sacred institutions. He is the creator of sacred objects and the interpreter of symbolic effects. His product embodies the ambivalent principles of male and female orientations to life, and it is his vision which integrates and expresses them as powerful representations of the sacred. He is, to a considerable extent, the conscious recreator of his own status; for he manipulates the symbolic content of his role through the continual re-enactment of the private drama of spiritual guidance. This private drama represents his individual and subjective mastery of the powers which his society as a whole seeks to control in the cycle of Poro and Sande activities, and in the communal myth of ancestral commerce with sentient nature.

REFERENCES

d'Azevedo, W. L., "Some Historical Problems in the Delineation of a Central West Atlantic Region," *Annals of the New York Academy of Sciences,* vol. 96, 1962 (1), pp. 512–38.

———, "Common Principles of Variant Kinship Structures Among the Gola of Western Liberia," *American Anthropologist,* vol. 64, 1962 (2), pp. 504–20.

———, "The Sources of Gola Artistry," in W. L. d'Azevedo (ed.), *The Traditional Artist in African Societies,* Indiana, 1973.

Dalby, D., "The Mel Languages: A Reclassification of the Southern 'West Atlantic,'" *African Languages Studies,* vol. VI, 1965, pp. 1–17.

Harley, G. W. "Notes on Poro in Liberia," *Papers of the Peabody Museum,* vol. 19, no. 2, 1941.

———, "Masks as Agents of Social Control in Northeast Liberia," *Papers of the Peabody Museum,* vol. 32, no. 2, 1950.

———, and G. Schwab, "Tribes of the Liberian Hinterland," *Papers of the Peabody Museum,* vol. 31, 1947.

Welmers, W. E., "The Mande Languages," *Georgetown University Monograph Series,* no. 11, 1958.

Self-decoration offers one of the best examples of the difficulties of abstracting a mode of aesthetic expression from the cultural context in which it is created. The art of personal adornment is not exempt from the generalization that art rarely exists for "art's sake" alone. How people decorate themselves always depends on the prevailing style culturally defined as appropriate for their status—age, sex, social position—and for the activity they are engaged in. The jeans, Earth Shoes, and old Mexican nightgowns recently worn at American weddings, highly stylized innovations approved within their wearers' subculture; the selected items of working-class clothing worn by upper-middle-class youth; or the sateen and glitter favored by those vicariously nostalgic for vintage decadence are all forms of aesthetically expressive behavior that reflect the wearer's response to an often subtle complex of sociocultural circumstances. According to the Stratherns it is much the same in Mount Hagen, New Guinea.

Self-Decoration in Mount Hagen

Andrew and Marilyn Strathern

Informal and Formal Decoration

The most important occasions on which decorations are worn are formal ones, when dancers display themselves publicly before spectators; and our main interest is in these formal occasions. But ornaments are also worn for less formal affairs, and people often casually decorate themselves in their everyday activities. However, if we look at the contexts in which informal decorations are worn, we find that many of them reveal elements of display and ceremonial which link them to the more formal ones.

Hageners say that they decorate themselves for everyday affairs, courting parties, warfare, religious cults, and exchange festivals. Only the latter two are said to merit important decorations. The Melpa term which we represent here as "decoration" is *moke*. It refers to the whole process of wearing special clothing, plumes, grasses, shells, and so on, and to carrying accessories such as spears and axes. A second word, *waep*, refers to painting of designs, particularly on the face.

The only major occasion at which decorations are inappropriate is a funeral. Mourning behavior is in some ways the opposite to that of festivals. For example, at festivals men and women don wigs, paint their faces, and grease their bodies; when mourning they tear off their wigs, smear mud or clay over the body and face, and may be covered in ashes as well: mud and ashes make the skin "bad" and "dry," which is the reverse of the effect desired in applying grease. Mourners also tear out their hair; old men sometimes wear their hair permanently unkempt and un-bewigged from grief for a dead son.

Smearing mud and ashes over the body is not regarded as "decorating" (*moke*) at all, for decorating always implies the attempt of a person to make himself more impressive and attractive. The situation with regard to warfare is interesting here. For warfare, decorations were put on, but fights could easily result in death and mourning, and this seems reflected in ambiguous attitudes to war ornaments themselves.

We can make a rough scheme of contexts, ranging from those in which least decoration is worn to those in which it is most elaborate. We should emphasize, before describing these in more detail, that not everyone wears the same amount of decoration, especially in everyday affairs. Variations in the precise items chosen and their arrangements seem, in fact, to be a way of expressing individuality. Our account simply indicates the kinds of items from which people are expected to choose their assemblages.

INFORMAL OCCASIONS. For ordinary garden work or jobs round the house little attention is paid to clothing. Men wear a bark belt, with an old string apron in front and leaves behind; their heads may be uncovered. Women's regular wear, besides a long, corded genital apron, is a large string netbag suspended from the forehead and hanging over the back. It is a mark of correct behavior in women to wear a covering of this kind for their head and back.[1] In their netbags women carry up to fifty pounds of food and perhaps a baby as well.

Women . . . spend much more time on household tasks than do men. Hageners speak of them as staying at home to work, while their husbands walk about visiting and obtaining valuables. Correspondingly, men are much more likely to decorate themselves: they wear ornaments to impress their friends and get the wealth items they want. It is rather the same with young girls, who are expected to visit places away from their own settlements to attend courting parties: their decorations are put on to impress potential husbands and to attract a good bridewealth payment. The daughters of big-men are likely to be those most adorned.

Source: From Andrew and Marilyn Strathern, *Self-Decoration in Mount Hagen* (Toronto: University of Toronto Press; London: Gerald Duckworth & Co. Ltd., 1971). Used by permission of the publisher and the authors.

[1] Cf. Strauss 1962:319.

When they smarten themselves up, men first pay attention to their hair, putting on a wig covered with a knitted head-net, trimmed with grass and leaves, perhaps a marsupial fur and a topknot of old feathers. Nowadays a bright handkerchief frequently replaces the fur. Boys sometimes wear flowers in place of feathers. Round the neck men suspend a pearl shell or a set of bamboo tally sticks (*omak*), which indicate how many times they have given away sets of eight or ten shells in *moka*.[2] Fresh cordyline leaves are stuck in the rear of their bark belt.

Pearl shell pendants are the commonest form of ornament for women, given to them by their fathers, brothers or husbands.[3] Younger women, newly married or still unmarried, wear trade-store bangles and beads as armlets and necklaces. Courting girls amass rows of bead necklaces, given to them mainly by senior kinsfolk, but also partly by boys as favors. They wear bright trade-cloth as a cloak over the back, where an older woman has a traditional net covering or an old blanket.

For visiting, girls may in addition put a little grease or oil on their foreheads, while men may blacken their faces. Both sexes wear good aprons —men choose ones that are ample and not ragged with age; women and girls wear specially oiled and blackened ones. Men usually add feathers, or perhaps a tall marsupial tail, to their wig. A standard type of second-best plume is the cassowary, worn either as a cropped pompom or in a larger form in which the plumes spray and trail out. It is suitable for some formal occasions, too, if men lack the right kinds of "best" feathers. Visitors at a *moka* who come simply to watch should also wear cassowary or some other second-best type of feather. It goes regularly with a charcoaled, but not otherwise painted, face.

Most often visits are connected with *moka* or bridewealth exchanges, or with trading. Frequently such "trading" is subsumed under a kin relationship. Northern Melpa men, for example, visit kinsmen in the Jimi Valley, in order to obtain special forest products as well as decorations. The Jimi men also catch and rear cassowaries, which have been hatched wild in the forest, and exchange these with their kinsmen for shells, money, pigs and tree-oil. Live cassowaries are an important valuable, used as bridewealth and *moka* gifts. In cash terms, an adult bird is worth about $A100; a chick some $A10.

For courting parties there is more overt emphasis on decoration than for visiting (except for visits at times of festivals). The parties are held regularly, at night-time, in women's houses. Unmarried girls and youths from about fifteen onwards, and also young married men, take part as protagonists. Especially when a new women's house is built, girls and men are invited to come and sing in it, as a kind of house-warming. At least one older married woman acts as chaperone, greeting the men as they arrive, stirring up the fire and watching the performance. Often, there are further spectators, married folk and younger boys, who join in the singing. The girls at first stay in a back compartment of the house, while the men sing romantic songs in a loud, nasal voice, to attract them out. At length the girls emerge and kneel at one end of the room, while two men sit cross-legged on either side of each one. After waving their heads in a stylized preliminary motion, partners press noses together, duck heads down while turning on to the cheek, swing back, turn their heads together twice, retaining contact on the nose and forehead, then duck again. This is the "turn-head"[4] movement. A girl "turns" alternately with partners on either side of her. Men replace each other in relays. Courting is supposed to continue till daylight, when the girls have a right to chase their partners out, threatening them with mud and stinging nettles. If a man turns head with a favorite girl several times, he should give her beads, feathers, furs, knives, or money as a compliment; and such gifts can be a preliminary to bridewealth payments.

Men display little overt concern with success at courting parties. Despite their obvious enjoyment of turning-head and their interest in sex, men sometimes say that it is a "rubbish" activity.

[2] Each stick records that eight or ten pearl shells have been exchanged as a set in return for two shells and a pig. Sometimes a son or a daughter may wear the father's sticks; or a woman her husband's.

[3] Women may be said to own these pearl shell crescents in their own name, as they do their aprons, netbags, beads, and fur pendants. More valuable ornaments (mounted pearl shells, cowrie or nassa shells in the past, plumes) are owned by men. A woman may wear, on occasion, decorations belonging to her husband, and thereby display his wealth; or she may borrow decorations for a dance from male kinsmen.

[4] In Melanesian pidgin, this sequence is known as *tanim-hed*.

One reason may be that courting is neither a necessary nor a sufficient means of obtaining a bride, since marriages are often arranged by senior kin and must be accompanied by bridewealth payments. Another may be that prowess in courting does not itself bring high status, as prowess in exchange does. It is significant that men claim they do not pray to family ghosts to help them in courting, and that courting decorations are not so elaborate as those for *moka*. Nevertheless, they are keen to wear some feathers and furs for turning-head.

For a big party, men and youths gather forest leaves and grasses; for a smaller occasion they simply pick greenery near to their houses. They can wear a variety of feathers: Red bird, eagle, black cassowary, cockatoo, hawk's wing. They can partly charcoal or paint their faces, rub grease on their bodies, insert shells in the nose, and bind marsupial fur round the forehead. All kinds of leaves and grasses (perhaps twenty kinds are regularly used) fringe the beard and wig. Shreds of colored paper from tin-labels are nowadays popular as topknots. These accessories are worn for the pleasant swishing sound they make as the wearer sways his head. But the feathers should not be too fine, men say, for they are spoilt by fire-smoke and by rubbish on the floor. They add that it is not worthwhile decorating too well for an event that occurs at night, when people cannot see properly. This remark underlines the point that dancing and decorations are intended primarily for public display, hence the major occasions take place in large, cleared spaces and during the daytime.

For turning-head, girls may wear a pearl shell crescent between their breasts, cowrie necklaces and beads, all of which they cover with trade-cloth cloaks knotted in front. They oil their hair, charcoal their foreheads or paint them with a red band, put multicolored spots or triangles of paint on their cheeks. Girls are supposed to mix love-magic with their pigments and men to do the same with their grease. Such magic is meant to attract the opposite sex by its perfume, and nowadays trade-store scent and talcum powder are used by both sexes for the same purpose. Men can also wear leaves of the resin-bearing *kilt* tree (Rutaceae *Evodielle* sp.),[5] which they invoke in charms to make them attractive. Girls tend not to wear so many leaves and grasses as men, though they often tuck flowers in the hair as a fringe for the forehead.

Although men usually dress a little more elaborately for courting than girls, in the past a big-man might decorate a young female relative for a courting party with some care, giving her white marsupial fur and a nassa shell band for her brow, and a fine head-dress of brown cassowary feathers. This would be done with a view to sharing in the subsequent bridewealth obtained at her marriage.

Girls may also be permanently tattooed. Designs are usually (though not always) confined to the face, and they resemble those applied with ochre and trade-store paints, although we do not know if they are called by special names as the latter are. Most commonly they consist of dots over the forehead or arching over the eyebrows, and under-eye dots or short streaks at the top of the cheek. Tattoo marks are made by pricking the skin and rubbing in charcoal and blue dye. A mother may tattoo her young daughter; or a man his wife's sister (no doubt other relatives and friends may perform this service also).[6]

Occasions at which bridewealth payments are made are much more elaborate public affairs than courting parties, but are not marked by noticeably more elaborate decorations. The main exchanges between the kin of the bride and groom take place in two stages.[7] First, the groom's sub-clan mates, headed by his father, display live pigs, mounted pearl shells, and money to the bride's kin. Discussion centers on those items which are to be exchanged for equivalents provided by the bride's people. Male participants at this stage rarely bother to decorate themselves. They discuss the "deal" in a small courtyard at the groom's place.

Although many of the items are for direct ex-

[5] Cf. Strathern, A. J. and A. M. 1968: 180. We discuss the *kilt* tree again later, in connection with the manufacture of special kinds of wigs.

[6] Vicedom, the German missionary-anthropologist who worked in Hagen between 1934 and 1939, reports (1943–8, vol. 1, 101) that at this time the Hageners did not practice tattooing, although it was mentioned in one of the folk-tales which he collected. It is hard to tell whether tattooing has been introduced to Hagen through copying other peoples, such as Chimbu or Papuans, or whether it has been simply revived. The copying, if it is such, is not exact: Hagen facial tattooing is much slighter and more restricted than that of Chimbu, for example. Young men as well as girls may be lightly tattooed.

[7] For a fuller account of bridewealth see Strathern, A. J. and A. M., 1969.

change the bride's kin hope that a large initial bridewealth will be offered, for this will make a better display at the more public second stage; and to this end they decorate the girl with shells and cook a pig with prayers to the ancestors before sending her to the groom's settlement at the stage of the overtures. They take grease from this pig to rub her with so that her body gleams and appears healthy, and they divine by the way fat drips over her forehead whether the bridewealth will be good or not.[8] The custom reveals an association between bodily appearance, grease, and the ability to attract valuables which we shall find again later.

At the second stage the groom's kinsmen cook further pigs and take them to the bride's place, for display and formal presentation to her kin at the same time as the exchange of shells and live pigs. For the last part of the journey the bride is ceremonially laden with most of the meat and carries it over to her people, who await the visitors at a ceremonial ground. (Her folk later distribute the meat to segments of her clan and to clusters of other kin and in-laws.) Both sides wish to make a good impression on their new friends: men wear second-best feathers, striped possum tails, furs or clean handkerchiefs round their foreheads, fresh cordylines, and a decent apron, and they may oil their skins. Married women may have a new piece of cloth; and marriageable girls dress in the same way as for courting parties, their faces stippled with bright paint, perhaps leaves tucked in their armbands. The bride decorates herself as the girls do, but also dons a large netbag as a sign of her impending work as a married woman. The groom, if this is his first marriage, is not likely to play a prominent part in the proceedings nor is he especially decorated.

Men make speeches on either side when the meat is handed over and the exchanges of wealth are announced. But the occasion does not require full-scale competitive displays by whole clans such as occur at festivals. Perhaps this is why it is not marked by elaborate self-decoration. We could express the point by saying that bridewealth occasions fall half-way between the domestic and the political spheres of action. Other events also, at which a similar range of decorations is worn, fall into the same category. These events are: preliminary meetings for *moka* festivals, special work occasions, Local Government Council meetings and elections, and market days.

Preliminary debates to a *moka* are numerous and lengthy. Sometimes they take place between a few men inside their houses, sometimes more men are present and discussions are held at ceremonial grounds. Prominent leaders deliver speeches, often accompanying their arguments with more or less good-humored taunts. Donors eventually make overt promises by setting up sticks to represent pigs they will give. Finally, they hold a "showing" of all the pigs to be transferred, ideally at a single ceremonial ground, as a sign that they are ready for the festival.

Spectators do not attend these preliminaries to a *moka* and women have no part in them.

Special work occasions sometimes involve something closer to public competition between clans than is evinced at bridewealths and *moka* preliminaries, and the competition is accompanied by a greater emphasis on decorations. The work involved is usually the pulling of huge tree-trunks for bridge-building and the cutting of new road sections.[9] It is especially when a home group invites one of its traditionally allied clans to help it that excitment rises. The two groups vie with each other to heave a trunk or complete a section of road. Women and girls may come as spectators, painted and greased as for a dance. Men march to work in ranks holding long-handled spades, like warriors with spears, and may wear decorations close in style to those appropriate for *moka*.

At one work party, for example, several men had painted their faces with charcoal, and added outlines in white round the eyes, nose, or mouth. They wore various types of feather, predominantly cassowary plumes. At another occasion we took some details of 50 men's decorations. We divided the items into six categories: leaves and grasses, paint and charcoal, feathers, fur, shells, and additional miscellanea. We found that 14 men wore items from four or more categories, 36 from three or fewer. The 50 workers had 23 different combinations of the

[8] If the grease trickles straight down her nose, this is a good omen. It is the ancestors who send the omen.

[9] These are Administration-introduced tasks. Most of the work on side roads is still done by hand. The logs support plank bridges.

categories. Despite an overall impression of uniformity, no two men were decorated exactly alike.

Elections,[10] council meetings,[11] and markets[12] are public events but are less marked by intergroup competition. However, they draw throngs of people from a wide area, and everyone is, in a sense, on display. It is especially young men and girls who like to dress up for markets. There is always the chance of impressing the crowd and meeting an old or making a new acquaintance. The girls put on their beads, bangles, cloth, talcum powder, shells and flowers as usual, but probably not paint; the men have neat cassowary, cockatoo, eagle, or marsupial tail headdresses.

In summary, we can say that on these informal occasions decorations are worn either to express group competition, or to make oneself sexually attractive,[13] or simply in recognition of a public event. These are precisely the reasons for self-decoration on formal occasions also. For informal affairs people have rather more choice about whether to decorate themselves and how. Nevertheless, choice is not random. Many specific assemblages of items are reserved for the more formal *moka* and cult festivals, as we shall see.

FORMAL OCCASIONS. Formal decorations are worn at festivals for ceremonial gifts of pigs and shells and at cult performances. In chapter one we have given some idea of the preparations for dancing at a festival. Here we must describe the rationale for the festivals and patterns of dancing at them.

The main types of exchange are those resulting from warfare in the past and those which we can designate as "pure *moka*."

The first type includes enemy-compensation and ally-reparation payments, which we can best describe with stereotyped examples. If group A killed a man of group B it may later compensate its enemies for the death, in order to restore good relations. This occurs only if the two groups are not major enemies. Again, if group A asked group B to help it as an ally against group C, and a man of B was killed, A should make reparations to B for this, or else face the loss of the alliance and also a possible threat of violence from B. Payments are made with both pigs and shells.

The second type (pure *moka*) also includes gifts of shells and pigs. In shell-*moka* sets of mounted pearl shells[14] are given away to exchange partners by the men of a donor group or a single big-man. Recipients receive the shells in sets of eight or ten, and for each set they privately (not on the occasion of the main festival) return a pig and two shells. The latter items can sometimes be looked on as soliciting the main gift. Pig-*moka* takes a similar form: sets of pigs are given away in return for smaller "solicitory" gifts of pigs. An alternative is to kill pigs and present their meat to exchange partners.

In practice pure *moka* and warfare exchanges become intertwined. An important feature of all ceremonial exchange relations in Hagen is that they are expected to continue over a number of years. If one group compensates, reparates, or gives *moka* to another it expects that the recipients will reciprocate after a few years. *Moka* relations are explicitly based on this norm of reciprocity; war payments come to follow the same pattern since it is often the case that there have been reciprocal killings or reciprocal ally-losses between clans. Thus A pays B for losses and later B pays A, much as is done in *moka* itself.

War payments are also supposed to follow a sequence, starting from the time when a killing or loss has newly occurred. They begin with gifts of cooked pig, pass through presentations of pearl shells, and end with live pigs. Through a number of years they become converted into forms which resemble *moka* more and more closely. When the stage of exchanging live pigs is reached, participants say, "Now we are making a road of *moka* between us."

Moreover, there is a further factor involved

10 These are elections of Local Government Councillors or of Members of the Papua and New Guinea House of Assembly.

11 Native Local Government Councils were established by the Administration in the early 1960s.

12 There are two main markets in the area, neither of them traditional: the Hagen town market and one set up by Dei Council (Northern Melpa).

13 A jealous husband may tear off his wife's decorations; to show her that she should not philander as if she were a young girl.

14 In the past bailer, nassa, and green-snail as well. A fuller account of *moka* is given in Strathern, A. J. 1966b and forthcoming.

in the relations between exchanging groups, which is important for us here: where groups are in reciprocal exchange relations they are likely to have been both allies and enemies to each other on different occasions in the past. They are rivals. and in their exchanges they try to outdo each other by the total size of their gifts. Rivalry is built into the *moka* transaction as a premise, since the main gift should exceed the solicitory gifts in value and should also exceed previous *moka* gifts given by those now receiving. We are dealing with groups which confront and test each other over time with demonstrations of their wealth.

The style of dancing adopted seems to fit this accent on rivalry. It is very simple in movement, but effectively shows off the numbers of men and their decorations. Men don feathers, shells, leaves and grasses, face-paint and charcoal, and their finest wigs, belts, and aprons. If women and girls are dancing formally, they are decked out with a profusion of items of the same general kind as those worn by the men, with long sweeping reed aprons, although they do not charcoal their faces or carry weapons. Girls and younger women who come as spectators are dressed in second-best attire, but their faces will almost certainly be painted.

There are two main dances for men, *mør* and *kanan.* Married women decorate themselves and dance formally only for pig-*moka,* and then not always, but only if the display is to be a large one. For such an occasion their dance is called *werl;* at other times they, or more particularly unmarried girls, perform *mørli,* quite different in character, which requires little more decoration than is worn for courting parties.

In *mør,* male dancers form in a single line or extend into a horseshoe round the ceremonial ground with donors and recipients facing each other. Drum and whistle notes may punctuate the dancing. With a sharp, opening yodel, all begin to sing. The dance consists of a stately, rhythmic genuflection, the drums beaten just as the legs are straightened and the body reaches an upward crescendo. After a few minutes a faster rhythm is adopted, involving constant pivoting on the toes. Then there is a rest, till someone starts singing or drumming again. Those without drums hold spears, which, lifting up and down in unison, they point at the spectators. As the men move, their plumes sway backwards, and light catches on the feathers and on their shell ornaments, while the long aprons billow out in front.

For *kanan*[15] men form into ranks, consisting of rows of four or more across, and stamp round the ceremonial ground in time with each other. They maintain rows by locking arms or by holding a spear horizontally in front of them. Or they may space out further from each other and grasp bow and arrows in the left hand, an axe in the right. *Kanan* is favored for impressive group entrances, or to wind up a session of *mør,* or it can be performed on its own.

In both types of dance the men concentrate on their posture, staring out unseeingly at the crowd of jostling spectators. Their decorations, they say, help them by making them harder to recognize as individuals. This point seems surprising, in view of the stress which is also laid on individual rivalry between the dancers. One can resolve the paradox, perhaps, by suggesting that men do not aim at making it *impossible* to recognize them, but only at making it difficult, so that recognition comes with some surprise. It is also the case that as clansmen they can recognize and appraise each other easily enough under their "disguise"; while outsiders who do not know them well will simply evaluate their performance as a whole group. The individual rivalry is internal to the group of dancers themselves.

At festivals where pigs are actually killed and cooked for distribution, another dance, *ware,* may traditionally be performed. Dancing then takes place for three days before the pigs are slaughtered, and on the fourth men take off their decorations and work at preparing the meat. Each man distributes meat to his individual exchange partners. Decorations for *ware* and a similar dance called simply "cooked pig dance" (*kng kui*) sometimes resemble those of non-Melpa-speaking Wahgi Valley people. (At smaller pig-kills, for which a block gift of pigmeat is handed over by one group to another, there may be no dancing at all, and if so there is correspondingly less emphasis on decorations.)

Married women do not dance in the *mør* and *kanan* sequences, but a few unmarried girls

[15] Called *nde mbo kanan,* "ceremonial tree dance," by Vicedom (1943–8, vol. 1, 245–6), from the fact that the dancers encircle the ceremonial tree planted at the head of the dancing ground. See also Strauss 1962: 115.

occasionally join the *mør*. Either they enter the line spontaneously, as a mark of favor for a particular dancer, or they take part on a formal basis and their decorations closely parallel those of their male clanmates, except in their face-paint, wigs, and aprons. In the latter case they are on display for potential husbands to see. If a man has no sons, his eldest unmarried daughter can also dance in the *kanan* (but does not hold weapons, which are exclusive to men).[16]

Married women, as we have mentioned, dance in elaborate decorations only for pig-*moka*, and they do so specifically to celebrate their success in rearing pigs which their husbands are giving away to exchange partners. Shell payments are exclusively men's affairs; but when men achieve renown by the size of their *moka* pigs, they are expected to recognize the wives' contribution by making them glamorous for a day. Men say that women dirty themselves in muddy paths and gardens and bear the brunt of food-getting and pig-rearing; and that hence their husbands are sorry for them and help them gather decorations for the final *moka* dance.[17]

For a pig-*moka* dance, then, while men line up for *mør* or stamp round in *kanan* formation, heavily decorated women appear one by one at the edge of the ceremonial ground. Each holds a drum (little daughters may be decorated, too, but do not always have drums). The women dance *werl*, which consists of a measured bowing from side to side, in time with drum-beats and singing. Gradually they swing more in one direction, until they turn right around and display their backs to spectators (mainly other women and girls). Their backs are profusely decorated with shells and leaves, to an extent greater than in the case of men. Whereas women ornament their whole bodies with equal elaborateness, the emphasis for men tends to be on the head. We shall return later to the significance of head decorations for Hageners.

The men complete the day by charging aggressively up and down the ceremonial ground where pigs are tethered to stakes, weapons in hand, and by making formal speeches in a special chanting style, ending each phrase with a long-drawn-out oh—oh—oh.[18] They explain the reasons for the gift, announce further plans and boast of their prowess. The wives of the donors, who have been dancing *werl*, move more slowly up and down the row of pigs, beating their drums, as a sign that it is really they who have enabled the *moka* to take place. Finally, one of the donors walks down the row and gives each pig a ceremonial kick, saying, "Kill this and cook it!" as an act of completing the transfer.

At other types of exchange festival women and girls dance only the *mørli*, for which they wear much less decoration, as it is peripheral to the main business of display by men. In *mørli* the dancers gather intimately in one or more circles, linking arms, and enclose other females as spectators. One of them leads a chanting song, and as this reaches a shrieking crescendo they jump up and down lustily, and the circle moves around. *Mørli* is thus a dance carried out with high spirits, in which young women draw attention to themselves; it is, in fact, a kind of group invitation to young men to turn-head when the main transactions are over. The songs are really courting songs, whereas women dancing *werl*, like the men executing *mør* or *kanan*, sing refrains which have political themes—commenting on the display of strength and wealth, throwing taunts at rivals or enemies. *Mørli* is to do with sex; *werl* is concerned with the serious world of pigs and exchange.

For *mørli* girls paint their faces in triangles, stipples, and streaks, of blue, yellow, and red, with eyes ringed in white. They remove their netbags but may retain a bright red trade-cloth over their backs. They may wear a cassowary quill through the septum, for this is thought to be sexually alluring. They have oiled their bodies and perhaps put crinkled red cordylines over their aprons. The aprons themselves they tie between the legs, giving a kind of horse-tail appearance, by which means they preserve a little modesty while they dance. They have no feathers, and few shells or furs; and the absence of these decoration items indicates how peripheral they are to the main business of the day. Married women who join in may not be decorated at all.

While men are dancing or speech-making they appear to ignore the *mørli*, except for occasionally shouting to the girls to be less noisy or to move away. Meanwhile the *mørli* circle grows in size. When important matters are over,

16 Vicedom (1943–8, vol. 1, 246) makes this point.
17 Contrast Kuma (Wahgi Valley) practice (Reay 1959:156).
18 Cf. Reay 1959:118 for a similar oratorical style in Kuma.

the younger and more energetic men doff their tall plumes and begin a rival dance called *yap*.[19] Their circle swells till it dominates the ceremonial ground; they move round fast and continuously, without the ecstatic shrieks and jumps of the girls. Songs usually become ribald, and dialogue develops through them between the rival circles of men and girls. Young men may now even join the women's circle, perhaps to dance with a turning-head partner.

Mørli episodes, although they are aside from the actual exchanges of wealth at a *moka,* do relate clearly to one of the aims of self-decoration, that is to make oneself sexually attractive. A sequence of exchange festivals, in fact, triggers off courting parties; after a day's dancing young men frequently spend the night turning-head; and during the formal dance itself, as we have mentioned, girls may break into the line of men and link arms with a dancer they admire, jogging up and down with him. This is a mark of favor and it brings some prestige to the man chosen.

At a deeper level, attracting the opposite sex is thought of as cognate with the ability to attract wealth to oneself. That is why dancers have to be not only impressive but also "attractive."

There is one other context in which women play a part at *moka* dances: this is called the display of "women with netbags full of greens." [20] It is performed only occasionally, when a particular "message" is to be relayed to spectators. For it, women are deliberately dressed in a reversal of what would constitute good decorations. They wear no feathers, begrime their faces and bodies with charcoal, making themselves "dark," and may even smear their heads with earth. They fill netbags with scraps of greens, nuts, and pig-tusks, and march silently, with heads down, around the men doing *mør*. The message involved in these decorations is a part of inter-clan politics and is an aggressive one. If a clan related to the donors at the festival has been taunted for not making *moka,* its men may decorate some of their wives and sisters in this way and send them to the dance. The decorations are meant to say: "All right, you our critics claim that we are 'rubbish men.' You whisper this behind our backs but we have heard it and so send our women along in rubbishy decorations, carrying nuts instead of shells, tusks instead of real pigs, scraps instead of true food. But later we shall show you this is just a pretense. We have good ground, excellent food, plenty of wealth, and we shall make *moka* and eclipse your prestige—so look out!"

This example reminds us that exchange festivals are meant to be demonstrations of strength and prosperity on the part of the donor clan. The political commentary of dancers' songs can be overtly hostile towards other groups.

Religious cults are similar demonstrations, but in addition their explicit aim is to promote prosperity and fertility by ritual action. Currently the two main cults practiced in Hagen are the Female and Male Spirit cults (*Amb Kor* and *Kor Wøp*).[21]

Performances of these cults circulate from group to group, but any single clan group holds one only at intervals of many years. The chief cult objects are decorated stones. These are in fact water-worn river stones or else prehistoric

[19] This is Northern Melpa usage. The Central Melpa call both the men's and the women's circular dances *morli*. It is this dance which Leahy and Crain illustrate (1937:opp. p. 193).

[20] Melpa *amb mui pukl wal.* There are two variations of this. In one (*amb mui pukl wal* proper) the emphasis is on the earth which the woman smothers over her head and the scraps of food (rind, peelings, leaves) she has in her netbag. The import is a reminder to enemies or rivals of their taunts that the group's land is bad, its produce poor, and the food they eat is offal (i.e. they have no wealth). In the other (*wur wur*) the woman may carry more direct symbols of wealth: the pig-tusks and nuts, along with leaves associated with magic for drawing in valuables. The group's enemies have accused them of being weak like women, so it is their women that the men decorate, implying that they have riches enough, which they will display in good time. These messages may be directed at traditional major enemies, or else at allies, impatient for the expected exchanges, who have accused the clan of having no resources.

[21] Female Spirit is a literal rendering of the Melpa *Amb Kor;* the *Wop* Spirit is thought of as male. The Northern Melpa do not perform the *Wop,* or have not so far performed it. In the circulation of cults between clans, the performing clan pays ritual experts for knowledge of the cult spells and actions. In the lower Nebilyer Valley, a variety of other cults is practiced (e.g. *Palyim, Kopiaka, Engawakl*), but we cannot discuss these here. An important pair-cult of the *Wop,* the *Eimb,* seems not to be planned currently by any group. Mission activity may cut short the progress of these cults through all the Hagen groups. Fairly detailed accounts of the two we discuss here are given in Vicedom and Tischner 1943–8, vol. 2, 423ff., and Strauss 1962:425ff. Our account is based on our own observations also. We give only enough detail to establish the rough meaning of the cults and the sequence of events in them.

mortars and pestles of the kind which are commonly enough found throughout the New Guinea Highlands.[22] Men discover these stones while digging garden ditches or walking by rivers, or they inherit custodianship of them from their fathers. They keep them buried inside an enclosure marked by trees, at the back of a ceremonial ground. The Spirit connected with the stones shows its power by sending sickness to the clansmen who own them. Ritual experts diagnose the situation and prescribe a cult performance to satisfy and control the Spirit and to ensure future health. A sequence of sacrifices takes place within the enclosure, which is shut off by a number of high cane fences. The experts officiate, and see to the building of houses for the rituals and the digging of earth ovens. After what is often years of specific preparations, there is a final sacrificial cooking in the enclosure, the participants decorate themselves and dance, viewed by hundreds of spectators, many of whom receive gifts of pork.

The decorations worn for these cults are essentially similar in scale and magnificence to those worn for *moka* exchanges and war payments. They are similar also in style. But the cults have additional stylistic elements of their own. . . . We end this account by briefly discussing the meaning of the cult rituals themselves.

The Female Spirit cult is concerned both with fertility and with male purification. The Spirit is said to appear to men in dreams as a beautifully adorned young bride. Although she appears as a bride, she does not stay to bear children, but remains a virgin. It is perhaps this combination of femininity and purity that makes her an appropriate object for a cult which includes a ritual to protect men against the threat of menstrual pollution from their actual human wives. Protection is obtained by eating, within the cult enclosure, a ritual meal of forest herbs mixed with pig's kidneys. The theme of general fertility appears in another ritual sequence, in which pig-suet is taken and placed in a trench within the house where the cult stones are displayed; here the suet is described as "grease" which helps to fertilize the earth. The ritual experts accompany every action with a spell. Most of the pig-meat is cooked in a long oven, covered with forest moss, which runs the length of one of the cult houses. This meat the performers then distribute, partly to the experts in payment for their services, and later partly to male exchange partners outside the enclosure. Women are in theory not supposed to eat this meat; nor should they enter even the first part of the cult enclosure.[23] Although the cult centers on a Female Spirit it is emphatically an affair of the men.

In the inner part of the enclosure men practice their Spirit-dance. They line up in pairs, each man holding a twist of ferns before him in place of the pearl shells he will later hold, and, with a quick shuffle-cum-stamp of the feet, move in a train round the cult house. On the final day they decorate themselves fully in secret, dance out of the cult place, and stream round the ceremonial ground. As they flash out of the enclosure door, displaying their shells and waving their white plumes, the crowd shouts, "The Spirit is coming!" They circle three times, then re-enter the enclosure, remove their feathers, and reappear on high platforms at the sides of the ceremonial area to distribute strips of pork among the upturned spears of visitors. This distribution over, the crowd rapidly disperses.

The *Wøp* cult centers on actions designed to ensure clan strength and fertility. Like the Female Spirit cult, it can be performed only by men, but it stresses relations between the sexes rather than male purification from the polluting power of women.

Some months before the final performance, ritual experts sacrifice pigs, take examples of the cult stones which resemble pestles and place them in mortars as a symbol of sexual intercourse; they wrap all the stones in moss saturated with pig's blood and bury them underneath a tall "pole-house" with open sides and a bark roof, inside the cult enclosure. At the same time they divide out pig's liver to the initiates. Both of these ritual actions are to produce fertility and health.

Near by in the enclosure is a spring of water, called the "Spirit's eye," which is regarded as a source of the same virtues. In front of the main sacrifice-pit there is a stake which represents the group of male participants themselves, and their penises are supposed to be made by the cult

22 Cf. Bulmer, R. and S., 1964.

23 At one performance in 1964 they did both. The mission had weakened taboos in this area.

actions as erect as the stake itself is. The experts also plant a garden of tall sugar-cane and taro. Each small subgroup involved in the cult performance brings plants for this garden, which is set up at night-time. Next morning it is torn down and the pieces are thrown into the spring, with a libation of tree-oil. This is an offering of food and grease to the earth, again for fertility, which is reminiscent of the action of burying suet in the Female cult. Finally, the performers place their feather head-dresses inside the tall pole-house, where spirits of clan ancestors are supposed to cluster, to make the plumes bright before they don them and dance out.

The stress on fertility and sexuality shown in this cult seems consistent with the fact that women may take part in the climactic dance for it. They should strictly keep to the outer part of the enclosure (away from the chief ritual objects), and then precede the men out into the ceremonial ground over the main fence, which is hacked down at this time. (At a performance in 1965[24] the women actually marched right through to the inner enclosure, to the disgust of the ritual experts.) Two or three men, beating drums and weaving from side to side, accompany women, who trot and stamp in time, then once they are outside fall into the *werl* dance, as for an exchange festival. Behind them comes a solid mass of men, in rows of perhaps six across, thumping out an orthodox *kanan* or a more lively version, proper to the cult, called *poke*. After making a procession about the ceremonial ground the men settle to a *mør* dance, continuing till the afternoon.

Both of these cults, then, end with massive public displays just as the exchange festivals do. Indeed they may be preceded by actual *moka* transactions and followed by distributions of meat. Rituals performed within the enclosure are inward-looking, designed to promote group well-being. The final dance, when the enclosure fence has been broken down, is a display by the group to show that they have achieved the cult aims. In the Female Spirit cult only men perform; but in the *Wøp* men and women dance together.

In this account of situations in which decorations are worn we have pointed to a general theme. The act of decorating is symbolic: it is a gesture of self-display, and what is being displayed is a person in an enhanced or ideal state. On formal occasions the dancers assert group prosperity and health; when people dress up informally they assert their personal well-being. This is the general "message" which decorations convey, and in a very real sense they are both the medium in which the message is communicated and the message itself. An examination of the details of decoration will show us, further, that a whole battery of messages can be transmitted through different combinations of items.

24 By the Ep^{e}kla-Eilya pair of tribes, in the Kulir part of the Nebilyer Valley, west of the Nebilyer river.

SECTION II

Oral Tradition, Music, Dance, and Drama

Of the major nontangible forms of aesthetic expression, oral tradition and music have so far received the most anthropological attention. Again, both illustrate the recurrent closeness of art to the other aspects of culture. Anthropologists, folklorists, and ethnomusicologists have been collecting for years. In the last decades the availability of increasingly good recording equipment has made this basic aspect of their task much easier. Now increasing attention is being directed to the cultural meaning of what has been collected and to analysis of the context in which these forms of aesthetic expression are created and then usually repeatedly performed.

A people's oral traditions—their proverbs, jokes, legends, myths, and riddles, to make only the sparsest listing—offer the ethnographer valuable insights into the cognitive system of another culture, the world view and values of another people. The study of music as symbolic action and cultural behavior has become a highly specialized subfield within anthropology, one that combines an almost mathematical attention to musicological analysis with a humanistic approach that points up the frequent alliance between anthropology and the arts. Anthropologists are less well along in successfully devising a way to analyze dance.

Drama, as we know it, exists in other cultures as a distinct and discrete aesthetic form. But most often it is part of all the other kinds of artistic expression so far described, combining oral tradition, music, and dance with graphic and plastic forms of aesthetic expression. In the proletarian theater of parts of the Third World economic issues, especially instances of economic injustice, are a recurrent dramatic theme. Universally, drama mirrors major social concerns. Political behavior often seems coterminous with drama. And the place of drama in religious ritual is perhaps most evident of all. Because none of these assertions seems particularly startling, it is dismaying that the cross-cultural study of drama is not more advanced. Some of the best work on the subject has been done by students of folklore.

As a folklorist with a long and close association with anthropology, Ben-Amos is exceptionally well suited to define his field further and to place it in a sociocultural context.

Toward a Definition of Folklore in Context

Dan Ben-Amos

Definitions of folklore are as many and varied as the versions of a well-known tale. Both semantic and theoretical differences have contributed to this proliferation. The German *Volkskunde,* the Swedish *folkminne,* and the Indian *lok sahitya* all imply slightly different meanings that the English term "folklore" cannot syncretize completely.[1] Similarly, anthropologists and students of literature have projected their own bias into their definitions of folklore. In fact, for each of them folklore became the exotic topic, the green grass on the other side of the fence, to which they were attracted but which, alas, was not in their own domain. Thus, while anthropologists regarded folklore as literature, scholars of literature defined it as culture.[2] Folklorists themselves resorted to enumerative,[3] intuitive,[4] and operational[5] definitions; yet, while all these certainly contributed to the clarification of the nature of folklore, at the same time they circumvented the main issue, namely, the isolation of the unifying thread that joins jokes and myths, gestures and legends, costumes and music into a single category of knowledge.

The difficulties experienced in defining folklore are genuine and real. They result from the nature of folklore itself and are rooted in the historical development of the concept. Early definitions of folklore were clouded by romantic mist and haunted by the notion of "popular antiquities," which Thoms sought to replace. Implicit in these definitions are criteria of the antiquity of the material, the anonymity or collectiveness of composition, and the simplicity of the folk—all of which are circumstantial and not essential to folklore. The age of a song, for example, establishes it chronologically; the identification of the composer describes it historically; and its association with a particular group defines it socially. Each of these factors has an explanatory and interpretive value, but none of them defines the song as folklore. Thus, the principles that united "customs, observance, superstitions, ballads, proverbs, etc." in Thoms' initial definition of folklore were not intrinsic to these items and could only serve as a shaky framework for the development of a scientific discipline concentrating upon them.

Subsequent attempts to construct a definition that would hold together all these apparently diversified phenomena encountered a difficulty inherent in the nature of folklore. On the one hand, folklore forms—like mentifacts and artifacts—are superorganic in the sense that once created their indigenous environment and cultural context are not required for their con-

Source: From Dan Ben-Amos, "Toward a Definition of Folklore in Context," *Toward New Perspectives in Folklore,* edited by Paredes and Bauman (Austin: American Folklore Society, 1972). Used by permission of the publisher and the author.

1 For a discussion of each of these terms see respectively Gerhard Lutz, *Volkskunde: Ein Handbuch zur Geschichte ihrer Probleme* (Berlin, 1958); Åke Hultkrantz, *General Ethnological Concepts* (Copenhagen, 1960), 243–247; Manne Eriksson, "Problems of Ethnological and Folkloristic Terminology with Regard to Scandinavian Material and Languages," in *Papers of the International Congress of European and Western Ethnology Stockholm* 1951, ed. Sigurd Erixon (Stockholm, 1955), 37–40; Trilochan Pande, "The Concept of Folklore in India and Pakistan," *Schweizerisches Archiv für Volkskunde,* 59 (1963), 25–30. For a general survey of this problem see Elisée Legros, *Sur les noms et les tendances du folklore* (Liège, 1962).

2 Compare, for example, the definitions of Melville J. Herskovits and William R. Bascom with those of Aurelio Espinosa and MacEdward Leach in *The Funk and Wagnalls Standard Dictionary of Folklore, Mythology, and Legend,* ed. Maria Leach and Jerome Fried (New York, 1949), 398–400.

3 William Thoms, "Folklore," in *The Study of Folklore,* ed. Alan Dundes (Englewood Cliffs, N.J., 1965), 5; Alan Dundes, "What Is Folklore?" in *The Study of Folklore,* 1–3; Samuel P. Bayard, "The Materials of Folklore," *Journal of American Folklore,* 66 (1953), 9–10.

4 Benjamin A. Botkin, *A Treasury of American Folklore* (New York, 1944), xxi; Francis Lee Utley, "A Definition of Folklore," in *Our Living Traditions: An Introduction to American Folklore,* ed. Tristram P. Coffin (New York, 1968), 3–14.

5 Francis Lee Utley, "Folk Literature: An Operational Definition," *Journal of American Folklore,* 74 (1961), 193–206. Reprinted in Dundes, *The Study of Folklore,* 7–24.

tinuous existence.[6] Background information may be essential for the analytical interpretation of the materials, but none of it is crucial for the sheer existence of the folklore forms. Tales and songs can shift media, cross language boundaries, pass from one culture to another, and still retain sufficient traces of similarity to enable us to recognize a core of sameness in all their versions. Folk art objects can outlive their users and even exist when their culture as a whole has become extinct, so that they are literally survivals of ancient times. A folk musician nowadays can perform for millions of people on a television network, in a style and manner that approximate his own singing and playing in the midst of his own small group, thus extending his art far beyond his social circle. In sum, the materials of folklore are mobile, manipulative, and transcultural.

On the other hand, folklore is very much an organic phenomenon in the sense that it is an integral part of culture. Any divorce of tales, songs, or sculptures from their indigenous locale, time, and society inevitably introduces qualitative changes into them. The social context, the cultural attitude, the rhetorical situation, and the individual aptitude are variables that produce distinct differences in the structure, text, and texture of the ultimate verbal, musical, or plastic product. The audience itself, be it children or adults, men or women, a stable society or an accidental grouping, affects the kind of folklore genre and the manner of presentation.[7] Moreover, the categorization of prose narratives into different genres depends largely upon the cultural attitude toward the tales and the indigenous taxonomy of oral tradition. Thus, in the process of diffusion from one culture to another, tales may also cross narrative categories; and the same story may be myth for one group and *Märchen* for another. In that case the question of the actual generic classification of the tale is irrelevant, since it does not depend on any autonomous intrinsic features but rather on the cultural attitude toward it. Finally, unlike written literature, music, and fine art, folklore forms and texts are performed repeatedly by different peoples on various occasions. The performance situation, in the final analysis, is the crucial context for the available text. The particular talent of the professional or lay artist, his mood at the moment of recitation, and the response of his audience may all affect the text of his tale or song.

Thus, definitions of folklore have had to cope with this inherent duality of the subject and often did so by placing the materials of folklore in different, even conflicting perspectives. In spite of this diversification, it is possible to distinguish three basic conceptions of the subject underlying many definitions; accordingly, folklore is one of these three: a body of knowledge, a mode of thought, or a kind of art. These categories are not completely exclusive of each other. Very often the difference between them is a matter of emphasis rather than of essence; for example, the focus on knowledge and thought implies a stress on the contents of the materials and their perception, whereas the concentration on art puts the accent on the forms and the media of transmission. Nevertheless, each of these three foci involves a different range of hypotheses, relates to a distinct set of theories about folklore, and consequently leads toward divergent research directions.

However, since knowledge, thought, and art are broad categories of culture, folklorists have had to concentrate mainly on distinguishing their subject matter from other phenomena of the same kind. For that purpose, they have qualified folklore materials in terms of their social context, time depth, and medium of transmission. Thus, folklore is not thought of as existing without or apart from a structured group. It is not a phenomenon *sui generis.* No matter how defined, its existence depends on its social context, which may be either a geographic, linguistic, ethnic, or occupational grouping. In addition, it has required distillation through the mills of time. Folklore may be "old wine in new bottles" and also "new wine in old bottles" [8] but rarely has it been conceived of as new wine in new bottles. Finally, it has to pass through time at least partially via the channels of oral transmission. Any other medium is liable to disqualify the material from being folklore.

[6] For a discussion of the implications of the concept of the superorganic see David Bidney, *Theoretical Anthropology* (New York, 1953), 129–131.

[7] See Linda Dégh, "Some Questions of the Social Function of Story-telling," *Acta Ethnographica,* (1957), 91–147.

[8] Botkin, xxi–xxii.

Further, folklorists have constructed their definitions on the basis of sets of relations between the social context, the time depth, and the medium of transmission on the one hand, and the conception of folklore as a body of knowledge, mode of thought, and kind of art on the other, as illustrated in the following table.

	Social Context	*Time Depth*	*Medium of Transmission*
Knowledge	Communal possession	Antiquity	Verbal or imitative
Thought	Collective representation	Survival	Verbal
Art	Communal creation or re-creation	Antiquity	Verbal or imitative

It is possible to distinguish three types of relations between the social context and folklore: possession, representation, and creation or re-creation. Basically, a literal interpretation of the term "folklore" sets up the first type of relationship. Accordingly, folklore is "the learning of the people," [9] "the wisdom of the people, the people's knowledge," [10] or more fully, "the lore, erudition, knowledge or teaching of a folk." [11] This view of folklore as the lore shared by the whole group communally applies, in practice and theory, to different degrees of public possession. First, folklore can be the sum total of knowledge in a society. Since no single member of the community has a complete command of all its facets, folklore in this sense must be an abstract construct based upon the collective information as it is stored with many individuals, "the whole body of people's traditionary beliefs and customs." [12]

Secondly, and in contrast, folklore has been considered only that knowledge shared by every member of the group. This definition excludes any esoteric information to which only selected experts in the community have access, since it restricts folklore to "popular knowledge" [13] alone. In that case, folklore is the real "common property" [14] of the community. Thirdly, this real communal lore can be expressed by the group at large in "collective actions of the multitude," as Frazer defines it,[15] including public festivities, rituals, and ceremonies in which every member of the group partakes. Lastly, folklore can be restricted to customs and observances that each individual adheres to in the privacy of his home, though all the people in the society abide by them. Although this last interpretation is theoretically possible, no definition has limited the scope of folklore so narrowly.

The construction of the second set of relations between folklore and its social context is based upon British evolutionary theory and French sociological anthropology. Accordingly, folklore represents a particular mode of collective and spontaneous thought, as André Varagnac has formulated his definition: "Le folklore, ce sont des croyances collectives sans doctrine, des pratiques collectives sans théorie." [16] In that case, the actual customs, rituals, and other observances are representations of the mode of thought that underlies them. The notion of collective thought in the context of definitions of folklore has several connotations. First it refers to the average, unexceptional thought that lacks any marks of individuality, "conventional models of human thought." [17] Secondly, it implies the particular thinking patterns of primitive man, as they were conceived by early folklorists and anthropologists. Edwin Sidney Hartland, for example, defined tradition, the subject matter of the science of fairy tales, as "the sum total of

9 Charlotte Sophia Burne, *The Handbook of Folklore* (London, 1931), 1.
10 Y. M. Sokolov, *Russian Folklore* (New York, 1950), 1.
11 Ralph Steele Boggs, "Folklore: Materials, Science, Art," *Folklore Americas,* 3 (1943), 1.
12 James G. Frazer, *Folklore in the Old Testament,* vol. 1 (London, 1919), vii.
13 Espinosa, 399.
14 Bayard, 8.
15 Frazer, vii.
16 André Varagnac, *Définition du Folklore* (Paris, 1938), 18.
17 Boggs, 1.

the psychological phenomena of uncivilized man."[18] In that sense, folklore is "the expression of the psychology of early man" as it concerns any field, either philosophy, religion, science or history.

All these aspects of thought are represented collectively in the folklore of the people. The conception of a special mode of thinking pertaining to primitive people was developed by Lévi-Bruhl as "the collective representation." Folklore, as other social facts, is a manifestation of this particular mode of thought. It expresses the particular mystique that characterizes primitive mentality in its perception of natural and social reality. Although Lévi-Bruhl's theories are no longer accepted without reservations, they still serve as a basis for defining folklore, as exemplified in Joseph Rysan's, "Folklore can be defined as the collective objectifications of basic emotions, such as awe, fear, hatred, reverence, and desire, on the part of the social group."[19]

When the principle of collectivity or communality is applied to the definition of folklore as art, reference is made particularly to the creation of folk literature. Two concepts have been developed in that regard: communal creation and re-creation. The first—whose main exponent in America was Francis Gummere—implies that folk songs, especially ballads, are a product of communal creation.[20] This notion, long discarded, is not as absurd as Miss Louise Pound would have liked us to believe.[21] Although its particular application to the origin of the ballad is rather doubtful, it is possible to conceive of such a process in relation to other kinds of folklore. Paul Bohannan reports a case of communal creation in the decoration of a walking stick and of other objects. Many members of the group, including the anthropologist himself, contributed to the formation of the wooden pieces.[22] Some of my own informants, composers of songs from Benin City, Midwestern Nigeria, admitted readily, and without perceiving the theoretical difficulties such admissions impose upon us, that they often composed a song alone, but that the group of singers to whom they belonged reworked it afterwards until everybody was pleased. However, by now the notion of communal creation has been completely discarded from any definition of folklore and replaced, when applicable, by the concept of communal re-creation. Archer Taylor, for example, incorporated the concept explicitly into his definition of folklore.[23] Actually this process is implied in the notion of oral transmission and the variability of the text. The concept of re-creation differs from that of creation only in regard to the duration of the creative moment. The main feature of folklore remains the same: verbal art is the sum total of creation of a whole community over time. Actually, when this hypothesis itself is challenged, the notion of passive creativity is introduced. Accordingly, the audience reaction is as much a part of the act of creation as the active imagination of the folk artist.[24]

By its very nature, the notion of communal re-creation involves a relationship between folklore and a second factor—time depth. The persistence of the materials in circulation in a culture, "bequeathed from generation to generation,"[25] has become the determining criterion for the identification of folklore items. For Thompson "the idea of tradition is the touchstone for everything that is to be included in the term folklore."[26] According to this notion, however, there cannot be any innovation in tradition, and if there is, it still has to "live in people's mouths for at least several generations."[27] This conception of folklore was con-

[18] Edwin Sidney Hartland, *The Science of Fairy Tales* (London, 1891), 34.

[19] Joseph Rysan, "Is Our Civilization Able to Create a New Folklore?" *South Atlantic Bulletin*, 18 (1952), 10.

[20] Francis B. Gummere, *The Popular Ballad* (New York, 1908).

[21] Louise Pound, *Poetic Origins and the Ballad* (New York, 1921).

[22] Paul Bohannan, "Artist and Critic in an African Society," in *The Artist in Tribal Society*, ed. Marian W. Smith (New York, 1961), 85–94.

[23] Archer Taylor, "Folklore," *Funk and Wagnalls Standard Dictionary of Folklore, Mythology, and Legend*, I, 402.

[24] See C. W. von Sydow, *Selected Papers on Folklore*, ed. Laurits Bødker (Copenhagen, 1948), 11–43; Walter Anderson, *Kaiser und Abt, die Geschichte eines Schwanks*, FFC No. 42 (Helsinki, 1923), 397–403.

[25] Boggs, 1.

[26] Stith Thompson, "Folklore at Midcentury," *Midwest Folklore*, 1 (1951), 11.

[27] Richard M. Dorson, *Bloodstoppers and Bearwalkers: Folk Traditions of the Upper Peninsula* (Cambridge, Mass., 1952), 7.

tained in the original definition of Thoms and maintained by folklorists up to the present time. Francis Utley, who made a content analysis of the definitions in the *Funk and Wagnalls Standard Dictionary of Folklore, Mythology, and Legend,* found the great preponderance of the term "tradition" to be unchallenged by any other concept.[28] The idea of tradition refers to folklore both as knowledge (the "wisdom" of the past) and as art (old songs and tales). In relation to thoughts and beliefs, the relative time depth qualifies folklore even further. It designates the materials as survivals, as implied by the evolutionary theories of Edward Tylor[29] and Andrew Lang.[30] In that case, "folklore" applies only to that item in culture that had vital currency in previous stages of human evolution and either survived the changes of time and became "a lively fossil" [31] or remained alive among those segments of society least exposed to the light of civilization.

Of the three factors, it is the medium of transmission that has been the most persistent in folklore definitions. Almost from the beginning, the most accepted characteristic of folklore—whether conceived of as knowledge, thought, or art—has been its transmission by oral means. In order for an item to qualify as folklore, the prime prerequisite is that it have been in oral circulation and passed from one person to another without the aid of any written texts. When a visual, musical, or kinetic form is considered, the transmission can be through imitation.[32] The basic assumption is that this particular form of transmission introduces some distinct qualities into the materials, that would be lost otherwise. In this sense, folklore as a discipline preceded Marshall McLuhan in declaring "the medium is the message." [33]

The criterion of oral tradition has become the last citadel of folklore scholars in defending the uniqueness of their materials. When the theories about communal creation collapsed and the doctrine of survivals fell through, scholars were able to hold firm to the idea that folklore is "verbal art," "unrecorded mentifacts," and "literature orally transmitted." [34] This conception of folklore was hailed both by anthropologists who worked in nonliterate societies and by scholars of literature, who found it an operational distinction separating folklore from literature. Although folklorists concede that the purity of this transmission has often been contaminated by literary texts, the final standard for the identification of materials as folklore is the actual circulation, even once, through verbal media.

In spite of its popularity, the criterion of medium of transmission has not defined what folklore really is; it has merely provided a qualifying statement about the form of circulation. Moreover, such definitions impose a preconceived framework upon folklore. Rather than define it, they establish certain ideals as to what folklore should be. These attempts to reconcile romantic with empirical approaches actually have held back scientific research in the field and are partially responsible for the fact that, while other disciplines that emerged during the nineteenth century have made headway, folklore is still suffering growing pains.

It is still necessary to ask, "What is it that circulates verbally and is transmitted through time within a distinct social entity?" This rhetorical question in itself reflects the wrong direction that various attempts to define folklore have taken. They have searched for a way to describe folklore as a static, tangible object. The enumerative definitions consisted of lists of objects, while the substantive definitions regarded folklore as art, literature, knowledge, or belief. In actuality, it is none of these and all of them together. Folklore does contain knowledge, it is an expression of thought, formulated artistically, but at the same time it is also a unique phenomenon which is irreducible to any of these categories.

In order to discern the uniqueness of folk-

28 Utley, "Folk Literature: An Operational Definition," 193.

29 *The Origins of Culture,* paperback edition, vol. 1 (New York, 1958), 70–159.

30 "Introduction," in *Grimm's Household Tales,* vol. 1, trans., Margaret Hunt (London, 1884), xi–lxxv.

31 Charles Francis Potter, "Folklore," *Funk and Wagnalls Standard Dictionary of Folklore, Mythology, and Legend,* 401.

32 Boggs, 1.

33 Marshall McLuhan, *Understanding Media: The Extensions of Man,* paperback edition (New York, 1964), 23–39.

34 See Bascom, "Verbal Art," *Journal of American Folklore,* 68 (1955), 245–252; Elli-Kaija Köngäs-Maranda, "The Concept of Folklore," *Midwest Folklore,* 13 (1963), 85: Utley, "Folk Literature: An Operational Definition," 204.

lore, it is first necessary to change the existing perspective we have of the subject. So far, most definitions have conceived of folklore as a collection of things. These could be either narratives, melodies, beliefs, or material objects. All of them are completed products or formulated ideas; it is possible to collect them. In fact this characteristic has been at the base of the major portion of folklore research since its inception. The collection of things requires a methodological abstraction of objects from their actual context. No doubt this can be done; often it is essential for research purposes. Nevertheless, this abstraction is only methodological and should not be confused with, or substituted for, the true nature of the entities. Moreover, any definition of folklore on the basis of these abstracted things is bound to mistake the part for the whole. To define folklore, it is necessary to examine the phenomena as they exist. In its cultural context, folklore is not an aggregate of things, but a process—a communicative process, to be exact.

It should be pointed out that this conception of folklore differs substantially from previous views of folklore as a process. Focusing upon the dynamics of transmission, modification, and textual variation,[35] such views perpetuated the dichotomy between processes and things. They stressed the transmission of objects in time and society and allowed for a methodological and theoretical separation between the narrators and their tales. These views of folklore are logically justified, since after all there is a distinction between the man and his songs, the child and his games. But the ever increasing emphasis on the situational background of tales, songs, and proverbs that developed from Malinowski's functionalism into Hymes' "ethnography of speaking," [36] enables us not only to study but to define folklore in its context. And in this framework, which is the real habitat of all folklore forms, there is no dichotomy between processes and products. The telling is the tale; therefore the narrator, his story, and his audience are all related to each other as components of a single continuum, which is the communicative event.

Folklore is the action that happens at that time. It is an artistic action. It involves creativity and esthetic response, both of which converge in the art forms themselves. Folklore in that sense is a social interaction via the art media and differs from other modes of speaking and gesturing. This distinction is based upon sets of cultural conventions, recognized and adhered to by all the members of the group, which separate folklore from nonart communication. In other words, the definition of folklore is not merely an analytical construct, depending upon arbitrary exclusion and inclusion of items; on the contrary, it has a cultural and social base. Folklore is not "pretty much what one wants to make out of it"; [37] it is a definite realistic, artistic, and communicative process. The locus of the conventions marking the boundaries between folklore and nonfolklore is in the text, texture, and context of the forms, to apply Dundes' three levels for the analysis of folklore in somewhat modified form.[38]

The textual marks that set folklore apart as a particular kind of communication are the opening and closing formulas of tales and songs and the structure of actions that happen in-between. The opening and closing formulas designate the events enclosed between them as a distinct category of narration, not to be confused with reality. As the Ashanti storyteller states most explicitly, "We don't really mean to say so, we don't really mean to say so," referring to the imaginary nature of the story.[39] Tales, however, do not necessarily relate to denotative speech as fiction does to truth. A folkloristic historical narrative, such as a legend,[40] is nevertheless formally distinct from a chronology of events. This contention, admittedly, requires further research. However, the phrase "it is like in a folktale"—

[35] See for example Francis Lee Utley, "The Study of Folk Literature: Its Scope and Use," *Journal of American Folklore,* 71 (1958), 139; Roger D. Abrahams, "Folklore in Culture: Notes toward an Analytical Method," *Texas Studies in Literature and Language,* 5 (1963), 102; Kenneth S. Goldstein, "Experimental Folklore: Laboratory vs. Field," in *Folklore International: Essays in Traditional Literature, Belief, and Custom in Honor of Wayland Debs Hand,* ed. D. K. Wilgus and Carol Sommer (Hatboro, 1967), 71–82.

[36] Dell Hymes, "The Ethnography of Speaking," in *Anthropology and Human Behavior,* ed. Thomas Gladwin and William C. Sturtevant (Washington, D.C., 1962), 15–53.

[37] George M. Foster, "Folklore," *Funk and Wagnalls Standard Dictionary of Folklore, Mythology and Legend,* I, 399.

[38] Alan Dundes, "Text, Texture and Context," *Southern Folklore Quarterly,* 28 (1964), 251–265.

[39] R. S. Rattray, *Akan-Ashanti Folk-Tales* (Oxford, 1930), x.

[40] As defined by William Bascom, "The Forms of Folklore: Prose Narratives," *Journal of American Folklore,* 78 (1965), 3–20.

which people employ whenever reality duplicates the sequence of actions in an artistic narration—attests to the awareness of a particular folktale structure. Also, other genres such as proverbs and riddles have distinct syntactic and semantic structures that separate them from the regular daily speech into which they are interspersed. Furthermore, these artistic forms are culturally recognized categories of communication. They have special names or identifying features distinguishing them from each other and from other modes of social interaction, pointing to the cultural awareness of their unique character.

Each of these forms may also have distinct textural qualities that separate them from other kinds of communication. These can be rhythmical speech, musical sounds, melodic accompaniment, or patterned design. In a sense, this is a reverse argument for the arts. Accordingly, a message is not considered artistic because it possesses these qualities, but it is these textural features that serve as markers to distinguish it as artistic. Since folklore forms are often interspersed in the midst of other modes of social interaction, they require such textural marks to single them out and prevent mistaking them for what they are not. Thus the telling of a story may necessitate a distinct speech pattern, such as recitative, and the saying of a proverb may involve a shift in intonation.[41]

Finally, there are contextual conventions that set folklore apart. These are specifications as to time, place, and company in which folklore actions happen. "To everything there is a season and a time to every purpose" (Eccles. 3:1). Narratives can be told during the daytime in the market place, the country store, and the street corner; or at night in the village square, the parlor, and the coffee-house. Songs and music have other occasions when they are performed. Although such specifications may have other functions, such as confining folklore to leisure and ceremonial activities, they also separate art from nonart in cultures that otherwise lack a complex division of time, space, and labor. In a sense, they provide a spatial, temporal, and social definition for folklore in culture.

These communicative marks of folklore do not necessarily exist on all three levels—text, texture, and context. The identification of social interaction as folklore by the people who tell the stories, sing the songs, play the music, and paint the pictures may be in terms of only one or all of these three. In any case, for them folklore is a well-defined cultural category.

Although folklore is a distinct category in terms of social interaction patterns and communication media, it is not necessarily recognized by the culture as a separate concept. In fact, within the cognitive system its forms may be classified into such apparently unrelated categories as history, tradition, dance, music, games, and tales. The reason for this categorization is inherent in the nature of the folkloristic communication itself. Folklore, like any other art, is a symbolic kind of action. Its forms have symbolic significance reaching far beyond the explicit content of the particular text, melody, or artifact. The very syntactic and semantic structure of the text, the special recitative rhythm of presentation, and the time and locality in which the action happens may have symbolic implications for which the text itself cannot account. Consequently, it is quite plausible that in their classification of these materials people will use as a criterion not the symbolic mode of the form but its reference. Legend, for example, often signifies a chronological truth; myth symbolizes a religious truth; and parable implies a moral truth. A definition, according to these references, would regard them as history, religion, and ethics respectively. However, if their actual cultural mode of communication is the key for definition, then all these forms are different phases in the same process of folklore.

The allowance for a possible disparity between ethnic taxonomy and behavior implies that, in a certain instance, the definition of folklore in its context depends upon actual modes of communication and not necessarily upon the particular cultural concept of them. There may be an overlap between the analytical view, which depends upon observation, and the internal interpretation, which results from participation; however, for the purpose of a cross-cultural application of this definition the analytical approach to the material must have methodological priority.

Similarly, the acceptance of the possible disparity between the analytical and the cultural views in regard to processes of social interaction

41 See George Herzog and Charles G. Glooah, *Jabo Proverbs from Liberia: Maxims in the Life of a Native Tribe* (London, 1936), 8.

permits the extension of the scope of folklore beyond the limits imposed upon it by the concept of verbal art. As an artistic process, folklore may be found in any communicative medium: musical, visual, kinetic, or dramatic. Theoretically, it is not necessary for the people themselves to make the conceptual connection between their melodies, masks, and tales. From the cultural point of view, these may well be separate phenomena unrelated to each other and not even existing in the same situation. Sufficient is the cultural recognition of their qualitative uniqueness in relation to other modes of communication in the respective media of sound, motion, and vision. The factor of rhythm changes human noise to music, movement and gesture to dance, and object to sculpture. Thus, they are artistic communication by their very essence. Furthermore, they are recognized as such by the people, since there are definite contexts of time and place in culture in which these actions are permissible. In the case of music and dance, there is no need to differentiate them from nonart communication. Their artistic qualities are intrinsic and essential to their very existence. There is, however, some necessity to distinguish these media as folklore. The distinguishing factor would be the particular social context of folklore.

As a communicative process, folklore has a social limitation as well, namely, the small group. This is the particular context of folklore. The concept of the small group, so popular among sociologists in the early fifties,[42] somehow bypassed the ranks of folklorists, who preferred the more romantic, even corny, term "folk." Since, in America at least, the connotations of marginality and low socio-economic status that once were associated with the term "folk" have long been abandoned,[43] the concept of "folk" has become almost synonymous with the group concept. A group is "a number of persons who communicate with one another, often over a span of time, and who are few enough so that each person is able to communicate with all the others, not at second-hand through other people, but face-to-face."[44] A group could be a family, a street-corner gang, a roomful of factory workers, a village, or even a tribe. These are social units of different orders and qualities, yet all of them exhibit to a larger or smaller extent the characteristics of a group. For the folkloric act to happen, two social conditions are necessary: both the performers and the audience have to be in the same situation and be part of the same reference group. This implies that folklore communication takes place in a situation in which people confront each other face to face and relate to each other directly.

It is necessary to remember at this point that even when a certain literary theme or musical style is known regionally, nationally, or internationally, its actual existence depends upon such small group situations. In these cases the tellers know their audience and relate specifically to them, and the listeners know the performer and react to his particular way of presentation. Of course this familiarity is often relative to the size of the general reference group. A storyteller who has a regional reputation may entertain people whom he does not know as intimately as he knows the people in his own village. Yet, even in such cases, both the performers and the audience belong to the same reference group; they speak the same language, share similar values, beliefs, and background knowledge, have the same system of codes and signs for social interaction. In other words, for a folklore communication to exist as such, the participants in the small group situation have to belong to the same reference group, one composed of people of the same age or the same professional, local, religious, or ethnic affiliation. In theory and in practice tales can be narrated and music can be played to foreigners. Sometimes this accounts for diffusion. But folklore is true to its own nature when it takes place within the group itself. In sum, folklore is artistic communication in small groups.

Two key folklore terms are absent from this definition, namely, tradition and oral transmission. This omission is not accidental. The cultural use of tradition as a sanction is not necessarily dependent upon historical fact. Very often it is merely a rhetorical device or a socially instrumental convention. The combination of

[42] For a critical survey of these studies see Robert T. Golembiewski, *The Small Group: An Analysis of Research Concepts and Operations* (Chicago, 1962).

[43] See Boggs, 1–8; Kenneth W. and Mary W. Clarke, *Introducing Folklore* (New York, 1963), 1; Dundes, "The American Concept of Folklore," *Journal of the Folklore Institute,* 3 (1966), 229–233.

[44] George C. Homans, *The Human Group* (New York, 1950), 1.

a narrative content concerned with olden times with the cultural conviction in the historicity of tales necessitates a presentation of the stories as if they were handed down from antiquity. Further, in past-oriented cultures, the sanction of tradition may be instrumental to the introduction of new ideas; and tales may serve as the vehicle for that purpose. Thus, the traditional character of folklore is an accidental quality, associated with it in some cases, rather than an objectively intrinsic feature of it. In fact, some groups specifically divorce the notion of antiquity from certain folklore forms and present them as novelty instead. Thus, for example, the lore of children derives its efficacy from its supposed newness. Often children consider their rhymes as fresh creations of their own invention.[45] Similarly, riddles have to be unfamiliar to the audience. A known riddle is a contradiction in terms and cannot fulfill its rhetorical function any more. In fact, riddles may disappear from circulation exactly because they are traditional and recognized as such by the members of the group.[46]

In both cases the traditional character of folklore is an analytical construct. It is a scholarly and not a cultural fact. The antiquity of the material has been established after laborious research, and the tellers themselves are completely ignorant of it. Therefore, tradition should not be a criterion for the definition of folklore in its context.

There are methodological reasons as well for releasing folklore from the burden of tradition. The focus on those items alone that have stood the test of time cannot provide us with a systematic understanding of the principles of diachronic transmission, selection, and memorization of folklore. Since the criterion of tradition determines a priori the selection of items, any research into these problems lacks the "control data" to check its conclusions. After all, the study of transmission requires the inquiry into the principles both of forgetting and of remembering. Thus, even the study of tradition itself should demand that we broaden the scope of folklore and not limit it to time-proven tales and songs alone. The artistic forms that are part of the communicative processes of small groups are significant, without regard to the time they have been in circulation. The statement that "all folklore is traditional, but not all traditions are folklore"[47] might well be revised to "some traditions are folklore, but not all folklore is traditional."

Furthermore, if folklore as a discipline focuses on tradition only, it "contradicts its own raison d'être."[48] If the initial assumption of folklore research is based on the disappearance of its subject matter, there is no way to prevent the science from following the same road. If the attempt to save tradition from oblivion remains the only function of the folklorist, he returns to the role of the antiquarian from which he tried so hard to escape. In that case, it is in the interest of folklore scholarship that we change the definition of the subject to allow broader and more dynamic research in the field.

The same applies to the notion of oral transmission; an insistence on the "purity" of all folklore texts can be destructive in terms of folklore scholarship. Because of the advent of modern means of communication, folklorists who insist upon this criterion actually saw off the branch they are sitting on. They inevitably concentrate upon isolated forms and ignore the real social and literary interchange between cultures and artistic media and channels of communication. In reality, oral texts cross into the domain of written literature and the plastic and musical arts; conversely, the oral circulation of songs and tales has been affected by print. This has long been recognized, and yet it has been a source of constant frustration for folklorists who searched for materials uncontaminated by print or broadcast. The notion of folklore as a process may provide a way out of this dilemma. Accordingly, it is not the life history of the text that determines its folkloristic quality but its present mode of existence. On the one hand, a popular melody, a current joke, or a political anecdote that has been incorporated into the

45 See Iona and Peter Opie, *The Lore and Language of Schoolchildren* (Oxford, 1959), 12.

46 Kenneth S. Goldstein, "Riddling Traditions in Northeastern Scotland," *Journal of American Folklore*, 76 (1963), 330–336.

47 Compare William R. Bascom, "Folklore and Anthropology," *Journal of American Folklore*, 66 (1953), 285.

48 Dell Hymes, "Review of *Indian Tales of North America—An Anthology for the Adult Reader*, by Tristram P. Coffin," *American Anthropologist*, 64 (1962), 678.

artistic process in small group situations is folklore, no matter how long it has existed in that context. On the other hand, a song, a tale, or a riddle that is performed on television or appears in print ceases to be folklore because there is a change in its communicative context.

This definition may break away from some scholarly traditions, but at the same time it may point to possible new directions. A major factor that prevented folklore studies from becoming a full-fledged discipline in the academic community has been the tendency toward thing-collecting projects. The tripodal scheme of folklore research as collecting, classifying, and analyzing emphasizes this very point. This procedure developed as a nineteenth-century positivistic reaction to some of the more speculative ideas about folklore that prevailed at that time. Since then, however, the battle for empiricism has been won twice over. Folklore scholarship—which developed since the rejection of unilinear cultural evolutionism and the solar and psychoanalytical universal symbolism—has had its own built-in limitations and misconceptions. These resulted in part from the focus on facts. Because of the literary and philological starting point of folklore studies, the empirical fact was an object, a text of a tale, song, or proverb, or even an isolated word. This approach limited the research possibilities in folklore and narrowed the range of generalizations that could be induced from the available data. It might have been suitable for Krappe's notion of folklore as an historical science that purported to reconstruct the spiritual history of man, but it completely incapacitated the development of any other thesis about the nature of folklore in society. Consequently, when social sciences such as anthropology, sociology, and psychology came of age, they incorporated folklore into their studies only as a reflection and projection of other phenomena. Folklore was "a mirror of culture" but not a dynamic factor in it, a projection of basic personality, but not personality in action. Once viewed as a process, however, folklore does not have to be a marginal projection or reflection; it can be considered a sphere of interaction in its own right.[49]

49 A shorter version of this paper, titled "Folklore: The Definition Game Once Again," was read at the American Folklore Society Annual Meeting in Toronto, November 1967. My wife, Paula, helped me in many ways in preparing this paper for print.

Music is an accompaniment to most human activities, joyous, solemn, and sad. There is music at weddings nearly everywhere. Music almost invariably has a part to play in the ceremonies surrounding important political events. Generally, music is an important aspect of rituals of mourning and separation.

The link to most other aspects of culture is apparent. Forms of musical expression are affected by the level of a people's technological development. We would not expect hunter-gatherers to support full symphony orchestras, for example, although the music of such people is often subtle, complex, and lovely even to the unconditioned ear of an outsider. But the possibility of a grand piano or of a full set of woodwinds and strings is out, for obvious material reasons.

As for the relationship between music and economic organization: in our culture music is reported to improve workers' efficiency. Where labor is cooperative, music is often used to call laborers to their work, to set the pace of their collective efforts, to entertain them, and to diminish the tedium of their tasks. The many-faceted role of music as an adjunct to religious ritual as well as other forms of ideology is evident everywhere.

That the social role of music is perhaps most complicated of all is suggested by this description of its cultural meaning in several contiguous communities in Latin America. Increasingly, ethnomusicological interest focuses upon the study of music as a form of cultural behavior; Whitten offers an illustrative case.

Musical Contexts in the Pacific Lowlands of Colombia and Ecuador

Norman E. Whitten, Jr.

Introduction

This article seeks to analyze the symbolic expression of social relationships. I wish to demonstrate, with reference to a particular part-society, the way in which flexible interpersonal networks are expressed, and to some degree formed, through activities within musical contexts. The focus for analysis is the lower class Negro segment of the Pacific littoral of Colombia and Ecuador. The Negro segment, consisting of approximately 250,000 persons, constitutes 90 per cent of the population of the Pacific littoral extending north from the Esmeraldas River in northern Ecuador to the San Juan River, Colombia, and including the Province of Esmeraldas, Ecuador and the coastal sectors of the Departments of Nariño, Cauca, and Valle, Colombia.[1] The Colombian Chocó is not included in this analysis.

Lower class Negroes in the Pacific lowlands must continually adjust their activities to the vicissitudes of a fluctuating money economy, these fluctuations resulting from a sporadic exploitation of forest and sea resources. At any time, in any area, the money economy is best portrayed as a succession of boom and depression periods. For example, there have been booms in different places, at different periods, centering on gold, rubber, bananas, tagua, timber, fish and shellfish, and sometimes on secondary booms such as those brought about by road, railroad and port construction.

Social relationships considered to be adaptive to a fluctuating money economy are those which can be "activated" (Peranio 1961:95) in times of individual need, and in times of economic expansion, but which can remain "un-tapped" or dormant in times of relative depression. In the Pacific lowlands, activities establishing and reinforcing adaptable social relationships are most apparent in social contexts where music is the dominant mode of expression. For this reason, I will focus on adaptable social relationships which are portrayed through the activities of lower class Negroes in musical contexts.[2] Re-

Source: From Norman E. Whitten, Jr., "Personal Networks and Musical Contexts in the Pacific Lowlands of Colombia and Ecuador," *Man*, Vol. 3 (1968), pp. 50–61. Used by permission of the author and the Royal Anthropological Society of Great Britain and Ireland.

Data for this article were gathered in north-west Ecuador during the summer of 1961 and the winter and summer of 1963 under the auspices of two supplemental NIMH grants to Fellowship No. 14,333. The Colombian data were collected under the auspices of Tulane University and the Universidad del Valle while I was at the International Center for Medical Research and Training, Cali, Colombia during 1964–5. Grateful acknowledgement is made to these sources of funds. Parts of the article are presented, in a different manner and with different emphasis, in the author's book (1965). Permission to reprint such portions, and to discuss the material in a new light, is granted by Stanford University Press.

This article, a condensed version of which was read at the 1966 American Anthropological Association meetings, has benefited from several critical readings by Dorothea Scott Whitten. Lee Rainwater, Charles A. Valentine and Robert C. Hunt made critical and perceptive comments, without which the article would have suffered. I also wish to thank Jerome Stromberg and Kenneth Little for their comments. No faults, of course, can be attributed to anyone other than the author.

1 For an analysis of the material culture and ecology of the region see West (1957). Illustrative studies of two particular towns are given in Whitten (1965) and Price (1955). General historical sources include King (1945), West (1952), Hudson (1964), Merizalde del Carmen (1921), Paredes Borja (1963) and Hernández de Alba (1946). Pavy (1967) has recently tried to work out some of the tribal origins of Negroes entering the region.

2 The music of the Pacific lowlands is, to the outsider, the most striking complex of the culture area, and in some respects, aspects of the music are strikingly African. I wish to note in passing that the greatest complex of African musical traits exists in a *secular context* (in the *currulao,* or marimba dance), discussed below. This is offered as a striking exception to the point most recently propounded by Nettl (1965:174) that African styles tend to be retained in sacred contexts, in association with African cults. In the Pacific lowlands, at least, African musical styles have not been "retained"—that is, have not "survived"

inforcement of such activities is continually made through community gossip. People gossip about the behavior of participants in recent musical events, and, through daily gossip, individuals assert strings of debts incurred by coactors in various encounters within the context of musical occurrences.

The social relationships of the Pacific littoral make up "quasi-groups" (Mayer 1966:97–102) which involve one "categorical relationship" (Mitchell 1966:52), apparently providing a social resource for the establishment of "personal networks." The categorical relationship is that of female sexual solidarity. The personal network relationship, defined by Mitchell as ". . . the network of personal links which individuals have built up around themselves in towns" (1966:54), is adaptable to the money economy.

These concepts will be amplified and illustrated during the discussion of musical contexts in which the personal networks and the categorical relationship are symbolically portrayed, reinforced, and constructed. I will proceed by considering in turn five musical contexts: the *currulao,* or marimba dance; the *chigualo* (wake for a dead child); the *alabado* and *novenario* (wake and post-interment rites for a dead adult); the arrullo for a saint (or propitiation rites for a special saint); and the saloon and dance hall situation.

Music and Social Relationships

1. The currulao, or marimba dance, is held on most weekends and at special secular events. The music is produced by six or seven male musicians, two of whom play the marimba and the other four, drums; and two or three females shaking tube-rattles (called *guasás*). Most of the patterns of African music described by Waterman (1952:211–12), Merriam (1959:49–86) and Lomax (1962:433, 446–9) are clearly and strongly present.

The ambience of the marimba dance is tense, and the dancing stylized with an "advance-retreat" pattern between men and women being the prevalent style. A woman (or sometimes two women) takes the initiative in inviting the man to dance. The man and woman move towards one another, and then the man retreats and the woman pursues. She then turns her back and retreats, but as soon as he begins to follow she again turns towards him and he again retreats. This pattern is repeated again and again. The woman steadily advances, pivots, retreats, while the man becomes more and more excited, leaps into the air, stamps his feet in time with the drums, shouts and waves his handkerchief or hat. He may even open his arms as if to grab the woman, but as she turns to him, he retreats (Whitten 1965:124–6; Whitten & Fuentes C. 1966).

Sometimes, when only the male singer performs and relates snatches of a stylized story about a journey there is no dancing and people listen to the text.

The currulao is attended by a variety of persons from a community, and sometimes from adjacent communities. Usually, husband and wife, or even lovers, do not attend the marimba dance at the same time. When couples do attend the same dance they do not dance with one another, and they do not acknowledge each other's presence.

One of the most prominent themes taken from texts in the marimba dance refers to the freedom and necessity of men to move when they wish, to leave their women. The female counter-theme which matches that of the men (and which is sung in vigorous counterpoint to the male theme about travel and leaving women) is that of the ability to hold a particular man, while other men are moving on.

For example, the lead male singer, called *glosador,* always begins singing with stylized shouts, which are followed by established and improvised verses. The female singers, *respondedoras,* harmonize with his long notes and sing set choruses to his verses. In the music's crescendo, the glosador and the respondedoras sing together. While the glosador improvises, yodels and shouts, the respondedoras frequently sing choruses and verses like these:[3] "Good-bye, Berejú, Good-bye, Berejú—I don't want, I don't want, I don't want to love; Because whenever I love, they will desert me." Or, the respondedoras

---

in the face of change in other parts of the system—but rather have been adapted to function in secular contexts. By symbolically portraying relationships which are adaptive, the style of portrayal has continued. Although the style of music is often African in rhythm and melody, a Spanish content endures throughout (cf. texts in Whitten 1967 and in Whitten & Fuentes C. 1966).

[3] The actual transcriptions are published in Whitten (1967) and Whitten & Fuentes C. (1966).

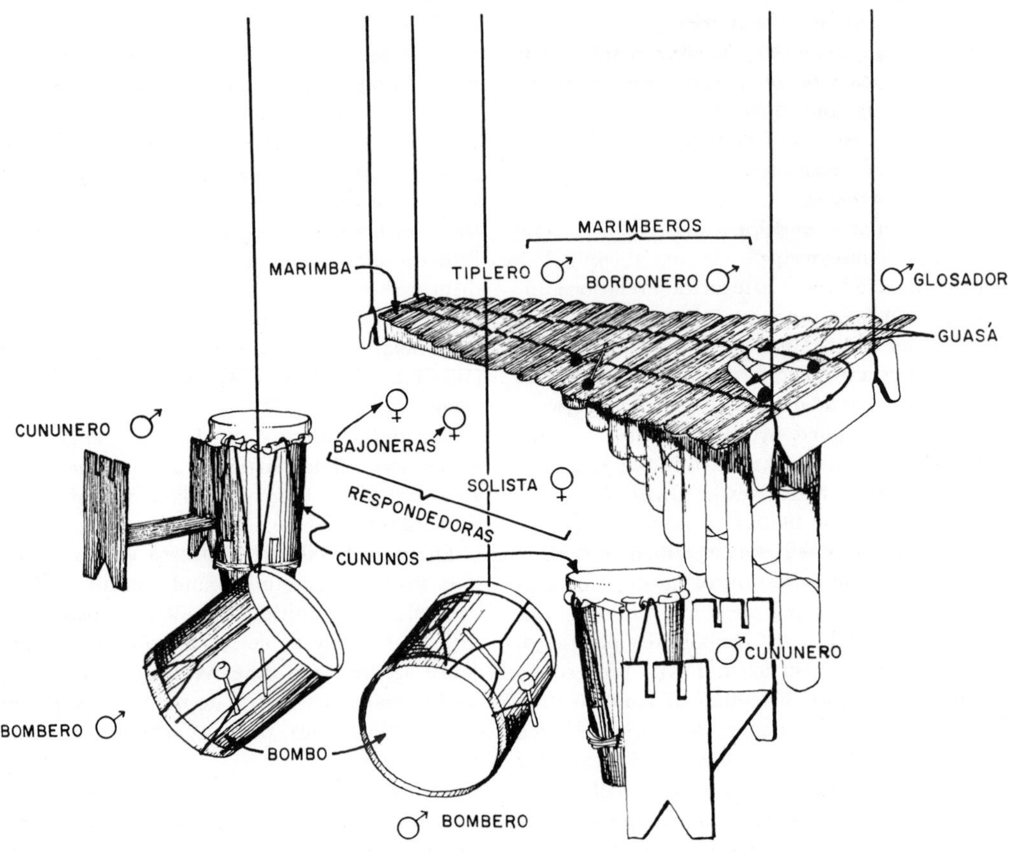

may sing lines like these (indicating that a man is leaving his wife—usually related to an actual happening in the community): "Good-bye by the man, I now have my man"; or, "Ay, man, wait for me, man." While the respondedoras are singing, the glosador sings the following strophes (or similar strophes): "Those who are dancing, let them dance with care; For under the house, the Devil is standing; Don't arouse my desire to dance with you; Because when I dance, my belly button hurts." Such strophes are variations on common themes in the marimba dance. In one very popular combination of these themes, the glosador sings this sequence in the course of about twenty minutes: "Come hear the marimba; It chases the Devil; I am the Devil; I am going on a trip; Do not dance with me, Because I might decide to stay with you." In response to this, or simultaneously with it, the respondedoras sing these lines: "The Devil is coming; Good-bye by a man; I now hold my man."

Elsewhere (Whitten & Fuentes C. 1966) it has been suggested that the marimba dance reenacts potential problems between the sexes arising from the practice of serial polygyny. Such problems are re-enacted until dancers and musicians are too exhausted to continue. Unlike dancing in a saloon (discussed below), marimba dancing does not end in a night of new sexual alliances. Household structure is not rearranged afterwards, but the *normative portrayal* of rearrangement is expressed through the texts and activities in the currulao.

Although serial polygyny is normatively portrayed in the texts and activities, activities to implement the norm are prohibited in the context of the currulao. Dancers and musicians insist that the dance is a *baile de respecto* (dance of respect). People are not supposed to touch one another during the currulao. They do, however, even dancing in a loose embrace in some dances (such as the *torbellino*). I suggest that the idea of respect and the insistence that people should not touch during the dance is a way of prohibiting sexual liaisons. People not only symbolically represent the existing prohibition against fulfilling the normative prerogative, they also explicitly state that the currulao is not the place to seek a new partner, and severely criticize outsiders (usually highlanders) who mistake the currulao activities for saloon activities and attempt sexual liaisons.

In terms of social relationships we can say that the *viability of attenuated affinal links*[4] is recognized and maintained in the context of the currulao. By symbolically emphasising and portraying men's prerogative to change wives, together with an emphasis on women's attempt to hold men, a certain stability to the dynamic phases of the structure of serial polygyny (Freilich 1961:960–1) is given cultural expression, is symbolized and is tolerated.

Figure 1 represents the idea of "attenuated affinity" as this functions in the broader system. Individuals A and B consider themselves "related" to one another through bond X. In the daily life of the people, attenuated affinal bonds provide major reference points around which a person builds his own network of obligations and responsibilities. Women, though "left" in the physical sense, are not "left" in a social sense. A man who has moved on and set up another household still co-operates, not only with his former wife in the care of children, but also with her relatives, and with his immediate kinsmen by involving them in a network of reciprocity.

In the Pacific lowlands the lattice of persons "related" by links of attenuated affinity ties together most people within a town, as well as those in the town and the rural hinterland. It is the currulao which gives the cultural expression and symbolic portrayal to such a lattice.

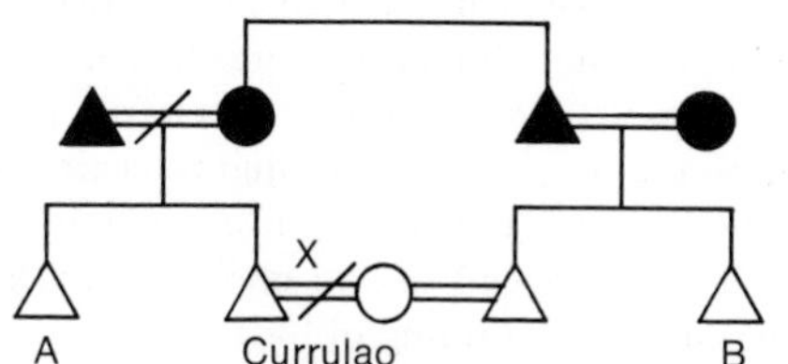

Figure 1. A and B consider themselves related through relationship X. The relationship is portrayed in the currulao. (≠ represents attenuated affinity.)

The process of portrayal, together with cultural restriction in the context of portrayal, gives symbolic sanction to links of attenuated affinity, and in so doing culturally reinforces a loose but adaptable lattice of interpersonal ties. The lattice itself provides a broad foundation for co-operation between individuals in economic and political pursuits (for an example see Whitten 1965:167–8, 183–94).

2. The chigualo is a simple ceremony which expresses assurance that a dead child travels directly to heaven. Texts from the spirituals (*arrullos*) sung during the wake are full of certainty that the "little angel" (*angelito*) goes directly to heaven and will never return. The music is produced by between three and eight well known women singers (*cantadoras*) together with a number of male drummers related to the father of the child, to the mother, and/or to her husband. The cantadoras stand on one side of the table displaying the corpse, while a large chorus of young women sits on the other side. The singers and the chorus alternate in their songs, each group following a leader-response pattern. The singers are not paid but the mother and other close relatives obligate themselves to the singers—if they are served sufficient liquor (*aguardiente*) at the wake the obligation is dissolved; if not, reciprocity in kind will be expected. The ambience is cordial, men may even flirt with the young women, provided that these are not relatives of the mother of the child.

Two classes of people attend the chigualo: those who are considered to be significant kinsmen of the mother and father and/or mother's current husband, and others who simply wish to extend their sympathy. To those who are considered significant kinsmen, women in the kinship network of the mother serve aguardiente. Occasionally, one who wishes to reciprocate as a kinsman in the future asks for a drink, thereby expressing his willingness to co-operate with the network of kinsmen who are seen, in the context of the chigualo, as radiating from the couple. Those who make up, in effect, the localized segment of the personal kindred (Davenport 1959:563) of the mother and her husband and/or father of the child spend the entire night at the chigualo; others do not. Some

[4] Briefly, attenuated affinity refers to a broken marital bond which is used as a decisive reference point in the establishment of meaningful relationships between members in a kinship network. The attenuated affinal bond functions just as an affinal or consanguineous bond in allying individuals, or networks of individuals.

close friends of the father of the child and/or of the mother's husband will stay all night, provided the father and/or the mother's husband themselves remain. Normally, such men alternate as drummers.

It should be noted at this point that it is musical expression, as well as death, that establishes the meaningful context in which these social relationships develop and are maintained. I have seen people simply sit and look at the dead child for several hours (after dressing and arranging it) because the cantadoras had not yet arrived, or because a drummer could not control his beat. No aguardiente was passed, no conversations developed, no attempt to sort out important from residual visitors took place *until the music began.* Also, I have repeatedly noted that all of the above relationships were activated without a dead child, when well-known cantadoras were paid by the ethnographer to "stage" a chigualo in a variety of towns and settings in western Colombia. Finally, in support of my contention that music, as well as death, is necessary for establishing a context portraying reciprocity within the personal kindred, Catholic priests report "confusion" over the symbolism attached to Baby Jesus. The Negroes interpret pictures of Baby Jesus wrapped in swaddling as being evidence of infant death, and hold ritual chigualos at Christmas time. During these chigualos the same patterns are manifest, except that the "mother" is replaced by the female head of the household (*jefe de la casa*), or the wife of the household head if there is a man in the position of husband-father.

The personal network which is reinforced during the chigualo is the localised segment of the personal kindred—particularly as this focuses on the mother of the child, but also as it involves kinsmen of her husband and/or the father of the child. Given the high infant mortality rate, most parents are assured several gatherings of significant kinsmen before they reach middle age.

Figure 2 represents the portrayal of social relationships in the context of the chigualo. In this case A and B portray their kinship relationship to one another by reinforcing relationship Y. This relationship may be further reinforced through *compadrazgo men*, either before the child dies, or, as is often the case, after the child dies. In the case where relationship Y is reinforced through a compadrazgo tie the compadres A and B may assume responsibility for the performance of the chigualo. However, compadrazgo is not necessary for the portrayal and reinforcement of relationship Y.

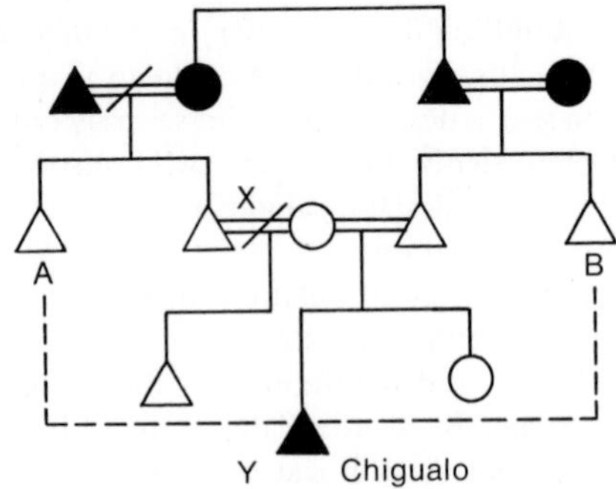

Figure 2. A and B consider themselves related through relationship Y. The relationship is portrayed in the chigualo.

3. When an adult dies the wake and burial are more solemn affairs than when a child dies. Only local members of the deceased's kindred plus other friends and neighbors ordinarily attend the first wake, or alabado. Well known cantadoras sing verses and choruses sometimes similar to those which are sung in the chigualo, but slowly, with a different rhythm, and with different inflections. No assurance is expressed at this time as to where the ghost goes, and it is believed that it remains around the house and community. There is no drumming. The whole ambience is one of mourning. Aguardiente is passed by members of the deceased's household to the various members of the localized segment of the deceased's personal kindred.

After a week or nine days (custom varies) the dispersed members of the dead person's personal kindred join the local members at one of their homes (not necessarily the home of the deceased) to hold the most important rite, frequently referred to as *último alabado*, or *novenario.* People come to the house when the singing begins; and it is the beginning of singing in some household that defines the end of the ghost's sojourn on earth, and the beginning of his departure.

At this second wake everyone sings dirges. The singing of these dirges is led by a well known female singer, usually not related to the deceased, and continues for a matter of hours or up to several days, the length depending upon *how important the deceased was to his personal network of kinsmen.* Importance of a person to his network of kinsmen refers to how central he was as a locus for economic and political co-operation and redistribution of surplus capital. The rise of kindreds in the local class hierarchies of western Ecuador and Colombia begins with the localisation of a siblingship and proceeds through a series of expanding ties to kinsmen as the siblingship solidifies its position in terms of upward socio-economic mobility. By transferring the centricity of ties from parents to some children, the upwardly mobile kindred tends to perpetuate itself, and takes on the character of a "stem kindred" (Davenport 1959: 565) or "nodal kindred" (Goodenough 1962:10–11). Those individuals in any community who are in the central position of a dominant stem kindred (see Whitten 1965: 155–61) are the most important. Normally, such persons are not only important to the recognised members of the stem kindred but also to others in the community, for they usually control certain crucial aspects of the community's political and economic resources.

The cantadora who leads the singing of dirges usually begins with the phrase: "Good-bye first cousin, first cousin good-bye," and is then joined by the chorus which sings "You go and leave me, alone with God." The ensuing dirge themes tell of demons coming for the deceased, the "Virgen Pura" mediating with Jesus for leave of this world, the departure of the spirit, and the strength of saints and God to take the spirit. The final dirge is usually this: "Holy spirit, powerful saint, Holy spirit, powerful and mortal." The emphasis in this singing is not on the intensification of ties but rather the *dismissal* of the dead person and the dismissal of the idea that he ever owned anything, or figured prominently in any network. In other words, Murdock's (1949:106) "criterion of decadence" is culturally recognized in the Pacific lowlands.

It seems to me that, more than anything else, the último alabado asserts the necessity of a living individual as a locus for a network of kinsmen. People are very concerned that the ghost be dismissed, for if he returns he may well be displeased with the conduct of the young—particularly those in the process of establishing sexual liaisons—and with the disposal of property (e.g. house, canoe, clothes, machete, axe, net), which normally takes place on a consensus basis wherein the occupant of the house is regarded as owner of everything in the house, and where those who normally worked with the deceased "own" the implements with which they worked (axe, machete, canoe, net).

Just as individuals are concerned with dismissing the ghost, and the idea that the deceased was ever important in maintaining a network of individuals, so are they equally concerned with maintaining the network itself. The alabado provides a mechanism for efficient re-sorting of network ties. Some individuals at the último alabado do break links of reciprocity by saying that they are not really kinsmen to other participants for the link has gone. But most individuals engage in exchanges of aguardiente and compliments, and co-operate in discussions relating to the dismissal of the ghost (e.g. by discussing how the ghost must now be gone, how difficult it will be for him to return, and by symbolically "forgetting" who the person was). During such discussions the importance of various individuals in the economic and political life of the community is discussed and people stress whatever socially recognized bonds they may have to important living individuals. In some cases the important people are the children, or some of the children, of the deceased, in other cases not. But in asserting new relationships to important individuals, people *do not refer to any bond necessitating reference to a dead person.*

In asserting relationship to an important person, individuals within any town are forced to find a series of links which connect them through living people. The most frequently discussed links are those developed through attenuated affinity. By denying genealogical links necessitating reference to a dead person, and by asserting "relationship" through past sexual and sexual-plus-economic alliances and liaisons, the *viability of networks maintained through attenuated affinity is reinforced,* and any network which might be based on a concept of descent is discouraged. Because it is fairly easy to re-arrange one's personal network to meet new contingencies, it seems to me that a flexible, adaptable kinship system is maintained.

Figure 3 represents the process in simplified form. A and B, in the context of the alabado, dismiss relationship Z at the death of either of their parents. In seeking a socially recognizable relationship through which to continue patterned co-operation they recognize the viability of relationship X. This relationship may also be

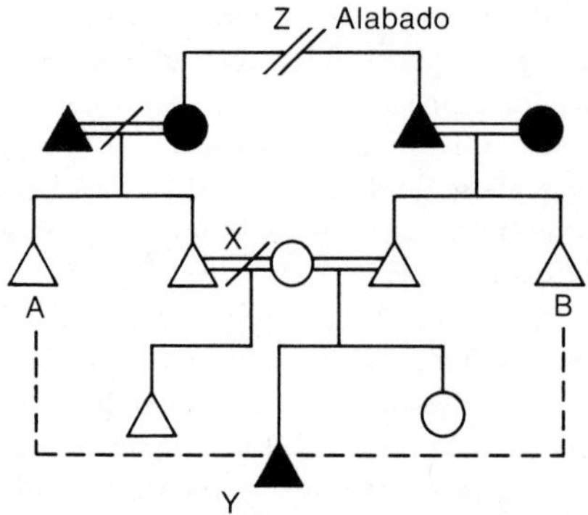

Figure 3. In the context of the alabado, A and B, who were once related through relationship Z, break the genealogical bond between them and seek a new bond, which is normally bond X, often supported by relationship Y.

reflected in relationship Y and might even be supported through a compadrazgo tie. However, if A and B did not have relationship X, then there would not normally be reason to continue a compadrazgo tie.

The context of music relating to final dirges dismisses the individual who might represent the continuance of property and network loci. By stressing dismissal, persons may remain in networks but must find support from other individuals involved in contemporary economic pursuits. The immediacy of life is apparent; and the other world and members of it are not to be involved in the practical day-to-day contingencies of reciprocating with kinsmen or other community members.

4. The fourth context of musical expression is that defined by a special day devoted to the propitiation of a saint. Such saints' days occur irregularly in the Pacific littoral and the degree and intensity of musical expression is also variable.[5]

Organizing and performing the music for a saint's day, and indeed remembering just when the day is to be, is strictly a female responsibility. In communities where clergymen object to the holding of saints' arrullos, women hold a secret arrullo well away from the center of town, and away from the Catholic church.

Essentially, the music is made by a group of women with *maracas* and/or tubeshakers who sing in a rotating leader-response pattern and move in rhythm, clapping their hands for added rhythm. They normally get one or two of their male relatives, perhaps their sons, to play one or two drums, but may sometimes supply their own rhythm and dispense with the drums. They may be accompanied by a marimba, over whose playing they keep close supervision. The older women are in turn the leaders, the younger are always respondents.

In general, older women are in charge of the arrullo, although most women in a community or in a neighborhood participate at some time or another during the day. Normally no aguardiente is passed around, and men are discouraged from turning the saint's day into a fiesta with national music and aguardiente, though this sometimes happens. Where it does, however, groups of women still hold their own singing of arrullos in semi-private fashion.

The social relationships portrayed in the activities and sentiments may be termed *categorical*: they relate to solidarity and intra-sexual co-operation among women. No particular networks are portrayed, or reinforced, and co-operation at an arrullo does not seem to ally particular networks of participants in other contexts of life; nor are enduring groups reinforced or established. This is a time when women decide on the musical event, design the context, and wihdraw to continue their own musical context if the situation begins to take on the character of saloon–dance hall interaction.

5. Our final context of musical expression is that of the saloon or dance hall. Here we find either a dance band or gramophone playing popular national music.[6] Although people go to saloons to drink and to dance at any time, I shall discuss only the weekend or fiesta pattern where a large segment of lower class Negroes of both sexes gathers.

In the context of saloon music Negro men of the Pacific littoral further solidify relationships within an actual cash-labor group (e.g. a dock gang, steady saw-mill employees, a group of railway workers) by sitting together, spending the same amount of money on one another, by passing drinks nearly exclusively within the circle

[5] Prominent saints (apart from Mary, Joseph and Jesus) include San Antonio, the Virgen de Carmen, the Virgen de La Laja, the Virgen de Atocha and the Virgen de Belén (who is not the same as María, "La Virgen Pura").

[6] E.g. *cumbia, gaita, merecumbea, guaracha,* etc.

of co-operating men, and by letting others know that it is the cash which they make at the same job which is important, not other ties to community members not engaged in steady wage work. Other men drain off the economic capital of a head of a traditional work group, or the focus of a politically or economically important kindred, by insisting that he buy something for everyone since he has more money than the rest.

Besides solidifying relationships within an actual cash-labor work group and "leveling" the head of a traditional work group or focus for an important kindred, men also establish and intensify dyadic contracts by the exchange of aguardiente and dancing partners.[7] By so doing, they also set up a situation which facilitates household fission. In this article I want to focus on this third social relationship—the establishment of relatively brittle symmetrical dyadic contracts (Foster 1961:1174) through the ritualized exchange of aguardiente and female dancing partners. I will also illustrate the process whereby household composition can be tactically rearranged in the context of saloon activities.

Men with some money enter the saloon and sit alone or in small groups. Men with no money do not sit within the saloon, but rather bring a woman in to dance. Men with money give a drink to friends and relatives sitting in the saloon and to those entering to dance. The drink is handed; neither man looks at the other—the recipient gulps it, shakes the last drop or two out, spits on the floor, and hands the glass back without proffering thanks. Should he proffer verbal thanks, equal exchange is made, thereby eliminating a basis for continuing an exchange pattern. The dyadic contract is closed by verbal thanks. If the man is sitting within the saloon he returns to his table; if entering to dance he dances with the woman and then goes back outside, or stands against the door or wall. The woman goes out after the dance.

Sometimes, the recipient becomes a donor by giving the drink accepted from one man to yet another man. If a woman asks her dancing partner for a drink he indicates that the man offering him a drink should give it to her. Rarely does a man take a drink from another man and then give it to the woman with whom he is about to dance, or with whom he is dancing. In this context women may receive a drink *for* a man, but not directly (symbolically) *from* a person—it is not up to the woman to receive a prestation and thereby be in the position of agreeing to reciprocate (by not thanking the one who proffers the drink) or refusing to do so (by thanking the man and thereby making immediate exchange). Rather, she must symbolise a prestation *to* a man, and this is normally the man with whom she is dancing at the moment. The gift to the woman is regarded by the giver as a prestation to the man with whom she is dancing.

Women, except for a few being courted, or for a few prostitutes working within the saloon, remain outside during the earlier part of the night, where they wait for a man to take them inside to dance. They usually accept all invitations to dance, but normally do not dance with their husbands, even on the rare occasions when they attend the saloon together.

While dancing, a man may suggest that he and the woman spend the night together; she will frequently consent, especially if she has no husband in residence. It is common for the couple to continue residing together. In this sense, sexual associations in saloon contexts, unlike those in the currulao, serve to change the structure of particular households. Ordinarily, before a man asks a woman, he is aware of her current situation and will not attempt to "steal" her from another man—for such an attempt will normally result in violence.

A man frequently takes a woman by the hand and leads her to another man; he offers her hand, none of the people look at one another, and the woman and man dance. At the end of the dance the man walks the woman back outside or back to the giver. The offer of a woman to dance with is not an offer of the woman herself. The man who accepts the invitation to dance is expected not to make sexual overtures of his own.

In the context of the saloon a dance and a drink are equivalent tokens of exchange. Verbal personal compliments and proffered thanks are also tokens equivalent to a drink and a dance, but the quality is different. A drink and a dance are prestations with implied contingencies for

[7] For a full socio-psychological and sociological treatment of processes of exchange see Thibault & Kelley (1959) and Blau (1964). These dyadic contracts may strengthen existing kinship and compadrazgo ties, or lead to the establishment of new ties which may eventually lead to kinship or compadrazgo relations. For an analysis of compadrazgo see Whitten (1965: 69–74).

reciprocity, while verbal personal compliments and proffered thanks for a drink and a dance are terminal (closed) exchanges. By accepting a shot of aguardiente (or a glass of beer when affluence is particularly high) and/or by dancing with a proffered woman *without returning thanks,* the recipient indebts himself to the donor. Payment can easily be made by immediate reciprocity, or it can be withheld and made in other ways in contexts involving economic return for those reciprocating.

Such loaning of dance partners and giving of alcohol continues throughout the night in a saloon, and people are careful to remember what is given to whom (though not necessarily what is received from whom). In daily gossip, people frequently remind individuals to whom they have given something how much they are doing for them; not uncommonly, one not reminded "forgets" what he has received, though he remembers his own generosity to individuals from whom he wants something.

The network of personal ties established in saloons is apparent primarily when there is economic gain to be had for group labour on a short term basis. The social relationships themselves are long term, but they are activated only on the basis of short term group labour. Particular groups organised to exploit a situation for economic profit (e.g. a lumber gang, political party, temporary dock gang) vary in composition through time, but the broader networks vary little through time, except by actual migration. The network of reciprocating men bound through mutual exchange of the tokens of a drink and a dance can be activated by individuals to whom a number of people owe favors. To stimulate such networks lumber buyers, budding politicans and traders, among others, make it a point to buy a whole bottle of aguardiente for an interacting group of men. The buyer of the bottle, however, does not sit with the men or speak to them if he wishes to obligate them—for if they have a chance to thank him profusely and to pour for him, or in other ways to express subservience, the incipient asymmetrical contract (Foster 1961:1174; 1963:1281) can be closed, or terminated.[8]

In the context of saloon music it can be said that the social components of household structure may realign as men seek new partners and women accept new overtures; and that men intensify the potential for co-operation among themselves by the exchange of dance partners and aguardiente as tokens for future economic co-operation.

Summary and Discussion

In summary, this article may be taken as a preliminary attempt to go a bit beyond the point well expressed by Merriam (1964:226) in his discussion of the functions of music: ". . . it is clear that in providing a solidarity point around which members of society congregate, music does indeed function to integrate society." Merriam is talking about the function of music in terms of general intra-societal integration; I am attempting to speak about musical contexts within a particular marginal social system as they support the development of personal networks, adaptable to economic fluctuations in a larger money economy.

Women express their sexual solidarity through the various arrullos to saints, by their leading roles in chigualos and alabados, and by serving as constant "antagonists" in their role during the currulao in which the singers collectively express their particular ability to hold particular men. Such solidarity seems to provide a basis from which men move, manipulate, and strive to involve themselves in personal networks which are strategic to the larger money economy.

The chigualo helps to establish the relative boundaries of the local personal kindred and reinforces networks of kinsmen around the bereaved parents of a dead child. At the same time, however, it becomes apparent that networks are shifting and overlapping as the central actors for one chigualo become more peripheral participants in the next. The idea of a living, tangible locus for personal networks is strongly expressed in the dismissal of the dead in the last alabado for the deceased adult.

We can regard the currulao and saloon musical contexts as being in symbolic opposition, and regard the other three contexts as supporting social relationships which form the basis for symbolic strategies portrayed in the currulao and saloon contexts. The currulao provides an expressive context which allows for realignments of household and marital structure when neces-

[8] For a discussion of the labour groups which are activated by economic middlemen see Whitten (1965: 69–74, 105–7, 148–54, 157–8, 164–5, 185–6).

sity demands it, but also provides stability for the particular structure at the time of the currulao. The saloon, on the other hand, provides the instrumental context of actual facile fission in domestic units, and at the same time establishes an expressive context in which economically feasible reciprocity can be established, or portrayed, through the exchange of acceptable tokens.

Symbolic opposition seems to be increasing with developing urbanism, and with incipient urbanization. In the large towns of the Pacific lowlands (Esmeraldas, Limones, San Lorenzo, Tumaco and Buenaventura) where race lines appear to be stiffening, the intensity of saloon dancing is matched by the growth of marimba houses.[9] On Saturday night individuals may choose to attend one or the other. In the saloon there is the potential for future co-operation, and for household fission, but there is also a certain cost in reciprocity, and the potential risk of an unsatisfactory new spouse. In the marimba house, on the other hand, stability of the particular structure is guaranteed, but the gain in terms of the future is nonexistent.

Interestingly enough, although men and women make this choice week by week (that is, choose to attend the currulao or the saloon) they are not consistent in their choices. It is generally difficult, and in some places impossible, to differentiate aggregates in terms of attendance. Usually people attend one or the other, seldom both in the same weekend. While they are acting in one context they deride the other, as if they would "never" attend; but they do attend at another time, and in so doing again deride the other. In towns, it appears that the instrumental and expressive contexts for household fission and fusion are regarded as being in symbolic opposition; the choice made in favor of one context generates a negative sentiment toward the opposite alternative.

In the rural hinterland, there seems to be either a marimba or a saloon context on a given weekend. People either play national music and engage in activities described above for the saloon context, or they go to the marimba house and hold a currulao. When acting in one context, hinterland Negroes normally deny that they *ever* act in the other. They say for example, when engaging in saloon activities, that "no one ever holds a currulao on this particular river." But the same people, when holding a currulao, deny that anyone knows how to play national music.

This suggests that the musical patterns in hinterland and town parallel one another, but that the greater diversity within a town exerts a pressure towards individual choice in terms of musical context. In the Pacific lowlands musical contexts, whatever the settlement pattern and proximity to the cash economic loci, do seem central in reinforcing and maintaining adaptable social relationships through a process of symbolic portrayal.

It is within contexts dominated by musical expression that one finds the greatest evidence for the reinforcement and maintenance of flexible personal networks within the Pacific littoral of south-west Colombia and north-west Ecuador. These personal networks can serve an individual in times of personal need, or can be activated for general economic return during boom periods. During times of relative depression the manipulations within musical contexts continue as men establish and break links in networks of kinsmen and friends, fortifying a system of links to individual persons which may be strategic as opportunities for economic gain develop.

[9] In 1963 San Lorenzo seemed atypical of this pattern. The marimba appeared to be in decline both in this port town and in the rural hinterland. However, this was a time in which a potential advantage in upward socio-economic mobility was perceived by most people in the town and, in the context of potential upward mobility, the marimba dance is negatively valued. However, by 1965 the currulao in San Lorenzo again manifested the characteristics and fitted the generalizations here offered. It seems that with a stiffening of race lines in the process of expanding capital resources, an adaptive mode is strengthened instead of a direct competitive mode of interaction in a money economy.

REFERENCES

Blau, Peter M. 1964. *Exchange and power in social life*. New York: Wiley.

Davenport, William 1959. Nonunilinear descent and descent groups. *Am. Anthrop.* 61, 557–72.

Foster, George 1961. The dyadic contract: a model for the social structure of a Mexican peasant village. *Am. Anthrop.* 63, 1137–92.

——— 1963. The dyadic contract in Tzintzuntzan II: patron-client relationships. *Am. Anthrop.* 65, 1280–94.

Freilich, Morris 1961. Serial polygyny, Negro peasants and model analysis. *Am. Anthrop.* 63, 955–75.

Goodenough, Ward H. 1962. Kindred and hamlet in Lakalai. *Ethnology* 1, 5–12.

Hernández de Alba, Gregorio 1946. The highland tribes of southern Colombia. *In Handbook of American Indians* 2 (ed.) J. H. Steward (Bur. Am. Ethnol. Bull. 143). Washington: Smithsonian Institution.

Hudson, Randall O. 1964. The status of the Negro in northern South America, 1820–1860. *J. Negro Hist.* 49, 225–39.

King, J. F. 1945. Negro slavery in New Granada. In *Greater America.* Berkeley: Univ. of California Press.

Lomax, Alan 1962. Song structure and social structure. *Ethnology* 1, 425–51.

Mayer, Adrian C. 1966. The significance of quasi-groups in the study of complex societies. In *The social anthropology of complex societies* (ed.) M. Banton (Ass. social Anthrop. Monogr. 4). New York: Praeger.

Merizalde del Carmen, B. 1921. *Estudio de la costa colombiana del Pacifico.* Bogotá: Imp. del Estado Mayor General.

Merriam, Alan P. 1959. African music. In *Continuity and change in African cultures* (eds) W. R. Bascom & M. J. Herskovits. Chicago: Univ. Press.

——— 1964. *The anthropology of music.* Evanston: Northwestern Univ. Press.

Mitchell, J. Clyde 1966. Theoretical orientations in African urban studies. In *The social anthropology of complex societies* (ed.) M. Banton (Ass. social Anthrop. Monogr. 4). New York: Praeger.

Murdock, George P. 1949. *Social structure.* New York: Macmillan.

Nettl, Bruno 1965. *Folk and traditional music of the western continents.* Englewood Cliffs: Prentice-Hall.

Paredes Borja, Virgilio 1963. Suma de la historia de los conocimientos médicos en el Ecuador: 1 (?–1914). *Med. Cienc. biol. Quito* 1, 43–51.

Pavy, David 1967. The provenience of Colombian Negroes. *J. Negro Hist.* 47, 36–58.

Peranio, Roger 1961. Descent, descent line and descent group in cognatic social systems. *Proc. Am. ethnol. Soc.* 1961, 93–114.

Price, Thomas J. Jr. 1955. *Saints and spirits: a study of differential acculturation in Colombian Negro communities.* Ann Arbor: University Microfilms.

Thibault, John W. & Harold H. Kelley 1959. *The social psychology of groups.* New York: Wiley.

Waterman, Richard A. 1952. African influence on the music of the Americas. In *Acculturation in the Americas* (ed.) Sol Tax (Proc. int. Congr. Am. 29). Chicago: Univ. Press.

West, Robert C. 1952. *Colonial placer mining in Colombia.* Baton Rouge: Louisiana State Univ. Press.

——— 157. *The Pacific lowlands of Colombia: a Negroid area of the American tropics.* Baton Rouge: Louisiana State Univ. Press.

Whitten, Norman E. Jr. 1965. *Class, kinship and power in an Ecuadorian town: the Negroes of San Lorenzo.* Stanford: Univ. Press.

——— 1967. *Afro-Hispanic music from western Colombia and Ecuador.* Ethnic Folkways Library: FE 4376.

——— & Aurelio Fuentes C. 1966. ¡Baile marimba! Negro folk music in northwest Ecuador. *J. Folkl. Inst.* 3, 168–91.

All the art forms we have examined so far are incorporated in drama. And typically drama itself is part of some larger production—a harvest festival, any one of the rites that mark the individual's passage through the stages of the life cycle, important events in the life of the community, a political pageant, a religious observance. All often combine the graphic and plastic arts, oral tradition, music, and dance in an overall production that provides a many-channeled means of aesthetic expression conveying with dramatic impact a complex message reflecting the participants' perception of one or more facets of the "human condition."

Only so rarely as to seem almost unnatural is drama a thing apart, an art form that ostensibly exists only for the sake of art. Usually, as among the Maya described by Nash, drama assumes an important cultural role.

The Maya Passion Play

June Nash

The dramatic re-enactment of an event compresses in symbolic form psychological and social processes. For this reason, ritual dramas are useful events for the study of transmission of culture and reformulation of tradition. Dramatization as a communication strategy has a special importance for solidarity groups, as Young (1965:2) has pointed out. The potential for transforming given attitudes and values has not been explored by social scientists although playwriters, actors, and directors have consciously or unconsciously attempted this in dramaturgy.

The Spanish missionaries employed dramatic techniques in introducing Catholicism into the New World.[1] The most significant of these dramas was the Passion Play, which contained the central core of Catholic ideology. Because the priests did not control the ideological or social context in which the ceremonial events they scheduled took place, a transformation of significance attached to rituals and roles has taken place. The play has become a vehicle for expressing indigenous social themes. In the cultural interpretation of roles, both the Indians and their spiritual conquerors have identified protagonists of the original drama with pre-Columbian mythological antecedents. This has given them a link to the past. In addition the Indians have projected conflicts of the contemporary society in the dramatic action. In this aspect they reveal a sense of their oppression, a definition of the dominant Ladino group as oppressor and an imagined victory over their masters. The ritual drama thus encapsulates modes of cultural and social translations which are continually in a process of reinterpretation and change.

This paper is concerned with variations in the role interpretation and selection of symbolic acts in the re-enactment of the Passion Play in three highland Maya Indian communities. Easter week is a peak period for the participation of all the religious organizations of the communities. The ritual dramas provide a focus for analyzing internal conflicts and accommodations. The following religious systems come into competition: (1) folk Catholicism, represented by traditional religious hierarchies, (2) formal Catholicism, organized in the recent reaction by missionary priests against "pagan" elements, (3) Protestantism, representing a reaction against both folk and formal Catholicism, and (4) esoteric cults associated with curers and shamans. These represent the organizations which are shaping the present religious beliefs and behavior in the communities of Middle America.

The Passion Play as conceived by colonial Spanish missionaries involved three major components: (1) the contest of good and evil personified in Christ and the anti-Christ, (2) the redemption of humanity from original sin through the sacrifice of the martyr, and (3) the temporal contest between infidels and the universal church (Bishop Nuñez de la Vega, 1692).

In the recreation of the drama of the Passion in Middle American communities today, there is a differential selective emphasis on the themes from the Spanish prototypes. The basis for selection will be discussed first in terms of role analysis of the dramatic personages and second in terms of structural analysis of the religious organizations responsible for producing the dramas.

I. Role Analysis

The selection of social identities assigned to the chief protagonists derives both from identifi-

Source: Reprinted from "The Passion Play in Maya Indian Communities," by June Nash, in *Comparative Studies in Society and History,* 1968, 10 (3):318–327, by permission of Cambridge University Press and the author.

* Research in the community of Amatenango del Valle was done under a grant from the National Institute of Mental Health in 1964 and 1965. A grant by the Archbold Expeditions, American Museum of Natural History, made possible a return trip to the field in April, 1966, during Semana Santa. The original version was read at the American Anthropological Association meetings in 1966. I am grateful for comments made by Norman Klein and Constance Sutton which have improved it.

[1] Cardoza y Aragon (1929) points out in the preface to the Cortezian drama "Rabinal Achi" that missionaries took advantage of the New World Indians' passion for drama in presenting dramatizations of biblical stories.

cation with preconquest Maya cosmological figures, and from projections of social roles in the contemporary communities.

I have selected three communities in which to analyze these variations: Amatenango del Valle in Chiapas, Mexico, and Cantel, Guatemala, where I have done field work, and Santiago Atitlán, Guatemala. Material from the last community is drawn from Michael Mendelson (1965).

In Amatenango del Valle the mythological kernel which defines the relationships between Jesus Christ, the Virgin Mary, and Judas is contained in a tale entitled "How Jesus Gained Control Over the World." Judas (called *Hurio*, or the Jew) is alternately identified with the devil (*Pukuh*) and the kader of the Jews (*Stâtal Hurioetik*). He prevents the corn plants from growing by making them come out with one "arm" and one "leg" so that they fall over. Jesus and Mary outwit him by enticing the leader of the Jews to a fiesta. Mary dances with the Jew and plies him with liquor so that he forgets the fields. Jesus meanwhile goes to the fields of corn and guards them so that the corn grows straight and tall. In this role he is identified with a preconquest deity, Cananlum, caretaker of the earth (Nuñez de la Vega, 1692:9). The people then recognized Jesus as their commander lord (*Kahwaltik Tios*). Mary is identified with Meʔtikcic, Our Grandmother the Moon, who also has charge of crops.

Jesus, in the role of the martyred hero, is not perfectly identified as an Indian. During the Caste War in Chiapas in 1868 the Indians felt that they would be able to overcome the Ladino oppressors if they made their own martyr. During Holy Week, they hung a live Indian from a cross and crucified him in the hope that they would find their own savior (Colby and Van den Berghe, 1961). The attitude toward Jesus is ambivalent: they repeat the priest's words that he saved humanity by this act of martyrdom. But he is undeniably a loser. In this community, men are killed when they violate the social mores either by theft or witchcraft (Nash, n.d.). A dead man is referred to as "the guilty one" (*a stukel smul*) even when information is lacking. Lacking the conceptualized role of martyr, the Indians have a hard time accepting such a deity even without identifying with him.[2]

Similarly, there is imperfect identification with the Virgin's role of the grief-stricken mother. During the Holy Week ritual of crucifixion in the church when the Priest admonished the people to cry as Jesus was lowered from the cross and presented to the tear-stained Madonna, there was no response in the congregation except for the wail of a visiting Ladina. In contrast to this absence of affect, when the Indians were called back to life by Our Grandmother the Moon on the occasion of an eclipse I observed signs of consternation and distress. Ritual wailing at death is conventionally established behavior for women.

In the role of the anti-Christ in the Passion Play in Amatenango, Judas is unequivocally identified with Ladinos. His figure, made of hay stuffed into a pair of Ladino style pants, shirt and boots, with a mask tied to his head and a felt hat such as that worn only by non-Indians, is a caricature of the Ladino.

On Thursday of Holy Week, Judas is hauled up by ropes and hung from the bell tower "to show the world that he killed Christ." As he is raised aloft the mayordomos on the ground, who are assisting those up in the bell tower, jab him with long poles. In this horseplay they symbolically castrate him; I heard one mayordomo say "Meʔčunun" (transvestite) as one well-directed blow struck Judas. On Saturday, he is let down and given a ride on horseback around town. Formerly, riding a horse was the prerogative only of Ladinos in the department of San Cristobal Las Casas (Colby and Van den Berghe, 1961). Placing Judas on a horse has possibly a rhetorical value in identifying this man as one of the hated dominant group who asserted this privilege. As he rides around town, the mayordomos solicit gifts from the people. Everyone gives fruits except the curers who donate money. This transaction may indicate an obligation they feel toward Judas as one source of their power over witchcraft-derived illnesses. The money is used to buy liquor, called "the washing of the arms and legs of our Lord Esquipulas," a reference to an origin myth which indicates that liquor was

[2] When San Pedro Martyr was introduced as patron saint into the town, the Indians transposed him into patron of the witches who gave them power for their evil work. His image, showing a skull split by a bloody hatchet, inspired fear and avoidance rather than respect and admiration. The Indians burned the church in which he was housed and cut off his head in the 18th century. His image was, however, replaced, and today he is respected—and feared—as Lord of the Lightning.

derived from the water used to bathe Christ when he was lowered from the cross. The drinking is mandatory for all the religious officials who have participated in the hanging of Judas.

The Judas figure, which was the church's symbol of the hated semite, is subverted by the Indians to appear as their enemy, the Ladino. In the acts in which he figures he symbolizes the sexual license of Ladinos with Indian women, the oppression of Indians, and the killer of Christ. In retaliation, the Indians symbolically castrate and hang him, and finally burn his body, thus dramatically vanquishing the alien in their midst. The subversive implications of these acts are not recognized by the priest. However, he prevented the ride of Judas through town during his presence because of its pagan association. The Indians rescheduled the act after his departure.

In Cantel, Guatemala,[3] where I spent the year 1953–54, Judas, or San Simón, is the patron of a cult organization sponsored by the traditional religious figures. He is permanently ensconced in the house of the brotherhood of San Buenaventura. The caricature of a Ladino in a black wool suit, felt hat, and Ladino shoes, is embellished with a wooden mask equipped with a pair of sunglasses. A rubber stomach is attached to a tube at his mouth to receive contributions of liquor. He visits all of the shops and is given donations of $5 by the owners to ensure luck in their commercial operations throughout the year. After the round of the shops, he is put in the local jail on the premise that his stay will attract many drunks and result in fines for the town. On the following day, he is ceremonially seated on the bandstand in the plaza in a chair with a table set before him. Donations of cooked food are placed before him by people who wish to succeed in their negotiations throughout the year.

In their icon of Judas, the Canteleños have symbolized the transaction in which Judas deceived Christ for the payment of thirty pieces of silver. In San Simón, they recognize the commercial superiority of Ladinos and cultivate his patronage in order to secure luck in business.

The many-faceted character of Judas in Santiago Atitlán, Guatemala, has been described by Michael Mendelson (1965) in his monograph, *Los Escandalos de Maximón*. The figure of Judas, called Maximón, is not as clearly an icon of Ladinos as in Amatenango or Cantel. He wears a shirt, pants and belt similar to that worn by the Atiteco Indian, but a blue jacket, boots, and broad brimmed hat distinguish him from other Indians, as does a large cigar firmly placed in his mouth. Maximón is said to be the oldest of the *nahwales*, or animal spirits. He is called *akitz*, the black magician who is the patron of *ajkunes*, the prayermakers who divine the cause of illness (Mendelson, 122). An origin myth suggests the ambivalence in reference to his sexuality. Some say that the ancient authorities decided to make a talking figure to scare men away from their wives, who had been seduced during their husbands' absence when the latter made trips to the capital (*ibid.*, 132). Created as a guardian of sexual morality, he became the principal transgressor. He could impregnate a woman who would then give birth to a child who looked like him, or perhaps show some deformity. Or he would transform himself into a woman and lure men into sexual relations after which they would die in three days (*ibid.*, 129).

Maximón is the patron of romantic love, an unstabilizing emotion which threatens parental control over the selection of mates. Young men ask the *ajkunes* to intercede for them with Maximón. The positive aspect of sexuality in the fertility of human beings and crops is symbolized in the corn cobs hung on his image during the cult celebrations, and in the fruit offerings displayed on his altar.

Maximón is one of a trinity of deities with preconquest counterparts. San Martín represents continuity with the past and is identified with the elders *Mamaletik*, who were responsible for the life-renewal ceremonies. Jesus Christ is included, more as an act of courtesy, since he is not integral to the earth renewal myth, as Mendelson points out (*ibid.*, 103) or perhaps by semantic confusion because of his manifestation as the *Santo Entierro*, or the Holy Buried One. During the Holy Week, the personality and rituals surrounding Maximón eclipse those for Jesus. In Maximón, the Atitecos have restored the positive aspects of sex—fertility—negated in the Christian identification of sexuality with sin (*ibid.*, 135). Christ may have redeemed man from original sin, but he exposed the world to sterility. In one of the myths retold by Atitecos, God cooperated with the ancient kings to sow the world with good things, but something hap-

[3] Material is drawn from the field notes of Manning and June Nash, 1953–54.

pened, and the world died. Maximón, the anti-Christ, maintains the balance of fertility and purity (*ibid.*, 136).

In the character transformation of the chief figures of the passion play, Indians provide a cognitive frame based on pre-conquest mythology. The logico-meaningful integration (Sorokin, 1937) in roles was promoted by the priests, who had in their cultural translations of the Bible a special dispensation to adopt "some similes used by Indians' (*Doctrina Christiana,* Lima, 1584 III, 3, *Recopilación de Leyes,* Ley 22, Lib V cited in Lamb, 1956:531). The dynamic aspect of role transformation is contained in the projection of social relations between Indians and Ladinos. Jesus and Mary are weakly identified with Indian culture, and the significance of voluntary sacrifice is never fully assimilated. Judas, however, is clearly identified with Ladinos in all three communities.[4] The Indians, with all the subtlety and intensity of the dominated, have transmogrified the despised villain of the anti-Semitic Christian passion into an icon of their own oppressor, the Christian Ladino. The very characteristics of Ladinos by which they have dominated the Indian—commercial chicanery, sexual license with Indian women, prerogatives of social dominance—are caricatured with different emphasis in the portrayal of Judas. However, they do not seem to be condemning these features as much as they are assimilating them. The offerings to Judas by the shopkeepers of Cantel, the farmers of Santiago and the curers of Amatenango are given in expectation of receiving the power that he symbolizes. Before the eyes of their conquerors, sometimes, as in the case of Santiago Atitlán, in the bosom of the "Holy Mother Church" in which their defeat and spiritual domination is institutionalized, the Indians subversively act out their incorporation of Ladino power and their triumph over the source.

II. Structural Opposition in the Enactment of the Passion Play

The full spectrum of religious organizations mentioned in the introduction, traditional indigenous Catholicism, orthodox Catholicism, Protestantism and folk culture, is present in the Guatemalan communities of Cantel and Santiago Atitlán. Amatenango has representatives of only traditional and orthodox Catholicism and the priest, representing the latter, is not in residence all the time.

Both of the Guatemalan communities have representatives of all four religious organizations. The variety of ritual presentations during Easter Week is directly related to the size of the community and the number of religious organizations. Conflict between the various organizations is only indirectly related to these factors since it depends upon the explicitness of the competition and ideological interpretations of the situation. The drama of the passion is presented at three levels, each sponsored by different religious organizations. Each of these levels is differentiated by the degree of openness and sanctioning by official religious authorities. The first level is that which takes place in the context of the church with the images of the saints playing the roles of the protagonists. This action is controlled by the official, orthodox ideology of the church. The priest directs the action, assisted by lay sisters and the local Indian *fiscal* or assistant. In this context, conflict is minimized, the anti-Christ is absent from the scene and his action is known only by the effects on Christ and the Virgin. The second level is the enactment of the passion by the people of the town. The entire community becomes the theater for the recreation of the crucifixion on Calvary and the action takes place in the same chronology as given in the New Testament, beginning with the search for Christ by the "Jews" on Wednesday and continuing until Sunday. In this context the conflict between "the Mother Church" and Judaism is given by laymen to a lay audience. Although this play was fostered by missionaries in colonial times, it is now opposed by the reform church which objected to the antics of the "Jews" running through the streets, shouting obscenities and attacking people as they looked for Christ in all the liquor shops. The third level is that of the drama enacted by the cult of Judas. This takes place on Thursday of Holy Week and is climaxed on Saturday with the destruction of the "Jew." This performance may be sponsored by a special cult and given

[4] Diaz de Salas (1963) points out that in Venustiano Carranza, Chiapas, Ladinos are called the "children of the devil." Judas is often equated with the devil by the Indians of highland Chiapas.

support by the traditional hierarchy as in Santiago Atitlán, or it may be undertaken by the traditional religious official themselves as in Cantel. Protestant religious competition exists in the communities, but it did not come into open conflict during Easter Week because the Protestants are not fighting for the domain of the church. However, competition for an audience exists, and Protestants may make alliances with any one of the other groups, as in Santiago.

In Amatenango, only the first and the third level performances were enacted. The Priest took the opportunity presented by the Holy Week rituals to assert his control over the scheduling of activities. This year for the first time he prevented the peregrination of Judas throughout the town. His growing influence has been only weakly resisted by the traditional hierarchy. The absence of a cult organization related to Judas meant that there was little reaction to this decision. The mayordomos, under the direction of the *fiscal* and the priest, have no religious organization independent of the church. The last open confrontation of traditional leaders and the priest occurred in 1957. At this time the priest successfully prevented the mayordomos from drinking in the churchyard during a fiesta. This prohibition is recognized so long as the priest is in residence. Hostility is latent, not absent. Disapproval of the priest's control over the church has been voiced during town meetings at which he has been accused of expropriating funds from the donation boxes. The overt expression of conflict was avoided during Holy Week by scheduling events disapproved by the priest when he was absent from the town.

Conflict of religious organizations was polarized in Santiago Atitlán at the time of Mendelson's study in 1950 with the priest and catechists opposing the cult ritual during Holy Week. The cult of Maximón is supported by the shamans, or *ajkunes* and the traditional religious officials (Mendelson, 1965:129). The Protestants, who were not directly threatened by continued existence of the cult of Maximón, aligned themselves with the traditional side in the controversy over whether the rituals would be carried out that year. They took the rational position that Maximón was a tourist attraction and much desired by the people and therefore should be tolerated. The leader of the Protestants was looking for an opportunity to demonstrate that they were more tolerant than were the Catholics. Paradoxically, they were defending in the name of religious freedom a figure whom they had denounced when they had been converted to Protestantism (Mendelson, 1965:69).

The indecision within the ranks of the traditionalists prevented the conflict from breaking into the open during the events of Holy Week in Santiago Atitlán. The ambivalence resulted from the feeling of uncertainty as to whether Maximón was identified with evil or with good. Similarly, the *ajkunes* or shamans whose power derives from him are being assimilated with the enemies of man and are more frequently called witches than magicians.

In the heterogeneous community of Cantel, the spectrum of religious organizations included the entire range of ideological and practical diversity. There were three Protestant sects, formal and folk Catholicism and an esoteric cult of Judas. All three levels in the dramatic performances of the Passion Play were carried out. Conflict during the events of Easter Week was never polarized since there was not enough agreement among the fragmented groups to find alliances. Sporadic friction was engendered as the competing religious organizations vied for space and audience during key performances of the Easter Week proceedings. Open conflict between folk and orthodox Catholicism broke out on two occasions during the week: when the priest shut the doors of the church on the procession of the Just Judge (Christ carrying the cross) on Wednesday evening and again on the morning of Good Friday. On this occasion, when the priest emerged from the church to point out the stations of the cross, he had to push his way through the crowd of over a thousand people gathered in the square to watch the hanging of Judas. There was tension, but no incident other than pushing and frowning.

III. Conclusions

The cultural significance of the Passion Play is coded in the staging, the costuming, the postures and gestures of respect or derision. Each element is an interpretative comment by those who direct and act the play. We are told that the Jew is the anti-Christ, but we learn that he is also a Ladino through the props with which he is caricatured: the clothing, sunglasses, cigar or cigarette, and the horse-back ride.[5] The Indians do not state that they castrate him in hoisting him upon the church, but their comments reveal this and their actions betray the intent. The spatial location of the actors or of the images are a clue to the position of the referent in the belief system: Maximón's presence in the church is an important statement of his position in the belief system of Santiago Atitlán as is San Simón's permanent position in the *cofradia,* or religious brotherhood house in Cantel. The selection of traits to characterize the Ladino-Jew is related to the cultural emphasis of the community. In Cantel his appearance as the commercial trickster is supported by the growing number of shopkeepers and those who wish luck in business. In Santiago Atitlán, Maximón as a symbol of fertility relates to anxiety in maintaining earth renewal rites. In Amatenango animosity toward the Ladino as oppressor, once openly expressed in the Caste War, is subversively projected in symbolic castration and annihilation of the "Jew." In the Passion Play, the Indians have found a means of expressing what they want to say about their world in a form given to them by their conquerors.

The ritual events of Easter Week are a period when stress for structural realignment comes to the fore. In each community, competing organizations attempt to assert their control or improve their status. Polarization of interest groups makes the conflict explicit, as in Santiago Atitlán. Fragmentation of religious segments limits the expression of conflict, as in Cantel. In Amatenango, conflict is latent since the potential opposition of the traditional leaders to the padre does not come into the open. The Indians comply with the orders of the priest while he is present, and carry out their objectives in his absence. It is only in the observation of the rituals that such dynamic processes become explicit. People cannot verbalize readily such emergent conflicts, nor can the analyst imagine the questions which would evoke them. As an event provides a microcosm of the real world, the dramatic re-enactment of an event concentrates in symbolic form the essence of social relations in the society.

[5] Siegel (1941–42) accepts the representation of the Jews as an anti-Semitic portrayal, thus missing the cultural re-interpretation in the scene and action.

BIBLIOGRAPHY

Cardoza y Aragon, Luis, 1929
"Prefacis" *Rabinal Achi. Anales de la Sociedad de Geografía e Historia,* Año V. toma VI, Num. 1, Guatemala.

Diaz de Salas, Marcelo, 1963
"Notas sobre la visión del mundo entre los tzotziles de Venustiano Carranza, Chiapas, *La palabra y el hombre," Revista de la Universidad Veracruzana* (Jalapa), 2 epoca 26, 253–68.

Lamb, Ursula, 1956
"Religious Conflicts in the Conquest of Mexico," *Journal of the History of Ideas,* 17,4:526–39.

Mendelson, E. Michael, 1965
Los Escandalos de Maximón, Seminario de Integración Social Guatemalteca.

Nash, June, n.d.
Death as a Way of Life; The Increasing Resort to Homicide in a Mexican Town. In Press.

Nash, June, and Manning, 1953–54
Field Notes.

Nuñez de la Vega, D. Francisco, 1692
Constituciones Diocesanas del Obispado de Chiappa.

Siegel, Morris, 1941–42
"Horns, Tails and Easter Sport, A Study of a Stereotype," *Social Forces,* 20:352–86.

Sorokin, P., 1937
Social and Cultural Dynamics, three volumes. New York.

Young, Frank W., 1965
Initiation Ceremonies: A Cross Cultural Study of Status Dramatization. New York, The Bobbs-Merrill Co.

PART EIGHT
Language

The Sociocultural Setting of Linguistic Behavior

Our ability to use language—to translate our perception of reality into abstract symbols, words; to hold them in the head, to think; and to communicate our thoughts—is an attribute unique to our species. And this ability is shared by us all. There are no "primitive" languages or linguistically inferior dialects. There is only language, varied in its forms but unitary in function, providing everywhere equally well for the transformation of experience into the symbols essential for imagination, speculation, categorization, discrimination, evaluation; for communication; and for benefiting from the accumulated experience of others, adding to it and passing it on to future generations.

The capacity to use language and culture evolved together. Neither could have developed without the other. Gradually they emerged, over millions of years, out of the signaling systems of our socially more successful prehuman ancestors.

Although general linguistics, the scientific study of language, exists as a separate discipline (many linguists are not anthropologists and ignore the subject almost entirely), anthropologists cannot ignore the study of language. Without language there could be neither human society nor culture. The capacity to communicate is essential both for social functioning and for the use of culture. And without society and culture we could not live.

Although language evolved out of some simpler form of communication that at the outset may have been rather like the systems or calls of some of the contemporary primates, before we had become fully human language must already have developed in incipient form the major attributes that set it apart from the often surprisingly complex and efficient communication systems of the other social animals. One of the most important of these attributes is the capacity to convey abstract concepts. Like our own apelike antecedents, modern apes can vocally warn of danger, beckon and scold their young, express friendliness, and threaten aggression. But none of them can utter, understand, or communicate with others about next Thursday, the product of $\pi \times$ the diameter, or the subtle distinctions between hip and cool.

Another equally profound difference between human language and animal communication systems derives from the capacity of our species to form and to understand an infinite number of grammatically correct utterances. This fact that it is grammatically possible to say or to find a way to say literally anything in any language with equal efficiency (and that there are, thus, no "primitive" languages) opens up for theoretical speculation a range of issues touched upon in several of the selections that follow.

Every language consists of three analytically distinct aspects: (1) a finite number of meaningfully distinctive sounds, *phonemes*, which combine in certain characteristic sequences into (2) *morphemes*, one or more sounds with a unitary meaning, which are arranged in accordance with the rules of (3) the *grammar* of the language into words, phrases, and sentences. Sounds, meanings, and their arrangement are the universal elements of language. The scientific study of their development and diversity is the subject of linguistics.

SECTION I

Anthropological Linguistics

Originally the division between general linguistics and anthropological linguistics derived from general linguistics' greater concern with the description and comparison of languages in the Indo-European family. Anthropological linguistics was traditionally most involved with the more "exotic" languages, those of aboriginal America, Africa, Asia, and the Pacific.

Today the two quasi-separate disciplines are increasingly convergent: in recognition of the universal attributes that unite all languages and of the similar processes by which they have evolved; in common speculation upon the ways language reflects culture; and in a shared interest in uncovering the still elusive causes of ongoing linguistic change.

Although it is no longer contended that some languages are more primitive than others, it does not follow that all languages are mutually translatable with equal facility (it is easier to translate from French to Italian than it is from Albanian to Amharic, for example). Nor do all languages lend themselves at a given time to coping with equal efficiency with the exigencies of communicating culturally unfamiliar data. In this sense a particular language clearly reflects the culture of which it is a part.

For example, it is no surprise that there are more words for car parts in German than there are in Nama Hottentot and more words for savannah pasturage in Nama Hottentot than there are in German. It is not that African speakers of the former language could not develop a grammatically correct way of communicating about automobile parts, or that German is grammatically impeded from generating the utterances necessary to discuss the vagaries of cattle keeping on the edges of the desert. Given the cultural need either language is grammatically capable of coming up with the necessary new words and phrases. But this does not mean that they will always do so.

Any Nama Hottentot speaker permitted to study auto mechanics would probably be trained in either English or Afrikaans and with time he would incorporate the foreign words he needed into his native tongue, changing their pronunciation to fit the sound system of his indigenous idiom. In this limited sense, his aboriginal language, Nama Hottentot, might be impeded from evolving a way of its own for communicating about this new field of cultural experience. It is frequently easier to borrow words than to invent them—but this says nothing about the relative primitivism or superiority of either language.

As for the somewhat separate issue alluded to earlier, the greater ease of translating from French to Italian as opposed to the considerable difficulty of changing an Albanian utterance into understandable Amharic, the reason for the difference is simple. French and Italian have both emerged comparatively recently from a single parent tongue, Latin. They are still much alike. The strong evidence of grammatical and lexical similarities is supported by an extensive record of earlier writing in the two languages that literally chronicles their gradual divergence from a common source. The same sort of evidence supports the theory that Albanian and Amharic are only distantly related. Grammatical and lexical comparisons of the two languages combine with what is known of the rate at which languages change to point to a very ancient parting of their respective linguistic ways.

In brief, assertion of the fundamental equality of all languages refers to grammatical capability. Equality in this sense does not imply similarity.

Currently much of the anthropologists' interest in linguistics is in the study of language in sociocultural context, of language as a form of cultural behavior. But this and other lines of inquiry into the relations between language and culture could never have developed had it not been for the solid methodological and theoretical foundation provided by general linguistics.

Greenberg, an anthropologist whose major work has been in linguistics, surveys the field with particular emphasis upon the complex interrelationships between language and culture, and upon the relevance of the study of language to understanding what ethnology is about.

The Science of Linguistics

Joseph H. Greenberg

All the sciences and humanities deal in some manner with data which are linguistic; to cite but a few examples, the documents of the historian, the informant statements of the ethnologists, the very materials of folklorist and literary studies are linguistic in form. Even the physical sciences share at least one linguistic preoccupation with disciplines concerned with human and therefore largely verbal behavior: namely, a concern with the language of science itself. However, all these other areas of study deal with language as a means to an end. Only linguistics studies languages as an end in itself. The distinction between the linguistic system as such, describable by a set of rules, and the system in actual use has been variously phrased as *langue* versus *parole*, code versus message or competence versus performance (transformational approach). However stated, it serves to delimit in a general way the province of linguistics as against the linguistic aspects of all other fields of study.

Linguistics is a social science. The very notion of language presupposes a social group which employs it as a means of communication. Linguistics, therefore, deals with the speech of an individual as representative of that of a social group, often called the speech community. Further, language as a highly complex body of learned behavior forms a part of the cultural heritage of the community which uses it. Indeed it has a central role as the fundamental vehicle of transmission of other cultural traits within and across social groups. From this point of view, linguistics may be considered a specialized branch of cultural anthropology.

The primary interest of the linguist is in spoken language. Writing and similar systems are viewed by virtually all linguists as derivative phenomena. Speech has priority over writing in the life history both of the individual and of the race. Writing always implies some spoken form, but the converse does not hold. A further reason for assigning priority to the study of spoken language has to do with the study of language change. Writing systems are highly stable whereas spoken languages constantly change. Hence the changes in a writing system can be understood by reference to the spoken language but not vice versa. The effect of writing on speech in the form of spelling pronunciations is a real but relatively insignificant factor. Although his attention is thus centered on the spoken language, the linguist cannot but be concerned with the relation between spoken and written forms. Almost all our knowledge of past languages comes from texts which must be subject to linguistic interpretation in terms of a primary written source. In setting forth the results of descriptive analysis, moreover, the linguist himself employs a written description. He may also become involved in the practical problem of devising orthographies.

Linguistics is divided into two main branches: descriptive and historical—or, as they are sometimes called, synchronic and diachronic. Linguistics in its recognizably modern form arose in the first decades of the nineteenth century as a basically historical discipline chiefly concerned with the specific problem of the reconstruction of the ancestral Indo-European language. Interest tended to shift to problems of language description with the rise of various "structural" schools from approximately 1920 onwards. The relation between these two main fields of study is complementary, not hostile. The degree of success of historical inquiry is in the final analysis dependent on the reliability and completeness of descriptive data. On the other hand, while a language can be described without reference to its own past, and this has been an ideal of the structuralist approach with its strict separation of the synchronic and diachronic aspects of language, it is now becoming apparent that the very description of a language is more revealing if it incorporates dynamic statements which parallel the historical processes which gave rise to it. Moreover, the historical mode of explanation inherited from the earlier linguistics of the nineteenth century still plays a fundamental role in the understanding of synchronic phenomena.

The aim of a scientific language description is to state as accurately, completely and economically as possible the structure of a language at a particular time. There are a number of differing theoretic approaches to the problem of language description characteristic of various "schools" of linguistics. In spite of these differences the descriptions are largely convertible from one framework to another.

In view of these differences of approach, any attempt to describe linguistic theory for the specialist must steer between the Scylla of all-inclusiveness, going far beyond the purpose and scope of the present exposition, and the Charybdis of a biased presentation based on a single theory. The orientation will be towards problems rather than specific solutions. The overall purpose will be to sharpen the non-linguist reader's awareness regarding some of the fundamental issues debated by linguists and to acquaint him with some frequently encountered linguistic terms and concepts.

Descriptive Linguistics

There are three main aspects of any language description, and it would seem that, on any showing, they have a certain irreducible distinctiveness which cannot be eliminated theoretically and in practice lead to quite different sets of problems. These are *phonology* (the study of sound systems), *grammar* (the study of rules governing the arrangement of meaningful elements), and *semantics* (the study of meaning). There are, of course, interconnections. Morphophonemics is the aspect of language which has as its subject matter the variations in the phonological and representations of meaningful units. In English, for example, the rules regarding the occurrence of the three phonologically different forms of the -s plural: [s] as in "hats," [z] as in "bags" and [əz] as in "roses" belong to morphophonemics which thus has relations both to phonology and to grammar. Again, semantics is concerned not merely with dictionary or "lexical" meanings of individual items but with the wider task of sentence interpretation, a process which involves the grammatical structure of the sentence as well as specific lexical meanings. The structuralist approach in American linguistics has tended to treat each of the three main aspects of language as autonomously as possible and to view semantics, since it necessarily involves extra-linguistic considerations, as external to, or even not to be included in, linguistics. The transformational approach to be discussed later does not shrink from "mixing levels" and seeks to integrate the three basic aspects of linguistics into a single integrated pattern of description.

Phonology

All contemporary schools distinguish in some manner between a level of description based on sounds (phonetics) and a more abstract level of description in terms of functioning units of the language structure (phonological level).

The basis of any description of this aspect of language is an accurate description of the sounds of the language. An indispensable tool for accomplishing this is training in the theory and practice of articulatory phonetics. The theoretical framework of this phonetics developed in its essentials in the course of the nineteenth century. In effect, this system provides a set of coordinates, almost all stated in terms of articulatory processes, that is, positions and movements of the speech organs, by means of which all possible speech sounds may be defined. Thus the English *b* sound in this system would be described (in an oversimplified fashion for purposes of illustration) as a bilabial voiced stop, each of these three terms referring to features of articulation, contact of the lips (bilabial), vibration of the vocal chords (voiced) and completeness of the closure (stop). A very few features are, however, *faute de mieux,* described in terms of acoustic impression rather than articulations. Thus pitch or fundamental frequency depends in its articulation upon the frequency of vibration of the vocal cords; this cannot be measured by non-instrumental methods. Hence pitch, in traditional phonetics, is described on the basis of acoustic impression as high, low, falling, etc.

The training of the practical phonetician includes the understanding of the theoretical framework of this system and the ability to place any sound accurately within it. The technique is largely one of mimicking and introspective analysis of the matching sound thus produced. Visual observation, e.g., of the lip movements, plays a definite but minor role. The tape recorder, by providing a virtually permanent, indefinitely repeatable, record of speech sounds, has been of great practical importance in the more accurate application of such methods. Finally, the practical phonetician must learn to apply a standard method of transcription in order to codify his results and make them understandable to others.

A second set of fundamental methods is that of laboratory phonetics. To a certain degree, these methods simply provide more objective data about articulation. By the use, for example, of the palatogram—essentially an artificial palate covered with a removable substance—it is possible to discover what part of the palate has been subject to contact in a specific articulation. In particular, recent developments in X-ray photography promise much in the area of the objective observation of speech articulations. The heart of laboratry phonetics, however, is acoustic analysis of the sound wave itself as employed in speech: a source of information obviously not available without instrumental means. Fundamental advances have occurred during the last two decades through the invention of the sound spectograph. From a sound input this instrument produced a spectogram in which the relative power within each of a number of frequency bands is indicated by the darkness of the impression on the paper. The subsequent invention of a speech synthesizer, by which the process is reversed so that hand-painted spectograms are utilized as inputs with synthetic sound as output, provides another basic tool in acoustic research.

Such laboratory methods are obviously of considerable relevance to the linguist-phonetician involved in the description of specific languages. However, if only for practical reasons of time, expense and the absence of servicing facilities under field conditions, such instrumental methods cannot as yet replace the traditional methods of practical phonetics. No one has yet been able to analyze the sounds of a language by purely instrumental means, although individual points of doubt in the analysis can often be clarified by such methods. Outside of any such practical help in linguistic analysis, it is clear that research into the acoustic nature of speech is of fundamental importance to linguistics and communication in studies.

A method very different from those already described is required in those cases where the only evidence regarding a language is in the form of written texts from a past period. The methods employed consist of highly complex inferences based on comparative linguistic methods, transcriptions of loan words into and borrowings from other languages, and the contemporary phonetic facts when study is being made of an earlier stage of a language still spoken. The results are necessarily both more uncertain and less detailed than when direct observation is possible.

The fundamental unit of phonological structure has usually been the phoneme, the basic principle of which is foreshadowed in the prescientific invention of alphabet writing. It might be thought that a single principle would suffice: namely, the consistent assignment to each individual sound of a symbol. In this case the phonologic unit would correspond in a simple one-to-one fashion to the phonetic notion of a distinct sound as defined by the coordinates of phonetics as described earlier. In fact, however, there is often a multiplicity of sounds, consistently distinguishable by a trained phonetician but intuitively regarded as the same sound unit by the average speaker. For example, the average speaker of English, untrained in phonetics, is unlikely ever to have noticed that the sound spelled *t* in "stop" (unaspirated) is distinct from the *t* in "top" (aspirated). It is not enough to say that the difference is small, for this precise difference of aspiration or lack of aspiration of *t* and other stops is evidently phonemic in Hindi, Chinese and many other languages.

If the approach to a foreign language is naive, a response will be made only to those sound differences which are structurally relevant in the investigator's language. He will thus ignore relevant differences in the foreign language where he is not accustomed to respond to them and will sometimes erroneously assume that the differences are relevant when they coincide with differences familiar to him from his own language. Thus an untrained observer will tend to arrive at essentially the same sound system for any language he describes and two untrained observers with different first languages will describe the same foreign language in different ways.

The concentration on those differences which are functionally relevant in each language has significant theoretic byproducts. It becomes evident that the sound system of every language is in a quite precise sense an organized whole. For example, the significance of aspiration in the Hindi *t* sound and its lack of significance in English is not an isolated phenomenon in either language. In Hindi it extends to a whole series of sounds which are paired as aspirate versus non-aspirate while in English there are no such pairs. The example of aspiration in Hindi will serve to illustrate another essential point about phonologic structures, namely, that what is involved is not so much the property of aspiration but a significant opposition, aspiration versus non-aspiration, which functions as part of the system of Hindi but not as part of English. In fact, it turns out that all sound units (phonemes) can be defined in terms of the recurrent oppositions in which they participate. This procedure is known as distinctive feature analysis.

Since, as in the instance of aspiration versus non-aspiration, such distinctive principles of contrast are binary, that is, consist of two terms, the attempt has been made to reduce all oppositions to binary ones. This approach which was pioneered by Jakobson is at present quite influential. It further seeks to reduce the total number of such binary oppositions to a relatively small number, commonly twelve, which are considered to be sufficient to account for all the sound contrast of the languages of the world. This is in part accomplished by exploiting recent advances in acoustic theory in order to use acoustic criteria of similarity alongside of the mainly articulatory rubrics of traditional phonetics.

The following is an example of this approach. A single binary opposition flat versus non-flat encompasses several contrasts which differ from the articulatory point of view. For example, the contrasts velarized versus non-velarized and pharyngealized versus non-pharyngealized are included under the opposition flat versus non-flat. In spite of their articulatory differences, they have in common acoustic characteristics. Moreover, it is found that no language employs a contrast between them. Thus we may say that in two different languages the same feature flat versus non-flat exists but that it is implemented as velarization in one language and pharyngealization in another.

Even in the present brief presentation, it is necessary to point out that an analysis which seeks to account for all structurally relevant differences in sound sequences must reckon with additional entities beyond the phoneme. Along with the succession of discrete sound units are various elements characteristic of the syllable, word, phrase or sentence which are, as it were, superimposed on this underlying sequence and can only arbitrarily be assigned a position within it. In American structural linguistics, such units have been called prosodic features, in contrast to the segmental units or phonemes proper. In England, the "prosodic" school of J. R. Firth has emphasized such phenomena and tended to reduce the role of segmental entities, called "phonematic units" in their terminology. Because sentence, phrase and words are grammatical units, we have here once again a linguistic phenomenon involving the relation of two fundamental aspects, the phonological and grammatical.

Grammar

The basic strategy of phonological analysis has been described as the attempt to develop a method which exhibits the functionally relevant feature of the sound system as an organized whole. It might be maintained that the most significant advances of grammatical theory have been along the same lines. The aim has been to develop techniques through which the functional categories of each language emerge in place of an *a priori* set derived from traditional models of Latin grammar as applied to Western languages. It was, indeed, the challenge of "exotic languages" differing drastically in type from European languages, which exposed the inadequacies of traditional methods of grammatical analysis. At the same time, by representing each language as a unique structure, there is the danger that the basic similarities among languages may be overlooked. As with distinctive feature analysis in phonology, it is possible in this more objective and non-ethnocentric framework to isolate general characteristics of grammatical structure common to all languages. There has in recent years, therefore, been a revival of interest in such universal properties of language.

The basic problem of grammatical theory as it relates to the structure of individual languages may be characterized as the generation of an infinity of grammatically possible sentences based on a necessarily finite set of given utterances and by means of a necessarily finite set of rules.

If the number of grammatical sentences in a language were finite, they could be ordered in degree of length, and there would be some one or more finite number of sentences of maximum length. But from a sentence of any length a still longer sentence can always be formed by the addition of co-ordinate clauses, additional modifiers, e.g. adjectives, and by still other methods. Although each sentence is itself of finite length, the number of sentences in any language forms what mathematicians call a countable infinity. Grammars, therefore, cannot take the form of a simple finite enumeration of sentences. This is confirmed by everyday experiences in that speakers constantly understand and make up sentences which they have never encountered in their previous experience.

The possibility of a grammar which generates an infinity of sentences arises through the existence of constructions in which the same finite class of words can occur repeatedly without limit (e.g. adjectives modifying a single noun), as well as by more complex indefinitely repeatable processes (e.g. coordination of clauses). It follows, then, that in one guise or other, at least some grammatical statements must be in terms of such classes of finite membership. Traditional grammar has made us familiar with the most inclusive of such classes, the so-called parts of speech. The most common variant of traditional grammar, based on a fixed set of parts of speech and even on a fixed order of treatment among them, has furnished the ground plan of innumerable grammars.

Such a grammar consists of two kinds of statements. The first, or morphological, concerns variations in form, that is, constituent sounds, particularly those connected with the functioning of the same part of speech in different constructions (inflection). Here then belong the tables of conjugation and declension. The second type of statement has to do with the use rather than the form of parts of speech. In fact, it becomes a statement regarding the meanings of inflectional categories. The two types of statement define a dichotomy between form (morphology) and use (syntax). Thus, in a traditional Latin grammar a morphological section states, say, that the ablative singular of *vir* ("man") is *viro* while the syntactic section includes a description of the uses of the ablative under such rubrics as "the ablative of separation," "the ablative of instrument," etc.

The heart of this doctrine is obviously the

notion of parts of speech. It presupposes a universally valid set of categories (noun, verb, etc.) believed to be present in all languages because they are necessary to human thinking. The definition is thus necessarily semantic.

The reaction against this scheme largely developed in terms of a rejection of universal *a priori* semantically based definitions for isolating the classes of elements to be employed in grammatical description. In consequence a formal (i.e. non-semantic) approach to the definition of grammatical categories arose. Such classes were defined in terms of morphological behavior; for example, by their occurrence in certain inflectional categories as marked by afformatives of specified phonemic shapes, or by their occurrence in the same or similar environments. To say that elements occur in the same environment is tantamount to saying that one can substitute for another. Hence the definition of classes by substitution became a key operation in structural linguistics, particularly in its American version. These techniques often led to the isolation of classes of meaningful elements which departed widely from the traditional model, even for familiar languages, e.g. English.

Still other procedures of structuralism undermined even more decisively the very concept of parts of speech which constitutes the core of the traditional schemes. It is obvious that traditional analysis requires that the basic unit of grammatical description be the "word." Morphology is the study of the formal (phonologic) internal structure of the word, and syntax has reference to its use in the sentence. It should be noted that in this usage some term such as paradigm is perhaps more appropriate than word. Thus in the traditional view *man, man's, men* and *men's* are all variants (accidents or inflectional forms) of the same underlying word. But the search for a minimal unit corresponding to the phoneme in phonology led to the postulation of a unit smaller than the word as a basis for grammatical theory. This unit, first introduced by Bloomfield, was the morpheme, defined by him as the minimum meaningful unit. Thus, a word such as "farmers" would consist of three morphemes: *farm-*, *-er-* and *-s*. In this way, inflectional elements likewise become morphemes, so that the above-mentioned paradigm of *man* is dissolved into morpheme combinations.

A consistent attempt was made to develop an overall theory of linguistic description based on the phoneme and morpheme as the two basic units and with a good deal of parallelism in the analytic procedures involved in both. This finds its classic expression in a paper by Z. Harris, in which, by repeated substitution procedures on higher and higher levels, there is a *gradus ad Parnassum* from the morpheme to the sentence. The word level appears here only tacitly, so that for all practical purposes, the old morphology-syntax division disappears. Form variations formerly handled in declensional and conjugational tables with words as units are treated as allomorphs (i.e. variants) of the same morphemic unit, e.g. *-en* is an allomorph of the plural morpheme in the environment . . . *ox-* . . . .

The morphophonemics of the language is then comprised in a set of statements describing all such varying shapes of morphemes and constitutes, in this scheme, a distinctive compartment of the grammar. The connection with phonology is via what Hockett called the principle of accountability, according to which, as far as possible, every phoneme is assigned to one and only one allomorph in a specific context.

The model sketched is, basically, one of several distinct levels, each with minimal units and with rules which describe the variants of each unit and the combinations in which it occurs with units on the same level. This general model which has numerous variations in theory and practice has been widely influential and many grammars have been written in accordance with it. In particular the type known as tagmemic and developed chiefly by K. Pike has been employed by linguistic workers affiliated with the missionary-oriented Summer Institute of Linguistics in the description of many languages throughout the world.

A fundamentally different model, commonly known as the transformational, first attracted attention in 1957 with the publication of N. Chomsky's *Syntactic Structures* and, at the time of writing, had clearly assumed a dominant position within American linguistics. During the first ten years of existence it has itself undergone considerable changes and it seems clear that its development is by no means closed. Hence any discussion of its basic outlines at the present time is subject to the promise that this model is quite likely to undergo further drastic changes in the future.

A transformational grammar is a subclass of the generative type of grammar. In general, the notion of a generative grammar requires use at the start of a set of primitive symbols, normally a single one, symbolized S (= sentence). For any particular language, by various rewritings and further manipulations in accordance with the given rules, a succession of strings, each consisting of a sequence of symbols, is generated. As constituted at present, such a grammar consists of base rules, a lexicon, a transformational component, and sets of phonological and semantic interpretation rules. The base consists of the base rules and the lexicon. It produces the abstract underlying structure of the sentence, the so-called deep structure. In principle, this is sufficient for semantic interpretation of the sentence since it contains all the relevant grammatical and lexical information required for sentence interpretation. The transformational component, whose form of rules is different from that of the base, produces a "surface structure" from the deep structure of any sentence. This in turn undergoes the phonological rules to produce a sequence of symbols subject to phonetic interpretation. As currently practiced, binary feature analysis is employed in phonological representations and semantic feature analysis in the lexicon and in the semantic interpretation. Semantic features will be briefly described in a subsequent section.

This scheme has not yet been applied in its entirety to any language but a fair number of partial descriptions have been produced in accordance with the earlier forms of the transformational model. In general, this approach differs from the phoneme–morpheme model in a number of ways. In the former, there are units which are supposed to be discoverable by procedures applied, ideally at least, in a mechanical way from a given body of actual utterances. Hence sentences in their overt forms as sound sequences are ultimately described and classified in terms of such units and their combinations. In the generative approach, there is rather a sequence of abstract structures which do not assume the form of the actual sentence until the operation of semantic and phonological interpretation. The adequacy of particular alternative formulations is judged in relation to the overall structure of rules for the entire language with the aim of incorporating to the maximum extent the possibilities of generalization within the description. The ultimate aim is the justification of such choices in terms of their applicability in principle to all linguistic descriptions, i.e. their universality.

Levels are distinguished not in terms of the nature of the units which occur in them but on the logical form of the rules of which they consist. By incorporating semantic interpretation rules as well as phonological rules, this model seeks an overall integrated theory of linguistic description. The grammatical aspect, here generally called the syntactic, has, as can be seen, the central position in that it generates the underlying structures subject to semantic and phonological interpretation.

Semantics

A central problem in semantics, traditionally *the* basic problem, is the statement of meanings in terms of definitions, whether the language is the same (periphrasis) or different from (translation) the object language. This has been primarily the task of the lexicographer or dictionary-maker. The division between the written productions commonly called grammars and dictionaries, however, does not completely coincide with the division of the subject into grammar and semantics. Certain kinds of meanings, e.g. those of inflections, are treated in grammars, at least in traditional ones, and are almost never found in dictionaries. On the other hand, the assignment of words to paradigm class, e.g. the gender of nouns in French and irregularities or morphological formation, particularly the former, are regularly included in dictionaries. Thus, a grammar of French will describe the phenomenon of grammatical gender and give rules relating to agreement in gender, but it will not normally list all masculine and feminine nouns.

Lexicography is still very much an art learned by apprenticeship or unguided imitation of existing dictionaries with relatively little in the way of codified principles or theoretical elaboration. It is significant to note that the lexicographic aspects of hitherto unwritten languages or of those with a minimal written literature are quite different from those of established or standardized literary languages. Oral information from informants rather than published texts provides the basis for entries. Moreover, the languages are frequently parts of non-Western cultures with which the dictionary-maker or the non-indigenous user may not be familiar. The lexicographer, in these instances, finds his task extraordinarily close to that of the ethnographic fieldworker. Indeed, a really first-rate dictionary cannot be compiled under these circumstances without coincident investigation of non-linguistic culture and is itself an ethnographic document of first-rate importance.

There is, then, an absence of an organized theoretical framework in the actual practice of the dictionary-maker. Nevertheless, there have been important developments in recent semantic theory, none of these as yet incorporated in full-fledged dictionaries, which bid fair ultimately to alter this situation. The most important development here has been a notable gain in the precision of methods based on the semantic analysis by features, which was inherited from the earlier theoretical literature of semantics. These methods have been employed with particular success in the area of kinship terminologies and the basic principles have been adopted into the program for semantics being developed by transformational theorists as noted earlier.

Some of the basic notions of semantic feature analysis can be illustrated from the set of kinship terms in the English language. Each particular term, e.g. "brother," "aunt," can be defined by reference to a set of features which recur elsewhere in the system. Most of these features are, as in phonology, binary. A simple and not entirely adequate model which will, however, illustrate these principles is the following. We have a set of the following features: sex of the person referred to, lineal versus collateral, consanguineal versus affinal, generation. All except the last of these is binary. The term "uncle" is then defined as male, collateral, consanguineal, first-ascending generation. Just as in phonology, there is a restricted universal set of features and every language utilizes only some of them. For example, English does not use the feature "sex of the speaker" but for some Bantu languages, this category appears in the existence of distinct terms of reference for a male sibling in relation to a male sibling as against a female sibling in relation to a male sibling. On the other hand, many systems, unlike English, do not distinguish lineal from collateral relatives.

Comparative Linguistics

Great as is the value of descriptions of the thousands of the world's languages from both the practical and the theoretic point of view, it can be argued that description is but the initial task of linguistic science. Only by comparisons of languages can either law-like generalizations or specific historical conclusions be derived from linguistic study.

Historical Method. One basic type of comparison is that of two or more historical stages of the same language. This, the direct historical method, depends on the existence of documentation for the earlier periods of the language. Historical depth can also be attained by the comparative method, which involves the systematic comparison of related languages in order to reconstruct the ancestral language from which they have sprung. A specialized aspect of the comparative historical method is the intensive study of dialect variation within a single language, for such inter-dialectal relationship can be considered the limiting case of closest relationship. This field, which has a highly developed set of techniques, is called dialect geography. Its characteristic production is the dialect atlas, in which the geographical distribution of linguistic features within the total language area is mapped. In principle, social stratification of linguistic forms on class and occupational lines is likewise an aspect of linguistic variability within the bounds of a single language, but this area of study is still in its infancy.

The concept of genetic relationship of languages, the basis of comparative historical linguistics, is an extension of the notion of dialectic divergence over a longer time span. The dialects of one period become the separate but related languages of a later time. Language is always changing, and no language spoken over an extensive area can maintain full and equal communication within the entire speech community. A further factor in language change is migration, which may result in a community of speakers who are permanently removed from frequent and easy communication with the home community, i.e. Dutch in South Africa which evolved into a separate language, Afrikaans. Under the conditions just outlined, linguistic innovations, which may occur in all aspects of language, tend not to diffuse over the communication barriers; the results are local differentiation or dialects, as they are called. As the process continues, the dialects shift further apart beyond the point of mutual intelligibility. Each of the new languages which arises in this way may itself once more undergo the same splitting process.

The recovery of this sequence of events leads to the postulation of a family tree or genetic classification of languages. Hypotheses of this kind are based on shared resemblances which are retentions, though often in a modified form, from the original period of linguistic unity. The systematic comparison of such related languages leads to the reconstruction, as far as may be possible, of the traits of the ancestral language and the processes of change in the languages during the intervening period. A fundamental part of this method is the technique of determining sound correspondences. Sound change is regular in that a phoneme in a particular language changes to another phoneme virtually without exception under stated conditions, these conditions themselves being phonetic. Sometimes all instances of a phoneme change under all conditions (so-called unconditioned sound change). An example of a conditioned change is the shift from earlier *t* in German to *s* (written *ss*) in non-initial position and to *ts* (written *z*) in initial position. Since in English *t* did not change under these circumstances, there have resulted two sets of correspondences between English and German. Initially, German *ts* = English *t*, as in *zwei: two; Zunge: tongue,* etc.; non-initially, German *s* = English *t*, as in *beissen: bite; schiessen: shoot,* etc. An example of an unconditioned change is the shift of Anglo-Saxon ā to modern English *o*, e.g. *hām: home; stān: stone,* etc.

An understanding of regular sound changes and a number of other processes of change permits, by a kind of triangulation, the determination of features of the parent language. Such comparative study is most advanced in the case of the Indo-European languages, but it has been applied successfully to closely related groups of languages in many parts of the world, even in the absence of earlier written records. An incidental but important by-product is the sorting out of resemblances among both related and non-related languages which result from borrowing rather than descent with modification from a form in the ancestral language.

It is evident that the most important contributions of linguistics to historical research lie in this area. Until recently, conclusions of this kind have lacked the all-important aspect of absolute chronology. Since about 1950, however, Swadesh and others have developed a method called glottochronology, which attempts to fill this gap. The fundamental assumption of glottochronology is that the rate of change by replacement within a standard vocabulary list is reasonably constant for all languages. The absolute value is calculated from a number of documented cases from earlier and later stages of the same languages in Europe and the Near East. If it is hypothesized that attrition in related languages is occurring independently at this rate, then there will be an expected number of common retentions, the so-called cognate forms. From the percentage of cognates in such cases it is possible to derive an estimate of the chronological date at which divergence within the original unified speech community began. Recently both the empirical and mathematical bases of the theory have come under sharp attack.

Typologic Method. Another type of comparison has come into renewed prominence in recent years. This is typologic comparison and classification in which the criteria employed refer to similarities which may arise without any necessary implication or historical connection through either contact or common origin. Languages can have noun case systems, for example, which considerably resemble each other in the semantic categories but which do not have corresponding similarities in the sound sequences which express these categories. Thus certain Australian, Caucasian, Indo-European, Amerind, and other languages in all probability have independently developed systems of case inflection in the nouns. To cite but a few instances of a widespread phenomenon in phonology: Ewe in West Africa, Chinese in Eastern Asia, and Zapotecan in Mexico, make use of pitch distinctions in their phonemic systems although the languages have had no historic connection.

Non-historical comparison using such criteria leads to classification of languages into types. The complete absence of certain logically possible types and the significantly different frequencies of others evidently lead to generalizations about human language as a whole. In the past there has been a tendency to confuse typological and genetic criteria for resemblances, but the growing clarification of this problem has tended to elucidate the legitimate role of typological comparison in the development of both synchronic law-like generalizations and diachronic regularities governing the change of type.

Other Linguistic Disciplines

In addition to the two core fields of descriptive and comparative linguistics just outlined, a number of more or less peripheral, though definitely related, topics possess the common characteristic of having fairly direct relevance to other disciplines. In certain instances the area of common interest is sufficiently extensive to have given rise to nascent subdisciplines, notably psycholinguistics and ethnolinguistics. In the present context the emphasis is on common ground with other social sciences, and no consideration need be given to such fields as semantic analysis, an important joint interest of linguistics with logic.

Because language is a part of culture, and linguistics, from this point of view, may be considered a branch of cultural anthropology, the relationship between language and other aspects of culture has naturally become a concern of anthropological linguistics. This rather vague area of knowledge is often called *ethnolinguistics.* Among its basic problems is the determination of the role of language in the transmission of culture from one generation to another (enculturation) and from one culture to another (acculturation). Studies have been made, for example, of the changes induced in one language by contact with another in the context of the general culture-contact situation, including its non-linguistic aspects. Another set of problems has to do with possible correlations between language, particularly in its semantic aspect of classification of concepts, and non-linguistic cultural behavior. The by now classic anthropological topic of the relation between kinship terminology and patterned kinship behavior is an example of this. But the sharpest issues in this area have been raised through the largely posthumous interest in the writings of Benjamin Whorf. The Whorfian thesis or "linguistic Weltanschauung hypothesis," as it has been called, in its most extreme interpretation would assert that the general "world view" of its speakers is determined by, or at least mirrored in, the categories of the language which they speak. This thesis has aroused wide interest and has been the stimulus both for analytic discussion and for cross-cultural psychological experimentation.

Like ethnolinguistics, the merging subdiscipline of *psycholinguistics* does not as yet have a clearly delineated set of problems or techniques. In order to give a general [illegible] contents, a number of topics gene[illegible] sidered relevant may be mentioned here. [illegible] include the psychological processes in langu[illegible] learning, whether of first or subsequent la[illegible] guages, and in language-loss in the pathological condition known as aphasia; the study of sound perceptions in speech; and the psychological aspects of meaning interpreted as the reaction of subjects to words operating as stimulus objects. This last type of interest has given rise to the semantic differential as an instrument to measure meaning as response along a set of dimensions.

Even more recent is the interest in what has come to be called *sociolinguistics,* including such topics as: the relation of language differences to social class; the differential social roles of different languages coexisting in the same society; the development and spread of lingua francas as auxiliary languages in multilingual situations; the factors involved in the differential prestige ratings of languages; the role of language as a sign of ethnic identification; language in relation to nationalism; and problems of language policy, e.g. in education. This area has become a focus of interest largely because of problems arising in developing areas.

Still another aspect of language, namely its employment as a *medium of aesthetic expression,* must also be considered. There is a purely linguistic side to the characterization of individual and folk style in written and unwritten literature. Linguistic considerations also enter into the description and analysis of differences between prose and various poetic types of language. One particular poetic device, meter, cannot be analyzed without reference to strictly linguistic factors. The use of language in song, for example, the relation between linguistic and musical pitch patterns in tone languages, raises at least partly linguistic considerations. Departing somewhat from the strictly aesthetic aspect, one may also consider the ritual use of language, secret languages, the linguistic aspect of drum and other communication based on language and the playful modification of language involved in tongue-twisters, dog-Latin and similar devices.

SECTION II

Language in Context

For a long time study of the interplay between language and culture has focused primarily upon the way cultural experience may be reflected in language structure, and conversely, upon the ways the structure of language may condition both perception and behavior. How a language is organized, it is argued, may influence how its speakers organize their experience. Language is perceived as standing between the individual and his environment, acting as a sort of interpretive filter, not just reporting experience but categorizing and defining it.

The subfield within anthropological linguistics most concerned with gaining a better understanding of the differentiating role of language in shaping human perception is so important it has its own name. (Unfortunately, in fact, it has several, including psycholinguistics and sociolinguistics.) Usually, however, it is called ethnolinguistics. It is currently a very hot specialization, one in which the relations between linguistic and sociocultural phenomena overlap so clearly that there is no question about the appropriateness of its place within the field of anthropology.

But the role of language in categorizing experience, conditioning perception, and affecting cultural action has been of interest not only to anthropologists and linguists, but to philosophers such as Henle as well.

Language, Thought, and Culture

Paul Henle

Ordinarily, language is taken for granted. Its fluent and easy use leads to the assumption that it is a transparent medium for the transmission of thought. Because it offers no apparent obstacle to our customary flow of ideas, one assumes that it is a vehicle equally fitted to convey any beliefs. Scientifically, it is assumed to be of interest to linguists and perhaps to psychologists interested in child development or aphasia, but that is all. Such a conception of

Source: From Paul Henle, "Language, Thought, and Culture," *Language, Thought, and Culture,* Ann Arbor. © University of Michigan Press, 1958. Reprinted by permission.

language has been challenged by a number of linguists and anthropologists. Edward Sapir, more than twenty years ago, maintained that:

> The relation between language and experience is often misunderstood. Language is not merely a more or less systematic inventory of the various items of experience which seem relevant to the individual, as is so often naively assumed, but is also a self-contained, creative symbolic organization, which not only refers to experience largely-acquired without its help but actually defines experience for us by reason of its formal completeness and because of our unconscious projection of its implicit expectations into the field of experience.

Sapir added that the force of this claim could be realized only when the relatively similar Indo-European languages were compared with widely differing languages such as those indigenous to Africa and America.

Benjamin Lee Whorf in a series of papers has developed Sapir's claim, maintaining that a language constitutes a sort of logic, a general frame of reference, and so molds the thought of its habitual users. He claimed also that, where a culture and a language have developed together, there are significant relationships between the general aspects of the grammar and the characteristics of the culture taken as a whole. To substantiate these theses, Whorf made a comparison of American Indian languages, notably Hopi, with European languages. Among the latter, he found the differences so insignificant in comparison to the differences from Hopi that he grouped them all together under the general title of SAE (Standard Average European).

If Whorf and his followers are right, the study of language takes on a new importance in the social sciences. Its place in psychology is greatly expanded, and it becomes of primary significance in all studies of culture. It may even provide the focal point about which the social sciences can best be integrated. For this reason we shall devote the present chapter to an examination of the thesis, beginning with a consideration of terms and then proceeding to discussions first of the relation of language to thought and then of the connection between language and culture.

Since the connections which can be established between language, thought, and culture depend in part, of course, on the definitions of the terms involved, it is to this problem that we first turn. Such an analysis is particularly necessary before trying to establish relationships between thought and language. Ordinarily, language is the chief evidence for the existence and character of thought and, if Whorf's claim is to be anything more than a truism, the relevant aspects of the two must be clearly distinguished and kept separate.

We may begin by looking for aspects of language which are clearly separable from thought and which may be compared to it. Vocabulary, meaning by this simply the list of words to be found in the language, would clearly be one such item. Comparing this with the vocabulary of another language one might obtain some idea of the peculiarities of the language in question, or, at least, of the difference in the two vocabularies. These differences might be compared with differences in ideas and opinions commonly expressed in the two languages. Another even more striking characteristic of languages is the mode of inflection, and diverse languages may be compared to see if differences here are connected with differences in what is expressed in the language. Again, the manner of sentence formation is a linguistic element, isolable from the content of a language and comparable with it. In some cases, also, terms in different languages, designating the same phenomena, belong to different word classes, so that, for example, what is represented by a noun in one language may be represented by a verb in another. This again is a concrete difference capable of being compared with the content of the two languages.

In the category which we have generically referred to as thought, perception must be included, as well as what may be called the conceptual organization of experience. Thus Whorf reports that in Shawnee the cleaning of a gun with a ramrod is described by something close to directing "a hollow moving dry spot by means of a tool." This certainly shows a difference in organization—the emphasis in English being on the things, the physical objects, and the emphasis in Shawnee being elsewhere. According to some theories, differences in organization of this sort, if carried far enough, result in differences in philosophies. In any case they would show a difference in thought to be related to differences of language.

This enumeration of elements of language and thought would hardly be controversial. On bringing culture into the problem, however, one is faced with an anthropological controversy as to just what culture includes. We shall not attempt to settle the dispute, but shall merely outline the view which is most useful for comparison with language, without making any claims for this view in any other connection. A good statement of it makes culture "all those historically created designs for living, explicit and implicit, rational, irrational and nonrational, which exist at any given time as potential guides for the behavior of men." From this standpoint, culture constitutes the set of modes of procedure or the guides to living which are dominant in a group. These are thought of not as isolated but as functionally interrelated, clustering together to form certain *themes*, a theme being a higher-level generalization. Generalizations of the lower level are simply those directly based on instances of conduct, constituting patterns of behavior. Generalizations of these patterns constitute themes, each theme containing notions exemplified in a number of patterns of behavior. Themes need not be consistent and as Opler has noticed such themes as "old age is desired and respected" and "all persons must continually validate their positions by participation in activities defined as peculiar to that position" may both be operative in the same culture. Indeed the limitation of one theme by the operation of another conflicting one may be necessary to the survival of the society.

The problem, then, which Whorf poses may be restated a little more explicitly: What is the relationship between the mechanisms of language such as vocabulary, inflection, and sentence formation on the one hand and either perception and organization of experience or the broad patterns of behavior on the other? This question is reasonably specific, except for the sort of relation involved. Obviously, the most desirable and least controversial goal would be simply to set up correlations to show that certain linguistic elements vary, say, with certain aspects of culture. Given the correlations, it would not be necessary to assign causal priority, but there still could be inferences from one side to the other. In dealing with the relationship between vocabulary and the interests of a society there is enough direct evidence to indicate such a correlation, but hardly so with any of the other relationships. In these cases, collateral evidence must enter and, in part, must take the form of showing reason to believe that a correlation would be found if more evidence were available. This prediction of the correlation is made by claiming causal connections between various factors. Even in the case of the relationship between vocabulary and culture, this sort of evidence helps substantiate the evidence of direct correlation. We see every reason to believe, as part of our commonsense psychology, that a people should have words for objects with which they are concerned and that they should lack words for objects with which they have fewer dealings. We are therefore more ready to accept as adequate the evidence which exists for the connection between the two.

To claim a causal relation between language and culture is not, of course, to say which influences the other. Either may be the causal agent, both may be joint effects of a common cause, or there may be mutual causal action. Indeed this latter is to be expected with continuing factors such as language and culture. The connections which we shall investigate in the next section will be largely causal.

With this brief discussion of the factors involved, we may turn to the evidence for relationships. It will be convenient to begin with the evidence for a connection between language and thought and to open the discussion with a consideration of the relationship between vocabulary and perception. Languages differ notoriously in vocabulary, and this difference is generally correlated with a difference in environment. Thus, Whorf notices that Eskimo languages have a variety of words for different kinds of snow where we have only one. Aztec is even poorer than we in this respect, using the same word stem for cold, ice, and snow. Sapir gives detailed evidence over a broader field in claiming that the vocabulary of a language clearly reflects the physical and social environment of a people. Indeed, the complete vocabulary of a language would be "a complex inventory of all the ideas, interests, and occupations that take up the attention of the community. . . ." He notices that among the Nootka of the northwest coast, marine animals are defined and symbolized with precise detail. Some desert people reserve the detailed lexicon for berries and other edible food plants. Similarly, the Paiute, a desert people, speak a language which permits the most detailed description of topographical features, a necessity in a country where complex directions may be required for the location of water holes. Sapir points out that what holds for the physical environment, holds even more clearly for the social. Status systems in various cultures, however complex, and differentiations due to occupations are all mirrored in languages.

So far, the argument merely shows that vocabulary reflects the environment of a people. Since the culture is largely dependent on this environment, especially where technology is relatively undeveloped, we have an argument suggesting at least that vocabulary and general ways of acting are effects of a common cause, so one may be an index to the other.

All this still says nothing concerning perception and would have little to do with it, if perception were merely a matter of recording what is presented. This is not the case, however, and there is abundant evidence to show that perception is influenced by mental set. Such effects of mental set have been summarized by Bruner and Goodman in a now classical paper. They say:

> . . . subjects can be conditioned to see and hear things in much the same way as they can be conditioned to perform such overt acts as knee jerking, eye blinking, or salivating. Pair a sound and a faint image frequently enough, fail to present the image, and the subject sees it anyway when the sound is presented. Any student of suggestion, whether or not he has pursued Bird's exhaustive bibliography of the literature on the subject, knows that. Not perception? Why not? The subject sees what he reports as vividly as he sees the phi-phenomenon.

In addition, they point out, reward and punishment, experience, and social factors may all be of influence. Their own research goes on to show that children overestimate the size of coins, that the amount of overestimation is, in general, dependent upon the value of the coin, that the error is greater with coins than with cardboard discs of the same size, and that it is greater with poor than with rich children. Clearly, as they say, it will not do to consider a perceiver as a "passive recording instrument of rather complex design."

The question then becomes one of whether knowing an item of vocabulary—at least one which has application to sense experience—constitutes a set directed toward perceiving in terms of this word. The existence of such a set would mean noticing those aspects of the environment which pertained to the application of the term and tending to neglect others. Direct evidence on the point is not available, but it seems reasonable to conjecture that there is such a set. There is strong motivation to learn the language of a society on the part of children and newcomers, for only through knowing the language can wants be satisfied and communication be established. Ability to use the words of a language is thus prized, and this desire is reinforced by the discovery that the vocabulary is useful in dealing with the environment. Given the motivation to learn the language it is reasonable to infer a set favoring the application of it and so an influence on perception.

It would seem then to be consistent with what we know of mental set on other grounds to assume that the world appears different to a person using one vocabulary than it would to a person using another. The use of language would call attention to different aspects of the environment in the one case than it would in the other. Numerous illustrations of this sort may be given. The Navaho, for example, possess color terms corresponding roughly to our "white," "red," and "yellow" but none which are equivalent to our "black," "gray," "brown," "blue," and "green." They have two terms corresponding to "black," one denoting the black of darkness, the other the black of such objects as coal. Our "gray" and "brown," however, correspond to a single term in their language and likewise our "blue" and "green." As far as vocabulary is concerned, they divide the spectrum into segments different from ours. It would seem probable that on many occasions of casual perception they would not bother to notice whether an object were brown or gray, and that they would merely avoid discussions as to whether a shade of color in a trying light was blue or green, but they would not even make the distinction.

This example must not be taken as showing that the Navahos are incapable of making color distinctions which are familiar to us. They do not suffer from a peculiar form of color-blindness any more than we do since we lack words for the two sorts of black which they distinguish. The point is rather that their vocabulary tends to let them leave other distinctions unnoticed which we habitually make.

If we are right in claiming an influence of vocabulary on perception, it might be expected that vocabulary would influence other aspects of thought as well. The divisions we make in our experience depend on how we perceive and so would be subject to the same linguistic influence as perception. Once again, one would expect the influence to run in both directions. If, in thinking about the world, one has occasion to use certain ideas, one would expect them to be added to the vocabulary, either directly or through metaphor; this is probably the primary influence. Once the term is in the vocabulary, however, it would constitute an influence both on perception and conception.

Inflections also were listed among the linguistic items which might have an influence on thought. Since grammatical forms are less subject to change than vocabulary, such an influence, if it exists, would be far more pervasive than that of vocabulary. We shall contend that there is an influence and that it is similar to that of vocabulary, influencing perception by calling attention to certain aspects of experience rather than to others.

The way in which inflections most often operate may be illustrated by means of a hypothetical example. Suppose we have a verb-stem, say *A*, and suppose that, at some early stage of the language, *A* is used by itself. At a later stage, let us suppose that it seemed desirable to add tense indicators to the verb, representing, say, past, present, and future. These might be suffixed and might be schematized by *Ax*, *Ay*, and *Az*. Since every situation in which *A* was formerly used was one in which a suffix was applicable, a simplification would naturally suggest itself. The stem form was no longer needed by itself, since one of the suffixed forms would always be appropriate, yet it was easier to pronounce than any of them. It would naturally, therefore, be used in place of one of the suffixed forms with the meaning of that form. Thus, *Ax* might be abbreviated to *A*. Although this would be a convenience in conversation it would have the effect of depriving the language of any word having the old meaning of *A*. This might be no loss, but it would require an increase in thought in order to use the language. No longer could one simply notice that the conditions for the application of the stem word were present and proceed to use it. One would be required to notice in addition which of the suffixes applied. In order to speak of one aspect of experience, it would be necessary to notice—and speak of—another as well. This might be called a *forced observation* induced by inflection. Tense, discussed above, represents only one sort of forced observation, and it is apparent that the use of an English verb requires observations regarding number and person as well.

The use of the term "forced observation" must not be construed to imply that a speaker of a language is conscious of being compelled to notice certain aspects of his environment. Most often he makes these observations naturally, almost unconsciously, and certainly with no feeling of constraint. Nor, of course, is the force actual or physical. A person can use the English vocabulary, disregarding distinctions of tense and person, and, under favorable circumstances, make himself understood. Under usual, and less favorable circumstances, however, he will not be understood and, in any case, he risks ridicule. This is the only external compulsion. Habitual use of the language provides an internal compulsion.

The observations which are forced differ in different languages. Thus Kluckhohn and Leighton comparing English with Navaho say:

> English stops with what from the Navaho point of view is a very vague statement—"I drop it." The Navaho must specify four particulars which the English leaves either unsettled or to inference from context:
>
> 1. The form must make clear whether "it" is definite or just "something."
> 2. The verb stem used will vary depending upon whether the object is round, or long, or fluid, or animate, etc., etc.
> 3. Whether the act is in progress, or just about to start, or just about to stop, or habitually carried on, or repeatedly carried on, must be rigorously specified. . . .
> 4. The extent to which the agent controls the fall must be indicated. . . .

Dorothy Lee has noticed that, in a similar fashion, Wintu requires the indication in suffixes of the evidence on which a statement is based thus forcing an observation. She says:

> He (the Wintu) cannot say simply *the salmon is good*. That part of *is good* which implies the tense (now) and the person (it) further has to contain one of the following implications: (the salmon is good) I see, I taste (or know through some sense other than sight), I infer, I judge, I am told.

Just as is the case with vocabulary, one may claim that the forced observations imposed by inflections constitute a mental set. Because it must be mentioned in speaking, the time of an action is more likely to receive the attention of a user of English than of a user of Wintu. Again, it is easy to make a statement in English without considering the evidence for it. A Wintu might be expected to be more perceptive in this respect. The influence here is similar to that exerted by vocabulary except that it is concentrated on relatively fewer items—those which form the basis of inflection—and so is stronger with regard to these.

Finally, under the heading of language comes the factor of sentence structure. While again one would expect that the primary influence runs from thought and social needs to sentence structure, there may be a reciprocal influence as well.

To take the case of English and the SAE languages generally, there seem to be two dominant forms of sentence: first, what may be called the subject-predicate type of statement, of which "The book is red" may be taken as a paradigm; and second, what may be called the actor-action type, of which "John runs" or "John loves Mary" are typical. In the first type there is no action, merely a quality attributed to a subject, in the second the subject is thought of as taking an action. In either case, however, the subject typically is an enduring object—something recognizable through time. Even when the subject is not an object in this sense, the tendency is to speak of it as if it were. Thus, an automobile mechanic will talk of fixing the timing on a car in much the same terms that he speaks of fixing the tire, even though the timing is simply a relation of events while the tire is an object. One may claim that speaking of fixing the timing in this way is metaphorical, and this may be, but the point is that the metaphor proceeds via the conception of a stable physical object.

This tendency is pervasive in our language. In general, events are spoken of as if they were stable objects, and, in speech at least, much of the fluidity of passing experience seems to be lost. This tendency, as Whorf has noticed, extends even to time itself. We speak of it and even think of it as a substance of indefinite extent. We may isolate a segment of it in the same sense that we may cut a link of sausage, and we may save five minutes in something like the sense that we save a scrap of meat.

Such ways of looking at the world are of importance, not merely in the organization of the details of experience, but also for philosophy, in particular for logic and metaphysics. Classic logic took the subject-predicate form of statement as basic and insisted that any logical manipulations must be confined to this form. Sentences of the form "John loves Mary" had to be twisted until loving Mary was considered a predicate of John. Various arguments were classified and tested in terms of the relations between subject and predicate. While this conception of logic is almost completely rejected at present, there is no doubt that it was a major influence on thought up to the present century.

In metaphysics the notion of subject and predicate appears in a somewhat different form. One of the classic philosophic problems has been that of explaining the integration and organization of our sense-perception. It makes no difference whether one considers sensations given in isolation or presented in Gestalten, the problem still remains of relating the observations of one time with those of another. The classic answer to the problem, already fully developed in Aristotle, is that the universe is composed of *substances* and that everything perceived is an attribute of some substance. Substances or substance—whether there was only one substance in the universe, or many, depended on the philosopher—were thought of as continuing through time and, in some cases, even as lasting forever, and so connecting the perceptions of one time with those of another. Thus the broadest description of the universe according to most of the Western philosophic tradition would be to say that the world consists of substances and their attributes. The parallel between the metaphysical substance, which had, or was modified by, qualities, and the logical subject, which had, or was modified by, predicates, was apparent—so much so that substance was often defined as that which is always subject and never predicate. By the same parallel, attributes corresponded to predicates.

Much of the philosophy of this century has been a polemic against these conceptions. The older logic has been displaced by one which allows a predicate to connect several subjects and in which the whole notion of subject has nothing like its classical importance. In metaphysics, such otherwise divergent writers as Whitehead, Russell, and Bergson have agreed in rejecting the classical formulations of substance. Both the close parallel between substance and subject and the connection between classical logic and grammar have been deprecated. Thus Russell has insisted: " 'Substance,' in a word, is a metaphysical mistake, due to the transference to the world-structure of the structure of sentences composed of a subject and a predicate." Having noticed this connection between SAE language and philosophy, we may turn to the contrast of both of them to the thought and language of the Hopi which Whorf has pointed out in considerable detail. There are five principal points of divergence, and it will be seen that they represent differences either in grammar or in the conception of time. These major linguistic differences occur in the following points: (1) plurality and numeration, (2) nouns of physical quantity, (3) phases of cycles, (4) temporal forms of verbs, and (5) duration, intensity, and tendency. Each of these calls for some discussion.

1. SAE uses plurals and cardinal numbers, not merely for actual aggregates given all at once, but also for aggregates which Whorf calls "imaginary" such as ten days, which cannot be given in one perception. Hopi does not use plurals in this latter case and where we would speak of ten days as an aggregate, the Hopi would say "until the eleventh day" or "after the tenth day."

There is a temptation to dismiss this difference between SAE and Hopi modes of speaking merely as a difference in idiom, having no significance for the underlying thought. If the preference for "ten days" rather than "after the tenth day" were considered alone, this would undoubtedly be the proper explanation. A difference in thought-pattern of the sort that Whorf is trying to show cannot rest on any single instance of linguistic usage, however striking it may be. Only the multiplication of instances makes it less probable that one is faced with a casual difference in manner of speaking and more probable that one is dealing with a difference in the mode of thought. Thus the total weight of evidence which Whorf presents is of importance rather than any single item.

2. Whorf distinguishes two sorts of SAE nouns, individual nouns, denoting bodies with definite outlines (e.g., a tree, a stick, a man) and mass nouns, denoting "homogeneous continua without implied boundaries" (e.g., water, wood, meat, etc.). Where it is desirable to indicate boundaries for a mass noun, we do so by such phrases as "pane of glass," "piece of soap," "cup of coffee," "bag of flour," etc. The prevalence in such phrases of a combination of a term for a container with one for contents paves the way, Whorf thinks, for the philosophic notion of the world as a combination of form and matter. Such a theory he claims is instantly acceptable to common sense: "It is so through linguistic habit. Our language patterns often require us to name a physical thing by a binomial that splits the reference into a formless item plus a form."

Hopi nouns, in contrast, always have an individual sense, even though the boundaries of some objects are vague or indefinite. There is no contrast between individual and mass nouns, hence no reference to container or body-type, and no analogy to provide the dichotomy of form and matter.

3. In SAE terms like "summer," "morning," and "hour" which indicate phases of cycles are treated in much the same way as other nouns. They may serve as grammatical subjects and objects and may be pluralized and used with number-terms in the same way as nouns for physical objects. Even "time" is treated as a mass-noun. Hopi is quite different in this respect. Terms denoting phases of cycles are linguistically distinct from nouns and constitute a separate form-class called temporals. Whorf says: "There is no objectification as a region, an extent, a quantity, of the subjective duration-feeling. Nothing is suggested about time except the perpetual "getting later" of it. And so there is no basis here for a formless item answering to our 'time.'"

4. Our system of tenses divides time into three distinct sections, past, present, and future and thereby aids in the objectification of time which is conceived by analogy to space. There are some difficulties with the scheme, notable in the variety of uses to which the present tense is put, and these, Whorf claims, are responsible for confusions of thought.

Hopi verbs have no tenses but only validity-forms, aspects and modal forms linking clauses. There are three validity-forms: one indicating simply that the speaker is reporting a past or present event, another indicating the speaker's expectation, and a third showing that he is making a statement generally recognized to be true. Aspect forms report differing degrees of duration in respect to the event, and the modal forms, employed only when an utterance includes two verbs or clauses, show relations, including temporal relations, between the two clauses. This grammatical structure, according to Whorf, avoids the objectification of time.

5. SAE languages express duration, intensity, and tendency through spatial metaphors. Thus:

> We express duration by long, short, great, much, quick, slow, etc.; intensity by large, great, much, heavy, light, high, low, sharp, faint, etc.; tendency by more, increase, grow, turn, get, approach, go,

come, rise, fall, stop, smooth, even, rapid, slow, and so on through an almost inexhaustible list of metaphors that we hardly recognize as such since they are virtually the only linguistic media available. The non-metaphorical terms in this field, like early, late, soon, lasting, intense, very, tending are a mere handful, quite inadequate to the needs.

Hopi on the contrary has no such metaphors, but expresses duration, intensity, and tendency literally, without any trace of the spatial figures found in SAE. There is even a special class of terms, the "tensors," constituting a separate part of speech, to express these factors, and it is a very large class of terms. Other linguistic devices are used as well.

Whorf sums up the influence of these linguistic differences on thought by saying that speakers of SAE tend to see the world in terms of things, the things themselves built up of a formless stuff given a determinate form. Non-spatial entities are conceived by spatial metaphor. The Hopi, on the other hand, seem

> . . . to have analyzed reality largely in terms of *events* (or better "eventing"), referred to in two ways, objective and subjective. Objectively, and only if perceptible physical experience, events are expressed mainly as outlines, colors, movements, and other perceptive reports. Subjectively, for both the physical and non-physical, events are considered the expression of invisible intensity-factors, on which depend their stability and persistence, or their fugitiveness and proclivities. It implies that existents do not "become later and later" all in the same way; but some do so by growing, like plants, some by diffusing and vanishing, some by a procession of metamorphoses, some by enduring in one shape till affected by violent forces. In the nature of each existent able to manifest as a definite whole is the power of its own mode of duration; its growth, decline, stability, cyclicity, or creativeness.

A similar connection between grammatical forms and prevalent modes of thought has been noticed in Wintu by Dorothy Lee. Each Wintu verb has two related forms to be used under different circumstances. The first category of stems, she finds, indicates among other things, that the subject participates as a free agent in the activity described by the verb. In contrast to this:

> . . . to this stem of Category II is attached a suffix whose underlying meaning seems to be that of natural necessity and which corresponds to the modal suffixes of Category I. This suffix is used to express, all in one, futurity, causality, potentiality, probability, necessity; to refer to an inevitable future which might, can and must be, in the face of which the individual is helpless. Category II has reference to a state of being in which the individual is not a free agent.

This difference in verb categories is significant as mirroring the prevalent conception of the universe. In part, the Wintu feels he can control his environment; for the rest, it is completely beyond him. This underlying metaphysics is summed up as follows:

> The Wintu has a small sphere wherein he can choose and do, can feel and think and make decisions. Cutting through this and circumscribing it is the world of natural necessity wherein all things that are potential and probable are also inevitable, wherein existence is unknowable and ineffable.

Here again, then, is a parallel between thought about the world in its broadest aspects and major grammatical categories. The aspect of grammar emphasized is different from the aspects prominent in Whorf's investigation, but the major conclusion is the same.

Before leaving this topic of the relation between language and thought, it may be well to notice what we have and have not sought to establish. We have looked for connections and causal relationships between language on the one hand and thought on the other. We have claimed an influence of vocabulary and inflection, acting primarily on perception, and an influence of methods of combination, affecting thought primarily at a more abstract level. In neither case have we claimed, nor would we want to claim, that language is the sole influence or even the primary influence. In neither case have we claimed that the causal relationship does not also run in the other direction as well. Because of the enduring character of language and the fact that a population changes in time, it well may be that language considered in the large is molded by environmental conditions, social organization, and prevalent modes of thought. This would not prevent language being an influence on thought in the development of the individual, and this is all we have claimed. Next, we have made no claim that a study of a language by itself would suffice to show the general character of thought of its users. Some general knowledge of the culture of the speakers would be required, and, indeed, it is doubtful that one could get the necessary intimacy with the language without this broader knowledge of the culture.

Neither, finally, have we argued that there is

any compulsive influence of language upon thought, that language makes impossible all but certain modes of perception and organization of expression. Since perception and the organization of experience are ordinarily manifested only through language, the point being made here may be made in another way. In natural languages, the elements we have been considering—vocabulary, inflection and modes of sentence structure—do not make it impossible to express certain things, they merely make it more difficult to express them. In artificial languages of the sort with which a logician deals, the vocabulary is fixed. The rules for combination of symbols are explicit and the types of manipulation permissible are specified. In such model languages, one can often show that a given expression cannot be stated in the language. The situation is different in natural languages, however. Vocabulary may grow by the addition of new words or metaphorical extension of old ones, syntactical rules may sometimes be sacrificed without loss of intelligibility, and it would be difficult to show that any given expression cannot go into the language. At least it need be no part of the present argument that there are such impossibilities of expression. All we have contended is that certain linguistic features make certain modes of perception more prevalent or more probable, not that they completely rule out others. Similarly, in showing metaphysical implications of language, we have not meant to say that conflicting views would be inexpressible in the language. After all, Whorf, while arguing that the prevailing Hopi metaphysics is radically different from that inherent in the SAE languages, has given his account of the Hopi philosophy in an SAE language. Bergson, whose thought in retrospect appears to have greater affinities to typical Hopi modes of thought than to SAE, was highly successful in expressing himself in an SAE language.

It should be noted parenthetically, that in showing a connection between linguistic forms and metaphysics, we have not, of course, intended any implication concerning the truth of the rival systems. If Aristotle comes closer to the inherent SAE metaphysics than Bergson, it does not follow that he is more—or less—likely to be correct. The fact, which we have just seen, that a metaphysics may run counter to that typical of the language in which it is written shows, moreover, that metaphysical thought cannot be entirely linguistically conditioned.

The contention of this section, then, is that language is one of the factors influencing perception and the general organization of experience. This influence need not be primary or unique or compelling, but neither is it negligible.

In the discussion of the relations of language to culture there is at least the advantage of greater objectivity over the preceding section. There, in discussing the relation of language to thought, it was exceedingly difficult to determine the thought side of the comparison. In discussion of the influence of various linguistic elements on perception, the evidence was indirect and consisted in contending that, from what we know of mental set, we would expect these factors to constitute sets influencing perception. The only likely alternative to this procedure would be some sort of projective technique used to test whether speakers of different languages perceived ambiguous figures in radically different ways. Even here, the perception would be marked by its linguistic formulation, and it would probably be necessary to ask the subject to reproduce what was seen after an interval of time rather than to state what was seen. Even if users of different languages showed markedly different results, there would still be the problem of showing that the difference depends on language rather than on a set induced by other environmental factors. The extreme difficulty of administering such tests, as well as their inconclusive nature, leaves the kind of evidence we have cited as good as any which is likely to become available in the near future.

In discussing the relationship between language and the broader aspects of thought, the situation was somewhat, though not a great deal, better. There was at least direct evidence, a connection between grammatical forms and general characteristics of Western thought and philosophy. Here the grammatical forms could be described with relative assurance, but the evidence as to the dominant trends of Western philosophy, while a very widely held view, is merely an interpretation of an historical record. Similarly, when Whorf contrasted SAE and Hopi characteristic modes of thought, these represented interpretations, and interpretations based on a feeling for a social atmosphere rather than on anything so definite as a written record. While it represents the work of a sensitive observer based on long acquaintance with the people studied, and so constitutes valuable evidence, still, it is the sort of evidence characteristic of the beginning of a science rather than of an advanced stage.

In tracing the connection of language and culture, it is easier to give the evidence in a precise form. As in any scientific work there is, of course, an element of interpretation in generalizing from specific acts to patterns and from patterns to broader themes, but at least there are interpretations of individual acts which are public and verifiable. Though this line of investigation presents great difficulties and lacks the precision which it may later acquire, still it has a more hopeful outlook. Since, moreover, thought is concerned with, and so influenced by, general aspects of culture, this latter investigation of the relation of language to culture may be the key to the problem of the preceding section.

As before, we may consider vocabulary, inflections, and the building of compounds as the elements of language to be compared with patterns of culture. We have noticed before that there is a close relationship between vocabulary and environment, and, since the general patterns of behavior which we have taken as definitive of culture are equally a function of environment, one would expect a correlation with vocabulary. Certainly, one needs words for the objects involved in habitual action and, conversely, words which have no use in discourse are not likely to remain long in any active sort of vocabulary. Because of the very function of language, it may be taken for granted that language and culture are related in this way, and this conclusion would not generally be regarded as controversial.

With regard to the role played by inflections and modes of word-combination, there is, however, more room for dispute. In a discussion of the Hopi language which embraces both these points, Whorf has argued that differences between SAE and Hopi grammar correspond, not merely to differences in modes of thought, but to differences in the cultures as well. These differences center about differences in the conception of time.

In Hopi, we have noticed, days are not totaled by use of cardinal numbers, but are referred to by their order. It is as if, Whorf says, different days were thought of as successive reappearances of the same entity rather than as completely separate and distinct slices of time. Since time is viewed as having this sort of continuity, special importance attached to preparations for what is done at one time might be expected to leave its impress on reappearances of the same time. Preparation constitutes a relatively important part of Hopi life and involves such factors as prayer, practicing, rehearsing, as well as various magic rites and even mere good wishes to a project, to say nothing of the types of preparation considered relevant in SAE. Whorf says:

> Hopi "preparing" activities again show a result of their linguistic thought background in an emphasis on persistence and constant insistent repetition. A sense of the cumulative value of innumerable small momenta is dulled by an objectified, spatialized view of time like ours, enhanced by a way of thinking close to the subjective awareness of duration, of the ceaseless "latering" of events.

And this difference in views of time, as we have seen, he holds to be a direct consequence of the structures of the languages.

In complete contrast to the Hopi treatment of time is the quantified, spatialized view involved in the SAE languages. Whorf finds correlated with this the prevalence of:

> 1. Records, diaries, book-keeping, accounting, mathematics stimulated by accounting;
> 2. Interest in exact sequence, dating, calendars, chronology, clocks, time wages, time graphs, time as used in physics;
> 3. Annals, histories, the historical attitude, interest in the past, archaeology, attitudes of introjection towards past periods, e.g., classicism, romanticism.

Whorf also attributes interest in speed and in saving time to this quantitative treatment of time. Some of the differences between Hopi and SAE cultures, therefore, seem explicable in terms of the differing treatments of time and this, as was argued in the preceding section, depends on differences in the grammatical structures of the languages.

Hoijer, in working with the Navaho, has reached a similar conclusion as to the relation of grammatical categories to culture. He dealt, first of all, with Navaho verb forms and found in them a parallel to general traits of the society. Navaho verbs may be divided into two types, the neuter and the active. The neuter verbs represent states or conditions and show an absence of movement or action. Some represent qualities, such as being blue, or thin, or tall. Active verbs, on the other hand, represent events, actions, and movements. While at first sight the two kinds appear quite different, Hoijer finds in analyzing the types of neuter verbs that each represents a withdrawal of motion of a certain sort. He summarizes his results as follows:

> . . . it would appear that Navaho verb categories center very largely about the reporting of events, or better, "eventings." These eventings are divided into neuters, eventings solidified, as it were, into states of being by virtue of the withdrawal of motion, and actives, eventings in motion. . . .
>
> But this is not all. A careful analysis of the meanings of Navaho verb bases, neuter and active, reveals that eventings themselves are conceived, not abstractly for the most part, but very concretely in terms of the movements of corporeal bodies, or of entities metaphorically linked with corporeal bodies. Movement itself is reported in painstaking detail, even to the extent of classifying as semantically different the movement of one, two, or several bodies, and sometimes distinguishing as well between movements of bodies differentiated by their shape and distribution in space.

Extending the discussion to other aspects of the language, Hoijer finds a similar emphasis on motion and notices a strong cultural parallel. He says:

> To summarize: in three broad speech patterns, illustrated by the conjugation of active verbs, the reporting of actions and events, and the framing of substantive concepts, Navaho emphasized movement and specifies the nature, direction, and status of such movement in considerable detail. Even the neuter category is relatable to the dominant conception of a universe in motion, for, just as some one is reported to have described architecture as frozen music, so the Navaho define position as a resultant of the withdrawal of motion.
>
> Parallels to this semantic theme may be found in almost every aspect of Navaho culture taken as a whole. Even today the Navaho are fundamentally a wandering, nomadic folk, following their flocks from one pasturage to another. Myths and legends reflect this emphasis most markedly, for both Gods and culture heroes move restlessly from one holy place to the next, seeking by their motion to perfect and repair the dynamic flux which is the universe.

Hoijer also finds an additional parallel between the Navaho language and culture, which this time involves a somewhat different aspect of the grammar, the sentence structure. He finds that the actor-action pattern of sentence so common in SAE is foreign to Navaho. A person is associated with an action, rather than being the author or cause of it. Motion and position are treated as being inherent in an object, rather than as being induced by some agent. Hoijer notices how consonant this is with the general Navaho attitude toward nature as reported by Kluckhohn and Leighton. They say that the Navaho does not seek to control nature or believe in doing so; rather, he attempts to influence it, often through songs and ritual. This lack of agency toward nature, as shown in practice, is mirrored in the grammatical construction which does not speak in terms of acting upon an object.

While this evidence adduced by Whorf and Hoijer is certainly striking, there is a question as to just how much it shows. Whorf himself was quite modest in his claims, maintaining that "there are connections but not correlations or diagnostic correspondences between cultural norms and linguistic patterns." Hoijer, however, wishes to go farther and claims that Whorf has understated his case, that more can be made of the correspondence. The attempt to establish correlations would certainly present a program for future investigations, though it is unlikely that more can be claimed for it at present as a general method. Hoijer, as we have just observed, found a striking parallel between the movement expressed in Navaho verb-forms and the general mobility of Navaho life, but it is doubtful that one would be even tempted to generalize and expect such correlations with mobility among all peoples. Certainly, many more studies like Hoijer's are required, extending over a wide range of languages, before much warrant could be given such a generalization. It is worth noticing also that Whorf's study of Hopi does not give verb-forms anything like the prominence that Hoijer gives them. The point would seem to be that every culture may, perhaps, be correlated with some aspect of the language accompanying it, but there is not yet enough evidence to suggest what this aspect may be without actual examination of the case. For the present it is necessary to study both the language and the culture to trace parallels, and so there can be no diagnostic employment of the correlations discovered. Only after many more studies of this sort would it be possible even to suggest which features of a grammar might in general be expected to correlate with a culture. This is not, of course, to condemn the investigations which have been made, but merely to point out that they stand at the beginning of a vast inquiry. More data are required before it is even possible to formulate specific hypotheses; but this is often the case at the start of a new science.

Just as no languages are more primitive than others, it is also true that no dialect of a particular language—whether based on region, social status, or ethnicity—is inferior to any other. All provide equally well for the expression of any idea necessary to their speakers. All are equally valuable as modes for conveying and altering meaning. All are equally effective at categorizing and making logical distinctions. And all are equally "rich" as means of verbal expression.

The solidly supported scientific fact of the fundamental equality of all languages and dialects must be explicitly distinguished from culturally derived criteria for evaluating language; that is, from the greater prestige that is culturally ascribed to the dialect or language of those who enjoy the highest social status. Such judgments are usually based on differences in relative socioeconomic or political power. Colonialist governments in particular and dominant nations in general have consistently asserted the superiority of their languages to those of the subordinate "natives." Similarly, when a society is stratified, the dialect of the high status group invariably carries more prestige and is defined as "better." Those lower down in the social hierarchy are consistently described as speaking more "badly" than those at the top.

An argument against this sort of biased evaluation is provided by such essays as this one by Kochman, which both reveals the richness of a "nonstandard" form of speech and demonstrates the tenacity of the ties that bind language and culture within the component subcultures of a single society.

Toward an Ethnography of Black American Speech Behavior

Thomas Kochman

In the black idiom of Chicago and elsewhere, there are several words that refer to talking; *rapping, shucking, jiving, running it down, gripping, copping a plea, signifying,* and *sounding*. Led by the assumption that these terms, as used by the speakers, referred to different kinds of verbal behavior, this writer has attempted to discover which features of form, style, and function distinguish one type of talk from the other. In this pursuit, we would hope to be able to identify the variable threads of the communication situation: speaker, setting and audience, and how they influence the use of language within the social context of the black community. We also expect that some light would be shed on the black perspective behind a speech event, on those orientating values and attitudes of the speaker that cause him to behave or perform in one way as opposed to another.

The guidelines and descriptive framework for the type of approach used here have been articulated most ably by Hymes in his introduction to the publication *The Ethnography of Communication* (Gumperz and Hymes 1964:2ff.), from which I quote:

> In short, "ethnography of communication" implies two characteristics that an adequate approach to the problems of language which engage anthropologists must have. Firstly, such an approach cannot simply take results from linguistics, psychology, sociology, ethnology, as given, and seek to correlate them, however partially useful such work is. It must call attention to the need for fresh kinds of data, to the need to investigate directly the use of language in contexts of situation so as to discern patterns proper to speech activity, patterns which escape separate studies of grammar, of personality, of religion, of kinship and the like, each abstracting from the patterning of speech activity as such into some other frame of reference. Secondly, such an approach cannot take linguistic form, a given code, or speech

Source: Reprinted with permission of the author and Macmillan Publishing Co., Inc., from *Afro-American Anthropology* edited by Norman E. Whitten, Jr., and John F. Szwed.

itself, as frame of reference. It must take as context a community, investigating its communicative habits as a whole, so that any given use of channel and code takes its place as but part of the resources upon which the members of the community draw.

It is not that linguistics does not have a vital role. Well analyzed linguistic materials are indispensable, and the logic of linguistic methodology is a principal influence in the ethnographic perspective of the approach. It is rather that it is not linguistics, but ethnography—not language, but communication—which must provide the frame of reference within which the place of language in culture and society is to be described.

The following description and analysis is developed from information supplied mainly by blacks living within the inner city of Chicago. Their knowledge of the above terms, their ability to recognize and categorize the language behavior of others (e.g., "Man, stop shucking!"), and on occasion, to give examples themselves, established them as reliable informants. Although a general attempt has been made here to illustrate the different types of language behavior from field sources, I have had, on occasion, to rely on published material to provide better examples, such as the writings of Malcolm X, Robert Conot, Iceberg Slim, and others. Each example cited from these authors, however, is regarded as authentic by my informants. In my own attempts at classification and analysis I have sought confirmation from the same group.

Rapping, while used synonymously to mean ordinary conversation, is distinctively a fluent and lively way of talking which is always characterized by a high degree of personal narration, a colorful rundown of some past event. A recorded example of this type of rap follows, an answer from a Chicago gang member to a youth worker who asked how his group became organized.

Now I'm goin tell you how the jive really started. I'm goin tell you how the club got this big. 'Bout 1956 there used to be a time when the Jackson Park show was open and the Stony show was open. Sixty-six street, Jeff, Gene, all of 'em, little bitty dudes, little bitty. . . . Gene wasn't with 'em then. Gene was cribbin (living) over here. Jeff, all of 'em, real little bitty dudes, you dig? All of us were little.

Sixty-six (the gang on sixty sixth street), they wouldn't allow us in the Jackson Park show. That was when the parky (?) was headin it. Everybody say, If we want to go to the show, we go! One day, who was it? Carl Robinson. He went up to the show . . . and Jeff fired on him. He came back and all this was swelled up 'bout yay big, you know. He come back over to the hood (neighborhood). He told (name unclear) and them dudes went up there. That was when mostly all the main sixty-six boys was over here like Bett Riley. All of 'em was over here. People that quit gang-bangin [fighting, especially as a group], Marvell Gates, people like that.

They went on up there, John, Roy and Skeeter went in there. And they start humbuggin (fighting) in there. That's how it all started. Sixty-six found out they couldn't beat us, at *that* time. They couldn't *whup* seven-o (70). Am I right Leroy? You was cribbin over here then. Am I right? We were dynamite! Used to be a time, you ain't have a passport, Man, you couldn't walk through here. And if didn't nobody know you it was worse than that. . . .

Rapping to a woman is a colorful way of "asking for some pussy." "One needs to throw a lively rap when he is 'putting the make' on a broad" (Horton 1967:6).

According to one informant the woman is usually someone he had seen or just met, looks good, and might be willing to have sexual intercourse with him. My informant remarked that the term would not be descriptive of talk between a couple "who have had a relationship over any length of time." Rapping, then, is used by the speaker at the beginning of a relationship to create a favorable impression and be persuasive at the same time. The man who has the reputation for excelling at this is the pimp, or mack man. Both terms describe a person of considerable status in the street hierarchy, who, by his lively and persuasive rapping (*macking* is also used in this context), has acquired a stable of girls to hustle for him and give him money. For most street men and many teenagers he is the model whom they try to emulate. Thus, within the community you have a pimp walk, pimp style boots and clothes, and perhaps most of all "pimp talk." A colorful literary example of a telephone rap, which one of my informants regards as extreme, but agrees that it illustrates the language, style, and technique of rapping, is set forth in Iceberg Slim's book *Pimp: The Story of My Life* (© 1967 Holloway House, Los Angeles; used by permission), p. 179. "Blood" is rapping to an ex-whore named Christine in an effort to trap her into his stable.

Now try to control yourself baby. I'm the tall stud with the dreamy bedroom eyes across the hall in four-twenty. I'm the guy with the pretty towel wrapped around his sexy hips. I got the same hips on now that you x-rayed. Remember that hump of sugar your peepers feasted on?

She said, "Maybe, but you shouldn't call me. I don't want an incident. What do you want? A lady doesn't accept phone calls from strangers."

I said, "A million dollars and a trip to the moon with a bored, trapped, beautiful bitch, you dig? I'm no stranger. I've been popping the elastic in your panties ever since you saw me in the hall. . . ."

Field examples of this kind of rapping were difficult to obtain primarily because talk of this nature generally occurs in private, and when occurring in public places such as parties and taverns, it is carried on in an undertone. However, the first line of a rap, which might be regarded as introductory, is often overheard. What follows are several such lines collected by two of my students in and around the south and west side of Chicago:

Say pretty, I kin tell you need lovin' by the way you wiggle your ass when you walk—and I'm jus' the guy what' kin put out yo' fire.

Let me rock you mamma, I kin satisfy your soul.

Say, baby, give me the key to your pad. I want to play with your cat.

Baby, you're fine enough to make me spend my rent money.

Baby, I sho' dig your mellow action.

Rapping between men and women often is competitive and leads to a lively repartee, with the woman becoming as adept as the men. An example follows:

A man coming from the bathroom forgot to zip his pants. An unescorted party of women kept watching him and laughing among themselves. The man's friends "hip" [inform] him to what's going on. He approaches one woman—"Hey baby, did you see that big black Cadillac with the full tires ready to roll in action just for you?" She answers—"No motherfucker, but I saw a little gray Volkswagen with two flat tires."

Everybody laughs. His rap was *capped* (excelled, topped).

When "whupping the game" on a "trick" or "lame" (trying to get goods or services from someone who looks like he can be swindled), rapping is often descriptive of the highly stylized verbal part of the maneuver. In well established "con games" the verbal component is carefully prepared and used with great skill in directing the course of the transaction. An excellent illustration of this kind of "rap" came from an adept hustler who was playing the "murphy" game on a white trick. The maneuvers in the "murphy" game are designed to get the *trick* to give his money to the hustler, who in this instance poses as a "steerer" (one who directs or steers customers to a brothel), to keep the whore from stealing it. The hustler then skips with the money (Iceberg Slim 1967:38).

Look Buddy, I know a fabulous house not more than two blocks away. Brother you ain't never seen more beautiful, freakier broads than are in that house. One of them, the prettiest one, can do more with a swipe than a monkey can with a banana. She's like a rubber doll; she can take a hundred positions.

At this point the sucker is wild to get to this place of pure joy. He entreats the con player to take him there, not just direct him to it.

The "murphy" player will prat him (pretend rejection) to enhance his desire. He will say, "Man, don't be offended, but Aunt Kate, that runs the house don't have nothing but highclass white men coming to her place. . . . you know, doctors, lawyers, big-shot politicians. You look like a clean-cut white man, but you ain't in that league are you?

After a few more exchanges of the "murphy" dialogue, "the mark is separated from his scratch."

An analysis of rapping indicates a number of things. For instance, it is revealing that one raps *to* rather than *with* a person, supporting the impression that rapping is to be regarded more as a performance than a verbal exchange. As with other performances, rapping projects the personality, physical appearance, and style of the performer. In each of the examples given above, in greater or lesser degree, the intrusive "I" of the speaker was instrumental in contributing to the total impression of the rap.

The relative degree of the personality-style component of rapping is generally highest when "asking for some pussy" (rapping 2) and lower when "whupping the game" on someone (rapping 3) or "running something down" (rapping 1). In each instance, however, the personality-style component is higher than any other in producing the total effect on the listener.

In asking "for some pussy," for example, where personality and style might be projected through non-verbal means (stance, clothing, walking, looking), one can speak of a "silent rap" where the woman is won without the use of words, or rather, with the words being implied that would generally accompany the non-verbal components.

As a lively way of "running it down" the verbal element consists of two parts: the personality-style component and the information component. Someone *reading* my example of the gang member's narration might get the impression that the information component would be more influential in directing the audience response—that the youth worker would say "So that's how the gang got so big," in which case he would be responding to the information component, instead of saying "Man, that gang member is *bad* (strong, brave)," in which instance he would be responding to the personality-style component of the rap. However, if the reader would *listen* to the gang member on tape or could have been present (*watching-listening*) when the gang member spoke, he more likely would have reacted more to the personality-style component, as my informants did.

Supporting this hypothesis is the fact that in attendance with the youth worker were members of the gang who *already knew* how the gang got started (e.g., "Am I right, Leroy? You was cribbin over there then"), and for whom the information component by itself would have little interest. Their attention was held by the *way* the information was presented—i.e., directed toward the personality-style component.

The verbal element in "whupping the game" on someone, in the above illustration, was an integral part of an overall deception in which the information component and the personality-style component were skillfully manipulated to control the "trick's" response. But again, greater weight must be given to the personality-style component. In the "murphy game," for example, it was this element which got the trick to *trust* the hustler and to leave his money with him for "safekeeping."

The function of rapping in each of the forms discussed above is *expressive*. By this I mean that the speaker raps to project his personality onto the scene or to evoke a generally favorable response from another person or group. In addition, when rapping is used to "ask for some pussy" (rapping 2) or to "whup the game" on someone (rapping 3), its function is *directive*. By this I mean that rapping here becomes the instrument used to manipulate and control people to get them to give up or do something. The difference between rapping to a *fox* (pretty girl) for the purpose of "getting inside her pants" and rapping to a *lame* to get something from him is operational rather than functional. The latter rap contains a concealed motivation whereas the former does not. A statement made by one of my high school informants illustrates this distinction. "If I wanted something from a guy I would try to *trick* him out of it. If I wanted something from a girl I would try to *talk* her out of it (emphasis mine).

Shucking, shucking it, shucking and jiving, S-ing and J-ing or just *jiving,* are terms that refer to one form of language behavior practiced by the black when interacting with "the Man" (the white man, the establishment, or *any* authority figure), and to another form of language behavior practiced by blacks when interacting with each other on the peer group level.

When referring to the black's dealings with the white man and the power structure, the above terms are descriptive of the talk and accompanying physical movements of the black that are appropriate to some momentary guise, posture, or facade.

Originally in the South, and later in the North, the black learned that American society had assigned to him a restrictive role and status. Among whites his behavior had to conform to this imposed station and he was constantly reminded to "keep his place." He learned that before white people it was not acceptable to show feelings of indignation, frustration, discontent, pride, ambition, or desire; that real feelings had to be concealed behind a mask of innocence, ignorance, childishness, obedience, humility, and deference. The terms used by the black to describe the role he played before white folks in the South was "tomming" or "jeffing." Failure to accommodate the white southerner in this respect was almost certain to invite psychological and often physical brutality. The following description by black psychiatrist Alvin F. Poussaint (1967:53) is typical and revealing:

> Once last year as I was leaving my office in Jackson, Miss., with my Negro secretary, a white policeman yelled, "Hey, boy! Come here!" Somewhat bothered, I retorted: "I'm no boy!" He then rushed at me, inflamed and stood towering over me, snorting "What d'ja say, boy?" Quickly he frisked me and demanded "What's your name, boy?" Frightened, I replied, "Dr. Poussaint, I'm a physician." He angrily chuckled and hissed, "What's your first name, boy?" When I hesitated he assumed a threatening stance and clenched his fists. As my heart palpitated, I muttered in profound humiliation, "Alvin."
>
> He continued his psychological brutality, bellowing, "Alvin, the next time I call you, you come right away, you hear? You hear?" I hesitated. "You hear me, boy?" My voice trembling with helplessness, but *following my instincts of self-preservation,* I murmured, "Yes, sir." *Now fully satisfied that I had performed and acquiesced to my "boy" status,* he dis-

missed me with, "Now boy, go on and get out of here or next time we'll take you for a little ride down to the station house! (emphasis mine)."

In northern cities the black encountered authority figures equivalent to the southern "crackers": policemen, judges, probation officers, truant officers, teachers, and "Mr. Charlies" (bosses), and soon learned that the way to get by and avoid difficulty was to *shuck*. Thus, he learned to accommodate "the Man," to use the total orchestration of speech, intonation, gesture, and facial expression to produce whatever appearance would be acceptable. It was a technique and ability that was developed from fear, a respect for power, and a will to survive. This type of accommodation is exemplified by the "Yes sir, Mr. Charlie," or "Anything you say, Mr. Charlie," "Uncle Tom" type "Negro" of the North. The language and behavior of accommodation was the prototype out of which other slightly modified forms of shucking evolved.

Through accommodation, many blacks became adept at concealing and controlling their emotions and at assuming a variety of postures. They became competent actors in the process. Many developed a keen perception of what affected, motivated, appeased, or satisfied the authority figures with whom they came into contact. What became an accomplished and effective coping mechanism for many blacks to "stay out of trouble" became for others a useful artifice for avoiding arrest or "getting out of trouble" when apprehended. *Shucking it* with a judge, for example, would be to feign repentance in the hope of receiving a lighter or suspended sentence, with a probation officer to give the impression of being serious and responsible so that if you violate probation, you would not be sent back to jail. Robert Conot reports an example of the latter in his book (1967:333):

> Joe was found guilty of possession of narcotics. But he did an excellent job of shucking it with the probation officer.

The probation officer interceded for Joe with the judge as follows:

> His own attitude toward the present offense appears to be serious and responsible and it is believed that the defendant is an excellent subject for probation.

Some field illustrations of *shucking* to get out of trouble after having been caught come from some seventh grade children from an inner city school in Chicago. The children were asked to "talk their way out of" a troublesome situation. Examples of the situation and their impromptu responses follow:

> **Situation:** You're cursing at this old man and your mother comes walking down the stairs. She hears you. Response to "talk your way out of this," "I'd tell her that I was studying a scene in school for a play."
>
> **Situation:** What if you were in a store and were stealing something and the manager caught you. Responses: "I would tell him that I was used to putting things in my pocket and then going to pay for them and show the cashier."
> "I'd tell him that some of my friends was outside and they wanted some candy so I was goin to put it in my pocket to see if it would fit before I bought it."
> "I would start stuttering. Then I would say, 'Oh, Oh, I forgot. Here the money is.' "
>
> **Situation:** What do you do when you ditch school and you go to the beach and a truant officer walks up and says, "Are you having fun?" and you say, "Yeah," and you don't know he is a truant officer and then he says, "I'm a truant officer, what are you doing out of school?" Responses: "I'd tell him that I had been expelled from school, that I wasn't supposed to go back to school for seven days."
> "I'd tell him that I had to go to the doctor to get a checkup and that my mother said I might as well stay out of school the whole day and so I came over here."
>
> **Situation:** You're at the beach and they've got posted signs all over the beach and floating on the water and you go past the swimming mark and the sign says "Don't go past the mark!" How do you talk your way out of this to the lifeguard? Responses: "I'd tell him that I was having so much fun in the water that I didn't pay attention to the sign."
> "I'd say that I was swimming under water and when I came back up I was behind the sign."

One literary and one field example of shucking to avoid arrest follow. The literary example of shucking comes from Iceberg Slim's autobiography, already cited above (1967:294). Iceberg, a pimp, shucks before "two red-faced Swede rollers (detectives)" who catch him in a motel room with his whore. My underlining identifies which elements of the passage constitute the shuck.

> I put my shaking hands into the pajama pockets. . . . *I hoped I was keeping the fear out of my face. I gave them a wide toothy smile.* They came in and stood in the middle of the room. Their eyes were racing about the room. Stacy was open mouthed in the bed.

I said, *"Yes gentlemen, what can I do for you?"* Lanky said, "We wanta see your I. D."

I went to the closet and got the phony John Cato Fredrickson I. D. I put it in his palm. I felt cold sweat running down my back. They looked at it, then looked at each other.

Lanky said, "You are in violation of the law. You signed the motel register improperly. Why didn't you sign your full name? What are you trying to hide? What are you doing here in town? It says here you're a dancer. We don't have a club in town that books entertainers."

I said, *"Officers, my professional name is Johnny Cato. I've got nothing to hide. My full name had always been too long for the marquees. I've fallen into the habit of using the shorter version. My legs went out last year. I don't dance anymore. My wife and I decided to go into business. We are making a tour of this part of the country. We think that in your town we've found the ideal site for a southern fried chicken shack. My wife has a secret recipe that should make us rich here."*

The following example from the field was related to me by one of my colleagues. One Negro gang member was coming down the stairway from the club room with seven guns on him and encountered some policemen coming up the same stairs. If they stopped and frisked him, he and others would have been arrested. A paraphrase of his shuck follows: "Man, I gotta get away from up there. There's gonna be some trouble and I don't want no part of it." This shuck worked on the minds of the policemen. It anticipated their questions as to why he was leaving the club room, and why he would be in a hurry. He also gave *them* a reason for wanting to get up to the room fast.

It ought to be mentioned at this point that there was not uniform agreement among my informants in characterizing the above examples as shucking. One informant used shucking only in the sense in which it is used among the black peer group—viz., bull-shitting—and characterized the above examples as *jiving* or *whupping game*. Others, however, identified the above examples as shucking and reserved *jiving* and *whupping game* for more offensive maneuvers. In fact, one of the apparent criterial features of shucking is that the posture of the black when interacting with members of the establishment be a *defensive* one. Some of my informants, for example, regarded the example of a domestic who changed into older clothing than she could afford before going to work in a white household as shucking, provided that she were doing it to keep her job. On the other hand, if she would be doing it to get a raise in pay, they regarded the example as *whupping the game*. Since the same guise and set of maneuvers are brought into play in working on the mind and feeling of the domestic's boss, the difference would seem to be whether the reason behind the pose were to protect oneself or to gain some advantage. Since this distinction is not always so clearly drawn, opinions are often divided. The following example is clearly ambiguous in this respect. Frederick Douglass (1968:57), in telling of how he taught himself to read, would challenge a white boy with whom he was playing by saying that he could write as well as the white boy, whereupon he would write down all the letters he knew. The white boy would then write down more letters than Douglass did. In this way, Douglass eventually learned all the letters of the alphabet. Some of my informants regarded the example as whupping game. Others regarded it as shucking. The former were perhaps focusing on the maneuver rather than the language used. The latter may have felt that any maneuvers designed to learn to read were justifiably defensive. One of my informants said Douglass was "shucking *in order to* whup the game." This latter response seems to be the most revealing. Just as one can *rap* to whup the game on someone, so one can *shuck* or *jive* for the same purpose—i.e., assume a guise or posture or perform some action in a certain way that is designed to work on someone's mind to get him to give up something. The following examples from Malcolm X (1965:87) illustrate the use of *shucking* and *jiving* in this context, though *jive* is the term used. Today, *whupping game* might also be the term used to describe the operation.

Whites who came at night got a better reception; the several Harlem nightclubs they patronized were geared to entertain and *jive* (flatter, cajole) the night white crowd to get their money.

The maneuvers involved here are clearly designed to obtain some benefit or advantage.

Freddie got on the stand and went to work on his own shoes. Brush, liquid polish, brush, paste wax, shine rag, lacquer sole dressing . . . step by step, Freddie showed me what to do.

"But you got to get a whole lot faster. You can't waste time!" Freddie showed me how fast on my own shoes. Then because business was tapering off, he had time to give me a demonstration of how to make the shine rag pop like a firecracker. "Dig the action?"

he asked. He did it in slow motion. I got down and tried it on his shoes. I had the principle of it. "Just got to do it faster," Freddie said. *"It's a jive noise, that's all. Cats tip better, they figure you're knocking yourself out!"* (Malcolm X 1965:48, emphasis mine).

I was involved in a field example in which an eight-year-old boy whupped the game on me as follows:

My colleague and I were sitting in a room listening to a tape. The door to the room was open and outside was a soda machine. Two boys came up in the elevator, stopped at the soda machine, and then came into the room and asked: "Do you have a dime for two nickels?" Presumably, the soda machine would not accept nickels. I took out the change in my pocket, found a dime and gave it to the boy for two nickels. After accepting the dime, he looked at the change in my hand and asked, "Can I have two cents? I need carfare to get home." I gave him the two cents.

At first I assumed the verbal component of the maneuver was the rather weak, transparently false reason for wanting the two cents. Actually, as was pointed out to me later, the maneuver began with the first question, which was designed to get me to show my money. He could then ask me for something that he knew I had, making my refusal more difficult. He apparently felt that the reason need not be more than plausible because the amount he wanted was small. Were the amount larger, he would no doubt have elaborated on the verbal element of the game. The form of the verbal element could be directed toward *rapping* or *shucking and jiving*. If he were to rap, the eight-year-old might say, "Man, you know a cat needs to have a little bread to keep the girls in line." Were he to shuck and jive he might make the reason for needing the money more compelling: look hungry, or something similar.

The function of shucking and jiving as it refers to transactions involving confrontation between blacks and "the Man" is both expressive and directive. It is language behavior designed to work on the mind and emotions of the authority figure to get him to feel a certain way or give up something that will be to the other's advantage. When viewed in its entirety, shucking must be regarded as a performance. Words and gestures become the instruments for promoting a certain image, or posture. In the absence of words, shucking would be descriptive of the *actions* which constitute the deception, as in the above example from Malcolm X, where the movement of the shine rag in creating the "jive noise" was the deceptive element. Similarly, in another example, a seventh grade boy recognized the value of stuttering before saying, "Oh, I forgot. Here the money is," knowing that stuttering would be an invaluable aid in presenting a picture of innocent intent. Iceberg showed a "toothy smile" which said to the detective, "I'm glad to see you" and "Would I be glad to see you if I had something to hide?" When the maneuvers seem to be defensive, most of my informants regarded the language behavior as shucking. When the maneuvers were offensive, my informants tended to regard the behavior as "whupping the game." The difference in perception is culturally significant.

Also significant is the fact that the first form of shucking which I have described above, which developed out of accommodation, is becoming less frequently used today by many blacks, as a result of a new found self-assertiveness and pride, challenging the system "that is so brutally and unstintingly suppressive of self-assertion" (Poussaint 1967:52). The willingness on the part of many blacks to accept the psychological and physical brutality and general social consequences of not "keeping one's place" is indicative of the changing self-concept of the black man. Ironically, the shocked reaction of the white power structure to the present militancy of the black is partly due to the fact that the black has been so successful at "putting whitey on" via shucking in the past—i.e., compelling a belief in whatever posture the black chose to assume. The extent to which this attitude has penetrated the black community can be seen from a conversation I recently had with a shoe shine attendant at O'Hare airport in Chicago.

I was having my shoes shined and the black attendant was using a polishing machine instead of the rag that was generally used in the past. I asked whether the machine made his work any easier. He did not answer me until about ten seconds had passed and then responded in a loud voice that he "never had a job that was easy, that he would give me one hundred dollars for any *easy* job I could offer him, that the machine made his job 'faster' but not 'easier.'" I was startled at the response because it was so unexpected and I realized that here was a new "breed of cat" who was not going to *shuck* for a big tip or ingratiate himself with "whitey" anymore. A few years ago his response would have been different.

The contrast between this "shoe-shine" scene and the one illustrated earlier from Malcolm X's autobiography, when "shucking whitey" was the common practice, is striking.

Shucking, jiving, shucking and jiving, or *S-ing and J-ing,* when referring to language behavior practiced by blacks when interacting with one another on the peer group level, is descriptive of the talk and gestures that are appropriate to "putting someone on" by creating a false impression, conveying false information, and the like. The terms seem to cover a range from simply telling a lie, to bull-shitting, to subtly playing with someone's mind. An important difference between this form of shucking and that described earlier is that the same talk and gestures that are deceptive to "the Man" are often transparent to those members of one's own group who are able practitioners at shucking themselves. As Robert Conot has pointed out (1967:161), "The Negro who often fools the white officer by 'shucking it' is much less likely to be successful with another Negro. . . ." Also, S-ing and J-ing within the group often has play overtones in which the person being "put on" is aware of the attempts being made and goes along with it for the enjoyment of it or in appreciation of the style involved. As example from Iceberg Slim illustrates this latter point (1967:162):

> He said, "Ain't you the little shit ball I chased outta the Roost?"
>
> I said, "Yeah, I'm one and the same. I want to beg your pardon for making you salty (angry) that night. Maybe I coulda gotten a pass if I had told you I'm your pal's nephew. I ain't got no sense, Mr. Jones. I took after my idiot father."

Mr. Jones, perceiving Iceberg's shuck, says,

> "Top, this punk ain't hopeless. He's silly as a bitch grinning all the time, but dig how he butters the con to keep his balls outta the fire."

Other citations showing the use of *shucking* and *jiving* to mean simply *lying* follow:

> It was a *jive* (false) tip but there were a lot of cats up there on humbles (framed up charges) (Brown 1965:142).
>
> How would you like to have half a "G" ($500) in your slide (pocket)?
>
> I said, "All right, give me the poison and take me to the baby."
>
> He said, "I ain't *shucking* (lying). It's cream-puff work" (Iceberg Slim 1967:68).

Running it down is the term used by ghetto dwellers when they intend to communicate information, either in the form of an explanation, narrative, giving advice, and the like. The information component in the field example cited under rapping (1) would constitute the "run down." In the following literary example, Sweet Mac is "running this Edith broad down" to his friends (King 1965:24):

> Edith is the "saved" broad who can't marry out of her religion . . . or do anything else out of her religion for that matter, especially what I wanted her to do. A bogue religion, man! So dig, for the last couple weeks I been quoting the Good Book and all that stuff to her; telling her I am now saved myself, you dig.

The following citation from Claude Brown (1965:390) uses the term with the additional sense of giving advice:

> If I saw him (Claude's brother) hanging out with cats I knew were weak, who might be using drugs sooner or later, I'd *run it down* to him.

Iceberg Slim (1967:79) asks a bartender regarding a prospective whore:

> Sugar, *run her down* to me. Is the bitch qualified? Is she a whore? Does she have a man?

It seems clear that running it down has simply an informative function, telling somebody something that he doesn't already know.

Gripping is of fairly recent vintage, used by black high school students in Chicago to refer to the talk and facial expression that accompanies a *partial* loss of face or self-possession, or displaying of fear. Its appearance alongside *copping a plea,* which refers to a total loss of face, in which one begs one's adversary for mercy, is a significant new perception. Linking it with the street code which acclaims the ability to "look tough and inviolate, fearless, secure, 'cool,'" (Horton 1967:11) suggests that even the slightest weakening of this posture will be held up to ridicule and contempt. There are always contemptuous overtones attached to the use of the term when applied to others' behavior. One is tempted to link it further with the degree of violence and level of toughness that is required to survive on the street. The intensity of both seems to be increasing. As one of my informants noted, "Today, you're *lucky* if you end up in the hospital" (i.e., are not killed).

Both *gripping* and *copping a plea* refer to behavior that stems from fear and a respect for superior power. An example of gripping comes from the record *Street and Gangland Rhythms* (Band 4, Dumb boy). Lennie meets Calvin and asks him what happened to his lip. Calvin tells Lennie that a boy named Pierre hit him for copying off him in school. Lennie, pretending to be Calvin's brother, goes to confront Pierre. Their dialogue follows:

Lennie: "Hey you! What you hit my little brother for?"
Pierre: "Did he tell you what happen man?"
Lennie: "Yeah, he told me what happen."
Pierre: "But you . . . but you . . . but you should tell your people to teach him to go to school, man. (Pause) I . . . I know . . . I know I didn't have a right to hit him."

Pierre, anticipating a fight with Lennie if he continued to justify his hitting of Calvin, tried to avoid it by "gripping" with the last line.

Copping a plea, originally used to mean "to plead guilty to a lesser charge to save the state the cost of a trial," (Wentworth and Flexner 1960:123) (with the hope of receiving a lesser or suspended sentence), but is now generally used to mean "to beg, plead for mercy," as in the example "Please cop, don't hit me. I give" (*Street and Gangland Rhythms,* Band 1, Gang fight). This change of meaning can be seen from its use by Piri Thomas (1967:316) in *Down These Mean Streets.*

The night before my hearing, I decided to make a prayer. It had to be on my knees, cause if I was gonna *cop a plea* to God, I couldn't play it cheap.

For the original meaning, Thomas (1967:245) uses "deal for a lower plea."

I was three or four months in the Tombs, waiting for a trial, going to court, waiting for adjournments, trying to *deal for a lower plea,* and what not.

The function of gripping and copping a plea is obviously expressive. One evinces noticeable feelings of fear and insecurity which result in a loss of status among one's peers. At the same time one may arouse in one's adversary feelings of contempt.

An interesting point to consider with respect to copping a plea is whether the superficial features of the form may be borrowed to mitigate one's punishment, in which case it would have the same directive function as shucking, and would be used to arouse feelings of pity, mercy, and the like. The question whether one can arouse such feelings among one's street peers by copping a plea is unclear. In the example cited above from the record *Street and Gangland Rhythms,* which records the improvisations of eleven- and twelve-year-old boys, one of the boys convincingly *acts out* the form of language behavior, which was identified by all my informants as "copping a plea" with the police officer: "Please cop, don't hit me. I give." In this example it was clearly an artifice with a directive function and here we have the familiar dynamic opposition of black vs. authority figure discussed under shucking.

"Signifying" is the term used to describe the language behavior that, as Abrahams has defined it, attempts to "imply, goad, beg, boast by indirect verbal or gestural means" (1964:267). In Chicago it is also used as a synonym to describe a form of language behavior which is more generally known as "sounding" elsewhere and will be discussed under the latter heading below.

Some excellent examples of signifying as well as of other forms of language behavior discussed above come from the well known "toast" (narrative form) "The signifying monkey and the lion" which was collected by Abrahams from black street corner bards in Philadelphia. In the above toast the monkey is trying to get the lion involved in a fight with the elephant (Abrahams 1964:150ff.):

Now the lion came through the jungle one peaceful day,
When the signifying monkey stopped him, and that is what he started to say:
He said, "Mr. Lion," he said, "A bad-assed motherfucker down your way,"
He said, "Yeah! The way he talks about your folks is a certain shame.
"I've even heard him curse when he mentioned your grandmother's name."
The lion's tail shot back like a forty-four
When he went down that jungle in all uproar.

Thus the monkey has goaded the lion into a fight with the elephant by "signifying," indicating that the elephant has been "sounding on" (insulting) the lion. When the lion comes back, thoroughly beaten up, the monkey again "signifies" by making fun of the lion:

. . . a lion came back through the jungle more dead than alive,

When the monkey started some more of that signifying jive.
He said, "Damn, Mr. Lion, you went through here yesterday, the jungle rung.
"Now you come back today, damn near hung."

The monkey, of course, is delivering this taunt from a safe distance away on the limb of a tree when his foot slips and he falls to the ground, at which point

Like a bolt of lightning, a stripe of white heat,
The lion was on the monkey with all four feet.

In desperation the monkey quickly resorts to "copping a plea":

The monkey looked up with a tear in his eyes.
He said, "Please, Mr. Lion, I apologize."

His "plea," however, fails to move the lion to any show of pity or mercy so the monkey tries another verbal ruse: "shucking:"

He said, "You lemme get my head out of the sand
Ass out of the grass, I'll fight you like a natural man."

In this he is more successful as

The lion jumped back and squared for a fight.
The motherfucking monkey jumped clear out of sight.

A safe distance away again, the monkey returns to "signifying":

He said, "Yeah, you had me down, you had me at last.
But you left me free, now you can still kiss my ass."

The above example illustrates the methods of provocation, goading, and taunting as artfully practiced by the signifier. Interestingly, when the *function* of signifying is *directive*, the *tactic* which is employed is one of *indirection*—i.e., the signifier reports or repeats what someone else has said about the listener; the "report" is couched in plausible language designed to compel belief and arouse feelings of anger and hostility. There is also the implication that if the listener fails to do anything about it—what has to be "done" is usually quite clear—his status will be seriously compromised. Thus the lion is compelled to vindicate the honor of his family by fighting or else leave the impression that he is afraid, and that he is not "king" of the jungle. When used to direct action, "signifying" is like "shucking" in also being deceptive and subtle in approach and depending for success on the naivete or gullibility of the person being "put on."

When the function of signifying is only expressive (i.e., to arouse feelings of embarrassment, shame, frustration or futility, for the purpose of diminishing someone's status, but without directive implication), the tactic employed is direct in the form of a taunt, as in the above example where the monkey is making fun of the lion. Signifying frequently occurs when things are dull and someone wishes to generate some excitement and interest within the group. This is shown in another version of the above toast:

There hadn't been no disturbin in the jungle for quite a bit,
For up jumped the monkey in the tree one day and laughed, "I guess I'll start some shit."

Sounding is the term which is today most widely known for the game of verbal insult known in the past as "playing the dozens," "the dirty dozens," or just "the dozens." Other current names for the game have regional distribution: *signifying* or "sigging" (Chicago), *joning* (Washington, D.C.), *screaming* (Harrisburg), and so on. In Chicago, the term "sounding" would be descriptive of the initial remarks which are designed to "sound" out the other person to see whether he will play the game. The verbal insult is also subdivided, the term "signifying" applying to insults which are hurled directly at the person and the "dozens" applying to insults hurled at your opponent's family, especially, the mother.

Sounding is often catalyzed by "signifying" remarks referred to earlier, such as "Are you going to let him say that about your mama?" in order to spur on an exchange between two (or more) other members of the group. It is begun on a relatively low key and built up by means of verbal exchanges.

Abrahams (1962b:209–10) describes the game:

One insults a member of another's family; others in the group make disapproving sounds to spur on the coming exchange. The one who has been insulted feels at this point that he must reply with a slur on the protagonist's family which is clever enough to defend his honor (and therefore that of his family). This, of course, leads the other (once again, more due to pressure from the crowd than actual insult) to make further jabs. This can proceed until everyone is bored with the whole affair, until one hits the other (fairly rare), or until some other subject comes up that interrupts the proceedings (the usual state of affairs).

McCormick (1960:8) describes the dozens as a verbal contest

. . . in which the players strive to bury one another with vituperation. In the play, the opponent's mother is especially slandered . . . then, in turn fathers are identified as queer and syphilitic. Sisters are whores, brothers are defective, cousins are "funny" and the opponent is himself diseased.

An example of the "game" collected by one of my students goes as follows:

Frank looked up and saw Leroy enter the Outpost. Leroy walked past the room where Quinton, "Nap," "Pretty Black," "Cunny," Richard, Haywood, "Bull," and Reese sat playing cards. As Leroy neared the T. V. room, Frank shouted to him.

Frank: "Hey, Leroy, your mama—calling you man."

Leroy turned and walked toward the room where the sound came from. He stood in the door and looked at Frank.

Leroy: "Look motherfuckers, I don't play that shit."

Frank, signifying: "Man, I told you cats 'bout that mama jive" (as if he were concerned about how Leroy felt).

Leroy: "That's all right Frank; you don't have to tell those funky motherfuckers nothing; I'll fuck me up somebody yet."

Frank's face lit up as if he were ready to burst his side laughing. "Cunny" became pissed at Leroy.

"Cunny": "Leroy, you stupid bastard, you let Frank make a fool of you. *He* said that 'bout your mama."

"Pretty Black": "Aw, fat ass head, 'Cunny' shut up."

"Cunny": "Ain't that some shit. This black slick head motor flicker got nerve 'nough to call somebody 'fathead.' Boy, you so black, you sweat super Permalube Oil."

This eased the tension of the group as they burst into loud laughter.

"Pretty Black": "What 'chu laughing 'bout 'Nap,' with your funky mouth smelling like dog shit."

Even Leroy laughed at this.

"Nap": "Your mama motherfucker."

"Pretty Black": "Your funky mama too."

"Nap" strongly: "It takes twelve barrels of water to make a steamboat run; it takes an elephant's dick to make your Grandmammy come; she been elephant fucked, camel fucked and hit side the head with your Grandpappy's nuts."

Reese: "Goddor damn; go on and rap motherfucker."

Reese began slapping each boy in his hand, giving his positive approval of "Nap's" comment. "Pretty Black," in an effort not to be outdone but directing his verbal play elsewhere, stated:

"Pretty Black": "Reese, what you laughing 'bout? You so square you shit bricked shit."

Frank: "Whoooowee!"

Reese sounded back: "Square huh, what about your nappy ass hair before it was stewed; that shit was so bad till, when you went to bed at night, it would leave your head and go on the corner and meddle."

The boys slapped each other in the hand and cracked up.

"Pretty Black": "On the streets meddling, bet Dinky didn't offer me no pussy and I turned it down."

Frank: "Reese scared of pussy."

"Pretty Black": "Hell yeah; the greasy mother rather fuck old, ugly, funky cock Sue Willie than get a piece of ass from a decent broad."

Frank: "Goddor damn! Not Sue Willie."

"Pretty Black": "Yeah ol' meat beating Reese rather screw that cross-eyed, clapsy bitch, who when she cry, tears drip down her ass."

Haywood: "Don't be so mean, Black."

Reese: "Aw shut up, you half-white bastard."

Frank: "Wait man, Haywood ain't gonna hear much more of that half-white shit; he's a brother too."

Reese: "Brother, my black ass; that white ass landlord gotta be this motherfucker's paw."

"Cunny": "Man, you better stop foolin with Haywood; he's turning red."

Haywood: "Fuck yall" (as he withdrew from the "sig" game).

Frank: "Yeah, fuck yall; let's go to the stick hall."

The above example of "sounding" is an excellent illustration of the "game" as played by fifteen-, sixteen-, and seventeen-year-old Negro boys, some of whom have already acquired the verbal skill which for them is often the basis for having a high "rep." Abrahams (1964:62) observed that ". . . the ability with words is as highly valued as physical strength." In the sense that the status of one of the participants in the game is diminished if he has to resort to fighting to answer a verbal attack, verbal ability may be even more highly regarded than physical ability. However, age within the peer group may be a factor in determining the relative value placed on verbal vis-à-vis physical ability.

Nevertheless, the relatively high value placed on verbal ability must be clear to most black boys at an early age in their cognitive development. Abrahams (1964:53) is probably correct in linking "sounding" to the taunt which is learned and practiced as a child and is part of "signifying," which has its origins in childlike behavior. The taunts of the "Signifying Monkey," illustrated above, are good examples of this.

Most boys begin their activity in "sounding" by compiling a repertoire of "one liners." When the game is played among this age group the one who has the greatest number of such remarks wins. Here are some examples of "one liners" collected from fifth and sixth grade black boys in Chicago:

> Yo mama is so bowlegged, she looks like the bite out of a donut.
>
> You mama sent her picture to the lonely hearts club, and they sent it back and said "We ain't that lonely"!
>
> Your family is so poor the rats and roaches eat lunch out.
>
> Your house is so small the roaches walk single file.
>
> I walked in your house and your family was running around the table. I said, "Why you doin that?" Your mama say, "First one drops, we eat."

Real proficiency in the game comes to only a small percentage of those who play it, as might be expected. These players have the special skill in being able to turn what their opponents have said and attack them with it. Thus, when someone indifferently said "fuck you" to Concho, his retort was immediate and devastating: "Man, you haven't even kissed me yet."

The "best talkers" from this group often become the successful street-corner, barber shop, and pool hall story tellers who deliver the long, rhymed, witty narrative stories called "toasts." A portion of the toast "The Signifying Monkey and the Lion" was given above. However, it has also produced entertainers, such as Dick Gregory and Redd Foxx, who are virtuosos at repartee, and preachers, whose verbal power has been traditionally esteemed.

The function of the "dozens" or "sounding" is invariably self-assertive. The speaker borrows status from his opponent through an exercise of verbal power. The opponent feels compelled to regain his status by "sounding" back on the speaker or some other member of the group whom he regards as more vulnerable. The social interaction of the group at the Outpost, for example, demonstrated less an extended verbal barrage between two people than a "pecking order." Frank "sounds" on Leroy; "Cunny" "signifies" on Leroy; "Pretty Black" "sounds" on "Cunny"; "Cunny" "sounds" back on "Pretty Black" who (losing) turns on "Nap"; "Nap" "sounds" (winning) back on "Pretty Black"; "Pretty Black" finally borrows back his status by "sounding" on Reese. Reese "sounds" back on "Pretty Black" but gets the worst of the exchange and so borrows back his status from Haywood. "Cunny" also "sounds" on Haywood. Haywood defaults. Perhaps by being "half-white," Haywood feels himself to be the most vulnerable.

The presence of a group seems to be especially important in controlling the game. First of all, one does not "play" with just anyone since the subject matter is concerned with things that in reality one is quite sensitive about. It is precisely *because* "Pretty Black" has a "black slick head" that makes him vulnerable to "Cunny's" barb, especially now when the Afro-American "natural" hair style is in vogue. It is precisely *because* Reese's girl-friend *is* ugly that makes him vulnerable to "Pretty Black's" jibe that Reese can't get a "piece of ass from a decent broad." It is *because* the living conditions are so poor and intolerable that they can be used as subject matter for "sounding." Without the control of the group "sounding" will frequently lead to a fight. This was illustrated by a tragic epilogue concerning Haywood; when Haywood was being "sounded" on in the presence of two girls by his best friend (other members of the group were absent), he refused to tolerate it. He went home, got a rifle, came back, and shot and killed his friend. In the classroom from about the fourth grade on fights among black boys invariably are caused by someone "sounding" on the other person's mother.

Significantly, the subject matter of "sounding" is changing with the changing self-concept of the black with regard to those physical characteristics that are characteristically "Negro," and which in the past were vulnerable points in the black psyche: blackness and "nappy" hair.

They still occur, as in the above example: from the Outpost, and the change in the above illustration is notably more by what has been added than subtracted—viz., the attack on black *slick* hair and half-white color. With regard to the latter, however, it ought to be said that for many blacks, blackness was always highly esteemed and it might be more accurate to regard the present sentiment of the black community toward skin color as reflecting a shifted attitude for only a *portion* of the black community. This suggests that "sounding" on someone's light skin color is not new. Nevertheless, one can regard the previously favorable attitude toward light skin color and "good hair" as the prevailing one. "Other things being equal, the more closely a woman approached her white counterpart, the more attractive she was considered to be, by both men and women alike. 'Good hair' (hair that is long and soft) and light skin were the chief criteria" (Liebow 1966: 138). Also, children's rhymes which before "black power" were

> If you like black
> Keep your black ass back

and

> If you like white
> You're all right

have respectively changed to

> If you like black
> You have a Cadillac

and

> If you like white
> You're looking for a fight.

Both Abrahams and McCormick link the "dozens" to the over-all psychosocial growth of the black male. McCormick has stated that a "single round of a dozen or so exchanges frees more pent-up aggressions than will a dose of sodium pentothal." The fact that one permits a kind of abuse within the rules of the game and within the confines of the group which would otherwise not be tolerated is filled with psychological importance, and this aspect is rather fully discussed by Abrahams. It also seems important, however, to view its function from the perspective of the non-participating members of the group. Its function for them may be directive: i.e., they incite and prod individual members of the group to combat for the purpose of energizing the elements, of simply relieving the boredom of just "hanging around" and the malaise of living in a static and restrictive environment. One of my informants remarked that he and other members of the group used to feed insults to one member to hurl back at another if they felt that the contest was too uneven, "to keep the game going." In my above illustration from the Outpost, for example, Frank seemed to be the precipitating agent as well as chorus for what was going on and "Bull" did not directly participate at all. For them the "dozens" may have had the social function of "having a little fun," or as Loubee said to Josh of just "passing the time" (Shorris 1966:65).

A summary analysis of the different forms of language behavior which have been discussed permit the following generalizations.

The prestige norms which influence black speech behavior are those which have been successful in manipulating and controlling people and situations. The function of all of the forms of language behavior discussed above, with the exception of "running it down," was either expressive or expressive-directive. Specifically, this means that language was used to project personality, assert oneself, or arouse emotion, frequently with the additional purpose of getting the person to give up or do something which will be of some benefit to the speaker. Only "running it down" has as its primary function to communicate information and often here, too, the personality and style of the speaker in the form of "rapping" is projected along with the information.

The purpose for which language is used suggests that the speaker views the social situations into which he moves as essentially agonistic, by which I mean that he sees his environment as consisting of a series of transactions which require that he be continually ready to take advantage of a person or situation or defend himself against being victimized. He has absorbed what Horton (1967:8) has called "street rationality." As one of Horton's respondents put it: "The good hustler . . . conditions his mind and must never put his guard down too far, to relax, or he'll be taken."

I have carefully avoided, throughout this paper, delimiting the group within the black community of whom the language behavior and perspective of their environment is characteristic. While I have no doubt that it is true of those who are generally called "street people" I am not certain of the extent to which it is also true of a much larger portion of the black community, especially the male segment. My informants consisted of street people, high school students, and blacks, who by their occupation as community and youth workers possess what has been described as a "sharp sense of the streets." Yet it is difficult to find a black male in the community who has *not* witnessed or participated in the "dozens" or heard of "signifying," or "rapping," or "shucking and jiving" at some time while he was growing up. It would be equally difficult to imagine a high school student in a Chicago inner city school not being touched by what is generally regarded a "street culture" in some way.

In conclusion, by blending style and verbal power, through "rapping," "sounding," and "running it down," the black in the ghetto establishes his personality; through "shucking," "gripping," and "copping a plea" he shows his respect for power; through "jiving" and "signifying" he stirs up excitement. With all of the above, he hopes to manipulate and control people and situations to give himself a winning edge.

REFERENCES CITED

Abrahams, D., 1962, "Playing the Dozens," *Journal of American Folklore,* 75:209–20.

——— 1964, *Deep Down in the Jungle,* Folklore Associates, Hatboro, Pennsylvania.

Brown, C., 1965, *Manchild in the Promised Land,* Macmillan, New York.

Conot, R., 1967, *Rivers of Blood, Years of Darkness,* Bantam, New York.

Douglass, F., 1968, *Narrative of the Life of an American Slave,* New American Library, New York.

Gumperz, J. and D. Hymes (ed.), 1964, *The Ethnography of Communication, American Anthropologist,* 66, No. 6, part 2.

Horton, J., 1967, "Time and Cool People," *Trans-action,* 4:5–12.

King, W., 1965, "The Game," *The Liberator,* 5:20–25.

Liebow, E., 1967, *Tally's Corner,* Little Brown, Boston.

McCormick, M., 1960, *The Dirty Dozens, The Unexpurgated Folksongs of Men,* Arhoolie Record Album.

Pouissaint, A., 1967, "A Negro Psychiatrist Explains the Negro Psyche," *The New York Times,* August 20, Section 6:52ff.

Shorris, E., 1966, *Ofay,* Dell, New York.

PART NINE
Method and Theory

Perspectives on the Collection and Analysis of Ethnographic Data

That acquisition of a better understanding of human behavior anywhere can contribute to better understanding human behavior everywhere is probably the most basic premise in ethnology. It is derived from belief in both the fundamental biologically determined similarity of all human beings and in their common reliance upon sociocultural means of coping with the problems of survival. It follows that we can learn more about *all* people from properly studying *any* people in the present or in the past; the more dissimilar their ways of life, the better the perspective we can gain upon the total range of behavioral variation of which our species is capable, and looking at these variations over time can help us to identify both the causes and the patterns of those collective alterations in behavior that we know of as social and cultural change.

Understanding how others have dealt or are dealing with problems common to us all helps to place our own way of life in cross-cultural perspective. As such understanding grows, it contributes to the gradual development of a general theory of human behavior. In building such a theory emphasis upon the search for an ever more accurate comprehension of causality allows for the advanced, experience-based planning and prediction that can enable us to avoid repeating past errors and to find a more harmonious accommodation to the laws that govern the sociocultural processes upon which our survival depends. In this quest for fuller comprehension few issues are "purely academic"; the theoretical and practical implications of an improved understanding of human behavior are totally merged.

So far most of the data anthropologists have collected on human behavior have been gathered among the aboriginal peoples of the non-Western world, the indigenous inhabitants of Asia, Africa, the Pacific, and Native America. Much early fieldwork was done under the auspices of various prevailing colonial regimes and with only the most perfunctory attention to obtaining the consent of the usually powerless people who were studied. Unable to protect their private lives, their traditions, and their persons from inquisitive outsiders handsomely backed by grants, with several years of graduate study, and equipped with tape recorders, cameras, notebooks, and letters of introduction to the local white administration, "the natives" could only fight back indirectly. Often they were startlingly successful. Fieldwork literature is full of fascinating accounts of aboriginal ingenuity in eluding the anthropologists' quest for data. But more frequently anthropologists have encountered trust, acceptance, cooperation, and extraordinary unselfishness from the indigenous peoples they have lived among and whose ways of life they have studied.

Quite a lot has been learned. Some data have proved faulty, but most have stood the test of restudying and crosschecking and now offer us a fine beginning example of the many ways other people cope with the human problems common to us all, of the ways their sociocultural systems are organized and how they change in response to ceaselessly shifting circumstances. We now possess a sufficiently adequate sampling of the processes of sociocultural variation to begin to state some generalizations and even to formulate tentatively a few laws.

Anthropologists differ in the strength of their confidence in the likelihood of early success in identifying the general laws that govern both individual human behavior, the form and content of sociocultural systems, and the processes by which they change. Some prefer to work solely on the careful study of specific small-scale problems—the diffusion of the harpoon in the Eastern Arctic, kinship terminology in aboriginal Hawaii, varieties of Central African feudalism, or Andean textile designs. Others are more eager to generalize. Although both propensities are valuable, it is the willingness to theorize, to set up hypotheses for testing, that contributes most strongly to the development of ethnology as a science.

SECTION I

Problems of Method

Although anthropologists have by no means perfected their techniques for studying other cultures, so far they have been more successful working elsewhere than they have been at working closer to home. Many scholars now recognize that it is time for a change, and that some methodological retooling needs to be done.

Neatly delimited, still unstudied island communities and isolated forest bands are in increasingly short supply. It is crucial to study those that remain before they change forever, and the chance to learn from them is forever lost as well. But we also need more data on our own society and culture, and upon those of other European and New World peoples. This will require a shift in methodological emphasis and the development of more efficient techniques for studying large-scale societies. For major problems arise in data collection and sampling when a lone anthropologist takes on the task of trying to study even a single facet of the culture of a society whose population may number in the millions. Village mapping, taking a census of household heads, getting together with the elders, interviewing key informants, and just generally sitting around absorbing the raw material for field notes do not work well enough. Some of these methods have to be modified.

It is probably not accidental that anthropologists who have worked at home have selected for study groups whose status was still at least semicolonial, in the sense of their relative powerlessness in relation to the dominant majority. Most anthropological work in North America, for example, has been done among Indians, blacks, and the white poor (with Chicano and Asian American studies moving up fast). Studies of higher status, less "ethnic" American groups have been left largely to sociologists. This partly derives from a traditional division of labor between the two disciplines that will have to be renegotiated if we are ever to become more responsive to the pressing need for a better understanding of our own sociocultural system, how it works, how it changes, and how likely it is to survive.

At home or away, we need a model for fieldwork that will provide for a more honest, mutually beneficial relationship between the ethnographer and the people he studies. Hatfield has one to suggest.

Fieldwork: Toward a Model of Mutual Exploitation

Colby R. Hatfield, Jr.

Introduction

In salubrious contrast to views that the "public relations" side of research is best left up to the informal ingenuity of researchers, a number of anthropologists have recently displayed their willingness to explore this "mysterious art" by publishing frank accounts of their own fieldwork experiences. Fortes, for example, gives his notion of the "public relations" side of fieldwork preparation, "I regard them as peripheral . . . Our experience is that the best way of dealing with them is to leave it to the research student to soak up clues, in part from the literature and largely from fellow students who are recently back from the field" (Fortes 1963:433). There are several current examples of attempts to systematize "soaking up clues" (Williams 1967; Henry and Saberwell 1969; Spindler 1970; Freilich 1970; and Golde 1970). While perhaps the primary aim is to provide the novice with some degree of comfort in undertaking his first research exercise and the professional with a comparative framework in which to weigh his own experiences, an equally important goal is the attempt to understand the field experience in contexts consonant with current theories of human social behavior.

One of the more fruitful approaches is a model of fieldwork based upon the economics of human interaction. The writings of Homans (1961) and Blau (1964) emphasize the dynamics of cost and reward as fundamental to human interaction. Thus Wax (1952:35) considers field relations in a setting of reciprocities, the actors ". . . consciously or unconsciously giving each other something they both desire or need." Lundberg (1968:47) concentrates on "transactions" in which partners seek just ratios of rewards by exchanging information and confirmation. Freilich (1970:540f) discusses rapport as a "conditional agreement to communicate," determined by factors of risk, time costs, and communication net profit.

The model introduces the anthropologist to a self-image more desirable than Malinowski's (1961:8) ". . . necessary evil or nuisance, mitigated by donations of tobacco." First, it places the field experience in a context of actions and motivations claimed common to all interaction, albeit transferred to unfamiliar settings to which the researcher brings special training. Second, by appreciating the economic aspects in interpersonal relations, he has the opportunity to utilize better what Freilich (1970:539) called an "engineering" approach to fieldwork.

Yet this model contains a major shortcoming. In focusing on interaction as a contest for "just exchanges," balancing personal investment with reward, it implies that indeed a happy equilibrium is achievable. That there is doubt of this even in normal conditions of life should lead those embarking on fieldwork to be wary of achieving it in another society. Blau (1964:25ff) considers symmetries in human exchange basically impossible, for the very attempt to balance effort and reward on one level of interaction implies or induces imbalances on others. I believe the fieldwork situation denies just exchanges, that within the relationship of "stranger" to "insider" are inherent tendencies towards unjust (asymmetrical) transactions or simply exploitation, with the stranger often as the loser.

Those presently concerned with ethics and exploitation in cultural anthropology will hardly find this contention startling. Not only do subjects of inquiry claim that researchers usurp their time, patience, and good will, giving little in return, but many anthropologists accuse their peers of using or permitting the use of data in ways harmful to the people from whom it was collected. Obviously exploitation in these circumstances is very much a one-sided affair. It is not my purpose to add to the debate over the exploiting anthropologist (I am concerned at the moment with the exploited anthropologist), but it would be naive to think them unrelated.

Source: From Colby R. Hatfield, Jr., "Fieldwork: Toward a Model of Mutual Exploitation," *Anthropological Quarterly,* Vol. 46 (1973), pp. 15–29. Used by permission of the publisher and the author.

A researcher might endure the most difficult of experiences because he knows it will bring him a commensurate reward—professional status. The justice in this human exchange may come a long time after actual interaction has ceased. He may also feel he has so dearly paid for his data that it becomes his outright possession. What then may be viewed as exploitation from one view is the ultimate balancing of the exchange from another. My point is simply that while explorations into the anthropologist as exploiter serve to remind researchers of their human and professional responsibilities and to sensitize them to the ease with which data can be misused, they tend to obscure the basic problems in the field where exploitation is unavoidable. The idealism of the transactional and the idealistic goals of the exploitation models ignore the dialemma of anthropologist as stranger and friend and in so doing tend to intensify his personal and technical problems. What follows is an exploration into three sets of statuses (usually ascribed) viz. *Incompetent, Fort Knox,* and *Sahib,* in which the anthropologist is either hopelessly exploited or must exploit to survive personally and professionally. I divide Incompetent into *Dope, Child,* and *Pawn*; Sahib into two subtypes: *Technician* and *Social Expert.* In conclusion I will discuss those characteristics of anthropological training which I feel make the researcher less able to cope with the vicissitudes of exploitation in the field.

The Anthropologist as Incompetent

THE INCOMPETENT DOPE. A newcomer is anxious to please and not offend. Being on his best professional behavior and playing the "nice guy" role, he is often unaware of the intensity and scope of challenges to his tolerance and social skills. Freilich (1970:501) points out that the nice guy role is a mask by which ". . . natives, by and large, are not deceived." It is the anthropologist who fools himself. The nice guy ". . . appears ready to do favors for everyone; he is always interested in everything that is going on, concerned with everyone's welfare, and is rarely angry, upset, or hostile. He is almost goodness personified." Once the strictures of politeness and official protection dissipate and he begins penetrating community life, he becomes fair game for a collection of outrages, the butt of everyone's humor and deception. Evans-Pritchard (1968:12f, 182) complained about Nuer genius for confounding interviews and their pleasure in lying to him. "You are a foreigner, why should we tell you the right way?" Williams (1967:19) reeled from house to house politely gulping two cups of wine at each until the headman informed him it was a Dusun joke.

The nice guy suffers various forms of scapegoatism. In the early stages he is too green to know the rules of daily intercourse and sanctions for their infringement. Later he may avoid imposing them, fearing to estrange potentially valuable contacts. Thus insiders can subject him to a gamut of harrassments with impunity. After a decimating attack on my true motives for being in East Africa, using the Sukuma to make money, and alleged subversiveness, guised in apparently polite inquiries of an itinerant chicken salesman before twenty Sukuma elders, I learned how great a dope I could be as a stranger whose poverty of social resources and linguistic facility had provided a little amusement on a hot afternoon. Although Berreman (1962:7–8) was able to triumph over a similar adversary, his was a Pyrrhic victory, for it brought him no more rapport or information.

The researcher as petitioner, unaware of proper channels and social forms can be trapped in bureaucratic games of broken appointments, red tape, office referrals, and persecution (Whitten 1970:270ff; Schwab 1970:104–5; Landes 1970:130ff). In 1963 local permission was necessary to work in Sukumaland. Although tedious, the procedure mollified highly suspicious officials in newly independent Tanzania. But the flimsy fabric of legitimacy was almost completely rent when an important officer caught a researcher from the institute (of which I was Acting Director) visiting friends in an area without permission. On returning, he subjected us to a long harangue about American intervention in the Congo, our disregard of government policies, and other observations of our defects including the questionable value of our researches. He dismissed us with the warning that we could have been on the next plane out of the country. My compatriot had been wrong in not asking permission, but he was also not given the chance to explain that his visit was not research-centered. We felt that the official had welcomed the occasion to vent personal animosities towards Americans. Yet, in spite of the humiliation, we could only express our gratitude at being let off so easily.

Some asymmetries diminish after the initiations of strangerhood, but while playing a Dope, the anthropologist cannot escape the embarrassments of being the town fool, the paralysis of bureaucratic runarounds, and the sometimes unsubtle persecutions reserved for the unintegrated.

THE INCOMPETENT CHILD. Insiders often find it convenient to call the stranger a child (Middleton 1970:12; Bowen 1964:142). The anthropologist also finds it a convenient device for initiating his learning. Yet it is a pseudostatus, a status of convenience, with inherent contradictions. Williams (1967:43–44) calls "false status-roles" assignments which tend to disrupt a researcher's social position as government informant, tax collector, spy, etc. The anthropologist's position as child is not false in these terms but merely partial, based not upon error but on convenience or design. The stranger is only like a child in lacking certain knowledge, otherwise he is an adult. In ideal transactions a community accepts the responsibility to train the child and the anthropologist agrees to be a conscientious learner. Rewards for the deal range from outright gifts to the prestige of teacherhood for the one, and knowledge and personal friendships for the other. In reality a learner discovers he has little control over what or how he is to learn in spite of what he knows he wants to learn. He also experiences that deep frustration centered on being treated as more incompetent than he really is. Bohannan echoes a familiar plaint:

> Far from having the docile informants whom I could train, I found myself in spare-time amusement of people who told me what they considered it good for me to know and what they were interested in at the moment . . . I longed to make a stand. I knew of no grounds on which to make one. In cold blood I could find little reason for complaint, yet I found myself watching and waiting for an opportunity for self-assertion, an occasion when I would be so clearly in the right that I could have my own way and call it justice (Bowen 1964:38).

In 1963 I tried to be a proper apprentice to Sukuma religious specialists. But in spite of my willingness, I was still regarded as a stranger or European (*mzungu*) judged stupider than a child and incapable of bearing stresses of daily life; "weak," they said. My teachers felt it necessary to keep me out of the sun, adhere to my feeding times, and not overtax me with information. Should a religious quest begin before my breakfast, I would not be invited or all would wait until "Nkwabi" (my local name) had eaten. In trying to assist in extinguishing a grass fire, I was peremptorily ordered into my hut for fear I would burn myself. On another occasion, after insisting on attending a search for magical stone, I was entertained well-apart from the proceedings by a huge guard who made me toy arrows. My escape to some rocks for a better view caused the hunt to cease until I was firmly back in custody. I learned that, as a proper child I was at a true learning disadvantage, for to obtain the knowledge I deemed necessary in the time allotted to me I would have to break the rules of apprenticeship. Finally, banking on my statuses of stranger and dope, I infiltrated groups and events, painfully aware that I was not welcome and in their eyes a very bad mannered stranger indeed.

The pseudo-status of child can be useful once the researcher learns to manipulate it. Otherwise he is at the mercy of those who teach when and what they wish. Opportunities for balanced exchanges are minimized, because the learner, caught in his dual status of nice guy stranger and proper child, is unable to develop a status more consonant with what he really is or must achieve.

THE INCOMPETENT PAWN. The anthropologist can also be a social resource, a celebrity enhancing his friend's prestige or a pawn in a mean game of power. After initial motorcycle parades with my first medicine-father, I realized that a part of my apprenticeship was to tolerate participating in his publicity scheme, his special asset for achieving renown. Living in the household of my second teacher, I became the official entertainer of visitors he disliked, feared, or wanted to impress, until he swept the guest away for a talk to which I was pointedly not invited: "Nkwabi has to write, Nkwabi has to rest," etc. Sometimes I was the *pièce de résistence* of elaborate rituals designed for local potentates, produced like a pet monkey at the crucial moment to toss medicine on the fire.

Pawnship in other situations can be deeply disturbing. Bohannan was innocently enmeshed in the power struggles between two elders until she learned its advantages for her work (Bowen 1964:99). Powdermaker (1967:277ff, 253ff) was the victim of rumors by vengeful former aides and Europeans who resented her social cutting of racial lines. A young worker, whom I was about to dismiss, slyly insinuated that he could see that my request to enter a district of great importance to my work was refused, claiming the official concerned was his uncle.

Two asymmetries are involved here; the emotional strain of knowing one is being manipulated with little possibility of redress and the imbalance of rewards in permitting its use. I did not gain greater depths of data from being a pet monkey, nor had I any basis for refusal—a proper apprentice obeyed his teacher. In the latter examples, immediate action was required to save oneself from disaster; yet often situations are ambiguous enough to make any course of action risky. I solved my problem by lying. I fired the assistant, telling him I had already written his uncle of his misdeeds. And I did receive permission to work in my important area three months after I had departed the country. Caught in these exchanges the anthropologist becomes more of a social dupe than a social dope.

The Anthropologist as Fort Knox

The most obvious manifestation of the exploited anthropologist is in allocating his resources. Few researchers expect to obtain privileges of participation gratis. But few today desire to pay other than assistants or interpreters directly. Information, rapport, and friendship are reciprocated by gifts, making available one's services and facilities, and providing "confirmation" (Lundberg 1968:47). Maxwell's (1970:476) Samoan informants refused payment but accepted presents from beer to racing bicycles. Nader (1970:104) minimized individual gifts by giving to her host town; Williams (1967:16–17) held parties for the neighborhood. Bowen (1964:36f) and Powdermaker (1967:77) conducted clinics. Saberwal (1969:56–57) offered his car as an ambulance; and Yengoyan (1970:414) initiated an informal men's club. But attempts at generosity or *quid pro quo* often deteriorate into burdensome and unrewarding demands. Saberwal's ambulance service, for example, operating on a twenty-four hour basis, still did not bring him universal popularity. The Lugbara were never convinced that Middleton (1970:27) could not distribute more cash, since they were invincibly certain he had complete access to all he wanted from the government. Beals records his reaction to incessant demands: "They demanded their rights. Tempers flared. We said we were poor. . . . Finally we drove everyone out and locked the door" (Beals 1970:42).

Having no door to lock when demands got intolerable, I escaped to my camp bed making full use of my mzungu weakness for rest. In truth I found little more exhausting than trying to say "no" without saying it, or saying "yes" without meaning it—an art which my informants had mastered. The situation was intolerable less from my fear of being reduced to rags as from what it signified. Not being able to mean "no" while saying "yes," I became more conscious of my strangerhood. I had not learned how to use devices which spared the Sukuma the embarrassment and loss of social credit which faced me. And this knowledge led to a more stinging question: if I could not master them, then how could I aspire to participate in their lifeways, how ultimately could I hope to be an anthropologist? Equally decimating were the inroads such occasions made into my self-image as honest and forthright, capable of cultural transvestism. In order to protect my own possessions and interests I had to resort to more devious deceptions than the Sukuma themselves. I knew at least that in Sukumaland one does not refuse outright, for to refuse is to embarrass and thus to hurt; and for me, as a stranger, to hurt is to endanger the tenuous artifice of rapport and security. So I survived through hypocrisy.

As I became more sophisticated—or perhaps cold blooded—about the game of asking and refusing, I also realized that neither knowledge of the system of avoidances nor acceptance by the Sukuma was sufficient to balance exchanges. The rules of social life could never completely apply to me. I would not be in Sukumaland long enough for a transactional equilibrium to develop. Besides, in spite of my modest stipend, I was so obviously affluent in their eyes (and in my own) as to transcend all local rules.

The Anthropologist as Sahib

Appearances are deceiving. Surrounded by the accoutrements of his own technology, the fieldworker is thought to possess the knowledge that creates and maintains them. As a visitor from afar he is a store of news and information. These superior qualities are enhanced by his apparent class-hopping skills; he seems to penetrate the sacrosanct realms of government and mission and with the same ease impose himself on the community. His own self-image as world traveler, cultural transvestite, and encyclopedia of knowledge often merges with that of his informants. The result is a superficial inflation of his technical and socio-political competencies.

THE TECHNICIAN. Although I claimed to be expert at nothing, my Sukuma friends assumed that my possessions (motorcycle, typewriter, taperecorder, camera, medicines) indicated I had the skills necessary for their maintenance. I was periodically probed for these talents and usually found wanting. First I failed to negotiate the household's ancient malfunctioning lorry out of the rut into which I jostled teacher and fellow apprentices. I was not asked to drive again, it being rumored that I was responsible for its demise a bit later. When I proved incapable of a simple motorcycle repair, their hopes of my technical aid were demolished. In trying to remove a tick from my teacher's chest with a hot match I failed my medical exam as well, even though some apprentices still came for bandaids, aspirin, and malaria pills.

I found it hopelessly difficult to explain how airplanes remained in the air and how their pilots navigated, what contributed to world political crises, and the value of smallpox inoculations over native treatment (we were in the midst of an epidemic at the time). In 1970 the discrepancy between expectations and reality of my competence was even more pronounced, for farmers assumed that I, as a member of a technical aid team, knew how to do all the things reserved for animal production officers in the job descriptions. My job seemed in their eyes to be asking irrelevant questions.

THE SOCIAL EXPERT. Miscalculations of a person's social and political competence can operate in two ways (Colson 1967:93). Early in fieldwork the anthropologist is prone to overestimate the abilities of informants and assistants. Weidman (1970:249), for example, had the misfortune to hire a Christian Karen totally ignorant of proper conduct in a Burmese Buddhist village. Once I overcame the charisma of lion skin and amulets, I realized my first medicine-father hardly lived up to the reputation his grandiose equipment signified.

Obversely, the anthropologist can also be a victim of informants' overassessment of his social skills. He too can only succeed in proving his true abilities when he fails to achieve what his hosts want from him. The Taiwanese hoped that Diamond (1970:130) had the connections and influence which would initiate a flood of economic aid to them; yet she was barely surviving on a small grant. Both Gulick (1970:148–150) and Middleton (1970:26) were expected to use non-existent connections to obtain favors from school and government officials. When Kloos (1969:511) refused Surinamese demands that he rear one of their children in the arts of leadership, hostility marked the remainder of his visit. Despite lack of contacts, I was continually asked for aid in getting students into American schools or in obtaining posts by tapping what connections I possessed, by writing letters of recommendation, and occasionally by playing gatekeeper between official and petitioner.

As technical and social expert, the anthropologist is placed in statuses not of his making (although he may unconsciously support them). He is then expected to demonstrate the skills which they imply. False statuses are common to the field experience. They are tiresome disadvantages which a researcher eventually dispels through trust. But these statuses are destroyed only when the anthropologist fails to accomplish what they demand. Rapport constructed on such a basis requires more of the anthropologist than he can give with little reward for his efforts, but great rejection once the truth is revealed.

The Paradox of Professional and Human Competence

I have argued that exploitations in the field are unavoidable because the anthropologist is a stranger caught in a variety of ascribed statuses hampering his activities, an imagined fund of monetary and other resources, and socially outside the sanctions of local life. But another consideration aggravates the problem: the stranger as anthropologist. My purpose is not to criticize participation observation as a valid technique for data collection. Rather I am concerned with airing the human—not the scientific—problems of being an anthropologist in the field. I am not examining the effects of the technique used upon the data but upon the person who obtains the data.

Professional competence demands first that a student become an effective research instrument.

He must not only master techniques of data collection, but must be disciplined to accept nothing at face value, be excessively curious, a perfect interrogator, listener, and skilled judge of human reliability and truthfulness. Second, he must be trained in cultural relativism, which from one stance means cultivating the ability to tolerate cultural differences even when they may disgust him (Williams 1967:50). The anthropologist as human prides himself on being a cultural transvestite, as a research instrument cultural relativism ensures his control of bias.

But most anthropological research is accomplished in a milieu of participation, where the fieldworker must ally technical competence with skills in the arts of human interaction. The key word in fieldwork is rapport. In spite of efforts of Freilich and others to place the concept on a more technical level, achieving and maintaining rapport still demands an expansion of one's capacities for empathy, understanding, patience, tolerance, fearlessness, and friendliness as well as their distillation into effective tools. At the same time deeply concerned with the potential dangers he might bring to his host community, the fieldworker attempts to use the gentler of these skills lest he alienate, or be accused of exploiting his host people.

Professional competence also requires cultivation of rapport skills because fieldwork, at least initially, is more than doing research. It is a *rite de passage*, a transformation. From Freilich's discussion of the meaning of subsequent fieldtrips one might conclude that they have characteristics of rites of intensification. As Eggan states, "Fieldwork is an essential ingredient to the student's own training . . . it is a period when the student is largely on his own, with the opportunity to make mistakes and to be frustrated, but also with the opportunity to achieve personal successes and to come to grips with reality" (Eggan 1963:94). The fieldworker participates not simply to be a better assessor of information or to obtain an in-depth picture of community life, but also because he is supposed to enjoy it or at least to be moulded into a professional by it. But most anthropologists do not take courses in "How to Win Friends . . ." nor do they necessarily have natural gifts in the arts of human interaction. Some writers would claim that the anthropologist indeed does have natural skills or at least tendencies toward cross-cultural adventures (Powdermaker 1967:19; Evans-Pritchard 1964:81–82; Wintrob 1969:75–76). As strangers, defenseless and alone, they want to use their resources to make others like them, gain respect and achieve mutual trust.

The paradox then arises from incompatible expectations that the anthropologist be a perfect research machine, posing as a human being and at the same time be truly human. I began fieldwork with an image of perfect researcher, rapport gainer, and ideal human, not as myself. My role image did not include the less gentle qualities inherent to human transactions: guile, manipulation, exploitation, one-upsmanship, breaking promises, bullying, anger, etc. Certainly I did not think to find these as responses to my ideal image. My wife opines part of the reason for creating so ideal an image and its generalization into field relations is fear. It is always better to anticipate a perfect world of human transactions if the world itself is unknown. It is tragic that Kloos (1969:511) must confess, ". . . any fieldworker has to suppress a lot of his own identity, because it interferes with his smooth integration." In constructing my ideal self I committed a great crime of superiority. I presumed the Sukuma to act as I thought I should act, hoping to repress the fact that paths of human interaction require different—and often inconsistent, contradictory—responses. I was not prepared to see myself and them in a contest of who exploits whom or games of hide-and-seek with data, and thus I was not prepared to utilize resulting asymmetries nor accept them stoically as part of my experience.

I suggest that the concept of transaction, which has done so much to put anthropological fieldwork on a realistic plane, needs an even more realistic emendation through an acceptance of exploitation as inherent to the art. Those most vociferous about the exploiting anthropologist need to bring in the fuller picture for clarification. Both are modeled on ideal and extreme situations: the former in a perfect state of exchanges (a perfect market); the latter in an absolute state of asymmetry.

Exploitation in its simplest form means to achieve or turn to practical account. It is inherent to daily life, for participants measure the cost of their participation, calculating the means by which these can be turned into short- or long-range profits. Only the child, the incompetent, and the stranger suffer because they are either ignorant of or cannot play the game. In cross-cultural contexts, where fieldwork demands intense interaction between stranger and insider, exploitations are bound to occur. But the anthropologist, determined to play a role of perfect machine and man, hoping to soar above the complexities of being human by not playing the game, suffers the consequences of his perfection, like Alcestis.

I have focused on the negative side of fieldwork neither out of pessimism nor disillusionment, but because I feel that the experience is often marred by greater difficulties than there need be. Prepared from the onset to suffer inconsistency, to assume contradictory roles, to manipulate when necessary and in turn tolerate manipulation, the anthropologist can indeed survive his professionalization with greater justice to himself and his hosts. In some cases he may find himself the object of Evans-Pritchard's (1964:79) accusation that "an anthropologist has failed unless, when he says goodbye to the natives, there is on both sides the sorrow of parting." But he may take comfort in Jarvie's (1969) claim that it is possible to be a scientist and to treat everyone (including oneself) as an end, a human being.

REFERENCES CITED

Beals, Alan R.
1970—Gopalpur. 1958–1960. *In* Being an anthropologist: fieldwork in eleven cultures. G. Spindler, ed., New York: Holt, Rinehart & Winston.
Berreman, Gerald
1962—Behind many masks: ethnology and impression management in a Himalayan village. Society for Applied Anthropology, Monograph 4.
Blau, Peter M.
1964—Exchange and power in social life. New York: John Wiley & Sons.
Bowen, Elenore S.
1964—Return to laughter: an anthropological novel. Garden City, N.Y.: Anchor.
Colson, Elizabeth
1967—Competence and incompetence in context of independence. Current Anthropology 8:92–99.
Diamond, Norma
1970—Fieldwork in a complex society: Taiwan. *In* Being an anthropologist: fieldwork in eleven cultures. G. Spindler, eds., New York: Holt, Rinehart & Winston.
Eggan, Fred
1963—The graduate program. *In* The teaching of anthropology, AAA Memoir 94. D. Mandelbaum, G. Lasker, and E. Albert, eds.
Evans-Pritchard, E. E.
1964—Social anthropology and other essays. Glencoe: The Free Press.
1968—The Nuer: a description of the modes of livelihood and political institutions of a Nilotic people. Oxford: Clarendon.
Fortes, Meyer
1963—Graduate study and research. *In* The teaching of anthropology, AAA Memoir 94. D. Mandelbaum, G. Lasker, and E. Albert, eds.
Freilich, Morris, Ed.
1970—Marginal natives: anthropologists at work. New York: Harper and Row.
Golde, Peggy, Ed.
1970—Women in the field: anthropological experiences. Chicago: Aldine.
Gulick, John
1970—Village and city: fieldwork in Lebanon. *In* Marginal natives: anthropologists at work. Morris Freilich, ed., New York: Harper and Row.
Henry, Frances & S. Saberwal, Eds.
1969—Stress and response in fieldwork. New York: Holt, Rinehart and Winston.
Homans, George C.
1961—Social behavior: its elementary forms. New York: Harcourt Brace.
Jarvie, I. C.
1969—The problem of ethical integrity in participant observation. Current Anthropology 10:5:505–508.
Kloos, Peter
1969—Role conflicts in social fieldwork. Current Anthropology 10:509–11.
Landes, Ruth
1970—A woman anthropologist in Brazil. *In* Women in the field: anthropological experiences. Peggy Golde, ed., Chicago: Aldine.

Lundberg, Craig C.
1968—A transactional conception of fieldwork. Human Organization 27:45–49.
Malinowski, Bronislaw
1961—Argonauts of the Western Pacific: an account of native enterprise and adventure in the archipelagoes of Melanesian New Guinea. New York: E. P. Dutton.
Maxwell, Robert J.
1970—A comparison of field research in Canada and Polynesia. *In* Marginal natives: anthropologists at work. Morris Freilich, ed., New York: Harper and Row.
Middleton, John
1970—The study of the Lugbara: expectation and paradox in anthropological research. New York: Holt, Rinehart and Winston.
Nader, Laura
1970—From anguish to exultation. *In* Women in the field: anthropological experiences. Peggy Golde, ed., Chicago: Aldine.
Powdermaker, Hortense
1967—Stranger and friend: the way of an anthropologist. New York: W. W. Norton.
Saberwal, Salish
1969—Rapport and resistance among the Embu of Central Kenya (1963–1964). *In* Stress and response in fieldwork. Frances Henry and S. Saberwal, eds., New York: Harper and Row.
Schwab, William
1970—Comparative field techniques in urban research in Africa. *In* Marginal natives: anthropologists at work. Morris Freilich, ed., New York: Harper and Row.
Spindler, George Ed.
1970—Being an anthropologist: fieldwork in eleven cultures. New York: Holt, Rinehart and Winston.
Wax, Rosalie
1952—Field methods and techniques: reciprocity as a field technique. Human Organization 11:34–37.
Weidman, Hazel H.
1970—On ambivalence in the field. *In* Women in the field: anthropological experiences. Peggy Golde, ed., Chicago: Aldine.
Whitten, Norman E., Jr.
1970—Network analysis and processes of adaptation among Ecuadorian and Novascotian Negroes. *In* Marginal natives: anthropologists at work. Morris Freilich, ed., New York: Harper and Row.
Williams, Thomas R.
1967—Field methods in the study of culture. New York: Holt, Rinehart and Winston.
Wintrob, Ronald M.
1969—An inward focus: a consideration of psychological stress in fieldwork. *In* Stress and response in fieldwork. Frances Henry and Satish Saberwal, eds., New York: Holt, Rinehart and Winston.
Yengoyan, Aram
1970—Open networks and native formalism: the Mandaya and Pitjandara cases. *In* Marginal natives: anthropologists at work. Morris Freilich, ed., New York: Harper and Row.

Anthropology and history have always been closely connected, it is difficult to understand any contemporary sociocultural system without knowledge of the circumstances that contributed to its development. Only by studying sociocultural events through time do we get the depth of perception that will enable us to engage in theoretical generalizing. To identify causality we first have to know the order of events: what happened first and may therefore have affected what happened next.

The chief difference between the anthropologist's and the historian's approach to the study of history is that the former must usually reconstruct the past of a people without writing, without the documentary record of earlier events that is other historians' first resource. Vansina is in the advance guard among ethnohistorians who have ingeniously contributed to overcoming this lack.

Studying Cultures Through Time

Jan Vansina

Two types of building blocks can be used in the construction of anthropological theory. The first and obvious one is the ethnographic monograph, usually based on field work by a trained anthropologist. The data gathered are presumed to apply all to one point in time, the "ethnographic present." In fact the fiction goes farther and most studies are timeless. Such a synchronic analysis usually shows the intricate patterns of integration in society just as descriptive grammars trace the forms of language. To achieve this result the anthropologist has had to pick and choose from his notes, all of which to begin with represented only a fraction of reality. This is best expressed in Evans-Pritchard 1940:261, e.g., ". . . but in case it be said that we have only described the facts in relation to a theory of them and as exemplifications of it and have subordinated description to analysis, we reply that this was our intention." The facts are used to illustrate a pattern, a pattern which can either be superimposed from the start—and this is bad ethnography—or stems from the data as interpreted by the ethnographer. Thus the monograph always represents a descriptive model.

The second building block is the historical monograph. It describes the evolution of a culture and abolishes the zero-time fiction. It is then complementary to and indeed follows from synchronic analysis. Such studies are still rare and have been left, by and large, to the care of historians. Our contention is that these diachronic monographs are important to the development of anthropology and research energy should be devoted to this approach. First, as will be seen, it is technically possible to gather the necessary data and put them together for a reconstruction of the past. Secondly, from this material diachronic models can then be elaborated. Such models have subsidiary uses; they provide a check on synchronic models and also provide a means to overcome the prison of the single culture unit. Their major usefulness however is that they lend themselves to comparative study *sui generis.* These comparisons then lead by step-by-step progression to those regularities in society, which all anthropologists worth their salt are trying to discover. Historical monographs as diachronic models are therefore of critical importance for theoretical anthropology.

Assembling the Data

The techniques to gather and evaluate historical data are generally well established. The most common sources are written, iconographic, monumental, archaeological, oral, linguistic, ethnographic or biological in relation to ethnography (McCall 1964 in relation to Africa). Precise rules for applying historical critique to written sources have been formulated by the positivistic historians of the nineteenth century (Bernheim 1908) and updated or adapted by later theorists (Bauer 1928, Bloch 1952, Carr 1664, Feder 1924, Marrou 1961). The major point here is that it is only through a careful appreciation of the document in its full context that its intrinsic value can be appreciated. In this respect some anthropologists have shown a rather remarkable lack of understanding of the nature of historiography. Kroeber (1939) offers probably the most celebrated case of this when he dismisses documents by Spanish missionaries in California in favor of his own observations, made a century and a half later. This certainly shows how ingrained the zerotime notion is among anthropologists!

Oral tradition and eyewitness accounts are sources which usually make the cultural anthropologist feel much more at home. Here again the essence of criticism or historiography is to place the source in its cultural and linguistic milieu, but this milieu happens to be the society the anthropologist is studying at the time he is studying it. In recent years this type of documentation has received much attention (cf., e.g.,

Source: "Cultures Through Time" by Jan Vansina from the book *A Handbook of Method in Cultural Anthropology,* copyright © 1970 by Raoul Naroll and Ronald Cohen. Reprinted by permission of Doubleday & Company, Inc., and the author.

contributions in *Journal of African History;* Vansina 1961).

Monumental and iconographic sources can be considered along with archaeology, and methods for the use and interpretation of all these data are well established (Atkinson 1953, Leroi Gourhan 1950, Childe 1956). For the important dating methods the journal *Radiocarbon* supplements the more standard accounts. In many parts of the world monuments and iconographic materials have not been fully used yet. An obvious example can be seen in the fact that no one as yet has described material culture and daily life at the court of Benin during the seventeenth century despite the availability of hundreds of bronze plaques which could be used as documents. Also it is often forgotten that cherished objects may be archaeological monuments. In many cases copies will be made when these artifacts are worn out (e.g., in the case of wooden statues, masks and the like), but many of these do not wear out so easily, as seen by the dating of a Dogon (West Africa) mask to 1470 ± 150 A.D. (*Radiocarbon* 1964:4:243; wood). Wooden objects for instance can be used both as a monument and sometimes as a source for iconography concerning dress, decoration patterns, etc.

Historical linguistics and its related techniques have been researched since the early nineteenth century and one can consult the classic by Paul (1909) along with more recent studies such as Bloomfield 1933, Sturtevant 1917, Greenberg 1957, Lehmann 1962, and Sapir 1916. The latter is a classic of its kind and set the pattern for ethnohistorical research in the U.S.A. for the next three or four decades.

Ethnographic data cannot be evaluated so easily since this is the outstanding area where much more work needs to be done regarding methods. The works of the *Kulturhistorische Schule,* Graebner 1911, Van Bulck 1931, Schmidt 1939 and some of the earlier studies in North America, including even Sapir 1916, suffer from two basic defects: the lack of realization that there are no cultural traits similar to molecules in the physical world (Herskovits 1956:170–174) and that every culture is a strongly integrated whole. Under no circumstance can a culture be seen as a Neapolitan cake consisting of layers of cultural sedimentation, because the integrating forces of a culture and the cultural environment which exercises constant (and not interrupted) contact preclude such an evolution. Nevertheless some studies (Spier 1921) show that ethnographic sources can indeed be used. This situation in relation to methodology is best discussed by Herskovits (1956:461–560). We may simply underline here that the very integration of cultures means that no people can mix two cultures in equal proportions at one moment in time. Thus *Mischkulturen* like *Mischsprachen* are nonexistent. Therefore each culture goes back, with regard to its core, to one ancestral culture. The difficulty is that, unlike the linguistic core where phonology and morphology always are at the heart of it, in cultures anything can belong at a given time to the core and the core changes from one culture to another and from one period in time to another. The most that can be said is that usually structures of kinship and territoriality are present as core aspects. On the other hand it is also known that cultures can exhibit some extreme conservatism. In the Middle East archaeologists have found the function of some tools and objects from their diggings by comparison with present-day practice. A hunting camp site of central Africa dated to 2340–2750 B.C. shows a technology which can be paralleled almost perfectly with similar items of Bushman culture in the general area today (Gabel 1965); other examples could be multiplied.

The problem then is to identify what are borrowed features in a culture and if possible put these in a chronological sequence; what are internal innovations and in what order they occurred; and what features were inherited from an ancestral culture whose "reflexes" today would all contribute to this evidence (Vansina 1964b). Obviously if this were to be successfully and completely achieved one would have told the history of cultural change. However, it is only partially possible to achieve this result. The relative chronologies yielded by this type of data are so limited that it becomes difficult even to put them in a common grid for the chronology of even one culture.

The techniques used for construction of chronologies include the tracing of survivals even if metataxis has taken place. Other techniques include distribution patterns of cultural items of which the age area hypothesis is only one variety, and the reconstruction, through comparison, of cultures that are known to have descended from a common ancestral culture, as well as several minor techniques of interpolation and inference. Ethnological data go beyond the status of "conjectural history" and the "40% hypothesis" when they are used in tandem with linguistics and the results confirm one another. In any case the technique of counterproof should be used by which all other explanations could be shown to be much more involved (Ockham's razor) or otherwise much less likely than the selected one. Finally, hypotheses based on cultural evidence should be stated in such a fashion that they can eventually be strengthened by archaeology and/or eventually written data.

The use of biological techniques requires a high degree of competence and detailed discussion is best left to specialists. In general these methods draw conclusions from distribution maps plotting such items as: (a) the wild relatives of domesticated plants and animals; (b) the centers of greatest diversity in domesticated species; and (c) the center of greatest diversity or wild relatives of associated weeds, animal ticks and other parasites. In all cases, including human biology, the genetic situation is at the heart of such reasoning and therefore techniques of population genetics are central to the method. The best the cultural anthropologist can do is to check the data and the general reasoning. Generally his own competence does not go far enough so that he can invent fruitful hypotheses with such data on his own.

The technical question which has been most neglected with regard to historical data is the problem of historical synthesis. How does one draw together data from many different disciplines into a single body of historical reconstruction?

It is not merely a matter of avoiding primary errors of logic such as anachronisms, faulty collection or interpretation of the data, use *pars pro toto,* theological selection of arguments and the like. An example of most of these errors can be found in Heyerdahl 1950, 1952, 1958. Some of these are also discussed in Suggs (1960:212–224). Heyerdahl's work exemplifies the misuse of evidence which has bred such suspicion of reconstructions based on sets of diverse data. One major error has been too strict an application of Collingwood's imaginative reconstruction. The way in which such a process works is illustrated by the last chapter of *Aku-Aku* in which Heyerdahl shows how romantic daydreaming can lead to an uncontrolled and uncritical selection of data.

The first question to arise in any synthesis is to ask what weight should be given to one piece of evidence in relation to another. Many scholars have felt that whole sets of evidence were *a priori* better than others because the discipline they derived from was somehow more trustworthy. We are a long way from Munro's "The materials with which the archaeologist deals are absolutely free from the bias and the ignorance which so frequently distort the statements of the historian" (Piggott 1965:4). Still Herskovits could say, "The ethnohistorian, in fact, draws on four kinds of resources, those of history, archaeology, oral tradition, and ethnolgy. The first two may be thought of as giving him his "hard" materials, which can be taken as much at face value as any of the data of history or archaeology and are subject to the same reservations with regard to their interpretation" Herskovits (1959:230). He argues that "in terms of any index of certainty, the conclusions derived from the ethnographic data must be lodged on a far lower level than those derived from the study of historical documents" (i.e., written materials). What is being weighed are bits of evidence, one pitted against or along another, in a particular situation. But situations vary and it would not be difficult to show cases in which the so often maligned ethnographic materials come out as "hard" evidence, or where any other bit derived from another discipline would make a good show. Thus there is no simple rule of "hard" as opposed to "soft" data for ethnohistory.

In general terms one can only compare the characteristics of the sets of evidence and actually show their complementarity. In most cultures without writing, written sources give accurate dates for the absolute chronology, but they are written by outsiders and often present an external view of a culture in its most visible aspects only. Iconography, monuments and archaeology yield a somewhat vaguer absolute chronology whilst dealing with evidence relating to environment, economics, and visible artifacts, with some possible data about social structure, political life and religious institutions. Oral tradition is weaker on chronology. It gives us ordinarily a relative chronology whose universe is the people or a subset of that society and it does not go as far back in the past as archaeology does. But its data cover all conscious changes in the culture and this means often some economic, political and even religious changes whereas some slow drifts, in social structure for instance, will not be noticed. Linguistic and ethnographic data are the best tools available to uncover unconscious change in the nonmaterial aspects of a culture and they can be applied to all aspects of culture. However, as chronologies they are always relative and the temporal dimension is often limited such that only two events or situations make up the chronological field. One is earlier than the other is all that can be said, and these situations often cannot be related to other chronologies. This of course is a serious weakness since absolute chronology is the grid of history[1] and relative chronologies will be the more useful the wider their geographical and cultural scale. Still this does not mean that linguistic, ethnographic and biological data are to be set aside, only that the intermeshing of their relative chronologies with wider chronologies must eventually be possible if they are going to contribute to ultimate historical syntheses.

To summarize the real complementarity of ethnohistorical data it may be pointed out that usually only written documents tell us something about the role of an individual in a set of events, oral documents tell us about the motivations leading to events, e.g., wars and present idealized images of individuals involved, whereas impersonal slower changes are better shown in archaeological, cultural and linguistic data. In fact the latter three disciplines usually tell us about succeeding situations whereas the first two deal mainly with events. A practical example is the way in which these data can help to determine the origin of a culture and a people. Oral tradition often gives straightforward detailed data. But they may apply only to leaders, not to the majority of the population. Archaeology adds to this by tracing bulk changes in the culture from its artifacts, and linguistics tells us where the language, and presumably the bulk of the ancestors of the present-day speakers,[2] came from. Written data in cultures without writing are usually simply the repositories of oral tradition at one particular point in time. Ethnological data do not tell us much because they presuppose knowledge from other sources, but once this knowledge exists then ethnological materials can be used to describe the processes by which a particular culture originated from its ancestor(s).

Given then that in every individual case the evidence should be weighed without reference to an *a priori* statement about the value of disciplines, how are such reconstructions made? Usually the synthesis centers heavily around one set of data while others are merely complementary. Thus Suggs' reconstruction of Marquesan history is built around archaeology (Suggs 1962) and the author's *Kuba History* revolve heavily around oral traditions (Vansina 1963). This type of reconstruction is only an intermediate synthesis to be replaced by a genuinely full reconstruction later on when the work is redone.

An ultimate synthesis must take *all* the available evidence into account. All evidence implies that all of the disciplines mentioned above will be used (others as well) if they can throw light on the reconstruction such that it becomes eventually a thorough mix of all these data. This can be achieved more easily than it might at first appear. When any evidence of this nature is presented a conscious effort should be made to make out what it represents in terms of other disciplines. For instance, if the cultural data indicate that people in the ancestral society were polygynous and did not share the same house, one would expect archaeologists to find clusters of houses with hearths in each house except the main one in each cluster. That major house was then the dwelling of the husband. If linguistics postulates that several migrations occurred in a small area the correlative evidence from archaeology would be an exact correspondence, say, in successive pottery types. That this actually can be done is well illustrated by the case of the inter-lacustrine Bantu area, where oral tradition suggests that Nilotic invaders entered the area in the second half of the fifteenth century. This conclusion was not arrived at by relative chro-

1 Lévi-Strauss (1962:342–348) details the characteristics of the chronological grid and points out the important fact that several grids are involved, and thus several sorts of history result.

2 As is known, this is no absolute rule. Still, in most cases language, culture and people evolve together. The cultural ancestors are also the physical and linguistic ancestors of the bulk of the people and their modern tongue respectively. Culture and language are more closely tied to each other than any of them to physical population. Yet even in the latter case the link is strong. High prestige, political dominance and a long period of time is necessary for the language of a minority to impose itself on a majority. We believe that this also can happen when population density is low but the minority lives in clusters so that in their immediate environment they are the majority. Given a great length of time they might impose their language and culture on the majority in the whole larger area. Apart from these two situations, though, it is not possible to see how the bulk of a population could lose its language or culture.

nology alone since there was available a selection of absolute dates based on sun eclipses mentioned in the traditions. Archaeological work helped to confirm the date and added some weight to the theory of Nilotic origin because of the type of artifact found, and added strong confirmation to the idea of an invasion (Posnansky 1966).

In this fashion it turns out that the weak chronology of tradition can be bolstered by the use of astronomy and archaeology. Furthermore, this can also be done as well using linguistics and ethnography, whenever items are referred to that can be traced by some artifact or material trace. On the other hand, the interpretation of archaeological data is made within a context of ethnography which often assumes the persistence of features over long periods (Gabel 1965). Such an assumption may be tested by ethnographic studies of the distribution of crucial features involved. Wider distribution generally means longer time depth, although this is not always the case; thus the test is only partial.

If all the data dovetail and confirm one another the result is gratifying because by the principle of independent confirmation, the probability reached by the convergence of independent sources is many times greater than the probability of one line of data only and amounts in practice to certainty. However, care should be exercised to see to it that the data compared are really independent. For instance, if a people say that archaeological deposits such and such are the product of an ancient people named X and Y, oral tradition may depend upon the archaeology. For, if the people knew the sites beforehand they could, and very likely would, have made up an explanation for them and if they had not and human artifacts were discovered, they might conclude logically by themselves that these ought to belong to their predecessors whose name they knew from other oral evidence! The best case of independence is when the oral tradition says that X or Y lived on site A, where nothing is visible today, and then digging on that site uncovers archaeological materials. Similar difficulties can arise for instance between oral tradition and modern ethnographic data. For example, a story has the king of Burundi coming to found the kingdom from the south and passing through places A, B, C, etc., where he founded royal estates of a special kind. It is quite likely that the storyteller, who knows where these sites are today, will have adjusted his story to this knowledge. He thus mentions sites which may not really be mentioned in the original traditions. A detailed comparison of variant stories taken from many informants actually indicates "contamination" of this sort. Thus we can tell when the distribution of archaeological sites and the oral tradition are not truly independent.

It happens also, all too frequently, that data do contradict each other or simply "pass by" each other (McCall 1964:146–148). The first case is rather like the two different results obtained in making a simple sum, and as in that case, one of the results obtained must be wrong. It is not enough that one set of data is wrong; one should show as well, why it is wrong. For instance, an oral tradition may be wrong about the origin of a people because it refers only to the ruling family. It then is not really in flat contradiction with the other data but in fact adds something to them, qualifies them by suggesting that the ruling group is intrusive. This is a very frequent situation which generally indicates that the investigator who complains of the contradiction has not interpreted his data correctly. It is very rare indeed that two types of data will contradict one another when both of them are interpreted rightly. In fact we know of no such case except where the evidence is deliberately falsified, which could happen with both written and oral data.

The "passing-by" of sets of data happens often enough. It means that data which were supposed to cross-check each other are shown not to. For instance, Imbangala traditions in Central Africa include something about a governor or a Portuguese chief Manuel or Miguel. Several interpretations are possible, but in none of these is there any correspondence between events narrated in the traditions and those available in written documents. But as we have already mentioned, written documents do not focus on the same type of events as oral ones. In such cases the result of the confrontation must be limited to show the particular characteristics and inadequacies of each set of data involved, and compared for verification purposes only when truly comparable contents are shown to exist in each.

Historical Reconstruction: A Diachronic Model

Treatises on historical method are usually laconic about both heuristics (how to find the data) and historical synthesis or reconstruction of the past. This is because the personality and especially the imagination of the investigator loom so large in these operations. He "sees" a problem, gathers the data by imagining where they could be and after evaluation he "puts them together" by imagining how things happened in the past. This process of reconstruction is an abstraction. The vulture in its manifestations acts like discourse in language. The realization of the potentials inherent in cultural "structure" are infinite, and even the most prolix study will never exhaust its content. Which means first that new data can always be adduced to refine a reconstruction and second that any reconstruction of the past, like any description of a culture, has to be a model.

This amounts to saying that all historical monographs are models. This is obviously true for works such as Marc Bloch's study of feudalism or Fustel de Coulanges' *Ancient City*. It is also true of such seemingly true-to-life works as memoirs or biographies. Underlying each of these is a hidden framework which determines that only "relevant" data have been included. The principles of relevance are also those which have presided over the construction of the model. The words of Evans-Pritchard quoted earlier in relation to the anthropological monograph apply just as well here. The most remarkable case is certainly that of Viollet LeDuc who built his models in stone when he restored the French Gothic cathedrals to a point where they represented an ideal which he acknowledged had probably never existed at any given moment of the past (Hubert 1961:1229)!

In practice the scholar feels that a study is "finished" when all the "significant" data have been put into some satisfactory relation with each other. For the culture historian this comes when it is sensed that an answer to the question "What were the major lines of development of this culture?" is provided by his interpretation and synthesis. By "major" is understood what the investigator thinks is major, and this subjective element, present in both anthropology and history, has to be squarely recognized. If only pains are taken to explain what is deemed to be "major," to reveal, in other words, what the postulates are, which presided over the construction of the framework of the model, nothing is really wrong. But the trouble is that it is impossible to provide an overt statement of all the premises and assumptions utilized on an *a priori* basis. We are not consciously aware of all of them. Many are bound to a scholar's *Zeitgeist* and he is no more aware of them than the fish is of the water in which it swims. And yet this unconscious structuring is a major characteristic of all sociological and historical models.

The major difference between a synchronic and a dynamic model stems necessarily from the time element. The diachronic one works with the one "law" in history: that what happened later cannot have influenced what happened earlier although what *could* happen later often influences earlier action!). A situation A′ at a later period in time cannot be a *cause* of an earlier situation A. But A can or cannot be a *cause* of A′.

Historical causality is most correctly described as a chain of related antecedents and consequents. The chain is endless but has to be cut if an analysis is to be made possible. Usually one item or variable in a situation is not the cause of the next situation but a number of interacting variables are. Some of these are known and some, indeed most, are not. Thus to attempt to pinpoint a particular thing and say that this alone was responsible for a particular change is wrong. Instead we say that a bundle of antecedents, a "situation," was responsible for a bundle of consequents in a later "situation." Indeed the assumption of cultural integration opens the door to the possibility that any or all facets of culture, be it a hair style or a worldwide war, involve each other and thus every aspect of culture may be a possible antecedent to a consequent change.

Given this point, what is actually said when historical causes are expressed is that situation A became situation A′ because of the known variables (*a, b, c, d . . . n*) plus a number of unknown ones in A all of which together produced the identifiable cluster (*a′, b′, c′, d′ . . . n′*) and other unknowns in A′. In a practical case it looks like this: In a congeries of autonomous chiefdoms with similar structure, the central one stood out because it included more people, was bigger and was more central than the others. Later the others were subordinated to the central one. Clearly the change from autonomy to dependence was dependent upon the factors of size, numbers of people, centricity, and maybe some others. This is the story of the Kuba peoples of Central Africa and the central Bushoong chiefdom. But further factors must be added: different and better military institutions for the center and the ideology that one chiefdom should dominate the rest. The obvious next question must then deal with the development of these military institutions, involving antecedents of the antecedents (the introduction of age groups for one) and bringing to light some new antecedents hidden among the unknown factors as well as asking the same questions about the ideology. Clearly a chain of events is involved and the point of departure for the analysis is in practice an arbitrary one. There is also a field or set of unknown factors, and the point at which one decides to limit the investigation is also arbitrary. To travel down the road of intensifying the investigation yields a diminishing return for greater and greater efforts after a certain point, given present data, method, and theory.

At this point, then, other tactics must be utilized. As we shall see, the notion of historical cause is valuable because it complements synchronic causality shown by covariant correlations. The trick is to keep the unknown factors in the historical equations constant. It then becomes quite clear that the known antecedents ($a \ldots n$) caused ($a' \ldots n'$). This is sound practice and is in fact the cardinal rule of the inductive method used by the natural and physical sciences. It is important to note that the historical method allows us to keep unknown factors more constant than does the synchronic method. This results from the fact that in any given culture the physical environment and the structural framework may not change much over a short time span, whereas in synchronic analysis both are likely to vary. The other advantage of historical causality is that under these circumstances it directly yields a statement in which we can say that a cluster of factors A *caused* the later cluster B whereas the synchronic statement of relationship can only say (without further analysis) that when A changes B also changes. But there is no way of knowing at this stage which of the two sets of factors really controls the other. For these reasons, then, painstaking care should be taken to etch these chains of events clearly in any reconstruction, for they are the "why" of the diachronic model. In other words, whenever a diachronic model is constructed, it is not simply the order of succession of synchronic situations which must be worked out—let us say, describing Mexico in 1492, and the same situation again in 1592. Rather it is to show the chain of events which led from Mexico in 1492 to Mexico in 1592 and justifying the terminal dates in the sequence by showing that they represent periods of comparatively slower change in the chain of events studied.

Perhaps the sources may provide enough information directly when they narrate events, but even so, the picture is usually so complex that at least part of the factors involved have to be inferred. For instance the history of Burundi tells us how Ntare II doubled the national territory between 1800 and 1850—but not why it happened or how it was possible at that particular time. The chain of causal factors must then be inferred by some form of hypothesis. Maybe the kingdom had changed and become stronger than its neighbors, or maybe the neighbors had weakened? One must then go back to the data and check what indications are available. It is then noted that some neighbors had become weaker and that Burundi had not shown signs of becoming stronger through internal reorganization. This provides a "why" answer, but only in the rough. A full explanation must assume events not recorded in the sources.

Such assumed chains of events are generally recurrent ones. When they are recognized as such they are called "processes" and the more current ones are baptized by labels: "population explosion," "migration," "conquest," "ecological adaptation," to name but a few that grace the current literature. Obviously these labels are simplified expressions describing complex phenomena and should never be tagged to an historical model without the most careful scrutiny. Vagueness in this can lead to quite unwarranted generalizations or even impossible sequences. In fact dynamic models can often be judged by the sophisticated or naive way they tackle such processes. Errors in these matters are most often due to preconceptions or general notions held by the scholar about the nature of culture change. Conversely this means that any historical reconstruction is very much affected by the empirical and theoretical knowledge of culture change held by the scholar at the time of his investigations. Such understanding should of course not be expressed in *a priori* structuring of a process of change which then leads to an *a posteriori* "discovery." The obvious course to follow when a general process applies to a particular situation of change is to investigate if all the conditions of the hypothesis are present and all the antecedents and consequents postulated by the theory of social change are manifest in ways consonant with the theory.

Another major cause of errors in the construction of dynamic models stems from the problem of biased data. The underplaying of the role of the individual or the unique event which occurred where there are no written or oral records is an obvious one. Often, for example, economic factors are overdone simply because more is known about them than about socio-political evolution. Above all there is a tendency to simplify the total picture of a culture as one goes farther into the past and the sources become scarcer. The latter tendency usually results in the construction of a model showing an increase in over-all culture complexity, a picture which satisfies us because it coincides with our equation: complexity = progress = trend of history. Such notions as early, developmental, formative, militaristic, expansion, classical, postclassical, in archaeology are illustrations of this level of generalization. However, this notion of progress in history is as much a myth of our culture as the notion of cyclical time, four dynastic reigns deep, is to Burundi or the structural condensation of time in two or three generations to the Australian aborigines. In practice the notion is all the more dangerous in that it is perfectly valid for long time periods and in a world-wide setting. But when the cast is reduced to one culture or one area, and the time to a few centuries, even up to two millennia or so, reality can be quite different. Thus the smaller the time period, the greater the care that should be given to distinguish between the unsupported assumption of a simple-to-complex progression in a diachronic model and clear-cut evidence for such increasing complexity. Only the latter is acceptable.

Dynamic models can be built basically in two ways and in both cases the type of model produced is a structural one. This results from the assumption that the sociostructural framework and the environment condition culture just as morphology and phonemics condition language. They are the framework to be described in a model, that can be either "mechanical" or "statistical," using Lévi-Strauss' terms (1958), but which is always structural.[3] In the first method the scholar may ponder over what happened, recreate the past, fit in the evidence and explain all of it with the simplest and most elegant hypothesis. He then can take his thesis as the outline of his exposé and present all the facts in their appropriate places. But to be thorough he must take the contrary hypotheses into account and then explain why they are less adequate. Only then does this basically narrative form become acceptable, because the assumptions are stated, even though all the reasoning behind the model is not spelled out in detail and the structure of the model often has to be discovered underneath the narrative. Most historians do it this way. The advantage is to underline the subjective aspects of the reconstruction, stress the unique and focus clearly on the chain of causalities. A major disadvantage is that the model itself and the regularities and processes in it may be somewhat obscured, and this is what anthropologists are most interested in.

The second method is to set a starting situation and a final situation, possibly with intermediary situation floors, and then to adduce the necessary evidence for each of these situations. In effect this becomes a succession of synchronic models. Then the stages are tied one to another by showing how the functional loads were shifted from one synchronic situation to the next one and thereby change occurred, or how structural conflict created changes as conflicts were resolved. Similarly, the investigator may work out how the structure allowed room or opportunity for the entry and acceptance of new elements through diffusion or innovation, or again how readaptation to changed environmental factors took place. Although this is a rather popular approach in anthropology, it has a number of drawbacks. For one thing, it is surrounded by an unnecessary gantry of sophistry and definitions aimed at making certain that all assumptions made are conscious (which is, strictly speaking, impossible) and that purely logical argument be observed at all times. It often underplays the determinative power of the unique, and finally it tends to reduce artificially

[3] Lévi-Strauss (1958:311–317) distinguished between history, which uses, he says, statistical models, and anthropology, which uses mechanical ones. In fact we believe both use statistical models in a descriptive stage and mechanical ones later. Note I, page 313, gives a bibliography of the dissenters to Lévi-Strauss' view. He expanded these in *La pensée sauvage,* Chap, IX.

the chains of antecedent and consequent relations into convenient and often therefore simplified processes. The more theoretical the model the more divorced it becomes from the abstracted reality of the particular case involved and the more assumptions have to be read into the data. But these drawbacks can be avoided as shown by some studies (Smith 1960) and the approach may not be inherently inferior to the previous one. Nor is it superior. My personal inclination, however, lies with the first type of model. Whatever the presentation, the elegance of a dynamic model lies in the way it is able to bring out in all its shadings what the chains of change are, while still preserving the horizontal perspectives of the structure at almost any moment in the period. This is not an easy recipe and in practice the exposition of a dynamic model usually takes a book-length study.

The Use of Dynamic Models

To build up the history of a culture one must start from some sort of synchronic model. But during the operation the emerging historical view helps to correct the synchronic perspective which in turn leads to more refined interpretations of the diachronic system. The relation between the two types of models is that of a dialogue which operates in the form of a dialectic. For instance, an analysis of contemporary government may indicate that effective governing cabinets in modern states usually have ten members or less. One may then propose an hypothesis that only a restricted number of persons can efficiently constitute the final decision-making body in a government. The diachronic analysis shows that indeed whenever the cabinet tended to become larger a new "inner" cabinet arose from it and that whenever institutions lost their crucial functions of government they were then allowed to swell to any size, e.g., the House of Lords in Great Britain. The diachronic analysis thus confirms the synchronic statement and in addition illuminates the process by which the size of the crucial "inner cabinet" evolves (Parkinson 1958:39, Table I; *The Coefficient of Inefficiency*, Chap. IV).

In other cases the dynamic view helps to explain some oddities of the synchronic one. When the Bushoong (Congo) political structure is analyzed, it appears that the authority of the king is balanced by his councils. Yet in the actual operation of the political system during 1953, the king obviously held the upper hand. There was a glaring discrepancy between the structure and the practice. A diachronic analysis, however, clearly indicates that this is a recent innovation resulting from the power of the king which developed because he had become a recognized agent of the colonial state. In other words, we are obliged to redraw the synchronic equation of 1953 and take the colonial situation into account (Vansina 1964b).

In some cases two interpretations of a synchronic situation are possible and the diachronic view enables us to see which one is more acceptable. About 80% of Rwanda's population, the Hutu, used to be serfs ruled by an upper caste, the Tutsi. One theory had it that the Hutu accepted their inferior status because a basic premise or configuration, sanction, or theme of society was the inequality of the castes and the mental and hereditary superiority of the upper caste (Maquet 1954:184–196). The other theory was simply that the status of inferiority was accepted because it had been enforced by superior military means. It stresses a structural rather than a mental attitude, and holds that the Hutu do not really accept the premise of inequality (Codere 1962). Rwanda's history shows that the second hypothesis comes closer to reality. Before 1900 much of what is now Rwanda was not under strict Tutsi control and inferiority was not accepted. In the center of the country, on the other hand, the long subservience of the Hutu to the Tutsi, enforced by effective military structures, had led to a common pattern of life in which many Hutu accepted the premise postulated by Maquet. But the chain of causality started from the institutions (military domination) and led to a mental attitude; thus the premise came later rather than the reverse. This implies that as soon as the institutions of dominance decay (as they did under the colonial regime) the mental attitudes might change with some time lag, which they did. The original model then was wrong in the sequence of mental attitude and structure and erred also by considering regional cultural variations to be unimportant. Another instance of the reinterpretation and choice between models through the help of history is the study by Codere (1950) of the Kwakiutl *potlatch*.

Another contribution of diachronic models is that they help to describe the boundaries of a culture unit when it is used in a synchronic model. The problem of defining culture units is a vexing one (Naroll 1964). Generally they have been defined either by postulating an "objective" culture unit from the outside or from the inside. In the first case the anthropologist decides which local communities are more similar in culture and/or language to each other, when this set is compared to others in the area. The congeries are then called a "tribe." Typical examples of these procedures are the Bushmen, Semang, Pygmies, and Lapps. In all these cases members of these "tribes" do not know about the full extent of the ethnic unit and recognize only a smaller unit as their "universe." The subjective view of insiders turns out to be based either on the largest political units (Schapera 1956, e.g., in relation to the South African chief and kingdoms) or on the largest autonomous community felt by insiders to share a similar culture, to be "we" and not "they." By contrast, this definition will make for difficulties in any segmentary society since there is little of a hard and fast line between insiders and outsiders. The arbitrariness of such procedures is shown as well by a case such as Ashanti, where objective similarities lead the investigator to talk about one over-all "Akan tribe" including, among others, the Ashanti. But the kingdom was too big and important so it was made into a separate culture unit. The other Akan are however often labeled Akan because they constitute a number of minor chiefdoms in this area. To confuse things even further, when Akan is used in this latter sense it is often meant to include Ashanti as well!

Whatever culture unit is chosen as the starting point for a diachronic study, it may be assumed that analysis will soon lead to redefinition of the unit almost as a side product of working out its history. If the unit is political the territorial growth or shrinking of the state will show what changes have occurred in the boundaries over time. If it is an "objective" unit, history may show that the unit is not real because the groups which make it up have no common past at all or it may confirm and clarify the unit by showing the exact extent of the common past. If the unit is an insider's point of view it is sometimes possible to show the fluctuations in time of local identification. For instance, the Kongo people of 1600 began to be subdivided, after 1675, by "tribe" into subunits such as the Solongo, Zombo, Soso. This is not a case of better information being available at the later dates. A process of decay occurred in the Kongo kingdom about this time and local loyalties overcame the *esprit de corps* of the one Kongo "nation." Very often it is not feasible to trace the origins of such "subjective" culture units, when no written documents are available, because the shifts in opinion are largely unconscious and intangible and do not tend to be reported by any corroborative sources. But the concept leaves a trace in local cultural life. If it was really a unit, those who felt themselves insiders should have acted together some time against outsiders and some record of this unity may be available.

Whatever the ethnic unit may be, the major job of a diachronic technique is not to decide pro and con, but to help overcome the tyranny inherent in the very notion of units derived from synchronic analysis. Descriptive anthropology may have stressed the study of cultures in isolation far too much and has certainly missed useful interpretations and limited our understanding of situations: for example, the demonstration by Lévi-Strauss (1949) after Radcliffe-Brown (1930) that a form of transformational theory (Lévi-Strauss 1958:Chap. 3) makes the Australian kinship systems more understandable and certainly shows a logic within them not clearly seen before. On a synchronic level there is no simple way to go beyond a unit which is also the universe of description. The only natural and genuine way to overcome the unit and handle an "area" is an historical one. Even Lévi-Strauss has to admit as much (1964: 9) when he says that such comparisons can take place only if historical or geographical (diffusion) ties can be reasonably postulated. Diachronic documentation is the best guide to know how to enlarge one's field of inquiry from one particular "universe" to a larger one, from "village" to "tribe" to "area." It is a guide and it is often used as the justification for doing this. To help overcome the ethnic unit problem is an important contribution that a diachronic approach can make to the comparative study of cultures. In fact, synchronic analysis may already involve the comparative use of diachronic models whose existence is more or less understood as the causal basis for the contemporary unit distributions.

It is hard to exaggerate the contributions that can be made to anthropology by the technique of comparing diachronic models. This is an inductive comparative method, differing from the cross-cultural survey in a *sui generis* way. The steps of the method are: the building of a single larger diachronic model which includes several societies known to descend from a single common ancestral culture (Vansina 1964a). In the model the diversity of the cultures involved in the comparison is totally preserved and no elements are wrenched out of context as they sometimes are in synchronic cross-cultural comparisons. This explains why even for a comparison of two cultures only, it may require a book to set forth a good diachronic model.

The central Kuba and the Lele of Congo are a "simple" case of this sort. Both speak the same language, live in the same environment and superficially at least many features of their cultures are very similar, such as dress, houses, carving, etc. But a sociological analysis shows that the underlying structures are very different one from the other. For example the Kuba are organized in centralized chiefdoms, the Lele in autonomous villages. Even on the level of food production in a similar environment there are differences. The Kuba reap two crops of maize a year, the Lele one; the Kuba fish, the Lele do not; the Lele make finer cloth than the Kuba whose designs are more ornate, etc. (Douglas 1962, 1963; Vasina 1964b). There are good data showing the general evolution of the Kuba since *circa* 1600, especially their political development (Vansina 1963). There is little direct information about the Lele but a number of ethnographic distributions confirm that they have been major innovators in the area. They either invented or (more likely) adopted a system of age-sets and this is correlated with new forms of village government, and polyandry (new). The distribution of the latter institution on the fringes of all peoples bordering on the Lele and throughout Lele land makes it likely that they are the innovators. It is possible to show with present material how the Kuba and Lele cultures have diverged from a common ancestral pattern. This proto-Lele-Kuba society was a type of small and rather weak chiefdom. Each of them (Kuba and Lele) reintegrated constantly new internal or foreign elements into their societies and differentiated eventually from the parent society. It is obvious that cases such as these (and they are, I believe, *legio*) do enrich our knowledge of the dynamics of social change considerably. But such work requires separate treatment. Apart from the two books already devoted to describing synchronic models for Kuba and Lele, a third one is needed to build a satisfying, rich diachronic one showing Kuba and Lele as descendant ethnic groups from a common ancestor.

There is a natural transition from the previous type of comparison to a real one. The Mongo peoples of the Congo basin (numbering at least twenty-five "tribes") are all related one to another and one could presumably try to build up a single diachronic model or a history for all of them. The difference from the Lele-Kuba would be merely one of scope. The same could be done for, e.g., the Western interlacustrine cultures of East Africa. One goes almost unwittingly a step further when an area is considered in which whatever ancestral society there may have been lies much farther back in time. For instance the Lele-Kuba probably separated from the parent culture in the sixteenth century or so. But they belong to a larger congeries of people, which was well differentiated long before that. It would not be wise to reconstruct an ancestral society for the larger group, because it would have to be based on several already reconstructed cultures, which means that the resulting hypothesis would be second or third or *n*th degrees removed from data. For instance, to describe a common ancestral Bantu society about two thousand years ago by this method would be quite unreal! But an over-all examination of all the cultures in an area would yield specific features about them, realized differently in each culture but still belonging to a common theme. The evidence would show that probably a single ancestral institution might lay at the bottom of these variations on one theme, or it might turn out that diffusion was to be considered. In practice the different realizations of the common theme would be handled as transformations and one would show why each transformation was adopted by each culture, rather than to try to reconstruct the Ur-institution! In such a fashion areas can be enlarged as long as there are good ethnographic and historical reasons for it. One can consider Australia or Bantu Africa or lowland South America or ultimately even the whole of the Americas as one area. In each case the variations of the socio-political structures, religious life, economics, etc., could be recorded and tentative rules about social change, valid for the area, could be set up, rather like those laws in physics which apply only in a given environment.

Another complementary form of a real comparison occurs when the histories of cultures or parts of the cultures in the area are known. We have argued that one of the major steps in handling historical causality is to preserve the unknowns in the equation of the antecedent and subsequent situations, keeping them as constant as possible. If the culture area investigated lies within a single environment such that basic economic production is rather similar, and there are many similarities in the basic social and political patterns, then many of the unknowns in a comparison are held constant. . . . A comparison of the separate cultural histories will then show whether the interpretations used to explain one of the cases has more general application to other cases. In practice it is fairly easy to sort out processes which are unique from more general ones even though there may be unknown antecedents working in all cases whose comparability is beyond our reach at this point. For instance, in the Central African kingdoms monarchy was the keystone to the political structure: it was a common antecedent everywhere. So, in most cases, was matrilinearity, except for the Luba among whom patrilinearity made for some unique antecedents. The common factor of kingship, the common ideology of kingship by which the personality of a ruler was so important that fluctuations in the fortunes of the state were closely associated with the succession of personalities on the throne more than to anything else led to remarkably similar profiles in the political history of most of these states. Linked to this was a system of succession whereby frequent civil wars led to a weakening of the state during the *inter regna*, and in many cases states succumbed to foreign intervention during civil wars of this sort. Everywhere too decentralization was so marked that the outer provinces were often semi-autonomous, which explains the lack of a balance of power between the great states and the impossibility of a struggle for the "hegemony." It resulted also in the frequent splitting off of peripheral provinces, whenever the nuclear area was under great stress (Vansina 1966). All of these remarks about Central African states can be said to form a set of regularities or "laws" valid for the area.

A next step might be to compare one area with another where the backgrounds were somewhat different and historical relationship would be nil or remote. For example we might compare the Central African kingdoms with those of Indonesia. If regularities held up after this comparison one could then say about the Central African cases that certain of their common "unknown" factors could be discarded because they did not occur in Indonesia. A good illustration of this sort of comparison is the comparison of Meso-America and the Middle East by Adams (1966). Here regularities are detected quite skillfully and at the same time an explanation is given for differences in the "realization" of the underlying regularities, i.e., in the way they manifest themselves in each area.

Comparisons of some areas with others that are close to them geographically but where no recent historical relationship is involved yields results in between those obtained from intra-areal comparisons and comparisons between areas far away from each other. To compare Central African states with interlacustrine states or West African kingdoms will yield more regularities, and these may be more specific, than in a comparison between Central Africa and Indonesia. The point is that, depending on the problem, there is available a marvelously graduated scale of comparisons from very close and similar cultures to the very distant ones. Inductive reasoning can be followed step by step throughout a set of ever-widening "universes" or the researcher can jump steps to test a regularity he suspects to be more fundamental and try it out in a comparison between very different cultures far apart from one another.

By and large there is no doubt that real gains will be made only by a natural progression from the smallest to the biggest levels of universes. For only in this way are regularities tested gradually, refined and retested whilst the cultural data are never wrenched out of context. Theoretically the ultimate level would be the world and conclusions might be reached that whenever antecedents (a . . . n) obtain, x follows. With that would have been established what all anthropologists strive for: a statement with predictive value.

In practice though, it is known that so many variables are at work in human affairs that any particular global constellation of factors will hardly ever occur twice. It is still not certain that what we call the "unique" (*das Einmalige*) is not merely a unique combination of factors which are not unique in themselves. However, this is quite likely, and the consequences of uniqueness must be faced up to. Only in a few fields of history has there been systematic utilization of historical regularities in which decisions are based on such knowledge. The use by the military men of the history of war is a case in point;

prediction is achieved by computers who program the several possible initial situations and give a series of probable outcomes.

From the military example and some practice of history, it is obvious that when regularities are proposed as laws this almost never takes the form of: given factors *a, b, c,* the result will be *x, y, z.* But rather: given *a, b, c,* and unknowns, the result will be *x, y, z,* or *t, u, v;* and if *x, y, z,* this will develop into *z';* if *t, u, v,* into *t',* etc. Such a statement looks like this:

Given the general conditions of the Central African states, the relation between the leadership of the territorial upper level posts and the future evolution of the state will be: first, if these posts are filled with members of the royal lineage they can either become hereditary and lead to another type of territorial control; or the posts are filled every generation by new members of the royal lineage, more closely related to the new rulers, in which case the system can become one of an appointed bureaucracy in which non-royals begin to be appointed, or can persist as before. But, *no case of persistence is known as yet.* Secondly, if the posts are filled by an hereditary principle, the autonomy of the provinces increases and the kingdom can fall apart rather easily. This is also a possible outcome in the first variant of the first case. As long as there is a strong nucleus, however, the system can persist. Thirdly, if an appointed bureaucracy rules, the system is likely to persist as long as tendencies toward inheritance are checked by the court. Since this is difficult to achieve with the powerful royal lineages, a bureaucracy staffed by royals will not last and that is the reason no persistence has been noted.

This set of rules applies to the Central African states. It looks very much like the "rules" one finds in handbooks of chess. And in fact we suspect strongly that all "historical laws" will have to be expressed in the form of a game theory.

One must point out however that even if predictions could be made, the prediction would not be able to come true any longer in the future because in almost all the situations the antecedents would specify a pre-industrial economy, and would not apply to a modern state. Even if control areas were set aside from which no data could be used in the formulation of the rule, such a situation would still hold. If the rule did not apply, a reason for its non-application would have to be stated and incorporated into the rule. No possible predictive test can then be used for those cases. But although it is disappointing, it does not invalidate the procedure.

It has been argued that diachronic models can be built and are worth building not only because they help to improve synchronic models or overcome the difficulties arising from the use of culture units, but mainly because they can be used inductively and comparatively without any loss whatsoever of the fascinating complexity of reality, and without any tearing of features from their natural backgrounds. This method leads to the statement of rules about process, thus fulfilling an essential aim of anthropology. It is however also obvious that much humble collecting of ethnographic data, and much piecing together of "simple" histories and limited diachronic comparisons, will be necessary before any solidly based general rules can be uncovered. And here, as the history of anthropology shows, there is no shortcut.[4]

[4] Most of the illustrations have been drawn from Africa, not that none could be found elsewhere, but because of our greater familiarity with this area. Comparable examples might be adduced from any area in the world.

BIBLIOGRAPHY

Adams, R. M.

1966 *The evolution of urban society: early Mesopotamia and Prehispanic Mexico.* Chicago, Aldine.

Atkinson, R. J. C.

1953 *Field archaeology.* London, Methuen.

Bauer, W.

1928 *Einführung in das studium der geschichte.* Tübingen, J. C. B. Mohr.

Bernheim, E.

1908 *Lehrbuch der historischen methode und der geschichtsphilosophie.* Leipzig, Duncker and Humbolt.

Bloch, M.

1952 Apologie de l'histoire ou le métier d'historien. *Cahiers des annales* 3.

Bloomfield, L.

1933 *Language*. New York, Holt.

Carr, E. H.

1964 *What is history?* New York, Knopf.

Childe, V. G.

1956 *A short introduction to archaeology*. London, Muller.

Codere, H.

1950 *Fighting with property*. Monographs of the American Ethnological Society, Vol. 18.

1962 Power in Ruanda. In R. Cohen, ed., Power in complex societies in Africa. Anthropologica 4:45–85.

Douglas, M.

1962 Lele economy compared with the Bushong: a study of economic backwardness. In Bohannan and Dalton, eds., *Markets in Africa*. Evanston, Northwestern University Press.

1963 *The Lele of Kasai*. London, Oxford University Press.

Evans-Pritchard, E. E.

1940 *The Nuer*. Oxford, Clarendon Press.

Feder, A.

1924 *Lehrbuch der geschichtlichen methodik*. Regensburg, München, Verlag J. Kossel and F. Pustet.

Gabel, C.

1965 *Stone age hunters of the Kafue: the Gwisho A site*. Boston University African Research Studies No. 6. Boston, Boston University Press.

Graebner, F.

1911 *Methode der ethnologie*. Heidelberg, C. Winter.

Greenberg, J. H.

1957 *Essays in linguistics*. New York, Wenner-Gren Foundation for Anthropological Research.

Herskovits, M.J.

1956 *Man and his works*. New York, Knopf.

1959 Anthropology and Africa: a wider perspective. *Africa,* 29 (3):225–238.

Heyerdahl, T.

1950 *Kon-Tiki*. London, G. Allen.

1952 *American Indians in the South Pacific*. London, Allen and Unwin.

1958 *Aku-Aku*. Chicago, Rand McNally.

Hubert, J.

1961 Archéologie Médiévale. In C. Samaran, ed. *L'histoire et ses méthodes,* pp. 275–238, 1226–1241. Paris, Gallimard.

Journal of African History

1960–1966 Cambridge University Press.

Kroeber, A. L.

1939 *Cultural and natural areas of North America*. University of California Publications in American Archaeology and Ethnology, Vol. 48. Berkeley, University of California Press.

Lehmann, W. P.

1962 *Historical linguistics: an introduction*. New York, Holt, Rinehart and Winston.

Leroi Gourhan, A.

1950 *Les fouilles préhistoriques: techniques et méthodes*. Paris, Picard.

Lévi-Strauss, C.

1949 *Les structures élémentaires de la parenté*. Paris, Presses Universitaires de France.

1958 *Anthropologie structurale*. Paris, Plon.

1962 *La pensée sauvage*. Paris, Plon.

1964 *Mythologiques: le cru et le cuit*. Paris, Plon.

Maquet, J. J.

1954 *Le système des relations sociales dans le Ruanda ancien*. Annales du musée royal du Congo belge. Sciences de l'homme. Ethnologie, Vol. 1.

Marrou, C. I.

1961 Qu'est-ce que l'histoire? In C. Samaran, ed., *L'histoire et ses méthodes,* pp. 3–36. Paris, Gallimard.

1961 Comment comprendre le métier d'historien. In C. Samaran, ed., *L'historie et ses méthodes,* pp. 1465–1540. Paris, Gallimard.

McCall, D.

1964 *African in time perspective*. Boston, Boston University Press.

Naroll, R.
1964 On ethnic unit classification. *Current Anthropology* 5 (4):283–312.
Parkinson, C. Northcote
1958 *Parkinson's law*. London, J. Murray.
Paul, H.
1909 *Prinzipien der sprachgeschichte*. Halle, M. Niemeyer.
Piggott, S.
1965 *Ancient Europe*. Chicago, Aldine.
Posnansky, M.
1966 *Prelude to East African history*. London, Oxford University Press.
Radcliffe-Brown, A. R.
1930–1931 The social organization of Australian tribes. *Oceania* 1 (2).
Sapir, E.
1916 *Time perspective in aboriginal American culture: a study in method*. Department of mines, geological survey, anthropological series. Memoir 90, Series No. 13. Reprinted in D. Mandelbaum, ed., *Selected writings of Edward Sapir,* 1949. Berkeley, University of California Press.
Schapera, I.
1956 *Government and politics in tribal societies*. London, Watts.
Schmidt, W.
1939 *The cultural historical method of ethnology*. Translated by S. A. Sieber. New York, Fortuny's.
Smith, M. G.
1960 *Government in Zazzau*. London, Oxford University Press.
Spier, L.
1921 The sun dance of the Plains Indians: its development and diffusion. *Anthropological Papers, American Museum of Natural History* 16 (7):451–527.
Sturtevant, E. H.
1917 *Linguistic change*. Chicago. Reprinted 1962, Chicago, University of Chicago Press.
Suggs, R. C.
1960 *The island civilizations of Polynesia*. New York, New American Library.
1962 *The hidden worlds of Polynesia*. New York, Harcourt, Brace.
Van Bulck, G.
1931 *Beiträge zur methodik der völkerkunde*. Wiener beiträge zur kulturgeschichte und linguistick, Vol. 2.
Vansina, J.
1961 *De la tradition orale*. Translated by H. M. Wright, *Oral tradition*. Chicago, Aldine.
1963 *Geschiedenis van de kuba*. Annales du musée royal de l'Afrique Centrale, sciences humaines, No. 44.
1964a The use of process-models in African history. In J. Vansina, R. Mauny, and L. Thomas, eds., *The historian in tropical Africa*. London, Oxford University Press.
1964b *Le royaume kuba*. Annales du musée royal de l'Afrique Centrale, sciences humaines, No. 49.
1965 *Oral tradition*. Chicago, Aldine.
1966 *Kingdoms of the savanna*. Madison, University of Wisconsin Press.

To theorize about causality in human behavior, about what actions or events recurrently precipitate what consequences, there are two methodological problems that must be dealt with after a worthwhile theoretical question has been properly posed. The first entails collecting a sample that is adequately representative to permit generalization. The other involves undertaking the statistical manipulations necessary to assure that the sampling results are theoretically useful.

Statistics is a standard part of most anthropologists' training. Many of the techniques they employ in cross-cultural analysis were first developed in the other behavioral sciences, particularly in sociology and psychology. Udy is a sociologist who has lent his skills to some of the most theoretically productive intersocietal comparisons that have so far been made.

Cross-Cultural Analysis

Stanley H. Udy, Jr.

Any comparative study of social phenomena across two or more different societies is, in the broadest sense of the term, "cross-cultural." Current usage, however, ordinarily distinguishes "cross-cultural" from "cross-national" research, with the former referring only to comparisons among nonindustrial societies of the variety traditionally studied by anthropologists, and the latter, to comparisons among modern nations. It is also usually presumed that "cross-cultural analysis" is directed, at least in part, toward generalizations, and is thereby distinguished from piecemeal comparisons seeking only to describe one society by contrasting it with others, though this distinction has by no means always been approved (Lewis 14). The trend of recent years has thus favored an increasingly specialized conception of cross-cultural analysis, and for good reason. As a research activity, the comparative study of nonindustrial societies with a view to discovering or testing general principles is distinctive, and in fact quite different theoretically, conceptually, and methodologically from both cross-national research and piecemeal comparison. Our discussion will thus be confined to cross-cultural analysis, conceived in this narrower, more specialized, sense.

Despite the fact that the ultimate objectives of cross-cultural analysis would seem to be central to both anthropology and sociology, its basic patterns of operations, as well as the skills it demands, are very different from those of any other type of research habitually carried on in either field. The typical cross-cultural study is directed toward the analysis of a relatively small number of traits over a relatively large number of societies. The number and type of societies studied, as well as the range and kinds of data required from each society, are determined by the nature of the generalizations sought, rather than by a desire to study any society in particular. If only because several or many societies are involved, the cross-cultural researcher is almost always obliged to rely on secondary source materials for most of his information. Since the sample of societies is usually fairly large, it is likely to prove convenient, and possibly necessary, to manipulate the data through aggregative statistical techniques. Cross-cultural analysis therefore typically emerges as a scholarly and statistical enterprise carried on largely in the library, office, and laboratory, rather than in the field. Generally speaking, it involves studying secondary ethnographic and historical sources in large numbers of nonindustrial societies, coding relevant data from these sources, and manipulating these data so that they will yield fairly abstract, theoretical conclusions.

There certainly would seem to be nothing terribly strange about all this. Indeed, if one wishes to develop general theories about the nature of human society from empirical data, it is difficult to imagine how else one could do it. Yet this "package" of activities does not contain very many things that anthropologists or sociologists have been, or are, normally trained to do. This situation seems rather curious, and the historical circumstances that brought it about lie at the root of many current problems faced by cross-cultural research. We shall thus begin our review with a brief discussion of these circumstances and the intellectual situation in which they have left us. We shall then be in a position to comment not only on the kinds of research problems to which cross-cultural analysis is appropriate, but also on its practical limitations in dealing with these problems. This discussion will lead us to a more explicit consideration of the difficulties currently faced by cross-cultural analysis, together with some suggestions as to how such difficulties might be resolved or at least coped with. Throughout the entire review, our references to the literature will be illustrative rather than exhaustive. Unlike many social scientists, cross-cultural researchers are frequently assiduous bibliographers, with the result that fairly complete bibliographies of this field are readily available else-

Source: Reprinted, with permission of the author and the publisher, from "Cross-Cultural Analysis: Methods and Scope," *Annual Review of Anthropology*. Vol. 2, pp. 253–270.

where. We shall thus not replicate them here. Excellent, complete, current, and cumulative bibliographies are provided by O'Leary (27, 28). The journal, *Behavior Science Notes,* proposes to publish annual supplements to these bibliographies. A fine selective bibliography is provided by Textor (39, pp. 189–208). Marsh's *Comparative Sociology* (15, pp. 375–496) contains a comprehensive selection, not limited, however, to cross-cultural comparative research as that area is here defined.

The Historical Legacy

Cross-cultural analysis makes sense only in an intellectual context that stresses the fundamental general similarities among separate societies that are different in detail. "Classical" evolutionism provided such a context (Tylor 40), as does—to some extent—contemporary sociological theory (Parsons 29), but what happened in between did not. As a result, the current theoretical situation of cross-cultural analysis is rather weak, and the data base from which such analysis must usually proceed is not especially well suited for comparative purposes.

CULTURAL RELATIVISM. This situation had its origin in the severity of the cultural relativist reaction to classical evolutionism. Some of our humanist colleagues even today have never quite forgiven us for the excesses of nineteenth and early twentieth century social evolutionism. Nevertheless, whatever their faults, the evolutionists did emphasize cross-cultural research using a framework based on analytic similarities assumed to be universal to all societies. Unfortunately, in their righteous indignation at the frequently both grandiose and incorrect formulations of the evolutionists, the cultural relativists virtually cast out the comparative method along with evolutionism. Each society became unique. The comparison of different societies, therefore, made no sense. The proper task of social anthropology became the explanation of traits by tracing their configuration within a single, presumptively unique, culture.

The widespread acceptance of this position discouraged the explanation of culture traits not only by the general evolutionistic theories it was meant to avoid, but by any general theory whatever. Yet at the same time it provided a major stimulus to the development of a rich and valuable tradition of descriptive empirical field research in anthropology, a tradition which continues, and without which cross-cultural research would today be impossible for want of data. The cultural relativist reaction thus has the mixed consequence of making cross-cultural analysis possible today while at the same time being responsible for many of its most serious difficulties. It generated a veritable flood of ethnographic field studies. At the same time, its atheoretical and anticomparative bias meant that most of these studies were not carried on with a view to their possible use as sources in cross-cultural research, and they were quite likely to have been conducted with the underlying idea that they could not be so used (Eggan 6, pp. 747–49). As a result, the cross-cultural analyst today is likely to have to cope with fairly uneven data and must face some exceedingly difficult problems in adapting these data for comparative purposes without distorting them.

MITIGATING INFLUENCES. The situation might be worse were it not for two more or less independent mitigating elements in the situation. The first was a lack of consistency among the cultural relativists in their insistence that each society is unique. Furthermore, this lack of consistency fortunately followed quite consistent patterns and thus laid some groundwork for later comparative taxonomy. The cultural relativists particularly stressed fieldwork and developed standard strategies for doing it, which resulted in some comparability, unintended or not, among different ethnographic reports. They also continued, by and large, to utilize fairly uniform sets of topical headings in presenting their findings. Certain entire models from the earlier comparative tradition were preserved as well and continued to be uniformly applied in different societies. The most elaborate and frequently used was Morgan's model of the kinship system (16), and it is noteworthy that the comparability of data thereby achieved subsequently made kinship one of the most fruitful areas of cross-cultural research. To be sure, these seemingly arbitrary, albeit systematic, deviations from a strict relativist doctrine imposed an occasionally odd structure of criteria of relevance on anthropology. The presumed centrality of kinship to social structure is a case in point. One wonders what anthropology might look like today had Morgan happened to write, for example, on Forms of Coordination and Authority in Human Work. What is important, however, is that some measure of uniformity and standardization was maintained in both research and reporting in the face of strong opposing pressures.

The second mitigating element in the situation was the fact that cultural relativism in the last analysis represented more a shift of emphasis than a total abandonment of comparison per se. Lewis (14) argues this point in some detail, pointing out that "comparison is a generic aspect of human thought rather than a special method of anthropology or of any other discipline." As part of this picture, comparative studies of even the extensive cross-cultural variety we have in mind here continued to surface from time to time. Perhaps the most notable examples were those of Hobhouse, Wheeler & Ginsberg (12) and of Sumner & Keller (37).[1] In the heyday of cultural relativism, however, such comprehensive efforts were neither particularly appreciated nor admired. To a great extent this still remains the case; a legacy of three decades is very difficult to escape, particularly if one is in the position of having to continue to depend on much of what it has left behind: However, the situation has basically changed. The current state of social theory is such that cross-cultural analysis again makes sense and at the very least is difficult not to tolerate in some form.

THE "RETURN" TO COMPARATIVE RESEARCH. Every systematic empiricist enterprise, if at all sophisticated, is soon in search of a theoretical rationale. Cultural relativism found such a rationale in functionalism. The effect of early functionalism, whatever may have been its intent, was not to generalize but rather to particularize by portraying any given culture as a unique network of interdependent concrete traits. In its actual application, however, the analytic procedure following from this position implied the presence of some general model against which the description of the society in question was being projected. In the course of time, therefore, functionalism did a complete about face, moving from a collection of discrete empirical systems of concrete traits, each describing a particular society, to a generalized model relating structural categories allegedly common to all societies (Levy 13). Whatever special problems this model may involve, it denies that each culture is truly unique and stresses general cultural similarities. It thus not only provides justification for cross-cultural analysis on a basis different from that of evolutionism, but also lends itself to the formulation of conceptual frameworks specifically designed for that purpose.

By the late 1940s, therefore, the stage had been set for the reconstitution of cross-cultural analysis as an intellectually respectable enterprise. Indeed, such reconstitution may be regarded as having been initiated by the publication in 1949 of Murdock's *Social Structure* (17), and has proceeded since that time. It has proceeded at something less than breakneck speed, however, for the legacy of cultural relativism is still very much with us. In many quarters, descripive field research is still regarded as being much more important than comparative analysis. Of more significance, because it is more unavoidably durable, is the fact that most of the data available for use in cross-cultural research were collected under the influence of strongly anticomparative intellectual persuasions. At best, considerable adaptation, with many attendant risks and problems, is necessary to render these data usable for comparative purposes. Finally, in view of the excursion away from theory for the better part of three decades, it is not surprising that contemporary cross-cultural analysis is likely to suffer frequently from ad hoc conceptualization and highly eclectic and opportunistic taxonomy. Placed in this context, our earlier observations that cross-cultural analysis is less popular than one might logically expect it to be, and that it involves a style of work quite different from the current norm in both anthropology and sociology, become more readily understood. Yet the fact remains that the objectives of cross-cultural analysis are not only central to both of these fields, but embody certain kinds of research problems that are very difficult to attack by any other method.

Problems Appropriate to Cross-Cultural Analysis

Cross-cultural analysis is not only appropriate, but in principle necessary, whenever one is studying phenomena whose total relevant range

[1] The latter eventually led to the establishment at Yale University of the Cross-Cultural Index, later to become the Human Relations Area Files (Ford 7).

of variation exceeds the degree of variation ever found within any given society. This condition is regularly encountered in two research situations, and may be encountered in a third. The first situation occurs in very broadly conceived research designed to achieve generalizations about the nature of human society as such. The second occurs in the generalizing study of narrower institutional structures which, however, regularly permeate entire human societies. Both of these situations are similar in that entire societies are the basic units of observation—in the case of the first because society is itself the object of investigation, and in the case of the second because some of the boundaries of social institutions always at least presumptively extend to the boundaries of the society in which they are found. The third situation is different. It is the study of organizations of one type or another by means of cross-cultural analysis. The difference lies in the fact that the basic units of observation are organizations of the type being studied, rather than societies, with the latter along with institutional structures emerging as contextual rather than primary objects of investigation. Cross-cultural analysis in principle is always a possible response to this type of research situation, but it becomes essential only if the research problem requires the systematic introduction of more contextual variation than can be achieved in the context of a single society. In practice, the cross-cultural study of organizations is quite rare.

Almost any given cross-cultural study can be classified as primarily involving some one of these three research situations, on the basis of what it is essentially about (i.e. what the structural reference is of the dependent variables it is ultimately trying to explain). Such classification is useful because the precise nature of certain fundamental theoretical and methodological problems depends specifically on the locus of the ultimate dependent variables. It is not, however, uncommon for a given study to involve, in a secondary way, more than one of these research situations. Any cross-cultural study of organizations, for example, will almost invariably entail some analysis of the nature of institutions or entire societies in order to develop independent contextual variables (Udy 45). The basic problems encountered, however, will remain those of a study of organizations, rather than of institutions or societies.

The Study of Society. Though standard fare for the earlier evolutionists, comprehensive cross-cultural research about the general nature of human society is not too frequently encountered today as an end in itself. Rather, it usually appears as a means for developing independent contextual variables to aid in explaining something less general, such as institutions or organizations. Cross-cultural analyses focusing broadly on the nature of human society thus ordinarily appear as parts of studies primarily concerned with something else. Even those that stand alone usually clearly imply that they were carried out with the aim of systematizing the context of lower order phenomena to be studied in the future (Freeman & Winch 8, Schuessler & Driver 34). The only consistent exceptions are occasional comprehensive, neo-evolutionist efforts, though there are other unique examples (Carneiro & Tobias 3).

Although this variety of cross-cultural research may be explicitly directed toward stating general propositions and of course implicitly always involves doing so, it is more frequently carried on with a view to devising classification schemes or constructing taxonomies, given its usual purpose. It almost always follows one of two major approaches. The first seeks to discover principal dimensions of social structure inductively through the use of cluster or factor analysis. Relationships among the dimensions thus yielded can then be explored and propositionalized, with the end result, presumably, of a set of principles about the general nature of human society (Driver & Schuessler 5, Gouldner & Peterson 9, Gregg & Banks 11, Sawyer & LeVine 32, Schuessler & Driver 34, Stewart & Jones 36). Although this approach has yielded some extremely interesting pieces of work, it emerges with a final closed model of society consisting of interrelated basic dimensions of variation among the traits studied. One must therefore be prepared to argue that the list of traits studied is a theoretically defensible operational definition of "any society." The present state of theory combined with the highly empiricist character of most ethnographic materials make such an argument very difficult. Criteria of relevance for the selection of traits to be included in such an analysis are very likely to be insufficiently developed, and efforts to overcome this problem by an "everything but the kitchen sink" solution will not suffice. One is thus faced with a model describing a somewhat arbitrary collection of culture traits, purporting to be a model of any society, and constructed in such a way that traits cannot be added without, in effect, starting all over again. Reliable results are difficult to achieve; this approach yields an inflexible solution to a problem that, given the current state of the field, may require a more flexible solution. It has proved more useful as an exploratory aid to discovering contextual correlates of variation in particular institutions where "finality" of results may be exactly what is desired (Russell 31).

The second major cross-cultural approach to the study of entire societies is that of ordering societies on a Guttman scale according to whether or not they possess certain culture traits, or to utilize some other similar form of index construction. It has proved possible, at least empirically, to do this from a number of points of view, with the resulting scale, in one way or another, usually roughly indicative of variations in structural complexity (Carneiro 2, Carneiro & Tobias 3, Freeman & Winch 8, Naroll 23, Schwartz & Miller 35). In principle, of course, this approach suffers from many of the same problems as the first. However, in our view, it has fared somewhat better in practice. It lends itself to evolutionistic formulations—most notably the "surplus" model of development—and can hence benefit from criteria of relevance derived from evolutionistic models. In this connection, it also has the fortunate capability of often yielding pragmatically fruitful results even when the model on which it is based proceeds from questionable or incorrect assumptions. For example, one of the controversies surrounding this approach is whether or not a scale so derived describes an actual developmental sequence. Our position, which we and others have argued elsewhere, is that one cannot answer this question on the basis of an inductive inspection of the scale pattern alone (Graves, Graves & Kobrin 10, Udy 43). The answer, however, may be quite irrelevant in many applications of this method. In fact, it may not even matter whether the resulting "scale" is really a scale at all, as opposed to a simple typology of qualitatively different kinds of societies which fit a pattern that merely looks like a scale. What is important is that through scaling one can systematically order societies according to degree of complexity, degree of affinity to the characteristics of industrialism, and so forth, in such a way as to generate independent contextual variables in connection with the study of institutions and organizations. To be sure, if one is interested in social change at the societal level, the developmental sequence problem remains. In such instances, scaling undoubtedly can be used to advantage, but, we would argue, only in combination with other historical evidence.

Social Institutions. The study of the general nature of human society is rather ambitious, and it is thus perhaps not surprising that the most frequent application of cross-cultural analysis lies in a less comprehensive area—the study of particular social institutions. By "institution" in this context we understand a more or less internally consistent system of values, norms, and folk models defining a pattern of aspects of social activity. An "institutional structure" is a complex of institutions, culturally defined as systematically interrelated, although occasionally this term is also used to refer to a single institution as well. These conventions of usage lead one to a superorganic view of culture; the totality of institutional structures in any society would constitute the "culture" of that society. One may thus think, for example, of "debt relations" as an institution, forming part of a broader institutional structure called the "economic system," which in turn combines with other similarly broad institutional structures such as the political and religious systems to form the culture of the society. It is apparent that some institutional structures are more comprehensive than others, and that the more comprehensive ones are frequently intertwined by virtue of the high probability that particular institutions may have simultaneous reference to more than one broader institutional structure. Debt relations, for example, are very likely to have political as well as economic relevance in any society. Since institutions define aspects of action rather than concrete unit acts, it is conceptually possible to assume that any given institution at least potentially permeates the entire society, and most cross-cultural studies make this assumption. It thus becomes possible for the researcher to discuss any social activity, or set of social activities, from the standpoint of potential relevance to any institutional structure.

It is likewise evident that the number, type, and arrangement of institutions may vary considerably from one society to another. In societies very close to the subsistence level, for example, the political system may emerge as essentially a substructure of the kinship system, or it may not even exist as a separate culturally defined entity. Such questions are ordinarily left to empirical determination, and, in one form or another, are often part of the cross-cultural research problem itself.

Institutional cross-cultural studies vary enormously in scope, as one might expect, since institutional structures themselves vary greatly in complexity and comprehensiveness. Some such studies focus narrowly on particular sets of customs, such as, for example, child-rearing practices, menstrual taboos, or specific forms of witchcraft. Others are broadly conceived and focus on comprehensive institutional structures, such as the economy, religious system, or kinship system. The bibliography of such studies is very extensive, and the reader is referred to O'Leary (27, 28) for references. Two particularly thorough examples which illustrate almost polar variations in scope are Whiting & Child (47) and Swanson (38).

The typical institutional research strategy seeks to explain variations in the institutional structure focused upon by concomitant variations in (*a*) other institutions, (*b*) physical environmental conditions, and/or (*c*) general measures of social-organizational characteristics. With dependent and independent variables thus conceptualized, their values are coded over a sample of societies, a correlational analysis of some type is made, and an explanatory causal model imposed on the results. The last step is potentially the most productive, yet at the same time often the weakest, as the researcher is here frequently obliged to draw on—and try to create—theoretical resources greater than the field realistically provides at the present time. Two general kinds of causal models are commonly found in the literature, sometimes separately and sometimes together. One is ecological and adaptive; an institution is structured the way it is, regardless of specific motivations involved, because no other adaptation would be viable in view of some presumed set of functional requirements or structural properties. The other is psychological and motivational; an institution is structured the way it is as a result of people being motivated by orientations to other institutions or organizational problems. Neither of these models can be applied except in conjunction with the other one, at least to the extent of making some assumptions, explicit or implicit, about its state. The mechanism implied by the first does not alone really provide a causal explanation. The mechanism implied by the second is likewise incomplete. It can operate only in a structural context and also invites questions about the consequences of its operations for presumed viable structural properties.

The fact that the cross-cultural researcher is forcibly pushed into confronting the causative problem in principle renders cross-cultural institutional analysis a potentially very powerful tool for theoretical development. In practice, however, it has proved extremely difficult to realize this potential, owing to the character of the data ordinarily at the disposal of the cross-cultural analyst. In order to trace social causation through both of these models simultaneously, it is necessary to move between the cultural, morphological, and interpersonal levels of social structure, at the very least (Udy 44). Most ethnographic sources available for cross-cultural research, however, report only cultural—and perhaps some morphological—data with any degree of consistency or completeness. Most cross-cultural analyses are thus constrained to predict to dependent variables deriving from prevailing normative patterns, folk models, or gross morphological characteristics, from independent variables in these same areas. Emphasis on kinship terminology, as such, is a case in point. Intervening behavioral or interpersonal structural patterns cannot consistently be "observed." One must therefore either make assumptions about them or remain content with no more than a correlational or cross-tabular description of what seems somehow to go with what.

This situation combines with the lack of a temporal dimension in most cross-cultural data to make it impossible to test hypotheses concerning specific causal mechanisms directly. Even with the lack of a temporal dimension, one could come closer to such a test if one could at least make some cross-sectional observations of presumed intervening mechanisms. Without this possibility, the researcher is reduced, at best, to observing the starting points and end points only. To be sure, this is not wholly without value, since it is of course possible to try imposing various models on such observations with a view to selecting those which seem best to relate the starting and end points. That potentialities are restricted by having to proceed in this manner, however, is evident.

Some Theoretical Problems. It is thus apparent that cross-cultural analysis is subject in practice to rather severe restrictions and requires certain quite far-reaching theoretical assumptions. This is especially true of the two general kinds of research situation just discussed; namely, where the object is to generalize about the nature of entire societies or the nature of institutional structures assumed potentially to permeate entire societies. Some of these restrictions result from the character of the data usually available. The lack of much material describing change through time, plus the lack of much information of even a cross-sectional nature on behavioral and interpersonal patterns, render assumptions about causal mechanisms necessary, as we have just seen. The entire cross-cultural enterprise further demands the assumption that separate societies exist as independent entities and that they are enough alike so that they can be meaningfully compared as different instances of essentially the same thing. In practice, if not necessarily in principle, this assumption is closely related to the first one about causal mechanism, since both assumptions are satisfied by a general functionalist model of "any society" as a self-subsistent boundary-maintaining social system, which handles all of its functional problems internally. Such a model describes any society as an independent entity, and provides at least a formal "solution" to the problem of causality by stipulating a general tendency toward stable functional integration which—if it exists—makes knowledge of specific causal mechanisms somewhat superfluous. It is thus perhaps not surprising that this model underlies most cross-cultural research. It is also necessary to point out, however, that this model flies in the face of common sense and is in fact quite unrealistic much of the time. Given diffusion and an ongoing network of intersocietal relations, few if any societies are now or ever were actually independent. This model also does not allow for discontinuities in social structure; society is portrayed as culturally homogeneous. As a result, the similarities between very small and very large societies are almost certainly exaggerated. We all know, for example, that Tikopia and China are actually very different; they may be so different that they are not, in fact, by any reasonable standard, separate instances of the same phenomenon. It is likewise well known that societies are almost never functionally integrated stable entities. This assumption has, on the whole, probably proved more difficult to stomach than either of the other two, at least judging by the frequency and vigor of the criticism directed against it. But much of this criticism misses the mark. The real problem is that in the absence of the possibility of directly investigating causal mechanisms, some assumptions about structural tendencies are necessary, and this one is not demonstrably any more unrealistic than any similar alternative assumption might be, say, to the effect that all societies tend to be conflict ridden and to fall apart, which is not true either. Most societies, though, do change through time, and the systematic general study of societal change will remain difficult until more comparative temporal data, and more comparative data on behavioral and interpersonal process, are available. It will then be possible to develop alternative assumptions, or perhaps consider a different model altogether.

Meanwhile, cross-cultural analysis is stuck with a basically functionalist model, both as a way of identifying "society," and as a way of coping with problems of social causation. The problem thus becomes one of devising research strategies which will, insofar as possible, avoid the consequences of the defects of this model. One such strategy, which we are following in this discussion in response to a general trend in the field as a whole, is to separate "cross-cultural" from "cross-national" research. Whatever one might say about the functionalist model of "any society," it is generally conceded to fit the small—or even large—traditional society familiar to ethnography better than it fits any contemporary industrial nation. It thus seems prudent to pursue these two modes of comparative investigation separately, comparing and contrasting their results when appropriate, rather than trying to combine them in a single over-all analysis. A second strategy is to design one's sampling frame so as to result, insofar as possible, in the selection of societies known to be maximally independent of one another historically, and we shall have more to say about this presently. A third strategy, which obviously cannot be followed all or even most of the time, is to attenuate the effects of the functionalist model by defining one's research problem in such a way that the society is no longer the basic unit of observation. This strategy coincides with a third general type of research situation to which cross-cultural analysis is often appropriate, and which deserves special discussion.

THE STUDY OF ORGANIZATIONAL FORMS. The cross-cultural study of organizations is theoretically quite a different matter from the cross-cultural study of either societies or institutions. An "organization" is a bounded system of roles, existing within the context of some society, and performed at any given time by a specifiable group of persons. Unlike an institution, which is a concrete system of symbols on the cultural level defining aspects of action on the social level, an organization is a concrete unit on the social level oriented to aspects of different institutions on the cultural level. Just as an institution may be predominantly but not completely manifested in certain organizations, so may any given organization be oriented predominantly but not completely to some one institutional structure. In our own society, for example, the government is undoubtedly predominantly politically oriented, but it is also oriented to economic and other institutional considerations as well. The pattern of institutional orientations of a given organizational form is, furthermore, very likely to vary from one society to another. Work organizations in our own society are almost always predominantly economically oriented, but in other societies they may be predominantly oriented to political or kinship considerations, with economic considerations distinctly secondary.

Most organizational research is, of course, not cross-cultural. Indeed, there is every reason why it should not be if the research problem calls for holding institutional orientations constant. However, if one is interested in exploring the relationship of organizational structure to institutional orientation, a cross-cultural analysis may be called for as a means of introducing sufficient variation into the social context (Nimkoff & Middleton 26; Udy 41, 45). The resulting research situation is quite different from that of studying entire societies or social institutions, for in the last analysis, one is comparing organizations rather than cultures. Typically, one is faced with a complex of independent and dependent variables concerning internal organization structure, together with certain contextual control variables having to do with the social and ecological setting. The unit of investigation is the organization, not the total society; the aim in sampling societies is not really to sample societies as such, but to introduce systematic variations in those contextual control variables with which one is working. One is sampling contexts rather than units. Thus the possible consequences of some of the theoretical problems we have indicated earlier, stemming from possible lack of independence of societies from one another, and the kind of model of "society" one is obliged to use, are at least attenuated in practice, even if they are not formally resolved in principle. In almost any sample of societies, especially a very large sample, there is, as we have seen, always some question of whether the societies sampled are really independent of one another. But if one samples organizations by first drawing societies and then drawing one organization from each society, there is considerable chance that the organizations drawn will be independent in all relevant ways even where the societies are not. Furthermore, since most cross-cultural studies of organizations are concerned with exploring specified ranges of contextual variation on organization structure, it is much more important, and also likely to be much more arguable, that the societies sampled provide the desired range of contextual variation than that they be representative of some total population of all possible societies. The fact that one is studying the structure of organizations rather than the structure of societies also renders much less important the question of what model of "society" one is assuming. What is important is what model of organization one is using, and that is a problem of organization theory not of cross-cultural analysis. It is also more easily handled.

The cross-cultural study of organizations thus offers several theoretical and methodological advantages over the cross-cultural study of either entire societies or social institutions, if only because it enables one to duck some rather difficult questions. However, it involves some problems of its own. The fact that it operationally equates sampling relevant social and technical contexts of organizations with sampling societies is, we think, not terribly serious, although for some purposes it does render difficult the precise specification of what population of organizations one's eventual sample represents, even if one has followed an impeccable strategy in selecting societies. A much more difficult practical problem is that standard categories of ethnographic reporting generally have to do with culture and institutions, rather than with organizational forms. It is thus necessary to do much "cutting and pasting" to retrieve the necessary information needed to locate organizations in the first place, let alone to discover how they actually function or are basically structured. To some degree one is saved by the probability that organizations will be described under the headings of their predominant institutional orientations, but there are still gaps. In the study of work organization, for example, one seldom finds much information usable for comparative purposes about actual interpersonal behavior patterns, or even about the numbers of people present in a work situation. One is obliged, for the most part, to work with descriptions couched in terms of generalized cultural models. The range of areas researchable by this method is thus limited to rather broad problems. This does not mean that such research is without value. An abiding problem with conventional, non-cross-cultural, organizational research is that it often proceeds with no clear conception of total possible ranges of variation. General cross-cultural research can aid in providing some such conception, which can serve as a backdrop against which comparative organizational studies confined to one society, or case studies of particular organizations, can be projected. There is value in knowing the layout of the ball park.

SUMMARY. Inherent in each of the three major applications of cross-cultural analysis discussed are several rather difficult theoretical and methodological problems. These problems are actually quite similar, with different kinds of applications varying largely in the precise forms the problems take and the probable severity of their consequences. In all cross-cultural research the investigator is tied to an essentially functionalist model of human society from which it is hard to escape, inasmuch as the available data seldom admit of adequate exploration of causal mechanisms operating through time and across different structural levels. The state of theory is such that most cross-cultural studies are perforce exploratory, not only with respect to relationships among variables, but with regard to exactly what the specific variables and categories should be in the first place. The data themselves derive from an almost radically empiricist tradition, are descriptive and qualitative, and are at best ordered according to criteria of relevance that are frequently arbitrary and sometimes downright whimsical. They were also almost always gathered by someone other than the cross-cultural researcher and for purposes utterly removed from those of any cross-cultural analyst. All of these data must be coded, not only to fit a cross-cultural research problem, but usually also in such a way as to be of exploratory assistance in defining the problem in the first place and in specifying the variables relevant to it. When one combines this situation with the fact that the peculiar library-cum-statistical character of cross-cultural analysis does not conform closely to the current training traditions of either anthropology or sociology, it is no wonder that cross-cultural research is considerably less popular than its apparent theoretical centrality might lead one to expect it to be. It simply entails too many barriers and pitfalls. Nonetheless, the fact remains that cross-cultural analysis is, in principle, central to both anthropology and sociology, to the extent that these fields involve interest in developing any very general theories about their subject matter. It is also possible, despite limitations, to do cross-cultural analysis and in fact achieve some results. The remainder of our discussion will be devoted to an appraisal of available methods for conducting such analysis.

Methods

Most literature on cross-cultural methodology deals either with the problem of selecting a representative sample of independent societies or with the question of validity and reliability of coding. These two topics represent only a part of the picture, however, and we shall treat them in the more general contexts of sampling and analysis procedures, respectively.

SAMPLING. The first problem to be confronted in cross-cultural sampling is what the size of the sample should be. If one is so fortunate as to be working with a tight research model and conducting classical tests of hypotheses of relationships among known variables, one can readily achieve a retrospective experimental design, and the problem of sample size becomes trivial. One matches societies on control variables, systematically varies the independent variables with the number of societies required following mechanically from the complexity of the model and the dictates of statistical significance. Very few cross-cultural studies, however, do or can involve very much classical hypothesis testing given the current state of theoretical knowledge. Rather, most are exploratory and are directed toward trying to discover what relationships, if any, exist among very broad structural areas. Frequently, the relevant specific variables are not known; part of the problem is precisely to discover what the variables are, i.e. which ones will work the best in characterizing relationships among the broad areas being studied. Having inductively extracted from the data variables which work, one then investigates and describes their interrelations. The results, when stated in propositional form, may superficially resemble a set of tested hypotheses. In fact, they are usually a series or possibly a system of result-guided descriptions.

There is nothing wrong with this provided one does not forget it, but one must face the difficulty that little is known of the formal properties of exploratory research. It is thus often difficult to choose among alternative procedures; it is no accident that cross-cultural research exhibits so many different approaches. Despite occasional assertions to the contrary, it is impossible to accept the contention that simply because the research is exploratory, "anything goes." Some guidelines would appear desirable, even if they may later prove somewhat arbitary, if only to enable readers of the research to know how it was done and to insure some degree of consistency. As regards sample size, it is of course impossible formally to "solve for *n*" in exploratory research, since one does not know exactly what relationships one will ultimately wish to explore. It therefore seems desirable to draw the largest number of societies possible, known to be independent and representative according to criteria to be described presently, and for which the desired data are available. If this number seems, or later proves to be, larger than feasible or necessary, an alternative procedure is to extract variables at intervals while drawing the sample in such a way as to maintain representativeness throughout, and to stop drawing societies are yielding no new information.

The next sampling problem faced by the cross-cultural researcher is that of assuring maximum independence among the societies drawn, together with some arguable modicum or representativeness of the sample.[2] Unlike the question of size, this problem is similar in both hypothesis testing and exploratory research. The central difficulty is that one is of course limited to societies that have actually been studied, and among those, to societies on which adequate data are available relative to one's research problem. Since there is no valid way of determining how this rather restricted population might relate to the total universe of all societies, a straight random sampling procedure is unrealistic. In order to maximize the probability of finding the total possible range of variation in the variables one is studying, it is necessary to resort to a planned "quota sample," wherein one's final sample is distributed as evenly as possible over ethnographically recognized world culture areas, choosing at random within areas or subareas, where a choice exists. In the process, one can also maximize independence by selecting societies from different areas preferably, or at least from different subareas if the former procedure would result in too small a sample. Fortunately, this problem has received a great deal of attention in the literature, most notably at the hands of Murdock and his associates. As a result, several excellent procedural guides are available, and the reader is referred to them for further information and assistance (Barry 1, Murdock 18–20, Murdock & White 22, White 46).

ANALYSIS PROCEDURE. Having drawn a sample, one next faces the question of precisely what categories and variables the data are to be ordered into. In the case of hypothesis testing, the answer to this question is of course already known, but in the case of exploratory analysis, it usually is not, and methods textbooks have little or nothing to say about precisely what to do in such circumstances. Given broad areas of interest, a useful general convention is to proceed as far as one can on theoretical grounds, and beyond that to aim for categories which reflect the widest ranges of observed variation in the data. Procedures such as factor analysis may be useful here, but, as we have seen, they have various

[2] The question of independence, under the heading "Galtons problem," though certainly important, has been discussed *ad nauseam* in the cross-cultural methodological literature, receiving a really incredible amount of attention particularly when one considers that other problems of equal or greater importance are scarcely discussed at all. For recent summary statements of the vast "Galton's problem" literature, see Naroll (25) and Schaefer et al. (33).

practical limitations. It may be better simply to try one system of theoretically defensible categories after another, and to choose that system which gives the best empirical results. It is usually desirable to carry out such trials by initially using a small number—say six or seven—of ethnographic sources known to be especially accurate and complete, and then apply the results to one's larger sample (Udy 42). At this stage the Human Relations Area Files become a facility of inestimable value, because the data in them are already ordered according to a generalized, yet detailed, classification scheme (Murdock et al. 21). To the extent that one's sample has been contrived to include societies processed in the Files, one can at this point, by dint of another series of trials, discover how the Files can be searched so as to retrieve the data one needs. One can then formalize one's procedures and collect one's data, using the Files whenever possible, saving countless hours of work thereby, as well as being enabled to make use of the special bibliographical and critical information the Files provide.

A word or two of caution, however, is in order about the Human Relations Area Files. Except in rare fortuitious circumstances, where one's own categories happen to coincide with those of the Files, one cannot just "look things up" in them. Rather, one must code initially from monographs on a few given societies, then discover that pattern of search in the Files which yields the same information, with a view finally to applying that pattern to other societies. It is a question of "translating" the categories of the Files into one's own system of categories. The raw category system of the Files itself is derived ultimately from Sumner & Keller's *The Science of Society* (37), plus an elaborate variety of systematic and ad hoc emendations, and is, in principle, open to an infinitude of theoretical criticisms. Nonetheless, in our experience it works surprisingly well when used as we have described. The only comment we can offer on this score is that Sumner & Keller, adumbrated by years of practical ethnographic experience, might well bear revisiting.

Armed with a system of categories one may now code one's data. The most serious problems encountered in the actual procedure of cross-cultural analysis, whether one is testing hypotheses or exploring the material, are those of data validity and coding reliability. Various ways of coping with both problems have been proposed, all of which, according even to the claims of the proponents themselves, are, at best, merely somewhat helpful. The Human Relations Area Files seeks to code sources according to their probable accuracy. Naroll (24) has set forth and demonstrated a rather elaborate method which in effect weights variables in any given study according to both probable validity and observed coder reliability with respect to the traits comprising the variables, and takes such weights into account in the analysis. Much can be said in favor of such schemes, but their rigorous use does involve a "trade-off" in that it materially reduces the number of potentially available sources, and at times seems to do so quite artificially. Restricting oneself to those societies offering several ethnographic sources is open to the same objection. A more usual procedure is to utilize two or more judges in coding the material, together with possible group discussions to achieve consensus about coding or throwing out the source in cases of doubt (Swanson 38, Udy 45). A particularly severe problem on this score occurs when one is attempting to code some trait as "present" or "absent," and encounters a source where the trait is simply not mentioned. Under such circumstances, the question is whether to code the trait as "absent" or "don't know." Given the empiricist character of much ethnography, consistently—and, in a way, properly—coding "don't know" will result in an overreporting of "present" cases if one then eliminates the "don't know" cases from the analysis. For our part, we have adopted the convention of consistently coding such cases as "absent" if the ethnographer discusses other matters related to the trait in detail without mentioning the trait itself. Obviously, none of the foregoing "solutions" is very satisfactory. At some point one is obliged simply to believe what the ethnographer says, resign oneself to gaps in the data, propose results as tentative, and embrace the dictum that the ultimate test of cross-cultural research results lies in their successful application in other areas.

If one has succeeded in coping with the problems of sampling, category and variable construction, validity, and coding, we would contend that the remaining analysis problems in cross-cultural research are trivial, in that they do not differ at this point from those of any social science research problem characterized by essentially rectangular data sets. One simply runs one's data by any suitable standard statistical procedure (Driver 4). If the sample is very small, one may instead choose to proceed with words rather than numbers. There is no essential methodological difference in doing so; one cannot avoid statistical problems by using words. It seems necessary to point this out, since at one time the "words vs numbers" option was a matter of some controversy, albeit for reasons which we confess we have never been able to understand. It should be pointed out, however, that in the case of exploratory analysis, statistical (or equivalent verbal) procedures merely summarize and describe the results, despite the fact that they may superficially resemble tests of hypotheses. Such devices as tests of significance are therefore, in such instances, open to various technical criticisms. They may perhaps be defended as providing descriptions of how the investigator was thinking about the material, in that they project the findings against a random model.

Conclusions

In this review we have tried to show that cross-cultural analysis is neither ideal nor impossible. It suffers from a plethora of theoretical and methodological problems, many of which stem from intellectual-historical accident, some of which arise from the current state of theory, and perhaps the most serious of which derive from the character of available data. Indeed, some of the last-named problems are unquestionably forever inherent, as many of these data cannot now be changed. Because of this situation, cross-cultural analysis suffers from intrinsic and probably permanent limitations. The methodological history of the field has in great part been a history of compiling and archiving data combined with a history of efforts to evade these limitations. The latter efforts have not always been wholly successful and, as we have seen, have often consisted of conventions rather than formally defensible procedures.

However, the fact remains that one can carry out cross-cultural research and achieve results. The fact that some of these results can be successfully tested in other ways lends confidence in other results that must stand alone. Furthermore, cross-cultural analysis, despite its problems, is essential if one wishes to develop general theories about social structure while remaining in touch with empirical data. On this score, cross-cultural analysis has achieved something that few other specialties in social science have; namely, cumulative findings. It is possible to merge cross-cultural studies together when their samples overlap, and thereby construct new studies. The most comprehensive and ambitious effort to do this to date is that of Textor (39). Aided by the development and application of new computer routines, such effort could well lead to new and fruitful theoretical perspectives. If nothing else, cross-cultural analysis is surely dedicated to the proposition that ethnography is good for something apart from its own sake.

LITERATURE CITED

1. Barry, H. 1969. Cross-cultural research with matched pairs of societies. *J. Soc. Psychol.* 79:25–33.
2. Carneiro, R. L. 1970. Scale analysis, evolutionary sequences, and the rating of cultures. *Handbook of Method in Cultural Anthropology,* ed. R. Naroll, R. Cohen, 834–71. Garden City: Natural History Press.
3. Carneiro, R. L., Tobias, S. R. 1963. The application of scale analysis to the study of cultural evolution. *Trans. N.Y. Acad. Sci. Ser. 2* 26:196–207.
4. Driver, H. E. 1961. Introduction to statistics for comparative research. *Readings in Cross-Cultural Methodology,* ed. F. W. Moore, 303–31. New Haven: HRAF Press.
5. Driver, H. E., Schuessler, K. F. 1957. Factor analysis of ethnographic data. *Am. Anthropol.* 59:655–63.
6. Eggan, F. 1954. Social anthropology and the method of controlled comparison. *Am. Anthropol.* 56: 743–63.
7. Ford, C. S. 1970. Human relations area files: 1949–1969. *Behav. Sci. Notes* 5:1–61.
8. Freeman, L. C., Winch, R. F. 1957. Social complexity: an empirical test of a typology of societies. *Am. J. Sociol.* 62:461–66.
9. Gouldner, A. W., Peterson, R. A. 1962. *Notes on Technology and the Moral Order.* Indianapolis: Bobbs-Merrill.
10. Graves, T. D., Graves, N. B., Kobrin, M. J. 1969. Historical inferences from Guttman scales. *Curr. Anthropol.* 10:317–38.
11. Gregg, P. M., Banks, A. S. 1965. Dimensions of political systems. *Am. Pol. Sci. Rev.* 59:602–14.

12. Hobhouse, L. T., Wheeler, G. C., Ginsberg, M. 1915. *The Material Culture and Social Institutions of the Simpler Peoples*. London: Chapman and Hall.
13. Levy, M. J. Jr. 1925. *The Structure of Society*. Princeton Univ. Press.
14. Lewis, O. 1956. Comparisons in cultural anthropology. *Current Anthropology: A Supplement to Anthropology Today*, ed. W. L. Thomas Jr., 259–92. Univ. Chicago Press.
15. Marsh, R. M. 1967. *Comparative Sociology*. New York: Harcourt, Brace and World.
16. Morgan, L. H. 1870. *Systems of Consanguinity and Affinity in the Human Family*. Washington, D.C.: Smithsonian Inst.
17. Murdock, G. P. 1949. *Social Structure*. New York: Macmillan.
18. Murdock, G. P. 1957. World ethnographic sample. *Am. Anthropol.* 59:664–87.
19. Murdock, G. P. 1967. *Ethnographic Atlas: A Summary*. Univ. Pittsburgh Press.
20. Murdock, G. P. 1969. *Outline of World Cultures*. New Haven: HRAF Press.
21. Murdock, G. P. et al 1969. *Outline of Cultural Materials*. New Haven: HRAF Press. 4th rev. ed.
22. Murdock, G. P., White, D. R. 1969. Standard cross-cultural sample. *Ethnology* 8:329–69.
23. Naroll, R. 1956. A preliminary index of social development. *Am. Anthropol.* 58:687–715.
24. Naroll, R. 1962. *Data Quality Control*. Glencoe: Free Press.
25. Naroll, R. 1970. Galton's problem. *A Handbook of Method in Cultural Anthropology*, ed. R. Naroll, R. Cohen, 974–89. Garden City: Natural History Press.
26. Nimkoff, M. F., Middleton, R. 1968. Types of family and types of economy. *Man in Adaptation*, ed. Y. A. Cohen, 384–93. Chicago: Aldine.
27. O'Leary, T. J. 1969. A preliminary bibliography of cross-cultural studies. *Behav. Sci. Notes* 4:95–115.
28. Ibid 1971. Bibliography of cross-cultural studies: supplement I. 6:191–203.
29. Parsons, T. 1966. *Societies: Evolutionary and Comparative Perspectives*. Englewood Cliffs: Prentice-Hall.
30. Radcliffe-Brown, A. R. 1952. *Structure and Function in Primitive Society*. Glencoe: Free Press.
31. Russell, E. W. 1972. Factors of human aggression. *Behav. Sci. Notes* 7:275–312.
32. Sawyer, J., LeVine, R. A. 1966. Cultural dimensions. *Am. Anthropol.* 68:708–31.
33. Schaefer, J. M. et al 1971. Sampling methods, functional associations, and Galton's problem. *Behav. Sci. Notes* 6:229–74.
34. Schuessler, K. F., Driver, H. E. 1956. A factor analysis of sixteen primitive societies. *Am. Sociol. Rev.* 21:493–99.
35. Schwartz, R. D., Miller, J. C. 1964. Legal evolution and societal complexity. *Am. J. Sociol.* 70:159–69.
36. Stewart, R. A. C., Jones, K. J. 1972. Cultural dimensions. *Behav. Sci. Notes* 7: 37–81.
37. Sumner, W. G., Keller, A. G. 1927. *The Science of Society*. 4 vols. New Haven: Yale Univ. Press.
38. Swanson, G. E. 1960. *The Birth of the Gods*. Ann Arbor: Univ. Michigan Press.
39. Textor, R. B. 1967. *A Cross-Cultural Summary*. New Haven: HRAF Press.
40. Tylor, E. B. 1889. On a method of investigating the development of institutions. *J. Roy. Anthropol. Inst.* 18:245–72.
41. Udy, S. H. Jr. 1959. *Organization of Work*. New Haven: HRAF Press.
42. Udy, S. H. Jr. 1964. Cross-cultural analysis: a case study. *Sociologists at Work*, ed. P. E. Hammond, 161–83. New York: Basic Books.
43. Udy, S. H. Jr. 1965. Dynamic inferences from static data. *Am. J. Sociol.* 70:625–27.
44. Udy, S. H. Jr. 1968. Social structural analysis. *Int. Encycl. Soc. Sci.* 13:489–95.
45. Udy, S. H. Jr. 1970. *Work in Traditional and Modern Societies*. Englewood Cliffs: Prentice-Hall.
46. White, D. R. 1970. Societal research archives system. *A Handbook of Method in Cultural Anthropology*, ed. R. Naroll, R. Cohen, 676–85. Garden City: Natural History Press.
47. Whiting, J. W. M., Child, I. L. 1953. *Child Training and Personality*. New Haven: Yale Univ. Press.

Most ethnographers have so far been satisfied that their systems for categorizing culture—usually in accordance with some variant on the one used in this book (technology, economic organization, social organization, and so on)—were sufficiently valid to be applied cross-culturally. Recently, however, a number of prominent anthropologists have been arguing against the scientific efficacy of imposing our own inevitably culture-bound categories upon the life experience of other peoples. To do so, they have argued, is to distort the data from the start. They correctly contend that every people categorizes its experience in accordance with its cultural conditioning: attributing significance to some phenomena, ignoring others, classifying events, objects, places, and other people in conformity with indigenous notions of cause and effect, using its own standards for determining what is significant and what can be ignored.

It is further asserted that it is the anthropologist's responsibility to uncover how such indigenous systems of categorization work, that it is only when he has done so that he can approach understanding another people's world as they perceive it themselves, and can thus properly comprehend the differing patterns of cognition that give impetus to their distinctive patterns of sociocultural behavior. But, as Kay indicates, the ethnoscientific approach (sometimes termed the *new ethnography*) is too complex to synthesize in a few words.

Ethnoscience[1]

Paul Kay

The familiar material objects may not be all that is real, but they are admirable examples.

W. V. O. Quine [1960:3]

I think Quine's caution to the philosopher in search of the nature of ultimate reality can be adapted for the anthropologist in search of the nature of culture: *The informant's most careful statements about the nature of his world may not be all the ethnographic data, but they are admirable examples.* Neither statement is exclusivist. Quine does not limit the real things to familiar material objects; nor does the "new ethnographer" so-called limit his data to the verbal formulations of his informants.[2] Practitioners of the new ethnography do many things besides ethnosemantics, depending on their problems and their tastes. They may take censuses, count yams, take aerial photographs, learn to identify several thousand plant species and so on. They also just sit around and watch and listen and empathize, as all ethnographers do. But whatever else they may do, they always do ethnosemantics. That is, the new ethnography seeks through interview, observation and, when possible, experiment, to discover some part of the system of meanings by which people organize the world. The goal is the raw cognition if you will, but since the major realization of this cognition is in the words people speak, semantics is considered an integral part of ethnography.[3]

The task of establishing some sector of the culture bearer's tacit theory of the world is a necessary part of the new ethnography. Many specialized techniques are used in the attempt, and new ones are constantly developed. This is not the time or place to present a catalogue of those methods. Rather our business here is to discuss the findings of ethnoscience rather than

Source: From Paul Kay, "Some Theoretical Implications of Ethnographic Semantics." Reproduced by permission of the American Anthropological Association from *Current Directions in Anthropology,* Vol. 3, 170, and by permission of the author.

[1] This paper is Working Paper no. 24, Language-Behavior Research Laboratory, University of California, Berkeley. The Language-Behavior Research Laboratory is funded by a grant from the Institute of International Studies, University of California, Berkeley.

[2] The "new ethnography," as Marvin Harris accurately points out, is not all that new. Rather, it is a recent development which adds a measure of methodological and theoretical precision to a venerated anthropological tradition stretching back through Kluckhohn, Malinowski and Lowie to Durkheim and even Dilthey—a tradition which, it appears, Harris feels is more honored in the breach than the observance (Harris 1968: 597–98). Nevertheless, rather than add yet another term to an already overcrowded lexical domain, I will continue to use the incompletely felicitous term "new ethnography."

[3] It has long been claimed in anthropology, and correctly so, that not all culturally important categories are directly reflected in the lexicon. Significantly, the actual demonstration of this claim awaited the work of ethnosemanticists, especially Berlin and Black (Berlin, Breedlove and Raven 1968; Black 1969). The significance of this finding is first that most of the culturally important cognitive categories are represented directly in lexicon and, secondly, that the best way to arrive at the linguistically covert categories is to use as input for that search the output of a semantic analysis of the lexically encoded concepts.

its methods, and particularly the theoretical findings and general theoretical position of the field.

Above and in what follows, I use the expressions *ethnographic semantics, ethnosemantics* and *ethnoscience* synonymously and interchangeably to refer to the systematic study of the meanings of words and the role of these meanings in cognitive systems. I would contrast *ethnography*, new or old. The new ethnography (or linguistic or cognitive ethnography) is that approach to ethnography which includes ethnosemantic study as a necessary part. Practitioners of the new ethnography employ many methods other than ethnosemantic ones, in particular all the traditional techniques of anthropological field work, including participant observation; they also use a host of specialized techniques ranging from soil analysis to multidimensional scaling.

I have argued that ethnosemantics does not exhaust the content of the new ethnography. It is equally true that the theoretical relevance of ethnosemantics is not limited to the field of ethnography or even to anthropology. Ethnographic semantics is that discipline which seeks to understand human cognition through analysis of the cognitive content of linguistic expressions. It is therefore, in principle at least, as much a part of linguistics and psychology as of anthropology. Should any anthropologist be inclined to interpret the last statement as an admission of guilt, I would suggest to him that anthropology is unlikely to profit from a self-imposed jurisdictional isolationism. I hope we can all agree that science is advanced when we define scientific disciplines in terms of natural groupings of phenomena, rather than the other way around. The system of meanings—the tacit theory of the world—lying behind a language and its usage is a natural phenomenon worthy of scientific study. Ethnographic semantics is that study. The results of ethnographic semantics are variously relevant to ethnography, cultural anthropology, linguistics and psychology.

One of the major methodological principles of ethnoscience is the method of contrast. One establishes the meaning of a word (that is, the concept realized by a lexical item) by exploring the features that cause it to contrast in usage with any word that can be substituted for it. One discovers what the concept is by systematically exploring what it is not. In a loose way, I will apply that method here. I will try to make clear what I believe ethnosemantics to be by talking for a bit about what it is not. This strategy particularly recommends itself because in recent years there has appeared a fair amount of literature and a large amount of conversation which indicates that some anthropologists, who do not themselves do ethnosemantics, harbor some specific misconceptions about the nature of that field.[4] I should hasten to add that the critics of ethnoscience do not bear the full blame for their misunderstandings of the field. Not infrequently the misunderstandings revealed in criticisms of ethnoscience are attributable less to obtuseness on the part of the critics than to opaqueness in the writings being criticized. Some of the more important work in ethnosemantics has been presented in a confusing and/or confused style, and the fact of its being misunderstood must be considered at least as much the authors' as the critics' fault. A logician has said in speaking of the *Principia Mathematica* that when Bertrand Russell *does* logic he is always right and when he talks *about* logic he is almost always wrong. Ethnoscientists, like logicians, are not infalliable when they interpret the significance of their own technical accomplishments.

I would also like to call attention at the outset to an obvious fact: namely, that it is just as easy to do ethnosemantics badly as to do anything else badly. (Upon occasion I have personally found it distressingly easy.) Inaccurate or trivial work can be done in ethnosemantics as in any other field. When, in attempting to set straight some erroneous criticisms that have been made against ethnosemantics, I speak of what ethnosemantics is, I mean what it is when it's done right.

On the other hand, none of us wishes to evaluate an entire field in terms of its worst productions. A criticism of a field based on an artful selection of its errors and trivia is a criticism itself devoid of much accuracy or importance. In the growth of a science, it is the peaks of achievement that count, not the troughs of error. In the evaluation of progress, let us look not at the twisted trial of false starts and needless detours, but at where in fact we have got to.

There are at least 6 important misconceptions

[4] Most of these misconceptions, although not all, may be found in Harris (1968:568–604) and Berreman (1966).

about ethnographic semantics extant in the literature. It is perhaps worthy of passing note that several pairs of these misconceptions are mutually contradictory; for example, that ethnographic semantics is anti-empirical on the one hand, yet anti-theoretical and exclusively concerned with trivial methods for data shuffling on the other. When we have considered how and why ethnoscience is not each of these things, I think we will have a fair idea of what it is.

1. Ethnosemantics does not take native generalizations at face value. Some anthropologists have criticized the cognitive approach to ethnography in the mistaken belief that (1) ethnoscientists believe everything their informants tell them and (2) ethnoscientists believe only what their informants tell them. According to this view, the cognitively oriented ethnographer presents as his model of the culture or society just a summary of the explicit ideological statements of the local establishment. As Marvin Harris (1968:590) has suggested, this approach would produce an ethnography of the contemporary United States in which race is irrelevant to economic opportunity, adultery never occurs and the major purpose of the meetings of learned societies is intellectual intercourse.

There are at least two errors here, one obvious and one subtle. In the first place there is the tacit assumption that an ethnographer who pays careful attention to the local ideology is *ipso facto* a maniacal super-Platonist who can't tell the difference between ideology and practice. Perhaps there does exist some confusion in British social anthropology on this point, for example in the interminable debate on "jural rules" and related matters. But the position of the new ethnography is straightforward. Cognition is cognition and behavior is behavior. If the native's cognitive world is populated by 72 different kinds of yams and 36 different kinds of ghosts, then that's that. I know of no case where an ethnosemanticist has confused a native's beliefs about ghosts with actual ghosts.

A somewhat more subtle error is the notion that the ethnoscientist equates the explicit ideology with the culture, i.e., wih he native's system of belief, his cognition. According to this slightly more refined view, the semantic ethnographer of the United States would describe it as a place in which adultery and racial discrimination indeed flourish but in which the natives are unaware of these facts. The accusation is that ethnoscientists tend to give excessive credence to natives' broad generalizations, producing descriptions of cultures that contain a spurious homogeneity, simplicity and harmony—ethnographies, to use Harris's felicitous phrase, "in which the rules of behavior dominate the rules for breaking rules."

The fact that Harris and similar critics ignore is that the very notion of "rules for breaking rules" has come from the new ethnography. The confusion is apparent when Harris (1968:590–91) attacks Goodenough (1965) on this issue for his treatment of the now famous incident in which a Trukese father strikes his married daughter, "thus violating five of the six rules in Goodenough's emic 'Duty Scale.'" Harris remarks scornfully that "Goodenough takes comfort from the fact that the woman in question had in turn been breaking another series of rules!" and he concludes, "So blatant a failure of a set of rules to predict behavior requires a rewriting of the rules." But, what Goodenough has in fact presented is an instance of actual behavior in conformity with a rule for breaking the rules. Goodenough's argument is that Trukese culture prohibits fathers from hitting their married daughters *except* when the daughter has violated certain cultural rules to an extent which is unconscionable from the Trukese point of view. Goodenough has uncovered a Trukese cultural rule which is formally analogous to the American cultural rule prohibiting homicide *except* in self defense. When Goodenough characterizes the father's blow as "poetic justice" and "just what she deserved," he is not expressing his personal moral judgment, as Harris appears to think; he is underlining the facts that Trukese cultural rules provide for fathers striking their married daughters just on one set of narrowly defined occasions, and that this is one of those occasions.

The moral of Goodenough's story is precisely that cultures, seen as cognitive systems, are extremely complex, and that cultural rules characteristically contain *except* and *unless* clauses. Goodenough's (1956) early paper on residence rules in Nakanai makes the same point. He lists half a dozen or so variables which are evaluated by an individual in deciding where to reside postmaritally. The actual decision procedure is represented by a set of contingency statements to which are inputted the evaluations on the relevant variables. The set of contingency statements forms a rather complex network, formally analogous to a switching circuit diagram or the flow diagram of a computer algorithm. The central idea is that global characterizations such as *matrilocality* or *patrilocality* do not cut fine enough to match the complexity of the native cognitive system.

It is the appreciation of the detail and complexity in human cognitive systems that has been one of the major contributions of ethnoscience to cultural anthropology. The realization of just how complex even a small area of culture can be has led ethnosemanticists frequently to restrict their study to individual lexical and cognitive domains, which has in turn led to the charge that ethnoscience studies trivialities.

2. *Ethnosemantics is not concerned with methodology for its own sake.* The basic working assumptions of ethnoscience are (1) that human behavior cannot be understood without taking into account human cognition and (2) that human cognition is complex. These beliefs lead naturally to the methodological hypothesis that traditional anthropological techniques of recording and analyzing native systems of belief are insufficiently rigorous and detailed to capture the fine complexity of cultural systems. We really know very little about how people organize their cultural knowledge and we need new techniques for finding out. It is this attitude that has led to the series of methodological studies associated with the names of Goodenough, Lounsbury, Metzger, Williams, Conklin, Frake, Romney, D'Andrade and others. I am not at the moment defending the substantive assumptions which lead to the conviction that anthropology needs some new methods (although I certainly agree with these assumptions); I am just arguing that the methodological concerns of ethnographic semantics are not fortuitous but are derived from a substantive theoretical position. The major outlines of that position can, I think, be delineated as follows:

1. Culture is essentially a matter of shared cognition.
2. Human cognition is not in principle unamenable to rational inquiry.
3. Among the relatively concrete and understandable phenomena at our disposal, language and speech appear to most directly express what we suspect may be the organizing principles of human thought.

If one accepts the above 3 assumptions, then I think it becomes clear why ethnosemanticists have been vitally concerned with the development of new research strategies and have looked especially toward linguistics and cognitive psychology for candidates. The critic may still legitimately object "I do not believe in the importance of cognition and language and therefore I have no use for research methods which are founded on this belief." But it is not a valid criticism of ethnosemantics to characterize it as concerned with rigorous method for its own sake.

3. *Ethnoscience is not anti-theoretical or anti-comparative.* As suggested above, much of the impetus to the formation of the new ethnography was a growing dissatisfaction with traditional ethnological categories such as *matriliny, patrilocality, unilineal descent* and so on. This imposition of an *a priori* classificational scheme on richly complex cultural materials is precisely what Leach refers to in his article on "butterfly collecting" (1961:1–27).[4] Ethnoscience shares with a certain segment of British social anthropology the conviction that intercultural comparisons based on such gross classificational schemes are likely to be no more meaningful than comparisons of nominal systems in grammar in terms of the Latin categories nominative, genitive, dative, accusative and ablative. In short, one has to isolate comparable units before one can engage in reasonable comparison. Hence, the emphasis in ethnoscience on emics, so-called, the analysis of a cultural system or subsystem in its own terms as a precondition to the comparison of different systems.

But to say that one should compare only things that are truly comparable is not to say that one should not compare. The very provenience of the emic/etic distinction, namely phonology, should make it clear that the guiding spirit of an emic approach is to rid oneself of his *pre*conceptions about universal structures so that the data may be analyzed objectively to reveal the true universal structures. Phonology is in fact an excellent case in point. Far from becoming (or remaining) a particularizing discipline, phonology has enjoyed a lively debate about universal laws of sound structure ever since the discovery of the phonemic principle. The phonemic principle was in fact a very strong empirical hypothesis about the universal

[4] I must confess that although I agree totally with Leach's statement of the problem in that article, I am hard pressed to make much out of his proposed solution.

structure of sound systems. This hypothesis led to the intensive investigation of sound systems of many languages in their own terms and to the continual comparison of the results of these analyses in the search for stronger universal hypotheses of sound structure. The result of these investigations has been a great enrichment of general phonological theory; the principle of systematic phonological opposition is retained and applied at new levels while the traditionally basic substantive unit (the autonomous phoneme of Bloomfield) plays a diminished role. The principal change, however, is that phonological generalizations are now expressed as rules, analogous to syntactic rules, in contrast to traditional practice in which such generalizations were expressed more implicitly through a listing of items with appended distributional information.

Phonology today is a field rich in general theory including Greenberg's implicational universals and the Jacobsonian and other distinctive feature systems and their formal incorporation into the theoretical framework of generative phonology. The emic approach in ethnography as in phonology is fundamentally the very opposite of a particularizing, antitheoretical position. Rather it incorporates a firm belief in the existence of universal structural principles in the phenomenon under study and a commitment to the diligent search for those universal, pan-human structures, unimpeded by preconceptions as to the outcome.

Ethnographic semantics, although not nearly so well developed a field as phonology, is already beginning to produce just such universal hypotheses of human cognitive structure. Lounsbury's theory of kinship extensions is one example. The axiomatization of human cognitive structures involved in taxonomic systems growing out of the work of Conklin, Berlin and myself is another. Greenberg's work on semantic universals, especially semantic marking, is another case in point. Berlin's findings on formal and substantive semantic universals in the growth of ethnobiological vocabulary are additional examples, as are some of his findings on universals in the lexical classification of shapes and textures. Geoghegan's axiomatic theory of cultural systems for the processing of classificatory information is yet another example. Additional examples could be cited and I apologize in advance for the inevitable slights. I also apologize for being unable to present a detailed discussion of these findings and theories, but even an adequate summary of any one would require almost the full time allotted to me here. However, Berlin has discussed some of these findings already.

4. Ethnographic semantics is not limited to domains[5] *in which there are preexisting etic grids; nor are its methods inapplicable to domains of social organization not involving genealogical relationships.* Some of the successes —or excesses, depending on your point of view —of the semantic analysis of kinship systems have led to the mistaken conclusion that objective semantic analyses can be performed only in a small class of semantic domains, namely those domains for which we possess *a priori* a classification that is so fine it necessarily incorporates all the distinctions made in any native system. Such an *a priori* classification is sometimes called an etic grid. The traditional notation of biological kin-types, so called, and its various recent modifications and improvements embodies one such classificational device. The international phonetic alphabet and the Jacobsonian distinctive feature framework are linguistic prototypes.

The belief that semantic analysis can only be performed when an etic grid is available seems to be connected with an odd misconception about the history of phonology that appears to be widespread in anthropology.[6] The idea seems to be that the development of an adequate universal phonetic grid temporally preceded the successful emic description of individual phonological systems; only after linguists were able to figure out all the possible sounds and sound contrasts that people could make were they able to perform phonemic analyses. The historical facts are quite to the contrary. Linguists first achieved a large number of emic analyses of the sound systems of various languages and, as evidence from a wide number of emic studies accumulated, the general outlines of the universal phonetic possibilities began to emerge. In fact, there is probably much less agreement right

[5] A semantic domain is a set of linguistic forms and meanings where the meanings are closely related.

[6] I must confess that I do not recall having seen this stated explicitly in print, but it seems implicit in much anthropological discourse on these matters both written and spoken.

now within linguistics on the general outlines of universal phonetics than many anthropologists imagine.

In any case, presence of an etic grid is not a precondition to successful semantic analysis. It can often be a help but can never be taken for granted. Berlin's experience in Tzeltal ethnobotany has shown that using Western botanical classification as an etic grid handles most of the data, but not all. Tzeltal botanical classification, with respect both to plant classes and the features defining and distinguishing the classes, usually "makes sense," so to speak, in Western botanical terms. But there are occasions where Tzeltal cognition of the botanical realm does not make sense in Western terms, as when, for example, two taxa are distinguished on the basis of what is in Western terms a botanically irrelevant attribute such as size or color of fruit.

Closely related to the idea that ethnographic semantic analysis always requires an etic grid, and intimately involved in the accusation that ethnosemantics is "the science of trivia" (Harris 1968:591), is the notion that semantic analysis is inapplicable in any cognitive domain of social importance. Lounsbury's work on Trobriand kinship and on Crow-Omaha systems in general is a sufficient counter-example to this claim, although this work does employ the genealogical etic grid. However, much of Keesing's excellent work on the Kwaio employs semantic analysis not based on an etic grid, as do several significant studies of residence including Goodenough's on Nakanai and Geoghegan's (1968) on Samal. (Again, apologies to colleagues I may have slighted.)

A particularly interesting example of an ethnosemantic analysis not employing an etic grid and of unquestionable sociological significance is that performed by Irving Zaretsky on the religious argot of San Francisco Spiritualist Churches (Zaretsky 1969). Zaretsky found that many common English words were being used in ways that were clearly not the normal meanings of those words. An ethnosemantic analysis of all such words revealed a subset with the following interesting properties. Words belonging to this set have unmistakable although vague connotations of supernatural "spirit forces" at work in the world, and in particular through the agency of the medium. However, the referential meanings of these forms are extremely nebulous. This is not a question of the investigator's being unable to discover the referential meanings but rather that Zaretsky has shown through detailed comparison of the contexts in which these expressions are employed that the referential meanings are in fact very vague. He then goes on to show two important ways in which the very referential vagueness of these words contributes to perpetuation of the social organization in which they are employed. First, referential vagueness permits the medium to transmit acceptable messages from the spirits to a parishioner who has written down a specific question that the medium has not seen. For example,

Ethnographer: Can you recall any message you received in church recently?

Informant: Well, let's see . . . She told me I was going to get drafted . . .

Ethnographer: Did she actually come right out and tell you you will get drafted, just like that?

Informant: Well, not exactly. She kept muttering about how I have *upset conditions* around me and how she saw the color green in my *vibration* . . . She just went on like that for a while . . . Well, I know what she was talking about because I waited to hear from my draft board all this time . . . But I certainly didn't want her to tell me that I will be drafted . . .

Ethnographer: How did you know what she meant by *condition, vibration, environment*?

Informant: Well I didn't . . . No, actually, it was obvious . . . I guess she could tell psychically what bothered me . . . Well, I don't know, but I think it was pretty obvious what she meant . . . [Zaretsky 1969:124].

This referential vagueness of the terms employed permits the ardent parishioner to endow them with whatever particular referential interpretation he wishes in each occasion of use. Secondly, this same referential vagueness protects the medium from the possible legal charge that she is engaged in the illicit activity of forecasting specific future events for money.

5. *Ethnosemantics, despite its emphasis on research techniques that take account of local variations in emic structures, is not anti-evolutionary, anti-historical or anti-etic.* I will dwell only briefly on this point, as Berlin's talk has treated some of the relevant data in considerable detail. It is certainly true that most empirical work in ethnographic semantics has until recently been devoted to synchronic emic studies. This fact has convinced some people that the field is inherently anti-historical and committed to an unyielding form of the doctrine of extreme cultural relativity. One cannot help but be re-

minded of the accusation frequently leveled against generative grammar until about 5 years ago that it was anti-historical or at least incapable of dealing with the data of language change. (I think it was at about that time that a noted Neo-Bloomfieldian is reported to have remarked, "My God, I hear they're going to invade historical linguistics next.") In the last 5 years a large number of historical studies by generative linguists have appeared, the most recent of which is a comprehensive theoretical treatise on historical linguistics from the generative point of view (King 1969).

Ethnosemantics has never been anti-etic. In fact, as I have argued above, the guiding spirit of the emic methodology has always been to take objective account of the local emic organization of cultural materials precisely in order to discover both the universal formal structures that dictate the shape of all emic cultural systems and to crack through the local emic codes to the etic semantic universals that underly them. There has never been any question in ethnosemantics about belief in the psychic unity of mankind. This has always been taken for granted. The discovery of as much as possible about the nature of the human psyche has always been the ultimate goal. The concern with emic methods has been dictated by the obvious fact that our common human psyche chooses, at least on the surface, to organize itself very differently in different cultural systems.

Linguistics is beginning now, only after years of careful analysis of individual emic systems, always with an eye to possible universal generalizations, to achieve some fairly clear and powerful general theories of the universal structure and sound content of language. But it is unlikely that the important results of modern linguistic theory with respect to universals of language would have been achieved if that discipline had refused to take account of the irrefutable facts of the emic diversity of languages.[7]

A concrete example of the use of emic method being confused with the notion that the user is committed to an ultimate emic nominalism with respect to semantic and cognitive systems is illustrated by recent work on color terminologies. Conklin (1955) showed convincingly that Hanunóo color terminology in fact encodes much noncolorimetric information. In fact, there is some question, as Conklin points out, whether from the point of view of Hanunóo culture it makes any sense to talk about "color" terminology at all. What Conklin demonstrated is that there is an emic structure to cognitive domains that must be taken account of methodologically if one is to arrive at anything like a meaningful crosscultural generalization. In commencing our search for semantic universals in color terminology, Berlin and I never doubted for a moment the validity of Conklin's findings, and our results in no way—I repeat, in no way—contradict his. We knew we had to employ a method that would first uncover the local emic organization of the domain of color and then find some way to get behind or beyond that to see if there were in fact etic universals at another level of structure. I think it is no accident that these etic universals were stumbled upon by people trained in ethnoscientific method and firmly committed to a procedure that takes account of the inconvenient but unalterable fact of emic cultural diversity.

In addition, it turned out that our findings had historical and evolutionary implications. I will not recapitulate the details here. I wish only to point out that this constitutes a counterexample to the claim that ethnographic semantics is necessarily anti-historical.

6. Ethnoscience is neither anti-statistical nor unconcerned with prediction. I have insisted on the distinction between ethnosemantics on the one hand and an approach to ethnography that includes an ethnosemantic component on the other. Some critics of the new ethnography have been unaware of this distinction and have consequently criticized ethnosemantics for not being all of ethnography. The most usual form this criticism takes is the accusation that the new ethnography so-called is either unwilling or unable (or both) to deal with the statistical facts of the distributions of persons and resources in a society, that is, with social organization.

It is true that a cardinal tenet of cognitively oriented ethnography is that one must take careful account of the cognitive devices that constitute the culture bearer's decision making process

[7] Notwithstanding some of Chomsky's more extreme statements in *Cartesian Linguistics* (1966), from which some have inferred his position to be that generative grammar has no historical roots in linguistics of the period between, say, 1700 and 1950.

if one is to arrive at a successful description of the outcomes of these decisions. Resources, including human resources, do not allocate *themselves* to various slots in the social economy but rather resource allocation is achieved as the result of myriad individual decisions made in accordance with the cognitive structure we call the local culture (or subcultures). There are at least two ways of checking empirically that one's construction of the native actors' decision making process is correct. First, one can assess native actors' reactions to actions on the part of their fellows. The cognitive model predicts which actions will be judged appropriate under which circumstances. We have already considered an example of this type; Trukese find a man's striking his married daughter inappropriate, if not downright insane, *except* under certain specified conditions.

However, this is not the only kind of test one can make of a cognitive model. The stronger test requires that one predict not only the natives' judgments of appropriateness after the behavioral facts but that one predict actual behaviors before the fact. To do so one obviously has to have information outside of the cognitive model, namely, the inputs to that model. For example, suppose a cultural rule states in part "reside post-maritally with the husband's matri-sib if that sib (a) is localized (i.e., is in possession of territory) and (b) owns uncultivated land." If we wish to predict where a given individual X will reside after marriage, we will have to know, in addition to the fragment of a cultural rule just given, the sex of X, which matri-sib X (or X's husband) belongs to, whether that matri-sib is localized, if so where, and whether or not that matri-sib controls unused land, among other things.

To predict distributions of actual residence patterns on an aggregate scale, we have to furnish as input to the postulated cognitive model the joint distributions of matri-sib membership, matri-sib localization, wealth in land and so on, for the entire population. This approach has been successfully employed to predict several sorts of statistical distributions of economic and demographic data reflecting the outcomes of individual applications of cultural rules. For example, the varying frequencies with which Society Islanders in diverse communities adopt members of different kin and non-kin social categories have been successfully predicted by a model that posits a uniform set of cultural rules into which are plugged the appropriate local demographic and economic parameters in each community (Kay 1963; Hooper and Kay 1965; Hooper 1969).

A more recent and complete example is Geoghegan's (1969) study of "Decision-Making and Residence on Tagtabon Island" in the southern Philippines.

On the basis of controlled elicitation and semantic analysis, Geoghegan posits a cognitive model of how an individual Samal decides how to reside. The model takes into account various emically defined attributes of the age, sex, social status, economic status, kin relationship and so on, of the person making the decision and of various other persons related to him. The outputs of the model are diverse modes and locales of residence; for example, "I shall live in my own house, and locate it near my father's house," or "I shall live alternately in the house of my wife's mother and the house of my own father." The model applies not only to residence choice at marriage, which may be a more or less conscious affair, but also to the tacit decision which may be attributed to every individual by virtue of the fact that he is residing somewhere. This model, constructed exclusively from data obtained through systematic elicitation from selected informants, nevertheless applies to the entire population in that it takes into account the relevant social identities of the native user. We may note in passing that the model itself is a rather intricate mathematical object, which Geoghegan derived directly from his analysis of natives' statements; it is certainly not consciously articulated by any one informant or group of informants.

The model is tested as follows. Detailed census data give the actual distributions of residence modes and locales in the population. The census data also give distributions of age, sex, social status of various types and so on. From the latter type of data, Geoghegan estimates the probability that an arbitrary individual will answer yes to each of the many questions implied by the cognitive decision model (for example, "yes, I am adult"; "yes, my spouse is living," etc). To simplify greatly, let us suppose that the cognitive model specifies a particular mode of residence (call it A) for an adult male whose spouse is living. Estimating from the census data the individual probabilities that an arbitrary person is male, adult and possessed of a living spouse, Geoghegan multiplies these 3 numbers together to get an estimate of the probability that an arbitrary person will choose residence of type A. (Actually the individual conditional probabilities are employed.) Geoghegan then multiplies the probability of each type of residence decision by the number of persons in the total population. The result is the hypothetical distribution of residence types in the population that is predicted by the cultural rule. This predicted distribution is then compared to the actual distribution of residence types taken directly from census data. The two distributions are virtually identical. The largest proportional error in prediction (11 percent) involves a predicted frequency of 8 cases against an observed frequency of 9 cases. The average proportional error of prediction is about 6 percent.

I know of no case in anthropology where this fine a prediction of comparably significant behavioral data has been achieved. Not only is ethnoscience not opposed in principle to prediction, but I think it is fair to say that it has achieved substantial practical results in that direction.

Conclusion

Having discussed ethnosemantics by contrasting it with a number of things which it is not, let me summarize in a more positive vein. Ethnographic semantics is the study of the meanings of the expressions of a language, the system formed by the interrelations of these meanings, and the cognitive system which lies behind the system of meanings and which is realized in large part through them. As such, ethnosemantics is part of anthropology as well as part of linguistics and psychology. It is part of anthropology in that the culture shared by a group of people consists essentially in the cognitive system that makes the actions of one intelligible to another and makes possible all truly social intercourse, including competition, regulated conflict, and insult, as well as gentler modes of transaction.

Ethnosemantics is employed in ethnography as a means of arriving at the cognitive system, or systems, employed by people as a device for classifying their environment, evaluating various states of that environment, predicting what the outcomes of the various behavioral possibilities open to them will have on that environment, and ultimately selecting a course of action. As we have seen, cognitive models alone do not predict overt behavior. But when the cognitive model is supplied with the information it specifies as necessary for reaching a decision, it can predict overt behavior accurately.

There is also a point at which the disciplines of anthropology, linguistics and psychology coalesce, the study of the human mind. I am sorry if that word offends anyone, but to pretend that human beings do not have minds because a mind has never been seen or touched would require that we reject virtually all highly abstract and therefore useful scientific concepts, including, for example, gravity, relativity and probability. The theoretical implications of ethnosemantics to the study of mind are twofold. First, we are beginning to get a glimpse of the formal structure of semantic and cognitive domains, and even of their articulation into larger subsystems of the total cognitive system. I refer here specifically to the theoretical work of Goodenough (e.g., 1965), Geoghegan (1968) and its empirical applications by Goodenough, Geoghegan, Keesing and others in representing formally not only individual cognitive domains but their mutual integration into larger cognitive systems.

Secondly, in the emergence of substantive and formal semantic universals, we are perhaps seeing the first glimpses of an explicit and empirically motivated description of that "psychic unity of mankind" in which anthropologists have so long believed. Lounsbury's work strongly suggests that we may soon attain a fixed finite vocabulary of universally recognized basic kin relations which are variously elaborated into the widely differing emically defined kinship systems of the world by a set of orderly and precisely describable processes. It is hard to resist an analogy between this and the recent findings on color terminology. Once again we see a universal set of fixed focal points underlying the apparent randomness of the distribution of color concept boundaries in various cultures. The recurrent themes are that emic diversity and relativity are underlain by certain universal etic semantic constants and that the ways in which each emic system defines its own genius out of the universal vocabulary of basic concepts are orderly and subject to rational discovery.

REFERENCES CITED

Berlin, B., D. E. Breedlove and P. H. Raven

1968 Covert categories and folk taxonomies. American Anthropologist 70:290–99.

Berreman, G. D.

1966 Anemic and emetic analyses in social anthropology. American Anthropologist 68:346–54.

Black, M. B.

1969 Eliciting folk taxonomy in Ojibwa. *In* Cognitive anthropology. S. A. Tyler, ed. New York: Holt, Rinehart and Winston.

Chomsky, N.

1966 Cartesian linguistics. New York: Harper and Row.

Conklin, H. C.

1955 Hanunóo color categories. Southwestern Journal of Anthropology 11:339–44.

Geoghegan, W.

1968 Information processing systems in culture. Working Paper no. 6, Language-Behavior Research Laboratory, University of California, Berkeley. *To appear in* Explorations in mathematical anthropology. P. Kay, ed. Cambridge: MIT Press. Forthcoming.

1969 Decision-making and residence on Tagtabon Island. Working Paper no. 17, Language-Behavior Research Laboratory, University of California, Berkeley.

Goodenough, W. H.

1956 Residence rules. Southwestern Journal of Anthropology 12:22–37.

1965 Rethinking "status" and "role." *In* The relevance of models in social anthropology. New York: Praeger.

Harris, M.

1968 The rise of anthropological theory. New York: Crowell.

Hooper, A. B.

1969 Adoption in the Society Islands. *In* Adoption in Eastern Oceania. V. Carroll, ed. ASAEO Monograph no. 1. Honolulu: University of Hawaii Press.

Hooper, A., and P. Kay

1965 Tahitian fosterage, cultural rules, and "social structure." Paper presented at the Annual Meeting of the American Anthropological Association.

Kay, P.

1963 Tahitian fosterage and the form of ethnographic models. American Anthropologist 65:1027–44.

King, R. P.

1969 Historical linguistics and generative grammar. Englewood Cliffs: Prentice-Hall.

Leach, E. R.

1961 Rethinking anthropology. London: Athlone Press.

Quine, W. V. O.

1960 Word and object. Cambridge: MIT Press.

Zaretsky, I. I.

1969 The message is the medium: an ethnosemantic study of the language of spiritualist churches. PhD dissertation, University of California, Berkeley.

SECTION II

Questions of Theory

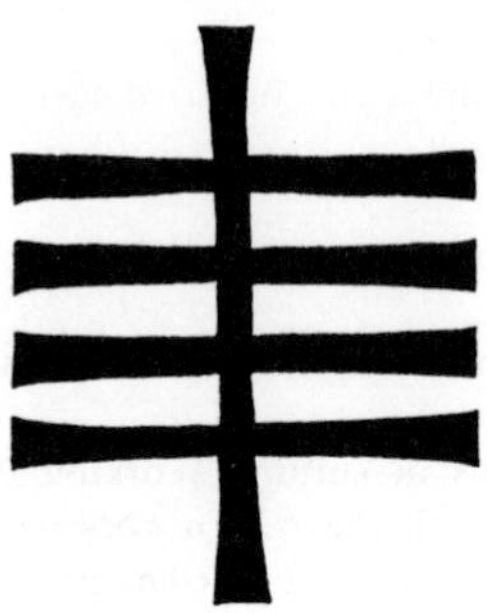

The following are prominent among the major theoretical contentions that characterize contemporary cultural and social anthropology.

- Society and culture are systems to be studied with special attention to the structure and function of their component parts, especially as these contribute to the survival of the sociocultural system as an integrated totality.
- Society and culture are in an ongoing state of evolution, in accordance with a process similar to biological evolution, in which the inexorable emergence of ever greater levels of technological complexity inevitably precipitates social, economic, political, and ideological changes. Those sociocultural systems that fail to make the necessary adaptive changes risk increasing vulnerability in competition with those that have succeeded.
- Society and culture are radically affected in form and content by the patterns of techno-environmental adaptation that provide their material base.
- Society and culture play major formative roles in the development of both normal and deviant personality. Consequently societies can be distinguished on the basis of the relative prevalence of particular character types among their members.

To begin with the first of these several theoretical contentions, it is now a very basic assumption in ethnology that all aspects of culture are interrelated in meaningful ways. It is thus always a fundamental part of the anthropologist's task to keep in mind the functional relationship of any particular aspect of society or culture to the total sociocultural system of which it is an integral part. In other words, it is assumed that no people's way of life, no matter how apparently "primitive" or bizarre, is ever a haphazard jumble of unrelated parts. Rather, each component is functionally integrated with all the others. And most parts must be so structured and function in such a way as to contribute to the continued survival of the sociocultural system as a totality.

Also entailed is the idea that the function of aspects of culture may be either *positive* (a type of family organization well adapted to prevailing techno-environmental conditions, for example), or *negative*, threatening to societal stability or survival (a political system so rigidly structured that it functions to repress needed economic change).

Although any aspect of culture can be abstracted for analysis—farming techniques, work organization, kinship terminology, art forms—it must always be so interpreted as to remain analytically replaceable in sociocultural context. For it is only there that it can be fully understood, only there that the implications of the way it works can be fully assessed as they may affect the survival chances of the total system of which they are always an integrated part. Sometimes their function is of major significance. Sometimes it is not. Sometimes their function is negative in relation to certain aspects of the system (crime as a threat to societal stability) and positive in relation to others (crime as a source of income for criminals and the police).

British social anthropologists were among the first to develop a cross-cultural interest in studying the structure of society and the function of its component parts. So it is appropriate that Mair, a prominent English anthropologist, should describe this approach further.

The Concept of Function

Lucy Mair

A good many anthropologists in Britain, and some in America, describe the kind of studies of society that they make as "functional," and the theory that guides them as "functionalism." A number of different meanings have been given to the word "function."

In everyday language we speak of a machine, and sometimes of a person, "functioning" if it, or he, "works"; does adequately what is expected of it, or him; and the noun "function" means, among other things, a kind of activity that is appropriate to the agency performing it, a meaning that implies that we know what machines or social arrangements are *for*.

We generally conceive of a machine or a living organism as consisting of interrelated parts, each of which must *function* properly if the machine is to keep running or the organism to keep alive, and most of the writers who have made "function" a key-word in discussions of society have had this analogy in mind. None of them invites his readers to picture society as a machine (though people often write about "social mechanisms"), but most of them compare it to a living organism. Some push the metaphor further than others.[1]

Herbert Spencer, the first British sociologist (1820–1903), was the first to use "function" as a technical term for the analysis of society. He saw close parallels between human societies and biological organisms, both in the way they might be supposed to have evolved and in the way they kept themselves in being. Their existence, he argued, is maintained by the "functional dependence of parts."[2] In a society, as in an organism, there is "a perpetual removal and replacement of parts joined with a continued integrity of the whole." In this comparison the individual members of the society correspond to the cells of the organism.[3] This is more than a metaphor; Spencer believed that the laws of biology should be equally applicable to aggregations of cells and aggregations of individuals. Societies, he believed, developed through the differentiation of functions as biological organisms had been shown to do. He not only de-

Source: From Lucy Mair, *An Introduction to Social Anthropology*, second edition, © 1972 Oxford University Press and by permission of The Clarendon Press, Oxford. Used with permission of the author and the publisher.

[1] The word "function" is also used in a mathematical sense: to say that x is a function of y means that the relation between x and y is constant, so that when y changes x changes. This metaphor has occasionally been used by social anthropologists, but it is not what most of them intend to convey by the word.

[2] "The Social Organism," in *Essays Scientific, Political, and Speculative,* 1884, Vol. I, pp. 1396 ff. The essay was written in 1860.

[3] Readers of literary bent may be interested to note that Marcel Proust in his great novel, when writing of the 1914–18 war, pictures the opposing nations in terms very similar to these, though his biographers do not mention Spencer among the writers who influenced him.

scribed the functions of different members of a human society as "duties," but used this word for the functions even of cells in organisms showing the very minimum of differentiation. When he began to draw analogies between the differentiation of function in evolving organisms and in evolving societies, he remarked that an organ increased in bulk as a result of "actively discharging the duties which the body at large requires of it"; and here the social counterpart of the biological organ was "any class of laborers or artisans, any manufacturing centre, or any official agency." Railways in his picture of society corresponded to veins and arteries: profits to the excess of nutrition over waste which makes growth possible. By using for both biological and social functions a word—"duty"—which is really applicable only to social relationships, Spencer evaded some of the problems connected with the concept of function that later writers have had to wrestle with.

It will be seen that the writers who have sought to attribute functions to different parts of a social system (to use the broadest possible term) have been far from unanimous in their choice of analogies. To make an analogy of our own, we might say that each has dissected society in a different way.

Whereas Spencer drew his comparisons from the lowest forms of life, later writers made theirs with organs of the human body. Thus Durkheim (1858–1917) when he elaborated his principles of sociological method,[4] said that to explain a social phenomenon one must seek both the cause that produced it and "the function that it fulfilled." He preferred the idea of function to that of "end" or "aim" because, as he remarked, social phenomena do not owe their existence to the results that they produce. We should look for the relation between the phenomenon we are considering and "the general needs of the social organism." Whether it was created intentionally or not is not important. Durkheim adds, however, that even though social phenomena do not come into being because they are useful, they would not continue to exist unless they were useful in some way. Useless social arrangements (a non-technical word may make the meaning clearer) are harmful by the mere fact of being useless; society is burdened with them without getting any good from them. Therefore, we should ask how the phenomena that together constitute social life combine to produce harmony within the society and a satisfactory adaptation to the environment. Examples of social phenomena given in this context are the punishment of crime and the division of labor. Durkheim was primarily interested in the maintenance of *order*, and since most people would agree that order is essential to any arrangement of persons which can be called a society, one could say that his idea of function did not beg many questions.

Of the social anthropologists who drew inspiration from Durkheim, Malinowski developed the conception of function to its greatest elaboration, and even (partly in joke) gave to himself and his pupils the title of "the Functional School." His starting-point is contained in Durkheim's argument summarized above. Useless and meaningless customs just do not continue to exist; therefore a student of society, when he is confronted with a way of doing things that seems peculiar at first sight, should ask what it does for the people who practise it. This advice is obviously of even greater value to anthropologists working in societies very different from their own than it was to Durkheim's readers, who were only being urged to ask new questions about the world of their own experience.

Malinowski found his answers in the relation of social organization to biological needs. Man, he argued, cannot survive without food and shelter; the species cannot survive unless it reproduces its kind. In this respect man resembles other animals, but he differs from most of them in that he meets these essential needs indirectly through co-operation with his fellows in an organized society; and because he is endowed with speech and conceptual thought, he is able to pass on experience so that every society has an accumulated heritage of knowledge, values and rules of conduct which is further developed in every generation. In the possession of this heritage man differs even from the social animals, who do co-operate to meet their basic needs. It is this, indeed, that has enabled him to evolve the roundabout ways of procuring the economic necessities of life, and regulating sex relations and procreation, that we find in every human society. But these roundabout ways necessitate obedience to rules and restrictions, in contrast to a simple response to instinctive drives. Therefore *society*—no longer merely the indi-

4 *Règles de la Méthode Sociologique*, 1895.

vidual or the species—has further needs. It needs arrangements for the transmission of its heritage of knowledge and moral values, that is some system of education. It needs, also, some source of confidence in the rightness of its rules and the worthwhileness of its continued existence; this it derives from religion.

This scheme of needs has been criticized on the ground that it confuses the needs of an individual organism, which cannot survive without food, or a species, which cannot survive without reproduction, and those of a society, which can survive—that is continue to exist—even if large numbers of its members die of hunger in famines or for some other reason do not produce offspring. Malinowski's most elaborate scheme included other biological needs for which human society makes provision; for example shelter, warmth, freedom of movement. But his actual discussion of the relation of social institutions to biological needs was pretty well confined to those concerned with subsistence and those concerned with marriage and the family; quite rightly, since these occupy the greater part of the life of the simpler societies.

E. R. Leach,[5] a contemporary Cambridge anthropologist, has contrasted Malinowski's use of the idea of needs with Durkheim's. Whereas Malinowski sought to relate *social* arrangements to *biological* needs, what Durkheim did was to draw the same analogy as Spencer between the *biological* function of a *biological* organ and the *social* function of a form of regularly recurring *social* behavior (what he called a "social fact"). So far from seeking to interpret social behavior as a response to biological needs, Durkheim insisted, as was indicated earlier, that social facts were *sui generis*. "The social can be explained only by the social," he said; in other words, the explanation of social behavior is not to be sought either in man's biological constitution or, as is commoner among laymen, in individual psychology.

Radcliffe-Brown, drawing on Spencer, liked to elaborate the analogy between biological systems and social organisms. "The function of a recurrent physiological process," he wrote, "is a correspondence between it and the necessary conditions of existence of the organism."[6] In social life "the function of a recurrent activity, such as the punishment of a crime or a funeral ceremony, is the part it plays in the social life as a whole and therefore the contribution it makes to the maintenance of the structural continuity." More specifically, he said "the function of a particular social usage is the contribution it makes to the total social life as the functioning of the total social system." But he expressly insisted that "function" should not be used to mean "aim," "purpose" or "meaning,"[7] and neither he nor the other writers quoted would have dreamed of equating it with "duty." One may note too that he confined his analogy to usages and did not bring in the objects which men make and use. Such a treatment assumes that the usage under discussion is *good for* the society in which it is found; and this assumption having been made, the next step is to explain *what good* it does. The proposition that every social usage has a function can then only too easily become the proposition that whatever is, is good, but this assumption is not made by social anthropologists today.

Not much attention has been given to the question what kind of social usage we should consider when we are looking for functions; a social usage might be anything from blowing one's nose with a handkerchief to the duty of avenging a slain kinsman. Malinowski's scheme did designate *institutions* as the social arrangements that can be said to meet needs and therefore have functions—and an institution was, for him, a complex of organized activities in which particular persons are expected to co-operate. Other writers have been concerned with rules of conduct, such as those which forbid marriage between persons in certain relationships. Malinowski himself used the rule of exogamy (no intermarriage within a descent group) as an example. He said its function was to eliminate sexual rivalries from a group which is expected to co-operate; others might say with Tylor that its function was to create a network of alliances between different descent groups (which is certainly its *effect*).

[5] "The Epistemological Background to Malinowski's Empiricism," in R. W. Firth ed., *Man and Culture*, 1957, p. 123 n.

[6] *Structure and Function in Primitive Society*, 1952, p. 179.

[7] Ibid., p. 200.

It is clear that the people who practise the usages examined by the anthropologist do not ascribe to them functions of this kind. They may say, for example, "We perform mortuary rituals so that the dead man's spirit will go to the place of spirits and not come back to trouble us"; but they certainly would not say with Malinowski that they perform mortuary rituals to meet the need for reassurance in the face of death. This led Merton[8] to distinguish between "manifest functions," as the conscious aims of people participating in some prescribed action, and "latent functions" which are apparent only to the observer.

It is indeed extremely difficult to use the metaphor of "function" without implying some notion of fitness for ends which itself implies some idea of purpose. But students of society do not explicitly endorse such ideas. Most of them would repudiate the notion of design in the universe, and all would agree that the institutions of the simpler societies have not been deliberately created by the members of these societies. One could then fall back on the Darwinian analogy, once so popular, with species which die out because they cannot hold their own in competition with others better adapted to their environment. But human societies differ from organisms less because, as Spencer and Radcliffe-Brown said, they persist while their members change, than because their members continue to reproduce the species while the society changes. We do not often see societies "going under in the struggle"; and in the rare cases where this has happened the reason is to be found not in the kind of inadequate adaptation to environment that would explain the extinction of a biological species, but much more crudely in the inadequacy of weapons of defence.

Moreover, though the exaggeration of functionalist theory can lead to the absurdity of assuming that what the fieldworker sees is a system so perfectly balanced that any change must be for the worse, it is certain that it is preferable to begin by looking for "function" or "meaning" in social usages rather than assume, as earlier anthropologists did, that, if they are hard to understand, they must be anachronisms that have lost their meaning—"survivals" from earlier states of society. Most of the customs that used to be explained as survivals have proved to have adequate functional explanations; and any fieldworker, however much he may try to exclude from his own interpretations such notions as "purpose" or "meaning," will hardly be able to avoid feeling that they are implicit in the attitudes of the people among whom he is working. We should not deny the possibility that certain customs—particularly perhaps rituals—have survived into the present without retaining much meaning, or with their meaning greatly changed; and what is perhaps even more important is that we should recognize social anachronisms in periods of rapid change, such as all societies are experiencing at the present day. But the ideas of survival and anachronism must be used circumspectly, and not as a tool for the invention of imaginary histories.

It may seem that the concept of function has been given too many different meanings to be really very useful, and certainly it is possible to get on quite well without ever using the word. But the attitude towards the study of society which gave it currency is fundamental to modern social anthropology, and that is why many anthropologists who have given up trying to find functions for particular usages still describe their kind of study as functionalism. The assumption they make is that what one is looking for in social behavior is a system, or systems, of interrelated activities which have, as Radcliffe-Brown put it, "a certain kind of unity which we may speak of as functional unity"; that what one is primarily interested in is how this system works rather than how it came to be what it is; and that for this kind of study one must see at first hand what actually goes on, not merely ask questions to elicit general statements about what ought to happen. As Fortes pointed out in his inaugural lecture as William Wyse Professor of Social Anthropology at Cambridge, one can see this unity only by living in the society and observing its parts "working together contemporaneously."[9] For another contemporary, Gellner,[10] the essence of a functional study is that the usages we are looking at should not be divorced from their context. The question then arises, how wide is the context? For Malinowski the context of any one custom extended all through the society in which it was found (and

8 R. K. Merton, *Social Theory and Social Structure*, 2nd edn., 1957, p. 51.
9 *Social Anthropology at Cambridge since 1900*, 1953, p. 25.
10 "Concepts and Society," *Transactions of the Fifth World Congress of Sociology*, 1962, pp. 155–8.

there was really no reason why it should not extend through the whole world). This insistence on the inter-connections of the facts we were discussing was what made his teaching so intensely stimulating. But as a guide to the fieldworker it was a counsel of perfection, and it becomes more unattainable, not less, as fieldwork methods become more intensive. The fieldworker just has to judge for himself how much context is relevant; there will be critics to take him up if he judges badly. What people mean by a functional study today is selecting a particular problem for intensive examination and looking at it in the context of a wider whole, the structure of which must be understood in its essentials.

All along, the organization of this reader has reflected the assumption that society and culture, and their component parts, can be usefully examined in an evolutionary perspective that sees the emergence of more complex sociocultural forms as developing out of or replacing simpler ones in response to the compelling requirement for new systems for dealing with the new economic, social, political, and ideological needs that result from what has been, from the Old Stone Age to the present, the inexorable evolution of technology.

Evidence supporting this approach is derived both from archaeology and from comparative ethnography. Literally the further down you dig the simpler become the remains of our ancestors' material culture, in a straight line back through time from modern nuclear-powered generators through the use of steam, windmills, and water wheels to the most rudimentary hand tools of our most ancient antecedents. By combining the conclusions derived from this evidence with what has been learned of the causal connections between particular levels of technological development and the nontangible aspects of culture (economic organization, social organization, and so on) among contemporary peoples, it becomes possible to plot both the evolution of material culture and the new economic, social, and political institutions that marked each succeeding stage of our species' ongoing technological progression. Ribeiro, a distinguished Brazilian anthropologist, develops this theme more fully.

Sociocultural Evolution

Darcy Ribeiro

In recent years, most anthropologists have readopted an evolutionary point of view, but have rephrased it in multilinear terms and disassociated it from the more conjectural earlier attempts to trace the origin of customs and institutions. There is not yet available, however, a global scheme for the stages of sociocultural evolution that is based on the most recent contributions from archeology, ethnology, and history—one that permits the placement of any society, whether living or extinct, into the continuum of sociocultural development.

The absence of such a scheme creates at least four kinds of deformation in social science theory. First, there is a tendency to apply theories of limited scope to problems like social development and modernization, which by their very nature require a broader and more comprehensive handling. Second, studies of cultural dynamics—especially those involving acculturation

Source: From Darcy Ribeiro, *The Civilizational Process,* translated by Betty J. Meggers (Washington, D.C.: Smithsonian Institution Press, 1968). Used by permission of the publisher, the author, and the translator.

—are approached on the level of microanalysis, which contributes practically nothing to the knowledge of the processes by which cultural traditions are shaped and by which ethnic groups are formed and transformed. Third, functional studies are given prominence, obliging anthropologists to formulate theoretical explanations in terms of the interaction between elements present within each culture, and depriving them of the advantage inherent in the search for generalizations in the older diachronic perspective. Fourth, a theory of sociocultural evolution is implicit in many studies without being openly discussed or exposed to critical examination. Furthermore, even studies explicitly based on cultural evolutionary methodology are frequently formulated within such narrow limits that they do not provide a causal explanation of cultural dynamics, nor do they lead to the formulation of theories that explain the composition and interaction of contemporary societies as the result of long and complicated historical processes.

The filling of this theoretical gap, although obviously too large a task for one person, motivates this preliminary formulation of a theory of sociocultural evolution. It will focus on the evolution of human societies during the last ten millennia, in other words, since the appearance of the first agricultural communities. Earlier stages will be considered only to the minimal degree necessary to lay the foundation for later developments.

Theoretical Postulates

The history of human societies during the past ten millennia can be explained in terms of successive technological revolutions and civilizational processes, by means of which the majority of mankind has passed from a generalized hunting-and-gathering condition to diverse modes of subsistence, social organization, and self-explanation. Although these ways of life differ widely in cultural content, their variation is not arbitrary because of the underlying existence of three orders of imperatives. The first is the cumulative character of technological progress, which advances from simpler to more complex forms in an irreversible sequence. The second is the reciprocal relations between the technological equipment employed by a society in dealing with its natural environment and the size of its population, as well as the way in which those relations are organized both internally and with other societies. The third is the interaction of the forces used to control nature and to organize human relations with the rest of the culture; namely, the standardized ways of producing and thinking that are manifested materially in artifacts and property, behaviorally in social conduct, and ideologically in symbolic communication and the formulation of social experience into bodies of knowledge, beliefs, and values.

The existence of these three orders of interacting imperatives—technological, social, and ideological—means that a classification of evolutionary stages based on technological distinctions should bring to light complementary sequences of patterns in social organization and ideological configuration. The result should be a general evolutionary typology valid for all three imperatives, although derived primarily from the first of them. Such a typology should make it possible to fit all human societies into a limited number of structural categories, which in turn can be seriated into a sequence of more general evolutionary stages.

There is a high degree of agreement among students that the technological imperative exercises a determinative influence over the social and ideological aspects of culture and that progressive stages of technological evolution can be discerned. It is also generally agreed that the technological, social, and ideological sectors of a society are interconnected. There is much less unanimity regarding the possibility of equating these patterns of relationship with evolutionary stages that combine a certain level of technological development with specific features of social organization and particular kinds of ideological configuration. To many observers, the possible number of sociocultural responses to a particular technological system seems too large or too arbitrary to make a correlation between them practical, or to permit the creation of a universally applicable typology. Other students, while admitting the possibility of arriving at such a framework of stages, consider that it would have no operative value because universal stages would have to be formulated in such generic terms that they would be "neither very arguable nor very useful" (Steward, 1955, p. 17).

Even if this were true, however, the elaboration of a global scheme of sociocultural evolution is justifiable in terms of its value in explaining cultural dynamics. It is highly probable, moreover, that such a scheme would have a practical value, since it would permit the subdivision of sociocultural evolution into segments, each possessing specific characteristics relevant to concrete situations. Actually, as long as this kind of general perspective is missing, social scientists cannot frame problems that will lead to an understanding of the relationships between the concrete level of historical, archeological, and ethnographical studies and the abstract level of anthropological and sociological explanations. A general theory of sociocultural evolution is also a prerequisite to the elaboration of scientific generalizations from analysis of synchronic or functional relationships.

The basic concept underlying theories of sociocultural evolution is that human societies, over long periods of time, were affected by two simultaneous and mutually complementary processes, one of them responsible for diversification and the other for homogenization. Under the influence of the former, societies tend to multiply their population contingents, to expand the ethnic entities into which they agglutinate, and to diversify their cultural heritages. Because of the second process, however, this diversification does not lead to increasing differentiation between human groups, but rather to a homogenization of ways of life via the fusion of ethnic entities into ever larger units and the development of their cultural characteristics along parallel lines.

The first process, diversifying in character, is a response to the differing requirements of ecological adaptation, which impart unique qualities to each culture by channeling it toward specialization to a particular environment. It is also a consequence of the impact of unique historical events, which deflect the path of development. These individual qualities, although relevant to an explanation of the content of a particular society, are only of concern in an examination of the evolutionary process when they represent general modes of human adaptation utilizable by other societies.

The second process, which is integrating and homogenizing in character, is sociocultural evolution. It could be said that sociocultural evolution proceeds by a realization of the limited possibilities for response to similar fundamental imperatives under similar conditions. This leads to the repetition of cultural forms and to the creation of uniformities in structure, which make it possible to establish a universal typology.

Examination of the varied composition of those human societies for which we have adequate documentation reveals that they can be categorized according to their degree of efficiency in achieving a mastery over nature. This categorization implies the existence of a developmental process that, while it does not operate with the same intensity on all societies, neither does it act arbitrarily. On the contrary, it is both regulated and directional because of the existence of a series of causal forces, including one general imperative and three basic contingencies that are extra-cultural in character, as well as several factors of a cultural nature.

The general imperative is the uniformity of the natural environment within which man operates, and which obliges him to adjust to physicochemical and biological factors that are not modifiable by culture. The leveling effect of this imperative is most evident in technology which, because of its direct involvement with nature, must of necessity respond to its requirements. As a consequence of this imperative, we find in all cultures a minimum body of objective knowledge and a standardized means of production, and these exercise a determinative influence on the other aspects of the culture.

The three basic contingencies of an extra-cultural nature combine with this general imperative to stamp all cultures with similar guidelines. All three can be subsumed under the label "human nature." The first kind stems from man's biological structure, and sets him apart from other species; it includes intelligence, flexibility, individuality, and sociability—traits that result from the process of biological evolution. This biological uniformity is reflected in the universal development of cultural norms of action upon the environment for the extraction of those materials essential to human survival and reproduction (collecting, hunting, fishing, etc.). Secondly, there are the contingencies of group living, which require the creation of cultural guidelines for the maintenance of group solidarity (family, kinship, clan, etc.) and for economic production (division of labor, stratification, etc.). Thirdly, there are contingencies of a psychological nature, which are more difficult to define, but which reflect the essential unity of the neuropsychological and mental structure of human beings, and which lead to independent discovery of similar responses to the same kinds of challenges.

In addition to the general imperative and these three contingencies—all of an extra-cultural nature—there is another imperative that is cultural. This is the uniquely human capacity for symbolic communication, which is responsible for enveloping social life in a fabric of cultural tradition transmitted from generation to generation, and which makes all developments dependent on the characteristics of the preexisting heritage.

Within the limitations set by these various factors, the accumulation of communal knowledge and the exercise of options have produced human culture in all its variations. The necessity of developing within this restrictive framework makes cultural evolution directional. Instead of always beginning anew, human activities are linked across generations into evolutionary sequences that are equivalent to those in biological evolution, but are both more variable and more uniform than the latter. Nature, evolving by genetic mutation, cannot return to an earlier state and is held to a relatively slow rate of transformation. Culture, on the other hand, evolves by the addition of bodies of information and ways of acting, and is disseminated by learning, thus making possible rapid change, the spread of new ideas with minimal spatial or temporal limitations, and the creation of increasingly larger and more homogeneous configurations.

The anthropological literature exhaustively demonstrates the universal character of these factors as well as the uniformity of the cultural response by documenting the presence of the same classes of elements in the basic structure of different cultures. This repetitive character of the responses made during the course of history to the causal challenges that confront all societies is attested by the occurrence of many similar forms of social stratification, political institutions, religious behavior, etc. There is also ample evidence not only for the existence of a succession of technological systems—based on the same physico-chemical and biological principles, but endowed with increasing efficiency both in productivity and the capacity to support ever larger groups of people—but for the power of some societies to gain domination over others. In short, all the data indicate that the evolutionary process must be viewed as both homogenizing and directional.

Sociocultural evolution has been considered thus far as an internal process of transformation that operates within the extra-cultural limitations already mentioned. In reality, however, cultures are not developed and maintained in isolation, but in a continuous interrelation with one another. Consequently, the internal creativity responsible for cultural innovations is supplemented by diffusion, which adds new traits, and by social compulsions of external origin, which may alter the course of evolutionary development. Although it is possible to isolate conceptually the variations that result from specialized ecological adaptation, the same is not true of variations brought about by diffusion or external pressures. The importance of the latter two factors is so great, however, that a satisfactory theory of sociocultural evolution must recognize their existence.

The present analysis attempts to show: (1) that the development of societies and cultures is regulated by an orientational principle originating from the cumulative development of productive and military technology; (2) that certain advances in this technology represent quantitative changes of a radical character that make it possible to distinguish stages or phases of sociocultural evolution; and (3) that these progressive technological stages correlate with necessary, and consequently uniform, alterations in social organization and ideological configuration.

The attribution of determinative power to technological innovations of a productive or military nature does not exclude the presence of other dynamic forces. On the contrary, over short periods of time social organization can bring about a realization of the potentialities inherent in technological advances, and a beneficial or adverse influence can also be exerted by ideological elements (such as scientific knowledge) on technology and through the latter, on social structure. Examples include the dynamic roles played by the phenomena of solidarity (Kropotkin, 1955) or conflict between economic classes (Marx, 1967); or between social units structured around cultural loyalties, such as national ethnic groups (Znaniecki, 1944) or religious groups (M. Weber, 1948). Even though these forms of solidarity and conflict are linked with technology, they are not reducible to technology, nor is their variety of form and function explainable in its terms. White (1949, p. 382) expressed this same point when he asserted that "every social system rests upon and is determined by a technological system. But every technological system functions *within* a social system, and therefore is conditioned by it."

Recognition of the interaction between these various orders of determinants makes it possible to achieve a realistic comprehension of the process of sociocultural evolution, which combines a more abstract global perspective with complementary perspectives of an historical nature, derived from the interplay between currents of cultural diffusion and acculturative pressures. Such a conceptual integration makes it unnecessary to choose between the relativistic doctrines of diffusionism, parallelism, and convergence, and the more radical evolutionistic explanations, which are based on the psychic unity of mankind or an exaggeration of the frequency of independent invention. Adoption of such a broad analytic perspective also permits us to view the diversification and homogenization of societies and cultures as resulting from local inventions (the rarer alternative), from the acquisition of advances diffused from elsewhere, and from responses to stresses created either by pressures for ecological adaptation or by the necessity to maintain an integration between the various cultural segments.

Recognition of the developmental phenomena that promote the homogeneity of cultural configurations on a global scale is facilitated by creating the concept of the civilizational process. Reference to such a concept also permits evaluation both of the differential effects of adaptation to specific ecological and historical situations, and of the degree to which the posing of alternative responses to similar basic challenges is permitted. This concept is in some ways similar to the cultural circles and strata of the diffusionists (Schmidt and Koppers, 1924; Graebner, 1924; Montandon, 1934), to culture area formulations (Wissler, 1938; Murdock, 1951; Kroeber, 1939, 1944), and even to cultural typologies (Redfield, 1956; Linton, 1936; Benedict, 1934). All of these, however, have an anti-evolutionistic bias, as well as other limitations. Complexes of traits that compose the *Kulturkreise,* for example, are fanciful in character; the culture areas are tied to geography; the search for culture types is often psychological in emphasis. Our approach is closer to the culture type concept as reformulated by Steward (1955, Ch. 11), who also made an effort to supersede earlier notions of culture areas and evolutionary stages. Our general civilizational process, however, overcomes the causal limitations of Steward's culture type, since it combines the concepts of technological revolution as the basic causal factor, sociocultural formations as theoretical models of cultural response to these revolutions, and civilizations as concrete historical entities that are crystallized out of the formations.

This perspective also achieves a higher plane of abstraction than the one on which Steward operated, and this makes it possible to examine diachronically large groups or classes of societies such as the nomadic pastoral hordes and the irrigation civilizations. This higher level of generalization obviously requires a correspondingly larger degree of abstraction in the definition of the diagnostic traits of each formation. It remains to be seen whether this will permit both the derivation of generalizations that can explain global sociocultural evolution and the classification into a scale of general evolutionary stages of the individual societies that are the concrete components. It is our belief that even under the limitations of this preliminary study, we can demonstrate this to be the case.

Conceptual Scheme

The greatest difficulty confronting an attempt to formulate a global evolutionary scheme is the need to combine different temporal and functional approaches, and to invest them with the appropriate degree of congruity and reliability, so as to permit comprehension both of the grand current of human cultural evolution and of the tumultuous steps in its historical progress and regression. In the following pages we will attempt to make explicit the foundations and limitations within which we propose to formulate such a general evolutionary scheme. The analysis will involve several levels of abstraction and make use of the concepts of *general civilizational process,* whose meaning approximates that of A. Weber's (1935) "civilizing process"; of *individual civilizational processes,* with the significance that Sorokin (1937–1941) gave to the term "cultural supersystems"; of *technological revolutions,* but in a more restricted sense than that given to the concept of "cultural revolutions" by Childe (1936, 1951) and White (1959); of *sociocultural formations,* with the meaning that Marx (1904, 1965, 1967) gave to the expression "socio-economic formations"; of *structural models and types* in the sense of M. Weber (1954); and finally of *cultural historical configurations,* with a significance close to that of Steward's (1955) "cultural types." We will also make use of the concepts of *progress, regression, stagnation, historical incorporation,* and *evolutionary acceleration* in special ways that will be precisely defined. It will also be necessary to redefine, in terms of the proposed conceptualization, the notions of *civilization,* of *genuine* and *spurious culture* (Sapir, 1924); of *cultural autonomy* and *cultural anachronism* (Ogburn, 1926); of *cultural traumatization, restoration,* and *crystallization* (Foster, 1962); of *acculturation* and *deculturation;* and of *ethnos, macro-ethnos,* and *national ethnos,* as well as sociological concepts like *assimilation, development,* and *modernization.*

We conceive of sociocultural evolution as a temporal pattern of alteration in the ways of life of human groups. This alteration is created by the impact of successive technological revolutions (agricultural, industrial, etc.) on specific societies, tending to transform them from one evolutionary stage to another, or from one sociocultural formation to another. Sociocultural formations are conceptual models of social life, each of which combines a specific level of development in productive technology with a generic form of social regulation and with an ideological configuration that represents a greater or lesser degree of lucidity and rationality.

Each sociocultural formation is thus a particular constellation of certain aspects of mode of environmental adaptation, certain attributes of social organization, and certain qualities of world view. These three orders of phenomena correspond to three systems: adaptive, associative, and ideological. The *adaptive system* is composed of the cultural means of manipulating nature for the production and reproduction of the material requirements of a society. The *associative system* includes standardized means of regulating interpersonal relations that involve subsistence activities and biological reproduction. At certain stages of sociocultural evolution, tendencies toward the institutionalization of social life beyond the family and of elementary kinds of division of labor express themselves in new forms of property, in social stratification in terms of differentiated roles in the productive process, and in the emergence of regulative institutions of a political, religious, or educational character. The third order of elements making up a sociocultural formation is its *ideological system,* which includes not only abstract knowledge about techniques of production and social norms, but all forms of symbolic communication —such as language, explicit formulations of knowledge, bodies of beliefs, and systems of values—which are developed to explain and justify a people's behavior and way of life. These three systems comprise the culture of a society. In a sufficiently homogeneous group of societies, they assume a generic character that permits the recognition of a culture type, as in the case of pastoral societies or, when there is geographic continuity, of a culture area; for example, the indigenous horticulturists of the South American tropical forest.

The concept of *sociocultural formation* applies to a higher level of abstraction; one in which, for example, all hunting-and-gathering tribal groups are combined into a single category. As a result, the degree of specificity characterizing the adaptive, associative, and ideological systems that correspond to a particular sociocultural formation must be relatively low, although not so low as to make the scheme valueless for classificatory purposes. The great difficulty in constructing theoretical paradigms of sociocultural formations is thus the recognition of distinctive aspects, which because of their crucial nature and their influential role constitute a minimum definition. An allied problem arises from the wide variation in cultural traditions, which makes it improbable that all the diagnostic traits will occur in every society assigned to a given formation. Rather, incomplete representation is likely to be more frequent than a faithful reproduction of the theoretical model.

The ideal way to define sociocultural formations would be to identify a body of homogeneous diagnostic traits that not only represent the adaptive, associative, and ideological systems and traverse all the sociocultural formations, but which also embrace all significant modifications. This ideal cannot be realized, however, because of the range of variation in the content of each culture. As a consequence, each stage or formation must be defined in its own terms and without the requirement that the same kinds of elements must form part of the definition of an earlier or later stage. Even such specific definitions cannot be constructed with the desirable degree of homogeneity, however, because the choice of criteria is limited by practical considerations, including ease of correlation with designations prevalent in the classical bibliography on the subject. We will, therefore, draw upon existing terms that refer to productive activities (hunting-and-gathering, pastoral, agricultural, rural craftsman, irrigation, industrial), to social stratification, and labor and property relations (undifferentiated—as opposed to stratified—collectivistic, privatistic, slavistic, mercantile, capitalistic, socialistic), to political entities (tribe, horde, village, chiefdom, state, empire, colony), and to ideological systems and special attributes thereof (theocratic, salvationistic, despotic, revolutionary, evolutionary, modernizing).

The theoretical construction of sociocultural formations also presents two additional difficulties, both of which derive from the abstract nature of the analytical categories. The first is the reconciliation of their developmental aspect, as stages in an evolutionary continuum, with their nonchronological nature, which permits the coexistence of societies that are classifiable into the most disparate evolutionary stages. This ambivalent situation, which led Huxley (1955) to characterize evolutionary stages as "nonsynchronic homotaxa," creates special problems since relations between contrasting formations frequently produce ambiguous results in the form of societies incorporating traits that normally correspond to distinct "moments" in evolution. This frequently results from the implantation of modern industries in backward areas, as with the recently pacified Xavante Indians of Brazil who, although primitive in most respects, use metal tools. Such situations, far from invalidating the deterministic nature of the evolutionary framework, help to confirm it. They require us, however, to consider in all their complexity not only the autonomous processes of development and the effects of diffusion and acculturation, but also the consequences of both kinds of phenomena for the peoples that experience them.

The second problem stems from the dynamic nature of the sociocultural formations, which makes them more comparable to a directional continuum than to a series of discrete stages. As a result, it becomes necessary to recognize an incipient (formative) aspect that may be little differentiated from the preceding formation, and a mature (florescent) aspect that results from intensification of the diagnostic characteristics. Thus when a transition takes place between two successive stages, the florescent aspect of the earlier one may often be difficult to distinguish from the formative aspect of the later one. Such confusion is inevitable, and is characteristic not only of evolutionary situations, but also of societies undergoing cultural trauma as a result of external pressures. The recognition of such a transitional, incipient stage, however, permits the classification and incorporation into the proposed typology of those societies in which archaic survivals are combined with new qualities that have not yet assumed a dominant role.

Only under exceptional conditions do societies move continually upward in evolution, passing through all the successive stages. Their course is usually interrupted by a variety of factors, which may lead either to stagnation and cultural regression, or to cycles of advances and declines. In fact, there seems to be a correlation between the maturity of a formation and a tendency toward regression. This is explainable in some cases by the fact that maturity coincides with saturation in the exploitation of the creative potential of the technology, and in others by expansionistic tendencies that emerge with maturation. The latter bring about extremely tense dominance relations, the oppressive nature of which can rupture a sociocultural constellation by reversing the roles of the dominated peoples and the dominating center. This situation leads to the development of militarism and colonialism at a certain point in the maturation of all advanced formations, and thus eliminates these features from inclusion among the general diagnostic traits used to define a specific evolutionary stage. Their universality, however, makes them of decisive importance in the general study of one basic motivating force of evolution; namely, the acculturative social compulsion that is primarily responsible for the creation and modification of ethnic entities.

All concrete societies are continually undergoing alterations, as a consequence both of interaction between their constituent parts and of influence from other societies and, therefore, they inevitably exhibit more or less severe disconformities. In this respect, they differ from the conceptual formulations, which express an ideal state of maturity and equilibrium seldom encountered in real situations. Conditions commonly classified as "structural duality" reflect a similar kind of disconformity, resulting from differences in the rhythms of transformation in various sectors of a culture.

All of this means that classification of concrete societies into evolutionary schemes can only be done after they have been conceptually stripped of any unique aspects, leaving only those features diagnostic of the model for each formation. The focus must also be on long periods of time so that the significance of alterations can more easily be perceived.

Technological Revolutions and Civilizational Processes

The concept of technological revolution is employed here to designate those transformations in man's ability to exploit nature or to make war that are prodigious enough to produce qualitative alterations in the whole way of life of societies. Consequently, it is assumed that the unleashing of each technological revolution, or the multiplication of its effects in different sociocultural contexts via the civilizational processes, will tend to correlate with the emergence of new sociocultural formations.

Most students accept the classification of Childe (1936), which distinguishes three "cultural revolutions." The first is the *Agricultural Revolution,* which introduced the cultivation of plants and the domestication of animals into the subsistence system, transforming man's situation from that of an exploiter of nature's spontaneous bounty to that of an active agent of food production. The succeeding *Urban Revolution,* which stemmed from innovations in subsistence production and the invention of metallurgy and writing, led to the internal dichotomization of societies into rural and urban segments, to social stratification into classes, and to other profound alterations in social life and cultural heritage. Finally, the *Industrial Revolution,* which began in western Europe with the harnessing of inanimate energy to operate mechanical devices, was responsible for new and fundamental changes in social stratification, political organization, and world view.

When an effort was made to correlate technological revolutions with sociocultural formations, however, it became obvious that a larger number of revolutions had to be recognized. As a consequence, the Urban Revolution is followed in our scheme by the *Irrigation Revolution,* which provided the technological basis for the appearance of the first regional civilizations. Significant technological advances include construction of large canals for irrigation and navigation, new types of watercraft, systems of roads, and cities with large public buildings (pyramids, temples, and palaces), as well as ideographic writing, systems of weights and measures, and scientific developments, especially in the realms of mathematics and astronomy. Following it, we have added the *Metallurgical Revolution,* which equates generally with the Iron Age of archeological sequences. During its course, the alphabet and decimal notation were invented, and iron forging, the manufacture of tools, and coinage were perfected and diffused. With the succeeding *Pastoral Revolution,* some of the earlier innovations were applied to harnessing animals for traction and warfare, and to improvements in the use of wind and water for productive purposes. In our view, furthermore, the Industrial Revolution was preceded by the *Mercantile Revolution,* which was based on the technology of oceanic navigation and firearms, and was responsible for the breakdown of European feudalism. Finally, we have recognized the *Thermonuclear Revolution,* which is underway at the present time with the application of electronics, atomic energy, automation, laser beams, etc. It holds potentialities for the transformation of human life as radical as those of any previous technological revolution.

In summary, therefore, we recognize eight technological revolutions that are characterized by major transformations in productive capacity and military might, and which lead to fundamental modifications in the adaptive, associative, and ideological systems of the people that experience them, whether they do so indirectly or directly. Yet without a recognition of the complementary concept of the civilizational process, this series of technological revolutions is not sufficient to explain the whole evolutionary process. The reason for this is that it is not the invention itself that produces consequences, but rather its dissemination into various sociocultural contexts and its application to different sectors of production. Thus, for each technological revolution there may be one or more civilizational processes through which its potentialities for the transformation of material life and the transfiguration of sociocultural formations are realized (Figure 1).

The first of these civilizational processes spread the technology of plant domestication, destroying the nomadic hunting-and-gathering way of life, and giving rise to a new sociocultural formation, the *Undifferentiated Horticultural Villages.* Under the influence of the second civilizational process, which corresponds to animal domestication and the functional specialization of some groups in this subsistence activity (Pastoral Expansion), another formation was generated that can be termed *Nomadic Pastoral Hordes.*

The Urban Revolution incorporates the third, fourth, and fifth civilizational processes. The third corresponds to the rise of cities and states, to the stratification of societies into social classes, to the first experiments in irrigation agriculture, and to copper and bronze metallurgy, ideographic writing, numbers, and the calendar. It resulted in the crystallization of the *Rural Craftsman States* formation. Maturation of the fourth civilizational process is expressed by the adoption of private property and the enslavement of the labor force in some Rural Craftsman States, which transformed them from a *Collectivistic* to a *Privatistic* form. Finally, elaboration of certain technological developments, such as the use of copper and its application to pastoral activities, during the course of the fifth civilizational process (alternatively designated as the Second Pastoral Expansion), brought into existence the *Nomadic Pastoral Chiefdoms.*

Maturation of the basic technology that produced the Urban Revolution, especially that relating to the construction of large irrigation works, led to the Irrigation Revolution. With it came the sixth civilizational process, which created the first regional civilizations, the *Theocratic Irrigation Empires,* as a new sociocultural formation. The seventh civilizational process originated from the Metallurgical Revolution, based on generalization of technological innovations like iron forging. This permitted the development of a more productive agriculture in forested regions, the manufacture of a variety of new tools, and the improvement of sailing vessels. Other significant inventions were coinage, which facilitated external commerce, the phonetic alphabet, and decimal notation. This technological base led to the maturation of a new sociocultural formation in the form of the *Mercantile Slavistic Empires.*

The eighth civilizational process was set in motion by the Pastoral Revolution. It was founded on the application of certain elements of the same basic technology (especially forged iron) to production and warfare, including a generalized use of saddles, stirrups, and horseshoes (all of which increased the efficiency of animals for riding and traction) and swords and rigid armor. These technological improvements led to the development of a messianic expansionistic movement among some of the Nomadic Pastoral Chiefdoms, which attacked areas occupied by early feudal civilizations and incorporated them into *Despotic Salvationist Empires.*

The ninth civilizational process equates with the Mercantile Revolution and the first world civilizations. It gave rise to two sociocultural formations, the *Salvationistic Mercantile Empires* and their reciprocals, the *Slavistic Colonies.* The tenth civilizational process reflects the progressive elaboration of this same technological revolution, and led to the appearance of the *Capitalistic Mercantile Empires* and two reciprocal formations, *Trading Colonies* and *Immigrant Colonies.* The Industrial Revolution brought about a restructuring into *Imperialistic Industrial Powers* and *Neo-Colonial Dependencies* under the influence of the eleventh civilizational process. Rational intervention or social planning constitutes the twelfth civilizational process, which created the *Socialistic Revolutionary, Socialistic Evolutionary,* and *Nationalistic Modernizing States.*

The emerging Thermonuclear Revolution, with its immense potential for transformation of the material life of peoples the world over, will accelerate the evolution of backward groups and produce new sociocultural formations. These *Future Societies* will probably render obsolete both existing types of social stratification and the dependence on warfare in international relations.

The conceptual framework proposed here makes it possible to distinguish between a *global civilizational process,* largely synonymous with sociocultural evolution, and general and individual civilizational processes, which are contained within the global process and contribute to its formation, but which also produce individual civilizations. The global view derives from the perspective provided by the present over the past. It permits us to appreciate retrospectively how varying particular cultural traditions, developed at different times and places, have become interlinked, interfertilizing, or destroying one another, but in so doing advancing a great cultural tradition and contributing to the creation of the universal human civilization now beginning to take shape.

The *general civilizational processes* correspond to generic evolutionary sequences resulting from the effects on the lives of diverse peoples of

Figure 1. Basic sequences of sociocultural evolution in terms of technological revolutions, civilizational processes, and sociocultural formations. (The italicized formations result from processes of historical incorporation and are the most significant of the many that have been produced in this way.)

Technological Revolutions
I Agricultural Revolution
II Urban Revolution
III Irrigation Revolution
IV Metallurgical Revolution
V Pastoral Revolution
VI Mercantile Revolution
VII Industrial Revolution
VIII Thermonuclear Revolution

cultural innovations unleashed by a technological revolution. Dissemination of each of these processes causes racial mixture and cultural unification of divergent groups, and brings about new sociocultural formations, either by simple historical incorporation or by evolutionary acceleration. This occurred, for example, with the expansion of irrigation agriculture, which although it energized the lives of different groups in distinct places and at different times, remodeled their societies and cultures along similar general lines. In contrast, the *individual civilizational processes* as conceived here are concrete historical expressions of the general civilizational processes. For example, the expansion of irrigation in Mesopotamia was an individual civilizational process, which led to the maturation of several local civilizations based on irrigation; parallel developments occurred both in Egypt and India.

This conceptual framework requires the redefinition of the concepts of ethnos (ethnic group) and civilization. *Civilizations* are the crystallizations of individual civilizational processes. Each civilization expands from its metropolitan centers, bringing the surrounding area under economic and political domination and cultural influence (e.g., the Egyptian, Aztec, and Greek civilizations). The *ethnos* (ethnic groups) are the operative units of the civilizational process, each of which corresponds to a unique human group united by a common language and culture (e.g., the Tupinambá or Germanic ethnic group). We can speak of a *national ethnos* when linguistic, cultural, and national political boundaries coincide, and of a *macro-ethnos* when such states expand to incorporate populations of different ethnic origins. An ethnos may be a hunting band, composed of family groups that move over a defined territory, or a national minority that is segregated by its common language and traditions, and has aspirations toward autonomy. Or it may be a group that preserves certain common integrative traditions and whose members are united by strong in-group loyalties, like the Gypsies or the Jews. When two or more such groups are combined by imperialistic domination in an attempt to amalgamate them into a larger entity, they form part of a macro-ethnos (e.g., Roman, Inca, or Spanish Colonial).

When conceived as a succession of general civilizational processes, sociocultural evolution has a progressive character that corresponds to man's rise from a tribal condition to modern national macro-societies. As conceptualized here, general civilizational processes are also evolutionary expansions by which progressively more complex sociocultural formations are produced.

General Civilizational Processes	Sociocultural Formations	Historic Examples
1 Agricultural Revolution	Undifferentiated Horticultural Villages	Jarmo (5th mil. B.C.) Tupinambá (16th century)
2 Pastoral Expansion	Nomadic Pastoral Hordes	Guaikurú (18th century) Kirghiz (20th century)
3 Urban Revolution	Rural Craftsman States (Collectivist type)	Urartu (10th century B.C.) Mochica (2nd century B.C.)
4 Slavistic Expansion	Rural Craftsman States (Privatistic type)	Phoenicians (2nd mil. B.C.) Kushan (5th century B.C.)
5 Second Pastoral Expansion	Nomadic Pastoral Chiefdoms	Hyksos (18th century B.C.) Huns (3–5th century)
6 Irrigation Revolution	Theocratic Irrigation Empires	Egypt (3rd mil. B.C.) Inca (15th century)
7 Metallurgical Revolution	Mercantile Slavistic Empires	Greece (5th century B.C.) Rome (1st century B.C.)
8 Pastoral Revolution	Despotic Salvationist Empires	Islam (7th century) Ottoman (15th century)
9 Mercantile Revolution	Salvationistic Mercantile Empires	Iberia (16th century) Russia (16th century)
	Slavistic Colonies	Brazil (16th century) Cuba (18th century)
10 Capitalistic Expansion	Capitalistic Mercantile Empires	Holland (17th century) England (17th century)
	Trading Colonies	Indonesia (19th century) Guianas (20th century)
	Immigrant Colonies	North America (17th century) Australia (19th century)
11 Industrial Revolution	Imperialistic Industrial Powers	England (19th century) United States (20th century)
	Neo-Colonial Dependencies	Brazil (20th century) Venezuela (20th century)
12 Socialistic Expansion	Socialistic Revolutionary Nations	USSR (1917) China (1949)
	Socialistic Evolutionary Nations	Sweden (1945) England (1965)
	Nationalistic Modernizing States	Egypt (1953) Algeria (1962)
	Future Societies	

By contrast, individual civilizational processes are concrete historical expansions that may vitalize wide areas and crystallize into diverse civilizations, but which tend to have a cyclical history. Civilizations thus rise, fall into periods of regression or "dark ages," and rebuild themselves along similar lines—until the cycle is broken by the unfolding of a new general civilizational process, which in turn gives rise to specific civilizational processes from which a new type of civilization emerges.

Diffusion and acculturation studies achieve increased clarity when examined in terms of the individual civilizational processes. The concept of *diffusion* does not require special definition because it will be employed here in the usual sense; i.e., to refer to the direct or indirect transfer of cultural traits of any type without necessitating the subordination of the receiver by the donor. The concept of *acculturation*, however, will not be restricted to situations involving contact between autonomous cultural entities—which is the most common usage in the anthropological literature (e.g., Herskovits, 1938;

Redfield and others, 1936; Beals, 1953; Barnett and others, 1954). If strictly adhered to, such a definition would limit application of the concept to intertribal relations, because only in such cases are the cultures autonomous and able to adopt foreign cultural traits without a loss of independence. In the interest of wider applicability, therefore, acculturation will be expanded here to include both the amalgamation of advanced cultural traditions and their expansion over less-developed cultural complexes.

Historical Incorporation and Evolutionary Acceleration

When viewed within the framework of a broad historical perspective, several aspects of cultural development become evident. Among them are the transitory character of institutions, the attitude displayed by various interests toward social change, and the progressive or regressive character of tensions prevalent in transitional societies. The difficulties inherent in dealing with problems of social dynamics on the basis of theories of limited scope and functionalist methodology—both of which attempt to explain sociocultural problems in terms of the interaction of constituent elements as though the societies did not have a past history, or on the assumption that all elements have an equal determinative potential—can be surmounted with the perspective provided by the civilizational processes. This perspective also helps to overcome the tendency to view the most highly developed societies of today as the ideal sociocultural system and the objective toward which all peoples are moving (e.g., Lerner, 1958; Balandier, Ed., 1956; Perroux, 1958; Gerschenkron, 1962; Eisenstadt, 1963a; Baran, 1957). In order to deal with such problems, several other concepts should be defined, among them historical incorporation, evolutionary acceleration, cultural stagnation, and historical backwardness or regression.

Historical incorporation will be used here to designate the process by which backward peoples are forcibly integrated into more highly evolved technological systems, with consequent loss of autonomy or even the destruction of their ethnic distinctness. This took place, for example, with the incorporation into colonial American slavistic formations of subjugated indigenous people and of transplanted African populations for slave labor in mines and on plantations. Thus the concept of incorporation refers both to situations that are of a regressive character from the standpoint of the enslaved ethnic entities, which may be traumatized or even destroyed, and to those of a progressive nature in the sense that they incorporate retarded peoples into more advanced socio-economic systems. The most significant characteristic of the process of historical incorporation is its reflex action, which inflicts loss of autonomy and the risk of ethnic disintegration on the incorporated groups.

The process of historical incorporation also includes cases in which a society suffers the indirect consequences of alterations produced in the adaptive systems of other societies. Although profound transformations of a progressive nature often take place, a dependent relationship is also inevitably established. This is a frequent result of the diffusion of products of the Industrial Revolution such as railroads and ports, which have "modernized" large sectors of the non-European world to make them more efficient producers of certain kinds of articles, but in so doing have also made these sectors increasingly dependent on the exporters of the industrial goods. Because of this process, the populations of Latin America extricated themselves from the status of colonial areas in a Salvationistic Mercantile formation, only to become Neo-Colonial Dependencies of Imperialistic Industrial formations.

The concept of *evolutionary acceleration* will be used to refer to progress that is achieved without loss of autonomy or ethnic identity. For example, a society may undergo a technological revolution as a result of internal creativity, or by the autonomous adoption of technological innovations achieved by other societies, or by a combination of the two. Other kinds of evolutionary acceleration occur in societies that were at one time subjugated by processes of historical incorporation, but which have regained their lost political autonomy, as was the case with the former colonial populations of North America. Evolutionary acceleration may also be produced by a political vanguard that operates in the name of the subordinate classes, and which brings about a restructuring of the society in accord with the interests of the latter by removing forces hostile to the adoption and general application of a more efficient productive technology. In the same category, although less effective, are efforts to bring about socio-economic progress through governmental programs of planned development, which are always directed toward the reinforcement of political and economic autonomy.

Viewed within this framework, the developed and underdeveloped peoples of the modern world do not represent distinct and unequally advanced stages of cultural evolution. On the contrary, they are interacting and mutually complementary components of broad systems of domination, linked by a symbiotic relationship that tends to perpetuate their status as poles of progress and retardation within a single civilization. The developed societies of the contemporary world are those that have integrated themselves into industrial civilization by evolutionary acceleration. The underdeveloped ones are those that were drawn in by historical incorporation as "external proletariats," which are destined to provide not only the necessities of life but prosperity for the developed peoples to which they are related.

Still to be defined are the concepts of *cultural stagnation* and *historical regression*. The former refers to the condition of societies that remain without notable alterations in their way of life over long periods of time, during which other societies advance. Examples are the pre-agricultural tribes and tropical forest horticulturists of South America, which remained in the same cultural stage for millennia while other peoples of the continent rose to the level of urban civilization. Stagnation has been explained in terms of anti-progressive elements, such as the oppressive or nonstimulating condition of a humid forest environment; or, contrarywise, its generous productivity, which offers no incentive to increased efforts. It has also been attributed to the absence of dynamic factors like domesticable animals, and as a consequence, the absence of aggressive pastoral groups; or to isolation from external contacts. Another explanation has been that extreme specialization brings about so satisfactory an adaptation to the environment that societies achieving it are rendered incapable of further advance.

Among the numerous examples of stagnation are certain super-specialized cultures of the arctic regions or the steppes, which represent generic modes of adaptation by societies that are very diverse in other characteristics. Groups like the polar Eskimo or the Timbira of the Brazilian scrub forest (cerrado) exhibit extreme cultural specialization toward a particular type of environment. This adaptation was achieved by deviating from rather than following a path of progressive cultural development. The excellence of some of these adaptations, which permit creation, reproduction, and expansion of human communities under highly adverse ecological conditions, does not alter the fact that the complexes they represent are marginal and consequently condemned at a certain stage in general cultural evolution either to retardation or to stagnation. The correctness of this analysis is shown by the fact that both in the arctic and in the scrub forest modern scientific technology has brought about much more efficient adaptations, evidenced by increase in size of the populations that can be supported.

Although it is possible to recognize several secondary agents of stagnation, the primary explanations are historical and ecological. Stagnating cultures are relevant to a general study of the civilizational process only as representatives of peoples still outside its sphere of influence, but who will inevitably be drawn in, either by historical incorporation or by evolutionary acceleration, depending on the conditions under which they enter into contact with more advanced peoples who penetrate their territories.

Examples of sociocultural *regression* can also be explained by a variety of factors. Some are the result of the impact of a more highly developed society on more backward peoples, who avoid ethnic disintegration by retreating to an inhospitable region where their former system of adaptation does not function efficiently. This happened to a number of New World peoples when Europeans invaded their territories. Regression can also result from internal trauma like insurrection and destruction of the old social order, if a new and more progressive one does not emerge. Among many such cases is the situation in ancient Egypt around 2200 B.C., when Memphis was paralyzed and fell into decline, never to flourish again. Another is Haiti following its independence; here, only a complete and intentional reorganization of the entire social structure, which was beyond its capabilities, would have permitted the creation of an economic structure as efficient as the former slavistic colonialism, and able at the same time to fulfill the aspirations of the population for liberty and progress.

Another factor leading to regression is reactionary behavior on the part of the dominant class which, when menaced in its hegemony, adopts measures that have an involutional effect. For example, the obsession to retain domination over a slavistic context produced the Spartan caricature of Greek culture. Similarly, both Nazi Germany and Fascist Italy were disfigured by their desperate efforts to suppress emergent socialistic movements, and by their transformation into centers of imperialistic domination. All such anti-historical interruptions slide into decadent militaristic and despotic regimes, which first degrade the social and cultural life of their people, and subsequently propel them into disastrous wars. A further cause of cultural regression is over-utilization of an efficient technology like irrigation agriculture, which at the level of saturation becomes destructive of the environment. This occurred in the valleys of the Indus, Tigris and Euphrates, Hwang-ho, and Yangtse, where millions of hectares of agricultural land were lost by erosion or by increasing alkalinity or salinity of the soil resulting from deficient drainage during long periods of flood cultivation (Revelle, 1963).

The principal cause of cultural regression, however, is exhaustion of the potentialities of a sociocultural formation, which toward the end of its existence solidifies the social structure and creates conflicts between classes. When this occurs, continued social life depends on the development of despotic institutions for strict control of the labor force and for repression of lower class rebellions. In this form of regression, a special role is played by the attacks of culturally backward peoples, who succeed in defeating and subjugating more advanced societies that have been made vulnerable by their structural rigidity and internal crises. This situation gives rise to one of the most important forms of sociocultural regression; namely, the plunge of relatively advanced societies into so-called "dark ages." Such is our conceptualization of feudalism; we do not view it as a sociocultural formation or an evolutionary stage, but rather as a regression produced by disintegration of the associative, the centralized political and administrative, and the commercial systems within an area once integrated by a civilization, so that it falls back into a subsistence economy. When a feudal regression takes place, the cities also lose their dynamism, and the erudite cultural tradition that once radiated from them tends to be replaced by an orally transmitted folk tradition. The arts and crafts also decline, and occupational specialists return to rural pursuits. During this process, the old forms of labor conscription, such as bondage and slavery, give way to new methods of controlling the subordinate classes under local military fiefs. Feudal regressions of this type followed all civilizational expansions prior to the emergence of the Mercantile Revolution, The latter, which was succeeded almost immediately by the Industrial Revolution, caused progressive changes in human societies of such an intensity that feudal regressions occurred only in exceptional societies. Some of the latter remained economically marginal only for short periods, while others had a social structure that was too rigid to permit technological renovation and the corresponding social reorganization.

Actually, human history records more regressive steps of the various kinds just reviewed than steps forward. In spite of their prevalence, however, regressions are only temporary setbacks stemming from an exhaustion of the potentialities of a productive system or of a particular form of social organization. By contrast, evolutionary steps are cultural renovations which once achieved and dispersed, permanently enlarge the human capacity to produce and consume energy, to create increasingly inclusive forms of social organization, and to achieve ever more reliable conceptualizations of the external world.

In summary, sociocultural evolution is viewed here in two ways: (1) as a series of evolutionary stages expressed in a sequence of sociocultural formations, each generated by the action of a cultural revolution via one of its civilizational processes, and (2) as an interplay between cultural progressions and regressions, and between historical incorporations and evolutionary accelerations. This conceptualization replaces the prevailing and much criticized view of evolution as a sequence of fixed and necessary stages (either unilinear or multilinear) with a broader and more varied perspective; it envisages evolution as a dialectic movement in which both progress and regression are necessary constituents. This view also implies that each technological revolution will follow a different history in a new context from that of its original context. Thus a great variety in expression is to be expected since (1) change is more often brought about by diffusion than it is generated internally; (2) diffusion does not make available to receiving societies all the elements originally developed, nor are these elements acquired in their original order or with the same associated elements; (3)

the civilizational processes are propelled by technological revolutions that give an advantage to the groups that first experience them, permitting their expansion as centers of domination; and (4) peoples influenced by the same civilizational process through historical incorporation, lose command of their destiny and are reduced to a state of subjugation and dependency that severely limits their possibilities for subsequent development.

In addition, the point of view adopted here provides for the conceptual integration of the various individual civilization processes corresponding to divergent lines of multilinear evolution into a global process, which is the historical reality. This permits an evaluation of both positive and negative aspects of the interaction between the individual processes. It also permits generalized reconstruction of the relationships between modern peoples throughout the world and the civilizational processes that have shaped the great cultural traditions within which their present cultures have been crystallized. Finally, this viewpoint makes possible the erection of a typology of technological revolutions, civilizational processes, and sociocultural formations that is applicable to the classification both of past societies at varying levels of development and of contemporary societies with differing degrees of complexity.

REFERENCES CITED

Balandier, G., 1956, (ed.), *Le "Tiers Monde" Sous-Développement et Developpement,* Presses Universitaires de France, Paris.

Baran, P. 1957, *The Political Economy of Growth,* Monthly Review Press, New York.

Barnett, H., 1963, *Innovation: The Basis of Cultural Change,* McGraw-Hill, New York.

Beals, R., 1953, "Acculturation," in A. Kroeber, (ed.), *Anthropology Today,* Chicago U.P., Chicago, 621–641.

Benedict, R., 1934, *Patterns of Culture,* Houghton Mifflin, New York.

Childe, V., 1936, *Man Makes Himself,* Watts, London.

——— 1951, *Social Evolution,* Watts, London.

Eisenstadt, S., 1963, *Modernization: Growth and Diversity,* Department of Government, Indiana University.

Foster, G., 1962, *Traditional Cultures and the Impact of Technological Change,* Harper, New York.

Gerschenkron, A., 1962, *Economic Backwardness in Historical Perspective,* Harvard U.P., Cambridge.

Graeburn, F., 1924, *Das Weltbild der Primitiven,* Reinhardt, Munich.

Herskovits, M., 1938, *Acculturation,* Augustin, New York.

Huxley, J., 1955, "Evolution, Cultural and Biological," *Yearbook of Anthropology,* Wenner-Gren Foundation, New York, 3–25.

Kropotkin, P., 1955, *Mutual Aid,* Extending Horizons Books, Boston.

Kroeber, A., 1939, *Cultural and Natural Areas of Native North America,* California U.P., Berkeley.

——— 1946, "The Chibcha," *Handbook of South American Indians,* Bureau of American Ethnology, Bulletin 143, Vol. 2, 887–909, Washington, D.C.

Lerner, D., 1958, *The Passing of Traditional Society,* Free Press, Glencoe.

Linton, R., 1936, *The Study of Man,* Appleton-Century, New York.

Marx, K., 1904, *A Contribution to the Critique of Political Economy,* International Library, New York.

——— 1965, *Pre-Capitalist Economic Formations,* International Publishers, New York.

——— 1967, *Capital: A Critique of Political Economy,* International Publishers, New York.

Murdock, G., 1951, *Outline of South American Cultures,* Human Relations Area Files, New Haven.

Montandon, G., 1934, *L'Ologénèse Culturelle,* Payot, Paris.

Ogburn, W., 1926, *Social Change,* Huebsch, New York.

Perroux, F., 1958, *La Coexistence Pacifique,* Presses Universitaires de France, Paris.

Redfield, R., *Peasant Society and Culture,* Chicago U.P., Chicago.

Sapir, E., 1924, "Culture, Genuine and Spurious," *American Journal of Sociology,* 29:401–429.

Schmidt, W. and W. Koppers, 1924, *Volker und Kulturen,* Regensburg.

Sorokin, P., 1937–41, *Social and Cultural Dynamics,* American Book Company, New York.

Steward, J., 1955, (ed.), *Irrigation Civilizations,* Pan American Union, Washington, D.C.

Weber, A., 1935, *Kulturgeschichte als Kultursoziologie,* Sijthoff, Leiden.

Weber, M., 1948, *The Protestant Ethic and the Spirit of Capitalism,* Scribner, New York.

White, L., 1949, *The Science of Culture,* Farrar, Strauss, New York.
——— 1959, *The Evolution of Culture,* McGraw-Hill, New York.
Wissler, C., 1938, *The American Indian,* Oxford U.P., New York.
Znaniecki, F., 1944, *Las Sociedades de Cultura Nacional y Sus Relaciones,* Fondo de Cultura Ecónomica, Mexico.

Ideas taken from cultural ecology have affected the organization of this reader as strongly as the cultural evolutionary approach just described. There was a time when the two theories were regarded as being in conflict. Now not only are they regarded as being analytically compatible, they are often hard to tell apart. Cultural evolutionary theory is more general; focus is often more upon the overall evolution of culture and less upon the evolutionary development of particular societies.

Cultural ecology as a theoretical approach is more attentive to the causal role of particular sets of environmental circumstances in affecting both the ways people make a living and how these ways shape, in turn, the other major aspects of their society and culture.

Emphasis is upon the role of environmental factors as they may impede or facilitate particular types of sociocultural development—it would be difficult to develop a way of life based on date cultivation in the Arctic, for example, whereas one based on hunting has worked out very well. A Saharan oasis is often a fine place for raising dates; it would be a terrible place to try to make a living or support a way of life based on hunting seals.

An adequate look at the role of the setting in shaping sociocultural forms must take into account not only topographical, geological, and climatic factors, and the flora and fauna (including disease-producing bacteria), but also the presence of other peoples, friendly or hostile, and the possible role of geographic isolation. All must be analyzed to place correctly a particular sociocultural system in ecological context.

Harris has played a major innovative role in synthesizing the complementary aspects of cultural ecological and cultural evolutionary theory within the broader framework of an approach he terms cultural materialism.

Cultural Materialism: Cultural Ecology

Marvin Harris

The attempt to reconcile Steward with White does not require further elaborations of a typology of evolutionism. The central question is to what extent the strategy employed by Steward corresponds to the cultural-materialist formulation which underlies White's evolutionary and energetistic pronouncements. It can be shown that Steward has led his contemporaries in actually applying cultural-materialist principles to the solution of concrete questions concerning cultural differences and similarities. Unlike White, Steward has sought to identify the material condition of sociocultural life in terms of the articulation between production processes and habitat. His cultural materialism resides in this pragmatic venture to which he himself gives the title "the method of cultural ecology."

It will obviously not be possible to review any significant proportion of the anthropological research which has been undertaken in conformity with ecological versions of cultural materialism. Even to give summary treatment to the work carried out by those who have been directly influenced by Steward—Sidney Mintz

Source: From *The Rise of Anthropological Theory* by Marvin Harris. Copyright, 1968. New York: Thomas Y. Crowell Company. Used by permission of the publisher and the author.

(1956), Eric Wolf (1957; 1966), Morton Fried (1952; 1967), Elman Service (1955; 1962), René Millon (1967), Andrew Vayda (1956; 1961c), Robert Manners (1956), F. Lehman (1963)—could prove an exhausting task.

The list of anthropologists who have benefited indirectly from Steward's treatment of techno-environmental and techno-economic interactions is proportionally larger and includes, at this date, many younger figures who take their cultural ecology for granted, and who acknowledge Steward's contribution only by means of criticism aimed at disproving some of his specific ecological explanations on the basis of new data.

Nothing would be more contrary to the general frame of reference advocated in this book than to explain the recent prominence of ecological studies as a result of Steward's personal influence. The mounting interest in techno-environmental and techno-economic relationships reflects a broad movement aimed at strengthening the scientific credentials of cultural anthropology within the prestigious and well-funded natural sciences. Cultural ecology, precisely because it links emic phenomena with the etic conditions of "nature," strengthens the association between social science and the "harder" disciplines. In a synchronic mode it thus promotes research involving cooperation with the general medical sciences, biology, nutrition, demography, and agronomy, all of which enjoy high levels of economic support. Applied diachronically, the ecological approach establishes a similar set of ties between archaeology and numerous specialties within geology and paleontology. The contemporary premium upon scientism thus makes the expansion of cultural ecological research almost inevitable. Predictably, however, the movement to take up the cultural-materialist option in the guise of cultural ecology has failed to link itself with the historical precedent of Marx's proposals. Indeed, one of the most fascinating aspects of Steward's contribution to the revival of nomothetic inquiry is the slow but unacknowledged rediscovery or reinvention of principles long ago made explicit in Marx's "Preface" to *The Critique of Political Economy.*

Multilinear Evolutionism Not a Methodology

The link betwen cultural ecology and cultural materialism has been obscured by the spurious issue of evolutionism. This has provided Steward with the impetus to think of cultural ecology as a kind of evolutionism rather than as a kind of determinism. Inded, he would have us believe that "Cultural evolution may be regarded as a special type of historical reconstruction or as a particular methodology or approach" (1955:27). "Multilinear evolution is essentially a methodology based on the assumption that significant regularities in cultural change occur, and it is concerned with the determination of cultural laws" (*ibid.*). Now, the establishment of the lines of cultural evolution might be an important result of research oriented by the assumption that there are regularities in cultural change. Such regularities would presumably eventuate in certain lines occurring repeatedly in separate regions of the world in which similar conditions obtain. But to call multilinear evolutionism the *method* by which this assumption is brought to the research phase is a malapropism which has the unfortunate consequence of distracting us from the true nature of Steward's methodological contribution. In contrast to that method and its brilliant concrete results, to which we shall turn in a moment, Steward's concept of multilinear evolution is all the more regrettable.

How Many Is Multi-?

Multilinear evolution, Steward says, "deals only with those limited parallels of form, function, and sequence which have empirical reality" (*ibid.*:19). This is equivalent to the statement that other forms of evolutionism have not been rigorously empirical and have as a result discovered too many parallels. Where have we heard it before? Is this not precisely the message which Boas delivered from Morningside Heights?

> Multilinear evolution, therefore, has no a priori scheme or laws. It recognizes that the cultural traditions of different areas may be wholly or partly distinctive, and it simply poses the question of whether any genuine or meaningful similarities between certain cultures exist and whether these lend themselves to formulation [*ibid.*].

This misnomered "methodology" is scarcely a decisive invention. It is encumbered by a lingering acceptance of the possibility that endless diversity may still turn out to be the best model of cultural evolution.

> A taxonomic scheme designed to facilitate the determination of parallels and regularities in terms of concrete characteristics and developmental processes will have to distinguish innumerable culture types, many of which have not as yet been recognized [*ibid.*:24].

If the "innumerable" tends toward the infinity side, we have historical particularism. Moving in the other direction, we have multilinear evolutionism. But it must be remembered that even in the biological model of the tree of life, "innumerable" convergences and parallelisms have their place. Furthermore, the so-called unilinear evolutionists, despite their emphasis upon parallelism, certainly did not deny "innumerable" divergences. Finally, Steward himself questioned the utility and not the validity of White's universal sequence.

The question of how much parallelism has existed during the course of culture history is a logico-empirical matter which cannot be settled by adhering to one or another brand of evolutionism. The most important considerations here are the operations by which judgments of similarity or difference are rendered. It should be possible to demonstrate the similarities of band organization among the Arunta and Bushmen regardless of the type of evolutionism adhered to by the community of observers. This of course is not to say that the identification of parallel sequences is equally possible under all research options. In the case of historical particularism, differences are deliberately enumerated until they overwhelm similarities, and we should not expect the discovery of many parallels. I must repeat, however, that the issue here is not evolutionism, but rather the triumph of the nomothetic mode over the idiographic. In this respect, both Steward and White stand opposed to the Boasian school, regardless of their differences of opinion concerning the kind of evolutionism one ought to "practice." They both believe that causal explanations of cultural phenomena are within our grasp.

The Significance of Parallel and Convergent Cases

One of the most unfortunate consequences of the subordination of the question of causality to that of "evolution" is that it has deflected our attention away from an understanding of the central importance of parallel cases in the social sciences. To look for and collect parallel sequences is not a methodology; the methodology comes in when one looks for parallel cases in order to establish the causal principles which account for both parallel and divergent evolution. If the evolutionary trajectory consequent upon the introduction of irrigation agriculture were associated with the development of "oriental despotism" in Egypt and nowhere else, it would be difficult to establish any kind of causal relation betwen the two phenomena. It is the fact that a similar sequence is repeated in several different cases that makes it possible for us to talk about nomothetic causal relationships. The special significance of parallel developmental sequences therefore is that they provide the natural history analogues to laboratory controls in the experimental sciences. In this respect they potentially offer a highly satisfactory form of cross-cultural correlation analysis since actual chronological sequence may be invoked to determine the direction of causality.

Although Steward has not participated in the development of statistically oriented cross-cultural theories, his understanding of the methodological function of parallelisms actually assumes both diachronic and synchronic forms of correlation:

> . . . it is our basic premise that the crucial methodological feature of evolution is the determination of recurrent causal relationships in independent cultural traditions. . . . Whether it requires ten, twenty, or several hundred years for the relationship to become established, development through time must always take place. Therefore parallel developments which require only a few years and involve only a limited number of features are no less evolutionary from a scientific point of view than sequences involving whole cultures and covering millennia [*ibid.*:27].

Removing the emphasis from the sterile question of whether a phenomenon is or is not evolution, we may rephrase Steward's point to read as follows: cross-culturally valid correlations indicate that causality is operative. As we shall see in a moment, one of Steward's most important contributions, namely the ecological analysis of hunting and gathering bands, actually follows the paradigm of synchronic correlation analysis, rather than a diachronic model.

Steward as Cultural Materialist

In order to show that cultural ecology is a subcase of cultural materialism, two points must be established: (1) in the cultural-ecological strategy, techno-environmental and techno-economic variables are accorded research priority; (2) this is done in conformity with the hypothesis that social organization and ideology tend to be the dependent variables in any large diachronic sample of sociocultural systems.

It is clear that Steward is the author of many statements which conform to the definition of cultural materialism. One of the most succinct is embedded in the discussion which led him to revise the culture area classification in the *Handbook of the South American Indians.* In explaining why a diffusionist interpretation of South American culture is unsatisfactory, he states that the acceptance or rejection of diffused items "was always contingent upon local potentialities." These "potentialities" are

> . . . a function of the local ecology, that is, the interaction of environment, exploitative devices, the socioeconomic habits. In each case, the exigencies of making a living in a given environment with a specific set of devices and methods for obtaining, transporting, and preparing food and other essential goods set limits to the dispersal or grouping of the people and to the composition of settlements, and it strongly influenced many of their modes of behavior [Steward 1949a, V:674].

There will be critics of this interpretation who will fix upon the phrase "strongly influenced many of their modes of behavior" to prove that Steward's position is not that of "cultural materialism." But if provision for "accident," "historical factors," and short-run and relatively rare reversals of causality from superstructure to base remove one from the heritage of cultural-materialist theory, then Marx as well as Steward must be so removed.

Dogmatic and otherwise degraded versions of historical materialism may insist on a one-to-one absolute correlation betwen material base and the rest of the social system. But our interest does not encompass such aberrations. Any rejection of cultural materialism on the grounds that it represents a less empirical, less skeptical, less operational or, in brief, an inferior scientific method is unworthy of serious consideration. Empiricism, skepticism, operationalism are scarcely the exclusive property of any particular anthropological school or theoretical orientation. These are the minimum conditions of science in general. If they are not met, as is frequently enough the case, it is a disaster regardless of the theoretical orientation in whose name the lapse has occurred.

The essence of cultural materialism is that it directs attention to the interaction between behavior and environment as mediated by the human organism and its cultural apparatus. It does so as an order of priority in conformity with the prediction that group structure and ideology are responsive to these classes of material conditions. Turning to Steward's statement of the research strategy of cultural ecology, we find all of these attributes of cultural materialism clearly delineated. He states that there are three fundamental procedures of cultural ecology:

> First, the interrelationship of exploitative or productive technology and environment must be analyzed. . . . Second, the behavior patterns involved in the exploitation of a particular area by means of a particular technology must be analyzed. . . . The third procedure is to ascertain the extent to which the behavior patterns entailed in exploiting the environment affect other aspects of culture [Steward 1955: 40–41].

This is Steward's research strategy. It is the procedure actually followed in his substantive work to which we turn in a moment.

Core, Base, Superstructure

In connection with his misnomered "method of multilinear evolution," Steward attempts to set up a taxonomy of the empirically identified instances of parallel lines of development. By what congeries of traits shall we identify these sequences? Steward's answer is that they should be classified in accordance with the kinds of "cultural cores" which they manifest. Such cores he defines as "the constellation of features which are most closely related to subsistence activities and economic arrangements" (*ibid.*:37). It is inevitable that this definition of "cultural core" should summon up comparison with Marx's distinction between base and superstructure. One thinks immediately that the core is that part of the sociocultural system which in the long run determines all the other parts. Steward's explication, however, leads to other conclusions:

> *cultural core*—the constellation of features which are most closely related to subsistence activities and economic arrangements. The core includes such social, political, and religious patterns as are empirically determined to be closely connected with these arrangements. Innumerable other features may have great potential variability because they are less

> strongly tied to the core. These latter, or secondary features, are determined to a greater extent by purely cultural-historical factors—by random innovations or by diffusion—and they give the appearance of outward distinctiveness to cultures with similar cores. Cultural ecology pays primary attention to those features which empirical analysis shows to be most closely involved in the utilization of environment in culturally prescribed ways [*ibid.*].

If we proceed on the assumption that "core" is analogous to "base," we shall find on closer inspection that the logic of the above statement leaves much to be desired.

On this assumption, the core would be essential to the understanding of the causality responsible for a type, yet it would not determine the type's secondary features. These are determined by purely chance cultural-historical factors, that is, by variables which cannot be put into nomothetic generalizations. What about the subsistence activities, economic arrangements, the social, political, and religious patterns, all of which are to be included in the core? Is there any indication that we are to regard some of these factors as causally more significant than the others? None at all. Why then, we may very well wonder, should certain types tend to occur frequently enough to produce the parallel sequences which constitute the subject matter of multilinear evolution? How can we speak of "causality" when it appears to be a matter of indifference whether it is one, several, or all of the respective subsistence, economic, political, or religious variables which can summon into existence the whole pattern of the cultural-ecological type? But this quandary has not exhausted itself.

> Obviously, the diagnostic features of any given era —*the cultural core*—will depend in part upon particular research interest, upon what is considered important; and there is still a healthy if somewhat confusing disagreement regarding these matters. It should be noted, however, that functionally interrelated economic, social, political, religious, and military patterns as well as technological and esthetic features have become the basis for developmental taxonomies. These features do not constitute total cultures. They form *culture cores*, which are defined according to the empirical facts of *cross-cultural type* and level [*ibid.*:93].

Not only must we now admit military and aesthetic features into the culture core, thus rounding out the entire universal pattern, but the reasons for including some and excluding others may depend upon what each anthropologist appears to consider important!

The Core of Confusion

It is clear that the interests of coherent and systematic theory cannot be served by the interpretation of Steward's "cultural core" as a statement of causal relations. The concept of cultural core makes sense only in relation to the misguided polemic surrounding the multilinearity of cultural evolution. It cannot be reconciled with Steward's cultural-ecological method. Steward has confused the causal implications of the cultural-ecological stategy with the typological requirements of multilinear sequences. The stress on multilinearity, in turn, is intelligible only as a counterweight to dogmatized versions of Marxism, as a means of dissociating cultural ecology from the political stigma attached to historical materialism. We do not otherwise require to be told over and over again that cultural ecology cannot explain everything, that there are exceptions, that not all cultures conform to the same type, and that there is divergence as well as convergence and parallelism in human history. What anthropologists can deny these challenges to nomothetic understanding?

But that is not the issue. Rather, the issue is what kinds of results have been achieved by following historical particularism, culture and personality, and the other emic and idealist alternatives? Let those who know how to explain what the cultural-materialist strategy has thus far failed to explain step forward with their nomothetic alternatives. We do not demean a theory by its failures to explain everything, but rather by its failure to explain as much as its nearest rivals. In this frame of reference, the alternatives to cultural materialism have failed and have as often obscured as enlightened our understanding of sociocultural evolution.

Early Influences on Steward

When we turn to the substantive applications of Steward's cultural-ecological method, the confusion associated with his concept of cultural core is somewhat attenuated. In each of his major undertakings he has stressed the techno-economic and techno-environmental parameters as the first order of business and has demonstrated the advantages of such a strategy by rendering intelligible cultural phenomena which are otherwise inscrutable. It will obviously not be possible to recount all of Steward's achievements; only those of the highest theoretical significance can be touched upon.

Steward was trained at Berkeley, where he received his Ph.D. in 1931, and his earlier work was dominated by particularist influences emanating from Kroeber and Lowie. One must also reckon with the influence of Carl Sauer, whose interest in human geography helped to strengthen Kroeber's awareness of environmental factors.

Steward's own interest in environmental factors was first consolidated by fieldwork among the Eastern Mono and Paiute of Owens Valley, California, in 1927 and 1928. Up to the publication of his "The Economic and Social Basis of Primitive Bands," however, Steward's position corresponded essentially to that of a rather large number of anthropologists who regarded the natural environment as a vaguely limiting or enabling factor in culture history. Let us pause for a moment to consider the background.

Earlier Treatments of the Relationship Between Culture and Environment: Wissler

The salient feature of the anthropological discussions of the influence of environment on culture prior to Steward's essay was that they were carried out within the particularist frame of culture area classifications, and hence did not rise to nomothetic status. Both Kroeber and Clark Wissler for example, basing themselves on the still earlier formulations of Otis Mason (1895a), were convinced that there was a correspondence between cultural and natural areas over the entire New World. Wissler in particular indicated that some kind of determinist influence had to be operating from environment to culture. He was especially impressed by the fact that when a map of North American "ecological" areas was placed over a map of the cultural areas, not only did the two line up, but the centers of the respective areas were the same for both the cultural and natural features. He was baffled, however, as to why this should be so.

> We have, then, made progress in our search for the environmental factor, since it appears the rule that, wherever in aboriginal America, a well marked ecological area can be delineated, there one will find a culture area and that the centers of distribution for the constituent traits will fall in the heart of the ecological area. There must then be some determining condition that produces this uniformity, some ecological relation here, and no doubt a mechanism involved, which when laid bare, will give an adequate scientific explanation of the phenomenon. This discussion has at least set us on the trail of this mechanism, for its place of function is the ecological area, and it is most in evidence at the center [Wissler 1926:216–17].

Wissler was further convinced that in so far as the environment influenced the formation of cultural areas, it was through effects of food production.

> In a large measure the particular economic type followed by the community shapes the entire mode of life. . . . As we have stated repeatedly, the most basic of all economic conditions are those related to food, and the specific food habits of a people are among the most resistant to change [Wissler 1929:79].

But Wissler was also capable of such statements as: "The influence of the environment thus appears as a passive limiting agency rather than as a causal factor in tribal life" (*ibid.*:339), and his notion of determinism becomes utterly befuddled when he tries to explain the uniformity of subsistence practices within a cultural area. This he attributed not to the adaptive advantages of a particular mode of subsistence but rather to the alleged advantage which accrues to the tribes of a region when they all exploit the same resources:

> The environment really holds together the tribes occupying a region, and develops a community of interest and concentrates leadership within itself. The tendency for a bison-hunting tribe is, first, to confine its wanderings to the bison range; secondly, to observe and to fraternize with other bison-hunting tribes. Under such circumstances, it seems inevitable that the tribes within a region should follow much the same round of life [*ibid.*:338–39].

Wissler was thus unable to formulate the essential ingredients in a nomothetic approach to the culture-environment relationship. Such an approach can be stated only in terms of relationships that are found in different culture areas—indeed, on different continents—as a result of recurrent ecological exigencies. Furthermore, Wissler had no idea how, in general, the techno-environmental conditions could be nomothetically related to social organization and ideology. All in all, Wissler's approach represented only a slight advance over the work of Ratzel, to whom he himself attributed many of his ideas.

Culture and Environment: C. Daryll Forde

One additional approach to the culture-environment problem must be mentioned, namely that of C. Daryll Forde. Like Wissler, Forde was convinced that the environment was important, but he was also incapable of and disinclined toward expressing the relationship in nomothetic terms. In effect, his main contribution was to warn geographers that they could not hope to understand cultures as mere reflexes of environment since each culture had the power to take out of the environment or to stress those aspects of it which historical (i.e., cultural) events inclined it to take into consideration:

> Physical conditions enter intimately into every cultural development and pattern, not excluding the most abstract and non-material; they enter not as determinants, however, but as one category of the raw material of cultural elaboration. The study of the relations between cultural patterns and physical conditions is of the greatest importance for an understanding of human society, but it cannot be undertaken in terms of simple geographical controls alleged to be identifiable on sight. It must proceed inductively from the minute analysis of each actual society. The culture must in the first place be studied as an entity, and as an historical development; there can be no other effective approach to interrelations of such complexity. The most meticulous knowledge of physical geography, whether of great regions or of small areas, will not serve to elucidate these problems unless the nature of cultural development is grasped. The geographer who is unversed in the culture of the people of the land he studies, or in the lessons which ethnology as a whole has to teach, will, as soon as he begins to consider the mainspring of human activity, find himself groping uncertainly for geographical factors whose significance he cannot truly assess [Forde 1934:464–65].

What we have here is merely a restatement of the historical-particularist position with an emphasis upon accumulating techno-environmental data instead of folktales. The failure to reach a nomothetic point of view is yet more evident when Forde goes on to say that even if we could discover determinist principles by which techno-economic patterns could be related to the environment, we should still confront an impasse in trying to relate these patterns to the rest of the culture. One more citation is required at this point in order that the full measure of Steward's achievement may be taken:

> But if geographical determinism fails to account for the existence and distribution of economies, economic determinism is equally inadequate in accounting for the social and political organizations, the religious beliefs and the psychological attitudes, which may be found in cultures based on those economies. . . . The tenure and transmission of land and other property, the development and relations of social classes, the nature of government, the religious and ceremonial life—all these are parts of a social superstructure, the development of which is conditioned not only by the foundations of habitat and economy, but by complex interactions within its own fabric and by external contacts, often largely indifferent to both the physical background and to the basic economy alike [*ibid.*].

The phrase "complex interactions within its own fabric" is a noteworthy example of how an admission of ignorance, properly celebrated, can convey a sense of wisdom.

Economic and Social Basis of Primitive Bands

Against this background, Steward's "The Economic and Social Basis of Primitive Bands" must be reckoned among the important achievements of modern anthropology. It constitutes the first coherent statement of how the interaction between culture and environment could be studied in causal terms without reverting to a simple geographical determinism or without lapsing into historical particularism. This achievement has a double focus: first, the identification of a cross-culturally valid form of social organization, the "primitive band"; second, its explanation. The band occurs among widely separated hunting and gathering peoples in many different parts of the world. It is a type of social organization distinguished in its most general form by political autonomy and a small population, in that it consists of several nuclear families whose access to land is controlled by ownership privileges vested in the larger group. Incidentally, in defining this unit Steward had to cut through the issue of family and individual land ownership which Boas' student Speck (1928) had succeeded in bringing to a point of almost complete confusion by his failure to separate acculturation effects from aboriginal patterns. Having established the existence of the major type by reference to several dozen recorded cases, Steward classified them into three subtypes: patrilineal, composite, and matrilineal. He then proceeded to supply causal explanations for the existence of the major type and its three subtypes. These explanations involve a consideration of the relationship between the productive capacity of low-level technologies applied to various types of habitats. Where Steward triumphed over the earlier expressions of determinism linking habitat and social organization going back as far as Turgot was in being able to explain how, despite the diversity of environments and technologies associated with band-organized societies, there remained underlying ecological commonalities which gave rise to the general type and other commonalities which gave rise to the subtypes. Where the older tradition of geographical determinism was baffled by the fact that similar organizations occurred among the desert-dwelling Arunta, the Negritoes of the Congo rain forest, and the California Miwok, Steward's analysis focused attention on the structural similarities which resulted from the interaction of habitats and cultures whose specific content masked a fundamentally similar ecologic adjustment.

The nature of this adjustment may be summed up in reference to the low productivity of hunting and gathering techniques in adverse environments with a consequent limitation of population density to less than one person per square mile. Social aggregates are therefore necessarily small (averaging thirty to fifty persons per band) yet they are larger than the nuclear family because of the greater efficiency of the larger group in "subsistence insurance" and "security in warfare and feuds" (Steward 1936:332–33). According to Steward, the patrilineal type results from patrilocal residence which in turn is associated with the subsistence and defense advantages stemming from organizing the local group around a core of resident males. Composite forms of the band result from the intrusion of factors which reduce the advantages of patrilocality, as when subsistence depends on migratory animals.

Not only did this formulation surpass crude environmental determinism, which makes no provision for cultural variables, but it also surpassed that form of human geography known as "possibilism," in which the recognition of the cultural factor ends in a morass of indeterminacy. Steward was not merely saying that a particular combination of technology and environment made it possible for man to create a particular type of social organization; the whole weight of his argument was in the direction of insisting that a similar techno-environmental relationship regularly caused a similar effect (i.e., made it highly probable) regardless of whether the people involved were "creatively inclined" or not. Despite subsequent critical evaluations of certain aspects of Steward's data (*cf.* Service 1962; Meggitt 1962), the strategy of Steward's explanation continues to warrant approval.

Some Superfluous Limitations

It should not be concluded, however, that Steward had in one stroke severed his ties to particularism. In the actual listing of causal factors responsible for the band and its subtypes, Steward included a number of fortuitous and quixotic ingredients which, if taken as integral to the argument, greatly reduce its novelty. Thus in his summary of the factors responsible for the patrilineal band, Steward noted that band size is something restricted not by ecological relations but rather by "some social factor which nevertheless has brought about occupation of small parcels of territory by correspondingly small groups" (*ibid.*: 343). Similarly in the explanation of the conditions responsible for composite bands he included such intrusive factors as "adoption of children between bands" and legitimacy of parallel cousin marriages; for matrilocal bands he listed: "Desire to secure the assistance of the wife's mother in child rearing"; and "strength of borrowed matrilineal institutions" (*ibid.*). Despite these lapses, there is no doubt that Steward intended to produce a statement of nomothetic causality based upon techno-environmental regularities. In his own words:

> Underlying this paper is the assumption that every cultural phenomenon is the product of some definite cause or causes. This is a necessary presupposition if anthropology is considered a science. The method of this paper has been first to ascertain the causes of primitive bands through analysis of the inner functional or organic connection of the components of a culture and their environmental basis. Next, through comparisons, it endeavored to discover what degree of generalization is possible. It is not assumed, of course, that generalizations may be made concerning all culture traits. On the contrary, it is entirely possible that the very multiplicity of antecedents of many traits or complexes will preclude satisfactory

generalization and that the conclusion with respect to some things will be that "history never repeats itself." The extent, however, to which generalizations can be made may be ascertained by further application of the methods followed here [*ibid.*].

What Steward failed to realize is that the idiosyncratic, social, and ideational factors included among the determinants of band organization preclude "satisfactory generalization" and thus should have been removed from the statement of the lawful conditions.

Consequences of Nonstatistical Generalization

It is regrettable that Steward operates with a nonstatistical concept of causality: "The method will be to analyze functional or necessary relationships. It will not undertake statistics or correlations" (*ibid.*:331). Had he approached the statement of ecological causality in terms of statistical probabilities, then we might have been spared a long series of curiously self-defeating theoretical forays, each of which undermines an important substantive nomothetic achievement by putting back into the ecological formula the indeterminacy which it was designed to overcome.

The significance of Steward's analysis of bands is that it showed how the interaction between technology and environment could explain *most* of the important structural and ideological features of low-energy hunters and gatherers in *most* of the known examples without utilizing historical or other idiographic modes of explanation. If we do not clearly state that the issue is a matter of probabilities, then before long we find ourselves retreating to the cupboard of eclecticism in order to achieve an explanation of *all* of the important structural and ideational features in *all* of the known cases. But such explanation ceases to be nomothetically viable. We already know beforehand that if we could be given an account of all of the events in the history of each of the peoples who have band organization, we should be able to offer an explanation which would be more "complete" than that which can be obtained through the nomothetic option. But such a program is the antithesis of science, and we do not improve our nomothetic formulations by tacking on the additional bit of advice that the exceptions to our rules can be understood by dragging in other factors, *unless these additional considerations are couched in nomothetic terms.*

Ecology of the Southwest

In his analysis of the development of multimatrisib villages among the Pueblos and multipatrisib villages among the Yuman tribes of the Colorado River, Steward repeated the performance which made his treatment of the origin of bands a landmark. Rejecting the prevailing theories which derived the Yuman sib organization from the Pueblos, he emphasized instead the effect which the introduction of agriculture had upon the population density of the Colorado groups. This combined with pressure of warfare produced the evolution of the Yuman groups from patrilineal bands to multi-patrisib villages. Similar processes account for the gradual conversion of the semisedentary seed gatherers of Basket Maker times into the multimatrisib villages of the late Basket Maker and Pueblo times.

It is noteworthy for an assessment of Steward's total impact upon anthropological theory during the last three decades that his utilization of archaeological data for the reconstruction of the Pueblo sequence helped to usher in a new era of archaeological interpretations, one whose influence continues to expand exponentially at the moment of writing. But I shall return to the interrelationship between cultural ecology and archaeology in a moment.

First we must record Steward's reiteration of the importance of the cultural-ecological approach:

> The present analysis of Southwestern society assumes that cultural process, and therefore sound historical reconstruction, can be understood only if due attention is paid to the economic and ecological factors that shape society. This requires analysis of the degree and manner in which economic factors have combined with kinship, ceremonialism, inheritance, and other factors to produce observed social patterns [1955:155].

Once again, however, we confront not only the nomothetic factors but the peculiar idiographic ones which negate the entire effort if we accord them their literal significance. In explaining the concentration of formerly localized and independent units in Pueblo III times, for example, Steward asserts that the change was "made possible but not caused by ecological factors" (*ibid.*: 166–67).

Village concentration must, therefore, have been produced by a factor of a nonecological order. Many causes are conceivable but in this instance it does not seem imperative to seek beyond the need for defense; for, whatever the danger, increasing pains taken to choose impregnable dwelling sites attest an important motive for banding together. This tendency to concentrate in large villages, aided by the development of multistoried architecture and probably stimulated by some threat, began to spread. But at this time the total Pueblo area also began to shrink. The communal dwelling has persisted to the present, but now that the motives for constructing it have vanished, the reverse tendency has set in, houses becoming more widely scattered. The unilateral organization presumed to have been created during the original concentration of the Pueblo population continues in effect to the present day [*ibid.*:167].

A slight amount of reflection should suffice for establishing the point that an increase in warfare in the Pueblo area could easily have resulted from factors consistent with Steward's notion of ecology, namely from population increase. Once again, it should be emphasized that the peculiarly hesitant formulation would be rendered redundant by rephrasing the determinism to accord with statistical notions of causality. What Steward was really saying in this paper on the formation of multisib communities is that given a certain set of environmental and technological conditions, the transition from band to sib is highly predictable in a sufficiently large sample. But this is all we can ask of nomothetic statements in any realm of science.

Cultural Law and Causality

We turn now to an historically decisive paper, Steward's "Cultural Causality and Law; A Trial Formulation of Early Civilization." This article elaborated on Steward's contribution to the 1947 Viking Fund Conference on Peruvian Archaeology at which the first stratigraphically based syntheses of the independent evolution of civilization in the New World had been set forth. . . . Juxtaposing the New World sequences as known from northern Peru and central Mexico with available summaries of events in Mesopotamia, Egypt, and North China, Steward demonstrated a degree of developmental parallelism which dwarfed all of the "stupendous" phenomena referred to by Sapir. . . . In all five regions Steward identified a sequence which involved a roughly parallel development through the following stages: Hunting and Gathering; Incipient Agriculture; Formative; Regional Florescent; Cyclical Conquests. The importance of this synthesis will emerge from the following discussion of the background of Steward's theory. We shall have to consider first the relationship of Steward's formulation to the "hydraulic hypothesis" as proposed by the comparative historian and sinologist Karl Wittfogel. Second, the relationship between Wittfogel, Steward, and Marxist theory must also be considered. And finally we shall have to assess the relationship between archaeological research and the rise of cultural-materialist theories.

Wittfogel and the Hydraulic Theory

Steward's trial formulation of the developmental sequence in the five centers of ancient civilization was not intended to exhaust all of the possible routes which cultures have followed toward complex state-organizations. Rather, the trajectories he outlined were those assumed to be the characteristic sequences of one particular type, namely, irrigation, or "hydraulic civilizations."

The formulation here offered excludes all areas except the arid and semiarid centers of ancient civilizations. In the irrigation areas, environment, production, and social patterns had similar functional and developmental interrelationships [Steward 1949b:17].

Steward's ideas at this point converged with the theories of Karl Wittfogel.

As early as 1926 Wittfogel had begun to apply a cultural-ecological approach to the explanation of the peculiarities of Chinese and other "Asiatic" societies. In Wittfogel's early formulation these systems were characterized as "mighty hydraulic bureaucracies" whose despotic control over the densely populated ancient states in China, India, and Egypt arose from the techno-environmental exigencies of large-scale irrigation and other forms of water control in regions of scant rainfall. Although inspired by Max Weber, this analysis owed its central thrust, its clarity, and its success to Marx. The realization that the evolution of Oriental societies had followed a path substantially different from those of Europe was quite common among the scholars of the Enlightenment. Marx accepted this difference and postulated an Oriental mode of production.

As Wittfogel tells us, he employed "Marx's concept," in conformity with what he understood to be Marx's own conclusions (Wittfogel 1957:5–6). Wittfogel's analysis of the functional interdependence of the main features of the social organization and techno-economic patterns of irrigation civilization led him to stress the general importance of environmental parameters in the application of historical materialism to the understanding of social systems. His proposal to emphasize the interplay between economics and environment to account for phenomena which had baffled Marx was published in the Marxist journal *Unter dem Banner der Marxismus* (1929), and was clearly conceived as an expansion of the scope and effectiveness of the historical-materialist strategy.

Wittfogel Abandons Cultural Materialism

Wittfogel's views on hydraulic society clashed with several cardinal items of dogma in the Stalinist version of world history. Marx's notion of an Asiatic mode of production indicated a degree of divergence in sociopolitical evolution which the international Communist parties were unwilling to accept. The Asiatic mode of production with its despotic centralized bureaucratic state was the very opposite of European feudal society. If there could be no feudalism in the evolutionary careers of the hydraulic civilizations, how could they develop capitalism? And without capitalism, how could they develop communism? As a result of the communist expurgation of Marx's ideas on the multilinearity of sociocultural evolution, Wittfogel's research and writing gradually took on the coloration of a crusade against communism and totalitarianism in general. Initially this crusade was closely linked with a defense of the cultural-materialist strategy and was inspired by "Marx's insistence on an unbiased pursuit of truth" (1957:6). Gradually, however, Wittfogel came to see the phenomena of Oriental despotism as capable of surviving in, and diffusing to, societies whose techno-economic relationships bore little resemblance to the conditions underlying the pristine state. Oriental society, he has recently declared, "cannot be explained in purely ecological or economic terms; and the spread of Oriental despotism to areas lacking a hydraulic agriculture underlines the limitations of such an explanation" (Wittfogel 1964:46).

Disturbed by a vision of the Soviet Union and Communist China as new installments in an age-old pattern, Wittfogel permitted himself to serve as a government witness in the McCarran committee's investigation of the Institute of Pacific Studies. Tragedies resulting from this episode have ill-served the cause of scholarship and have contributed to the suppression of the cultural-materialist strategy in American social science. Wittfogel's crusade to prove the multilinearity of evolution has centered more and more on the alleged moral implications of closed and open models of history:

> Marx and Engels' acceptance of Asiatic society as a separate and stationary conformation shows the doctrinal insincerity of those who, in the name of Marx, peddle the unilinear construct. And the comparative study of societal conformations demonstrates the empirical untenability of their position. Such a study brings to light a complex sociohistorical pattern, which includes stagnation as well as progress. By revealing the opportunities, and the pitfalls, of open historical situations, this concept assigns to man a profound moral responsibility, for which the unilinear scheme, with its ultimate fatalism, has no place [1957:7–8].

The Politics of Hydraulics

Although Wittfogel's model of history is more correct than anything proposed in the name of Stalinist orthodoxy, it is regrettable that the issue of moral responsibility should be employed in support of multilinear evolutionism. One could argue that there is not the slightest evidence that a world view in which human behavior is determined by material processes leads to any greater or lesser amount of "fatalism" than is to be found among peoples who believe in the determinism of an omnipotent God. Under either alternative mature individuals learn to accept responsibility for their actions. But I shall not elaborate on this aspect of the issue, because we have before us not a question of morality but one of scientific fact and theory. If we want to know to what extent human history is determined along parallel and convergent lines, we must turn to our measuring instruments and to our evidence and not to the moral premises of theologians, philosophers, and politicians.

Wittfogel's concern with the need to defeat the Stalinist world view has led him away from the cultural-materialist strategy—the strategy which was responsible for the formulation of his original theory of Oriental despotism. The irony of this situation is that in the meantime the evidence in favor of his theory has accumulated far beyond that which was available in the 1920's. Wittfogel's emigration to the United States corresponded to the period during which the revival of interest in large-scale nomothetic formulations was just getting under way. And by the end of the 1930's, this interest could for the first time in history avail itself of an abundance of archaeological facts adequate to the scientific solution of some of the most formidable riddles of human life.

Anthropological Contributions to the Strategy of Cultural Materialism

As we shall see, the central hypothesis in Steward's "Cultural Causality and Law" was taken over bodily from Wittfogel. It would appear that knowingly or unknowingly, Steward had thus succeeded in wedding anthropology to the materialist strategy of which Marx had been the pioneer. But "Cultural Causality and Law" also represents the coming together of a number of distinctively anthropological achievements, whose substance and nature must now be set forth.

There was first of all the heritage of research carried out among non-European and precivilized groups with all its advantages in terms of the relative simplicity of the techno-environmental and techno-economic feedbacks. Field techniques applied to living people in their natural habitat gave anthropologists an advantage over the scholars who like Marx and his orthodox followers depended upon documents and historiography as their principal source of information about the structure and dynamics of sociocultural systems. Steward himself was an important contributor to this heritage, having carried out additional field studies in 1934–36 among the Great Basin Shoshone seed gatherers.

Secondly, anthropology was rapidly expanding the scope of its ethnographic studies over areas which provided maximum contrast with the cases most familiar to the European historians and even to scholars such as Wittfogel, whose great knowledge of Chinese history freed him from the typical Eurocentric parochialism of Western historiography.

Steward, for example, enjoyed an especially advantageous ethnological perspective as editor of the six-volume *Handbook of South American Indians* (1946–50). This monumental collection immersed him in ethnographic material covering an entire continent with an extraordinary variety of environments and sociopolitical types.

In his struggle to organize the contributions of some ninety collaborators from a dozen different countries, Steward had at first accepted the historical-particularist trait-inventory frame of culture areas. In the fifth volume, however, he expressed his dissatisfaction with the definition of the four culture areas which provided the typological basis for one of each of the preceding volumes: *Marginal, Tropical Forest, Circum-Caribbean/Sub-Andean*, and *Andean*. In retrospect, he announced, "it is evident that many tribes were improperly classified" (1940a:670–71), and he called for and carried out a reclassification in accordance with patterns "which integrate the institutions of the sociopolitical unit" (*ibid.*:672).

The resulting reclassification corresponded roughly to the levels of sociocultural development which Elman Service (1962) later came to designate as band, tribe, chiefdom, and state. Steward himself was obliged to continue to speak of the culture types in question in terms of the continental-specific rubrics in the titles of the first four volumes. Within the *Handbook*, Steward (1949a:674) refrained from pressing "the developmental implications" of his classification, preferring instead, in a work so clearly a product of many different collaborators, to offer a more conventional historical reconstruction of diffusionist routes within South America. "Cultural Causality and Law," however, was a direct outgrowth of this revised classification since it answers the question of the origin of the Andean civilization in nomothetic rather than historical terms.

The Link with Archaeology

The third great anthropological contribution to the cultural-materialist approach was perhaps the most important. It was largely through cultural-ecological reconstructions, first of the Southwest and then in regard to the hydraulic hypothesis, that a link was established between cultural materialism and the discoveries of New World archaeologists. This relationship was beneficial in two directions; that is, it played a key role both in bringing the results of archaeology to bear upon nomothetic issues as well as in bringing the benefits of cultural-materialist strategy to the conduct and interpretation of archaeological research.

To appreciate the scope of this contribution and to understand the strategic significance of "Cultural Causality and Law," we must digress for a moment and consider the condition into which archaeology had lapsed during the Boasian period.

Archaeology During the Reign of Particularism

If the hand of historical particularism rested heavily upon the study of cultural regularities among ethnologists, its weight was even more deadening among the archaeologists. If each ethnologist had his tribe, each archaeologist had his "site." If the ethnologist described his tribe in terms peculiar to and literally borrowed from the lexicon of the people he was studying, the archaeologist concentrated upon the pattern of rim sherd incisions found at his site and possibly at one or two adjacent localities. If culture was a thing of shreds and patches to Lowie, to the majority of his contemporaries working in archaeology it was a thing of sherds and scrapers and little else.

Speaking of the period from 1910 to 1936, the archaeologist Alfred Kidder lamented the particularism into which archaeology had lapsed as a result of what he called "pre-1910 speculations about the vast antiquity of the American Indians" with its consequent loss of "historical perspective" and its "taboo" on questions concerning origins:

> Archaeology accordingly became preponderantly descriptive; effort was directed toward identification of ancient sites with modern tribes; research upon American prehistory, striking forward rather than back, upward rather than downward, was left without foundations . . . many of us merely dodged the issue of origins and comforted ourselves by working in the satisfactorily clear atmosphere of the late periods [Kidder 1936:146].

The Problem of New World Origins

What kind of attitude prevailed concerning the universally accepted belief (ushered in with the defeat of the Morgan-Bandelier reconstruction of Aztec "democracy") that highly elaborate state-organized societies existed in the New World as well as the Old? We have already seen that the Boasians tended to adopt an ambivalent position on this question. On the one hand almost all the Boasians were convinced that the attempts by the diffusionists to explain the native American civilizations exclusively by migrations and contact processes across either the Atlantic or Pacific were without foundation in fact. On the other hand, the Boasians were willing to admit that it was by no means unlikely that transoceanic influences had occurred. The task of separating the diffused from the independently invented items was regarded as an empirical question, the unraveling of which might require many years of research for each item in the list of parallels. There was certainly slight expectation that when the final balance was reckoned, any of the major tenets of the Boasian position would require restatement.

In the reiterated assurance that no one doubted that certain technological events would have to precede others and that civilization could result only from an increasingly more stable food supply and enlarged population, the Boasians thought that they had already exhausted the entire inventory of generalizations which the further study of the origin of New World civilizations could make possible. From their eclectic and particularist viewpoint they were willing to concede that states and empires had to have a basis in "surplus" production and "leisure time" made available by intensive agriculture. But since cultural evolution was conceived of as a hodgepodge of independent inventions and capricious diffusions, it was of no special importance that similar traits such as supreme god-priest rulers, monumental architecture, standing armies, state corvee, urbanization, astronomical and mathematical specialists, writing and calendars, and hundreds of other traits and institutions should appear in a number of different places throughout the world.

Kroeber, it will be recalled, explicitly warned against any expectation that any but the vaguest resemblance of sequence could be expected. The discussion of the theoretical significance of the New World civilizations thus remained in a state of suspended animation.

New Techniques, New Data

The foundation of this murky mixture of diffusion and invention, however, rested upon a precarious situation in the archaeological realm. Here vast uncertainties of chronology and seriation fed the prevailing fashions of particularism. In this connection, it must be recalled that techniques of excavation adequate to an understanding of nongeologically stratified sites were not perfected and certainly were not widely used until the mid-twenties. The new techniques and their consequences have been outlined by the archaeologist Gordon Willey:

> The method was applicable to refuse deposits which had grown by occupational accretion. Marked physical stratification of deposits was not necessary. The technique consisted of removing detritus and artifacts from arbitrary depth levels. In studying artifact change by levels, percentage fluctuations of types were noted from level to level, so that rising or declining percentage frequencies of types were correlated with time. Deriving in large part from the mechanical nature of the operation, "continuous stratigraphy" of this kind had important theoretical repercussions on the nature of culture continuity and change. With the continuous depositional record of a site occupation before his eyes, the archaeologist could not help being impressed with the evidence for culture dynamics [Willey 1953:365].

During the twenties and early thirties, the impact of the numerous but far-flung applications of these new techniques on both simple and complex societies was obscured by an inability to establish a coordinated chronology for the entrance of man into the New World and his subsequent dispersal to the southernmost limits of the hemisphere. Although, as J. A. Mason (1966) has pointed out, many archaeologists accepted a Pleistocene date for the migration from Siberia, providing for some 10,000 years of evolution, diffusion, and migration, it was not until 1926, with the discovery of a point embedded between the ribs of an extinct form of bison at Folsom, New Mexico, that really convincing evidence could be brought forth to buttress the logical arguments for the time span in question.

Time and the Significance of the New World Civilizations

Few archaeologists appreciated the theoretical significance of the possibility of an independent origin for New World civilizations. An exception was Herbert Spinden, who, during the course of his arguments with the doctrinaire diffusionists, remained alert to the theoretical import of the independent inventionist position. If America "was the home of a family of civilizations independent of the family of civilizations in the Old World," observed Spinden, this fact would ". . . have a tremendous bearing on the innate potentialities of mankind, and thus, in turn, on the future course of political and social evolution" (Spinden 1927:60–61). In very general terms, Spinden's view of evolution in the New World appears to have anticipated Steward's treatment of the subject:

> The American record indicates in very complete fashion the natural history of civilizations, from the family hunting band type of association up through the farmer's and fisherman's villages to nationalities, including all the members of a language group and even to empires based on conquest and tribute [*ibid.*: 62].

Spinden, however, was far from having achieved a clear understanding of the scope and pattern of the evolution of New World culture. This is shown by his curious change of heart about the antiquity of the Paleo-Indian migration. In his 1936 presidential address to the American Anthropological Association he insisted that the Amerindian migration from the Old to the New World could not have occurred before 2500 B.C. Few anthropologists were willing to compress the entire sequence from the first appearance of Folsom-type hunters, their dispersal over the hemisphere, and the appearance of the first civilizations into such a short time period. Spinden's theory nonetheless reveals how doubtful the whole chronology of the New World continued to be as late as the mid-thirties. Clark Wissler, writing in 1933, summed up the situation in the following words:

> While it is true that the great number of living tribal units and their various cultures suggest a fair lapse of time, no satisfactory way has been found to express this interval in years or even in the relative terms of Old World chronology [Wissler 1933:216].

The picture was especially unclear precisely in those areas such as the Valley of Mexico and the Central Andean highlands in which the best known of the New World civilizations had flourished at the time of conquest. Thus, the archaeologist Alfred Kidder observed in 1936 that "Kroeber and Vaillant believe that the oldest remains so far discovered in Peru and Mexico are not older than the time of Christ" (1936:146). Indeed, even in 1949, the entire Incipient Agricultural phase in Steward's chart was supported by nothing more than a question mark.

Discovery of the Energy Basis of the New World Civilizations

The turning point in the relationship between archaeological data and cultural materialism came in the late thirties and early forties with the excavations in Peru carried out by W. D. Strong, Steward's classmate at Berkeley, and Gordon Willey, one of Strong's students at Columbia. In the Viru Valley, a complex of domesticated beans, squash, and cotton was identified at the base of a large mound with an estimated date of 2500 B.C. A continuous evolutionary sequence was obtained in the mound and in adjacent sites leading from Incipient Agriculture through several stages of village life up to the lowland irrigation states which were ultimately absorbed by the Inca Empire. Of special interest in this sequence was the phase identified by Steward as the Formative, when maize was introduced and irrigation techniques took over the main subsistence load. The entire sequence is wholly intelligible as a product of endogenous forces; increasing productivity, increasing population density, multiplication of village sites, warfare, intervillage and later intervalley coordination of productive processes, increasing social stratification and bureaucratic control of production and distribution, centralization of power, feedback to greater productivity, and population density. If contacts with the Old World had occurred during the 2500 to 3000 years which were required for the shift from autonomous village to state organization, nothing vital to the dynamic of the process seems to have resulted therefrom.

The only possible exception was maize, which obviously had not been domesticated on the Peruvian coast. At the time of Steward's analysis of the New World irrigation sequence the wild ancestors of the plant had yet to be identified. A few die-hard diffusionists continued to insist that it was not a native American cultigen, despite the fact that it was grown nowhere outside of the New World prior to the European conquest. In recent years not only have the wild ancestors of corn been identified in highland Mexico, but radiocarbon 14 dates have confirmed a period of gradual experimentation with domesticated varieties extending back to 7000 B.C. in the Tehuacán Valley of Central Mexico and in southern Tamaulipas (Mangelsdorf, Macneish, and Galinat 1964; Macneish 1964a; 1964b)! Proof that the Amerindians domesticated corn is tantamount to proof that they were capable of achieving every other technological innovation associated with the New World sequence independently of diffusion from the Old. Given the combination Homo sapiens, a nutritive and hardy grain, semiarid valleys, ample sources of water, terrain adaptable to irrigation, it was highly probable that irrigation civilizations would evolve, not once, but again and again.

Steward's provisional comparison of the main evolutionary sequences in the Old and New World was thus an epochal event because it marked the beginning of the use of the New World archaeological evidence to support a cultural-materialist interpretation of the origin of civilization. Hitherto, few archaeologists had accepted cultural materialism as a valid strategy. There were, of course, a number of exceptions, one of whom, V. Gordon Childe, must now be considered.

V. Gordon Childe and the Strategy of Cultural Materialism

A key figure in English archaeology, Childe was a Marxist who, like Leslie White, staunchly supported the validity of Morgan's stages of Savagery, Barbarism, and Civilization. But when it came to the specific sequences of the Middle East and of Europe, Childe actually seems closer to historical particularism than to historical materialism. As previously discussed . . . , Childe's working model of evolution was that of the divergent Darwinian tree of life. Despite his explicit Marxist leanings, Childe was unsuccessful in achieving a reconciliation between the abstract overall transition from savagery to civilization and his superb knowledge of the specific developmental sequences in the Middle East and Europe. He did of course recognize certain parallels in the end product, but he saw these as resulting more from diffusion than from parallel evolution. "The intervening steps in development did not exhibit even abstract parallelism" (1951a:161).

> So the observed developments in rural economy do not run parallel; they cannot therefore be used to define stages common to all the sequences examined. . . . In fine, the development of barbarians' rural economies in the regions surveyed exhibits not parallelism but divergence and convergence [*ibid.*:162].

Childe's Position on the Irrigation Question

Childe was not unfamiliar with the importance of irrigation in Mesopotamia and Egypt both from the perspective of productivity and organizational exigencies and controls:

> Conditions of life in a river valley or other oasis place in the hands of society an exceptional power for coercing its members; the community can refuse a recalcitrant access to water and can close the channels that irrigate his fields. Rain falleth upon the just and the unjust alike, but irrigating waters reach the fields by channels that the community has constructed. And what society has provided, society can also withdraw from the unjust and confine to the just alone. The social solidarity needed by irrigators can thus be imposed owing to the very circumstances that demand it. And young men cannot escape the restraint of their elders by founding fresh villages when all beyond the oasis is waterless desert. So when the social will comes to be expressed through a chief or a king, he is invested not merely with moral authority, but with coercive force too; he can apply sanctions against the disobedient [Childe 1946:90].

Childe's views on irrigation were transmitted by Pedro Armillas (1948) to the Conference on Peruvian Archaeology sponsored by the Viking Fund. It was at the same conference that Steward read a paper entitled "A Functional-Developmental Classification of American High Cultures" (1948), which provided an outline of the sequence that was incorporated, one year later, in "Cultural Causality and Law." However, Steward at this point made no mention of the hydraulic hypothesis. Armillas, on the other hand, citing Childe, gave extensive attention to the possible role of irrigation in the Formative and Regional Florescent, but he rather tended to postpone and limit its influence to the later Classic and post-Classic periods. That he was far from postulating a hydraulic base for the Formative as Steward was to do after adapting Wittfogel's theories to the Meso-American sequence may be seen from the following passage:

> In considering the role which irrigation works may have played in the social development of Meso-America it is necessary to note that water for irrigation was obtained from many local sources–various rivers and arroyos, springs and also wells—making unnecessary the constitution of large political entities. In fact, irrigation in Meso-America may have favored cantonalism, making each valley self-sufficient in nearly all of its basic economic products [Armillas 1948:107].

We shall turn to the question of irrigation in Meso-America in just a moment.

The Significance of the Second Earth

Childe's most serious shortcoming was his lack of interest in the civilizational sequences outside of the Middle East and Europe. Having concluded correctly at an early point in his career that there was little resemblance between the specific steps involved in the development of civilization in Europe, on the one hand, and in Mesopotamia and Egypt on the other, he was unprepared to look for parallels in Mexico or Peru.

Childe's views are extremely instructive with respect to our understanding of Steward's relationship to Marxism and historical materialism. Observe the irony: Both Steward and Wittfogel appear embarrassed by the relationship between Marxism and cultural materialism. Childe, on the other hand, openly pleads for the importance of a cultural-materialist strategy. Yet it is Childe who argues that environmental differences are too great in the earliest centers of civilization to expect parallel sequences, while it is Steward and Wittfogel—the cultural ecologists and doctrinaire multilinear evolutionists—who propose that hydraulic types, wherever they occur, tend to evolve through a similar series of stages.

Thus it was in Steward's trial formulation that for the first time archaeological evidence from the New World was harnessed to the task of providing a cultural-materialist interpretation of cultural evolution on a global scale. At last, it could be seen through archaeological data that American Indian populations, starting with paleolithic tool kits and restricted to a life of hunting and gathering, had slowly advanced through various degrees of complexity in a direction fundamentally similar to that taken by racially and culturally separate populations in the Old World. There was no longer any possibility that either area had depended on the other for any of the vital steps in the sequence. The New World in other words had finally emerged as the equivalent of a second earth; and on that second earth, due to the fact that in the psychocultural realm, as in all others, similar causes under similar conditions lead to similar results, hominid cultures tended to evolve along essentially similar paths when they were confronted with similar techno-environmental situations.

The New Archaeology

We have already seen that the analysis of the development of the sibs in the Southwest and California integrated a knowledge of both ethnographic and archaeological facts. We also should note in this connection that Steward himself had been trained in seriational stratigraphy by Kroeber and that he had worked with William Duncan Strong in a project at The Dalles on the Columbia River in 1926 (Strong, Schenck, and Steward 1930). Firsthand familiarity with the techniques of modern archaeological research gave Steward both the authority and the motivation for criticizing the failure of his colleagues to articulate their findings with significant nomothetic issues:

> When complexes have been identified and history in the narrow sense reconstructed, what task remains for archaeology? Some day world culture history will be known as far as archaeological materials and human intelligence permit. Every possible element of culture will be placed in time and space. . . . When taxonomy and history are thus complete, shall we cease our labors and hope that the future Darwin of anthropology will interpret the great historical scheme that will have been erected? There has been a marked tendency to avoid these questions on the assumption that they are unimportant at present. It is held that the urgent need of the moment is to record data which are rapidly vanishing. . . . We believe that it is unfortunate that attempts to state broad objectives which are basic to all cultural anthropology . . . should be relegated to a future time of greater leisure and fullness of data.
>
> One wonders whether the frequent limitations of interest to measurements and tabulations of data and refinement of technique is an unwillingness to grapple with the problem of objectives. And it is by no means improbable that inspite of our refined techniques of excavation, ceramic studies, and classification, we are actually overlooking important data, even when doing field work.
>
> Often ten pages are devoted to the minutiae of pottery types . . . while one page or less describes subsistence and the relationship of the culture to the geographical environment. . . . Even less space is usually accorded data concerning social groups and population distribution and concentration which are indicated by such elements as house remains and village locations [Steward and Seltzer 1938:5–7].

To a marked degree, Steward's image of what archaeology should have been doing in the 1930's has become true in the fifties and sixties. The dominant orientation in contemporary American anthropological archaeology now conforms to Steward's understanding of cultural ecology. Whether it be shell middens on Long Island, ancient burial grounds in Peru, or pyramids in Mexico, the questions now being asked and the theories being framed to answer them reflect a growing convergence toward the strategy of cultural materialism.

Mere dating and classification have ceased to guarantee respectability in archaeological circles. The demands of the moment are to be met by data on population size, density, minima and maxima in short- and long-time runs; seasonal and climatic cycles; response of settlement pattern; rate of population increase; food production techniques; total exploited habitat; short- and long-run changes in natural biota; techno-environmental effects; size of food producing and non-food producing groups; incidence of warfare; contribution of disease vectors to mortality; nature of social organization defined in terms of house groups, village or town units; and intercommunity organization (Binford 1962; 1967; Steward 1967). These interests link archaeology to ethnology in a powerful new symbiosis, providing the two disciplines with a common set of assumptions emphasizing etic events and a joint strategy which has already begun to yield a better understanding of evolutionary processes.

Testing of the Hydraulic Hypothesis

One of the most interesting manifestations of the new strategy of archaeological research is the attempt to test the hydraulic hypothesis. Research has centered on the role of irrigation in the evolution of Classic period Meso-American urban civilizations. The case of the Valley of Teotihuacán, a short distance to the north of the Valley of Mexico, is a good example of recent efforts along these lines. It was in this valley that one of the largest man-made structures in the world, the great Pyramid of the Sun, was erected a thousand years before Columbus' voyage. In 1948, when Steward formulated his developmental typology, very little was known about the circumstances which had led to the construction of this great pyramid, or of any of the other monuments which were part of the total Teotihuacán complex. Very little was known, either, about the role of irrigation in the formation of Meso-American civilizations. Although there was no doubt that the Aztecs had carried out extensive hydraulic projects in connection with *chinampa* cultivation (misnomered "floating gardens") and the drainage of Lake Texcoco, the date at which these installations were introduced and their causal significance remained uncertain.

In the case of Teotihuacán, nothing at all was known about the agricultural practices which had provided the energy for building the great monuments. Excavations carried out under the direction of René Millon (1967) of the University of Rochester have now established the fact that Teotihuacán was the site of one of the New World's largest aboriginal cities. Its estimated population of 70,000 to 100,000 people could only have been surpassed, if at all, by Tenochtitlán, capital of the Aztecs. Like Tenochtitlán, Teotihuacán was the center of an empire that covered a large part of Central Mexico. The question of whether it was based on hydraulic modes of production appears now to have been settled. Studies carried out by William Sanders of Pennsylvania State University show that the change from rainfall farming to irrigation was correlated with rapid population growth, nucleation, monument construction, intense social stratification, and expansionist warfare. "The water for the permanent irrigation systems derives from 80 springs, all located within a single very small area (20 hectares). This was the most significant single ecological resource" (Sanders 1965:201). Sanders and Price (1968) have gone on to interpret the difference between Maya civilizations and the Highland Mexican hydraulic empires. The former were based not on irrigation agriculture but on slash-and-burn (swidden) farming. These were true civilizations, but they lacked the nucleated settlements of urban civilization. The hierarchical divisions within the lowland Maya states appear to have been much less severe than those in Teotihuacán.

Mexico and Mesopotamia

It would be unreasonable to suppose that substantial criticisms of the details of Steward's irrigation sequence would not have been forthcoming from archaeologists and historians with specialized knowledge of the areas in question. Nor should the impression be conveyed that Wittfogel's hydraulic hypothesis has everywhere received support from our rapidly expanding knowledge of prehistory. It is not possible to review all the negative and positive bits of information and favorable and unfavorable interpretations which are accumulating around this vital question. I shall mention only the most recent attempt by Robert Adams (1966) to compare the evolution of Meso-American and Mesopotamian urban civilizations.

Although Adams acknowledges the existence of irrigation agriculture in Early Dynastic times in Mesopotamia, he does not believe that its scale was large enough to account for the concentration of political power which is characteristic of the later or Classic phases. He is also skeptical of the organizational role of irrigation in Meso-America although his argument is based more on the Aztec than on the Teotihuacán situation. A major difficulty appears to be the lack of coordinating measures of the irrigation works and size of polity in the two regions through successive periods of growth and expansion. Adams' position is weakened when we consider that there is, in the long run, a step-by-step increase in the size of the Mesopotamian waterworks and the size and power of the ruling bureaucracy. Thus, even if Adams is correct in maintaining that the first consolidation of political power was achieved independently of the organizational requisites of the hydraulic system, the achievement of Wittfogel's Oriental despotic type remains closely associated with maximum hydraulic dependency.

But the most interesting aspect of Adams' critique lies elsewhere. Despite his rejection of the hydraulic theory, his entire perspective on the Mesopotamian data bears the imprint of the nomothetic revival, and everywhere implicitly acknowledges the inspiration of the search for law and causality. Indeed, in the final reckoning, Adams reaches conclusions that vindicate Steward's method to a remarkable extent if we reflect how fragmentary were the data upon which Steward was obliged to base his "trial formulation":

> What seems overwhelmingly most important about these differences is how small they bulk even in aggregate, when considered against the mass of similarities in form and process. In short, the parallels in the Mesopotamian and Mexican "careers to state-

hood," in the forms that institutions ultimately assumed as well as in the processes leading to them, suggest that both instances are most significantly characterized by a common core of regularly occurring features. We discover anew that social behavior conforms not merely to laws but to a limited number of such laws, which perhaps has always been taken for granted in the case of cultural subsystems (e.g., kinship) and among "primitives" (e.g., hunting bands). Not merely as an abstract article of faith but as a valid starting point for detailed, empirical analysis, it applies equally well to some of the most complex and creative of human societies [Adams 1966:174–75].

We may note that Adams, who deals with time scales on the order of millennia, appears to have misunderstood recent anthropological history in suggesting that elements of the nomothetic revival were always "taken for granted." It has been a long hard struggle all the way. In concluding our review of this centuries-old struggle to achieve a science of history, it cannot be overemphasized that the vindication of the strategy of cultural materialism does not depend on the verification of the hydraulic hypothesis or of any other particular techno-environmental, techno-economic theory. Rather, it lies in the capacity of the approach to generate major explanatory hypotheses which can be subjected to the tests of ethnographic and archaeological research, modified if necessary, and made part of a corpus of theory equally capable of explaining the most generalized features of universal history and the most exotic specialties of particular cultures.

REFERENCES CITED

Adams, R., McC., 1966, *The Evolution of Urban Society,* Aldine, Chicago.

Armillas, P., 1948, "A Sequence of Cultural Development in Meso-America," in W. Bennett (ed.), *A Reappraisal of Peruvian Archaeology,* Memoirs of the Society for American Archaeology, 4:105–11.

Binford, L., 1962, "Archaeology as Anthropology," *American Antiquity,* 28:217–25.

——— 1967, Comment on K. C. Chang, "Major Aspects of the Interrelationship of Archaeology and Ethnology," *Current Anthropology,* 8:234–35.

Childe, V., 1946, *What Happened in History,* Pelican, New York.

——— 1951, *Social Evolution,* Schuman, New York.

Forde, C. D., 1934, *Habitat, Economy, and Society,* Methuen, London.

Fried, M., 1952, "Land Tenure, Geography and Ecology in the Contact of Cultures," *American Journal of Economics and Sociology,* 11:1.

Kidder, A., 1936, "Speculations on New World Prehistory," R. Lowie (ed.), *Essays in Anthropology,* California U.P., Berkeley, 143–51.

Lehman, W., 1963, *The Structure of Chin Society,* Illinois Studies in Anthropology, Number 3, Illinois U.P., Urbana.

Mangelsdorf, P., R. MacNeish, and W. Galinat, 1964, "Domestication of Corn," *Science,* 143:538–45.

MacNeish, R., 1964a, "Ancient Mesoamerican Civilization," *Science,* 143:531–37.

——— 1964b, "The Origins of New World Civilization," *Scientific American,* 211:5, 29–37.

Manners, R., 1956, "Tabara: Subculture of a Tobacco and Mixed Crop Municipality," in J. Steward (ed.), *The People of Puerto Rico,* Illinois U.P., Urbana, 93–170.

Marx, K., 1904 (orig. 1859), *The Critique of Political Economy,* I. Stone (trans.), International Library Publication Co., Chicago.

———, and F. Engels, 1957, *Marx and Engels on Religion,* Foreign Languages Publishers, Moscow.

Mason, J., 1966, "Pre-Folsom Estimates of the Ages of Man in America," *American Anthropologist,* 68: 193–96.

Mason, O., 1895, "Influence of Environment upon Human Industries or Arts," *Annual Report of the Smithsonian Institution,* 639–65.

Meggitt, M., 1962, *Desert People; A Study of the Walbiri Aborigines of Central Australia,* Angus and Robertson, Sydney.

Millon, R., 1967, "Teotihuacán," *Scientific American,* 216:38–48.

Mintz, S., "Cañamelar, the Sub-Culture of a Rural Sugar Plantation Proletariat, in J. Steward (ed.), *The People of Puerto Rico,* Illinois U.P., Urbana, 314–17.

Sanders, W., 1965, *The Cultural Ecology of the Teotihuacán Valley,* Unpublished manuscript.

———, and B. Price, 1968, *Mesoamerica: The Evolution of a Civilization,* Random, New York.

Service, E., 1955, "Indian-European Relations in Colonial Latin America," *American Anthropologist,* 57: 411–25.

——— 1962, Primitive Social Organization, Random, New York.

Spinden, H., 1927, "The Prosaic vs. the Romantic School in Anthropology, in E. Smith (ed.), *Culture: The Diffusion Controversy,* Norton, New York, 47–98.

Steward, J., 1936, "The Economic and Social Basis of Primitive Bands," in R. Lowie (ed.), *Essays in Anthropology Presented to A. L. Kroeber,* California U.P., Berkeley, 331–45.

——— 1949a, "The Native Populations of South America," in J. Steward (ed.), *Handbook of the South American Indians,* Bureau of American Ethnology, Bull. 143, Vol. 5:655–88.

——— 1949b, "Cultural Causality and Law; A Trial Formulation of Early Civilization," *American Anthropologist,* 51:1–27.

——— 1955, *Theory of Culture Change,* Illinois U.P., Urbana.

——— 1967, Comment on K. C. Chang, "Major Aspects of the Interrelationship of Archaeology and Ethnology," *Current Anthropology* 8:239–40.

———, and F. Seltzer, 1938, "Function and Configuration in Archaeology," *American Antiquity,* 4:4–10.

Strong, W., W. Schenck, and J. Steward, 1930, "Archaeology of the Dallas-Deschutes Region," *University of California Publications in American Archaeology and Ethnology,* 29:1–154.

Vayda, A., 1956, "Maori Conquests in Relation to the New Zealand Environment," *Journal of the Polynesian Society,* 65:204–11.

——— 1961, "Expansion and Warfare Among Swidden Agriculturalists," *American Anthropologist,* 63:346–58.

Willey, G., 1953, "Archaeological Theories and Interpretation: New World," in A. Kroeber (ed.), *Anthropology Today,* Chicago U.P., 361–85.

Wittfogel, K., 1957, *Oriental Despotism,* Yale U.P., New Haven.

——— 1964, "Ideas and the Power Structure," W. de Bary and A. Embree (eds.), *Approaches to Asian Civilizations,* Columbia U.P., New York, 86–97.

Wolf, E., 1957, "Closed Corporate Peasant Communities in Mesoamerica and Central Java," *Southwestern Journal of Anthropology,* 1–18.

If society and culture provide the means by which all humans meet their most basic needs, then it is the individual's specific sociocultural milieu that determines specifically how he will behave and how his particular personality will gradually be formed. From this essential premise has developed the study of personality and culture, one of the best established subfields in contemporary anthropology; and from it, two further assumptions follow.

First, it is assumed that all people who have shared a similar culturally derived pattern of child-rearing and adolescent experience will grow up to behave quite similarly, so similarly that they can be readily distinguished as a group from other groups whose members have been raised differently. These differences are often so marked that it is possible to refer to the "national character," a shared cluster of specific personality traits that literally characterize an entire population. Second, as it is assumed that sociocultural conditioning plays a major role in the formation of whatever personality type is culturally designated as "normal," it is also contended that societies differ in the relative incidence of particular types of behavioral disorders, presumably as a consequence of the specific kind and intensity of the stress they impose.

Given the attention to the processes of individual personality development that is necessary in this field, LeVine's placement of culture and personality studies in evolutionary perspective is a particularly welcome contribution.

Personality and Culture: Basic Concepts in an Evolutionary Model

Robert A. LeVine

The attempt to construct an evolutionary model of personality-culture relations analogous to those that have proved fruitful in the comparative aspects of population biology was originally based on the assumption that, as in that more advanced field, our subject matter concerns statistical distributions of individual characteristics and the selective operation of environments. Intergenerational transmission of characteristics, selective pressures on individuals and populations, processes of adaptive equilibrium and adaptive change, are additional foci of common concern. The first part of an evolutionary model designed especially for relations between personality and the sociocultural system is presented in this chapter. Initially the focus is on the processes of personality development and socialization, and the basic concepts are personality genotype,[1] personality phenotype, and deliberate socialization.

The Personality Genotype

This refers to a set of enduring individual behavioral dispositions that may or may not find socially acceptable expression in the customary (or institutionalized) behavior of a population. Its major characteristics are early acquisition (through the interaction of constitution and early experience); resistance to elimination in subsequent experience; and capacity for inhibition, generalization, and other transformations under the impact of experiential pressures. It acts as a set of constraints on later learning and on the adaptive flexibility of the individual.

The personality genotype has its origins in certain distinctive features of human ontogeny: an extended period of psychological as well as physical immaturity, in which the environment is mediated by caretakers, and a capacity for acquiring ideational representations of experience from the earliest years of life. The higher-order capacities for logically processing environmental information do not mature, according to Piaget, until the years from seven to eleven. Long before that time the child has acquired a stable psychological organization for regulating tension and adapting to his caretakers. This intellectually primitive organization is subordinated by the higher-order processes that govern adult adaptation but continues as an active substratum of motivation and a reservoir of affective imagery for expressive and creative activities.

Three broad classes of dispositions comprise the personality genotype:

(1) Basic, probably genetically determined, parameters of individual functioning, such as general activity level and thresholds for perceiving, discriminating, and reacting to stimuli (*e.g.*, arousal and irritability thresholds). These dispositions set gross limits on the quantities of behavioral output and stimulus input characteristic of one individual compared with another.

(2) The motivational residues of early experience. The child's representations of his wishes and fears concerning other persons in his early life provide unconscious prototypes for his emotional response to others in subsequent environments. These early social motives, developed by the cognitively immature organism in coping with his interpersonal environment and

Source: Reprinted from Robert A. LeVine, *Culture, Behavior, and Personality* (Chicago: Aldine Publishing Company, 1973); copyright © 1973 by Robert A. LeVine. Reprinted by permission of the author and Aldine Publishing Company.

[1] The terms *phenotype* and *genotype* were introduced into personality psychology by Kurt Lewin (1935) to distinguish the "immediate perceptible appearance" from "the properties that determine the object's dynamic relations" (p. 11). It is in this sense rather than in the biological sense related to genes that the terms are used here. *Genotype* refers to the individual's personality dispositions and their organization . . . ; *phenotype* refers to the consistencies in individual behavior that are accessible to observation by the community and by the investigator making inferences about the underlying dispositions. It should also be noted that I use the word *genetic* to refer to the action and transmission of the genes in the biological sense, rather than using it as psychoanalysts do to mean "developmental" or "pertaining to ontogeny." (They use *genic* in referring to the biological genes and their action.)

inner needs, become stabilized long before they are integrated into a mature adaptive organization, and they continue as influences on adult behavior. In their original emotional intensity, these wishes and fears must be defended against to maintain the child's sense of well-being, and these primitive defensive resolutions are experienced in adulthood as deeply felt preferences and aversions.

(3) Adaptive organizations that monitor and regulate responses to stimuli coming from the external environment and from internal needs. These include a basic perceptual organization (*e.g.*, self-other differentiation, reality-testing), a drive organization (*e.g.*, capacities for stable affective responses to human objects including the self), and the functions of information processing (perceptual discrimination, memory, thinking, learning), control (*e.g.*, delay of gratification, moral restraints), and synthesis (ability to mediate between drives, controls, and environmental demands).

The personality genotype is complexly formed but has at least the following sources: genetic constitution; patterns of stimulation, gratification, frustration, and attachment to caretakers in infancy; patterns of childhood separation (temporary and permanent) and perceptions of threatened separation from love objects causing fear and hatred of others in the immediate environment and giving rise to intrapsychic conflicts, their representations in unconscious fantasies, defenses against the conflicts, and identifications with objects perceived as lost; traumatic experiences—the influx of greater stimulation than the child can master, causing developmental arrest or regression and the subsequent formation of a repressed motivational complex.

These influences act to form the personality genotype as an organization of motives, cognitions, and adaptive habits during the first five or six years of life, but many of their separate effects are manifested in infancy and early childhood as individual differences in activity or passivity, irritability, dependence, hostility, sociability, inhibitions, imitativeness, masculinity-femininity, and other observable (phenotypic) behaviors. Determinants acting earlier form constraints on subsequent development. For example, genetic differences in perceptual thresholds may determine whether a given amount of stimulation will be traumatic. In like manner, if we assume that self-other differentiation and capacity for delay of gratification, in their most developed forms, are contingent on optimal frustration during a critical period of infancy, then it follows that infants who do not experience optimal frustration at that time will develop defects in cognitive and control functions that will affect the way they perceive and experience separation and potential traumata during childhood. A proper understanding of the development of the personality genotype would include a telescoping series of developmental constraints as one form (among many) of interaction between innate and environmental, and earlier and later, determinants. In its final form the personality genotype is itself an organized set of constraints on the later development of the individual.

These sources of the personality genotype are, with the exception of genetic constitution, social stimuli impinging on the infant and child and are parts of larger patterns of social interaction that are in turn aspects of social structure. The events in infant care and child life that lead to attachments, aversions, separations, traumata, and their complex psychological residues can be seen as outgrowths of social structure and therefore as varying concomitantly with structural variations among populations. For example, the number of nuclear families sharing a courtyard and cooperating in domestic tasks may determine the likelihood of multiple mothering of infants. The presence, absence, or frequency of polygyny and its associated rules of husband-wife relations may determine the time interval between births and therefore the average age at which children experience the birth of the next sibling. The clustering or dispersal of residences in local communities, and the density of settlement, may determine the availability of children from outside the family as playmates. The degree of mother's participation in occupational roles such as cultivator and trader may determine the amount of time she has available to attend to her children and the likelihood of her using supplementary caretakers. The marriage pattern, particularly the frequency of stable unions, may determine the number of households in which fathers are available as objects for love, hate, and identification; and the rate of divorce or conjugal separation may determine the number of children who become separated from one or both parents. In these (and many other) cases, abrupt or recurrent events having an impact on the child's experience, and consequently on his personality development, are unplanned and usually unconscious byproducts of variations in the structure of family, community, and occupation.

The relations between social structure and typical patterns of childhood experience pose two important problems: Are such relations accidental, evolved through an adaptive variation-selection process, or the product of purposive social policy? Do they reduce variation among the personality genotypes of a population?

In dealing with the first of these problems we return briefly to the question of consciousness and purpose discussed in the preceding chapter. At the most superficial level, an answer is easy. Adults respond to the coercive pressures of their social and economic environment—for example, the need to grow food or find a job in the face of potential scarcity, the need to cluster and cooperate for mutual defense against invaders—and they create living arrangements designed first and foremost to solve these practical problems of survival. Child rearing must be adjusted accordingly, fitted into a pattern of family and community life already fashioned for other purposes. From this point of view the resultant patterns of childhood experience are accidental consequences of socio-economic adaptation. But there are limits inherent in the raising of children: Each generation must survive the high mortality period of infancy and early childhood characteristic of most human populations until recently (and of many today), and they must be capable of carrying on basic subsistence tasks as their elders decline in vigor. If these conditions are not met the population will not survive, no matter how successful their mode of production or defense.

It seems altogether plausible that some populations have at times reacted to ecological shifts with new structural arrangements that failed to meet these conditions—for example, an organization of work in which infants and children were neglected physically and emotionally, with a consequent rise in infant mortality and decline in the educability of children for their occupational roles. There would then have to be a modification in the new structure to allow better child care, or the population would be threatened with demographic and economic collapse and eventually disappear or become absorbed into neighboring populations that had better adapted child-care practices. In other words, selection would operate, across both historical and interpopulation variation, to eliminate structural variants incompatible with the basic conditions for child care and to propagate structural variants that do meet those conditions. If this has indeed happened in human history, we would be justified in stating that customary patterns of childhood experience are not entirely accidental byproducts of social structure but have adaptively evolved through haphazard variation and selective retention. To put it more accurately, limits on the impact of social structure on childhood experience have probably been evolved through variation-selection. Within these broad limits, so long as structural arrangements do not endanger the survival or occupational trainability of children, social structures are free to vary in accordance with ecological demands and to alter the shape of childhood experience in a nonpurposive way.

A further qualification on the proposition that childhood experience is an accidental byproduct of social structure is required for those populations in which the basic conditions of infant and child care are self-consciously planned to achieve developmental goals dictated by a general ideology. The analogy with eugenics is apposite here, for eugenicists desire central and selective control over what is normally a rather haphazard process. Societies that have consciously organized the social experience of the infant and child in accordance with ideological goals are not so hard to find as those that have adopted eugenic policies, but they are the exceptions that prove the rule. The rule, the normal state of affairs in most human societies, is that infant and child care is conducted in multi-functional social units (such as the family) by persons having other tasks and responsibilities, so that child rearing takes place in a social context largely established for other purposes. Although for ideological reasons, mothers in some societies more than their counterparts elsewhere may seek to stimulate, gratify or frustrate their infants and children, no more than a fraction of the significant social-emotional experience in early life can be attributed to purposive manipulation. Present evidence does not allow us to say with any certainty how influential this fraction may be in personality development. What we can say, however, is that the effects of early influences on the complex structure of motives, cognitive patterns, and capacities, here called the personality genotype, are still so imperfectly known, even by scientific investigators of child development, that manipulative intent on the part of parents is no guarantee of success.

It is inherently difficult to discover what the preverbal child perceives and experiences and what parts of his environment are particularly significant to him, and this lack of feedback reduces the advantage that deliberate manipulation of early environment has over unconsciously evolved practices in achieving long-range developmental goals. (In this regard, the emphasis put on the early development of speech in the child by modern parents, with their consciously manipulative intent, should be especially noted.) Thus, though populations vary widely in the extent to which they aspire to manipulate the preverbal environment of the child, and though sociocultural evolution seems to have set limits on the range of child-rearing possibilities, the social-structural sources of influence on development of the personality genotype are predominantly unplanned consequences of small group interaction patterns. Parents, in their social roles (as husband, wife, kinsman, producer, consumer, etc.) and social behavior, are unwittingly generating an environment that profoundly affects the emotional development of their children.

The other question posed by relations between social structure and childhood experience is whether the structural determination of childhood environments tends to homogenize the early experiences that form personality genotypes in a population. In general, social structure operates to make social behavior more uniform. When an aspect of behavior comes under normative regulation, it may no longer be varied freely without being stigmatized as deviant and punished by social sanctions. In the absence of normative regulation of family life, characteristics such as legitimized marriage, divorce, polygyny, birth spacing, father absence, might be randomly distributed. The fact is they are not randomly distributed; there are sharp discontinuities among human populations in norms of marriage and family life, and the frequency distribution curves for relevant behavioral characteristics are distinctly different in different populations. Most frequently, such curves are either J-curves in which a large majority conform to a norm (*e.g.*, legitimized marriage among middle-class Americans) or bell-shaped curves in which variation is normally distributed around a population mean that represents a normative ideal (*e.g.*, family size among middle-class Americans). There may be no variation among population members in their recognition of a normative ideal, but there is always variation in the incidence of actual social behavior patterns. Thus, in a population universally regarding polygynous marriage as ideal, there will be some men who remain monogamists because of poverty, causing variation in the social experience of their children. Conformity to social norms does not in practice mean uniformity of childhood social environment.

The timing of structurally patterned events in a family also creates variations in childhood experience. For example, the oldest children in a polygynous family may spend their first few years of life in a monogamous unit, whereas those born after their father has several wives are exposed to a very different environment. The developmental cycle through which domestic groups pass in many societies (see Goody, 1958, and Gray and Gulliver, 1964) diversifies the experience of children in the "same" family. A population may have a high divorce rate, but any particular divorce, occurring at a different point in the life of each of the several children of the union, is likely to affect them differently. Potentially traumatic events and separations, though caused by widespread patterns of family structure, are likely to have different effects even on children in the same family. Environmental differences among siblings is even greater where norms select first or last children (or sons) for special treatment, as in primogeniture or the practice of keeping the last child home. When we consider the preexisting genetic variations among siblings with which these environmental variables interact, we can see that the number of combinations and permutations among factors influencing the personality genotype is very great indeed. Structural determinants narrow the range of variation but they do not eliminate it. Thus, we might expect a given trauma or separation experience to be more "characteristic" of (more frequent in) one population than another but not uniform within it.

In sum, the personality genotype is an enduring organization of drives, cognitions, and adaptive capacities; is formed early in life; varies widely among individuals and (in frequency and central tendency) between populations; and acts as a series of constraints on later development and learning. Many of the formative influences on the personality genotype can be seen as indirect outcomes or byproducts of social structure, to which certain survival-oriented limits have probably evolved, and which necessarily narrow the range of genotypic dispositions in a population sharing a social-structural environment. Nevertheless, these formative influences are in most societies sufficiently variable in their impact on individual experience and sufficiently free of manipulative intent to be considered unplanned and nonnormative sources of personality variation.

The dispositions comprising the personality genotype are by definition latent and do not always find socially acceptable expression. It is as generalizable constraints on later learning and performance that their influence is manifested. The constraints stemming from the drive residues of infancy and childhood (as shaped by patterns of stimulation, attachment, and separation) act as internal motivational pressures for gratification, provide a symbolic interpretation of later social experience, and give direction and content to free choice behavior (as in interpersonal relations and fantasy). The constraints resulting from early ego development act as limits on the complexity and intensity of stimuli (external and internal) to which the individual can respond effectively and, therefore, constitute thresholds of perceptual discrimination and stress tolerance.

The Personality Phenotype

This refers to the observable regularities of behavior characterizing an adult functioning in the variety of settings comprising his environment. The personality phenotype of an individual includes his patterns of performance in social roles, in formal and informal settings, in interaction and alone, in coercive and free-choice situations, under stressful and relaxed conditions, in verbalization and actual behavior. It includes his conscious attitudes and values, his skills, competence and knowledge, and his preferences and tastes in recreational and hedonistic activities. If the individual is functioning normally, his phenotypic personality is a stable organization of characteristics that affords him satisfaction of his perceived needs, enables him to meet social demands and take advantage of sociocultural opportunities, and protects him from excessive anxiety.

The phenotype is not independent of the genotype; in a sense, it *is* the personality genotype modified by prolonged normative experience, through the deliberate socialization by parents and through direct participation in the wider social system. The phenotypic personality develops within the constraints of the genotype and, when formed, allows the unconscious motivational components of the latter normatively regulated expression in overt behavior. The most noticeable expressions in phenotypic behavior are idiosyncratic mannerisms, inhibitions, and other facets of distinctive behavioral style. These character traits, as they are called by psychoanalysts, are fixed stabilized expressions of defenses against unconscious impulses, and they frequently incorporate into their content some of the original impulse that is being defended against.

We are aware of the unconscious motivation of character traits when they are idiosyncratic and approach the limits of social acceptability, but we are generally incapable of seeing them in members of our own population when the behavior patterns involved are very common and completely acceptable. It takes a foreigner to point out to us the arbitrary, irrational, and perhaps compulsive quality of the behavior and make us realize that what we had seen as "natural," "normal," "rational," or "adaptive," because of its familiarity and normative acceptability, might be as unconscious in origin and defensive in function as an idiosyncratic mannerism. (For a general discussion of the "phenomenal absolutism" underlying cultural-bound perception, see Segall *et al.*, 1966; for the use of outsiders' judgments in group personality assessment, see LeVine, 1966b.) It is not only idiosyncratic character traits that are defensive expressions of genotypic conflicts but also character traits widespread in the population; this is what Fromm (1941) and others have referred to as "social character." In the present perspective, social character refers to all character traits positively valued and relatively frequent in a population, and includes nondefensive (conflict-free) dispositions of the personality genotype that become enduring features of social behavior.

One of the most important integrating characteristics of the personality phenotype is a self-concept, an internal mental representation of the self that includes boundaries between, and identities with, the self and other individuals, groups, and ideologies. In his functioning as a member of society, the individual uses this enduring self-concept to monitor his own behavior and to determine the extent to which each of his behavior patterns is ego-syntonic, that is, consistent with his image of himself. This self-concept, having been produced in part through normative social experience, represents social norms as its selects among possible behaviors (in a manner analogous to other forms of variation and selection) those that are consistent with the socially acceptable image the individual wants to present to the world. In the category of unacceptable are behaviors seen as immoral, impolite, childish, stupid, crazy (or their nearest equivalents in other cultures); these are viewed as ego-dystonic, except under especially permissive conditions, and are eliminated in favor of more acceptable behaviors. When the individual loses the capacity to suppress certain behavior that he himself regards as unacceptable in one of those senses, when he is unable to keep his behavior ego-syntonic, he develops a neurotic symptom. When he alters his self-concept to include the defensive contents of a neurotic symptom (e.g., develops a rationalized inhibition out of a phobia), he has developed a neurotic character trait.

The distinction between genotypic and phenotypic personality contains elements of familiar behavioral science polarities—unconscious versus conscious, latent versus manifest, subjective versus objective, general versus specialized—but two other elements require further emphasis. First, the phenotypic personality is responsive to contemporaneous environmental pressures—in the form of real, threatened, or promised social rewards, punishments, incentives—whereas the genotype is the relatively unchanging "internal environment" of the personality, responsive only to its own past, and can be used for or against adaptation without altering its direction and content. In their phenotypic expression, genotypic dispositions may be suppressed and disguised for purposes of social adaptation and conformity but are not thereby eliminated.

Second, the personality genotype is inherently more variable and heterogeneous in a population than the phenotype; the former reflects individual constitution and experience, whereas the latter reflects the normative consensus of society. Insofar as populations have intact functioning social structures, there must be such a consensus represented in the phenotypic personalities of its members, no matter how diverse their underlying genotypic dispositions. In measuring these dispositions, the closer the investigator comes to what is explicitly prescribed by norms, the more agreement and homogeneity he finds in a population, whereas the closer he comes to normatively permissive areas of behavior—in which "free," (genotypically expressive) choice is possible—the more heterogeneity of response within the population. This has been less clear than it might be because terms such as *values* have been used to cover dispositions varying widely in their degree of normative prescriptiveness; hence some (usually sociological) investigators, measuring individuals' perceptions or expectations of norms, find populations homogenous on values, while other (usually psychological) investigators, measuring personal interests and tastes, find a heterogeneity of values. It is in the nature of genotype-phenotype relations, as conceptualized here, that the former will be more variable than the latter unless a radical breakdown in social consensus has occurred.

Deliberate Socialization

This refers to the intentions and actions of the parents (or substitutes) in training the child. In this process there are several factors: the child and his presocialized behavior, the goals of the parents, the means they use to achieve their goals, and the consequences of applying these means.

The argument can be anticipated briefly as follows: Parents use reward, punishment, and instruction to shape the child's behavior, already genotypically influenced, in the direction of social norms; the typical result is a phenotypic personality involving both preparedness for adaptation to the adult environment and unsatisfied needs stemming from conflicts between personality genotype and normative demands. The model of training is that of behavioristic response-reinforcement theory, with the added assumptions that the major formative influences on the child's personality are ordinarily outside parental control and have acted before deliberate parental training and that parental reinforcement schedules, whether effective or not, have unintended motivational consequences of great importance for personality-culture interaction.

The Child. No matter how early parents begin deliberate training, they find neither a *tabula rasa* nor a passive receiving instrument in their child. Even the infant is an active organism, striving and exploring within the constraints of his constitutional dispositions and developmental immaturity. Parental training must deal with the child's unprovoked behavioral output, and it must be geared to his perceptual thresholds and his tolerance limits for particular types of stimulation. Some active infants seem intractable to their parents; others are resistant to manipulation in more passive ways, and parents may find the difficulties so great that they postpone training to a later age. With the exception of the most consciously manipulative and ideologized parents, most parents in most societies postpone the first onset of serious behavioral manipulation until the child can talk, and they begin more intensive training in useful skills when the child has "sense," usually at about five or six years of age. (In some societies there are clear-cut phases of this type, while in others the intensity of training is gradually increased.)

The child's behavioral development goes on regardless of whether anyone is attempting to manipulate it and to produce desirable habits. Maturational processes make new forms of behavior possible; and the child is continuously interacting with his environment, experiencing gratification and frustration, suffering trauma and separation, acquiring attachments and avoidances, observing the behavior of others, spontaneously imitating what he sees, developing pleasant and frightening fantasies and increasingly differentiated patterns of thought and action. Anyone who has observed two- and three-year-old children in a society where socialization in any serious purposive sense begins later than that, has seen behavior patterns of personal and cultural distinctiveness, obvious precursors of adult behavioral styles. These are early phenotypic expressions of the personality genotype, preceding the onset of manipulative training. Whenever the parent begins deliberate training of his child, be it at two or six years of age, he confronts not a completely unformed mass of clay ready to be shaped, but a set of genotypic dispositions that already give the child's behavior shape and purpose of its own not necessarily consistent with the parents' purposes. The parent, unlike the animal experimenter, cannot dispose of his subject and obtain a more tractable one; he must render the child tractable and amenable to training by persistent effort, by increasing reward and punishment as seems necessary, and by finding within the child dispositional allies that can be harnessed to the parent's goals. The personality genotype of the child sets the stage for impending conflict in the socialization process. And since each child in a family has a different personality genotype, each poses for its parents a different set of training problems.

Parental Goals. The parent (assisted by other socializing agents and agencies) has the task of directing the behavioral (phenotypic) development of the child toward normative socially valued goals. Insofar as he performs this task, the parent is acting as a feedback mechanism, the mediator of environmental information to his child, implicitly communicating messages about discrepancies between the child's current behavior and environmental norms of behavior as he attempts to eliminate those discrepancies through training. More immediately, however, the parent's training program is determined by his phenomenal field, a field in which environmental information is only one of several forces and may be muted in its effect on parental behavior.

The phenomenal field of the parent is his view of the child-training situation as influenced by factors internal and external to that situation. In such a field of forces, a number of determinants contribute (positively and negatively) to a few resultant outcomes. The outcomes in this case are decisions concerning child training; the determinants are all the sources of pressure, constraint, belief, and value that influence his training decisions. Some of these sources are in the parent's personality; some are in the social system in which he participates; and some are in the behavior of the child with whom he interacts. Research into parental phenomenal fields has been fragmentary and incomplete so that we do not have a clear picture of how the diverse forces combine, or what their valences are, or how they are assigned valences that account for their relative contributions to the resultant decisions. We do have some idea of the range of forces involved. Brim (1959) has referred to this complexity:

> With respect to the six causes of parent behavior considered here, one recognizes that the individual operates or behaves in his parent role as part of a social system. The parent engages in behavior vis-a-vis the child in interaction situations which are reg-

ulated by social norms or rules as to what is appropriate and inappropriate. As an individual, the parent is also restricted by repressed and unconscious motives which work to determine his behavior in parent role performance in ways unknown to him. Moreover, the pressures of time and the demands of the conflicting social situations involved in a large family as well as restrictions placed upon behavior by the absence of certain economic goods, whether these be living space, the absence of toys, or more generally, the simple absence of money, all work to limit the rational and self-controlled performance of the role (p. 55).

Some of the influences on child-training decisions are enduring parameters of the parent's personality: his intelligence, his internalized moral and social values (reflecting in part normative information from the environment in which he grew up); his preferences, sensitivities, and aversions derived from unconscious genotypic dispositions. Other influences originate in relatively permanent aspects of his life situation: concepts of competence based on his occupational experience, concepts of his social and economic environment based on the breadth of his experience (including travel), the structure of housing and settlement in which he is raising his child, and traditional folk beliefs concerning child training. Still other influences are long-term but recurrent pressures generated by the life situation: work fatigue, marital adjustment, other family relationships. Then there are influences that change with the development of the family, including the number of other children and their ages, the parent's experience as a trainer of children, and the generalizations he has drawn from observing the effects of previous child training. Finally, there are the immediate, but not necessarily recurrent or developmental, pressures such as short-run economic necessity, which may give one parent less time to spend with the child or make the child's early occupational maturity seem more important, current child-care fashions, and other potentially relevant persuasive communications to which the parent is exposed (*e.g.*, through the mass media). All of these interact with the child as perceived by the parent, who may attempt to tailor his training program to what he sees as this particular child's individual characteristics. The complexity of this interaction can be illustrated by the case of the parent whose first male child, being particularly demanding, reactivates in the parent jealousy from his own early experience with a younger brother, and who therefore is particularly punitive in training this child, affecting the entire training process with this inappropriate emotion.

These influences on the parent's definition of the child-training situation operate, as Brim suggests, to limit his role as a simple mediator of environmental norms; they act as a filter through which environmental information must pass if it is to affect the training of the child. The parent lacking in the ability to think abstractly may see no connection between environmental events and his child's behavior; the ignorant or provincial parent may be simply unaware of the broader environmental context of his life; the parent engaged in marital conflict may not pay attention to external events and norms; the parent dominated by unconscious wishes and fears may misperceive environmental cues or inaccurately transform them into child-training practices. If a parent is under intense pressure to adjust to difficult domestic or economic conditions, these may come to dominate his thinking to such an extent that he thinks only of his child's adaptation to similar conditions, neglecting other goals. The parent, then, is often not a smoothly operating child-preparation machine.

Given so many possibilities for faulty transmission between adult performance criteria and child-training goals, one might wonder how parents are able to perform this function at all. They are able to do so in relatively stable societies because the more enduring influences on their phenomenal fields are not independent of contemporaneous environmental information concerning future adaptation of their child; the parents' internalized values and life experience and their current life pressures approximate the child's future environment well enough to act as adaptive guides to training even in the absence of accurate and conscious parental transmission of environmental information, and child training is thus overdetermined. In rapidly changing societies or immigration situations, however, discontinuities between past, present, and future environments force parents to attune themselves to the environment and seek from it novel information about adult performance criteria or see their children suffer the effects of serious maladaptation as adults (see Inkeles, 1955; Miller and Swanson, 1958). It should be no surprise, then, that rapidly changing societies provide our best examples of parents attempting to rationalize their child training in terms of feedback from the environment, as well as our most familiar instances of maladaptation, for example among rural immigrants to the city who fail to change their child-training goals rapidly enough to provide their children the competence they need for economic viability and mobility in urban industrial society (see Inkeles, 1966a).

Despite the complex determination of parental phenomenal fields and the equally complex variations in the filtration they provide for environmental information, the theoretical model of parental mediation is a simple one. Parents want their children to be able to meet societal demands and to take advantage of the opportunities for personal success or fulfillment (social, economic, political) that the sociocultural environment offers. These are their most general training objectives. To attain them, the parents must anticipate what demands and opportunities the child will face in adulthood, through generalization of their own direct and vicarious experience as participant observers in a sociocultural system approximating that of the future adult, or through a conscious search for new information about social norms and payoffs, or both. This information about the normative environment as the parent sees it gives him a view of what he is preparing the child for, and can be translated into criteria for evaluating behavior patterns manifested by the child. Although there can be a good deal of slippage between the objective sociocultural environment and evaluative decisions made by the parent, parental mediation is at least theoretically self-correcting in that, in situations where the parent's own past experience is not an adequate guide for the child, the social payoffs for adaptation and penalties for maladaptation increase in value and hence in salience for parents, increasing the pressure on them to notice discrepancies between their children's behavior and societal norms.

One set of conclusions the parent draws from participant observation in his normative environment concerns the kinds of personality traits and types that lead to respectable, righteous, and pragmatically successful adult behavior. He sees persons varying in personality characteristics receive varying amounts of endorsement or resistance from the sociocultural system, and he aggregates these instances and arrives at inductive generalizations concerning personality ideals that, if compatible with other parts of his cognitive structure, will act as a guide to the qualities he will attempt to reinforce and eliminate in his child.

Parental Means. To give normative shape to the child's behavior, the parent has a number of means at his disposal. First is his power to reward and punish the child, based not only on control of resources seen by the child as necessary or desirable to his welfare but also on the child's emotional attachment to and dependence on the parent. No less important is his knowledge of adaptive skills in which to instruct the willing child. Since the parent, especially in the more differentiated societies, does not himself command all the skills he wants his child to learn, he delegates part of the training task to specialists—as tutors, and in schools and institutionalized apprenticeships. Although he certainly uses reinforcement procedures himself, the parent is not simply an administrator of rewards and punishments but an executive of sorts, making decisions about what kind of training is needed, who should give it to the child, and what level of performance the child should reach.

The role of verbal and behavioral feedback is critical in distinguishing the processes of deliberate socialization from the unplanned acquisition of behavioral dispositions through early experience. In deliberate socialization, the parent is specific enough in his goals and the child developed enough in his responses that it is possible for the trainer to gauge his immediate success or failure in attaining a training goal and then modify the quantity or quality of his reinforcement accordingly. The feedback permits establishment of a self-correcting system of training, with parental training being varied in response to the child's performance until the desired performance is achieved, a highly efficient way of shaping behavior. As mentioned before, parents who seek to extend purposive manipulation into the early life of the child are particularly concerned that their children acquire language skills as early as possible so that they can obtain verbal feedback as to the effectiveness of their training procedures. But feedback from nonverbal behavior also enables the parent to adjust his training to the child's performance and improves his ability to obtain desired results. Feedback is also essential in parental decisions concerning nonparental training: a parent who sees his child doing badly in school may decide that special tutoring is required to insure the child's admission to a higher school later on. The ultimate in self-regulation is achieved if the child acts on the basis of his own feedback to correct his mistakes and improve his performance, which children do when they have internalized adult standards of performance.

Through these conditioning processes the child acquires a range of adaptive skills that, along with earlier patterns of social behavior, become habitualized in a normative direction. It must be emphasized, however, that deliberate socialization operates predominantly on overt behavior, on the behavioral phenotype, and modifies only the overt expressions of the personality genotype—suppressing some genotypic tendencies, permitting restricted expression of others, disguising some for socially sanctioned behavior, and using others for adaptive purposes. The resultant character structure is thus based on but not reducible to the personality genotype that, in the process of deliberate socialization, has its first but far from last encounter with the normative pressures of the sociocultural environment.

Consequences. Socialization has intended and unintended products. Its intended products are skills and inhibitions, skills for adaptive performance, inhibitions of genotypic tendencies incompatible with normative demands. Unintended products include the various motivational side-effects of suppressing or attenuating genotypic tendencies.

The cross-cultural evidence taken as a whole indicates how extremely effective deliberate socialization is in producing adaptive skills in growing individuals. At the level of skills related to subsistence activity and dominant cultural values, the old idea that "culture" can turn the child into anything "it" wants seems to receive strong support: In groups to whom waterways are importantly involved in subsistence, children learn to swim early and well (Mead, 1930); in some agricultural groups, six-year-old children can cultivate fields (LeVine & LeVine, 1966); children of political elites learn respect behavior when they are tiny (Read, 1959). The evidence concerning the acquisition of skills in children so strongly suggests their great malleability that it is virtually taken for granted that if pressures are exerted in a given aspect of training, the majority of children in a population will comply even if the tasks are complex.

The matter of inhibitions is more complex. At one level, this type of socialization is highly effective, too, in producing compliance with social constraints. There is little question that if enough negative pressure is brought to bear in the socialization process, highly motivated behaviors such as sexuality and aggression can be suppressed so thoroughly in most of the population that they seem almost nonexistent to the casual observer. But suppression is not elimination, and while phenotypic expressions can be brought into line even with strict cultural prohibitions, the underlying genotypic dispositions, both motivational and cognitive, cannot be "extinguished." Indeed, Whiting and Child (1953) have argued that the inhibition of a motive through socialization actually increases its strength, although altering its direction in favor of objects dissimilar to those that were culturally prohibited (displacement).

The impossibility of eliminating common genotypic motives through socialization of the child is frequently encountered in studies of particular cultures. For example, in my own work (LeVine, 1959) I found that the Gusii, although known among the peoples of Western Kenya for their sexual prudishness, and although maintaining strict sexual prohibitions in many areas of life, had a very high frequency of rape by local and cross-cultural standards. Gusii socialization of sex, being strict and repressive concerning public manifestations of sexuality but relatively permissive concerning sexual feelings and clandestine sexual acts, was predicated on the existence of enforcement procedures (inter-clan feuding) that had broken down during British colonial administration. At the time of my field work, the strict sex-training practices, although still effective in maintaining conformity to intra-clan prohibitions, did nothing to prevent inter-clan sex offenses and could even be seen as promoting rape by raising the average level of male sexual frustration and making females resistant to heterosexual advances. Hence the paradox of an ethnic group notorious for both its prudery and its sex crimes. Whiting *et al.* (1966) present another example in the case of the Zuni Indians, whose well known emphasis on harmony and peaceful solidarity is belied by their intense and frequent malicious intrigues over witchcraft. The authors argue that the strict socialization of aggression in Zuni children is necessitated by the crowded housing conditions in which they are raised but that their aggressive motivations find an outlet in witchcraft beliefs and clandestine intrigues.

In both these instances, socialization of the child brings about overt conformity to prohibitive standards in one arena of social life but leads to unintended consequences based on the suppressed genotypic dispositions in other arenas. The social system "pays" for social control in visible primary group relations with a certain amount of disruption and strain behind the scenes or beyond the confines of the primary group. This social "cost" factor appears to be present wherever social norms require suppression of motives in the socialization of the child. Parents are then put in the position of unwittingly fostering deviant behavior as they consciously attempt to build into their children the inhibitions that will enable them to conform to institutional demands, although quite possibly institutional functioning gains more from the conformity than it loses in the deviant behavior; an evolutionary model would require this for a stable system. Where socialization of the child's impulse life is so thorough that he becomes a self-policing individual, it may be, as Freud proposed, that the cost is paid not by the social system but by the individual, who turns his socially unacceptable impulses against himself and suffers self-punishment, painful neurotic symptoms, and crippling inhibitions. This situation may be optimal for institutional functioning, unless the incidence of psychopathology and discontent becomes so great as to exact its own toll from the social system.

Thus adaptation of the individual to his sociocultural environment begins in the process of child socialization but is not successfully completed there, partly because the parent is an imperfect mediator of environmental pressures and often cannot anticipate them accurately, and partly because deliberate socialization can have unintended consequences that are maladaptive. This means that adaptation must be a continuing process in adult life, although many of the basic patterns of adaptive behavior are established in the training of the child. But there are, as we have seen, limits to the modification of individual behavior in the interests of adaptation to institutional environment, limits stemming from the personality genotype as a highly resistant organization of motives and cognitive dispositions. The genotypic tendencies can be suppressed, disguised, and diverted, but they are hardly ever eliminated in socialization through the life cycle. They seek expression in overt behavior, and no social system is so prescriptive and coercive as to prevent such expressions; there are always loopholes in normative prescriptions for role performance, areas for choice, and alternative possibilities. Therefore, the sociocultural environment must bend at points before these inflexibilities of the personality system, and adaptation is achieved through compromise. Institutionalized forms of adaptation between personality and sociocultural systems can be seen as compromise formations in which constraints and demands of both the personality genotype and the normative environment are represented. They have evolved from the interaction of environmental and genotypic pressures operating over time. Although movement is toward a steady state in which the more pressing demands of both sides are adequately satisfied, many particular institutionalized adaptations are "bad" compromises, in which one side or another is overrepresented. The forms of institutionalized adaptation and the processes of stability and change constitute the second part of this evolutionary model and are presented in the next two chapters.

Conclusions. On the basis of this first part of an evolutionary model of culture-personality relations, it is possible to locate those points at which processes analogous to the Darwinian mechanisms of variation and selection seem to be operating and to identify relevant problems for empirical research.

1. *The adaptation of early child-care customs to ecological pressures.* Since infants must survive a period of high mortality and acquire basic adaptive skills for a population to survive, it is reasonable to assume that the infant-care customs of stable or growing populations are a product of an evolutionary process in which poorly adapted populations failed to survive, were absorbed into better adapted populations, or radically changed their customs of infant care. This process requires evolving limits on the extent to which the structure of primary groups in which children are raised can be altered in accordance with the requirements of the wider

social structure. It may be, however, that this process makes more positive contributions to personality-environment adaptation. For example, Nimkoff and Middleton (1960) have shown that families in hunting and gathering societies are smaller than in agricultural societies, and we know from studies within our own culture (see Clausen, 1966) that smaller families produce children different in certain behavioral dimensions (*e.g.*, higher on achievement even with social class held constant). This accords with the finding of Barry, Child, and Bacon (1959) that parents in hunting and gathering societies emphasize self-reliance and achievement in child training, but it does not necessarily support their assumption that it is the deliberate socialization of the parents that produces requisite amounts of these dispositions in their children to maintain the subsistence economy.

Could it be that children raised in small families have early experiences that equip them with genotypic dispositions making them easier to train in self-reliance and achievement? That this greater potential for self-reliance and achievement helped give small families a selective advantage in hunting and gathering groups? Or perhaps more reasonably, could it be that the greater potential for obedience and responsibility of children raised in large families contributed to the selective advantage of large domestic groups once the food-producing revolution had occurred? These are difficult problems to study, but they raise the possibility that the structure of the primary groups in which children are raised may be more tightly adapted to ecological pressures than is readily apparent, with the personality outcome of early primary group experience being a factor in the evolution of more adaptive forms. Although the mechanisms involved are far from clear, this type of evolutionary conceptualization, closer to the original Darwinian model, is a challenging source of rival hypotheses for theorists who tend to assign to conscious parental mediation and deliberate socialization the central roles in child rearing.

2. *The initial adaptation of genotypically varying personalities to normative pressures through deliberate socialization.* In this process, the distribution of personality genotypes provides the unplanned variation, and the parent's values and decisions concerning child training constitute the selective criteria. The variation-selection model fits at the level of the population, in which normatively agreeing parents act selectively on the randomly varying personality genotypes of their children, and at the level of the parent-child dyad, in which the child's behavioral output, at first haphazardly compatible and incompatible with parental goals, is shaped toward greater compatibility by the differential reinforcement of the parent. To a degree not adequately documented and undoubtedly variable cross culturally, the parent acts as an agent of society and in response to its changing norms, so that child training helps prepare the child for future normative environments. This preparation cannot be completed in childhood because child training cannot anticipate in all their specificity the micro- and macroenvironments to which the future adult will adapt. So this is initial adaptation, in which the child develops some skills and inhibitory controls that will facilitate his subsequent adaptive behavior.

3. *The secondary adaptations of individual personality to normative environments through selective social behavior.* This has to do with differing genotype-phenotype relations within the personality of the individual as he occupies differing normative environments (including social roles) successively or simultaneously. The personality genotype is a continual source of impulses, wishes, and ideas that constitute unplanned variation from the viewpoint of performance in social roles. The individual has in the normatively shaped self-image that is central to his phenotypic social character a set of criteria for selecting among these genotypic impulses. Furthermore, each role or other ecological niche he occupies provides its own criteria for evaluating and administering rewards and punishments for behavior of varying degrees of compatibility with his genotypic dispositions. Operating within the limits set by his own (perhaps temporarily) stabilized self-image, he responds to the demand characteristics of the micro-environment, experiencing or anticipating reward and punishment for genotypically derived behaviors until some of the underlying dispositions are selected for expression in overt behavior, others for suppression, displacement, or disguise, in a stabilized adaptation to the niche. On a similarly experimental basis he selectively regulates the amount and kind of genotypic expression in the various environmental

niches that comprise his life situation, until a total life adaptation is reached. If he moves from one role or status position to another or otherwise alters his life situation, the selective process will be repeated.

4. *The adaptation of aggregate personality characteristics of populations to normative environments through the selective pressure of social sanctions.* This refers to the means by which the frequency distributions of phenotypic character traits in a population come to fit the society-wide normative ideals of role performance, or at least to be skewed in that direction, compared to societies with other normative ideals. The details of this . . . can be dealt with only briefly here. Phenotypic character traits, although normatively influenced and shaped, are still highly variable in a population because they are embedded in different personality structures, with varying genotypic capacities for approximating ideal role performance. Some persons have genotypic personality traits that are favored by the normative environment in which they function; in consequence they manifest greater talent, skill, and fluency in role performance, are able to take greater advantage of opportunities, and achieve greater success and other social rewards. Other persons, though able to acquire normatively sanctioned character traits through socialization and subsequent secondary adaptation, have a harder time conforming and performing in roles because their genotypic dispositions are less compatible with environmental demands and opportunities; in consequence they do not manifest excellence in role performance, are less able to gain success and social rewards, and are more likely to engage in deviant behavior and incur negative sanctions. This variation in social competence (see Inkeles, 1966a) is constantly being acted upon by social sanctions, with the effect of differentially distributing social rewards and punishments (*e.g.*, success and failure, upward and downward mobility, honor and stigma, prestige and disgrace) in accordance with demonstrated levels of competence on a more or less permanent basis.

In addition, the operation of this selective procedure is highly visible to actors in the social system, particularly in societies in which status mobility is possible, so that knowledge of which character traits are associated with competence becomes widespread and affects the deliberate socialization of children. There is thus a feedback from the selective pressure of social sanctions on adults to parental training of children, inducing parents to train their children to meet operative standards of competence. Over time, this feedback, if consistent, results in the production through socialization of a higher frequency of persons with character traits labeled as competent, until some stable state is reached. In societies where relatively little mobility is possible, stability may have been reached such a long time before that the feedback is no longer necessary, since parents' internalized norms are an adequate guide to socially approved competence without redundant observation of environmental selection. This conception of personality-environment adaptation is applied by LeVine (1966a) to relations between status-mobility systems and frequency of achievement motivation in research on three Nigerian ethnic groups.

The Darwinian variation-selection model provides a plausible conceptualization of culture-personality relations in adaptive terms, so long as one identifies those junctures in social and psychological functioning at which unplanned variation and cumulative selection can reasonably be thought to operate. Rather than a single adaptive process bringing personality and sociocultural environment into some kind of fit, there are variation and selection mechanisms operating at numerous levels toward stable integration of individual dispositions and social norms. The fact that human adaptation of this kind is not attained through a single fixed mechanism probably permits greater flexibility and efficiency of adaptation and more rapid adjustment to environmental change.

In terms of research implications, this model permits great variability among populations in responsiveness to environmental feedback and in tightness of conscious control over selection, and assigns a central role to the purposive behavior of parents and other socializing agents. It is parents who decide how to organize relations between environments and children, and we need to know much more about the cognitive and other bases for their decisions before we can understand how these relations are organized in culturally differing populations.

From this theoretical perspective, then, the most urgent objective for empirical research on socialization is to understand the relation between the planned and unplanned aspects of social learning, how this relation varies among societies, and the kinds of adaptations that are made possible with varying degrees of conscious linkage between environmental feedback and deliberate socialization. In their central position as socializing agents, parents are able to act on their perceptions of the child's personality and the environment's demands and opportunities to create the basis for adaptive fit between personality and culture; it is essential that we investigate more intensively what these perceptions are and how parents organize their perceptions to arrive at training decisions.

REFERENCES CITED

Barry, H., I. Child, and M. Bacon, 1959, "Relation of Childhood to Subsistence Economy," *American Anthropologist* 61:51–63.

Brim, O., 1959, *Education for Child Rearing,* Russell Sage, New York.

Clausen, J., 1966, "Family Structure, Socialization, and Personality," in W. Hoffman and M. Hoffman (eds.), *Review of Child Development Research,* Volume 2, Russell Sage, New York.

Fromm, E., 1941, *Escape from Freedom,* Farrar and Rinehart, New York.

Goody, J., 1958 (ed.), *The Developmental Cycle in Domestic Groups,* Cambridge U.P., Cambridge.

Gray, R., and P. Tulliver (eds.), *The Family Estate in Africa,* Routledge and Kegan Paul, London.

Inkeles, A., 1955, "Social Change and Social Character: The Role of Parental Mediation," *Journal of Social Issues* 11:12–23.

——— 1966, "Social Structure and the Socialization of Competence," *Harvard Educational Review* 36:265–283.

LeVine, R., 1959, "Gusii Sex Offenses: A Study in Social Control," *American Anthropologist* 61:965–990.

——— 1966a, *Dreams and Deeds: Achievement Motivation in Nigeria,* Chicago U.P., Chicago.

———, 1966b, "Outsiders' Judgements: An Ethnographic Approach to Group Differences in Personality," *Southwestern Journal of Anthropology* 22:101–116.

——— and B. LeVine, 1966, *Nyansongo: A Gusii Community in Kenya,* Wiley, New York.

Lewin, K., 1935, *A Dynamic Theory of Personality,* McGraw-Hill, New York.

Mead, M., 1930, *Growing Up in New Guinea,* Morrow, New York.

Miller, D., and G. Swanson, 1958, *The Changing American Parent,* Wiley, New York.

Nimkoff, M., and R. Middleton, 1960, "Types of Family and Types of Economy," *American Journal of Sociology* 66:215–225.

Read, M., 1959, *Children of Their Fathers: Growing Up Among the Ngoni of Nyasaland,* Yale, U.P., New Haven.

Segall, M., D. Campbell, and M. Herskovits, 1966, *The Influence of Culture on Visual Perception,* Bobbs-Merrill, Indianapolis.

Whiting, J., and I. Child, 1953, "Child Training and Personality: A Cross-Cultural Study," Yale U.P., New Haven.

——— E. Chasdi, H. Antonovsky, and B. Ayres, 1966, "The Learning of Values," in E. Vogt and E. Albert (eds.), *People of the Rimrock: A Study of Values in Five Cultures,* Harvard U.P., Cambridge.

SECTION III

The Issue of Ethics

Recently in these troubled times, anthropologists have begun to undertake an intensive, long-overdue re-examination of their professional ethics, especially as they relate to their responsibilities to the peoples whose privacy they often invade, to study their ways of life for purposes of publication, professional advancement, and the growth of a discipline that has so far had little beneficial effect on the usually poor, relatively powerless "non-Western" peoples themselves. At *best* they have been left unaffected. Given the problems of individual and cultural survival most such peoples face, perhaps this is not enough.

However, even benevolent intervention can have sinister consequences and anthropological findings have often been used as data in making action decisions that neither the subjects of the studies nor the anthropologists have been able to control.

Exploitative relationships have frequently marked not only the anthropologists' contacts with native peoples, but those with indigenous scholars as well. Rarely have they had the opportunity to benefit from collaboration with anthropologists working among their people, to say nothing of participating in deciding on research priorities and standards of research conduct.

Particularly now, during the current war years in many parts of the Third World, overly interested government agencies have been willing to sponsor anthropological research for reasons that have been by no means necessarily in the subject people's best interest. Recently the "tribal" peoples of Southeast Asia have been an especially popular research subject, for example. Because such study is frequently "classified" (and may be undertaken by anthropologists who are only marginally qualified), naïve if not disastrous political decisions may be made on the basis of ethnographic data that cannot be critically scrutinized by other scholars because it is kept secret.

Honest anthropologists are finding their continued access to the field increasingly threatened by all this, and controversy continues to be heated and heavy. Fortunately it is not only in the traditional "field" but at home as well that the ethics of the anthropologist's objectives are being rethought. Wolf has been on the natives' side from the start.

American Anthropologists and American Society

Eric R. Wolf

I shall argue that in the period of the last hundred years there have been three major phases of American anthropology, and that these three phases in the development of our discipline correspond largely to three phases in the development of American society. Such a triadic scheme represents, of course, an oversimplification, but the oversimplification will serve its purpose if it leads us to think about problem-setting in our discipline, not merely in terms of the truth and falsity of answers to questions asked, but about our whole intellectual enterprise as a form of social action, operating within and against a certain societal and cultural context. I must also caution that in this attempt I cannot help but be idiosyncratic, though common acquaintance with our professional literature renders my idosyncrasy intersubjective, that is, amenable to discussion by others who, in turn, hold their own idiosyncratic positions. My purpose in this presentation is not to defend a new interpretation of American anthropology, but to generate an interest in the sociology of anthropological knowledge.

The oversimplified periods into which I want to break down the development of American society during the last century are, first, the period of Capitalism Triumphant, lasting roughly from the end of the Civil War into the last decade of the nineteenth century; second, the period of intermittent Liberal Reform, beginning in the last decade of the nineteenth century and ending with the onset of World War II; and third, the America of the present, characterized by what President Eisenhower first called "the military-industrial complex" in his farewell address of January 17, 1961. Each of these periods has been characterized by a central problem and a central set of responses to that problem. There were, of course, numerous subsidiary and peripheral problems and subsidiary and peripheral responses to them; and there were more often than not divergent and contradictory responses. But I want to argue that even the divergent and contradictory responses possessed a common denominator in that they addressed themselves to the same central issue of the day and that they were marked by a common intellectual mood, even when directly opposed to each other in suggesting possible solutions.

The phase of Capitalism Triumphant witnessed the construction of American industry by our untrammeled entrepreneurs; its dominant mode of intellectural response was Social Darwinism. The period of reform was marked by the drive to democratize America; the dominant mode of intellectual response was to explain and justify the entry of "new" and previously unrepresented groups into the American scene and to adumbrate the outlines of a pluralistic and liberal America. The period of the present is marked by the extension into all spheres of public life of a set of civil and military bureaucracies, connected through contracts to private concerns. I shall argue that the dominant intellectual issue of the present is the nature of public power and its exercise, wise or unwise, responsible or irresponsible.

To each of these three phases American anthropology has responded in its own way: it responded to the intellectual mood of Social Darwinism with the elaboration of evolutionist theory; it responded to Liberal Reform with theories which stressed human flexibility and plasticity; and it responds to the present phase with uncertainties and equivocations about power. Intellectual responses fed theory, and theory, in turn, fed practice; concern with the central issues of each period did not mean that anthropologists abandoned their technical tasks.

Source: From Eric R. Wolf, "American Anthropologists and American Society," in *Concepts and Assumptions in Contemporary Anthropology,* Stephen A. Tyler, ed., Southern Anthropological Society Proceedings, No. 3 (Athens, Ga.: University of Georgia Press, 1969). Used by permission of the publisher and the author.

Under the impetus of an evolutionist philosophy, Lewis Henry Morgan studied the Iroquois and collected the data which underwrote *Systems of Consanguinity and Affinity* (1870), just as John Wesley Powell embarked on a vast effort to study Indian languages, institutions, arts, and philosophies (cf. Darrah, 1951; and on both men, Hallowell, 1960, pp. 48–58). The emphasis on human plasticity and flexibility similarly prompted numerous technical investigations, especially in the field of culture and personality, a mode of inquiry which made American ethnology distinct from the ethnological efforts of other nations. Nor does the character of the present inhibit technical skill and cumulation; indeed, I shall argue that it is the very character of the present which causes us to emphasize technique and to de-emphasize ideas or ideology. Yet in no case could American anthropology escape the dominant issue of the time, and its intellectual responses could not and cannot help but direct themselves to answering it, or to escaping from it. To that extent, at least, the problems of the day enter into how we construct the picture of reality around which we organize our common understandings. As that reality shifts and changes, so our responses to it must shift and change.

Of Social Darwinism, the intellectual response of the first phase, its historian, Richard Hofstadter, has written that

> Darwinism had from the first this dual potentiality; intrinsically, it was a neutral instrument, capable of supporting opposite ideologies. How, then, can one account for the ascendancy, until the 1890's, of the rugged individualist interpretation of Darwinism? The answer is that American society saw its own image in the tooth-and-claw version of natural selection, and that its dominant groups were therefore able to dramatize this vision of competition as a thing good in itself. Ruthless business rivalry and unprincipled politics seemed to be justified by the survival philosophy. As long as the dream of personal conquest and individual assertion motivated the middle class, this philosophy seemed tenable, and its critics remained a minority. (1959, p. 201)

To the extent that American anthropologists were primarily concerned with the Indian, this general view also informed their own. It was anthropology, above all, which had contributed the realization that "savagery is not inchoate civilization; it is a distinct status of society with its own institutions, customs, philosophy, and religion," but "all these must necessarily be overthrown before new institutions, customs, philosophy, and religion can be introduced" (John Wesley Powell, quoted in Darrah, 1951, p. 256).

Such an overthrow of one status of society by another involves numerous processes—the process of power among them—but it is a hallmark of Social Darwinism that it focused the scientific spotlight, not on the actual processes—the fur trade, the slave trade, the colonization of the Plains—but on the outcome of the struggle. This allowed Americans—and American anthropologists among them—to avert their eyes from the actual processes of conflict both morally and scientifically. Hence the problem of power, of its forms and their exercise, remained unattended. Unattended also remained the problem of the power relationship which would link victor and defeated even after savagery had yielded to civilization. This basic paradigm did not change even when it was extended from Indians to Negroes, immigrants, Mexicans, or Filipinos by equating the spread of civilization with the spread of the Anglo-Saxons. When Theodore Roosevelt exclaimed (quoted in Hofstadter, 1959, pp. 171–72) that "the Mexican race now see in the fate of the aborigines of the north their own inevitable destiny. They must amalgamate or be lost in the superior vigor of the Anglo-Saxon race, or they must utterly perish," he was merely elaborating an already familiar argument. The civilized are more virtuous than the uncivilized; the Anglo-Saxons are the most capable agents of civilization; *ergo*, the non-Anglo-Saxons must yield to their superior vigor. Here moral judgment masked, as it so often does, the realities of power, and Americans, including American anthropologists, emerged into the next phase of their intellectual endeavors with appreciably less concern and understanding of power than their British confreres. The victim could be censured, or he could be pitied (Pearce, 1953, p. 53), but as an object of censure or pity he was merely an object lesson of history, not an object himself.

We have said that the next stage in American history was the movement toward reform. It began around the turn of the century and found its most substantial expression in the New Deal. On the one hand, it asserted the claims of society as a whole against the rights of the untrammeled and individualistic entrepreneur. On the other hand, it sponsored the social and political mobility of groups not hitherto represented in the social and political arena. On the wider intellectual scene, the assertion of a collectivity of common men against the anarchistic captains of industry was represented by Beard, Turner, Veblen, Commons, Dewey, Brandeis, and Holmes; in American anthropology, the reaction against Social Darwinism found its main spokesman in Franz Boas. Boas' work in physical anthropology furnished some of the initial arguments against a racism linked to Social Darwinist arguments. In his historical particularism he validated a shift of interest away from the grand evolutionary schemes to concern with the panoply of particular cultures in their historically conditioned setting. If we relate these anthropological interests to the tenor of the times, we can say that the renewed interest in cultural plurality and relativity had two major functions. It called into question the moral and political monopoly of an elite which had justified their rule with the claim that their superior virtue was the outcome of the evolutionary process; it was their might which made their right. If other races were shown to be equipotential with the Caucasians in general and the Anglo-Saxons in particular, if other cultures could be viewed as objects in themselves and not merely as object lessons in history, then other races and other cultures could claim an equal right to participate in the construction of an America more pluralist and more cooperative in its diversity. For the intellectual prophets of the times the preeminent instruments for the achievement of this cooperative participation among new and diverse elements were to be scientific education and liberal reform achieved through social engineering. The major protagonist of this faith in education as a means of liberaing men from the outworn canons of the past was John Dewey, who saw in the union of education and science the basis for a true association of equals, sustained through the freely given cooperation of the participants. In anthropology, this concern found its expression in the variety of approaches to culture and personality. These celebrated the malleability of man, thus celebrating also his vast potential for change; and they pointed to the socialization or enculturation process as the way in which societies produced viable adults. Each culture was seen, in fact, as one large schoolhouse instead of a little red one; the plurality of cultures constituted a plurality of educational institutions. The tool for the discovery of the manifold educational processes—and hence also for a more adequate approach to the engineering of pluralistic education—was science, that is, anthropology. The faith in social engineering and in the possibility of a new educational pluralism also underwrote the action programs among American Indians, who by means of the new techniques were to become autonomous participants in a more pluralistic and tolerant America.

But like the anthropology of Social Darwinism before it, the anthropology of Liberal Reform did not address itself, in any substantive way, to the problem of power. Human-kind was seen as infinitely malleable, and the socialization processes of personalities in different cultures as enormously diverse in their means as well as in their ends. But only rarely—if at all—did anthropologists shift their scientific focus to the constraints impeding both human malleability and malleability in socialization from the outside. At the risk of overstating my case, I would say that the anthropology of the period of Liberal Reform placed the burden for change on freely volunteering participants, drawn from both the culture under consideration and from among their neighbors. It might no longer deal with a given culture as an object lesson in history, but as an object in itself. Yet just as the Social Darwinists had made a moral paradigm of the evolutionary process, so the culture-and-personality schools of the thirties and forties made a moral paradigm of each individual culture. They spoke of patterns, themes, world view, ethos, and values, but not of power. In seeing culture as more or less of an organic whole, they asserted some of the claims of earlier intellectual predecessors who had seen in "political economy" an organic model for the explanation of a vast range of cultural phenomena. But where "political economy" explicitly emphasized the processes by which an organization of power is equipped with economic resources as central to the organic constellation to be explained, the anthropologist's culture of the thirties and forties was "political economy" turned inside out, all ideology and morality, and neither power nor economy. Neither in the nineteenth century nor in the first half of the twentieth century, therefore, did American anthropology as such come to grips with the phenomenon of power. It is with this legacy of unconcern that we enter the period of the present, a period in which the phenomenon of power is uppermost in men's minds.

This period, it seems to me, is characterized by two opposing and yet interconnected trends. The first of these is the growth of a war machine which is becoming the governing mechanism of our lives. Whether we are radicals or liberals or conservatives, we have a prevailing sense that knowledge is not sufficient to put things right; we have come up against institutional restraints which may have to be removed before changes can occur. Gone is the halcyon feeling that knowledge alone, including anthropological knowledge, will set men free. On the other hand, the pacific or pacified objects of our investigation, primitives and peasants alike, are ever more prone to define our field situation gun in hand. A new vocabulary is abroad in the world. It speaks of "imperialism," "colonialism," "neo-colonialism," and "internal colonialism," rather than just of primitives and civilized, or even of developed and underdeveloped. Yet anthropology has in the past always operated among pacified or pacific natives; when the native "hits back" we are in a very different situation from that in which we found ourselves only yesterday. Thus the problem of power has suddenly come to the fore for us; and it exists in two ways—as power exerted within our own system and as power exerted from the outside, often against us, by populations we so recently thought incapable of renewed assertion and resistance.

Yet neither the intellectual endeavors of Social Darwinism nor the period of Liberal Reform has equipped us to deal with the phenomenon of power. In these matters we are babes in the woods, indeed, "babes in the darkling woods," as H. G. Wells entitled one of his last novels. We confront the problem of understanding power at a time when the very signposts of understanding are growing confused and irrelevant.

This is not only our own situation. Stillmann and Pfaff, political scientists, write of this as an age in which

> the world practices politics, originated in the Western historical experience, whose essentially optimistic and rationalistic assumptions fail utterly to account for the brutality and terror which are the principal public experiences of the twentieth century. . . . neither tragedy nor irrationality are to be understood in terms of the political philosophies by which the West, and now the world, conducts its public life. (1964, p. 238)

Daniel Bell, in a similar vein of ambiguity, entitles a book of essays *The End of Ideology,* and subtitles it *On the Exhaustion of Political Ideas in the Fifties*; and John Higham summarizes the mood of present-day American historians by saying:

> Most of the major postwar scholars seem to be asking, in one way or another, what (if anything) is so deeply rooted in our past that we can rely on its survival. This has become, perhaps, the great historical question in a time of considerable moral confusion, when the future looks precarious and severely limited in its possibilities. (1965, p. 226)

Yet where some are lost in doubt, others assert a brutal return to Machiavellianism, to a naked power politics, abstracted from the social realities which underlie it. "The modern politician," write Stephen Rousseas and James Farganis,

> is the man who understands how to manipulate and how to operate in a Machiavellian world which divorces ethics from politics. Modern democracy becomes, in this view, transformed into a system of techniques sans *telos.* And democratic politics is reduced to a constellation of self-seeking pressure groups peaceably engaged in a power struggle to determine the allocation of privilege and particular advantage. (1965, pp. 270–71)

On the international plane, this has meant recourse to a "new realism," most evident in the application of game theory to what the Germans so charmingly call the international *"Chickenspiel."* This new realism emphasized technique over purpose, the *how* of political relations over their *whys* and *wherefores.* Where opponents of this approach argue that such a new emphasis sacrifices the hope of understanding the causes of such politics, its defenders argue, as true American pragmatists, that what matters is the world as given, and what counts is the most rational deployment of our resources to respond to present-day dilemmas. What counts in Vietnam is not how "we" got there, but that "we" are there. Two kinds of rationality thus oppose each other: a substantive rationality, which aims at a critical understanding of the world, and perhaps even at critical action; and a formal or technical rationality, which understands the world in terms of technical solutions.

In this argument social scientists find themselves heavily involved. Some feel, with Ithiel de Sola Pool (1967, pp. 268–69):

> The only hope for humane government in the future is through the extensive use of the social sciences by government. . . . The McNamara revolution is essentially the bringing of social science

analysis into the operation of the Department of Defense. It has remade American defense policy in accordance with a series of ideas that germinated in the late 1950's in the RAND Corporation among people like Schelling, Wohlstetter, Kahn, and Kaufmann. These were academic people playing their role as social scientists (whatever their early training may have been). They were trying to decide with care and seriousness what would lead to deterrence and what would undermine it. While one might argue with their conclusions at any given point, it seems to me that it is the process that has been important. The result has been the humanization of the Department of Defense. That is a terribly important contribution to the quality of American life.

Others will echo C. Wright Mills when he described the selfsame set of social scientists as

> crackpot realists, who, in the name of realism, have constructed a paranoid reality all their own and in the name of practicality have projected a utopian image of capitalism. They have replaced the responsible interpretation of events by the disguise of meaning in a maze of public relations, respect for public debate by unshrewd notions of psychological warfare, intellectual ability by the agility of the sound and mediocre judgment, and the capacity to elaborate alternatives and to gauge their consequences by the executive stance. (1963, pp. 610–11)

Anthropologists, like other social scientists, cannot evade the dilemmas posed by the return to Machiavellian politics. Yet our major response has been one of retreat. This retreat is all the more notable when we realize that wholly anthropological ideas have suddenly been taken over and overtaken by other disciplines. Political scientists have appropriated the anthropological concept of "tradition" and used it to build a largely fictitious polarity between traditional and modern societies; Marshall McLuhan has made use of largely anthropological insights to project the outlines of the communication revolution of the present and future. In contrast to the thirties and forties when anthropology furnished the cutting edge of innovation in social science, we face at the moment a descent into triviality and irrelevance. This descent into triviality seems to me, above all, marked by an increasing concern for pure technique. Important as our technical heritage is for all of us, it cannot in and of itself quicken the body of our discipline without the accession of new ideas. Technique without ideas grows sterile; the application of improved techniques to inherited ideas is the mark of the epigone. This is true regardless of whether anthropologists put themselves at the service of the new realists, or whether they seek refuge in an uncertain ivory tower.

Someone who diagnoses an illness should also prescribe remedies. If I am correct in saying that anthropology has reached its present impasse because it has so systematically disregarded the problems of power, then we must find ways of educating ourselves in the realities of power. One way I can think of to accomplish this is to engage ourselves in the systematic writing of a history of the modern world in which we spell out the processes of power which created the present-day cultural systems and the linkages between them. I do not mean history in the sense of "one damned thing after another"; I mean a critical and comprehensive history of the modern world. It is not irrelevant to the present state of American anthropology that the main efforts at analyzing the interplay of societies and cultures on a world scale in anthropological terms have come from Peter Worsley (1964), an Englishman, and from Darcy Ribeiro (1968), a Brazilian. Where, in our present-day anthropological literature, are the comprehensive studies of the slave trade, the fur trade, of colonial expansion, of forced and voluntary acculturation, of rebellion and accommodation in the modern world, which would provide us with the intellectual grid needed to order the massive data we now possess on individual societies and cultures engulfed by these phenomena? We stand in need of such a project, I believe, not only as a learning experience for ourselves, but also as a responsible intellectual contribution to the world in which we live, so that we may act to change it.

REFERENCES

Bell, Daniel. 1960. *The End of Ideology*. Glencoe, Ill.: Free Press.

Darrah, William C. 1951. *Powell of the Colorado*. Princeton, N.J.: Princeton University Press.

Hallowell, A. Irving. 1960. "The Beginnings of Anthropology in America." In *Selected Papers from the American Anthropologist, 1888–1920,* ed. Frederica de Laguna. Evanston, Ill.: Row, Peterson & Co. Pp. 1–90.

Higham, John. 1965. *History*. Englewood Cliffs, N.J.: Prentice-Hall.

Hofstadter, Richard. 1959. *Social Darwinism in American Thought*. New York: George Braziller.

Mills, C. Wright. 1963. *Power, Politics, and People: The Collected Essays of C. Wright Mills,* ed. Irving L. Horowitz. New York: Ballantine Books.

Morgan, Lewis Henry. 1870. *Systems of Consanguinity and Affinity of the Human Family*. Smithsonian Contributions to Knowledge, No. 16. Washington, D.C.

Pearce, Roy Harvey. 1953. *The Savages of America*. Baltimore: Johns Hopkins Press.

Pool, Ithiel de Sola. 1967. "The Necessity for Social Scientists Doing Research for Government." In *The Rise and Fall of Project Camelot*. ed. Irving L. Horowitz. Cambridge, Mass.: M.I.T. Press. Pp. 267–80.

Ribeiro, Darcy. 1968. *The Civilizational Process*. Washington, D.C.: Smithsonian Institution Press.

Rousseas, Stephen, and James Farganis. 1965. "American Politics and the End of Ideology." In *The New Sociology,* ed. Irving L. Horowitz. New York: Oxford University Press, Pp. 268–89.

Stillmann, Edmund, and William Pfaff. 1964. *The Politics of Hysteria*. New York: Harper & Row, Colophon Books.

Worsley, Peter. 1964. *The Third World*. London: Weidenfeld & Nicholson.

Glossary

Aardvark. African anteater.

Aboriginal. Indigenous or native; pertaining to the original inhabitants of a region, country, or continent.

Acculturation. The process by which a society undergoes profound cultural change as the result of prolonged contact with the culture of another society.

Adjudication. A judicial decision.

Adumbrate. To indicate vaguely.

Adz. A tool with a heavy chisel-like end, usually mounted on a wooden handle.

Affinal. Related by marriage.

Afformative. An affix; one or more letters or syllables added at either end of a word.

Agaric. Any gill fungus; including the edible mushroom.

Age-grade. A group whose members' assigned roles are determined by the socially designated age category to which they belong; typically part of an age organization composed of several such grades.

Agnate. A kinsman whose connection is exclusively through males; one related by descent through the male line.

Agouti. A rodent of the guinea pig family.

Agriculture. In anthropology, cultivation with the use of draft animals, irrigation, and fertilizers; usually distinguished from horticulture by reliance on these generally more productive techniques.

Aguardiente. A strong brandy.

Ahaggar. A plateau in the central Sahara desert.

Animatism. The attribution of consciousness to inanimate objects and natural phenomena.

Animism. Belief in spirits and other supernatural beings.

Apochryphal. Of doubtful authenticity.

Aphorism. A short statement of a general truth.

A priori. Designating that which can be known by reason alone and not through experience.

A posteriori. Designating that which can be known from the observation of facts.

Arracha. A plant with a thick edible root.

Arrullo. A lullaby.

Association. A social group usually formed on the basis of shared interests and/or attributes.

Aspiration. The breathing sound made in pronouncing the letter "h."

Asymetrical. Lacking symmetry or balance.

Autonomous. Independent, self-sufficient.

Attrition. Wearing down.

Avunculocal. Usually pertaining to residence with an uncle.

Axiomatization. The process of making self-evident.

Band. A small, territorially based social group most of whose members are related.

Bantu. Speakers of any one of the major related languages of Central and Southern Africa.

Baraka. In Islam, the popular belief in the supernatural power of events, objects, or actions associated with supernaturally favored persons.

Bifurcate. To divide or fork into two separate branches.

Bigha. A measure of land, approximately ¼ of an acre.

Bichrome. Consisting of two colors.

Bilateral descent. A system for reckoning descent in which the individual is related almost equally to all the close kinsmen of both parents.

Bilocal. Relating to residence in or near the parental home of one spouse or the other, with no strongly expressed preference for either.

Binary. Consisting of two parts.

Biotic. Relating to life; biological.

Boasian. Pertaining to the historical approach in American anthropology developed by Franz Boas.

Bond friendship. A close reciprocal association between two persons of the same age and sex.

Bride price. Or bridewealth; goods, usually property or money, given by a prospective husband and his kinsmen to the family of his bride.

Bride service. Labor or other service rendered to a woman's kinsmen by her husband, before or after marriage.

Bronze Age. The period that followed the discovery of metallurgy about 3100 B.C.

Bustard. Any of several large terrestrial birds of the family Otididae; related to the cranes.

Caiman. A tropical American alligator.

Calabash. A gourd.

Capybara. South American rodent related to the Guinea pig.

Carapace. The hard covering of the back, or a portion of the back, of an animal.

Caribou. Reindeer of North America and Greenland.

Cassava. A starchy edible root.

Cassowary. A large, ostrichlike bird, native to New Guinea.

Caste. An hereditary, endogamous group usually identified with a specific occupation; typically one of several such groups, all of which are ranked hierarchically.

Cathartic. Pertaining to the reduction of tension through the expressive release of strong pent-up emotions.

Chaff. The husks of grain separated from the seed by threshing or winnowing, etc.

Charybdis. A female monster in Greek mythology.

Chickenspiel. "Chicken-talk."

Chilliasm. Belief in Christ's return to earth to reign during the Millennium.

Churinga. An object, usually elliptical, and decorated with surface designs, made of wood or stone and considered the symbol or repository of supernatural power.

Clan. A unilineal descent group whose members claim descent from a remote common ancestor, often a mythical figure; sometimes used to refer to a residential kin group organized around a core of unilineally related persons and their wives or husbands.

Class. A social stratum composed of people sharing basically similar economic, social, and other cultural characteristics and having the same social position; one of several such strata within a ranked system.

Coati. Raccoonlike mammal of tropical America.

Cognate. A word related to another word by common origin.

Cognition. Knowledge, or a way of perceiving and thinking about reality.

Collateral. Referring to relationship through nondirect, or horizontal links, as in the instance of one's "uncles," "aunts," and "cousins."

Compadrazgo. The Spanish term for the institution of ritual co-parenthood.

Conjugal. Pertaining to marriage or marital relations.

Consanguinity. Pertaining to kinship based on common descent; of the same "blood."

Cordyline. A palm.

Corporate. Pertaining to a group of individuals whose organization and actions are continuous and independent of the existence of individual members.

Cosmography. A general description of the cosmos, or universe.

Creolization. The process by which a new language is developed as the result of prolonged contact between speakers of very different languages.

Cross-cousin. The offspring of siblings of unlike sex; i.e., the child of a father's sister or a mother's brother.

Cucurbits. A plant of the gourd family.

Culture area. A geographical region in which the cultures tend to be similar in a number of significant aspects.

Declension. Inflection of nouns, adjectives, and so on, according to a definite sequence of their case forms.

Demography. The statistical study of populations.

Diachronic. Pertaining to events or phenomena as they change through time.

Diffusion. The transmission of a culture trait from one group to another in the absence of face-to-face contact.

Diglossia. Pertaining to two languages.

Divination. A practice aimed at foretelling the course of future events by supernatural means.

Double descent. Pertaining to the coexistence in a single society of patrilateral and matrilateral systems for tracing descent.

Dyadic. Pertaining to two units treated as one; a couple or pair.

Ecological. Pertaining to the natural relations between organisms and their environment.

Ethnosemantics. The systematic study of the meanings of words and of the role of these meanings in cognitive systems.

Ego. The "I" in kinship analysis; designation for the hypothetical person used as the point of reference in analyzing kinship relations.

Eleusine. A small seeded cereal grass.

Emics. Domains or operations that are real or meaningful (but not necessarily conscious) to the natives themselves (see *etics*).

Empirical. Pertaining to experience; to information that can be verified by evidence or experience.

Encapsulate. To enclose.

Enclitic. Pertaining to a word which, losing its own accent, is attached in pronunciation to another word.

Enculturation. The process by which a person gradually learns and assimilates the patterns of cultural behavior expected by the members of his society.

Endogamy. The custom or law requiring or encouraging a person to marry within some particular social group to which he belongs.

Ethnic group. A group of people identifiable by a common cultural or "racial" background.

Ethnocentric. Pertaining to the use of the learned values of one's own culture as a standard against which other patterns of behavior are invidiously compared.

Ethnography. That aspect of cultural and social anthropology devoted to the objective, first-hand description of a particular culture.

Ethnology. The division of anthropology devoted to the theoretical analysis and description of ethnographic data.

Ethnomusicology. The anthropological study of music, particularly the study of the music of nonliterate peoples, with emphasis upon the place of music in sociocultural context.

Etics. Domains or operations whose validity does not depend upon the demonstration of conscious or unconscious significance or validity in the minds of the native (see *emics*.).

Etiology. The systematic study of the causes of particular developments.

Exogamy. The socially enforced requirement that a person marry outside some culturally defined group to which he belongs.

Expiate. To seek supernatural purification and atonement by ritual means.

Extended family. Two or more nuclear families affiliated through an extension of the parent-child relationship; e.g., a family comprised of a man and his wife and his sons and their wives.

Febrile. Feverish.

Feral. Wild.

Fission. In kinship studies, division of a descent group into two or more parts.

Fulani. West African pastoral nomads.

Genealogical. A record or account of the ancestry of a person or kin group.

Generative. Having the capability of generating or producing.

Generic. Pertaining to a basic, general descriptive term.

Glottal. Pertaining to an utterance modified by movement of the glottis.

Glottochronology. The chronological study of linguistic change, especially of the rate of change in written languages, to establish their relationship to other languages.

Gradus ad Parnassum. Latin title of a dictionary of prosody, concerning meter, versification, stress, and intonation.

Grammar. Study of the structure of words and of the rules by which they are combined to form longer utterances, sentences, etc.

Groundnuts. Peanuts.

Hierarchy. Organization on the basis of ranked groups of unequal status.

Hijara. The flight of Mohammad from Mecca; any journey to a more desirable or congenial place.

Homotaxis. Similarity of arrangement, as of genealogical strata.

Horticulture. In anthropology, the cultivation of plants without the use of draft animals, fertilizers, irrigation, or the plow; generally a less productive system of cultivation than agriculture (although this is not always true in the tropics.).

Incest. Sexual relations with a kinsman with whom such relations are prohibited by custom or law.

Iconographic. Pertaining to representation by pictures or images.

Incubus. A demon, or evil spirit.

Indo-European. Pertaining to the family of languages found over most of Europe and parts of the Middle East and India.

Inter alia. Among other things.
Ipso facto. By the fact itself.
Isomorphism. Pertaining to superficial structural similarity.

Jajman. A high-caste landowner in an Indian farming community.
Jati. The Hindi word for caste.
Jural. Pertaining to legal rights or obligations.

Kindred. An "ego-focused" group of close bilaterally related kinsmen.
Kula ring. The system of intertribal ceremonial exchange of shell armbands and necklaces in certain parts of southwestern Melanesia.
Kulturkreise. Culture-circles, complexes of traits dispersed throughout the world.
Kynomorphic. Cowlike.

Language family. A group of languages whose systematic resemblance to each other suggests their descent from a common ancestral language.
Lineage. A group of kinsmen who share unilateral descent from a common known ancestor; such a group usually spans at least three generations.
Lingua franca. A common language.
Lexicon. Usually, a dictionary-like listing of meanings.
Levirate. The custom whereby a widow marries her deceased husband's brother.

Maize. Corn.
Mana. A Malayo-Polynesian term for an impersonal supernatural force believed to be concentrated in a particular person or object.
Manioc. Cassava; a tropical plant cultivated for its tuberous roots, which yield a nutritious starch.
Märchen. A type of fairy tale.
Matrilocal. Pertaining to postmarital residence of the husband within or near the household of his wife's parents.
Matrilocal family. A family in which the mother maintains the household and is the principal source of economic, social, and emotional support and from which the father is frequently or always absent.
Matrilineage. A lineage based on descent traced exclusively through females.
Matrisib. A descent group with a tradition of shared descent through the female line from a remote ancestress.
Maund. A unit of weight in India varying from about 25 to 82 pounds.
Mayordomo. Mayor.
Metate. A flat or grooved grinding stone that functions as a mortar.
Mesoamerica. Middle America, from Mexico to Panama.
Melanesia. A major cultural and geographical area in the South and Southwest Pacific.
Meiji. Name of the period of the reign of the Japanese Emperor Mutshuhito, 1868–1912.
Mesolithic. A transitional postglacial period between the Old Stone Age and the Neolithic, or New Stone Age.
Millet. A small seeded cereal grain.
Millennium. Pertaining to a future period of great happiness brought about by supernatural means.
Milieu. Environment.
Mischsprachen. Mixed language.
Mischkulturen. Mixed culture.
Morphology. In linguistics, the aspect of grammar concerned with the patterns of word formation.
Moiety. Half; the social group formed when a community is divided into halves on the basis of kinship affiliation.
Morpheme. One or more phonemes having a unitary meaning.
Moka. Exchange resulting from warfare, enemy-compensation and ally-reparation payments.
Mughal. Mongol.
Mythopoeic. Giving rise to myth.

Paca. A large white-spotted rodent.
Paleolithic. The Old Stone Age.
Panseri. 1/22nd of a maund of .82 pounds.
Paradigm. A model or pattern.
Parallel cousin. The child of a father's brother or of a mother's sister; cousins whose related parents are of like sex.
Patriclan. A clan based upon descent traced exclusively through males.
Patrilineage. A group of kinsmen related exclusively through the male (agnatic) line to a common known male ancestor.
Patrilocal. Pertaining to the establishment of postnuptial residence with or near the kinsmen of the husband.
Peccary. A piglike mammal.
Peregrination. A journey, or pilgrimage.
Peyote. A variety of cactus ingested to induce visions as part of a religious ritual.

Phenotype. A type determined by common visible characteristics.

Phoneme. A minimal unit of spoken sound, a change in which produces an alteration of meaning in the utterance.

Phonemics. Pertaining to a phoneme.

Phonetics. The scientific study of speech sounds.

Pharynx. The space between the mouth cavity and the esophagus.

Phonology. The study of speech sounds with emphasis upon the rules governing their sequence and upon the theoretical analysis of sound changes.

Phratry. A social unit consisting of two or more clans united by an often mythical belief that they share a common ancestor.

Pidgin. A new language developed as the result of contact between the speakers of very different languages.

Plantain. A kind of banana.

Platonist. An adherent of the philosophy of Plato.

Pleistocene. The Ice Age.

Plethora. State of being overfull; excess.

Polyandry. A form of marriage that allows a woman to have more than one husband at the same time.

Polygamy. The practice of having more than one spouse at a time.

Polygyny. A form of polygamy that allows a husband to have two or more wives at a time.

Poro. A men's secret society in West Africa.

Potlatch. Ceremonial, often competitive gift giving among the Indians of the Northwest Pacific Coast.

Polynesia. The cultural area of the Central Pacific that falls within a triangle formed by Hawaii, Easter Island, and New Zealand.

Predatory. Plundering, preying upon others.

Prognosis. Outlook or forecast.

Pronominal. Having the nature of a pronoun.

Prosodic. Versification. the systematic study of metrical structure.

Putative. Supposed.

Radical. In linguistics, an uncompounded word, a root.

Reciprocity. In anthropology, the institutionalized exchange of goods of roughly equivalent value among persons of similar social status.

Redistribution. In anthropology, an exchange system in which goods move toward an allocative center and out again, e.g., taxation.

Retroflex. Pertaining to sounds made with the tongue raised and bent back.

Rite de passage. Ritual accompanying a change in status.

Role. A part; the behavior culturally defined as appropriate to a particular status or position.

Sacerdotal. Pertaining to the priestly activities of a religious functionary.

Salubrious. Healthy.

Sanction. A reaction operating to induce conformity to a culturally defined standard of behavior.

Sapiens. Latin word meaning "wise" or "knowing."

Savannah. A tropical or subtropical grasslands country with scattered trees.

Scylla. A monster of partly human form in Greek and Roman mythology.

Segmentary. Pertaining to a descent group in which internal divisions result in the frequent emergence of new and separate descent groups.

Semantic. Pertaining to meaning in language.

Shaman. One who acts as a ritual intermediary between others and the spirit world.

Sibling. One of two or more children of the same parents.

Sir. An Indian unit of weight varying from ½ to 2 pounds.

Socialization. The early stages of the learning process during which the young child internalizes the behaviors required of him by society.

Society. A generally large group of people who share a common culture and a sense of common identity; also, the system of interpersonal and intergroup relationships among members of such a group.

Sodality. Fellowship or association.

Sorcery. The use of supernatural power for aggressive purposes.

Sorghum. A tropical cereal grass.

Sororate. A practice whereby a woman marries the husband of her deceased sister.

Status. The position of an individual in relation to others within a society.

Strophe. A turning, or the first part of a choral ode.

Strychnos. Pertaining to styrchnine, a colorless poison.

Succubus. A demon that assumes female form to have sexual intercourse with men in their sleep.

Swidden. Shifting cultivation.

Syncretism. The fusion of two distinct systems of belief and practice.

Synchronic. Concerned with events within a limited time period, usually ignoring historical processes.

Syntax. The study of how words and significant features of intonation are arranged in phrases or sentences, and of how sentences relate to each other.

Taboo (or tapu). Usually pertaining to a certain kind of ritually prohibited activity punishable by supernatural sanctions.

Tabula rasa. Clean slate.

Tagmeme. Any of the minimal units of grammatical construction embodying distinctive word order, grammatical agreement, and choice of determiners.

Tokugawa. Name of a powerful family that ruled Japan from 1603 to 1867.

Tallensi. A farming people who live in the northern part of Ghana.

Tapa. Polynesian bark cloth.

Tapir. A nocturnal mammal of tropical America distantly related to the horse.

Tar. A Tiv word for the territory occupied by the descendants of a single ancestor.

Taro. A tropical plant cultivated for its tuberous, starchy, edible root.

Taxonomy. The systematic classification of things according to scientific principles.

Tenure. Pertaining to holding the right to land.

Transformational generative grammar. The technique of linguistic analysis by which one can account systematically for the processes that generate all the possible well-formed sentences in a language.

Transhumance. The regular movement of livestock in response to seasonal shifts in the availability of pasturage.

Transmogrify. To transform.

Transmutation. The conversion of one thing into another.

Tribe. An autonomous but not necessarily centrally or politically organized group with a distinctive culture, a distinctive language or dialect, and usually a sense of common identity and shared territory.

Trophic. Pertaining to nutrition.

Tsantsa. A shrunken head trophy.

Tyro. A beginner or novice.

Unilateral. Referring to descent through one line of relatives only.

Unilineal descent. The tracing of kinship through kinsmen of one sex only, i.e., a line of descent traced exculsively through males or through females.

Untouchable. An English term for certain members of Hindu society who are categorized as outside the formal structure of the caste system.

Uxorilocal. Or matrilocal, pertaining to the practice of establishing postnuptial residence in or near the domicile of the wife's family.

Varna. Any of the four main Hindu castes.

Velarize. To modify an utterance by raising the back of the tongue toward the velum, or soft palate, as in the *l* of *pool.*

Virilocal. Or patrilocal, pertaining to the practice of establishing postnuptial residence in or near the household of the husband's family.

Wattle. Stakes or rods interwoven with twigs or tree branches.

Winnow. To separate the chaff from the grain by fanning or passing it through the air.

THIRTEENTH EDITION

VANDER'S Human Physiology

THE MECHANISMS OF BODY FUNCTION

ERIC P. WIDMAIER
BOSTON UNIVERSITY

HERSHEL RAFF
MEDICAL COLLEGE OF WISCONSIN
AURORA ST. LUKE'S MEDICAL CENTER

KEVIN T. STRANG
UNIVERSITY OF WISCONSIN–MADISON

The McGraw-Hill Companies

VANDER'S HUMAN PHYSIOLOGY: THE MECHANISMS OF BODY FUNCTION, THIRTEENTH EDITION

Published by McGraw-Hill, a business unit of The McGraw-Hill Companies, Inc., 1221 Avenue of the Americas, New York, NY 10020.

This book is printed on acid-free paper.

4 5 6 7 8 9 0 DOW/DOW 1 0 9 8 7 6 5 4

ISBN 978–0–07–337830–5
MHID 0–07–337830–5

Senior Vice President, Products & Markets: *Kurt L. Strand*
Vice President, General Manager, Products & Markets: *Marty Lange*
Vice President, Content Production & Technology Services: *Kimberly Meriwether David*
Managing Director: *Michael S. Hackett*
Director: *James F. Connely*
Brand Manager: *Marija Magner*
Senior Developmental Editor: *Fran Simon*
Director, Content Production: *Terri Schiesl*
Project Manager: *Sherry L. Kane*
Senior Buyer: *Sandy Ludovissy*
Designer: *Tara McDermott*
Cover/Interior Designer: *Elise Lansdon*
Cover Images: *(girl drinking water) © JGI/Blend Images LLC/RF; (MRI midsagittal section) © ISM/Phototake; (freeze fractured bundle) © Steve Gschmeissner/Photo Researchers; (stress test) © Michael Krasowitz/Getty Images; (leather spine) © Siede Preis/Getty Images/RF*
Senior Content Licensing Specialist: *John C. Leland*
Photo Research: *David Tietz/Editorial Image, LLC*
Compositor: *Laserwords Private Limited*
Typeface: *10/12 Janson Text LT Std*
Printer: *R. R. Donnelley*

Library of Congress Cataloging-in-Publication Data

Widmaier, Eric P.
Vander's human physiology : the mechanisms of body function. – Thirteenth edition / Eric P. Widmaier, Department of Biology, Boston University, Hershel Raff, Medical College of Wisconsin, Aurora St. Luke's Medical Center, Kevin T. Strang, Department of Neuroscience, University of Wisconsin.
pages cm
Includes index.
ISBN 978–0–07–337830–5 — ISBN 0–07–337830–5 (hard copy : alk. paper) 1. Human physiology. I. Raff, Hershel, 1953- II. Strang, Kevin T. III. Vander, Arthur J., 1933– Human physiology. IV. Title. V. Title: Human physiology.
QP34.5.W47 2014
612–dc23

2012041775

www.mhhe.com

Meet the Authors

ERIC P. WIDMAIER received his Ph.D. in 1984 in Endocrinology from the *University of California at San Francisco.* His postdoctoral training was in endocrinology and physiology at the *Worcester Foundation for Experimental Biology* and *The Salk Institute* in La Jolla, California. His research is focused on the control of body mass and metabolism in mammals, the mechanisms of hormone action, and molecular mechanisms of intestinal and hypothalamic adaptation to high-fat diets. He is currently Professor of Biology at *Boston University,* where he teaches Human Physiology and has been recognized with the Gitner Award for Distinguished Teaching by the College of Arts and Sciences, and the Metcalf Prize for Excellence in Teaching by Boston University. He is the author of numerous scientific and lay publications, including books about physiology for the general reader. He lives outside Boston with his wife Maria and children Caroline and Richard.

HERSHEL RAFF received his Ph.D. in Environmental Physiology from the *Johns Hopkins University* in 1981 and did postdoctoral training in Endocrinology at the *University of California at San Francisco.* He is now a Professor of Medicine (Endocrinology, Metabolism, and Clinical Nutrition), Surgery, and Physiology at the *Medical College of Wisconsin* and Director of the Endocrine Research Laboratory at *Aurora St. Luke's Medical Center.* At the *Medical College of Wisconsin,* he teaches physiology and pharmacology to medical and graduate students, and is the Endocrinology/Reproduction Unit Director for the new integrated curriculum. He was an inaugural inductee into the Society of Teaching Scholars, received the Beckman Basic Science Teaching Award three times, received the Outstanding Teacher Award from the Graduate School, and has been one of the MCW's Outstanding Medical Student Teachers for each year the award has been given. He is also an Adjunct Professor of Biomedical Sciences at *Marquette University.* He is the former Associate Editor of *Advances in Physiology Education.* Dr. Raff's basic research focuses on the adaptation to low oxygen (hypoxia). His clinical interest focuses on pituitary and adrenal diseases, with a special focus on laboratory tests for the diagnosis of Cushing's syndrome. He resides outside Milwaukee with his wife Judy and son Jonathan.

KEVIN T. STRANG received his Master's Degree in Zoology (1988) and his Ph.D. in Physiology (1994) from the *University of Wisconsin at Madison.* His research area is cellular mechanisms of contractility modulation in cardiac muscle. He teaches a large undergraduate systems physiology course as well as first-year medical physiology in the *UW-Madison School of Medicine and Public Health.* He was elected to UW-Madison's Teaching Academy and as a Fellow of the Wisconsin Initiative for Science Literacy. He is a frequent guest speaker at colleges and high schools on the physiology of alcohol consumption. He has twice been awarded the UW Medical Alumni Association's Distinguished Teaching Award for Basic Sciences, and also received the University of Wisconsin System's Underkofler/Alliant Energy Excellence in Teaching Award. In 2012 he was featured in *The Princeton Review* publication, *"The Best 300 Professors."* Interested in teaching technology, Dr. Strang has produced numerous animations of figures from *Vander's Human Physiology* available to instructors and students. He lives in Madison with his wife Sheryl and his children Jake and Amy.

TO OUR FAMILIES: MARIA, RICHARD, AND CAROLINE; JUDY AND JONATHAN; SHERYL, JAKE, AND AMY

Brief Contents

Table of Contents

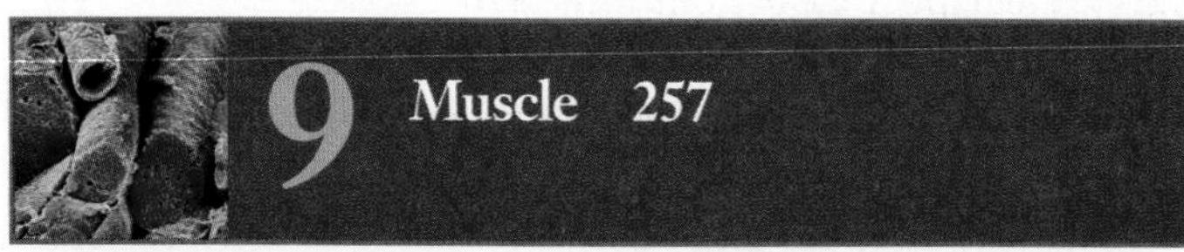

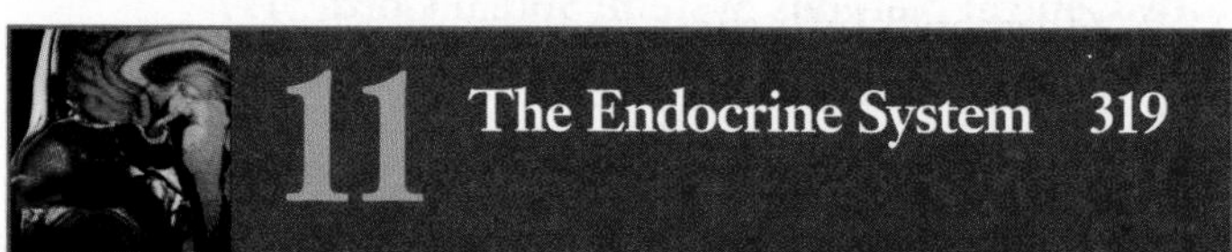

17 Reproduction 602

SECTION A Gametogenesis, Sex Determination, and Sex Differentiation; General Principles of Reproductive Endocrinology 603

SECTION B Male Reproductive Physiology 612

SECTION C Female Reproductive Physiology 622

18 The Immune System 652

Index of Exercise Physiology

From the Authors

It is with great pleasure that we present the thirteenth edition of *Vander's Human Physiology*. The cover of this edition reflects some of the major themes of the textbook: homeostasis, exercise, pathophysiology, and cellular and molecular mechanisms of body function. These themes and others have now been introduced in Chapter 1, called "General Principles of Physiology." These principles have been integrated throughout the remaining chapters in order to continually reinforce their importance. Each chapter opens with a preview of those principles that are particularly relevant for the material covered in that chapter. The principles are then reinforced when specific examples arise within a chapter. Finally, assessments are provided at the end of each chapter to provide immediate feedback for students to gauge their understanding of the chapter material and its relationship to physiological principles. These assessments tend to require analytical and critical thinking; answers are provided in an appendix.

Users of the book will also benefit from expanded assessments of the traditional type, such as multiple choice and thought questions, as well as additional Physiological Inquiries associated with various key figures. In total, approximately 70 new assessment questions have been added to the textbook; this is in addition to the several hundred test questions available on the McGraw-Hill Connect site associated with the book.

As in earlier editions, there is extensive coverage of exercise physiology (see the special exercise index that follows the detailed Table of Contents), and special attention to the clinical relevance of much of the basic science (see the Index of Clinical Terms in Appendix B). This index is organized according to disease; infectious or causative agents; and the treatments, diagnostics, and therapeutic drugs used to treat disease. This is a very useful resource for instructors and students interested in the extensive medical applications of human physiology that are covered in this book.

As textbooks become more integrated with digital content, we are pleased that McGraw-Hill has provided ***Vander's Human Physiology*** with cutting-edge digital content that continues to expand and develop. Students will again find a Connect Plus site associated with the text. The assessments have been updated and are now authored by one of the author team, Kevin Strang. For the first time we also have LearnSmart! McGraw-Hill LearnSmart™ is an adaptive diagnostic tool that constantly assesses student knowledge of course material.

We are always grateful to receive e-mail messages from instructors and students worldwide who are using the book and wish to offer suggestions regarding content. Finally, no textbook such as this could be written without the expert and critical eyes of our many reviewers; we are thankful to those colleagues who took time from their busy schedules to read all or a portion of a chapter (or more) and provide us with their insights and suggestions for improvements.

Guided Tour Through a Chapter

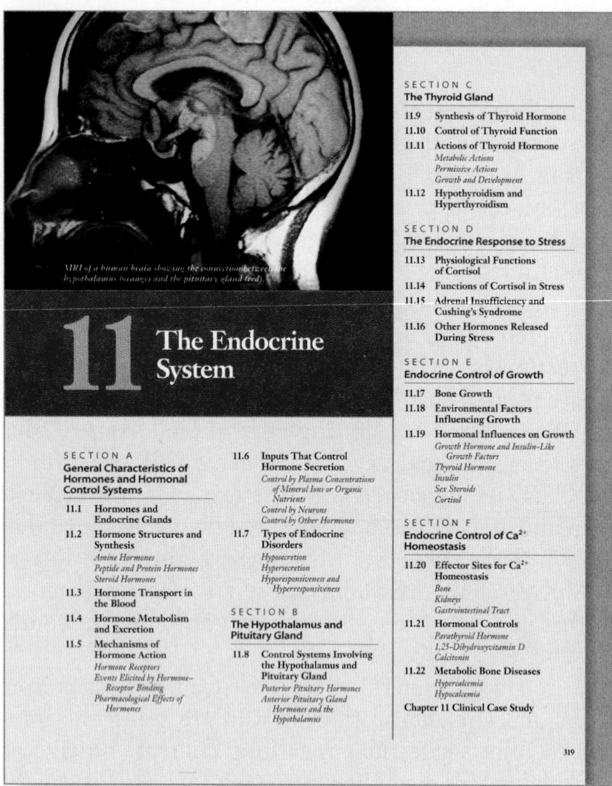

MRI of a human brain showing the connection between the hypothalamus (orange) and the pituitary gland (red).

11 The Endocrine System

319

Chapter Outline

Every chapter starts with an introduction giving the reader a brief overview of what is to be covered in that chapter. Included in the introduction for the thirteenth edition is a new feature that provides students with a preview of those General Principles of Physiology (introduced in Chapter 1) that will be covered in the chapter.

General Principles of Physiology—NEW!

General Principles of Physiology have been integrated throughout each chapter in order to continually reinforce their importance. Each chapter opens with a preview of those principles that are particularly relevant for the material covered in that chapter. The principles are then reinforced when specific examples arise within a chapter.

In Chapters 6–8 and 10, you learned that the nervous system is one of the two major control systems of the body, and now we turn our attention to the other—the endocrine system. The **endocrine system** consists of all those glands, called **endocrine glands**, that secrete **hormones**, as well as hormone-secreting cells located in various organs such as the heart, kidneys, liver, and stomach. Hormones are chemical messengers that enter the blood, which carries them from their site of secretion to the cells upon which they act. The cells a particular hormone influences are known as the target cells for that hormone. The aim of this chapter is to first present a detailed overview of endocrinology—that is, a structural and functional analysis of general features of hormones—followed by a more detailed analysis of several important hormonal systems. Before continuing, you should review the principles of ligand-receptor interactions and cell signaling that were described in Chapter 3 (Section C) and Chapter 5, because they pertain to the mechanisms by which hormones exert their actions.

Hormones functionally link various organ systems together. As such, several of the general principles of physiology first introduced in Chapter 1 apply to the study of the endocrine system, including the principle that the functions of organ systems are coordinated with each other. This coordination is key to the maintenance of homeostasis, another important general principle of physiology that will be covered in Sections C, D, and F. In many cases, the actions of one hormone can be potentiated, inhibited, or counterbalanced by the actions of another. This illustrates the general principle of physiology that most physiological functions are controlled by multiple regulatory systems, often working in opposition. It will be especially relevant in the sections on the endocrine control of metabolism and the control of pituitary gland function. Finally, this chapter exemplifies the general principle of physiology that information flow between cells, tissues, and organs is an essential feature of homeostasis and allows for integration of physiological processes.

Clinical Case Studies

The authors have drawn from their teaching and research experiences and the clinical experiences of colleagues to provide students with real-life applications through clinical case studies in each chapter.

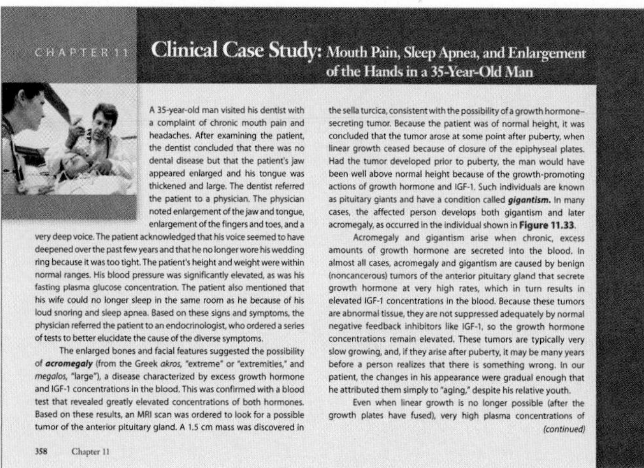

CHAPTER 11 **Clinical Case Study:** Mouth Pain, Sleep Apnea, and Enlargement of the Hands in a 35-Year-Old Man

A 35-year-old man visited his dentist with a complaint of chronic mouth pain and headaches. After examining the patient, the dentist concluded that there was no dental disease but that the patient's jaw appeared enlarged and his tongue was thickened and large. The dentist referred the patient to a physician. The physician noted enlargement of the jaw and tongue, enlargement of the fingers and toes, and a very deep voice. The patient acknowledged that his voice seemed to have deepened over the past few years and that he no longer wore his wedding ring because it was too tight. The patient's height and weight were within normal ranges. His blood pressure was significantly elevated, as was his fasting plasma glucose concentration. The patient also mentioned that his wife could no longer sleep in the same room as he because of his loud snoring and sleep apnea. Based on these signs and symptoms, the physician referred the patient to an endocrinologist, who ordered a series of tests to better elucidate the cause of the diverse symptoms.

The enlarged bones and facial features suggested the possibility of ***acromegaly*** (from the Greek *akros*, "extreme" or "extremities," and *megalos*, "large"), a disease characterized by excess growth hormone and IGF-1 concentrations in the blood. This was confirmed with a blood test that revealed greatly elevated concentrations of both hormones. Based on these results, an MRI scan was ordered to look for a possible tumor of the anterior pituitary gland. A 1.5 cm mass was discovered in the sella turcica, consistent with the possibility of a growth hormone–secreting tumor. Because the patient was of normal height, it was concluded that the tumor arose at some point after puberty, when linear growth ceased because of closure of the epiphyseal plates. Had the tumor developed prior to puberty, the man would have been well above normal height because of the growth-promoting actions of growth hormone and IGF-1. Such individuals are known as pituitary giants and have a condition called ***gigantism.*** In many cases, the affected person develops both gigantism and later acromegaly, as occurred in the individual shown in **Figure 11.33**.

Acromegaly and gigantism arise when chronic, excess amounts of growth hormone are secreted into the blood. In almost all cases, acromegaly and gigantism are caused by benign (noncancerous) tumors of the anterior pituitary gland that secrete growth hormone at very high rates, which in turn results in elevated IGF-1 concentrations in the blood. Because these tumors are abnormal tissue, they are not suppressed adequately by normal negative feedback inhibitors like IGF-1, so the growth hormone concentrations remain elevated. These tumors are typically very slow growing, and, if they arise after puberty, it may be many years before a person realizes that there is something wrong. In our patient, the changes in his appearance were gradual enough that he attributed them simply to "aging," despite his relative youth.

Even when linear growth is no longer possible (after the growth plates have fused), very high plasma concentrations of

(continued)

358 Chapter 11

(continued)

Figure 11.33 Appearance of an individual with gigantism and acromegaly.

growth hormone and IGF-1 result in the thickening of many bones in the body, most noticeably in the hands, feet, and head. The jaw, particularly, enlarges to give the characteristic facial appearance called ***prognathism*** (from the Greek *pro*, "forward," and *gnathos*, "jaw") that is associated with acromegaly. This was likely the cause of our patient's chronic mouth pain. The enlarged sinuses that resulted from the thickening of his skull bones may have been responsible in part for his headaches. In addition, many internal organs—such as the heart—also become enlarged due to growth hormone and IGF-1-induced hypertrophy, and this can interfere with their ability to function normally. In some acromegalics, the tissues comprising the larynx enlarge, resulting in a deepening of the voice as in our subject. The enlarged and deformed tongue was likely a contributor to the sleep apnea and snoring reported by the patient; this is called obstructive sleep apnea because the tongue base weakens and, consequently, the tongue obstructs the upper airway (see Chapter 13 for a discussion of sleep apnea). Finally, roughly half of all people with acromegaly have elevated blood pressure (hypertension). The cause of the hypertension is uncertain, but it is a serious medical condition that requires treatment with antihypertensive drugs.

As described earlier, adults continue to make and secrete growth hormone even after growth ceases. That is because growth hormone has metabolic actions in addition to its effects on growth. The major actions of growth hormone in metabolism are to increase the concentrations of glucose and fatty acids in the blood and decrease the sensitivity of skeletal muscle and adipose tissue to insulin. Not surprisingly, therefore, one of the stimuli that increases growth hormone concentrations in the healthy adult is a decrease in blood glucose or fatty acids. The secretion of growth hormone during these metabolic crises, however, is transient; once glucose or fatty acid concentrations are restored to normal, growth hormone concentrations decrease to baseline. In acromegaly, however, growth hormone concentrations are almost always increased. Consequently, acromegaly is often associated with increased plasma concentrations of glucose and fatty acids, in some cases even reaching the concentrations observed in diabetes mellitus. As in Cushing's syndrome (Section D), therefore, the presence of chronically increased concentrations of growth hormone may result in diabetes-like symptoms. This explains why our patient had a high fasting plasma glucose concentration.

Our subject was fortunate to have had a quick diagnosis. This case study illustrates one of the confounding features of endocrine disorders. The rarity of some endocrine diseases (e.g., acromegaly occurs in roughly 4 per million individuals), together with the fact that the symptoms of a given endocrine disease can be varied and insidious in their onset, often results in a delayed diagnosis. This means that in many cases, a patient is subjected to numerous tests for more common disorders before a diagnosis of endocrine disease is made.

Treatment of gigantism and acromegaly usually requires surgical removal of the pituitary tumor. The residual normal pituitary tissue is then sufficient to maintain baseline growth hormone concentrations. If this treatment is impossible or not successful, treatment with long-acting analogs of somatostatin is sometimes necessary. (Recall that somatostatin is the hypothalamic hormone that inhibits GH secretion.) Our patient elected to have surgery. This resulted in a reduction in his plasma growth hormone and IGF-1 concentrations. With time, several of his symptoms were reduced, including the increased plasma glucose concentrations. However, within 2 years, his growth hormone and IGF-1 concentrations were three times higher than the normal range for his age and a follow-up MRI revealed that the tumor had regrown. Not wanting a second surgery, the patient was treated with radiation therapy focused on the pituitary tumor, followed by regular administration of somatostatin analogs. This treatment decreased but did not completely normalize his hormone concentrations. His blood pressure remained elevated and was treated with two different antihypertensive drugs (see Chapter 12).

Clinical terms: acromegaly, gigantism, prognathism

See Chapter 19 for complete, integrative case studies.

TABLE 11.6	Major Hormones Influencing Growth
Hormone	**Principal Actions**
Growth hormone	Major stimulus of postnatal growth: Induces precursor cells to differentiate and secrete insulin-like growth factor 1 (IGF-1), which stimulates cell division Stimulates liver to secrete IGF-1 Stimulates protein synthesis
Insulin	Stimulates fetal growth Stimulates postnatal growth by stimulating secretion of IGF-1 Stimulates protein synthesis
Thyroid hormone	Permissive for growth hormone's secretion and actions Permissive for development of the central nervous system
Testosterone	Stimulates growth at puberty, in large part by stimulating the secretion of growth hormone Causes eventual epiphyseal closure Stimulates protein synthesis in male
Estrogen	Stimulates the secretion of growth hormone at puberty Causes eventual epiphyseal closure
Cortisol	Inhibits growth Stimulates protein catabolism

Summary Tables

Summary tables are used to bring together large amounts of information that may be scattered throughout the book or to summarize small or moderate amounts of information. The tables complement the accompanying figures to provide a rapid means of reviewing the most important material in the chapter.

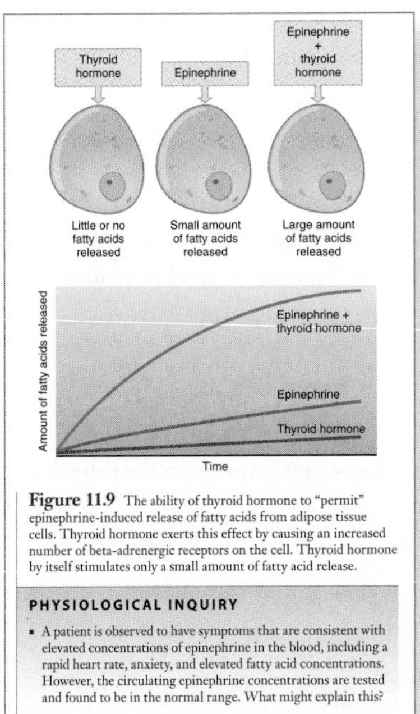

Figure 11.9 The ability of thyroid hormone to "permit" epinephrine-induced release of fatty acids from adipose tissue cells. Thyroid hormone exerts this effect by causing an increased number of beta-adrenergic receptors on the cell. Thyroid hormone by itself stimulates only a small amount of fatty acid release.

PHYSIOLOGICAL INQUIRY

- A patient is observed to have symptoms that are consistent with elevated concentrations of epinephrine in the blood, including a rapid heart rate, anxiety, and elevated fatty acid concentrations. However, the circulating epinephrine concentrations are tested and found to be in the normal range. What might explain this?

Answer can be found at end of chapter.

Physiological Inquiries

The authors have continued to refine and expand the number of critical-thinking questions based on many figures from all chapters. These concept checks were introduced in the eleventh edition and continue to prove extremely popular with users of the textbook. They are designed to help students become more engaged in learning a concept or process depicted in the art. These questions challenge a student to analyze the content of the figure, and occasionally to recall information from previous chapters. Many of the questions also require quantitative skills. Many instructors find that these Physiological Inquiries make great exam questions.

Anatomy and Physiology Revealed (APR) Icon—NEW!

APR icons are found in figure legends. These icons indicate that there is a direct link to APR available in the eBook provided with Connect Plus for this title! AP|R

Descriptive Art Style

A realistic three-dimensional perspective is included in many of the figures for greater clarity and understanding of concepts presented.

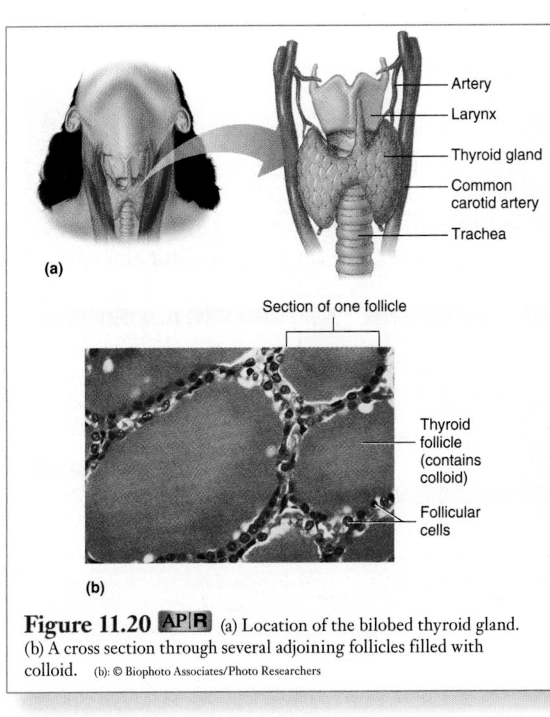

Figure 11.20 AP|R (a) Location of the bilobed thyroid gland. (b) A cross section through several adjoining follicles filled with colloid. (b): © Biophoto Associates/Photo Researchers

Guided Tour Through a Chapter

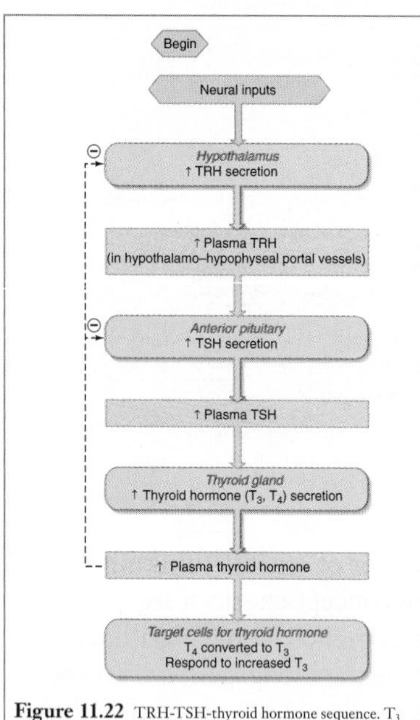

Figure 11.22 TRH-TSH-thyroid hormone sequence. T_3 and T_4 inhibit secretion of TSH and TRH by negative feedback, indicated by the ⊖ symbol.

Flow Diagrams

Long a hallmark of this book, extensive use of flow diagrams is continued in this edition. They have been updated to assist in learning.

Key to Flow Diagrams

- The beginning boxes of the diagrams are color-coded green.
- Other boxes are consistently color-coded throughout the book.
- Structures are always shown in three-dimensional form.

Uniform Color-Coded Illustrations

Color-coding is effectively used to promote learning. For example, there are specific colors for extracellular fluid, the intracellular fluid, muscle filaments, and transporter molecules.

Multilevel Perspective

Illustrations depicting complex structures or processes combine macroscopic and microscopic views to help students see the relationships between increasingly detailed drawings.

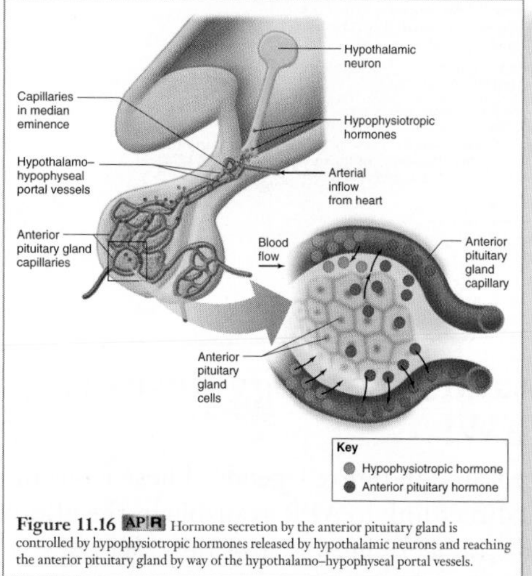

Figure 11.16 APIR Hormone secretion by the anterior pituitary gland is controlled by hypophysiotropic hormones released by hypothalamic neurons and reaching the anterior pituitary gland by way of the hypothalamo–hypophyseal portal vessels.

End of Section

At the end of sections throughout the book, you will find a summary, review questions, key terms, and clinical terms.

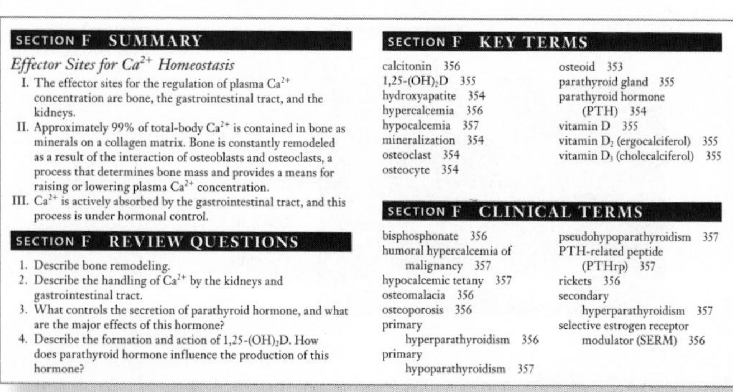

SECTION F SUMMARY

Effector Sites for Ca^{2+} Homeostasis

I. The effector sites for the regulation of plasma Ca^{2+} concentration are bone, the gastrointestinal tract, and the kidneys.
II. Approximately 99% of total-body Ca^{2+} is contained in bone as minerals on a collagen matrix. Bone is constantly remodeled as a result of the interaction of osteoblasts and osteoclasts, a process that determines bone mass and provides a means for raising or lowering plasma Ca^{2+} concentration.
III. Ca^{2+} is actively absorbed by the gastrointestinal tract, and this process is under hormonal control.

SECTION F REVIEW QUESTIONS

1. Describe bone remodeling.
2. Describe the handling of Ca^{2+} by the kidneys and gastrointestinal tract.
3. What controls the secretion of parathyroid hormone, and what are the major effects of this hormone?
4. Describe the formation and action of 1,25-$(OH)_2$D. How does parathyroid hormone influence the production of this hormone?

SECTION F KEY TERMS

calcitonin 356
1,25-$(OH)_2$D 355
hydroxyapatite 354
hypercalcemia 356
hypocalcemia 357
mineralization 354
osteoclast 354
osteocyte 354
osteoid 353
parathyroid gland 355
parathyroid hormone (PTH) 354
vitamin D 355
vitamin D_2 (ergocalciferol) 355
vitamin D_3 (cholecalciferol) 355

SECTION F CLINICAL TERMS

bisphosphonate 356
humoral hypercalcemia of malignancy 357
hypocalcemic tetany 357
osteomalacia 356
osteoporosis 356
primary hyperparathyroidism 356
primary hypoparathyroidism 357
pseudohypoparathyroidism 357
PTH-related peptide (PTHrp) 357
rickets 356
secondary hyperparathyroidism 357
selective estrogen receptor modulator (SERM) 356

End of Chapter

At the end of the chapters, you will find

- Test Questions that are designed to test student comprehension of key concepts.
- *NEW!*—General Principles Assessment questions that test the student's ability to relate the material covered in a given chapter to one or more of the General Principles of Physiology described in Chapter 1. This provides a powerful unifying theme to understanding all of physiology, and is also an excellent gauge of a student's progress from the beginning to the end of a semester.
- Quantitative and Thought Questions that challenge the student to go beyond the memorization of facts, to solve problems and to encourage thinking about the meaning or broader significance of what has just been read.
- Answers to the Physiological Inquiries in that chapter.

CHAPTER 11 TEST QUESTIONS *Answers found in Appendix A.*

1–5: Match the hormone with the function or feature (choices a–e).

Hormone:
1. vasopressin
2. ACTH
3. oxytocin
4. prolactin
5. luteinizing hormone

Function:
a. tropic for the adrenal cortex
b. is controlled by an amine-derived hormone of the hypothalamus
c. antidiuresis
d. stimulation of testosterone production
e. stimulation of uterine contractions during labor

6. In the following figure, which hormone (A or B) binds to receptor X with higher affinity?

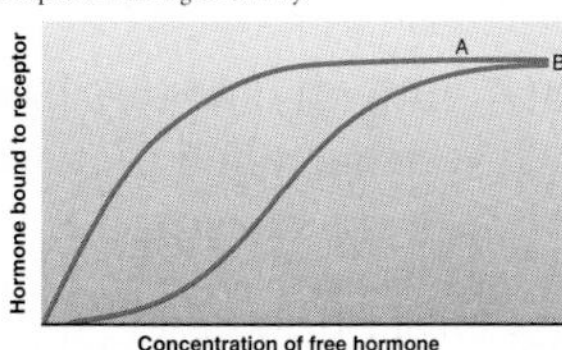

7. Which is *not* a symptom of Cushing's disease?
a. high blood pressure
b. bone loss
c. suppressed immune function
d. goiter
e. hyperglycemia (increased blood glucose)

8. Tremors, nervousness, and increased heart rate can all be symptoms of
a. increased activation of the sympathetic nervous system.
b. excessive secretion of epinephrine from the adrenal medulla.
c. hyperthyroidism.
d. hypothyroidism.
e. answers a, b, and c (all are correct).

9. Which of the following could theoretically result in short stature?
a. pituitary tumor making excess thyroid-stimulating hormone
b. mutations that result in inactive IGF-1 receptors
c. delayed onset of puberty
d. decreased hypothalamic concentrations of somatostatin
e. normal plasma GH but decreased feedback of GH on GHRH

10. Choose the correct statement.
a. During times of stress, cortisol acts as an anabolic hormone in muscle and adipose tissue.
b. A deficiency of thyroid hormone would result in increased cellular concentrations of Na^+/K^+-ATPase pumps in target tissues.
c. The posterior pituitary is connected to the hypothalamus by long portal vessels.
d. Adrenal insufficiency often results in increased blood pressure and increased plasma glucose concentrations.
e. A lack of iodide in the diet will have no significant effect on the concentration of circulating thyroid hormone for at least several weeks.

11. A lower-than-normal concentration of plasma Ca^{2+} causes
a. a PTH-mediated increase in 25-OH D.
b. a decrease in renal 1-hydroxylase activity.
c. a decrease in the urinary excretion of Ca^{2+}.
d. a decrease in bone resorption.
e. an increase in vitamin D release from the skin.

12. Which of the following is *not* consistent with primary hyperparathyroidism?
a. hypercalcemia
b. elevated plasma 1,25-$(OH)_2$D
c. increased urinary excretion of phosphate ions
d. a decrease in Ca^{2+} resorption from bone
e. an increase in Ca^{2+} reabsorption in the kidney

True or False

13. T_4 is the chief circulating form of thyroid hormone but is less active than T_3.
14. Acromegaly is usually associated with hypoglycemia and hypotension.
15. Thyroid hormone and cortisol are both permissive for the actions of epinephrine.

CHAPTER 11 GENERAL PRINCIPLES ASSESSMENT *Answers found in Appendix A.*

1. Referring back to Tables 11.3, 11.4, and 11.5, explain how certain of the actions of epinephrine, cortisol, and growth hormone illustrate in part the general principle of physiology that *most physiological functions are controlled by multiple regulatory systems, often working in opposition.*
2. Another general principle of physiology is that *structure is a determinant of—and has coevolved with—function.* The structure of the thyroid gland is very unlike other endocrine glands. How is the structure of this gland related to its function?
3. *Homeostasis is essential for health and survival.* How do parathyroid hormone, ADH, and thyroid hormone contribute to homeostasis? What might be the consequence of having too little of each of those hormones?

CHAPTER 11 QUANTITATIVE AND THOUGHT QUESTIONS *Answers found at www.mhhe.com/widmaier13.*

1. In an experimental animal, the sympathetic preganglionic fibers to the adrenal medulla are cut. What happens to the plasma concentration of epinephrine at rest and during stress?
2. During pregnancy, there is an increase in the liver's production and, consequently, the plasma concentration of the major plasma binding protein for thyroid hormone. This causes a sequence of events involving feedback that results in an increase in the plasma concentrations of T_3 but no evidence of hyperthyroidism. Describe the sequence of events.
3. A child shows the following symptoms: deficient growth, failure to show sexual development, decreased ability to respond to stress. What is the most likely cause of all these symptoms?
4. If all the neural connections between the hypothalamus and pituitary gland below the median eminence were severed, the secretion of which pituitary gland hormones would be affected? Which pituitary gland hormones would not be affected?
5. Typically, an antibody to a peptide combines with the peptide and renders it nonfunctional. If an animal were given an antibody to somatostatin, the secretion of which anterior pituitary gland hormone would change and in what direction?
6. A drug that blocks the action of norepinephrine is injected directly into the hypothalamus of an experimental animal, and the secretion rates of several anterior pituitary gland hormones are observed to change. How is this possible, given the fact that norepinephrine is not a hypophysiotropic hormone?

CHAPTER 11 ANSWERS TO PHYSIOLOGICAL INQUIRIES

Figure 11.3 By storing large amounts of hormone in an endocrine cell, the plasma concentration of the hormone can be increased within seconds when the cell is stimulated. Such rapid responses may be critical for an appropriate response to a challenge to homeostasis. Packaging peptides in this way also prevents intracellular degradation.

Figure 11.5 Because steroid hormones are derived from cholesterol, they are lipophilic. Consequently, they can freely diffuse through lipid bilayers, including those that constitute secretory vesicles. Therefore, once a steroid hormone is synthesized, it diffuses out of the cell.

Figure 11.9 One explanation for this patient's symptoms may be that his or her circulating concentration of thyroid hormone was elevated. This might occur if the person's thyroid was overstimulated due, for example, to thyroid disease. The control of the anterior pituitary gland by a very small number of discrete neurons within the hypothalamus.

Figure 11.21 Iodine is not widely found in foods; in the absence of iodized salt, an acute or chronic deficiency in dietary iodine is possible. The colloid permits a long-term store of iodinated thyroglobulin that can be used during times when dietary iodine intake is reduced or absent.

Figure 11.24 Plasma cortisol concentrations would increase. This would result in decreased ACTH concentrations in the systemic blood, and CRH concentrations in the portal vein blood, due to increased negative feedback at the pituitary gland and hypothalamus, respectively. The right adrenal gland would shrink in size (atrophy) as a consequence of the decreased ACTH concentrations (decreased "trophic" stimulation of the adrenal cortex).

Figure 11.28 Note from the figure that a decrease in plasma glucose concentrations results in an increase in growth hormone concentrations. This makes sense, because one of the metabolic actions of growth hormone is to increase the concentrations will decrease. This is a form of secondary hypoparathyroidism.

Visit this book's website at **www.mhhe.com/widmaier13** for chapter quizzes, interactive learning exercises, and other study tools.

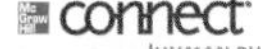

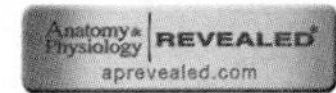

Updates and Additions

In addition to updating material throughout the text to reflect cutting-edge changes in physiology and medicine, the authors have introduced the following:

- A new unifying theme has been integrated into all chapters based on fundamental, key principles of physiology. These are outlined in Chapter 1 in a new section called General Principles of Physiology, and include such things as homeostasis, structure/function relationships, information flow, and several others. Beginning with Chapter 2, the introduction to each chapter provides a preview for the student of the general principles that will be covered in that chapter. Within the chapter, the principles are reinforced where appropriate. At the end of each chapter, one or more assessments are provided that enable the student to relate the material in that chapter to an understanding of unifying physiological themes.
- The number of Test Questions and Quantitative and Thought Questions has been expanded. These assessments complement the many test questions available free of charge to students on the McGraw-Hill website that accompanies the textbook.
- The Physiological Inquiries feature has been retained and expanded. Continued positive feedback from users of the text indicated that this learning tool is extremely valuable, and thus we have added additional inquiries associated with key figures.

In addition to new assessments, and the usual editing to make sure the text remains even more reader-friendly, up-to-date, and accurate, approximately 25 new pieces of art have been added, and another 25 existing pieces of art have been considerably modified to provide updated information. A sampling of substantive changes to each chapter follows.

Chapter 1 **Homeostasis: A Framework for Human Physiology**

New section introducing and describing the important General Principles of Physiology, providing an instructional framework that unifies all the chapters.

Chapter 2 **Chemical Composition of the Body**

Increased emphasis on the physiological relevance of chemical principles; expanded discussion of the use of isotopes in physiology with a new PET scan figure; ionic bonds treated in a new section.

Chapter 3 **Cellular Structure, Proteins, and Metabolism**

Importance of cholesterol in determining membrane fluidity is now discussed and illustrated.

Chapter 4 **Movement of Molecules Across Cell Membranes**

Compensatory endocytosis now discussed.

Chapter 5 **Control of Cells by Chemical Messengers**

Illustrations of receptor conformations with and without bound ligand are now depicted to emphasize binding-induced shape changes linked to receptor activation; IP_3 receptor/ion channel now depicted in illustration of cell signaling.

Chapter 6 **Neuronal Signaling and the Structure of the Nervous System**

New discussion about the use of adult stem cells to treat neurological diseases; new figure illustrating the way in which synapses that increase chloride conductance stabilize the membrane potential.

Chapter 7 **Sensory Physiology**

A new table has been added summarizing the general principles of sensory stimulus processing; discussion of Müller cells added to section on retinal function; expanded discussion and illustration of the mechanism by which retinal dissociates from its opsin and is enzymatically reassociated.

Chapter 8 **Consciousness, the Brain, and Behavior**

A comparison between PET, MRI, and EEG as effective tools for assessing tumors, clots, or hemorrhages in the brain has been added; new discussion of high-frequency gamma-wave patterns; updated the NREM designations to the new Phase N1–N3 nomenclature; discussion of hypnic jerk movements added; new section added describing the neural basis of the conscious state, including the role of RAS monoamine, orexins/hypocretins, and the "sleep center" of the brain; discussion of narcolepsy; new discussion regarding the role of the right cerebral hemisphere in the emotional context of language; new figure illustrating brain regions involved in consciousness; a new figure showing a model of the regulation of sleep/wake transitions; new figure of a CT scan of the brain of a person with an epidural hemorrhage.

Chapter 9 **Muscle**

A new figure illustrating cardiac muscle excitation–contraction coupling; reorganization of the first two sections of the chapter such that events are described in the order in which they occur: excitation, E–C coupling, sliding filament mechanism; updated discussion about muscle fatigue; new discussion about myostatin and its role in muscle mass; new discussion about caldesmon's role in smooth muscle function.

Chapter 10 **Control of Body Movement**

Interconnections of structures participating in the motor control hierarchy have been updated; new example demonstrating the importance of association areas in motor control.

Chapter 11 **The Endocrine System**

Role of pendrin in thyroid hormone synthesis now introduced and illustrated; steroid synthetic pathway simplified to illustrate major events; improved illustration of anatomical relationship between hypothalamus and anterior pituitary gland; addition of numerous specific examples to highlight general principles, such as hyporesponsiveness; new figure showing production of insulin from proinsulin.

Chapter 12 **Cardiovascular Physiology**

Numerous figures have been updated or improved for clarity, or modified to include additional important information; discussion added about internodal pathways between the SA and AV nodes; new description about transient outward K^+ channels in myocytes; new table added comparing hemodynamics of systemic and pulmonary circuits; new discussion about VEGF antibodies and angiogenesis; section on hypertension has been updated to include the latest information about the effects of a high-salt diet, the findings of the DASH diet study, and other environmental causes or links to hypertension.

Chapter 13 **Respiratory Physiology**

New information about the cystic fibrosis channel mutation and treatment of cystic fibrosis; new figure showing the muscles of respiration; new improved illustration of respiratory cycle; enhanced illustration of the factors that change the shape of the O_2 dissociation curve including a panel on fetal hemoglobin; new figure on brainstem respiratory control centers and simplification of the description of respiratory control.

Chapter 14 **The Kidneys and Regulation of Water and Inorganic Ions**

New figure showing major anatomical structures of the kidney; new figure and text describing the effects of vasopressin on the volume and osmolarity of the filtrate along the length of the nephron; revised and expanded discussion of the local and central control of micturition.

Chapter 15 **The Digestion and Absorption of Food**

New figure and text updating the control of bicarbonate secretion in the pancreatic duct cells and the role of the cystic fibrosis transmembrane conductance regulator (CFTR) in this process; reorganization of portions of the text to improve the flow of the chapter.

Chapter 16 **Regulation of Organic Metabolism and Energy Balance**

New figure on energy expenditure during common activities; streamlined text with greater emphasis on general principles of physiology.

Chapter 17 **Reproduction**

Reorganization of first two sections into a single new section entitled Gametogenesis, Sex Determination, and Sex Differentiation; General Principles of Reproductive Endocrinology; several new figures illustrating the events of gametogenesis, embryonic development of the male and female reproductive tracts, development of external genitalia in males and females, and synthesis of gonadal steroids; new section on anabolic steroid use.

Chapter 18 **The Immune System**

Additional artwork and photographs including a new micrograph of a human blood smear, a new micrograph of a leukocyte undergoing diapedesis, and a computer model of an immunoglobulin.

Chapter 19 **Medical Physiology: Integration Using Clinical Cases**

This chapter reinforces the General Physiological Principles introduced in Chapter 1 by demonstrating how these principles relate to human disease.

Teaching and Learning Supplements

NEW! McGraw-Hill LearnSmart™

McGraw-Hill LearnSmart™ is an online diagnostic learning system that determines the level of student knowledge, and feeds the students suitable content for their physiology course. Students learn faster and study more effectively. As a student works within the system, LearnSmart develops a personal learning path adapted to what the student has learned and retained. LearnSmart is able to recommend additional study resources to help the student master topics. This innovative and outstanding study tool also has features for instructors where they can see exactly what students have accomplished, and a built-in assessment tool for graded assignments.

For more information, go to www.mhlearnsmart.com.

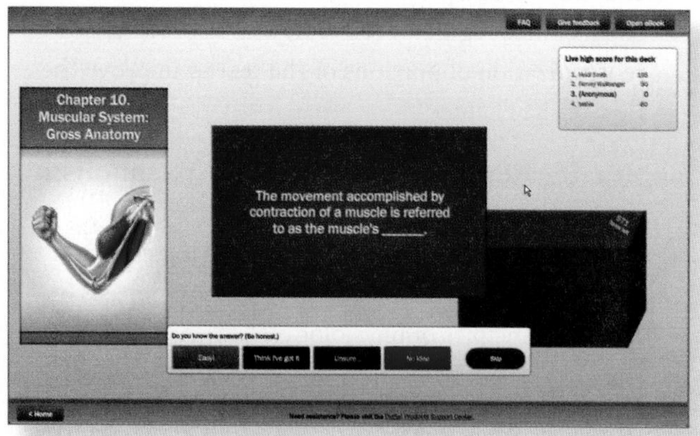

McGraw-Hill Connect™ Anatomy & Physiology

This Web-based assignment and assessment platform that gives students the means to better connect with their coursework, with their instructors, and with the important concepts that they will need to know for success now and in the future.

With Connect, instructors can deliver assignments, quizzes, and tests online. Questions are presented in an auto-gradable format and tied to the organization of the textbook. Instructors can edit existing questions and author entirely new problems; track individual student performance—by question, assignment, or in relation to the class overall—with detailed grade reports; integrate grade reports easily with learning management systems (LMS) such as WebCT and Blackboard; and much more. By choosing Connect, instructors are providing their students with a powerful tool for improving academic performance and truly mastering course material. Connect allows students to practice important skills at their own pace and on their own schedule.

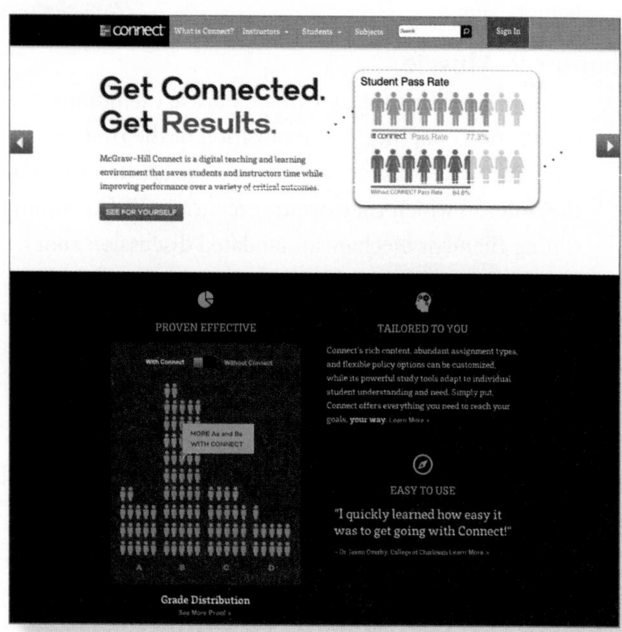

Importantly, students' assessment results and instructors' feedback are all saved online—so students can continually review their progress and plot their course to success.

Some instructors may also choose ConnectPlus™ for their students. Like Connect, ConnectPlus provides students with online assignments and assessments, plus 24/7 online access to an eBook—an online edition of the text—to aid them in successfully completing their work, wherever and whenever they choose.

Physiology Interactive Lab Simulations (Ph.I.L.S.)

NEW! Ph.I.L.S. 4.0 has been updated! Users have requested and we are providing ***five new exercises*** (Respiratory Quotient, Weight & Contraction, Insulin and Glucose Tolerance, Blood Typing, and Anti-Diuretic Hormone).

Ph.I.L.S. 4.0 is the perfect way to reinforce key physiology concepts with powerful lab experiments. Created by Dr. Phil Stephens at Villanova University, this program offers ***42 laboratory simulations*** that may be used to supplement or substitute for wet labs. All 42 labs are self-contained experiments—no lengthy instruction manual required. Users can adjust variables, view outcomes, make predictions, draw conclusions, and print lab reports. This easy-to-use software offers the flexibility to change the parameters of the lab experiment. There is no limit!

Craft your teaching resources to match the way you teach! With McGraw-Hill Create™, www.mcgrawhillcreate.com, you can easily rearrange chapters, combine material from other content sources, and quickly upload content you have written, like your course syllabus or teaching notes. Find the content you need in Create by searching through thousands of leading McGraw-Hill textbooks. Arrange your book to fit your teaching style. Create even allows you to personalize your book's appearance by selecting the cover and adding your name, school, and course information. Order a Create book and you'll receive a complimentary print review copy in 3–5 business days or a complimentary electronic review copy (eComp) via e-mail in minutes. Go to www.mcgrawhillcreate.com today and register to experience how McGraw-Hill Create™ empowers you to teach *your* students *your* way.

Text Website—www.mhhe.com/widmaier13

The text website that accompanies this text offers an extensive array of learning and teaching tools.

- Interactive Activities—Fun and exciting learning experiences await the student at *Vander's Human Physiology* text website. Chapters offer a series of interactive activities like art labeling, animations, vocabulary flashcards, and more!
- Practice Quizzes at the *Vander's Human Physiology* text website contain hundreds of test questions that gauge student mastery of chapter content. Each chapter quiz is specifically constructed to test student comprehension of key concepts. Immediate feedback to student responses explains why an answer is correct or incorrect.
- Presentation Center is an online digital library containing assets such as photos, artwork, animations, and PowerPoints that can be used to create customized lectures, visually enhanced tests and quizzes, compelling course website, or attractive printed support materials.

Test Bank

Written by the textbook authors, a computerized test bank that uses testing software to quickly create customized exams is available for this text. The user-friendly program allows instructors to search for questions by topic or format, edit existing questions or add new ones, and scramble questions for multiple versions of the same test. Word files of the test bank questions are provided for those instructors who prefer to work outside the test-generator software.

Instructor's Manual

The Instructor's Manual is available on the text website (www.mhhe.com/widmaier13). It contains teaching/learning objectives, sample lecture outlines, and the answers to Review Questions for each chapter.

The Best of Both Worlds

McGraw-Hill and Blackboard®
McGraw-Hill Higher Education and Blackboard have teamed up. What does this partnership mean for you? Blackboard users will find the single sign-on and deep Integration of ConnectPlus within their Blackboard course an invaluable benefit. Even if your school is not using Blackboard, we have a solution for you. Learn more at www.domorenow.com.

Acknowledgments

The authors are deeply indebted to the following individuals for their contributions to the thirteenth edition of *Vander's Human Physiology.* Their feedback on the twelfth edition or their critique of the revised text provided invaluable assistance and greatly improved the final product. Any errors that may remain are solely the responsibility of the authors.

Allan Albig, *Indiana State University*
Lisa Carney Anderson, *University of Minnesota*
Heather Wilson-Ashworth, *Utah Valley University*
Kim Barrett, *University of California, San Diego*
Daniel Bergman, *Grand Valley State University*
Nicole Berthelemy, *Weber State University*
Robert W. Blair, *University of Oklahoma Health Sciences Center*
Eric Blough, *Marshall University*
Carol A. Britson, *University of Mississippi*
George A. Brooks, *University of California–Berkeley*
Martin G. Burg, *Grand Valley State University*
Patricia Cai, *Brooklyn College of CUNY*
Edwin R. Chapman, *University of Wisconsin–Madison*
Pat Clark, *IUPUI*
Maria Elena de Bellard, *CSUN*
Lee D. Faucher, *University of Wisconsin–Madison SMPH*
James S. Ferraro, *Southern Illinois University–School of Medicine*
Margaret Flanigan Skinner, *University of Wyoming*
Kennon M. Garrett, *University of Oklahoma Health Sciences Center*
Nicholas Geist, *Sonoma State University*
Brian Geraghty, *CUNY @ Brooklyn College & Kingsborough Community College*
Chaya Gopalan, *St. Louis College of Pharmacy*
Marion Greaser, *University of Wisconsin–Madison*
Eric Green, *Salt Lake Community College*
Chi-Ming Hai, *Brown University*
Janet L. Haynes, *Long Island University*
Steve Henderson, *California State University*
David W. Johnson, *University of New England*
Kelly Johnson, *Kansas University*
Tim Juergens, *University of Wisconsin–Madison SMPH*
Kenneth Kaloustian, *Quinnipiac University*
David King, *Nova Southeastern University*
Brian H. Kipp, *Grand Valley State University*
Sumana Koduri, *Medical College of Wisconsin*
Dean V. Lauritzen, *City College of San Francisco*
Mingyu Liang, *Medical College of Wisconsin*
Christian Lytle, *University of California, Riverside*
Steven Magill, *Medical College of Wisconsin*
David L. Mattson, *Medical College of Wisconsin*
Donald W. Michielli, *Brooklyn College of the City University of New York*
Kevin Middleton, *California State University*
Paul Nealen, *Indiana University of PA*
Lisa Parks, *North Carolina State University*
Mark Paternostro, *West Virginia University*
Timothy Plagge, *San Diego Mesa College*
Jocelyn Parks Ramos, *Ivy Tech Community College*
Laurel B. Roberts, *University of Pittsburgh*
Angela M. Seliga, *Boston University*
Virginia K. Shea, *University of North Carolina*
Mark Smith, *Santiago Canyon College*
Andrea Sobieraj, *Brown University*
Nadja Spitzer, *Marshall University*
Ruy Tchao, *University of the Sciences*
Dana K. Vaughan, *University of Wisconsin–Oshkosh*
Gordon M. Wahler, *Midwestern University*
R. Douglas Watson, *University of Alabama at Birmingham*
Eliot Williams, *University of Wisconsin–Madison SMPH*
Loren E. Wold, *The Research Institute at Nationwide Children's Hospital/The Ohio State University*
Yuri Zagvazdin, *Nova Southeastern University*

The authors are indebted to the many individuals who assisted with the numerous digital and ancillary products associated with these text. Thank you to Beth Altschafl, Patti Atkins, Janet Casagrand, Patricia Clark, Mike Griffin, David Johnson, Tami Mau, Carla Reinstadtl, Laurel Bridges Roberts, Rebecca Sheller, Andrea Jeanne Sobieraj, Nadja Spitzer, and Melanie Waite-Wright.

The authors are also indebted to the editors and staff at McGraw-Hill Higher Education who contributed to the development and publication of this text, particularly Developmental Editor Fran Simon, Brand Manager Marija Magner, Project Manager Sherry Kane, Production Supervisor Sandy Ludovissy, Designer Tara McDermott, and Photo Researcher John Leland. We also thank freelance copy editor C. Jeanne Patterson and freelance proofreader Beatrice Sussman. As always, we are grateful to the many students and faculty who have provided us with critiques and suggestions for improvement.

Eric P. Widmaier
Hershel Raff
Kevin T. Strang

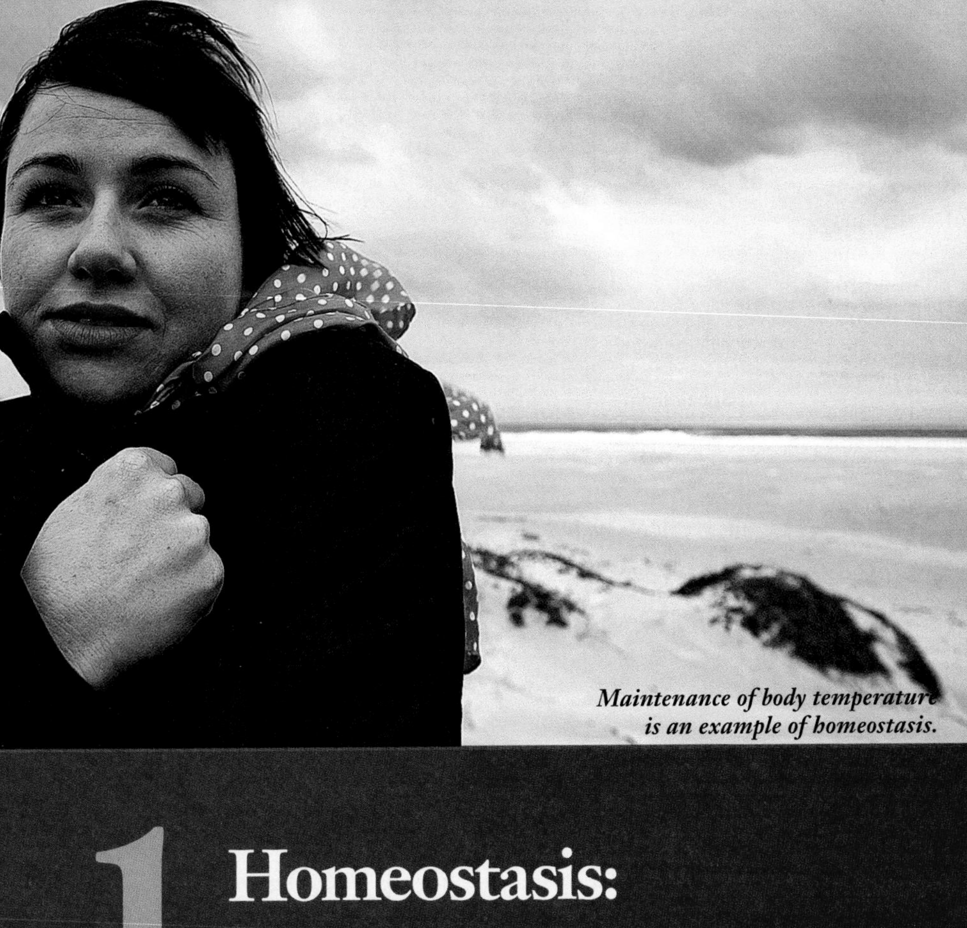

Maintenance of body temperature is an example of homeostasis.

1 Homeostasis:

A FRAMEWORK FOR HUMAN PHYSIOLOGY

The purpose of this chapter is to provide an orientation to the subject of human physiology and the central role of homeostasis in the study of this science. An understanding of the functions of the body also requires knowledge of the structures and relationships of the body parts. For this reason, this chapter also introduces the way the body is organized into cells, tissues, organs, and organ systems. Lastly, several "General Principles of Physiology" are introduced. These serve as unifying themes throughout the textbook, and the student is encouraged to return to them often to see how they apply to the material covered in subsequent chapters.

1.1 The Scope of Human Physiology

Physiology is the study of how living organisms function. As applied to human beings, its scope is extremely broad. At one end of the spectrum, it includes the study of individual molecules—for example, how a particular protein's shape and electrical properties allow it to function as a channel for ions to move into or out of a cell. At the other end, it is concerned with complex processes that depend on the integrated functions of many organs in the body—for example, how the heart, kidneys, and several glands all work together to cause the excretion of more sodium ions in the urine when a person has eaten salty food.

Physiologists are interested in function and integration—how parts of the body work together at various levels of organization and, most importantly, in the entire organism. Even when physiologists study parts of organisms, all the way down to individual molecules, the intention is ultimately to apply the information they gain to understanding the function of the whole body. As the nineteenth-century physiologist Claude Bernard put it, "After carrying out an analysis of phenomena, we must . . . always reconstruct our physiological synthesis, so as to see the *joint action* of all the parts we have isolated. . . ."

In this regard, a very important point must be made about the present and future status of physiology. It is easy for a student to gain the impression from a textbook that almost everything is known about the subject, but nothing could be farther from the truth for physiology. Many areas of function are still only poorly understood, such as how the workings of the brain produce conscious thought and memory.

Finally, in many areas of this text, we will relate physiology to medicine. Some disease states can be viewed as physiology "gone wrong," or **pathophysiology,** which makes an understanding of physiology essential for the study and practice of medicine. Indeed, many physiologists are actively engaged in research on the physiological bases of a wide range of diseases. In this text, we will give many examples of pathophysiology to illustrate the basic physiology that underlies the disease. A handy index of all the diseases and medical conditions discussed in this text appears in Appendix B. We begin our study of physiology by describing the organization of the structures of the human body.

1.2 How Is the Body Organized?

Before exploring how the human body works, it is necessary to understand the components of the body and their anatomical relationships to each other. The simplest structural units into which a complex multicellular organism can be divided and still retain the functions characteristic of life are called **cells** (**Figure 1.1**). Each human being begins as a single cell, a fertilized egg, which divides to create two cells, each of which divides in turn to result in four cells, and so on. If cell multiplication were the only event occurring, the end result would be a spherical mass of identical cells. During development, however, each cell

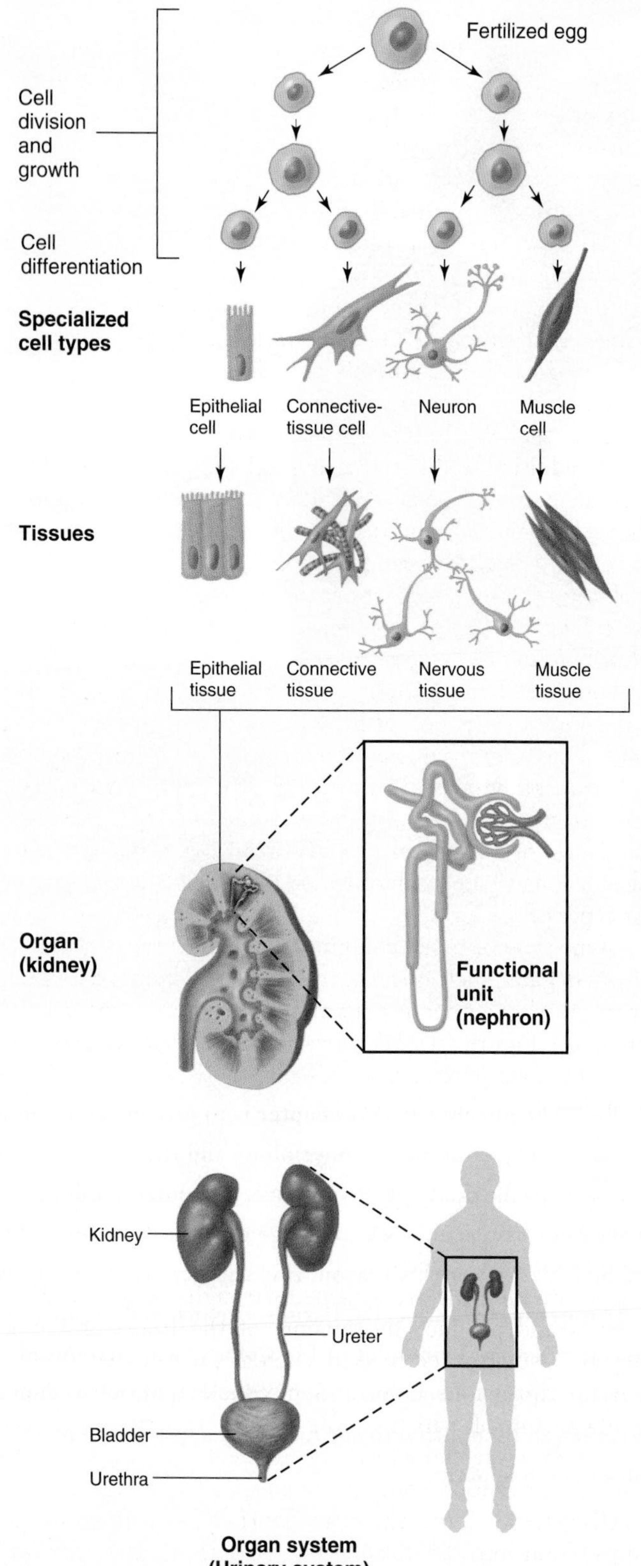

Figure 1.1 Levels of cellular organization. The nephron is not drawn to scale.

becomes specialized for the performance of a particular function, such as producing force and movement or generating electrical signals. The process of transforming an unspecialized cell into a specialized cell is known as **cell**

differentiation, the study of which is one of the most exciting areas in biology today. About 200 distinct kinds of cells can be identified in the body in terms of differences in structure and function. When cells are classified according to the broad types of function they perform, however, four major categories emerge: (1) muscle cells, (2) neurons, (3) epithelial cells, and (4) connective-tissue cells. In each of these functional categories, several cell types perform variations of the specialized function. For example, there are three types of muscle cells—skeletal, cardiac, and smooth. These cells differ from each other in shape, in the mechanisms controlling their contractile activity, and in their location in the various organs of the body, but each of them is a muscle cell.

In addition to differentiating, cells migrate to new locations during development and form selective adhesions with other cells to produce multicellular structures. In this manner, the cells of the body arrange themselves in various combinations to form a hierarchy of organized structures. Differentiated cells with similar properties aggregate to form **tissues.** Corresponding to the four general categories of differentiated cells, there are four general types of tissues: (1) **muscle tissue,** (2) **nervous tissue,** (3) **epithelial tissue,** and (4) **connective tissue.** The term *tissue* is used in different ways. It is formally defined as an aggregate of a single type of specialized cell. However, it is also commonly used to denote the general cellular fabric of any organ or structure—for example, kidney tissue or lung tissue, each of which in fact usually contains all four types of tissue.

One type of tissue combines with other types of tissues to form **organs,** such as the heart, lungs, and kidneys. Organs, in turn, work together as **organ systems,** such as the urinary system (see Figure 1.1). We turn now to a brief discussion of each of the four general types of cells and tissues that make up the organs of the human body.

Muscle Cells and Tissue

As noted earlier, there are three types of muscle cells. These cells form skeletal, cardiac, or smooth muscle tissue. All **muscle cells** are specialized to generate mechanical force. Skeletal muscle cells are attached through other structures to bones and produce movements of the limbs or trunk. They are also attached to skin, such as the muscles producing facial expressions. Contraction of skeletal muscle is under voluntary control, which simply means that you can choose to contract a skeletal muscle whenever you wish. Cardiac muscle cells are found only in the heart. When cardiac muscle cells generate force, the heart contracts and consequently pumps blood into the circulation. Smooth muscle cells surround many of the tubes in the body—blood vessels, for example, or the tubes of the gastrointestinal tract—and their contraction decreases the diameter or shortens the length of these tubes. For example, contraction of smooth muscle cells along the esophagus—the tube leading from the pharynx to the stomach—helps "squeeze" swallowed food down to the stomach. Cardiac and smooth muscle tissues are said to be "involuntary" muscle, because you cannot consciously alter the activity of these types of muscle. You will learn about the structure and function of each of the three types of muscle cells in Chapter 9.

Neurons and Nervous Tissue

A **neuron** is a cell of the nervous system that is specialized to initiate, integrate, and conduct electrical signals to other cells, sometimes over long distances. A signal may initiate new electrical signals in other neurons, or it may stimulate a gland cell to secrete substances or a muscle cell to contract. Thus, neurons provide a major means of controlling the activities of other cells. The incredible complexity of connections between neurons underlies such phenomena as consciousness and perception. A collection of neurons forms nervous tissue, such as that of the brain or spinal cord. In some parts of the body, cellular extensions from many neurons are packaged together along with connective tissue (described shortly); these neuron extensions form a nerve, which carries the signals from many neurons between the nervous system and other parts of the body. Neurons, nervous tissue, and the nervous system will be covered in Chapter 6.

Epithelial Cells and Epithelial Tissue

Epithelial cells are specialized for the selective secretion and absorption of ions and organic molecules, and for protection. These cells are characterized and named according to their unique shapes, including cuboidal (cube-shaped), columnar (elongated), squamous (flattened), and ciliated. Epithelial tissue (known as an epithelium) may form from any type of epithelial cell. Epithelia may be arranged in single-cell-thick tissue, called a simple epithelium, or a thicker tissue consisting of numerous layers of cells, called a stratified epithelium. The type of epithelium that forms in a given region of the body reflects the function of that particular epithelium. For example, the epithelium that lines the inner surface of the main airway, the trachea, consists of ciliated epithelial cells (see Chapter 13). The beating of these cilia helps propel mucus up the trachea and into the mouth, which aids in preventing airborne particles and pollutants from reaching the sensitive lung tissue.

Epithelia are located at the surfaces that cover the body or individual organs, and they line the inner surfaces of the tubular and hollow structures within the body, such as the trachea just mentioned. Epithelial cells rest on an extracellular protein layer called the **basement membrane,** which (among other functions) anchors the tissue (**Figure 1.2**). The side of the cell anchored to the basement membrane is called the basolateral side; the opposite side, which typically faces the interior (called the lumen) of a structure such as the trachea or the tubules of the kidney (see Figure 1.1), is called the apical side. A defining feature of many epithelia is that the two sides of all the epithelial cells in the tissue may perform different physiological functions. In addition, the cells are held together along their lateral surfaces by extracellular barriers called tight junctions (look ahead to Figure 3.9, b and c, for a depiction of tight junctions). Tight junctions enable epithelia to form boundaries between body compartments and to function as selective barriers regulating the exchange of molecules. For

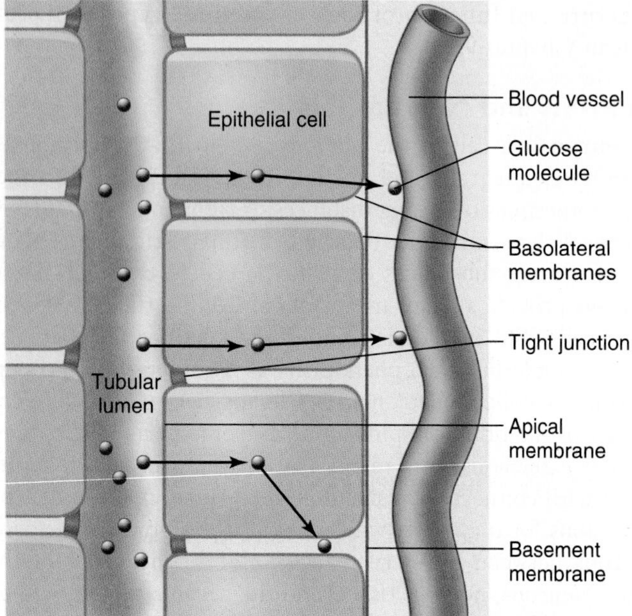

Figure 1.2 Epithelial tissue lining the inside of a structure such as a kidney tubule. The basolateral side of the cell is attached to a basement membrane. Each side of the cell can perform different functions, as in this example in which glucose is moved across the epithelium, first directed into the cell, and then directed out of the cell.

example, the epithelial cells at the surface of the skin form a barrier that prevents most substances in the external environment from entering the body through the skin. In the kidney tubules, the apical membranes transport useful solutes such as the sugar glucose from the tubule lumen into the epithelial cell; the basolateral sides of the cells transport glucose out of the cell and into the surrounding fluid where it can reach the bloodstream. The tight junctions prevent glucose from leaking "backward."

Connective-Tissue Cells and Connective Tissue

Connective-tissue cells, as their name implies, connect, anchor, and support the structures of the body. Some connective-tissue cells are found in the loose meshwork of cells and fibers underlying most epithelial layers; this is called loose connective tissue. Another type called dense connective tissue includes the tough, rigid tissue that makes up tendons and ligaments. Other types of connective tissue include bone, cartilage, and adipose (fat-storing) tissue. Finally, blood is a type of fluid connective tissue. This is because the cells in the blood have the same embryonic origin as other connective tissue, and because the blood connects the various organs and tissues of the body through the delivery of nutrients, removal of wastes, and transport of chemical signals from one part of the body to another.

An important function of some connective tissue is to form the **extracellular matrix** (ECM) around cells. The immediate environment that surrounds each individual cell in the body is the **extracellular fluid.** Actually, this fluid is interspersed within a complex ECM consisting of a mixture of proteins; polysaccharides (chains of sugar molecules); and, in some cases, minerals, specific for any given tissue. The matrix serves two general functions: (1) it provides a scaffold for cellular attachments; and (2) it transmits information in the form of chemical messengers to the cells to help regulate their activity, migration, growth, and differentiation.

The proteins of the extracellular matrix consist of proteins called **fibers**—ropelike **collagen fibers** and rubberband-like **elastin fibers**—and a mixture of nonfibrous proteins that contain carbohydrate. In some ways, the extracellular matrix is analogous to reinforced concrete. The fibers of the matrix, particularly collagen, which constitutes as much as one-third of all bodily proteins, are like the reinforcing iron mesh or rods in the concrete. The carbohydrate-containing protein molecules are analogous to the surrounding cement. However, these latter molecules are not merely inert packing material, as in concrete, but function as adhesion or recognition molecules between cells. Thus, they are links in the communication between extracellular messenger molecules and cells.

Organs and Organ Systems

Organs are composed of two or more of the four kinds of tissues arranged in various proportions and patterns, such as sheets, tubes, layers, bundles, and strips. For example, the kidneys consist of (1) a series of small tubes, each composed of a simple epithelium; (2) blood vessels, whose walls contain varying quantities of smooth muscle and connective tissue; (3) extensions from neurons that end near the muscle and epithelial cells; (4) a loose network of connective-tissue elements that are interspersed throughout the kidneys and include the protective capsule that surrounds the organ.

Many organs are organized into small, similar subunits often referred to as **functional units,** each performing the function of the organ. For example, the functional unit of the kidney, the nephron, contains the small tubes mentioned in the previous paragraph. The total production of urine by the kidneys is the sum of the amounts produced by the 2 million or so individual nephrons.

Finally, we have the organ system, a collection of organs that together perform an overall function. For example, the kidneys; the urinary bladder; the ureters, the tubes leading from the kidneys to the bladder; and the urethra, the tube leading from the bladder to the exterior, constitute the urinary system. **Table 1.1** lists the components and functions of the organ systems in the body.

To sum up, the human body can be viewed as a complex society of differentiated cells that combine structurally and functionally to carry out the functions essential to the survival of the entire organism. The individual cells constitute the basic units of this society, and almost all of these cells individually exhibit the fundamental activities common to all forms of life, such as metabolism and replication. Key to the survival of all body cells is the **internal environment** of the body; this refers to the fluids that surround cells and exist in the blood. These fluid compartments and one other—that which exists inside cells—are described next.

TABLE 1.1	Organ Systems of the Body	
System	**Major Organs or Tissues**	**Primary Functions**
Circulatory	Heart, blood vessels, blood	Transport of blood throughout the body
Digestive	Mouth, salivary glands, pharynx, esophagus, stomach, small and large intestines, anus, pancreas, liver, gallbladder	Digestion and absorption of nutrients and water; elimination of wastes
Endocrine	All glands or organs secreting hormones: Pancreas, testes, ovaries, hypothalamus, kidneys, pituitary, thyroid, parathyroids, adrenals, stomach, small intestine, liver, adipose tissue, heart, and pineal gland; and endocrine cells in other organs	Regulation and coordination of many activities in the body, including growth, metabolism, reproduction, blood pressure, water and electrolyte balance, and others
Immune	White blood cells and their organs of production	Defense against pathogens
Integumentary	Skin	Protection against injury and dehydration; defense against pathogens; regulation of body temperature
Lymphatic	Lymph vessels, lymph nodes	Collection of extracellular fluid for return to blood; participation in immune defenses; absorption of fats from digestive system
Musculoskeletal	Cartilage, bone, ligaments, tendons, joints, skeletal muscle	Support, protection, and movement of the body; production of blood cells
Nervous	Brain, spinal cord, peripheral nerves and ganglia, sense organs	Regulation and coordination of many activities in the body; detection of and response to changes in the internal and external environments; states of consciousness; learning; memory; emotion; others
Reproductive	Male: Testes, penis, and associated ducts and glands Female: Ovaries, fallopian tubes, uterus, vagina, mammary glands	Male: Production of sperm; transfer of sperm to female Female: Production of eggs; provision of a nutritive environment for the developing embryo and fetus; nutrition of the infant
Respiratory	Nose, pharynx, larynx, trachea, bronchi, lungs	Exchange of carbon dioxide and oxygen; regulation of hydrogen ion concentration in the body fluids
Urinary	Kidneys, ureters, bladder, urethra	Regulation of plasma composition through controlled excretion of salts, water, and organic wastes

1.3 Body Fluid Compartments

Water is present within and around the cells of the body, and within all the blood vessels. When we refer to "body fluids," we are referring to a watery solution of dissolved substances such as oxygen, nutrients, and wastes. Body fluids exist in two major compartments, intracellular fluid and extracellular fluid. **Intracellular fluid** is the fluid contained within all the cells of the body and accounts for about 67% of all the fluid in the body. Collectively, the fluid present in the blood and in the spaces surrounding cells is called **extracellular fluid,** that is, all the fluid that is outside of cells. Of this, only about 20%–25% is in the fluid portion of blood, which is called the **plasma,** in which the various blood cells are suspended. The remaining 75%–80% of the extracellular fluid, which lies around and between cells, is known as the **interstitial fluid.** The space containing interstitial fluid is called the **interstitium.** Therefore, the total volume of extracellular fluid is the sum of the plasma and interstitial volumes. **Figure 1.3** summarizes the relative volumes of water in the different fluid compartments of the body. Water accounts for about 55%–60% of body weight in an adult.

As the blood flows through the smallest of blood vessels in all parts of the body, the plasma exchanges oxygen, nutrients, wastes, and other substances with the interstitial fluid. Because of these exchanges, concentrations of dissolved substances are virtually identical in the plasma and interstitial fluid, except for protein concentration (which, as you will learn in Chapter 12, remains higher in plasma than in interstitial fluid). With this major exception, the entire extracellular fluid may be considered to have a homogeneous solute composition. In contrast, the composition of the extracellular

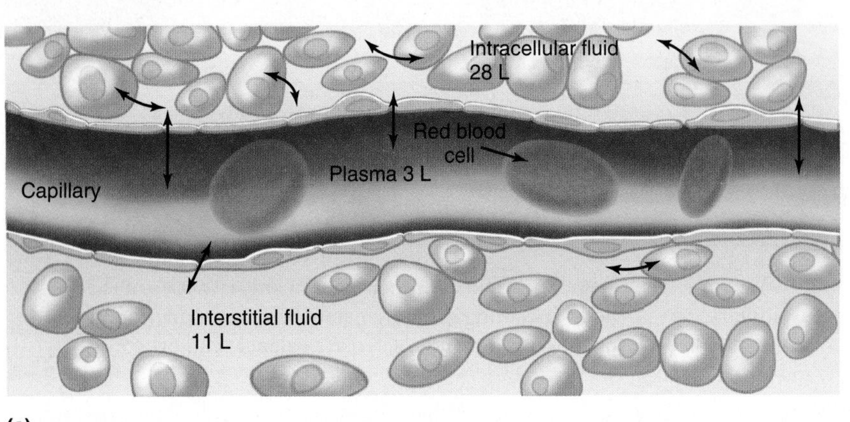

(a)

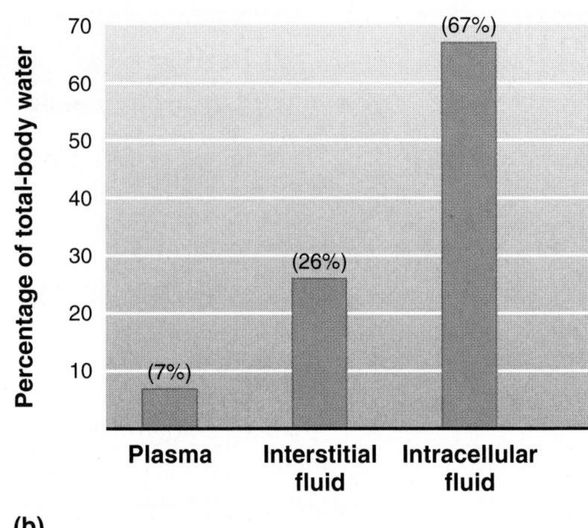

(b)

Figure 1.3 Fluid compartments of the body. Volumes are for an average 70-kilogram (kg) (154-pound [lb]) person. (a) The bidirectional arrows indicate that fluid can move between any two adjacent compartments. Total-body water is about 42 liters (L), which makes up about 55%–60% of body weight. (b) The approximate percentage of total-body water normally found in each compartment.

PHYSIOLOGICAL INQUIRY

- What fraction of total-body water is extracellular? Assume that water constitutes 60% of a person's body weight. What fraction of this person's body weight is due to extracellular body water?

Answer can be found at end of chapter.

fluid is very different from that of the intracellular fluid. Maintaining differences in fluid composition across the cell membrane is an important way in which cells regulate their own activity. For example, intracellular fluid contains many different proteins that are important in regulating cellular events such as growth and metabolism. These proteins must be retained within the intracellular fluid and are not required in the extracellular fluid.

Compartmentalization is an important feature of physiology and is achieved by barriers between the compartments. The properties of the barriers determine which substances can move between compartments. These movements, in turn, account for the differences in composition of the different compartments. In the case of the body fluid compartments, plasma membranes that surround each cell separate the intracellular fluid from the extracellular fluid. Chapters 3 and 4 describe the properties of plasma membranes and how they account for the profound differences between intracellular and extracellular fluid. In contrast, the two components of extracellular fluid—the interstitial fluid and the plasma—are separated by the wall of the blood vessels. Chapter 12 discusses how this barrier normally keeps 75%–80% of the extracellular fluid in the interstitial compartment and restricts proteins mainly to the plasma.

With this understanding of the structural organization of the body, we turn to a description of how balance is achieved in the internal environment of the body.

1.4 Homeostasis: A Defining Feature of Physiology

From the earliest days of physiology—at least as early as the time of Aristotle—physicians recognized that good health was somehow associated with a balance among the multiple life-sustaining forces ("humours") in the body. It would take millennia, however, for scientists to determine what it was that was being balanced and how this balance was achieved. The advent of modern tools of science, including the ordinary microscope, led to the discovery that the human body is composed of trillions of cells, each of which can permit movement of certain substances—but not others—across the cell membrane. Over the course of the nineteenth and twentieth centuries, it became clear that most cells are in contact with the interstitial fluid. The interstitial fluid, in turn, was found to be in a state of flux, with water and solutes such as ions and gases moving back and forth through it between the cell interiors and the blood in nearby capillaries (see Figure 1.3).

It was further determined by careful observation that most of the common physiological variables found in healthy organisms such as humans—blood pressure; body temperature; and blood-borne factors such as oxygen, glucose, and sodium ions, for example—are maintained within a predictable range. This is true despite external environmental conditions that may be far from constant. Thus was born the idea, first put forth by Claude Bernard, of a constant internal environment that is a prerequisite for good health, a concept later refined by the American physiologist Walter Cannon, who coined the term *homeostasis*.

Originally, **homeostasis** was defined as a state of reasonably stable balance between physiological variables such as those just described. However, this simple definition cannot give one a complete appreciation of what homeostasis entails. There probably is no such thing as a physiological variable that is constant over long periods of time. In fact, some variables undergo fairly dramatic swings around an average value during the course of a day, yet are still considered to be in balance. That is because homeostasis is a *dynamic*, not a static, process.

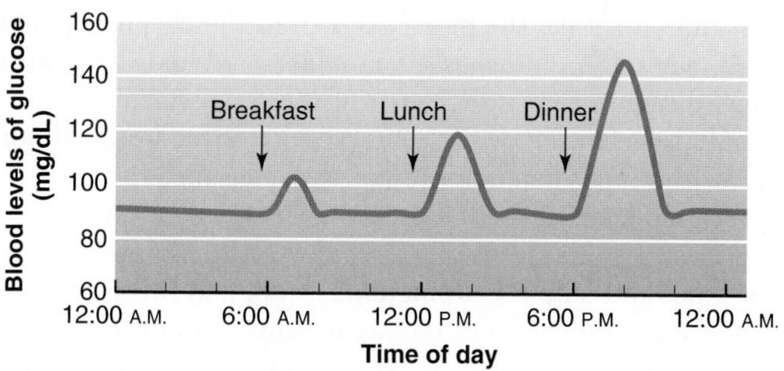

Figure 1.4 Changes in blood glucose concentrations during a typical 24 h period. Note that glucose concentration increases after each meal, more so after larger meals, and then returns to the premeal concentration in a short while. The profile shown here is that of a person who is homeostatic for blood glucose, even though concentrations of this sugar vary considerably throughout the day.

Consider swings in the concentration of glucose in the blood over the course of a day (**Figure 1.4**). After a typical meal, carbohydrates in food are broken down in the intestines into glucose molecules, which are then absorbed across the intestinal epithelium and released into the blood. As a consequence, blood glucose concentrations increase considerably within a short time after eating. Clearly, such a large change in the blood concentration of glucose is not consistent with the idea of a stable or static internal environment. What is important is that once the concentration of glucose in the blood increases, compensatory mechanisms restore it toward the concentration it was before the meal. These homeostatic compensatory mechanisms do not, however, overshoot to any significant degree in the opposite direction. That is, the blood glucose usually does not decrease below the premeal concentration, or does so only slightly. In the case of glucose, the endocrine system is primarily responsible for this adjustment, but a wide variety of control systems may be initiated to regulate other processes. In later chapters, we will see how every organ and tissue of the human body contributes to homeostasis, sometimes in multiple ways, and usually in concert with each other.

Homeostasis, therefore, does not imply that a given physiological function or variable is rigidly constant with respect to time but that it fluctuates within a predictable and often narrow range. When disturbed above or below the normal range, it is restored to normal.

What do we mean when we say that something varies within a normal range? This depends on just what we are monitoring. If the oxygen level in the blood of a healthy person breathing air at sea level is measured, it barely changes over the course of time, even if the person exercises. Such a system is said to be tightly controlled and to demonstrate very little variability or scatter around an average value. Blood glucose concentrations, as we have seen, may vary considerably over the course of a day. Yet, if the daily average glucose concentration was determined in the same person on many consecutive days, it would be much more predictable over days or even years than random, individual measurements of glucose over the course of a single day. In other words, there may be considerable variation in glucose values over short time periods, but less when they are averaged over long periods of time. This has led to the concept that homeostasis is a state of **dynamic constancy.** In such a state, a given variable like blood glucose may vary in the short term but is stable and predictable when averaged over the long term.

It is also important to realize that a person may be homeostatic for one variable but not homeostatic for another. Homeostasis must be described differently, therefore, for each variable. For example, as long as the concentration of sodium ions in the blood remains within a few percentage points of its normal range, sodium homeostasis exists. However, a person whose sodium ion concentrations are homeostatic may suffer from other disturbances, such as abnormally high carbon dioxide levels in the blood resulting from lung disease, a condition that could be fatal. Just one nonhomeostatic variable, among the many that can be described, can have life-threatening consequences. Often, when one variable becomes dramatically out of balance, other variables in the body become nonhomeostatic as a consequence. For example, when you exercise strenuously and begin to get warm, you perspire to help maintain body temperature homeostasis. This is important, because many cells (notably neurons) malfunction at elevated temperatures. However, the water that is lost in perspiration creates a situation in which total-body water is no longer in balance. In general, if all the major organ systems are operating in a homeostatic manner, a person is in good health. Certain kinds of disease, in fact, can be defined as the loss of homeostasis in one or more systems in the body. To elaborate on our earlier definition of *physiology*, therefore, when homeostasis is maintained, we refer to physiology; when it is not, we refer to pathophysiology (from the Greek *pathos*, meaning "suffering" or "disease").

1.5 General Characteristics of Homeostatic Control Systems

The activities of cells, tissues, and organs must be regulated and integrated with each other so that any change in the extracellular fluid initiates a reaction to correct the change. The compensating mechanisms that mediate such responses are performed by **homeostatic control systems.**

Consider again an example of the regulation of body temperature. This time, our subject is a resting, lightly clad man in a room having a temperature of 20°C and moderate humidity. His internal body temperature is 37°C, and he is losing heat to the external environment because it is at a lower temperature. However, the chemical reactions occurring within the cells of his body are producing heat at a rate equal to the rate of heat loss. Under these conditions, the body undergoes no *net* gain or loss of heat, and the body temperature remains constant. The system is in a **steady state,** defined as a system in which a particular variable—temperature, in this case—is not changing but in which energy—in this case, heat—must be added continuously to maintain a constant condition. (Steady state differs from **equilibrium,** in which a particular variable is not changing but no input of energy is required to maintain the constancy.) The steady-state temperature in our example is known as the **set point** of the thermoregulatory system.

This example illustrates a crucial generalization about homeostasis. Stability of an internal environmental variable is achieved by the balancing of inputs and outputs. In the previous example, the variable (body temperature) remains constant because metabolic heat production (input) equals heat loss from the body (output).

Now imagine that we rapidly reduce the temperature of the room, say to 5°C, and keep it there. This immediately increases the loss of heat from our subject's warm skin, upsetting the balance between heat gain and loss. The body temperature therefore starts to decrease. Very rapidly, however, a variety of homeostatic responses occur to limit the decrease. **Figure 1.5** summarizes these responses. *The reader is urged to study Figure 1.5 and its legend carefully because the figure is typical of those used throughout the remainder of the book to illustrate homeostatic systems, and the legend emphasizes several conventions common to such figures.*

The first homeostatic response is that blood vessels to the skin become constricted (narrowed), reducing the amount of blood flowing through the skin. This reduces heat loss from the blood to the environment and helps maintain body temperature. At a room temperature of 5°C, however, blood vessel constriction cannot completely eliminate the extra heat loss from the skin. Like the person shown in the chapter opening photo, our subject hunches his shoulders and folds his arms in order to reduce the surface area of the skin available for heat loss. This helps somewhat, but excessive heat loss still continues, and body temperature keeps decreasing, although at a slower rate. Clearly, then, if excessive heat loss (output) cannot be prevented, the only way of restoring the balance between heat input and output is to increase input, and this is precisely what occurs. Our subject begins to shiver, and the chemical reactions responsible for the skeletal muscle contractions that constitute shivering produce large quantities of heat.

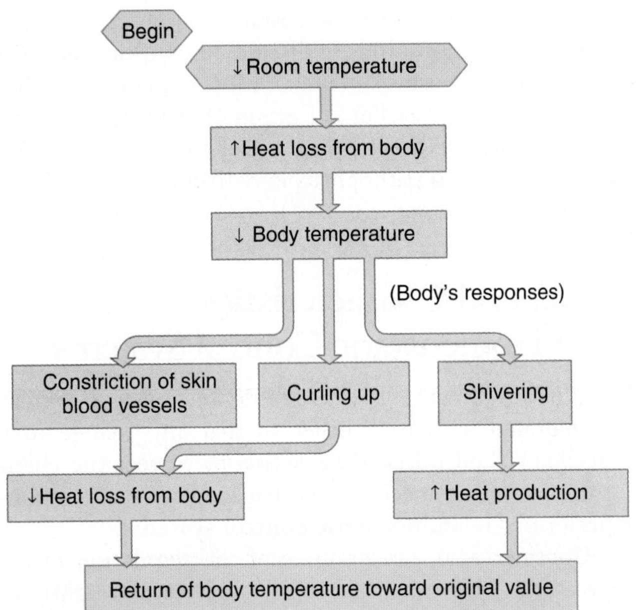

Figure 1.5 A homeostatic control system maintains body temperature when room temperature decreases. This flow diagram is typical of those used throughout this book to illustrate homeostatic systems, and several conventions should be noted. The "Begin" sign indicates where to start. The arrows next to each term within the boxes denote increases or decreases. The arrows connecting any two boxes in the figure denote cause and effect; that is, an arrow can be read as "causes" or "leads to." (For example, decreased room temperature "leads to" increased heat loss from the body.) In general, you should add the words "tends to" in thinking about these cause-and-effect relationships. For example, decreased room temperature tends to cause an increase in heat loss from the body, and curling up tends to cause a decrease in heat loss from the body. Qualifying the relationship in this way is necessary because variables like heat production and heat loss are under the influence of many factors, some of which oppose each other.

Feedback Systems

The thermoregulatory system just described is an example of a **negative feedback** system, in which an increase or decrease in the variable being regulated brings about responses that tend to move the variable in the direction opposite ("negative" to) the direction of the original change. Thus, in our example, a decrease in body temperature led to responses that tended to increase the body temperature—that is, move it toward its original value.

Without negative feedback, oscillations like some of those described in this chapter would be much greater and, therefore, the variability in a given system would increase. Negative feedback also prevents the compensatory responses to a loss of homeostasis from continuing unabated. Details of the mechanisms and characteristics of negative feedback in different systems will be addressed in later chapters. For now, it is important to recognize that negative feedback plays a vital part in the checks and balances on most physiological variables.

Negative feedback may occur at the organ, cellular, or molecular level. For instance, negative feedback regulates many enzymatic processes, as shown in schematic form in **Figure 1.6.** (An enzyme is a protein that catalyzes chemical reactions.) In this example, the product formed from a substrate by an enzyme negatively feeds back to inhibit further action of the enzyme. This may occur by several processes, such as chemical modification of the enzyme by the product of the reaction. The production of adenosine triphosphate (ATP) within cells is a good example of a chemical process regulated by feedback. Normally, glucose molecules are enzymatically broken down inside cells to release some of the chemical energy that was contained in the bonds of the molecule. This energy is then stored in the bonds of ATP. The energy from ATP can later be tapped by cells to power such functions as muscle contraction, cellular secretions, and transport of molecules across cell membranes. As ATP accumulates in the cell, however, it inhibits the activity of some of the enzymes involved in the breakdown of glucose. Therefore, as ATP concentrations increase within a cell, further production of ATP slows down due to negative feedback. Conversely, if ATP concentrations decrease within a cell, negative feedback is removed and more glucose is broken down so that more ATP can be produced.

Not all forms of feedback are negative. In some cases, **positive feedback** accelerates a process, leading to an "explosive" system. This is counter to the principle of homeostasis, because positive feedback has no obvious means of stopping. Not surprisingly, therefore, positive feedback is much less

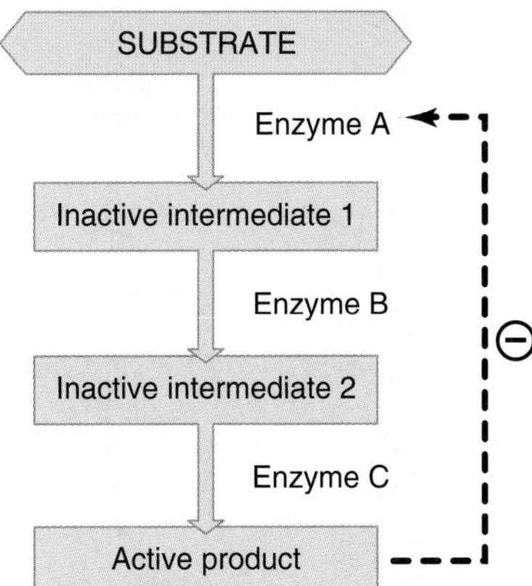

Figure 1.6 Hypothetical example of negative feedback (as denoted by the circled minus sign and dashed feedback line) occurring within a set of sequential chemical reactions. By inhibiting the activity of the first enzyme involved in the formation of a product, the product can regulate the rate of its own formation.

PHYSIOLOGICAL INQUIRY

- What would be the effect on this pathway if negative feedback was removed?

Answer can be found at end of chapter.

common in nature than negative feedback. Nonetheless, there are examples in physiology in which positive feedback is very important. One well-described example, which you will learn about in Chapter 17, is the process of parturition (birth). As the uterine muscles contract and a baby's head is pressed against the mother's cervix during labor, signals are relayed via nerves from the cervix to the mother's brain. The brain initiates the secretion into the blood of a molecule called oxytocin from the mother's pituitary gland. Oxytocin is a potent stimulator of further uterine contractions. As the uterus contracts even harder in response to oxytocin, the baby's head is pushed harder against the cervix, causing it to stretch more; this stimulates yet more nerve signals to the mother's brain, resulting in yet more oxytocin secretion. This self-perpetuating cycle continues until finally the baby pushes through the stretched cervix and is born.

Resetting of Set Points

As we have seen, changes in the external environment can displace a variable from its set point. In addition, the set points for many regulated variables can be physiologically reset to a new value. A common example is fever, the increase in body temperature that occurs in response to infection and that is somewhat analogous to raising the setting of a thermostat in a room. The homeostatic control systems regulating body temperature are still functioning during a fever, but they maintain the temperature at an increased value. This regulated increase in body temperature is adaptive for fighting the infection, because elevated temperature inhibits proliferation of some pathogens. In fact, this is why a fever is often preceded by chills and shivering. The set point for body temperature has been reset to a higher value, and the body responds by shivering to generate heat.

The example of fever may have left the impression that set points are reset only in response to external stimuli, such as the presence of pathogens, but this is not the case. Indeed, the set points for many regulated variables change on a rhythmic basis every day. For example, the set point for body temperature is higher during the day than at night.

Although the resetting of a set point is adaptive in some cases, in others it simply reflects the clashing demands of different regulatory systems. This brings us to one more generalization. It is not possible for everything to be held constant by homeostatic control systems. In our earlier example, body temperature was maintained despite large swings in ambient temperature, but only because the homeostatic control system brought about large changes in skin blood flow and skeletal muscle contraction. Moreover, because so many properties of the internal environment are closely interrelated, it is often possible to keep one property relatively stable only by moving others away from their usual set point. This is what we mean by "clashing demands," which explains the phenomenon mentioned earlier about the interplay between body temperature and water balance during exercise.

The generalizations we have given about homeostatic control systems are summarized in **Table 1.2.** One additional point is that, as is illustrated by the regulation of body temperature, multiple systems usually control a single parameter. The adaptive value of such redundancy is that it provides much greater fine-tuning and also permits regulation to occur even when one of the systems is not functioning properly because of disease.

Feedforward Regulation

Another type of regulatory process often used in conjunction with feedback systems is *feedforward.* Let us give an example of feedforward and then define it. The temperature-sensitive neurons that trigger negative feedback regulation of body temperature when

TABLE 1.2 Some Important Generalizations About Homeostatic Control Systems
Stability of an internal environmental variable is achieved by balancing inputs and outputs. It is not the absolute magnitudes of the inputs and outputs that matter but the balance between them.
In negative feedback, a change in the variable being regulated brings about responses that tend to move the variable in the direction opposite the original change—that is, back toward the initial value (set point).
Homeostatic control systems cannot maintain complete constancy of any given feature of the internal environment. Therefore, any regulated variable will have a more or less narrow range of normal values depending on the external environmental conditions.
The set point of some variables regulated by homeostatic control systems can be reset—that is, physiologically raised or lowered.
It is not always possible for homeostatic control systems to maintain every variable within a narrow normal range in response to an environmental challenge. There is a hierarchy of importance, so that certain variables may be altered markedly to maintain others within their normal range.

it begins to decrease are located inside the body. In addition, there are temperature-sensitive neurons in the skin; these cells, in effect, monitor outside temperature. When outside temperature decreases, as in our example, these neurons immediately detect the change and relay this information to the brain. The brain then sends out signals to the blood vessels and muscles, resulting in heat conservation and increased heat production. In this manner, compensatory thermoregulatory responses are activated *before* the colder outside temperature can cause the internal body temperature to decrease. In another familiar example, the smell of food triggers nerve responses from odor receptors in the nose to the cells of the digestive system. The effect is to prepare the digestive system for the arrival of food before we even consume it, for example by inducing saliva to be secreted in the mouth and causing the stomach to churn and produce acid. Thus, **feedforward** regulation anticipates changes in regulated variables such as internal body temperature or energy availability, improves the speed of the body's homeostatic responses, and minimizes fluctuations in the level of the variable being regulated—that is, it reduces the amount of deviation from the set point.

In our examples, feedforward regulation utilizes a set of external or internal environmental detectors. It is likely, however, that many examples of feedforward regulation are the result of a different phenomenon—learning. The first times they occur, early in life, perturbations in the external environment probably cause relatively large changes in regulated internal environmental factors, and in responding to these changes the central nervous system learns to anticipate them and resist them more effectively. A familiar form of this is the increased heart rate that occurs in an athlete just before a competition begins.

1.6 Components of Homeostatic Control Systems

Reflexes

The thermoregulatory system we used as an example in the previous section and many of the other homeostatic control systems belong to the general category of stimulus–response sequences known as *reflexes*. Although in some reflexes we are aware of the stimulus and/or the response, many reflexes regulating the internal environment occur without our conscious awareness.

In the narrowest sense of the word, a **reflex** is a specific, involuntary, unpremeditated, "built-in" response to a particular stimulus. Examples of such reflexes include pulling your hand away from a hot object or shutting your eyes as an object rapidly approaches your face. Many responses, however, appear automatic and stereotyped but are actually the result of learning and practice. For example, an experienced driver performs many complicated acts in operating a car. To the driver, these motions are, in large part, automatic, stereotyped, and unpremeditated, but they occur only because a great deal of conscious effort was spent learning them. We term such reflexes **learned** or **acquired reflexes.** In general, most reflexes, no matter how simple they may appear to be, are subject to alteration by learning.

The pathway mediating a reflex is known as the **reflex arc,** and its components are shown in **Figure 1.7**. A **stimulus** is defined as a detectable change in the internal or external environment, such as a change in temperature, plasma potassium concentration, or blood pressure. A **receptor** detects the environmental change. A stimulus acts upon a receptor to produce a signal that is relayed to an **integrating center.** The signal travels between the receptor and the integrating center along the **afferent pathway** (the general term *afferent* means "to carry to," in this case, to the integrating center).

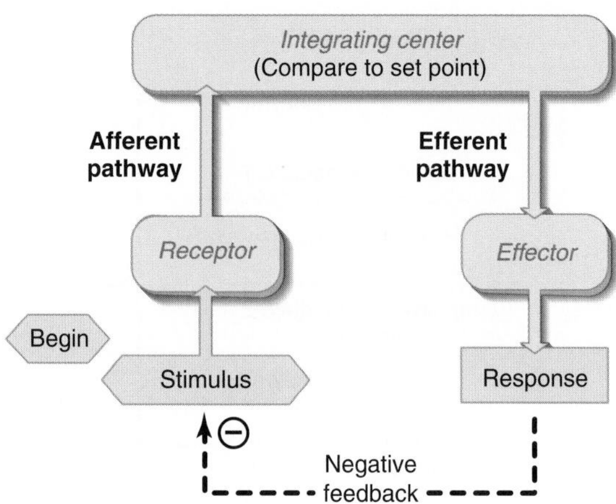

Figure 1.7 General components of a reflex arc that functions as a negative feedback control system. The response of the system has the effect of counteracting or eliminating the stimulus. This phenomenon of negative feedback is emphasized by the minus sign in the dashed feedback loop.

An integrating center often receives signals from many receptors, some of which may respond to quite different types of stimuli. Thus, the output of an integrating center reflects the net effect of the total afferent input; that is, it represents an integration of numerous bits of information.

The output of an integrating center is sent to the last component of the system, whose change in activity constitutes the overall response of the system. This component is known as an **effector.** The information going from an integrating center to an effector is like a command directing the effector to alter its activity. This information travels along the **efferent pathway** (the general term *efferent* means "to carry away from," in this case, away from the integrating center).

Thus far, we have described the reflex arc as the sequence of events linking a stimulus to a response. If the response produced by the effector causes a decrease in the magnitude of the stimulus that triggered the sequence of events, then the reflex leads to negative feedback and we have a typical homeostatic control system. Not all reflexes are associated with such feedback. For example, the smell of food stimulates the stomach to secrete molecules that are important for digestion, but these molecules do not eliminate the smell of food (the stimulus).

Figure 1.8 demonstrates the components of a negative feedback homeostatic reflex arc in the process of thermoregulation. The temperature receptors are the endings of certain neurons in various parts of the body. They generate electrical signals in the neurons at a rate determined by the temperature. These electrical signals are conducted by nerves containing processes from the neurons—the afferent pathway—to the brain, where the integrating center for temperature regulation is located. The

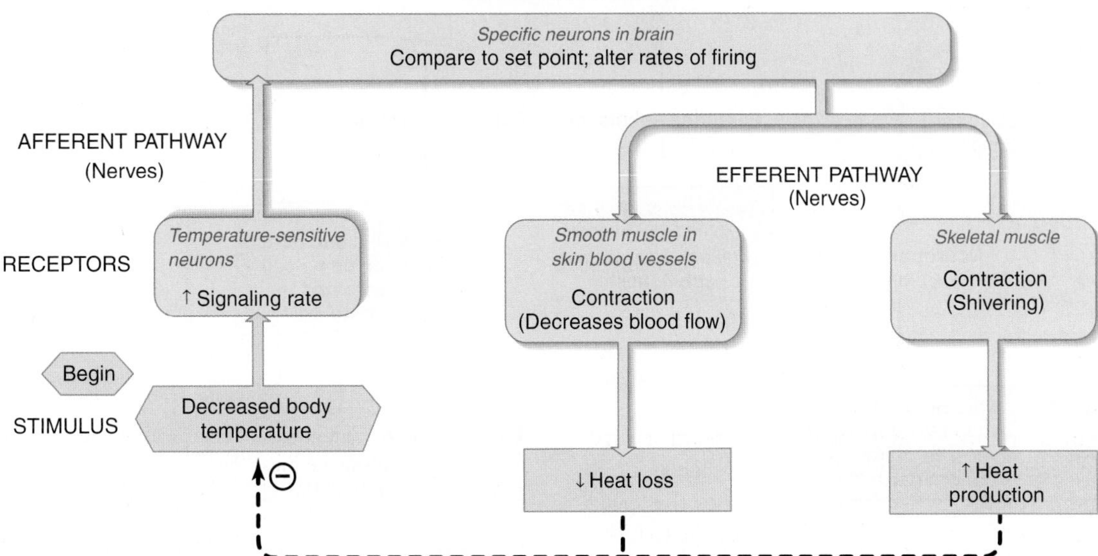

Figure 1.8 Reflex for minimizing the decrease in body temperature that occurs on exposure to a reduced external environmental temperature. This figure provides the internal components for the reflex shown in Figure 1.5. The dashed arrow and the ⊖ indicate the negative feedback nature of the reflex, denoting that the reflex responses cause the decreased body temperature to return toward normal. An additional flow-diagram convention is shown in this figure: blue boxes always denote events that are occurring in anatomical structures (labeled in blue italic type in the upper portion of the box).

PHYSIOLOGICAL INQUIRY

- What might happen to the efferent pathway in this control system if body temperature *increased* above normal?

Answer can be found at end of chapter.

integrating center, in turn, sends signals out along neurons that cause skeletal muscles and the muscles in skin blood vessels to contract. The neurons to the muscles are the efferent pathway, and the muscles are the effectors. The dashed arrow and the negative sign indicate the negative feedback nature of the reflex.

Almost all body cells can act as effectors in homeostatic reflexes. Muscles and glands, however, are the major effectors of biological control systems. In the case of glands, for example, the effector may be a hormone secreted into the blood. A **hormone** is a type of chemical messenger secreted into the blood by cells of the endocrine system (see Table 1.1). Hormones may act on many different cells simultaneously because they circulate throughout the body.

Traditionally, the term *reflex* was restricted to situations in which the receptors, afferent pathway, integrating center, and efferent pathway were all parts of the nervous system, as in the thermoregulatory reflex. However, the principles are essentially the same when a blood-borne chemical messenger, rather than a nerve, serves as the efferent pathway, or when a hormone-secreting gland serves as the integrating center.

In our use of the term *reflex*, therefore, we include hormones as reflex components. Moreover, depending on the specific nature of the reflex, the integrating center may reside either in the nervous system or in a gland. In addition, a gland may act as both receptor and integrating center in a reflex. For example, the gland cells that secrete the hormone insulin, which *decreases* plasma glucose concentration, also detect *increases* in the plasma glucose concentration.

Local Homeostatic Responses

In addition to reflexes, another group of biological responses, called **local homeostatic responses,** is of great importance for homeostasis. These responses are initiated by a change in the external or internal environment (that is, a stimulus), and they induce an alteration of cell activity with the net effect of counteracting the stimulus. Like a reflex, therefore, a local response is the result of a sequence of events proceeding from a stimulus. Unlike a reflex, however, the entire sequence occurs only in the area of the stimulus. For example, when cells of a tissue become very metabolically active, they secrete substances into the interstitial fluid that dilate (widen) local blood vessels. The resulting increased blood flow increases the rate at which nutrients and oxygen are delivered to that area, and the rate at which wastes are removed. The significance of local responses is that they provide individual areas of the body with mechanisms for local self-regulation.

1.7 The Role of Intercellular Chemical Messengers in Homeostasis

Essential to reflexes and local homeostatic responses—and therefore to homeostasis—is the ability of cells to communicate with one another. In this way, cells in the brain, for example, can be made aware of the status of activities of structures outside the brain, such as the heart, and help regulate those activities to meet new homeostatic challenges. In the majority of cases, intercellular

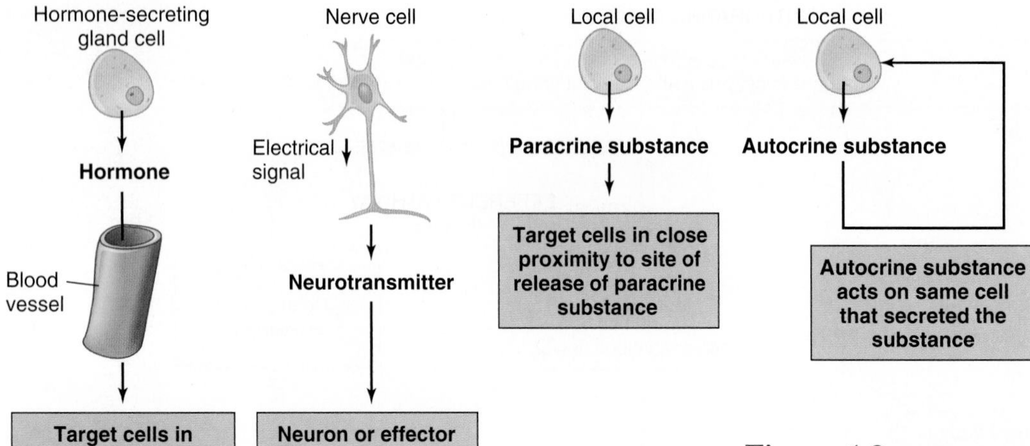

Figure 1.9 Categories of chemical messengers. With the exception of autocrine messengers, all messengers act between cells—that is, *inter*cellularly.

communication is performed by chemical messengers. There are three categories of such messengers: hormones, neurotransmitters, and paracrine or autocrine substances (**Figure 1.9**).

As noted earlier, a hormone functions as a chemical messenger that enables the hormone-secreting cell to communicate with cells acted upon by the hormone—its **target cells**—with the blood acting as the delivery system. Hormones are produced in and secreted from **endocrine glands** or in scattered cells that are distributed throughout another organ. They play key roles in essentially all physiological processes, including growth, reproduction, metabolism, mineral balance, and blood pressure, and are often produced whenever homeostasis is threatened.

In contrast to hormones, **neurotransmitters** are chemical messengers that are released from the endings of neurons onto other neurons, muscle cells, or gland cells. A neurotransmitter diffuses through the extracellular fluid separating the neuron and its target cell; it is not released into the blood like a hormone. Neurotransmitters and their roles in neuronal signaling and brain function will be covered in Chapter 6. In the context of homeostasis, they form the signaling basis of some reflexes, as well as playing a vital role in the compensatory responses to a wide variety of challenges, such as the requirement for increased heart and lung function during exercise.

Chemical messengers participate not only in reflexes but also in local responses. Chemical messengers involved in local communication between cells are known as **paracrine substances** (or agents). Paracrine substances are synthesized by cells and released, once given the appropriate stimulus, into the extracellular fluid. They then diffuse to neighboring cells, some of which are their target cells. Given this broad definition, neurotransmitters could be classified as a subgroup of paracrine substances, but by convention they are not. Once they have performed their functions, paracrine substances are generally inactivated by locally existing enzymes and therefore they do not enter the bloodstream in large quantities. Paracrine substances are produced throughout the body; an example of their key role in homeostasis that you will learn about in Chapter 15 is their ability to fine-tune the amount of acid produced by cells of the stomach in response to eating food.

There is one category of local chemical messengers that are not *inter*cellular messengers—that is, they do not communicate *between* cells. Rather, the chemical is secreted by a cell into the extracellular fluid and then acts upon the very cell that secreted it. Such messengers are called **autocrine substances** (or agents) (see Figure 1.9). Frequently, a messenger may serve both paracrine and autocrine functions simultaneously—that is, molecules of the messenger released by a cell may act locally on adjacent cells as well as on the same cell that released the messenger.

A point of great importance must be emphasized here to avoid later confusion. A neuron, endocrine gland cell, and other cell type may all secrete the same chemical messenger. In some cases, a particular messenger may sometimes function as a neurotransmitter, a hormone, or a paracrine or autocrine substance. Norepinephrine, for example, is not only a neurotransmitter in the brain; it is also produced as a hormone by cells of the adrenal glands.

All types of intercellular communication described thus far in this section involve secretion of a chemical messenger into the extracellular fluid. However, there are two important types of chemical communication between cells that do not require such secretion. In the first type, which occurs via gap junctions (physical linkages connecting the cytosol between two cells; see Chapter 3), molecules move from one cell to an adjacent cell without entering the extracellular fluid. In the second type, the chemical messenger is not actually released from the cell producing it but rather is located in the plasma membrane of that cell. When the cell encounters another cell type capable of responding to the message, the two cells link up via the membrane-bound messenger. This type of signaling, sometimes termed *juxtacrine*, is of particular importance in the growth and differentiation of tissues as well as in the functioning of cells that protect the body against pathogens (Chapter 18).

1.8 Processes Related to Homeostasis

Adaptation and Acclimatization

The term **adaptation** denotes a characteristic that favors survival in specific environments. Homeostatic control systems are inherited biological adaptations. The ability to respond to a particular environmental stress is not fixed, however, but can be enhanced by prolonged exposure to that stress. This type of adaptation—the improved functioning of an already existing homeostatic system—is known as **acclimatization.**

Let us take sweating in response to heat exposure as an example and perform a simple experiment. On day 1, we expose a person for 30 minutes (min) to an elevated temperature and ask her to do a standardized exercise test. Body temperature increases, and sweating begins after a certain period of time. The sweating provides a mechanism for increasing heat loss from the body and therefore tends to minimize the increase in body temperature in a hot environment. The volume of sweat produced under these conditions is measured. Then, for a week, our subject enters the heat chamber for 1 or 2 hours (h) per day and exercises. On day 8, her body temperature and sweating rate are again measured during the same exercise test performed on day 1. The striking finding is that the subject begins to sweat sooner and much more profusely than she did on day 1. As a consequence, her body temperature does not increase to nearly the same degree. The subject has become acclimatized to the heat. She has undergone an adaptive change induced by repeated exposure to the heat and is now better able to respond to heat exposure.

Acclimatizations are usually reversible. If, in the example just described, the daily exposures to heat are discontinued, our subject's sweating rate will revert to the preacclimatized value within a relatively short time.

The precise anatomical and physiological changes that bring about increased capacity to withstand change during acclimatization are highly varied. Typically, they involve an increase in the number, size, or sensitivity of one or more of the cell types in the homeostatic control system that mediates the basic response.

Biological Rhythms

As noted earlier, a striking characteristic of many body functions is the rhythmic changes they manifest. The most common type is the **circadian rhythm,** which cycles approximately once every 24 h. Waking and sleeping, body temperature, hormone concentrations in the blood, the excretion of ions into the urine, and many other functions undergo circadian variation; an example of one type of rhythm is shown in **Figure 1.10**.

What do biological rhythms have to do with homeostasis? They add an anticipatory component to homeostatic control systems, in effect, a feedforward system operating without detectors. The negative feedback homeostatic responses we described earlier in this chapter are *corrective* responses. They are initiated *after* the steady state of the individual has been perturbed. In contrast, biological rhythms enable homeostatic mechanisms to be utilized immediately and automatically by activating them at times when a challenge is *likely* to occur but before it actually does occur. For example, body temperature increases prior to waking in a person on a typical sleep–wake cycle. This allows the metabolic machinery of the body to operate most efficiently immediately upon waking, because metabolism (chemical reactions) is to some extent temperature dependent. During sleep, metabolism is slower than during the active hours, and therefore body temperature decreases at that time. A crucial point concerning most body rhythms is that they are internally driven. Environmental factors do not drive the rhythm but rather provide the timing cues important for **entrainment,** or setting of the actual hours of the rhythm. A classic experiment will clarify this distinction.

Subjects were put in experimental chambers that completely isolated them from their usual external environment, including knowledge of the time of day. For the first few days, they were exposed to a 24 h rest–activity cycle in which the room lights were turned on and off at the same times each day. Under these conditions, their sleep–wake cycles were 24 h long. Then, all environmental time cues were eliminated, and the subjects were allowed to control the lights themselves. Immediately, their sleep–wake patterns began to change. On average, bedtime began about 30 min later each day, and so did wake-up time. Thus, a sleep–wake cycle persisted in the complete absence of environmental cues. Such a rhythm is called a **free-running rhythm.** In this case, it was approximately 24.5 h rather than 24. This indicates that cues are required to entrain or set a circadian rhythm to 24 h.

The light–dark cycle is the most important environmental time cue in our lives—but not the only one. Others include external environmental temperature, meal timing, and many social cues. Thus, if several people were undergoing the experiment just described in isolation from each other, their free-running rhythms would be somewhat different, but if they were all in the same room, social cues would entrain all of them to the same rhythm.

Environmental time cues also function to **phase-shift** rhythms—in other words, to reset the internal clock. Thus, if you fly west or east to a different time zone, your sleep–wake cycle and other circadian rhythms slowly shift to the new light–dark cycle. These shifts take time, however, and the disparity between external time and internal time is one of the causes of the symptoms of jet lag—a disruption of homeostasis that leads to gastrointestinal disturbances, decreased vigilance and attention span, sleep problems, and a general feeling of malaise.

Similar symptoms occur in workers on permanent or rotating night shifts. These people generally do not adapt

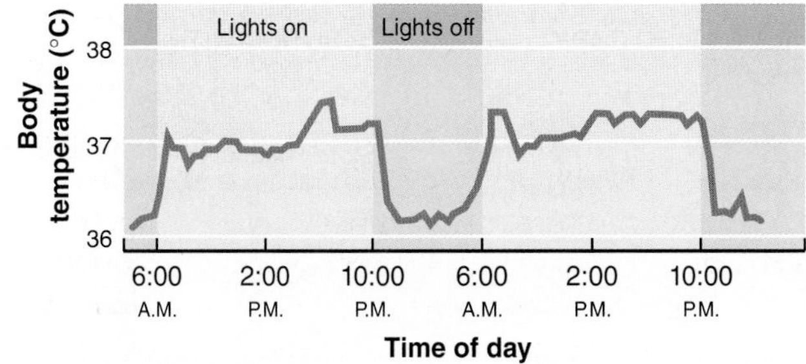

Figure 1.10 Circadian rhythm of body temperature in a human subject with room lights on (open bars at top) for 16 h, and off (blue bars at top) for 8 h. Note the increase in body temperature that occurs just prior to lights on, in anticipation of the increased activity and metabolism that occur during waking hours.
Adapted from Moore-Ede and Sulzman.

to their schedules even after several years because they are exposed to the usual outdoor light–dark cycle (normal indoor lighting is too dim to function as a good entrainer). In recent experiments, night-shift workers were exposed to extremely bright indoor lighting while they worked and they were exposed to 8 h of total darkness during the day when they slept. This schedule produced total adaptation to night-shift work within 5 days.

What is the neural basis of body rhythms? In the part of the brain called the hypothalamus, a specific collection of neurons (the suprachiasmatic nucleus) functions as the principal **pacemaker,** or time clock, for circadian rhythms. How it keeps time independent of any external environmental cues is not fully understood, but it appears to involve the rhythmic turning on and off of critical genes in the pacemaker cells.

The pacemaker receives input from the eyes and many other parts of the nervous system, and these inputs mediate the entrainment effects exerted by the external environment. In turn, the pacemaker sends out neural signals to other parts of the brain, which then influence the various body systems, activating some and inhibiting others. One output of the pacemaker goes to the **pineal gland,** a gland within the brain that secretes the hormone **melatonin.** These neural signals from the pacemaker cause the pineal gland to secrete melatonin during darkness but not during daylight. It has been hypothesized, therefore, that melatonin may act as an important mediator to influence other organs either directly or by altering the activity of the parts of the brain that control these organs.

Balance of Chemical Substances in the Body

Many homeostatic systems regulate the balance between addition and removal of a chemical substance from the body. **Figure 1.11** is a generalized schema of the possible pathways involved in maintaining such balance. The **pool** occupies a position of central importance in the balance sheet. It is the body's readily available quantity of the substance and is often identical to the amount present in the extracellular fluid. The pool receives substances and redistributes them to all the pathways.

The pathways on the left of Figure 1.11 are sources of net gain to the body. A substance may enter the body through the gastrointestinal (GI) tract or the lungs. Alternatively, a substance may be synthesized within the body from other materials.

The pathways on the right of the figure are causes of net loss from the body. A substance may be lost in the urine, feces, expired air, or menstrual fluid, as well as from the surface of the body as skin, hair, nails, sweat, or tears. The substance may also be chemically altered by enzymes and thus removed by metabolism.

The central portion of the figure illustrates the distribution of the substance within the body. The substance may be taken from the pool and accumulated in storage depots—such as the accumulation of fat in adipose tissue. Conversely, it may leave the storage depots to reenter the pool. Finally, the substance may be incorporated reversibly into some other molecular structure, such as fatty acids into plasma membranes. Incorporation is reversible because the substance is liberated again whenever the more complex structure is broken down. This pathway is distinguished from storage in that the incorporation of the substance into other molecules produces new molecules with specific functions.

Substances do not necessarily follow all pathways of this generalized schema. For example, minerals such as Na^+ cannot be synthesized, do not normally enter through the lungs, and cannot be removed by metabolism.

The orientation of Figure 1.11 illustrates two important generalizations concerning the balance concept: (1) during any period of time, total-body balance depends upon the relative rates of net gain and net loss to the body; and (2) the pool concentration depends not only upon the total amount of the substance in the body but also upon exchanges of the substance *within* the body.

For any substance, three states of total-body balance are possible: (1) loss exceeds gain, so that the total amount of the substance in the body is decreasing, and the person is in **negative balance;** (2) gain exceeds loss, so that the total amount of the substance in the body is increasing, and the person is in **positive balance;** and (3) gain equals loss, and the person is in **stable balance.**

Clearly, a stable balance can be upset by a change in the amount being gained or lost in any single pathway in the schema. For example, increased sweating can cause severe negative water balance. Conversely, stable balance can be restored by homeostatic control of water intake and output.

Let us take the balance of calcium ions as another example. The concentration of calcium ions (Ca^{2+}) in the extracellular fluid is critical for normal cellular functioning, notably muscle cells and neurons, but also for the formation and maintenance of the skeleton. The vast majority of the body's Ca^{2+} is present in bone. The control systems for Ca^{2+} balance target the intestines and kidneys such that the amount of Ca^{2+} absorbed from the diet is balanced with the amount excreted in the urine. During infancy and childhood, however, the net balance of Ca^{2+} is positive, and Ca^{2+} is deposited in growing bone. In later life, especially in women after

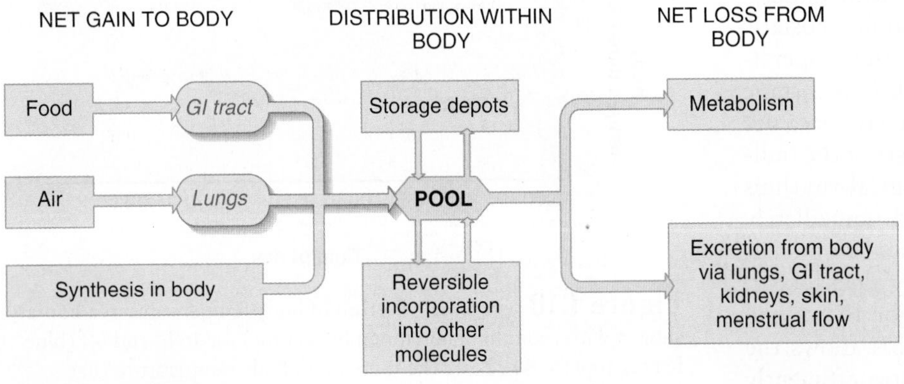

NET GAIN TO BODY | DISTRIBUTION WITHIN BODY | NET LOSS FROM BODY

Food → GI tract; Air → Lungs; Synthesis in body → POOL ↔ Storage depots; POOL ↔ Reversible incorporation into other molecules; POOL → Metabolism; POOL → Excretion from body via lungs, GI tract, kidneys, skin, menstrual flow

Figure 1.11 Balance diagram for a chemical substance.

menopause (see Chapter 17), Ca^{2+} is released from bones faster than it can be deposited, and that extra Ca^{2+} is lost in the urine. Consequently, the bone pool of Ca^{2+} becomes smaller, the rate of Ca^{2+} loss from the body exceeds the rate of intake, and Ca^{2+} balance is negative.

In summary, homeostasis is a complex, dynamic process that regulates the adaptive responses of the body to changes in the external and internal environments. To work properly, homeostatic systems require a sensor to detect the environmental change, and a means to produce a compensatory response. Because compensatory responses require muscle activity, behavioral changes, or synthesis of chemical messengers such as hormones, homeostasis is achieved by the expenditure of energy. The nutrients that provide this energy, as well as the cellular structures and chemical reactions that release the energy stored in the chemical bonds of the nutrients, are described in the following two chapters.

1.9 General Principles of Physiology

When you undertake a detailed study of the functions of the human body, several fundamental, general principles are repeatedly observed. Recognizing these principles and how they manifest in the different organ systems can provide a deeper understanding of the integrated function of the human body. To help you gain this insight, beginning with Chapter 2, the introduction to each chapter will highlight the general principles demonstrated in that chapter. Your understanding of how to apply the following general principles of physiology to a given chapter's content will then be tested with assessments at the end of the chapter.

1. ***Homeostasis is essential for health and survival.*** The ability to maintain physiological variables such as body temperature and blood sugar concentrations within normal ranges is the underlying principle upon which all physiology is based. Keys to this principle are the processes of feedback and feedforward, first introduced in this chapter. Challenges to homeostasis may result from disease or from environmental factors such as famine or exposure to extremes of temperature.
2. ***The functions of organ systems are coordinated with each other.*** Physiological mechanisms operate and interact at the level of cells, tissues, organs, and organ systems. Furthermore, the different organ systems in the human body do not function independently of each other. Each system typically interacts with one or more others to control a homeostatic variable. A good example that you will learn about in Chapters 12 and 14 is the coordinated activity of the circulatory and urinary systems in regulating blood pressure. This type of coordination is often referred to as "integration" in physiological contexts.
3. ***Most physiological functions are controlled by multiple regulatory systems, often working in opposition.*** Typically, control systems in the human body operate such that a given variable, such as heart rate, receives both stimulatory and inhibitory signals. As you will learn in detail in Chapter 6, for example, the autonomic nervous system sends both types of signals to the heart; adjusting the ratio of stimulatory to inhibitory signals allows for fine-tuning of the heart rate under changing conditions such as rest or exercise.
4. ***Information flow between cells, tissues, and organs is an essential feature of homeostasis and allows for integration of physiological processes.*** Cells can communicate with nearby cells via locally secreted chemical signals; a good example of this is the signaling between cells of the stomach that results in acid production, a key feature of the digestion of proteins (see Chapter 15). Cells in one structure can also communicate long distances using electrical signals or chemical messengers such as hormones. Electrical and hormonal signaling will be discussed throughout the textbook and particularly in Chapters 6, 7, and 11.
5. ***Controlled exchange of materials occurs between compartments and across cellular membranes.*** The movement of water and solutes—such as ions, sugars, and other molecules—between the extracellular and intracellular fluid is critical for the survival of all cells, tissues, and organs. In this way, important biological molecules are delivered to cells and wastes are removed and eliminated from the body. In addition, regulation of ion movements creates the electrical properties that are crucial to the function of many cell types. These exchanges occur via several different mechanisms, which are introduced in Chapter 4 and are reinforced where appropriate for each organ system throughout the book.
6. ***Physiological processes are dictated by the laws of chemistry and physics.*** Throughout this textbook, you will encounter some simple chemical reactions, such as the reversible binding of oxygen to the protein hemoglobin in red blood cells (Chapter 13). The basic mechanisms that regulate such reactions are reviewed in Chapter 3. Physical laws, too, such as gravity, electromagnetism, and the relation between the diameter of a tube and the flow of liquid through the tube, help explain things like why we may feel lightheaded upon standing too suddenly (Chapter 12, but also see the Clinical Case Study that follows in this chapter), how our eyes detect light (Chapter 7), and how we inflate our lungs with air (Chapter 13).
7. ***Physiological processes require the transfer and balance of matter and energy.*** Growth and the maintenance of homeostasis require regulation of the movement and transformation of energy-yielding nutrients and molecular building blocks between the body and the environment and between different regions of the body. Nutrients are ingested (Chapter 15), stored in various forms (Chapter 16), and ultimately metabolized to provide energy that can be stored in the bonds of ATP (Chapters 2, 3, and 16). The concentrations of many inorganic molecules must also be regulated to maintain body structure and function,

for example, the calcium found in bones (Chapter 11). One of the most important functions of the body is to respond to changing demands, such as the increased requirement for nutrients and oxygen in exercising muscle. This requires a coordinated allocation of resources to regions that most require them at a particular time. The mechanisms by which the organ systems of the body recognize and respond to changing demands is a theme you will encounter repeatedly in Chapters 6 through 19.

8. ***Structure is a determinant of—and has coevolved with—function.*** The form and composition of cells, tissues, organs, and organ systems determine how they interact with each other and with the physical world. Throughout the text, you will see examples of how different body parts converge in their structure to accomplish similar functions. For example, enormous elaborations of surface areas to facilitate membrane transport and diffusion can be observed in the circulatory (Chapter 12), respiratory (Chapter 13), urinary (Chapter 14), digestive (Chapter 15), and reproductive (Chapter 17) systems.

SUMMARY

The Scope of Human Physiology

I. Physiology is the study of how living organisms work. Physiologists are interested in the regulation of body function.
II. Disease states are physiology "gone wrong" (pathophysiology).

How Is the Body Organized?

I. Cells are the simplest structural units into which a complex multicellular organism can be divided and still retain the functions characteristic of life.
II. Cell differentiation results in the formation of four general categories of specialized cells:
  a. Muscle cells generate the mechanical activities that produce force and movement.
  b. Neurons initiate and conduct electrical signals.
  c. Epithelial cells form barriers and selectively secrete and absorb ions and organic molecules.
  d. Connective-tissue cells connect, anchor, and support the structures of the body.
III. Specialized cells associate with similar cells to form tissues: muscle tissue, nervous tissue, epithelial tissue, and connective tissue.
IV. Organs are composed of two or more of the four kinds of tissues arranged in various proportions and patterns. Many organs contain multiple, small, similar functional units.
V. An organ system is a collection of organs that together perform an overall function.

Body Fluid Compartments

I. The body fluids are enclosed in compartments.
  a. The extracellular fluid is composed of the interstitial fluid (the fluid between cells) and the blood plasma. Of the extracellular fluid, 75%–80% is interstitial fluid, and 20%–25% is plasma.
  b. Interstitial fluid and plasma have essentially the same composition except that plasma contains a much greater concentration of protein.
  c. Extracellular fluid differs markedly in composition from the fluid inside cells—the intracellular fluid.
  d. Approximately one-third of body water is in the extracellular compartment, and two-thirds is intracellular.
II. The differing compositions of the compartments reflect the activities of the barriers separating them.

Homeostasis: A Defining Feature of Physiology

I. The body's internal environment is the extracellular fluid.
II. The function of organ systems is to maintain a stable internal environment—this is called homeostasis.
III. Numerous variables within the body must be maintained homeostatically. When homeostasis is lost for one variable, it may trigger a series of changes in other variables.

General Characteristics of Homeostatic Control Systems

I. Homeostasis denotes the stable condition of the internal environment that results from the operation of compensatory homeostatic control systems.
  a. In a negative feedback control system, a change in the variable being regulated brings about responses that tend to push the variable in the direction opposite to the original change. Negative feedback minimizes changes from the set point of the system, leading to stability.
  b. Homeostatic control systems minimize changes in the internal environment but cannot maintain complete constancy.
  c. Feedforward regulation anticipates changes in a regulated variable, improves the speed of the body's homeostatic responses, and minimizes fluctuations in the level of the variable being regulated.

Components of Homeostatic Control Systems

I. The components of a reflex arc are the receptor, afferent pathway, integrating center, efferent pathway, and effector. The pathways may be neural or hormonal.
II. Local homeostatic responses are also stimulus–response sequences, but they occur only in the area of the stimulus, with neither nerves nor hormones involved.

The Role of Intercellular Chemical Messengers in Homeostasis

I. Intercellular communication is essential to reflexes and local responses and is achieved by neurotransmitters, hormones, and paracrine or autocrine substances. Less common is intercellular communication through either gap junctions or cell-bound messengers.

Processes Related to Homeostasis

I. Acclimatization is an improved ability to respond to an environmental stress. The improvement is induced by prolonged exposure to the stress with no change in genetic endowment.
II. Biological rhythms provide a feedforward component to homeostatic control systems.
  a. The rhythms are internally driven by brain pacemakers but are entrained by environmental cues, such as light, which also serve to phase-shift (reset) the rhythms when necessary.
  b. In the absence of cues, rhythms free-run.

III. The balance of substances in the body is achieved by matching inputs and outputs. Total-body balance of a substance may be negative, positive, or stable.

General Principles of Physiology

I. Several fundamental, general principles of physiology are important in understanding how the human body functions at all levels of structure, from cells to organ systems. These include, among others, such things as homeostasis, information flow, coordination between the function of different organ systems, and the balance of matter and energy.

REVIEW QUESTIONS

1. Describe the levels of cellular organization and state the four types of specialized cells and tissues.
2. List the organ systems of the body and give one-sentence descriptions of their functions.
3. Name the two fluids that constitute the extracellular fluid. What are their relative proportions in the body, and how do they differ from each other in composition?
4. State the relative volumes of water in the body fluid compartments.
5. Describe several important generalizations about homeostatic control systems.
6. Contrast feedforward and negative feedback.
7. List the components of a reflex arc.
8. What is the basic difference between a local homeostatic response and a reflex?
9. List the general categories of intercellular messengers.
10. Describe the conditions under which acclimatization occurs. Are acclimatizations passed on to a person's offspring?
11. Under what conditions do circadian rhythms become free running?
12. How do phase shifts occur?
13. What is the most important environmental cue for entrainment of body rhythms?
14. Draw a figure illustrating the balance concept in homeostasis.
15. Make a list of the General Principles of Physiology, without the paragraphs that accompany each one. See if you can explain what is meant by each principle. To really see how well you've learned physiology at the end of your course, remember to return to the list you've made and try this exercise again at that time.

KEY TERMS

acclimatization 13
acquired reflex 10
adaptation 12
afferent pathway 10
autocrine substance 12
basement membrane 3
cell 2
cell differentiation 2
circadian rhythm 13
collagen fiber 4
connective tissue 3
connective-tissue cell 4
dynamic constancy 7
effector 10
efferent pathway 10
elastin fiber 4
endocrine gland 12
entrainment 13
epithelial cell 3
epithelial tissue 2
equilibrium 7
extracellular fluid 5
extracellular matrix 4
feedforward 10
fiber 4
free-running rhythm 13
functional unit 4
homeostasis 6
homeostatic control system 7
hormone 11
integrating center 10
internal environment 4
interstitial fluid 5
interstitium 5
intracellular fluid 5
learned reflex 10
local homeostatic response 11
melatonin 14
muscle cell 3
muscle tissue 3
negative balance 14
negative feedback 8
nervous tissue 3
neuron 3
neurotransmitter 12
organ 3
organ system 3
pacemaker 14
paracrine substance 12
pathophysiology 2
phase-shift 13
physiology 2
pineal gland 14
plasma 5
pool 14
positive balance 14
positive feedback 8
receptor 10
reflex 10
reflex arc 10
set point 7
stable balance 14
steady state 7
stimulus 10
target cell 12
tissue 3

CHAPTER 1 Clinical Case Study: Loss of Consciousness in a 64-Year-Old Man While Gardening on a Hot Day

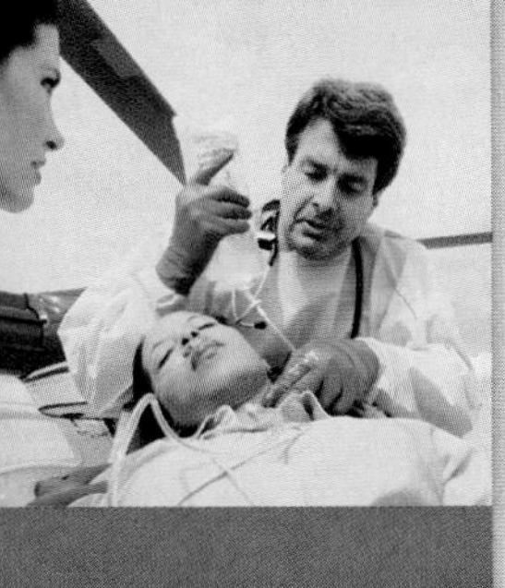

Throughout this text, you will find a feature at the end of each chapter called the "Clinical Case Study." These segments reinforce what you have learned in that chapter by applying it to real-life examples of different medical conditions. The clinical case studies will increase in complexity as you progress through the text and will enable you to integrate recent material from a given chapter with information learned in previous chapters. In this first clinical case study, we examine a serious and potentially life-threatening condition that can occur in individuals in whom body temperature homeostasis is disrupted. All of the material presented in this clinical case study will be explored in depth in subsequent chapters, as you learn the mechanisms that underlie the pathologies and compensatory responses illustrated here in brief. Notice as you read that the first two general principles of physiology described earlier are particularly relevant to this case. *It is highly recommended that you return to this case study as a benchmark at the end of your semester; we are certain that you will be amazed at how your understanding of physiology has grown in that time.*

A 64-year-old, fair-skinned man in good overall health spent a very hot, humid summer day gardening in his backyard. After several hours in the sun, he began to feel light-headed and

(continued)

(continued)

confused as he knelt over his vegetable garden. Although earlier he had been perspiring profusely, his sweating had eventually stopped. Because he also felt confused and disoriented, he could not recall for how long he had not been perspiring, or even how long it had been since he had taken a drink of water. He called to his wife, who was alarmed to see that his skin had turned a pale-blue color. She asked her husband to come indoors, but he fainted as soon as he tried to stand. The wife called for an ambulance, and the man was taken to a hospital and diagnosed with a condition called heatstroke. What happened to this man that would explain his condition? How does it relate to homeostasis?

As you learned in this chapter, body temperature is a physiological function that is under homeostatic control. If body temperature decreases, heat production increases and heat loss decreases, as illustrated in Figures 1.5 and 1.8. Conversely, as in our example here, if body temperature increases, heat production decreases and heat loss increases. When our patient began gardening on a hot, humid day, his body temperature began to increase. At first, he perspired heavily. As you will learn in Chapter 16, perspiration is an important mechanism by which the body loses heat; it takes considerable heat to evaporate water from the surface of the skin, and the source of that heat is from the body. However, as you likely know from personal experience, evaporation of water from the body is less effective in humid environments, which makes it more dangerous to exercise when it is not only hot but also humid.

The sources of perspiration are the sweat glands, which are located beneath the skin and which secrete a salty solution through ducts to the surface of the skin. The fluid in sweat comes from the extracellular fluid compartment, which, as you have learned, consists of the plasma and interstitial fluid compartments (see Figure 1.3). Consequently, the profuse sweating that initially occurred in this man caused his extracellular fluid levels to decrease. In fact, the fluid levels decreased so severely that the amount of blood available to be pumped out of his heart with each heartbeat also decreased. The relationship between fluid volume and blood pressure is an important one that you will learn about in detail in Chapter 12. Generally speaking, if extracellular fluid levels decrease, blood pressure decreases as a consequence. This explains why our patient felt light-headed, particularly when he suddenly tried to stand up. As his blood pressure decreased, the ability of his heart to pump sufficient blood against gravity up to his brain also decreased; when brain cells are deprived of blood flow, they begin to malfunction. Standing suddenly only made matters worse. Perhaps you have occasionally experienced a little of this light-headed feeling when you have jumped out of a chair or bed and stood up too quickly. Normally, your nervous system quickly compensates for the effects of gravity on blood flowing up to the brain, as will be described in Chapters 6 and 12. In a person with decreased blood volume and pressure, however, this compensation may not happen and the person can lose consciousness. After fainting and falling, the man's head and heart were at the same horizontal level; consequently, blood could more easily reach his brain.

Another concern is that the salt concentrations in the body fluids changed. If you have ever tasted the sweat on your upper lip on a hot day, you know that it is somewhat salty. That is because sweat is derived from extracellular fluid, which as you have learned is a watery solution of ions (derived from salts, such as NaCl) and other substances. Sweat, however, is slightly more dilute than extracellular fluid because more water than ions is secreted from sweat glands. Consequently, the more heavily one perspires, the more concentrated the extracellular fluid becomes. In other words, the total amount of water and ions in the extracellular fluid decreases with perspiration, but the remaining fluid is "saltier." Heavy perspiration, therefore, not only disrupts fluid balance and blood pressure homeostasis but also has an impact on the balance of the ions in the body fluids, notably Na^+, K^+, and Cl^-. A homeostatic balance of ion concentrations in the body fluids is absolutely essential for normal heart and brain function, as you will learn in Chapters 4 and 6. As the man's ion concentrations changed, therefore, the change affected the activity of the cells of his brain.

Why did the man stop perspiring and why did his skin turn pale? To understand this, we must consider that several homeostatic variables were disrupted by his activities. His body temperature increased, which initially resulted in heavy sweating. As the sweating continued, it resulted in an imbalance in fluid levels and ion concentrations in his body; this contributed to a decrease in mental function, and he became confused. As his body fluid levels continued to decrease, his blood pressure also decreased, further endangering brain function. At this point, the homeostatic control systems were essentially in competition. Though it is potentially life threatening for body temperature to increase too much, it is also life threatening for blood pressure to decrease too much. Eventually, many of the blood vessels in regions of the body that are not immediately required for survival, such as the skin, began to close off. By doing so, the more vital organs of the body—such as the brain—could receive sufficient blood. This is why the man's skin turned a pale blue, because the amount of oxygen-rich blood flowing to the surface of his skin was decreased. Unfortunately, although this compensatory mechanism helped save the man's brain and other vital organs, reducing the amount of blood flowing to the skin made it impossible for the sweat glands under the skin to extract extracellular fluid and make more sweat. The man stopped perspiring, therefore, and a key mechanism to controlling his body temperature was lost. At that point, his body temperature spiraled out of control and he was hospitalized.

This case illustrates a critical feature of homeostasis that you will encounter throughout this textbook and that was emphasized in this chapter. Often, when one physiological variable such as body temperature is disrupted, the compensatory responses initiated to correct that disruption cause, in turn, imbalances in other variables. These secondary imbalances must also be compensated for, and the significance of each imbalance must be "weighed" against the others. In this example, the man was treated with intravenous fluids made up of a salt solution to restore his fluid levels and concentrations, and he was immersed in a cool bath and given cool compresses to help reduce his body temperature. Although he recovered, many people do not survive heatstroke because of its profound impact on homeostasis.

See Chapter 19 for complete, integrative case studies.

CHAPTER 1 TEST QUESTIONS

Answers found in Appendix A.

1. Which of the following is one of the four basic cell types in the body?
   a. respiratory
   b. epithelial
   c. endocrine
   d. integumentary
   e. immune
2. Which of the following is incorrect?
   a. Equilibrium requires a constant input of energy.
   b. Positive feedback is less common in nature than negative feedback.
   c. Homeostasis does not imply that a given variable is unchanging.
   d. Fever is an example of resetting a set point.
   e. Efferent pathways carry information away from the integrating center of a reflex arc.
3. In a reflex arc initiated by touching a hand to a hot stove, the effector belongs to which class of tissue?
   a. nervous
   b. connective
   c. muscle
   d. epithelial
4. In the absence of any environmental cues, a circadian rhythm is said to be
   a. entrained.
   b. in phase.
   c. free running.
   d. phase-shifted.
   e. no longer present.
5. Most of the water in the human body is found in
   a. the interstitial fluid compartment.
   b. the intracellular fluid compartment.
   c. the plasma compartment.
   d. the total extracellular fluid compartment.

CHAPTER 1 QUANTITATIVE AND THOUGHT QUESTIONS

Answers found in Appendix A.

1. The Inuit of Alaska and Canada have a remarkable ability to work in the cold without gloves and not suffer decreased skin blood flow. Does this prove that there is a genetic difference between the Inuit and other people with regard to this characteristic?
2. Explain how an imbalance in any given physiological variable may produce a change in one or more *other* variables.

CHAPTER 1 ANSWERS TO PHYSIOLOGICAL INQUIRIES

Figure 1.3 Approximately one-third of total-body water is in the extracellular compartments. If water makes up 60% of a person's body weight, then the water in extracellular fluid makes up approximately 20% of body weight (because $0.33 \times 0.60 = 0.20$).

Figure 1.6 Removing negative feedback in this example would result in an increase in the amount of active product formed, and eventually the amount of available substrate would be greatly depleted.

Figure 1.8 If body temperature were to increase, the efferent pathway shown in this diagram would either turn off or become reversed. For example, shivering would not occur (muscles may even become more relaxed than usual), and blood vessels in the skin would not constrict. Indeed, in such a scenario, skin blood vessels would dilate to bring warm blood to the skin surface, where the heat could leave the body across the skin. Heat loss, therefore, would be increased.

Visit this book's website at **www.mhhe.com/widmaier13** for chapter quizzes, interactive learning exercises, and other study tools.

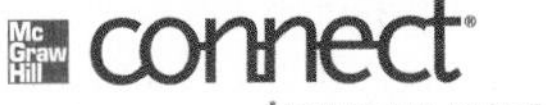

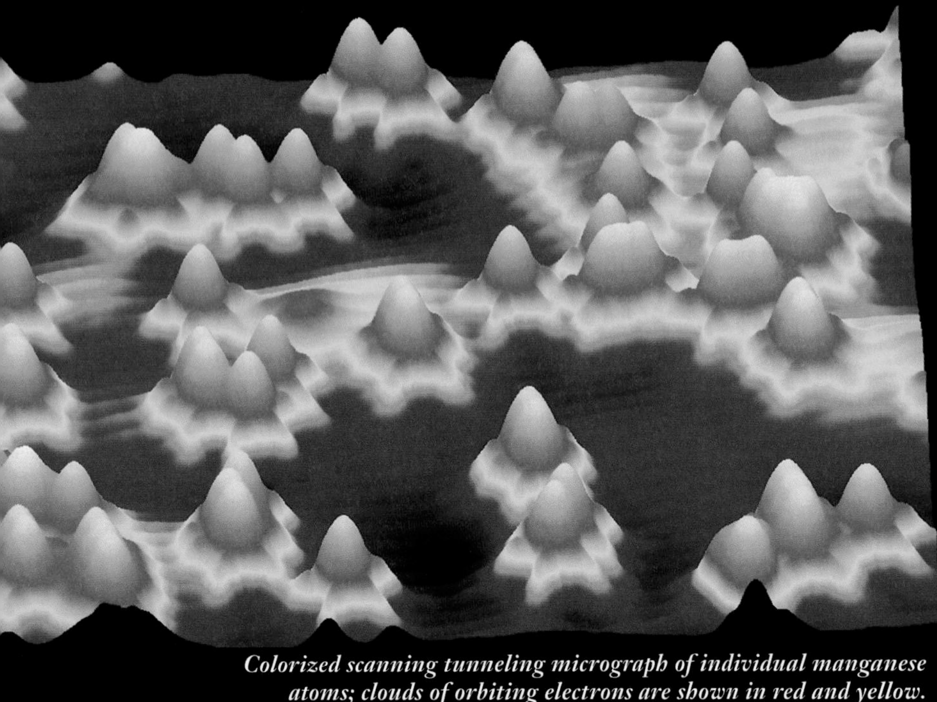

Colorized scanning tunneling micrograph of individual manganese atoms; clouds of orbiting electrons are shown in red and yellow.

2 Chemical Composition of the Body

In Chapter 1, you were introduced to the concept of homeostasis, and how chemistry plays an important role in the maintenance of homeostasis, particularly at the cellular level. To fully appreciate the importance of chemistry to physiology, it is necessary to briefly review some of the key features of atoms and molecules that contribute to their ability to interact with one another. Such interactions form the basis for processes as diverse as maintaining a healthy pH of the body fluids, determining which molecules will bind to or otherwise influence the function of other molecules, forming functional proteins that mediate numerous physiological processes, and maintaining energy homeostasis.

In this chapter, we describe the distinguishing characteristics of some of the major molecules in the human body. The specific roles of these substances in physiology will be introduced here and discussed more fully in subsequent chapters where appropriate. This chapter will provide you with the knowledge required to best appreciate the significance of one of the general principles of physiology introduced in Chapter 1, namely that physiological processes are dictated by the laws of chemistry and physics.

2.1 Atoms

The units of matter that form all chemical substances are called **atoms.** Each type of atom—carbon, hydrogen, oxygen, and so on—is called a **chemical element.** A one- or two-letter symbol is used as an abbreviated identification for each element. Although more than 100 elements occur naturally or have been synthesized in the laboratory, only 24 (**Table 2.1**) are known to be essential for the structure and function of the human body and are therefore of particular interest to physiologists.

Components of Atoms

The chemical properties of atoms can be described in terms of three subatomic particles—**protons, neutrons,** and **electrons.** The protons and neutrons are confined to a very small volume at the center of an atom called the **atomic nucleus.** The electrons revolve in orbitals at various distances from the nucleus. Each orbital can hold up to two electrons and no more. The larger the atom, the more electrons it contains, and therefore the more orbitals that exist around the nucleus. Orbitals are found in regions known as electron shells; additional shells exist at greater and greater distances from the nucleus as atoms get bigger. An atom such as carbon has more shells than does hydrogen with its lone electron, but fewer than an atom such as iron, which has a greater number of electrons. The first, innermost shell of any atom can hold up to two electrons in a single, spherical ("*s*") orbital (**Figure 2.1a**). Once the innermost shell is filled, electrons begin to fill the second shell. The second shell can hold up to eight electrons; the first two electrons fill a spherical orbital, and subsequent electrons fill three additional, propeller-shaped ("*p*") orbitals. Additional shells can accommodate further orbitals; this will happen once the inner shells are filled. For simplicity, we will ignore the distinction between *s* and *p* orbitals and represent the shells of an atom in two dimensions as shown in **Figure 2.1b** for nitrogen.

An atom is most stable when all of the orbitals in its outermost shell are filled with two electrons each. If one or more orbitals do not have their capacity of electrons, the atom can react with other atoms and form molecules, as described later. For many of the atoms that are most important for physiology, the outer shell requires eight electrons in its orbitals in order to be filled to capacity.

TABLE 2.1 Essential Chemical Elements in the Body (neo-Latin terms in italics)

Element	Symbol
Major Elements: 99.3% of Total Atoms in the Body	
Hydrogen	H (63%)
Oxygen	O (26%)
Carbon	C (9%)
Nitrogen	N (1%)
Mineral Elements: 0.7% of Total Atoms in the Body	
Calcium	Ca
Phosphorus	P
Potassium	K (*kalium*)
Sulfur	S
Sodium	Na (*natrium*)
Chlorine	Cl
Magnesium	Mg
Trace Elements: Less than 0.01% of Total Atoms in the Body	
Iron	Fe (*ferrum*)
Iodine	I
Copper	Cu (*cuprum*)
Zinc	Zn
Manganese	Mn
Cobalt	Co
Chromium	Cr
Selenium	Se
Molybdenum	Mo
Fluorine	F
Tin	Sn (*stannum*)
Silicon	Si
Vanadium	V

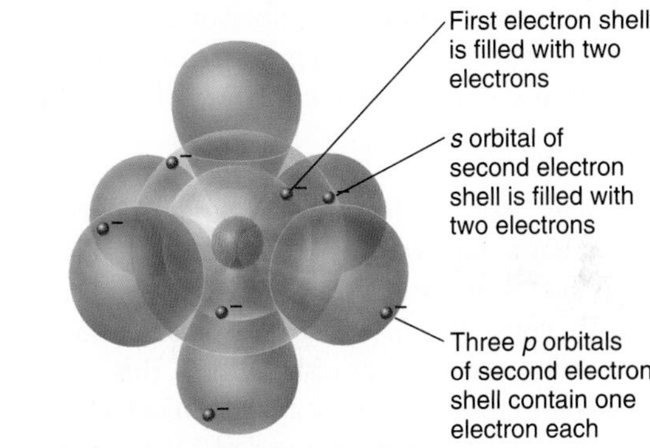

(a) Nitrogen atom showing electrons in orbitals

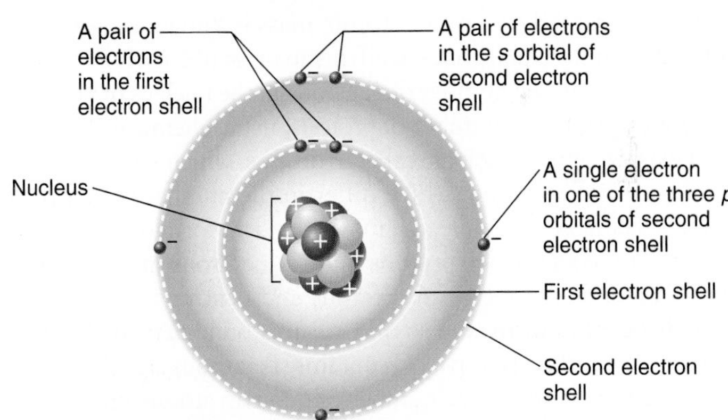

(b) Simplified depiction of a nitrogen atom (seven electrons; two electrons in first electron shell, five in second electron shell)

Figure 2.1 APR Arrangement of subatomic particles in an atom, shown here for nitrogen. (a) Negatively charged electrons orbit around a nucleus consisting of positively charged protons and (except for hydrogen) uncharged neutrons. Up to two electrons may occupy an orbital, shown here as regions in which an electron is likely to be found. The orbitals exist within electron shells at progressively greater distances from the nucleus as atoms get bigger. Different shells may contain a different number of orbitals. (b) Simplified, two-dimensional depiction of a nitrogen atom, showing a full complement of two electrons in its innermost shell and five electrons in its second, outermost shell. Orbitals are not depicted using this simplified means of illustrating an atom.

Each of the subatomic particles has a different electrical charge. Protons have one unit of positive charge, electrons have one unit of negative charge, and neutrons are electrically neutral. Because the protons are located in the atomic nucleus, the nucleus has a net positive charge equal to the number of protons it contains. One of the fundamental principles of physics is that opposite electrical charges attract each other and like charges repel each other. It is the attraction between the positively charged protons and the negatively charged electrons that serves as a major force that forms an atom. The entire atom has no net electrical charge, however, because the number of negatively charged electrons orbiting the nucleus equals the number of positively charged protons in the nucleus.

Atomic Number

Each chemical element contains a unique and specific number of protons, and it is this number, known as the **atomic number,** that distinguishes one type of atom from another. For example, hydrogen, the simplest atom, has an atomic number of 1, corresponding to its single proton. As another example, calcium has an atomic number of 20, corresponding to its 20 protons. Because an atom is electrically neutral, the atomic number is also equal to the number of electrons in the atom.

Atomic Mass

Atoms have very little mass. A single hydrogen atom, for example, has a mass of only 1.67×10^{-24} g. The **atomic mass** scale indicates an atom's mass relative to the mass of other atoms. By convention, this scale is based upon assigning the carbon atom a mass of exactly 12. On this scale, a hydrogen atom has an atomic mass of approximately 1, indicating that it has about one-twelfth the mass of a carbon atom. A magnesium atom, with an atomic mass of 24, has twice the mass of a carbon atom. The unit of atomic mass is known as a dalton. One dalton (d) equals one-twelfth the mass of a carbon atom.

Although the number of neutrons in the nucleus of an atom is often equal to the number of protons, many chemical elements can exist in multiple forms, called **isotopes,** which have identical numbers of protons but which differ in the number of neutrons they contain. For example, the most abundant form of the carbon atom, ^{12}C, contains six protons and six neutrons and therefore has an atomic number of 6. Protons and neutrons are approximately equal in mass, and so ^{12}C has an atomic mass of 12. The radioactive carbon isotope ^{14}C contains six protons and eight neutrons, giving it an atomic number of 6 but an atomic mass of 14. The value of atomic mass given in the standard Periodic Table of the Elements is actually an average mass that reflects the relative abundance in nature of the different isotopes of a given element.

Many isotopes are unstable; they will spontaneously emit energy or even release components of the atom itself, such as part of the nucleus. This process is known as radiation, and such isotopes are called **radioisotopes.** The special qualities of radioisotopes are of great practical benefit in the practice of medicine and the study of physiology. In one example, high-energy radiation can be focused onto cancerous areas of the body to kill cancer cells. Radioisotopes may also be useful in making diagnoses. In one common method, the sugar glucose can be chemically modified so that it contains a radioactive isotope of fluorine. When injected into the blood, all of the organs of the body take up the radioactive glucose just as they would ordinary glucose. Special imaging techniques such as ***PET (positron emission tomography) scans*** can then be used to detect how much of the radioactive glucose appears in different organs (**Figure 2.2**); because glucose is a key source of energy used by all cells, this information can be used to determine if a given organ is functioning normally or at an increased or decreased rate. For example, a PET scan that revealed decreased uptake of radioactive glucose into the heart might indicate that the blood vessels of the heart were diseased, thereby depriving the heart of nutrients. PET scans can also reveal the presence of cancer—a disease characterized by uncontrolled cell growth and increased glucose uptake.

The **gram atomic mass** of a chemical element is the amount of the element, in grams, equal to the numerical value of its atomic mass. Thus, 12 g of carbon (assuming it is all ^{12}C) is 1 gram atomic mass of carbon, and 1 g of hydrogen is 1 gram atomic mass of hydrogen. *One gram atomic mass of any element contains the same number of atoms.* For example, 1 g of hydrogen contains 6×10^{23} atoms; likewise, 12 g of carbon, whose atoms have 12 times the mass of a hydrogen atom, also has 6×10^{23} atoms (this value is often called Avogadro's constant, or Avogadro's number, after the nineteenth-century Italian scientist Amedeo Avogadro).

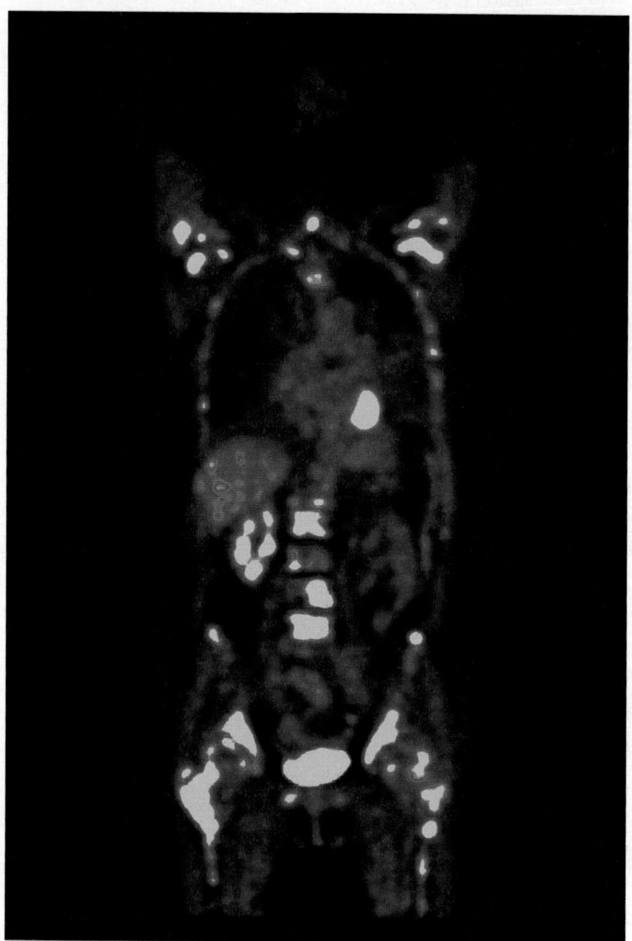

Figure 2.2 Positron emission tomography (PET) scan of a human body. In this image, radioactive glucose that has been taken up by the body's organs appears as a false color; the greater the uptake, the more intense the color. The brightest regions were found to be areas of cancer in this particular individual.

Ions

As mentioned earlier, a single atom is electrically neutral because it contains equal numbers of negative electrons and positive protons. There are instances, however, in which certain atoms may gain or lose one or more electrons; in such cases, they will then acquire a net electrical charge and become an **ion.** This may happen, for example, if an atom has an outer shell that contains only one or a few electrons; losing those electrons would mean that the next innermost shell would then become the outermost shell. This shell is complete with a full capacity of electrons and is therefore very stable (recall that each successive shell does not begin to acquire electrons until all the preceding inner shells are filled). For example, when a sodium atom (Na), which has 11 electrons, loses one electron, it becomes a sodium ion (Na^+) with a net positive charge; it still has 11 protons, but it now has only 10 electrons, two in its first shell and a full complement of eight in its second, outer shell. On the other hand, a chlorine atom (Cl), which has 17 electrons, is one electron shy of a full outer shell. It can gain an electron and become a chloride ion (Cl^-) with a net negative charge—it now has 18 electrons but only 17 protons. Some atoms can gain or lose more than one electron to become ions with two or even three units of net electrical charge (for example, the calcium ion Ca^{2+}).

Hydrogen and many other atoms readily form ions. **Table 2.2** lists the ionic forms of some of these elements that are found in the body. Ions that have a net positive charge are called **cations,** and those that have a net negative charge are called **anions.** Because of their charge, ions are able to conduct electricity when dissolved in water; consequently, the ionic forms of mineral elements are collectively referred to as **electrolytes.** This is extremely important in physiology, because electrolytes are used to carry electrical charge across cell membranes; in this way, they serve as the source of electrical current in certain cells. You will learn in Chapters 6, 9, and 12 that such currents are critical to the ability of muscle cells and neurons to function in their characteristic ways.

Atomic Composition of the Body

Just four of the body's essential elements (see Table 2.1)—hydrogen, oxygen, carbon, and nitrogen—account for over 99% of the atoms in the body.

The seven essential **mineral elements** are the most abundant substances dissolved in the extracellular and intracellular fluids. Most of the body's calcium and phosphorus atoms, however, make up the solid matrix of bone tissue.

The 13 essential **trace elements,** so-called because they are present in extremely small quantities, are required for normal growth and function. For example, iron plays a critical role in the blood's transport of oxygen, and iodine is required for the production of thyroid hormone.

Many other elements, in addition to the 24 listed in Table 2.1, may be detected in the body. These elements enter in the foods we eat and the air we breathe but are not essential for normal body function and may even interfere with normal body chemistry. For example, ingested arsenic has poisonous effects.

2.2 Molecules

Two or more atoms bonded together make up a **molecule.** A molecule made up of two or more different elements is called a compound, but the two terms are often used interchangeably. For example, a molecule of oxygen gas consists of two atoms of oxygen bonded together. By contrast, water is a compound that contains two hydrogen atoms and one oxygen atom. For simplicity, we will simply use the term *molecule* in this textbook. Molecules can be represented by their component atoms. In the two examples just given, a molecule of oxygen can be represented as O_2 and water as H_2O. The atomic composition of glucose, a sugar, is $C_6H_{12}O_6$, indicating that the molecule contains 6 carbon atoms, 12 hydrogen atoms, and 6 oxygen atoms. Such formulas, however, do not indicate how the atoms are linked together in the molecule. This occurs by means of chemical bonds, as described next.

Covalent Chemical Bonds

Chemical bonds between atoms in a molecule form when electrons transfer from the outer electron shell of one atom to that of another, or when two atoms with partially unfilled electron orbitals share electrons. The strongest chemical bond between two atoms is called a **covalent bond,** which forms when one or more electrons in the outer electron orbitals of each atom are shared between the two atoms (**Figure 2.3**). In the example shown in Figure 2.3, a carbon atom with two electrons in its innermost shell and four in its outer shell forms covalent bonds with four hydrogen atoms. Recall that the second shell of atoms can hold up to eight electrons. Carbon has six total electrons

TABLE 2.2 Ionic Forms of Elements Most Frequently Encountered in the Body

Chemical Atom	Symbol	Ion	Chemical Symbol	Electrons Gained or Lost
Hydrogen	H	Hydrogen ion	H^+	1 lost
Sodium	Na	Sodium ion	Na^+	1 lost
Potassium	K	Potassium ion	K^+	1 lost
Chlorine	Cl	Chloride ion	Cl^-	1 gained
Magnesium	Mg	Magnesium ion	Mg^{2+}	2 lost
Calcium	Ca	Calcium ion	Ca^{2+}	2 lost

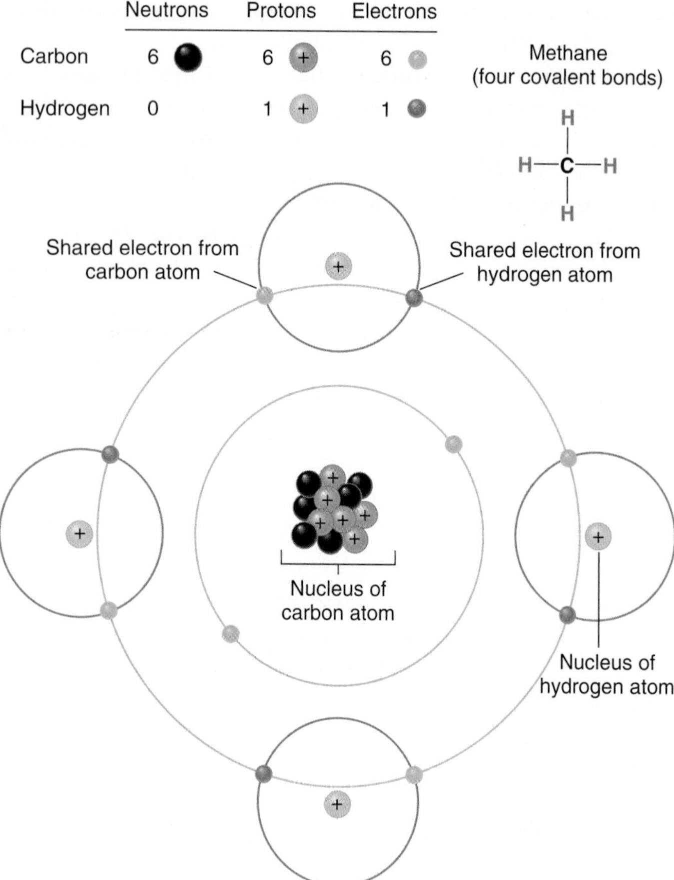

Figure 2.3 AP|R A covalent bond formed by sharing electrons. Hydrogen atoms have room for one additional electron in their sole orbital; carbon atoms have four electrons in their second shell, which can accommodate up to eight electrons. Each of the four hydrogen atoms in a molecule of methane (CH_4) forms a covalent bond with the carbon atom by sharing its one electron with one of the electrons in carbon. Each shared pair of electrons—one electron from the carbon and one from a hydrogen atom—forms a covalent bond. The sizes of protons, neutrons, and electrons are not to scale.

and only four in the second shell, because two electrons are used to fill the first shell. Therefore, it has "room" to acquire four additional electrons in its outer shell. Hydrogen has only a single electron, but like all orbitals, its single orbital can hold up to two electrons. Therefore, hydrogen also has room for an additional electron. In this example, a single carbon atom shares its four electrons with four different hydrogen atoms, which in turn share their electrons with the carbon atom. The shared electrons orbit around both atoms, bonding them together into a molecule of methane (CH_4). These covalent bonds are the strongest type of bonds in the body; once formed, they usually do not break apart unless acted upon by an energy source (heat) or an enzyme (see Chapter 3 for a description of enzymes).

As mentioned, the atoms of some elements can form more than one covalent bond and thus become linked simultaneously to two or more other atoms. Each type of atom forms a characteristic number of covalent bonds, which depends on the number of electrons in its outermost orbit. The number of chemical bonds formed by the four most abundant atoms in the body are hydrogen, one; oxygen, two; nitrogen, three; and carbon, four. When the structure of a molecule is diagrammed, each covalent bond is represented by a line indicating a pair of shared electrons. The covalent bonds of the four elements just mentioned can be represented as

$$\text{H—} \quad \text{—O—} \quad \text{—}\overset{|}{\text{N}}\text{—} \quad \text{—}\underset{|}{\overset{|}{\text{C}}}\text{—}$$

A molecule of water, H_2O, can be diagrammed as

$$\text{H—O—H}$$

In some cases, two covalent bonds—a double bond—form between two atoms when they share two electrons from each atom. Carbon dioxide (CO_2), a waste product of metabolism, contains two double bonds:

$$\text{O=C=O}$$

Note that in this molecule the carbon atom still forms four covalent bonds and each oxygen atom only two.

Polar Covalent Bonds

Not all atoms have the same ability to attract shared electrons. The measure of an atom's ability to attract electrons in a covalent bond is called its **electronegativity.** Electronegativity generally increases as the total positive charge of a nucleus increases but decreases as the distance between the shared electrons and the nucleus increases. When two atoms with different electronegativities combine to form a covalent bond, the shared electrons will tend to spend more time orbiting the atom with the higher electronegativity. This creates a polarity across the bond (think of the poles of a magnet; only in this case the polarity refers to a difference in charge).

Due to the polarity in electron distribution just described, the more electronegative atom acquires a slight negative charge, whereas the other atom, having partly lost an electron, becomes slightly positive. Such bonds are known as **polar covalent bonds** (or, simply, polar bonds) because the atoms at each end of the bond have an opposite electrical charge. For example, the bond between hydrogen and oxygen in a **hydroxyl group** (—OH) is a polar covalent bond in which the oxygen is slightly negative and the hydrogen slightly positive:

$$\text{R—}\overset{(\delta^-)}{\text{O}}\text{—}\overset{(\delta^+)}{\text{H}}$$

The δ^- and δ^+ symbols refer to atoms with a partial negative or positive charge, respectively. The R symbolizes the remainder of the molecule; in water, for example, R is simply another hydrogen atom carrying another partial positive charge. The electrical charge associated with the ends of a polar bond is considerably less than the charge on a fully ionized atom. Polar bonds do not have a *net* electrical charge, as do ions, because they contain overall equal amounts of negative and positive charge.

Atoms of oxygen, nitrogen, and sulfur, which have a relatively strong attraction for electrons, form polar bonds with hydrogen atoms (**Table 2.3**). One of the characteristics of polar bonds that is important in our understanding of physiology is that molecules that contain such bonds tend to be more soluble in water than molecules containing the other major type of covalent bond, described next. Consequently, these molecules—called **polar molecules**—readily dissolve in the blood, interstitial fluid,

TABLE 2.3 Examples of Nonpolar and Polar Bonds and Ionized Chemical Groups

Nonpolar Bonds	$-\overset{\vert}{\underset{\vert}{C}}-H$	Carbon–hydrogen bond
	$-\overset{\vert}{\underset{\vert}{C}}-\overset{\vert}{\underset{\vert}{C}}-$	Carbon–carbon bond
Polar Bonds	$R-\overset{(\delta^-)}{O}-\overset{(\delta^+)}{H}$	Hydroxyl group (R—OH)
	$R-\overset{(\delta^-)}{S}-\overset{(\delta^+)}{H}$	Sulfhydryl group (R—SH)
	$H^{(\delta^+)}$ bonded to $N^{(\delta^-)}$ in R—N—R	Nitrogen–hydrogen bond
Ionized Groups	$R-\overset{\overset{O}{\Vert}}{C}-O^-$	Carboxyl group (R—COO$^-$)
	$R-\overset{\overset{H}{\vert +}}{\underset{\underset{H}{\vert}}{N}}-H$	Amino group (R—NH_3^+)
	$R-O-\overset{\overset{O}{\Vert}}{\underset{\underset{O^-}{\vert}}{P}}-O^-$	Phosphate group (R—PO_4^{2-})

and intracellular fluid. Indeed, water itself is the classic example of a polar molecule, with a partially negatively charged oxygen atom and two partially positively charged hydrogen atoms.

Nonpolar Covalent Bonds

In contrast to polar covalent bonds, bonds between atoms with similar electronegativities are said to be **nonpolar covalent bonds.** In such bonds, the electrons are equally or nearly equally shared by the two atoms, such that there is little or no unequal charge distribution across the bond. Bonds between carbon and hydrogen atoms and between two carbon atoms are electrically neutral, nonpolar covalent bonds (see Table 2.3). Molecules that contain high proportions of nonpolar covalent bonds are called **nonpolar molecules;** they tend to be less soluble in water than those with polar covalent bonds. Consequently, such molecules are often found in the lipid bilayers of the membranes of cells and intracellular organelles. When present in body fluids such as the blood, they may associate with a polar molecule that serves as a sort of "carrier" to prevent the nonpolar molecule from coming out of solution. The characteristics of molecules in solution will be covered later in this chapter.

Ionic Bonds

As noted earlier, some elements, such as those that make up table salt (NaCl), can form ions. NaCl is a solid crystalline substance because of the strong electrical attraction between positive sodium ions and negative chloride ions. This strong attraction between two oppositely charged ions is known as an **ionic bond.** When a crystal of sodium chloride is placed in water, the highly polar water molecules with their partial positive and negative charges are attracted to the charged sodium and chloride ions (**Figure 2.4**). Clusters of water molecules surround the ions, allowing the sodium and chloride ions to separate from each other and enter the water—that is, to dissolve.

Hydrogen Bonds

When two polar molecules are in close contact, an electrical attraction may form between them. For example, the hydrogen atom in a polar bond in one molecule and an oxygen or nitrogen atom in a polar bond of another molecule attract each other forming a type of bond called a **hydrogen bond.** Such bonds may also form between atoms within the same molecule. Hydrogen bonds are represented in diagrams by dashed or dotted lines to distinguish them from covalent bonds, as illustrated in the bonds between water molecules (**Figure 2.5**). Hydrogen bonds are very weak, having only about 4% of the strength of the polar bonds between the hydrogen and oxygen atoms in a single molecule of water. Although hydrogen bonds are weak individually, when present in large numbers, they play an extremely important role in molecular interactions and in determining the shape of large molecules. This is of great importance for physiology, because the shape of large molecules often determines their

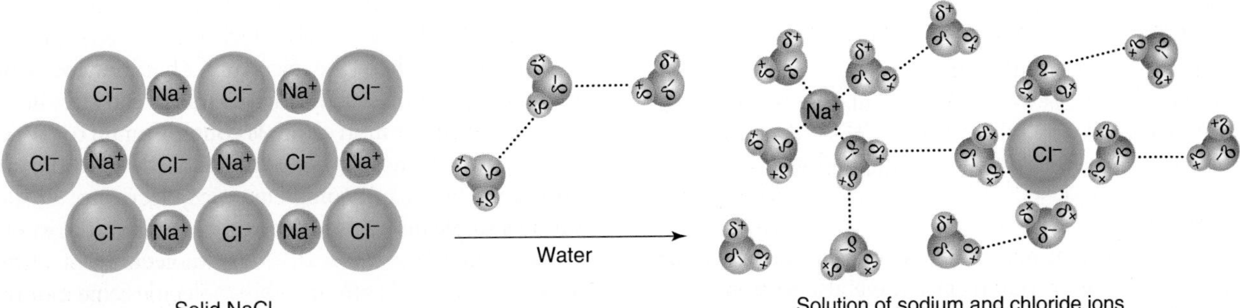

Figure 2.4 APIR The electrical attraction between the charged sodium and chloride ions forms ionic bonds in solid NaCl. The attraction of the polar, partially charged regions of water molecules breaks the ionic bonds and the sodium and chloride ions dissolve.

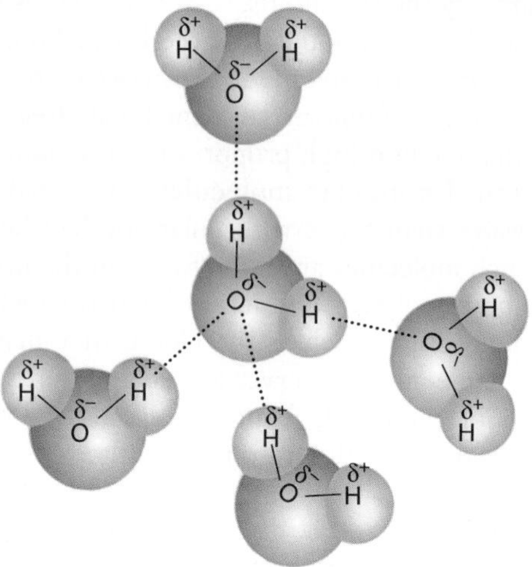

Figure 2.5 Five water molecules. Note that polar covalent bonds link the hydrogen and oxygen atoms within each molecule and that hydrogen bonds occur between adjacent molecules. Hydrogen bonds are represented in diagrams by dashed or dotted lines, and covalent bonds by solid lines.

PHYSIOLOGICAL INQUIRY

- What effect might hydrogen bonds have on the temperature at which liquid water becomes a vapor?

Answer can be found at end of chapter.

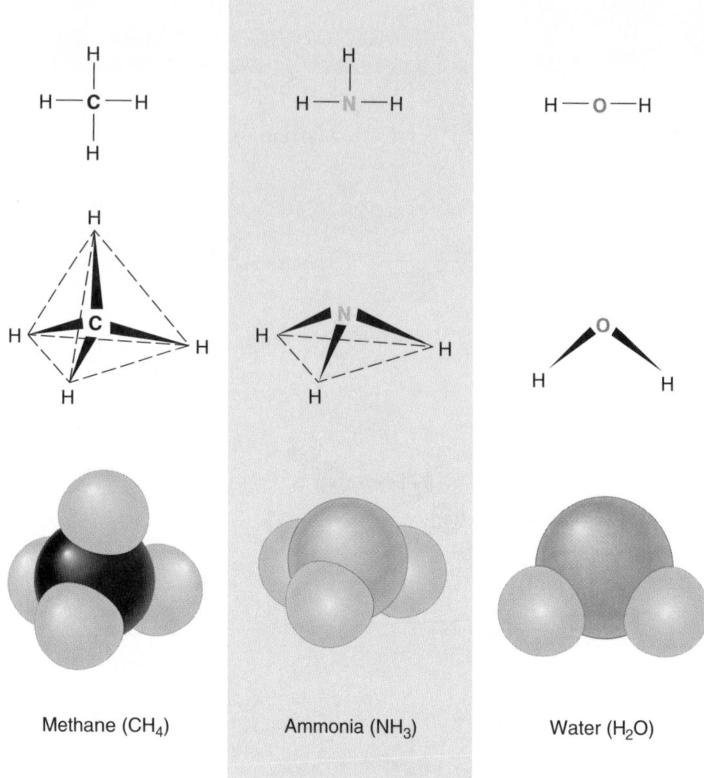

Figure 2.6 Three different ways of representing the geometric configuration of covalent bonds around the carbon, nitrogen, and oxygen atoms bonded to hydrogen atoms.

functions and their ability to interact with other molecules. For example, some molecules interact with a "lock-and-key" arrangement that can only occur if both molecules have precisely the correct shape, which in turn depends in part upon the number and location of hydrogen bonds.

Molecular Shape

As just mentioned, when atoms are linked together they form molecules with various shapes. Although we draw diagrammatic structures of molecules on flat sheets of paper, molecules are three-dimensional. When more than one covalent bond is formed with a given atom, the bonds are distributed around the atom in a pattern that may or may not be symmetrical (**Figure 2.6**).

Molecules are not rigid, inflexible structures. Within certain limits, the shape of a molecule can be changed without breaking the covalent bonds linking its atoms together. A covalent bond is like an axle around which the joined atoms can rotate. As illustrated in **Figure 2.7**, a sequence of six carbon atoms can assume a number of shapes by rotating around various covalent bonds. As we will see in subsequent chapters, the three-dimensional, flexible shape of molecules is one of the major factors governing molecular interactions.

Ionic Molecules

The process of ion formation, known as ionization, can occur not only in single atoms, as stated earlier, but also in atoms that are covalently linked in molecules. Two commonly encountered groups of atoms that undergo ionization in molecules are the **carboxyl group** (—COOH) and the **amino group** ($—NH_2$). The shorthand formula for only a portion of a molecule can be written as R—COOH or $R—NH_2$, with R being the remainder of the molecule. The carboxyl group ionizes when the oxygen linked to the hydrogen captures the hydrogen's only electron to form a carboxyl ion ($R—COO^-$), releasing a hydrogen ion (H^+):

$$R—COOH \rightleftharpoons R—COO^- + H^+$$

The amino group can bind a hydrogen ion to form an ionized amino group ($R—NH_3^+$):

$$R—NH_2 + H^+ \rightleftharpoons R—NH_3^+$$

The ionization of each of these groups can be reversed, as indicated by the double arrows; the ionized carboxyl group can combine with a hydrogen ion to form a nonionized carboxyl group, and the ionized amino group can lose a hydrogen ion and become a nonionized amino group.

Free Radicals

As described earlier, the electrons that revolve around the nucleus of an atom occupy energy shells, each of which can be occupied by one or more orbitals containing up to two electrons each. An atom is most stable when each orbital in the outer shell is occupied by its full complement of electrons. An atom containing a single (unpaired) electron in an orbital of its outer shell is known as a **free radical,** as are molecules containing such atoms. Free radicals are unstable molecules that can react with other atoms, through the process known as oxidation. When a free radical oxidizes another atom, the free radical gains an electron and the other atom usually becomes a new free radical.

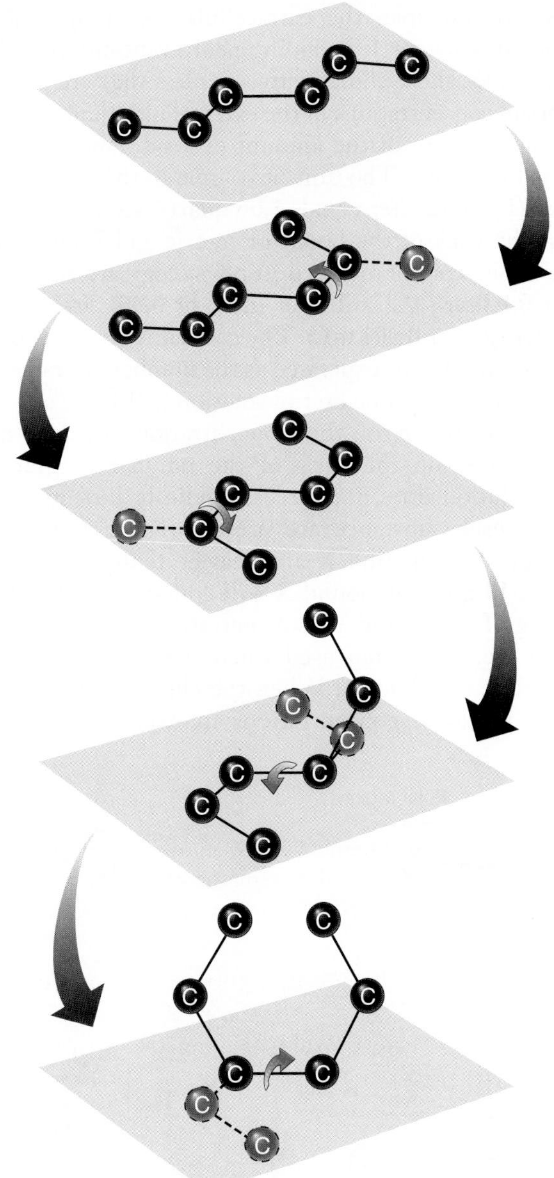

Figure 2.7 Changes in molecular shape occur as portions of a molecule rotate around different carbon-to-carbon bonds, transforming this molecule's shape, for example, from a relatively straight chain (top) into a ring (bottom).

Free radicals are formed by the actions of certain enzymes in some cells, such as types of white blood cells that destroy pathogens. The free radicals are highly reactive, removing electrons from the outer shells of atoms within molecules present in the pathogen cell wall or membrane, for example. This mechanism begins the process whereby the pathogen is destroyed.

In addition, however, free radicals can be produced in the body following exposure to radiation or toxin ingestion. These free radicals can do considerable harm to the cells of the body. For example, oxidation due to long-term buildup of free radicals has been proposed as one cause of several different human diseases, notably eye, cardiovascular, and neural diseases associated with aging. Thus, it is important that free radicals be inactivated by molecules that can donate electrons to free radicals without becoming dangerous free radicals themselves. Examples of such protective molecules are the antioxidant vitamins C and E.

Free radicals are diagrammed with a dot next to the atomic symbol. Examples of biologically important free radicals are superoxide anion, $O_2 \cdot^-$; hydroxyl radical, $OH \cdot$; and nitric oxide, $NO \cdot$. Note that a free radical configuration can occur in either an ionized (charged) or a nonionized molecule.

We turn now to a discussion of solutions and molecular solubility in water. We begin with a review of some of the properties of water that make it so suitable for life.

2.3 Solutions

Substances dissolved in a liquid are known as **solutes,** and the liquid in which they are dissolved is the **solvent.** Solutes dissolve in a solvent to form a **solution.** Water is the most abundant solvent in the body, accounting for ≈60% of total body weight. A majority of the chemical reactions that occur in the body involve molecules that are dissolved in water, either in the intracellular or extracellular fluid. However, not all molecules dissolve in water.

Water

Out of every 100 molecules in the human body, about 99 are water. The covalent bonds linking the two hydrogen atoms to the oxygen atom in a water molecule are polar. Therefore, as noted earlier, the oxygen in water has a partial negative charge, and each hydrogen has a partial positive charge. The positively polarized regions near the hydrogen atoms of one water molecule are electrically attracted to the negatively polarized regions of the oxygen atoms in adjacent water molecules by hydrogen bonds (see Figure 2.5).

At temperatures between 0°C and 100°C, water exists as a liquid; in this state, the weak hydrogen bonds between water molecules are continuously forming and breaking, and occasionally some water molecules escape the liquid phase and become a gas. If the temperature is increased, the hydrogen bonds break more readily and molecules of water escape into the gaseous state. However, if the temperature is reduced, hydrogen bonds break less frequently, so larger and larger clusters of water molecules form until at 0°C, water freezes into a solid crystalline matrix—ice. Body temperature in humans is normally close to 37°C, and therefore water exists in liquid form in the body. Nonetheless, even at this temperature, some water leaves the body as a gas (water vapor) each time we exhale during breathing. This water loss in the form of water vapor has considerable importance for total-body-water homeostasis and must be replaced with water obtained from food or drink.

Water molecules take part in many chemical reactions of the general type:

$$R_1{-}R_2 + H{-}O{-}H \rightleftharpoons R_1{-}OH + H{-}R_2$$

In this reaction, the covalent bond between R_1 and R_2 and the one between a hydrogen atom and oxygen in water are broken, and the hydroxyl group and hydrogen atom are transferred to R_1 and R_2, respectively. Reactions of this type are known as hydrolytic reactions, or **hydrolysis.** Many large molecules in the body are broken down into smaller molecular units by hydrolysis, usually with the assistance of a class of molecules called enzymes. These reactions are usually reversible, a process known as condensation or **dehydration.** In dehydration, one net water molecule is removed to combine two small molecules into one larger one. Dehydration reactions are responsible for, among other things, building proteins and other large molecules required by the body.

Other properties of water that are of importance in physiology include the colligative properties—those that depend on the *number* of dissolved substances, or solutes, in water. For example, water moves between fluid compartments by the process of osmosis, which you will learn about in detail in Chapter 4. In osmosis, water moves from regions of low solute concentrations to regions of high solute concentrations, regardless of the specific type of solute. Osmosis is the mechanism by which water is absorbed from the intestinal tract (Chapter 15) and from the kidney tubules into the blood (Chapter 14).

Having presented this brief survey of some of the physiologically relevant properties of water, we turn now to a discussion of how molecules dissolve in water. Keep in mind as you read on that most of the chemical reactions in the body take place between molecules that are in watery solution. Therefore, the relative solubilities of different molecules influence their abilities to participate in chemical reactions.

Molecular Solubility

Molecules having a number of polar bonds and/or ionized groups will dissolve in water. Such molecules are said to be **hydrophilic,** or "water-loving." Therefore, the presence of ionized groups such as carboxyl and amino groups or of polar groups such as hydroxyl groups in a molecule promotes solubility in water. In contrast, molecules composed predominantly of carbon and hydrogen are poorly or almost completely insoluble in water because their electrically neutral covalent bonds are not attracted to water molecules. These molecules are **hydrophobic,** or "water-fearing."

When hydrophobic molecules are mixed with water, two phases form, as occurs when oil is mixed with water. The strong attraction between polar molecules "squeezes" the nonpolar molecules out of the water phase. Such a separation is rarely if ever 100% complete, however, so very small amounts of nonpolar solutes remain dissolved in the water phase.

A special class of molecules has a polar or ionized region at one site and a nonpolar region at another site. Such molecules are called **amphipathic,** derived from Greek terms meaning "love both." When mixed with water, amphipathic molecules form clusters, with their polar (hydrophilic) regions at the surface of the cluster where they are attracted to the surrounding water molecules. The nonpolar (hydrophobic) ends are oriented toward the interior of the cluster (**Figure 2.8**). This arrangement provides the maximal interaction between water molecules and the polar ends of the amphipathic molecules. Nonpolar molecules can dissolve in the central nonpolar regions of these clusters and thus exist in aqueous solutions in far greater amounts than would otherwise be possible based on their decreased solubility in water. As we will see, the orientation of amphipathic molecules plays an important role in plasma membrane structure (Chapter 3) and in both the absorption of nonpolar molecules from the intestines and their transport in the blood (Chapter 15).

Concentration

Solute **concentration** is defined as the amount of the solute present in a unit volume of solution. The concentrations of solutes in a solution are key to their ability to produce physiological actions. For example, the extracellular signaling molecules described in Chapter 1, including neurotransmitters and hormones, cannot alter cellular activity unless they are present in appropriate concentrations in the extracellular fluid.

One measure of the amount of a substance is its mass expressed in grams. The unit of volume in the metric system is a liter (L). (One liter equals 1.06 quarts; see the conversion table at the back of the book for metric and English units.) Smaller units commonly used in physiology are the deciliter (dL, or 0.1 liter), the milliliter (mL, or 0.001 liter), and the microliter (μL, or 0.001 mL). The concentration of a solute in a solution can then be expressed as the number of grams of the substance present in one liter of solution (g/L).

A comparison of the concentrations of two different substances on the basis of the number of grams per liter of solution does not directly indicate how many molecules of each substance are present. For example, if the molecules of compound X are heavier than those of compound Y, 10 g of compound X will contain fewer molecules than 10 g of compound Y. Concentrations in units of grams per liter are most often used when the chemical structure of the solute is unknown. When the chemical structure of a molecule is known, concentrations are expressed based upon

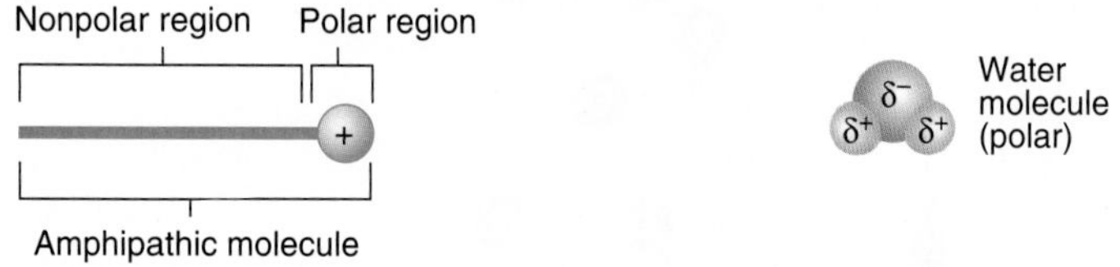

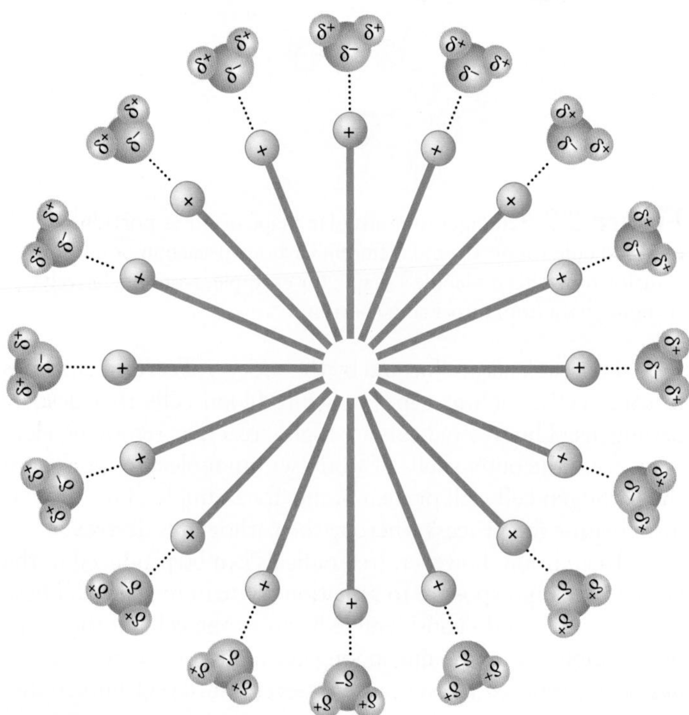

Figure 2.8 In water, amphipathic molecules aggregate into spherical clusters. Their polar regions form hydrogen bonds with water molecules at the surface of the cluster, whereas the nonpolar regions cluster together and exclude water.

the number of solute molecules in solution, using a measure of mass called the molecular weight. The **molecular weight** of a molecule is equal to the sum of the atomic masses of all the atoms in the molecule. For example, glucose ($C_6H_{12}O_6$) has a molecular weight of 180 because $[(6 \times 12) + (12 \times 1) + (6 \times 16)] = 180$. One **mole** (mol) of a compound is the amount of the compound in grams equal to its molecular weight. A solution containing 180 g glucose (1 mol) in 1 L of solution is a 1 molar solution of glucose (1 mol/L). If 90 g of glucose were dissolved in 1 L of water, the solution would have a concentration of 0.5 mol/L. Just as a 1 g atomic mass of any element contains the same number of atoms, 1 mol of any molecule will contain the same number of molecules—6×10^{23} (Avogadro's number). Thus, a 1 mol/L solution of glucose contains the same number of solute molecules per liter as a 1 mol/L solution of any other substance.

The concentrations of solutes dissolved in the body fluids are much less than 1 mol/L. Many have concentrations in the range of millimoles per liter (1 mmol/L = 0.001 mol/L), whereas others are present in even smaller concentrations—micromoles per liter (1 μmol/L = 0.000001 mol/L) or nanomoles per liter (1 mol/L = 0.000000001 mol/L). By convention, the liter (L) term is sometimes dropped when referring to concentrations. Thus, a 1 mmol/L solution is often written as 1 mM (the capital "M" stands for "molar" and is defined as mol/L).

An example of the importance of solute concentrations is related to a key homeostatic variable, that of the pH of the body fluids, as described next. Maintenance of a narrow range of pH (that is, hydrogen ion concentration) in the body fluids is absolutely critical to most physiological processes, in part because enzymes and other proteins depend on pH for their normal shape and activity.

Hydrogen Ions and Acidity

As mentioned earlier, a hydrogen atom consists of a single proton in its nucleus orbited by a single electron. The most common type of hydrogen ion (H^+) is formed by the loss of the electron and is, therefore, a single free proton. Molecules that release protons (hydrogen ions) in solution are called **acids,** for example:

$$\underset{\text{hydrochloric acid}}{HCl} \longrightarrow H^+ + \underset{\text{chloride}}{Cl^-}$$

$$\underset{\text{carbonic acid}}{H_2CO_3} \rightleftharpoons H^+ + \underset{\text{bicarbonate}}{HCO_3^-}$$

$$\underset{\text{lactic acid}}{CH_3\text{—}\overset{\overset{\displaystyle OH}{|}}{\underset{\underset{\displaystyle H}{|}}{C}}\text{—}COOH} \rightleftharpoons H^+ + \underset{\text{lactate}}{CH_3\text{—}\overset{\overset{\displaystyle OH}{|}}{\underset{\underset{\displaystyle H}{|}}{C}}\text{—}COO^-}$$

Conversely, any substance that can accept a hydrogen ion (proton) is termed a **base.** In the reactions shown, bicarbonate and lactate are bases because they can combine with hydrogen ions (note the two-way arrows in the two reactions). Also, note that by convention, separate terms are used for the acid forms—*lactic acid* and *carbonic acid*—and the bases derived from the acids—*lactate* and *bicarbonate.* By combining with hydrogen ions, bases decrease the hydrogen ion concentration of a solution.

When hydrochloric acid is dissolved in water, 100% of its atoms separate to form hydrogen and chloride ions, and these ions do not recombine in solution (note the one-way arrow in the preceding reaction). In the case of lactic acid, however, only a fraction of the lactic acid molecules in solution release hydrogen ions at any instant. Therefore, if a 1 mol/L solution of lactic acid is compared with a 1 mol/L solution of hydrochloric acid, the hydrogen ion concentration will be lower in the lactic acid solution than in the hydrochloric acid solution. Hydrochloric acid and other acids that are completely or nearly completely ionized in solution are known as **strong acids,** whereas carbonic and lactic acids and other acids that do not completely ionize in solution are **weak acids.** The same principles apply to bases.

It is important to understand that the hydrogen ion concentration of a solution refers only to the hydrogen ions that are free in solution and not to those that may be bound, for example, to amino groups ($R\text{—}NH_3^+$). The **acidity** of a solution thus refers to the *free* (unbound) hydrogen ion concentration in the solution; the greater the hydrogen ion concentration, the greater the acidity. The hydrogen ion concentration is often expressed as the solution's **pH,** which is defined as the negative logarithm to the base 10 of the hydrogen ion concentration. The brackets around the symbol for the hydrogen ion in the following formula indicate concentration:

$$pH = -\log [H^+]$$

As an example, a solution with a hydrogen ion concentration of 10^{-7} mol/L has a pH of 7. Pure water, due to the ionization of some of the molecules into H^+ and OH^-, has hydrogen ion and hydroxyl ion concentrations of 10^{-7} mol/L (pH = 7.0) at 25°C. The product of the concentrations of H^+ and OH^- in pure water is always 10^{-14} M at 25°C. A solution of pH 7.0 is termed a **neutral solution. Alkaline solutions** have a lower hydrogen ion concentration (a pH greater than 7.0), whereas those with a greater hydrogen ion concentration (a pH lower than 7.0) are **acidic solutions.** Note that as the acidity *increases,* the pH *decreases;* a change in pH from 7 to 6 represents a 10-fold increase in the hydrogen ion concentration. The extracellular fluid of the body has a hydrogen ion concentration of about 4×10^{-8} mol/L (pH = 7.4), with a homeostatic range of about pH 7.35 to 7.45, and is thus slightly alkaline. Most intracellular fluids have a slightly greater hydrogen ion concentration (pH 7.0 to 7.2) than extracellular fluids.

As we saw earlier, the ionization of carboxyl and amino groups involves the release and uptake, respectively, of hydrogen ions. These groups behave as weak acids and bases. Changes in the acidity of solutions containing molecules with carboxyl and amino groups alter the net electrical charge on these molecules by shifting the ionization reaction to the right or left according to the general form:

$$R\text{—}COO^- + H^+ \rightleftharpoons R\text{—}COOH$$

For example, if the acidity of a solution containing lactate is increased by adding hydrochloric acid, the concentration of lactic acid will increase and that of lactate will decrease.

If the electrical charge on a molecule is altered, its interaction with other molecules or with other regions within the same molecule changes, and thus its functional characteristics change. In the extracellular fluid, *hydrogen ion concentrations beyond the 10-fold pH range of 7.8 to 6.8 are incompatible with life if maintained for more than a brief period of time.* Even small changes in the hydrogen ion concentration can produce large changes in molecular interaction. For example, many enzymes in the body operate efficiently within very narrow ranges of pH. Should pH vary from the normal homeostatic range due to disease, these enzymes work at reduced rates, creating an even worse pathological situation.

This concludes our overview of atomic and molecular structure, water, and pH. We turn now to a description of the molecules essential for life in all living organisms, including humans. These are the carbon-based molecules required for forming the building blocks of cells, tissues, and organs; providing energy; and forming the genetic blueprints of all life.

2.4 Classes of Organic Molecules

Because most naturally occurring carbon-containing molecules are found in living organisms, the study of these compounds is known as organic chemistry. (Inorganic chemistry refers to the study of non-carbon-containing molecules.) However, the chemistry of living organisms, or biochemistry, now forms only a portion of the broad field of organic chemistry.

One of the properties of the carbon atom that makes life possible is its ability to form four covalent bonds with other atoms, including with other carbon atoms. Because carbon atoms can also combine with hydrogen, oxygen, nitrogen, and sulfur atoms, a vast number of compounds can form from relatively few chemical elements. Some of these molecules are extremely large (**macromolecules**), composed of thousands of atoms. In some cases, such large molecules form when many identical smaller molecules, called subunits or monomers (literally, "one part"), link together. These large molecules are known as **polymers** ("many parts"). The structure of any polymer depends upon the structure of the subunits, the number of subunits bonded together, and the three-dimensional way in which the subunits are linked.

Most of the organic molecules in the body can be classified into one of four groups: carbohydrates, lipids, proteins, and nucleic acids (**Table 2.4**). We will consider each of these groups separately, but it is worth mentioning here that many molecules in the body are made up of two or more of these groups. For example, glycoproteins are composed of a protein covalently bonded to one or more carbohydrates.

Carbohydrates

Although carbohydrates account for only about 1% of body weight, they play a central role in the chemical reactions that provide cells with energy. As you will learn later in this chapter and in greater detail in Chapter 3, energy is stored in the chemical bonds in glucose molecules; this energy can be released within cells when required and stored in the bonds of another molecule called adenosine triphosphate (ATP). The energy stored in the bonds in ATP is used to power many different reactions in the body, including those necessary for cell survival, muscle contraction, protein synthesis, and many others.

Carbohydrates are composed of carbon, hydrogen, and oxygen atoms. Linked to most of the carbon atoms in a carbohydrate are a hydrogen atom and a hydroxyl group:

$$\begin{array}{c} | \\ \text{H—C—OH} \\ | \end{array}$$

The presence of numerous polar hydroxyl groups makes most carbohydrates readily soluble in water.

TABLE 2.4 Major Categories of Organic Molecules in the Body

Category	Percentage of Body Weight	Predominant Atoms	Subclass	Subunits
Carbohydrates	1	C, H, O	Polysaccharides (and disaccharides)	Monosaccharides
Lipids	15	C, H	Triglycerides	3 fatty acids + glycerol
			Phospholipids	2 fatty acids + glycerol + phosphate + small charged nitrogen-containing group
			Steroids	None
Proteins	17	C, H, O, N	Peptides and polypeptides	Amino acids
Nucleic acids	2	C, H, O, N	DNA	Nucleotides containing the bases adenine, cytosine, guanine, thymine; the sugar deoxyribose; and phosphate
			RNA	Nucleotides containing the bases adenine, cytosine, guanine, uracil; the sugar ribose; and phosphate

Many carbohydrates taste sweet, particularly the carbohydrates known as sugars. The simplest sugars are the monomers called **monosaccharides** (from the Greek for "single sugars"), the most abundant of which is **glucose,** a six-carbon molecule ($C_6H_{12}O_6$). Glucose is often called "blood sugar" because it is the major monosaccharide found in the blood.

Glucose may exist in an open chain form, or, more commonly, a cyclic structure as shown in **Figure 2.9**. Five carbon atoms and an oxygen atom form a ring that lies in an essentially flat plane. The hydrogen and hydroxyl groups on each carbon lie above and below the plane of this ring. If one of the hydroxyl groups below the ring is shifted to a position above the ring, a different monosaccharide is produced.

Most monosaccharides in the body contain five or six carbon atoms and are called **pentoses** and **hexoses,** respectively. Larger carbohydrates can be formed by joining a number of monosaccharides together. Carbohydrates composed of two monosaccharides are known as **disaccharides. Sucrose,** or table sugar, is composed of two monosaccharides, glucose and fructose (**Figure 2.10**). The linking together of most monosaccharides involves a dehydration reaction in which a hydroxyl group is removed from one monosaccharide and a hydrogen atom is removed from the other, giving rise to a molecule of water and covalently bonding the two sugars together through an oxygen atom. Conversely, hydrolysis of the disaccharide breaks this linkage by adding back the water and thus uncoupling the two monosaccharides. Other disaccharides frequently encountered are maltose (glucose–glucose), formed during the digestion of large carbohydrates in the intestinal tract, and lactose (glucose–galactose), present in milk.

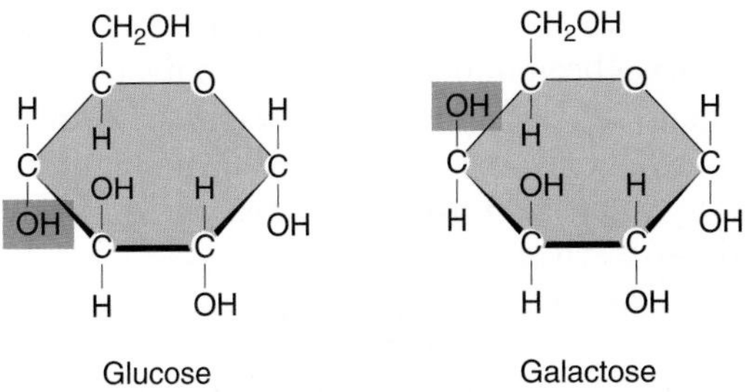

Figure 2.9 The structural difference between the monosaccharides glucose and galactose is based on whether the hydroxyl group at the position indicated lies below or above the plane of the ring.

When many monosaccharides are linked together to form polymers, the molecules are known as **polysaccharides.** Starch, found in plant cells, and **glycogen,** present in animal cells, are examples of polysaccharides (**Figure 2.11**). Both of these polysaccharides are composed of thousands of glucose molecules linked together in long chains, differing only in the degree of branching along the chain. Glycogen exists in the body as a reservoir of available energy that is stored in the chemical bonds within individual glucose monomers. Hydrolysis of glycogen, as occurs during periods of fasting, leads to release of the glucose monomers into the blood, thereby preventing blood glucose from decreasing to dangerously low concentrations.

Lipids

Lipids are molecules composed predominantly (but not exclusively) of hydrogen and carbon atoms. These atoms are linked by nonpolar covalent bonds; therefore, lipids are nonpolar and have a very low solubility in water. Lipids, which account for about 40% of the organic matter in the average body (15% of the body weight), can be divided into four subclasses: fatty

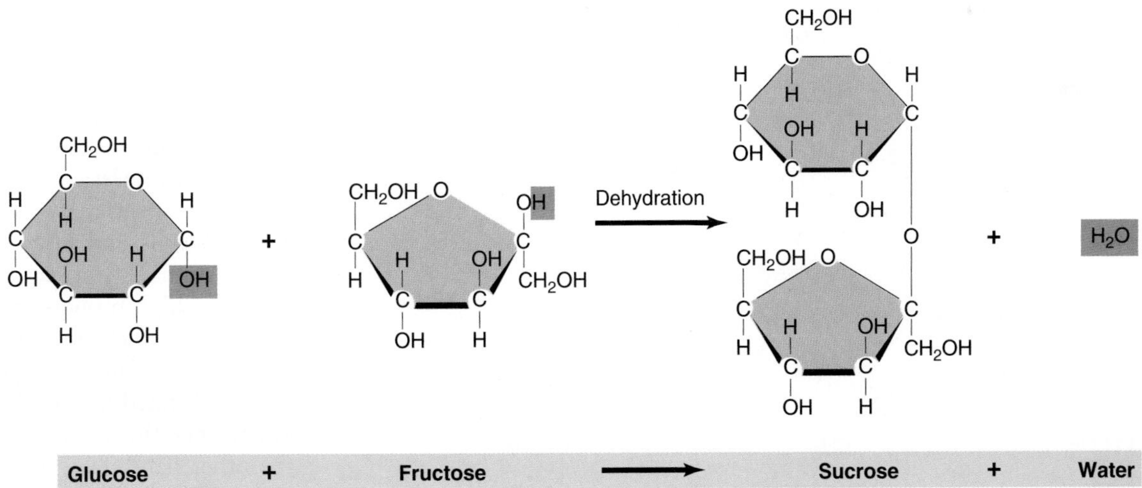

Figure 2.10 APR Sucrose (table sugar) is a disaccharide formed when two monosaccharides, glucose and fructose, bond together through a dehydration reaction.

PHYSIOLOGICAL INQUIRY

- What is the reverse reaction called?

Answer can be found at end of chapter.

acids, triglycerides, phospholipids, and steroids. Like carbohydrates, lipids are important in physiology partly because some of them provide a valuable source of energy. Other lipids are a major component of all cellular membranes, and still others are important signaling molecules.

Fatty Acids

A **fatty acid** consists of a chain of carbon and hydrogen atoms with an acidic carboxyl group at one end (**Figure 2.12a**). Therefore, fatty acids contain two oxygen atoms in addition to their complement of carbon and hydrogen. Fatty acids are synthesized in cells by the covalent bonding together of two-carbon fragments, resulting most commonly in fatty acids of 16 or 18 carbon atoms. When all the carbons in a fatty acid are linked by single covalent bonds, the fatty acid is said to be a **saturated fatty acid,** because both of the remaining available bonds in each carbon atom are occupied—or saturated—with covalently bound H. Some fatty acids contain one or more double bonds between carbon atoms, and these are known as **unsaturated fatty acids** (they have fewer C—H bonds than a saturated fatty acid). If one double bond is present, the fatty acid is **monounsaturated,** and if there is more than one double bond, it is **polyunsaturated** (see Figure 2.12a).

Most naturally occurring unsaturated fatty acids exist in the cis position, with both hydrogens on the same side of the double-bonded carbons (see Figure 2.12a). It is possible, however, to modify fatty acids during the processing of certain fatty foods, such that the hydrogens are on opposite sides of the double bond. These chemically altered fatty acids are known as **trans fatty acids.** The trans configuration imparts stability to the food for longer storage and alters the food's flavor and consistency. However, trans fatty acids have recently been linked with a number of serious health conditions, including elevated blood concentrations of cholesterol; current health guidelines recommend against the consumption of foods containing trans fatty acids.

Fatty acids have many important functions in the body, including but not limited to providing energy for cellular metabolism. The bonds between carbon and hydrogen atoms in a fatty acid can be broken to release chemical energy that can be stored in the chemical bonds of ATP. Like glucose, therefore, fatty acids are an extremely important source of energy. In addition, some fatty acids can be altered to produce a special class of molecules that regulate a number of cell functions by acting as cell signaling molecules. These modified fatty acids—collectively termed *eicosanoids*—are derived from the 20-carbon, polyunsaturated fatty acid arachidonic acid. They have been implicated in the control of blood pressure (Chapter 12), inflammation (Chapters 12 and 18), and smooth muscle contraction (Chapter 9), among other things. Finally, fatty acids form part of the structure of triglycerides, described next.

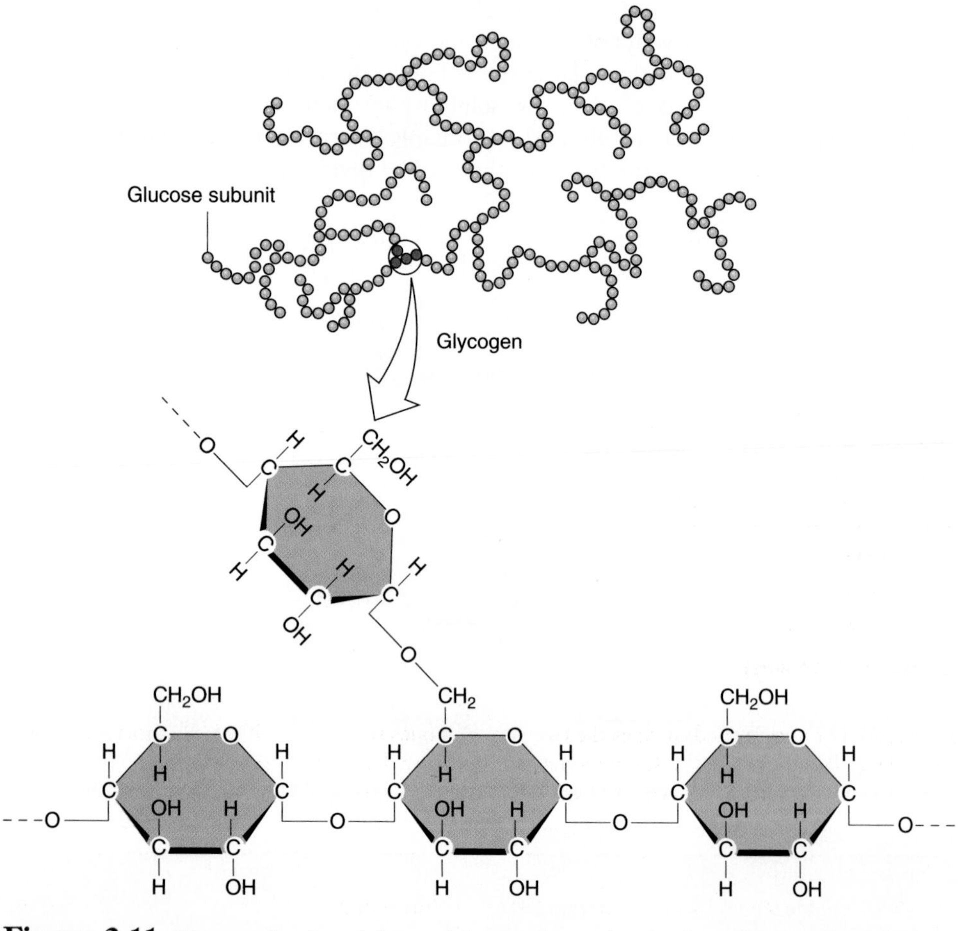

Figure 2.11 Many molecules of glucose joined end to end and at branch points form the branched-chain polysaccharide glycogen, shown here in diagrammatic form. The four red subunits in the glycogen molecule correspond to the four glucose subunits shown at the bottom.

Triglycerides

Triglycerides (also known as *triacylglycerols*) constitute the majority of the lipids in the body; these molecules are generally referred to simply as "fats." Triglycerides form when **glycerol,** a three-carbon sugar-alcohol, bonds to three fatty acids (**Figure 2.12b**). Each of the three hydroxyl groups in glycerol is bonded to the carboxyl group of a fatty acid by a dehydration reaction.

The three fatty acids in a molecule of triglyceride are usually not identical. Therefore, a variety of triglycerides can be formed with fatty acids of different chain lengths and degrees of saturation. Animal triglycerides generally contain a high proportion of saturated fatty acids, whereas vegetable triglycerides contain more unsaturated fatty acids. Saturated fats tend to be solid at low temperatures. Unsaturated fats, on the other hand, have a very low melting point, and thus they are liquids (oil) even at low temperatures. In a familiar example, heating a hamburger on the stove melts the saturated animal fats, leaving grease in the frying pan. When allowed to cool, however, the oily grease returns to its solid form.

Triglycerides are present in the blood and can be synthesized in the liver.

(a)

Saturated fatty acid (stearic acid)

$HO{-}\overset{O}{\overset{\|}{C}}{-}(CH_2)_{16}{-}CH_3$ (Shorthand formula)

Cis double bonds

Polyunsaturated fatty acid (linoleic acid)

$HO{-}\overset{O}{\overset{\|}{C}}{-}(CH_2)_7{-}C{=}C{-}CH_2{-}C{=}C{-}(CH_2)_4{-}CH_3$ (Shorthand formula)

(b)

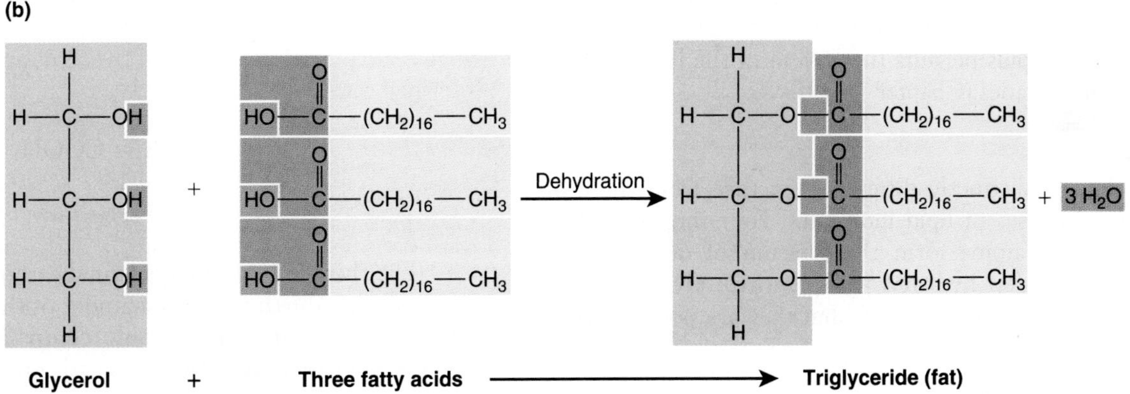

(c)

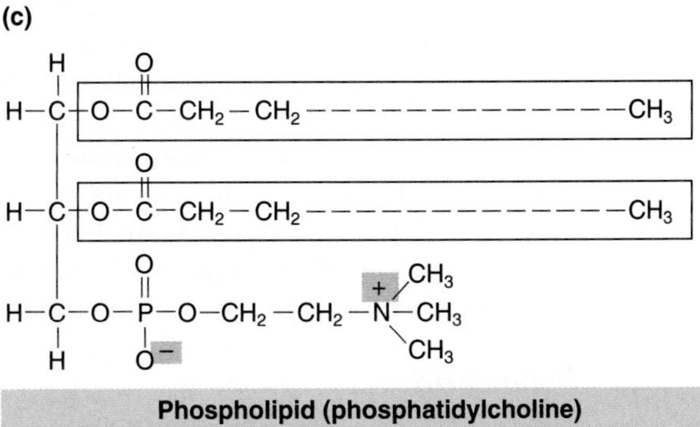

Figure 2.12 Lipids. (a) Fatty acids may be saturated or unsaturated, such as the two common ones shown here. Note the shorthand way of depicting the formula of a fatty acid. (b) Glycerol and fatty acids are the subunits that combine by a dehydration reaction to form triglycerides and water. (c) Phospholipids are formed from glycerol, two fatty acids, and one or more charged groups.

PHYSIOLOGICAL INQUIRY

- Which portion of the phospholipid depicted in Figure 2.12c would face the water molecules as shown in Figure 2.8?

Answer can be found at end of chapter.

They are stored in great quantities in adipose tissue, where they serve as an energy reserve for the body, particularly during times when a person is fasting or requires additional energy (exercise, for example). This occurs by hydrolysis, which releases the fatty acids from triglycerides in adipose tissue; the fatty acids enter the blood and are carried to the tissues and organs where they can be metabolized to provide energy for cell functions. Therefore, as with polysaccharides, storing energy in the form of triglycerides requires dehydration reactions, and both polysaccharides and triglycerides can be broken down by hydrolysis reactions to usable forms of energy.

Phospholipids

Phospholipids are similar in overall structure to triglycerides, with one important difference. The third hydroxyl group of glycerol, rather than being attached to a fatty acid, is linked to phosphate. In addition, a small polar or ionized nitrogen-containing molecule is usually attached to this phosphate (**Figure 2.12c**). These groups constitute a polar (hydrophilic) region at one end of the phospholipid, whereas the two fatty acid chains provide a nonpolar (hydrophobic) region at the opposite end. Therefore, phospholipids are amphipathic. In aqueous solution, they become organized into clusters, with their polar ends attracted to the water molecules. This property of phospholipids permits them to form the lipid bilayers of cellular membranes (Chapter 3).

Steroids

Steroids have a distinctly different structure from those of the other subclasses of lipid molecules. Four interconnected rings of carbon atoms form the skeleton of every steroid (**Figure 2.13**). A few hydroxyl groups, which are polar, may be attached to this ring structure, but they are not numerous enough to make a steroid water-soluble. Examples of steroids are cholesterol, cortisol from the adrenal glands, and female and male sex hormones (estrogen and testosterone, respectively) secreted by the gonads.

(a) Steroid ring structure

(b) Cholesterol

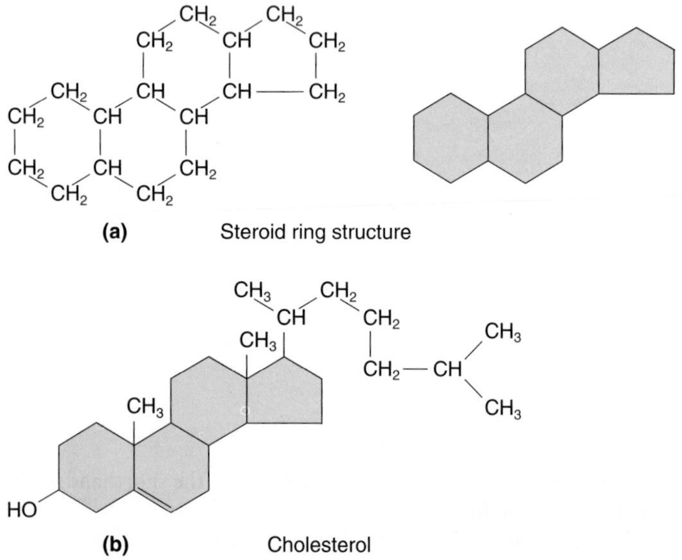

Figure 2.13 (a) Steroid ring structure, shown with all the carbon and hydrogen atoms in the rings and again without these atoms to emphasize the overall ring structure of this class of lipids. (b) Different steroids have different types and numbers of chemical groups attached at various locations on the steroid ring, as shown by the structure of cholesterol.

Proteins

The term **protein** comes from the Greek *proteios* ("of the first rank"), which aptly describes their importance. Proteins account for about 50% of the organic material in the body (17% of the body weight), and they play critical roles in almost every physiological and homeostatic process (summarized in **Table 2.5**). Proteins are composed of carbon, hydrogen, oxygen, nitrogen, and small amounts of other elements, notably sulfur. They are macromolecules, often containing thousands of atoms; they are formed when a large number of small subunits (monomers) bond together via dehydration reactions to create a polymer.

Amino Acid Subunits

The subunit monomers of proteins are **amino acids;** therefore, proteins are polymers of amino acids. Every amino acid except one (proline) has an amino (—NH_2) and a carboxyl (—COOH) group bound to the terminal carbon atom in the molecule:

$$\begin{array}{c} \mathrm{H} \\ | \\ \mathrm{R—C—COOH} \\ | \\ \mathrm{NH_2} \end{array}$$

The third bond of this terminal carbon is to a hydrogen atom and the fourth to the remainder of the molecule, which is known as the **amino acid side chain** (R in the formula). These side chains are relatively small, ranging from a single hydrogen atom to nine carbon atoms with their associated hydrogen atoms.

The proteins of all living organisms are composed of the same set of 20 different amino acids, corresponding to 20 different side chains. The side chains may be nonpolar (eight amino acids), polar but not ionized (seven amino acids), or polar and ionized (five amino acids) (**Figure 2.14**). The human body can synthesize many amino acids, but several must be obtained in the diet; the latter are known as essential amino acids. This term does not imply that these amino acids are somehow more important than others, only that they must be obtained in the diet.

Polypeptides

Amino acids are joined together by linking the carboxyl group of one amino acid to the amino group of another. As in the formation of glycogen and triglycerides, a molecule of water is formed by dehydration (**Figure 2.15**). The bond formed between the amino and carboxyl group is called a **peptide bond.** Although peptide bonds are covalent, they can be enzymatically broken by hydrolysis to yield individual amino acids, as happens in the stomach and intestines, for example, when we digest protein in our diet.

Notice in Figure 2.15 that when two amino acids are linked together, one end of the resulting molecule has a

TABLE 2.5 Major Categories and Functions of Proteins		
Category	**Functions**	**Examples**
Proteins that regulate gene expression	Make RNA from DNA; synthesize polypeptides from RNA	Transcription factors activate genes; RNA polymerase transcribes genes; ribosomal proteins are required for translation of mRNA into protein.
Transporter proteins	Mediate the movement of solutes such as ions and organic molecules across plasma membranes	Ion channels in plasma membranes allow movement across the membrane of ions such as Na^+ and K^+.
Enzymes	Accelerate the rate of specific chemical reactions, such as those required for cellular metabolism	Pancreatic lipase, amylase, and proteases released into the small intestine break down macromolecules into smaller molecules that can be absorbed by the intestinal cells; protein kinases modify other proteins by the addition of phosphate groups, which changes the function of the protein.
Cell signaling proteins	Enable cells to communicate with each other, themselves, and with the external environment	Plasma membrane receptors bind to hormones or neurotransmitters in extracellular fluid.
Motor proteins	Initiate movement	Myosin, found in muscle cells, provides the contractile force that shortens a muscle.
Structural proteins	Support, connect, and strengthen cells, tissues, and organs	Collagen and elastin provide support for ligaments, tendons, and certain large blood vessels; actin makes up much of the cytoskeleton of cells.
Defense proteins	Protect against infection and disease due to pathogens	Cytokines and antibodies attack foreign cells and proteins, such as those from bacteria and viruses.

free amino group and the other has a free carboxyl group. Additional amino acids can be linked by peptide bonds to these free ends. A sequence of amino acids linked by peptide bonds is known as a **polypeptide.** The peptide bonds form the backbone of the polypeptide, and the side chain of each amino acid sticks out from the chain. Strictly speaking, the term *polypeptide* refers to a structural unit and does not necessarily suggest that the molecule is functional. By convention, if the number of amino acids in a polypeptide is about 50 or fewer and has a known biological function, the molecule is often referred to simply as a **peptide,** a term we will use throughout the text where relevant. When one or more polypeptides are folded into a characteristic shape forming a functional molecule, that molecule is called a protein.

As mentioned earlier, one or more monosaccharides may become covalently attached to the side chains of specific amino acids in a protein; such proteins are known as **glycoproteins.** These proteins are present in plasma membranes; are major components of connective tissue; and are also abundant in fluids like mucus, where they play a protective or lubricating role.

All proteins have multiple levels of structure that give each protein a unique shape; these are called the primary, secondary, tertiary, and—in some proteins—quaternary structure.

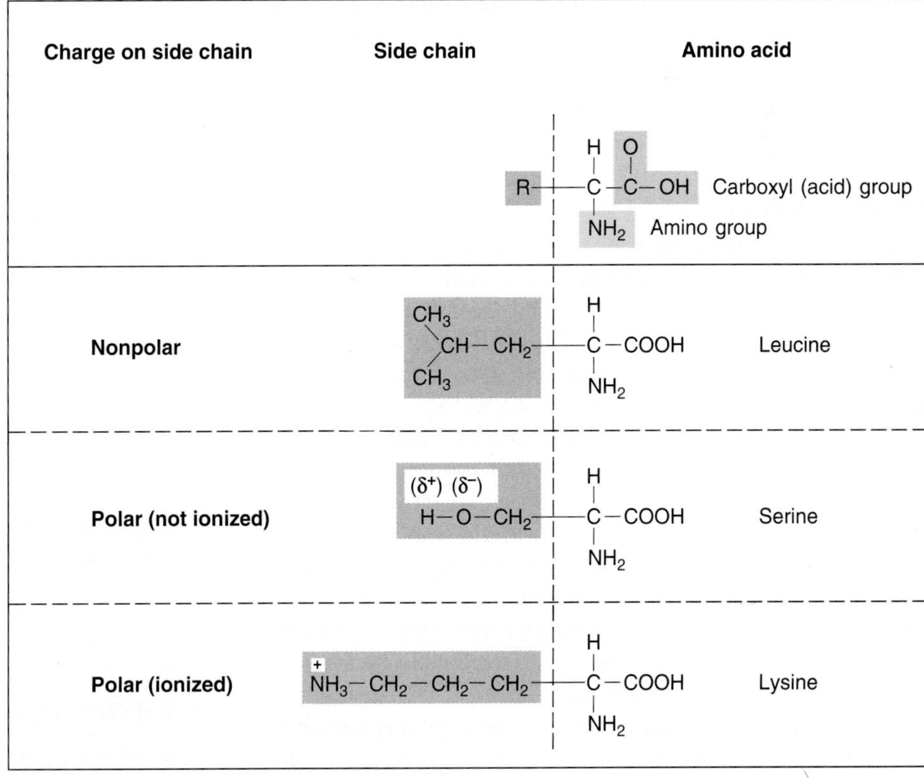

Figure 2.14 Representative structures of each class of amino acids found in proteins.

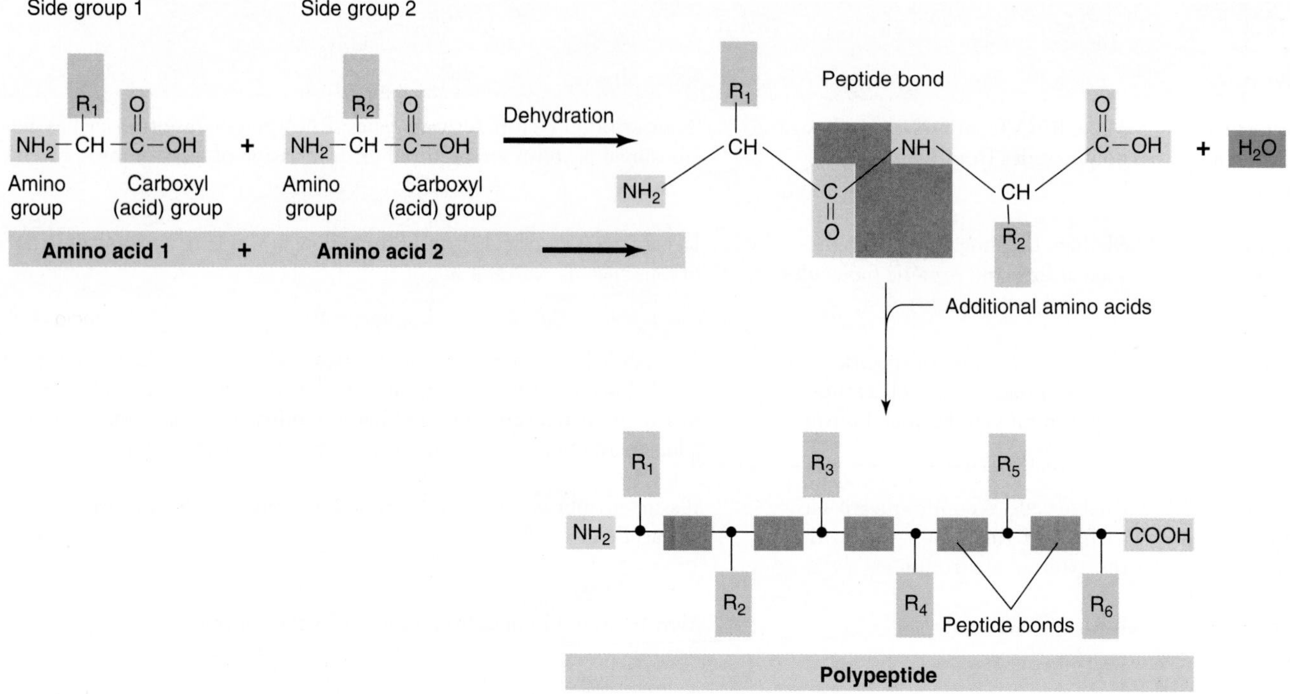

Figure 2.15 Linkage of amino acids by peptide bonds to form a polypeptide.

A general principle of physiology is that structure and function are linked. This is true even at the molecular level. The shape of a protein determines its physiological activity. In all cases, a protein's shape depends on its amino acid sequence, known as the *primary structure* of the protein.

Primary Structure

Two variables determine the **primary structure** of a protein: (1) the number of amino acids in the chain, and (2) the specific type of amino acid at each position along the chain (**Figure 2.16**). Each position along the chain can be occupied by any one of the 20 different amino acids.

Secondary Structure

A polypeptide can be envisioned as analogous to a string of beads, each bead representing one amino acid (see Figure 2.16). Moreover, because amino acids can rotate around bonds within a polypeptide chain, the chain is flexible and can bend into a number of shapes, just as a string of beads can be twisted into many configurations. Proteins do not appear in nature like a linear string of beads on a chain; interactions between side groups of each amino acid lead to bending, twisting, and folding of the chain into a more compact structure. The final shape of a protein is known as its **conformation.**

The attractions between various regions along a polypeptide chain create **secondary structure** in a protein. For example, hydrogen bonds can occur between a hydrogen linked to the nitrogen atom in one peptide bond and the double-bonded oxygen atom in another peptide bond (**Figure 2.17**). Because peptide bonds occur at regular intervals along a polypeptide chain, the hydrogen bonds between them tend to force the chain into a coiled conformation known as an **alpha helix.** Hydrogen bonds can also form between peptide bonds when extended regions of a polypeptide chain run approximately parallel to each other, forming a relatively straight, extended region known as a **beta pleated sheet** (see Figure 2.17). However, for several reasons,

Figure 2.16 The primary structure of a polypeptide chain is the sequence of amino acids in that chain. The polypeptide illustrated contains 223 amino acids. Different amino acids are represented by different-colored circles. The numbering system begins with the amino terminal (NH_2).

PHYSIOLOGICAL INQUIRY

- What is the difference between the terms *polypeptide* and *protein?*

Answer can be found at end of chapter.

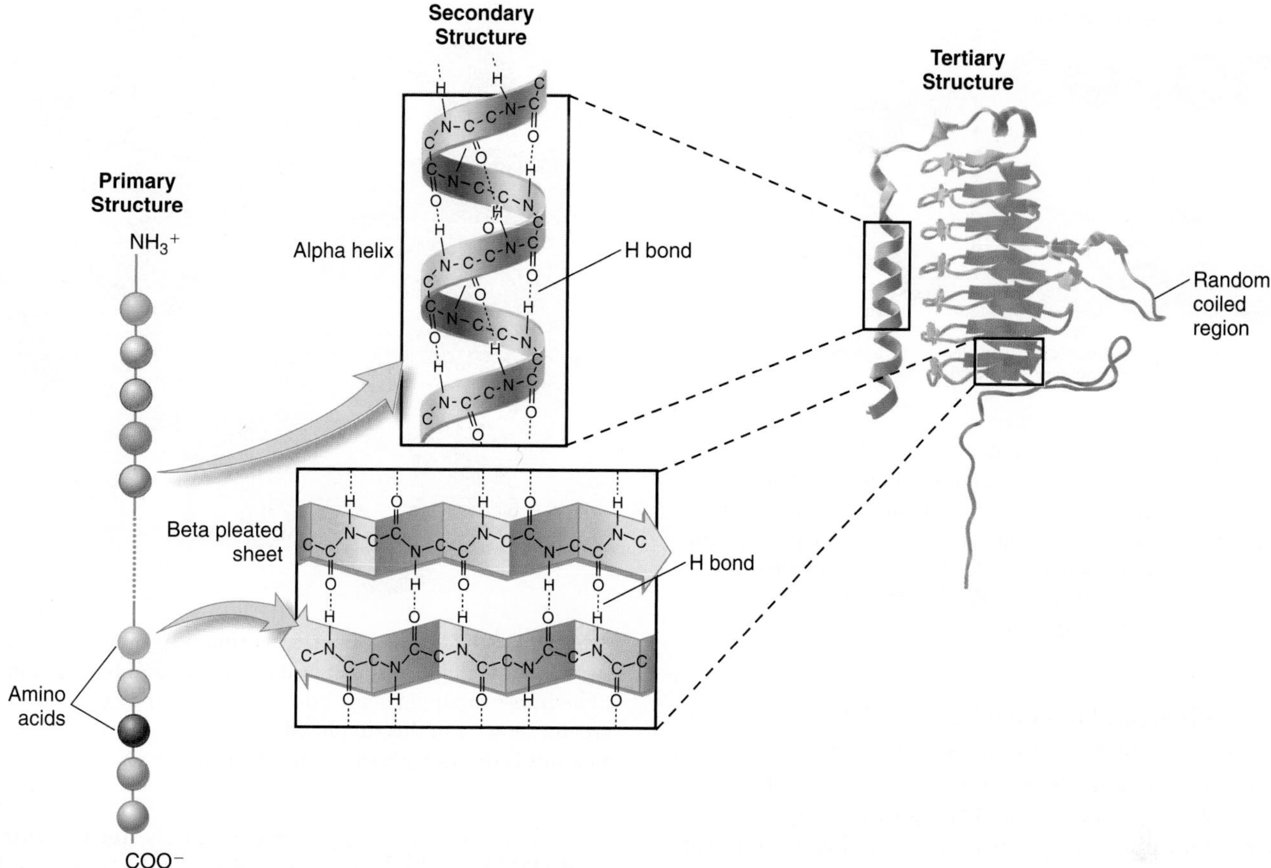

Figure 2.17 Secondary structure of a protein forms when regions of a polypeptide chain fold and twist into either an alpha-helical or beta pleated sheet conformation. The folding occurs largely through hydrogen bonds between nearby amino acid side groups. Further folding of the polypeptide chain produces tertiary structure, which is the final conformation of the protein.

a given region of a polypeptide chain may not assume either a helical or beta pleated sheet conformation. For example, the sizes of the side chains and the presence of ionic bonds between side chains with opposite charges can interfere with the repetitive hydrogen bonding required to produce these shapes. These irregular regions, known as random coil conformations, occur in regions linking the more regular helical and beta pleated sheet patterns (see Figure 2.17).

Beta pleated sheets and alpha helices tend to impart upon a protein the ability to anchor itself into a lipid bilayer, like that of a plasma membrane, because these regions of the protein usually contain amino acids with hydrophobic side chains. The hydrophobicity of the side chains makes them more likely to remain in the lipid environment of the plasma membrane.

Tertiary Structure

Once secondary structure has been formed, associations between additional amino acid side chains become possible. For example, two amino acids that may have been too far apart in the linear sequence of a polypeptide to interact with each other may become very near each other once secondary structure has changed the shape of the molecule. These interactions fold the polypeptide into its final three-dimensional conformation, making it a functional protein (see Figure 2.17). Five major factors determine the final conformation, or **tertiary structure,** of a polypeptide chain once the amino acid sequence (primary structure) has been formed: (1) hydrogen bonds between portions of the chain or with surrounding water molecules; (2) ionic bonds between polar and ionized regions along the chain; (3) attraction between nonpolar (hydrophobic) regions; (4) covalent **disulfide bonds** linking the sulfur-containing side chains of two cysteine amino acids; and (5) **van der Waals forces,** which are very weak and transient electrical interactions between the electrons in the outer shells of two atoms that are in close proximity to each other (**Figure 2.18**).

Quaternary Structure

Some proteins are composed of more than one polypeptide chain; they are said to have **quaternary structure** and are known as **multimeric** ("many parts") **proteins.** The same factors that influence the conformation of a single polypeptide also determine the interactions between the polypeptides in a multimeric protein. Therefore, the chains can be held together by interactions between various ionized, polar, and nonpolar side chains, as well as by disulfide covalent bonds between the chains.

Multimeric proteins have many diverse functions. The polypeptide chains in a multimeric protein may be

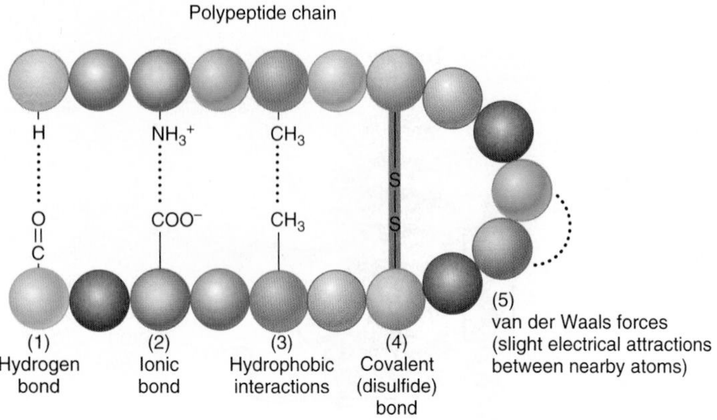

Figure 2.18 Factors that contribute to the folding of polypeptide chains and thus to their conformation are (1) hydrogen bonds between side chains or with surrounding water molecules, (2) ionic bonds between polar or ionized side chains, (3) hydrophobic attractive forces between nonpolar side chains, (4) disulfide bonds between side chains, and (5) van der Waals forces between atoms in the side chains of nearby amino acids.

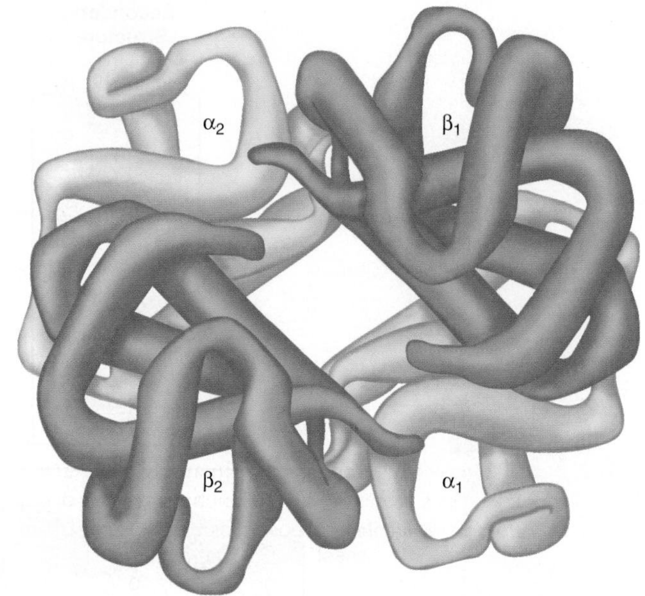

Figure 2.19 Hemoglobin, a multimeric protein composed of two identical alpha (α) subunits and two identical beta (β) subunits. (The iron-containing heme groups attached to each globin chain are not shown.) In this simplified view, the overall arrangement of subunits is shown without details of secondary structure.

identical or different. For example, hemoglobin, the protein that transports oxygen in the blood, is a multimeric protein with four polypeptide chains, two of one kind and two of another (**Figure 2.19**). Each subunit can transport one oxygen molecule. Other multimeric proteins that you will learn of in this textbook play a role in creating pores, or channels, in plasma membranes to allow movement of small solutes in and out of cells.

The primary structures (amino acid sequences) of a large number of proteins are known, but three-dimensional conformations have been determined for only a small number. Because of the multiple factors that can influence the folding of a polypeptide chain, it is not yet possible to accurately predict the conformation of a protein from its primary amino acid sequence. However, it should be clear that a change in the primary structure of a protein may alter its secondary, tertiary, and quaternary structures. Such an alteration in primary structure is called a **mutation.** Even a single amino acid change resulting from a mutation may have devastating consequences, as occurs when a molecule of valine replaces a molecule of glutamic acid in the beta chains of hemoglobin. The result of this change is a serious disease called ***sickle-cell disease*** (formerly called *sickle-cell anemia*). When red blood cells in a person with this disease are exposed to decreased oxygen levels, their hemoglobin precipitates. This contorts the red blood cells into a crescent shape, which makes the cells fragile and unable to function normally.

Nucleic Acids

Nucleic acids account for only 2% of body weight, yet these molecules are extremely important because they are responsible for the storage, expression, and transmission of genetic information. The expression of genetic information in the form of specific proteins determines whether one is a human or a mouse, or whether a cell is a muscle cell or an epithelial cell.

There are two classes of nucleic acids, **deoxyribonucleic acid (DNA)** and **ribonucleic acid (RNA)**. DNA molecules store genetic information coded in the sequence of their genes, whereas RNA molecules are involved in decoding this information into instructions for linking together a specific sequence of amino acids to form a specific polypeptide chain.

Both types of nucleic acids are polymers and are therefore composed of linear sequences of repeating subunits. Each subunit, known as a **nucleotide,** has three components: a phosphate group, a sugar, and a ring of carbon and nitrogen atoms known as a base because it can accept hydrogen ions (**Figure 2.20**). The phosphate group of one nucleotide is linked to the sugar of the adjacent nucleotide to form a chain, with the bases sticking out from the side of the phosphate–sugar backbone (**Figure 2.21**).

DNA

The nucleotides in DNA contain the five-carbon sugar **deoxyribose** (hence the name "deoxyribonucleic acid"). Four different nucleotides are present in DNA, corresponding to the four different bases that can be bound to deoxyribose. These bases are divided into two classes: (1) the **purine** bases, **adenine** (A) and **guanine** (G), which have double rings of nitrogen and carbon atoms; and (2) the **pyrimidine** bases, **cytosine** (C) and **thymine** (T), which have only a single ring (see Figure 2.21).

A DNA molecule consists of not one but two chains of nucleotides coiled around each other in the form of a double helix (**Figure 2.22**). The two chains are held together by hydrogen bonds between a purine base on one chain and a pyrimidine base on the opposite chain. The ring structure of

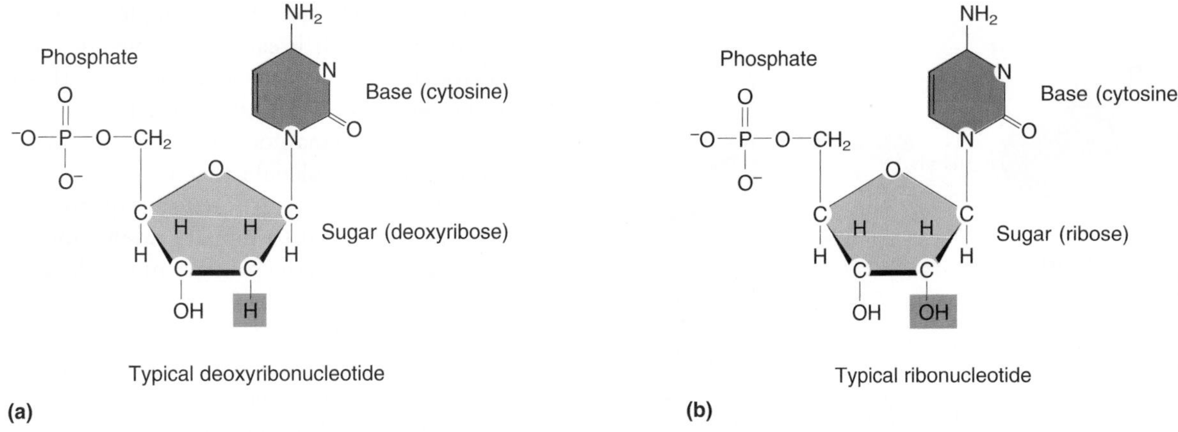

Figure 2.20 Nucleotide subunits of DNA and RNA. Nucleotides are composed of a sugar, a base, and a phosphate group. (a) Deoxyribonucleotides present in DNA contain the sugar deoxyribose. (b) The sugar in ribonucleotides, present in RNA, is ribose, which has an OH at a position in which deoxyribose has only a hydrogen atom.

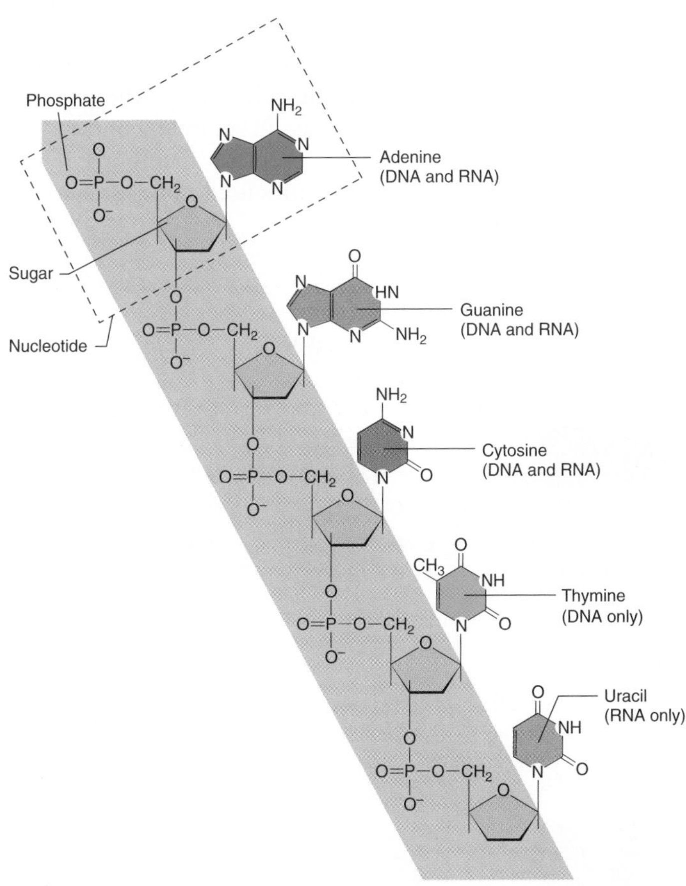

Figure 2.21 AP|R Phosphate–sugar bonds link nucleotides in sequence to form nucleic acids. Note that the pyrimidine base thymine is only found in DNA, and uracil is only present in RNA.

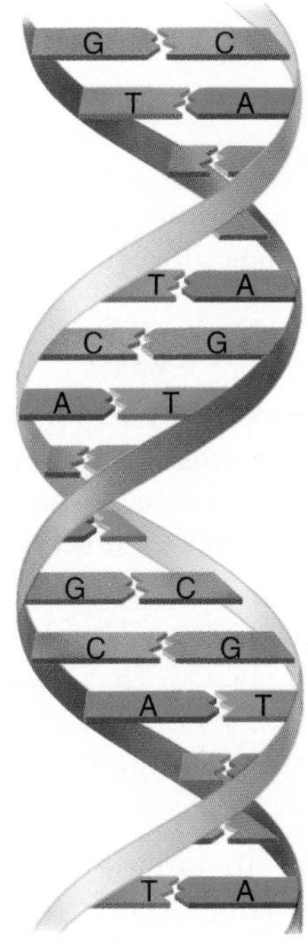

Figure 2.22 AP|R Base pairings between a purine and pyrimidine base link the two polynucleotide strands of the DNA double helix.

each base lies in a flat plane perpendicular to the phosphate–sugar backbone, like steps on a spiral staircase. This base pairing maintains a constant distance between the sugar–phosphate backbones of the two chains as they coil around each other.

Specificity is imposed on the base pairings by the location of the hydrogen-bonding groups in the four bases (**Figure 2.23**). Three hydrogen bonds form between the purine guanine and the pyrimidine cytosine (G–C pairing), whereas only two hydrogen bonds can form between the purine adenine and the pyrimidine thymine (A–T pairing). As a result, G is always paired with C, and A with T. This specificity provides the mechanism for duplicating and transferring genetic information.

The hydrogen bonds between the bases can be broken by enzymes. This separates the double helix into two strands; such DNA is said to be denatured. Each single strand can be replicated to form two new molecules of DNA. This occurs during cell division such that each daughter cell has a full complement of DNA. The bonds can also be broken by heating DNA in a test tube, which provides a convenient way for researchers to examine such processes as DNA replication.

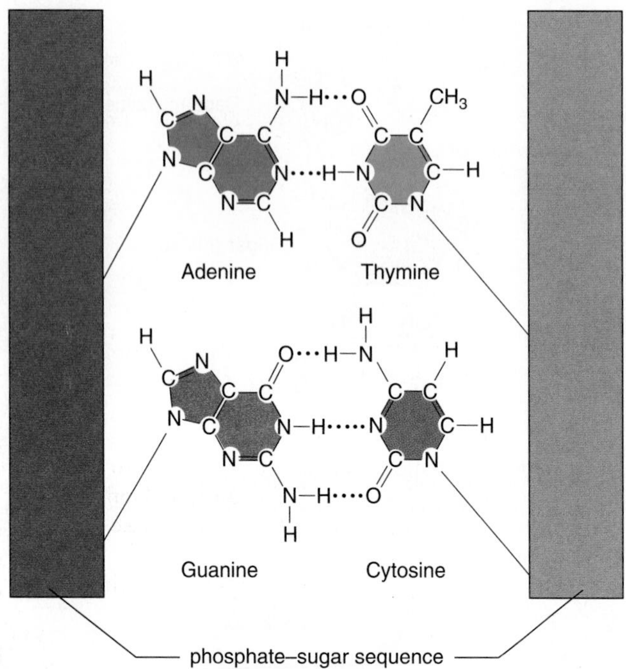

Figure 2.23 AP|R Hydrogen bonds between the nucleotide bases in DNA determine the specificity of base pairings: adenine with thymine, and guanine with cytosine.

PHYSIOLOGICAL INQUIRY

- When a DNA molecule is heated to an extreme temperature in a test tube, the two chains break apart. Which type of DNA molecule would you expect to break down at a reduced temperature, one with more G–C bonds, or one with more A–T bonds?

Answer can be found at end of chapter.

RNA

RNA molecules differ in only a few respects from DNA: (1) RNA consists of a single (rather than a double) chain of nucleotides; (2) in RNA, the sugar in each nucleotide is **ribose** rather than deoxyribose; and (3) the pyrimidine base thymine in DNA is replaced in RNA by the pyrimidine base **uracil** (U) (see Figure 2.21), which can base-pair with the purine adenine (A–U pairing). The other three bases—adenine, guanine, and cytosine—are the same in both DNA and RNA. Because RNA contains only a single chain of nucleotides, portions of this chain can bend back upon themselves and undergo base pairing with nucleotides in the same chain or in other molecules of DNA or RNA.

ATP

The purine bases are important not only in DNA and RNA synthesis but also in a molecule that serves as the molecular energy source for all cells.

The functioning of a cell depends upon its ability to extract and use the chemical energy in the organic molecules discussed in this chapter. For example, when, in the presence of oxygen, a cell breaks down glucose to carbon dioxide and water, energy is released. Some of this energy is in the form of heat, but a cell cannot use heat energy to perform its functions. The remainder of the energy is transferred to another important molecule that can in turn transfer it to yet another molecule or to energy-requiring processes. In all cells, from bacterial to human, **adenosine triphosphate (ATP)** (**Figure 2.24**) is the primary molecule that receives the transfer of energy from the breakdown of fuel molecules—carbohydrates, fats, and proteins.

Energy released from organic molecules is used to add phosphate groups to molecules of adenosine. This stored energy can then be released upon hydrolysis:

$$ATP + H_2O \longrightarrow ADP + P_i + H^+ + \text{energy}$$

The products of the reaction are **adenosine diphosphate (ADP)**, inorganic phosphate (P_i), and H^+.

Among other things, the energy derived from the hydrolysis of ATP is used by the cells for (1) the production of force and movement, as in muscle contraction; (2) active transport of molecules across membranes; and (3) synthesis of the organic molecules used in cell structures and functions. ■

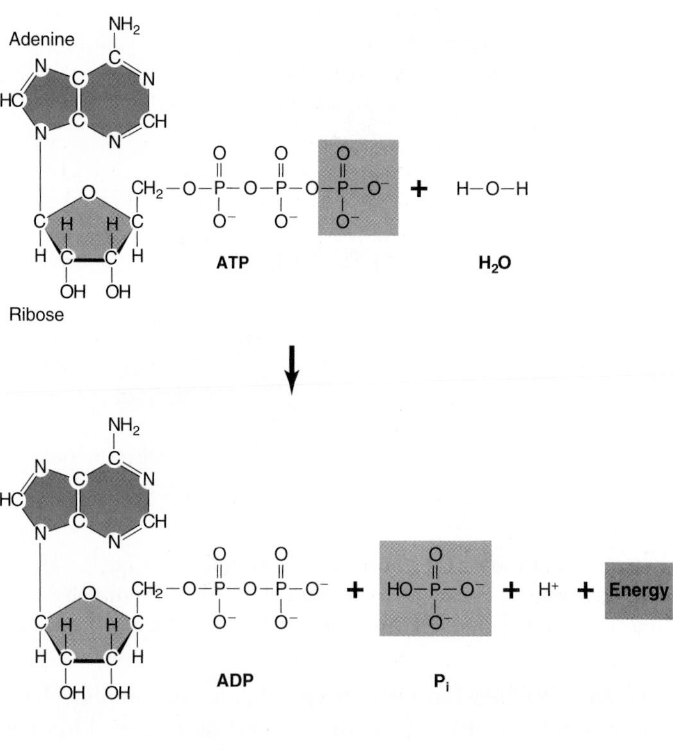

Figure 2.24 Chemical structure of ATP. Its breakdown to ADP and P_i is accompanied by the release of energy.

SUMMARY

Atoms

I. Atoms are composed of three subatomic particles: positive protons and neutral neutrons, both located in the nucleus, and negative electrons revolving around the nucleus in orbitals contained within electron shells.

II. The atomic number is the number of protons in an atom, and because atoms (except ions) are electrically neutral, it is also the number of electrons.

III. The atomic mass of an atom is the ratio of the atom's mass relative to that of a carbon-12 atom.

IV. One gram atomic mass is the number of grams of an element equal to its atomic mass. One gram atomic mass of any element contains the same number of atoms: 6×10^{23}.

V. When an atom gains or loses one or more electrons, it acquires a net electrical charge and becomes an ion.

Molecules

I. Molecules are formed by linking atoms together.

II. A covalent bond forms when two atoms share a pair of electrons. Each type of atom can form a characteristic number of covalent bonds: hydrogen forms one; oxygen, two; nitrogen, three; and carbon, four. In polar covalent bonds, one atom attracts the bonding electrons more than the other atom of the pair. Nonpolar covalent bonds are between two atoms of similar electronegativities.

III. Molecules have characteristic shapes that can be altered within limits by the rotation of their atoms around covalent bonds.

IV. The electrical attraction between hydrogen and an oxygen or nitrogen atom in a separate molecule, or between different regions of the same molecule, forms a hydrogen bond.

V. Molecules may have ionic regions within their structure.

VI. Free radicals are atoms or molecules that contain atoms having an unpaired electron in their outer electron orbital.

Solutions

I. Water, a polar molecule, is attracted to other water molecules by hydrogen bonds. Water is the solvent in which most of the chemical reactions in the body take place.

II. Substances dissolved in a liquid are solutes, and the liquid in which they are dissolved is the solvent.

III. Substances that have polar or ionized groups dissolve in water by being electrically attracted to the polar water molecules.

IV. In water, amphipathic molecules form clusters with the polar regions at the surface and the nonpolar regions in the interior of the cluster.

V. The molecular weight of a molecule is the sum of the atomic weights of all its atoms. One mole of any substance is its molecular weight in grams and contains 6×10^{23} molecules.

VI. Substances that release a hydrogen ion in solution are called acids. Those that accept a hydrogen ion are bases.
   a. The acidity of a solution is determined by its free hydrogen ion concentration; the greater the hydrogen ion concentration, the greater the acidity.
   b. The pH of a solution is the negative logarithm of the hydrogen ion concentration. As the acidity of a solution increases, the pH decreases. Acid solutions have a pH less than 7.0, whereas alkaline solutions have a pH greater than 7.0.

Classes of Organic Molecules

I. Carbohydrates are composed of carbon, hydrogen, and oxygen atoms.
   a. The presence of the polar hydroxyl groups makes carbohydrates soluble in water.
   b. The most abundant monosaccharide in the body is glucose ($C_6H_{12}O_6$), which is stored in cells in the form of the polysaccharide glycogen.

II. Most lipids have many fewer polar and ionized groups than carbohydrates, a characteristic that makes them nearly or completely insoluble in water.
   a. Triglycerides (fats) form when fatty acids are bound to each of the three hydroxyl groups in glycerol.
   b. Phospholipids contain two fatty acids bound to two of the hydroxyl groups in glycerol, with the third hydroxyl bound to phosphate, which in turn is linked to a small charged or polar compound. The polar and ionized groups at one end of phospholipids make these molecules amphipathic.
   c. Steroids are composed of four interconnected rings, often containing a few hydroxyl and other groups.
   d. One fatty acid (arachidonic acid) can be converted to a class of signaling substances called eicosanoids.

III. Proteins, macromolecules composed primarily of carbon, hydrogen, oxygen, and nitrogen, are polymers of 20 different amino acids.
   a. Amino acids have an amino (—NH_2) and a carboxyl (—COOH) group bound to their terminal carbon atom.
   b. Amino acids are bound together by peptide bonds between the carboxyl group of one amino acid and the amino group of the next.
   c. The primary structure of a polypeptide chain is determined by (1) the number of amino acids in sequence and (2) the type of amino acid at each position.
   d. Hydrogen bonds between peptide bonds along a polypeptide force much of the chain into an alpha helix or beta pleated sheet (secondary structure).
   e. Covalent disulfide bonds can form between the sulfhydryl groups of cysteine side chains to hold regions of a polypeptide chain close to each other; together with hydrogen bonds, ionic bonds, hydrophobic interactions, and van der Waals forces, this creates the final conformation of the protein (tertiary structure).
   f. Multimeric proteins have multiple polypeptide chains (quaternary structure).

IV. Nucleic acids are responsible for the storage, expression, and transmission of genetic information.
   a. Deoxyribonucleic acid (DNA) stores genetic information.
   b. Ribonucleic acid (RNA) is involved in decoding the information in DNA into instructions for linking amino acids together to form proteins.
   c. Both types of nucleic acids are polymers of nucleotides, each containing a phosphate group; a sugar; and a base of carbon, hydrogen, oxygen, and nitrogen atoms.
   d. DNA contains the sugar deoxyribose and consists of two chains of nucleotides coiled around each other in a double helix. The chains are held together by hydrogen bonds between purine and pyrimidine bases in the two chains.
   e. Base pairings in DNA always occur between guanine and cytosine and between adenine and thymine.

f. RNA consists of a single chain of nucleotides, containing the sugar ribose and three of the four bases found in DNA. The fourth base in RNA is the pyrimidine uracil rather than thymine. Uracil base-pairs with adenine.
g. In all cells, energy from the catabolism of organic molecules is transferred to ATP. Hydrolysis of ATP to ADP + P_i then transfers this energy to power cell functions. ATP consists of the purine adenine coupled by high-energy bonds to three phosphate groups.

REVIEW QUESTIONS

1. Describe the electrical charge, mass, and location of the three major subatomic particles in an atom.
2. Which four kinds of atoms are most abundant in the body?
3. Describe the distinguishing characteristics of the three classes of essential chemical elements found in the body.
4. How many covalent bonds can be formed by atoms of carbon, nitrogen, oxygen, and hydrogen?
5. What property of molecules allows them to change their three-dimensional shape?
6. Define *ion* and *ionic bond.*
7. Draw the structures of an ionized carboxyl group and an ionized amino group.
8. Define *free radical.*
9. Describe the polar characteristics of a water molecule.
10. What determines a molecule's solubility or lack of solubility in water?
11. Describe the organization of amphipathic molecules in water.
12. What is the molar concentration of 80 g of glucose dissolved in sufficient water to make 2 L of solution?
13. What distinguishes a weak acid from a strong acid?
14. What effect does increasing the pH of a solution have upon the ionization of a carboxyl group? An amino group?
15. Name the four classes of organic molecules in the body.
16. Describe the three subclasses of carbohydrate molecules.
17. What properties are characteristic of lipids?
18. Describe the subclasses of lipids.
19. Describe the linkages between amino acids that form polypeptide chains.
20. What distinguishes the terms *peptide, polypeptide,* and *protein?*
21. What two factors determine the primary structure of a polypeptide chain?
22. Describe the types of interactions that determine the conformation of a polypeptide chain.
23. Describe the structure of DNA and RNA.
24. Describe the characteristics of base pairings between nucleotide bases.

KEY TERMS

CLINICAL TERMS

CHAPTER 2 Clinical Case Study: A Young Man with Severe Abdominal Pain While Mountain Climbing

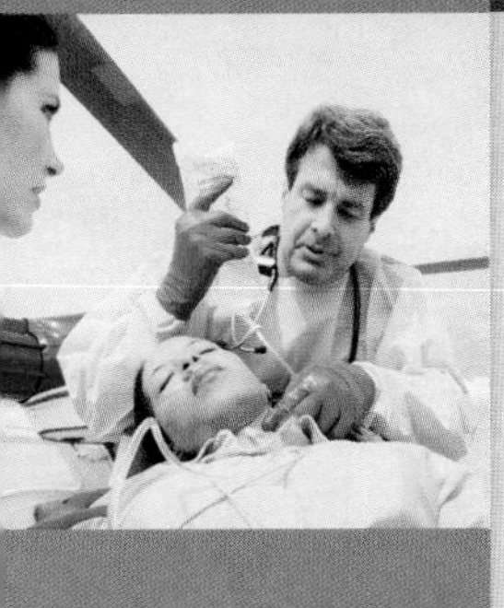

An athletic, 21-year-old African-American male in good health spent part of the summer before his senior year in college traveling with friends in the western United States. Although not an experienced mountain climber, he joined his friends in a professionally guided climb partway up Mt. Rainier in Washington. Despite his overall fitness, the rigors of the climb were far greater than he expected, and he found himself breathing heavily. At an elevation of around 6000 feet, he began to feel twinges of pain on the left side of his upper abdomen. By the time he reached 9000 feet, the pain worsened to the point that he stopped climbing and descended the mountain. However, the pain did not go away and in fact became very severe during the days after his climb. At that point, he went to a local emergency room, where he was subjected to a number of tests that revealed a disorder in his red blood cells due to an abnormal form of the protein hemoglobin.

Recall from Figure 2.19 that hemoglobin is a protein with quaternary structure. Each subunit in hemoglobin is noncovalently bound to the other subunits by the forces described in Figure 2.18. The three-dimensional (tertiary) structure of each subunit spatially aligns the individual amino acids in such a way that the bonding forces exert themselves between specific amino acid side groups. Therefore, anything that disrupts the tertiary structure of hemoglobin also disrupts the way in which subunits bond with one another. The patient described here had a condition called ***sickle-cell trait*** (SCT). Such individuals are carriers of the gene that causes sickle-cell disease (SCD), formerly called sickle-cell anemia. Individuals with SCT have one normal gene inherited from one parent and one gene with a mutation inherited from the other parent. The SCT/SCD gene is prevalent in several regions of the world, particularly in sub-Saharan Africa. In SCD, a mutation in the gene for the beta subunits of hemoglobin results in the replacement of a single glutamic acid residue with one of valine. Glutamic acid has a charged, polar side group, whereas valine has a nonpolar side group. Thus, in hemoglobin containing the mutation, one type of intermolecular bonding force is replaced with a completely different one, and this can lead to abnormal bonding of hemoglobin subunits with each other. In fact, the hydrophobic interactions created by the valine side groups cause multiple hemoglobin molecules to bond with each other, forming huge polymer-like structures that precipitate out of solution within the cytoplasm of the red blood cell resulting in a deformation of the entire cell. This happens most noticeably when the amount of oxygen in the red blood cell is decreased. Such a situation can occur at high altitude, where the atmospheric pressure is low and consequently the amount of oxygen that diffuses into the lung circulation is also low. (You will learn about the relationship between altitude, oxygen, and atmospheric pressure in Chapter 13.)

When red blood cells become deformed into the sicklelike shape characteristic of SCD, they are removed from the circulation by the spleen, an organ that lies in the upper left quadrant of the abdomen and plays an important role in eliminating dead or damaged red blood cells from the circulation. However, in the event of a sudden, large increase in the number of sickled cells, the spleen can become overfilled with damaged cells and painfully enlarged. Moreover, some of the sickled cells can block some of the small blood vessels in the spleen, which also causes pain and damage to the organ. This may begin quickly but may also continue for several days, which is why our subject's pain did not become very severe until a day or two after his climb.

Why would our patient attempt to climb a mountain to high altitude, knowing that the available amount of oxygen in the air is decreased at such altitudes? Recall that we said that the patient had sickle-cell *trait,* not sickle-cell disease. Individuals with sickle-cell trait produce enough normal hemoglobin to be symptom free their entire lives and may never know that they are carriers of a mutated gene. However, when pushed to the limits of oxygen deprivation by high altitude and exercise, as our patient was, the result is sickling of some of the red blood cells. Once the young man's condition was confirmed, he was given analgesics (painkillers) and advised to rest for the next 2 to 3 weeks until his spleen returned to normal. His spleen was carefully monitored during this time, and he recovered fully. Our patient was lucky; numerous deaths due to unrecognized SCT have occurred throughout the world as a result of situations just like the one described here. It is a striking example of how a protein's overall structure and function depend upon its primary structure, and how protein–protein interactions are critically dependent on the bonding forces described in this chapter. This theme will be explored in more detail in Sections B–D of Chapter 3.

Clinical term: sickle-cell trait (SCT)

See Chapter 19 for complete, integrative case studies.

CHAPTER 2 TEST QUESTIONS

Answers found in Appendix A.

1. A molecule that loses an electron to a free radical
   a. becomes more stable.
   b. becomes electrically neutral.
   c. becomes less reactive.
   d. is permanently destroyed.
   e. becomes a free radical itself.

2. Of the bonding forces between atoms and molecules, which are strongest?
   a. hydrogen bonds
   b. bonds between oppositely charged ionized groups
   c. bonds between nearby nonpolar groups
   d. covalent bonds
   e. bonds between polar groups

3. The process by which monomers of organic molecules are made into larger units
   a. requires hydrolysis.
   b. results in the generation of water molecules.
   c. is irreversible.
   d. occurs only with carbohydrates.
   e. results in the production of ATP.
4. Which of the following is/are not found in DNA?
   a. adenine
   b. uracil
   c. cytosine
   d. deoxyribose
   e. both b and d
5. Which of the following statements is incorrect about disulfide bonds?
   a. They form between two cysteine amino acids.
   b. They are noncovalent.
   c. They contribute to the tertiary structure of some proteins.
   d. They contribute to the quaternary structure of some proteins.
   e. They involve the loss of two hydrogen atoms.
6. Match the following compounds with choices (a) monosaccharide, (b) disaccharide, or (c) polysaccharide:
   Sucrose
   Glucose
   Glycogen
   Fructose
   Starch
7. Which of the following reactions involve/involves hydrolysis?
   a. formation of triglycerides
   b. formation of proteins
   c. breakdown of proteins
   d. formation of polysaccharides
   e. a, b, and d

CHAPTER 2 GENERAL PRINCIPLES ASSESSMENT

Answers found in Appendix A.

1. Proteins play important roles in many physiological processes. Using Figures 2.17 through 2.19 as your guide, explain how protein structure is an example of the general physiological principle that *physiological processes are dictated by the laws of chemistry and physics.*

CHAPTER 2 QUANTITATIVE AND THOUGHT QUESTIONS

Answers found in Appendix A.

1. What is the molarity of a solution with 100 g fructose dissolved in 0.7 L water? (See Figure 2.10 for the chemical structure of fructose.)
2. The pH of the fluid in the human stomach following a meal is generally around 1.5. What is the hydrogen ion concentration in such a fluid?
3. Potassium has an atomic number of 19 and an atomic mass of 39 (ignore the possibility of isotopes for this question). How many neutrons and electrons are present in potassium in its nonionized (K) and ionized (K^+) forms?

CHAPTER 2 ANSWERS TO PHYSIOLOGICAL INQUIRIES

Figure 2.5 The presence of hydrogen bonds helps stabilize water in its liquid form such that less water escapes into the gaseous phase.

Figure 2.10 The reverse of a dehydration reaction is called hydrolysis, which is derived from Greek words for "water" and "break apart." In hydrolysis, a molecule of water is added to a complex molecule that is broken down into two smaller molecules.

Figure 2.12 The portion of the phospholipid containing the charged phosphate and nitrogen groups would face the water, and the two fatty acid tails would exclude water.

Figure 2.16 *Polypeptide* refers to a structural unit of two or more amino acids bonded together by peptide bonds and does not imply anything about function. A *protein* is a functional molecule formed by the folding of a polypeptide into a characteristic shape, or conformation.

Figure 2.23 Because adenine and thymine are bonded by two hydrogen bonds, whereas guanine and cytosine are held together by three hydrogen bonds, A–T bonds would be more easily broken by heat.

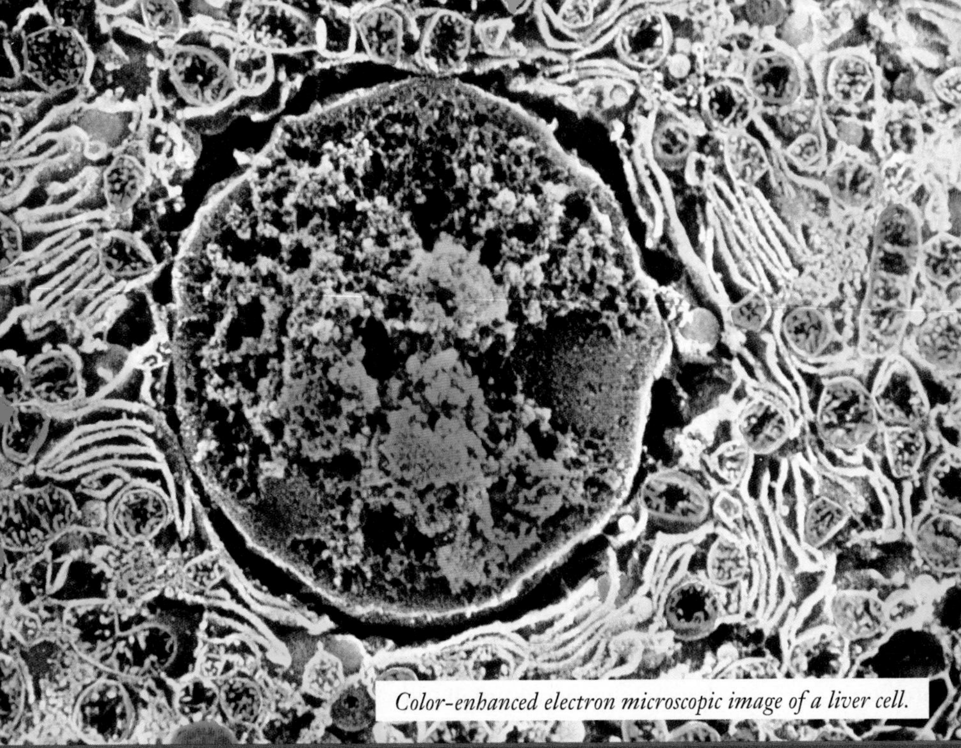

Color-enhanced electron microscopic image of a liver cell.

3 Cellular Structure, Proteins, and Metabolism

Cells are the structural and functional units of all living organisms and comprise the tissues and organs that physiologists study. The human body is composed of trillions of cells with highly specialized structures and functions, but you learned in Chapter 1 that most cells can be included in one of four major functional and morphological categories: muscle, connective, nervous and epithelial cells. In this chapter, we briefly describe the structures that are common to most of the cells of the body regardless of the category to which they belong.

Having learned the basic structures that comprise cells, we next turn our attention to how cellular proteins are synthesized, secreted, and degraded, and how proteins participate in the chemical reactions required for cells to survive. Proteins are associated with practically every function living cells perform. As described in Chapter 2, proteins have a unique shape or conformation that is established by their primary, secondary, tertiary, and—in some cases—quaternary structures. This conformation enables them to bind specific molecules on portions of their surfaces known as binding sites. This chapter includes a discussion of the properties of protein-binding sites that apply to all proteins, as well as a description of how these properties are involved in one special class of protein functions—the ability of enzymes to accelerate specific chemical reactions. We then apply this information to a description of the multitude of biochemical reactions involved in metabolism and cellular energy balance.

As you read this chapter, think about where the following general principles of physiology apply. The general principle that structure is a determinant of—and has coevolved with—function was described at the molecular level in Chapter 2; in Section A of this chapter, you will see how that principle is important at the cellular level, and in Sections C and D at the protein level. Also in Sections C and D, you will see how the general principle that physiological processes are dictated by the laws of chemistry and physics applies to protein function. The general principle that homeostasis is essential for health and survival will be explored in Sections D and E. Finally, the general principle that physiological processes require the transfer and balance of matter and energy will be explored in Section E.

SECTION A
Cell Structure

3.1 Microscopic Observations of Cells

The smallest object that can be resolved with a microscope depends upon the wavelength of the radiation used to illuminate the specimen—the shorter the wavelength, the smaller the object that can be seen. Whereas a light microscope can resolve objects as small as 0.2 μm in diameter, an electron microscope, which uses electron beams instead of light rays, can resolve structures as small as 0.002 μm. Typical sizes of cells and cellular components are illustrated in **Figure 3.1**.

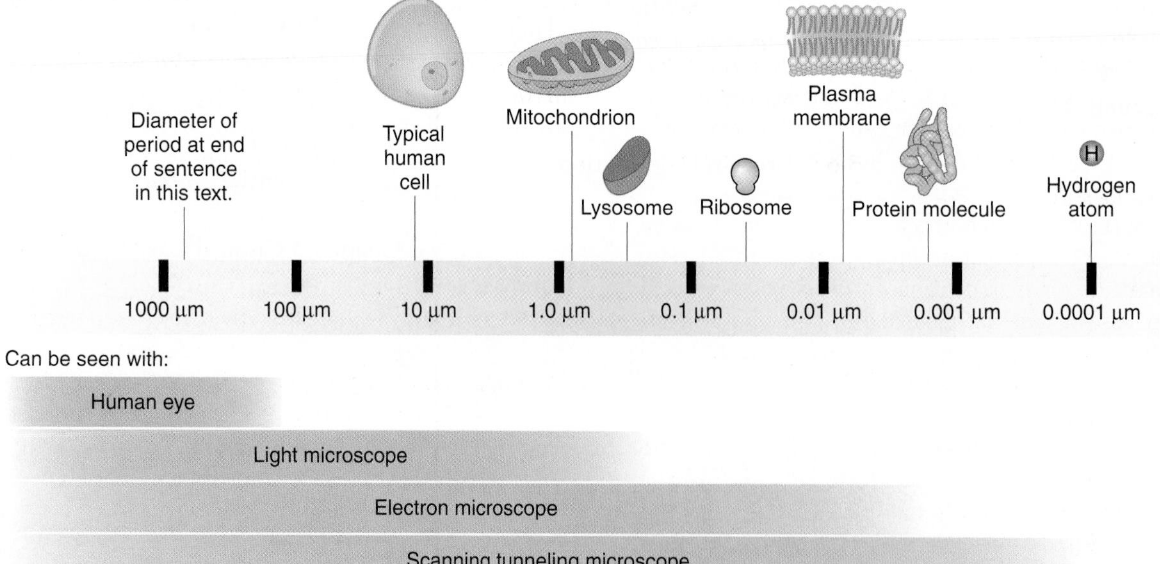

Figure 3.1 Typical sizes of cell structures, plotted on a logarithmic scale.

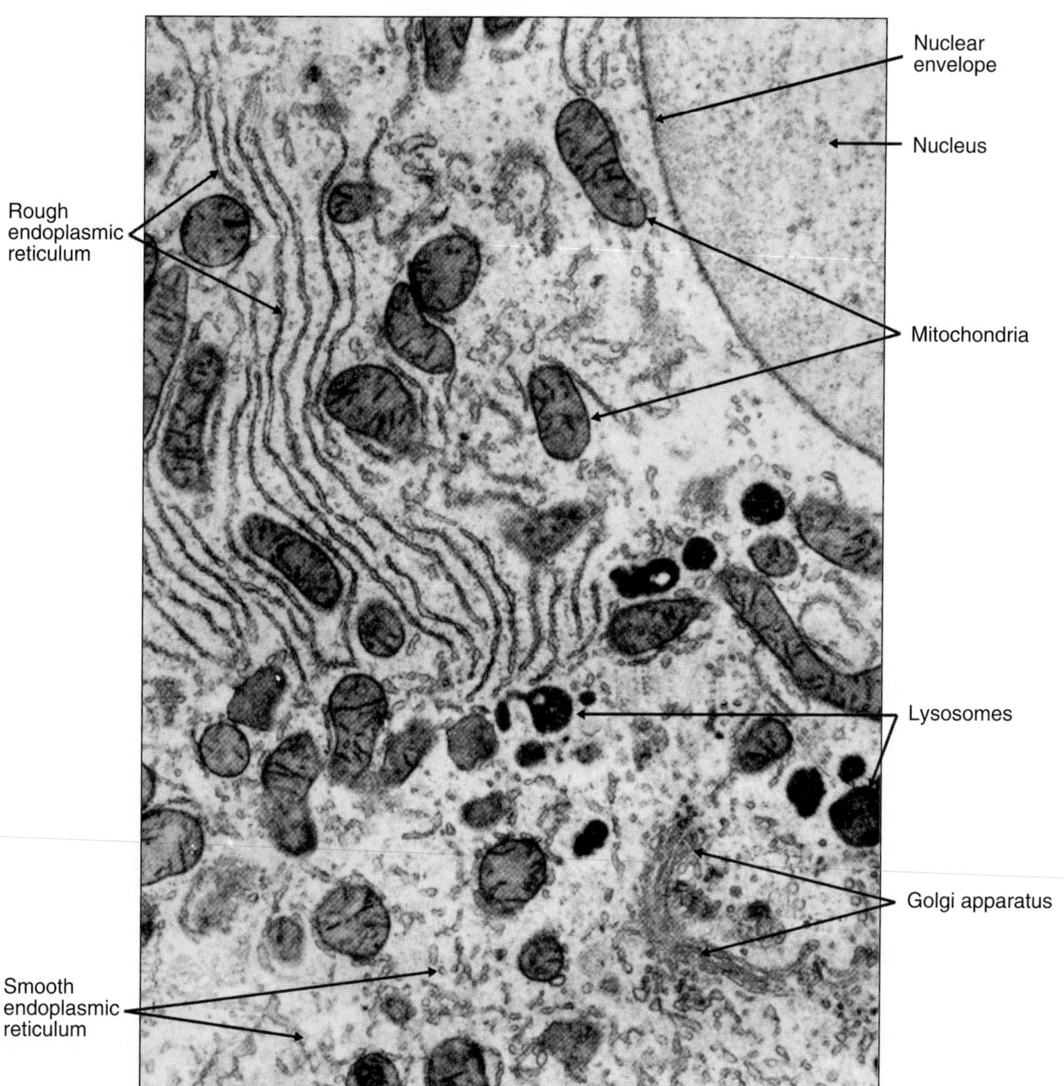

Figure 3.2 APIR Electron micrograph of a thin section through a portion of a human adrenal cell, showing the appearance of intracellular organelles.

Although living cells can be observed with a light microscope, this is not possible with an electron microscope. To form an image with an electron beam, most of the electrons must pass through the specimen, just as light passes through a specimen in a light microscope. However, electrons can penetrate only a short distance through matter; therefore, the observed specimen must be very thin. Cells to be observed with an electron microscope must be cut into sections on the order of 0.1 μm thick, which is about one-hundredth of the thickness of a typical cell.

Because electron micrographs, such as the one in **Figure 3.2**, are images of very thin sections of a cell, they can sometimes be misleading. Structures that appear as separate objects in the electron micrograph may actually be continuous structures connected through a region lying outside the plane of the section. As an analogy, a thin section through a ball of string would appear to be a collection of separate lines and disconnected dots even though the piece of string was originally continuous.

Two classes of cells, **eukaryotic cells** and **prokaryotic cells,** can be distinguished by their structure. The cells of the human body, as well as those of other multicellular animals and plants, are eukaryotic (true-nucleus) cells. These cells contain a nuclear membrane surrounding the cell nucleus and also contain numerous other membrane-bound structures. Prokaryotic cells, such as bacteria, lack these membranous structures. This chapter describes the structure of eukaryotic cells only.

Compare an electron micrograph of a section through a cell (see Figure 3.2) with a diagrammatic illustration of a typical human cell (**Figure 3.3**). What is immediately obvious from both figures is the extensive structure inside the cell. Cells are surrounded by a limiting barrier, the **plasma membrane** (also called the cell membrane), which covers the cell surface. The cell interior is divided into a number of compartments surrounded by membranes. These membrane-bound compartments, along with some particles and filaments, are known as **cell organelles.** Each cell organelle performs specific functions that contribute to the cell's survival.

The interior of a cell is divided into two regions: (1) the **nucleus,** a spherical or oval structure usually near the center of the cell, and (2) the **cytoplasm,** the region outside the nucleus (**Figure 3.4**). The cytoplasm contains cell organelles and fluid surrounding the organelles, known as the **cytosol.** As described in Chapter 1, the term **intracellular fluid** refers to *all* the fluid inside a cell—in other words, cytosol plus the fluid inside all the organelles, including the nucleus. The chemical compositions of the fluids in cell organelles may differ from that of the cytosol. The cytosol is by far the largest intracellular fluid compartment.

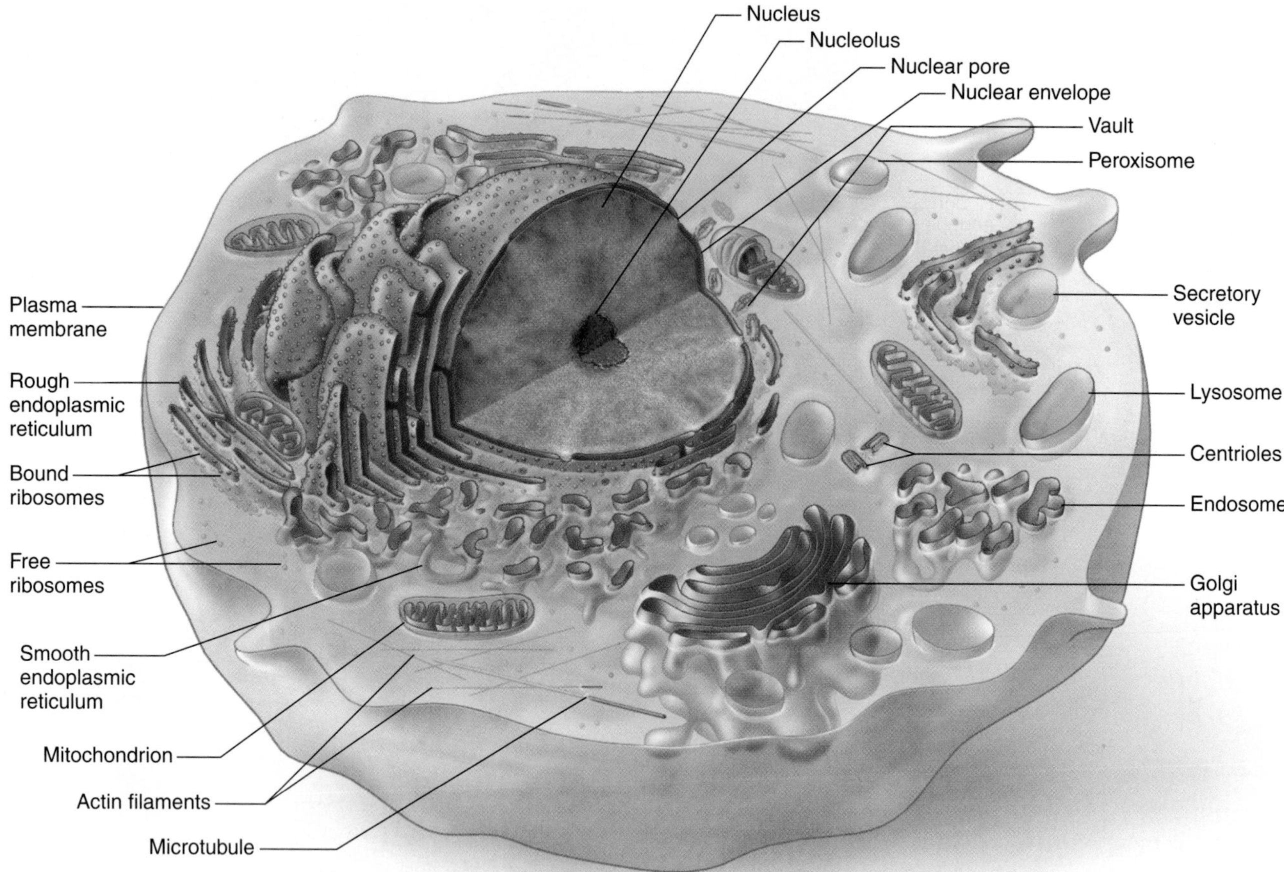

Figure 3.3 APIR Structures found in most human cells. Not all structures are drawn to scale.

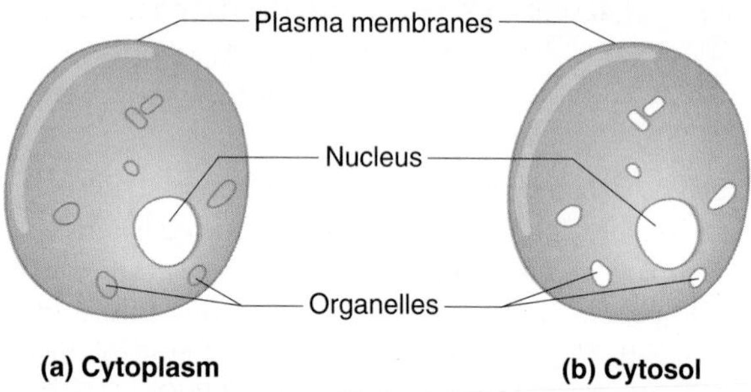

Figure 3.4 APIR Comparison of cytoplasm and cytosol. (a) Cytoplasm (shaded area) is the region of the cell outside the nucleus. (b) Cytosol (shaded area) is the fluid portion of the cytoplasm outside the cell organelles.

PHYSIOLOGICAL INQUIRY

- What compartments constitute the entire intracellular fluid?

Answer can be found at end of chapter.

3.2 Membranes

Membranes form a major structural element in cells. Although membranes perform a variety of functions that are important in physiology (**Table 3.1**), their most universal role is to act as a selective barrier to the passage of molecules, allowing some molecules to cross while excluding others. The plasma membrane regulates the passage of substances into and out of the cell, whereas the membranes surrounding cell organelles allow the selective movement of substances between the organelles and the cytosol. One of the advantages of restricting the movements of molecules across membranes is confining the products of chemical reactions to specific cell organelles. The hindrance a membrane offers to the passage of substances can be altered to allow increased or decreased flow of molecules or ions across the membrane in response to various signals.

In addition to acting as a selective barrier, the plasma membrane plays an important role in detecting chemical signals from other cells and in anchoring cells to adjacent cells and to the extracellular matrix of connective-tissue proteins.

TABLE 3.1 Functions of Plasma Membranes
Regulate the passage of substances into and out of cells and between cell organelles and cytosol.
Detect chemical messengers arriving at the cell surface.
Link adjacent cells together by membrane junctions.
Anchor cells to the extracellular matrix.

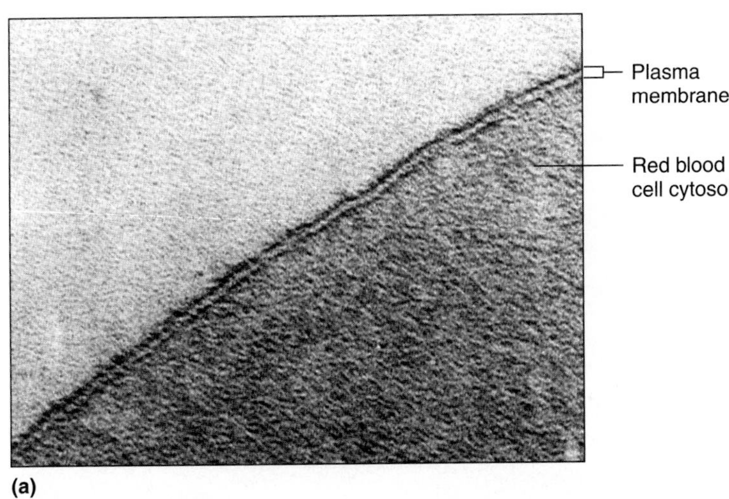

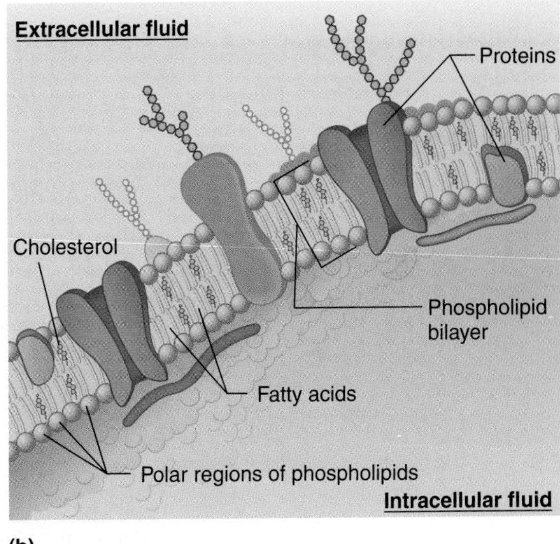

Figure 3.5 AP|R (a) Electron micrograph of a human red blood cell plasma membrane. Plasma membranes are 6 to 10 nm thick, too thin to be seen without the aid of an electron microscope. In an electron micrograph, a membrane appears as two dark lines separated by a light interspace. The dark lines correspond to the polar regions of the proteins and lipids, whereas the light interspace corresponds to the nonpolar regions of these molecules. (b) Schematic arrangement of the proteins, phospholipids and cholesterol in a membrane. Some proteins have carbohydrate molecules attached to their extracellular surface. From J. D. Robertson in Michael Locke (ed.), *Cell Membranes in Development*, Academic Press, Inc., New York.

Membrane Structure

The structure of membranes determines their function. For example, all membranes consist of a double layer of lipid molecules containing embedded proteins (**Figure 3.5**). The major membrane lipids are **phospholipids.** One end of a phospholipid has a charged or polar region, and the remainder of the molecule, which consists of two long fatty acid chains, is nonpolar; therefore, phospholipids are amphipathic (see Chapter 2). The phospholipids in plasma membranes are organized into a bilayer with the nonpolar fatty acid chains in the middle. The polar regions of the phospholipids are oriented toward the surfaces of the membrane as a result of their attraction to the polar water molecules in the extracellular fluid and cytosol. The lipid bilayer acts as a barrier to the movement of polar molecules into and out of cells.

With some exceptions, chemical bonds do not link the phospholipids to each other or to the membrane proteins. Therefore, each molecule is free to move independently of the others. This results in considerable random lateral movement of both membrane lipids and proteins parallel to the surfaces of the bilayer. In addition, the long fatty acid chains can bend and wiggle back and forth. As a consequence, the lipid bilayer has the characteristics of a fluid, much like a thin layer of oil on a water surface, and this makes the membrane quite flexible. This flexibility, along with the fact that cells are filled with fluid, allows cells to undergo moderate changes in shape without disrupting their structural integrity. Like a piece of cloth, a membrane can be bent and folded but cannot be significantly stretched without being torn. As you will learn in Chapter 4, these structural features of membranes permit cells to undergo processes such as exocytosis and endocytosis, and to withstand slight changes in volume due to osmotic imbalances.

The plasma membrane also contains cholesterol, whereas intracellular membranes contain very little. Cholesterol is slightly amphipathic because of a single polar hydroxyl group (see Figure 2.13) attached to its relatively rigid, nonpolar ring structure. Like the phospholipids, therefore, cholesterol is inserted into the lipid bilayer with its polar region at the bilayer surface and its nonpolar rings in the interior in association with the fatty acid chains. The polar hydroxyl group forms hydrogen bonds with the polar regions of phospholipids. The close association of the nonpolar rings of cholesterol with the fatty acid tails of phospholipids tends to limit the ordered packing of fatty acids in the membrane. A more highly ordered, tightly packed arrangement of fatty acids tends to reduce membrane fluidity. Thus, cholesterol and phospholipids play a coordinated role in maintaining an intermediate membrane fluidity. At high temperatures, cholesterol reduces membrane fluidity, possibly by limiting lateral movement of phospholipids. At low temperatures, cholesterol minimizes the decrease in fluidity that would otherwise occur. The latter effect most likely is due to the reduced ability of fatty acid chains to form tightly packed, ordered structures. Cholesterol also may associate with certain classes of plasma membrane phospholipids and proteins, forming organized clusters that work together to pinch off portions of the plasma membrane to form vesicles that deliver their contents to various intracellular organelles, as Chapter 4 will describe.

There are two classes of membrane proteins: integral and peripheral. **Integral membrane proteins** are closely associated with the membrane lipids and cannot be extracted from the membrane without disrupting the lipid bilayer. Like the phospholipids, the integral proteins are amphipathic, having polar amino acid side chains in one region of the molecule and nonpolar side chains clustered together in a separate region. Because they are amphipathic, integral proteins are arranged in the membrane with the same orientation as amphipathic lipids—the polar regions are at the surfaces in association with polar water molecules, and the nonpolar regions are in the interior in

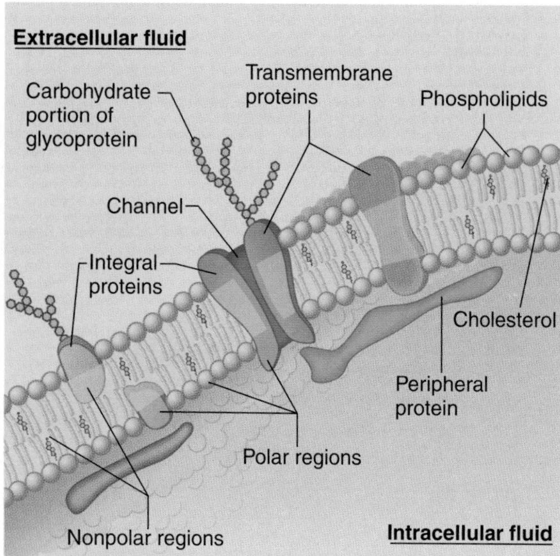

Figure 3.6 AP|R Arrangement of integral and peripheral membrane proteins in association with a bimolecular layer of phospholipids.

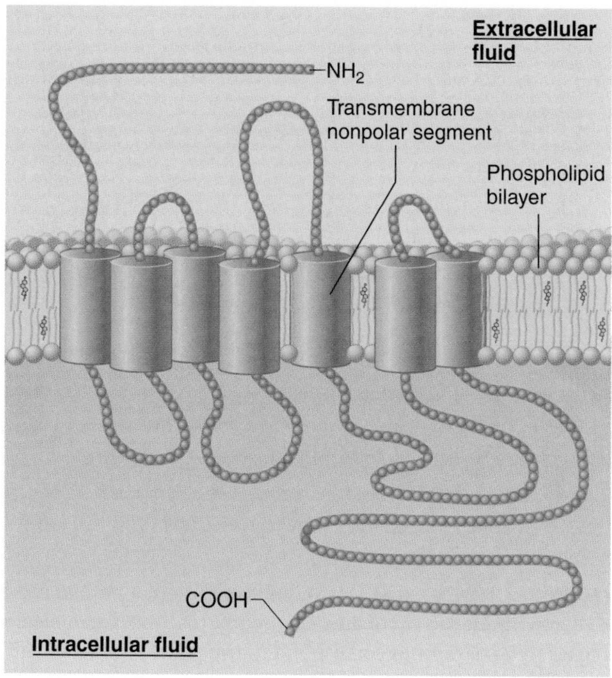

Figure 3.7 A typical transmembrane protein with multiple hydrophobic segments traversing the lipid bilayer. Each transmembrane segment is composed of nonpolar amino acids spiraled in an alpha-helical conformation (shown as cylinders).

association with nonpolar fatty acid chains (**Figure 3.6**). Like the membrane lipids, many of the integral proteins can move laterally in the plane of the membrane, but others are immobilized because they are linked to a network of peripheral proteins located primarily at the cytosolic surface of the membrane.

Most integral proteins span the entire membrane and are referred to as **transmembrane proteins.** The polypeptide chains of many of these transmembrane proteins cross the lipid bilayer several times (**Figure 3.7**). These proteins have polar regions connected by nonpolar segments that associate with the nonpolar regions of the lipids in the membrane interior. The polar regions of transmembrane proteins may extend far beyond the surfaces of the lipid bilayer. Some transmembrane proteins form channels through which ions or water can cross the membrane, whereas others are associated with the transmission of chemical signals across the membrane or the anchoring of extracellular and intracellular protein filaments to the plasma membrane.

Peripheral membrane proteins are not amphipathic and do not associate with the nonpolar regions of the lipids in the interior of the membrane. They are located at the membrane surface where they are bound to the polar regions of the integral membrane proteins (see Figure 3.6) and also in some cases to the charged polar regions of membrane phospholipids. Most of the peripheral proteins are on the cytosolic surface of the plasma membrane where they may perform one of several different types of actions. For example, some peripheral proteins are enzymes that mediate metabolism of membrane components; others are involved in local transport of small molecules along the membrane or between the membrane and cytosol. Many are associated with cytoskeletal elements that influence cell shape and motility.

The extracellular surface of the plasma membrane contains small amounts of carbohydrate covalently linked to some of the membrane lipids and proteins. These carbohydrates consist of short, branched chains of monosaccharides that extend from the cell surface into the extracellular fluid, where they form a layer known as the **glycocalyx.** These surface carbohydrates play important roles in enabling cells to identify and interact with each other.

The lipids in the outer half of the bilayer differ somewhat in kind and amount from those in the inner half, and, as we have seen, the proteins or portions of proteins on the outer surface differ from those on the inner surface. Many membrane functions are related to these asymmetries in chemical composition between the two surfaces of a membrane.

All membranes have the general structure just described, which is known as the **fluid-mosaic model** because a "mosaic" or mix of membrane proteins are free to move in a sea of lipid (**Figure 3.8**). However, the proteins and, to a lesser extent, the

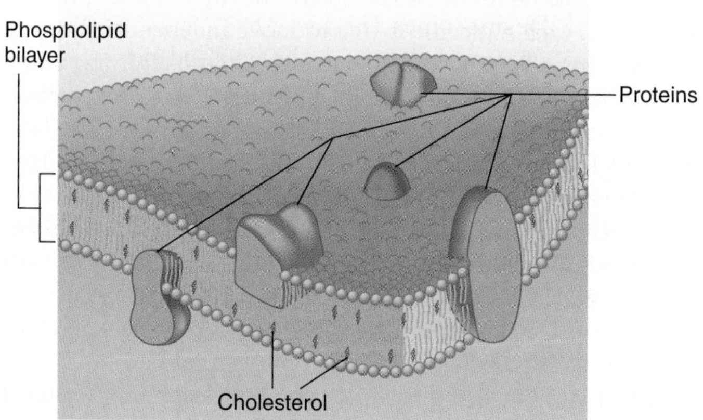

Figure 3.8 Fluid-mosaic model of plasma membrane structure. The proteins and lipids may move within the bilayer; cholesterol helps maintain an intermediate membrane fluidity through the interactions of its polar and nonpolar regions with phospholipids.

lipids in the plasma membrane differ from those in organelle membranes—for example, in the distribution of cholesterol. Therefore, the special functions of membranes, which depend primarily on the membrane proteins, may differ in the various membrane-bound organelles and in the plasma membranes of different types of cells.

The fluid-mosaic model is a useful way of visualizing cellular membranes. However, isolated regions within some cell membranes do not conform to this model. These include regions in which certain membrane proteins are anchored to cytoplasmic proteins, for example, or covalently linked with membrane lipids to form structures called "lipid rafts." **Lipid rafts** are cholesterol-rich regions of reduced membrane fluidity that are believed to serve as organizing centers for the generation of complex intracellular signals. Such signals may arise when a cell binds a hormone or paracrine molecule, for example (see Chapter 1), and lead to changes in cellular activities such as secretion, cell division, and many others. Another example in which cellular membranes do not entirely conform to the fluid-mosaic model is found when proteins in a plasma membrane are linked together to form specialized patches of membrane junctions, as described next.

Membrane Junctions

In addition to providing a barrier to the movements of molecules between the intracellular and extracellular fluids, plasma membranes are involved in the interactions between cells to form tissues. Most cells are packaged into tissues and are not free to move around the body. Even in tissues, however, there is usually a space between the plasma membranes of adjacent cells. This space, filled with extracellular (interstitial) fluid (see Figure 1.3), provides a pathway for substances to pass between cells on their way to and from the blood.

The way that cells become organized into tissues and organs depends, in part, on the ability of certain transmembrane proteins in the plasma membrane, known as **integrins,** to bind to specific proteins in the extracellular matrix and link them to membrane proteins on adjacent cells.

Many cells are physically joined at discrete locations along their membranes by specialized types of junctions, including desmosomes, tight junctions, and gap junctions. These junctions provide an excellent example of the physiological principle that structure and function are related, in this case at the cellular level. **Desmosomes** (**Figure 3.9a**) consist of a region between two adjacent cells where the apposed plasma membranes are separated by about 20 nm. Desmosomes are characterized by accumulations of protein known as "dense plaques" along the cytoplasmic surface of the plasma membrane. These proteins serve as anchoring points for cadherins. **Cadherins** are proteins that extend from the cell into the extracellular space, where they link up and bind with cadherins from an adjacent cell. In this way, two adjacent cells can be firmly attached to each other. The presence of numerous desmosomes between cells helps to provide the structural integrity of tissues in the body. In addition, other proteins such as keratin filaments anchor the cytoplasmic surface of desmosomes to interior structures of the cell. It is believed that this helps secure the desmosome in place and also provides structural support for the cell. Desmosomes hold adjacent cells firmly together in areas that are subject to considerable stretching, such as the skin. The specialized area of the membrane in the region of a desmosome is usually disk-shaped; these membrane junctions could be likened to rivets or spot welds.

A second type of membrane junction, the **tight junction** (**Figure 3.9b**), forms when the extracellular surfaces of two adjacent plasma membranes join together so that no extracellular space remains between them. Unlike the desmosome, which is limited to a disk-shaped area of the membrane, the tight junction occurs in a band around the entire circumference of the cell. Most epithelial cells are joined by tight junctions near their apical surfaces. For example, epithelial cells line the inner surface of the small intestine, where they come in contact with the digestion products in the cavity (or lumen) of the intestine. During absorption, the products of digestion move across the epithelium and enter the blood. This movement could theoretically take place either through the extracellular space between the epithelial cells or through the epithelial cells themselves. For many substances, however, movement through the extracellular space is blocked by the tight junctions; this forces organic nutrients to pass through the cells rather than between them. In this way, the selective barrier properties of the plasma membrane can control the types and amounts of substances absorbed. The ability of tight junctions to impede molecular movement between cells is not absolute. Ions and water can move through these junctions with varying degrees of ease in different epithelia. **Figure 3.9c** shows both a tight junction and a desmosome near the apical (luminal) border between two epithelial cells.

A third type of junction, the **gap junction,** consists of protein channels linking the cytosols of adjacent cells (**Figure 3.9d**). In the region of the gap junction, the two opposing plasma membranes come within 2 to 4 nm of each other, which allows specific proteins (called connexins) from the two membranes to join, forming small, protein-lined channels linking the two cells. The small diameter of these channels (about 1.5 nm) limits what can pass between the cytosols of the connected cells to small molecules and ions, such as Na^+ and K^+, and excludes the exchange of large proteins. A variety of cell types possess gap junctions, including the muscle cells of the heart, where they play a very important role in the transmission of electrical activity between the cells.

3.3 Cell Organelles

In this section, we highlight some of the major structural and functional features of the organelles found in nearly all the cells of the human body. The reader should use this brief overview as a reference to help with subsequent chapters in the textbook.

Nucleus

Almost all cells contain a single nucleus, the largest of the membrane-bound cell organelles. A few specialized cells, such as skeletal muscle cells, contain multiple nuclei, whereas mature red blood cells have none. The primary function of the nucleus is the storage and transmission of genetic information to the next generation of cells. This information, coded in molecules of DNA, is also used to synthesize the proteins that determine the structure and function of the cell, as described later in this chapter.

Surrounding the nucleus is a barrier, the **nuclear envelope,** composed of two membranes. At regular intervals

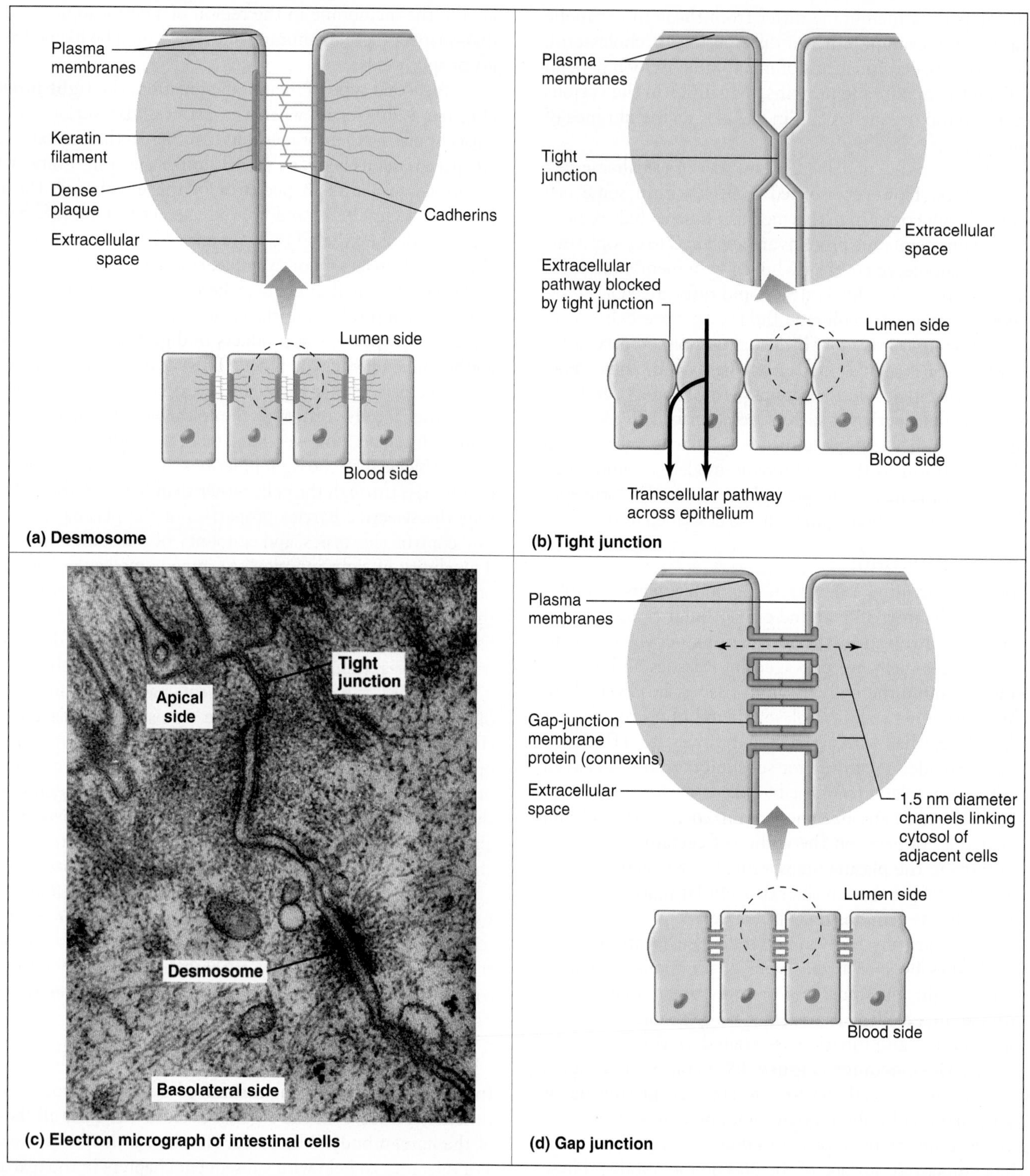

Figure 3.9 APIR Three types of specialized membrane junctions: (a) desmosome; (b) tight junction; (c) electron micrograph of two intestinal epithelial cells joined by a tight junction near the apical (luminal) surface and a desmosome below the tight junction; and (d) gap junction. Electron micrograph from M. Farquhar and G. E. Palade, *J. Cell. Biol.*, 17:375–412.

PHYSIOLOGICAL INQUIRY

- What physiological function might tight junctions serve in the epithelium of the intestine, as shown in part (c) of this figure?

Answer can be found at end of chapter.

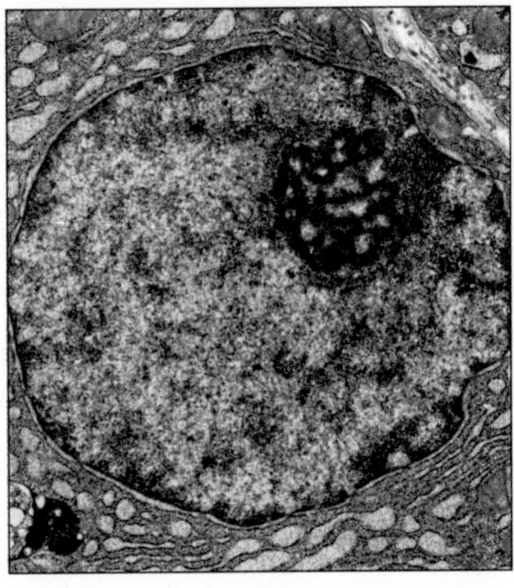

Nucleus

Structure: Largest organelle. Round or oval body located near the cell center. Surrounded by a nuclear envelope composed of two membranes. Envelope contains nuclear pores; messenger molecules pass between the nucleus and the cytoplasm through these pores. No membrane-bound organelles are present in the nucleus, which contains coiled strands of DNA known as chromatin. These condense to form chromosomes at the time of cell division.

Function: Stores and transmits genetic information in the form of DNA. Genetic information passes from the nucleus to the cytoplasm, where amino acids are assembled into proteins.

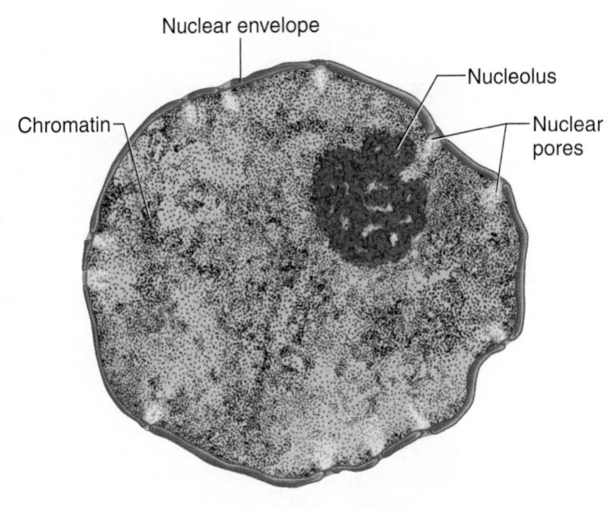

Nucleolus

Structure: Densely stained filamentous structure within the nucleus. Consists of proteins associated with DNA in regions where information concerning ribosomal proteins is being expressed.

Function: Site of ribosomal RNA synthesis. Assembles RNA and protein components of ribosomal subunits, which then move to the cytoplasm through nuclear pores.

Figure 3.10 APR
Nucleus and nucleolus.
Electron micrograph courtesy of K. R. Porter.

along the surface of the nuclear envelope, the two membranes are joined to each other, forming the rims of circular openings known as **nuclear pores** (**Figure 3.10**). RNA molecules that determine the structure of proteins synthesized in the cytoplasm move between the nucleus and cytoplasm through these nuclear pores. Proteins that modulate the expression of various genes in DNA move into the nucleus through these pores.

Within the nucleus, DNA, in association with proteins, forms a fine network of threads known as **chromatin.** The threads are coiled to a greater or lesser degree, producing the variations in density seen in electron micrographs of the nucleus (see Figure 3.10). At the time of cell division, the chromatin threads become tightly condensed, forming rodlike bodies known as **chromosomes.**

The most prominent structure in the nucleus is the **nucleolus,** a densely staining filamentous region without a membrane. It is associated with specific regions of DNA that contain the genes for forming the particular type of RNA found in cytoplasmic organelles called ribosomes. This RNA and the protein components of ribosomes are assembled in the nucleolus, then transferred through the nuclear pores to the cytoplasm, where they form functional ribosomes.

Ribosomes

Ribosomes are the protein factories of a cell. On ribosomes, protein molecules are synthesized from amino acids, using genetic information carried by RNA messenger molecules from DNA in the nucleus. Ribosomes are large particles, about 20 nm in diameter, composed of about 70 to 80 proteins and several RNA molecules. As described in Section B, ribosomes consist of two subunits that either are floating free in the cytoplasm or combine during protein synthesis. In the latter case, the ribosomes bind to the organelle called rough endoplasmic reticulum (described next). A typical cell may contain as many as 10 million ribosomes.

The proteins synthesized on the free ribosomes are released into the cytosol, where they perform their varied functions. The proteins synthesized by ribosomes attached to the rough endoplasmic reticulum pass into the lumen of the reticulum and are then transferred to yet another organelle, the Golgi apparatus. They are ultimately secreted from the cell or distributed to other organelles.

Endoplasmic Reticulum

The most extensive cytoplasmic organelle is the network (or "reticulum") of membranes that form the **endoplasmic reticulum** (**Figure 3.11**). These membranes enclose a space that is continuous throughout the network.

Two forms of endoplasmic reticulum can be distinguished: rough, or granular, and smooth, or agranular. The rough endoplasmic reticulum has ribosomes bound to its cytosolic surface, and it has a flattened-sac appearance. Rough endoplasmic reticulum is involved in packaging proteins that, after processing in the Golgi apparatus, are secreted by the cell or distributed to other cell organelles.

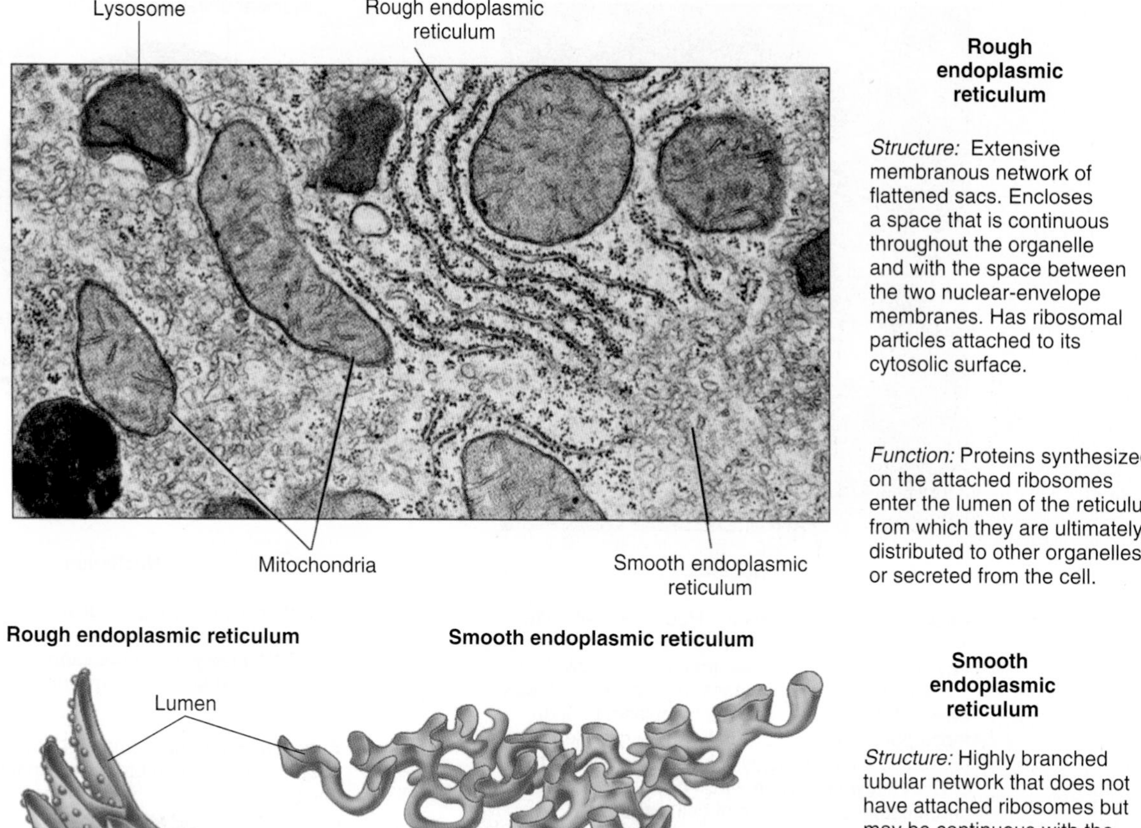
Lysosome
Rough endoplasmic reticulum
Mitochondria
Smooth endoplasmic reticulum
Rough endoplasmic reticulum
Structure: Extensive membranous network of flattened sacs. Encloses a space that is continuous throughout the organelle and with the space between the two nuclear-envelope membranes. Has ribosomal particles attached to its cytosolic surface.
Function: Proteins synthesized on the attached ribosomes enter the lumen of the reticulum from which they are ultimately distributed to other organelles or secreted from the cell.
Rough endoplasmic reticulum
Smooth endoplasmic reticulum
Lumen
Ribosomes
Smooth endoplasmic reticulum
Structure: Highly branched tubular network that does not have attached ribosomes but may be continuous with the rough endoplasmic reticulum.
Function: Contains enzymes for fatty acid and steroid synthesis. Stores and releases calcium, which controls various cell activities.

Figure 3.11 AP|R Endoplasmic reticulum. Electron micrograph from D. W. Fawcett, *The Cell, An Atlas of Fine Structure*, W. B. Saunders Company, Philadelphia.

The smooth endoplasmic reticulum has no ribosomal particles on its surface and has a branched, tubular structure. It is the site at which certain lipid molecules are synthesized, it plays a role in detoxification of certain hydrophobic molecules, and it also stores and releases calcium ions involved in controlling various cell activities.

Golgi Apparatus

The **Golgi apparatus** is a series of closely apposed, flattened membranous sacs that are slightly curved, forming a cup-shaped structure (**Figure 3.12**). Associated with this organelle, particularly near its concave surface, are a number of roughly spherical, membrane-enclosed vesicles.

Proteins arriving at the Golgi apparatus from the rough endoplasmic reticulum undergo a series of modifications as they pass from one Golgi compartment to the next. For example, carbohydrates are linked to proteins to form glycoproteins, and the length of the protein is often shortened by removing a terminal portion of the polypeptide chain. The Golgi apparatus sorts the modified proteins into discrete classes of transport vesicles that will travel to various cell organelles or to the plasma membrane, where the protein contents of the vesicle are released to the outside of the cell. Vesicles containing proteins to be secreted from the cell are known as **secretory vesicles.** Such vesicles are found, for example, in certain endocrine gland cells, where protein hormones are released into the extracellular fluid to modify the activities of other cells.

Endosomes

A number of membrane-bound vesicular and tubular structures called **endosomes** lie between the plasma membrane and the Golgi apparatus. Certain types of vesicles that pinch off the plasma membrane travel to and fuse with endosomes. In turn, the endosome can pinch off vesicles that then move to other cell organelles or return to the plasma membrane. Like the Golgi apparatus, endosomes are involved in sorting, modifying, and directing vesicular traffic in cells.

Mitochondria

Mitochondria (singular, *mitochondrion*) participate in the chemical processes that transfer energy from the chemical bonds of nutrient molecules to newly created adenosine triphosphate (ATP) molecules, which are then made available to cells. Most of the ATP that cells use is formed in the mitochondria by a process called cellular respiration, which consumes oxygen and produces carbon dioxide, heat, and water.

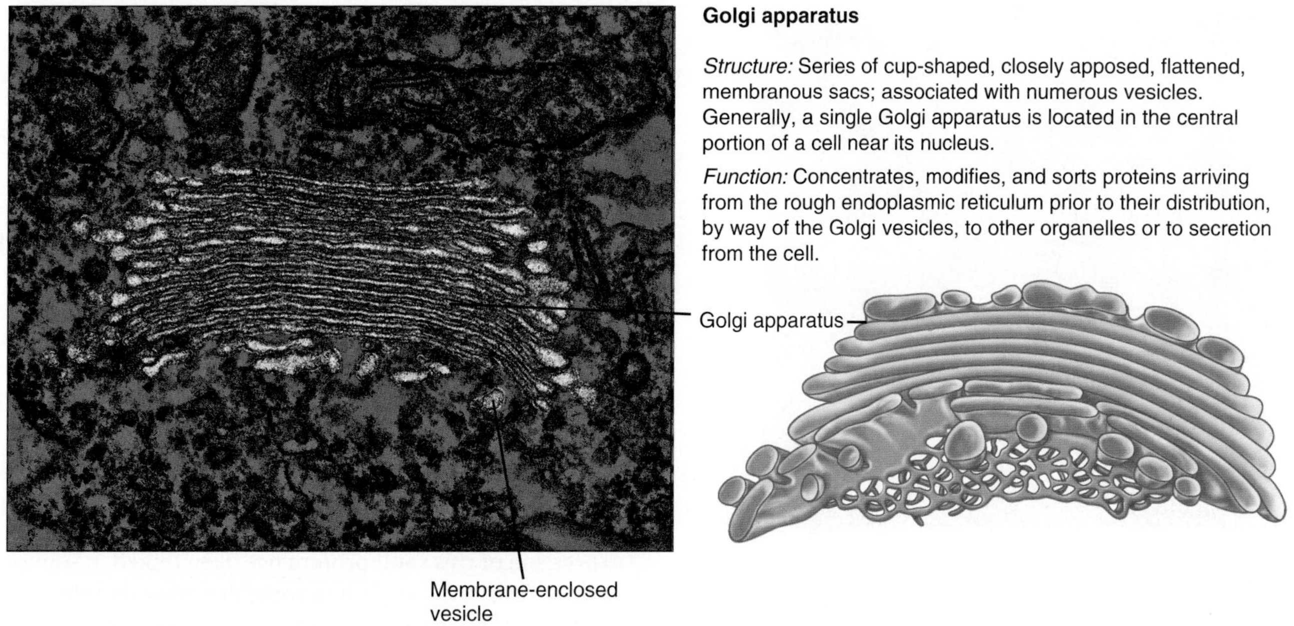

Golgi apparatus
Structure: Series of cup-shaped, closely apposed, flattened, membranous sacs; associated with numerous vesicles. Generally, a single Golgi apparatus is located in the central portion of a cell near its nucleus.
Function: Concentrates, modifies, and sorts proteins arriving from the rough endoplasmic reticulum prior to their distribution, by way of the Golgi vesicles, to other organelles or to secretion from the cell.
Golgi apparatus
Membrane-enclosed vesicle

Figure 3.12 APIR Golgi apparatus. Electron micrograph from W. Bloom and D. W. Fawcett, *Textbook of Histology*, 9th ed. W. B. Saunders Company, Philadelphia.

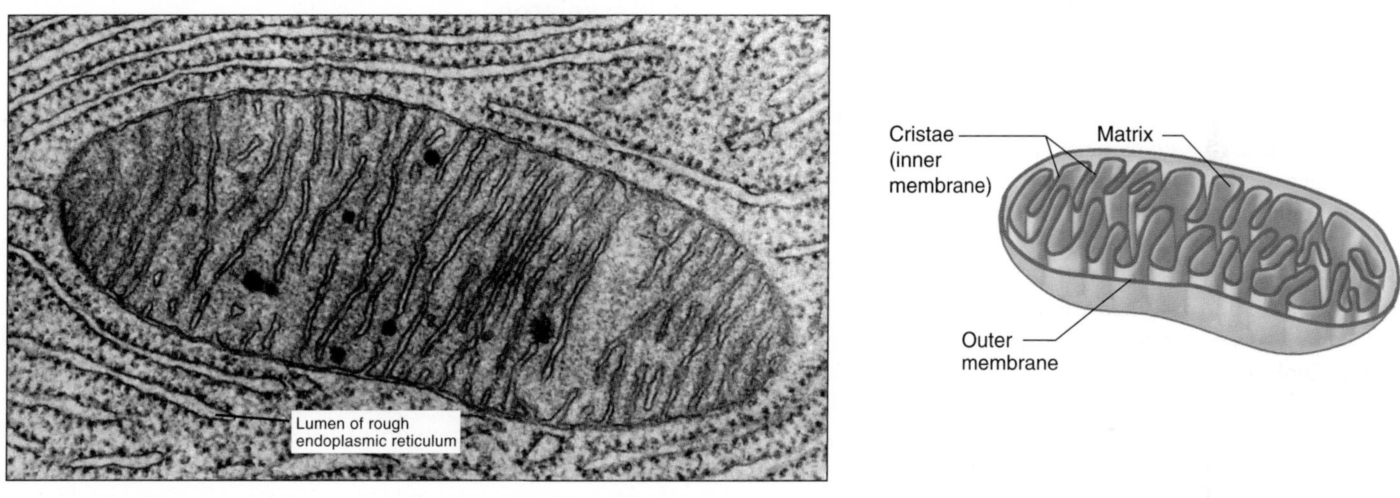

Mitochondrion

Structure: Rod- or oval-shaped body surrounded by two membranes. Inner membrane folds into matrix of the mitochondrion, forming cristae.

Function: Major site of ATP production, O_2 utilization, and CO_2 formation. Contains enzymes active in Krebs cycle and oxidative phosphorylation.

Figure 3.13 APIR Mitochondrion. Electron micrograph courtesy of K. R. Porter.

Mitochondria are spherical or elongated, rodlike structures surrounded by an inner and an outer membrane (**Figure 3.13**). The outer membrane is smooth, whereas the inner membrane is folded into sheets or tubules known as **cristae,** which extend into the inner mitochondrial compartment, the **matrix.** Mitochondria are found throughout the cytoplasm. Large numbers of them, as many as 1000, are present in cells that utilize large amounts of energy, whereas less active cells contain fewer. Our modern understanding of mitochondrial structure and function has evolved, however, from the idea that each mitochondrion is physically and functionally isolated from others. In all cell types that have been examined, mitochondria appear to exist at least in part in a reticulum (**Figure 3.14**). This interconnected network of mitochondria may be particularly important in the distribution of oxygen and energy sources (notably, fatty acids) throughout the mitochondria within a cell. Moreover, the extent of the reticulum may change in different physiological settings; more mitochondria may fuse, or split apart, or even destroy themselves as the energetic demands of cells change.

In addition to providing most of the energy required to power physiological events such as muscle contraction, mitochondria also play a role in the synthesis of certain lipids, such as the hormones estrogen and testosterone (Chapter 11).

Lysosomes

Lysosomes are spherical or oval organelles surrounded by a single membrane (see Figure 3.3). A typical cell may contain several hundred lysosomes. The fluid within a lysosome is

Figure 3.14 Mitochondrial reticulum in skeletal muscle cells. The mitochondria are indicated by the letter *m;* other labels refer to structures found in skeletal muscle and will be described in later chapters. Electron micrograph courtesy G. A. Brooks et al., *Exercise Physiology: Human Bioenergetics and its Applications*, McGraw-Hill Higher Education, New York.

acidic and contains a variety of digestive enzymes. Lysosomes act to break down bacteria and the debris from dead cells that have been engulfed by a cell. They may also break down cell organelles that have been damaged and no longer function normally. They play an especially important role in the various cells that make up the defense systems of the body (Chapter 18).

Peroxisomes

Like lysosomes, **peroxisomes** are moderately dense oval bodies enclosed by a single membrane. Like mitochondria, peroxisomes consume molecular oxygen, although in much smaller amounts. This oxygen is not used in the transfer of energy to ATP, however. Instead, it undergoes reactions that remove hydrogen from organic molecules including lipids, alcohol, and potentially toxic ingested substances. One of the reaction products is hydrogen peroxide, H_2O_2, thus the organelle's name. Hydrogen peroxide can be toxic to cells in high concentrations, but peroxisomes can also destroy hydrogen peroxide and thereby prevent its toxic effects. Peroxisomes are also involved in the process by which fatty acids are broken down into two-carbon fragments, which the cell can then use as a source for generating ATP.

Vaults

Vaults are cytoplasmic structures composed of protein and a type of untranslated RNA called vault RNA (vRNA). These tiny structures have been described as barrel-shaped but also as resembling vaulted cathedrals, from which they get their name. Although the functions of vaults are not certain, studies using electron microscopy and other methods have revealed that vaults tend to be associated with nuclear pores. This has led to the hypothesis that vaults are important for transport of molecules between the cytosol and the nucleus. In addition, at least one vault protein is believed to function in regulating a cell's sensitivity to certain drugs. For example, increased expression of this vault protein has been linked in some studies to drug resistance, including some drugs used in the treatment of cancer. If true, then vaults may someday provide a target for modulating the effectiveness of such drugs in human patients.

Cytoskeleton

In addition to the membrane-enclosed organelles, the cytoplasm of most cells contains a variety of protein filaments. This filamentous network is referred to as the cell's **cytoskeleton,** and, like the bony skeleton of the body, it is associated with processes that maintain and change cell shape and produce cell movements.

The three classes of cytoskeletal filaments are based on their diameter and the types of protein they contain. In order of size, starting with the thinnest, they are (1) actin filaments (also called microfilaments), (2) intermediate filaments, and (3) microtubules (**Figure 3.15**). Actin filaments and microtubules can be assembled and disassembled rapidly, allowing a cell to alter these components of its cytoskeletal framework according to changing requirements. In contrast, intermediate filaments, once assembled, are less readily disassembled.

Actin filaments are composed of monomers of the protein **G-actin** (or "globular actin"), which assemble into a

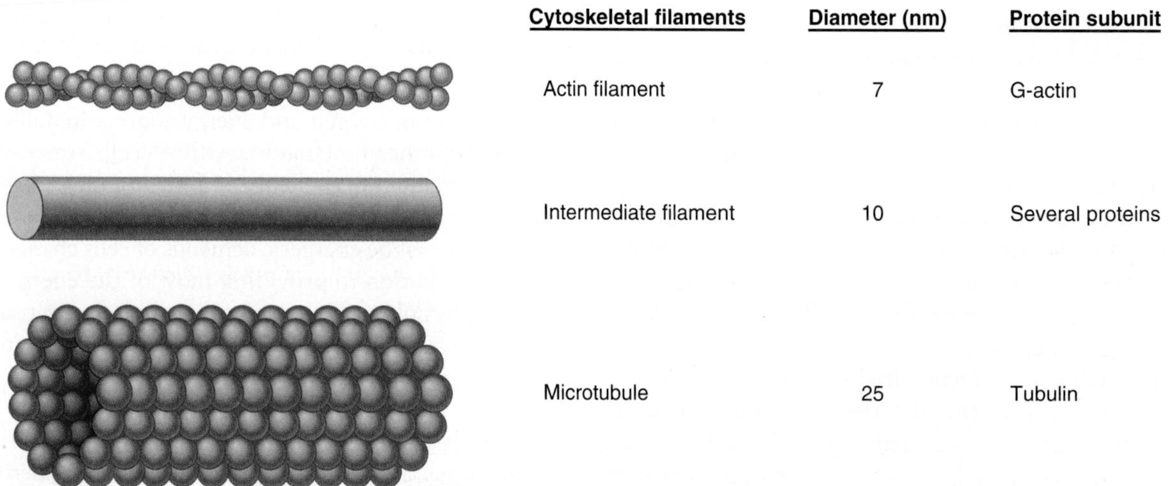

Cytoskeletal filaments
Diameter (nm)
Protein subunit
Actin filament
7
G-actin
Intermediate filament
10
Several proteins
Microtubule
25
Tubulin

Figure 3.15 APIR Cytoskeletal filaments associated with cell shape and motility.

polymer of two twisting chains known as **F-actin** (for "filamentous"). These filaments make up a major portion of the cytoskeleton in all cells. They play important roles in determining cell shape, the ability of cells to move by amoeboid-like movements, cell division, and muscle cell contraction.

Intermediate filaments are composed of twisted strands of several different proteins, including keratin, desmin, and lamin. These filaments also contribute to cell shape and help anchor the nucleus. They provide considerable strength to cells and consequently are most extensively developed in the regions of cells subject to mechanical stress (for example, in association with desmosomes).

Microtubules are hollow tubes about 25 nm in diameter, whose subunits are composed of the protein **tubulin.** They are the most rigid of the cytoskeletal filaments and are present in the long processes of neurons, where they provide the framework that maintains the processes' cylindrical shape. Microtubules also radiate from a region of the cell known as the **centrosome,** which surrounds two small, cylindrical bodies called **centrioles,** composed of nine sets of fused microtubules. The centrosome is a cloud of amorphous material that regulates the formation and elongation of microtubules. During cell division, the centrosome generates the microtubular spindle fibers used in chromosome separation. Microtubules and actin filaments have also been implicated in the movements of organelles within the cytoplasm. These fibrous elements form tracks, and organelles are propelled along these tracks by contractile proteins attached to the surface of the organelles. **Cilia,** the hairlike motile extensions on the surfaces of some epithelial cells, have a central core of microtubules organized in a pattern similar to that found in the centrioles. These microtubules, in combination with a contractile protein, produce movements of the cilia. In hollow organs lined with ciliated epithelium, the cilia wave back and forth, propelling the luminal contents along the surface of the epithelium. An example of this is the cilia-mediated movement of mucus up the trachea, which helps remove inhaled particles that could damage the lungs.

SECTION A SUMMARY

Microscopic Observations of Cells

I. All living matter is composed of cells.
II. There are two types of cells: prokaryotic cells (bacteria) and eukaryotic cells (plant and animal cells).

Membranes

I. Every cell is surrounded by a plasma membrane.
II. Within each eukaryotic cell are numerous membrane-bound compartments, nonmembranous particles, and filaments, known collectively as cell organelles.
III. A cell is divided into two regions, the nucleus and the cytoplasm. The latter is composed of the cytosol and cell organelles other than the nucleus.
IV. The membranes that surround the cell and cell organelles regulate the movements of molecules and ions into and out of the cell and its compartments.
  a. Membranes consist of a bimolecular lipid layer, composed of phospholipids with embedded proteins.
  b. Integral membrane proteins are amphipathic proteins that often span the membrane, whereas peripheral membrane proteins are confined to the surfaces of the membrane.
V. Three types of membrane junctions link adjacent cells.
  a. Desmosomes link cells that are subject to considerable stretching.
  b. Tight junctions, found primarily in epithelial cells, limit the passage of molecules through the extracellular space between the cells.
  c. Gap junctions form channels between the cytosols of adjacent cells.

Cell Organelles

I. The nucleus transmits and expresses genetic information.
  a. Threads of chromatin, composed of DNA and protein, condense to form chromosomes when a cell divides.
  b. Ribosomal subunits are assembled in the nucleolus.
II. Ribosomes, composed of RNA and protein, are the sites of protein synthesis.
III. The endoplasmic reticulum is a network of flattened sacs and tubules in the cytoplasm.
  a. Rough endoplasmic reticulum has attached ribosomes and is primarily involved in the packaging of proteins to be secreted by the cell or distributed to other organelles.
  b. Smooth endoplasmic reticulum is tubular, lacks ribosomes, and is the site of lipid synthesis and calcium accumulation and release.
IV. The Golgi apparatus modifies and sorts the proteins that are synthesized on the rough or granular endoplasmic reticulum and packages them into secretory vesicles.
V. Endosomes are membrane-bound vesicles that fuse with vesicles derived from the plasma membrane and bud off vesicles that travel to other cell organelles.
VI. Mitochondria are the major cell sites that consume oxygen and produce carbon dioxide in chemical processes that transfer energy to ATP, which can then provide energy for cell functions.
VII. Lysosomes digest particulate matter that enters the cell.
VIII. Peroxisomes use oxygen to remove hydrogen from organic molecules and in the process form hydrogen peroxide.
IX. Vaults are cytoplasmic structures made of protein and RNA and may be involved in cytoplasmic-nuclear transport.
X. The cytoplasm contains a network of three types of filaments that form the cytoskeleton: (a) actin filaments, (b) intermediate filaments, and (c) microtubules. These filaments are involved in determining cell shape, regulating cell motility and division, and regulating cell contractility, among other functions.

SECTION A REVIEW QUESTIONS

1. Identify the location of cytoplasm, cytosol, and intracellular fluid within a cell.
2. Identify the classes of organic molecules found in plasma membranes.
3. Describe the orientation of the phospholipid molecules in a membrane.
4. Which plasma membrane components are responsible for membrane fluidity?
5. Describe the location and characteristics of integral and peripheral membrane proteins.
6. Describe the structure and function of the three types of junctions found between cells.

7. What function does the nucleolus perform?
8. Describe the location and function of ribosomes.
9. Contrast the structure and functions of the rough and smooth endoplasmic reticulum.
10. What function does the Golgi apparatus perform?
11. What functions do endosomes perform?
12. Describe the structure and primary function of mitochondria.
13. What functions do lysosomes and peroxisomes perform?
14. List the three types of filaments associated with the cytoskeleton. Identify the structures in cells that are composed of microtubules.

SECTION A KEY TERMS

SECTION B
Protein Synthesis, Degradation, and Secretion

3.4 Genetic Code

The importance of proteins in physiology cannot be overstated. Proteins are involved in all physiological processes, from cell signaling to tissue remodeling to organ function. This section describes how cells synthesize, degrade, and, in some cases, secrete proteins. We begin with an overview of the genetic basis of protein synthesis.

As noted previously, the nucleus of a cell contains DNA, which directs the synthesis of all proteins in the body. Molecules of DNA contain information, coded in the sequence of nucleotides, for protein synthesis. A sequence of DNA nucleotides containing the information that specifies the amino acid sequence of a single polypeptide chain is known as a **gene.** A gene is thus a unit of hereditary information. A single molecule of DNA contains many genes.

The total genetic information coded in the DNA of a typical cell in an organism is known as its **genome.** The human genome contains roughly 20,000 genes. Scientists have determined the nucleotide sequence of the entire human genome (approximately 3 billion nucleotides). This is only a first step, however, because the function and regulation of most genes in the human genome remain unknown.

It is easy to misunderstand the relationship between genes, DNA molecules, and chromosomes. In all human cells other than eggs or sperm, there are 46 separate DNA molecules in the cell nucleus, each molecule containing many genes. Each DNA molecule is packaged into a single chromosome composed of DNA and proteins, so there are 46 chromosomes in each cell. A chromosome contains not only its DNA molecule but also a special class of proteins called **histones.** The cell's nucleus is a marvel of packaging. The very long DNA molecules, with lengths a thousand times greater than the diameter of the nucleus, fit into the nucleus by coiling around clusters of histones at frequent intervals to form complexes known as **nucleosomes.** There are about 25 million of these complexes on the chromosomes, resembling beads on a string.

Although DNA contains the information specifying the amino acid sequences in proteins, it does not itself participate directly in the assembly of protein molecules. Most of a cell's DNA is in the nucleus, whereas most protein synthesis occurs in the cytoplasm. The transfer of information from DNA to the site of protein synthesis is accomplished by RNA molecules, whose synthesis is governed by the information coded in DNA. Genetic information flows from DNA to RNA and then to protein (**Figure 3.16**). The process of transferring genetic information from DNA to RNA in the nucleus is known as **transcription.** The process that uses the coded information in RNA to assemble a protein in the cytoplasm is known as **translation.**

$$\text{DNA} \xrightarrow{\text{transcription}} \text{RNA} \xrightarrow{\text{translation}} \text{Protein}$$

As described in Chapter 2, a molecule of DNA consists of two chains of nucleotides coiled around each other to form a double helix. Each DNA nucleotide contains one of four bases—adenine (A), guanine (G), cytosine (C), or thymine (T)—and each of these bases is specifically paired by hydrogen bonds with a base on the opposite chain of the double helix. In this base pairing, A and T bond together and G and C bond together. Thus, both nucleotide chains contain a specifically ordered sequence of bases, with one chain complementary to the other. This specificity of base pairing forms the basis of the transfer of information from DNA to RNA and of the duplication of DNA during cell division.

The genetic language is similar in principle to a written language, which consists of a set of symbols, such as A, B, C, D, that form an alphabet. The letters are arranged in specific sequences to form words, and the words are arranged in linear sequences to

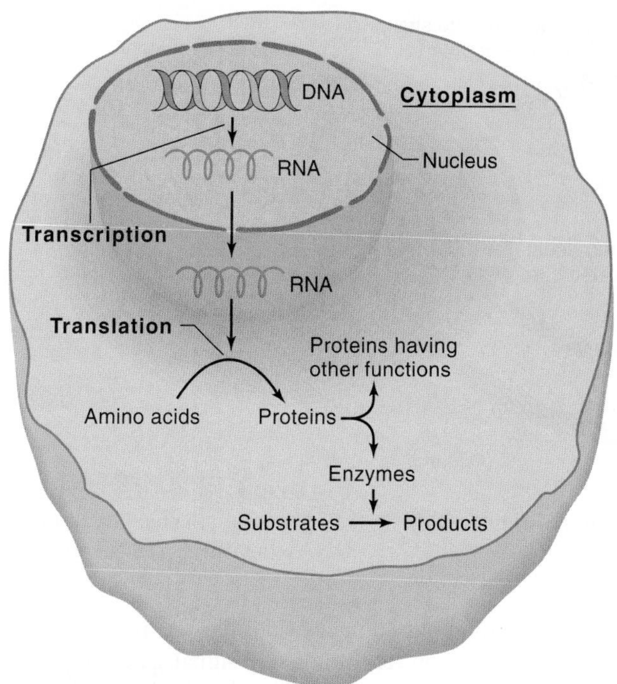

Figure 3.16 APR The expression of genetic information in a cell occurs through the *transcription* of coded information from DNA to RNA in the nucleus, followed by the *translation* of the RNA information into protein synthesis in the cytoplasm. The proteins then perform the functions that determine the characteristics of the cell.

form sentences. The genetic language contains only four letters, corresponding to the bases A, G, C, and T. The genetic words are three-base sequences that specify particular amino acids—that is, each word in the genetic language is only three letters long. This is termed a *triplet code*. The sequence of three-letter code words (triplets) along a gene in a single strand of DNA specifies the sequence of amino acids in a polypeptide chain (**Figure 3.17**). In this way, a gene is equivalent to a sentence, and the genetic information in the human genome is equivalent to a book containing about 20,000 sentences. Using a single letter (A, T, C, or G) to specify each of the four bases in the DNA nucleotides, it would require about 550,000 pages, each equivalent to this text page, to print the nucleotide sequence of the human genome.

The four bases in the DNA alphabet can be arranged in 64 different three-letter combinations to form 64 triplets ($4 \times 4 \times 4 = 64$). Therefore, this code actually provides more than enough words to code for the 20 different amino acids that are found in proteins. This means that a given amino acid is usually specified by more than one triplet. For example, the four DNA triplets C—C—A, C—C—G, C—C—T, and C—C—C all specify the amino acid glycine. Only 61 of the 64 possible triplets are used to specify amino acids. The triplets that do not specify amino acids are known as **stop signals.** They perform the same function as a period at the end of a sentence—they indicate that the end of a genetic message has been reached.

The genetic code is a universal language used by all living cells. For example, the triplets specifying the amino acid tryptophan are the same in the DNA of a bacterium, an amoeba, a plant, and a human being. Although the same triplets are used by all living cells, the messages they spell out—the sequences of triplets that code for a specific protein—vary from gene to gene in each organism. The universal nature of the genetic code supports the concept that all forms of life on earth evolved from a common ancestor.

Before we turn to the specific mechanisms by which the DNA code operates in protein synthesis, an important qualification is required. Although the information coded in genes is always first transcribed into RNA, there are several classes of RNA required for protein synthesis—including messenger RNA, ribosomal RNA, and transfer RNA. Only messenger RNA *directly* codes for the amino acid sequences of proteins, even though the other RNA classes participate in the overall process of protein synthesis.

3.5 Protein Synthesis

To repeat, the first step in using the genetic information in DNA to synthesize a protein is called transcription, and it involves the synthesis of an RNA molecule containing coded information that corresponds to the information in a single gene. The class of RNA molecules that specifies the amino acid sequence of a protein and carries this message from DNA to the site of protein synthesis in the cytoplasm is known as **messenger RNA (mRNA)**.

Transcription: mRNA Synthesis

Recall from Chapter 2 that ribonucleic acids are single-chain polynucleotides whose nucleotides differ from DNA because they contain the sugar ribose (rather than deoxyribose) and the base uracil (rather than thymine). The other three bases—adenine, guanine, and cytosine—occur in both DNA and RNA. The subunits used to synthesize mRNA are free (uncombined) ribonucleotide triphosphates: ATP, GTP, CTP, and UTP.

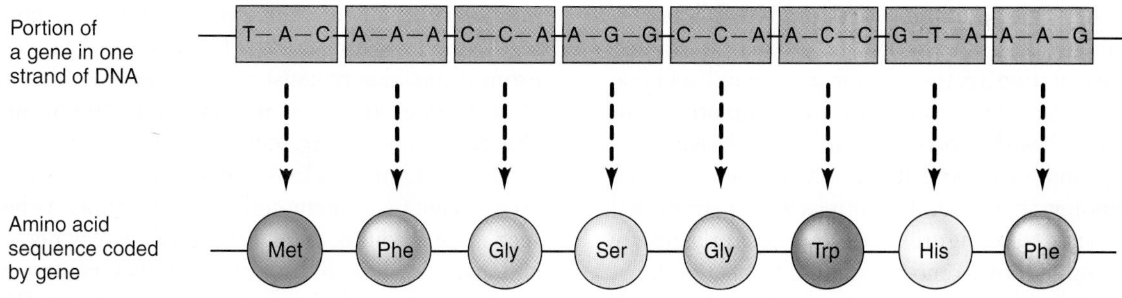

Figure 3.17 APR The sequence of three-letter code words in a gene determines the sequence of amino acids in a polypeptide chain. The names of the amino acids are abbreviated. Note that more than one three-letter code sequence can specify the same amino acid; for example, the amino acid phenylalanine (Phe) is coded by two triplet codes, A—A—A and A—A—G.

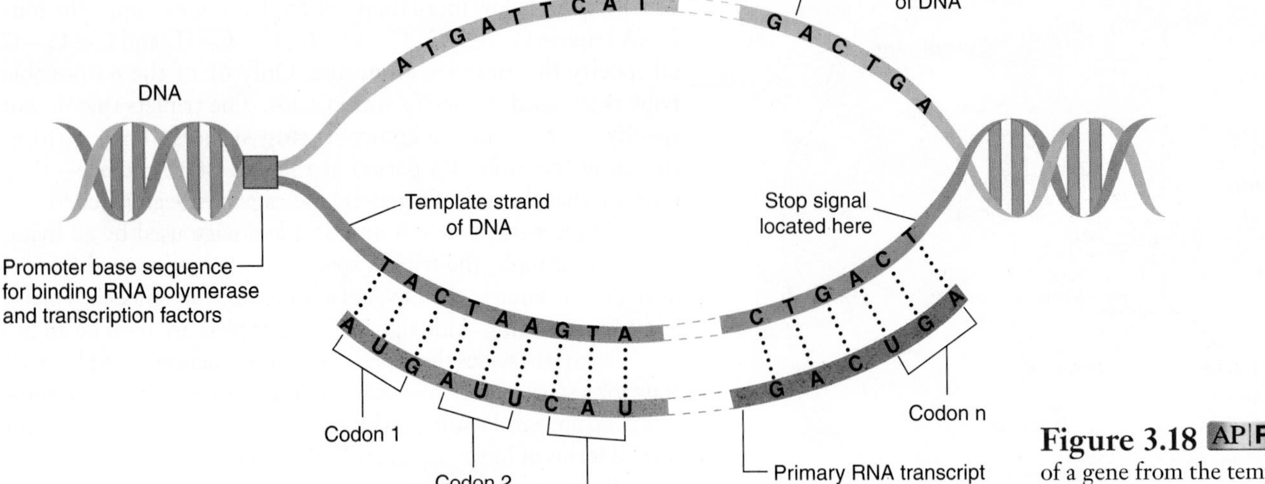

Figure 3.18 AP|R Transcription of a gene from the template strand of DNA to a primary mRNA transcript.

Recall also that the two polynucleotide chains in DNA are linked together by hydrogen bonds between specific pairs of bases: A—T and C—G. To initiate RNA synthesis, the two antiparallel strands of the DNA double helix must separate so that the bases in the exposed DNA can pair with the bases in free ribonucleotide triphosphates (**Figure 3.18**). Free ribonucleotides containing U bases pair with the exposed A bases in DNA; likewise, free ribonucleotides containing G, C, or A bases pair with the exposed DNA bases C, G, and T, respectively. Note that uracil, which is present in RNA but not DNA, pairs with the base adenine in DNA. In this way, the nucleotide sequence in one strand of DNA acts as a template that determines the sequence of nucleotides in mRNA.

The aligned ribonucleotides are joined together by the enzyme **RNA polymerase,** which hydrolyzes the nucleotide triphosphates, releasing two of the terminal phosphate groups and joining the remaining phosphate in covalent linkage to the ribose of the adjacent nucleotide.

DNA consists of two strands of polynucleotides that run antiparallel to each other based on the orientation of their phosphate–sugar backbone. Because both strands are exposed during transcription, it should theoretically be possible to form two individual RNA molecules, one complementary to each strand of DNA. However, only one of the two potential RNAs is typically formed. This is because RNA polymerase binds to DNA only at specific sites of a gene, adjacent to a sequence called the **promoter.** The promoter is a specific sequence of DNA nucleotides, including some that are common to most genes. The promoter directs RNA polymerase to proceed along a strand in only one direction that is determined by the orientation of the phosphate–sugar backbone. Thus, for a given gene, one strand, called the **template strand** or antisense strand, has the correct orientation relative to the location of the promoter to bind RNA polymerase. The location of the promoter, therefore, determines which strand will be the template strand (see Figure 3.18). Consequently, for any given gene, only one DNA strand typically is transcribed.

Thus, the transcription of a gene begins when RNA polymerase binds to the promoter region of that gene. This initiates the separation of the two strands of DNA. RNA polymerase moves along the template strand, joining one ribonucleotide at a time (at a rate of about 30 nucleotides per second) to the growing RNA chain. Upon reaching a stop signal specifying the end of the gene, the RNA polymerase releases the newly formed RNA transcript, which is then translocated out of the nucleus where it binds to ribosomes in the cytoplasm.

In a given cell, typically only 10% to 20% of the genes present in DNA are transcribed into RNA. Genes are transcribed only when RNA polymerase can bind to their promoter sites. Cells use various mechanisms to either block or make accessible the promoter region of a particular gene to RNA polymerase. Such regulation of gene transcription provides a means of controlling the synthesis of specific proteins and thereby the activities characteristic of a particular type of cell. Collectively, the specific proteins expressed in a given cell at a particular time constitute the **proteome** of the cell. The proteome determines the structure and function of the cell at that time.

Note that the base sequence in the RNA transcript is not identical to that in the template strand of DNA, because the formation of RNA depends on the pairing between *complementary*, not identical, bases (see Figure 3.18). A three-base sequence in RNA that specifies one amino acid is called a **codon.** Each codon is complementary to a three-base sequence in DNA. For example, the base sequence T—A—C in the template strand of DNA corresponds to the codon A—U—G in transcribed RNA.

Although the entire sequence of nucleotides in the template strand of a gene is transcribed into a complementary sequence of nucleotides known as the **primary RNA transcript** or **pre-mRNA,** only certain segments of most genes actually code for sequences of amino acids. These regions of the gene, known as **exons** (expression regions), are separated by noncoding sequences of nucleotides known as **introns** (from "intragenic region" and also called intervening sequences). It is estimated that as much as 98.5% of human DNA is composed of intron sequences that do not contain protein-coding information. What role, if any, such large amounts of noncoding DNA may perform is unclear, although they have been postulated to exert some transcriptional regulation. In addition, a class of very short RNA molecules called microRNAs are transcribed in some cases from noncoding DNA. MicroRNAs are not themselves translated into protein but, rather, prevent the translation of specific mRNA molecules.

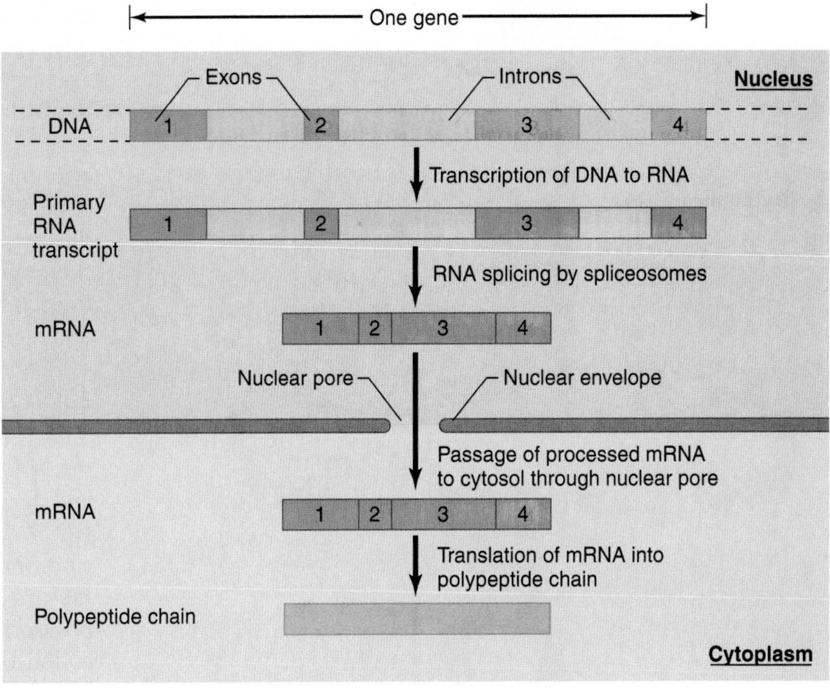

Figure 3.19 Spliceosomes remove the noncoding intron-derived segments from a primary RNA transcript (or pre-mRNA) and link the exon-derived segments together to form the mature mRNA molecule that passes through the nuclear pores to the cytosol. The lengths of the intron- and exon-derived segments represent the relative lengths of the base sequences in these regions.

PHYSIOLOGICAL INQUIRY

- Using the format of this diagram, draw an mRNA molecule that might result from alternative splicing of the primary RNA transcript.

Answer can be found at end of chapter.

Before passing to the cytoplasm, a newly formed primary RNA transcript must undergo splicing (**Figure 3.19**) to remove the sequences that correspond to the DNA introns. This allows the formation of the continuous sequence of exons that will be translated into protein. Only after this splicing occurs is the RNA termed *mature messenger RNA*, or *mature mRNA*.

Splicing occurs in the nucleus and is performed by a complex of proteins and small nuclear RNAs known as a **spliceosome.** The spliceosome identifies specific nucleotide sequences at the beginning and end of each intron-derived segment in the primary RNA transcript, removes the segment, and splices the end of one exon-derived segment to the beginning of another to form mRNA with a continuous coding sequence. In many cases during the splicing process, the exon-derived segments from a single gene can be spliced together in different sequences or some exon-derived segments can be deleted entirely; this is called alternative splicing and is estimated to occur in more than half of all genes. These processes result in the formation of different mRNA sequences from the same gene and give rise, in turn, to proteins with different amino acid sequences. Thus, there are more different proteins in the human body than there are genes.

Translation: Polypeptide Synthesis

After splicing, the mRNA moves through the pores in the nuclear envelope into the cytoplasm. Although the nuclear pores allow the diffusion of small molecules and ions between the nucleus and cytoplasm, they have specific energy-dependent mechanisms for the selective transport of large molecules such as proteins and RNA.

In the cytoplasm, mRNA binds to a ribosome, the cell organelle that contains the enzymes and other components required for the translation of mRNA into protein. Before describing this assembly process, we will examine the structure of a ribosome and the characteristics of two additional classes of RNA involved in protein synthesis.

Ribosomes and rRNA

A ribosome is a complex particle composed of about 70 to 80 different proteins in association with a class of RNA molecules known as **ribosomal RNA (rRNA)**. The genes for rRNA are transcribed from DNA in a process similar to that for mRNA except that a different RNA polymerase is used. Ribosomal RNA transcription occurs in the region of the nucleus known as the nucleolus. Ribosomal proteins, like other proteins, are synthesized in the cytoplasm from the mRNAs specific for them. These proteins then move back through nuclear pores to the nucleolus, where they combine with newly synthesized rRNA to form two ribosomal subunits, one large and one small. These subunits are then individually transported to the cytoplasm, where they combine to form a functional ribosome during protein translation.

Transfer RNA

How do individual amino acids identify the appropriate codons in mRNA during the process of translation? By themselves, free amino acids do not have the ability to bind to the bases in mRNA codons. This process of identification involves the third major class of RNA, known as **transfer RNA (tRNA)**. Transfer RNA molecules are the smallest (about 80 nucleotides long) of the major classes of RNA. The single chain of tRNA loops back upon itself, forming a structure resembling a cloverleaf with three loops (**Figure 3.20**).

Like mRNA and rRNA, tRNA molecules are synthesized in the nucleus by base-pairing with DNA nucleotides at specific tRNA genes; then they move to the cytoplasm. The key to tRNA's role in protein synthesis is its ability to combine with both a specific amino acid and a codon in ribosome-bound mRNA specific for that amino acid. This permits tRNA to act as the link between an amino acid and the mRNA codon for that amino acid.

A tRNA molecule is covalently linked to a specific amino acid by an enzyme known as aminoacyl-tRNA synthetase. There are 20 different aminoacyl-tRNA synthetases, each of which catalyzes

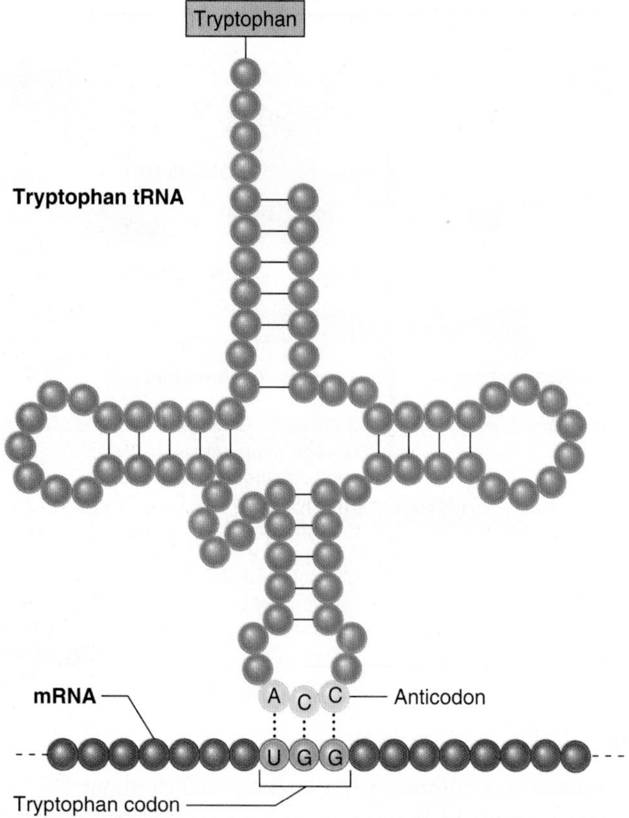

Figure 3.20 AP|R Base pairing between the anticodon region of a tRNA molecule and the corresponding codon region of an mRNA molecule.

the linkage of a specific amino acid to a specific type of tRNA. The next step is to link the tRNA, bearing its attached amino acid, to the mRNA codon for that amino acid. This is achieved by the base pairing between tRNA and mRNA. A three-nucleotide sequence at the end of one of the loops of tRNA can base-pair with a complementary codon in mRNA. This tRNA three-letter code sequence is appropriately known as an **anticodon.** Figure 3.20 illustrates the binding between mRNA and a tRNA specific for the amino acid tryptophan. Note that tryptophan is covalently linked to one end of tRNA and does not bind to either the anticodon region of tRNA or the codon region of mRNA.

Protein Assembly

The process of assembling a polypeptide chain based on an mRNA message involves three stages—initiation, elongation, and termination. The initiation of synthesis occurs when a tRNA containing the amino acid methionine binds to the small ribosomal subunit. A number of proteins known as **initiation factors** are required to establish an initiation complex, which positions the methionine-containing tRNA opposite the mRNA codon that signals the start site at which assembly is to begin. The large ribosomal subunit then binds, enclosing the mRNA between the two subunits. This initiation phase is the slowest step in protein assembly, and factors that influence the activity of initiation factors can regulate the rate of protein synthesis.

Following the initiation process, the protein chain is elongated by the successive addition of amino acids (**Figure 3.21**). A ribosome has two binding sites for tRNA. Site 1 holds the tRNA linked to the portion of the protein chain that has been assembled up to this point, and site 2 holds the tRNA containing the

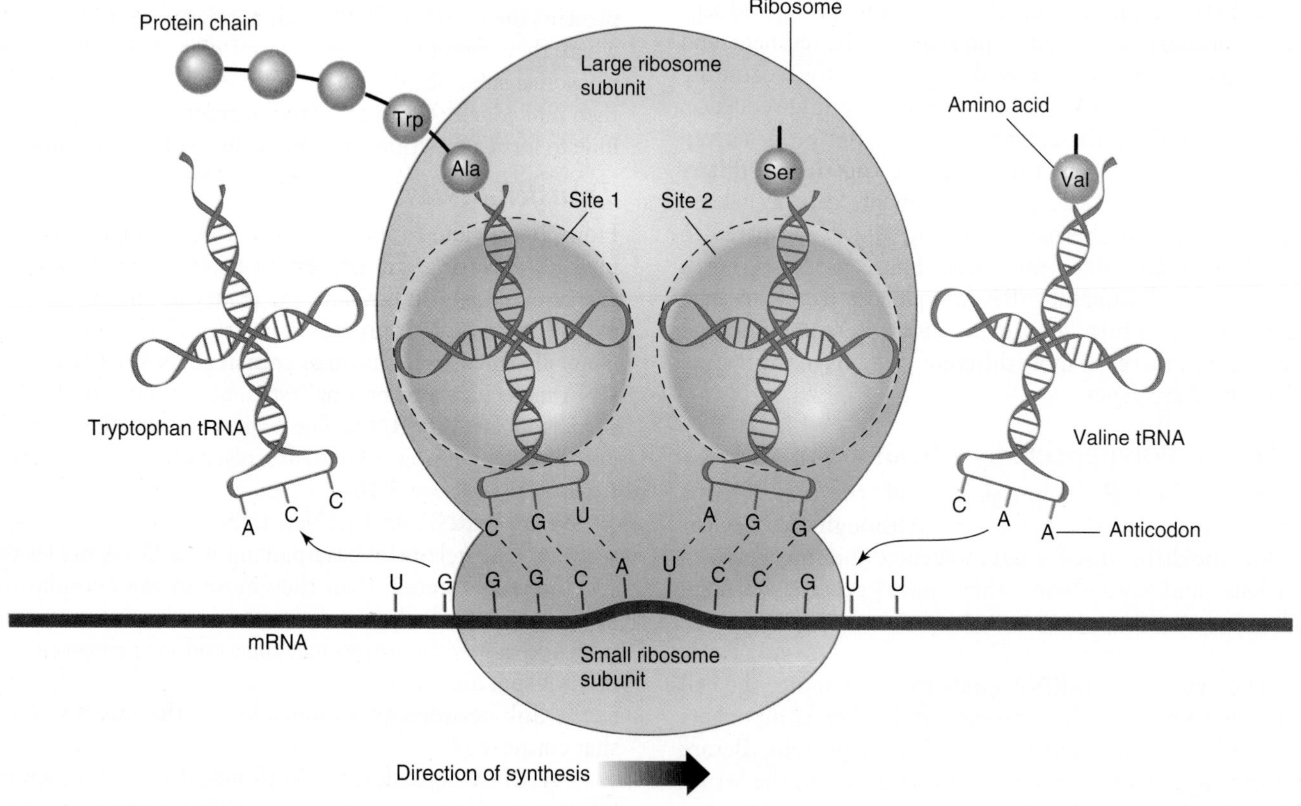

Figure 3.21 AP|R Sequence of events during protein synthesis by a ribosome.

next amino acid to be added to the chain. Ribosomal enzymes catalyze the linkage of the protein chain to the newly arrived amino acid. Following the formation of the peptide bond, the tRNA at site 1 is released from the ribosome, and the tRNA at site 2—now linked to the peptide chain—is transferred to site 1. The ribosome moves down one codon along the mRNA, making room for the binding of the next amino acid–tRNA molecule. This process is repeated over and over as amino acids are added to the growing peptide chain, at an average rate of two to three per second. When the ribosome reaches a termination sequence in mRNA (called a stop codon) specifying the end of the protein, the link between the polypeptide chain and the last tRNA is broken, and the completed protein is released from the ribosome.

Messenger RNA molecules are not destroyed during protein synthesis, so they may be used to synthesize many more protein molecules. In fact, while one ribosome is moving along a particular strand of mRNA, a second ribosome may become attached to the start site on that same mRNA and begin the synthesis of a second identical protein molecule. Therefore, a number of ribosomes—as many as 70—may be moving along a single strand of mRNA, each at a different stage of the translation process (**Figure 3.22**).

Molecules of mRNA do not, however, remain in the cytoplasm indefinitely. Eventually, cytoplasmic enzymes break them down into nucleotides. Therefore, if a gene corresponding to a particular protein ceases to be transcribed into mRNA, the protein will no longer be formed after its cytoplasmic mRNA molecules have broken down.

Once a polypeptide chain has been assembled, it may undergo posttranslational modifications to its amino acid sequence. For example, the amino acid methionine that is used to identify the start site of the assembly process is cleaved from the end of most proteins. In some cases, other specific peptide bonds within the polypeptide chain are broken, producing a number of smaller peptides, each of which may perform a different function. For example, as illustrated in **Figure 3.23**, five different proteins can be derived from the same mRNA as a result of posttranslational cleavage. The same initial polypeptide may be split at different points in different cells depending on the specificity of the hydrolyzing enzymes present.

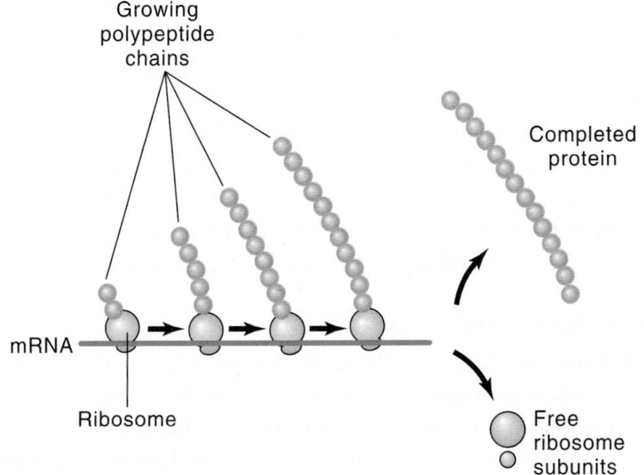

Figure 3.22 AP|R Several ribosomes can simultaneously move along a strand of mRNA, producing the same protein in different stages of assembly.

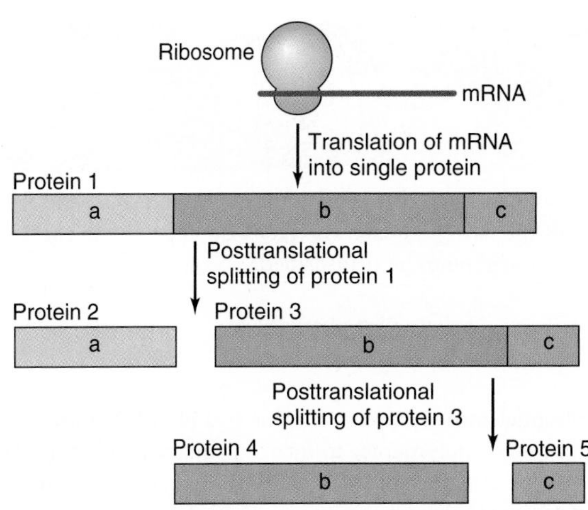

Figure 3.23 Posttranslational splitting of a protein can result in several smaller proteins, each of which may perform a different function. All these proteins are derived from the same gene.

Carbohydrates and lipid derivatives are often covalently linked to particular amino acid side chains. These additions may protect the protein from rapid degradation by proteolytic enzymes or act as signals to direct the protein to those locations in the cell where it is to function. The addition of a fatty acid to a protein, for example, can lead the protein to anchor to a membrane as the nonpolar portion of the fatty acid inserts into the lipid bilayer.

The steps leading from DNA to a functional protein are summarized in **Table 3.2**.

Regulation of Protein Synthesis

As noted earlier, in any given cell, only a small fraction of the genes in the human genome are ever transcribed into mRNA and translated into proteins. Of this fraction, a small number of genes are continuously being transcribed into mRNA. The transcription of other genes, however, is regulated and can be turned on or off in response to either signals generated within the cell or external signals the cell receives. In order for a gene to be transcribed, RNA polymerase must be able to bind to the promoter region of the gene and be in an activated configuration.

Transcription of most genes is regulated by a class of proteins known as **transcription factors,** which act as gene switches, interacting in a variety of ways to activate or repress the initiation process that takes place at the promoter region of a particular gene. The influence of a transcription factor on transcription is not necessarily all or none, on or off; it may simply slow or speed up the initiation of the transcription process. The transcription factors, along with accessory proteins, form a **preinitiation complex** at the promoter that is needed to carry out the process of separating the DNA strands, removing any blocking nucleosomes in the region of the promoter, activating the bound RNA polymerase, and moving the complex along the template strand of DNA. Some transcription factors bind to regions of DNA that are far removed from the promoter region of the gene whose transcription they regulate. In this case, the DNA containing the bound transcription factor forms a loop that brings the transcription factor into contact with the promoter region, where it may then activate or repress transcription (**Figure 3.24**).

Many genes contain regulatory sites that a common transcription factor can influence; there does not need to be a

TABLE 3.2	Events Leading from DNA to Protein Synthesis
Transcription	
RNA polymerase binds to the promoter region of a gene and separates the two strands of the DNA double helix in the region of the gene to be transcribed.	
Free ribonucleotide triphosphates base-pair with the deoxynucleotides in the template strand of DNA.	
The ribonucleotides paired with this strand of DNA are linked by RNA polymerase to form a primary RNA transcript containing a sequence of bases complementary to the template strand of the DNA base sequence.	
RNA splicing removes the intron-derived regions, which contain noncoding sequences, in the primary RNA transcript and splices together the exon-derived regions, which code for specific amino acids, producing a molecule of mature mRNA.	
Translation	
The mRNA passes from the nucleus to the cytoplasm, where one end of the mRNA binds to the small subunit of a ribosome.	
Free amino acids are linked to their corresponding tRNAs by aminoacyl-tRNA synthetase.	
The three-base anticodon in an amino acid–tRNA complex pairs with its corresponding codon in the region of the mRNA bound to the ribosome.	
The amino acid on the tRNA is linked by a peptide bond to the end of the growing polypeptide chain.	
The tRNA that has been freed of its amino acid is released from the ribosome.	
The ribosome moves one codon step along mRNA.	
The previous four steps are repeated until a termination sequence is reached, and the completed protein is released from the ribosome.	
In some cases, the protein undergoes posttranslational processing in which various chemical groups are attached to specific side chains and/or the protein is split into several smaller peptide chains.	

different transcription factor for every gene. In addition, more than one transcription factor may interact to control the transcription of a given gene.

Because transcription factors are proteins, the activity of a particular transcription factor—that is, its ability to bind to DNA or to other regulatory proteins—can be turned on or off by allosteric or covalent modulation in response to signals a cell either receives or generates. Thus, specific genes can be regulated in response to specific signals.

To summarize, the rate of a protein's synthesis can be regulated at various points: (1) gene transcription into mRNA; (2) the initiation of protein assembly on a ribosome; and (3) mRNA degradation in the cytoplasm.

Mutation

Any alteration in the nucleotide sequence that spells out a genetic message in DNA is known as a **mutation.** Certain chemicals and various forms of ionizing radiation, such as x-rays, cosmic rays, and atomic radiation, can break the chemical bonds in DNA. This can result in the loss of segments of DNA or the incorporation of the wrong base when the broken bonds re-form. Environmental factors that increase the rate of mutation are known as **mutagens.**

Types of Mutations

The simplest type of mutation, known as a point mutation, occurs when a single base is replaced by a different one. For example, the base sequence C—G—T is the DNA triplet for the amino acid alanine. If guanine (G) is replaced by adenine (A), the sequence becomes C—A—T, which is the code for valine. If, however, cytosine (C) replaces thymine (T), the sequence becomes C—G—C, which is another code for alanine, and the amino acid sequence transcribed from the mutated gene would not be altered. On the other hand, if an amino acid code mutates to one of the termination triplets, the translation of the mRNA message will cease when this triplet is reached, resulting in the synthesis of a shortened, typically nonfunctional protein.

Assume that a mutation has altered a single triplet code in a gene, for example, alanine C—G—T changed to valine C—A—T, so that it now codes for a protein with one different amino acid. What effect does this mutation have upon the cell? The answer depends upon where in the gene the mutation has occurred. Although proteins are composed of many amino acids, the properties of a protein often depend upon a very small region of the total molecule, such as the binding site of an enzyme. If the mutation does not alter the conformation of the binding site, there may be little or no change in the protein's properties. On the other hand, if the mutation alters the binding site, a marked change in the protein's properties may occur.

What effects do mutations have upon the functioning of a cell? If a mutated, nonfunctional protein is part of a chemical reaction supplying most of a cell's chemical energy, the loss of the protein's function could lead to the death of the cell. In contrast, if the active protein were involved in the synthesis of a particular amino acid, and if the cell could also obtain that amino acid from the extracellular fluid, the cell function would not be impaired by the absence of the protein.

To generalize, a mutation may have any one of three effects upon a cell: (1) it may cause no noticeable change in cell function; (2) it may modify cell function but still be compatible with cell growth and replication; or (3) it may lead to cell death.

Mutations and Evolution

Mutations contribute to the evolution of organisms. Although most mutations result in either no change or an impairment of cell function, a very small number may alter the activity of a protein in such a way that it is more, rather than less, active; or they may introduce an entirely new type of protein activity into a cell. If an organism carrying such a mutant gene is able to perform some function more effectively than an organism lacking the

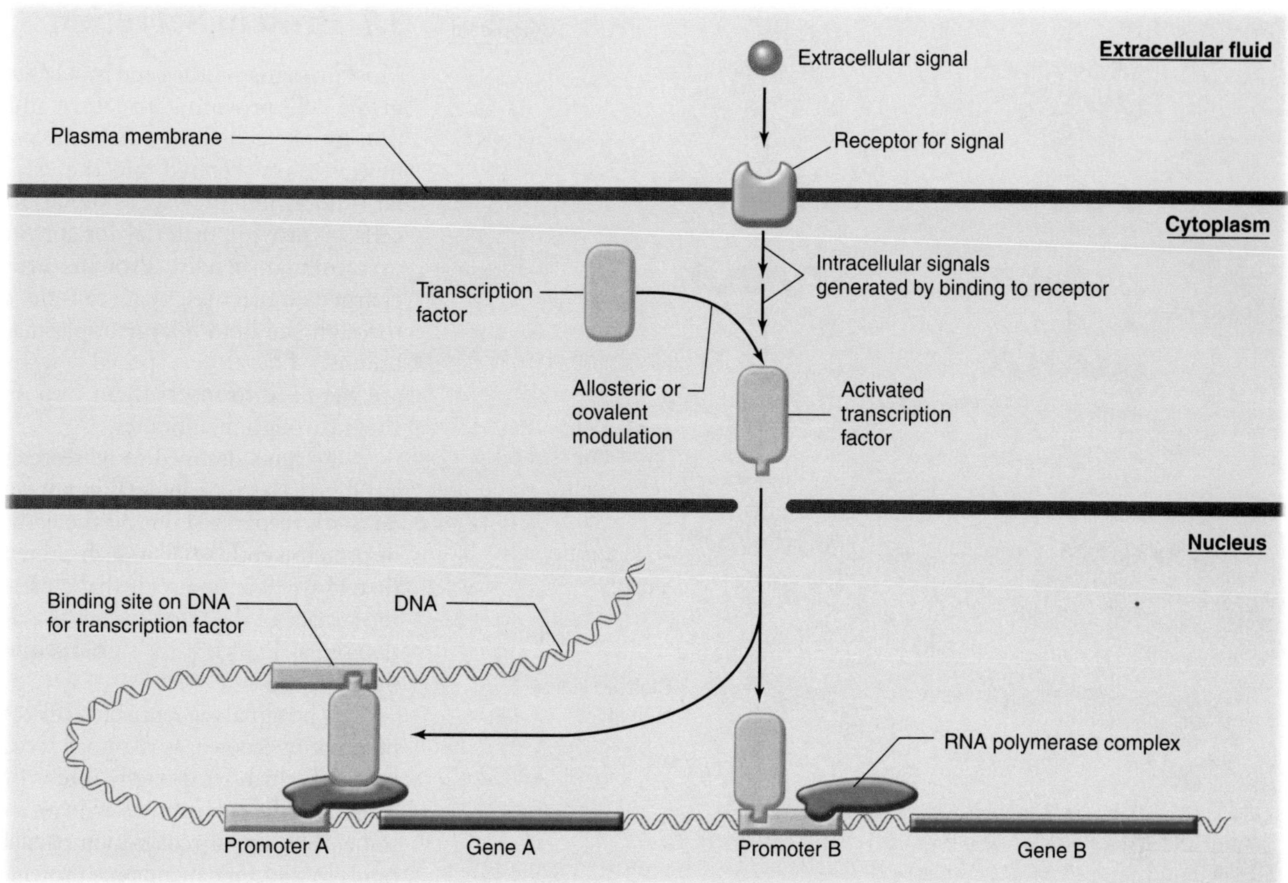

Figure 3.24 APIR Transcription of gene B is modulated by the binding of an activated transcription factor directly to the promoter region. In contrast, transcription of gene A is modulated by the same transcription factor, which, in this case, binds to a region of DNA considerably distant from the promoter region.

mutant gene, the organism has a better chance of reproducing and passing on the mutant gene to its descendants. On the other hand, if the mutation produces an organism that functions less effectively than organisms lacking the mutation, the organism is less likely to reproduce and pass on the mutant gene. This is the principle of **natural selection.** Although any one mutation, if it is able to survive in the population, may cause only a very slight alteration in the properties of a cell, given enough time, a large number of small changes can accumulate to produce very large changes in the structure and function of an organism.

3.6 Protein Degradation

We have thus far emphasized protein synthesis, but the concentration of a particular protein in a cell at a particular time depends upon not only its rate of synthesis but also its rates of degradation and/or secretion.

Different proteins degrade at different rates. In part, this depends on the structure of the protein, with some proteins having a higher affinity for certain proteolytic enzymes than others. A denatured (unfolded) protein is more readily digested than a protein with an intact conformation. Proteins can be targeted for degradation by the attachment of a small peptide, **ubiquitin,** to the protein. This peptide directs the protein to a protein complex known as a **proteasome,** which unfolds the protein and breaks it down into small peptides. Degradation is an important mechanism for confining the activity of a given protein to a precise window of time.

In summary, there are many steps in the path from a gene in DNA to a fully active protein, which allow the rate of protein synthesis or the final active form of the protein to be altered (**Table 3.3**). By controlling these

TABLE 3.3 Factors That Alter the Amount and Activity of Specific Cell Proteins

Process Altered	Mechanism of Alteration
Transcription of DNA	Activation or inhibition by transcription factors
Splicing of RNA	Activity of enzymes in spliceosome
mRNA degradation	Activity of RNase
Translation of mRNA	Activity of initiating factors on ribosomes
Protein degradation	Activity of proteasomes
Allosteric and covalent modulation	Signal ligands, protein kinases, and phosphatases

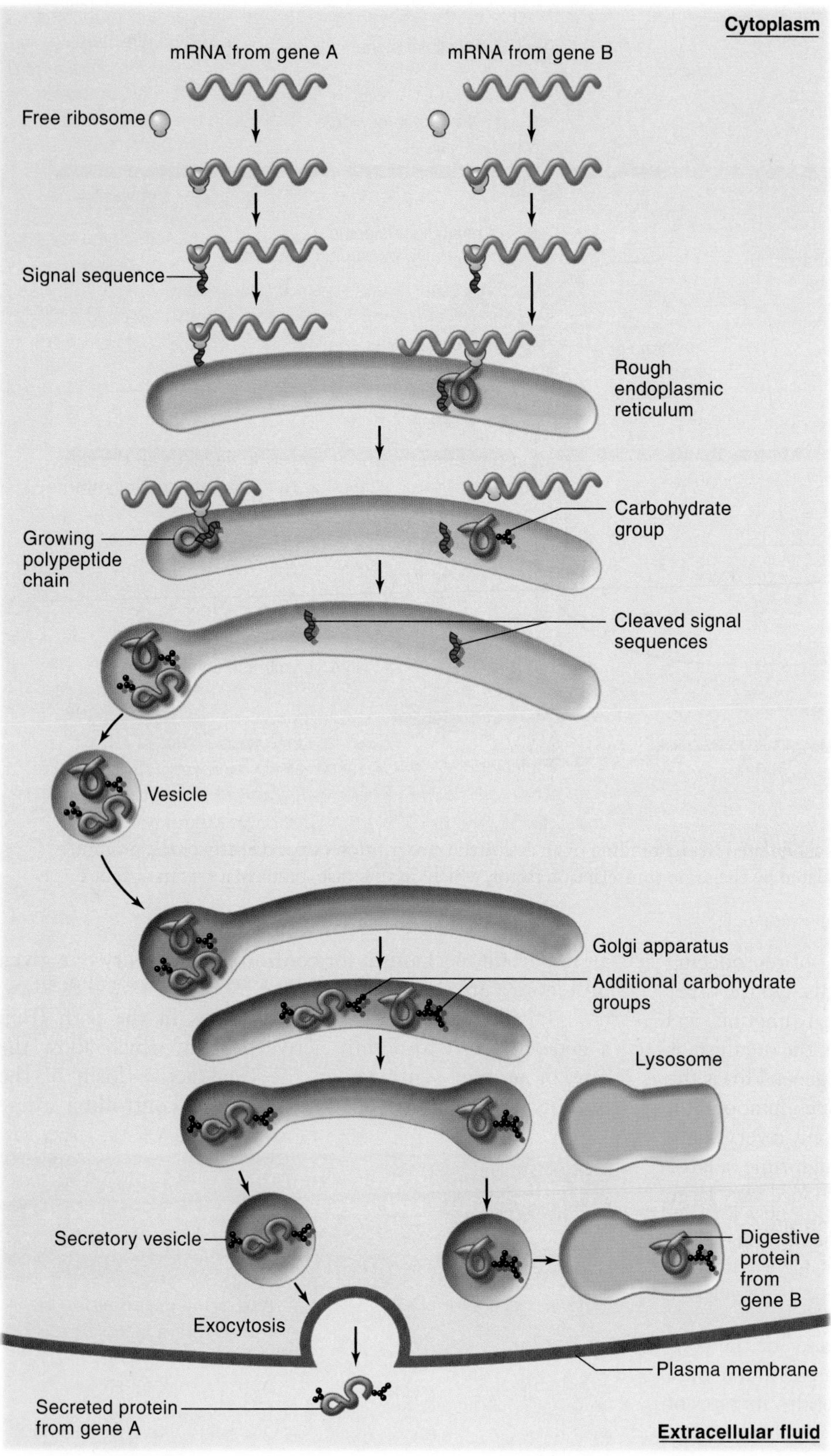

Figure 3.25 Pathway of proteins destined to be secreted by cells or transferred to lysosomes. An example of the latter might be a protein important in digestive functions in which a cell degrades other intracellular molecules.

steps, extracellular or intracellular signals, as described in Chapter 5, can regulate the total amount of a specific protein in a cell.

3.7 Protein Secretion

Most proteins synthesized by a cell remain in the cell, providing structure and function for the cell's survival. Some proteins, however, are secreted into the extracellular fluid, where they act as signals to other cells or provide material for forming the extracellular matrix. Proteins are large, charged molecules that cannot diffuse through the lipid bilayer of plasma membranes. Therefore, special mechanisms are required to insert them into or move them through membranes.

Proteins destined to be secreted from a cell or to become integral membrane proteins are recognized during the early stages of protein synthesis. For such proteins, the first 15 to 30 amino acids that emerge from the surface of the ribosome act as a recognition signal, known as the **signal sequence** or signal peptide.

The signal sequence binds to a complex of proteins known as a signal recognition particle, which temporarily inhibits further growth of the polypeptide chain on the ribosome. The signal recognition particle then binds to a specific membrane protein on the surface of the rough endoplasmic reticulum. This binding restarts the process of protein assembly, and the growing polypeptide chain is fed through a protein complex in the endoplasmic reticulum membrane into the lumen of the reticulum (**Figure 3.25**). Upon completion of protein assembly, proteins that are to be secreted end up in the lumen of the rough endoplasmic reticulum. Proteins that are destined to function as integral membrane proteins remain embedded in the reticulum membrane.

Within the lumen of the endoplasmic reticulum, enzymes remove the signal sequence from most proteins, so this portion is not present in the final protein. In addition, carbohydrate groups are sometimes linked to various side chains in the proteins.

Following these modifications, portions of the reticulum membrane bud off, forming vesicles that contain the newly synthesized proteins. These vesicles migrate to the Golgi apparatus (see Figure 3.25) and fuse with the Golgi membranes.

Within the Golgi apparatus, the protein may undergo further modifications. For example, additional carbohydrate groups may be added; these groups are typically important as recognition sites within the cell.

While in the Golgi apparatus, the many different proteins that have been funneled into this organelle are sorted out according to their final destinations. This sorting involves the binding of regions of a particular protein to specific proteins in the Golgi membrane that are destined to form vesicles targeted to a particular destination.

Following modification and sorting, the proteins are packaged into vesicles that bud off the surface of the Golgi membrane. Some of the vesicles travel to the plasma membrane, where they fuse with the membrane and release their contents to the extracellular fluid, a process known as exocytosis. Other vesicles may dock and fuse with lysosome membranes, delivering digestive enzymes to the interior of this organelle. Specific docking proteins on the surface of the membrane where the vesicle finally fuses recognize the specific proteins on the surface of the vesicle.

In contrast to this entire story, if a protein does not have a signal sequence, synthesis continues on a free ribosome until the completed protein is released into the cytosol. These proteins are not secreted but are destined to function within the cell. Many remain in the cytosol, where they function as enzymes, for example, in various metabolic pathways. Others are targeted to particular cell organelles. For example, ribosomal proteins are directed to the nucleus, where they combine with rRNA before returning to the cytosol as part of the ribosomal subunits. The specific location of a protein is determined by binding sites on the protein that bind to specific sites at the protein's destination. For example, in the case of the ribosomal proteins, they bind to sites on the nuclear pores that control access to the nucleus.

SECTION B SUMMARY

Genetic Code

I. Genetic information is coded in the nucleotide sequences of DNA molecules. A single gene contains either (a) the information that, via mRNA, determines the amino acid sequence in a specific protein; or (b) the information for forming rRNA, tRNA, or small nuclear RNAs, which assist in protein assembly.

II. Genetic information is transferred from DNA to mRNA in the nucleus (transcription); then mRNA passes to the cytoplasm, where its information is used to synthesize protein (translation).

III. The "words" in the DNA genetic code consist of a sequence of three nucleotide bases that specify a single amino acid. The sequence of three-letter codes along a gene determines the sequence of amino acids in a protein. More than one triplet can specify a given amino acid.

Protein Synthesis

I. Table 3.2 summarizes the steps leading from DNA to protein synthesis.

II. Transcription involves forming a primary RNA transcript by base-pairing with the template strand of DNA containing a single gene. Transcription also involves the removal of intron-derived segments by spliceosomes to form mRNA, which moves to the cytoplasm.

III. Translation of mRNA occurs on the ribosomes in the cytoplasm when the anticodons in tRNAs, linked to single amino acids, base-pair with the corresponding codons in mRNA.

IV. Protein transcription factors activate or repress the transcription of specific genes by binding to regions of DNA that interact with the promoter region of a gene.

V. Mutagens alter DNA molecules, resulting in the addition or deletion of nucleotides or segments of DNA. The result is an altered DNA sequence known as a mutation. A mutation may (a) cause no noticeable change in cell function, (b) modify cell function but still be compatible with cell growth and replication, or (c) lead to the death of the cell.

Protein Degradation

I. The concentration of a particular protein in a cell depends on (a) the rate of the corresponding gene's transcription; (b) the rate of initiating protein assembly on a ribosome; (c) the rate at which mRNA is degraded; (d) the rate of protein digestion by enzymes associated with proteasomes; and (e) the rate of secretion, if any, of the protein from the cell.

Protein Secretion

I. Targeting of a protein for secretion depends on the signal sequence of amino acids that first emerge from a ribosome during protein synthesis.

SECTION B REVIEW QUESTIONS

1. Describe how the genetic code in DNA specifies the amino acid sequence in a protein.
2. List the four nucleotides found in mRNA.
3. Describe the main events in the transcription of genetic information from DNA into mRNA.
4. Explain the difference between an exon and an intron.
5. What is the function of a spliceosome?
6. Identify the site of ribosomal subunit assembly.
7. Describe the role of tRNA in protein assembly.
8. Describe the events of protein translation that occur on the surface of a ribosome.
9. Describe the effects of transcription factors on gene transcription.
10. List the factors that regulate the concentration of a protein in a cell.
11. What is the function of the signal sequence of a protein? How is it formed, and where is it located?
12. Describe the pathway that leads to the secretion of proteins from cells.
13. List the three general types of effects a mutation can have on a cell's function.

SECTION B KEY TERMS

anticodon 62
codon 60
exon 60
gene 58
genome 58
histone 58
initiation factor 62
intron 60
messenger RNA (mRNA) 59
mutagen 64
mutation 64
natural selection 65
nucleosome 58
preinitiation complex 63
pre-mRNA 60
primary RNA transcript 60
promoter 60
proteasome 65
proteome 60
ribosomal RNA (rRNA) 61
RNA polymerase 60
signal sequence 66
spliceosome 61
stop signal 59
template strand 60
transcription 58
transcription factor 63
transfer RNA (tRNA) 61
translation 58
ubiquitin 65

SECTION C

Interactions Between Proteins and Ligands

3.8 Binding Site Characteristics

In the previous sections, we learned how the cellular machinery synthesizes and processes proteins. We now turn our attention to how proteins physically interact with each other and with other molecules and ions. These interactions are fundamental to nearly all physiological processes, clearly illustrating the general principle that physiological processes are dictated by the laws of chemistry and physics.

The ability of various molecules and ions to bind to specific sites on the surface of a protein forms the basis for the wide variety of protein functions (refer back to Table 2.5 for a summary of protein functions). A **ligand** is any molecule (including another protein) or ion that is bound to a protein by one of the following physical forces: (1) electrical attractions between oppositely charged ionic or polarized groups on the ligand and the protein, or (2) weaker attractions due to hydrophobic forces between nonpolar regions on the two molecules. These types of binding do not involve covalent bonds; in other words, binding is generally reversible. The region of a protein to which a ligand binds is known as a **binding site** or a ligand-binding site. A protein may contain several binding sites, each specific for a particular ligand, or it may have multiple binding sites for the same ligand. Typically, the binding of a ligand to a protein changes the conformation of the protein. When this happens, the protein's specific function may either be activated or inhibited, depending on the ligand. In the case of an enzyme, for example, the change in conformation may make the enzyme more active until the ligand is removed.

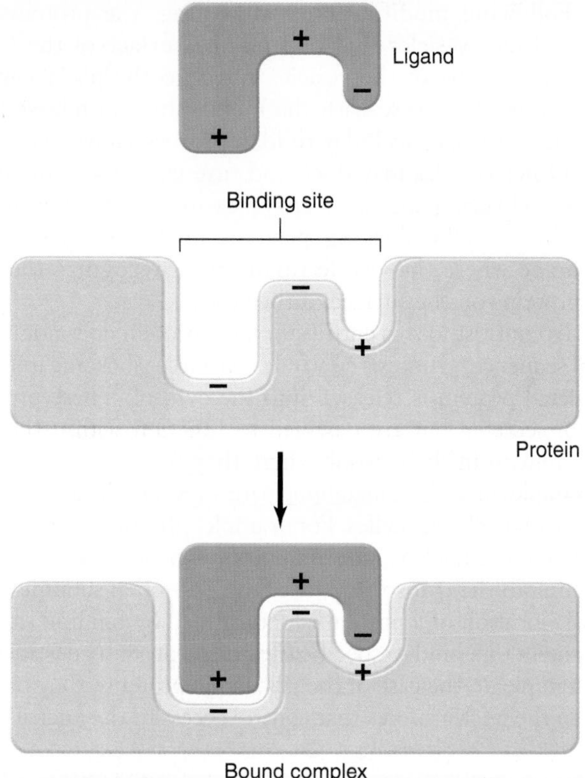

Figure 3.26 APIR The complementary shapes of ligand and the protein-binding site determine the chemical specificity of binding.

Chemical Specificity

A principle of physics states that the force of electrical attraction between oppositely charged particles decreases exponentially as the distance between them increases. This applies to charges within proteins and their ligands, as well. The even weaker hydrophobic forces act only between nonpolar groups that are very close to each other. Therefore, for a ligand to bind to a protein, the ligand must be close to the protein surface. This proximity occurs when the shape of the ligand is complementary to the shape of the protein's binding site, so that the two fit together like pieces of a jigsaw puzzle, illustrating the importance of structure to function at the molecular level (**Figure 3.26**).

The binding between a ligand and a protein may be so specific that a binding site can bind only one type of ligand and no other. Such selectivity allows a protein to identify (by binding) one particular molecule in a solution containing hundreds of different molecules. This ability of a protein-binding site to bind specific ligands is known as **chemical specificity,** because the binding site determines the type of chemical that is bound.

In Chapter 2, we described how the conformation of a protein is determined by the sequence of the various amino acids along the polypeptide chain. Accordingly, proteins with different amino acid sequences have different shapes and, therefore, differently shaped binding sites, each with its own chemical specificity. As illustrated in **Figure 3.27**, the amino acids that interact with a ligand at a binding site do not need to be adjacent to each other along the polypeptide chain, because the three-dimensional folding of the protein may bring various segments of the molecule into close contact.

Although some binding sites have a chemical specificity that allows them to bind only one type of ligand, others are less specific and thus can bind a number of related ligands. For example, three different ligands can combine with the binding site of protein X in **Figure 3.28**, because a portion of each ligand is complementary to the shape of the binding site. In contrast, protein Y has a greater chemical specificity and can bind only one of the three ligands. It is the degree of specificity of proteins that determines, in part, the side effects of therapeutic drugs. For example, a drug (ligand) designed to treat high blood pressure may act by binding to and thereby activating certain proteins that, in turn, help restore pressure to normal. The same drug, however, may also bind to a lesser degree to other proteins, whose functions may be completely unrelated to blood pressure. Changing the activities of these other proteins may lead to unwanted side effects of the medication.

Affinity

The strength of ligand–protein binding is a property of the binding site known as **affinity.** The affinity of a binding site for a ligand determines how likely it is that a bound ligand will

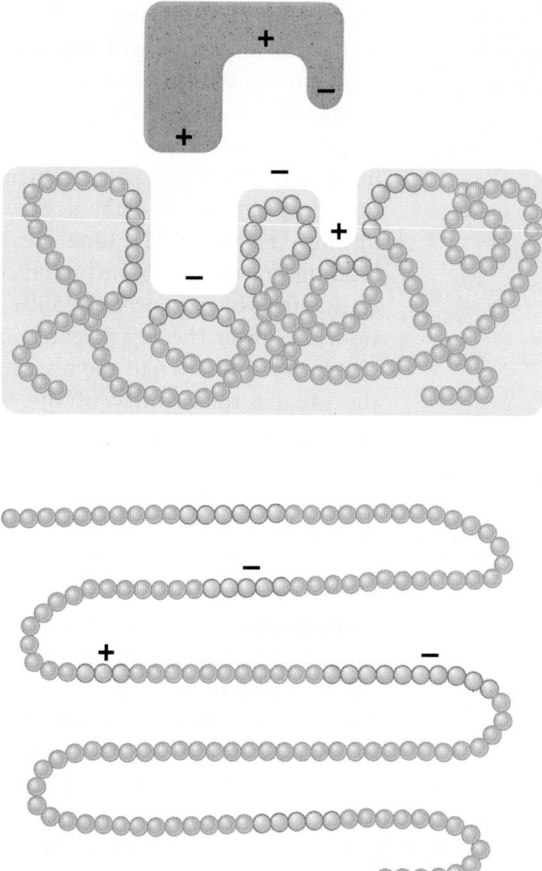

Figure 3.27 Amino acids that interact with the ligand at a binding site need not be at adjacent sites along the polypeptide chain, as indicated in this model showing the three-dimensional folding of a protein. The unfolded polypeptide chain appears at the bottom.

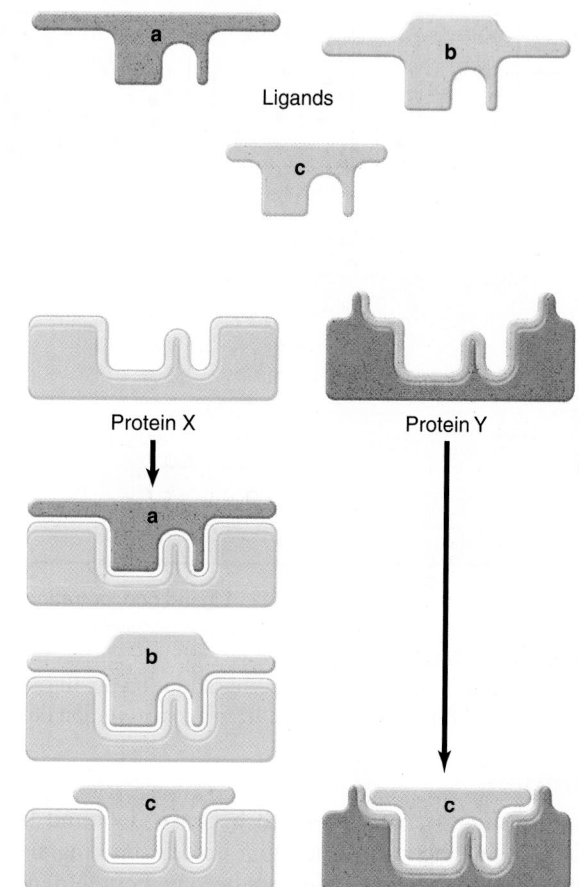

Figure 3.28 Protein X can bind all three ligands, which have similar chemical structures. Protein Y, because of the shape of its binding site, can bind only ligand c. Protein Y, therefore, has a greater chemical specificity than protein X.

PHYSIOLOGICAL INQUIRY

- Assume that both proteins X and Y have been linked with disease in humans. For which protein do you think it would be easier to design therapeutic drugs?

Answer can be found at end of chapter.

leave the protein surface and return to its unbound state. Binding sites that tightly bind a ligand are called high-affinity binding sites; those that weakly bind the ligand are low-affinity binding sites.

Affinity and chemical specificity are two distinct, although closely related, properties of binding sites. Chemical specificity, as we have seen, depends only on the shape of the binding site, whereas affinity depends on the strength of the attraction between the protein and the ligand. Consequently, different proteins may be able to bind the same ligand—that is, may have the same chemical specificity—but may have different affinities for that ligand. For example, a ligand may have a negatively charged ionized group that would bind strongly to a site containing a positively charged amino acid side chain but would bind less strongly to a binding site having the same shape but no positive charge (**Figure 3.29**). In addition, the closer the surfaces of the ligand and binding site are to each other, the stronger the attractions. Thus, the more closely the ligand shape matches the binding site shape, the greater the affinity. In other words, shape can influence affinity as well as chemical specificity. Affinity has great importance in physiology and medicine, because when a protein has a high-affinity binding site for a ligand, very little of the ligand is required to bind to the protein. For example, a therapeutic drug may act by binding to a protein; if the protein has a high-affinity

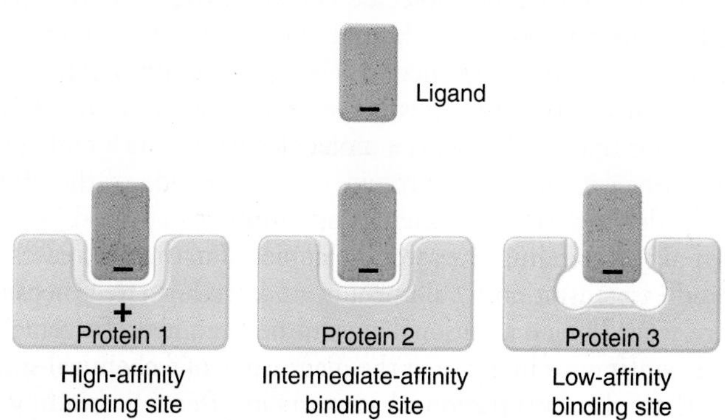

Figure 3.29 Three binding sites with the same chemical specificity but different affinities for a ligand.

binding site for the drug, then only very small quantities of the drug are usually required to treat an illness. This reduces the likelihood of unwanted side effects.

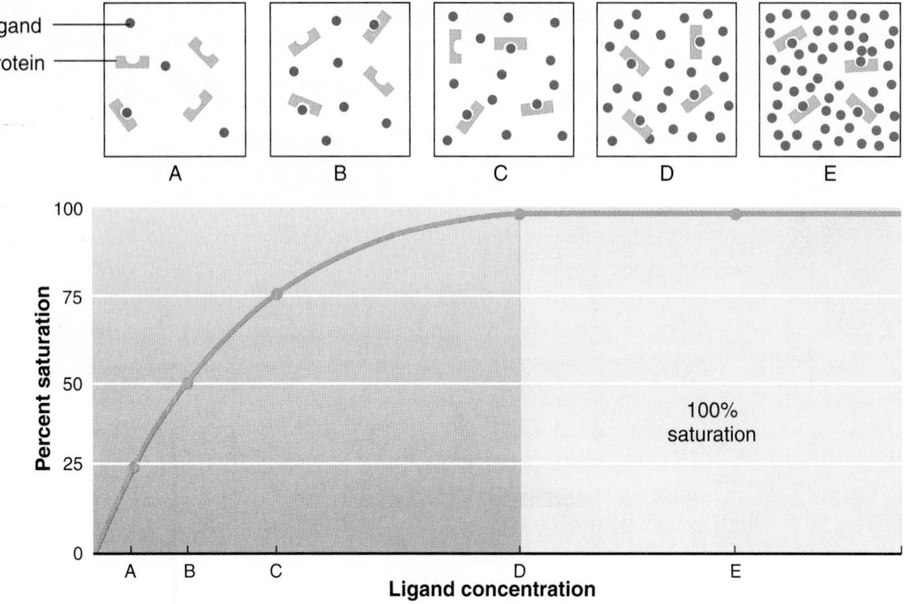

Figure 3.30 Increasing ligand concentration increases the number of binding sites occupied—that is, it increases the percent saturation. At 100% saturation, all the binding sites are occupied, and further increases in ligand concentration do not increase the number bound.

Saturation

An equilibrium is rapidly reached between unbound ligands in solution and their corresponding protein-binding sites. At any instant, some of the free ligands become bound to unoccupied binding sites, and some of the bound ligands are released back into solution. A single binding site is either occupied or unoccupied. The term **saturation** refers to the fraction of total binding sites that are occupied at any given time. When all the binding sites are occupied, the population of binding sites is 100% saturated. When half the available sites are occupied, the system is 50% saturated, and so on. A *single* binding site would also be 50% saturated if it were occupied by a ligand 50% of the time. The percent saturation of a binding site depends upon two factors: (1) the concentration of unbound ligand in the solution, and (2) the affinity of the binding site for the ligand.

The greater the ligand concentration, the greater the probability of a ligand molecule encountering an unoccupied binding site and becoming bound. Therefore, the percent saturation of binding sites increases with increasing ligand concentration until all the sites become occupied (**Figure 3.30**). Assuming that the ligand is a molecule that exerts a biological effect when it binds to a protein, the magnitude of the effect would also increase with increasing numbers of bound ligands until all the binding sites were occupied. Further increases in ligand concentration would produce no further effect because there would be no additional sites to be occupied. To generalize, a continuous increase in the magnitude of a chemical stimulus (ligand concentration) that exerts its effects by binding to proteins will produce an increased biological response until the point at which the protein-binding sites are 100% saturated.

The second factor determining the percent saturation of a binding site is the affinity of the binding site. Collisions between molecules in a solution and a protein containing a bound ligand can dislodge a loosely bound ligand, just as tackling a football player may cause a fumble. If a binding site has a high affinity for a ligand, even a reduced ligand concentration will result in a high degree of saturation because, once bound to the site, the ligand is not easily dislodged. A low-affinity site, on the other hand, requires a higher concentration of ligand to achieve the same degree of saturation (**Figure 3.31**). One measure of binding site affinity is the ligand concentration necessary to produce 50% saturation; the lower the ligand concentration required to bind to half the binding sites, the greater the affinity of the binding site (see Figure 3.31).

Competition

As we have seen, more than one type of ligand can bind to certain binding sites (see Figure 3.28). In such cases, **competition** occurs between the ligands for the same binding site. In other words, the presence of multiple ligands able to bind to the same binding site affects the percentage of binding sites occupied by any one ligand. If two competing ligands, A and B, are present, increasing the concentration of A will increase the amount of A that is bound, thereby decreasing the number of sites available to B and decreasing the amount of B that is bound.

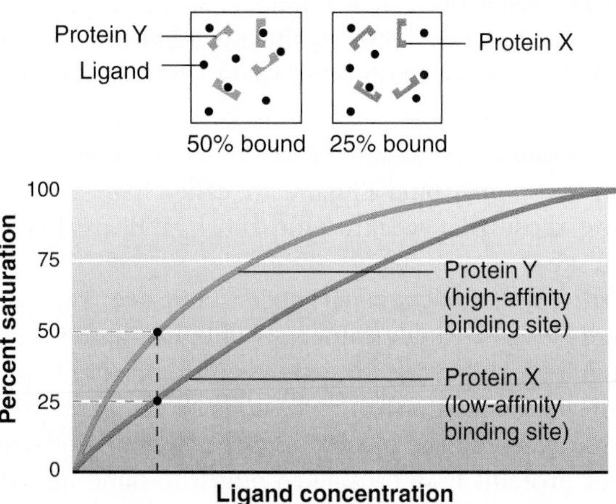

Figure 3.31 When two different proteins, X and Y, are able to bind the same ligand, the protein with the higher-affinity binding site (protein Y) has more bound sites at any given ligand concentration up to 100% saturation.

PHYSIOLOGICAL INQUIRY

- Assume that the function of protein Y in the body is to increase blood pressure by some amount and that of protein X is to decrease blood pressure by about the same amount. These effects only occur, however, if the protein binds the ligand shown in this figure. Predict what might happen if the ligand were administered to a person with normal blood pressure.

Answer can be found at end of chapter.

As a result of competition, the biological effects of one ligand may be diminished by the presence of another. For example, many drugs produce their effects by competing with the body's natural ligands for binding sites. By occupying the binding sites, the drug decreases the amount of natural ligand that can be bound.

3.9 Regulation of Binding Site Characteristics

Because proteins are associated with practically everything that occurs in a cell, the mechanisms for controlling these functions center on the control of protein activity. There are two ways of controlling protein activity: (1) changing protein shape, which alters the binding of ligands; and (2) as described earlier in this chapter, regulating protein synthesis and degradation, which determines the types and amounts of proteins in a cell.

As described in Chapter 2, a protein's shape depends partly on electrical attractions between charged or polarized groups in various regions of the protein. Therefore, a change in the charge distribution along a protein or in the polarity of the molecules immediately surrounding it will alter its shape. The two mechanisms found in cells that selectively alter protein shape are known as allosteric modulation and covalent modulation, though only certain proteins are regulated by modulation. Many proteins are not subject to either of these types of modulation.

Allosteric Modulation

Whenever a ligand binds to a protein, the attracting forces between the ligand and the protein alter the protein's shape. For example, as a ligand approaches a binding site, these attracting forces can cause the surface of the binding site to bend into a shape that more closely approximates the shape of the ligand's surface.

Moreover, as the shape of a binding site changes, it produces changes in the shape of *other* regions of the protein, just as pulling on one end of a rope (the polypeptide chain) causes the other end of the rope to move. Therefore, when a protein contains *two* binding sites, the noncovalent binding of a ligand to one site can alter the shape of the second binding site and, therefore, the binding characteristics of that site. This is termed **allosteric** (other shape) **modulation** (**Figure 3.32a**), and such proteins are known as **allosteric proteins.**

One binding site on an allosteric protein, known as the **functional** (or active) **site,** carries out the protein's physiological function. The other binding site is the **regulatory site.** The ligand that binds to the regulatory site is known as a **modulator molecule,** because its binding allosterically modulates the shape, and therefore the activity, of the functional site. Here again is a physiologically important example of how structure and function are related at the molecular level.

The regulatory site to which modulator molecules bind is the equivalent of a molecular switch that controls the functional site. In some allosteric proteins, the binding of the modulator molecule to the regulatory site turns on the functional site by changing its shape so that it can bind the functional ligand. In other cases, the binding of a modulator molecule turns off the functional site by preventing the functional site from binding its ligand. In still other cases, binding of the modulator molecule may decrease or increase the affinity of the functional site. For example, if the functional site is 75% saturated at a particular ligand concentration, the binding of a modulator molecule that decreases the affinity of the functional site may decrease its saturation to 50%. This concept will be especially important when we consider how carbon dioxide acts as a modulator molecule to lower the affinity of the protein hemoglobin for oxygen (Chapter 13).

To summarize, the activity of a protein can be increased without changing the concentration of either the protein or the functional ligand. By controlling the concentration of the modulator molecule, and therefore the percent saturation of the regulatory site, the functional activity of an allosterically regulated protein can be increased or decreased.

We have described thus far only those interactions between regulatory and functional binding sites. There is, however, a way that functional sites can influence each other in certain proteins. These proteins are composed of more than one polypeptide chain held together by electrical attractions between the chains. There may be only one binding site, a functional binding site, on each chain. The binding of

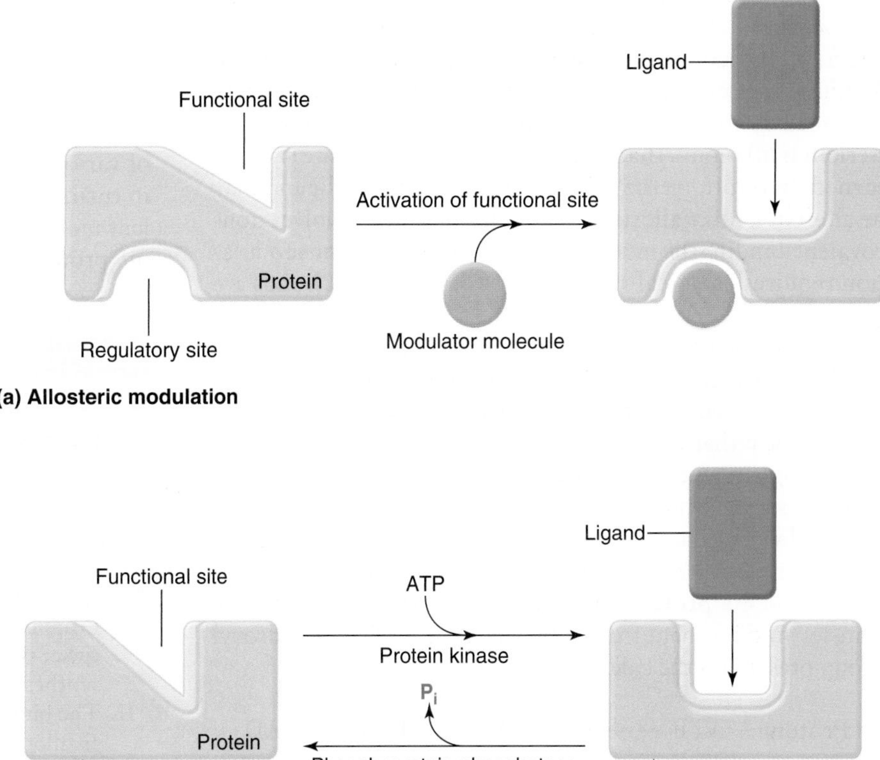

Figure 3.32 (a) Allosteric modulation and (b) covalent modulation of a protein's functional binding site.

a functional ligand to one of the chains, however, can result in an alteration of the functional binding sites in the other chains. This happens because the change in shape of the chain that holds the bound ligand induces a change in the shape of the other chains. The interaction between the functional binding sites of a multimeric (more than one polypeptide chain) protein is known as **cooperativity.** It can result in a progressive increase in the affinity for ligand binding as more and more of the sites become occupied. Hemoglobin again provides a useful example. As described in Chapter 2, hemoglobin is a protein composed of four polypeptide chains, each containing one binding site for oxygen. When oxygen binds to the first binding site, the affinity of the other sites for oxygen increases, and this continues as additional oxygen molecules bind to each polypeptide chain until all four chains have bound an oxygen molecule (see Chapter 13 for a description of this process and its physiological importance).

Covalent Modulation

The second way to alter the shape and therefore the activity of a protein is by the covalent bonding of charged chemical groups to some of the protein's side chains. This is known as **covalent modulation.** In most cases, a phosphate group, which has a net negative charge, is covalently attached by a chemical reaction called **phosphorylation,** in which a phosphate group is transferred from one molecule to another. Phosphorylation of one of the side chains of certain amino acids in a protein introduces a negative charge into that region of the protein. This charge alters the distribution of electrical forces in the protein and produces a change in protein conformation (**Figure 3.32b**). If the conformational change affects a binding site, it changes the binding site's properties. Although the mechanism is completely different, the effects produced by covalent modulation are similar to those of allosteric modulation—that is, a functional binding site may be turned on or off, or the affinity of the site for its ligand may be altered. Unlike allosteric modulation, which involves noncovalent binding of modulator molecules, covalent modulation requires chemical reactions in which covalent bonds are formed.

Most chemical reactions in the body are mediated by a special class of proteins known as enzymes, whose properties will be discussed in Section D of this chapter. For now, suffice it to say that enzymes accelerate the rate at which reactant molecules, called substrates, are converted to different molecules called products. Two enzymes control a protein's activity by covalent modulation: one adds phosphate, and one removes it. Any enzyme that mediates protein phosphorylation is called a **protein kinase.** These enzymes catalyze the transfer of phosphate from a molecule of ATP to a hydroxyl group present on the side chain of certain amino acids:

$$\text{Protein} + \text{ATP} \xrightarrow{\text{protein kinase}} \text{Protein} - PO_4^{2-} + \text{AD}$$

The protein and ATP are the substrates for protein kinase, and the phosphorylated protein and adenosine diphosphate (ADP) are the products of the reaction.

There is also a mechanism for removing the phosphate group and returning the protein to its original shape. This dephosphorylation is accomplished by a second class of enzymes known as **phosphoprotein phosphatases:**

$$\text{Protein} - PO_4^{2-} + H_2O \xrightarrow{\text{phosphoprotein phosphatase}} \text{Protein} + HPO_4^{2-}$$

The activity of the protein will depend on the relative activity of the kinase and phosphatase that controls the extent of the protein's phosphorylation. There are many protein kinases, each with specificities for different proteins, and several kinases may be present in the same cell. The chemical specificities of the phosphoprotein phosphatases are broader; a single enzyme can dephosphorylate many different phosphorylated proteins.

An important interaction between allosteric and covalent modulation results from the fact that protein kinases are themselves allosteric proteins whose activity can be controlled by modulator molecules. Therefore, the process of covalent modulation is itself indirectly regulated by allosteric mechanisms. In addition, some allosteric proteins can also be modified by covalent modulation.

In Chapter 5, we will describe how cell activities can be regulated in response to signals that alter the concentrations of various modulator molecules. These modulator molecules, in turn, alter specific protein activities via allosteric and covalent modulations. **Table 3.4** summarizes the factors influencing protein function.

TABLE 3.4 Factors That Influence Protein Function

I. Changing protein shape
   A. Allosteric modulation
   B. Covalent modulation
      1. Protein kinase activity
      2. Phosphoprotein–phosphatase activity

II. Changing protein concentration
   A. Protein synthesis
   B. Protein degradation

SECTION C SUMMARY

Binding Site Characteristics

I. Ligands bind to proteins at sites with shapes complementary to the ligand shape.
II. Protein-binding sites have the properties of chemical specificity, affinity, saturation, and competition.

Regulation of Binding Site Characteristics

I. Protein function in a cell can be controlled by regulating either the shape of the protein or the amounts of protein synthesized and degraded.
II. The binding of a modulator molecule to the regulatory site on an allosteric protein alters the shape of the functional binding site, thereby altering its binding characteristics and the activity of the protein. The activity of allosteric proteins is regulated by varying the concentrations of their modulator molecules.
III. Protein kinase enzymes catalyze the addition of a phosphate group to the side chains of certain amino acids in a protein, changing the shape of the protein's functional binding site and

thus altering the protein's activity by covalent modulation. A second enzyme is required to remove the phosphate group, returning the protein to its original state.

SECTION C REVIEW QUESTIONS

1. List the four characteristics of a protein-binding site.
2. List the types of forces that hold a ligand on a protein surface.
3. What characteristics of a binding site determine its chemical specificity?
4. Under what conditions can a single binding site have a chemical specificity for more than one type of ligand?
5. What characteristics of a binding site determine its affinity for a ligand?
6. What two factors determine the percent saturation of a binding site?
7. How is the activity of an allosteric protein modulated?
8. How does regulation of protein activity by covalent modulation differ from that by allosteric modulation?

SECTION C KEY TERMS

affinity 68
allosteric modulation 71
allosteric protein 71
binding site 68
chemical specificity 68
competition 70
cooperativity 72
covalent modulation 72
functional site 71
ligand 68
modulator molecule 71
phosphoprotein phosphatase 72
phosphorylation 72
protein kinase 72
regulatory site 71
saturation 70

SECTION D Enzymes and Chemical Energy

Thus far, we have discussed the synthesis and regulation of proteins. In this section, we describe some of the major functions of proteins, specifically those that relate to facilitating chemical reactions.

Thousands of chemical reactions occur each instant throughout the body; this coordinated process of chemical change is termed *metabolism* (Greek, "change"). **Metabolism** involves the synthesis and breakdown of organic molecules required for cell structure and function and the release of chemical energy used for cell functions. The synthesis of organic molecules by cells is called **anabolism,** and their breakdown, **catabolism.** For example, the synthesis of a triglyceride is an anabolic reaction, whereas the breakdown of a triglyceride to glycerol and fatty acids is a catabolic reaction.

The organic molecules of the body undergo continuous transformation as some molecules are broken down while others of the same type are being synthesized. Molecularly, no person is the same at noon as at 8:00 A.M. because during even this short period, some of the body's structure has been broken down and replaced with newly synthesized molecules. In a healthy adult, the body's composition is in a steady state in which the anabolic and catabolic rates for the synthesis and breakdown of most molecules are equal. In other words, homeostasis is achieved as a result of a balance between anabolism and catabolism.

3.10 Chemical Reactions

Chemical reactions involve (1) the breaking of chemical bonds in reactant molecules, followed by (2) the making of new chemical bonds to form the product molecules. Take, for example, a chemical reaction that occurs in the blood in the lungs, which permits the lungs to rid the body of carbon dioxide. In the following reaction, carbonic acid is transformed into carbon dioxide and water. Two of the chemical bonds in carbonic acid are broken, and the product molecules are formed by establishing two new bonds between different pairs of atoms:

$$\underset{\text{broken}}{\mathrm{H{-}O}}{-}\overset{\mathrm{O}\atop\|}{\underset{\text{broken}}{\mathrm{C{-}O}}}{-}\mathrm{H} \longrightarrow \underset{\text{formed}}{\mathrm{O{=}}}\overset{\mathrm{O}\atop\|}{\mathrm{C}} + \underset{\text{formed}}{\mathrm{H{-}O}}{-}\mathrm{H}$$

$$\underset{\text{carbonic acid}}{H_2CO_3} \longrightarrow \underset{\text{carbon dioxide}}{CO_2} + \underset{\text{water}}{H_2O} + \text{Energy}$$

Because the energy contents of the reactants and products are usually different, and because it is a fundamental law of physics that energy can neither be created nor destroyed, energy must either be added or released during most chemical reactions. For example, the breakdown of carbonic acid into carbon dioxide and water releases energy because carbonic acid has a higher energy content than the sum of the energy contents of carbon dioxide and water.

The released energy takes the form of heat, the energy of increased molecular motion, which is measured in units of calories. One **calorie** (1 cal) is the amount of heat required to raise the temperature of 1 g of water 1°C. Energies associated with most chemical reactions are several thousand calories per mole and are reported as **kilocalories** (1 kcal = 1000 cal; 1 kcal is sometimes written as 1 Calorie with a capital "C").

Determinants of Reaction Rates

The rate of a chemical reaction (in other words, how many molecules of product form per unit of time) can be determined by measuring the change in the concentration of reactants or products per unit of time. The faster the product concentration increases or the reactant concentration decreases, the greater the rate of the reaction. Four factors (**Table 3.5**) influence the reaction rate: reactant concentration, activation energy, temperature, and the presence of a catalyst.

The lower the concentration of reactants, the slower the reaction simply because there are fewer molecules available to react and the likelihood of any two reactants encountering

TABLE 3.5	Determinants of Chemical Reaction Rates
Reactant concentrations (greater concentrations: faster reaction rate)	
Activation energy (greater activation energy: slower reaction rate)	
Temperature (higher temperature: faster reaction rate)	
Catalyst (presence of catalyst: faster reaction rate)	

each other is low. Conversely, the higher the concentration of reactants, the faster the reaction rate.

Given the same initial concentrations of reactants, however, not all reactions occur at the same rate. Each type of chemical reaction has its own characteristic rate, which depends upon what is called the activation energy for the reaction. For a chemical reaction to occur, reactant molecules must acquire enough energy—the **activation energy**—to overcome the mutual repulsion of the electrons surrounding the atoms in each molecule. The activation energy does not affect the difference in energy content between the reactants and final products because the activation energy is released when the products are formed.

How do reactants acquire activation energy? In most of the metabolic reactions we will be considering, the reactants obtain activation energy when they collide with other molecules. If the activation energy required for a reaction is large, then the probability of a given reactant molecule acquiring this amount of energy will be small, and the reaction rate will be slow. Thus, the greater the activation energy required, the slower the rate of a chemical reaction.

Temperature is the third factor influencing reaction rates. The higher the temperature, the faster molecules move and the greater their impact when they collide. Therefore, one reason that increasing the temperature increases a reaction rate is that reactants have a better chance of acquiring sufficient activation energy such that when they collide, bonds can be broken or formed. In addition, faster-moving molecules collide more often.

A **catalyst** is a substance or molecule that interacts with one or more reactants by altering the distribution of energy between the chemical bonds of the reactants, resulting in a decrease in the activation energy required to transform the reactants into products. Catalysts may also bind two reactants and thereby bring them in close proximity and in an orientation that facilitates their interaction; this, too, reduces the activation energy. Because less activation energy is required, a reaction will proceed at a faster rate in the presence of a catalyst. The chemical composition of a catalyst is not altered by the reaction, so *a single catalyst molecule can act over and over again to catalyze the conversion of many reactant molecules to products.* Furthermore, a catalyst does not alter the difference in the energy contents of the reactants and products.

Reversible and Irreversible Reactions

Every chemical reaction is, in theory, reversible. Reactants are converted to products (we will call this a "forward reaction"), and products are converted to reactants (a "reverse reaction"). The overall reaction is a **reversible reaction:**

$$\text{Reactants} \underset{\text{reverse}}{\overset{\text{forward}}{\rightleftharpoons}} \text{Products}$$

As a reaction progresses, the rate of the forward reaction decreases as the concentration of reactants decreases. Simultaneously, the rate of the reverse reaction increases as the concentration of the product molecules increases. Eventually, the reaction will reach a state of **chemical equilibrium** in which the forward and reverse reaction rates are equal. At this point, there will be no further change in the concentrations of reactants or products even though reactants will continue to be converted into products and products converted into reactants.

Consider our previous example in which carbonic acid breaks down into carbon dioxide and water. The products of this reaction, carbon dioxide and water, can also recombine to form carbonic acid. This occurs outside the lungs and is a means for safely transporting CO_2 in the blood in a nongaseous state.

$$CO_2 + H_2O + \text{Energy} \rightleftharpoons H_2CO_3$$

Carbonic acid has a greater energy content than the sum of the energies contained in carbon dioxide and water; therefore, energy must be added to the latter molecules to form carbonic acid. This energy is not activation energy but is an integral part of the energy balance. This energy can be obtained, along with the activation energy, through collisions with other molecules.

When chemical equilibrium has been reached, the concentration of products does not need to be equal to the concentration of reactants even though the forward and reverse reaction rates are equal. The ratio of product concentration to reactant concentration at equilibrium depends upon the amount of energy released (or added) during the reaction. The greater the energy released, the smaller the probability that the product molecules will be able to obtain this energy and undergo the reverse reaction to re-form reactants. Therefore, in such a case, the ratio of product concentration to reactant concentration at chemical equilibrium will be large. If there is no difference in the energy contents of reactants and products, their concentrations will be equal at equilibrium.

Thus, although all chemical reactions are reversible to some extent, reactions that release large quantities of energy are said to be **irreversible reactions** because almost all of the reactant molecules are converted to product molecules when chemical equilibrium is reached. The energy released in a reaction determines the degree to which the reaction is reversible or irreversible. This energy is not the activation energy and it does not determine the reaction rate, which is governed by the four factors discussed earlier. The characteristics of reversible and irreversible reactions are summarized in **Table 3.6**.

Law of Mass Action

The concentrations of reactants and products play a very important role in determining not only the rates of the forward and reverse reactions but also the direction in which the *net* reaction proceeds—whether reactants or products are accumulating at a given time.

TABLE 3.6	Characteristics of Reversible and Irreversible Chemical Reactions
Reversible Reactions	A + B $\rightleftharpoons$ C + D + Small amount of energy At chemical equilibrium, product concentrations are only slightly higher than reactant concentrations.
Irreversible Reactions	E + F $\longrightarrow$ G + H + Large amount of energy At chemical equilibrium, almost all reactant molecules have been converted to product.

Consider the following reversible reaction that has reached chemical equilibrium:

$$\underset{\text{Reactants}}{A + B} \underset{\text{reverse}}{\overset{\text{forward}}{\rightleftharpoons}} \underset{\text{Products}}{C + D}$$

If at this point we increase the concentration of one of the reactants, the rate of the forward reaction will increase and lead to increased product formation. In contrast, increasing the concentration of one of the product molecules will drive the reaction in the reverse direction, increasing the formation of reactants. The direction in which the net reaction is proceeding can also be altered by *decreasing* the concentration of one of the participants. Therefore, decreasing the concentration of one of the products drives the net reaction in the forward direction because it decreases the rate of the reverse reaction without changing the rate of the forward reaction.

These effects of reaction and product concentrations on the direction in which the net reaction proceeds are known as the **law of mass action.** Mass action is often a major determining factor controlling the direction in which metabolic pathways proceed because reactions in the body seldom come to chemical equilibrium. More typically, new reactant molecules are added and product molecules are simultaneously removed by other reactions.

3.11 Enzymes

Most of the chemical reactions in the body, if carried out in a test tube with only reactants and products present, would proceed at very slow rates because they have large activation energies. To achieve the fast reaction rates observed in living organisms, catalysts must lower the activation energies. These particular catalysts are called **enzymes.** Enzymes are protein molecules, so an enzyme can be defined as a protein catalyst. (Although some RNA molecules possess catalytic activity, the number of reactions they catalyze is very small, so we will restrict the term *enzyme* to protein catalysts.)

To function, an enzyme must come into contact with reactants, which are called **substrates** in the case of enzyme-mediated reactions. The substrate becomes bound to the enzyme, forming an enzyme–substrate complex, which then breaks down to release products and enzyme. The reaction between enzyme and substrate can be written:

$$\underset{\text{Substrate}}{S} + \underset{\text{Enzyme}}{E} \rightleftharpoons \underset{\text{Enzyme–substrate complex}}{ES} \rightleftharpoons \underset{\text{Product}}{P} + \underset{\text{Enzyme}}{E}$$

At the end of the reaction, the enzyme is free to undergo the same reaction with additional substrate molecules. The overall effect is to accelerate the conversion of substrate into product, with the enzyme acting as a catalyst. An enzyme increases both the forward and reverse rates of a reaction and thus does not change the chemical equilibrium that is finally reached.

The interaction between substrate and enzyme has all the characteristics described previously for the binding of a ligand to a binding site on a protein—specificity, affinity, competition, and saturation. The region of the enzyme the substrate binds to is known as the enzyme's **active site** (a term equivalent to "binding site"). The shape of the enzyme in the region of the active site provides the basis for the enzyme's chemical specificity. Two models have been proposed to describe the interaction of an enzyme with its substrate(s). In one, the enzyme and substrate(s) fit together in a "lock-and-key" configuration. In another model, the substrate itself induces a shape change in the active site of the enzyme, which results in a highly specific binding interaction ("induced-fit model"), a good example of the dependence of function on structure at the protein level (**Figure 3.33**).

A typical cell expresses several thousand different enzymes, each capable of catalyzing a different chemical reaction. Enzymes are generally named by adding the suffix *-ase* to the name of either the substrate or the type of reaction the enzyme catalyzes. For example, the reaction in which carbonic acid is broken down into carbon dioxide and water is catalyzed by the enzyme **carbonic anhydrase.**

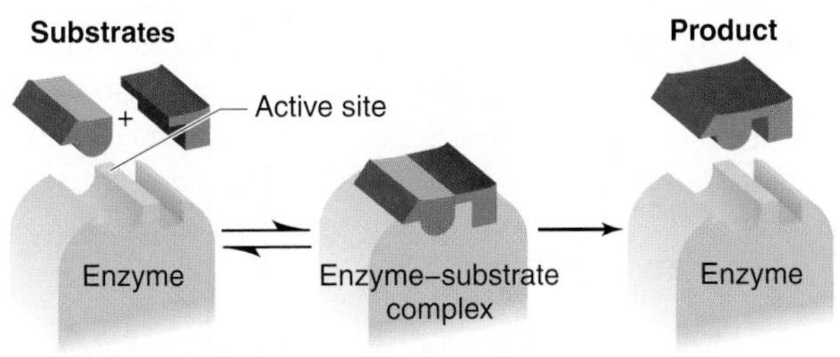

(a) Lock-and-key model

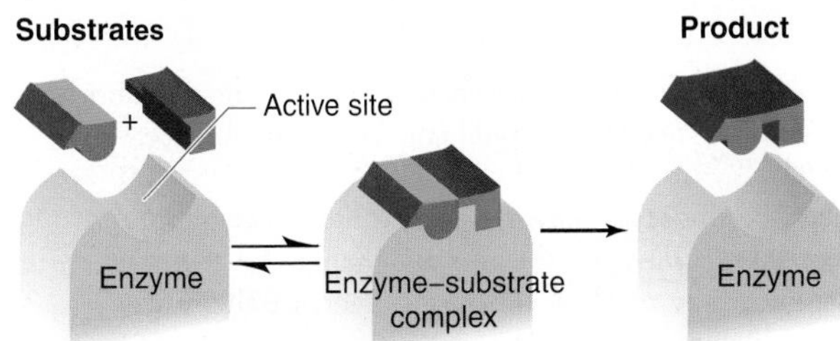

(b) Induced-fit model

Figure 3.33 APIR Binding of substrate to the active site of an enzyme catalyzes the formation of products. From M. S. Silberberg, *Chemistry: The Molecular Nature of Matter and Change*, 3rd ed., p. 701. The McGraw-Hill Companies, Inc., New York.

The catalytic activity of an enzyme can be extremely large. For example, one molecule of carbonic anhydrase can catalyze the conversion of about 100,000 substrate molecules to products in one second! The major characteristics of enzymes are listed in **Table 3.7**.

Cofactors

Many enzymes are inactive without small amounts of other substances known as **cofactors.** In some cases, the cofactor is a trace metal, such as magnesium, iron, zinc, or copper. Binding of one of the metals to an enzyme alters the enzyme's conformation so that it can interact with the substrate; this is a form of allosteric modulation. Because only a few enzyme molecules need be present to catalyze the conversion of large amounts of substrate to product, very small quantities of these trace metals are sufficient to maintain enzyme activity.

In other cases, the cofactor is an organic molecule that directly participates as one of the substrates in the reaction, in which case the cofactor is termed a **coenzyme.** Enzymes that require coenzymes catalyze reactions in which a few atoms (for example, hydrogen, acetyl, or methyl groups) are either removed from or added to a substrate. For example,

$$\text{R—2H} + \text{Coenzyme} \xrightarrow{\text{Enzyme}} \text{R} + \text{Coenzyme—2H}$$

What distinguishes a coenzyme from an ordinary substrate is the fate of the coenzyme. In our example, the two hydrogen atoms that transfer to the coenzyme can then be transferred from the coenzyme to another substrate with the aid of a second enzyme. This second reaction converts the coenzyme back to its original form so that it becomes available to accept two more hydrogen atoms. A single coenzyme molecule can act over and over again to transfer molecular fragments from one reaction to another. Therefore, as with metallic cofactors, only small quantities of coenzymes are necessary to maintain the enzymatic reactions in which they participate.

Coenzymes are derived from several members of a special class of nutrients known as **vitamins.** For example, the coenzymes **NAD^+** (nicotinamide adenine dinucleotide) and **FAD** (flavin adenine dinucleotide) are derived from the B vitamins niacin and riboflavin, respectively. As we will see, they play major roles in energy metabolism by transferring hydrogen from one substrate to another.

TABLE 3.7 Characteristics of Enzymes
An enzyme undergoes no net chemical change as a consequence of the reaction it catalyzes.
The binding of substrate to an enzyme's active site has all the characteristics—chemical specificity, affinity, competition, and saturation—of a ligand binding to a protein.
An enzyme increases the rate of a chemical reaction but does not cause a reaction to occur that would not occur in its absence.
Some enzymes increase both the forward and reverse rates of a chemical reaction and thus do not change the chemical equilibrium finally reached. They only increase the rate at which equilibrium is achieved.
An enzyme lowers the activation energy of a reaction but does not alter the net amount of energy that is added to or released by the reactants in the course of the reaction.

3.12 Regulation of Enzyme-Mediated Reactions

The rate of an enzyme-mediated reaction depends on substrate concentration and on the concentration and activity (defined later in this section) of the enzyme that catalyzes the reaction. Body temperature is normally nearly constant, so changes in temperature do not directly alter the rates of metabolic reactions. Increases in body temperature can occur during a fever, however, and around muscle tissue during exercise; such increases in temperature increase the rates of all metabolic reactions, including enzyme-catalyzed ones, in the affected tissues.

Substrate Concentration

Substrate concentration may be altered as a result of factors that alter the supply of a substrate from outside a cell. For example, there may be changes in its blood concentration due to changes in diet or the rate of substrate absorption from the intestinal tract. Intracellular substrate concentration can also be altered by cellular reactions that either utilize the substrate, and thus decrease its concentration, or synthesize the substrate, and thereby increase its concentration.

The rate of an enzyme-mediated reaction increases as the substrate concentration increases, as illustrated in **Figure 3.34**, until it reaches a maximal rate, which remains constant despite further increases in substrate concentration. The maximal rate is reached when the enzyme becomes saturated with substrate—that is, when the active binding site of every enzyme molecule is occupied by a substrate molecule.

Enzyme Concentration

At any substrate concentration, including saturating concentrations, the rate of an enzyme-mediated reaction can be increased by increasing the enzyme concentration. In most metabolic reactions, the substrate concentration is much greater than the concentration of enzyme available to catalyze the reaction. Therefore, if the number of enzyme molecules is doubled,

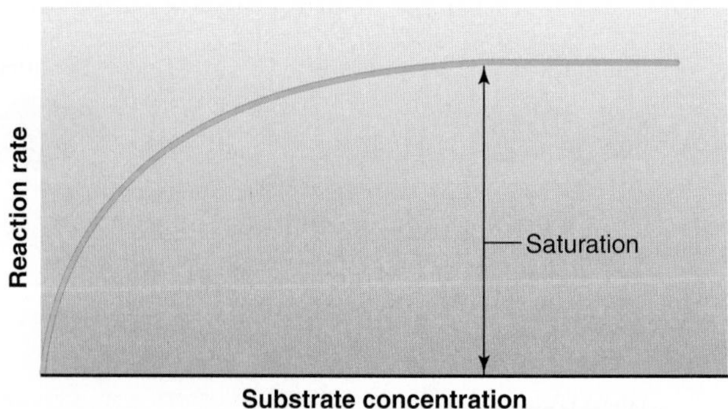

Figure 3.34 Rate of an enzyme-catalyzed reaction as a function of substrate concentration.

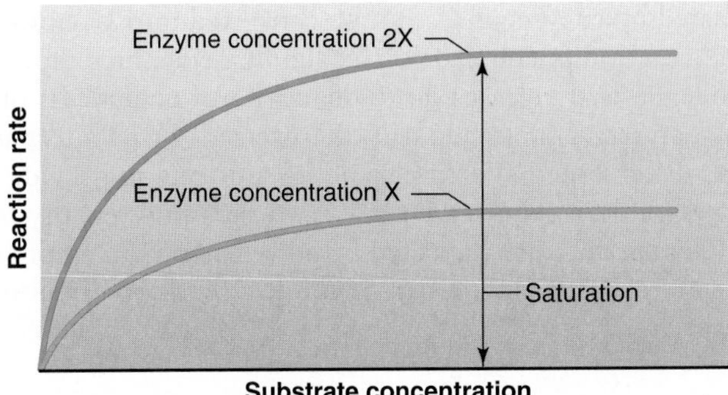

Figure 3.35 Rate of an enzyme-catalyzed reaction as a function of substrate concentration at two enzyme concentrations, X and 2X. Enzyme concentration 2X is twice the enzyme concentration of X, resulting in a reaction that proceeds twice as fast at any substrate concentration.

twice as many active sites will be available to bind substrate and twice as many substrate molecules will be converted to product (**Figure 3.35**). Certain reactions proceed faster in some cells than in others because more enzyme molecules are present.

To change the concentration of an enzyme, either the rate of enzyme synthesis or the rate of enzyme breakdown must be altered. Because enzymes are proteins, this involves changing the rates of protein synthesis or breakdown.

Enzyme Activity

In addition to changing the rate of enzyme-mediated reactions by changing the *concentration* of either substrate or enzyme, the rate can be altered by changing **enzyme activity.** A change in enzyme activity occurs when either allosteric or covalent modulation alters the properties (for example, the structure) of the enzyme's active site. Such modulation alters the rate at which the binding site converts substrate to product, the affinity of the binding site for substrate, or both.

Figure 3.36 illustrates the effect of increasing the affinity of an enzyme's active site without changing the substrate or enzyme concentration. If the substrate concentration is less than the saturating concentration, the increased affinity of the enzyme's binding site results in an increased number of active sites bound to substrate and, consequently, an increase in the reaction rate.

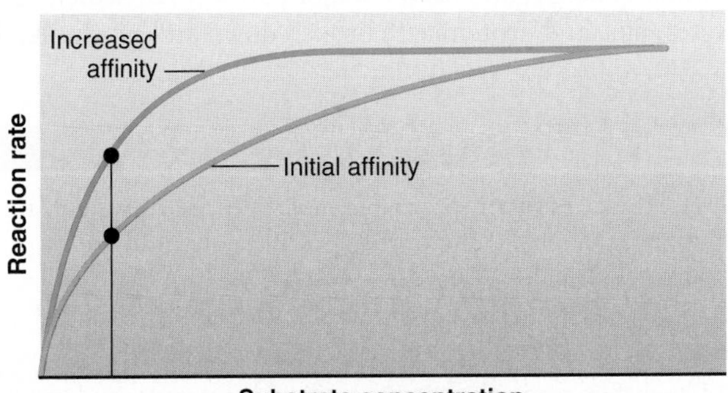

Figure 3.36 At a constant substrate concentration, increasing the affinity of an enzyme for its substrate by allosteric or covalent modulation increases the rate of the enzyme-mediated reaction. Note that increasing the enzyme's affinity does not increase the *maximal* rate of the enzyme-mediated reaction.

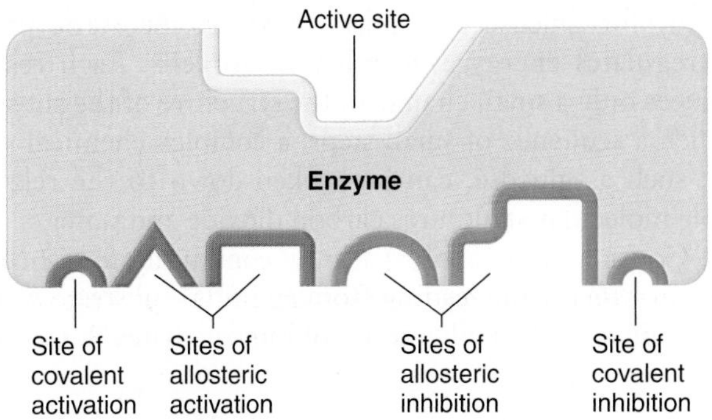

Figure 3.37 APIR On a single enzyme, multiple sites can modulate enzyme activity, and therefore the reaction rate, by allosteric and covalent activation or inhibition.

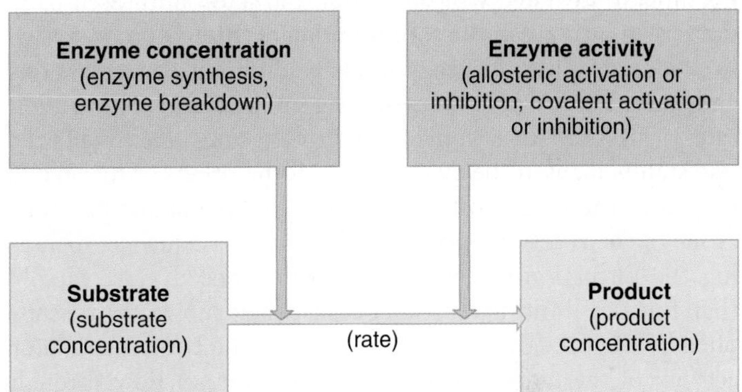

Figure 3.38 Factors that affect the rate of enzyme-mediated reactions.

PHYSIOLOGICAL INQUIRY

- What would happen in an enzyme-mediated reaction if the product formed was immediately used up or converted to another product by the cell?

Answer can be found at end of chapter.

The regulation of metabolism through the control of enzyme activity is an extremely complex process because, in many cases, more than one agent can alter the activity of an enzyme (**Figure 3.37**). The modulator molecules that allosterically alter enzyme activities may be product molecules of other cellular reactions. The result is that the overall rates of metabolism can adjust to meet various metabolic demands. In contrast, covalent modulation of enzyme activity is mediated by protein kinase enzymes that are themselves activated by various chemical signals the cell receives from, for example, a hormone.

Figure 3.38 summarizes the factors that regulate the rate of an enzyme-mediated reaction.

3.13 Multienzyme Reactions

The sequence of enzyme-mediated reactions leading to the formation of a particular product is known as a **metabolic pathway.** For example, the 19 reactions that break glucose down to carbon dioxide and water constitute the metabolic pathway for glucose catabolism, a key homeostatic process that regulates energy availability in all cells. Each reaction produces only a small change in the structure of the substrate. By such a sequence of small steps, a complex chemical structure, such as glucose, can be broken down to the relatively simple molecular structures carbon dioxide and water.

Consider a metabolic pathway containing four enzymes (e_1, e_2, e_3, and e_4) and leading from an initial substrate A to the end-product E, through a series of intermediates B, C, and D:

$$A \overset{e_1}{\rightleftharpoons} B \overset{e_2}{\rightleftharpoons} C \overset{e_3}{\rightleftharpoons} D \overset{e_4}{\longrightarrow} E$$

The irreversibility of the last reaction is of no consequence for the moment. By mass action, increasing the concentration of A will lead to an increase in the concentration of B (provided e_1 is not already saturated with substrate), and so on until eventually there is an increase in the concentration of the end-product E.

Because different enzymes have different concentrations and activities, it would be extremely unlikely that the reaction rates of all these steps would be exactly the same. Consequently, one step is likely to be slower than all the others. This step is known as the **rate-limiting reaction** in a metabolic pathway. None of the reactions that occur later in the sequence, including the formation of end product, can proceed more rapidly than the rate-limiting reaction because their substrates are supplied by the previous steps. By regulating the concentration or activity of the rate-limiting enzyme, the rate of flow through the whole pathway can be increased or decreased. Thus, it is not necessary to alter all the enzymes in a metabolic pathway to control the rate at which the end product is produced.

Rate-limiting enzymes are often the sites of allosteric or covalent regulation. For example, if enzyme e_2 is rate-limiting in the pathway just described, and if the end-product E inhibits the activity of e_2, **end-product inhibition** occurs (**Figure 3.39**). As the concentration of the product increases, the inhibition of further product formation increases. Such inhibition, which is a form of negative feedback (Chapter 1), frequently occurs in synthetic pathways in which the formation of end product is effectively shut down when it is not being utilized. This prevents unnecessary excessive accumulation of the end product and contributes to the homeostatic balance of the product.

Control of enzyme activity also can be critical for *reversing* a metabolic pathway. Consider the pathway we have been discussing, ignoring the presence of end-product inhibition of enzyme e_2. The pathway consists of three reversible reactions mediated by e_1, e_2, and e_3, followed by an irreversible reaction

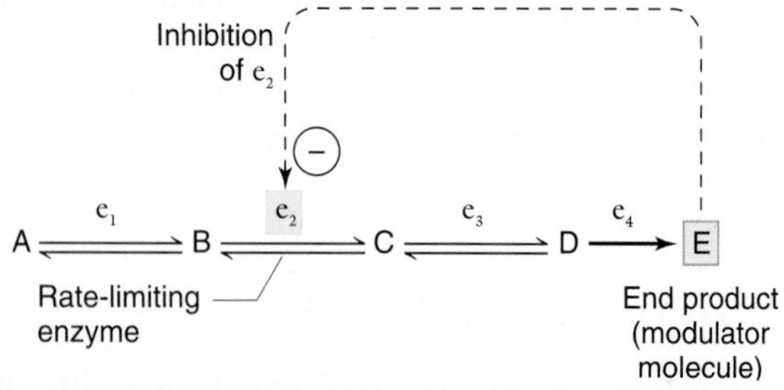

Figure 3.39 End-product inhibition of the rate-limiting enzyme in a metabolic pathway. The end-product E becomes the modulator molecule that produces inhibition of enzyme e_2.

mediated by enzyme e_4. E can be converted into D, however, if the reaction is coupled to the simultaneous breakdown of a molecule that releases large quantities of energy. In other words, an irreversible step can be "reversed" by an alternative route, using a second enzyme and its substrate to provide the large amount of required energy. Two such high-energy irreversible reactions are indicated by bowed arrows to emphasize that two separate enzymes are involved in the two directions:

$$A \overset{e_1}{\rightleftharpoons} B \overset{e_2}{\rightleftharpoons} C \overset{e_3}{\rightleftharpoons} D \underset{e_5 \;(X \rightarrow Y)}{\overset{e_4}{\rightleftarrows}} E$$

The direction of flow through the pathway can be regulated by controlling the concentration and/or activities of e_4 and e_5. If e_4 is activated and e_5 inhibited, the flow will proceed from A to E; whereas inhibition of e_4 and activation of e_5 will produce flow from E to A.

Another situation involving the differential control of several enzymes arises when there is a branch in a metabolic pathway. A single metabolite C may be the substrate for more than one enzyme, as illustrated by the pathway:

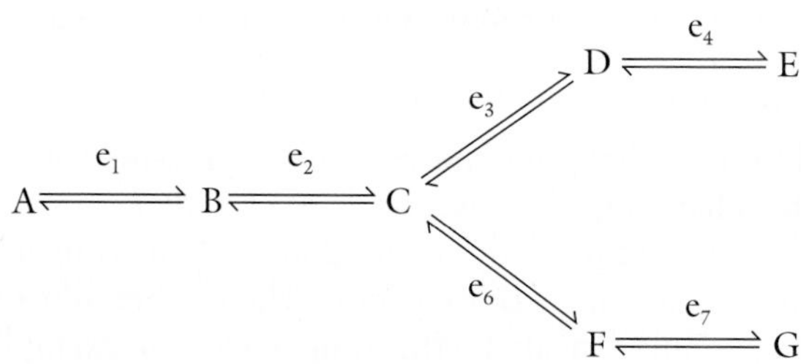

Altering the concentration and/or activities of e_3 and e_6 regulates the flow of metabolite C through the two branches of the pathway.

Considering the thousands of reactions that occur in the body and the permutations and combinations of possible control points, the overall result is staggering. The details of regulating the many metabolic pathways at the enzymatic level are beyond the scope of this book. In the remainder of this chapter, we consider only (1) the overall characteristics of the pathways by which cells obtain energy; and (2) the major pathways by which carbohydrates, fats, and proteins are broken down and synthesized.

SECTION D SUMMARY

In adults, the rates at which organic molecules are continuously synthesized (anabolism) and broken down (catabolism) are approximately equal.

Chemical Reactions

I. The difference in the energy content of reactants and products is the amount of energy (measured in calories) released or added during a reaction.

II. The energy released during a chemical reaction is either released as heat or transferred to other molecules.

III. The four factors that can alter the rate of a chemical reaction are listed in Table 3.5.

IV. The activation energy required to initiate the breaking of chemical bonds in a reaction is usually acquired through collisions between molecules.
V. Catalysts increase the rate of a reaction by lowering the activation energy.
VI. The characteristics of reversible and irreversible reactions are listed in Table 3.6.
VII. The net direction in which a reaction proceeds can be altered, according to the law of mass action, by increases or decreases in the concentrations of reactants or products.

Enzymes

I. Nearly all chemical reactions in the body are catalyzed by enzymes, the characteristics of which are summarized in Table 3.7.
II. Some enzymes require small concentrations of cofactors for activity.
   a. The binding of trace metal cofactors maintains the conformation of the enzyme's binding site so that it is able to bind substrate.
   b. Coenzymes, derived from vitamins, transfer small groups of atoms from one substrate to another. The coenzyme is regenerated in the course of these reactions and can do its work over and over again.

Regulation of Enzyme-Mediated Reactions

I. The rates of enzyme-mediated reactions can be altered by changes in temperature, substrate concentration, enzyme concentration, and enzyme activity. Enzyme activity is altered by allosteric or covalent modulation.

Multienzyme Reactions

I. The rate of product formation in a metabolic pathway can be controlled by allosteric or covalent modulation of the enzyme mediating the rate-limiting reaction in the pathway. The end product often acts as a modulator molecule, inhibiting the rate-limiting enzyme's activity.
II. An "irreversible" step in a metabolic pathway can be reversed by the use of two enzymes, one for the forward reaction and one for the reverse direction via another, energy-yielding reaction.

SECTION D REVIEW QUESTIONS

1. How do molecules acquire the activation energy required for a chemical reaction?
2. List the four factors that influence the rate of a chemical reaction and state whether increasing the factor will increase or decrease the rate of the reaction.
3. What characteristics of a chemical reaction make it reversible or irreversible?
4. List five characteristics of enzymes.
5. What is the difference between a cofactor and a coenzyme?
6. From what class of nutrients are coenzymes derived?
7. Why are small concentrations of coenzymes sufficient to maintain enzyme activity?
8. List three ways to alter the rate of an enzyme-mediated reaction.
9. How can an "irreversible step" in a metabolic pathway be reversed?

SECTION D KEY TERMS

activation energy 74
active site 75
anabolism 73
calorie 73
carbonic anhydrase 75
catabolism 73
catalyst 74
chemical equilibrium 74
coenzyme 76
cofactor 76
end-product inhibition 78
enzyme 75
enzyme activity 77
FAD 76
irreversible reaction 74
kilocalorie 73
law of mass action 75
metabolic pathway 77
metabolism 73
NAD^+ 76
rate-limiting reaction 78
reversible reaction 74
substrate 75
vitamin 76

SECTION E Metabolic Pathways

Enzymes are involved in many important physiological reactions that together promote a homeostatic state. For example, enzymes are vital for the regulated production of cellular energy (ATP), which, in turn, is needed for such widespread events as muscle contraction, nerve cell function, and chemical signal transduction.

Cells use three distinct but linked metabolic pathways to transfer the energy released from the breakdown of nutrient molecules to ATP. They are known as (1) glycolysis, (2) the Krebs cycle, and (3) oxidative phosphorylation (**Figure 3.40**). In the following section, we will describe the major characteristics of these three pathways, including the location of the pathway enzymes in a cell, the relative contribution of each pathway to ATP production, the sites of carbon dioxide formation and oxygen utilization, and the key molecules that enter and leave each pathway. Later, in Chapter 16, we will refer to these pathways when we describe the physiology of energy balance in the human body.

Several facts should be noted in Figure 3.40. First, glycolysis operates only on carbohydrates. Second, all the categories of macromolecular nutrients—carbohydrates, fats, and proteins—contribute to ATP production via the Krebs cycle and oxidative phosphorylation. Third, mitochondria are the sites of the Krebs cycle and oxidative phosphorylation. Finally, one important generalization to keep in mind is that glycolysis can occur in either the presence or absence of oxygen, whereas both the Krebs cycle and oxidative phosphorylation require oxygen.

3.14 Cellular Energy Transfer

Glycolysis

Glycolysis (from the Greek *glycos*, "sugar," and *lysis*, "breakdown") is a pathway that partially catabolizes carbohydrates, primarily glucose. It consists of 10 enzymatic reactions that convert a six-carbon molecule of glucose into two three-carbon

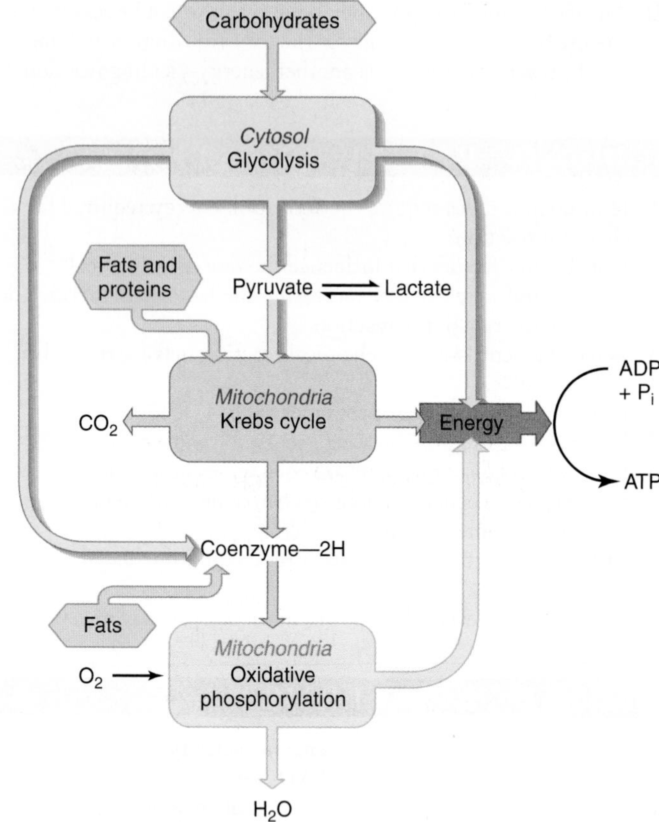

Figure 3.40 APIR Pathways linking the energy released from the catabolism of nutrient molecules to the formation of ATP.

molecules of **pyruvate,** the ionized form of pyruvic acid (**Figure 3.41**). The reactions produce a net gain of two molecules of ATP and four atoms of hydrogen, two transferred to NAD^+ and two released as hydrogen ions:

$$\text{Glucose} + 2\ \text{ADP} + 2\ P_i + 2\ \text{NAD}^+ \longrightarrow 2\ \text{Pyruvate} + 2\ \text{ATP} + 2\ \text{NADH} + 2\ H^+ + 2\ H_2O$$

These 10 reactions, *none of which utilizes molecular oxygen,* take place in the cytosol. Note (see Figure 3.41) that all the intermediates between glucose and the end product pyruvate contain one or more ionized phosphate groups. Plasma membranes are impermeable to such highly ionized molecules; therefore, these molecules remain trapped within the cell.

The early steps in glycolysis (reactions 1 and 3) each *use,* rather than produce, one molecule of ATP to form phosphorylated intermediates. In addition, note that reaction 4 splits a six-carbon intermediate into two three-carbon molecules and reaction 5 converts one of these three-carbon molecules into the other. Thus, at the end of reaction 5, we have two molecules of 3-phosphoglyceraldehyde derived from one molecule of glucose. Keep in mind, then, that from this point on, *two* molecules of each intermediate are involved.

The first formation of ATP in glycolysis occurs during reaction 7, in which a phosphate group is transferred to ADP to form ATP. Because two intermediates exist at this point, reaction 7 produces two molecules of ATP, one from each intermediate. In this reaction, the mechanism of forming ATP is known as **substrate-level phosphorylation** because the phosphate group is transferred from a substrate molecule to ADP.

A similar substrate-level phosphorylation of ADP occurs during reaction 10, in which again two molecules of ATP are formed. Thus, reactions 7 and 10 generate a total of four molecules of ATP for every molecule of glucose entering the pathway. There is a net gain, however, of only two molecules of ATP during glycolysis because two molecules of ATP are used in reactions 1 and 3.

The end product of glycolysis, pyruvate, can proceed in one of two directions. If oxygen is present—that is, if **aerobic** conditions exist—much of the pyruvate can enter the Krebs cycle and be broken down into carbon dioxide, as described in the next section. Pyruvate is also converted to **lactate** (the ionized form of lactic acid) by a single enzyme-mediated reaction. In this reaction (**Figure 3.42**), two hydrogen atoms derived from $NADH^+ + H^+$ are transferred to each molecule of pyruvate to form lactate, and NAD^+ is regenerated. These hydrogens were originally transferred to NAD^+ during reaction 6 of glycolysis, so the coenzyme NAD^+ shuttles hydrogen between the two reactions during glycolysis. The overall reaction for the breakdown of glucose to lactate is

$$\text{Glucose} + 2\ \text{ADP} + 2\ P_i \longrightarrow 2\ \text{Lactate} + 2\ \text{ATP} + 2\ H_2O$$

As stated in the previous paragraph, under aerobic conditions, some of the pyruvate is not converted to lactate but instead enters the Krebs cycle. Therefore, the mechanism just described for regenerating NAD^+ from $NADH^+ + H^+$ by forming lactate does not occur to as great a degree. The hydrogens of NADH are transferred to oxygen during oxidative phosphorylation, regenerating NAD^+ and producing H_2O, as described in detail in the discussion that follows.

In most cells, the amount of ATP produced by glycolysis from one molecule of glucose is much smaller than the amount formed under aerobic conditions by the other two ATP-generating pathways—the Krebs cycle and oxidative phosphorylation. In special cases, however, glycolysis supplies most—or even all—of a cell's ATP. For example, erythrocytes contain the enzymes for glycolysis but have no mitochondria, which are required for the other pathways. All of their ATP production occurs, therefore, by glycolysis. Also, certain types of skeletal muscles contain considerable amounts of glycolytic enzymes but few mitochondria. During intense muscle activity, glycolysis provides most of the ATP in these cells and is associated with the production of large amounts of lactate. Despite these exceptions, most cells do not have sufficient concentrations of glycolytic enzymes or enough glucose to provide by glycolysis alone the high rates of ATP production necessary to meet their energy requirements.

What happens to the lactate that is formed during glycolysis? Some of it is released into the blood and taken up by the heart, brain, and other tissues where it is converted back to pyruvate and used as an energy source. Another portion of the secreted lactate is taken up by the liver where it is used as a precursor for the formation of glucose, which is then released into the blood where it becomes available as an energy source for all cells. The latter reaction is particularly important

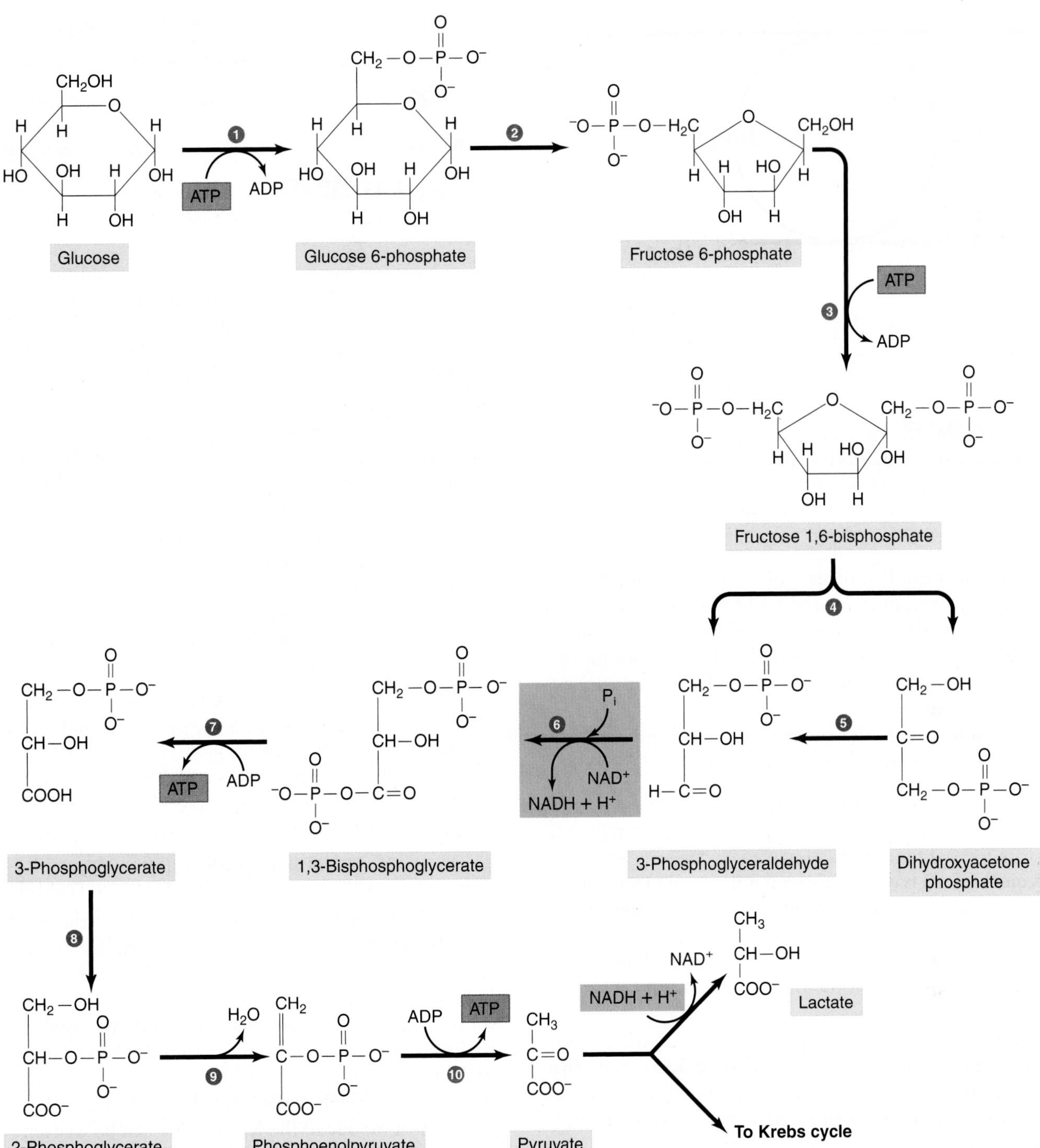

Figure 3.41 APIR Glycolytic pathway. During glycolysis, every molecule of glucose that enters the pathway produces a net synthesis of two molecules of ATP. Note that at the pH existing in the body, the products produced by the various glycolytic steps exist in the ionized, anionic form (pyruvate, for example). They are actually produced as acids (pyruvic acid, for example) that then ionize. Pyruvate is converted to lactate or enters the Krebs cycle; production of lactate is increased when the ATP demand of cells increases, as during exercise. *Note:* Beginning with step 5, two molecules of each intermediate are present even though only one is shown for clarity.

during periods in which energy demands are high, such as during exercise.

Our discussion of glycolysis has focused upon glucose as the major carbohydrate entering the glycolytic pathway. However, other carbohydrates such as fructose, derived from the disaccharide sucrose (table sugar), and galactose, from the disaccharide lactose (milk sugar), can also be catabolized by glycolysis because these carbohydrates are converted into several of the intermediates that participate in the early portion of the glycolytic pathway.

Krebs Cycle

The **Krebs cycle,** named in honor of Hans Krebs, who worked out the intermediate steps in this pathway (also known as the **citric acid cycle** or **tricarboxylic acid cycle**), is the second of the three pathways involved in nutrient catabolism

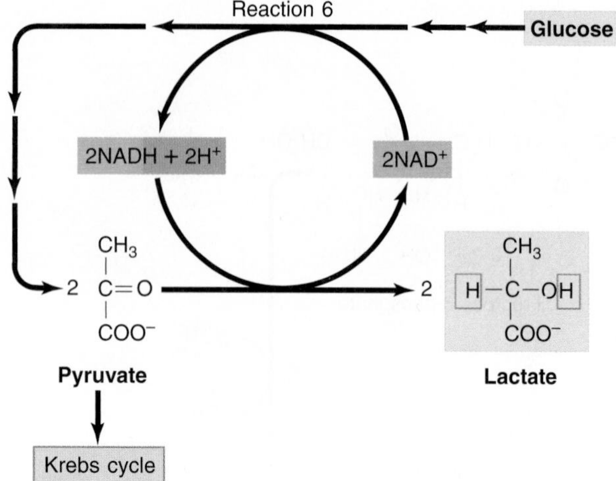

Figure 3.42 **AP|R** The coenzyme NAD^+ utilized in the glycolytic reaction 6 (see Figure 3.41) is regenerated when it transfers its hydrogen atoms to pyruvate during the formation of lactate. These reactions are increased in times of energy demand.

and ATP production. It utilizes molecular fragments formed during carbohydrate, protein, and fat breakdown; it produces carbon dioxide, hydrogen atoms (half of which are bound to coenzymes), and small amounts of ATP. The enzymes for this pathway are located in the inner mitochondrial compartment, the matrix.

The primary molecule entering at the beginning of the Krebs cycle is **acetyl coenzyme A (acetyl CoA)**:

$$CH_3—\overset{\overset{\displaystyle O}{\|}}{C}—S—CoA$$

Coenzyme A (CoA) is derived from the B vitamin pantothenic acid and functions primarily to transfer acetyl groups, which contain two carbons, from one molecule to another. These acetyl groups come either from pyruvate—the end product of aerobic glycolysis—or from the breakdown of fatty acids and some amino acids.

Pyruvate, upon entering mitochondria from the cytosol, is converted to acetyl CoA and CO_2 (**Figure 3.43**). Note that this reaction produces the first molecule of CO_2 formed thus far in the pathways of nutrient catabolism, and that the reaction also transfers hydrogen atoms to NAD^+.

The Krebs cycle begins with the transfer of the acetyl group of acetyl CoA to the four-carbon molecule oxaloacetate to form the six-carbon molecule citrate (**Figure 3.44**). At the third step in the cycle, a molecule of CO_2 is produced—and again at the fourth step. Therefore, two carbon atoms entered the cycle as part of the acetyl group attached to CoA, and two carbons (although not the same ones) have left in the form of CO_2. Note also that the oxygen that appears in the CO_2 is derived not from molecular oxygen but from the carboxyl groups of Krebs-cycle intermediates.

In the remainder of the cycle, the four-carbon molecule formed in reaction 4 is modified through a series of reactions to produce the four-carbon molecule oxaloacetate, which becomes available to accept another acetyl group and repeat the cycle.

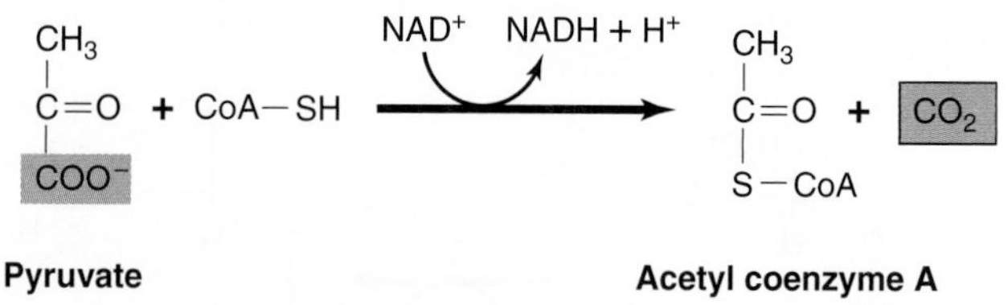

$$\underset{\text{Pyruvate}}{\begin{matrix} CH_3 \\ | \\ C=O \\ | \\ COO^- \end{matrix}} + CoA—SH \xrightarrow{NAD^+ \;\; NADH + H^+} \underset{\text{Acetyl coenzyme A}}{\begin{matrix} CH_3 \\ | \\ C=O \\ | \\ S—CoA \end{matrix}} + CO_2$$

Figure 3.43 **AP|R** Formation of acetyl coenzyme A from pyruvate with the formation of a molecule of carbon dioxide.

Now we come to a crucial fact: In addition to producing carbon dioxide, intermediates in the Krebs cycle generate hydrogen atoms, most of which are transferred to the coenzymes NAD^+ and FAD to form NADH and $FADH_2$. This hydrogen transfer to NAD^+ occurs in each of steps 3, 4, and 8, and to FAD in reaction 6. These hydrogens will be transferred from the coenzymes, along with the free H^+, to oxygen in the next stage of nutrient metabolism—oxidative phosphorylation. Because oxidative phosphorylation is necessary for regeneration of the hydrogen-free form of these coenzymes, *the Krebs cycle can operate only under aerobic conditions.* There is no pathway in the mitochondria that can remove the hydrogen from these coenzymes under anaerobic conditions.

So far, we have said nothing of how the Krebs cycle contributes to the formation of ATP. In fact, the Krebs cycle *directly* produces only one high-energy nucleotide triphosphate. This occurs during reaction 5 in which inorganic phosphate is transferred to guanosine diphosphate (GDP) to form guanosine triphosphate (GTP). The hydrolysis of GTP, like that of ATP, can provide energy for some energy-requiring reactions. In addition, the energy in GTP can be transferred to ATP by the reaction

$$GTP + ADP \rightleftharpoons GDP + ATP$$

The formation of ATP from GTP is the only mechanism by which ATP is formed within the Krebs cycle. Why, then, is the Krebs cycle so important? The reason is that the hydrogen atoms transferred to coenzymes during the cycle (plus the free hydrogen ions generated) are used in the next pathway, oxidative phosphorylation, to form large amounts of ATP.

The net result of the catabolism of one acetyl group from acetyl CoA by way of the Krebs cycle can be written

$$\text{Acetyl CoA} + 3\ NAD^+ + FAD + GDP + P_i + 2\ H_2O \longrightarrow 2\ CO_2 + CoA + 3\ NADH + 3\ H^+ + FADH_2 + GTP$$

Table 3.8 summarizes the characteristics of the Krebs-cycle reactions.

Oxidative Phosphorylation

Oxidative phosphorylation provides the third, and quantitatively most important, mechanism by which energy derived from nutrient molecules can be transferred to ATP. The basic principle behind this pathway is simple: The energy transferred to ATP is derived from the energy released when hydrogen ions combine with molecular oxygen to form water. The hydrogen comes from the NADH + H^+ and $FADH_2$ coenzymes generated by the Krebs cycle, by the metabolism

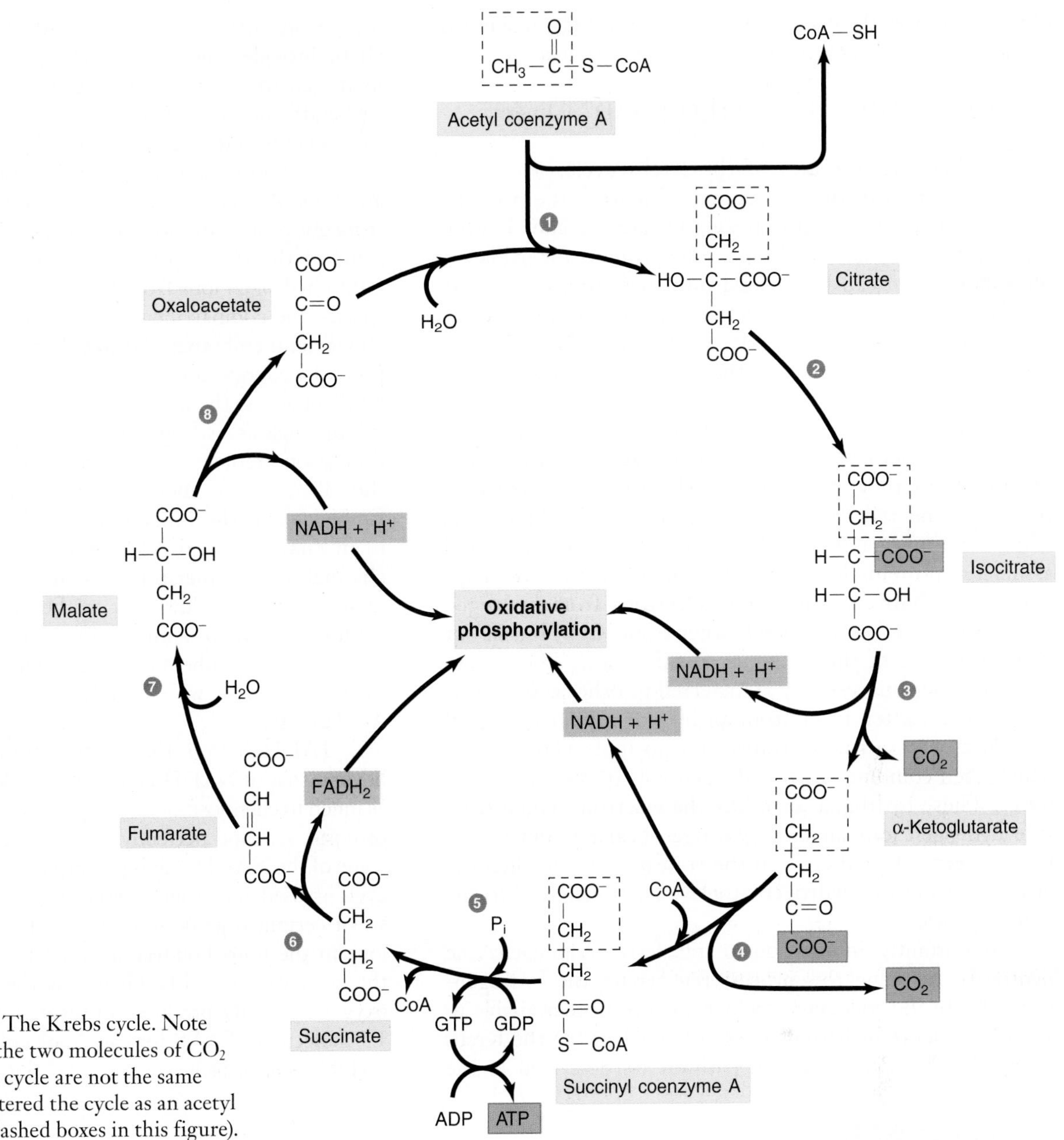

Figure 3.44 AP|R The Krebs cycle. Note that the carbon atoms in the two molecules of CO_2 produced by a turn of the cycle are not the same two carbon atoms that entered the cycle as an acetyl group (identified by the dashed boxes in this figure).

TABLE 3.8	Characteristics of the Krebs Cycle
Entering substrate	Acetyl coenzyme A—acetyl groups derived from pyruvate, fatty acids, and amino acids Some intermediates derived from amino acids
Enzyme location	Inner compartment of mitochondria (the mitochondrial matrix)
ATP production	1 GTP formed directly, which can be converted into ATP Operates only under aerobic conditions even though molecular oxygen is not used directly in this pathway
Coenzyme production	3 NADH + 3 H^+ and 2 $FADH_2$
Final products	2 CO_2 for each molecule of acetyl coenzyme A entering pathway Some intermediates used to synthesize amino acids and other organic molecules required for special cell functions
Net reaction	Acetyl CoA + 3 NAD^+ + FAD + GDP + P_i + 2 $H_2O \longrightarrow$ 2 CO_2 + CoA + 3 NADH + 3 H^+ + $FADH_2$ + GTP

of fatty acids (see the discussion that follows), and—to a much lesser extent—during glycolysis. The net reaction is

$$\frac{1}{2} O_2 + NADH + H^+ \longrightarrow H_2O + NAD^+ + \text{Energy}$$

Unlike the enzymes of the Krebs cycle, which are soluble enzymes in the mitochondrial matrix, the proteins that mediate oxidative phosphorylation are embedded in the inner mitochondrial membrane. The proteins for oxidative phosphorylation can be divided into two groups: (1) those that mediate the series of reactions that cause the transfer of hydrogen ions to molecular oxygen, and (2) those that couple the energy released by these reactions to the synthesis of ATP.

Some of the first group of proteins contain iron and copper cofactors and are known as **cytochromes** (because in pure form they are brightly colored). Their structure resembles the red iron-containing hemoglobin molecule, which binds oxygen in red blood cells. The cytochromes and associated proteins form the components of the **electron-transport chain,** in which two electrons from hydrogen atoms are initially transferred either from NADH + H^+ or $FADH_2$ to one of the elements in this chain. These electrons are then successively transferred to other compounds in the chain, often to or from an iron or copper ion, until the electrons are finally transferred to molecular oxygen, which then combines with hydrogen ions (protons) to form water. These hydrogen ions, like the electrons, come from free hydrogen ions and the hydrogen-bearing coenzymes, having been released early in the transport chain when the electrons from the hydrogen atoms were transferred to the cytochromes.

Importantly, in addition to transferring the coenzyme hydrogens to water, this process regenerates the hydrogen-free form of the coenzymes, which then become available to accept two more hydrogens from intermediates in the Krebs cycle, glycolysis, or fatty acid pathway (as described in the discussion that follows). Therefore, the electron-transport chain provides the *aerobic* mechanism for regenerating the hydrogen-free form of the coenzymes, whereas, as described earlier, the *anaerobic* mechanism, which applies only to glycolysis, is coupled to the formation of lactate.

At certain steps along the electron-transport chain, small amounts of energy are released. As electrons are transferred from one protein to another along the electron-transport chain, some of the energy released is used by the cytochromes to pump hydrogen ions from the matrix into the intermembrane space—the compartment between the inner and outer mitochondrial membranes (**Figure 3.45**). This creates a source of potential energy in the form of a hydrogen-ion-concentration gradient across the membrane. As you will learn in Chapter 4, solutes such as hydrogen ions move—or diffuse—along concentration gradients, but the presence of a lipid bilayer blocks the diffusion of most water-soluble molecules and ions. Embedded in the inner mitochondrial membrane, however, is an enzyme called **ATP synthase.** This enzyme forms a channel in the inner mitochondrial membrane, allowing the hydrogen ions to flow back to the matrix side, a process that is known as **chemiosmosis.** In the process, the energy of the concentration gradient is converted into chemical bond energy by ATP synthase, which catalyzes the formation of ATP from ADP and P_i.

$FADH_2$ enters the electron-transport chain at a point beyond that of NADH and therefore does not contribute quite as much to chemiosmosis. The processes associated with chemiosmosis are not perfectly stoichiometric, however, because some of the NADH that is produced in glycolysis and the Krebs cycle is used for other cellular activities, such as the synthesis of certain organic molecules. Also, some of the hydrogen ions in the mitochondria are used for other activities besides the generation of ATP. Therefore, the transfer of electrons to oxygen typically produces on average approximately 2.5 and 1.5 molecules of ATP for each molecule of NADH + H^+ and $FADH_2$, respectively.

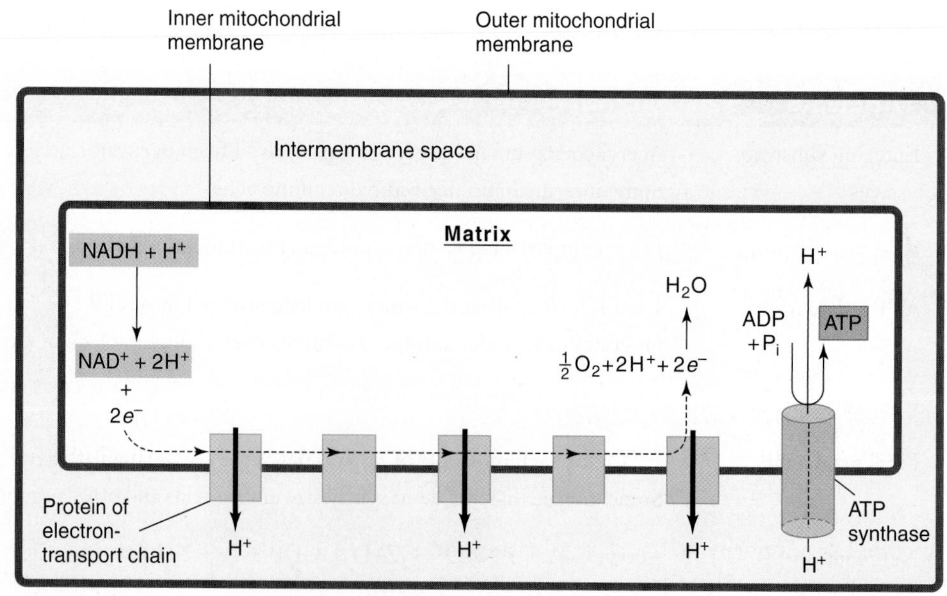

Figure 3.45 AP|R ATP is formed during oxidative phosphorylation by the flow of electrons along a series of proteins shown here as blue rectangles on the inner mitochondrial membrane. Each time an electron hops from one site to another along the transport chain, it releases energy, which is used by three of the transport proteins to pump hydrogen ions into the intermembrane space of the mitochondria. The hydrogen ions then flow down their concentration gradient across the inner mitochondrial membrane through a channel created by ATP synthase, shown here in red. The energy derived from this concentration gradient and flow of hydrogen ions is used by ATP synthase to synthesize ATP from ADP + P_i. A maximum of two to three molecules of ATP can be produced per pair of electrons donated, depending on the point at which a particular coenzyme enters the electron-transport chain. For simplicity, only the coenzyme NADH is shown.

TABLE 3.9	Characteristics of Oxidative Phosphorylation
Entering substrates	Hydrogen atoms obtained from NADH + H^+ and $FADH_2$ formed (1) during glycolysis, (2) by the Krebs cycle during the breakdown of pyruvate and amino acids, and (3) during the breakdown of fatty acids Molecular oxygen
Enzyme location	Inner mitochondrial membrane
ATP production	2–3 ATP formed from each NADH + H^+ 1–2 ATP formed from each $FADH_2$
Final products	H_2O—one molecule for each pair of hydrogens entering pathway
Net reaction	$\frac{1}{2}\,O_2 + NADH + H^+ + 3\,ADP + 3\,P_i \longrightarrow H_2O + NAD^+ + 3\,ATP$

In summary, most ATP formed in the body is produced during oxidative phosphorylation as a result of processing hydrogen atoms that originated largely from the Krebs cycle during the breakdown of carbohydrates, fats, and proteins. The mitochondria, where the oxidative phosphorylation and the Krebs-cycle reactions occur, are thus considered the powerhouses of the cell. In addition, most of the oxygen we breathe is consumed within these organelles, and most of the carbon dioxide we exhale is produced within them as well.

Table 3.9 summarizes the key features of oxidative phosphorylation.

3.15 Carbohydrate, Fat, and Protein Metabolism

Now that we have described the three pathways by which energy is transferred to ATP, let's consider how each of the three classes of energy-yielding nutrient molecules—carbohydrates, fats, and proteins—enters the ATP-generating pathways. We will also consider the synthesis of these molecules and the pathways and restrictions governing their conversion from one class to another. These anabolic pathways are also used to synthesize molecules that have functions other than the storage and release of energy. For example, with the addition of a few enzymes, the pathway for fat synthesis is also used for synthesis of the phospholipids found in membranes.

The material presented in this section should serve as a foundation for understanding how the body copes with changes in nutrient availability. The physiological mechanisms that regulate appetite, digestion, and absorption of food; transport of energy sources in the blood and across plasma membranes; and the body's responses to fasting and starvation are covered in Chapter 16.

Carbohydrate Metabolism

Carbohydrate Catabolism

In the previous sections, we described the major pathways of carbohydrate catabolism: the breakdown of glucose to pyruvate or lactate by way of the glycolytic pathway, and the metabolism of pyruvate to carbon dioxide and water by way of the Krebs cycle and oxidative phosphorylation.

The amount of energy released during the catabolism of glucose to carbon dioxide and water is 686 kcal/mol of glucose:

$$C_6H_{12}O_6 + 6\,O_2 \longrightarrow 6\,H_2O + 6\,CO_2 + 686\text{ kcal/mol}$$

About 40% of this energy is transferred to ATP. **Figure 3.46** summarizes the points at which ATP forms during glucose catabolism. A net gain of two ATP molecules occurs by substrate-level phosphorylation during glycolysis, and two more are formed during the Krebs cycle from GTP, one from each of the two molecules of pyruvate entering the cycle. The majority of ATP molecules glucose catabolism produces—up to 34 ATP per molecule—form during oxidative phosphorylation from the hydrogens generated at various steps during glucose breakdown.

Because in the absence of oxygen only two molecules of ATP can form from the breakdown of glucose to lactate, the evolution of aerobic metabolic pathways greatly increases the amount of energy available to a cell from glucose catabolism. For example, if a muscle consumed 38 molecules of ATP during a contraction, this amount of ATP could be supplied by the breakdown of one molecule of glucose in the presence of oxygen or 19 molecules of glucose under anaerobic conditions.

However, although only two molecules of ATP are formed per molecule of glucose under anaerobic conditions, large amounts of ATP can still be supplied by the glycolytic pathway if large amounts of glucose are broken down to lactate. This is not an efficient utilization of nutrients, but it does permit continued ATP production under anaerobic conditions, such as occur during intense exercise.

Glycogen Storage

A small amount of glucose can be stored in the body to provide a reserve supply for use when glucose is not being absorbed into the blood from the small intestine. Recall from Chapter 2 that it is stored as the polysaccharide **glycogen,** mostly in skeletal muscles and the liver.

Glycogen is synthesized from glucose by the pathway illustrated in **Figure 3.47**. The enzymes for both glycogen synthesis and glycogen breakdown are located in the cytosol. The first step in glycogen synthesis, the transfer of phosphate from a molecule of ATP to glucose, forming glucose 6-phosphate, is the same as the first step in glycolysis. Thus, glucose 6-phosphate can either be broken down to pyruvate or used to form glycogen.

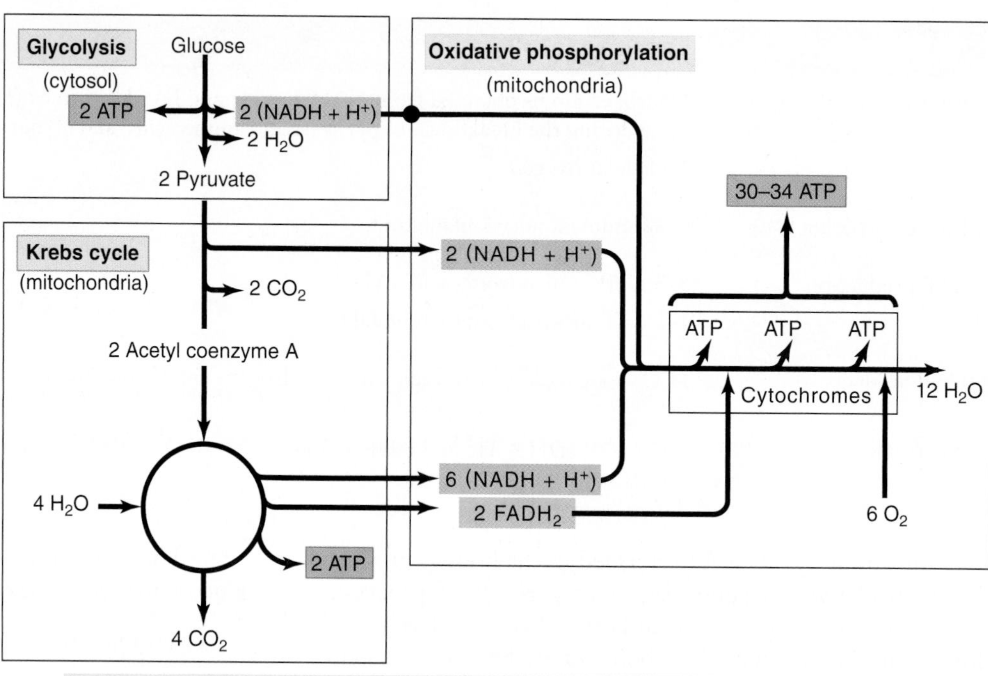

Figure 3.46 APIR Pathways of glycolysis and aerobic glucose catabolism and their linkage to ATP formation. The value of 38 ATP molecules is a theoretical maximum assuming that all molecules of NADH produced in glycolysis and the Krebs cycle enter into the oxidative phosphorylation pathway, and all of the free hydrogen ions are used in chemiosmosis for ATP synthesis.

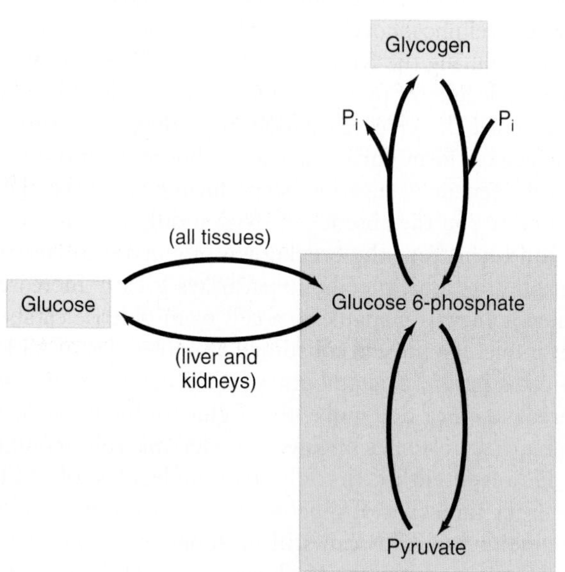

Figure 3.47 Pathways for glycogen synthesis and breakdown. Each bowed arrow indicates one or more irreversible reactions that require different enzymes to catalyze the reaction in the forward and reverse directions.

As indicated in Figure 3.47, different enzymes synthesize and break down glycogen. The existence of two pathways containing enzymes that are subject to both covalent and allosteric modulation provides a mechanism for regulating the flow between glucose and glycogen. When an excess of glucose is available to a liver or muscle cell, the enzymes in the glycogen-synthesis pathway are activated and the enzyme that breaks down glycogen is simultaneously inhibited. This combination leads to the net storage of glucose in the form of glycogen.

When less glucose is available, the reverse combination of enzyme stimulation and inhibition occurs, and net breakdown of glycogen to glucose 6-phosphate (known as **glycogenolysis**) ensues. Two paths are available to this glucose 6-phosphate: (1) in most cells, including skeletal muscle, it enters the glycolytic pathway where it is catabolized to provide the energy for ATP formation; (2) in liver and kidney cells, glucose 6-phosphate can be converted to free glucose by removal of the phosphate group, and the glucose is then able to pass out of the cell into the blood to provide energy for other cells.

Glucose Synthesis

In addition to being formed in the liver from the breakdown of glycogen, glucose can be synthesized in the liver and kidneys from intermediates derived from the catabolism of glycerol (a sugar alcohol) and some amino acids. This process of generating new molecules of glucose from noncarbohydrate precursors is known as **gluconeogenesis.** The major substrate in gluconeogenesis is pyruvate, formed from lactate as described earlier, and from several amino acids during protein breakdown. In addition, glycerol derived from the hydrolysis of triglycerides can be converted into glucose via a pathway that does not involve pyruvate.

The pathway for gluconeogenesis in the liver and kidneys (**Figure 3.48**) makes use of many but not all of the enzymes used in glycolysis because most of these reactions are reversible. However, reactions 1, 3, and 10 (see Figure 3.41) are irreversible, and additional enzymes are required, therefore, to form glucose from pyruvate. Pyruvate is converted to phosphoenolpyruvate by a series of mitochondrial reactions in which CO_2 is added to pyruvate to form the four-carbon Krebs-cycle intermediate oxaloacetate. An additional series of reactions leads to the transfer of a four-carbon intermediate derived from oxaloacetate out of the mitochondria and its conversion to phosphoenolpyruvate in the cytosol. Phosphoenolpyruvate then reverses the steps of glycolysis back to the level of reaction 3, in which a different enzyme from that used in glycolysis is required to convert fructose 1,6-bisphosphate to fructose 6-phosphate. From this point on, the reactions are again reversible, leading to glucose

6-phosphate, which can be converted to glucose in the liver and kidneys or stored as glycogen. Because energy in the form of heat and ATP generation is released during the glycolytic breakdown of glucose to pyruvate, energy must be added to reverse this pathway. A total of six ATP are consumed in the reactions of gluconeogenesis per molecule of glucose formed.

Many of the same enzymes are used in glycolysis and gluconeogenesis, so the questions arise: What controls the direction of the reactions in these pathways? What conditions determine whether glucose is broken down to pyruvate or whether pyruvate is converted into glucose? The answers lie in the concentrations of glucose or pyruvate in a cell and in the control the enzymes exert in the irreversible steps in the pathway. This control is carried out via various hormones that alter the concentrations and activities of these key enzymes. For example, if blood glucose concentrations fall below normal, certain hormones are secreted into the blood and act on the liver. There, the hormones preferentially induce the expression of the gluconeogenic enzymes, thereby favoring the formation of glucose.

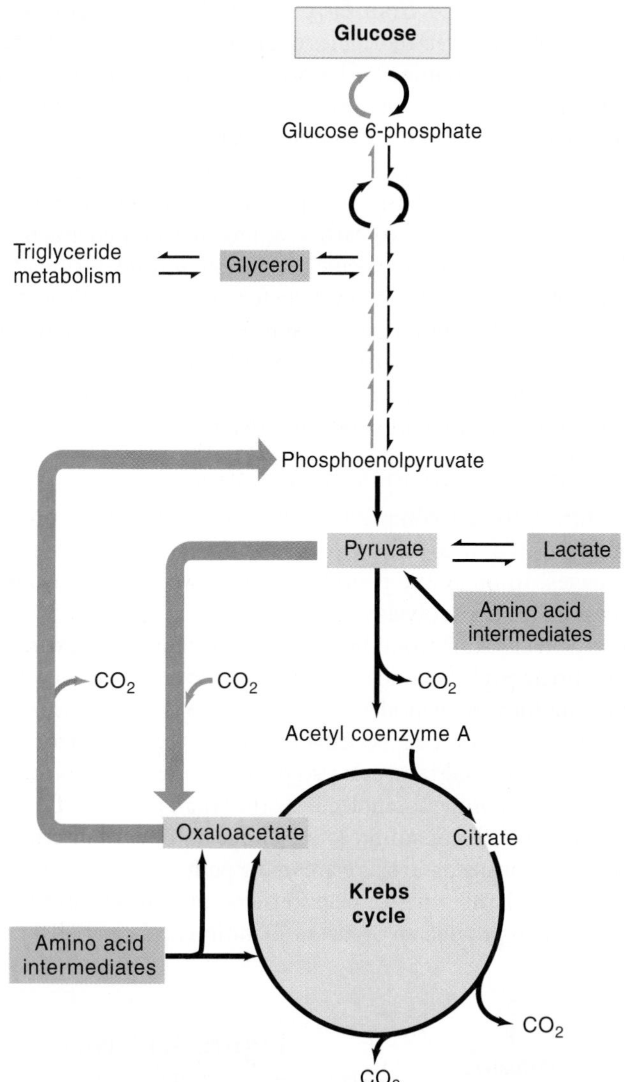

Figure 3.48 Gluconeogenic pathway by which pyruvate, lactate, glycerol, and various amino acid intermediates can be converted into glucose in the liver (and kidneys). Note the points at which each of these precursors, supplied by the blood, enters the pathway.

Fat Metabolism

Fat Catabolism

Triglyceride (fat) consists of three fatty acids bound to glycerol (Chapter 2). Fat typically accounts for approximately 80% of the energy stored in the body (**Table 3.10**). Under resting conditions, approximately half the energy used by muscle, liver, and the kidneys is derived from the catabolism of fatty acids.

Although most cells store small amounts of fat, most of the body's fat is stored in specialized cells known as **adipocytes.** Almost the entire cytoplasm of each of these cells is filled with a single, large fat droplet. Clusters of adipocytes form **adipose tissue,** most of which is in deposits underlying the skin or surrounding internal organs. The function of adipocytes is to synthesize and store triglycerides during periods of food uptake and then, when food is not being absorbed from the small intestine, to release fatty acids and glycerol into the blood for uptake and use by other cells to provide the energy needed for ATP formation. The factors controlling fat storage and release from adipocytes during different physiological states will be described in Chapter 16. Here, we will emphasize the pathway by which most cells catabolize fatty acids to provide the energy for ATP synthesis, and the pathway by which other molecules are used to synthesize fatty acids.

Figure 3.49 shows the pathway for fatty acid catabolism, which is achieved by enzymes present in the mitochondrial matrix. The breakdown of a fatty acid is initiated by linking a molecule of coenzyme A to the carboxyl end of the fatty acid. This initial step is accompanied by the breakdown of ATP to AMP and two P_i.

The coenzyme-A derivative of the fatty acid then proceeds through a series of reactions, collectively known as **beta oxidation,** which splits off a molecule of acetyl coenzyme A from the end of the fatty acid and transfers two pairs of hydrogen atoms to coenzymes (one pair to FAD and the other to NAD^+). The hydrogen atoms from the coenzymes then enter the oxidative-phosphorylation pathway to form ATP.

When an acetyl coenzyme A is split from the end of a fatty acid, another coenzyme A is added (ATP is not required for this step), and the sequence is repeated. Each passage through this sequence shortens the fatty acid chain by two carbon atoms until all the carbon atoms have transferred to coenzyme-A molecules. As we saw, these molecules then lead to production of CO_2 and ATP via the Krebs cycle and oxidative phosphorylation.

How much ATP is formed as a result of the total catabolism of a fatty acid? Most fatty acids in the body contain 14 to

TABLE 3.10 Energy Content of a 70 kg Person

	Total-Body Content (kg)	Energy Content (kcal/g)	Total-Body Energy Content (kcal)	%
Triglycerides	15.6	9	140,000	78
Proteins	9.5	4	38,000	21
Carbohydrates	0.5	4	2000	1

22 carbons, 16 and 18 being most common. The catabolism of one 18-carbon saturated fatty acid yields 146 ATP molecules. In contrast, as we have seen, the catabolism of one glucose molecule yields a maximum of 38 ATP molecules. Thus, taking into account the difference in molecular weight of the fatty acid and glucose, the amount of ATP formed from the catabolism of a gram of fat is about 2½ times greater than the amount of ATP produced by catabolizing 1 gram of carbohydrate. If an average person stored most of his or her energy as carbohydrate rather than fat, body weight would have to be approximately 30% greater in order to store the same amount of usable energy, and the person would consume more energy moving this extra weight around. Thus, a major step in energy economy occurred when animals evolved the ability to store energy as fat.

Fat Synthesis

The synthesis of fatty acids occurs by reactions that are almost the reverse of those that degrade them. However, the enzymes in the synthetic pathway are in the cytosol, whereas (as we have just seen) the enzymes catalyzing fatty acid breakdown are in the mitochondria. Fatty acid synthesis begins with cytoplasmic acetyl coenzyme A, which transfers its acetyl group to another molecule of acetyl coenzyme A to form a four-carbon chain. By repetition of this process, long-chain fatty acids are built up two carbons at a time. This accounts for the fact that all the fatty acids synthesized in the body contain an even number of carbon atoms.

Once the fatty acids are formed, triglycerides can be synthesized by linking fatty acids to each of the three hydroxyl groups in glycerol, more specifically, to a phosphorylated form of glycerol called **α-glycerol phosphate.** The synthesis of triglyceride is carried out by enzymes associated with the membranes of the smooth endoplasmic reticulum.

Compare the molecules produced by glucose catabolism with those required for synthesis of both fatty acids and α-glycerol phosphate. First, acetyl coenzyme A, the starting material for fatty acid synthesis, can be formed from pyruvate, the end product of glycolysis. Second, the other ingredients required for fatty acid synthesis—hydrogen-bound coenzymes and ATP—are produced during carbohydrate catabolism. Third, α-glycerol phosphate can be formed from a glucose intermediate. It should not be surprising, therefore, that much of the carbohydrate in food is converted into fat and stored in adipose tissue shortly after its absorption from the gastrointestinal tract.

Importantly, fatty acids—or, more specifically, the acetyl coenzyme A derived from fatty acid breakdown—cannot be used to synthesize *new* molecules of glucose. We can see the reasons for this by examining the pathways for glucose synthesis (see Figure 3.48). First, because the reaction in which pyruvate is broken down to acetyl coenzyme A and carbon dioxide is irreversible, acetyl coenzyme A cannot be converted into pyruvate, a molecule that could lead to the production of glucose. Second, the equivalents of the two carbon atoms in acetyl coenzyme A are converted into two molecules of carbon dioxide during their passage through the Krebs cycle before reaching oxaloacetate, another takeoff point for glucose synthesis; therefore, they cannot be used to synthesize *net* amounts of oxaloacetate.

Therefore, *glucose can readily be converted into fat, but the fatty acid portion of fat cannot be converted to glucose.*

Protein and Amino Acid Metabolism

In contrast to the complexities of protein synthesis, protein catabolism requires only a few enzymes, collectively called **proteases**, to break the peptide bonds between amino acids (a process called **proteolysis**). Some of these enzymes remove one amino acid at a time from the ends of the protein chain, whereas others break peptide bonds between specific amino acids within the chain, forming peptides rather than free amino acids.

Amino acids can be catabolized to provide energy for ATP synthesis, and they can also provide intermediates for the synthesis of a number of molecules other than proteins. Because there are 20 different amino acids, a large number of intermediates can be formed, and there are many pathways for processing them. A few basic types of reactions common to most of these pathways can provide an overview of amino acid catabolism.

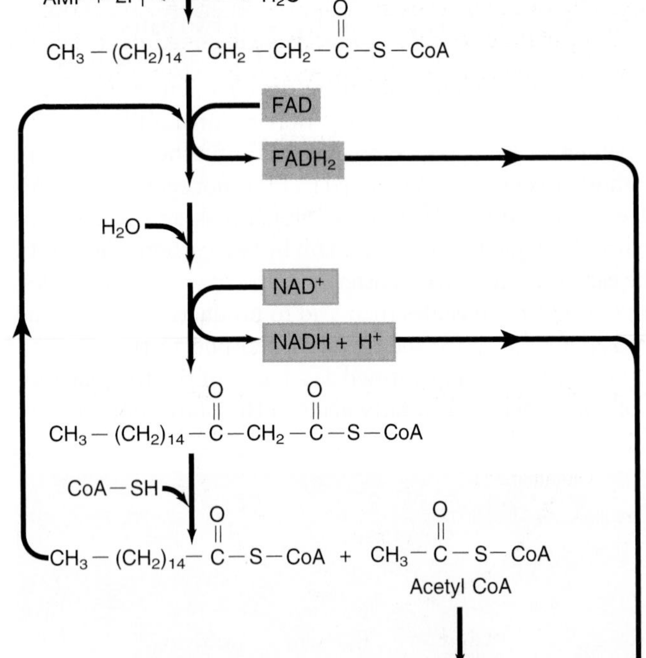

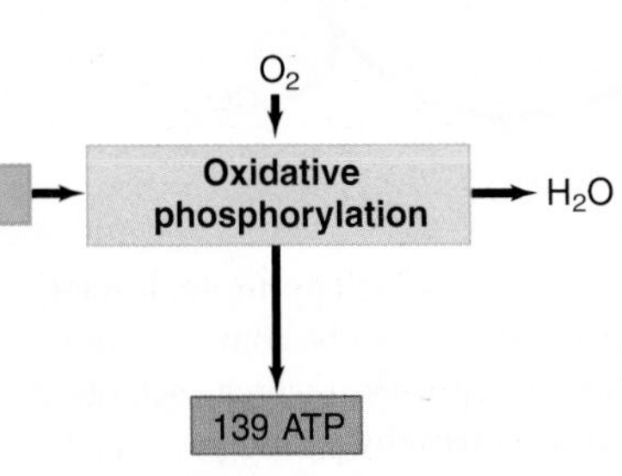

Figure 3.49 Pathway of fatty acid catabolism in mitochondria. The energy equivalent of two ATP is consumed at the start of the pathway, for a *net* gain of 146 ATP for this C18 fatty acid.

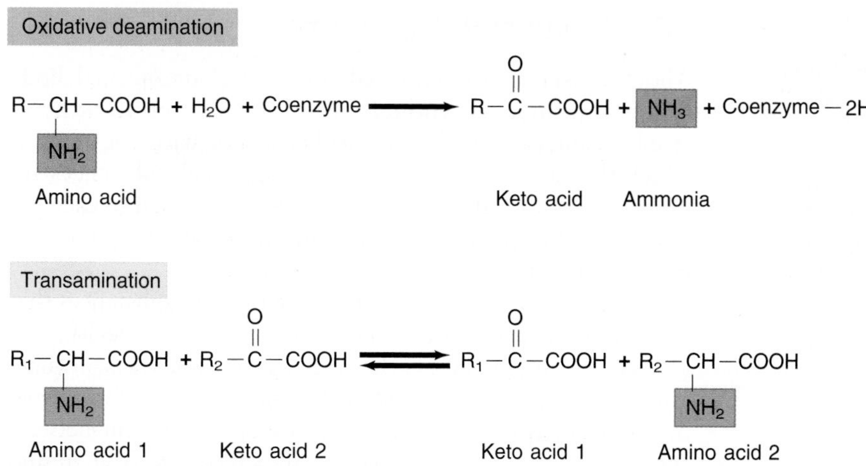

Figure 3.50 Oxidative deamination and transamination of amino acids.

Unlike most carbohydrates and fats, amino acids contain nitrogen atoms (in their amino groups) in addition to carbon, hydrogen, and oxygen atoms. Once the nitrogen-containing amino group is removed, the remainder of most amino acids can be metabolized to intermediates capable of entering either the glycolytic pathway or the Krebs cycle.

Figure 3.50 illustrates the two types of reactions by which the amino group is removed. In the first reaction, **oxidative deamination,** the amino group gives rise to a molecule of ammonia (NH_3) and is replaced by an oxygen atom derived from water to form a **keto acid,** a categorical name rather than the name of a specific molecule. The second means of removing an amino group is known as **transamination** and involves transfer of the amino group from an amino acid to a keto acid. Note that the keto acid to which the amino group is transferred becomes an amino acid. Cells can also use the nitrogen derived from amino groups to synthesize other important nitrogen-containing molecules, such as the purine and pyrimidine bases found in nucleic acids.

Figure 3.51 illustrates the oxidative deamination of the amino acid glutamic acid and the transamination of the amino acid alanine. Note that the keto acids formed are intermediates either in the Krebs cycle (α-ketoglutaric acid) or glycolytic pathway (pyruvic acid). Once formed, these keto acids can be metabolized to produce carbon dioxide and form ATP, or they can be used as intermediates in the synthetic pathway leading to the formation of glucose. As a third alternative, they can be used to synthesize fatty acids after their conversion to acetyl coenzyme A by way of pyruvic acid. Therefore, amino acids can be used as a source of energy, and some can be converted into carbohydrate and fat.

The ammonia that oxidative deamination produces is highly toxic to cells if allowed to accumulate. Fortunately, it passes through plasma membranes and enters the blood, which carries it to the liver. The liver contains enzymes that can combine two molecules of ammonia with carbon dioxide to form **urea,** which is relatively nontoxic and is the major nitrogenous waste product of protein catabolism. It enters the blood from the liver and is excreted by the kidneys into the urine.

Thus far, we have discussed mainly amino acid catabolism; now we turn to amino acid synthesis. The keto acids pyruvic acid and α-ketoglutaric acid can be derived from the breakdown of glucose; they can then be transaminated, as described previously, to form the amino acids glutamate and alanine. Therefore, glucose can be used to produce certain amino acids, provided other amino acids are available in the diet to supply amino groups for transamination. However, only 11 of the 20 amino acids can be formed by this process because nine of the specific keto acids cannot be synthesized from other intermediates. We have to obtain the nine amino acids corresponding to these keto acids from the food we eat; consequently, they are known as **essential amino acids.**

Figure 3.52 provides a summary of the multiple routes by which the body handles amino acids. The amino acid pools, which consist of the body's total free amino acids, are derived from (1) ingested protein, which is degraded to amino acids during digestion in the small intestine; (2) the synthesis of nonessential amino acids from the keto acids derived from carbohydrates and fat; and (3) the continuous breakdown of body proteins. These pools are the source of amino acids for the resynthesis of body protein and a host of specialized amino acid derivatives, as well as for conversion to carbohydrate and fat. A very small quantity of amino acids and protein is lost from the body via the urine; skin; hair; fingernails; and, in women, the menstrual fluid. The major route for the loss of amino acids is not their excretion but rather their deamination, with the eventual excretion of the nitrogen atoms as urea in the urine. The terms **negative nitrogen balance** and **positive nitrogen balance** refer to whether there is a net loss or gain, respectively, of amino acids in the body over any period of time.

If any of the essential amino acids are missing from the diet, a negative nitrogen balance—that is, loss greater than gain—always

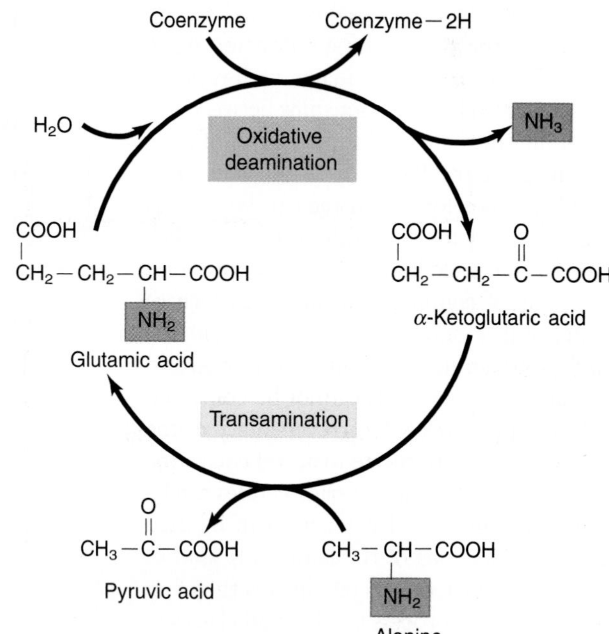

Figure 3.51 Oxidative deamination and transamination of the amino acids glutamic acid and alanine produce keto acids that can enter the carbohydrate pathways.

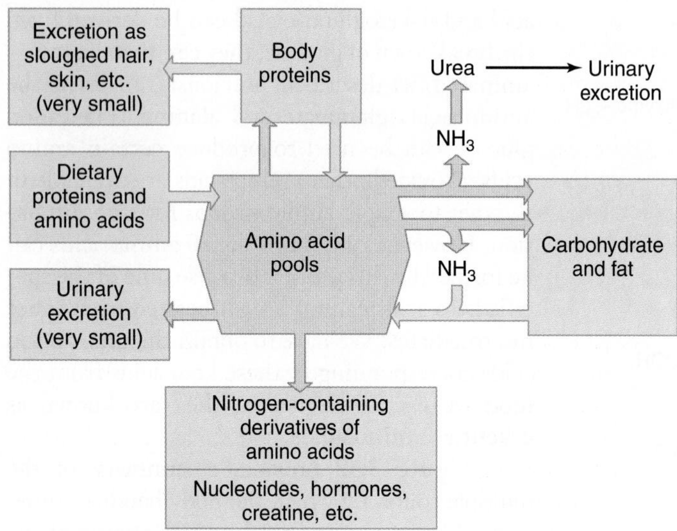

Figure 3.52 Pathways of amino acid metabolism.

results. The proteins that require a missing essential amino acid cannot be synthesized, and the other amino acids that would have been incorporated into these proteins are metabolized. This explains why a dietary requirement for protein cannot be specified without regard to the amino acid composition of that protein. Protein is graded in terms of how closely its relative proportions of essential amino acids approximate those in the average body protein. The highest-quality proteins are found in animal products, whereas the quality of most plant proteins is lower. Nevertheless, it is quite possible to obtain adequate quantities of all essential amino acids from a mixture of plant proteins alone.

Metabolism Summary

Having discussed the metabolism of the three major classes of organic molecules, we can now briefly review how each class is related to the others and to the process of synthesizing ATP. **Figure 3.53** illustrates the major pathways we have discussed and the relationships between the common intermediates. All three classes of molecules can enter the Krebs cycle through some intermediate; therefore, all three can be used as a source of energy for the synthesis of ATP. Glucose can be converted into fat or into some amino acids by way of common intermediates such as pyruvate, oxaloacetate, and acetyl coenzyme A. Similarly, some amino acids can be converted into glucose and fat. Fatty acids cannot be converted into glucose because of the irreversibility of the reaction converting pyruvate to acetyl coenzyme A, but the glycerol portion of triglycerides can be converted into glucose. Fatty acids can be used to synthesize portions of the keto acids used to form some amino acids. Metabolism is therefore a highly integrated process in which all classes of nutrient macromolecules can be used to provide energy and in which each class of molecule can be used to synthesize most but not all members of other classes.

3.16 Essential Nutrients

About 50 substances required for normal or optimal body function cannot be synthesized by the body or are synthesized in amounts inadequate to keep pace with the rates at which they are broken down or excreted. Such substances are known as **essential nutrients (Table 3.11)**. Because they are all removed from the body at some finite rate, they must be continually supplied in the foods we eat.

The term *essential nutrient* is reserved for substances that fulfill two criteria: (1) they must be essential for health, and (2) they must not be synthesized by the body in adequate amounts. Therefore, glucose, although "essential" for normal metabolism, is not classified as an essential nutrient because the body normally can synthesize all it requires, from amino acids, for example. Furthermore, the quantity of an essential nutrient that must be present in the diet to maintain health is not a criterion for determining whether the substance is essential. Approximately 1500 g of water, 2 g of the amino acid methionine, and only about 1 mg of the vitamin thiamine are required per day.

Water is an essential nutrient because the body loses far more water in the urine and from the skin and respiratory tract than it can synthesize. (Recall that water forms as an end product of oxidative phosphorylation as well as from several other metabolic reactions.) Therefore, to maintain water balance, water intake is essential.

The mineral elements are examples of substances the body cannot synthesize or break down but that the body continually loses in the urine, feces, and various secretions. The major

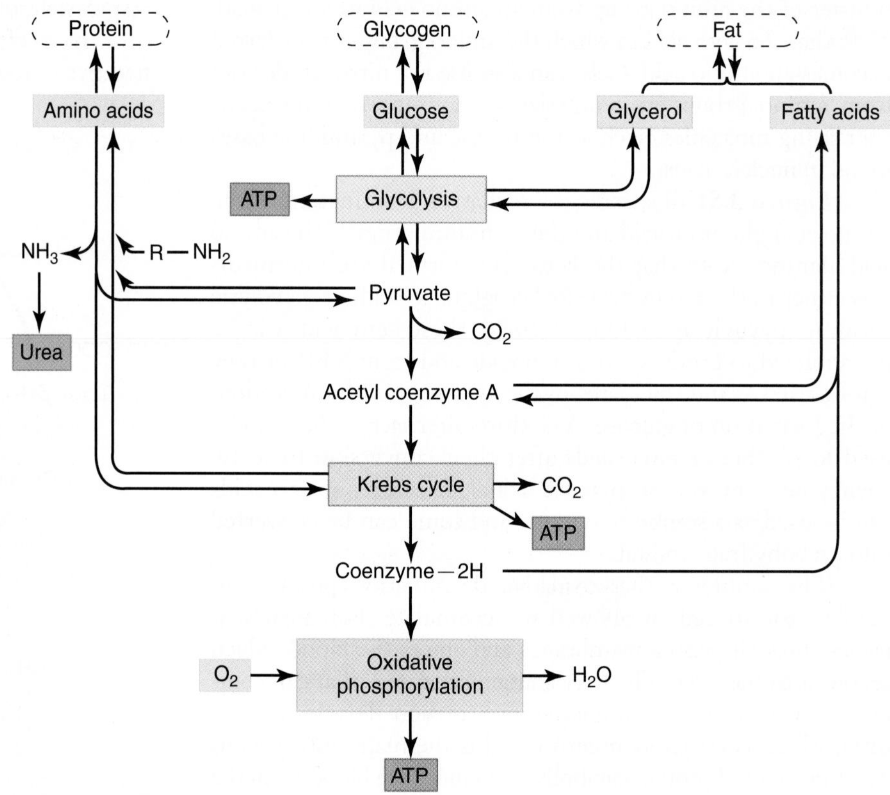

Figure 3.53 The relationships between the pathways for the metabolism of protein, carbohydrate (glycogen), and fat (triglyceride).

TABLE 3.11 Essential Nutrients	
Water	
Mineral Elements	
7 major mineral elements (see Table 2.1)	
13 trace elements (see Table 2.1)	
Essential Amino Acids	
Histidine	
Isoleucine	
Leucine	
Lysine	
Methionine	
Phenylalanine	
Threonine	
Tryptophan	
Valine	
Essential Fatty Acids	
Linoleic acid	
Linolenic acid	
Vitamins	
Water-soluble vitamins	
B_1: thiamine	Vitamin B complex
B_2: riboflavin	Vitamin B complex
B_6: pyridoxine	Vitamin B complex
B_{12}: cobalamine	Vitamin B complex
Niacin	Vitamin B complex
Pantothenic acid	Vitamin B complex
Folic acid	Vitamin B complex
Biotin	Vitamin B complex
Lipoic acid	
Vitamin C	
Fat-soluble vitamins	
Vitamin A	
Vitamin D	
Vitamin E	
Vitamin K	
Other Essential Nutrients	
Inositol	
Choline	
Carnitine	

minerals must be supplied in fairly large amounts, whereas only small quantities of the trace elements are required.

We have already noted that nine of the 20 amino acids are essential. Two fatty acids, linoleic and linolenic acid, which contain a number of double bonds and serve important roles in chemical messenger systems, are also essential nutrients. Three additional essential nutrients—inositol, choline, and carnitine—have functions that will be described in later chapters but do not fall into any common category other than being essential nutrients. Finally, the class of essential nutrients known as vitamins deserves special attention.

Vitamins

Vitamins are a group of 14 organic essential nutrients required in very small amounts in the diet. The exact chemical structures of the first vitamins to be discovered were unknown, and they were simply identified by letters of the alphabet. Vitamin B turned out to be composed of eight substances now known as the vitamin B complex. Plants and bacteria have the enzymes necessary for vitamin synthesis, and we get our vitamins by eating either plants or meat from animals that have eaten plants.

The vitamins as a class have no particular chemical structure in common, but they can be divided into the **water-soluble vitamins** and the **fat-soluble vitamins.** The water-soluble vitamins form portions of coenzymes such as NAD^+, FAD, and coenzyme A. The fat-soluble vitamins (A, D, E, and K) in general do not function as coenzymes. For example, vitamin A (retinol) is used to form the light-sensitive pigment in the eye, and lack of this vitamin leads to night blindness. The specific functions of each of the fat-soluble vitamins will be described in later chapters.

The catabolism of vitamins does not provide chemical energy, although some vitamins participate as coenzymes in chemical reactions that release energy from other molecules. Increasing the amount of a vitamin in the diet beyond a certain minimum does not necessarily increase the activity of those enzymes for which the vitamin functions as a coenzyme. Only very small quantities of coenzymes participate in the chemical reactions that require them, and increasing the concentration above this level does not increase the reaction rate.

The fate of large quantities of ingested vitamins varies depending upon whether the vitamin is water-soluble or fat-soluble. As the amount of water-soluble vitamins in the diet is increased, so is the amount excreted in the urine; therefore, the accumulation of these vitamins in the body is limited. On the other hand, fat-soluble vitamins can accumulate in the body because they are poorly excreted by the kidneys and because they dissolve in the fat stores in adipose tissue. The intake of very large quantities of fat-soluble vitamins can produce toxic effects.

SECTION E SUMMARY

Cellular Energy Transfer

I. The end products of glycolysis under aerobic conditions are ATP and pyruvate; the end products under anaerobic conditions are ATP and lactate.
   a. Carbohydrates are the only major nutrient molecules that can enter the glycolytic pathway, and the enzymes that facilitate this pathway are located in the cytosol.
   b. Hydrogen atoms generated by glycolysis are transferred either to NAD^+, which then transfers them to pyruvate to form lactate, thereby regenerating the original coenzyme molecule; or to the oxidative-phosphorylation pathway.
   c. The formation of ATP in glycolysis occurs by substrate-level phosphorylation, a process in which a phosphate group is transferred from a phosphorylated metabolic intermediate directly to ADP.

II. The Krebs cycle catabolizes molecular fragments derived from nutrient molecules and produces carbon dioxide, hydrogen atoms, and ATP. The enzymes that mediate the cycle are located in the mitochondrial matrix.
   a. Acetyl coenzyme A, the acetyl portion of which is derived from all three types of nutrient macromolecules, is the major substrate entering the Krebs cycle. Amino acids can also enter at several places in the cycle by being converted to cycle intermediates.

b. During one rotation of the Krebs cycle, two molecules of carbon dioxide are produced, and four pairs of hydrogen atoms are transferred to coenzymes. Substrate-level phosphorylation produces one molecule of GTP, which can be converted to ATP.

III. Oxidative phosphorylation forms ATP from ADP and P_i, using the energy released when molecular oxygen ultimately combines with hydrogen atoms to form water.
   a. The enzymes for oxidative phosphorylation are located on the inner membranes of mitochondria.
   b. Hydrogen atoms derived from glycolysis, the Krebs cycle, and the breakdown of fatty acids are delivered, most bound to coenzymes, to the electron-transport chain. The electron-transport chain then regenerates the hydrogen-free forms of the coenzymes NAD^+ and FAD by transferring the hydrogens to molecular oxygen to form water.
   c. The reactions of the electron-transport chain produce a hydrogen ion gradient across the inner mitochondrial membrane. The flow of hydrogen ions back across the membrane provides the energy for ATP synthesis.

Carbohydrate, Fat, and Protein Metabolism

I. The aerobic catabolism of carbohydrates proceeds through the glycolytic pathway to pyruvate. Pyruvate enters the Krebs cycle and is broken down to carbon dioxide and hydrogens, which are then transferred to coenzymes.
   a. About 40% of the chemical energy in glucose can be transferred to ATP under aerobic conditions; the rest is released as heat.
   b. Under aerobic conditions, a maximum of 38 molecules of ATP can form from one molecule of glucose: up to 34 from oxidative phosphorylation, two from glycolysis, and two from the Krebs cycle.
   c. Under anaerobic conditions, two molecules of ATP can form from one molecule of glucose during glycolysis.

II. Carbohydrates are stored as glycogen, primarily in the liver and skeletal muscles.
   a. Different enzymes synthesize and break down glycogen. The control of these enzymes regulates the flow of glucose to and from glycogen.
   b. In most cells, glucose 6-phosphate is formed by glycogen breakdown and is catabolized to produce ATP. In liver and kidney cells, glucose can be derived from glycogen and released from the cells into the blood.

III. New glucose can be synthesized (gluconeogenesis) from some amino acids, lactate, and glycerol via the enzymes that catalyze reversible reactions in the glycolytic pathway. Fatty acids cannot be used to synthesize new glucose.

IV. Fat, stored primarily in adipose tissue, provides about 80% of the stored energy in the body.
   a. Fatty acids are broken down, two carbon atoms at a time, in the mitochondrial matrix by beta oxidation to form acetyl coenzyme A and hydrogen atoms, which combine with coenzymes.
   b. The acetyl portion of acetyl coenzyme A is catabolized to carbon dioxide in the Krebs cycle, and the hydrogen atoms generated there, plus those generated during beta oxidation, enter the oxidative-phosphorylation pathway to form ATP.
   c. The amount of ATP formed by the catabolism of 1 g of fat is about 2½ times greater than the amount formed from 1 g of carbohydrate.
   d. Fatty acids are synthesized from acetyl coenzyme A by enzymes in the cytosol and are linked to α-glycerol phosphate, produced from carbohydrates, to form triglycerides by enzymes in the smooth endoplasmic reticulum.

V. Proteins are broken down to free amino acids by proteases.
   a. The removal of amino groups from amino acids leaves keto acids, which can be either catabolized via the Krebs cycle to provide energy for the synthesis of ATP or converted into glucose and fatty acids.
   b. Amino groups are removed by (i) oxidative deamination, which gives rise to ammonia; or by (ii) transamination, in which the amino group is transferred to a keto acid to form a new amino acid.
   c. The ammonia formed from the oxidative deamination of amino acids is converted to urea by enzymes in the liver and then excreted in the urine by the kidneys.

VI. Some amino acids can be synthesized from keto acids derived from glucose, whereas others cannot be synthesized by the body and must be provided in the diet.

Essential Nutrients

I. Approximately 50 essential nutrients are necessary for health but cannot be synthesized in adequate amounts by the body and must therefore be provided in the diet.

II. A large intake of water-soluble vitamins leads to their rapid excretion in the urine, whereas a large intake of fat-soluble vitamins leads to their accumulation in adipose tissue and may produce toxic effects.

SECTION E REVIEW QUESTIONS

1. What are the end products of glycolysis under aerobic and anaerobic conditions?
2. What are the major substrates entering the Krebs cycle, and what are the products formed?
3. Why does the Krebs cycle operate only under aerobic conditions even though it does not use molecular oxygen in any of its reactions?
4. Identify the molecules that enter the oxidative-phosphorylation pathway and the products that form.
5. Where are the enzymes for the Krebs cycle located? The enzymes for oxidative phosphorylation? The enzymes for glycolysis?
6. How many molecules of ATP can form from the breakdown of one molecule of glucose under aerobic conditions? Under anaerobic conditions?
7. What molecules can be used to synthesize glucose?
8. Why can't fatty acids be used to synthesize glucose?
9. Describe the pathways used to catabolize fatty acids to carbon dioxide.
10. Why is it more efficient to store energy as fat than as glycogen?
11. Describe the pathway by which glucose is converted into fat.
12. Describe the two processes by which amino groups are removed from amino acids.
13. What can keto acids be converted into?
14. What is the source of the nitrogen atoms in urea, and in what organ is urea synthesized?
15. Why is water considered an essential nutrient whereas glucose is not?
16. What is the consequence of ingesting large quantities of water-soluble vitamins? Fat-soluble vitamins?

SECTION E KEY TERMS

acetyl coenzyme A (acetyl CoA) 82
adipocyte 87
adipose tissue 87
aerobic 80
α-glycerol phosphate 88
ATP synthase 84
beta oxidation 87
chemiosmosis 84
citric acid cycle 81
cytochrome 84
electron-transport chain 84
essential amino acid 89
essential nutrient 90
fat-soluble vitamin 91
gluconeogenesis 87
glycogen 86
glycogenolysis 86
glycolysis 79
keto acid 89
Krebs cycle 81
lactate 80
negative nitrogen balance 89
oxidative deamination 89
oxidative phosphorylation 82
positive nitrogen balance 89
protease 88
proteolysis 88
pyruvate 80
substrate-level phosphorylation 80
transamination 89
tricarboxylic acid cycle 81
urea 89
water-soluble vitamin 91

CHAPTER 3 Clinical Case Study: An Elderly Man Develops Muscle Damage After Changing His Diet

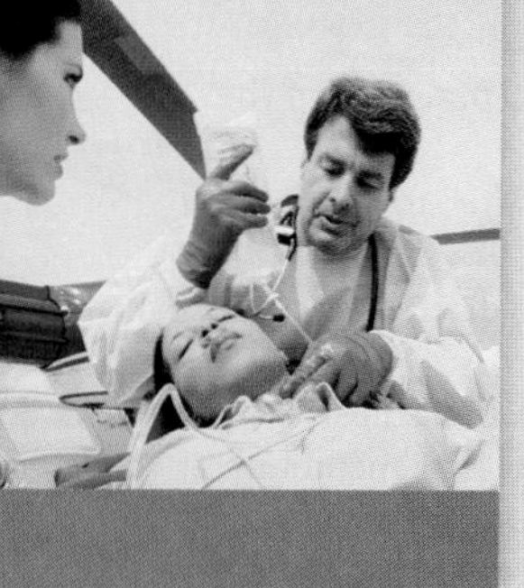

An elderly man and his wife moved from New Jersey to Florida to begin their retirement. The husband had recently been told by his physician in New Jersey that he needed to lose weight and start exercising or he ran the risk of developing type 2 diabetes mellitus. As part of his effort to become healthier, the man began walking daily and adding more fruits and vegetables to his diet in place of red meats and other fatty foods. About 2 weeks after making these changes, he began to feel weakness, tenderness, and cramps in his legs and arms. Eventually, the cramps developed into severe pain, and he also noticed a second alarming change, that his urine had become reddish brown in color. He was admitted into the hospital, where it was determined that he had widespread damage to his skeletal muscles. The dying muscle cells were releasing their intracellular contents into the man's blood; as these substances were filtered by the man's kidneys, they entered the urine and turned the urine a dark color.

After questioning the man, his Florida physician determined that the only change in the man's life and routine—apart from his move to Florida—were the changes in his diet and exercise level. Partly because the exercise (slow walks around the block) was deemed to be very mild, it was ruled out as a contributor to the muscle damage. His medical history revealed that the man had been taking a medication called a "statin" every day for 15 years to decrease his concentration of blood cholesterol. (You will learn more about cholesterol and statins in Chapters 12 and 16.) A rare side effect of statins is damage to skeletal muscle; however, why should this side effect appear suddenly after 15 years, and how could it be linked with this man's change in diet?

Further questioning revealed that the man and his wife had moved to a town that happened to have a large grapefruit orchard in which local residents typically picked their own grapefruits. This seemed like a fortuitous way to supplement his diet with a healthy and fresh citrus fruit, and consequently the man had been drinking up to five large glasses a day of freshly squeezed grapefruit juice since his arrival in town. This information solved the puzzle of what had happened to this man. Grapefruit juice contains a number of compounds called furanocoumarins. These compounds are inhibitors of a very important enzyme located in the small intestine and liver, called cytochrome P450 3A4 (or CYP3A4). The function of CYP3A4 is to metabolize substances in the body that are potentially toxic, including compounds ingested in the diet. Many oral medications are metabolized by this enzyme; you can think of this as the body's way of rejecting ingested compounds that it does not recognize. Recall from Figures 3.37 and 3.38 that one of the key features of enzymes is that their activity can be regulated in several ways. Furanocoumarins inhibit CYP3A4 by covalent inhibition.

Some of the statins, including the one our patient was taking, are metabolized by CYP3A4 in the small intestine. This must be factored into the amount, or dose, of the drug that is given to patients, so that enough of the drug gets into the bloodstream to exert its beneficial effect on decreasing cholesterol concentrations. When the man began drinking grapefruit juice, however, the furanocoumarins inhibited his CYP3A4. Therefore, when he took his usual dose of statin, the amount of the drug entering the blood was greater than normal, and this continued each day as he continued taking his medication. Eventually, the blood concentrations of the statin became very high, and he started to experience muscle damage and other side effects. Once this was determined, the man was advised to substitute other citrus drinks (most of which do not contain furanocoumarins) for grapefruit juice and to stop taking his cholesterol medication until his blood concentrations returned to normal. Additional treatments were initiated to treat his muscle damage.

This case is a fascinating study of how enzymes are regulated and what may happen when an enzyme that should be active instead is inhibited. It also points out the importance of reading the labels on all medications about possibly harmful drug and food interactions.

See Chapter 19 for complete, integrative case studies

CHAPTER 3 TEST QUESTIONS

Answers found in Appendix A.

1. Which cell structure contains the enzymes required for oxidative phosphorylation?
   a. inner membrane of mitochondria
   b. smooth endoplasmic reticulum
   c. rough endoplasmic reticulum
   d. outer membrane of mitochondria
   e. matrix of mitochondria
2. Which sequence regarding protein synthesis is correct?
   a. translation ⟶ transcription ⟶ mRNA synthesis
   b. transcription ⟶ splicing of primary RNA transcript ⟶ translocation of mRNA ⟶ translation
   c. splicing of introns ⟶ transcription ⟶ mRNA synthesis translation
   d. transcription ⟶ translation ⟶ mRNA production
   e. tRNA enters nucleus ⟶ transcription begins ⟶ mRNA moves to cytoplasm ⟶ protein synthesis begins
3. Which is *incorrect* regarding ligand–protein binding reactions?
   a. Allosteric modulation of the protein's binding site occurs directly at the binding site itself.
   b. Allosteric modulation can alter the affinity of the protein for the ligand.
   c. Phosphorylation of the protein is an example of covalent modulation.
   d. If two ligands can bind to the binding site of the protein, competition for binding will occur.
   e. Binding reactions are either electrical or hydrophobic in nature.
4. According to the law of mass action, in the following reaction,

$$CO_2 + H_2O \rightleftharpoons H_2CO_3$$

   a. Increasing the concentration of carbon dioxide will slow down the forward (left-to-right) reaction.
   b. Increasing the concentration of carbonic acid will accelerate the rate of the reverse (right-to-left) reaction.
   c. Increasing the concentration of carbon dioxide will speed up the reverse reaction.
   d. Decreasing the concentration of carbonic acid will slow down the forward reaction.
   e. No enzyme is required for either the forward or reverse reaction.
5. Which of the following can be converted to glucose by gluconeogenesis in the liver?
   a. fatty acid
   b. triglyceride
   c. glycerol
   e. glycogen
   d. ATP
6. Which of the following is true?
   a. Triglycerides have the least energy content per gram of the three major energy sources in the body.
   b. Fat catabolism generates new triglycerides for storage in adipose tissue.
   c. By mass, the total-body content of carbohydrates exceeds that of total triglycerides.
   d. Catabolism of fatty acids occurs in two-carbon steps.
   e. Triglycerides are the major lipids found in plasma membranes.

CHAPTER 3 GENERAL PRINCIPLES ASSESSMENT

Answers found in Appendix A.

1. How does the general principle that *structure is a determinant of—and has coevolved with—function* pertain to cells or cellular organelles? For example, what might be the significance of the extensive folds of the inner mitochondrial membranes shown in Figure 3.13? (See Figure 3.45 for a hint.) How do the illustrations in Figures 3.28 and 3.32b apply to the relationship between structure and function at the molecular (protein) level?
2. *Physiological processes are dictated by the laws of chemistry and physics.* Referring back to Figure 3.27, explain how this principle applies to the interaction between proteins and ligands.
3. *Physiological processes require the transfer and balance of matter and energy.* How is this general principle illustrated in Figure 3.53, and how does this relate to another key physiological principle that *homeostasis is essential for health and survival?* (You may want to refer back to Figure 1.6 and imagine that the box labeled "Active product" is "ATP.")

CHAPTER 3 QUANTITATIVE AND THOUGHT QUESTIONS

Answers found in Appendix A.

1. A base sequence in a portion of one strand of DNA is A—G—T—G—C—A—A—G—T—C—T. Predict
   a. the base sequence in the complementary strand of DNA.
   b. the base sequence in RNA transcribed from the sequence shown.
2. The triplet code in DNA for the amino acid histidine is G—T—A. Predict the mRNA codon for this amino acid and the tRNA anticodon.
3. If a protein contains 100 amino acids, how many nucleotides will be present in the gene that codes for this protein?

4. A variety of chemical messengers that normally regulate acid secretion in the stomach bind to proteins in the plasma membranes of the acid-secreting cells. Some of these binding reactions lead to increased acid secretion, others to decreased secretion. In what ways might a drug that causes decreased acid secretion be acting on these cells?
5. In one type of diabetes, the plasma concentration of the hormone insulin is normal but the response of the cells that insulin usually binds to is markedly decreased. Suggest a reason for this in terms of the properties of protein-binding sites.
6. The following graph shows the relation between the amount of acid secreted and the concentration of compound X, which stimulates acid secretion in the stomach by binding to a membrane protein. At a plasma concentration of 2 pM, compound X produces an acid secretion of 20 mmol/h.

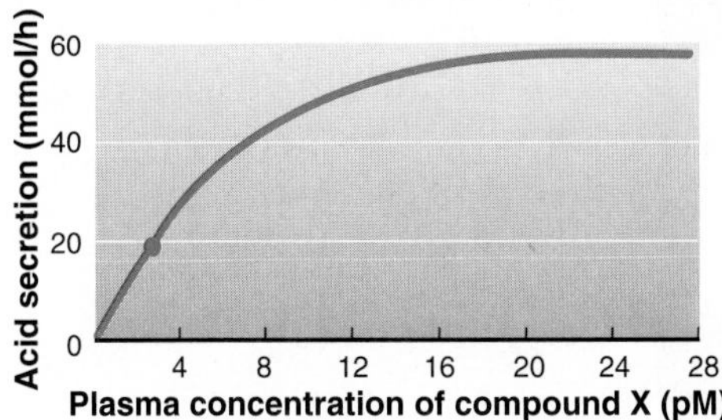

   a. Specify two ways in which acid secretion by compound X could be increased to 40 mmol/h.
   b. Why will increasing the concentration of compound X to 28 pM fail to produce more acid secretion than increasing the concentration of X to 20 pM?
7. In the following metabolic pathway, what is the rate of formation of the end-product E if substrate A is present at a saturating concentration? The maximal rates (products formed per second) of the individual steps are indicated.

$$A \xrightarrow{30} B \xrightarrow{5} C \xrightarrow{20} D \xrightarrow{40} E$$

8. If the concentration of oxygen in the blood delivered to a muscle is increased, what effect will it have on the muscle's rate of ATP production?
9. During prolonged starvation, when glucose is not being absorbed from the gastrointestinal tract, what molecules can be used to synthesize new glucose?
10. How might certain forms of liver disease produce an increase in the blood concentrations of ammonia?

CHAPTER 3 ANSWERS TO PHYSIOLOGICAL INQUIRIES

Figure 3.4 The intracellular fluid compartment includes all of the water in the cytoplasm plus the water in the nucleus. See Chapter 1 for a discussion of the different water compartments in the body.

Figure 3.9 Because tight junctions form a barrier to the transport of most substances across an epithelium, the food you consume remains in the intestine until it is digested into usable components. Thereafter, the digested products can be absorbed across the epithelium in a controlled manner.

Figure 3.19 An example of an alternatively spliced mRNA might appear as follows, where exon number 2 is missing from the mRNA.

Figure 3.28 It would be easier to design drugs to interact with protein X because it has less chemical specificity. Any of a number of similar-shaped ligands (drugs) could theoretically interact with the protein.

Figure 3.31 Unless the dose of the ligand was sufficiently high to fully saturate both proteins X and Y, the effect of the ligand would probably be to increase blood pressure because at any given ligand concentration, protein Y would have a higher percent saturation than protein X. However, because protein X also binds the ligand to some extent, it would counteract some of the effects of protein Y.

Figure 3.38 If the product were rapidly removed or converted to another product, then the rate of conversion of the substrate into product would increase according to the law of mass action. This is actually typical of what happens in cells.

Visit this book's website at **www.mhhe.com/widmaier13** for chapter quizzes, interactive learning exercises, and other study tools.

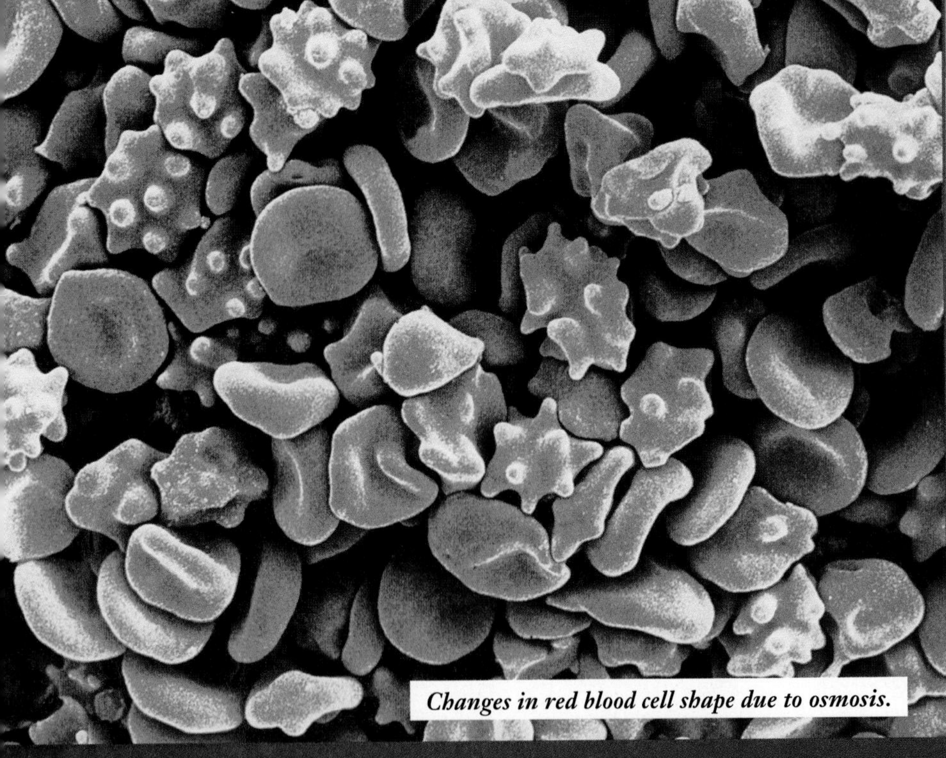
Changes in red blood cell shape due to osmosis.

4 Movement of Molecules Across Cell Membranes

You learned in Chapter 3 that the contents of a cell are separated from the surrounding extracellular fluid by a thin bilayer of lipids and protein, which forms the plasma membrane. You also learned that membranes associated with mitochondria, endoplasmic reticulum, lysosomes, the Golgi apparatus, and the nucleus divide the intracellular fluid into several membrane-bound compartments. The movements of molecules and ions between the various cell organelles and the cytosol, and between the cytosol and the extracellular fluid, depend on the properties of these membranes. The rates at which different substances move through membranes vary considerably and in some cases can be controlled—increased or decreased—in response to various signals. This chapter focuses upon the transport functions of membranes, with emphasis on the plasma membrane. The controlled movement of solutes such as ions, glucose, and gases, as well as the movement of water across membranes, is of profound importance in physiology. As just a few examples, such transport mechanisms are essential for cells to maintain their size and shape, energy balance, and their ability to send and respond to electrical or chemical signals from other cells.

As you read the first section, think how diffusion is a good example of the general principle introduced in Chapter 1 that physiological processes are dictated by the laws of chemistry and physics. In the subsequent sections, consider how the principles of homeostasis and of controlled exchange of materials apply.

4.1 Diffusion

One of the fundamental physical features of molecules of any substance, whether solid, liquid, or gas, is that they are in a continuous state of movement or vibration. The energy for this movement comes from heat; the warmer a substance is, the faster its molecules move. In solutions, such rapidly moving molecules cannot travel very far before colliding with other molecules, undergoing millions of collisions every second. Each collision alters the direction of the molecule's movement, so that the path of any one molecule becomes unpredictable. Because a molecule may at any instant be moving in any direction, such movement is random, with no preferred direction of movement.

The random thermal motion of molecules in a liquid or gas will eventually distribute them uniformly throughout a container. Thus, if we start with a solution in which a solute is more concentrated in one region than another (**Figure 4.1a**), random thermal motion will redistribute the solute from regions of higher concentration to regions of lower concentration until the solute reaches a uniform concentration throughout the solution (**Figure 4.1b**). This movement of molecules from one location to another solely as a result of their random thermal motion is known as **simple diffusion.**

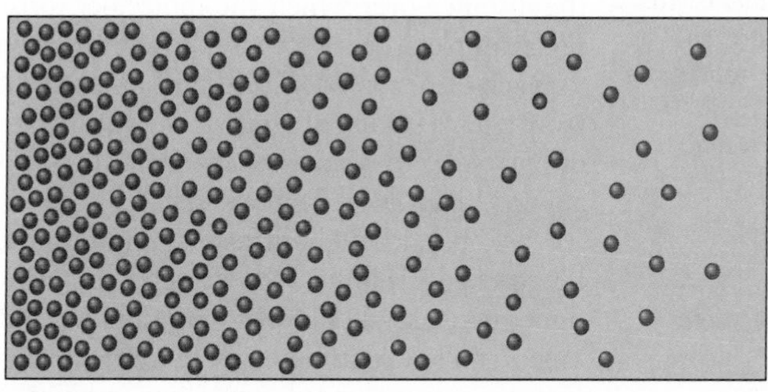

(a)

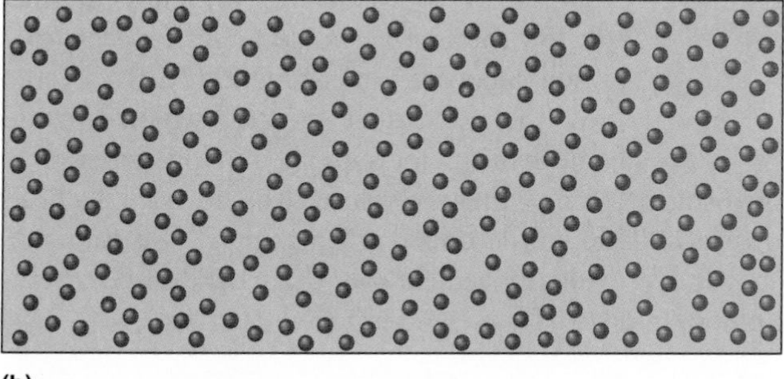

(b)

Figure 4.1 APIR Simple diffusion. (a) Molecules initially concentrated in one region of a solution will, due to their random thermal motion, undergo a net diffusion from the region of higher concentration to the region of lower concentration. (b) With time, the molecules will become uniformly distributed throughout the solution.

Many processes in living organisms are closely associated with simple diffusion. For example, oxygen, nutrients, and other molecules enter and leave the smallest blood vessels (capillaries) by simple diffusion, and the movement of many substances across plasma membranes and organelle membranes occurs by simple diffusion. In this way, simple diffusion is one of the key mechanisms by which cells maintain homeostasis. For the remainder of the text, we will often follow convention and refer only to "diffusion" when describing simple diffusion. You will learn later about another type of diffusion called facilitated diffusion.

Magnitude and Direction of Diffusion

Figure 4.2 illustrates the diffusion of glucose between two compartments of equal volume separated by a permeable barrier. Initially, glucose is present in compartment 1 at a concentration of 20 mmol/L, and there is no glucose in compartment 2. The random movements of the glucose molecules in compartment 1 move some of them into compartment 2. The amount of material crossing a surface in a unit of time is known as a **flux.** This one-way flux of glucose from compartment 1 to compartment 2 depends on the concentration of glucose in compartment 1. If the number of molecules in a unit of volume is doubled, the flux of molecules across the surface of the unit will also be doubled because twice as many molecules will be moving in any direction at a given time.

After a short time, some of the glucose molecules that have entered compartment 2 will randomly move back into compartment 1 (see Figure 4.2, time B). The magnitude of the glucose flux from compartment 2 to compartment 1 depends upon the concentration of glucose in compartment 2 at any time.

The **net flux** of glucose between the two compartments at any instant is the difference between the two one-way fluxes. The net flux determines the net gain of molecules in compartment 2 per unit time and the net loss from compartment 1 per unit time.

Eventually, the concentrations of glucose in the two compartments become equal at 10 mmol/L. Glucose molecules continue to move randomly, and some will find their way from one compartment to the other. However, the two one-way fluxes are now equal in magnitude but opposite in direction; therefore, the *net* flux of glucose is zero (see Figure 4.2, time C). The system has now reached **diffusion equilibrium.** No further change in the glucose concentrations of the two compartments will occur because of the equal rates of diffusion of glucose molecules in both directions between the two compartments.

Several important properties of diffusion can be emphasized using this example. Three fluxes can be identified—the

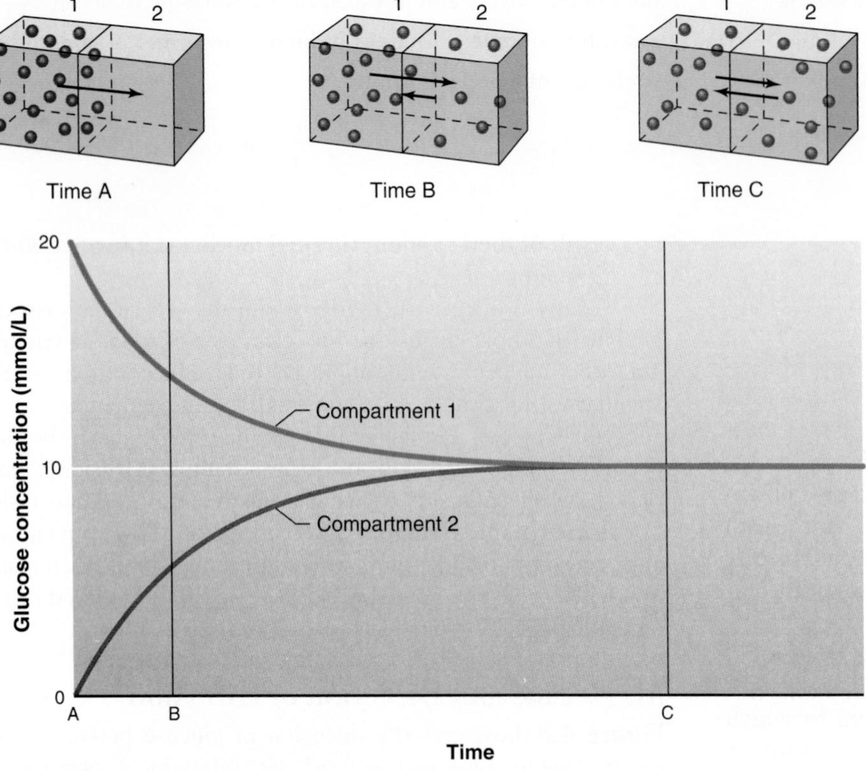

Figure 4.2 AP|R Diffusion of glucose between two compartments of equal volume separated by a barrier permeable to glucose. Initially, time A, compartment 1 contains glucose at a concentration of 20 mmol/L, and no glucose is present in compartment 2. At time B, some glucose molecules have moved into compartment 2, and some of these are moving back into compartment 1. The length of the arrows represents the magnitudes of the one-way movements. At time C, diffusion equilibrium has been reached, the concentrations of glucose are equal in the two compartments (10 mmol/L), and the *net* movement is zero. In the graph at the bottom of the figure, the green line represents the concentration in compartment 1, and the purple line represents the concentration in compartment 2. Note that at time C, glucose concentration is 10 mmol/L in both compartments. At that time, diffusion equilibrium has been reached.

PHYSIOLOGICAL INQUIRY

- If at time C, additional glucose could be added to compartment 1 such that its concentration was instantly increased to 15 mmol/L, what would the graph look like following time C? Draw the new graph on the figure and indicate the glucose concentrations in compartments 1 and 2 at diffusion equilibrium. (*Note:* It is not actually possible to instantly change the concentration of a substance in this way because it will immediately begin diffusing to the other compartment as it is added.)

Answer can be found at end of chapter.

two one-way fluxes occurring in opposite directions from one compartment to the other, and the net flux, which is the difference between them (**Figure 4.3**). The net flux is the most important component in diffusion because it is the net rate of material transfer from one location to another. Although the movement of individual molecules is random, *the net flux is always greater from regions of higher concentration to regions of lower concentration.* For this reason, we often say that substances move "downhill" by diffusion. The greater the difference in concentration between any two regions, the greater the magnitude of the net flux. Therefore, the concentration difference determines both the direction and the magnitude of the net flux.

At any concentration difference, however, the magnitude of the net flux depends on several additional factors: (1) temperature—the more elevated the temperature, the greater the speed of molecular movement and the faster the net flux; (2) mass of the molecule—large molecules such as proteins have a greater mass and lower speed than smaller molecules such as glucose and, consequently, have a slower net flux; (3) surface area—the greater the surface area between two regions, the greater the space available for diffusion and, therefore, the faster the net flux; and (4) the medium through which the molecules are moving—molecules diffuse more rapidly in air than in water. This is because collisions are less frequent in a gas phase, and, as we will see, when a membrane is involved, its chemical composition influences diffusion rates.

Diffusion Rate Versus Distance

The distance over which molecules diffuse is an important factor in determining the rate at which they can reach a cell from the blood or move throughout the interior of a cell after crossing the plasma membrane. Although individual molecules travel at high speeds, the number of collisions they undergo prevents them from traveling very far in a straight line. Diffusion times increase in proportion to the *square* of the distance over which the molecules diffuse. For example, it takes glucose only a few seconds to reach diffusion equilibrium at a point 10 μm away from a source of glucose, but it would take over 11 years to reach the same concentration at a point 10 cm away from the source.

Thus, although diffusion equilibrium can be reached rapidly over distances of cellular dimensions, it takes a very long time when distances of a few centimeters or more are involved. For an organism as large as a human being, the diffusion of oxygen and nutrients from the body surface to tissues located only a few centimeters below the surface would be far too slow to provide adequate nourishment. This is overcome by the circulatory system, which provides a mechanism for rapidly moving materials over large distances using a pressure source (the heart). This process, known as bulk flow, is described in Chapter 12. Diffusion, on the other hand, provides movement over the short distances between the blood, interstitial fluid, and intracellular fluid.

Diffusion Through Membranes

The rate at which a substance diffuses across a plasma membrane can be measured by monitoring the rate at which its intracellular concentration approaches diffusion equilibrium with its concentration in the extracellular fluid. For simplicity's sake, assume that because the volume of extracellular fluid

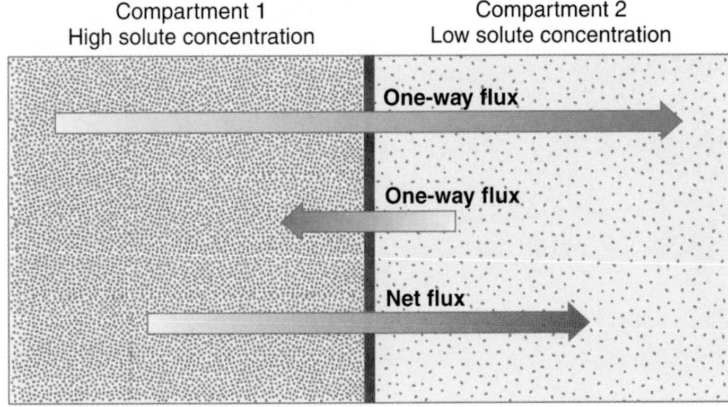

Figure 4.3 APIR The two one-way fluxes occurring during the simple diffusion of solute across a boundary and the net flux, which is the difference between the two one-way fluxes. The net flux always occurs in the direction from higher to lower concentration. The length of the arrows indicates the magnitude of the flux.

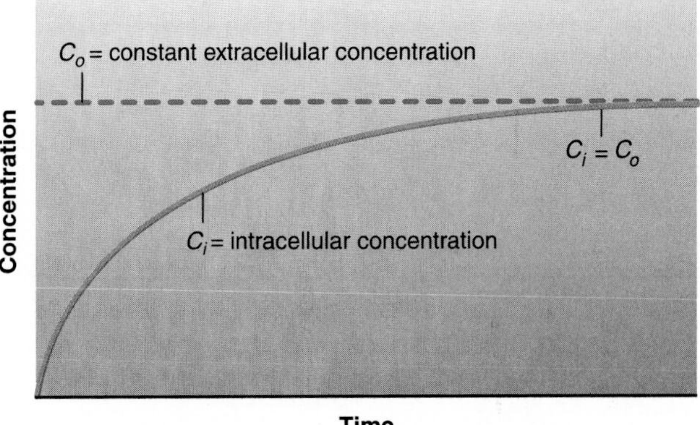

Figure 4.4 The increase in intracellular concentration as a solute diffuses from a constant extracellular concentration until diffusion equilibrium ($C_i = C_o$) is reached across the plasma membrane of a cell.

is large, its solute concentration will remain essentially constant as the substance diffuses into the intracellular volume (**Figure 4.4**). As with all diffusion processes, the net flux J of material across the membrane is from the region of greater concentration (the extracellular solution in this case) to the region of less concentration (the intracellular fluid). The magnitude of the net flux is directly proportional to the difference in concentration across the membrane ($C_o - C_i$, where o and i stand for concentrations outside and inside the cell), the surface area of the membrane A, and the membrane permeability coefficient P as described by the Fick diffusion equation:

$$J = PA(C_o - C_i)$$

The numerical value of the permeability coefficient P is an experimentally determined number for a particular type of molecule at a given temperature; it reflects the ease with which the molecule is able to move through a given membrane. In other words, the greater the permeability coefficient, the faster the net flux across the membrane for any given concentration difference and membrane surface area. Due to the magnitude of their permeability coefficients, molecules typically diffuse a thousand to a million times slower through membranes than through a water layer of equal thickness. Membranes, therefore, act as barriers that considerably slow the diffusion of molecules across their surfaces. The major factor limiting diffusion across a membrane is its chemical composition, namely the hydrophobic interior of its lipid bilayer, as described next.

Diffusion Through the Lipid Bilayer

When the permeability coefficients of different organic molecules are examined in relation to their molecular structures, a correlation emerges. Whereas most polar molecules diffuse into cells very slowly or not at all, nonpolar molecules diffuse much more rapidly across plasma membranes—that is, they have large permeability constants. The reason is that nonpolar molecules can dissolve in the nonpolar regions of the membrane occupied by the fatty acid chains of the membrane phospholipids. In contrast, polar molecules have a much lower solubility in the membrane lipids. Increasing the lipid solubility of a substance by decreasing the number of polar or ionized groups it contains will increase the number of molecules dissolved in the membrane lipids. This will increase the flux of the substance across the membrane. Oxygen, carbon dioxide, fatty acids, and steroid hormones are examples of nonpolar molecules that diffuse rapidly through the lipid portions of membranes. Most of the organic molecules that make up the intermediate stages of the various metabolic pathways (Chapter 3) are ionized or polar molecules, often containing an ionized phosphate group; therefore, they have a low solubility in the lipid bilayer. Most of these substances are retained within cells and organelles because they cannot diffuse across the lipid bilayer of membranes, unless the membrane contains special proteins such as channels, as we see next. This is an excellent example of the general principle that physiological processes are dictated by the laws of chemistry and physics.

Diffusion of Ions Through Protein Channels

Ions such as Na^+, K^+, Cl^-, and Ca^{2+} diffuse across plasma membranes at much faster rates than would be predicted from their very low solubility in membrane lipids. Also, different cells have quite different permeabilities to these ions, whereas nonpolar substances have similar permeabilities in nearly all cells. Moreover, artificial lipid bilayers containing no protein are practically impermeable to these ions; this indicates that the protein component of the membrane is responsible for these permeability differences.

As we have seen (Chapter 3), integral membrane proteins can span the lipid bilayer. Some of these proteins form **ion channels** that allow ions to diffuse across the membrane. A single protein may have a conformation resembling that of a doughnut, with the hole in the middle providing the channel for ion movement. More often, several proteins aggregate, each forming a subunit of the walls of a channel (**Figure 4.5**). The diameters of ion channels are very small, only slightly larger than those of the ions that pass through them. The small size of the channels prevents larger molecules from entering or leaving.

An important characteristic of ion channels is that they can show selectivity for the type of ion or ions that can diffuse through them. This selectivity is based on the channel diameter, the charged and polar surfaces of the protein subunits

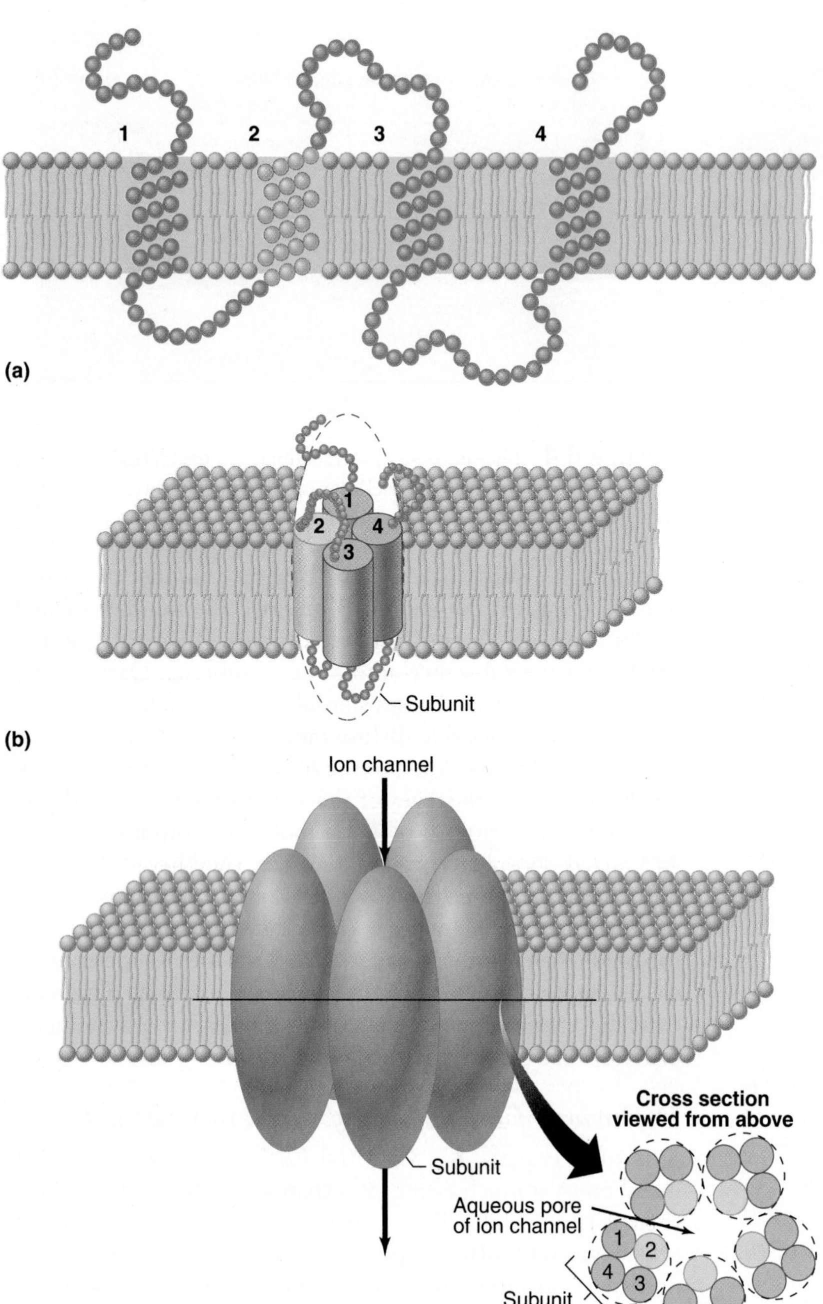

Figure 4.5 Model of an ion channel composed of five polypeptide subunits. Individual amino acids are represented as beads. (a) A channel subunit consisting of an integral membrane protein containing four transmembrane segments (1, 2, 3, and 4), each of which has an alpha-helical configuration within the membrane. Although this model has only four transmembrane segments, some channel proteins have as many as 12. (b) The same subunit as in (a) shown in three dimensions within the membrane, with the four transmembrane helices aggregated together and shown as cylinders. (c) The ion channel consists of five of the subunits illustrated in (b), which form the sides of the channel. As shown in cross section, the helical transmembrane segment 2 (light purple) of each subunit forms each side of the channel opening. The presence of ionized amino acid side chains along this region determines the selectivity of the channel to ions. Although this model shows the five subunits as identical, many ion channels are formed from the aggregation of several different types of subunit polypeptides.

PHYSIOLOGICAL INQUIRY

- In Chapter 2, you learned that proteins have several levels of structure. Which levels of structures are evident in the drawing of the ion channel in this figure?

Answer can be found at end of chapter.

that form the channel walls and electrically attract or repel the ions, and on the number of water molecules associated with the ions (so-called waters of hydration). For example, some channels (K^+ channels) allow only potassium ions to pass, whereas others are specific for Na^+ (Na^+ channels). Still others allow diffusion of both Na^+ and K^+ but not other ions. For this reason, two membranes that have the same permeability to K^+ because they have the same number of K^+ channels may have quite different permeabilities to Na^+ if they contain different numbers of Na^+ channels.

Role of Electrical Forces on Ion Movement

Thus far, we have described the direction and magnitude of solute diffusion across a membrane in terms of the solute's concentration difference across the membrane, its solubility in the membrane lipids, the presence of membrane ion channels, and the area of the membrane. When describing the diffusion of ions, because they are charged, one additional factor must be considered: the presence of electrical forces acting upon the ions.

A separation of electrical charge exists across plasma membranes of all cells. This is known as a **membrane potential** (**Figure 4.6**), the magnitude of which is measured in units of millivolts. (The origin of a membrane potential will be described in Chapter 6 in the context of neuronal function.) The membrane potential provides an electrical force that influences the movement of ions across the membrane. A simple principle of physics is that like charges repel each other, whereas opposite charges attract. For example, if the inside of a cell has a net negative charge with respect to the outside, as

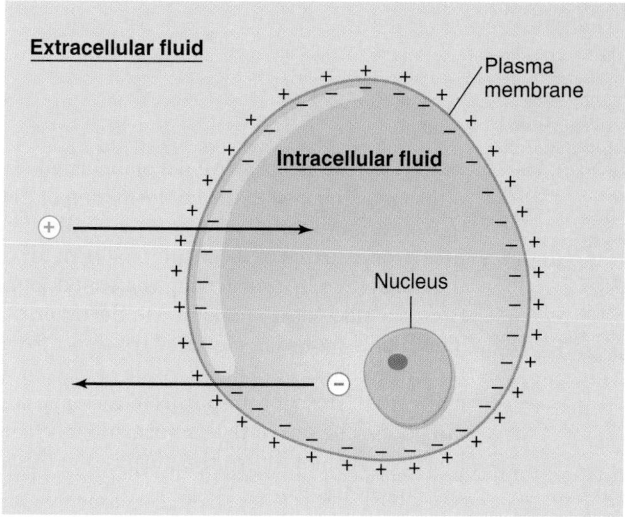

Figure 4.6 The separation of electrical charge across a plasma membrane (the membrane potential) provides the electrical force that drives positive ions (+) into a cell and negative ions (−) out.

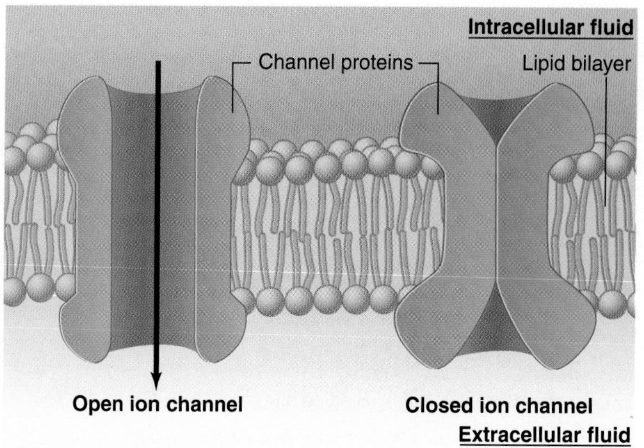

Figure 4.7 As a result of conformational changes in the proteins forming an ion channel, the channel may be open, allowing ions to diffuse across the membrane, or may be closed. The conformational change is grossly exaggerated for illustrative purposes. The actual conformational change is more likely to be just sufficient to allow or prevent an ion to fit through.

is generally true, there will be an electrical force attracting positive ions into the cell and repelling negative ions. Even if no difference in ion concentration existed across the membrane, there would still be a net movement of positive ions into and negative ions out of the cell because of the membrane potential. Consequently, the direction and magnitude of ion fluxes across membranes depend on both the concentration difference *and* the electrical difference (the membrane potential). These two driving forces are collectively known as the **electrochemical gradient** across a membrane.

The two forces that make up the electrochemical gradient may in some cases oppose each other. For example, the membrane potential may be driving potassium ions in one direction across the membrane while the concentration difference for K^+ is driving these ions in the opposite direction. The net movement of K^+ in this case would be determined by the relative magnitudes of the two opposing forces—that is, by the electrochemical gradient across the membrane.

Regulation of Diffusion Through Ion Channels

Ion channels can exist in an open or closed state (**Figure 4.7**), and changes in a membrane's permeability to ions can occur rapidly as these channels open or close. The process of opening and closing ion channels is known as **channel gating,** like the opening and closing of a gate in a fence. A single ion channel may open and close many times each second, suggesting that the channel protein fluctuates between these conformations. Over an extended period of time, at any given electrochemical gradient, the total number of ions that pass through a channel depends on how often the channel opens and how long it stays open.

Three factors can alter the channel protein conformations, producing changes in how long or how often a channel opens. First, the binding of specific molecules to channel proteins may directly or indirectly produce either an allosteric or covalent change in the shape of the channel protein. Such channels are termed **ligand-gated channels,** and the ligands that influence them are often chemical messengers. Second, changes in the membrane potential can cause movement of certain charged regions on a channel protein, altering its shape—these are **voltage-gated channels.** Third, physically deforming (stretching) the membrane may affect the conformation of some channel proteins—these are **mechanically gated channels.**

A single type of ion may pass through several different types of channels. For example, a membrane may contain ligand-gated K^+ channels, voltage-gated K^+ channels, and mechanically gated K^+ channels. Moreover, the same membrane may have several types of voltage-gated K^+ channels, each responding to a different range of membrane voltage, or several types of ligand-gated K^+ channels, each responding to a different chemical messenger. The roles of these gated channels in cell communication and electrical activity will be discussed in Chapters 5 through 7.

4.2 Mediated-Transport Systems

As stated in Chapter 1, a general principle of physiology is that controlled exchange of materials occurs between compartments and across cellular membranes. Although diffusion through gated channels accounts for some of the controlled transmembrane movement of ions, it does not account for all of it. Moreover, a number of other molecules, including amino acids and glucose, are able to cross membranes yet are too polar to diffuse through the lipid bilayer and too large to diffuse through channels. The passage of these molecules and the nondiffusional movements of ions are mediated by integral membrane proteins known as **transporters** (or carriers). The movement of substances through a membrane by these mechanisms is called **mediated transport,** which depends on conformational changes in these transporters.

The transported solute must first bind to a specific site on a transporter, a site exposed to the solute on one surface of the membrane (**Figure 4.8**). A portion of the transporter then undergoes a change in shape, exposing this same binding site to the solution on the opposite side of the membrane.

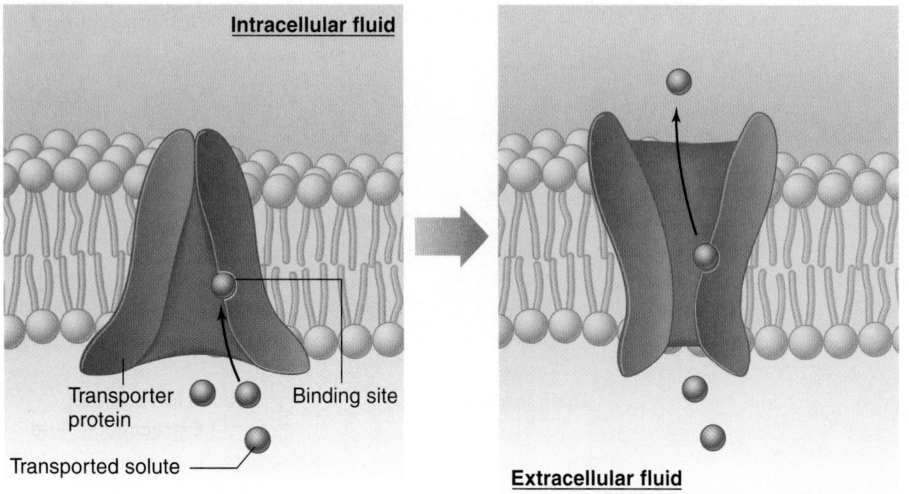

Figure 4.8 APIR Model of mediated transport. A change in the conformation of the transporter exposes the transporter binding site first to one surface of the membrane then to the other, thereby transferring the bound solute from one side of the membrane to the other. This model shows net mediated transport from the extracellular fluid to the inside of the cell. In many cases, the net transport is in the opposite direction. The size of the conformational change is exaggerated for illustrative purposes in this and subsequent figures.

The dissociation of the substance from the transporter binding site completes the process of moving the material through the membrane. Using this mechanism, molecules can move in either direction, getting on the transporter on one side and off at the other. The diagram of the transporter in Figure 4.8 is only a model, because the specific conformational changes of any transport protein are still uncertain.

Many of the characteristics of transporters and ion channels are similar. Both involve membrane proteins and show chemical specificity. They do, however, differ in the number of molecules or ions crossing the membrane by way of these membrane proteins. Ion channels typically move several thousand times more ions per unit time than do transporters. In part, this is because a transporter must change its shape for each molecule transported across the membrane, whereas an open ion channel can support a continuous flow of ions without a change in conformation. Imagine, for example, how many more cars can move over a bridge than can be shuttled back and forth by a ferry boat.

Many types of transporters are present in membranes, each type having binding sites that are specific for a particular substance or a specific class of related substances. For example, although both amino acids and sugars undergo mediated transport, a protein that transports amino acids does not transport sugars, and vice versa. Just as with ion channels, the plasma membranes of different cells contain different types and numbers of transporters; consequently, they exhibit differences in the types of substances transported and in their rates of transport.

Three factors determine the magnitude of solute flux through a mediated-transport system. The first of these is the extent to which the transporter binding sites are saturated, which depends on both the solute concentration and the affinity of the transporters for the solute. Second, the number of transporters in the membrane determines the flux at any level of saturation. The third factor is the rate at which the conformational change in the transport protein occurs. The flux through a mediated-transport system can be altered by changing any of these three factors.

For any transported solute, a finite number of specific transporters reside in a given membrane at any particular moment. As with any binding site, as the concentration of the solute to be transported is increased, the number of occupied binding sites increases until the transporters become saturated—that is, until all the binding sites are occupied. When the transporter binding sites are saturated, the maximal flux across the membrane has been reached and no further increase in solute flux will occur with increases in solute concentration. Contrast the solute flux resulting from mediated transport with the flux produced by diffusion through the lipid portion of a membrane (**Figure 4.9**). The flux due to diffusion increases in direct proportion to the increase in extracellular concentration, and there is no limit because diffusion does not involve binding to a fixed number of sites. (At very high ion concentrations, however, diffusion through ion channels may approach a limiting value because of the fixed number of channels available, just as an upper limit determines the rate at which cars can move over a bridge.)

When transporters are saturated, however, the maximal transport flux depends upon the rate at which the conformational changes in the transporters can transfer their binding sites from one surface to the other. This rate is much slower than the rate of ion diffusion through ion channels.

Thus far, we have described mediated transport as though all transporters had similar properties. In fact, two types of mediated transport exist—facilitated diffusion and active transport.

Facilitated Diffusion

As in simple diffusion, in **facilitated diffusion** the net flux of a molecule across a membrane always proceeds from higher to lower concentration, or "downhill" across a membrane; the key difference between these processes is that facilitated diffusion uses a transporter to move solute, as in Figure 4.8. Net facilitated diffusion continues until the concentrations of the solute on the two sides of the membrane become equal. At this point, equal numbers of molecules are binding to the transporter at the outer surface of the cell and moving into the cell as are binding at the inner surface and moving out. Neither simple diffusion nor facilitated diffusion is directly coupled to energy (ATP) derived from metabolism. For this reason, they are incapable of producing a net flux of solute from a lower to a higher concentration across a membrane.

Among the most important facilitated-diffusion systems in the body are those that mediate the transport of glucose across plasma membranes. Without such glucose transporters, or GLUTs as they are abbreviated, cells would be virtually

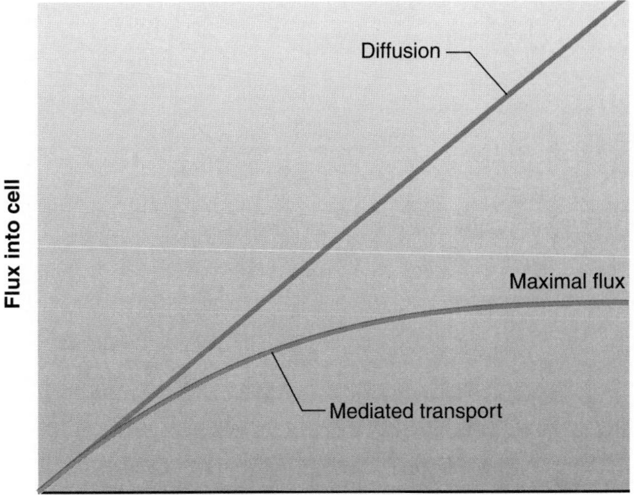

Figure 4.9 The flux of molecules diffusing into a cell across the lipid bilayer of a plasma membrane (green line) increases continuously in proportion to the extracellular concentration, whereas the flux of molecules through a mediated-transport system (purple line) reaches a maximal value.

PHYSIOLOGICAL INQUIRY

- What might determine the value for maximal flux of a mediated-transport system as shown here?

Answer can be found at end of chapter.

impermeable to glucose, which is a polar molecule. It might be expected that as a result of facilitated diffusion the glucose concentration inside cells would become equal to the extracellular concentration. This does not occur in most cells, however, because glucose is metabolized in the cytosol to glucose 6-phosphate almost as quickly as it enters (refer back to Figure 3.41). Consequently, the intracellular glucose concentration remains lower than the extracellular concentration, and there is a continuous net flux of glucose into cells.

Several distinct GLUTs are known to mediate the facilitated diffusion of glucose across cell membranes. Each GLUT is coded for by a different gene, and these genes are expressed in different types of cells. The transporters differ in the affinity of their binding sites for glucose; their maximal rates of transport when saturated; and the modulation of their transport activity by various chemical signals, such as the hormone insulin. As you will learn in Chapter 16, although glucose enters all cells by means of GLUTs, insulin primarily affects the type of transporter expressed in skeletal and cardiac muscle and adipose tissue. Insulin increases the recruitment of these glucose transporters from intracellular vesicles to the plasma membrane. The insertion of the GLUTs into the plasma membrane increases the rate of glucose movement into those cells. When insulin is not available, as in the disease ***type 1 diabetes mellitus,*** muscle and adipose cells cannot efficiently transport glucose into their cells because fewer GLUTs exist in the plasma membranes of those cells. This contributes to the accumulation of glucose in the extracellular fluid, which is a hallmark of the disease (described in detail in Chapter 16).

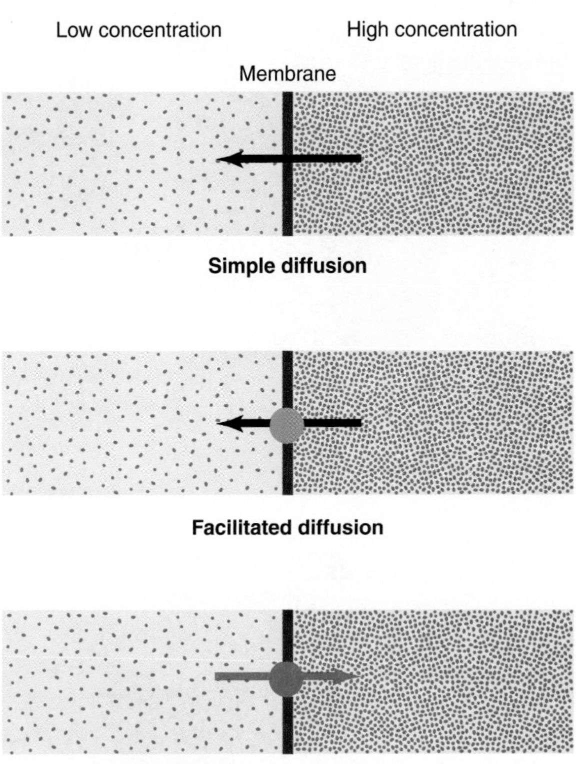

Figure 4.10 Direction of net solute flux crossing a membrane by simple diffusion (high to low concentration), facilitated diffusion (high to low concentration), and active transport (low to high concentration). The colored circles represent transporter molecules.

Active Transport

Active transport differs from facilitated diffusion in that it uses energy to move a substance *uphill* across a membrane—that is, against the substance's concentration gradient (**Figure 4.10**). As with facilitated diffusion, active transport requires a substance to bind to the transporter in the membrane. Because these transporters move the substance *uphill,* they are often referred to as pumps. As with facilitated-diffusion transporters, active-transport transporters exhibit specificity and saturation—that is, the flux via the transporter is maximal when all transporter binding sites are occupied.

The net movement from lower to higher concentrations and the maintenance of a higher steady-state concentration on one side of a membrane can be achieved only by the continuous input of energy into the active-transport process. Two means of coupling energy to transporters are known: (1) the direct use of ATP in **primary active transport,** and (2) the use of an electrochemical gradient across a membrane to drive the process in **secondary active transport.**

Primary Active Transport

The hydrolysis of ATP by a transporter provides the energy for primary active transport. The transporter itself is an enzyme called *ATPase* that catalyzes the breakdown of ATP and, in the process, phosphorylates itself. Phosphorylation of the transporter protein is a type of covalent modulation that changes the conformation of the transporter and the affinity of the transporter's solute binding site.

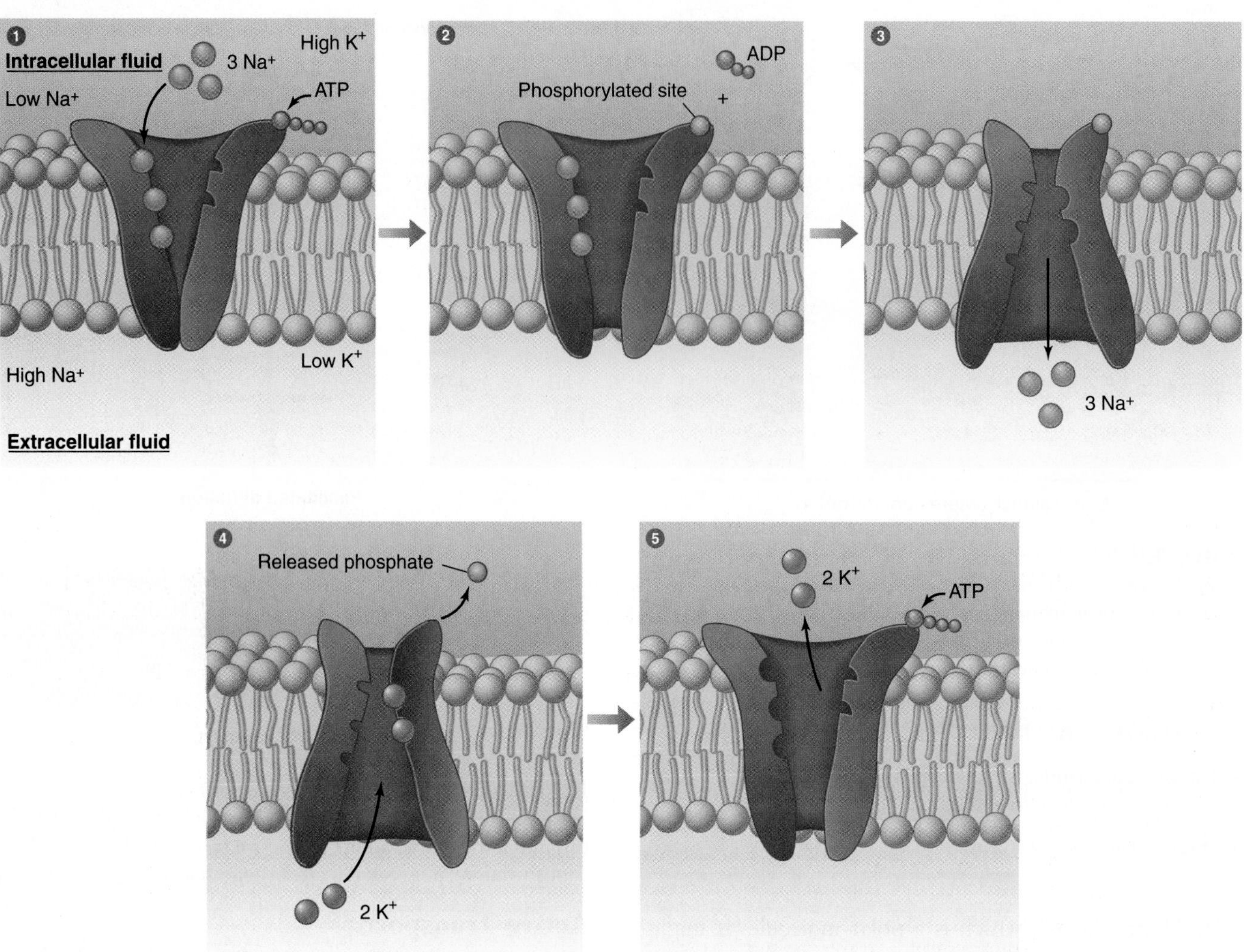

Figure 4.11 AP|R Active transport of Na^+ and K^+ mediated by the Na^+/K^+-ATPase pump. See text for the numbered sequence of events occurring during transport.

One of the best-studied examples of primary active transport is the movement of sodium and potassium ions across plasma membranes by the Na^+/K^+-ATPase pump. This transporter, which is present in all cells, moves sodium ions from intracellular to extracellular fluid, and potassium ions in the opposite direction. In both cases, the movements of the ions are against their respective concentration gradients. **Figure 4.11** illustrates the sequence the Na^+/K^+-ATPase pump is believed to use to transport these two ions in opposite directions. (1) Initially, the transporter, with an associated molecule of ATP, binds three sodium ions at high-affinity sites on the intracellular surface of the protein. Two binding sites also exist for K^+, but at this stage they are in a low-affinity state and therefore do not bind intracellular K^+. (2) Binding of Na^+ results in activation of an inherent ATPase activity of the transporter protein, causing phosphorylation of the cytosolic surface of the transporter and releasing a molecule of ADP. (3) Phosphorylation results in a conformational change of the transporter, exposing the bound sodium ions to the extracellular fluid and, at the same time, reducing the affinity of the binding sites for Na^+. The sodium ions are released from their binding sites. (4) The new conformation of the transporter results in an increased affinity of the two binding sites for K^+, allowing two molecules of K^+ to bind to the transporter on the extracellular surface. (5) Binding of K^+ results in dephosphorylation of the transporter. This returns the transporter to its original conformation, resulting in reduced affinity of the K^+ binding sites and increased affinity of the Na^+ binding sites. K^+ is therefore released into the intracellular fluid, allowing new molecules of Na^+ (and ATP) to be bound at the intracellular surface.

The pumping activity of the Na^+/K^+-ATPase primary active transporter establishes and maintains the characteristic distribution of high intracellular K^+ and low intracellular Na^+ relative to their respective extracellular concentrations (**Figure 4.12**). For each molecule of ATP hydrolyzed, this transporter moves three sodium ions out of a cell and two potassium ions into a cell. This results in a net transfer of positive charge to the outside of the cell; therefore, this transport process is not electrically neutral, a point that will be described in detail in Chapter 6 when we consider the electrical charge across plasma membranes of neurons. The Na^+/K^+-ATPase primary active transporter is found in every cell and helps establish and maintain the membrane potential of the cell.

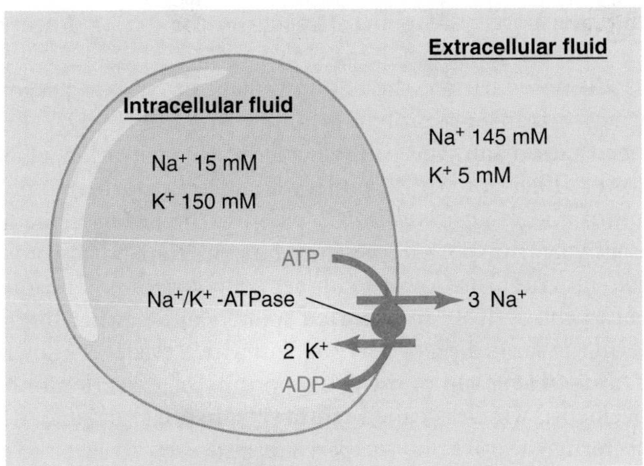

Figure 4.12 AP|R The primary active transport of sodium and potassium ions in opposite directions by the Na^+/K^+-ATPase in plasma membranes is responsible for the low Na^+ and high K^+ intracellular concentrations. For each ATP hydrolyzed, three sodium ions move out of a cell and two potassium ions move in.

In addition to the Na^+/K^+-ATPase transporter, the major primary active-transport proteins found in most cells are (1) Ca^{2+}-ATPase; (2) H^+-ATPase; and (3) H^+/K^+-ATPase. Together, the activities of these and other active-transport systems account for a significant share of the total energy usage of the human body. Ca^{2+}-ATPase is found in the plasma membrane and several organelle membranes, including the membranes of the endoplasmic reticulum. In the plasma membrane, the direction of active calcium transport is from cytosol to extracellular fluid. In organelle membranes, it is from cytosol into the organelle lumen. Thus, active transport of Ca^{2+} out of the cytosol, via Ca^{2+}-ATPase, is one reason that the cytosol of most cells has a very low Ca^{2+} concentration, about 10^{-7} mol/L, compared with an extracellular Ca^{2+} concentration of 10^{-3} mol/L, 10,000 times greater. These transport mechanisms help ensure intracellular calcium ion homeostasis, an important function because of the many physiological activities in cells that are regulated by changes in calcium ion concentration (for example, release of cell secretions from storage vesicles into the extracellular fluid).

H^+-ATPase is in the plasma membrane and several organelle membranes, including the inner mitochondrial and lysosomal membranes. In the plasma membrane, the H^+-ATPase moves hydrogen ions out of cells and in this way helps maintain cellular pH. All enzymes in the body require a narrow range of pH for optimal activity; consequently, this active-transport process is vital for cell metabolism and survival.

H^+/K^+-ATPase is in the plasma membranes of the acid-secreting cells in the stomach and kidneys, where it pumps one hydrogen ion out of the cell and moves one K^+ in for each molecule of ATP hydrolyzed. The hydrogen ions enter the stomach lumen where they play an important role in the digestion of proteins.

Secondary Active Transport

In secondary active transport, the movement of an ion down its electrochemical gradient is coupled to the transport of another molecule, such as a nutrient like glucose or an amino acid. Thus, transporters that mediate secondary active transport have two binding sites, one for an ion—typically but not always Na^+—and another for the cotransported molecule. An example of such transport is shown in **Figure 4.13**. In this example, the electrochemical gradient for Na^+ is directed into the cell because of the higher concentration of Na^+ in the extracellular fluid and the excess negative charges inside the cell. The other solute to be transported, however, must move *against* its concentration gradient, uphill into the cell. High-affinity binding sites for Na^+ exist on the extracellular surface of the transporter. Binding of Na^+ increases the affinity of the binding site for the transported solute. The transporter then undergoes a conformational change, which exposes both binding sites to the intracellular side of the membrane. When the transporter

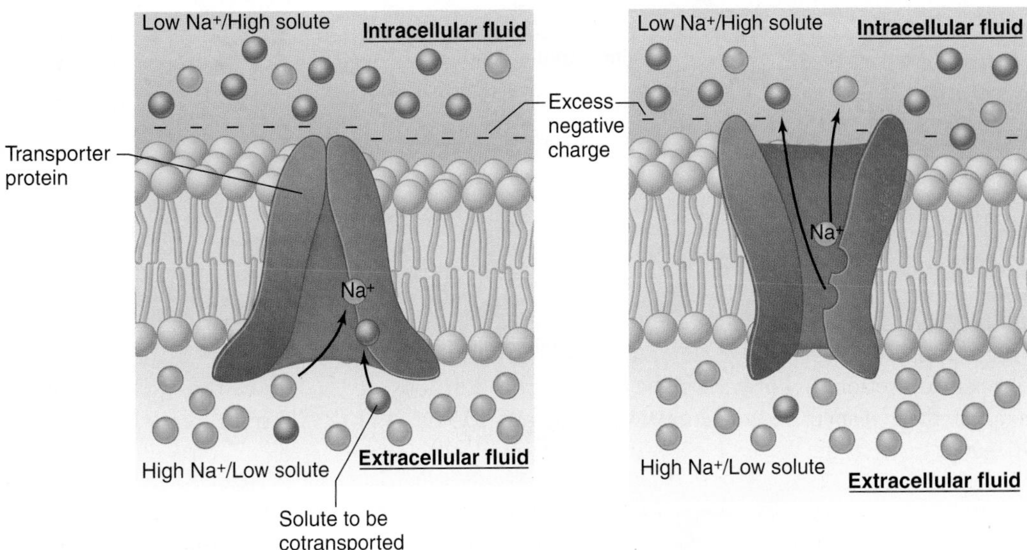

Figure 4.13 AP|R Secondary active-transport model. In this example, the binding of a sodium ion to the transporter produces an allosteric increase in the affinity of the solute binding site at the extracellular surface of the membrane. Binding of Na^+ and solute causes a conformational change in the transporter that exposes the binding sites to the intracellular fluid. Na^+ diffuses down its electrochemical gradient into the cell, which returns the solute binding site to a low-affinity state.

PHYSIOLOGICAL INQUIRY

- Is ATP hydrolyzed in the process of transporting solutes with secondary active transport?

Answer can be found at end of chapter.

changes conformation, Na^+ moves into the intracellular fluid by simple diffusion down its electrochemical gradient. At the same time, the affinity of the solute binding site decreases, which releases the solute into the intracellular fluid. The solute can be thought of as entering the cell by "piggyback" with the sodium ion. Once the transporter releases both molecules, the protein assumes its original conformation. The most important distinction, therefore, between primary and secondary active transport is that secondary active transport uses the stored energy of an electrochemical gradient to move both an ion and a second solute across a plasma membrane. The creation and maintenance of the electrochemical gradient, however, depend on the action of primary active transporters.

The creation of a Na^+ concentration gradient across the plasma membrane by the primary active transport of Na^+ is a means of indirectly "storing" energy that can then be used to drive secondary active-transport pumps linked to Na^+. Ultimately, however, the energy for secondary active transport is derived from metabolism in the form of the ATP that is used by the Na^+/K^+-ATPase to create the Na^+ concentration gradient. If the production of ATP were inhibited, the primary active transport of Na^+ would cease and the cell would no longer be able to maintain an Na^+ concentration gradient across the membrane. This, in turn, would lead to a failure of the secondary active-transport systems that depend on the Na^+ gradient for their source of energy.

As noted earlier, the net movement of Na^+ by a secondary active-transport protein is always from high extracellular concentration into the cell, where the concentration of Na^+ is lower. Therefore, in secondary active transport, the movement of Na^+ is always *downhill*, whereas the net movement of the actively transported solute on the same transport protein is *uphill*, moving from lower to higher concentration. The movement of the actively transported solute can be either into the cell (in the same direction as Na^+), in which case it is known as **cotransport,** or out of the cell (opposite the direction of Na^+ movement), which is called **countertransport** (**Figure 4.14**). The terms *symport* and *antiport* are also used to refer to the processes of cotransport and countertransport, respectively.

In summary, the distribution of substances between the intracellular and extracellular fluid is often unequal (**Table 4.1**) due to the presence in the plasma membrane of primary and secondary active transporters, ion channels, and the membrane potential. **Table 4.2** provides a summary of the major characteristics of the different pathways by which substances move through cell membranes, whereas **Figure 4.15** illustrates the variety of commonly encountered channels and transporters associated with the movement of substances across a typical plasma membrane.

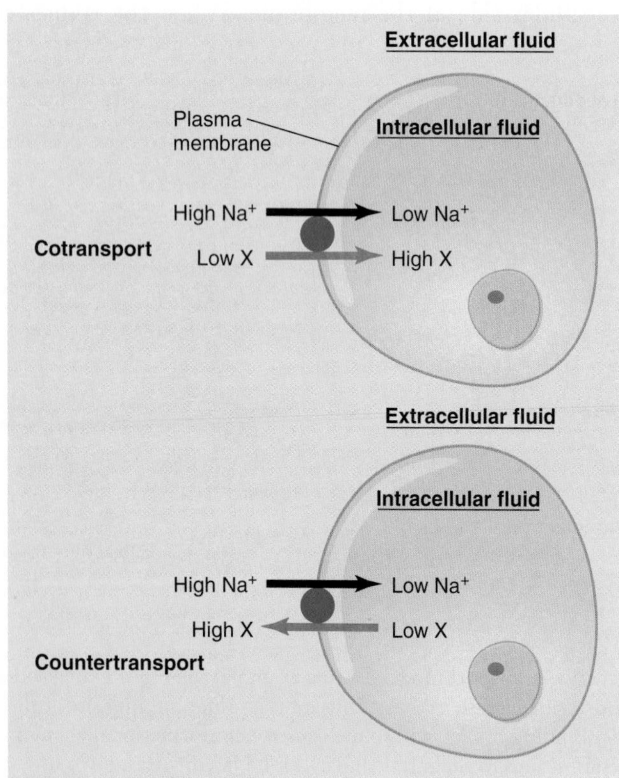

Figure 4.14 APIR Cotransport and countertransport during secondary active transport driven by Na^+. Sodium ions always move *down* their concentration gradient into a cell, and the transported solute always moves *up* its gradient. Both Na^+ and the transported solute X move in the same direction during cotransport, but in opposite directions during countertransport.

TABLE 4.1 Composition of Extracellular and Intracellular Fluids

	Extracellular Concentration (mM)	Intracellular Concentration (mM)*
Na^+	145	15
K^+	5	150
Ca^{2+}	1	0.0001
Mg^{2+}	1.5	12
Cl^-	100	7
HCO_3^-	24	10
P_i	2	40
Amino acids	2	8
Glucose	5.6	1
ATP	0	4
Protein	0.2	4

*The intracellular concentrations differ slightly from one tissue to another, depending on the expression of plasma membrane ion channels and transporters. The intracellular concentrations shown in the table are typical of most cells. For Ca^{2+}, values represent free concentrations. Total calcium levels, including the portion sequestered by proteins or in organelles, approach 2.5 mM (extracellular) and 1.5 mM (intracellular).

TABLE 4.2 Major Characteristics of Pathways by Which Substances Cross Membranes

	Diffusion		*Mediated Transport*		
	Through Lipid Bilayer	**Through Protein Channel**	**Facilitated Diffusion**	**Primary Active Transport**	**Secondary Active Transport**
Direction of net flux	High to low concentration	High to low concentration	High to low concentration	Low to high concentration	Low to high concentration
Equilibrium or steady state	$C_o = C_i$	$C_o = C_i$*	$C_o = C_i$	$C_o \neq C_i$	$C_o \neq C_i$
Use of integral membrane protein	No	Yes	Yes	Yes	Yes
Maximal flux at high concentration (saturation)	No	No	Yes	Yes	Yes
Chemical specificity	No	Yes	Yes	Yes	Yes
Use of energy and source	No	No	No	Yes: ATP	Yes: ion gradient (often Na^+)
Typical molecules using pathway	Nonpolar: O_2, CO_2, fatty acids	Ions: Na^+, K^+, Ca^{2+}	Polar: glucose	Ions: Na^+, K^+, Ca^{2+}, H^+	Polar: amino acids, glucose, some ions

*In the presence of a membrane potential, the intracellular and extracellular ion concentrations will not be equal at equilibrium.

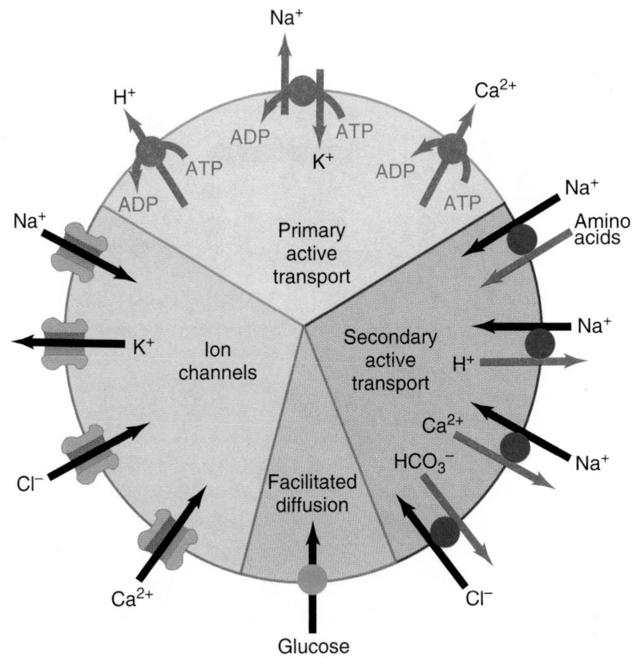

Figure 4.15 Movement of solutes across a typical plasma membrane involving membrane proteins. A specialized cell may contain additional transporters and channels not shown in this figure. Many of these membrane proteins can be modulated by various signals, leading to a controlled increase or decrease in specific solute fluxes across the membrane. The stoichiometry of cotransporters is not shown.

Not included in Table 4.2 is the mechanism by which water moves across membranes. The special case whereby this polar molecule moves between body fluid compartments is covered next.

4.3 Osmosis

Water is a polar molecule and yet it diffuses across the plasma membranes of most cells very rapidly. This process is mediated by a family of membrane proteins known as **aquaporins** that form channels through which water can diffuse. The type and number of these water channels differ in different membranes. Consequently, some cells are more permeable to water than others. In some cells, the number of aquaporin channels—and, therefore, the permeability of the membrane to water—can be altered in response to various signals. This is especially important in the epithelial cells that line certain ducts in the kidneys. As you will learn in Chapter 14, one of the major functions of the kidneys is to regulate the amount of water that gets excreted in the urine; this helps keep the total amount of water in the body fluid compartments homeostatic. The epithelial cells of the kidney ducts contain numerous aquaporins that can be increased or decreased in number depending on the water balance of the body at any time. For example, in an individual who is dehydrated, the numbers of aquaporins in the kidney epithelial cells will increase; this will permit additional water to move from the urine that is being formed in the renal ducts back into the blood. That is why the volume of urine decreases whenever an individual becomes dehydrated.

The net diffusion of water across a membrane is called **osmosis.** As with any diffusion process, a concentration difference must be present in order to produce a net flux. How can a difference in water concentration be established across a membrane?

The addition of a solute to water decreases the concentration of water in the solution compared to the concentration of pure water. For example, if a solute such as glucose is dissolved in water, the concentration of water in the resulting solution is less than that of pure water. A given volume of a glucose solution contains fewer water molecules than an equal volume of pure water because each glucose molecule occupies space formerly occupied by a water molecule (**Figure 4.16**). In quantitative terms, a liter of pure water weighs about 1000 g, and the molecular weight of water is 18. Thus, the concentration of water in pure water is 1000/18 = 55.5 M. The decrease in water concentration in a solution is approximately equal to the concentration of added solute. In other words, one solute molecule will displace one water molecule. The water concentration in a 1 M glucose solution is therefore approximately 54.5 M rather than 55.5 M. Just as adding water to a solution will dilute the solute, adding solute to water will "dilute" the water. The greater the solute concentration, the lower the water concentration.

The degree to which the water concentration is decreased by the addition of solute depends upon the *number* of particles (molecules or ions) of solute in solution (the solute concentration) and not upon the *chemical nature* of the solute. For example, 1 mol of glucose in 1 L of solution decreases the water concentration to the same extent as does 1 mol of an amino acid, or 1 mol of urea, or 1 mol of any other molecule that exists as a single particle in solution. On the other hand, a molecule that ionizes in solution decreases the water concentration in proportion to the number of ions formed. For example, many simple salts dissociate nearly completely in water. For simplicity's sake, we will assume the dissociation is 100% at body temperature and at concentrations found in the blood. Therefore, 1 mol of sodium chloride in solution gives rise to 1 mol of sodium ions and 1 mol of chloride ions, producing 2 mol of solute particles. This lowers the water concentration twice as much as 1 mol of glucose. By the same reasoning, if a 1 M $MgCl_2$ solution were to dissociate completely, it would lower the water concentration three times as much as would a 1 M glucose solution.

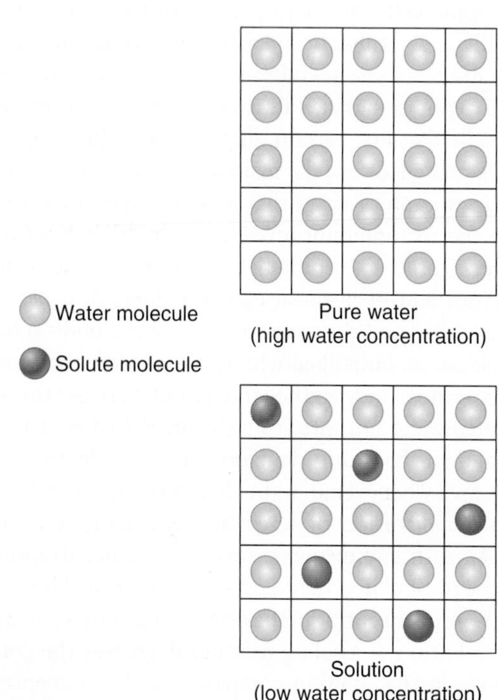

Figure 4.16 The addition of solute molecules to pure water lowers the water concentration in the solution.

Because the water concentration in a solution depends upon the number of solute particles, it is useful to have a concentration term that refers to the total concentration of solute particles in a solution, regardless of their chemical composition. The total solute concentration of a solution is known as its **osmolarity.** One **osmol** is equal to 1 mol of solute particles. Therefore, a 1 M solution of glucose has a concentration of 1 Osm (1 osmol per liter), whereas a 1 M solution of sodium chloride contains 2 osmol of solute per liter of solution. A liter of solution containing 1 mol of glucose and 1 mol of sodium chloride has an osmolarity of 3 Osm. A solution with an osmolarity of 3 Osm may contain 1 mol of glucose and 1 mol of sodium chloride, or 3 mol of glucose, or 1.5 mol of sodium chloride, or any other combination of solutes as long as the total solute concentration is equal to 3 Osm.

Although *osmolarity* refers to the concentration of solute particles, it also determines the water concentration in the solution because the higher the osmolarity, the lower the water concentration. The concentration of water in any two solutions having the same osmolarity is the same because the total number of solute particles per unit volume is the same.

Let us now apply these principles governing water concentration to osmosis of water across membranes. **Figure 4.17** shows two 1 L compartments separated by a membrane permeable to *both* solute and water. Initially, the concentration of solute is 2 Osm in compartment 1 and 4 Osm in compartment 2. This difference in solute concentration means there is also a difference in water concentration across the membrane: 53.5 M

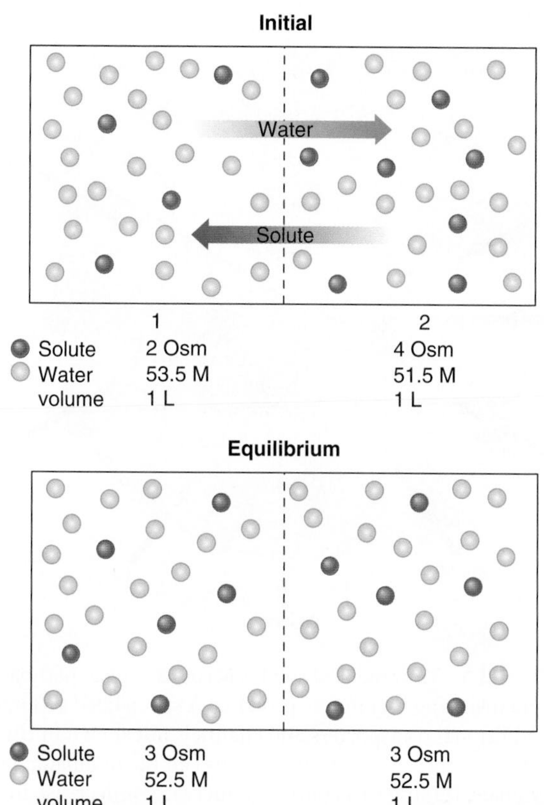

Figure 4.17 APIR Between two compartments of equal volume, the net diffusion of water and solute across a membrane permeable to both leads to diffusion equilibrium of both, with no change in the volume of either compartment. (For clarity's sake, not all water molecules are shown in this figure or in Figure 4.18.)

in compartment 1 and 51.5 M in compartment 2. Therefore, a net diffusion of water from the higher concentration in compartment 1 to the lower concentration in compartment 2 will take place, and a net diffusion of solute in the opposite direction, from 2 to 1. When diffusion equilibrium is reached, the two compartments will have identical solute and water concentrations, 3 Osm and 52.5 M, respectively. One mol of water will have diffused from compartment 1 to compartment 2, and 1 mol of solute will have diffused from 2 to 1. Because 1 mol of solute has replaced 1 mol of water in compartment 1, and vice versa in compartment 2, no change in the volume occurs for either compartment.

If the membrane is now replaced by one *permeable to water but impermeable to solute* (**Figure 4.18**), the same *concentrations* of water and solute will be reached at equilibrium as before, but a change in the *volumes* of the compartments will also occur. Water will diffuse from 1 to 2, but there will be no solute diffusion in the opposite direction because the membrane is impermeable to solute. Water will continue to diffuse into compartment 2, therefore, until the water concentrations on the two sides become equal. The solute concentration in compartment 2 decreases as it is diluted by the incoming water, and the solute in compartment 1 becomes more concentrated as water moves out. When the water reaches diffusion equilibrium, the osmolarities of the compartments will be equal; therefore, the solute concentrations must also be equal. To reach this state of equilibrium, enough water must pass from compartment 1 to 2 to increase the volume of compartment 2 by one-third and decrease the volume of compartment 1 by an equal amount. Note that it is the presence of a membrane impermeable to solute that leads to the volume changes associated with osmosis.

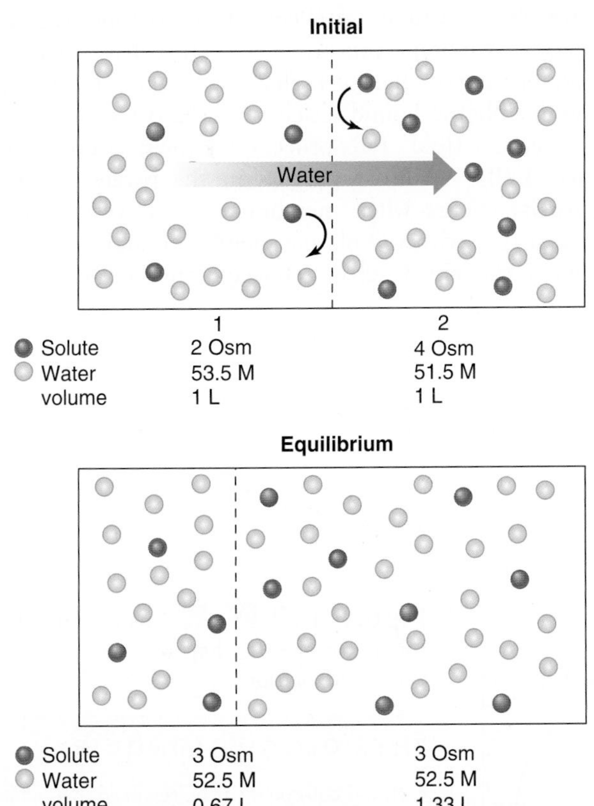

Figure 4.18 APIR The movement of water across a membrane that is permeable to water but not to solute leads to an equilibrium state involving a change in the volumes of the two compartments. In this case, a net diffusion of water (0.33 L) occurs from compartment 1 to 2. (We will assume that the membrane in this example stretches as the volume of compartment 2 increases so that no significant change in compartment pressure occurs.)

The two compartments in our example were treated as if they were infinitely expandable, so the net transfer of water did not create a pressure difference across the membrane. In contrast, if the walls of compartment 2 in Figure 4.18 had only a limited capacity to expand, as occurs across plasma membranes, the movement of water into compartment 2 would raise the pressure in compartment 2, which would oppose further net water entry. Thus, the movement of water into compartment 2 can be prevented by the application of pressure to compartment 2. This leads to an important definition. When a solution containing solutes is separated from pure water by a **semipermeable membrane** (a membrane permeable to water but not to solutes), the pressure that must be applied to the solution to prevent the net flow of water into it is known as the **osmotic pressure** of the solution. The greater the osmolarity of a solution, the greater the osmotic pressure. It is important to recognize that osmotic pressure does not push water molecules into a solution. Rather, it represents the amount of pressure that would have to be applied to a solution to *prevent* the net flow of water into the solution. Like osmolarity, the osmotic pressure associated with a solution is a measure of the solution's water concentration—the lower the water concentration, the higher the osmotic pressure.

Extracellular Osmolarity and Cell Volume

We can now apply the principles learned about osmosis to cells, which meet all the criteria necessary to produce an osmotic flow of water across a membrane. Both the intracellular and extracellular fluids contain water, and cells are surrounded by a membrane that is very permeable to water but impermeable to many substances. Substances that cannot cross the plasma membrane are called **nonpenetrating solutes;** that is, they do not penetrate through the lipid bilayer.

Most of the extracellular solute particles are sodium and chloride ions, which can diffuse into the cell through ion channels in the plasma membrane or enter the cell during secondary active transport. As we have seen, however, the plasma membrane contains Na^+/K^+-ATPase pumps that actively move sodium ions out of the cell. Therefore, Na^+ moves into cells and is pumped back out, behaving as if it never entered in the first place. For this reason, extracellular Na^+ behaves as a nonpenetrating solute. Any chloride ions that enter cells are also removed as quickly as they enter, due to the electrical repulsion generated by the membrane potential and the action of secondary transporters. Like Na^+, therefore, extracellular chloride ions behave as if they were nonpenetrating solutes.

Inside the cell, the major solute particles are potassium ions and a number of organic solutes. Most of the latter are large polar molecules unable to diffuse through the plasma membrane. Although potassium ions can diffuse out of a cell through K^+ channels, they are actively transported back by the Na^+/K^+-ATPase pump. The net effect, as with extracellular Na^+ and Cl^-, is that K^+ behaves as if it were a nonpenetrating solute, but in this case one confined to the intracellular fluid.

Therefore, Na^+ and Cl^- outside the cell and K^+ and organic solutes inside the cell behave as nonpenetrating solutes on the two sides of the plasma membrane.

The osmolarity of the extracellular fluid is normally in the range of 285–300 mOsm (we will round off to a value of 300 for the rest of this text unless otherwise noted). Because water can diffuse across plasma membranes, water in the intracellular and extracellular fluids will come to diffusion equilibrium. At equilibrium, therefore, the osmolarities of the intracellular and extracellular fluids are the same—approximately 300 mOsm. Changes in extracellular osmolarity can cause cells, such as the red blood cells shown in the chapter-opening photo, to shrink or swell as water molecules move across the plasma membrane.

If cells with an intracellular osmolarity of 300 mOsm are placed in a solution of nonpenetrating solutes having an osmolarity of 300 mOsm, they will neither swell nor shrink because the water concentrations in the intracellular and extracellular fluids are the same, and the solutes cannot leave or enter. Such solutions are said to be **isotonic** (**Figure 4.19**), meaning any solution that does not cause a change in cell size. Isotonic solutions have the same concentration of *nonpenetrating* solutes as normal extracellular fluid. By contrast, **hypotonic** solutions have a nonpenetrating solute concentration lower than that found in cells; therefore, water moves by osmosis into the cells, causing them to swell. Similarly, solutions containing greater than 300 mOsm of nonpenetrating solutes (**hypertonic** solutions) cause cells to shrink as water diffuses out of the cell into the fluid with the lower water concentration. The concentration of *nonpenetrating* solutes in a solution, not the total osmolarity, determines its tonicity—isotonic, hypotonic, or hypertonic. Penetrating solutes do not contribute to the tonicity of a solution.

Another set of terms—**isoosmotic, hypoosmotic,** and **hyperosmotic**—denotes the osmolarity of a solution relative to that of normal extracellular fluid without regard to whether the solute is penetrating or nonpenetrating. The two sets of terms are therefore not synonymous. For example, a 1 L solution containing 150 mOsm each of nonpenetrating Na^+ and Cl^- and 100 mOsm of urea, which can rapidly cross plasma membranes, would have a total osmolarity of 400 mOsm and would be hyperosmotic. It would, however, also be an isotonic solution, producing no change in the equilibrium volume of cells immersed in it. *Initially*, cells placed in this solution would shrink as water moved into the extracellular fluid. However, urea would quickly diffuse into the cells and reach the same concentration as the urea in the extracellular solution; consequently, both the intracellular and extracellular solutions would soon reach the same osmolarity. Therefore, at equilibrium, there would be no difference in the water concentration across the membrane and thus no change in final cell volume; this would be the case even though the extracellular fluid would remain hyperosmotic relative to the normal value of 300 mOsm. **Table 4.3** provides a comparison of the various terms used to describe the osmolarity and tonicity of solutions.

4.4 Endocytosis and Exocytosis

In addition to diffusion and mediated transport, there is another pathway by which substances can enter or leave cells, one that does not require the molecules to pass through the structural matrix of the plasma membrane. When sections of cells are observed under an electron microscope, regions of the plasma membrane can often be seen to have folded into the cell, forming small pockets that pinch off to produce intracellular, membrane-bound vesicles that enclose a small volume of extracellular fluid. This process is known as **endocytosis** (**Figure 4.20**). A similar process in the reverse direction, **exocytosis,** occurs when membrane-bound vesicles in the cytoplasm fuse with the plasma membrane and release their contents to the outside of the cell (see Figure 4.20).

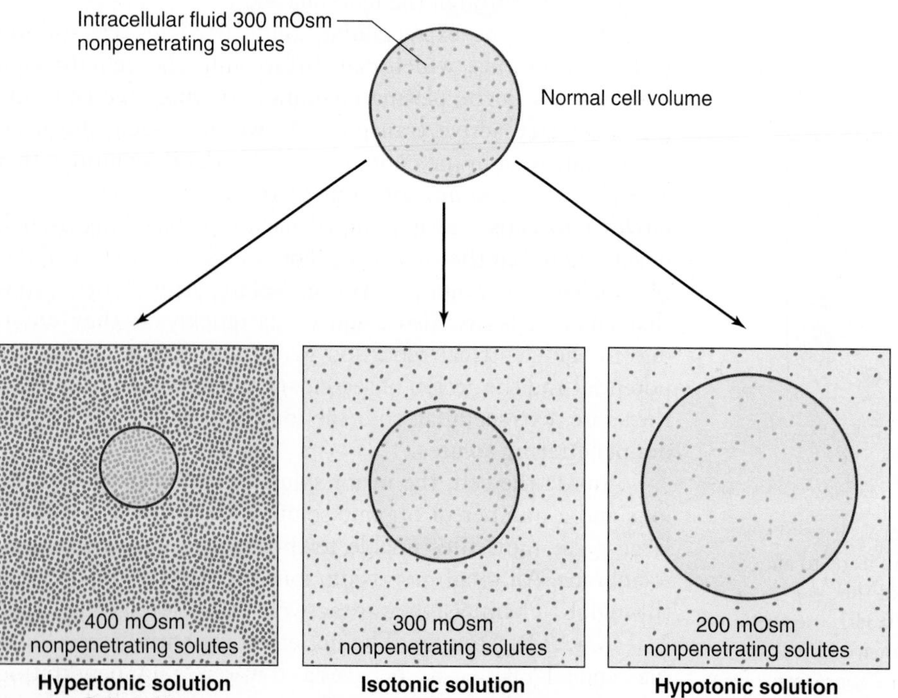

Figure 4.19 AP|R Changes in cell volume produced by hypertonic, isotonic, and hypotonic solutions.

PHYSIOLOGICAL INQUIRY

- Blood volume must be restored in a person who has lost large amounts of blood due to serious injury. This is often accomplished by infusing isotonic NaCl solution into the blood. Why is this better than infusing an isoosmotic solution of a penetrating solute, such as urea?

Answer can be found at end of chapter.

TABLE 4.3	Terms Referring to the Osmolarity and Tonicity of Solutions*
Isotonic	A solution that does not cause a change in cell volume; one that contains 300 mOsmol/L of nonpenetrating solutes, regardless of the concentration of membrane-penetrating solutes present
Hypertonic	A solution that causes cells to shrink; one that contains greater than 300 mOsmol/L of nonpenetrating solutes, regardless of the concentration of membrane-penetrating solutes present
Hypotonic	A solution that causes cells to swell; one that contains less than 300 mOsmol/L of nonpenetrating solutes, regardless of the concentration of membrane-penetrating solutes present
Isoosmotic	A solution containing 300 mOsmol/L of solute, regardless of its composition of membrane-penetrating and nonpenetrating solutes
Hyperosmotic	A solution containing greater than 300 mOsmol/L of solutes, regardless of its composition of membrane-penetrating and nonpenetrating solutes
Hypoosmotic	A solution containing less than 300 mOsmol/L of solutes, regardless of its composition of membrane-penetrating and nonpenetrating solutes

*These terms are defined using an intracellular osmolarity of 300 mOsm, which is within the range for human cells but not an absolute fixed number.

Endocytosis

Three general types of endocytosis may occur in a cell. These are pinocytosis ("cell drinking"), phagocytosis ("cell eating"), and receptor-mediated endocytosis (**Figure 4.21**).

In **pinocytosis,** also known as **fluid endocytosis,** an endocytotic vesicle encloses a small volume of extracellular fluid. This process is nonspecific because the vesicle simply engulfs the water in the extracellular fluid along with whatever solutes are present. These solutes may include ions, nutrients, or any other small extracellular molecule. Large macromolecules, other cells, and cell debris do not normally enter a cell via this process.

In **phagocytosis,** cells engulf bacteria or large particles such as cell debris from damaged tissues. In this form of endocytosis, extensions of the plasma membrane called pseudopodia fold around the surface of the particle, engulfing it entirely. The pseudopodia, with their engulfed contents, then fuse into large vesicles called **phagosomes** that are internalized into the cell. Phagosomes migrate to and fuse with lysosomes in the cytoplasm, and the contents of the phagosomes are then destroyed by lysosomal enzymes and other molecules. Whereas most cells undergo pinocytosis, only a few special types of cells, such as those of the immune system (Chapter 18), carry out phagocytosis.

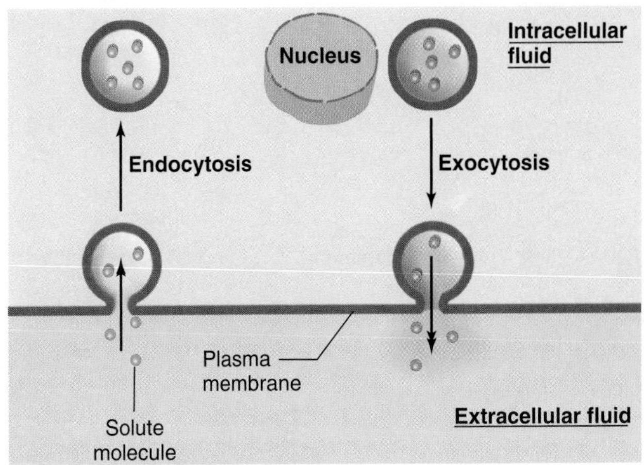

Figure 4.20 APIR Endocytosis and exocytosis.

In contrast to pinocytosis and phagocytosis, most cells have the capacity to *specifically* take up molecules that are important for cellular function or structure. In **receptor-mediated endocytosis,** certain molecules in the extracellular fluid bind to specific proteins on the outer surface of the plasma membrane. These proteins are called **receptors,** and each one recognizes one ligand with high affinity (see Section C of Chapter 3 for a discussion of ligand–protein interactions). In one form of receptor-mediated endocytosis, the receptor undergoes a conformational change when it binds a ligand. Through a series of steps, a cytosolic protein called **clathrin** is recruited to the plasma membrane. A class of proteins called adaptor proteins links the ligand-receptor complex to clathrin. The entire complex then forms a cagelike structure that leads to the aggregation of ligand-bound receptors into a localized region of membrane, forming a depression, or **clathrin-coated pit,** which then invaginates and pinches off to form a clathrin-coated vesicle. By localizing ligand-receptor complexes to discrete patches of plasma membrane prior to endocytosis, cells may obtain concentrated amounts of ligands without having to engulf large amounts of extracellular fluid from many different sites along the membrane. Receptor-mediated endocytosis, therefore, leads to a selective concentration in the endocytotic vesicle of a specific ligand bound to one type of receptor.

Cholesterol is one example of a ligand that enters cells via clathrin-dependent, receptor-mediated endocytosis. Cholesterol is an important building block for plasma and intracellular membranes, and most cells require a steady supply of this molecule. Cholesterol circulates in the blood, bound with proteins in particles called lipoproteins. The protein components of lipoproteins are recognized by plasma membrane receptors. When the receptors bind the lipoproteins, endocytosis ensues and the cholesterol is delivered to the intracellular fluid. The rate at which this occurs can be regulated. For example, if a cell has sufficient supplies of cholesterol, the rate at which it replenishes its supply of lipoprotein receptors may decrease. Conversely, receptor production increases when cholesterol supplies are low. This is a type of negative feedback that acts to maintain the cholesterol content of the cell within a homeostatic range.

Once an endocytotic vesicle pinches off from the plasma membrane in receptor-mediated endocytosis, the clathrin coat

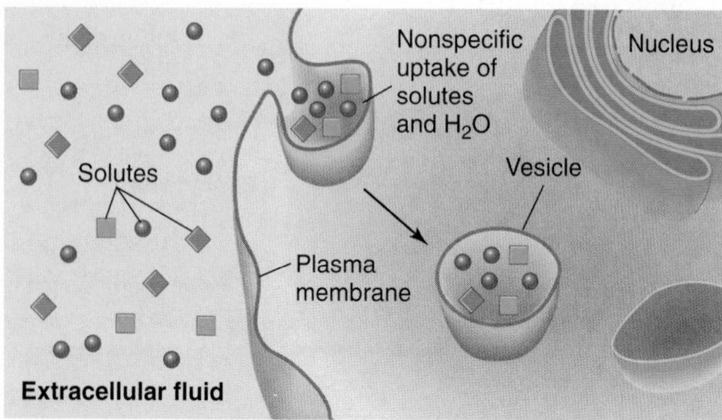

(a) Fluid endocytosis

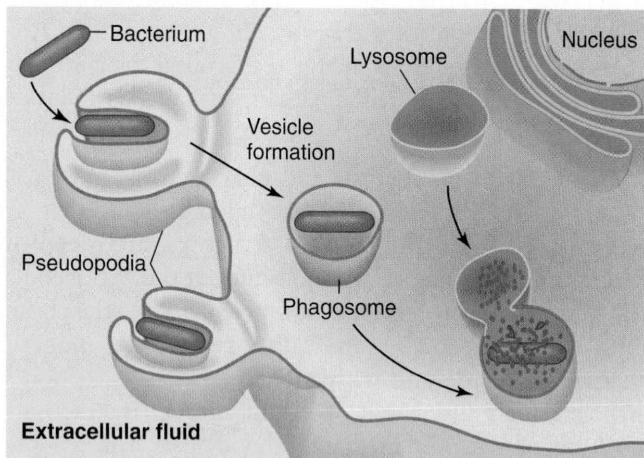

(b) Phagocytosis

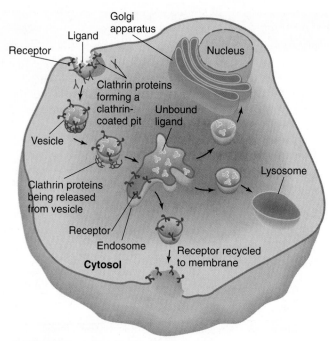

(c) Receptor-mediated endocytosis

Figure 4.21 **AP|R** Pinocytosis, phagocytosis, and receptor-mediated endocytosis. (a) In pinocytosis, solutes and water are nonspecifically brought into the cell from the extracellular fluid via endocytotic vesicles. (b) In phagocytosis, specialized cells form extensions of the plasma membrane called pseudopodia, which engulf bacteria or other large objects such as cell debris. The vesicles that form fuse with lysosomes, which contain enzymes and other molecules that destroy the vesicle contents. (c) In receptor-mediated endocytosis, a cell recognizes a specific extracellular ligand that binds to a plasma membrane receptor. The binding triggers endocytosis. In the example shown here, the ligand-receptor complexes are internalized via clathrin-coated vesicles, which merge with endosomes (for simplicity, adapter proteins are not shown). Ligands may be routed to the Golgi apparatus for further processing, or to lysosomes. The receptors are typically recycled to the plasma membrane.

is removed and clathrin proteins are recycled back to the membrane. The vesicles then have several possible fates, depending upon the cell type and the ligand that was engulfed. Some vesicles fuse with the membrane of an intracellular organelle, adding the contents of the vesicle to the lumen of that organelle. Other endocytotic vesicles pass through the cytoplasm and fuse with the plasma membrane on the opposite side of the cell, releasing their contents to the extracellular space. This provides a pathway for the transfer of large molecules, such as proteins, across the layers of cells that separate two fluid compartments in the body (for example, the blood and interstitial fluid). A similar process allows small amounts of macromolecules to move across the intestinal epithelium.

Most endocytotic vesicles fuse with a series of intracellular vesicles and tubular elements known as endosomes (Chapter 3), which lie between the plasma membrane and the Golgi apparatus. Like the Golgi apparatus, the endosomes perform a sorting function, distributing the contents of the vesicle and its membrane to various locations. Some of the contents of endocytotic vesicles are passed from the endosomes to the Golgi apparatus, where the ligands are modified and processed. Other vesicles fuse with lysosomes, organelles that contain digestive enzymes that break down large molecules such as proteins, polysaccharides, and nucleic acids. The fusion of endosomal vesicles with the lysosomal membrane exposes the contents of the vesicle to these digestive enzymes. Finally, in many cases, the receptors that were internalized with the vesicle get recycled back to the plasma membrane.

Another fate of endocytotic vesicles is seen in a special type of receptor-mediated endocytosis called potocytosis. **Potocytosis** is similar to other types of receptor-mediated endocytosis in that an extracellular ligand typically binds to a plasma membrane receptor, initiating formation of an intracellular vesicle. In potocytosis, however, the ligands appear to be primarily restricted to low-molecular-weight molecules such as certain vitamins, but have also been found to include the lipoprotein complexes just described. Potocytosis differs from clathrin-dependent, receptor-mediated endocytosis in the fate of the endocytotic vesicle. In potocytosis, tiny vesicles called **caveolae** (singular: *caveolus*, "little cave") pinch off from the plasma membrane and deliver their contents directly to the cell cytosol rather than merging with lysosomes or other organelles. The small molecules within the caveolae may diffuse into the cytosol via channels or be transported by carriers. Although their functions are still being actively investigated, caveolae have been implicated in a variety of important cellular functions, including cell signaling, transcellular transport, and cholesterol homeostasis.

Each episode of endocytosis removes a small portion of the membrane from the cell surface. In cells that have a great deal of endocytotic activity, more than 100% of the plasma membrane may be internalized in an hour, yet the membrane surface area remains constant. This is because the membrane is replaced at about the same rate by vesicle membrane that fuses with the plasma membrane during *exocytosis.* Some of the plasma membrane proteins taken into the cell during endocytosis are stored in the membranes of endosomes and, upon receiving the appropriate signal, can be returned to fuse with the plasma membrane during exocytosis.

Exocytosis

Exocytosis performs two functions for cells: (1) it provides a way to replace portions of the plasma membrane that endocytosis has removed and, in the process, a way to add new membrane components as well; and (2) it provides a route by which membrane-impermeable molecules (such as protein hormones) that the cell synthesizes can be secreted into the extracellular fluid.

How does the cell package substances that are to be secreted by exocytosis into vesicles? Chapter 3 described the entry of newly formed proteins into the lumen of the endoplasmic reticulum and the protein's processing through the Golgi apparatus. From the Golgi apparatus, the proteins to be secreted travel to the plasma membrane in vesicles from which they can be released into the extracellular fluid by exocytosis. In some cases, substances enter vesicles via mediated transporters in the vesicle membrane.

The secretion of substances by exocytosis is triggered in most cells by stimuli that lead to an increase in cytosolic calcium concentration in the cell. As will be described in Chapters 5 and 6, these stimuli open calcium channels in the plasma membrane and/or the membranes of intracellular organelles. The resulting increase in cytosolic calcium concentration activates proteins required for the vesicle membrane to fuse with the plasma membrane and release the vesicle contents into the extracellular fluid. Material stored in secretory vesicles is available for rapid secretion in response to a stimulus, without delays that might occur if the material had to be synthesized after the stimulus arrived. Exocytosis is the mechanism by which most neurons communicate with each other through the release of neurotransmitters stored in secretory vesicles that merge with the plasma membrane. It is also a major way in which many types of hormones are released from endocrine cells into the extracellular fluid.

Cells that actively undergo exocytosis recover bits of membrane via a process called compensatory endocytosis. This process, the mechanisms of which are still uncertain but that may involve both clathrin- and non-clathrin-mediated events, restores membrane material to the cytoplasm that can be made available for the formation of new secretory vesicles. It also helps prevent the plasma membrane's unchecked expansion.

4.5 Epithelial Transport

As described in Chapter 1, epithelial cells line hollow organs or tubes and regulate the absorption or secretion of substances across these surfaces. One surface of an epithelial cell generally faces a hollow or fluid-filled chamber, and the plasma membrane on this side is referred to as the **apical membrane** (also known as the luminal or mucosal membrane) of the epithelium (refer back to Figures 1.2 and 3.9). The plasma membrane on the opposite surface, which is usually adjacent to a network of blood vessels, is referred to as the **basolateral membrane** (also known as the serosal membrane).

The two pathways by which a substance can cross a layer of epithelial cells are (1) the **paracellular pathway,** in which diffusion occurs *between* the adjacent cells of the epithelium; and (2) the **transcellular pathway,** in which a substance moves *into* an epithelial cell across either the apical or basolateral membrane, diffuses through the cytosol, and exits across the opposite membrane. Diffusion through the paracellular pathway is limited by the presence of tight junctions between adjacent cells, because these junctions form a seal around the apical end of the epithelial cells (Chapter 3). Although small ions and water can diffuse to some degree through tight junctions, the amount of paracellular diffusion is limited by the tightness of the junctional seal and the relatively small area available for diffusion.

During transcellular transport, the movement of molecules through the plasma membranes of epithelial cells occurs via the pathways (diffusion and mediated transport) already described for movement across membranes. However, the transport and permeability characteristics of the apical and basolateral membranes are not the same. These two membranes often contain different ion channels and different transporters for mediated transport. As a result of these differences, substances can undergo a net movement from a low concentration on one side of an epithelium to a higher concentration on the other side. Examples include the absorption of material from the gastrointestinal tract into the blood, the movement of substances between the kidney tubules and the blood during urine formation, and the secretion of salts and water by glands such as sweat glands.

Figure 4.22 and **Figure 4.23** illustrate two examples of active transport across an epithelium. Na^+ is actively transported across most epithelia from lumen to blood side in absorptive processes, and from blood side to lumen during secretion. In our example, the movement of Na^+ from the lumen into the epithelial cell occurs by diffusion through Na^+ channels in the apical membrane (see Figure 4.22). Na^+ diffuses into the cell because the intracellular concentration of Na^+ is kept low by the active transport of Na^+ back out of the cell across the basolateral membrane on the opposite side, where all of the Na^+/K^+-ATPase pumps are located. In other words, Na^+ moves downhill into the cell and then uphill out of it. The net result is that Na^+ can be moved from lower to higher concentration across the epithelium.

Figure 4.23 illustrates the active absorption of organic molecules across an epithelium. In this case, the entry of an organic molecule X across the luminal plasma membrane occurs via a secondary active transporter linked to the downhill movement of Na^+ into the cell. In the process, X moves from a lower concentration in the luminal fluid to a higher concentration in the cell. The substance exits across the basolateral membrane by facilitated diffusion, which moves the material from its higher concentration in the cell to a lower concentration in the extracellular fluid on the blood side. The

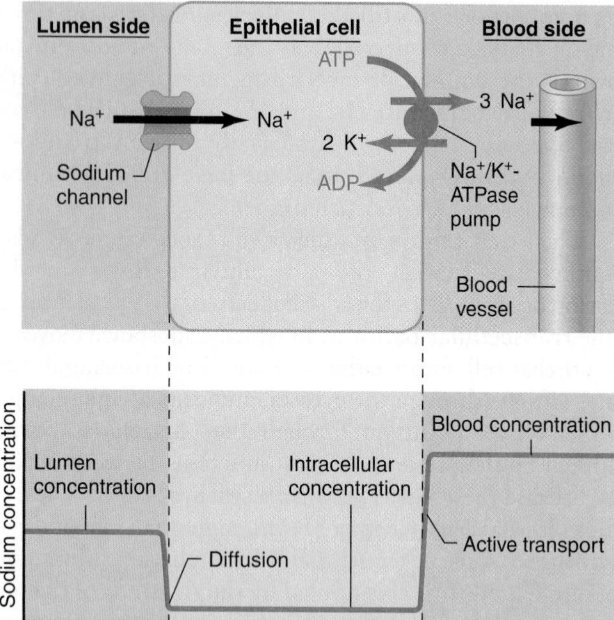

Figure 4.22 Active transport of Na^+ across an epithelial cell. The transepithelial transport of Na^+ always involves primary active transport out of the cell across one of the plasma membranes, typically via an Na^+/K^+-ATPase pump as shown here. The movement of Na^+ into the cell across the plasma membrane on the opposite side is always downhill. Sometimes, as in this example, it is by diffusion through Na^+ channels, whereas in other epithelia this downhill movement occurs through a secondary active transporter. Shown below the cell is the concentration profile of the transported solute across the epithelium.

PHYSIOLOGICAL INQUIRY

- What would happen in this situation if the cell's ATP supply decreased significantly?

Answer can be found at end of chapter.

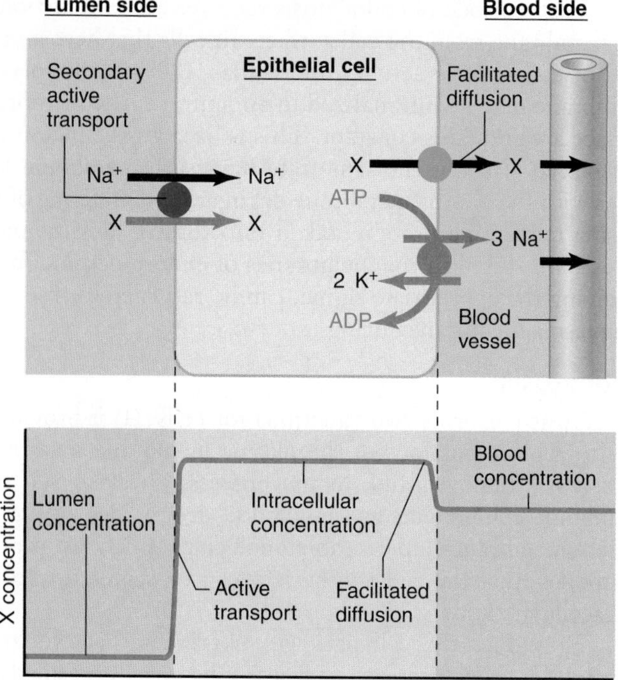

Figure 4.23 The transepithelial transport of most organic solutes (X) involves their movement into a cell through a secondary active transport driven by the downhill flow of Na^+. The organic substance then moves out of the cell at the blood side down a concentration gradient by means of facilitated diffusion. Shown below the cell is the concentration profile of the transported solute across the epithelium.

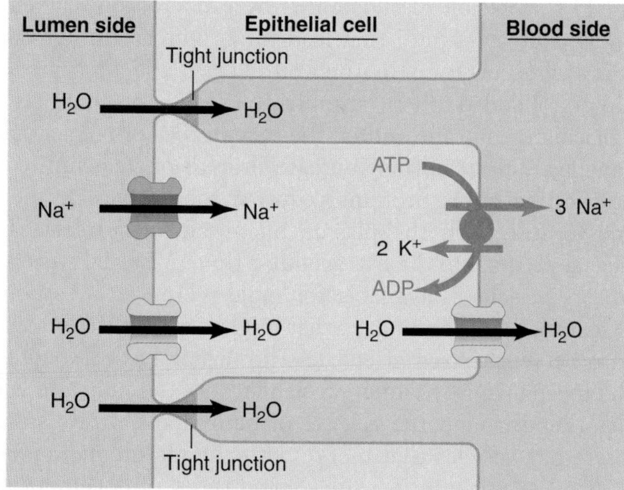

Figure 4.24 Net movements of water across an epithelium are dependent on net solute movements. The active transport of Na^+ across the cells and into the surrounding interstitial spaces produces an elevated osmolarity in this region and a decreased osmolarity in the lumen. This leads to the osmotic flow of water across the epithelium in the same direction as the net solute movement. The water diffuses through water channels in the membrane and across the tight junctions between the epithelial cells.

concentration of the substance may be considerably higher on the blood side than in the lumen because the blood-side concentration can approach equilibrium with the high intracellular concentration created by the apical membrane entry step.

Although water is not actively transported across cell membranes, net movement of water across an epithelium can occur by osmosis as a result of the active transport of solutes, notably Na^+, across the epithelium. The active transport of Na^+, as previously described, results in a decrease in the Na^+ concentration on one side of an epithelial layer (the luminal side in our example) and an increase on the other. These changes in solute concentration are accompanied by changes in the water concentration on the two sides because a change in solute concentration, as we have seen, produces a change in water concentration. The water concentration difference will cause water to move by osmosis from the low-Na^+ side to the high-Na^+ side of the epithelium (**Figure 4.24**). Therefore, net movement of solute across an epithelium is accompanied by a flow of water in the same direction. If the epithelial cells are highly permeable to water, large net movements of water can occur with very small differences in osmolarity. As you will learn in Chapter 14, this is a major way in which epithelial cells of the kidney absorb water from the urine back into the blood. It is also the major way in which water is absorbed from the intestines into the blood (Chapter 15).

SUMMARY

Diffusion

I. Simple diffusion is the movement of molecules from one location to another by random thermal motion.
  a. The net flux between two compartments always proceeds from higher to lower concentrations.
  b. Diffusion equilibrium is reached when the concentrations of the diffusing substance in the two compartments become equal.

II. The magnitude of the net flux J across a membrane is directly proportional to the concentration difference across the membrane $C_o - C_i$, the surface area of the membrane A, and the membrane permeability coefficient P.

III. Nonpolar molecules diffuse through the hydrophobic portions of membranes much more rapidly than do polar or ionized molecules because nonpolar molecules can dissolve in the fatty acyl tails in the lipid bilayer.

IV. Ions diffuse across membranes by passing through ion channels formed by integral membrane proteins.
  a. The diffusion of ions across a membrane depends on both the concentration gradient and the membrane potential.
  b. The flux of ions across a membrane can be altered by opening or closing ion channels.

Mediated-Transport Systems

I. The mediated transport of molecules or ions across a membrane involves binding the transported solute to a transporter protein in the membrane. Changes in the conformation of the transporter move the binding site to the opposite side of the membrane, where the solute dissociates from the protein.
  a. The binding sites on transporters exhibit chemical specificity, affinity, and saturation.
  b. The magnitude of the flux through a mediated-transport system depends on the degree of transporter saturation, the number of transporters in the membrane, and the rate at which the conformational change in the transporter occurs.

II. Facilitated diffusion is a mediated-transport process that moves molecules from higher to lower concentrations across a membrane by means of a transporter until the two concentrations become equal. Metabolic energy is not required for this process.

III. Active transport is a mediated-transport process that moves molecules against an electrochemical gradient across a membrane by means of a transporter and an input of energy.
  a. Primary active transport uses the phosphorylation of the transporter by ATP to drive the transport process.
  b. Secondary active transport uses the binding of ions (often Na^+) to the transporter to drive the secondary-transport process.
  c. In secondary active transport, the downhill flow of an ion is linked to the uphill movement of a second solute either in the same direction as the ion (cotransport) or in the opposite direction of the ion (countertransport).

Osmosis

I. Water crosses membranes by (a) diffusing through the lipid bilayer, and (b) diffusing through protein channels in the membrane.

II. Osmosis is the diffusion of water across a membrane from a region of higher water concentration to a region of lower water concentration. The osmolarity—total solute concentration in a solution—determines the water concentration: the higher the osmolarity of a solution, the lower the water concentration.

III. Osmosis across a membrane that is permeable to water but impermeable to solute leads to an increase in the volume of the compartment on the side that initially had the higher osmolarity, and a decrease in the volume on the side that initially had the lower osmolarity.

IV. Application of sufficient pressure to a solution will prevent the osmotic flow of water into the solution from a compartment of pure water. This pressure is called the osmotic pressure. The greater the osmolarity of a solution, the greater its osmotic pressure. Net water movement occurs from a region of lower osmotic pressure to one of higher osmotic pressure.

V. The osmolarity of the extracellular fluid is about 300 mOsm. Because water comes to diffusion equilibrium across cell membranes, the intracellular fluid has an osmolarity equal to that of the extracellular fluid.
  a. Na^+ and Cl^- ions are the major effectively nonpenetrating solutes in the extracellular fluid; potassium ions and various organic solutes are the major effectively nonpenetrating solutes in the intracellular fluid.
  b. Table 4.3 lists the terms used to describe the osmolarity and tonicity of solutions containing different compositions of penetrating and nonpenetrating solutes.

Endocytosis and Exocytosis

I. During endocytosis, regions of the plasma membrane invaginate and pinch off to form vesicles that enclose a small volume of extracellular material.
  a. The three classes of endocytosis are (i) fluid endocytosis, (ii) phagocytosis, and (iii) receptor-mediated endocytosis.
  b. Most endocytotic vesicles fuse with endosomes, which in turn transfer the vesicle contents to lysosomes for digestion by lysosomal enzymes.
  c. Potocytosis is a special type of receptor-mediated endocytosis in which vesicles called caveolae deliver their contents directly to the cytosol.

II. Exocytosis, which occurs when intracellular vesicles fuse with the plasma membrane, provides a means of adding components to the plasma membrane and a route by which membrane-impermeable molecules, such as proteins the cell synthesizes, can be released into the extracellular fluid.

Epithelial Transport

I. Molecules can cross an epithelial layer of cells by two pathways: (a) through the extracellular spaces between the cells—the paracellular pathway; and (b) through the cell, across both the luminal and basolateral membranes as well as the cell's cytoplasm—the transcellular pathway.

II. In epithelial cells, the permeability and transport characteristics of the apical and basolateral plasma membranes differ, resulting in the ability of cells to actively transport a substance between the fluid on one side of the cell and the fluid on the opposite side.

III. The active transport of Na^+ through an epithelium increases the osmolarity on one side of the cell and decreases it on the other, causing water to move by osmosis in the same direction as the transported Na^+.

REVIEW QUESTIONS

1. What determines the direction in which net diffusion of a nonpolar molecule will occur?
2. In what ways can the net solute flux between two compartments separated by a permeable membrane be increased?
3. Why are membranes more permeable to nonpolar molecules than to most polar and ionized molecules?
4. Ions diffuse across cell membranes by what pathway?
5. When considering the diffusion of ions across a membrane, what driving force, in addition to the ion concentration gradient, must be considered?
6. Describe the mechanism by which a transporter of a mediated-transport system moves a solute from one side of a membrane to the other.
7. What determines the magnitude of flux across a membrane in a mediated-transport system?
8. What characteristics distinguish simple diffusion from facilitated diffusion?
9. What characteristics distinguish facilitated diffusion from active transport?
10. Describe the direction in which sodium ions and a solute transported by secondary active transport move during cotransport and countertransport.
11. How can the concentration of water in a solution be decreased?
12. If two solutions with different osmolarities are separated by a water-permeable membrane, why will a change occur in the volumes of the two compartments if the membrane is impermeable to the solutes but no change in volume will occur if the membrane is permeable to solutes?
13. Why do sodium and chloride ions in the extracellular fluid and potassium ions in the intracellular fluid behave as though they were nonpenetrating solutes?
14. What is the approximate osmolarity of the extracellular fluid? Of the intracellular fluid?
15. What change in cell volume will occur when a cell is placed in a hypotonic solution? In a hypertonic solution?
16. Under what conditions will a hyperosmotic solution be isotonic?
17. How do the mechanisms for actively transporting glucose and Na^+ across an epithelium differ?
18. By what mechanism does the active transport of Na^+ lead to the osmotic flow of water across an epithelium?

KEY TERMS

CLINICAL TERMS

CHAPTER 4 Clinical Case Study: A Novice Marathoner Collapses After a Race

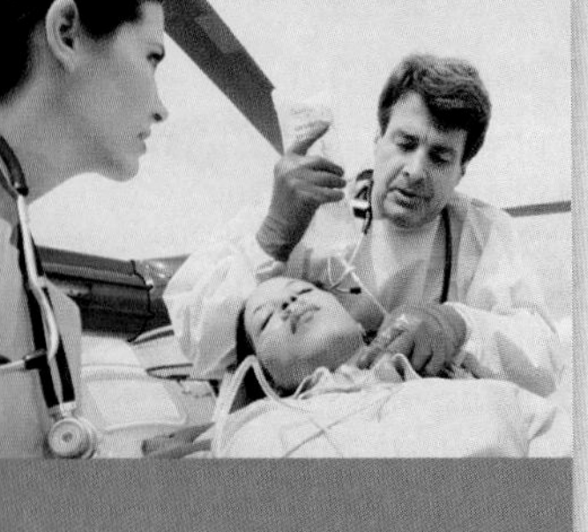

A 22-year-old, 102-pound (46.4 kg) woman who had occasionally competed in short-distance races, decided to compete in her first marathon. She was in good health but was completely inexperienced in long-distance runs. During the hour before the race, she drank two 20-ounce bottles of water (about 1.2 liters) in anticipation of the water loss she expected to occur due to perspiration over the next few hours. The race took place on an unseasonably cool day in April. As she ran, she was careful to drink a cup of water (5–10 ounces) at each water station, roughly each mile along the course. Being a newcomer to competing in marathons, she had already been running for 3 hours at the 20-mile mark and was beginning to feel extremely fatigued. Soon after, her leg muscles began cramping and she felt slightly sick to her stomach. Thinking she was losing too much fluid, she stopped for a moment at a water station and drank several cups of water, then continued on. After another 2 miles, she became nauseated and consumed a full 20-ounce bottle of water; a mile later, she began to feel confused and disoriented and developed a headache. At that point, she became panicked that she would not finish the race; even though she did not feel thirsty, she finished yet another bottle of water. Twenty minutes later, she collapsed, lost consciousness, and was taken by ambulance to a local hospital. She was diagnosed with ***exercise-associated hyponatremia*** (EAH), a condition in which the concentration of Na^+ in the blood decreases to dangerously low levels (in her case, to 115 mM; see Table 4.1 for comparison).

(continued)

(continued)

It was clear to her physicians what caused the EAH. When we exercise, perspiration helps cool us down. Perspiration is a dilute solution of several ions, particularly Na^+ (the other major ones being Cl^- and K^+). The result of excessive sweating is that the total amount of water and Na^+ in the body becomes depleted. Our patient was exercising very hard and for a very long time but was not losing as much fluid as she had anticipated because of the cold weather. She was wise to be aware of the potential for fluid loss, but she was not aware that drinking pure water in such quantities could significantly dilute her body fluids. As the concentration of Na^+ in her extracellular fluid decreased, the electrochemical gradient for Na^+ across her cells—including her muscle and brain cells—also decreased as a consequence. As noted in this chapter and described in detail in Chapters 6 and 9, the electrochemical gradient for Na^+ is part of what regulates the function of skeletal muscle and brain cells. As a result of disrupting this gradient, our patient's muscles and neurons began to malfunction, accounting in part for the cramps and mental confusion.

In addition, however, recall from Figure 4.19 what happens to cells when the concentrations of nonpenetrating solutes across the cell membrane are changed. As our patient's extracellular fluid became more dilute than her intracellular fluid, water moved by osmosis into her cells. Many types of cells, including those of the brain, are seriously damaged when they swell due to water influx. It is even worse in the brain than elsewhere because there is no room for the brain to expand within the skull. As brain cells swell, the fluid pressure in the brain increases, compressing blood vessels and restricting blood flow. When blood flow is reduced, oxygen and nutrient levels decrease and metabolic waste products build up, further contributing to brain cell malfunction. Thus, the combination of water influx, increased pressure, and changes in the electrochemical gradient for Na^+ all contributed to the mental disturbances and subsequent loss of consciousness in our patient.

Interestingly, the nausea triggered by the EAH probably is responsible in part for activating the release of a hormone called antidiuretic hormone (ADH) from the pituitary gland. You will learn about this hormone and gland in Chapters 11, 12, and 14, but for now it is worth noting that the primary function of ADH is to stimulate the kidneys to retain water in the body by producing less urine. This might happen, for example, when someone is dehydrated, as was described earlier in this chapter. In the case of our subject, however, this hormone was counterproductive, because she was already overhydrated. The decrease in urine production caused by nausea-induced increases in antidiuretic hormone only made things worse.

What do you think would be an appropriate way to treat EAH? Remember, the patient is not dehydrated. In fact, one of the best predictors of EAH in patients like ours is weight *gain* during a marathon; such individuals actually weigh more at the end of a race than at the beginning because of all the water they drink! The treatment is an intravenous infusion of an isotonic solution of NaCl to bring the total levels of Na^+ in the body fluids back toward normal. At the same time, however, the extracellular fluid volume is reduced with a diuretic (a medication that increases urine production). In addition, patients may also receive medications to prevent or stop seizures. As you will learn in Chapters 6 and 8, a seizure is uncontrolled, unregulated activity of the neurons in the brain; one potential cause of a seizure is a large imbalance in extracellular ion concentrations in the brain. In our patient, gradual restoration of Na^+ levels and treatment for the nausea and headache were sufficient to save her life, but careful monitoring of her progress over the course of a 24-hour hospital stay was required.

Clinical term: exercise-associated hyponatremia (EAH)

See Chapter 19 for complete, integrative case studies.

CHAPTER 4 TEST QUESTIONS

Answers found in Appendix A.

1. Which properties are characteristic of ion channels?
   a. They are usually lipids.
   b. They exist on one side of the plasma membrane, usually the intracellular side.
   c. They can open and close depending on the presence of any of three types of "gates."
   d. They permit movement of ions against concentration gradients.
   e. They mediate facilitated diffusion.
2. Which of the following does *not* directly or indirectly require an energy source?
   a. primary active transport
   b. operation of the Na^+/K^+-ATPase pump
   c. the mechanism used by cells to produce a calcium ion gradient across the plasma membrane
   d. facilitated transport of glucose across a plasma membrane
   e. secondary active transport
3. If a small amount of urea were added to an isoosmotic saline solution containing cells, what would be the result?
   a. The cells would shrink and remain that way.
   b. The cells would first shrink but then be restored to normal volume after a brief period of time.
   c. The cells would swell and remain that way.
   d. The cells would first swell but then be restored to normal volume after a brief period of time.
   e. The urea would have no effect, even transiently.
4. Which is/are true of epithelial cells?
   a. They can only move uncharged molecules across their surfaces.
   b. They may have segregated functions on apical (luminal) and basolateral surfaces.
   c. They cannot form tight junctions.
   d. They depend upon the activity of Na^+/K^+-ATPase pumps for much of their transport functions.
   e. Both b and d are correct.
5. Which is *incorrect?*
   a. Diffusion of a solute through a membrane is considerably quicker than diffusion of the same solute through a water layer of equal thickness.
   b. A single ion, such as K^+, can diffuse through more than one type of channel.
   c. Lipid-soluble solutes diffuse more readily through the phospholipid bilayer of a plasma membrane than do water-soluble ones.

d. The rate of facilitated diffusion of a solute is limited by the number of transporters in the membrane at any given time.
e. A common example of cotransport is that of an ion and an organic molecule.

6. In considering diffusion of ions through an ion channel, which driving force/forces must be considered?
   a. the ion concentration gradient
   b. the electrical gradient
   c. osmosis
   d. facilitated diffusion
   e. both a and b

CHAPTER 4 GENERAL PRINCIPLES ASSESSMENT

Answers found in Appendix A.

1. How does the information presented in Figures 4.8–4.10 and 4.17 illustrate the general principle that *homeostasis is essential for health and survival?*
2. Give two examples from this chapter that illustrate the general principle that *controlled exchange of materials occurs between compartments and across cellular membranes.*
3. Another general physiological principle states that *physiological processes are dictated by the laws of chemistry and physics.* How does this relate to the movement of solutes through lipid bilayers and its dependence on electrochemical gradients? How is heat related to solute movement?

CHAPTER 4 QUANTITATIVE AND THOUGHT QUESTIONS

Answers found in Appendix A.

1. In two cases (A and B), the concentrations of solute X in two 1 L compartments separated by a membrane through which X can diffuse are

Case	*Concentration of X (mM)* Compartment 1	Compartment 2
A	3	5
B	32	30

   a. In what direction will the net flux of X take place in case A and in case B?
   b. When diffusion equilibrium is reached, what will the concentration of solute in each compartment be in case A and in case B?
   c. Will A reach diffusion equilibrium faster, slower, or at the same rate as B?
2. When the extracellular concentration of the amino acid alanine is increased, the net flux of the amino acid leucine into a cell is decreased. How might this observation be explained?
3. If a transporter that mediates active transport of a substance has a lower affinity for the transported substance on the extracellular surface of the plasma membrane than on the intracellular surface, in what direction will there be a net transport of the substance across the membrane? (Assume that the rate of transporter conformational change is the same in both directions.)
4. Why will inhibition of ATP synthesis by a cell lead eventually to a decrease and, ultimately, cessation in secondary active transport?
5. Given the following solutions, which has the lowest water concentration? Which two have the same osmolarity?

Solution	*Concentration (mM)* Glucose	Urea	NaCl	$CaCl_2$
A	20	30	150	10
B	10	100	20	50
C	100	200	10	20
D	30	10	60	100

6. Assume that a membrane separating two compartments is permeable to urea but not permeable to NaCl. If compartment 1 contains 200 mmol/L of NaCl and 100 mmol/L of urea, and compartment 2 contains 100 mmol/L of NaCl and 300 mmol/L of urea, which compartment will have increased in volume when osmotic equilibrium is reached?
7. What will happen to cell volume if a cell is placed in each of the following solutions?

Solution	*Concentration of X, mM* NaCl (Nonpenetrating)	Urea (Penetrating)
A	150	100
B	100	150
C	200	100
D	100	50

8. Characterize each of the solutions in question 7 as isotonic, hypotonic, hypertonic, isoosmotic, hypoosmotic, or hyperosmotic.
9. By what mechanism might an increase in intracellular Na^+ concentration lead to an increase in exocytosis?

ANSWERS TO PHYSIOLOGICAL INQUIRIES

Figure 4.2 As shown in the accompanying graph, there would be a net flux of glucose from compartment 1 to compartment 2, with diffusion equilibrium occurring at 12.5 mmol/L.

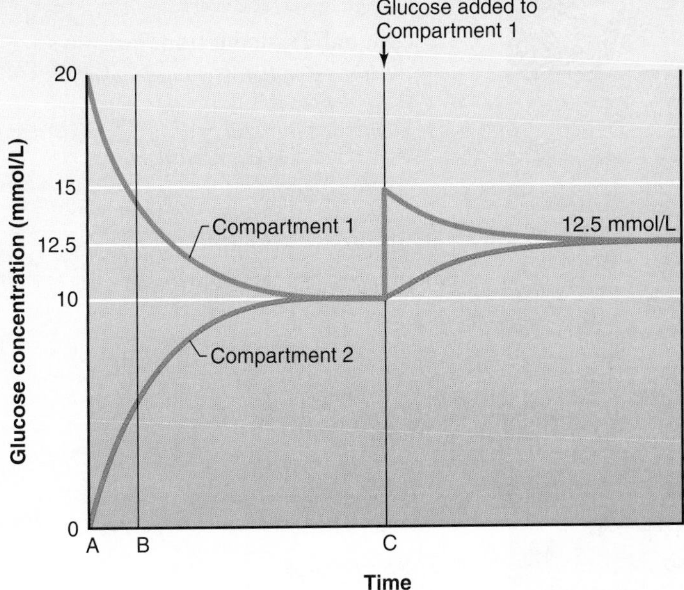

Figure 4.5 The primary structure of the protein is represented by the beads—the amino acid sequence shown in (a). The secondary structure includes all the helical regions in the lipid bilayer, shown in (a) and (b). The tertiary structure is the folded conformation shown in (b). The quaternary structure is the association of the five subunit polypeptides into one protein, shown in (c).

Figure 4.9 Maximal flux depends on the number of transporter molecules in the membrane and their inherent rate of conformational change when binding solute. If we assume that the rate of conformational change stays constant, then the greater the number of transporters, the greater the maximal flux that can occur.

Figure 4.13 ATP is not hydrolyzed when a solute moves across a membrane by secondary active transport. However, ATP *is* hydrolyzed by an ion pump (typically the Na^+/K^+-ATPase primary active transporter) to establish the ion concentration gradient that is used during secondary active transport. Therefore, secondary active transport *indirectly* requires ATP.

Figure 4.19 Because it is a nonpenetrating solute, infusion of isotonic NaCl restores blood volume without causing a redistribution of water between body fluid compartments due to osmosis. An isoosmotic solution of a penetrating solute, however, would only partially restore blood volume because some water would enter the intracellular fluid by osmosis as the solute enters cells. This could also result in damage to cells as their volume expands beyond normal.

Figure 4.22 Active transport of Na^+ across the basolateral (blood side) membrane would decrease, resulting in an increased intracellular concentration of Na^+. This would reduce the rate of Na^+ diffusion into the cell through the Na^+ channel on the lumen side because the diffusion gradient would be smaller.

Visit this book's website at **www.mhhe.com/widmaier13** for chapter quizzes, interactive learning exercises, and other study tools.

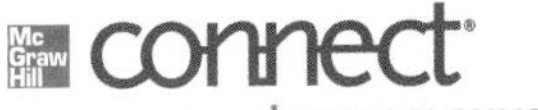

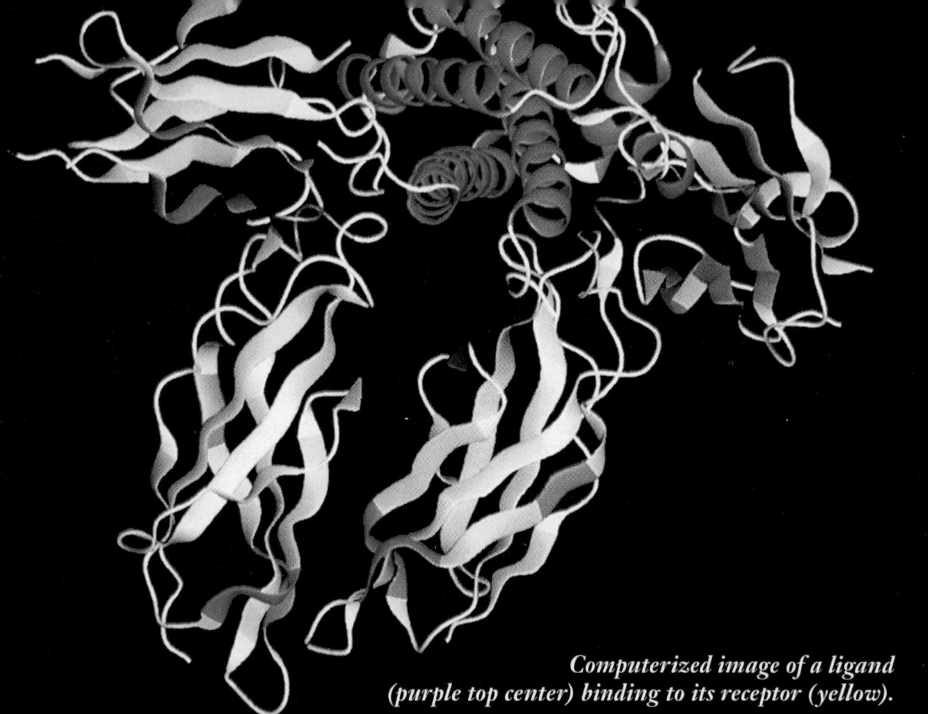

Computerized image of a ligand (purple top center) binding to its receptor (yellow).

5 Control of Cells by Chemical Messengers

You learned in Chapter 1 how homeostatic control systems help maintain a normal balance of the body's internal environment. The operation of control systems requires that cells be able to communicate with each other, often over long distances. Much of this intercellular communication is mediated by chemical messengers. This chapter describes how these messengers interact with their target cells and how these interactions trigger intracellular signals that lead to the cell's response. Throughout this chapter, you should carefully distinguish *inter*cellular (between cells) and *intra*cellular (within a cell) chemical messengers and communication. The material in this chapter will provide a foundation for understanding how the nervous, endocrine, and other organ systems function. Before starting, you should review the material covered in Section C of Chapter 3 for background on ligand–protein interactions.

The material in this chapter illustrates the general physiological principle that information flow between cells, tissues, and organs is an essential feature of homeostasis and allows for integration of physiological processes. These many and varied processes will be covered in detail beginning in Chapter 6 and will continue throughout the book, but the mechanisms of information flow that link different structures and processes share many common features, as described here.

5.1 Receptors

In Chapter 1, you learned that several classes of chemical messengers can communicate a signal from one cell to another. These messengers include molecules such as neurotransmitters, whose signals are mediated rapidly and over a short distance. Other messengers, such as hormones, communicate more slowly and over greater distances. Whatever the chemical messenger, however, the cell receiving the signal must have a way to detect the signal's presence. Once a cell detects a signal, a mechanism is required to transduce that signal into a biologically meaningful response, such as the cell-division response to the delivery of growth-promoting signals.

The first step in the action of any intercellular chemical messenger is the binding of the messenger to specific target-cell proteins known as **receptors** or **receptor proteins.** In the general language of Chapter 3, a chemical messenger is a ligand, and the receptor has a binding site for that ligand. The binding of a messenger to a receptor activates the receptor; this initiates a sequence of events in the cell leading to the cell's response to that messenger, a process called **signal transduction.** In this section, we consider some general features common to many receptors, describe the interactions between receptors and their ligands, and give some examples of how receptors are regulated.

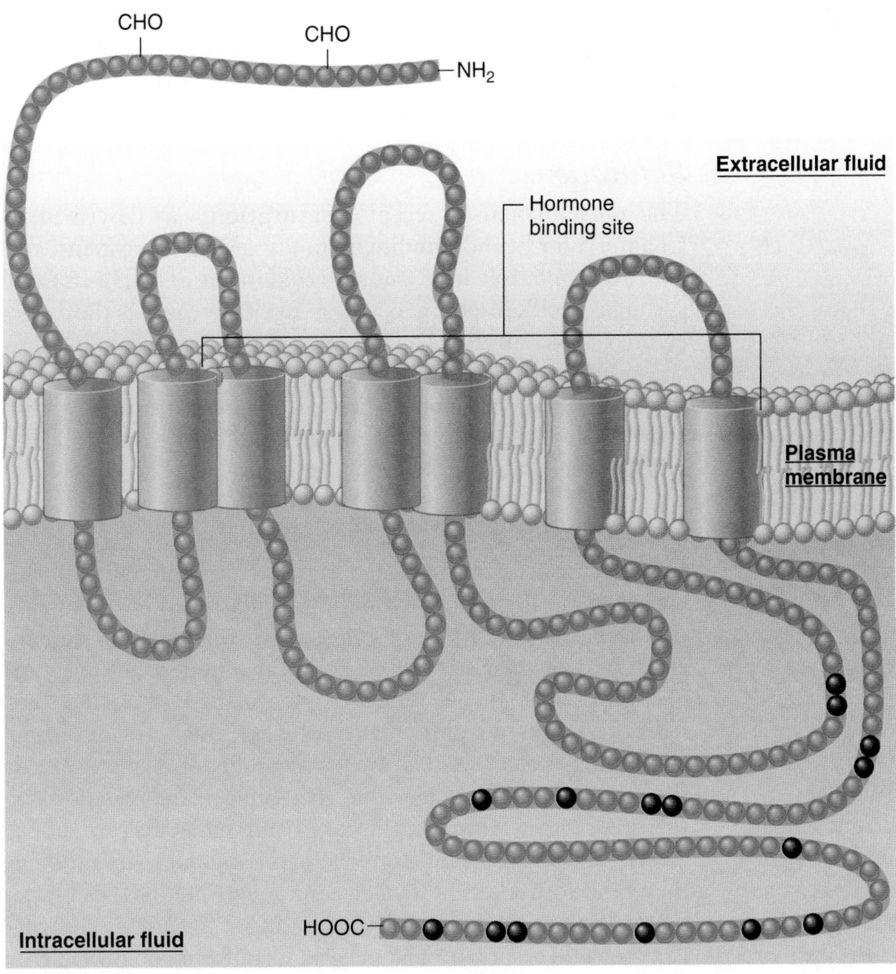

Figure 5.1 Structure of a receptor that binds the hormone epinephrine. The seven clusters of amino acids embedded in the phospholipid bilayer represent hydrophobic portions of the protein's alpha helix (shown here as cylinders). Note that the binding site for the hormone includes several of the segments that extend into the extracellular fluid. Portions of the extracellular segments can be linked to carbohydrates (CHO). The amino acids denoted by black circles represent some of the sites at which intracellular enzymes can phosphorylate, and thereby regulate, the receptor.

Receptors and Their Interactions with Ligands

What is the nature of the receptors that bind intercellular chemical messengers? They are proteins or glycoproteins located either in the cell's plasma membrane or inside the cell, either in the cytosol or the nucleus. The plasma membrane is the much more common location, because a very large number of messengers are water-soluble and therefore cannot diffuse across the lipid-rich (hydrophobic) plasma membrane. In contrast, a much smaller number of lipid-soluble messengers pass through membranes (mainly by diffusion but in some cases assisted by mediated transport) to bind to their receptors located inside the cell.

Plasma membrane receptors are transmembrane proteins; that is, they span the entire membrane thickness. A typical plasma membrane receptor is illustrated in **Figure 5.1.** Like other transmembrane proteins, a plasma membrane receptor has hydrophobic segments within the membrane, one or more hydrophilic segments extending out from the membrane into the extracellular fluid, and other hydrophilic segments extending into the intracellular fluid. Arriving chemical messengers bind to the extracellular parts of the receptor.

Specificity

The binding of a chemical messenger to its receptor initiates the events leading to the cell's response. The existence of receptors explains a very important characteristic of intercellular communication—**specificity** (see **Table 5.1** for a glossary of terms concerning receptors). Although a given chemical messenger may come into contact with many different cells, it influences certain cell types and not others. This is because cells differ in the types of receptors they possess. Only certain cell types—sometimes just one—express the specific receptor required to bind a given chemical messenger (**Figure 5.2**). In many cases, the receptor proteins for a group of messengers are structurally related. For example, there are "superfamilies" of hormone receptors such as the steroid hormone receptors.

Even though different cell types may possess the receptors for the same messenger, the responses of the various cell types to that messenger may differ from each other.

TABLE 5.1	A Glossary of Terms Concerning Receptors
Receptor (receptor protein)	A specific protein in either the plasma membrane or the interior of a target cell that a chemical messenger binds with, thereby invoking a biologically relevant response in that cell.
Specificity	The ability of a receptor to bind only one type or a limited number of structurally related types of chemical messengers.
Saturation	The degree to which receptors are occupied by messengers. If all are occupied, the receptors are fully saturated; if half are occupied, the saturation is 50%, and so on.
Affinity	The strength with which a chemical messenger binds to its receptor.
Competition	The ability of different molecules to compete with a ligand for binding to its receptor. Competitors generally are similar in structure to the natural ligand.
Antagonist	A molecule that competes with a ligand for binding to its receptor but does not activate signaling normally associated with the natural ligand. Therefore, an antagonist prevents the actions of the natural ligand. Antihistamines are examples of antagonists.
Agonist	A chemical messenger that binds to a receptor and triggers the cell's response; often refers to a drug that mimics a normal messenger's action. Decongestants are examples of agonists.
Down-regulation	A decrease in the total number of target-cell receptors for a given messenger; may occur in response to chronic high extracellular concentration of the messenger.
Up-regulation	An increase in the total number of target-cell receptors for a given messenger; may occur in response to a chronic low extracellular concentration of the messenger.
Increased sensitivity	The increased responsiveness of a target cell to a given messenger; may result from up-regulation of receptors.

For example, the neurotransmitter norepinephrine causes the smooth muscle of certain blood vessels to contract but, via the same type of receptor, inhibits insulin secretion from the pancreas. In essence, then, the receptor functions as a molecular switch that elicits the cell's response when "switched on" by the messenger binding to it. Just as identical types of switches can be used to turn on a light or a radio, a single type of receptor can be used to produce different responses in different cell types.

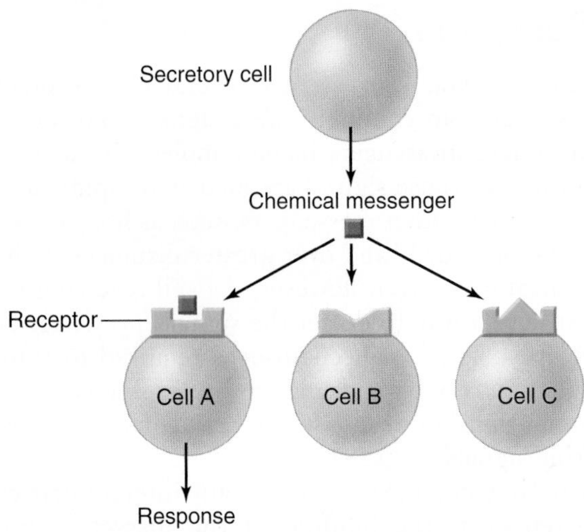

Figure 5.2 Specificity of receptors for chemical messengers. Only cell A has the appropriate receptor for this chemical messenger; therefore, it is the only one among the group that is a target cell for the messenger.

Affinity

The degree to which a particular messenger binds to its receptor is determined by the **affinity** of the receptor for the messenger. A receptor with high affinity will bind at lower concentrations of a messenger than will a receptor of low affinity (refer back to Figure 3.36). Differences in affinity of receptors for their ligands have important implications for the use of therapeutic drugs in treating illness; receptors with high affinity for a ligand require much less of the ligand (that is, a lower dose) to become activated.

Saturation

The phenomenon of receptor **saturation** was described in Chapter 3 for ligands binding to binding sites on proteins, and are fully applicable here (summarized in **Figure 5.3**). In most systems, a cell's response to a messenger increases as the extracellular concentration of the messenger increases, because the number of receptors occupied by messenger molecules increases. There is an upper limit to this responsiveness, however, because only a finite number of receptors are available, and they become fully saturated at some point.

Competition

Competition refers to the ability of a molecule to compete with a natural ligand for binding to its receptor. Competition typically occurs with messengers that have a similarity in part of their structures, and it also underlies the action of many drugs. If researchers or physicians wish to interfere with the action of a particular messenger, they can administer competing molecules that are structurally similar enough to the endogenous messenger that they bind to the receptors for that messenger. However, the competing molecules are different enough in structure from the native ligand that, although they bind to the receptor, they cannot activate it. This blocks the endogenous messenger from binding and yet does not trigger the cell's response. The general term for a compound that

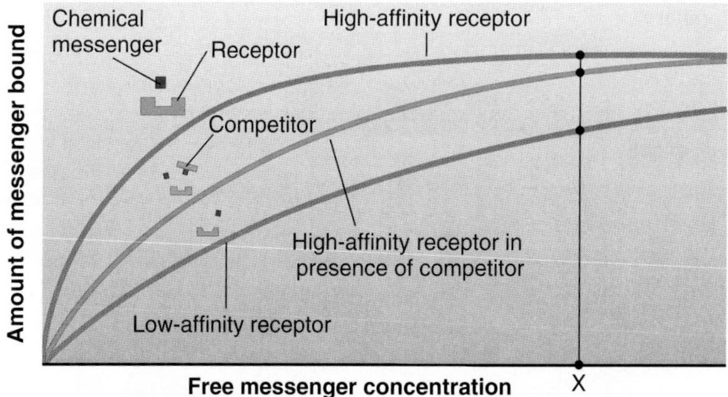

Figure 5.3 Characteristics of receptors binding to messengers. The receptors with high affinity will have more bound messenger at a given messenger concentration (e.g., concentration X). The presence of a competitor will reduce the amount of messenger bound, until at very high concentrations the receptors become saturated with messenger. Note in the illustration that the low-affinity receptor in this case has a slightly different shape in its ligand-binding region compared to the high-affinity receptor. Also note the similarity in parts of the shapes of the natural messenger and its competitor.

blocks the action of a chemical messenger is **antagonist;** when an antagonist works by competing with a chemical messenger for its binding site, it is known as a competitive antagonist. One example is a type of drug called a beta-blocker, which is sometimes used in the treatment of high blood pressure and other diseases. Beta-blockers antagonize the ability of epinephrine and norepinephrine to bind to one of their receptors—the beta-adrenergic receptor. Because epinephrine and norepinephrine normally act to increase blood pressure (Chapter 12), beta-blockers tend to decrease blood pressure by acting as antagonists. Antihistamines are another example and are useful in treating allergic symptoms brought on due to excess histamine secretion from cells known as mast cells (Chapter 18). Antihistamines are antagonists that block histamine from binding to its receptors on cells and triggering an allergic response.

On the other hand, some drugs that compete with natural ligands for a particular receptor type do trigger the cell's response exactly as if the true (endogenous) chemical messenger had combined with the receptor. Such drugs, known as **agonists,** are used therapeutically to mimic the messenger's action. For example, the common decongestant drugs ***phenylephrine*** and ***oxymetazoline***, found in many types of nasal sprays, mimic the action of epinephrine on a different class of receptors, called alpha-adrenergic receptors, in blood vessels. When alpha-adrenergic receptors are activated, the smooth muscles of inflamed, dilated blood vessels in the nose contract, resulting in constriction of those vessels in the nasal passages and fewer sniffles.

Regulation of Receptors

Receptors are themselves subject to physiological regulation. The number of receptors a cell has, or the affinity of the receptors for their specific messenger, can be increased or decreased in certain systems. An important example is the phenomenon of **down-regulation.** When a high extracellular concentration of a messenger is maintained for some time, the total number of the target cell's receptors for that messenger may decrease—that is, down-regulate. Down-regulation has the effect of reducing the target cells' responsiveness to frequent or intense stimulation by a messenger—that is, desensitizing them—and thus represents a local negative feedback mechanism.

Change in the opposite direction, called **up-regulation,** also occurs. Cells exposed for a prolonged period to very low concentrations of a messenger may come to have many more receptors for that messenger, thereby developing increased sensitivity to it. The greater the number of receptors available to bind a ligand, the greater the likelihood that such binding will occur. For example, when the nerves to a muscle are damaged, the delivery of neurotransmitters from those nerves to the muscle is decreased or eliminated. With time, under these conditions, the muscle will contract in response to a much smaller amount of neurotransmitter than normal. This happens because the receptors for the neurotransmitter have been up-regulated, resulting in increased sensitivity.

Up-regulation and down-regulation are possible because there is a continuous synthesis and degradation of receptors. The main cause of down-regulation of plasma membrane receptors is **internalization.** The binding of a messenger to its receptor can stimulate the internalization of the complex; that is, the messenger-receptor complex is taken into the cell by receptor-mediated endocytosis (see Chapter 4). This increases the rate of receptor degradation inside the cell. Consequently, at elevated hormone concentrations, the number of plasma membrane receptors of that type gradually decreases during down-regulation.

The opposite events also occur and contribute to up-regulation. The cell may contain stores of receptors in the membranes of intracellular vesicles. These are then inserted into the plasma membrane during up-regulation. Receptor regulation is an excellent example of the general physiological principle of homeostasis, because it acts to return signal strength toward normal when the concentration of messenger molecules varies above or below normal.

5.2 Signal Transduction Pathways

What are the sequences of events by which the binding of a chemical messenger to a receptor causes the cell to respond in a specific way?

The combination of messenger with receptor causes a change in the conformation (three-dimensional shape) of the receptor. This event, known as **receptor activation,** is the initial step leading to the cell's responses to the messenger. These cellular responses can take the form of changes in (1) the permeability, transport properties, or electrical state of the plasma membrane; (2) metabolism; (3) secretory activity; (4) rate of proliferation and differentiation; or (5) contractile or other activities.

Despite the seeming variety of responses, there is a common denominator: they are all directly due to alterations of particular cell proteins. Let us examine a few examples of messenger-induced responses, all of which are described more fully in subsequent chapters. The neurotransmitter-induced generation of electrical signals in neurons reflects the altered conformation of membrane proteins (ion channels) through which ions can diffuse between extracellular and intracellular fluid. Similarly, changes in the rate of glucose secretion by the liver induced by the hormone epinephrine reflect the altered activity and concentration of enzymes in the metabolic pathways for glucose synthesis. Finally, muscle contraction induced by the neurotransmitter acetylcholine results from the altered conformation of contractile proteins.

Thus, receptor activation by a messenger is only the first step leading to the cell's ultimate response (contraction, secretion, and so on). The diverse sequences of events that link receptor activation to cellular responses are termed **signal transduction pathways.** The "signal" is the receptor activation, and "transduction" denotes the process by which a stimulus is transformed into a response.

Signal transduction pathways differ between lipid-soluble and water-soluble messengers. As described earlier, the receptors for these two broad chemical classes of messenger are in different locations—the former inside the cell and the latter in the plasma membrane of the cell. The rest of this chapter describes the major features of the signal transduction pathways that these two broad categories of receptors initiate.

Pathways Initiated by Lipid-Soluble Messengers

Lipid-soluble messengers usually act on cells by binding to intracellular receptor proteins. Lipid-soluble messengers include all steroid hormones and the thyroid hormones. Chemically, these hormones are all hydrophobic, and the steroid receptors constitute the **steroid-hormone-receptor superfamily.** Although plasma membrane receptors for a few of these messengers have been identified, most of the receptors in this superfamily are intracellular. When not bound to a messenger, the receptors are inactive. In a few cases, the inactive receptors are located in the cytosol and move into the nucleus after binding their hormone. Most of the inactive receptors, however, already reside in the cell nucleus, where they bind to and are activated by their respective ligands. In both cases, receptor activation leads to altered rates of the transcription of one or more genes in a particular cell.

The messenger diffuses out of capillaries from plasma to the interstitial fluid. From there, the messenger diffuses across the plasma membrane and nuclear envelope to enter the nucleus and bind to the receptor there (**Figure 5.4**). The activated receptor complex then functions in the nucleus as a transcription factor, defined as a regulatory protein that directly influences gene transcription. The hormone–receptor complex binds to DNA at a regulatory region of a gene, an event that typically increases the rate of that gene's transcription into mRNA. The mRNA molecules move out of the nucleus to direct the synthesis, on ribosomes, of the protein the gene encodes. The result is an increase in the cellular concentration of the protein and/or its rate of secretion, accounting for the cell's ultimate response to the messenger. For example, if the protein encoded by the gene is an enzyme, the cell's response is an increase in the rate of the reaction catalyzed by that enzyme.

Two other points are important. First, more than one gene may be subject to control by a single receptor type. For example, the glucocorticoid hormone cortisol acts via its intracellular receptor to activate numerous genes involved in the coordinated control of cellular metabolism and energy balance. Second, in some cases, the transcription of a gene or genes may be *decreased* rather than increased by the activated receptor. Cortisol, for example, inhibits transcription of several genes whose protein products mediate inflammatory responses that occur following injury or infection; for this reason, cortisol has important anti-inflammatory effects.

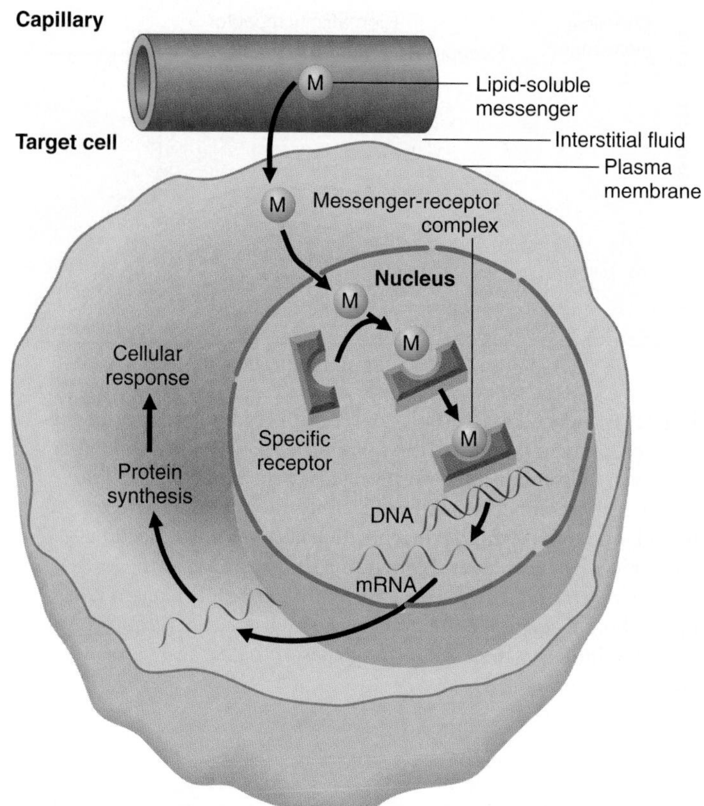

Figure 5.4 AP|R Mechanism of action of lipid-soluble messengers. This figure shows the receptor for these messengers in the nucleus. In some cases, the unbound receptor is in the cytosol rather than the nucleus, in which case the binding occurs there, and the messenger-receptor complex moves into the nucleus. For simplicity, a single messenger is shown binding to a single receptor. In many cases, however, two messenger-receptor complexes must bind together in order to activate a gene.

Pathways Initiated by Water-Soluble Messengers

Water-soluble messengers cannot readily enter cells by diffusion through the lipid bilayer of the plasma membrane. Instead, they exert their actions on cells by binding to the extracellular portion of receptor proteins embedded in the plasma membrane. Water-soluble messengers include most peptide and protein hormones, neurotransmitters, and paracrine–autocrine compounds. On the basis of the signal transduction pathways they initiate, plasma membrane receptors can be classified into the types listed in **Table 5.2** and illustrated in **Figure 5.5**.

Some notes on general terminology are essential for this discussion. First, the extracellular chemical messengers that reach the cell and bind to their specific plasma membrane

TABLE 5.2 Classification of Receptors Based on Their Locations and the Signal Transduction Pathways They Use

I. Intracellular receptors (Figure 5.4) (for lipid-soluble messengers): Function in the nucleus as transcription factors or suppressors to alter the rate of transcription of particular genes

II. Plasma membrane receptors (Figure 5.5) (for water-soluble messengers)
  A. Receptors that are ligand-gated ion channels
  B. Receptors that themselves function as enzymes, such as receptor tyrosine kinases
  C. Receptors that are bound to and activate cytoplasmic janus kinases
  D. G-protein-coupled receptors that activate G proteins, which in turn act upon effector proteins—either ion channels or enzymes—in the plasma membrane

receptors are often referred to as **first messengers. Second messengers,** then, are substances that enter or are generated in the cytoplasm as a result of receptor activation by the first messenger. The second messengers diffuse throughout the cell to serve as chemical relays from the plasma membrane to the biochemical machinery inside the cell. The third essential general term is **protein kinase,** which is the name for an enzyme that phosphorylates other proteins by transferring a phosphate group to them from ATP. Phosphorylation of a protein changes its three-dimensional conformation and, consequently, alters the protein's activity. There are many different protein kinases, and each type is able to phosphorylate only specific proteins. The important point is that a variety of protein kinases are involved in signal transduction pathways. These pathways may involve a series of reactions in which a particular inactive protein kinase is activated by phosphorylation and then catalyzes the phosphorylation of another inactive protein kinase, and so on. At the ends of these sequences, the ultimate phosphorylation of key proteins, such as transporters, metabolic enzymes, ion channels, and contractile proteins, underlies the cell's biochemical response to the first messenger. Different proteins respond differently to phosphorylation; some are activated and some are inactivated (inhibited).

As described in Chapter 3, other enzymes do the reverse of protein kinases; that is, they dephosphorylate proteins. These enzymes, termed protein phosphatases, also participate in signal transduction pathways, but their roles are less understood than those of the protein kinases and will not be described further in this chapter.

Receptors That Are Ligand-Gated Ion Channels

In the first type of plasma membrane receptor listed in Table 5.2, the protein that acts as the receptor is also an ion channel. Activation of the receptor by a first messenger (the ligand) results in a conformational change of the receptor such that it forms an open channel through the plasma membrane (**Figure 5.5a**). Because the opening of ion channels has been compared to the opening of a gate in a fence, these types of channels are known as **ligand-gated ion channels.** They are particularly prevalent in the plasma membranes of neurons, as you will learn in Chapter 6.

The opening of ligand-gated ion channels in response to binding of a first messenger results in an increase in the net diffusion across the plasma membrane of one or more types of ions specific to that channel. As you will see in Chapter 6, such a change in ion diffusion results in a change in the electrical charge, or membrane potential, of a cell. This change in membrane potential constitutes the cell's response to the messenger. In addition, when the channel is a Ca^{2+} channel, its opening results in an increase by diffusion in cytosolic Ca^{2+} concentration. Increasing cytosolic Ca^{2+} is another essential event in the transduction pathway for many signaling systems.

Receptors That Function as Enzymes

The receptors in the second category of plasma membrane receptors listed in Table 5.2 have intrinsic enzyme activity. With one major exception (discussed later), the many receptors that possess intrinsic enzyme activity are all protein kinases (**Figure 5.5b**). Of these, the great majority specifically phosphorylate tyrosine residues. Consequently, these receptors are known as **receptor tyrosine kinases.**

The typical sequence of events for receptors with intrinsic tyrosine kinase activity is as follows. The binding of a specific messenger to the receptor changes the conformation of the receptor so that its enzymatic portion, located on the cytoplasmic side of the plasma membrane, is activated. This results in autophosphorylation of the receptor; that is, the receptor phosphorylates some of its own tyrosine residues. The newly created phosphotyrosines on the cytoplasmic portion of the receptor then serve as docking sites for cytoplasmic proteins. The bound docking proteins then bind and activate other proteins, which in turn activate one or more signaling pathways within the cell. The common denominator of these pathways is that they all involve activation of cytoplasmic proteins by phosphorylation. Most of the receptors with intrinsic tyrosine kinase activity bind first messengers that typically influence cell proliferation and differentiation, and are often called growth factors.

There is one physiologically important exception to the generalization that plasma membrane receptors with inherent enzyme activity function as protein kinases. In this exception, the receptor functions both as a receptor and as a **guanylyl cyclase** to catalyze the formation, in the cytoplasm, of a molecule known as **cyclic GMP (cGMP).** In turn, cGMP functions as a second messenger to activate a protein kinase called **cGMP-dependent protein kinase.** This kinase phosphorylates specific proteins that then mediate the cell's response to the original messenger. As described in Chapter 7, receptors that function both as ligand-binding molecules and as guanylyl cyclases are abundantly expressed in the retina of the eye, where they are important for processing visual inputs. This

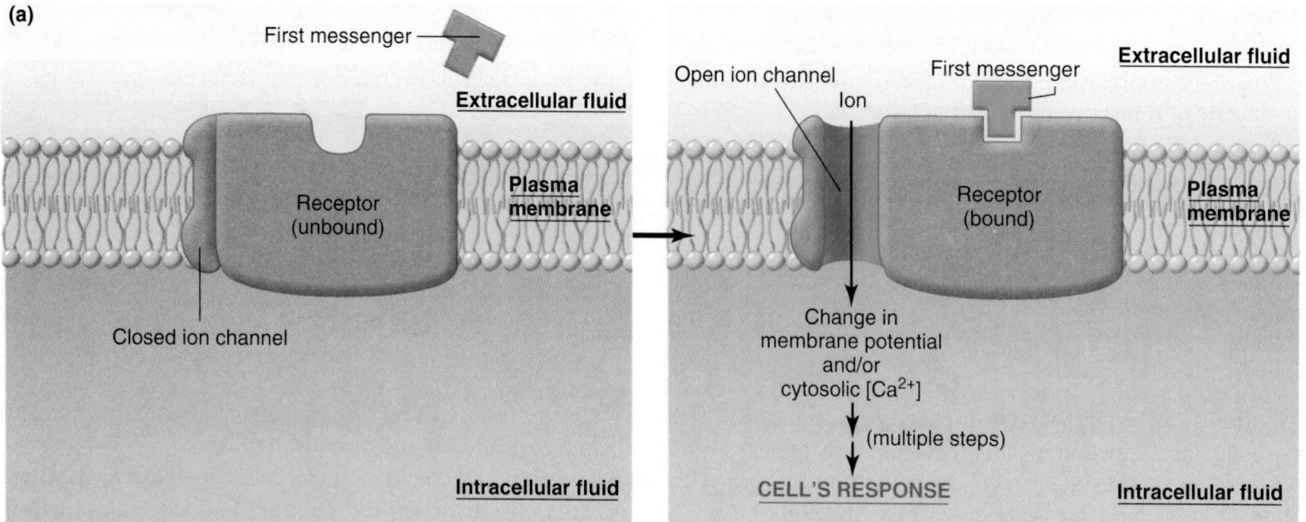

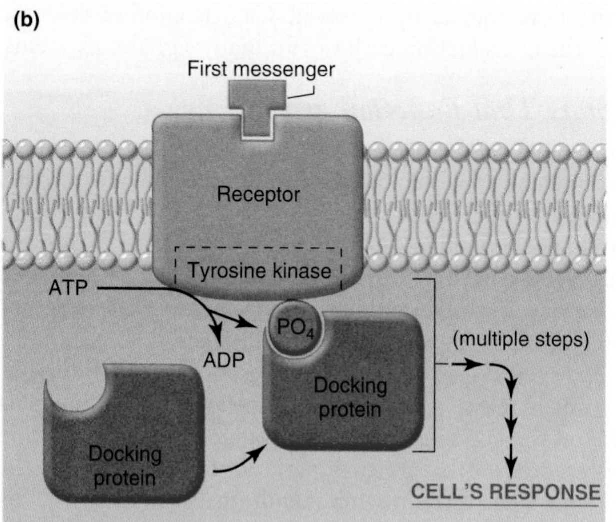

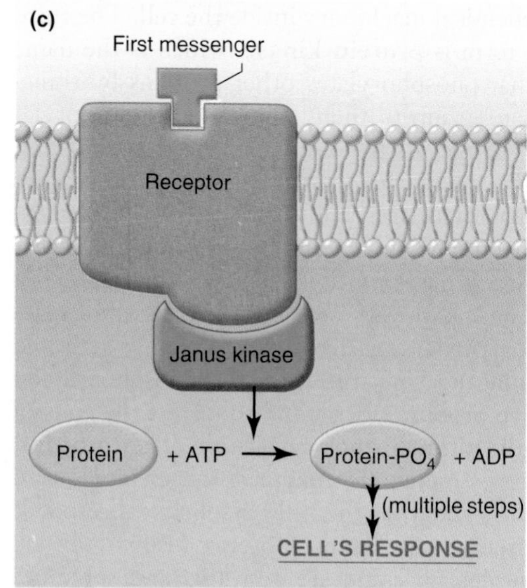

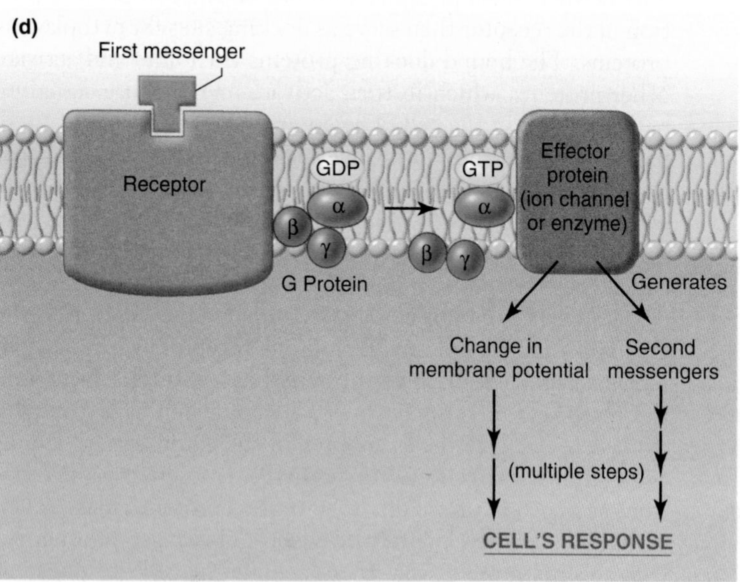

Figure 5.5 **AP|R** Mechanisms of action of water-soluble messengers (noted as "first messengers" in this and subsequent figures). (a) Signal transduction mechanism in which the receptor complex includes an ion channel. Note that the receptor exists in two conformations in the unbound and bound states. It is the binding of the first messenger to its receptor that triggers the conformational change that leads to opening of the channel. *Note: Conformational changes also occur in panels b–d but only the bound state is shown for simplicity.* (b) Signal transduction mechanism in which the receptor itself functions as an enzyme, usually a tyrosine kinase. (c) Signal transduction mechanism in which the receptor activates a janus kinase in the cytoplasm. (d) Signal transduction mechanism involving G proteins. When GDP is bound to the alpha subunit of the G protein, the protein exists as an inactive trimeric molecule. Binding of GTP to the alpha subunit causes dissociation of the alpha subunit, which then activates the effector protein.

PHYSIOLOGICAL INQUIRY

- Many cells express more than one of the four types of receptors depicted in this figure. Why might this be?

Answer can be found at end of chapter.

signal transduction pathway is used by only a small number of messengers and should not be confused with the much more prevalent cAMP system to be described in a later section. Also, in certain cells, guanylyl cyclase enzymes are present in the cytoplasm. In these cases, a first messenger—the gas nitric oxide (NO)—diffuses into the cytosol of the cell and combines with the guanylyl cyclase to trigger the formation of cGMP. Nitric oxide is a lipid-soluble gas produced from the amino acid arginine by the action of an enzyme called nitric oxide synthase, which is present in numerous cell types including the cells that line the interior of blood vessels. When released from such cells, NO acts locally in a paracrine fashion to relax the smooth muscle component of certain blood vessels, which allows the blood vessel to dilate, or open, more. As you will learn in Chapter 12, the ability of certain blood vessels to dilate is an important part of the homeostatic control of the circulation of blood and of blood pressure.

Receptors That Interact with Cytoplasmic Janus Kinases

Recall that in the previous category, the receptor itself has intrinsic enzyme activity. In the next category of receptors (see Table 5.2 and **Figure 5.5c**), the enzymatic activity—again, tyrosine kinase activity—resides not in the receptor but in a family of separate cytoplasmic kinases, called **janus kinases (JAKs),** which are associated with the receptor. In these cases, the receptor and its associated janus kinase function as a unit. The binding of a first messenger to the receptor causes a conformational change in the receptor that leads to activation of the janus kinase. Different receptors associate with different members of the janus kinase family, and the different janus kinases phosphorylate different target proteins, many of which act as transcription factors. The result of these pathways is the synthesis of new proteins, which mediate the cell's response to the first messenger. One significant example of signals mediated primarily via receptors linked to janus kinases are those of the cytokines—proteins secreted by cells of the immune system that play a critical role in immune defenses (Chapter 18).

G-Protein-Coupled Receptors

The fourth category of plasma membrane receptors in Table 5.2 is by far the largest, including hundreds of distinct receptors (**Figure 5.5d**). Bound to the inactive receptor is a protein complex located on the cytosolic surface of the plasma membrane and belonging to the family of proteins known as **G proteins.** G proteins contain three subunits, called the alpha, beta, and gamma subunits. The alpha subunit can bind GDP and GTP. The beta and gamma subunits help anchor the alpha subunit in the membrane. The binding of a first messenger to the receptor changes the conformation of the receptor. This activated receptor increases the affinity of the alpha subunit of the G protein for GTP. When bound to GTP, the alpha subunit dissociates from the beta and gamma subunits of the trimeric G protein. This dissociation allows the activated alpha subunit to link up with still another plasma membrane protein, either an ion channel or an enzyme. These ion channels and enzymes are effector proteins that mediate the next steps in the sequence of events leading to the cell's response.

In essence, then, a G protein serves as a switch to couple a receptor to an ion channel or to an enzyme in the plasma membrane. Consequently, these receptors are known as **G-protein-coupled receptors.** The G protein may cause the ion channel to open, with a resulting change in electrical signals or, in the case of Ca^{2+} channels, changes in the cytosolic Ca^{2+} concentration. Alternatively, the G protein may activate or inhibit the membrane enzyme with which it interacts. Such enzymes, when activated, cause the generation of second messengers inside the cell.

Once the alpha subunit of the G protein activates its effector protein, a GTPase activity inherent in the alpha subunit cleaves the GTP into GDP and P_i. This cleavage renders the alpha subunit inactive, allowing it to recombine with its beta and gamma subunits.

There are several subfamilies of plasma membrane G proteins, each with multiple distinct members, and a single receptor may be associated with more than one type of G protein. Moreover, some G proteins may couple to more than one type of plasma membrane effector protein. In this way, a first-messenger-activated receptor, via its G-protein couplings, can call into action a variety of plasma membrane proteins such as ion channels and enzymes. These molecules can, in turn, induce a variety of cellular events.

To illustrate some of the major points concerning G proteins, plasma membrane effector proteins, second messengers, and protein kinases, the next two sections describe the two most common effector protein enzymes regulated by G proteins—adenylyl cyclase and phospholipase C. In addition, the subsequent portions of the signal transduction pathways in which they participate are described.

Adenylyl Cyclase and Cyclic AMP

In this pathway (**Figure 5.6**), activation of the receptor by the binding of the first messenger (for example, the hormone epinephrine) allows the receptor to activate its associated G protein, in this example known as G_s (the subscript *s* denotes "stimulatory"). This causes G_s to activate its effector protein, the membrane enzyme called **adenylyl cyclase** (also known as adenylate cyclase). The activated adenylyl cyclase, with its catalytic site located on the cytosolic surface of the plasma membrane, catalyzes the conversion of cytosolic ATP to cyclic 3′,5′-adenosine monophosphate, or **cyclic AMP (cAMP)** (**Figure 5.7**). Cyclic AMP then acts as a second messenger (see Figure 5.6). It diffuses throughout the cell to trigger the sequence of events leading to the cell's ultimate response to the first messenger. The action of cAMP eventually terminates when it is broken down to AMP, a reaction catalyzed by the enzyme **cAMP phosphodiesterase** (see Figure 5.7). This enzyme is also subject to physiological control. Thus, the cellular concentration of cAMP can be changed either by altering the rate of its messenger-mediated synthesis or the rate of its phosphodiesterase-mediated breakdown. Caffeine and theophylline, the active ingredients of coffee and tea, are widely consumed stimulants that work partly by inhibiting phosphodiesterase activity, thereby prolonging the actions of cAMP within cells.

What does cAMP actually do inside the cell? It binds to and activates an enzyme known as **cAMP-dependent protein kinase,** also called protein kinase A (see Figure 5.6). Recall that

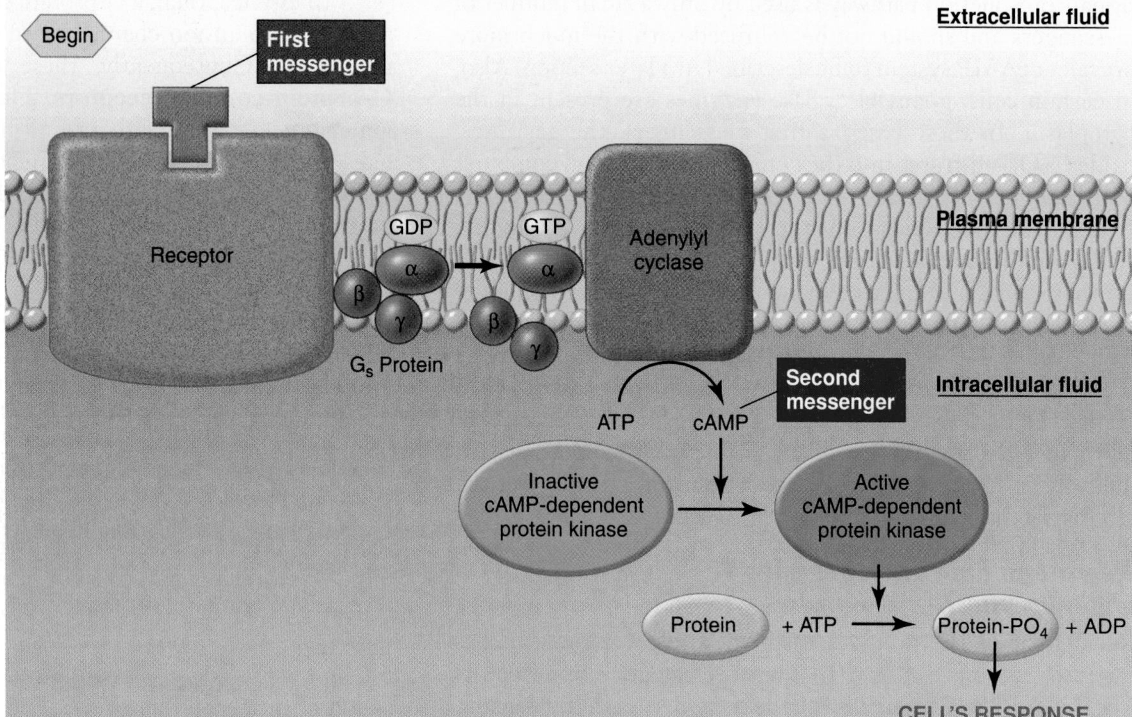

Figure 5.6 APIR Cyclic AMP second-messenger system. Not shown in the figure is the existence of another regulatory protein, G_i, which certain receptors can react with to cause inhibition of adenylyl cyclase.

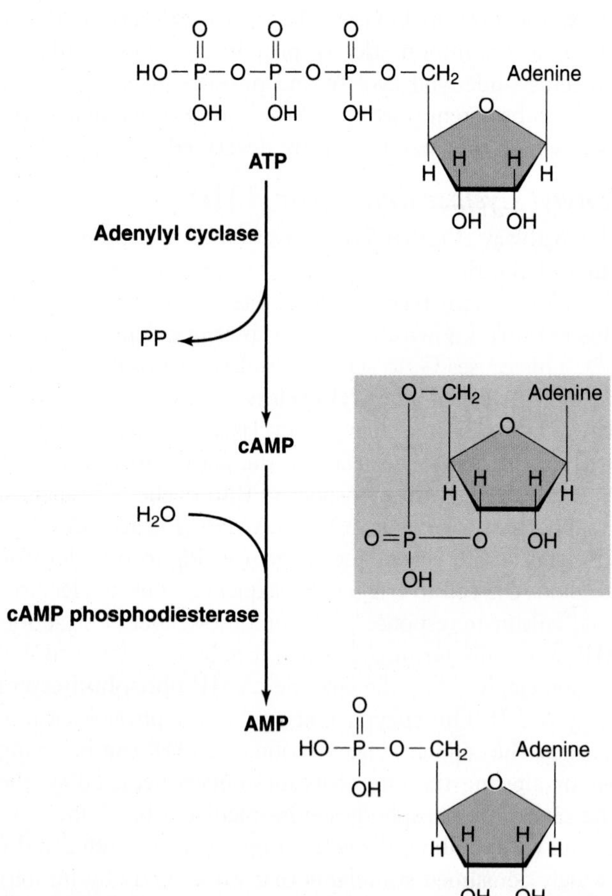

Figure 5.7 Structure of ATP, cAMP, and AMP. ATP is converted to cAMP by the action of the plasma membrane enzyme adenylyl cyclase. cAMP is inactivated by the cytosolic enzyme cAMP phosphodiesterase, which converts cAMP into the noncyclized form AMP.

protein kinases phosphorylate other proteins—often enzymes—by transferring a phosphate group to them. The changes in the activity of proteins phosphorylated by cAMP-dependent protein kinase bring about the cell's response (secretion, contraction, and so on). Again, recall that each of the various protein kinases that participate in the multiple signal transduction pathways described in this chapter has its own specific substrates.

In essence, then, the activation of adenylyl cyclase by a G protein initiates an "amplification cascade" of events that converts proteins in sequence from inactive to active forms. **Figure 5.8** illustrates the benefit of such a cascade. While it is active, a single enzyme molecule is capable of transforming into product not one but many substrate molecules, let us say 100. Therefore, one active molecule of adenylyl cyclase may catalyze the generation of 100 cAMP molecules. At each of the two subsequent enzyme-activation steps in our example, another 100-fold amplification occurs. Therefore, the end result is that a single molecule of the first messenger could, in this example, cause the generation of 1 million product molecules. This helps to explain how hormones and other messengers can be effective at extremely low extracellular concentrations. To take an actual example, one molecule of the hormone epinephrine can cause the liver to generate and release 10^8 molecules of glucose.

In addition, activated cAMP-dependent protein kinase can diffuse into the cell nucleus, where it can phosphorylate a protein that then binds to specific regulatory regions of certain genes. Such genes are said to be cAMP-responsive. Therefore, the effects of cAMP can be rapid and independent of changes in gene activity, as in the example of epinephrine and glucose production, or slower and dependent upon the formation of new gene products.

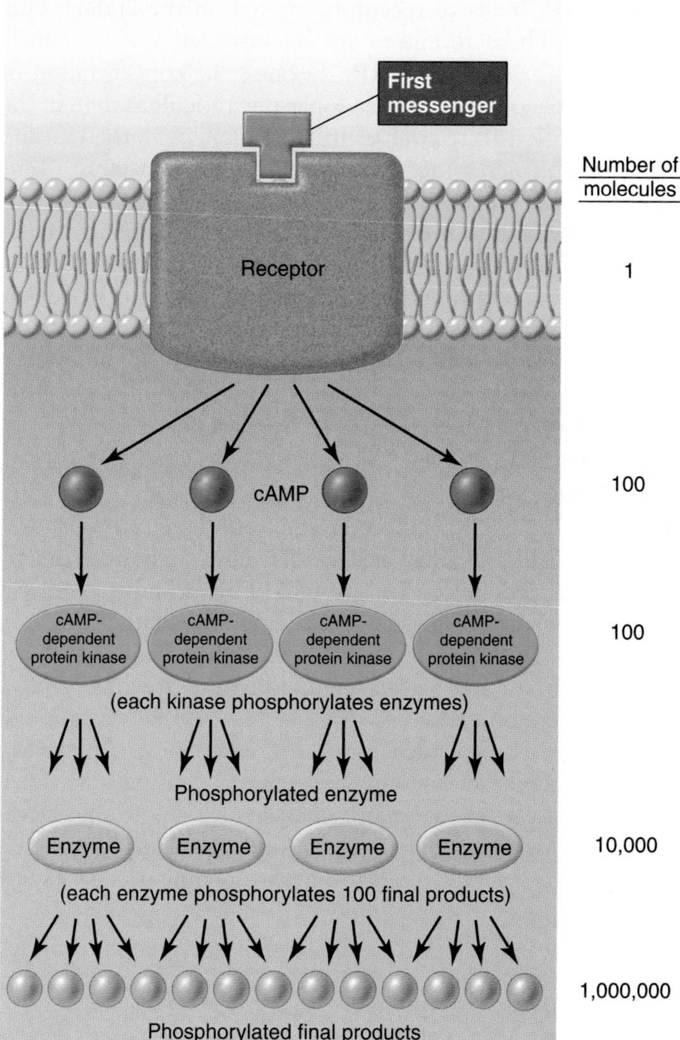

Figure 5.8 AP|R Example of signal amplification. In this example, a single molecule of a first messenger results in 1 million final products. Other second-messenger pathways have similar amplification processes. The steps between receptor activation and cAMP generation are omitted for simplicity.

PHYSIOLOGICAL INQUIRY

- What are the advantages of having an enzyme like adenylyl cyclase involved in the initial response to receptor activation by a first messenger?

Answer can be found at end of chapter.

How can cAMP's activation of a single molecule, cAMP-dependent protein kinase, be common to the great variety of biochemical sequences and cell responses initiated by cAMP-generating first messengers? The answer is that cAMP-dependent protein kinase can phosphorylate a large number of different proteins (**Figure 5.9**). In this way, activated cAMP-dependent protein kinase can exert multiple actions within a single cell and different actions in different cells. For example, epinephrine acts via the cAMP pathway on fat cells to stimulate the breakdown of triglyceride, a process that is mediated by one particular phosphorylated enzyme that is chiefly expressed in adipose cells. In the liver, epinephrine acts via cAMP to stimulate both glycogenolysis and gluconeogenesis, processes that are mediated by phosphorylated enzymes that differ from those in fat cells.

Whereas phosphorylation mediated by cAMP- dependent protein kinase activates certain enzymes, it inhibits others. For example, the enzyme catalyzing the rate-limiting step in glycogen synthesis is inhibited by phosphorylation. This explains how epinephrine inhibits glycogen synthesis at the same time it stimulates glycogen breakdown by activating the enzyme that catalyzes the latter response.

Not mentioned thus far is the fact that receptors for some first messengers, upon activation by their messengers, *inhibit* adenylyl cyclase. This inhibition results in less, rather than more, generation of cAMP. This occurs because these receptors are associated with a different G protein known as G_i

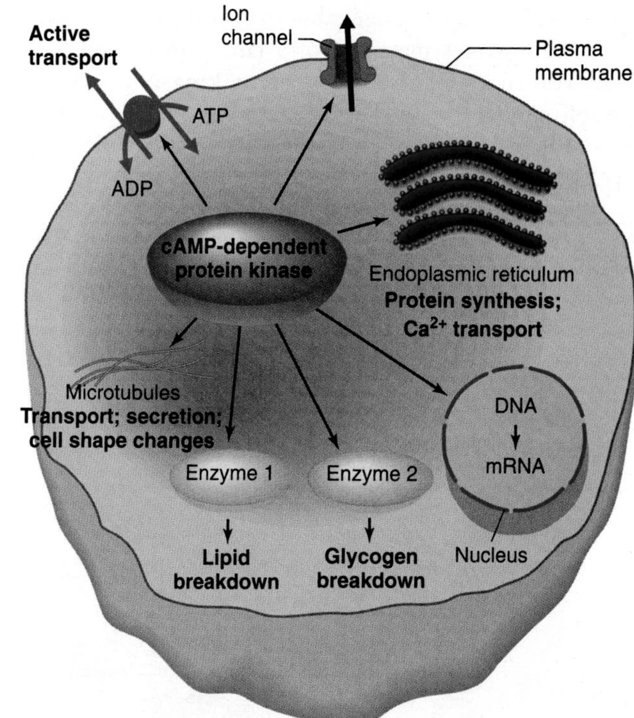

Figure 5.9 AP|R The variety of cellular responses induced by cAMP is due mainly to the fact that activated cAMP-dependent protein kinase can phosphorylate many different proteins, activating or inhibiting them. In this figure, the protein kinase is shown phosphorylating seven different proteins—a microtubular protein, an ATPase, an ion channel, a protein in the endoplasmic reticulum, a protein involved in stimulating the transcription of a gene into mRNA, and two enzymes.

PHYSIOLOGICAL INQUIRY

- Does a given protein kinase, such as cAMP-dependent protein kinase, phosphorylate the same proteins in all cells in which the kinase is present?

Answer can be found at end of chapter.

(the subscript *i* denotes "inhibitory"). Activation of G_i causes the inhibition of adenylyl cyclase. The result is to decrease the concentration of cAMP in the cell and thereby the phosphorylation of key proteins inside the cell. Many cells express both stimulatory and inhibitory G proteins in their membranes, providing a means of tightly regulating intracellular cAMP concentrations. This common cellular feature highlights the general principle that most physiological functions are controlled by multiple regulatory systems, often working in opposition.

Phospholipase C, Diacylglycerol, and Inositol Trisphosphate

In this system, a G protein called G_q is activated by a receptor bound to a first messenger. Activated G_q then activates a plasma membrane effector enzyme called **phospholipase C.** This enzyme catalyzes the breakdown of a plasma membrane phospholipid known as phosphatidylinositol bisphosphate, abbreviated PIP_2, to **diacylglycerol (DAG)** and **inositol trisphosphate (IP_3)** (**Figure 5.10**). Both DAG and IP_3 then function as second messengers but in very different ways.

DAG activates members of a family of related protein kinases known collectively as **protein kinase C,** which, in a fashion similar to cAMP-dependent protein kinase, then phosphorylates a large number of other proteins, leading to the cell's response.

IP_3, in contrast to DAG, does not exert its second-messenger role by directly activating a protein kinase. Rather, cytosolic IP_3 binds to receptors located on the endoplasmic reticulum. These receptors are ligand-gated Ca^{2+} channels that open when bound to IP_3. Because the concentration of Ca^{2+} is much greater in the endoplasmic reticulum than in the cytosol, Ca^{2+} diffuses out of this organelle into the cytosol, significantly increasing cytosolic Ca^{2+} concentration. This increased Ca^{2+} concentration then continues the sequence of events leading to the cell's response to the first messenger. We will pick up this thread in more detail in a later section. However, it is worth noting that one of the actions of Ca^{2+} is to help activate some forms of protein kinase C (which is how this kinase got its name—*C* for "calcium").

Control of Ion Channels by G Proteins

A comparison of Figure 5.5d and Figure 5.9 emphasizes one more important feature of G-protein function—the ability to both directly and indirectly gate ion channels. As shown in Figure 5.5d and described earlier, an ion channel can be the effector protein for a G protein. This is known as direct G-protein gating of plasma membrane ion channels because the G protein interacts directly with the channel. All the events occur in the plasma membrane and are independent of second messengers. Now look at Figure 5.9, and you will see that cAMP-dependent protein kinase can phosphorylate a plasma membrane ion channel, thereby causing it to open. As we have seen, the sequence of events leading to the activation of cAMP-dependent protein kinase proceeds through a G protein, so it should be clear that the opening of this channel

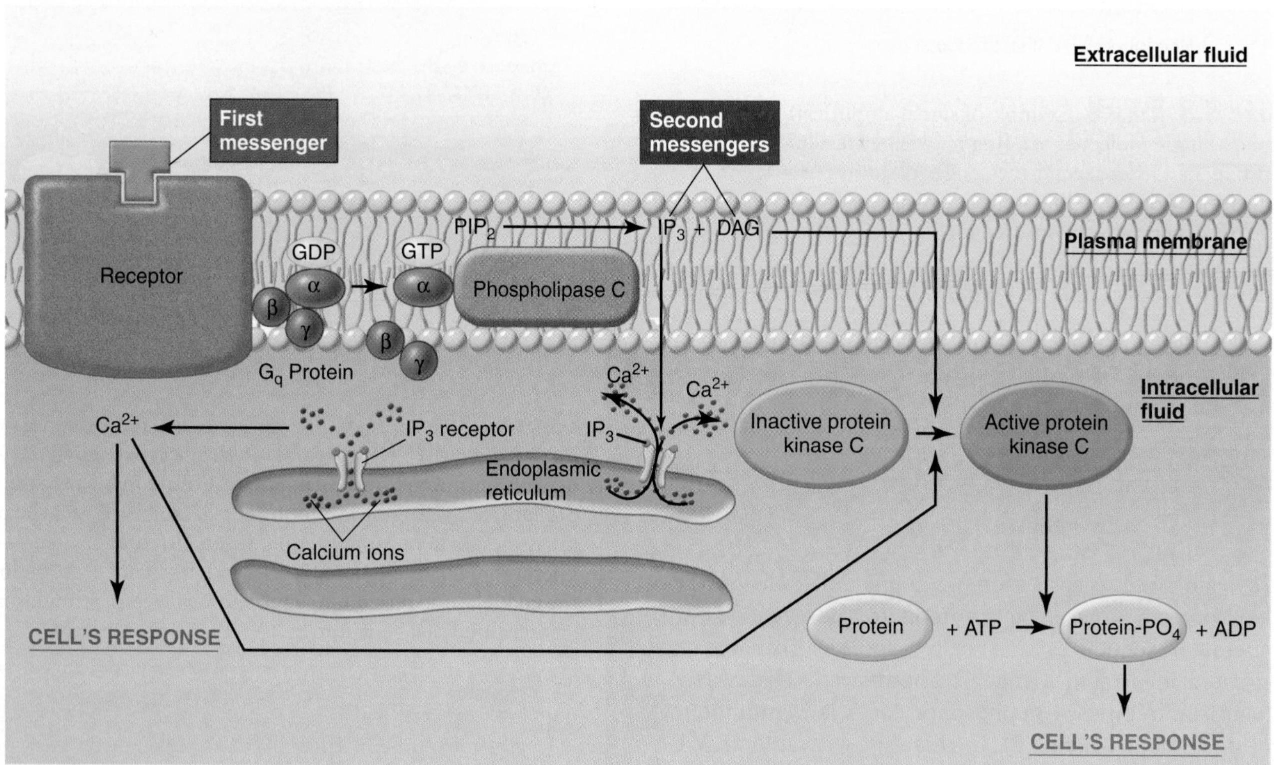

Figure 5.10 AP|R Mechanism by which an activated receptor stimulates the enzymatically mediated breakdown of PIP_2 to yield IP_3 and DAG. IP_3 then binds to a receptor on the endoplasmic receptor. This receptor is a ligand-gated ion channel that, when opened, allows the release of calcium ions from the endoplasmic reticulum into the cytosol. Together with DAG, Ca^{2+} activates protein kinase C.

TABLE 5.3	Summary of Mechanisms by Which Receptor Activation Influences Ion Channels
The ion channel is part of the receptor.	
A G protein directly gates the channel.	
A G protein gates the channel indirectly via a second messenger.	

TABLE 5.4	Ca^{2+} as a Second Messenger
Common Mechanisms by Which Stimulation of a Cell Leads to an Increase in Cytosolic Ca^{2+} Concentration	
I. Receptor activation A. Plasma-membrane Ca^{2+} channels open in response to a first messenger; the receptor itself may contain the channel, or the receptor may activate a G protein that opens the channel via a second messenger. B. Ca^{2+} is released from the endoplasmic reticulum; this is typically mediated by IP_3. C. Active Ca^{2+} transport out of the cell is inhibited by a second messenger. II. Opening of voltage-gated Ca^{2+} channels	
Major Mechanisms by Which an Increase in Cytosolic Ca^{2+} Concentration Induces the Cell's Responses	
I. Ca^{2+} binds to calmodulin. On binding Ca^{2+}, the calmodulin changes shape, which allows it to activate or inhibit a large variety of enzymes and other proteins. Many of these enzymes are protein kinases. II. Ca^{2+} combines with Ca^{2+}-binding intermediary proteins other than calmodulin. These proteins then act in a manner analogous to calmodulin. III. Ca^{2+} combines with and alters response proteins directly, without the intermediation of any specific Ca^{2+}-binding protein.	

is indirectly dependent on that G protein. To generalize, the *indirect G-protein gating* of ion channels utilizes a second-messenger pathway for the opening or closing of the channel. Not just cAMP-dependent protein kinase but protein kinases involved in other signal transduction pathways can participate in reactions leading to such indirect gating. **Table 5.3** summarizes the three ways by which receptor activation by a first messenger leads to opening or closing of ion channels, causing a change in membrane potential.

Ca^{2+} as a Second Messenger

The calcium ion (Ca^{2+}) functions as a second messenger in a great variety of cellular responses to stimuli, both chemical and electrical. The physiology of Ca^{2+} as a second messenger requires an analysis of two broad questions: (1) How do stimuli cause the cytosolic Ca^{2+} concentration to increase? (2) How does the increased Ca^{2+} concentration elicit the cells' responses? Note that, for simplicity, our two questions are phrased in terms of an *increase* in cytosolic concentration. There are, in fact, first messengers that elicit a *decrease* in cytosolic Ca^{2+} concentration and therefore a decrease in calcium's second-messenger effects. Now for the answer to the first question.

By means of active-transport systems in the plasma membrane and cell organelles, Ca^{2+} is maintained at an extremely low concentration in the cytosol. Consequently, there is always a large electrochemical gradient favoring diffusion of Ca^{2+} into the cytosol via Ca^{2+} channels found in both the plasma membrane and the endoplasmic reticulum. A stimulus to the cell can alter this steady state by influencing the active-transport systems and/or the ion channels, resulting in a change in cytosolic Ca^{2+} concentration. The most common ways that receptor activation by a first messenger increases the cytosolic Ca^{2+} concentration have already been presented in this chapter and are summarized in the top part of **Table 5.4**.

Now we turn to the question of how the increased cytosolic Ca^{2+} concentration elicits the cells' responses (see bottom of Table 5.4). The common denominator of Ca^{2+} actions is its ability to bind to various cytosolic proteins, altering their conformation and thereby activating their function. One of the most important of these is a protein found in most cells known as **calmodulin** (**Figure 5.11**). On binding with Ca^{2+}, calmodulin changes shape, and this allows calcium–calmodulin to activate or inhibit a large variety of enzymes and other proteins, many of them protein kinases. Activation or inhibition of **calmodulin-dependent protein kinases** leads, via phosphorylation, to activation or inhibition of proteins involved in the cell's ultimate responses to the first messenger.

Calmodulin is not, however, the only intracellular protein influenced by Ca^{2+} binding. For example, you will learn in Chapter 9 how Ca^{2+} binds to a protein called troponin in certain types of muscle to initiate contraction.

As a final note, it was described earlier in this chapter that the receptors for lipid-soluble messengers, once activated by hormone binding, act in the nucleus as transcription factors to increase or decrease the rate of gene transcription. There are many other transcription factors inside cells, however, and the signal transduction pathways initiated by plasma membrane receptors often activate these transcription factors, typically by phosphorylation. Therefore, many first messengers that bind to plasma membrane receptors can also alter gene transcription via second messengers. For example, several of the proteins that cAMP-dependent protein kinase phosphorylates function as transcription factors.

Other Messengers

In a few places in this text, you will learn about messengers that are not as readily classified as those just described. Among these are the eicosanoids. The **eicosanoids** are a family of molecules produced from the polyunsaturated fatty acid **arachidonic acid,** which is present in plasma membrane phospholipids. The eicosanoids include the **cyclic endoperoxides,** the **prostaglandins,** the **thromboxanes,** and the **leukotrienes** (**Figure 5.12**). They are generated in many

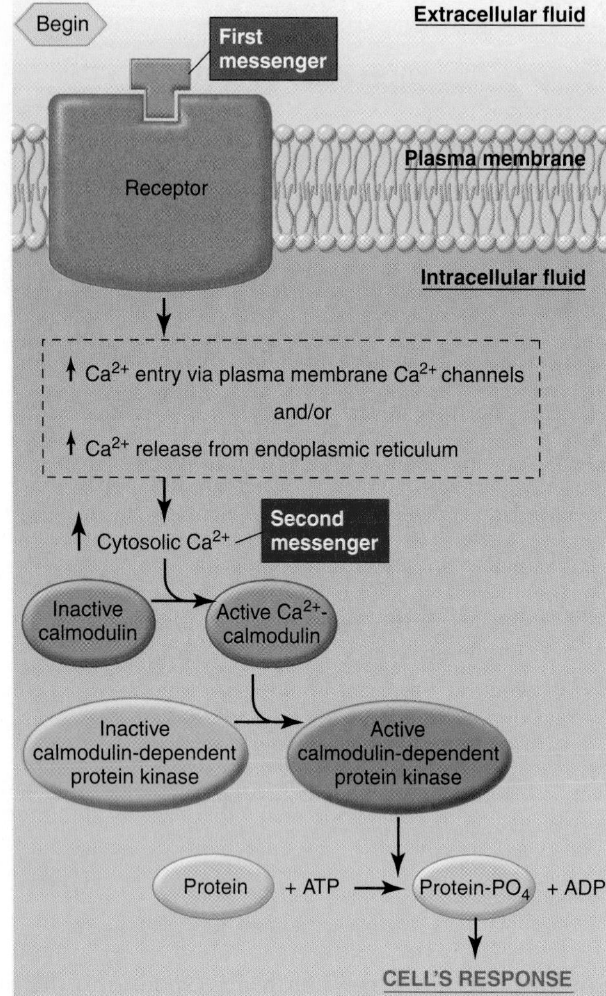

Figure 5.11 Ca^{2+}, calmodulin, and the calmodulin-dependent protein kinase system. (There are multiple calmodulin-dependent protein kinases.) Table 5.4 summarizes the mechanisms for increasing cytosolic Ca^{2+} concentration.

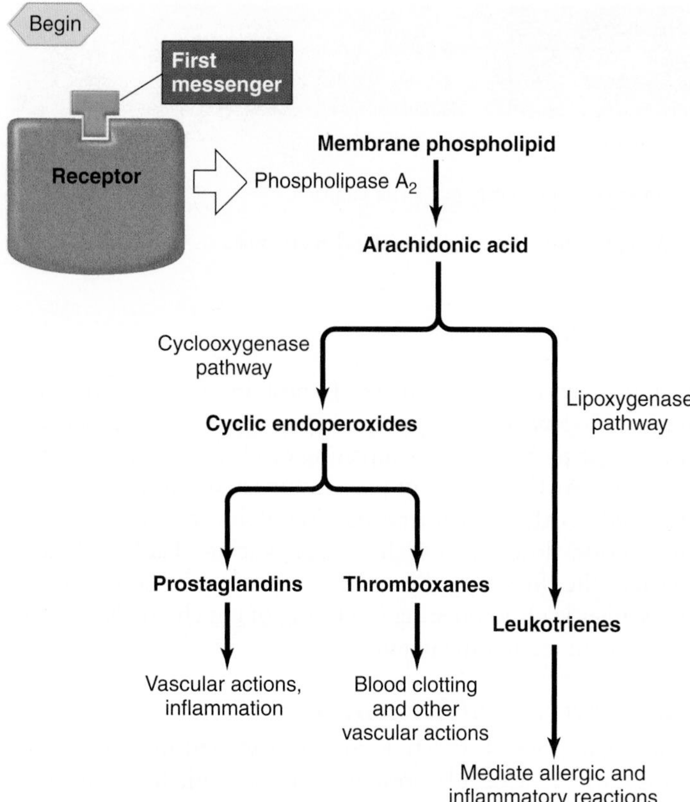

Figure 5.12 Pathways for eicosanoid synthesis and some of their major functions. Phospholipase A_2 is the one enzyme common to the formation of all the eicosanoids; it is the site at which stimuli act. Anti-inflammatory steroids inhibit phospholipase A_2. The step mediated by cyclooxygenase is inhibited by aspirin and other nonsteroidal anti-inflammatory drugs (NSAIDs). There are also drugs available that inhibit the lipoxygenase enzyme, thereby blocking the formation of leukotrienes. These drugs may be helpful in controlling asthma, in which excess leukotrienes have been implicated in the allergic and inflammatory components of the disease.

PHYSIOLOGICAL INQUIRY

- Based on the pathways shown in this figure, why are people advised to avoid taking aspirin or other NSAIDs prior to a surgical procedure?

Answer can be found at end of chapter.

kinds of cells in response to different types of extracellular signals; these include a variety of growth factors, immune defense molecules, and even other eicosanoids. Thus, eicosanoids may act as both extracellular and intracellular messengers, depending on the cell type.

The synthesis of eicosanoids begins when an appropriate stimulus—hormone, neurotransmitter, paracrine substance, drug, or toxic agent—binds its receptor and activates **phospholipase A_2,** an enzyme localized to the plasma membrane of the stimulated cell. As shown in Figure 5.12, this enzyme splits off arachidonic acid from the membrane phospholipids, and the arachidonic acid can then be metabolized by two pathways. One pathway is initiated by an enzyme called **cyclooxygenase (COX)** and leads ultimately to formation of the cyclic endoperoxides, prostaglandins, and thromboxanes. The other pathway is initiated by the enzyme **lipoxygenase** and leads to formation of the leukotrienes. Within both of these pathways, synthesis of the various specific eicosanoids is enzyme-mediated. Thus, beyond phospholipase A_2, the eicosanoid-pathway enzymes expressed in a particular cell determine which eicosanoids the cell synthesizes in response to a stimulus.

Each of the major eicosanoid subdivisions contains more than one member, as indicated by the use of the plural in referring to them (*prostaglandins,* for example). On the basis of structural differences, the different molecules within each subdivision are designated by a letter—for example, PGA and PGE for prostaglandins of the A and E types, which then may be further subdivided—for example, PGE_2.

Once they have been synthesized in response to a stimulus, the eicosanoids may in some cases act as intracellular messengers, but more often they are released immediately and act locally. For this reason, the eicosanoids are usually categorized as paracrine and autocrine substances. After they act, they are quickly metabolized by local enzymes to inactive forms. The eicosanoids exert a wide array of effects, particularly on blood vessels and in inflammation. Many of these will be described in future chapters.

Certain drugs influence the eicosanoid pathway and are among the most commonly used in the world today. ***Aspirin***, for example, inhibits cyclooxygenase and, therefore, blocks the synthesis of the endoperoxides, prostaglandins, and thromboxanes. It and other drugs that also block cyclooxygenase are collectively termed ***nonsteroidal anti-inflammatory drugs (NSAIDs)***. Their major uses are to reduce pain, fever, and inflammation. The term *nonsteroidal* distinguishes them from synthetic glucocorticoids (analogs of steroid hormones made by the adrenal glands) that are used in large doses as anti-inflammatory drugs; these steroids inhibit phospholipase A_2 and therefore block the production of all eicosanoids.

Cessation of Activity in Signal Transduction Pathways

Once initiated, signal transduction pathways are eventually shut off, preventing chronic overstimulation of a cell, which can be detrimental. The key event is usually the cessation of receptor activation. Responses to messengers are transient events that persist only briefly and subside when the receptor is no longer bound to the first messenger. A major way that receptor activation ceases is by a decrease in the concentration of first-messenger molecules in the region of the receptor. This occurs as enzymes in the vicinity metabolize the first messenger, as the first messenger is taken up by adjacent cells, or as it simply diffuses away.

In addition, receptors can be inactivated in at least three other ways: (1) the receptor becomes chemically altered (usually by phosphorylation), which may reduce its affinity for a first messenger, and so the messenger is released; (2) phosphorylation of the receptor may prevent further G-protein binding to the receptor; and (3) plasma membrane receptors may be removed when the combination of first messenger and receptor is taken into the cell by endocytosis. The processes described here are physiologically controlled. For example, in many cases the inhibitory phosphorylation of a receptor is mediated by a protein kinase that was initially activated in response to the first messenger. This receptor inactivation constitutes negative feedback.

This concludes our description of the basic principles of signal transduction pathways. It is essential to recognize that the pathways do not exist in isolation but may be active simultaneously in a single cell, undergoing complex interactions. This is possible because a single first messenger may trigger changes in the activity of more than one pathway and, much more importantly, because many different first messengers—often dozens—may simultaneously influence a cell. Moreover, a great deal of "cross talk" can occur at one or more levels among the various signal transduction pathways. For example, active molecules generated in the cAMP pathway can alter the activity of receptors and signaling molecules generated by other pathways.

Finally, for reference purposes, **Table 5.5** summarizes the biochemistry of the second messengers described in this chapter.

TABLE 5.5 Reference Table of Important Second Messengers

Substance	Source	Effects
Ca^{2+}	Enters cell through plasma membrane ion channels or is released from endoplasmic reticulum.	Activates calmodulin and other Ca^{2+}-binding proteins; calcium–calmodulin activates calmodulin-dependent protein kinases. Also activates protein kinase C.
Cyclic AMP (cAMP)	A G protein activates plasma membrane adenylyl cyclase, which catalyzes the formation of cAMP from ATP.	Activates cAMP-dependent protein kinase (protein kinase A).
Cyclic GMP (cGMP)	Generated from guanosine triphosphate in a reaction catalyzed by a plasma membrane receptor with guanylyl cyclase activity.	Activates cGMP-dependent protein kinase (protein kinase G).
Diacylglycerol (DAG)	A G protein activates plasma membrane phospholipase C, which catalyzes the generation of DAG and IP_3 from plasma membrane phosphatidylinositol bisphosphate (PIP_2).	Activates protein kinase C.
Inositol trisphosphate (IP_3)	See DAG above.	Releases Ca^{2+} from endoplasmic reticulum.

SUMMARY

Receptors

I. Receptors for chemical messengers are proteins or glycoproteins located either inside the cell or, much more commonly, in the plasma membrane. The binding of a messenger by a receptor manifests specificity, saturation, and competition.

II. Receptors are subject to physiological regulation by their own messengers. This includes down- and up-regulation.

III. Different cell types express different types of receptors; even a single cell may express multiple receptor types.

Signal Transduction Pathways

I. Binding a chemical messenger activates a receptor, and this initiates one or more signal transduction pathways leading to the cell's response.

II. Lipid-soluble messengers bind to receptors inside the target cell. The activated receptor acts in the nucleus as a transcription factor to alter the rate of transcription of specific genes, resulting in a change in the concentration or secretion of the proteins the genes encode.

III. Water-soluble messengers bind to receptors on the plasma membrane. The pathways induced by activation of the receptor often involve second messengers and protein kinases.

a. The receptor may be a ligand-gated ion channel. The channel opens, resulting in an electrical signal in the membrane and, when Ca^{2+} channels are involved, an increase in the cytosolic Ca^{2+} concentration.

b. The receptor may itself be an enzyme. With one exception, the enzyme activity is that of a protein kinase, usually a tyrosine kinase. The exception is the receptor that functions as a guanylyl cyclase to generate cyclic GMP.

c. The receptor may activate a cytosolic janus kinase associated with it.

d. The receptor may interact with an associated plasma membrane G protein, which in turn interacts with plasma membrane effector proteins—ion channels or enzymes.

e. Very commonly, the receptor may stimulate, via a G_s protein, or inhibit, via a G_i protein, the membrane effector enzyme adenylyl cyclase, which catalyzes the conversion of cytosolic ATP to cyclic AMP. Cyclic AMP acts as a second messenger to activate intracellular cAMP-dependent protein kinase, which phosphorylates proteins that mediate the cell's ultimate responses to the first messenger.

f. The receptor may activate, via a G_q protein, the plasma membrane enzyme phospholipase C, which catalyzes the formation of diacylglycerol (DAG) and inositol trisphosphate (IP_3). DAG activates protein kinase C, and IP_3 acts as a second messenger to release Ca^{2+} from the endoplasmic reticulum.

IV. The receptor, via a G protein, may directly open or close (gate) an adjacent ion channel. This differs from indirect G-protein gating of channels, in which a second messenger acts upon the channel.

V. The calcium ion is one of the most widespread second messengers.

a. An activated receptor can increase cytosolic Ca^{2+} concentration by causing certain Ca^{2+} channels in the plasma membrane and/or endoplasmic reticulum to open.

b. Ca^{2+} binds to one of several intracellular proteins, most often calmodulin. Calcium-activated calmodulin activates or inhibits many proteins, including calmodulin-dependent protein kinases.

VI. Eicosanoids are derived from arachidonic acid, which is released from phospholipids in the plasma membrane. They exert widespread intracellular and extracellular effects on cell activity.

VII. The signal transduction pathways triggered by activated plasma membrane receptors may influence genetic expression by activating transcription factors.

VIII. Cessation of receptor activity occurs when the first-messenger molecule concentration decreases or when the receptor is chemically altered or internalized, in the case of plasma membrane receptors.

REVIEW QUESTIONS

1. What is the chemical nature of receptors? Where are they located?
2. Explain why different types of cells may respond differently to the same chemical messenger.
3. Describe how the metabolism of receptors can lead to down-regulation or up-regulation.
4. What is the first step in the action of a messenger on a cell?
5. Describe the signal transduction pathway that lipid-soluble messengers use.
6. Classify plasma membrane receptors according to the signal transduction pathways they initiate.
7. What is the result of opening a membrane ion channel?
8. Contrast receptors that have intrinsic enzyme activity with those associated with cytoplasmic janus kinases.
9. Describe the role of plasma membrane G proteins.
10. Draw a diagram describing the adenylyl cyclase–cAMP system.
11. Draw a diagram illustrating the phospholipase C/DAG/IP_3 system.
12. How does the calcium–calmodulin system function?

KEY TERMS

adenylyl cyclase 127
affinity 122
agonist 123
antagonist 123
arachidonic acid 131
calmodulin 131
calmodulin-dependent protein kinase 131
cAMP-dependent protein kinase 127
cAMP phosphodiesterase 127
cGMP-dependent protein kinase 125
competition 122
cyclic AMP (cAMP) 127
cyclic endoperoxide 131
cyclic GMP (cGMP) 125
cyclooxygenase (COX) 132
diacylglycerol (DAG) 130
down-regulation 123
eicosanoid 131
first messenger 125
G protein 127
G-protein-coupled receptor 127
guanylyl cyclase 125
inositol trisphosphate (IP_3) 130
internalization 123
janus kinase (JAK) 127
leukotriene 131
ligand-gated ion channel 125
lipoxygenase 132
phospholipase A_2 132
phospholipase C 130
prostaglandin 131
protein kinase 125
protein kinase C 130
receptor 121
receptor activation 123
receptor protein 121
receptor tyrosine kinase 125
saturation 122
second messenger 125
signal transduction 121
signal transduction pathway 124
specificity 121
steroid-hormone-receptor superfamily 124
thromboxane 131
up-regulation 123

CLINICAL TERMS

aspirin 133
nonsteroidal anti-inflammatory drug (NSAID) 133
oxymetazoline 123
phenylephrine 123
pseudohypoparathyroidism 134

Clinical Case Study: A Child with Unexplained Weight Gain and Calcium Imbalance

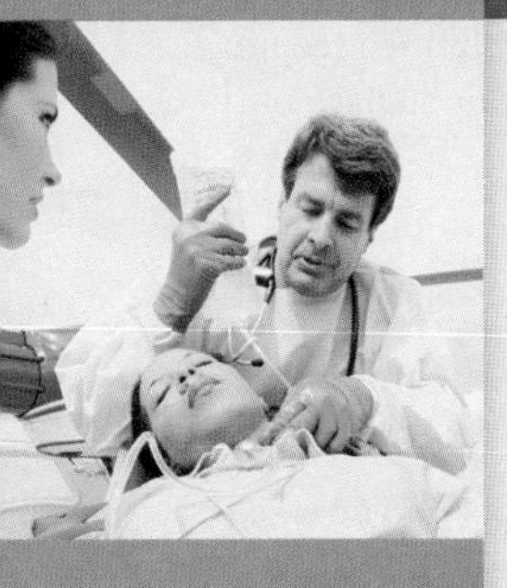

A 3-year-old girl was seen by her pediatrician to determine the cause of a recent increase in the rate of her weight gain. Her height was normal (95 cm/37.4 inches) but she weighed 16.5 kg (36.3 pounds), which is in the 92nd percentile for her age. The girl's mother—who was very short and overweight—stated that the child seemed listless at times and was rarely very active. She was also prone to muscle cramps and complained to her mother that her fingers and toes "felt funny," which the pediatrician was able to interpret as tingling sensations. She had a good appetite but not one that appeared unusual or extreme. The doctor suspected that the child had developed a deficiency in the amount of thyroid hormone in her blood. This hormone is produced by the thyroid gland in the neck (see Chapter 11) and is responsible in part for normal metabolism, that is, the rate at which calories are expended. Too little thyroid hormone typically results in weight gain and may also cause fatigue or lack of energy. A blood test was performed, and indeed the girl's thyroid hormone concentration was low. Because there are several conditions that may result in a deficiency of thyroid hormone, an additional exam was performed. During that exam, the physician noticed that the fourth metacarpals on each of the girl's hands were shorter than normal, and he could feel hard bumps (nodules) just beneath the girl's skin at various sites on her body. He ordered a blood test for Ca^{2+} and another hormone called parathyroid hormone (PTH).

PTH gets its name because the glands that produce it lie adjacent (*para*) to the thyroid gland. PTH normally acts on the kidneys and bones to maintain calcium ion homeostasis in the blood. For example, should Ca^{2+} concentrations in the blood decrease for any reason, PTH secretion will increase and stimulate the release of Ca^{2+} from bones into the blood. It also stimulates the retention of Ca^{2+} by the kidneys, such that less Ca^{2+} is lost in the urine. These two factors help to restore blood Ca^{2+} concentrations—a classic example of homeostasis through negative feedback. The doctor suspected that the nodules he felt were Ca^{2+} deposits and that the shortened fingers were the result of improper bone formation during development due to a Ca^{2+} imbalance. Abnormally low blood Ca^{2+} concentrations would also explain the cramps and tingling sensations. This is because extracellular Ca^{2+} concentration is critical for normal function of muscles and nerves, as well as for healthy bones and growth. The results of the blood test confirmed that Ca^{2+} concentrations were lower than normal. A logical explanation for why Ca^{2+} levels were low would be because PTH concentrations were low. Paradoxically, however, PTH concentrations were increased in the girl's blood. This means that PTH was present but was unable to act on its targets—the bones and kidneys—to maintain Ca^{2+} balance in the blood. What could prevent PTH from doing its job? How might this be related to the thyroid hormone imbalance that was responsible for the weight gain?

A genetic condition in which PTH concentrations in the blood are high but Ca^{2+} concentrations are low is ***pseudohypoparathyroidism.*** The prefix *hypo* in this context refers to "less than normal amounts of" PTH in the blood. This girl's condition seemed to fit a diagnosis of hypoparathyroidism, because her Ca^{2+} concentrations were low and she consequently demonstrated several symptoms characteristic of low Ca^{2+}. However, because her PTH concentrations were *not* low—in fact, they were higher than normal—the condition is called *pseudo,* or "false," hypoparathyroidism. A blood sample was taken from the girl and the white blood cells were subjected to DNA analysis. That analysis revealed that the girl was heterozygous for a mutation in the *GNAS1* gene, which encodes the alpha subunit of the stimulatory G protein (G_s alpha). Recall from Figure 5.6 that G_s couples certain plasma membrane receptor proteins to adenylyl cyclase and the production of cAMP, an important second messenger in many cells. PTH is known to act by binding to a cell surface receptor and activating adenylyl cyclase via this pathway. Because the girl had reduced expression of normal G_s alpha, her cells were unable to respond adequately to PTH, and consequently her blood concentrations of Ca^{2+} could not be maintained within the normal range.

PTH, however, is not the only signaling molecule in the body that acts through a G_s-coupled receptor; as you have learned in this chapter, there are many other such molecules. One of them is a hormone from the pituitary gland that stimulates thyroid hormone production by the thyroid gland. This explains why our patient had low thyroid hormone concentrations in addition to her PTH/Ca^{2+} imbalance.

Pseudohypoparathyroidism is a rare disorder, but it illustrates a larger and extremely important medical concern called target-organ resistance. Such diseases are characterized by normal or even elevated blood concentrations of signaling molecules such as PTH but insensitivity (that is, resistance) of a target organ (or organs) to the molecule. In our patient, the cause of the resistance was insufficient G_s-alpha action due to an inherited mutation; in other cases (such as type 2 diabetes mellitus, described in Chapter 16), it may result from defects in other aspects of cell signaling pathways. It is likely that the girl inherited the mutation from her mother, who showed some similar symptoms.

The girl was treated with a thyroid hormone pill each day, calcium tablets twice per day, and a derivative of vitamin D (which helps the intestines absorb Ca^{2+}) twice per day. She will need to remain on this treatment plan for the rest of her life. In addition, it will be important for her physician to monitor other physiological functions mediated by other hormones that are known to act via G_s alpha.

Clinical term: pseudohypoparathyroidism

See Chapter 19 for complete, integrative case studies.

CHAPTER 5 TEST QUESTIONS

Answers found in Appendix A.

1–3: Match a receptor feature (a–e) with each choice.

1. Defines the situation when all receptor binding sites are occupied by a messenger
2. Defines the strength of receptor binding to a messenger
3. Reflects the fact that a receptor normally binds only to a single messenger

Receptor feature:

a. affinity
b. saturation
c. competition
d. down-regulation
e. specificity

4. Which of the following intracellular or plasma membrane proteins require/requires Ca^{2+} for full activity?
   a. calmodulin
   b. janus kinase (JAK)
   c. cAMP-dependent protein kinase
   d. guanylyl cyclase
   e. all of the above

5. Which is correct?
   a. cAMP-dependent protein kinase phosphorylates tyrosine residues.
   b. Protein kinase C is activated by cAMP.
   c. The subunit of G_s proteins that activates adenylyl cyclase is the beta subunit.
   d. Lipid-soluble messengers typically act on receptors in the cell cytosol or nucleus.
   e. The binding site of a typical plasma membrane receptor for its messenger is located on the cytosolic surface of the receptor.

6. Inhibition of which enzyme/enzymes would inhibit the conversion of arachidonic acid to leukotrienes?
   a. cyclooxygenase
   b. lipoxygenase
   c. phospholipase A_2
   d. adenylyl cyclase
   e. both b and c

7–10: Match each type of molecule with the correct choice (a–e); a given choice may be used once, more than once, or not at all.

Molecule:

7. second messenger
8. example of a first messenger
9. part of a trimeric protein in membranes
10. enzyme

Choices:

a. neurotransmitter or hormone
b. cAMP-dependent protein kinase
c. calmodulin
d. Ca^{2+}
e. alpha subunit of G proteins

CHAPTER 5 GENERAL PRINCIPLES ASSESSMENT

Answers found in Appendix A.

1. What examples from this chapter demonstrate the general physiological principle that *controlled exchange of materials occurs between compartments and across cell membranes?* Specifically, how is this related to another general principle, namely, *information flow between cells, tissues, and organs is an essential feature of homeostasis and allows for integration of physiological processes?*
2. Another principle states that *physiological processes require the transfer and balance of matter and energy.* How is energy balance related to intracellular signaling?

CHAPTER 5 QUANTITATIVE AND THOUGHT QUESTIONS

Answers found in Appendix A.

1. Patient A is given a drug that blocks the synthesis of all eicosanoids, whereas patient B is given a drug that blocks the synthesis of leukotrienes but none of the other eicosanoids. What enzymes do these drugs most likely block?
2. Certain nerves to the heart release the neurotransmitter norepinephrine. If these nerves are removed in experimental animals, the heart becomes extremely sensitive to the administration of a drug that is an agonist of norepinephrine. Explain why this may happen, in terms of receptor physiology.
3. A particular hormone is known to elicit—completely by way of the cyclic AMP system—six different responses in its target cell. A drug is found that eliminates one of these responses but not the other five. Which of the following, if any, could the drug be blocking: the hormone's receptors, G_s protein, adenylyl cyclase, or cyclic AMP?
4. If a drug were found that blocked all Ca^{2+} channels directly linked to G proteins, would this eliminate the role of Ca^{2+} as a second messenger? Why or why not?
5. Explain why the effects of a first messenger do not immediately cease upon removal of the messenger.

CHAPTER 5 ANSWERS TO PHYSIOLOGICAL INQUIRIES

Figure 5.5 Expressing more than one type of receptor allows a cell to respond to more than one type of first messenger. For example, one first messenger might activate a particular biochemical pathway in a cell by activating one type of receptor and signaling pathway. By contrast, another first messenger acting on a different receptor and activating a different signaling pathway might inhibit the same biochemical process. In this way, the biochemical process can be tightly regulated.

Figure 5.8 Enzymes can generate large amounts of product without being consumed. This is an extremely efficient way to generate a second messenger like cAMP. Enzymes have many other advantages (see Table 3.7), including the ability to have their activities fine-tuned by other inputs (see Figures 3.36 to 3.38). This enables the cell to adjust its response to a first messenger depending on the other conditions present.

Figure 5.9 Not necessarily. In some cases, a kinase may phosphorylate the same protein in many different types of cells. However, many cells also express certain cell-specific proteins that are not found in all tissues, and some of these proteins may be substrates for cAMP-dependent protein kinase. Thus, the proteins that are phosphorylated by a given kinase depend upon the cell type, which makes the cellular response tissue-specific. As an example, in the kidneys, cAMP-dependent protein kinase phosphorylates proteins that insert water channels in cell membranes and thereby reduce urine volume, whereas in heart muscle the same kinase phosphorylates Ca^{2+} channels that increase the strength of muscle contraction.

Figure 5.12 Aspirin and NSAIDs block the cyclooxygenase pathway. This includes the pathway to the production of thromboxanes, which as shown in the figure are important for blood clotting. Because of the risk of bleeding that occurs with any type of surgery, the use of such drugs prior to the surgery may increase the likelihood of excessive bleeding.

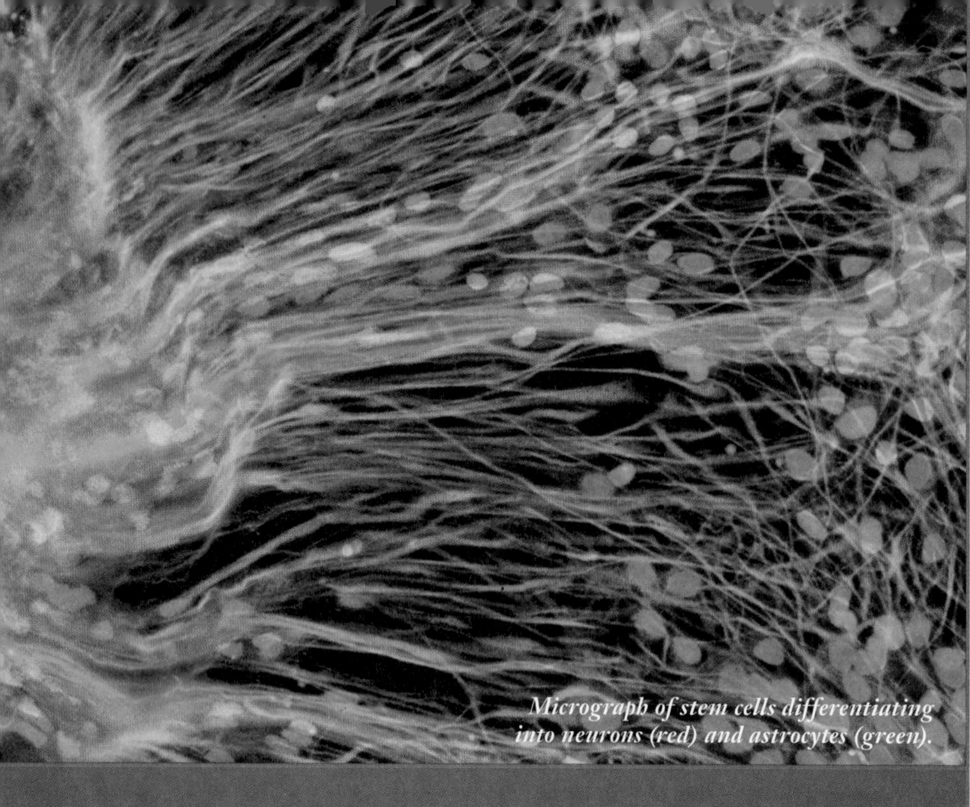

Micrograph of stem cells differentiating into neurons (red) and astrocytes (green).

6 Neuronal Signaling and the Structure of the Nervous System

Chapters 1–5 examined the principle of homeostasis, the basic chemistry of the body, and the general structure and function of all body cells. Now we turn our attention to the structure and function of a specific organ system and its cells—the nervous system. The nervous system is composed of trillions of cells distributed in a network throughout the brain, spinal cord, and periphery. It plays a key role in the maintenance of homeostasis. It does this by mediating information flow that coordinates the activity of widely dispersed cells, tissues, and organs, both internally and with the external environment. Among its many functions are activation of muscle contraction (Chapters 9 and 10), integration of blood oxygen, carbon dioxide, and pH levels with respiratory system activity (Chapter 13), regulation of volumes and pressures in the circulation by acting on the cardiovascular system (Chapter 12) and urinary system (Chapter 14), and modulating digestive system motility and secretion (Chapter 15). The nervous system is one of the two major control systems of the body; the other is the endocrine system (Chapter 11). Unlike the relatively slow, long-lasting signals of the endocrine system, the nervous system sends rapid electrical signals along nerve cell membranes.

As you read about the structure and function of neurons and the nervous system in this chapter, you will encounter numerous examples of the general principles of physiology that were outlined in Chapter 1. Section A highlights how the structure of neurons contributes to their specialized functions in mediating the information flow between organs and integration of homeostatic processes. In Section B, controlled exchange of materials (ions) across cellular membranes and the laws of chemistry and physics will be key principles underlying the electrical properties of neurons. Information flow that allows for integration of physiological processes between cells of the nervous system is the theme of Section C; and in Section D, you will see how the nervous system illustrates the general principle of physiology that most physiological functions are controlled by multiple regulatory systems, often working in opposition.

SECTION A Neural Tissue

The various structures of the nervous system are intimately interconnected, but for convenience we divide them into two parts: (1) the **central nervous system (CNS)**, composed of the brain and spinal cord; and (2) the **peripheral nervous system (PNS)**, consisting of the nerves that connect the brain and spinal cord with the body's muscles, glands, sense organs, and other tissues.

The basic unit of the nervous system is the individual nerve cell, or **neuron.** Neurons operate by generating electrical signals that move from one part of the cell to another part of the same cell or to neighboring cells. In most neurons, the electrical signal causes the release of chemical messengers—**neurotransmitters**—to communicate with other cells. Most neurons serve as integrators because their output reflects the balance of inputs they receive from up to hundreds of thousands of other neurons.

6.1 Structure and Maintenance of Neurons

Neurons occur in a wide variety of sizes and shapes, but all share features that allow cell-to-cell communication. Long extensions, or **processes,** connect neurons to each other and perform the neurons' input and output functions. As shown in **Figure 6.1**, most neurons contain a cell body and two types of processes—dendrites and axons.

As in other types of cells, a neuron's **cell body** (or **soma**) contains the nucleus and ribosomes and thus has the genetic information and machinery necessary for protein synthesis. The **dendrites** are a series of highly branched outgrowths of the cell body. In the PNS, dendrites receive incoming sensory information and transfer it to integrating regions of sensory neurons. In the CNS, dendrites and the cell body receive most of the inputs from other neurons, with the dendrites generally taking a more important role. Branching dendrites increase a cell's surface area—some neurons may have as many as 400,000 dendrites. Knoblike outgrowths called **dendritic spines** increase the surface area of dendrites still further, and there are often ribosomes present. The presence of protein-synthesis machinery allows dendritic spines to remodel their shape in response to variation in synaptic activity, which may play a key role in complex processes like learning and memory. Thus, the structure of dendrites in the CNS increases a cell's capacity to receive signals from many other neurons.

The **axon,** sometimes also called a **nerve fiber,** is a long process that extends from the cell body and carries outgoing signals to its target cells. In humans, axons range in length from a few microns to over a meter. The region of the axon that arises from the cell body is known as the **initial segment** (or **axon hillock**). The initial segment is the "trigger zone" where, in most neurons, propagated electrical signals are generated. These signals then propagate away from the cell body along the axon or, sometimes, back along the dendrites. The axon may have branches, called **collaterals.** Near their ends, both the axon and its collaterals undergo further branching (see Figure 6.1). The greater the degree of branching of the axon and axon collaterals, the greater the cell's sphere of influence.

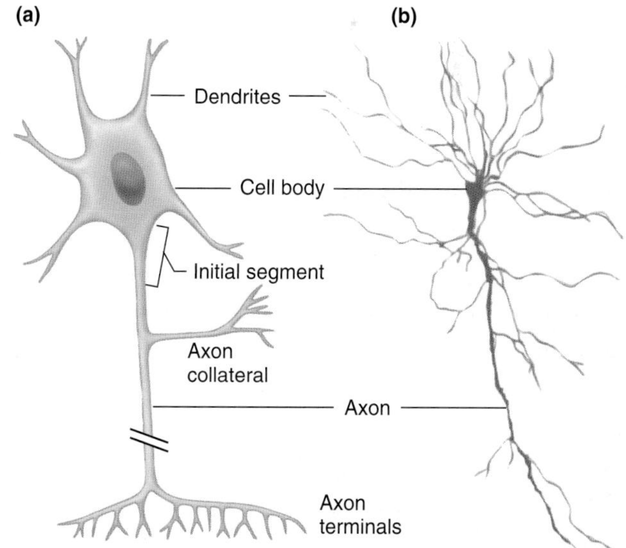

Figure 6.1 APIR (a) Diagrammatic representation of one type of neuron. The break in the axon indicates that axons may extend for long distances; in fact, they may be 5000 to 10,000 times longer than the cell body is wide. This neuron is a common type, but there is a wide variety of neuronal morphologies, some of which have no axons. (b) A neuron as observed through a microscope. The axon terminals cannot be seen at this magnification.

Each branch ends in an **axon terminal,** which is responsible for releasing neurotransmitters from the axon. These chemical messengers diffuse across an extracellular gap to the cell opposite the terminal. Alternatively, some neurons release their chemical messengers from a series of bulging areas along the axon known as **varicosities.**

The axons of many neurons are covered by sheaths of **myelin** (**Figure 6.2**), which usually consists of 20 to 200 layers of highly modified plasma membrane wrapped around the axon by a nearby supporting cell. In the brain and spinal cord, these myelin-forming cells are the **oligodendrocytes.** Each oligodendrocyte may branch to form myelin on as many as 40 axons. In the PNS, cells called **Schwann cells** form individual myelin sheaths surrounding 1- to 1.5-mm-long segments at regular intervals along some axons. The spaces between adjacent sections of myelin where the axon's plasma membrane is exposed to extracellular fluid are called the **nodes of Ranvier.** As we will see, the myelin sheath speeds up conduction of the electrical signals along the axon and conserves energy.

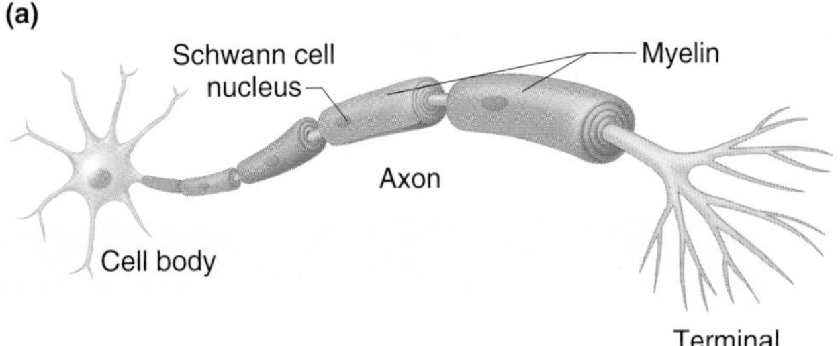

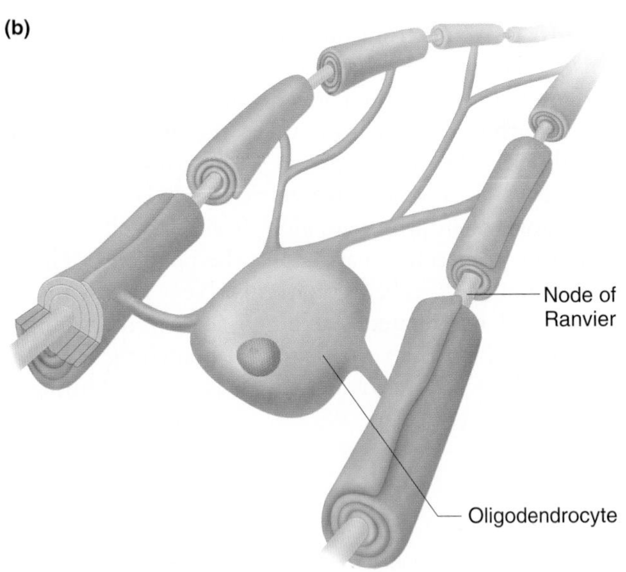

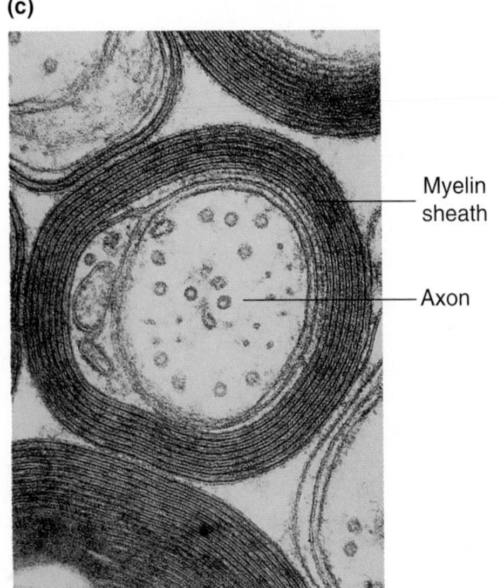

Figure 6.2 APIR (a) Myelin formed by Schwann cells, and (b) oligodendrocytes on axons. (c) Electron micrograph of transverse sections of myelinated axons in brain.

To maintain the structure and function of the cell axon, various organelles and other materials must move as far as 1 meter between the cell body and the axon terminals. This movement, termed **axonal transport,** depends on a scaffolding of microtubule "rails" running the length of the axon and specialized types of motor proteins known as **kinesins** and **dyneins** (**Figure 6.3**). At one end, these double-headed motor proteins bind to their cellular cargo, and the other end uses energy derived from the hydrolysis of ATP to "walk" along the microtubules. Kinesin transport mainly occurs from the cell body toward the axon terminals (**anterograde**) and is important in moving nutrient molecules, enzymes, mitochondria, neurotransmitter-filled vesicles, and other organelles. Dynein movement is in the other direction (**retrograde**), carrying recycled membrane vesicles, growth factors, and other chemical signals that can affect the neuron's morphology, biochemistry, and connectivity. Retrograde transport is also the route by which some harmful agents invade the CNS, including tetanus toxin and the herpes simplex, rabies, and polio viruses.

6.2 Functional Classes of Neurons

Neurons can be divided into three functional classes: afferent neurons, efferent neurons, and interneurons (**Figure 6.4**). **Afferent neurons** convey information from the tissues and organs of the body *toward* the CNS. **Efferent neurons** convey information *away from* the CNS to effector cells like muscle, gland, or other cell types. **Interneurons** connect neurons *within* the CNS. As a rough estimate, for each afferent neuron entering the CNS, there are 10 efferent neurons and 200,000 interneurons. Thus, the great majority of neurons are interneurons.

At their peripheral ends (the ends farthest from the CNS), afferent neurons have **sensory receptors,** which respond to various physical or chemical changes in their environment by generating electrical signals in the neuron. The receptor region may be a specialized portion of the plasma membrane or a separate cell closely associated with the neuron ending. (Recall from Chapter 5 that the term *receptor* has two distinct meanings, the one defined here and the other referring to the specific proteins a chemical messenger combines with to exert its effects on a target cell.) Afferent neurons propagate electrical signals from their receptors into the brain or spinal cord.

Afferent neurons have a shape that is distinct from that diagrammed in Figure 6.1, because they have only a single process associated with the cell body, usually considered an axon. Shortly after leaving the cell body, the axon divides. One branch, the peripheral process, begins where the dendritic branches converge from the receptor endings. The other branch, the

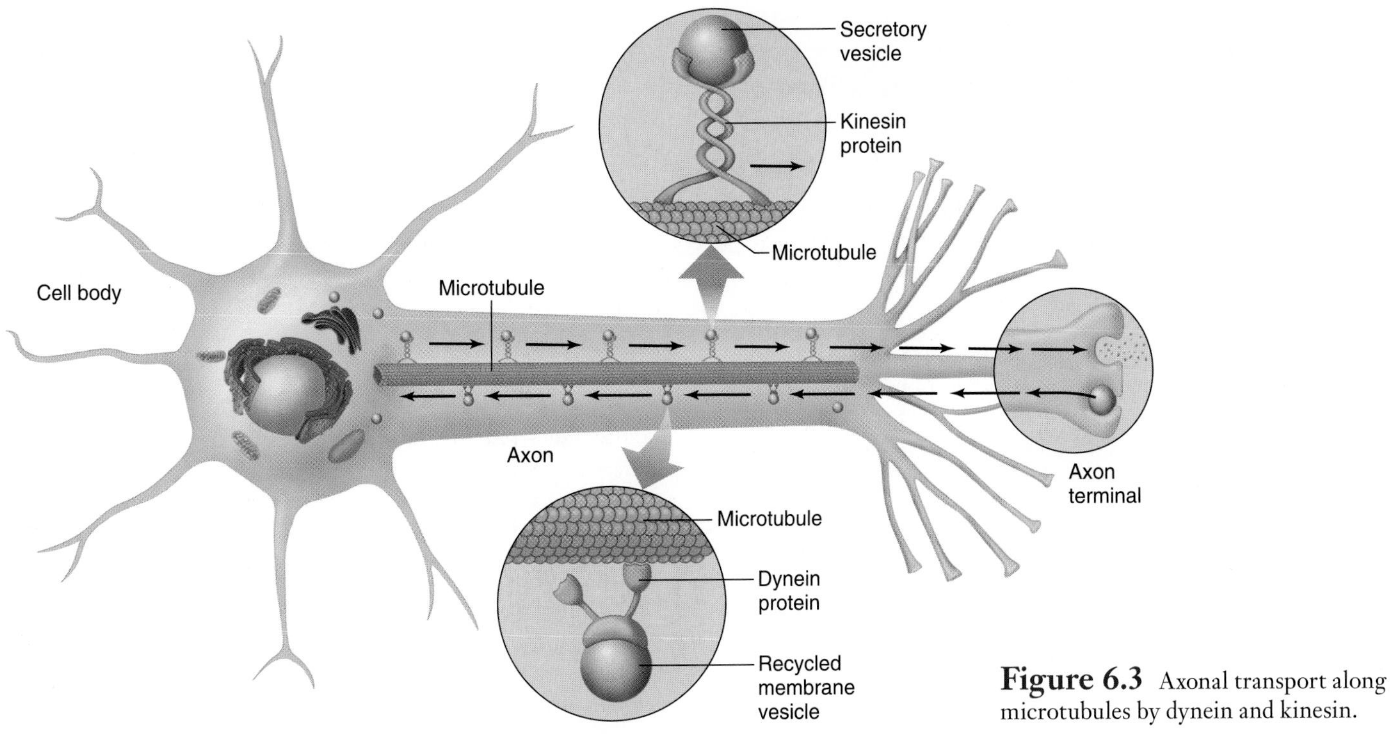

Figure 6.3 Axonal transport along microtubules by dynein and kinesin.

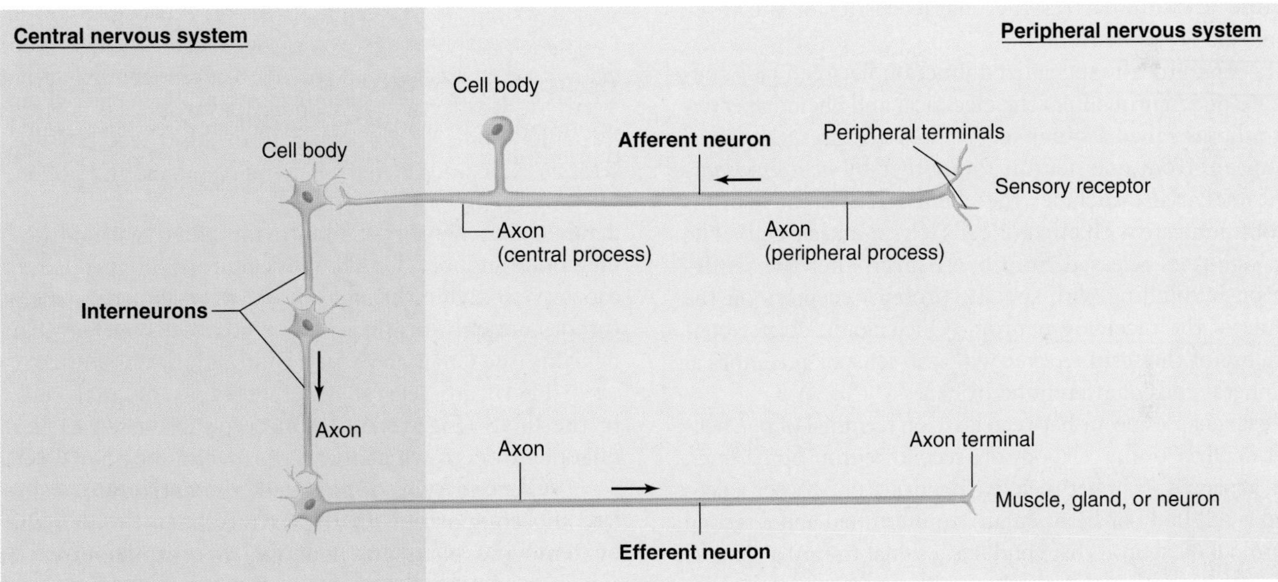

Figure 6.4 AP|R Three classes of neurons. The arrows indicate the direction of transmission of neural activity. Afferent neurons in the PNS generally receive input at sensory receptors. Efferent components of the PNS may terminate on muscle, gland, neuron, or other effector cells. Both afferent and efferent components may consist of two neurons, not one as shown here.

central process, enters the CNS to form junctions with other neurons. Note in Figure 6.4 that for afferent neurons, both the cell body and the long axon are outside the CNS and only a part of the central process enters the brain or spinal cord.

Efferent neurons have a shape like that shown in Figure 6.1. Generally, their cell bodies and dendrites are within the CNS, and the axons extend out to the periphery. There are exceptions, however, such as in the enteric nervous system of the gastrointestinal tract described in Chapter 15. Groups of afferent and efferent neuron axons, together with connective tissue and blood vessels, form the **nerves** of the PNS. Note that *nerve fiber* is a term sometimes used to refer to a single axon, whereas a *nerve* is a bundle of axons (fibers) bound together by connective tissue.

Interneurons lie entirely within the CNS. They account for over 99% of all neurons and have a wide range of physiological properties, shapes, and functions. The number of interneurons interposed between specific afferent and efferent neurons varies according to the complexity of the action they control. The knee-jerk reflex elicited by tapping below the kneecap activates thigh muscles without interneurons—the afferent neurons interact directly with efferent neurons. In contrast, when you

TABLE 6.1	Characteristics of Three Classes of Neurons

I. Afferent neurons
   A. Transmit information into the CNS from receptors at their peripheral endings
   B. Single process from the cell body splits into a long peripheral process (axon) that is in the PNS and a short central process (axon) that enters the CNS

II. Efferent neurons
   A. Transmit information out of the CNS to effector cells, particularly muscles, glands, neurons, and other cells
   B. Cell body with multiple dendrites and a small segment of the axon are in the CNS; most of the axon is in the PNS

III. Interneurons
   A. Function as integrators and signal changers
   B. Integrate groups of afferent and efferent neurons into reflex circuits
   C. Lie entirely within the CNS
   D. Account for > 99% of all neurons

hear a song or smell a certain perfume that evokes memories of someone you know, millions of interneurons may be involved.

Table 6.1 summarizes the characteristics of the three functional classes of neurons.

The anatomically specialized junction between two neurons where one neuron alters the electrical and chemical activity of another is called a **synapse.** At most synapses, the signal is transmitted from one neuron to another by *neurotransmitters*, a term that also includes the chemicals efferent neurons use to communicate with effector cells (e.g., a muscle cell). The neurotransmitters released from one neuron alter the receiving neuron by binding with specific protein receptors on the membrane of the receiving neuron. (Once again, do not confuse this use of the term *receptor* with the sensory receptors at the peripheral ends of afferent neurons.)

Most synapses occur between an axon terminal of one neuron and a dendrite or the cell body of a second neuron. Sometimes, however, synapses occur between two dendrites or between a dendrite and a cell body or between an axon terminal and a second axon terminal. A neuron that conducts a signal toward a synapse is called a **presynaptic neuron,** whereas a neuron conducting signals away from a synapse is a **postsynaptic neuron. Figure 6.5** shows how, in a multineuronal pathway, a single neuron can be postsynaptic to one cell and presynaptic to another. A postsynaptic neuron may have thousands of synaptic junctions on the surface of its dendrites and cell body, so that signals from many presynaptic neurons can affect it. Interconnected in this way, the many millions of neurons in the nervous system exemplify the general principle of physiology that information flow between cells, tissues, and organs is an essential feature of homeostasis and allows for complex integration of physiological processes.

6.3 Glial Cells

According to recent analyses, neurons account for only about half of the cells in the human CNS. The remainder are **glial cells** (*glia*, "glue"). Glial cells surround the soma, axon, and

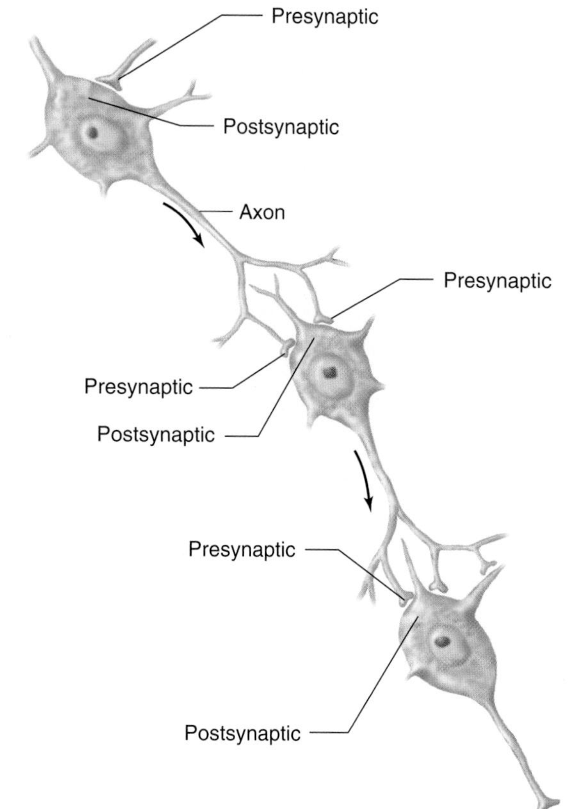

Figure 6.5 APR A neuron postsynaptic to one cell can be presynaptic to another. Arrows indicate direction of neural transmission.

dendrites of neurons and provide them with physical and metabolic support. Unlike most neurons, glial cells retain the capacity to divide throughout life. Consequently, many CNS tumors actually originate from glial cells rather than from neurons (see Chapter 19 for a thorough discussion).

There are several different types of glial cells found in the CNS (**Figure 6.6**). One type discussed earlier is the oligodendrocyte, which forms the myelin sheath of CNS axons.

A second type of glial cell, the **astrocyte,** helps regulate the composition of the extracellular fluid in the CNS by removing potassium ions and neurotransmitters around synapses. Another important function of astrocytes is to stimulate the formation of tight junctions (review Figure 3.9) between the cells that make up the walls of capillaries found in the CNS. This forms the **blood–brain barrier,** which is a much more selective filter for exchanged substances than is present between the blood and most other tissues. Astrocytes also sustain the neurons metabolically—for example, by providing glucose and removing ammonia. In developing embryos, astrocytes guide neurons as they migrate to their ultimate destination, and they stimulate neuronal growth by secreting growth factors. In addition, astrocytes have many neuronlike characteristics. For example, they have ion channels, receptors for certain neurotransmitters and the enzymes for processing them, and the capability of generating weak electrical responses. Thus, in addition to all their other roles, it is speculated that astrocytes may take part in information signaling in the brain.

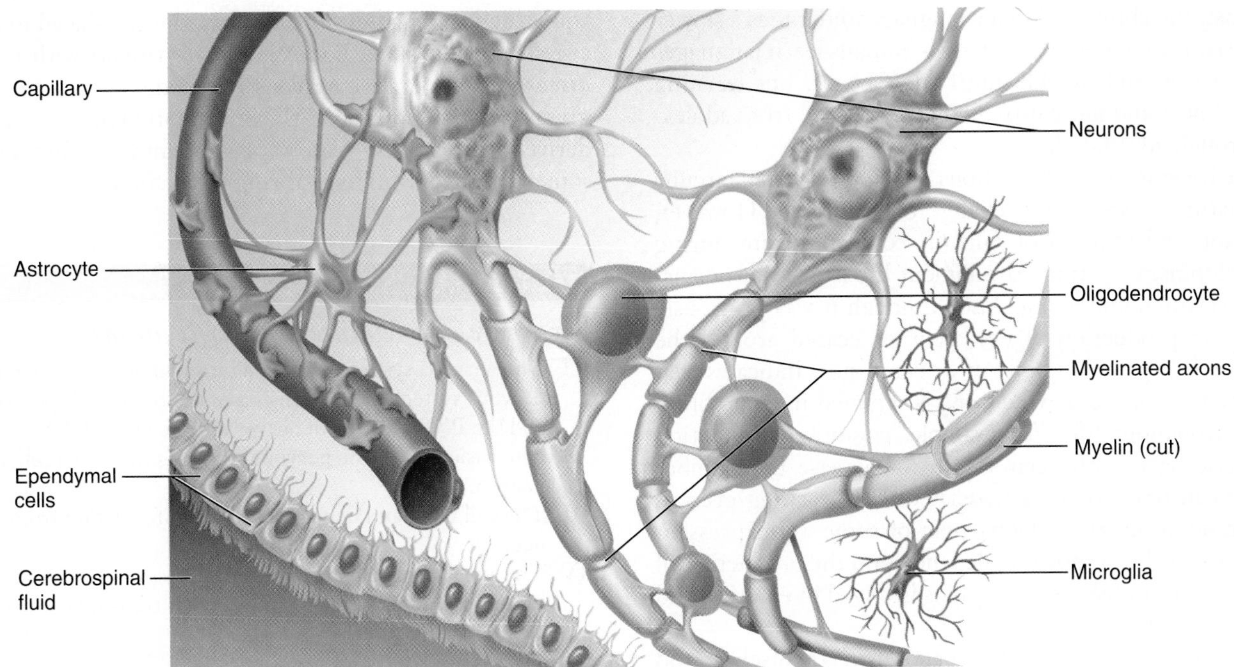

Figure 6.6 APIR Glial cells of the central nervous system.

The **microglia,** a third type of glial cell, are specialized, macrophage-like cells (Chapter 18) that perform immune functions in the CNS, and may also contribute to synapse remodeling and plasticity. Lastly, **ependymal cells** line the fluid-filled cavities within the brain and spinal cord and regulate the production and flow of cerebrospinal fluid, which will be described later.

Schwann cells, the glial cells of the PNS, have most of the properties of the CNS glia. As mentioned earlier, Schwann cells produce the myelin sheath of the axons of the peripheral neurons.

6.4 Neural Growth and Regeneration

The elaborate networks of neuronal processes that characterize the nervous system are remarkably similar in all human beings and depend upon the outgrowth of specific axons to specific targets.

Development of the nervous system in the embryo begins with a series of divisions of undifferentiated precursor cells (**stem cells**) that can develop into neurons or glia. After the last cell division, each neuronal daughter cell differentiates, migrates to its final location, and sends out processes that will become its axon and dendrites. A specialized enlargement, the **growth cone,** forms the tip of each extending axon and is involved in finding the correct route and final target for the process.

As the axon grows, it is guided along the surfaces of other cells, most commonly glial cells. Which route the axon follows depends largely on attracting, supporting, deflecting, or inhibiting influences exerted by several types of molecules. Some of these molecules, such as cell adhesion molecules, reside on the membranes of the glia and embryonic neurons. Others are soluble **neurotrophic factors** (growth factors for neural tissue) in the extracellular fluid surrounding the growth cone or its distant target.

Once the target of the advancing growth cone is reached, synapses form. The synapses are active, however, before their final maturation. This early activity, in part, determines their final function. During these early stages of neural development, which occur during all trimesters of pregnancy and into infancy, alcohol and other drugs, radiation, malnutrition, and viruses can exert effects that cause permanent damage to the developing fetal nervous system.

A surprising aspect of development of the nervous system occurs after growth and projection of the axons. Many of the newly formed neurons and synapses degenerate. In fact, as many as 50% to 70% of neurons undergo a programmed self-destruction called **apoptosis** in the developing CNS. Exactly why this seemingly wasteful process occurs is unknown, although neuroscientists speculate that this refines or fine-tunes connectivity in the nervous system.

Throughout the life span, our brain has an amazing ability to modify its structure and function in response to stimulation or injury, a characteristic known as **plasticity.** This involves both the generation of new neurons and remodeling of synaptic connections, and is stimulated by exercise and by engaging in cognitively challenging activities.

The degree of neural plasticity varies with age. For example, an infant suffering from seizures (uncontrolled excessive neural activity) can have nearly half of the brain removed, and because of extensive remodeling the brain can recover full functionality into adulthood. If the same procedure were performed on an adult, it would result in permanent deficits in the functions served by the excised brain regions. For many neural systems, the critical time window for development occurs at a fairly young age. In visual pathways, for example, regions of the brain involved in processing visual stimuli are permanently impaired if no visual stimulation is received during a critical time, which peaks between 1 and 2 years of age.

By contrast, the ability to learn a language undergoes a slower and more subtle change in plasticity—humans learn languages relatively easily and quickly until adolescence, but learning becomes slower and more difficult as we proceed from adolescence through adulthood.

The basic shapes and locations of major neuronal circuits in the mature CNS do not change once formed. However, the creation and removal of synaptic contacts begun during fetal development continue throughout life as part of normal growth, learning, and aging. Also, although it was previously thought that production of new neurons ceased around the time of birth, a growing body of evidence now indicates that the ability to produce new neurons is retained in some brain regions throughout life. For example, cognitive stimulation and exercise have both been shown to increase the number of neurons in brain regions associated with learning even in adults. In addition, the effectiveness of some antidepressant medications has been shown to depend upon the production of new neurons in limbic system regions involved in emotion and motivation (Chapter 8).

If axons are severed, they can repair themselves and restore significant function provided that the damage occurs outside the CNS and does not affect the neuron's cell body. After such an injury, the axon segment that is separated from the cell body degenerates. The part of the axon still attached to the cell body then gives rise to a growth cone, which grows out to the effector organ so that function can be restored. Return of function following a peripheral nerve injury is delayed because axon regrowth proceeds at a rate of only 1 mm per day. So, for example, if afferent neurons from your thumb were damaged by an injury in the area of your shoulder, it might take 2 years for sensation in your thumb to be restored.

Spinal injuries typically crush rather than cut the tissue, leaving the axons intact. In this case, a primary problem is self-destruction (apoptosis) of the nearby oligodendrocytes. When these cells die and their associated axons lose their myelin sheath, the axons cannot transmit information effectively. Severed axons within the CNS may grow small new extensions, but no significant regeneration of the axon occurs across the damaged site, and there are no well-documented reports of significant return of function. Functional regeneration is prevented either by some basic difference of CNS neurons or some property of their environment, such as inhibitory factors associated with nearby glia.

Researchers are trying a variety of ways to provide an environment that will support axonal regeneration in the CNS. They are creating tubes to support regrowth of the severed axons, redirecting the axons to regions of the spinal cord that lack growth-inhibiting factors, preventing apoptosis of the oligodendrocytes so myelin can be maintained, and supplying neurotrophic factors that support recovery of the damaged tissue.

Medical researchers are also attempting to restore function to damaged or diseased spinal cords and brains by implanting undifferentiated stem cells that will develop into new neurons and replace missing neurotransmitters or neurotrophic factors. Initial stem cell research focused on the use of embryonic and fetal stem cells which, while yielding promising results, raises ethical concerns. Recently, however, researchers have developed promising techniques using stem cells isolated from adults, and using adult cells that have been induced to revert to a stem-cell-like state. For example, in patients with ***Parkinson disease***, a degenerative nervous system disease resulting in progressive loss of movement, the implantation of neural stem cells derived from healthy regions of a patient's own brain has been somewhat successful in restoring motor function.

SECTION A SUMMARY

Structure and Maintenance of Neurons

I. The nervous system is divided into two parts. The central nervous system (CNS) consists of the brain and spinal cord, and the PNS consists of nerves outside of the CNS.

II. The basic unit of the nervous system is the nerve cell, or neuron.

III. The cell body and dendrites receive information from other neurons.

IV. The axon (nerve fiber), which may be covered with sections of myelin separated by nodes of Ranvier, transmits information to other neurons or effector cells.

Functional Classes of Neurons

I. Neurons are classified in three ways:
   a. *Afferent neurons* transmit information into the CNS from receptors at their peripheral endings.
   b. *Efferent neurons* transmit information out of the CNS to effector cells.
   c. *Interneurons* lie entirely within the CNS and form circuits with other interneurons or connect afferent and efferent neurons.

II. Neurotransmitters, which are released by a presynaptic neuron and combine with protein receptors on a postsynaptic neuron, transmit information across a synapse.

Glial Cells

I. The CNS also contains glial cells, which help regulate the extracellular fluid composition, sustain the neurons metabolically, form myelin and the blood–brain barrier, serve as guides for developing neurons, provide immune functions, and regulate cerebrospinal fluid.

Neural Growth and Regeneration

I. Neurons develop from stem cells, migrate to their final locations, and send out processes to their target cells.

II. Cell division to form new neurons and the plasticity to remodel after injury markedly decrease between birth and adulthood.

III. After degeneration of a severed axon, damaged peripheral neurons may regrow the axon to their target organ. Functional regeneration of severed CNS axons does not usually occur.

SECTION A REVIEW QUESTIONS

1. Describe the direction of information flow through a neuron in response to input from another neuron. What is the relationship between the presynaptic neuron and the postsynaptic neuron?
2. Contrast the two uses of the word *receptor.*
3. Where are afferent neurons, efferent neurons, and interneurons located in the nervous system? Are there places where all three could be found?

SECTION A KEY TERMS

afferent neuron 140
anterograde 140
apoptosis 143
astrocyte 142
axon 139
axon hillock 139
axon terminal 140
axonal transport 140
blood–brain barrier 142
cell body 139
central nervous system (CNS) 139
collateral 139
dendrite 139
dendritic spines 139
dynein 140
efferent neuron 140
ependymal cell 143
glial cell 142
growth cone 143
initial segment 139
interneuron 140
kinesin 140
microglia 143
myelin 140
nerve 141
nerve fiber 139
neuron 139
neurotransmitter 139
neurotrophic factor 143
node of Ranvier 140
oligodendrocyte 140
peripheral nervous system (PNS) 139
plasticity 143
postsynaptic neuron 142
presynaptic neuron 142
process 139
retrograde 140
Schwann cell 140
sensory receptor 140
soma 139
stem cell 143
synapse 142
varicosity 140

SECTION A CLINICAL TERMS

Parkinson disease 144

SECTION B Membrane Potentials

6.5 Basic Principles of Electricity

This section provides an excellent demonstration of the general principle of physiology that physiological processes are dictated by the laws of chemistry and physics, notably those that determine the net flux of charged molecules. As discussed in Chapter 4, the predominant solutes in the extracellular fluid are sodium and chloride ions. The intracellular fluid contains high concentrations of potassium ions and ionized nonpenetrating molecules, particularly phosphate compounds and proteins with negatively charged side chains. Electrical phenomena resulting from the distribution of these charged particles occur at the cell's plasma membrane and play a significant role in signal integration and cell-to-cell communication, the two major functions of the neuron.

A fundamental physical principle is that charges of the same type repel each other—positive charge repels positive charge, and negative charge repels negative charge. In contrast, oppositely charged substances attract each other and will move toward each other if not separated by some barrier (**Figure 6.7**).

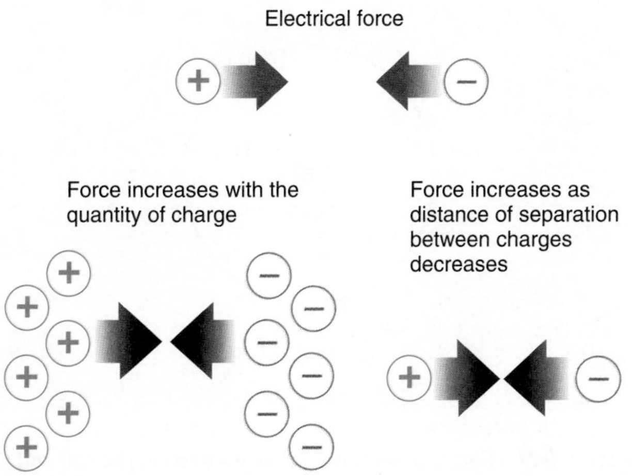

Figure 6.7 The electrical force of attraction between positive and negative charges increases with the quantity of charge and with decreasing distance between charges.

Separated electrical charges of opposite sign have the potential to do work if they are allowed to come together. This potential is called an **electrical potential** or, because it is determined by the difference in the amount of charge between two points, a **potential difference.** The electrical potential difference is often referred to simply as the **potential.** The units of electrical potential are volts. The total charge that can be separated in most biological systems is very small, so the potential differences are small and are measured in millivolts (1 mV = 0.001 V).

The movement of electrical charge is called a **current.** The electrical potential between charges tends to make them flow, producing a current. If the charges are opposite, the current brings them toward each other; if the charges are alike, the current increases the separation between them. The amount of charge that moves—in other words, the current—depends on the potential difference between the charges and on the nature of the material or structure through which they are moving. The hindrance to electrical charge movement is known as **resistance.** If resistance is high, the current flow will be low. The effect of voltage V and resistance R on current I is expressed in **Ohm's law:**

$$I = \frac{V}{R}$$

Materials that have a high electrical resistance reduce current flow and are known as insulators. Materials that have a low resistance allow rapid current flow and are called conductors.

Water that contains dissolved ions is a relatively good conductor of electricity because the ions can carry the current. As we have seen, the intracellular and extracellular fluids contain many ions and can therefore carry current. Lipids, however, contain very few charged groups and cannot carry current. Therefore, the lipid layers of the plasma membrane are regions of high electrical resistance separating the intracellular fluid and the extracellular fluid, two low-resistance aqueous compartments.

6.6 The Resting Membrane Potential

All cells under resting conditions have a potential difference across their plasma membranes, with the inside of the cell negatively charged with respect to the outside (**Figure 6.8**). This potential is the **resting membrane potential.**

By convention, extracellular fluid is designated as the voltage reference point, and the polarity (positive or negative) of the membrane potential is stated in terms of the sign of the excess charge on the inside of the cell by comparison. For example, if the intracellular fluid has an excess of negative charge and the potential difference across the membrane has a magnitude of 70 mV, we say that the membrane potential is −70 mV (inside relative to outside).

The magnitude of the resting membrane potential varies from about −5 to −100 mV, depending upon the type of cell. In neurons, it is generally in the range of −40 to −90 mV.

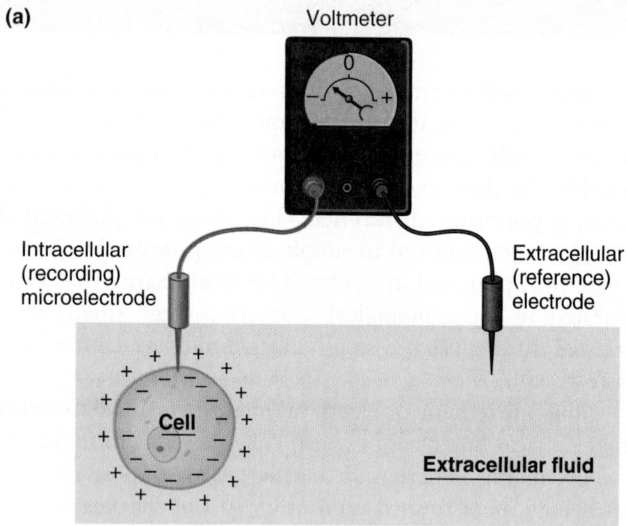

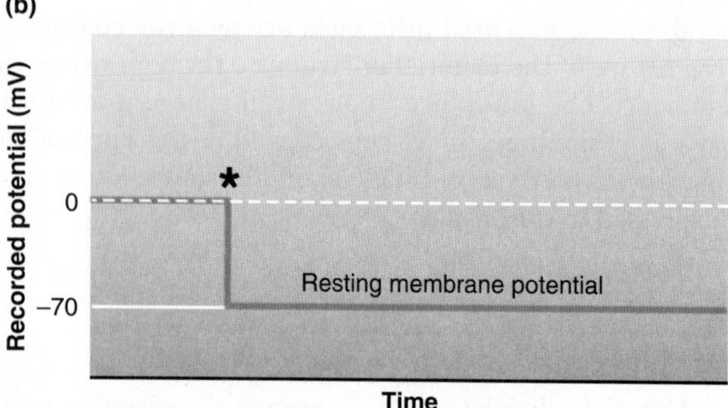

Figure 6.8 (a) Apparatus for measuring membrane potentials. The voltmeter records the difference between the intracellular and extracellular electrodes. (b) The potential difference across a plasma membrane as measured by an intracellular microelectrode. The asterisk indicates the moment the electrode entered the cell.

PHYSIOLOGICAL INQUIRY

- If you reversed the position of these two electrodes, would the graph in part (b) look different?

Answer can be found at end of chapter.

The resting membrane potential holds steady unless changes in electrical current alter the potential.

The resting membrane potential exists because of a tiny excess of negative ions inside the cell and an excess of positive ions outside. The excess negative charges inside are electrically attracted to the excess positive charges outside the cell, and vice versa. Thus, the excess charges (ions) collect in a thin shell tight against the inner and outer surfaces of the plasma membrane (**Figure 6.9**), whereas the bulk of the intracellular and extracellular fluid remains electrically neutral. Unlike the diagrammatic representation in Figure 6.9, the number of positive and negative charges that have to be separated across a membrane to account for the potential is actually an infinitesimal fraction of the total number of charges in the two compartments.

Table 6.2 lists the concentrations of sodium, potassium, and chloride ions in the extracellular fluid and in the intracellular fluid of a representative neuron. Each of these ions has a 10- to 30-fold difference in concentration between the inside and the outside of the cell. Although this table appears to contradict our earlier assertion that the bulk of the intracellular and extracellular fluid is electrically neutral, there are many other ions not listed, including Mg^{2+}, Ca^{2+}, H^+, HCO_3^-, HPO_4^{2-}, SO_4^{2-}, amino acids, and proteins. When all ions are accounted for, each solution is indeed electrically neutral. Of the ions that can flow across the membrane and affect its electrical potential, Na^+, K^+, and Cl^- are present in the highest concentrations, and the membrane permeability to each is independently determined. Na^+ and K^+ generally play the most important roles in generating the resting membrane potential, but in some cells Cl^- is also a factor. Notice that the Na^+ and Cl^- concentrations are lower inside the cell than outside, and that the K^+ concentration is greater inside the cell. The concentration differences for Na^+ and K^+ are established by the action of the sodium–potassium ion pump (Na^+/K^+-ATPase, Chapter 4) that pumps Na^+ out of the cell and K^+ into it. The reason for the Cl^- distribution varies between cell types, as will be described later.

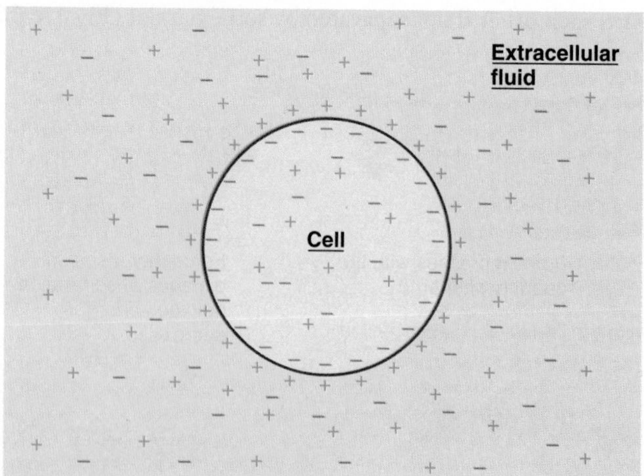

Figure 6.9 The excess positive charges outside the cell and the excess negative charges inside collect in a tight shell against the plasma membrane. In reality, these excess charges are only an extremely small fraction of the total number of ions inside and outside the cell.

TABLE 6.2	Distribution of Major Mobile Ions Across the Plasma Membrane of a Typical Nerve Cell	
	Concentration (mmol/L)	
Ion	**Extracellular**	**Intracellular**
Na^+	145	15
Cl^-	100	7*
K^+	5	150

A more accurate measure of electrical driving force can be obtained using mEq/L, which factors in ion valence. Because all the ions in this table have a valence of 1, the mEq/L is the same as the mmol/L concentration.

*Intracellular Cl^- concentration varies significantly between neurons due to differences in expression of membrane transporters and channels.

The magnitude of the resting membrane potential depends mainly on two factors: (1) differences in specific ion concentrations in the intracellular and extracellular fluids; and (2) differences in membrane permeabilities to the different ions, which reflect the number of open channels for the different ions in the plasma membrane.

To understand how concentration differences for Na^+ and K^+ create membrane potentials, first consider what happens when the membrane is permeable (has open channels) to only one ion (**Figure 6.10**). In this hypothetical situation, it is assumed that the membrane contains K^+ channels but no Na^+ or Cl^- channels. Initially, compartment 1 contains 0.15 M NaCl, compartment 2 contains 0.15 M KCl, and no ion movement occurs because the channels are closed (**Figure 6.10a**). There is no potential difference across the membrane because the two compartments contain equal numbers of positive and negative ions. The positive ions are different—Na^+ versus K^+, but the *total* numbers of positive ions in the two compartments are the same, and each positive ion balances a chloride ion.

However, if these K^+ channels are opened, K^+ will diffuse down its concentration gradient from compartment 2 into compartment 1 (**Figure 6.10b**). Sodium ions will not be able to move across the membrane. After a few potassium ions have moved into compartment 1, that compartment will have an excess of positive charge, leaving behind an excess of negative charge in compartment 2 (**Figure 6.10c**). Thus, a potential difference has been created across the membrane.

This introduces another major factor that can cause net movement of ions across a membrane: an electrical potential. As compartment 1 becomes increasingly positive and compartment 2 increasingly negative, the membrane potential difference begins to influence the movement of the potassium ions. The negative charge of compartment 2 tends to attract them back into their original compartment, and the positive charge of compartment 1 tends to repulse them (**Figure 6.10d**).

As long as the flux or movement of ions due to the K^+ concentration gradient is greater than the flux due to the membrane potential, net movement of K^+ will occur from compartment 2 to compartment 1 (see Figure 6.10d) and the membrane potential will progressively increase. However, eventually, the

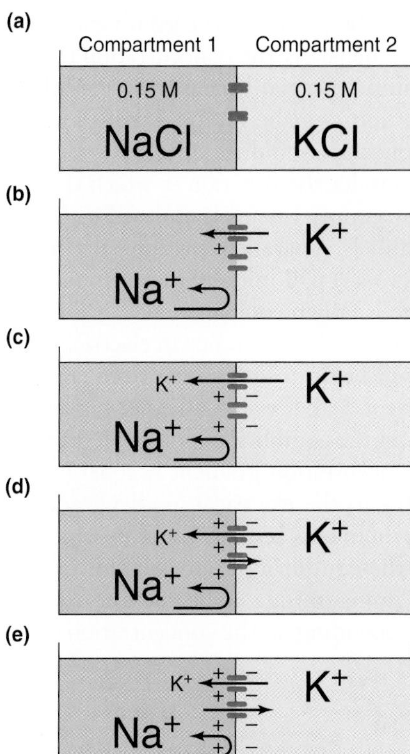

Figure 6.10 Generation of a potential across a membrane due to diffusion of K^+ through K^+ channels (red). Arrows represent ion movements; as in Figure 4.3, arrow length represents the magnitude of the flux. So few K^+ ions cross the membrane that ion concentrations do not change significantly on either side of the membrane from step (a) to step (e). See the text for a complete explanation of the steps a–e.

PHYSIOLOGICAL INQUIRY

- In setting up this experiment, 0.15 mole of NaCl was placed in compartment 1, 0.15 mole of KCl was placed in compartment 2, and each compartment has a volume of 1 liter. What is the approximate total solute concentration in each compartment at equilibrium?

Answer can be found at end of chapter.

membrane potential will become negative enough to produce a flux equal but opposite to the flux produced by the concentration gradient (**Figure 6.10e**). The membrane potential at which these two fluxes become equal in magnitude but opposite in direction is called the **equilibrium potential** for that ion—in this case, K^+. At the equilibrium potential for an ion, there is no *net* movement of the ion because the opposing fluxes are equal, and the potential will undergo no further change. It is worth emphasizing once again that the number of ions crossing the membrane to establish this equilibrium potential is insignificant compared to the number originally present in compartment 2, so there is no significant change in the K^+ concentration in either compartment between step (a) and step (e).

The magnitude of the equilibrium potential (in mV) for any type of ion depends on the concentration gradient for that ion across the membrane. If the concentrations on the two sides were equal, the flux due to the concentration gradient would be zero and the equilibrium potential would also be zero. The larger the concentration gradient, the larger the equilibrium potential because a larger, electrically driven movement of ions will be required to balance the movement due to the concentration difference.

Now consider the situation in which the membrane separating the two compartments is replaced with one that contains only Na^+ channels. A parallel situation will occur (**Figure 6.11**). Sodium ions (Na^+) will initially move from compartment 1 to compartment 2. When compartment 2 is positive with respect to compartment 1, the difference in electrical charge across the membrane will begin to drive Na^+ from compartment 2 back to compartment 1 and, eventually, net movement of Na^+ will cease. Again, at the equilibrium potential, the movement of ions due to the concentration gradient is equal but opposite to the movement due to the electrical gradient, and an insignificant number of sodium ions actually move in achieving this state.

Thus, the equilibrium potential for one ion species can be different in magnitude *and* direction from those for other ion species, depending on the concentration gradients between the intracellular and extracellular compartments for each ion. If the concentration gradient for any ion is known, the equilibrium potential for that ion can be calculated by means of the Nernst equation.

The **Nernst equation** describes the equilibrium potential for any ion species—that is, the electrical potential necessary to balance a given ionic concentration gradient across a membrane so that the net flux of the ion is zero. The Nernst equation is

$$E_{ion} = \frac{61}{Z}\log\left(\frac{C_{out}}{C_{in}}\right)$$

where

E_{ion} = equilibrium potential for a particular ion, in mV
C_{in} = intracellular concentration of the ion
C_{out} = extracellular concentration of the ion
Z = the valence of the ion

61 = a constant value that takes into account the universal gas constant, the temperature (37°C), and the Faraday electrical constant

Using the concentration gradients from Table 6.2, the equilibrium potentials for Na^+ (E_{Na}) and K^+ (E_K) are

$$E_{Na} = \frac{61}{+1}\log\left(\frac{145}{15}\right) = +60\text{ mV}$$

$$E_K = \frac{61}{+1}\log\left(\frac{5}{150}\right) = -90\text{ mV}$$

Thus, at these typical concentrations, Na^+ flux through open channels will tend to bring the membrane potential toward +60 mV, whereas K^+ flux will bring it toward −90 mV. If the concentration gradients change, the equilibrium potentials will change.

The hypothetical situations presented in Figures 6.10 and 6.11 are useful for understanding how individual permeating ions like Na^+ and K^+ influence membrane potential, but keep in mind that real cells are far more complicated. Many charged molecules contribute to the overall electrical properties of cell membranes. For example, most of the negative charge inside neurons is accounted for not by chloride ions but by impermeable organic anions—in particular, proteins and phosphate compounds. Thus, when there is a net flux of K^+ out of a cell, these are the main ion species contributing to the negative charge on the inside of the membrane. Another complication in real cells is that they are rarely permeable to only a single ion at a time.

When channels for more than one ion species are open in the membrane at the same time, the permeabilities and concentration gradients for all the ions must be considered when accounting for the membrane potential. For a given concentration gradient, the greater the membrane permeability to an ion species, the greater the contribution that ion species will make to the membrane potential. Given the concentration gradients and relative membrane permeabilities (P_{ion}) for Na^+, K^+, and Cl^-, the potential of a membrane (V_m) can be calculated using the **Goldman-Hodgkin-Katz (GHK) equation:**

$$V_m = 61\log\frac{P_K[K_{out}] + P_{Na}[Na_{out}] + P_{Cl}[Cl_{in}]}{P_K[K_{in}] + P_{Na}[Na_{in}] + P_{Cl}[Cl_{out}]}$$

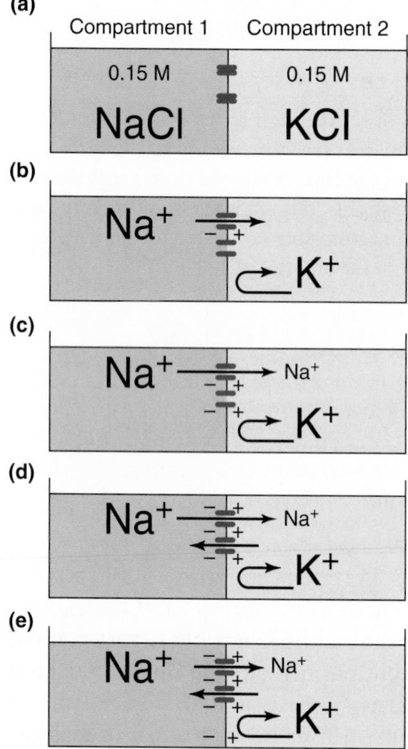

Figure 6.11 Generation of a potential across a membrane due to diffusion of Na^+ through Na^+ channels (blue). Arrows represent ion movements; as in Figure 4.3, arrow length indicates the magnitude of the flux. So few Na^+ ions cross the membrane that ion concentrations do not change significantly from step (a) to step (e). See the text for a more complete explanation.

PHYSIOLOGICAL INQUIRY

- In this hypothetical system, what equilibrium state would result if open channels for both Na^+ and K^+ were present?

Answer can be found at end of chapter.

The GHK equation is essentially an expanded version of the Nernst equation that takes into account individual ion permeabilities. In fact, setting the permeabilities of any two ions to zero gives the equilibrium potential for the remaining ion. Note that the Cl^- concentrations are reversed as compared to Na^+ and K^+ (the inside concentration is in the numerator and the outside in the denominator), because Cl^- is an anion and its movement has the opposite effect on the membrane potential. Ion gradients and permeabilities vary widely in different excitable cells of the human body and in other animals, and yet the GHK equation can be used to determine the resting membrane potential of any cell if the conditions are known. For example, if the relative permeability values of a cell were $P_K = 1$, $P_{Na} = 0.04$, and $P_{Cl} = 0.45$ and the ion concentrations were equal to those listed in Table 6.2, the resting membrane potential would be

$$V_m = 61 \log \frac{(1)(5) + (.04)(145) + (.45)(7)}{(1)(150) + (.04)(15) + (.45)(100)} = -70 \text{ mV}$$

The contributions of Na^+, K^+ and Cl^- to the overall membrane potential are thus a function of their concentration gradients and relative permeabilities. The concentration gradients determine their equilibrium potentials, and the relative permeability determines how strongly the resting membrane potential is influenced toward those potentials. In mammalian neurons, the K^+ permeability may be as much as 100 times greater than that for Na^+ and Cl^-, so neuronal resting membrane potentials are typically fairly close to the equilibrium potential for K^+ (**Figure 6.12**). The value of the Cl^- equilibrium potential is also near the resting membrane potential in many neurons, but for reasons we will return to shortly, Cl^- actually has minimal importance in determining neuronal resting membrane potentials compared to K^+ and Na^+.

In summary, the resting potential is generated across the plasma membrane largely because of the movement of K^+ out of the cell down its concentration gradient through open K^+ channels (called **leak K^+ channels**). This makes the inside of the cell negative with respect to the outside. Even though K^+ flux has more impact on the resting membrane potential than does Na^+ flux, the resting membrane potential is not *equal* to the K^+ equilibrium potential, because having a small number of open Na^+ channels does pull the membrane potential slightly toward the Na^+ equilibrium potential. Thus, at the resting membrane potential, ion channels allow net movement both of Na^+ into the cell and K^+ out of the cell.

Over time, the concentrations of intracellular sodium and potassium ions do not change, however, because of the action of the Na^+/K^+-ATPase pump. In a resting cell, the number of ions the pump moves equals the number of ions that leak down their concentration and/or electrical gradients (described collectively in Chapter 4 as the *electrochemical gradient*). As long as the concentration gradients remain stable and the ion permeabilities of the plasma membrane do not change, the electrical potential across the resting membrane will also remain constant.

Thus far, we have described the membrane potential as due purely and directly to the passive movement of ions down their electrochemical gradients, with the concentration gradients maintained by membrane pumps. However, the Na^+/K^+-ATPase pump not only maintains the concentration gradients for these ions but also helps to establish the membrane potential more directly. The Na^+/K^+-ATPase pumps actually move three sodium ions out of the cell for every two potassium ions that they bring in. This unequal transport of positive ions makes the inside of the cell more negative than it would be from ion diffusion alone. When a pump moves net charge across the membrane and contributes directly to the membrane potential, it is known as an **electrogenic pump.**

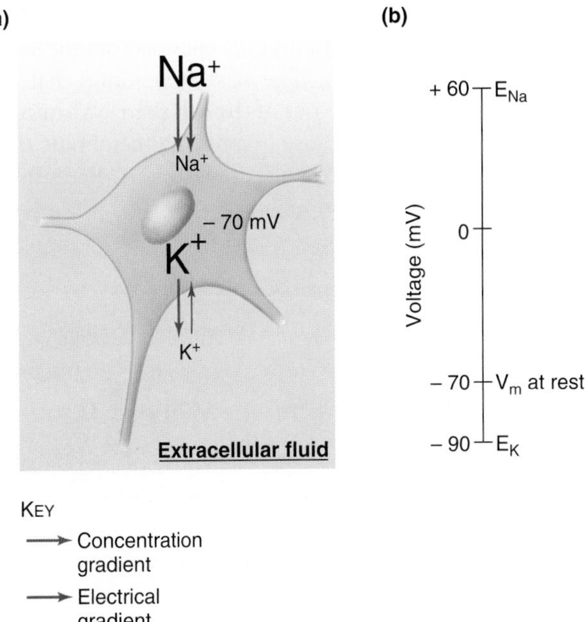

Figure 6.12 Forces influencing sodium and potassium ions at the resting membrane potential. (a) At a resting membrane potential of −70 mV, both the concentration and electrical gradients favor inward movement of Na^+, whereas the K^+ concentration and electrical gradients are in opposite directions. (b) The greater permeability and movement of K^+ maintain the resting membrane potential at a value near E_K.

PHYSIOLOGICAL INQUIRY

- Would decreasing a neuron's intracellular fluid $[K^+]$ by 1 mM have the same effect on resting membrane potential as raising the extracellular fluid $[K^+]$ by 1 mM?

Answer can be found at end of chapter.

In most cells, the electrogenic contribution to the membrane potential is quite small. Even though the electrogenic contribution of the Na^+/K^+-ATPase pump is small, the pump always makes an essential *indirect* contribution to the membrane potential because it maintains the concentration gradients that result in ion diffusion and charge separation.

Figure 6.13 summarizes the development of a resting membrane potential in three conceptual steps. First, the action of the Na^+/K^+-ATPase pump sets up the concentration gradients for Na^+ and K^+ (**Figure 6.13a**). These concentration gradients determine the equilibrium potentials for the two ions—that is, the value to which each ion would bring the membrane potential if it were the only permeating ion. Simultaneously, the pump has a small electrogenic effect on the membrane due to the fact that three sodium ions are pumped out for every two potassium ions pumped in. The next step shows that initially there is a greater flux of K^+ out of the cell than Na^+ into the cell (**Figure 6.13b**). This is because in a resting membrane there is a greater permeability to K^+ than there is to Na^+. Because there is greater net efflux than influx of positive ions during this step, a significant negative membrane potential develops, with the value approaching that of the K^+ equilibrium potential. In the steady-state resting neuron, the flux of ions across the membrane reaches a dynamic balance (**Figure 6.13c**). Because the membrane potential is not equal to the equilibrium potential for either ion, there is a small but steady leak of Na^+ into the cell and K^+ out of the cell. The concentration gradients do not dissipate over time, however, because ion movement by the Na^+/K^+-ATPase pump exactly balances the rate at which the ions leak in the opposite direction.

Now let's return to the behavior of chloride ions in excitable cells. The plasma membranes of many cells also have Cl^- channels but do not contain chloride ion pumps. Therefore, in these cells, Cl^- concentrations simply shift until the equilibrium potential for Cl^- is equal to the resting membrane potential. In other words, the negative membrane potential determined by Na^+ and K^+ moves Cl^- out of the cell, and the Cl^- concentration inside the cell becomes lower than that outside. This concentration gradient produces a diffusion of Cl^- back into the cell that exactly opposes the movement out because of the electrical potential.

In contrast, some cells have a nonelectrogenic active-transport system that moves Cl^- out of the cell, generating a strong concentration gradient. In these cells, the Cl^- equilibrium potential is negative to the resting membrane potential, and net Cl^- diffusion into the cell contributes to the excess negative charge inside the cell; that is, net Cl^- diffusion makes the membrane potential more negative than it would be if only Na^+ and K^+ were involved.

6.7 Graded Potentials and Action Potentials

You have just learned that all cells have a resting membrane potential due to the presence of ion pumps and leak channels in the cell membrane. In addition, however, some cells have another group of ion channels that can be gated (opened or closed) under certain conditions. Such channels give a cell the ability to produce electrical signals that can transmit information between different regions of the membrane. This property is known as **excitability,** and such membranes are called **excitable membranes.** Cells of this type include all neurons and muscle cells, as well as some endocrine, immune, and reproductive cells. The electrical signals occur in two forms: graded potentials and action potentials. Graded potentials are important in signaling over short distances, whereas action potentials are long-distance signals that are particularly important in neuronal and muscle cell membranes.

(a)

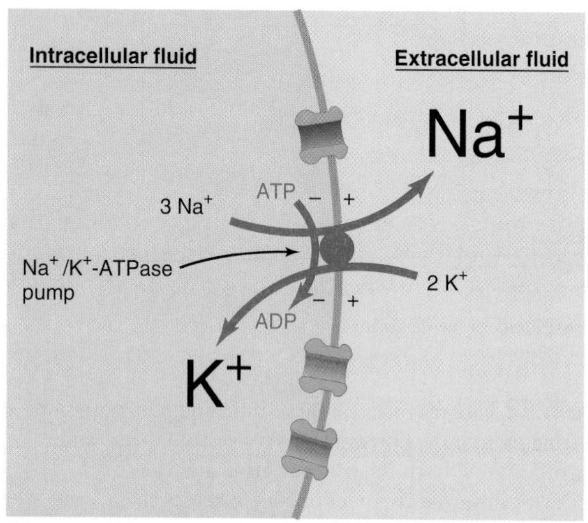

(b)

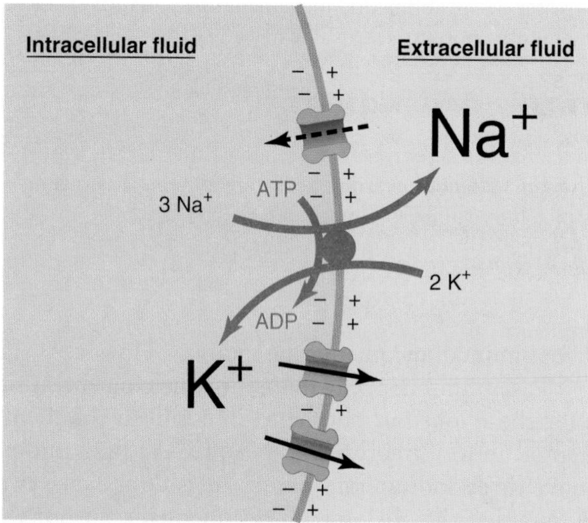

(c)

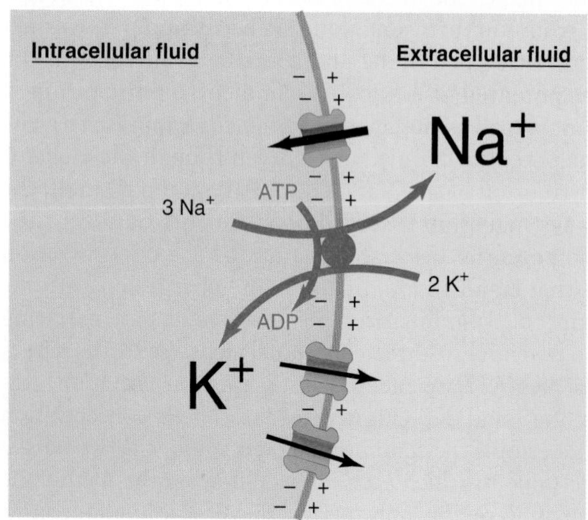

Figure 6.13 AP|R Summary of steps establishing the resting membrane potential. (a) An Na^+/K^+-ATPase pump establishes concentration gradients and generates a small negative potential. (b) Greater net movement of K^+ than Na^+ makes the membrane potential more negative on the inside. (c) At a steady negative resting membrane potential, ion fluxes through the channels and pump balance each other. The K^+ permeability (shown in red) is mainly due to K^+ leak channels, while Na^+ permeability (purple) is due mainly to other transport processes (see Figure 4.15).

The terms *depolarize*, *repolarize*, and *hyperpolarize* are used to describe the direction of changes in the membrane potential relative to the resting potential (**Figure 6.14**). The resting membrane potential is "polarized," simply meaning that the outside and inside of a cell have a different net charge. The membrane is **depolarized** when its potential becomes less negative (closer to zero) than the resting level. **Overshoot** refers to a reversal of the membrane potential polarity—that is, when the inside of a cell becomes positive relative to the outside. When a membrane potential that has been depolarized is returning toward the resting value, it is **repolarizing.** The membrane is **hyperpolarized** when the potential is more negative than the resting level.

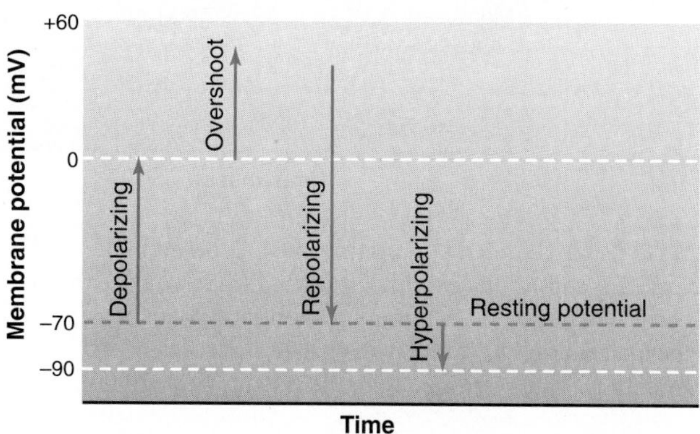

Figure 6.14 Depolarizing, repolarizing, hyperpolarizing, and overshoot changes in membrane potential relative to the resting potential.

The changes in membrane potential that the neuron uses as signals occur because of changes in the permeability of the cell membrane to ions. Recall from Chapter 4 that gated channels in a membrane may be opened or closed by mechanical, electrical, or chemical stimuli. When a neuron receives a chemical signal from a neighboring neuron, for instance, some gated channels will open, allowing greater ionic current across the membrane. The greater movement of ions down their electrochemical gradient alters the membrane potential so that it is either depolarized or hyperpolarized relative to the resting state. We will see that particular characteristics of these gated channels play a role in determining the nature of the electrical signal generated.

Graded Potentials

Graded potentials are changes in membrane potential that are confined to a relatively small region of the plasma membrane. They are usually produced when some specific change in the cell's environment acts on a specialized region of the membrane. They are called graded potentials simply because the magnitude of the potential change can vary (is "graded"). Graded potentials are given various names related to the location of the potential or the function they perform—for instance, receptor potential, synaptic potential, and pacemaker potential are all different types of graded potentials (**Table 6.3**).

Whenever a graded potential occurs, charge flows between the place of origin of this potential and adjacent regions of the plasma membrane, which are still at the resting potential. In **Figure 6.15a**, a small region of a membrane

TABLE 6.3 A Miniglossary of Terms Describing the Membrane Potential

Term	Definition
Potential or potential difference	The voltage difference between two points
Membrane potential or transmembrane potential	The voltage difference between the inside and outside of a cell
Equilibrium potential	The voltage difference across a membrane that produces a flux of a given ion species that is equal but opposite to the flux due to the concentration gradient of that same ion species
Resting membrane potential or resting potential	The steady transmembrane potential of a cell that is not producing an electrical signal
Graded potential	A potential change of variable amplitude and duration that is conducted decrementally; has no threshold or refractory period
Action potential	A brief all-or-none depolarization of the membrane, which reverses polarity in neurons; has a threshold and refractory period and is conducted without decrement
Synaptic potential	A graded potential change produced in the postsynaptic neuron in response to the release of a neurotransmitter by a presynaptic terminal; may be depolarizing (an excitatory postsynaptic potential or EPSP) or hyperpolarizing (an inhibitory postsynaptic potential or IPSP)
Receptor potential	A graded potential produced at the peripheral endings of afferent neurons (or in separate receptor cells) in response to a stimulus
Pacemaker potential	A spontaneously occurring graded potential change that occurs in certain specialized cells
Threshold potential	The membrane potential at which an action potential is initiated

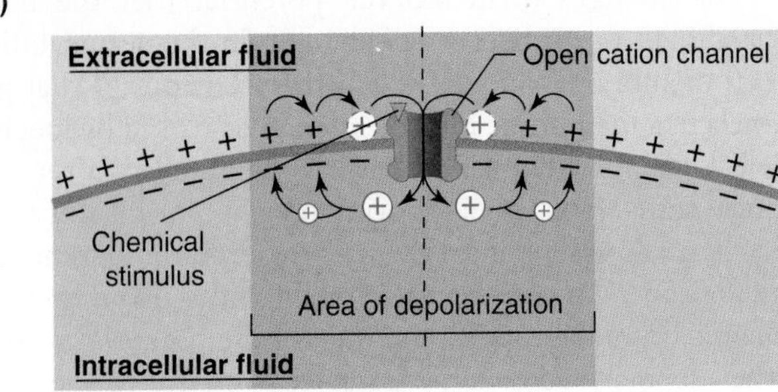

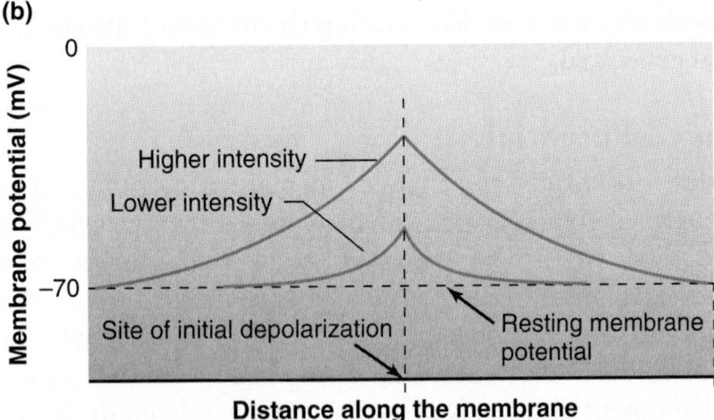

Figure 6.15 Depolarization and graded potential caused by a chemical stimulus. (a) Inward positive current through ligand-gated cation channels depolarizes a region of the membrane, and local currents spread the depolarization to adjacent regions. (b) The intensity of the initial stimulus determines the magnitude of membrane depolarization, and at increasing distances from the initial site the amount of depolarization is less.

PHYSIOLOGICAL INQUIRY

- If the ligand-gated ion channel allowed only the outward flow of K^+ from the cell, how would this figure and graph be different?

Answer can be found at end of chapter.

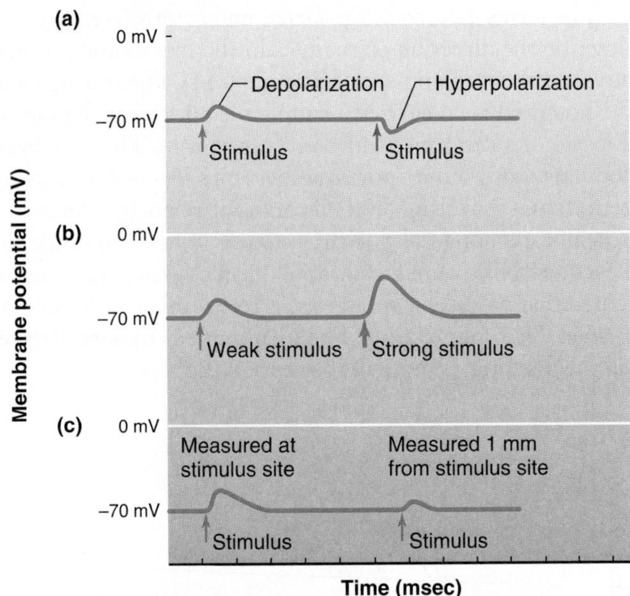

Figure 6.16 Graded potentials can be recorded under experimental conditions in which the stimulus strength can vary. Such experiments show that graded potentials (a) can be depolarizing or hyperpolarizing, (b) can vary in size, (c) are conducted decrementally. The resting membrane potential is −70 mV.

has been depolarized by transient application of a chemical signal, briefly opening membrane cation channels and producing a potential less negative than that of adjacent areas. Positive charges inside the cell (mainly K^+ ions) will move through the intracellular fluid away from the depolarized region and toward the more negative, resting regions of the membrane. Simultaneously, outside the cell, positive charge will move from the more positive region of the resting membrane toward the less positive regions the depolarization just created. Note that this local current moves positive charges toward the depolarization site along the outside of the membrane and away from the depolarization site along the inside of the membrane. Thus, it produces a decrease in the amount of charge separation in the membrane regions surrounding the open ion channel. In other words, depolarization spreads to adjacent areas along the membrane.

Depending upon the initiating event, graded potentials can occur in either a depolarizing or a hyperpolarizing direction (**Figure 6.16a**), and their magnitude is related to the magnitude of the initiating event (**Figure 6.15b, Figure 6.16b**).

In addition to the movement of ions on the inside and the outside of the cell, charge is lost across the membrane because the membrane is permeable to ions through open membrane channels. The result is that the change in membrane potential decreases as the distance increases from the initial site of the potential change (Figure 6.15b, **Figure 6.16c**). Current flows much like water flows through a leaky hose, decreasing just as water flow decreases the farther along the hose you are from the faucet. In fact, plasma membranes are so leaky to ions that these currents die out almost completely within a few millimeters of their point of origin. Because of this, local current is **decremental;** that is, the flow of charge decreases as the distance from the site of origin of the graded potential increases (**Figure 6.17**).

Because the electrical signal decreases with distance, graded potentials (and the local current they generate) can function as signals only over very short distances (a few millimeters). However, if additional stimuli occur before the graded potential has died away, these can add to the depolarization from the first stimulus. This process, termed **summation,** is particularly important for sensation, as Chapter 7 will discuss. Graded potentials are the only means of communication used by some neurons, whereas in other neurons, graded potentials initiate signals that travel longer distances, as described next.

Action Potentials

Action potentials are very different from graded potentials. They are large alterations in the membrane potential; the membrane potential may change by as much as 100 mV. For example, a cell might depolarize from −70 to +30 mV, and then repolarize to its resting potential. Action potentials are generally very rapid (as brief as 1–4 milliseconds) and may

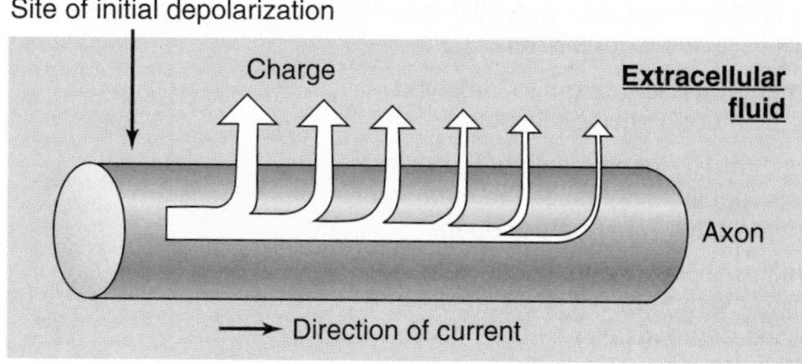

Figure 6.17 Leakage of charge (predominately potassium ions) across the plasma membrane reduces the local current at sites farther along the membrane from the site of initial depolarization.

repeat at frequencies of several hundred per second. The propagation of action potentials down the axon is the mechanism the nervous system uses to communicate over long distances.

What properties of ion channels allow them to generate these large, rapid changes in membrane potential, and how are action potentials propagated along an excitable membrane? These questions are addressed in the following sections.

Voltage-Gated Ion Channels

As described in Chapter 4, there are many types of ion channels and several different mechanisms that regulate the opening of the different types. **Ligand-gated channels** open in response to the binding of signaling molecules (as shown in Figure 6.15), and **mechanically gated channels** open in response to physical deformation (stretching) of the plasma membranes. Whereas these types of channels often cause graded potentials that can serve as the initiating stimulus for an action potential, it is **voltage-gated channels** that give a membrane the ability to undergo action potentials. There are dozens of different types of voltage-gated ion channels, varying by which ion they conduct (for example, Na^+, K^+, Ca^{2+}, or Cl^-) and in how they behave as the membrane voltage changes. For now, we will focus on the particular types of Na^+ and K^+ channels that mediate most neuronal action potentials.

Figure 6.18 summarizes the relevant characteristics of these channels. Na^+ and K^+ channels are similar in having sequences of charged amino acid residues in their structure that make the channels reversibly change shape in response to changes in membrane potential. When the membrane is at a negative potential (for example, at the resting membrane potential), both types of channels tend to close, whereas membrane depolarization tends to open them. Two key differences, however, allow these channels to play different roles in the production of action potentials. First, Na^+ channels respond much faster to changes in membrane voltage. When an area of a membrane is suddenly depolarized, local Na^+ channels open before the K^+ channels do, and if the membrane is then repolarized to negative voltages, the K^+ channels are also slower to close. The second key difference is that Na^+ channels have an extra feature in their structure known as an **inactivation gate.** This structure, sometimes visualized as a "ball and chain," limits the flux of sodium ions by blocking the channel shortly after depolarization opens it. When the membrane

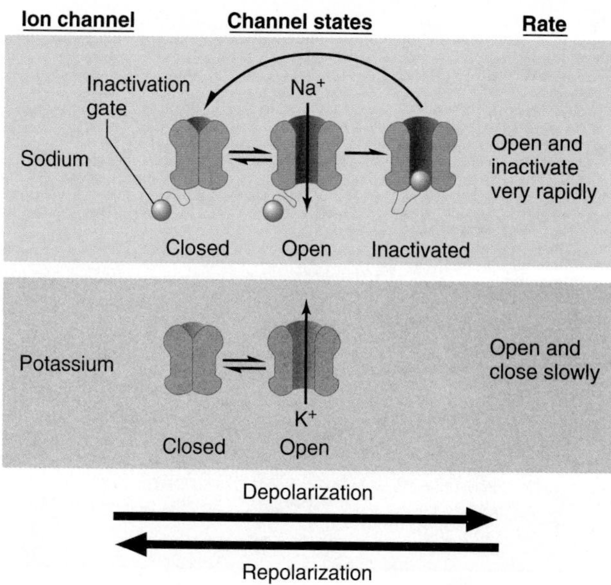

Figure 6.18 APIR Behavior of voltage-gated Na^+ and K^+ channels. Depolarization of the membrane causes Na^+ channels to rapidly open, then undergo inactivation followed by the opening of K^+ channels. When the membrane repolarizes to negative voltages, both channels return to the closed state.

repolarizes, the channel closes, forcing the inactivation gate back out of the pore and allowing the channel to return to the closed state. Integrating these channel properties with the basic principles governing membrane potentials, we can now explain how action potentials occur.

Action Potential Mechanism

In our previous coverage of resting membrane potential and graded potentials, we saw that the membrane potential depends upon the concentration gradients and membrane permeabilities of different ions, particularly Na^+ and K^+. This is true of the action potential as well. During an action potential, transient changes in membrane permeability allow sodium and potassium ions to move down their electrochemical gradients. **Figure 6.19** illustrates the steps that occur during an action potential.

In step 1 of the figure, the resting membrane potential is close to the K^+ equilibrium potential because there are more open K^+ channels than Na^+ channels. Note that these leak channels are distinct from the voltage-gated channels just described. An action potential begins with a depolarizing stimulus—for example, when a neurotransmitter binds to a specific ligand-gated ion channel and allows Na^+ to enter the cell (review Figure 6.15). This initial depolarization stimulates the opening of some voltage-gated Na^+ channels, and further entry of Na^+ through those channels adds to the local membrane depolarization. When the membrane reaches a critical **threshold potential** (step 2), depolarization becomes a **positive feedback** loop. Na^+ entry causes depolarization, which opens more voltage-gated Na^+ channels, which causes more depolarization, and so on. This process is represented as a rapid depolarization of the membrane potential (step 3), and it overshoots so that the membrane actually becomes positive

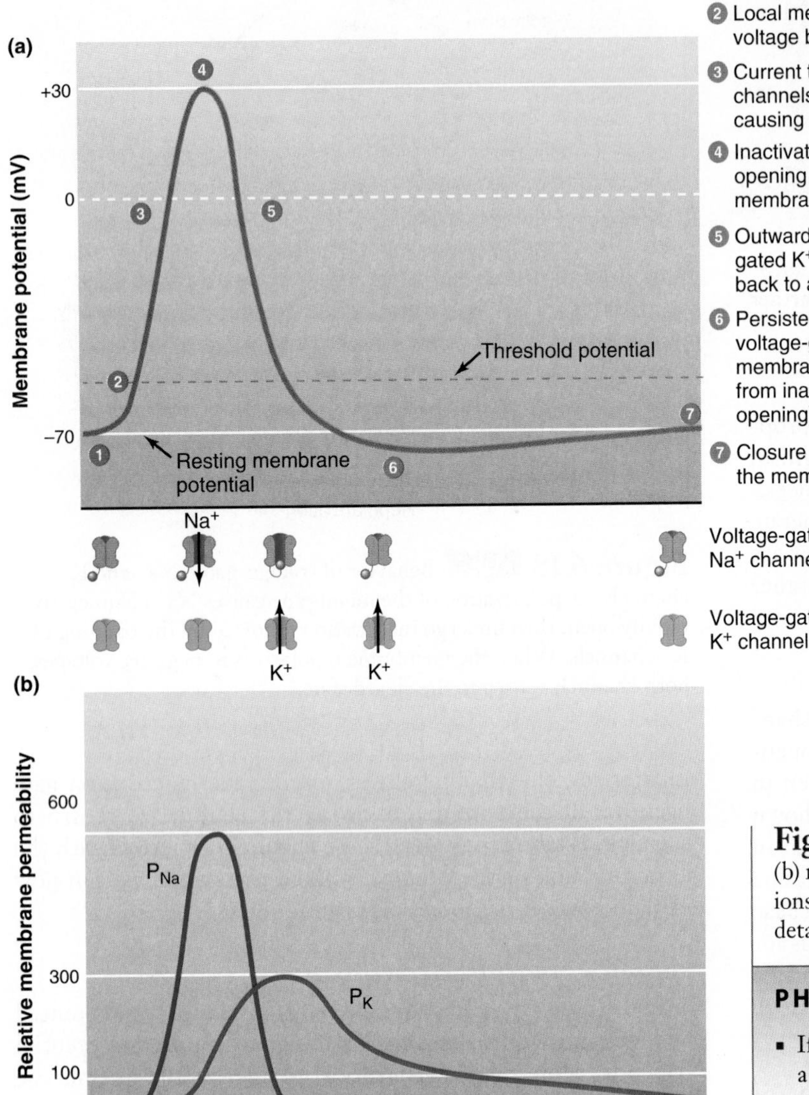

1. Steady resting membrane potential is near E_K, $P_K > P_{Na}$, due to leak K^+ channels.
2. Local membrane is brought to threshold voltage by a depolarizing stimulus.
3. Current through opening voltage-gated Na^+ channels rapidly depolarizes the membrane, causing more Na^+ channels to open.
4. Inactivation of Na^+ channels and delayed opening of voltage-gated K^+ channels halt membrane depolarization.
5. Outward current through open voltage-gated K^+ channels repolarizes the membrane back to a negative potential.
6. Persistent current through slowly closing voltage-gated K^+ channels hyperpolarizes membrane toward E_K; Na^+ channels return from inactivated state to closed state (without opening).
7. Closure of voltage-gated K^+ channels returns the membrane potential to its resting value.

Voltage-gated Na^+ channel

Voltage-gated K^+ channel

Figure 6.19 The changes in (a) membrane potential (mV) and (b) relative membrane permeability (*P*) to sodium and potassium ions during an action potential. Steps 1–7 are described in more detail in the text.

PHYSIOLOGICAL INQUIRY

- If extracellular $[Na^+]$ is elevated (and you ignore any effects of a change in osmolarity), how would the resting potential and action potential of a neuron change?

Answer can be found at end of chapter.

on the inside and negative on the outside. In this phase, the membrane approaches but does not quite reach the Na^+ equilibrium potential (+60 mV).

As the membrane potential approaches its peak value (step 4), the Na^+ permeability abruptly declines as inactivation gates break the cycle of positive feedback by blocking the open Na^+ channels. Meanwhile, the depolarized state of the membrane has begun to open the relatively sluggish voltage-gated K^+ channels, and the resulting elevated K^+ flux out of the cell rapidly repolarizes the membrane toward its resting value (step 5). The return of the membrane to a negative potential causes voltage-gated Na^+ channels to go from their inactivated state back to the closed state (without opening, as described earlier) and K^+ channels to also return to the closed state. Because voltage-gated K^+ channels close relatively slowly, immediately after an action potential there is a period when K^+ permeability remains above resting levels and the membrane is transiently hyperpolarized toward the K^+ equilibrium potential (step 6). This portion of the action potential is known as the **afterhyperpolarization.** Once the voltage-gated K^+ channels finally close, however, the resting membrane potential is restored (step 7). Whereas voltage-gated Na^+ channels operate in a positive feedback mode at the beginning of an action potential, voltage-gated K^+ channels bring the action potential to an end and induce their own closing through a **negative feedback** process (**Figure 6.20**).

You may think that large movements of ions across the membrane are required to produce such large changes in membrane potential. Actually, the number of ions that cross the membrane during an action potential is extremely small compared to the total number of ions in the cell, producing only infinitesimal changes in the intracellular ion concentrations. Yet, if this tiny number of additional ions crossing the membrane with repeated action potentials were not eventually moved back across the membrane, the concentration gradients of Na^+ and K^+ would gradually dissipate and action potentials

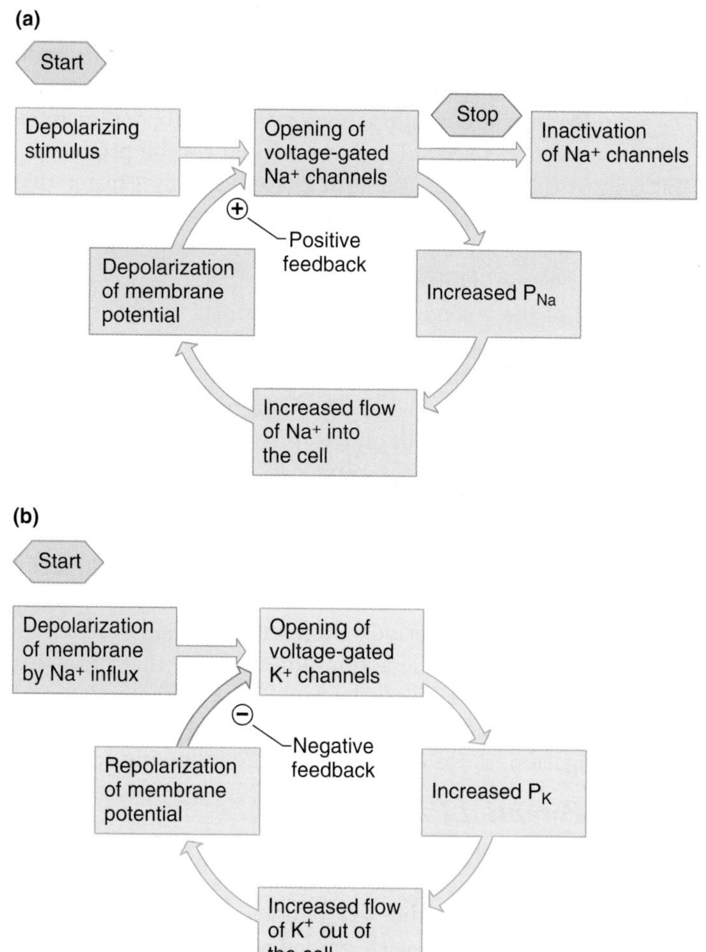

Figure 6.20 Feedback control in voltage-gated ion channels. (a) Na^+ channels exert positive feedback on membrane potential. (b) K^+ channels exert negative feedback.

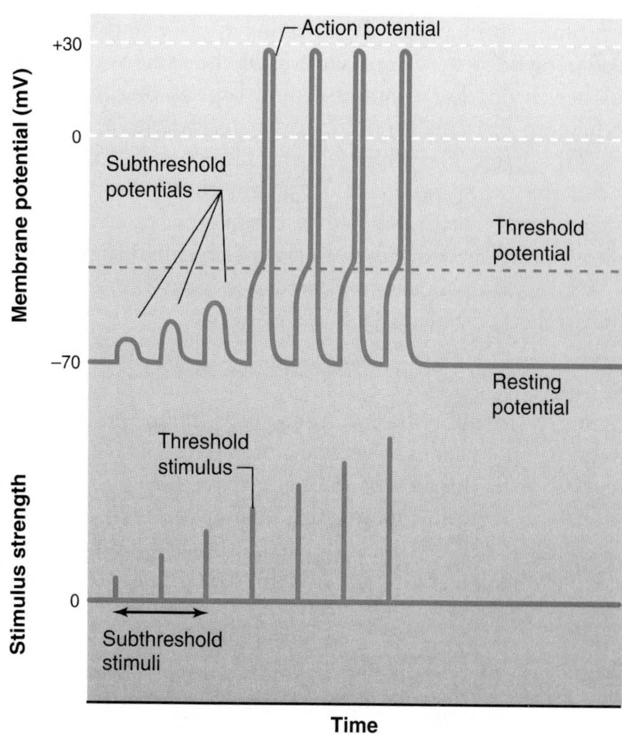

Figure 6.21 Changes in the membrane potential with increasing strength of excitatory stimuli. When the membrane potential reaches threshold, action potentials are generated. Increasing the stimulus strength above threshold level does not cause larger action potentials. (The afterhyperpolarization has been omitted from this figure for clarity, and the absolute value of threshold is not indicated because it varies from cell to cell.)

could no longer be generated. As may be expected, cellular accumulation of Na^+ and loss of K^+ are prevented by the continuous action of the membrane Na^+/K^+-ATPase pumps.

As explained previously, not all membrane depolarizations in excitable cells trigger the positive feedback process that leads to an action potential. Action potentials occur only when the initial stimulus plus the current through the Na^+ channels it opens are sufficient to elevate the membrane potential beyond the threshold potential. Stimuli that are just strong enough to depolarize the membrane to this level are **threshold stimuli** (**Figure 6.21**). The threshold of most excitable membranes is about 15 mV less negative than the resting membrane potential. Thus, if the resting potential of a neuron is −70 mV, the threshold potential may be −55 mV. At depolarizations less than threshold, the positive feedback cycle cannot get started. In such cases, the membrane will return to its resting level as soon as the stimulus is removed and no action potential will be generated. These weak depolarizations are called **subthreshold potentials,** and the stimuli that cause them are **subthreshold stimuli.**

Stimuli stronger than those required to reach threshold elicit action potentials, but as can be seen in Figure 6.21, the action potentials resulting from such stimuli have exactly the same amplitude as those caused by threshold stimuli. This is because once threshold is reached, membrane events are no longer dependent upon stimulus strength. Rather, the depolarization generates an action potential because the positive feedback cycle is operating. Action potentials either occur maximally or they do not occur at all. Another way of saying this is that action potentials are **all-or-none.**

The firing of a gun is a mechanical analogy that shows the principle of all-or-none behavior. The magnitude of the explosion and the velocity at which the bullet leaves the gun do not depend on how hard the trigger is squeezed. Either the trigger is pulled hard enough to fire the gun, or it is not; the gun cannot be fired halfway.

Because the amplitude of a single action potential does not vary in proportion to the amplitude of the stimulus, an action potential cannot convey information about the magnitude of the stimulus that initiated it. How then do you distinguish between a loud noise and a whisper, a light touch and a pinch? This information, as we will discuss later, depends upon the number and patterns of action potentials transmitted per unit of time (i.e., their frequency) and not upon their magnitude.

The generation of action potentials is prevented by ***local anesthetics*** such as ***procaine*** (*Novocaine*) and ***lidocaine*** (*Xylocaine*) because these drugs block voltage-gated Na^+ channels, preventing them from opening in response to depolarization. Without action potentials, graded signals generated in sensory neurons—in response to injury, for example—cannot reach the brain and give rise to the sensation of pain.

Some animals produce toxins (poisons) that work by interfering with nerve conduction in the same way that local anesthetics do. For example, some organs of the pufferfish produce an extremely potent toxin, ***tetrodotoxin***, that binds to voltage-gated Na^+ channels and prevents the Na^+ component of the action potential. In Japan, chefs who prepare this delicacy are specially trained to completely remove the toxic organs before serving the pufferfish dish called fugu. Individuals who eat improperly prepared fugu may die, even if they ingest only a tiny quantity of tetrodotoxin.

Refractory Periods

During the action potential, a second stimulus, no matter how strong, will not produce a second action potential (**Figure 6.22**). That region of the membrane is then said to be in its **absolute refractory period.** This occurs during the period when the voltage-gated Na^+ channels are either already open or have proceeded to the inactivated state during the first action potential.

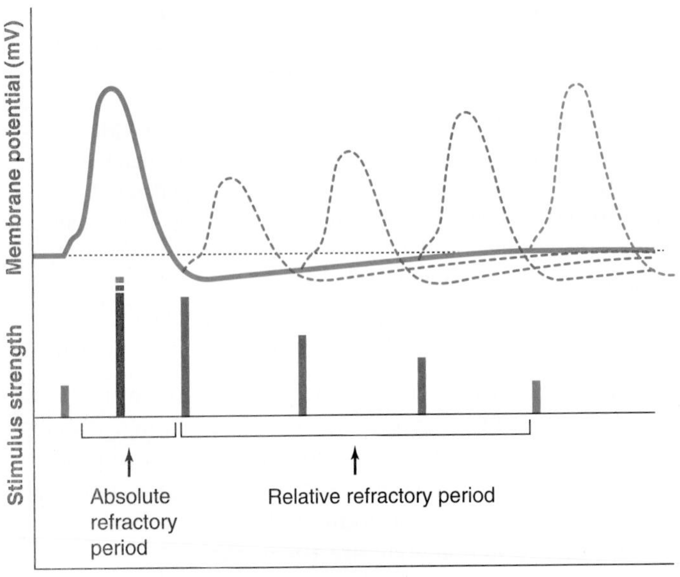

Figure 6.22 Absolute and relative refractory periods of the action potential determined by a paired-pulse protocol. After a threshold stimulus that results in an action potential (first stimulus and solid voltage trace), a second stimulus given at various times after the first can be used to determine refractory periods. All stimuli shown are of the minimum size needed to stimulate an action potential. During the absolute refractory period, a second stimulus (black), no matter how strong, will not produce a second action potential. In the relative refractory period (stimuli and action potentials shown in red), a second action potential can be triggered, but a larger stimulus is required to reach threshold, mainly because K^+ permeability is still above resting levels. Action potentials are reduced in size during the relative refractory period, due both to the inactivation of some Na^+ channels and the persistence of some open K^+ channels.

The inactivation gate that has blocked these channels must be removed by repolarizing the membrane and closing the pore before the channels can reopen to the second stimulus.

Following the absolute refractory period, there is an interval during which a second action potential can be produced—but only if the stimulus strength is considerably greater than usual. This is the **relative refractory period,** which can last 1 to 15 msec or longer and coincides roughly with the period of afterhyperpolarization. During the relative refractory period, some but not all of the voltage-gated Na^+ channels have returned to a resting state and some of the K^+ channels that repolarized the membrane are still open. From this relative refractory state, it is possible for a new stimulus to depolarize the membrane above the threshold potential, but only if the stimulus is large in magnitude or outlasts the relative refractory period.

The refractory periods limit the number of action potentials an excitable membrane can produce in a given period of time. Most neurons respond at frequencies of up to 100 action potentials per second, and some may produce much higher frequencies for brief periods. Refractory periods contribute to the separation of these action potentials so that individual electrical signals pass down the axon. The refractory periods also are the key in determining the direction of action potential propagation, as we will discuss in the following section.

Action Potential Propagation

The action potential can only travel the length of a neuron if each point along the membrane is depolarized to its threshold potential as the action potential moves down the axon (**Figure 6.23**). As with graded potentials (refer back to Figure 6.15a), the membrane is depolarized at each point along the way with respect to the adjacent portions of the membrane, which are still at the resting membrane potential. The difference between the potentials causes current to flow, and this local current depolarizes the adjacent membrane where it causes the voltage-gated Na^+ channels located there to open. The current entering during an action potential is sufficient to easily depolarize the adjacent membrane to the threshold potential.

The new action potential produces local currents of its own that depolarize the region adjacent to it (Figure 6.23b), producing yet another action potential at the next site, and so on, to cause **action potential propagation** along the length of the membrane. Thus, there is a sequential opening and closing of Na^+ and K^+ channels along the membrane. It is like lighting a trail of gunpowder—the action potential does not move, but it "sets off" a new action potential in the region of the axon just ahead of it. Because each regeneration of the action potential depends on the positive feedback cycle of a new group of Na^+ channels where the action potential is occurring, the action potential arriving at the end of the membrane is virtually identical in form to the initial one. Thus, action potentials do not decrease in magnitude with distance like graded potentials.

Because a membrane area that has just undergone an action potential is refractory and cannot immediately undergo another, the only direction of action potential propagation is away from a region of membrane that has recently been active. This is again similar to a burning trail of gunpowder—the fire can only spread in the forward direction where the gunpowder is fresh, and not backward where the gunpowder has already burned.

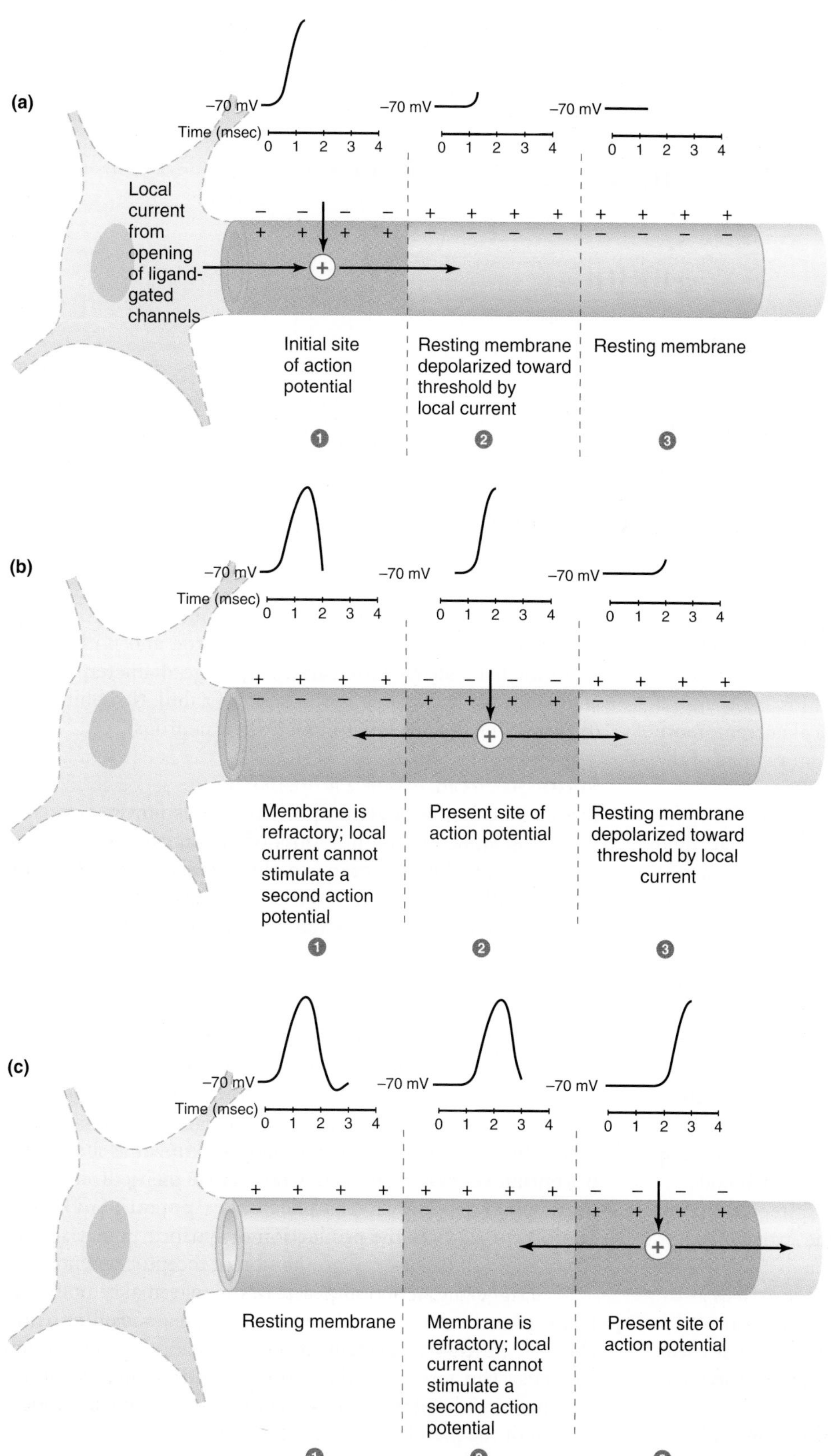

Figure 6.23 APIR One-way propagation of an action potential. For simplicity, potentials are shown only on the upper membrane, local currents are shown only on the inside of the membrane, and repolarizing currents are not shown. (a) Local current from the opening of ligand-gated ion channels in the cell body and dendrites causes an action potential to be initiated in region 1, and local current depolarizes region 2. (b) Action potential in region 2 generates local currents; region 3 is depolarized toward threshold, but region 1 is refractory. (c) Action potential in region 3 generates local currents, but region 2 is refractory.

PHYSIOLOGICAL INQUIRY

- Striking the ulnar nerve in your elbow against a hard surface (sometimes called "hitting your funny bone") initiates action potentials near the midpoint of sensory and motor axons traveling in that nerve. In which direction will those action potentials propagate?

Answer can be found at end of chapter.

If the membrane through which the action potential must travel is not refractory, excitable membranes can conduct action potentials in either direction, with the direction of propagation determined by the stimulus location. For example, the action potentials in skeletal muscle cells are initiated near the middle of the cells and propagate toward the two ends. In most neurons, however, action potentials are initiated at one end of the cell and propagate toward the other end, as shown in Figure 6.23. The propagation ceases when the action potential reaches the end of an axon.

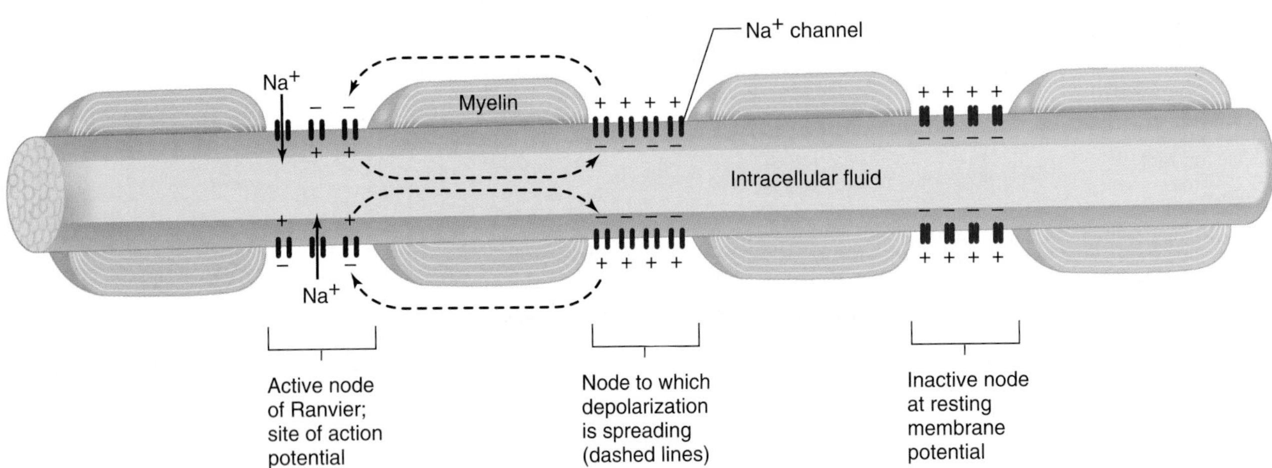

Figure 6.24 Myelinization and saltatory conduction of action potentials. K^+ channels are not depicted.

The velocity with which an action potential propagates along a membrane depends upon fiber diameter and whether or not the fiber is myelinated. The larger the fiber diameter, the faster the action potential propagates. This is because a large fiber offers less internal resistance to local current; more ions will flow in a given time, bringing adjacent regions of the membrane to threshold faster.

Myelin is an insulator that makes it more difficult for charge to flow between intracellular and extracellular fluid compartments. Because there is less "leakage" of charge across the myelin, a local current can spread farther along an axon. Moreover, the concentration of voltage-gated Na^+ channels in the myelinated region of axons is low. Therefore, action potentials occur only at the nodes of Ranvier, where the myelin coating is interrupted and the concentration of voltage-gated Na^+ channels is high (**Figure 6.24**). Action potentials appear to jump from one node to the next as they propagate along a myelinated fiber; for this reason, such propagation is called **saltatory conduction** (Latin, *saltare*, "to leap"). However, it is important to understand that an action potential does not, in fact, jump from region to region but rather is regenerated at each node.

Propagation via saltatory conduction is faster than propagation in nonmyelinated fibers of the same axon diameter. This is because less charge leaks out through the myelin-covered sections of the membrane, more charge arrives at the node adjacent to the active node, and an action potential is generated there sooner than if the myelin were not present. Moreover, because ions cross the membrane only at the nodes of Ranvier, the membrane pumps need to restore fewer ions. Myelinated axons are therefore metabolically more efficient than unmyelinated ones. Thus, myelin adds speed, reduces metabolic cost, and saves room in the nervous system because the axons can be thinner.

Conduction velocities range from about 0.5 m/sec (1 mi/h) for small-diameter, unmyelinated fibers to about 100 m/sec (225 mi/h) for large-diameter, myelinated fibers. At 0.5 m/sec, an action potential would travel the distance from the toe to the brain of an average-sized person in about 4 sec; at a velocity of 100 m/sec, it only takes about 0.02 sec. Perhaps you've dropped a heavy object on your toe and noticed that an immediate, sharp pain (carried by large-diameter, myelinated neurons) occurs before the onset of a dull, throbbing ache (transmitted along small, unmyelinated neurons).

Generation of Action Potentials

In our description of action potentials thus far, we have spoken of "stimuli" as the initiators of action potentials. These stimuli bring the membrane to the threshold potential, and voltage-gated Na^+ channels initiate the action potential. How is the threshold potential attained, and how do various types of neurons actually generate action potentials?

In afferent neurons, the initial depolarization to threshold is achieved by a graded potential—here called a **receptor potential.** Receptor potentials are generated in the sensory receptors at the peripheral ends of the neurons, which are at the ends farthest from the CNS. In all other neurons, the depolarization to threshold is due either to a graded potential generated by synaptic input to the neuron, known as a **synaptic potential,** or to a spontaneous change in the neuron's membrane potential, known as a **pacemaker potential.** The next section will address the production of synaptic potentials, and Chapter 7 will discuss the production of receptor potentials.

Triggering of action potentials by pacemaker potentials is an inherent property of certain neurons (and other excitable cells, including certain smooth muscle and cardiac muscle cells). In these cells, the activity of different types of ion channels in the plasma membrane causes a graded depolarization of the membrane—the pacemaker potential. If threshold is reached, an action potential occurs; the membrane then repolarizes and again begins to depolarize. There is no stable, resting membrane potential in such cells because of the continuous change in membrane permeability. The rate at which the membrane depolarizes to threshold determines the action potential frequency. Pacemaker potentials are implicated in many rhythmic behaviors, such as breathing, the heartbeat, and movements within the walls of the stomach and intestines.

TABLE 6.4 Differences Between Graded Potentials and Action Potentials

Graded Potential	Action Potential
Amplitude varies with size of the initiating event.	All-or-none. Once membrane is depolarized to threshold, amplitude is independent of the size of the initiating event.
Can be summed.	Cannot be summed.
Has no threshold.	Has a threshold that is usually about 15 mV depolarized relative to the resting potential.
Has no refractory period.	Has a refractory period.
Amplitude decreases with distance.	Is conducted without decrement; the depolarization is amplified to a constant value at each point along the membrane.
Duration varies with initiating conditions.	Duration is constant for a given cell type under constant conditions.
Can be a depolarization or a hyperpolarization.	Is only a depolarization.
Initiated by environmental stimulus (receptor), by neurotransmitter (synapse), or spontaneously.	Initiated by a graded potential.
Mechanism depends on ligand-gated channels or other chemical or physical changes.	Mechanism depends on voltage-gated channels.

Because of the effects of graded changes in membrane potential on action potential generation, a review of graded and action potentials is recommended. The differences between graded potentials and action potentials are listed in **Table 6.4**.

SECTION B SUMMARY

Basic Principles of Electricity

I. Separated electrical charges create the potential to do work, as occurs when charged particles produce an electrical current as they flow down a potential gradient. The lipid barrier of the plasma membrane is a high-resistance insulator that keeps charged ions separated, whereas ionic current flows readily in the aqueous intracellular and extracellular fluids.

The Resting Membrane Potential

I. Membrane potentials are generated mainly by the diffusion of ions and are determined by both the ionic concentration differences across the membrane and the membrane's relative permeability to different ions.
   a. Plasma membrane Na^+/K^+-ATPase pumps maintain low intracellular Na^+ concentration and high intracellular K^+ concentration.
   b. In almost all resting cells, the plasma membrane is much more permeable to K^+ than to Na^+, so the membrane potential is close to the K^+ equilibrium potential—that is, the inside is negative relative to the outside.
   c. The Na^+/K^+-ATPase pumps directly contribute a small component of the potential because they are electrogenic.

Graded Potentials and Action Potentials

I. Neurons signal information by graded potentials and action potentials (APs).

II. Graded potentials are local potentials whose magnitude can vary and that die out within 1 or 2 mm of their site of origin.

III. An AP is a rapid change in the membrane potential during which the membrane rapidly depolarizes and repolarizes. At the peak, the potential reverses and the membrane becomes positive inside. APs provide long-distance transmission of information through the nervous system.
   a. APs occur in excitable membranes because these membranes contain many voltage-gated Na^+ channels. These channels open as the membrane depolarizes, causing a positive feedback opening of more voltage-gated Na^+ channels and moving the membrane potential toward the Na^+ equilibrium potential.
   b. The AP ends as the Na^+ channels inactivate and K^+ channels open, restoring resting conditions.
   c. Depolarization of excitable membranes triggers an AP only when the membrane potential exceeds a threshold potential.
   d. Regardless of the size of the stimulus, if the membrane reaches threshold, the AP generated is the same size.
   e. A membrane is refractory for a brief time following an AP.
   f. APs are propagated without any change in size from one site to another along a membrane.
   g. In myelinated nerve fibers, APs are regenerated at the nodes of Ranvier in saltatory conduction.
   h. APs can be triggered by depolarizing graded potentials in sensory neurons, at synapses, or in some cells by pacemaker potentials.

SECTION B REVIEW QUESTIONS

1. Describe how negative and positive charges interact.
2. Contrast the abilities of intracellular and extracellular fluids and membrane lipids to conduct electrical current.
3. Draw a simple cell; indicate where the concentrations of Na^+, K^+, and Cl^- are high and low and the electrical potential difference across the membrane when the cell is at rest.
4. Explain the conditions that give rise to the resting membrane potential. What effect does membrane permeability have on this potential? What role do Na^+/K^+-ATPase membrane pumps play in the membrane potential? Is this role direct or indirect?
5. Which two factors involving ion diffusion determine the magnitude of the resting membrane potential?
6. Explain why the resting membrane potential is not equal to the K^+ equilibrium potential.
7. Draw a graded potential and an action potential on a graph of membrane potential versus time. Indicate zero membrane potential, resting membrane potential, and threshold potential; indicate when the membrane is depolarized, repolarizing, and hyperpolarized.
8. List the differences between graded potentials and action potentials.
9. Describe how ion movement generates the action potential.
10. What determines the activity of the voltage-gated Na^+ channel?
11. Explain threshold and the relative and absolute refractory periods in terms of the ionic basis of the action potential.
12. Describe the propagation of an action potential. Contrast this event in myelinated and unmyelinated axons.
13. List three ways in which action potentials can be initiated in neurons.

SECTION B KEY TERMS

absolute refractory period 156
action potential 152
action potential propagation 156
afterhyperpolarization 154
all-or-none 155
current 145
decremental 152
depolarized 151
electrical potential 145
electrogenic pump 149
equilibrium potential 147
excitability 150
excitable membrane 150
Goldman-Hodgkin-Katz (GHK) equation 148
graded potential 151
hyperpolarized 151
inactivation gate 153
leak K^+ channels 149
ligand-gated channels 153
mechanically gated channels 153
negative feedback 154
Nernst equation 148
Ohm's law 145
overshoot 151
pacemaker potential 158
positive feedback 153
potential 145
potential difference 145
receptor potential 158
relative refractory period 156
repolarizing 151
resistance 145
resting membrane potential 146
saltatory conduction 158
subthreshold potential 155
subthreshold stimulus 155
summation 152
synaptic potential 158
threshold potential 153
threshold stimulus 155
voltage-gated channels 153

SECTION B CLINICAL TERMS

lidocaine (Xylocaine) 155
local anesthetics 155
procaine (Novocaine) 155
tetrodotoxin 156

SECTION C
Synapses

As defined earlier, a synapse is an anatomically specialized junction between two neurons, at which the electrical activity in a presynaptic neuron influences the electrical activity of a postsynaptic neuron. Anatomically, synapses include parts of the presynaptic and postsynaptic neurons and the extracellular space between these two cells. According to recent estimates, there are more than 10^{14} (100 trillion!) synapses in the CNS.

Activity at synapses can increase or decrease the likelihood that the postsynaptic neuron will fire action potentials by producing a brief, graded potential in the postsynaptic membrane. The membrane potential of a postsynaptic neuron is brought closer to threshold (depolarized) at an **excitatory synapse,** and it is either driven farther from threshold (hyperpolarized) or stabilized at its resting potential at an **inhibitory synapse.**

Hundreds or thousands of synapses from many different presynaptic cells can affect a single postsynaptic cell (**convergence**), and a single presynaptic cell can send branches to affect many other postsynaptic cells (**divergence, Figure 6.25**). Convergence allows information from many sources to influence a cell's activity; divergence allows one cell to affect multiple pathways.

The level of excitability of a postsynaptic cell at any moment (i.e., how close its membrane potential is to threshold) depends on the number of synapses active at any one time and the number that are excitatory or inhibitory. If the membrane of the postsynaptic neuron reaches threshold, it will generate action potentials that are propagated along its axon to the terminal branches, which in turn influence the excitability of other cells.

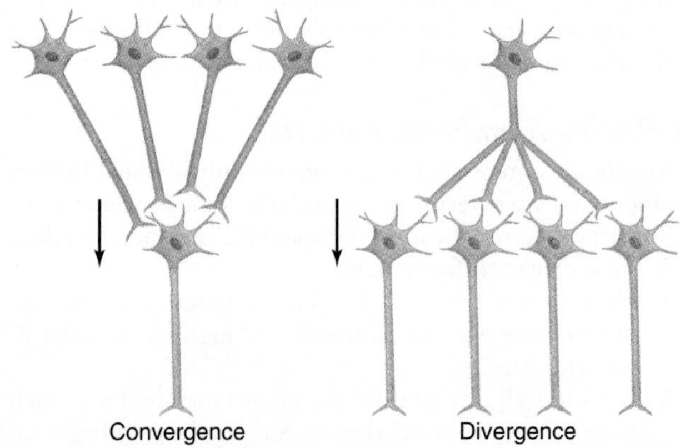

Figure 6.25 Convergence of neural input from many neurons onto a single neuron, and divergence of output from a single neuron onto many others. Arrows indicate the direction of transmission of neural activity.

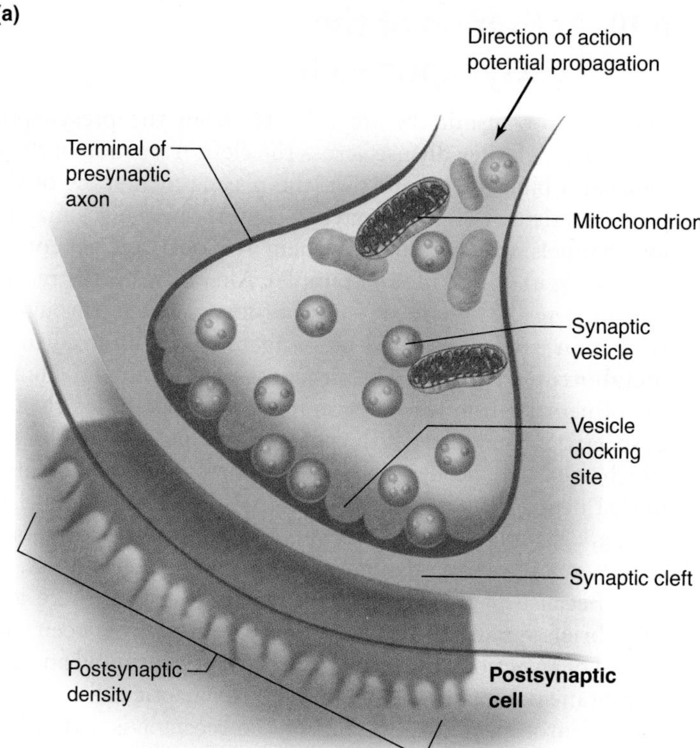

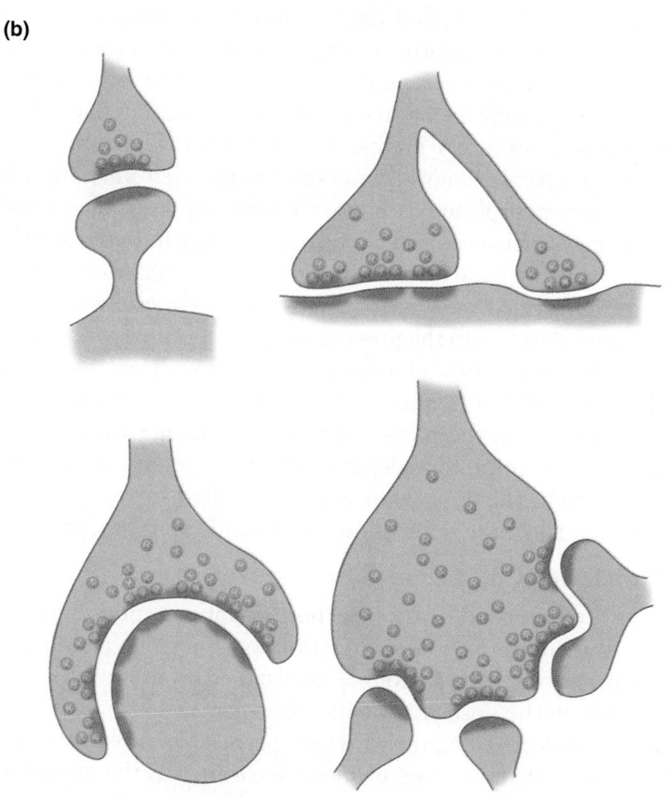

Figure 6.26 APIR (a) Diagram of a chemical synapse. Some vesicles are docked at the presynaptic membrane, ready for release. The postsynaptic membrane is distinguished microscopically by the postsynaptic density, which contains proteins associated with the receptors. (b) Synapses appear in many forms, as demonstrated here. The presynaptic terminals all contain synaptic vesicles. Redrawn from Walmsley et al.

6.8 Functional Anatomy of Synapses

There are two types of synapses: electrical and chemical. At **electrical synapses,** the plasma membranes of the presynaptic and postsynaptic cells are joined by gap junctions (Chapter 3). These allow the local currents resulting from arriving action potentials to flow directly across the junction through the connecting channels from one neuron to the other. This depolarizes the membrane of the second neuron to threshold, continuing the propagation of the action potential. Communication between cells via electrical synapses is extremely rapid. Until recently, it was thought that electrical synapses were rare in the adult mammalian nervous system. However, they have now been described in widespread locations, and neuroscientists suspect they may play important roles. Among the possible functions are synchronization of electrical activity of neurons clustered in local CNS networks and communication between glial cells and neurons. Multiple isoforms of gap-junction proteins have been described, and the conductance of some of these is modulated by factors such as membrane voltage, intracellular pH, and Ca^{2+} concentration. More research will be required to gain a complete understanding of this modulation and all of the complex roles of electrical synapses in the nervous system. Their function is better understood in cardiac and smooth muscle tissues, where they are also numerous (see Chapter 9).

Figure 6.26a shows the basic structure of a typical **chemical synapse.** The axon of the presynaptic neuron ends in a slight swelling, the axon terminal, which holds the **synaptic vesicles** that contain neurotransmitter molecules. The postsynaptic membrane adjacent to the axon terminal has a high density of membrane proteins that make up a specialized area called the **postsynaptic density.** Note that in actuality the size and shape of the presynaptic and postsynaptic elements can vary greatly (**Figure 6.26b**). A 10 to 20 nm extracellular space, the **synaptic cleft,** separates the presynaptic and postsynaptic neurons and prevents *direct* propagation of the current from the presynaptic neuron to the postsynaptic cell. Instead, signals are transmitted across the synaptic cleft by means of a chemical messenger—a neurotransmitter—released from the presynaptic axon terminal. Sometimes more than one neurotransmitter may be simultaneously released from an axon, in which case the additional neurotransmitter is called a **cotransmitter.** These neurotransmitters have different receptors on the postsynaptic cell.

6.9 Mechanisms of Neurotransmitter Release

As indicated in **Figure 6.27,** neurotransmitters are stored in small vesicles with lipid bilayer membranes. Prior to activation, many vesicles are docked on the presynaptic membrane at release regions known as **active zones,** whereas others are dispersed within the terminal. Neurotransmitter release is initiated when an action potential reaches the presynaptic terminal membrane. A key feature of neuron terminals is that in addition to the Na^+ and K^+ channels found elsewhere in the neuron, they also possess voltage-gated Ca^{2+} channels. Depolarization during the action potential opens these Ca^{2+} channels, and because the electrochemical gradient favors Ca^{2+} influx, Ca^{2+} flows into the axon terminal.

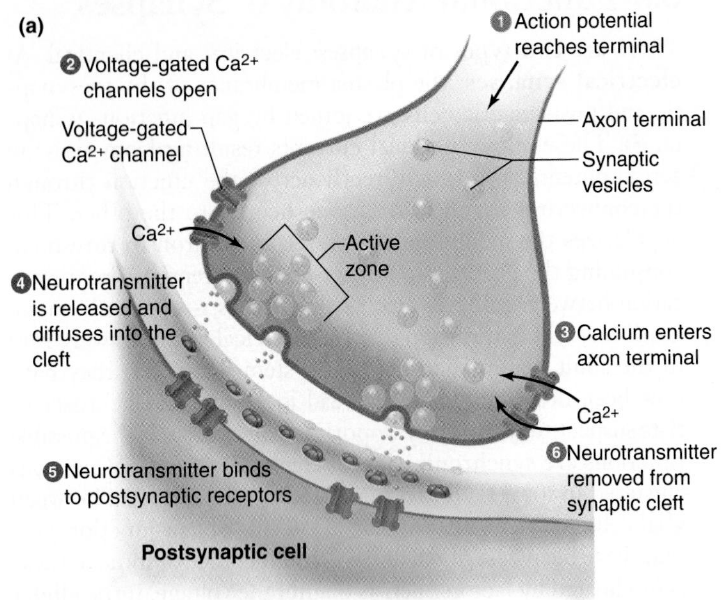
(a)
1 Action potential reaches terminal
2 Voltage-gated Ca2+ channels open
Voltage-gated Ca2+ channel
Axon terminal
Synaptic vesicles
Ca2+
Active zone
4 Neurotransmitter is released and diffuses into the cleft
3 Calcium enters axon terminal
Ca2+
6 Neurotransmitter removed from synaptic cleft
5 Neurotransmitter binds to postsynaptic receptors
Postsynaptic cell

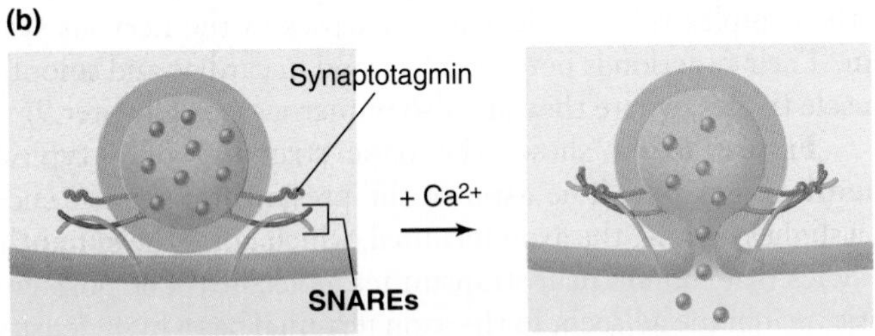
(b)
Synaptotagmin
+ Ca2+
SNAREs

Figure 6.27 APIR (a) Mechanisms of signaling at a chemical synapse. (b) Magnified view showing details of neurotransmitter release. Calcium ions trigger synaptotagmin and SNARE proteins to induce membrane fusion and neurotransmitter release. (SNARE = Soluble *N*-ethylmaleimide-sensitive factor attachment protein receptor)

Calcium ions activate processes that lead to the fusion of docked vesicles with the synaptic terminal membrane (**Figure 6.27b**). Prior to the arrival of an action potential, vesicles are loosely docked in the active zones by the interaction of a group of proteins, some of which are anchored in the vesicle membrane and others that are found in the membrane of the terminal. These are collectively known as **SNARE proteins** (soluble *N*-ethylmaleimide-sensitive factor attachment protein receptors). Calcium ions entering during depolarization bind to a separate family of proteins associated with the vesicle, **synaptotagmins,** triggering a conformational change in the SNARE complex that leads to membrane fusion and neurotransmitter release. After fusion, vesicles can undergo at least two possible fates. At some synapses, vesicles completely fuse with the membrane and are later recycled by endocytosis from the membrane at sites outside the active zone (see Figure 4.21). At other synapses, especially those at which action potential firing frequencies are high, vesicles may fuse only briefly while they release their contents and then reseal the pore and withdraw back into the nerve terminal (a mechanism called "kiss-and-run fusion").

6.10 Activation of the Postsynaptic Cell

Once neurotransmitters are released from the presynaptic axon terminal, they diffuse across the cleft. A fraction of these molecules bind to receptors on the plasma membrane of the postsynaptic cell. The activated receptors themselves may be ion channels, which designates them as **ionotropic receptors** (review Figure 6.15a for an example). Alternatively, the receptors may act indirectly on separate ion channels through a G protein and/or a second messenger, a type referred to as **metabotropic receptors.** In either case, the result of the binding of neurotransmitter to receptor is the opening or closing of specific ion channels in the postsynaptic plasma membrane, which eventually leads to changes in the membrane potential in that neuron. These channels belong, therefore, to the class of ligand-gated channels controlled by receptors, as discussed in Chapter 5, and are distinct from voltage-gated channels.

Because of the sequence of events involved, there is a very brief **synaptic delay**—about 0.2 msec—between the arrival of an action potential at a presynaptic terminal and the membrane potential changes in the postsynaptic cell.

Neurotransmitter binding to the receptor is a transient and reversible, noncovalent event. As with any binding site, the bound ligand—in this case, the neurotransmitter—is in equilibrium with the unbound form. Thus, if the concentration of unbound neurotransmitter in the synaptic cleft decreases, the number of occupied receptors will decrease. The ion channels in the postsynaptic membrane return to their resting state when the neurotransmitters are no longer bound. Unbound neurotransmitters are removed from the synaptic cleft when they (1) are actively transported back into the presynaptic axon terminal (in a process called **reuptake**) or, in some cases, into nearby glial cells; (2) diffuse away from the receptor site; or (3) are enzymatically transformed into inactive substances, some of which are transported back into the presynaptic axon terminal for reuse.

The two kinds of chemical synapses—excitatory and inhibitory—are differentiated by the effects of the neurotransmitter on the postsynaptic cell. Whether the effect is excitatory or inhibitory depends on the type of ion channel influenced by the signal transduction mechanism brought into operation when the neurotransmitter binds to its receptor.

Excitatory Chemical Synapses

At an excitatory synapse, the postsynaptic response to the neurotransmitter is a depolarization, bringing the membrane potential closer to threshold. The usual effect of the activated receptor on the postsynaptic membrane at such synapses is to open nonselective channels that are permeable to Na^+ and K^+. These ions then are free to move according to the electrical and chemical gradients across the membrane.

Both electrical and concentration gradients drive Na^+ into the cell, whereas for K^+, the electrical gradient opposes the concentration gradient (review Figure 6.12). Opening channels that are permeable to both ions therefore results in the simultaneous movement of a relatively small number of potassium ions out of the cell and a larger number of sodium ions into the cell. Thus, the *net* movement of positive ions is into the postsynaptic cell, causing a slight depolarization. This membrane potential

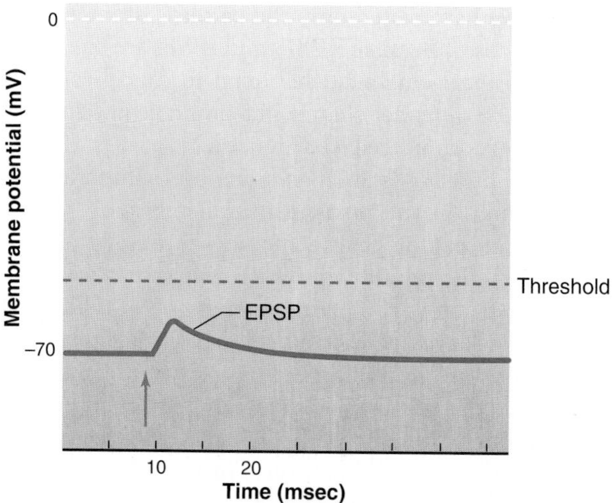

Figure 6.28 Excitatory postsynaptic potential (EPSP). Stimulation of the presynaptic neuron is marked by the green arrow. (Drawn larger than normal; typical EPSP = 0.5 mV)

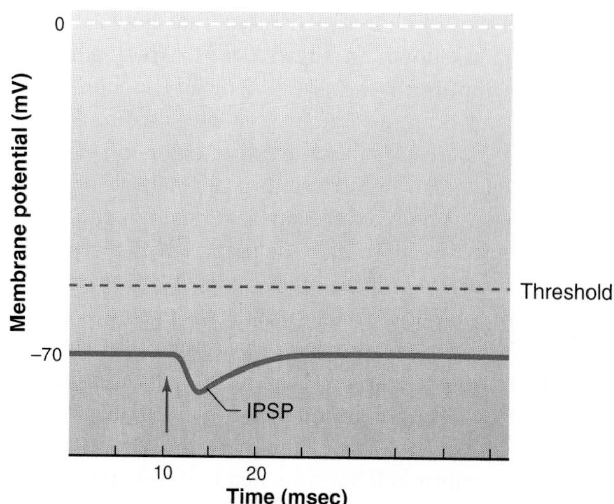

Figure 6.29 Inhibitory postsynaptic potential (IPSP). Stimulation of the presynaptic neuron is marked by the red arrow. (This hyperpolarization is drawn larger than a typical IPSP.)

change is called an **excitatory postsynaptic potential (EPSP, Figure 6.28)**. The EPSP is a graded potential that decreases in magnitude as it spreads away from the synapse by local current. Its only function is to bring the membrane potential of the postsynaptic neuron closer to threshold.

Inhibitory Chemical Synapses

At inhibitory synapses, the potential change in the postsynaptic neuron is generally a hyperpolarizing graded potential called an **inhibitory postsynaptic potential (IPSP, Figure 6.29)**. Alternatively, there may be no IPSP but rather *stabilization* of the membrane potential at its existing value. In either case, activation of an inhibitory synapse lessens the likelihood that the postsynaptic cell will depolarize to threshold and generate an action potential.

At an inhibitory synapse, the activated receptors on the postsynaptic membrane open Cl^- or K^+ channels; Na^+ permeability is not affected. In those cells that actively regulate intracellular Cl^- concentrations via active transport out of the cell, the Cl^- equilibrium potential is more negative than the resting potential. Therefore, as Cl^- channels open, Cl^- enters the cell, producing a hyperpolarization—that is, an IPSP. In cells that do not actively transport Cl^-, the equilibrium potential for Cl^- is equal to the resting membrane potential. Therefore, an increase in Cl^- permeability does not change the membrane potential but is able to increase chloride's influence on the membrane potential. This makes it more difficult for excitatory inputs from other synapses to change the potential when these chloride channels are simultaneously open (**Figure 6.30**). Increased K^+ permeability, when it occurs in the postsynaptic cell, also produces an IPSP. Earlier, we noted that if a cell membrane were permeable only to potassium ions, the resting membrane potential would equal the K^+ equilibrium potential; that is, the resting membrane potential would be about −90 mV instead of −70 mV. Thus, with increased K^+ permeability, more potassium ions leave the cell and the membrane moves closer to the K^+ equilibrium potential, causing a hyperpolarization.

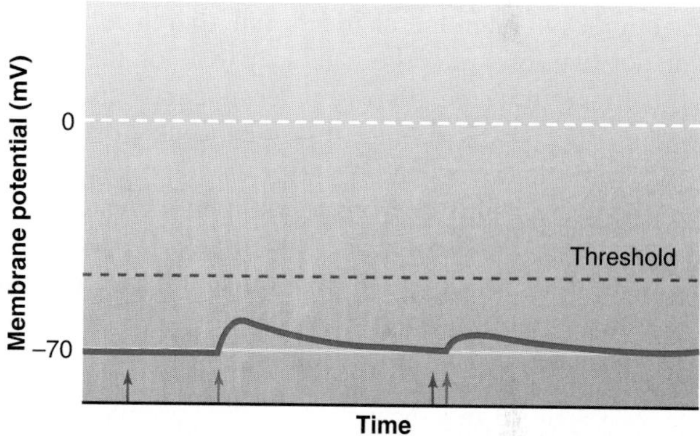

Figure 6.30 Synaptic inhibition of postsynaptic cells where E_{Cl} is equal to the resting membrane potential. Stimulation of a presynaptic neuron releasing a neurotransmitter that opens chloride channels (red arrows) has no direct effect on the postsynaptic membrane potential. However, when an excitatory synapse is simultaneously activated (green arrows), chloride movement into the cell diminishes the EPSP.

6.11 Synaptic Integration

In most neurons, one excitatory synaptic event by itself is not enough to reach threshold in the postsynaptic neuron. For example, a single EPSP may be only 0.5 mV, whereas changes of about 15 mV are necessary to depolarize the neuron's membrane to threshold. This being the case, an action potential can be initiated only by the combined effects of many excitatory synapses.

Of the thousands of synapses on any one neuron, probably hundreds are active simultaneously or close enough in time that the effects can add together. The membrane potential of the postsynaptic neuron at any moment is, therefore, the result of all the synaptic activity affecting it at that moment. A depolarization of the membrane toward threshold occurs when excitatory synaptic input predominates, and either a hyperpolarization or stabilization occurs when inhibitory input predominates.

A simple experiment can demonstrate how EPSPs and IPSPs interact, as shown in **Figure 6.31**. Assume there are three synaptic inputs to the postsynaptic cell. The synapses from axons A and B are excitatory, and the synapse from axon C is inhibitory. There are laboratory stimulators on axons A, B, and C so that each can be activated individually. An electrode is placed in the cell body of the postsynaptic neuron that will record the membrane potential. In part 1 of the experiment, we will test the interaction of two EPSPs by stimulating axon A and then, after a short time, stimulating it again. Part 1 of Figure 6.31 shows that no interaction occurs between the two EPSPs. The reason is that the change in membrane potential associated with an EPSP is fairly short-lived. Within a few milliseconds (by the time we stimulate axon A for the second time), the postsynaptic cell has returned to its resting condition.

In part 2, we stimulate axon A for the second time before the first EPSP has died away; the second synaptic potential adds to the previous one and creates a greater depolarization than from one input alone. This is called **temporal summation** because the input signals arrive from the same presynaptic cell at different *times*. The potentials summate because there are a greater number of open ion channels and, therefore, a greater flow of positive ions into the cell. In part 3 of Figure 6.31, axon B is first stimulated alone to determine its response, and then axons A and B are stimulated simultaneously. The EPSPs resulting from input from the two separate neurons also summate in the postsynaptic neuron, resulting in a greater degree of depolarization. Although it clearly is necessary that stimulation of A and B occur closely in time for summation to occur, this is called **spatial summation** because the two inputs occurred at different *locations* on the cell. The interaction of multiple EPSPs through spatial and temporal summation can increase the inward flow of positive ions and bring the postsynaptic membrane to threshold so that action potentials are initiated (see part 4 of Figure 6.31).

So far, we have tested only the patterns of interaction of excitatory synapses. Because EPSPs and IPSPs are due to oppositely directed local currents, they tend to cancel each other, and there is little or no net change in membrane potential when both A and C are stimulated (see Figure 6.31, part 5). Inhibitory potentials can also show spatial and temporal summation.

Depending on the postsynaptic membrane's resistance and on the amount of charge moving through the ligand-gated channels, the synaptic potential will spread to a greater or lesser degree across the plasma membrane of the cell. The membrane of a large area of the cell becomes slightly depolarized during activation of an excitatory synapse and slightly hyperpolarized or stabilized during activation of an inhibitory synapse, although these graded potentials will decrease with distance from the synaptic junction (**Figure 6.32**). Inputs from more than one synapse can result in summation of the synaptic potentials, which may then trigger an action potential.

In the previous examples, we referred to the threshold of the postsynaptic neuron as though it were the same for all parts of the cell. However, different parts of the neuron have different thresholds. In general, the initial segment has a more negative threshold (i.e., much closer to the resting potential) than the membrane of the cell body and dendrites. This is due to a higher density of voltage-gated Na^+ channels in this area of the membrane. Therefore, the initial segment is most responsive to small changes in the membrane potential that occur in response to synaptic potentials on the cell body and dendrites. The initial segment reaches threshold whenever enough EPSPs summate. The resulting action potential is then propagated from this point down the axon.

The fact that the initial segment usually has the lowest threshold explains why the locations of individual synapses on the postsynaptic cell are important. A synapse located near the initial segment will produce a greater voltage change in the initial segment than will a synapse on the outermost branch of a

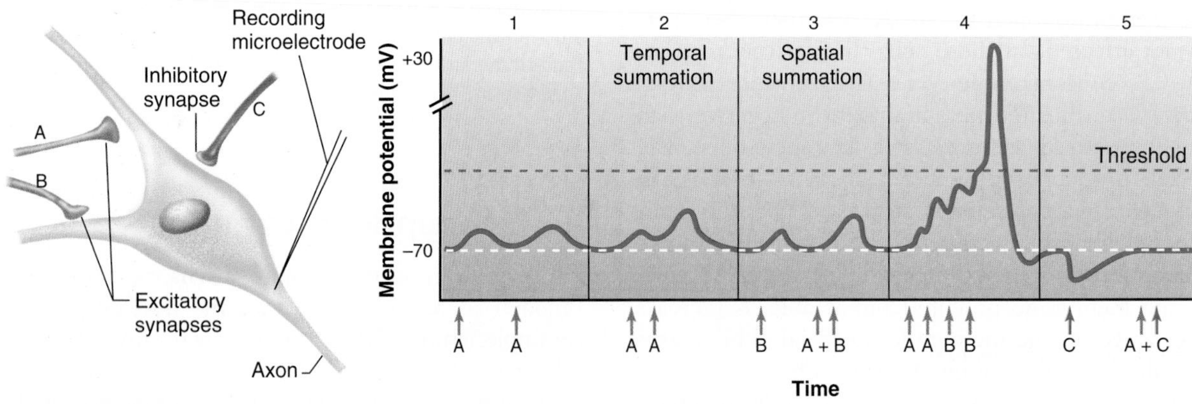

Figure 6.31 Interaction of EPSPs and IPSPs at the postsynaptic neuron. Presynaptic neurons (A–C) were stimulated at times indicated by the arrows, and the resulting membrane potential was recorded in the postsynaptic cell by a recording microelectrode.

PHYSIOLOGICAL INQUIRY

- How might the traces in panel 5 be different if the excitatory synapse (A) was much closer to the initial segment than the inhibitory synapse (C)?

Answer can be found at end of chapter.

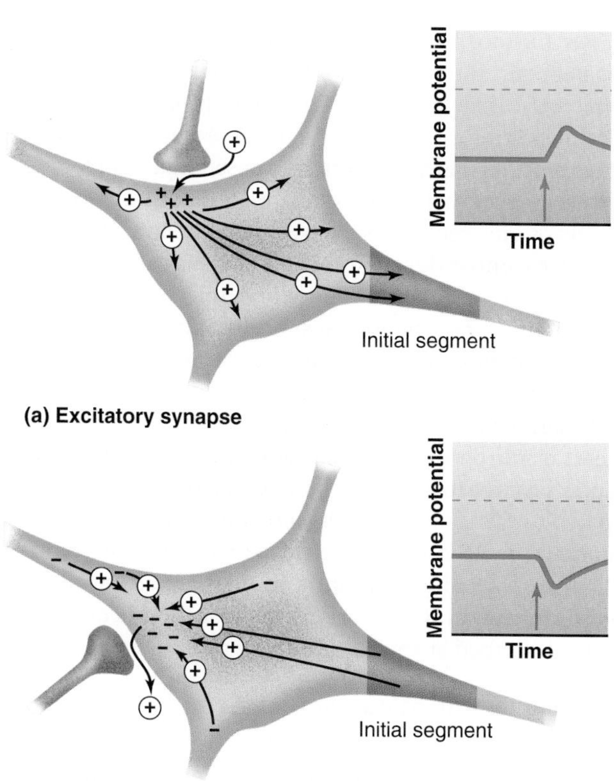

Figure 6.32 Comparison of excitatory and inhibitory synapses, showing current direction through the postsynaptic cell following synaptic activation. (a) Current through the postsynaptic cell is away from the excitatory synapse and may depolarize the initial segment. (b) Current through the postsynaptic cell is toward the inhibitory synapse and may hyperpolarize the initial segment. The arrow on the graph indicates moment of stimulus.

dendrite because it will expose the initial segment to a larger local current. In some neurons, however, signals from dendrites distant from the initial segment may be boosted by the presence of some voltage-gated Na^+ channels in parts of those dendrites.

Postsynaptic potentials last much longer than action potentials. In the event that cumulative EPSPs cause the initial segment to still be depolarized to threshold after an action potential has been fired and the refractory period is over, a second action potential will occur. In fact, as long as the membrane is depolarized to threshold, action potentials will continue to arise. Neuronal responses almost always occur in bursts of action potentials rather than as single, isolated events.

6.12 Synaptic Strength

Individual synaptic events—whether excitatory or inhibitory—have been presented as though their effects are constant and reproducible. Actually, enormous variability occurs in the postsynaptic potentials that follow a presynaptic input. The effectiveness or strength of a given synapse is influenced by both presynaptic and postsynaptic mechanisms.

A presynaptic terminal does not release a constant amount of neurotransmitter every time it is activated. One reason for this variation involves Ca^{2+} concentration. Calcium ions that have entered the terminal during previous action potentials are pumped out of the cell or (temporarily) into intracellular organelles. If Ca^{2+} removal does not keep up with entry, as can occur during high-frequency stimulation, Ca^{2+} concentration in the terminal, and consequently the amount of neurotransmitter released upon subsequent stimulation, will be greater than usual. The greater the amount of neurotransmitter released, the greater the number of ion channels opened in the postsynaptic membrane and the larger the amplitude of the EPSP or IPSP in the postsynaptic cell.

The neurotransmitter output of some presynaptic terminals is also altered by activation of membrane receptors on the terminals themselves. Activation of these presynaptic receptors influences Ca^{2+} influx into the terminal and thus the number of neurotransmitter vesicles that release neurotransmitter into the synaptic cleft. These presynaptic receptors may be associated with a second synaptic ending known as an **axo–axonic synapse,** in which an axon terminal of one neuron ends on an axon terminal of another. For example, in **Figure 6.33**, the neurotransmitter released by A binds with receptors on B, resulting in a change in the amount of neurotransmitter released from B in response to action potentials. Thus, neuron A has no direct effect on neuron C, but it has an important influence on the ability of B to influence C. Neuron A is thus exerting a presynaptic effect on the synapse between B and C. Depending upon the type of presynaptic receptors activated by the neurotransmitter from neuron A, the presynaptic effect may decrease the amount of neurotransmitter released from B (**presynaptic inhibition**) or increase it (**presynaptic facilitation**).

Axo–axonic synapses such as A in Figure 6.33 can alter the Ca^{2+} concentration in axon terminal B or even affect neurotransmitter synthesis there. The mechanisms bringing about these effects vary from synapse to synapse. The receptors on the

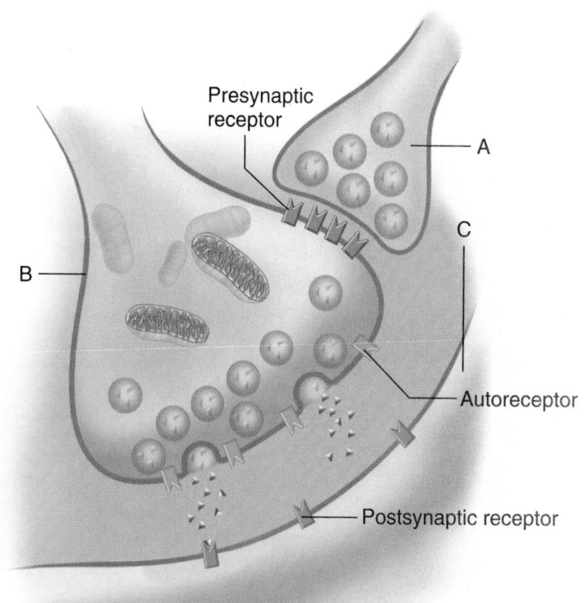

Figure 6.33 AP|R A presynaptic (axo–axonic) synapse between axon terminal A and axon terminal B. Cell C is postsynaptic to cell B.

axon terminal of neuron B could be ionotropic, in which case the membrane potential of the terminal is rapidly and directly affected by neurotransmitter from A; or they might be metabotropic, in which case the alteration of synaptic machinery by second messengers is generally slower in onset and longer in duration. In either case, if the Ca^{2+} concentration in axon terminal B increases, the number of vesicles releasing neurotransmitter from B increases. Decreased Ca^{2+} reduces the number of vesicles releasing transmitter. Axo–axonic synapses are important because they selectively control one specific input to the postsynaptic neuron C. This type of synapse is particularly common in the modulation of sensory input, for example, in the modulation of pain pathways (discussed in the next chapter, see Figure 7.16).

Some receptors on the presynaptic terminal are not associated with axo–axonic synapses. Instead, they are activated by neurotransmitters or other chemical messengers released by nearby neurons or glia or even by the axon terminal itself. In the last case, the receptors are called **autoreceptors** (see Figure 6.33) and provide an important feedback mechanism that the neuron can use to regulate its own neurotransmitter output. In most cases, the released neurotransmitter acts on autoreceptors to decrease its own release, thereby providing negative feedback control.

Postsynaptic mechanisms for varying synaptic strength also exist. For example, as described in Chapter 5, many types and subtypes of receptors exist for each kind of neurotransmitter. The different receptor types operate by different signal transduction mechanisms and can have different—sometimes even opposite—effects on the postsynaptic mechanisms they influence. A given signal transduction mechanism may be regulated by multiple neurotransmitters, and the various second-messenger systems affecting a channel may interact with each other.

Recall, too, from Chapter 5 that the number of receptors is not constant, varying with up- and down-regulation, for example. Also, the ability of a given receptor to respond to its neurotransmitter can change. Thus, in some systems, a receptor responds normally when first exposed to a neurotransmitter but then eventually fails to respond despite the continued presence of the receptor's neurotransmitter, a phenomenon known as **receptor desensitization.** This is part of the reason that drug abusers sometimes develop a tolerance to drugs that elevate certain brain neurotransmitters, forcing them to take increasing amounts of the drug to get the desired effect (see Chapter 8).

Imagine the complexity when a cotransmitter (or several cotransmitters) is released with the neurotransmitter to act upon postsynaptic receptors and maybe upon presynaptic receptors as well! Clearly, the possible variations in transmission are great at even a single synapse, and these provide mechanisms by which synaptic strength can be altered in response to changing conditions, part of the phenomenon of *plasticity* described at the beginning of this chapter.

Modification of Synaptic Transmission by Drugs and Disease

The great majority of therapeutic, illicit, and so-called "recreational" drugs that act on the nervous system do so by altering synaptic mechanisms and thus synaptic strength. Drugs act by interfering with or stimulating normal processes in the neuron involved in neurotransmitter synthesis, storage, and release, and in receptor activation. The synaptic mechanisms labeled in **Figure 6.34** are important to synaptic function and are vulnerable to the effects of drugs.

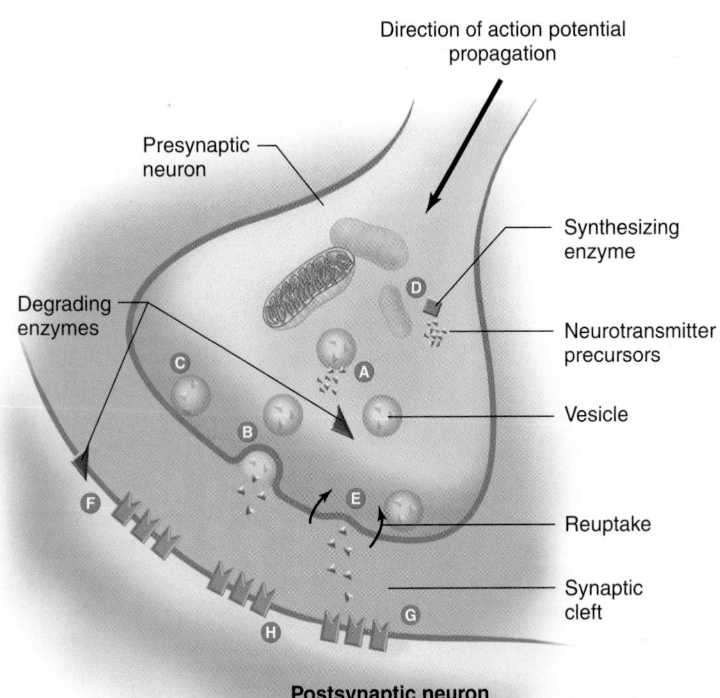

A drug might

- **A** increase leakage of neurotransmitter from vesicle to cytoplasm, exposing it to enzyme breakdown.
- **B** increase transmitter release into cleft.
- **C** block transmitter release.
- **D** inhibit transmitter synthesis.
- **E** block transmitter reuptake.
- **F** block cleft enzymes that metabolize transmitter.
- **G** bind to receptor on postsynaptic membrane to block (antagonist) or mimic (agonist) transmitter action.
- **H** inhibit or stimulate second-messenger activity within postsynaptic cell.

Figure 6.34 APIR Possible actions of drugs on a synapse.

The long-term effects of drugs are sometimes difficult to predict because the imbalances the initial drug action produces are soon counteracted by feedback mechanisms that normally regulate the processes. For example, if a drug interferes with the action of a neurotransmitter by inhibiting the rate-limiting enzyme in its synthetic pathway, the neurons may respond by increasing the rate of precursor transport into the axon terminals to maximize the use of any available enzyme.

Recall from Chapter 5 that drugs that bind to a receptor and produce a response similar to the normal activation of that receptor are called **agonists,** and drugs that bind to the receptor but are unable to activate it are **antagonists.** By occupying the receptors, antagonists prevent binding of the normal neurotransmitter at the synapse. Specific agonists and antagonists can affect receptors on both presynaptic and postsynaptic membranes.

Diseases can also affect synaptic mechanisms. For example, the neurological disorder tetanus is caused by the bacillus *Clostridium tetani,* which produces a toxin (***tetanus toxin***). This toxin is a protease that destroys SNARE proteins in the presynaptic terminal so that fusion of vesicles with the membrane is prevented, inhibiting neurotransmitter release. Tetanus toxin specifically affects inhibitory neurons in the CNS that normally are important in suppressing the neurons that lead to skeletal muscle activation. Therefore, tetanus toxin results in an increase in muscle contraction and a rigid, or spastic paralysis. Toxins of the *Clostridium botulinum* bacilli, which cause ***botulism,*** also block neurotransmitter release from synaptic vesicles by destroying SNARE proteins. However, they target the excitatory synapses that activate skeletal muscles; consequently, botulism is characterized by reduced muscle contraction, or a flaccid paralysis. Low doses of one type of botulinum toxin (***Botox***) are injected therapeutically to treat a number of conditions, including facial wrinkles, severe sweating, uncontrollable blinking, misalignment of the eyes, and others.

Table 6.5 summarizes the factors that determine synaptic strength.

TABLE 6.5 Factors That Determine Synaptic Strength

I. Presynaptic factors
   A. Availability of neurotransmitter
      1. Availability of precursor molecules
      2. Amount (or activity) of the rate-limiting enzyme in the pathway for neurotransmitter synthesis
   B. Axon terminal membrane potential
   C. Axon terminal Ca^{2+}
   D. Activation of membrane receptors on presynaptic terminal
      1. Axo–axonic synapses
      2. Autoreceptors
      3. Other receptors
   E. Certain drugs and diseases, which act via the above mechanisms A–D

II. Postsynaptic factors
   A. Immediate past history of electrical state of postsynaptic membrane (e.g., excitation or inhibition from temporal or spatial summation)
   B. Effects of other neurotransmitters or neuromodulators acting on postsynaptic neuron
   C. Up- or down-regulation and desensitization of receptors
   D. Certain drugs and diseases

III. General factors
   A. Area of synaptic contact
   B. Enzymatic destruction of neurotransmitter
   C. Geometry of diffusion path
   D. Neurotransmitter reuptake

6.13 Neurotransmitters and Neuromodulators

We have emphasized the role of neurotransmitters in eliciting EPSPs and IPSPs. However, certain chemical messengers elicit complex responses that cannot be described as simply EPSPs or IPSPs. The word *modulation* is used for these complex responses, and the messengers that cause them are called **neuromodulators.** The distinctions between neuromodulators and neurotransmitters are not always clear. In fact, certain neuromodulators are often synthesized by the presynaptic cell and coreleased with the neurotransmitter. To add to the complexity, many hormones, paracrine factors, and messengers used by the immune system serve as neuromodulators.

Neuromodulators often modify the postsynaptic cell's response to specific neurotransmitters, amplifying or dampening the effectiveness of ongoing synaptic activity. Alternatively, they may change the presynaptic cell's synthesis, release, reuptake, or metabolism of a transmitter. In other words, they alter the effectiveness of the synapse.

In general, the receptors for neurotransmitters influence ion channels that directly affect excitation or inhibition of the postsynaptic cell. These mechanisms operate within milliseconds. Receptors for neuromodulators, on the other hand, more often bring about changes in metabolic processes in neurons, often via G proteins coupled to second-messenger systems. Such changes, which can occur over minutes, hours, or even days, include alterations in enzyme activity or, through influences on DNA transcription, in protein synthesis. Thus, neurotransmitters are involved in rapid communication, whereas neuromodulators tend to be associated with slower events such as learning, development, motivational states, and some types of sensory or motor activities.

The number of substances known to act as neurotransmitters or neuromodulators is large and still growing. **Table 6.6** provides a framework for categorizing that list. A huge amount of information has accumulated concerning the synthesis, metabolism, and mechanisms of action of these messengers—material well beyond the scope of this book. The following sections will therefore present only some basic generalizations about some of the neurotransmitters that are deemed most important. For simplicity's sake, we use the term *neurotransmitter* in a general sense, realizing that sometimes the messenger may be described more appropriately as a neuromodulator. A note on terminology should also be included here. Neurons are often referred to using the suffix *-ergic;* the missing prefix is the type of neurotransmitter the neuron releases. For example, *dopaminergic* applies to neurons that release the neurotransmitter dopamine.

TABLE 6.6	Classes of Some of the Chemicals Known or Presumed to Be Neurotransmitters or Neuromodulators
I. Acetylcholine (ACh)	
II. Biogenic amines A. Catecholamines 1. Dopamine (DA) 2. Norepinephrine (NE) 3. Epinephrine (Epi) B. Serotonin (5-hydroxytryptamine, 5-HT) C. Histamine	
III. Amino acids A. Excitatory amino acids; for example, glutamate B. Inhibitory amino acids; for example, gamma-aminobutyric acid (GABA) and glycine	
VI. Neuropeptides For example, endogenous opioids, oxytocin, tachykinins	
V. Gases For example, nitric oxide, carbon monoxide, hydrogen sulfide	
VI. Purines For example, adenosine and ATP	

Acetylcholine

Acetylcholine (ACh) is a major neurotransmitter in the PNS at the neuromuscular junction (Chapter 9) and in the brain. Neurons that release ACh are called **cholinergic** neurons. The cell bodies of the brain's cholinergic neurons are concentrated in relatively few areas, but their axons are widely distributed.

Acetylcholine is synthesized from choline (a common nutrient found in many foods) and acetyl coenzyme A in the cytoplasm of synaptic terminals and stored in synaptic vesicles. After it is released and activates receptors on the postsynaptic membrane, the concentration of ACh at the postsynaptic membrane decreases (thereby stopping receptor activation) due to the action of the enzyme **acetylcholinesterase.** This enzyme is located on the presynaptic and postsynaptic membranes and rapidly destroys ACh, releasing choline and acetate. The choline is then transported back into the presynaptic axon terminals where it is reused in the synthesis of new ACh. The ACh concentration at the receptors is also reduced by simple diffusion away from the synapse and eventual breakdown of the molecule by an enzyme in the blood. Some chemical weapons, such as the nerve gas ***Sarin,*** inhibit acetylcholinesterase, causing a buildup of ACh in the synaptic cleft. This results in overstimulation of postsynaptic ACh receptors, initially causing uncontrolled muscle contractions but ultimately leading to receptor desensitization and paralysis.

There are two general types of ACh receptors, and they are distinguished by their responsiveness to two different chemicals. Recall that although a receptor is considered specific for a given ligand, such as ACh, most receptors will recognize natural or synthetic compounds that exhibit some degree of chemical similarity to that ligand. Some ACh receptors respond not only to acetylcholine but to the drug nicotine and have therefore come to be known as **nicotinic receptors.** ***Nicotine*** is a plant alkaloid compound that constitutes 1% to 2% of tobacco products. It is also contained in treatments for smoking cessation, such as nasal sprays, chewing gums, and transdermal patches. Nicotine's hydrophobic structure allows rapid absorption through lung capillaries, mucous membranes, skin, and the blood–brain barrier. The nicotinic acetylcholine receptor is an excellent example of a receptor that contains an ion channel (i.e., a ligand-gated channel). In this case, the channel is permeable to both sodium and potassium ions, but because Na^+ has the larger electrochemical driving force, the net effect of opening these channels is depolarization. Nicotinic receptors are present at the neuromuscular junction and, as Chapter 9 will explain, several nicotinic receptor antagonists are toxins that induce paralysis. Nicotinic receptors in the brain are important in cognitive functions and behavior. For example, one cholinergic system that employs nicotinic receptors plays a major role in attention, learning, and memory by reinforcing the ability to detect and respond to meaningful stimuli. The presence of nicotinic receptors on presynaptic terminals in reward pathways of the brain explains why tobacco products are among the most highly addictive substances known.

The other general type of cholinergic receptor is stimulated not only by acetylcholine but by the mushroom poison muscarine; therefore, these are called **muscarinic receptors.** These receptors couple with G proteins, which then alter the activity of a number of different enzymes and ion channels. They are prevalent at some cholinergic synapses in the brain and at junctions where a major division of the PNS innervates peripheral glands and organs, like salivary glands and the heart. ***Atropine*** is an antagonist of muscarinic receptors with many clinical uses, such as in eyedrops that relax the muscles of the iris, thereby dilating the pupils for an eye exam.

Neurons associated with the ACh system degenerate in people with ***Alzheimer disease*** (also called *Alzheimer's disease*), a brain disease that is usually age related and is the most common cause of declining intellectual function in late life. Alzheimer disease affects 10% to 15% of people over age 65, and 50% of people over age 85. Because of the degeneration of cholinergic neurons, this disease is associated with a decreased amount of ACh in certain areas of the brain and even the loss of the postsynaptic neurons that would have responded to it. These defects and those in other neurotransmitter systems that are affected in this disease are related to the declining language and perceptual abilities, confusion, and memory loss that characterize Alzheimer disease sufferers. Several genetic mechanisms have been identified as potential contributors to increased risk of developing Alzheimer disease. One example is a gene on chromosome 19 that codes for a protein involved in carrying cholesterol in the bloodstream. Mutations of genes on chromosomes 1, 14, and 21 are associated with abnormally increased concentrations of ***beta-amyloid protein,*** which is associated with neuronal cell death in a severe form of the disease that can begin as early as 30 years of age. This emerging picture of genetic risk factors is complex, and in some cases it appears that multiple genes are simultaneously involved. Some research also suggests that lifestyle factors like diet, exercise, social engagement, and mental stimulation may play a role in determining whether cholinergic neurons are lost and Alzheimer disease develops.

Biogenic Amines

The **biogenic amines** are small, charged molecules that are synthesized from amino acids and contain an amino group (R—NH_2). The most common biogenic amines are dopamine, norepinephrine, serotonin, and histamine. Epinephrine, another biogenic amine, is not a common neurotransmitter in the CNS but is the major *hormone* secreted by the adrenal medulla. Norepinephrine is an important neurotransmitter in both the central and peripheral components of the nervous system.

Catecholamines

Dopamine, norepinephrine (NE), and **epinephrine** all contain a catechol ring (a six-carbon ring with two adjacent hydroxyl groups) and an amine group, which is why they are called **catecholamines.** The catecholamines are formed from the amino acid tyrosine and share the same two initial steps in their synthetic pathway (**Figure 6.35**). Synthesis of catecholamines begins with the uptake of tyrosine by the axon terminals and its conversion to another precursor, L-dihydroxy-phenylalanine (**L-dopa**) by the rate-limiting enzyme in the pathway, tyrosine hydroxylase. Depending on the enzymes present in the terminals, any one of the three catecholamines may ultimately be released. Autoreceptors on the presynaptic terminals strongly modulate synthesis and release of the catecholamines.

After activation of the receptors on the postsynaptic cell, the catecholamine concentration in the synaptic cleft declines, mainly because a membrane transporter protein actively transports the catecholamine back into the axon terminal. The catecholamine neurotransmitters are also broken down in both the extracellular fluid and the axon terminal by enzymes such as **monoamine oxidase (MAO).** Drugs known as MAO inhibitors increase the amount of norepinephrine and dopamine in a synapse by slowing their metabolic degradation. They are used in the treatment of mood disorders such as some types of depression.

Within the CNS, the cell bodies of the catecholamine-releasing neurons lie in parts of the brain called the brainstem and hypothalamus. Although these neurons are relatively few in number, their axons branch greatly and go to virtually all parts of the brain and spinal cord. These neurotransmitters play essential roles in states of consciousness, mood, motivation, directed attention, movement, blood pressure regulation, and hormone release, functions that will be covered in more detail in Chapters 8, 10, 11, and 12.

For historical reasons having to do with nineteenth-century British physiologists referring to secretions of the adrenal gland as "adrenaline," the adjective "**adrenergic**" is commonly used to describe neurons that release norepinephrine or epinephrine and also to describe the receptors to which those chemicals bind. There are two major classes of receptors for norepinephrine and epinephrine: **alpha-adrenergic receptors** and **beta-adrenergic receptors** (also called alpha-adrenoceptors and beta-adrenoceptors). All catecholamine receptors are metabotropic, and thus use second messengers to transfer a signal from the surface of the cell to the cytoplasm. Beta-adrenoceptors act via stimulatory G proteins to increase cAMP in the postsynaptic cell. There are three subclasses of beta-receptors, β_1, β_2, and β_3, which function in different ways in different tissues (as will be described in Section D and Table 6.11). Alpha-adrenoceptors exist in two subclasses, α_1 and α_2. They act presynaptically to inhibit norepinephrine release (α_2) or postsynaptically to either stimulate or inhibit the activity of different types of K^+ channels (α_1). The subclasses of alpha- and beta-receptors are distinguished by the drugs that influence them and their second-messenger systems.

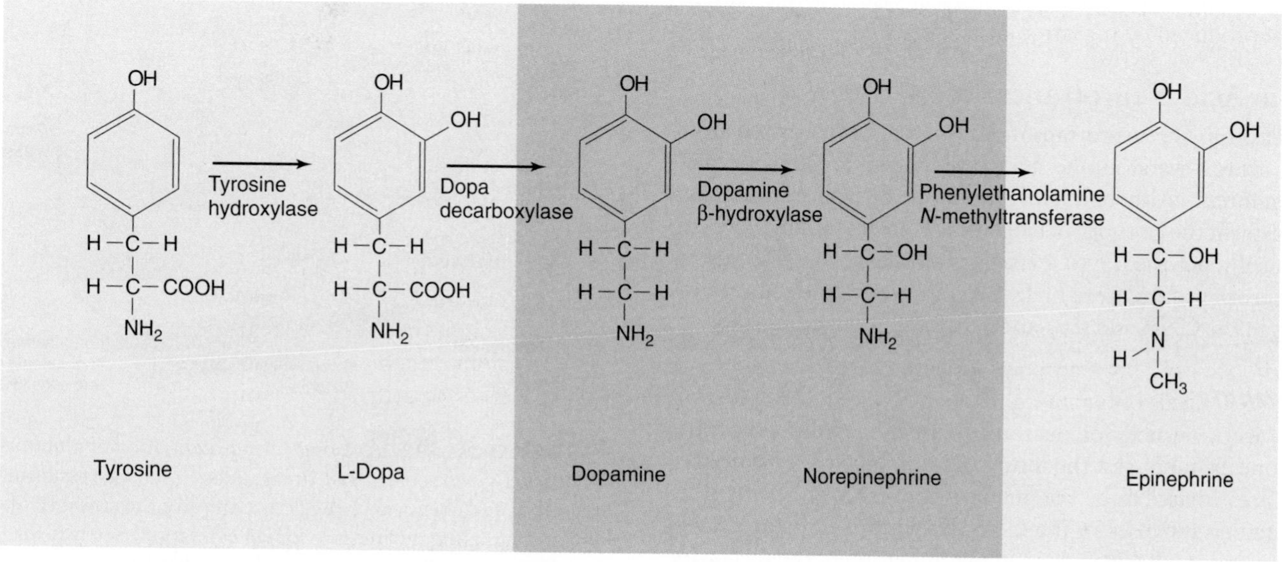

Figure 6.35 Catecholamine biosynthetic pathway. Tyrosine hydroxylase is the rate-limiting enzyme, but which neurotransmitter is ultimately released from a neuron depends on which of the other three enzymes are present in that cell. The dark-colored box indicates the more common CNS catecholamine neurotransmitters.

Serotonin

Though not a catecholamine, **serotonin** (5-hydroxy-tryptamine, or 5-HT) is an important biogenic amine. It is produced from tryptophan, an essential amino acid. Its effects generally have a slow onset, indicating that it works as a neuromodulator. Serotonergic neurons innervate virtually every structure in the brain and spinal cord and operate via at least 16 different receptor types.

In general, serotonin has an excitatory effect on pathways that are involved in the control of muscles, and an inhibitory effect on pathways that mediate sensations. The activity of serotonergic neurons is lowest or absent during sleep and highest during states of alert wakefulness. In addition to their contributions to motor activity and sleep, serotonergic pathways also function in the regulation of food intake, bone remodeling, reproductive behavior, and emotional states such as mood and anxiety.

Selective serotonin reuptake inhibitors such as ***paroxetine*** (***Paxil***) are thought to aid in the treatment of depression by inactivating the 5-HT transporter and increasing the synaptic concentration of the neurotransmitter. Interestingly, such drugs are often associated with decreased appetite but paradoxically cause weight gain due to disruption of enzymatic pathways that regulate fuel metabolism. Recent reports also suggest that bone density may be reduced in people taking this class of drugs. This is one example of how the use of reuptake inhibitors for a specific neurotransmitter—one with widespread actions—can cause unwanted side effects. Serotonin is found in both neural and nonneural cells, with the majority located outside of the CNS. In fact, approximately 90% of the body's total serotonin is found in the digestive system, 8% is in blood platelets and immune cells, and only 1% to 2% is found in the brain.

The drug lysergic acid diethylamide (***LSD***) stimulates the 5-HT_{2A} subtype of serotonin receptor and alters its interaction with glutamate receptors in the brain. Though the mechanism is not completely understood, alteration of this receptor complex produces the intense visual hallucinations that are produced by ingestion of LSD.

Amino Acid Neurotransmitters

In addition to the neurotransmitters that are synthesized from amino acids, several amino acids themselves function as neurotransmitters. Although the amino acid neurotransmitters chemically fit the category of biogenic amines, neurophysiologists traditionally put them into a category of their own. The amino acid neurotransmitters are by far the most prevalent neurotransmitters in the CNS, and they affect virtually all neurons there.

Glutamate

There are a number of **excitatory amino acids, aspartate** being one example, but the most common by far is **glutamate,** which is estimated to be the primary neurotransmitter at 50% of excitatory synapses in the CNS. As with other neurotransmitter systems, pharmacological manipulation of the receptors for glutamate has permitted identification of specific receptor subtypes by their ability to bind natural and synthetic ligands. Although metabotropic glutamate receptors do exist, the vast majority are ionotropic, with two important subtypes being found in postsynaptic membranes. They are designated as **AMPA receptors** (identified by their binding to α-amino-3 hydroxy-5 methyl-4 isoxazole propionic acid) and **NMDA receptors** (which bind *N*-methyl-D-aspartate).

Cooperative activity of AMPA and NMDA receptors has been implicated in one type of a phenomenon called **long-term potentiation (LTP)**. This mechanism couples frequent activity across a synapse with lasting changes in the strength of signaling across that synapse, and is thus thought to be one of the major cellular processes involved in learning and memory. **Figure 6.36** outlines the mechanism in stepwise fashion. When a presynaptic neuron fires action potentials (step 1), glutamate is released from presynaptic terminals (step 2) and binds to both AMPA and NMDA receptors on postsynaptic membranes (step 3). AMPA receptors function just like the excitatory postsynaptic receptors discussed earlier—when glutamate binds, the channel becomes permeable to both Na^+ and K^+, but the larger entry of Na^+ creates a depolarizing EPSP of the postsynaptic cell (step 4). By contrast, NMDA-receptor channels also mediate a substantial Ca^{2+} flux, but opening them requires more than just glutamate binding. A magnesium ion blocks NMDA channels when the membrane voltage is near the negative resting potential, and to drive it out of the way the membrane must be significantly depolarized by the current through AMPA channels (step 5). This explains why it requires a high frequency of presynaptic action potentials to complete

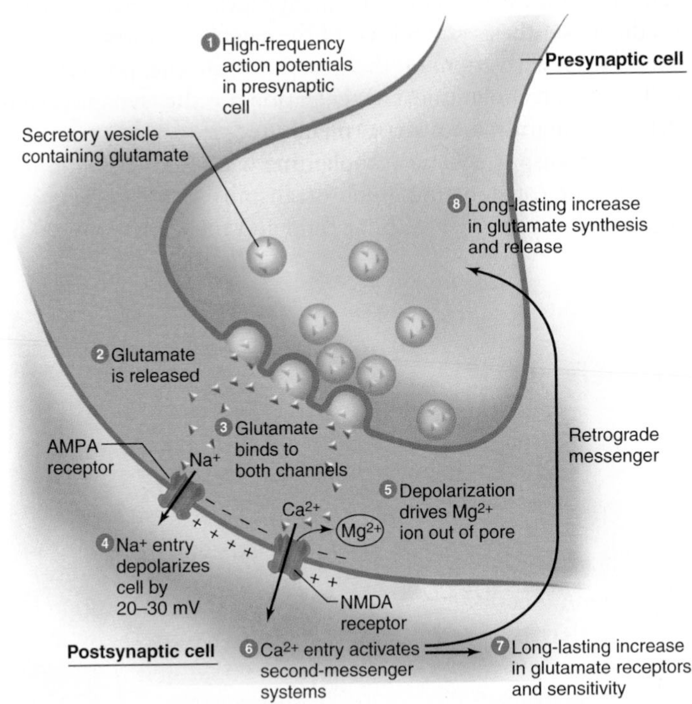

Figure 6.36 AP|R Long-term potentiation at glutamatergic synapses. Episodes of intense firing across a synapse result in structural and chemical changes that amplify the strength of synaptic signaling during subsequent activation. See text for description of each step; details of the mechanism linking steps 1 and 2 were described in Figure 6.27. Note that both AMPA and NMDA receptors are nonspecific cation channels that also allow K^+ flux, but the net Na^+ and Ca^{2+} fluxes indicated are most relevant to the LTP mechanism, as described in the text.

the long-term potentiation mechanism. At low frequencies, there is insufficient temporal summation of AMPA-receptor EPSPs to provide the 20–30 mV of depolarization needed to move the magnesium ion, and so the NMDA receptors do not open. When the depolarization is sufficient, however, NMDA receptors do open, allowing Ca^{2+} to enter the postsynaptic cell (step 6). Calcium ions then activate a second-messenger cascade in the postsynaptic cell that includes persistent activation of multiple different protein kinases, stimulation of gene expression and protein synthesis, and ultimately a long-lasting increase in the sensitivity of the postsynaptic neuron to glutamate (step 7). This second-messenger system can also activate long-term enhancement of presynaptic glutamate release via retrograde signals that have not yet been identified (step 8). Each subsequent action potential arriving along this presynaptic cell will cause a greater depolarization of the postsynaptic membrane. Thus, repeatedly and intensely activating a particular pattern of synaptic firing (as you might when studying for an exam) causes chemical and structural changes that facilitate future activity along those same pathways (as might occur when recalling what you learned).

NMDA receptors have also been implicated in mediating **excitotoxicity.** This is a phenomenon in which the injury or death of some brain cells (due, for example, to blocked or ruptured blood vessels) rapidly spreads to adjacent regions. When glutamate-containing cells die and their membranes rupture, the flood of glutamate excessively stimulates AMPA and NMDA receptors on nearby neurons. The excessive stimulation of those neurons causes the accumulation of toxic concentrations of intracellular Ca^{2+}, which in turn kills those neurons and causes *them* to rupture, and the wave of damage progressively spreads. Recent experiments and clinical trials suggest that administering NMDA receptor antagonists may help minimize the spread of cell death following injuries to the brain.

GABA

GABA (gamma-aminobutyric acid) is the major inhibitory neurotransmitter in the brain. Although it is not one of the 20 amino acids used to build proteins, it is classified with the amino acid neurotransmitters because it is a modified form of glutamate. With few exceptions, GABA neurons in the brain are small interneurons that dampen activity within neural circuits. Postsynaptically, GABA may bind to ionotropic or metabotropic receptors. The ionotropic receptor increases Cl^- flux into the cell, resulting in hyperpolarization of the postsynaptic membrane. In addition to the GABA binding site, this receptor has several additional binding sites for other compounds, including steroids, barbiturates, and benzodiazepines. Benzodiazepine drugs such as ***alprazolam*** **(*Xanax*)** and ***diazepam*** **(*Valium*)** reduce anxiety, guard against seizures, and induce sleep by increasing Cl^- flux through the GABA receptor.

Synapses that use GABA are also among the many targets of the ethanol (ethyl alcohol) found in alcoholic beverages. Ethanol stimulates GABA synapses and simultaneously inhibits excitatory glutamate synapses, with the overall effect being global depression of the electrical activity of the brain. Thus, as a person's blood alcohol content increases, there is a progressive reduction in overall cognitive ability, along with sensory perception inhibition (hearing and balance, in particular), loss of motor coordination, impaired judgment, memory loss, and unconsciousness. Very high doses of ethanol are sometimes fatal, due to suppression of brainstem centers responsible for regulating the cardiovascular and respiratory systems. Dopaminergic and endogenous opioid signaling pathways (discussed in the next section) are also affected by ethanol, which results in short-term mood elevation or euphoria. The involvement of these pathways underlies the development of long-term alcohol dependence in some people.

Glycine

Glycine is the major neurotransmitter released from inhibitory interneurons in the spinal cord and brainstem. It binds to ionotropic receptors on postsynaptic cells that allow Cl^- to enter, thus preventing them from approaching the threshold for firing action potentials. Normal function of glycinergic neurons is essential for maintaining a balance of excitatory and inhibitory activity in spinal cord integrating centers that regulate skeletal muscle contraction. This becomes apparent in cases of poisoning with the neurotoxin ***strychnine,*** an antagonist of glycine receptors sometimes used to kill rodents. Victims experience hyperexcitability throughout the nervous system, which leads to convulsions, spastic contraction of skeletal muscles, and ultimately death due to impairment of the muscles of respiration.

Neuropeptides

The **neuropeptides** are composed of two or more amino acids linked together by peptide bonds. About 100 neuropeptides have been identified, but their physiological roles are not all known. It seems that evolution has selected the same chemical messengers for use in widely differing circumstances, and many of the neuropeptides have been previously identified in nonneural tissue where they function as hormones or paracrine substances. They generally retain the name they were given when first discovered in the nonneural tissue.

The neuropeptides are formed differently than other neurotransmitters, which are synthesized in the axon terminals by very few enzyme-mediated steps. The neuropeptides, in contrast, are derived from large precursor proteins, which in themselves have little, if any, inherent biological activity. The synthesis of these precursors, directed by mRNA, occurs on ribosomes, which exist only in the cell body and large dendrites of the neuron, often a considerable distance from axon terminals or varicosities where the peptides are released.

In the cell body, the precursor protein is packaged into vesicles, which are then moved by axonal transport into the terminals or varicosities (review Figure 6.3), where the protein is cleaved by specific peptidases. Many of the precursor proteins contain multiple peptides, which may be different or be copies of one peptide. Neurons that release one or more of the peptide neurotransmitters are collectively called **peptidergic.** In many cases, neuropeptides are cosecreted with another type of neurotransmitter and act as neuromodulators.

The amount of peptide released from vesicles at synapses is significantly lower than the amount of nonpeptidergic neurotransmitters such as catecholamines. In addition, neuropeptides can diffuse away from the synapse and affect other neurons at some distance, in which case they are referred to as neuromodulators. The actions of these neuromodulators are longer lasting (on the order of several hundred milliseconds) than when peptides or other molecules act as neurotransmitters. After release, peptides can interact with either ionotropic or metabotropic receptors. They are eventually broken down by peptidases located in neuronal membranes.

Endogenous opioids—a group of neuropeptides that includes **beta-endorphin,** the **dynorphins,** and the **enkephalins**—have attracted much interest because their receptors are the sites of action of opiate drugs such as ***morphine*** and ***codeine.*** The opiate drugs are powerful ***analgesics*** (that is, they relieve pain without loss of consciousness), and the endogenous opioids undoubtedly play a role in regulating pain. The opioids have been implicated as a possible contributor to a runner's "second wind," when the athlete feels a boost of energy and a decrease in pain and effort, and in the general feeling of well-being experienced after a bout of strenuous exercise, the so-called "runner's high." There is also evidence that the opioids play a role in eating and drinking behavior, in regulation of the cardiovascular system, and in mood and emotion.

Substance P, another of the neuropeptides, is a transmitter released by afferent neurons that relay sensory information into the CNS. It is known to be involved in pain sensation.

Gases

Surprisingly, certain very short-lived gases also serve as neurotransmitters. **Nitric oxide** is the best understood, but recent research indicates that **carbon monoxide** and **hydrogen sulfide** are also emitted by neurons as signals. Gases are not released by exocytosis of presynaptic vesicles, nor do they bind to postsynaptic plasma membrane receptors. They are produced by enzymes in axon terminals (in response to Ca^{2+} entry) and simply diffuse from their sites of origin in one cell into the intracellular fluid of other neurons or effector cells, where they bind to and activate proteins. For example, nitric oxide released from neurons activates guanylyl cyclase in recipient cells, which increases the concentration of the second-messenger cyclic GMP.

Nitric oxide plays a role in a bewildering array of neurally mediated events—learning, development, drug tolerance, penile and clitoral erection, and sensory and motor modulation, to name a few. Paradoxically, it is also implicated in neural damage that results, for example, from the stoppage of blood flow to the brain or from a head injury. In later chapters, we will see that nitric oxide is produced not only in the central and peripheral nervous systems but also by a variety of nonneural cells; it also plays an important paracrine role in the cardiovascular and immune systems, among others.

Purines

Other nontraditional neurotransmitters include the purines, **ATP** and **adenosine,** which act principally as neuromodulators. ATP is present in all presynaptic vesicles and is coreleased with one or more other neurotransmitters in response to Ca^{2+} influx into the terminal. Adenosine is derived from ATP via enzyme activity occurring in the extracellular compartment. Both presynaptic and postsynaptic receptors have been described for adenosine, and the roles these substances play in the nervous system and other tissues are active areas of research.

6.14 Neuroeffector Communication

Thus far, we have described the effects of neurotransmitters released at synapses between neurons. Many neurons of the PNS end, however, not at synapses on other neurons but at neuroeffector junctions on muscle, gland, and other cells. The neurotransmitters released by these efferent neurons' terminals or varicosities provide the link by which electrical activity of the nervous system regulates effector cell activity.

The events that occur at neuroeffector junctions are similar to those at synapses between neurons. The neurotransmitter is released from the efferent neuron upon the arrival of an action potential at the neuron's axon terminals or varicosities. The neurotransmitter then diffuses to the surface of the effector cell, where it binds to receptors on that cell's plasma membrane. The receptors may be directly under the axon terminal or varicosity, or they may be some distance away so that the diffusion path the neurotransmitter follows is long. The receptors on the effector cell may be either ionotropic or metabotropic. The response (such as altered muscle contraction or glandular secretion) of the effector cell will be described in later chapters. As we will see in the next section, the major neurotransmitters released at neuroeffector junctions are acetylcholine and norepinephrine.

SECTION C SUMMARY

I. An excitatory synapse brings the membrane of the postsynaptic cell closer to threshold. An inhibitory synapse prevents the postsynaptic cell from approaching threshold by hyperpolarizing or stabilizing the membrane potential.

II. Whether a postsynaptic cell fires action potentials depends on the number of synapses that are active and whether they are excitatory or inhibitory.

III. Neurotransmitters are chemical messengers that pass from one neuron to another and modify the electrical or metabolic function of the recipient cell.

Functional Anatomy of Synapses

I. Electrical synapses consist of gap junctions that allow current to flow between adjacent cells.

II. In chemical synapses, neurotransmitter molecules are stored in synaptic vesicles in the presynaptic axon terminal, and when released transmit the signal from a presynaptic to a postsynaptic neuron.

Mechanisms of Neurotransmitter Release

I. Depolarization of the axon terminal increases the Ca^{2+} concentration within the terminal, which causes the release of neurotransmitter into the synaptic cleft.

II. The neurotransmitter diffuses across the synaptic cleft and binds to receptors on the postsynaptic cell; the activated receptors usually open ion channels.

Activation of the Postsynaptic Cell

I. At an excitatory synapse, the electrical response in the postsynaptic cell is called an excitatory postsynaptic potential (EPSP). At inhibitory synapses, it is either an inhibitory postsynaptic potential (IPSP) or a stabilization of the membrane potential near resting levels.

II. Usually at an excitatory synapse, channels in the postsynaptic cell that are permeable to Na^+, K^+, and other small positive ions open, but Na^+ flux dominates, because it has the largest electrochemical gradient. At inhibitory synapses, channels to Cl^- or K^+ open.

Synaptic Integration

I. The postsynaptic cell's membrane potential is the result of temporal and spatial summation of the EPSPs and IPSPs at the many active excitatory and inhibitory synapses on the cell.
II. Action potentials are generally initiated by the temporal and spatial summation of many EPSPs.

Synaptic Strength

I. Synaptic strength is modified by presynaptic and postsynaptic events, drugs, and diseases (see Table 6.5).

Neurotransmitters and Neuromodulators

I. In general, neurotransmitters cause EPSPs and IPSPs, and neuromodulators cause, via second messengers, more complex metabolic effects in the postsynaptic cell.
II. The actions of neurotransmitters are usually faster than those of neuromodulators.
III. A substance can act as a neurotransmitter at one type of receptor and as a neuromodulator at another.
IV. The major classes of known or suspected neurotransmitters and neuromodulators are listed in Table 6.6.

Neuroeffector Communication

I. The synapse between a neuron and an effector cell is called a neuroeffector junction.
II. The events at a neuroeffector junction (release of neurotransmitter into an extracellular space, diffusion of neurotransmitter to the effector cell, and binding with a receptor on the effector cell) are similar to those at synapses between neurons.

SECTION C REVIEW QUESTIONS

1. Describe the structure of presynaptic axon terminals, and the mechanism of neurotransmitter release.
2. Contrast the postsynaptic mechanisms of excitatory and inhibitory synapses.
3. Explain how synapses allow neurons to act as integrators; include the concepts of facilitation, temporal and spatial summation, and convergence in your explanation.
4. List at least eight ways in which the effectiveness of synapses may be altered.
5. Discuss differences between neurotransmitters and neuromodulators.
6. List the major classes of neurotransmitters, and give examples of each.
7. Detail the mechanism of long-term potentiation, and explain what role it might play in learning and memory.

SECTION C KEY TERMS

acetylcholine (ACh) 168
acetylcholinesterase 168
active zones 161
adenosine 172
adrenergic 169
agonist 167
alpha-adrenergic receptor 169
AMPA receptor 170
antagonist 167
aspartate 170
ATP 172
autoreceptor 166
axo–axonic synapse 165
beta-adrenergic receptor 169
beta-endorphin 172
biogenic amine 169
carbon monoxide 172
catecholamine 169
chemical synapse 161
cholinergic 168
convergence 160
cotransmitter 161
divergence 160
dopamine 169
dynorphin 172
electrical synapse 161
endogenous opioid 172
enkephalin 172
epinephrine 169
excitatory amino acid 170
excitatory postsynaptic potential (EPSP) 163
excitatory synapse 160
excitotoxicity 171
GABA (gamma-aminobutyric acid) 171
glutamate 170
glycine 171
hydrogen sulfide 172
inhibitory postsynaptic potential (IPSP) 163
inhibitory synapse 160
ionotropic receptor 162
L-dopa 169
long-term potentiation (LTP) 170
metabotropic receptor 162
monoamine oxidase (MAO) 169
muscarinic receptor 168
neuromodulator 167
neuropeptide 171
nicotinic receptor 168
nitric oxide 172
NMDA receptor 170
norepinephrine (NE) 169
peptidergic 171
postsynaptic density 161
presynaptic facilitation 165
presynaptic inhibition 165
receptor desensitization 166
reuptake 162
serotonin 170
SNARE proteins 162
spatial summation 164
substance P 172
synaptic cleft 161
synaptic delay 162
synaptic vesicle 161
synaptotagmin 162
temporal summation 164

SECTION C CLINICAL TERMS

alprazolam 171
Alzheimer disease 168
analgesics 172
atropine 168
beta-amyloid protein 168
Botox 167
botulism 167
codeine 172
diazepam 171
LSD 170
morphine 172
nicotine 168
paroxetine (Paxil) 170
Sarin 168
strychnine 171
tetanus toxin 167
Valium 171
Xanax 171

SECTION **D**

Structure of the Nervous System

We now survey the anatomy and broad functions of the major structures of the central and peripheral nervous systems. **Figure 6.37** provides a conceptual overview of the organization of the nervous system for you to refer to as we discuss the various subdivisions in this section and in later chapters.

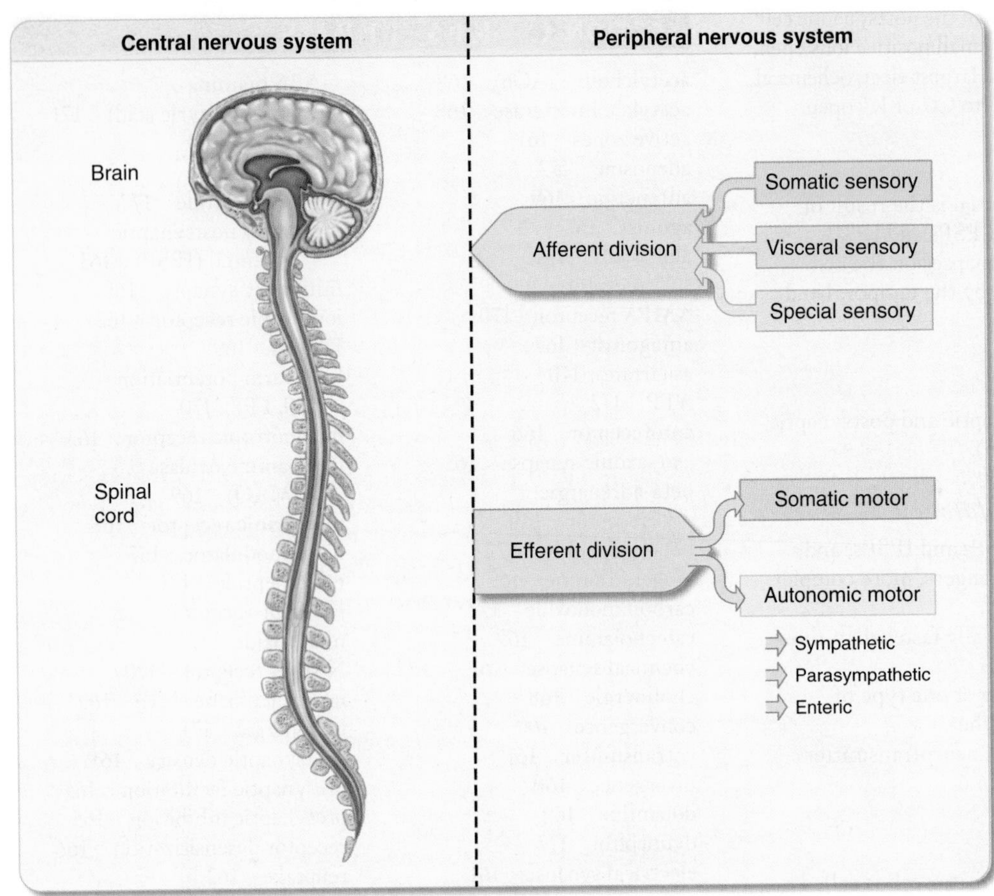

Figure 6.37 Overview of the structural and functional organization of the nervous system.

First, we must introduce some important terminology. Recall that a long extension from a single neuron is called an axon or a nerve fiber and that the term *nerve* refers to a group of many axons that are traveling together to and from the same general location in the PNS. There are no nerves in the CNS. Rather, a group of axons traveling together in the CNS is called a **pathway,** a **tract,** or, when it links the right and left halves of the CNS, a **commissure.** Two general types of pathways occur in the CNS. The first are sometimes referred to as *long neural pathways* and consist of neurons with relatively long axons that carry information directly between the brain and spinal cord or between large regions of the brain. The second type are *multisynaptic pathways* and include many neurons with branching axons and many synaptic connections. Because synapses are the sites where new information can be integrated into neural messages, these pathways perform complex neural processing, while long neural pathways transmit signals with relatively less alteration. The cell bodies of neurons with similar functions are often clustered together. Groups of neuron cell bodies in the PNS are called ganglia (singular, **ganglion**). In the CNS, they are called nuclei (singular, **nucleus**), not to be confused with cell nuclei.

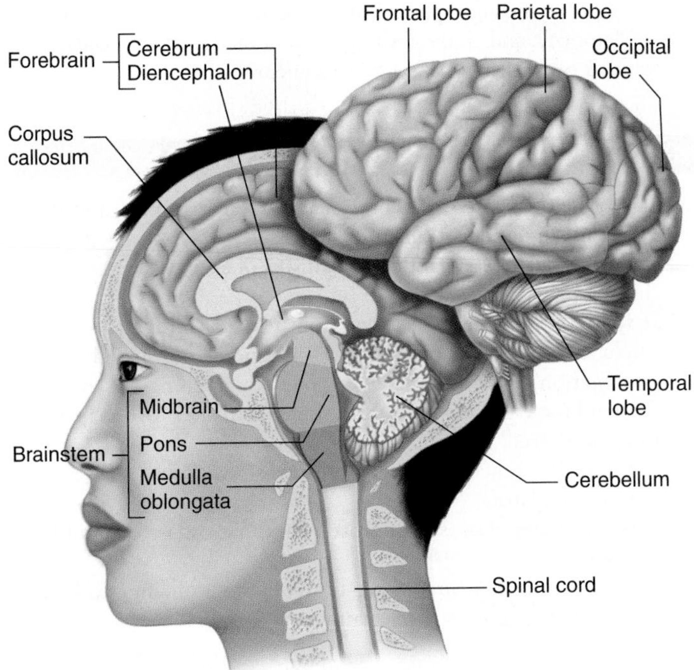

Figure 6.38 APIR The surface of the cerebral cortex and the divisions of the brain shown in sagittal section. The outer surface of the cerebrum (cortex) is divided into four lobes as shown.

6.15 Central Nervous System: Brain

During development, the CNS forms from a long tube. As the anterior part of the tube, which becomes the brain, folds during its continuing formation, four different regions become apparent. These regions become the four subdivisions of the brain: the **cerebrum, diencephalon, brainstem,** and **cerebellum** (**Figure 6.38**). The cerebrum and diencephalon together constitute the **forebrain.** The brainstem consists of the **midbrain, pons,** and **medulla oblongata.** The brain also

TABLE 6.7 Summary of Functions of the Major Parts of the Brain

I. Forebrain
- A. Cerebral hemispheres
  1. Contain the cerebral cortex, which participates in perception (Chapter 7); the generation of skilled movements (Chapter 10); reasoning, learning, and memory (Chapter 8)
  2. Contain subcortical nuclei, including those that participate in coordination of skeletal muscle activity (Chapter 10)
  3. Contain interconnecting fiber pathways
- B. Thalamus
  1. Acts as a synaptic relay station for sensory pathways on their way to the cerebral cortex (Chapter 7)
  2. Participates in control of skeletal muscle coordination (Chapter 10)
  3. Plays a key role in awareness (Chapter 8)
- C. Hypothalamus
  1. Regulates anterior pituitary gland function (Chapter 11)
  2. Regulates water balance (Chapter 14)
  3. Participates in regulation of autonomic nervous system (Chapters 6 and 16)
  4. Regulates eating and drinking behavior (Chapter 16)
  5. Regulates reproductive system (Chapters 11 and 17)
  6. Reinforces certain behaviors (Chapter 8)
  7. Generates and regulates circadian rhythms (Chapters 1, 7, and 16)
  8. Regulates body temperature (Chapter 16)
  9. Participates in generation of emotional behavior (Chapter 8)
- D. Limbic system
  1. Participates in generation of emotions and emotional behavior (Chapter 8)
  2. Plays essential role in most kinds of learning (Chapter 8)

II. Cerebellum
- A. Coordinates movements, including those for posture and balance (Chapter 10)
- B. Participates in some forms of learning (Chapter 8)

III. Brainstem
- A. Contains all the fibers passing between the spinal cord, forebrain, and cerebellum
- B. Contains the reticular formation and its various integrating centers, including those for cardiovascular and respiratory activity (Chapters 12 and 13)
- C. Contains nuclei for cranial nerves III through XII

contains four interconnected cavities, the **cerebral ventricles,** which are filled with fluid.

Overviews of the brain subdivisions are included here and in **Table 6.7**, but details of their functions are given more fully in Chapters 7, 8, and 10.

Forebrain

The larger component of the forebrain, the cerebrum, consists of the right and left **cerebral hemispheres** as well as some associated structures on the underside of the brain. The central core of the forebrain is formed by the diencephalon.

The cerebral hemispheres (**Figure 6.39**) consist of the **cerebral cortex**—an outer shell of **gray matter** composed primarily of cell bodies that give the area a gray appearance—and an inner layer of **white matter,** composed primarily of myelinated fiber tracts. This in turn overlies cell clusters, which are also gray matter and are collectively termed the **subcortical nuclei.** The fiber tracts consist of the many nerve fibers that bring information into the cerebrum, carry information out, and connect different areas within a hemisphere. The cortex layers of the left and right cerebral hemispheres, although largely separated by a deep longitudinal division, are connected by a massive bundle of nerve fibers known as the **corpus callosum.**

The cortex of each cerebral hemisphere is divided into four lobes, named after the overlying skull bones covering the brain: the **frontal, parietal, occipital,** and **temporal lobes.** Although it averages only 3 mm in thickness, the cortex is highly folded. This results in an area containing cortical neurons that is four times larger than it would be if unfolded, yet does not appreciably increase the volume of the brain. Such elaboration of structural surface area to enhance function in organs throughout the body affirms the general principle of physiology that structure and function are related. This folding also results in the characteristic external appearance of the human cerebrum, with its sinuous ridges called gyri (singular, **gyrus**) separated by grooves called sulci (singular, **sulcus**). The cells of the human cerebral cortex are organized in six distinct layers, composed of varying sizes and numbers of two basic types: pyramidal cells (named for the shape of their cell bodies) and nonpyramidal cells. The **pyramidal cells** form the major output cells of the cortex, sending their axons to other parts of the cortex and to other parts of the CNS. Nonpyramidal cells are mostly involved in receiving inputs into the cortex and in local processing of information. This elaboration of the human cerebral cortex into multiple cell layers, like its highly folded structure, allows for an increase in the number and integration of neurons for signal processing. This is supported by the fact that an increase in the number of cell layers in the cerebral cortex has paralleled the increase in behavioral and cognitive complexity in vertebrate evolution. For example, reptiles have just three layers in the cortex, and dolphins have five. Some regions of the human brain with ancient evolutionary origins, such as the olfactory cortex, persist in having only three cell layers.

The cerebral cortex is one of the most complex integrating areas of the nervous system. In the cerebral cortex, basic afferent information is collected and processed into meaningful perceptual images, and control over the systems that govern the movement of the skeletal muscles is refined. Nerve fibers enter the cortex predominantly from the diencephalon, specifically from a region known as the thalamus as well as from other regions of the cortex and areas of the brainstem. Some of the input fibers convey information about specific events in the environment, whereas others control levels of cortical excitability, determine states of arousal, and direct attention to specific stimuli.

The subcortical nuclei are heterogeneous groups of gray matter that lie deep within the cerebral hemispheres. Predominant among them are the **basal nuclei** (often, but less correctly referred to as **basal ganglia**), which play an important role in controlling movement and posture and in more complex aspects of behavior.

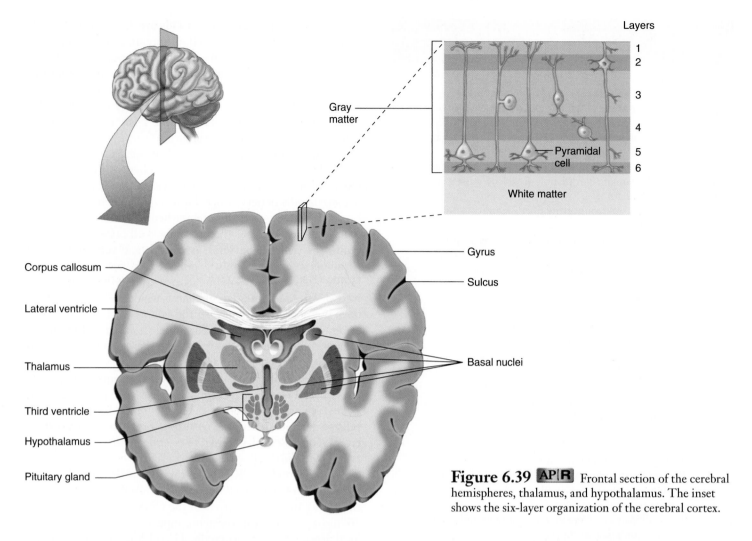

Figure 6.39 AP|R Frontal section of the cerebral hemispheres, thalamus, and hypothalamus. The inset shows the six-layer organization of the cerebral cortex.

The diencephalon, which is divided in two by the narrow third cerebral ventricle, is the second component of the forebrain. It contains the thalamus, hypothalamus, and epithalamus. The **thalamus** is a collection of several large nuclei that serve as synaptic relay stations and important integrating centers for most inputs to the cortex, and it plays a key role in general arousal. The thalamus also is involved in focusing attention. For example, it is responsible for filtering out extraneous sensory information such as might occur when you try to concentrate on a private conversation at a loud, crowded party.

The **hypothalamus** lies below the thalamus and is on the undersurface of the brain. Although it is a tiny region that accounts for less than 1% of the brain's weight, it contains different cell groups and pathways that form the master command center for neural and endocrine coordination. Indeed, the hypothalamus is the single most important control area for homeostatic regulation of the internal environment. Behaviors having to do with preservation of the individual (for example, eating and drinking) and preservation of the species (reproduction) are among the many functions of the hypothalamus. The hypothalamus lies directly above and is connected by a stalk to the **pituitary gland,** an important endocrine structure that the hypothalamus regulates (Chapter 11).

The **epithalamus** is a small mass of tissue that includes the **pineal gland,** which has a role in regulating circadian rhythms through release of the hormone melatonin.

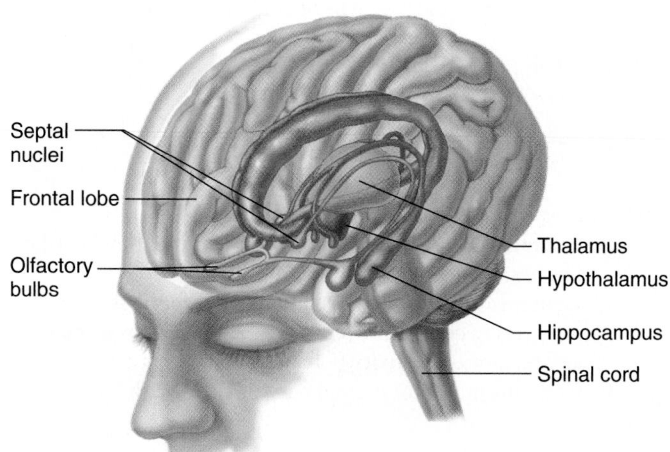

Figure 6.40 AP|R Structures of the limbic system (violet) and their anatomical relation to the hypothalamus (purple) are shown in this partially transparent view of the brain.

Thus far, we have described discrete anatomical areas of the forebrain. Some of these forebrain areas, consisting of both gray and white matter, are also classified together in a functional system called the **limbic system.** This interconnected group of brain structures includes portions of frontal-lobe cortex, temporal lobe, thalamus, and hypothalamus, as well as the fiber pathways that connect them (**Figure 6.40**).

Besides being connected with each other, the parts of the limbic system connect with many other parts of the CNS. Structures within the limbic system are associated with learning, emotional experience and behavior, and a wide variety of visceral and endocrine functions (see Chapter 8). In fact, the hypothalamus coordinates much of the output of the limbic system into behavioral and endocrine responses.

Cerebellum

The cerebellum consists of an outer layer of cells, the cerebellar cortex (do not confuse this with the cerebral cortex), and several deeper cell clusters. Although the cerebellum does not initiate voluntary movements, it is an important center for coordinating movements and for controlling posture and balance. To carry out these functions, the cerebellum receives information from the muscles and joints, skin, eyes, vestibular apparatus, viscera, and the parts of the brain involved in control of movement. Although the cerebellum's function is almost exclusively motor, it also may be involved in some forms of learning.

Brainstem

All the nerve fibers that relay signals between the forebrain, cerebellum, and spinal cord pass through the brainstem. Running through the core of the brainstem and consisting of loosely arranged neuron cell bodies intermingled with bundles of axons is the **reticular formation,** the one part of the brain absolutely essential for life. It receives and integrates input from all regions of the CNS and processes a great deal of neural information. The reticular formation is involved in motor functions, cardiovascular and respiratory control, and the mechanisms that regulate sleep and wakefulness and that focus attention. Most of the biogenic amine neurotransmitters are released from the axons of cells in the reticular formation and, because of the far-reaching projections of these cells, these neurotransmitters affect all levels of the nervous system.

Some reticular formation neurons send axons for considerable distances up or down the brainstem and beyond to most regions of the brain and spinal cord. This pattern explains the very large scope of influence that the reticular formation has over other parts of the CNS and explains the widespread effects of the biogenic amines.

The pathways that convey information from the reticular formation to the upper portions of the brain stimulate arousal and wakefulness. They also direct attention to specific events by selectively stimulating neurons in some areas of the brain while inhibiting others. The fibers that descend from the reticular formation to the spinal cord influence activity in both efferent and afferent neurons. Considerable interaction takes place between the reticular pathways that go up to the forebrain, down to the spinal cord, and to the cerebellum. For example, all three components function in controlling muscle activity.

The reticular formation encompasses a large portion of the brainstem, and many areas within the reticular formation serve distinct functions. For example, some reticular formation neurons are clustered together, forming brainstem nuclei and integrating centers. These include the cardiovascular, respiratory, swallowing, and vomiting centers, all of which we will discuss in later chapters. The reticular formation also has nuclei important in eye-movement control and the reflexive orientation of the body in space.

In addition, the brainstem contains nuclei involved in processing information for 10 of the 12 pairs of **cranial nerves.** These are the peripheral nerves that connect directly with the brain and innervate the muscles, glands, and sensory receptors of the head, as well as many organs in the thoracic and abdominal cavities.

6.16 Central Nervous System: Spinal Cord

The spinal cord lies within the bony vertebral column (**Figure 6.41**). It is a slender cylinder of soft tissue about as big around as your little finger. The central butterfly-shaped area (in cross section) of gray matter is composed of interneurons, the cell bodies and dendrites of efferent neurons, the entering axons of afferent neurons, and glial cells. The regions of gray matter projecting toward the back of the body are called the **dorsal horns,** whereas those oriented toward the front are the **ventral horns.**

The gray matter is surrounded by white matter, which consists of groups of myelinated axons. These groups of fiber tracts run longitudinally through the cord, some descending to relay information *from* the brain to the spinal cord, others ascending to transmit information *to* the brain. Pathways also transmit information between different levels of the spinal cord.

Groups of afferent fibers that enter the spinal cord from the peripheral nerves enter on the dorsal side of the cord via the **dorsal roots.** Small bumps on the dorsal roots, the

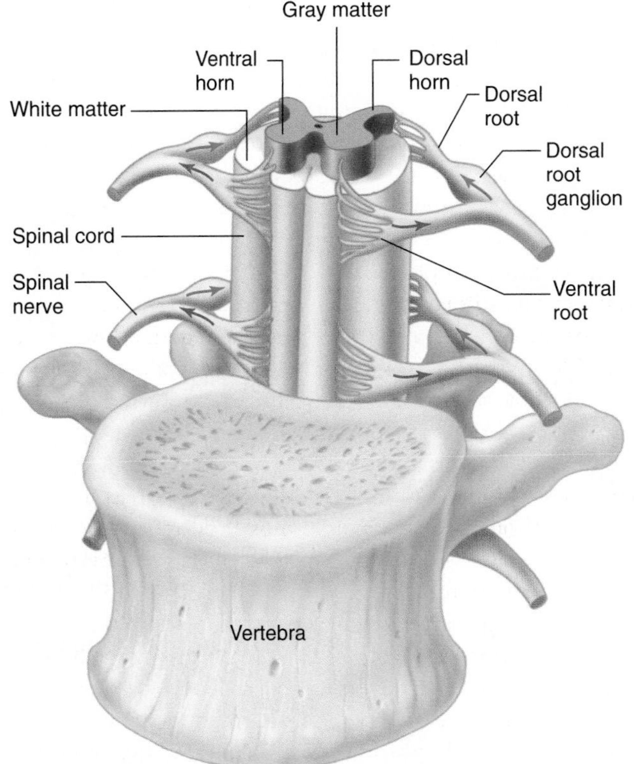

Figure 6.41 AP|R Section of the spinal cord, ventral view. The arrows indicate the direction of transmission of neural activity.

dorsal root ganglia, contain the cell bodies of these afferent neurons. The axons of efferent neurons leave the spinal cord on the ventral side via the **ventral roots.** A short distance from the cord, the dorsal and ventral roots from the same level combine to form a **spinal nerve,** one on each side of the spinal cord.

6.17 Peripheral Nervous System

Neurons in the PNS transmit signals between the CNS and receptors and effectors in all other parts of the body. As noted earlier, the axons are grouped into bundles called nerves. The PNS has 43 pairs of nerves: 12 pairs of cranial nerves and 31 pairs of spinal nerves that connect with the spinal cord. **Table 6.8** lists the cranial nerves and summarizes the information they transmit. The 31 pairs of spinal nerves are designated by the vertebral levels from which they exit: cervical, thoracic, lumbar, sacral, and coccygeal (**Figure 6.42**). Neurons in the spinal nerves at each level generally communicate with nearby structures, controlling muscles and glands as well as receiving sensory input. The eight pairs of cervical nerves innervate the neck, shoulders, arms, and hands. The 12 pairs of thoracic nerves are associated with the chest and upper abdomen. The five pairs of lumbar nerves are associated with the lower abdomen, hips, and legs; the five pairs of sacral nerves are associated with the genitals and lower digestive tract. A single pair of coccygeal nerves associated with the tailbone brings the total to 31 pairs.

These peripheral nerves can contain nerve fibers that are the axons of efferent neurons, afferent neurons, or both. Therefore, fibers in a nerve may be classified as belonging to the **efferent** or the **afferent division** of the PNS (refer back to Figure 6.37). All the spinal nerves contain both afferent and efferent fibers, whereas some of the cranial nerves contain only afferent fibers (the optic nerves from the eyes, for example) or only efferent fibers (the hypoglossal nerve to muscles of the tongue, for example).

As noted earlier, afferent neurons convey information from sensory receptors at their peripheral endings to the CNS. The long part of their axon is outside the CNS and is part of the PNS. Afferent neurons are sometimes called primary afferents or first-order neurons because they are the first cells entering the CNS in the synaptically linked chains of neurons that handle incoming information.

TABLE 6.8 The Cranial Nerves

Name	Fibers	Comments
I. Olfactory	Afferent	Carries input from receptors in olfactory (smell) neuroepithelium*
II. Optic	Afferent	Carries input from receptors in eye*
III. Oculomotor	Efferent	Innervates skeletal muscles that move eyeball up, down, and medially, and raise upper eyelid; innervates smooth muscles that constrict pupil and alter lens shape for near and far vision
	Afferent	Transmits information from receptors in muscles
IV. Trochlear	Efferent	Innervates skeletal muscles that move eyeball downward and laterally
	Afferent	Transmits information from receptors in muscles
V. Trigeminal	Efferent	Innervates skeletal chewing muscles
	Afferent	Transmits information from receptors in skin; skeletal muscles of face, nose, and mouth; and teeth sockets
VI. Abducens	Efferent	Innervates skeletal muscles that move eyeball laterally
	Afferent	Transmits information from receptors in muscles
VII. Facial	Efferent	Innervates skeletal muscles of facial expression and swallowing; innervates nose, palate, and lacrimal and salivary glands
	Afferent	Transmits information from taste buds in front of tongue and mouth
VIII. Vestibulocochlear	Afferent	Transmits information from receptors in inner ear
IX. Glossopharyngeal	Efferent	Innervates skeletal muscles involved in swallowing and parotid salivary gland
	Afferent	Transmits information from taste buds at back of tongue and receptors in auditory-tube skin
X. Vagus	Efferent	Innervates skeletal muscles of pharynx and larynx and smooth muscle and glands of thorax and abdomen
	Afferent	Transmits information from receptors in thorax and abdomen
XI. Accessory	Efferent	Innervates sternocleidomastoid and trapezius muscles in the neck
XII. Hypoglossal	Efferent	Innervates skeletal muscles of tongue

*The olfactory and optic pathways are CNS structures so are not technically "nerves."

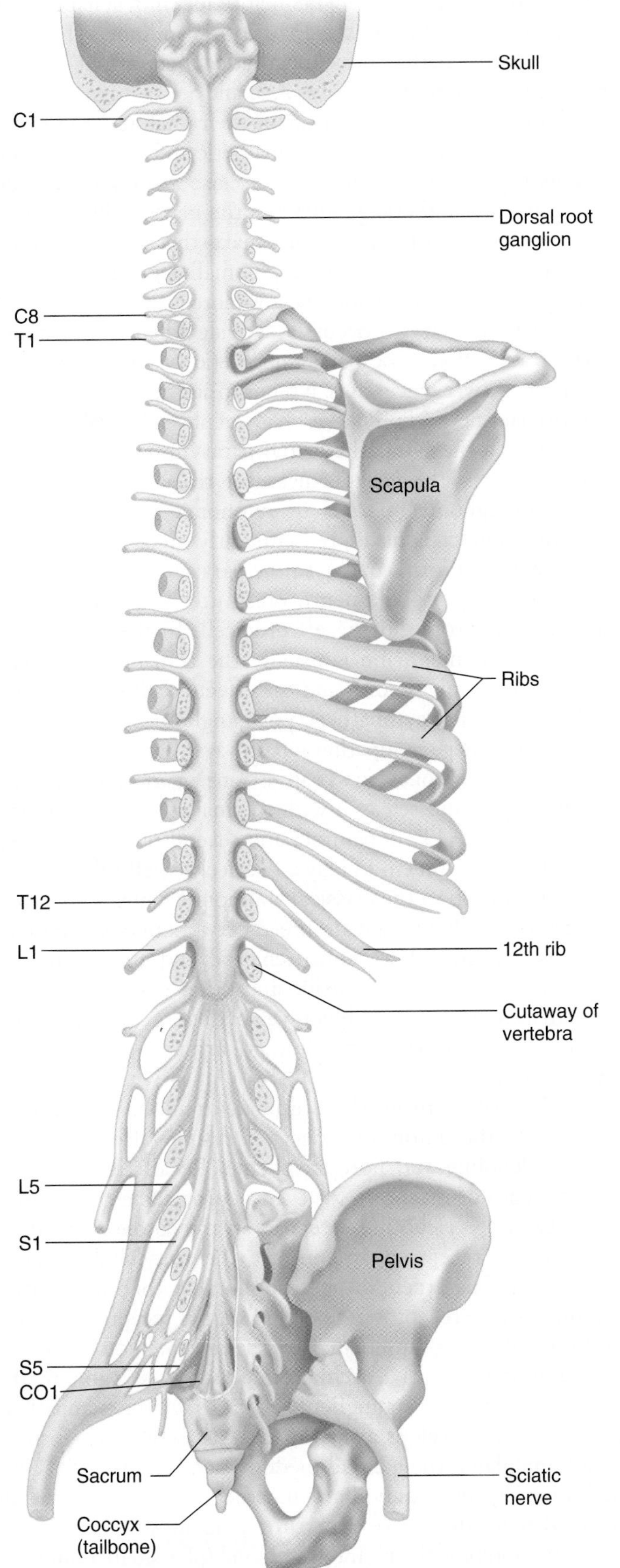

Efferent neurons carry signals out from the CNS to muscles, glands, and other tissues. The efferent division of the PNS is more complicated than the afferent, being subdivided into a **somatic nervous system** and an **autonomic nervous system.** These terms are somewhat misleading because they suggest the presence of additional nervous systems distinct from the central and peripheral systems. Keep in mind that these terms together make up the efferent division of the PNS.

The simplest distinction between the somatic and autonomic systems is that the neurons of the somatic division innervate skeletal muscle, whereas the autonomic neurons innervate smooth and cardiac muscle, glands, neurons in the gastrointestinal tract, and other tissues. Other differences are listed in **Table 6.9**.

The somatic portion of the efferent division of the PNS is made up of all the nerve fibers going from the CNS to skeletal muscle cells. The cell bodies of these neurons are located in groups in the brainstem or the ventral horn of the spinal cord. Their large-diameter, myelinated axons leave the CNS and pass without any synapses to skeletal muscle cells. The neurotransmitter these neurons release is acetylcholine. Because activity in the somatic neurons leads to contraction of the innervated skeletal muscle cells, these neurons are called **motor neurons.** Excitation of motor neurons leads only to the *contraction* of skeletal muscle cells; there are no somatic neurons that inhibit skeletal muscles. Muscle relaxation involves the inhibition of the motor neurons in the spinal cord.

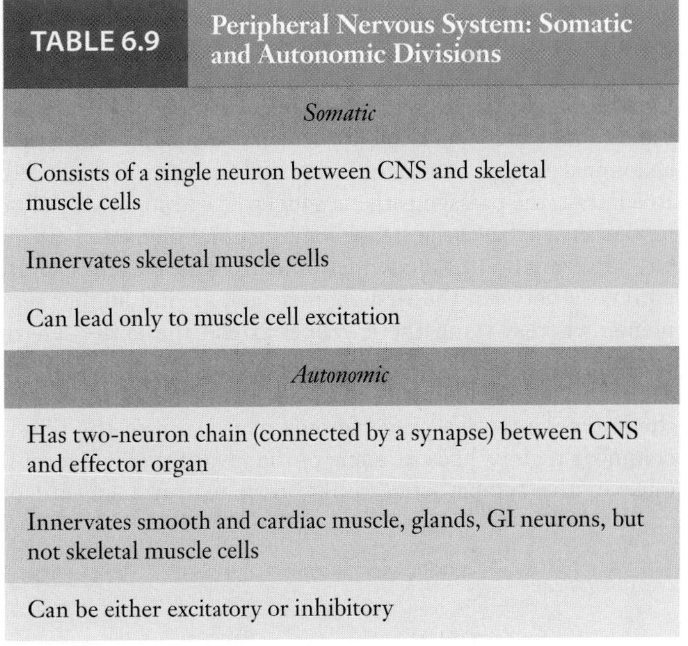

TABLE 6.9 Peripheral Nervous System: Somatic and Autonomic Divisions

Somatic
Consists of a single neuron between CNS and skeletal muscle cells
Innervates skeletal muscle cells
Can lead only to muscle cell excitation
Autonomic
Has two-neuron chain (connected by a synapse) between CNS and effector organ
Innervates smooth and cardiac muscle, glands, GI neurons, but not skeletal muscle cells
Can be either excitatory or inhibitory

Figure 6.42 APIR Dorsal view of the spinal cord and spinal nerves. Parts of the skull and vertebrae have been cut away; the ventral roots of the spinal nerves are not visible. In general, the eight cervical nerves (C) control the muscles and glands and receive sensory input from the neck, shoulders, arms, and hands. The 12 thoracic nerves (T) are associated with the shoulders, chest, and upper abdomen. The five lumbar nerves (L) are associated with the lower abdomen, hips, and legs; and the five sacral nerves (S) are associated with the genitals and lower digestive tract. Redrawn from *Fundamental Neuroanatomy* by Walle J. H. Nauta and Michael Fiertag. Copyright © 1986 by W. H. Freeman and Company. Reprinted by permission.

6.18 Autonomic Nervous System

The efferent innervation of tissues other than skeletal muscle is by way of the autonomic nervous system. A special case occurs in the gastrointestinal tract, where autonomic neurons innervate a nerve network in the wall of the intestinal tract. This network is called the **enteric nervous system,** and although often classified as a subdivision of the autonomic efferent nervous system, it also includes sensory neurons and interneurons. Chapter 15 will describe this network in more detail.

In contrast to the somatic nervous system, the autonomic nervous system is made up of two neurons in series that connect the CNS and the effector cells (**Figure 6.43**). The first neuron has its cell body in the CNS. The synapse between the two neurons is outside the CNS in a cell cluster called an **autonomic ganglion.** The neurons passing between the CNS and the ganglia are called **preganglionic neurons;** those passing between the ganglia and the effector cells are **postganglionic neurons.**

Anatomical and physiological differences within the autonomic nervous system are the basis for its further subdivision into **sympathetic** and **parasympathetic divisions** (review Figure 6.37). The neurons of the sympathetic and parasympathetic divisions leave the CNS at different levels—the sympathetic fibers from the thoracic (chest) and lumbar regions of the spinal cord, and the parasympathetic fibers from the brainstem and the sacral portion of the spinal cord (**Figure 6.44**). Therefore, the sympathetic division is also called the thoracolumbar division, and the parasympathetic division is called the craniosacral division.

The two divisions also differ in the location of ganglia. Most of the sympathetic ganglia lie close to the spinal cord and form the two chains of ganglia—one on each side of the cord—known as the **sympathetic trunks** (see Figure 6.44 and **Figure 6.45**). Other sympathetic ganglia, called collateral ganglia—the celiac, superior mesenteric, and inferior mesenteric ganglia—are in the abdominal cavity, closer to the innervated organ (see Figure 6.44). In contrast, the parasympathetic ganglia lie within, or very close to, the organs that the postganglionic neurons innervate.

Preganglionic sympathetic neurons leave the spinal cord only between the first thoracic and second lumbar segments, whereas sympathetic *trunks* extend the entire length of the cord, from the cervical levels high in the neck down to the sacral levels. The ganglia in the extra lengths of sympathetic trunks receive preganglionic neurons from the thoracolumbar regions because some of the preganglionic neurons, once in the sympathetic trunks, turn to travel upward or downward for several segments before forming synapses with postganglionic neurons (see Figure 6.45, numbers 1 and 4). Other possible paths the sympathetic fibers might take are shown in Figure 6.45, numbers 2, 3, and 5.

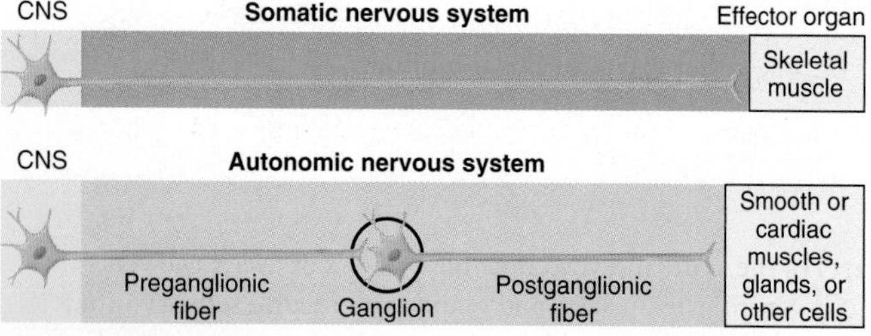

Figure 6.43 Efferent division of the PNS, including an overall plan of the somatic and autonomic nervous systems.

Due in part to differences in their anatomy, the overall activation pattern within the sympathetic and parasympathetic systems tends to be different. The close anatomical association of the sympathetic ganglia and the marked divergence of presynaptic sympathetic neurons make that division tend to respond as a single unit. Although small segments are occasionally activated independently, it is more typical for increased sympathetic activity to occur body-wide when circumstances warrant activation. The parasympathetic system, in contrast, exhibits less divergence; thus, it tends to activate specific organs in a pattern finely tailored to each given physiological situation.

In both the sympathetic and parasympathetic divisions, acetylcholine is the neurotransmitter released between pre- and postganglionic neurons in autonomic ganglia, and the postganglionic cells have predominantly nicotinic acetylcholine receptors (**Figure 6.46**). In the parasympathetic division, acetylcholine is also the neurotransmitter between the postganglionic neuron and the effector cell. In the sympathetic division, norepinephrine is usually the transmitter between the postganglionic neuron and the effector cell. We say "usually" because a few sympathetic postganglionic endings release acetylcholine (e.g., sympathetic pathways that regulate sweating). At many autonomic synapses, one or more cotransmitters are stored and released with the major neurotransmitter. These include ATP, dopamine, and several of the neuropeptides, all of which seem to play a relatively small role.

In addition to the classical autonomic neurotransmitters just described, there is a widespread network of postganglionic neurons recognized as nonadrenergic and noncholinergic. These neurons use nitric oxide and other neurotransmitters to mediate some forms of blood vessel dilation and to regulate various gastrointestinal, respiratory, urinary, and reproductive functions.

Many of the drugs that stimulate or inhibit various components of the autonomic nervous system affect receptors for acetylcholine and norepinephrine. Recall that there are several types of receptors for each neurotransmitter. A great majority of acetylcholine receptors in the autonomic ganglia are nicotinic receptors. In contrast, the acetylcholine receptors on cellular targets of postganglionic autonomic neurons are muscarinic receptors. The cholinergic receptors on skeletal muscle fibers, innervated by the *somatic* motor neurons, not autonomic neurons, are nicotinic receptors (**Table 6.10**).

One set of postganglionic neurons in the sympathetic division never develops axons. Instead, these neurons form an endocrine gland, the adrenal medulla (see Figure 6.46). Upon activation by preganglionic sympathetic axons, cells of the **adrenal medulla** release a mixture of about 80% epinephrine and 20% norepinephrine into the blood (plus small amounts of other substances, including dopamine, ATP, and neuropeptides). These catecholamines, properly called *hormones* rather than *neurotransmitters* in this circumstance, are transported via the blood to effector cells having receptors sensitive to them. The receptors may be the same adrenergic receptors that are located near the release sites of sympathetic postganglionic neurons

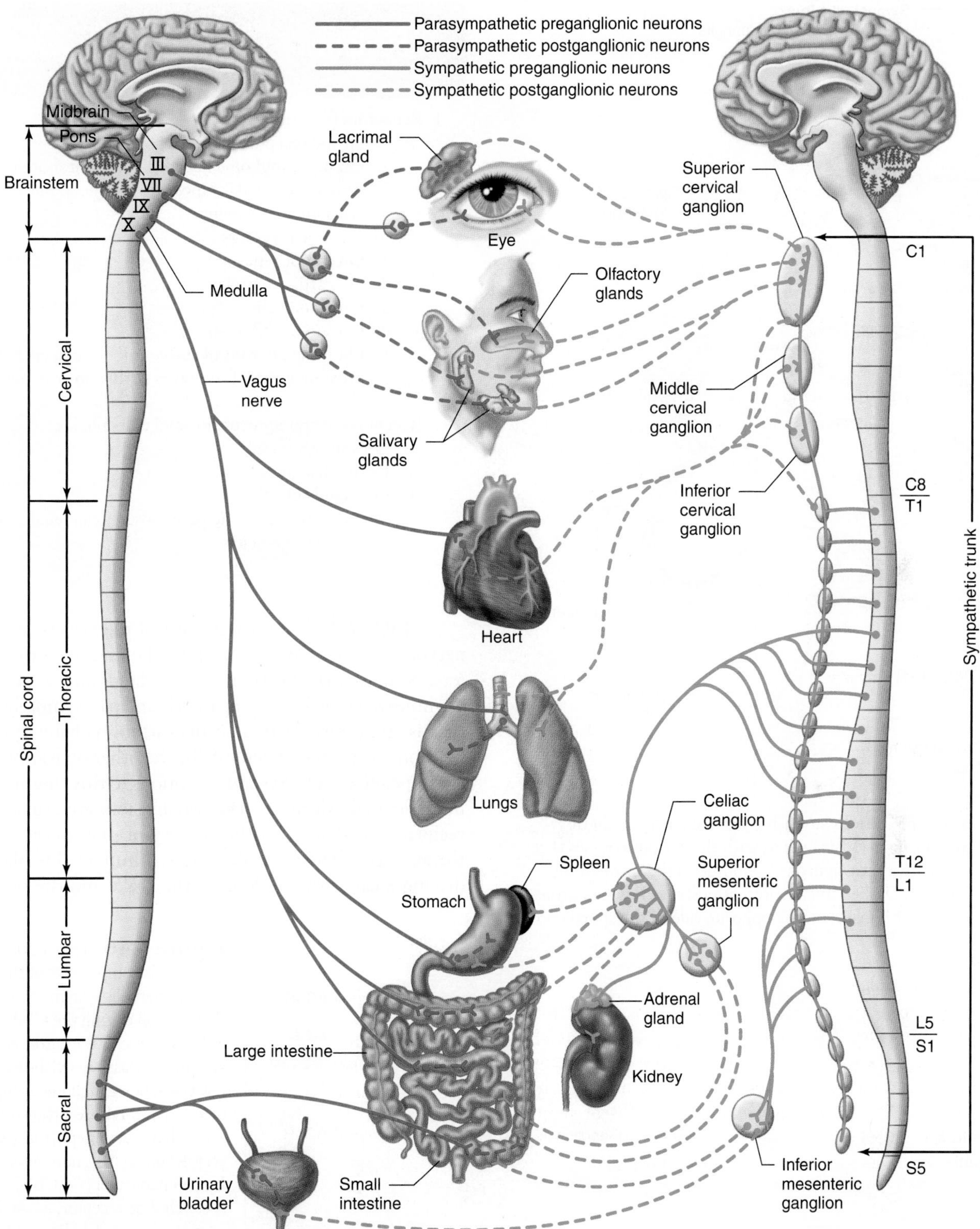

Figure 6.44 APIR The parasympathetic (at left) and sympathetic (at right) divisions of the autonomic nervous system. Although single nerves are shown exiting the brainstem and spinal cord, all represent paired (left and right) nerves. Only one sympathetic trunk is indicated, although there are two, one on each side of the spinal cord. The celiac, superior mesenteric, and inferior mesenteric ganglia are collateral ganglia. Not shown are the fibers passing to the liver, blood vessels, genitalia, and skin glands.

and are normally activated by the norepinephrine released from these neurons. In other cases, the receptors may be located in places that are not near the neurons and are therefore activated only by the circulating epinephrine or norepinephrine. The overall effect of these catecholamines is slightly different due to the fact that some adrenergic receptor subtypes have a higher affinity for epinephrine (e.g., β_2), whereas others have a higher affinity for norepinephrine (e.g., α_1).

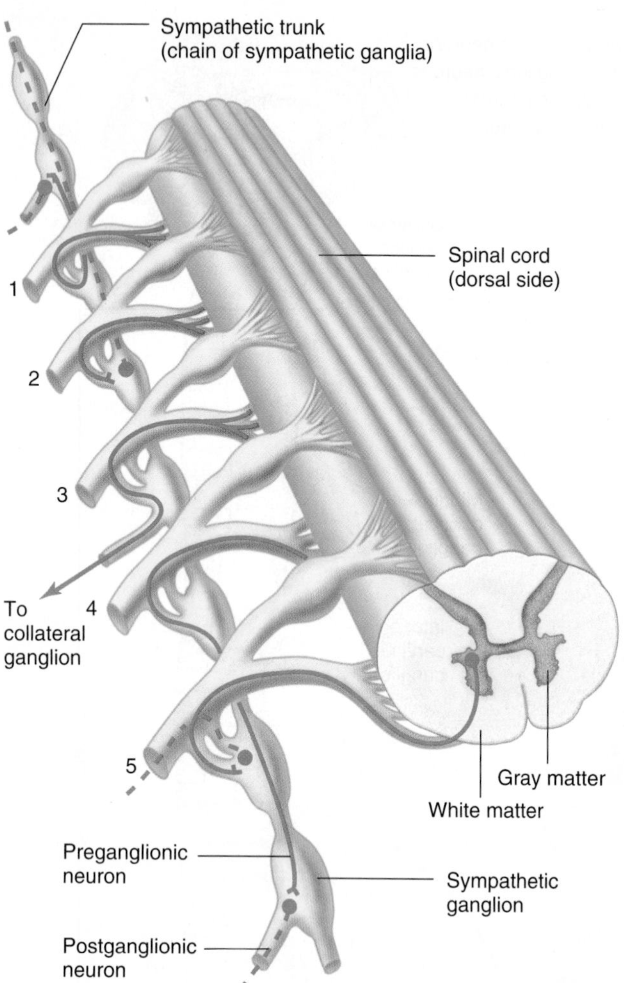

Figure 6.45 APIR Relationship between a sympathetic trunk and spinal nerves (1 through 5) with the various courses that preganglionic sympathetic neurons (solid lines) take through the sympathetic trunk. Dashed lines represent postganglionic neurons. A mirror image of this exists on the opposite side of the spinal cord.

TABLE 6.10	Locations of Receptors for Acetylcholine, Norepinephrine, and Epinephrine

I. Receptors for acetylcholine
- A. Nicotinic receptors
  1. On postganglionic neurons in the autonomic ganglia
  2. At neuromuscular junctions of skeletal muscle
  3. On some CNS neurons
- B. Muscarinic receptors
  1. On smooth muscle
  2. On cardiac muscle
  3. On gland cells
  4. On some CNS neurons
  5. On some neurons of autonomic ganglia (although the great majority of receptors at this site are nicotinic)

II. Receptors for norepinephrine and epinephrine
- A. On smooth muscle
- B. On cardiac muscle
- C. On gland cells
- D. On other tissue cells (e.g., adipose, bone, renal tubules)
- E. On some CNS neurons

Table 6.11 is a reference list of the effects of autonomic nervous system activity, which will be described in later chapters. Note that the heart and many glands and smooth muscles are innervated by both sympathetic and parasympathetic fibers; that is, they receive **dual innervation.** Whatever effect one division has on the effector cells, the other division usually has the opposite effect. (Several exceptions to this rule are indicated in Table 6.11.) Moreover, the two divisions are usually activated reciprocally; that is, as the activity of one division increases, the activity of the other decreases. Think of this like a person driving a car with one foot on the brake and the other on the

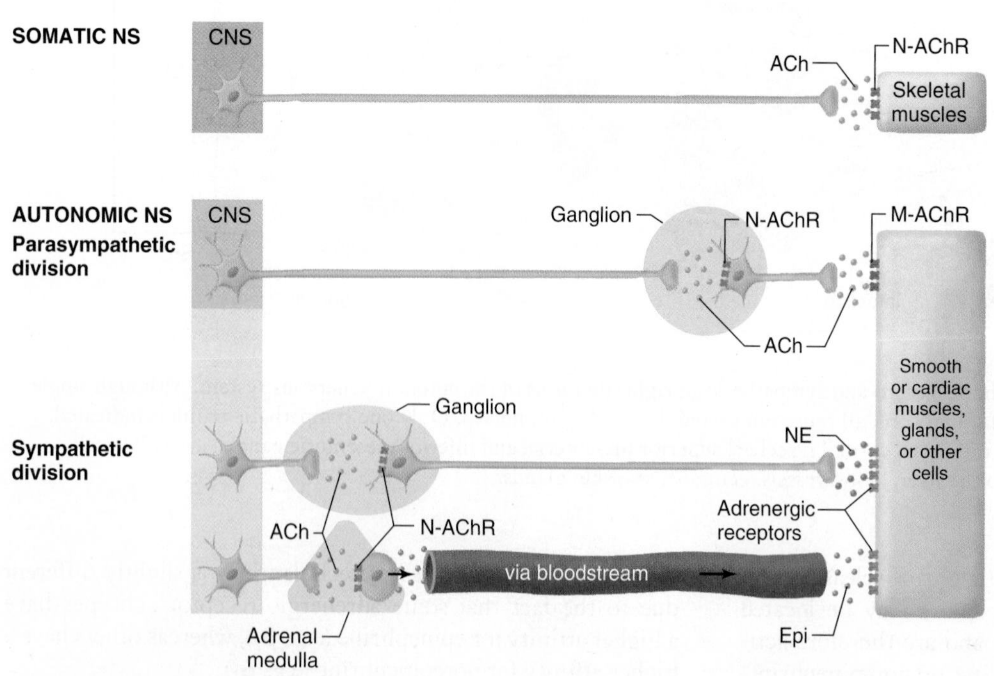

Figure 6.46 Transmitters used in the various components of the peripheral efferent nervous system. Notice that the first neuron exiting the CNS—whether in the somatic or the autonomic nervous system—releases acetylcholine. In a very few cases, postganglionic sympathetic neurons may release a transmitter other than norepinephrine. (ACh, acetylcholine; NE, norepinephrine; Epi, epinephrine; N-AChR, nicotinic acetylcholine receptor; M-AChR, muscarinic acetylcholine receptor)

PHYSIOLOGICAL INQUIRY

- How would the effects differ between a drug that blocks muscarinic acetylcholine receptors and one that blocks nicotinic acetylcholine receptors?

Answer can be found at end of chapter.

TABLE 6.11	Some Effects of Autonomic Nervous System Activity	
Effector Organ	**Sympathetic Nervous System Effect and Receptor Types***	**Parasympathetic Nervous System Effect (All M-ACh Receptors)**
Eyes		
Iris muscle	Contracts radial muscle (widens pupil), α_1	Contracts sphincter muscle (makes pupil smaller)
Ciliary muscle	Relaxes (flattens lens for far vision), β_2	Contracts (allows lens to become more convex for near vision)
Heart		
SA node	Increases heart rate, β_1	Decreases heart rate
Atria	Increases contractility, β_1, β_2	Decreases contractility
AV node	Increases conduction velocity, β_1, β_2	Decreases conduction velocity
Ventricles	Increases contractility, β_1, β_2	Decreases contractility slightly
Arterioles		
Coronary	Constricts, α_1, α_2	—†
	Dilates, β_2	
Skin	Constricts, α_1, α_2	—
Skeletal muscle	Constricts, α_1	—
	Dilates, β_2	
Abdominal viscera	Constricts, α_1	—
Kidneys	Constricts, α_1	—
Salivary glands	Constricts, α_1, α_2	Dilates
Veins	Constricts, α_1, α_2	—
	Dilates, β_2	
Lungs		
Bronchial muscle	Relaxes, β_2	Contracts
Salivary glands	Stimulates secretion, α_1	Stimulates watery secretion
	Stimulates enzyme secretion, β_1	
Stomach		
Motility, tone	Decreases, α_1, α_2, β_2	Increases
Sphincters	Contracts, α_1	Relaxes
Secretion	Inhibits (?)	Stimulates
Intestine		
Motility	Decreases, α_1, α_2, β_1, β_2	Increases
Sphincters	Contracts (usually), α_1	Relaxes (usually)
Secretion	Inhibits, $x\alpha_2$	Stimulates
Gallbladder	Relaxes, β_2	Contracts
Liver	Glycogenolysis and gluconeogenesis, α_1, β_2	—
Pancreas		
Exocrine glands	Inhibits secretion, α	Stimulates secretion
Endocrine glands	Inhibits secretion, α_2	—
	Stimulates secretion, β_2	
Fat cells	Increases fat breakdown, α_2, β_3	—
Kidneys	Increases renin secretion, β_1	—
Urinary bladder		
Bladder wall	Relaxes, β_2	Contracts
Sphincter	Contracts, α_1	Relaxes
Uterus	Contracts in pregnancy, α_1	Variable
	Relaxes, β_2	
Reproductive tract (male)	Ejaculation, α_1	Erection
Skin		
Muscles causing hair erection	Contracts, α_1	—
Sweat glands	Secretion from hands, feet, and armpits, α_1	—
	Generalized abundant, dilute secretion, M-AChR	—
Lacrimal glands	Minor secretion, α_1	Major secretion
Nasopharyngeal glands	—	Secretion

*Note that many effector organs contain both alpha-adrenergic and beta-adrenergic receptors. Activation of these receptors may produce either the same or opposing effects. For simplicity, except for the arterioles and a few other cases, only the dominant sympathetic effect is given when the two receptors oppose each other.

† A dash means these cells are not innervated by this branch of the autonomic nervous system or that these nerves do not play a significant physiological role.

Table adapted from Laurence L. Brunton, John S. Lazo, and Keither L. Parker, eds., *Goodman and Gilman's The Pharmacological Basis of Therapeutics*, 11th ed., McGraw-Hill, New York, 2006.

accelerator. Either depressing the brake (parasympathetic) or relaxing the accelerator (sympathetic) will slow the car. Dual innervation by neurons that cause opposite responses provides a very fine degree of control over the effector organ; this is perhaps one of the most obvious examples of the general principle of physiology that most physiological functions are controlled by multiple regulatory systems, often working in opposition.

A useful generalization is that the sympathetic system increases its activity under conditions of physical or psychological stress. Indeed, a generalized activation of the sympathetic system is called the **fight-or-flight response,** describing the situation of an animal forced to either challenge an attacker or run from it. All resources for physical exertion are activated: heart rate and blood pressure increase; blood flow increases to the skeletal muscles, heart, and brain; the liver releases glucose; and the pupils dilate. Simultaneously, the activity of the gastrointestinal tract and blood flow to it are inhibited by sympathetic firing. In contrast, when the parasympathetic system is activated, a person is in a **rest-or-digest state** in which homeostatic functions are predominant.

The two divisions of the autonomic nervous system rarely operate independently, and autonomic responses generally represent the regulated interplay of both divisions. Autonomic responses usually occur without conscious control or awareness, as though they were indeed autonomous (in fact, the autonomic nervous system has been called the "involuntary" nervous system). However, it is wrong to assume that this is always the case, for some visceral or glandular responses can be learned and thus, to an extent, voluntarily controlled.

A complex pattern of stimulation and desensitization of the nicotinic acetylcholine receptors at autonomic ganglia underlies many of the physiological effects of *nicotine.* At low doses, nicotine activates autonomic ganglia and stimulates the release of catecholamines from the adrenal medulla. The sympathetic components of these pathways dominate control of the cardiovascular system under these conditions, and so heart rate and blood pressure increase. Persistent high blood pressure and increased work on the heart are part of the reason that chronic nicotine use contributes to cardiovascular disease. In the gastrointestinal system, parasympathetic effects tend to dominate, leading to activation of intestinal smooth muscle motor activity. At higher doses of nicotine, brainstem control centers that regulate gastrointestinal functions can be overactivated and vomiting or diarrhea can sometimes occur, especially in individuals who have had little prior nicotine exposure. After initial activation, nicotinic acetylcholine receptors eventually become desensitized by high nicotine doses, which results in depression of all autonomic signaling pathways.

6.19 Blood Supply, Blood–Brain Barrier, and Cerebrospinal Fluid

As mentioned earlier, the brain lies within the skull, and the spinal cord lies within the vertebral column. Between the soft neural tissues and the bones that house them are three types of membranous coverings called **meninges:** the thick **dura mater** next to the bone, the **arachnoid mater** in the middle, and the thin **pia mater** next to the nervous tissue (**Figure 6.47**). The **subarachnoid space** between the arachnoid mater and pia mater is filled with **cerebrospinal fluid** (**CSF**). The meninges and their specialized parts protect and support the CNS, and they circulate and absorb the cerebrospinal fluid. ***Meningitis*** is an infection of the meninges that occurs in the CSF of the subarachnoid space and that can result in increased intracranial pressure, seizures, and loss of consciousness.

Ependymal cells make up a specialized epithelial structure called the **choroid plexus,** which produces CSF at a rate that completely replenishes it about three times per day. The black arrows in Figure 6.47 show the flow of CSF. It circulates through the interconnected ventricular system to the brainstem, where it passes through small openings out to the subarachnoid space surrounding the brain and spinal cord. Aided by circulatory, respiratory, and postural pressure changes, the fluid ultimately flows to the top of the outer surface of the brain, where most of it enters the bloodstream through one-way valves in large veins. CSF can provide important diagnostic information for diseases of the nervous system, such as meningitis. Fluid samples are generally obtained by inserting a large needle into the spinal canal below the level of the second lumbar vertebra, where the spinal cord ends (see Figure 6.42).

Thus, the CNS literally floats in a cushion of cerebrospinal fluid. Because the brain and spinal cord are soft, delicate tissues, they are somewhat protected by this shock-absorbing fluid from sudden and jarring movements. If the outflow is obstructed, cerebrospinal fluid accumulates, causing ***hydrocephalus*** ("water on the brain"). In severe, untreated cases, the resulting elevation of pressure in the ventricles causes compression of the brain's blood vessels, which may lead to inadequate blood flow to the neurons, neuronal damage, and cognitive dysfunction.

Under normal conditions, glucose is the only substrate metabolized by the brain to supply its energy requirements, and most of the energy from the oxidative breakdown of glucose is transferred to ATP. The brain's glycogen stores are negligible, so it depends upon a continuous blood supply of glucose and oxygen. In fact, the most common form of brain damage is caused by a decreased blood supply to a region of the brain. When neurons in the region are without a blood supply and deprived of nutrients and oxygen for even a few minutes, they cease to function and die. This neuronal death, when it results from vascular disease, is called a ***stroke.***

Although the adult brain makes up only 2% of the body weight, it receives 12% to 15% of the total blood supply, which supports its high oxygen utilization. If the blood flow to a region of the brain is reduced to 10% to 25% of its normal level, energy-dependent membrane ion pumps begin to fail, membrane ion gradients decrease, extracellular K^+ concentration increases, and membranes depolarize.

The exchange of substances between blood and extracellular fluid in the CNS is different from the more-or-less unrestricted diffusion of nonprotein substances from blood to extracellular fluid in the other organs of the body. A complex group of **blood–brain barrier** mechanisms closely control both the kinds of substances that enter the extracellular fluid of the brain and the rates at which they enter. These mechanisms minimize the ability of many harmful substances to reach the neurons, but they also reduce the access of some potentially helpful therapeutic drugs.

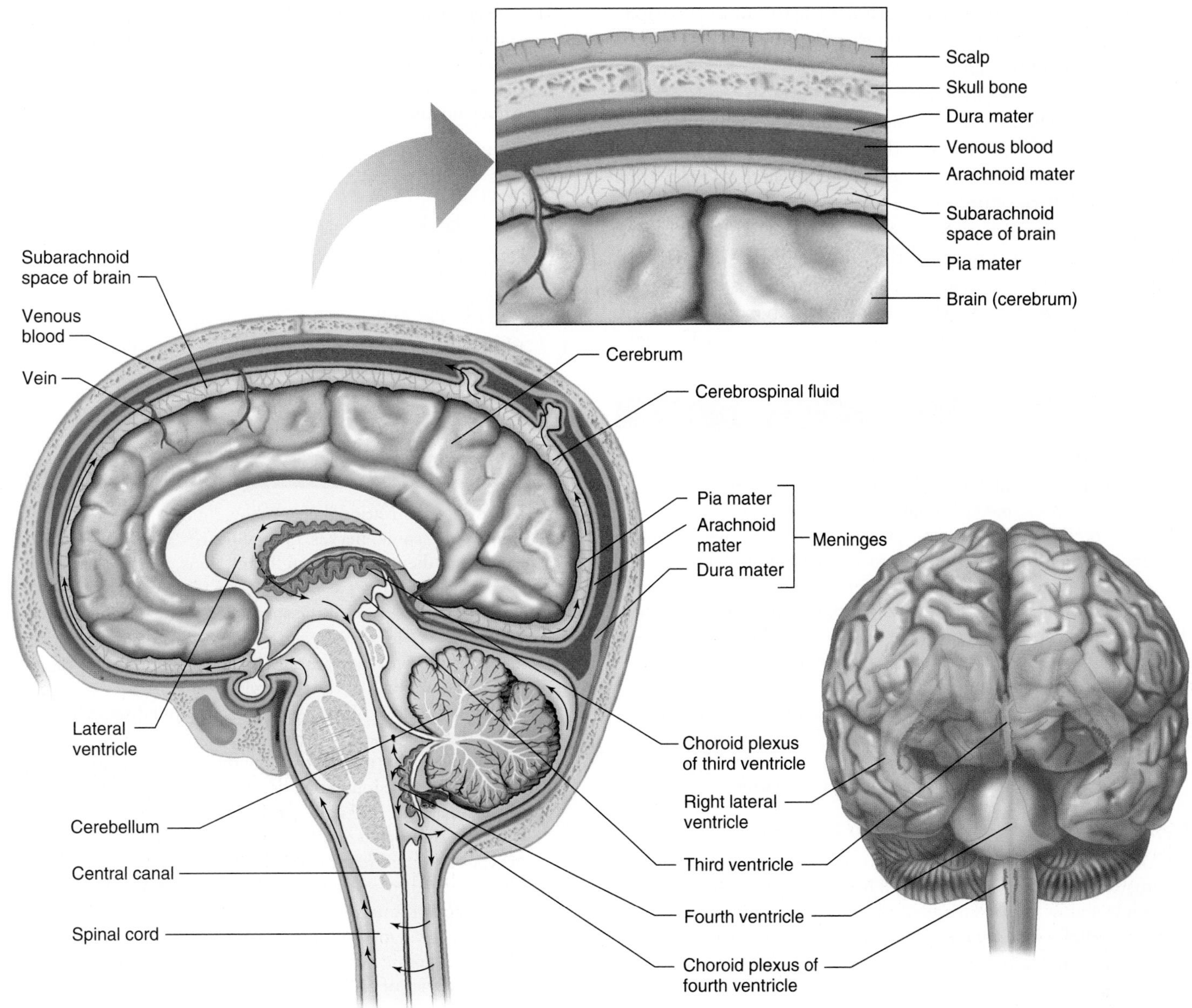

Figure 6.47 APIR The four interconnected ventricles of the brain. The lateral ventricles form the first two. The choroid plexus forms the cerebrospinal fluid (CSF), which flows out of the ventricular system at the brainstem (arrows).

The blood–brain barrier is formed by the cells that line the smallest blood vessels in the brain. It has anatomical structures, such as tight junctions, and physiological transport systems that handle different classes of substances in different ways. Substances that dissolve readily in the lipid components of the plasma membranes enter the brain quickly. Therefore, the extracellular fluid of the brain and spinal cord is a product of—but chemically different from—the blood.

The blood–brain barrier accounts for some drug actions, too, as we can see from the following scenario. Morphine differs chemically from heroin only slightly: morphine has two hydroxyl groups, whereas heroin has two acetyl groups ($—COCH_3$). This small difference renders heroin more lipid-soluble and able to cross the blood–brain barrier more readily than morphine. As soon as heroin enters the brain, however, enzymes remove the acetyl groups from heroin and change it to morphine. The morphine, less soluble in lipid, is then effectively trapped in the brain, where it may have prolonged effects. Other drugs that have rapid effects in the CNS because of their high lipid solubility are barbiturates, nicotine, caffeine, and alcohol.

Many substances that do not dissolve readily in lipids, such as glucose and other important substrates of brain metabolism, nonetheless enter the brain quite rapidly by combining with membrane transport proteins in the cells that line the smallest brain blood vessels. Similar transport systems also move substances out of the brain and into the blood, preventing the buildup of molecules that could interfere with brain function.

A barrier is also present between the blood in the capillaries of the choroid plexuses and the cerebrospinal fluid, and cerebrospinal fluid is thus a selective secretion. For example, K^+ and Ca^{2+} concentrations are slightly lower in cerebrospinal fluid than in plasma, whereas the Na^+ and Cl^- concentrations are slightly higher. The choroid plexus vessel walls also have limited permeability to toxic heavy metals such as lead, thus affording a degree of protection to the brain.

The cerebrospinal fluid and the extracellular fluid of the CNS are, over time, in diffusion equilibrium. Thus, the restrictive, selective barrier mechanisms in the capillaries and choroid plexuses regulate the extracellular environment of the neurons of the brain and spinal cord.

SECTION D SUMMARY

Central Nervous System: Brain

I. The brain is divided into six regions: cerebrum, diencephalon, midbrain, pons, medulla oblongata, and cerebellum.

II. The cerebrum, made up of right and left cerebral hemispheres, and the diencephalon together form the forebrain. The cerebral cortex forms the outer shell of the cerebrum and is divided into the parietal, frontal, occipital, and temporal lobes.

III. The diencephalon contains the thalamus and hypothalamus.

IV. The limbic system is a set of deep forebrain structures associated with learning and emotion.

V. The cerebellum plays a role in posture, movement, and some kinds of memory.

VI. The midbrain, pons, and medulla oblongata form the brainstem, which contains the reticular formation.

Central Nervous System: Spinal Cord

I. The spinal cord is divided into two areas: central gray matter, which contains nerve cell bodies and dendrites; and white matter, which surrounds the gray matter and contains myelinated axons organized into ascending or descending tracts.

II. The axons of the afferent and efferent neurons form the spinal nerves.

Peripheral Nervous System

I. The PNS consists of 43 paired nerves—12 pairs of cranial nerves and 31 pairs of spinal nerves, as well as neurons found in the gastrointestinal tract wall. Most nerves contain the axons of both afferent and efferent neurons.

II. The efferent division of the PNS is divided into somatic and autonomic parts. The somatic fibers innervate skeletal muscle cells and release the neurotransmitter acetylcholine.

Autonomic Nervous System

I. The autonomic nervous system innervates cardiac and smooth muscle, glands, gastrointestinal tract neurons, and other tissue cells. Each autonomic pathway consists of a preganglionic neuron with its cell body in the CNS and a postganglionic neuron with its cell body in an autonomic ganglion outside the CNS.

II. The autonomic nervous system is divided into sympathetic and parasympathetic components. Enteric neurons within the walls of the GI tract are also sometimes considered as a separate subcategory of the autonomic system. Preganglionic neurons in both the sympathetic and parasympathetic divisions release acetylcholine; the postganglionic parasympathetic neurons release mainly acetylcholine; and the postganglionic sympathetic neurons release mainly norepinephrine.

III. The adrenal medulla is a hormone-secreting part of the sympathetic nervous system and secretes mainly epinephrine.

IV. Many effector organs that the autonomic nervous system innervates receive dual innervation from the sympathetic and parasympathetic division of the autonomic nervous system.

Blood Supply, Blood–Brain Barrier, and Cerebrospinal Fluid

I. Inside the skull and vertebral column, the brain and spinal cord are enclosed in and protected by the meninges.

II. Brain tissue depends on a continuous supply of glucose and oxygen for metabolism.

III. The brain ventricles and the space within the meninges are filled with cerebrospinal fluid, which is formed in the ventricles.

IV. The blood–brain barrier closely regulates the chemical composition of the extracellular fluid of the CNS.

SECTION D REVIEW QUESTIONS

1. Make an organizational chart showing the CNS, PNS, brain, spinal cord, spinal nerves, cranial nerves, forebrain, brainstem, cerebrum, diencephalon, midbrain, pons, medulla oblongata, and cerebellum.
2. Draw a cross section of the spinal cord showing the gray and white matter, dorsal and ventral roots, dorsal root ganglion, and spinal nerve. Indicate the general locations of pathways.
3. List two functions of the thalamus.
4. List the functions of the hypothalamus, and discuss how they relate to homeostatic control.
5. Make a PNS chart indicating the relationships among afferent and efferent divisions, somatic and autonomic nervous systems, and sympathetic and parasympathetic divisions.
6. Contrast the somatic and autonomic divisions of the efferent nervous system; mention at least three characteristics of each.
7. Name the neurotransmitter released at each synapse or neuroeffector junction in the somatic and autonomic systems.
8. Contrast the sympathetic and parasympathetic components of the autonomic nervous system; mention at least four characteristics of each.
9. Explain how the adrenal medulla can affect receptors on various effector organs despite the fact that its cells have no axons.
10. The chemical composition of the CNS extracellular fluid is different from that of blood. Explain how this difference is achieved.

SECTION D KEY TERMS

SECTION D CLINICAL TERMS

CHAPTER 6 Clinical Case Study: A Woman Develops Pain, Visual Problems, and Tingling in Her Legs

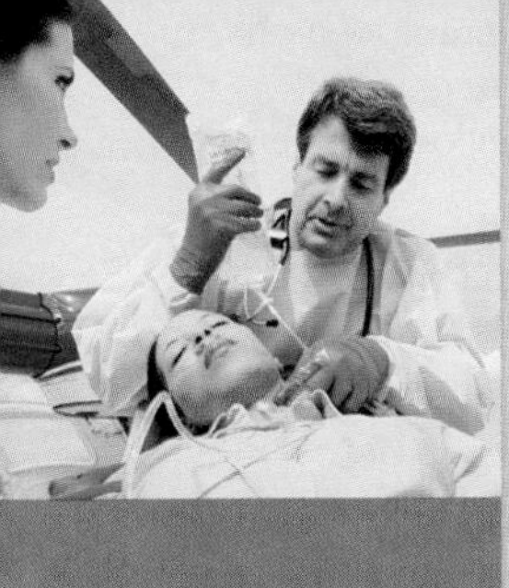

A 37-year-old female visits her doctor because of back pain and numbness and tingling in her legs. Sensory tests also show reduced ability to sense light touch and to feel a pinprick on both legs. X-rays show no abnormalities of the vertebrae or her spinal canal that might obstruct or damage nerve pathways. She is prescribed anti-inflammatory medications and sent home, and her symptoms gradually subside. Three months later, she comes back to the clinic because her symptoms have returned. In addition to back pain and sensory disturbances in her legs, however, she now also reports experiencing double vision when she looks to one side, and persistent dizziness. A sample of her cerebrospinal fluid obtained by lumbar puncture shows the presence of an abnormally high concentration of the disease-fighting proteins called antibodies (see Chapter 18), which suggests excess immune system activity within her CNS. Magnetic resonance imaging (MRI) is used to visualize her nervous system tissues, and several abnormal spots, or lesions, are noted in her mid-thoracic spinal cord, in her brainstem, and near the ventricles of her brain (see Figure 19.6 for an explanation of MRI). Her condition is tentatively diagnosed as multiple sclerosis, which is confirmed when a follow-up MRI performed 4 months later shows an increase in the number and size of lesions in her nervous system.

In the disease ***multiple sclerosis*** (***MS***), a loss of myelin occurs at one or several places in the nervous system. Multiple sclerosis ranks second only to trauma as a cause of neurological disability arising in young and middle-aged adults. It most commonly strikes between the ages of 20 and 50 and twice as often in females as in males. It currently affects approximately 400,000 Americans and as many as 3 million people worldwide. Multiple sclerosis is an autoimmune condition in which the myelin sheaths surrounding axons in the CNS are attacked and destroyed by antibodies and cells of the immune system. The loss of insulating myelin sheaths results in increased leak of K^+ through newly exposed channels. This results in hyperpolarization and failure of action potential conduction of neurons in the brain and spinal cord. Depending upon the location of the affected neurons, symptoms can include muscle weakness, fatigue, decreased motor coordination, slurred speech, blurred or hazy vision, bladder dysfunction, pain or other sensory disturbances, and cognitive dysfunction. In many patients, the symptoms are markedly worsened when body temperature is elevated, for example, by exercise, a hot shower, or hot weather.

The severity and rate of progression of MS vary enormously among individuals, ranging from isolated, episodic attacks with complete recovery in between to steadily progressing neurological disability. In the latter case, MS can ultimately be fatal as brainstem centers responsible for respiratory and cardiovascular function are destroyed. Because of the variability in presentation, diagnosing MS can be difficult. A person having several of these symptoms on two or more occasions separated by more than a month is a candidate for further testing. Nerve-conduction tests can detect slowed or failed action potential conduction in the motor, sensory, and visual systems. Cerebrospinal fluid analysis can reveal the presence of an abnormal immune reaction against myelin. The most definitive evidence, however, is usually the visualization by MRI of multiple, progressive, scarred (sclerotic) areas within the brain and spinal cord, from which this disease derives its name.

The cause of multiple sclerosis is not known, but it appears to result from a combination of genetic and environmental factors. It tends to run in families and is more common among Caucasians than in other racial groups. The involvement of environmental triggers is suggested by occasional clusters of disease outbreaks and also by the observation that the prevalence of MS in people of Japanese descent rises significantly when they move to the United States. Among the suspects for the environmental trigger is infection early in life with a virus, such as those that cause measles, cold sores, chicken pox, or influenza. There is presently no cure for multiple sclerosis, but anti-inflammatory agents and drugs that suppress the immune response have been proven to reduce the severity and slow the progression of the disease.

Clinical term: multiple sclerosis (MS)

See Chapter 19 for complete, integrative case studies.

TEST QUESTIONS

Answers found in Appendix A.

1. Which best describes an afferent neuron?
   a. The cell body is in the CNS and the peripheral axon terminal is in the skin.
   b. The cell body is in the dorsal root ganglion and the central axon terminal is in the spinal cord.
   c. The cell body is in the ventral horn of the spinal cord and the axon ends on skeletal muscle.
   d. The dendrites are in the PNS and the axon terminal is in the dorsal root.
   e. All parts of the cell are within the CNS.

2. Which incorrectly pairs a glial cell type with an associated function?
   a. astrocytes; formation of the blood–brain barrier
   b. microglia; performance of immune function in the CNS
   c. oligodendrocytes; formation of myelin sheaths on axons in the PNS
   d. ependymal cells; regulation of production of cerebrospinal fluid
   e. astrocytes; removal of potassium ions and neurotransmitters from the brain's extracellular fluid

3. If the extracellular Cl^- concentration is 110 mmol/L and a particular neuron maintains an intracellular Cl^- concentration of 4 mmol/L, at what membrane potential would Cl^- be closest to electrochemical equilibrium in that cell?
   a. +80 mV
   b. +60 mV
   c. 0 mV
   d. −86 mV
   e. −100 mV

4. Consider the following five experiments in which the concentration gradient for Na^+ was varied. In which case(s) would Na^+ tend to leak out of the cell if the membrane potential was experimentally held at +42 mV?

Experiment	Extracellular Na^+ (mmol/L)	Intracellular Na^+ (mmol/L)
A	50	15
B	60	15
C	70	15
D	80	15
E	90	15

   a. A only
   b. B only
   c. C only
   d. A, B, and C
   e. D and E

5. Which is a true statement about the resting membrane potential in a typical neuron?
   a. The membrane potential is closer to the Na^+ equilibrium potential than to the K^+ equilibrium potential.
   b. The Cl^- permeability is higher than that for Na^+ or K^+.
   c. The membrane potential is at the equilibrium potential for K^+.
   d. There is no ion movement at the steady resting membrane potential.
   e. Ion movement by the Na^+/K^+-ATPase pump is equal and opposite to the leak of ions through Na^+ and K^+ channels.

6. If a ligand-gated channel permeable to both Na^+ and K^+ was briefly opened at a specific location on the membrane of a typical resting neuron, what would result?
   a. Local currents on the inside of the membrane would flow away from that region.
   b. Local currents on the outside of the membrane would flow away from that region.
   c. Local currents would travel without decrement all along the cell's length.
   d. A brief local hyperpolarization of the membrane would result.
   e. Fluxes of Na^+ and K^+ would be equal, so no local currents would flow.

7. Which ion channel state correctly describes the phase of the action potential it is associated with?
   a. Voltage-gated Na^+ channels are inactivated in a resting neuronal membrane.
   b. Open voltage-gated K^+ channels cause the depolarizing upstroke of the action potential.
   c. Open voltage-gated K^+ channels cause afterhyperpolarization.
   d. The sizable leak through voltage-gated K^+ channels determines the value of the resting membrane potential.
   e. Opening of voltage-gated Cl^- channels is the main factor causing rapid repolarization of the membrane at the end of an action potential.

8. Two neurons, A and B, synapse onto a third neuron, C. If neurotransmitter from A opens ligand-gated channels permeable to Na^+ and K^+ and neurotransmitter from B opens ligand-gated Cl^- channels, which of the following statements is true?
   a. An action potential in neuron A causes a depolarizing EPSP in neuron B.
   b. An action potential in neuron B causes a depolarizing EPSP in neuron C.
   c. Simultaneous action potentials in A and B will cause hyperpolarization of neuron C.
   d. Simultaneous action potentials in A and B will cause less depolarization of neuron C than if only neuron A fired an action potential.
   e. An action potential in neuron B will bring neuron C closer to its action potential threshold than would an action potential in neuron A.

9. Which correctly associates a neurotransmitter with one of its characteristics?
   a. Dopamine is a catecholamine synthesized from the amino acid tyrosine.
   b. Glutamate is released by most inhibitory interneurons in the spinal cord.
   c. Serotonin is an endogenous opioid associated with "runner's high."
   d. GABA is the neurotransmitter that mediates long-term potentiation.
   e. Neuropeptides are synthesized in the axon terminals of the neurons that release them.

10. Which of these synapses does not have acetylcholine as its primary neurotransmitter?
   a. synapse of a postganglionic parasympathetic neuron onto a heart cell
   b. synapse of a postganglionic sympathetic neuron onto a smooth muscle cell
   c. synapse of a preganglionic sympathetic neuron onto a postganglionic neuron
   d. synapse of a somatic efferent neuron onto a skeletal muscle cell
   e. synapse of a preganglionic sympathetic neuron onto adrenal medullary cells

CHAPTER 6 GENERAL PRINCIPLES ASSESSMENT

Answers found in Appendix A.

1. One of the general principles of physiology introduced in Chapter 1 is, *Most physiological functions are controlled by multiple regulatory systems, often working in opposition.* How do the structure and function of the autonomic nervous system demonstrate this principle?
2. What general principles of physiology are demonstrated by the mechanisms underlying neuronal resting membrane potentials?
3. Another general principle of physiology states, ***Structure is a determinant of—and has coevolved with—function.*** A common theme in humans and other organisms is elaboration of surface area of a structure to maximize its ability to perform some function. What structures of the human nervous system demonstrate this principle?

CHAPTER 6 QUANTITATIVE AND THOUGHT QUESTIONS

Answers found in Appendix A.

1. Neurons are treated with a drug that instantly and permanently stops the Na^+/K^+-ATPase pumps. Assume for this question that the pumps are not electrogenic. What happens to the resting membrane potential immediately and over time?
2. Extracellular K^+ concentration in a person is increased with no change in intracellular K^+ concentration. What happens to the resting potential and the action potential?
3. A person has received a severe blow to the head but appears to be all right. Over the next week, however, he develops loss of appetite, thirst, and loss of sexual capacity but no loss in sensory or motor function. What part of the brain do you think may have been damaged?
4. A person is taking a drug that causes, among other things, dryness of the mouth and speeding of the heart rate but no impairment of the ability to use the skeletal muscles. What type of receptor does this drug probably block? (Table 6.11 will help you answer this.)
5. Some cells are treated with a drug that blocks Cl^- channels, and the membrane potential of these cells becomes slightly depolarized (less negative). From these facts, predict whether the plasma membrane of these cells actively transports Cl^- and, if so, in what direction.
6. If the enzyme acetylcholinesterase was blocked with a drug, what malfunctions would occur in the heart and skeletal muscle?
7. The compound tetraethylammonium (TEA) blocks the voltage-gated changes in K^+ permeability that occur during an action potential. After experimental treatment of neurons with TEA, what changes would you expect in the action potential? In the afterhyperpolarization?
8. A resting neuron has a membrane potential of −80 mV (determined by Na^+ and K^+ gradients), there are no Cl^- pumps, the cell is slightly permeable to Cl^-, and ECF $[Cl^-]$ is 100 mM. What is the intracellular $[Cl^-]$?

CHAPTER 6 ANSWERS TO PHYSIOLOGICAL INQUIRIES

Figure 6.8 If the electrodes were reversed, the graph would start at 0 mV as before, but when the electrode was inserted the potential difference recorded would jump to +70 mV rather than −70 mV.

Figure 6.10 NaCl and KCl ionize in solution virtually completely, so initially each compartment would have a total solute concentration of approximately 0.3 osmols per liter (see Chapter 4 to review the difference between moles and osmols). Because an insignificant number of potassium ions actually move in establishing the equilibrium potential, the final solute concentrations of the compartments would not be significantly different.

Figure 6.11 Na^+ and K^+ would move down their concentration gradients in opposite directions, each canceling charge carried by the other. Thus, at equilibrium, there would be no membrane potential and both compartments would have 0.15 M Cl^-, 0.075 M Na^+, and 0.075 M K^+.

Figure 6.12 No. Changing the ECF [K^+] has a greater effect on E_K (and thus the resting membrane potential). This is because the ratio of external to internal K^+ is changed more when ECF concentration goes from 5 to 6 mM (a 20% increase) than when ICF concentration is decreased from 150 to 149 mM (a 0.7% decrease). You can confirm this with the Nernst equation. Inserting typical values, when $[K_{out}] = 5$ mM and $[K_{in}] = 150$ mM, the calculated value of $E_K = -90.1$ mV. If you change $[K_{in}]$ to 149 mM, the calculated value of $E_K = -89.9$ mV, which is not very different. By comparison, changing $[K_{out}]$ to 6 mM causes a greater change, with the resulting $E_K = -85.3$ mV.

Figure 6.15 Because the exit of K^+ from the cell would make the inside of the cell more negative in the area of the channel, positive current would flow toward the channel's location on the inside of the cell and away from the channel on the outside. The graph would simply be inverted; there would be hyperpolarization at the initial site of the channel, which would be smaller in magnitude at increasing distances from the site.

Figure 6.19 The value of the resting potential would change very little because the permeability of resting membranes to Na^+ is very low. However, during an action potential, the membrane voltage would rise more steeply and reach a more positive value due to the larger electrochemical gradient for Na^+ entry through open voltage-gated channels.

Figure 6.23 In all of the neurons, action potentials will propagate in both directions from the elbow—up the arm toward the spinal cord and down the arm toward the hand. Action potentials traveling upward along afferent pathways will continue through synapses into the CNS to be perceived as pain, tingling, vibration, and other sensations of the lower arm. In contrast, action potential signals traveling backward up motor axons will die out once they reach the cell bodies because synapses found there are "one way" in the opposite direction.

Figure 6.31 The greater the distance between the synapse and the initial segment (the location of the electrode), the greater the decrement of a graded potential. Therefore, if synapse A were closer to the axon hillock than synapse C, summing the two would most likely result in a small depolarizing potential. The farther from the hillock synapse C is, the more closely the depolarization would come to resemble the trace occurring in response to synapse A firing alone.

Figure 6.46 The muscarinic receptor blocker would only inhibit parasympathetic pathways, where acetylcholine released from postganglionic neurons binds to muscarinic receptors on target organs. This would reduce the ability to stimulate "rest-or-digest" processes and leave the sympathetic "fight-or-flight" response intact. On the other hand, a nicotinic acetylcholine receptor blocker would inhibit all autonomic control of target organs because those receptors are found at the ganglion in both parasympathetic and sympathetic pathways.

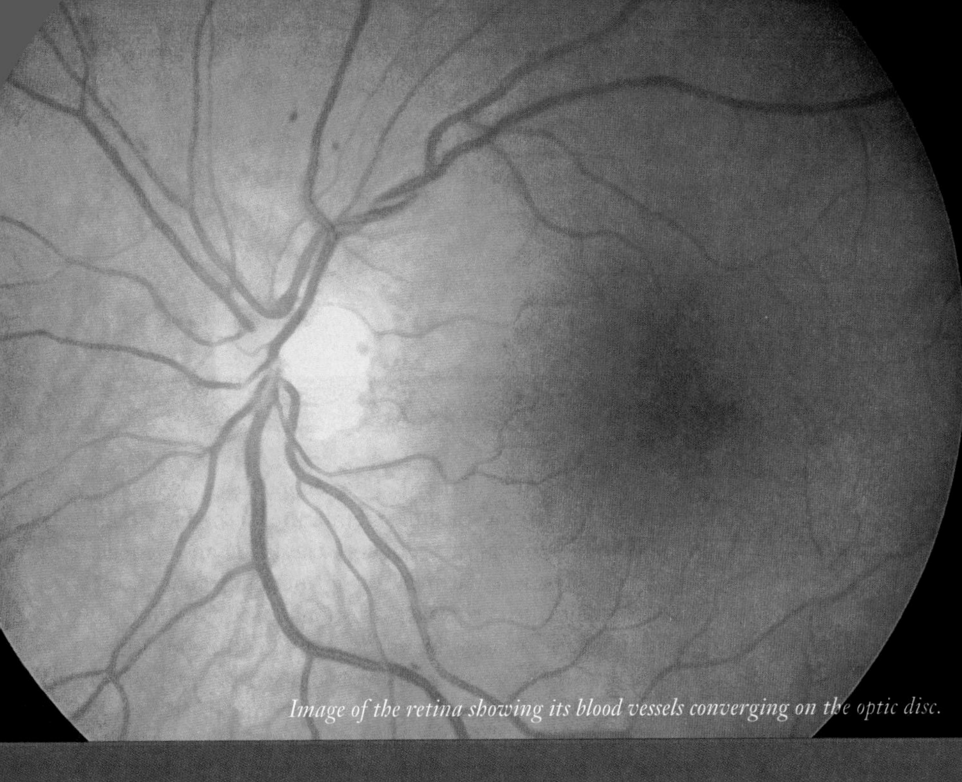

Image of the retina showing its blood vessels converging on the optic disc.

7 Sensory Physiology

SECTION A
General Principles

SECTION B
Specific Sensory Systems

Chapter 6 provided an overview of the structure and function of the nervous system, and explained in detail how electrical signals are generated and transmitted by excitable membranes. It also generally described two functional divisions of the nervous system: the afferent division, by which the CNS receives information, and the efferent division, which transmits outgoing commands. In this chapter, you will learn in more detail about the structure and function of sensory systems comprising the afferent division of the nervous system. In addition, you will learn how those systems help maintain homeostasis by providing the CNS with information about conditions in the external and internal environments. Such information is communicated to the CNS from the skin, muscles, and viscera as well as from the visual, auditory, vestibular, and chemical sensory systems.

A number of general principles of physiology will be evident in this discussion of sensory systems. One is that information flow between cells, tissues and organs is an essential feature of homeostasis that allows for integration of physiological processes. Sensory systems gather information in the form of various physical and chemical stimuli and convert those stimuli into action potentials that are conducted to integrating centers for processing. An amazing variety of examples of the relationship between structure and function will be apparent in the form of specialized

receptors that allow the different sensory systems to detect specific types of stimuli, such as pressure, light, or airborne chemicals. An understanding of some simple laws of chemistry and physics is important for appreciating how some stimuli are detected and encoded, as will be evident in the discussions of how the eye detects electromagnetic radiation of particular wavelengths, and how the ear detects sound waves.

SECTION **A**

General Principles

A **sensory system** is a part of the nervous system that consists of sensory receptors that receive stimuli from the external or internal environment, the neural pathways that conduct information from the receptors to the brain or spinal cord, and those parts of the brain that deal primarily with processing the information. Information that a sensory system processes may or may not lead to conscious awareness of the stimulus. For example, whereas you would immediately notice a change when leaving an air-conditioned house on a hot summer day, your blood pressure can fluctuate significantly without your awareness. Regardless of whether the information reaches consciousness, it is called **sensory information.** If the information does reach consciousness, it can also be called a **sensation.** A person's awareness of the sensation (and, typically, understanding of its meaning) is called **perception.** For example, feeling pain is a sensation, but awareness that a tooth hurts is a perception. Sensations and perceptions occur after the CNS modifies or processes sensory information. This processing can accentuate, dampen, or otherwise filter sensory afferent information.

The initial step of sensory processing is the transduction of stimulus energy first into graded potentials—the receptor potentials—and then into action potentials in afferent neurons. The pattern of action potentials in particular neurons is a code that provides information about the stimulus such as its intensity, its location, and the specific type of input that is being sensed. Primary sensory areas of the central nervous system that receive this input then communicate with other regions of the brain or spinal cord in further processing of the information, which may include determination of reflexive efferent responses, perception, storage into memory, comparison with past memories, and assignment of emotional significance.

7.1 Sensory Receptors

Information about the external world and about the body's internal environment exists in different forms—pressure, temperature, light, odorants, sound waves, chemical concentrations, and so on. **Sensory receptors** at the peripheral ends of afferent neurons change this information into graded potentials that can initiate action potentials, which travel into the central nervous system. The receptors are either specialized endings of the primary afferent neurons themselves (**Figure 7.1a**) or separate receptor cells (some of which are actually specialized neurons) that signal the primary afferent neurons by releasing neurotransmitters (**Figure 7.1b**).

To avoid confusion, be aware that the term *receptor* has two completely different meanings. One meaning is that of "sensory receptor," as just defined. The second usage is for the individual proteins in the plasma membrane or inside a cell that bind specific chemical messengers, triggering an intracellular signal transduction pathway or influencing gene transcription, culminating in the cell's response (see Chapter 5). The potential confusion between these two meanings is magnified by the fact that the stimuli for some sensory receptors (e.g., those involved in taste and smell) are chemicals that bind to receptor proteins in the plasma membrane of the sensory receptor. If you are in doubt as to which meaning is intended, add the modifier "sensory" or "protein" to see which makes sense in the context.

The energy or chemical that impinges upon and activates a sensory receptor is known as a **stimulus.** There are many types of sensory receptors, each of which responds much more readily to one form of stimulus than to others. The type of stimulus to which a particular receptor responds in normal functioning is known as its **adequate stimulus.** In addition, within the general stimulus type that serves as a receptor's adequate stimulus, a particular receptor may respond best (i.e., at lowest threshold) to a limited subset of stimuli. For example, different individual receptors in the eye respond best to light (the adequate stimulus) of different wavelengths.

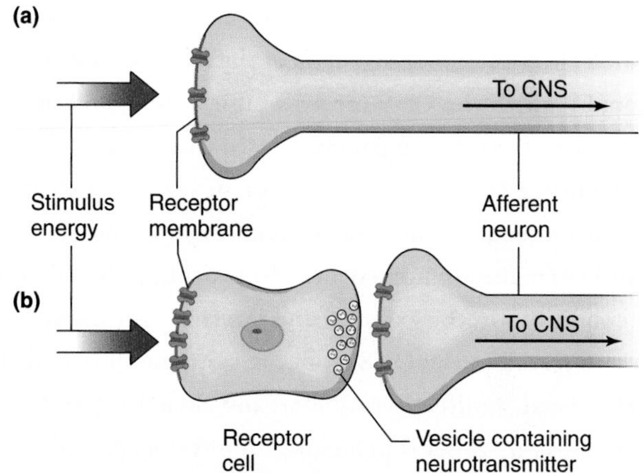

Figure 7.1 Schematic diagram of two types of sensory receptors. The sensitive membrane region that responds to a stimulus is either (a) an ending of an afferent neuron or (b) on a separate cell adjacent to an afferent neuron. Ion channels (shown in purple) on the receptor membrane alter ion flux and initiate stimulus transduction. Note that in some cases the stimulus (red arrows) does not act directly on ion channels but activates them indirectly through mechanisms specific to that sensory system.

Most sensory receptors are exquisitely sensitive to their specific adequate stimulus. For example, some olfactory receptors respond to as few as three or four odor molecules in the inspired air, and visual receptors can respond to a single photon, the smallest quantity of light.

Virtually all sensory receptors, however, can be activated by different types of stimuli if the intensity is sufficient. For example, the receptors of the eye normally respond to light, but they can be activated by an intense mechanical stimulus. For example, a poke in the eye can result in "seeing stars"—the sensation of *light* is still perceived even though the photoreceptors are stimulated by a mechanical stimulus. Regardless of how the receptor is stimulated, any given receptor gives rise to only one sensation.

Several general classes of receptors are characterized by the type of stimulus to which they are sensitive. As the name indicates, **mechanoreceptors** respond to mechanical stimuli, such as pressure or stretch, and are responsible for many types of sensory information, including touch, blood pressure, and muscle tension. These stimuli alter the permeability of ion channels on the receptor membrane, changing the membrane potential. **Thermoreceptors** detect sensations of cold or warmth, and **photoreceptors** respond to particular ranges of light wavelengths. **Chemoreceptors** respond to the binding of particular chemicals to the receptor membrane. This type of receptor provides the senses of smell and taste and detects blood pH and oxygen concentration. **Nociceptors** are a general category of detectors that sense pain due to actual or potential tissue damage. They can be activated by a variety of stimuli such as heat, mechanical stimuli like excess stretch, or chemical substances in the extracellular fluid of damaged tissues.

The Receptor Potential

Regardless of the original form of the signal that activates sensory receptors, the information must be translated into the language of graded potentials or action potentials. The process by which a stimulus—a photon of light, say, or the mechanical stretch of a tissue—is transformed into an electrical response is known as **sensory transduction.** The transduction process in all sensory receptors involves the opening or closing of ion channels that receive information about the internal and external world, either directly or through a second-messenger system. The ion channels are present in a specialized region of the receptor membrane located at the distal tip of the cell's single axon or on associated specialized sensory cells (see Figure 7.1). The gating of these ion channels allows a change in ion flux across the receptor membrane, which in turn produces a change in the membrane potential. This change is a graded potential called a **receptor potential.** (See Figure 6.16 to review the general properties of graded potentials.) The different mechanisms that affect ion channels in the various types of sensory receptors are described throughout this chapter.

In afferent neurons with specialized receptor tips, the receptor membrane region where the initial ion channel changes occur does not generate action potentials. Instead, local current flows a short distance along the axon to a region where the membrane has voltage-gated ion channels and can generate action potentials. In myelinated afferent neurons, this region is usually at the first node of Ranvier. The receptor potential, like the synaptic potential discussed in Chapter 6, is a graded response to different stimulus intensities (**Figure 7.2**) and diminishes as it travels along the membrane.

If the receptor membrane is on a separate cell, the receptor potential there alters the release of neurotransmitter from that cell. The neurotransmitter diffuses across the extracellular cleft between the receptor cell and the afferent neuron and binds to receptor proteins on the afferent neuron. Thus, this junction is a synapse. The combination of neurotransmitter with its binding sites generates a graded potential in the afferent neuron analogous to either an excitatory postsynaptic potential or, in some cases, an inhibitory postsynaptic potential.

As is true of all graded potentials, the magnitude of a receptor potential (or a graded potential in the axon adjacent to the receptor cell) decreases with distance from its origin. However, if the amount of depolarization at the first excitable patch of membrane in the afferent neuron (e.g., at the first node of Ranvier)

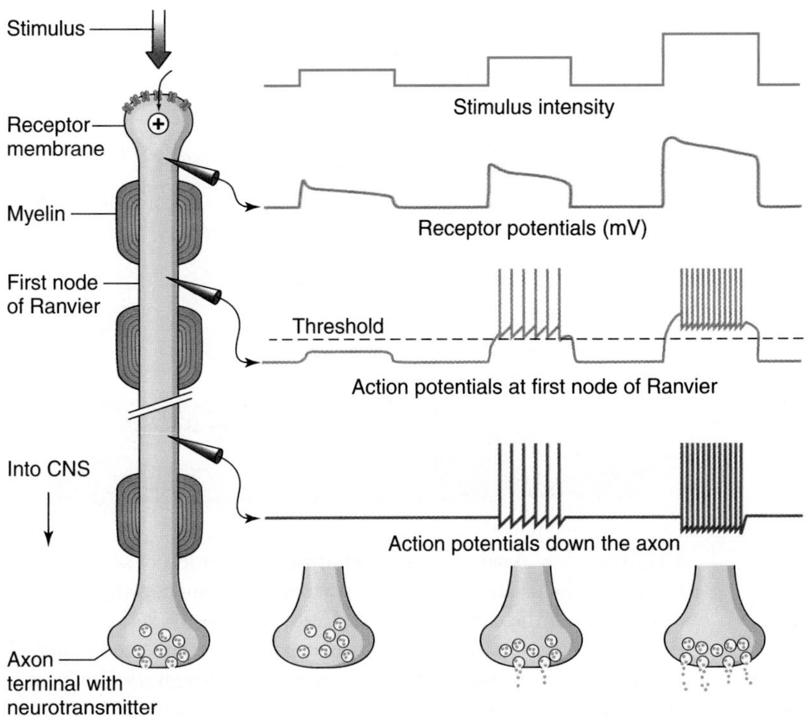

Figure 7.2 Stimulation of an afferent neuron with a receptor ending. Electrodes measure graded potentials and action potentials at various points in response to different stimulus intensities. Action potentials arise at the first node of Ranvier in response to a suprathreshold stimulus, and the action potential frequency and neurotransmitter release increase as the stimulus and receptor potential become larger.

PHYSIOLOGICAL INQUIRY

- How would this afferent pathway be affected by exposing this entire neuron to a drug that blocks voltage-gated Ca^{2+} channels?

Answer can be found at end of chapter.

is large enough to bring the membrane to threshold, action potentials are initiated, which then propagate along the afferent neuron (see Figure 7.2).

As long as the receptor potential keeps the afferent neuron depolarized to a level at or above threshold, action potentials continue to fire and propagate along the afferent neuron. Moreover, an increase in the graded potential magnitude causes an increase in the action potential frequency in the afferent neuron (up to the limit imposed by the neuron's refractory period) and an increase in neurotransmitter release at the afferent neuron's central axon terminal (see Figure 7.2). Although the magnitude of the receptor potential determines the *frequency* of the action potentials, it does not determine the *amplitude* of those action potentials. Factors that control the magnitude of the receptor potential include stimulus strength, rate of change of stimulus strength, temporal summation of successive receptor potentials (see Figure 6.31), and a process called adaptation.

Adaptation is a decrease in receptor sensitivity, which results in a decrease in action potential frequency in an afferent neuron despite the continuous presence of a stimulus. Degrees of adaptation vary widely among different types of sensory receptors (**Figure 7.3**). **Slowly adapting receptors** maintain a persistent or slowly decaying receptor potential during a constant stimulus, initiating action potentials in afferent neurons for the duration of the stimulus. These receptors are common in systems sensing parameters that need to be constantly monitored, such as joint and muscle receptors that participate in the maintenance of steady postures. Conversely, **rapidly adapting receptors** generate a receptor potential and action potentials at the onset of a stimulus but very quickly cease responding. Adaptation may be so rapid that only a single action potential is generated. Some rapidly adapting receptors only initiate action potentials at the onset of a stimulus—a so-called "on response"—whereas others respond with a burst at the beginning of the stimulus and again upon its removal—called "on–off responses." Rapidly adapting receptors are important for monitoring sensory stimuli that move or change quickly (like receptors in the skin that sense vibration) and those that persist but do not need to be monitored closely (like receptors that detect the pressure of a chair only when you first sit down).

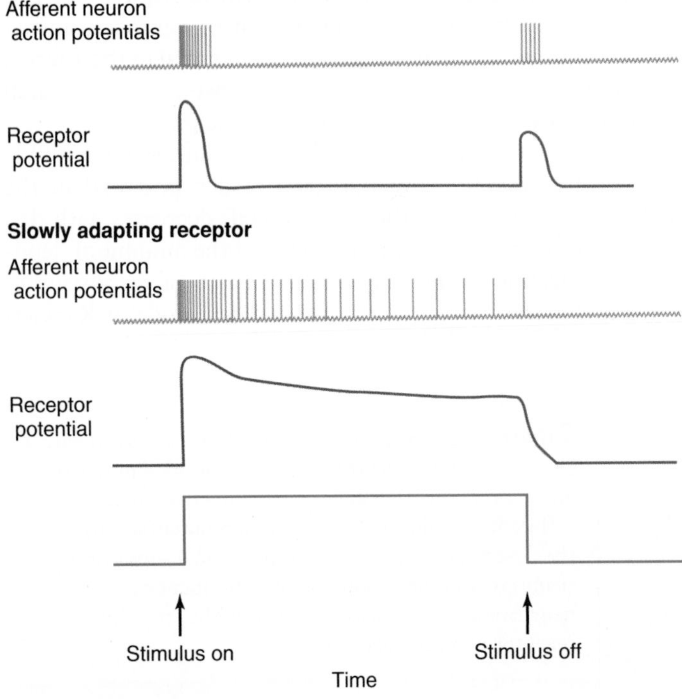

Figure 7.3 Responses of slowly adapting and rapidly adapting receptors to a prolonged, constant stimulus. Rapidly adapting receptors respond only briefly before adapting to a constant stimulus, whereas slowly adapting receptors have persistent receptor potentials and afferent neuronal action potentials. The rapidly adapting receptor shown has an "off response" at the end of the stimulus, which is not always the case.

7.2 Primary Sensory Coding

Coding is the conversion of stimulus energy into a signal that conveys the relevant sensory information to the central nervous system. Important characteristics of a stimulus include the type of input it represents, its intensity, and the location of the body it affects. Coding begins at the receptive neurons in the peripheral nervous system.

A single afferent neuron with all its receptor endings makes up a **sensory unit.** In a few cases, the afferent neuron has a single receptor, but generally the peripheral end of an afferent neuron divides into many fine branches, each terminating with a receptor.

The area of the body that leads to activity in a particular afferent neuron when stimulated is called the **receptive field** for that neuron (**Figure 7.4**). Receptive fields of neighboring afferent neurons usually overlap so that stimulation of a single point activates several sensory units. Thus, activation of

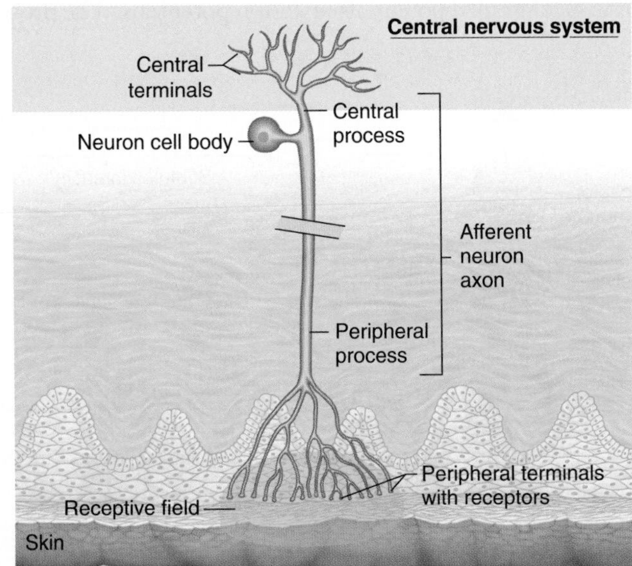

Figure 7.4 A sensory unit including the location of sensory receptors, the processes reaching peripherally and centrally from the cell body, and the terminals in the CNS. Also shown is the receptive field of this neuron. Afferent neuron cell bodies are located in dorsal root ganglia of the spinal cord for sensory inputs from the body and cranial nerve ganglia for sensory inputs from the head.

a single sensory unit almost never occurs. As we will see, the degree of overlap varies in different parts of the body.

Stimulus Type

Another term for stimulus type (heat, cold, sound, or pressure, for example) is stimulus **modality.** Modalities can be divided into submodalities. Cold and warm are submodalities of temperature, whereas salty, sweet, bitter, and sour are submodalities of taste. The type of sensory receptor a stimulus activates plays the primary role in coding the stimulus modality.

As mentioned earlier, a given receptor type is particularly sensitive to one stimulus modality—the adequate stimulus—because of the signal transduction mechanisms and ion channels incorporated in the receptor's plasma membrane. For example, receptors for vision contain pigment molecules whose shapes are transformed by light, which in turn alters the activity of membrane ion channels and generates a receptor potential. In contrast, receptors in the skin do not have light-sensitive pigment molecules, so they cannot respond to light.

All the receptors of a single afferent neuron are preferentially sensitive to the same type of stimulus; for example, they are all sensitive to cold or all to pressure. Adjacent sensory units, however, may be sensitive to different types of stimuli. Because the receptive fields for different modalities overlap, a single stimulus, such as an ice cube on the skin, can simultaneously give rise to the sensations of touch and temperature.

Stimulus Intensity

How do we distinguish a strong stimulus from a weak one when the information about both stimuli is relayed by action potentials that are all the same amplitude? The frequency of action potentials in a single afferent neuron is one way, because increased stimulus strength means a larger receptor potential, and this in turn leads to more frequent action potentials (review Figure 7.2).

As the strength of a local stimulus increases, receptors on adjacent branches of an afferent neuron are activated, resulting in a summation of their local currents. **Figure 7.5** shows an experiment in which increased stimulus intensity to the receptors of a sensory unit is reflected in increased action potential frequency in its afferent neuron.

In addition to increasing the firing frequency in a single afferent neuron, stronger stimuli usually affect a larger area and activate similar receptors on the endings of *other* afferent neurons. For example, when you touch a surface lightly with a finger, the area of skin in contact with the surface is small, and only the receptors in that skin area are stimulated. Pressing down firmly increases the area of skin stimulated. This "calling in" of receptors on additional afferent neurons is known as **recruitment.**

Stimulus Location

A third type of information to be signaled is the location of the stimulus—in other words, where the stimulus is being applied. It should be noted that in vision, hearing, and smell, stimulus location is interpreted as arising from the site from which the stimulus originated rather than the place on our body where the stimulus was actually applied. For example, we interpret the sight and sound of a barking dog as arising from the dog in the yard rather than in a specific region of our eyes and ears. We will have more to say about this later; we deal here with the senses in which the stimulus is localized to a site on the body.

Stimulus location is coded by the site of a stimulated receptor, as well as by the fact that action potentials from each

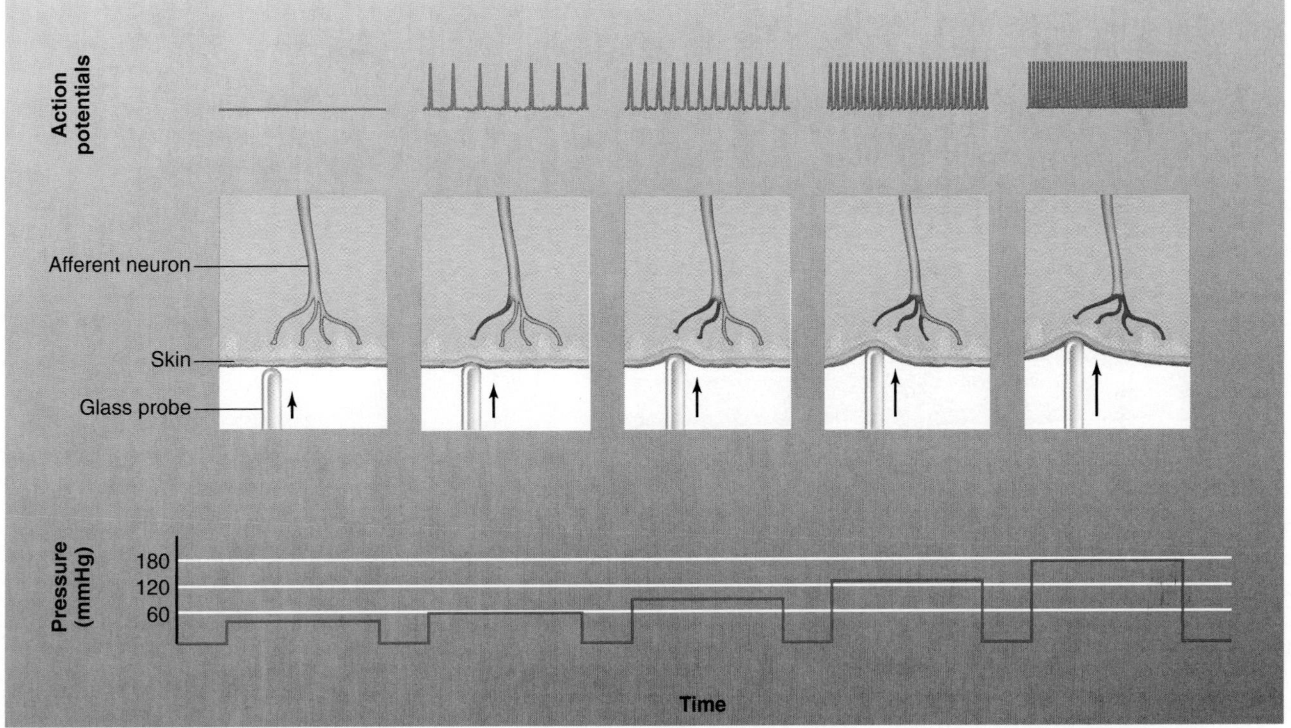

Figure 7.5 Action potentials in an afferent fiber leading from the pressure receptors of a slowly adapting, single sensory unit increase in frequency as more branches of the afferent neuron are stimulated by pressures of increasing magnitude.

receptor travel along unique pathways to a specific region of the CNS associated only with that particular modality and body location. These distinct anatomical pathways are sometimes referred to as **labeled lines.** The precision, or **acuity,** with which we can locate and discern one stimulus from an adjacent one depends upon the amount of convergence of neuronal input in the specific ascending pathways. The greater the convergence, the less the acuity. Other factors affecting acuity are the size of the receptive field covered by a single sensory unit (**Figure 7.6a**), the density of sensory units, and the amount of overlap in nearby receptive fields. For example, it is easy to discriminate between two adjacent stimuli (two-point discrimination) applied to the skin on your lips, where the sensory units are small and numerous, but it is harder to do so on the back, where the relatively few sensory units are large and widely spaced (**Figure 7.6b**). Locating sensations from internal organs is less precise than from the skin because there are fewer afferent neurons in the internal organs and each has a larger receptive field.

It is fairly easy to see why a stimulus to a neuron that has a small receptive field can be located more precisely than a stimulus to a neuron with a large receptive field (see Figure 7.6). However, more subtle mechanisms also exist that allow us to localize distinct stimuli within the receptive field of a single neuron. In some cases, receptive field overlap aids stimulus localization even though, intuitively, overlap would seem to "muddy" the image. In the next few paragraphs, we will examine how this works.

An afferent neuron responds most vigorously to stimuli applied at the center of its receptive field because the receptor density—that is, the number of its receptor endings in a given area—is greatest there. The response decreases as the stimulus is moved toward the receptive field periphery. Thus, a stimulus activates more receptors and generates more action potentials in its associated afferent neuron if it occurs at the center of the receptive field (point A in **Figure 7.7**). The firing frequency of the afferent neuron is also related to stimulus strength, however. Thus, a high frequency of impulses in the single afferent nerve fiber of Figure 7.7 could mean either that a moderately intense stimulus was applied to the center at point A or that a stronger stimulus was applied near the periphery at point B. Therefore, neither the intensity nor the location of the stimulus can be detected precisely with a single afferent neuron.

Because the receptor endings of different afferent neurons overlap, however, a stimulus will trigger activity in more than one sensory unit. In **Figure 7.8,** neurons A and C, stimulated near the edges of their receptive fields where the receptor density is low, fire action potentials less frequently than does neuron B, stimulated at the center of its receptive field. A high action potential frequency in neuron B occurring

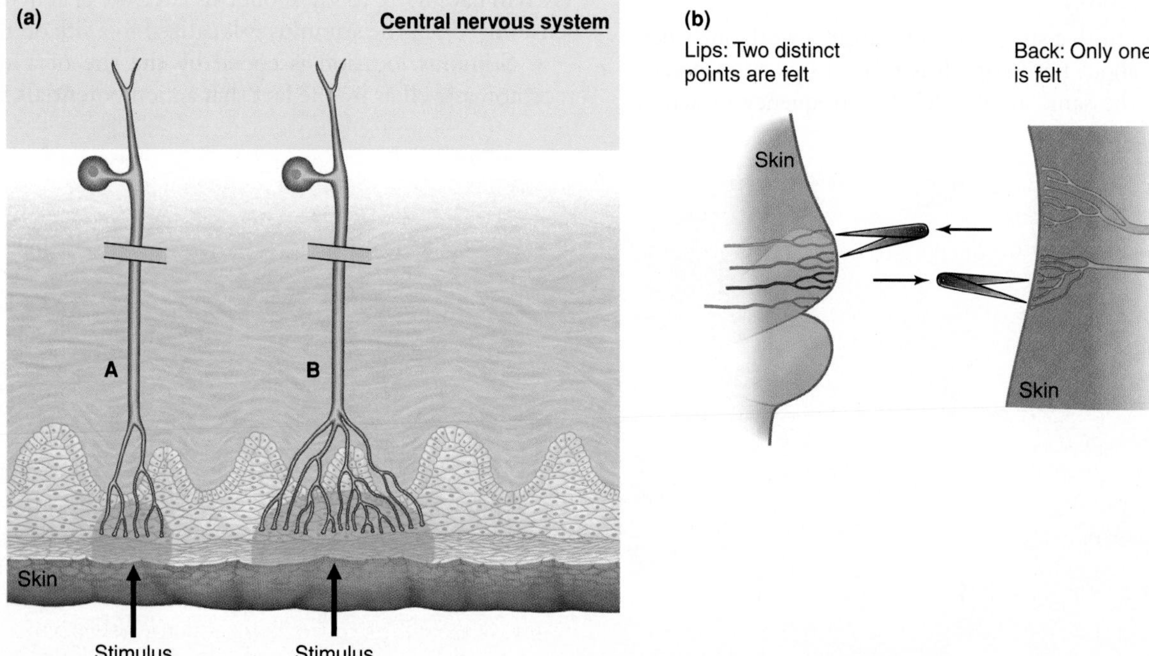

Figure 7.6 The influence of sensory unit size and density on acuity. (a) The information from neuron A indicates the stimulus location more precisely than does that from neuron B because A's receptive field is smaller. (b) Two-point discrimination is finer on the lips than on the back, due to the lips' numerous sensory units with small receptive fields.

PHYSIOLOGICAL INQUIRY

- Referring to part (b) of the figure, make a prediction about the relative size of the brain region devoted to processing lip sensations versus that for the brain region that processes sensations from the skin of your back.

Answer can be found at end of chapter.

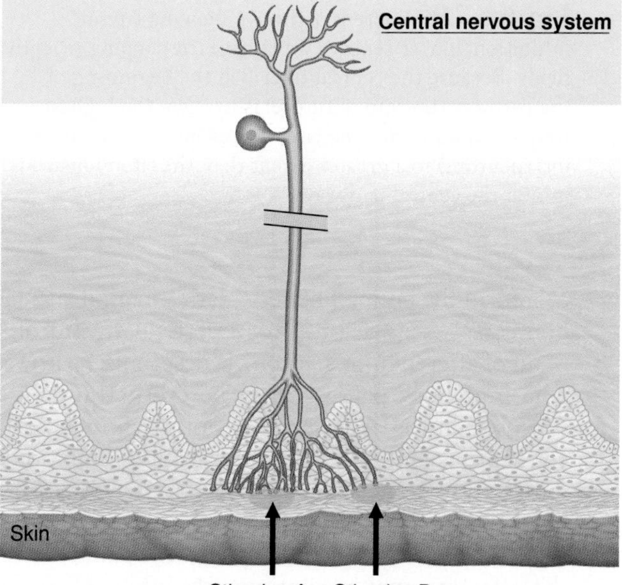

Figure 7.7 Two stimulus points, A and B, in the receptive field of a single afferent neuron. The density of receptor terminals around area A is greater than around B, so the frequency of action potentials in response to a stimulus in area A will be greater than the response to a similar stimulus in B.

simultaneously with lower frequencies in A and C provides the brain with a more accurate localization of the stimulus near the center of neuron B's receptive field. Once this location is known, the brain can interpret the firing frequency of neuron B to determine stimulus intensity.

Lateral Inhibition

The phenomenon of **lateral inhibition** is an important mechanism enabling the localization of a stimulus site for some sensory systems. In lateral inhibition, information from afferent neurons whose receptors are at the edge of a stimulus is strongly inhibited compared to information from the stimulus's center. **Figure 7.9** shows one neuronal arrangement that accomplishes lateral inhibition. The afferent neuron in the center (B) has a higher initial firing frequency than do the neurons on either side (A and C). The number of action potentials transmitted in the lateral pathways is further decreased by inhibitory inputs from inhibitory interneurons stimulated by the central neuron. Although the lateral afferent neurons (A and C) also exert inhibition on the central pathway, their lower initial firing frequency has a smaller inhibitory effect on the central pathway. Thus, lateral inhibition enhances the *contrast* between the center and periphery of a stimulated region, thereby increasing the brain's ability to localize a sensory input. Lateral inhibition can occur at different levels in the sensory pathways but typically happens at an early stage.

Lateral inhibition can be demonstrated by pressing the tip of a pencil against your finger. With your eyes closed, you can localize the pencil point precisely, even though the region around the pencil tip is also indented, activating mechanoreceptors within this region (**Figure 7.10**). Exact localization is possible because lateral inhibition removes the information from the peripheral regions.

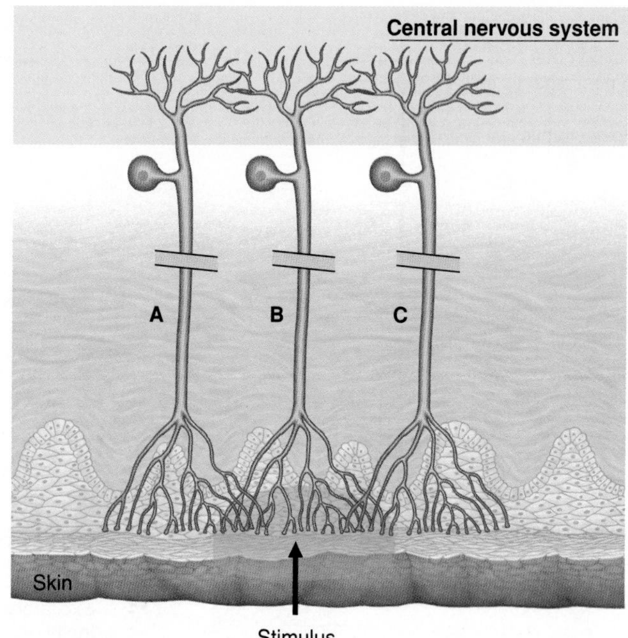

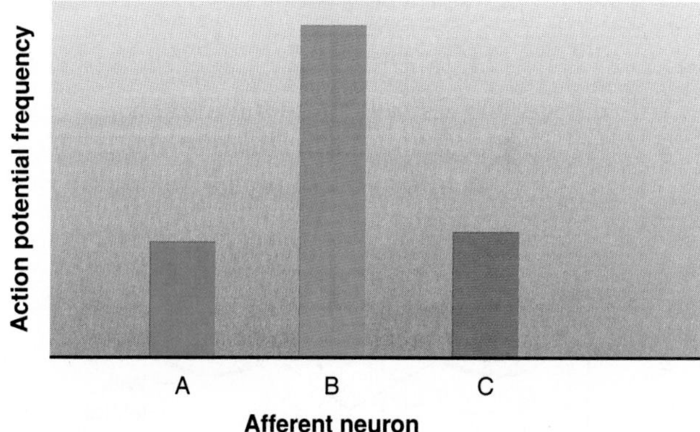

Figure 7.8 A stimulus point falls within the overlapping receptive fields of three afferent neurons. Note the difference in receptor response (i.e., the action potential frequency in the three neurons) due to the difference in receptor distribution under the stimulus (fewer receptor endings for A and C than for B).

Lateral inhibition is utilized to the greatest degree in the pathways providing the most accurate localization. For example, lateral inhibition within the retina of the eye creates amazingly sharp visual acuity, and skin hair movements are also well-localized due to lateral inhibition between parallel pathways ascending to the brain. On the other hand, neuronal pathways carrying temperature and pain information do not have significant lateral inhibition, so we locate these stimuli relatively poorly.

Central Control of Afferent Information

All sensory signals are subject to extensive modification at the various synapses along the sensory pathways before they reach higher levels of the central nervous system. Inhibition from collaterals from other ascending neurons (e.g., lateral inhibition) reduces or even abolishes much of the incoming information, as can inhibitory pathways descending from higher

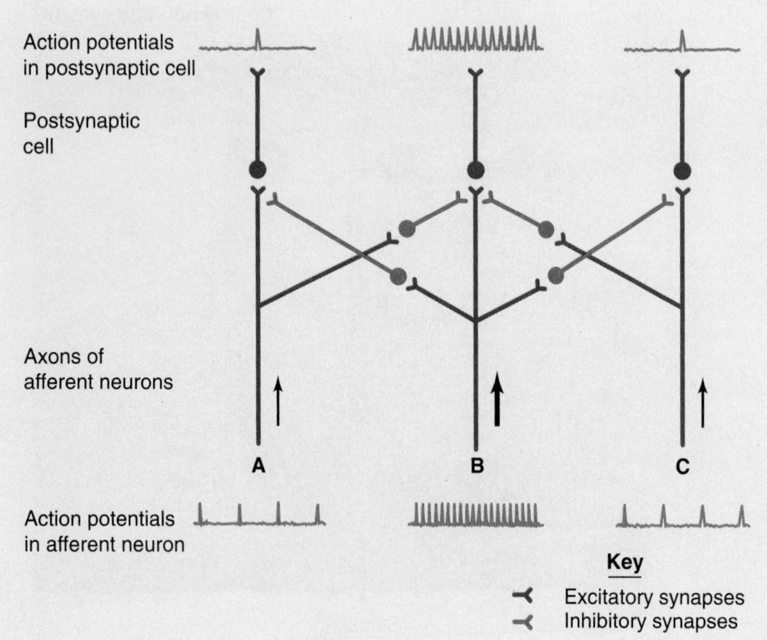

Figure 7.9 Afferent pathways showing lateral inhibition. Three sensory units have overlapping receptive fields. Because the central fiber B at the beginning of the pathway (bottom of figure) is firing at the highest frequency, it inhibits the lateral neurons (via inhibitory interneurons) to a greater extent than the lateral neurons inhibit the central pathway.

centers in the brain. The reticular formation and cerebral cortex (see Chapter 6), in particular, control the input of afferent information via descending pathways. The inhibitory controls may be exerted directly by synapses on the axon terminals of the primary afferent neurons (an example of presynaptic inhibition) or indirectly via interneurons that affect other neurons in the sensory pathways (**Figure 7.11**).

In some cases, for example, in the pain pathways, the afferent input is continuously inhibited to some degree. This provides the flexibility of either removing the inhibition, so as to allow a greater degree of signal transmission, or increasing the inhibition, so as to block the signal more completely.

Therefore, the sensory information that reaches the brain is significantly modified from the basic signal originally transduced into action potentials at the sensory receptors. The neuronal pathways within which these modifications take place are described next.

7.3 Ascending Neural Pathways in Sensory Systems

Afferent **sensory pathways** are generally formed by chains of three or more neurons connected by synapses. These chains of neurons travel in bundles of parallel pathways carrying information into the central nervous system. Some pathways terminate in parts of the cerebral cortex responsible for conscious recognition of the incoming information; others carry information not consciously perceived. Sensory pathways are also called **ascending pathways** because they project "up" to the brain.

The central processes of the afferent neurons enter the brain or spinal cord and synapse upon interneurons there. The central processes may diverge to terminate on several, or many, interneurons (**Figure 7.12a**) or converge so that the processes of many afferent neurons terminate upon a single interneuron (**Figure 7.12b**). The interneurons upon which the afferent neurons synapse are called second-order neurons, and these in turn synapse with third-order neurons, and so on, until the information (coded action potentials) reaches the cerebral cortex.

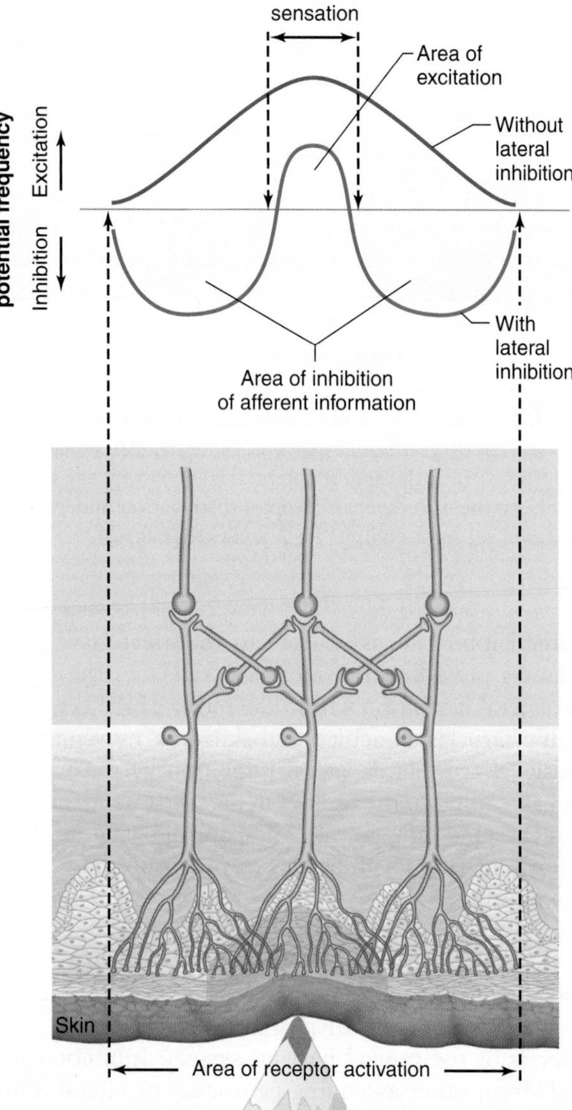

Figure 7.10 A pencil tip pressed against the skin activates receptors under the pencil tip and in the adjacent tissue. The sensory unit under the tip inhibits additional stimulated units at the edge of the stimulated area. Lateral inhibition produces a central area of excitation surrounded by an area in which the afferent information is inhibited. The sensation is localized to a more restricted region than that in which all three units are actually stimulated.

Most sensory pathways convey information about only a single type of sensory information. For example, one pathway conveys information only from mechanoreceptors, whereas another is influenced by information only from thermoreceptors. This allows the brain to distinguish the different types of sensory information even though all of it is being transmitted by essentially the same signal, the action potential. The ascending pathways in the spinal cord and brain that carry information about single types of stimuli

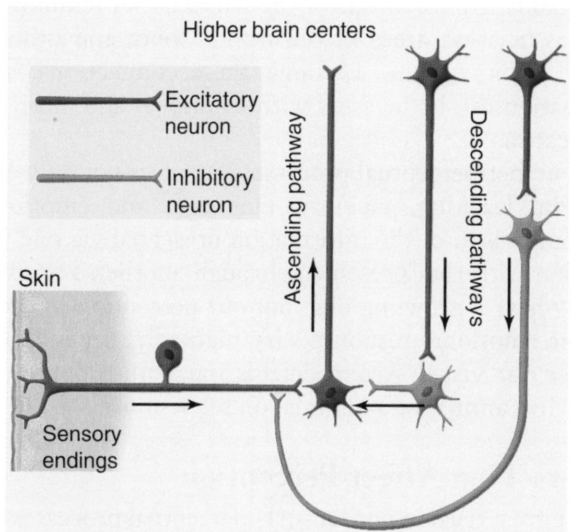

Figure 7.11 Descending pathways may influence sensory information by directly inhibiting the central terminals of the afferent neuron (an example of presynaptic inhibition) or via an interneuron that affects the ascending pathway by inhibitory synapses. Arrows indicate the direction of action potential transmission.

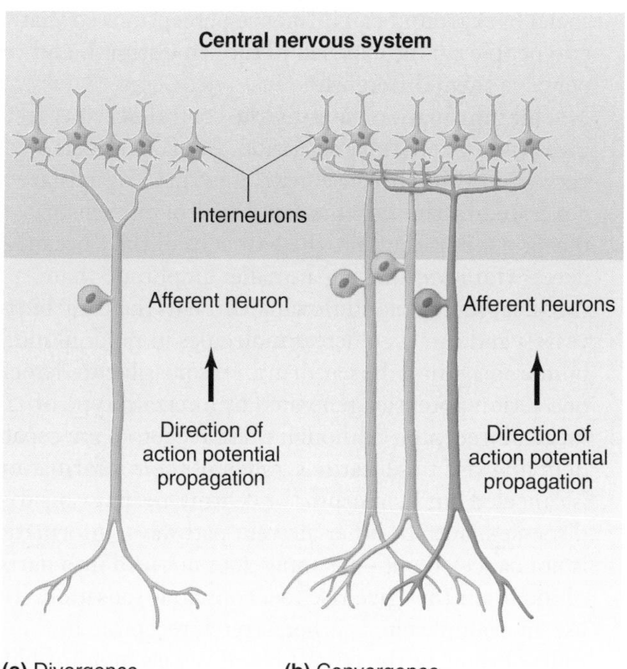

Figure 7.12 (a) Divergence of an afferent neuron onto many interneurons. (b) Convergence of input from several afferent neurons onto single interneurons.

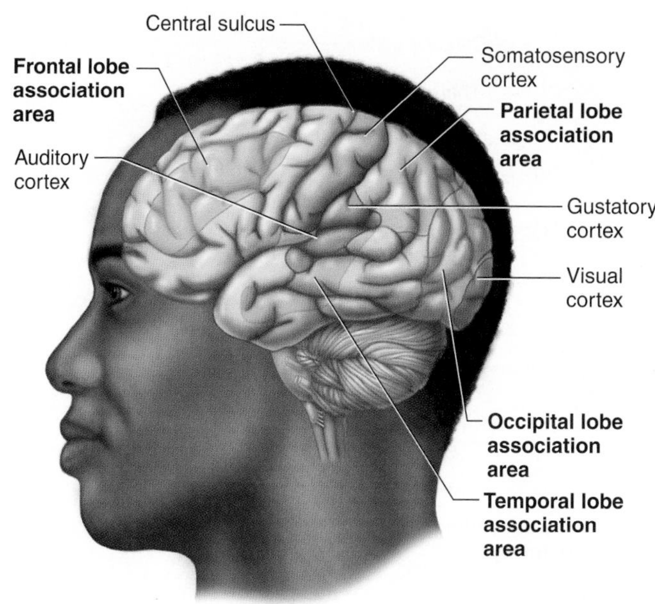

Figure 7.13 AP|R Primary sensory areas and areas of association cortex. The olfactory cortex is located toward the midline on the undersurface of the frontal lobes (not visible in this picture).

are known as the **specific ascending pathways.** The specific ascending pathways pass to the brainstem and thalamus, and the final neurons in the pathways go from there to specific sensory areas of the cerebral cortex (**Figure 7.13**). (The olfactory pathways do not send pathways to the thalamus, instead sending some branches directly to the olfactory cortex and others to the limbic system.) For the most part, the specific pathways cross to the side of the central nervous system that is opposite to the location of their sensory receptors. Thus, information from receptors on the right side of the body is transmitted to the left cerebral hemisphere, and vice versa.

The specific ascending pathways that transmit information from somatic receptors project to the somatosensory cortex. **Somatic receptors** are those carrying information from the skin, skeletal muscle, bones, tendons, and joints. The **somatosensory cortex** is a strip of cortex that lies in the parietal lobe of the brain just posterior to the **central sulcus,** which separates the parietal and frontal lobes (see Figure 7.13). The specific ascending pathways from the eyes connect to a different primary cortical receiving area, the **visual cortex,** which is in the occipital lobe. The specific ascending pathways from the ears go to the **auditory cortex,** which is in the temporal lobe. Specific ascending pathways from the taste buds pass to the **gustatory cortex** adjacent to the region of the somatosensory cortex where information from the face is processed. The pathways serving olfaction project to portions of the limbic system and the **olfactory cortex,** which is located on the undersurface of the frontal and temporal lobes. Finally, the processing of afferent information does not end in the primary cortical receiving areas but continues from these areas to association areas in the cerebral cortex where complex integration occurs.

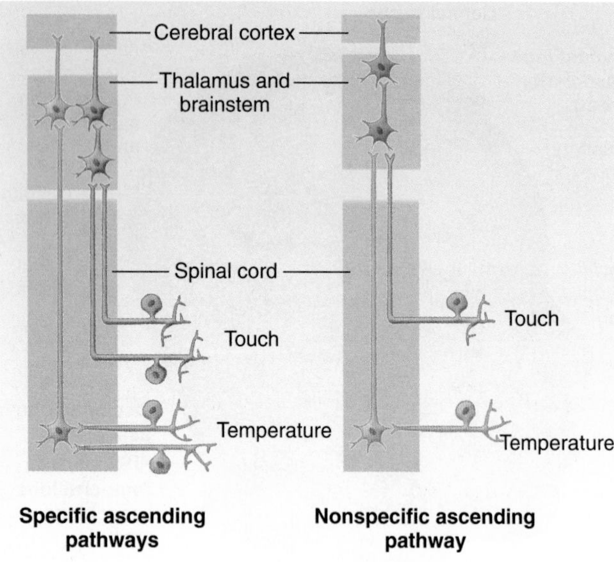

Figure 7.14 Diagrammatic representation of two specific ascending sensory pathways and a nonspecific ascending sensory pathway.

In contrast to the specific ascending pathways, neurons in the **nonspecific ascending pathways** are activated by sensory units of several different types and therefore signal general information (**Figure 7.14**). In other words, they indicate that *something* is happening, without specifying just what or where. A given ascending neuron in a nonspecific ascending pathway may respond, for example, to input from several afferent neurons, each activated by a different stimulus, such as maintained skin pressure, heating, and cooling. Such pathway neurons are called **polymodal neurons.** The nonspecific ascending pathways, as well as collaterals from the specific ascending pathways, end in the brainstem reticular formation and regions of the thalamus and cerebral cortex that are not highly discriminative but are important in controlling alertness and arousal.

7.4 Association Cortex and Perceptual Processing

The **cortical association areas** presented in Figure 7.13 lie outside the primary cortical sensory or motor areas but are adjacent to them. The cortical association areas are not considered part of the sensory pathways, but they play a role in the progressively more complex analysis of incoming information.

Although neurons in the earlier stages of the sensory pathways are necessary for perception, information from the primary sensory cortical areas undergoes further processing after it is relayed to a cortical association area. The region of association cortex closest to the primary sensory cortical area processes the information in fairly simple ways and serves basic sensory-related functions. Regions farther from the primary sensory areas process the information in more complicated ways. These include, for example, greater contributions from areas of the brain serving arousal, attention, memory, and language. Some of the neurons in these latter regions also integrate input concerning two or more types of sensory stimuli. Thus, an association area neuron receiving input from both the visual cortex and the "neck" region of the somatosensory cortex may integrate visual information with sensory information about head position. In this way, for example, a viewer understands a tree is vertical even if the viewer's head is tipped sideways.

Axons from neurons of the parietal and temporal lobes go to association areas in the frontal lobes and other parts of the limbic system. Through these connections, sensory information can be invested with emotional and motivational significance.

Further perceptual processing involves not only arousal, attention, learning, memory, language, and emotions but also comparison of the information presented via one type of sensation with that presented through another. For example, we may hear a growling dog, but our perception of the event and our emotional response vary markedly, depending upon whether our visual system detects the sound source to be a nearby live animal or an animal on television.

Factors That Affect Perception

We put great trust in our sensory–perceptual processes despite the inevitable modifications we know the nervous system makes. Several factors are known to affect our perceptions of the real world:

1. Sensory receptor mechanisms (e.g., adaptation) and processing of the information along afferent pathways can influence afferent information.
2. Factors such as emotions, personality, experience, and social background can influence perceptions so that two people can be exposed to the same stimuli and yet perceive them differently.
3. Not all information entering the central nervous system gives rise to conscious sensation. Actually, this is a very good thing because many unwanted signals are generated by the extreme sensitivity of our sensory receptors. For example, the hair cells of the ear can detect vibrations having a smaller amplitude than those caused by blood flowing through the ears' blood vessels and can even detect molecules in random motion bumping against the ear drum. It is possible to detect one action potential generated by a certain type of mechanoreceptor. Although these receptors are capable of giving rise to sensations, much of their information is canceled out by receptor or central mechanisms to be discussed later. In other afferent pathways, information is not canceled out—it simply does not feed into parts of the brain that give rise to a conscious sensation. To use an example cited earlier, stretch receptors in the walls of some of the largest blood vessels monitor blood pressure as part of reflex regulation of this pressure, but people usually do not have a conscious awareness of their blood pressure.

4. We lack suitable receptors for many types of potential stimuli. For example, we cannot directly detect ionizing radiation or radio waves.
5. Damaged neural networks may give faulty perceptions as in the phenomenon known as ***phantom limb***, in which a limb lost by accident or amputation is experienced as though it were still in place. The missing limb is perceived to be the site of tingling, touch, pressure, warmth, itch, wetness, pain, and even fatigue. It seems that the sensory neural networks in the central nervous system that are normally triggered by receptor activation are, instead, activated independently of peripheral input. The activated neural networks continue to generate the usual sensations, which the brain perceives as arising from the missing receptors.
6. Some drugs alter perceptions. In fact, the most dramatic examples of a clear difference between the real world and our perceptual world can be found in drug-induced hallucinations.
7. Various types of mental illness can alter perceptions of the world, like the hallucinations that can occur in the disease ***schizophrenia*** (discussed in detail in Chapter 8).

In summary, for perception to occur, there can be no separation of the three processes involved—transducing stimuli into action potentials by the receptor, transmitting information through the nervous system, and interpreting those inputs. Sensory information is processed at each synapse along the afferent pathways and at many levels of the central nervous system, with the more complex stages receiving input only after the more elementary systems have processed the information. This hierarchical processing of afferent information along individual pathways is an important organizational feature of sensory systems. As we will see, a second important feature is that information is processed by *parallel* pathways, each of which handles a limited aspect of the neural signals generated by the sensory transducers. A third feature is that information at each stage along the pathway is modified by "top-down" influences serving the emotions, attention, memory, and language. Every synapse along the afferent pathway adds an element of organization and contributes to the sensory experience so that what we perceive is not a simple—or even an absolutely accurate—image of the stimulus that originally activated our receptors.

We conclude our introduction to sensory system pathways and coding with a summary of the general principles of sensory stimulus processing (**Table 7.1**). In the next section, we will take a detailed look at mechanisms involved in specific sensory systems.

TABLE 7.1 Summary of General Principles of Sensory Stimulus Processing

Stimulus Feature	Stimulus Processing
Modality	The structure of specific sensory receptor types allows them to best detect certain modalities and submodalities. General classes of receptor types include mechanoreceptors, thermoreceptors, photoreceptors, and chemoreceptors. The type of stimulus that specifically activates a given receptor is called that receptor's adequate stimulus. Information in sensory pathways is organized such that initial cortical processing of the various modalities occurs in different parts of the brain.
Duration	Detecting stimulus duration occurs in two general ways, determined by a receptor property called adaptation. Some sensory receptors respond and generate receptor potentials the entire time that a stimulus is applied (slowly adapting, or tonic receptors), while others respond only briefly when a stimulus is first applied and sometimes again when the stimulus is removed (rapidly adapting, or phasic receptors).
Intensity	Sensory receptor potential amplitude tends to be graded according to the size of the stimulus applied, but action potential amplitude does not change with stimulus intensity. Rather, increasing stimulus intensity is encoded by the activation of increasing numbers of sensory neurons (recruitment) and by an increase in the frequency of action potentials propagated along sensory pathways.
Location	Stimuli of a given modality from a particular region of the body generally travel along dedicated, specific neural pathways to the brain, referred to as labeled lines. The acuity with which a stimulus can be localized depends on the size and density of receptive fields in each body region. A synaptic processing mechanism called lateral inhibition enhances localization as sensory signals travel through the CNS. Most specific ascending pathways synapse in the thalamus on the way to the cerebral cortex after crossing the midline, such that sensory information from the right side of the body is generally processed on the left side of the brain, and vice versa.
Sensation and perception	A consciously perceived stimulus is referred to as a sensation, and awareness of a stimulus combined with understanding of its meaning is called perception. This higher processing of sensory information occurs in association areas of the cerebral cortex.

SECTION A SUMMARY

I. Sensory processing begins with the transformation of stimulus energy into graded potentials and then into action potentials in neurons.

II. Information carried in a sensory system may or may not lead to a conscious awareness of the stimulus.

Sensory Receptors

I. Receptors translate information from the external and internal environments into graded potentials.
   a. Receptors may be either specialized endings of afferent neurons or separate cells that form synapses with the afferent neurons.
   b. Receptors respond best to one form of stimulus, but they may respond to other forms if the stimulus intensity is abnormally high.
   c. Regardless of how a specific receptor is stimulated, activation of that receptor can only lead to perception of one type of sensation. However, not all receptor activations lead to conscious sensations.

II. The transduction process in all sensory receptors involves—either directly or indirectly—the opening or closing of ion channels in the receptor. Ions then flow across the membrane, causing a receptor potential.
   a. Receptor potential magnitude and action potential frequency increase as stimulus strength increases.
   b. Receptor potential magnitude varies with stimulus strength, rate of change of stimulus application, temporal summation of successive receptor potentials, and adaptation.

Primary Sensory Coding

I. The type of stimulus perceived is determined in part by the type of receptor activated. All receptors of a given sensory unit respond to the same stimulus modality.

II. Stimulus intensity is coded by the rate of firing of individual sensory units and by the number of sensory units activated.

III. Localization of a stimulus depends on the size of the receptive field covered by a single sensory unit and on the overlap of nearby receptive fields. Lateral inhibition is a means by which ascending pathways increase sensory acuity.

IV. Information coming into the nervous system is subject to modification by both ascending and descending pathways.

Ascending Neural Pathways in Sensory Systems

I. A single afferent neuron with all its receptor endings is a sensory unit.
   a. Afferent neurons, which usually have more than one receptor of the same type, are the first neurons in sensory pathways.
   b. The receptive field for a neuron is the area of the body that causes activity in a sensory unit or other neuron in the ascending pathway of that unit.

II. Neurons in the specific ascending pathways convey information about only a single type of stimulus to specific primary receiving areas of the cerebral cortex.

III. Nonspecific ascending pathways convey information from more than one type of sensory unit to the brainstem reticular formation and regions of the thalamus that are not part of the specific ascending pathways.

Association Cortex and Perceptual Processing

I. Information from the primary sensory cortical areas is elaborated after it is relayed to a cortical association area.
   a. The primary sensory cortical area and the region of association cortex closest to it process the information in fairly simple ways and serve basic sensory-related functions.
   b. Regions of association cortex farther from the primary sensory areas process the sensory information in more complicated ways.
   c. Processing in the association cortex includes input from areas of the brain serving other sensory modalities, arousal, attention, memory, language, and emotions.

SECTION A REVIEW QUESTIONS

1. Distinguish between a sensation and a perception.
2. Define the term *adequate stimulus.*
3. Describe the general process of transduction in a receptor that is a cell separate from the afferent neuron. Include in your description the following terms: *specificity, stimulus, receptor potential, synapse, neurotransmitter, graded potential,* and *action potential.*
4. List several ways in which the magnitude of a receptor potential can vary.
5. Differentiate between the function of rapidly adapting and slowly adapting receptors.
6. Describe the relationship between sensory information processing in the primary cortical sensory areas and in the cortical association areas.
7. List several ways in which sensory information can be distorted.
8. How does the nervous system distinguish between stimuli of different types?
9. How does the nervous system code information about stimulus intensity?
10. Describe the general mechanism of lateral inhibition and explain its importance in sensory processing.
11. Make a diagram showing how a specific ascending pathway relays information from peripheral receptors to the cerebral cortex.

SECTION A KEY TERMS

acuity 196
adaptation 194
adequate stimulus 192
ascending pathway 198
auditory cortex 199
central sulcus 199
chemoreceptor 193
coding 194
cortical association area 200
gustatory cortex 199
labeled lines 196
lateral inhibition 197
mechanoreceptor 193
modality 195
nociceptor 193
nonspecific ascending pathway 200
olfactory cortex 199
perception 192
photoreceptor 193
polymodal neuron 200
rapidly adapting receptor 194
receptive field 194
receptor potential 193
recruitment 195
sensation 192
sensory information 192
sensory pathway 198
sensory receptor 192
sensory system 192
sensory transduction 193
sensory unit 194
slowly adapting receptor 194
somatic receptor 199
somatosensory cortex 199
specific ascending pathway 199
stimulus 192
thermoreceptor 193
visual cortex 199

SECTION A CLINICAL TERMS

phantom limb 201
schizophrenia 201

SECTION **B**

Specific Sensory Systems

7.5 Somatic Sensation

Sensation from the skin, skeletal muscles, bones, tendons, and joints—**somatic sensation**—is initiated by a variety of sensory receptors collectively called somatic receptors (**Figure 7.15**). Some of these receptors respond to mechanical stimulation of the skin, hairs, and underlying tissues, whereas others respond to temperature or chemical changes. Activation of somatic receptors gives rise to the sensations of touch, pressure, awareness of the position of the body parts and their movement, temperature, and pain. The receptors for visceral sensations, which arise in certain organs of the thoracic and abdominal cavities, are the same types as the receptors that give rise to somatic sensations. Some organs, such as the liver, have no sensory receptors at all. Each sensation is associated with a specific receptor type. In other words, distinct receptors exist for heat, cold, touch, pressure, limb position or movement, and pain.

Touch and Pressure

Stimulation of different types of mechanoreceptors in the skin (see Figure 7.15) leads to a wide range of touch and pressure experiences—hair bending, deep pressure, vibrations, and superficial touch, for example. These mechanoreceptors are highly specialized neuron endings encapsulated in elaborate cellular structures. The details of the mechanoreceptors vary, but, in general, the neuron endings are linked to networks of collagen fibers within a capsule that is often filled with fluid. These networks transmit the mechanical tension in the fluid-filled capsule to ion channels in the neuron endings and activate them.

The skin mechanoreceptors adapt at different rates. About half of them adapt rapidly, firing only when the stimulus is changing. Other types of mechanoreceptors adapt more slowly. Activation of rapidly adapting receptors gives rise to the sensations of touch, movement, and vibration, whereas slowly adapting receptors give rise to the sensation of pressure.

In both categories, some receptors have small, well-defined receptive fields and can provide precise information about the contours of objects indenting the skin. As might be expected, these receptors are concentrated at the fingertips. In contrast, other receptors have large receptive fields with obscure boundaries, sometimes covering a whole finger or a large part of the palm. These receptors are not involved in detailed spatial discrimination but signal information about skin stretch and joint movement.

Senses of Posture and Movement

The senses of posture and movement are complex. The major receptors responsible for these senses are the muscle-spindle stretch receptors and Golgi tendon organs. These mechanoreceptors occur in skeletal muscles and the fibrous tendons that connect them to bone. Muscle-spindle stretch receptors respond both to the absolute magnitude of muscle stretch and to the rate at which the stretch occurs, and Golgi tendon organs monitor muscle tension (both of these receptors are

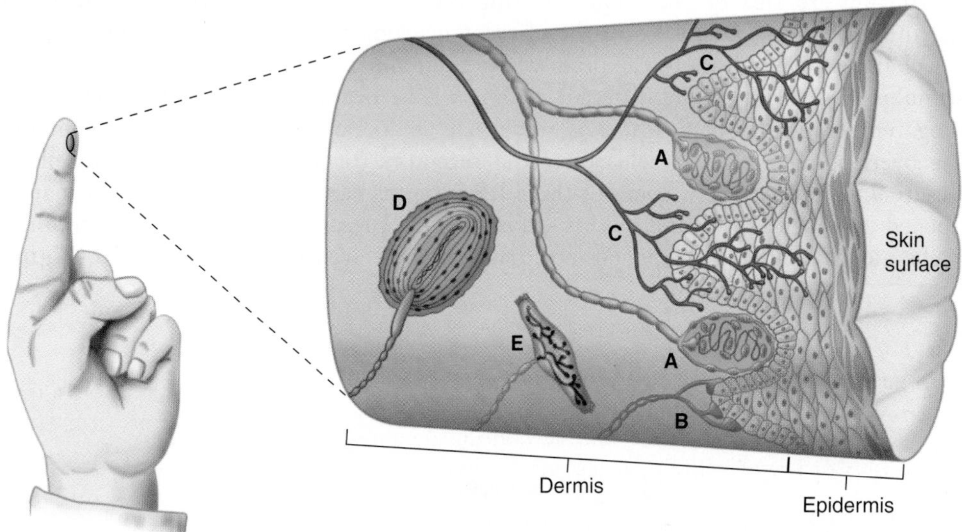

A. Meissner's corpuscle—rapidly adapting mechanoreceptor, touch and pressure
B. Merkel's corpuscle—slowly adapting mechanoreceptor, touch and pressure
C. Free neuron ending—slowly adapting, some are nociceptors, some are thermoreceptors, and some are mechanoreceptors
D. Pacinian corpuscles—rapidly adapting mechanoreceptor, vibration and deep pressure
E. Ruffini corpuscle—slowly adapting mechanoreceptor, skin stretch

Figure 7.15 APR Skin receptors. Some nerve fibers have free endings not related to any apparent receptor structure. Thicker, myelinated axons, on the other hand, end in receptors that have a complex structure. Not drawn to scale; for example, Pacinian corpuscles are actually four to five times larger than Meissner's corpuscles. In skin with hair (like the back of the hand), there are receptors made up of free neuron endings wrapped around the hair follicles, and Meissner's corpuscles are absent.

PHYSIOLOGICAL INQUIRY

- Applying a pressure stimulus to the fluid-filled capsule of an isolated Pacinian corpuscle causes a brief burst of action potentials in the afferent neuron, which ceases until the pressure is removed, at which time another brief burst of action potentials occurs. If an experimenter removes the capsule and applies pressure directly to the afferent neuron ending, action potentials are continuously fired during the stimulus. Explain these results.

Answer can be found at end of chapter.

described in Chapter 10). Vision and the vestibular organs (the sense organs of balance) also support the senses of posture and movement. Mechanoreceptors in the joints, tendons, ligaments, and skin also play a role. The term **kinesthesia** refers to the sense of movement at a joint.

Temperature

Information about temperature is transmitted along small-diameter, afferent neurons with little or no myelination. These neurons originate in the tissues as free neuron endings—that is, they lack the elaborate capsular endings commonly seen in tactile receptors. The actual temperature sensors are ion channels in the plasma membranes of the axon terminals that belong to a family of proteins called **transient receptor potential (TRP) proteins.** Different isoforms of TRP channels have gates that open in different temperature ranges. When activated, all of these channel types allow flux of a nonspecific cation current that is dominated by a depolarizing inward flux of Na^+. The resulting receptor potential initiates action potentials in the afferent neuron, which travel along labeled lines to the brain where the temperature stimulus is perceived. The different channels have overlapping temperature ranges, which is somewhat analogous to the overlapping receptive fields of tactile receptors (review Figure 7.8). Interestingly, some of the TRP proteins can be opened by chemical ligands. This explains why capsaicin (a chemical found in chili peppers) and ethanol are perceived as being hot when ingested and menthol feels cool when applied to the skin. Some afferent neurons, especially those stimulated at the extremes of temperature, have proteins in their receptor endings that also respond to painful stimuli. These multipurpose neurons are therefore included among the polymodal neurons described earlier in relation to the nonspecific ascending pathways and are in part responsible for the perception of pain at extreme temperatures. These neurons represent only a subset of the pain receptors, which are described next.

Pain

Most stimuli that cause, or could potentially cause, tissue damage elicit a sensation of pain. Receptors for such stimuli are known as nociceptors. Nociceptors, like thermoreceptors, are free axon terminals of small-diameter afferent neurons with little or no myelination. They respond to intense mechanical deformation, extremes of temperature, and many chemicals. Examples of the latter include H^+, neuropeptide transmitters, bradykinin, histamine, cytokines, and prostaglandins, several of which are released by damaged cells. Some of these chemicals are secreted by cells of the immune system (described in Chapter 18) that have moved into the injured area. These substances act by binding to specific ligand-gated ion channels on the nociceptor plasma membrane.

The primary afferents having nociceptor endings synapse on ascending neurons after entering the central nervous system (**Figure 7.16a**). Glutamate and the neuropeptide

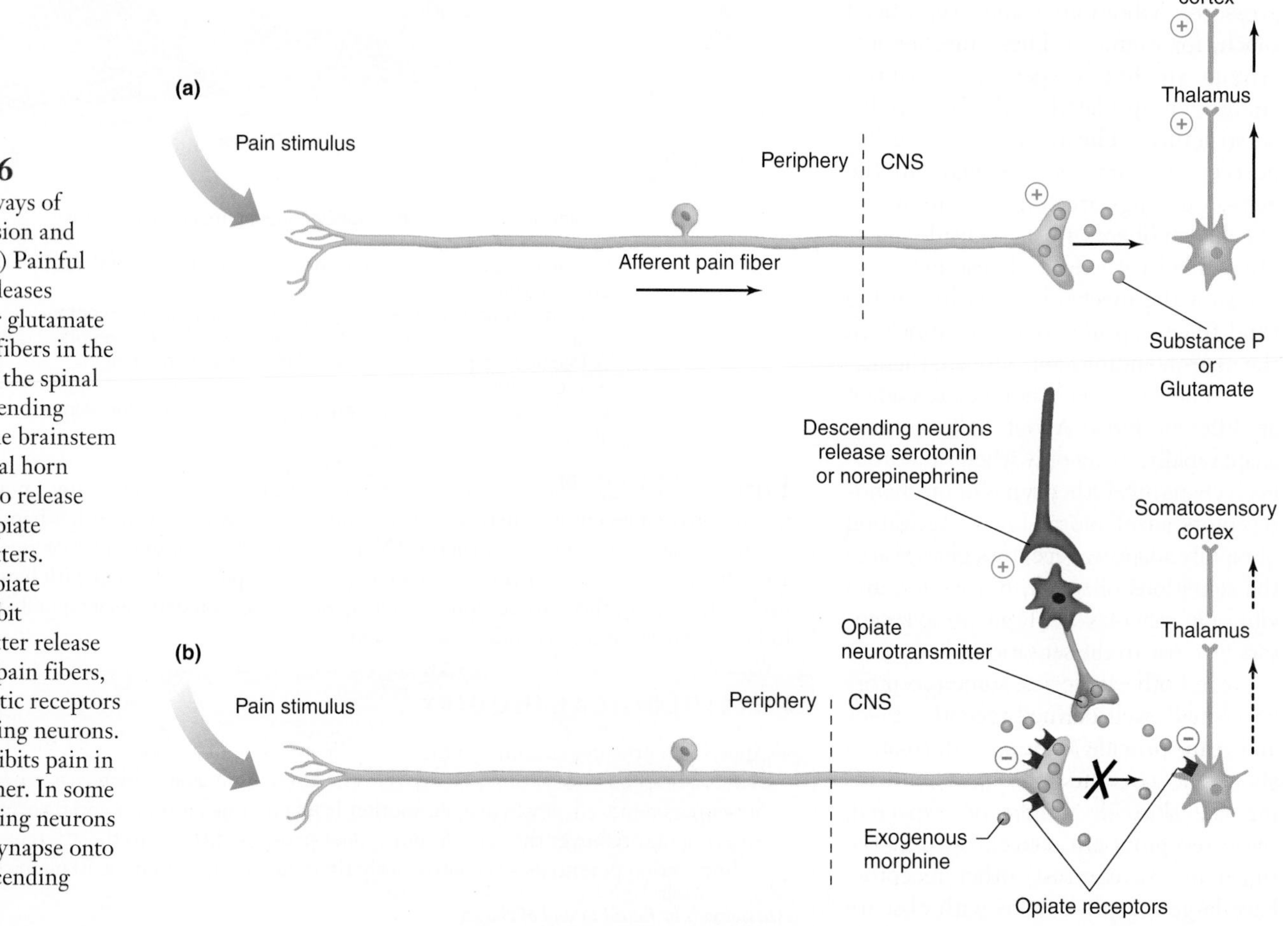

Figure 7.16 Cellular pathways of pain transmission and modulation. (a) Painful stimulation releases substance P or glutamate from afferent fibers in the dorsal horn of the spinal cord. (b) Descending inputs from the brainstem stimulate dorsal horn interneurons to release endogenous opiate neurotransmitters. Presynaptic opiate receptors inhibit neurotransmitter release from afferent pain fibers, and postsynaptic receptors inhibit ascending neurons. Morphine inhibits pain in a similar manner. In some cases, descending neurons may directly synapse onto and inhibit ascending neurons.

substance P are among the neurotransmitters released at these synapses.

When incoming nociceptive afferents activate interneurons, it may lead to the phenomenon of ***referred pain***, in which the sensation of pain is experienced at a site other than the injured or diseased tissue. For example, during a heart attack, a person often experiences pain in the left arm. Referred pain occurs because both visceral and somatic afferents often converge on the same neurons in the spinal cord (**Figure 7.17**). Excitation of the somatic afferent fibers is the more usual source of afferent discharge, so we "refer" the location of receptor activation to the somatic source even though, in the case of visceral pain, the perception is incorrect. **Figure 7.18** shows the typical distribution of referred pain from visceral organs.

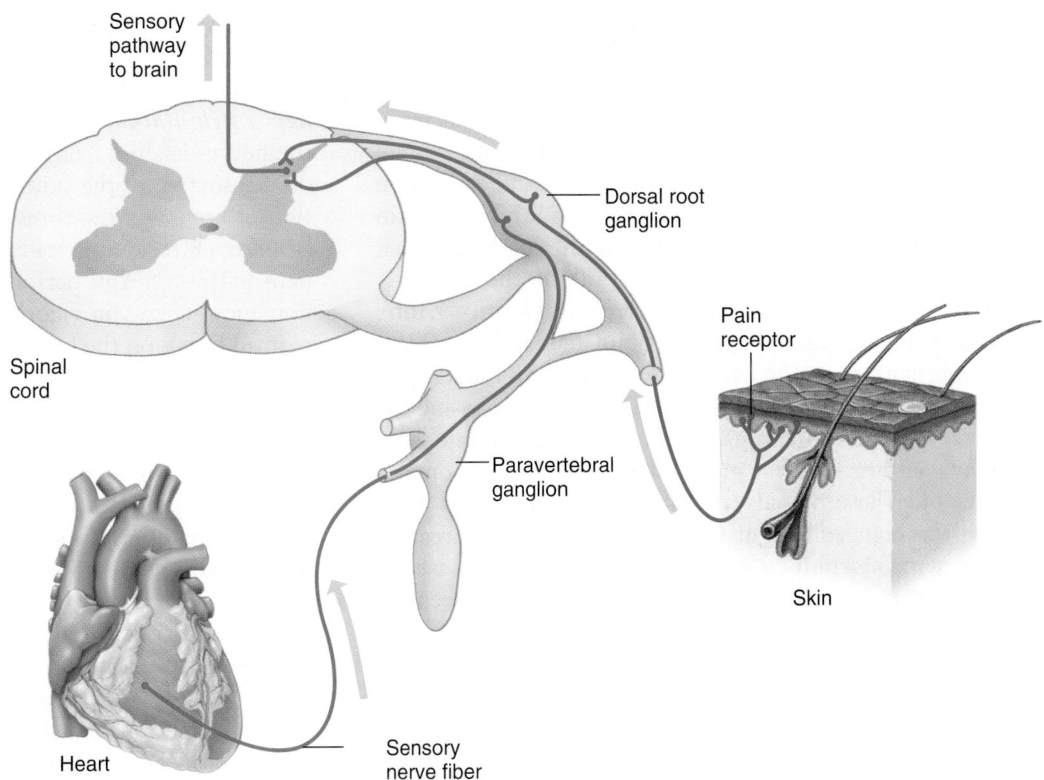

Figure 7.17 Convergence of visceral and somatic afferent neurons onto ascending pathways produces the phenomenon of referred pain.

Pain differs significantly from the other somatosensory modalities. After transduction of a first noxious stimulus into action potentials in the afferent neuron, a series of changes can occur in components of the pain pathway—including the ion channels in the nociceptors themselves—that alters the way these components respond to subsequent stimuli. Both increased and decreased sensitivity to painful stimuli can occur. When these changes result in an increased sensitivity to painful stimuli, known as ***hyperalgesia***, the pain can last for hours after the original stimulus is gone. Therefore, the pain experienced in response to stimuli that occur even a short time after the original stimulus (and the reactions to that pain) can be more intense than the initial pain. This type of pain response is common with severe burn injuries. Moreover, probably more than any other type of sensation, pain can be altered by past experiences, suggestion, emotions (particularly anxiety), and the simultaneous activation of other sensory

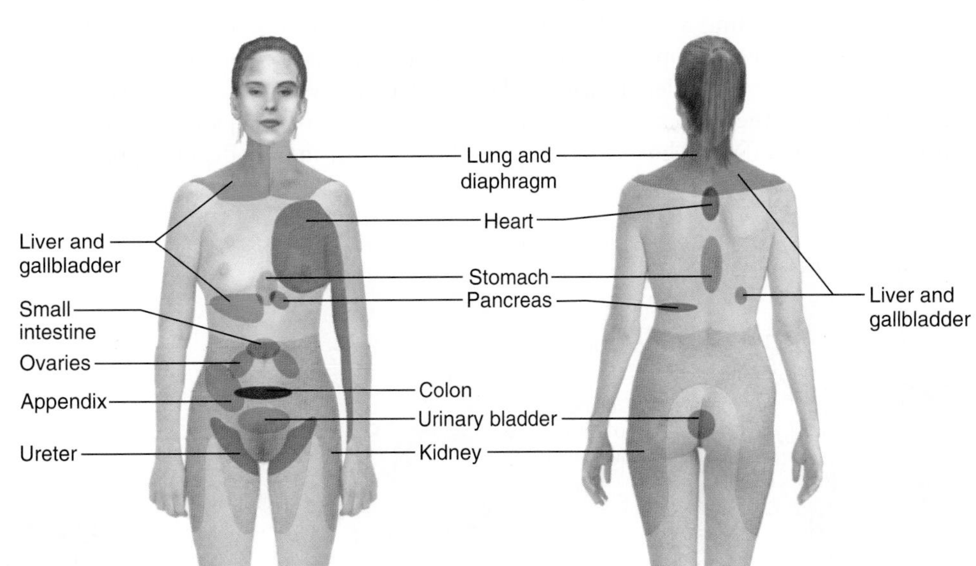

Figure 7.18 Regions of the body surface where we typically perceive referred pain from visceral organs.

PHYSIOLOGICAL INQUIRY

- A woman has had a sore neck for a few days. Why might a clinician listen carefully to her chest and upper back with a stethoscope during the examination?

Answer can be found at end of chapter.

modalities. Thus, the level of pain experienced is not solely a physical property of the stimulus.

Analgesia is the selective suppression of pain without effects on consciousness or other sensations. Electrical stimulation of specific areas of the central nervous system can produce a profound reduction in pain—a phenomenon called ***stimulation-produced analgesia***—by inhibiting pain pathways. This occurs because descending pathways that originate in these brain areas selectively inhibit the transmission of information originating in nociceptors (**Figure 7.16b**). The descending axons end at lower brainstem and spinal levels on interneurons in the pain pathways and inhibit synaptic transmission between the afferent nociceptor neurons and the secondary ascending neurons. Some of the neurons in these inhibitory pathways release morphinelike endogenous opioids (Chapter 6). These opioids inhibit the propagation of input through the higher levels of the pain system. Thus, treating a patient with morphine can provide relief in many cases of intractable pain by binding to and activating opioid receptors at the level of entry of the active nociceptor neurons. This is distinct from morphine's effect on the brain.

The endogenous-opioid systems also mediate other phenomena known to relieve pain. In clinical studies, 55% to 85% of patients experienced pain relief when treated with ***acupuncture,*** an ancient Chinese therapy involving the insertion of needles into specific locations on the skin. This success rate was similar to that observed when patients were treated with morphine (70%). In studies comparing morphine to a ***placebo*** (injections of sugar that patients *thought* was the drug), as many as 35% of those receiving the placebo experienced pain relief. Acupuncture is thought to activate afferent neurons leading to spinal cord and midbrain centers that release endogenous opioids and other neurotransmitters implicated in pain relief. It seems likely that pathways descending from the cortex activate those same regions to exert the placebo effect. Thus, exploiting the body's built-in analgesia mechanisms can be an effective means of controlling pain.

Also of use for lessening pain is ***transcutaneous electrical nerve stimulation*** (***TENS***), in which the painful site itself or the nerves leading from it are stimulated by electrodes placed on the surface of the skin. TENS works because the stimulation of nonpain, low-threshold afferent fibers (e.g., the fibers from touch receptors) leads to the inhibition of neurons in the pain pathways. You perform a low-tech version of this phenomenon when you vigorously rub your scalp at the site of a painful bump on the head.

Neural Pathways of the Somatosensory System

After entering the central nervous system, the afferent nerve fibers from the somatic receptors synapse on neurons that form the specific ascending pathways projecting primarily to the somatosensory cortex via the brainstem and thalamus. They also synapse on interneurons that give rise to the nonspecific ascending pathways. There are two major types of somatosensory pathways from the body; these pathways are organized differently from each other in the spinal cord and brain (**Figure 7.19**). The ascending **anterolateral pathway,** also called the spinothalamic pathway, makes its first synapse between the sensory receptor neuron and a second neuron located in the gray matter of the spinal cord (**Figure 7.19a**). This second neuron immediately crosses to the opposite side of the spinal cord and then ascends through the anterolateral column of the cord to the thalamus, where it synapses on cortically projecting neurons. The anterolateral pathway processes pain and temperature information. The second major pathway for somatic sensation is the **dorsal column pathway** (**Figure 7.19b**). This, too, is named for the section of white matter (the dorsal columns of the spinal cord) through which the sensory receptor neurons project. In the dorsal column pathway, sensory neurons do not cross over or synapse immediately upon entering the spinal cord. Rather, they ascend on

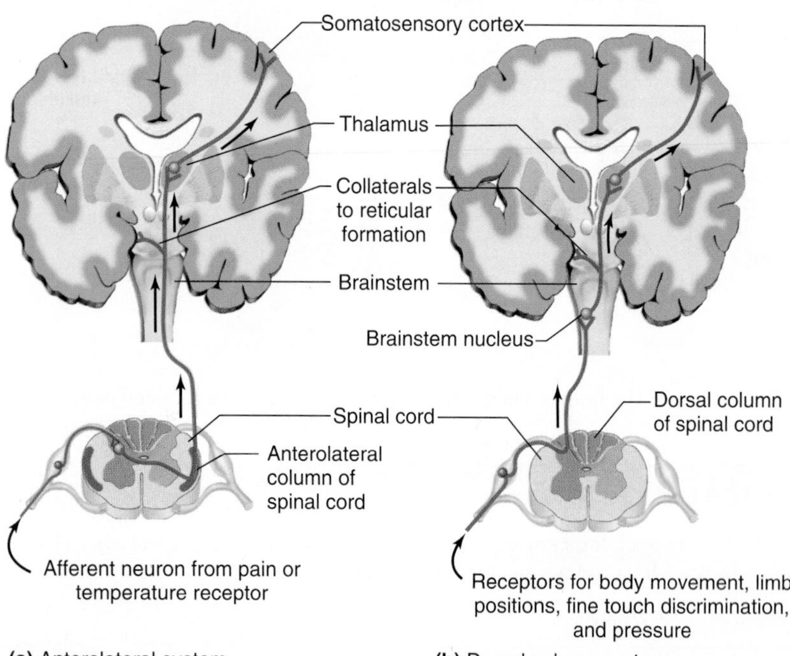

Figure 7.19 (a) The anterolateral system. (b) The dorsal column system. Information carried over collaterals to the reticular formation in (a) and (b) contribute to alertness and arousal mechanisms.

PHYSIOLOGICAL INQUIRY

- If an accident severed the left half of a person's spinal cord at the mid-thoracic level but the right half remained intact, what pattern of sensory deficits would occur?

Answer can be found at end of chapter.

the same side of the cord and make the first synapse in the brainstem. The secondary neuron then crosses in the brainstem as it ascends. As in the anterolateral pathway, the second synapse is in the thalamus, from which projections are sent to the somatosensory cortex.

Note that both pathways cross from the side where the afferent neurons enter the central nervous system to the opposite side either in the spinal cord (anterolateral system) or in the brainstem (dorsal column system). Consequently, sensory pathways from somatic receptors on the left side of the body terminate in the somatosensory cortex of the right cerebral hemisphere. Somatosensory information from the head and face does not travel to the brain within these two spinal cord pathways; it enters the brainstem directly via cranial nerves (review Table 6.8).

In the somatosensory cortex, the endings of the axons of the specific somatic pathways are grouped according to the peripheral location of the receptors that give input to the pathways (**Figure 7.20**). The parts of the body that are most densely innervated—fingers, thumb, and face—are represented by the largest areas of the somatosensory cortex. There are qualifications, however, to this seemingly precise picture. There is considerable overlap of the body part representations, and the sizes of the areas can change with sensory experience. The phantom limb phenomenon described in the first section of this chapter provides a good example of the dynamic nature of the somatosensory cortex. Studies of upper-limb amputees have shown that cortical areas formerly responsible for a missing arm and hand are commonly "rewired" to respond to sensory inputs originating in the face (note the proximity of the cortical regions representing these areas in Figure 7.20). As the somatosensory cortex undergoes this reorganization, a touch on a person's cheek might be perceived as a touch on his or her missing arm.

7.6 Vision

Vision is perhaps the most important sense for the day-to-day activities of humans. Perceiving a visual signal requires an organ—the eye—capable of focusing and responding to light, and the appropriate neural pathways and structures to interpret the signal. We begin with an overview of light energy and eye structure.

Light

The receptors of the eye are sensitive only to that tiny portion of the vast spectrum of electromagnetic radiation that we call visible light (**Figure 7.21a**). Radiant energy is described in terms of wavelengths and frequencies. The **wavelength** is the distance between two successive wave peaks of the electromagnetic radiation (**Figure 7.21b**). Wavelengths vary from several kilometers at the long-wave radio end of the spectrum to trillionths of a meter at the gamma-ray end. The **frequency** (in hertz, the number of cycles per second) of the radiation wave varies inversely with wavelength. The wavelengths capable of stimulating the receptors of the eye—the **visible spectrum**—are between about 400 and 750 nm. Different wavelengths of light within this band are perceived as different colors.

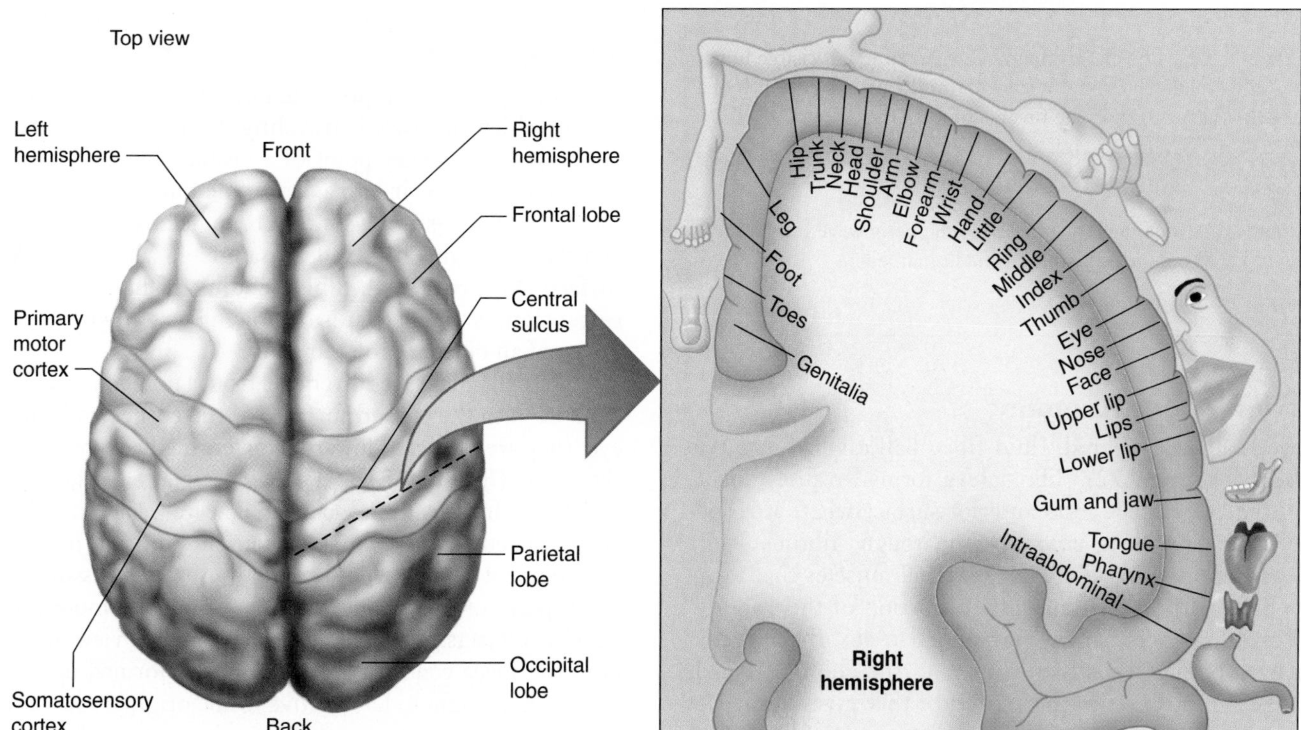

Figure 7.20 The location of pathway terminations for different parts of the body in somatosensory cortex, although there is actually much overlap between the cortical regions. The left half of the body is represented on the right hemisphere of the brain, and the right half of the body is represented on the left hemisphere, which is not shown here.

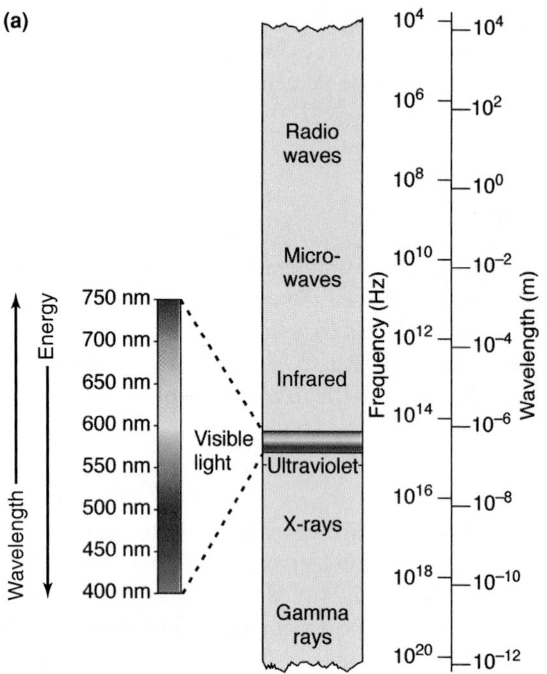

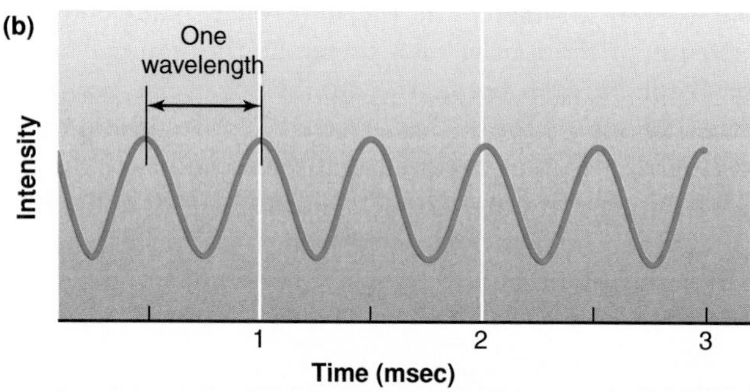

Figure 7.21 The electromagnetic spectrum. (a) Visible light ranges in wavelength from 400 to 750 nm (1 nm = 1 billionth of a meter). (b) Wavelength is the inverse of frequency.

PHYSIOLOGICAL INQUIRY

- What is the frequency of the electromagnetic wave shown in panel (b)? Would it be visible to the human eye?

Answer can be found at end of chapter.

Overview of Eye Anatomy

The eye is a three-layered, fluid-filled ball divided into two chambers (**Figure 7.22**). The **sclera** forms a white capsule around the eye, except at its anterior surface where it is specialized into the clear **cornea.** The tough, fibrous sclera serves as the insertion point for external muscles that move the eyeballs within their sockets. A portion of the underlying **choroid** layer is darkly pigmented to absorb light rays at the back of the eyeball. In the front, the choroid layer is specialized into the **iris** (the structure that gives your eyes their color), the **ciliary muscle,** and the **zonular fibers.** Circular and radial smooth muscle fibers of the iris determine the diameter of the **pupil,** the anterior opening that allows light into the eye. Activity of the ciliary muscle and the resulting tension on the zonular fibers determine the shape and consequently the focusing power of the crystalline **lens** just behind the iris.

The **retina** is formed from an extension of the developing brain in fetal life. It forms the inner, posterior surface of the eye, containing numerous types of neurons including the sensory cells of the eyes, called **photoreceptors.** Features of the retina can be viewed through the pupil with an ***ophthalmoscope,*** a handheld device that uses a light source and lenses to illuminate and magnify the image of the back of the eye. These features include

1. the **macula lutea** (Latin for "yellow spot"; often simply referred to as the macula): a small region at the center of the retina that is relatively free of blood vessels;
2. the **fovea centralis:** a central, shallow pit within the macula containing a high density of cones but relatively few light-obstructing retinal neurons—this region is specialized to deliver the highest visual acuity;
3. the **optic disc:** a distinct, circular region toward the nasal side of the retina where neurons carrying information from the photoreceptors exit the eye as the **optic nerve;** and
4. blood vessels: these enter the eye at the optic disc and branch extensively over the inner surface of the retina.

The eye is divided into two fluid-filled spaces. The anterior chamber of the eye, between the iris and the cornea, is filled with a clear fluid called **aqueous humor.** The posterior chamber of the eye, between the lens and the retina, is filled with a viscous, jellylike substance known as **vitreous humor.**

The Optics of Vision

A ray of light can be represented by a line drawn in the direction in which the wave is traveling. Light waves diverge in all directions from every point of a visible object. When a light wave crosses from air into a denser medium like glass or water, the wave changes direction at an angle that depends on the density of the medium and the angle at which it strikes the surface (**Figure 7.23a**). This bending of light waves, called **refraction,** is the mechanism allowing us to focus an accurate image of an object onto the retina.

When light waves diverging from a point on an object pass from air into the curved surfaces of the cornea and lens of the eye, they are refracted inward, converging back into a point on the retina (**Figure 7.23b**). The cornea plays a larger quantitative role than the lens in focusing light waves because the waves are refracted more in passing from air into the much denser environment of the cornea than they are when passing between fluid spaces of the eye and the lens, which are more similar in density. Objects in the center of the field of view are focused onto the fovea centralis, with the image formed upside down and reversed right to left relative to the original source. One of the fascinating features of the brain, however, is that it restores our perception of the image to its proper orientation.

Light waves from objects close to the eye strike the cornea at greater angles and must be refracted more in order to

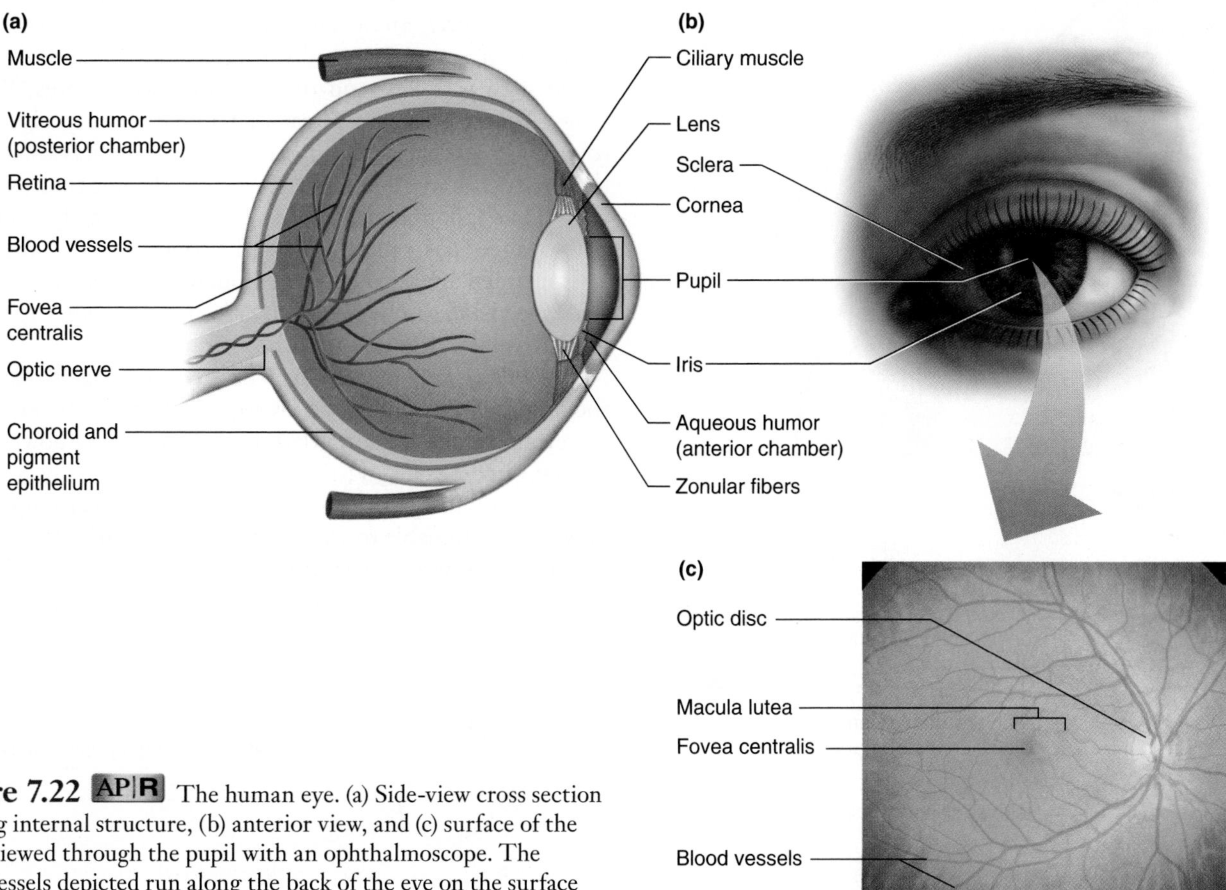

Figure 7.22 APIR The human eye. (a) Side-view cross section showing internal structure, (b) anterior view, and (c) surface of the retina viewed through the pupil with an ophthalmoscope. The blood vessels depicted run along the back of the eye on the surface of the retina.

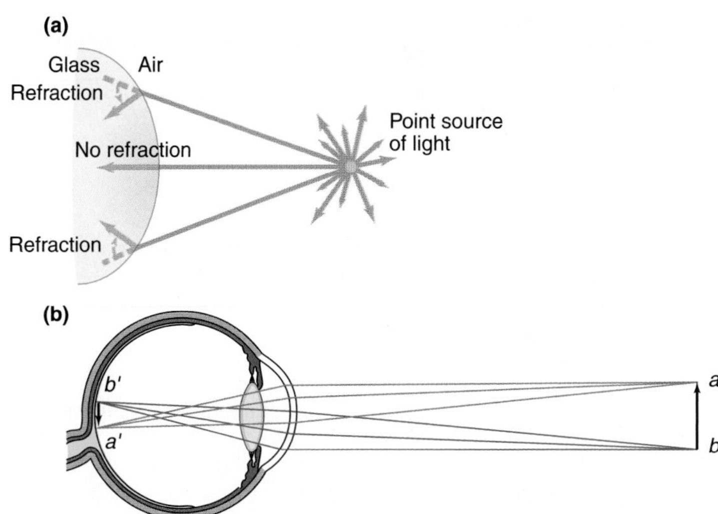

Figure 7.23 APIR Focusing point sources of light. (a) When diverging light rays enter a dense medium at an angle to its convex surface, refraction bends them inward. (b) Refraction of light by the lens system of the eye. For simplicity, we show light refraction only at the surface of the cornea, where the greatest refraction occurs. Refraction also occurs in the lens and at other sites in the eye. Incoming light from *a* (above) and *b* (below) is bent in opposite directions, resulting in *b′* being above *a′* on the retina.

reconverge on the retina. Although, as previously noted, the cornea performs the greater part quantitatively of focusing the visual image on the retina, all *adjustments* for distance are made by changes in lens shape. Such changes are part of the process known as **accommodation.**

The shape of the lens is controlled by the ciliary muscle and the tension it applies to the zonular fibers, which attach the ciliary muscle to the lens (**Figure 7.24**). The ciliary muscle, which is stimulated by parasympathetic nerves, is circular, so that it draws nearer to the central lens as it contracts. As the muscle contracts, it lessens the tension on the zonular fibers. Conversely, when the ciliary muscle relaxes, the diameter of the ring of muscle increases and the tension on the zonular fibers also increases. Therefore, the shape of the lens is altered by contraction and relaxation of the ciliary muscle. To focus on distant objects, the ciliary muscle relaxes and the zonular fibers pull the lens into a flattened, oval shape. Contraction of the ciliary muscles focuses the eye on near objects by releasing the tension on the zonular fibers, which allows the natural elasticity of the lens to return it to a more spherical shape (**Figure 7.25**). The shape of the lens determines to what degree the light waves are refracted and how they project onto the retina. Constriction of the pupil also occurs when the ciliary muscle contracts, which helps sharpen the image further.

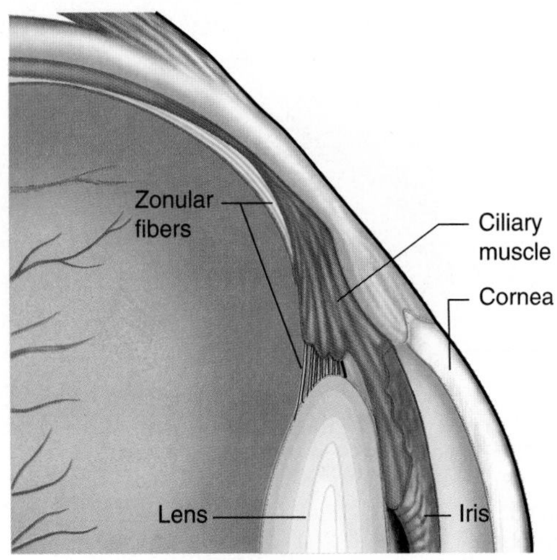

Figure 7.24 AP|R Ciliary muscle, zonular fibers, and lens of the eye.

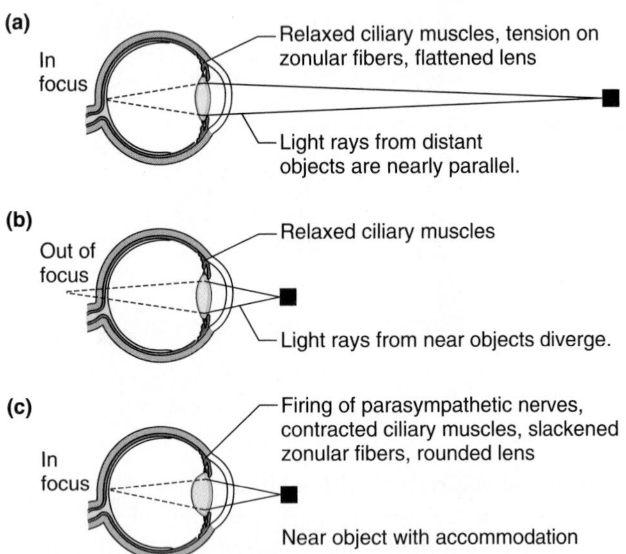

Figure 7.25 Accommodation for near vision. (a) Light rays from distant objects are more parallel, and they focus onto the retina when the lens is less curved. (b) Diverging light rays from near objects do not focus on the retina when the ciliary muscles are relaxed. (c) Accommodation increases the curvature of the lens, focusing the image of near objects onto the retina.

As people age, the lens tends to lose elasticity, reducing its ability to assume a spherical shape. The result is a progressive decline in the ability to accommodate for near vision. This condition, known as ***presbyopia,*** is a normal part of the aging process and is the reason that people around 45 years of age may have to begin wearing reading glasses or bifocals for close work.

The cells that make up most of the lens lose their internal membranous organelles early in life and are therefore transparent, but they lack the ability to replicate. The only lens cells that retain the capacity to divide are on the lens surface, and as new cells form, older cells come to lie deeper within the lens. With increasing age, the central part of the lens becomes denser and stiffer and may acquire a coloration that progresses from yellow to black.

Another change in lens color that sometimes occurs with aging is ***cataract,*** an opacity (clouding) of the lens that is one of the most common eye disorders. Cataracts are also associated with smoking and diseases such as diabetes. Because long-term exposure to ultraviolet radiation may also play a role, many experts recommend wearing sunglasses to delay the onset. Early changes in lens color do not interfere with vision, but vision is impaired as the process slowly continues. The opaque lens can be removed surgically. With the aid of an implanted artificial lens or compensating corrective lenses, effective vision can be restored, although the ability to accommodate is lost.

Cornea and lens shape and eyeball length determine the point where light rays converge. Defects in vision occur if the eyeball is too long in relation to the focusing power of the lens (**Figure 7.26a**). In this case, the images of faraway objects focus at a point in front of the retina. This ***nearsighted,*** or ***myopic,*** eye is unable to see distant objects clearly. Near objects are clear to a person with this condition but without the normal rounding of the lens that occurs via accommodation. In

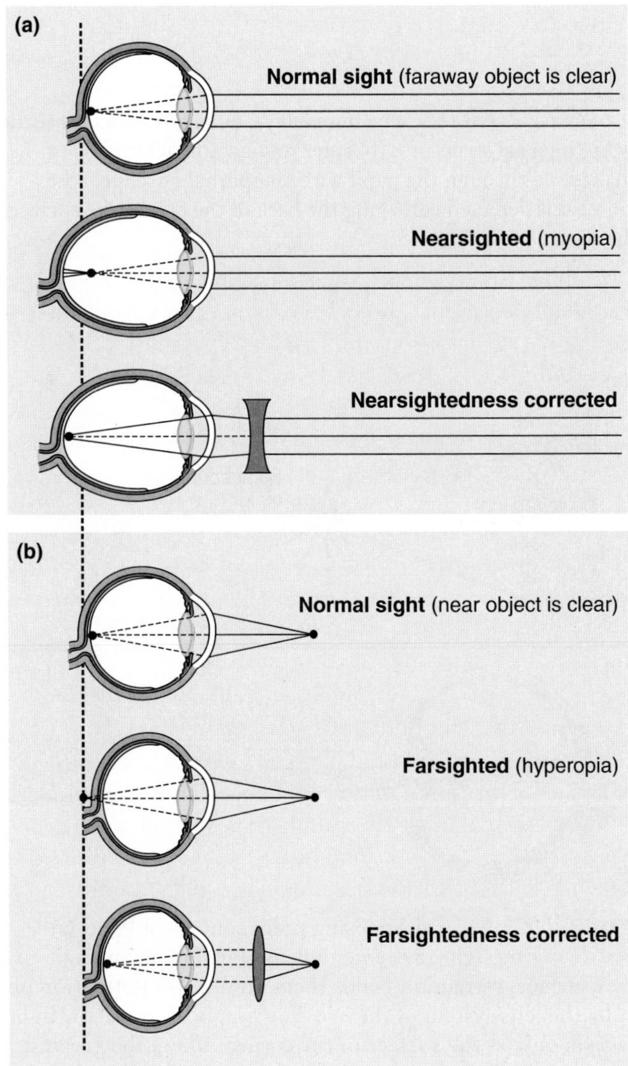

Figure 7.26 Correction of vision defects. (a) Nearsightedness (myopia). (b) Farsightedness (hyperopia).

contrast, if the eye is too short for the lens, images of near objects are focused behind the retina (**Figure 7.26b**). This eye is ***farsighted,*** or ***hyperopic;*** though a person with this condition has poor near vision, distant objects can be seen if the accommodation reflex is activated to increase the curvature of the lens. These visual defects are easily correctable by manipulating the refraction of light entering the eye. The use of corrective lenses (such as glasses or contact lenses) for near- and farsighted vision is shown in Figure 7.26. In recent years, major advances in refractive surgery have involved reshaping the cornea with the use of lasers.

Defects in vision also occur when the lens or cornea does not have a smoothly spherical surface, a condition known as ***astigmatism.*** Corrective lenses can usually compensate for these surface imperfections.

The size and shape of a person's eye over time depend in part on the volume of the aqueous humor and vitreous humor. These two fluids are colorless and permit the transmission of light from the front of the eye to the retina. The aqueous humor is constantly formed by special vascular tissue that overlies the ciliary muscle and drains away through a canal in front of the iris at the edge of the cornea. In some instances, the aqueous humor forms faster than it is removed, which results in increased pressure within the eye. ***Glaucoma,*** a major cause of irreversible blindness, is a disease in which retinal cells are damaged as a result of increased pressure within the eye.

Just as the aperture of a camera can be varied to alter the amount of light that enters, the iris regulates the diameter of the pupil. The color of the iris is of no importance as long as the tissue is sufficiently opaque to prevent the passage of light. The iris is composed of two layers of smooth muscle that are innervated by autonomic nerves. Stimulation of sympathetic nerves to the iris enlarges the pupil by causing radially arranged muscle fibers to contract. Stimulation of parasympathetic fibers to the iris makes the pupil smaller by causing the muscle fibers that circle around the pupil to contract.

These neurally induced changes occur in response to light-sensitive reflexes integrated in the midbrain. Bright light causes a decrease in the diameter of the pupil, which reduces the amount of light entering the eye and restricts the light to the central part of the lens for more accurate vision. The constriction of the pupil also protects the retina from damage induced by very bright light, such as direct rays from the sun. Conversely, the pupil enlarges in dim light, when maximal light entry is needed. Changes also occur as a result of emotion or pain. For example, activation of the sympathetic nervous system dilates the pupils of a person who is angry (review Table 6.11). Abnormal or absent response of the pupil to changes in light can indicate damage to the midbrain from trauma or tumors or can also be a telltale sign when a person is under the influence of narcotics like heroin.

Photoreceptor Cells and Phototransduction

The retina, an extension of the central nervous system, contains photoreceptors and several other cell types that function in the transduction of light waves into visual information (**Figure 7.27**). The photoreceptor cells have a tip, or **outer segment,** composed of stacked layers of membrane called **discs.** The discs house the molecular machinery that responds to light. The photoreceptors also have an **inner segment,** which contains mitochondria and other organelles, and a synaptic terminal that connects the photoreceptor to other neurons in the retina. The two types of photoreceptors are called **rods** and **cones** because of the shapes of their light-sensitive outer segments. The rods are extremely sensitive and respond to very low levels of illumination, whereas the cones are considerably less sensitive and respond only when the light is bright. In cones, the light-sensitive discs are formed from in-foldings of the surface plasma membrane, whereas in rods, the disc membranes are intracellular structures.

Note that the light-sensitive portions of the photoreceptor cells face *away* from the incoming light, and the light must pass through all the cell layers of the retina before reaching and stimulating the photoreceptors. A remarkable specialization of the vertebrate retina prevents light rays from being blocked or scattered as they pass through these layers. Approximately 20% of the volume of the retina is taken up by a type of glial cells called **Müller cells** (not shown in Figure 7.27). These elongated, funnel-shaped cells span the distance from the inner surface of the retina directly to the photoreceptors, with an estimated abundance of 1:1 with cone cells and one per 10 rod cells. In addition to metabolically supporting retinal neurons and mediating neurotransmitter degradation, they appear to act like fiber-optic cables that deliver light rays through the retinal layers directly to the photoreceptor cells.

Two pigmented layers, the choroid and the **pigment epithelium** of the back of the retina, absorb light rays that bypass the photoreceptors. This prevents reflection and scattering of photons back through the rods and cones, which would cause the visual image to blur.

The photoreceptors contain molecules called **photopigments,** which absorb light. **Rhodopsin** is a unique photopigment in the retina for the rods, and there are also unique photopigments for each of three different types of cones. Photopigments consist of membrane-bound proteins called **opsins** bound to a **chromophore** molecule. The chromophore in all types of photopigments is **retinal** (reh-tin-AL), a derivative of vitamin A. This is the part of the photopigment that is light-sensitive. The opsin in each of the photopigments is different and binds to the chromophore in a different way. Because of this, each photopigment absorbs light most effectively at a specific part of the visible spectrum. For example, the photopigment found in one type of cone cell absorbs light most effectively at long wavelengths (designated as "red" cones), whereas another absorbs short wavelengths ("blue" cones).

The membranous discs of the outer segment are stacked perpendicular to the path of incoming light rays. This layered arrangement maximizes the membrane surface area, a relationship between structure and function that is a general principle of physiology observable in many body systems. In fact, each photoreceptor may contain over a billion molecules of photopigment, providing an extremely effective trap for light.

The photoreceptor is unique because it is the only type of sensory cell that is relatively depolarized (about −35 mV) when it is at rest (i.e., in the dark) and *hyperpolarized* (to about −70 mV) in response to its adequate stimulus. The mechanisms involved in mediating these membrane potential changes are shown in **Figure 7.28.** In the absence of light, action of the enzyme **guanylyl cyclase** converts GTP into a high intracellular concentration of the second-messenger molecule, cyclic GMP (cGMP). The cGMP maintains outer segment ligand-gated cation channels in an open state, and a persistent influx of Na^+ and Ca^{2+} results. Thus, in the dark, cGMP concentrations are high and the photoreceptor cell is maintained in a relatively depolarized state.

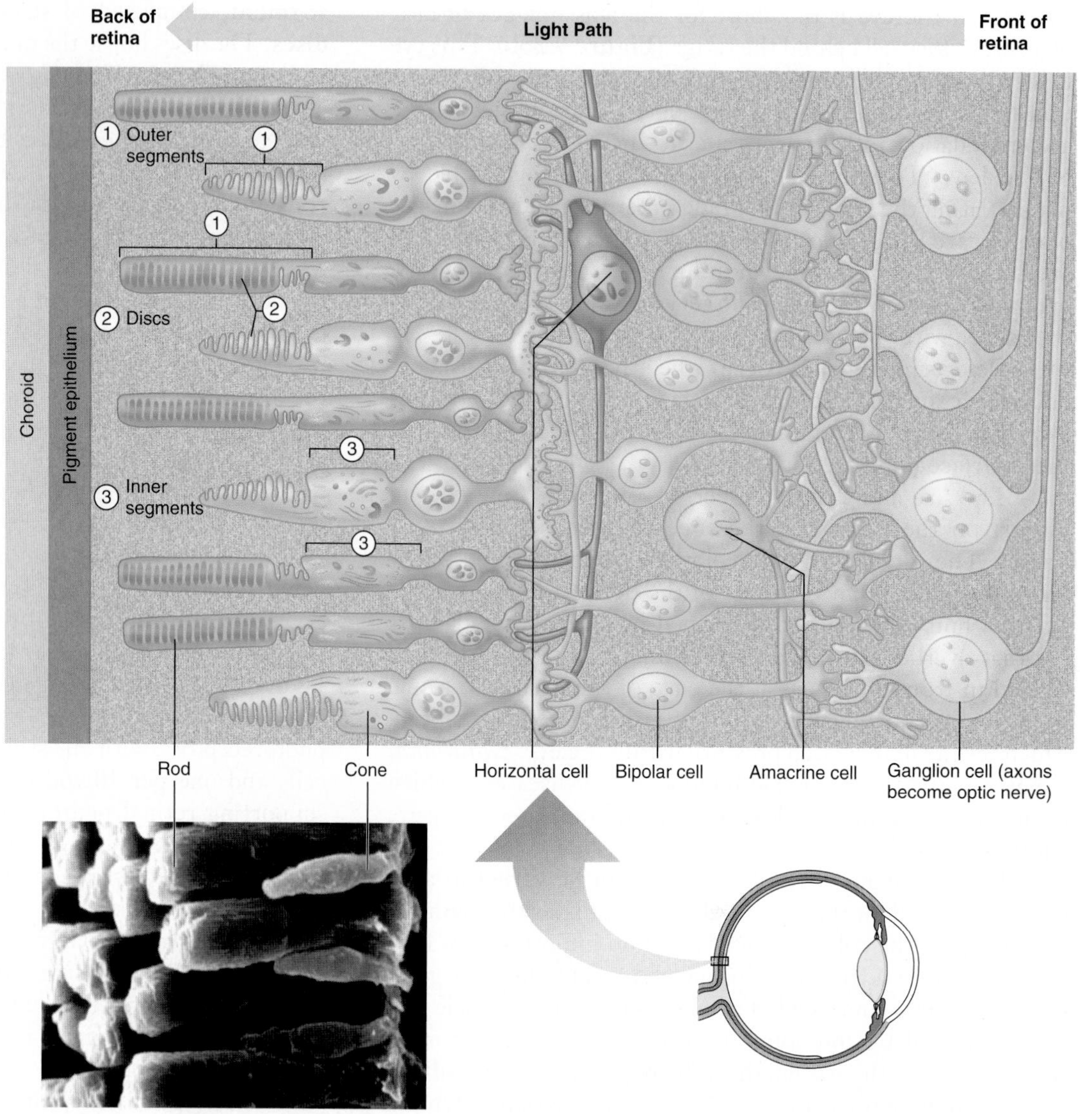

When light of an appropriate wavelength shines on a photoreceptor cell, a cascade of events leads to hyperpolarization of the photoreceptor cell membrane. Molecules of retinal in the disc membrane assume a new conformation induced by the absorption of energy from photons and dissociate from the opsin. This, in turn, alters the shape of the opsin protein and promotes an interaction between the opsin and a protein called **transducin** that belongs to the G-protein family (see Chapter 5). Transducin activates the enzyme **cGMP-phosphodiesterase,** which rapidly degrades cGMP. The decrease in cytoplasmic cGMP concentration allows the cation channels to close, and the loss of depolarizing current allows the membrane potential to hyperpolarize. After its activation by light, the retinal molecule changes back to its resting shape and is reassociated with the opsin by an enzyme-mediated mechanism.

If you move from a place of bright sunlight into a darkened room, a temporary "blindness" takes place until the photoreceptors can undergo **dark adaptation.** In the low levels of illumination of the darkened room, vision can only be supplied by the rods, which have greater sensitivity than the cones. During the exposure to bright light, however, the rhodopsin in the rods has been completely activated and retinal has dissociated from the opsin, making the rods insensitive to further stimulation by light. Rhodopsin cannot respond fully again until it is restored to its resting state by enzymatic reassociation of retinal with the opsin, a process requiring several minutes. Obtaining sufficient dietary vitamin A is essential for good night vision because it provides the chromophore retinal for rhodopsin.

Light adaptation occurs when you step from a dark place into a bright one. Initially, the eye is extremely sensitive to light as rods are overwhelmingly activated, and the visual image is too bright and has poor contrast. However, the rhodopsin is soon inactivated (sometimes said to be "bleached") as retinal dissociates from rhodopsin. As long as you remain

Figure 7.27 APR Organization of the retina. Light enters through the cornea and passes through the aqueous humor, pupil, vitreous humor, and the front surface of the retina before reaching the photoreceptor cells. The membranes that contain the light-sensitive proteins form discrete discs in the rods but are continuous with the plasma membrane in the cones, which accounts for the comblike appearance of these latter cells. Horizontal and amacrine cells, depicted here in purple and orange, provide lateral integration between neurons of the retina. Not shown are Müller cells, funnel-shaped glial cells that act as fiber-optic pathways for light from the front surface of the retina to the photoreceptors. At the lower left is a scanning electron micrograph of rods and cones. Redrawn from Dowling and Boycott.

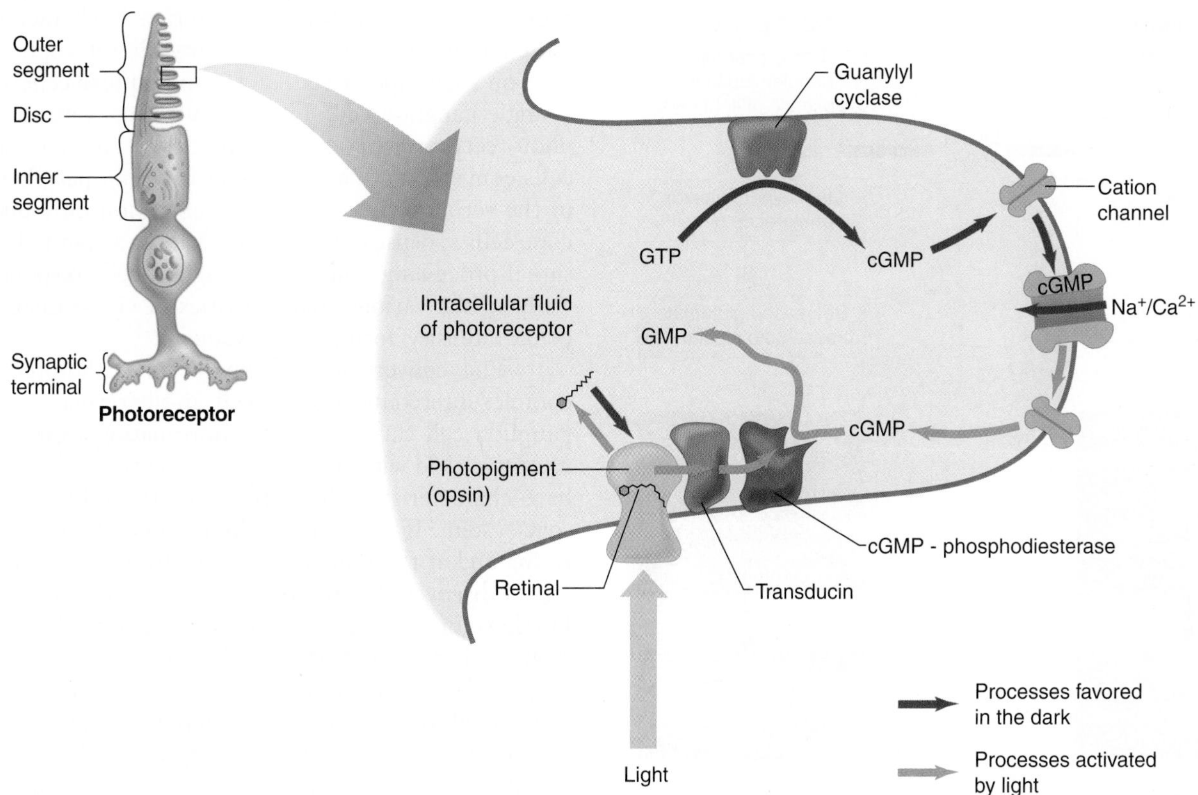

Figure 7.28 Phototransduction in a cone cell. In the absence of a light stimulus, cGMP binds to cation channels and opens them. When light strikes the chromophore (retinal) of the photopigment, it changes conformation and dissociates from the opsin. As a result, cGMP-phosphodiesterase in the membrane of the disc is stimulated, which decreases cGMP and thus closes the cation channels. For simplicity, the proteins are shown widely spaced in the membrane. In fact, all of these proteins are densely interspersed within the cone disc membrane. Phototransduction in rods is basically identical, except the membranous discs are contained completely within the cell's cytosol (see Figure 7.27), and the cGMP-gated ion channels are in the surface membrane rather than the disc membranes.

PHYSIOLOGICAL INQUIRY

- Explain why one early symptom of vitamin A deficiency is impaired vision at night (often called night blindness).

Answer can be found at end of chapter.

in bright light, the rods are unresponsive so that only the less-sensitive cones are operating, and the image is sharp and not overwhelmingly bright.

Neural Pathways of Vision

The distinct characteristics of the visual image are transmitted through the visual system along multiple, parallel pathways. The neural pathway of vision begins with the rods and cones. We just described in detail how the presence or absence of light influences photoreceptor cell membrane potential, and we will now consider how this information is encoded, processed, and transmitted to the brain.

Light signals are converted into action potentials through the interaction of photoreceptors with **bipolar cells** and **ganglion cells.** Photoreceptor and bipolar cells only undergo graded responses because they lack the voltage-gated channels that mediate action potentials in other types of neurons (review Figure 6.19). Ganglion cells have those channels and are therefore the first cells in the pathway where action potentials can be initiated. Photoreceptors interact with bipolar and ganglion cells in two distinct ways, designated as "ON-pathways" and "OFF-pathways." In both pathways, photoreceptors are depolarized in the absence of light, causing the neurotransmitter glutamate to be released onto bipolar cells. Light striking the photoreceptors of either pathway hyperpolarizes the photoreceptors, resulting in a decrease in glutamate release onto bipolar cells. Two key differences in the two pathways are that (1) bipolar cells of the ON-pathway spontaneously depolarize in the absence of input, whereas bipolar cells of the OFF-pathway hyperpolarize in the absence of input; and (2) glutamate receptors of ON-pathway bipolar cells are inhibitory, whereas glutamate receptors of OFF-pathway bipolar cells are excitatory. The net result is that the two pathways respond exactly the opposite in the presence and absence of light (**Figure 7.29**).

Glutamate released onto ON-pathway bipolar cells binds to metabotropic receptors that cause enzymatic breakdown of cGMP, which hyperpolarizes the bipolar cells by a mechanism

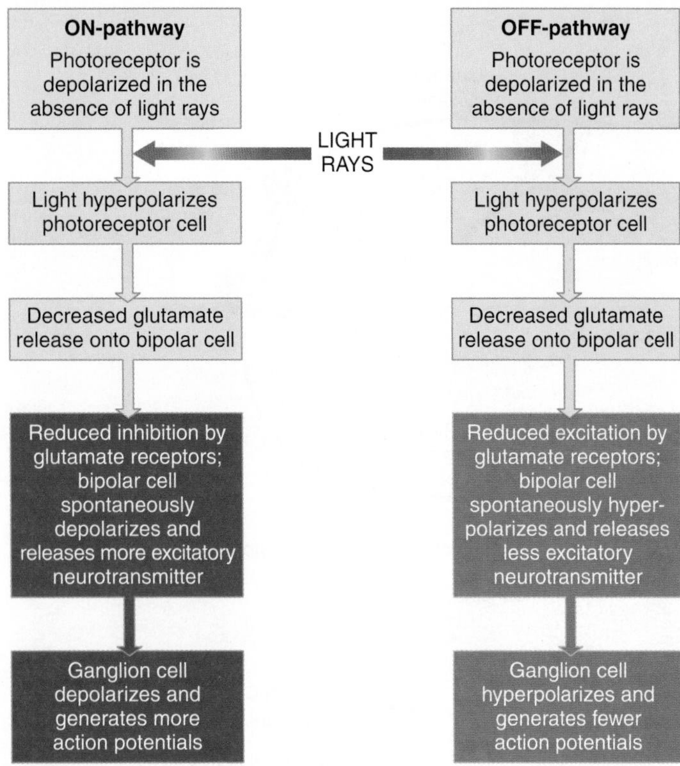
ON-pathway
Photoreceptor is depolarized in the absence of light rays
OFF-pathway
Photoreceptor is depolarized in the absence of light rays
LIGHT RAYS
Light hyperpolarizes photoreceptor cell
Light hyperpolarizes photoreceptor cell
Decreased glutamate release onto bipolar cell
Decreased glutamate release onto bipolar cell
Reduced inhibition by glutamate receptors; bipolar cell spontaneously depolarizes and releases more excitatory neurotransmitter
Reduced excitation by glutamate receptors; bipolar cell spontaneously hyper-polarizes and releases less excitatory neurotransmitter
Ganglion cell depolarizes and generates more action potentials
Ganglion cell hyperpolarizes and generates fewer action potentials

Figure 7.29 Effects of light on signaling in ON-pathway ganglion cells and OFF-pathway ganglion cells.

similar to that occurring when light strikes a photoreceptor cell. When the bipolar cells are hyperpolarized, they are prevented from releasing excitatory neurotransmitter onto their associated ganglion cells. Thus, in the absence of light, ganglion cells of the ON-pathway are not stimulated to fire action potentials. These processes reverse, however, when light strikes the photoreceptors: glutamate release from photoreceptors declines, ON-bipolar cells depolarize, excitatory neurotransmitter is released, the ganglion cells are depolarized, and an increased frequency of action potentials propagates to the brain.

OFF-pathway bipolar cells have ionotropic glutamate receptors that are nonselective cation channels, which depolarize the bipolar cells when glutamate binds. Depolarization of these bipolar cells stimulates them to release excitatory neurotransmitter onto their associated ganglion cells, stimulating them to fire action potentials. Thus, the OFF-pathway generates action potentials in the absence of light, and reversal of these processes inhibits action potentials when light does strike the photoreceptors. The coexistence of these ON- and OFF-pathways in each region of the retina greatly improves image resolution by increasing the brain's ability to perceive contrast at edges or borders.

Stimulation of ganglion cells is actually far more complex than just described—a significant amount of signal processing occurs within the retina before action potentials actually travel to the brain. Synapses between photoreceptors, bipolar cells, and ganglion cells are interconnected by a layer of **horizontal cells** and a layer of **amacrine cells,** which pass information between adjacent areas of the retina (review Figure 7.27). Furthermore, the retina is characterized by a large amount of convergence; many photoreceptors can synapse on each bipolar cell, and many bipolar cells synapse on a single ganglion cell. The amount of convergence varies by photoreceptor type and retinal region. As many as 100 rod cells converge onto a single bipolar cell in peripheral regions of the retina, whereas in the fovea region only one or a few cone cells synapse onto a bipolar cell. As a result of this retinal signal processing, individual ganglion cells respond differentially to the various characteristics of visual images, such as color, intensity, form, and movement.

The convergence of inputs from photoreceptors and complex interconnections of cells in the retina mean that each ganglion cell carries encoded information from a particular receptive field within the retina. Receptive fields in the retina have characteristics that differ from those in the somatosensory system. If you were to shine pinpoints of light onto the retina and at the same time record from a ganglion cell, you would discover that the receptive field for that cell is round. Furthermore, the response of the ganglion cell could demonstrate either an increased or decreased action potential frequency, depending on the location of the stimulus within that single field. Because of different inputs from bipolar cell pathways to the ganglion cell, each receptive field has an inner core ("center") that responds differently than the area around it (the "surround"). There can be "ON center/OFF surround" or "OFF center/ON surround" ganglion cells, so named because the responses are either depolarization (ON) or hyperpolarization (OFF) in the two areas of the field (**Figure 7.30**). The usefulness of this organization is that the existence of a clear edge between the "ON" and "OFF" areas of the receptive field increases the contrast between the area that is receiving light and the area around it, increasing visual acuity. As a result, a

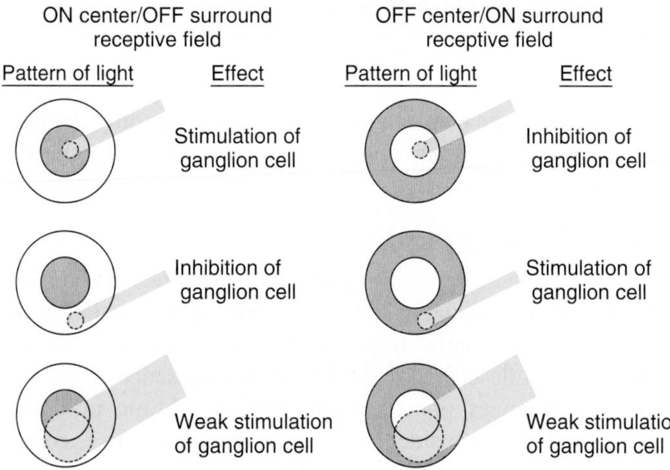
Ganglion Cell Receptive Fields
ON center/OFF surround receptive field
OFF center/ON surround receptive field
Pattern of light
Effect
Pattern of light
Effect
Stimulation of ganglion cell
Inhibition of ganglion cell
Inhibition of ganglion cell
Stimulation of ganglion cell
Weak stimulation of ganglion cell
Weak stimulation of ganglion cell

Figure 7.30 Types of ganglion cell receptive fields. ON center/OFF surround ganglion cells are stimulated when a pinpoint of light strikes the center of the receptive field and are inhibited when light strikes the surrounding area. The opposite occurs in OFF center/ON surround cells. In either case, light striking both regions results in intermediate activation due to offsetting influences. This is an example of lateral inhibition and enhances the detection of the edges of a visual stimulus, thus increasing visual acuity.

great deal of information processing takes place at this early stage of the sensory pathway.

The axons of the ganglion cells form the output from the retina—the optic nerve, which is cranial nerve II (**Figure 7.31a**). The two optic nerves meet at the base of the brain to form the **optic chiasm,** where some of the axons cross and travel within the **optic tracts** to the opposite side of the brain, providing both cerebral hemispheres with input from each eye. With both eyes open, the outer regions of our total visual field is perceived by only one eye (zones of **monocular vision**). In the central portion, the fields from the two eyes overlap (the zone of **binocular vision**) (**Figure 7.31b**). The ability to compare overlapping information from the two eyes in this central region allows for depth perception and improves our ability to judge distances.

Parallel processing of information continues all the way to and within the cerebral cortex to the highest stages of visual neural networks. Cells in this pathway respond to electrical signals that are generated initially by the photoreceptors' response to light. Optic nerve fibers project to several structures in the brain, the largest number passing to the thalamus (specifically to the lateral geniculate nucleus of the thalamus; see Figure 7.31), where the information (color, intensity, shape, movement, etc.) from the different ganglion cell types is kept distinct. In addition to the input from the retina, many neurons of the lateral geniculate nucleus also receive input from the brainstem reticular formation and input relayed back from the visual cortex, the primary visual area of the cerebral cortex. These nonretinal inputs can control the transmission of information from the retina to the visual cortex and may be involved in our ability to shift attention between vision and the other sensory modalities.

The lateral geniculate nucleus sends action potentials to the visual cortex (see Figures 7.13 and 7.31). Different aspects of visual information continue along in the parallel pathways coded by the ganglion cells, then are processed simultaneously in a number of independent ways in different parts of the cerebral cortex before they are reintegrated to produce the conscious sensation of sight and the perceptions associated with it. The cells of the visual pathways are organized to handle information about line, contrast, movement, and color. They do not, however, form a picture in the brain but only generate a spatial and temporal pattern of electrical activity that we *perceive* as a visual image.

We mentioned earlier that some neurons of the visual pathway project to regions of the brain other than the visual cortex. For example, a recently discovered class of ganglion cells containing an opsinlike pigment called **melanopsin** carries visual information to the **suprachiasmatic nucleus,** which lies just above the optic chiasm and functions as part of the "biological clock." It appears that information about the daily cycle of light intensity from these ganglion cells is used

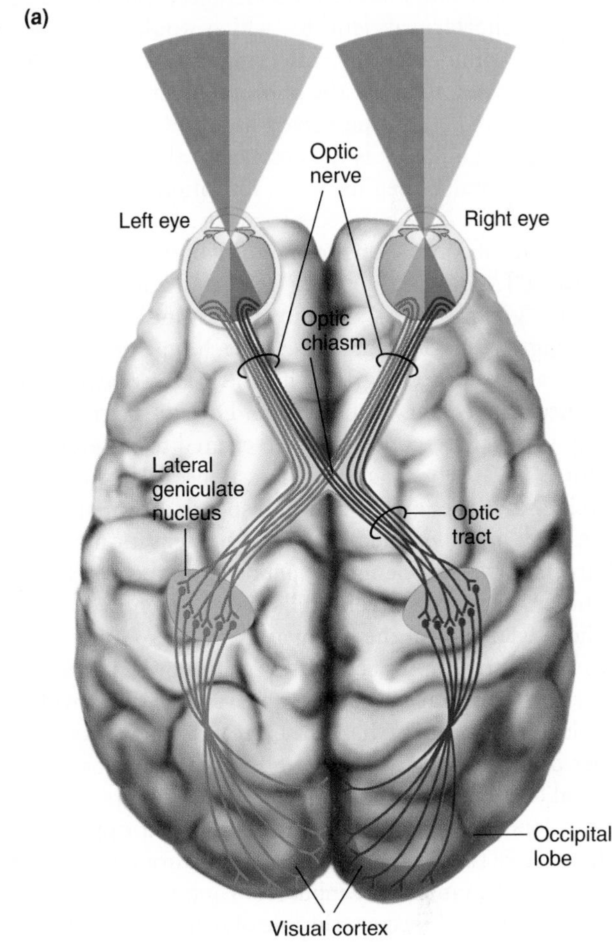

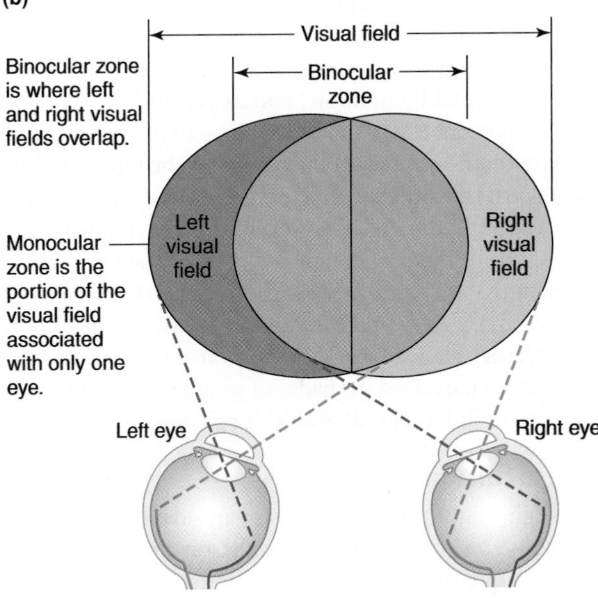

Figure 7.31 AP|R Visual pathways and fields. (a) Visual pathways viewed from above show how visual information from each eye field is distributed to the visual cortex of both occipital lobes. (b) Overlap of visual fields from the two eyes creates a binocular zone of vision, which allows for perception of depth and distance.

PHYSIOLOGICAL INQUIRY

- Three patients have suffered destruction of different portions of their visual pathway. Patient 1 has lost the right optic tract, patient 2 has lost the nerve fibers that cross at the optic chiasm, and patient 3 has lost the left occipital lobe. Draw a picture of what each person would perceive through each eye when looking at a white wall.

Answer can be found at end of chapter.

to entrain this neuronal clock to a 24-hour day—the circadian rhythm (review Figure 1.10). Other visual information passes to the brainstem and cerebellum, where it is used in the coordination of eye and head movements, fixation of gaze, and change in pupil size.

Color Vision

The colors we perceive are related to the wavelengths of light that the pigments in the objects of our visual world reflect, absorb, or transmit. For example, an object appears red because it absorbs shorter wavelengths, which would be perceived as blue, while simultaneously reflecting the longer wavelengths, perceived as red, to excite the photopigment of the retina most sensitive to red. Light perceived as white is a mixture of all wavelengths, and black is the absence of all light.

Color vision begins with activation of the photopigments in the cone photoreceptor cells. Human retinas have three kinds of cones—one responding optimally at long wavelengths ("L" or "red" cones), one at medium wavelengths ("M" or "green" cones), and the other stimulated best at short wavelengths ("S" or "blue" cones). Each type of cone is excited over a range of wavelengths, with the greatest response occurring near the center of that range. For any given wavelength of light, the three cone types are excited to different degrees (**Figure 7.32**). For example, in response to light of 531 nm wavelengths, the green cones respond maximally, the red cones less, and the blue not at all. Our sensation of the shade of green at this wavelength depends upon the relative outputs of these three types of cone cells and the comparison made by higher-order cells in the visual system.

The pathways for color vision follow those that Figure 7.31 describes. Ganglion cells of one type respond to a broad band of wavelengths. In other words, they receive input from all three types of cones, and they signal not a specific color but, rather, general brightness. Ganglion cells of a second type code for specific colors. These latter cells are also called **opponent color cells** because they have an excitatory input from one type of cone receptor and an inhibitory input from another. For example, the cell in **Figure 7.33** increases its rate of firing when viewing a blue light but decreases it when a yellow light replaces the blue. The cell gives a weak response when stimulated with a white light because the light contains both blue and yellow wavelengths. Other more complicated patterns also exist. The output from these cells is recorded by multiple, and as yet unclear, mechanisms in visual centers of the brain. Our ability to discriminate color also depends on the *intensity* of light striking the retina. In brightly lit conditions, the differential response of the cones allows for good color vision. In dim light, however, only the highly sensitive rods are able to respond. Though rods are activated over a range of wavelengths that overlap with those that activate the cones (see Figure 7.32), there is no mechanism for distinguishing between frequencies. Thus, objects that appear vividly colored in bright daylight are perceived in shades of gray as night falls and lighting becomes so dim that only rods can respond.

Color Blindness

At high light intensities, as in daylight vision, most people—92% of the male population and over 99% of the female population—have normal color vision. However, there are several types of defects in color vision that result from mutations in the cone pigments. The most common form of ***color blindness***, red–green color blindness, is present predominantly in men, affecting 1 out of 12. Color blindness in women is much rarer (1 out of 200). Men with red–green color blindness lack either the red or the green cone pigments entirely or have them in an abnormal form. Because of this, the discrimination between shades of these colors is poor.

Color blindness results from a recessive mutation in one or more genes encoding the cone pigments. Genes encoding the red and green cone pigments are located very close to each other on the X chromosome, whereas the gene encoding the blue chromophore is located on chromosome 7. Because of this close association of the red and green genes on the X chromosome, there is a greater likelihood that genetic recombination will occur during meiosis (see Chapter 17, Section A),

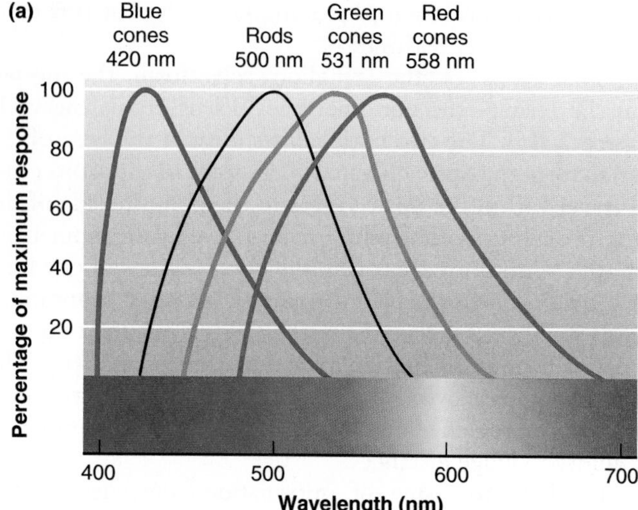

(b)

Figure 7.32 The sensitivities of the photopigments in the normal human retina. (a) The frequency of action potentials in the optic nerve is directly related to a photopigment's absorption of light. Under bright lighting conditions, the three types of cones respond over different frequency ranges. In dim light, only the rods respond. (b) Demonstration of cone cell fatigue and afterimage. Hold very still and stare at the triangle inside the yellow circle for 30 seconds. Then, shift your gaze to the square and wait for the image to appear around it.

PHYSIOLOGICAL INQUIRY

- What color was the image you saw while you stared at the square? Why did you perceive that particular color?

Answer can be found at end of chapter.

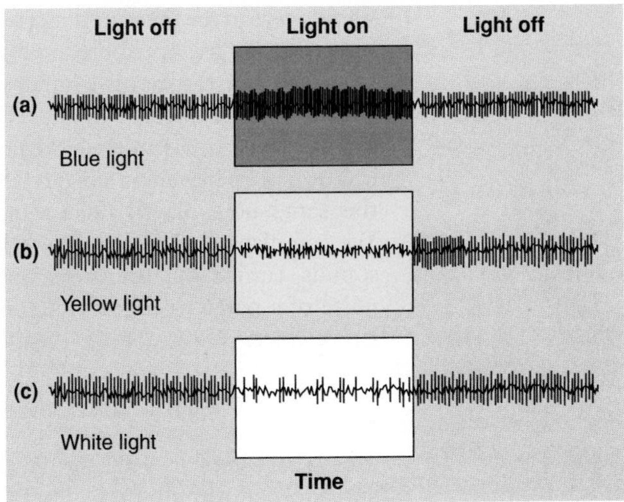

Figure 7.33 Response of a single opponent color ganglion cell to blue, yellow, and white lights. Redrawn from Hubel and Wiesel.

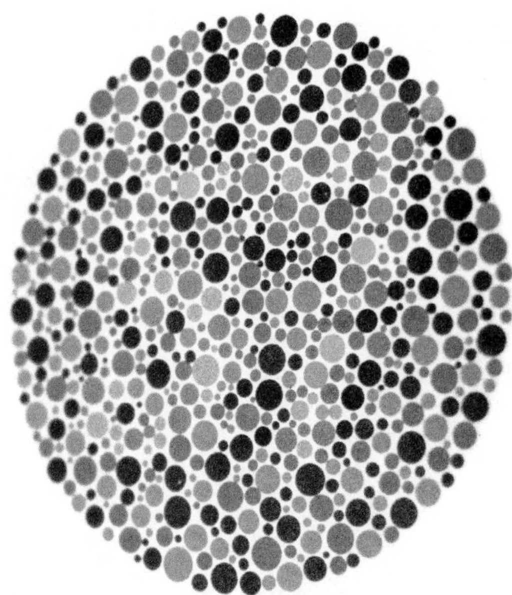

Figure 7.34 Image used for testing red–green color vision. With normal color vision, the number 57 is visible; no number is apparent to those with a red–green defect.

thus eliminating or changing the spectral characteristics of the red and green pigments produced. This, in part, accounts for the fact that red–green defects are not always complete and that some color-blind individuals under some conditions can distinguish shades of red or green. In males, the presence of only a single X chromosome means that a single recessive allele from the mother will result in color blindness, even though the mother herself may have normal color vision due to having one normal X chromosome. It also means that 50% of the male offspring of that mother will be expected to be color blind. Individuals who have red–green color blindness will not be able to see the number in **Figure 7.34.**

Eye Movement

The macula lutea region of the retina, within which the fovea centralis is located, is specialized in several ways to provide the highest visual acuity. It is comprised of densely packed cones with minimal convergence through the bipolar and ganglion cell layers. In addition, light rays are scattered less on the way to the outer segment of those cones than in other retinal regions, because the interneuron layers and the blood vessels are displaced to the edges. This central region becomes impaired in a condition known as ***macular degeneration,*** producing a defect characterized by loss of vision in the center of the visual field. The most common form of this disease increases with age, occurring in approximately 30% of individuals over the age of 75, and is therefore referred to as ***age-related macular degeneration*** (***AMD***).

To focus the most important point in the visual image (the fixation point) on the fovea and keep it there, the eyeball must be able to move. Six skeletal muscles attached to the outside of each eyeball (identified in **Figure 7.35**) control its movement. These muscles perform two basic movements, fast and slow.

The fast movements, called **saccades,** are small, jerking movements that rapidly bring the eye from one fixation point to another to allow a search of the visual field. In addition, saccades move the visual image over the receptors, thereby preventing adaptation that would result from persistent photobleaching of photoreceptors in a given region of the retina. Saccades also occur during certain periods of sleep when dreaming occurs, though these movements are not thought to be involved in "watching" the visual imagery of dreams.

Slow eye movements are involved both in tracking visual objects as they move through the visual field and during compensation for movements of the head. The control centers for these compensating movements obtain their information about head movement from the vestibular system, which we will describe shortly. Control systems for the other slow movements of the eyes require the continuous feedback of visual information about the moving object.

7.7 Hearing

The sense of hearing (**audition**) is based on the physics of sound and the physiology of the external, middle, and inner ear. In addition, there is complex neural processing along pathways to the brain and within brain regions involved in sensing and perceiving acoustic information.

Sound

Sound energy is transmitted through a gaseous, liquid, or solid medium by setting up a vibration of the medium's molecules, air being the most common medium in which we hear sound energy. When there are no molecules, as in a vacuum, there can be no sound. Anything capable of disturbing molecules—for example, vibrating objects—can serve as a sound source. **Figure 7.36, a–d**, demonstrates the basic mechanism of sound production using a tuning fork as an example. When struck, the tuning fork vibrates, creating disturbances of air molecules that make up the sound wave. The sound wave consists of zones of compression, in which the molecules are close together and the pressure is increased, alternating with zones of rarefaction, in which the molecules are farther apart and the pressure is lower.

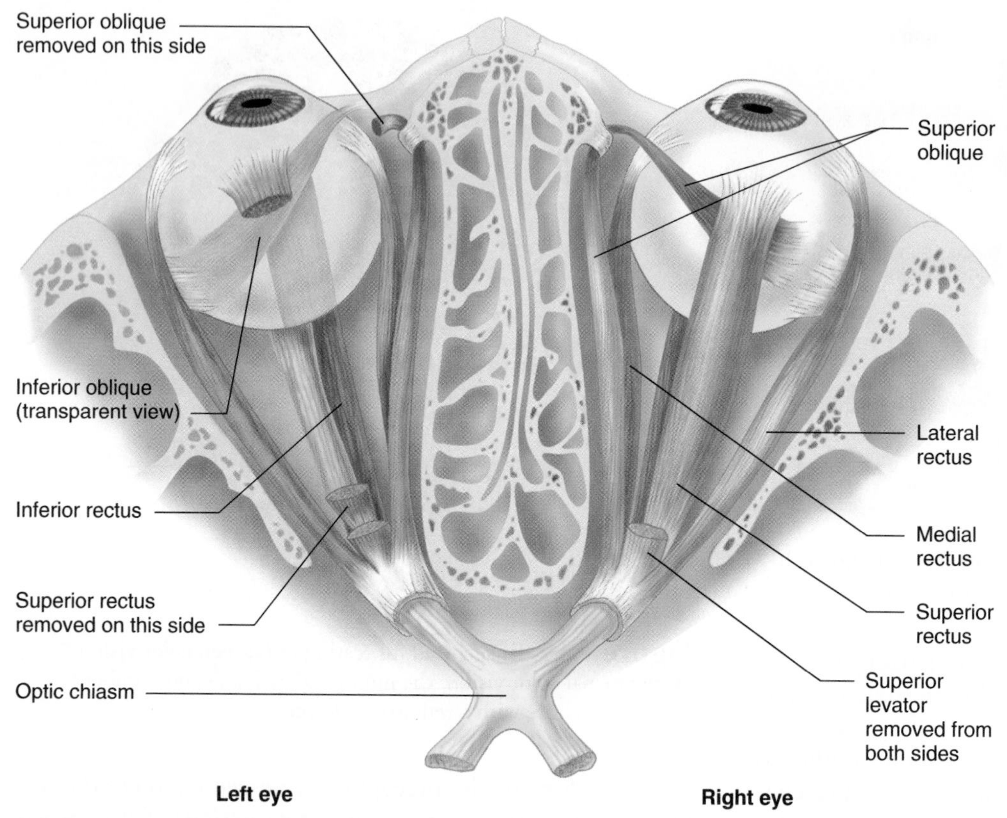

Figure 7.35 AP|R A superior view of the muscles that move the eyes to direct the gaze and provide convergence.

As the air molecules bump against each other, the zones of compression and rarefaction ripple outward and the sound wave is transmitted over distance.

A sound wave measured over time (**Figure 7.36e**) consists of rapidly alternating pressures that vary continuously from a high during compression of molecules, to a low during rarefaction, and back again. The difference between the pressure of molecules in zones of compression and rarefaction determines the wave's amplitude, which is related to the loudness of the sound; the greater the amplitude, the louder the sound. The human ear can detect volume variations over an enormous range, from the sound of someone breathing in the room to a jet taking off on a nearby runway. Because of this incredible range, sound loudness is measured in decibels (dB), which are a logarithmic function of sound pressure. The threshold for human hearing is assigned a value of 0 dB, and an increase of 30 dB, for example, would represent a 1000-fold increase in sound intensity.

The frequency of vibration of the sound source (the number of zones of compression or rarefaction in a given time) determines the pitch we hear; the faster the vibration, the higher the pitch. The sounds heard most keenly by human ears are those from sources vibrating at frequencies between 1000 and 4000 Hz (hertz, or cycles per second), but the entire range of frequencies audible to human beings extends from 20 to 20,000 Hz. Most sounds are not pure tones but are mixtures of tones of a variety of frequencies. Sequences of pure tones of varying frequencies are generally perceived as musical. The addition of other frequencies, called overtones, to a pure tone's sound wave gives the sound its characteristic quality, or timbre.

We can distinguish hundreds of thousands of different sounds. For example, we can distinguish the note C (261.63 Hz) played on a piano from the same note played on a violin. We can also selectively *not* perceive sounds, tuning out the background noise of a party to concentrate on a single voice.

Sound Transmission in the Ear

The first step in hearing is the entrance of sound waves into the **external auditory canal (Figure 7.37)**. The shapes of the outer ear (the pinna, or auricle) and the external auditory canal help to amplify and direct the sound. The sound waves reverberate from the sides and end of the external auditory canal, filling it with the continuous vibrations of pressure waves.

The **tympanic membrane** (eardrum) is stretched across the end of the external auditory canal, and as air molecules push against the membrane, they cause it to vibrate at the same frequency as the sound wave. Under higher pressure during a zone of compression, the tympanic membrane bows inward. The distance the membrane moves, although always very small, is a function of the force with which the air molecules hit it and is related to the sound pressure and therefore its loudness. During the subsequent zone of rarefaction, the membrane bows outward; when the sound ceases, it returns toward a midpoint. The exquisitely sensitive tympanic membrane responds to all the varying pressures of the sound waves, vibrating slowly in response to low-frequency sounds and rapidly in response to high-frequency sounds.

The tympanic membrane separates the external auditory canal from the **middle ear,** an air-filled cavity in the temporal bone of the skull. The pressures in the external auditory canal and middle ear cavity are normally equal to atmospheric pressure. The middle ear cavity is exposed to atmospheric pressure through the **eustachian tube,** which connects the middle ear to the pharynx. The slitlike ending of this tube in the pharynx is normally closed, but muscle movements open the tube during yawning, swallowing, or sneezing. A difference in pressure can be produced with sudden changes in altitude (as in an ascending or descending elevator or airplane). When the pressures outside the ear and in the ear canal change, the pressure in the middle ear initially remains constant because the eustachian tube is closed. This pressure difference can stretch the tympanic membrane and cause pain. This problem is relieved by voluntarily yawning or swallowing, which opens the eustachian tube and allows the pressure in the middle ear to equilibrate with the new atmospheric pressure.

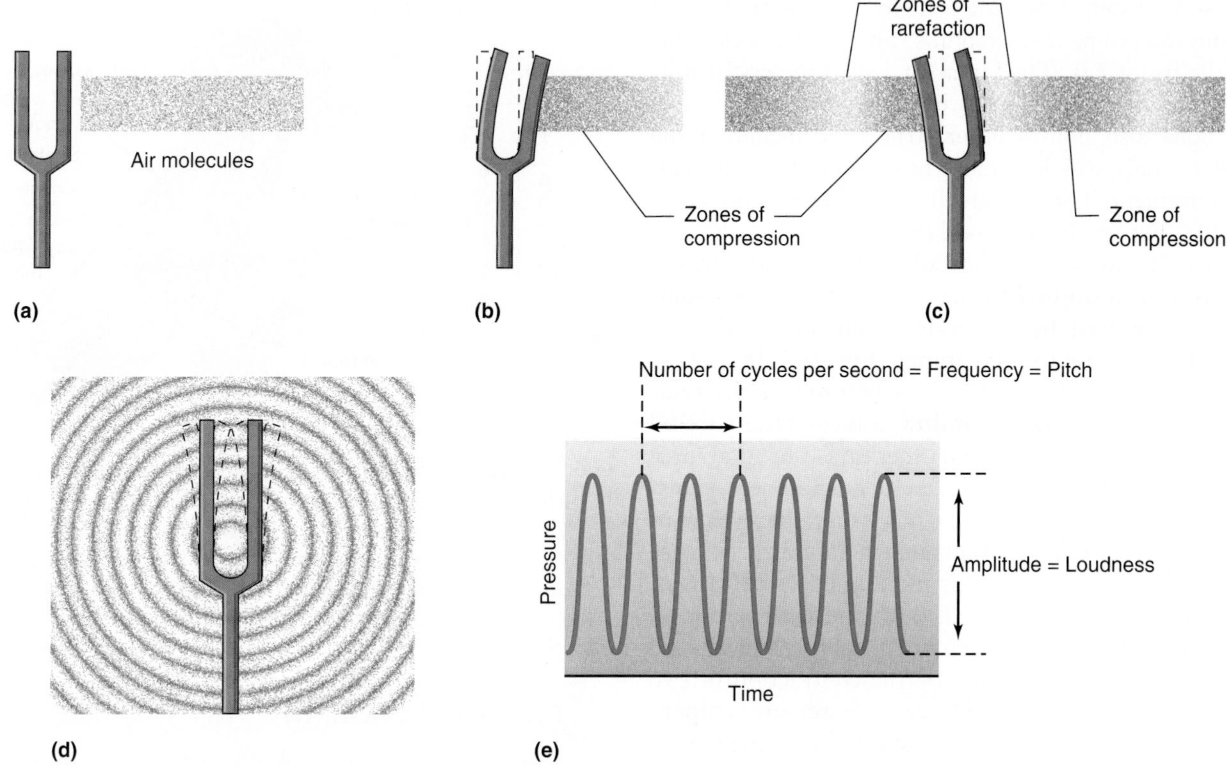

Figure 7.36 Formation of sound waves from a vibrating tuning fork.

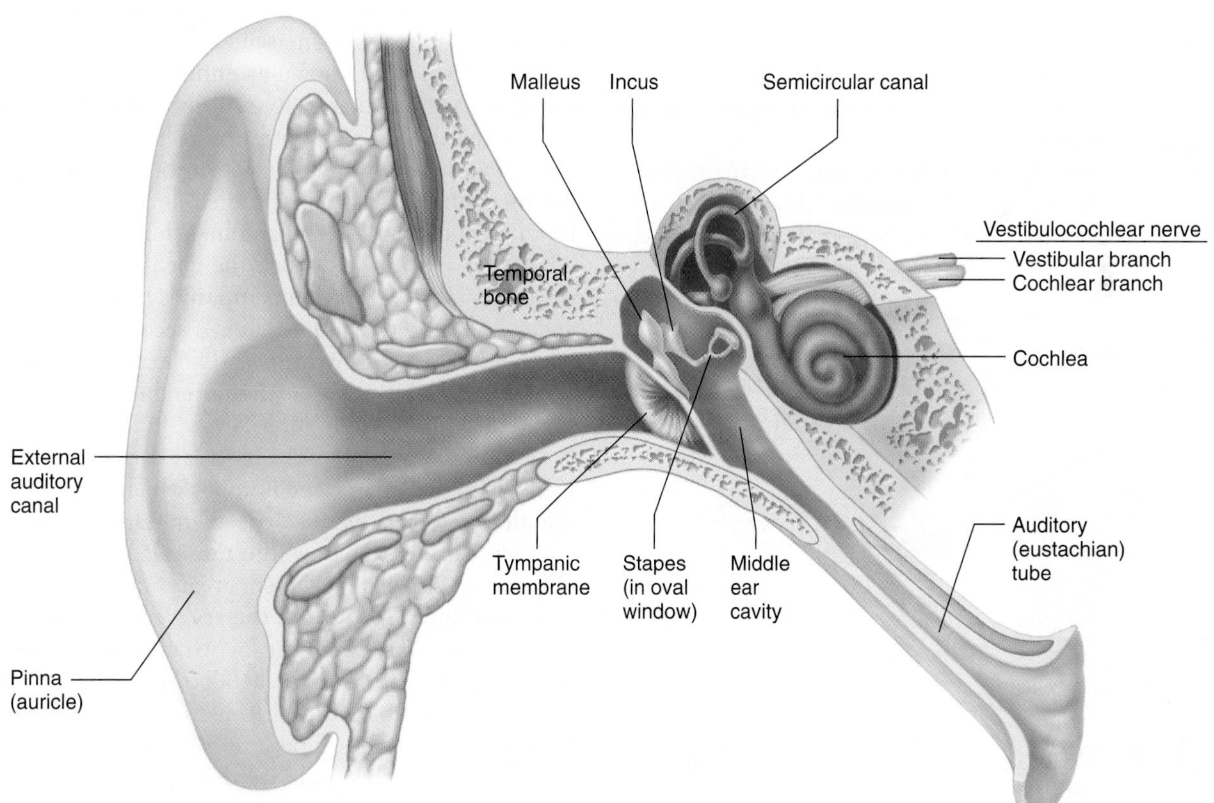

Figure 7.37 APIR The human ear. In this and the following two figures, violet indicates the outer ear, green the middle ear, and blue the inner ear. The malleus, incus, and stapes are bones and components of the middle ear compartment. The eustachian tube is generally closed except during pharynx movements such as swallowing or yawning.

The second step in hearing is the transmission of sound energy from the tympanic membrane through the middle ear cavity to the **inner ear.** The inner ear, called the **cochlea,** is a spiral-shaped, fluid-filled space in the temporal bone. The temporal bone also houses other structures, including the semicircular canals, which contain the sensory organs for balance and movement. These fluid-filled passages are connected to the cochlea but will be discussed later.

Because liquid is more difficult to move than air, the sound pressure transmitted to the inner ear must be amplified. This is achieved by a movable chain of three small bones, the **malleus, incus,** and **stapes** (**Figure 7.38**). These bones act as a piston and couple the vibrations of the tympanic membrane to the **oval window,** a membrane-covered opening separating the middle and inner ears. The total force of a sound wave applied to the tympanic membrane is transferred to the oval window; however, because the oval window is much smaller than the tympanic membrane, the force per unit area (i.e., the pressure) is increased 15 to 20 times. Additional advantage is gained through the lever action of the middle ear bones. The amount of energy transmitted to the inner ear can be lessened by the contraction of two small skeletal muscles in the middle ear. The **tensor tympani muscle** attaches to the malleus, and contraction of the muscle dampens the bone's movement. The **stapedius** attaches to the stapes and similarly controls its mobility. These muscles contract reflexively to protect the delicate receptor apparatus of the inner ear from continuous, loud sounds. They cannot, however, protect against sudden, intermittent loud sounds, which is why it is crucial for people to wear ear protection in environments like a gun firing range. These muscles also contract reflexively when you vocalize to reduce the perception of loudness of your own voice, and optimize hearing over certain frequency ranges.

The entire system described thus far involves the transmission of sound energy into the cochlea. The cochlea is almost completely divided lengthwise by a membranous tube called the **cochlear duct,** which contains the sensory receptors of the auditory system (see Figure 7.38). The cochlear duct is filled with a fluid known as **endolymph,** a compartment of extracellular fluid that is atypical in that its K^+ concentration is high and its Na^+ concentration is low, like the intracellular fluid of most cells. On either side of the cochlear duct are compartments filled with a fluid called **perilymph,** which is similar in composition to cerebrospinal fluid (review Figure 6.47). The **scala vestibuli** is above the cochlear duct and begins at the oval window; the **scala tympani** is below the cochlear duct and connects to the middle ear at a second membrane-covered opening, the **round window.** The scala vestibuli and scala tympani are continuous at the far end of the cochlear duct at the **helicotrema** (see Figure 7.38).

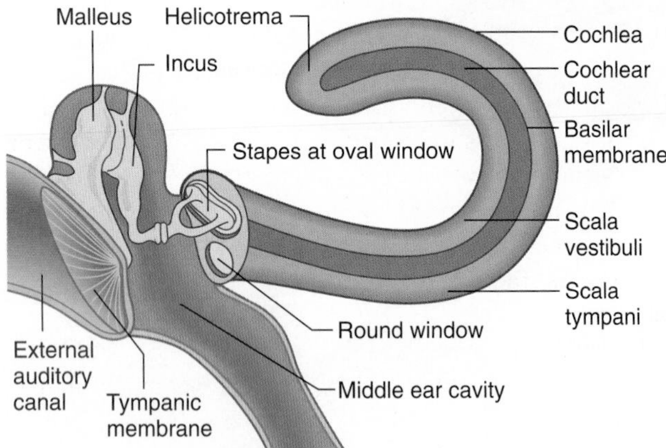

Figure 7.38 AP|R Relationship between the middle ear bones and the cochlea. The stapes attaches to the oval window, on the other side of which is the fluid-filled scala vestibuli. At the far end of this compartment is the helicotrema, an opening leading directly into the fluid-filled scala tympani. The membranous round window is between the scala tympani and middle ear. The cochlea is shown uncoiled for clarity. Redrawn from Kandel and Schwartz.

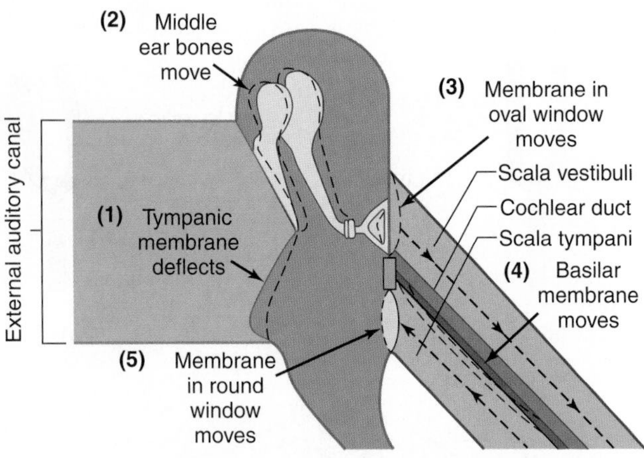

Figure 7.39 AP|R Transmission of sound vibrations through the middle and inner ear. (1) Sound waves coming through the external auditory canal move the tympanic membrane, which (2) moves the bones of the middle ear, (3) vibrates the membrane in the oval window, (4) causes oscillation of specific regions of the basilar membrane, and (5) causes pressure-relieving oscillations of the round window membrane. Redrawn from Davis and Silverman.

PHYSIOLOGICAL INQUIRY

- How might sounding an 80 dB warning tone just before the firing of an artillery gun (140 dB) reduce hearing damage?

Answer can be found at end of chapter.

Sound waves in the ear canal cause in-and-out movement of the tympanic membrane, which moves the chain of middle ear bones against the membrane covering the oval window, causing it to bow into the scala vestibuli and back out (**Figure 7.39**). This movement creates waves of pressure in the scala vestibuli. The wall of the scala vestibuli is largely bone, and there are only two paths by which the pressure waves can dissipate. One path is to the helicotrema, where the waves pass around the end of the cochlear duct into the scala tympani. However, most of the pressure is transmitted from the scala vestibuli across the cochlear duct. Pressure changes in the scala tympani are relieved by movements of the membrane within the round window.

The side of the cochlear duct nearest to the scala tympani is formed by the **basilar membrane** (**Figure 7.40**), upon which sits the **organ of Corti,** which contains the

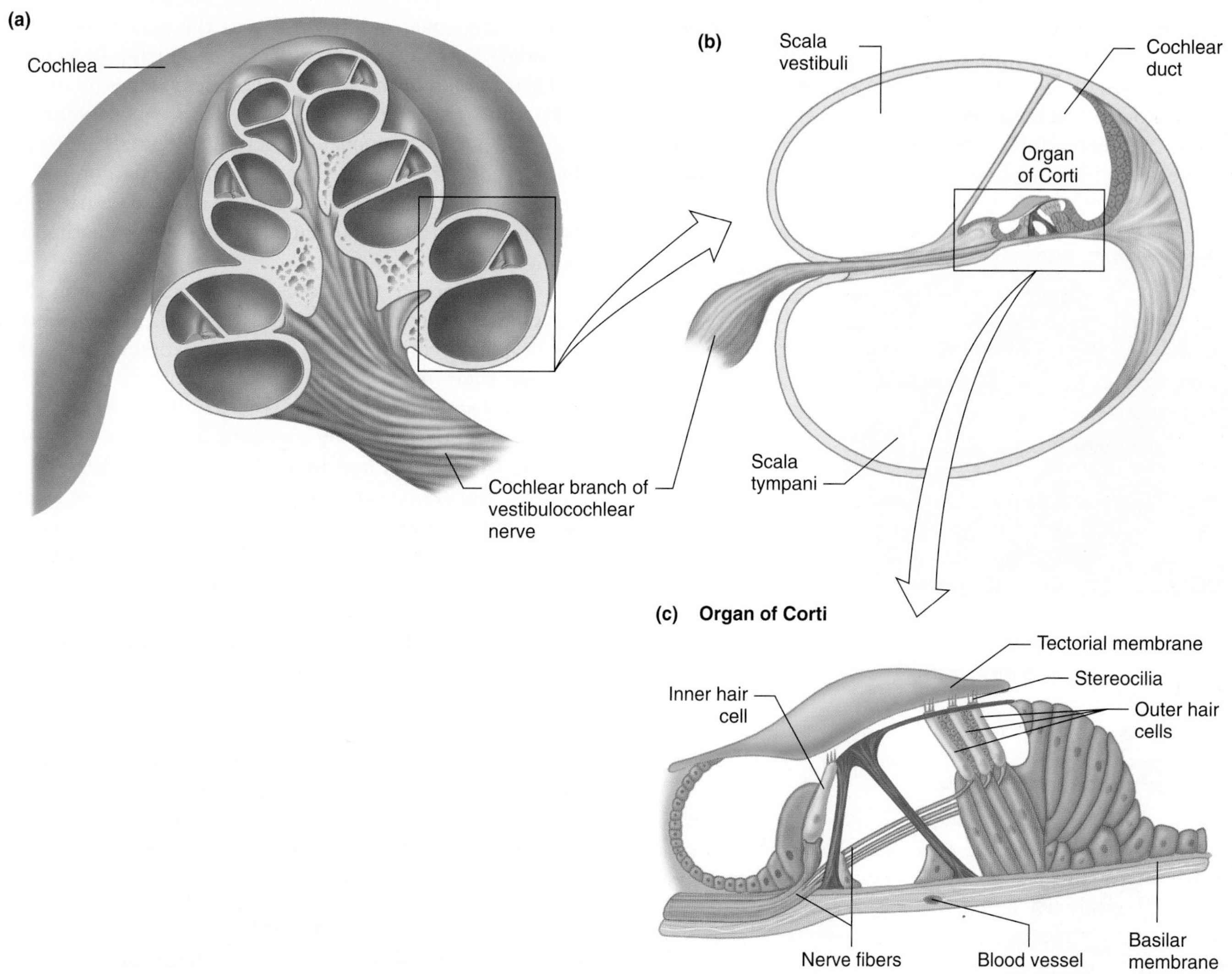

Figure 7.40 APIR Cross section of the membranes and compartments of the inner ear with detailed view of the hair cells and other structures on the basilar membrane. Views (a), (b), and (c) show increasing magnification. Redrawn from Rasmussen.

ear's sensitive receptor cells. Pressure differences across the cochlear duct cause the basilar membrane to vibrate.

The region of maximal displacement of the vibrating basilar membrane varies with the frequency of the sound source. Nearest to the middle ear, the basilar membrane is relatively narrow and stiff, predisposing it to vibrate most easily—that is, it undergoes the greatest movement—in response to high-frequency (high-pitched) tones. The basilar membrane becomes progressively wider and less stiff toward the far end. Thus, as the frequency of received sound waves is lowered, the point of maximal vibrational movement occurs progressively farther along the membrane toward the helicotrema. The basilar membrane is thus a sort of frequency-analyzing map, with high pitches being detected nearest the middle ear and low pitches detected toward the far end.

Hair Cells of the Organ of Corti

The receptor cells of the organ of Corti are called **hair cells.** These cells are mechanoreceptors that have hairlike **stereocilia** protruding from one end (**Figure 7.41a**). There are two anatomically separate groups of hair cells, a single row of **inner hair cells** and three rows of **outer hair cells.** Stereocilia of inner hair cells extend into the endolymph fluid and actually transduce pressure waves caused by fluid movement in the cochlear duct into receptor potentials. The stereocilia of outer hair cells are embedded in an overlying **tectorial membrane** and mechanically alter its movement in a complex way that sharpens frequency tuning at each point along the basilar membrane.

The tectorial membrane overlies the organ of Corti. As pressure waves displace the basilar membrane, the hair cells move in relation to the stationary tectorial membrane, and, consequently, the stereocilia bend. When the stereocilia are bent toward the tallest member of a bundle, fibrous connections called **tip links** pull open mechanically gated cation channels, and the resulting charge influx from the K^+-rich endolymph fluid depolarizes the membrane (see Figure 7.41). This opens voltage-gated Ca^{2+} channels near the base of the cell, which triggers neurotransmitter release. Bending the hair cells in the opposite direction slackens the tip links, closing the channels and allowing the cell to rapidly repolarize. Thus, as sound waves vibrate the basilar membrane, the stereocilia are bent back and forth, the membrane potential of the hair cells rapidly oscillates, and bursts of neurotransmitter are released onto afferent neurons.

The neurotransmitter released from each hair cell is glutamate (just like in photoreceptor cells), which binds to and activates protein-binding sites on the terminals of 10 or so afferent neurons. This causes the generation of action potentials in the neurons, the axons of which join to form the cochlear branch of the **vestibulocochlear nerve** (cranial nerve VIII). The greater the energy (loudness) of the sound wave, the greater the frequency of action potentials generated in the afferent nerve fibers. Because of its position on the basilar membrane, each hair cell responds to a limited range of sound frequencies, with one particular frequency stimulating it most strongly.

In addition to the protective reflexes involving the tensor tympani and stapedius muscles, efferent nerve fibers from the brainstem regulate the activity of outer hair cells and dampen their response, which also protects them. Despite these protective mechanisms, the hair cells are easily damaged or even destroyed by exposure to high-intensity sounds such as those generated by rock concert speakers, jet plane engines, and construction equipment. Lesser noise levels also cause damage if exposure is chronic. The general mechanism of loud-sound-induced hair cell damage is thought to be due to breakage of the delicate tips of stereocilia caused by high-amplitude movements of the basilar membrane. Hearing impairment may be temporary at intermediate levels of exposure, because stereocilia tips can regenerate. However, if the sound is excessively loud or prolonged, the hair cells themselves die and are not replaced. In either temporary or permanent hearing loss, it is common for a person to experience ***tinnitis***, or "ringing in the ears," from persistent, inappropriate activation of afferent cochlear neurons following hair cell damage or loss. **Table 7.2** lists the volume level of common sounds and their effects on hearing.

Neural Pathways in Hearing

Cochlear nerve fibers enter the brainstem and synapse with interneurons there. Fibers from both ears often converge on the same neuron. Many of these interneurons are influenced by the different arrival times and intensities of the input from the two ears. The different arrival times of low-frequency sounds and the different intensities of high-frequency sounds are used to determine the direction of the sound source. If, for example, a sound is louder in the right ear or arrives sooner at the right ear than at the left, we assume that the sound source

(a)

(b)

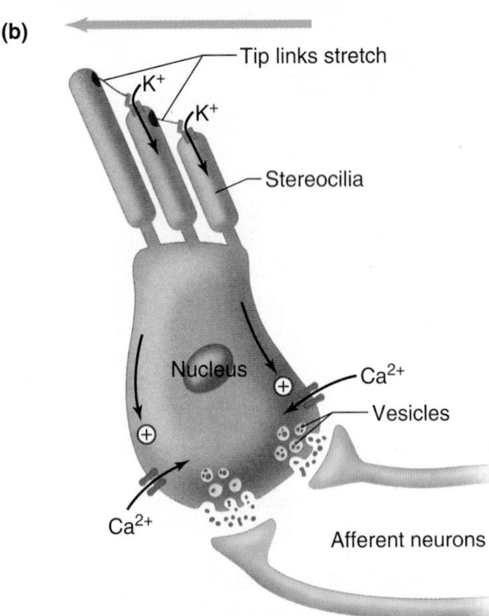

(c)

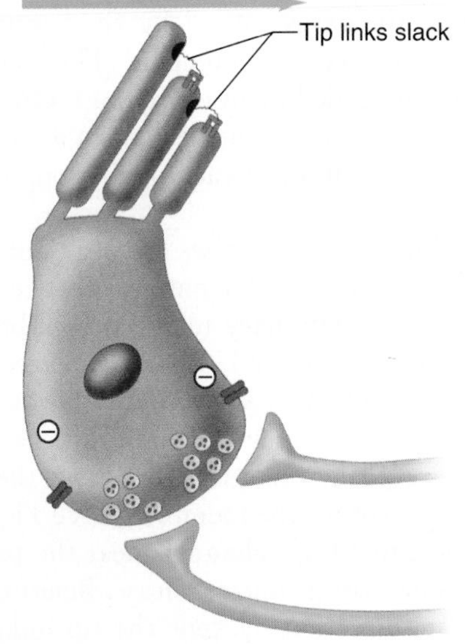

Figure 7.41 Mechanism for neurotransmitter release in a hair cell of the auditory system. (a) Scanning electron micrograph shows the size gradation in a bundle of outer hair cell stereocilia at the top of a single hair cell (tectorial membrane removed). (b) Bending stereocilia in one direction depolarizes the cell and stimulates neurotransmitter release. (c) Bending in the opposite direction repolarizes the cell and stops the release.

PHYSIOLOGICAL INQUIRY

- Furosemide is commonly used to treat high blood pressure because it increases the production of urine (it is a diuretic). It acts in the kidney by inhibiting a membrane protein responsible for pumping K^+, Na^+, and Cl^- across an epithelial membrane. Based on this information, propose a mechanism that might explain why one of the drug's side effects is hearing loss.

Answer can be found at end of chapter.

TABLE 7.2	Decibel Levels of Common Sounds and Their Effects	
Sound Source	**Decibel Level**	**Effects**
Breathing	10	Just audible
Rustling leaves	20	
Whisper	30	Very quiet
Refrigerator humming	40	
Quiet office conversation	50–60	Comfortable hearing level below 60 dB
Vacuum cleaner, hair dryer	70	Intrusive; interferes with telephone conversation
City traffic, garbage disposal	80	Annoying; constant exposure could damage hearing
Lawnmower, blender	90	Above 85 dB, 8 hours exposure causes hearing damage
Farm tractor	100	To prevent hearing loss, recommendation is for less than 15 minutes unprotected exposure
Chain saw	110	Regular exposure of more than 1 minute risks permanent hearing loss
Rock concert	110–140	Threshold of pain begins at around 125 dB
Shotgun blast, jet take-off (200-foot distance)	130	Some permanent hearing loss likely
Jet take-off (75-foot distance)	150	Tympanic membrane rupture, permanent damage

Adapted from National Institute on Deafness and Other Communication Disorders, National Institutes of Health, www.nidcd.nih.gov.

is on the right. The shape of the outer ear (the pinna; see Figure 7.37) and movements of the head are also important in localizing the sound source.

From the brainstem, the information is transmitted via a polysynaptic pathway to the thalamus and on to the auditory cortex in the temporal lobe (see Figure 7.13). The neurons responding to different pitches (frequencies) are mapped along the auditory cortex in a manner that corresponds to regions along the basilar membrane, much as stimuli from different regions of the body are represented at different sites in the somatosensory cortex. Different areas of the auditory system is further specialized; some neurons respond best to complex sounds such as those used in verbal communication. Others signal the location, movement, duration, or loudness of a sound. Descending influences on auditory nerve pathways modulate sound perception in complex ways, allowing us to selectively focus on particular sounds. For example, we can focus on a soloist's efforts above an orchestra's accompaniment and selectively suppress the echoes of a sound off of walls and floors when attempting to localize the sound's source.

Electronic devices can help compensate for damage to the intricate middle ear, cochlea, or neural structures. ***Hearing aids*** amplify incoming sounds, which then pass via the ear canal to the same cochlear mechanisms used for normal sound. When substantial damage has occurred, however, and hearing aids cannot correct the deafness, electronic devices known as ***cochlear implants*** may in some cases partially restore functional hearing. In response to sound, cochlear implants directly stimulate the cochlear nerve with tiny electrical currents so that sound signals are transmitted directly to the auditory pathways, bypassing the cochlea.

7.8 Vestibular System

Hair cells are also found in the **vestibular apparatus** of the inner ear. The vestibular apparatus is a connected series of endolymph-filled, membranous tubes that also connect with the cochlear duct (**Figure 7.42**). The hair cells detect changes in the motion and position of the head by a stereocilia transduction mechanism similar to that just discussed for cochlear hair cells. The vestibular apparatus consists of three membranous **semicircular canals** and two saclike swellings, the **utricle** and

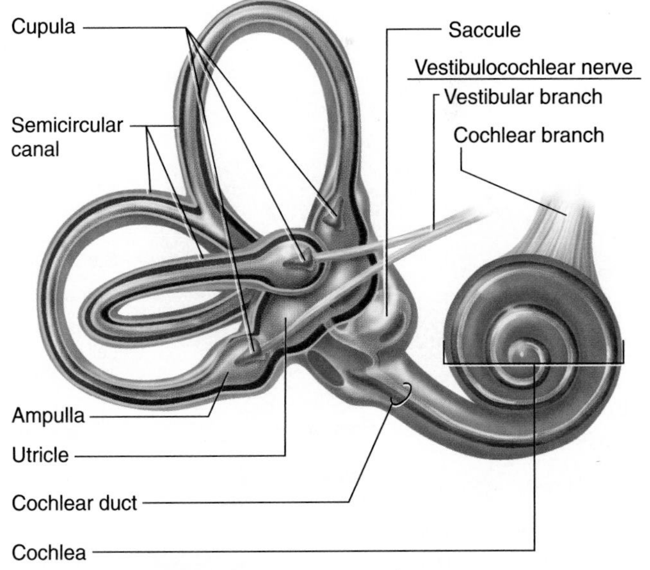

Figure 7.42 AP|R A tunnel in the temporal bone contains a fluid-filled membranous duct system. The semicircular canals, utricle, and saccule make up the vestibular apparatus. This system is connected to the cochlear duct. The purple structures within the ampullae are the cupulae (singular, *cupula*), which contain the hair (receptor) cells. Redrawn from Hudspeth.

saccule, all of which lie in tunnels in the temporal bone on each side of the head. The bony tunnels of the inner ear, which house the vestibular apparatus and cochlea, have such a complicated shape that they are sometimes called the **labyrinth.**

The Semicircular Canals

The semicircular canals detect angular acceleration during *rotation* of the head along three perpendicular axes. The three axes of the semicircular canals are those activated while nodding the head up and down as in signifying "yes," shaking the head from side to side as in signifying "no," and tipping the head so the ear touches the shoulder (**Figure 7.43**).

Receptor cells of the semicircular canals, like those of the organ of Corti, contain stereocilia. These stereocilia are encapsulated within a gelatinous mass, the **cupula,** which extends across the lumen of each semicircular canal at the **ampulla,** a slight bulge in the wall of each duct (**Figure 7.44**). Whenever the head moves, the semicircular canal within its bony enclosure and the attached bodies of the hair cells all move with it. The fluid filling the duct, however, is not attached to the skull and, because of inertia, tends to retain its original position. Thus, the moving ampulla is pushed against the stationary fluid, which causes bending of the stereocilia and alteration in the rate of release of neurotransmitter from the hair cells. This neurotransmitter crosses the synapse and activates the neurons associated with the hair cells, initiating the propagation of action potentials toward the brain.

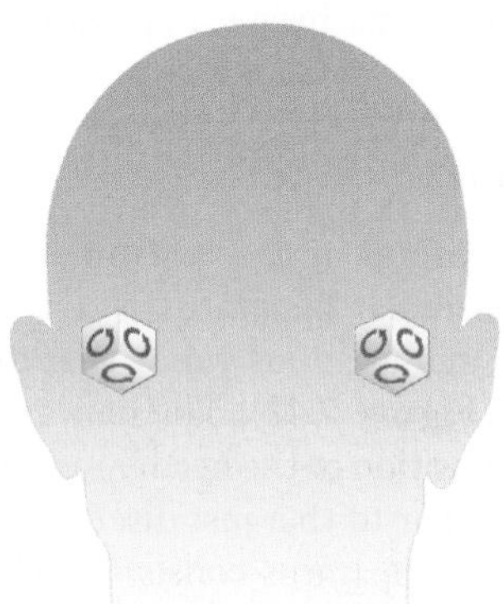

Figure 7.43 Orientation of the semicircular canals within the labyrinth. Each plane of orientation is perpendicular to the others. Together, they allow detection of movements in all directions.

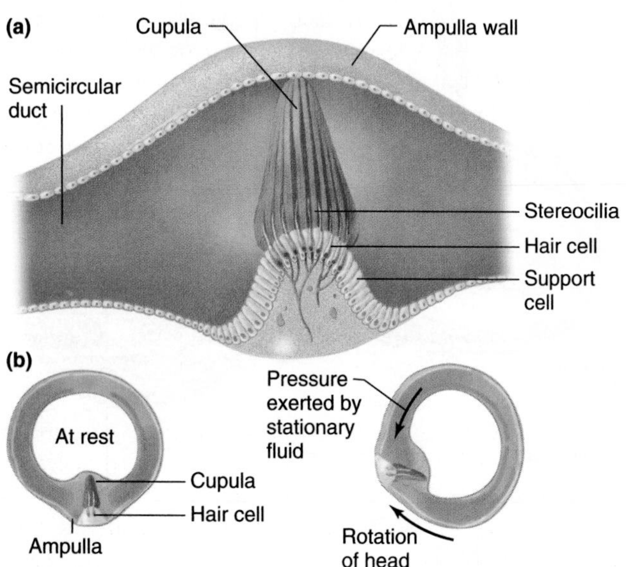

Figure 7.44 (a) Organization of a cupula and ampulla. (b) Relation of the cupula to the ampulla when the head is at rest and when it is accelerating.

The speed and magnitude of rotational head movements determine the direction in which the stereocilia are bent and which hair cells are stimulated. Movement of these mechanoreceptors causes changes in the membrane potential of the hair cell and neurotransmitter release by a mechanism similar to that in cochlear hair cells (review Figure 7.41). Neurotransmitter is released from the hair cells at rest, and the release increases or decreases from this resting rate according to the direction in which the hairs are bent. Each hair cell receptor has one direction of maximum neurotransmitter release; when its stereocilia are bent in this direction, the receptor cell depolarizes (**Figure 7.45**). When the stereocilia are bent in the opposite direction, the cell hyperpolarizes. The frequency of action potentials in the afferent nerve fibers that synapse with the hair cells is related to both the amount of force bending the stereocilia on the receptor cells and the direction in which this force is applied.

When the head continuously rotates at a steady velocity (like a figure skater's head during a spin), the duct fluid begins to move at the same rate as the rest of the head, and the stereocilia slowly return to their resting position. For this reason, the hair cells are stimulated only during acceleration or deceleration in the rate of rotation of the head.

The Utricle and Saccule

The utricle and saccule (see Figure 7.42) provide information about *linear* acceleration of the head, and about changes in head position relative to the forces of gravity. Here, too, the receptor cells are mechanoreceptors sensitive to the displacement of projecting hairs. The hair cells in the utricle point nearly

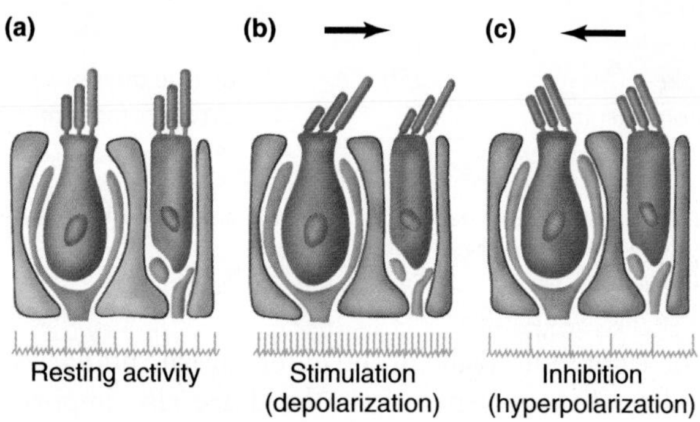

Figure 7.45 The relationship between the position of hairs in the ampulla and action potential firing in afferent neurons. (a) Resting activity. (b) Movement of hairs in one direction increases the action potential frequency in the afferent nerve activated by the hair cell. (c) Movement in the opposite direction decreases the rate relative to the resting state.

straight up when you stand, and they respond when you tip your head away from the horizontal plane, or to linear accelerations in the horizontal plane. In the saccule, hair cells project at right angles to those in the utricle, and they respond when you move from a lying to a standing position, or to vertical accelerations like those produced when you jump on a trampoline.

The utricle and saccule are slightly more complex than the ampullae. The stereocilia projecting from the hair cells are covered by a gelatinous substance in which tiny stones, or **otoliths,** are embedded. The otoliths, which are calcium carbonate crystals, make the gelatinous substance heavier than the surrounding fluid. In response to a change in position, the gelatinous otolithic material moves according to the forces of gravity and pulls against the hair cells so that the stereocilia on the hair cells bend and the receptor cells are stimulated. **Figure 7.46** demonstrates how otolith organs are stimulated by a change in head position.

Vestibular Information and Pathways

Vestibular information is used in three ways. One is to control the eye muscles so that, in spite of changes in head position, the eyes can remain fixed on the same point. ***Nystagmus*** is a large, jerky, back-and-forth movement of the eyes that can occur in response to unusual vestibular input in healthy people; it can also be a sign of pathology. Nystagmus is noticeable when a person spins in a swiveling chair for about 20 seconds, then abruptly stops the chair. For a short time after the motion ceases, the fluid in the semicircular canals continues to spin and the person's eyes will involuntarily move as though attempting to track objects spinning past the field of view. High blood alcohol concentrations disrupt functioning of the vestibular apparatus, leading to a type of nystagmus that traffic patrol officers commonly use as evidence of driving while intoxicated.

The second use of vestibular information is in reflex mechanisms for maintaining upright posture and balance. The vestibular apparatus plays a role in the support of the head during movement, orientation of the head in space, and reflexes accompanying locomotion. Very few postural reflexes, however, depend exclusively on input from the vestibular system despite the fact that the vestibular organs are sometimes called the sense organs of balance.

The third use of vestibular information is in providing conscious awareness of the position and acceleration of the body, perception of the space surrounding the body, and memory of spatial information.

Information about hair cell stimulation is relayed from the vestibular apparatus to nuclei within the brainstem via the vestibular branch of the vestibulocochlear nerve. It is transmitted via a polysynaptic pathway through the thalamus to a system of vestibular centers in the parietal lobe. Descending projections are also sent from the brainstem nuclei to the spinal cord to influence postural reflexes. Vestibular information is integrated with information from the joints, tendons, and skin, leading to the sense of posture (**proprioception**) and movement. A good example of this occurs when you try to maintain your posture while standing on a moving train or subway.

A mismatch in information from the various sensory systems can create feelings of nausea and dizziness. For example, many amusement parks feature widescreen virtual thrill rides in which your eyes take you on a dizzying helicopter ride, while your vestibular system signals that you are not moving at all. ***Motion sickness*** also involves the vestibular system, occurring when you experience unfamiliar patterns of linear and rotational acceleration and adaptation to them has not yet occurred.

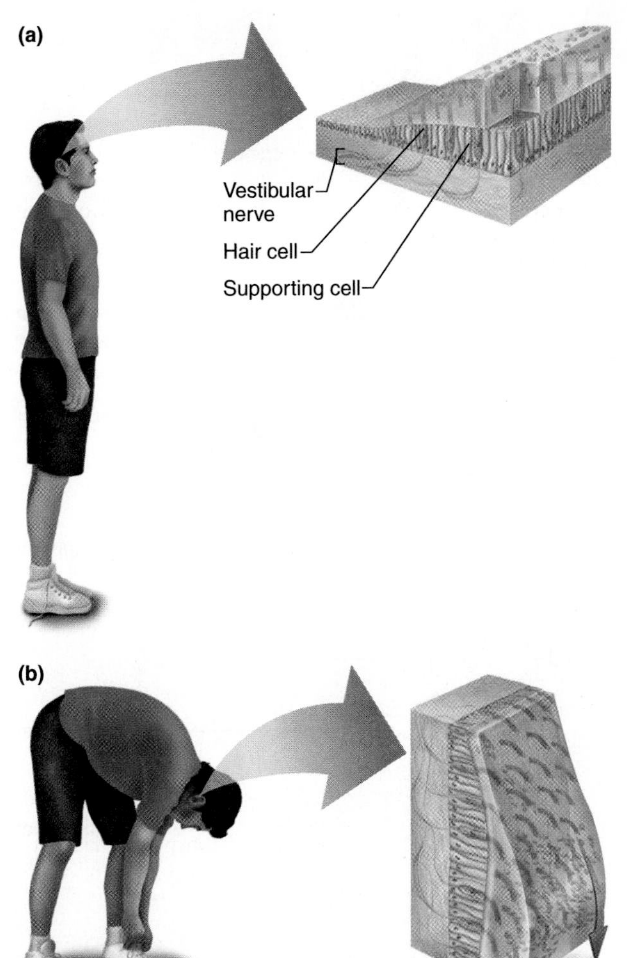

Figure 7.46 Effect of head position on otolith organ of the utricle. (a) Upright position: hair cells are not bent. (b) Gravity bends the hair cells when the head tilts forward.

7.9 Chemical Senses

Recall that receptors sensitive to specific chemicals are chemoreceptors. Some of these respond to chemical changes in the internal environment; two examples are receptors that sense oxygen and hydrogen ion concentration in the blood, which you will learn more about in Chapter 13. Others respond to external chemical changes. In this category are the receptors for taste and smell, which affect a person's appetite, saliva flow, gastric secretions, and avoidance of harmful substances.

Taste

The specialized sense organs for taste (also called **gustation**) are the 10,000 or so **taste buds** found in the mouth and throat, the vast majority on the upper surface and sides of the tongue. Taste buds are small groups of cells arranged like orange slices around a hollow pore and are found in the walls of visible structures called **lingual papillae** (**Figure 7.47**). Some of the cells serve mainly as supporting cells, but others are specialized epithelial cells that act as receptors for various chemicals in the food we eat. Small, hairlike microvilli increase the surface area of taste receptor cells and contain integral membrane proteins that transduce the presence of a given chemical into a receptor potential. At the bottom of taste buds are **basal cells,** which divide and differentiate to continually replace taste receptor cells damaged in the occasionally harsh environment of the mouth. To enter the pores of the taste buds and come into contact with taste receptor cells, food molecules must be dissolved in liquid—either ingested or provided by secretions of the salivary glands. Try placing sugar or salt on your tongue after thoroughly drying it; little or no taste sensation occurs until saliva begins to flow and dissolves the substance.

Many different chemicals can generate the sensation of taste by differentially activating a few basic types of taste receptors. Taste submodalities generally fall into five different categories according to the receptor type most strongly activated: sweet, sour, salty, bitter, and **umami** (oo-MAH-mee). This latter category gets its name from a Japanese word that can be roughly translated as "delicious." This taste is associated with the taste of glutamate and similar amino acids and is sometimes described as conveying the sense of savoriness or flavorfulness. Glutamate (or monosodium glutamate, MSG) is a common additive used to enhance the flavor of foods in traditional Asian cuisine. In addition to these known taste receptors, there are likely others yet to be discovered. For example, recent experiments suggest that a fatty

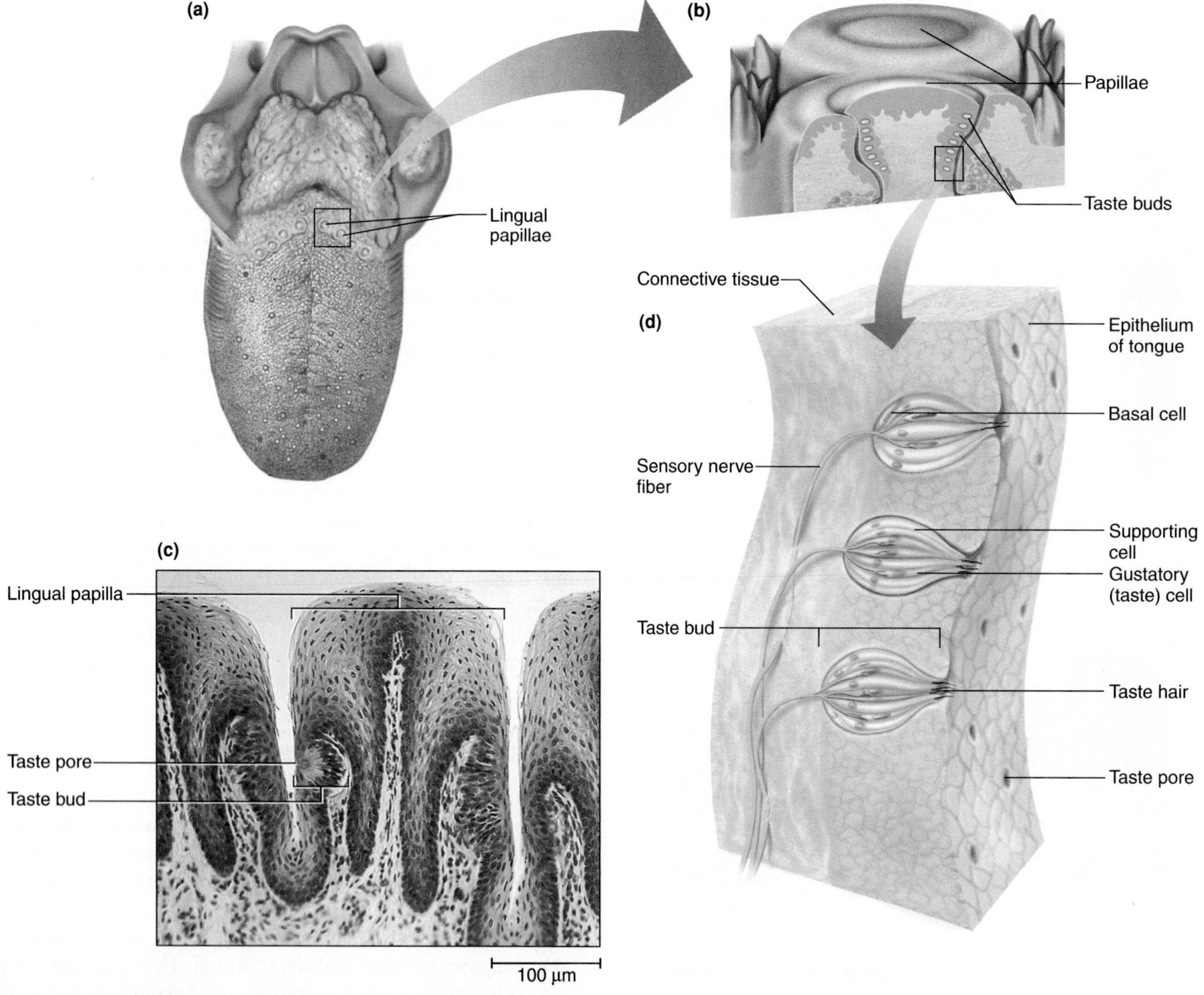

Figure 7.47 APIR Taste receptors. (a) Top view of the tongue showing lingual papillae. (b and c) Cross section of one type of papilla with taste buds. (d) Pores in the sides of papillae open into taste buds, which are composed of supporting cells, taste receptor cells, and basal cells.

acid transport protein first identified in the lingual papillae of rodents may soon be added to the list. Research has shown that blocking these transporters inhibits the preference for the taste of foods with high lipid content and reduces the production of fat-digesting enzymes by the gastrointestinal system. If confirmed in humans, this fatty acid transporter could become the sixth member of the taste receptor family and might help explain our tendency to overindulge on high-calorie, high-fat foods.

Each group of tastes has a distinct signal transduction mechanism. Salt taste is detected by a simple mechanism in which ingested sodium ions enter channels in the receptor cell membrane, depolarizing the cell and stimulating the production of action potentials in the associated sensory neuron. Sour taste is stimulated by foods with high acid content, such as lemons, which contain citric acid. Hydrogen ions block K^+ channels in the sour receptors, and the loss of the hyperpolarizing K^+ leak current depolarizes the receptor cell. Sweet receptors have integral membrane proteins that bind natural sugars like glucose, as well as artificial sweetener molecules like saccharin and aspartame. Binding of sugars to these receptors activates a G-protein-coupled second-messenger pathway (Chapter 5) that ultimately blocks K^+ channels and thus generates a depolarizing receptor potential. Bitter flavor is associated with many poisonous substances, especially certain elements such as arsenic, and plant alkaloids like strychnine. There is an obvious evolutionary advantage in recognizing a wide variety of poisonous substances, and thus there are many varieties of bitter receptors. All of those types, however, generate receptor potentials via G-protein-mediated second-messenger pathways and ultimately evoke the negative sensation of bitter flavor. Umami receptor cells also depolarize via a G-protein-coupled receptor mechanism.

Each afferent neuron synapses with more than one receptor cell, and the taste system is organized into independent coded pathways into the central nervous system. Single receptor cells, however, respond in varying degrees to substances that fall into more than one taste category. This property is analogous to the overlapping sensitivities of photoreceptors to different wavelengths. Awareness of the specific taste of a substance depends also upon the pattern of firing in other types of sensory neurons. For example, sensations of pain (hot spices), texture, and temperature contribute to taste.

The pathways for taste in the central nervous system project to the gustatory cortex, near the "mouth" region of the somatosensory cortex (see Figure 7.13).

Smell

A major part of the flavor of food is actually contributed by the sense of smell, or **olfaction.** This is illustrated by the common experience of finding that food lacks taste when a head cold blocks your nasal passages. The odor of a substance is directly related to its chemical structure. We can recognize and identify thousands of different odors with great accuracy. Thus, neural circuits that deal with olfaction must encode information about different chemical structures, store (learn) the different code patterns that represent the different structures, and at a later time recognize a particular neural code to identify the odor.

The olfactory receptor neurons, the first cells in the pathways that give rise to the sense of smell, lie in a small patch of epithelium called the **olfactory epithelium** in the upper part of the nasal cavity (**Figure 7.48a**). Olfactory receptor neurons survive for only about 2 months, so they are constantly being replaced by new cells produced from stem cells in the olfactory epithelium. The mature cells are specialized afferent neurons that have a single, enlarged dendrite that extends to the surface of the epithelium. Several long, nonmotile cilia extend from the tip of the dendrite and lie along the surface of the olfactory

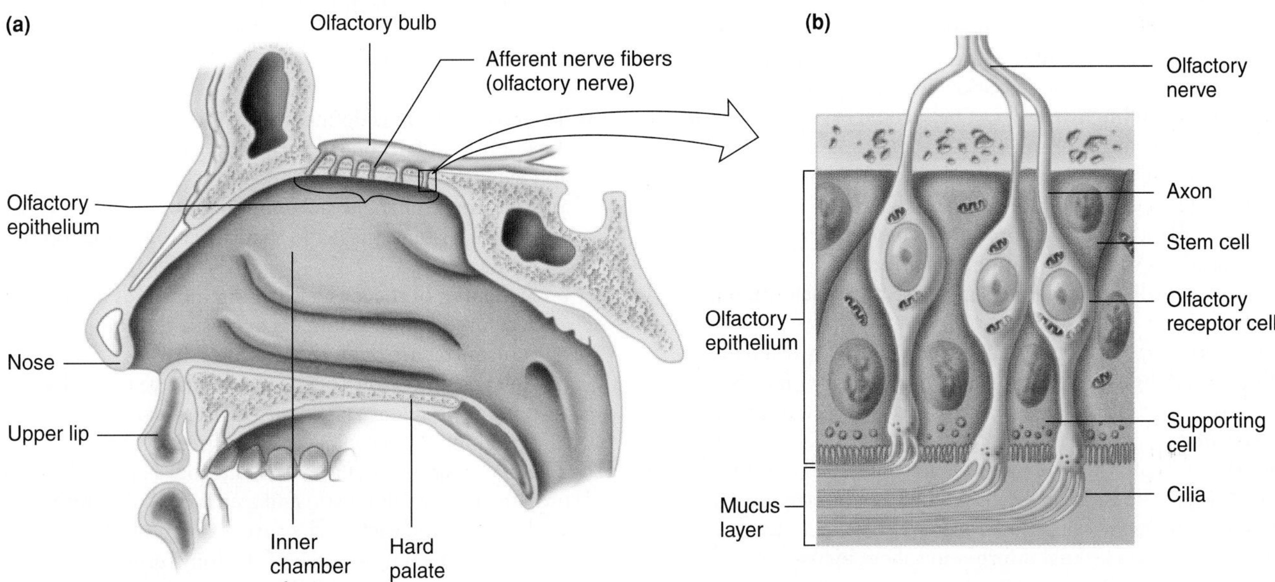

Figure 7.48 APIR (a) Location and (b) enlargement of a portion of the olfactory epithelium showing the structure of the olfactory receptor cells. In addition to these cells, the olfactory epithelium contains stem cells, which give rise to new receptors and supporting cells.

epithelium (**Figure 7.48b**) where they are bathed in mucus. The cilia contain the receptor proteins that provide the binding sites for odor molecules. The axons of the neurons form the olfactory nerve, which is cranial nerve I.

For us to detect an odorous substance (an **odorant**), molecules of the substance must first diffuse into the air and pass into the nose to the region of the olfactory epithelium. Once there, they dissolve in the mucus that covers the epithelium and then bind to specific odorant receptors on the cilia. Proteins in the mucus may interact with the odorant molecules, transport them to the receptors, and facilitate their binding to the receptors. Stimulated odorant receptors activate a G-protein-mediated pathway that increases cAMP, which in turn opens nonselective cation channels and depolarizes the cell.

Although there are many thousands of olfactory receptor cells, each contains only one of the 1000 or so different plasma membrane odorant receptor types. In turn, each of these types responds only to a specific chemically related group of odorant molecules. Each odorant has characteristic chemical groups that distinguish it from other odorants, and each of these groups activates a different plasma membrane odorant receptor type. Thus, the identity of a particular odorant is determined by the activation of a precise combination of plasma membrane receptors, each of which is contained in a distinct group of olfactory receptor cells.

The axons of the olfactory receptor cells synapse in a pair of brain structures known as **olfactory bulbs,** which lie on the undersurface of the frontal lobes. Axons from olfactory receptor cells that share a common receptor specificity synapse together on certain olfactory bulb neurons, thereby maintaining the specificity of the original stimulus. In other words, specific odorant receptor cells activate only certain olfactory bulb neurons, allowing the brain to determine which receptors have been stimulated. The codes used to transmit olfactory information probably use both spatial (which specific neurons are firing) and temporal (the frequency of action potentials in each neuron) components.

The olfactory system is the only sensory system that does not synapse in the thalamus prior to reaching the cortex. Information passes from the olfactory bulbs directly to the olfactory cortex and parts of the limbic system. The limbic system and associated hypothalamic structures are involved with emotional, food-getting, and sexual behaviors; the direct connection from the olfactory system explains why the sense of smell has such an important influence on these activities. Some areas of the olfactory cortex then send projections to other regions of the frontal cortex. Different odors elicit different patterns of electrical activity in several cortical areas, allowing humans to discriminate between some 10,000 different odorants even though they have only 1000 or so different olfactory receptor types.

Olfactory discrimination varies with attentiveness, hunger (sensitivity is greater in hungry subjects), gender (women in general have keener olfactory sensitivities than men), smoking (decreased sensitivity has been repeatedly associated with smoking), age (the ability to identify odors decreases with age, and a large percentage of elderly persons cannot detect odors at all), and state of the olfactory mucosa (as we have mentioned, the sense of smell decreases when the mucosa is congested, as in a head cold). Some individuals are born with genetic defects resulting in a total lack of the ability to smell (***anosmia***). For example, defects in genes on the X chromosome, as well as in chromosomes 8 and 20, can cause ***Kallmann syndrome.*** This is a condition in which the olfactory bulbs fail to form, as do regions of the brain associated with regulation of sex hormones.

SECTION B SUMMARY

Somatic Sensation

I. A variety of receptors sensitive to one or a few stimulus types provide sensory function of the skin and underlying tissues.

II. Information about somatic sensation enters both specific and nonspecific ascending pathways. The specific pathways cross to the opposite side of the brain.

III. The somatic sensations include touch, pressure, the senses of posture and movement, temperature, and pain.

   a. Rapidly adapting mechanoreceptors of the skin give rise to sensations such as vibration, touch, and movement, whereas slowly adapting ones give rise to the sensation of pressure.

   b. Skin receptors with small receptive fields are involved in fine spatial discrimination, whereas receptors with larger receptive fields signal less spatially precise touch or pressure sensations.

   c. A major receptor type responsible for the senses of posture and kinesthesia is the muscle-spindle stretch receptor.

   d. Cold receptors are sensitive to decreasing temperature; warmth receptors signal information about increasing temperature.

   e. Tissue damage and immune cells release chemical agents that stimulate specific receptors that give rise to the sensation of pain.

   f. Stimulation-produced analgesia, transcutaneous electrical nerve stimulation (TENS), and acupuncture control pain by blocking transmission in the pain pathways.

Vision

I. The color of light is defined by its wavelength or frequency.

II. The light that falls on the retina is focused by the cornea and lens.

   a. Lens shape changes (accommodation) to permit viewing near or distant images so that they are focused on the retina.

   b. Stiffening of the lens with aging interferes with accommodation. Cataracts decrease the amount of light transmitted through the lens.

   c. An eyeball too long or too short relative to the focusing power of the lens and cornea causes nearsighted (myopic) or farsighted (hyperopic) vision, respectively.

III. The photopigments of the rods and cones are made up of a protein component (opsin) and a chromophore (retinal).

   a. The rods and each of the three cone types have different opsins, which make each of the four receptor types sensitive to different ranges of light wavelengths.

   b. When light strikes retinal, it changes shape, triggering a cascade of events leading to hyperpolarization of photoreceptors and decreased neurotransmitter release from them. When exposed to darkness, the rods and cones are depolarized and therefore release more neurotransmitter than in light.

IV. The rods and cones synapse on bipolar cells, which synapse on ganglion cells.
  a. Ganglion cell axons form the optic nerves, which exit the eyeballs.
  b. The optic nerve fibers from the medial half of each retina cross to the opposite side of the brain in the optic chiasm. The fibers from the optic nerves terminate in the lateral geniculate nuclei of the thalamus, which sends fibers to the visual cortex.
  c. Photoreceptors also send information to areas of the brain dealing with biological rhythms.

V. Coding in the visual system occurs along parallel pathways in which different aspects of visual information, such as color, form, movement, and depth, are kept separate from each other.

VI. The colors we perceive are related to the wavelength of light. The three cone photopigments vary in the strength of their response to light over differing ranges of wavelengths.
  a. Certain ganglion cells are excited by input from one type of cone cell and inhibited by input from a different cone type.
  b. Our sensation of color depends on the output of the various opponent color cells and the processing of this output by brain areas involved in color vision.
  c. Color blindness is due to abnormalities of the cone pigments resulting from genetic mutations.

VII. Six skeletal muscles control eye movement to scan the visual field for objects of interest, keep the fixation point focused on the fovea centralis despite movements of the object or the head, and prevent adaptation of the photoreceptors.

Hearing

I. Sound energy is transmitted by movements of pressure waves.
  a. Sound wave frequency determines pitch.
  b. Sound wave amplitude determines loudness.

II. The sequence of sound transmission follows.
  a. Sound waves enter the external auditory canal and press against the tympanic membrane, causing it to vibrate.
  b. The vibrating membrane causes movement of the three small middle ear bones; the stapes vibrates against the oval window membrane.
  c. Movements of the oval window membrane set up pressure waves in the fluid-filled scala vestibuli, which cause vibrations in the cochlear duct wall, setting up pressure waves in the fluid there.
  d. These pressure waves cause vibrations in the basilar membrane, which is located on one side of the cochlear duct.
  e. As this membrane vibrates, the hair cells of the organ of Corti move in relation to the tectorial membrane.
  f. Movement of the hair cells' stereocilia stimulates the hair cells to release glutamate, which activates receptors on the peripheral ends of the afferent nerve fibers.

III. Separate parts of the basilar membrane vibrate maximally in response to particular sound frequencies; high frequency is detected near the oval window and low frequency toward the far end of the cochlear duct.

Vestibular System

I. A vestibular apparatus lies in the temporal bone on each side of the head and consists of three semicircular canals, a utricle, and a saccule.

II. The semicircular canals detect angular acceleration during rotation of the head, which causes bending of the stereocilia on their hair cells.

III. Otoliths in the gelatinous substance of the utricle and saccule (a) move in response to changes in linear acceleration and the position of the head relative to gravity and (b) stimulate the stereocilia on the hair cells.

Chemical Senses

I. The receptors for taste lie in taste buds throughout the mouth, principally on the tongue. Different types of taste receptors have different sensory transduction mechanisms.

II. Olfactory receptors, which are part of the afferent olfactory neurons, lie in the upper nasal cavity.
  a. Odorant molecules, once dissolved in the mucus that bathes the olfactory receptors, bind to specific receptors (protein-binding sites). Each olfactory receptor cell has one or at most a few of the 1000 different receptor types.
  b. Olfactory pathways go directly to the olfactory cortex and limbic system, rather than to the thalamus.

SECTION B REVIEW QUESTIONS

1. Describe the similarities between pain and the other somatic sensations. Describe the differences.
2. Explain the mechanism of sensory transduction in temperature-sensing neurons.
3. What are the sensory implications of the different crossover points of the anterolateral and dorsal column ascending pathways in patients with injuries that damage half of the spinal cord at a given level?
4. List at least two ways the retina has adapted to minimize the potential problem caused by the photoreceptors being the last layer of the retina that light reaches.
5. Describe the events that take place during accommodation for near vision.
6. Detail the separate mechanisms activated in photoreceptor cells in the presence and in the absence of light.
7. Beginning with the photoreceptor cells of the retina, describe the interactions with bipolar and ganglion cells in the ON- and OFF-pathways of the visual system.
8. List the sequence of events that occurs between the entry of a sound wave into the external auditory canal and the firing of action potentials in the cochlear nerve.
9. Describe the functional relationship between the scala vestibuli, scala tympani, and the cochlear duct.
10. What is the relationship between head movement and cupula movement in a semicircular canal?
11. What causes the release of neurotransmitter from the utricle and saccule receptor cells?
12. In what ways are the sensory systems for taste and olfaction similar? In what ways are they different?

SECTION B KEY TERMS

accommodation 209
amacrine cell 214
ampulla 224
anterolateral pathway 206
aqueous humor 208
audition 217
basal cell 226
basilar membrane 220
binocular vision 215
bipolar cell 213
cGMP-phosphodiesterase 212
choroid 208
chromophore 211
ciliary muscle 208
cochlea 220
cochlear duct 220
cone 211
cornea 208
cupula 224
dark adaptation 212

disc 211
dorsal column pathway 206
endolymph 220
eustachian tube 218
external auditory canal 218
fovea centralis 208
frequency 207
ganglion cell 213
guanylyl cyclase 212
gustation 226
hair cell 221
helicotrema 220
horizontal cell 214
incus 220
inner ear 220
inner hair cells 221
inner segment 211
iris 208
kinesthesia 204
labyrinth 224
lens 208
light adaptation 212
lingual papillae 226
macula lutea 208
malleus 220
melanopsin 215
middle ear 218
monocular vision 215
Müller cells 211
odorant 228
olfaction 227
olfactory bulb 228
olfactory epithelium 227
opponent color cell 216
opsin 211
optic chiasm 215
optic disc 208
optic nerve 208
optic tracts 215
organ of Corti 220
otolith 225
outer hair cells 221
outer segment 211
oval window 220
perilymph 220
photopigment 211
photoreceptor 208
pigment epithelium 211
proprioception 225
pupil 208
refraction 208
retina 208
retinal 211
rhodopsin 211
rod 211
round window 220
saccade 217
saccule 224
scala tympani 220
scala vestibuli 220
sclera 208
semicircular canal 223
somatic sensation 203
stapedius 220
stapes 220
stereocilia 221
suprachiasmatic nucleus 215
taste bud 226
tectorial membrane 221
tensor tympani muscle 220
tip link 221
transducin 212
transient receptor potential (TRP) proteins 204
tympanic membrane 218
umami 226
utricle 223
vestibular apparatus 223
vestibulocochlear nerve 222
visible spectrum 207
vitreous humor 208
wavelength 207
zonular fiber 208

SECTION B CLINICAL TERMS

acupuncture 206
age-related macular degeneration (AMD) 217
analgesia 206
anosmia 228
astigmatism 211
cataract 210
cochlear implant 223
color blindness 216
farsighted 211
glaucoma 211
hearing aid 223
hyperalgesia 205
hyperopic 211
Kallmann syndrome 228
macular degeneration 217
motion sickness 225
myopic 210
nearsighted 210
nystagmus 225
ophthalmoscope 208
placebo 206
presbyopia 210
referred pain 205
stimulation-produced analgesia 206
tinnitis 222
transcutaneous electrical nerve stimulation (TENS) 206

CHAPTER 7 Clinical Case Study: Severe Dizzy Spells in a Healthy, 65-Year-Old Farmer

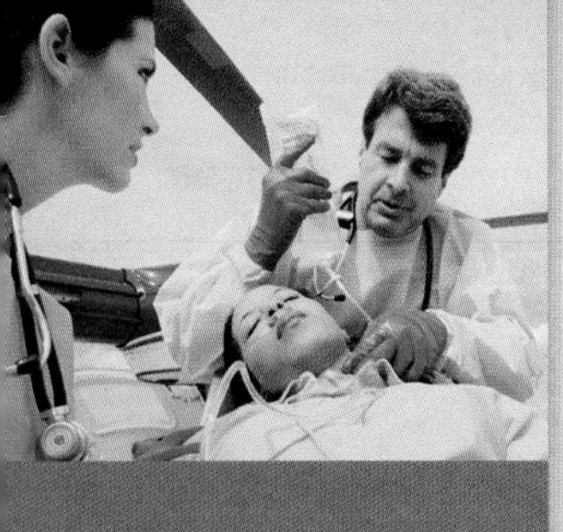

Just after 6:00 A.M. on a Sunday morning, a large man in overalls staggered into the emergency room leaning heavily for support on his wife's shoulder. He held a bloody towel pressed tightly to the right side of his head, and his skin was pale and sweaty. The towel was removed to reveal a 1-inch scalp laceration above his right ear. As the emergency room physician cleaned and stitched the wound, the man and his wife explained what had happened. A dairy farmer, he was arising to do his chores that morning when he became dizzy, fell, and struck his head on the dresser. When the doctor commented that it wasn't that unusual for a transient decrease in blood pressure to cause fainting upon standing up too quickly, the man's wife stated that this was something different. Over the past 3 months, he had experienced a number of occasions when he suddenly became dizzy. These dizzy spells also seemed to be becoming more severe, and they were not always associated with standing up; indeed, sometimes they happened even when he was lying down. Lasting anywhere from a few minutes to a few hours, the episodes were sometimes accompanied by headaches, nausea, and vomiting. Not one to complain, the man had not previously sought treatment. Because these could be signs of serious underlying illness, the physician elected to do a more thorough examination.

The patient was 65 years old and appeared relatively muscular and fit for his age. At the time of the examination, he had trouble sitting or standing without support and reported feeling dizzy and nauseated. His only known chronic medical problem was high blood pressure, which had been diagnosed 10 years earlier and had been well-controlled by medication since that time. When questioned about alcohol use, both he and his wife assured the doctor that he only drank one or two beers at a time and only on weekends.

One of the first things the physician needed to determine was whether the patient suffered from vertigo or from light-headedness. "Dizziness" is one of the most common symptoms reported by patients seeing primary care physicians, but that generic description does not discriminate between the actual underlying mechanisms of the sensation and their causes. Light-headedness is a sensation

(continued)

(continued)

of beginning to lose consciousness (becoming faint, also called ***presyncope***). Actual loss of consciousness is referred to as ***syncope.*** ***Vertigo*** is a sensation of environmental movement when lying, sitting, or standing still (e.g., a feeling that the room is spinning) and results from a disruption of the vestibular systems but usually not from disruption of cerebral blood supply. Interruption of blood flow to the brain can cause a light-headed sensation because brain cells deprived of oxygen or nutrients for even brief periods of time begin to malfunction. This is the cause of the commonly observed phenomenon in which a person can become light-headed in the moments after standing up. Lying down, the brain is level with the heart and blood delivery requires very little work, whereas in the standing position, the heart must pump more strongly to maintain blood flow to the brain against gravity. Even a slight delay in increasing cardiac contraction strength upon standing can reduce brain blood flow enough to cause light-headedness.

Reduced blood flow to the brain can also be caused by dehydration, low blood pressure, interruption of the normal rhythm of the heartbeat, and blockage of the arteries in the neck that carry blood to the brain. Even if brain blood flow is adequate, brain cells can also malfunction and cause light-headedness if the concentrations of oxygen or glucose in the blood are below normal. However, a thorough assessment of the farmer's circulatory system function, blood oxygen concentration, and blood glucose concentration showed no abnormalities. These results, combined with the fact that the patient's symptoms were not always linked to suddenly standing up, seemed to indicate that the sensation of dizziness the patient reported was most likely not light-headedness due to a problem with the blood supply to his brain.

The doctor next examined the patient's eyes, ears, nose, and throat. There was no evidence of infection of the man's nose, throat, or tympanic membranes. This suggested that he was not suffering from an infection that could cause sinus pressure or fluid buildup in the middle ear, both of which can be associated with headaches, dizziness, and nausea. Viewed with an ophthalmoscope, his retinas also appeared normal. In cases in which patients have rapidly growing brain tumors that increase the intracranial pressure and cause dizziness and disorientation, the optic discs are often observed to bulge from the surface of the retina. When asked to focus on the doctor's finger as it was held in some positions in his visual field (far left, up, down), the man's eyes remained fixated without abnormality, but they developed rapid, rhythmic, jerking movements when the finger was brought to the patient's far right. This eye-movement pattern is called nystagmus and is frequently associated with abnormalities of the vestibular apparatus of the inner ear or the neural pathways involved in reflexive integration of head and eye movements. Excess alcohol consumption can disrupt vestibular function and cause nystagmus, but the evidence did not suggest that was the cause in this case.

One condition leading to malfunction of the vestibular system is ***Ménière's disease,*** in which an abnormal buildup of pressure in the inner ear disrupts the function of the cochlea and semicircular canals. This disease often manifests as periodic bouts of vertigo and loss of balance, accompanied by nausea and vomiting; each bout may last from minutes to many hours. Because the cochlea is also involved, this condition sometimes also results in auditory symptoms including tinnitus ("ringing in the ears") and/or loss of hearing. The lack of auditory symptoms in this case led the doctor to question the patient further; when asked in more detail about what he thought triggered his dizzy spells, the patient said it tended to occur only after rapid movements of his head, especially when turning his head to the right. This statement was an essential clue leading to the correct diagnosis.

The man was suffering from ***benign paroxysmal positional vertigo*** (***BPPV***), which involves disruption of function of the vestibular apparatus or its neural pathways. This particular type of vertigo, as the name suggests, is not associated with serious or permanent damage, occurs sporadically, and is associated with changes in head position. It may occur at any age but occurs most frequently in elderly persons; this is of great concern because of the likelihood of falling when dizzy and the fragility of the bones of many elderly persons. Though the cause of BPPV is not clear in most cases, the leading hypothesis is that loose calcium carbonate crystals (otoliths) associated with the vestibular apparatus float into the semicircular canals and interrupt normal fluid movement. Otoliths may be dislodged by head injury or infection or due to the normal degeneration of aging.

One treatment that has achieved some success for reducing the symptoms of BPPV is a series of carefully choreographed manipulations of head position called the ***Epley maneuver.*** The head movements are designed to use the force of gravity to dislodge loose otoliths from the semicircular canals and move them back into the gelatinous membranes within the utricle and saccule. Patients undergoing this or similar manipulations are cured of BPPV about 80% of the time. After two times through the procedure, the farmer's vertigo went away and he was able to stand on his own. Because multiple treatments are sometimes required, he was given instructions on how to self-administer a modified Epley maneuver at home; within 3 weeks, his vertigo was gone.

Clinical terms: benign paroxysmal positional vertigo (BPPV), Epley maneuver, Ménière's disease, presyncope, syncope, vertigo

See Chapter 19 for complete, integrative case studies.

CHAPTER 7 TEST QUESTIONS

Answers found in Appendix A.

1. Choose the *true* statement:
   a. The modality of energy a given sensory receptor responds to in normal functioning is known as the "adequate stimulus" for that receptor.
   b. Receptor potentials are "all or none," that is, they have the same magnitude regardless of the strength of the stimulus.
   c. When the frequency of action potentials along sensory neurons is constant as long as a stimulus continues, it is called "adaptation."
   d. When sensory units have large receptive fields, the acuity of perception is greater.
   e. The "modality" refers to the intensity of a given stimulus.

2. Using a single intracellular recording electrode, in what part of a sensory neuron could you simultaneously record both receptor potentials and action potentials?
   a. in the cell body
   b. at the node of Ranvier nearest the peripheral end
   c. at the receptor membrane where the stimulus occurs
   d. at the central axon terminals within the CNS
   e. There is no single point where both can be measured.
3. Which best describes "lateral inhibition" in sensory processing?
   a. Presynaptic axo–axonal synapses reduce neurotransmitter release at excitatory synapses.
   b. When a stimulus is maintained for a long time, action potentials from sensory receptors decrease in frequency with time.
   c. Descending inputs from the brainstem inhibit afferent pain pathways in the spinal cord.
   d. Inhibitory interneurons decrease action potentials from receptors at the periphery of a stimulated region.
   e. Receptor potentials increase in magnitude with the strength of a stimulus.
4. What region of the brain contains the primary visual cortex?
   a. the occipital lobe
   b. the frontal lobe
   c. the temporal lobe
   d. the somatosensory cortex
   e. the parietal lobe association area
5. Which type of receptor does *not* encode a somatic sensation?
   a. muscle-spindle stretch receptor
   b. nociceptor
   c. Pacinian corpuscle
   d. thermoreceptor
   e. cochlear hair cell
6. Which best describes the vision of a person with uncorrected nearsightedness?
   a. The eyeball is too long; far objects focus on the retina when the ciliary muscle contracts.
   b. The eyeball is too long; near objects focus on the retina when the ciliary muscle is relaxed.
   c. The eyeball is too long; near objects cannot be focused on the retina.
   d. The eyeball is too short; far objects cannot be focused on the retina.
   e. The eyeball is too short; near objects focus on the retina when the ciliary muscle is relaxed.
7. If a patient suffers a stroke that destroys the optic tract on the right side of the brain, which of the following visual defects will result?
   a. Complete blindness will result.
   b. There will be no vision in the left eye, but vision will be normal in the right eye.
   c. The patient will not perceive images of objects striking the left half of the retina in the left eye.
   d. The patient will not perceive images of objects striking the right half of the retina in the right eye.
   e. Neither eye will perceive objects in the right side of the patient's field of view.
8. Which correctly describes a step in auditory signal transduction?
   a. Displacement of the basilar membrane with respect to the tectorial membrane stimulates stereocilia on the hair cells.
   b. Pressure waves on the oval window cause vibrations of the malleus, which are transferred via the stapes to the round window.
   c. Movement of the stapes causes oscillations in the tympanic membrane, which is in contact with the endolymph.
   d. Oscillations of the stapes against the oval window set up pressure waves in the semicircular canals.
   e. The malleus, incus, and stapes are found in the inner ear, within the cochlea.
9. A standing subject looking over her left shoulder suddenly rotates her head to look over her right shoulder. How does the vestibular system detect this motion?
   a. The utricle goes from a vertical to a horizontal position, and otoliths stimulate stereocilia.
   b. Stretch receptors in neck muscles send action potentials to the vestibular apparatus, which relays them to the brain.
   c. Fluid within the semicircular canals remains stationary, bending the cupula and stereocilia as the head rotates.
   d. The movement causes endolymph in the cochlea to rotate from right to left, stimulating inner hair cells.
   e. Counterrotation of the aqueous humor activates a nystagmus response.
10. Which category of taste receptor cells does MSG (monosodium glutamate) most strongly stimulate?
   a. salty
   b. bitter
   c. sweet
   d. umami
   e. sour

CHAPTER 7 GENERAL PRINCIPLES ASSESSMENT

Answers found in Appendix A.

1. A key general principle of physiology is that *homeostasis is essential for health and survival.* How might sensory receptors responsible for detecting painful stimuli (nociceptors) contribute to homeostasis?
2. How does the sensory transduction mechanism in the vestibular and auditory systems demonstrate the importance of the general principle of physiology that *controlled exchange of materials occurs between compartments and across cellular membranes?*
3. Elaboration of surface area to maximize functional capability is a common motif in the body illustrating the general principle of physiology that *structure is a determinant of—and has coevolved with—function.* Cite an example from this chapter.

CHAPTER 7 QUANTITATIVE AND THOUGHT QUESTIONS

Answers found in Appendix A.

1. Describe several mechanisms by which pain could theoretically be controlled medically or surgically.
2. At what two sites would central nervous system injuries interfere with the perception that heat is being applied to the right side of the body? At what single site would a central nervous system injury interfere with the perception that heat is being applied to either side of the body?
3. What would vision be like after a drug has destroyed all the cones in the retina?
4. Damage to what parts of the cerebral cortex could explain the following behaviors? (a) A person walks into a chair placed in her path. (b) The person does not walk into the chair, but she does not know what the chair can be used for.
5. How could the concept of referred pain potentially complicate the clinical assessment of the source of a patient's somatic pain?

CHAPTER 7 ANSWERS TO PHYSIOLOGICAL INQUIRIES

Figure 7.2 Receptor potentials would not be affected because they are not mediated by voltage-gated channels. Action potential propagation to the central nervous system would also be normal because it depends only on voltage-gated Na^+ and K^+ channels. The drug would inhibit neurotransmitter release from the central axon terminal, however, because vesicle exocytosis requires Ca^{2+} entry through voltage-gated channels.

Figure 7.6 Although the skin area of your lips is much smaller than that of your back, the much larger number of sensory neurons originating in your lips requires a larger processing area within the somatosensory cortex of your brain. See Figure 7.20 for a diagrammatic representation of cortical areas involved in sensory processing.

Figure 7.15 Pacinian corpuscles are rapidly adapting receptors, and that property is conferred by the fluid-filled connective tissue capsule that surrounds them. When pressure is initially applied, the fluid in the capsule compresses the nerve ending, opening mechanically gated nonspecific cation channels and causing depolarization and action potentials. However, fluid then redistributes within the capsule, taking the pressure off the nerve ending; consequently, the channels close and the neuron repolarizes. When the pressure is removed, redistribution of the capsule back to its original shape briefly deforms the nerve ending once again and a brief depolarization results. Without the specialized capsule, the afferent nerve ending becomes a slowly adapting receptor; as long as pressure is applied, the mechanoreceptors remain open and the receptor potential and action potentials persist.

Figure 7.18 Because the referred pain field for the lungs and diaphragm is the neck and shoulder, it is not unusual for individuals suffering from lower respiratory infections to complain of neck stiffness or pain. Lung infections are often accompanied by an accumulation of fluid in the lungs, which is detectable with a stethoscope as crackling or bubbling sounds during breathing.

Figure 7.19 Sensation of all body parts above the level of the injury would be normal. Below the level of the injury, however, there would be a mixed pattern of sensory loss. Fine touch, pressure, and body position sensation would be lost from the left side of the body below the level of the injury because that information ascends in the spinal cord on the side that it enters without crossing the midline until it reaches the brainstem. Pain and temperature sensation would be lost from the right side of the body below the injury because those pathways cross immediately upon entry and ascend in the opposite side of the spinal cord.

Figure 7.21 The frequency of this electromagnetic wave is 2×10^3 Hz (2000 cycles/sec). It would not be visible, because visible light frequencies are in the range of 10^{14} to 10^{15} Hz.

Figure 7.28 Vitamin A is the source of the chromophore retinal, which is the portion of the rhodopsin photopigment that triggers the response of rod cells to light. Because retinal is also used in cone photopigments, a severe vitamin A deficiency eventually results in impairment of vision under all lighting conditions, being generally most noticeable at night when less light is available.

Figure 7.31

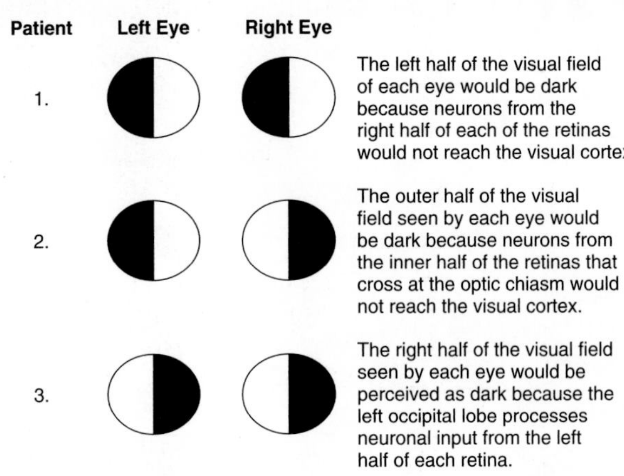

Patient
Left Eye
Right Eye
1.
The left half of the visual field of each eye would be dark because neurons from the right half of each of the retinas would not reach the visual cortex.
2.
The outer half of the visual field seen by each eye would be dark because neurons from the inner half of the retinas that cross at the optic chiasm would not reach the visual cortex.
3.
The right half of the visual field seen by each eye would be perceived as dark because the left occipital lobe processes neuronal input from the left half of each retina.

Figure 7.32 Most people who stare at the yellow background perceive an afterimage of a blue circle around the square. This is because prolonged staring at the color yellow activates most of the available retinal in the photopigments of both red and green cones (see Figure 7.32a), effectively fatiguing them into a state of reduced sensitivity. When you shift your gaze to the white background (white light contains all wavelengths of light), only the blue cones are available to respond, so you perceive a blue circle until the red and green cones recover.

Figure 7.39 Though an 80 dB warning tone is not loud enough to cause hearing damage, it can activate the contraction of the stapedius and tensor tympani muscles. With those muscles contracted, the movement of the middle ear bones is dampened during the 140 dB gun blast, thus reducing the transmission of that harmfully loud sound to the inner ear.

Figure 7.41 The transport protein responsible for reabsorbing K^+ (along with Na^+ and Cl^-) in the kidney is also present in epithelial cells surrounding the cochlear duct. It appears to play a role in generating the unusually high K^+ concentration found in the endolymph. Inhibiting this transporter with furosemide reduces the K^+ concentration in the endolymph, which reduces the ability of hair cells to depolarize when sound waves bend the tip links. Less depolarization reduces Ca^{2+} entry, glutamate release, and action potentials in the cochlear nerve, which in turn would reduce the perception of sound.

Visit this book's website at **www.mhhe.com/widmaier13** for chapter quizzes, interactive learning exercises, and other study tools.

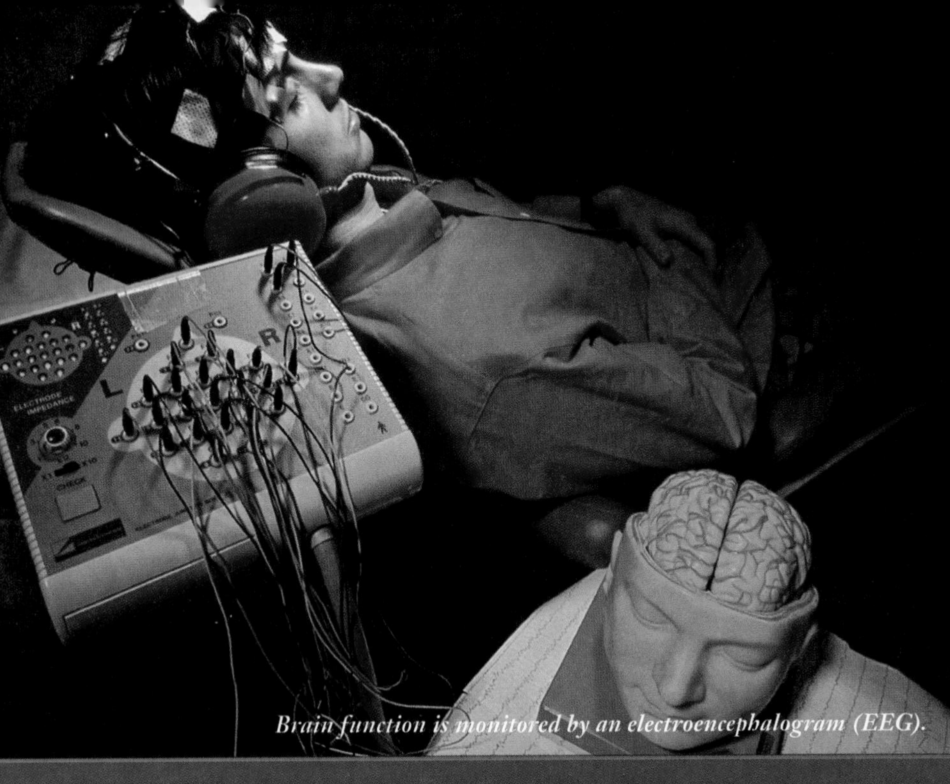

Brain function is monitored by an electroencephalogram (EEG).

8 Consciousness, the Brain, and Behavior

Chapters 6 and 7 introduced some of the fundamental mechanisms underlying the processing of information in the nervous system. The focus was on the transmission of information within neurons, between neurons, and from the peripheral nervous system (PNS) to the central nervous system (CNS). In this chapter, you will learn about higher-order functions and more complex processing of information that occurs within the CNS. We discuss the general phenomenon of consciousness and its variable states of existence, as well some of the important neural mechanisms involved in the processing of our experiences. Although advances in electrophysiological and brain-imaging techniques are yielding fascinating insights, there is still much that we do not know about these topics. If you can imagine that, for any given neuron, there may be as many as 200,000 other neurons connecting to it through synapses, you can begin to appreciate the complexity of the systems that control even the simplest behavior.

The general principle of physiology most obviously on display in this chapter is that information flow between cells, tissues, and organs is an essential feature of homoeostasis and allows for integration of physiological processes. The nervous system "information" discussed previously involved phenomena like chemical and electrical gradients, graded potentials, and

action potentials. Those are the essential physiological building blocks for the higher-order processes discussed in this chapter, which include our abilities to consciously pay attention, be motivated, learn, remember, and communicate with others. These abilities are essential determinants of many complex behaviors that help us maintain homeostasis.

8.1 States of Consciousness

The term *consciousness* includes two distinct concepts: **states of consciousness** and **conscious experiences.** The first concept refers to levels of alertness such as being awake, drowsy, or asleep. The second refers to experiences a person is aware of—thoughts, feelings, perceptions, ideas, dreams, reasoning—during any of the states of consciousness.

A person's state of consciousness is defined in two ways: (1) by behavior, covering the spectrum from maximum attentiveness to comatose, and (2) by the pattern of brain activity that can be recorded electrically. This record, known as the **electroencephalogram (EEG)**, portrays the electrical potential difference between different points on the surface of the scalp. The EEG is such a useful tool in identifying the different states of consciousness that we begin with it.

Electroencephalogram

Neural activity is manifested by the electrical signals known as graded potentials and action potentials (Chapter 6). It is possible to record the electrical activity in the brain's neurons—particularly those in the cortex near the surface of the brain—from the outside of the head. Electrodes, which are wires attached to the head by a salty paste that conducts electricity, pick up electrical signals generated in the brain and transmit them to a machine that records them as the EEG.

Though we often think of electrical activity in neurons in terms of action potentials, action potentials do not usually contribute directly to the EEG. Action potentials in individual neurons are also far too small to be picked up on an EEG recording. Rather, EEG patterns are largely due to synchronous graded potentials—in this case, summed postsynaptic potentials (see Chapter 6) in the many hundreds of thousands of brain neurons that underlie the recording electrodes. The majority of the electrical signal recorded in the EEG originates in the pyramidal cells of the cortex (review Figure 6.39). The processes of these large cells lie close to and perpendicular to the surface of the brain, and the EEG records postsynaptic potentials in their dendrites.

EEG patterns are complex waveforms with large variations in both amplitude and frequency (**Figure 8.1**). (The properties of a wave are summarized in Figure 7.21.) The wave's amplitude, measured in microvolts (μV), indicates how much electrical activity of a similar type is occurring beneath the recording electrodes at any given time. A large amplitude indicates that many neurons are being activated simultaneously. In other words, it indicates the degree of synchronous firing of the neurons that are generating the synaptic activity. On the other hand, a small amplitude indicates that these neurons are less activated or are firing asynchronously. The amplitude may range from 0.5 to 100 μV, which is about 1000 times smaller than the amplitude of an action potential.

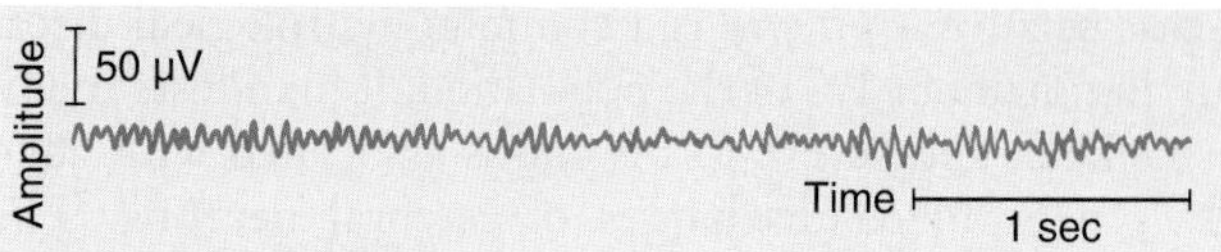

Figure 8.1 EEG patterns are wavelike. This represents a typical EEG recorded from the parietal or occipital lobe of an awake, relaxed person, with a frequency of approximately 20 Hz and an average amplitude of 20 μV.

PHYSIOLOGICAL INQUIRY

- What is the approximate duration of each wave in this recording?

Answer can be found at end of chapter.

The frequency of the wave indicates how often it cycles from the maximal to the minimal amplitude and back. The frequency is measured in hertz (Hz, or cycles per second) and may vary from 0.5 to 40 Hz or higher. Four distinct frequency ranges that define different states of consciousness are characteristic of EEG patterns. In general, lower EEG frequencies indicate less responsive states, such as sleep, whereas higher frequencies indicate increased alertness. As we will see, one stage of sleep is an exception to this general relationship.

The neuronal networks underlying the wavelike oscillations of the EEG and how they function are still not completely understood. Wave patterns vary not only as a function of state of consciousness but also according to where on the scalp they are recorded. Current thinking is that clusters of neurons in the thalamus play a critical role; they provide a fluctuating action potential frequency output through neurons leading from the thalamus to the cortex. This output, in turn, causes a rhythmic pattern of synaptic activity in the pyramidal neurons of the cortex. As noted previously, the cortical synaptic activity—not the activity of the deep thalamic structures—comprises most of a recorded EEG signal. The synchronicity of the cortical synaptic activity (in other words, the amplitude of the EEG) reflects the degree of synchronous firing of the thalamic neuronal clusters that are generating the EEG. These clusters receive input from brain areas involved in controlling the conscious state. Research is also beginning to identify and measure waves of coordinated EEG activity that spread between particular regions of the somatosensory and motor cortex in response to sensory inputs and during the performance of motor tasks.

The EEG is useful clinically in the diagnosis of and treatment of the disease epilepsy, as well as in the diagnosis of coma and brain death. It was formerly also used in the detection of brain areas damaged by tumors, blood clots, or hemorrhage. However, the much greater spatial resolution of modern imaging techniques such as ***positron emission tomography (PET)*** and ***magnetic resonance imaging (MRI)*** make them far superior for detecting and localizing damaged brain areas in such cases (see Figures 19.6 and 19.7).

A shift from a less synchronized pattern of electrical activity (small-amplitude EEG) to a highly synchronized pattern can be a prelude to the electrical storm that signifies an epileptic seizure. ***Epilepsy*** is a common neurological disease, occurring in about 1% of the population. It manifests in mild, intermediate, and severe forms and is associated with abnormally synchronized discharges of cerebral neurons. These discharges are reflected in the EEG as recurrent waves having distinctive large amplitudes (up to 1000 μV) and individual spikes or combinations of spikes and waves (**Figure 8.2**). Epilepsy is also associated with changes in behavior that vary according to the part of the brain affected and severity and can include involuntary muscle contraction and a temporary loss of consciousness. In most cases, the cause of epilepsy cannot be determined. Among the known triggers are traumatic brain injury, abnormal prenatal brain development, diseases that alter brain blood flow, heavy alcohol and illegal drug use, infectious diseases like meningitis and viral encephalitis, extreme stress, sleep deprivation, and exposure to environmental toxins such as lead or carbon monoxide.

The Waking State

Behaviorally, the waking state is far from homogeneous, reflecting the wide variety of activities you may be engaged in at any given moment. The most prominent EEG wave pattern of an awake, relaxed adult whose eyes are closed is an oscillation of 8 to 13 Hz, known as the **alpha rhythm** (**Figure 8.3a**). The alpha rhythm is recorded best over the parietal and occipital lobes and is associated with decreased levels of attention. When alpha rhythms are generated, subjects commonly report that they feel relaxed and happy. However, people who normally experience more alpha rhythm than usual have not been shown to be psychologically different from those with less.

When people are attentive to an external stimulus or are thinking hard about something, the alpha rhythm is replaced by smaller-amplitude, higher-frequency (>12 Hz) oscillations, the **beta rhythm** (**Figure 8.3b**). This transformation, known as the **EEG arousal,** is associated with the act of paying attention to a stimulus rather than with the act of perception itself. For example, if people open their eyes in a completely dark room and try to see, EEG arousal occurs even though they perceive no visual input. With decreasing attention to repeated stimuli, the EEG pattern reverts to the alpha rhythm.

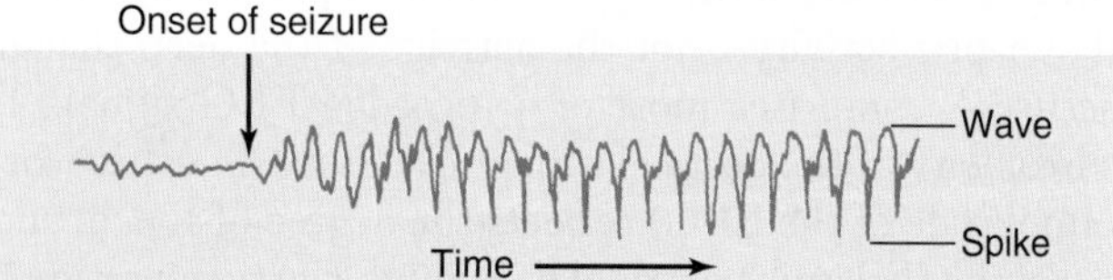

Figure 8.2 Spike-and-wave pattern in the EEG of a patient during an epileptic seizure. Scale is the same as in Figure 8.1.

PHYSIOLOGICAL INQUIRY

- Suppose the patient from which this trace was recorded had a mild form of epilepsy, with the only symptom being vivid visual hallucinations. Where on the patient's head was this measurement most likely taken?

Answer can be found at end of chapter.

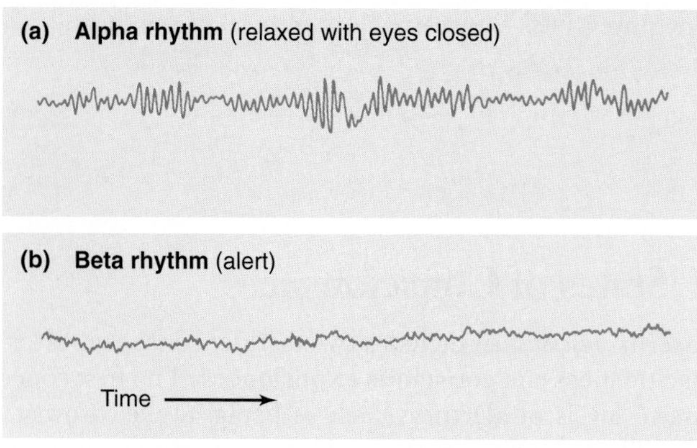

Figure 8.3 EEG recordings of (a) alpha and (b) beta rhythms. Alpha waves vary from 8 to 13 Hz and have larger amplitudes than beta waves, which have frequencies above 13 Hz. Scale is the same as Figure 8.1. Not shown are higher-frequency EEG waves known as gamma waves (30–100 Hz), which have been observed in awake individuals processing sensory inputs.

More recent research has described another EEG pattern known as **gamma rhythm.** These are high-frequency oscillations (30–100 Hz) that spread across large regions of the cortex, which seem in some cases to emanate from the thalamus. They often coincide with the occurrence of combinations of stimuli like hearing noises and seeing objects and are thought to be evidence of large numbers of neurons in the brain actively tying together disparate parts of an experienced scene or event.

Sleep

The EEG pattern changes profoundly in sleep, as demonstrated in **Figure 8.4**. As a person becomes increasingly drowsy, his or her wave pattern transitions from a beta rhythm to a predominantly alpha rhythm. When sleep actually occurs, the EEG shifts toward lower-frequency, larger-amplitude wave patterns known as the **theta rhythm** (4–8 Hz) and the **delta rhythm** (slower than 4 Hz). Relaxation of posture, decreased ease of arousal, increased threshold for sensory stimuli, and decreased motor neuron output accompany these EEG changes.

There are two phases of sleep, the names of which depend on whether or not the eyes move behind the closed eyelids: **NREM** (non–rapid eye movement) and **REM** (rapid eye movement) **sleep.** The initial phase of sleep—NREM sleep—is subdivided into three stages. Each successive stage is characterized by an EEG pattern with a lower frequency and larger amplitude than the preceding one. In stage N1 sleep, theta waves begin to be interspersed among the alpha pattern. In stage N2, high-frequency bursts called **sleep spindles** and large-amplitude **K complexes** occasionally interrupt the theta rhythm. Delta waves first appear along with the theta rhythm in stage N3 sleep; as this stage continues, the dominant

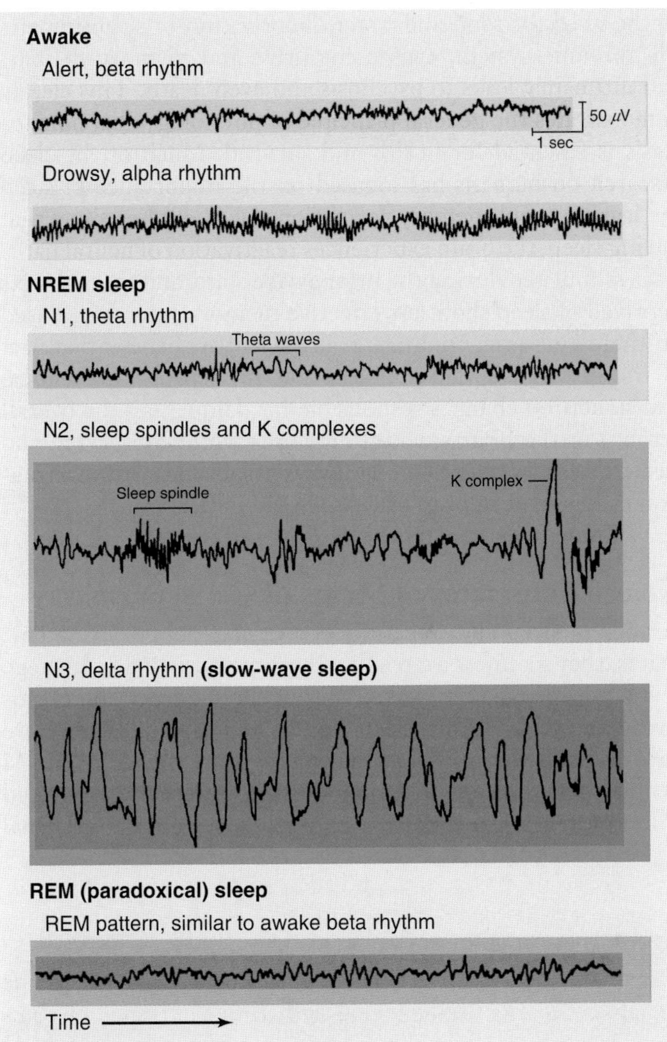

Figure 8.4 The EEG record of a person passing from an awake state through the various stages of sleep. The large-amplitude delta waves of slow-wave sleep demonstrate the synchronous activity pattern in cortical neurons. The asynchronous pattern during REM sleep is similar to that observed in awake individuals.

pattern becomes a delta rhythm N3, sometimes referred to as slow-wave sleep.

Sleep begins with the progression from stage N1 to stage N3 of NREM sleep, which normally takes 30 to 45 min. The process then reverses itself; the EEG ultimately resumes a small-amplitude, high-frequency, asynchronous pattern that looks very similar to the alert, awake state (see Figure 8.4, bottom trace). Instead of the person waking, however, the behavioral characteristics of sleep continue at this time, but this sleep also includes rapid eye movement (REM).

REM sleep is also called **paradoxical sleep,** because even though a person is asleep and difficult to arouse, his or her EEG pattern shows intense activity that is similar to that observed in the alert, awake state. In fact, brain O_2 consumption is higher during REM sleep than during the NREM or awake states. When awakened during REM sleep, subjects frequently report that they have been dreaming. This is true even in people who usually do not remember dreaming when they awaken on their own.

If uninterrupted, the stages of sleep occur in a cyclical fashion, tending to move from NREM stages N1 to N2 to N3, then back up to N2, and then to an episode of REM sleep. Continuous recordings of adults show that the average total night's sleep comprises four or five such cycles, each lasting 90 to 100 min (**Figure 8.5**). Significantly more time is spent in NREM during the first few cycles, but time spent in REM sleep increases toward the end of an undisturbed night. In young adults, REM sleep constitutes 20% to 25% of the total sleeping time; this fraction tends to decline progressively with aging. Initially, as you transition from drowsiness to stage N1 sleep, there is a considerable tension in the postural muscles, and brief muscle twitches called **hypnic jerks** sometimes occur. Eventually, the muscles become progressively more relaxed as NREM sleep progresses. Sleepers awakened during NREM sleep report dreaming less frequently than sleepers awakened during REM sleep. REM dreams also tend to seem more "real" and be more emotionally intense than those occurring in NREM sleep.

With several exceptions, skeletal muscle tension, already decreased during NREM sleep, is markedly inhibited during REM sleep. Exceptions include the eye muscles, which undergo rapid bursts of contractions and cause the sweeping eye movements that give this sleep stage its name. The significance of these eye movements is not understood. Experiments suggest that they do not seem to rigorously correlate with the content of dreams; that is, what the sleeper is "seeing" in a dream does not seem to affect the eye movements. Furthermore, eye movements also occur during REM sleep in animals and humans that have been blind since birth and thus have no experience tracking objects with eye movements. Other groups of muscles that are active during REM sleep are the respiratory muscles; in fact, the rate of breathing is frequently increased compared to the awake, relaxed state. In one form of a disease known as ***sleep apnea,*** however, stimulation of the respiratory muscles temporarily ceases, sometimes hundreds of times during a night. The resulting decreases in oxygen levels repeatedly awaken the apnea sufferer, who is deprived of both slow-wave and REM sleep. As a result, this disease is associated with excessive—and sometimes dangerous—sleepiness during the day (refer to Chapter 13 for a more complete discussion of sleep apnea).

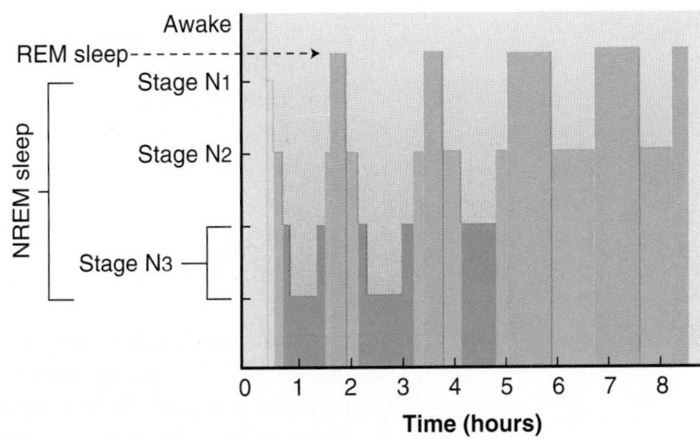

Figure 8.5 Schematic representation of the timing of sleep stages in a young adult. Bar colors correspond to the EEG traces shown in Figure 8.4.

During the sleep cycle, many changes occur throughout the body in addition to altered muscle tension, providing an excellent example of the general principle of physiology that the functions of organ systems are coordinated with each other. During NREM sleep, for example, there are pulsatile releases of hormones from the anterior pituitary gland such as growth hormone and the gonadotropic hormones (Chapter 11), so adequate sleep is essential for normal growth in children and for regulation of reproductive function in adults. Decreases in blood pressure, heart rate, and respiratory rate also occur during NREM sleep. REM sleep is associated with an increase and irregularity in blood pressure, heart rate, and respiratory rate. Moreover, twitches of the facial muscles or limb muscles may occur—despite the generalized lack of skeletal muscle tone—as may erection of the penis and engorgement of the clitoris. The occurrence of erections during REM sleep in patients being assessed for ***erectile dysfunction*** (***ED***) indicates that the cause of ED (see Chapter 17) may be psychological rather than physical.

Although we spend about one-third of our lives sleeping, the functions of sleep are not completely understood. Many lines of research, however, suggest that sleep is a fundamental necessity of a complex nervous system. Sleep, or a sleeplike state, is a characteristic found throughout the animal kingdom, including insects, reptiles, birds, mammals, and others. Studies of sleep deprivation in humans and other animals suggest that sleep is a homeostatic requirement, similar to the need for food and water. Deprivation of sleep impairs the immune system, causes cognitive and memory deficits, and ultimately leads to psychosis and even death. This clearly demonstrates the general principle of physiology that homeostasis is essential for health and survival. Much of the sleep research on humans has focused on the importance of sleep for learning and memory formation. EEG studies show that during sleep, the brain experiences reactivation of neural pathways stimulated during the prior awake state, and that subjects deprived of sleep show less effective memory retention. Based on these and other findings, many scientists believe that part of the restorative value of sleep lies in facilitating chemical and structural changes responsible for dampening the overall activity in the brain's neural networks while conserving and strengthening synapses in pathways associated with information that is important to learn and remember.

Table 8.1 summarizes the sleep states.

Neural Substrates of States of Consciousness

Periods of sleep and wakefulness alternate about once a day; that is, they manifest a circadian rhythm consisting on average of 8 h asleep and 16 h awake. Within the sleep portion of this circadian cycle, NREM sleep and REM sleep alternate, as we have seen. As we shift from the waking state through NREM sleep to REM sleep, attention shifts to internally generated stimuli (dreams) so that we are largely insensitive to external

TABLE 8.1 Sleep–Wakefulness Stages

Stage	Behavior	EEG (See Figures 8.3 and 8.4)
Alert wakefulness	Awake, alert with eyes open.	Beta rhythm (greater than 13 Hz).
Relaxed wakefulness	Awake, relaxed with eyes closed.	Mainly alpha rhythm (8–13 Hz) over the parietal and occipital lobes. Changes to beta rhythm in response to internal or external stimuli.
Relaxed drowsiness	Fatigued, tired, or bored; eyelids may narrow and close; head may start to droop; momentary lapses of attention and alertness. Sleepy but not asleep.	Decrease in alpha-wave amplitude and frequency.
NREM (slow-wave) sleep		
Stage N1	Light sleep; easily aroused by moderate stimuli or even by neck muscle jerks triggered by muscle stretch receptors as head nods; continuous lack of awareness.	Alpha waves reduced in frequency, amplitude, and percentage of time present; gaps in alpha rhythm filled with theta (4–8 Hz) and delta (slower than 4 Hz) activity.
Stage N2	Further lack of sensitivity to activation and arousal.	Alpha waves replaced by random waves of greater amplitude.
Stage N3	Deep sleep; in stage N3, activation and arousal occur only with vigorous stimulation.	Much theta and delta activity; progressive increase in amount of delta.
REM (paradoxical) sleep	Greatest muscle relaxation and difficulty of arousal; begins 50–90 min after sleep onset, episodes repeated every 60–90 min, each episode lasting about 10 min; dreaming frequently occurs, rapid eye movements behind closed eyelids; marked increase in brain O_2 consumption.	EEG resembles that of alert awake state.

stimuli. Although sleep facilitates our ability to retain memories of experiences occurring in the waking state, dreams are generally forgotten relatively quickly. The tight rules for determining reality also become relaxed during dreaming, sometimes allowing for bizarre dreams.

What physiological processes drive these cyclic changes in states of consciousness? Nuclei in both the brainstem and hypothalamus are involved.

Recall from Chapter 6 that a diverging network of neurons called the reticular formation connects the brainstem with widespread regions of the brain and spinal cord. This network is essential for life and integrates a large number of physiological functions, including motor control, cardiovascular and respiratory control, and—relevant to the present discussion—states of consciousness. The components involved in regulating consciousness are sometimes referred to as the **reticular activating system (RAS)**. This system consists of clusters of neurons and neural pathways originating in the brainstem and hypothalamus, distinguished by both their anatomical distribution and the neurotransmitters they release (**Figure 8.6**). Neurons of the RAS project widely throughout the cortex, as well as to areas of the thalamus that influence the EEG. Varying activation and inhibition of distinct groups of these neurons mediate transitions between waking and sleeping states.

The awake state is characterized by widespread activation of the cortex and thalamus by ascending pathways of the RAS (see Figure 8.6). Neurons originating in the brainstem release the monoaminergic neurotransmitters norepinephrine, serotonin, and histamine, which in this case function principally as neuromodulators (see Chapter 6). Their nerve terminals are distributed widely throughout the brain, where they enhance excitatory synaptic activity. The drowsiness that occurs in people using antihistamines may be a result of blocking the histaminergic inputs of this system. In addition, acetylcholine from neurons in the pons and basal forebrain facilitates transmission of ascending sensory information through the thalamus and also enhances communication between the thalamus and cortex.

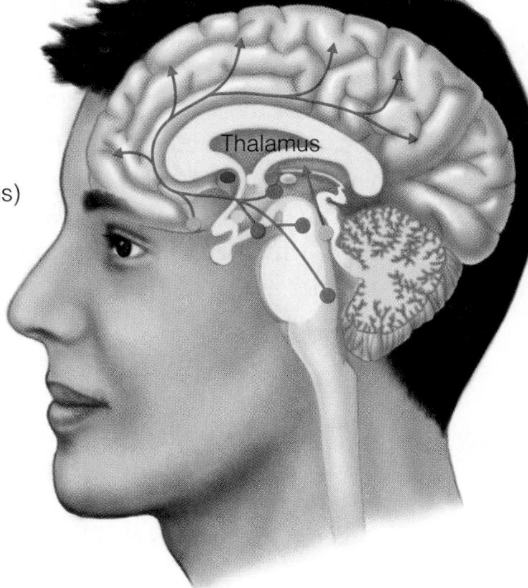

Figure 8.6 AP|R Brain regions involved in regulating states of consciousness. Red arrows indicate principal pathways of ascending activation of the thalamus and cortex by the reticular activating system (RAS) during the awake state. Additional pathways not shown that are important in maintaining cortical arousal include excitatory inputs to the monoaminergic RAS nuclei from orexinergic neurons, and inhibitory inputs to the sleep center from the monoaminergic RAS nuclei. Monoamines from the RAS nuclei include histamine, norepinephrine, and serotonin. Orexin neurons and GABAergic neurons of the sleep center are hypothalamic nuclei, and the acetylcholine neurons are in the basal forebrain and pons.

PHYSIOLOGICAL INQUIRY

- Explain why some drugs prescribed to treat allergic reactions cause drowsiness as a side effect.

Answer can be found at end of chapter.

Recently discovered neuropeptides called **orexins** (a name meaning "to stimulate appetite") also play an important role in maintaining the awake state. They are produced by neurons in the hypothalamus that have widespread projections throughout the cortex and thalamus. (Some scientists also refer to these peptides as **hypocretins** because they are made in the *hypo*thalamus and are similar to the hormone se*cretin*.) Orexin-secreting neurons also densely innervate and stimulate action potential firing by the monoaminergic neurons of the RAS. Experimental animals and humans that lack orexins or their receptors suffer from ***narcolepsy***, a condition characterized by sudden attacks of sleepiness that unpredictably occur during the normal wakeful period. The importance of orexins in wakefulness has been recently validated by experiments showing that sleep is promoted in people ingesting a drug that blocks binding of orexins to their receptors. Loss of orexinergic neurons that occurs with age may explain why older people sometimes have difficulty sleeping.

Sleep is characterized by a markedly different pattern of neuronal activity and neurotransmitter release. Of central importance is the active firing of neurons in the "sleep center," a group of neurons in the ventrolateral preoptic nucleus of the hypothalamus (see Figure 8.6). These neurons release the inhibitory neurotransmitter GABA (gamma-aminobutyric acid) onto neurons throughout the brainstem and hypothalamus, including those that secrete orexins and monoamines. Inhibition of these regions reduces the levels of orexin, norepinephrine, serotonin, and histamine throughout the brain. Each of these substances has been associated with alertness and arousal; therefore, inhibition of their secretion by GABA tends to promote sleep. This accounts for the sleep-inducing effects of ***benzodiazepines*** such as ***diazepam*** (***Valium***) and ***alprazolam*** (***Xanax***), which are GABA agonists and are used to treat anxiety and insomnia in some people.

The pattern of acetylcholine release varies in different sleep stages. It is reduced in NREM sleep, but in REM sleep it is increased to levels similar to those in the awake state. The increase in acetylcholine during REM sleep facilitates communication between the thalamus and cortex and increases the cortical activity and dreaming that occur in this state.

Figure 8.7 shows a model of factors involved in regulating the transition between waking and sleeping states. Transition to the wakeful state is favored by three main inputs to orexin-secreting cells: (1) action potential firing from the suprachiasmatic nucleus (SCN), (2) indicators of negative energy balance, and (3) arousing emotional states signaled by the limbic system (see Figure 6.40 and Section 8.3 of this chapter). The SCN is the principle circadian pacemaker of the body (see Chapters 1 and 7). Entrained to a 24-hour cycle by light and other daily stimuli, it activates orexin cells in the morning. It also triggers the secretion of melatonin at night (see Chapters 1 and 11). Although melatonin has been used as a "natural" substance for treating insomnia and jet lag, it has not yet been demonstrated unequivocally to be effective as a sleeping pill. It has, however, been shown to induce a decrease in body temperature, a key event in falling asleep.

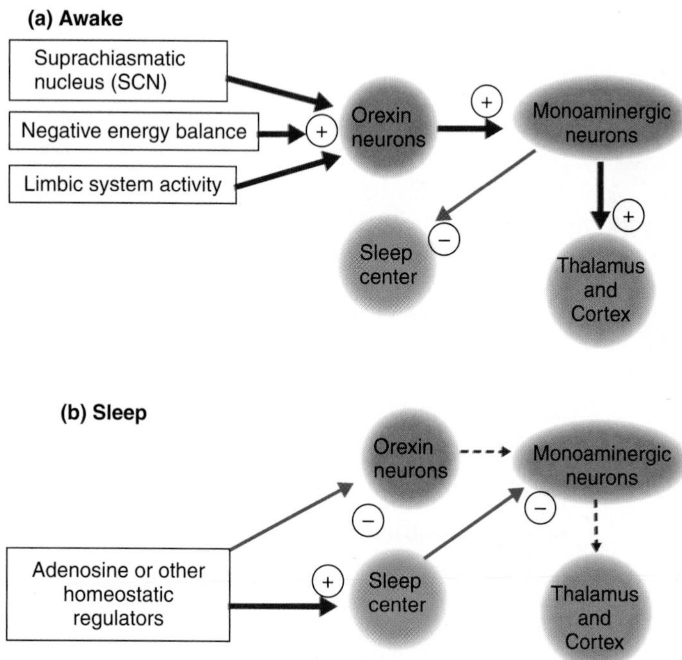

Figure 8.7 A model for the regulation of transitions to (a) the awake state and (b) sleep. Red arrows and "+" indicate stimulatory influences, blue arrows and "–" indicate inhibitory pathways. Orexin neurons and the sleep center are in the hypothalamus. Monoaminergic neurons release norepinephrine, serotonin, and histamine. Adapted from Sakurai, Takeshi. Nature Reviews, *Neuroscience* (8): pp. 171–181, March 2007.

PHYSIOLOGICAL INQUIRY

- Interleukin 1, a fever-inducing cytokine that increases in the circulation during an infection, promotes the sleep state. Speculate about some possible adaptive advantages of such a mechanism.

Answer can be found at end of chapter.

The metabolic and limbic system inputs to orexinergic neurons provide adaptive behavioral flexibility to the initiation of wakefulness, so that under special circumstances our sleep and wake patterns can vary from the typical pattern of sleeping at night and being awake during the day. Metabolic indicators of negative energy balance resulting from a prolonged fast include decreased blood glucose concentration, increased plasma concentrations of the appetite-stimulating hormone called ghrelin, and decreased concentrations of the appetite-suppressing hormone leptin (see Chapter 16 for a detailed description of these hormones). These conditions all stimulate orexin release, which may be adaptive because the resulting arousal would allow you to seek out food at times when you would otherwise be asleep. This link between metabolism and wakefulness is an excellent example of the general principle of physiology that the functions of organ systems are coordinated with each other. Limbic system inputs coding strong emotions such as fear or anger also stimulate orexin neurons. This may be adaptive by interrupting sleep at times when we need to respond to situations affecting our well-being and survival.

The factors that activate the sleep center are not completely understood, but it is thought that homeostatic regulation by one or more chemicals plays a role. The need for sleep behaves like other homeostatic demands of the body. Individuals deprived of sleep for a prolonged period will subsequently experience prolonged bouts of "catch-up" sleep, as though the body needs to rid itself of some chemical that has built up. Adenosine (a metabolite of ATP) is one likely candidate. Its concentration is increased in the brain after a prolonged waking period, and it has been shown to reduce firing by orexinergic neurons. This in part explains the stimulatory effect of caffeine, which blocks adenosine receptors. Buildup of adenosine or other homeostatic regulators can also facilitate the transition to the sleep state at times when you may normally be awake, like when you take an afternoon nap after being up late studying for an exam. Another potential sleep-inducing chemical candidate is interleukin 1, one of the cytokines in a family of intercellular messengers having an important role in the immune defense system (Chapter 18). It fluctuates in parallel with normal sleep–wake cycles and has also been shown to facilitate the sleep state.

Coma and Brain Death

The term ***coma*** describes an extreme decrease in mental function due to structural, physiological, or metabolic impairment of the brain. A person in a coma exhibits a sustained loss of the capacity for arousal even in response to vigorous stimulation. There is no outward behavioral expression of any mental function, the eyes are usually closed, and sleep–wake cycles disappear. Coma can result from extensive damage to the cerebral cortex; damage to the brainstem arousal mechanisms; interruptions of the connections between the brainstem and cortical areas; metabolic dysfunctions; brain infections; or an overdose of certain drugs, such as sedatives, sleeping pills, narcotics, or ethanol. Comas may be reversible or irreversible, depending on the type, location, and severity of brain damage. Experiments using high-density EEG arrays in some coma patients suggest that even though they exhibit no outward behaviors or responses, they may have some level of consciousness. For example, talking to a patient about tennis may evoke increased

EEG activity over motor areas of the cortex that would be active if the person were actually playing tennis.

Patients in an irreversible coma often enter a ***persistent vegetative state*** in which sleep–wake cycles are present even though the patient is unaware of his or her surroundings. Individuals in a persistent vegetative state may smile, cry, or seem to react to elements of their environment. However, there is no definitive evidence that they can comprehend these behaviors.

A coma—even when irreversible—is not equivalent to death. We are left, then, with the question, When is a person actually dead? This question often has urgent medical, legal, and social consequences. For example, with the need for viable tissues for organ transplantation, it becomes important to know just when a donor is legally dead so that the organs can be removed as soon after death as possible.

Brain death is currently accepted by the medical and legal establishment as the criterion for death, despite the viability of other organs. Brain death occurs when the brain no longer functions and appears to have no possibility of functioning again.

The problem now becomes practical. How do we know when a person (e.g., someone in a coma) is brain-dead? Although there is some variation in how different hospitals and physicians determine brain death, the criteria listed in **Table 8.2** lists the generally agreed-upon standards. Notice that the cause of a coma must be known, because comas due to drug poisoning and other conditions are often reversible. Also, the criteria specify that there be no evidence of functioning neural tissues above the spinal cord because fragments of spinal reflexes may remain for several hours or longer after the brain is dead (see Chapter 10 for spinal reflex examples). The criterion for lack of spontaneous respiration (apnea) must be assessed with caution. Machines supplying artificial respiration must be turned off, and arterial blood gas levels monitored carefully (see Figure 13.21 and Table 13.6). Although arterial carbon dioxide levels must be allowed to increase above a critical point for the test to be valid, it is of course not advisable to allow arterial oxygen levels to decrease too much because of the danger of further brain damage. Therefore, apnea tests are generally limited to a duration of 8 to 10 minutes.

TABLE 8.2 Criteria for Brain Death
I. The nature and duration of the coma must be known. A. Known structural damage to brain or irreversible systemic metabolic disease B. No chance of drug intoxication, especially from paralyzing or sedative drugs C. No severe electrolyte, acid–base, or endocrine disorder that could be reversible D. Patient not suffering from hypothermia E. Peak arterial blood pressure above 100 mmHg
II. Cerebral and brainstem function are absent. A. No response to painful stimuli other than spinal cord reflexes B. Pupils unresponsive to light C. No eye movement in response to stimulation of the vestibular reflex or corneal touch D. Apnea (no spontaneous breathing) for 8–10 minutes when ventilator is removed and arterial carbon dioxide levels are allowed to increase above 60 mmHg E. No gag or cough reflex; purely spinal reflexes may be retained F. Confirmatory neurological exam after 6 hours
III. Supplementary (optional) criteria A. Flat EEG for 30 min (wave amplitudes less than 2 mV) B. Responses absent in vital brainstem structures C. Greatly reduced cerebral circulation

Table adapted from American Academy of Neurology, *Neurology* 74: 1911–1918 (2010).

8.2 Conscious Experiences

Conscious experiences are those things we are aware of—either internal, such as an idea, or external, such as an object or event. The most obvious aspect of this phenomenon is sensory awareness, but we are also aware of inner states such as fatigue, thirst, and happiness. We are aware of the passing of time, of what we are presently thinking about, and of consciously recalling a fact learned in the past. We are aware of reasoning and exerting self-control, and we are aware of directing our attention to specific events. Not least, we are aware of "self."

Basic to the concept of conscious experience is the question of attention.

Selective Attention

The term **selective attention** means avoiding the distraction of irrelevant stimuli while seeking out and focusing on stimuli that are momentarily important. Both voluntary and reflex mechanisms affect selective attention. An example of voluntary control of selective attention familiar to students is ignoring distracting events in a busy library while studying there.

Another example of selective attention occurs when a novel stimulus is presented to a relaxed subject showing an alpha EEG pattern. This causes the EEG to shift to the beta rhythm. If the stimulus has meaning for the individual, behavioral changes also occur. The person stops what he or she is doing, listens intently, and turns toward the stimulus source, a behavior called the **orienting response.** If the person is concentrating hard and is not distracted by the novel stimulus, the orienting response does not occur. It is also possible to focus attention on a particular stimulus without making any behavioral response.

For attention to be directed only toward stimuli that are meaningful, the nervous system must have the means to evaluate the importance of incoming sensory information. Thus, even before we focus attention on an object in our sensory world and become aware of it, a certain amount of processing has already occurred. This so-called **preattentive processing** directs our attention toward the part of the sensory world that is of particular interest and prepares the brain's perceptual processes for it.

If a stimulus is repeated but is found to be irrelevant, the behavioral response to the stimulus progressively decreases, a process known as **habituation.** For example, when a loud bell is sounded for the first time, it may evoke an orienting response because the person may be frightened by or curious about the novel stimulus. After several rings, however, the individual has a progressively smaller response and eventually may ignore the bell altogether. An extraneous stimulus of another type or the same stimulus at a different intensity can restore the orienting response.

Habituation involves a depression of synaptic transmission in the involved pathway, possibly related to a prolonged inactivation of Ca^{2+} channels in presynaptic axon terminals. Such inactivation results in a decreased Ca^{2+} influx during depolarization and, therefore, a decrease in the amount of neurotransmitter released by a terminal in response to action potentials.

Neural Mechanisms for Selective Attention

Directing our attention to an object involves several distinct neurological processes. First, our attention must be disengaged from its present focus. Then, attention must be moved to the new focus. Attention must then be engaged at the new focus. Finally, there must be an increased level of arousal that produces prolonged attention to the new focus.

An area that plays an important role in orienting and selective attention is in the brainstem, where the interaction of various sensory modalities in single cells can be detected experimentally. The receptive fields of the different modalities overlap. For example, a visual and auditory input from the same location in space will significantly enhance the firing rates of certain of these so-called multisensory cells, whereas the same type of stimuli originating at different places will have little effect on or may even inhibit their response. Thus, weak clues can add together to enhance each other's significance so we pay attention to the event, whereas we may ignore an isolated small clue.

The locus ceruleus is one of the monoaminergic RAS nuclei. It is located in the pons, projects to the parietal cortex and many other parts of the central nervous system, and is also implicated in selective attention. The system of fibers leading from the locus ceruleus helps determine which brain area is to gain temporary predominance in the ongoing stream of the conscious experience. These neurons release norepinephrine, which acts as a neuromodulator to enhance the signals transmitted by certain sensory inputs. The effect is to increase the difference between the sensory inputs and other, weaker signals. Thus, neurons of the locus ceruleus improve information processing during selective attention.

The thalamus is another brain region involved in selective attention. It is a synaptic relay station for the majority of ascending sensory pathways (see Figure 7.19). Inputs from regions of the cerebral cortex and brainstem can modulate synaptic activity in the thalamus, making it a filter that can selectively influence the transmission of sensory information.

There are also multisensory neurons in association areas of the cerebral cortex (see Figure 7.13). Whereas the brainstem neurons are concerned with the orienting movements associated with paying attention to a specific stimulus, the cortical multisensory neurons are more involved in the perception of the stimulus. Neuroscientists are only beginning to understand how the various areas of the attentional system interact.

Some insights into neural mechanisms of selective attention are being gained from the study of individuals diagnosed with ***attention-deficit/hyperactivity disorder*** (***AD/HD***). This condition typically begins early in childhood and is the most common neurobehavioral problem in school-aged children (estimates range from 3% to 7%). AD/HD is characterized by abnormal difficulty in maintaining selective attention and/or impulsiveness and hyperactivity. Investigation has yet to reveal clear environmental causes, but there is some evidence for a genetic basis because AD/HD tends to run in families. Functional imaging studies of the brains of children with AD/HD have indicated dysfunction of brain regions in which catecholamine signaling is prominent, including the basal nuclei and prefrontal cortex. In support of this, the most effective medication used to treat AD/HD is ***methylphenidate*** (***Ritalin***), a drug that increases synaptic concentrations of dopamine and norepinephrine.

Neural Mechanisms of Conscious Experiences

Conscious experiences are popularly attributed to the workings of the "mind," a word that conjures up the image of a nonneural "me," a phantom interposed between afferent and efferent impulses. The implication is that the mind is something more than neural activity. Most experts would agree that the mind represents a summation of neural activity at any given moment and does not require anything more. However, scientists are only beginning to understand the mechanisms that give rise to mind or to conscious experiences.

We will speculate about this problem in this section. The thinking begins with the assumption that conscious experience requires neural processes—either graded potentials or action potentials—somewhere in the brain. At any moment, certain of these processes correlate with conscious awareness, and others do not. A key question here is, What is different about the processes we are aware of?

A further assumption is that the neural activity that corresponds to a conscious experience resides not in a single anatomical cluster of "consciousness neurons" but rather in a set of neurons that are temporarily functioning together in a specific way. Because we can become aware of many different things, we further assume that this grouping of neurons can vary—shifting, for example, among parts of the brain that deal with visual or auditory stimuli, memories or new ideas, emotions, or language.

Consider the visual perception of an object. As we discussed in Chapter 7, different aspects of something we see are processed by different areas of the visual cortex—the object's color by one part, its motion by another, its location in the visual field by another, and its shape by still another—but we see *one* object. Not only do we perceive it; we may also know its name and function. Moreover, as we see an object, we can sometimes also hear or smell it, which requires participation of brain areas other than the visual cortex.

The simultaneous participation of different groups of neurons in a conscious experience can also be inferred for the olfactory system. Repugnant and alluring odors evoke different reactions, although they are both processed in the olfactory pathway. Neurons involved in emotion are also clearly involved in this type of perception.

Neurons from the various parts of the brain that simultaneously process different aspects of the information related to the object we see are said to form a "temporary set" of neurons. It is suggested that the synchronous activity of the neurons in the temporary set leads to conscious awareness of the object we are seeing.

As we become aware of still other events—perhaps a memory related to the object—the set of neurons involved in the synchronous activity shifts, and a different temporary set forms. In other words, it is suggested that specific relevant neurons in many areas of the brain function together to form the unified activity that corresponds to awareness.

What parts of the brain may be involved in such a temporary neuronal set? Clearly, the cerebral cortex is involved. Removal of specific areas of the cortex abolishes awareness of only specific types of consciousness. For example, in a syndrome called ***sensory neglect,*** damage to association areas of the parietal cortex causes the injured person to neglect parts of the body or parts of the visual field as though they do not exist. Stroke patients with parietal lobe damage often do not acknowledge the presence of a paralyzed part of their body or will only be able to describe some but not all elements in a visual field. **Figure 8.8** shows an example of sensory neglect as shown in drawings made by a patient with parietal lobe damage on the right side of the brain. Patients such as these are completely unaware of the left-hand parts of the visual image. Subcortical areas such as the thalamus and basal ganglia may also be directly involved in conscious experience, but it seems that the hippocampus and cerebellum are not.

Saying that we can use one set of neurons and then shift to a new set at a later time may be the same as saying we can focus attention on—that is, bring into conscious awareness—one object or event and then shift our focus of attention to another object or event at a later time. Thus, the mechanisms of conscious awareness and attention are intimately related.

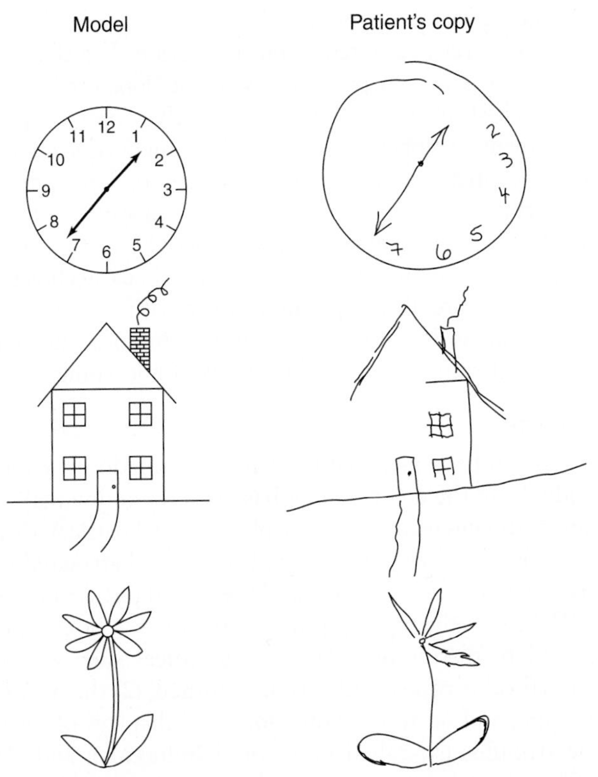

Figure 8.8 Unilateral visual neglect in a patient with right parietal lobe damage. Although patients such as these are not impaired visually, they do not perceive part of their visual world. The drawings on the right were copied by the patient from the drawings on the left.

8.3 Motivation and Emotion

Motivation is a factor in most, if not all, behaviors, and emotions accompany many of our conscious experiences. Motivated behaviors such as sexual behaviors play a part in controlling much of our day-to-day behavior, and emotions may help us to achieve the goals we set for ourselves as well as express our feelings.

Motivation

Those processes responsible for the goal-directed quality of behavior are the **motivations,** or "drives," for that behavior. Motivation can lead to hormonal, autonomic, and behavioral responses. **Primary motivated behavior** is behavior related directly to homeostasis—that is, the maintenance of a relatively stable internal environment, such as getting something to drink when you are thirsty. In such homeostatic goal-directed behavior, specific body "needs" are satisfied. Thus, in our example, the perception of need results from a decrease in total body water, and the correlate of need satisfaction is the return of body water concentration to normal. We will discuss the neurophysiological integration of much homeostatic goal-directed behavior later (thirst and drinking, Chapter 14; food intake and temperature regulation, Chapter 16).

In many kinds of behavior, however, the relation between the behavior and the primary goal is indirect. For example, the selection of a particular flavor of beverage has little if any apparent relation to homeostasis. The motivation in this case is secondary. Much of human behavior fits into this latter category and is influenced by habit, learning, intellect, and emotions—factors that can be lumped together under the term "incentives." Often, it is difficult to distinguish between primary and secondary goals. For instance, although some salt in the diet is required for survival, most of your drive to eat salt is hedonistic (for enjoyment). Sometimes the primary homeostatic goals and secondary goals conflict, as, for example, during a religious fast.

The concepts of reward and punishment are inseparable from motivation. Rewards are things that organisms work for or things that make the behavior that leads to them occur more often—in other words, positive reinforcement. Punishments are the opposite.

The neural system subserving reward and punishment is part of the reticular activating system, which you will recall arises in the brainstem and comprises several components. The component involved in motivation is known as the **mesolimbic dopamine pathway:** *meso-* because it arises in the midbrain (mesencephalon) area of the brainstem; *limbic* because it sends its fibers to areas of the limbic system, such as the prefrontal cortex, the nucleus accumbens, and the undersurface of the frontal lobe (**Figure 8.9**); and *dopamine* because its fibers release the neurotransmitter dopamine. The mesolimbic dopamine pathway is implicated in evaluating the availability of incentives and reinforcers (asking, Is it worth it? for example) and translating the evaluation into action.

Much of the available information concerning the neural substrates of motivation has been obtained by studying behavioral responses of animals to rewarding or punishing stimuli. One way in which this can be done is by using the technique of **brain self-stimulation.** In this technique, an awake experimental animal regulates the rate at which electrical stimuli are

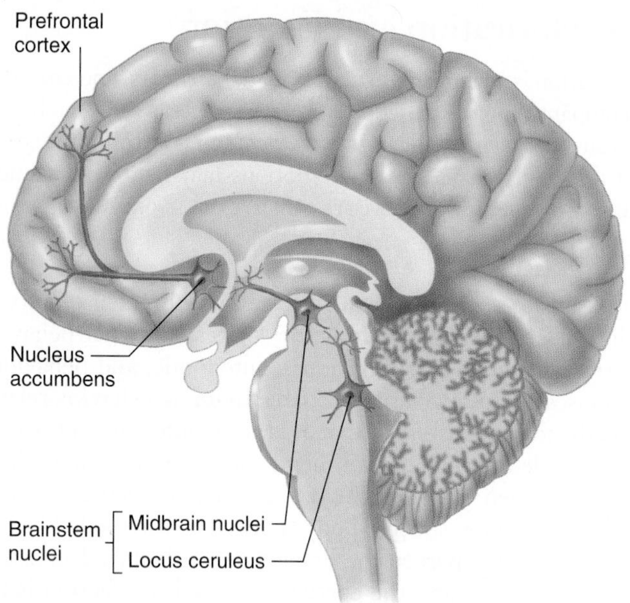

Figure 8.9 AP|R Schematic drawing of the mesolimbic dopamine pathway. Various psychoactive substances are thought to work in these areas to enhance brain reward.

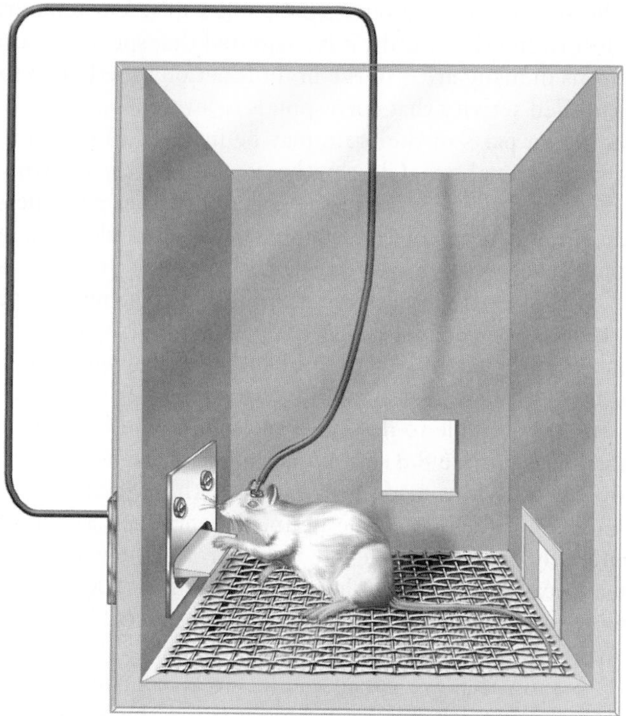

Figure 8.10 Apparatus for self-stimulation experiments. Rats like the one shown here do not appear to be bothered by the implanted electrode. In fact, they work hard to get the electrical stimulation. Adapted from Olds.

delivered through electrodes implanted in discrete brain areas. The small electrical charges given to the brain cause the local neurons to depolarize, thus mimicking what may happen if these neurons were to fire spontaneously. The experimental animal is placed in a box containing a lever it can press (**Figure 8.10**). If no stimulus is delivered to the brain when the bar is pressed, the animal usually presses it occasionally at random.

However, if a stimulus is delivered to the brain as a result of a bar press, different behaviors occur, depending on the location of the electrodes. If the animal increases the bar-pressing rate above the level of random presses, the electrical stimulus is by definition rewarding. If the animal decreases the press rate below the random level, the stimulus is punishing. Thus, the rate of bar pressing with the electrode in different brain areas is taken to be a measure of the effectiveness of the reward or punishment. Different pressing rates are found for different brain regions.

Scientists expected the hypothalamus to play a role in motivation because the neural centers for the regulation of eating, drinking, temperature control, and sexual behavior are there (Chapter 6). Indeed, it was found that brain self-stimulation of the lateral regions of the hypothalamus serves as a positive reward. Animals with electrodes in these areas have been known to press a bar to stimulate their brains 2000 times per hour continuously for 24 h until they collapse from exhaustion. In fact, electrical stimulation of the lateral hypothalamus is more rewarding than external rewards. Hungry rats, for example, often ignore available food for the sake of stimulating their brains at that location.

Although the rewarding sites—particularly those for primary motivated behavior—are more densely packed in the lateral hypothalamus than anywhere else in the brain, self-stimulation can occur in a large number of brain areas. Motivated behaviors based on learning also involve additional integrative centers, including the cortex, and limbic system, brainstem, and spinal cord—in other words, all levels of the nervous system can be involved.

Chemical Mediators

Dopamine is a major neurotransmitter in the pathway that mediates the brain reward systems and motivation. For this reason, drugs that increase synaptic activity in the dopamine pathways increase self-stimulation rates—that is, they provide positive reinforcement. Amphetamines are an example of such a drug because they increase the presynaptic release of dopamine. Conversely, drugs such as chlorpromazine, an antipsychotic drug that blocks dopamine receptors and lowers activity in the catecholamine pathways, are negatively reinforcing. The catecholamines, as we will see, are also implicated in the pathways involved in learning. This is not unexpected, because rewards and punishments are believed to constitute incentives for learning.

Emotion

Emotion can be considered in terms of a relation between an individual and the environment based on the individual's evaluation of the environment (is it pleasant or hostile?), disposition toward the environment (am I happy and attracted to the environment or fearful of it?), and the actual physical response to it. While analyzing the physiological bases of emotion, it is helpful to distinguish (1) the anatomical sites where the emotional value of a stimulus is determined; (2) the hormonal, autonomic, and outward expressions and displays of response to the stimulus (so-called **emotional behavior**); and (3) the conscious experience, or **inner emotions,** such as feelings of fear, love, anger, joy, anxiety, hope, and so on.

Emotional behavior can be studied more easily than the anatomical systems or inner emotions because it includes responses that can be measured externally (in terms of behavior). For example, stimulation of certain regions of the lateral hypothalamus causes an experimental animal to arch its back, puff out the fur on its tail, hiss, snarl, bare its claws and teeth, flatten its ears, and strike. Simultaneously, its heart rate, blood pressure, respiration, salivation, and plasma concentrations of epinephrine and fatty acids all increase. Clearly, this behavior typifies that of an enraged or threatened animal. Moreover, the animal's behavior can be changed from savage to docile and back again simply by activating different areas of the limbic system (**Figure 8.11**).

An early case study that shed light on neurological structures involved in emotional behavior was that of a patient known as S.M. This patient suffered from a rare disorder (***Urbach–Wiethe disease***) in which the anterior and medial portions of the temporal lobe atrophied, essentially destroying the amygdala bilaterally. Intelligence and memory formation remained intact. However, this individual lacked the ability to express fear in appropriate situations and could not recognize fearful expressions on other people's faces. Therefore, in humans, the amygdala is important for the emotion of fear.

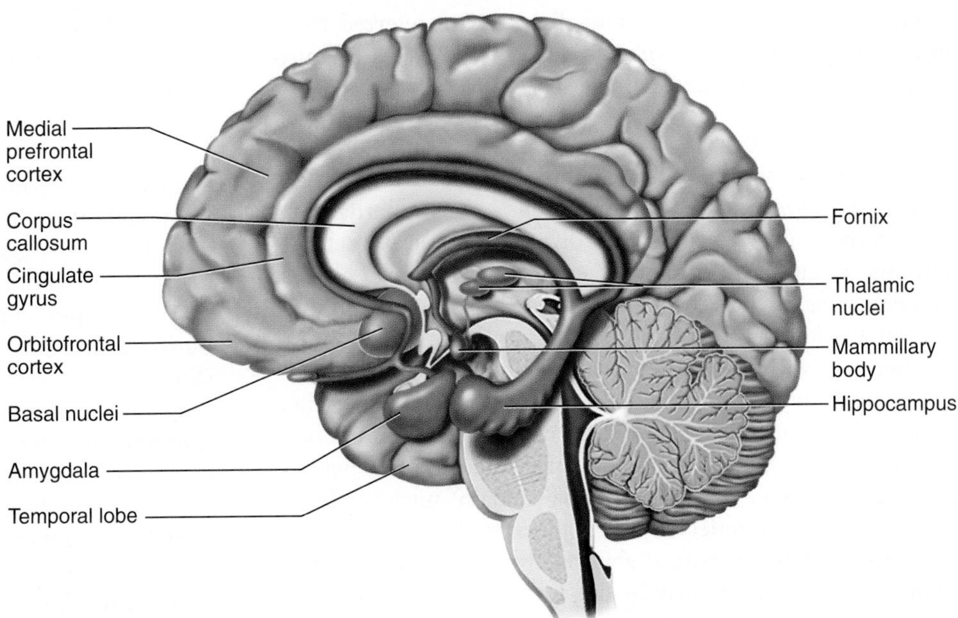

Figure 8.11 APIR Brain structures involved in emotion, motivation, and the affective disorders. The limbic system is shaded purple; individual basal nuclei are not shown in this view.

PHYSIOLOGICAL INQUIRY

- What might have favored the evolution of emotions?

Answer can be found at end of chapter.

Emotional behavior includes such complex behaviors as the passionate defense of a political ideology and such simple actions as laughing, sweating, crying, or blushing. Emotional behavior is achieved by the autonomic and somatic nervous systems under the influence of integrating centers such as those we just mentioned, and provides an outward sign that the brain's "emotion systems" are activated.

The cerebral cortex plays a major role in directing many of the motor responses during emotional behavior (for example, whether you approach or avoid a situation). Moreover, forebrain structures, including the cerebral cortex, account for the modulation, direction, understanding, or even inhibition of emotional behaviors.

Although limbic areas of the brain seem to handle inner emotions, there is no single "emotional system." The amygdala (see Figure 8.11), and the region of association cortex on the lower surface of the frontal lobe, however, are central to most emotional states (**Figure 8.12**). The amygdala, in addition to being responsible for the emotion of fear, interacts with other parts of the brain via extensive reciprocal connections that can influence emotions about external stimuli, decision making, memory, attention, homeostatic processes, and behavioral responses. For example, it sends output to the hypothalamus, which is central to autonomic and hormonal homeostatic processes.

The limbic areas have been stimulated in awake human beings undergoing neurosurgery. These patients reported vague feelings of fear or anxiety during periods of stimulation to certain areas. Stimulation of other areas induced pleasurable sensations that the subjects found hard to define precisely. In normal functioning, the cerebral cortex allows us to connect such inner emotions with the particular experiences or thoughts that cause them.

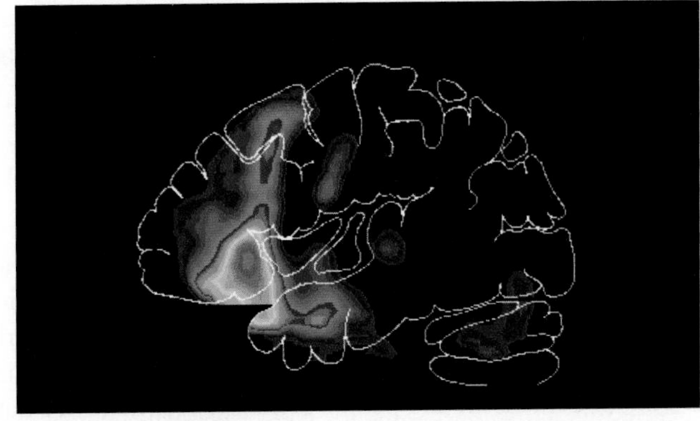

Figure 8.12 APIR Computer image showing increased activity (red and yellow areas) in the prefrontal cortex during a sad thought. Marcus E. Raichle, M.D., Washington University School of Medicine.

8.4 Altered States of Consciousness

States of consciousness may be different from the commonly experienced ones like wakefulness and drowsiness. Other, more unusual sensations, such as those occurring with hypnosis, mind-altering drugs, and certain diseases, are referred to as ***altered states of consciousness.*** These altered states are also characteristic of psychiatric illnesses.

Schizophrenia

One of the diseases that induces altered states of consciousness is ***schizophrenia,*** in which information is not properly regulated in the brain. The amazingly diverse symptoms of schizophrenia include hallucinations, especially "hearing" voices, and delusions, such as the belief that one has been chosen for a special mission or is being persecuted by others. Schizophrenics become withdrawn, are emotionally unresponsive, and experience inappropriate moods. They may also experience abnormal motor behavior, which can include total immobilization (***catatonia***). The symptoms vary from person to person.

The causes of schizophrenia remain unclear. Studies suggest that it reflects a developmental disorder in which neurons migrate or mature abnormally during brain formation. The abnormality may be due to a genetic predisposition or multiple environmental factors such as viral infections and malnutrition during fetal life or early childhood. The brain abnormalities involve diverse neural circuits and neurotransmitter systems that regulate basic cognitive processes. A widely accepted explanation for schizophrenia suggests that certain mesocortical dopamine pathways are overactive. This hypothesis is supported by the fact that amphetamine-like drugs, which enhance dopamine signaling, make the symptoms worse, as well as by the fact that the most therapeutically beneficial drugs used in treating schizophrenia block dopamine receptors.

Schizophrenia affects approximately 1% of people over the age of 18, with the typical age of onset in the late teens or early 20s just as brain development nears completion. Currently, there is no prevention or cure for the disease, although drugs can often control the symptoms. In a small number of cases, there has been complete recovery.

The Mood Disorders: Depressions and Bipolar Disorders

The term **mood** refers to a pervasive and sustained inner emotion that affects a person's perception of the world. In addition to being part of the conscious experience of the person, others can observe it. In healthy people, moods can be normal, elevated, or depressed, and people generally feel that they have some degree of control over their moods. That sense of control is lost, however, in the ***mood disorders,*** which include depressive disorders and bipolar disorders. Along with schizophrenia, the mood disorders represent the major psychiatric illnesses.

Some of the prominent features of ***depressive disorder*** (***depression***) are a pervasive feeling of emptiness or sadness; a loss of energy, interest, or pleasure; anxiety; irritability; an increase or decrease in appetite; disturbed sleep; and thoughts of death or suicide. Depression can occur on its own, independent of any other illness, or it can arise secondary to other medical disorders. It is associated with decreased neuronal activity and metabolism in the anterior part of the limbic system and nearby prefrontal cortex. These same brain regions show abnormalities, albeit inconsistent ones, in bipolar disorders.

The term ***bipolar disorder*** describes swings between mania and depression. Episodes of ***mania*** are characterized by an abnormally and persistently elevated mood, sometimes with euphoria (that is, an exaggerated and unrealistic sense of well-being), racing thoughts, excessive energy, overconfidence, impulsiveness, significantly decreased time spent sleeping, and irritability.

Although the major biogenic amine neurotransmitters (norepinephrine, dopamine, and serotonin) and acetylcholine have all been implicated, the causes of the mood disorders are unknown.

Current treatment of the mood disorders emphasizes drugs and psychotherapy. The classical antidepressant drugs are of three types. The ***tricyclic antidepressant drugs*** such as ***amitriptyline*** (***Elavil***), ***desipramine*** (***Norpramin***), and ***doxepin*** (***Sinequan***) interfere with serotonin and/or norepinephrine reuptake by presynaptic endings. The ***monoamine oxidase inhibitors*** interfere with the enzyme responsible for the breakdown of these same two neurotransmitters. A third class of antidepressant drugs, the ***serotonin-specific reuptake inhibitors*** (***SSRIs***), includes the most widely used antidepressant drugs—including ***escitalopram*** (***Lexapro***), ***fluoxetine*** (***Prozac***), ***paroxetine*** (***Paxil***), and ***sertraline*** (***Zoloft***). As the name of this class of drugs suggests, they selectively inhibit serotonin reuptake by presynaptic terminals. In all three classes, the result is an increased concentration of serotonin and (except for the third class) norepinephrine in the extracellular fluid at synapses. SSRIs are currently the most commonly prescribed of the three types, due to a better safety record and fewer side effects and interactions with other medications. Recent research suggests that combining psychotherapy with drug therapy provides the maximum benefit to most patients with depression.

The biochemical effects of antidepressant medications occur immediately, but the beneficial antidepressant effects usually appear only after several weeks of treatment. Thus, the known biochemical effect must be only an early step in a complex sequence that leads to a therapeutic effect of these drugs. Consistent with the long latency of the antidepressant effect is the recent evidence that these drugs may ultimately stimulate the growth of new neurons in the hippocampus. Chronic stress is a known trigger of depression in some people, and it has also been shown to inhibit neurogenesis in animals. In addition, careful measurements of the hippocampus in chronically depressed patients show that it tends to be smaller than in matched, nondepressed individuals. Finally, though antidepressant drugs normally have measurable effects on behavior in animal models of depression, it was recently shown that those effects disappear completely when steps are taken to prevent neurogenesis.

Alternative treatments used when drug therapy and psychotherapy are not effective include electrical stimulation of the brain. One such treatment is ***electroconvulsive therapy*** (***ECT***). As the name suggests, pulses of electrical current applied through the skull are used to activate a large number of neurons in the brain simultaneously, thereby inducing a convulsion, or seizure. The patient is under anesthesia and prepared with a muscle relaxant to minimize the effects of the convulsion on the musculoskeletal system. A series of ECT treatments is believed to act via changes in neurotransmitter function by causing changes in the sensitivity of certain serotonin and adrenergic postsynaptic receptors. Despite good evidence that it can be an effective treatment, ECT tends to be utilized as a treatment of last resort in patients with depression or bipolar disorder who do not respond to medication.

A more recent alternative to drug therapy used to treat depression involves stimulation of the brain with electromagnets and is called ***repetitive transcranial magnetic stimulation (rTMS)***. In rTMS, circular or figure-eight-shaped metallic coils are placed against the skull overlying specific brain regions; then, brief, powerful electrical currents are applied at frequencies between 1 and 25 pulses per second. The resulting magnetic field induces current to flow through cortical neuronal networks directly beneath the coil. The immediate effect is similar to ECT—neural activity is transiently disordered or sometimes silenced in that brain region. However, no anesthesia is required and no pain, convulsion, or memory loss occurs. Depending on the frequency and treatment regimen applied, the lasting effects of rTMS can cause either an increase or a decrease in the overall activity of the targeted area. In recent clinical trials, 2 to 4 weeks of daily rTMS stimulation of the left prefrontal cortex resulted in marked improvement of patients with major depression who had not responded to medication. However, rTMS has not yet shown the same level of clinical effectiveness as ECT. Medical scientists are hopeful that refinements in rTMS techniques in the future could lead to breakthroughs in the treatment of obsessive-compulsive disorder, mania, schizophrenia, and other psychiatric illnesses.

Another nondrug therapy used for the type of annual depression known as ***seasonal affective depressive disorder (SADD)*** is ***phototherapy,*** which exposes the patient to bright light for several hours per day during the winter months. Although light is thought to relieve depression by suppressing melatonin secretion from the pineal gland, as yet there is little evidence to support this claim.

A major drug used in treating patients with bipolar disorder is the chemical element ***lithium*** (***Eskalith, Lithobid***), sometimes given in combination with anticonvulsant drugs. It is highly specific, normalizing both the manic and depressed moods and slowing down thinking and motor behavior without causing sedation. In addition, it decreases the severity of the swings between mania and depression that occur in the bipolar disorders. In some cases, lithium is even effective in depression not associated with mania. Although it has been used for more than 50 years, the mechanisms of lithium action are not completely understood. It may help because it interferes with the formation of signaling molecules of the inositol phosphate family, thereby decreasing the response of postsynaptic neurons to neurotransmitters that utilize this signal transduction pathway (Chapter 5). Lithium has also been found to chronically increase the rate of glutamate uptake at excitatory synapses, which would be expected to reduce excessive nervous system activity during manic episodes.

Psychoactive Substances, Dependence, and Tolerance

In the previous sections, we mentioned several drugs used to combat altered states of consciousness. Psychoactive substances are also used as "recreational" drugs in a deliberate attempt to elevate mood and produce unusual states of consciousness ranging from meditative states to hallucinations. Virtually all the psychoactive substances exert their actions either directly or indirectly by altering neurotransmitter–receptor interactions in the biogenic amine pathways, particularly those of dopamine. For example, the primary effect of cocaine comes from its ability to block the reuptake of dopamine into the presynaptic axon terminal. Psychoactive substances are often chemically similar to neurotransmitters such as dopamine, serotonin, and norepinephrine, and they interact with the receptors activated by these transmitters (**Figure 8.13**).

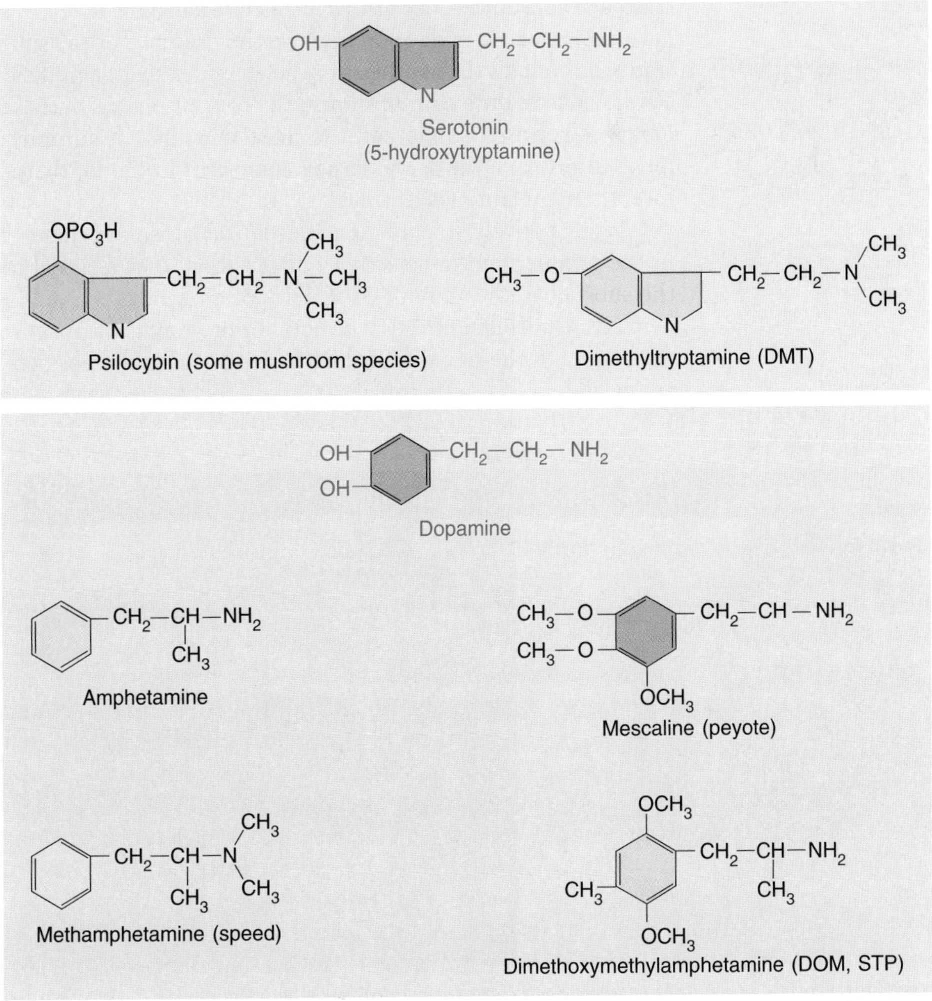

Serotonin (5-hydroxytryptamine)

Psilocybin (some mushroom species)

Dimethyltryptamine (DMT)

Dopamine

Amphetamine

Mescaline (peyote)

Methamphetamine (speed)

Dimethoxymethylamphetamine (DOM, STP)

Figure 8.13 Molecular similarities between neurotransmitters (orange) and some substances that elevate mood. At high doses, these substances can cause hallucinations.

PHYSIOLOGICAL INQUIRY

- How would you expect dimethyltryptamine (DMT) to affect sleeping behavior?

Answer can be found at end of chapter.

Dependence

Substance dependence, the term now preferred to *addiction,* has two facets that may occur either together or independently: (1) a ***psychological dependence*** that is experienced as a craving for a substance and an inability to stop using the substance at will; and (2) a ***physical dependence*** that requires one to take the substance to avoid ***withdrawal,*** which is the spectrum of unpleasant physiological symptoms that occur with cessation of substance use. Substance dependence is diagnosed if three or more of the characteristics listed in **Table 8.3** occur within a 12-month period. **Table 8.4** lists rates of use and risk of dependence for some commonly used substances.

TABLE 8.3 Diagnostic Criteria for Substance Dependence

Substance dependence is indicated when three or more of the following occur within a 12-month period.

I. Tolerance, as indicated by
   A. a need for increasing amounts of the substance to achieve the desired effect, or
   B. decreasing effects when continuing to use the same amount of the substance.

II. Withdrawal, as indicated by
   A. appearance of the characteristic withdrawal symptoms upon terminating use of the substance, or
   B. use of the substance (or one closely related to it) to relieve or avoid withdrawal symptoms.

III. Use of the substance in larger amounts or for longer periods of time than intended.

IV. Persistent desire for the substance; unsuccessful attempts to cut down or control use of the substance.

V. A great deal of time is spent in activities necessary to obtain the substance, use it, or recover from its effects.

VI. Occupational, social, or recreational activities are given up or reduced because of substance use.

VII. Use of the substance is continued despite knowledge that one has a physical or psychological problem that the substance is likely to exacerbate.

Table adapted from *The Diagnostic and Statistical Manual of Mental Disorders,* 4th ed., American Psychiatric Association, Arlington, VA, 2000.

Several neuronal systems are involved in substance dependence, but most psychoactive substances act on the mesolimbic dopamine pathway (see Figure 8.9). In addition to the actions of this system mentioned earlier in the context of motivation and emotion, the mesolimbic dopamine pathway allows a person to experience pleasure in response to pleasurable events or in response to certain substances. Although the major neurotransmitter implicated in substance dependence is dopamine, other neurotransmitters, including GABA, enkephalin, serotonin, and glutamate, can also be involved.

Tolerance

Tolerance to a substance occurs when increasing doses of the substance are required to achieve effects that initially occurred in response to a smaller dose. That is, it takes more of the substance to do the same job. Moreover, tolerance can develop to another substance as a result of taking the initial substance, a phenomenon called ***cross-tolerance.*** Cross-tolerance may develop if the physiological actions of the two substances are similar. Tolerance and cross-tolerance can occur with many classes of substances, not just psychoactive substances.

Tolerance may develop because the presence of the substance stimulates the synthesis of the enzymes that degrade it. With persistent use of a substance, the concentrations of these enzymes increase, so more of the substance must be administered to produce the same plasma concentrations and, therefore, the same initial effect.

Alternatively, tolerance can develop as a result of changes in the number and/or sensitivity of receptors that respond to the substance, the amount or activity of enzymes involved in neurotransmitter synthesis, the activity of reuptake transport molecules, or the signal transduction pathways in the postsynaptic cell.

TABLE 8.4 Substance Use and Dependence

Substance	Percentage of Population Using at Least Once	Percentage of Population Who Meet Dependence Criteria	Percentage of Those Using Who Become Dependent
Tobacco	75.6	24.1	31.9
Heroin	1.5	0.4	23.1
Cocaine	16.2	2.7	16.7
Alcohol	91.5	14.1	15.4
Amphetamines	15.3	1.7	11.2
Marijuana	46.3	4.2	9.1

Table adapted from Laurence L. Brunton, John S. Lazo, and Keither L. Parker, eds., *Goodman and Gilman's The Pharmacological Basis of Therapeutics,* 11th ed., McGraw-Hill, NY, 2006.

8.5 Learning and Memory

Learning is the acquisition and storage of information as a consequence of experience. It is measured by an increase in the likelihood of a particular behavioral response to a stimulus. Generally, rewards or punishments are crucial ingredients of learning, as are contact with and manipulation of the environment. **Memory** is the relatively permanent storage form of learned information, although, as we will see, it is not a single, unitary phenomenon. Rather, the brain processes, stores, and retrieves information in different ways to suit different needs.

Memory

The term **memory encoding** defines the neural processes that change an experience into the memory of that experience—in other words, the physiological events that lead to memory formation. This section addresses three questions. First, are there different kinds of memories? Second, where do they occur in the brain? Third, what happens physiologically to make them occur?

New scientific information about memory are being generated at a tremendous pace; there is as yet no unifying theory as to how memory is encoded, stored, and retrieved. However, memory can be viewed in two broad categories called declarative and procedural memory. **Declarative memory** (sometimes also referred to as "explicit" memory) is the retention and recall of conscious experiences that can be put into words (declared). One example is the memory of having perceived an object or event and, therefore, recognizing it as familiar and maybe even knowing the specific time and place when the memory originated. A second example would be the general knowledge of the world, such as names and facts. The hippocampus, amygdala, and other parts of the limbic system are required for the formation of declarative memories.

The second broad category of memory, **procedural memory,** can be defined as the memory of how to do things (sometimes this is also called "implicit" or "reflexive" memory). This is the memory for skilled behaviors independent of conscious understanding, as, for example, riding a bicycle. Individuals can suffer severe deficits in declarative memory but have intact procedural memory. One case study describes a pianist who learned a new piece to accompany a singer at a concert but had no recollection the following morning of having performed the composition. He could remember how to play the music but could not remember having done so. The category of procedural memory also includes learned emotional responses, such as fear of spiders, and the classic example of Pavlov's dogs, which learned to salivate at the sound of a bell after the sound had previously been associated with food. The primary areas of the brain involved in procedural memory are regions of sensorimotor cortex, the basal nuclei, and the cerebellum.

Another way to classify memory is in terms of duration—does it last for a long or only a short time? **Working memory,** also known as **short-term memory,** registers and retains incoming information for a short time—a matter of seconds to minutes—after its input. In other words, it is the memory that we use when we keep information consciously "in mind." For example, you may hear a telephone number in a radio advertisement and remember it only long enough to reach for your phone and enter the number. Working memory makes possible a temporary impression of one's present environment in a readily accessible form and is an essential ingredient of many forms of higher mental activity. Short-term memories may be converted into **long-term memories,** which may be stored for days to years and recalled at a later time. The process by which short-term memories become long-term memories is called **consolidation.**

Focusing attention is essential for many memory-based skills. The longer the span of attention in working memory, the better the chess player, the greater the ability to reason, and the better a student is at understanding complicated sentences and drawing inferences from texts. In fact, there is a strong correlation between working memory and standard measures of intelligence. Conversely, the specific memory deficit that occurs in the early stages of ***Alzheimer disease*** (also called Alzheimer's disease), a condition marked by dementia and serious memory losses, may be in this attention-focusing component of working memory.

The Neural Basis of Learning and Memory

The neural mechanism and parts of the brain involved vary for different types of memory. Short-term encoding and long-term memory storage occur in different brain areas for both declarative and procedural memories (**Figure 8.14**).

What is happening during memory formation on a cellular level? Conditions such as coma, deep anesthesia, electroconvulsive shock, and insufficient blood supply to the brain, all of which interfere with the electrical activity of the brain, also interfere with working memory. Therefore, it is assumed that

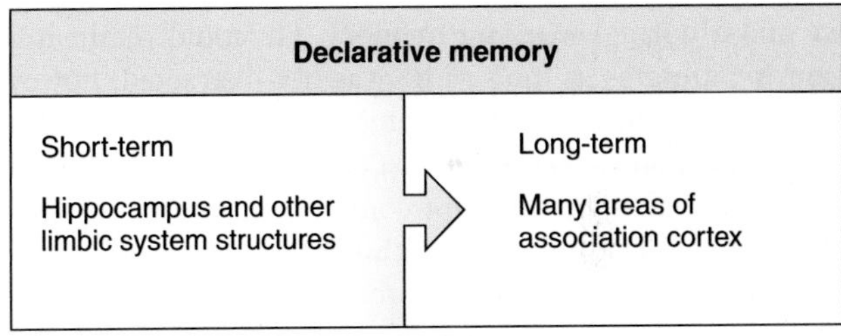

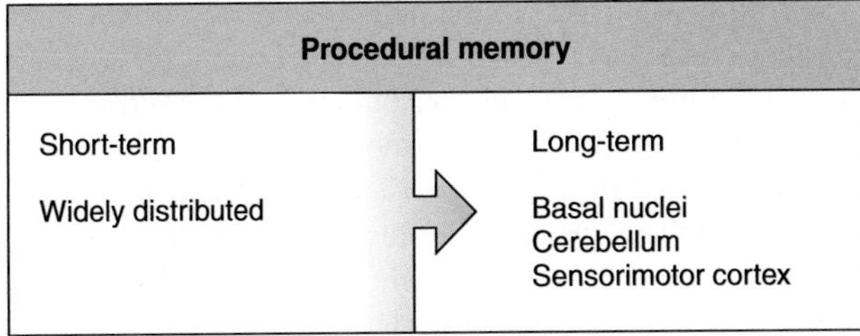

Figure 8.14 Brain areas involved in encoding and storage of declarative and procedural memories.

PHYSIOLOGICAL INQUIRY

- After a brief meeting, you are more likely to remember the name of someone you are strongly attracted to than the name of someone for whom you have no feelings. Propose a mechanism.

Answer can be found at end of chapter.

working memory requires ongoing graded or action potentials. Working memory is interrupted when a person becomes unconscious from a blow on the head, and memories are abolished for all that happened for a variable period of time before the blow, a condition called ***retrograde amnesia.*** (***Amnesia*** is the loss of memory.) Working memory is also susceptible to external interference, such as an attempt to learn conflicting information. On the other hand, long-term memory can survive deep anesthesia, trauma, or electroconvulsive shock, all of which disrupt the normal patterns of neural conduction in the brain. Thus, working memory requires electrical activity in the neurons.

Another type of amnesia is referred to as ***anterograde amnesia.*** It results from damage to the limbic system and associated structures, including the hippocampus, thalamus, and hypothalamus. Patients with this condition lose their ability to consolidate short-term declarative memories into long-term memories. Although they can remember stored information and events that occurred before their brain injury, after the injury they can only retain information as long as it exists in working memory. This type of amnesia is sometimes transiently induced pharmacologically during medical procedures for which patients are required to remain conscious, such as colonoscopy (see Chapter 15). The most common drugs used to produce this "conscious sedation" stimulate GABA receptors.

The case of a patient known as H.M. illustrates that formation of declarative and procedural memories involves distinct neural processes and that limbic system structures are essential for consolidating declarative memories. In 1953, H.M. underwent bilateral removal of the amygdala and large parts of the hippocampus as a treatment for persistent, debilitating epilepsy. Although his epileptic condition improved after this surgery, it resulted in anterograde amnesia. He still had a normal intelligence and a normal working memory. He could retain information for minutes as long as he was not distracted; however, he could not form long-term memories. If he was introduced to someone on one day, on the next day he did not recall having previously met that person. Nor could he remember any events that occurred after his surgery, although his memory for events prior to the surgery was intact. Interestingly, H.M. had normal procedural memory and could learn new puzzles and motor tasks as readily as normal individuals. This case was the first to draw attention to the critical importance of temporal lobe structures of the limbic system in consolidating short-term declarative memories into long-term memories. Additional cases since have demonstrated that the hippocampus is the primary structure involved in this process. Because H.M. retained memories from before the surgery, his case showed that the hippocampus is not involved in the *storage* of declarative memories.

The problem of exactly how memories are stored in the brain is still unsolved, but some of the pieces of the puzzle are falling into place. One model for memory is **long-term potentiation (LTP)**, in which certain synapses undergo a long-lasting increase in their effectiveness when they are heavily used. Review Figure 6.36, which details how this occurs at glutamatergic synapses. An analogous process, **long-term depression (LTD)**, *decreases* the effectiveness of synaptic contacts between neurons. The mechanism of this suppression of activity appears to be mainly via changes in the channels in the postsynaptic membrane.

It is generally accepted that long-term memory formation involves processes that alter gene expression. This is achieved by a cascade of second messengers and transcription factors that ultimately leads to the production of new cellular proteins. These new proteins may be involved in the increased number of synapses that have been demonstrated after long-term memory formation. They may also be involved in structural changes in individual synapses (e.g., by an increase in the number of receptors on the postsynaptic membrane). This ability of neural tissue to change because of activation is known as **plasticity.**

Certain types of learning depend not only on factors such as attention, motivation, and various neurotransmitters but also on certain hormones. For example, the hormones epinephrine, ACTH, and vasopressin affect the retention of learned experiences. These hormones are normally released in stressful or mildly stimulating circumstances, suggesting that the hormonal consequences of our experiences affect our memories of them.

Two of the opioid peptides, enkephalin and endorphin (see Chapter 6, Section C), interfere with learning and memory, particularly when the lesson involves a painful stimulus. They may inhibit learning simply because they decrease the emotional (fear, anxiety) component of the painful experience associated with the learning situation, thereby decreasing the motivation necessary for learning to occur.

Table 8.5 summarizes some general principles about learning and memory.

8.6 Cerebral Dominance and Language

The two cerebral hemispheres appear to be nearly symmetrical, but each has anatomical, chemical, and functional specializations. We have already mentioned that the left hemisphere deals with the somatosensory and motor functions of the right side of the body, and vice versa. In addition, specific aspects of language use tend to be controlled by predominantly one cerebral hemisphere or the other. In 90% of the population, the left hemisphere is specialized to handle specific tasks involved in

TABLE 8.5 General Principles of Learning and Memory
There are multiple memory systems in the brain.
Short-term and long-term forms of learning and memory involve changes in existing neural circuits.
These changes may involve multiple cellular mechanisms within individual neurons.
Second-messenger systems play a role in mediating cellular changes.
Changes in membrane channels are often correlated with learning and memory.
Long-term memory requires new protein synthesis, whereas short-term memory does not.

Table adapted from John H. Byrne, "Learning and Memory: Basic Mechanisms," in Larry R. Squire, Darwin Berg, Floyd E. Bloom, Sascha du Lac, Anirvan Ghosh, and Nicholas C. Spitzer, eds., *Fundamental Neuroscience*, Academic Press, San Diego, CA, 2008.

producing and comprehending language—the conceptualization of the words you want to say or write, the neural control of the act of speaking or writing, and recent verbal memory. This is even true of the sign language used by some deaf people. Conversely, the right cerebral hemisphere in most people tends to have dominance in determining the ability to understand and express affective, or emotional aspects of language.

Language is a complex code that includes the acts of listening, seeing, reading, speaking, and expressing emotion. The major centers for the technical aspects of language function are in the left hemisphere in the temporal, parietal, and frontal cortex next to the **Sylvian fissure,** which separates the temporal lobe from the frontal and parietal lobes (**Figure 8.15**). Each of the various regions deals with a separate aspect of language. For example, distinct areas are specialized for hearing, seeing, speaking, and generating words (**Figure 8.16**). There are even distinct brain networks for different categories of things, such as "animals" and "tools." Although the regions responsible for the affective components of language have not been as specifically mapped, it appears they are in the same general region of the right cerebral hemisphere. There is variation between individuals in the regional processing of language, and some research even suggests that males and females may process language slightly differently. Females are more likely to involve areas of both hemispheres for some language tasks, whereas males generally show activity mainly on the left side (**Figure 8.17**). The cerebellum is also important in speaking and writing, because those tasks involve coordinated muscle contractions.

Much of our knowledge about how language is produced has been obtained from patients who have suffered brain damage and, as a result, have one or more defects in language, including ***aphasia*** (from the Greek, "speechlessness") and ***aprosodia.*** (**Prosody** includes aspects of communication such as intonation, rhythm, pitch, emphasis, gestures, and accompanying facial expressions, so aprosodia refers to the absence of those aspects.)

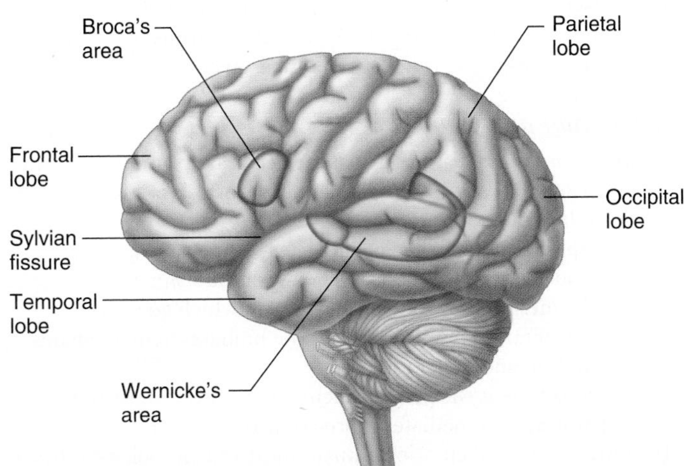

Figure 8.15 AP|R Areas of the left cerebral hemisphere found clinically to be involved in the comprehension (Wernicke's area) and motor (Broca's area) aspects of language. Blue lines indicate divisions of the cortex into frontal, parietal, temporal, and occipital lobes. Similar regions on the right side of the brain are involved in understanding and expressing affective (emotional) aspects of language.

The specific defects that occur vary according to the region of the brain that is damaged. For example, damage to the left temporal region known as **Wernicke's area** (see Figure 8.15) generally results in aphasias that are more closely related to *comprehension*—the individuals have difficulty understanding spoken or written language even though their hearing and vision are unimpaired. Although they may have fluent speech, they scramble words so that their sentences make no sense, often adding unnecessary words, or even creating made-up words. For example, they may intend to ask someone on a date but say, "If when going movie by fleeble because have to watch would."

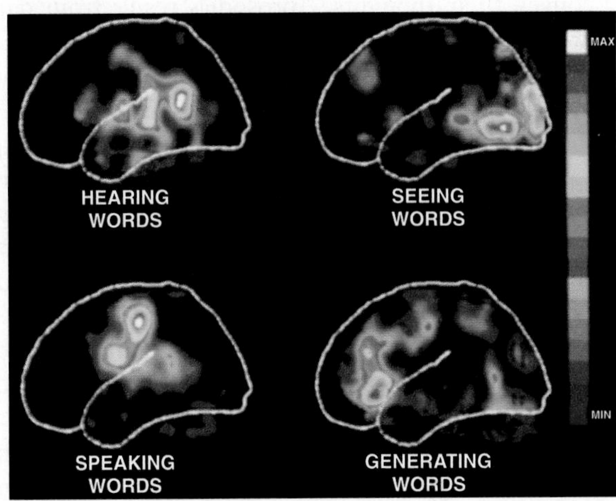

Figure 8.16 AP|R PET scans reveal areas of increased blood flow in specific parts of the temporal, occipital, parietal, and frontal lobes during various language-based activities. Courtesy of Dr. Marcus E. Raichle.

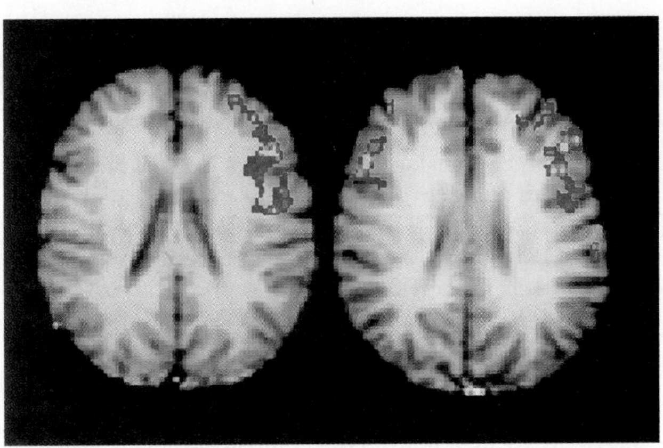

Figure 8.17 AP|R Images of the active areas of the brain in a male (left) and a female (right) during a language task. (In scans of this type, the patient's left is displayed on the right of the image.) Note that both sides of the woman's brain are used in processing language, but the man's brain is more compartmentalized. Shaywitz et al., 1995 NMR Research/Yale Medical School.

PHYSIOLOGICAL INQUIRY

- Based on typical patterns of cerebral dominance of language tasks, how may you explain the difference in how these two individuals processed this task?

Answer can be found at end of chapter.

They are often unaware that they are not speaking in clear sentences. In contrast, damage to **Broca's area,** the language area in the frontal cortex responsible for the articulation of speech, can cause *expressive* aphasias. Individuals with this condition have difficulty carrying out the coordinated respiratory and oral movements necessary for language even though they can move their lips and tongues. They understand spoken language and know what they want to say but have trouble forming words and sentences. For example, instead of fluidly saying, "I have two sisters," they may hesitantly utter, "Two . . . sister . . . sister." Patients with damage to Broca's area can become frustrated because they generally are aware that their words do not accurately convey their thoughts. Aprosodias result from damage to language areas in the right cerebral hemisphere or to neural pathways connecting the left and right hemispheres. Though they can form and understand words and sentences, people with these conditions have impaired ability to interpret or express emotional intentions, and their social interactions suffer greatly as a result. For example, they may not be able to distinguish whether a person who said "thank you very much" was expressing genuine appreciation for a thoughtful compliment or delivering a sarcastic retort after feeling insulted.

The potential for the development of language-specific mechanisms in the two hemispheres is present at birth, but the assignment of language functions to specific brain areas is fairly flexible in the early years of life. Thus, for example, damage to the language areas of the left hemisphere during infancy or early childhood causes temporary, minor language impairment until the right hemisphere can take over. However, similar damage acquired during adulthood typically causes permanent, devastating language deficits. By puberty, the brain's ability to transfer language functions between hemispheres is less successful, and often language skills are lost permanently.

Differences between the two hemispheres are usually masked by the integration that occurs via the corpus callosum and other pathways that connect the two sides of the brain. However, the separate functions of the left and right hemispheres have been uncovered by studying patients in whom the two hemispheres have been separated surgically for treatment of severe epilepsy. These so-called **split-brain** patients participated in studies in which they were asked to hold and identify an object such as a ball in their left or right hand behind a barrier that prevented them from seeing the object. Subjects who held the ball in their right hand were able to say that it was a ball, but persons who held the ball in their left hand were unable to name it. Because the processing of sensory information occurs on the side of the brain opposite to the sensation, this result demonstrated conclusively that the left hemisphere contains a language center that is not present in the right hemisphere.

Although language skills emerge spontaneously in children in all societies, there is a critical period during childhood when exposure to language is necessary for these skills to develop, just as the ability to see depends upon effective visual input early in life. The critical period is thought to end at puberty or earlier. The dramatic change at puberty in the possibility of learning language, or the ease of learning a second language, occurs as the brain attains its structural, biochemical, and functional maturity at that time.

SUMMARY

States of Consciousness

I. The electroencephalogram (EEG) provides one means of defining the states of consciousness.
   a. Electrical currents in the cerebral cortex due predominantly to summed postsynaptic potentials are recorded as the EEG.
   b. Slower EEG wave frequencies correlate with less responsive behaviors.
   c. Rhythm generators in the thalamus are probably responsible for the wavelike nature of the EEG.
   d. EEGs are used to diagnose brain disease and damage.

II. Alpha rhythms and, during EEG arousal, beta rhythms characterize the EEG of an awake person.

III. NREM sleep progresses from stage N1 (higher-frequency, smaller-amplitude waves) through stage N3 (lower-frequency, larger-amplitude waves) and then back again, followed by an episode of REM sleep. There are generally four or five of these cycles per night.

IV. Wakefulness is stimulated by regulated by groups of neurons originating in the brainstem and hypothalamus that activate cortical arousal by releasing orexins, norepinephrine, serotonin, histamine, and acetylcholine. A sleep center in the hypothalamus releases GABA and inhibits these activating centers.

V. Extensive damage to the cerebral cortex or brainstem arousal mechanisms can result in coma or brain death.

Conscious Experiences

I. Brain structures involved in selective attention determine which brain areas gain temporary predominance in the ongoing stream of conscious experience.

II. Conscious experiences may occur because a set of neurons temporarily function together, with the neurons that compose the set changing as the focus of attention changes.

Motivation and Emotion

I. Behaviors that satisfy homeostatic needs are primary motivated behaviors. Behavior not related to homeostasis is a result of secondary motivation.
   a. Repetition of a behavior indicates it is rewarding, and avoidance of a behavior indicates it is punishing.
   b. The mesolimbic dopamine pathway, which goes to prefrontal cortex and parts of the limbic system, mediates emotion and motivation.
   c. Dopamine is the primary neurotransmitter in the brain pathway that mediates motivation and reward.

II. Three aspects of emotion—anatomical and physiological bases for emotion, emotional behavior, and inner emotions—can be distinguished. The limbic system integrates inner emotions and behavior.

Altered States of Consciousness

I. Hyperactivity in a brain dopaminergic system is implicated in schizophrenia.

II. Mood disorders may be caused by disturbances in transmission at brain synapses mediated by dopamine, norepinephrine, serotonin, and acetylcholine.
III. Many psychoactive drugs, which are often chemically related to neurotransmitters, result in substance dependence, withdrawal, and tolerance. The mesolimbic dopamine pathway is implicated in substance abuse.

Learning and Memory

I. The brain processes, stores, and retrieves information in different ways to suit different needs.
II. Memory encoding involves cellular or molecular changes specific to different memories.
III. Declarative memories are involved in remembering facts and events. Procedural memories are memories of how to do things.
IV. Short-term memories are converted into long-term memories by a process known as consolidation.
V. Prefrontal cortex and limbic regions of the temporal lobe are important brain areas for some forms of memory.
VI. Formation of long-term memory probably involves changes in second-messenger systems and protein synthesis.

Cerebral Dominance and Language

I. The two cerebral hemispheres differ anatomically, chemically, and functionally. In 90% of the population, the left hemisphere dominates the technical aspects of language production and comprehension such as word meanings and sentence structure, while the right hemisphere dominates in mediating the emotional content of language.
II. The development of language functions occurs in a critical period that ends around the time of puberty.
III. After damage to the dominant hemisphere, the opposite hemisphere can acquire some language function—the younger the patient, the greater the transfer of function.

REVIEW QUESTIONS

1. State the two criteria used to define one's state of consciousness.
2. What type of neural activity is recorded as the EEG?
3. Draw EEG records that show alpha and beta rhythms, the stages of NREM sleep, and REM sleep. Indicate the characteristic wave frequencies of each.
4. Distinguish NREM sleep from REM sleep.
5. Briefly describe a neural mechanism that determines the states of consciousness.
6. Name the criteria used to distinguish brain death from coma.
7. Describe the orienting response as a form of directed attention.
8. Distinguish primary from secondary motivated behavior.
9. Explain how rewards and punishments are anatomically related to emotions.
10. Explain what brain self-stimulation can tell about emotions and rewards and punishments.
11. Name the primary neurotransmitter that mediates the brain reward systems.
12. Distinguish inner emotions from emotional behavior. Name the brain areas involved in each.
13. Describe the role of the limbic system in emotions.
14. Name the major neurotransmitters involved in schizophrenia and the mood disorders.
15. Describe a mechanism that could explain tolerance and withdrawal.
16. Distinguish the types of memory.

KEY TERMS

alpha rhythm 236
beta rhythm 236
brain self-stimulation 243
Broca's area 252
conscious experience 235
consolidation 249
declarative memory 249
delta rhythm 236
EEG arousal 236
electroencephalogram (EEG) 235
emotional behavior 244
gamma rhythm 236
habituation 241
hypnic jerk 237
hypocretins 239
inner emotion 244
K complex 236
learning 249
long-term depression (LTD) 250
long-term memory 249
long-term potentiation (LTP) 250
memory 249
memory encoding 249
mesolimbic dopamine pathway 243
mood 246
motivation 243
NREM sleep 236
orexins 239
orienting response 241
paradoxical sleep 237
plasticity 250
preattentive processing 241
primary motivated behavior 243
procedural memory 249
prosody 251
REM sleep 236
reticular activating system (RAS) 239
selective attention 241
short-term memory 249
sleep spindles 236
states of consciousness 235
Sylvian fissure 251
theta rhythm 236
Wernicke's area 251
working memory 249

CLINICAL TERMS

alprazolam (Xanax) 239
altered states of consciousness 246
Alzheimer disease 249
amitriptyline (Elavil) 246
amnesia 250
anterograde amnesia 250
aphasia 251
aprosodia 251
attention-deficit/hyperactivity disorder (AD/HD) 242
benzodiazepines 239
bipolar disorder 246
brain death 241
catatonia 246
coma 240
concussion 253
cross-tolerance 248
Cushing's phenomenon 253
depressive disorder (depression) 246
desipramine (Norpramin) 246
diazepam (Valium) 239
doxepin (Sinequan) 246
electroconvulsive therapy (ECT) 246
epidural hematoma 253
epilepsy 236
erectile dysfunction (ED) 238
escitalopram (Lexapro) 246
fluoxetine (Prozac) 246
intracranial hemorrhage 253
lithium (Eskalith, Lithobid) 247
magnetic resonance imaging (MRI) 236
mania 246
methylphenidate (Ritalin) 242
monoamine oxidase inhibitor 246
mood disorder 246
narcolepsy 239
paroxetine (Paxil) 246
persistent vegetative state 241
phototherapy 247
physical dependence 248
positron emission tomography (PET) 236
psychological dependence 248
repetitive transcranial magnetic stimulation (rTMS) 247
retrograde amnesia 250
schizophrenia 246
seasonal affective depressive disorder (SADD) 247
sensory neglect 243
serotonin-specific reuptake inhibitor (SSRI) 246
sertraline (Zoloft) 246
sleep apnea 237
split brain 252
subdural hematoma 253
substance dependence 248
tolerance 248
tricyclic antidepressant drug 246
Urbach–Wiethe disease 245
withdrawal 248

Clinical Case Study: Head Injury in a Teenage Soccer Player

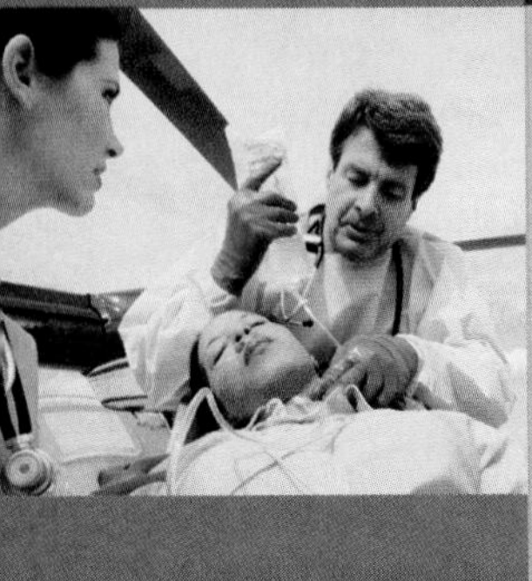

In the final minute of the high-school state championship match, with the score tied 1 to 1, the corner kick sailed toward the far post. Lunging for a header and the win, the 17-year-old midfielder was kicked solidly in the right side of her head by a defender. She crumpled to the ground and lay motionless. The team physician rushed onto the field, where the girl lay on her back with her eyes closed. She was breathing normally but failed to respond to the sound of her name or a touch on her arm. An ambulance was immediately summoned. After a few moments, her eyes fluttered open, and she looked up at the doctor and her teammates with a confused expression on her face. Asked how she was feeling, she said "fine" and attempted to sit up but winced in pain and put her hand to her head as the physician told her to remain lying down. It was an encouraging sign that all four limbs and her trunk muscles had moved normally in her attempt to sit up, suggesting she did not have a serious injury to her spinal cord.

The physician then asked her a series of questions. Did she remember how she had been injured? She responded with a blank look and a small shake of her head. Did she know what day this was and where she was? After a long pause and a look at her surroundings, she replied that it was Saturday and this was the championship soccer match. How much time was left in the game, and what was the score? Another long pause, and then "It's almost halftime, and it's zero to zero." Before he could ask the next question, her eyes rolled back in their sockets and her body stiffened for several seconds, after which she once again looked around with a confused expression.

These signs suggested that she had suffered an injury to her brain and should undergo a thorough neurological exam. The ambulance arrived, she was placed on a rigid backboard with her head supported and restrained, and she was transported to the hospital for further assessment and observation.

By the time she reached the emergency room, she was less disoriented and had no nausea but still complained that her head hurt. Her pulse rate and blood pressure were normal. A series of neurological tests was then performed. When a light was shone into either eye, both pupils constricted equally. She was also able to smoothly track a moving object with her eyes. Her sense of balance was good, and she was able to feel a vibrating tuning fork, light pinpricks, and warm and cold objects on the skin of all of her extremities. Muscle tone, strength, and reflexes were also normal. Asked again about the collision, she still was unsure what had happened. However, suddenly straightening in her chair, she said, "Wait—the game was almost over and we were tied one to one. . . . Did we win?"

The blow to this soccer player's head resulted in a ***concussion,*** an injury suffered by more than 300,000 athletes each year in the United States. Concussion is a usually brief loss of consciousness that occurs after some form of head trauma. It sometimes results in temporary retrograde amnesia, which varies in extent with the severity of the injury, and also in brief epileptic-like seizures. The mechanism of the loss of consciousness, amnesia, and seizures is thought to be a transient electrophysiological dysfunction of the reticular activating system in the upper midbrain caused by rotation of the cerebral hemispheres on the relatively fixed brainstem. The relatively large size and inertia of the brains of humans and other primates make them especially susceptible to such injuries. By comparison, animals adapted for cranial impact like goats, rams, and woodpeckers are able to withstand 100-fold greater force than humans without sustaining injury. Computed tomography and magnetic resonance imaging scans of most concussion patients show no abnormal swelling or vascular injury of the brain. However, widespread reports of persistent memory and concentration problems have increasingly raised concerns that in some cases concussion injuries may involve lasting damage in the form of microscopic shearing lesions in the brain. Quantitative analysis of EEG recordings is currently under investigation for its usefulness in the acute diagnosis of concussion and for the post-concussion monitoring of brain function.

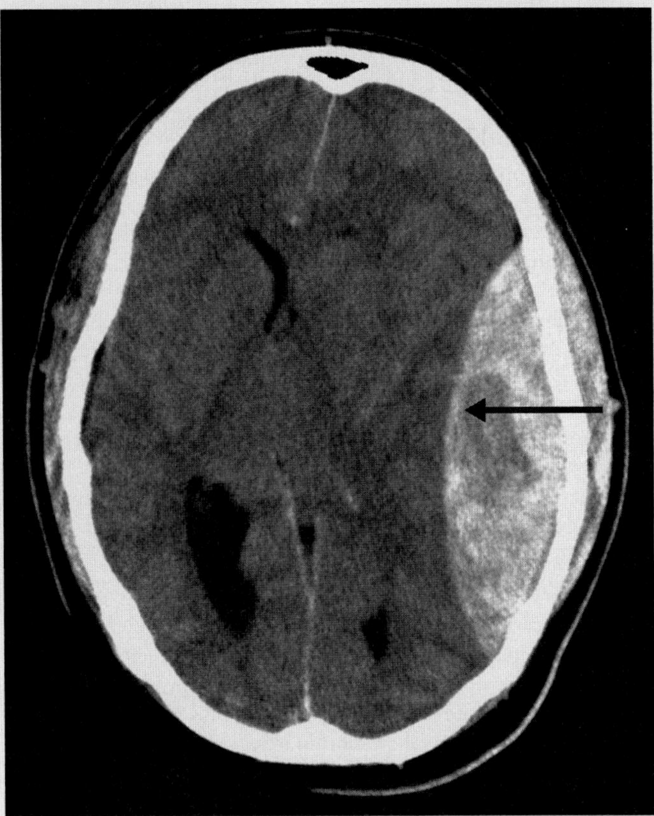

Figure 8.18 CT scan of a large, left-side epidural hematoma resulting from a motorcycle crash in which the rider was not wearing a helmet. Arrow shows where blood pooling within the cranium has compressed the brain tissue. Patient's left side is on the right side of the image. Courtesy of Lee Faucher, M.D., University of Wisconsin SMPH.

More serious than a concussion is ***intracranial hemorrhage,*** which results from damage to blood vessels in and around the brain. It can be associated with skull fracture, violent shaking, and sudden accelerative forces such as those that would occur during an automobile accident. Blood may collect between the skull and the dura mater (an ***epidural hematoma,* Figure 8.18**), or between the arachnoid mater and the surrounding meninges or within the brain (***subdural hematoma***). Intracranial hemorrhage often occurs without loss of consciousness; symptoms such as nausea, headache,

(continued)

(continued)

motor dysfunction, and loss of pupillary reflexes may not occur until several hours or days afterward. Another symptom of brain swelling after vascular trauma is ***Cushing's phenomenon,*** in which systemic blood pressure is markedly elevated (see Chapter 12, Section D). It is treated when necessary by drainage of the blood from the affected area. One reason that it is important to closely monitor the condition of a person with concussion for some time after the injury is to be able to recognize whether the initial trauma has resulted in an intracranial hemorrhage.

The soccer player in this case was given pain medication and kept in the hospital overnight for observation. She suffered no further seizures, and by morning her memory had completely returned and other neurological test results were normal. She was sent home with instructions to return for a follow-up examination the next week, or sooner if her headache did not steadily improve. She was also advised to avoid competing for a minimum of 2 weeks. A person who receives a second blow to the head prior to complete healing of a first concussion injury has an elevated risk of suffering life-threatening brain swelling.

Concussion injuries in sports are receiving increased attention. Some neurologists suspect that concussions have the potential to cause long-term physical, cognitive, and psychological changes, and that the risk is magnified in those who experience multiple concussions. Suspicions have been fueled by high-profile cases of professional boxers who have developed symptoms similar to those seen in the neurodegenerative conditions Parkinson disease (see Chapter 10) and Alzheimer disease (see Chapter 6). Recent histological studies of the brains of deceased professional football players have shown significant microscopic damage in those who have suffered multiple concussions. Even more disconcerting are the recent findings in teenage football players, that milder repetitive blows to the head that do not meet the clinical criteria of a concussion may also lead to lasting brain damage. To address issues such as these, research is currently under way in which athletes are being assessed for attention span, memory, processing speed, and reaction time—both before and after suffering concussions. Other initiatives include developing more sensitive diagnostic tests, creating guidelines on when to allow athletes to return to competition following a head injury, and the design of protective headgear.

Clinical terms: concussion, Cushing's phenomenon, epidural hematoma, intracranial hemorrhage, subdural hematoma

See Chapter 19 for complete, integrative case studies.

CHAPTER 8 TEST QUESTIONS

Answers found in Appendix A.

1–4: Match the state of consciousness (a–d) with the correct electroencephalogram pattern (use each answer once).

State of consciousness:

a. relaxed, awake, eyes closed
b. stage N3 non–rapid eye movement (NREM) sleep
c. rapid eye movement (REM) sleep
d. epileptic seizure

Electroencephalogram pattern:

1. Very large-amplitude, recurrent waves, associated with sharp spikes
2. Small-amplitude, high-frequency waves, similar to the attentive awake state
3. Irregular, slow-frequency, large-amplitude, "alpha" rhythm
4. Regular, very slow-frequency, very large-amplitude "delta" rhythm
5. Which pattern of neurotransmitter activity is most consistent with the awake state?
   a. high histamine, orexins and GABA; low norepinephrine
   b. high norepinephrine, histamine and serotonin; low orexins
   c. high histamine and serotonin; low GABA and orexins
   d. high histamine, GABA and orexins; low serotonin
   e. high orexins, histamine and norepinephrine; low GABA
6. Which best describes "habituation"?
   a. seeking out and focusing on momentarily important stimuli
   b. decreased behavioral response to a persistent irrelevant stimulus
   c. halting current activity and orienting toward a novel stimulus
   d. evaluation of the importance of sensory stimuli that occur prior to focusing attention
   e. strengthening of synapses that are repeatedly stimulated during learning
7. The mesolimbic dopamine pathway is most closely associated with
   a. shifting between states of consciousness.
   b. emotional behavior.
   c. motivation and reward behaviors.
   d. perception of fear.
   e. primary visual perception.
8. Antidepressant medications most commonly target what neurotransmitter?
   a. acetylcholine
   b. dopamine
   c. histamine
   d. serotonin
   e. glutamate
9. Which is a true statement about memory?
   a. Consolidation converts short-term memories into long-term memories.
   b. Working memory stores information for years, perhaps indefinitely.
   c. In retrograde amnesia, the ability to form new memories is lost.
   d. The cerebellum is an important site of storage for declarative memory.
   e. Destruction of the hippocampus erases all previously stored memories.

10. Broca's area
    a. is in the parietal association cortex and is responsible for language comprehension.
    b. is in the right frontal lobe and is responsible for memory formation.
    c. is in the left frontal lobe and is responsible for articulation of speech.
    d. is in the occipital lobe and is responsible for interpreting body language.
    e. is part of the limbic system and is responsible for the perception of fear.

CHAPTER 8 GENERAL PRINCIPLES ASSESSMENT

Answers found in Appendix A.

1. Review the general principles of physiology presented in Chapter 1. Which of those eight principles is best demonstrated by the two parts of Figure 8.7, and why?
2. How does the regulation of sleep exemplify the general principle of physiology that *homeostasis is essential for health and survival?*

CHAPTER 8 QUANTITATIVE AND THOUGHT QUESTIONS

Answers found in Appendix A.

1. Explain why patients given drugs to treat Parkinson disease (Chapter 6) sometimes develop symptoms similar to those of schizophrenia.
2. Explain how clinical observations of individuals with various aphasias help physiologists understand the neural basis of language.

CHAPTER 8 ANSWERS TO PHYSIOLOGICAL INQUIRIES

Figure 8.1 If the frequency of the waveform is 20 Hz (20 waves per second), then the duration of each wave is 1/20 sec, or 50 msec.

Figure 8.2 The primary visual cortex and related association areas are in the occipital lobes of the brain (review Figure 7.13), so it is most likely that this abnormal rhythm was recorded by electrodes placed on the scalp at the back of the patient's head.

Figure 8.6 Among the drugs used to treat allergic reactions are antihistamines. They are prescribed because of their ability to block histamine's contributions to the inflammatory response, which include vasodilation and leakiness of small blood vessels (see Table 18.12). Because a decrease in histamine is associated with the induction of NREM sleep, drowsiness is a common side effect of antihistamines. Fortunately, antihistamines have been developed that do not cross the blood–brain barrier and thus do not have this side effect (e.g., loratadine [Claritin, Alavert]).

Figure 8.7 There are a number of possible reasons it may be adaptive for cytokines to induce sleep. For example, the decreased physical activity associated with sleep may conserve metabolic energy when running a fever and fighting an infection. Sleeping more and eating less may also help by decreasing intake and plasma concentrations of specific nutrients needed by invading organisms to replicate, like iron (see Chapter 1). From a population health perspective, more time spent in sleep may be adaptive by reducing the number of others with which an infected person comes into contact.

Figure 8.11 There are many ways emotions could potentially contribute to survival and reproduction. The perception of fear aids survival by stimulating avoidance or caution in potentially dangerous situations, like coming into contact with potentially venomous spiders or snakes or walking near the edge of a high cliff. Our tendency to be disgusted by the smell of rotting food and fecal matter might have evolved as a protection against infection by potentially harmful bacteria or pathogens. Anger and rage could contribute to both survival and reproduction by facilitating our ability to fight for mates or territory or for self-defense. Emotions like happiness and love might have been selected for because of the advantage they provided in kinship safety and pair bonding with mates.

Figure 8.13 An increase in serotonin concentrations is associated with the waking state (refer back to Figure 8.7), so sleep is inhibited by DMT and other drugs that simulate serotonin action. For this same reason, sleeplessness is also a common side effect of antidepressant medications discussed earlier in the text (e.g., serotonin-specific reuptake inhibitors) because they increase serotonin levels in the brain.

Figure 8.14 The involvement of the limbic system in the formation of declarative memories (like remembering names) provides a clue. Experiences that generate strong emotional responses cause greater activity in the limbic system and are more likely to be remembered than emotionally neutral experiences. Also, much like a rat that repeatedly presses a bar to stimulate the mesolimbic dopamine pathway (see Figure 8.10), you may internally rehearse the name of a person who attracts you.

Figure 8.17 The left side of the brain is responsible for technical aspects of language like the definitions of words, sentence construction, and motor programs for speaking; the right side of the brain is responsible for encoding and expressing affective, or emotional, aspects. The individual showing right-hemisphere activity might have invested greater emotional content in the language task than the individual showing only left-hemisphere activity.

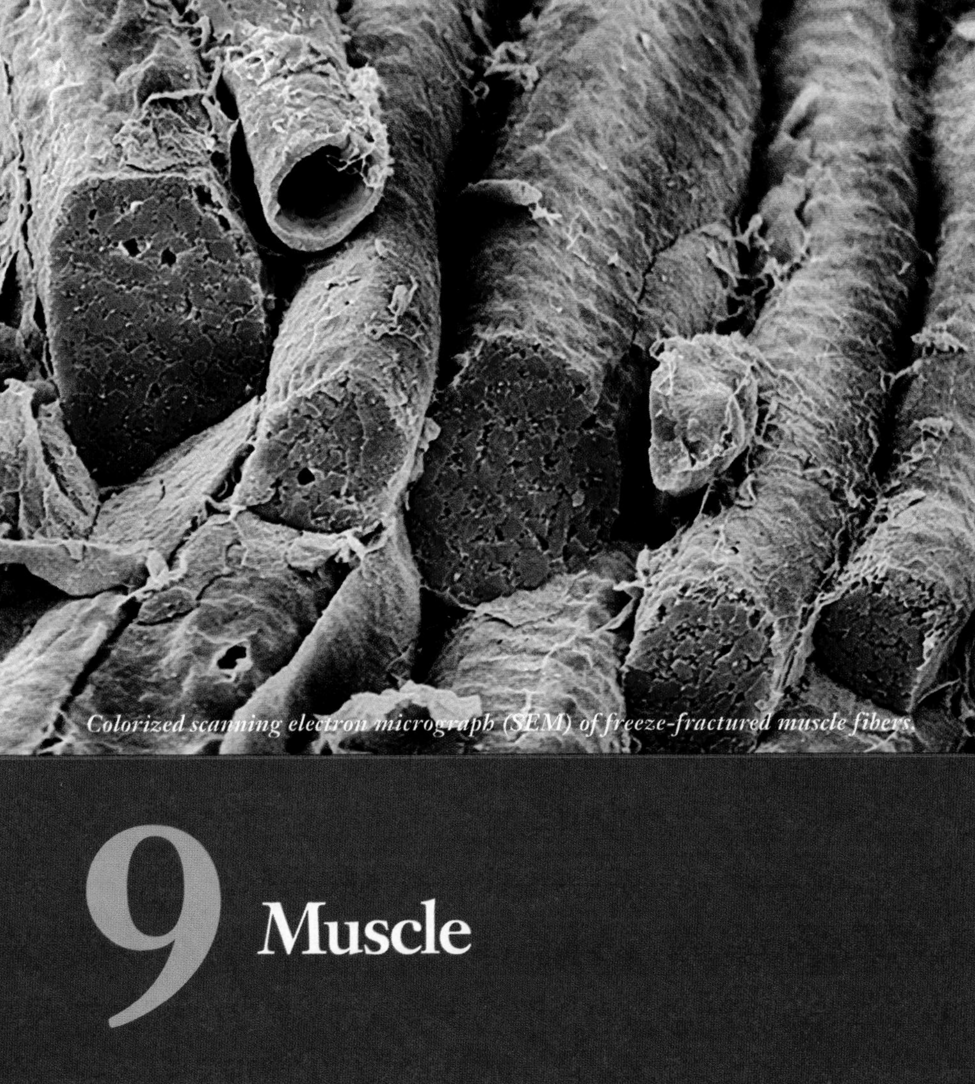

Colorized scanning electron micrograph (SEM) of freeze-fractured muscle fibers.

9 Muscle

SECTION A
Skeletal Muscle

SECTION B
Smooth and Cardiac Muscle

Muscle was introduced in Chapter 1 as one of the four principal tissue types that make up the human body. The ability to use chemical energy to produce force and movement is present to a limited extent in most cells, but in muscle cells it has become dominant. Muscles generate force and movements used to regulate the internal environment, and they also produce movements of the body in relation to the external environment. In humans, the ability to communicate, whether by speech, writing, or artistic expression, also depends on muscle contractions. Indeed, it is only by controlling muscle activity that the human mind ultimately expresses itself.

Three types of muscle tissue can be identified on the basis of structure, contractile properties, and control mechanisms—skeletal muscle, smooth muscle, and cardiac muscle. Most skeletal muscle, as the name implies, is attached to bone, and its contraction is responsible for supporting and moving the skeleton. As described in Chapter 6, contraction of skeletal muscle is initiated by action potentials in neurons of the somatic motor division of the nervous system, and is usually under voluntary control.

Sheets of smooth muscle surround various hollow organs and tubes, including the stomach, intestines, urinary bladder, uterus, blood vessels, and airways in the lungs. Contraction of smooth muscle may propel the luminal contents through the hollow organs, or it may regulate internal flow by changing the tube diameter. In addition, contraction of smooth muscle cells makes the hairs of the skin stand up and the pupil of the eye change diameter. In contrast to skeletal muscle, smooth muscle contraction is not normally under voluntary control. It occurs autonomously in some cases, but frequently it occurs in response to signals from the autonomic nervous system, hormones, autocrine or paracrine signals, and other local chemical factors.

Cardiac muscle is the muscle of the heart. Its contraction generates the pressure that propels blood through the circulatory system. Like smooth muscle, it is regulated by the autonomic nervous system, hormones, and autocrine or paracrine signals; and it can undergo spontaneous contractions.

Several of the general principles of physiology described in Chapter 1 are demonstrated in this chapter. One of these principles, that structure is a determinant of—and has coevolved with—function, is apparent in the elaborate specialization of muscle cells and whole muscles that enable them to generate force and movement. The principle that controlled exchange of materials occurs between compartments and across cellular membranes is exemplified by the movements of Ca^{2+} that underlie the regulation of activation and relaxation of muscle. The laws of chemistry and physics are fundamental to the molecular mechanism by which muscle cells convert chemical energy into force, and also to the mechanics governing bone–muscle lever systems. Finally, the transfer and balance of matter and energy are demonstrated by the ability of muscle cells to generate, store, and utilize energy via multiple metabolic pathways.

This chapter will describe skeletal muscle first, followed by smooth and cardiac muscle. Cardiac muscle, which combines some of the properties of both skeletal and smooth muscle, will be described in more depth in Chapter 12 in association with its role in the circulatory system.

SECTION A

Skeletal Muscle

9.1 Structure

The most striking feature seen when viewing **skeletal muscle** through a microscope is a distinct series of alternating light and dark bands perpendicular to the long axis. Because **cardiac muscle** shares this characteristic striped pattern, these two types are both referred to as **striated muscle.** The third basic muscle type, **smooth muscle,** derives its name from the fact that it lacks this striated appearance. **Figure 9.1** compares the appearance of skeletal muscle cells to cardiac and smooth muscle cells.

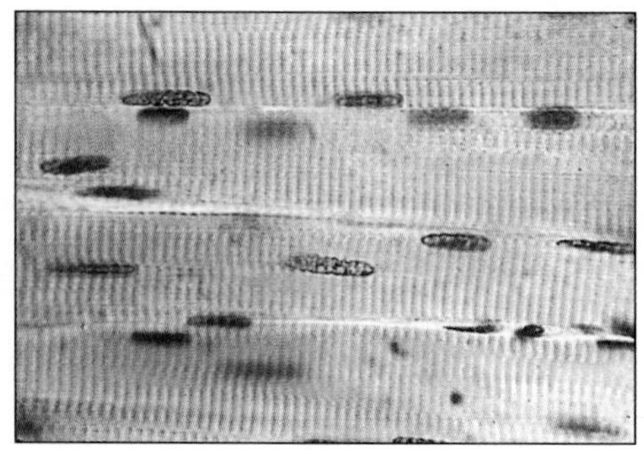

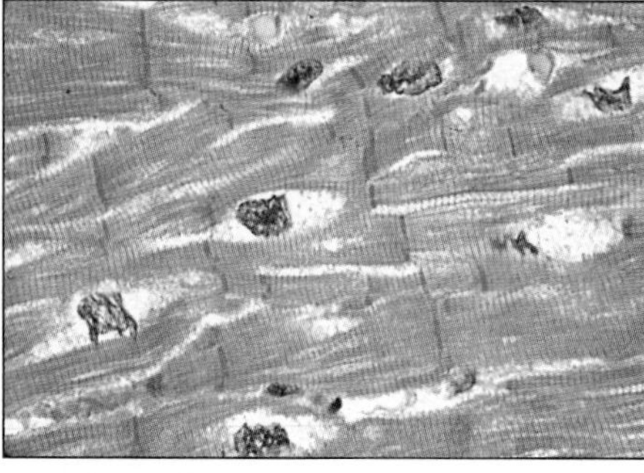

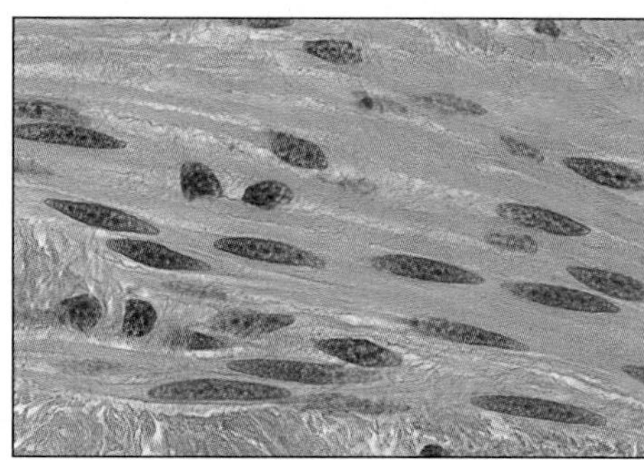

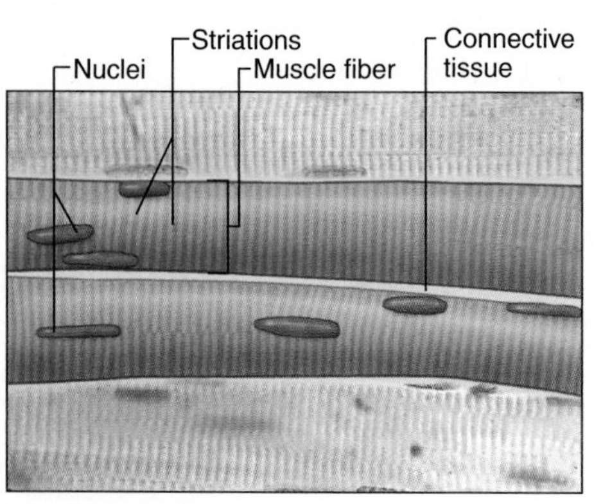

(a) Skeletal muscle

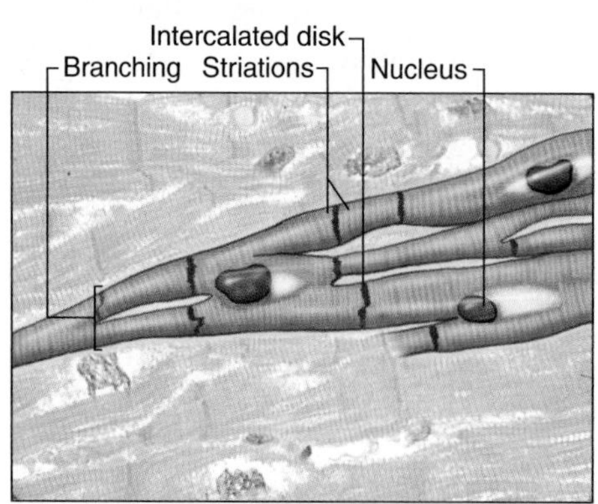

(b) Cardiac muscle

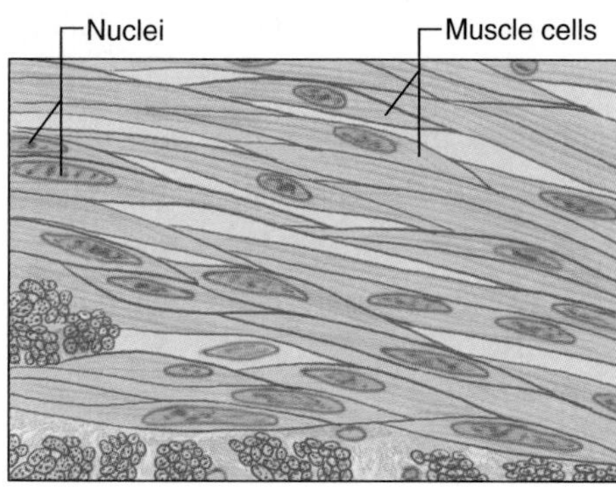

(c) Smooth muscle

Figure 9.1 APIR Comparison of (a) skeletal muscle to (b) cardiac and (c) smooth muscle as seen with light microscopy (top panels) and in schematic form (bottom panels). Both skeletal and cardiac muscle have a striated appearance. Cardiac and smooth muscle cells generally have a single nucleus, but skeletal muscle fibers are multinucleated.

Due to its elongated shape and the presence of multiple nuclei, a skeletal muscle cell is also referred to as a **muscle fiber.** Each muscle fiber is formed during development by the fusion of a number of undifferentiated, mononucleated cells known as **myoblasts** into a single, cylindrical, multinucleated cell. Skeletal muscle differentiation is completed around the time of birth, and these differentiated fibers continue to increase in size from infancy to adulthood. Compared to other cell types, skeletal muscle fibers are extremely large. Adult skeletal muscle fibers have diameters between 10 and 100 μm and lengths that may extend up to 20 cm. Key to the maintenance and function of such large cells is the retention of the nuclei from the original myoblasts. Spread throughout the length of the muscle fiber, each participates in regulation of gene expression and protein synthesis within its local domain.

If skeletal muscle fibers are damaged or destroyed after birth as a result of injury, they undergo a repair process involving a population of undifferentiated stem cells known as **satellite cells.** Satellite cells are normally quiescent, located between the plasma membrane and surrounding basement membrane along the length of muscle fibers. In response to strain or injury, they become active and undergo mitotic proliferation. Daughter cells then differentiate into myoblasts that can either fuse together to form new fibers or fuse with stressed or damaged muscle fibers to reinforce and repair them. The capacity for forming new skeletal muscle fibers is considerable but may not restore a severely damaged muscle to the original number of muscle fibers. Some of the compensation for a loss of muscle tissue also occurs through a satellite cell-mediated increase in the size (**hypertrophy**) of the remaining muscle fibers. Muscle hypertrophy also occurs in response to heavy exercise. Evidence suggests that this occurs through a combination of hypertrophy of existing fibers, splitting of existing fibers, and satellite cell proliferation, differentiation, and fusion. Many hormones and growth factors are involved in regulating these processes, such as growth hormone, insulin-like growth factor, and sex hormones (see Chapter 11).

The term **muscle** refers to a number of muscle fibers bound together by connective tissue (**Figure 9.2**). The relationship between a single muscle fiber and a muscle is analogous to that between a single neuron and a nerve, which is composed of

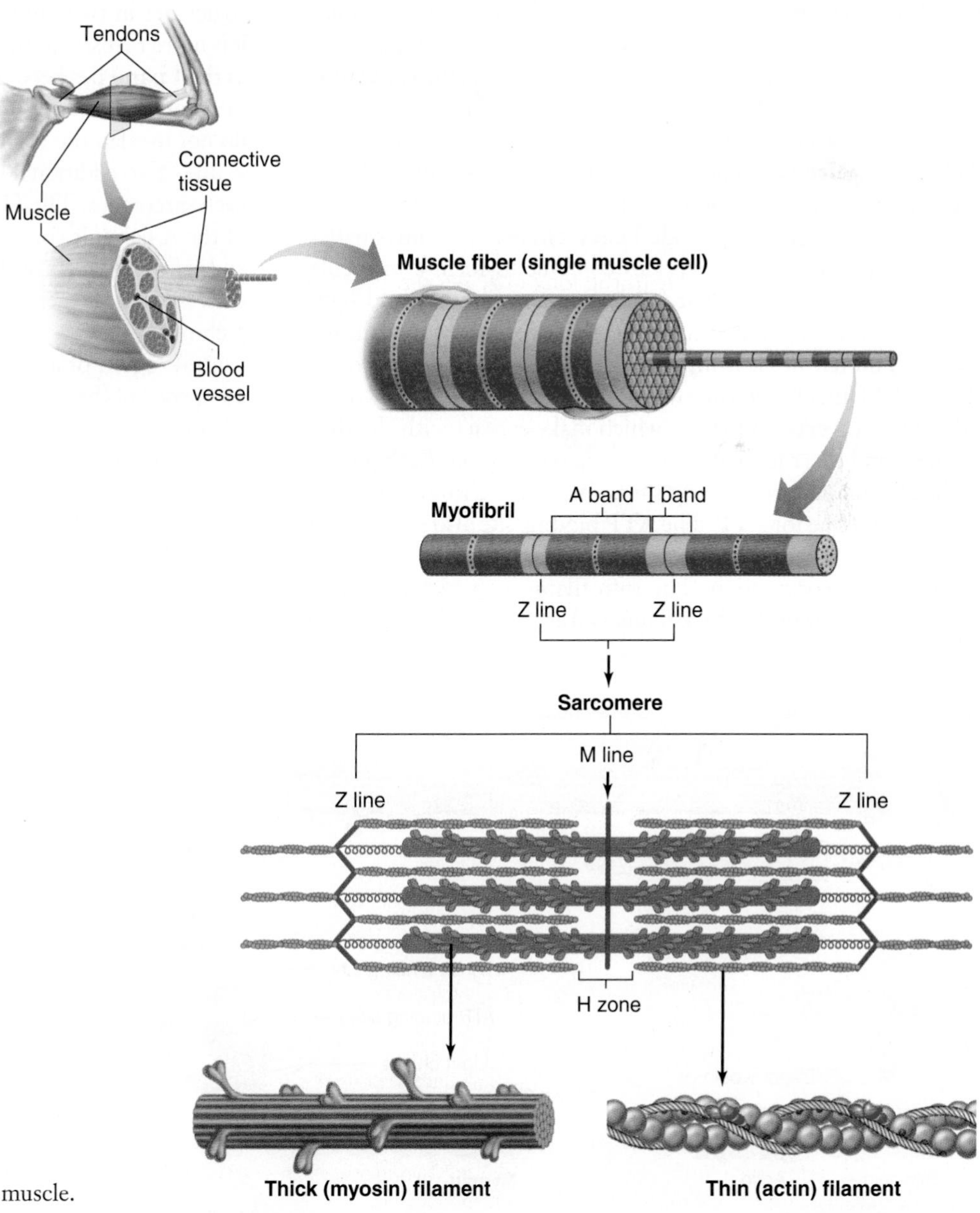

Figure 9.2 APIR Structure of skeletal muscle.

the axons of many neurons. Skeletal muscles are usually attached to bones by bundles of collagen fibers known as **tendons.**

In some muscles, the individual fibers extend the entire length of the muscle, but in most, the fibers are shorter, often oriented at an angle to the longitudinal axis of the muscle. The transmission of force from muscle to bone is like a number of people pulling on a rope, each person corresponding to a single muscle fiber and the rope corresponding to the connective tissue and tendons.

Some tendons are very long, with the site where the tendon attaches to the bone far removed from the end of the muscle. For example, some of the muscles that move the fingers are in the forearm (wiggle your fingers and feel the movement of the muscles just below your elbow). These muscles are connected to the fingers by long tendons.

The striated pattern in skeletal (and cardiac) muscle results from the arrangement of two types of filaments within the cytoplasm, the larger referred to as **thick filaments** and the smaller as **thin filaments.** These filaments are part of cylindrical bundles called **myofibrils,** which are approximately 1 to 2 μm in diameter (see Figure 9.2). Most of the cytoplasm of a fiber is filled with myofibrils, each extending from one end of the fiber to the other and linked to the tendons at the ends of the fiber. One unit of this repeating pattern of thick and thin filaments is known as a **sarcomere** (from the Greek *sarco,* "muscle," and *mer,* "part").

The molecular structure of thick and thin filaments is shown in **Figure 9.3**. The thick filaments are composed almost entirely of the protein **myosin.** The myosin molecule is composed of two large polypeptide **heavy chains** and four smaller **light chains.** These polypeptides combine to form a molecule that consists of two globular heads (containing heavy and light chains) and a long tail formed by the two intertwined heavy chains. The tail of each myosin molecule lies along the axis of the thick filament, and the two globular heads extend out to the sides, forming **cross-bridges,** which make contact with the thin filament and exert force during muscle contraction. Each globular head contains two binding sites, one for attaching to the thin filament and one for ATP. The ATP binding site also serves as an enzyme—an ATPase that hydrolyzes the bound ATP, harnessing its energy for contraction. The thin filaments (which are about half the diameter of the thick filaments) are principally composed of the protein **actin,** as well as two other proteins—**troponin** and **tropomyosin**—that play important roles in regulating contraction. An actin molecule is a globular protein composed of a single polypeptide (a monomer) that polymerizes with other actin monomers to form a polymer made up of two intertwined, helical chains. These chains make up the core of a thin filament. Each actin molecule contains a binding site for myosin.

The alternating dark and light bands produced by the orderly, parallel arrangement of thick and thin filaments are apparent in a microscopic view of skeletal muscle (**Figure 9.4**). The thick filaments are located in the middle of each sarcomere, where they create a wide, dark band known as the **A band** (see the Figure 9.4 legend for an explanation of the naming of the bands and zones of the sarcomere).

Each sarcomere contains two sets of thin filaments, one at each end. One end of each thin filament is anchored to a network of interconnecting proteins known as the **Z line,** whereas the other end overlaps a portion of the thick filaments. Two successive Z lines define the limits of one sarcomere. Thus, thin filaments from two adjacent sarcomeres are anchored to the two sides of each Z line. (The term *line* refers to the appearance of these structures in two dimensions. Because myofibrils are cylindrical, it is more realistic to think of them as *Z disks.*) A light band known as the **I band** lies between the ends of the A bands of two adjacent sarcomeres and contains those portions of the thin filaments that do not overlap the thick filaments. The I band is bisected by the Z line. Two additional bands are present in the A-band region of each sarcomere. The **H zone** is a narrow, light band in the center of the A band. It corresponds to the space between the opposing ends of the two sets of thin filaments in each sarcomere. A narrow, dark band in the center of the H zone, known as the **M line** (also technically a disk), corresponds to proteins that link together the central region of adjacent thick filaments. In addition, filaments composed of the elastic protein **titin** extend from the Z line to the M line and are linked to both the M-line proteins and the thick filaments. Both the M-line linkage between thick filaments and the titin filaments act to maintain the alignment of thick filaments in the middle of each sarcomere. A cross section through the A bands (**Figure 9.5**) shows the regular arrangement of overlapping thick and thin filaments. Each thick filament is surrounded by a hexagonal array of six thin filaments, and each thin filament is

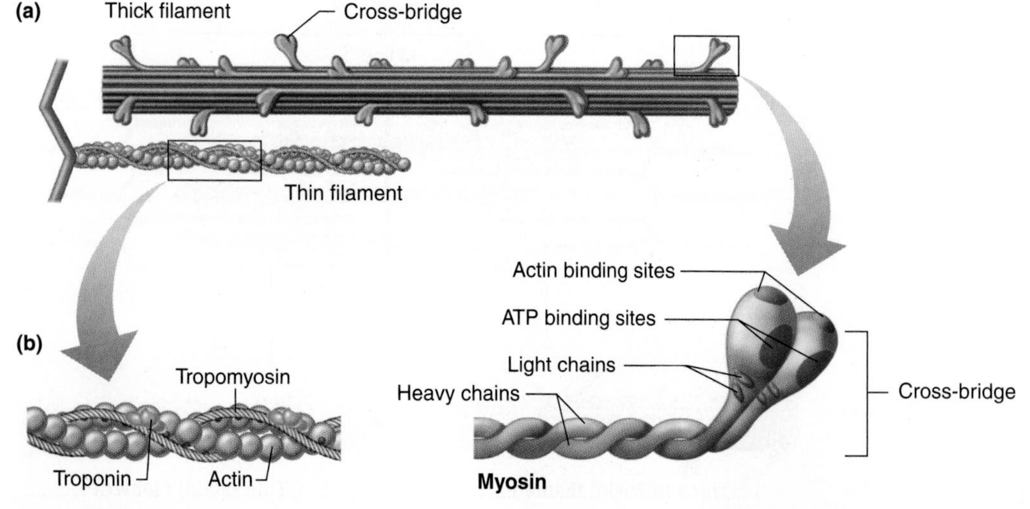

Figure 9.3 APIR (a) The heavy chains of myosin molecules form the core of a thick filament. The myosin molecules are oriented in opposite directions in either half of a thick filament. (b) Structure of thin filament and myosin molecule. Cross-bridge binding sites on actin are covered by tropomyosin. The two globular heads of each myosin molecule extend from the sides of a thick filament, forming a cross-bridge.

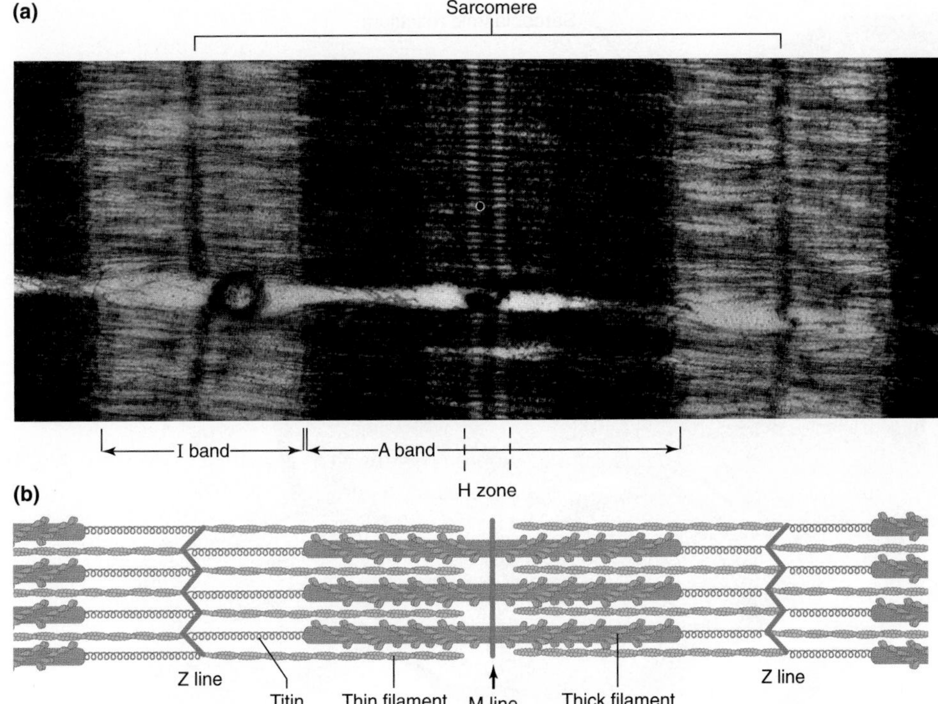

Figure 9.4 APR (a) High magnification of a sarcomere within myofibrils. (b) Arrangement of the thick and thin filaments in the sarcomere shown in (a). The names of the I and A bands come from "isotropy" and "anisotropy," terms from physics indicating that the I band has uniform appearance in all directions and the A band has a nonuniform appearance in different directions. The names for the Z line, M line, and H zone are from their initial descriptions in German: *zwischen* ("between"), *mittel* ("middle"), and *heller* ("light").

surrounded by a triangular arrangement of three thick filaments. Altogether, there are twice as many thin as thick filaments in the region of filament overlap.

In addition to force-generating mechanisms, skeletal muscle fibers have an elaborate system of membranes that play important roles in the activation of contraction (**Figure 9.6**). The **sarcoplasmic reticulum** in a muscle fiber is homologous to the endoplasmic reticulum found in most cells. This structure forms a series of sleevelike segments around each myofibril. At the end of each segment are two enlarged regions, known as **terminal cisternae** (sometimes also referred to as "lateral sacs"), that are connected to each other by a series of smaller tubular elements. Ca^{2+} is stored in the terminal cisternae and is released into the cytosol following membrane excitation.

A separate tubular structure, the **transverse tubule** (**T-tubule**), lies directly between—and is intimately associated with—the terminal cisternae of adjacent segments of the sarcoplasmic reticulum. The T-tubules and terminal cisternae surround the myofibrils at the region of the sarcomeres where the A bands and I bands meet. T-tubules are continuous with the plasma membrane (which in muscle cells is sometimes referred to as the **sarcolemma**), and action potentials propagating along the surface membrane also travel throughout the interior of the muscle fiber by way of the T-tubules. The lumen of the T-tubule is continuous with the extracellular fluid surrounding the muscle fiber.

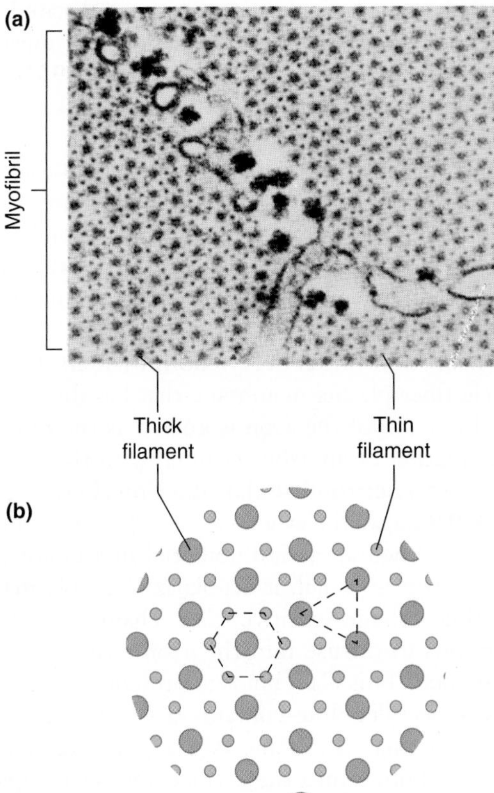

Figure 9.5 APR (a) Electron micrograph of a cross section through three myofibrils in a single skeletal muscle fiber. (b) Hexagonal arrangements of the thick and thin filaments in the overlap region in a single myofibril. Six thin filaments surround each thick filament, and three thick filaments surround each thin filament. Titin filaments and cross-bridges are not shown. From H. E. Huxley, *J. Mol. Biol.*, 37:507–520 (1968).

PHYSIOLOGICAL INQUIRY

- Draw a cross-section diagram like the one in part (b) for a slice taken (1) in the H zone, (2) in the I band, (3) at the M line, and (4) at the Z line (ignore titin).

Answer can be found at end of chapter.

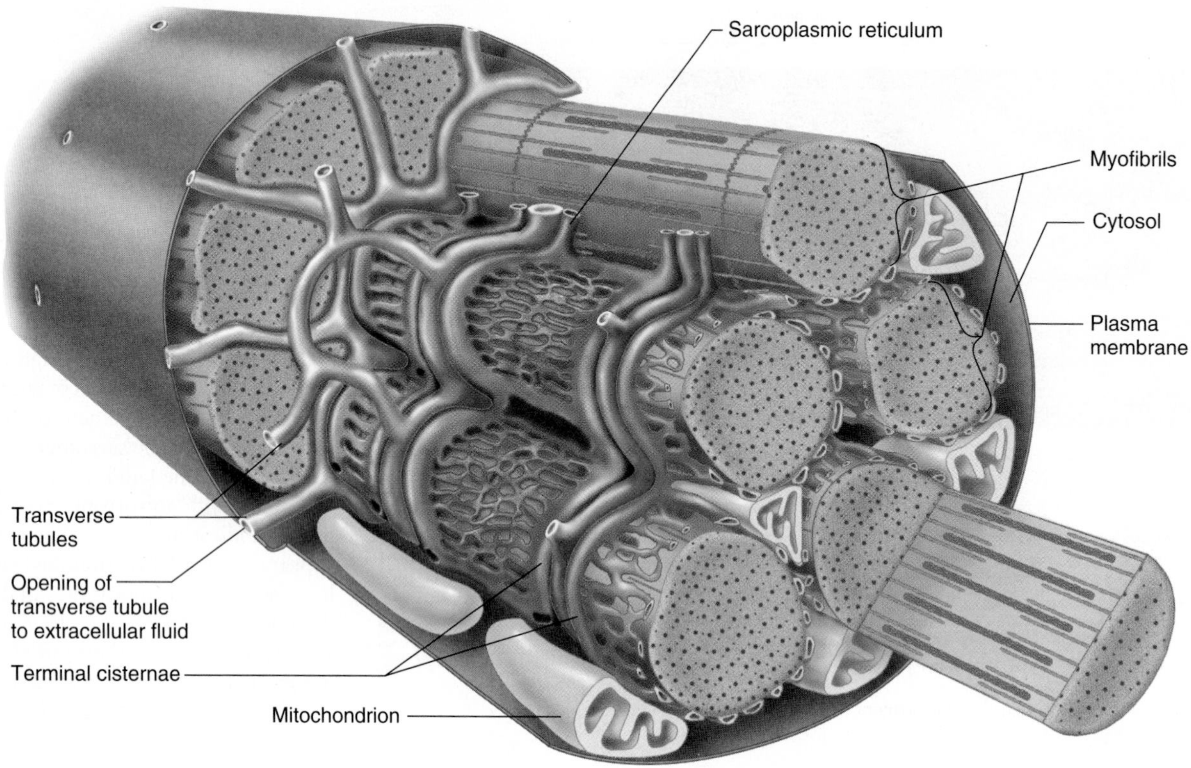

Figure 9.6 APR Transverse tubules and sarcoplasmic reticulum in a single skeletal muscle fiber.

9.2 Molecular Mechanisms of Skeletal Muscle Contraction

The term **contraction,** as used in muscle physiology, does not necessarily mean "shortening." It simply refers to activation of the force-generating sites within muscle fibers—the cross-bridges. For example, holding a dumbbell steady with your elbow bent requires muscle contraction but not muscle shortening. Following contraction, the mechanisms that generate force are turned off and tension declines, allowing **relaxation** of muscle fibers. We now begin our explanation of how skeletal muscles contract by describing the mechanism by which they are activated by neurons.

Membrane Excitation: The Neuromuscular Junction

Stimulation of the neurons to a skeletal muscle is the only mechanism by which action potentials are initiated in this type of muscle. In subsequent sections, you will see additional mechanisms for activating cardiac and smooth muscle contraction.

The neurons whose axons innervate skeletal muscle fibers are known as **motor neurons** (or somatic efferent neurons), and their cell bodies are located in the brainstem and the spinal cord. The axons of motor neurons are myelinated (see Figure 6.2) and are the largest-diameter axons in the body. They are therefore able to propagate action potentials at high velocities, allowing signals from the central nervous system to travel to skeletal muscle fibers with minimal delay (review Figure 6.24).

Upon reaching a muscle, the axon of a motor neuron divides into many branches, each branch forming a single junction with a muscle fiber. A single motor neuron innervates many muscle fibers, but each muscle fiber is controlled by a branch from only one motor neuron. A motor neuron plus the muscle fibers it innervates is called a **motor unit** (**Figure 9.7a**). The muscle fibers in a single motor unit are located in one muscle, but they are distributed throughout the muscle and are not necessarily adjacent to each other (**Figure 9.7b**). When an action potential occurs in a motor neuron, all the muscle fibers in its motor unit are stimulated to contract.

The myelin sheath surrounding the axon of each motor neuron ends near the surface of a muscle fiber, and the axon divides into a number of short processes that lie embedded in grooves on the muscle fiber surface (**Figure 9.8a**). The axon terminals of a motor neuron contain vesicles similar to those found at synaptic junctions between two neurons. The vesicles contain the neurotransmitter **acetylcholine** (**ACh**). The region of the muscle fiber plasma membrane that lies directly under the terminal portion of the axon is known as the **motor end plate.** The junction of an axon terminal with the motor end plate is known as a **neuromuscular junction** (**Figure 9.8b**).

Figure 9.9 shows the events occurring at the neuromuscular junction. When an action potential in a motor neuron arrives at the axon terminal, it depolarizes the plasma membrane, opening voltage-sensitive Ca^{2+} channels and allowing calcium ions to diffuse into the axon terminal from the extracellular fluid. This Ca^{2+} binds to proteins that enable the membranes of acetylcholine-containing vesicles to fuse with the neuronal plasma membrane (see Figure 6.27), thereby releasing acetylcholine into the extracellular cleft separating the axon terminal and the motor end plate.

(a) Single motor unit

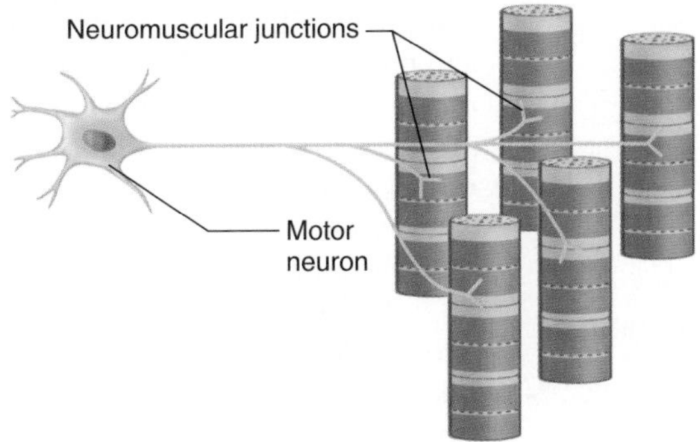

(b) Two motor units

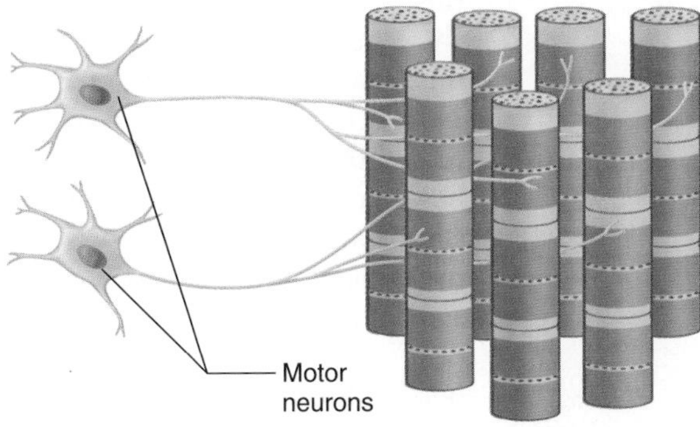

Figure 9.7 (a) Single motor unit consisting of one motor neuron and the muscle fibers it innervates. (b) Two motor units and their intermingled fibers in a muscle.

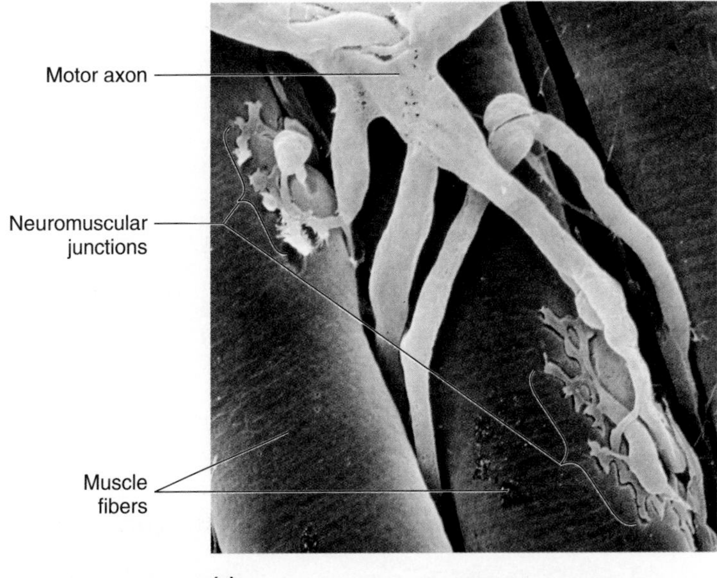

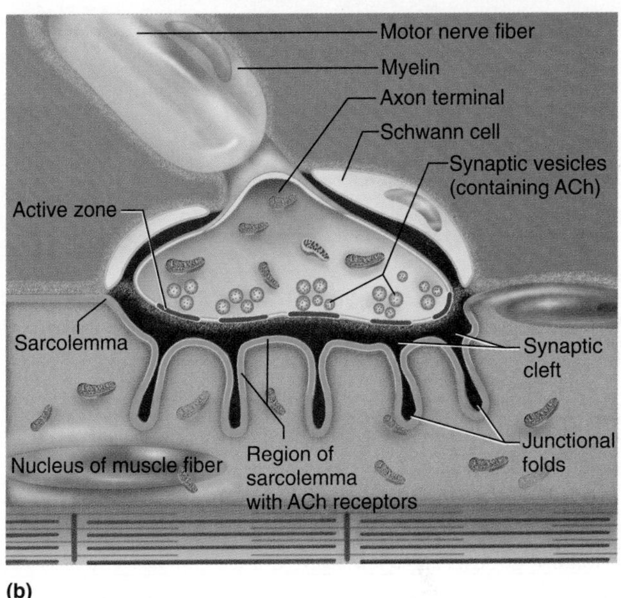

Figure 9.8 AP|R The neuromuscular junction. (a) Scanning electron micrograph showing branching of motor neuron axons, with axon terminals embedded in grooves in the muscle fiber's surface. (b) Structure of a neuromuscular junction.

ACh diffuses from the axon terminal to the motor end plate where it binds to ionotropic receptors of the nicotinic type (see Chapter 6). The binding of ACh opens an ion channel in each receptor protein; both sodium and potassium ions can pass through these channels. Because of the differences in electrochemical gradients across the plasma membrane (see Figure 6.12), more Na^+ moves in than K^+ out, producing a local depolarization of the motor end plate known as an **end-plate potential (EPP)**. Thus, an EPP is analogous to an EPSP (excitatory postsynaptic potential) at a neuron–neuron synapse (see Figure 6.28).

The magnitude of a single EPP is, however, much larger than that of an EPSP because neurotransmitter is released over a larger surface area, binding to many more receptors, and opening many more ion channels. For this reason, one EPP is normally more than sufficient to depolarize the muscle plasma membrane adjacent to the end-plate membrane to its threshold potential, initiating an action potential. This action potential is then propagated over the surface of the muscle fiber and into the T-tubules by the same mechanism shown in Figure 6.23 for the propagation of action potentials along unmyelinated axon membranes. Most neuromuscular junctions are located near the middle of a muscle fiber, and newly generated muscle action potentials propagate from this region in both directions toward the ends of the fiber.

Every action potential in a motor neuron normally produces an action potential in each muscle fiber in its motor unit. This is quite different from synaptic junctions between neurons, where multiple EPSPs must occur in order for threshold to be reached and an action potential elicited in the postsynaptic membrane.

There is another difference between interneuronal synapses and neuromuscular junctions. As we saw in Chapter 6, IPSPs (inhibitory postsynaptic potentials) are produced at some synaptic junctions. They hyperpolarize or stabilize the postsynaptic membrane and decrease the probability of its firing an action potential. In contrast, inhibitory potentials do not occur in human skeletal muscle; *all neuromuscular junctions are excitatory.*

In addition to receptors for ACh, the synaptic junction contains the enzyme **acetylcholinesterase,** which breaks down ACh, just as it does at ACh-mediated synapses in the nervous system. Choline is then transported back into the axon terminals,

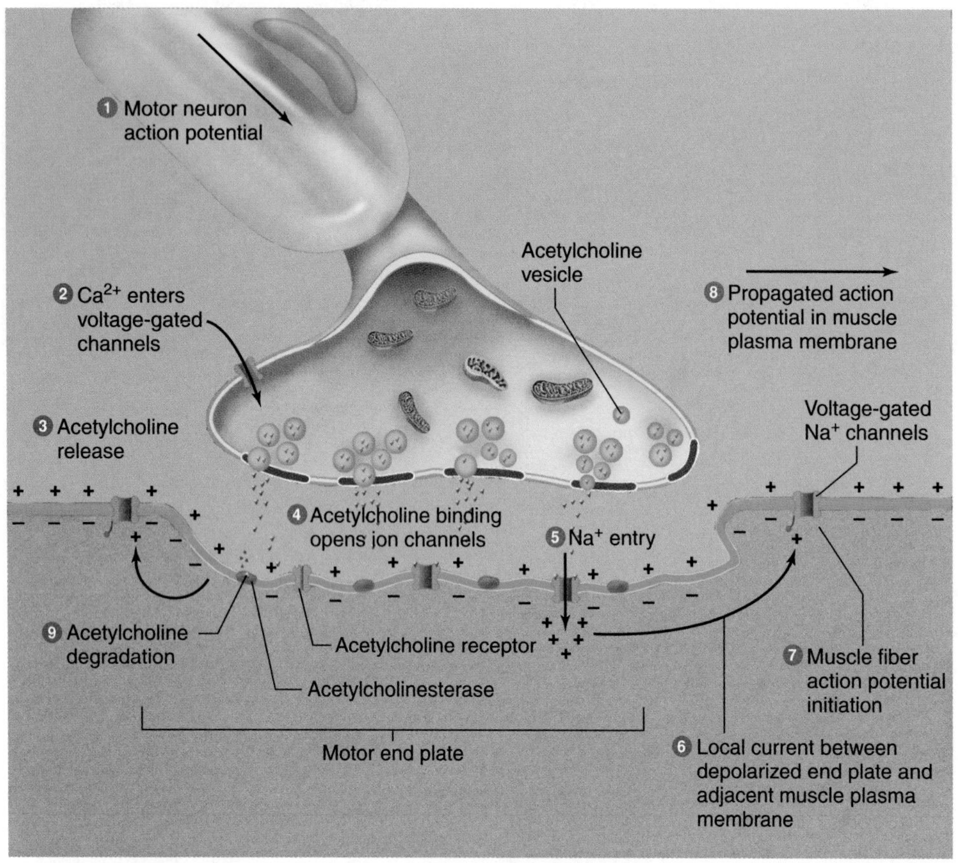

Figure 9.9 APIR Events at the neuromuscular junction that lead to an action potential in the muscle fiber plasma membrane. Although K^+ also exits the muscle cell when ACh receptors are open, Na^+ entry and depolarization dominate, as shown here.

PHYSIOLOGICAL INQUIRY

- If the ACh receptor channel is equally permeable to Na^+ and K^+, why does Na^+ influx dominate? (*Hint:* Review Figure 6.12.)

Answer can be found at end of chapter.

where it is reused in the synthesis of new ACh. ACh bound to receptors is in equilibrium with free ACh in the cleft between the neuronal and muscle membranes. As the concentration of free ACh decreases because of its breakdown by acetylcholinesterase, less ACh is available to bind to the receptors. When the receptors no longer contain bound ACh, the ion channels in the end plate close. The depolarized end plate returns to its resting potential and can respond to the subsequent arrival of ACh released by another neuron action potential.

Disruption of Neuromuscular Signaling

There are many ways by which disease or drugs can modify events at the neuromuscular junction. For example, ***curare***, a deadly arrowhead poison used by indigenous peoples of South America, binds strongly to nicotinic ACh receptors. It does not open their ion channels, however, and is resistant to destruction by acetylcholinesterase. When a receptor is occupied by curare, ACh cannot bind to the receptor. Therefore, although the motor neurons still conduct normal action potentials and release ACh, there is no resulting EPP in the motor end plate and no contraction. Because the skeletal muscles responsible for breathing, like all skeletal muscles, depend upon neuromuscular transmission to initiate their contraction, curare poisoning can cause death by asphyxiation.

Neuromuscular transmission can also be blocked by inhibiting acetylcholinesterase. Some organophosphates, which are the main ingredients in certain pesticides and "nerve gases" (the latter developed for chemical warfare), inhibit this enzyme. In the presence of these chemicals, ACh is released normally upon the arrival of an action potential at the axon terminal and binds to the end-plate receptors. The ACh is not destroyed, however, because the acetylcholinesterase is inhibited. The ion channels in the end plate therefore remain open, producing a maintained depolarization of the end plate and the muscle plasma membrane adjacent to the end plate. A skeletal muscle membrane maintained in a depolarized state cannot generate action potentials because the voltage-gated Na^+ channels in the membrane become inactivated, which requires repolarization to reverse. After prolonged exposure to ACh, the receptors of the motor end plate become insensitive to it, preventing any further depolarization. Thus, the muscle does not contract in response to subsequent nerve stimulation, and the result is skeletal muscle paralysis and death from asphyxiation. Nerve gases also cause ACh to build up at muscarinic synapses (see Chapter 6, Section C), for example, where parasympathetic neurons inhibit cardiac pacemaker cells (see Chapter 12). This can result in an extreme slowing of the heart rate, virtually halting blood flow through the body. Thus, the antidote for organophosphate and nerve gas exposure includes both ***pralidoxime,*** which reactivates acetylcholinesterase, and ***atropine,*** the muscarinic receptor antagonist.

Drugs that block neuromuscular transmission are sometimes used in small amounts to prevent muscular contractions during certain types of surgical procedures, when it is necessary to immobilize the surgical field. One example is ***succinylcholine,*** which actually acts as an agonist to the ACh receptors and produces a depolarizing/desensitizing block similar to acetylcholinesterase inhibitors. It has a rapid onset of action (about 1 minute) and relatively short duration (7 to 8 minutes). Nondepolarizing neuromuscular junction blocking drugs that act more like curare and last longer are also used, such as ***rocuronium*** and ***vecuronium.*** The use of such paralytic agents in surgery reduces the required dose of general anesthetic, allowing patients to recover faster and with fewer complications. Patients must be artificially ventilated, however, to maintain respiration until the drugs have cleared from their bodies.

Another group of substances, including the toxin produced by the bacterium *Clostridium botulinum*, blocks the release of acetylcholine from axon terminals. Botulinum toxin is an enzyme that breaks down proteins of the SNARE complex that are required for the binding and fusion of ACh vesicles with the plasma membrane of the axon terminal (review Figure 6.27). This toxin, which produces the food poisoning called ***botulism***, is one of the most potent poisons known. Application of botulinum toxin to block ACh release is increasingly being used for clinical and cosmetic procedures, including the inhibition of overactive extraocular muscles, prevention of excessive sweat gland activity, treatment of migraine headaches, and reduction of aging-related skin wrinkles.

Having described how action potentials in motor neurons initiate action potentials in skeletal muscle cells, we will now examine how that excitation results in muscle contraction.

Excitation–Contraction Coupling

Excitation–contraction coupling refers to the sequence of events by which an action potential in the plasma membrane activates the force-generating mechanisms. An action potential in a skeletal muscle fiber lasts 1 to 2 msec and is completed before any signs of mechanical activity begin (**Figure 9.10**). Once begun, the mechanical activity following an action potential may last 100 msec or more. The electrical activity in the plasma membrane does not directly act upon the contractile proteins but instead produces a state of increased cytosolic Ca^{2+} concentration, which continues to activate the contractile apparatus long after the electrical activity in the membrane has ceased.

How does the presence of Ca^{2+} in the cytoplasm initiate force generation by the thick and thin filaments? The answer requires a closer look at the thin filament proteins, troponin and tropomyosin (**Figure 9.11**). Tropomyosin is a rod-shaped molecule composed of two intertwined polypeptides with a length approximately equal to that of seven actin monomers. Chains of tropomyosin molecules are arranged end to end along the actin thin filament. These tropomyosin molecules partially cover the myosin-binding site on each actin monomer, thereby preventing the cross-bridges from making contact with actin. Each tropomyosin molecule is held in this blocking position by the smaller globular protein, troponin. Troponin, which interacts with both actin and tropomyosin, is composed of three subunits designated by the letters I (inhibitory), T (tropomyosin-binding) and C (Ca^{2+}-binding). One molecule of troponin binds to each molecule of tropomyosin and regulates the access to myosin-binding sites on the seven actin monomers in contact with that tropomyosin. This is the status of a resting muscle fiber; troponin and tropomyosin cooperatively block the interaction of cross-bridges with the thin filament.

To allow cross-bridges from the thick filament to bind to the thin filament, tropomyosin molecules must move away from their blocking positions on actin. This happens when Ca^{2+} binds to specific binding sites on the Ca^{2+}-binding subunit of troponin. The binding of Ca^{2+} produces a change in the

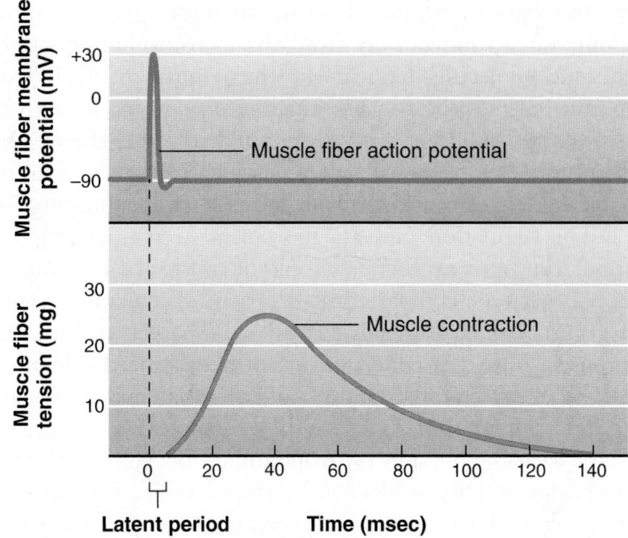

Figure 9.10 Time relationship between a skeletal muscle fiber action potential and the resulting contraction and relaxation of the muscle fiber. The latent period is the delay between the beginning of the action potential and the initial increase in tension.

PHYSIOLOGICAL INQUIRY

- Following a single action potential, cytosolic Ca^{2+} concentration increases and then decreases back to resting levels by about 50 msec. Why does the force last so much longer?

Answer can be found at end of chapter.

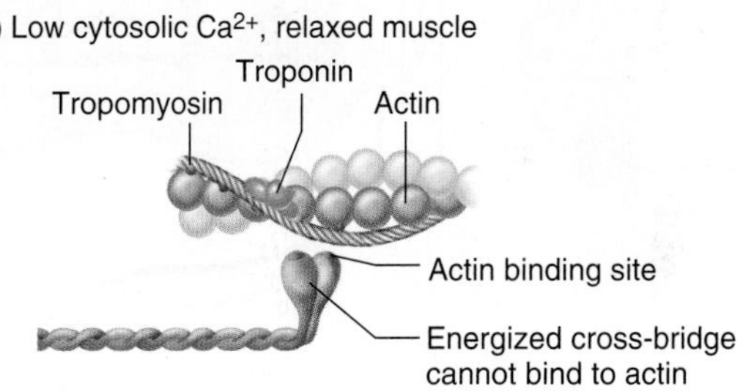

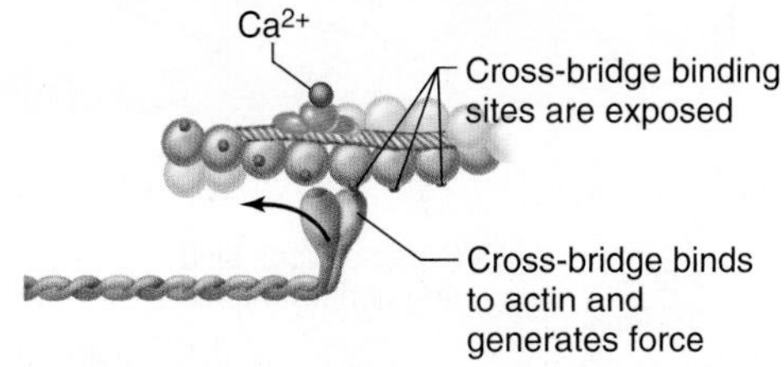

Figure 9.11 APIR Activation of cross-bridge cycling by Ca^{2+}. (a) Without calcium ions bound, troponin holds tropomyosin over cross-bridge binding sites on actin. (b) When Ca^{2+} binds to troponin, tropomyosin is allowed to move away from cross-bridge binding sites on actin, and cross-bridges can bind to actin.

shape of troponin, which relaxes its inhibitory grip and allows tropomyosin to move away from the myosin-binding site on each actin molecule. Conversely, the removal of Ca^{2+} from troponin reverses the process, turning off contractile activity. Thus, the cytosolic Ca^{2+} concentration determines the number of troponin sites occupied by Ca^{2+}, which in turn determines the number of actin sites available for cross-bridge binding.

The regulation of Ca^{2+} movement in the activation of muscle cells is an excellent example of controlled exchange of materials between compartments and across membranes, which is a general principle of physiology (see Chapter 1). In a resting muscle fiber, the concentration of free, ionized calcium in the cytosol surrounding the thick and thin filaments is very low, only about 10^{-7} mol/L. At this low Ca^{2+} concentration, very few of the Ca^{2+}-binding sites on troponin are occupied and, thus, cross-bridge activity is blocked by tropomyosin. Following an action potential, there is a rapid increase in cytosolic Ca^{2+} concentration and Ca^{2+} binds to troponin, removing the blocking effect of tropomyosin and allowing myosin cross-bridges to bind actin. The source of the increased cytosolic Ca^{2+} is the sarcoplasmic reticulum within the muscle fiber.

A specialized mechanism couples T-tubule action potentials with Ca^{2+} release from the sarcoplasmic reticulum (**Figure 9.12**, step 2). The T-tubules are in intimate contact with the terminal cisternae of the sarcoplasmic reticulum, connected by structures known as **junctional feet,** or **foot processes.** This junction involves two integral membrane proteins, one in the T-tubule membrane and the other in the membrane of the sarcoplasmic reticulum. The T-tubule protein is a modified voltage-sensitive Ca^{2+} channel known as the **dihydropyridine (DHP) receptor** (so named because it binds the class of drugs called dihydropyridines). The main role of the DHP receptor, however, is not to conduct Ca^{2+} but rather to act as a voltage sensor. The protein embedded in the sarcoplasmic reticulum membrane is known as the **ryanodine receptor** (because it binds to the plant alkaloid ryanodine). This large molecule not only includes the foot process but also forms a Ca^{2+} channel. During a T-tubule action potential, charged amino acid residues

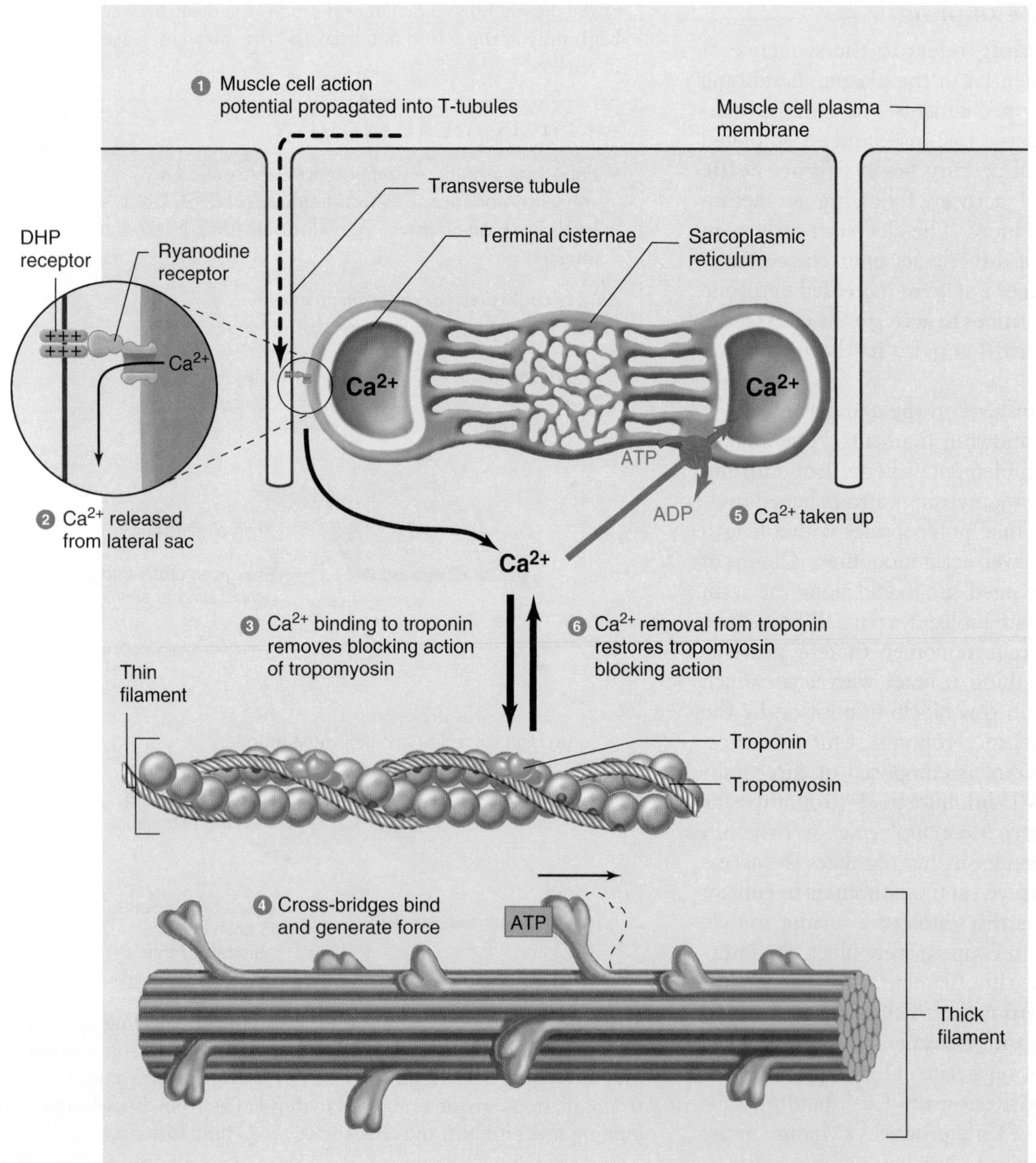

Figure 9.12 AP|R Release and uptake of Ca^{2+} by the sarcoplasmic reticulum during contraction and relaxation of a skeletal muscle fiber.

within the DHP receptor protein induce a conformational change, which acts via the foot process to open the ryanodine receptor channel. Ca^{2+} is thus released from the terminal cisternae of the sarcoplasmic reticulum into the cytosol, where it can bind to troponin. The increase in cytosolic Ca^{2+} in response to a single action potential is normally enough to briefly saturate all troponin-binding sites on the thin filaments.

A contraction is terminated by removal of Ca^{2+} from troponin, which is achieved by lowering the Ca^{2+} concentration in the cytosol back to its prerelease level. The membranes of the sarcoplasmic reticulum contain primary active-transport proteins—Ca^{2+}-ATPases—that pump calcium ions from the cytosol back into the lumen of the reticulum. As we just saw, Ca^{2+} is released from the reticulum when an action potential begins in the T-tubule, but the pumping of the released Ca^{2+} back into the reticulum requires a much longer time. Therefore, the cytosolic Ca^{2+} concentration remains elevated, and the contraction continues for some time after a single action potential.

To reiterate, just as contraction results from the release of Ca^{2+} stored in the sarcoplasmic reticulum, so contraction ends and relaxation begins as Ca^{2+} is pumped back into the reticulum (see Figure 9.12). ATP is required to provide the energy for the Ca^{2+} pump.

Sliding-Filament Mechanism

When force generation produces shortening of a skeletal muscle fiber, the overlapping thick and thin filaments in each sarcomere move past each other, propelled by movements of the cross-bridges. During this shortening of the sarcomeres, there is no change in the lengths of either the thick or thin filaments. This is known as the **sliding-filament mechanism** of muscle contraction.

During shortening, each myosin cross-bridge attached to a thin filament actin molecule moves in an arc much like an oar on a boat. This swiveling motion of many cross-bridges forces the thin filaments attached to successive Z lines to move toward the center of the sarcomere, thereby shortening the sarcomere (**Figure 9.13**). One stroke of a cross-bridge produces only a very small movement of a thin filament relative to a thick filament. As long as binding sites on actin remain exposed, however, each cross-bridge repeats its swiveling motion many times, resulting in large displacements of the filaments. It is worth noting that a common pattern of muscle shortening involves one end of the muscle remaining at a fixed position while the other end shortens toward it. In this case, as filaments slide and each sarcomere shortens internally, the center of each sarcomere also slides toward the fixed end of the muscle (this is depicted in **Figure 9.14**).

The sequence of events that occurs between the time a cross-bridge binds to a thin filament, moves, and then is set to repeat the process is known as a **cross-bridge cycle.** Each cycle consists of four steps: (1) attachment of the cross-bridge to a thin filament; (2) movement of the cross-bridge, producing tension in the thin filament; (3) detachment of the cross-bridge from the thin filament; and (4) energizing the cross-bridge so it can again attach to a thin filament and repeat the cycle. Each cross-bridge undergoes its own cycle of movement independently of other cross-bridges. At any instant during contraction, only some of the cross-bridges

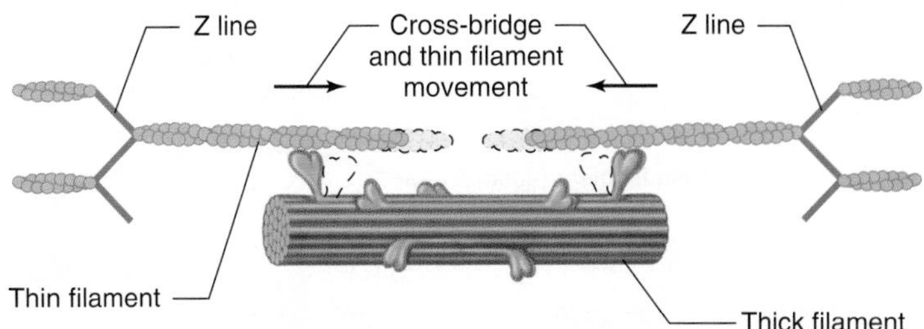

Figure 9.13 APIR Cross-bridges in the thick filaments bind to actin in the thin filaments and undergo a conformational change that propels the thin filaments toward the center of a sarcomere. (Only a few of the approximately 200 cross-bridges in each thick filament are shown.)

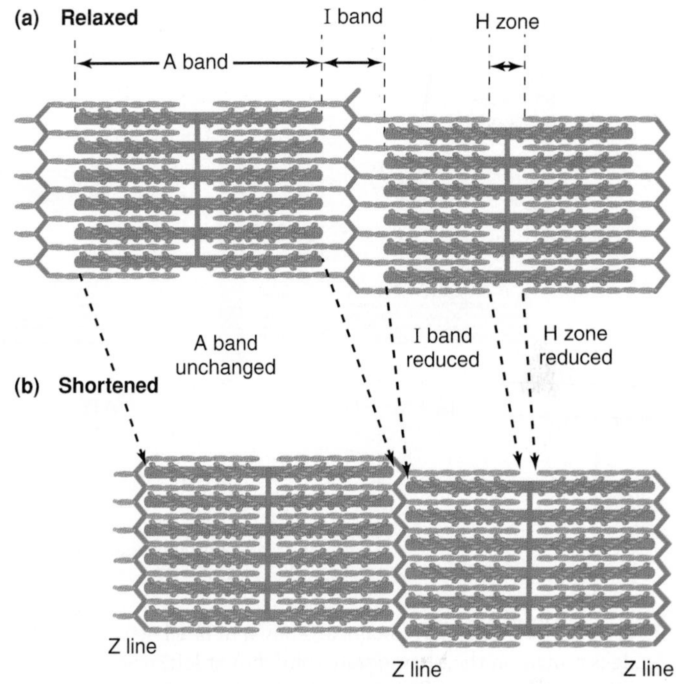

Figure 9.14 APIR The sliding of thick filaments past overlapping thin filaments shortens the sarcomere with no change in thick or thin filament length. The I band and H zone are reduced.

PHYSIOLOGICAL INQUIRY

- Sphincter muscles are circular and generally not attached to bones. How would this diagram differ if the sarcomeres shown were part of a sphincter muscle?

Answer can be found at end of chapter.

are attached to the thin filaments, producing tension, while others are simultaneously in a detached portion of their cycle.

A general principle of physiology states that physiological processes are dictated by the laws of chemistry and physics (see Chapter 1), and the details of the cross-bridge mechanism are an excellent example. **Figure 9.15** illustrates the chemical and physical events during the four steps of the cross-bridge cycle. The cross-bridges in a resting muscle fiber are in an energized state resulting from the splitting of ATP, and the hydrolysis products ADP and inorganic phosphate (P_i) are still bound

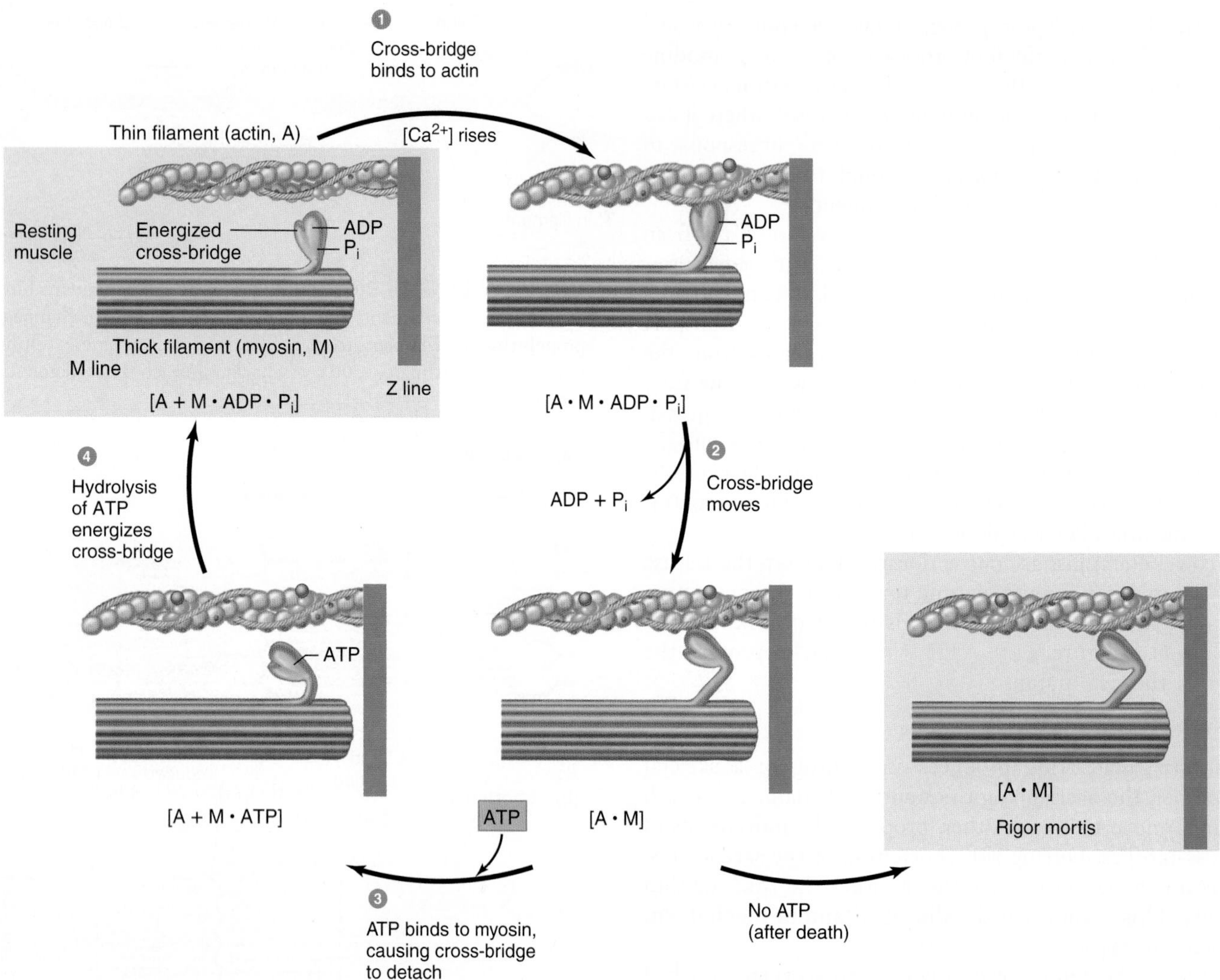

Figure 9.15 APIR Chemical (shown in brackets) and mechanical representations of the four stages of a cross-bridge cycle. Cross-bridges remain in the resting state (pink box at left) when Ca^{2+} remains low. In the rigor mortis state (pink box at right), cross-bridges remain rigidly bound when ATP is absent. In the chemical representation, A = actin, M = myosin, dots are between bound components, and plus signs are between detached components.

PHYSIOLOGICAL INQUIRY

- Under certain experimental conditions, it is possible to extract the protein troponin from a skeletal muscle fiber. Predict how cross-bridge cycling in a skeletal muscle fiber would be affected in the absence of troponin.

Answer can be found at end of chapter.

to myosin (in the chemical representation, bound elements are separated by a dot, while detached elements are separated by a plus sign). This energy storage in myosin is analogous to the storage of potential energy in a stretched spring.

Cross-bridge cycling is initiated when the excitation–contraction coupling mechanism elevates cytosolic Ca^{2+} and the binding sites on actin are exposed. The cycle begins with the binding of an energized myosin cross-bridge (M) to a thin filament actin molecule (A):

$$\text{Step 1} \quad A + M\cdot ADP\cdot P_i \xrightarrow[\text{actin binding}]{} A\cdot M\cdot ADP\cdot P_i$$

The binding of energized myosin to actin triggers the release of the strained conformation of the energized cross-bridge, which produces the movement of the bound cross-bridge (sometimes called the **power stroke**) and the release of P_i and ADP:

$$\text{Step 2} \quad A\cdot M\cdot ADP\cdot P_i \xrightarrow[\text{cross-bridge movement}]{} A\cdot M + ADP + P_i$$

This sequence of energy storage and release by myosin is analogous to the operation of a mousetrap: Energy is stored in the trap by cocking the spring (ATP hydrolysis) and released after springing the trap (binding to actin).

During the cross-bridge movement, myosin is bound very firmly to actin, but this linkage must be broken to allow the cross-bridge to be reenergized and repeat the cycle. The binding of a new molecule of ATP to myosin breaks the link between actin and myosin:

$$\text{Step 3} \quad \text{A}\cdot\text{M} + \text{ATP} \xrightarrow[\text{dissociation from actin}]{\text{cross-bridge}} \text{A} + \text{M}\cdot\text{ATP}$$

The dissociation of actin and myosin by ATP is an example of allosteric regulation of protein activity (see Figure 3.32a). The binding of ATP at one site on myosin decreases myosin's affinity for actin bound at another site. Note that ATP is not split in this step; that is, it is not acting as an energy source but only as an allosteric modulator of the myosin head that weakens the binding of myosin to actin.

Following the dissociation of actin and myosin, the ATP bound to myosin is hydrolyzed, thereby re-forming the energized state of myosin and returning the cross-bridge to its pre-power-stroke position:

$$\text{Step 4} \quad \text{A} + \text{M}\cdot\text{ATP} \xrightarrow[\text{ATP hydrolysis}]{} \text{A} + \text{M}\cdot\text{ADP}\cdot\text{P}_i$$

Note that the hydrolysis of ATP (step 4) and the movement of the cross-bridge (step 2) are not simultaneous events. If binding sites on actin are still exposed after a cross-bridge finishes its cycle, the cross-bridge can reattach to a new actin monomer in the thin filament and the cross-bridge cycle repeats. (In the event that the muscle is generating force without actually shortening, the cross-bridge will reattach to the same actin molecule as in the previous cycle.)

Thus, in addition to being used to maintain membrane excitability and regulate cytosolic Ca^{2+}, ATP performs two distinct roles in the cross-bridge cycle: (1) The energy released from ATP *hydrolysis* ultimately provides the energy for cross-bridge movement; and (2) ATP *binding* (not hydrolysis) to myosin breaks the link formed between actin and myosin during the cycle, allowing the next cycle to begin. **Table 9.1** summarizes the functions of ATP in skeletal muscle contraction.

TABLE 9.1 Functions of ATP in Skeletal Muscle Contraction
Hydrolysis of ATP by the Na^+/K^+-ATPase in the plasma membrane maintains Na^+ and K^+ gradients, which allows the membrane to produce and propagate action potentials (review Figure 6.13).
Hydrolysis of ATP by the Ca^{2+}-ATPase in the sarcoplasmic reticulum provides the energy for the active transport of calcium ions into the reticulum, lowering cytosolic Ca^{2+} to prerelease concentrations, ending the contraction, and allowing the muscle fiber to relax.
Hydrolysis of ATP by myosin energizes the cross-bridges, providing the energy for force generation.
Binding of ATP to myosin dissociates cross-bridges bound to actin, allowing the bridges to repeat their cycle of activity.

The importance of ATP in dissociating actin and myosin during step 3 of a cross-bridge cycle is illustrated by **rigor mortis,** the gradual stiffening of skeletal muscles that begins several hours after death and reaches a maximum after about 12 hours. The ATP concentration in cells, including muscle cells, declines after death because the nutrients and oxygen the metabolic pathways require to form ATP are no longer supplied by the circulation. In the absence of ATP, the breakage of the link between actin and myosin does not occur (see Figure 9.15). The thick and thin filaments remain bound to each other by immobilized cross-bridges, producing a rigid condition in which the thick and thin filaments cannot be pulled past each other. The stiffness of rigor mortis disappears about 48 to 60 hours after death as the muscle tissue decomposes.

Table 9.2 summarizes the sequence of events that lead from an action potential in a motor neuron to the contraction and relaxation of a skeletal muscle fiber.

9.3 Mechanics of Single-Fiber Contraction

The force exerted on an object by a contracting muscle is known as muscle **tension,** and the force exerted on the muscle by an object (usually its weight) is the **load.** Muscle tension and load are opposing forces. Whether a fiber shortens depends on the relative magnitudes of the tension and the load. For muscle fibers to shorten and thereby move a load, muscle tension must be greater than the opposing load.

When a muscle develops tension but does not shorten or lengthen, the contraction is said to be an **isometric** (constant length) **contraction.** Such contractions occur when the muscle supports a load in a constant position or attempts to move an otherwise supported load that is greater than the tension developed by the muscle. A contraction in which the muscle changes length while the load on the muscle remains constant is an **isotonic** (constant tension) **contraction.**

Depending on the relative magnitudes of muscle tension and the opposing load, isotonic contractions can be associated with either shortening or lengthening of a muscle. When tension exceeds the load, shortening occurs and it is referred to as **concentric contraction.** When an unsupported load is greater than the tension generated by cross-bridges, the result is an **eccentric contraction** (lengthening contraction). In this situation, the load pulls the muscle to a longer length in spite of the opposing force produced by the cross-bridges. Such lengthening contractions occur when an object being supported by muscle contraction is lowered, as when the knee extensors in your thighs are used to lower you to a seat from a standing position. It must be emphasized that in these situations the lengthening of muscle fibers is not an active process produced by the contractile proteins but a consequence of the external forces being applied to the muscle. In the absence of external lengthening forces, a fiber will only *shorten* when stimulated; it will never lengthen. All three types of contractions—isometric, concentric, and eccentric—occur in the natural course of everyday activities.

During each type of contraction, the cross-bridges repeatedly go through the four steps of the cross-bridge cycle illustrated in Figure 9.15. During step 2 of a concentric isotonic contraction,

TABLE 9.2	Sequence of Events Between a Motor Neuron Action Potential and Skeletal Muscle Fiber Contraction
1.	Action potential is initiated and propagates to motor neuron axon terminals.
2.	Ca^{2+} enters axon terminals through voltage-gated Ca^{2+} channels.
3.	Ca^{2+} entry triggers release of ACh from axon terminals.
4.	ACh diffuses from axon terminals to motor end plate in muscle fiber.
5.	ACh binds to nicotinic receptors on motor end plate, increasing their permeability to Na^+ and K^+.
6.	More Na^+ moves into the fiber at the motor end plate than K^+ moves out, depolarizing the membrane and producing the end-plate potential (EPP).
7.	Local currents depolarize the adjacent muscle cell plasma membrane to its threshold potential, generating an action potential that propagates over the muscle fiber surface and into the fiber along the T-tubules.
8.	Action potential in T-tubules induces DHP receptors to pull open ryanodine receptor channels, allowing release of Ca^{2+} from terminal cisternae of sarcoplasmic reticulum.
9.	Ca^{2+} binds to troponin on the thin filaments, causing tropomyosin to move away from its blocking position, thereby uncovering cross-bridge binding sites on actin.
10.	Energized myosin cross-bridges on the thick filaments bind to actin: $A + M \cdot ADP \cdot P_i \rightarrow A \cdot M \cdot ADP \cdot P_i$
11.	Cross-bridge binding triggers release of ATP hydrolysis products from myosin, producing an angular movement of each cross-bridge: $A \cdot M \cdot ADP \cdot P_i \rightarrow A \cdot M + ADP + P_i$
12.	ATP binds to myosin, breaking linkage between actin and myosin and thereby allowing cross-bridges to dissociate from actin: $A \cdot M + ATP \rightarrow A + M \cdot ATP$
13.	ATP bound to myosin is split, energizing the myosin cross-bridge: $M \cdot ATP \rightarrow M \cdot ADP \cdot P_i$
14.	Cross-bridges repeat steps 10 to 13, producing movement (sliding) of thin filaments past thick filaments. Cycles of cross-bridge movement continue as long as Ca^{2+} remains bound to troponin.
15.	Cytosolic Ca^{2+} concentration decreases as Ca^{2+}-ATPase actively transports Ca^{2+} into sarcoplasmic reticulum.
16.	Removal of Ca^{2+} from troponin restores blocking action of tropomyosin, the cross-bridge cycle ceases, and the muscle fiber relaxes.

the cross-bridges bound to actin rotate through their power stroke, causing shortening of the sarcomeres. In contrast, during an isometric contraction, the bound cross-bridges do exert a force on the thin filaments but they are unable to move it. Rather than the filaments sliding, the rotation during the power stroke is absorbed within the structure of the cross-bridge in this circumstance. If isometric contraction is prolonged, cycling cross-bridges repeatedly rebind to the same actin molecule. During a lengthening contraction, the load pulls the cross-bridges in step 2 backward toward the Z lines while they are still bound to actin and exerting force. The events of steps 1, 3, and 4 are the same in all three types of contractions. Thus, the chemical changes in the contractile proteins during each type of contraction are the same. The end result (shortening, no length change, or lengthening) is determined by the magnitude of the load on the muscle.

Contraction terminology applies to both single fibers and whole muscles. In this section, we describe the mechanics of single-fiber contractions. Later, we will discuss the factors controlling the mechanics of whole-muscle contraction.

Twitch Contractions

The mechanical response of a muscle fiber to a single action potential is known as a **twitch. Figure 9.16a** shows the main features of an isometric twitch. Following the action potential, there is an interval of a few milliseconds known as the **latent period** before the tension in the muscle fiber begins to increase. During this latent period, the processes associated with excitation–contraction coupling are occurring. The time interval from the beginning of tension development at the end of the latent period to the peak tension is the **contraction time.**

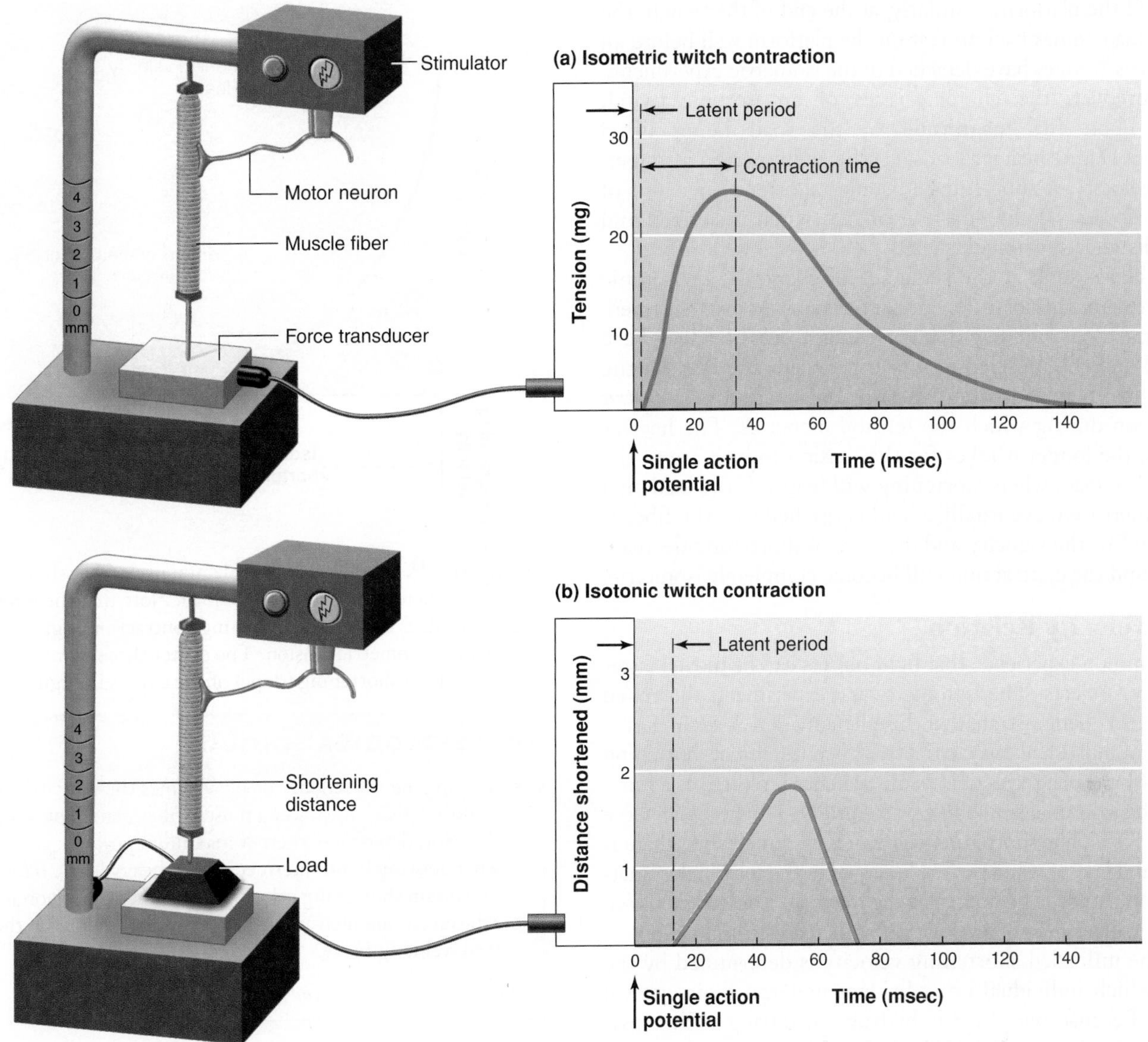

Figure 9.16 (a) Measurement of tension during a single isometric twitch contraction of a skeletal muscle fiber. (b) Measurement of shortening during a single isotonic twitch contraction of a skeletal muscle fiber.

PHYSIOLOGICAL INQUIRY

- Assuming that the same muscle fiber is used in these two experiments, estimate the magnitude of the load (in mg) being lifted in the isotonic experiment.

Answer can be found at end of chapter.

Not all skeletal muscle fibers have the same twitch contraction time. Some fibers have contraction times as short as 10 msec, whereas slower fibers may take 100 msec or longer. The total duration of a contraction depends in part on the time that cytosolic Ca^{2+} remains elevated so that cross-bridges can continue to cycle. This is closely related to the Ca^{2+}-ATPase activity in the sarcoplasmic reticulum; activity is greater in fast-twitch fibers and less in slow-twitch fibers. Twitch duration also depends on how long it takes for cross-bridges to complete their cycle and detach after the removal of Ca^{2+} from the cytosol.

Comparing isotonic and isometric twitches in the same muscle fiber, you can see from **Figure 9.16b** that the latent period in an isotonic twitch contraction is longer than that in an isometric twitch contraction. However, the duration of the mechanical event—shortening—is briefer in an isotonic twitch than the duration of force generation in an isometric twitch. The reason for these differences is most easily explained by referring to the measuring devices shown in Figure 9.16. In the isometric twitch experiment, twitch tension begins to increase as soon as the first cross-bridge attaches, so the latent period is due only to the excitation–contraction coupling delay. By contrast, in the isotonic twitch experiment, the latent period includes both the time for excitation–contraction coupling and the extra time it takes to accumulate enough attached cross-bridges to lift the load off of the platform. Similarly, at the end of the twitch, the isotonic load comes back to rest on the platform well before all of the cross-bridges have detached in the isometric experiment.

Moreover, the characteristics of an isotonic twitch depend upon the magnitude of the load being lifted (**Figure 9.17**). At heavier loads, (1) the latent period is longer, (2) the velocity of shortening (distance shortened per unit of time) is slower, (3) the duration of the twitch is shorter, and (4) the distance shortened is less.

A closer look at the sequence of events in an isotonic twitch explains this load-dependent behavior. As just explained, shortening does not begin until enough cross-bridges have attached and the muscle tension just exceeds the load on the fiber. Thus, before shortening, there is a period of *isometric* contraction during which the tension increases. The heavier the load, the longer it takes for the tension to increase to the value of the load, when shortening will begin. If the load on a fiber is increased, eventually a load is reached that the fiber is unable to lift, the velocity and distance of shortening decrease to zero, and the contraction will become completely isometric.

Load–Velocity Relation

It is a common experience that light objects can be moved faster than heavy objects. The isotonic twitch experiments illustrated in Figure 9.17 demonstrate that this phenomenon arises in part at the level of individual muscle fibers. When the initial shortening velocity (slope) of a series of isotonic twitches is plotted as a function of the load on a single fiber, the result is a hyperbolic curve (**Figure 9.18**). The shortening velocity is maximal when there is no load and is zero when the load is equal to the maximal isometric tension. At loads greater than the maximal isometric tension, the fiber will *lengthen* at a velocity that increases with load.

The unloaded shortening velocity is determined by the rate at which individual cross-bridges undergo their cyclical activity. Because one ATP is hydrolyzed during each cross-bridge cycle, the rate of ATP hydrolysis determines the shortening velocity. Increasing the load on a cross-bridge, however, slows its forward movement during the power stroke. This reduces the overall rate of ATP hydrolysis and, thus, decreases the velocity of shortening.

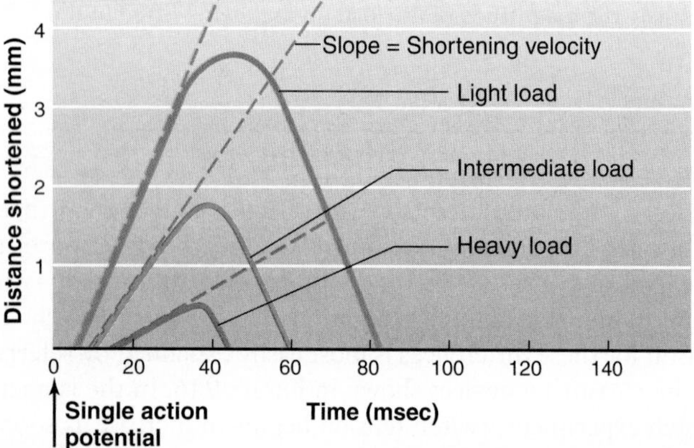

Figure 9.17 Isotonic twitch contractions with different loads. The distance shortened, velocity of shortening, and duration of shortening all decrease with increased load, whereas the time from stimulation to the beginning of shortening increases with increasing load.

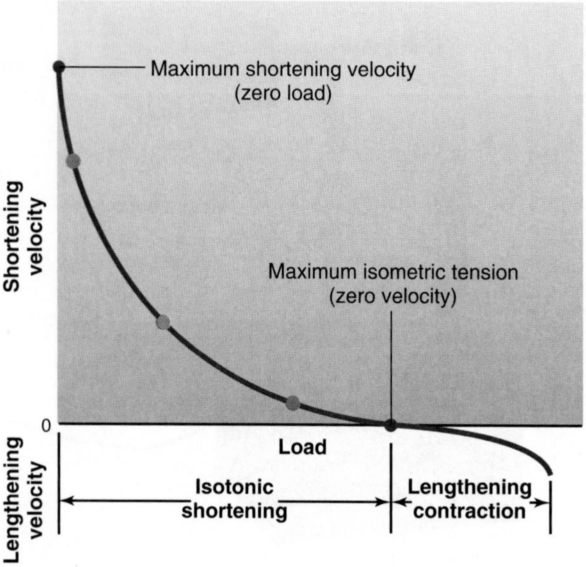

Figure 9.18 Velocity of skeletal muscle fiber shortening and lengthening as a function of load. Note that the force on the cross-bridges during a lengthening contraction is greater than the maximum isometric tension. The center three points correspond to the rate of shortening (slope) of the curves in Figure 9.17.

PHYSIOLOGICAL INQUIRY

- Multiplying the amount of a load times the velocity the load is moved gives the power a muscle fiber generates. From this plot, determine whether maximum power is generated when moving light, intermediate, or heavy loads. (*Hint:* Set maximum shortening velocity and isometric tension to an arbitrary value such as 10, and interpolate values on the load–velocity curve.)

Answer can be found at end of chapter.

Frequency–Tension Relation

Because a single action potential in a skeletal muscle fiber lasts only 1 to 2 msec but the twitch may last for 100 msec, it is possible for a second action potential to be initiated during the period of mechanical activity. **Figure 9.19** illustrates the tension generated during isometric contractions of a muscle fiber in response to multiple stimuli. The isometric twitch following the first stimulus, S_1, lasts 150 msec. The second stimulus, S_2, applied to the muscle fiber 200 msec after S_1, when the fiber has completely relaxed, causes a second identical twitch. When a stimulus is applied before a fiber has completely relaxed from a twitch, it induces a contractile response with a peak tension greater than that produced in a single twitch (S_3 and S_4). If the interval between stimuli is reduced further, the resulting peak tension is even greater (S_5 and S_6). Indeed, the mechanical response to S_6 is a smooth continuation of the mechanical response already induced by S_5.

The increase in muscle tension from successive action potentials occurring during the phase of mechanical activity is known as **summation.** Do not confuse this with the summation of neuronal postsynaptic potentials described in Chapter 6. Postsynaptic potential summation involves additive voltage effects on the membrane, whereas here we are observing the effect of additional attached cross-bridges. A maintained contraction in response to repetitive stimulation is known as a **tetanus** (tetanic contraction). At low stimulation frequencies, the tension may oscillate as the muscle fiber partially relaxes between stimuli, producing an **unfused tetanus.** A **fused tetanus,** with no oscillations, is produced at higher stimulation frequencies (**Figure 9.20**).

As the frequency of action potentials increases, the level of tension increases by summation until a maximal fused tetanic tension is reached, beyond which tension no longer increases even with further increases in stimulation frequency. This maximal tetanic tension is about three to five times greater than the isometric twitch tension. Different muscle fibers have different contraction times, so the stimulus frequency that will produce a maximal tetanic tension differs from fiber to fiber.

Why is tetanic tension so much greater than twitch tension? We can explain summation of tension in part by considering the relative timing of Ca^{2+} availability and cross-bridge binding. The isometric tension produced by a muscle fiber at any instant depends mainly on the total number of cross-bridges bound to actin and undergoing the power stroke of the cross-bridge cycle. Recall that a single action potential in a skeletal muscle fiber briefly releases enough Ca^{2+} to saturate troponin, and all the myosin-binding sites on the thin filaments are therefore *initially* available. However, the binding of energized cross-bridges to these sites (step 1 of the cross-bridge cycle) takes time, whereas the Ca^{2+} released into the cytosol begins to be pumped back into the sarcoplasmic reticulum almost immediately. Thus, after a single action potential, the Ca^{2+} concentration begins to decrease and the troponin–tropomyosin complex reblocks many binding sites before cross-bridges have had time to attach to them.

In contrast, during a tetanic contraction, the successive action potentials each release Ca^{2+} from the sarcoplasmic reticulum before all the Ca^{2+} from the previous action potential has been pumped back into the sarcoplasmic reticulum. This results in a persistent elevation of cytosolic Ca^{2+} concentration, which prevents a decline in the number of available binding sites on the thin filaments. Under these conditions, more binding sites remain available and many more cross-bridges become bound to the thin filaments.

Other causes of the lower tension seen in a single twitch are elastic structures, such as muscle tendons and the protein titin, which delay the transmission of cross-bridge force to the ends of a fiber. Because a single twitch is so brief, cross-bridge activity is already declining before force has been fully transmitted through these structures. This is less of a factor during tetanic stimulation because of the much longer duration of cross-bridge activity and force generation.

Length–Tension Relation

The springlike characteristic of the protein titin (see Figure 9.4), which is attached to the Z line at one end and the thick filaments at the other, is responsible for most of the *passive* elastic properties of relaxed muscle fibers. With increased stretch, the passive

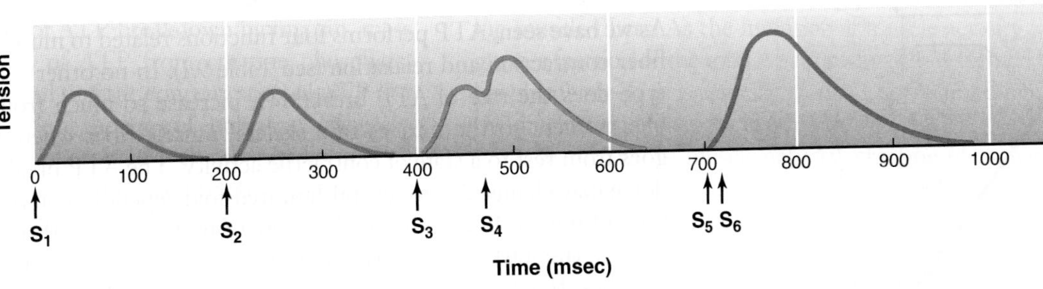

Figure 9.19 Summation of isometric contractions produced by shortening the time between stimuli.

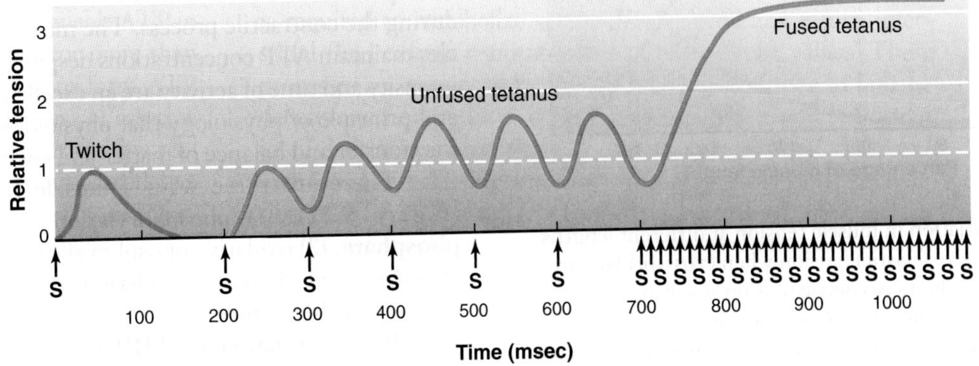

Figure 9.20 Isometric contractions produced by multiple stimuli (S) at 10 stimuli per second (unfused tetanus) and 100 stimuli per second (fused tetanus), as compared with a single twitch.

PHYSIOLOGICAL INQUIRY

- If the twitch contraction time is 35 msec and twitch duration is 150 msec, estimate the range of stimulation frequencies (stimuli per second) over which unfused tetanic contractions will occur.

Answer can be found at end of chapter.

tension in a rel
cross-bridge m
ments. If the st
librium length,
rubber band. I
tension a musc
altered by chan
fiber to various
the magnitude
ure 9.21 shows.
est isometric act

When a r
fiber develops
increased from
increased up to
decrease in tensi
develops no acti
elastic tension w

When mo
tic properties ke
mal length for f
be altered by th
muscles that str
the relaxed leng
ments to bones.

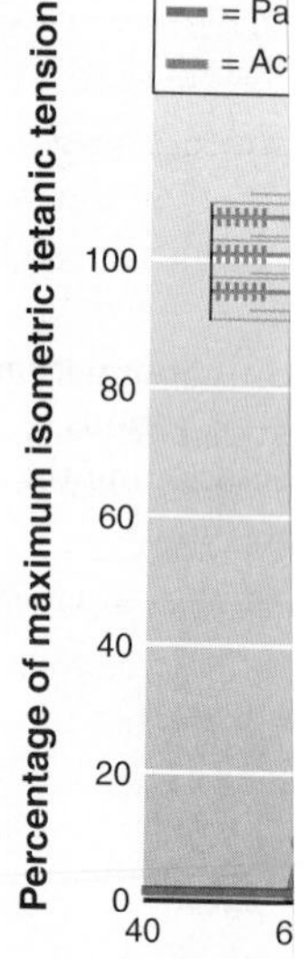

Figure 9.21
Red curve shows
inactive. Green
cross-bridge acti
indicated length.
of length change

PHYSIOLOG

- If this muscle f
and then tetan
measured by t
isometric tensi

Answer can be fou

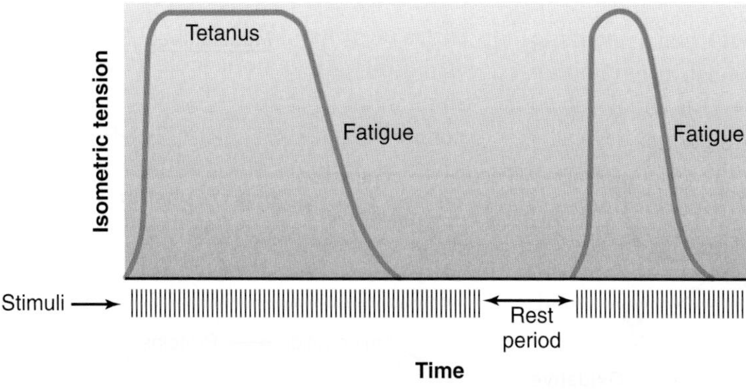

Figure 9.23 Muscle fatigue during a maintained isometric tetanus and recovery following a period of rest.

If a muscle is allowed to rest after the onset of fatigue, it can recover its ability to contract upon restimulation (see Figure 9.23). The rate of recovery also depends upon the duration and intensity of the previous activity. Some muscle fibers fatigue rapidly if continuously stimulated but also recover rapidly after only a few seconds of rest. This type of fatigue accompanies high-intensity, short-duration exercise, such as lifting up and continuously holding a very heavy weight for as long as possible. During this type of activity, blood flow through muscles can cease due to blood vessel compression. In contrast, fatigue develops more slowly with low-intensity, long-duration exercise, such as long-distance running, which includes cyclical periods of contraction and relaxation. Recovery from fatigue after such repetitive activities can take from minutes to hours. After exercise of extreme duration, like running a marathon, it may take days or weeks before muscles achieve complete recovery, likely due to a combination of fatigue and muscle damage.

The causes of acute muscle fatigue following various types of contractions in different types of muscle cells have been the subject of much research, but our understanding is still incomplete. Metabolic changes that occur in active muscle cells include a decrease in ATP concentration and increases in the concentrations of ADP, P_i, Mg^{2+}, H^+ (from lactic acid), and oxygen free radicals (see Chapter 2). Individually, and in combination, those metabolic changes have been shown to

1. decrease the rate of Ca^{2+} release, reuptake, and storage by the sarcoplasmic reticulum;
2. decrease the sensitivity of the thin filament proteins to activation by Ca^{2+}; and
3. directly inhibit the binding and power-stroke motion of the myosin cross-bridges.

Each of these mechanisms has been demonstrated to be important under particular experimental conditions, but their exact relative contributions to acute fatigue in intact human muscle has yet to be resolved.

A number of different processes have been implicated in the persistent fatigue that follows low-intensity, long-duration exercise. The acute effects just listed may play minor roles in this type of exercise as well, but at least two other mechanisms are thought to be more important. One involves changes in the regulation of the ryanodine receptor channels through which Ca^{2+} exits the sarcoplasmic reticulum. During prolonged exercise, these channels become leaky to Ca^{2+}, and persistent elevation of cytosolic Ca^{2+} activates proteases that degrade contractile proteins. The result is muscle soreness and weakness that lasts until the synthesis of new proteins can replace those that are damaged. It appears that depletion of fuel substrates could also play a role in fatigue that occurs during long-duration exercise. ATP depletion does not seem to be a direct cause of this type of fatigue, but a decrease in muscle glycogen, which supplies much of the fuel for contraction, correlates closely with fatigue onset. In addition, low blood glucose (hypoglycemia) and dehydration have been demonstrated to increase fatigue. Thus, a certain level of carbohydrate metabolism may be necessary to prevent fatigue during low-intensity exercise, but the mechanism of this requirement is unknown.

Another type of fatigue quite different from muscle fatigue occurs when the appropriate regions of the cerebral cortex fail to send excitatory signals to the motor neurons. This is called **central command fatigue,** and it may cause a person to stop exercising even though the muscles are not fatigued. An athlete's performance depends not only on the physical state of the appropriate muscles but also upon the mental ability to initiate central commands to muscles during a period of increasingly distressful sensations. Intriguingly, recent experiments have revealed a connection between fuel status and central command mechanisms. Subjects who rinse their mouths with solutions of carbohydrates are able to exercise significantly longer before exhaustion than subjects who rinse with water alone. This may represent a feedforward mechanism in which central command fatigue is inhibited when carbohydrate sensors in the mouth notify brain centers involved in motivation that more fuel is on the way.

9.5 Types of Skeletal Muscle Fibers

Skeletal muscle fibers do not all have the same mechanical and metabolic characteristics. Different types of fibers can be classified on the basis of (1) their maximal velocities of shortening—fast or slow—and (2) the major pathway they use to form ATP—oxidative or glycolytic.

Fast and slow fibers contain forms of myosin that differ in the maximal rates at which they use ATP. This, in turn, determines the maximal rate of cross-bridge cycling and thus the maximal shortening velocity. Fibers containing myosin with low ATPase activity are classified as **slow fibers** and are also sometimes referred to as type I fibers. By contrast, fibers containing myosin with higher ATPase activity are called **fast fibers** or type II fibers. Several subtypes of fast myosin can be distinguished based on small variations in their structure. Although the rate of cross-bridge cycling is about four times faster in fast fibers than in slow fibers, the force produced by both types of cross-bridges is about the same.

The second means of classifying skeletal muscle fibers is according to the type of enzymatic machinery available for synthesizing ATP. Some fibers contain numerous mitochondria and thus have a high capacity for oxidative phosphorylation. These fibers are classified as **oxidative fibers.** Most of the ATP such fibers produce is dependent upon blood flow to deliver oxygen and fuel molecules to the muscle. Not surprisingly, therefore, these fibers are surrounded by many small blood vessels.

They also contain large amounts of an oxygen-binding protein known as **myoglobin,** which increases the rate of oxygen diffusion into the fiber and provides a small store of oxygen. The large amounts of myoglobin present in oxidative fibers give the fibers a dark red color; thus, oxidative fibers are often referred to as **red muscle fibers.** Myoglobin is similar in structure and function to hemoglobin (see Figures 2.20 and 13.25 to 13.29).

In contrast, **glycolytic fibers** have few mitochondria but possess a high concentration of glycolytic enzymes and a large store of glycogen. Corresponding to their limited use of oxygen, these fibers are surrounded by relatively few blood vessels and contain little myoglobin. The lack of myoglobin is responsible for the pale color of glycolytic fibers and their designation as **white muscle fibers.**

On the basis of these two characteristics, three principal types of skeletal muscle fibers can be distinguished:

1. **Slow-oxidative fibers** (type I) combine low myosin-ATPase activity with high oxidative capacity.
2. **Fast-oxidative-glycolytic fibers** (type IIa) combine high myosin-ATPase activity with high oxidative capacity and intermediate glycolytic capacity.
3. **Fast-glycolytic fibers** (type IIb) combine high myosin-ATPase activity with high glycolytic capacity.

In addition to these biochemical differences, there are also size differences. Glycolytic fibers generally have larger diameters than oxidative fibers (**Figure 9.24**). This fact has significance for tension development. The number of thick and thin filaments per unit of cross-sectional area is about the same in all types of skeletal muscle fibers. Therefore, the larger the diameter of a muscle fiber, the greater the total number of thick and thin filaments acting in parallel to produce force, and the greater the maximum tension it can develop. Accordingly, the average glycolytic fiber, with its larger diameter, develops more tension when it contracts than does an average oxidative fiber.

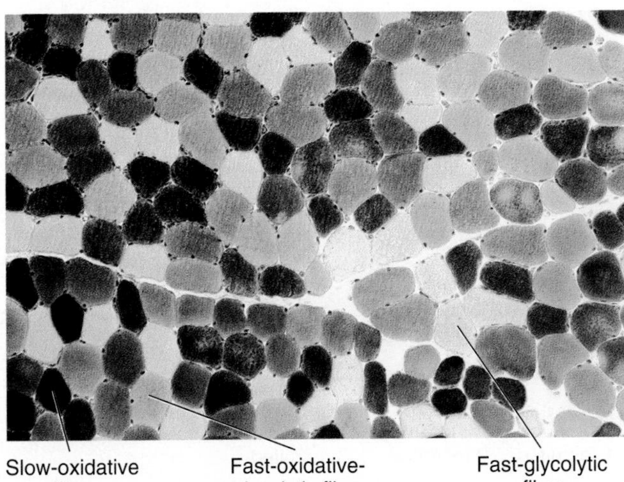

Figure 9.24 Muscle fiber types in normal human muscle, prepared using ATPase stain. Darkest fibers are slow-oxidative type; lighter-colored fibers are fast-oxidative-glycolytic and fast-glycolytic fibers. Note that the fourth theoretical possibility—slow-glycolytic fibers—is not found.

These three types of fibers also differ in their capacity to resist fatigue. Fast-glycolytic fibers fatigue rapidly, whereas slow-oxidative fibers are very resistant to fatigue, which allows them to maintain contractile activity for long periods with little loss of tension. Fast-oxidative-glycolytic fibers have an intermediate capacity to resist fatigue (**Figure 9.25**).

Table 9.3 summarizes the characteristics of the three types of skeletal muscle fibers.

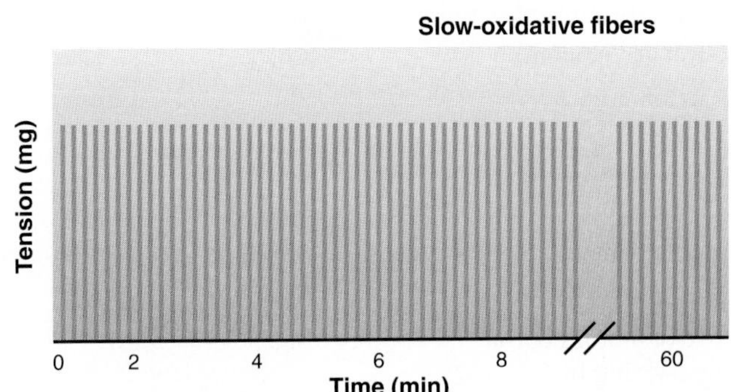

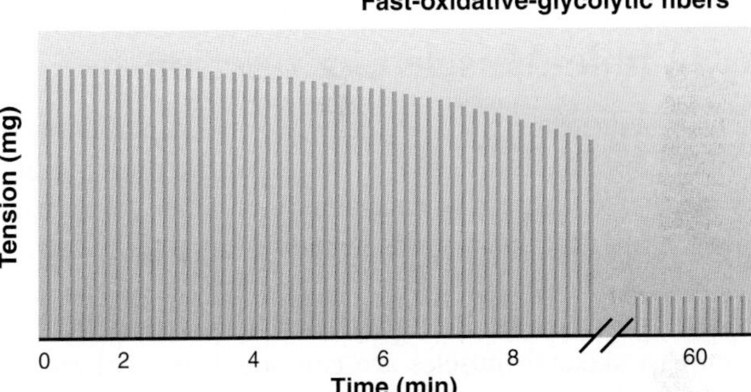

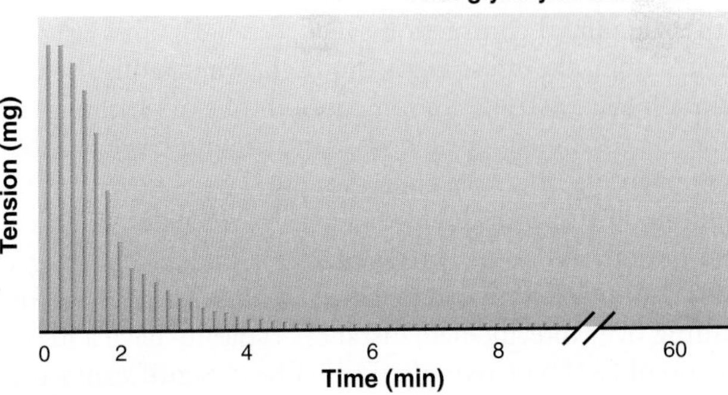

Figure 9.25 The rate of fatigue development in the three fiber types. Each vertical line is the contractile response to a brief tetanic stimulus and relaxation. The contractile responses occurring between about 9 min and 60 min are not shown on the figure.

PHYSIOLOGICAL INQUIRY

- Why is it logical that there are no muscle fibers classified as slow-glycolytic?

Answer can be found at end of chapter.

TABLE 9.3	Characteristics of the Three Types of Skeletal Muscle Fibers		
	Slow-Oxidative Fibers (Type I)	Fast-Oxidative-Glycolytic Fibers (Type IIa)	Fast-Glycolytic Fibers (Type IIb)*
Primary source of ATP production	Oxidative phosphorylation	Oxidative phosphorylation	Glycolysis
Mitochondria	Many	Many	Few
Capillaries	Many	Many	Few
Myoglobin content	High (red muscle)	High (red muscle)	Low (white muscle)
Glycolytic enzyme activity	Low	Intermediate	High
Glycogen content	Low	Intermediate	High
Rate of fatigue	Slow	Intermediate	Fast
Myosin-ATPase activity	Low	High	High
Contraction velocity	Slow	Fast	Fast
Fiber diameter	Small	Large	Large
Motor unit size	Small	Intermediate	Large
Size of motor neuron innervating fiber	Small	Intermediate	Large

*Type IIb fibers are sometimes designated as type IIx in the human muscle physiology literature.

9.6 Whole-Muscle Contraction

As described earlier, whole muscles are made up of many muscle fibers organized into motor units. All the muscle fibers in a single motor unit are of the same fiber type. Thus, you can apply the fiber designation to the motor unit and refer to slow-oxidative motor units, fast-oxidative-glycolytic motor units, and fast-glycolytic motor units.

Most skeletal muscles are composed of all three motor unit types interspersed with each other (**Figure 9.26**). No muscle has only a single fiber type. Depending on the proportions of the fiber types present, muscles can differ considerably in their maximal contraction speed, strength, and fatigability. For example, the muscles of the back, which must be able to maintain their activity for long periods of time without fatigue while supporting an upright posture, contain large numbers of slow-oxidative fibers. In contrast, muscles in the arms that are called upon to produce large amounts of tension over a short time period, as when a boxer throws a punch, have a greater proportion of fast-glycolytic fibers. Leg muscles used for fast running over intermediate distances typically have a high proportion of fast-oxidative-glycolytic fibers. Significant variation occurs between individuals, however. For example, elite distance runners on average have greater than 75% slow-twitch fibers in the gastrocnemius muscle of the lower leg, whereas in elite sprinters the same muscle has 75% fast-twitch fibers.

We will next use the characteristics of single fibers to describe whole-muscle contraction and its control.

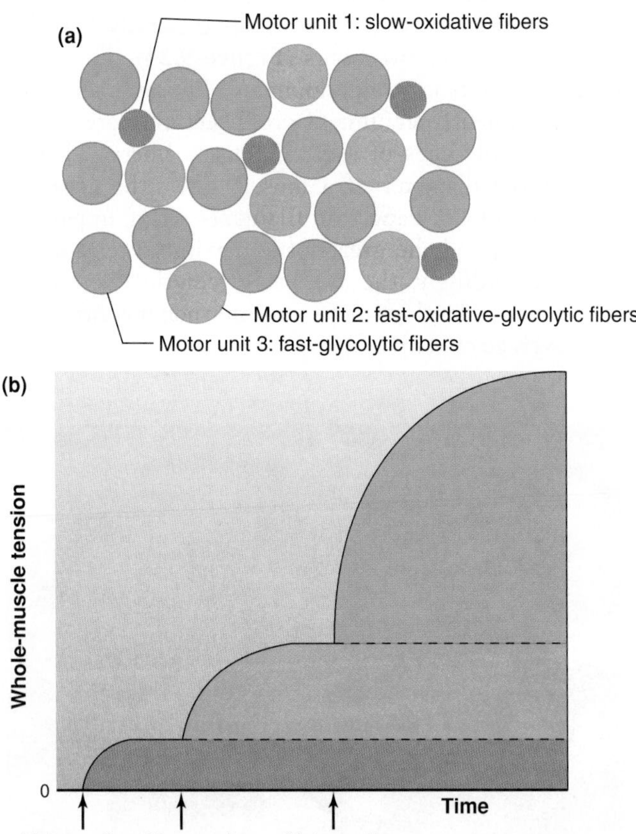

Figure 9.26 (a) Diagram of a cross section through a muscle composed of three types of motor units. (b) Tetanic muscle tension resulting from the successive recruitment of the three types of motor units. Note that motor unit 3, composed of fast-glycolytic fibers, produces the greatest increase in tension because it is composed of large-diameter fibers with the largest number of fibers per motor unit.

Control of Muscle Tension

The total tension a muscle can develop depends upon two factors: (1) the amount of tension developed by each fiber, and (2) the number of fibers contracting at any time. By controlling these two factors, the nervous system controls whole-muscle

TABLE 9.4	Factors Determining Muscle Tension
I. Tension developed by each fiber	
A. Action potential frequency (frequency–tension relation)	
B. Fiber length (length–tension relation)	
C. Fiber diameter	
D. Fatigue	
II. Number of active fibers	
A. Number of fibers per motor unit	
B. Number of active motor units	

tension as well as shortening velocity. The conditions that determine the amount of tension developed in a single fiber have been discussed previously and are summarized in **Table 9.4**.

The number of fibers contracting at any time depends on (1) the number of fibers in each motor unit (motor unit size), and (2) the number of active motor units.

Motor unit size varies considerably from one muscle to another. The muscles in the hand and eye, which produce very delicate movements, contain small motor units. For example, one motor neuron innervates only about 13 fibers in an eye muscle. In contrast, in the more coarsely controlled muscles of the legs, each motor unit is large, containing hundreds and in some cases several thousand fibers. When a muscle is composed of small motor units, the total tension the muscle produces can be increased in small steps by activating additional motor units. If the motor units are large, large increases in tension will occur as each additional motor unit is activated. Thus, finer control of muscle tension is possible in muscles with small motor units.

The force a single fiber produces, as we have seen earlier, depends in part on the fiber diameter—the greater the diameter, the greater the force. We have also noted that fast-glycolytic fibers have the largest diameters. Thus, a motor unit composed of 100 fast-glycolytic fibers produces more force than a motor unit composed of 100 slow-oxidative fibers. In addition, fast-glycolytic motor units tend to have more muscle fibers. For both of these reasons, activating a fast-glycolytic motor unit will produce more force than activating a slow-oxidative motor unit.

The process of increasing the number of motor units that are active in a muscle at any given time is called **recruitment.** It is achieved by activating excitatory synaptic inputs to more motor neurons. The greater the number of active motor neurons, the more motor units recruited and the greater the muscle tension.

Motor neuron size plays an important role in the recruitment of motor units. The size of a motor neuron refers to the diameter of the neuronal cell body, which usually correlates with the diameter of its axon. Given the same number of sodium ions entering a cell at a single excitatory synapse in a large and in a small motor neuron, the small neuron will undergo a greater depolarization because these ions will be distributed over a smaller membrane surface area. Accordingly, given the same level of synaptic input, the smallest neurons will be recruited first—that is, they will begin to generate action potentials first. The larger neurons will be recruited only as the level of synaptic input increases. Because the smallest motor neurons innervate the slow-oxidative motor units (see Table 9.3), these motor units are recruited first, followed by fast-oxidative-glycolytic motor units, and finally, during very strong contractions, by fast-glycolytic motor units (see Figure 9.26).

Thus, during moderate-strength contractions, such as those that occur in most endurance types of exercise, relatively few fast-glycolytic motor units are recruited, and most of the activity occurs in the more fatigue-resistant oxidative fibers. The large, fast-glycolytic motor units, which fatigue rapidly, begin to be recruited when the intensity of contraction exceeds about 40% of the maximal tension the muscle can produce.

In summary, the neural control of whole-muscle tension involves (1) the frequency of action potentials in individual motor units (to vary the tension generated by the fibers in that unit) and (2) the recruitment of motor units (to vary the number of active fibers). Most motor neuron activity occurs in bursts of action potentials, which produce tetanic contractions of individual motor units rather than single twitches. Recall that the tension of a single fiber increases only threefold to fivefold when going from a twitch to a maximal tetanic contraction. Therefore, varying the frequency of action potentials in the neurons supplying them provides a way to make only threefold to fivefold adjustments in the tension of the recruited motor units. The force a whole muscle exerts can be varied over a much wider range than this, from very delicate movements to extremely powerful contractions, by recruiting motor units. Thus, recruitment provides the primary means of varying tension in a whole muscle. Recruitment is controlled by the central commands from the motor centers in the brain to the various motor neurons (see Chapter 10).

Control of Shortening Velocity

As we saw earlier, the velocity at which a single muscle fiber shortens is determined by (1) the load on the fiber and (2) whether the fiber is a fast or slow fiber. Translated to a whole muscle, these characteristics become (1) the load on the whole muscle and (2) the types of motor units in the muscle. For the whole muscle, however, recruitment becomes a third very important factor, one that explains how the shortening velocity can be varied from very fast to very slow even though the load on the muscle remains constant. Consider for the sake of illustration a muscle composed of only two motor units of the same size and fiber type. One motor unit by itself will lift a 4 g load more slowly than a 2 g load because the shortening velocity decreases with increasing load. When both units are active and a 4 g load is lifted, each motor unit bears only half the load and its fibers will shorten as if it were lifting only a 2 g load. In other words, the muscle will lift the 4 g load at a higher velocity when both motor units are active. Recruitment of motor units thus leads to increases in both force and velocity.

Muscle Adaptation to Exercise

The regularity with which a muscle is used—as well as the duration and intensity of its activity—affects the properties of the muscle. If the neurons to a skeletal muscle are destroyed or the neuromuscular junctions become nonfunctional, the denervated muscle fibers will become progressively smaller in diameter and the amount of contractile proteins they contain will decrease. This condition is known as ***denervation atrophy.*** A muscle can also atrophy with its nerve supply intact if the muscle is not used for a long period of time, as when a broken arm or leg is immobilized in a cast. This condition is known as ***disuse atrophy.***

In contrast to the decrease in muscle mass that results from a lack of neural stimulation, increased amounts of contractile activity—in other words, exercise—can produce an increase in the size (hypertrophy) of muscle fibers as well as changes in their capacity for ATP production.

Exercise that is of relatively low intensity but long duration (popularly called "aerobic exercise"), such as distance running, produces increases in the number of mitochondria in the fibers that are recruited in this type of activity. In addition, the number of capillaries around these fibers also increases. All these changes lead to an increase in the capacity for endurance activity with a minimum of fatigue. (Surprisingly, fiber diameter decreases slightly, and thus there is a small decrease in the maximal strength of muscles as a result of endurance training.) As we will see in later chapters, endurance exercise produces changes not only in the skeletal muscles but also in the respiratory and circulatory systems, changes that improve the delivery of oxygen and fuel molecules to the muscle.

In contrast, short-duration, high-intensity exercise (popularly called "strength training") such as weight lifting affects primarily the fast-twitch fibers, which are recruited during strong contractions. These fibers undergo an increase in diameter (hypertrophy) due to satellite cell activation and increased synthesis of actin and myosin filaments, which form more myofibrils. In addition, glycolytic activity is increased by increasing the synthesis of glycolytic enzymes. The result of such high-intensity exercise is an increase in the strength of the muscle and the bulging muscles of a conditioned weight lifter. Such muscles, although very powerful, have little capacity for endurance and they fatigue rapidly. It should be noted that not all of the gains in strength with resistance exercise are due to muscle hypertrophy. It has frequently been observed, particularly in women, that strength can almost double with training without measurable muscle hypertrophy. The most likely mechanisms are modifications of neural pathways involved in motor control. For example, regular weight training is hypothesized to cause increased synchronization in motor unit recruitment, enhanced ability to recruit fast-glycolytic motor neurons, and a reduction in inhibitory afferent inputs from tendon sensory receptors (described in Chapter 10).

Exercise produces limited change in the types of myosin enzymes the fibers form and thus little change in the proportions of fast and slow fibers in a muscle. Research suggests that even with extreme exercise training, the change in ratio between slow and fast myosin types in muscle fibers is less than 10%. As described previously, however, exercise does change the rates at which metabolic enzymes are synthesized, leading to changes in the proportion of oxidative and glycolytic fibers within a muscle. With endurance training, there is a decrease in the number of fast-glycolytic fibers and an increase in the number of fast-oxidative-glycolytic fibers as the oxidative capacity of the fibers increases.

The signals responsible for all these changes in muscle with different types of activity are just beginning to be understood by researchers. They are related to the frequency and intensity of the contractile activity in the muscle fibers and, thus, to the pattern of action potentials and tension produced in the muscle over an extended period of time. Though multiple neural and chemical factors are likely involved, evidence is accumulating that locally produced insulin-like growth factor-1 (see Chapter 11) may play a central role. Anabolic steroids (androgens) also exert an influence on muscle strength and growth, which is discussed in Chapter 17. Recently, a regulatory protein called **myostatin** was discovered in the blood, which is produced by skeletal muscle cells and binds to receptors on those same cells. It appears to exert a negative feedback effect to prevent excessive muscle hypertrophy. Humans and other mammals with genetic mutations leading to deficiencies of myostatin or its receptors show exceptional muscle growth. Researchers are currently seeking ways to block myostatin activity to treat diseases that cause muscle atrophy, like muscular dystrophy (discussed at the end of this section).

Because different types of exercise training produce quite different changes in the strength and endurance capacity of a muscle, an individual performing regular exercise to improve muscle performance must choose a type of exercise compatible with the type of activity he or she ultimately wishes to perform. For example, lifting weights will not improve the endurance of a long-distance runner, and jogging will not produce the increased strength a weight lifter desires. Most types of exercise, however, produce some effect on both strength and endurance. These changes in muscle in response to repeated periods of exercise occur slowly over a period of weeks. If regular exercise ceases, the muscles will slowly revert to their unexercised state.

The maximum force a muscle generates decreases by 30% to 40% between the ages of 30 and 80. This decrease in tension-generating capacity is due primarily to a decrease in average fiber diameter. Some of the change is simply the result of diminishing physical activity and can be prevented by regular exercise. The ability of a muscle to adapt to exercise, however, decreases with age. The same intensity and duration of exercise in an older individual will not produce the same amount of change as in a younger person.

This effect of aging, however, is only partial; there is no question that even in elderly people, increases in exercise can produce significant adaptation. Aerobic training has received major attention because of beneficial effects on the cardiovascular system (see Chapter 12). Strength training to even a modest degree, however, can partially prevent the loss of muscle tissue that occurs with aging. Moreover, it helps maintain stronger bones and joints.

Extensive exercise by an individual whose muscles have not been used in performing that particular type of exercise leads to muscle soreness the next day. This soreness is thought to be the result of structural damage to muscle cells and their membranes, which activates the inflammation response (see Chapter 18). As part of this response, substances such as histamine released by cells of the immune system activate the endings of pain neurons in the muscle. Soreness most often results from lengthening contractions, indicating that the lengthening of a muscle fiber by an external force produces greater muscle damage than does either shortening or isometric contraction. Thus, exercising by gradually lowering weights will produce greater muscle soreness than an equivalent amount of weight

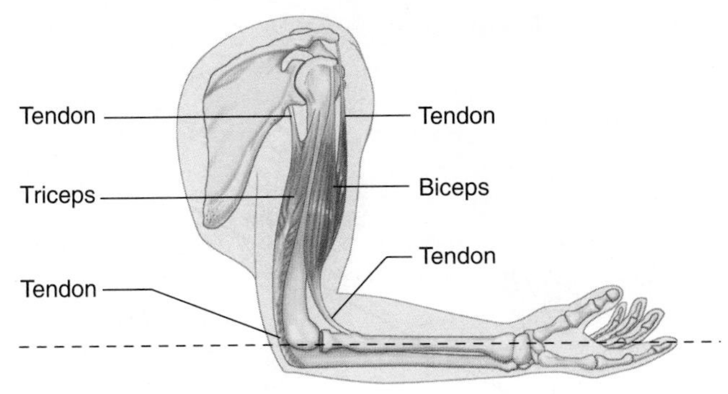

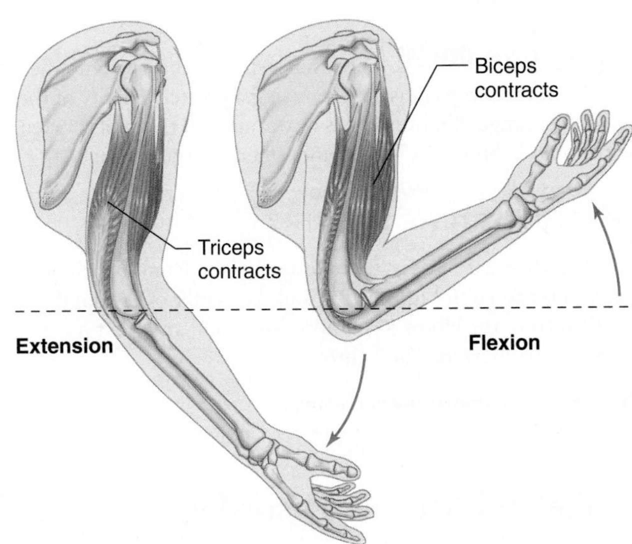

Figure 9.27 AP|R Antagonistic muscles for flexion and extension of the forearm.

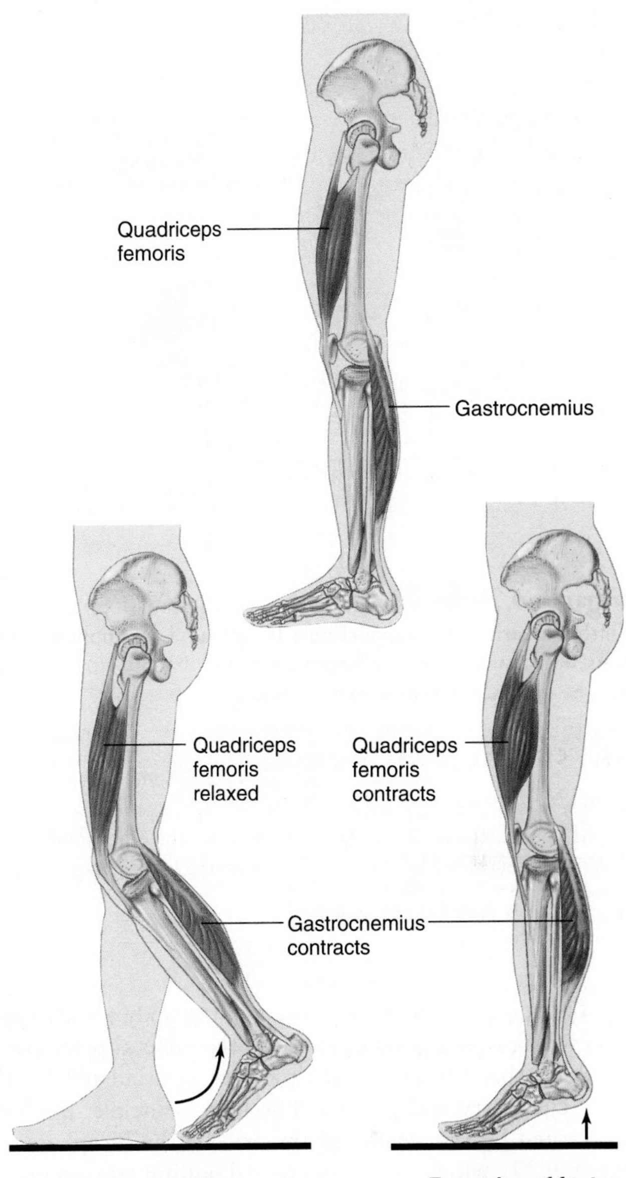

Figure 9.28 AP|R Contraction of the gastrocnemius muscle in the calf can lead either to flexion of the leg, if the quadriceps femoris muscle is relaxed, or to extension of the foot, if the quadriceps is contracting, preventing the knee joint from bending.

lifting. This explains a phenomenon well-known to athletic trainers: The shortening contractions of leg muscles used to run *up* flights of stairs result in far less soreness than the lengthening contractions used for running *down*. Interestingly, it has been demonstrated that most of the strength gains during weight lifting is due to the eccentric portion of the movement. It therefore seems that the mechanisms underlying muscle soreness and muscle adaptation to exercise are related.

Lever Action of Muscles and Bones

A contracting muscle exerts a force on bones through its connecting tendons. When the force is great enough, the bone moves as the muscle shortens. A contracting muscle exerts only a pulling force, so that as the muscle shortens, the bones it is attached to are pulled toward each other. **Flexion** refers to the *bending* of a limb at a joint, whereas **extension** is the *straightening* of a limb (**Figure 9.27**). These opposing motions require at least two muscles, one to cause flexion and the other extension. Groups of muscles that produce oppositely directed movements at a joint are known as **antagonists.** For example, from Figure 9.27 we can see that contraction of the biceps causes flexion of the arm at the elbow, whereas contraction of the antagonistic muscle, the triceps, causes the arm to extend. Both muscles exert only a pulling force upon the forearm when they contract.

Sets of antagonistic muscles are required not only for flexion–extension but also for side-to-side movements or rotation of a limb. The contraction of some muscles leads to two types of limb movement, depending on the contractile state of other muscles acting on the same limb. For example, contraction of the gastrocnemius muscle in the calf causes a flexion of the leg at the knee, as in walking (**Figure 9.28**). However, contraction of the gastrocnemius muscle with the simultaneous contraction of the quadriceps femoris (which causes extension of the lower leg) prevents the knee joint from bending, leaving only the ankle joint capable of moving. The foot is extended, and the body rises on tiptoe.

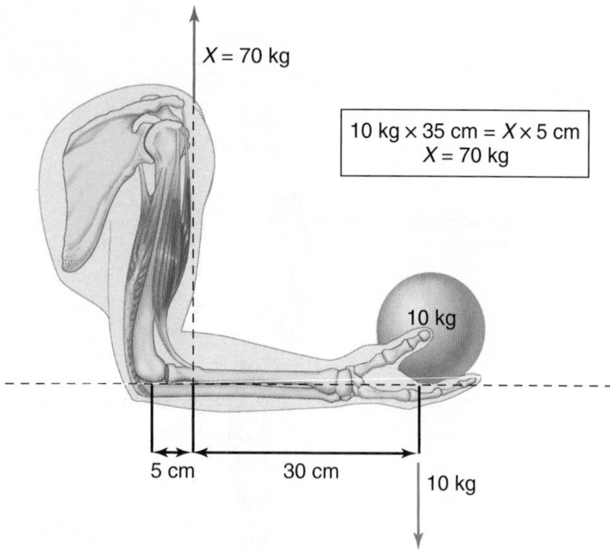

Figure 9.29 AP|R Mechanical equilibrium of forces acting on the forearm while supporting a 10 kg load. For simplicity, mass is used as a measure of the force here rather than newtons, which are the standard scientific units of force.

PHYSIOLOGICAL INQUIRY

- Describe what would happen if this weight was mounted on a rod that moved it 10 cm farther away from the elbow and the tension generated by the muscle was increased to 85 kg.

Answer can be found at end of chapter.

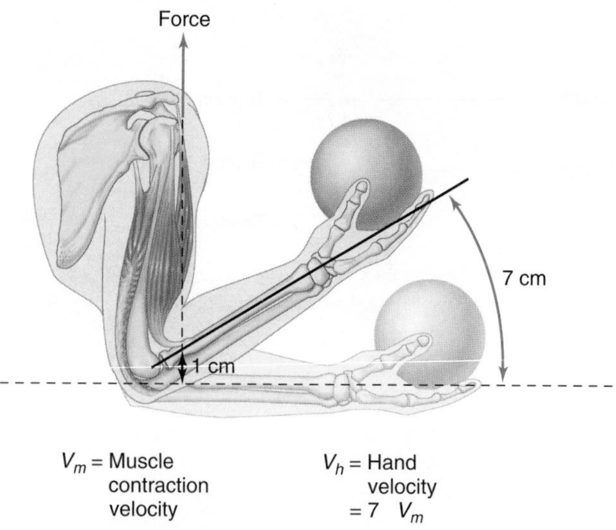

Figure 9.30 AP|R The lever system of the arm amplifies the velocity of the biceps muscle, producing a greater velocity of the hand. The range of movement is also amplified (1 cm of shortening by the muscle produces 7 cm of movement by the hand).

PHYSIOLOGICAL INQUIRY

- If an individual's biceps insertion was 5 cm from the elbow joint (as shown in Figure 9.29) and the center of the hand was 45 cm from the elbow joint, how fast would an object move if the biceps shortened at 2 cm/sec?

Answer can be found at end of chapter.

The muscles, bones, and joints in the body are arranged in lever systems—a good example of the general principle of physiology that physiological processes are dictated by the laws of chemistry and physics. The basic principle of a lever is illustrated by the flexion of the arm by the biceps muscle (**Figure 9.29**), which exerts an upward pulling tension on the forearm about 5 cm away from the elbow joint. In this example, a 10 kg weight held in the hand exerts a downward load of 10 kg about 35 cm from the elbow. A law of physics tells us that the forearm is in mechanical equilibrium when the product of the downward load (10 kg) and its distance from the elbow (35 cm) is equal to the product of the isometric tension exerted by the muscle (X) and its distance from the elbow (5 cm); that is, $10 \times 35 = X \times 5$. Thus, $X = 70$ kg. The important point is that this system is working at a mechanical disadvantage because the tension exerted by the muscle (70 kg) is considerably greater than the load (10 kg) it is supporting.

However, the mechanical disadvantage that most muscle lever systems operate under is offset by increased maneuverability. As illustrated in **Figure 9.30**, when the biceps shortens 1 cm, the hand moves through a distance of 7 cm. Because the muscle shortens 1 cm in the same amount of time that the hand moves 7 cm, the velocity at which the hand moves is seven times greater than the rate of muscle shortening. The lever system amplifies the velocity of muscle shortening so that short, relatively slow movements of the muscle produce faster movements of the hand. Thus, a pitcher can throw a baseball at 90 to 100 mph even though his muscles shorten at only a small fraction of this velocity.

9.7 Skeletal Muscle Disorders

A number of conditions and diseases can affect the contraction of skeletal muscle. Many of them are caused by defects in the parts of the nervous system that control contraction of the muscle fibers rather than by defects in the muscle fibers themselves. For example, ***poliomyelitis*** is a viral disease that destroys motor neurons, leading to the paralysis of skeletal muscle, and may result in death due to respiratory failure.

Muscle Cramps

Involuntary tetanic contraction of skeletal muscles produces ***muscle cramps.*** During cramping, action potentials fire at abnormally high rates, a much greater rate than occurs during maximal voluntary contraction. The specific cause of this high activity is uncertain, but it is probably related to electrolyte imbalances in the extracellular fluid surrounding both the muscle and nerve fibers. These imbalances may arise from overexercise or persistent dehydration, and they can directly induce action potentials in motor neurons and muscle fibers. Another theory is that chemical imbalances within the muscle stimulate sensory receptors in the muscle, and the motor neurons to the area are activated by reflex when those signals reach the spinal cord.

Hypocalcemic Tetany

Hypocalcemic tetany is the involuntary tetanic contraction of skeletal muscles that occurs when the extracellular Ca^{2+} concentration decreases to about 40% of its normal value. This may seem surprising, because we have seen that Ca^{2+} is required for excitation–contraction coupling. However, recall that this Ca^{2+} is sarcoplasmic reticulum Ca^{2+}, not extracellular Ca^{2+}. The effect of changes in extracellular Ca^{2+} is exerted not on the sarcoplasmic reticulum Ca^{2+} but directly on the plasma membrane. Low extracellular Ca^{2+} (**hypocalcemia**) increases the opening of Na^{+} channels in excitable membranes, leading to membrane depolarization and the spontaneous firing of action potentials. This causes the increased muscle contractions, which are similar to muscular cramping. Chapter 11 discusses the mechanisms controlling the extracellular concentration of calcium ions.

Muscular Dystrophy

Muscular dystrophy is a common genetic disease, affecting an estimated one in every 3500 males (but many fewer females). It is associated with the progressive degeneration of skeletal and cardiac muscle fibers, weakening the muscles and leading ultimately to death from respiratory or cardiac failure.

Muscular dystrophy is caused by the absence or defect of one or more proteins that make up the costameres in striated muscle. **Costameres** (*costa* = "rib") are clusters of structural and regulatory proteins that link the Z disks of the outermost myofibrils to the sarcolemma and extracellular matrix (**Figure 9.31a**). Proteins of the costameres serve multiple roles, including lateral transmission of force from the sarcomeres to the extracellular matrix and neighboring muscle fibers, stabilization of the sarcolemma against physical forces during muscle fiber contraction or stretch, and initiation of intracellular signals that link contractile activity with regulation of muscle cell remodeling. Defects in a number of specific costamere proteins have been demonstrated to cause various types of muscular dystrophy.

Duchenne muscular dystrophy is a sex-linked recessive disorder caused by a mutation in a gene on the X chromosome that codes for the protein **dystrophin.** Dystrophin was the first costamere protein discovered to be related to a muscular dystrophy, which is how it earned its name. As described in Chapter 17, females have two X chromosomes and males only one. Consequently, a female with one abnormal X chromosome and one normal one generally will not develop the disease, but males with an abnormal X chromosome always will. The defective gene can result in either a nonfunctional or missing protein. Dystrophin is an extremely large protein that normally forms a link between the contractile filament actin and proteins embedded in the overlying sarcolemma. In its absence, fibers subjected to repeated structural deformation during contraction are susceptible to membrane rupture and cell death. Therefore, the condition progresses with muscle use and age. Symptoms of weakness in the muscles of the hips and trunk become evident at about 2 to 6 years of age, and most affected individuals do not survive much beyond the age of 20 (**Figure 9.31b**). Preliminary attempts are being made to treat the disease by inserting the normal gene into dystrophic muscle cells.

Myasthenia Gravis

Myasthenia gravis is a collection of neuromuscular disorders characterized by muscle fatigue and weakness that progressively worsen as the muscle is used. Myasthenia gravis affects about one out of every 7500 Americans, occurring more often in women than men. The most common cause is the destruction of nicotinic ACh-receptor proteins of the motor end plate, mediated by antibodies of a person's own immune system (see Chapter 18 for a description of autoimmune diseases). The release of ACh from the axon terminals is normal, but

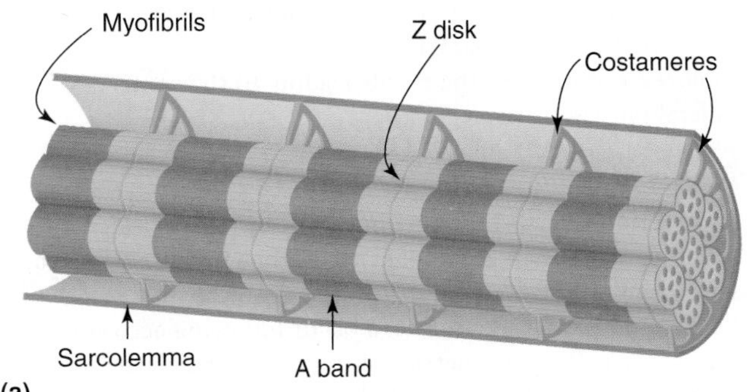

Figure 9.31 (a) Schematic diagram showing costamere proteins that link Z disks with membrane and extracellular matrix proteins. (b) Boy with Duchenne muscular dystrophy. Muscles of the hip girdle and trunk are the first to weaken, requiring patients to use their arms to "climb up" the legs in order to go from lying to standing. Part (a) is redrawn from James Ervasti, "Costameres: The Achilles' heel of Herculean muscle," *Journal of Biological Chemistry*, 278(16): 13591–13594 (2003).

the magnitude of the end-plate potential is markedly reduced because of the decreased availability of receptors. Even in normal muscle, the amount of ACh released with each action potential decreases with repetitive activity, and thus the magnitude of the resulting end-plate potential (EPP) decreases. In normal muscle, however, the EPP remains well above the threshold necessary to initiate a muscle action potential. In contrast, after a few motor nerve impulses in a myasthenia gravis patient, the magnitude of the EPP decreases below the threshold for initiating a muscle action potential.

A number of approaches are currently used to treat the disease. One is to administer acetylcholinesterase inhibitors (e.g., ***pyridostigmine***). This can partially compensate for the reduction in available ACh receptors by prolonging the time that acetylcholine is available at the synapse. Other therapies aim at blunting the immune response. Treatment with glucocorticoids is one way that immune function is suppressed (see Chapter 11). Removal of the thymus gland (***thymectomy***) reduces the production of antibodies and reverses symptoms in about 50% of patients. ***Plasmapheresis*** is a treatment that involves replacing the liquid fraction of blood (plasma) that contains the offending antibodies. A combination of these treatments has greatly reduced the mortality rate for myasthenia gravis.

SECTION A SUMMARY

There are three types of muscle—skeletal, smooth, and cardiac. Skeletal muscle is attached to bones and moves and supports the skeleton. Smooth muscle surrounds hollow cavities and tubes. Cardiac muscle is the muscle of the heart.

Structure

I. Skeletal muscles, composed of cylindrical muscle fibers (cells), are linked to bones by tendons at each end of the muscle.
II. Skeletal muscle fibers have a repeating, striated pattern of light and dark bands due to the arrangement of the thick and thin filaments within the myofibrils.
III. Actin-containing thin filaments are anchored to the Z lines at each end of a sarcomere. Their free ends partially overlap the myosin-containing thick filaments in the A band at the center of the sarcomere.
IV. Myosin molecules form the backbone of the thick filament and also have extensions called cross-bridges that span the gap between the thick and thin filaments. Each cross-bridge has two globular heads that contain a binding site for actin and an enzymatic site that splits ATP.
V. Skeletal muscle fibers have an elaborate membrane system in which the plasma membrane (sarcolemma) sends tubular extensions (T-tubules) throughout the cross section of the cell. T-tubules interact with terminal cisternae of the sarcoplasmic reticulum, in which Ca^{2+} is stored.

Molecular Mechanisms of Skeletal Muscle Contraction

I. Branches of a motor neuron axon form neuromuscular junctions with the muscle fibers in its motor unit. Each muscle fiber is innervated by a branch from only one motor neuron.
   a. Acetylcholine released by an action potential in a motor neuron binds to receptors on the motor end plate of the muscle membrane, opening ion channels that allow the passage of sodium and potassium ions, which depolarize the end-plate membrane.
   b. A single action potential in a motor neuron is sufficient to produce an action potential in a skeletal muscle fiber.
   c. Figure 9.9 summarizes events at the neuromuscular junction.
   d. Signaling at the neuromuscular junction can be disrupted by a number of different toxins, drugs, and disease processes.
II. In a resting muscle, tropomyosin molecules that are in contact with the actin subunits of the thin filaments block the attachment of cross-bridges to actin.
III. Contraction is initiated by an increase in cytosolic Ca^{2+} concentration. The calcium ions bind to troponin, producing a change in its shape that is transmitted via tropomyosin to uncover the binding sites on actin, allowing the cross-bridges to bind to the thin filaments.
   a. The increase in cytosolic Ca^{2+} concentration is triggered by an action potential in the plasma membrane. The action potential is propagated into the interior of the fiber along the transverse tubules to the region of the sarcoplasmic reticulum, where dihydropyridine receptors sense the voltage change and pull open ryanodine receptors, releasing calcium ions from the reticulum.
   b. Relaxation of a contracting muscle fiber occurs as a result of the active transport of cytosolic calcium ions back into the sarcoplasmic reticulum.
IV. When a skeletal muscle fiber actively shortens, the thin filaments are propelled toward the center of their sarcomere by movements of the myosin cross-bridges that bind to actin.
   a. The four steps occurring during each cross-bridge cycle are summarized in Figure 9.15. The cross-bridges undergo repeated cycles during a contraction, each cycle producing only a small increment of movement.
   b. The functions of ATP in muscle contraction are summarized in Table 9.1.
V. Table 9.2 summarizes the events leading to the contraction of a skeletal muscle fiber.

Mechanics of Single-Fiber Contraction

I. Contraction refers to the turning on of the cross-bridge cycle. Whether there is an accompanying change in muscle length depends upon the external forces acting on the muscle.
II. Three types of contractions can occur following activation of a muscle fiber: (1) an isometric contraction in which the muscle generates tension but does not change length; (2) an isotonic contraction in which the muscle shortens (concentric), moving a load; and (3) a lengthening (eccentric) contraction in which the external load on the muscle causes the muscle to lengthen during the period of contractile activity.
III. Increasing the frequency of action potentials in a muscle fiber increases the mechanical response (tension or shortening) up to the level of maximal tetanic tension.
IV. Maximum isometric tetanic tension is produced at the optimal sarcomere length L_0. Stretching a fiber beyond its optimal length or decreasing the fiber length below L_0 decreases the tension generated.
V. The velocity of muscle fiber shortening decreases with increases in load. Maximum velocity occurs at zero load.

Skeletal Muscle Energy Metabolism

I. Muscle fibers form ATP by the transfer of phosphate from creatine phosphate to ADP, by oxidative phosphorylation of ADP in mitochondria, and by substrate-level phosphorylation of ADP in the glycolytic pathway.
II. At the beginning of exercise, muscle glycogen is the major fuel consumed. As the exercise proceeds, glucose and fatty acids from the blood provide most of the fuel, and fatty acids

become progressively more important during prolonged exercise. When the intensity of exercise exceeds about 70% of maximum, glycolysis begins to contribute an increasing fraction of the total ATP generated.

III. A variety of factors may contribute to muscle fatigue, including a decrease in ATP concentration and increases in the concentrations of ADP, P_i, Mg^{2+}, H^+, and oxygen free radicals. Individually and in combination, those changes have effects such as decreasing Ca^{2+} uptake and storage by the sarcoplasmic reticulum, decreasing the sensitivity of the thin filaments to Ca^{2+}, and inhibiting the binding and power-stroke motion of the cross-bridges.

Types of Skeletal Muscle Fibers

I. Three types of skeletal muscle fibers can be distinguished by their maximal shortening velocities and the predominate pathway they use to form ATP: slow-oxidative, fast-oxidative-glycolytic, and fast-glycolytic fibers.
   a. Differences in maximal shortening velocities are due to different myosin enzymes with high or low ATPase activities, giving rise to fast and slow fibers.
   b. Fast-glycolytic fibers have a larger average diameter than oxidative fibers and therefore produce greater tension, but they also fatigue more rapidly.

II. All the muscle fibers in a single motor unit belong to the same fiber type, and most muscles contain all three types.

III. Table 9.3 summarizes the characteristics of the three types of skeletal muscle fibers.

Whole-Muscle Contraction

I. The tension produced by whole-muscle contraction depends on the amount of tension each fiber develops and the number of active fibers in the muscle (Table 9.4).

II. Muscles that produce delicate movements have a small number of fibers per motor unit, whereas large powerful muscles have much larger motor units.

III. Fast-glycolytic motor units not only have large-diameter fibers but also tend to have large numbers of fibers per motor unit.

IV. Increases in muscle tension are controlled primarily by increasing the number of active motor units in a muscle, a process known as recruitment. Slow-oxidative motor units are recruited first; then fast-oxidative-glycolytic motor units are recruited; and finally, fast-glycolytic motor units are recruited only during very strong contractions.

V. Increasing motor-unit recruitment increases the velocity at which a muscle will move a given load.

VI. Exercise can alter a muscle's strength and susceptibility to fatigue.
   a. Long-duration, low-intensity exercise increases a fiber's capacity for oxidative ATP production by increasing the number of mitochondria and blood vessels in the muscle, resulting in increased endurance.
   b. Short-duration, high-intensity exercise increases fiber diameter as a result of increased synthesis of actin and myosin, resulting in increased strength.

VII. Movement around a joint generally involves groups of antagonistic muscles; some flex a limb at the joint and others extend the limb.

VIII. The lever system of muscles and bones generally requires muscle tension far greater than the load in order to sustain a load in an isometric contraction, but the lever system produces a shortening velocity at the end of the lever arm that is greater than the muscle-shortening velocity.

Skeletal Muscle Disorders

I. Muscle cramps are involuntary tetanic contractions related to heavy exercise and may be due to dehydration and electrolyte imbalances in the fluid surrounding muscle and nerve fibers.

II. When extracellular Ca^{2+} concentration decreases below normal, Na^+ channels of nerve and muscle open spontaneously, which causes the excessive muscle contractions of hypocalcemic tetany.

III. Muscular dystrophies are commonly occurring genetic disorders that result from defects of muscle-membrane-stabilizing proteins such as dystrophin. Muscles of individuals with Duchenne muscular dystrophy progressively degenerate with use.

IV. Myasthenia gravis is an autoimmune disorder in which destruction of ACh receptors of the motor end plate causes progressive loss of the ability to activate skeletal muscles.

SECTION A REVIEW QUESTIONS

1. List the three types of muscle cells and their locations.
2. Diagram the arrangement of thick and thin filaments in a striated muscle sarcomere, and label the major bands that give rise to the striated pattern.
3. Describe the organization of myosin, actin, tropomyosin, and troponin molecules in the thick and thin filaments.
4. Describe the location, structure, and function of the sarcoplasmic reticulum in skeletal muscle fibers.
5. Describe the structure and function of the transverse tubules.
6. Define *motor unit* and describe its structure.
7. Describe the sequence of events by which an action potential in a motor neuron produces an action potential in the plasma membrane of a skeletal muscle fiber.
8. What is an end-plate potential, and what ions produce it?
9. Compare and contrast the transmission of electrical activity at a neuromuscular junction with that at a synapse.
10. What prevents cross-bridges from attaching to sites on the thin filaments in a resting skeletal muscle?
11. Describe the role and source of calcium ions in initiating contraction in skeletal muscle.
12. Describe the four steps of one cross-bridge cycle.
13. Describe the physical state of a muscle fiber in rigor mortis and the conditions that produce this state.
14. What three events in skeletal muscle contraction and relaxation depend on ATP?
15. Describe the events that result in the relaxation of skeletal muscle fibers.
16. Describe isometric, concentric, and eccentric contractions.
17. What factors determine the duration of an isotonic twitch in skeletal muscle? An isometric twitch?
18. What effect does increasing the frequency of action potentials in a skeletal muscle fiber have upon the force of contraction? Explain the mechanism responsible for this effect.
19. Describe the length–tension relationship in skeletal muscle fibers.
20. Describe the effect of increasing the load on a skeletal muscle fiber on the velocity of shortening.
21. What is the function of creatine phosphate in skeletal muscle contraction?
22. What fuel molecules are metabolized to produce ATP during skeletal muscle activity?
23. List the factors responsible for skeletal muscle fatigue.
24. What component of skeletal muscle fibers accounts for the differences in the fibers' maximal shortening velocities?

25. Summarize the characteristics of the three types of skeletal muscle fibers.
26. Upon what three factors does the amount of tension developed by a whole skeletal muscle depend?
27. Describe the process of motor-unit recruitment in controlling (a) whole-muscle tension and (b) velocity of whole-muscle shortening.
28. During increases in the force of skeletal muscle contraction, what is the order of recruitment of the different types of motor units?
29. What happens to skeletal muscle fibers when the motor neuron to the muscle is destroyed?
30. Describe the changes that occur in skeletal muscles following a period of (a) long-duration, low-intensity exercise training; and (b) short-duration, high-intensity exercise training.
31. How are skeletal muscles arranged around joints so that a limb can push or pull?
32. What are the advantages and disadvantages of the muscle-bone-joint lever system?

SECTION A KEY TERMS

A band 260
acetylcholine (ACh) 262
acetylcholinesterase 263
actin 260
antagonist 281
cardiac muscle 258
central command fatigue 276
concentric contraction 269
contraction 262
contraction time 270
costameres 283
creatine phosphate 274
cross-bridge 261
cross-bridge cycle 267
dihydropyridine (DHP) receptor 266
dystrophin 283
eccentric contraction 269
end-plate potential (EPP) 263
excitation–contraction coupling 265
extension 281
fast fiber 276
fast-glycolytic fiber 277
fast-oxidative-glycolytic fiber 277
flexion 281
foot process 266
fused tetanus 273
glycolytic fiber 277
H zone 260
heavy chains 260
hypertrophy 259
hypocalcemia 283
I band 260
isometric contraction 269
isotonic contraction 269
junctional feet 266
latent period 270
light chains 260
load 269
M line 260
motor end plate 262
motor neuron 262
motor unit 262
muscle 259
muscle fatigue 275
muscle fiber 259
myoblast 259
myofibril 260
myoglobin 277
myosin 260
myostatin 280
neuromuscular junction 262
optimal length (L_0) 274
oxidative fiber 276
oxygen debt 275
power stroke 268
recruitment 279
red muscle fiber 277
relaxation 262
rigor mortis 269
ryanodine receptor 266
sarcolemma 261
sarcomere 260
sarcoplasmic reticulum 261
satellite cell 259
skeletal muscle 258
sliding-filament mechanism 267
slow fiber 276
slow-oxidative fiber 277
smooth muscle 258
striated muscle 258
summation 272
tendon 260
tension 269
terminal cisternae 261
tetanus 273
thick filament 260
thin filament 260
titin 260
transverse tubule (T-tubule) 260
tropomyosin 260
troponin 261
twitch 270
unfused tetanus 273
white muscle fiber 277
Z line 260

SECTION A CLINICAL TERMS

atropine 264
botulism 265
curare 264
denervation atrophy 279
disuse atrophy 280
Duchenne muscular dystrophy 283
hypocalcemic tetany 282
muscle cramp 282
muscular dystrophy 283
myasthenia gravis 283
plasmapheresis 284
poliomyelitis 282
pralidoxime 264
pyridostigmine 284
rocuronium 264
succinylcholine 264
thymectomy 284
vecuronium 264

SECTION B

Smooth and Cardiac Muscle

We now turn our attention to the other muscle types, beginning with smooth muscle. Two characteristics are common to all smooth muscles. They lack the cross-striated banding pattern found in skeletal and cardiac fibers (which makes them "smooth"), and the nerves to them are part of the autonomic division of the nervous system rather than the somatic division. Thus, smooth muscle is not normally under direct voluntary control.

Smooth muscle, like skeletal muscle, uses cross-bridge movements between actin and myosin filaments to generate force, and calcium ions to control cross-bridge activity. However, the organization of the contractile filaments and the process of excitation–contraction coupling are quite different in smooth muscle. Furthermore, there is considerable diversity among smooth muscles with respect to the excitation–contraction coupling mechanism.

9.8 Structure of Smooth Muscle

Each smooth muscle cell is spindle-shaped, with a diameter between 2 and 10 μm, and length ranging from 50 to 400 μm. They are much smaller than skeletal muscle fibers, which are 10 to 100 μm wide and can be tens of centimeters long (see Figure 9.1). Skeletal muscle fibers are sometimes large enough to run the entire length of the muscles in which they are found, whereas many individual smooth muscle cells are generally interconnected to form sheetlike layers of cells (**Figure 9.32**). Skeletal muscle fibers are multinucleate cells with limited ability to

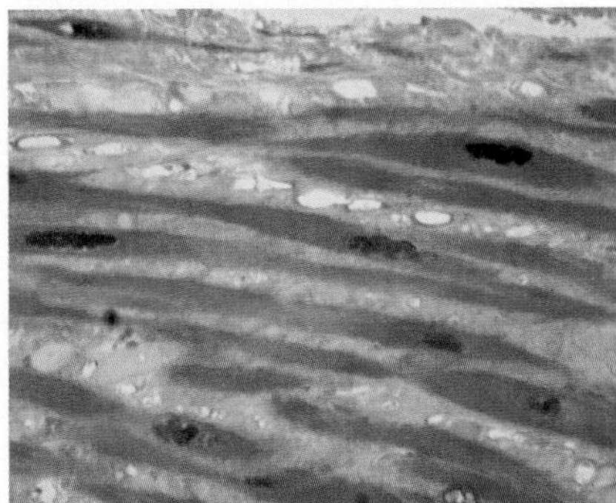

Figure 9.32 APIR Photomicrograph of a sheet of smooth muscle cells stained with a dye for visualization. Note the spindle shape, single nucleus, and lack of striations.

divide once they have differentiated; smooth muscle cells have a single nucleus and have the capacity to divide throughout the life of an individual. A variety of paracrine factors can stimulate smooth muscle cells to divide, often in response to tissue injury.

Just like skeletal muscle fibers, smooth muscle cells have thick myosin-containing filaments and thin actin-containing filaments. Although tropomyosin is present in the thin filaments, the regulatory protein troponin is absent. A protein called **caldesmon** also associates with the thin filaments; in some types of muscle, it may play a role in regulating contraction. The thin filaments are anchored either to the plasma membrane or to cytoplasmic structures known as **dense bodies,** which are functionally similar to the Z lines in skeletal muscle fibers. Note in **Figure 9.33** that the filaments are oriented diagonally to the long axis of the cell. When the fiber shortens, the regions of the plasma membrane between the points where actin is attached to the membrane balloon out. The thick and thin filaments are not organized into myofibrils, as in striated muscles, and there is no regular alignment of these filaments into sarcomeres, which accounts for the absence of a banding pattern. Nevertheless, smooth muscle contraction occurs by a sliding-filament mechanism.

The concentration of myosin in smooth muscle is only about one-third of that in striated muscle, whereas the actin content can be twice as great. In spite of these differences, the maximal tension per unit of cross-sectional area developed by smooth muscles is similar to that developed by skeletal muscle.

The isometric tension produced by smooth muscle fibers varies with fiber length in a manner qualitatively similar to that observed in skeletal muscle—tension development is highest at intermediate lengths and lower at shorter or longer lengths. However, in smooth muscle, significant force is generated over a relatively broad range of muscle lengths compared to that of skeletal muscle. This property is highly adaptive because most smooth muscles surround hollow structures and organs that undergo changes in volume with accompanying changes in the lengths of the smooth muscle fibers in their walls. Even with relatively large increases in volume, as during the accumulation of large amounts of urine in the bladder, the smooth muscle fibers in the wall retain some ability to develop tension, whereas such distortion might stretch skeletal muscle fibers beyond the point of thick and thin filament overlap.

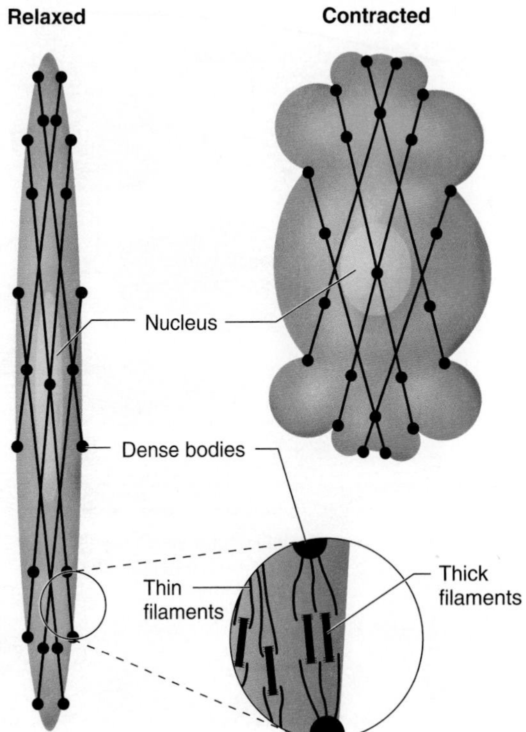

Figure 9.33 APIR Thick and thin filaments in smooth muscle are arranged in diagonal chains that are anchored to the plasma membrane or to dense bodies within the cytoplasm. When activated, the thick and thin filaments slide past each other, causing the smooth muscle fiber to shorten and thicken.

9.9 Smooth Muscle Contraction and Its Control

Changes in cytosolic Ca^{2+} concentration control the contractile activity in smooth muscle fibers, as in striated muscle. However, there are significant differences in the way Ca^{2+} activates cross-bridge cycling and in the mechanisms by which stimulation leads to alterations in Ca^{2+} concentration.

Cross-Bridge Activation

Because smooth muscle lacks the Ca^{2+}-binding protein troponin, tropomyosin is never held in a position that blocks cross-bridge access to actin. Thus, the thin filament is not the main switch that regulates cross-bridge cycling. *Instead, cross-bridge cycling in smooth muscle is controlled by a Ca^{2+}-regulated enzyme that phosphorylates myosin.* Only the phosphorylated form of smooth muscle myosin can bind to actin and undergo cross-bridge cycling.

The following sequence of events occurs after an increase in cytosolic Ca^{2+} in a smooth muscle fiber (**Figure 9.34**): (1) Ca^{2+} binds to calmodulin, a Ca^{2+}-binding protein that is present in the cytosol of most cells (see Chapter 5) and whose structure is related to that of troponin. (2) The Ca^{2+}–calmodulin complex binds to another cytosolic protein, **myosin light-chain kinase,** thereby activating the enzyme. (3) Active myosin light-chain kinase then uses ATP to phosphorylate myosin light chains in the globular head of myosin. (4) Phosphorylation of myosin drives the cross-bridge away from the thick filament backbone, allowing it to bind to actin.

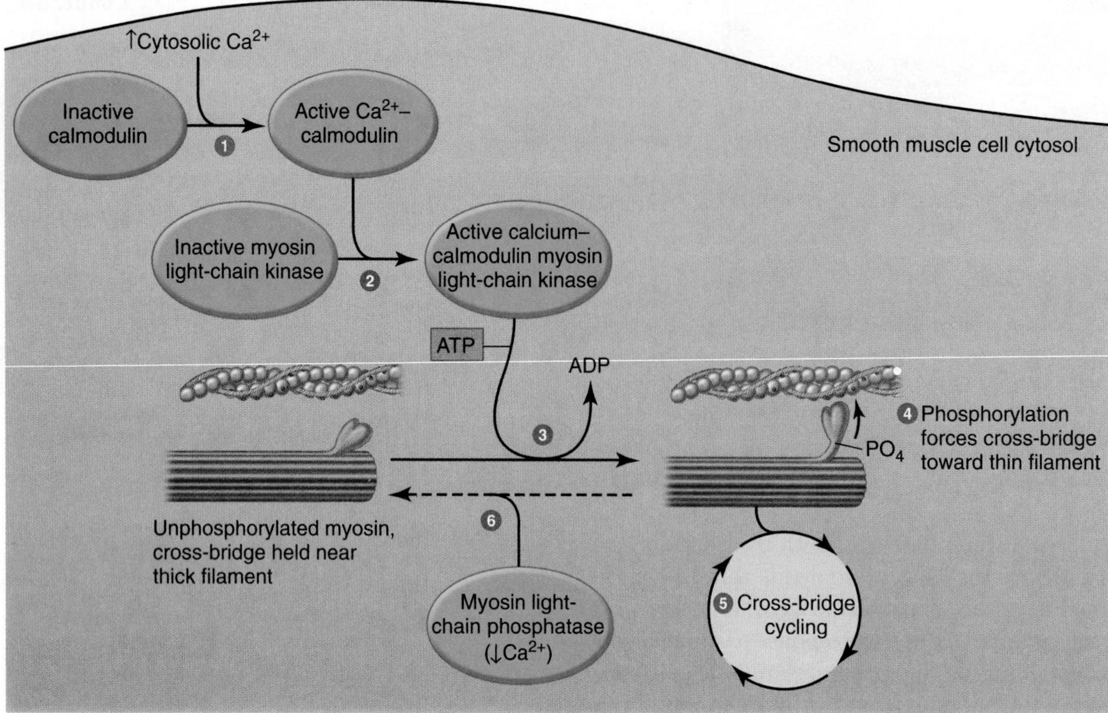

Figure 9.34 Activation of smooth muscle contraction by Ca^{2+}. See text for description of the numbered steps.

(5) Cross-bridges go through repeated cycles of force generation as long as myosin light chains are phosphorylated. A key difference here is that Ca^{2+}-mediated changes in the thick filaments turn on cross-bridge activity in smooth muscle, whereas in striated muscle, Ca^{2+} mediates changes in the thin filaments. However, recent research suggests that in some types of smooth muscle there may also be some Ca^{2+}-dependent regulation of the thin filament mediated by the protein caldesmon.

The smooth muscle form of myosin has a very low rate of ATPase activity, on the order of 10 to 100 times less than that of skeletal muscle myosin. Because the rate of ATP hydrolysis determines the rate of cross-bridge cycling and shortening velocity, smooth muscle shortening is much slower than that of skeletal muscle. Due to this slow rate of energy usage, smooth muscle does not undergo fatigue during prolonged periods of activity. Note the distinction between the two roles of ATP in smooth muscle: Hydrolyzing one ATP to transfer a phosphate onto a myosin light chain (*phosphorylation*) starts a cross-bridge cycling, after which one ATP per cycle is hydrolyzed to provide the energy for force generation.

To relax a contracted smooth muscle, myosin must be dephosphorylated because dephosphorylated myosin is unable to bind to actin. This dephosphorylation is mediated by the enzyme **myosin light-chain phosphatase,** which is continuously active in smooth muscle during periods of rest and contraction (step 6 in Figure 9.34). When cytosolic Ca^{2+} concentration increases, the rate of myosin phosphorylation by the activated kinase exceeds the rate of dephosphorylation by the phosphatase and the amount of phosphorylated myosin in the cell increases, producing an increase in tension. When the cytosolic Ca^{2+} concentration decreases, the rate of phosphorylation decreases below that of dephosphorylation and the amount of phosphorylated myosin decreases, producing relaxation.

In some smooth muscles, when stimulation is persistent and the cytosolic Ca^{2+} concentration remains elevated, the rate of ATP hydrolysis by the cross-bridges declines even though isometric tension is maintained. This condition is known as the **latch state** and a smooth muscle in this state can maintain tension in an almost rigorlike state without movement. Dissociation of cross-bridges from actin does occur in the latch state, but at a much slower rate. The net result is the ability to maintain tension for long periods of time with a very low rate of ATP consumption. A good example of the usefulness of this mechanism is seen in sphincter muscles of the gastrointestinal tract, where smooth muscle must maintain contraction for prolonged periods. **Figure 9.35** compares the activation of smooth and skeletal muscles.

Sources of Cytosolic Ca^{2+}

Two sources of Ca^{2+} contribute to the increase in cytosolic Ca^{2+} that initiates smooth muscle contraction: (1) the sarcoplasmic reticulum and (2) extracellular Ca^{2+} entering the cell through plasma membrane Ca^{2+} channels. The amount of Ca^{2+} each of these two sources contributes differs among various smooth muscles.

First, we will examine the role of the sarcoplasmic reticulum. The total quantity of this organelle in smooth muscle is smaller than in skeletal muscle, and it is not arranged in any specific pattern in relation to the thick and thin filaments. Moreover, there are no T-tubules continuous with the plasma membrane in smooth muscle. The small cell diameter and the slow rate of contraction do not require such a rapid mechanism for getting an excitatory signal into the muscle cell. Portions of the sarcoplasmic reticulum are located near the plasma membrane, however, forming associations similar to the relationship between T-tubules and the terminal cisternae

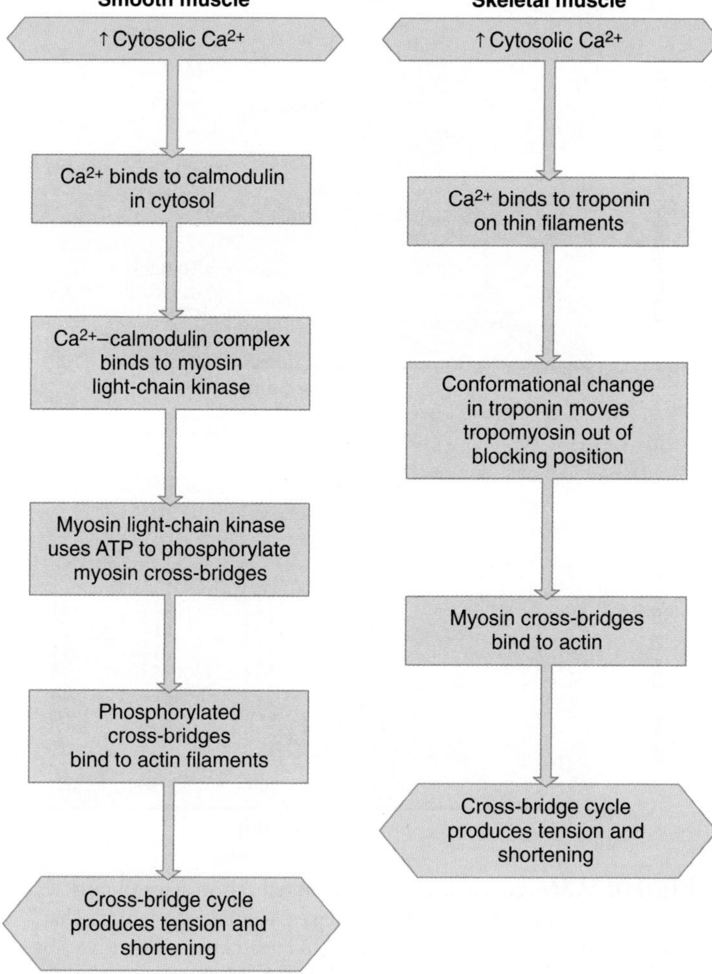

Figure 9.35 Pathways leading from increased cytosolic Ca^{2+} to cross-bridge cycling in smooth and skeletal muscle fibers.

in skeletal muscle. Action potentials in the plasma membrane can be coupled to the release of sarcoplasmic reticulum Ca^{2+} at these sites. In some types of smooth muscles, action potentials are not necessary for Ca^{2+} release. Instead, second messengers released from the plasma membrane, or generated in the cytosol in response to the binding of extracellular chemical messengers to plasma membrane receptors, can trigger the release of Ca^{2+} from the more centrally located sarcoplasmic reticulum (review Figure 5.10 for a specific example).

What about extracellular Ca^{2+} in excitation–contraction coupling? There are voltage-sensitive Ca^{2+} channels in the plasma membranes of smooth muscle cells, as well as Ca^{2+} channels controlled by extracellular chemical messengers. The Ca^{2+} concentration in the extracellular fluid is 10,000 times greater than in the cytosol; thus, the opening of Ca^{2+} channels in the plasma membrane results in an increased flow of Ca^{2+} into the cell. Because of the small cell size, the entering Ca^{2+} does not have far to diffuse to reach binding sites within the cell.

Removal of Ca^{2+} from the cytosol to bring about relaxation is achieved by the active transport of Ca^{2+} back into the sarcoplasmic reticulum as well as out of the cell across the plasma membrane. The rate of Ca^{2+} removal in smooth muscle is much slower than in skeletal muscle, with the result that a single twitch lasts several seconds in smooth muscle compared to a fraction of a second in skeletal muscle.

The degree of activation also differs between muscle types. In skeletal muscle, a single action potential releases sufficient Ca^{2+} to saturate all troponin sites on the thin filaments, whereas only a portion of the cross-bridges are activated in a smooth muscle fiber in response to most stimuli. Therefore, the tension generated by a smooth muscle cell can be *graded* by varying cytosolic Ca^{2+} concentration. The greater the increase in Ca^{2+} concentration, the greater the number of cross-bridges activated and the greater the tension.

In some smooth muscles, the cytosolic Ca^{2+} concentration is sufficient to maintain a low level of basal cross-bridge activity in the absence of external stimuli. This activity is known as **smooth muscle tone.** Factors that alter the cytosolic Ca^{2+} concentration also vary the intensity of smooth muscle tone.

Membrane Activation

Many inputs to a smooth muscle plasma membrane can alter the contractile activity of the muscle (**Table 9.5**). This contrasts with skeletal muscle, in which membrane activation depends only upon synaptic inputs from somatic neurons. Some inputs to smooth muscle increase contraction, and others inhibit it. Moreover, at any one time, the smooth muscle plasma membrane may be receiving multiple inputs, with the contractile state of the muscle dependent on the relative intensity of the various inhibitory and excitatory stimuli. All these inputs influence contractile activity by altering cytosolic Ca^{2+} concentration as described in the previous section.

Some smooth muscles contract in response to membrane depolarization, whereas others can contract in the absence of any membrane potential change. Interestingly, in smooth muscles in which action potentials occur, calcium ions, rather than sodium ions, carry a positive charge into the cell during the rising phase of the action potential—that is, depolarization of the membrane opens voltage-gated Ca^{2+} channels, producing Ca^{2+}-mediated rather than Na^{+}-mediated action potentials.

Smooth muscle is different from skeletal muscle in another important way with regard to electrical activity and cytosolic Ca^{2+} concentration. Smooth muscle cytosolic Ca^{2+} concentration can be increased (or decreased) by graded depolarizations (or hyperpolarizations) in membrane potential, which increase or decrease the number of open Ca^{2+} channels.

TABLE 9.5	Inputs Influencing Smooth Muscle Contractile Activity
Spontaneous electrical activity in the plasma membrane of the muscle cell	
Neurotransmitters released by autonomic neurons	
Hormones	
Locally induced changes in the chemical composition (paracrine factors, acidity, oxygen, osmolarity, and ion concentrations) of the extracellular fluid surrounding the cell	
Stretch	

Spontaneous Electrical Activity

Some types of smooth muscle cells generate action potentials spontaneously in the absence of any neural or hormonal input. The plasma membranes of such cells do not maintain a constant resting potential. Instead, they gradually depolarize until they reach the threshold potential and produce an action potential. Following repolarization, the membrane again begins to depolarize (**Figure 9.36a**), so that a sequence of action potentials occurs, producing a rhythmic state of contractile activity. The membrane potential change occurring during the spontaneous depolarization to threshold is known as a **pacemaker potential.**

Other smooth muscle pacemaker cells have a slightly different pattern of activity. The membrane potential drifts up and down due to regular variation in ion flux across the membrane. These periodic fluctuations are called **slow waves** (**Figure 9.36b**). When an excitatory input is superimposed, slow waves are depolarized above threshold, and action potentials lead to smooth muscle contraction.

Pacemaker cells are found throughout the gastrointestinal tract; thus, gut smooth muscle tends to contract rhythmically even in the absence of neural input. Some cardiac muscle cells and some neurons in the central nervous system also have pacemaker potentials and can spontaneously generate action potentials in the absence of external stimuli.

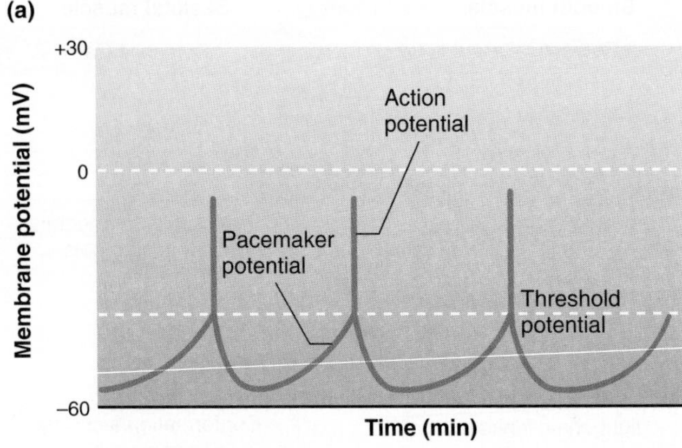

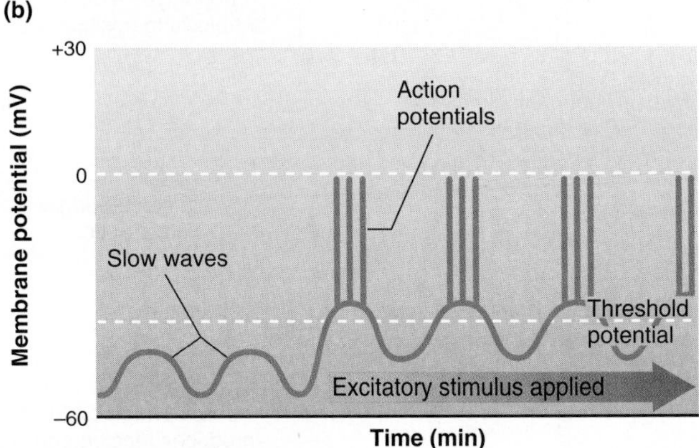

Figure 9.36 Generation of action potentials in smooth muscle fibers. (a) Some smooth muscle cells have pacemaker potentials that drift to threshold at regular intervals. (b) Pacemaker cells with a slow-wave pattern drift periodically toward threshold; excitatory stimuli can depolarize the cell to reach threshold and fire action potentials.

Nerves and Hormones

The contractile activity of smooth muscles is influenced by neurotransmitters released by autonomic neuron endings. Unlike skeletal muscle fibers, smooth muscle cells do not have a specialized motor end-plate region. As the axon of a postganglionic autonomic neuron enters the region of smooth muscle cells, it divides into many branches, each branch containing a series of swollen regions known as **varicosities** (**Figure 9.37**). Each varicosity contains many vesicles filled with neurotransmitter, some of which are released when an action potential passes the varicosity. Varicosities from a single axon may be located along several muscle cells, and a single muscle cell may be located near varicosities belonging to postganglionic fibers of both sympathetic and parasympathetic neurons. Therefore, a number of smooth muscle cells are influenced by the neurotransmitters released by a single neuron, and a single smooth muscle cell may be influenced by neurotransmitters from more than one neuron.

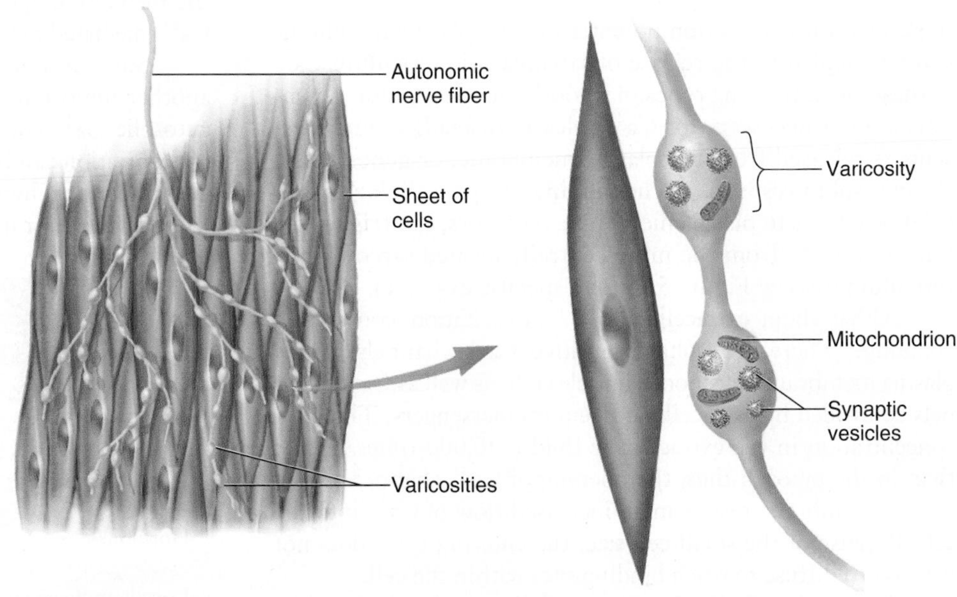

Figure 9.37 Innervation of smooth muscle by a postganglionic autonomic neuron. Neurotransmitter, released from varicosities along the branched axon, diffuses to receptors on muscle cell plasma membranes. Both sympathetic and parasympathetic neurons follow this pattern, often overlapping in their distribution. Note that the size of the varicosities is exaggerated compared to the cell at right.

Whereas some neurotransmitters enhance contractile activity, others decrease contractile activity. This is different than in skeletal muscle, which receives only excitatory input from its motor neurons; smooth muscle tension can be either increased or decreased by neural activity.

Moreover, a given neurotransmitter may produce opposite effects in different smooth muscle tissues. For example, norepinephrine, the neurotransmitter released from most postganglionic sympathetic neurons, enhances contraction of most vascular smooth muscle by acting on α-adrenergic receptors. By contrast, the same neurotransmitter produces relaxation of airway (bronchiolar) smooth muscle by acting on β_2-adrenergic receptors. Thus, the type of response (excitatory or inhibitory) depends not on the chemical messenger, per se, but on the receptors the chemical messenger binds to in the membrane and on the intracellular signaling mechanisms those receptors activate.

In addition to receptors for neurotransmitters, smooth muscle plasma membranes contain receptors for a variety of hormones. Binding of a hormone to its receptor may lead to either increased or decreased contractile activity.

Although most changes in smooth muscle contractile activity induced by chemical messengers are accompanied by a change in membrane potential, this is not always the case. Second messengers—for example, inositol trisphosphate—can cause the release of Ca^{2+} from the sarcoplasmic reticulum, producing a contraction without a change in membrane potential (review Figure 5.10).

Local Factors

Local factors, including paracrine signals, acidity, oxygen and carbon dioxide concentration, osmolarity, and the ionic composition of the extracellular fluid, can also alter smooth muscle tension. Responses to local factors provide a means for altering smooth muscle contraction in response to changes in the muscle's immediate internal environment, which can lead to regulation that is independent of long-distance signals from nerves and hormones.

Many of these local factors induce smooth muscle relaxation. Nitric oxide (NO) is one of the most commonly encountered paracrine compounds that produce smooth muscle relaxation. NO is released from some axon terminals as well as from a variety of epithelial and endothelial cells. Because of the short life span of this reactive molecule, it acts in a paracrine manner, influencing only those cells that are very near its release site.

Some smooth muscles can also respond by contracting when they are stretched. Stretching opens mechanically gated ion channels, leading to membrane depolarization. The resulting contraction opposes the forces acting to stretch the muscle.

At any given moment, smooth muscle cells in the body receive many simultaneous signals. The state of contractile activity that results depends on the net magnitude of the signals promoting contraction versus those promoting relaxation. This is a classic example of the general principle of physiology that most physiological functions are controlled by multiple regulatory systems, often working in opposition.

Types of Smooth Muscle

The great diversity of the factors that can influence the contractile activity of smooth muscles in various organs has made it difficult to classify smooth muscle fibers. Many smooth muscles can be placed, however, into one of two groups, based on the electrical characteristics of their plasma membrane: **single-unit smooth muscles** and **multiunit smooth muscles.**

Single-Unit Smooth Muscle

The muscle cells in a single-unit smooth muscle undergo synchronous activity, both electrical and mechanical; that is, the whole muscle responds to stimulation as a single unit. This occurs because each muscle cell is linked to adjacent fibers by gap junctions, which allow action potentials occurring in one cell to propagate to other cells by local currents. Therefore, electrical activity occurring anywhere within a group of single-unit smooth muscle cells can be conducted to all the other connected cells (**Figure 9.38**).

Some of the cells in a single-unit muscle are pacemaker cells that spontaneously generate action potentials. These action potentials are conducted by way of gap junctions to the rest of the cells, most of which are not capable of pacemaker activity.

Nerves, hormones, and local factors can alter the contractile activity of single-unit smooth muscles using the variety of mechanisms described previously for smooth muscles in general. The extent to which these muscles are innervated varies considerably in different organs. The axon terminals are often restricted to the regions of the muscle that contain pacemaker cells. The activity of the entire muscle can be controlled by regulating the frequency of the pacemaker cells' action potentials.

One additional characteristic of single-unit smooth muscles is that a contractile response can often be induced by stretching the muscle. In several hollow organs—the stomach, for example—stretching the smooth muscles in the walls of the organ as a result of increases in the volume of material in the lumen initiates a contractile response.

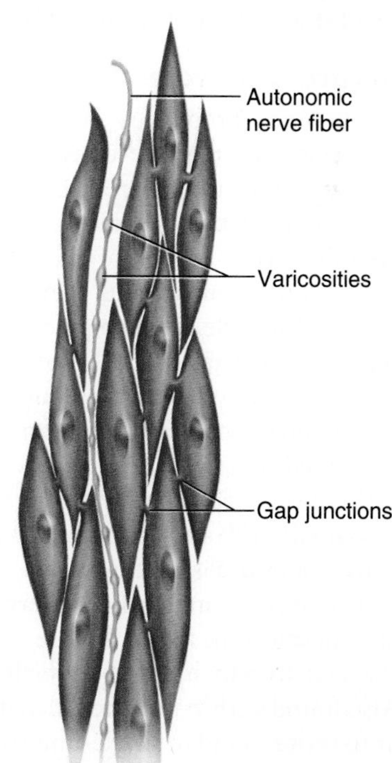

Figure 9.38 Innervation of a single-unit smooth muscle is often restricted to only a few cells in the muscle. Electrical activity is conducted from cell to cell throughout the muscle by way of the gap junctions between the cells.

The smooth muscles of the intestinal tract, uterus, and small-diameter blood vessels are examples of single-unit smooth muscles.

Multiunit Smooth Muscle

Multiunit smooth muscles have no or few gap junctions. Each cell responds independently, and the muscle behaves as multiple units. Multiunit smooth muscles are richly innervated by branches of the autonomic nervous system. The contractile response of the whole muscle depends on the number of muscle cells that are activated and on the frequency of nerve stimulation. Although stimulation of the muscle by neurons leads to some degree of depolarization and a contractile response, action potentials do not occur in most multiunit smooth muscles. Circulating hormones can increase or decrease contractile activity in multiunit smooth muscle, but stretching does not induce contraction in this type of muscle. The smooth muscles in the large airways to the lungs, in large arteries, and attached to the hairs in the skin are multiunit smooth muscles.

It must be emphasized that most smooth muscles do not show all the characteristics of either single-unit or multiunit smooth muscles. These two prototypes represent the two extremes in smooth muscle characteristics, with many smooth muscles having overlapping characteristics.

9.10 Cardiac Muscle

The third general type of muscle, cardiac muscle, is found only in the heart. Although many details about cardiac muscle will be discussed in the context of the cardiovascular system in Chapter 12, a brief explanation of its function and how it compares to skeletal and smooth muscle is presented here.

Cellular Structure of Cardiac Muscle

Cardiac muscle combines properties of both skeletal and smooth muscle. Like skeletal muscle, it has a striated appearance due to regularly repeating sarcomeres composed of myosin-containing thick filaments interdigitating with thin filaments that contain actin. Troponin and tropomyosin are also present in the thin filament, and they have the same functions as in skeletal muscle. Cellular membranes include a T-tubule system and associated Ca^{2+}-loaded sarcoplasmic reticulum. The mechanism by which these membranes interact to release Ca^{2+} is different than in skeletal muscle, however, as will be discussed shortly.

Like smooth muscle cells, individual cardiac muscle cells are relatively small (100 μm long and 20 μm in diameter) and generally contain a single nucleus. Adjacent cells are joined end to end at structures called **intercalated disks,** within which are desmosomes (see Figure 3.9) that hold the cells together and to which the myofibrils are attached (**Figure 9.39**). Also found within the intercalated disks are gap junctions similar to those found in single-unit smooth muscle. Cardiac muscle cells also are arranged in layers and surround hollow cavities—in this case, the blood-filled chambers of the heart. When muscle in the walls of cardiac chambers contracts, it acts like a squeezing fist and exerts pressure on the blood inside.

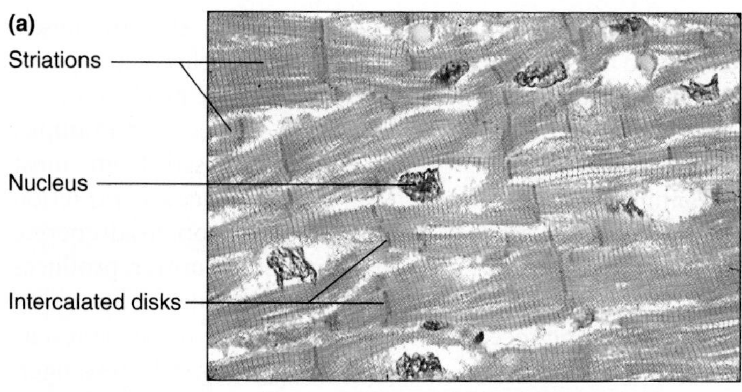

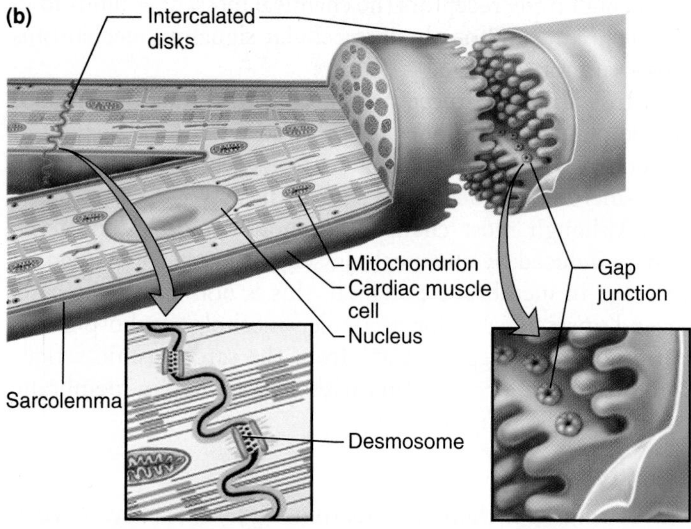

Figure 9.39 APIR Cardiac muscle. (a) Light micrograph. (b) Cardiac muscle cells and intercalated disks.

Excitation–Contraction Coupling in Cardiac Muscle

As in skeletal muscle, contraction of cardiac muscle cells occurs in response to a membrane action potential that propagates through the T-tubules, but the mechanisms linking that excitation to the generation of force exhibit features of both skeletal and smooth muscles (**Figure 9.40**). Depolarization during cardiac muscle cell action potentials is in part due to an influx of Ca^{2+} through specialized voltage-gated channels. These Ca^{2+} channels are known as **L-type Ca^{2+} channels** (named for their Long-lasting current) and are modified versions of the dihydropyridine (DHP) receptors that act as the voltage sensor in skeletal muscle cell excitation–contraction coupling. Not only does this entering Ca^{2+} participate in depolarization of the plasma membrane and cause a small increase in cytosolic Ca^{2+} concentration, but it also serves as a trigger for the release of a much larger amount of Ca^{2+} from the sarcoplasmic reticulum. This occurs because ryanodine receptors in the cardiac sarcoplasmic reticulum terminal cisternae are Ca^{2+} channels; but rather than being opened directly by voltage as in skeletal muscle, they are opened by the binding of trigger Ca^{2+} in the cytosol. Once cytosolic Ca^{2+} is elevated, thin filament activation, cross-bridge cycling, and force generation occur by the same basic mechanisms described for skeletal muscle (review Figures 9.11 and 9.15).

Thus, even though most of the Ca^{2+} that initiates cardiac muscle contraction comes from the sarcoplasmic

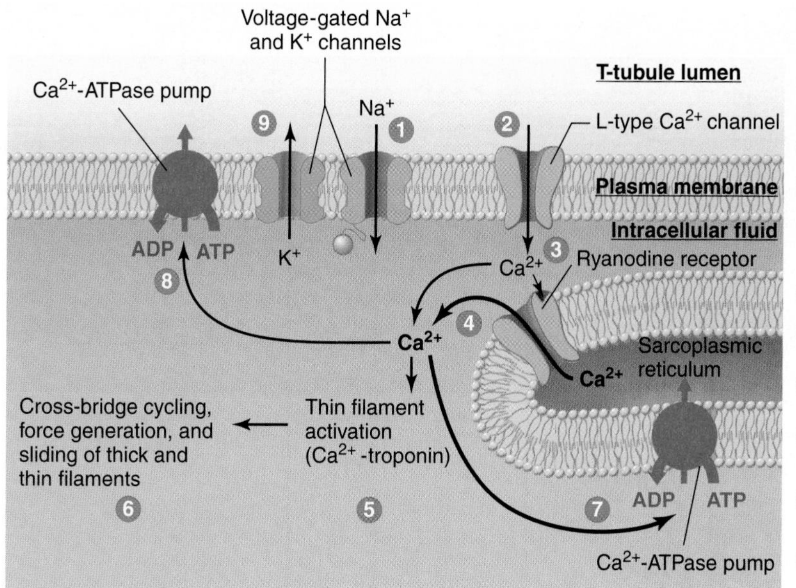

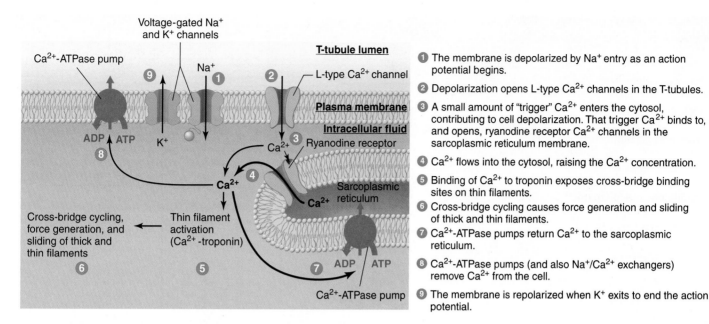

1. The membrane is depolarized by Na^+ entry as an action potential begins.
2. Depolarization opens L-type Ca^{2+} channels in the T-tubules.
3. A small amount of "trigger" Ca^{2+} enters the cytosol, contributing to cell depolarization. That trigger Ca^{2+} binds to, and opens, ryanodine receptor Ca^{2+} channels in the sarcoplasmic reticulum membrane.
4. Ca^{2+} flows into the cytosol, raising the Ca^{2+} concentration.
5. Binding of Ca^{2+} to troponin exposes cross-bridge binding sites on thin filaments.
6. Cross-bridge cycling causes force generation and sliding of thick and thin filaments.
7. Ca^{2+}-ATPase pumps return Ca^{2+} to the sarcoplasmic reticulum.
8. Ca^{2+}-ATPase pumps (and also Na^+/Ca^{2+} exchangers) remove Ca^{2+} from the cell.
9. The membrane is repolarized when K^+ exits to end the action potential.

Figure 9.40 Excitation–contraction coupling in cardiac muscle.

reticulum, the process—unlike that in skeletal muscle—is dependent on the movement of extracellular Ca^{2+} into the cytosol. Contraction ends when the cytosolic Ca^{2+} concentration is restored to its original extremely low resting value by primary active Ca^{2+}-ATPase pumps in the sarcoplasmic reticulum and sarcolemma and Na^+/Ca^{2+} countertransporters in the sarcolemma. The amount of Ca^{2+} returned to the extracellular fluid and into the sarcoplasmic reticulum exactly matches the amounts that entered the cytosol during excitation. During a single twitch contraction of cardiac muscle in a person at rest, the amount of Ca^{2+} entering the cytosol is only sufficient to expose about 30% of the cross-bridge attachment sites on the thin filament. As Chapter 12 will describe, however, hormones and neurotransmitters of the autonomic nervous system modulate the amount of Ca^{2+} released during excitation–contraction coupling, enabling the strength of cardiac muscle contractions to be varied. Cardiac muscle contractions are thus graded in a manner similar to that of smooth muscle contractions.

The prolonged duration of L-type Ca^{2+} channel current underlies an important feature of this muscle type—cardiac muscle cannot undergo tetanic contractions. Unlike skeletal muscle, in which the membrane action potential is extremely brief (1–2 msec) and force generation lasts much longer (20–100 msec), in cardiac muscle the action potential and twitch are both prolonged due to the long-lasting Ca^{2+} current (**Figure 9.41**). Because the plasma membrane remains refractory to additional stimuli as long as it is depolarized (review

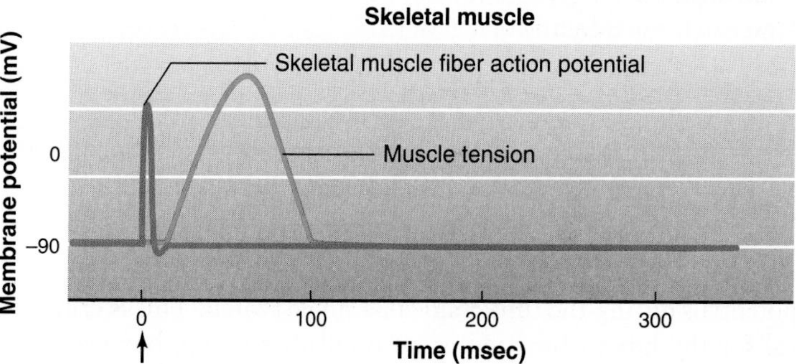

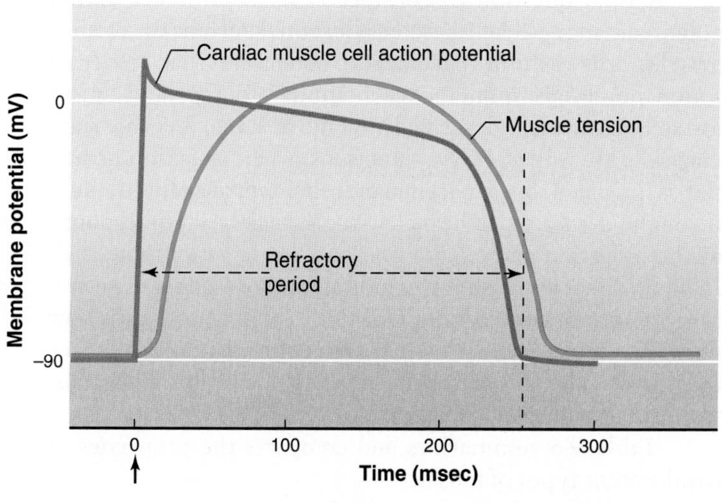

Figure 9.41 Timing of action potentials and twitch tension in skeletal and cardiac muscles. Muscle tension not drawn to scale.

PHYSIOLOGICAL INQUIRY

- The single-fiber twitch experiments shown here were generated by stimulating the muscle cell membranes to threshold with an electrode and measuring the resulting action potential and force. How would the results differ if Ca^{2+} were removed from the extracellular solution just before the electrical stimulus was applied?

Answer can be found at end of chapter.

TABLE 9.6 Characteristics of Muscle Cells

Characteristic	Skeletal Muscle	Smooth Muscle		Cardiac Muscle
		Single Unit	Multiunit	
Thick and thin filaments	Yes	Yes	Yes	Yes
Sarcomeres—banding pattern	Yes	No	No	Yes
Transverse tubules	Yes	No	No	Yes
Sarcoplasmic reticulum (SR)*	++++	+	+	++
Gap junctions between cells	No	Yes	Few	Yes
Source of activating Ca^{2+}	SR	SR and extracellular	SR and extracellular	SR and extracellular
Site of Ca^{2+} regulation	Troponin	Myosin	Myosin	Troponin
Speed of contraction	Fast–slow	Very slow	Very slow	Slow
Spontaneous production of action potentials by pacemakers	No	Yes	No	Yes, in a few specialized cells, but most not spontaneously active
Tone (low levels of maintained tension in the absence of external stimuli)	No	Yes	No	No
Effect of nerve stimulation	Excitation	Excitation or inhibition	Excitation or inhibition	Excitation or inhibition
Physiological effects of hormones on excitability and contraction	No	Yes	Yes	Yes
Stretch of cell produces contraction	No	Yes	No	No

*Number of plus signs (+) indicates the relative amount of sarcoplasmic reticulum present in a given muscle type.

Figure 6.22), it is not possible to initiate multiple cardiac action potentials during the time frame of a single twitch. This is critical for the heart's function as an oscillating pump, because it must alternate between being relaxed—and filling with blood—and contracting to eject blood.

A final question to consider is, What initiates action potentials in cardiac muscle? Certain specialized cardiac muscle cells exhibit pacemaker potentials that generate action potentials spontaneously, similar to the mechanism for smooth muscle described in Figure 9.36a. Because cardiac cells are linked via gap junctions, when an action potential is initiated by a pacemaker cell, it propagates rapidly throughout the entire heart. A single heartbeat corresponds to the initiation and conduction of a single action potential. In addition to discussing the modulation of Ca^{2+} release and the strength of contraction, Chapter 12 will also discuss how hormones and autonomic neurotransmitters modify the frequency of cardiac pacemaker cell depolarization and, thus, vary the heart rate.

Table 9.6 summarizes and compares the properties of the different types of muscle.

SECTION B SUMMARY

Structure of Smooth Muscle

I. Smooth muscle cells are spindle-shaped, lack striations, have a single nucleus, and are capable of cell division. They contain actin and myosin filaments and contract by a sliding-filament mechanism.

Smooth Muscle Contraction and Its Control

I. An increase in cytosolic Ca^{2+} leads to the binding of Ca^{2+} by calmodulin. The Ca^{2+}–calmodulin complex then binds to myosin light-chain kinase, activating the enzyme, which uses ATP to phosphorylate smooth muscle myosin. Only phosphorylated myosin can bind to actin and undergo cross-bridge cycling.

II. Smooth muscle myosin has a low rate of ATP splitting, resulting in a much slower shortening velocity than in striated muscle. However, the tension produced per unit cross-sectional area is equivalent to that of skeletal muscle.

III. Two sources of the cytosolic calcium ions that initiate smooth muscle contraction are the sarcoplasmic reticulum and extracellular Ca^{2+}. The opening of Ca^{2+} channels in the smooth muscle plasma membrane and sarcoplasmic reticulum, mediated by a variety of factors, allows calcium ions to enter the cytosol.

IV. The increase in cytosolic Ca^{2+} resulting from most stimuli does not activate all the cross-bridges. Therefore, smooth muscle tension can be increased by agents that increase the concentration of cytosolic calcium ions.

V. Table 9.5 summarizes the types of stimuli that can initiate smooth muscle contraction by opening or closing Ca^{2+} channels in the plasma membrane or sarcoplasmic reticulum.

VI. Most, but not all, smooth muscle cells can generate action potentials in their plasma membrane upon membrane depolarization. The rising phase of the smooth muscle action potential is due to the influx of calcium ions into the cell through voltage-gated Ca^{2+} channels.

VII. Some smooth muscles generate action potentials spontaneously, in the absence of any external input, because of pacemaker potentials in the plasma membrane that repeatedly depolarize the membrane to threshold. Slow waves are a pattern of spontaneous, periodic depolarization of the membrane potential seen in some smooth muscle pacemaker cells.

VIII. Smooth muscle cells do not have a specialized end-plate region. A number of smooth muscle cells may be influenced by neurotransmitters released from the varicosities on a single nerve ending, and a single smooth muscle cell may be influenced by neurotransmitters from more than one neuron. Neurotransmitters may have either excitatory or inhibitory effects on smooth muscle contraction.

IX. Smooth muscles can be classified broadly as single-unit or multiunit smooth muscles.

Cardiac Muscle

I. Cardiac muscle combines features of skeletal and smooth muscles. Like skeletal muscle, it is striated, is composed of myofibrils with repeating sarcomeres, has troponin in its thin filaments, has T-tubules that conduct action potentials, and has sarcoplasmic reticulum terminal cisternae that store Ca^{2+}. Like smooth muscle, cardiac muscle cells are small and single-nucleated, arranged in layers around hollow cavities, and connected by gap junctions.

II. Cardiac muscle excitation–contraction coupling involves entry of a small amount of Ca^{2+} through L-type Ca^{2+} channels, which triggers opening of ryanodine receptors that release a larger amount of Ca^{2+} from the sarcoplasmic reticulum. Ca^{2+} activates the thin filament and cross-bridge cycling as in skeletal muscle.

III. Cardiac contractions and action potentials are prolonged, tetany does not occur, and both the strength and frequency of contraction are modulated by autonomic neurotransmitters and hormones.

IV. Table 9.6 summarizes and compares the features of skeletal, smooth, and cardiac muscles.

SECTION B REVIEW QUESTIONS

1. How does the organization of thick and thin filaments in smooth muscle fibers differ from that in striated muscle fibers?
2. Compare the mechanisms by which an increase in cytosolic Ca^{2+} concentration initiates contractile activity in skeletal, smooth, and cardiac muscle cells.
3. What are the two sources of Ca^{2+} that lead to the increase in cytosolic Ca^{2+} that triggers contraction in smooth muscle?
4. What types of stimuli can trigger an increase in cytosolic Ca^{2+} in smooth muscle cells?
5. What effect does a pacemaker potential have on a smooth muscle cell?
6. In what ways does the neural control of smooth muscle activity differ from that of skeletal muscle?
7. Describe how a stimulus may lead to the contraction of a smooth muscle cell without a change in the plasma membrane potential.
8. Describe the differences between single-unit and multiunit smooth muscles.
9. Compare and contrast the physiology of cardiac muscle with that of skeletal and smooth muscles.
10. Explain why cardiac muscle cannot undergo tetanic contractions.

SECTION B KEY TERMS

caldesmon 287
dense body 287
intercalated disk 292
latch state 288
L-type Ca^{2+} channel 292
multiunit smooth muscle 291
myosin light-chain kinase 287
myosin light-chain phosphatase 288
pacemaker potential 290
single-unit smooth muscle 291
slow waves 290
smooth muscle tone 289
varicosity 290

CHAPTER 9 Clinical Case Study: A Dangerous Increase in Body Temperature in a Boy During Surgery

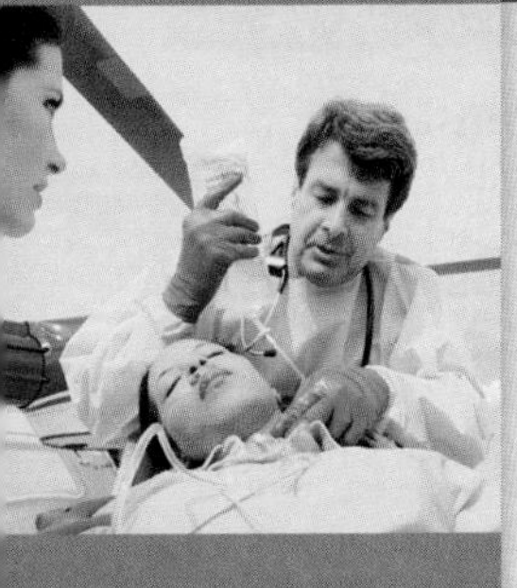

A 17-year-old boy lay on an operating table undergoing a procedure to repair a fractured jaw. In addition to receiving the local anesthetic ***lidocaine*** (which blocks voltage-gated Na^+ channels and therefore action potential propagation), he was breathing ***sevofluorane,*** an inhaled general anesthetic that induces unconsciousness. An hour into the procedure, the anesthesiologist suddenly noticed that the patient's face was red and beads of sweat were forming on his forehead. The patient's monitors revealed that his heart rate had almost doubled since the beginning of the procedure and that there had been significant increases in his body temperature and in the carbon dioxide concentration in his exhaled breath. The oral surgeon reported that the patient's jaw muscles had gone rigid. The patient was exhibiting all of the signs of a rare but deadly condition called ***malignant hyperthermia,*** and quick action would be required to save his life.

(continued)

(continued)

Most patients who suffer from malignant hyperthermia inherit an autosomal dominant mutation of a gene found on chromosome 19. This gene encodes the ryanodine receptors—the ion channels involved in releasing calcium ions from the sarcoplasmic reticulum in skeletal muscle. Although the channels function normally under most circumstances, they malfunction when exposed to some types of inhalant anesthetics or to drugs that depolarize and block skeletal muscle neuromuscular junctions (like succinylcholine). In some cases, the malfunction does not occur until the second exposure to the triggering agent.

The mechanism of malignant hyperthermia involves an excessive opening of the ryanodine receptor channel, with massive release of Ca^{2+} from the sarcoplasmic reticulum into the cytosol of skeletal muscle cells. The rate of Ca^{2+} release is so great that sarcoplasmic reticulum Ca^{2+}-ATPase pumps are unable to work fast enough to re-sequester it. The excess Ca^{2+} results in persistent activation of cross-bridge cycling and muscle contraction and also stimulates Ca^{2+}-activated proteases that degrade muscle proteins. The metabolism of ATP by muscle cells is increased enormously during an episode, with a number of consequences, some of which will be discussed in greater detail in later chapters:

1. ATP is depleted, causing cross-bridges to enter the rigor state, and therefore muscle rigidity ensues.
2. Muscle cells must resort to anaerobic metabolism to produce ATP because oxygen cannot be delivered to muscles fast enough to maintain aerobic production of ATP, so patients develop lactic acidosis (acidified blood due to the buildup of lactic acid).
3. CO_2 production increases, generating carbonic acid that contributes to acidosis (see Chapter 13).
4. Muscles generate a tremendous amount of heat as a by-product of ATP breakdown and production, producing the hyperthermia characteristic of this condition.
5. The drive to maintain homeostasis of body temperature, pH, and oxygen and carbon dioxide levels triggers an increase in heart rate to support an increase in the rate of blood circulation (see Chapter 12).
6. Flushing of the skin and sweating occur to help dissipate excess heat (see Chapter 16).

The anesthesiologist immediately halted the surgical procedure, then substituted 100% oxygen for the sevofluorane in the boy's breathing tube. Providing a high concentration of inspired oxygen increases the blood oxygen delivery to help muscles reestablish aerobic ATP production. The patient was then hyperventilated to help rid the body of excess CO_2, and ice bags were placed on his body to keep his temperature from increasing further. He was also given multiple injections of dantrolene until his condition began to improve. ***Dantrolene,*** a drug originally developed as a muscle relaxant, blocks the flux of Ca^{2+} through the ryanodine receptor. Since its introduction as a treatment, the mortality rate from malignant hyperthermia has decreased from greater than 70% to approximately 5%.

The boy was transferred to the intensive care unit, and his condition was monitored closely. Laboratory tests showed elevated blood H^+, K^+, Ca^{2+}, creatine kinase, and myoglobin concentrations, all of which are released during the rapid breakdown of muscle tissue (***rhabdomyolysis***). Among the dangers faced by such patients are malfunction of cardiac and other excitable cells, from abnormal pH and electrolyte levels, and kidney failure resulting from the overwhelming load of waste products released from damaged muscle cells. Over the next several days, the boy's condition improved and his blood chemistries returned to normal. Because the recognition and reaction by the medical team had been swift, the boy only suffered from sore muscles for the next few weeks but had no lasting damage to vital organs.

Malignant hyperthermia has a relatively low incidence, about one in 15,000 children and one in 50,000 adults. Because of its potentially lethal nature, however, it has become common practice to assess a given patient's risk of developing the condition. Although definitive proof of malignant hyperthermia can be determined by taking a muscle biopsy and assessing its response to anesthetics, the test is invasive and only available in a few clinical laboratories, so it is not usually performed. Risk is more commonly assessed by taking a detailed history that includes whether the patient or a genetic relative has ever had an adverse reaction to anesthesia. Even if the family history is negative, surgical teams need to have dantrolene on hand and be prepared. Advances in our understanding of the genetic basis of this disease make it likely that a reliable genetic screening test for malignant hyperthermia will someday be available.

Clinical terms: dantrolene, lidocaine, malignant hyperthermia, rhabdomyolysis, sevofluorane

See Chapter 19 for complete, integrative case studies.

CHAPTER 9 TEST QUESTIONS

Answers found in Appendix A.

1. Which is a *false* statement about skeletal muscle structure?
   a. A myofibril is composed of multiple muscle fibers.
   b. Most skeletal muscles attach to bones by connective-tissue tendons.
   c. Each end of a thick filament is surrounded by six thin filaments.
   d. A cross-bridge is a portion of the myosin molecule.
   e. Thin filaments contain actin, tropomyosin, and troponin.
2. Which is correct regarding a skeletal muscle sarcomere?
   a. M lines are found in the center of the I band.
   b. The I band is the space between one Z line and the next.
   c. The H zone is the region where thick and thin filaments overlap.
   d. Z lines are found in the center of the A band.
   e. The width of the A band is equal to the length of a thick filament.

3. When a skeletal muscle fiber undergoes a concentric isotonic contraction,
   a. M lines remain the same distance apart.
   b. Z lines move closer to the ends of the A bands.
   c. A bands become shorter.
   d. I bands become wider.
   e. M lines move closer to the end of the A band.
4. During excitation–contraction coupling in a skeletal muscle fiber,
   a. the Ca^{2+}-ATPase pumps Ca^{2+} into the T-tubule.
   b. action potentials propagate along the membrane of the sarcoplasmic reticulum.
   c. Ca^{2+} floods the cytosol through the dihydropyridine (DHP) receptors.
   d. DHP receptors trigger the opening of terminal cisternae ryanodine receptor Ca^{2+} channels.
   e. acetylcholine opens the DHP receptor channel.
5. Why is the latent period longer during an isotonic twitch of a skeletal muscle fiber than it is during an isometric twitch?
   a. Excitation–contraction coupling is slower during an isotonic twitch.
   b. Action potentials propagate more slowly when the fiber is shortening, so extra time is required to activate the entire fiber.
   c. In addition to the time for excitation–contraction coupling, it takes extra time for enough cross-bridges to attach to make the tension in the muscle fiber greater than the load.
   d. Fatigue sets in much more quickly during isotonic contractions, and when muscles are fatigued the cross-bridges move much more slowly.
   e. The latent period is longer because isotonic twitches only occur in slow (type I) muscle fibers.
6. What prevents a drop in muscle fiber ATP concentration during the first few seconds of intense contraction?
   a. Because cross-bridges are pre-energized, ATP is not needed until several cross-bridge cycles have been completed.
   b. ADP is rapidly converted back to ATP by creatine phosphate.
   c. Glucose is metabolized in glycolysis, producing large quantities of ATP.
   d. The mitochondria immediately begin oxidative phosphorylation.
   e. Fatty acids are rapidly converted to ATP by oxidative glycolysis.
7. Which correctly characterizes a "fast-oxidative" type of skeletal muscle fiber?
   a. few mitochondria and high glycogen content
   b. low myosin ATPase rate and few surrounding capillaries
   c. low glycolytic enzyme activity and intermediate contraction velocity
   d. high myoglobin content and intermediate glycolytic enzyme activity
   e. small fiber diameter and fast onset of fatigue
8. Which is *false* regarding the structure of smooth muscle?
   a. The thin filament does not include the regulatory protein troponin.
   b. The thick and thin filaments are not organized in sarcomeres.
   c. Thick filaments are anchored to dense bodies instead of Z lines.
   d. The cells have a single nucleus.
   e. Single-unit smooth muscles have gap junctions connecting individual cells.
9. The role of myosin light-chain kinase in smooth muscle is to
   a. bind to calcium ions to initiate excitation–contraction coupling.
   b. phosphorylate cross-bridges, thus driving them to bind with the thin filament.
   c. split ATP to provide the energy for the power stroke of the cross-bridge cycle.
   d. dephosphorylate myosin light chains of the cross-bridge, thus relaxing the muscle.
   e. pump Ca^{2+} from the cytosol back into the sarcoplasmic reticulum.
10. Single-unit smooth muscle differs from multiunit smooth muscle because
    a. single-unit muscle contraction speed is slow, and multiunit is fast.
    b. single-unit muscle has T-tubules, and multiunit muscle does not.
    c. single-unit muscles are not innervated by autonomic nerves.
    d. single-unit muscle contracts when stretched, whereas multiunit muscle does not.
    e. single-unit muscle does not produce action potentials spontaneously, but multiunit muscle does.
11. Which of the following describes a similarity between cardiac and smooth muscle cells?
    a. An action potential always precedes contraction.
    b. The majority of the Ca^{2+} that activates contraction comes from the extracellular fluid.
    c. Action potentials are generated by slow waves.
    d. An extensive system of T-tubules is present.
    e. Ca^{2+} release and contraction strengths are graded.

CHAPTER 9 GENERAL PRINCIPLES ASSESSMENT

Answers found in Appendix A.

1. Some cardiac muscle cells are specialized to serve as pacemaker cells that generate action potentials at regular intervals. Stimulation by sympathetic neurotransmitters increases the frequency of action potentials generated, while parasympathetic stimulation reduces the frequency. Which of the general principles of physiology described in Chapter 1 does this best demonstrate?
2. A general principle of physiology states that *physiological processes are dictated by the laws of chemistry and physics.* The chemical law of mass action tells us that the rate of a chemical reaction will slow down when there is a buildup in concentration of products of the reaction. How can this principle be applied as a contributing factor in muscle fatigue?
3. Explain how the process of skeletal muscle excitation–contraction coupling demonstrates the general principle of physiology that *controlled exchange of materials occurs between compartments and across cellular membranes.*

CHAPTER 9 QUANTITATIVE AND THOUGHT QUESTIONS

Answers found in Appendix A.

1. Which of the following corresponds to the state of myosin (M) under resting conditions, and which corresponds to rigor mortis? (a) M · ATP (b) M · ADP · P_i (c) A · M · ADP · P_i (d) A · M
2. If the insertion of a person's biceps muscle is 3 cm from the elbow joint, and the center of her hand is 27 cm from the insertion of the biceps, how fast will her hand move when her biceps contracts at 2 m/sec?
3. When a small load is attached to a skeletal muscle that is then tetanically stimulated, the muscle lifts the load in an isotonic contraction over a certain distance but then stops shortening and enters a state of isometric contraction. With a heavier load, the distance shortened before entering an isometric contraction is shorter. Explain these shortening limits in terms of the length–tension relation of muscle.
4. What conditions will produce the maximum tension in a skeletal muscle fiber?
5. A skeletal muscle can often maintain a moderate level of active tension for long periods of time, even though many of its fibers become fatigued. Explain.
6. If the blood flow to a skeletal muscle were markedly decreased, which types of motor units would most rapidly undergo a severe reduction in their ability to produce ATP for muscle contraction? Why?
7. As a result of an automobile accident, 50% of the muscle fibers in the biceps muscle of a patient were destroyed. Ten months later, the biceps muscle was able to generate 80% of its original force. Describe the changes that took place in the damaged muscle that enabled it to recover.
8. In the laboratory, if an isolated skeletal muscle is placed in a solution that contains no calcium ions, will the muscle contract when it is stimulated (a) directly by depolarizing its membrane, or (b) by stimulating the nerve to the muscle? What would happen if it was a smooth muscle?
9. The following experiments were performed on a single-unit smooth muscle in the gastrointestinal tract.
   a. Stimulating the parasympathetic nerves to the muscle produced a contraction.
   b. Applying a drug that blocks the voltage-sensitive Na^+ channels in most plasma membranes led to a failure to contract upon stimulating the parasympathetic nerves.
   c. Applying a drug that blocks muscarinic ACh receptors (see Chapter 6) did not prevent the muscle from contracting when the parasympathetic nerve was stimulated.

   From these observations, what might you conclude about the mechanism by which parasympathetic nerve stimulation produces a contraction of the smooth muscle?
10. Some endocrine tumors secrete a hormone that leads to elevation of extracellular fluid Ca^{2+} concentrations. How might this affect cardiac muscle?
11. If a single twitch of a skeletal muscle fiber lasts 40 msec, what action potential stimulation frequency (in action potentials per second) must be exceeded to produce an unfused tetanus?

CHAPTER 9 ANSWERS TO PHYSIOLOGICAL INQUIRIES

Figure 9.5

1 Only thick filaments are seen
2 Only thin filaments are seen

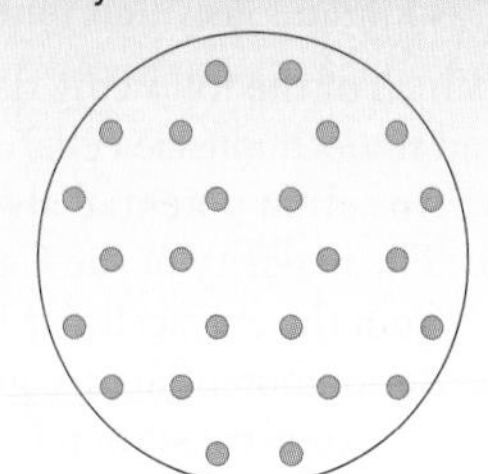

3 Thick filaments interconnected by a protein mesh

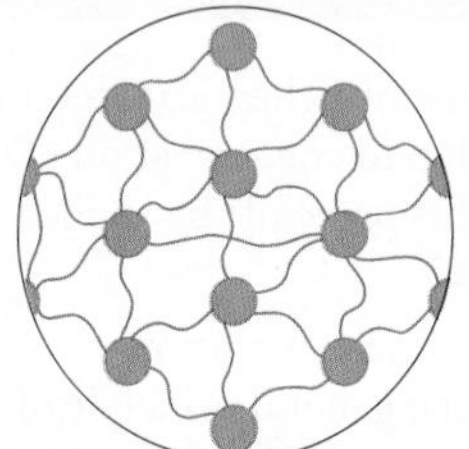

4 Thin filaments interconnected by a protein mesh

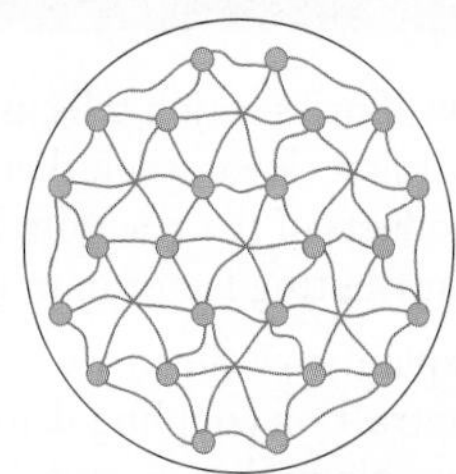

Figure 9.9 Na^+ current dominates when the ACh channels open because it has both a large inward diffusion gradient and, at the muscle cell's resting membrane potential, a large inward electrical gradient. Although the diffusion gradient for K^+ to leave the cell is large, the electrical gradient actually opposes its movement out of the cell. See Figure 6.12.

Figure 9.10 Tension takes longer to return to resting levels because all of the cross-bridges that attached to actin when Ca^{2+} was elevated require time to complete their power stroke and detach from actin.

Figure 9.14 Changes in the width of the I bands and H zone would be the same, but the sarcomeres would not slide toward the fixed Z line at the right side of the diagram. They would shorten uniformly and pull both of the outer Z lines toward the center one.

Figure 9.15 As long as ATP is available, cross-bridges would cycle continuously regardless of whether Ca^{2+} was present.

Figure 9.16 The weight in the isotonic experiment is approximately 14 mg. This can be estimated by determining the time at which the isotonic load begins to move on the lower graph (approximately 12 msec), then using the upper graph to assess the amount of tension generated by the fiber at that point in time.

Figure 9.18 Peak power generation by muscle fibers occurs at intermediate loads, usually at about one-third of their maximum isometric tension load. Using the arbitrary scale of 10 for the maximum velocity and load in this plot, for the points shown in this figure the power at the light load would be approximately $0.5 \times 7.5 = 3.75$. At the heavy load, it would be $7 \times 1 = 7$. At the intermediate load, the approximate power would be $3 \times 3 = 9$.

Figure 9.20 Unfused tetanic contractions will occur at between 6.7 and 28.6 stimuli per second. In order for an unfused tetanus to occur, the interval between stimuli must be less than 150 msec but greater than 35 msec. (If the interval was greater than 150 msec, twitches would not summate, and if less than 35 msec, a fused tetanus would occur.) To calculate the corresponding frequencies:

1 stimulus/150 msec × 1000 msec/sec = 6.7 stimuli/sec

1 stimulus/35 msec × 1000 msec/sec = 28.6 stimuli/sec

Figure 9.21 The passive tension at 150% of muscle length would be about 35% of the maximum isometric tension (see the red curve). When stimulated at that length, the active tension developed would be an additional 35% (see the green curve). The total tension measured would therefore be approximately 70% of the maximum isometric tetanic tension.

Figure 9.25 Muscle fibers containing the slow isoform of myosin contract and hydrolyze ATP relatively slowly. Their requirement for ATP can thus be satisfied by aerobic/oxidative mechanisms that, although slow, are extremely efficient (a yield of 38 ATP per glucose molecule with water and carbon dioxide as waste products—see Chapter 3). It would not be efficient for a slow fiber to produce its ATP predominantly by glycolysis, a process that is extremely rapid and relatively inefficient (only 2 ATP per glucose and lactic acid as a waste product).

Figure 9.29 The force acting upward on the forearm (85 × 5 = 425) would be less than the downward-acting force (10 × 45 = 450), so the muscle would undergo a lengthening (eccentric) contraction and the weight would move toward the ground.

Figure 9.30 The object would move nine times farther than the biceps in the same amount of time, or 18 cm/sec.

Figure 9.41 The skeletal muscle experiment would look the same. The calcium ions for contraction in skeletal muscle come from inside the sarcoplasmic reticulum. (*Note:* If the stimulus had been applied via a motor neuron, the lack of external Ca^{2+} would have prevented exocytosis of ACh and there would have been no action potential or contraction in the skeletal muscle cell.) Removing extracellular Ca^{2+} in the cardiac muscle experiment would eliminate both the prolonged plateau of the action potential and the contraction. Although the majority of the Ca^{2+} that activates contraction also comes from the sarcoplasmic reticulum in cardiac muscle, its release is triggered by entry of Ca^{2+} from the extracellular fluid through L-type channels during the action potential.

Visit this book's website at **www.mhhe.com/widmaier13** for chapter quizzes, interactive learning exercises, and other study tools.

Tracking and striking a tennis ball require a sophisticated system of motor control.

10 Control of Body Movement

Previous chapters described the complex structure and functions of the nervous system (Chapters 6–8) and skeletal muscles (Chapter 9). In this chapter, you will learn how those systems interact with each other in the initiation and control of body movements. Consider the events associated with reaching out and grasping an object. The trunk is inclined toward the object, and the wrist, elbow and shoulder are extended (straightened) and stabilized to support the weight of the arm and hand, as well as the object. The fingers are extended to reach around the object and then flexed (bent) to grasp it. The degree of extension will depend upon the size of the object, and the force of flexion will depend upon its weight and consistency (for example, you would grasp an egg less tightly than a rock). Through all this, the body maintains upright posture and balance despite its continuously shifting position.

The building blocks for these movements—as for all movements—are **motor units**, each comprising one motor neuron together with all the skeletal muscle fibers innervated by that neuron (Chapter 9). The motor neurons are the final common pathway out of the central nervous system because all neural influences on skeletal muscle converge on the motor neurons and can only affect skeletal muscle through them. All the motor neurons that supply a given muscle make up the **motor neuron pool** for the muscle. The cell bodies of the pool for a given muscle are close to each other either in the ventral horn of the spinal cord or in the brainstem.

Within the brainstem or spinal cord, the axon terminals of many neurons synapse on a motor neuron to control its activity. The precision and speed of normally coordinated actions are produced by a balance of excitatory and inhibitory inputs onto motor neurons. For example, if inhibitory synaptic input to a given motor neuron is decreased, the excitatory input to that neuron will be unopposed and the motor neuron firing will increase, leading to increased contraction. It is important to realize that movements—even simple movements such as flexing a finger—are rarely achieved by just one muscle. Body movements are achieved by activation, in a precise sequence, of many motor units in various muscles.

This chapter deals with the interrelated neural inputs that converge upon motor neurons to control their activity, and features several of the general principles of physiology described in Chapter 1. Throughout the chapter, signaling along individual neurons and within complex neural networks demonstrates the general principle of physiology that information flow between cells, tissues, and organs is an essential feature of homeostasis and allows for integration of physiological processes. Inputs to motor neurons can be either excitatory or inhibitory, a good example of the general principle of physiology that most physiological functions are controlled by multiple regulatory systems, often working in opposition. Finally, the challenge of maintaining posture and balance against gravity shows the general principle of physiology that physiological processes are dictated by the laws of chemistry and physics. We first present a general model of how the motor system functions and then describe each component of the model in detail. Keep in mind throughout this chapter that many of the contractions that skeletal muscles execute—particularly the muscles involved in postural support—are isometric (Chapter 9). These isometric contractions serve to stabilize body parts rather than to move them but are included in the discussion because they are essential in the overall control of body movements.

10.1 Motor Control Hierarchy

The neurons involved in controlling skeletal muscles can be thought of as being organized in a hierarchical fashion, with each level of the hierarchy having a certain task in motor control (**Figure 10.1**). To begin a consciously planned movement, a general intention such as "pick up sweater" or "write signature" or "answer telephone" is generated at the highest level of the motor control hierarchy. These higher centers include many regions of the brain, including sensorimotor areas and others involved in memory, emotions, and motivation.

Information is relayed from these higher-center "command" neurons to parts of the brain that make up the middle level of the motor control hierarchy. The middle-level structures specify the individual postures and movements needed to carry out the intended action. In our example of picking up a sweater, structures of the middle hierarchical level coordinate the commands that tilt the body and extend the arm and hand toward the sweater and shift the body's weight to maintain balance. The middle-level hierarchical structures are located in parts of the cerebral cortex as well as in the cerebellum, subcortical nuclei, and brainstem (see Figure 10.1 and **Figure 10.2**). These structures have extensive interconnections, as the arrows in Figure 10.1 indicate.

As the neurons in the middle level of the hierarchy receive input from the command neurons, they simultaneously receive afferent information from receptors in the muscles, tendons, joints, and skin, as well as from the vestibular apparatus and eyes. These afferent signals relay information to the middle-level

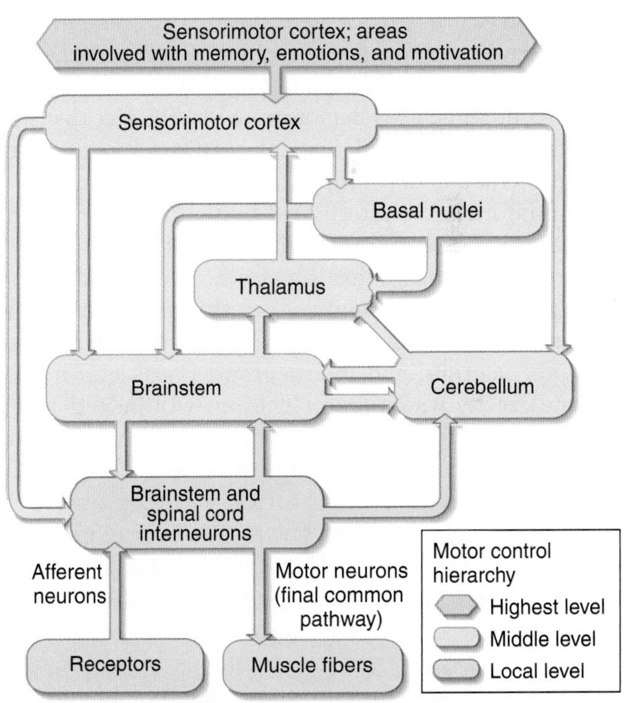

Figure 10.1 APIR The conceptual hierarchical organization of the neural systems controlling body movement. Motor neurons control all the skeletal muscles of the body. The sensorimotor cortex includes those parts of the cerebral cortex that act together to control skeletal muscle activity. The middle level of the hierarchy also receives input from the vestibular apparatus and eyes (not shown in the figure).

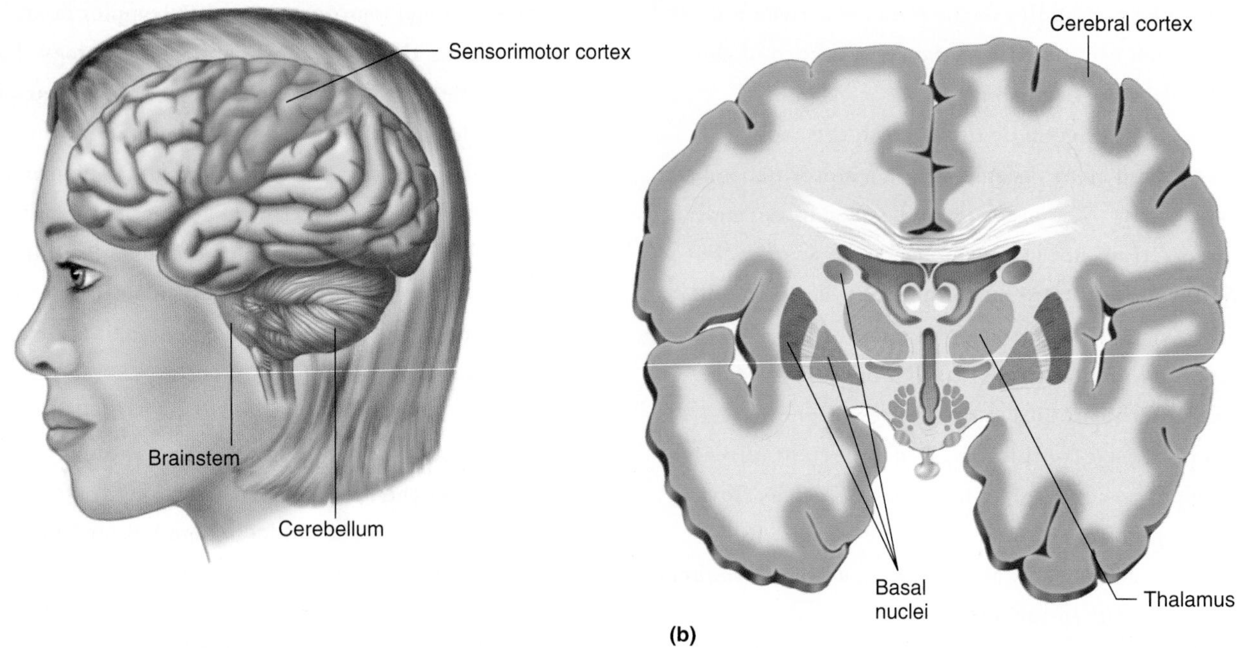

Figure 10.2 APIR (a) Side view of the brain showing three of the five components of the middle level of the motor control hierarchy. (Figure 10.10 shows details of the sensorimotor cortex.) (b) Cross section of the brain showing the thalamus and basal nuclei.

neurons about the starting positions of the body parts that are "commanded" to move. They also relay information about the nature of the space just outside the body in which a movement will take place. Neurons of the middle level of the hierarchy integrate all of this afferent information with the signals from the command neurons to create a **motor program**—defined as the pattern of neural activity required to properly perform the desired movement. The importance of sensory pathways in planning movements is demonstrated by the fact that when these pathways are impaired, a person has not only sensory deficits but also slow and uncoordinated voluntary movement.

The information determined by the motor program is transmitted via **descending pathways** to the local level of the motor control hierarchy. There, the axons of the motor neurons projecting to the muscles exit the brainstem or spinal cord. The local level of the hierarchy includes afferent neurons, motor neurons, and interneurons. Local-level neurons determine exactly which motor neurons will be activated to achieve the desired action and when this will happen. Note in Figure 10.1 that the descending pathways to the local level arise only in the sensorimotor cortex and brainstem. Other brain areas, notably the basal nuclei (also referred to as the basal ganglia), thalamus, and cerebellum, exert their effects on the local level only indirectly via the descending pathways from the cerebral cortex and brainstem.

The motor programs are continuously adjusted during the course of most movements. As the initial motor program begins and the action gets underway, brain regions at the middle level of the hierarchy continue to receive a constant stream of updated afferent information about the movements taking place. Afferent information about the position of the body and its parts in space is called **proprioception.** Say, for example, that the sweater you are picking up is wet and heavier than you expected so that the initially determined strength of muscle contraction is not sufficient to lift it. Any discrepancies between the intended and actual movements are detected, program corrections are determined, and the corrections are relayed to the local level of the hierarchy and the motor neurons. Reflex circuits acting entirely at the local level are also important in refining ongoing movements. Thus, many proprioceptive inputs are processed and influence ongoing movements without ever reaching the level of conscious perception.

If a complex movement is repeated often, learning takes place and the movement becomes skilled. Then, the initial information from the middle hierarchical level is more accurate and fewer corrections need to be made. Movements performed at high speed without concern for fine control are made solely according to the initial motor program.

Table 10.1 summarizes the structures and functions of the motor control hierarchy.

Voluntary and Involuntary Actions

Given such a highly interconnected and complicated neuroanatomical basis for the motor system, it is difficult to use the phrase **voluntary movement** with any real precision. We will use it, however, to refer to actions that have the following characteristics: (1) the movement is accompanied by a conscious awareness of what we are doing and why we are doing it, and (2) our attention is directed toward the action or its purpose.

The term *involuntary*, on the other hand, describes actions that do not have these characteristics. *Unconscious, automatic,* and *reflex* often serve as synonyms for *involuntary*, although in the motor system, the term *reflex* has a more precise meaning.

Despite our attempts to distinguish between voluntary and involuntary actions, almost all motor behavior involves both components, and it is not easy to make a distinction between the two. For example, even such a highly conscious act as walking involves many reflexive components, as the

TABLE 10.1	Conceptual Motor Control Hierarchy for Voluntary Movements

I. Higher centers
   A. Function: Forms complex plans according to individual's intention and communicates with the middle level via command neurons.
   B. Structures: Areas involved with memory, emotions and motivation, and sensorimotor cortex. All these structures receive and correlate input from many other brain structures.

II. The middle level
   A. Function: Converts plans received from higher centers to a number of smaller motor programs that determine the pattern of neural activation required to perform the movement. These programs are broken down into subprograms that determine the movements of individual joints. The programs and subprograms are transmitted through descending pathways to the local control level.
   B. Structures: Sensorimotor cortex, cerebellum, parts of basal nuclei, some brainstem nuclei.

III. The local level
   A. Function: Specifies tension of particular muscles and angle of specific joints at specific times necessary to carry out the programs and subprograms transmitted from the middle control levels.
   B. Structures: Brainstem or spinal cord interneurons, afferent neurons, motor neurons.

pattern of contraction of leg muscles is subconsciously varied to adapt to obstacles or uneven terrain.

Most motor behavior, therefore, is neither purely voluntary nor purely involuntary but has elements of both. Moreover, actions shift along this continuum according to the frequency with which they are performed. When a person first learns to drive a car with a manual transmission, for example, shifting gears requires a great deal of conscious attention. With practice, those same actions become automatic. On the other hand, reflex behaviors that are generally involuntary can, with special effort, sometimes be voluntarily modified or even prevented.

We now turn to an analysis of the individual components of the motor control system. We will begin with local control mechanisms because their activity serves as a base upon which the descending pathways exert their influence. Keep in mind throughout these descriptions that motor neurons always form the final common pathway to the muscles.

10.2 Local Control of Motor Neurons

The local control systems are the relay points for instructions to the motor neurons from centers higher in the motor control hierarchy. In addition, the local control systems play a major role in adjusting motor unit activity to unexpected obstacles to movement and to painful stimuli in the surrounding environment.

To carry out these adjustments, the local control systems use information carried by afferent fibers from sensory receptors in the muscles, tendons, joints, and skin of the body parts to be moved. As noted earlier, the afferent fibers also transmit information to higher levels of the hierarchy.

Interneurons

Most of the synaptic input to motor neurons from the descending pathways and afferent neurons does not go directly to motor neurons but, rather, goes to interneurons that synapse with the motor neurons. Interneurons comprise 90% of spinal cord neurons, and they are of several types. Some are near the motor neuron they synapse upon and thus are called local interneurons. Others have processes that extend up or down short distances in the spinal cord and brainstem, or even throughout much of the length of the central nervous system. The interneurons with longer processes are important for integrating complex movements such as stepping forward with your left foot as you throw a baseball with your right arm.

The interneurons are important elements of the local level of the motor control hierarchy, integrating inputs not only from higher centers and peripheral receptors but from other interneurons as well (**Figure 10.3**). They are crucial in determining which muscles are activated and when. This is especially important in coordinating repetitive, rhythmic activities like walking or running, for which spinal cord interneurons encode pattern generator circuits responsible for activating and inhibiting limb movements in an alternating sequence. Moreover, interneurons can act as "switches" that enable a movement to be turned on or off under the command of higher motor centers. For example, if you pick up a hot plate, a local reflex arc will be initiated by pain receptors in the skin of your hands, normally causing you to drop the plate. If it contains

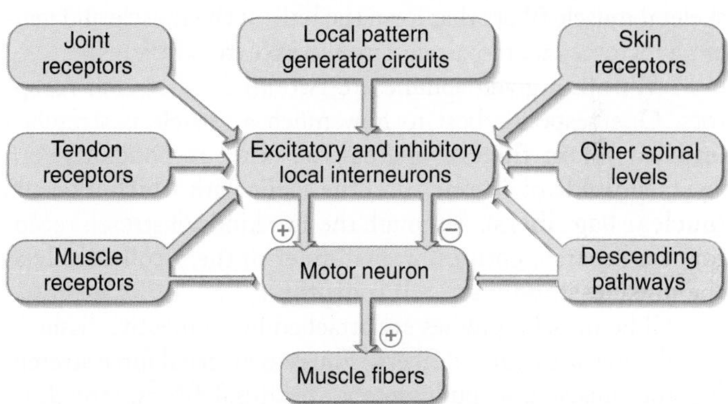

Figure 10.3 Converging inputs to local interneurons that control motor neuron activity. Plus signs indicate excitatory synapses and minus sign an inhibitory synapse. Neurons in addition to those shown may synapse directly onto motor neurons.

PHYSIOLOGICAL INQUIRY

- Many spinal cord interneurons release the neurotransmitter glycine, which opens chloride ion channels on postsynaptic cell membranes. Given that the plant-derived chemical strychnine blocks glycine receptors, predict the symptoms of strychnine poisoning.

Answer can be found at end of chapter.

your dinner, however, descending commands can inhibit the local activity, and you can hold onto the plate until you can put it down safely. The integration of various inputs by local interneurons is an excellent example of the general principle of physiology that most physiological functions are controlled by multiple regulatory systems, often working in opposition.

Local Afferent Input

As just noted, afferent fibers sometimes impinge on the local interneurons. (In one case that will be discussed shortly, they synapse directly on motor neurons.) The afferent fibers carry information from sensory receptors located in three places: (1) in the skeletal muscles controlled by the motor neurons; (2) in other nearby muscles, such as those with antagonistic actions; and (3) in the tendons, joints, and skin of body parts affected by the action of the muscle.

These receptors monitor the length and tension of the muscles, movement of the joints, and the effect of movements on the overlying skin. In other words, the movements themselves give rise to afferent input that, in turn, influences how the movement proceeds. As we will see next, their input sometimes provides negative feedback control over the muscles and also contributes to the conscious awareness of limb and body position.

Length-Monitoring Systems

Stretch receptors embedded within muscles monitor muscle length and the rate of change in muscle length. These receptors consist of peripheral endings of afferent nerve fibers wrapped around modified muscle fibers, several of which are enclosed in a connective-tissue capsule. The entire apparatus is collectively called a **muscle spindle** (**Figure 10.4**). The modified muscle fibers within the spindle are known as **intrafusal fibers.** The skeletal muscle fibers that form the bulk of the muscle and generate its force and movement are the **extrafusal fibers.**

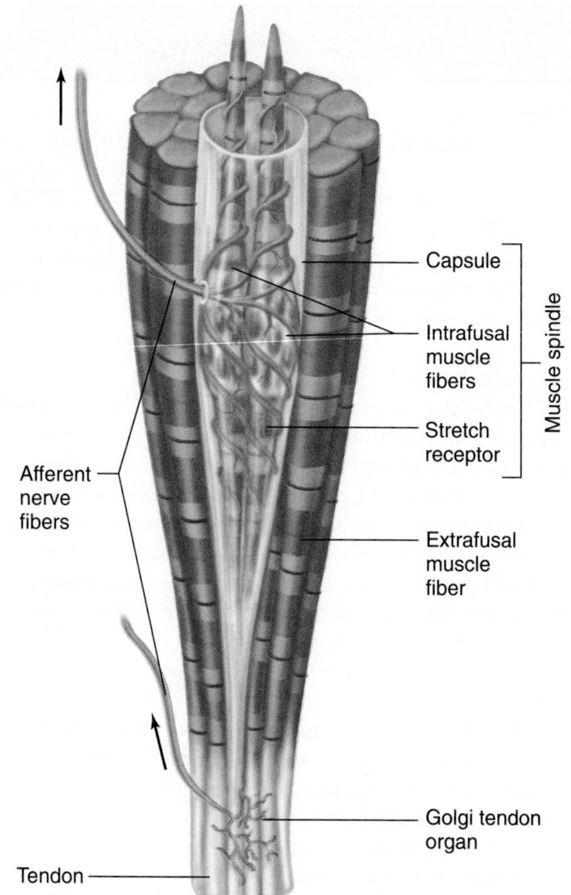

Figure 10.4 A muscle spindle and Golgi tendon organ. The muscle spindle is exaggerated in size compared to the extrafusal muscle fibers. The Golgi tendon organ will be discussed later in the chapter. Adapted from Elias, Pauly, and Burns.

Within a given spindle are two kinds of stretch receptors. One responds best to how much a muscle is stretched (**nuclear chain fibers**), whereas the other responds to both the magnitude of a stretch and the speed with which it occurs (**nuclear bag fibers**). Although the two kinds of stretch receptors are separate entities, we will refer to them collectively as the **muscle-spindle stretch receptors.**

The muscle spindles are attached by connective tissue in parallel to the extrafusal fibers. Thus, an external force stretching the muscle also pulls on the intrafusal fibers, stretching them and activating their receptor endings (**Figure 10.5a**). The more or the faster the muscle is stretched, the greater the rate of receptor firing. In contrast, if action potentials along motor neurons cause contraction of the extrafusal fibers, the resultant shortening of the muscle removes tension on the spindle and slows the rate of firing in the stretch receptor (**Figure 10.5b**).

If muscles were always activated as shown in Figure 10.5b, slackening of muscle spindles would reduce the available sensory information about muscle length during rapid shortening contractions. A mechanism called **alpha–gamma coactivation** prevents this loss of information. Extrafusal fibers of a muscle are activated by large-diameter **alpha motor neurons,** and the two ends of intrafusal muscle fibers are activated by smaller-diameter neurons called **gamma motor neurons.** The cell bodies of alpha and gamma motor neurons to a given muscle lie close together in the spinal cord or brainstem. Both types are activated by interneurons in their immediate vicinity and sometimes directly by neurons of the descending pathways. The contractile ends of intrafusal fibers are not large or strong enough to contribute to force or shortening of the whole muscle. However, they can maintain tension and stretch in the central receptor region of the intrafusal fibers. Activating gamma motor neurons alone therefore increases the sensitivity of a muscle to stretch. Coactivating gamma motor neurons along with alpha motor neurons prevents the central region of the muscle spindle from going slack during a shortening contraction (**Figure 10.5c**). This ensures that information about muscle length will be continuously available to provide for adjustment during ongoing actions and to plan and program future movements.

The Stretch Reflex

When the afferent fibers from the muscle spindle enter the central nervous system, they divide into branches that take different paths. In **Figure 10.6**, path A makes excitatory synapses directly onto motor neurons that return to the muscle that was stretched, thereby completing a reflex arc known as the **stretch reflex.**

This reflex is probably most familiar in the form of the **knee-jerk reflex,** part of a routine medical examination.

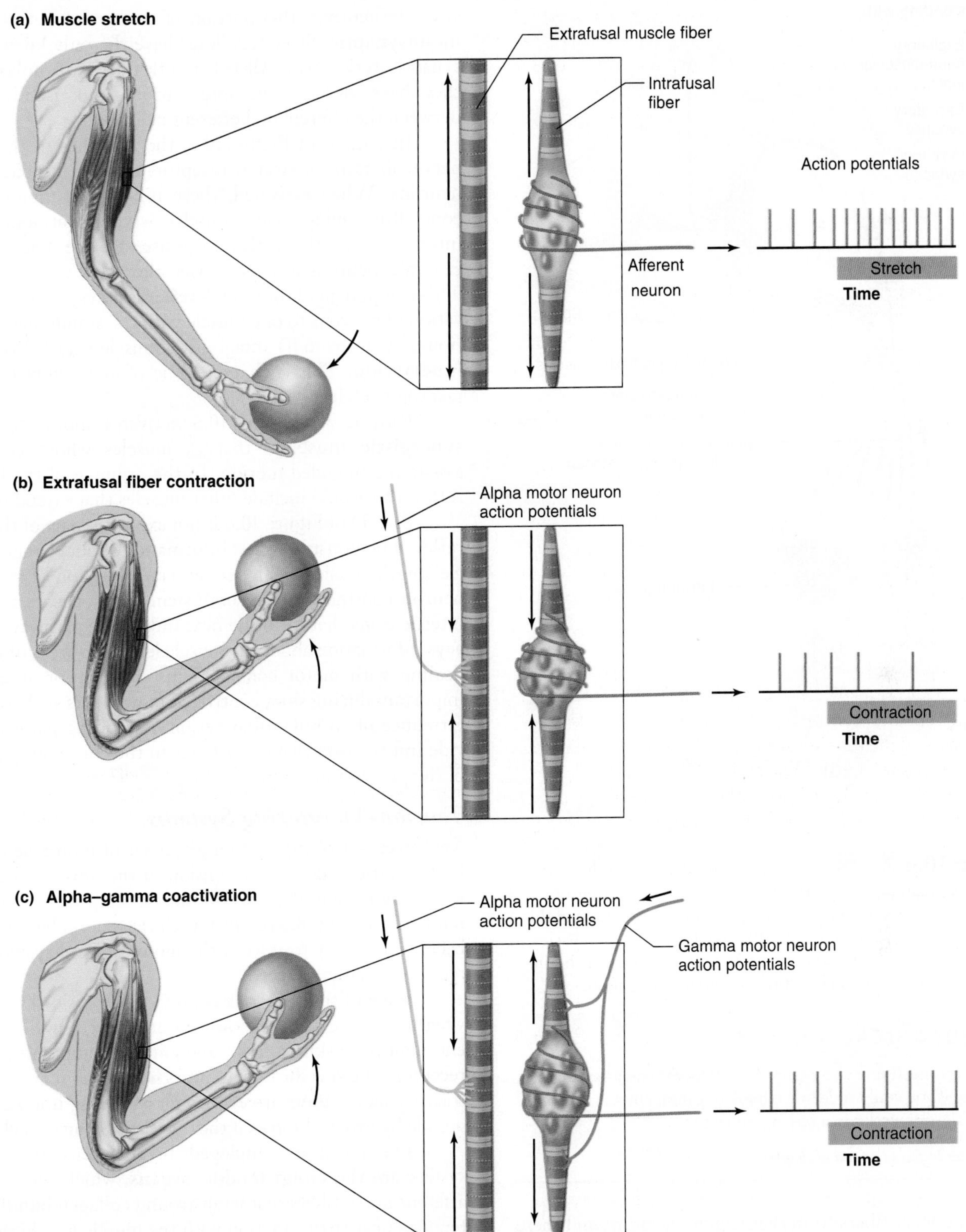

Figure 10.5 (a) Passive stretch of the muscle by an external load activates the spindle stretch receptors and causes an increased rate of action potentials in the afferent nerve. (b) Contraction of the extrafusal fibers removes tension on the stretch receptors and decreases the rate of action potential firing. (c) Simultaneous activation of alpha and gamma motor neurons results in maintained stretch of the central region of intrafusal fibers. Afferent information about muscle length continues to reach the central nervous system.

The examiner taps the patellar tendon (see Figure 10.6), which passes over the knee and connects extensor muscles in the thigh to the tibia in the lower leg. As the tendon is pushed in by tapping, the thigh muscles it is attached to are stretched, and all the stretch receptors within these muscles are activated. This stimulates a burst of action potentials in

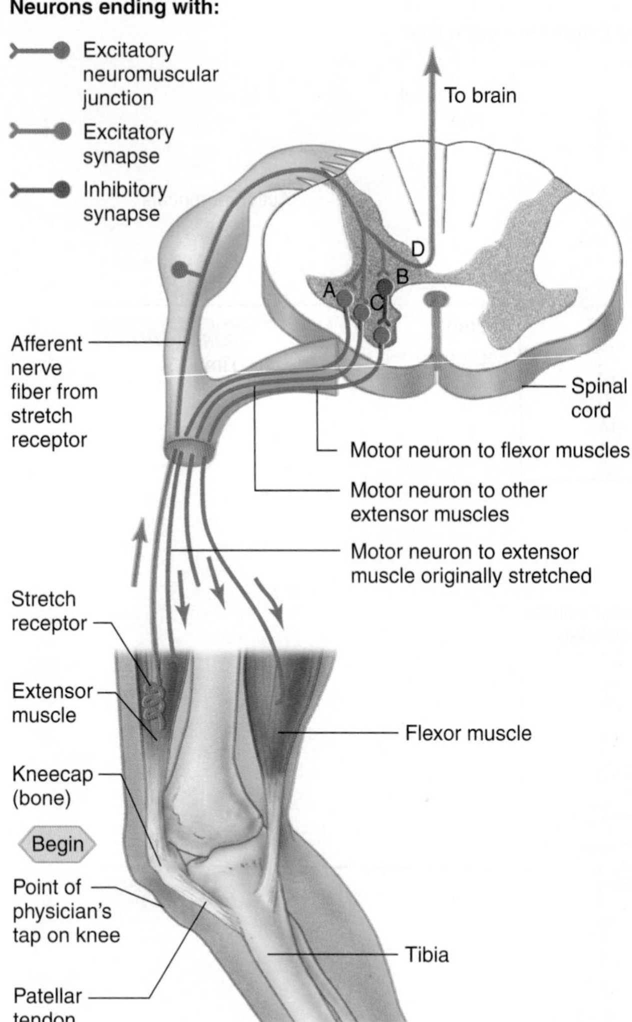

Figure 10.6 APIR Neural pathways involved in the knee-jerk reflex. Tapping the patellar tendon stretches the extensor muscle, causing (paths A and C) compensatory contraction of this and other extensor muscles, (path B) relaxation of flexor muscles, and (path D) information about muscle length to go to the brain. Arrows indicate direction of action potential propagation.

PHYSIOLOGICAL INQUIRY

- Based on this figure and Figure 10.5, hypothesize what might happen if you could suddenly stimulate gamma motor neurons to leg flexor muscles in a resting subject.

Answer can be found at end of chapter.

the afferent nerve fibers from the stretch receptors, and these action potentials activate excitatory synapses on the motor neurons that control these same muscles. The motor units are stimulated, the thigh muscles contract, and the patient's lower leg extends to give the knee jerk. The proper performance of the knee jerk tells the physician that the afferent fibers, the balance of synaptic input to the motor neurons, the motor neurons, the neuromuscular junctions, and the muscles themselves are functioning normally.

Because the afferent nerve fibers in the stretched muscle synapse directly on the motor neurons to that muscle without any interneurons, this portion of the stretch reflex is called **monosynaptic.** Stretch reflexes have the only known monosynaptic reflex arcs. All other reflex arcs are **polysynaptic;** they have at least one interneuron—and usually many—between the afferent and efferent neurons.

In path B of Figure 10.6, the branches of the afferent nerve fibers from stretch receptors end on inhibitory interneurons. When activated, these inhibit the motor neurons controlling antagonistic muscles whose contraction would interfere with the reflex response. In the knee jerk, for example, neurons to muscles that flex the knee are inhibited. This component of the stretch reflex is polysynaptic. The activation of neurons to one muscle with the simultaneous inhibition of neurons to its antagonistic muscle is called **reciprocal innervation.** This is characteristic of many movements, not just the stretch reflex.

Path C in Figure 10.6 activates motor neurons of **synergistic muscles**—that is, muscles whose contraction assists the intended motion. In the example of the knee-jerk reflex, this would include other muscles that extend the leg.

Path D of Figure 10.6 is not explicitly part of the stretch reflex; it demonstrates that information about changes in muscle length ascends to higher centers. The axon of the afferent neuron continues to the brainstem and synapses there with interneurons that form the next link in the pathway that conveys information about the muscle length to areas of the brain dealing with motor control. This information is especially important during slow, controlled movements such as the performance of an unfamiliar action. Ascending paths also provide information that contributes to the conscious perception of the position of a limb.

Tension-Monitoring Systems

Any given set of inputs to a given set of motor neurons can lead to various degrees of tension in the muscles they innervate. The tension depends on muscle length, the load on the muscles, and the degree of muscle fatigue. Therefore, feedback is necessary to inform the motor control systems of the tension actually achieved.

Some of this feedback is provided by vision (you can see whether you are lifting or lowering an object) as well as by afferent input from skin, muscle, and joint receptors. An additional receptor type specifically monitors how much tension the contracting motor units are exerting (or is being imposed on the muscle by external forces if the muscle is being stretched).

The receptors employed in this tension-monitoring system are the **Golgi tendon organs,** which are endings of afferent nerve fibers that wrap around collagen bundles in the tendons near their junction with the muscle (see Figure 10.4). These collagen bundles are slightly bowed in the resting state. When the muscle is stretched or the attached extrafusal muscle fibers contract, tension is exerted on the tendon. This tension straightens the collagen bundles and distorts the receptor endings, activating them. The tendon is typically stretched much more by an active contraction of the muscle than when the whole muscle is passively stretched (**Figure 10.7**). Therefore, the Golgi tendon organs discharge in response to the tension generated by the contracting muscle and initiate action potentials that are transmitted to the central nervous system.

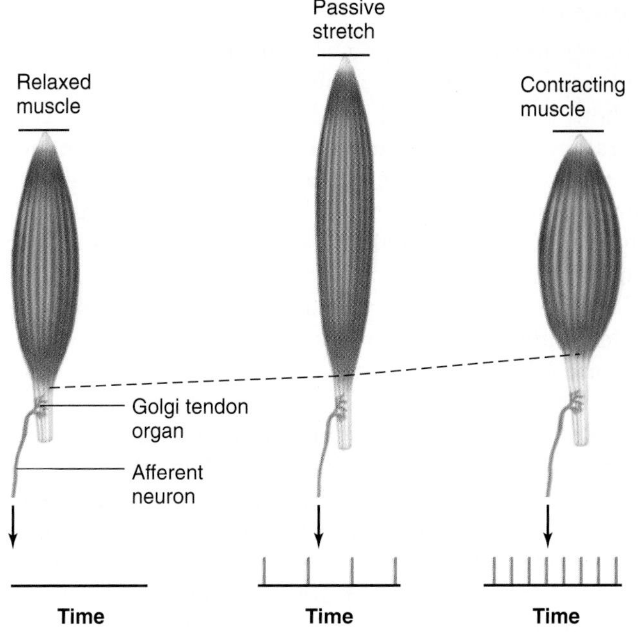

Figure 10.7 Activation of Golgi tendon organs. Compared to when a muscle is contracting, passive stretch of the relaxed muscle produces less stretch of the tendon and fewer action potentials from the Golgi tendon organ.

PHYSIOLOGICAL INQUIRY

- Which of these conditions would result in the greatest action potential frequency in afferent neurons from muscle-spindle receptors?

Answer can be found at end of chapter.

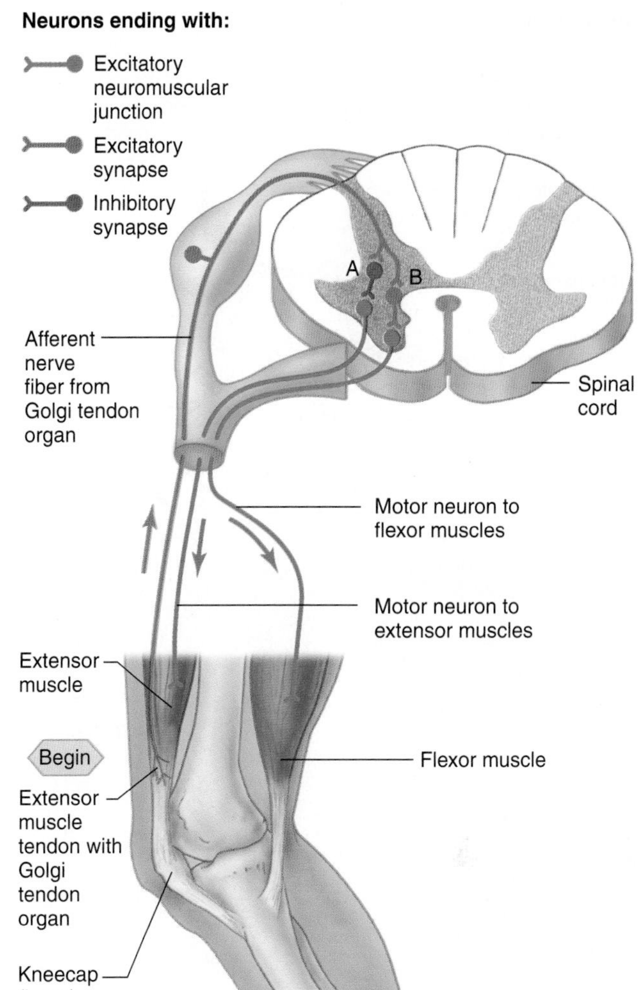

Figure 10.8 APR Neural pathways underlying the Golgi tendon organ component of the local control system. In this diagram, contraction of the extensor muscles causes tension in the Golgi tendon organ and increases the rate of action potential firing in the afferent nerve fiber. By way of interneurons, this increased activity results in (path A) inhibition of the motor neurons of the extensor muscle and its synergists and (path B) excitation of flexor muscle motor neurons. Arrows indicate the direction of action potential propagation.

PHYSIOLOGICAL INQUIRY

- Explain how the Golgi tendon organ protects against excessive force exertion that might tear a muscle or tendon.

Answer can be found at end of chapter.

Branches of the afferent neuron from the Golgi tendon organ cause widespread inhibition of the contracting muscle and its synergists via interneurons (path A in **Figure 10.8**). They also stimulate the motor neurons of the antagonistic muscles (path B in Figure 10.8). Note that this reciprocal innervation is the opposite of that produced by the muscle-spindle afferents. This difference reflects the different functional roles of the two systems: The muscle spindle provides local homeostatic control of muscle *length*, and the Golgi tendon organ provides local homeostatic control of muscle *tension*. In addition, the activity of afferent fibers from these two receptors supplies the higher-level motor control systems with information about muscle length and tension, which can be used to modify an ongoing motor program.

The Withdrawal Reflex

In addition to the afferent information from the spindle stretch receptors and Golgi tendon organs of the activated muscle, other input is transmitted to the local motor control systems. For example, painful stimulation of the skin, as occurs from stepping on a tack, activates the flexor muscles and inhibits the extensor muscles of the ipsilateral (on the same side of the body) leg. The resulting action moves the affected limb away from the harmful stimulus and is thus known as a **withdrawal reflex** (**Figure 10.9**). The same stimulus causes just the opposite response in the contralateral leg (on the opposite side of the body from the stimulus); motor neurons to the extensors are activated while the flexor muscle motor neurons are inhibited. This **crossed-extensor reflex** enables the contralateral leg to support the body's weight as the injured foot is lifted by flexion (see Figure 10.9). This concludes our discussion of the local level of motor control.

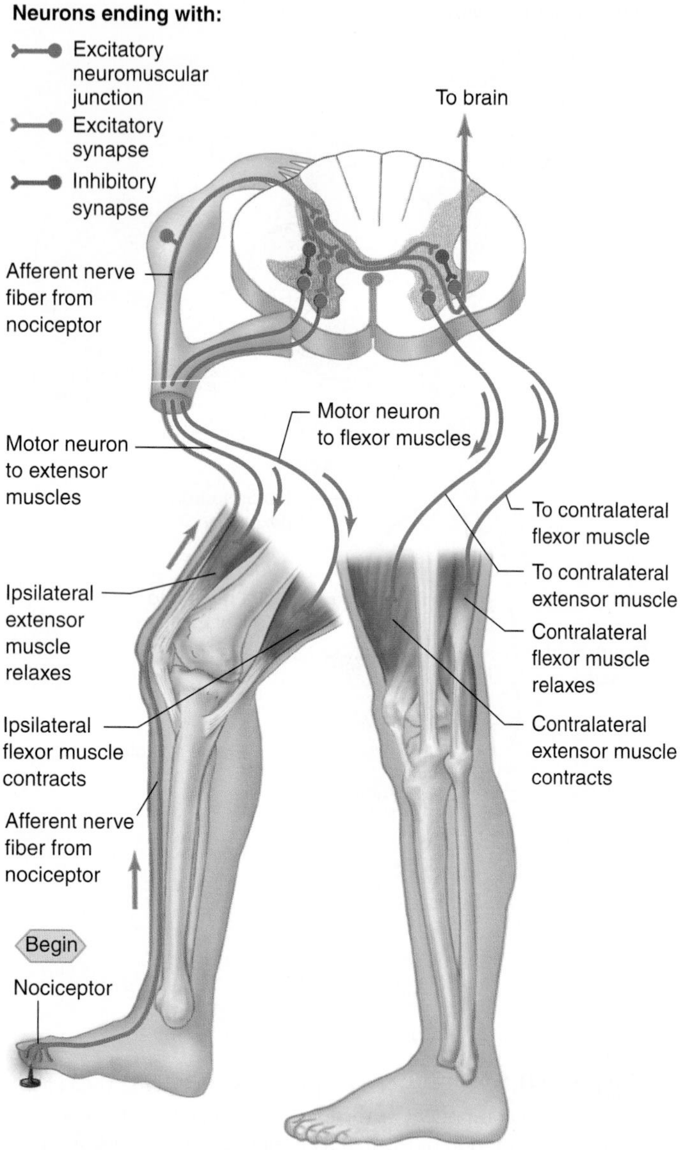

Figure 10.9 APIR In response to pain detected by nociceptors (Chapter 7), the ipsilateral flexor muscle's motor neuron is stimulated (withdrawal reflex). In the case illustrated, the opposite limb is extended (crossed-extensor reflex) to support the body's weight. Arrows indicate direction of action potential propagation.

PHYSIOLOGICAL INQUIRY

- While crawling across a floor, a child accidentally places her right hand onto a piece of broken glass. How will the flexor muscles of her left arm respond?

Answer can be found at end of chapter.

10.3 The Brain Motor Centers and the Descending Pathways They Control

We now turn our attention to the motor centers in the brain and the descending pathways that direct the local control system (review Figure 10.1).

Cerebral Cortex

The cerebral cortex plays a critical role in both the planning and ongoing control of voluntary movements, functioning in both the highest and middle levels of the motor control hierarchy. The term **sensorimotor cortex** is used to include all those parts of the cerebral cortex that act together to control muscle movement. A large number of neurons that give rise to descending pathways for motor control come from two areas of sensorimotor cortex on the posterior part of the frontal lobe: the **primary motor cortex** (sometimes called simply the **motor cortex**) and the **premotor area** (**Figure 10.10**).

Other areas of sensorimotor cortex shown in Figure 10.10 include the **supplementary motor cortex,** which lies mostly on the surface on the frontal lobe where the cortex folds down between the two hemispheres, the **somatosensory cortex,** and parts of the **parietal-lobe association cortex.** The neurons of the motor cortex that control muscle groups in various parts of the body are arranged anatomically into a **somatotopic map,** as shown in **Figure 10.11**.

Although these areas of the cortex are anatomically and functionally distinct, they are heavily interconnected, and individual muscles or movements are represented at multiple sites. Thus, the cortical neurons that control movement form a neural network, meaning that many neurons participate in each single movement. In addition, any one neuron may function in more than one movement. The neural networks can be distributed across multiple sites in parietal and frontal cortex, including the sites named in the preceding two paragraphs. The interactions of the neurons within the networks are flexible so that the neurons are capable of responding differently under different circumstances. This adaptability enhances the possibility of integrating incoming neural signals from diverse sources and the final coordination of many parts into a smooth, purposeful movement. It probably also accounts for the remarkable variety of ways in which we can approach a goal. For example, you can comb your hair with the right hand or the left, starting at the back of your head or the front. This same adaptability also accounts for some of the learning that occurs in all aspects of motor behavior.

We have described the various areas of sensorimotor cortex as giving rise, either directly or indirectly, to pathways descending to the motor neurons. However, additional brain areas are involved in the initiation of intentional movements, such as the areas involved in memory, emotion, and motivation.

Association areas of the cerebral cortex also play other roles in motor control. For example, neurons of the parietal association cortex are important in the visual control of reaching and grasping. These neurons play an important role in matching motor signals concerning the pattern of hand action with signals from the visual system concerning the three-dimensional features of the objects to be grasped. Imagine a glass of water sitting in front of you on your desk—you could reach out and pick it up much more smoothly with your eyes tracking your arm and hand movements than you could with your eyes closed. During activation of the cortical areas involved in motor control, subcortical mechanisms also become active. We now turn to these areas of the motor control system.

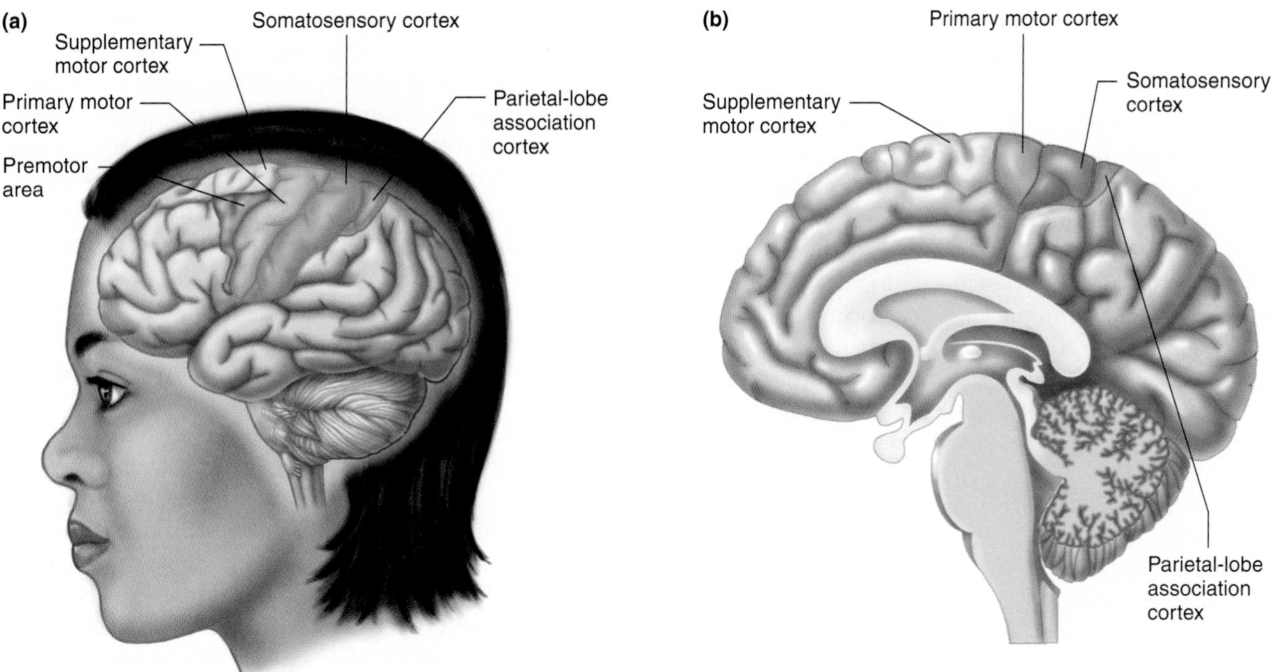

Figure 10.10 APIR (a) The major motor areas of the cerebral cortex. (b) Midline view of the right side of the brain showing the supplementary motor cortex, which lies in the part of the cerebral cortex that is folded down between the two cerebral hemispheres. Other cortical motor areas also extend onto this area. The premotor, supplementary motor, primary motor, somatosensory, and parietal-lobe association cortices together make up the sensorimotor cortex.

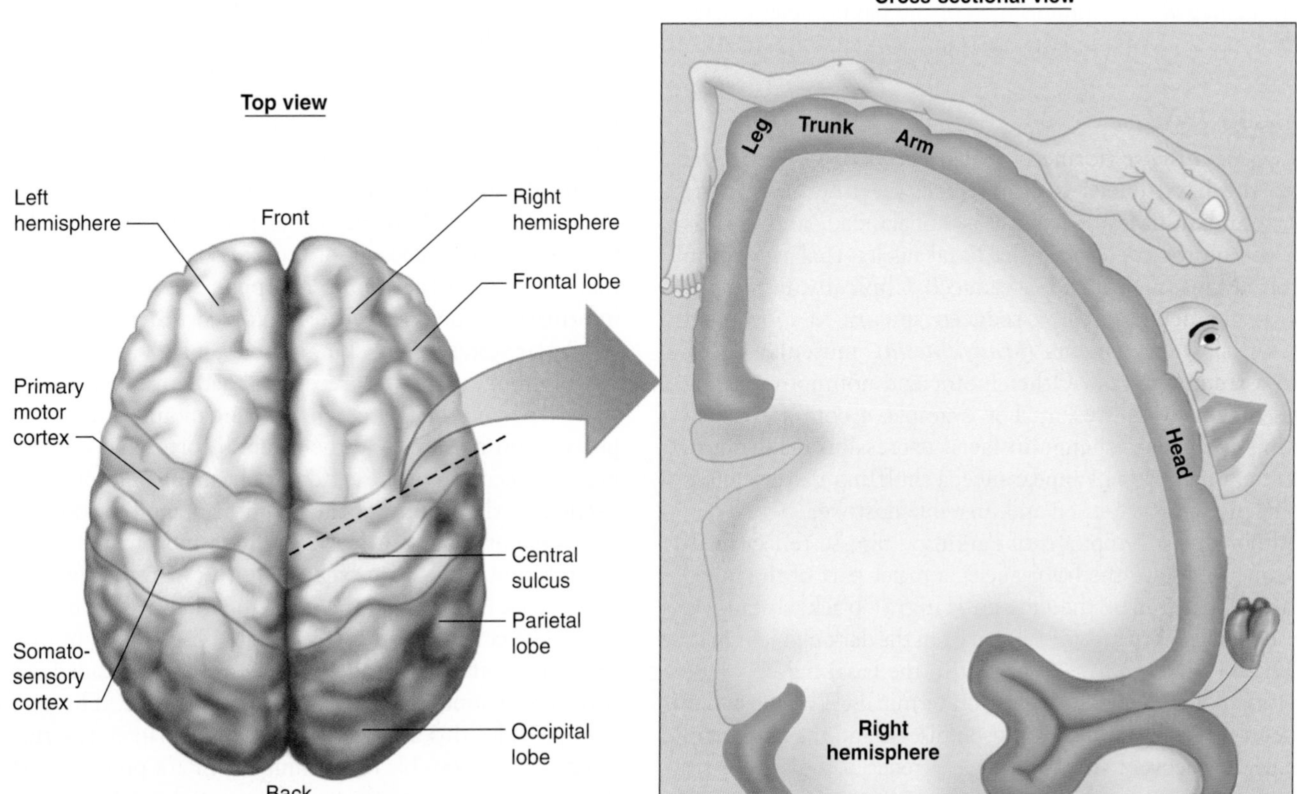

Figure 10.11 APIR Somatotopic map of major body areas in the primary motor cortex. Within the broad areas, no one area exclusively controls the movement of a single body region and there is much overlap and duplication of cortical representation. Relative sizes of body structures are proportional to the number of neurons dedicated to their motor control. Only the right motor cortex, which principally controls muscles on the left side of the body, is shown.

Subcortical and Brainstem Nuclei

Numerous highly interconnected structures lie in the brainstem and within the cerebrum beneath the cortex, where they interact with the cortex to control movements. Their influence is transmitted indirectly to the motor neurons both by pathways that ascend to the cerebral cortex and by pathways that descend from some of the brainstem nuclei.

It is not known to what extent—if any—these structures are involved in initiating movements, but they definitely play a prominent role in planning and monitoring them. Their role is to establish the programs that determine the specific sequence of movements needed to accomplish a desired action. Subcortical and brainstem nuclei are also important in learning skilled movements.

Prominent among the subcortical nuclei are the paired **basal nuclei** (see Figure 10.2b), which consist of a closely related group of separate nuclei. As described in Chapter 6, these structures are often referred to as basal ganglia, but their presence within the central nervous system makes the term *nuclei* more technically correct. They form a link in some of the looping parallel circuits through which activity in the motor system is transmitted from a specific region of sensorimotor cortex to the basal nuclei, from there to the thalamus, and then back to the cortical area where the circuit started (review Figure 10.1). Some of these circuits facilitate movements, and others suppress them. This explains why brain damage to subcortical nuclei following a stroke or trauma can result in either hypercontracted muscles or flaccid paralysis—it depends on which specific circuits are damaged. The importance of the basal nuclei is particularly apparent in certain disease states, as we discuss next.

Parkinson Disease

In ***Parkinson disease*** (formerly called *Parkinson's disease*), the input to the basal nuclei is diminished, the interplay of the facilitory and inhibitory circuits is unbalanced, and activation of the motor cortex (via the basal nuclei–thalamus limb of the circuit just mentioned) is reduced. Clinically, Parkinson disease is characterized by a reduced amount of movement (***akinesia***), slow movements (***bradykinesia***), muscular rigidity, and a tremor at rest. Other motor and nonmotor abnormalities may also be present. For example, a common set of symptoms includes a change in facial expression resulting in a masklike, unemotional appearance, a shuffling gait with loss of arm swing, and a stooped and unstable posture.

Although the symptoms of Parkinson disease reflect inadequate functioning of the basal nuclei, a major part of the initial defect arises in neurons of the **substantia nigra** ("black substance"), a brainstem nucleus that gets its name from the dark pigment in its cells. These neurons normally project to the basal nuclei, where they release dopamine from their axon terminals. The substantia nigra neurons degenerate in Parkinson disease and the amount of dopamine they deliver to the basal nuclei is reduced. This decreases the subsequent activation of the sensorimotor cortex.

It is not currently known what causes the degeneration of neurons of the substantia nigra and the development of Parkinson disease. In a small fraction of cases, there is evidence that it may have a genetic cause, based on observed changes in the function of genes associated with mitochondrial function, protection from oxidative stress, and removal of cellular proteins that have been targeted for metabolic breakdown. Scientists suspect that exposure to environmental toxins such as manganese, carbon monoxide, and some pesticides may also play a role. One chemical clearly linked to destruction of the substantia nigra is ***MPTP*** (***1-methyl-4-phenyl-1,2,3,6-tetrahydropyridine***). MPTP is an impurity sometimes created in the manufacture of a synthetic heroin-like opioid drug, which when injected leads to a Parkinson-like syndrome.

The drugs used to treat Parkinson disease are all designed to restore dopamine activity in the basal nuclei. They fall into three main categories: (1) agonists (stimulators) of dopamine receptors, (2) inhibitors of the enzymes that metabolize dopamine at synapses, and (3) precursors of dopamine itself. The most widely prescribed drug is ***Levodopa*** (***L-dopa***), which falls into the third category. L-dopa enters the bloodstream, crosses the blood–brain barrier, and is converted to dopamine. (Dopamine itself is not used as medication because it cannot cross the blood–brain barrier and it has too many systemic side effects.) The newly formed dopamine activates receptors in the basal nuclei and improves the symptoms of the disease. Side effects sometimes occurring with L-dopa include hallucinations, like those seen in individuals with schizophrenia who have excessive dopamine activity (see Chapter 8), and spontaneous, abnormal motor activity. Other therapies for Parkinson disease include the lesioning (destruction) of overactive areas of the basal nuclei and ***deep brain stimulation.*** The latter is accomplished with surgically implanted electrodes connected to an electrical pulse generator similar to a cardiac artificial pacemaker (Chapter 12); while in some cases it relieves symptoms, the mechanism is not understood. Injection of undifferentiated stem cells is also being explored as a possible treatment.

Cerebellum

The cerebellum is located dorsally to the brainstem (see Figure 10.2a). It influences posture and movement indirectly by means of input to brainstem nuclei and (by way of the thalamus) to regions of the sensorimotor cortex that give rise to pathways that descend to the motor neurons. The cerebellum receives information from the sensorimotor cortex, and also from the vestibular system, eyes, skin, muscles, joints, and tendons—that is, from some of the very receptors that movement affects.

One role of the cerebellum in motor functioning is to provide timing signals to the cerebral cortex and spinal cord for precise execution of the different phases of a motor program, in particular, the timing of the agonist/antagonist components of a movement. It also helps coordinate movements that involve several joints and stores the memories of these movements so they are easily achieved the next time they are tried.

The cerebellum also participates in planning movements—integrating information about the nature of an intended movement with information about the surrounding space. The cerebellum then provides this as a feedforward (see Chapter 1) signal to the brain areas responsible for refining the motor program. Moreover, during the course of the movement, the cerebellum compares information about what the muscles *should* be doing with information about what they actually *are* doing. If a discrepancy develops between the intended movement and the actual one, the cerebellum sends an error signal to the motor cortex and subcortical centers to correct the ongoing program.

The role of the cerebellum in programming movements can best be appreciated when observing its absence in individuals with ***cerebellar disease.*** They typically cannot perform limb or eye movements smoothly but move with a tremor—a so-called ***intention tremor*** that increases as a movement nears its final destination. This differs from patients with Parkinson disease, who have a tremor while at rest. People with cerebellar disease also cannot combine the movements of several joints into a single, smooth, coordinated motion. The role of the cerebellum in the precision and timing of movements can be appreciated when you consider the complex tasks it helps us accomplish. For example, a tennis player sees a ball fly over the net, anticipates its flight path, runs along an intersecting path, and swings the racquet through an arc that will intercept the ball with the speed and force required to return it to the other side of the court. People with cerebellar damage cannot achieve this level of coordinated, precise, learned movement.

Unstable posture and awkward gait are two other symptoms characteristic of cerebellar disease. For example, people with cerebellar damage walk with their feet wide apart, and they have such difficulty maintaining balance that their gait is similar to that seen in people who are intoxicated by ethanol. Visual input helps compensate for some of the loss of motor coordination—patients can stand on one foot with eyes open but not closed. A final symptom involves difficulty in learning new motor skills. Individuals with cerebellar disease find it hard to modify movements in response to new situations. Unlike damage to areas of sensorimotor cortex, cerebellar damage is not usually associated with paralysis or weakness.

Descending Pathways

The influence exerted by the various brain regions on posture and movement occurs via descending pathways to the motor neurons and the interneurons that affect them. The pathways are of two types: the **corticospinal pathways,** which, as their name implies, originate in the cerebral cortex; and a second group we will refer to as the **brainstem pathways,** which originate in the brainstem.

Neurons from both types of descending pathways end at synapses on alpha and gamma motor neurons or on interneurons that affect them. Sometimes these are the same interneurons that function in local reflex arcs, thereby ensuring that the descending signals are fully integrated with local information before the activity of the motor neurons is altered. In other cases, the interneurons are part of neural networks involved in posture or locomotion. The ultimate effect of the descending pathways on the alpha motor neurons may be excitatory or inhibitory.

Importantly, some of the descending fibers affect *afferent* systems. They do this via (1) presynaptic synapses on the terminals of afferent neurons as these fibers enter the central nervous system, or (2) synapses on interneurons in the ascending pathways. The overall effect of this descending input to afferent systems is to regulate their influence on either the local or brain motor control areas, thereby altering the importance of a particular bit of afferent information or sharpening its focus. For example, when performing an exceptionally delicate or complicated task, like brain surgery, descending inputs might facilitate signaling in afferent pathways carrying proprioceptive inputs monitoring hand and finger movements. This descending (motor) control over ascending (sensory) information provides another example to show that there is no real functional separation between the motor and sensory systems.

Corticospinal Pathway

The nerve fibers of the corticospinal pathways have their cell bodies in the sensorimotor cortex and terminate in the spinal cord. The corticospinal pathways are also called the **pyramidal tracts** or **pyramidal system** because of their triangular shape as they pass along the ventral surface of the medulla oblongata. In the medulla oblongata near the junction of the spinal cord and brainstem, most of the corticospinal fibers cross (known as decussation) to descend on the opposite side (**Figure 10.12**). The skeletal muscles on the left side of the body are therefore controlled largely by neurons in the right half of the brain, and vice versa.

As the corticospinal fibers descend through the brain from the cerebral cortex, they are accompanied by fibers of

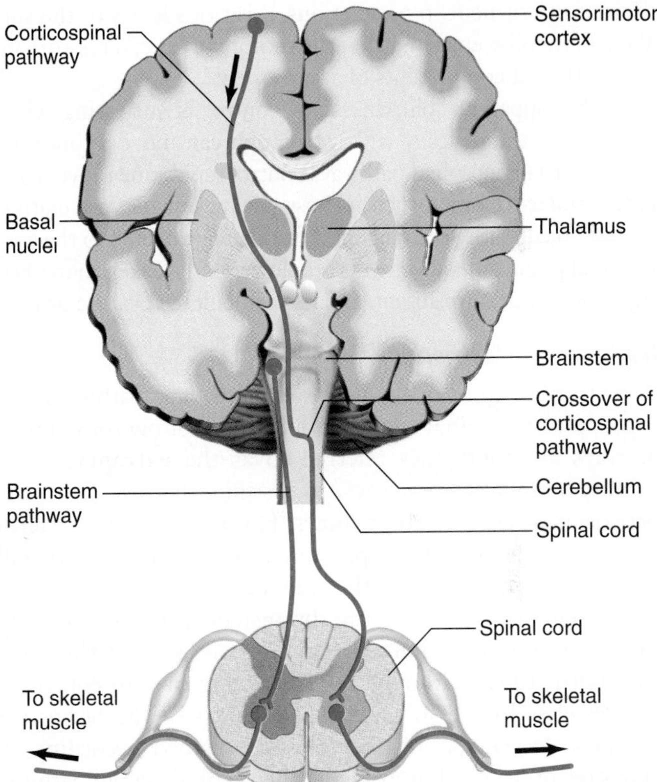

Figure 10.12 APIR The corticospinal and brainstem pathways. Most of the corticospinal fibers cross in the brainstem to descend in the opposite side of the spinal cord, but the brainstem pathways are mostly uncrossed. The descending neurons are shown synapsing directly onto motor neurons in the spinal cord, but they commonly synapse onto local interneurons. Adapted from Gardner.

PHYSIOLOGICAL INQUIRY

- If a blood clot blocked a cerebral blood vessel supplying a small region of the right cerebral cortex just in front of the central sulcus in the deep groove between the hemispheres, what symptoms might result? (*Hint:* See Figure 10.11.)

Answer can be found at end of chapter.

the **corticobulbar pathway** (*bulbar* means "pertaining to the brainstem"), a pathway that begins in the sensorimotor cortex and ends in the brainstem. The corticobulbar fibers control, directly or indirectly via interneurons, the motor neurons that innervate muscles of the eye, face, tongue, and throat. These fibers provide the main source of control for voluntary movement of the muscles of the head and neck, whereas the corticospinal fibers serve this function for the muscles of the rest of the body. For convenience, we will include the corticobulbar pathway in the general term *corticospinal pathways.*

Convergence and divergence are hallmarks of the corticospinal pathway. For example, a great number of different neuronal sources converge on neurons of the sensorimotor cortex, which is not surprising when you consider the many factors that can affect motor behavior. As for the descending pathways, neurons from wide areas of the sensorimotor cortex converge onto single motor neurons at the local level so that multiple brain areas usually control single muscles. Also, axons of single corticospinal neurons diverge markedly to synapse with a number of different motor neuron populations at various levels of the spinal cord, thereby ensuring that the motor cortex can coordinate many different components of a movement.

This apparent "blurriness" of control is surprising when you think of the delicacy with which you can move a fingertip, because the corticospinal pathways control rapid, fine movements of the distal extremities, such as those you make when you manipulate an object with your fingers. After damage occurs to the corticospinal pathways, movements are slower and weaker, individual finger movements are absent, and it is difficult to release a grip.

Brainstem Pathways

Axons from neurons in the brainstem also form pathways that descend into the spinal cord to influence motor neurons. These pathways are sometimes referred to as the **extrapyramidal system,** or indirect pathways, to distinguish them from the corticospinal (pyramidal) pathways. However, no general term is widely accepted for these pathways; for convenience, we will refer to them collectively as the brainstem pathways.

Axons of most of the brainstem pathways remain uncrossed and affect muscles on the same side of the body (see Figure 10.12), although a few do cross over to contralateral muscles. In the spinal cord, the fibers of the brainstem pathways descend as distinct clusters, named according to their sites of origin. For example, the vestibulospinal pathway descends to the spinal cord from the vestibular nuclei in the brainstem, whereas the reticulospinal pathway descends from neurons in the brainstem reticular formation. The brainstem pathways are especially important in controlling muscles of the trunk for upright posture, balance, and walking.

As stated previously, the corticospinal neurons generally have their greatest influence over motor neurons that control muscles involved in fine, isolated movements, particularly those of the fingers and hands. The brainstem descending pathways, in contrast, are involved more with coordination of the large muscle groups used in the maintenance of upright posture, in locomotion, and in head and body movements when turning toward a specific stimulus.

There is, however, much interaction between the descending pathways. For example, some fibers of the corticospinal pathway end on interneurons that play important roles in posture, whereas fibers of the brainstem descending pathways sometimes end directly on the alpha motor neurons to control discrete muscle movements. Because of this redundancy, one system may compensate for loss of function resulting from damage to the other system, although the compensation is generally not complete.

The distinctions between the corticospinal and brainstem descending pathways are not clear-cut. All movements, whether automatic or voluntary, require the continuous coordinated interaction of both types of pathways.

10.4 Muscle Tone

Even when a skeletal muscle is relaxed, there is a slight and uniform resistance when it is stretched by an external force. This resistance is known as **muscle tone,** and it can be an important diagnostic tool for clinicians assessing a patient's neuromuscular function.

Muscle tone is due both to the passive elastic properties of the muscles and joints and to the degree of ongoing alpha motor neuron activity. When a person is very relaxed, the alpha motor neuron activity does not make a significant contribution to the resistance to stretch. As the person becomes increasingly alert, however, more activation of the alpha motor neurons occurs and muscle tone increases.

Abnormal Muscle Tone

Abnormally high muscle tone, called ***hypertonia,*** accompanies a number of diseases and is seen very clearly when a joint is moved passively at high speeds. The increased resistance is due to an increased level of alpha motor neuron activity, which keeps a muscle contracted despite the attempt to relax it. Hypertonia usually occurs with disorders of the descending pathways that normally inhibit the motor neurons.

Clinically, the descending pathways and neurons of the motor cortex are often referred to as the **upper motor neurons** (a confusing misnomer because they are not really motor neurons). Abnormalities due to their dysfunction are classified, therefore, as ***upper motor neuron disorders.*** Thus, hypertonia usually indicates an upper motor neuron disorder. In this clinical classification, the alpha motor neurons—the true motor neurons—are termed **lower motor neurons.**

Spasticity is a form of hypertonia in which the muscles do not develop increased tone until they are stretched a bit, and after a brief increase in tone, the contraction subsides for a short time. The period of "give" occurring after a time of resistance is called the ***clasp-knife phenomenon.*** (When an examiner bends the limb of a patient with this condition, it is like folding a pocketknife—at first, the spring resists the bending motion, but once bending begins, it closes easily.) Spasticity may be accompanied by increased responses of motor reflexes such as the knee jerk and by decreased coordination and strength of voluntary actions. ***Rigidity*** is a form of hypertonia in which the increased muscle contraction is continual and the resistance to passive stretch is constant (as occurs in the disease tetanus, which is described in detail in the Clinical Case Study at the end of this chapter). Two other forms of hypertonia that can occur suddenly in individual or multiple muscles sometimes originate as problems in muscle and not nervous tissue: Muscle ***spasms*** are brief contractions, and muscle ***cramps*** are prolonged and painful contractions (see Chapter 9).

Hypotonia is a condition of abnormally low muscle tone accompanied by weakness, atrophy (a decrease in muscle bulk), and decreased or absent reflex responses. Dexterity and coordination are generally preserved unless profound weakness is present. Although hypotonia may develop after cerebellar disease, it more frequently accompanies disorders of the alpha motor neurons (lower motor neurons), neuromuscular junctions, or the muscles themselves. The term ***flaccid***, which means "weak" or "soft," is often used to describe hypotonic muscles.

10.5 Maintenance of Upright Posture and Balance

The skeleton supporting the body is a system of long bones and a many-jointed spine that cannot stand erect against the forces of gravity without the support provided through coordinated muscle activity. The muscles that maintain upright posture—that is, support the body's weight against gravity—are controlled by the brain and by reflex mechanisms "wired into" the neural networks of the brainstem and spinal cord. Many of the reflex pathways previously introduced (for example, the stretch and crossed-extensor reflexes) are active in posture control.

Added to the problem of maintaining upright posture is that of maintaining balance. A human being is a tall structure balanced on a relatively small base, with the center of gravity quite high, just above the pelvis. For stability, the center of gravity must be kept within the base of support the feet provide (**Figure 10.13**). Once the center of gravity has moved beyond this base, the body will fall unless one foot is shifted to broaden the base of support. Yet, people can operate under conditions of unstable equilibrium because complex interacting **postural reflexes** maintain their balance.

The afferent pathways of the postural reflexes come from three sources: the eyes, the vestibular apparatus, and the receptors involved in proprioception (joint, muscle, and touch receptors, for example). The efferent pathways are the alpha motor neurons to the skeletal muscles, and the integrating centers are neuron networks in the brainstem and spinal cord.

In addition to these integrating centers, there are centers in the brain that form an internal representation of the body's geometry, its support conditions, and its orientation with respect to vertical. This internal representation serves two purposes: (1) it provides a reference framework for the perception of the body's position and orientation in space and for planning actions, and (2) it contributes to stability via the motor controls involved in maintaining upright posture.

There are many familiar examples of using reflexes to maintain upright posture; one is the crossed-extensor reflex. As one leg is flexed and lifted off the ground, the other is extended more strongly to support the weight of the body, and the positions of various parts of the body are shifted to move the center of gravity over the single, weight-bearing leg. This shift in the center of gravity, as **Figure 10.14** demonstrates, is an important component in the stepping mechanism of locomotion.

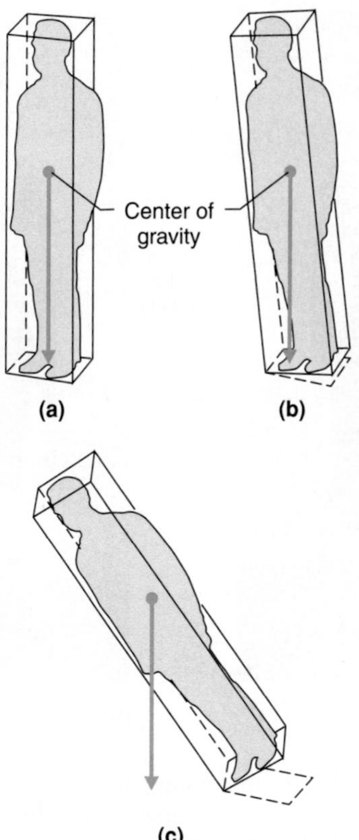

Figure 10.13 The center of gravity is the point in an object at which, if a string were attached and pulled up, all the downward force due to gravity would be exactly balanced. (a) The center of gravity must remain within the upward vertical projections of the object's base (the tall box outlined in the drawing) if stability is to be maintained. (b) Stable conditions. The box tilts a bit, but the center of gravity remains within the base area—the dashed rectangle on the floor—so the box returns to its upright position. (c) Unstable conditions. The box tilts so far that its center of gravity is not above any part of the object's base and the object will fall.

Afferent inputs from several sources are necessary for optimal postural adjustments, yet interfering with any one of these inputs alone does not cause a person to topple over. Blind people maintain their balance quite well with only a slight loss of precision, and people whose vestibular mechanisms have been destroyed can, with rehabilitation, have very little disability in everyday life as long as their visual system and somatic receptors are functioning.

The conclusion to be drawn from such examples is that the postural control mechanisms are not only effective and flexible but also highly adaptable.

10.6 Walking

Walking requires the coordination of many muscles, each activated to a precise degree at a precise time. We initiate walking by allowing the body to fall forward to an unstable position and then moving one leg forward to provide support. When the extensor muscles are activated on the supported side of the body to bear the body's weight, the contralateral extensors are inhibited by reciprocal innervation to allow the nonsupporting limb to flex and swing forward. The cyclical,

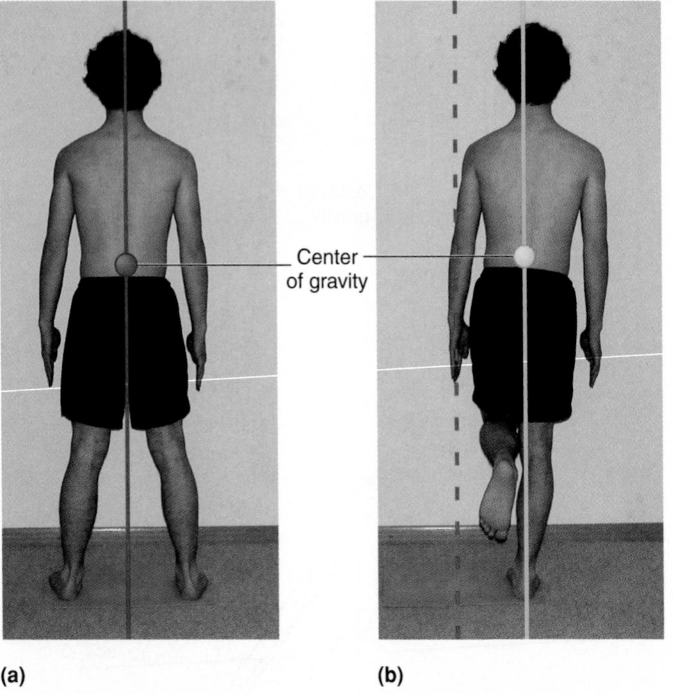

Figure 10.14 Postural changes with stepping. (a) Normal standing posture. The center of gravity falls directly between the two feet. (b) As the left foot is raised, the whole body leans to the right so that the center of gravity shifts over the right foot. Dashed line in part (b) indicates the location of the center of gravity when the subject was standing on both feet.

PHYSIOLOGICAL INQUIRY

- How might the posture shown in part (b) influence contractions of this individual's shoulder muscles?

Answer can be found at end of chapter.

alternating movements of walking are brought about largely by networks of interneurons in the spinal cord at the local level. The interneuron networks coordinate the output of the various motor neuron pools that control the appropriate muscles of the arms, shoulders, trunk, hips, legs, and feet.

The network neurons rely on both plasma membrane spontaneous pacemaker properties and patterned synaptic activity to establish their rhythms. At the same time, however, the networks are remarkably adaptable and a single network can generate many different patterns of neural activity, depending upon its inputs. These inputs come from other local interneurons, afferent fibers, and descending pathways.

These complex spinal cord neural networks can even produce the rhythmic movement of limbs in the absence of command inputs from descending pathways. This was demonstrated in classical experiments involving animals with their cerebrums surgically separated from their spinal cords just above the brainstem. Though sensory perception and voluntary movement were completely absent, when suspended in a position that brought the limbs into contact with a treadmill, normal walking and running actions were initiated by spinal reflexes arising from contact with the moving surface. This demonstrates that afferent inputs and local spinal cord neural networks contribute substantially to the coordination of locomotion.

Under normal conditions, neural activation occurs in the cerebral cortex, cerebellum, and brainstem, as well as in the spinal cord during locomotion. Moreover, middle and higher levels of the motor control hierarchy are necessary for postural control, voluntary override commands (like breaking stride to jump over a puddle), and adaptations to the environment (like walking across a stream on unevenly spaced stepping stones). Damage to even small areas of the sensorimotor cortex can cause marked disturbances in gait, which demonstrates its importance in locomotor control.

SUMMARY

Skeletal muscles are controlled by their motor neurons. All the motor neurons that control a given muscle form a motor neuron pool.

Motor Control Hierarchy

I. The neural systems that control body movements can be conceptualized as being arranged in a motor control hierarchy.
   a. The highest level determines the general intention of an action.
   b. The middle level establishes a motor program and specifies the postures and movements needed to carry out the intended action, taking into account sensory information that indicates the body's position.
   c. The local level ultimately determines which motor neurons will be activated.
   d. As the movement progresses, information about what the muscles are doing feeds back to the motor control centers, which make program corrections.
   e. Almost all actions have voluntary and involuntary components.

Local Control of Motor Neurons

I. Most direct input to motor neurons comes from local interneurons, which themselves receive input from peripheral receptors, descending pathways, and other interneurons.

II. Muscle-spindle stretch receptors monitor muscle length and the velocity of changes in length.
   a. Activation of these receptors initiates the stretch reflex, which inhibits motor neurons of ipsilateral antagonists and activates those of the stretched muscle and its synergists. This provides negative feedback control of muscle length.
   b. Tension on the stretch receptors is maintained during muscle contraction by activation of gamma motor neurons to the spindle muscle fibers.
   c. Alpha and gamma motor neurons are generally coactivated.

III. Golgi tendon organs monitor muscle tension. Through interneurons, they activate inhibitory synapses on motor neurons of the contracting muscle and excitatory synapses on motor neurons of ipsilateral antagonists. This provides negative feedback control of muscle tension.

IV. The withdrawal reflex excites the ipsilateral flexor muscles and inhibits the ipsilateral extensors. The crossed-extensor reflex excites the contralateral extensor muscles and inhibits the contralateral flexor muscles.

The Brain Motor Centers and the Descending Pathways They Control

I. Neurons in the motor cortex are anatomically arranged in a somatotopic map.
II. Different areas of sensorimotor cortex have different functions but much overlap in activity.
III. The basal nuclei form a link in a circuit that originates in and returns to sensorimotor cortex. These subcortical nuclei facilitate some motor behaviors and inhibit others.
IV. The cerebellum coordinates posture and movement and plays a role in motor learning.
V. The corticospinal pathways pass directly from the sensorimotor cortex to motor neurons in the spinal cord (or brainstem, in the case of the corticobulbar pathways) or, more commonly, to interneurons near the motor neurons.
   a. In general, neurons on one side of the brain control muscles on the other side of the body.
   b. Corticospinal pathways control predominantly fine, precise movements.
   c. Some corticospinal fibers affect the transmission of information in afferent pathways.
VI. Other descending pathways arise in the brainstem, control muscles on the same side of the body, and are involved mainly in the coordination of large groups of muscles used in posture and locomotion.
VII. There is significant interaction between the two descending pathways.

Muscle Tone

I. Hypertonia, as seen in spasticity and rigidity, usually occurs with disorders of the descending pathways.
II. Hypotonia can be seen with cerebellar disease or, more commonly, with disease of the alpha motor neurons or muscle.

Maintenance of Upright Posture and Balance

I. Maintenance of posture and balance depends upon inputs from the eyes, vestibular apparatus, and somatic proprioceptors.
II. To maintain balance, the body's center of gravity must be maintained over the body's base.
III. The crossed-extensor reflex is a postural reflex.

Walking

I. The activity of interneuron networks in the spinal cord brings about the cyclical, alternating movements of locomotion.
II. These pattern generators are controlled by corticospinal and brainstem descending pathways and affected by feedback and motor programs.

REVIEW QUESTIONS

1. Describe motor control in terms of the conceptual motor control hierarchy. Use the following terms: *highest, middle,* and *local levels; motor program; descending pathways;* and *motor neuron.*
2. List the characteristics of voluntary actions.
3. Picking up a book, for example, has both voluntary and involuntary components. List the components of this action and indicate whether each is voluntary or involuntary.
4. List the inputs that can converge on the interneurons active in local motor control.
5. Draw a muscle spindle within a muscle, labeling the spindle, intrafusal and extrafusal muscle fibers, stretch receptors, afferent fibers, and alpha and gamma efferent fibers.
6. Describe the components of the knee-jerk reflex (stimulus, receptor, afferent pathway, integrating center, efferent pathway, effector, and response).
7. Describe the major function of alpha–gamma coactivation.
8. Distinguish among the following areas of the cerebral cortex: sensorimotor, primary motor, premotor, and supplementary motor.
9. Contrast the two major types of descending motor pathways in terms of structure and function.
10. Describe the roles that the basal nuclei and cerebellum play in motor control.
11. Explain how hypertonia may result from disease of the descending pathways.
12. Explain how hypotonia may result from lower motor neuron disease.
13. Explain the role the crossed-extensor reflex plays in postural stability.
14. Explain the role of the interneuronal networks in walking, incorporating in your discussion the following terms: *interneuron, reciprocal innervation, synergist, antagonist,* and *feedback.*

KEY TERMS

alpha–gamma coactivation 304
alpha motor neuron 304
basal nuclei 310
brainstem pathway 311
corticobulbar pathway 312
corticospinal pathway 311
crossed-extensor reflex 307
descending pathway 302
extrafusal fiber 304
extrapyramidal system 312
gamma motor neuron 304
Golgi tendon organ 306
intrafusal fiber 304
knee-jerk reflex 304
lower motor neurons 312
monosynaptic 306
motor cortex 308
motor neuron pool 300
motor program 302
motor unit 300
muscle spindle 304
muscle-spindle stretch receptor 304
muscle tone 312
nuclear bag fiber 304
nuclear chain fiber 304
parietal-lobe association cortex 308
polysynaptic 306
postural reflex 313
premotor area 308
primary motor cortex 308
proprioception 302
pyramidal system 311
pyramidal tract 311
reciprocal innervation 306
sensorimotor cortex 308
somatosensory cortex 308
somatotopic map 308
stretch reflex 304
substantia nigra 310
supplementary motor cortex 308
synergistic muscle 306
upper motor neurons 312
voluntary movement 302
withdrawal reflex 307

CLINICAL TERMS

akinesia 310
bradykinesia 310
cerebellar disease 311
clasp-knife phenomenon 312
cramp 313
deep brain stimulation 310
flaccid 313
hypertonia 312
hypotonia 313
intention tremor 311
Levodopa (L-dopa) 310
MPTP (1-methyl-4-phenyl-1,2,3,6-tetrahydropyridine) 310
Parkinson disease 310
rigidity 312
spasm 313
spasticity 312
upper motor neuron disorders 312

CHAPTER 10 Clinical Case Study: A Woman Develops Stiff Jaw Muscles After a Puncture Wound

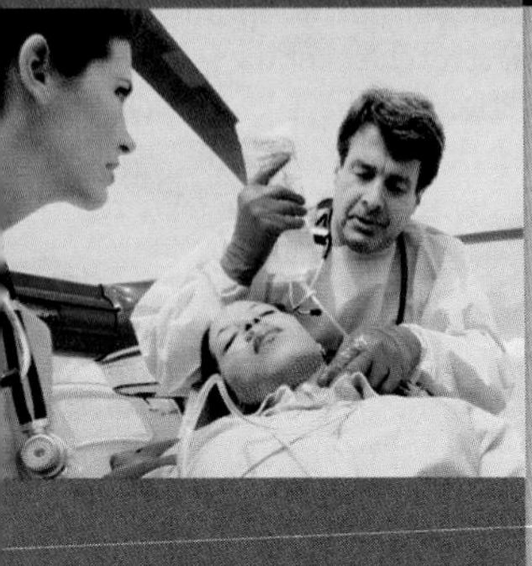

A 55-year-old woman with complaints of muscle pain was brought to an urgent-care clinic by her husband. The woman had trouble speaking, so her husband explained that over the previous 3 days, her back and jaw muscles had grown gradually stiffer and more painful. By the time of her visit, she could barely open her mouth wide enough to drink through a straw. Until that week, she had been extremely healthy, had no history of allergies or surgical procedures, and was not taking any medications. At the time of examination, her blood pressure was 122/70 mmHg and her temperature was 98.5°F. Other than a stiff jaw, findings from a head and neck exam were otherwise unremarkable, her lung sounds were clear, and her heart sounds were normal. Evaluating her extremities, the physician noticed that her right leg was bandaged just below the knee. A little over a week prior to this visit, she had been working in her garden and had stumbled and fallen onto a rake, puncturing her shin. The wound had not bled a great deal, so she had washed and bandaged it herself. Removal of the bandage revealed a raised, 5-cm-wide erythematous (reddened) region, surrounding a 1 cm puncture wound that had scabbed over. The doctor then asked a key question, When had she received her most recent tetanus booster shot? It had been so long ago that neither the woman nor her husband could remember exactly when it was—more than 20 years, they guessed. This piece of information, along with her leg wound and symptoms, led the physician to conclude that the woman had developed tetanus. Because this is a potentially fatal condition, she was admitted to the hospital.

Tetanus is a neurological disorder that results from a decrease in the inhibitory input to alpha motor neurons. It occurs when spores of *Clostridium tetani,* a bacterium commonly found in manure-treated soils, invade a poorly oxygenated wound. Proliferation of the bacterium under anaerobic conditions induces it to secrete a neurotoxin called ***tetanospasmin*** that targets inhibitory interneurons in the brainstem and spinal cord. Blockage of neurotransmitter release from these interneurons allows the normal excitatory inputs to dominate control of the alpha motor neurons, and the result is high-frequency action potential firing that causes increased muscle tone and spasms.

Because the toxin attacks interneurons by traveling backward along the axons of alpha motor neurons, muscles with short motor neurons are affected first. Muscles of the head are in this category, in particular those that move the jaw. The jaw rigidly clamps shut, because the muscles that close it are much stronger than those that open it. Appearance of this symptom early in the disease process explains the common name of this condition, ***lockjaw.*** Untreated tetanus is fatal, as progressive spastic contraction of all of the skeletal muscles eventually affects those involved in respiration, and asphyxia occurs.

Treatment for tetanus includes (1) cleaning and sterilizing wounds; (2) administering antibiotics to kill the bacteria; (3) injecting antibodies known as ***tetanus immune globulin (TIG)*** that bind the toxin, (4) providing neuromuscular blocking drugs to relax and/or paralyze spastic muscles; and (5) mechanically ventilating the lungs to maintain airflow despite spastic or paralyzed respiratory muscles. Treated promptly, 80% to 90% of tetanus victims recover completely. It can take several months, however, because inhibitory axon terminals damaged by the toxin must be regrown.

The patient in this case was fortunate to have had partial immunity from vaccinations received earlier in her life and to have received prompt treatment. Her disease was relatively mild as a result and did not require weeks of hospitalization with drug-induced paralysis and ventilation, as is necessary in more serious cases. She was immediately given intramuscular injections of TIG and a combination of strong antibiotics to be taken for the next 10 days. The leg wound was surgically opened, thoroughly cleaned, and monitored closely over the next week as the redness and swelling gradually subsided. Within 2 days, her jaw and back muscles had relaxed. She was released from the hospital with orders to continue the complete course of antibiotics and return immediately if any muscular symptoms returned. At the time of discharge, she was also vaccinated to stimulate production of her own antibodies against the tetanus toxin and was advised to receive booster shots against tetanus at least every 10 years.

Clinical terms: lockjaw, tetanospasmin, tetanus, tetanus immune globulin (TIG)

See Chapter 19 for complete, integrative case studies.

CHAPTER 10 TEST QUESTIONS

Answers found in Appendix A.

1. Which is a correct statement regarding the hierarchical organization of motor control?
   a. Skeletal muscle contraction can only be initiated by neurons in the cerebral cortex.
   b. The basal nuclei participate in the creation of a motor program that specifies the pattern of neural activity required for a voluntary movement.
   c. Neurons in the cerebellum have long axons that synapse directly on alpha motor neurons in the ventral horn of the spinal cord.
   d. The cell bodies of alpha motor neurons are found in the primary motor region of the cerebral cortex.
   e. Neurons with cell bodies in the basal nuclei can form either excitatory or inhibitory synapses onto skeletal muscle cells.
2. In the stretch reflex,
   a. Golgi tendon organs activate contraction in extrafusal muscle fibers connected to that tendon.
   b. lengthening of muscle-spindle receptors in a muscle leads to contraction in an antagonist muscle.

c. action potentials from muscle-spindle receptors in a muscle form monosynaptic excitatory synapses on motor neurons to extrafusal fibers within the same muscles.
d. slackening of intrafusal fibers within a muscle activates gamma motor neurons that form excitatory synapses with extrafusal fibers within that same muscle.
e. afferent neurons to the sensorimotor cortex stimulate the agonist muscle to contract and the antagonist muscle to be inhibited.

3. Which would result in reflex contraction of the extensor muscles of the right leg?
   a. stepping on a tack with the left foot
   b. stretching the flexor muscles in the right leg
   c. dropping a hammer on the right big toe
   d. action potentials from Golgi tendon organs in extensors of the right leg
   e. action potentials from muscle-spindle receptors in flexors of the right leg
4. If implanted electrodes were used to stimulate action potentials in gamma motor neurons to flexors of the left arm, which would be the most likely result?
   a. inhibition of the flexors of the left arm
   b. a decrease in action potentials from muscle-spindle receptors in the left arm
   c. a decrease in action potentials from Golgi tendon organs in the left arm
   d. an increase in action potentials along alpha motor neurons to flexors in the left arm
   e. contraction of flexor muscles in the right arm
5. Where is the primary motor cortex found?
   a. in the cerebellum
   b. in the occipital lobe of the cerebrum
   c. between the somatosensory cortex and the premotor area of the cerebrum
   d. in the ventral horn of the spinal cord
   e. just posterior to the parietal lobe association cortex

True or False

6. Neurons in the primary motor cortex of the right cerebral hemisphere mainly control muscles on the left side of the body.
7. Patients with upper motor neuron disorders generally have reduced muscle tone and flaccid paralysis.
8. Neurons descending in the corticospinal pathway control mainly trunk musculature and postural reflexes, whereas neurons of the brainstem pathways control fine motor movements of the distal extremities.
9. In patients with Parkinson disease, an excess of dopamine from neurons of the substantia nigra causes intention tremors when the person performs voluntary movements.
10. The disease tetanus results when a bacterial toxin blocks the release of inhibitory neurotransmitter.

CHAPTER 10 GENERAL PRINCIPLES ASSESSMENT

Answers found in Appendix A.

1. One of the general principles of physiology introduced in Chapter 1 states that *most physiological functions are controlled by multiple regulatory systems, often working in opposition.* However, skeletal muscle cells are only innervated by alpha motor neurons, which always release acetylcholine and always excite them to contract. By what mechanism are skeletal muscles induced to relax?
2. Another general principle of physiology is that *homeostasis is essential for health and survival.* How might the withdrawal reflex (see Figure 10.9) contribute to the maintenance of homeostasis?

CHAPTER 10 QUANTITATIVE AND THOUGHT QUESTIONS

Answers found in Appendix A.

1. What changes would occur in the knee-jerk reflex after destruction of the gamma motor neurons?
2. What changes would occur in the knee-jerk reflex after destruction of the alpha motor neurons?
3. Draw a cross section of the spinal cord and a portion of the thigh (similar to Figure 10.6) and "wire up" and activate the neurons so the leg becomes a stiff pillar, that is, so the knee does not bend.
4. Hypertonia is usually considered a sign of disease of the descending motor pathways. How might it also result from abnormal function of the alpha motor neurons?
5. What neurotransmitters/receptors might be effective targets for drugs used to prevent the muscle spasms characteristic of the disease tetanus?
6. A patient is told to relax, and her patellar tendon reflex is tested (see Figure 10.6). Next, the patient is instructed to hook the fingers of her two hands together and pull outward with her arms. While she is doing this, the patellar reflex is tested again, and the knee jerk is significantly greater. What are some possible explanations for this phenomenon?

CHAPTER 10 ANSWERS TO PHYSIOLOGICAL INQUIRIES

Figure 10.3 Recall that when chloride ion channels are opened, a neuron is inhibited from depolarizing to threshold (see Figure 6.29 and accompanying text). Thus, the neurons of the spinal cord that release glycine are inhibitory interneurons. By specifically blocking glycine receptors, strychnine shifts the balance of inputs to motor neurons in favor of excitatory interneurons, resulting in excessive excitation. Poisoning victims experience excessive and uncontrollable muscle contractions body-wide, and when the respiratory muscles are affected, asphyxiation can occur. These symptoms are similar to those observed in the disease state tetanus, which is described in the Clinical Case Study at the end of this chapter.

Figure 10.6 Stimulation of gamma motor neurons to leg flexor muscles would stretch muscle-spindle receptors in those muscles. That would trigger a monosynaptic reflex that would cause contraction of the flexor muscles and, through an interneuron, the extensor muscles would be inhibited. As a result, there would be a reflexive bending of the leg—the opposite of what occurs in the typical knee-jerk reflex.

Figure 10.7 Although the contracting muscle results in the greatest stretch of the tendon, the muscle itself (and consequently the intrafusal fibers) are stretched the most under passive stretch conditions. Action potentials from muscle-spindle receptors would therefore have the greatest frequency during passive stretch.

Figure 10.8 Tendons are stretched more by actively contracting muscles than when muscles are passively stretched (see Figure 10.7). Thus, during very intense contractions that have the potential to cause injury, Golgi tendon organs are strongly activated. The resulting high-frequency action potentials arriving in the spinal cord stimulate interneurons that inhibit motor neurons to the muscle associated with that tendon, thus reducing the force and protecting the muscle.

Figure 10.9 When crawling, the crossed-extensor reflex will occur for the arms just like it does in the legs during walking. Afferent pain pathways will stimulate flexor muscles and inhibit extensor muscles in the right arm, while stimulating extensor muscles and inhibiting flexor muscles in the left arm. This withdraws the right hand from the painful stimulus while the left arm straightens to bear the child's weight.

Figure 10.12 When a region of the brain is deprived of oxygen and nutrients for even a short time, it often results in a stroke—neuronal cell death (see Chapter 6, Section D). Because the right primary motor cortex was damaged in this case, the patient would have impaired motor function on the left side of the body. Given the midline location of the lesion, the leg would be most affected (see Figure 10.11).

Figure 10.14 To stand on the right foot, the hip extensors on the right side are activated while the hip flexors on the left side are activated. This is similar to what occurs when a walking person lifts the left leg and pushes forward with the right foot. In adults, spinal cord interneurons form locomotor pattern generators that connect the arms and legs, typically activating them in reciprocal fashion. Therefore, while standing on the right foot, the right shoulder flexor muscles and the left shoulder extensor muscles will tend to be activated.

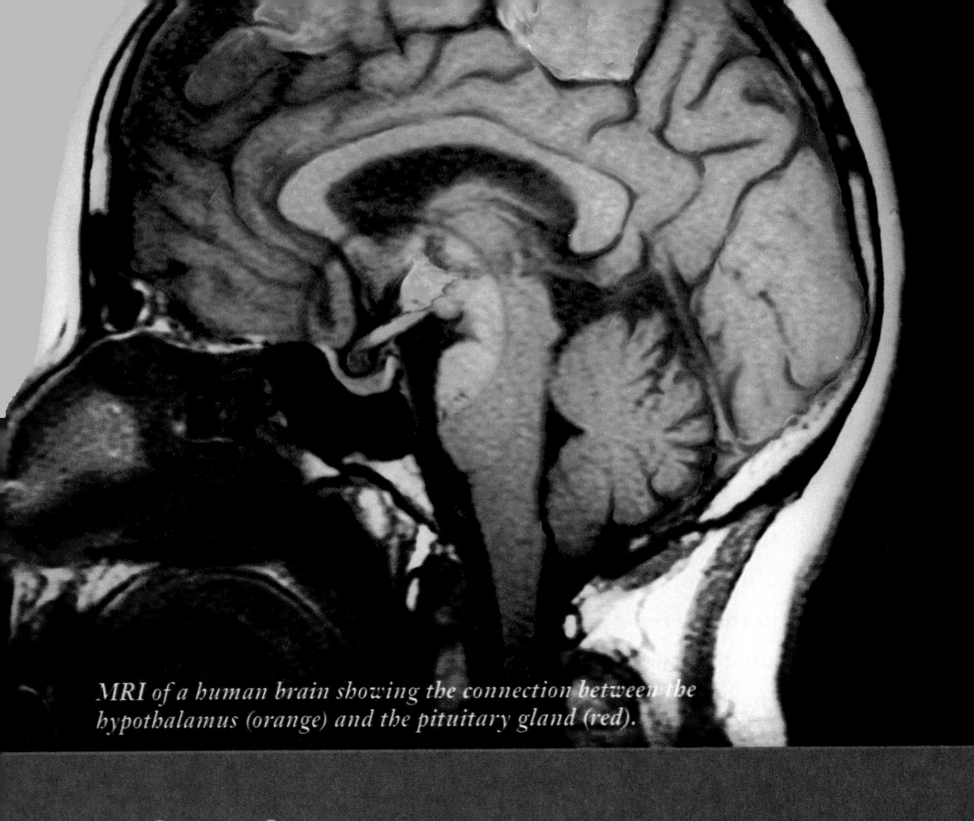

MRI of a human brain showing the connection between the hypothalamus (orange) and the pituitary gland (red).

11 The Endocrine System

In Chapters 6–8 and 10, you learned that the nervous system is one of the two major control systems of the body, and now we turn our attention to the other—the endocrine system. The **endocrine system** consists of all those glands, called **endocrine glands**, that secrete hormones, as well as hormone-secreting cells located in various organs such as the heart, kidneys, liver, and stomach. **Hormones** are chemical messengers that enter the blood, which carries them from their site of secretion to the cells upon which they act. The cells a particular hormone influences are known as the target cells for that hormone. The aim of this chapter is to first present a detailed overview of endocrinology—that is, a structural and functional analysis of general features of hormones—followed by a more detailed analysis of several important hormonal systems. Before continuing, you should review the principles of ligand-receptor interactions and cell signaling that were described in Chapter 3 (Section C) and Chapter 5, because they pertain to the mechanisms by which hormones exert their actions.

Hormones functionally link various organ systems together. As such, several of the general principles of physiology first introduced in Chapter 1 apply to the study of the endocrine system, including the principle that the functions of organ systems are coordinated with each other. This coordination is key to the maintenance of homeostasis, another important general principle of physiology that will be covered in Sections C, D, and F. In many cases, the actions of one hormone can be potentiated, inhibited, or counterbalanced by the actions of another. This illustrates the general principle of physiology that most physiological functions are controlled by multiple regulatory systems, often working in opposition. It will be especially relevant in the sections on the endocrine control of metabolism and the control of pituitary gland function. Finally, this chapter exemplifies the general principle of physiology that information flow between cells, tissues, and organs is an essential feature of homeostasis and allows for integration of physiological processes.

SECTION A
General Characteristics of Hormones and Hormonal Control Systems

11.1 Hormones and Endocrine Glands

Endocrine glands are distinguished from another type of gland in the body called exocrine glands. Exocrine glands secrete their products into a duct, from where the secretions either exit the body (as in sweat) or enter the lumen of another organ, such as the intestines. By contrast, endocrine glands are ductless and release hormones into the blood (**Figure 11.1**). Hormones are actually released first into interstitial fluid, from where they diffuse into the blood, but for simplicity we will often omit the interstitial fluid step in our discussion.

Table 11.1 summarizes most of the endocrine glands and other hormone-secreting organs, the hormones they secrete, and some of the major functions the hormones control. The endocrine system differs from most of the other organ systems of the body in that the various components are not anatomically connected; however, they do form a system in the functional sense. You may be puzzled to see some organs—the heart, for instance—that clearly have other functions yet are listed as part of the endocrine system. The explanation is that, in addition to the cells that carry out other functions, the organ also contains cells that secrete hormones.

Note also in Table 11.1 that the hypothalamus, a part of the brain, is considered part of the endocrine system. This is because the chemical messengers released by certain axon terminals in both the hypothalamus and its extension, the posterior pituitary, do not function as neurotransmitters affecting adjacent cells but, rather, enter the blood as hormones. The blood then carries these hormones to their sites of action.

Table 11.1 demonstrates that there are a large number of endocrine glands and hormones. This chapter is not all inclusive. Some of the hormones listed in Table 11.1 are best considered in the context of the control systems in which they participate. For example, the pancreatic hormones (insulin and glucagon) are described in Chapter 16 in the context of organic metabolism, and the reproductive hormones are extensively covered in Chapter 17.

Also evident from Table 11.1 is that a single gland may secrete multiple hormones. The usual pattern in such cases is that a single cell type secretes only one hormone, so that multiple-hormone secretion reflects the presence of different types of endocrine cells in the same gland. In a few cases, however, a single cell may secrete more than one hormone.

Finally, in some cases, a hormone secreted by an endocrine-gland cell may also be secreted by other cell types and serves in these other locations as a neurotransmitter or paracrine or autocrine substance. For example, somatostatin, a hormone produced by neurons in the hypothalamus, is also secreted by cells of the stomach and pancreas, where it has local paracrine actions.

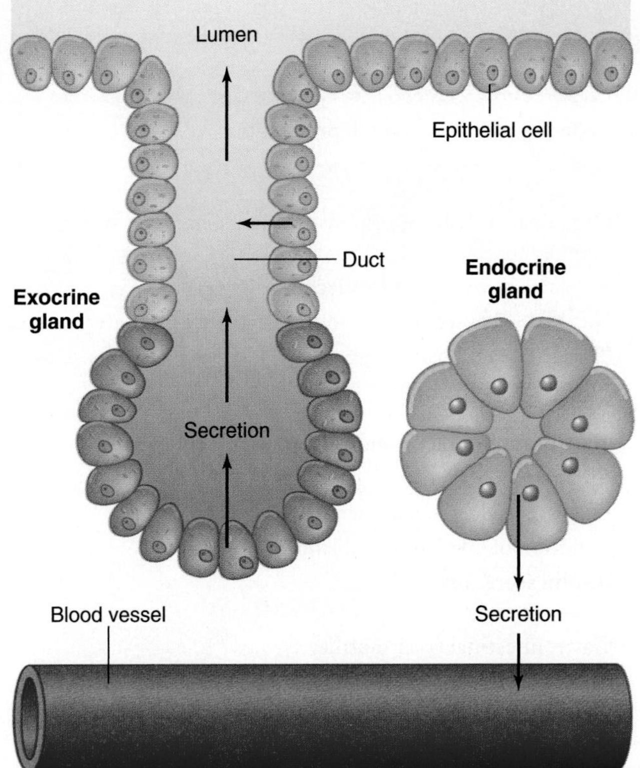

Figure 11.1 APIR Exocrine gland secretions enter ducts from where their secretions either exit the body or, as shown here, connect to the lumen of a structure such as the intestines or to the surface of the skin. By contrast, endocrine glands secrete hormones that enter the interstitial fluid and diffuse into the blood, from where they can reach distant target cells.

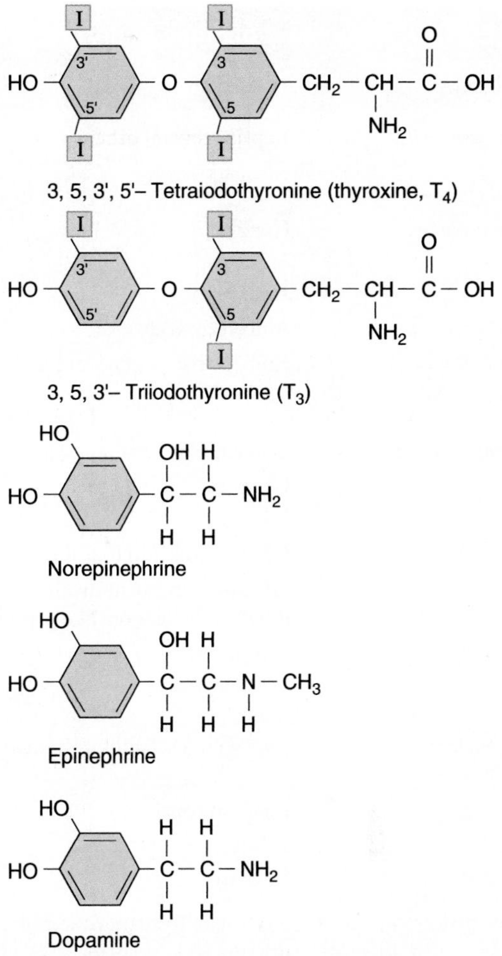

3, 5, 3', 5'– Tetraiodothyronine (thyroxine, T_4)

3, 5, 3'– Triiodothyronine (T_3)

Norepinephrine

Epinephrine

Dopamine

Figure 11.2 Chemical structures of the amine hormones: thyroxine, triiodothyronine, norepinephrine, epinephrine, and dopamine. The two thyroid hormones differ by only one iodine atom, a difference noted in the abbreviations T_3 and T_4. The position of the carbon atoms in the two rings of T_3 and T_4 are numbered; this provides the basis for the complete names of T_3 and T_4 as shown in the figure.

11.2 Hormone Structures and Synthesis

Hormones fall into three major structural classes: (1) amines, (2) peptides and proteins, and (3) steroids.

Amine Hormones

The **amine hormones** are derivatives of the amino acid tyrosine. They include the **thyroid hormones** (produced by the thyroid gland) and the catecholamines **epinephrine** and **norepinephrine** (produced by the adrenal medulla) and **dopamine** (produced by the hypothalamus). The structure and synthesis of the iodine-containing thyroid hormones will be described in detail in Section C of this chapter. For now, their structures are included in **Figure 11.2.** Chapter 6 described the structures of catecholamines and the steps of their synthesis; the structures are reproduced here in Figure 11.2.

There are two adrenal glands, one above each kidney. Each **adrenal gland** is composed of an inner **adrenal medulla,** which secretes amine hormones, and a surrounding **adrenal cortex,** which secretes steroid hormones. The adrenal medulla is really a modified sympathetic ganglion whose cell bodies do not have axons. Instead, they release their secretions into the blood, thereby fulfilling a criterion for an endocrine gland.

The adrenal medulla secretes mainly two amine hormones, epinephrine and norepinephrine. In humans, the adrenal medulla secretes approximately four times more epinephrine than norepinephrine. This is because the adrenal medulla expresses high amounts of an enzyme called phenylethanolamine-N-methyltransferase (PNMT), which catalyzes the reaction that converts norepinephrine to epinephrine. Epinephrine and norepinephrine exert actions similar to those of the sympathetic nerves, which, because they do not express PNMT, make only norepinephrine. These actions are described in various chapters and summarized in Section B of this chapter.

The other catecholamine hormone, dopamine, is synthesized by neurons in the hypothalamus. Dopamine is released into a special circulatory system called a portal system (see Section B), which carries the hormone to the pituitary gland; there, it acts to inhibit the activity of certain endocrine cells.

Peptide and Protein Hormones

Most hormones are polypeptides. Recall from Chapter 2 that short polypeptides with a known function are often referred to simply as peptides; longer polypeptides with

TABLE 11.1 Summary of Some Important Hormones

Site Produced	Hormone	Major Function* Is Control Of:
Adipose tissue cells	Leptin, several others	Appetite; metabolic rate; reproduction
Adrenal glands:		
Adrenal cortex	Cortisol	Organic metabolism; response to stress; immune system; development
	Androgens	Sex drive in women; adrenarche
	Aldosterone	Na^+ and K^+ excretion by kidneys; extracellular water balance
Adrenal medulla	Epinephrine and norepinephrine	Organic metabolism; cardiovascular function; response to stress ("fight-or-flight")
Gastrointestinal tract	Gastrin	Gastrointestinal tract motility and acid secretion
	Ghrelin	Appetite
	Secretin	Exocrine and endocrine secretions from pancreas
	Cholecystokinin (CCK)[†]	Secretion of bile from gallbladder
	Glucose-dependent insulinotropic peptide (GIP) and glucagon-like peptide 1 (GLP-1)	Insulin secretion
	Motilin	Gastrointestinal tract motility
Gonads:		
Ovaries: female	Estrogen (estradiol in humans)	Reproductive system; secondary sex characteristics; growth and development; development of ovarian follicles
	Progesterone	Endometrium and pregnancy
	Inhibin	Follicle-stimulating hormone (FSH) secretion
	Relaxin	Relaxation of cervix and pubic ligaments
Testes: male	Androgen (testosterone and dihydrotestosterone)	Reproductive system; secondary sex characteristics; growth and development; sex drive; gamete development
	Inhibin	FSH secretion
	Müllerian-inhibiting substance (MIS)	Regression of Müllerian ducts
Heart	Atrial natriuretic peptide (ANP)	Na^+ excretion by kidneys; blood pressure
Hypothalamus	Hypophysiotropic hormones:	Secretion of hormones by the anterior pituitary gland
	Corticotropin-releasing hormone (CRH)	Secretion of adrenocorticotropic hormone (ACTH)
	Thyrotropin-releasing hormone (TRH)	Secretion of thyroid-stimulating hormone (TSH)
	Growth hormone–releasing hormone (GHRH)	Secretion of growth hormone (GH)
	Somatostatin (SST)	Secretion of growth hormone
	Gonadotropin-releasing hormone (GnRH)	Secretion of luteinizing hormone (LH) and follicle-stimulating hormone (FSH)
	Dopamine (DA)	Secretion of prolactin (PRL)
Kidneys	Erythropoietin (EPO; also made in liver)	Erythrocyte production in bone marrow
	1,25-dihydroxyvitamin D	Ca^{2+} absorption in GI tract
Liver	Insulin-like growth factor 1 (IGF-1)	Cell division and growth of bone and other tissues
Pancreas	Insulin	Plasma glucose, amino acids, and fatty acids
	Glucagon	Plasma glucose
Parathyroid glands	Parathyroid hormone (PTH, parathormone)	Plasma Ca^{2+} and phosphate ion; synthesis of 1,25-dihydroxyvitamin D

(continued)

TABLE 11.1 Summary of Some Important Hormones *(Continued)*

Site Produced	Hormone	Major Function* Is Control Of:
Pineal	Melatonin	Possible role in circadian sleep-wake cycles
Pituitary gland:		
Anterior pituitary gland	Growth hormone (somatotropin)	Growth, mainly via local production of IGF-1; protein, carbohydrate, and lipid metabolism
	Thyroid-stimulating hormone (thyrotropin)	Thyroid gland activity and growth
	Adrenocorticotropic hormone (corticotropin)	Adrenal cortex activity and growth
	Prolactin	Milk production in breast
	Gonadotropic hormones:	
	Follicle-stimulating hormone	
	Males	Gamete production
	Females	Ovarian follicle growth
	Luteinizing hormone:	
	Males	Testicular production of testosterone
	Females	Ovarian production of estradiol; ovulation
	β-lipotropin and β-endorphin	Possibly fat mobilization and analgesia during stress
Posterior pituitary‡	Oxytocin	Milk secretion; uterine motility
	Vasopressin (antidiuretic hormone, ADH)	Blood pressure; water excretion by the kidneys
Placenta	Human chorionic gonadotropin (hCG)	Secretion of progesterone and estrogen by corpus luteum
	Estrogens	See Gonads: ovaries
	Progesterone	See Gonads: ovaries
	Human placental lactogen (hPL)	Breast development; organic metabolism
Thymus	Thymopoietin	T-lymphocyte function
Thyroid	Thyroxine (T_4) and triiodothyronine (T_3)	Metabolic rate; growth; brain development and function
	Calcitonin	Plasma Ca^{2+} in some vertebrates (role unclear in humans)
Other (produced in blood)	Angiotensin II	Blood pressure; production of aldosterone from adrenal cortex

*This table does not list all functions of all hormones.
†The names and abbreviations in parentheses are synonyms.
‡The posterior pituitary stores and secretes these hormones; they are synthesized in the hypothalamus.

tertiary structure and a known function are called proteins. Hormones in this class range in size from small peptides having only three amino acids to proteins, some of which contain carbohydrate and thus are glycoproteins. For convenience, we will simply refer to all these hormones as **peptide hormones.**

In many cases, peptide hormones are initially synthesized on the ribosomes of endocrine cells as larger molecules known as preprohormones, which are then cleaved to **prohormones** by proteolytic enzymes in the rough endoplasmic reticulum (**Figure 11.3a**). The prohormone is then packaged into secretory vesicles by the Golgi apparatus. In this process, the prohormone is cleaved to yield the active hormone and other peptide chains found in the prohormone. Consequently, when the cell is stimulated to release the contents of the secretory vesicles by exocytosis, the other peptides are secreted along with the hormone. In certain cases, these other peptides may also exert hormonal effects. In other words, instead of just one peptide hormone, the cell may secrete multiple peptide hormones—derived from the same prohormone—each of which differs in its effects on target cells. One well-studied example of this is the synthesis of insulin in the pancreas (**Figure 11.3b**). Insulin is synthesized as a single polypeptide preprohormone, then processed to the prohormone. Enzymes clip off a portion of the prohormone resulting in insulin and another product called C-peptide. Both insulin and C-peptide are secreted into the circulation in roughly equimolar amounts. Insulin is a key regulator of metabolism, while C-peptide has several actions on a variety of cell types.

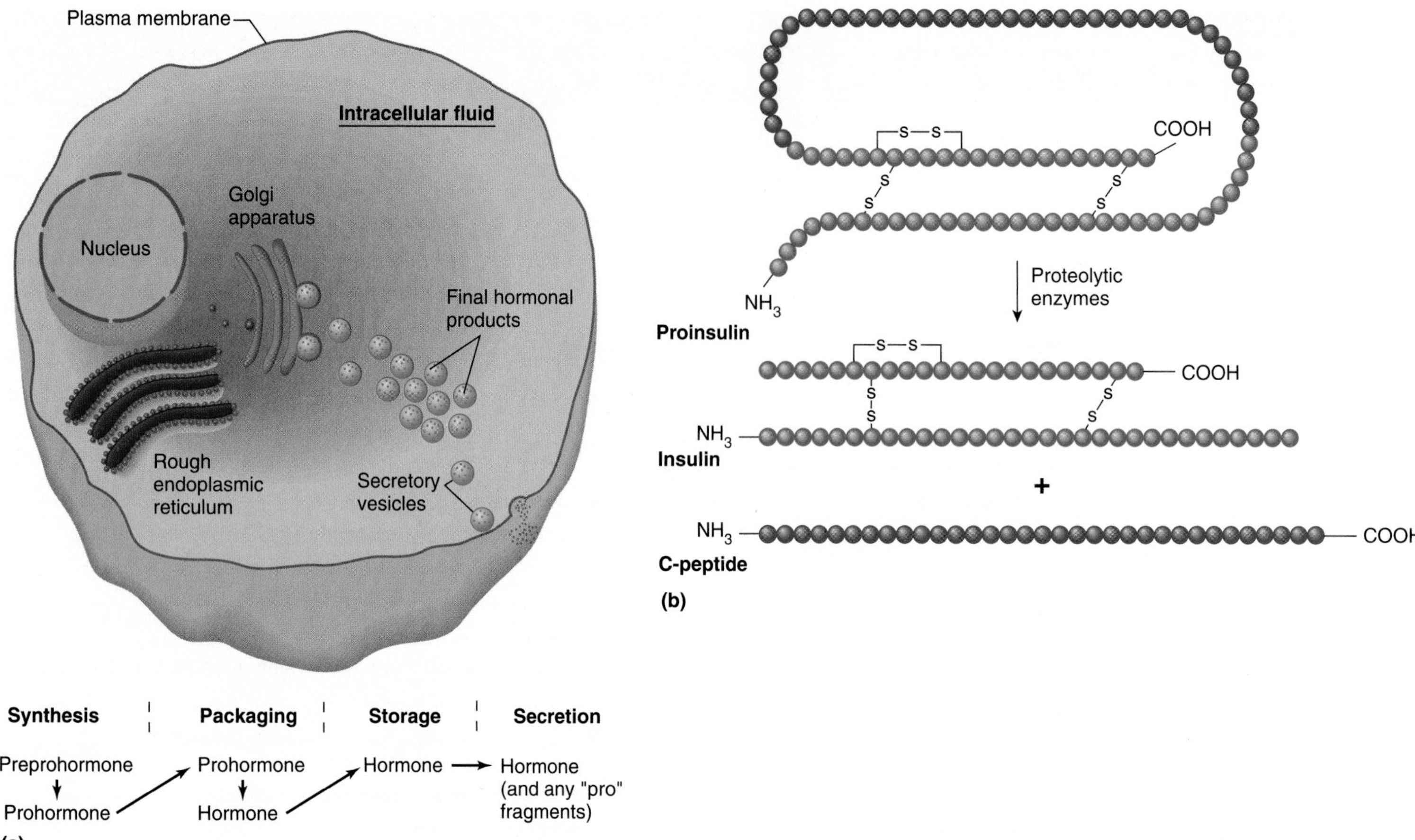

Figure 11.3 AP|R Typical synthesis and secretion of peptide hormones. (a) Peptide hormones typically are processed by enzymes from preprohormones containing a signal peptide, to prohormones; further processing results in one or more active hormones that are stored in secretory vesicles. Secretion of stored secretory vesicles occurs by the process of exocytosis. (b) An example of peptide hormone synthesis. Insulin is synthesized as a preprohormone (not shown) that is cleaved to the prohormone shown here. Each bead represents an amino acid. The action of proteolytic enzymes cleaves the prohormone into insulin and C-peptide. Note that this cleavage results in two chains of insulin, which are connected by disulfide bridges.

PHYSIOLOGICAL INQUIRY

- What is the advantage of packaging peptide hormones in secretory vesicles?

Answer can be found at end of chapter.

Steroid Hormones

Steroid hormones make up the third family of hormones. **Figure 11.4** shows some examples of steroid hormones; their ringlike structure was described in Chapter 2. Steroid hormones are primarily produced by the adrenal cortex and the **gonads** (testes and ovaries), as well as by the placenta during pregnancy. In addition, vitamin D is enzymatically converted by two hydroxylation reactions into the biologically active steroid hormone called **1,25-dihydroxyvitamin D** (also called 1,25-dihydroxycholecalciferol or calcitriol). These reactions occur in the liver and kidneys.

The general process of steroid hormone synthesis is illustrated in **Figure 11.5a.** In both the gonads and the adrenal cortex, the hormone-producing cells are stimulated by the binding of an anterior pituitary gland hormone to its plasma membrane receptor. These receptors are linked to G_s proteins (refer back to Figure 5.6), which activate adenylyl cyclase and cAMP production. The subsequent activation of protein kinase A by cAMP results in phosphorylation of numerous intracellular proteins, which facilitate the subsequent steps in the process.

All of the steroid hormones are derived from cholesterol, which is either taken up from the extracellular fluid by the cells or synthesized by intracellular enzymes. The final hormone product depends upon the cell type and the types and amounts of the enzymes it expresses. Cells in the ovary, for example, express large amounts of the enzyme needed to convert testosterone to estradiol, whereas cells in the testes do not express significant amounts of this enzyme and therefore make primarily testosterone.

Once formed, the steroid hormones cannot be stored in the cytosol in membrane-bound vesicles, because the lipophilic nature of the steroids allows them to freely diffuse across lipid bilayers. As a result, once they are synthesized, steroid hormones diffuse across the plasma membrane into the circulation. Because of their lipid nature, steroid hormones

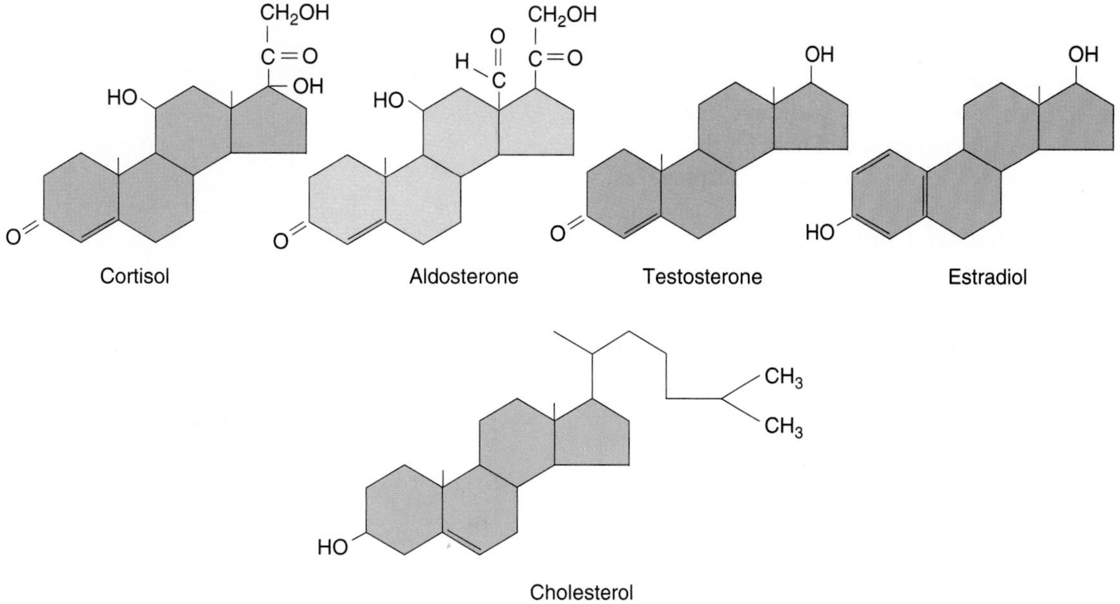

Figure 11.4 Structures of representative steroid hormones and their structural relationship to cholesterol.

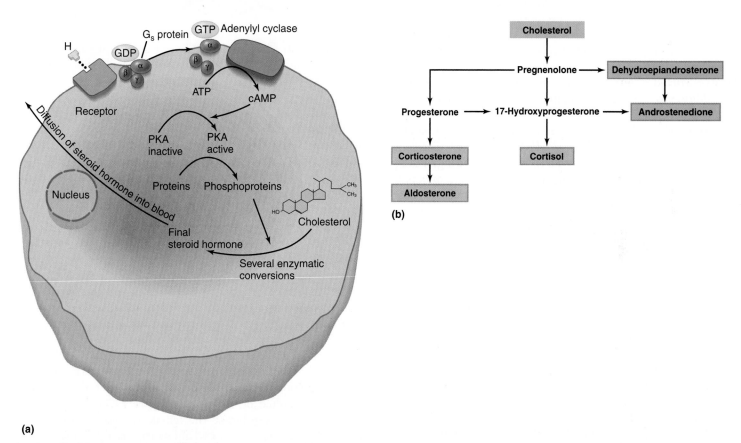

Figure 11.5 (a) Schematic overview of steps involved in steroid synthesis. (b) The five hormones shown in boxes are the major hormones secreted from the adrenal cortex. Dehydroepiandrosterone (DHEA) and androstenedione are androgens—that is, testosterone-like hormones. Cortisol and corticosterone are glucocorticoids, and aldosterone is a mineralocorticoid that is only produced by one part of the adrenal cortex. *Note:* For simplicity, not all enzymatic steps are indicated.

PHYSIOLOGICAL INQUIRY

- Why are steroid hormones not packaged into secretory vesicles, such as those depicted in Figure 11.3?

Answer can be found at end of chapter.

are not highly soluble in blood. The majority of steroid hormones are reversibly bound in plasma to carrier proteins such as albumin and various other proteins.

The next sections describe the pathways for steroid synthesis in the adrenal cortex and gonads. Those for the placenta are somewhat unusual and are briefly discussed in Chapter 17.

Hormones of the Adrenal Cortex

The five major hormones secreted by the adrenal cortex are aldosterone, cortisol, corticosterone, dehydroepiandrosterone (DHEA), and androstenedione (**Figure 11.5b**). **Aldosterone** is known as a **mineralocorticoid** because its effects are on salt (mineral) balance, mainly on the kidneys' handling of sodium, potassium, and hydrogen ions. Its actions are described in detail in Chapter 14. Briefly, production of aldosterone is under the control of another hormone called **angiotensin II,** which binds to plasma membrane receptors in the adrenal cortex to activate the inositol trisphosphate second-messenger pathway (see Chapter 5). This is different from the more common cAMP-mediated mechanism by which most steroid hormones are produced, as previously described. Once synthesized, aldosterone enters the circulation and acts on cells of the kidneys to stimulate Na^+ and H_2O retention, and K^+ and H^+ excretion in the urine.

Cortisol and corticosterone are called **glucocorticoids** because they have important effects on the metabolism of glucose and other organic nutrients. Cortisol is the predominant glucocorticoid in humans and is the only one we will discuss. In addition to its effects on organic metabolism, cortisol exerts many other effects, including facilitation of the body's responses to stress and regulation of the immune system (see Section D).

Dehydroepiandrosterone (DHEA) and androstenedione belong to the class of steroid hormones known as **androgens;** this class also includes the major male sex steroid **testosterone,** produced by the testes. All androgens have actions similar to those of testosterone. The adrenal androgens are much less potent than testosterone, and they are of little physiological significance in the adult male. They do, however, play roles in the adult female and in both sexes in the fetus and at puberty, as described in Chapter 17.

The adrenal cortex is not a homogeneous gland but is composed of three distinct layers (**Figure 11.6**). The cells of the outer layer—the zona glomerulosa—express the enzymes required to synthesize corticosterone and then convert it to aldosterone (see Figure 11.5b) but do *not* express the genes that code for the enzymes required for the formation of cortisol and androgens. Thus, this layer synthesizes and secretes aldosterone but not the other major adrenocortical hormones. In contrast, the zona fasciculata and zona reticularis have just the opposite enzyme profile. They secrete no aldosterone but do secrete cortisol and androgens. In humans, the zona fasciculata primarily produces cortisol and the zona reticularis primarily produces androgens, but both zones produce both types of steroid.

In certain diseases, the adrenal cortex may secrete decreased or increased amounts of various steroids. For example, the absence of an enzyme required for the formation of cortisol by the adrenal cortex can result in the shunting of the cortisol precursors into the androgen pathway. (Look at Figure 11.5b to imagine how this might happen.) One example of an inherited disease of this type is ***congenital adrenal hyperplasia*** (***CAH***) (see Chapter 17 for more details). In CAH, the excess adrenal androgen production results in virilization of the genitalia of female fetuses; at birth, it may not be obvious whether the baby is phenotypically male or female. Fortunately, the most common form of this disease is now routinely screened for at birth in many countries including certain states in the United States, and appropriate therapeutic measures can be initiated immediately.

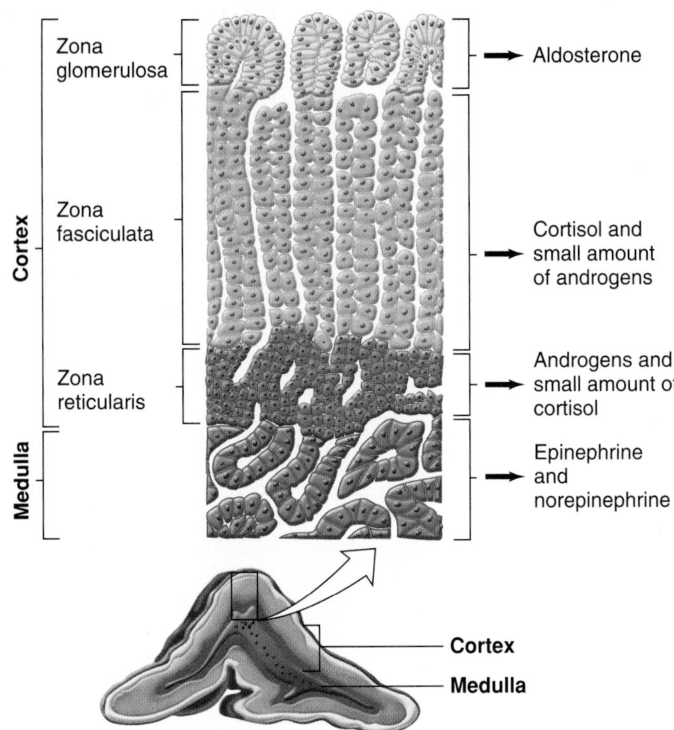

Figure 11.6 AP|R Section through an adrenal gland showing both the medulla and the zones of the cortex, as well as the hormones they secrete.

Hormones of the Gonads

Compared to the adrenal cortex, the gonads have very different concentrations of key enzymes in their steroid pathways. Endocrine cells in both the testes and the ovaries do not express the enzymes required to produce aldosterone and cortisol. They possess high concentrations of enzymes in the androgen pathways leading to androstenedione, as in the adrenal cortex. In addition, the endocrine cells in the testes contain a high concentration of the enzyme that converts androstenedione to testosterone, which is therefore the major androgen secreted by the testes (**Figure 11.7**). The ovarian endocrine cells synthesize the female sex hormones, which are collectively known as **estrogens** (primarily estradiol and estrone). **Estradiol** is the predominant estrogen present during a woman's lifetime. The ovarian endocrine cells have a high concentration of the enzyme aromatase, which catalyzes the conversion of androgens to estrogens (see Figure 11.7). Consequently, estradiol—rather than testosterone—is the major steroid hormone secreted by the ovaries.

Very small amounts of testosterone do diffuse out of ovarian endocrine cells, however, and very small amounts of estradiol are produced from testosterone in the testes. Moreover, following

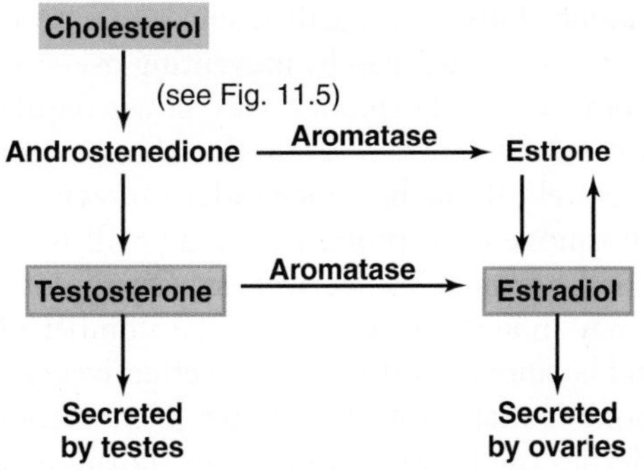

Figure 11.7 Gonadal production of steroids. Only the ovaries have high concentrations of the enzyme (aromatase) required to produce the estrogens estrone and estradiol.

their release into the blood by the gonads and the adrenal cortex, steroid hormones may undergo further conversion in other organs. For example, testosterone is converted to estradiol in some of its target cells. Consequently, the major male and female sex hormones—testosterone and estradiol, respectively—are not unique to males and females. The ratio of the concentrations of the hormones, however, is very different in the two sexes.

Finally, endocrine cells of the corpus luteum, an ovarian structure that arises following each ovulation, secrete another major steroid hormone, **progesterone.** This steroid is critically important for uterine maturation during the menstrual cycle and for maintaining a pregnancy (see Chapter 17). Progesterone is also synthesized in other parts of the body—notably, the placenta in pregnant women and in certain brain cells and the adrenal cortex in both males and females. It has been implicated in numerous functions unrelated to pregnancy, including water and ion balance; regulation of synaptic activity associated with mood, memory, and other brain activities; and immune function.

11.3 Hormone Transport in the Blood

Most peptide and all catecholamine hormones are water-soluble. Therefore, with the exception of a few peptides, these hormones are transported simply dissolved in plasma (**Table 11.2**). In contrast, the poorly soluble steroid hormones and thyroid hormones circulate in the blood largely bound to plasma proteins.

Even though the steroid and thyroid hormones exist in plasma mainly bound to large proteins, small concentrations of these hormones do exist dissolved in the plasma. The dissolved, or free, hormone is in equilibrium with the bound hormone:

$$\text{Free hormone} + \text{Binding protein} \rightleftharpoons \text{Hormone–protein complex}$$

The total hormone concentration in plasma is the sum of the free and bound hormones. However, only the *free* hormone can diffuse out of capillaries and encounter its target cells. Therefore, the concentration of the free hormone is what is biologically important rather than the concentration of the total hormone, most of which is bound. As we will see next, the degree of protein binding also influences the rate of metabolism and the excretion of the hormone.

11.4 Hormone Metabolism and Excretion

Once a hormone has been synthesized and secreted into the blood and has acted on a target tissue, the concentration of the hormone in the blood usually returns to normal. This is necessary to prevent excessive, possibly harmful effects from the prolonged exposure of target cells to hormones. A hormone's concentration in the plasma depends upon (1) its rate of secretion by the endocrine gland and (2) its rate of removal from the blood. Removal, or "clearance," of the hormone occurs either by excretion or by metabolic transformation. The liver and the kidneys are the major organs that metabolize or excrete hormones.

The liver and kidneys, however, are not the only routes for eliminating hormones. Sometimes a hormone is metabolized by the cells upon which it acts. In the case of some peptide hormones, for example, endocytosis of hormone–receptor complexes on plasma membranes enables cells to remove the hormones rapidly from their surfaces and catabolize them intracellularly. The receptors are then often recycled to the plasma membrane.

In addition, enzymes in the blood and tissues rapidly break down catecholamine and peptide hormones. These hormones therefore tend to remain in the bloodstream for only brief periods—minutes to an hour. In contrast, protein-bound

TABLE 11.2 Categories of Hormones

Chemical Class	Major Form in Plasma	Location of Receptors	Most Common Signaling Mechanisms*	Rate of Excretion/Metabolism
Peptides and catecholamines	Free (unbound)	Plasma membrane	1. Second messengers (e.g., cAMP, Ca^{2+}, IP_3) 2. Enzyme activation by receptor (e.g., JAK) 3. Intrinsic enzymatic activity of receptor (e.g., tyrosine autophosphorylation)	Fast (minutes)
Steroids and thyroid hormone	Protein-bound	Intracellular	Intracellular receptors directly alter gene transcription	Slow (hours to days)

*The diverse mechanisms of action of chemical messengers such as hormones were discussed in detail in Chapter 5.

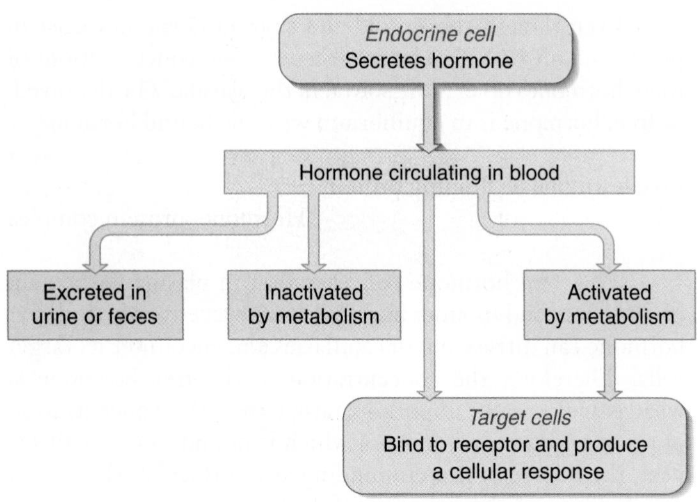

Figure 11.8 Possible fates and actions of a hormone following its secretion by an endocrine cell. Not all paths apply to all hormones.

hormones are protected from excretion or metabolism by enzymes as long as they remain bound. Therefore, removal of the circulating steroid and thyroid hormones generally takes longer, often several hours to days.

In some cases, metabolism of a hormone *activates* the hormone rather than inactivates it. In other words, the secreted hormone may be relatively inactive until metabolism transforms it. One example is one of the two major thyroid hormones, thyroxine, which is converted to a more active form upon entering a target cell.

Figure 11.8 summarizes the possible fates of hormones after their secretion.

11.5 Mechanisms of Hormone Action

Hormone Receptors

Because hormones are transported in the blood, they can reach all tissues. Yet, the response to a hormone is highly specific, involving only the target cells for that hormone. The ability to respond depends upon the presence of specific receptors for those hormones on or in the target cells.

As emphasized in Chapter 5, the response of a target cell to a chemical messenger is the final event in a sequence that begins when the messenger binds to specific cell receptors. As that chapter described, the receptors for water-soluble chemical messengers like peptide hormones and catecholamines are proteins located in the plasma membranes of the target cells. In contrast, the receptors for lipid-soluble chemical messengers like steroid and thyroid hormones are proteins located mainly *inside* the target cells.

Hormones can influence the response of target cells by regulating hormone receptors. Again, Chapter 5 described basic concepts of receptor modulation such as up-regulation and down-regulation. In the context of hormones, **up-regulation** is an increase in the number of a hormone's receptors in a cell, often resulting from a prolonged exposure to a low concentration of the hormone. This has the effect of increasing target-cell responsiveness to the hormone. **Down-regulation** is a decrease in receptor number, often from exposure to high concentrations of the hormone. This temporarily decreases target-cell responsiveness to the hormone, thereby preventing overstimulation.

In some cases, hormones can down-regulate or up-regulate not only their own receptors but the receptors for other hormones as well. If one hormone induces down-regulation of a second hormone's receptors, the result will be a reduction of the second hormone's effectiveness. On the other hand, a hormone may induce an increase in the number of receptors for a second hormone. In this case, the effectiveness of the second hormone is increased. This latter phenomenon, in some cases, underlies the important hormone–hormone interaction known as permissiveness. In general terms, **permissiveness** means that hormone A must be present in order for hormone B to exert its full effect. A low concentration of hormone A is usually all that is needed for this permissive effect, which may be due to A's ability to up-regulate B's receptors. For example, epinephrine causes a large release of fatty acids from adipose tissue, but only in the presence of permissive amounts of thyroid hormones (**Figure 11.9**). One reason is that thyroid hormones stimulate the synthesis of beta-adrenergic receptors for epinephrine in adipose tissue; as a result, the tissue becomes much more sensitive to epinephrine. However, receptor up-regulation does not explain all cases of permissiveness. Sometimes, the effect may be due to changes in the signaling pathway that mediates the actions of a given hormone.

Events Elicited by Hormone–Receptor Binding

The events initiated when a hormone binds to its receptor—that is, the mechanisms by which the hormone elicits a cellular response—are one or more of the signal transduction pathways that apply to all chemical messengers, as described in Chapter 5. In other words, there is nothing unique about the mechanisms that hormones initiate as compared to those used by neurotransmitters and paracrine or autocrine substances, and so we will only briefly review them here (see Table 11.2).

Effects of Peptide Hormones and Catecholamines

As stated previously, the receptors for peptide hormones and the catecholamine hormones are located on the outer surface of the target cell's plasma membrane. This location is important because these hormones are too hydrophilic to diffuse through the plasma membrane. When activated by hormone binding, the receptors trigger one or more of the signal transduction pathways for plasma membrane receptors described in Chapter 5. That is, the activated receptors directly influence (1) enzyme activity that is part of the receptor, (2) activity of cytoplasmic janus kinases associated with the receptor, or (3) G proteins coupled in the plasma membrane to effector proteins—ion channels and enzymes—that generate second messengers such as cAMP and Ca^{2+}. The opening or closing of ion channels changes the electrical potential across the membrane. When a Ca^{2+} channel is involved, the cytosolic concentration of this important ionic second messenger changes. The changes in enzyme activity are usually very rapid (e.g., due to phosphorylation) and produce changes in the activity of various cellular proteins. In some cases, the signal transduction pathways also lead to activation or inhibition of particular genes, causing a change in the synthesis rate of the proteins coded for by these genes. Thus, peptide hormones

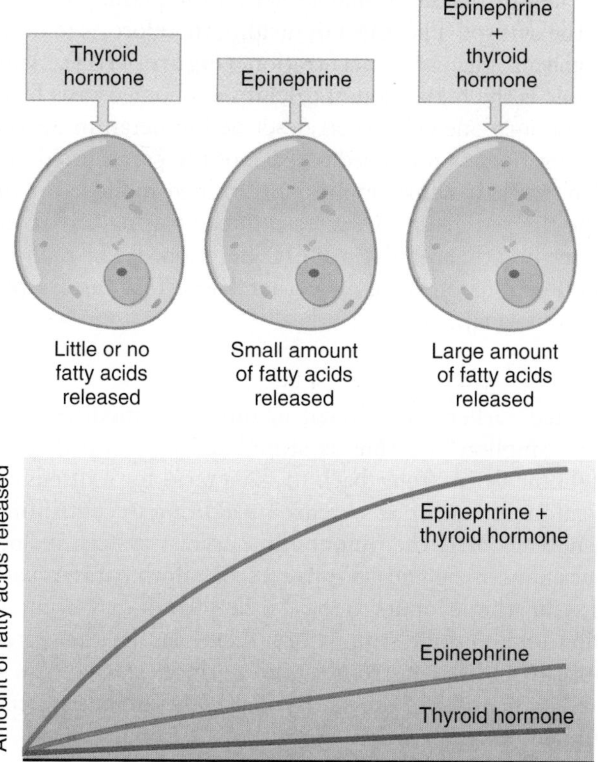

Figure 11.9 The ability of thyroid hormone to "permit" epinephrine-induced release of fatty acids from adipose tissue cells. Thyroid hormone exerts this effect by causing an increased number of beta-adrenergic receptors on the cell. Thyroid hormone by itself stimulates only a small amount of fatty acid release.

PHYSIOLOGICAL INQUIRY

- A patient is observed to have symptoms that are consistent with elevated concentrations of epinephrine in the blood, including a rapid heart rate, anxiety, and elevated fatty acid concentrations. However, the circulating epinephrine concentrations are tested and found to be in the normal range. What might explain this?

Answer can be found at end of chapter.

and catecholamines may exert both rapid (nongenomic) and slower (gene transcription) actions on the same target cell.

Effects of Steroid and Thyroid Hormone

The steroid hormones and thyroid hormone are all lipophilic, and their receptors, which are intracellular, constitute the steroid-hormone-receptor superfamily. As described for lipid-soluble messengers in Chapter 5, the binding of hormone to one of these receptors leads to the activation (or in some cases, inhibition) of the transcription of particular genes, causing a change in the synthesis rate of the proteins coded for by those genes. The ultimate result of changes in the concentrations of these proteins is an enhancement or inhibition of particular processes the cell carries out or a change in the cell's rate of protein secretion.

In addition to having intracellular receptors, some target cells also have plasma membrane receptors for certain of the steroid hormones, notably progesterone and estradiol. In such cases, the signal transduction pathways initiated by the plasma membrane receptors elicit rapid, nongenomic cell responses, whereas the intracellular receptors mediate a delayed response, requiring new protein synthesis. The physiological significance of the membrane receptors in humans is still under investigation, but it is clear from animal studies that these receptors are functional in other vertebrates.

Pharmacological Effects of Hormones

The administration of very large quantities of a hormone for medical purposes may have effects on an individual that are not usually observed in a healthy person. These ***pharmacological effects*** can also occur in diseases involving the secretion of excessive amounts of hormones. Pharmacological effects are of great importance in medicine because hormones are often used in large doses as therapeutic agents. Perhaps the most common example is that of very potent synthetic forms of cortisol, such as prednisone, which is administered to suppress allergic and inflammatory reactions. In such situations, a host of unwanted effects may be observed (as described in Section D).

11.6 Inputs That Control Hormone Secretion

Hormone secretion is mainly under the control of three types of inputs to endocrine cells (**Figure 11.10**): (1) changes in the plasma concentrations of mineral ions or organic nutrients, (2) neurotransmitters released from neurons ending on the endocrine cell, and (3) another hormone (or, in some cases, a paracrine substance) acting on the endocrine cell.

Before we look more closely at each category, we must stress that more than one input may influence hormone secretion. For example, insulin secretion is stimulated by the extracellular concentrations of glucose and other nutrients, and is either stimulated or inhibited by the different branches of the autonomic nervous system. Thus, the control of endocrine cells illustrates the general principle of physiology that most physiological functions are controlled by multiple regulatory systems, often working in opposition. The resulting output—the rate of hormone secretion—depends upon the relative amounts of stimulatory and inhibitory inputs.

The term *secretion* applied to a hormone denotes its release by exocytosis from the cell. In some cases, hormones such as steroid hormones are not secreted, per se, but instead diffuse through the cell's plasma membrane into the extracellular space. Secretion or release by diffusion is sometimes accompanied by increased synthesis of the hormone. For simplicity in this chapter and the rest of the book, we will

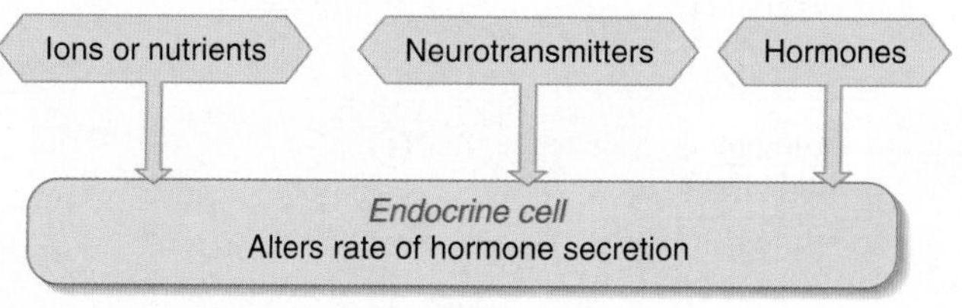

Figure 11.10 Inputs that act directly on endocrine gland cells to stimulate or inhibit hormone secretion.

generally not distinguish between these possibilities when we refer to stimulation or inhibition of hormone "secretion."

Control by Plasma Concentrations of Mineral Ions or Organic Nutrients

The secretion of several hormones is directly controlled—at least in part—by the plasma concentrations of specific mineral ions or organic nutrients. In each case, a major function of the hormone is to regulate through negative feedback (see Chapter 1) the plasma concentration of the ion or nutrient controlling its secretion. For example, insulin secretion is stimulated by an increase in plasma glucose concentration. Insulin, in turn, acts on skeletal muscle and adipose tissue to promote facilitated diffusion of glucose across the plasma membranes into the cytosol. The effect of insulin, therefore, is to decrease the plasma glucose concentration (**Figure 11.11**). Another example is the regulation of calcium ion homeostasis by parathyroid hormone (PTH), as described in detail in Section F. This hormone is produced by cells of the parathyroid glands, which, as their name implies, are located in close proximity to the thyroid gland. A decrease in the plasma Ca^{2+} concentration directly stimulates PTH secretion. PTH then exerts several actions on bone and other tissue that restore plasma Ca^{2+} to normal.

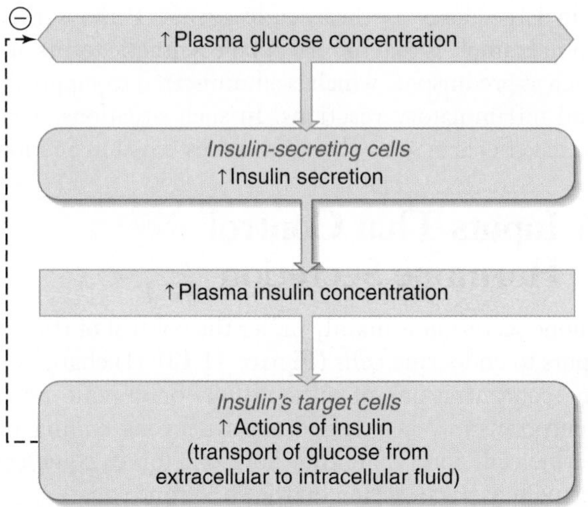

Figure 11.11 Example of how the direct control of hormone secretion by the plasma concentration of a substance—in this case, an organic nutrient—results in negative feedback control of the substance's plasma concentration. In other cases, the regulated plasma substance may be a mineral, such as Ca^{2+}.

Control by Neurons

As stated earlier, the adrenal medulla is a modified sympathetic ganglion and thus is stimulated by sympathetic preganglionic fibers (refer back to Chapter 6 for a discussion of the autonomic nervous system). In addition to controlling the adrenal medulla, the autonomic nervous system influences other endocrine glands (**Figure 11.12**). Both parasympathetic and sympathetic inputs to these other glands may occur, some inhibitory and some stimulatory. Examples are the secretions of insulin and the gastrointestinal hormones, which are stimulated by neurons of the parasympathetic nervous system and inhibited by sympathetic neurons.

One large group of hormones—those secreted by the hypothalamus and the posterior pituitary—is under the direct control not of autonomic neurons but of neurons in the brain itself (see Figure 11.12). This category will be described in detail in Section B.

Control by Other Hormones

In many cases, the secretion of a particular hormone is directly controlled by the blood concentration of another hormone. Often, the only function of the first hormone in a sequence is to stimulate the secretion of the next. A hormone that stimulates the secretion of another hormone is often referred to as a

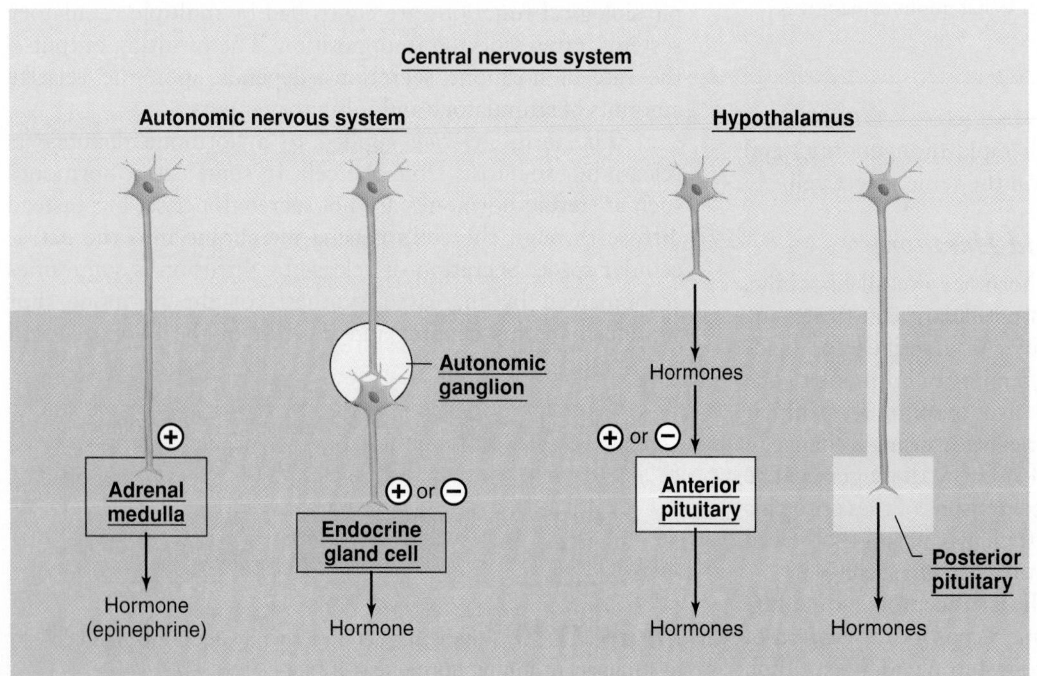

Figure 11.12 Pathways by which the nervous system influences hormone secretion. The autonomic nervous system controls hormone secretion by the adrenal medulla and many other endocrine glands. Certain neurons in the hypothalamus, some of which terminate in the posterior pituitary, secrete hormones. The secretion of hypothalamic hormones from the posterior pituitary and the effects of other hypothalamic hormones on the anterior pituitary gland are described later in this chapter. The ⊕ and ⊖ symbols indicate stimulatory and inhibitory actions, respectively.

tropic hormone. The tropic hormones usually stimulate not only secretion but also the growth of the stimulated gland. (When specifically referring to growth-promoting actions, the term *trophic* is often used, but for simplicity we will usually use only the general term *tropic*). These types of hormonal sequences are covered in detail in Section B. In addition to stimulatory actions, however, some hormones such as those in a multihormone sequence inhibit secretion of other hormones.

11.7 Types of Endocrine Disorders

Because there is such a wide variety of hormones and endocrine glands, disorders within the endocrine system may vary considerably in terms of symptoms. For example, endocrine disease may manifest as an imbalance in metabolism, leading to weight gain or loss; as a failure to grow or develop normally in early life; as an abnormally high or low blood pressure; as a loss of reproductive fertility; or as mental and emotional changes, to name a few. Despite these varied symptoms, which depend upon the particular hormone affected, essentially all endocrine diseases can be categorized in one of four ways. These include (1) too little hormone (***hyposecretion***), (2) too much hormone (***hypersecretion***), (3) decreased responsiveness of the target cells to hormone (***hyporesponsiveness***), and (4) increased responsiveness of the target cells to hormone (***hyperresponsiveness***).

Hyposecretion

An endocrine gland may be secreting too little hormone because the gland cannot function normally, a condition termed ***primary hyposecretion.*** Examples of primary hyposecretion include (1) partial destruction of a gland, leading to decreased hormone secretion; (2) an enzyme deficiency resulting in decreased synthesis of the hormone; and (3) dietary deficiency of iodine, specifically leading to decreased secretion of thyroid hormones. Many other causes, such as infections and exposure to toxic chemicals, have the common denominator of damaging the endocrine gland or reducing its ability to synthesize or secrete the hormone.

The other major cause of hyposecretion is ***secondary hyposecretion.*** In this case, the endocrine gland is not damaged but is receiving too little stimulation by its tropic hormone.

To distinguish between primary and secondary hyposecretion, one measures the concentration of the tropic hormone in the blood. If elevated, the cause is primary; if not increased, or lower than normal, the cause is secondary.

The most common means of treating hormone hyposecretion is to administer the missing hormone or a synthetic analog of the hormone. This is normally done either by oral (pill), topical (cream applied to skin), or nasal (spray) administration, or by injection. The route of administration typically depends upon the chemical nature of the hormone being replaced. For example, individuals with low thyroid hormone take a daily pill to restore normal hormone concentrations, because thyroid hormones are readily absorbed from the intestines. By contrast, people with diabetes mellitus who require insulin typically must obtain it via injection; insulin is a peptide that would be digested by the enzymes of the gastrointestinal tract if it were ingested.

Hypersecretion

A hormone can also undergo either ***primary hypersecretion*** (the gland is secreting too much of the hormone on its own) or ***secondary hypersecretion*** (excessive stimulation of the gland by its tropic hormone). One cause of primary or secondary hypersecretion is the presence of a hormone-secreting, endocrine-cell tumor. These tumors tend to produce their hormones continually at a high rate, even in the absence of stimulation.

When an endocrine tumor causes hypersecretion, the tumor can often be removed surgically or destroyed with radiation if it is confined to a small area. These procedures are also useful in certain cases where an endocrine gland is hypersecreting for reasons unrelated to the presence of a tumor. Both of these procedures can be used, for example, in treating hypersecretion from an overactive thyroid gland (see Section C). In many cases, drugs that inhibit a hormone's synthesis can block hypersecretion. Alternatively, the situation can be treated with drugs that do not alter the hormone's secretion but instead block the hormone's actions on its target cells.

Hyporesponsiveness and Hyperresponsiveness

In some cases, a component of the endocrine system may not be functioning normally, even though there is nothing wrong with hormone secretion. The problem is that the target cells do not respond normally to the hormone, a condition termed hyporesponsiveness, or hormone resistance. An important example of a disease resulting from hyporesponsiveness is the most common form of diabetes mellitus (called ***type 2 diabetes mellitus***), in which the target cells of the hormone insulin are hyporesponsive to this hormone.

One cause of hyporesponsiveness is deficiency of receptors—or abnormal, nonfunctional receptors—for the hormone. For example, some individuals who are genetically male have a defect manifested by the absence of receptors for androgens. Consequently, their target cells are unable to bind androgens, and the result is lack of development of certain male characteristics, as though the hormones were not being produced (see Chapter 17 for additional details).

In a second type of hyporesponsiveness, the receptors for a hormone may be normal but some signaling event that occurs within the cell after the hormone binds to its receptors may be defective. For example, the activated receptor may be unable to stimulate formation of cyclic AMP or another component of the signaling pathway for that hormone.

A third cause of hyporesponsiveness applies to hormones that require metabolic activation by some other tissue after secretion. There may be a deficiency of the enzymes that catalyze the activation. For example, some men secrete testosterone (the major circulating androgen) normally and have normal receptors for androgens. However, these men are missing the intracellular enzyme that converts testosterone to dihydrotestosterone, a potent metabolite of testosterone that binds to androgen receptors and mediates some of the actions of testosterone on secondary sex characteristics such as the growth of facial and body hair.

By contrast, hyperresponsiveness to a hormone can also occur and cause problems. For example, thyroid hormone causes an up-regulation of beta-adrenergic receptors for epinephrine; therefore, hypersecretion of thyroid hormone causes, in turn, a hyperresponsiveness to epinephrine. One result of this is the increased heart rate typical of people with elevated concentrations of thyroid hormones.

SECTION A SUMMARY

Hormones and Endocrine Glands

I. The endocrine system is one of the body's two major communications systems. It consists of all the glands and organs that secrete hormones, which are chemical messengers carried by the blood to target cells elsewhere in the body.

II. Endocrine glands differ from exocrine glands in that the latter secrete their products into a duct that connects with another structure, such as the intestines, or with the outside of the body.

III. A single gland may, in some cases, secrete multiple hormones.

Hormone Structures and Synthesis

I. The amine hormones are the iodine-containing thyroid hormones and the catecholamines secreted by the adrenal medulla and the hypothalamus.

II. The majority of hormones are peptides, many of which are synthesized as larger molecules, which are then cleaved into active fragments.

III. Steroid hormones are produced from cholesterol by the adrenal cortex and the gonads and by the placenta during pregnancy.
   a. The predominant steroid hormones produced by the adrenal cortex are the mineralocorticoid aldosterone; the glucocorticoid cortisol; and two androgens, DHEA and androstenedione.
   b. The ovaries produce mainly estradiol and progesterone, and the testes produce mainly testosterone.

Hormone Transport in the Blood

I. Peptide hormones and catecholamines circulate dissolved in the plasma, but steroid and thyroid hormones circulate mainly bound to plasma proteins.

Hormone Metabolism and Excretion

I. The liver and kidneys are the major organs that remove hormones from the plasma by metabolizing or excreting them.

II. The peptide hormones and catecholamines are rapidly removed from the blood, whereas the steroid and thyroid hormones are removed more slowly, in part because they circulate bound to plasma proteins.

III. After their secretion, some hormones are metabolized to more active molecules in their target cells or other organs.

Mechanisms of Hormone Action

I. The great majority of receptors for steroid and thyroid hormones are inside the target cells; those for the peptide hormones and catecholamines are on the plasma membrane.

II. Hormones can cause up-regulation and down-regulation of their own receptors and those of other hormones. The induction of one hormone's receptors by another hormone increases the first hormone's effectiveness and may be essential to permit the first hormone to exert its effects.

III. Receptors activated by peptide hormones and catecholamines utilize one or more of the signal transduction pathways available to plasma membrane receptors; the result is altered membrane potential or protein activity in the cell.

IV. Intracellular receptors activated by steroid and thyroid hormones typically function as transcription factors; the result is increased synthesis of particular proteins.

V. In pharmacological doses, hormones can have effects not seen under ordinary circumstances, some of which may be deleterious.

Inputs That Control Hormone Secretion

I. The secretion of a hormone may be controlled by the plasma concentration of an ion or nutrient that the hormone regulates, by neural input to the endocrine cells, and by one or more hormones.

II. The autonomic nervous system is the neural input controlling many hormones. Neuron endings from the sympathetic and parasympathetic nervous systems terminate directly on cells within some endocrine glands, thereby regulating hormone secretion.

Types of Endocrine Disorders

I. Endocrine disorders may be classified as hyposecretion, hypersecretion, and target-cell hyporesponsiveness or hyperresponsiveness.
   a. Primary disorders are those in which the defect is in the cells that secrete the hormone.
   b. Secondary disorders are those in which there is too much or too little tropic hormone.
   c. Hyporesponsiveness is due to an alteration in the receptors for the hormone, to disordered postreceptor events, or to failure of normal metabolic activation of the hormone in cases requiring such activation.

II. These disorders can be distinguished by measurements of the hormone and any tropic hormones under both basal conditions and during experimental stimulation of each hormone's secretion.

SECTION A REVIEW QUESTIONS

1. What distinguishes exocrine from endocrine glands?
2. What are the three general chemical classes of hormones?
3. What are the major hormones produced by the adrenal cortex? By the testes? By the ovaries?
4. Which classes of hormones are carried in the blood mainly as unbound, dissolved hormone? Mainly bound to plasma proteins?
5. Do protein-bound hormones diffuse out of capillaries?
6. Which organs are the major sites of hormone excretion and metabolic inactivation?
7. How do the rates of metabolism and excretion differ for the various classes of hormones?
8. List some metabolic transformations that prohormones and some hormones must undergo before they become biologically active.
9. Contrast the locations of receptors for the various classes of hormones.
10. How do hormones influence the concentrations of their own receptors and those of other hormones? How does this explain permissiveness in hormone action?
11. Describe the sequence of events when peptide or catecholamine hormones bind to their receptors.
12. Describe the sequence of events when steroid or thyroid hormones bind to their receptors.
13. What are the direct inputs to endocrine glands controlling hormone secretion?

14. How does control of hormone secretion by plasma mineral ions and nutrients achieve negative feedback control of these substances?
15. How would you distinguish between primary and secondary hyposecretion of a hormone? Between hyposecretion and hyporesponsiveness?

SECTION A KEY TERMS

SECTION A CLINICAL TERMS

SECTION B The Hypothalamus and Pituitary Gland

11.8 Control Systems Involving the Hypothalamus and Pituitary Gland

The **pituitary gland,** or **hypophysis** (from a Greek term meaning "to grow underneath"), lies in a pocket (called the sella turcica) of the sphenoid bone at the base of the brain (**Figure 11.13**) just below the **hypothalamus.** The pituitary gland is connected to the hypothalamus by the **infundibulum,** or pituitary stalk, containing axons from neurons in the hypothalamus and small blood vessels. In humans, the pituitary gland is composed of two adjacent lobes called the *anterior lobe*—usually referred to as the **anterior pituitary gland** or adenohypophysis—and the *posterior lobe*—usually called the **posterior pituitary** or neurohypophysis. The anterior pituitary gland arises embryologically from an invagination of the pharynx called Rathke's pouch, whereas the posterior pituitary is not actually a gland but, rather, an extension of the neural components of the hypothalamus.

The axons of two well-defined clusters of hypothalamic neurons (the supraoptic and paraventricular nuclei) pass down the infundibulum and end within the posterior pituitary in close proximity to capillaries (small blood vessels where exchange of solutes occurs between the blood and interstitium) (**Figure 11.13b**). Therefore, these neurons do not form a synapse with other neurons. Instead, their terminals end directly on capillaries. The terminals release hormones into these capillaries, which then collect into veins and the general circulation.

In contrast to the neural connections between the hypothalamus and posterior pituitary, there are no important neural connections between the hypothalamus and anterior pituitary gland. There is, however, a special type of circulatory connection (see Figure 11.13b). The junction of the hypothalamus and infundibulum is known as the **median eminence.** Capillaries in the median eminence recombine to form the **hypothalamo–hypophyseal portal vessels** (or portal veins). The term *portal* denotes veins that connect two sets of capillaries; normally, as you will learn in Chapter 12, capillaries drain into veins that return blood to the heart. Only in portal systems does one set of capillaries drain into veins that then form a *second* set of capillaries before eventually emptying again into veins that return to the heart. The hypothalamo–hypophyseal portal vessels pass down the infundibulum and enter the anterior pituitary gland, where they drain into a second set of capillaries, the anterior pituitary gland capillaries. Thus, the hypothalamo–hypophyseal portal vessels offer a local route for blood to be delivered directly from the hypothalamus to the cells of the anterior pituitary gland. As we will see shortly, this local blood system provides a mechanism for hormones of the hypothalamus to directly alter the activity of the cells of the anterior pituitary gland, bypassing the general circulation and thus efficiently regulating hormone release from that gland.

We begin our survey of pituitary gland hormones and their major physiological actions with the two hormones of the posterior pituitary.

Posterior Pituitary Hormones

We emphasized that the posterior pituitary is really a neural extension of the hypothalamus (see Figure 11.13). The hormones are synthesized not in the posterior pituitary itself but in the hypothalamus—specifically, in the cell bodies of the supraoptic and paraventricular nuclei, whose axons pass down the infundibulum and terminate in the posterior pituitary. Enclosed in small vesicles, the hormone moves down the axons to accumulate at the axon terminals in the posterior pituitary. Various stimuli activate inputs to these neurons, causing action potentials that propagate to the axon terminals and trigger the release of the stored hormone by exocytosis. The hormone then enters capillaries to be carried away by the blood returning to the heart. In this way, the brain can receive stimuli and respond as if it were an endocrine organ.

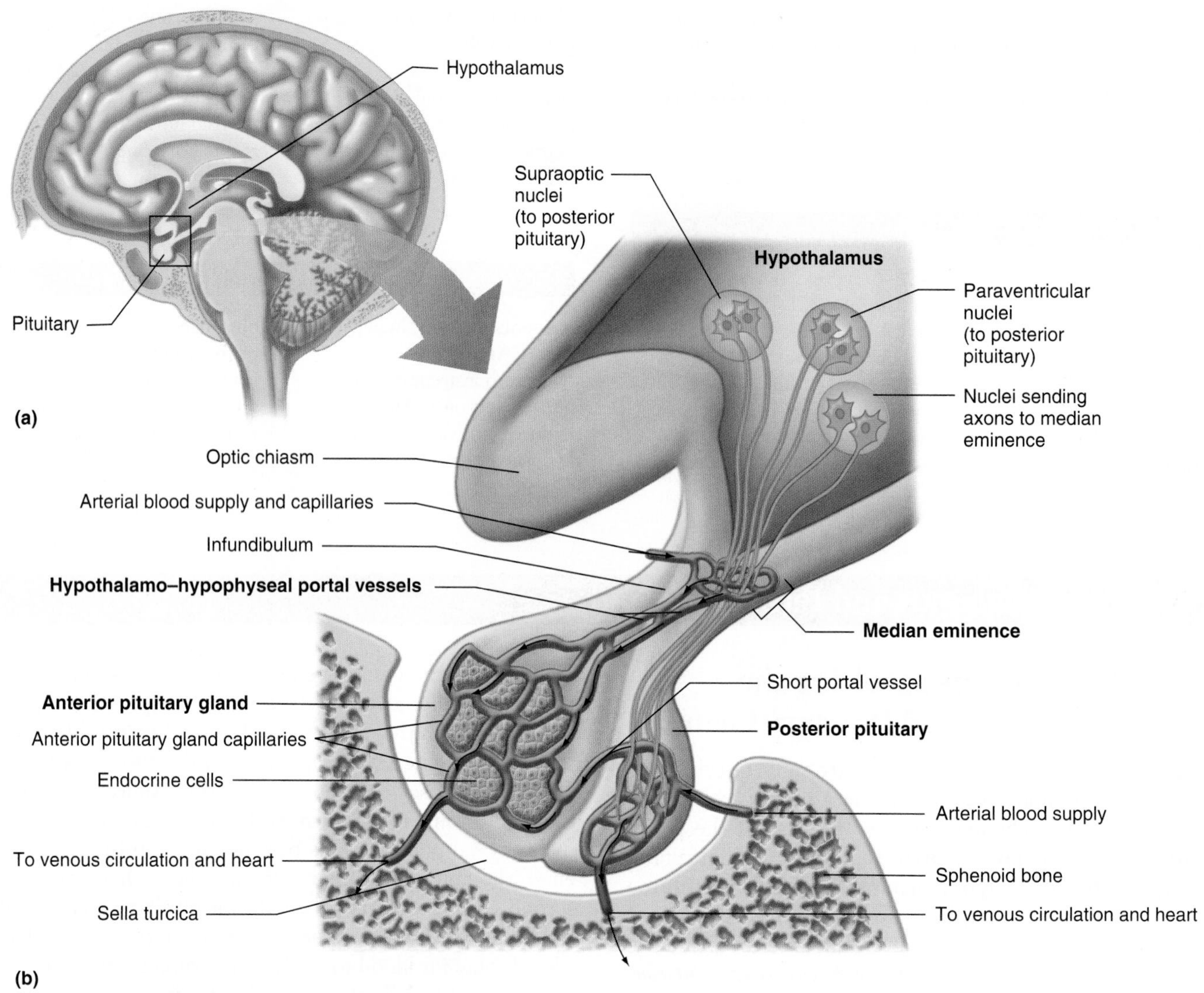

Figure 11.13 APR (a) Relation of the pituitary gland to the brain and hypothalamus. (b) Neural and vascular connections between the hypothalamus and pituitary gland. Hypothalamic neurons from the paraventricular and supraoptic nuclei travel down the infundibulum to end in the posterior pituitary, whereas others (shown for simplicity as a single nucleus, but in reality several nuclei, including some cells from the paraventricular nuclei) end in the median eminence. Almost the entire blood supply to the anterior pituitary gland comes via the hypothalamo–hypophyseal portal vessels, which originate in the median eminence. Long portal vessels connect the capillaries in the median eminence with those in the anterior pituitary gland. (The short portal vessels, which originate in the posterior pituitary, carry only a small fraction of the blood leaving the posterior pituitary and supply only a small fraction of the blood received by the anterior pituitary gland.) Arrows indicate direction of blood flow.

PHYSIOLOGICAL INQUIRY

- Why does it take only very small quantities of hypophysiotropic hormones to regulate anterior pituitary gland hormone secretion?

Answer can be found at end of chapter.

By releasing its hormones into the general circulation, the posterior pituitary can modify the functions of distant organs.

The two posterior pituitary hormones are the peptides **oxytocin** and **vasopressin.** Oxytocin is involved in two reflexes related to reproduction. In one case, oxytocin stimulates contraction of smooth muscle cells in the breasts, which results in milk ejection during lactation. This occurs in response to stimulation of the nipples of the breast during nursing of the infant. Sensory cells within the nipples send stimulatory neural signals to the brain that terminate on the hypothalamic cells that make oxytocin, causing their activation and thus release of the hormone. In a second reflex, one that occurs during labor in a pregnant woman, stretch receptors in the cervix send neural signals back to the hypothalamus, which releases oxytocin in response. Oxytocin then stimulates contraction of uterine smooth muscle cells, until eventually the baby is born (see Chapter 17 for details). Although oxytocin is also present in males, its systemic endocrine functions in males are uncertain. Recent research suggests that oxytocin may be involved in various aspects of behavior in male and female mammals, possibly including humans. These include such things as pair bonding, maternal behavior, and emotions such as love. If true in humans, this is likely due to oxytocin-containing neurons in other parts of the brain, as it is unclear whether any systemic oxytocin can cross the blood–brain barrier and enter the brain.

The other posterior pituitary hormone, vasopressin, acts on smooth muscle cells around blood vessels to cause their contraction, which constricts the blood vessels and thereby increases blood pressure. This may occur, for example, in response to a decrease in blood pressure that resulted from a loss of blood due to an injury. Vasopressin also acts within the kidneys to decrease water excretion in the urine, thereby retaining fluid in the body and helping to maintain blood volume. One way in which this would occur would be if a person were to become dehydrated. Because of its kidney function, vasopressin is also known as **antidiuretic hormone (ADH)**. (A loss of excess water in the urine is known as a *diuresis*, and because vasopressin decreases water loss in the urine, it has *anti*diuretic properties.)

Anterior Pituitary Gland Hormones and the Hypothalamus

Other nuclei of hypothalamic neurons secrete hormones that control the secretion of all the anterior pituitary gland hormones. For simplicity's sake, Figure 11.13 depicts these neurons as arising from a single nucleus, but in fact several hypothalamic nuclei send axons whose terminals end in the median eminence. The hypothalamic hormones that regulate anterior pituitary gland function are collectively termed **hypophysiotropic hormones** (recall that another name for the pituitary gland is *hypophysis*); they are also commonly called hypothalamic releasing or inhibiting hormones.

With one exception (dopamine), each of the hypophysiotropic hormones is the first in a three-hormone sequence: (1) A hypophysiotropic hormone controls the secretion of (2) an anterior pituitary gland hormone, which controls the secretion of (3) a hormone from some other endocrine gland (**Figure 11.14**). This last hormone then acts on its target cells. The adaptive value of such sequences is that they permit a variety of types of important hormonal feedback. They also allow amplification of a response of a small number of hypothalamic neurons into a large peripheral hormonal signal. We begin our description of these sequences in the middle—that is, with the anterior pituitary gland hormones—because the names of the hypophysiotropic hormones are mostly based on the names of the anterior pituitary gland hormones.

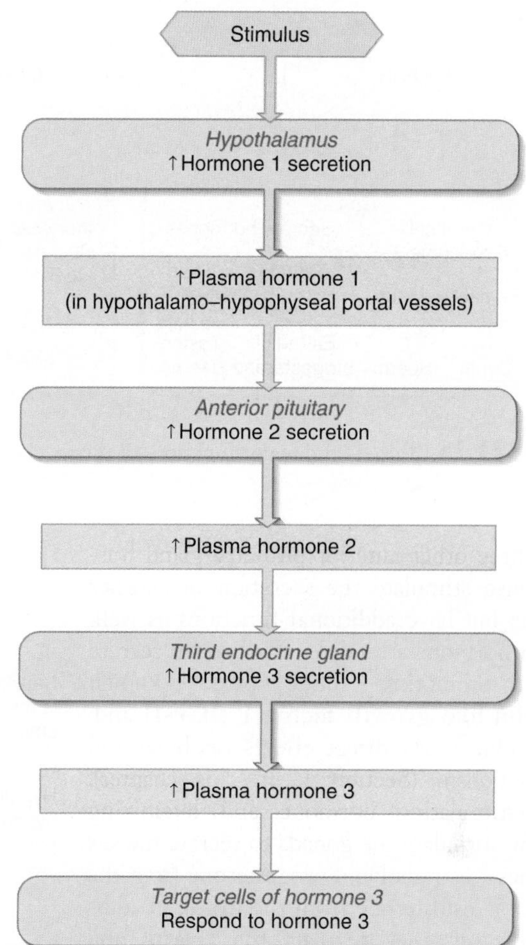

Figure 11.14 Typical sequential pattern by which a hypophysiotropic hormone (hormone 1 from the hypothalamus) controls the secretion of an anterior pituitary gland hormone (hormone 2), which in turn controls the secretion of a hormone by a third endocrine gland (hormone 3). The hypothalamo–hypophyseal portal vessels are illustrated in Figure 11.13.

Overview of Anterior Pituitary Gland Hormones

As shown in Table 11.1, the anterior pituitary gland secretes at least eight hormones, but only six have well-established functions in humans. These six hormones—all peptides—are **follicle-stimulating hormone (FSH)**, **luteinizing hormone (LH)**, **growth hormone (GH,** also known as *somatotropin*), **thyroid-stimulating hormone (TSH,** also known as *thyrotropin*), **prolactin,** and **adrenocorticotropic hormone (ACTH,** also known as *corticotropin*). Each of the last four is secreted by a distinct cell type in the anterior pituitary gland, whereas FSH and LH, collectively termed **gonadotropic hormones** (or gonadotropins) because they stimulate the gonads, are often secreted by the same cells.

The other two peptides—**beta-lipotropin** and **beta-endorphin**—are both derived from the same prohormone as ACTH, but in humans their physiological roles, if any, are unclear. In animal studies, however, beta-endorphin has been shown to have potent pain-killing effects, and beta-lipotropin can mobilize fats in the circulation to provide a source of energy. Both of these functions may contribute to the ability to cope with stressful challenges.

Figure 11.15 summarizes the target organs and major functions of the six classical anterior pituitary gland hormones. Note that the only major function of two of the six is to stimulate their target cells to synthesize and secrete other hormones (and to maintain the growth and function of these cells). Thyroid-stimulating hormone induces the thyroid to secrete the two major thyroid hormones, thyroxine and triiodothyronine. Adrenocorticotropic hormone stimulates the adrenal cortex to secrete cortisol.

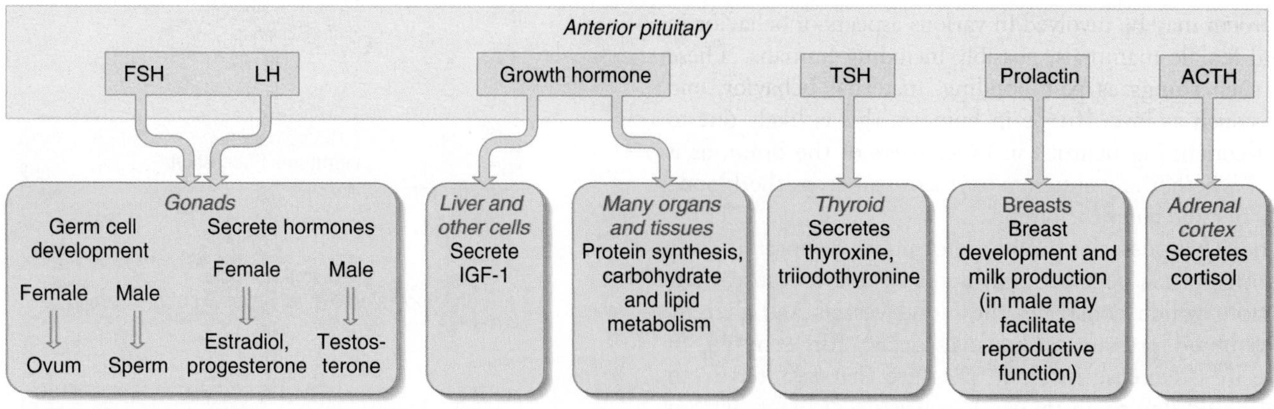

Figure 11.15 Targets and major functions of the six classical anterior pituitary gland hormones.

Three other anterior pituitary gland hormones also stimulate the secretion of another hormone but have additional functions as well. Growth hormone stimulates the liver to secrete a growth-promoting peptide hormone known as **insulin-like growth factor 1 (IGF-1)** and, in addition, exerts direct effects on bone and on metabolism (Section E in this chapter). Follicle-stimulating hormone and luteinizing hormone stimulate the gonads to secrete the sex hormones—estradiol and progesterone from the ovaries, or testosterone from the testes; in addition, however, they regulate the growth and development of ova and sperm. The actions of FSH and LH are described in detail in Chapter 17 and therefore are not covered further here.

Prolactin is unique among the six classical anterior pituitary gland hormones in that its major function is not to exert control over the secretion of a hormone by another endocrine gland. Its most important action is to stimulate development of the mammary glands during pregnancy and milk production when a woman is nursing (lactating); this occurs by direct effects upon gland cells in the breasts. During lactation, prolactin exerts a secondary action to inhibit gonadotropin secretion, thus decreasing fertility when a woman is nursing. In the male, the physiological functions of prolactin are still under investigation.

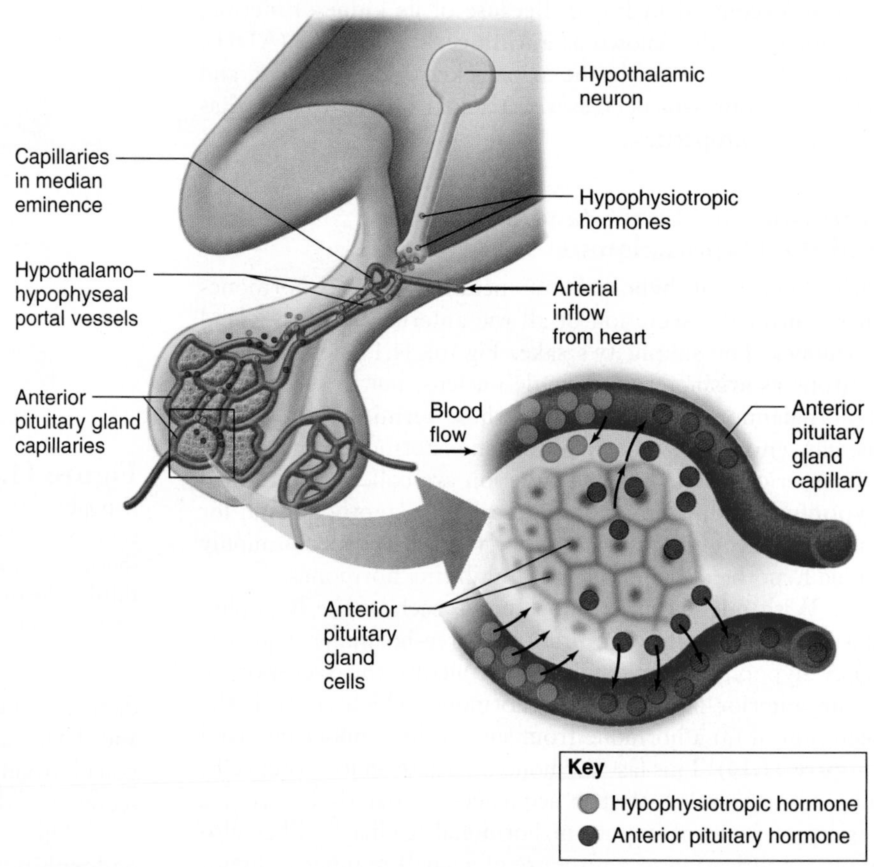

Figure 11.16 APR Hormone secretion by the anterior pituitary gland is controlled by hypophysiotropic hormones released by hypothalamic neurons and reaching the anterior pituitary gland by way of the hypothalamo–hypophyseal portal vessels.

Hypophysiotropic Hormones

As stated previously, secretion of the anterior pituitary gland hormones is largely regulated by hormones produced by the hypothalamus and collectively called hypophysiotropic hormones. These hormones are secreted by neurons that originate in discrete nuclei of the hypothalamus and terminate in the median eminence around the capillaries that are the origins of the hypothalamo–hypophyseal portal vessels. The generation of action potentials in these neurons causes them to secrete their hormones by exocytosis, much as action potentials cause other neurons to release neurotransmitters by exocytosis. Hypothalamic hormones, however, enter the median eminence capillaries and are carried by the hypothalamo–hypophyseal portal vessels to the anterior pituitary gland (**Figure 11.16**). There, they diffuse out of the anterior pituitary gland capillaries into the interstitial fluid surrounding the various anterior pituitary gland cells. Upon binding to specific membrane-bound receptors, the hypothalamic hormones act to stimulate or inhibit the secretion of the different anterior pituitary gland hormones.

Thus, these hypothalamic neurons secrete hormones in a manner identical to that described previously for the hypothalamic neurons whose axons end in the posterior pituitary. In both cases, the hormones are synthesized in hypothalamic neurons, pass down axons to the neuron terminals, and are released in response to action potentials in the neurons. Two crucial differences, however, distinguish the two systems. First, the axons of the hypothalamic neurons that secrete the posterior pituitary hormones leave the hypothalamus and end in the posterior pituitary, whereas those that secrete the hypophysiotropic hormones remain in the hypothalamus, ending in the median eminence. Second, most of the capillaries into which the posterior pituitary hormones are secreted immediately drain into the general circulation, which carries the hormones to the heart for distribution to the entire body. In contrast, the hypophysiotropic hormones enter capillaries in the median eminence of the hypothalamus that do not directly join the main bloodstream but empty into the hypothalamo–hypophyseal portal vessels, which carry them to the cells of the anterior pituitary gland.

When an anterior pituitary gland hormone is secreted, it will diffuse into the same capillaries that delivered the hypophysiotropic hormone. These capillaries then drain into veins, which enter the general blood circulation, where the anterior pituitary gland hormones can come into contact with their target cells. The portal circulatory system ensures that hypophysiotropic hormones can reach the cells of the anterior pituitary gland with very little delay. It also allows extremely small amounts of hypophysiotropic hormones from relatively few hypothalamic neurons to control the secretion of anterior pituitary hormones without dilution in the systemic circulation.

There are multiple hypophysiotropic hormones, each influencing the release of one or, in at least one case, two of the anterior pituitary gland hormones. For simplicity, **Figure 11.17** and the text of this chapter summarize only those hypophysiotropic hormones that have clearly documented physiological roles in humans.

Several of the hypophysiotropic hormones are named for the anterior pituitary gland hormone whose secretion they control. Thus, secretion of ACTH (corticotropin) is stimulated by **corticotropin-releasing hormone (CRH)**, secretion of growth hormone is stimulated by **growth hormone–releasing hormone (GHRH)**, secretion of thyroid-stimulating hormone (thyrotropin) is stimulated by **thyrotropin-releasing hormone (TRH)**, and secretion of both luteinizing hormone and follicle-stimulating hormone (the gonadotropins) is stimulated by **gonadotropin-releasing hormone (GnRH)**.

However, note in Figure 11.17 that two of the hypophysiotropic hormones do not *stimulate* the release of an anterior pituitary gland hormone but, rather, *inhibit* its release. One of them, **somatostatin (SST)**, inhibits the secretion of growth hormone. The other, **dopamine (DA)**, inhibits the secretion of prolactin.

As Figure 11.17 shows, growth hormone is controlled by *two* hypophysiotropic hormones—somatostatin, which inhibits its release, and growth hormone–releasing hormone, which stimulates it. The rate of growth hormone secretion depends, therefore, upon the relative amounts of the opposing hormones released by the hypothalamic neurons, as well as upon the relative sensitivities of the GH-producing cells of the anterior pituitary gland to them. This is a key example of the general principle of physiology that most physiological

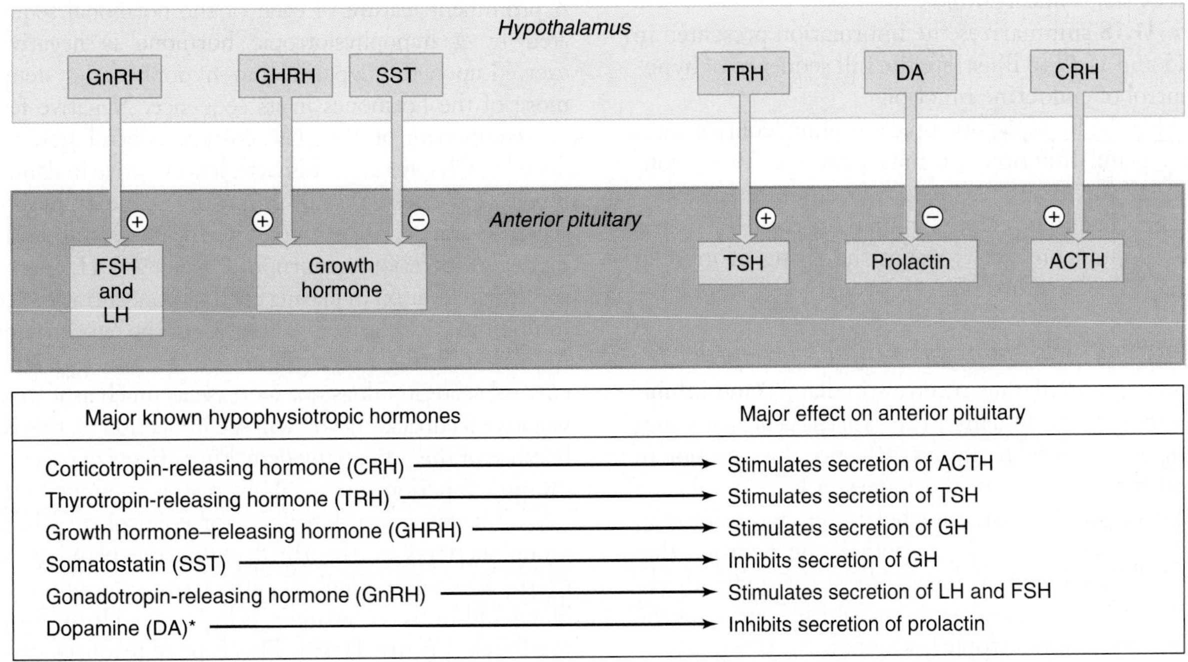

Major known hypophysiotropic hormones	Major effect on anterior pituitary
Corticotropin-releasing hormone (CRH)	Stimulates secretion of ACTH
Thyrotropin-releasing hormone (TRH)	Stimulates secretion of TSH
Growth hormone–releasing hormone (GHRH)	Stimulates secretion of GH
Somatostatin (SST)	Inhibits secretion of GH
Gonadotropin-releasing hormone (GnRH)	Stimulates secretion of LH and FSH
Dopamine (DA)*	Inhibits secretion of prolactin

*Dopamine is a catecholamine; all the other hypophysiotropic hormones are peptides. Evidence exists for PRL-releasing hormones, but they have not been unequivocally identified in humans. One possibility is that TRH serves this role in addition to its actions on TSH.

Figure 11.17 The effects of definitively established hypophysiotropic hormones on the anterior pituitary gland. The hypophysiotropic hormones reach the anterior pituitary gland via the hypothalamo–hypophyseal portal vessels. The ⊕ and ⊖ symbols indicate stimulatory and inhibitory actions, respectively.

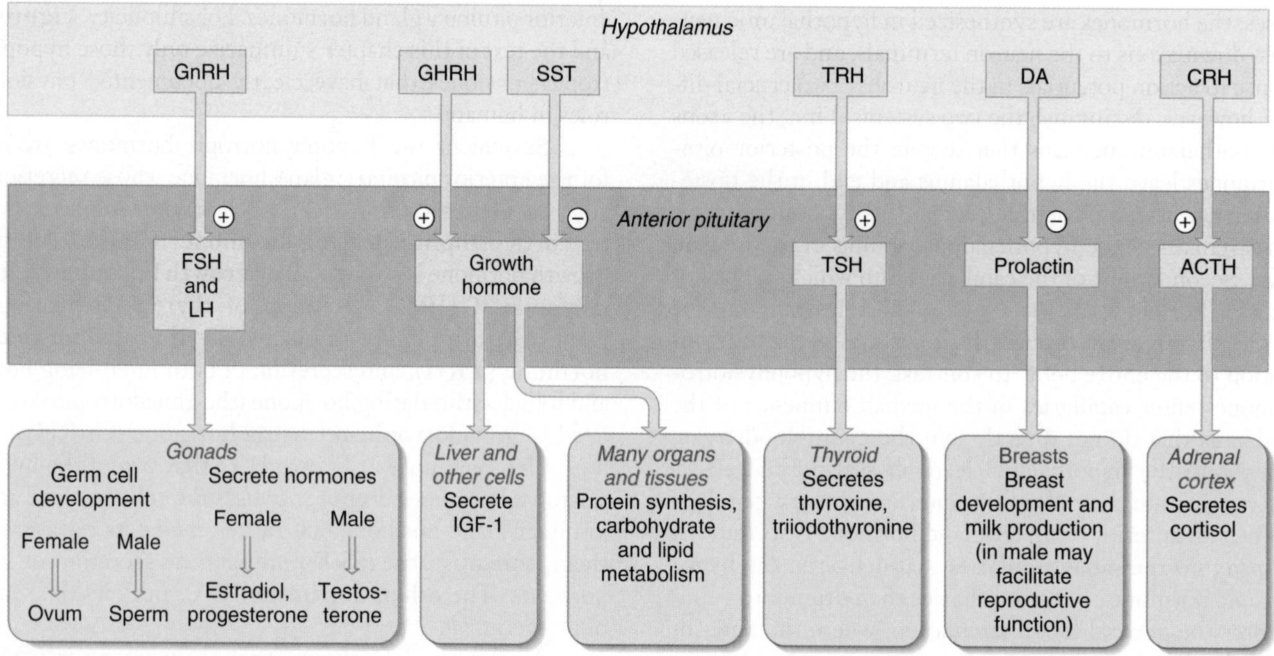

Figure 11.18 A combination of Figures 11.15 and 11.17 summarizes the hypothalamic–anterior pituitary gland system. The ⊕ and ⊖ symbols indicate stimulatory and inhibitory actions, respectively.

functions are controlled by multiple regulatory systems, often working in opposition. Such dual controls may also exist for the other anterior pituitary gland hormones. This is particularly true in the case of prolactin where the evidence for a prolactin-releasing hormone in laboratory animals is reasonably strong (the importance of such control for prolactin in humans, if it exists, is uncertain).

Figure 11.18 summarizes the information presented in Figures 11.15 and 11.17 to illustrate the full sequence of hypothalamic control of endocrine function.

Given that the hypophysiotropic hormones control anterior pituitary gland function, we must now ask, What controls secretion of the hypophysiotropic hormones themselves? Some of the neurons that secrete hypophysiotropic hormones may possess spontaneous activity, but the firing of most of them requires neural and hormonal input.

Neural Control of Hypophysiotropic Hormones

Neurons of the hypothalamus receive stimulatory and inhibitory synaptic input from virtually all areas of the central nervous system, and specific neural pathways influence the secretion of the individual hypophysiotropic hormones. A large number of neurotransmitters, such as the catecholamines and serotonin, are released at synapses on the hypothalamic neurons that produce hypophysiotropic hormones. Not surprisingly, therefore, drugs that influence these neurotransmitters can alter the secretion of the hypophysiotropic hormones.

In addition, there is a strong circadian influence (see Chapter 1) over the secretion of certain hypophysiotropic hormones. The neural inputs to these cells arise from other regions of the hypothalamus, which in turn are linked to inputs from visual pathways that recognize the presence or absence of light. A good example of this type of neural control is that of CRH, the secretion of which is tied to the day/night cycle in mammals. This pattern results in ACTH and cortisol concentrations in the blood that begin to increase just prior to the waking period.

Hormonal Feedback Control of the Hypothalamus and Anterior Pituitary Gland

A prominent feature of each of the hormonal sequences initiated by a hypophysiotropic hormone is negative feedback exerted upon the hypothalamo–hypophyseal system by one or more of the hormones in its sequence. Negative feedback is a key component of most homeostatic control systems, as introduced in Chapter 1. In this case, it is effective in dampening hormonal responses—that is, in limiting the extremes of hormone secretory rates. For example, when a stressful stimulus elicits increased secretion, in turn, of CRH, ACTH, and cortisol, the resulting elevation in plasma cortisol concentration feeds back to inhibit the CRH-secreting neurons of the hypothalamus and the ACTH-secreting cells of the anterior pituitary gland. Therefore, cortisol secretion does not increase as much as it would without negative feedback. As you will see in Section D, this is important because of the potentially damaging effects of excess cortisol on immune function and metabolic reactions, among others.

The situation described for cortisol, in which the hormone secreted by the third endocrine gland in a sequence exerts a negative feedback effect over the anterior pituitary gland and/or hypothalamus, is known as a **long-loop negative feedback** (**Figure 11.19**). This type of feedback exists for each of the three-hormone sequences initiated by a hypophysiotropic hormone.

Long-loop feedback does not exist for prolactin because this is one anterior pituitary gland hormone that does not have major control over another endocrine gland—that is, it does not participate in a three-hormone sequence. Nonetheless, there is negative feedback in the prolactin system, for this

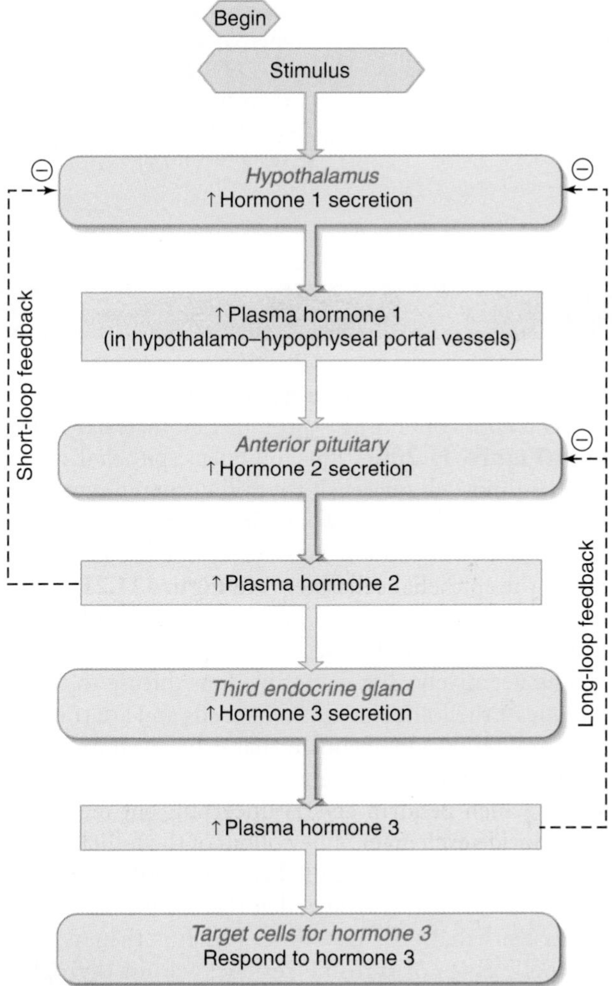

Figure 11.19 Short-loop and long-loop feedbacks. Long-loop feedback is exerted on the hypothalamus and/or anterior pituitary gland by the third hormone in the sequence. Short-loop feedback is exerted by the anterior pituitary gland hormone on the hypothalamus.

hormone itself acts upon the hypothalamus to *stimulate* the secretion of dopamine, which then *inhibits* the secretion of prolactin. The influence of an anterior pituitary gland hormone on the hypothalamus is known as a **short-loop negative feedback** (see Figure 11.19). Like prolactin, several other anterior pituitary gland hormones, including growth hormone, also exert such feedback on the hypothalamus.

The Role of "Nonsequence" Hormones on the Hypothalamus and Anterior Pituitary Gland

There are many stimulatory and inhibitory hormonal influences on the hypothalamus and/or anterior pituitary gland other than those that fit the feedback patterns just described. In other words, a hormone that is not itself in a particular hormonal sequence may nevertheless exert important influences on the secretion of the hypophysiotropic or anterior pituitary gland hormones in that sequence. For example, estradiol markedly enhances the secretion of prolactin by the anterior pituitary gland, even though estradiol secretion is not normally controlled by prolactin. Thus, the sequences we have been describing should not be viewed as isolated units.

SECTION B SUMMARY

Control Systems Involving the Hypothalamus and Pituitary Gland

I. The pituitary gland, comprising the anterior pituitary gland and the posterior pituitary, is connected to the hypothalamus by an infundibulum, or stalk, containing neuron axons and blood vessels.

II. Specific axons, whose cell bodies are in the hypothalamus, terminate in the posterior pituitary and release oxytocin and vasopressin.

III. The anterior pituitary gland secretes growth hormone (GH), thyroid-stimulating hormone (TSH), adrenocorticotropic hormone (ACTH), prolactin, and two gonadotropic hormones—follicle-stimulating hormone (FSH) and luteinizing hormone (LH). The functions of these hormones are summarized in Figure 11.15.

IV. Secretion of the anterior pituitary gland hormones is controlled mainly by hypophysiotropic hormones secreted into capillaries in the median eminence of the hypothalamus and reaching the anterior pituitary gland via the portal vessels connecting the hypothalamus and anterior pituitary gland. The actions of the hypophysiotropic hormones on the anterior pituitary gland are summarized in Figure 11.17.

V. The secretion of each hypophysiotropic hormone is controlled by neuronal and hormonal input to the hypothalamic neurons producing it.
   a. In each of the three-hormone sequences beginning with a hypophysiotropic hormone, the third hormone exerts negative feedback effects on the secretion of the hypothalamic and/or anterior pituitary gland hormone.
   b. The anterior pituitary gland hormone may exert a short-loop negative feedback inhibition of the hypothalamic releasing hormone(s) controlling it.
   c. Hormones not in a particular sequence can also influence secretion of the hypothalamic and/or anterior pituitary gland hormones in that sequence.

SECTION B REVIEW QUESTIONS

1. Describe the anatomical relationships between the hypothalamus and the pituitary gland.
2. Name the two posterior pituitary hormones and describe the site of synthesis and mechanism of release of each.
3. List all six well-established anterior pituitary gland hormones and their major functions.
4. List the major hypophysiotropic hormones and the anterior pituitary gland hormone(s) whose release each controls.
5. What kinds of inputs control secretion of the hypophysiotropic hormones?
6. What is the difference between long-loop and short-loop negative feedback in the hypothalamo–anterior pituitary gland system?

SECTION B KEY TERMS

adrenocorticotropic hormone (ACTH) 335
anterior pituitary gland 333
antidiuretic hormone (ADH) 335
beta-endorphin 335
beta-lipotropin 335
corticotropin-releasing hormone (CRH) 337
dopamine (DA) 337
follicle-stimulating hormone (FSH) 335
gonadotropic hormone 335
gonadotropin-releasing hormone (GnRH) 337
growth hormone (GH) 335
growth hormone–releasing hormone (GHRH) 337

SECTION **C**

The Thyroid Gland

11.9 Synthesis of Thyroid Hormone

Thyroid hormone exerts diverse effects throughout much of the body. The actions of this hormone are so widespread—and the consequences of imbalances in its concentration so significant—that it is worth examining thyroid gland function in additional detail.

The thyroid gland produces two iodine-containing molecules of physiological importance, **thyroxine** (called $\mathbf{T_4}$ because it contains four iodines) and **triiodothyronine** ($\mathbf{T_3}$, three iodines; review Figure 11.2). T_4 generally is converted into T_3 by enzymes known as deiodinases in target cells. We will therefore consider T_3 to be the major thyroid hormone, even though the concentration of T_4 in the blood is usually greater than that of T_3. (You may think of T_4 as a sort of reservoir for additional T_3.)

The thyroid gland sits within the neck straddling the trachea (**Figure 11.20a**). It first becomes functional early in fetal life. Within the thyroid gland are numerous **follicles,** each composed of an enclosed sphere of epithelial cells surrounding a core containing a protein-rich material called the **colloid** (**Figure 11.20b**). The follicular epithelial cells participate in almost all phases of thyroid hormone synthesis and secretion. Synthesis begins when circulating iodide is actively cotransported with sodium ions across the basolateral membranes of the epithelial cells (step 1 in **Figure 11.21**), a process known as **iodide trapping.** The Na^+ is pumped back out of the cell by Na^+/K^+-ATPases.

The negatively charged iodide ions diffuse to the apical membrane of the follicular epithelial cells and are transported into the colloid by a mechanism that is believed to require an integral membrane protein called **pendrin** (step 2). The mechanism by which pendrin acts is uncertain but may be as an iodide/chloride exchanger. The colloid of the follicles contains large amounts of a protein called **thyroglobulin.** Once in the colloid, iodide is rapidly oxidized at the luminal surface of the follicular epithelial cells to iodine, which is then attached to the phenolic rings of tyrosine residues within thyroglobulin (step 3). Thyroglobulin itself is synthesized by the follicular epithelial cells and secreted by exocytosis into the colloid. The enzyme responsible for oxidizing iodides and attaching them to tyrosines on thyroglobulin in the colloid is called **thyroid peroxidase,** and it, too, is synthesized by follicular epithelial cells. Iodine may be added to either of two positions on a given tyrosine within thyroglobulin. A tyrosine with one iodine attached is called **monoiodotyrosine** (**MIT**); if two iodines are attached, the product is **diiodotyrosine** (**DIT**). The precise mechanism of what happens next is still somewhat unclear. The phenolic ring of a molecule of MIT or DIT is removed from the remainder of its tyrosine and coupled to another DIT on the thyroglobulin molecule (step 4). This reaction may also be mediated by thyroid peroxidase. If two DIT molecules are coupled, the result is thyroxine (T_4). If one MIT and one DIT are coupled, the result is T_3.

Finally, for thyroid hormone to be secreted into the blood, extensions of the colloid-facing membranes of follicular epithelial cells engulf portions of the colloid (with its iodinated thyroglobulin) by endocytosis (step 5). The thyroglobulin, with its coupled MITs and DITs, is brought into contact with lysosomes in the cell interior (step 6). Proteolysis of thyroglobulin releases T_3 and T_4, which then diffuse out of the follicular epithelial cell into the interstitial fluid and from there to the blood (step 7). There is sufficient iodinated thyroglobulin stored within the follicles of the thyroid to provide thyroid hormone for several weeks even in the absence of dietary iodine. This storage capacity makes the thyroid gland

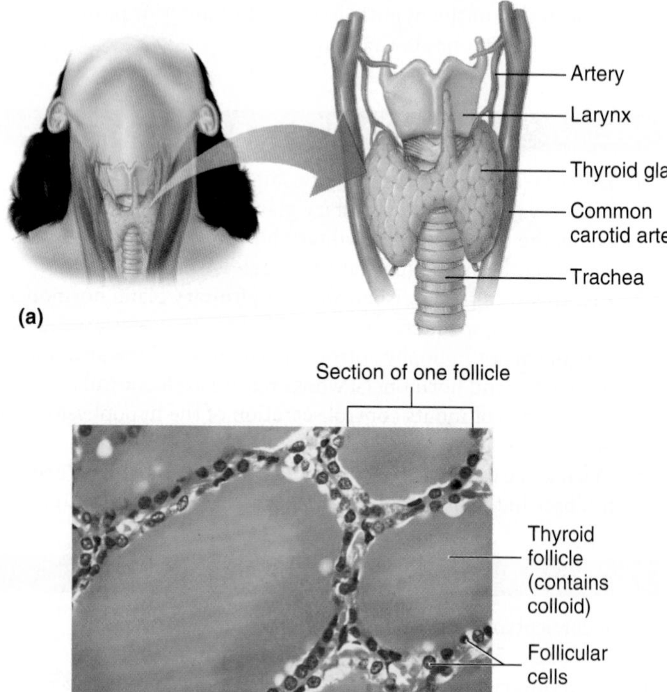

Figure 11.20 APIR (a) Location of the bilobed thyroid gland. (b) A cross section through several adjoining follicles filled with colloid. (b): © Biophoto Associates/Photo Researchers

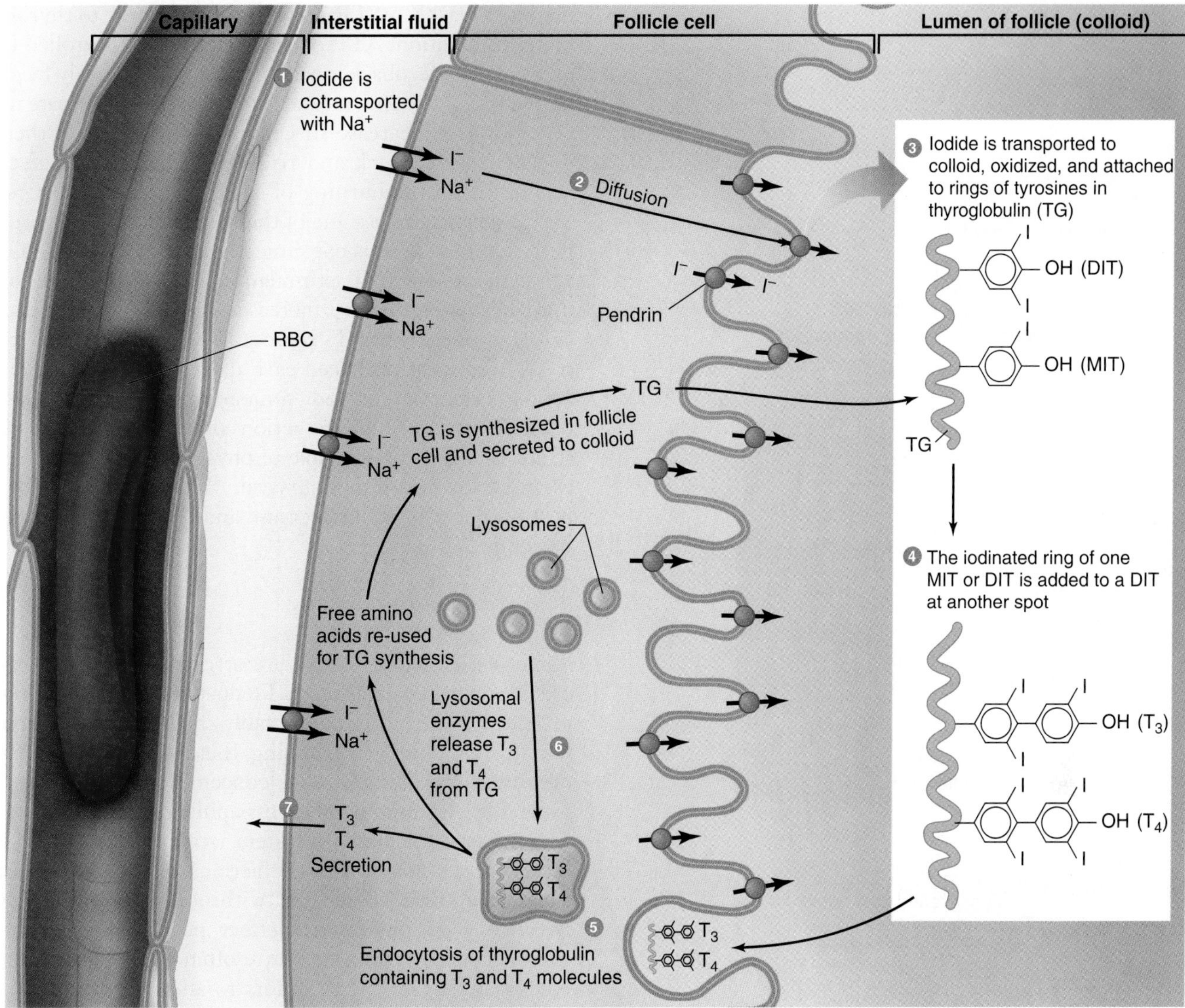

Figure 11.21 APIR Steps involved in T_3 and T_4 formation. Steps are keyed to the text.

PHYSIOLOGICAL INQUIRY

- What is the benefit of storing iodinated thyroglobulin in the colloid?

Answer can be found at end of chapter.

unique among endocrine glands but is an essential adaptation considering the unpredictable intake of iodine in the diets of most animals.

11.10 Control of Thyroid Function

Essentially all of the actions of the follicular epithelial cells just described are stimulated by TSH, which, as we have seen, is stimulated by TRH. The basic control mechanism of TSH production is the negative feedback action of T_3 and T_4 on the anterior pituitary gland and, to a lesser extent, the hypothalamus (**Figure 11.22**). However, TSH does more than just stimulate T_3 and T_4 production. TSH also increases protein synthesis in follicular epithelial cells, increases DNA replication and cell division, and increases the amount of rough endoplasmic reticulum and other cellular machinery required by follicular epithelial cells for protein synthesis. Therefore, if thyroid cells are exposed to greater TSH concentrations than normal, they will undergo **hypertrophy;** that is, they will increase in size. An enlarged thyroid gland from any cause is called a ***goiter.*** There are several ways in which goiters can occur, in addition to increased exposure of the thyroid gland to TSH, as will be described later in this section and in one of the case studies in Chapter 19.

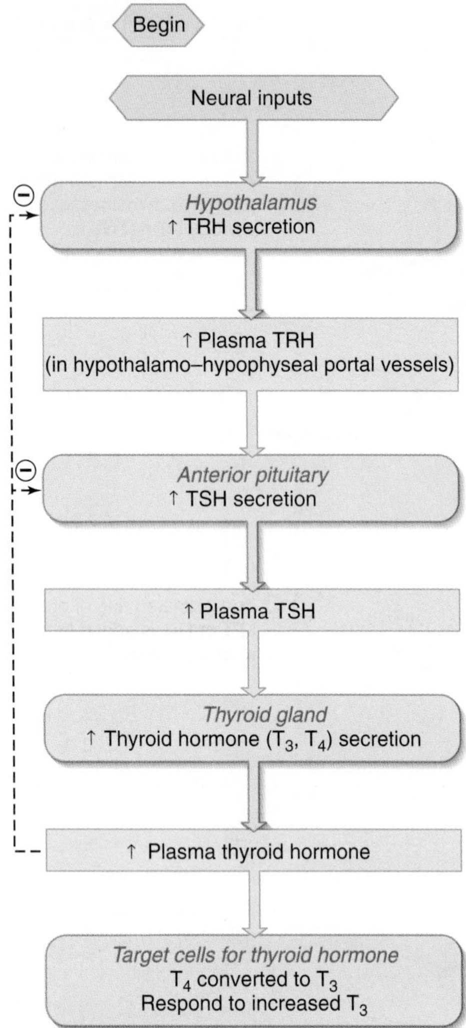

Figure 11.22 TRH-TSH-thyroid hormone sequence. T_3 and T_4 inhibit secretion of TSH and TRH by negative feedback, indicated by the ⊖ symbol.

11.11 Actions of Thyroid Hormone

Receptors for thyroid hormone are present in the nuclei of most of the cells of the body, unlike receptors for many other hormones, whose distribution is more limited. Thus, the actions of T_3 are widespread and affect many organs and tissues. Like steroid hormones, T_3 acts by inducing gene transcription and protein synthesis.

Metabolic Actions

T_3 has several effects on carbohydrate and lipid metabolism, although not to the extent as other hormones such as insulin. Nonetheless, T_3 stimulates carbohydrate absorption from the small intestine and increases fatty acid release from adipocytes. These actions provide energy that helps maintain metabolism at a high rate. Much of that energy is used to support the activity of Na^+/K^+-ATPases throughout the body; these enzymes are stimulated by T_3. The cellular concentration of ATP, therefore, is critical for the ability of cells to maintain Na^+/K^+-ATPase activity in response to thyroid hormone stimulation. ATP concentrations are controlled in part by a negative feedback mechanism; ATP negatively feeds back on the glycolytic enzymes within cells that participate in ATP generation. A decrease in cellular stores of ATP, therefore, releases the feedback and triggers an increase in glycolysis; this results in the burning of additional glucose that restores ATP concentrations. One of the by-products of this process is heat. Thus, as ATP is consumed in cells by Na^+/K^+-ATPases at a high rate due to T_3 stimulation, the cellular stores of ATP must be maintained by increased metabolism of fuels. This **calorigenic** action of T_3 represents a very significant fraction of the total heat produced each day in a typical person. This action is essential for body temperature homeostasis, just one of many ways in which the actions of thyroid hormone demonstrates the general principle of physiology that homeostasis is essential for health and survival. Without thyroid hormone, heat production would decrease and body temperature would be compromised.

Permissive Actions

Some of the actions of T_3 are attributable to its permissive effects on catecholamines. T_3 up-regulates beta-adrenergic receptors in many tissues, notably the heart and nervous system. It should not be surprising, therefore, that the symptoms of excess thyroid hormone concentration closely resemble some of the symptoms of excess epinephrine and norepinephrine (sympathetic nervous system activity). That is because the increased T_3 potentiates the actions of the catecholamines, even though the latter are within normal concentrations. Because of this potentiating effect, people with greater-than-normal concentrations of T_3 are often treated with drugs that block beta-adrenergic receptors to alleviate the anxiety, nervousness, and "racing heart" associated with excessive sympathetic activity.

Growth and Development

T_3 is required for normal production of growth hormone from the anterior pituitary gland. Therefore, in the absence of T_3, growth in children is decreased. In addition, though, T_3 is among the most important developmental hormones for the nervous system. During fetal life, T_3 exerts many effects on central nervous system development, including the formation of axon terminals and the production of synapses, the growth of dendrites and dendritic extensions (called "spines"), and the formation of myelin. Absence of T_3 during fetal life results in the syndrome called ***congenital hypothyroidism***. This syndrome is characterized by a poorly developed nervous system and severely compromised intellectual function (mental retardation). The most common cause of congenital hypothyroidism around the world (but rare in the United States) is dietary iodine deficiency in the mother. Without iodine in her diet, iodine is not available to the fetus. Thus, even though the fetal thyroid gland may be normal, it cannot manufacture sufficient T_3. If the condition is discovered and corrected with iodine and thyroid hormone administration shortly after birth, mental and physical abnormalities can be prevented. Some evidence suggests, however, that completely normal mental function may not be restored. Furthermore, if the treatment is not initiated in the early neonatal period, the intellectual impairment resulting from congenital hypothyroidism cannot be reversed. The availability of iodized salt products has essentially eliminated congenital hypothyroidism in many countries, but it is still a common disorder in some parts of the world where iodized salt is not available.

The effects of T_3 on nervous system function are not limited to fetal and neonatal life. For example, T_3 is required for proper nerve and muscle reflexes and for normal cognition in adults.

11.12 Hypothyroidism and Hyperthyroidism

Any condition characterized by plasma concentrations of T_3 that are chronically below normal is known as ***hypothyroidism.*** Most cases of hypothyroidism—about 95%—are primary defects resulting from damage to or loss of functional thyroid tissue or from inadequate iodine consumption.

In iodine deficiency, the synthesis of T_3 is compromised, leading to a decrease in the plasma concentration of this hormone. This, in turn, releases negative feedback on the hypothalamus and anterior pituitary gland, and TRH concentrations become chronically increased in the portal circulation that leads to the anterior pituitary gland. Plasma TSH concentration is increased due to the increased TRH and loss of thyroid hormone negative feedback on the anterior pituitary gland. The resulting overstimulation of the thyroid gland can produce goiters that can achieve astounding sizes if untreated (**Figure 11.23**). This form of hypothyroidism is reversible if iodine is added to the diet. As noted earlier, it is extremely rare in the United States because of the widespread use of iodized salt, in which a small fraction of NaCl molecules is replaced with NaI.

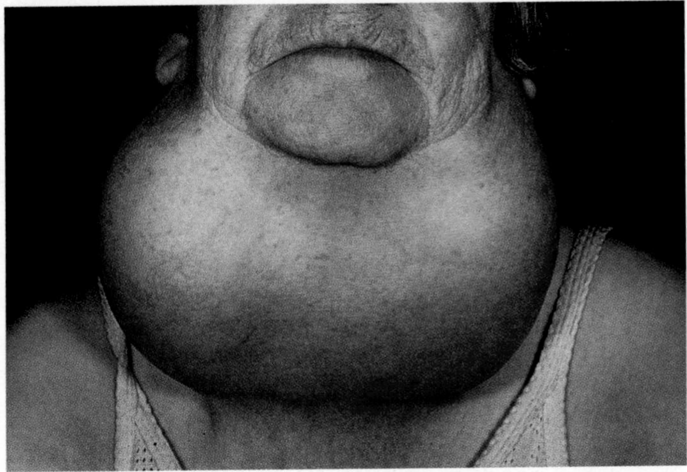

Figure 11.23 Goiter at an advanced stage.

The most common cause of hypothyroidism in the United States is autoimmune disruption of the normal function of the thyroid gland, a condition known as ***autoimmune thyroiditis.*** One form of autoimmune thyroiditis results from ***Hashimoto's disease,*** in which cells of the immune system attack and destroy thyroid tissue. Like many other autoimmune diseases, Hashimoto's disease is more common in women and can slowly progress with age. As thyroid hormone begins to decrease because of destruction of thyroid tissue, TSH concentrations increase due to the decreased negative feedback. The overstimulation of the thyroid gland results in cellular hypertrophy, and a goiter can develop. The usual treatment for autoimmune thyroiditis from any cause is daily replacement with a pill containing T_4 (most of which gets converted in the body to T_3). This causes the TSH concentration to decrease to normal due to negative feedback.

The signs and symptoms of hypothyroidism in adults may be mild or severe, depending on the degree of hormone deficiency. These include an increased sensitivity to cold (***cold intolerance***) and a tendency toward weight gain. Both of these symptoms are related to the decreased calorigenic actions normally produced by thyroid hormone. Many of the other symptoms appear to be diffuse and nonspecific, such as fatigue and changes in skin tone, hair, appetite, gastrointestinal function, and neurological function (for example, depression). The basis of the last effect in humans is uncertain, but it is now clear from work on laboratory animals that thyroid hormone has widespread effects on the adult mammalian brain. For example, thyroid hormone appears to be essential for maintaining cellular responsiveness to the neurotransmitter serotonin, and for stimulating neurogenesis in the adult hippocampus. Both serotonin and the hippocampus have been implicated in depressive disorders in humans (see Chapter 8).

In severe, untreated hypothyroidism, certain hydrophilic polymers called glycosaminoglycans accumulate in the interstitial space in scattered regions of the body. Normally, thyroid hormone acts to prevent overexpression of these extracellular compounds that are secreted by connective tissue cells. In the absence of T_3, therefore, these hydrophilic molecules accumulate and water tends to be trapped with them. This combination causes a characteristic puffiness of the face and other regions that is known as ***myxedema.***

As in the case of hypothyroidism, there are a variety of ways in which ***hyperthyroidism,*** or ***thyrotoxicosis,*** can develop. Among these are hormone-secreting tumors of the thyroid gland (rare), but the most common form of hyperthyroidism is an autoimmune disease called ***Graves' disease.*** This disease is characterized by the production of antibodies that bind to and activate the TSH receptors on thyroid gland cells, leading to chronic overstimulation of the growth and activity of the thyroid gland (see Chapter 19 for a case study related to this disease).

The signs and symptoms of thyrotoxicosis can be predicted in part from the previous discussion about hypothyroidism. Hyperthyroid patients tend to have ***heat intolerance,*** weight loss, and increased appetite, and often show signs of increased sympathetic nervous system activity (anxiety, tremors, jumpiness, increased heart rate).

Hyperthyroidism can be very serious, particularly because of its effects on the cardiovascular system (largely secondary to its permissive actions on catecholamines). It may be treated with drugs that inhibit thyroid hormone synthesis, by surgical removal of the thyroid gland, or by destroying a portion of the thyroid gland using radioactive iodine. In the last case, the radioactive iodine is ingested. Because the thyroid gland is the chief region of iodine uptake in the body, most of the radioactive iodine appears within the gland, where its high-energy radiation partly destroys the tissue.

SECTION C SUMMARY

Synthesis of Thyroid Hormone

I. T_3 and T_4 are synthesized by sequential iodinations of thyroglobulin in the thyroid follicle lumen, or colloid. Iodinated tyrosines on thyroglobulin are coupled to produce either T_3 or T_4. T_3 is the active hormone.

II. The enzyme responsible for T_3 and T_4 synthesis is thyroid peroxidase.

Control of Thyroid Function

I. All of the synthetic steps involved in T_3 synthesis are stimulated by TSH. TSH also stimulates uptake of iodide, where it is trapped in the follicle.

II. TSH causes growth (hypertrophy) of thyroid tissue. Excessive exposure of the thyroid gland to TSH can cause goiter.

Actions of Thyroid Hormone

I. T_3 increases the metabolic rate and therefore promotes consumption of calories (calorigenic effect). This results in heat production.

II. The actions of the sympathetic nervous system are potentiated by T_3. This is called the permissive action of T_3.

III. Thyroid hormone is essential for normal growth and development—particularly of the nervous system—during fetal life and childhood.

Hypothyroidism and Hyperthyroidism

I. Hypothyroidism most commonly results from autoimmune destruction of all or part of the thyroid gland. It is characterized by weight gain, fatigue, cold intolerance, and changes in skin tone and cognition. It may also result in goiter.

II. Hyperthyroidism is also typically the result of an autoimmune disorder. It is characterized by weight loss, heat intolerance, irritability and anxiety, and often goiter.

SECTION C REVIEW QUESTIONS

1. Describe the steps leading to T_3 and T_4 production, beginning with the transport of iodide into the thyroid follicular epithelial cell.
2. What are the major actions of TSH on thyroid function and growth?
3. What is the major way in which the TRH-TSH-TH pathway is regulated?
4. Explain why the symptoms of hyperthyroidism may be confused with a disorder of the autonomic nervous system.

SECTION C KEY TERMS

calorigenic 342
colloid 340
diiodotyrosine (DIT) 340
follicle 340
hypertrophy 341
iodide trapping 340
monoiodotyrosine (MIT) 340
pendrin 340
thyroglobulin 340
thyroid peroxidase 340
thyroxine (T_4) 340
triiodothyronine (T_3) 340

SECTION C CLINICAL TERMS

autoimmune thyroiditis 343
cold intolerance 343
congenital hypothyroidism 342
goiter 341
Graves' disease 343
Hashimoto's disease 343
heat intolerance 343
hyperthyroidism 343
hypothyroidism 343
myxedema 343
thyrotoxicosis 343

SECTION D
The Endocrine Response to Stress

Much of this book is concerned with the body's response to **stress** in its broadest meaning as a real or perceived threat to homeostasis. Thus, any change in external temperature, water intake, or other homeostatic factors sets into motion mechanisms designed to prevent a significant change in some physiological variable. In this section, the basic endocrine response to stress is described. These threats to homeostasis comprise an immense number of situations, including physical trauma, prolonged exposure to cold, prolonged heavy exercise, infection, shock, decreased oxygen supply, sleep deprivation, pain, and emotional stresses.

It may seem obvious that the physiological response to cold exposure must be very different from that to infection or emotional stresses such as fright, but in one respect the response to all these situations is the same: Invariably, the secretion from the adrenal cortex of the glucocorticoid hormone cortisol is increased. Activity of the sympathetic nervous system, including release of the hormone epinephrine from the adrenal medulla, also increases in response to most types of stress.

The increased cortisol secretion during stress is mediated by the hypothalamus–anterior pituitary gland system described earlier. As illustrated in **Figure 11.24,** neural input to the hypothalamus from portions of the nervous system responding to a particular stress induces secretion of CRH. This hormone is carried by the hypothalamo–hypophyseal portal vessels to the anterior pituitary gland, where it stimulates ACTH secretion. ACTH in turn circulates through the blood, reaches the adrenal cortex, and stimulates cortisol release.

The secretion of ACTH, and therefore of cortisol, is also stimulated to a lesser extent by vasopressin, which usually

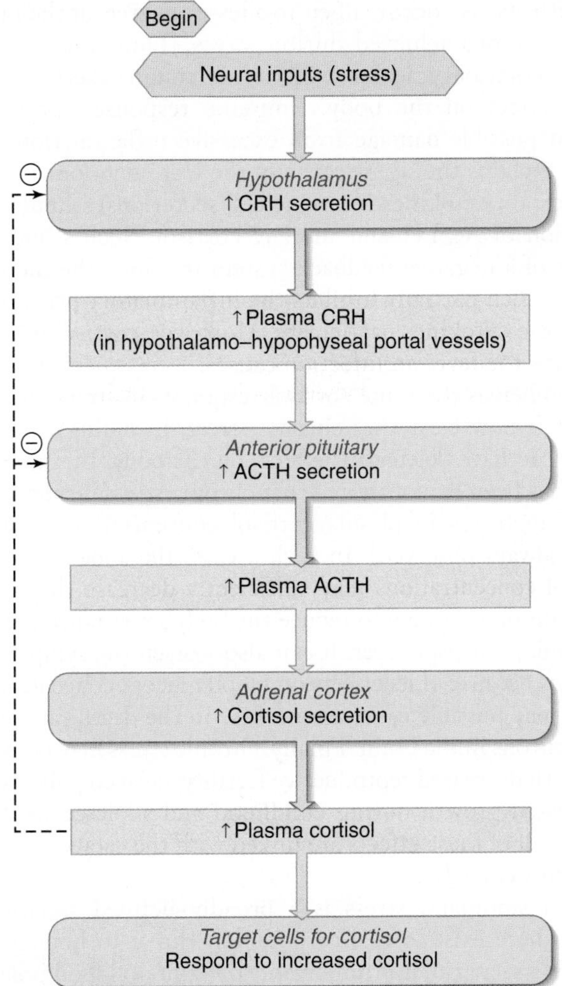

Figure 11.24 CRH-ACTH-cortisol pathway. Neural inputs include those related to stressful stimuli and nonstress inputs like circadian rhythms. Cortisol exerts a negative feedback control (⊖ symbols) over the system by acting on (1) the hypothalamus to inhibit CRH synthesis and secretion and (2) the anterior pituitary gland to inhibit ACTH production.

PHYSIOLOGICAL INQUIRY

- What hormonal changes in this pathway would be expected if a patient developed a benign tumor of the left adrenal cortex that secreted extremely large amounts of cortisol in the absence of external stimulation? What might happen to the right adrenal gland?

Answer can be found at end of chapter.

increases in response to stress and which may reach the anterior pituitary gland either from the general circulation or by the short portal vessels shown in Figure 11.13. Some of the cytokines (secretions from cells that comprise the immune system, Chapter 18) also stimulate ACTH secretion both directly and by stimulating the secretion of CRH. These cytokines provide a means for eliciting an endocrine stress response when the immune system is stimulated in, for example, systemic infection. The possible significance of this relationship for immune function is described next and in additional detail in Chapter 18.

11.13 Physiological Functions of Cortisol

Although the effects of cortisol are most dramatically illustrated during the response to stress, cortisol is always produced by the adrenal cortex and exerts many important actions even in nonstress situations. For example, cortisol has permissive actions on the reactivity to epinephrine and norepinephrine of smooth muscle cells that surround the lumen of blood vessels such as arterioles. Partly for this reason, therefore, cortisol helps maintain normal blood pressure. Likewise, cortisol is required to maintain the cellular concentrations of certain enzymes involved in metabolic homeostasis. These enzymes are expressed primarily in the liver, and they act to increase hepatic glucose production between meals, thereby preventing plasma glucose concentrations from significantly decreasing below normal.

Two important systemic actions of cortisol are its anti-inflammatory and anti-immune functions. The mechanisms by which cortisol inhibits immune system function are numerous and complex. Cortisol inhibits the production of leukotrienes and prostaglandins, both of which are involved in inflammation. Cortisol also stabilizes lysosomal membranes in damaged cells, preventing the release of their proteolytic contents. In addition, cortisol reduces capillary permeability in injured areas (thereby reducing fluid leakage to the interstitium), and it suppresses the growth and function of certain key immune cells such as lymphocytes. Thus, cortisol may serve as a "brake" on the immune system, which may overreact to minor infections in the absence of cortisol. Indeed, in diseases in which cortisol concentrations in the blood are greatly decreased, an increased incidence of autoimmune disease has been reported. Such diseases are characterized by a person's immune system launching an attack against one or more tissues of one's own body.

During fetal and neonatal life, cortisol is also an extremely important developmental hormone. It has been implicated in the proper differentiation of numerous tissues and glands, including various parts of the brain, the adrenal medulla, the intestine, and the lungs. In the last case, cortisol is very important for the production of surfactant, a substance that reduces surface tension in the lungs, thereby making it easier for the lungs to inflate (see Chapter 13).

Thus, although it is common to define the actions of cortisol in the context of the stress response, it is worth remembering that the maintenance of homeostasis in the absence of external stresses is also a critical function of cortisol.

11.14 Functions of Cortisol in Stress

Table 11.3 summarizes the major effects of increased plasma concentrations of cortisol during stress. The effects on organic metabolism are to mobilize energy sources to increase the plasma concentrations of amino acids, glucose, glycerol, and free fatty acids. These effects are ideally suited to meet a stressful situation. First, an animal faced with a potential threat is often forced to forgo eating, making these metabolic changes adaptive for coping with stress while fasting. Second, the amino acids liberated by catabolism of body protein not

TABLE 11.3	Effects of Increased Plasma Cortisol Concentration During Stress

I. Effects on organic metabolism
   A. Stimulation of protein catabolism in bone, lymph, muscle, and elsewhere
   B. Stimulation of liver uptake of amino acids and their conversion to glucose (gluconeogenesis)
   C. Maintenance of plasma glucose concentrations
   D. Stimulation of triglyceride catabolism in adipose tissue, with release of glycerol and fatty acids into the blood

II. Enhanced vascular reactivity (increased ability to maintain vasoconstriction in response to norepinephrine and other stimuli)

III. Unidentified protective effects against the damaging influences of stress

IV. Inhibition of inflammation and specific immune responses

V. Inhibition of nonessential functions (e.g., reproduction and growth)

only provide a potential source of glucose, via hepatic gluconeogenesis, but also constitute a potential source of amino acids for tissue repair should injury occur.

A few of the medically important implications of these cortisol-induced effects on organic metabolism are as follows. (1) Any patient who is ill or is subjected to surgery catabolizes considerable quantities of body protein; (2) a person with diabetes mellitus who suffers an infection requires more insulin than usual; and (3) a child subjected to severe stress of any kind may show a decreased rate of growth.

Cortisol has important effects during stress other than those on organic metabolism. For example, it increases the ability of vascular smooth muscle to contract in response to norepinephrine, thereby improving cardiovascular performance.

As item III in Table 11.3 notes, we still do not know the other reasons that increased cortisol is so important for the body's optimal response to stress, that is, for its ability to resist the damaging influences of stress. What is clear is that a person exposed to severe stress can die, usually of circulatory failure, if his or her plasma cortisol concentration is abnormally low; the complete absence of cortisol is always fatal.

Effect IV in Table 11.3 reflects the fact that administration of large amounts of cortisol or its synthetic analogs profoundly reduces the inflammatory response to injury or infection. Because of this effect, cortisol and its synthetic analogs are a valuable tool in the treatment of ***allergy***, ***arthritis*** (inflammation of the joints), other inflammatory diseases, and graft rejection (all of which are discussed in detail in Chapter 18). These anti-inflammatory and anti-immune effects have generally been classified among the various pharmacological effects of cortisol because it was assumed they could be achieved only by very large doses of administered glucocorticoids. It is now clear, however, that such effects also occur, albeit to a lesser degree, at the plasma concentrations achieved during stress. Thus, the increased plasma cortisol typical of infection or trauma exerts a dampening effect on the body's immune responses, protecting against possible damage from excessive inflammation. This effect explains the significance of the fact, mentioned earlier, that certain cytokines (immune cell secretions) stimulate the secretion of ACTH and thereby cortisol. Such stimulation is part of a negative feedback system in which the increased cortisol then partially inhibits the inflammatory processes in which the cytokines participate. Moreover, cortisol normally dampens the fever an infection causes.

Whereas the acute cortisol responses to stress are adaptive, it is now clear that chronic stress, including emotional stress, can have deleterious effects on the body. In some studies, it has been demonstrated that chronic stress results in sustained increases in plasma cortisol concentrations (but this is not always observed). In such a case, the abnormally high cortisol concentrations may sufficiently decrease the activity of the immune system to reduce the body's resistance to infection and, perhaps, cancer. It can also worsen the symptoms of diabetes because of its effects on blood glucose concentrations, and it may possibly cause an increase in the death rate of certain neurons in the brain. Finally, chronic stress may be associated with decreased reproductive fertility, delayed puberty, and suppressed growth during childhood and adolescence. Some but not all of these effects are linked with the catabolic actions of glucocorticoids.

In summary, stress is a broadly defined situation in which there exists a real or potential threat to homeostasis. In such a scenario, it is important to maintain blood pressure, to provide extra energy sources in the blood, and to temporarily shut down nonessential functions. Cortisol is the most important hormone that carries out these activities. Cortisol enhances vascular reactivity, catabolizes protein and fat to provide energy, and inhibits growth and reproduction. The price the body pays during stress is that cortisol is strongly catabolic. Thus, cells of the immune system, bone, muscles, skin, and numerous other tissues undergo catabolism to provide substrates for gluconeogenesis. In the short term, this is not of any major consequence. Chronic exposure to stress, however, can lead to severe decreases in bone density, immune function, and reproductive fertility.

11.15 Adrenal Insufficiency and Cushing's Syndrome

Cortisol is one of several hormones essential for life. The absence of cortisol leads to the body's inability to maintain homeostasis, particularly when confronted with a stress such as infection, which is usually fatal within days without cortisol. The general term for any situation in which plasma concentrations of cortisol are chronically lower than normal is ***adrenal insufficiency.*** Patients with adrenal insufficiency have a diffuse array of symptoms, depending on the severity and cause of the disease. These patients typically report weakness, fatigue, and loss of appetite and weight.

Examination may reveal low blood pressure (in part because cortisol is needed to permit the full extent of the cardiovascular actions of epinephrine) and low blood sugar, especially after fasting (because of the loss of the normal metabolic actions of cortisol).

There are several causes of adrenal insufficiency. ***Primary adrenal insufficiency*** is due to a loss of adrenal cortical function, as may rarely occur, for example, when infectious diseases such as ***tuberculosis*** infiltrate the adrenal glands and destroy them. The adrenals can also (rarely) be destroyed by invasive tumors. Most commonly by far, however, the syndrome is due to autoimmune attack in which the immune system mistakenly recognizes some component of a person's own adrenal cells as "foreign." The resultant immune reaction causes inflammation and eventually the destruction of many of the cells of the adrenal glands. Because of this, all of the zones of the adrenal cortex are affected. Thus, not only cortisol but also aldosterone concentrations are decreased below normal in primary adrenal insufficiency. This decrease in aldosterone concentration creates the additional problem of an imbalance in Na^+, K^+, and water in the blood because aldosterone is a key regulator of those variables. The loss of salt and water balance may lead to ***hypotension*** (low blood pressure). Primary adrenal insufficiency from any of these causes is also known as ***Addison's disease,*** after the nineteenth-century physician who first discovered the syndrome.

The diagnosis of primary adrenal insufficiency is made by measuring plasma concentrations of cortisol. In primary adrenal insufficiency, cortisol concentrations are well below normal, whereas ACTH concentrations are greatly increased due to the loss of the negative feedback actions of cortisol. Treatment of this disease requires daily oral administration of glucocorticoids and mineralocorticoids. In addition, the patient must carefully monitor his or her diet to ensure an adequate consumption of carbohydrates and controlled K^+ and Na^+ intake.

Adrenal insufficiency can also be due to a deficiency of ACTH—***secondary adrenal insufficiency,*** which may arise from pituitary disease. Its symptoms are often less dramatic than primary adrenal insufficiency because aldosterone secretion, which does not rely on ACTH, is maintained by other mechanisms.

Adrenal insufficiency can be life threatening if not treated aggressively. The flip side of this disorder—*excess* glucocorticoids—is usually not as immediately dangerous but can also be very severe. In ***Cushing's syndrome,*** even the nonstressed individual has excess cortisol in the blood. The cause may be a primary defect (e.g., a cortisol-secreting tumor of the adrenal) or may be secondary (usually due to an ACTH-secreting tumor of the anterior pituitary gland). In the latter case, the condition is known as ***Cushing's disease,*** which accounts for most cases of Cushing's syndrome. The increased blood concentrations of cortisol, particularly at night when cortisol is usually low, tend to promote uncontrolled catabolism of bone, muscle, skin, and other organs. As a result, bone strength diminishes and can even lead to ***osteoporosis*** (loss of bone mass), muscles weaken, and the skin becomes thinned and easily bruised. The increased catabolism may produce such a large quantity of precursors for hepatic gluconeogenesis that the blood sugar concentration increases to that observed in diabetes mellitus. A person with Cushing's syndrome, therefore, may show some of the same symptoms as a person with diabetes. Equally troubling is the possibility of ***immunosuppression,*** which may be brought about by the anti-immune actions of cortisol. Cushing's syndrome is often associated with loss of fat mass from the extremities and with redistribution of the fat in the trunk, face, and the back of the neck. Combined with an increased appetite, often triggered by high concentrations of cortisol, this results in obesity and a characteristic facial appearance in many patients (**Figure 11.25**). A further problem associated with Cushing's syndrome is the possibility of developing ***hypertension*** (high blood pressure). This is due not to increased aldosterone production but instead to the pharmacological effects of cortisol, because at high concentrations, cortisol exerts aldosterone-like actions on the kidney, resulting in salt and water retention, which contributes to hypertension.

Treatment of Cushing's syndrome depends on the cause. In Cushing's disease, for example, surgical removal of the pituitary tumor, if possible, is the best alternative.

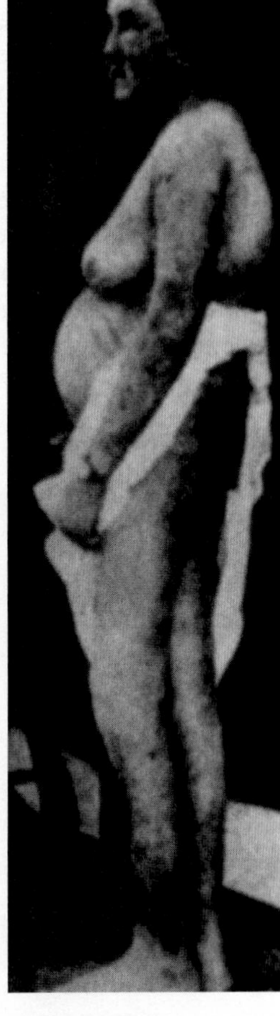

Figure 11.25 A young patient from the original series of Harvey Cushing. *Left:* Before onset of disease. *Right:* After development of Cushing's syndrome.

Of importance is the fact that glucocorticoids are often used therapeutically to treat inflammation, lung disease, and other disorders. If glucocorticoids are administered at a high enough dosage for long periods, the side effect of such treatment can be Cushing's syndrome.

11.16 Other Hormones Released During Stress

Other hormones that are usually released during many kinds of stress are aldosterone, vasopressin, growth hormone, glucagon, and beta-endorphin (which is coreleased from the anterior pituitary gland with ACTH). Insulin secretion usually decreases. Vasopressin and aldosterone act to retain water and Na^+ within the body, an important response in the face of potential losses by dehydration, hemorrhage, or sweating. The overall effects of the changes in growth hormone, glucagon, and insulin are, like those of cortisol and epinephrine, to mobilize energy stores and increase the plasma concentration of glucose. The role, if any, of beta-endorphin in stress may be related to its painkilling effects.

In addition, the sympathetic nervous system plays a key role in the stress response. Activation of the sympathetic nervous system during stress is often termed the fight-or-flight response, as described in Chapter 6. A list of the major effects of increased sympathetic activity, including secretion of epinephrine from the adrenal medulla, almost constitutes a guide to how to meet emergencies in which physical activity may be required and bodily damage may occur (**Table 11.4**).

This list of hormones whose secretion rates are altered by stress is by no means complete. It is likely that the secretion of almost every known hormone may be influenced by stress. For example, prolactin is increased, although the adaptive significance of this change is unclear. By contrast, the pituitary gonadotropins and the sex steroids are decreased. As noted previously, reproduction is not an essential function during a crisis.

TABLE 11.4 Actions of the Sympathetic Nervous System, Including Epinephrine Secreted by the Adrenal Medulla, During Stress
Increased hepatic and muscle glycogenolysis (provides a quick source of glucose)
Increased breakdown of adipose tissue triglyceride (provides a supply of glycerol for gluconeogenesis and of fatty acids for oxidation)
Increased cardiac function (e.g., increased heart rate)
Diversion of blood from viscera to skeletal muscles by means of vasoconstriction in the former beds and vasodilation in the latter
Increased lung ventilation by stimulating brain breathing centers and dilating airways

SECTION D SUMMARY

Physiological Functions of Cortisol

I. Cortisol is released from the adrenal cortex upon stimulation with ACTH. ACTH, in turn, is stimulated by the release of corticotropin-releasing hormone (CRH) from the hypothalamus.

II. The physiological functions of cortisol are to maintain the responsiveness of target cells to epinephrine and norepinephrine, to provide a "check" on the immune system, to participate in energy homeostasis, and to promote normal differentiation of tissues during fetal life.

Functions of Cortisol in Stress

I. The stimulus that activates the CRH-ACTH-cortisol pathway is stress, which encompasses a wide array of sensory and physical inputs that disrupt, or potentially disrupt, homeostasis.

II. In response to stress, the usual physiological functions of cortisol are enhanced as cortisol concentrations in the plasma increase. Thus, gluconeogenesis, lipolysis, and inhibition of insulin actions increase. This results in increased blood concentrations of energy sources (glucose, fatty acids) required to cope with stressful situations.

III. High cortisol concentrations also inhibit "nonessential" processes, such as reproduction, during stressful situations and inhibit immune function.

Adrenal Insufficiency and Cushing's Syndrome

I. Adrenal insufficiency may result from adrenal destruction (primary adrenal insufficiency, or Addison's disease) or from hyposecretion of ACTH (secondary adrenal insufficiency).

II. Adrenal insufficiency is associated with decreased ability to maintain blood pressure (due to loss of aldosterone) and blood sugar. It may be fatal if untreated.

III. Cushing's syndrome is the result of chronically elevated plasma cortisol concentration. When the cause of the increased cortisol is secondary to an ACTH-secreting pituitary tumor, the condition is known as Cushing's disease.

IV. Cushing's syndrome is associated with hypertension, high blood sugar, redistribution of body fat, obesity, and muscle and bone weakness. If untreated, it can also lead to immunosuppression.

Other Hormones Released During Stress

I. In addition to CRH, ACTH, and cortisol, several other hormones are released during stress. Beta-endorphin is coreleased with ACTH and may act to reduce pain. Vasopressin stimulates ACTH secretion and also acts on the kidney to increase water retention. Other hormones that are increased in the blood by stress are aldosterone, growth hormone, and glucagon. Insulin secretion, by contrast, decreases during stress.

II. Epinephrine is secreted from the adrenal medulla during stress in response to stimulation from the sympathetic nervous system. The norepinephrine from sympathetic neuron terminals, combined with the circulating epinephrine, prepare the body for stress in several ways. These include increased heart rate and heart pumping strength, increased ventilation, increased shunting of blood to skeletal muscle, and increased generation of energy sources that are released into the blood.

SECTION D REVIEW QUESTIONS

1. Diagram the CRH-ACTH-cortisol pathway.
2. List the physiological functions of cortisol.

3. Define *stress*, and list the functions of cortisol during stress.
4. List the major effects of activation of the sympathetic nervous system during stress.
5. Contrast the symptoms of adrenal insufficiency and Cushing's syndrome.

SECTION D KEY TERMS

stress 344

SECTION D CLINICAL TERMS

Addison's disease 347
adrenal insufficiency 346
allergy 346
arthritis 346
Cushing's disease 347
Cushing's syndrome 347
hypertension 347
hypotension 347
immunosuppression 347
osteoporosis 347
primary adrenal insufficiency 347
secondary adrenal insufficiency 347
tuberculosis 347

SECTION E Endocrine Control of Growth

One of the major functions of the endocrine system is to control growth. At least a dozen hormones directly or indirectly (e.g., hypophysiotropic hormones) play important roles in stimulating or inhibiting growth. This complex process is also influenced by genetics and a variety of environmental factors, including nutrition, and provides an illustration of the general principle of physiology that most physiological functions are controlled by multiple regulatory systems, often working in opposition. The growth process involves cell division and net protein synthesis throughout the body, but a person's height is determined specifically by bone growth, particularly of the vertebral column and legs. We first provide an overview of bone and the growth process before describing the roles of hormones in determining growth rates.

11.17 Bone Growth

Bone is a living tissue consisting of a protein (collagen) matrix upon which calcium salts, particularly calcium phosphates, are deposited. A growing long bone is divided, for descriptive purposes, into the ends, or **epiphyses,** and the remainder, the **shaft.** The portion of each epiphysis in contact with the shaft is a plate of actively proliferating cartilage (connective tissue composed of collagen and other fibrous proteins) called the **epiphyseal growth plate** (**Figure 11.26**). **Osteoblasts,** the bone-forming cells at the shaft edge of the epiphyseal growth plate, convert the cartilaginous tissue at this edge to bone, while cells called **chondrocytes** simultaneously lay down new cartilage in the interior of the plate. In this manner, the epiphyseal growth plate widens and is gradually pushed away from the center of the bony shaft as the shaft lengthens.

Linear growth of the shaft can continue as long as the epiphyseal growth plates exist but ceases when the growth plates themselves are converted to bone as a result of other hormonal influences at puberty. This is known as **epiphyseal closure** and occurs at different times in different bones. Thus, a person's **bone age** can be determined by x-raying the bones and determining which ones have undergone epiphyseal closure.

As shown in **Figure 11.27,** children manifest two periods of rapid increase in height, the first during the first 2 years of life and the second during puberty. Note that increase in height is not necessarily correlated with the rates of growth of specific organs.

The pubertal growth spurt lasts several years in both sexes, but growth during this period is greater in boys. In addition, boys grow more before puberty because they begin puberty approximately 2 years later than girls. These factors account for the differences in average height between men and women.

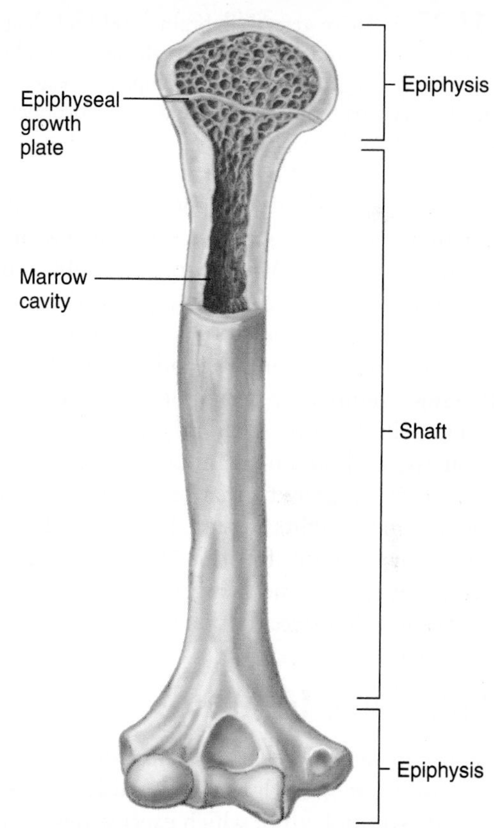

Figure 11.26 AP|R Anatomy of a long bone during growth.

11.18 Environmental Factors Influencing Growth

Adequate nutrition and good health are the primary environmental factors influencing growth. Lack of sufficient amounts of protein, fatty acids, vitamins, or minerals interferes with growth.

The growth-inhibiting effects of malnutrition can be seen at any time of development but are most profound when they occur early in life. For this reason, maternal malnutrition may cause growth retardation in the fetus. Because low birth

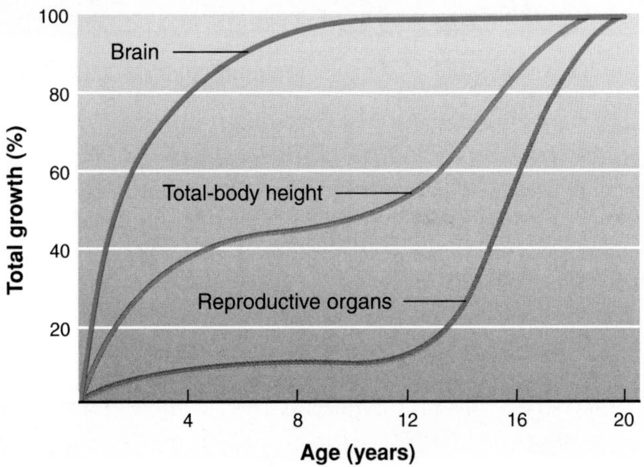

Figure 11.27 Relative growth in brain, total-body height (a measure of long-bone and vertebral growth), and reproductive organs. Note that brain growth is nearly complete by age 5, whereas maximal height (maximal bone lengthening) and reproductive-organ size are not reached until the late teens.

weight is strongly associated with increased infant mortality, prenatal malnutrition causes increased numbers of prenatal and early postnatal deaths. Moreover, irreversible stunting of brain development may be caused by prenatal malnutrition. During infancy and childhood, too, malnutrition can interfere with both intellectual development and total-body growth.

Following a temporary period of stunted growth due to malnutrition or illness, and given proper nutrition and recovery from illness, a child can manifest a remarkable growth spurt called **catch-up growth** that brings the child to within the range of normal heights expected for his or her age. The mechanisms that account for this accelerated growth are unknown, but recent evidence suggests that it may be related to the rate of stem cell differentiation within the growth plates.

11.19 Hormonal Influences on Growth

The hormones most important to human growth are growth hormone, insulin-like growth factors 1 and 2, T_3, insulin, testosterone, and estradiol, all of which exert widespread effects. In addition to all these hormones, a large group of peptide **growth factors** exert effects, most of them acting in a paracrine or autocrine manner to stimulate differentiation and/or cell division of certain cell types. The general term for a molecule that stimulates cell division is mitogen.

The various hormones and growth factors do not all stimulate growth at the same periods of life. For example, fetal growth is less dependent on fetal growth hormone, the thyroid hormones, and the sex steroids than are the growth periods that occur during childhood and adolescence.

Growth Hormone and Insulin-Like Growth Factors

Growth hormone, secreted by the anterior pituitary gland, has little effect on fetal growth but is the most important hormone for postnatal growth. Its major growth-promoting effect is stimulation of cell division in its many target tissues. Thus, growth hormone promotes bone lengthening by stimulating maturation and cell division of the chondrocytes in the epiphyseal plates, thereby continuously widening the plates and providing more cartilaginous material for bone formation.

Importantly, growth hormone exerts most of its mitogenic effect not *directly* on cells but *indirectly* through the mediation of the mitogenic hormone IGF-1, whose synthesis and release by the liver are induced by growth hormone. Despite some structural similarities to insulin (from which its name is derived), this messenger has its own unique effects distinct from those of insulin. Under the influence of growth hormone, IGF-1 is secreted by the liver, enters the blood, and functions as a hormone. In addition, growth hormone stimulates many other types of cells, including bone, to secrete IGF-1, where it functions as an autocrine or paracrine substance.

Current concepts of how growth hormone and IGF-1 interact on the epiphyseal plates of bone are as follows. (1) Growth hormone stimulates the chondrocyte precursor cells (prechondrocytes) and/or young differentiating chondrocytes in the epiphyseal plates to differentiate into chondrocytes. (2) During this differentiation, the cells begin both to secrete IGF-1 and to become responsive to IGF-1. (3) The IGF-1 then acts as an autocrine or paracrine substance (probably along with blood-borne IGF-1) to stimulate the differentiating chondrocytes to undergo cell division.

The importance of IGF-1 in mediating the major growth-promoting effect of growth hormone is illustrated by the fact that ***short stature*** can be caused not only by decreased growth hormone secretion but also by decreased production of IGF-1 or failure of the tissues to respond to IGF-1. For example, one rare form of short stature (called ***growth hormone–insensitivity syndrome***) is due to a genetic mutation that causes a change in the growth hormone receptor such that it fails to respond to growth hormone (an example of hyporesponsiveness). The result is failure to produce IGF-1 in response to growth hormone, and a consequent decreased growth rate in a child.

The secretion and activity of IGF-1 can be influenced by the nutritional status of the individual and by many hormones other than growth hormone. For example, malnutrition during childhood inhibits the production of IGF-1 even if plasma growth hormone concentration is increased.

In addition to its specific growth-promoting effect on cell division via IGF-1, growth hormone directly stimulates protein synthesis in various tissues and organs, particularly muscle. It does this by increasing amino acid uptake and both the synthesis and activity of ribosomes. All of these events are essential for protein synthesis. This anabolic effect on protein metabolism facilitates the ability of tissues and organs to enlarge. Growth hormone also plays a role in energy homeostasis. It does this in part by facilitating the breakdown of triglycerides that are stored in adipose cells, which then release fatty acids into the blood. It also stimulates gluconeogenesis in the liver and inhibits the ability of insulin to promote glucose transport into cells. Growth hormone, therefore, tends to increase circulating energy sources. Not surprisingly, therefore, situations such as exercise, stress, or fasting, for which increased energy availability is beneficial, result in stimulation of growth hormone secretion into the blood. The metabolic effects of growth hormone are important throughout life and continue in adulthood long after bone growth has ceased. **Table 11.5** summarizes some of the major effects of growth hormone.

Figure 11.28 shows the control of growth hormone secretion. Briefly, the control system begins with two of the hormones secreted by the hypothalamus. Growth hormone secretion is stimulated by growth hormone–releasing hormone (GHRH) and inhibited by somatostatin (SST). As a result of changes in these two signals, which are usually 180 degrees out of phase with each other (i.e., one is high when the other is low), growth hormone secretion occurs in episodic bursts and manifests a striking daily rhythm. During most of the day, little or no growth hormone is secreted, although bursts may be elicited by certain stimuli, including stress, hypoglycemia, and exercise. In contrast, 1 to 2 hours after a person falls asleep, one or more larger, prolonged bursts of secretion may occur. The negative feedback controls that growth hormone and IGF-1 exert on the hypothalamus and anterior pituitary gland are summarized in Figure 11.28.

TABLE 11.5 Major Effects of Growth Hormone

I. Promotes growth: Induces precursor cells in bone and other tissues to differentiate and secrete insulin-like growth factor 1 (IGF-1), which stimulates cell division. Also stimulates liver to secrete IGF-1.

II. Stimulates protein synthesis, predominantly in muscle.

III. Anti-insulin effects (particularly at high concentrations):
- A. Renders adipocytes more responsive to stimuli that induce breakdown of triglycerides, releasing fatty acids into the blood.
- B. Stimulates gluconeogenesis.
- C. Reduces the ability of insulin to stimulate glucose uptake by adipose and muscle cells, resulting in higher blood glucose concentrations.

In addition to the hypothalamic controls, a variety of hormones—notably, the sex steroids, insulin, and thyroid hormones—influence the secretion of growth hormone. The net result of all these inputs is that the secretion rate of growth hormone is highest during adolescence (the period of most rapid growth), next highest in children, and lowest in adults. The decreased growth hormone secretion associated with aging is responsible, in part, for the decrease in lean-body and bone mass, the expansion of adipose tissue, and the thinning of the skin that occur as people age.

The ready availability of human growth hormone produced by recombinant DNA technology has greatly facilitated the treatment of children with short stature due to growth hormone deficiency. Controversial at present is the administration of growth hormone to short children who do not have growth hormone deficiency, to athletes in an attempt to increase muscle mass, and to elderly persons to reverse growth hormone–related aging changes. It should be clear from Table 11.5 that administration of GH to an otherwise healthy individual (such as an athlete) can lead to serious side effects. Abuse of GH in such situations can lead to symptoms similar to those of diabetes mellitus, as well as numerous other problems. The consequences of chronically elevated growth

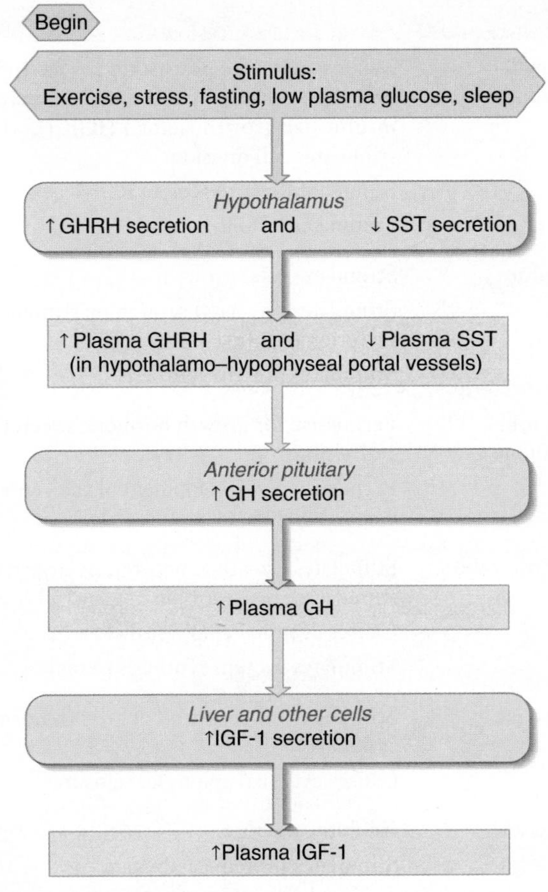

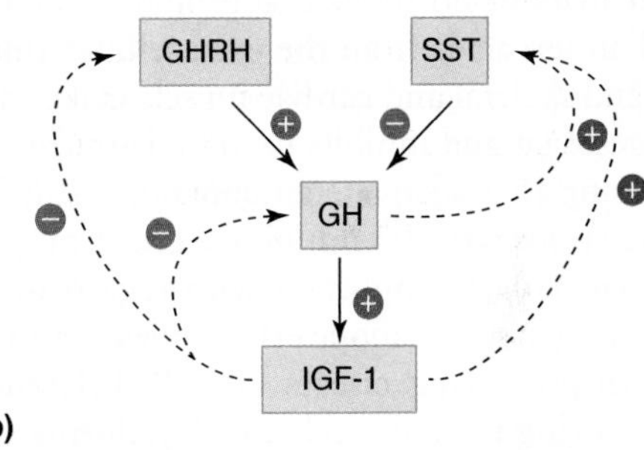

Figure 11.28 Hormonal pathways controlling the secretion of growth hormone (GH) and insulin-like growth factor 1 (IGF-1). (a) Various stimuli can increase GH and IGF-1 concentrations by increasing GHRH secretion and decreasing SST secretion. (b) Feedback control of GH and IGF-1 secretion is accomplished by inhibition (⊖ symbol) of GHRH and GH, and stimulation (⊕ symbol) of SST. Not shown in the figure is that several hormones not in the sequence (e.g., the thyroid hormones) influence growth hormone secretion via effects on the hypothalamus and/or anterior pituitary gland.

PHYSIOLOGICAL INQUIRY

- What might happen to plasma concentrations of GH in a person who was intravenously infused with a solution containing a high concentration of glucose, such that his plasma glucose concentrations were significantly increased?

Answer can be found at end of chapter.

hormone concentrations are dramatically illustrated in the disease called acromegaly (described later in this chapter).

As noted earlier, the role of GH in fetal growth, while still under investigation, appears not to be nearly as significant as at later stages of postnatal life. IGF-1, however, is required for normal fetal total-body growth and, specifically, for normal maturation of the fetal nervous system. The chief stimulus for IGF-1 secretion during prenatal life appears to be placental lactogen, a hormone released by cells of the placenta, which shares sequence similarity with growth hormone.

Finally, it should be noted that there is another messenger—**insulin-like growth factor 2 (IGF-2)**, which is closely related to IGF-1. IGF-2, the secretion of which is *independent* of growth hormone, is also a crucial mitogen during the prenatal period. It continues to be secreted throughout life, but its postnatal function is not definitively known. Recent evidence suggests a link between IGF-2 concentrations and the maintenance of skeletal muscle mass and strength in elderly persons.

Thyroid Hormone

Thyroid hormone is essential for normal growth because it is required for the synthesis of growth hormone. T_3 also has direct actions on bone, where it stimulates chondrocyte differentiation, growth of new blood vessels in developing bone, and responsiveness of bone cells to other growth factors such as fibroblast growth factor. Consequently, infants and children with hypothyroidism have slower growth rates than would be predicted.

Insulin

The major actions of insulin are described in Chapter 16. Insulin is an anabolic hormone that promotes the transport of glucose and amino acids from the extracellular fluid into adipose tissue and skeletal and cardiac muscle cells. Insulin stimulates storage of fat and inhibits protein degradation. Thus, it is not surprising that adequate amounts of insulin are necessary for normal growth. Its inhibitory effect on protein degradation is particularly important with regard to growth. In addition to this general anabolic effect, however, insulin exerts direct growth-promoting effects on cell differentiation and cell division during fetal life and, possibly, during childhood.

Sex Steroids

As Chapter 17 will explain, sex steroid secretion (testosterone in the male and estrogens in the female) begins to increase between the ages of 8 and 10 and reaches a plateau over the next 5 to 10 years. A normal pubertal growth spurt, which reflects growth of the long bones and vertebrae, requires this increased production of the sex steroids. The major growth-promoting effect of the sex steroids is to stimulate the secretion of growth hormone and IGF-1.

Unlike growth hormone, however, the sex steroids not only *stimulate* bone growth but ultimately *stop* it by inducing epiphyseal closure. The dual effects of the sex steroids explain the pattern seen in adolescence—rapid lengthening of the bones culminating in complete cessation of growth for life.

In addition to these dual effects on bone, testosterone—but not estrogen—exerts a direct anabolic effect on protein synthesis in many nonreproductive organs and tissues of the body. This accounts, at least in part, for the increased muscle mass of men in comparison to women. This effect of testosterone is also why athletes sometimes use androgens called ***anabolic steroids*** in an attempt to increase muscle mass and strength. These steroids include testosterone, synthetic androgens, and the hormones dehydroepiandrosterone (DHEA) and androstenedione. However, these steroids have multiple potential toxic side effects, such as liver damage, increased risk of prostate cancer, and infertility. Moreover, in females, they can produce virilization.

Cortisol

Cortisol, the major hormone the adrenal cortex secretes in response to stress, can have potent *antigrowth* effects under certain conditions. When present in high concentrations, it inhibits DNA synthesis and stimulates protein catabolism in many organs, and it inhibits bone growth. Moreover, it breaks down bone and inhibits the secretion of growth hormone. For all these reasons, in children, the increase in plasma cortisol that accompanies infections and other stressors is, at least in part, responsible for the decreased growth that occurs with chronic illness. One of the hallmarks of Cushing's syndrome in children is a dramatic decrease in the rate of linear growth. Furthermore, the administration of pharmacological glucocorticoid therapy for asthma or other disorders may decrease linear growth in children in a dose-related way.

This completes our survey of the major hormones that affect growth. **Table 11.6** summarizes their actions.

TABLE 11.6 Major Hormones Influencing Growth

Hormone	Principal Actions
Growth hormone	Major stimulus of postnatal growth: Induces precursor cells to differentiate and secrete insulin-like growth factor 1 (IGF-1), which stimulates cell division Stimulates liver to secrete IGF-1 Stimulates protein synthesis
Insulin	Stimulates fetal growth Stimulates postnatal growth by stimulating secretion of IGF-1 Stimulates protein synthesis
Thyroid hormone	Permissive for growth hormone's secretion and actions Permissive for development of the central nervous system
Testosterone	Stimulates growth at puberty, in large part by stimulating the secretion of growth hormone Causes eventual epiphyseal closure Stimulates protein synthesis in male
Estrogen	Stimulates the secretion of growth hormone at puberty Causes eventual epiphyseal closure
Cortisol	Inhibits growth Stimulates protein catabolism

SECTION E SUMMARY

Bone Growth

I. A bone lengthens as osteoblasts at the shaft edge of the epiphyseal growth plates convert cartilage to bone while new cartilage is simultaneously being laid down in the plates.

II. Growth ceases when the plates are completely converted to bone.

Environmental Factors Influencing Growth

I. The major environmental factors influencing growth are nutrition and disease.

II. Maternal malnutrition during pregnancy may produce irreversible growth stunting and mental deficiency in offspring.

Hormonal Influences on Growth

I. Growth hormone is the major stimulus of postnatal growth.
   a. It stimulates the release of IGF-1 from the liver and many other cells, and IGF-1 then acts locally (and perhaps also as a hormone) to stimulate cell division.
   b. Growth hormone also acts directly on cells to stimulate protein synthesis.
   c. Growth hormone secretion is highest during adolescence.

II. Because thyroid hormone is required for growth hormone synthesis and the growth-promoting effects of this hormone, it is essential for normal growth during childhood and adolescence. It is also permissive for brain development during infancy.

III. Insulin stimulates growth mainly during fetal life.

IV. Mainly by stimulating growth hormone secretion, testosterone and estrogen promote bone growth during adolescence, but these hormones also cause epiphyseal closure. Testosterone also stimulates protein synthesis.

V. High concentrations of cortisol inhibit growth and stimulate protein catabolism.

SECTION E REVIEW QUESTIONS

1. Describe the process by which bone lengthens.
2. What are the effects of malnutrition on growth?
3. List the major hormones that control growth.
4. Describe the relationship between growth hormone and IGF-1 and the roles of each in growth.
5. What are the effects of growth hormone on protein synthesis?
6. What is the status of growth hormone secretion at different stages of life?
7. State the effects of the thyroid hormones on growth.
8. Describe the effects of testosterone on growth, cessation of growth, and protein synthesis. Which of these effects does estrogen also exert?
9. What is the effect of cortisol on growth?
10. Give two ways in which short stature can occur.

SECTION E KEY TERMS

bone age 349
catch-up growth 350
chondrocyte 349
epiphyseal closure 349
epiphyseal growth plate 349
epiphysis 349
growth factor 350
insulin-like growth factor 2 (IGF-2) 352
osteoblast 349
shaft 349

SECTION E CLINICAL TERMS

anabolic steroid 352
growth hormone–insensitivity syndrome 350
short stature 350

SECTION F
Endocrine Control of Ca^{2+} Homeostasis

Many of the hormones of the body control functions that, though important, are not necessarily vital for survival, such as growth. By contrast, some hormones control functions so vital that the absence of the hormone would be catastrophic, even life threatening. One such function is calcium homeostasis. Calcium exists in the body fluids in its soluble, ionized form (Ca^{2+}) and bound to proteins. For simplicity in this chapter, we will refer hereafter to the physiologically active, ionic form of Ca^{2+}.

Extracellular Ca^{2+} concentration normally remains within a narrow homeostatic range. Large deviations in either direction can disrupt neurological and muscular activity, among others. For example, a low plasma Ca^{2+} concentration increases the excitability of neuronal and muscle plasma membranes. A high plasma Ca^{2+} concentration causes cardiac arrhythmias and depresses neuromuscular excitability via effects on membrane potential. In this section, we discuss the mechanisms by which Ca^{2+} homeostasis is achieved and maintained by actions of hormones.

11.20 Effector Sites for Ca^{2+} Homeostasis

Ca^{2+} homeostasis depends on the interplay among bone, the kidneys, and the gastrointestinal tract. The activities of the gastrointestinal tract and kidneys determine the net intake and output of Ca^{2+} for the entire body and, thereby, the overall Ca^{2+} balance. In contrast, interchanges of Ca^{2+} between extracellular fluid and bone do not alter total-body balance but instead change the *distribution* of Ca^{2+} within the body. We begin, therefore, with a discussion of the cellular and mineral composition of bone.

Bone

Approximately 99% of total-body calcium is contained in bone. Therefore, the movement of Ca^{2+} into and out of bone is critical in controlling the plasma Ca^{2+} concentration.

Bone is a connective tissue made up of several cell types surrounded by a collagen matrix called **osteoid,** upon which

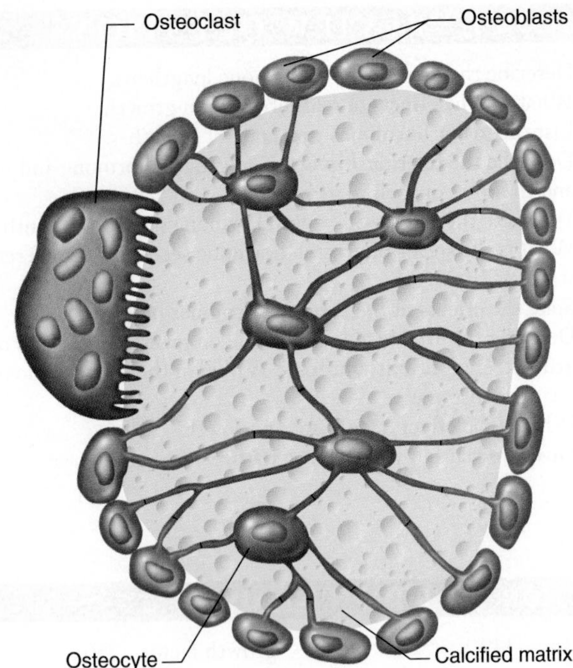

Figure 11.29 AP|R Cross section through a small portion of bone. The light tan area is mineralized osteoid. The osteocytes have long processes that extend through small canals and connect with each other and to osteoblasts via tight junctions. Adapted from Goodman.

are deposited minerals, particularly the crystals of calcium, phosphate, and hydroxyl ions known as **hydroxyapatite.** In some instances, bones have central marrow cavities where blood cells form. Approximately one-third of a bone, by weight, is osteoid, and two-thirds is mineral (the bone cells contribute negligible weight).

The three types of bone cells involved in bone formation and breakdown are osteoblasts, osteocytes, and osteoclasts (**Figure 11.29**). As described in Section E, osteoblasts are the bone-forming cells. They secrete collagen to form a surrounding matrix, which then becomes calcified, a process called **mineralization.** Once surrounded by calcified matrix, the osteoblasts are called **osteocytes.** The osteocytes have long cytoplasmic processes that extend throughout the bone and form tight junctions with other osteocytes. **Osteoclasts** are large, multinucleated cells that break down (resorb) previously formed bone by secreting hydrogen ions, which dissolve the crystals, and hydrolytic enzymes, which digest the osteoid.

Throughout life, bone is constantly remodeled by the osteoblasts (and osteocytes) and osteoclasts working together. Osteoclasts resorb old bone, and then osteoblasts move into the area and lay down new matrix, which becomes mineralized. This process depends in part on the stresses that gravity and muscle tension impose on the bones, stimulating osteoblastic activity. Many hormones, as summarized in **Table 11.7,** and a variety of autocrine or paracrine growth factors produced locally in the bone also play a role. Of the hormones listed, only parathyroid hormone (described later) is controlled primarily by the plasma Ca^{2+} concentration. Nonetheless, changes in the other listed hormones have important influences on bone mass and plasma Ca^{2+} concentration.

TABLE 11.7 Summary of Major Hormonal Influences on Bone Mass
Hormones That Favor Bone Formation and Increased Bone Mass
Insulin
Growth hormone
Insulin-like growth factor 1 (IGF-1)
Estrogen
Testosterone
Calcitonin
Hormones That Favor Increased Bone Resorption and Decreased Bone Mass
Parathyroid hormone (chronic elevations)
Cortisol
Thyroid hormone T_3

Kidneys

As you will learn in Chapter 14, the kidneys filter the blood and eliminate soluble wastes. In the process, cells in the tubules that make up the functional units of the kidneys recapture (reabsorb) most of the necessary solutes that were filtered, which minimizes their loss in the urine. Therefore, the urinary excretion of Ca^{2+} is the difference between the amount filtered into the tubules and the amount reabsorbed and returned to the blood. The control of Ca^{2+} excretion is exerted mainly on reabsorption. Reabsorption decreases when plasma Ca^{2+} concentration increases, and it increases when plasma Ca^{2+} decreases.

The hormonal controllers of Ca^{2+} also regulate phosphate ion balance. Phosphate ions, too, are subject to a combination of filtration and reabsorption, with the latter hormonally controlled.

Gastrointestinal Tract

The absorption of such solutes as Na^+ and K^+ from the gastrointestinal tract into the blood is normally about 100%. In contrast, a considerable amount of ingested Ca^{2+} is not absorbed from the small intestine and leaves the body along with the feces. Moreover, the active transport system that achieves Ca^{2+} absorption from the small intestine is under hormonal control. Thus, large regulated increases or decreases can occur in the amount of Ca^{2+} absorbed from the diet. Hormonal control of this absorptive process is the major means for regulating total-body-calcium balance, as we see next.

11.21 Hormonal Controls

The two major hormones that regulate plasma Ca^{2+} concentration are parathyroid hormone and 1,25-dihydroxyvitamin D. A third hormone, calcitonin, plays a limited role in humans, if any.

Parathyroid Hormone

Bone, kidneys, and the gastrointestinal tract are subject, directly or indirectly, to control by a protein hormone called **parathyroid hormone (PTH)**, which is produced

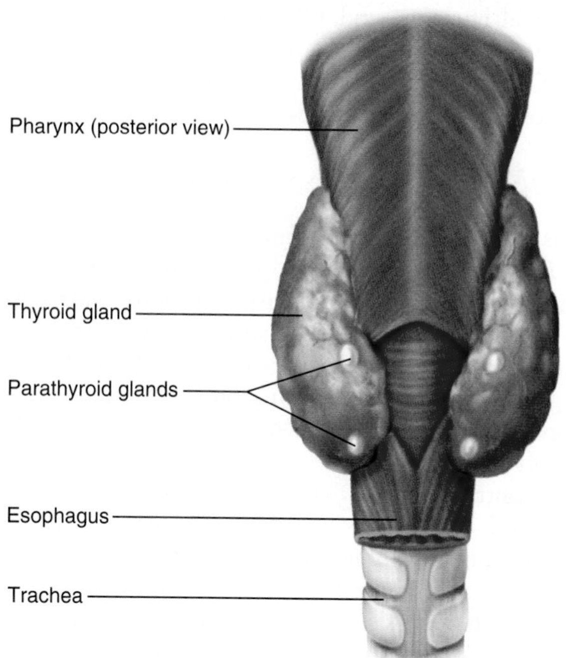

Figure 11.30 APR The parathyroid glands. There are usually four parathyroid glands embedded in the posterior surface of the thyroid gland.

by the **parathyroid glands.** These endocrine glands are in the neck, embedded in the posterior surface of the thyroid gland, but are distinct from it (**Figure 11.30**). Parathyroid hormone production is controlled by the extracellular Ca^{2+} concentration acting directly on the secretory cells via a plasma membrane Ca^{2+} receptor. *Decreased* plasma Ca^{2+} concentration *stimulates* parathyroid hormone secretion, and an *increased* plasma Ca^{2+} concentration does just the opposite.

Parathyroid hormone exerts multiple actions that increase extracellular Ca^{2+} concentration, thereby compensating for the decreased concentration that originally stimulated secretion of this hormone (**Figure 11.31**):

1. It directly increases the resorption of bone by osteoclasts, which causes calcium (and phosphate) ions to move from bone into extracellular fluid.
2. It directly stimulates the formation of 1,25-dihydroxyvitamin D, which then increases intestinal absorption of calcium (and phosphate) ions. Thus, the effect of parathyroid hormone on the intestines is indirect.
3. It directly increases Ca^{2+} reabsorption in the kidneys, thereby decreasing urinary Ca^{2+} excretion.
4. It directly *decreases* the reabsorption of phosphate ions in the kidneys, thereby increasing its excretion in the urine. This keeps plasma phosphate ions from increasing when parathyroid hormone causes an increased release of both calcium and phosphate ions from bone, and an increased production of 1,25-dihydroxyvitamin D leading to calcium and phosphate ion absorption in the intestine.

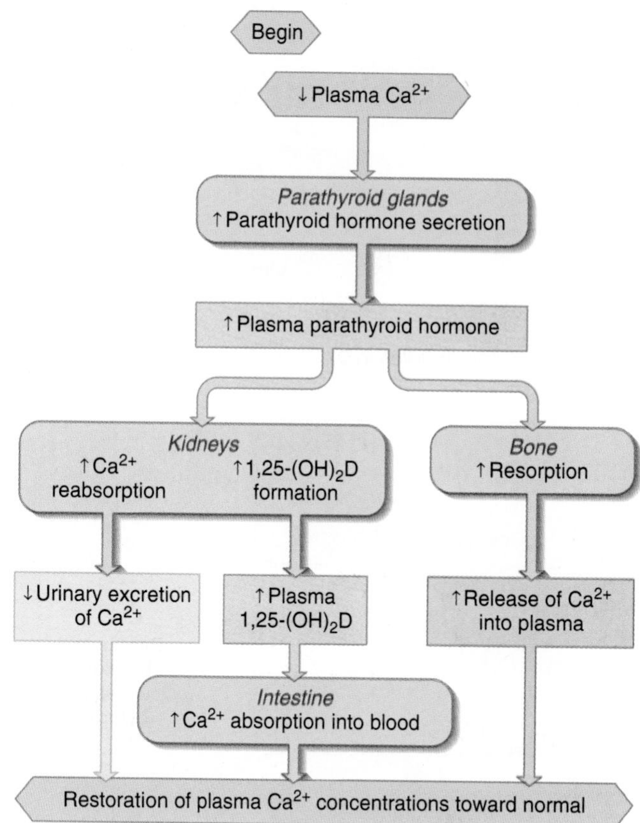

Figure 11.31 Mechanisms that allow parathyroid hormone to reverse a reduction in plasma Ca^{2+} concentration toward normal. See Figure 11.32 for a more complete description of 1,25-$(OH)_2D$ (1,25-dihydroxyvitamin D). Parathyroid hormone and 1,25- $(OH)_2D$ are also involved in the control of phosphate ion concentrations.

1,25-Dihydroxyvitamin D

The term **vitamin D** denotes a group of closely related compounds. **Vitamin D_3 (cholecalciferol)** is formed by the action of ultraviolet radiation from sunlight on a cholesterol derivative (7-dehydrocholesterol) in skin. **Vitamin D_2 (ergocalciferol)** is derived from plants. Both can be found in vitamin pills and enriched foods and are collectively called vitamin D.

Because of clothing, climate, and other factors, people are often dependent upon dietary vitamin D. For this reason, it was originally classified as a vitamin. Regardless of source, vitamin D is metabolized by the addition of hydroxyl groups, first in the liver by the enzyme 25-hydroxylase and then in certain kidney cells by 1-hydroxylase (**Figure 11.32**). The end result of these changes is 1,25-dihydroxyvitamin D (abbreviated **1,25-$(OH)_2D$**), the active hormonal form of vitamin D.

The major action of 1,25-$(OH)_2D$ is to stimulate the intestinal absorption of Ca^{2+}. Thus, the major consequence of vitamin D deficiency is decreased intestinal Ca^{2+} absorption, resulting in decreased plasma Ca^{2+}.

The blood concentration of 1,25-$(OH)_2D$ is subject to physiological control. The major control point is the second hydroxylation step that occurs primarily in the kidneys by the action of 1-hydroxylase, and which is stimulated by parathyroid hormone. Because a low plasma Ca^{2+} concentration stimulates the secretion of parathyroid hormone, the production of

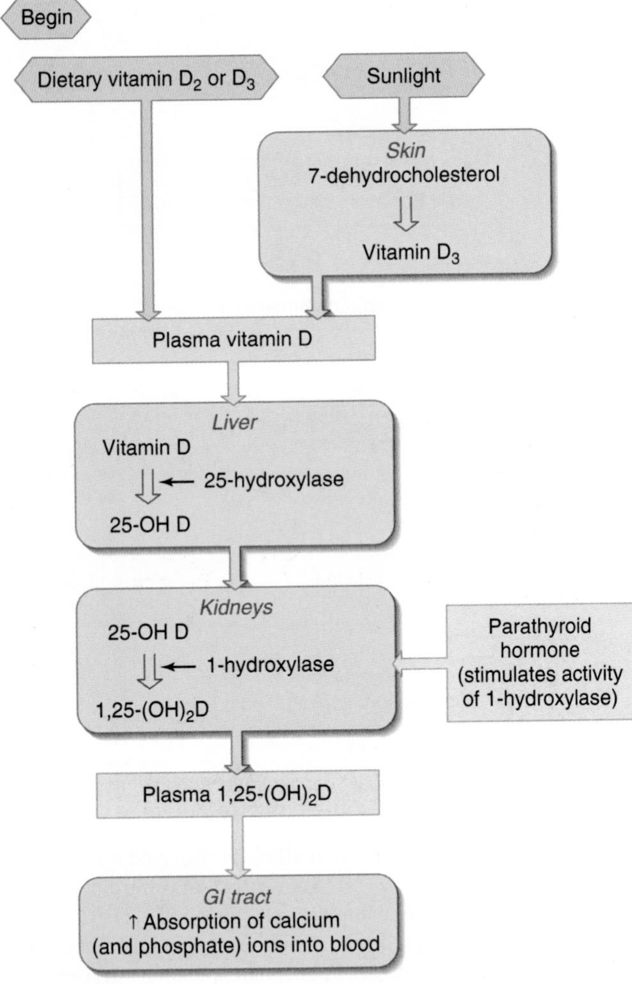

Figure 11.32 Metabolism of vitamin D to the active form, 1,25-$(OH)_2$D.

PHYSIOLOGICAL INQUIRY

- Sarcoidosis is a disease that affects a variety of organs (usually the lungs). It is characterized by the development of nodules of inflamed tissue known as granulomas. These granulomas can express significant 1-hydroxylase activity that is not controlled by parathyroid hormone. What will happen to plasma Ca^{2+} and parathyroid hormone concentrations under these circumstances?

Answer can be found at end of chapter.

1,25-$(OH)_2$D is increased as well under such conditions. Both hormones work together to restore plasma Ca^{2+} to normal.

Calcitonin

Calcitonin is a peptide hormone secreted by cells called parafollicular cells that are within the thyroid gland but are distinct from the thyroid follicles. Calcitonin decreases plasma Ca^{2+} concentration, mainly by inhibiting osteoclasts, thereby reducing bone resorption. Its secretion is stimulated by an increased plasma Ca^{2+} concentration, just the opposite of the stimulus for parathyroid hormone secretion. Unlike parathyroid hormone and 1,25-$(OH)_2$D, however, calcitonin appears to play no role in the normal day-to-day regulation of plasma Ca^{2+} in humans. It may be a factor in decreasing bone resorption when the plasma Ca^{2+} concentration is very high.

11.22 Metabolic Bone Diseases

Various diseases reflect abnormalities in the metabolism of bone. ***Rickets*** (in children) and ***osteomalacia*** (in adults) are conditions in which mineralization of bone matrix is deficient, causing the bones to be soft and easily fractured. In addition, a child suffering from rickets is typically severely bowlegged due to weight bearing on the weakened developing leg bones. A major cause of rickets and osteomalacia is deficiency of vitamin D.

In contrast to these diseases, in ***osteoporosis,*** both matrix and minerals are lost as a result of an imbalance between bone resorption and bone formation. The resulting decrease in bone mass and strength leads to an increased incidence of fractures. Osteoporosis can occur in people who are immobilized ("disuse osteoporosis"), in people who have an *excessive* plasma concentration of a hormone that favors bone resorption, and in people who have a *deficient* plasma concentration of a hormone that favors bone formation (see Table 11.7). It is most commonly seen, however, with aging. Everyone loses bone as he or she ages, but osteoporosis is more common in elderly women than in men for several reasons. Women have a smaller bone mass to begin with, and the loss that occurs with aging occurs more rapidly, particularly after menopause removes the bone-promoting influence of estrogen.

Prevention is the focus of attention for osteoporosis. Treatment of postmenopausal women with estrogen or its synthetic analogs is very effective in reducing the rate of bone loss, but long-term estrogen replacement can have serious consequences in some women (e.g., increasing the likelihood of breast cancer). A regular weight-bearing exercise program, such as brisk walking and stair climbing, is also helpful. Adequate dietary Ca^{2+} and vitamin D intake throughout life are important to build up and maintain bone mass. Several substances also provide effective therapy once osteoporosis is established. Most prominent is a group of drugs called ***bisphosphonates*** that interfere with the resorption of bone by osteoclasts. Other antiresorptive substances include calcitonin and ***selective estrogen receptor modulators*** (***SERMs***), which, as their name implies, act by interacting with (and activating) estrogen receptors, thereby compensating for the low estrogen after menopause.

A variety of pathophysiological disorders lead to abnormally high or low plasma Ca^{2+} concentrations—*hypercalcemia* or *hypocalcemia*, respectively— as described next.

Hypercalcemia

A relatively common cause of **hypercalcemia** is ***primary hyperparathyroidism.*** This is usually caused by a benign tumor (known as an adenoma) of one of the four parathyroid glands. These tumors are composed of abnormal cells that are not adequately suppressed by extracellular Ca^{2+}. As a result, the adenoma secretes parathyroid hormone in excess, leading to an increase in Ca^{2+} resorption from bone, increased kidney reabsorption of Ca^{2+}, and the increased production of 1,25-$(OH)_2D$ from the kidney. This results in an increase in Ca^{2+} absorption from the small intestine. Primary hyperparathyroidism is most effectively treated by surgical removal of the parathyroid tumor.

Certain types of cancer can lead to ***humoral hypercalcemia of malignancy.*** The cause of the hypercalcemia is often the release of a molecule that is structurally similar to PTH, called ***PTH-related peptide*** (***PTHrp***), that has effects similar to those of PTH. This peptide is produced by certain types of cancerous cells (e.g., some breast-cancer cells). However, authentic PTH release from the normal parathyroid glands is decreased due to the hypercalcemia caused by PTHrp released from the cancer cells. The most effective treatment of humoral hypercalcemia of malignancy is to treat the cancer that is releasing PTHrp. In addition, drugs such as bisphosphonates that decrease bone resorption can also provide effective treatment.

Finally, excessive ingestion of vitamin D can lead to hypercalcemia, as may happen in some individuals who consume vitamin D supplements far in excess of what is required.

Regardless of the cause, hypercalcemia causes significant symptoms primarily from its effects on excitable tissues. Among these symptoms are tiredness and lethargy with muscle weakness, as well as nausea and vomiting (due to effects on the GI tract).

Hypocalcemia

Hypocalcemia can result from a loss of parathyroid gland function (***primary hypoparathyroidism***). One cause of this is the removal of parathyroid glands, which may occur (though rarely) when a person with thyroid disease has his or her thyroid gland surgically removed. Because the concentration of PTH is low, 1,25-$(OH)_2D$ production from the kidney is also decreased. Decreases in both hormones lead to decreases in bone resorption, kidney Ca^{2+} reabsorption, and intestinal Ca^{2+} absorption.

Resistance to the effects of PTH in target tissue (hyporesponsiveness) can also lead to the symptoms of hypoparathyroidism, even though in such cases PTH concentrations in the blood tend to be elevated. This condition is called ***pseudohypoparathyroidism*** (see Chapter 5 Clinical Case Study).

Another interesting hypocalcemic state is ***secondary hyperparathyroidism.*** Failure to absorb vitamin D from the gastrointestinal tract, or decreased kidney 1,25-$(OH)_2D$ production, which can occur in kidney disease, can lead to secondary hyperparathyroidism. The decreased plasma Ca^{2+} that results from decreased intestinal absorption of Ca^{2+} results in stimulation of the parathyroid glands. Although the increased concentration of parathyroid hormone does act to restore plasma Ca^{2+} toward normal, it does so at the expense of significant loss of Ca^{2+} from bone and the acceleration of metabolic bone disease.

The symptoms of hypocalcemia are also due to its effects on excitable tissue. It increases the excitability of nerves and muscles, which can lead to CNS effects (seizures), muscle spasms (***hypocalcemic tetany***), and neuronal excitability. Long-term treatment of hypoparathyroidism involves giving calcium salts and 1,25-$(OH)_2D$ or vitamin D.

SECTION F SUMMARY

Effector Sites for Ca^{2+} Homeostasis

I. The effector sites for the regulation of plasma Ca^{2+} concentration are bone, the gastrointestinal tract, and the kidneys.

II. Approximately 99% of total-body Ca^{2+} is contained in bone as minerals on a collagen matrix. Bone is constantly remodeled as a result of the interaction of osteoblasts and osteoclasts, a process that determines bone mass and provides a means for raising or lowering plasma Ca^{2+} concentration.

III. Ca^{2+} is actively absorbed by the gastrointestinal tract, and this process is under hormonal control.

IV. The amount of Ca^{2+} excreted in the urine is the difference between the amount filtered and the amount reabsorbed, the latter process being under hormonal control.

Hormonal Controls

I. Parathyroid hormone (PTH) increases plasma Ca^{2+} concentration by influencing all of the effector sites.
   a. It stimulates kidney reabsorption of Ca^{2+}, bone resorption with release of Ca^{2+} into the blood, and formation of the hormone 1,25-dihydroxyvitamin D, which stimulates Ca^{2+} absorption by the intestine.
   b. It also inhibits the reabsorption of phosphate ions in the kidneys, leading to increased excretion of phosphate ions in the urine.

II. Vitamin D is formed in the skin or ingested and then undergoes hydroxylations in the liver and kidneys. The kidneys express the enzyme that catalyzes the production of the active form, 1,25-dihydroxyvitamin D. This process is greatly stimulated by parathyroid hormone.

Metabolic Bone Diseases

I. Osteomalacia (adults) and rickets (children) are diseases in which the mineralization of bone is deficient—usually due to inadequate vitamin D intake, absorption, or activation.

II. Osteoporosis is a loss of bone density (loss of matrix and minerals).
   a. Bone resorption exceeds formation.
   b. It is most common in postmenopausal (estrogen-deficient) women.
   c. It can be prevented by exercise, adequate Ca^{2+} and vitamin D intake, and medications (such as bisphosphonates).

III. Hypercalcemia (chronically elevated plasma Ca^{2+} concentrations) can occur from several causes.
   a. Primary hyperparathyroidism is usually caused by a benign adenoma, which produces too much PTH. Increased PTH causes hypercalcemia by increasing bone resorption of Ca^{2+}, increasing kidney reabsorption of Ca^{2+}, and increasing kidney production of 1,25-$(OH)_2D$, which increases Ca^{2+} absorption in the intestines.
   b. Humoral hypercalcemia of malignancy is often due to the production of PTH-related peptide (PTHrp) from cancer cells. PTHrp acts like PTH.
   c. Excessive vitamin D intake may also result in hypercalcemia.

IV. Hypocalcemia (chronically decreased plasma Ca^{2+} concentrations) can also be traced to several causes.
   a. Low PTH concentrations from primary hypoparathyroidism (loss of parathyroid function) lead to hypocalcemia by decreasing bone resorption of Ca^{2+}, decreasing urinary reabsorption of Ca^{2+}, and decreasing renal production of 1,25-$(OH)_2D$.
   b. Pseudohypoparathyroidism is caused by target-organ resistance to the action of PTH.
   c. Secondary hyperparathyroidism is caused by vitamin D deficiency due to inadequate intake, absorption, or activation in the kidney (e.g., in kidney disease).

SECTION F REVIEW QUESTIONS

1. Describe bone remodeling.
2. Describe the handling of Ca^{2+} by the kidneys and gastrointestinal tract.
3. What controls the secretion of parathyroid hormone, and what are the major effects of this hormone?
4. Describe the formation and action of 1,25-$(OH)_2D$. How does parathyroid hormone influence the production of this hormone?

SECTION F KEY TERMS

calcitonin 356
1,25-$(OH)_2D$ 355
hydroxyapatite 354
hypercalcemia 356
hypocalcemia 357
mineralization 354
osteoclast 354
osteocyte 354
osteoid 353
parathyroid gland 355
parathyroid hormone (PTH) 354
vitamin D 355
vitamin D_2 (ergocalciferol) 355
vitamin D_3 (cholecalciferol) 355

SECTION F CLINICAL TERMS

bisphosphonate 356
humoral hypercalcemia of malignancy 357
hypocalcemic tetany 357
osteomalacia 356
osteoporosis 356
primary hyperparathyroidism 356
primary hypoparathyroidism 357
pseudohypoparathyroidism 357
PTH-related peptide (PTHrp) 357
rickets 356
secondary hyperparathyroidism 357
selective estrogen receptor modulator (SERM) 356

CHAPTER 11 Clinical Case Study: Mouth Pain, Sleep Apnea, and Enlargement of the Hands in a 35-Year-Old Man

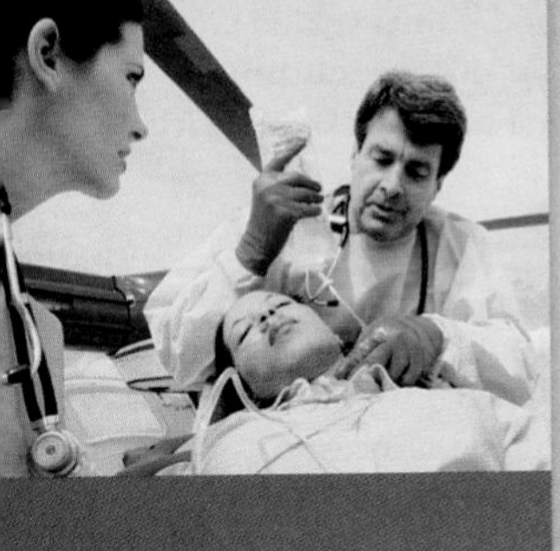

A 35-year-old man visited his dentist with a complaint of chronic mouth pain and headaches. After examining the patient, the dentist concluded that there was no dental disease but that the patient's jaw appeared enlarged and his tongue was thickened and large. The dentist referred the patient to a physician. The physician noted enlargement of the jaw and tongue, enlargement of the fingers and toes, and a very deep voice. The patient acknowledged that his voice seemed to have deepened over the past few years and that he no longer wore his wedding ring because it was too tight. The patient's height and weight were within normal ranges. His blood pressure was significantly elevated, as was his fasting plasma glucose concentration. The patient also mentioned that his wife could no longer sleep in the same room as he because of his loud snoring and sleep apnea. Based on these signs and symptoms, the physician referred the patient to an endocrinologist, who ordered a series of tests to better elucidate the cause of the diverse symptoms.

The enlarged bones and facial features suggested the possibility of ***acromegaly*** (from the Greek *akros,* "extreme" or "extremities," and *megalos,* "large"), a disease characterized by excess growth hormone and IGF-1 concentrations in the blood. This was confirmed with a blood test that revealed greatly elevated concentrations of both hormones. Based on these results, an MRI scan was ordered to look for a possible tumor of the anterior pituitary gland. A 1.5 cm mass was discovered in the sella turcica, consistent with the possibility of a growth hormone–secreting tumor. Because the patient was of normal height, it was concluded that the tumor arose at some point after puberty, when linear growth ceased because of closure of the epiphyseal plates. Had the tumor developed prior to puberty, the man would have been well above normal height because of the growth-promoting actions of growth hormone and IGF-1. Such individuals are known as pituitary giants and have a condition called ***gigantism.*** In many cases, the affected person develops both gigantism and later acromegaly, as occurred in the individual shown in **Figure 11.33**.

Acromegaly and gigantism arise when chronic, excess amounts of growth hormone are secreted into the blood. In almost all cases, acromegaly and gigantism are caused by benign (noncancerous) tumors of the anterior pituitary gland that secrete growth hormone at very high rates, which in turn results in elevated IGF-1 concentrations in the blood. Because these tumors are abnormal tissue, they are not suppressed adequately by normal negative feedback inhibitors like IGF-1, so the growth hormone concentrations remain elevated. These tumors are typically very slow growing, and, if they arise after puberty, it may be many years before a person realizes that there is something wrong. In our patient, the changes in his appearance were gradual enough that he attributed them simply to "aging," despite his relative youth.

Even when linear growth is no longer possible (after the growth plates have fused), very high plasma concentrations of

(continued)

(continued)

Figure 11.33 Appearance of an individual with gigantism and acromegaly.

growth hormone and IGF-1 result in the thickening of many bones in the body, most noticeably in the hands, feet, and head. The jaw, particularly, enlarges to give the characteristic facial appearance called ***prognathism*** (from the Greek *pro,* "forward," and *gnathos,* "jaw") that is associated with acromegaly. This was likely the cause of our patient's chronic mouth pain. The enlarged sinuses that resulted from the thickening of his skull bones may have been responsible in part for his headaches. In addition, many internal organs—such as the heart—also become enlarged due to growth hormone and IGF-1-induced hypertrophy, and this can interfere with their ability to function normally. In some acromegalics, the tissues comprising the larynx enlarge, resulting in a deepening of the voice as in our subject. The enlarged and deformed tongue was likely a contributor to the sleep apnea and snoring reported by the patient; this is called obstructive sleep apnea because the tongue base weakens and, consequently, the tongue obstructs the upper airway (see Chapter 13 for a discussion of sleep apnea). Finally, roughly half of all people with acromegaly have elevated blood pressure (hypertension). The cause of the hypertension is uncertain, but it is a serious medical condition that requires treatment with antihypertensive drugs.

As described earlier, adults continue to make and secrete growth hormone even after growth ceases. That is because growth hormone has metabolic actions in addition to its effects on growth. The major actions of growth hormone in metabolism are to increase the concentrations of glucose and fatty acids in the blood and decrease the sensitivity of skeletal muscle and adipose tissue to insulin. Not surprisingly, therefore, one of the stimuli that increases growth hormone concentrations in the healthy adult is a decrease in blood glucose or fatty acids. The secretion of growth hormone during these metabolic crises, however, is transient; once glucose or fatty acid concentrations are restored to normal, growth hormone concentrations decrease to baseline. In acromegaly, however, growth hormone concentrations are almost always increased. Consequently, acromegaly is often associated with increased plasma concentrations of glucose and fatty acids, in some cases even reaching the concentrations observed in diabetes mellitus. As in Cushing's syndrome (Section D), therefore, the presence of chronically increased concentrations of growth hormone may result in diabetes-like symptoms. This explains why our patient had a high fasting plasma glucose concentration.

Our subject was fortunate to have had a quick diagnosis. This case study illustrates one of the confounding features of endocrine disorders. The rarity of some endocrine diseases (e.g., acromegaly occurs in roughly 4 per million individuals), together with the fact that the symptoms of a given endocrine disease can be varied and insidious in their onset, often results in a delayed diagnosis. This means that in many cases, a patient is subjected to numerous tests for more common disorders before a diagnosis of endocrine disease is made.

Treatment of gigantism and acromegaly usually requires surgical removal of the pituitary tumor. The residual normal pituitary tissue is then sufficient to maintain baseline growth hormone concentrations. If this treatment is impossible or not successful, treatment with long-acting analogs of somatostatin is sometimes necessary. (Recall that somatostatin is the hypothalamic hormone that inhibits GH secretion.) Our patient elected to have surgery. This resulted in a reduction in his plasma growth hormone and IGF-1 concentrations. With time, several of his symptoms were reduced, including the increased plasma glucose concentrations. However, within 2 years, his growth hormone and IGF-1 concentrations were three times higher than the normal range for his age and a follow-up MRI revealed that the tumor had regrown. Not wanting a second surgery, the patient was treated with radiation therapy focused on the pituitary tumor, followed by regular administration of somatostatin analogs. This treatment decreased but did not completely normalize his hormone concentrations. His blood pressure remained elevated and was treated with two different antihypertensive drugs (see Chapter 12).

Clinical terms: acromegaly, gigantism, prognathism

See Chapter 19 for complete, integrative case studies.

CHAPTER 11 TEST QUESTIONS

Answers found in Appendix A.

1–5: Match the hormone with the function or feature (choices a–e).

Hormone:

1. vasopressin
2. ACTH
3. oxytocin
4. prolactin
5. luteinizing hormone

Function:

a. tropic for the adrenal cortex
b. is controlled by an amine-derived hormone of the hypothalamus
c. antidiuresis
d. stimulation of testosterone production
e. stimulation of uterine contractions during labor

6. In the following figure, which hormone (A or B) binds to receptor X with higher affinity?

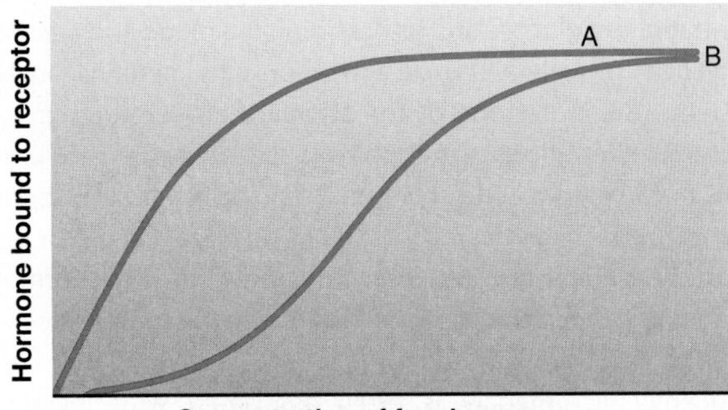

7. Which is *not* a symptom of Cushing's disease?
   a. high blood pressure
   b. bone loss
   c. suppressed immune function
   d. goiter
   e. hyperglycemia (increased blood glucose)
8. Tremors, nervousness, and increased heart rate can all be symptoms of
   a. increased activation of the sympathetic nervous system.
   b. excessive secretion of epinephrine from the adrenal medulla.
   c. hyperthyroidism.
   d. hypothyroidism.
   e. answers a, b, and c (all are correct).
9. Which of the following could theoretically result in short stature?
   a. pituitary tumor making excess thyroid-stimulating hormone
   b. mutations that result in inactive IGF-1 receptors
   c. delayed onset of puberty
   d. decreased hypothalamic concentrations of somatostatin
   e. normal plasma GH but decreased feedback of GH on GHRH
10. Choose the correct statement.
    a. During times of stress, cortisol acts as an anabolic hormone in muscle and adipose tissue.
    b. A deficiency of thyroid hormone would result in increased cellular concentrations of Na^+/K^+-ATPase pumps in target tissues.
    c. The posterior pituitary is connected to the hypothalamus by long portal vessels.
    d. Adrenal insufficiency often results in increased blood pressure and increased plasma glucose concentrations.
    e. A lack of iodide in the diet will have no significant effect on the concentration of circulating thyroid hormone for at least several weeks.
11. A lower-than-normal concentration of plasma Ca^{2+} causes
    a. a PTH-mediated increase in 25-OH D.
    b. a decrease in renal 1-hydroxylase activity.
    c. a decrease in the urinary excretion of Ca^{2+}.
    d. a decrease in bone resorption.
    e. an increase in vitamin D release from the skin.
12. Which of the following is *not* consistent with primary hyperparathyroidism?
    a. hypercalcemia
    b. elevated plasma 1,25-$(OH)_2D$
    c. increased urinary excretion of phosphate ions
    d. a decrease in Ca^{2+} resorption from bone
    e. an increase in Ca^{2+} reabsorption in the kidney

True or False

13. T_4 is the chief circulating form of thyroid hormone but is less active than T_3.
14. Acromegaly is usually associated with hypoglycemia and hypotension.
15. Thyroid hormone and cortisol are both permissive for the actions of epinephrine.

CHAPTER 11 GENERAL PRINCIPLES ASSESSMENT

Answers found in Appendix A.

1. Referring back to Tables 11.3, 11.4, and 11.5, explain how certain of the actions of epinephrine, cortisol, and growth hormone illustrate in part the general principle of physiology that *most physiological functions are controlled by multiple regulatory systems, often working in opposition.*
2. Another general principle of physiology is that *structure is a determinant of—and has coevolved with—function.* The structure of the thyroid gland is very unlike other endocrine glands. How is the structure of this gland related to its function?
3. *Homeostasis is essential for health and survival.* How do parathyroid hormone, ADH, and thyroid hormone contribute to homeostasis? What might be the consequence of having too little of each of those hormones?

CHAPTER 11 QUANTITATIVE AND THOUGHT QUESTIONS

Answers found in Appendix A.

1. In an experimental animal, the sympathetic preganglionic fibers to the adrenal medulla are cut. What happens to the plasma concentration of epinephrine at rest and during stress?
2. During pregnancy, there is an increase in the liver's production and, consequently, the plasma concentration of the major plasma binding protein for thyroid hormone. This causes a sequence of events involving feedback that results in an increase in the plasma concentrations of T_3 but no evidence of hyperthyroidism. Describe the sequence of events.
3. A child shows the following symptoms: deficient growth, failure to show sexual development, decreased ability to respond to stress. What is the most likely cause of all these symptoms?
4. If all the neural connections between the hypothalamus and pituitary gland below the median eminence were severed, the secretion of which pituitary gland hormones would be affected? Which pituitary gland hormones would not be affected?
5. Typically, an antibody to a peptide combines with the peptide and renders it nonfunctional. If an animal were given an antibody to somatostatin, the secretion of which anterior pituitary gland hormone would change and in what direction?
6. A drug that blocks the action of norepinephrine is injected directly into the hypothalamus of an experimental animal, and the secretion rates of several anterior pituitary gland hormones are observed to change. How is this possible, given the fact that norepinephrine is not a hypophysiotropic hormone?

7. A person is receiving very large doses of a synthetic glucocorticoid to treat her arthritis. What happens to her secretion of cortisol?
8. A person with symptoms of hypothyroidism (i.e., sluggishness and intolerance to cold) is found to have abnormally low plasma concentrations of T_4, T_3, and TSH. After an injection of TRH, the plasma concentrations of all three hormones increase. Where is the site of the defect leading to the hypothyroidism?
9. A full-term newborn infant is abnormally small. Is this most likely due to deficient growth hormone, deficient thyroid hormones, or deficient nutrition during fetal life?
10. Why might the administration of androgens to stimulate growth in a short, 12-year-old male turn out to be counterproductive?

CHAPTER 11 ANSWERS TO PHYSIOLOGICAL INQUIRIES

Figure 11.3 By storing large amounts of hormone in an endocrine cell, the plasma concentration of the hormone can be increased within seconds when the cell is stimulated. Such rapid responses may be critical for an appropriate response to a challenge to homeostasis. Packaging peptides in this way also prevents intracellular degradation.

Figure 11.5 Because steroid hormones are derived from cholesterol, they are lipophilic. Consequently, they can freely diffuse through lipid bilayers, including those that constitute secretory vesicles. Therefore, once a steroid hormone is synthesized, it diffuses out of the cell.

Figure 11.9 One explanation for this patient's symptoms may be that his or her circulating concentration of thyroid hormone was elevated. This might occur if the person's thyroid was overstimulated due, for example, to thyroid disease. The increased concentration of thyroid hormone would cause an even greater potentiation of the actions of epinephrine, making it appear as if the patient had excess concentrations of epinephrine.

Figure 11.13 Because the amount of blood into which the hypophysiotropic hormones are secreted is far less than would be the case if they were secreted into the general circulation of the body, the absolute amount of hormone required to achieve a given concentration is much less. This means that the cells of the hypothalamus need only synthesize a tiny amount of hypophysiotropic hormone to reach concentrations in the portal blood vessels that are physiologically active (i.e., can activate receptors on pituitary cells). This allows for the tight control of the anterior pituitary gland by a very small number of discrete neurons within the hypothalamus.

Figure 11.21 Iodine is not widely found in foods; in the absence of iodized salt, an acute or chronic deficiency in dietary iodine is possible. The colloid permits a long-term store of iodinated thyroglobulin that can be used during times when dietary iodine intake is reduced or absent.

Figure 11.24 Plasma cortisol concentrations would increase. This would result in decreased ACTH concentrations in the systemic blood, and CRH concentrations in the portal vein blood, due to increased negative feedback at the pituitary gland and hypothalamus, respectively. The right adrenal gland would shrink in size (atrophy) as a consequence of the decreased ACTH concentrations (decreased "trophic" stimulation of the adrenal cortex).

Figure 11.28 Note from the figure that a decrease in plasma glucose concentrations results in an increase in growth hormone concentrations. This makes sense, because one of the metabolic actions of growth hormone is to increase the concentrations of glucose in the blood. By the same reasoning, an *increase* in the concentration of glucose in the blood due to any cause, including an intravenous infusion as described here, would be expected to *decrease* circulating concentrations of growth hormone.

Figure 11.32 The 1-hydroxylase activity will stimulate the conversion of 25-OH D to 1,25-$(OH)_2$D in the granulomas themselves; the 1,25-$(OH)_2$D will then diffuse out of the granuloma cells and enter the plasma, leading to increased Ca^{2+} absorption in the gastrointestinal tract. This will increase plasma Ca^{2+}, which in turn will suppress parathyroid hormone production; consequently, plasma parathyroid hormone concentrations will decrease. This is a form of secondary hypoparathyroidism.

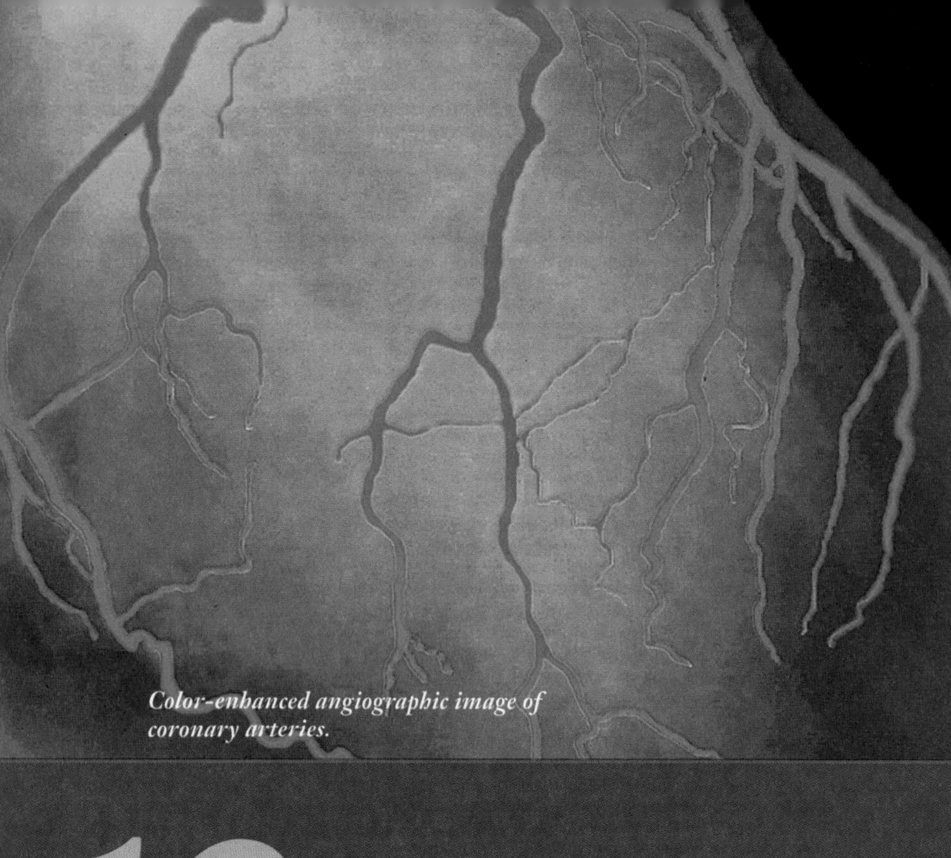

Color-enhanced angiographic image of coronary arteries.

12 Cardiovascular Physiology

Beyond a distance of a few cell diameters, the random movement of substances from a region of higher concentration to one of lower concentration (diffusion) is too slow to meet the metabolic requirements of cells. Because of this, our large, multicellular bodies require an organ system to transport molecules and other substances rapidly over the long distances between cells, tissues, and organs. This purpose is achieved by the **circulatory system** (also known as the **cardiovascular system**), which includes a pump (the **heart**); a set of interconnected tubes (**blood vessels** or **vascular system**); and a fluid connective tissue containing water, solutes, and cells that fills the tubes (the **blood**). Chapter 9 described the detailed mechanisms by which the cardiac and smooth muscle cells found in the heart and blood vessel walls, respectively, contract and generate force; in this chapter, you will learn how these contractions create pressures and move blood within the circulatory system.

The general principles of physiology described in Chapter 1 are abundantly represented in this chapter. In Section A, for example, you will learn about the relationships between blood pressure, blood flow, and resistance to blood flow, a classic illustration of the general principle of physiology that physiological processes are dictated by the laws of chemistry and physics. The general principle of physiology that structure is a determinant of—and has coevolved with—function is apparent throughout the chapter; as one example, you will learn how the structures of different types of blood vessels determine whether they participate in fluid exchange, regulate blood pressure, or provide a reservoir of blood (Section C). The general principle of physiology that most physiological functions are controlled by multiple regulatory systems, often working in opposition, is exemplified by the hormonal and neural regulation of blood vessel diameter and blood volume (Sections C and D), as well as by the opposing mechanisms that create and dissolve blood clots (Section F). Sections D and E explain how regulation of arterial blood pressure exemplifies that homeostasis is essential for health and survival, yet another general principle of physiology. Finally, multiple examples demonstrate the general principle of physiology that the functions of organ systems are coordinated with each other; for example, the circulatory and urinary systems work together to control blood pressure, blood volume, and sodium balance.

SECTION A
Overview of the Circulatory System

12.1 Components of the Circulatory System

We will begin with an overview of the components of the circulatory system and a discussion of some of the physical factors that determine its function.

Blood is composed of **formed elements** (cells and cell fragments) suspended in a liquid called **plasma.** Dissolved in the plasma are a large number of proteins, nutrients, metabolic wastes, and other molecules being transported between organ systems. The cells are the **erythrocytes** (red blood cells) and the **leukocytes** (white blood cells), and the cell fragments are the **platelets.** More than 99% of blood cells are erythrocytes, which carry oxygen. The leukocytes protect against infection and cancer, and the platelets function in blood clotting. The constant motion of the blood keeps all the cells dispersed throughout the plasma.

The **hematocrit** is defined as the percentage of blood volume that is erythrocytes. It is measured by centrifuging (spinning at high speed) a sample of blood. The erythrocytes are forced to the bottom of the centrifuge tube, the plasma remains on top, and the leukocytes and platelets form a very thin layer between them called the buffy coat (**Figure 12.1**). The normal hematocrit is approximately 45% in men and 42% in women.

The volume of blood in a 70 kg (154 lb) person is approximately 5.5 L. If we take the hematocrit to be 45%, then

$$\text{Erythrocyte volume} = 0.45 \times 5.5\text{ L} = 2.5\text{ L}$$

Because the volume occupied by leukocytes and platelets is usually negligible, the plasma volume equals the difference between blood volume and erythrocyte volume; therefore, in our 70 kg person,

$$\text{Plasma volume} = 5.5\text{ L} - 2.5\text{ L} = 3.0\text{ L}$$

The rapid flow of blood throughout the body is produced by pressures created by the pumping action of the heart. This type of flow is known as **bulk flow** because all constituents of the blood move together. The extraordinary degree of branching of blood vessels ensures that almost all cells in the body are within a few cell diameters of at least one of the smallest branches, the capillaries. Nutrients and metabolic end products move between capillary blood and the interstitial fluid by diffusion. Movements between the interstitial fluid and the cell interior are accomplished by both diffusion and mediated transport across the plasma membrane.

At any given moment, only about 5% of the total circulating blood is actually in the capillaries. Yet, it is this 5% that is performing the ultimate functions of the entire circulatory system: the supplying of nutrients and hormonal signals and the removal of metabolic end products and other cell secretions. All other components of the system serve the overall function of getting adequate blood flow through the capillaries.

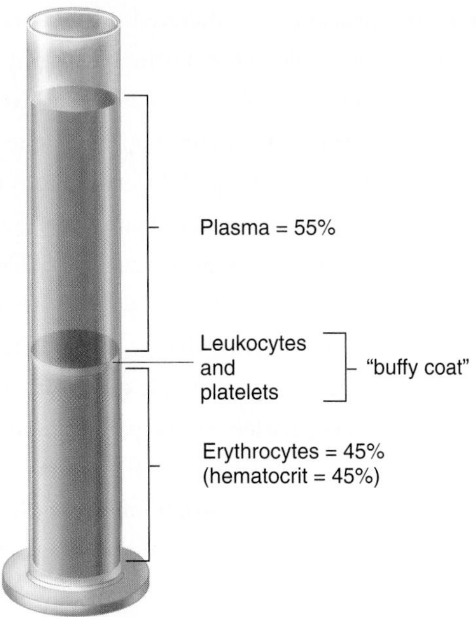

Figure 12.1 APIR Measurement of the hematocrit by centrifugation. The values shown are typical for a healthy male. Due to the presence of a thin layer of leukocytes and platelets between the plasma and red cells, the value for plasma is actually slightly less than 55%.

PHYSIOLOGICAL INQUIRY

- Estimate the hematocrit of a person with a plasma volume of 3 L and total blood volume of 4.5 L.

Answer can be found at end of chapter.

As British physiologist William Harvey reported in 1628, the circulatory system forms a closed loop, so that blood pumped out of the heart through one set of vessels returns to the heart by a different set. There are actually two circuits (**Figure 12.2**), both originating and terminating in the heart, which is divided longitudinally into two functional halves. Each half of the heart contains two chambers: an upper chamber—the **atrium**—and a lower chamber—the **ventricle.** The atrium on each side empties into the ventricle on that side, but there is usually no direct blood flow between the two atria or the two ventricles in the heart of a healthy adult.

The **pulmonary circulation** includes blood pumped from the right ventricle through the lungs and then to the left atrium. It is then pumped through the **systemic circulation** from the left ventricle through all the organs and tissues of the body—except the lungs—and then to the right atrium. In both circuits, the vessels carrying blood away from the heart are called **arteries;** those carrying blood from body organs and tissues back toward the heart are called **veins.**

In the systemic circuit, blood leaves the left ventricle via a single large artery, the **aorta** (see Figure 12.2). The arteries of the systemic circulation branch off the aorta, dividing into progressively smaller vessels. The smallest arteries branch into **arterioles,** which branch into a huge number (estimated at 10 billion) of very small vessels, the **capillaries,** which unite to form larger-diameter vessels, the **venules.** The arterioles, capillaries, and venules are collectively termed the **microcirculation.**

The venules in the systemic circulation then unite to form larger vessels, the veins. The veins from the various peripheral organs and tissues unite to produce two large veins, the **inferior vena cava,** which collects blood from below the heart, and the **superior vena cava,** which collects blood from above the heart (for simplicity, these are depicted as a single vessel in Figure 12.2). These two veins return the blood to the right atrium.

The pulmonary circulation is composed of a similar circuit. Blood leaves the right ventricle via a single large artery, the **pulmonary trunk,** which divides into the two **pulmonary arteries,** one supplying the right lung and the other the left. In the lungs, the arteries continue to branch and connect to arterioles, leading to capillaries that unite into venules and then veins. The blood leaves the lungs via four **pulmonary veins,** which empty into the left atrium.

As blood flows through the lung capillaries, it picks up oxygen supplied to the lungs by breathing. Therefore, the blood in the pulmonary veins, left side of the heart, and systemic arteries has a high oxygen content. As this blood flows through the capillaries of peripheral tissues and organs, some of this oxygen leaves the blood to enter and be used by cells, resulting in the lower oxygen content of systemic venous blood.

As shown in Figure 12.2, blood can pass from the systemic veins to the systemic arteries only by first being pumped through the lungs. Thus, the blood returning from the body's peripheral organs and tissues via the systemic veins is oxygenated before it is pumped back to them.

Note that the lungs receive all the blood pumped by the right side of the heart, whereas the branching of the systemic arteries results in a parallel pattern so that each of the peripheral organs and tissues receives only a fraction of the blood pumped by the left ventricle (see the three capillary beds shown in Figure 12.2). This arrangement (1) guarantees that all systemic tissues receive freshly oxygenated blood and (2) allows for independent variation in blood flow through different tissues as their metabolic activities change. For reference, the typical distribution of the blood pumped by the left ventricle in an adult at rest is given in **Figure 12.3.**

Finally, there are some exceptions to the usual anatomical pattern described in this section for the systemic circulation—for example, the liver and the anterior pituitary gland. In those organs, blood passes through two capillary beds, arranged in series and connected by veins, before returning to the heart. As described in Chapters 11 and 15, this pattern is known as a **portal system.**

12.2 Pressure, Flow, and Resistance

An important feature of the circulatory system is the relationship among blood pressure, blood flow, and the resistance to blood flow. As applied to blood, these factors are collectively referred to as **hemodynamics,** and they demonstrate the general principle of physiology that physiological processes are dictated by the laws of chemistry and physics. In all parts of the system, blood flow (F) is always from a region of higher pressure to one of lower pressure. The pressure exerted by any fluid is called a **hydrostatic pressure**, but this is usually shortened simply to "pressure" in descriptions of the cardiovascular system,

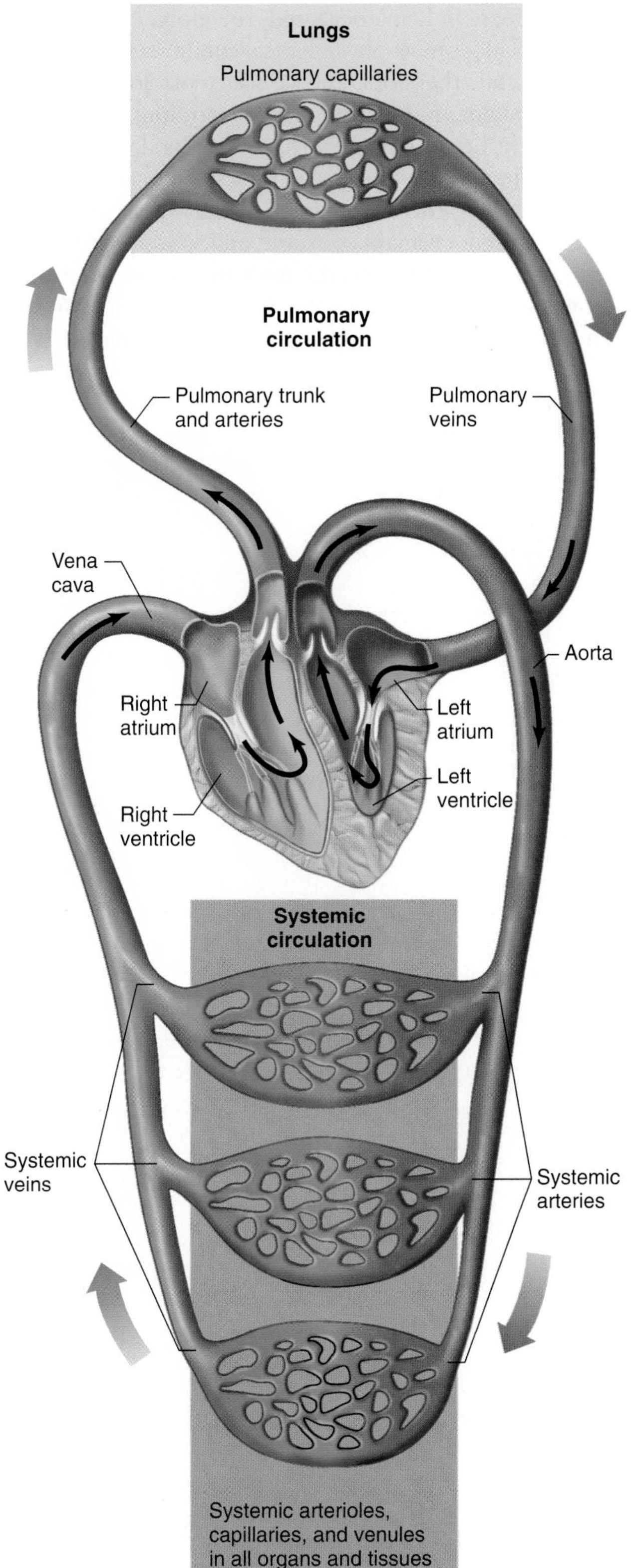

Organ	Flow at rest (mL/min)
Brain	650 (13%)
Heart	215 (4%)
Skeletal muscle	1030 (20%)
Skin	430 (9%)
Kidneys	950 (20%)
Abdominal organs	1200 (24%)
Other	525 (10%)
Total	5000 (100%)

Figure 12.3 Distribution of systemic blood flow to the various organs and tissues of the body at rest. (To see how blood flow changes during exercise, look ahead to Figure 12.61.) Adapted from Chapman and Mitchell.

PHYSIOLOGICAL INQUIRY

- Predict how the blood flow to these various areas might change in a resting person just after eating a large meal.

Answer can be found at end of chapter.

and it denotes the force exerted by the blood. This force is generated in the blood by the contraction of the heart, and its magnitude varies throughout the system for reasons that will be described later. The units for the rate of flow are volume per unit time, usually liters per minute (L/min). The units for the pressure difference (ΔP) driving the flow are millimeters of mercury (mmHg) because historically blood pressure was measured by determining how high the blood pressure could force a column of mercury. It is not the absolute pressure at any point in the cardiovascular system that determines flow rate but the difference in pressure between the relevant points (**Figure 12.4**).

Knowing only the pressure difference between two points will not tell you the flow rate, however. For this, you also need to know the **resistance** (***R***) to flow—that is, how difficult it is for blood to flow between two points at any given

Figure 12.2 APIR The systemic and pulmonary circulations. As depicted by the color change from blue to red, blood becomes fully oxygenated (red) as it flows through the lungs and then loses some oxygen (red to blue) as it flows through the other organs and tissues. Deoxygenated blood is shown as blue by convention throughout this book. In reality, it is more dark red or purple in color. Veins appear blue beneath the skin only because long-wavelength red light is absorbed by skin cells and subcutaneous fat, whereas short-wavelength blue light is transmitted. For simplicity, the arteries and veins leaving and entering the heart are depicted as single vessels; in reality, this is true for the arteries but there are multiple pulmonary veins and two venae cavae (see Figure 12.6).

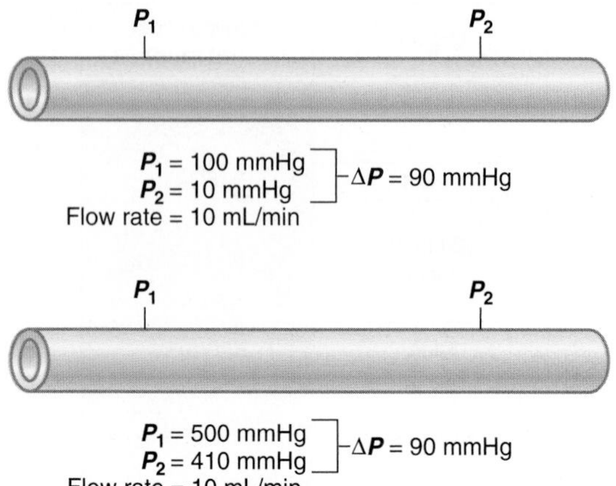

Figure 12.4 Flow between two points within a tube is proportional to the pressure difference between the points. The flows in these two identical tubes are the same (10 mL/min) because the pressure *differences* are the same.

pressure difference. Resistance is the measure of the friction that impedes flow. The basic equation relating these variables is

$$F = \Delta P/R \tag{12-1}$$

In words, flow rate is directly proportional to the pressure difference between two points and inversely proportional to the resistance. This equation applies not only to the cardiovascular system but to any system in which liquid or air moves by bulk flow (for example, in the urinary and respiratory systems).

Resistance cannot be measured directly, but it can be calculated from the directly measured F and ΔP. For example, in Figure 12.4, the resistances in both tubes can be calculated:

$$90 \text{ mmHg} \div 10 \text{ mL/min} = 9 \text{ mmHg/mL/min}$$

This example illustrates how resistance can be calculated, but what is it that actually determines the resistance? One determinant of resistance is the fluid property known as **viscosity,** which is a function of the friction between molecules of a flowing fluid; the greater the friction, the greater the viscosity. The other determinants of resistance are the length and radius of the tube through which the fluid is flowing, because these characteristics affect the surface area inside the tube and thus determine the amount of contact between the moving fluid and the stationary wall of the tube. The following equation defines the contributions of these three determinants:

$$R = \frac{8L\eta}{\pi r^4} \tag{12-2}$$

where η = fluid viscosity
L = length of the tube
r = inside radius of the tube
$8/\pi$ = a mathematical constant

In other words, resistance is directly proportional to both the fluid viscosity and the vessel's length, and inversely proportional to the fourth power of the vessel's radius.

Blood viscosity is not fixed but increases as hematocrit increases. Changes in hematocrit, therefore, can have significant effects on resistance to flow in certain situations. In extreme dehydration, for example, the reduction in body water leads to a relative increase in hematocrit and, therefore, in the viscosity of the blood. Under most physiological conditions, however, the hematocrit—and, therefore, the viscosity of blood—does not vary much and does not play a role in controlling resistance.

Similarly, because the lengths of the blood vessels remain constant in the body, length is also not a factor in the control of resistance along these vessels. In contrast, the radii of the blood vessels do not remain constant, and so vessel radius—the $1/r^4$ term in our equation—is the most important determinant of changes in resistance along the blood vessels. **Figure 12.5** demonstrates how radius influences the resistance and, as a

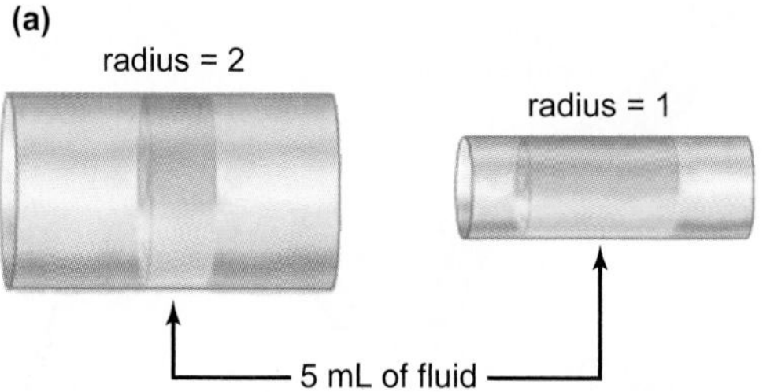

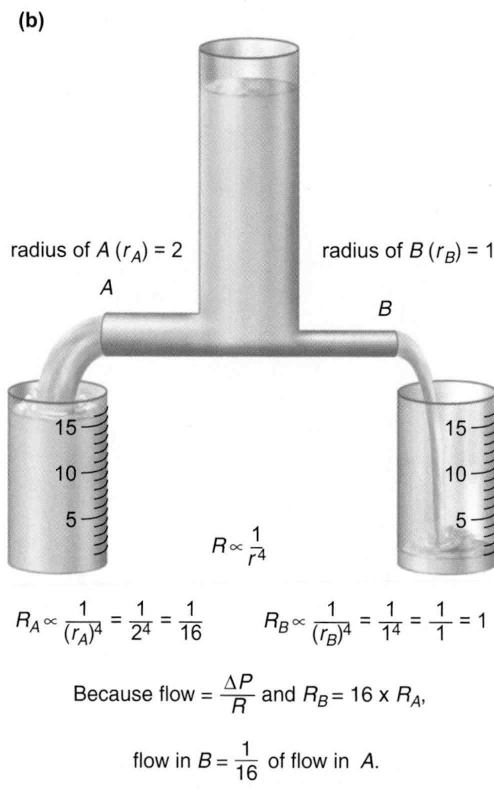

Figure 12.5 Effect of tube radius (r) on resistance (R) and flow. (a) A given volume of fluid is exposed to far more wall surface area and frictional resistance to blood flow in a smaller tube. (b) Given the same pressure gradient, flow through a tube is 16-fold less when the radius is half as large.

PHYSIOLOGICAL INQUIRY

- If outlet B in Figure 12.5b had two individual outlet tubes, each with a radius of 1, would the flow be equal to side A?

Answer can be found at end of chapter.

TABLE 12.1 The Circulatory System

Component	Function
Heart	
Atria	Chambers through which blood flows from veins to ventricles. Atrial contraction adds to ventricular filling but is not essential for it.
Ventricles	Chambers whose contractions produce the pressures that drive blood through the pulmonary and systemic vascular systems and back to the heart.
Vascular system	
Arteries	Low-resistance tubes conducting blood to the various organs with little loss in pressure. They also act as pressure reservoirs for maintaining blood flow during ventricular relaxation.
Arterioles	Major sites of resistance to flow; responsible for the pattern of blood-flow distribution to the various organs; participate in the regulation of arterial blood pressure.
Capillaries	Major sites of nutrient, metabolic end product, and fluid exchange between blood and tissues.
Venules	Sites of nutrient, metabolic end product, and fluid exchange between blood and tissues.
Veins	Low-resistance conduits for blood flow back to the heart. Their capacity for blood is adjusted to facilitate this flow.
Blood	
Plasma	Liquid portion of blood that contains dissolved nutrients, ions, wastes, gases, and other substances. Its composition equilibrates with that of the interstitial fluid at the capillaries.
Cells	Includes erythrocytes that function mainly in gas transport, leukocytes that function in immune defenses, and platelets (cell fragments) for blood clotting.

consequence, the flow of fluid through a tube. Decreasing the radius of a tube twofold increases its resistance 16-fold. If ΔP is held constant in this example, flow through the tube decreases 16-fold because $F = \Delta P/R$.

The equation relating pressure, flow, and resistance applies not only to flow through blood vessels but also to the flows into and out of the various chambers of the heart. These flows occur through valves, and the resistance of a valvular opening determines the flow through the valve at any given pressure difference across it.

As you read on, remember that *the ultimate function of the circulatory system is to ensure adequate blood flow through the capillaries of various organs.* Refer to the summary in **Table 12.1** as you read the description of each component to focus on how each contributes to this goal.

SECTION A SUMMARY

Components of the Circulatory System

I. The key components of the circulatory system are the heart, blood vessels, and blood.

II. The circulatory system consists of two circuits: the pulmonary circulation—from the right ventricle to the lungs and then to the left atrium—and the systemic circulation—from the left ventricle to all peripheral organs and tissues and then to the right atrium.

III. Arteries carry blood away from the heart, and veins carry blood toward the heart.

   a. In the systemic circuit, the large artery leaving the left side of the heart is the aorta, and the large veins emptying into the right side of the heart are the superior vena cava and inferior vena cava. The analogous vessels in the pulmonary circulation are the pulmonary trunk and the four pulmonary veins.
   b. The microcirculation consists of the vessels between arteries and veins: the arterioles, capillaries, and venules.

Pressure, Flow, and Resistance

I. Flow between two points in the cardiovascular system is directly proportional to the pressure difference between those points and inversely proportional to the resistance.

II. Resistance is directly proportional to the viscosity of a fluid and to the length of the tube. It is inversely proportional to the fourth power of the tube's radius, which is the major variable controlling changes in resistance.

SECTION A REVIEW QUESTIONS

1. What is the oxygen status of arterial and venous blood in the systemic versus the pulmonary circulation?
2. State the formula relating flow, pressure difference, and resistance.
3. What are the three determinants of resistance?
4. Which determinant of resistance is varied physiologically to alter blood flow?
5. How does variation in hematocrit influence the hemodynamics of blood flow?
6. Trace the path of a red blood cell through the entire circulatory system, naming all structures and vessel types it flows through, beginning and ending in a capillary of the left big toe.

SECTION A KEY TERMS

aorta 364
arteriole 364
artery 364
atrium 364
blood 363
blood vessels 363
bulk flow 363
capillary 364
cardiovascular system 363
circulatory system 363
erythrocytes 363
formed elements 363
heart 363
hematocrit 363
hemodynamics 364
hydrostatic pressure 364
inferior vena cava 364
leukocytes 363
microcirculation 364
plasma 363
platelet 363
portal system 364
pulmonary artery 364
pulmonary circulation 364
pulmonary trunk 364
pulmonary vein 364
resistance (R) 365
superior vena cava 364
systemic circulation 364
vascular system 363
vein 364
ventricle 364
venule 364
viscosity 366

SECTION B The Heart

12.3 Anatomy

The heart is a muscular organ enclosed in a protective fibrous sac, the **pericardium,** and located in the chest (**Figure 12.6**). A fibrous layer is also closely affixed to the heart and is called the **epicardium.** The extremely narrow space between the pericardium and the epicardium is filled with a watery fluid that serves as a lubricant as the heart moves within the sac.

The wall of the heart, the **myocardium,** is composed primarily of cardiac muscle cells. The inner surface of the cardiac chambers, as well as the inner wall of all blood vessels, is lined by a thin layer of cells known as **endothelial cells,** or **endothelium.**

As noted earlier, the human heart is divided into right and left halves, each consisting of an atrium and a ventricle. The two ventricles are separated by a muscular wall, the **interventricular septum.** Located between the atrium and ventricle in each half of the heart are the one-way **atrioventricular (AV) valves,** which permit blood to flow from atrium to ventricle but not backward from ventricle to atrium. The right AV valve is called the **tricuspid valve** because it has three fibrous flaps, or cusps (**Figure 12.7**). The left AV valve has two flaps and is therefore called the **bicuspid valve.** Its resemblance to a bishop's headgear (a "mitre") has earned the left AV valve another commonly used name, **mitral valve.**

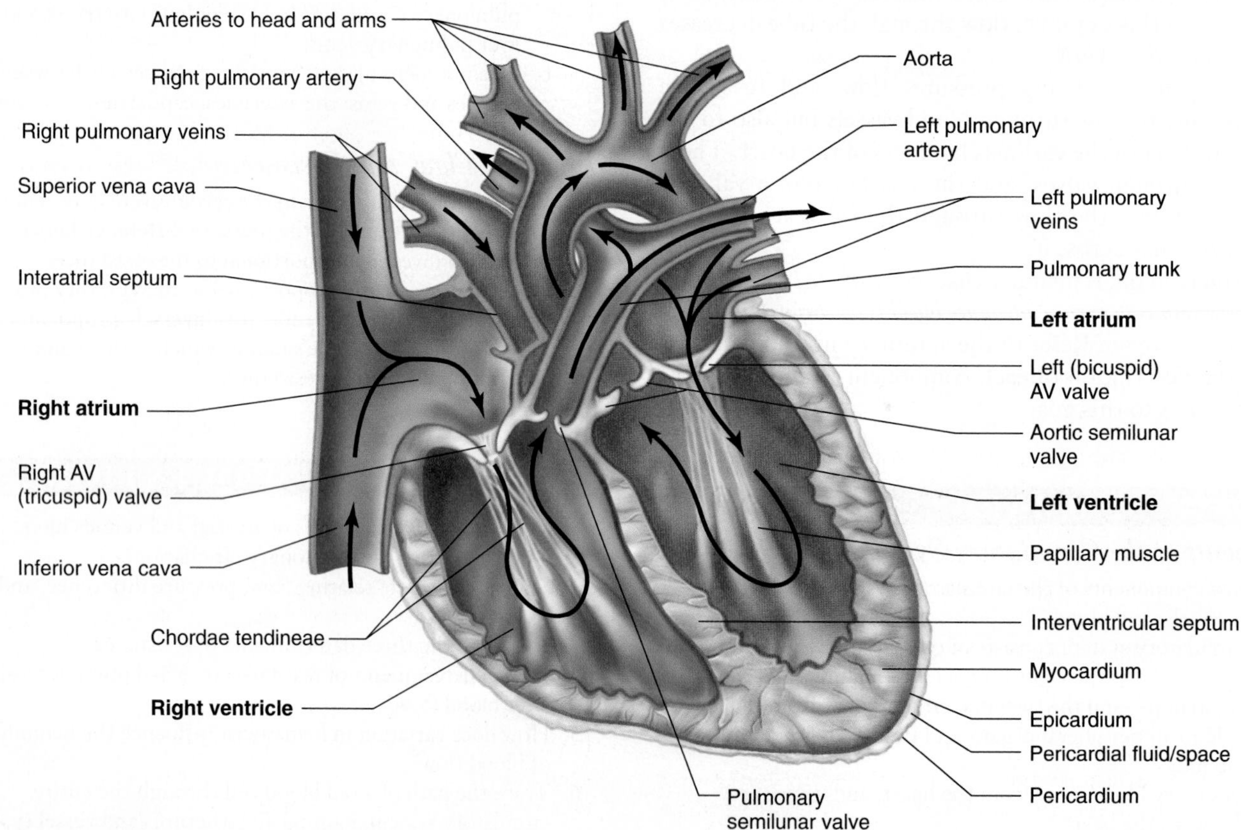

Figure 12.6 APIR Diagrammatic section of the heart. The arrows indicate the direction of blood flow.

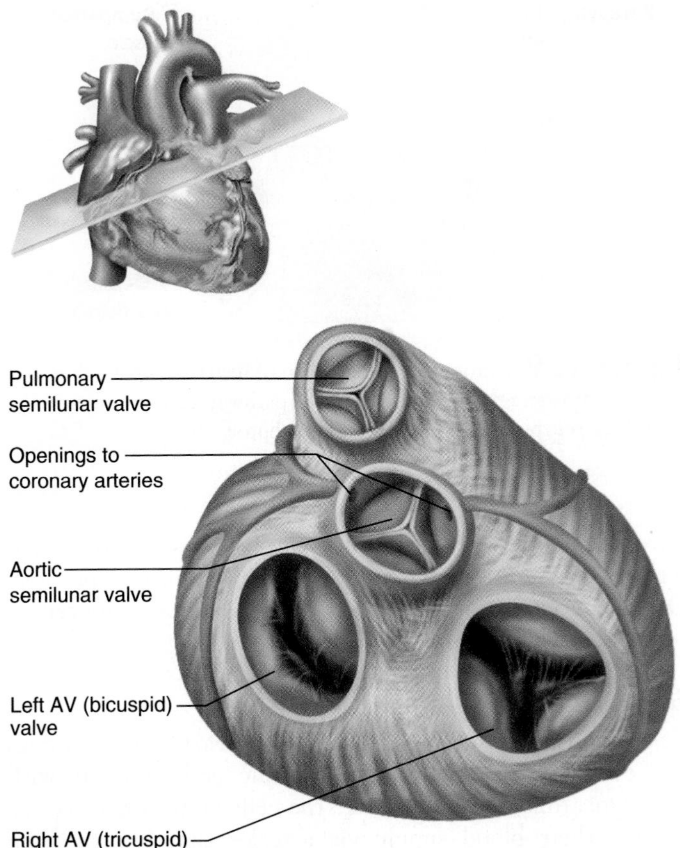

Figure 12.7 APIR Superior view of the heart with the atria removed, showing the heart valves. From R. Carola, J. P. Harley, and C. R. Noback, *Human Anatomy and Physiology*, McGraw-Hill, New York.

The opening and closing of the AV valves are passive processes resulting from pressure differences across the valves. When the blood pressure in an atrium is greater than in the corresponding ventricle, the valve is pushed open and blood flows from atrium to ventricle. In contrast, when a contracting ventricle achieves an internal pressure greater than that in its connected atrium, the AV valve between them is forced closed. Therefore, blood does not normally move back into the atria but is forced into the pulmonary trunk from the right ventricle and into the aorta from the left ventricle.

To prevent the AV valves from being pushed up and opening backward into the atria when the ventricles are contracting (a condition called ***prolapse***), the valves are fastened to muscular projections (**papillary muscles**) of the ventricular walls by fibrous strands (**chordae tendineae**). The papillary muscles do not open or close the valves. They act only to limit the valves' movements and prevent the backward flow of blood. Injury and disease of these tendons or muscles are two ways in which prolapse may occur in some individuals.

The openings of the right ventricle into the pulmonary trunk and of the left ventricle into the aorta also contain valves, the **pulmonary** and **aortic valves,** respectively (see Figures 12.6 and 12.7). These valves are also referred to as the semilunar valves, due to the half-moon shape of the cusps. These valves permit blood to flow into the arteries during ventricular contraction but prevent blood from moving in the opposite direction during ventricular relaxation. Like the AV valves, they act in a purely passive manner. Whether they are open or closed depends upon the pressure differences across them.

Another important point concerning the heart valves is that, when open, they offer very little resistance to flow. Consequently, very small pressure differences across them suffice to produce large flows. In disease states, however, a valve may become narrowed or not open fully so that it offers a high resistance to flow even when open. In such a state, the contracting cardiac chamber must produce an unusually high pressure to cause flow across the valve.

There are no valves at the entrances of the superior and inferior venae cavae (plural of *vena cava*) into the right atrium, and of the pulmonary veins into the left atrium. However, atrial contraction pumps very little blood back into the veins because atrial contraction constricts their sites of entry into the atria, greatly increasing the resistance to backflow. (Actually, a little blood is ejected back into the veins, and this accounts for the venous pulse that can often be seen in the neck veins when the atria are contracting.)

Figure 12.8 summarizes the path of blood flow through the entire cardiovascular system.

Cardiac Muscle

The bulk of the heart is comprised of specialized muscle cells with amazing resiliency and stamina. The cardiac muscle cells of the myocardium are arranged in layers that are tightly bound together and completely encircle the blood-filled chambers. When the walls of a chamber contract, they come together like a squeezing fist and exert pressure on the blood they enclose. Unlike skeletal muscle cells, which can be rested for prolonged periods and only a fraction of which are activated in a given muscle during most contractions, every heart cell contracts with every beat of the heart. Beating about once every second, cardiac muscle cells may contract almost 3 billion times in an average life span without resting! Remarkably, despite this enormous workload, the human heart has a limited ability to replace its muscle cells. Recent experiments suggest that only about 1% of heart muscle cells are replaced per year.

In other ways, cardiac muscle is similar to smooth and skeletal muscle. It is an electrically excitable tissue that converts chemical energy stored in the bonds of ATP into force generation. Action potentials propagate along cell membranes, Ca^{2+} enters the cytosol, and the cycling of force-generating cross-bridges is activated. Some details of the cellular structure and function of cardiac muscle were discussed in Chapter 9.

Approximately 1% of cardiac cells do not function in contraction but have specialized features that are essential for normal heart excitation. These cells constitute a network known as the **conducting system** of the heart and are in electrical contact with the cardiac muscle cells via gap junctions. The conducting system initiates the heartbeat and helps spread an action potential rapidly throughout the heart.

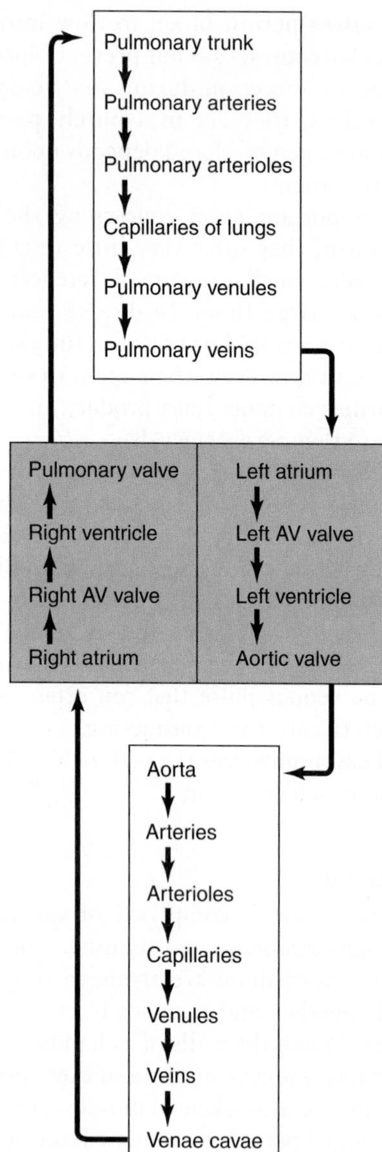

Figure 12.8 APR Path of blood flow through the entire cardiovascular system. All the structures within the colored box are located in the heart.

PHYSIOLOGICAL INQUIRY

- How would this diagram be different if it included a systemic portal vessel?

Answer can be found at end of chapter.

Innervation

The heart receives a rich supply of sympathetic and parasympathetic nerve fibers, the latter contained in the vagus nerves (**Figure 12.9**). The sympathetic postganglionic fibers innervate the entire heart and release norepinephrine, whereas the parasympathetic fibers terminate mainly on cells found in the atria and release primarily acetylcholine. The receptors for norepinephrine on cardiac muscle are mainly β-adrenergic. The hormone epinephrine, from the adrenal medulla, binds to the same receptors as

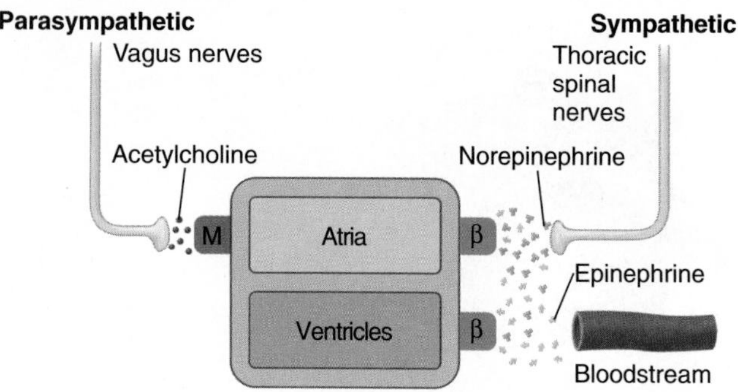

Figure 12.9 Autonomic innervation of heart. Neurons shown represent postganglionic neurons in the pathways. M = muscarinic-type ACh receptor; β = β-adrenergic receptor.

norepinephrine and exerts the same actions on the heart. The receptors for acetylcholine are of the muscarinic type. Details about the autonomic nervous system and its receptors were discussed in Chapter 6.

Blood Supply

The blood being pumped through the heart chambers does not exchange nutrients and metabolic end products with the myocardial cells. They, like the cells of all other organs, receive their blood supply via arteries that branch from the aorta. The arteries supplying the myocardium are the **coronary arteries,** and the blood flowing through them is the **coronary blood flow.** The coronary arteries exit from behind the aortic valve cusps in the very first part of the aorta (see Figure 12.7) and lead to a branching network of small arteries, arterioles, capillaries, venules, and veins similar to those in other organs. Most of the cardiac veins drain into a single large vein, the coronary sinus, which empties into the right atrium.

12.4 Heartbeat Coordination

The heart is a dual pump in that the left and right sides of the heart pump blood separately—but simultaneously—into the systemic and pulmonary vessels. Efficient pumping of blood requires that the atria contract first, followed almost immediately by the ventricles. Contraction of cardiac muscle, like that of skeletal muscle and many smooth muscles, is triggered by depolarization of the plasma membrane. Gap junctions interconnect myocardial cells and allow action potentials to spread from one cell to another. The initial excitation of one cardiac cell therefore eventually results in the excitation of all cardiac cells. This initial depolarization normally arises in a small group of conducting-system cells called the **sinoatrial (SA) node,** located in the right atrium near the entrance of the superior vena cava (**Figure 12.10**). The action potential then spreads from the SA node throughout the atria and then into and throughout the ventricles. This raises two questions: (1) What is the path of spread of excitation? (2) How does the SA node initiate an action potential? We will deal initially with the first question and then return to the second question in the next section.

Sequence of Excitation

The SA node is normally the pacemaker for the entire heart. Its depolarization generates the action potential that leads to depolarization of all other cardiac muscle cells. As we will see later, electrical excitation of the heart is coupled with contraction of cardiac muscle. Therefore, the discharge rate of the SA node determines the **heart rate,** the number of times the heart contracts per minute.

The action potential initiated in the SA node spreads throughout the myocardium, passing from cell to cell by way of gap junctions. Depolarization first spreads through the muscle cells of the atria, with conduction rapid enough that the right and left atria contract at essentially the same time.

The spread of the action potential to the ventricles involves a more complicated conducting system (see Figure 12.10 and **Figure 12.11**), which consists of modified cardiac cells that have lost contractile capability but that conduct action potentials with low resistance. The link between atrial depolarization and ventricular depolarization is a portion of the conducting system called the **atrioventricular (AV) node,** located at the base of the right atrium. The action potential is conducted relatively rapidly from the SA node to the AV node through **internodal pathways.** The AV node is an elongated structure with a particularly important characteristic: *The propagation of action potentials through the AV node is relatively slow* (requiring approximately 0.1 sec). This delay allows atrial contraction to be completed before ventricular excitation occurs.

After the AV node has become excited, the action potential propagates down the interventricular septum. This pathway has conducting-system fibers called the **bundle of His** (pronounced "hiss"), or atrioventricular bundle. The AV node and the bundle of His constitute the only electrical connection between the atria and the ventricles. Except for this pathway, the atria are completely separated from the ventricles by a layer of nonconducting connective tissue.

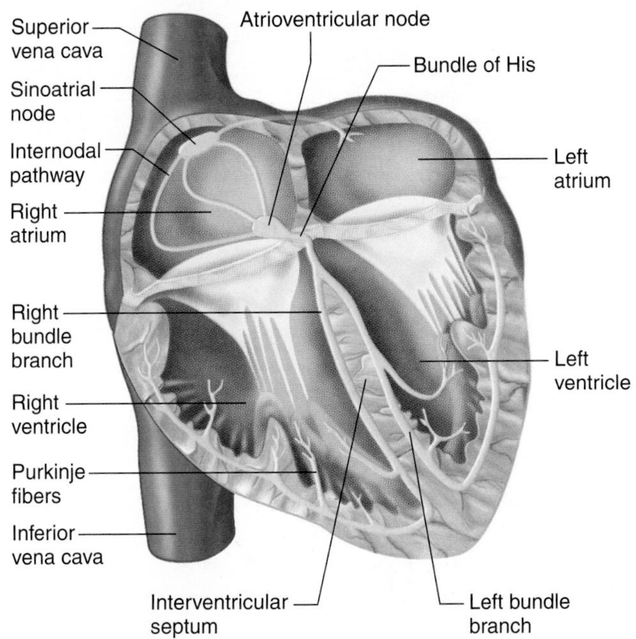

Figure 12.10 APR Conducting system of the heart (shown in yellow).

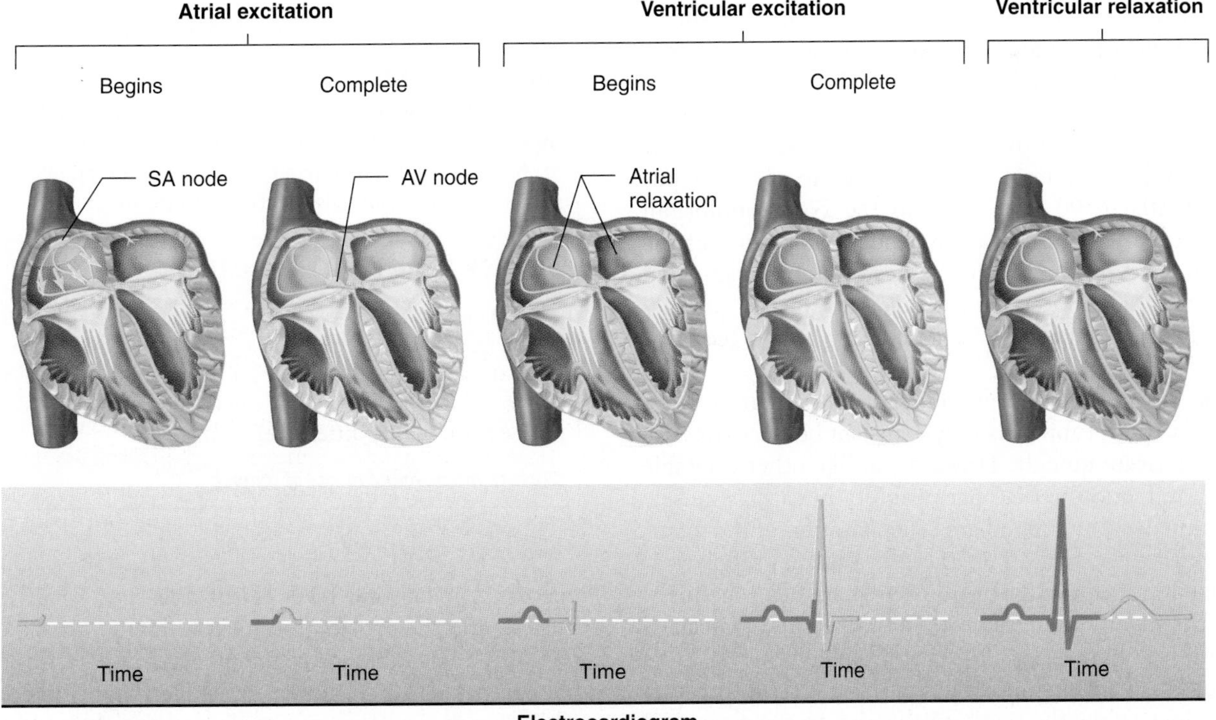

Figure 12.11 APR Sequence of cardiac excitation. The yellow color denotes areas that are depolarized. The electrocardiogram monitors the spread of the signal. Adapted from Rushmer.

Within the interventricular septum, the bundle of His divides into right and left **bundle branches,** conducting fibers that separate at the bottom (apex) of the heart and enter the walls of both ventricles. These fibers in turn make contact with **Purkinje fibers,** large-diameter conducting cells that rapidly distribute the impulse throughout much of the ventricles. Finally, the Purkinje fibers make contact with ventricular myocardial cells, which spread the action potential through the rest of the ventricles.

The rapid conduction along the Purkinje fibers and the diffuse distribution of these fibers cause depolarization of all right and left ventricular cells to occur nearly simultaneously and ensure a single coordinated contraction. Actually, though, depolarization and contraction do begin slightly earlier in the apex of the ventricles and then spread upward. The result is an efficient contraction that moves blood toward the exit valves, like squeezing a tube of toothpaste from the bottom up.

Cardiac Action Potentials and Excitation of the SA Node

The mechanism by which action potentials are conducted along the membranes of heart cells is basically similar to other excitable tissues like neurons and skeletal muscle cells. As was described in Chapters 6 and 9, it involves the controlled exchange of materials (ions) across cellular membranes, which is one of the general principles of physiology introduced in Chapter 1. However, different types of heart cells express unique combinations of ion channels that produce different action potential shapes. In this way, they are specialized for particular roles in the spread of excitation through the heart.

Figure 12.12a illustrates an idealized ventricular myocardial cell action potential. The changes in plasma membrane permeability that underlie it are shown in **Figure 12.12b.** As in skeletal muscle cells and neurons, the resting membrane is much more permeable to K^+ than to Na^+. Therefore, the resting membrane potential is much closer to the K^+ equilibrium potential (−90 mV) than to the Na^+ equilibrium potential (+60 mV). Similarly, the depolarizing phase of the action potential is due mainly to the opening of voltage-gated Na^+ channels. Sodium ion entry depolarizes the cell and sustains the opening of more Na^+ channels in positive feedback fashion.

Also, as in skeletal muscle cells and neurons, the increased Na^+ permeability is very transient because the Na^+ channels inactivate quickly. However, unlike other excitable tissues, the reduction in Na^+ permeability in cardiac muscle is not accompanied by immediate repolarization of the membrane to resting levels. Rather, there is a partial repolarization caused by a special class of transiently open K^+ channels, and then the membrane remains depolarized at a plateau of about 0 mV (see Figure 12.12a) for a prolonged period. The reasons for this continued depolarization are (1) K^+ permeability declines below the resting value due to the closure of the K^+ channels that were open in the resting state, and (2) a large increase in the cell membrane permeability to Ca^{2+} occurs. This second mechanism does not occur in skeletal muscle, and the explanation for it follows.

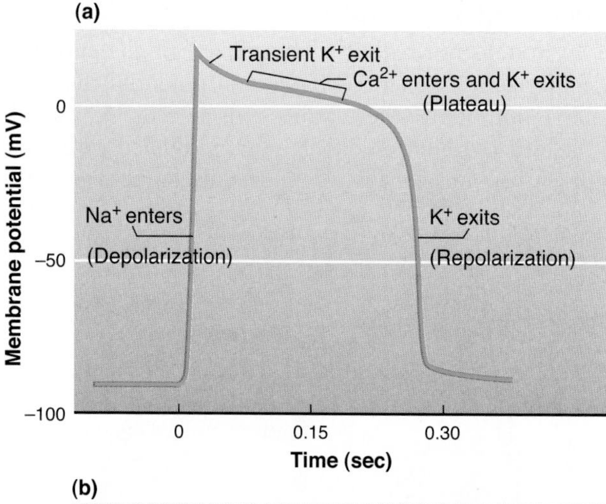

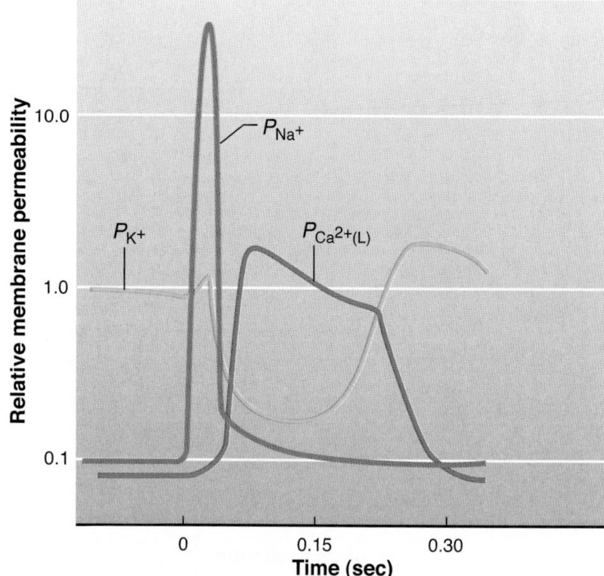

Figure 12.12 (a) Membrane potential recording from a ventricular muscle cell. Labels indicate key ionic movements in each phase. (b) Simultaneously measured permeabilities (P) to K^+, Na^+, and Ca^{2+} during the action potential of (a). Several subtypes of K^+ channels contribute to P_{K^+}.

PHYSIOLOGICAL INQUIRY

- The current due to outward K^+ movement is nearly equal to the current due to inward Ca^{2+} movement during the plateau of the action potential, and yet the membrane permeability to Ca^{2+} is much greater. How can the currents be similar despite the permeability difference?

Answer can be found at end of chapter.

In myocardial cells, membrane depolarization causes voltage-gated Ca^{2+} channels in the plasma membrane to open, which results in a flow of Ca^{2+} ions down their electrochemical gradient into the cell. These channels open much more slowly than do Na^+ channels, and, because they remain open for a prolonged period, they are often referred to as **L-type Ca^{2+} channels** (L = long lasting). These channels are modified versions of the dihydropyridine (DHP) receptors that function as voltage sensors in excitation–contraction coupling of skeletal muscle (see Figure 9.12). The flow of positive calcium ions into the cell just balances the flow of positive potassium ions out of the cell and keeps the membrane depolarized at the plateau value.

Ultimately, repolarization does occur due to the eventual inactivation of the L-type Ca^{2+} channels and the opening of another subtype of K^+ channels. These K^+ channels are similar to the ones described in neurons and skeletal muscle; they open in response to depolarization (but after a delay) and close once the K^+ current has repolarized the membrane to negative values.

The action potentials of atrial muscle cells are similar in shape to those just described for ventricular cells, but the duration of their plateau phase is shorter.

In contrast, there are extremely important differences between action potentials of cardiac muscle cells and those in nodal cells of the conducting system. **Figure 12.13a** illustrates the action potential of a cell from the SA node. Note that the SA node cell does not have a steady resting potential but, instead, undergoes a slow depolarization. This gradual depolarization is known as a **pacemaker potential;** it brings the membrane potential to threshold, at which point an action potential occurs.

Three ion channel mechanisms, which are shown in **Figure 12.13b**, contribute to the pacemaker potential. The first is a progressive reduction in K^+ permeability. The K^+ channels that opened during the repolarization phase of the previous action potential gradually close due to the membrane's return to negative potentials. Second, pacemaker cells have a unique set of channels that, unlike most voltage-gated channels, open when the membrane potential is at *negative* values. These nonspecific cation channels conduct mainly an inward, depolarizing, Na^+ current and, because of their unusual gating behavior, have been termed "funny," or **F-type channels.** The third pacemaker channel is a type of Ca^{2+} channel that opens only briefly but contributes inward Ca^{2+} current and an important final depolarizing boost to the pacemaker potential. These channels are called **T-type Ca^{2+} channels** (T = transient). Although SA node and AV node action potentials are basically similar in shape, the pacemaker currents of SA node cells bring them to threshold more rapidly than AV node cells, which is why SA node cells normally initiate action potentials and determine the pace of the heart.

Once the pacemaker mechanisms have brought a nodal cell to threshold, an action potential occurs. The depolarizing phase is caused not by Na^+ but rather by Ca^{2+} influx through L-type Ca^{2+} channels. These Ca^{2+} currents depolarize the membrane more slowly than voltage-gated Na^+ channels, and one result is that action potentials propagate more slowly along nodal-cell membranes than in other cardiac cells. This explains the slow transmission of cardiac excitation through the AV node. As in cardiac muscle cells, the long-lasting L-type Ca^{2+} channels prolong the nodal action potential, but eventually they close and K^+ channels open and the membrane is repolarized. The return to negative potentials activates the pacemaker mechanisms once again, and the cycle repeats.

Thus, the pacemaker potential provides the SA node with **automaticity,** the capacity for spontaneous, rhythmic self-excitation. The slope of the pacemaker potential—that is, how quickly the membrane potential changes per unit

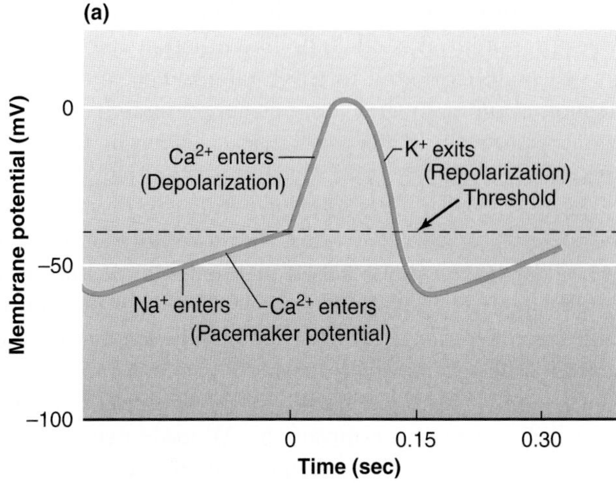

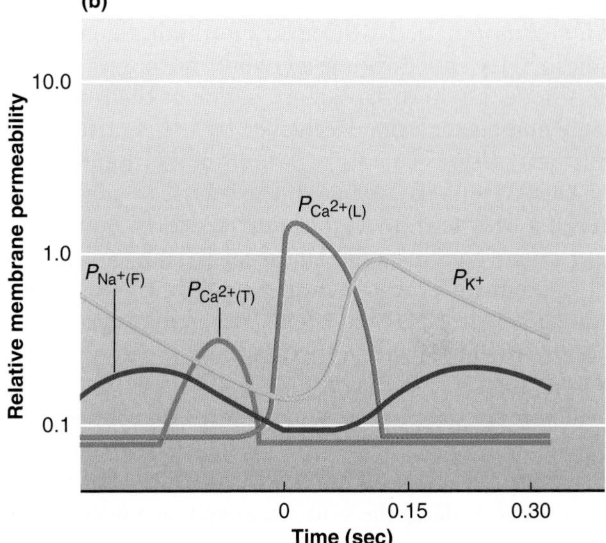

Figure 12.13 (a) Membrane potential recording from a cardiac nodal cell. Labels indicate key ionic movements in each phase. A gradual reduction in K^+ permeability also contributes to the pacemaker potential (not shown), and the Na^+ entry in this phase is through nonspecific cation channels. (b) Simultaneously measured permeabilities through four different ion channels during the action potential shown in (a).

PHYSIOLOGICAL INQUIRY

- Conducting cells of the ventricles contain all of the ion channel types found in both cardiac muscle cells and node cells. Draw a graph showing a Purkinje cell action potential.

Answer can be found at end of chapter.

time—determines how quickly threshold is reached and the next action potential is elicited. The inherent rate of the SA node—the rate exhibited in the total absence of any neural or hormonal input to the node—is approximately 100 depolarizations per minute. (We will discuss later why the resting heart rate in humans is typically slower than that.)

Because other cells of the conducting system have slower inherent pacemaker rates, they normally are driven to threshold by action potentials from the SA node and do not manifest their own rhythm. However, they can do so under certain circumstances and are then called ***ectopic pacemakers.*** Recall that excitation travels from the SA node to both ventricles only through the AV node; therefore, drug- or disease-induced malfunction of the AV node may reduce or completely eliminate the transmission of action potentials from the atria to the ventricles. This is known as an ***AV conduction disorder.*** If this occurs, autorhythmic cells in the bundle of His and Purkinje network, no longer driven by the SA node, begin to initiate excitation at their own inherent rate and become the pacemaker for the ventricles. Their rate is quite slow, generally 25 to 40 beats/min. Therefore, when the AV node is disrupted, the ventricles contract completely out of synchrony with the atria, which continue at the higher rate of the SA node. Under such conditions, the atria are less effective because they are often contracting when the AV valves are closed. Fortunately, atrial pumping is relatively unimportant for cardiac function except during strenuous exercise.

The current treatment for severe AV conduction disorders, as well as for many other abnormal rhythms, is permanent surgical implantation of an ***artificial pacemaker*** that electrically stimulates the ventricular cells at a normal rate.

The Electrocardiogram

The **electrocardiogram (ECG,** also abbreviated *EKG*—the *k* is from the German *elektrokardiogramm*) is a tool for evaluating the electrical events within the heart. When action potentials occur simultaneously in many individual myocardial cells, currents are conducted through the body fluids around the heart and can be detected by recording electrodes at the surface of the skin. **Figure 12.14a** illustrates an idealized normal ECG recorded as the potential difference between the right and left wrists. (Review Figure 12.11 for an illustration of how this waveform corresponds in time with the spread of an action potential through the heart.) The first deflection, the **P wave,** corresponds to current flow during atrial depolarization. The second deflection, the **QRS complex,** occurring approximately 0.15 sec later, is the result of ventricular depolarization. It is a complex deflection because the paths taken by the wave of depolarization through the thick ventricular walls differ from instant to instant, and the currents generated in the body fluids change direction accordingly. Regardless of its form (for example, the Q and/or S portions may be absent), the deflection is still called a QRS complex. The final deflection, the **T wave,** is the result of ventricular repolarization. Atrial repolarization is usually not evident on the ECG because it occurs at the same time as the QRS complex.

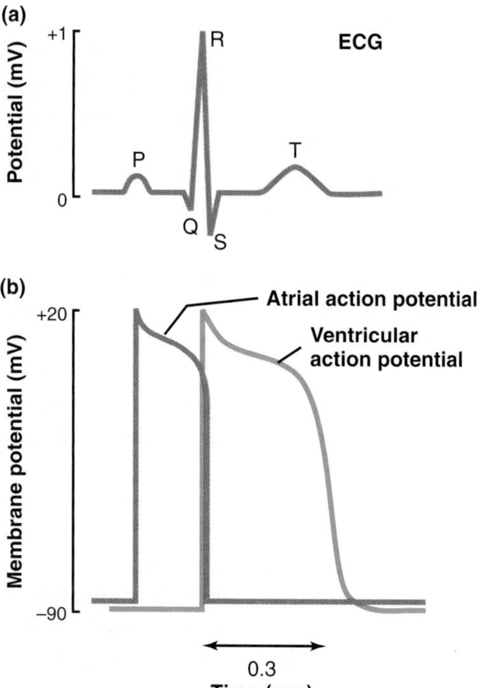

Figure 12.14 APIR (a) Idealized electrocardiogram recorded from electrodes placed on the wrists. (b) Action potentials recorded from a single atrial muscle cell and a single ventricular muscle cell, synchronized with the ECG trace in panel (a). Note the correspondence of the P wave with atrial depolarization, the QRS complex with ventricular depolarization, and the T wave with ventricular repolarization.

PHYSIOLOGICAL INQUIRY

- How would the timing of the waves in (a) be changed by a drug that reduces the L-type Ca^{2+} current in AV node cells?

Answer can be found at end of chapter.

A typical ECG makes use of multiple combinations of recording locations on the limbs and chest (called **ECG leads**) so as to obtain as much information as possible concerning different areas of the heart. The shapes and sizes of the P wave, QRS complex, and T wave vary with the electrode locations. For reference, see **Figure 12.15** and **Table 12.2,** which describe the placement of electrodes for the different ECG leads.

To reiterate, the ECG is not a direct record of the changes in membrane potential across individual cardiac muscle cells. Instead, it is a measure of the currents generated in the extracellular fluid by the changes occurring simultaneously in many cardiac cells. To emphasize this point, **Figure 12.14b** shows the simultaneously occurring changes in membrane potential in single atrial and ventricular muscle cells.

Because many myocardial defects alter normal action potential propagation, and thereby the shapes and timing of the waves, the ECG is a powerful tool for diagnosing certain

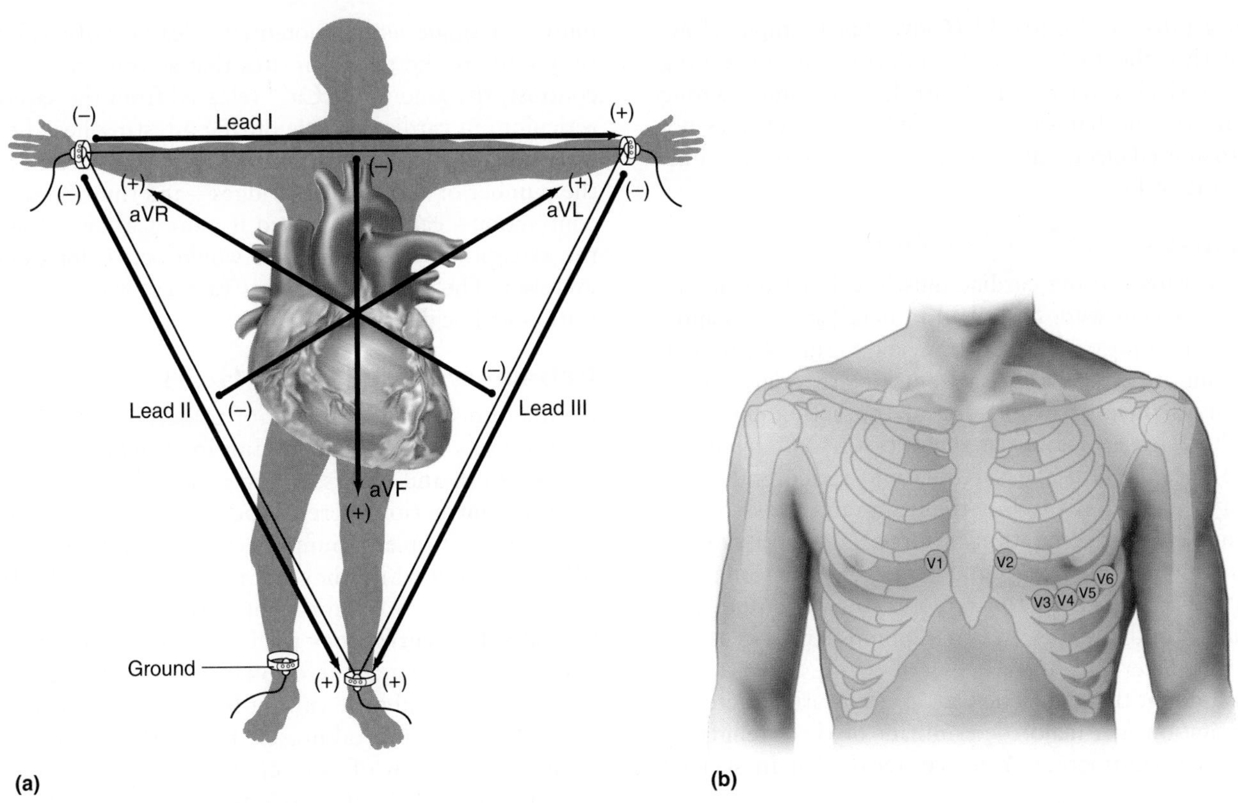

Figure 12.15 Placement of electrodes in electrocardiography. Each of the 12 leads uses a different combination of reference (negative pole) and recording (positive pole) electrodes, thus providing different angles for "viewing" the electrical activity of the heart. (a) The standard limb leads (I, II, and III) form a triangle between electrodes on the wrists and left leg (the right leg is a ground electrode). Augmented leads bisect the angles of the triangle by combining two electrodes as reference. (For example, for lead aVL, the right wrist and foot are combined as the negative pole, thus creating a reference point along the line between them, pointing toward the recording electrode on the left wrist.) (b) The precordial leads (V1 – V6) are recording electrodes placed on the chest as shown, with the limb leads combined into a reference point at the center of the heart.

TABLE 12.2 Electrocardiography Leads

Name of Lead	Electrode Placement	
Standard Limb Leads	*Reference (–) Electrode*	*Recording (+) Electrode*
Lead I	Right arm	Left arm
Lead II	Right arm	Left leg
Lead III	Left arm	Left leg
Augmented Limb Leads		
aVR	Left arm and left leg	Right arm
aVL	Right arm and left leg	Left arm
aVF	Right arm and left arm	Left leg
Precordial (Chest) Leads		
V1	Combined limb leads	4th intercostal space, right of sternum
V2	" " "	4th intercostal space, left of sternum
V3	" " "	5th intercostal space, left of sternum
V4	" " "	5th intercostal space, centered on clavicle
V5	" " "	5th intercostal space, left of V4
V6	" " "	5th intercostal space, under left arm

types of heart disease. **Figure 12.16** gives one example. However, note that the ECG provides information concerning only the electrical activity of the heart. If something is wrong with the heart's mechanical activity and the defect does not give rise to altered electrical activity, the ECG will be of limited diagnostic value.

Excitation–Contraction Coupling

The mechanisms linking cardiac muscle cell action potentials to contraction were described in detail in the chapter on muscle physiology (Chapter 9; review Figure 9.40). The small amount of extracellular Ca^{2+} entering through L-type Ca^{2+} channels during the plateau of the action potential triggers the release of a larger quantity of Ca^{2+} from the ryanodine receptors in the sarcoplasmic reticulum membrane. Ca^{2+} activation of thin filaments and cross-bridge cycling then lead to generation of force, just as in skeletal muscle (review Figures 9.15 and 9.11). Contraction ends when Ca^{2+} is returned to the sarcoplasmic reticulum and extracellular fluid by Ca^{2+}-ATPase pumps and Na^+/Ca^{2+} countertransporters.

The amount that cytosolic Ca^{2+} concentration increases during excitation is a major determinant of the strength of cardiac muscle contraction. You may recall that in skeletal muscle, a single action potential releases sufficient Ca^{2+} to fully saturate the troponin sites that activate contraction. By contrast, the amount of Ca^{2+} released from the sarcoplasmic reticulum in cardiac muscle during a resting heartbeat is not usually sufficient to saturate all troponin sites. Therefore, the number of active cross-bridges—and thus the strength of contraction—can be increased if more Ca^{2+} is released from the sarcoplasmic reticulum (as would occur, for example, in exercise). The mechanisms that vary cytosolic Ca^{2+} concentration will be discussed later.

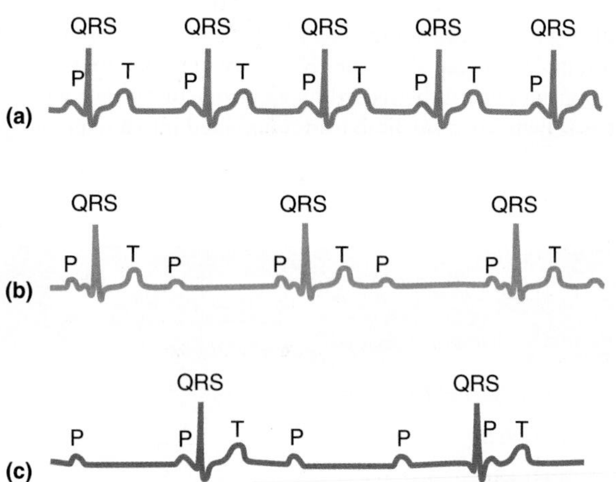

Figure 12.16 Electrocardiograms from a healthy person and from two people suffering from atrioventricular block. (a) A normal ECG. (b) Partial block. Damage to the AV node permits only every other atrial impulse to be transmitted to the ventricles. Note that every second P wave is not followed by a QRS and T. (c) Complete block. There is no synchrony between atrial and ventricular electrical activities, and the ventricles are being driven by a very slow pacemaker cell in the bundle of His.

PHYSIOLOGICAL INQUIRY

- Some people have a potentially lethal defect of ventricular muscle, in which the current through voltage-gated K^+ channels responsible for repolarization is delayed and reduced. How could this defect be detected on their ECG recordings?

Answer can be found at end of chapter.

Refractory Period of the Heart

Cardiac muscle is incapable of undergoing summation of contractions like that occurring in skeletal muscle (review Figure 9.19), and this is a very good thing. If a prolonged, tetanic contraction were to occur in the heart, it would cease to function as a pump because the ventricles can only fill with blood while they are relaxed. The inability of the heart to generate tetanic contractions is the result of the long **absolute refractory period** of cardiac muscle, defined as the period during and following an action potential when an excitable membrane cannot be re-excited. As in the case of neurons and skeletal muscle fibers, the main mechanism is the inactivation of Na^+ channels. The absolute refractory period of skeletal muscle is much shorter (1 to 2 msec) than the duration of contraction (20 to 100 msec), and a second action potential can therefore be elicited while the contraction resulting from the first action potential is still under way (see Figure 9.10). In contrast, because of the prolonged, depolarized plateau in the cardiac muscle action potential, the absolute refractory period of cardiac muscle lasts almost as long as the contraction (approximately 250 msec), and the muscle cannot be re-excited multiple times during an ongoing contraction (**Figure 12.17**; also review Figure 9.41).

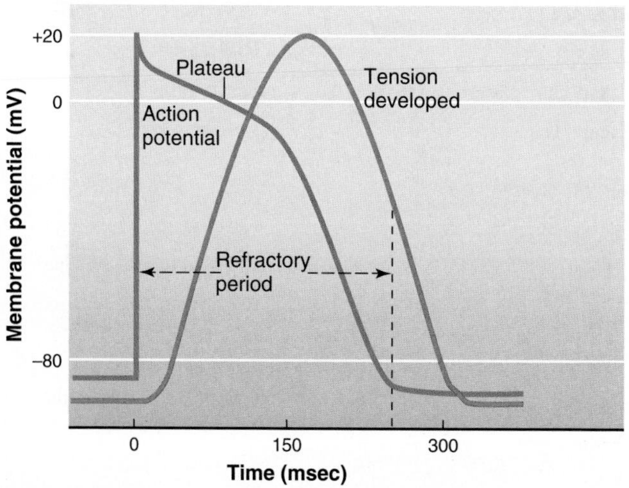

Figure 12.17 Relationship between membrane potential changes and contraction in a ventricular muscle cell. The refractory period lasts almost as long as the contraction. Tension scale not shown.

12.5 Mechanical Events of the Cardiac Cycle

The orderly process of depolarization described in the previous sections triggers a recurring **cardiac cycle** of atrial and ventricular contractions and relaxations (**Figure 12.18**). First, we will present an overview of the cycle, naming the phases and key events. A closer look at the cycle will follow, with a discussion of the pressure and volume changes that cause the events.

The cycle is divided into two major phases, both named for events in the ventricles: the period of ventricular contraction and blood ejection called **systole,** and the alternating period of ventricular relaxation and blood filling, **diastole.** For a typical heart rate of 72 beats/min, each cardiac cycle lasts approximately 0.8 sec, with 0.3 sec in systole and 0.5 sec in diastole.

As Figure 12.18 illustrates, both systole and diastole can be subdivided into two discrete periods. During the first part of systole, the ventricles are contracting but all valves in the heart are closed and so no blood can be ejected. This period is termed **isovolumetric ventricular contraction** because the ventricular volume is constant ("iso" means "equal" or in this context "unchanging"). The ventricular

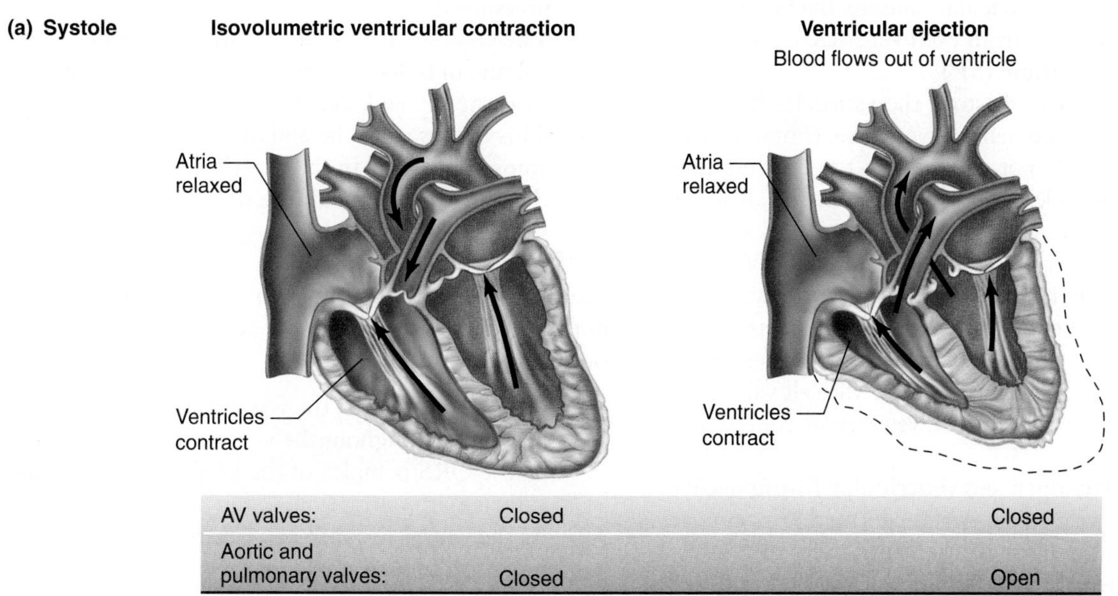

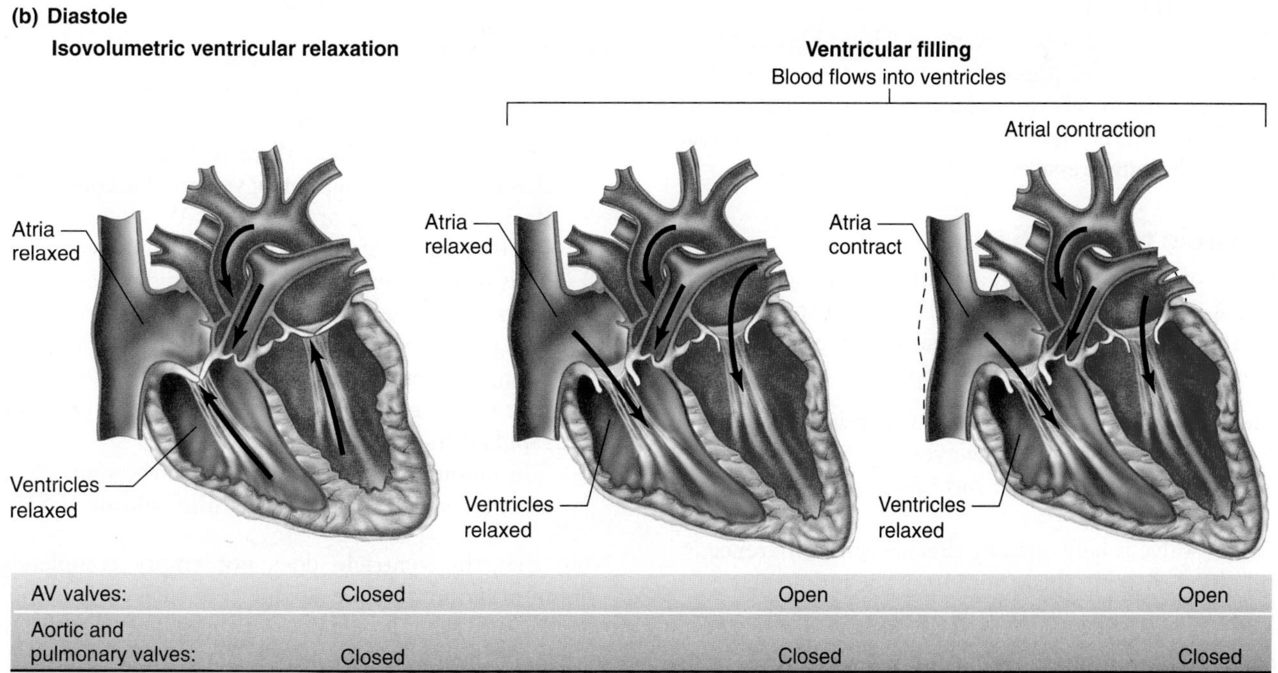

Figure 12.18 APIR Divisions of the cardiac cycle: (a) systole; (b) diastole. The phases of the cycle are identical in both halves of the heart. The direction in which the pressure difference *favors* flow is denoted by an arrow; note, however, that flow will not actually occur if a valve prevents it.

walls are developing tension and squeezing on the blood they enclose, increasing the ventricular blood pressure. However, because the volume of blood in the ventricles is constant and because blood, like water, is essentially incompressible, the ventricular muscle fibers cannot shorten. Thus, isovolumetric ventricular contraction is analogous to an isometric skeletal muscle contraction; the muscle develops tension, but it does not shorten.

Once the increasing pressure in the ventricles exceeds that in the aorta and pulmonary trunk, the aortic and pulmonary valves open and the **ventricular ejection** period of systole occurs. Blood is forced into the aorta and pulmonary trunk as the contracting ventricular muscle fibers shorten. The volume of blood ejected from each ventricle during systole is called the **stroke volume** (*SV*).

During the first part of diastole, the ventricles begin to relax and the aortic and pulmonary valves close. (Physiologists and clinical cardiologists do not all agree on the dividing line between systole and diastole; as presented here, the dividing line is the point at which ventricular contraction stops and the pulmonary and aortic valves close.) At this time, the AV valves are also closed; therefore, no blood is entering or leaving the ventricles. Ventricular volume is not changing, and this period is called **isovolumetric ventricular relaxation.** Note, then, that the only times during the cardiac cycle that all valves are closed are the periods of isovolumetric ventricular contraction and relaxation.

Next, the AV valves open and **ventricular filling** occurs as blood flows in from the atria. Atrial contraction occurs at the end of diastole, after most of the ventricular filling has taken place. The ventricle receives blood throughout most of diastole, not just when the atrium contracts. Indeed, in a person at rest, approximately 80% of ventricular filling occurs before atrial contraction.

This completes the basic orientation. Using **Figure 12.19**, we can now analyze the pressure and volume changes that occur in the left atrium, left ventricle, and aorta during the cardiac cycle. Events on the right side of the heart are very similar except for the absolute pressures.

Mid-Diastole to Late Diastole

Our analysis of events in the left atrium and ventricle and the aorta begins at the far left of Figure 12.19 with the events of mid- to late diastole. The numbers that follow correspond to the numbered events shown in that figure.

1. The left atrium and ventricle are both relaxed, but atrial pressure is slightly higher than ventricular pressure because the atrium is filled with blood that is entering from the veins.
2. The AV valve is held open by this pressure difference, and blood entering the atrium from the pulmonary veins continues on into the ventricle.

To reemphasize a point made earlier, all the valves of the heart offer very little resistance when they are open, so very small pressure differences across them are required to produce relatively large flows.

3. Note that at this time, and throughout all of diastole, the aortic valve is closed because the aortic pressure is higher than the ventricular pressure.
4. Throughout diastole, the aortic pressure is slowly decreasing because blood is moving out of the arteries and through the vascular system.
5. In contrast, ventricular pressure is increasing slightly because blood is entering the relaxed ventricle from the atrium, thereby expanding the ventricular volume.
6. Near the end of diastole, the SA node discharges and the atria depolarize, as signified by the P wave of the ECG.
7. Contraction of the atrium causes an increase in atrial pressure.
8. The elevated atrial pressure forces a small additional volume of blood into the ventricle, sometimes referred to as the "atrial kick."
9. This brings us to the end of ventricular diastole, so the amount of blood in the ventricle at this time is called the **end-diastolic volume** (*EDV*).

Systole

Thus far, the ventricle has been relaxed as it fills with blood. But immediately following the atrial contraction, the ventricles begin to contract.

10. From the AV node, the wave of depolarization passes into and throughout the ventricular tissue—as signified by the QRS complex of the ECG—and this triggers ventricular contraction.
11. As the ventricle contracts, ventricular pressure increases rapidly; almost immediately, this pressure exceeds the atrial pressure.
12. This change in pressure gradient forces the AV valve to close, thus preventing the backflow of blood into the atrium.
13. Because the aortic pressure still exceeds the ventricular pressure at this time, the aortic valve remains closed and the ventricle cannot empty despite its contraction. For a brief time, then, all valves are closed during this phase of isovolumetric ventricular contraction. Backward bulging of the closed AV valves causes a small upward deflection in the atrial pressure wave.
14. This brief phase ends when the rapidly increasing ventricular pressure exceeds aortic pressure.
15. The pressure gradient now forces the aortic valve to open, and ventricular ejection begins.
16. The ventricular volume curve shows that ejection is rapid at first and then slows down.
17. The amount of blood remaining in the ventricle after ejection is called the **end-systolic volume** (*ESV*).

Note that the ventricle does not empty completely. The amount of blood that does exit during each cycle is the difference between what it contained at the end of diastole and what remains at the end of systole. Thus,

$$\underset{SV}{\text{Stroke volume}} = \underset{EDV}{\text{End-diastolic volume}} - \underset{ESV}{\text{End-systolic volume}}$$

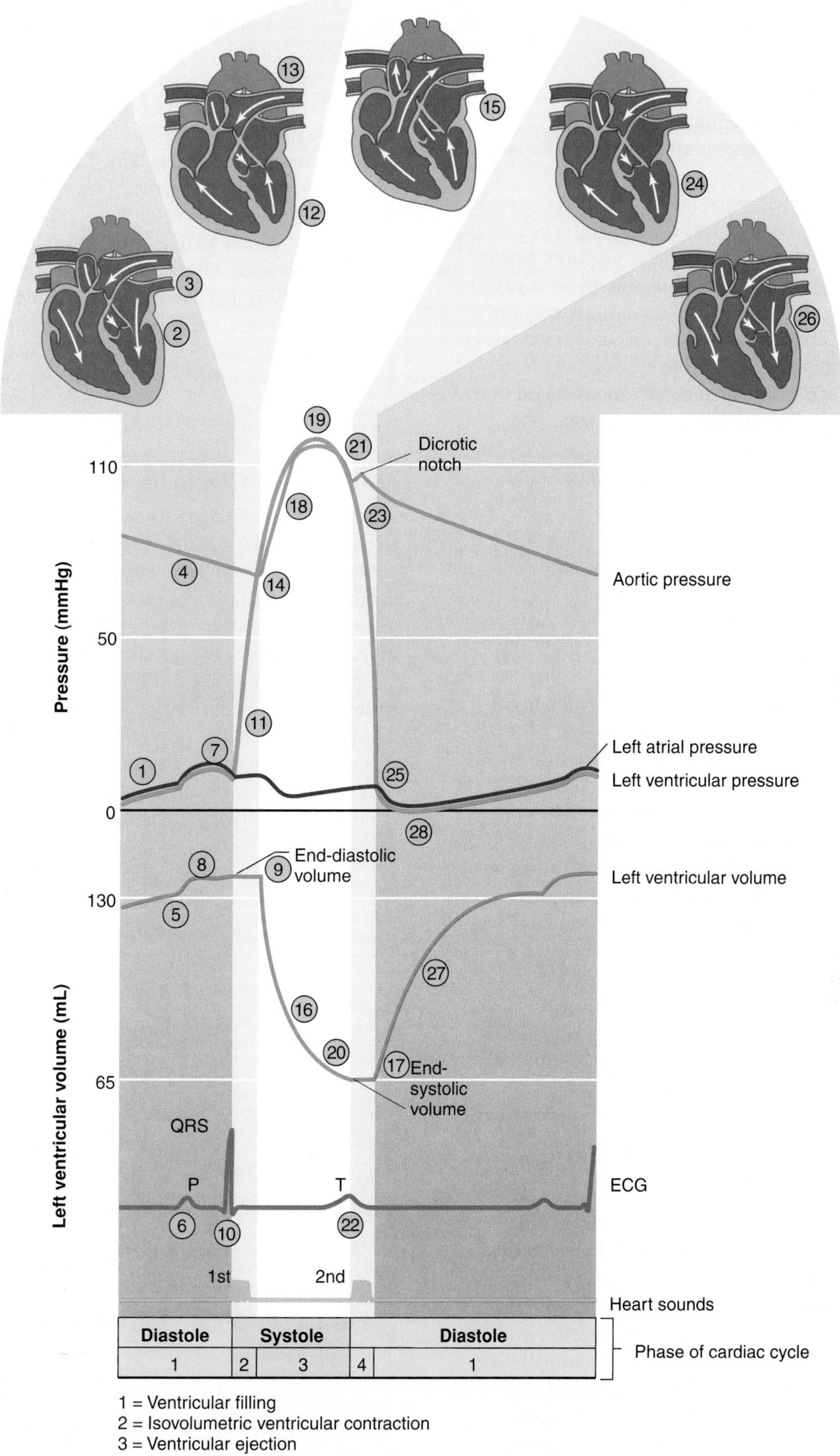

Figure 12.19 APIR Summary of events in the left atrium, left ventricle, and aorta during the cardiac cycle (sometimes called the "Wiggers" diagram). See text for a description of the numbered steps.

As Figure 12.19 shows, typical values for an adult at rest are end-diastolic volume = 135 mL, end-systolic volume = 65 mL, and stroke volume = 70 mL.

(18) As blood flows into the aorta, the aortic pressure increases along with the ventricular pressure. Throughout ejection, very small pressure differences exist between the ventricle and aorta because the open aortic valve offers little resistance to flow.

(19) Note that peak ventricular and aortic pressures are reached before the end of ventricular ejection; that is, these pressures start to decrease during the last part of systole despite continued ventricular contraction. This is because the strength of ventricular contraction diminishes during the last part of systole.

(20) This force reduction is evidenced by the reduced rate of blood ejection during the last part of systole.

(21) The volume and pressure in the aorta decrease as the rate of blood ejection from the ventricles becomes slower than the rate at which blood drains out of the arteries into the tissues.

Early Diastole

This phase of diastole begins as the ventricular muscle relaxes and ejection comes to an end.

(22) Recall that the T wave of the ECG corresponds to ventricular repolarization.

(23) As the ventricles relax, the ventricular pressure decreases below aortic pressure, which remains significantly elevated due to the volume of blood that just entered. The change in the pressure gradient forces the aortic valve to close. The combination of elastic recoil of the aorta and blood rebounding against the valve causes a rebound of aortic pressure called the **dicrotic notch.**

(24) The AV valve also remains closed because the ventricular pressure is still higher than atrial pressure. For a brief time, then, all valves are again closed during this phase of isovolumetric ventricular relaxation.

(25) This phase ends as the rapidly decreasing ventricular pressure decreases below atrial pressure.

(26) This change in pressure gradient results in the opening of the AV valve.

(27) Venous blood that had accumulated in the atrium since the AV valve closed flows rapidly into the ventricles.

(28) The rate of blood flow is enhanced during this initial filling phase by a rapid decrease in ventricular pressure. This occurs because the ventricle's previous contraction compressed the elastic elements of the chamber in such a way that the ventricle actually tends to recoil outward once systole is over. This expansion, in turn, lowers ventricular pressure more rapidly than would otherwise occur and may even create a negative (subatmospheric) pressure. Thus, some energy is stored within the myocardium during contraction, and its release during the subsequent relaxation aids filling.

The fact that most ventricular filling is completed during early diastole is of great importance. It ensures that filling is not seriously impaired during periods when the heart is beating very rapidly, and the duration of diastole and, therefore, total filling time are reduced. However, when heart rates of approximately 200 beats/min or more are reached, filling time becomes inadequate and the volume of blood pumped during each beat decreases. The clinical significance of this will be described in Section E.

Early ventricular filling also explains why the conduction defects that eliminate the atria as effective pumps do not seriously impair ventricular filling, at least in otherwise healthy individuals at rest. This is true, for example, of ***atrial fibrillation,*** a state in which the cells of the atria contract in a completely uncoordinated manner and so the atria fail to work as effective pumps.

Pulmonary Circulation Pressures

The pressure changes in the right ventricle and pulmonary arteries (**Figure 12.20**) are qualitatively similar to those just described for the left ventricle and aorta. There are striking quantitative differences, however. Typical pulmonary arterial systolic and diastolic pressures are 25 and 10 mmHg, respectively, compared to systemic arterial pressures of 120 and 80 mmHg. Thus, the pulmonary circulation is a low-pressure system, for reasons to be described later. This difference is clearly reflected in the ventricular anatomy—the right ventricular wall is much thinner than the left. Despite the difference in pressure during contraction, however, the stroke volumes of the two ventricles are the same.

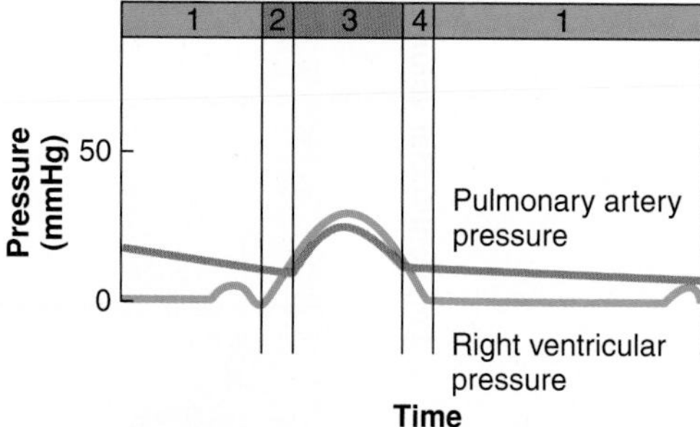

Figure 12.20 AP|R Pressures in the right ventricle and pulmonary artery during the cardiac cycle. Note that the pressures are lower than in the left ventricle and aorta.

PHYSIOLOGICAL INQUIRY

- If a person had a hole in the interventricular septum, would the blood ejected into the aorta have lower than normal oxygen levels?

Answer can be found at end of chapter.

Heart Sounds

Two **heart sounds** resulting from cardiac contraction are normally heard through a stethoscope placed on the chest wall. The first sound, a soft, low-pitched *lub*, is associated with closure of the AV valves; the second sound, a louder *dup*, is associated with closure of the pulmonary and aortic valves. Note in Figure 12.19 that the *lub* marks the onset of systole and the *dup* occurs at the onset of diastole. These sounds, which result from vibrations caused by the closing valves, are perfectly normal, but other sounds, known as ***heart murmurs,*** can be a sign of heart disease.

Murmurs can be produced by heart defects that cause blood flow to be turbulent. Normally, blood flow through valves and vessels is **laminar flow**—that is, it flows in smooth concentric layers (**Figure 12.21**). Turbulent flow can be caused by blood flowing rapidly in the usual direction through an abnormally narrowed valve (***stenosis***); by blood flowing backward through a damaged, leaky valve (***insufficiency***); or by blood flowing between the two atria or two ventricles through a small hole in the wall separating them (called a ***septal defect***).

The exact timing and location of the murmur provide the physician with a powerful diagnostic clue. For example, a murmur heard throughout systole suggests a stenotic pulmonary or aortic valve, an insufficient AV valve, or a hole in the interventricular septum. In contrast, a murmur heard during diastole suggests a stenotic AV valve or an insufficient pulmonary or aortic valve.

12.6 The Cardiac Output

The volume of blood each ventricle pumps as a function of time, usually expressed in liters per minute, is called the **cardiac output** (***CO***). In the steady state, the cardiac output flowing through the systemic and the pulmonary circuits is the same.

The cardiac output is calculated by multiplying the heart rate (*HR*)—the number of beats per minute—and the stroke volume (*SV*)—the blood volume ejected by each ventricle with each beat:

$$CO = HR \times SV$$

For example, if each ventricle has a rate of 72 beats/min and ejects 70 mL of blood with each beat, the cardiac output is

$$CO = 72 \text{ beats/min} \times 0.07 \text{ L/beat} = 5.0 \text{ L/min}$$

These values are typical for a resting, average-sized adult. Given that the average total blood volume is about 5.5 L, nearly all the blood is pumped around the circuit once each minute. During periods of strenuous exercise in well-trained athletes, the cardiac output may reach 35 L/min; the entire blood volume is pumped around the circuit almost seven times per minute! Even sedentary, untrained individuals can reach cardiac outputs of 20–25 L/min during exercise.

The following description of the factors that alter the two determinants of cardiac output—heart rate and stroke volume—applies in all respects to both the right and left sides of the heart because stroke volume and heart rate are the same for both under steady-state conditions. Heart rate and stroke volume do not always change in the same direction. For example, stroke volume decreases following blood loss, whereas heart rate increases. These changes produce opposing effects on cardiac output.

Control of Heart Rate

Rhythmic beating of the heart at a rate of approximately 100 beats/min will occur in the complete absence of any nervous or hormonal influences on the SA node. This is the inherent autonomous discharge rate of the SA node. The heart rate may be slower or faster than this, however, because the SA node is normally under the constant influence of nerves and hormones.

A large number of parasympathetic and sympathetic postganglionic neurons end on the SA node. Activity in the parasympathetic neurons (which travel within the vagus nerve) causes the heart rate to decrease, whereas activity in the sympathetic neurons causes an increase. In the resting state, there is considerably more parasympathetic activity to the heart than sympathetic, so the normal resting heart rate of about 70 beats/min is well below the inherent rate of 100 beats/min.

Figure 12.22 illustrates how sympathetic and parasympathetic activity influence SA node function. Sympathetic stimulation increases the slope of the pacemaker potential by increasing the F-type channel permeability. Because the

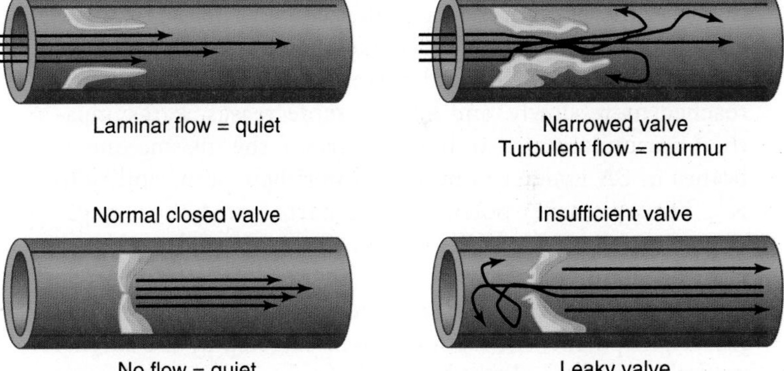

Figure 12.21 Heart valve defects causing turbulent blood flow and murmurs. (a) Normal valves allow smooth, laminar flow of blood in the forward direction when open and prevent backward flow of blood when closed. No sound is heard in either state. (b) Stenotic valves cause rapid, turbulent forward flow of blood, making a high-pitched, whistling murmur. Valve insufficiency results in turbulent backward flow when the valve should be closed, causing a low-pitched gurgling murmur.

PHYSIOLOGICAL INQUIRY

- What valve defect(s) would be indicated by the following sequence of heart sounds: *lub-whistle-dup-gurgle?*

Answer can be found at end of chapter.

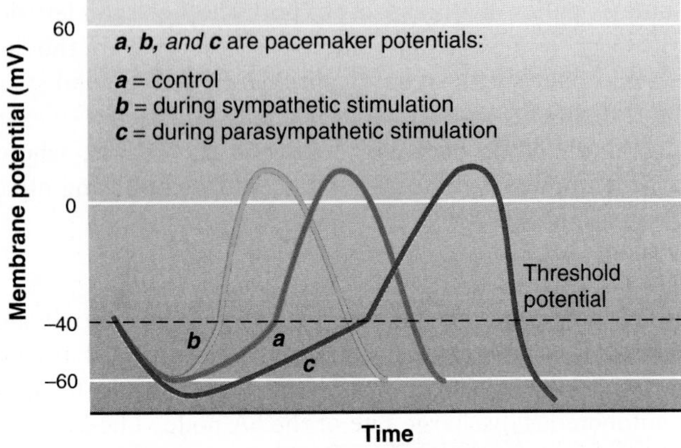

Figure 12.22 Effects of sympathetic and parasympathetic nerve stimulation on the slope of the pacemaker potential of an SA nodal cell. Note that parasympathetic stimulation not only reduces the slope of the pacemaker potential but also causes the membrane potential to be more negative before the pacemaker potential begins. Adapted from Hoffman and Cranefield.

PHYSIOLOGICAL INQUIRY

- Parasympathetic stimulation also increases the delay between atrial and ventricular contractions. What is the ionic mechanism?

Answer can be found at end of chapter.

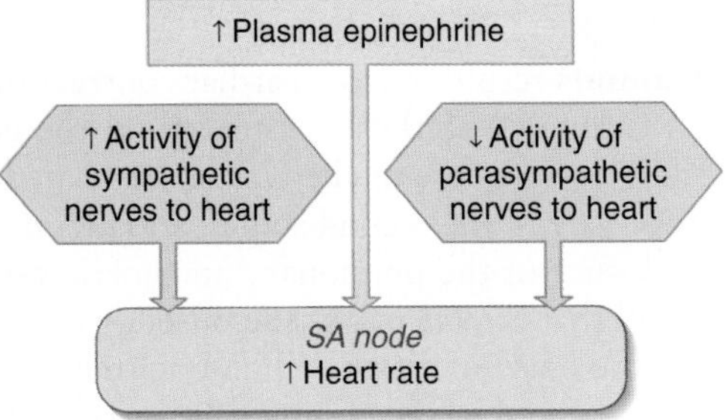

Figure 12.23 Major factors influencing heart rate. All effects are exerted upon the SA node. The figure shows how heart rate is increased; reversal of all the arrows in the boxes would illustrate how heart rate is decreased.

main current through these channels is Na^+ entering the cell, faster depolarization results. This causes the SA node cells to reach threshold more rapidly and the heart rate to increase. Increasing parasympathetic input has the opposite effect—the slope of the pacemaker potential decreases due to a reduction in the inward current. Threshold is therefore reached more slowly, and heart rate decreases. Parasympathetic stimulation also hyperpolarizes the plasma membranes of SA node cells by increasing their permeability to K^+. The pacemaker potential thus starts from a more negative value (closer to the K^+ equilibrium potential) and has a reduced slope.

Factors other than the cardiac nerves can also alter heart rate. Epinephrine, the main hormone secreted by the adrenal medulla, speeds the heart by acting on the same β-adrenergic receptors in the SA node as norepinephrine released from neurons. The heart rate is also sensitive to changes in body temperature, plasma electrolyte concentrations, hormones other than epinephrine, and adenosine—a metabolite produced by myocardial cells. These factors are normally of lesser importance, however, than the cardiac nerves. **Figure 12.23** summarizes the major determinants of heart rate.

As stated in the previous section on innervation, sympathetic and parasympathetic neurons innervate not only the SA node but other parts of the conducting system as well. Sympathetic stimulation increases conduction velocity through the entire cardiac conducting system, whereas parasympathetic stimulation decreases the rate of spread of excitation through the atria and the AV node. Autonomic regulation of heart rate is one of the best examples of the general principle of physiology that most physiological functions are controlled by multiple regulatory systems, often working in opposition.

Control of Stroke Volume

The second variable that determines cardiac output is stroke volume—the volume of blood each ventricle ejects during each contraction. Recall that the ventricles do not completely empty themselves during contraction. Therefore, a more forceful contraction can produce an increase in stroke volume by causing greater emptying. Changes in the force during ejection of the stroke volume can be produced by a variety of factors, but three are dominant under most physiological and pathophysiological conditions: (1) changes in the end-diastolic volume (the volume of blood in the ventricles just before contraction, sometimes referred to as the **preload**); (2) changes in the magnitude of sympathetic nervous system input to the ventricles; and (3) changes in **afterload** (i.e., the arterial pressures against which the ventricles pump).

Relationship Between Ventricular End-Diastolic Volume and Stroke Volume: The Frank–Starling Mechanism

The mechanical properties of cardiac muscle form the basis for an inherent mechanism for altering the strength of contraction and stroke volume; the ventricle contracts more forcefully during systole when it has been filled to a greater degree during diastole. In other words, all other factors being equal, the stroke volume increases as the end-diastolic volume increases. This is illustrated graphically as a **ventricular-function curve** (**Figure 12.24**). This relationship between stroke volume and end-diastolic volume is known as the **Frank–Starling mechanism** (also called *Starling's law of the heart*) in recognition of the two physiologists who identified it.

What accounts for the Frank–Starling mechanism? Basically, it is a length–tension relationship, as described for skeletal muscle in Figure 9.21, because end-diastolic volume is a major determinant of how stretched the ventricular sarcomeres are just before contraction: The greater the end-diastolic volume, the greater the stretch and the more forceful the contraction. However, a comparison of Figure 12.24 with Figure 9.21 reveals an important difference in the length–tension relationship between skeletal and cardiac muscle. The normal point for cardiac muscle in a resting individual is not at its optimal length for contraction, as it is for most resting

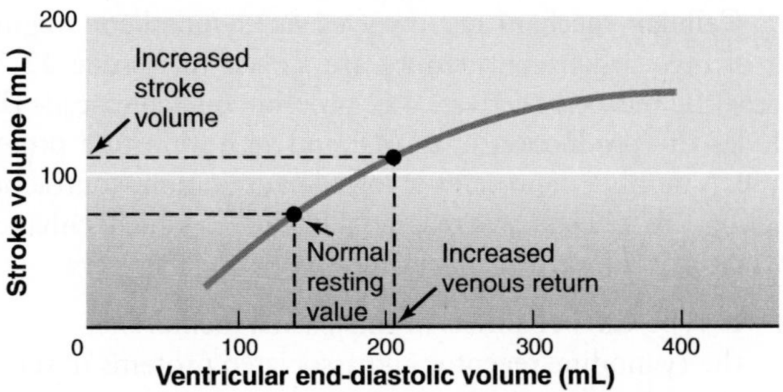

Figure 12.24 A ventricular-function curve, which expresses the relationship between end-diastolic ventricular volume and stroke volume (the Frank–Starling mechanism). The horizontal axis could have been labeled "sarcomere length" and the vertical "contractile force." In other words, this is a length–tension curve, analogous to that for skeletal muscle (see Figure 9.21). At very high volumes, force (and, therefore, stroke volume) declines as in skeletal muscle (not shown).

skeletal muscles, but is on the rising phase of the curve. For this reason, greater filling causes additional stretching of the cardiac muscle fibers and increases the force of contraction.

The mechanisms linking changes in muscle length to changes in muscle force are more complex in cardiac muscle than in skeletal muscle. In addition to changing the overlap of thick and thin filaments, stretching cardiac muscle cells toward their optimum length decreases the spacing between thick and thin filaments (allowing more cross-bridges to bind during a twitch), increases the sensitivity of troponin for binding Ca^{2+}, and increases Ca^{2+} release from the sarcoplasmic reticulum.

The significance of the Frank–Starling mechanism is as follows: At any given heart rate, an increase in the **venous return**—the flow of blood from the veins into the heart—automatically forces an increase in cardiac output by increasing end-diastolic volume and, therefore, stroke volume. One important function of this relationship is maintaining the equality of right and left cardiac outputs. For example, if the right side of the heart suddenly begins to pump more blood than the left, the increased blood flow returning to the left ventricle will automatically produce an increase in left ventricular output. This ensures that blood will not accumulate in the pulmonary circulation.

Sympathetic Regulation

Sympathetic nerves are distributed to the entire myocardium. The sympathetic neurotransmitter norepinephrine acts on β-adrenergic receptors to increase ventricular **contractility,** defined as the strength of contraction *at any given end-diastolic volume.* Plasma epinephrine acting on these receptors also increases myocardial contractility. Thus, the increased force of contraction and stroke volume resulting from sympathetic nerve stimulation or epinephrine are independent of a change in end-diastolic ventricular volume.

A change in contraction force due to increased end-diastolic volume (the Frank–Starling mechanism) does not reflect increased contractility. Increased contractility is specifically defined as an increased contraction force at *any* given end-diastolic volume.

The distinction between the Frank–Starling mechanism and sympathetic stimulation is illustrated in **Figure 12.25a.** The green ventricular-function curve is the same as that shown in Figure 12.24. The orange ventricular-function curve was

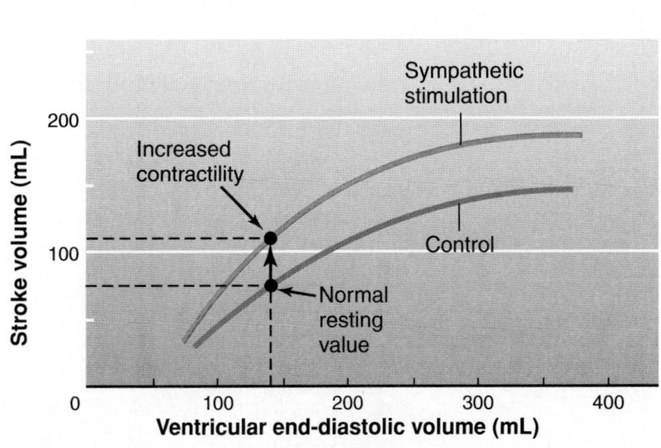

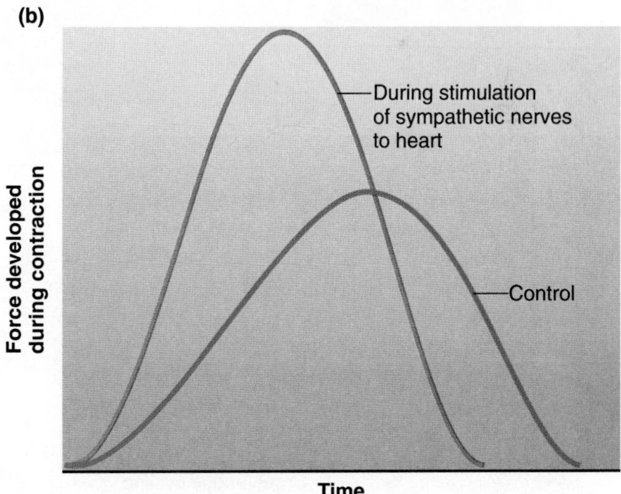

Figure 12.25 Sympathetic stimulation causes increased contractility of ventricular muscle. (a) Stroke volume is increased at any given end-diastolic volume. (b) Both the rate of force development and the rate of relaxation increase, as does the maximum force developed.

PHYSIOLOGICAL INQUIRY

- Estimate the ejection fraction and end-systolic volumes under control and sympathetic stimulation conditions at an end-diastolic volume of 140 mL.

Answer can be found at end of chapter.

obtained for the same heart during sympathetic nerve stimulation. The Frank–Starling mechanism still applies, but during sympathetic stimulation, the stroke volume is greater at any given end-diastolic volume. In other words, the increased contractility leads to a more complete ejection of the end-diastolic ventricular volume.

One way to quantify contractility is through the **ejection fraction (*EF*)**, defined as the ratio of stroke volume (*SV*) to end-diastolic volume (*EDV*):

$$EF = SV/EDV$$

Expressed as a percentage, the ejection fraction normally averages between 50% and 75% under resting conditions. Increased contractility causes an increased ejection fraction.

Not only does increased sympathetic stimulation of the myocardium cause a more powerful contraction, it also causes both the contraction and relaxation of the ventricles to occur more quickly (**Figure 12.25b**). These latter effects are quite important because, as described earlier, increased sympathetic activity to the heart also increases heart rate. As heart rate increases, the time available for diastolic filling decreases, but the quicker contraction and relaxation induced simultaneously by the sympathetic neurons partially compensate for this problem by permitting a larger fraction of the cardiac cycle to be available for filling.

Cellular mechanisms involved in sympathetic regulation of myocardial contractility are shown in **Figure 12.26**. Adrenergic receptors activate a G-protein-coupled cascade that includes the production of cAMP and activation of a protein kinase. A number of proteins involved in excitation–contraction coupling are phosphorylated by the kinase, which enhances contractility. These proteins include

1. L-type Ca^{2+} channels in the plasma membrane;
2. the ryanodine receptor and associated proteins in the sarcoplasmic reticulum membrane;
3. thin filament proteins—in particular, troponin;
4. thick filament proteins associated with the cross-bridges; and
5. proteins involved in pumping Ca^{2+} back into the sarcoplasmic reticulum.

Due to these alterations, cytosolic Ca^{2+} concentration increases more quickly and reaches a greater value during excitation, Ca^{2+} returns to its pre-excitation value more quickly following excitation, and the rates of cross-bridge activation and cycling are accelerated. The net result is the stronger, faster contraction observed during sympathetic activation of the heart.

There is little parasympathetic innervation of the ventricles, so the parasympathetic system normally has a negligible direct effect on ventricular contractility.

Table 12.3 summarizes the effects of the autonomic nerves on cardiac function.

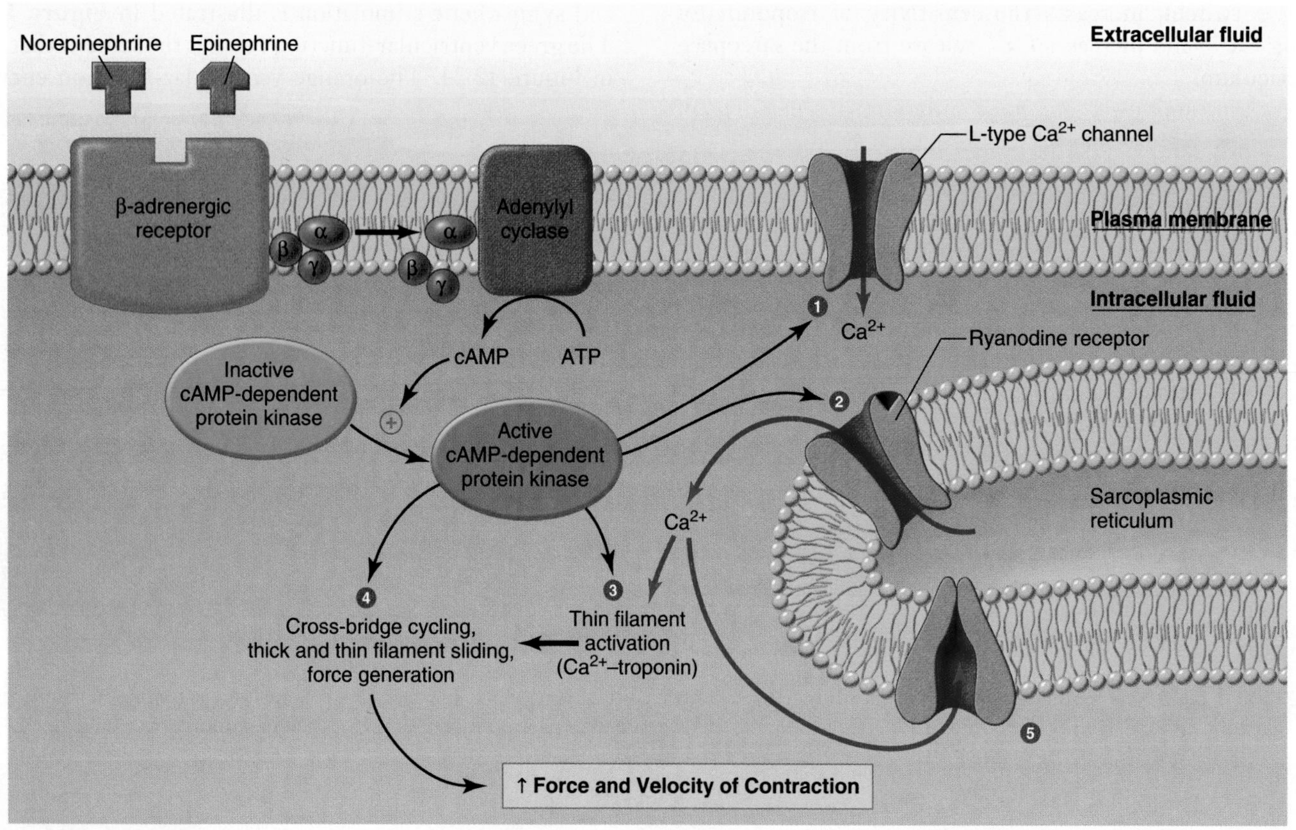

Figure 12.26 APIR Mechanisms of sympathetic effects on cardiac muscle cell contractility. In some of the pathways, the kinase phosphorylates accessory proteins that are not shown.

TABLE 12.3 Effects of Autonomic Nerves on the Heart		
Area Affected	Sympathetic Nerves (Norepinephrine on β-Adrenergic Receptors)	Parasympathetic Nerves (ACh on Muscarinic Receptors)
SA node	Increased heart rate	Decreased heart rate
AV node	Increased conduction rate	Decreased conduction rate
Atrial muscle	Increased contractility	Decreased contractility
Ventricular muscle	Increased contractility	No significant effect

Afterload

An increased arterial pressure tends to reduce stroke volume. This is because, like a skeletal muscle lifting a weight, the arterial pressure constitutes a "load" that contracting ventricular muscle must work against when it is ejecting blood. A term used to describe how hard the heart must work to eject blood is *afterload.* The greater the load, the less contracting muscle fibers can shorten at a given contractility (review Figure 9.17). This factor will not be dealt with further, because in the normal heart, several inherent adjustments minimize the overall influence of arterial pressure on stroke volume. However, in the sections on high blood pressure and heart failure, we will see that alterations in vascular resistance and long-term elevations of arterial pressure can weaken the heart and thereby influence stroke volume.

Figure 12.27 integrates the factors that determine stroke volume and heart rate into a summary of the control of cardiac output.

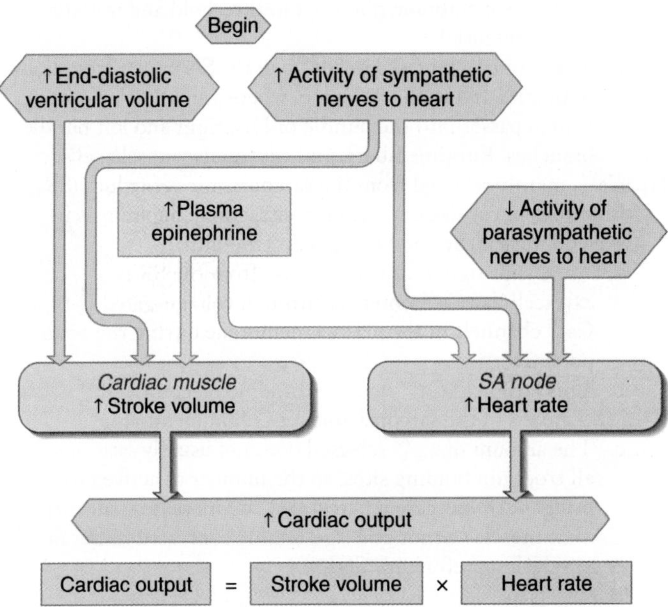

Figure 12.27 Major factors determining cardiac output. Reversal of all arrows in the boxes would illustrate how cardiac output is decreased.

PHYSIOLOGICAL INQUIRY

- Recall from Figure 12.9 that parasympathetic nerves do not innervate the ventricles. Is it therefore impossible for parasympathetic activity to influence stroke volume?

Answer can be found at end of chapter.

12.7 Measurement of Cardiac Function

Human cardiac output and heart function can be measured by a variety of methods. For example, ***echocardiography*** can be used to obtain two- and three-dimensional images of the heart throughout the entire cardiac cycle. In this procedure, ultrasonic waves are beamed at the heart and returning echoes are electronically plotted by computer to produce continuous images of the heart. It can detect the abnormal functioning of cardiac valves or contractions of the cardiac walls, and it can also be used to measure ejection fraction.

Echocardiography is a noninvasive technique because everything used remains external to the body. Other visualization techniques are invasive. One, ***cardiac angiography,*** requires the temporary threading of a thin, flexible tube called a catheter through an artery or vein into the heart. A liquid containing radiopaque contrast material is then injected through the catheter during high-speed x-ray videography. This technique is useful not only for evaluating cardiac function but also for identifying narrowed coronary arteries.

SECTION B SUMMARY

Anatomy

I. The atrioventricular (AV) valves prevent flow from the ventricles back into the atria.

II. The pulmonary and aortic valves prevent backflow from the pulmonary trunk into the right ventricle and from the aorta into the left ventricle, respectively.

III. Cardiac muscle cells are joined by gap junctions that permit the conduction of action potentials from cell to cell.

IV. The myocardium also contains specialized cells that constitute the conducting system of the heart, initiating cardiac action potentials and speeding their spread through the heart.

Heartbeat Coordination

I. Action potentials must be initiated in cardiac cells for contraction to occur.
   a. The rapid depolarization of the action potential in atrial and ventricular muscle cells is due mainly to a positive feedback increase in Na^+ permeability.
   b. Following the initial rapid depolarization, the cardiac muscle cell membrane remains depolarized (the plateau phase) for almost the entire duration of the contraction because of prolonged entry of Ca^{2+} into the cell through plasma membrane L-type Ca^{2+} channels.

II. The SA node generates the action potential that leads to depolarization of all other cardiac cells.
   a. The SA node manifests a pacemaker potential involving F-type cation channels and T-type Ca^{2+} channels, which brings its membrane potential to threshold and initiates an action potential.
   b. The action potential spreads from the SA node throughout both atria and to the AV node, where a small delay occurs. It then passes into the bundle of His, right and left bundle branches, Purkinje fibers, and ventricular muscle cells.

III. Ca^{2+}, mainly released from the sarcoplasmic reticulum (SR), functions in cardiac excitation–contraction coupling, as in skeletal muscle, by combining with troponin.
   a. The major signal for Ca^{2+} release from the SR is extracellular Ca^{2+} entering through voltage-gated L-type Ca^{2+} channels in the plasma membrane during the action potential.
   b. This "trigger" Ca^{2+} opens ryanodine receptor Ca^{2+} channels in the sarcoplasmic reticulum membrane.
   c. The amount of Ca^{2+} released does not usually saturate all troponin binding sites, so the number of active cross-bridges can increase if cytosolic Ca^{2+} increases still further.

IV. Cardiac muscle cannot undergo tetanic contractions because it has a very long refractory period.

Mechanical Events of the Cardiac Cycle

I. The cardiac cycle is divided into systole (ventricular contraction) and diastole (ventricular relaxation).
   a. At the onset of systole, ventricular pressure rapidly exceeds atrial pressure and the AV valves close. The aortic and pulmonary valves are not yet open, however, so no ejection occurs during this isovolumetric ventricular contraction.
   b. When ventricular pressures exceed aortic and pulmonary trunk pressures, the aortic and pulmonary valves open and the ventricles eject the blood.
   c. When the ventricles relax at the beginning of diastole, the ventricular pressures decrease significantly below those in the aorta and pulmonary trunk and the aortic and pulmonary valves close. Because the AV valves are also still closed, no change in ventricular volume occurs during this isovolumetric ventricular relaxation.
   d. When ventricular pressures decrease below the pressures in the right and the left atria, the AV valves open and the ventricular filling phase of diastole begins.
   e. Filling occurs very rapidly at first so that atrial contraction, which occurs at the very end of diastole, usually adds only a small amount of additional blood to the ventricles.

II. The amount of blood in the ventricles just before systole is the end-diastolic volume. The volume remaining after ejection is the end-systolic volume, and the volume ejected is the stroke volume.

III. Pressure changes in the systemic and pulmonary circulations have similar patterns, but the pulmonary pressures are much lower.

IV. The first heart sound is due to the closing of the AV valves, and the second is due to the closing of the aortic and pulmonary valves.

V. Murmurs can result from narrowed or leaky valves, as well as from holes in the interventricular septum.

The Cardiac Output

I. The cardiac output is the volume of blood each ventricle pumps per unit time, and equals the product of heart rate and stroke volume.
   a. Heart rate is increased by stimulation of the sympathetic neurons to the heart and by epinephrine; it is decreased by stimulation of the parasympathetic neurons to the heart.
   b. Stroke volume is increased mainly by an increase in end-diastolic volume (the Frank–Starling mechanism) and by an increase in contractility due to sympathetic stimulation or to epinephrine. Increased afterload can reduce stroke volume in certain situations.

Measurement of Cardiac Function

I. Methods of measuring cardiac function include echocardiography, for assessing wall and valve function, and cardiac angiography, for determining coronary blood flow.

SECTION B REVIEW QUESTIONS

1. List the structures through which blood passes from the systemic veins to the systemic arteries.
2. Contrast and compare the structure of cardiac muscle with that of skeletal and smooth muscle.
3. Describe the autonomic innervation of the heart, including the types of receptors involved.
4. Draw a ventricular muscle cell action potential. Describe the changes in membrane permeability that underlie the membrane potential changes.
5. Contrast action potentials in ventricular muscle cells with SA node action potentials. What is the pacemaker potential due to, and what is its inherent rate? By what mechanism does the SA node function as the pacemaker for the entire heart?
6. Describe the spread of excitation from the SA node through the rest of the heart.
7. Draw and label a normal ECG. Relate the P, QRS, and T waves to the atrial and ventricular action potentials.
8. Explain how the electrical activity of the heart can be viewed from different angles with electrocardiography.
9. What prevents the heart from undergoing summation of contractions?
10. Draw a diagram of the pressure changes in the left atrium, left ventricle, and aorta throughout the cardiac cycle. Show when the valves open and close, when the heart sounds occur, and the pattern of ventricular ejection.
11. Contrast the pressures in the right ventricle and pulmonary trunk with those in the left ventricle and aorta.
12. What causes heart murmurs in diastole? In systole?
13. Write the formula relating cardiac output, heart rate, and stroke volume; give normal values for a resting adult.
14. Describe the effects of sympathetic and parasympathetic neuronal stimulation on heart rate. Which is dominant at rest?
15. What are the major factors influencing force of contraction?
16. Draw a ventricular-function curve illustrating the Frank–Starling mechanism.

17. Describe the effects of sympathetic neuron stimulation on cardiac muscle during contraction and relaxation.
18. Draw a pair of curves relating end-diastolic volume and stroke volume, with and without sympathetic stimulation.
19. Summarize the effects of the autonomic nervous system on the heart.
20. Draw a flow diagram summarizing the factors determining cardiac output.

SECTION B KEY TERMS

absolute refractory period 376
afterload 382
aortic valve 369
atrioventricular (AV) node 371
atrioventricular (AV) valve 368
automaticity 373
bicuspid valve 368
bundle branches 372
bundle of His 371
cardiac cycle 377
cardiac output (*CO*) 381
chordae tendineae 369
conducting system 369
contractility 383
coronary artery 370
coronary blood flow 370
diastole 377
dicrotic notch 380
ECG lead 374
ejection fraction (*EF*) 384
electrocardiogram (ECG) 374
end-diastolic volume (*EDV*) 378
endothelial cell 368
endothelium 368
end-systolic volume (*ESV*) 378
epicardium 368
Frank–Starling mechanism 382
F-type channel 373
heart rate 371
heart sounds 381
internodal pathway 371
interventricular septum 368
isovolumetric ventricular contraction 377
isovolumetric ventricular relaxation 378
laminar flow 381
L-type Ca^{2+} channel 373
mitral valve 368
myocardium 368
pacemaker potential 373
papillary muscle 369
pericardium 368
preload 382
pulmonary valve 369
Purkinje fiber 372
P wave 374
QRS complex 374
sinoatrial (SA) node 370
stroke volume (*SV*) 378
systole 377
tricuspid valve 368
T-type Ca^{2+} channel 373
T wave 374
venous return 383
ventricular ejection 378
ventricular filling 378
ventricular-function curve 382

SECTION B CLINICAL TERMS

artificial pacemaker 374
atrial fibrillation 380
AV conduction disorders 374
cardiac angiography 385
echocardiography 385
ectopic pacemaker 374
heart murmur 381
insufficiency 381
prolapse 369
septal defect 381
stenosis 381

SECTION C
The Vascular System

Although the action of the muscular heart provides the overall driving force for blood movement, the vascular system plays an active role in regulating blood pressure and distributing blood flow to the various tissues. Elaborate branching and regional specializations of blood vessels enable efficient matching of blood flow to metabolic demand in individual tissues. This section will highlight repeatedly the general principle of physiology that structure is a determinant of function, as we examine the specialization of the different types of vessels that comprise the vascular system.

The structural characteristics of the blood vessels vary by region, as shown in **Figure 12.28**. However, the entire circulatory system, from the heart to the smallest capillary, has one structural component in common: a smooth, single-celled layer of endothelial cells (endothelium) that is in contact with the flowing blood. Capillaries consist only of endothelium and associated extracellular basement membrane, whereas all other vessels have one or more layers of connective tissue and smooth muscle. Endothelial cells have a large number of functions, which are summarized for reference in **Table 12.4** and are described in relevant sections of this chapter and others.

We have previously described the pressures in the aorta and pulmonary arteries during the cardiac cycle. **Figure 12.29** illustrates the pressure changes that occur along the rest of the systemic and pulmonary circulations. Text sections dealing with the individual vascular segments will describe the reasons for these changes in pressure. For the moment, note only that by the time the blood has completed its journey back to the atrium in each circuit, most of the pressure originally generated by the ventricular contraction has dissipated. The reason the average pressure at any point in the two circuits is lower than that upstream toward the heart is that the blood vessels offer resistance to the flow from one point to the next (review Figure 12.5).

12.8 Arteries

The aorta and other systemic arteries have thick walls containing large quantities of elastic tissue (see Figure 12.28). Although they also have smooth muscle, arteries can be viewed most conveniently as elastic tubes. The large radii of arteries suit their primary function of serving as low-resistance tubes conducting blood to the various organs. Their second major function, related to their elasticity, is to act as a "pressure reservoir" for maintaining blood flow through the tissues during diastole, as described next.

Arterial Blood Pressure

What are the factors determining the pressure within an elastic container, such as a balloon filled with water? The pressure inside the balloon depends on (1) the volume of water and (2) how easily the balloon can stretch. If the balloon is thin and stretchable, large quantities of water can be added with only a small increase in pressure. Conversely, the addition of even a small quantity of water causes a large pressure increase

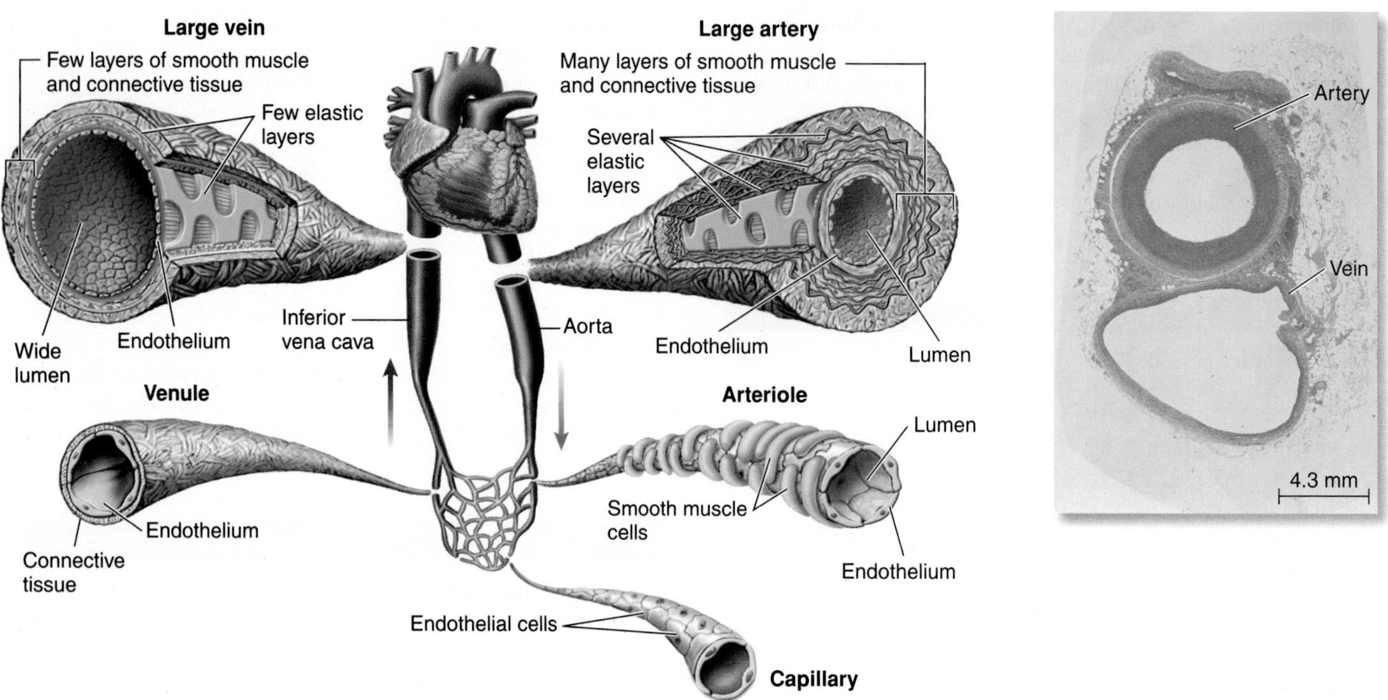

Figure 12.28 APIR Comparative features of blood vessels. Sizes are not drawn to scale. *Inset:* Light micrograph (enlarged four times) of a medium-sized artery near a vein. Note the difference between the two vessels in wall thickness and lumen diameter.

TABLE 12.4 Functions of Endothelial Cells
Serve as a physical lining that blood cells do not normally adhere to in heart and blood vessels
Serve as a permeability barrier for the exchange of nutrients, metabolic end products, and fluid between plasma and interstitial fluid; regulate transport of macromolecules and other substances
Secrete paracrine agents that act on adjacent vascular smooth muscle cells, including vasodilators such as prostacyclin and nitric oxide (endothelium-derived relaxing factor [EDRF]), and vasoconstrictors such as endothelin-1
Mediate angiogenesis (new capillary growth)
Play a central role in vascular remodeling by detecting signals and releasing paracrine agents that act on adjacent cells in the blood vessel wall
Contribute to the formation and maintenance of extracellular matrix
Produce growth factors in response to damage
Secrete substances that regulate platelet clumping, clotting, and anticlotting
Synthesize active hormones from inactive precursors (Chapter 14)
Extract or degrade hormones and other mediators (Chapters 11, 13)
Secrete cytokines during immune responses (Chapter 18)
Influence vascular smooth muscle proliferation in the disease atherosclerosis (Chapter 12, Section E)

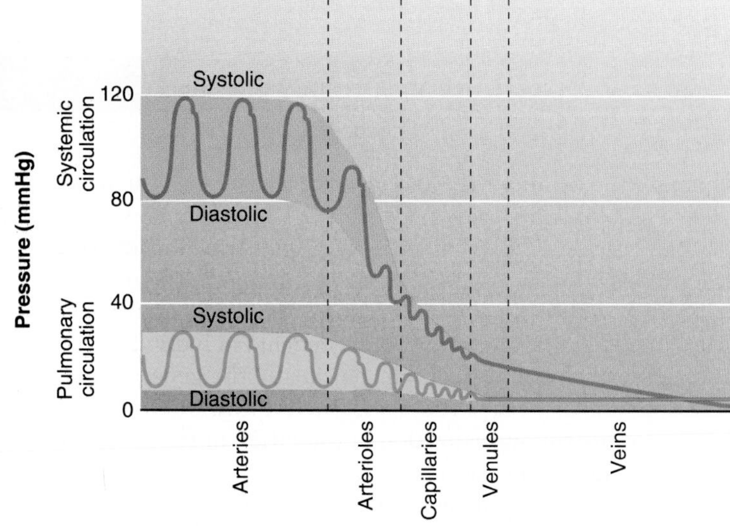

Figure 12.29 Pressures in the systemic and pulmonary vessels.

in a balloon that is thick and difficult to stretch. The term used to denote how easily a structure stretches is **compliance:**

$$\text{Compliance} = \Delta\text{Volume}/\Delta\text{Pressure}$$

The greater the compliance of a structure, the more easily it can be stretched.

These principles apply to an analysis of arterial blood pressure. The contraction of the ventricles ejects blood into the arteries during systole. If a precisely equal quantity of blood were to simultaneously drain out of the arteries into the arterioles during systole, the total volume of blood in the arteries would remain constant and arterial pressure would not change.

Such is not the case, however. As shown in **Figure 12.30,** a volume of blood equal to only about one-third of the stroke volume leaves the arteries during systole. The rest of the stroke volume remains in the arteries during systole, distending them and increasing the arterial pressure. When ventricular contraction ends, the stretched arterial walls recoil passively like a deflating balloon, and blood continues to be driven into the arterioles during diastole. As blood leaves the arteries, the arterial volume and pressure slowly decrease. The next ventricular contraction occurs while the artery walls are still stretched by the remaining blood. Therefore, the arterial pressure does not decrease to zero.

The aortic pressure pattern shown in **Figure 12.31a** is typical of the pressure changes that occur in all the large systemic arteries. The maximum arterial pressure reached during peak ventricular ejection is called **systolic pressure** (*SP*). The minimum arterial pressure occurs just before ventricular ejection begins and is called **diastolic pressure** (*DP*). Arterial pressure is generally recorded as systolic/diastolic, which would be 120/80 mmHg in the example shown. See **Figure 12.31b** for average values at different ages in the population of the United States. Both systolic pressure and diastolic pressure average about 10 mmHg lower in females than in males.

The difference between systolic pressure and diastolic pressure (120 − 80 = 40 mmHg in the example) is called the **pulse pressure.** It can be felt as a pulsation or throb in the arteries of the wrist or neck with each heartbeat. During diastole, nothing is felt over the artery, but the rapid increase in pressure at the next systole pushes out the artery wall; it is this expansion of the vessel that produces the detectable pulse.

The most important factors determining the magnitude of the pulse pressure are (1) stroke volume, (2) speed of ejection of the stroke volume, and (3) arterial compliance. Specifically, the pulse pressure produced by a ventricular ejection is greater if the volume of blood ejected increases, if the speed at which it is ejected increases, or if the arteries are less compliant. This last phenomenon occurs in ***arteriosclerosis,*** a stiffening of the arteries that progresses with age and accounts for the increasing pulse pressure that often occurs in older people (see Figure 12.31b).

It is evident from Figure 12.31a that arterial pressure is continuously changing throughout the cardiac cycle. The average pressure during the cycle, referred to as the **mean arterial pressure** (*MAP*), is not merely the value halfway between systolic pressure and diastolic pressure, because diastole lasts about twice as long as systole. The exact mean arterial pressure can be obtained by complex mathematical methods, but

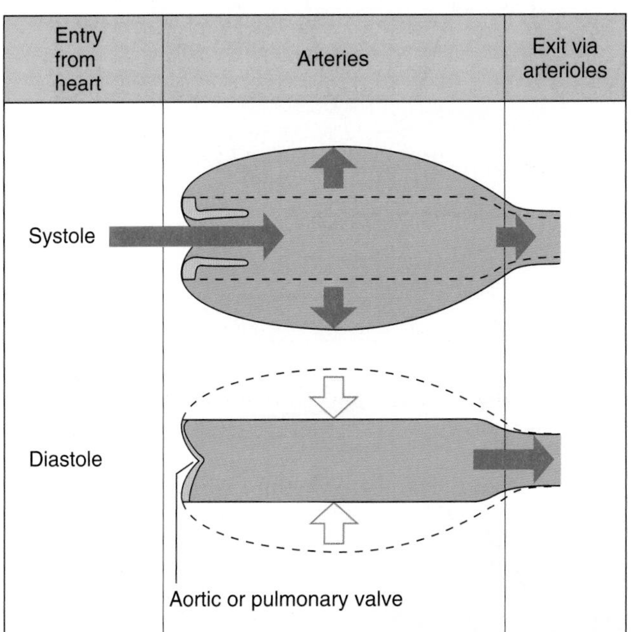

Figure 12.30 Movement of blood into and out of the arteries during the cardiac cycle. The lengths of the arrows denote relative quantities flowing into and out of the arteries and remaining in the arteries.

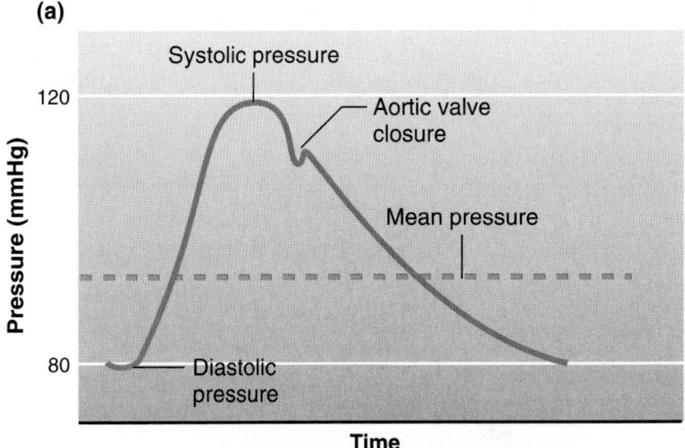

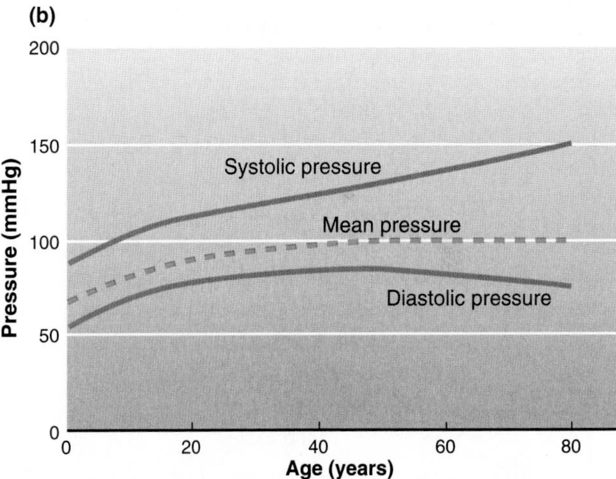

Figure 12.31 (a) Typical arterial pressure fluctuations during the cardiac cycle for a young adult male. Pressures average about 10 mmHg lower in females. (b) Changes in arterial pressure with age in the U.S. population. Adapted from National Institutes of Health Publication #04-5230, August 2004.

PHYSIOLOGICAL INQUIRY

- At an elevated heart rate, the amount of time spent in diastole is reduced more than the amount of time spent in systole. How would you estimate the mean arterial blood pressure at a heart rate elevated to the point at which the times spent in systole and diastole are roughly equal?

Answer can be found at end of chapter.

at a typical resting heart rate it is approximately equal to the diastolic pressure plus one-third of the pulse pressure:

$$MAP = DP + \frac{1}{3}(SP - DP)$$

Thus, in Figure 12.31a,

$$MAP = 80 + \frac{1}{3}(40) = 93 \text{ mmHg}$$

The *MAP* is important because it is the pressure driving blood into the tissues averaged over the entire cardiac cycle. We can say mean "arterial" pressure without specifying which artery we are referring to because the aorta and other large arteries have such large diameters that they offer negligible resistance to flow, and the mean pressures are therefore similar everywhere in the large arteries of a person who is lying down (gravitational effects in the upright posture will be considered in Section E).

One additional important point should be made: Although arterial compliance is an important determinant of pulse pressure, it does not have a major influence on the mean arterial pressure. As compliance changes, systolic and diastolic pressures also change but in opposite directions. For example, a person with a low arterial compliance (due to arteriosclerosis) but an otherwise normal cardiovascular system will have a large pulse pressure due to elevated systolic pressure and lowered diastolic pressure. The net result, however, is a mean arterial pressure that is close to normal. Pulse pressure is therefore a better diagnostic indicator of arteriosclerosis than mean arterial pressure. The determinants of mean arterial pressure are described in Section D. The method for measuring blood pressure is described next.

Measurement of Systemic Arterial Pressure

Both systolic and diastolic blood pressures are readily measured in human beings with the use of a device called a sphygmomanometer. An inflatable cuff containing a pressure gauge is wrapped around the upper arm, and a stethoscope is placed over the brachial artery just below the cuff.

The cuff is then inflated with air to a pressure greater than systolic blood pressure (**Figure 12.32**). The high pressure in the cuff is transmitted through the tissue of the arm and completely compresses the artery under the cuff, thereby preventing blood flow through the artery. The air in the cuff is then slowly released, causing the pressure in the cuff and on the artery to decrease. When cuff pressure has decreased

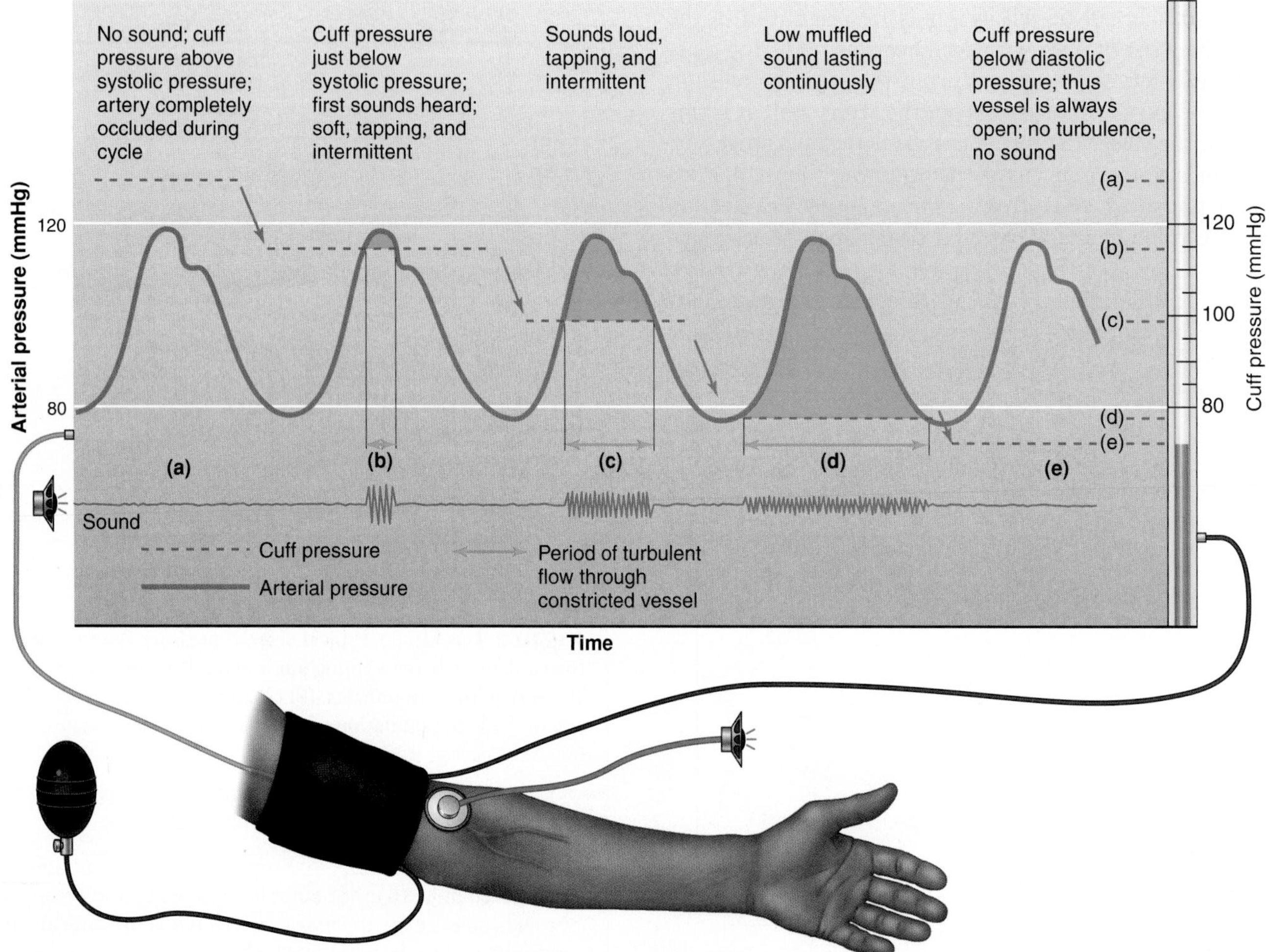

Figure 12.32 Sounds heard through a stethoscope as the cuff pressure of a sphygmomanometer is gradually lowered. Sounds are first heard when cuff falls just below systolic pressure, and they cease when cuff pressure falls below diastolic pressure.

to a value just below the systolic pressure, the artery opens slightly and allows blood flow for a brief time at the peak of systole. During this interval, the blood flow through the partially compressed artery occurs at a very high velocity because of the small opening and the large pressure difference across the opening. The high-velocity blood flow is turbulent and, therefore, produces vibrations called **Korotkoff's sounds** that can be heard through the stethoscope. Thus, the pressure at which sounds are first heard as the cuff pressure decreases is identified as the systolic blood pressure.

As the pressure in the cuff decreases further, the duration of blood flow through the artery in each cycle becomes longer. When the cuff pressure reaches the diastolic blood pressure, all sound stops because flow is continuous and nonturbulent through the open artery. Therefore, diastolic pressure is identified as the cuff pressure at which sounds disappear.

It should be clear from this description that the sounds heard during measurement of blood pressure are not the same as the heart sounds described earlier, which are due to closing of cardiac valves.

12.9 Arterioles

The arterioles play two major roles. (1) The arterioles in individual organs are responsible for determining the relative blood flows to those organs at any given mean arterial pressure. (2) The arterioles, all together, are the major factor in determining mean arterial pressure itself. The first function will be described now and the second in Section D.

Figure 12.33 illustrates the major principles of blood-flow distribution in terms of a simple model, a fluid-filled tank with a series of compressible outflow tubes. What determines the rate of flow through each exit tube? As stated in Section A of this chapter, flow (F) is a function of the pressure gradient (ΔP) and the resistance to flow (R):

$$F = \Delta P/R$$

Because the driving pressure (the height of the fluid column in the tank) is identical for each tube, differences in flow are completely determined by differences in the resistance to flow offered by each tube. The lengths of the tubes are the same and the viscosity of the fluid is constant, so differences in resistance are due solely to differences in the radii of the tubes. The widest tubes have the lowest resistance and, therefore, the greatest flows. If the radius of each tube can be independently altered, the blood flow through each is independently controlled.

This analysis can now be applied to the circulatory system. The tank is analogous to the major arteries, which serve as a pressure reservoir but are so large that they contribute little resistance to flow. Therefore, all the large arteries of the body can be considered a single pressure reservoir.

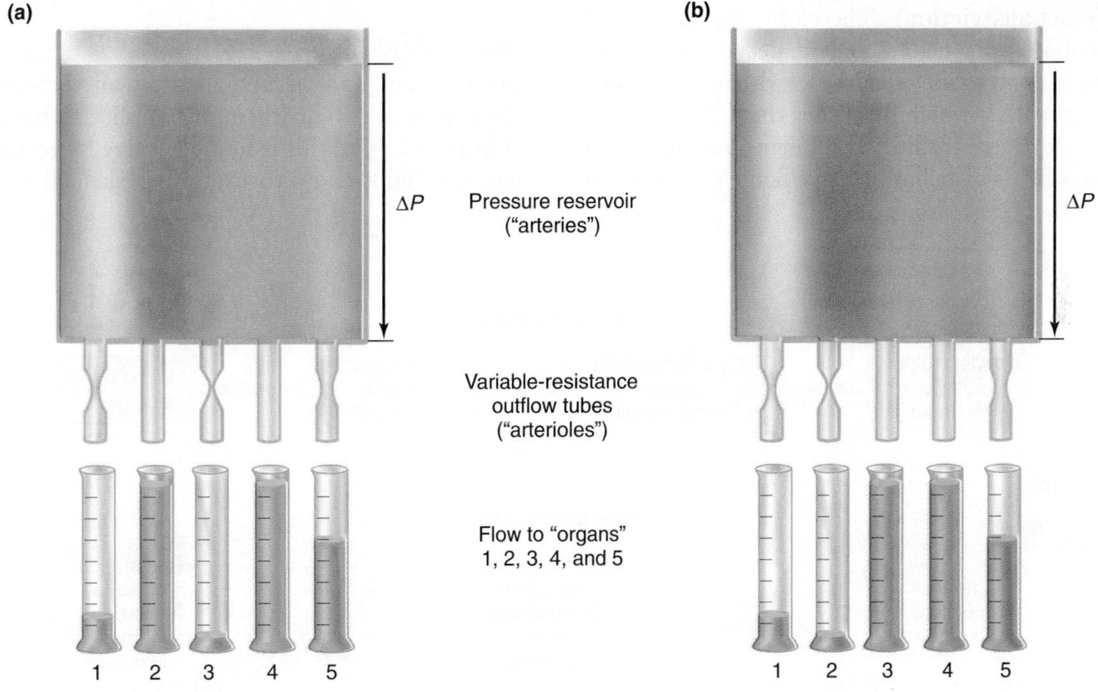

Figure 12.33 Physical model of the relationship between arterial pressure, arteriolar radius in different organs, and blood-flow distribution. In (a), blood flow is high through tube 2 and low through tube 3, whereas just the opposite is true for (b). This shift in blood flow was achieved by constricting tube 2 and dilating tube 3.

PHYSIOLOGICAL INQUIRY

- Assuming the reservoir is refilled at a constant rate, how would the flows shown in (b) be different if tube 2 remained the same as it was in condition (a)?

Answer can be found at end of chapter.

The arteries branch within each organ into progressively smaller arteries, which then branch into arterioles. The smallest arteries are narrow enough to offer significant resistance to flow, but the still narrower arterioles are the major sites of resistance in the vascular tree and are therefore analogous to the outflow tubes in the model. This explains the large decrease in mean pressure—from about 90 mmHg to 35 mmHg—as blood flows through the arterioles (see Figure 12.29). Pulse pressure also decreases in the arterioles, so flow is much less pulsatile in downstream capillaries, venules, and veins.

Like the model's outflow tubes (see Figure 12.33), the arteriolar radii in individual organs are subject to independent adjustment. The blood flow (F) through any organ is represented by the following equation:

$$F_{organ} = (MAP - \text{Venous pressure})/\text{Resistance}_{organ}$$

Venous pressure is normally close to zero, so we may write

$$F_{organ} = MAP/\text{Resistance}_{organ}$$

Because the *MAP* is the same throughout the body, differences in flows between organs depend entirely on the relative resistances of their respective arterioles. Arterioles contain smooth muscle, which can either relax and cause the vessel radius to increase (**vasodilation**), or contract and decrease the vessel radius (**vasoconstriction**). Therefore, the pattern of blood-flow distribution depends upon the degree of arteriolar smooth muscle contraction within each organ and tissue. Look back at Figure 12.3, which illustrates the distribution of blood flows at rest; these are due to differing resistances in the various organs. This distribution can change greatly when the various resistances are changed, as occurs during exercise (discussed in Section E).

How can resistance be changed? Arteriolar smooth muscle possesses a large degree of spontaneous activity (that is, contraction independent of any neural, hormonal, or paracrine input). This spontaneous contractile activity is called **intrinsic tone** (also called basal tone). It sets a baseline level of contraction that can be increased or decreased by external signals, such as neurotransmitters. These signals act by inducing changes in the cytosolic Ca^{2+} concentration of the smooth muscle cells (see Chapter 9 for a description of excitation–contraction coupling in smooth muscle). An increase in contractile force above the intrinsic tone causes vasoconstriction, whereas a decrease in contractile force causes vasodilation. The mechanisms controlling vasoconstriction and vasodilation in arterioles fall into two general categories: (1) local controls and (2) extrinsic (or reflex) controls.

Local Controls

The term **local controls** denotes mechanisms independent of nerves or hormones by which organs and tissues alter their own arteriolar resistances, thereby self-regulating their blood flows. This includes changes caused by autocrine and paracrine agents. This self-regulation is apparent in phenomena such as active hyperemia, flow autoregulation, reactive hyperemia, and local response to injury, which are described next.

Active Hyperemia

Most organs and tissues manifest an increased blood flow (**hyperemia**) when their metabolic activity is increased (**Figure 12.34a**); this is termed **active hyperemia.** For example, the blood flow to exercising skeletal muscle increases

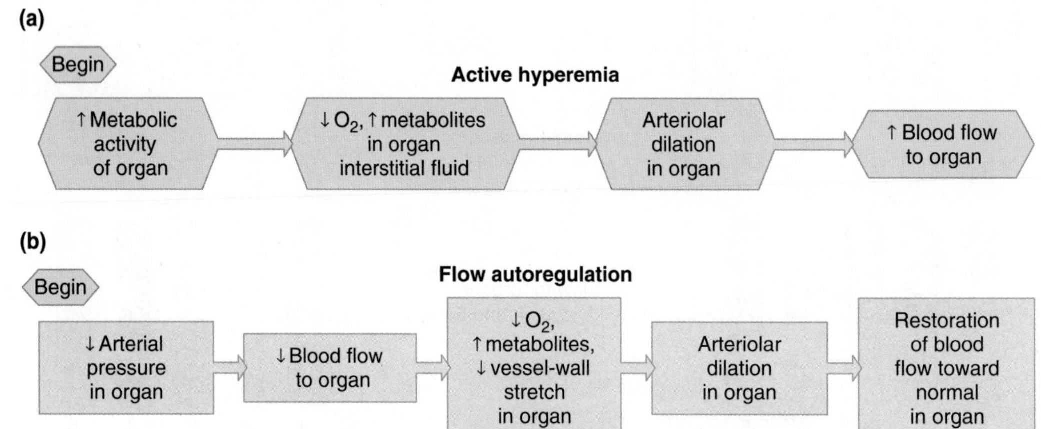

Figure 12.34 Local control of organ blood flow in response to (a) increases in metabolic activity and (b) decreases in blood pressure. Decreases in metabolic activity or increases in blood pressure would produce changes opposite those shown here.

PHYSIOLOGICAL INQUIRY

- An experiment is performed in which the blood flow through a single arteriole is measured. Initially, arterial pressure and flow through the arteriole are constant, but then the arterial pressure is experimentally increased and maintained at a higher level. How will blood flow through the arteriole change in the minutes that follow the increase in arterial pressure?

Answer can be found at end of chapter.

in direct proportion to the increased activity of the muscle. Active hyperemia is the direct result of arteriolar dilation in the more active organ or tissue.

The factors that cause arteriolar smooth muscle to relax in active hyperemia are local chemical changes in the extracellular fluid surrounding the arterioles. These result from the increased metabolic activity in the cells near the arterioles. The relative contributions of the different factors implicated vary, depending upon the organs involved and on the duration of the increased activity. Therefore, we will list—but not attempt to quantify—the local chemical changes that occur in the extracellular fluid.

Perhaps the most obvious change that occurs when tissues become more active is a decrease in the local concentration of oxygen, which is used in the production of ATP by oxidative phosphorylation. A number of other chemical factors *increase* when metabolism increases, including

1. carbon dioxide, an end product of oxidative metabolism;
2. hydrogen ions (decrease in pH), for example, from lactic acid;
3. adenosine, a breakdown product of ATP;
4. K^+ ions, accumulated from repeated action potential repolarization;
5. eicosanoids, breakdown products of membrane phospholipids;
6. osmotically active products from the breakdown of high-molecular-weight substances;
7. **bradykinin,** a peptide generated locally from a circulating protein called **kininogen** by the action of an enzyme, **kallikrein,** secreted by active gland cells; and
8. **nitric oxide,** a gas released by endothelial cells, which acts on the immediately adjacent vascular smooth muscle. Its action will be discussed in an upcoming section.

Local changes in all these chemical factors have been shown to cause arteriolar dilation under controlled experimental conditions, and they all probably contribute to the active-hyperemia response in one or more organs. It is likely, moreover, that additional important local factors remain to be discovered. All these chemical changes in the extracellular fluid act locally upon the arteriolar smooth muscle, causing it to relax. No nerves or hormones are involved.

It should not be too surprising that active hyperemia is most highly developed in skeletal muscle, cardiac muscle, and glands—tissues that show the widest range of normal metabolic activities in the body. It is highly efficient that their supply of blood is primarily determined locally.

Flow Autoregulation

During active hyperemia, increased metabolic activity of the tissue or organ is the initial event leading to local vasodilation. However, locally mediated changes in arteriolar resistance can also occur when a tissue or organ experiences a change in its blood supply resulting from a change in blood pressure (**Figure 12.34b**). The change in resistance is in the direction of maintaining blood flow nearly constant despite the pressure change, and is therefore termed **flow autoregulation.** For example, if arterial pressure to an organ is reduced because of a partial blockage in the artery supplying the organ, blood flow is reduced. In response, local controls cause arteriolar vasodilation, which tends to increase blood flow back toward normal levels.

What is the mechanism of flow autoregulation? One mechanism comprises the same metabolic factors described for active hyperemia. When a decrease in arterial pressure reduces blood flow to an organ, the supply of oxygen to the organ diminishes and the local extracellular oxygen concentration decreases. Simultaneously, the extracellular concentrations of carbon dioxide, hydrogen ions, and metabolites all increase because the blood cannot remove them as fast as they are produced. Therefore, the local metabolic changes occurring during decreased blood supply at constant metabolic activity are similar to those that occur during increased metabolic activity. This is because in both situations there is an imbalance between blood supply and level of cellular metabolic activity. Thus, the vasodilations of active hyperemia and of flow autoregulation in response to low arterial pressure involve the same metabolic mechanisms, even though they have different initiating events.

Flow autoregulation is not limited to circumstances in which arterial pressure decreases. The opposite events occur when, for various reasons, arterial pressure increases: The initial increase in flow due to the increase in pressure removes the local vasodilator chemical factors faster than they are produced and also increases the local concentration of oxygen. This causes the arterioles to constrict, thereby maintaining a relatively constant local flow despite the increased pressure.

Although our description has emphasized the role of local chemical factors in mediating flow autoregulation, another mechanism also participates in this phenomenon in certain tissues and organs. Arteriolar smooth muscle also responds directly, by contracting when increased arterial pressure causes increased wall stretch. Conversely, decreased stretch because of decreased arterial pressure causes this vascular smooth muscle to decrease its tone. These direct responses of arteriolar smooth muscle to stretch are termed **myogenic responses.** They are caused by changes in Ca^{2+} movement into the smooth muscle cells through Ca^{2+} channels in the plasma membrane.

Reactive Hyperemia

When an organ or tissue has had its blood supply completely occluded, a profound transient increase in its blood flow occurs if flow is reestablished. This phenomenon, known as **reactive hyperemia,** is essentially an extreme form of flow autoregulation. During the period of no blood flow, the arterioles in the affected organ or tissue dilate, owing to the local factors described previously. As soon as the occlusion to arterial flow is removed, blood flow increases greatly through these wide-open arterioles. This effect can be demonstrated by wrapping a string tightly around the base of your finger for 1–2 minutes. When it is removed, your finger will turn bright red due to the increase in blood flow.

Response to Injury

Tissue injury causes eicosanoids and a variety of other substances to be released locally from cells or generated from plasma precursors. These substances make arteriolar smooth muscle relax and cause vasodilation in an injured area. This phenomenon, a part of the general process known as inflammation, will be described in detail in Chapter 18.

Extrinsic Controls

Sympathetic Neurons

Most arterioles are richly innervated by sympathetic postganglionic neurons. These neurons release mainly norepinephrine, which binds to α-adrenergic receptors on the vascular smooth muscle to cause vasoconstriction.

In contrast, recall that the receptors for norepinephrine on heart muscle, including the conducting system, are mainly β-adrenergic. This permits the pharmacological use of β-adrenergic antagonists to block the actions of norepinephrine on the heart but not the arterioles, and vice versa for α-adrenergic antagonists.

Control of the sympathetic neurons to arterioles can also be used to produce vasodilation. Because the sympathetic neurons are seldom completely quiescent but discharge at some intermediate rate that varies from organ to organ, they always are causing some degree of tonic constriction in addition to the vessels' intrinsic tone. Dilation can be achieved by decreasing the rate of sympathetic activity to below this basal level.

The skin offers an excellent example of the role played by sympathetic regulation. At room temperature, skin arterioles are already under the influence of a moderate rate of sympathetic discharge. An appropriate stimulus—cold, fear, or loss of blood, for example—causes reflex enhancement of this sympathetic discharge, and the arterioles constrict further. In contrast, an increased body temperature reflexively inhibits sympathetic input to the skin, the arterioles dilate, and you radiate body heat.

In contrast to active hyperemia and flow autoregulation, the primary functions of sympathetic neurons to blood vessels are concerned not with the coordination of local metabolic needs and blood flow but with reflexes that serve whole-body needs. The most common reflex employing these pathways is that which regulates arterial blood pressure by influencing arteriolar resistance throughout the body (discussed in detail in the next section). Other reflexes redistribute blood flow to achieve a specific function (as in the previous example, to increase heat loss through the skin).

Parasympathetic Neurons

With few exceptions, there is little or no important parasympathetic innervation of arterioles. In other words, the great majority of blood vessels receive sympathetic but not parasympathetic input. This contrasts with the pattern of dual autonomic innervation of most tissues.

Noncholinergic, Nonadrenergic, Autonomic Neurons

As described in Chapter 6, there is a population of autonomic postganglionic neurons that are referred to as noncholinergic, nonadrenergic neurons because they release neither acetylcholine nor norepinephrine. Instead, they release other vasodilator substances—nitric oxide, in particular. These neurons are particularly prominent in the enteric nervous system, which plays a significant role in the control of the gastrointestinal system's blood vessels (see Chapter 15).

These neurons also innervate arterioles in other locations, for example, in the penis and clitoris, where they mediate erection. Some drugs used to treat erectile dysfunction in men, including ***sildenafil*** (***Viagra***) and ***tadalafil*** (***Cialis***), work by enhancing the nitric oxide signaling pathway and thus facilitating vasodilation.

Hormones

Epinephrine, like norepinephrine released from sympathetic neurons, can bind to α-adrenergic receptors on arteriolar smooth muscle and cause vasoconstriction. The story is more complex, however, because many arteriolar smooth muscle cells possess the β_2 subtype of adrenergic receptors as well as α-adrenergic receptors, and the binding of epinephrine to β_2 receptors causes the muscle cells to relax rather than contract (**Figure 12.35**).

In most vascular beds, the existence of β_2-adrenergic receptors on vascular smooth muscle is of little if any importance because the α-adrenergic receptors greatly outnumber them. The arterioles in skeletal muscle are an important exception, however. Because they have a significant number of β_2-adrenergic receptors, circulating epinephrine can contribute to vasodilation in muscle vascular beds.

Another hormone important for arteriolar control is **angiotensin II,** which constricts most arterioles. This peptide is part of the renin–angiotensin system, and drugs that prevent its action or formation are a major therapy for treating high blood pressure. Another hormone that causes arteriolar constriction is **vasopressin,** which is released into the blood by the posterior pituitary in response to a decrease in

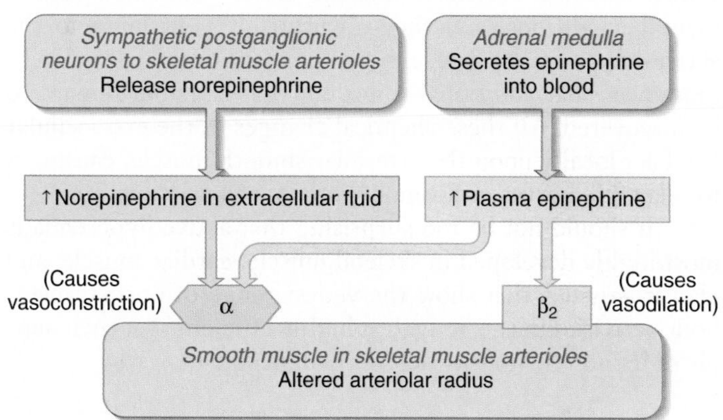

Figure 12.35 Effects of sympathetic nerves and plasma epinephrine on the arterioles in skeletal muscle. After its release from neuron terminals, norepinephrine diffuses to the arterioles, whereas epinephrine, a hormone, is blood-borne. Note that activation of α-adrenergic receptors and β_2-adrenergic receptors produces opposing effects. For simplicity, norepinephrine is shown binding only to α-adrenergic receptors; it can also bind to β_2-adrenergic receptors on the arterioles, but this occurs to a lesser extent.

blood pressure (Chapter 11). The functions of vasopressin and angiotensin II will be described more fully in Chapter 14.

Finally, the hormone secreted by the cardiac atria—**atrial natriuretic peptide**—is a potent vasodilator. It has not been established how important this effect is in the overall physiological control of arterioles. However, atrial natriuretic peptide does influence blood pressure by regulating Na^+ balance and blood volume, which also is described in Chapter 14.

Endothelial Cells and Vascular Smooth Muscle

It should be clear from the previous sections that many substances can induce the contraction or relaxation of vascular smooth muscle. Many of these substances do so by acting directly on the arteriolar smooth muscle, but others act indirectly via the endothelial cells adjacent to the smooth muscle. Endothelial cells, in response to these latter substances as well as certain mechanical stimuli, secrete several paracrine agents that diffuse to the adjacent vascular smooth muscle and induce either relaxation or contraction, resulting in vasodilation or vasoconstriction, respectively.

One very important paracrine vasodilator released by endothelial cells is nitric oxide. (*Note:* This refers to nitric oxide released from endothelial cells, not from neuronal endings as described earlier. Before the identity of the vasodilator paracrine factor released by the endothelium was determined to be nitric oxide, it was called endothelium-derived relaxing factor [EDRF], and this name is still often used because substances other than nitric oxide may also fit this general definition.) Nitric oxide is released continuously in significant amounts by endothelial cells in the arterioles and contributes to arteriolar vasodilation in the basal state. In addition, its secretion rapidly and markedly increases in response to a large number of the chemical mediators involved in both reflex and local control of arterioles. For example, nitric oxide release is stimulated by bradykinin and histamine, substances produced locally during inflammation.

Another vasodilator the endothelial cells release is the eicosanoid **prostacyclin** (also called **prostaglandin I_2 [PGI_2]**). Unlike the case for nitric oxide, there is little basal secretion of PGI_2, but secretion can increase markedly in response to various inputs. The roles of PGI_2 in the vascular responses to blood clotting are described in Section F of this chapter.

One of the important *vasoconstrictor* paracrine agents that the endothelial cells release in response to certain mechanical and chemical stimuli is **endothelin-1 (ET-1)**. Not only does ET-1 have paracrine actions, but under certain circumstances it can also achieve high enough concentrations in the blood to function as a hormone, causing widespread arteriolar vasoconstriction.

Arteriolar Control in Specific Organs

Figure 12.36 summarizes the factors that determine arteriolar radius. The importance of local and reflex controls varies from organ to organ, and **Table 12.5** lists for reference the key features of arteriolar control in specific organs. The variety of influences on arteriolar radius and their importance under various circumstances demonstrate the general principle of physiology that most physiological functions are controlled by multiple regulatory systems, often working in opposition.

12.10 Capillaries

As mentioned at the beginning of Section A, at any given moment, approximately 5% of the total circulating blood is flowing through the capillaries. It is this 5% that is performing the ultimate purpose of the entire cardiovascular system—the exchange of nutrients, metabolic end products, and cell secretions. Some exchange also occurs in the venules, which can be viewed as extensions of capillaries.

The capillaries permeate every tissue of the body except the cornea, the clear structure that allows light to enter the eye (see Chapter 7). Because most cells are no more than 0.1 mm (only a few cell widths) from a capillary, diffusion distances are very small and exchange is highly efficient. An adult has an estimated 25,000 miles (40,000 km) of capillaries, each individual capillary being only about 1 mm long with an inner diameter of about 8 μm, just wide enough for an erythrocyte

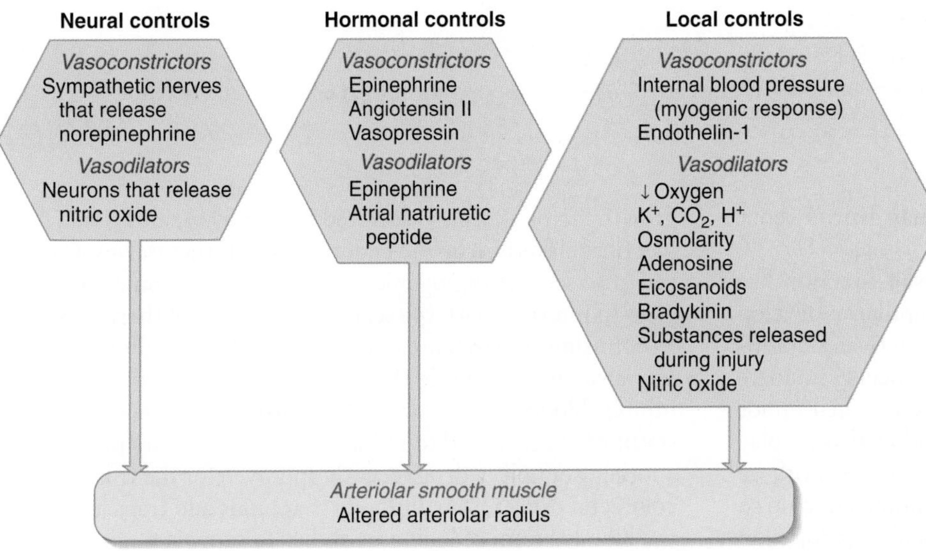

Figure 12.36 Major factors affecting arteriolar radius. Note that epinephrine can be a vasodilator or vasoconstrictor, depending on which adrenergic receptor subtype is present.

TABLE 12.5 Reference Summary of Arteriolar Control in Specific Organs

Heart

High intrinsic tone; oxygen extraction is very high at rest, so flow must increase when oxygen consumption increases if adequate oxygen supply is to be maintained.

Controlled mainly by local metabolic factors, particularly adenosine, and flow autoregulation; direct sympathetic influences are minor and normally overridden by local factors.

During systole, aortic semilunar cusps block the entrances to the coronary arteries, and vessels within the muscle wall are compressed; therefore, coronary flow occurs mainly during diastole.

Skeletal Muscle

Controlled by local metabolic factors during exercise.

Sympathetic activation causes vasoconstriction (mediated by α-adrenergic receptors) in reflex response to decreased arterial pressure.

Epinephrine causes vasodilation via β_2-adrenergic receptors when present in low concentration, and vasoconstriction via α-adrenergic receptors when present in high concentration.

GI Tract, Spleen, Pancreas, and Liver ("Splanchnic Organs")

Actually two capillary beds partially in series with each other; blood from the capillaries of the GI tract, spleen, and pancreas flows via the portal vein to the liver. In addition, the liver receives a separate arterial blood supply.

Sympathetic activation causes vasoconstriction, mediated by α-adrenergic receptors, in reflex response to decreased arterial pressure and during stress. In addition, venous constriction causes displacement of a large volume of blood from the liver to the veins of the thorax.

Increased blood flow occurs following ingestion of a meal and is mediated by local metabolic factors, neurons, and hormones secreted by the GI tract.

Kidneys

Flow autoregulation is a major factor.

Sympathetic stimulation causes vasoconstriction, mediated by α-adrenergic receptors, in reflex response to decreased arterial pressure and during stress. Angiotensin II is also a major vasoconstrictor. These reflexes help conserve sodium and water.

Brain

Excellent flow autoregulation.

Distribution of blood within the brain is controlled by local metabolic factors.

Vasodilation occurs in response to increased concentration of carbon dioxide in arterial blood.

Influenced relatively little by the autonomic nervous system.

Skin

Controlled mainly by sympathetic nerves, mediated by α-adrenergic receptors; reflex vasoconstriction occurs in response to decreased arterial pressure and cold, whereas vasodilation occurs in response to heat.

Substances released from sweat glands and noncholinergic, nonadrenergic neurons also cause vasodilation.

Venous plexus contains large volumes of blood, which contributes to skin color.

Lungs

Very low resistance compared to systemic circulation.

Controlled mainly by gravitational forces and passive physical forces within the lung.

Constriction mediated by local factors in response to low oxygen concentration—just the opposite of what occurs in the systemic circulation.

to squeeze through. (For comparison, a human hair is about 100 μm in diameter.)

The essential role of capillaries in tissue function has stimulated many questions concerning how capillaries develop and grow (**angiogenesis**). For example, what activates angiogenesis during wound healing and how do cancers stimulate growth of the new blood vessels required for continued tumor growth? It is known that the vascular endothelial cells play a central role in the building of a new capillary network by cell locomotion and cell division. They are stimulated to do so by a variety of **angiogenic factors** (e.g., vascular endothelial growth factor [VEGF]) secreted locally by various tissue cells like fibroblasts and by the endothelial cells themselves. Cancer cells also secrete angiogenic factors. The development of therapies to interfere with the secretion or action of these factors is a promising research area in anticancer therapy. For example, ***angiostatin*** is a peptide that occurs naturally in the body and inhibits blood vessel growth. Administering exogenous angiostatin has been found to reduce the size of tumors in mice. As another example, a drug recently approved for the treatment of colorectal cancer is an antibody that binds and traps VEGF in the bloodstream, reducing its ability to support angiogenesis.

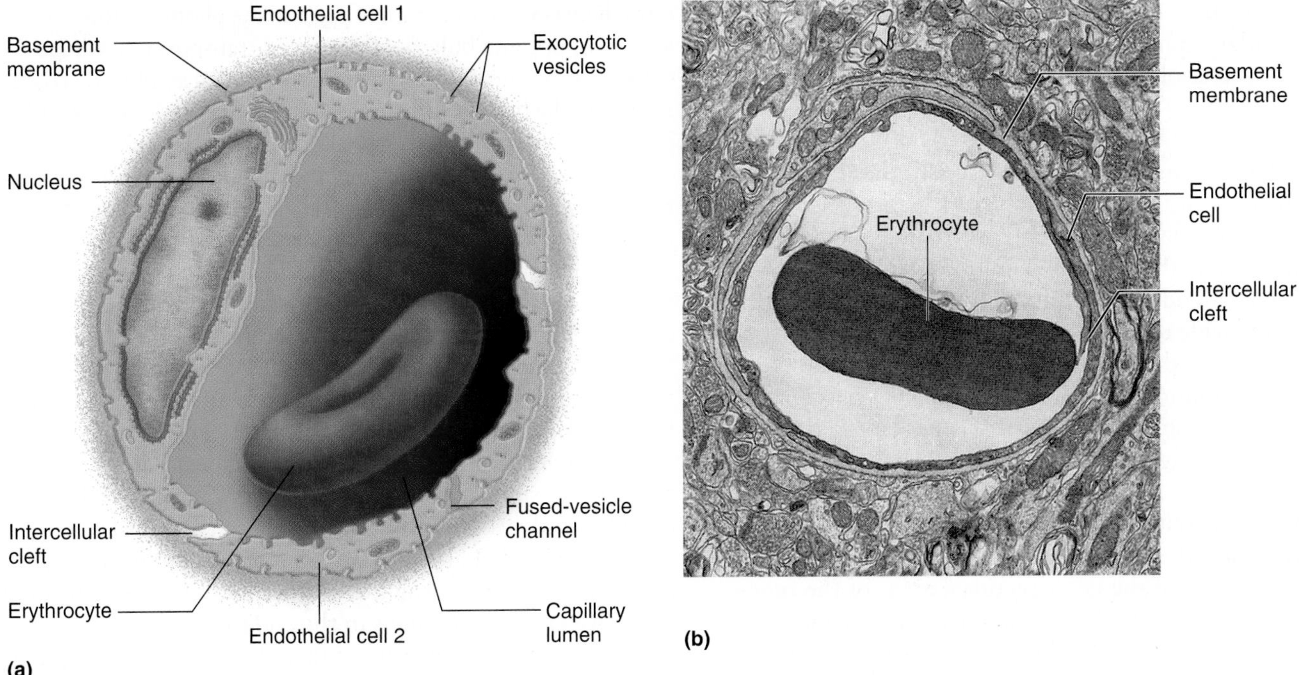

Figure 12.37 (a) Diagram of a capillary cross section. There are two endothelial cells in the figure, but the nucleus of only one is seen because the other is out of the plane of section. The fused-vesicle channel is part of endothelial cell 2. (b) Electron micrograph of a capillary containing a single erythrocyte; no nuclei are shown in this section. The long dimension of the blood cell is approximately 7 μm. Figure adapted from Lentz. EM courtesy of Dr. Michael Hart.

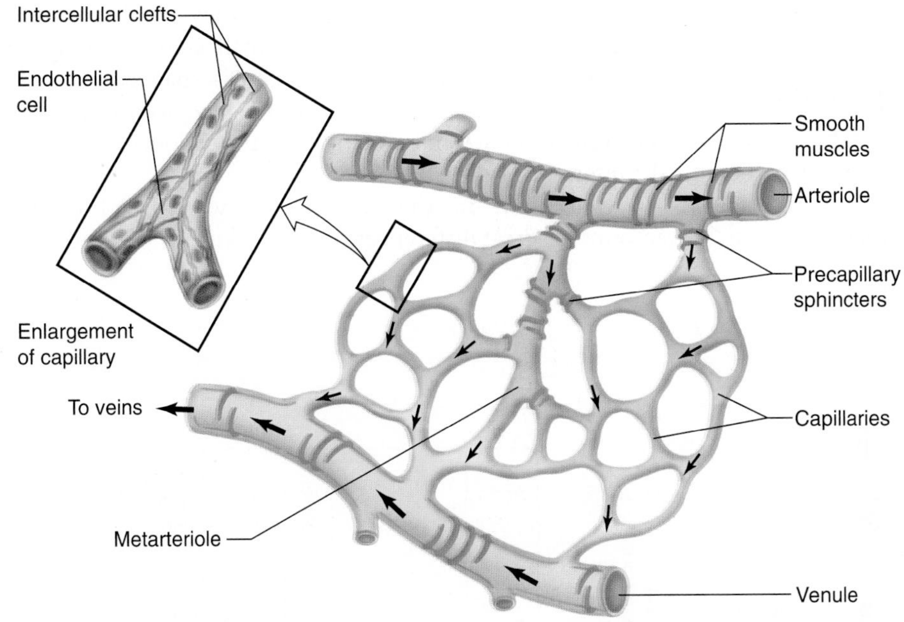

Figure 12.38 APIR Diagram of microcirculation. Note the absence of smooth muscle in the capillaries. Adapted from Chaffee and Lytle.

Anatomy of the Capillary Network

Capillary structure varies considerably from organ to organ, but the typical capillary (**Figure 12.37**) is a thin-walled tube of endothelial cells one layer thick resting on a basement membrane, without any surrounding smooth muscle or elastic tissue (review Figure 12.28). Capillaries in several organs (e.g., the brain) can have a second set of cells that surround the basement membrane that affect the ability of substances to diffuse across the capillary wall.

The flat cells that constitute the endothelial wall of a capillary are not attached tightly to each other but are separated by narrow, water-filled spaces termed **intercellular clefts.** The endothelial cells generally contain large numbers of endocytotic and exocytotic vesicles, and sometimes these fuse to form continuous **fused-vesicle channels** across the cell (**Figure 12.37a**).

Blood flow through capillaries depends very much on the state of the other vessels that constitute the microcirculation (**Figure 12.38**). For example, vasodilation of the arterioles supplying the capillaries causes increased capillary flow, whereas arteriolar vasoconstriction reduces capillary flow.

In addition, in some tissues and organs, blood enters capillaries not directly from arterioles but from vessels called **metarterioles,** which connect arterioles to venules. Metarterioles, like arterioles, contain scattered smooth muscle cells. The site at which a capillary exits from a metarteriole is surrounded by a ring of smooth muscle, the **precapillary sphincter,** which relaxes or contracts in response to local metabolic factors. When contracted, the precapillary sphincter closes the entry to the capillary completely. The more active the tissue, the more precapillary sphincters are open at any moment and the more capillaries in the network are receiving blood. Precapillary sphincters may also exist where the capillaries exit from arterioles.

Velocity of Capillary Blood Flow

Figure 12.39a is a simple mechanical model that illustrates how the branching of a tubular structure influences the velocity of fluid flow. A series of 1 cm diameter balls is being pushed down a single tube that branches into six narrower tubes. Although each individual tributary tube has a smaller cross section than the wide tube, the sum of the tributary cross sections is greater than that of the wide tube. In the wide tube, each ball moves 3 cm/min, but because the collective cross-sectional area of the small tubes is three times larger, the forward movement is only one-third as fast, or 1 cm/min.

This example illustrates the following important principle: When a continuous stream moves through consecutive sets of tubes arranged in parallel, the velocity of flow decreases as the sum of the cross-sectional areas of the tubes increases. This is precisely the case in the cardiovascular system (**Figure 12.39b**). The blood velocity is fast in the aorta, slows progressively in the arteries and arterioles, and then slows markedly as the blood passes through the huge cross-sectional area of the capillaries. Slow forward flow through the capillaries maximizes the time available for substances to exchange between the blood and interstitial fluid. The velocity of blood then progressively increases in the venules and veins because the cross-sectional area decreases. To reemphasize, blood velocity is dependent not on proximity to the heart but rather on total cross-sectional area of the vessel type.

Diffusion Across the Capillary Wall: Exchanges of Nutrients and Metabolic End Products

The extremely slow forward movement of blood through the capillaries maximizes the time for substance exchange across the capillary wall. Three basic mechanisms allow substances to move between the interstitial fluid and the plasma: diffusion, vesicle transport, and bulk flow. Mediated transport (see Chapter 4) constitutes a fourth mechanism in the capillaries of some tissues, including the brain. Diffusion and vesicle transport are described in this section, and bulk flow will be described in the next.

In all capillaries, excluding those in the brain, diffusion is the only important means by which net movement of nutrients, oxygen, and metabolic end products occurs across the capillary walls. The importance of diffusion in the exchange of substances between the blood and cells illustrates the general principle of physiology that physiological processes are dictated by the laws of chemistry and physics. As described in the next section, there is some movement of these substances by bulk flow, but the amount is negligible.

Chapter 4 described the factors determining diffusion rates. Lipid-soluble substances, including oxygen and carbon dioxide, easily diffuse through the plasma membranes of the capillary endothelial cells. In contrast, ions and other polar molecules are poorly soluble in lipid and must pass through small, water-filled channels in the endothelial lining.

The presence of water-filled channels in the capillary walls allows the rate of movement of ions and small polar molecules across the wall to be quite high, although not as high as that of lipid-soluble molecules. One location where these channels exist is in the intercellular clefts—that is, the narrow, water-filled spaces between adjacent cells. The fused-vesicle channels that penetrate the endothelial cells provide another set of water-filled channels.

The water-filled channels allow only small amounts of protein to diffuse through them. Small amounts of specific proteins—some hormones, for example—may also cross the endothelial cells by vesicle transport (endocytosis of plasma at the luminal border and exocytosis of the endocytotic vesicle at the interstitial side).

Variations in the size of the water-filled channels account for great differences in the "leakiness" of capillaries in

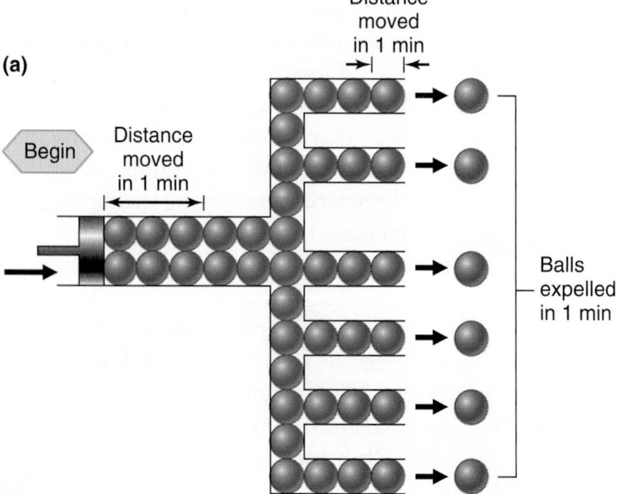

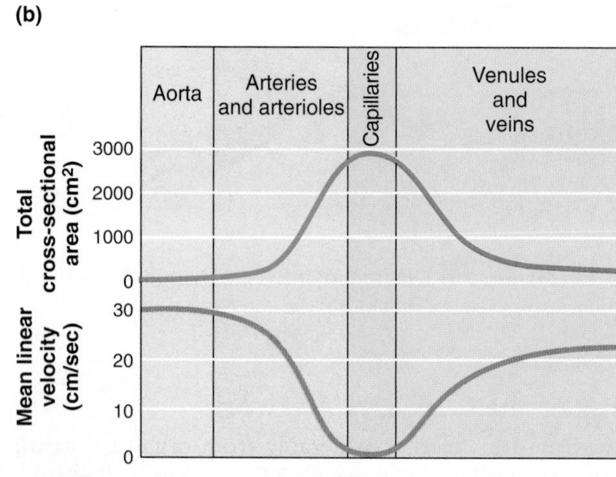

Figure 12.39 Relationship between total cross-sectional area and flow velocity. (a) The total cross-sectional area of the small tubes is three times greater than that of the large tube. Accordingly, flow velocity is one-third as great in the small tubes. (b) Cross-sectional area and velocity in the systemic circulation.

different organs. At one extreme are the "tight" capillaries of the brain, which have no intercellular clefts, only tight junctions. Therefore, water-soluble substances, even those of low molecular weight, can enter or exit the brain interstitial space only by carrier-mediated transport through the blood–brain barrier (see Chapter 6).

At the other end of the spectrum are liver capillaries, which have large intercellular clefts as well as large fused-vesicle channels through the endothelial cells, so that even protein molecules can readily pass across them. This is important because two of the major functions of the liver are the synthesis of plasma proteins and the metabolism of substances bound to plasma proteins. The leakiness of capillaries in most organs and tissues lies between these extremes of brain and liver capillaries.

Transcapillary diffusion gradients for oxygen and nutrients occur as a result of cellular utilization of the substance. Those for metabolic end products arise as a result of cellular production of the substance. Consider three examples: glucose, oxygen, and carbon dioxide in muscle (**Figure 12.40**). Glucose is continuously transported from interstitial fluid into the muscle cell by carrier-mediated transport mechanisms, and oxygen moves in the same direction by diffusion. The removal of glucose and oxygen from interstitial fluid lowers the interstitial fluid concentrations below those in capillary plasma and creates the gradient for their diffusion from the capillary into the interstitial fluid.

Simultaneously, carbon dioxide is continuously produced by muscle cells and diffuses into the interstitial fluid. This causes the carbon dioxide concentration in interstitial fluid to be greater than that in capillary plasma, producing a gradient for carbon dioxide diffusion from the interstitial fluid into the capillary.

Note that for substances moving in both directions, the local metabolic rate ultimately establishes the transcapillary diffusion gradients.

If a tissue increases its metabolic rate, it must obtain more nutrients from the blood and must eliminate more metabolic end products. One mechanism for achieving that is active hyperemia. The second important mechanism is increased diffusion gradients between plasma and tissue; increased cellular utilization of oxygen and nutrients lowers their tissue concentrations, whereas increased production of carbon dioxide and other end products raises their tissue concentrations. In both cases, the substance's transcapillary concentration difference increases, which also increases the rate of diffusion.

Bulk Flow Across the Capillary Wall: Distribution of the Extracellular Fluid

At the same time that the diffusional exchange of nutrients, oxygen, and metabolic end products is occurring across the capillaries, another, completely distinct process is also taking place across the capillary—the bulk flow of protein-free plasma. The function of this process is not the exchange of nutrients and metabolic end products but rather the distribution of the extracellular fluid volume (**Figure 12.41**). Recall that extracellular fluid includes the plasma and interstitial fluid. Normally, there is almost four times more interstitial fluid than plasma—11 L versus 3 L—in a 70 kg person. This distribution is not fixed, however, and the interstitial fluid functions as a reservoir that can supply fluid to or receive fluid from the plasma.

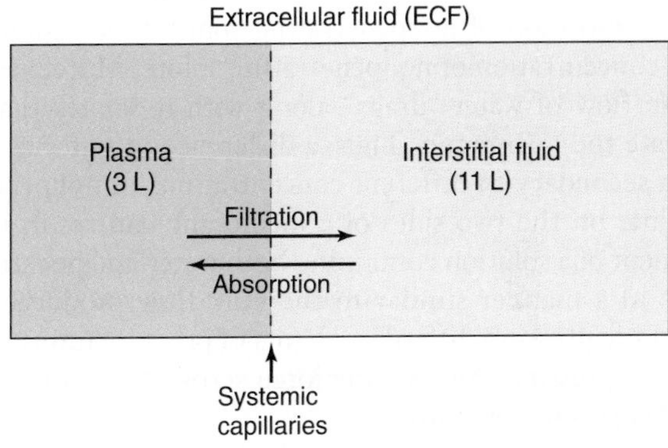

Figure 12.41 Distribution of the extracellular fluid by bulk flow.

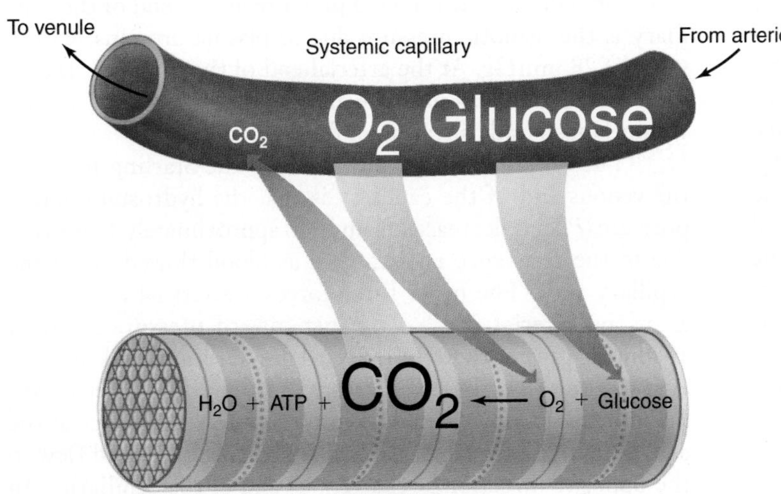

Figure 12.40 APR Diffusion gradients at a systemic capillary.

PHYSIOLOGICAL INQUIRY

- If cellular metabolism was not changed but the blood flow through a tissue's capillaries was reduced, how would the venous blood leaving that tissue differ compared to that before flow reduction?

Answer can be found at end of chapter.

As described in the previous section, most capillary walls are highly permeable to water and to almost all plasma solutes, except plasma proteins. Therefore, in the presence of a hydrostatic pressure difference across it, the capillary wall behaves like a porous filter, permitting protein-free plasma to move by bulk flow from capillary plasma to interstitial fluid through the water-filled channels. (This is technically termed *ultrafiltration*, but we will refer to it simply as *filtration*.) *The concentrations of all the plasma solutes except protein are virtually the same in the filtered fluid as in plasma.*

The magnitude of the bulk flow is determined, in part, by the difference between the capillary blood pressure and the interstitial fluid hydrostatic pressure. Normally, the former is much higher than the latter. Therefore, a considerable hydrostatic pressure difference exists to filter protein-free plasma out of the capillaries into the interstitial fluid, with the protein remaining behind in the plasma.

Why doesn't all the plasma filter out into the interstitial space? The explanation is that the hydrostatic pressure difference favoring filtration is offset by an osmotic force opposing filtration. To understand this, we must review the principle of osmosis.

In Chapter 4, we described how a net movement of water occurs across a semipermeable membrane from a solution of high water concentration to a solution of low water concentration. Stated another way, water moves from a region with a low concentration of nonpenetrating solute to a region with a high concentration of nonpenetrating solute. Moreover, this osmotic flow of water "drags" along with it solutes that can penetrate the membrane. Thus, a difference in water concentration secondary to different concentrations of nonpenetrating solute on the two sides of a membrane can result in the movement of a solution containing both water and penetrating solutes in a manner similar to the bulk flow produced by a hydrostatic pressure difference. Units of pressure (mmHg) are used in expressing this osmotic force across a membrane, just as for hydrostatic pressures.

This analysis can now be applied to osmotically induced flow across capillaries. The plasma within the capillary and the interstitial fluid outside it contain large quantities of low-molecular-weight solutes (also termed **crystalloids**) that easily penetrate capillary pores. Examples include Na^+, Cl^-, and K^+. Because these crystalloids pass easily through the capillary wall, their concentrations in the plasma and interstitial fluid are essentially identical. Consequently, the presence of the crystalloids causes no significant difference in water concentration. In contrast, the plasma proteins (also termed **colloids**) are unable to move through capillary pores (nonpenetrating) and have a very low concentration in the interstitial fluid. The difference in protein concentration between the plasma and the interstitial fluid means that the water concentration of the plasma is slightly lower (by about 0.5%) than that of interstitial fluid, creating an osmotic force that tends to cause the flow of water from the interstitial compartment into the capillary. Because the crystalloids in the interstitial fluid move along with water, flow that is driven by either osmotic or hydrostatic pressures across the capillary wall does not alter crystalloid concentrations in either plasma or interstitial fluid.

A key word in this last sentence is *concentrations*. The amount of water (the volume) and the amount of crystalloids in the two locations do change. Thus, an increased filtration of fluid from plasma to interstitial fluid increases the volume of the interstitial fluid and decreases the volume of the plasma, even though no changes in crystalloid concentrations occur.

In summary, opposing forces act to move fluid across the capillary wall (**Figure 12.42a**): (1) The difference between capillary blood hydrostatic pressure and interstitial fluid hydrostatic pressure favors filtration out of the capillary; and (2) the water-concentration difference between plasma and interstitial fluid, which results from differences in protein concentration, favors the **absorption** of interstitial fluid into the capillary. Therefore, the **net filtration pressure (*NFP*)** depends directly upon the algebraic sum of four variables: capillary hydrostatic pressure, P_c (favoring fluid movement out of the capillary); interstitial hydrostatic pressure, P_{IF} (favoring fluid movement into the capillary); the osmotic force due to plasma protein concentration, π_c (favoring fluid movement into the capillary); and the osmotic force due to interstitial fluid protein concentration, π_{IF} (favoring fluid movement out of the capillary). Thus,

$$NFP = P_c + \pi_{IF} - P_{IF} - \pi_c$$

Note that we have arbitrarily assigned a positive value to the forces directed out of the capillary and negative values to the inward-directed forces. The four factors that determine net filtration pressure are termed the **Starling forces** because Starling, the same physiologist who helped elucidate the Frank–Starling mechanism of the heart, was the first to describe these forces.

We may now consider this movement quantitatively in the systemic circulation (**Figure 12.42b**). Much of the arterial blood pressure has already dissipated as the blood flows through the arterioles, so that hydrostatic pressure tending to push fluid out of the arterial end of a typical capillary is only about 35 mmHg. The interstitial fluid protein concentration at this end of the capillary would produce a flow of fluid out of the capillary equivalent to a hydrostatic pressure of 3 mmHg. Because the interstitial fluid hydrostatic pressure is virtually zero, the only inward-directed pressure at this end of the capillary is the osmotic pressure due to plasma proteins, with a value of 28 mmHg. At the arterial end of the capillary, therefore, the net outward pressure exceeds the inward pressure by 10 mmHg, so bulk filtration of fluid will occur.

The only substantial difference in the Starling forces at the venous end of the capillary is that the hydrostatic blood pressure (P_c) has decreased from 35 to approximately 15 mmHg due to the resistance encountered as blood flowed along the capillary wall. The other three forces are virtually the same as at the arterial end, so the net inward pressure is about 10 mmHg greater than the outward pressure, and bulk absorption of fluid into the capillaries will occur. Thus, net movement of fluid from the plasma into the interstitial space at the arterial end of capillaries tends to be balanced by fluid flow in the opposite direction at the venous end of the capillaries. In

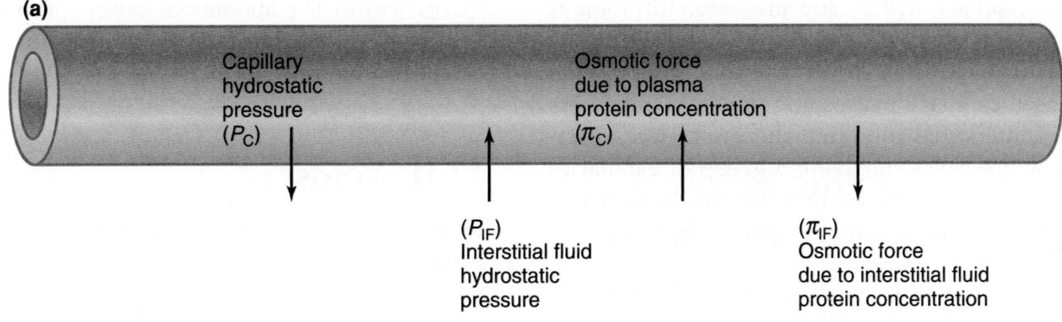

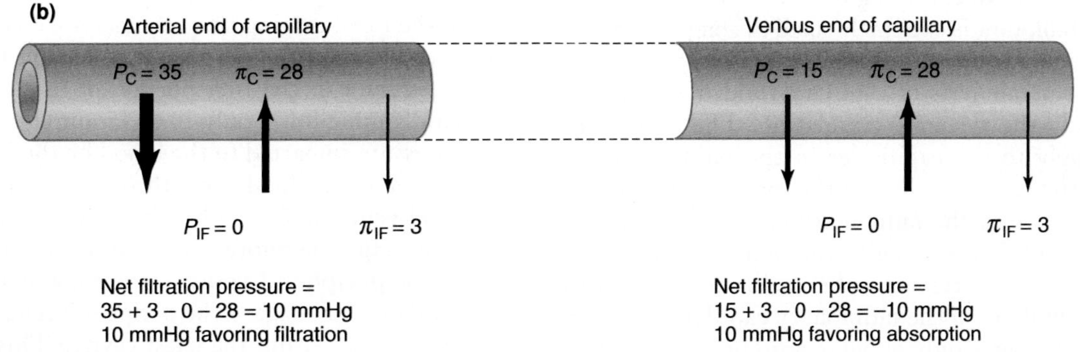

Figure 12.42 APIR (a) The four factors determining fluid movement across capillaries. (b) Quantification of forces causing filtration at the arterial end of the capillary and absorption at the venous end. Outward forces are arbitrarily assigned positive values, so a positive net filtration pressure favors filtration, whereas a negative pressure indicates that net absorption of fluid will occur. Arrows in (b) denote magnitude of forces. No arrow is shown for interstitial fluid hydrostatic pressure (P_{IF}) in (b) because it is approximately zero.

PHYSIOLOGICAL INQUIRY

- If an accident victim loses 1 L of blood, why would an intravenous injection of a liter of plasma be more effective for replacing the lost volume than injecting a liter of an equally concentrated crystalloid solution?

Answer can be found at end of chapter.

actuality, for the aggregate of capillaries in the body, the net outward force is normally slightly larger than the inward, so there is a net filtration amounting to approximately 4 L/day (this number does not include the capillaries in the kidneys). The fate of this fluid will be described in the section on the lymphatic system.

In our example, we have assumed a typical capillary hydrostatic pressure varying from 35 mmHg down to 15 mmHg. In reality, capillary hydrostatic pressures vary in different regions of the body and, as will be described in a later section, are strongly influenced by whether the person is lying down, sitting, or standing. Moreover, capillary hydrostatic pressure in any given region is subject to physiological regulation, mediated mainly by changes in the resistance of the arterioles in that region. As **Figure 12.43** shows, dilating the arterioles in a particular tissue raises capillary hydrostatic pressure in that region because less pressure is lost overcoming resistance between the arteries and the capillaries. Because

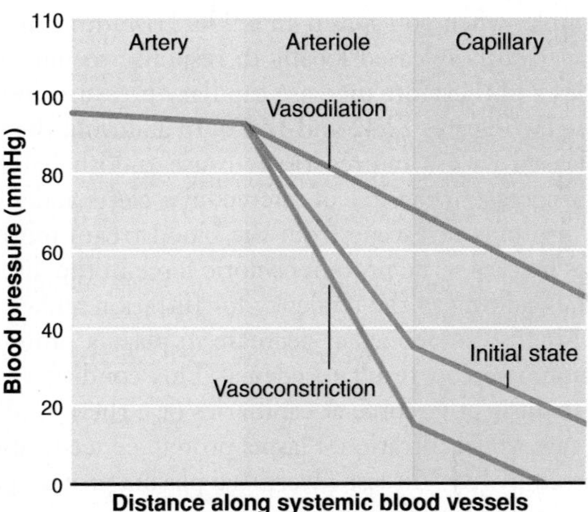

Figure 12.43 Effects of arteriolar vasodilation or vasoconstriction on capillary blood pressure in a single organ (under conditions of constant arterial pressure).

of the increased capillary hydrostatic pressure, filtration is increased and more protein-free fluid is transferred to the interstitial fluid. In contrast, marked arteriolar constriction produces decreased capillary hydrostatic pressure and favors net movement of interstitial fluid into the vascular compartment. Indeed, the arterioles supplying a group of capillaries may be so dilated or so constricted that the capillaries manifest only filtration or only absorption, respectively, along their entire length.

To reiterate an important point, capillary filtration and absorption play a minimal role in the exchange of nutrients and metabolic end products between capillaries and tissues. The reason is that the total quantity of a substance, such as glucose or carbon dioxide, moving into or out of a capillary as a result of net bulk flow is extremely small in comparison with the quantities moving by net diffusion.

Finally, this analysis of capillary fluid dynamics has considered only the systemic circulation. The same Starling forces apply to the capillaries in the pulmonary circulation, but the relative values of the four variables differ. In particular, because the pulmonary circulation is a low-resistance, low-pressure circuit, the normal pulmonary capillary hydrostatic pressure—the major force favoring movement of fluid out of the pulmonary capillaries into the interstitium—averages only about 7 mmHg. This is offset by a greater accumulation of proteins in lung interstitial fluid than is found in other tissues. Overall, the Starling forces in the lung slightly favor filtration as in other tissues, but extensive and active lymphatic drainage prevents the accumulation of extracellular fluid in the interstitial spaces and airways.

In some pathophysiological circumstances, imbalances in the Starling forces can lead to ***edema***—an abnormal accumulation of fluid in the interstitial spaces. Heart failure (discussed in detail in Section E) is a condition in which increased venous pressure reduces blood flow out of the capillaries, and the increased hydrostatic pressure (P_c) causes excess filtration and accumulation of interstitial fluid. The resulting edema can occur in either systemic or pulmonary tissues. A more common experience is the swelling that occurs with injury—for example, when you sprain an ankle. Histamine and other chemical factors released locally in response to injury dilate arterioles and therefore increase capillary pressure and filtration (review Figures 12.42 and 12.43). In addition, the chemicals released within injured tissue cause endothelial cells to distort, increasing the size of intercellular clefts and allowing plasma proteins to escape from the bloodstream more readily. This increases the protein osmotic force in the interstitial fluid (π_{IF}), adding to the tendency for filtration and edema to occur. Finally, an abnormal decrease in plasma protein concentration also can result in edema. This condition reduces the main absorptive force at capillaries (π_c), thereby allowing an increase in net filtration. Plasma protein concentration can be reduced by liver disease (decreased plasma protein production) or by kidney disease (loss of protein in the urine). In addition, as with liver disease, protein malnutrition (***kwashiorkor***) compromises the manufacture of plasma proteins. The resulting edema is particularly marked in the interstitial spaces within the abdominal cavity, producing the swollen-belly appearance commonly observed in people with insufficient protein in their diets.

12.11 Veins

Blood flows from capillaries into venules and then into veins. Some exchange of materials occurs between the interstitial fluid and the venules, just as in capillaries. Indeed, permeability to macromolecules is often greater for venules than for capillaries, particularly in damaged areas.

The veins are the last set of tubes through which blood flows on its way back to the heart. In the systemic circulation, the force driving this venous return is the pressure difference between the peripheral veins and the right atrium. The pressure in the first portion of the peripheral veins is generally quite low—only 10 to 15 mmHg—because most of the pressure imparted to the blood by the heart is dissipated by resistance as blood flows through the arterioles, capillaries, and venules. The right atrial pressure is normally close to 0 mmHg. Therefore, the total driving pressure for flow from the **peripheral veins** to the right atrium is only 10 to 15 mmHg on average. (The peripheral veins include all veins not contained within the chest cavity.) This pressure difference is adequate because of the low resistance to flow offered by the veins, which have large diameters. Thus, a major function of the veins is to act as low-resistance conduits for blood flow from the tissues to the heart. The peripheral veins of the arms and legs contain valves that permit flow only toward the heart.

In addition to their function as low-resistance conduits, the veins perform a second important function: Their diameters are reflexively altered in response to changes in blood volume, thereby maintaining peripheral venous pressure and venous return to the heart. In a previous section, we emphasized that the rate of venous return to the heart is a major determinant of end-diastolic ventricular volume and thereby stroke volume. We now see that peripheral venous pressure is an important determinant of stroke volume. We next describe how venous pressure is determined.

Determinants of Venous Pressure

The factors determining pressure in any elastic tube are the volume of fluid within it and the compliance of its walls. Consequently, total blood volume is one important determinant of venous pressure because, as we will see, most blood is in the veins. Also, the walls of veins are thinner and much more compliant than those of arteries (see Figure 12.28). Thus, veins can accommodate large volumes of blood with a relatively small increase in internal pressure. Approximately 60% of the total blood volume is present in the systemic veins (**Figure 12.44**), but the venous pressure is only about 10 mmHg on average. (In contrast, the systemic arteries contain less than 15% of the blood, at a pressure of nearly 100 mmHg.)

The walls of the veins contain smooth muscle innervated by sympathetic neurons. Stimulation of these neurons releases

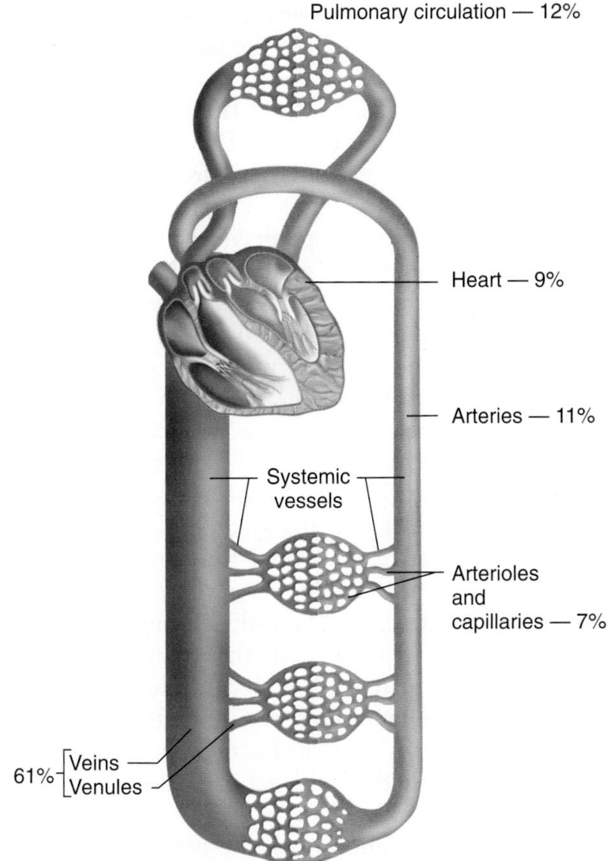

Figure 12.44 Distribution of the total blood volume in different parts of the cardiovascular system. Adapted from Guyton.

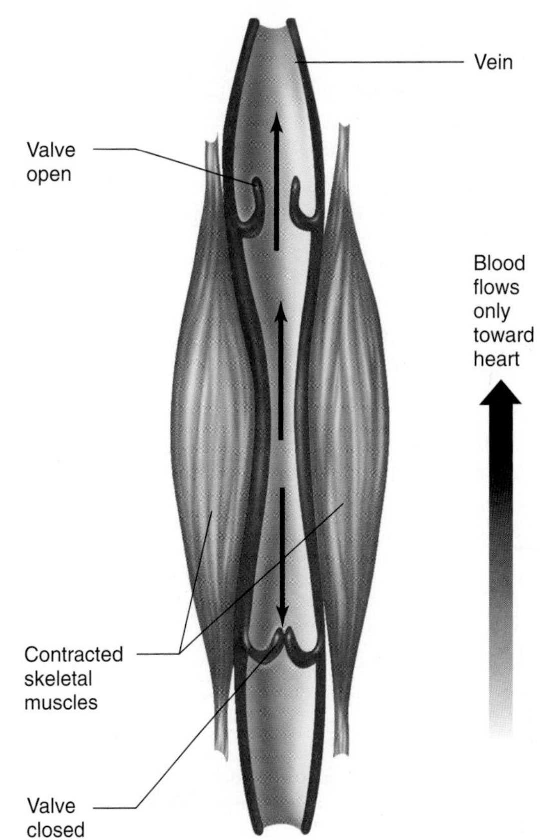

Figure 12.45 AP|R The skeletal muscle pump. During muscle contraction, venous diameter decreases and venous pressure increases. The increase in pressure forces the flow only toward the heart because backward pressure forces the valves in the veins to close.

norepinephrine, which causes contraction of the venous smooth muscle, decreasing the diameter and compliance of the vessels and increasing the pressure within them. Increased venous pressure then drives more blood out of the veins into the right side of the heart. Note the different effect of venous constriction compared to that of arterioles; when arterioles constrict, the constriction *reduces* forward flow through the systemic circuit, whereas constriction of veins *increases* forward flow. Although sympathetic neurons are the most important input, venous smooth muscle, like arteriolar smooth muscle, also responds to hormonal and paracrine vasodilators and vasoconstrictors.

Two other mechanisms, in addition to contraction of venous smooth muscle, can increase venous pressure and facilitate venous return. These mechanisms are the **skeletal muscle pump** and the **respiratory pump.** During skeletal muscle contraction, the veins running through the muscle are partially compressed, which reduces their diameter and forces more blood back to the heart. Now we can describe a major function of the peripheral vein valves; when the skeletal muscle pump increases local venous pressure, the valves permit blood flow only toward the heart and prevent flow back toward the capillaries (**Figure 12.45**).

The respiratory pump is somewhat more difficult to visualize. As Chapter 13 describes, at the base of the chest cavity (thorax) is a large muscle called the diaphragm, which separates the thorax from the abdomen. During inspiration of air, the diaphragm descends, pushing on the abdominal contents and increasing abdominal pressure. This pressure increase is transmitted passively to the intra-abdominal veins. Simultaneously, the pressure in the thorax decreases, thereby decreasing the pressure in the intrathoracic veins and right atrium. The net effect of the pressure changes in the abdomen and thorax is to increase the pressure difference between the peripheral veins and the heart. Thus, venous return is enhanced during inspiration (expiration would reverse this effect if not for the venous valves), and breathing deeply and frequently, as in exercise, helps blood flow toward the heart.

You might get the incorrect impression from these descriptions that venous return and cardiac output are independent entities. Rather, any change in venous return almost immediately causes equivalent changes in cardiac output, largely through the Frank–Starling mechanism. *Venous return and cardiac output therefore must be the same except for transient changes over brief periods of time.*

In summary (**Figure 12.46**), venous smooth muscle contraction, the skeletal muscle pump, and the respiratory pump all work to facilitate venous return and thereby enhance cardiac output by the same amount.

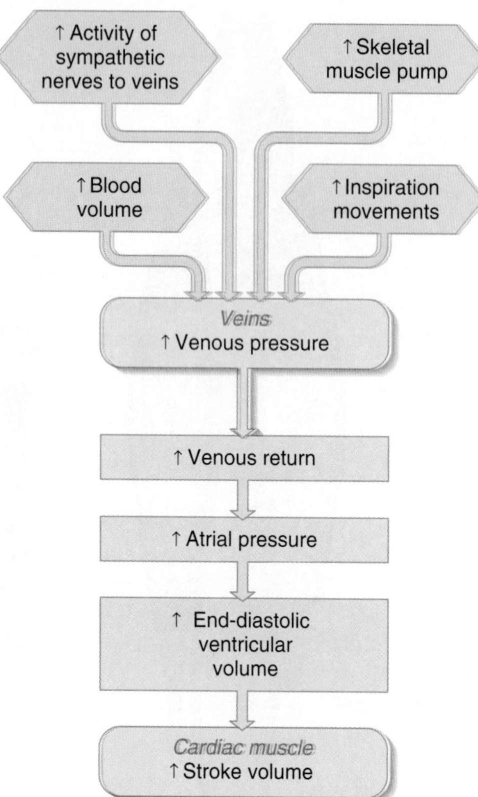

Figure 12.46 Major factors determining peripheral venous pressure, venous return, and stroke volume. Reversing the arrows in the boxes would indicate how these factors can decrease. The effects of increased inspiration on end-diastolic ventricular volume are actually quite complex, but for the sake of simplicity, they are shown here only as increasing venous pressure.

PHYSIOLOGICAL INQUIRY

- Figure 12.44 shows the typical distribution of blood in a normal, resting individual. How would the percentages change during vigorous exercise?

Answer can be found at end of chapter.

12.12 The Lymphatic System

The **lymphatic system** is a network of small organs (lymph nodes) and tubes (**lymphatic vessels** or simply "lymphatics") through which **lymph**—a fluid derived from interstitial fluid—flows. The lymphatic system is not technically part of the circulatory system, but it is described in this chapter because its vessels provide a route for the movement of interstitial fluid to the circulatory system (**Figure 12.47a**).

Present in the interstitium of virtually all organs and tissues are numerous **lymphatic capillaries** that are completely distinct from blood vessel capillaries. Like the latter, they are tubes made of only a single layer of endothelial cells resting on a basement membrane, but they have large water-filled channels that are permeable to all interstitial fluid constituents, including protein. The lymphatic capillaries are the first of the lymphatic vessels, for unlike the blood vessel capillaries, no tubes flow into them.

Small amounts of interstitial fluid continuously enter the lymphatic capillaries by bulk flow. This lymph fluid flows from the lymphatic capillaries into the next set of lymphatic vessels, which converge to form larger and larger lymphatic vessels. At various points in the body—in particular, the neck, armpits, groin, and around the intestines—the lymph flows through lymph nodes (**Figure 12.47b**), which are part of the immune system and are described in Chapter 18. Ultimately, the entire network ends in two large lymphatic ducts that drain into the veins near the junction of the jugular and subclavian veins in the upper chest. Valves at these junctions permit only one-way flow from lymphatic ducts into the veins. Thus, the lymphatic vessels carry interstitial fluid to the cardiovascular system.

The movement of interstitial fluid from the lymphatics to the cardiovascular system is very important because, as noted earlier, the amount of fluid filtered out of all the blood vessel capillaries (except those in the kidneys) exceeds that absorbed by approximately 4 L each day. This 4 L is returned to the blood via the lymphatic system. In the process, small amounts of protein that may leak out of blood vessel capillaries into the interstitial fluid are also returned to the cardiovascular system.

Under some circumstances, the lymphatic system can become occluded, which allows the accumulation of excessive interstitial fluid. For example, occlusion of lymph flow by infectious organisms can result in a condition called ***elephantiasis***, in which there is massive edema of the involved area (**Figure 12.48**). Surgical removal of lymph nodes and vessels during the treatment of breast cancer can similarly allow interstitial fluid to pool in affected tissues.

In addition to draining excess interstitial fluid, the lymphatic system provides the pathway by which fat absorbed from the gastrointestinal tract reaches the blood (see Chapter 15). The lymphatics can also be the route by which cancer cells spread from their area of origin to other parts of the body (which is why cancer treatment sometimes includes the removal of lymph nodes).

Mechanism of Lymph Flow

In large part, the lymphatic vessels beyond the lymphatic capillaries propel the lymph within them by their own contractions. The smooth muscle in the wall of the lymphatics exerts a pumplike action by inherent rhythmic contractions. Because the lymphatic vessels have valves similar to those in veins, these contractions produce a one-way flow toward the point at which the lymphatics enter the circulatory system. The lymphatic vessel smooth muscle is responsive to stretch, so when no interstitial fluid accumulates and, therefore, no lymph enters the lymphatics, the smooth muscle is inactive. However, when increased fluid filtration out of capillaries occurs, the increased fluid entering the lymphatics stretches the walls and triggers rhythmic contractions of the smooth muscle. This constitutes a negative feedback mechanism for adjusting the rate of lymph flow to the rate of lymph formation and thereby preventing edema.

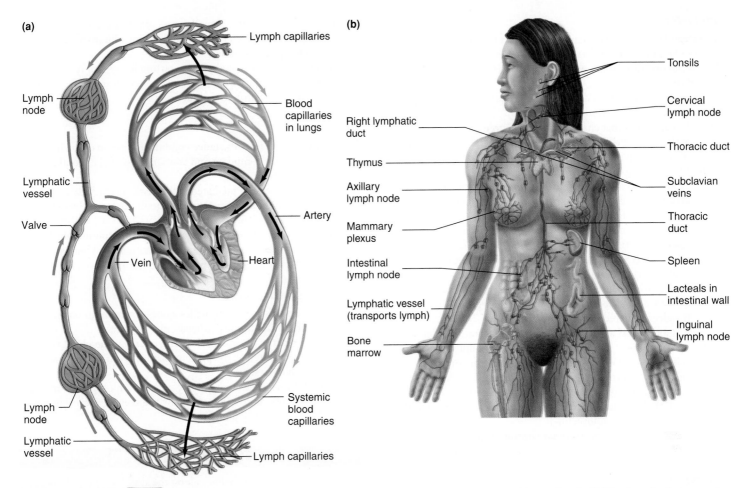

Figure 12.47 APR The lymphatic system (green) in relation to the cardiovascular system (blue and red). (a) The lymphatic system is a one-way system from interstitial fluid to the cardiovascular system. (b) Prior to reentering the blood at the subclavian veins, lymph flows through lymph nodes in the neck, armpits, groin, and around the intestines.

PHYSIOLOGICAL INQUIRY

- How might periodic ingestion of extra fluids be expected to increase the flow of lymph?

Answer can be found at end of chapter.

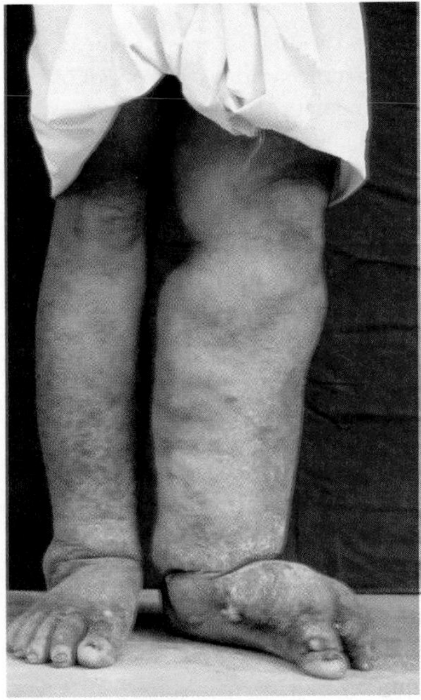

Figure 12.48 Elephantiasis is a disease resulting when mosquito-borne filarial worms block the return of lymph to the vascular system.

In addition, the smooth muscle of the lymphatic vessels is innervated by sympathetic neurons, and excitation of these neurons in various physiological states such as exercise may contribute to increased lymph flow. Forces external to the lymphatic vessels also enhance lymph flow. These include the same external forces we described for veins—the skeletal muscle pump and respiratory pump.

SECTION C SUMMARY

Arteries

I. The arteries function as low-resistance conduits and as pressure reservoirs for maintaining blood flow to the tissues during ventricular relaxation.

II. The difference between maximal arterial pressure (systolic pressure) and minimal arterial pressure (diastolic pressure) during a cardiac cycle is the pulse pressure.

III. Mean arterial pressure can be estimated as diastolic pressure plus one-third of the pulse pressure.

Arterioles

I. Arterioles are the dominant site of resistance to flow in the vascular system and play major roles in determining mean arterial pressure and in distributing flows to the various organs and tissues.

II. Arteriolar resistance is determined by local factors and by reflex neural and hormonal input.

a. Local factors that change with the degree of metabolic activity cause the arteriolar vasodilation and increased flow of active hyperemia.

b. Flow autoregulation involves local metabolic factors and arteriolar myogenic responses to stretch, and it changes arteriolar resistance to maintain a constant blood flow when arterial blood pressure changes.

c. Sympathetic neurons innervate most arterioles and cause vasoconstriction via α-adrenergic receptors. In certain cases, noncholinergic, nonadrenergic neurons that release nitric oxide or other vasodilators also innervate blood vessels.

d. Epinephrine causes vasoconstriction or vasodilation, depending on the proportion of α-adrenergic and β_2-adrenergic receptors in the organ.

e. Angiotensin II and vasopressin cause vasoconstriction.

f. Some chemical inputs act by stimulating endothelial cells to release vasodilator or vasoconstrictor paracrine agents, which then act on adjacent smooth muscle. These paracrine agents include the vasodilators nitric oxide (endothelium-derived relaxing factor), prostacyclin, and the vasoconstrictor endothelin-1.

III. Table 12.5 summarizes arteriolar control in specific organs.

Capillaries

I. Capillaries are the site at which nutrients and waste products are exchanged between blood and tissues.

II. Blood flows through the capillaries more slowly than through any other part of the vascular system because of the huge cross-sectional area of the capillaries.

III. Capillary blood flow is determined by the resistance of the arterioles supplying the capillaries and by the number of open precapillary sphincters.

IV. Diffusion is the mechanism that exchanges nutrients and metabolic end products between capillary plasma and interstitial fluid.

a. Lipid-soluble substances can move through the endothelial cells, whereas ions and polar molecules only move through water-filled intercellular clefts or fused-vesicle channels.

b. Plasma proteins do not easily move across capillary walls; specific proteins like certain hormones can be moved by vesicle transport.

c. The diffusion gradient for a substance across capillaries arises as a result of cell utilization or production of the substance. Increased metabolism increases the diffusion gradient and increases the rate of diffusion.

V. Bulk flow of protein-free plasma or interstitial fluid across capillaries determines the distribution of extracellular fluid between these two fluid compartments.

a. Filtration from plasma to interstitial fluid is favored by the hydrostatic pressure difference between the capillary and the interstitial fluid. Absorption from interstitial fluid to plasma is favored by the protein concentration difference between the plasma and the interstitial fluid.

b. Filtration and absorption do not change the concentrations of crystalloids in the plasma and interstitial fluid because these substances move together with water.

c. There is normally a small excess of filtration over absorption, which returns fluids to the bloodstream via lymphatic vessels.

d. Disease states that alter the Starling forces can result in edema (e.g., heart failure, tissue injury, liver disease, kidney disease, and protein malnutrition).

Veins

I. Veins serve as low-resistance conduits for venous return.

II. Veins are very compliant and contain most of the blood in the vascular system.

a. Sympathetically mediated vasoconstriction reflexively reduces venous diameter to maintain venous pressure and venous return.

b. The skeletal muscle pump and respiratory pump increase venous pressure and enhance venous return. Venous valves permit the pressure to produce flow only toward the heart.

The Lymphatic System

I. The lymphatic system provides a one-way route to return interstitial fluid to the cardiovascular system.

II. Lymph returns the excess fluid filtered from the blood vessel capillaries, as well as the protein that leaks out of the blood vessel capillaries.

III. Lymph flow is driven mainly by contraction of smooth muscle in the lymphatic vessels but also by the skeletal muscle pump and the respiratory pump.

SECTION C REVIEW QUESTIONS

1. Draw the pressure changes along the systemic and pulmonary vascular systems during the cardiac cycle.
2. What are the two main functions of the arteries?
3. What are normal values for systolic, diastolic, and mean arterial pressures in young adult males? Females? How is mean arterial pressure estimated?
4. What are two major factors that determine pulse pressure?
5. What denotes systolic and diastolic pressure in the measurement of arterial pressure with a sphygmomanometer?
6. What are the major sites of resistance in the systemic vascular system?
7. Name two functions of arterioles.
8. Write the formula relating flow through an organ to mean arterial pressure and to the resistance to flow that organ offers.
9. List the chemical factors that mediate active hyperemia.
10. Name a mechanism other than chemical factors that contributes to flow autoregulation.
11. What is the only autonomic innervation of most arterioles? What are the major adrenergic receptors influenced by these nerves? How can control of sympathetic nerves to arterioles achieve vasodilation?
12. Name four hormones that cause vasodilation or vasoconstriction of arterioles, and specify their effects.
13. Describe the role of endothelial paracrine agents in mediating arteriolar vasoconstriction and vasodilation, and give three examples.
14. Draw a flow diagram summarizing the factors affecting arteriolar radius.
15. What are the relative velocities of flow through the various vessel types of the systemic circulation?
16. Contrast diffusion and bulk flow. Which mechanism is most important in the exchange of nutrients, oxygen, and metabolic end products across the capillary wall?

17. What is the only solute that has a significant concentration difference across the capillary wall? How does this difference influence water concentration?
18. What four variables determine the net filtration pressure across the capillary wall? Give representative values for each of them at the arteriolar and venous ends of a systemic capillary.
19. How do changes in local arteriolar resistance influence downstream capillary pressure?
20. What is the relationship between cardiac output and venous return in the steady state? What is the force driving venous return?
21. Contrast the compliances and blood volumes of the veins and arteries.
22. What four factors influence venous pressure?
23. Approximately how much fluid do the lymphatics return to the blood each day?
24. Describe the mechanisms that cause lymph flow.

SECTION C KEY TERMS

absorption 400
active hyperemia 392
angiogenesis 396
angiogenic factors 396
angiotensin II 394
atrial natriuretic peptide 395
bradykinin 393
colloid 400
compliance 388
crystalloid 400
diastolic pressure (*DP*) 389
endothelin-1 (ET-1) 395
flow autoregulation 393
fused-vesicle channel 397
hyperemia 392
intercellular cleft 397
intrinsic tone 392
kallikrein 393
kininogen 393
Korotkoff's sounds 391
local control 392
lymph 404
lymphatic capillary 404
lymphatic system 404
lymphatic vessel 404
mean arterial pressure (*MAP*) 389
metarteriole 397
myogenic response 393
net filtration pressure (*NFP*) 400
nitric oxide 393
peripheral veins 402
precapillary sphincter 397
prostacyclin 395
prostaglandin I_2 (PGI_2) 395
pulse pressure 389
reactive hyperemia 393
respiratory pump 403
skeletal muscle pump 403
Starling force 400
systolic pressure (*SP*) 389
vasoconstriction 392
vasodilation 392
vasopressin 394

SECTION C CLINICAL TERMS

angiostatin 396
arteriosclerosis 389
edema 402
elephantiasis 404
kwashiorkor 402
sildenafil (Viagra) 394
tadalafil (Cialis) 394

SECTION D

Integration of Cardiovascular Function: Regulation of Systemic Arterial Pressure

In Chapter 1, we described the fundamental components of homeostatic control systems: (1) an internal environmental variable maintained in a relatively narrow range, (2) receptors sensitive to changes in this variable, (3) afferent pathways from the receptors, (4) an integrating center that receives and integrates the afferent inputs, (5) efferent pathways from the integrating center, and (6) effectors that act to change the variable when signals arrive along efferent pathways. The control and integration of cardiovascular function will be described in these terms.

The major cardiovascular variable being regulated is the mean arterial pressure in the systemic circulation. This should not be surprising because this pressure is the driving force for blood flow through all the organs except the lungs. Maintaining it is therefore a prerequisite for ensuring adequate blood flow to these organs. The importance of maintaining blood pressure within a normal range demonstrates the general principle of physiology that homeostasis is essential for health and survival. Without a homeostatic control system operating to maintain blood pressure, the tissues of the body would quickly die if pressure were to decrease significantly.

The mean systemic arterial pressure is the arithmetic product of two factors: (1) the cardiac output and (2) the **total peripheral resistance** (***TPR***), which is the combined resistance to flow of all the systemic blood vessels.

$$\underset{(MAP)}{\text{Mean systemic arterial pressure}} = \underset{(CO)}{\text{Cardiac output}} \times \underset{(TPR)}{\text{Total peripheral resistance}}$$

Cardiac output and total peripheral resistance set the mean systemic arterial pressure because they determine the average volume of blood in the systemic arteries over time; it is this blood volume that causes the pressure. This relationship cannot be emphasized too strongly: *All changes in mean arterial pressure must be the result of changes in cardiac output and/or total peripheral resistance.* Keep in mind that mean arterial pressure will change only if the arithmetic product of cardiac output and total peripheral resistance changes. For example, if cardiac output doubles and total peripheral resistance decreases by half, mean arterial pressure will not change because the product of cardiac output and total peripheral resistance has not changed. Because cardiac output is the volume of blood pumped into the arteries per unit time, it is fairly intuitive that it should be one of the two determinants of mean arterial volume and pressure. The contribution of total peripheral resistance to mean arterial pressure is less obvious, but it can be illustrated with the model introduced previously in Figure 12.33.

As shown in **Figure 12.49**, a pump pushes fluid into a container at the rate of 1 L/min. At steady state, fluid also leaves through the outflow tubes at a total rate of 1 L/min. Therefore, the height of the fluid column (ΔP), which is the driving pressure for outflow, remains stable. We then disturb the steady state by dilating outflow tube 1, thereby increasing its radius, reducing its resistance, and increasing its flow. The total outflow for the system immediately becomes greater than 1 L/min, and more fluid leaves the reservoir than enters

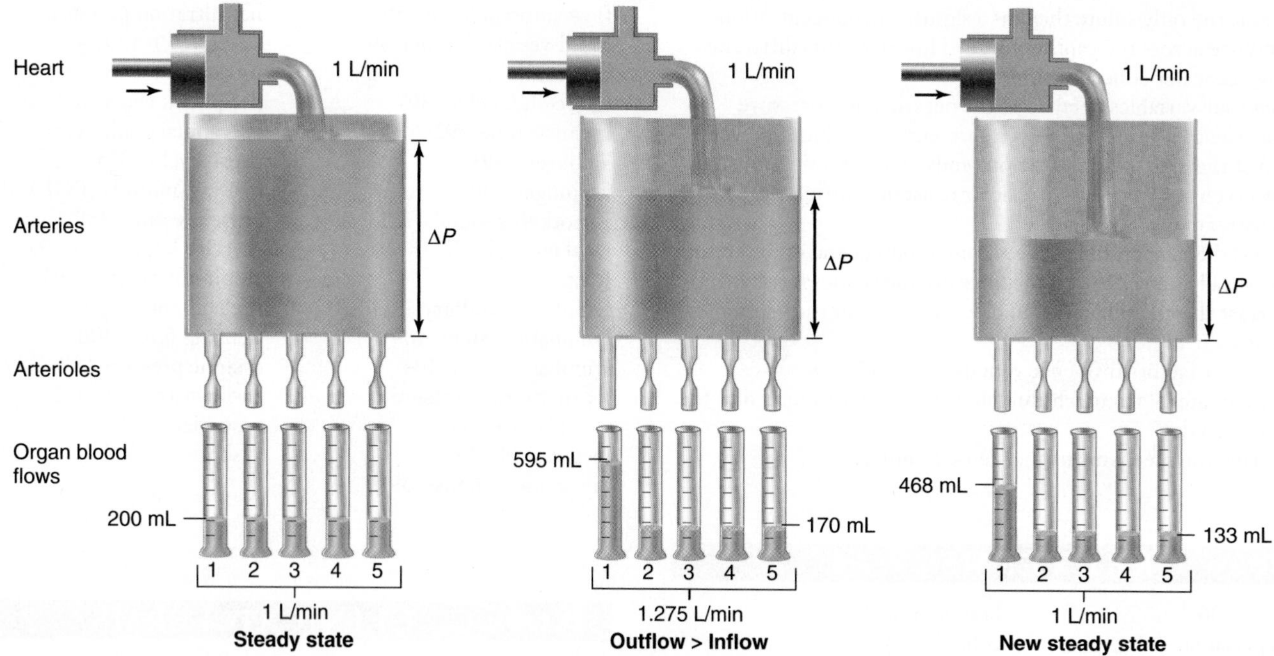

Figure 12.49 Dependence of arterial blood pressure upon total arteriolar resistance. Dilating one arteriolar bed affects arterial pressure and organ blood flow if no compensatory adjustments occur. The middle panel indicates a transient state before the new steady state occurs.

from the pump. Therefore, the volume and height of the fluid column begin to decrease until a new steady state between inflow and outflow is reached. In other words, at any given pump input, a change in total outflow resistance must produce changes in the volume and height (pressure) in the reservoir.

This analysis can be applied to the circulatory system by again equating the pump with the heart, the reservoir with the arteries, and the outflow tubes with various arteriolar beds. As described earlier, the major sites of resistance in the systemic circuit are the arterioles. Moreover, changes in total resistance are normally due to changes in the resistance of arterioles. Therefore, total peripheral resistance is determined by total arteriolar resistance.

A physiological analogy to opening outflow tube 1 is exercise. During exercise, the skeletal muscle arterioles dilate, thereby decreasing resistance. If the cardiac output and the arteriolar diameters of all other vascular beds were to remain unchanged, the increased runoff through the skeletal muscle arterioles would cause a decrease in systemic arterial pressure.

We must reemphasize that it is the *total* arteriolar resistance that influences systemic arterial blood pressure. The distribution of resistances among organs is irrelevant in this regard. **Figure 12.50** illustrates this point. On the right, outflow tube 1 has been opened, as in the previous example, while tubes 2 to 4 have been simultaneously constricted. The increased resistance in tubes 2 to 4 compensates for the decreased resistance in tube 1. Therefore, total resistance remains unchanged, and the reservoir pressure is unchanged. Total outflow remains 1 L/min, although the distribution of flows is such that flow through tube 1 increases, flow through tubes 2 to 4 decreases, and flow through tube 5 is unchanged. This is analogous to the alteration of systemic vascular resistances that occurs during exercise. When the skeletal muscle arterioles (tube 1) dilate, the total resistance of the systemic circulation can still be maintained if arterioles constrict in other organs, such as the kidneys, stomach, and intestine (tubes 2 to 4). In contrast, the brain arterioles (tube 5) remain unchanged, ensuring constant brain blood supply.

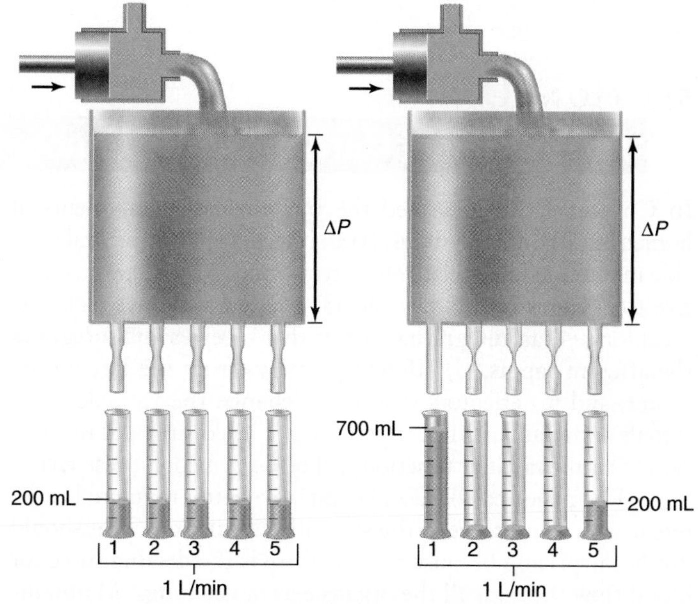

Figure 12.50 Compensation for dilation in one bed by constriction in others. When outflow tube 1 is opened, outflow tubes 2 to 4 are simultaneously tightened so that total outflow resistance, total runoff rate, and reservoir pressure all remain constant.

This type of resistance juggling can maintain total resistance only within limits, however. Obviously, if tube 1 opens too wide, even complete closure of the other tubes potentially might not prevent total outflow resistance from decreasing. In that situation, cardiac output must be

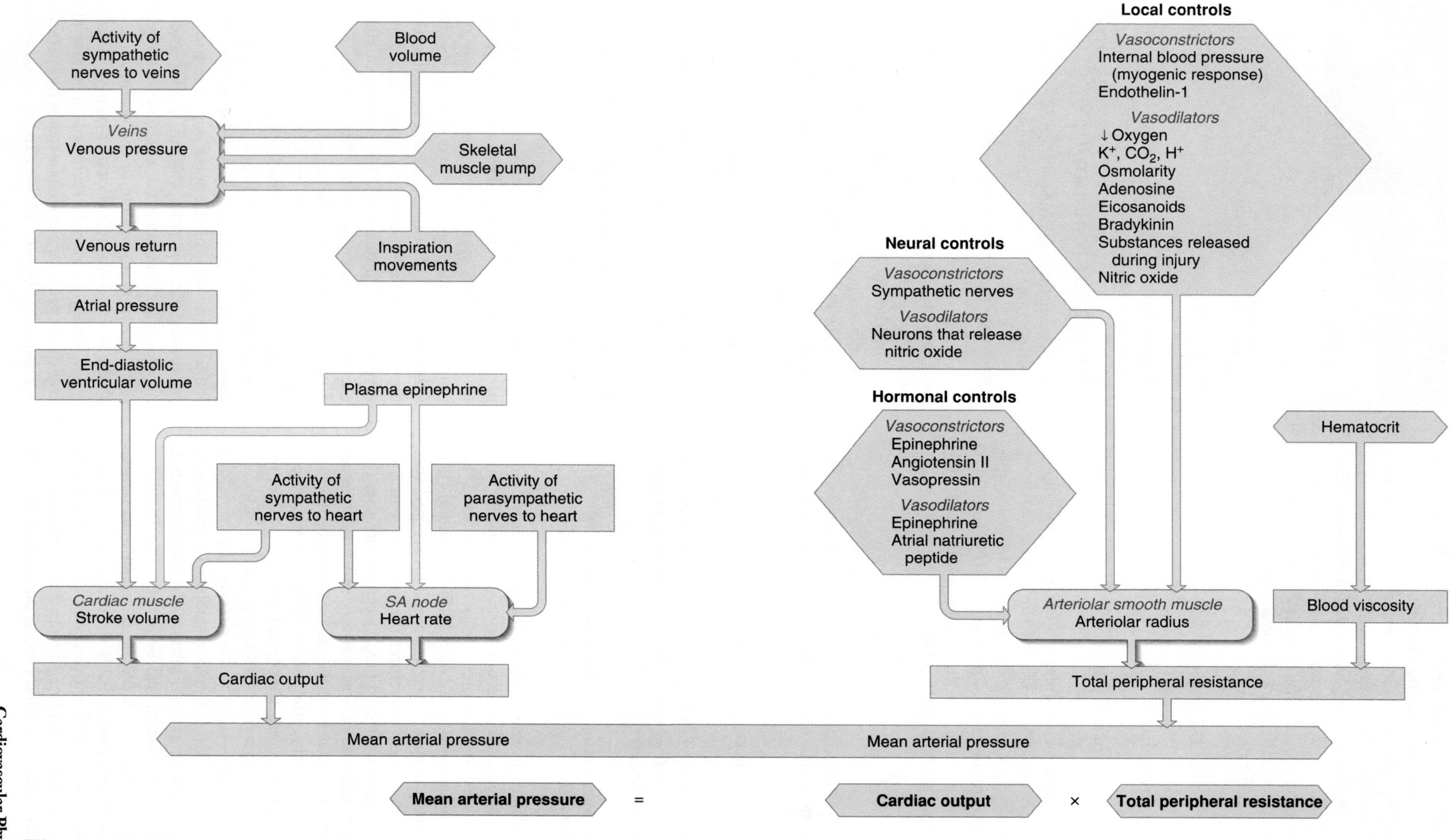

Figure 12.51 Summary of factors that determine systemic arterial pressure, a composite of Figures 12.27, 12.36, and 12.46, with the addition of the effect of hematocrit on resistance.

increased to maintain pressure in the arteries. We will see that this is actually the case during exercise.

We have so far explained in an intuitive way why cardiac output (*CO*) and total peripheral resistance (*TPR*) are the two variables that determine mean systemic arterial pressure. This intuitive approach, however, does not explain specifically why *MAP* is the arithmetic product of *CO* and *TPR*. This relationship can be derived formally from the basic equation relating flow, pressure, and resistance:

$$F = \Delta P / R$$

Rearranging terms algebraically,

$$\Delta P = F \times R$$

Because the systemic vascular system is a continuous series of tubes, this equation holds for the entire system—that is, from the arteries to the right atrium. Therefore, the ΔP term is mean systemic arterial pressure (*MAP*) minus the pressure in the right atrium, *F* is the cardiac output (*CO*), and *R* is the total peripheral resistance (*TPR*):

$$MAP - \text{Right atrial pressure} = CO \times TPR$$

Because the pressure in the right atrium is close to zero, we can drop this term and we are left with the equation presented earlier:

$$MAP = CO \times TPR$$

This equation is the fundamental equation of cardiovascular physiology. An analogous equation can also be applied to the pulmonary circulation:

$$\begin{matrix}\text{Mean pulmonary} \\ \text{arterial pressure}\end{matrix} = CO \times \begin{matrix}\text{Total pulmonary} \\ \text{vascular resistance}\end{matrix}$$

These equations provide a way to integrate information presented in this chapter. For example, we can now explain why mean pulmonary arterial pressure is much lower than mean systemic arterial pressure (**Table 12.6**). The blood flow (that is, the cardiac output) through the pulmonary and systemic arteries is the same. Therefore, the pressures can differ only if the resistances differ. Thus, we can deduce that the pulmonary vessels offer much less resistance to flow than do the systemic vessels. In other words, the total pulmonary vascular resistance is lower than the total peripheral resistance.

Figure 12.51 presents the grand scheme of factors that determine mean systemic arterial pressure. None of this information is new—all of it was presented in previous figures. A change in only a single variable will produce a change in mean systemic arterial pressure by altering either cardiac output or total peripheral resistance. For example, **Figure 12.52** illustrates how bleeding that results in significant blood loss (***hemorrhage***) leads to a decrease in mean arterial pressure. Conversely, any deviation in mean arterial pressure, such as that occurring during hemorrhage, will elicit homeostatic reflexes so that cardiac output and/or total peripheral resistance will change in the direction required to minimize the initial change in arterial pressure.

TABLE 12.6 Comparison of Hemodynamics in the Systemic and Pulmonary Circuits

	Systemic Circulation	Pulmonary Circulation
Cardiac output (L/min)	5	5
Systolic pressure (mmHg)	120	25
Diastolic pressure (mmHg)	80	10
Mean arterial pressure (mmHg)	93	15

PHYSIOLOGICAL INQUIRY

- Calculate the magnitude of the difference in total resistance between the systemic and pulmonary circuits.

Answer can be found at end of chapter.

In the short term—seconds to hours—these homeostatic adjustments to mean arterial pressure are brought about by reflexes called the *baroreceptor reflexes*. They utilize mainly changes in the activity of the autonomic neurons supplying the heart and blood vessels, as well as changes in the secretion of the hormones that influence these structures (epinephrine, angiotensin II, and vasopressin). Over longer time spans, the baroreceptor reflexes become less important and factors controlling blood volume play a dominant role in determining blood pressure. The next two sections describe these phenomena.

12.13 Baroreceptor Reflexes

Arterial Baroreceptors

The reflexes that homeostatically regulate arterial pressure originate primarily with arterial receptors that respond to changes in pressure. Two of these receptors are found where the left and right common carotid arteries divide into two smaller arteries that supply the head with blood (**Figure 12.53**). At this division, the wall of the artery is thinner than usual and contains a large number of branching, sensory neuronal processes. This portion of the artery is called the carotid sinus (the term *sinus* denotes a recess, space, or dilated channel), and the sensory neurons are highly sensitive to stretch or distortion. The degree of wall stretching is directly related to the pressure within the artery. Therefore, the carotid sinuses serve as pressure receptors, or **baroreceptors.** An area functionally similar to the carotid sinuses is found in the arch of the aorta and is termed the **aortic arch baroreceptor.** The two carotid sinuses and the aortic arch baroreceptor constitute the **arterial baroreceptors.** Afferent neurons travel from them to the brainstem and provide input to the neurons of cardiovascular control centers there.

Action potentials recorded in single afferent neurons from the carotid sinus demonstrate the pattern of baroreceptor response (**Figure 12.54a**). In this experiment, the pressure

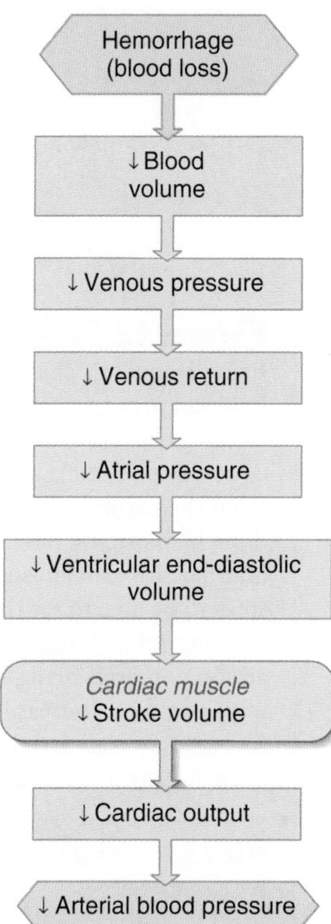

Figure 12.52 Sequence of events by which a decrease in blood volume leads to a decrease in mean arterial pressure.

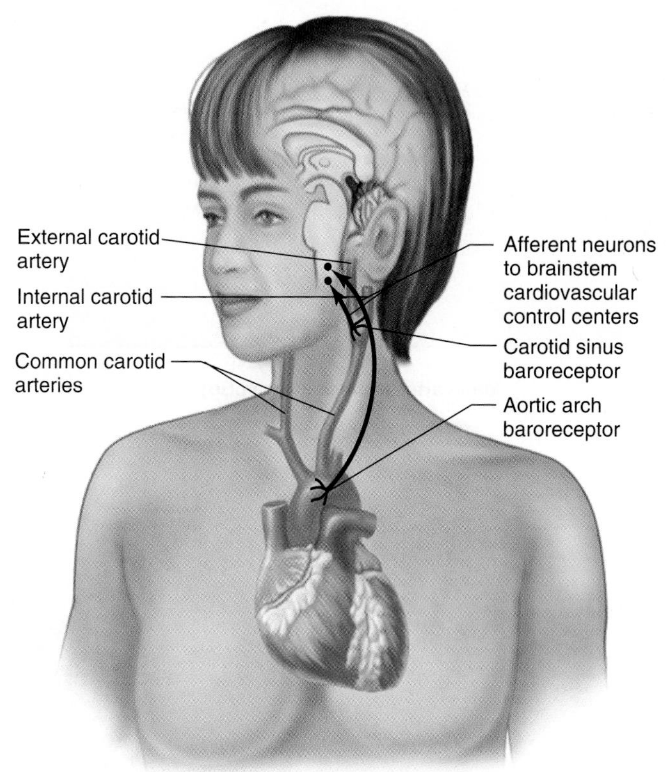

Figure 12.53 APR Locations of arterial baroreceptors.

PHYSIOLOGICAL INQUIRY

- When you first stand up after getting out of bed, how does the pressure detected by the carotid baroreceptors change?

Answer can be found at end of chapter.

in the carotid sinus is artificially controlled so that the pressure is steady, not pulsatile (i.e., not varying as usual between systolic and diastolic pressure). At a particular steady pressure, for example, 100 mmHg, there is a certain rate of discharge by the neuron. This rate can be increased by raising the arterial pressure, or it can be decreased by lowering the pressure. The rate of discharge of the carotid sinus is therefore directly proportional to the mean arterial pressure.

If the experiment is repeated using the same mean pressures as before but allowing pressure pulsations (**Figure 12.54b**), it is found that at any given mean pressure, the larger the pulse pressure, the faster the rate of firing by the carotid sinus. This responsiveness to pulse pressure adds a further element of information to blood pressure regulation, because small changes in factors such as blood volume may cause changes in arterial pulse pressure with little or no change in mean arterial pressure.

The Medullary Cardiovascular Center

The primary integrating center for the baroreceptor reflexes is a diffuse network of highly interconnected neurons called the **medullary cardiovascular center,** located in the medulla oblongata. The neurons in this center receive input from the various baroreceptors. This input determines the action potential frequency from the cardiovascular center along neural pathways that terminate upon the cell bodies and dendrites of the vagus (parasympathetic) neurons to the heart and the sympathetic neurons to the heart, arterioles, and veins. When the arterial baroreceptors increase their rate of discharge, the result is a decrease in sympathetic neuron activity and an increase in parasympathetic neuron activity (**Figure 12.55**). A decrease in baroreceptor firing rate results in the opposite pattern.

Angiotensin II generation and vasopressin secretion are also altered by baroreceptor activity and help restore blood pressure. Decreased arterial pressure elicits increased plasma concentrations of both these hormones, which increase arterial pressure by constricting arterioles.

Operation of the Arterial Baroreceptor Reflex

Our description of the arterial baroreceptor reflex is now complete. If arterial pressure decreases, as during a hemorrhage (**Figure 12.56**), the discharge rate of the arterial baroreceptors also decreases. Fewer action potentials travel up the afferent nerves to the medullary cardiovascular center, and this induces (1) increased heart rate because of increased sympathetic activity and decreased parasympathetic activity to the heart, (2) increased ventricular contractility because of increased sympathetic activity to the ventricular myocardium, (3) arteriolar constriction because of increased sympathetic activity to the arterioles (and increased plasma concentrations of angiotensin II and vasopressin), and (4) increased venous constriction because of increased sympathetic activity to the veins. The net result is an increased

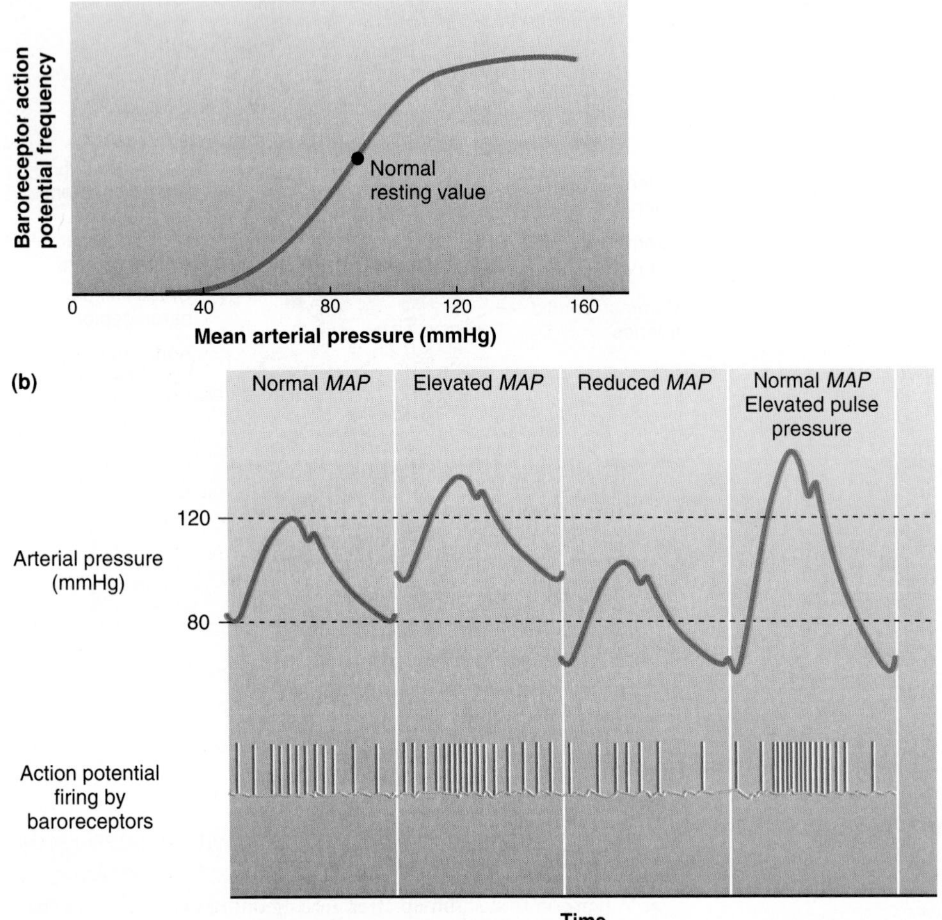

Figure 12.54 APIR Baroreceptor firing frequency changes with changes in blood pressure. (a) Effect of changing mean arterial pressure (*MAP*) on the firing of action potentials by afferent neurons from the carotid sinus. This experiment is done by pumping blood in a nonpulsatile manner through an isolated carotid sinus so as to be able to set the pressure inside it at any value desired. (b) Baroreceptor action potential firing frequency fluctuates with pressure. Increase in pulse pressure increases overall action potential frequency even at a normal *MAP*.

PHYSIOLOGICAL INQUIRY

- Note in part (a) that the normal resting value on this pressure–frequency curve is on the steepest, center part of the curve. What might be the physiological significance of this?

Answer can be found at end of chapter.

cardiac output (increased heart rate and stroke volume), increased total peripheral resistance (arteriolar constriction), and return of blood pressure toward normal. Conversely, an increase in arterial blood pressure for any reason causes increased firing of the arterial baroreceptors, which reflexively induces compensatory decreases in cardiac output and total peripheral resistance.

Having emphasized the importance of the arterial baroreceptor reflex, we must now add an equally important qualification. The baroreceptor reflex functions primarily as a short-term regulator of arterial blood pressure. It is activated instantly by any blood pressure change and functions to restore blood pressure rapidly toward normal. However, if arterial pressure remains increased from its normal set point for more than a few days, the arterial baroreceptors adapt to this new pressure and decrease their frequency of action potential firing at any given pressure. Thus, in patients who have chronically elevated blood pressure, the arterial baroreceptors continue to oppose minute-to-minute changes in blood pressure, but at a higher set point.

Other Baroreceptors

The large systemic veins, the pulmonary vessels, and the walls of the heart also contain baroreceptors, most of which function in a manner analogous to the arterial baroreceptors. By keeping brain cardiovascular control centers constantly informed about changes in the systemic venous, pulmonary, atrial, and ventricular pressures, these other baroreceptors provide a further degree of regulatory sensitivity. In essence, they contribute a feedforward component of arterial pressure control. For example, a slight decrease in ventricular pressure reflexively increases the activity of the sympathetic nervous system even before the change decreases cardiac output and arterial pressure enough to be detected by the arterial baroreceptors.

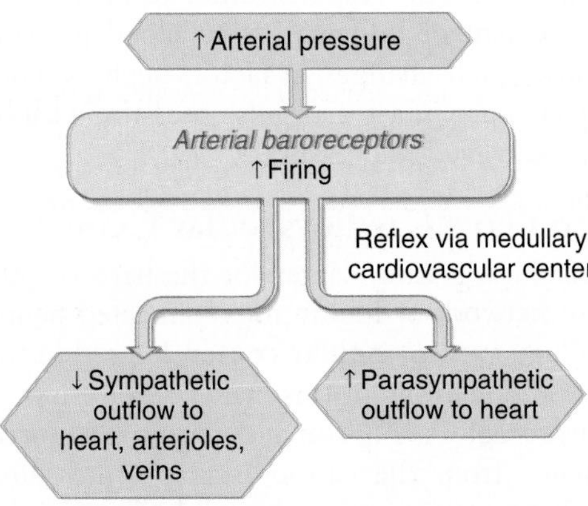

Figure 12.55 APIR Neural components of the arterial baroreceptor reflex. If the initial change were a decrease in arterial pressure, all the arrows in the boxes would be reversed.

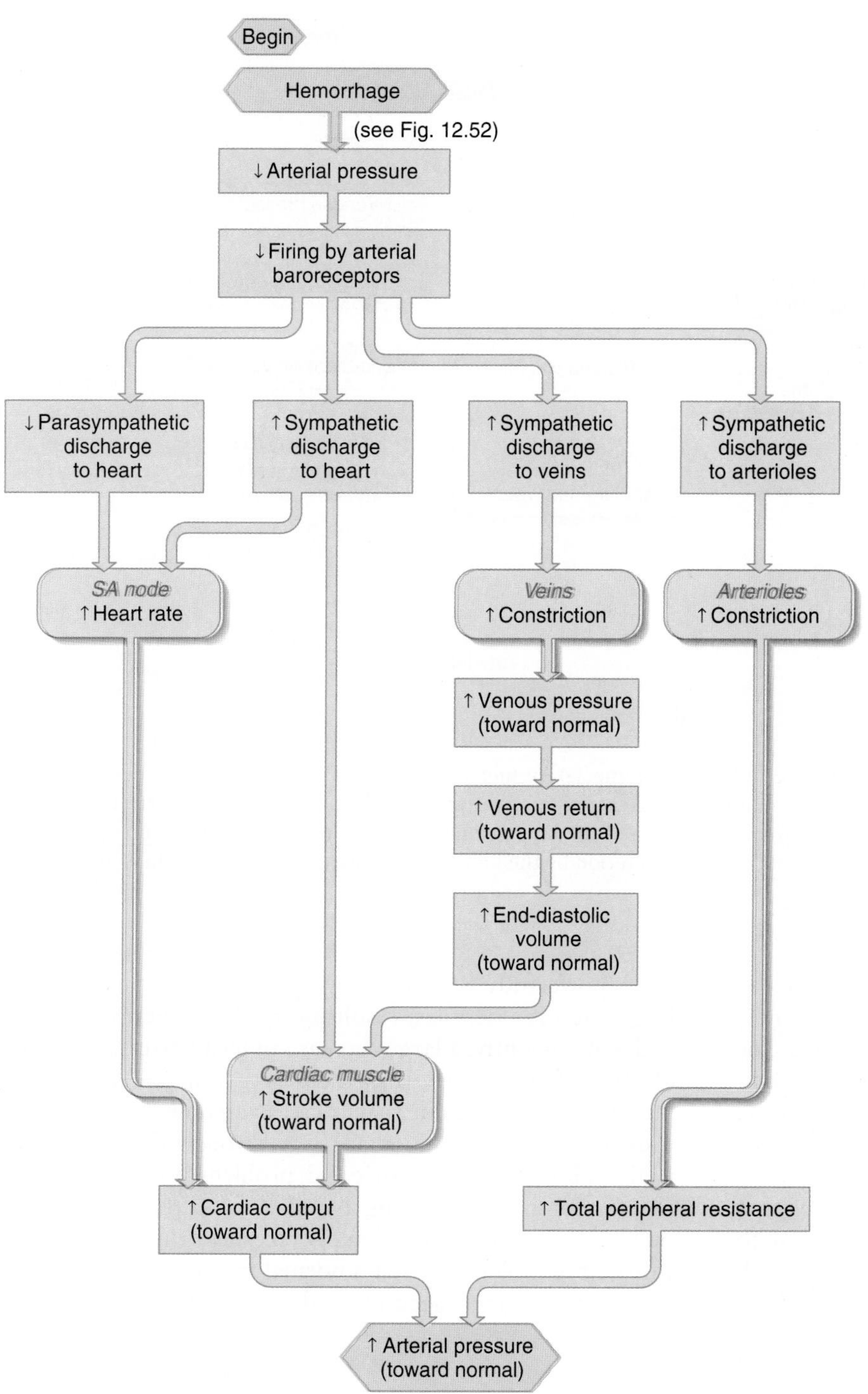

Figure 12.56 APR Arterial baroreceptor reflex compensation for hemorrhage. The compensatory mechanisms do not restore arterial pressure completely to normal. The increases designated "toward normal" are relative to prehemorrhage values; for example, the stroke volume is increased reflexively "toward normal" relative to the low point caused by the hemorrhage (i.e., before the reflex occurs), but it does not reach the level it had prior to the hemorrhage. For simplicity, the fact that plasma angiotensin II and vasopressin are also reflexively increased and help constrict arterioles is not shown.

12.14 Blood Volume and Long-Term Regulation of Arterial Pressure

The fact that the arterial baroreceptors (and other baroreceptors as well) adapt to prolonged changes in pressure means that the baroreceptor reflexes cannot set long-term arterial pressure. The major mechanism for long-term regulation occurs through the blood volume. As described earlier, blood volume is a major determinant of arterial pressure because it influences venous pressure, venous return, end-diastolic volume, stroke volume, and cardiac output. Thus, increased blood volume increases arterial pressure. However, the opposite causal chain also exists—an increased arterial pressure reduces blood volume (more specifically, the plasma component of the blood volume) by increasing the excretion of salt and water by the kidneys, as will be described in Chapter 14.

Figure 12.57 illustrates how these two causal chains constitute negative feedback loops that determine both blood volume and arterial pressure. An increase in blood pressure for any reason causes a decrease in blood volume, which tends to bring the blood pressure back down. An increase in the blood volume for any reason increases the blood pressure, which tends to bring the blood volume back down. The important point is this: Because arterial pressure influences blood volume but blood volume also influences arterial pressure, blood pressure can stabilize, in the long run, only at a value at which blood volume is also stable. Consequently, changes in steady-state blood volume are the single most important long-term determinant of blood pressure. The cooperation of the urinary and circulatory systems in the maintenance of blood volume and pressure is an excellent example of how the functions of organ systems are coordinated with each other—one of the general principles of physiology introduced in Chapter 1.

12.15 Other Cardiovascular Reflexes and Responses

Stimuli acting upon receptors other than baroreceptors can initiate reflexes that cause changes in arterial pressure. For example, the following stimuli all cause an increase in blood pressure: decreased arterial oxygen concentration, increased arterial carbon dioxide concentration, decreased blood flow to the brain, and pain originating in the skin. In contrast, pain originating in the viscera or joints may cause *decreases* in arterial pressure.

Many physiological states such as eating and sexual activity are also associated with changes in blood pressure. For example, attending a stressful business meeting may increase mean blood pressure by as much as 20 mmHg, walking increases it 10 mmHg, and sleeping decreases it 10 mmHg. Mood also has a significant effect on blood pressure, which tends to be lower when people report that they are happy than when they are angry or anxious.

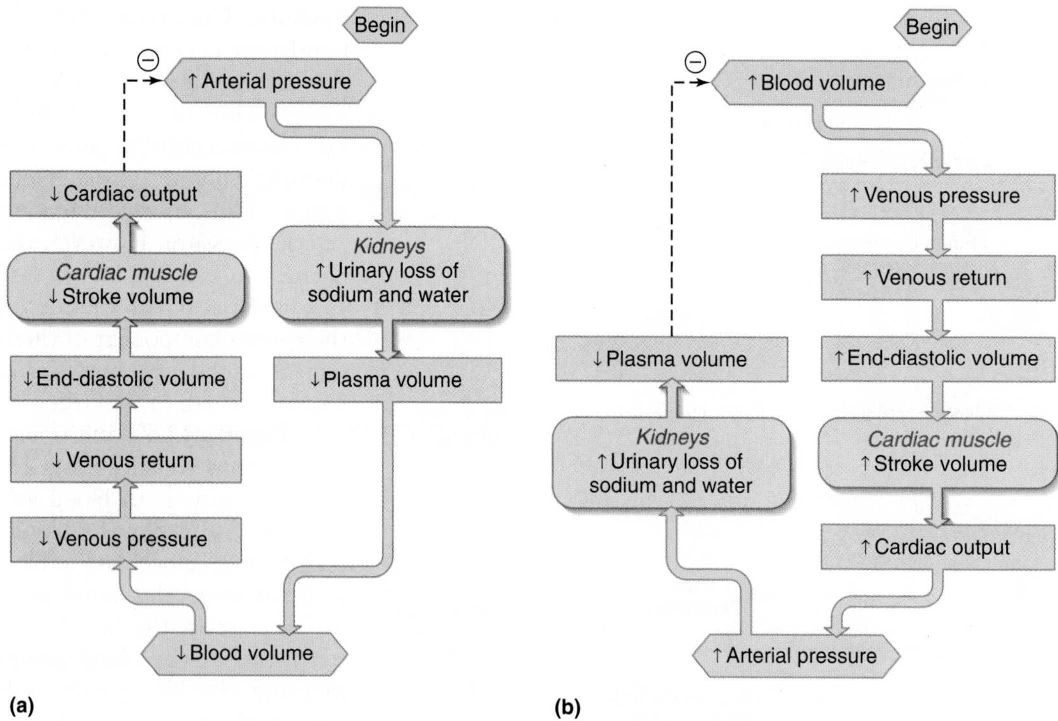

Figure 12.57 Causal relationships between arterial pressure and blood volume. (a) An increase in arterial pressure due, for example, to an increased cardiac output induces a decrease in blood volume by promoting fluid excretion by the kidneys. This tends to restore arterial pressure to its original value. (b) An increase in blood volume due, for example, to increased fluid ingestion induces an increase in arterial pressure, which tends to restore blood volume to its original value by promoting fluid excretion by the kidneys. Because of these relationships, blood volume is a major determinant of arterial pressure.

These changes are triggered by input from receptors or higher brain centers to the medullary cardiovascular center or, in some cases, to pathways distinct from these centers. For example, the fibers of certain neurons whose cell bodies are in the cerebral cortex and hypothalamus synapse directly on the sympathetic neurons in the spinal cord, bypassing the medullary center altogether.

An important clinical situation involving reflexes that regulate blood pressure is Cushing's phenomenon (not to be confused with Cushing's syndrome and disease, which are endocrine diseases discussed in Chapter 11). ***Cushing's phenomenon*** is a situation in which increased intracranial pressure causes a dramatic increase in mean arterial pressure. A number of different circumstances can cause increased pressure in the brain, including the presence of a rapidly growing cancerous tumor or a traumatic head injury that triggers internal hemorrhage or edema. What distinguishes these situations from similar problems elsewhere in the body is the fact that the enclosed bony cranium does not allow physical swelling toward the outside, so pressure is directed inward. This inward pressure exerts a collapsing force on intracranial vasculature, and the reduction in radius greatly increases the resistance to blood flow (recall that resistance increases as the fourth power of a decrease in radius). Blood flow is reduced below the level needed to satisfy metabolic requirements, brain oxygen concentration decreases, and carbon dioxide and other metabolic wastes increase. Accumulated metabolites in the brain interstitial fluid powerfully stimulate sympathetic neurons controlling systemic arterioles, resulting in a large increase in *TPR* and, consequently, a large increase in mean arterial pressure ($MAP = CO \times TPR$). In principle, this increased systemic pressure is adaptive, in that it can overcome the collapsing pressures and force blood to flow through the brain once again. However, if the original problem was an intracranial hemorrhage, restoring blood flow to the brain might only cause more bleeding and exacerbate the problem. To restore brain blood flow at a normal mean arterial pressure, the brain tumor or accumulated intracranial fluid must be removed.

SECTION D SUMMARY

I. Mean arterial pressure, the primary regulated variable in the cardiovascular system, equals the product of cardiac output and total peripheral resistance.

II. The factors that determine cardiac output and total peripheral resistance are summarized in Figure 12.51.

Baroreceptor Reflexes

I. The primary baroreceptors are the arterial baroreceptors, including the two carotid sinuses and the aortic arch. Other baroreceptors are located in the systemic veins, pulmonary vessels, and walls of the heart.

II. The firing rates of the arterial baroreceptors are proportional to mean arterial pressure and to pulse pressure.

III. An increase in firing of the arterial baroreceptors due to an increase in pressure causes, by way of the medullary cardiovascular center, an increase in parasympathetic outflow to the heart and a decrease in sympathetic outflow to the heart, arterioles, and veins. The result is a decrease in cardiac output, total peripheral resistance, and mean arterial pressure. The opposite occurs when the initial change is a decrease in arterial pressure.

Blood Volume and Long-Term Regulation of Arterial Pressure

I. The baroreceptor reflexes are short-term regulators of arterial pressure but adapt to a maintained change in pressure.
II. The most important long-term regulator of arterial pressure is the blood volume.

Other Cardiovascular Reflexes and Responses

I. Blood pressure can be influenced by many factors other than baroreceptors, including arterial blood gas concentrations, pain, emotions, and sexual activity.
II. Cushing's phenomenon is a clinical condition in which elevated intracranial pressure leads to decreased brain blood flow and a large increase in arterial blood pressure.

SECTION D REVIEW QUESTIONS

1. Write the equation relating mean arterial pressure to cardiac output and total peripheral resistance.
2. What variable accounts for the fact that mean pulmonary arterial pressure is lower than mean systemic arterial pressure?
3. Draw a flow diagram illustrating the factors that determine mean arterial pressure.
4. Identify the receptors, afferent pathways, integrating center, efferent pathways, and effectors in the arterial baroreceptor reflex.
5. When the arterial baroreceptors decrease or increase their rate of firing, what changes in autonomic outflow and cardiovascular function occur?
6. Describe the role of blood volume in the long-term regulation of arterial pressure.
7. Describe the cardiovascular response to a head injury that causes cerebral edema.

SECTION D KEY TERMS

aortic arch baroreceptor 409
arterial baroreceptors 409
baroreceptors 409
medullary cardiovascular center 412
total peripheral resistance (*TPR*) 407

SECTION D CLINICAL TERMS

Cushing's phenomenon 414
hemorrhage 409

SECTION E Cardiovascular Patterns in Health and Disease

12.16 Hemorrhage and Other Causes of Hypotension

The term ***hypotension*** means a low blood pressure, regardless of cause. One general cause of hypotension is a significant loss of blood volume as, for example, in a hemorrhage, which produces hypotension by the sequence of events shown previously in Figure 12.52. The most serious consequence of hypotension is reduced blood flow to the brain and cardiac muscle. The immediate counteracting response to hemorrhage is the arterial baroreceptor reflex, as summarized in Figure 12.56.

Figure 12.58, which shows how five variables change over time when blood volume decreases, adds a further degree of clarification to Figure 12.56. The values of factors changed as a direct result of the hemorrhage—stroke volume, cardiac output, and mean arterial pressure—are restored by the baroreceptor reflex toward, but not all the way to, normal. In contrast, values not altered directly by the hemorrhage but only by the reflex response to hemorrhage—heart rate and total peripheral resistance—increase above their prehemorrhage values. The increased peripheral resistance results from increases in sympathetic outflow to the arterioles in many vascular beds (but not those of the heart and brain). Thus, skin blood flow may decrease considerably because of arteriolar vasoconstriction; this is why the skin can become pale and cold following a significant hemorrhage. Kidney and intestinal blood flow also decrease because the usual functions of these organs are not immediately essential for life.

A second important type of compensatory mechanism (one not shown in Figure 12.56) involves the movement of interstitial fluid into capillaries. This occurs because both the decrease in blood pressure and the increase in arteriolar constriction decrease capillary hydrostatic pressure, thereby favoring the absorption of interstitial fluid (**Figure 12.59**). Thus, the initial events—blood loss and decreased blood volume—are in part compensated for by the movement of interstitial fluid into the vascular system. This mechanism, referred to as **autotransfusion,** can restore the blood volume to virtually normal levels within 12 to 24 hours after a moderate hemorrhage (**Table 12.7**). At this time, the entire restoration of blood volume is due to expansion of the plasma volume; therefore, the hematocrit actually decreases.

The early compensatory mechanisms for hemorrhage (the baroreceptor reflexes and interstitial fluid absorption) are

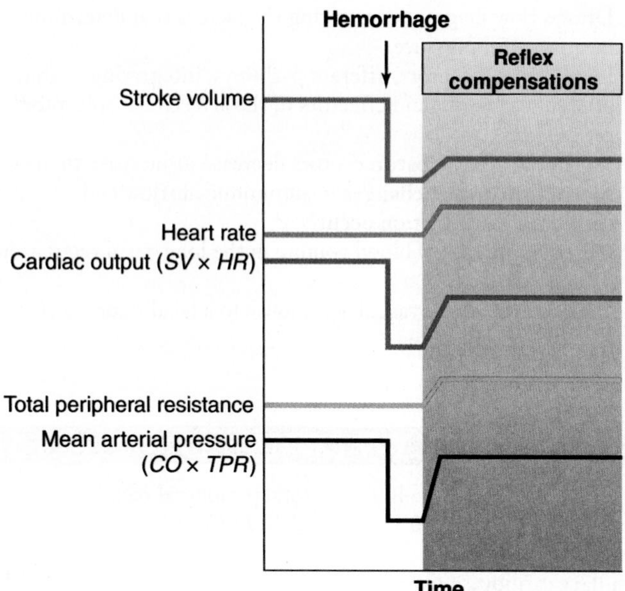

Figure 12.58 Five simultaneous graphs showing the time course of cardiovascular effects of hemorrhage. Note that the entire decrease in arterial pressure immediately following hemorrhage is secondary to the decrease in stroke volume and, therefore, cardiac output. This figure emphasizes the relative proportions of the "increase" and "decrease" arrows of Figure 12.56. All variables shown are increased relative to the state immediately following the hemorrhage, but they are not all increased compared to the state prior to the hemorrhage.

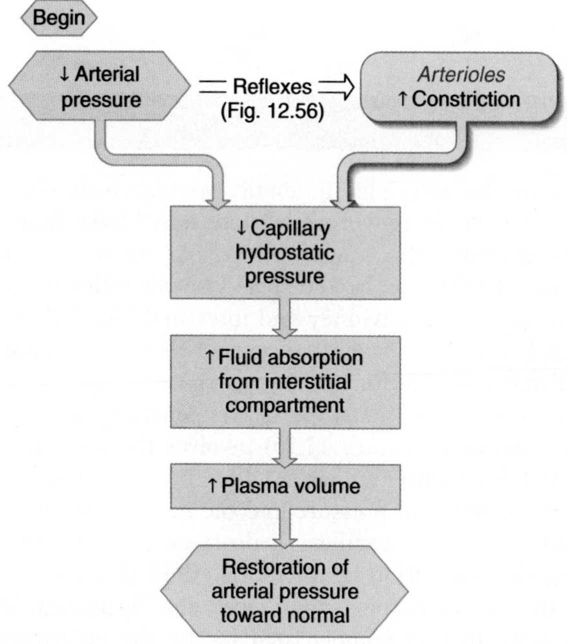

Figure 12.59 The autotransfusion mechanism compensates for blood loss by causing interstitial fluid to move into the capillaries.

highly efficient, so that losses of as much as 30% of total blood volume can be sustained with only slight reductions of mean arterial pressure or cardiac output.

We must emphasize that absorption of interstitial fluid only *redistributes* the extracellular fluid. Ultimate restoration of blood volume involves the control of fluid ingestion and

TABLE 12.7 Fluid Shifts After Hemorrhage

	Normal	Immediately After Hemorrhage	18 Hours After Hemorrhage
Total blood volume (mL)	5000	4000	4900
Erythrocyte volume (mL)	2300	1840	1840
Plasma volume (mL)	2700	2160	3060

PHYSIOLOGICAL INQUIRY

- Calculate the hematocrit before and 18 hours after the hemorrhage, and explain the changes that are observed.

Answer can be found at end of chapter.

minimizing water loss via the kidneys. These slower-acting compensations include an increase in thirst and a reduction in the excretion of salt and water in the urine. They are mediated by hormones, including renin, angiotensin, and aldosterone, and are described in Chapter 14. Replacement of the lost erythrocytes requires the hormone erythropoietin to stimulate erythropoiesis (maturation of immature red blood cells); this is described in detail in Section F of this chapter. These replacement processes require days to weeks in contrast to the rapidly occurring reflex compensations illustrated in Figure 12.59.

Hemorrhage is a striking example of hypotension due to a decrease in blood volume. There is a second way, however, that hypotension can occur due to volume depletion that does not result from loss of whole blood. It may occur through the skin, as in severe sweating or burns, or through the gastrointestinal tract, as in diarrhea or vomiting, or through the kidneys, as with unusually large urinary losses. By these various routes, the body can be depleted of water and ions such as Na^+, Cl^-, K^+, H^+, and HCO_3^-. Regardless of the route, the loss of fluid decreases circulating blood volume and produces symptoms and compensatory cardiovascular changes similar to those seen in hemorrhage.

Hypotension may also be caused by events other than blood or fluid loss. One major cause is a decrease in cardiac contractility (for example, during a heart attack). Another cause is strong emotion, which in rare cases can cause hypotension and fainting. The higher brain centers involved with emotions inhibit sympathetic activity to the cardiovascular system and enhance parasympathetic activity to the heart, resulting in a markedly decreased arterial pressure and brain blood flow. This whole process, known as ***vasovagal syncope,*** is usually transient. It should be noted that the fainting that sometimes occurs in a person donating blood is usually due to hypotension brought on by emotion, not due to the blood loss, because losing 0.5 L of blood will not generally cause serious hypotension. Massive release of endogenous substances that relax arteriolar smooth muscle may also cause hypotension by reducing total peripheral resistance. An important example is the hypotension that occurs during severe allergic responses (Chapter 18).

Shock

The term ***shock*** denotes any situation in which a decrease in blood flow to the organs and tissues damages them. Arterial pressure is usually, but not always, low in shock, and the classification of shock is quite similar to that used for hypotension. ***Hypovolemic shock*** is caused by a decrease in blood volume secondary to hemorrhage or loss of fluid other than blood. ***Low-resistance shock*** is due to a decrease in total peripheral resistance secondary to excessive release of vasodilators, as in allergy and infection. ***Cardiogenic shock*** is due to an extreme decrease in cardiac output from any of a variety of factors (for example, during a heart attack).

The circulatory system, especially the heart, suffers damage if shock is prolonged. As the heart deteriorates, cardiac output further declines and shock becomes progressively worse. Ultimately, shock may become irreversible even though blood transfusions and other appropriate therapy may temporarily restore blood pressure. See Chapter 19 for a case study of a person who experiences shock.

12.17 The Upright Posture

A decrease in the effective circulating blood volume occurs in the circulatory system when moving from a lying, horizontal position to a standing, vertical one. Why this is so requires an understanding of the action of gravity upon the long, continuous columns of blood in the vessels between the heart and the feet.

The pressures described in previous sections of this chapter are for an individual in the horizontal position, in which all blood vessels are at nearly the same level as the heart. In this position, the weight of the blood produces negligible pressure. In contrast, when a person is standing, the intravascular pressure everywhere becomes equal to the pressure generated by cardiac contraction plus an additional pressure equal to the weight of a column of blood from the heart to the point of measurement. In an average adult, for example, the weight of a column of blood extending from the heart to the feet would amount to 80 mmHg. In a foot capillary, therefore, the pressure could potentially increase from 25 (the average capillary pressure resulting from cardiac contraction) to 105 mmHg, the extra 80 mmHg being due to the weight of the column of blood.

This increase in pressure due to gravity influences the effective circulating blood volume in several ways. First, the increased hydrostatic pressure that occurs in the legs (as well as the buttocks and pelvic area) when a person is standing pushes outward on the highly distensible vein walls, causing marked distension. The result is pooling of blood in the veins; that is, some of the blood emerging from the capillaries simply goes into expanding the veins rather than returning to the heart. Simultaneously, the increase in capillary pressure caused by the gravitational force produces increased filtration of fluid out of the capillaries into the interstitial space. This is why our feet can swell during prolonged standing. The combined effects of venous pooling and increased capillary filtration reduce the effective circulating blood volume very similarly to the effects caused by a mild hemorrhage. Venous pooling explains why a person may sometimes feel faint when standing up suddenly. The reduced venous return causes a transient decrease in end-diastolic volume and therefore decreased stretch of the ventricles. This reduces stroke volume, which in turn reduces cardiac output and blood pressure. This feeling is normally very transient, however, because the decrease in arterial pressure immediately causes baroreceptor-reflex-mediated compensatory adjustments similar to those shown in Figure 12.56 for hemorrhage.

The effects of gravity can be offset by contraction of the skeletal muscles in the legs. Even gentle contractions of the leg muscles without movement produce intermittent, complete emptying of deep leg veins so that uninterrupted columns of venous blood from the heart to the feet no longer exist (**Figure 12.60**). The result is a decrease in both venous distension and pooling plus a significant reduction in capillary hydrostatic pressure and fluid filtration out of the capillaries. This phenomenon is illustrated by the fact that soldiers may faint while standing at attention for long periods of time

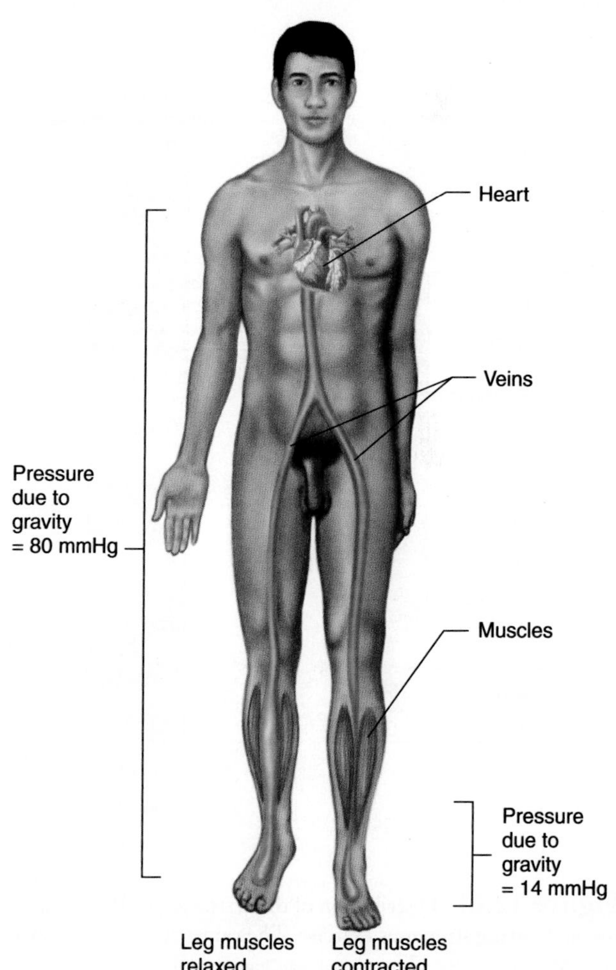

Figure 12.60 APIR Role of contraction of the leg skeletal muscles in reducing capillary pressure and filtration in the upright position. The skeletal muscle contraction compresses the veins, causing intermittent emptying so that the columns of blood are interrupted.

because of minimal leg muscle contractions. Fainting may be considered adaptive in this circumstance, because the venous and capillary pressure changes induced by gravity are eliminated. When a person who has fainted becomes horizontal, pooled venous blood is mobilized and fluid is absorbed back into the capillaries from the interstitial fluid of the legs and feet. Consequently, the wrong thing to do for a person who has fainted is to hold him or her upright.

12.18 Exercise

During exercise, cardiac output may increase from a resting value of about 5 L/min to a maximal value of about 35 L/min in trained athletes. **Figure 12.61** illustrates the distribution of this cardiac output during strenuous exercise. As expected, most of the increase in cardiac output goes to the exercising muscles. However, there are also increases in flow to the heart, to provide for the increased metabolism and workload as cardiac output increases, and to the skin, if it becomes necessary to dissipate heat generate by metabolism. The increases in flow through these three vascular beds are the result of arteriolar vasodilation in them. In both skeletal and cardiac muscle, local metabolic factors mediate the vasodilation, whereas the vasodilation in skin is achieved mainly by a decrease in the firing of the sympathetic neurons to the skin. At the same time that arteriolar vasodilation is occurring in these three beds, arteriolar vasoconstriction is occurring in the kidneys and gastrointestinal organs. This vasoconstriction is caused by increased activity of sympathetic neurons and manifests as decreased blood flow in Figure 12.61.

Vasodilation of arterioles in skeletal muscle, cardiac muscle, and skin causes a decrease in total peripheral resistance to blood flow. This decrease is partially offset by vasoconstriction of arterioles in other organs. This compensatory change in resistance, however, is not capable of compensating for the huge dilation of the muscle arterioles, and the net result is a decrease in total peripheral resistance.

What happens to arterial blood pressure during exercise? As always, the mean arterial pressure is simply the arithmetic product of cardiac output and total peripheral resistance. During most forms of exercise (**Figure 12.62** illustrates the case for mild exercise), the cardiac output tends to increase somewhat more than the total peripheral resistance decreases so that mean arterial pressure usually increases a small amount. Pulse pressure, in contrast, significantly increases because an increase in both stroke volume and the speed at which the stroke volume is ejected significantly increases systolic pressure. It should be noted that by "exercise," we are referring to cyclic contraction and relaxation of muscles occurring over a

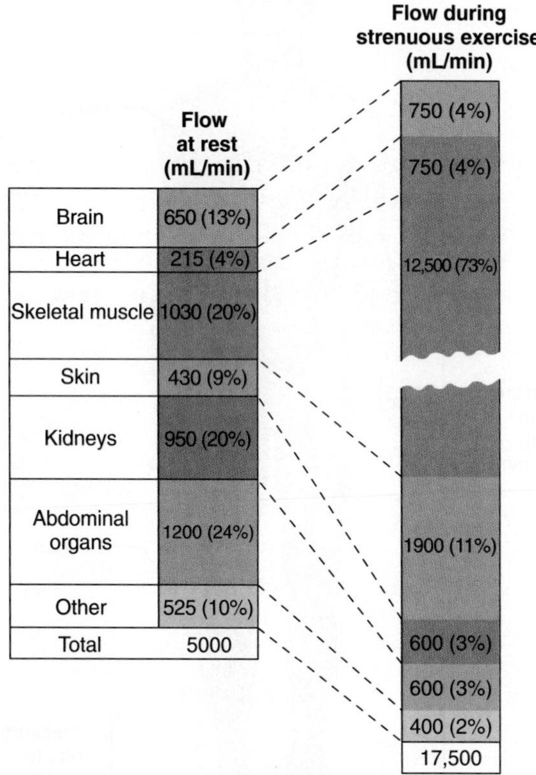

Figure 12.61 Distribution of the systemic cardiac output at rest and during strenuous exercise. The values at rest were previously presented in Figure 12.3. Adapted from Chapman and Mitchell.

PHYSIOLOGICAL INQUIRY

- Why might exercising on a very hot day result in fainting?

Answer can be found at end of chapter.

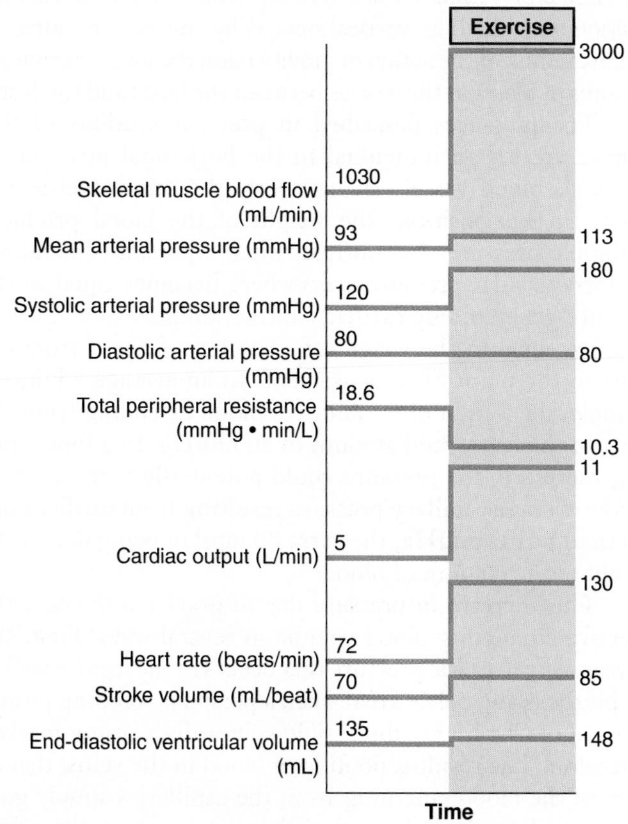

Figure 12.62 Summary of cardiovascular changes during mild upright exercise like jogging. The person was sitting quietly prior to the exercise. Total peripheral resistance was calculated from mean arterial pressure and cardiac output.

period of time, like jogging. A single, intense isometric contraction of muscles has a very different effect on blood pressure and will be described shortly.

The increase in cardiac output during exercise is supported by a large increase in heart rate and a small increase in stroke volume. The increase in heart rate is caused by a combination of decreased parasympathetic activity to the SA node and increased sympathetic activity. The increased stroke volume is due mainly to an increased ventricular contractility, manifested by an increased ejection fraction and mediated by the sympathetic neurons to the ventricular myocardium. Note in Figure 12.62, however, that there is a small increase (about 10%) in end-diastolic ventricular volume. Because of this increased filling, the Frank–Starling mechanism also contributes to the increased stroke volume, although not to the same degree as the increased contractility. We have focused our attention on factors that act directly upon the heart to alter cardiac output during exercise. By themselves, however, these factors are insufficient to account for the increased cardiac output. The fact is that cardiac output can be increased to high levels only if the peripheral processes favoring venous return to the heart are simultaneously activated to the same degree. Otherwise, the shortened filling time resulting from the high heart rate would decrease end-diastolic volume and, therefore, stroke volume (by the Frank–Starling mechanism).

Factors promoting venous return during exercise are (1) increased activity of the skeletal muscle pump, (2) increased depth and frequency of inspiration (the respiratory pump), (3) sympathetically mediated increase in venous tone, and (4) greater ease of blood flow from arteries to veins through the dilated skeletal muscle arterioles. **Figure 12.63** provides a summary of the control mechanisms that elicit the cardiovascular changes in exercise. As described previously, vasodilation of arterioles in skeletal and cardiac muscle once exercise is under way represents active hyperemia as a result of local metabolic factors within the muscle. But what drives the enhanced sympathetic outflow to most other arterioles, the heart, and the veins and the decreased parasympathetic outflow to the heart? The control of this autonomic outflow during exercise offers an excellent example of a preprogrammed pattern, modified by continuous afferent input. One or more discrete control centers in the brain are activated during exercise by output from the cerebral cortex, and descending pathways from these centers to the appropriate autonomic preganglionic neurons elicit the firing pattern typical of exercise. These centers become active, and changes to cardiac and vascular function occur even before exercise begins. Thus, this constitutes a feedforward system.

Once exercise is under way, if there is imperfect matching between blood flow and metabolic demands, local chemical changes in the muscle can develop, particularly during intense exercise. These changes activate chemoreceptors in the muscle. Afferent input from these receptors goes to the medullary cardiovascular center and facilitates the output reaching the autonomic neurons from higher brain centers. The result is a further increase in heart rate, myocardial contractility, and vascular resistance in the nonactive organs. Such a system permits a fine degree of matching between cardiac pumping and total oxygen and nutrients required by the exercising muscles. Mechanoreceptors in the exercising muscles are also stimulated and provide input to the medullary cardiovascular center.

Finally, the arterial baroreceptors also play a role in the altered autonomic outflow. Knowing that the mean and pulsatile pressures increase during exercise, you may logically assume that the arterial baroreceptors will respond to these elevated pressures and signal for increased parasympathetic and decreased sympathetic outflow, a pattern designed to counter the increase in arterial pressure. In reality, however, exactly the opposite occurs; the arterial baroreceptors play an important role in *increasing* the arterial pressure over that existing at rest. The reason is that one neural component of the

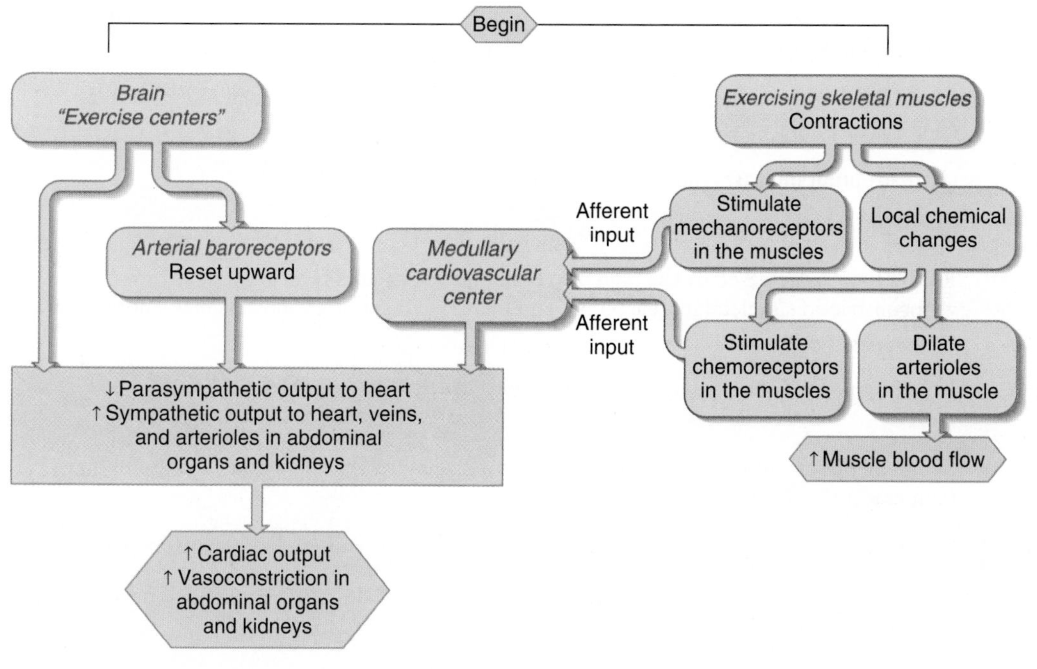

Figure 12.63 Control of the cardiovascular system during exercise. The primary outflow to the sympathetic and parasympathetic neurons is via pathways from "exercise centers" in the brain. Afferent input from mechanoreceptors and chemoreceptors in the exercising muscles and from reset arterial baroreceptors also influences the autonomic neurons by way of the medullary cardiovascular center.

central command output travels to the arterial baroreceptors and "resets" them upward as exercise begins. This resetting causes the baroreceptors to respond as though arterial pressure had decreased, and their output (decreased action potential frequency) signals for decreased parasympathetic and increased sympathetic outflow. **Table 12.8** summarizes the changes that occur during moderate exercise—that is, exercise (like jogging, swimming, or fast walking) that involves large muscle groups for an extended period of time.

In closing, we return to the other major category of exercise, which involves maintained high-force, slow-shortening-velocity contractions, as in weight lifting. Here, too, cardiac output and arterial blood pressure increase, and the arterioles in the exercising muscles undergo vasodilation due to local metabolic factors. However, there is a crucial difference. During maintained contractions, once the contracting muscles exceed 10% to 15% of their maximal force, the blood flow to the muscle is greatly reduced because the muscles are physically compressing the blood vessels that run through them. In other words, the arteriolar vasodilation is completely overcome by the physical compression of the blood vessels. Thus, the cardiovascular changes are ineffective in causing increased blood flow to the muscles, and these contractions can be maintained only briefly before fatigue sets in. Moreover, because of the compression of blood vessels, total peripheral resistance may increase considerably (instead of decreasing as it does in endurance exercise), contributing to a large increase in mean arterial pressure during the contraction. Frequent exposure of the heart to only this type of exercise can cause maladaptive changes in the left ventricle, including wall hypertrophy and diminished chamber volume.

Maximal Oxygen Consumption and Training

As the intensity of any endurance exercise increases, oxygen consumption also increases in exact proportion until reaching a point when it fails to increase despite a further increment in workload. This is known as **maximal oxygen consumption** (**$\dot{V}_{O_2}$ max**). After this point has been reached, work can be increased and sustained only briefly by anaerobic metabolism in the exercising muscles.

Theoretically, $\dot{V}_{O_2}$ max could be limited by (1) the cardiac output, (2) the respiratory system's ability to deliver oxygen to the blood, or (3) the exercising muscles' ability to use oxygen. In fact, in typical, healthy people (except for very highly trained athletes), cardiac output is the factor that determines $\dot{V}_{O_2}$ max. With increasing workload (**Figure 12.64**), heart rate increases progressively until it reaches a maximum. Stroke volume increases much less and tends to level off at 75% of $\dot{V}_{O_2}$ max (it actually starts to go back down in elderly people). The major factors responsible for limiting the increase in stroke volume and, therefore, cardiac output are (1) the very rapid heart rate, which decreases diastolic filling time; and (2) inability of the peripheral factors favoring venous return (skeletal muscle pump, respiratory pump, venous vasoconstriction, arteriolar vasodilation) to increase ventricular filling further during the very short time available.

TABLE 12.8 Cardiovascular Changes During Moderate Exercise

Variable	Change	Explanation
Cardiac output	Increases	Heart rate and stroke volume both increase, the former to a much greater extent.
Heart rate	Increases	Sympathetic stimulation of the SA node increases, and parasympathetic stimulation decreases.
Stroke volume	Increases	Contractility increases due to increased sympathetic stimulation of the ventricular myocardium; increased ventricular end-diastolic volume also contributes to increased stroke volume by the Frank–Starling mechanism.
Total peripheral resistance	Decreases	Resistance in heart and skeletal muscles decreases more than resistance in other vascular beds increases.
Mean arterial pressure	Increases	Cardiac output increases more than total peripheral resistance decreases.
Pulse pressure	Increases	Stroke volume and velocity of ejection of the stroke volume increase.
End-diastolic volume	Increases	Filling time is decreased by the high heart rate, but the factors favoring venous return—venoconstriction, skeletal muscle pump, and increased inspiratory movements—more than compensate for it.
Blood flow to heart and skeletal muscle	Increases	Active hyperemia occurs in both vascular beds, mediated by local metabolic factors.
Blood flow to skin	Increases	Sympathetic activation of skin blood vessels is inhibited reflexively by the increase in body temperature.
Blood flow to viscera	Decreases	Sympathetic activation of blood vessels in the abdominal organs and kidneys is increased.
Blood flow to brain	Increases slightly	Autoregulation of brain arterioles maintains constant flow despite the increased mean arterial pressure.

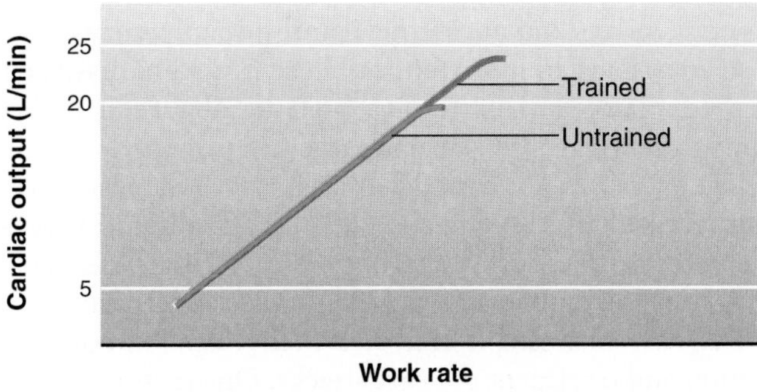

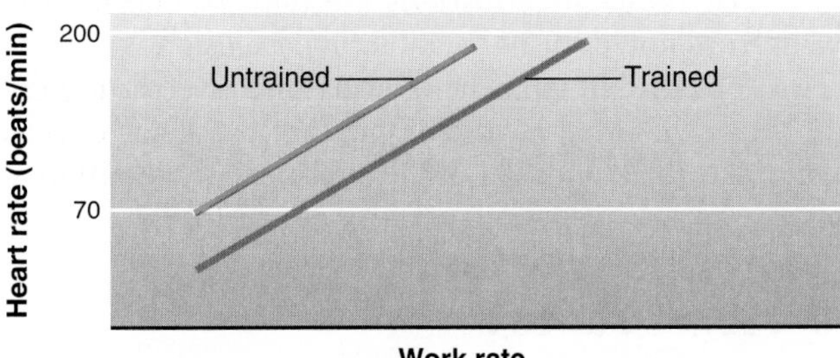

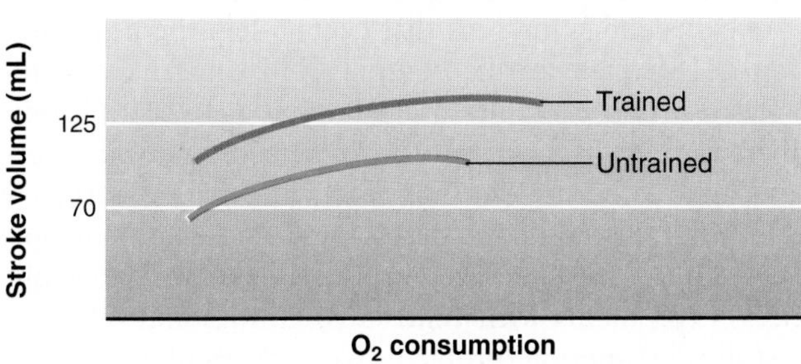

Figure 12.64 Changes in cardiac output, heart rate, and stroke volume with increasing workload in untrained and trained individuals.

An individual's $\dot{V}_{O_2}$ max is not fixed at any given value but can be altered by his or her habitual level of physical activity. For example, prolonged bed rest may decrease $\dot{V}_{O_2}$ max by 15% to 25%, whereas intense, long-term physical training may increase it by a similar amount. To be effective, the training must be endurance-type exercise and must reach certain minimal levels of duration, frequency, and intensity. For example, running 20 to 30 min three times weekly at 5 to 8 mi/h produces a significant training effect in most people.

At rest, compared to values prior to training, the trained individual has an increased stroke volume and decreased heart rate with no change in cardiac output (see Figure 12.64). At $\dot{V}_{O_2}$ max, cardiac output is increased compared to pretraining values; this is due entirely to an increased maximal stroke volume because training does not alter maximal heart rate (see Figure 12.64). The increase in stroke volume is due to a combination of (1) effects on the heart (remodeling of the ventricular walls produces moderate hypertrophy and an increase in chamber size); and (2) peripheral effects, including increased blood volume and increases in the number of blood vessels in skeletal muscle, which permit increased muscle blood flow and venous return.

Training also increases the concentrations of oxidative enzymes and mitochondria in the exercised muscles. These changes increase the speed and efficiency of metabolic reactions in the muscles and permit 200% to 300% increases in exercise endurance, but they do not increase $\dot{V}_{O_2}$ max because they were not limiting it in the untrained individuals.

Aging is associated with significant changes in the heart's performance during exercise. Most striking is a decrease in the maximum heart rate (and, therefore, cardiac output) achievable. This results, in particular, from increased stiffness of the heart that decreases its ability to rapidly fill during diastole.

12.19 Hypertension

Hypertension is defined as a chronically increased systemic arterial pressure. Although the clinical definition of hypertension is a blood pressure above 140/90 mmHg, new guidelines suggest that interventions to lower blood pressure should be instituted at systolic pressures of 130 to 139 mmHg and diastolic pressures of 85 to 89 mmHg.

Hypertension is a serious public-health problem. Over a billion people worldwide (26% of the adult population), and 76 million (34%) in the U.S. population are estimated to suffer from this condition. Hypertension is a contributing cause to some of the leading causes of disability and death. One of the organs most affected is the heart. Because the left ventricle in a hypertensive person must chronically pump against an increased arterial pressure (afterload), it develops an adaptive increase in muscle mass called ***left ventricular hypertrophy.*** In the early phases of the disease, this hypertrophy helps maintain the heart's function as a pump. With time, however, changes in the organization and properties of myocardial cells occur, and these result in diminished contractile function and heart failure. The presence of hypertension also enhances the possible development of atherosclerosis and heart attacks, kidney damage, and ***stroke***—the rupture of a cerebral blood vessel, causing localized brain damage. Long-term data on the link between blood pressure and health show that for every 20 mmHg increase in systolic pressure and every 10 mmHg increase in diastolic pressure, the risk of heart disease and stroke doubles.

Hypertension is categorized according to its causes. Hypertension of uncertain cause is diagnosed as ***primary hypertension*** (formerly called "essential hypertension"). ***Secondary hypertension*** is the term used when there are identified causes. Primary hypertension accounts for over 90% of all cases.

By definition, the causes of primary hypertension are unknown, though a number of genetic and environmental factors are suspected to be involved. In cases in which the condition appears to be inherited, a number of genes have been implicated, including some coding for enzymes involved in the renin-angiotensin-aldosterone pathway (see Chapter 14) and some involved in the regulation of endothelial cell function and arteriolar smooth muscle contraction. Although, theoretically, hypertension could result from an increase either in cardiac output or in total peripheral resistance, it appears that in most cases of well-established primary hypertension, increased total peripheral resistance caused by reduced arteriolar radius is the most significant factor.

A number of environmental risk factors contribute to the development of primary hypertension. Recent studies show that lifestyle changes that reduce those factors result in lowered blood pressure, both in hypertensive and healthy people. Obesity and the frequently associated insulin insensitivity (discussed in Chapter 16) are risk factors, and weight loss significantly reduces blood pressure in most people. Chronic, high salt intake is also associated with hypertension, and recent research has revealed mechanisms by which even slight elevations in plasma Na^+ levels lead to chronic overstimulation of the sympathetic nervous system, constriction of arterioles, and narrowing of the lumen of arteries. These vascular changes are the hallmark in many cases of primary hypertension. Significant reduction in blood pressure occurred in experimental subjects who ate a low-salt diet in a large, well-designed study known as DASH (Dietary Approaches to Stop Hypertension). In addition to obesity and excessive salt intake, other environmental factors hypothesized to contribute to primary hypertension include smoking; excess alcohol consumption; diets low in fruits, vegetables, and whole grains; diets low in vitamin D and calcium; lack of exercise; chronic stress; excess caffeine consumption; maternal smoking; low birth weight; and not being breast-fed as an infant.

There are a number of well-characterized causes of secondary hypertension. Damage to the kidneys or their blood supply can lead to ***renal hypertension,*** in which increased renin release leads to excessive concentrations of the potent vasoconstrictor angiotensin II and inappropriately decreased urine production by the kidneys, resulting in excessive extracellular fluid volume. Some individuals are genetically predisposed to excess renal Na^+ reabsorption. These patients respond well to a low-sodium diet or to drugs called ***diuretics,*** which cause increased Na^+ and water loss in the urine (see Chapter 14). A number of endocrine disorders result in hypertension, such as syndromes involving hypersecretion of cortisol or thyroid hormone (see Chapter 11). Medications such as oral contraceptives and nonsteroidal anti-inflammatory drugs can also contribute to hypertension. Recently, a link has been established between hypertension and the abnormal nighttime breathing pattern, sleep apnea (see Chapter 13).

The major categories of drugs used to treat hypertension are summarized in **Table 12.9.** These drugs all act in ways that decrease cardiac output and/or total peripheral resistance. You will note in subsequent sections of this chapter that these same drugs are also used to treat heart failure and in both the prevention and treatment of heart attacks. One reason for this overlap is that these three diseases are causally interrelated. For example, as noted in this section, hypertension is a major risk factor for the development of heart disease. In addition, though, the drugs often have multiple cardiovascular effects, which may play different roles in the treatment of the different diseases.

12.20 Heart Failure

Heart failure (also called ***congestive heart failure***) is a collection of signs and symptoms that occur when the heart fails to pump an adequate cardiac output. This may happen for many reasons; two examples are pumping against a chronically increased arterial pressure in hypertension, and structural damage to the myocardium due to decreased coronary blood flow. It has become standard practice to separate people with heart failure into two categories: (1) those with diastolic dysfunction (problems with ventricular filling) and (2) those with systolic dysfunction (problems with ventricular ejection). Many people with heart failure, however, exhibit elements of both categories.

In ***diastolic dysfunction,*** the wall of the ventricle has reduced compliance. Its abnormal stiffness results in a reduced ability to fill adequately at normal diastolic filling pressures. The result is a reduced end-diastolic volume (even though the end-diastolic pressure in the stiff ventricle may be quite high),

TABLE 12.9 Drugs Used to Treat Hypertension
Diuretics: These drugs increase urinary excretion of sodium and water (Chapter 14). They tend to decrease cardiac output with little or no change in total peripheral resistance.
β-adrenergic receptor blockers: These drugs exert their antihypertensive effects mainly by reducing cardiac output.
Ca^{2+} channel blockers: These drugs reduce the entry of Ca^{2+} into vascular smooth muscle cells, causing them to contract less strongly and lowering total peripheral resistance. (Surprisingly, it has been found that despite their effectiveness in lowering blood pressure, at least some of these drugs may significantly increase the risk of a heart attack. Consequently, their use as therapy for hypertension is under intensive review.)
Angiotensin-converting enzyme (ACE) inhibitors: As Chapter 14 will describe, the final step in the formation of angiotensin II, a vasoconstrictor, is mediated by an enzyme called angiotensin-converting enzyme. Drugs that block this enzyme therefore reduce the concentration of angiotensin II in plasma, which causes arteriolar vasodilation, lowering total peripheral resistance. The same effect can be achieved with drugs that block the receptors for angiotensin II. A reduction in plasma angiotensin II or blockage of its receptors is also protective against the development of heart wall changes that lead to heart failure.
Drugs that antagonize one or more components of the sympathetic nervous system: The major effect of these drugs is to reduce sympathetic mediated stimulation of arteriolar smooth muscle and thereby reduce total peripheral resistance. Examples include drugs that inhibit the brain centers that mediate the sympathetic outflow to arterioles, and drugs that block α-adrenergic receptors on the arterioles.

which results in a reduced stroke volume by the Frank–Starling mechanism. In pure diastolic dysfunction, ventricular compliance is decreased but ventricular contractility is normal.

Several situations may lead to decreased ventricular compliance, but by far the most common is the existence of systemic hypertension. As noted in the previous section, hypertrophy results when the left ventricle pumps against a chronically increased arterial pressure (afterload). The structural and biochemical changes associated with this hypertrophy make the ventricle stiff and less able to expand.

In contrast to diastolic dysfunction, ***systolic dysfunction*** results from myocardial damage, like that resulting from a heart attack (discussed next). This type of dysfunction is characterized by a decrease in cardiac contractility—a lower stroke volume at any given end-diastolic volume. This is manifested as a decrease in ejection fraction and, as illustrated in **Figure 12.65**, a downward shift of the ventricular-function curve. The affected ventricle does not hypertrophy, but note that the end-diastolic volume increases.

The reduced cardiac output of heart failure, regardless of whether it is due to diastolic or systolic dysfunction, triggers the arterial baroreceptor reflexes. In this situation, these reflexes are elicited more than usual because, for unknown reasons, the afferent baroreceptors are less sensitive. In other words, the baroreceptors discharge less rapidly than normal at any given mean or pulsatile arterial pressure and the brain interprets this decreased discharge as a larger-than-usual decrease in pressure. The results of the reflexes are that (1) heart rate is increased through increased sympathetic and decreased parasympathetic activation of the heart; and (2) total peripheral resistance is increased by increased sympathetic activation of systemic arterioles, as well as by increased plasma concentrations of the two major hormonal vasoconstrictors—angiotensin II and vasopressin. The reflex increases in heart rate and total peripheral resistance are initially beneficial in restoring cardiac output and arterial pressure, just as if the changes in these parameters had been triggered by hemorrhage.

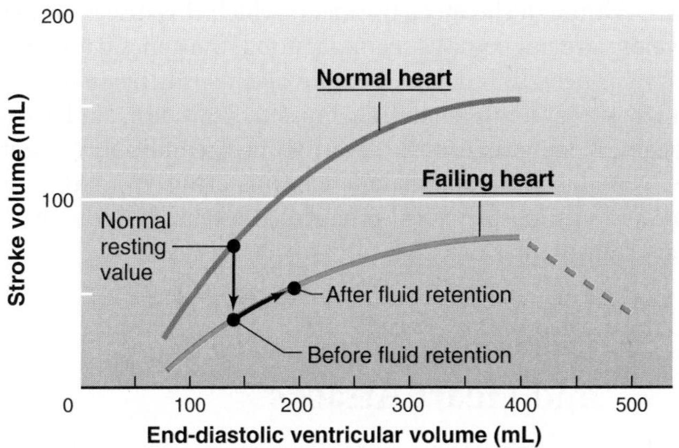

Figure 12.65 Relationship between end-diastolic ventricular volume and stroke volume in a normal heart and one with heart failure due to systolic dysfunction (decreased contractility). The normal curve was shown previously in Figure 12.24. With decreased contractility, the ventricular-function curve is displaced downward; that is, there is a lower stroke volume at any given end-diastolic volume. Fluid retention causes an increase in end-diastolic volume and restores stroke volume toward normal by the Frank–Starling mechanism. Note that this compensation occurs even though contractility—the basic defect—has not been altered by the fluid retention.

PHYSIOLOGICAL INQUIRY

- Estimate the ejection fraction of the failing heart at a typical normal end-diastolic volume.

Answer can be found at end of chapter.

Maintained chronically throughout the period of cardiac failure, the baroreceptor reflexes also bring about fluid retention and an expansion—often massive—of the extracellular volume. This is because, as Chapter 14 describes, the neuroendocrine efferent components of the reflexes cause the kidneys to reduce their excretion of sodium and water. The retained fluid then causes expansion of the extracellular volume. Because the plasma volume is part of the extracellular fluid volume, plasma volume also increases. This in turn increases venous pressure, venous return, and end-diastolic ventricular volume, which tends to restore stroke volume toward normal by the Frank–Starling mechanism (see Figure 12.65). Thus, fluid retention is also, at least initially, an adaptive response to decreased cardiac output.

However, problems emerge as the fluid retention progresses. For one thing, when a ventricle with systolic dysfunction (as opposed to a normal ventricle) becomes very distended with blood, its force of contraction actually decreases and the situation worsens. Second, the fluid retention, with its accompanying elevation in venous pressure, causes edema—accumulation of interstitial fluid. Why does an increased venous pressure cause edema? The capillaries drain via venules into the veins; so when venous pressure increases, the capillary pressure also increases and causes increased filtration of fluid out of the capillaries into the interstitial fluid (review Figure 12.42). Thus, most of the fluid retained by the kidneys ends up as extra interstitial fluid rather than extra plasma. Swelling of the legs and feet is particularly prominent.

Most important in this regard, failure of the *left* ventricle —whether due to diastolic or systolic dysfunction—leads to ***pulmonary edema***, the accumulation of fluid in the interstitial spaces of the lung or in the air spaces themselves. This impairs pulmonary gas exchange. The reason for such accumulation is that the left ventricle fails to pump blood to the same extent as the right ventricle, so the volume of blood in all the pulmonary vessels increases. The resulting engorgement of pulmonary capillaries increases the capillary pressure above its normally very low value, causing filtration to occur at a rate faster than the lymphatics can remove the fluid. This situation usually worsens at night. During the day, because of the patient's upright posture, fluid accumulates in the legs; then the fluid is slowly absorbed back into the capillaries when the patient lies down at night, thereby expanding the plasma volume and precipitating the development of pulmonary edema.

TABLE 12.10 Types of Drugs Used to Treat Heart Failure
Diuretics: Drugs that increase urinary excretion of sodium and water (Chapter 14). These drugs eliminate the excessive fluid accumulation contributing to edema and/or worsening myocardial function.
Cardiac inotropic drugs: Drugs that enhance β-adrenergic receptor pathways and drugs such as ***digitalis,*** which increases ventricular contractility by increasing cytosolic Ca^{2+} concentration in the myocardial cell, can increase cardiac output in the short term. The use of these drugs is currently controversial, however, because although they clearly improve the symptoms of heart failure, they do not prolong life and, in some studies, seem to have shortened it.
Vasodilator drugs: Drugs that lower total peripheral resistance and thus the arterial blood pressure (afterload) the failing heart must pump against. Some inhibit a component of the sympathetic nervous pathway to the arterioles (α-adrenergic receptor blockers), whereas others block the formation of angiotensin II (angiotensin-converting enzyme [ACE] inhibitors, see Chapter 14). In addition, the ACE inhibitors prevent or reverse the maladaptive remodeling of the myocardium that is mediated by the increased plasma concentration of angiotensin II in heart failure.
β-adrenergic receptor blockers: Drugs that block the major adrenergic receptors in the myocardium. The mechanism by which this action improves heart failure is unknown. You may predict that such an action, by blocking sympathetically induced increases in cardiac contractility, would be counterproductive (note above that *β-agonists* are sometimes used, which is more intuitive). One hypothesis is that excess sympathetic stimulation of the heart reflexively produced by the decreased cardiac output of heart failure may cause an excessive elevation of cytosolic Ca^{2+} concentration, which would lead to cell apoptosis and necrosis; β-adrenergic receptor blockers would prevent this.

Another component of the reflex response to heart failure that is at first beneficial but ultimately becomes maladaptive is the increase in total peripheral resistance, mediated by the sympathetic neurons to arterioles and by angiotensin II and vasopressin. By chronically maintaining the arterial blood pressure the failing heart must pump against, this increased resistance makes the failing heart work harder.

One obvious treatment for heart failure is to correct, if possible, the precipitating cause (for example, hypertension). **Table 12.10** lists the types of drugs most often used for treatment. Finally, although cardiac transplantation is often the treatment of choice, the paucity of donor hearts, the high costs, and the challenges of postsurgical care render it a feasible option for only a very small number of patients. Considerable research has also been directed toward the development of artificial hearts, though success has been limited to date.

12.21 Hypertrophic Cardiomyopathy

Hypertrophic cardiomyopathy is a condition that frequently leads to heart failure. It is one of the most common inherited cardiac diseases, occurring in about one out of 500 people. As the name implies, it is characterized by an increase in thickness of the heart muscle, in particular, the interventricular septum and the wall of the left ventricle. In conjunction with wall thickening, there is a disruption of the orderly array of myocytes and conducting cells within the walls. The thickening of the septum interferes with the ejection of blood through the aortic valve, particularly during exercise, which can prevent cardiac output from increasing sufficiently to meet tissue metabolic requirements. The heart itself is commonly a victim of this reduction in blood flow, and one symptom that can be an early warning sign is the associated chest pain (***angina pectoris*** or, more commonly, angina). Moreover, disruption of the conduction pathway can lead to dangerous, sometimes fatal arrhythmias. Many people with this disease have no symptoms, so it can go undetected until it has progressed to an advanced stage. For these reasons, hypertrophic cardiomyopathy is most often the cause in the rare circumstance when a young athlete suffers sudden, unexpected cardiac death. If it progresses without treatment, it can lead to heart failure, with all of the consequences discussed previously. Although the mechanisms by which this disease process develops are not completely understood, the genetic mutations that have been found to cause it involve mainly proteins of the contractile system, including myosin, troponin, and tropomyosin. Depending on the severity of the condition when it is discovered, treatments include administering drugs that prevent arrhythmias, surgical repair of the septum and valve, or heart transplantation.

12.22 Coronary Artery Disease and Heart Attacks

We have seen that the myocardium does not extract oxygen and nutrients from the blood within the atria and ventricles but depends upon its own blood supply via the coronary arteries. In ***coronary artery disease,*** changes in one or more of the coronary arteries cause insufficient blood flow (***ischemia***) to the heart. The result may be myocardial damage in the affected region, or even death of that portion of the heart—a ***myocardial infarction,*** or ***heart attack.*** Many patients with coronary artery disease experience recurrent transient episodes of inadequate coronary blood flow and angina, usually during exertion or emotional tension, before ultimately suffering a heart attack.

The symptoms of myocardial infarction include prolonged chest pain, often radiating to the left arm; nausea; vomiting; sweating; weakness; and shortness of breath. Diagnosis is made by ECG changes typical of infarction and by detection of specific cardiac muscle proteins in plasma. These proteins leak out into the blood when the muscle is damaged;

the most commonly detected are the myocardial-specific isoform of the enzyme creatine kinase, and cardiac troponin.

Approximately 1.1 million Americans have a new or recurrent heart attack each year, and over 40% of them die from it. Sudden cardiac deaths during myocardial infarction are due mainly to ***ventricular fibrillation,*** an abnormality in impulse conduction triggered by the damaged myocardial cells. This conduction pattern results in completely uncoordinated ventricular contractions that are ineffective in producing flow. (Note that ventricular fibrillation is usually fatal, whereas atrial fibrillation, as described earlier in this chapter, generally causes only minor cardiac problems.) A small fraction of individuals with ventricular fibrillation can be saved if emergency resuscitation procedures are applied immediately after the attack. This treatment is ***cardiopulmonary resuscitation*** (***CPR***), a repeated series of chest compressions sometimes accompanied by mouth-to-mouth respirations that circulate a small amount of oxygenated blood to the brain, heart, and other vital organs when the heart has stopped. CPR is then followed by definitive treatment, including ***defibrillation,*** a procedure in which electrical current is passed through the heart to try to halt the abnormal electrical activity causing the fibrillation. ***Automatic electronic defibrillators*** (***AEDs***) are now commonly found in public places. These devices make it relatively simple to render timely aid to victims of ventricular fibrillation.

The major cause of coronary artery disease is the presence of atherosclerosis in these vessels (**Figure 12.66**). ***Atherosclerosis*** is a disease of arteries characterized by a thickening of the portion of the arterial vessel wall closest to the lumen with plaques made up of (1) large numbers of cells, including smooth muscle cells, macrophages (derived from blood monocytes), and lymphocytes; (2) deposits of cholesterol and other fatty substances, both within cells and extracellularly; and (3) dense layers of connective tissue matrix. Such atherosclerotic plaques are one cause of aging-related arteriosclerosis.

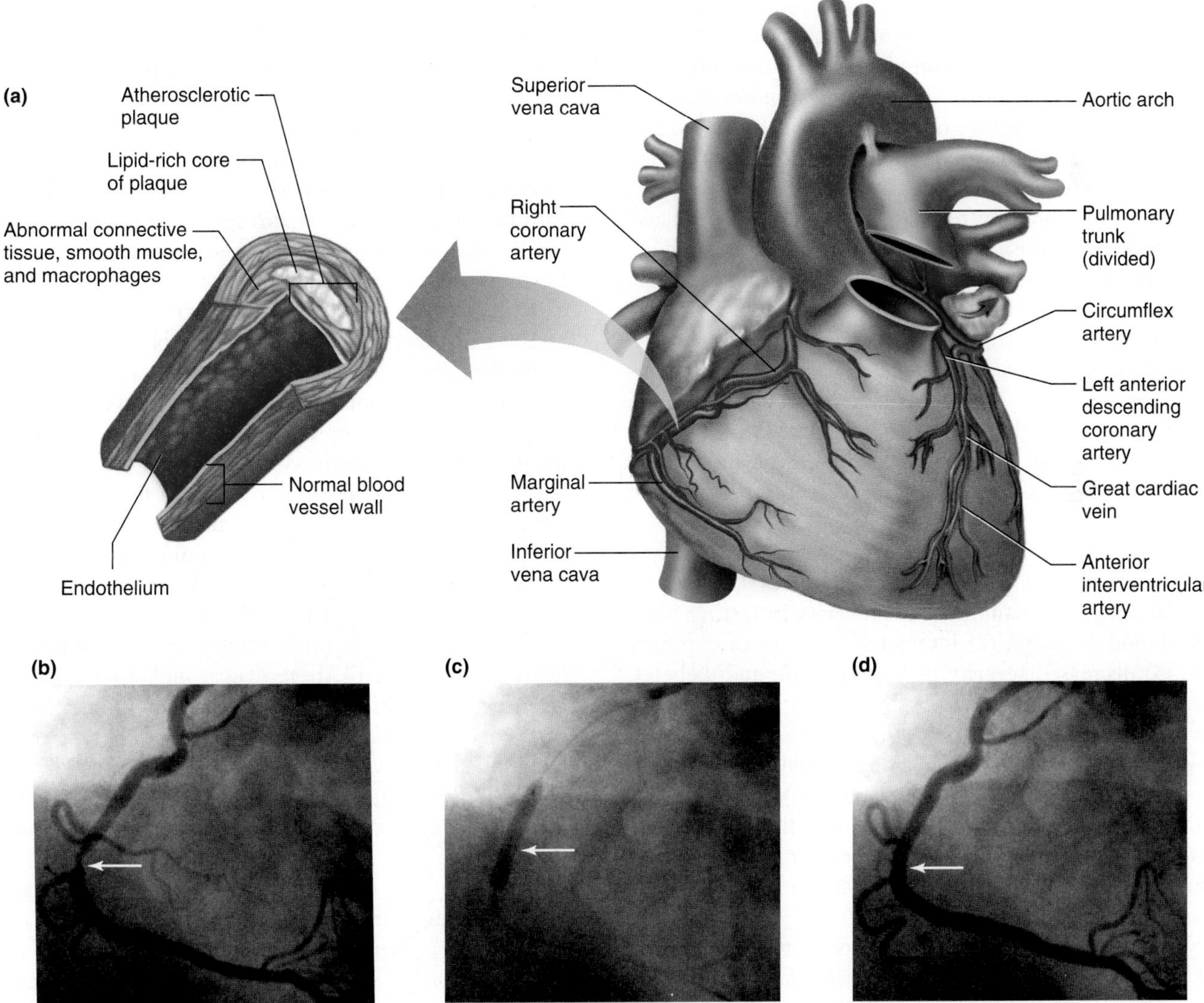

Figure 12.66 APIR Coronary artery disease and its treatment. (a) Anterior view of the heart showing the major coronary vessels. Inset demonstrates narrowing due to atherosclerotic plaque. (b) Dye-contrast x-ray angiography performed by injecting radiopaque dye shows a significant occlusion of the right coronary artery (arrow). (c) A guide wire is used to position and inflate a dye-filled balloon in the narrow region, and a wire-mesh stent is inserted. (d) Blood flows freely through the formerly narrowed region after the procedure. Photos (b), (c), and (d) courtesy of Matthew R. Wolff, M.D.

Atherosclerosis reduces coronary blood flow by several mechanisms. The extra muscle cells and various deposits in the wall bulge into the lumen of the vessel and increase resistance to flow. Also, dysfunctional endothelial cells in the atherosclerotic area release excess vasoconstrictors (e.g., endothelin-1) and lower-than-normal amounts of vasodilators (nitric oxide and prostacyclin). These processes are progressive, sometimes leading ultimately to complete occlusion. Total occlusion is usually caused, however, by the formation of a blood clot (***coronary thrombosis***) in the narrowed atherosclerotic artery, and this triggers the heart attack.

The processes that lead to atherosclerosis are complex and still not completely understood. It is likely that the damage is initiated by agents that injure the endothelium and underlying smooth muscle, leading to an inflammatory and proliferative response that may well be protective at first but ultimately becomes excessive.

Cigarette smoking, high blood concentrations of certain types of cholesterol and the amino acid homocysteine, hypertension, diabetes, obesity, a sedentary lifestyle, and stress are all risk factors that can increase the incidence and severity of the atherosclerotic process and coronary artery disease. Prevention efforts therefore focus on eliminating or minimizing these risk factors through lifestyle changes and/or medications. In a sense, menopause can also be considered a risk factor for coronary artery disease because the incidence of heart attacks in women is very low until after menopause.

A few words about exercise are warranted here because of some potential confusion. Although it is true that a sudden burst of strenuous physical activity can sometimes trigger a heart attack, the risk is greatly reduced in individuals who perform regular physical activity. The overall risk of heart attack at any time can be reduced as much as 35% to 55% by maintaining an active rather than sedentary lifestyle. In general, the more you exercise, the better the protective effect, but any exercise is better than none. For example, even moderately paced walking three to four times a week confers significant benefit.

Regular exercise is protective against heart attacks for a variety of reasons. Among other things, it induces (1) decreased myocardial oxygen demand due to decreases in resting heart rate and blood pressure; (2) increased diameter of coronary arteries; (3) decreased severity of hypertension and diabetes, two major risk factors for atherosclerosis; (4) decreased total plasma cholesterol concentration with simultaneous increase in the plasma concentration of a "good" cholesterol-carrying lipoprotein (HDL, discussed in Chapter 16); (5) decreased tendency of blood to clot and improved ability of the body to dissolve blood clots; and (6) better control of blood glucose due to increased sensitivity to the hormone insulin (see Chapter 16).

Nutrition can also play a role in protecting against heart attacks. Reduction in the intake of saturated fat (a type abundant in red meat) and regular consumption of fruits, vegetables, whole grains, and fish may help by reducing the concentration of "bad" cholesterol (LDLs, discussed in Chapter 16) in the blood. This form of cholesterol contributes to the buildup of atherosclerotic plaques in blood vessels. Supplements like folic acid (a B vitamin; also called folate or folacin) may also be protective, in this case because folic acid helps reduce the blood concentration of the amino acid homocysteine, one of the risk factors for heart attacks. Homocysteine is an intermediary in the metabolism of methionine and cysteine. In increased amounts, it exerts several proatherosclerotic effects, including damaging the endothelium of blood vessels. Folic acid is involved in a metabolic reaction that lowers the plasma concentration of homocysteine.

Finally, there is the question of alcohol and coronary artery disease. In many studies, moderate alcohol intake—red wine, in particular—has been shown to reduce the risk of dying from a heart attack. Likely contributing to this effect is the observed increase in HDL concentration and inhibition of blood clot formation that result from low doses of alcohol. However, alcohol—particularly at higher doses—increases the chances of an early death from a variety of other diseases (cancer and cirrhosis of the liver, for example) and accidents. Because of these complex health effects and the potential to develop alcohol dependence (see Chapter 8), doctors do not recommend that patients start drinking alcohol for health benefits. For those who do drink, the recommendation is to have no more than one standard drink per day. (One standard drink is approximately 12 ounces of beer, 5 ounces of wine, or 1.5 ounces of 80-proof liquor.)

A variety of drugs can be used for the prevention and treatment of angina and coronary artery disease. For example, vasodilator drugs such as ***nitroglycerin*** (which is a vasodilator because it is converted in the body to nitric oxide) help by dilating the coronary arteries and the systemic arterioles and veins. The arteriolar effect lowers total peripheral resistance, thereby lowering arterial blood pressure and the work the heart must do to eject blood. The venous dilation, by decreasing venous pressure, reduces venous return and thereby the stretch of the ventricle and its oxygen requirement during subsequent contraction. In addition, drugs that block β-adrenergic receptors are used to reduce the arterial pressure in people with hypertension. They reduce myocardial work and cardiac output by inhibiting the effect of sympathetic neurons on heart rate and contractility. Drugs that prevent or reverse clotting within hours of its occurrence are also extremely important in the treatment (and prevention) of heart attacks. Use of these drugs, including aspirin, will be described in Section F of this chapter. Finally, a variety of drugs decrease plasma cholesterol by influencing one or more metabolic pathways for cholesterol (Chapter 16). For example, one group of drugs, sometimes referred to as "statins," interferes with a critical enzyme involved in the liver's synthesis of cholesterol.

There are several interventions for coronary artery disease after cardiac angiography (described earlier in this chapter) identifies an area of narrowing or occlusion. ***Coronary balloon angioplasty*** involves threading a catheter with a balloon at its tip into the occluded artery and then expanding the balloon (Figure 12.66c). This procedure enlarges the lumen by stretching the vessel and breaking up abnormal tissue deposits. It is generally accompanied by the placement of ***coronary stents*** in the narrowed or occluded coronary vessel (Figure 12.66d). Stents are tubes made of a stainless steel lattice that provide a scaffold within a vessel to open it and keep it open. Researchers are testing stents made of a hardened, biodegradable polymer that is absorbed after 6 months to 1 year. Another surgical treatment is ***coronary bypass***, in which a new vessel is attached across an area of occluded coronary artery. The new vessel is often a vein taken from elsewhere in the patient's body. Despite the widespread use of these surgical interventions and their proven effectiveness in relieving the pain of angina, evidence accumulated over the past 20 years suggests that such procedures have a limited effect on long-term survival after a cardiac event or on the prevention of future events.

Atherosclerosis does not attack only the coronary vessels. Many arteries of the body are subject to this same occluding process, and wherever the atherosclerosis becomes severe, the resulting symptoms reflect the decrease in blood flow to the specific area. For example, occlusion of a cerebral artery due to atherosclerosis and its associated blood clotting can cause a stroke. (Recall that rupture of a cerebral vessel, as sometimes occurs in hypertension, is another cause of stroke.) People with atherosclerotic cerebral vessels may also suffer reversible neurological deficits known as ***transient ischemic attacks*** (***TIAs***), lasting minutes to hours, without actually experiencing a stroke at the time.

Finally, note that both myocardial infarcts and strokes due to occlusion may result when a fragment of blood clot or fatty deposit breaks off and then lodges elsewhere, completely blocking a smaller vessel. The fragment is called an ***embolus***, and the process is ***embolism***. See Chapter 19 for more information about embolisms.

SECTION E SUMMARY

Hemorrhage and Other Causes of Hypotension

I. The physiological responses to hemorrhage are summarized in Figures 12.52, 12.56, 12.58, and 12.59.

II. Hypotension can be caused by loss of body fluids, by cardiac malfunction, by strong emotion, and by liberation of vasodilator chemicals.

III. Shock is any situation in which blood flow to the tissues is low enough to cause damage to them.

The Upright Posture

I. In the upright posture, gravity acting upon unbroken columns of blood reduces venous return by increasing vascular pressures in the veins and capillaries in the limbs.
   a. The increased venous pressure distends the veins, causing venous pooling, and the increased capillary pressure causes increased filtration out of the capillaries.
   b. These effects are minimized by contraction of the skeletal muscles in the legs.

Exercise

I. The cardiovascular changes that occur in endurance-type exercise are illustrated in Figures 12.61, 12.62, and 12.64.

II. The changes are due to active hyperemia in the exercising skeletal muscles and heart; increased sympathetic outflow to the heart, arterioles, and veins; and decreased parasympathetic outflow to the heart.

III. The increase in cardiac output depends not only on the autonomic influences on the heart but on factors that help increase venous return.

IV. Training can increase a person's maximal oxygen consumption by increasing maximal stroke volume and thus cardiac output.

Hypertension

I. Hypertension is usually due to increased total peripheral resistance resulting from increased arteriolar vasoconstriction.

II. More than 90% of cases of hypertension are called *primary hypertension*, meaning that a specific cause of the increased arteriolar vasoconstriction is unknown. However, obesity, excessive salt intake, and a variety of other environmental factors clearly contribute to the development of hypertension.

Heart Failure

I. Heart failure can occur as a result of diastolic or systolic dysfunction; in both cases, cardiac output becomes inadequate.

II. This leads to fluid retention by the kidneys and formation of edema because of increased capillary pressure.

III. Pulmonary edema can occur when the left ventricle fails.

Hypertrophic Cardiomyopathy

I. Hypertrophic cardiomyopathy is a disease caused by genetic mutations in genes coding for cardiac contractile proteins.

II. It results in thickening of the left ventricle wall and septum, and disruption of the orderly array of myocytes and conducting cells.

III. If not successfully treated, it can result in sudden death by arrhythmia or heart failure.

Coronary Artery Disease and Heart Attacks

I. Insufficient coronary blood flow can cause damage to the heart.

II. Sudden death from a heart attack is usually due to ventricular fibrillation.

III. The major cause of reduced coronary blood flow is atherosclerosis, an occlusive disease of the arteries.

IV. People may suffer intermittent attacks of angina pectoris without actually suffering a heart attack at the time of the pain.

V. Atherosclerosis can also cause strokes and symptoms of inadequate blood flow in other areas.

VI. Coronary artery disease incidence is reduced by exercise, good nutrition, and avoiding smoking.

VII. Treatments for coronary artery disease include drugs that dilate blood vessels, reduce blood pressure, and prevent blood clotting. Balloon angioplasty and coronary bypass are surgical treatments.

SECTION E REVIEW QUESTIONS

1. Draw a flow diagram illustrating the reflex compensation for hemorrhage.
2. What happens to plasma volume and interstitial fluid volume following a hemorrhage?
3. What causes hypotension during a severe allergic response?
4. How does gravity influence effective blood volume?

5. Describe the role of the skeletal muscle pump in decreasing capillary filtration.
6. List the directional changes that occur during exercise for all relevant cardiovascular variables. What are the specific efferent mechanisms that bring about these changes?
7. What factors enhance venous return during exercise?
8. Diagram the control of autonomic outflow during exercise.
9. What is the limiting cardiovascular factor in endurance exercise?
10. What changes in cardiac function occur at rest and during exercise as a result of endurance training?
11. What is the abnormality in most cases of established hypertension? How does excess salt ingestion contribute?
12. State how fluid retention can help restore stroke volume in heart failure.
13. How does heart failure lead to edema in the pulmonary and systemic vascular beds?
14. Name the major risk factors for atherosclerosis.
15. Describe changes in lifestyle that may help prevent coronary artery disease.
16. List some ways that coronary artery disease can be treated.

SECTION E KEY TERMS

autotransfusion 415
maximal oxygen consumption ($\dot{V}_{O_2}$max) 420

SECTION E CLINICAL TERMS

angina pectoris 424
angiotensin-converting enzyme (ACE) inhibitors 422
atherosclerosis 425
automatic electronic defibrillator (AED) 425
β-adrenergic receptor blocker 424
Ca^{2+} channel blocker 422
cardiac inotropic drug 424
cardiogenic shock 417
cardiopulmonary resuscitation (CPR) 425
congestive heart failure 422
coronary artery disease 424
coronary balloon angioplasty 426
coronary bypass 427
coronary stent 426
coronary thrombosis 426
defibrillation 425
diastolic dysfunction 422
digitalis 424
diuretic 422
embolism 427
embolus 427
heart attack 424
heart failure 422
hypertension 421
hypertrophic cardiomyopathy 424
hypotension 415
hypovolemic shock 417
ischemia 424
left ventricular hypertrophy 421
low-resistance shock 417
myocardial infarction 424
nitroglycerin 426
primary hypertension 421
pulmonary edema 423
renal hypertension 422
secondary hypertension 421
shock 417
stroke 421
systolic dysfunction 423
transient ischemic attack (TIA) 427
vasodilator drug 424
vasovagal syncope 416
ventricular fibrillation 425

SECTION F Blood and Hemostasis

Blood was defined earlier as a mixture of cellular components suspended in a fluid called plasma. In this section, we will take a more detailed look at blood cells and plasma and then discuss the complex mechanisms that prevent excessive blood loss following injury.

12.23 Plasma

Plasma consists of a large number of organic and inorganic substances dissolved in water. A list of the major substances dissolved in plasma and their typical concentrations can be found inside the back cover of this book.

The **plasma proteins** constitute most of the plasma solutes, by weight. Their role in exerting an osmotic pressure that favors the absorption of extracellular fluid into capillaries was described in Section C of this chapter. They can be classified into three broad groups: the **albumins,** the **globulins,** and **fibrinogen.** The first two have many overlapping functions, which are discussed in relevant sections throughout the book. The albumins are the most abundant of the three plasma protein groups and are synthesized by the liver. Fibrinogen functions in clotting, discussed in detail in the latter part of this section. **Serum** is plasma with fibrinogen and other proteins involved in clotting removed. Cells normally do not take up plasma proteins; plasma proteins perform their functions in the plasma itself or in the interstitial fluid. In addition to proteins, plasma contains nutrients, metabolic waste products, hormones, and a variety of mineral electrolytes including Na^+, K^+, Cl^-, and others.

12.24 The Blood Cells

All blood cells are descended from a single population of cells called **pluripotent hematopoietic stem cells,** which are undifferentiated cells capable of giving rise to precursors (progenitors) of any of the different blood cells (**Figure 12.67**). When a pluripotent stem cell divides, its two daughter cells either remain pluripotent stem cells or become committed to a particular developmental pathway. The first branching yields either lymphoid stem cells, which give rise to the lymphocytes, or myeloid stem cells, the progenitors of all the other varieties. At some point, the proliferating offspring of the myeloid stem cells become committed to differentiating along only one path—for example, into erythrocytes.

Erythrocytes

The major function of erythrocytes is gas transport; they carry oxygen taken in by the lungs and carbon dioxide produced by the cells. Erythrocytes contain large amounts of the protein **hemoglobin** with which oxygen and, to a lesser extent, carbon dioxide reversibly combine. Oxygen binds to

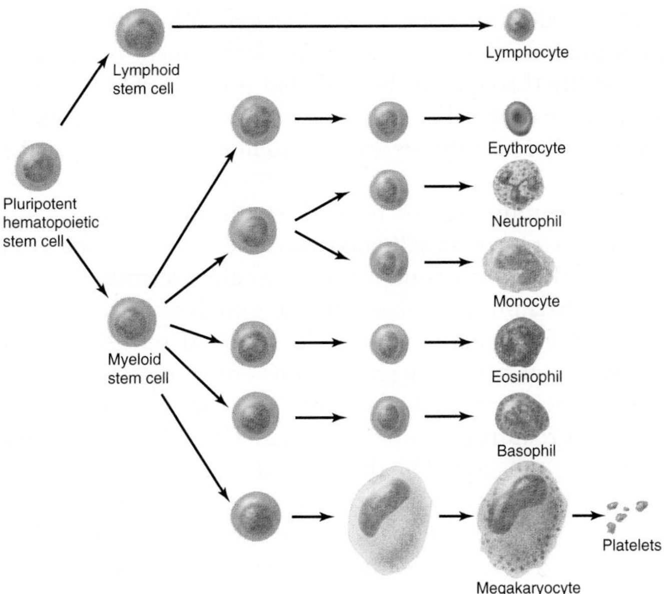

Figure 12.67 AP|R Production of blood cells by the bone marrow. For simplicity, no attempt has been made to differentiate the appearance of the various precursors. Adapted from Golde and Gasson.

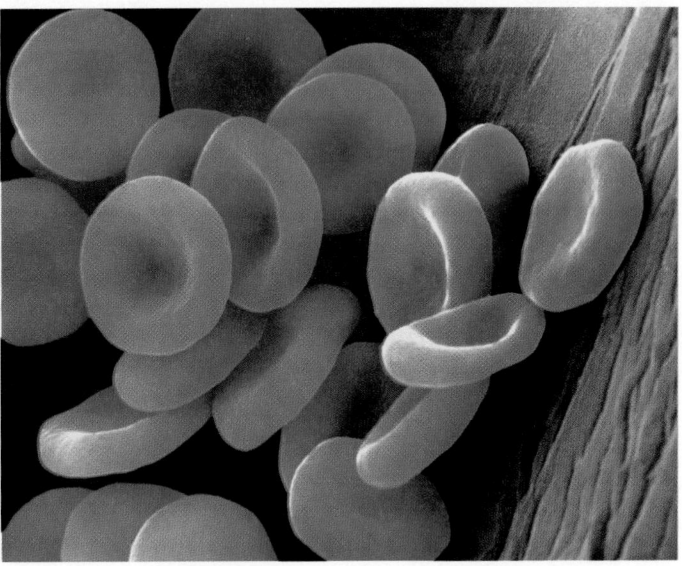

Figure 12.68 AP|R Electron micrograph of erythrocytes.

iron atoms (Fe^{2+}) in the hemoglobin molecules. The average concentration of hemoglobin is 14 g/100 mL blood in women and 15.5 g/100 mL in men. Chapter 13 further describes the structure and functions of hemoglobin.

Erythrocytes are an excellent example of the general principle of physiology that structure is a determinant of—and has coevolved with—function. They have the shape of a biconcave disk—that is, a disk thicker at the edges than in the middle, like a doughnut with a center depression on each side instead of a hole (**Figure 12.68**). This shape and their small size (7 μm in diameter) impart to the erythrocytes a high surface-area-to-volume ratio, so that oxygen and carbon dioxide can diffuse rapidly to and from the interior of the cell.

The site of erythrocyte production is the soft interior of certain bones called **bone marrow,** specifically, the red bone marrow. With differentiation, the erythrocyte precursors produce hemoglobin, but then they ultimately lose their nuclei and organelles—their machinery for protein synthesis. Young erythrocytes in the bone marrow still contain a few ribosomes, which produce a weblike (reticular) appearance when treated with special stains, an appearance that gives these young erythrocytes the name **reticulocyte.** Normally, erythrocytes lose these ribosomes about a day after leaving the bone marrow, so reticulocytes constitute only about 1% of circulating erythrocytes. In the presence of unusually rapid erythrocyte production, however, many more reticulocytes can be found in the blood, a phenomenon of clinically diagnostic usefulness.

Because erythrocytes lack nuclei and most organelles, they can neither reproduce themselves nor maintain their normal structure for very long. The average life span of an erythrocyte is approximately 120 days, which means that almost 1% of the erythrocytes are destroyed and must be replaced every day. This amounts to 250 billion cells per day! Destruction of damaged or dying erythrocytes normally occurs in the spleen and the liver. As we will later describe, most of the iron released in the process is conserved. The major breakdown product of hemoglobin is **bilirubin,** which is returned to the circulation and gives plasma its characteristic yellowish color (Chapter 15 will describe the fate of this substance).

Iron

As noted previously, iron is the element to which oxygen binds on a hemoglobin molecule within an erythrocyte. Small amounts of iron are lost from the body via the urine, feces, sweat, and cells sloughed from the skin. Women lose an additional amount via menstrual blood. In order to remain in iron balance, the amount of iron lost from the body must be replaced by ingestion of iron-containing foods. Particularly rich sources of iron are meat, liver, shellfish, egg yolk, beans, nuts, and cereals. A significant disruption of iron balance can result in either ***iron deficiency***, leading to inadequate hemoglobin production, or an excess of iron in the body (***hemochromatosis***), which results in abnormal iron deposits and damage in various organs, including the liver, heart, pituitary gland, pancreas, and joints.

The homeostatic control of iron balance resides primarily in the intestinal epithelium, which actively absorbs iron from ingested foods. Normally, only a small fraction of ingested iron is absorbed. However, this fraction is increased or decreased in a negative feedback manner, depending upon the state of the body's iron balance—the more iron in the body, the less ingested iron is absorbed (the mechanism will be described in Chapter 15).

The body has a considerable store of iron, mainly in the liver, bound up in a protein called **ferritin.** Ferritin serves as a buffer against iron deficiency. About 50% of the total body iron is in hemoglobin, 25% is in other heme-containing proteins (mainly the cytochromes) in the cells of the body, and 25% is in liver ferritin.

The recycling of iron is very efficient (**Figure 12.69**). As old erythrocytes are destroyed in the spleen (and liver), their iron is released into the plasma and bound to an iron-transport plasma protein called **transferrin.** Transferrin delivers almost all of this iron to the bone marrow to be incorporated into new erythrocytes. Recirculation of erythrocyte iron is very important because it involves 20 times more iron per day than the body absorbs and excretes.

Folic Acid and Vitamin B_{12}

Folic acid, a vitamin found in large amounts in leafy plants, yeast, and liver, is required for synthesis of the nucleotide base thymine. It is, therefore, essential for the formation of DNA and thus for normal cell division. When this vitamin is not present in adequate amounts, impairment of cell division occurs throughout the body but is most striking in rapidly proliferating cells, including erythrocyte precursors. As a result, fewer erythrocytes are produced when folic acid is deficient.

The production of normal erythrocyte numbers also requires extremely small quantities (one-millionth of a gram per day) of a cobalt-containing molecule, **vitamin B_{12}** (also called cobalamin), because this vitamin is required for the action of folic acid. Vitamin B_{12} is found only in animal products, and strictly vegetarian diets tend to be deficient in it. Also, the absorption of vitamin B_{12} from the gastrointestinal tract requires a protein called **intrinsic factor,** which is secreted by the stomach (see Chapter 15). Lack of this protein, therefore, causes vitamin B_{12} deficiency, and the resulting erythrocyte deficiency is known as ***pernicious anemia.***

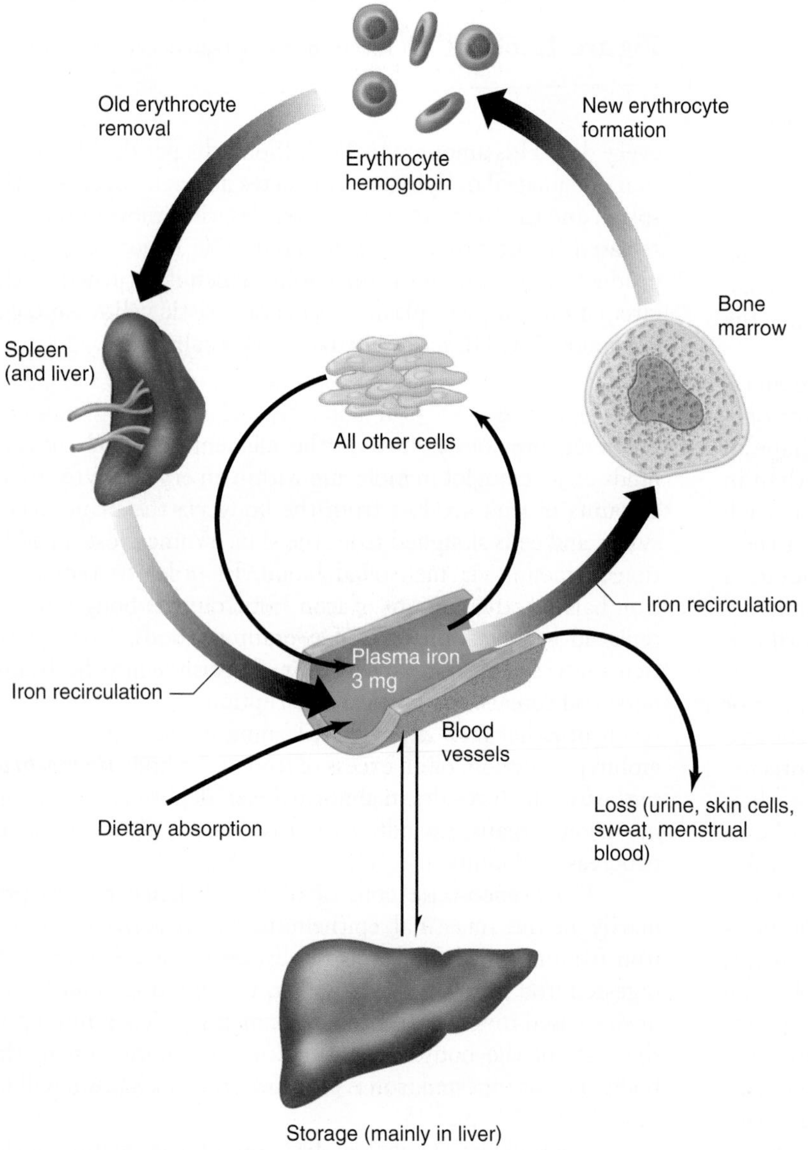

Regulation of Erythrocyte Production

In a typical person, the total volume of circulating erythrocytes remains remarkably constant because of reflexes that regulate the bone marrow's production of these cells. In the previous section, we stated that iron, folic acid, and vitamin B_{12} must be present for normal erythrocyte production, or **erythropoiesis.** However, none of these substances constitutes the signal that regulates the production rate.

The direct control of erythropoiesis is exerted primarily by a hormone called **erythropoietin,** which is secreted into the blood mainly by a particular group of hormone-secreting connective tissue cells in the kidneys. Erythropoietin acts on the bone marrow to stimulate the proliferation of erythrocyte progenitor cells and their differentiation into mature erythrocytes.

Erythropoietin is normally secreted in small amounts that stimulate the bone marrow to produce erythrocytes at a rate adequate to replace the usual loss. The erythropoietin secretion rate is increased markedly above basal values when there is a decreased oxygen delivery to the kidneys. Situations in which this occurs include insufficient pumping of blood by the heart, lung disease, anemia (a decrease in number of erythrocytes or in hemoglobin concentration), prolonged exercise, and exposure to high altitude. As a result of the increase in erythropoietin secretion, plasma erythropoietin concentration, erythrocyte production, and the oxygen-carrying capacity of the blood all increase. Therefore, oxygen delivery to the tissues returns toward normal (**Figure 12.70**). Testosterone, the male sex hormone, also stimulates the release of erythropoietin. This accounts in part for the higher hematocrit in men than in women.

Figure 12.69 Summary of iron balance. The thickness of the arrows correlates with the amount of iron involved. In the steady state, the rate of gastrointestinal iron absorption equals the rate of iron loss via urine, skin, and menstrual flow. Adapted from Crosby.

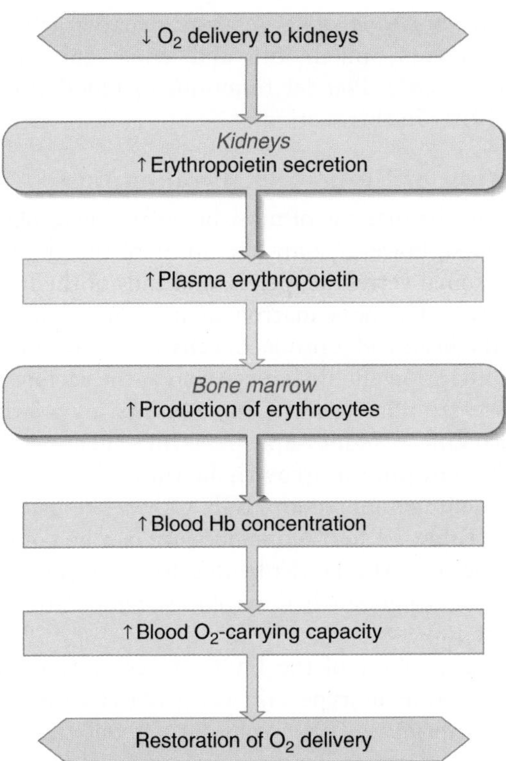

Figure 12.70 Reflex by which decreased oxygen delivery to the kidneys increases erythrocyte production via increased erythropoietin secretion.

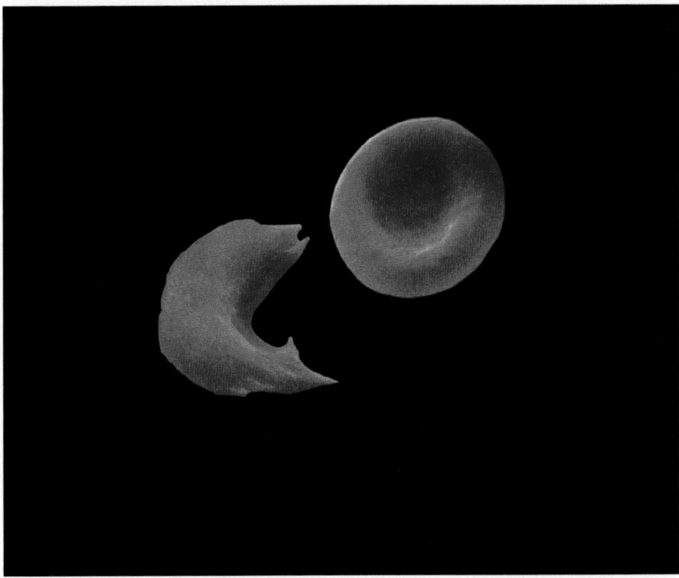

Figure 12.71 AP|R Digitally colorized scanning electron micrograph of red blood cells from a patient with sickle cell anemia. The cell at left assumed this sickle shape after exposure to low-oxygen conditions.

Anemia

As just described, ***anemia*** is defined as a decrease in the ability of the blood to carry oxygen due to (1) a decrease in the total number of erythrocytes, each having a normal quantity of hemoglobin; (2) a diminished concentration of hemoglobin per erythrocyte; or (3) a combination of both. Anemia has a wide variety of causes, some of which are listed in **Table 12.11.**

Sickle-cell disease (formerly called *sickle-cell anemia*) is due to a genetic mutation that alters one amino acid in the hemoglobin chain. At the low oxygen levels existing in many capillaries, the abnormal hemoglobin molecules interact with each other to form fiberlike polymers that distort the erythrocyte membrane and cause the cell to form sickle shapes or other bizarre forms (**Figure 12.71**). This causes both the blockage of capillaries, with consequent tissue damage and pain, and the destruction of the deformed erythrocytes, with consequent anemia. Sickle-cell disease is an example of a disease that is manifested fully only in people homozygous for the mutated gene (that is, they have two copies of the mutated gene, one from each parent). In heterozygotes (one mutated copy and one normal gene), people who are said to have sickle-cell trait, the normal gene codes for normal hemoglobin and the mutated gene for the abnormal hemoglobin. The erythrocytes in this case contain both types of hemoglobin, but symptoms are observed only when the oxygen level is unusually low, as at high altitude. The persistence of the sickle-cell mutation in humans is due to the fact that heterozygotes are more resistant to ***malaria***, a blood infection caused by a protozoan parasite that is spread by mosquitoes in tropical regions. See the Chapter 2 Clinical Case Study for a case discussion of sickle-cell trait.

TABLE 12.11 Major Causes of Anemia
Dietary deficiencies of iron (***iron-deficiency anemia***), vitamin B_{12}, or folic acid
Bone marrow failure due to toxic drugs or cancer
Blood loss from the body (hemorrhage)
Inadequate secretion of erythropoietin in kidney disease
Excessive destruction of erythrocytes (for example, sickle-cell disease)

Finally, there also exist conditions in which there are more erythrocytes than normal, a condition called ***polycythemia.*** An example, to be described in Chapter 13, is the polycythemia that occurs in high-altitude dwellers. In this case, the increased number of erythrocytes is an adaptive response because it increases the oxygen-carrying capacity of blood exposed to low oxygen levels. As discussed earlier, however, increasing the hematocrit increases the viscosity of blood. Therefore, polycythemia makes the flow of blood through blood vessels more difficult and puts a strain on the heart. Abuse of synthetic erythropoietin and the subsequent extreme polycythemia have resulted in the deaths of competitive bicyclists—one reason that such "blood doping" is banned in sports.

Leukocytes

Circulating in the blood and interspersed among various tissues are white blood cells, or leukocytes (see Figure 12.67). The leukocytes are all involved in immune defenses and include neutrophils, eosinophils, monocytes, macrophages, basophils, and lymphocytes. A brief description of their functions follows; these functions are detailed in Chapter 18.

- **Neutrophils** are phagocytes and the most abundant leukocytes. They are found in blood but leave capillaries and enter tissues during inflammation. After neutrophils engulf microbes such as bacteria by phagocytosis, the bacteria are destroyed within endocytotic vacuoles by proteases, oxidizing compounds, and antibacterial proteins called **defensins.** The production and release of neutrophils from bone marrow are greatly stimulated during the course of an infection.
- **Eosinophils** are found in the blood and in the mucosal surfaces lining the gastrointestinal, respiratory, and urinary tracts, where they fight off invasions by eukaryotic parasites. In some cases, eosinophils act by releasing toxic chemicals that kill parasites, and in other cases by phagocytosis.
- **Monocytes** are phagocytes that circulate in the blood for a short time, after which they migrate into tissues and organs and develop into macrophages.
- **Macrophages** are strategically located where they will encounter invaders, including epithelia in contact with the external environment, such as skin and the linings of respiratory and digestive tracts. Macrophages are large phagocytes capable of engulfing viruses and bacteria.
- **Basophils** are secretory cells. They secrete an anticlotting factor called heparin at the site of an infection, which helps the circulation flush out the infected site. Basophils also secrete histamine, which attracts infection-fighting cells and proteins to the site.
- **Lymphocytes** are comprised of several different types of cells that play key roles in protecting against specific pathogens, including viruses, bacteria, toxins, and cancer cells. Some lymphocytes directly kill pathogens, and others secrete antibodies into the circulation that bind to foreign molecules and begin the process of their destruction.

Platelets

The circulating platelets are colorless, nonnucleated cell fragments that contain numerous granules and are much smaller than erythrocytes. Platelets are produced when cytoplasmic portions of large bone marrow cells, termed **megakaryocytes,** pinch off and enter the circulation (see Figure 12.67). Platelet functions in blood clotting are described later in this section.

Regulation of Blood Cell Production

In children, the marrow of most bones produces blood cells. By adulthood, however, only the bones of the chest, base of the skull, spinal vertebrae, pelvis, and ends of the limb bones remain active. The bone marrow in an adult weighs almost as much as the liver, and it produces cells at an enormous rate.

Proliferation and differentiation of the various progenitor cells is stimulated, at multiple points, by a large number of protein hormones and paracrine agents collectively termed **hematopoietic growth factors (HGFs)**. Erythropoietin is one example of an HGF. Others are listed for reference in **Table 12.12.** (Nomenclature can be confusing in this area because the HGFs belong to a still larger general family of messengers called cytokines, which are described in Chapter 18.)

The physiology of the HGFs is very complex because (1) there are so many types, (2) any given HGF is often produced by a variety of cell types throughout the body, and (3) HGFs often exert other actions in addition to stimulating blood cell production. Moreover, there are many interactions of the HGFs on particular bone marrow cells and processes. For example, although erythropoietin is the major stimulator of erythropoiesis, at least 10 other HGFs cooperate in the process. Finally, in several cases, the HGFs not only stimulate differentiation and proliferation of progenitor cells but also inhibit the usual programmed death (apoptosis) of these cells.

The administration of specific HGFs is proving to be of considerable clinical importance. Examples are the use of erythropoietin in persons having a deficiency of this hormone due to kidney disease and the use of granulocyte colony-stimulating factor (G-CSF) to stimulate granulocyte production in individuals whose bone marrow has been damaged by anticancer drugs.

12.25 Hemostasis: The Prevention of Blood Loss

The stoppage of bleeding is known as **hemostasis** (do not confuse this word with *homeostasis*). Physiological hemostatic mechanisms are most effective in dealing with injuries in

TABLE 12.12 Reference Table of Major Hematopoietic Growth Factors (HGFs)

Name	Stimulates Progenitor Cells Leading To:
Erythropoietin	Erythrocytes
Colony-stimulating factors (CSFs) (example: granulocyte CSF)	Granulocytes and monocytes
Interleukins (example: interleukin 3)	Various leukocytes
Thrombopoietin	Platelets (from megakaryocytes)
Stem cell factor	Many types of blood cells

small vessels—arterioles, capillaries, and venules, which are the most common sources of bleeding in everyday life. In contrast, the body usually cannot control bleeding from a medium or large artery. Venous bleeding leads to less rapid blood loss because veins have low blood pressure. Indeed, the decrease in hydrostatic pressure induced by raising the bleeding part above the level of the heart level may stop hemorrhage from a vein. In addition, if the venous bleeding is internal, the accumulation of blood in the tissues may increase interstitial pressure enough to eliminate the pressure gradient required for continued blood loss. Accumulation of blood in the tissues can occur as a result of bleeding from any vessel type and is known as a ***hematoma.***

When a blood vessel is severed or otherwise injured, its immediate inherent response is to constrict. The mechanism is not completely understood but most likely involves changes in local vasodilator and constrictor substances released by endothelial cells and blood cells (see Figure 12.36). This short-lived response slows the flow of blood in the affected area. In addition, this constriction presses the opposed endothelial surfaces of the vessel together and this contact induces a stickiness capable of keeping them "glued" together.

Permanent closure of the vessel by constriction and contact stickiness occurs only in the very smallest vessels of the microcirculation, however, and the staunching of bleeding ultimately depends upon two other interdependent processes that occur in rapid succession: (1) formation of a platelet plug and (2) blood coagulation (clotting). The blood platelets are involved in both processes.

Formation of a Platelet Plug

The involvement of platelets in hemostasis requires their adhesion to a surface. Injury to a vessel disrupts the endothelium and exposes the underlying connective-tissue collagen fibers. Platelets adhere to collagen, largely via an intermediary called **von Willebrand factor (vWF)**, a plasma protein secreted by endothelial cells and platelets. This protein binds to exposed collagen molecules, changes its conformation, and becomes able to bind platelets. Thus, vWF forms a bridge between the damaged vessel wall and the platelets.

Binding of platelets to collagen triggers the platelets to release the contents of their secretory vesicles, which contain a variety of chemical agents. Many of these agents, including adenosine diphosphate (ADP) and serotonin, then act locally to induce multiple changes in the metabolism, shape, and surface proteins of the platelets, a process called **platelet activation.** Some of these changes cause new platelets to adhere to the old ones, a positive feedback phenomenon termed **platelet aggregation,** which rapidly creates a **platelet plug** inside the vessel.

Chemical agents in the platelets' secretory vesicles are not the only stimulators of platelet activation and aggregation. Adhesion of the platelets rapidly induces them to synthesize **thromboxane A_2,** a member of the eicosanoid family, from arachidonic acid in the platelet plasma membrane. Thromboxane A_2 is released into the extracellular fluid and acts locally to further stimulate platelet aggregation and release of their secretory vesicle contents (**Figure 12.72**).

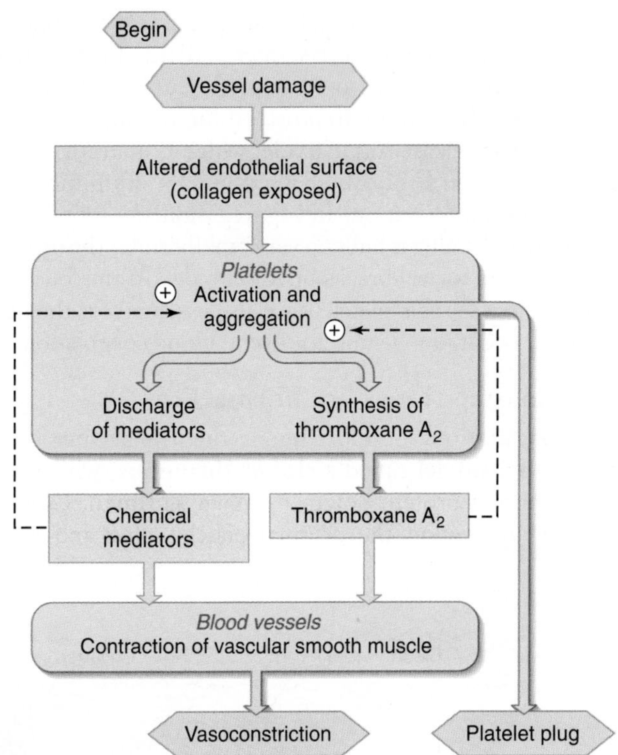

Figure 12.72 Sequence of events leading to formation of a platelet plug and vasoconstriction following damage to a blood vessel wall. Note the two positive feedbacks in the pathways.

Fibrinogen, a plasma protein whose essential role in blood clotting is described in the next section, also plays a crucial role in the platelet aggregation produced by the factors previously described. It does so by forming the bridges between aggregating platelets. The receptors (binding sites) for fibrinogen on the platelet plasma membrane become exposed and activated during platelet activation.

The platelet plug can completely seal small breaks in blood vessel walls. Its effectiveness is further enhanced by another property of platelets—contraction. Platelets contain a very high concentration of actin and myosin (see Chapter 9), which are stimulated to interact in aggregated platelets. This causes compression and strengthening of the platelet plug. (When they occur in a test tube, this contraction and compression are termed *clot retraction.*)

While the plug is being built up and compacted, the vascular smooth muscle in the damaged vessel is simultaneously being stimulated to contract (see Figure 12.72), thereby decreasing the blood flow to the area and the pressure within the damaged vessel. This vasoconstriction is the result of platelet activity, for it is mediated by thromboxane A_2 and by several chemicals contained in the platelet's secretory vesicles.

Once started, why does the platelet plug not continuously expand, spreading away from the damaged endothelium along intact endothelium in both directions? One important reason involves the ability of the adjacent undamaged endothelial cells to synthesize and release the eicosanoid known as **prostacyclin** (also termed **prostaglandin I_2 [PGI_2]**), which is a profound inhibitor of platelet aggregation. Thus, whereas platelets possess the enzymes that produce thromboxane A_2

from arachidonic acid, normal endothelial cells contain a different enzyme that converts intermediates formed from arachidonic acid not to thromboxane A_2 but to prostacyclin (**Figure 12.73**). In addition to prostacyclin, the adjacent endothelial cells also release **nitric oxide,** which is not only a vasodilator (see Section C of this chapter) but also an inhibitor of platelet adhesion, activation, and aggregation.

The platelet plug is built up very rapidly and is the primary mechanism used to seal breaks in vessel walls. In the following section, we will see that platelets are also essential for the next, more slowly occurring hemostatic event: blood coagulation.

Blood Coagulation: Clot Formation

Blood coagulation, or **clotting,** is the transformation of blood into a solid gel called a **clot** or **thrombus,** which consists mainly of a protein polymer known as **fibrin.** Clotting occurs locally around the original platelet plug and is the dominant hemostatic defense. Its function is to support and reinforce the platelet plug and to solidify blood that remains in the wound channel.

Figure 12.74 summarizes, in very simplified form, the events leading to clotting. These events, like platelet aggregation, are initiated when injury to a vessel disrupts the endothelium and permits the blood to contact the underlying tissue. This contact initiates a locally occurring cascade of chemical activations. At each step of the cascade, an inactive plasma protein, or "factor," is converted (activated) to a proteolytic enzyme, which then catalyzes the generation of the next enzyme in the sequence. Each of these activations results from the splitting of a small peptide fragment from the inactive plasma protein precursor, thereby exposing the active site of the enzyme. However, several of the plasma protein factors, following their activation, function not as enzymes but rather as cofactors for enzymes.

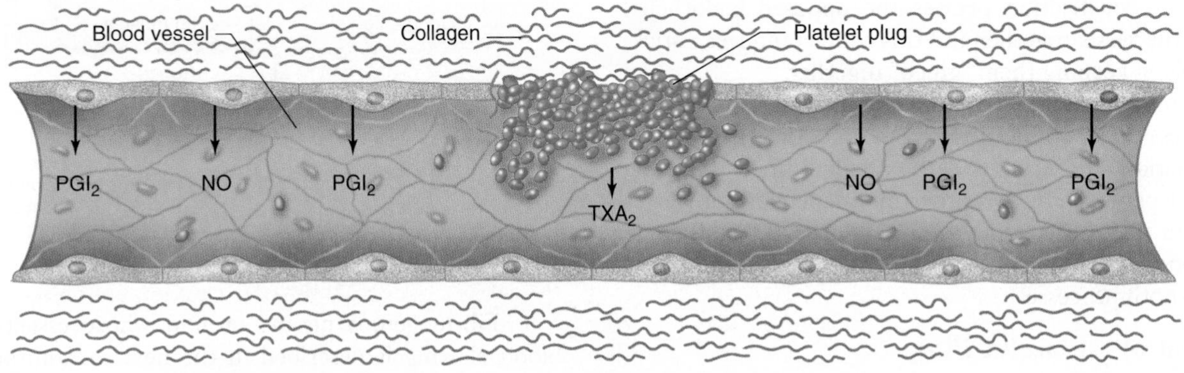

Figure 12.73 Prostacyclin (prostaglandin I_2 [PGI_2]) and nitric oxide (NO), both produced by endothelial cells, inhibit platelet aggregation and therefore prevent the spread of platelet aggregation from a damaged site. TXA_2 = Thromboxane A_2.

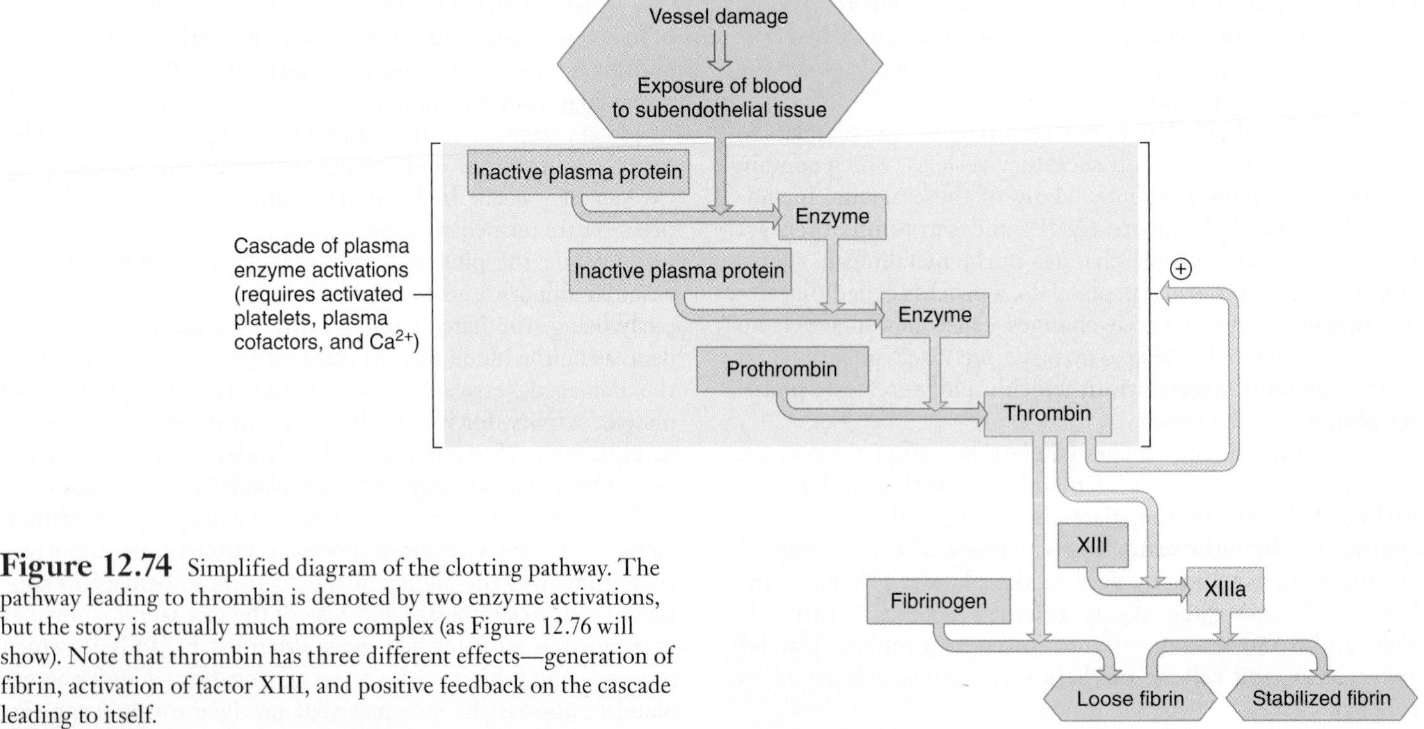

Figure 12.74 Simplified diagram of the clotting pathway. The pathway leading to thrombin is denoted by two enzyme activations, but the story is actually much more complex (as Figure 12.76 will show). Note that thrombin has three different effects—generation of fibrin, activation of factor XIII, and positive feedback on the cascade leading to itself.

For simplicity, Figure 12.74 gives no specifics about the cascade until the key point at which the plasma protein **prothrombin** is converted to the enzyme **thrombin.** Thrombin then catalyzes a reaction in which several polypeptides are split from molecules of the large, rod-shaped plasma protein fibrinogen. The fibrinogen remnants then bind to each other to form fibrin. The fibrin, initially a loose mesh of interlacing strands, is rapidly stabilized and strengthened by the enzymatically mediated formation of covalent cross-linkages. This chemical linking is catalyzed by an enzyme known as factor XIIIa, which is formed from plasma protein factor XIII in a reaction also catalyzed by thrombin.

Thus, thrombin catalyzes not only the formation of loose fibrin but also the activation of factor XIII, which stabilizes the fibrin network. However, thrombin does even more than this—it exerts a profound positive feedback effect on its own formation. It does so by activating several proteins in the cascade and also by activating platelets. Therefore, once thrombin formation has begun, reactions leading to much more thrombin generation are activated by this initial thrombin. We will make use of this crucial fact later when we describe the specifics of the cascade leading to thrombin.

In the process of clotting, many erythrocytes and other cells are trapped in the fibrin meshwork (**Figure 12.75**), but the essential component of the clot is fibrin, and clotting can occur in the absence of all cellular elements except platelets. Activated platelets are essential because several of the cascade reactions take place on the surface of the platelets. As noted earlier, platelet activation occurs early in the hemostatic response as a result of platelet adhesion to collagen, but in addition, thrombin is an important stimulator of platelet activation. The activation causes the platelets to display specific plasma membrane receptors that bind several of the clotting factors, and this permits the reactions to take place on the surface of the platelets. The activated platelets also display particular phospholipids, called **platelet factor** (**PF**), which functions as a cofactor in the steps mediated by the bound clotting factors.

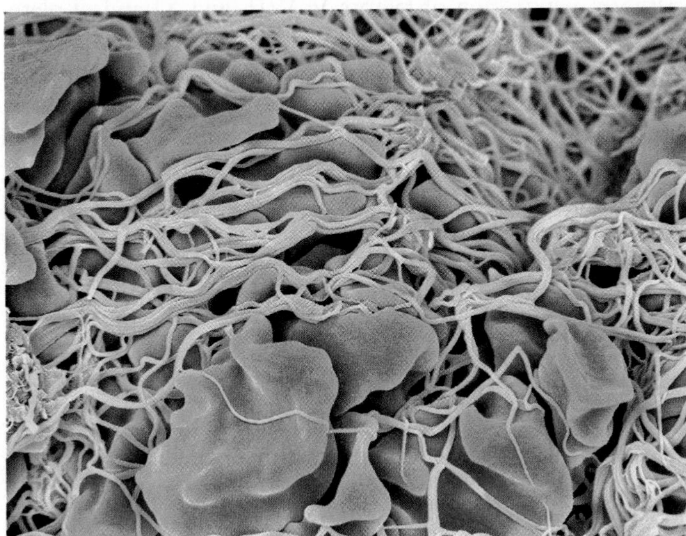

Figure 12.75 Scanning electron micrograph of erythrocytes enmeshed in fibrin.

In addition to protein factors, plasma Ca^{2+} is required at various steps in the clotting cascade. However, Ca^{2+} concentration in the plasma can never decrease enough to cause clotting defects because death would occur from muscle paralysis or cardiac arrhythmias before such low concentrations were reached.

Now we present the specifics of the early portions of the clotting cascade—those leading from vessel damage to the prothrombin–thrombin reaction. These early reactions consist of two seemingly parallel pathways that merge at the step just before the prothrombin–thrombin reaction. Under physiological conditions, however, the two pathways are not parallel but are actually activated sequentially, with thrombin serving as the link between them. There are also several points at which the two pathways interact. It will be clearer, however, if we first discuss the two pathways as though they were separate and then deal with their actual interaction. The pathways are called (1) the **intrinsic pathway,** so named because everything necessary for it is in the blood; and (2) the **extrinsic pathway,** so named because a cellular element outside the blood is needed. **Figure 12.76** will be an essential reference for this entire discussion. Also, **Table 12.13** is a reference list of the names of and synonyms for the substances in these pathways.

The first plasma protein in the intrinsic pathway (upper left of Figure 12.76) is called factor XII. It can become activated to factor XIIa when it contacts certain types of surfaces, including the collagen fibers underlying damaged endothelium. The contact activation of factor XII to XIIa is a complex process that requires the participation of several other plasma proteins not shown in Figure 12.76. Contact activation also explains why blood coagulates when it is taken from the body and put in a glass tube. This has nothing whatever to do with exposure to air but happens because the glass surface acts like collagen and induces the same activation of factor XII and aggregation of platelets as a damaged vessel surface. A silicone coating delays clotting by reducing the activating effects of the glass surface.

Factor XIIa then catalyzes the activation of factor XI to factor XIa, which activates factor IX to factor IXa. This last factor then activates factor X to factor Xa, which is the enzyme that converts prothrombin to thrombin. Note in Figure 12.76 that another plasma protein—factor VIIIa—serves as a cofactor (not an enzyme) in the factor IXa–mediated activation of factor X. The importance of factor VIII in clotting is emphasized by the fact that the disease ***hemophilia,*** characterized by excessive bleeding, is usually due to a genetic absence of this factor. (In a smaller number of cases, hemophilia is due to an absence of factor IX.)

Now we turn to the extrinsic pathway for initiating the clotting cascade (upper right of Figure 12.76). This pathway begins with a protein called **tissue factor,** which is not a plasma protein. It is located instead on the outer plasma membrane of various tissue cells, including fibroblasts and other cells in the walls of blood vessels outside the endothelium. The blood is exposed to these subendothelial cells when vessel damage disrupts the endothelial lining. Tissue factor on these cells then binds a plasma protein, factor VII, which becomes activated to factor VIIa. The complex of tissue factor and factor VIIa on the plasma membrane of the tissue cell then

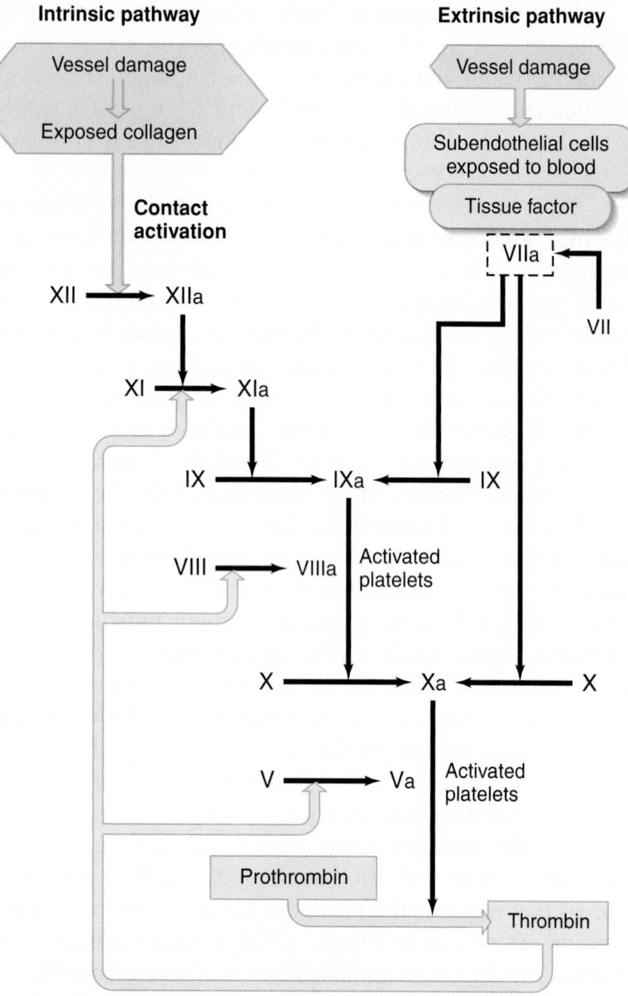

Figure 12.76 Two clotting pathways—intrinsic and extrinsic—merge and can lead to the generation of thrombin. Under most physiological conditions, however, factor XII and the contact-activation step that begins the intrinsic pathway probably play little, if any, role in clotting. Rather, clotting is initiated solely by the extrinsic pathway, as described in the text. You may think that factors IX and X were accidentally transposed in the intrinsic pathway, but this is not the case; the order of activation really is XI, IX, and X. For the sake of clarity, the roles Ca^{2+} plays in clotting are not shown.

PHYSIOLOGICAL INQUIRY

- Which would affect normal blood clotting more, a mutation that blocked the production of clotting factor XII, or one that blocked production of factor VII?

Answer can be found at end of chapter.

catalyzes the activation of factor X. In addition, it catalyzes the activation of factor IX, which can then help activate even more factor X by way of the intrinsic pathway.

In summary, clotting can theoretically be initiated either by the activation of factor XII or by the generation of the tissue factor–factor VIIa complex. The two paths merge at factor Xa, which then catalyzes the conversion of prothrombin to thrombin, which catalyzes the formation of fibrin. As shown in Figure 12.76, thrombin also contributes to the activation of

TABLE 12.13 Official Designations for Clotting Factors, Along with Synonyms More Commonly Used

Factor I (fibrinogen)
Factor Ia (fibrin)
Factor II (prothrombin)
Factor IIa (thrombin)
Factor III (tissue factor, tissue thromboplastin)
Factor IV (Ca^{2+})
Factors V, VII, VIII, IX, X, XI, XII, and XIII are the inactive forms of these factors; the active forms add an "a" (e.g., factor XIIa). There is no factor VI.
Platelet factor (PF)

(1) factors XI and VIII in the intrinsic pathway and (2) factor V, with factor Va then serving as a cofactor for factor Xa. Not shown in the figure is the fact that thrombin also activates platelets.

As stated earlier, under physiological conditions, the two pathways just described actually are activated sequentially. To understand how this works, turn again to Figure 12.76; hold your hand over the first part of the intrinsic pathway so that you can eliminate the contact activation of factor XII, and then begin the description in the next paragraph at the top of the extrinsic pathway in the figure.

The extrinsic pathway, with its tissue factor, is the usual way of initiating clotting in the body, and factor XII—the beginning of the full intrinsic pathway—normally plays little if any role (in contrast to its initiation of clotting in test tubes or within the body in several unusual situations). Thus, thrombin is initially generated only by the extrinsic pathway. The amount of thrombin is too small, however, to produce adequate, sustained coagulation. It *is* large enough, though, to trigger thrombin's positive feedback effects on the intrinsic pathway—activation of factors V, VIII, and XI and of platelets. This is all that is needed to trigger the intrinsic pathway independently of factor XII. This pathway then generates the large amounts of thrombin required for adequate coagulation. The extrinsic pathway, therefore, via its initial generation of small amounts of thrombin, provides the means for recruiting the more potent intrinsic pathway without the participation of factor XII. In essence, thrombin eliminates the need for factor XII. Moreover, thrombin not only recruits the intrinsic pathway but facilitates the prothrombin–thrombin step itself by activating factor V and platelets.

Finally, note that the liver plays several important indirect roles in clotting (**Figure 12.77**); as a result, persons with liver disease often have serious bleeding problems. First, the liver is the site of production for many of the plasma clotting factors. Second, the liver produces bile salts (Chapter 15), and these are important for normal intestinal absorption of the lipid-soluble substance **vitamin K.** The liver requires this vitamin to produce prothrombin and several other clotting factors.

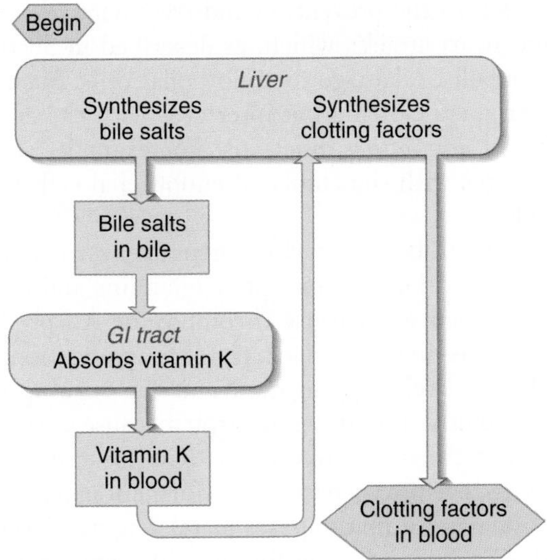

Figure 12.77 Roles of the liver in blood clotting.

PHYSIOLOGICAL INQUIRY

- How might prolonged treatment with antibiotics result in the side effect of impaired blood clotting? (*Hint:* Read about vitamin K in Chapter 15.)

Answer can be found at end of chapter.

Anticlotting Systems

Earlier, we described how the release of prostacyclin and nitric oxide by endothelial cells inhibits platelet aggregation. Because this aggregation is an essential precursor for clotting, these agents reduce the magnitude and extent of clotting. In addition, however, the body has mechanisms for limiting clot formation itself and for dissolving a clot after it has formed. The presence of mechanisms that both favor and limit blood clotting is a good example of the general principle of physiology that most physiological functions are controlled by multiple regulatory systems, often working in opposition.

Factors That Oppose Clot Formation

There are at least three different mechanisms that oppose clot formation, thereby helping to limit this process and prevent it from spreading excessively. Defects in any of these natural anticoagulant mechanisms are associated with abnormally high risk of clotting, a condition called ***hypercoagulability*** (see Chapter 19 for a case discussion of a patient with this condition).

The first anticoagulant mechanism acts during the initiation phase of clotting and utilizes the plasma protein called **tissue factor pathway inhibitor (TFPI)**, which is secreted mainly by endothelial cells. This substance binds to tissue factor–factor VIIa complexes and inhibits the ability of these complexes to generate factor Xa. This anticoagulant mechanism is the reason that the extrinsic pathway by itself can generate only small amounts of thrombin.

The second anticoagulant mechanism is triggered by thrombin. As illustrated in **Figure 12.78**, thrombin can bind to an endothelial cell receptor known as **thrombomodulin.** This binding eliminates all of thrombin's clot-producing effects and causes the bound thrombin to bind a particular plasma protein, **protein C** (distinguish this from protein kinase C, Chapter 5). The binding to thrombin activates protein C, which, in combination with yet another plasma protein, then inactivates factors VIIIa and Va. We saw earlier that thrombin directly activates factors VIII and V when the endothelium is damaged, and now we see that it indirectly inactivates them via protein C in areas where the endothelium is intact. **Table 12.14** summarizes the effects—both stimulatory and inhibitory—of thrombin on the clotting pathways.

A third naturally occurring anticoagulant mechanism is a plasma protein called **antithrombin III,** which inactivates thrombin and several other clotting factors. The activity of antithrombin III is greatly enhanced when it binds to **heparin,** a substance present on the surface of endothelial cells. Antithrombin III prevents the spread of a clot by rapidly inactivating clotting factors that are carried away from the immediate site of the clot by the flowing blood.

The Fibrinolytic System

TFPI, protein C, and antithrombin III all function to *limit* clot formation. The system to be described now, however, dissolves a clot *after* it is formed.

A fibrin clot is not designed to last forever. It is a temporary fix until permanent repair of the vessel occurs. The **fibrinolytic** (or thrombolytic) **system** is the principal effector of clot removal. The physiology of this system (**Figure 12.79**) is analogous to that of the clotting system; it constitutes a plasma

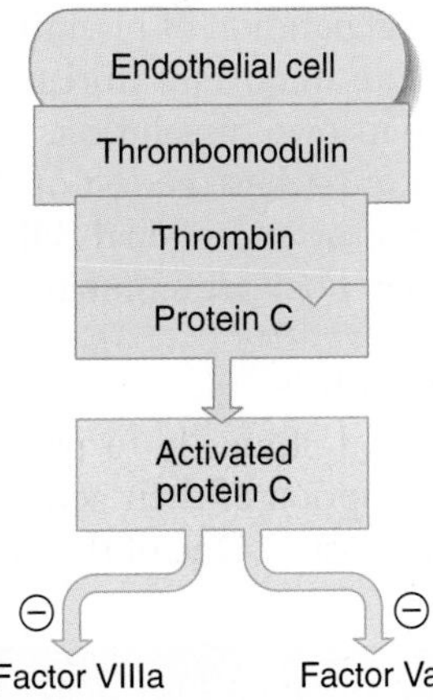

Figure 12.78 Thrombin indirectly inactivates factors VIIIa and Va via protein C. To activate protein C, thrombin must first bind to a thrombin receptor, thrombomodulin, on endothelial cells; this binding also eliminates thrombin's procoagulant effects. The ⊖ symbol indicates inactivation of factors Va and VIIIa.

TABLE 12.14	Actions of Thrombin
Procoagulant	Cleaves fibrinogen to fibrin Activates clotting factors XI, VIII, V, and XIII Stimulates platelet activation
Anticoagulant	Activates protein C, which inactivates clotting factors VIIIa and Va

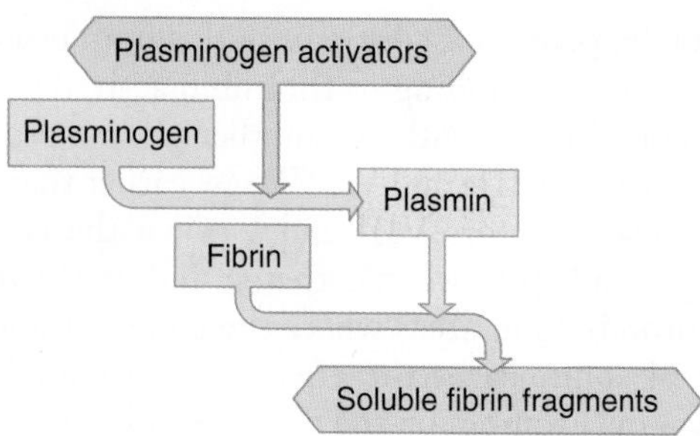

Figure 12.79 Basic fibrinolytic system. There are many different plasminogen activators and many different pathways for initiating their activity.

proenzyme, **plasminogen,** which can be activated to the active enzyme **plasmin** by protein **plasminogen activators.** Once formed, plasmin digests fibrin, thereby dissolving the clot.

The fibrinolytic system is proving to be every bit as complicated as the clotting system, with multiple types of plasminogen activators and pathways for generating them, as well as several inhibitors of these plasminogen activators. In describing how this system can be set into motion, we restrict our discussion to one example—the particular plasminogen activator known as **tissue plasminogen activator (t-PA),** which is secreted by endothelial cells. During clotting, both plasminogen and t-PA bind to fibrin and become incorporated throughout the clot. The binding of t-PA to fibrin is crucial because t-PA is a very weak enzyme in the absence of fibrin. The presence of fibrin profoundly increases the ability of t-PA to catalyze the generation of plasmin from plasminogen. Fibrin, therefore, is an important initiator of the fibrinolytic process that leads to its own dissolution.

The secretion of t-PA is the last of the various anticlotting functions exerted by endothelial cells that we have mentioned in this chapter. They are summarized in **Table 12.15**.

Anticlotting Drugs

Various drugs are used clinically to prevent or reverse clotting, and a brief description of their actions serves as a review of key clotting mechanisms. One of the most common uses of these drugs is in the prevention and treatment of myocardial infarction (heart attack), which, as described in Section E, is often the result of damage to endothelial cells. Such damage not only triggers clotting but interferes with the endothelial cells' normal *anticlotting* functions. For example, atherosclerosis interferes with the ability of endothelial cells to secrete nitric oxide.

Aspirin inhibits the cyclooxygenase enzyme in the eicosanoid pathways that generate prostaglandins and thromboxanes (see Chapter 5). Because thromboxane A_2, produced by the platelets, is important for platelet aggregation, aspirin reduces both platelet aggregation and the ensuing coagulation. Importantly, low doses of aspirin cause a steady-state decrease in *platelet* cyclooxygenase (COX) activity but not *endothelial-cell* cyclooxygenase; so the formation of prostacyclin—the prostaglandin that opposes platelet aggregation—is not impaired. (There is a reason for this difference between the responses of platelet and endothelial-cell cyclooxygenase to drugs. Platelets, once formed and released from megakaryocytes, have lost their ability to synthesize proteins. Therefore, when their COX is irreversibly blocked, thromboxane A_2 synthesis is gone for that platelet's lifetime. In contrast, the endothelial cells produce new COX molecules to replace the ones blocked by the drug.) Aspirin appears to be effective at preventing heart attacks. In addition, the administration of aspirin following a heart attack significantly reduces the incidence of sudden death and a recurrent heart attack.

A variety of drugs that interfere with platelet function by mechanisms different from those of aspirin also have great promise in the treatment or prevention of heart attacks. In particular, certain drugs block the binding of fibrinogen to platelets and thus interfere with platelet aggregation.

Drugs known collectively as ***oral anticoagulants*** interfere with clotting factors. One type interferes with the action of vitamin K, which in turn reduces the synthesis of clotting factors by the liver. Another type recently developed includes drugs that specifically inactivate factor Xa. Heparin, the naturally occurring endothelial-cell cofactor for antithrombin III, can also be administered as a drug, which then binds to endothelial cells and inhibits clotting.

TABLE 12.15 Anticlotting Roles of Endothelial Cells

Action	Result
Normally provide an intact barrier between the blood and subendothelial connective tissue	Platelet aggregation and the formation of tissue factor–factor VIIa complexes are not triggered.
Synthesize and release PGI_2 and nitric oxide	These inhibit platelet activation and aggregation.
Secrete tissue factor pathway inhibitor	This inhibits the ability of tissue factor–factor VIIa complexes to generate factor Xa.
Bind thrombin (via thrombomodulin), which then activates protein C	Active protein C inactivates clotting factors VIIIa and Va.
Display heparin molecules on the surfaces of their plasma membranes	Heparin binds antithrombin III, and this molecule then inactivates thrombin and several other clotting factors.
Secrete tissue plasminogen activator	Tissue plasminogen activator catalyzes the formation of plasmin, which dissolves clots.

In contrast to aspirin, the fibrinogen blockers, the oral anticoagulants, and heparin, all of which prevent clotting, the fifth type of drug—plasminogen activators—dissolves a clot after it is formed. The use of such drugs is termed ***thrombolytic therapy.*** Intravenous administration of ***recombinant t-PA*** within a few hours after myocardial infarction significantly reduces myocardial damage and mortality. Recombinant t-PA has also been effective in reducing brain damage following a stroke caused by blood vessel occlusion. In addition, exciting new clinical studies suggest that a plasminogen activator found in vampire bat saliva may be even more effective than t-PA at protecting the brain after an ischemic stroke. Its name includes the genus and species of the animal—***Desmodus rotundus salivary plasminogen activator (DSPA).***

SECTION F SUMMARY

Plasma

I. Plasma is the liquid component of blood; it contains proteins (albumins, globulins, and fibrinogen), nutrients, metabolic end products, hormones, and inorganic electrolytes.

II. Plasma proteins, synthesized by the liver, play many roles within the bloodstream, such as exerting osmotic pressure for absorption of interstitial fluid and participating in the clotting reaction.

The Blood Cells

I. The blood cells, which are suspended in plasma, include erythrocytes, leukocytes, and platelets.

II. Erythrocytes, which make up more than 99% of blood cells, contain hemoglobin, an oxygen-binding protein. Oxygen binds to the iron in hemoglobin.
   a. Erythrocytes are produced in the bone marrow and destroyed in the spleen and liver.
   b. Iron, folic acid, and vitamin B_{12} are essential for erythrocyte formation.
   c. The hormone erythropoietin, which is produced by the kidneys in response to low oxygen supply, stimulates erythrocyte differentiation and production by the bone marrow.

III. The leukocytes include neutrophils, eosinophils, basophils, monocytes, and lymphocytes.

IV. Platelets are cell fragments essential for blood clotting.

V. Blood cells are descended from stem cells in the bone marrow. Hematopoietic growth factors control their production.

Hemostasis: The Prevention of Blood Loss

I. The initial response to blood vessel damage is vasoconstriction and the sticking together of the opposed endothelial surfaces.

II. The next events are formation of a platelet plug followed by blood coagulation (clotting).

III. Platelets adhere to exposed collagen in a damaged vessel and release the contents of their secretory vesicles.
   a. These substances help cause platelet activation and aggregation.
   b. This process is also enhanced by von Willebrand factor, secreted by the endothelial cells, and by thromboxane A_2, produced by the platelets.
   c. Fibrin forms the bridges between aggregating platelets.
   d. Contractile elements in the platelets compress and strengthen the plug.

IV. The platelet plug does not spread along normal endothelium because the latter secretes prostacyclin and nitric oxide, both of which inhibit platelet aggregation.

V. Blood is transformed into a solid gel when, at the site of vessel damage, plasma fibrinogen is converted into fibrin molecules, which then bind to each other to form a mesh.

VI. This reaction is catalyzed by the enzyme thrombin, which also activates factor XIII, a plasma protein that stabilizes the fibrin meshwork.

VII. The formation of thrombin from the plasma protein prothrombin is the end result of a cascade of reactions in which an inactive plasma protein is activated and then enzymatically activates the next protein in the series.
   a. Thrombin exerts a positive feedback stimulation of the cascade by activating platelets and several clotting factors.
   b. Activated platelets, which display platelet factor and binding sites for several activated plasma factors, are essential for the cascade.

VIII. In the body, the cascade usually begins via the extrinsic clotting pathway when tissue factor forms a complex with factor VIIa. This complex activates factor X, which then catalyzes the conversion of small amounts of prothrombin to thrombin. This thrombin then recruits the intrinsic pathway by activating factor XI and factor VIII, as well as platelets, and this pathway generates large amounts of thrombin.

IX. The liver requires vitamin K for the normal production of prothrombin and other clotting factors.

X. Clotting is limited by three events:
   a. Tissue factor pathway inhibitor inhibits the tissue factor–factor VIIa complex.
   b. Protein C, activated by thrombin, inactivates factors VIIIa and Va.
   c. Antithrombin III inactivates thrombin and several other clotting factors.

XI. Clots are dissolved by the fibrinolytic system.
   a. A plasma proenzyme, plasminogen, is activated by plasminogen activators to plasmin, which digests fibrin.
   b. Tissue plasminogen activator is secreted by endothelial cells and is activated by fibrin in a clot.

SECTION F REVIEW QUESTIONS

1. Give average values for total blood volume, erythrocyte volume, plasma volume, and hematocrit.
2. What are the different classes of plasma proteins, and which are the most abundant?
3. Which solute is found in the highest concentration in plasma?
4. Summarize the production, life span, and destruction of erythrocytes.
5. What are the routes of iron gain, loss, and distribution? How is iron recycled when erythrocytes are destroyed?
6. Describe the control of erythropoietin secretion and the effect of this hormone.
7. State the relative proportions of erythrocytes and leukocytes in blood.
8. Diagram the derivation of the different blood cell types.
9. Describe the sequence of events leading to platelet activation and aggregation and the formation of a platelet plug. What helps keep this process localized?
10. Diagram the clotting pathway beginning with prothrombin.
11. What is the role of platelets in clotting?
12. List all the procoagulant effects of thrombin.
13. How is the clotting cascade initiated? How does the extrinsic pathway recruit the intrinsic pathway?

14. Describe the roles of the liver and vitamin K in clotting.
15. List three ways in which clotting is limited.
16. Diagram the fibrinolytic system.
17. How does fibrin help initiate the fibrinolytic system?
18. Which symptoms of pericarditis mimic a heart attack, and which symptoms differentiate the conditions? (See the Clinical Case Study.)

SECTION F KEY TERMS

albumin 428
antithrombin III 437
basophil 432
bilirubin 429
blood coagulation 434
bone marrow 429
clot 434
clotting 434
defensins 432
eosinophil 432
erythropoiesis 430
erythropoietin 430
extrinsic pathway 435
ferritin 429
fibrin 434
fibrinogen 428
fibrinolytic system 437
folic acid 430
globulin 428
hematopoietic growth factor (HGF) 432
hemoglobin 428
hemostasis 432
heparin 437
intrinsic factor 430
intrinsic pathway 435
lymphocyte 432
macrophage 432
megakaryocyte 432
monocyte 432
neutrophil 432
nitric oxide 434
plasma protein 428
plasmin 438
plasminogen 438
plasminogen activator 438
platelet activation 433
platelet aggregation 433
platelet factor (PF) 435
platelet plug 433
pluripotent hematopoietic stem cell 428
prostacyclin 433
prostaglandin I_2 (PGI_2) 433
protein C 437
prothrombin 435
reticulocyte 429
serum 428
thrombin 435
thrombomodulin 437
thromboxane A_2 433
thrombus 434
tissue factor 435
tissue factor pathway inhibitor (TFPI) 437
tissue plasminogen activator (t-PA) 438
transferrin 430
vitamin B_{12} 430
vitamin K 436
von Willebrand factor (vWF) 433

SECTION F CLINICAL TERMS

anemia 431
aspirin 438
Desmodus rotundus salivary plasminogen activator (DSPA) 439
hematoma 433
hemochromatosis 429
hemophilia 435
hypercoagulability 437
iron deficiency 429
iron-deficiency anemia 431
malaria 431
oral anticoagulants 438
pernicious anemia 430
polycythemia 431
recombinant t-PA 439
sickle-cell disease 431
thrombolytic therapy 439

CHAPTER 12 Clinical Case Study: Chest Pain in a 48-Year-Old Woman

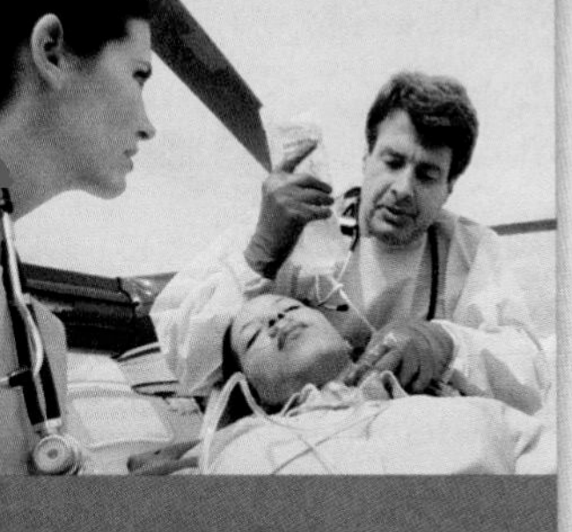

A 48-year-old woman arrived at the emergency room, complaining of chest pain. She reported being ill for about a week. At first, she just had a runny nose, cough, and sore throat. Over the past 4 days, she had developed pain in her chest and back that seemed worse with inspiration and when she was lying down. After getting into bed that evening, she had suddenly experienced sharp, stabbing pain in her chest and left shoulder, upon which she had called an ambulance.

Because the emergency room physician suspected the woman was experiencing a heart attack, an intravenous line was started, through which she was given nitroglycerin and heparin to prevent blood clot formation. Supplemental inspired oxygen was administered via a nasal tube while a history was taken and further tests were performed. Prior to this episode, she had been in good health; she reported no personal or family history of heart disease. Her heart rate was 105 beats/minute, blood pressure was 115/65 mmHg, and body temperature was 101°F (38.5°C) (normal = 98.6°F/37°C). Auscultation with a stethoscope detected rasping sounds associated with systole and diastole that obscured the normal heart sounds. A 12-lead electrocardiogram showed slight elevations of her ST segment in all of the leads except aVR and V1. A venous blood sample revealed normal hemoglobin and cardiac troponin concentrations, but the white blood cell count was mildly elevated. She was transferred to the cardiac catheterization lab for angiography, which showed minor atherosclerosis but no blocked coronary arteries. Her chest pain continued despite the nitroglycerin, and she also began to experience dizziness and a headache. When an additional measurement showed her blood pressure had decreased to 80/50 mmHg, the nitroglycerin and heparin were discontinued. What had seemed at first like a heart attack turned out to be a case of acute ***pericarditis.***

Pericarditis is an inflammation of the fibrous pericardial sac that surrounds the heart. It can be caused by viral, bacterial, or fungal infection and also by autoimmune conditions in which the body's own tissues come under immune attack (see Chapter 18). Normally, the pericardial space is extremely narrow and filled with a lubricating fluid that allows the heart to move within the thoracic cavity with a minimum of friction. In pericarditis, the membranes swell and roughen, and a large volume of fluid—either an

(continued)

(continued)

interstitial fluid exudate, blood, or pus—can build up inside the space. Friction between the roughened pericardial and epicardial membranes can produce grating or rasping sounds in concert with the heart's movements. These sounds are audible with a stethoscope and can be loud enough to make detection of the normal heart sounds difficult.

Some of the symptoms mimic those of a myocardial infarction (heart attack): chest, shoulder, or back pain; rapid heart rate; and changes in the appearance of the ST segment on an electrocardiogram. Because of the high potential for permanent cardiac damage or death from myocardial infarction, caretakers of patients with these symptoms often err on the side of immediately assuming a myocardial infarct is occurring. Nitroglycerin is given to dilate coronary arteries, and heparin or similar drugs may be given to inhibit blood clots that could occlude coronary arteries.

Information gradually emerged in this case, however, that suggested pericarditis as the correct diagnosis. Sharp chest pain that increases with inspiration (because pressure is placed on the heart when the lungs expand) and when lying down (because gravity presses the heart against the pericardial sac wall) are hallmark characteristics of pericarditis. Also, in myocardial infarction, there are changes in the ST segment only of those leads with vectors oriented through the ischemic areas; in pericarditis, ST segment changes are generally observed in most of the leads. The lack of coronary obstruction observed during angiography, combined with the failure of heparin and nitroglycerin to reduce the pain, also argued against cardiac ischemia and infarct in this case. (The decrease in this patient's blood pressure, dizziness, and headache were likely caused by a nitroglycerin-induced decrease in total peripheral resistance.) Finally, the blood concentration of cardiac troponin is generally increased beginning 8 hours after chest pain in a heart attack, but not in a patient with pericarditis.

Treatment of patients with pericarditis is directed toward pain management and addressing the cause of the inflammation. A nonsteroidal anti-inflammatory drug (see Chapter 5) or aspirin is generally prescribed; if the condition is secondary to autoimmune disease, corticosteroid treatment may also be administered (see Chapter 11). The early symptoms—elevated white blood cell count and fever in the present case—suggested the possibility of an infection, and a subsequent throat culture detected the presence of streptococcal bacteria. Therefore, in addition to pain medication, the woman was prescribed a course of antibiotics, after which she returned to good health.

Clinical term: pericarditis

See Chapter 19 for complete, integrative case studies.

CHAPTER 12 TEST QUESTIONS

Answers found in Appendix A.

1. Which of the following contains blood with the lowest oxygen content?
   a. aorta
   b. left atrium
   c. right ventricle
   d. pulmonary veins
   e. systemic arterioles
2. If other factors are equal, which of the following vessels would have the lowest resistance?
   a. length = 1 cm, radius = 1 cm
   b. length = 4 cm, radius = 1 cm
   c. length = 8 cm, radius = 1 cm
   d. length = 1 cm, radius = 2 cm
   e. length = 0.5 cm, radius = 2 cm
3. Which of the following correctly ranks pressures during isovolumetric contraction of a normal cardiac cycle?
   a. left ventricular > aortic > left atrial
   b. aortic > left atrial > left ventricular
   c. left atrial > aortic > left ventricular
   d. aortic > left ventricular > left atrial
   e. left ventricular > left atrial > aortic
4. Considered as a whole, the body's capillaries have
   a. smaller cross-sectional area than the arteries.
   b. less total blood flow than in the veins.
   c. greater total resistance than the arterioles.
   d. slower blood velocity than in the arteries.
   e. greater total blood flow than in the arteries.
5. Which of the following would *not* result in tissue edema?
   a. an increase in the concentration of plasma proteins
   b. an increase in the pore size of systemic capillaries
   c. an increase in venous pressure
   d. blockage of lymph vessels
   e. a decrease in the protein concentration of the plasma
6. Which statement comparing the systemic and pulmonary circuits is *true?*
   a. The blood flow is greater through the systemic.
   b. The blood flow is greater through the pulmonary.
   c. The absolute pressure is higher in the pulmonary.
   d. The blood flow is the same in both.
   e. The pressure gradient is the same in both.
7. What is mainly responsible for the delay between the atrial and ventricular contractions?
   a. the shallow slope of AV node pacemaker potentials
   b. slow action potential conduction velocity of AV node cells
   c. slow action potential conduction velocity along atrial muscle cell membranes
   d. slow action potential conduction in the Purkinje network of the ventricles
   e. greater parasympathetic nerve firing to the ventricles than to the atria
8. Which of the following pressures is closest to the mean arterial blood pressure in a person whose systolic blood pressure is 135 mmHg and pulse pressure is 50 mmHg?
   a. 110 mmHg c. 102 mmHg e. 85 mmHg
   b. 78 mmHg d. 152 mmHg

9. Which of the following would help restore homeostasis in the first few moments after a person's mean arterial pressure became elevated?
   a. a decrease in baroreceptor action potential frequency
   b. a decrease in action potential frequency along parasympathetic neurons to the heart
   c. an increase in action potential frequency along sympathetic neurons to the heart
   d. a decrease in action potential frequency along sympathetic neurons to arterioles
   e. an increase in total peripheral resistance
10. Which is *false* about L-type Ca^{2+} channels in cardiac ventricular muscle cells?
   a. They are open during the plateau of the action potential.
   b. They allow Ca^{2+} entry that triggers sarcoplasmic reticulum Ca^{2+} release.
   c. They are found in the T-tubule membrane.
   d. They open in response to depolarization of the membrane.
   e. They contribute to the pacemaker potential.
11. Which correctly pairs an ECG phase with the cardiac event responsible?
   a. P wave: Depolarization of the ventricles
   b. P wave: Depolarization of the AV node
   c. QRS wave: Depolarization of the ventricles
   d. QRS wave: Repolarization of the ventricles
   e. T wave: Repolarization of the atria
12. When a person engages in strenuous, prolonged exercise,
   a. blood flow to the kidneys is reduced.
   b. cardiac output is reduced.
   c. total peripheral resistance increases.
   d. systolic arterial blood pressure is reduced.
   e. blood flow to the brain is reduced.
13. Hematocrit is increased
   a. when a person has a vitamin B_{12} deficiency.
   b. by an increase in secretion of erythropoietin.
   c. when the number of white blood cells is increased.
   d. by a hemorrhage.
   e. in response to excess oxygen delivery to the kidneys.
14. The principal site of erythrocyte production is
   a. the liver.
   b. the kidneys.
   c. the bone marrow.
   d. the spleen.
   e. the lymph nodes.
15. Which is *not* part of the cascade leading to formation of a blood clot?
   a. contact between the blood and collagen found outside the blood vessels
   b. prothrombin converted to thrombin
   c. formation of a stabilized fibrin mesh
   d. activated platelets
   e. secretion of tissue plasminogen activator (t-PA) by endothelial cells

CHAPTER 12 GENERAL PRINCIPLES ASSESSMENT

Answers found in Appendix A.

1. A general principle of physiology states that *information flow between cells, tissues, and organs is an essential feature of homeostasis and allows for integration of physiological processes.* How is this principle demonstrated by the relationship between the circulatory and endocrine systems?
2. The left AV valve has only two large leaflets, while the right AV valve has three smaller leaflets. It is a general principle of physiology that *structure is a determinant of—and has coevolved with—function.* Although it is unknown why the two valves differ in structure in this way, what difference in the functional demands of the left side of the heart might explain why there is one less valve leaflet than on the right side?
3. Two of the body's important fluid compartments are those of the interstitial fluid and plasma. How does the liver's production of plasma proteins interact with those compartments to illustrate the general principle of physiology, *controlled exchange of materials occurs between compartments and across cellular membranes?*

CHAPTER 12 QUANTITATIVE AND THOUGHT QUESTIONS

Answers found in Appendix A.

1. A person is found to have a hematocrit of 35%. Can you conclude that there is a decreased volume of erythrocytes in the blood? Explain.
2. Which would cause a greater increase in resistance to flow, a doubling of blood viscosity or a halving of tube radius?
3. If all plasma membrane Ca^{2+} channels in contractile cardiac muscle cells were blocked with a drug, what would happen to the muscle's action potentials and contraction?
4. A person with a heart rate of 40 has no P waves but normal QRS complexes on the ECG. What is the explanation?
5. A person has a left ventricular systolic pressure of 180 mmHg and an aortic systolic pressure of 110 mmHg. What is the explanation?
6. A person has a left atrial pressure of 20 mmHg and a left ventricular pressure of 5 mmHg during ventricular filling. What is the explanation?
7. A patient is taking a drug that blocks β-adrenergic receptors. What changes in cardiac function will the drug cause?
8. What is the mean arterial pressure in a person with a systolic pressure of 160 mmHg and a diastolic pressure of 100 mmHg?
9. A person is given a drug that doubles the blood flow to her kidneys but does not change the mean arterial pressure. What must the drug be doing?
10. A blood vessel removed from an experimental animal dilates when exposed to acetylcholine. After the endothelium is scraped from the lumen of the vessel, it no longer dilates in response to this mediator. Explain.
11. A person is accumulating edema throughout the body. Average capillary pressure is 25 mmHg, and lymphatic function is normal. What is the most likely cause of the edema?
12. A person's cardiac output is 7 L/min and mean arterial pressure is 140 mmHg. What is the person's total peripheral resistance?

13. The following data are obtained for an experimental animal before and after administration of a drug.

 Before: Heart rate = 80 beats/min; Stroke volume = 80 mL/beat

 After: Heart rate = 100 beats/min; Stroke volume = 64 mL/beat

 Total peripheral resistance remains unchanged.

 What has the drug done to mean arterial pressure?

14. When the nerves from all the arterial baroreceptors are cut in an experimental animal, what happens to mean arterial pressure?
15. What happens to the hematocrit within several hours after a hemorrhage?
16. If a woman's mean arterial pressure is 85 mmHg and her systolic pressure is 105 mmHg, what is her pulse pressure?
17. When a heart is transplanted into a patient, it is not possible to connect autonomic neurons from the medullary cardiovascular centers to the new heart. Will such a patient be able to increase cardiac output during exercise?
18. The P wave records the spread of depolarization of the atria on a lead I ECG as an upright wave form. Referring to the orientation of the ECG leads in Figure 12.15, what difference in the shape of the P wave might you expect when recording with lead aVR?
19. Given the following cardiac performance data,

 Cardiac output (*CO*) = 5400 mL/min

 Heart rate (*HR*) = 75 beats/min

 End-systolic volume (*ESV*) = 60 mL

 calculate the ejection fraction (*EF*).

20. Which is potentially more dangerous, a small blood clot that forms within a systemic vein, or the same thing occurring in a pulmonary vein?

CHAPTER 12 ANSWERS TO PHYSIOLOGICAL INQUIRIES

Figure 12.1 The hematocrit would be 33% because the red blood cell volume is the difference between total blood volume and plasma volume (4.5 − 3.0 = 1.5 L), and hematocrit is determined by the fraction of whole blood that is red blood cells (1.5 L/4.5 L = 0.33, or 33%).

Figure 12.3 The major change in blood flow would be an increase to certain abdominal organs, notably the stomach and small intestines. This change would provide the additional oxygen and nutrients required to meet the increased metabolic demands of digestion and absorption of the breakdown products of food. Blood flow to the brain and other organs would not be expected to change significantly, but there might be a small increase in blood flow to the skeletal muscles associated with chewing and swallowing. Consequently, the total blood flow in a resting person during and following a meal would be expected to increase.

Figure 12.5 No. The flow on side *B* would be doubled, but still less than that on side *A*. The summed wall area would be the same in both sides. The formula for circumference of a circle is $2\pi r$; so the wall circumference in side *A* would be $2 \times 3.14 \times 2 = 12.56$; for the two tubes on side *B*, it would be $(2 \times 3.14 \times 1) + (2 \times 3.14 \times 1) = 12.56$. However, the total cross section through which flow occurs would be larger in side *A* than in side *B*. The formula for cross-sectional area of a circle is πr^2, so the area of side *A* would be $3.14 \times 2^2 = 12.56$, whereas the summed area of the tubes in side *B* would be $(3.14 \times 1^2) + (3.14 \times 1^2) = 6.28$. Thus, even with two outflow tubes on side *B*, there would be more flow through side *A*

Figure 12.8 A: If this diagram included a systemic portal vessel, the order of structures in the lower box would be: aorta → arteries → arterioles → capillaries → venules → portal vessel → capillaries → venules → veins → vena cava. Examples of portal vessels include the hepatic portal vein, which carries blood from the intestines to the liver (Chapter 15), and the hypothalamo–pituitary portal vessels (Figure 11.13).

Figure 12.12 The rate of ion flux across a membrane depends on both the permeability of the membrane to the ion, and the electrochemical gradient for the ion (see Chapter 6, Section B). During the plateau of the cardiac action potential, the membrane potential is positive and closer to the Ca^{2+} equilibrium potential (which also has a positive value) than it is to the K^+ equilibrium potential (which has a negative value). Thus, Ca^{2+} has a high permeability and a low electrochemical driving force, while K^+ has a lower permeability but a higher electrochemical driving force. These factors offset each other, and the oppositely directed currents end up being nearly the same.

Figure 12.13 Purkinje cell action potentials have a depolarizing pacemaker potential, like node cells (though the slope is much more gradual), and a rapid upstroke and broad plateau, like cardiac muscle cells.

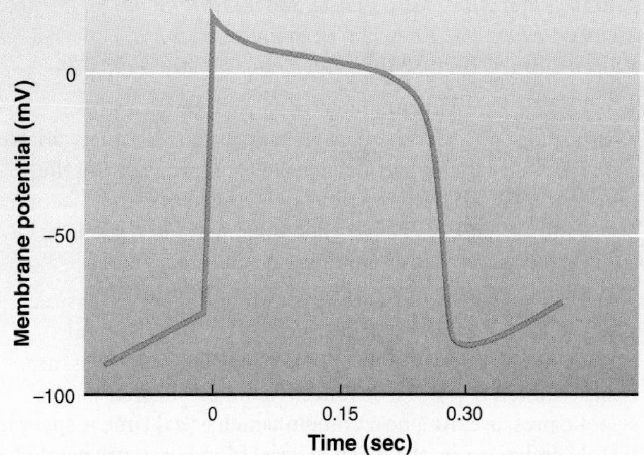

Figure 12.14 Reducing the L-type Ca^{2+} current in AV node cells would decrease the rate at which action potentials are conducted between the atria and ventricles. On the ECG tracing, this would be indicated by a longer interval between the P wave (atrial depolarization) and the QRS wave (ventricular depolarization).

Figure 12.16 A reduction in current through voltage-gated K^+ channels delays the repolarization of ventricular muscle cell action potentials. Thus, the T wave (ventricular repolarization) of the ECG wave is delayed relative to the QRS waves (ventricular depolarization). This fact gives the name to the condition "long QT syndrome."

Figure 12.20 Aortic blood would not have significantly lower-than-normal oxygen levels. Compare this figure with

Figure 12.19; the pressure in the left ventricle is higher than the right throughout the entire cardiac cycle. This pressure gradient would favor blood flow through the hole in the septum only from the left ventricle into the right. Thus, pulmonary artery blood would be higher in oxygen than normal (because blood in the left ventricle has just come from the lungs), but deoxygenated blood would not dilute the blood flowing into the aorta.

Figure 12.21 The patient most likely has a damaged semilunar valve that is stenotic and insufficient. A "whistling" murmur generally results from blood moving forward through a stenotic valve, whereas a lower-pitched "gurgling" murmur occurs when blood leaks backward through a valve that does not close properly. Systole and ejection occur between the two normal heart sounds, whereas diastole and filling occur after the second heart sound. Thus, a whistle between the heart sounds indicates a stenotic semilunar valve, and the gurgle following the second heart sound would arise from an insufficient semilunar valve. It is most likely that a single valve is both stenotic and insufficient in this case. Diagnosis could be confirmed by determining where on the chest wall the sounds were loudest and by diagnostic imaging techniques.

Figure 12.22 The delay between atrial and ventricular contractions is caused by slow propagation of the action potential through the AV node, which is a result of the relatively slow rate that the cells are depolarized by the L-type Ca^{2+} current. Parasympathetic stimulation slows AV node cell propagation further by reducing the current through L-type Ca^{2+} channels, which in turn increases the AV nodal delay.

Figure 12.25 Ejection fraction (EF) = Stroke volume (SV)/End-diastolic volume (EDV); End-systolic volume (ESV) = $EDV - SV$. Based on the graph, under control conditions, the SV is 75 mL and during sympathetic stimulation it is 110 mL. Thus: Control $ESV = 140 - 75 = 65$ mL, and $EF = 75/140 = 53.6\%$; Sympathetic $ESV = 140 - 110 = 30$ mL, and $EF = 110/140 = 78.6\%$.

Figure 12.27 Parasympathetic activity can influence stroke volume indirectly, via the effect on heart rate. If all other variables were held constant (in particular, venous return), slowing the heart rate would allow more time for the ventricles to fill between beats, and the greater end-diastolic volume would result in a larger stroke volume by the Frank–Starling mechanism.

Figure 12.31 At resting heart rate, the time spent in diastole is twice as long as that spent in systole (i.e., $\frac{1}{3}$ of the total cycle is spent near systolic pressures) and the mean pressure is approximately $\frac{1}{3}$ of the distance from diastolic pressure to systolic pressure. At a heart rate in which equal time is spent in systole and diastole, the mean arterial blood pressure would be approximately halfway between those two pressures.

Figure 12.33 If the only change from what is shown in (a) was dilation of tube 3, there would be a net decrease in the resistance to flow out of the pressure reservoir. If the rate of refilling the reservoir remains constant, then the height of fluid (hydrostatic pressure) in the reservoir would decrease to a new steady-state level. Compared to what (b) currently shows, tubes 1, 3, 4, and 5 would all have less flow because their resistance is the same but the pressure gradient would be less, whereas tube 2 would have greater flow because its diameter remained large and its resistance low. An analogous experiment is shown in Figure 12.49.

Figure 12.34 When the arterial pressure is increased, the blood flow through the arteriole will initially increase because the ΔP is higher but the resistance is unchanged (or the resistance might even be lower if the increased pressure stretches it). Within the next few minutes, however, the local oxygen concentration will increase and local metabolite concentrations will decrease, inducing vasoconstriction of the arteriole. This increases resistance, and blood flow will thus decrease toward the level it was prior to the increase in arterial pressure.

Figure 12.40 Venous blood leaving that tissue would be lower in oxygen and nutrients (like glucose) and higher in metabolic wastes (like carbon dioxide).

Figure 12.42 Injecting a liter of crystalloid to replace the lost blood would initially restore the volume (and, therefore, the capillary hydrostatic pressure), but it would dilute the plasma proteins remaining in the bloodstream. As a result, the main force opposing capillary filtration (π_c) would be reduced, causing an increase in net filtration of fluid from the capillaries into the interstitial fluid space. A plasma injection, however, restores the plasma volume as well as the plasma proteins. Thus, the Starling forces remain in balance, and more of the injected volume remains within the vasculature.

Figure 12.46 The increase in sympathetic activity and pumping of the skeletal and inspiratory muscles during vigorous exercise would increase the flow of blood out of the systemic veins and back to the heart, so the percentage of the total blood contained in the veins would decrease compared to the resting levels. At the same time, increased metabolic activity of the skeletal muscles would cause arteriolar dilation and increased blood flow (see Figure 12.34a), so the percentage of total blood in systemic arterioles and capillaries would be greater than at rest.

Figure 12.47 Ingestion of fluids supports the net filtration of fluid at capillaries by transiently elevating vascular pressure (and, therefore, P_c) and reducing the concentration of plasma proteins (and, therefore, π_c). Although reflex mechanisms described in the next section and in Chapter 14 minimize and eventually reverse changes in blood pressure and plasma osmolarity, you could expect a transient increase in interstitial fluid formation and lymph flow after ingesting extra fluids.

Table 12.6 The relative total resistance of the two circuits can be calculated using the equation, $MAP = CO \times TPR$. Rearranging, $TPR = MAP/CO$. Thus, for the systemic circuit, the total resistance = 93/5 = 18.6, while for the pulmonary circuit, $R = 15/5 = 3$. Relative to the total pulmonary resistance, then, the systemic resistance is 18.6/3 = 6.2 times greater.

Figure 12.53 There is a transient reduction in pressure at the baroreceptors when you first stand up. This occurs because gravity has a significant impact on blood flow. While lying down, the effect of gravity is minimal because baroreceptors and the rest of the vasculature are basically level with the heart. Upon standing, gravity resists the return of blood from below the heart (where the majority of the vascular volume exists). This transiently reduces cardiac output and, thus, blood pressure. Section E of this chapter provides a detailed description of this phenomenon and explains how the body compensates for the effects of gravity.

Figure 12.54 Because the normal resting value is in the center of the steepest part of the curve, baroreceptor action potential frequency is maximally sensitive to small changes in mean arterial pressure in either direction, and that sensitivity can be maintained with minor upward or downward changes in the homeostatic set point.

Table 12.7 The hematocrit is the fraction of the total blood volume that is made up of erythrocytes. Thus, the normal hematocrit in this case was $2300/5000 \times 100 = 46\%$.

Immediately after the hemorrhage, it was 1840/4000 × 100 = 46%; 18 h later, it was 1840/4900 × 100 = 37%. The hemorrhage itself did not change hematocrit because erythrocytes and plasma were lost in equal proportions. However, over the next 18 h, there was a net shift of interstitial fluid into the blood plasma due to a reduction in P_c. Because this occurs faster than does the production of new red blood cells, this "autotransfusion" resulted in a dilution of the remaining erythrocytes in the bloodstream. In the days and weeks that follow, increased erythropoietin will stimulate the replacement of the lost erythrocytes, and the lost ECF volume will be replaced by ingestion and decreased urine output.

Figure 12.61 Exercising in extreme heat can result in fainting due to an inability to maintain sufficient blood flow to the brain. This occurs because maintaining homeostasis of body temperature places demands on the cardiovascular system beyond those of exercising muscles alone. Sweat glands secrete fluid from the plasma onto the skin surface to facilitate evaporative cooling, and arterioles to the skin dilate, directing blood toward the surface for radiant cooling. With reduced blood volume and large amounts of blood flowing to the skeletal muscles and skin, cardiac output may not be sufficient to maintain flow to the brain and other tissues at adequate levels.

Figure 12.65 The normal end-diastolic volume is 135 mL, and the graph shows that the stroke volume is approximately 40 mL at this volume for the failing heart. The ejection fraction would thus be approximately 40/135 = 29.6%. This is significantly lower than the normal heart (70/135 = 51.8%).

Figure 12.76 Blood clotting would be inhibited significantly more without factor VII. Normal activation of blood clotting begins with activation of factor VII, which not only initiates the extrinsic pathway but also sequentially activates the intrinsic pathway when thrombin activates factors XI, VIII, and V. This sequence would not be disrupted by the absence of factor XII. Conversely, in the absence of factor VII, the extrinsic pathway cannot be activated at all.

Figure 12.77 As described in Chapter 15, production by gut bacteria can be a significant source of vitamin K when dietary intake is low. Antibiotic treatment kills not only harmful bacteria but also the beneficial gut bacteria that produce vitamin K. It is thus possible for a prolonged course of antibiotics to cause vitamin K deficiency and thus a deficiency of clotting factor synthesis.

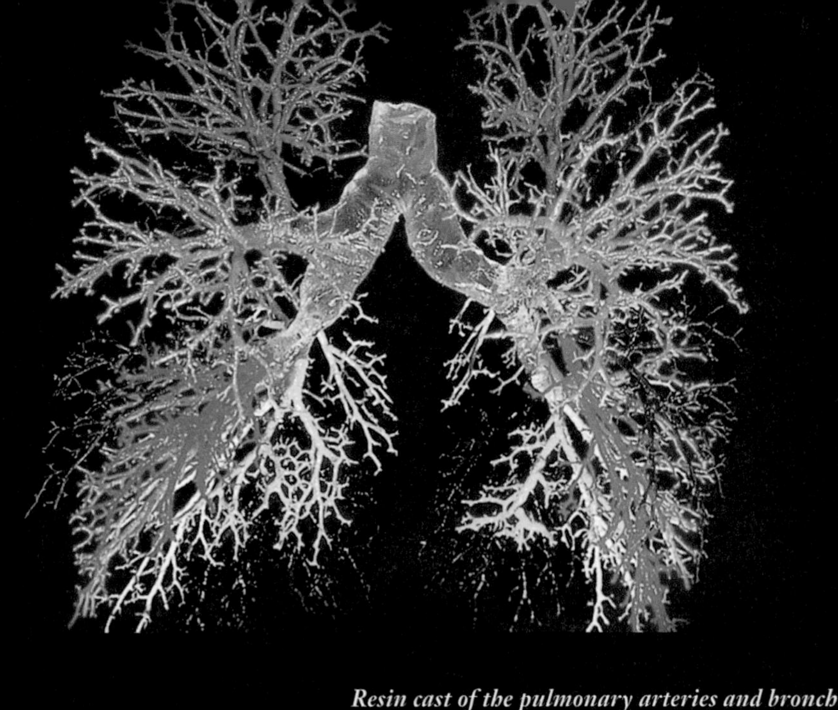

Resin cast of the pulmonary arteries and bronchi.

13 Respiratory Physiology

In the previous chapter, you learned that the major role of the cardiovascular system is to deliver nutrients and oxygen to the tissues and to remove carbon dioxide and other waste products of metabolism. In this chapter, you will learn how the respiratory system is intimately associated with the cardiovascular system and is responsible for taking up oxygen from the environment and delivering it to the blood, as well as eliminating carbon dioxide from the blood.

Respiration can have two quite different meanings: (1) utilization of oxygen in the metabolism of organic molecules by cells, often termed *internal* or *cellular respiration*, as described in Chapter 3; and (2) the exchange of oxygen and carbon dioxide between an organism and the external environment, often called *pulmonary physiology*. The adjective pulmonary refers to the lungs. The second meaning is the subject of this chapter. Human cells obtain most of their energy from chemical reactions involving oxygen. In addition, cells must be able to eliminate carbon dioxide, the major end product of oxidative metabolism. A unicellular organism can exchange oxygen and carbon dioxide directly with the external environment, but this is obviously impossible for most cells of a complex organism like a human being. Therefore, the evolution of large animals required the development of specialized structures for the entire animal to exchange oxygen and carbon dioxide with the external environment. In humans and other mammals, the respiratory system includes the oral and nasal cavities, the lungs, the series of tubes leading to the lungs, and the chest structures responsible for moving air into and out of the lungs during breathing.

As you read about the structure, function, and control of the respiratory system, you will encounter numerous examples of the general principles of physiology that were outlined in Chapter 1. The principle that physiological processes are governed by the laws of chemistry and physics is demonstrated when describing the binding of oxygen and carbon dioxide to hemoglobin, the handling by the blood of acid produced by metabolism, and the factors that control the inflation and deflation of the lungs. The diffusion of gases is an excellent example of the general principle of physiology that states that controlled exchange of materials occurs between compartments and across cellular membranes. You will learn how the functional units of the lung, the alveoli, are elegant examples of the general principle of physiology that structure is a determinant of—and has coevolved with—function. Finally, the central nervous system control of respiration is yet another example of how homeostasis is essential for health and survival.

13.1 Organization of the Respiratory System

There are two lungs, the right and left, each divided into lobes. The lungs consist mainly of tiny air-containing sacs called **alveoli** (singular, **alveolus**), which number approximately 300 million in an adult. The alveoli are the sites of gas exchange with the blood. The **airways** are the tubes that air flows through from the external environment to the alveoli and back.

Inspiration (inhalation) is the movement of air from the external environment through the airways into the alveoli during breathing. **Expiration** (exhalation) is movement in the opposite direction. An inspiration and expiration constitute a **respiratory cycle.** During the entire respiratory cycle, the right ventricle of the heart pumps blood through the pulmonary arteries and arterioles and into the capillaries surrounding each alveolus. In a healthy adult at rest, approximately 4 L of fresh air enters and leaves the alveoli per minute, while 5 L of blood, the cardiac output, flows through the pulmonary capillaries. During heavy exercise, the airflow can increase 20-fold, and the blood flow five- to sixfold.

The Airways and Blood Vessels

During inspiration, air passes through the nose or the mouth (or both) into the **pharynx,** a passage common to both air and food (**Figure 13.1**). The pharynx branches into two tubes: the esophagus, through which food passes to the stomach, and the **larynx,** which is part of the airways. The larynx houses the **vocal cords,** two folds of elastic tissue stretched horizontally across its lumen. The flow of air past the vocal cords causes them to vibrate, producing sounds. The nose, mouth, pharynx, and larynx are collectively termed the **upper airways.**

The larynx opens into a long tube, the **trachea,** which in turn branches into two **bronchi** (singular, **bronchus**),

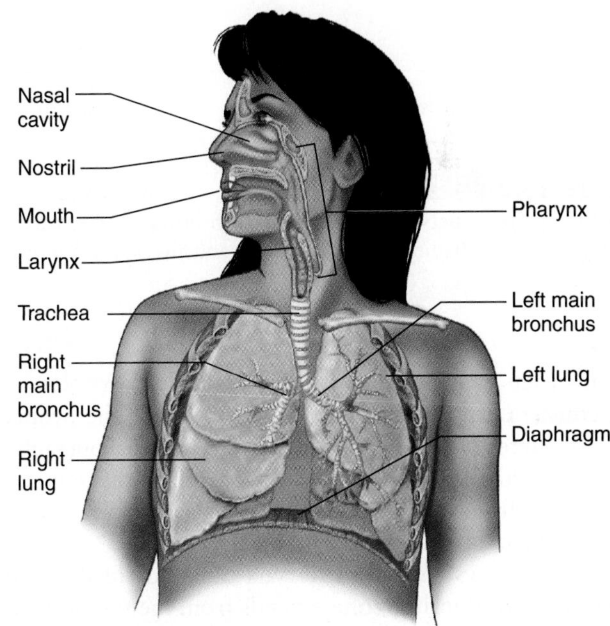

Figure 13.1 APIR Organization of the respiratory system. The ribs have been removed in front, and the lungs are shown in a way that makes visible the major airways within them. *Not shown:* The pharynx continues posteriorly to the esophagus.

one of which enters each lung. Within the lungs, there are more than 20 generations of branchings, each resulting in narrower, shorter, and more numerous tubes; their names are summarized in **Figure 13.2.** The walls of the trachea and bronchi contain rings of cartilage, which give them their cylindrical shape and support them. The first airway branches that no longer contain cartilage are termed **bronchioles,** which branch into the smaller, **terminal bronchioles.** Alveoli first begin to appear attached to the walls of the **respiratory bronchioles.** The number of alveoli increases in the alveolar ducts (see Figure 13.2), and the

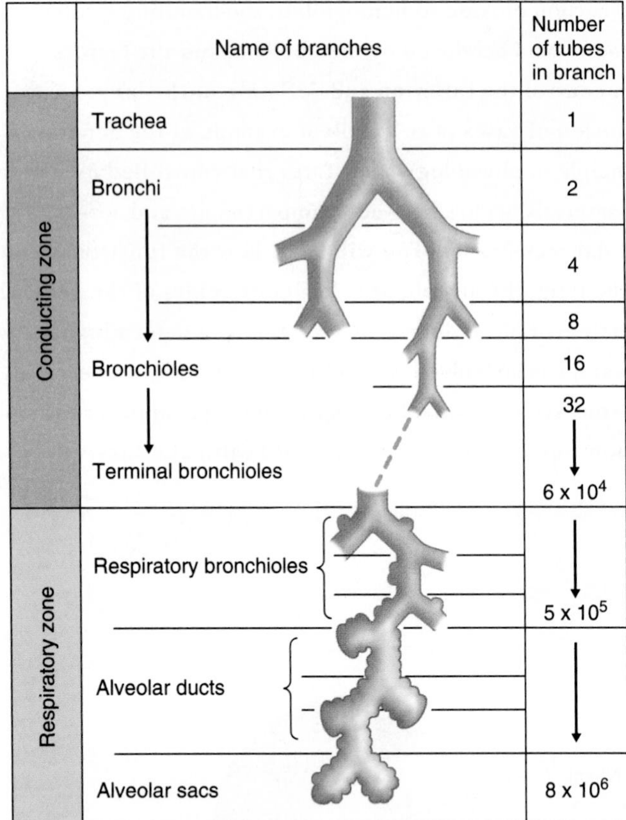

Figure 13.2 APIR Airway branching. Asymmetries in branching patterns between the right and left bronchial trees are not depicted. The diameters of the airways and alveoli are not drawn to scale.

airways then end in grapelike clusters called **alveolar sacs** that consist entirely of alveoli (**Figure 13.3**). The bronchioles are surrounded by smooth muscle, which contracts or relaxes to alter bronchiolar radius, in much the same way that the radius of small blood vessels (arterioles) is controlled, as you learned in Chapter 12.

The airways beyond the larynx can be divided into two zones. The **conducting zone** extends from the top of the trachea to the beginning of the respiratory bronchioles. This zone contains no alveoli and does not exchange gases with the blood. The **respiratory zone** extends from the respiratory bronchioles down. This zone contains alveoli and is the region where gases exchange with the blood.

The oral and nasal cavities trap airborne particles in nasal hairs and mucus. The epithelial surfaces of the airways, to the end of the respiratory bronchioles, contain cilia that constantly beat upward toward the pharynx. They also contain glands and individual epithelial cells that secrete mucus, and macrophages which can phagocytize inhaled pathogens. Particulate matter, such as dust contained in the inspired air, sticks to the mucus, which is continuously and slowly moved by the cilia to the pharynx and then swallowed. This so-called mucous escalator is important in keeping the lungs clear of particulate matter and the many bacteria that enter the body on dust particles. Ciliary activity and number can be decreased by many noxious agents, including the smoke from chronic cigarette smoking. This is why smokers often cough up mucus that the cilia would normally have cleared.

The airway epithelium also secretes a watery fluid upon which the mucus can ride freely. The production of this fluid is impaired in the disease ***cystic fibrosis*** (***CF***), the most common lethal genetic disease among Caucasians, in which the mucous layer becomes thick and dehydrated, obstructing the airways. CF is caused by an autosomal recessive mutation in an epithelial chloride channel called the **CF transmembrane conductance regulator** (**CFTR**) protein. This results in problems with salt and water movement across cell membranes, which leads to thickened secretions and a high incidence of lung infection. It is usually treated with (1) therapy to improve clearance of mucus from the lung and (2) the aggressive use of antibiotics to prevent pneumonia. Although the treatment of CF has improved over the past few decades, median life expectancy is still only about 35 years. Ultimately, lung transplantation may be required. In addition to the lungs, other organs are usually affected—particularly in the secretory components of the gastrointestinal tract (for example, the exocrine pancreas).

Constriction of bronchioles in response to irritation helps to prevent particulate matter and irritants from entering the sites of gas exchange. Another protective mechanism against infection is provided by cells called macrophages that are present in the airways and alveoli. These cells engulf and destroy inhaled particles and bacteria that have reached the alveoli. Macrophages, like the ciliated epithelium of the airways, are injured by cigarette smoke and air pollutants. The physiology of the conducting zone is summarized in **Table 13.1**.

The pulmonary blood vessels generally accompany the airways and also undergo numerous branchings. The smallest of these vessels branch into networks of capillaries that richly supply the alveoli (see Figure 13.3). As you learned in Chapter 12, the pulmonary circulation has a very low resistance to the flow of blood compared to the systemic circulation, and for this reason the pressures within all pulmonary blood vessels are low. This is an important adaptation that minimizes accumulation of fluid in the interstitial spaces of the lungs (see Figure 12.42 for a description of Starling forces and the movement of fluid across capillaries).

Site of Gas Exchange: The Alveoli

The alveoli are tiny, hollow sacs whose open ends are continuous with the lumens of the airways (**Figure 13.4a**). Typically, a single alveolar wall separates the air in two adjacent alveoli. Most of the air-facing surfaces of the wall are lined by a continuous layer, one cell thick, of flat epithelial cells termed **type I alveolar cells.** Interspersed between these cells are thicker, specialized cells termed **type II alveolar cells** (**Figure 13.4b**) that produce a detergent-like substance called surfactant.

The alveolar walls contain capillaries and a very small interstitial space, which consists of interstitial fluid and a loose meshwork of connective tissue (see Figure 13.4b). In many places, the interstitial space is absent altogether, and the basement membranes of the alveolar-surface epithelium and

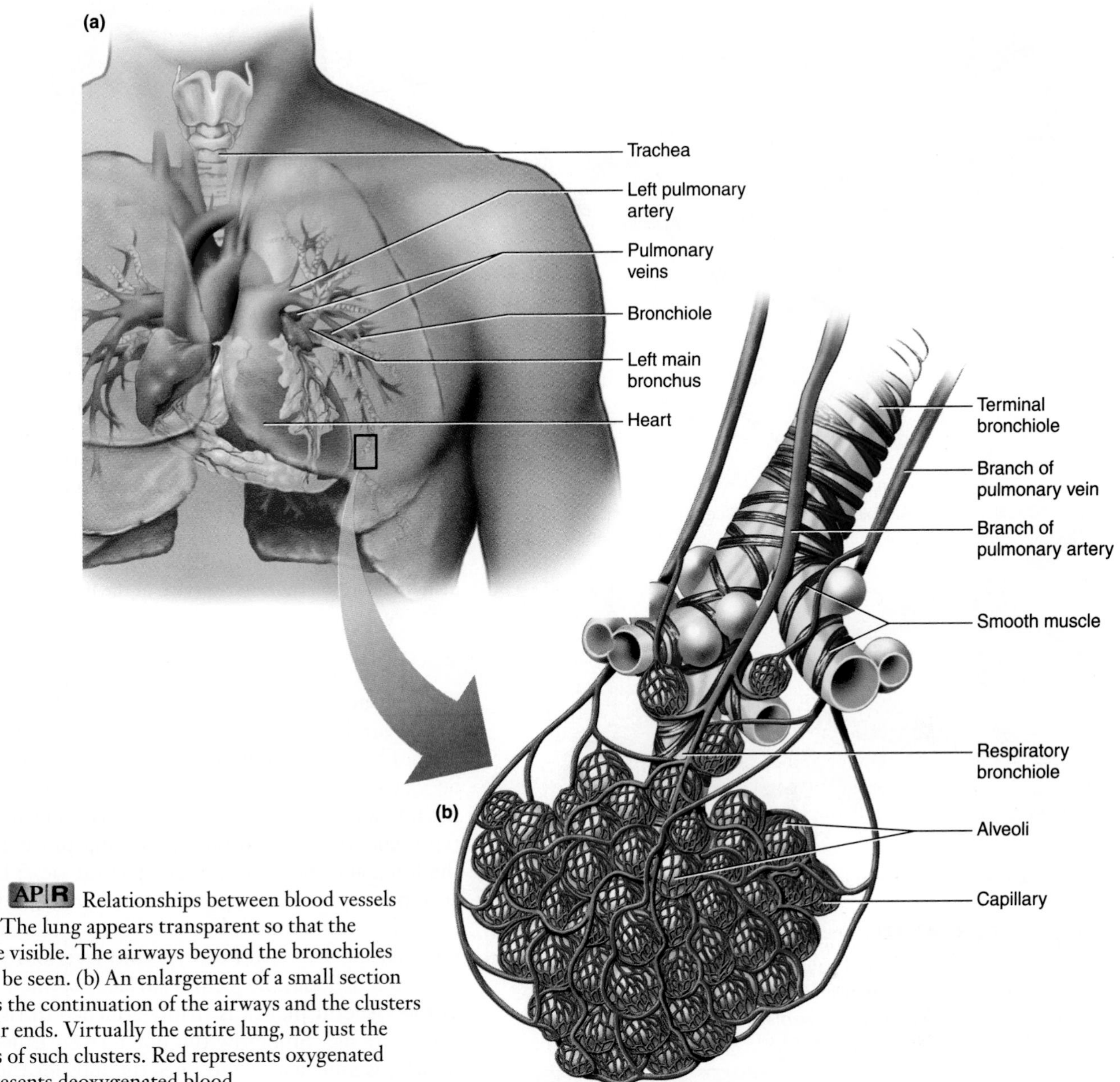

Figure 13.3 APIR Relationships between blood vessels and airways. (a) The lung appears transparent so that the relationships are visible. The airways beyond the bronchioles are too small to be seen. (b) An enlargement of a small section of part (a) shows the continuation of the airways and the clusters of alveoli at their ends. Virtually the entire lung, not just the surface, consists of such clusters. Red represents oxygenated blood; blue represents deoxygenated blood.

the capillary-wall endothelium fuse. Thus, the blood within an alveolar-wall capillary is separated from the air within the alveolus by an extremely thin barrier (0.2 μm, compared with the 7 μm diameter of an average red blood cell). The total surface area of alveoli in contact with capillaries is roughly the size of a tennis court. This extensive area and the thinness of the barrier permit the rapid exchange of large quantities of oxygen and carbon dioxide by diffusion. These are excellent examples of two of the general principles of physiology—that physiological processes require the transfer and balance of matter (in this case, oxygen and carbon dioxide) and energy between compartments, and that structure (in this case, the thinness of the diffusion barrier and the enormous surface area for gas exchange) is a determinant of—and has coevolved with—function (the transfer of oxygen and carbon dioxide between the alveolar air and the blood in the pulmonary capillaries).

In some of the alveolar walls, pores permit the flow of air between alveoli. This route can be very important when the airway leading to an alveolus is occluded by disease, because some air can still enter the alveolus by way of the pores between it and adjacent alveoli.

TABLE 13.1 Functions of the Conducting Zone of the Airways
Provides a low-resistance pathway for airflow. Resistance is physiologically regulated by changes in contraction of bronchiolar smooth muscle and by physical forces acting upon the airways.
Defends against microbes, toxic chemicals, and other foreign matter. Cilia, mucus, and macrophages perform this function.
Warms and moistens the air.
Phonates (vocal cords).

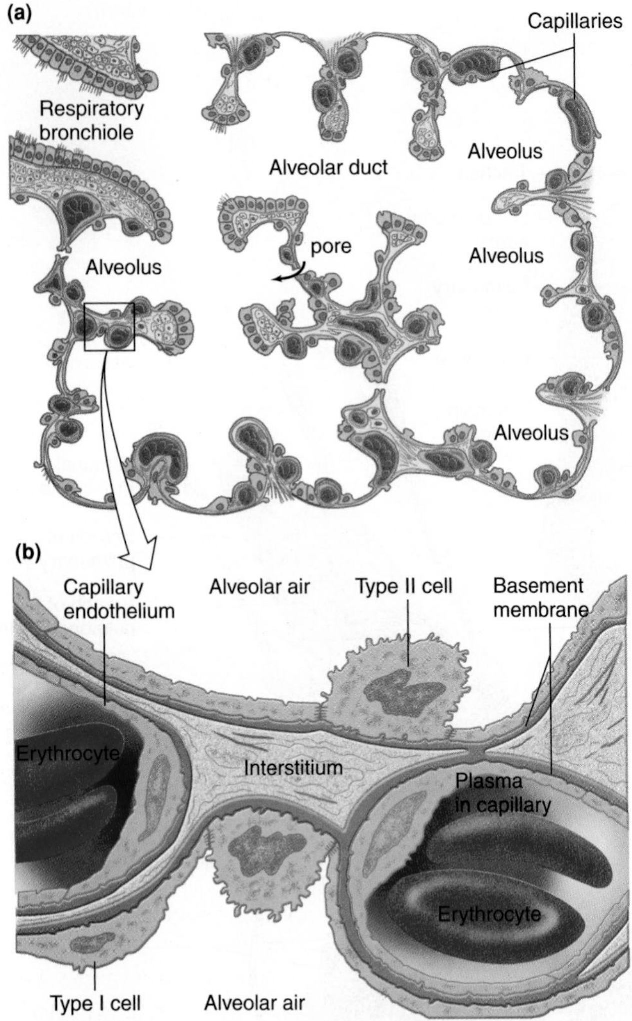

Figure 13.4 APIR (a) Cross section through an area of the respiratory zone. There are 18 alveoli in this figure, only four of which are labeled. Two often share a common wall. (b) Schematic enlargement of a portion of an alveolar wall. (a) From R. O. Greep and L. Weiss, *Histology*, 3rd ed., McGraw-Hill, New York. (b) Adapted from Gong and Drage.

PHYSIOLOGICAL INQUIRY

- What consequences would result if inflammation caused a buildup of fluid in the alveoli and interstitial spaces?

Answer can be found at end of chapter.

Relation of the Lungs to the Thoracic (Chest) Wall

The lungs, like the heart, are situated in the **thorax,** the compartment of the body between the neck and abdomen. *Thorax* and *chest* are synonyms. The thorax is a closed compartment bounded at the neck by muscles and connective tissue and completely separated from the abdomen by a large, dome-shaped sheet of skeletal muscle called the **diaphragm** (see Figure 13.1). The wall of the thorax is formed by the spinal column, the ribs, the breastbone (sternum), and several groups of muscles that run between the ribs that are collectively called the **intercostal muscles.** The thoracic wall also contains large amounts of connective tissue with elastic properties.

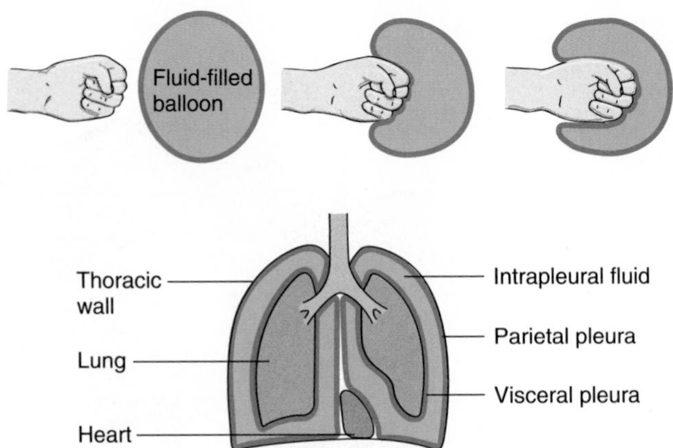

Figure 13.5 APIR Relationship of lungs, pleura, and thoracic wall, shown as analogous to pushing a fist into a fluid-filled balloon. Note that there is no communication between the right and left intrapleural fluids. For purposes of illustration, the volume of intrapleural fluid is greatly exaggerated. It normally consists of an extremely thin layer of fluid between the pleural membrane lining the inner surface of the thoracic wall (the parietal pleura) and the membrane lining the outer surface of the lungs (the visceral pleura).

Each lung is surrounded by a completely closed sac, the **pleural sac,** consisting of a thin sheet of cells called **pleura.** The pleural sac of one lung is separate from that of the other lung. The relationship between a lung and its pleural sac can be visualized by imagining what happens when you push a fist into a fluid-filled balloon. The arm shown in **Figure 13.5** represents the major bronchus leading to the lung, the fist is the lung, and the balloon is the pleural sac. The fist becomes coated by one surface of the balloon. In addition, the balloon is pushed back upon itself so that its opposite surfaces lie close together but are separated by a thin layer of fluid. Unlike the hand and balloon, the pleural surface coating the lung known as the **visceral pleura** is firmly attached to the lung by connective tissue. Similarly, the outer layer, called the **parietal pleura,** is attached to and lines the interior thoracic wall and diaphragm. The two layers of pleura in each sac are very close but not attached to each other. Rather, they are separated by an extremely thin layer of **intrapleural fluid,** the total volume of which is only a few milliliters. The intrapleural fluid totally surrounds the lungs and lubricates the pleural surfaces so that they can slide over each other during breathing. As we will see in the next section, changes in the hydrostatic pressure of the intrapleural fluid—the **intrapleural pressure** (P_{ip})—cause the lungs and thoracic wall to move in and out together during normal breathing.

A way to visualize the apposition of the two pleural surfaces is to put a drop of water between two glass microscope slides. The two slides can easily slide over each other but are very difficult to pull apart.

13.2 Ventilation and Lung Mechanics

This section highlights that physiological processes are dictated by the laws of chemistry and physics, one of the general principles of physiology described in Chapter 1.

Understanding the forces that control the inflation and deflation of the lung and the flow of air between the lung and the environment requires some knowledge of several fundamental physical laws. Furthermore, understanding of these forces is necessary to appreciate several pathophysiological events, such as the collapse of a lung due to an air leak into the chest cavity. We begin with an overview of these physical processes and the steps involved in respiration (**Figure 13.6**) before examining each step in detail.

Ventilation is defined as the exchange of air between the atmosphere and alveoli. Like blood, air moves by *bulk flow* from a region of high pressure to one of low pressure. Bulk flow can be described by the equation

$$F = \Delta P/R \qquad \text{(13–1)}$$

Stated differently, flow (F) is proportional to the pressure difference (ΔP) between two points and inversely proportional to the resistance (R). (Notice that this equation is the same one used to describe the movement of blood through blood vessels, described in Chapter 12.) For airflow into or out of the lungs, the relevant pressures are the gas pressure in the alveoli—the **alveolar pressure (P_{alv})**—and the gas pressure at the nose and mouth, normally **atmospheric pressure (P_{atm})**, which is the pressure of the air surrounding the body:

$$F = (P_{alv} - P_{atm})/R \qquad \text{(13–2)}$$

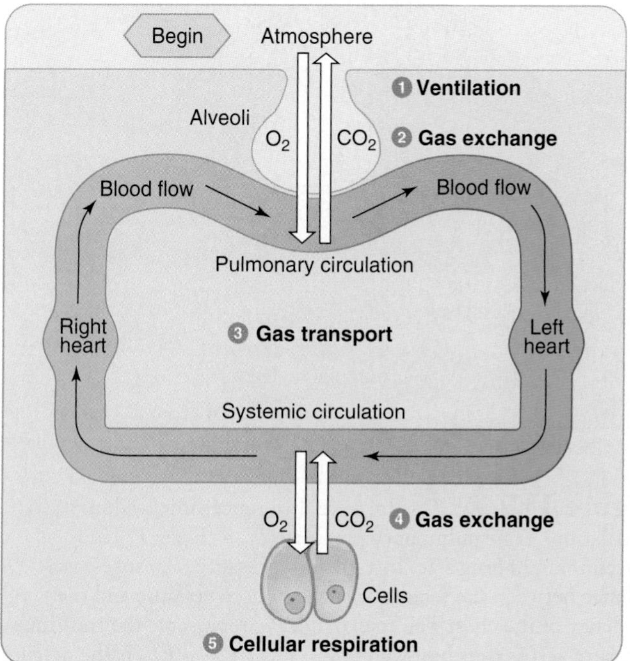

Figure 13.6 The steps of respiration.

A very important point must be made here: All pressures in the respiratory system, as in the cardiovascular system, are given *relative to atmospheric pressure*, which is 760 mmHg at sea level but which decreases in proportion to an increase in altitude. For example, the alveolar pressure between breaths is said to be 0 mmHg, which means that it is the same as atmospheric pressure at any given altitude. From equation 13–2, when there is no airflow, $F = 0$; therefore, $P_{alv} - P_{atm} = 0$, and $P_{alv} = P_{atm}$.

During ventilation, air moves into and out of the lungs because the alveolar pressure is alternately less than and greater than atmospheric pressure (**Figure 13.7**). In accordance with equation 13.2 describing airflow, a negative value reflects an inward-directed pressure gradient and a positive value indicates an outward-directed gradient. Thus, when P_{alv} is less than P_{atm}, $P_{alv} - P_{atm}$ is negative and airflow is inward (inspiration). When P_{alv} is greater than P_{atm}, $P_{alv} - P_{atm}$ is positive and airflow is outward (expiration). These alveolar pressure changes are caused, as we will see, by changes in the dimensions of the chest wall and lungs.

To understand how a change in lung dimensions causes a change in alveolar pressure, you need to learn one more basic physical principle described by **Boyle's law,** which is represented by the equation $P_1V_1 = P_2V_2$ (**Figure 13.8**). At constant temperature, the relationship between the pressure (P) exerted by a fixed number of gas molecules and the volume (V) of their container is as follows: An increase in the volume of the container decreases the pressure of the gas, whereas a decrease in the container volume increases the pressure. In other words, in a closed system, the pressure of a gas and the volume of its container are inversely proportional.

It is essential to recognize the correct sequence of events that determine the inspiration and then expiration of a breath. During inspiration and expiration, the volume of the "container"—the lungs—is made to change, and these changes then cause, by Boyle's law, the alveolar pressure changes that drive airflow into or out of the lungs. Our descriptions of ventilation must focus, therefore, on how the changes in lung dimensions are brought about.

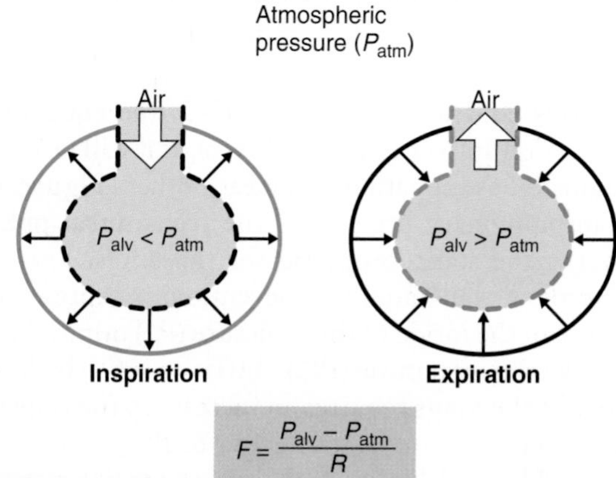

Figure 13.7 APIR Relationships required for ventilation. When the alveolar pressure (P_{alv}) is less than atmospheric pressure (P_{atm}), air enters the lungs. Flow (F) is directly proportional to the pressure difference ($P_{alv} - P_{atm}$) and inversely proportional to airway resistance (R). Black lines show lung's position at beginning of inspiration or expiration, and blue lines show position at end of inspiration or expiration.

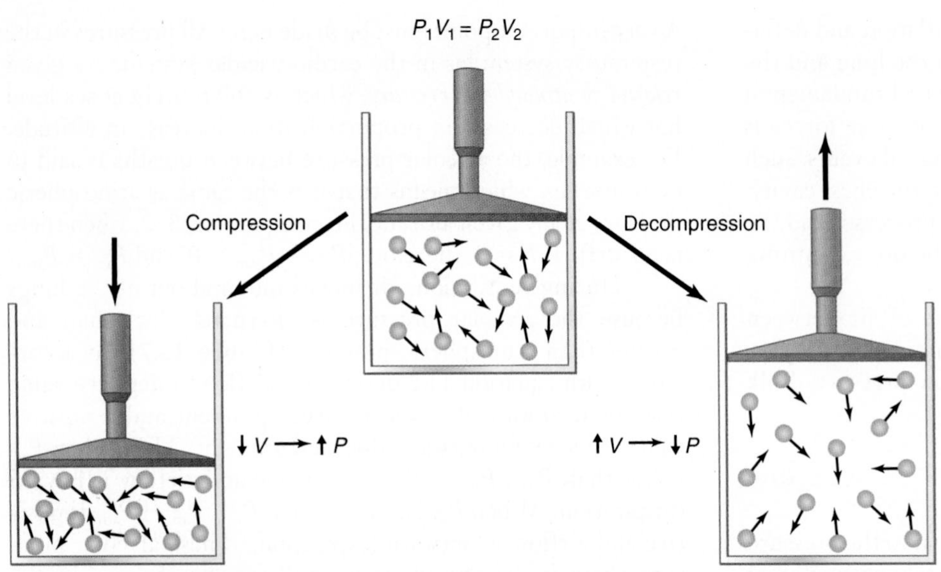

Figure 13.8 APIR Boyle's law: The pressure exerted by a constant number of gas molecules (at a constant temperature) is inversely proportional to the volume of the container. As the container is compressed, the pressure in the container increases. When the container is decompressed, the pressure inside decreases.

There are no muscles attached to the lung surface to pull the lungs open or push them shut. Rather, the lungs are passive elastic structures—like balloons—and their volume, therefore, depends on other factors. The first of these is the difference in pressure between the inside and outside of the lung, termed the **transpulmonary pressure (P_{tp})**. The second is how stretchable the lungs are, which determines how much they expand for a given change in P_{tp}. The rest of this section and the next three sections focus on transpulmonary pressure; stretchability will be discussed later in the section on lung compliance.

The pressure inside the lungs is the air pressure inside the alveoli (P_{alv}), and the pressure outside the lungs is the pressure of the intrapleural fluid surrounding the lungs (P_{ip}). Thus,

$$\text{Transpulmonary pressure} = P_{alv} - P_{ip} \qquad \textbf{(13–3)}$$
$$P_{tp} = P_{alv} - P_{ip}$$

Compare this equation to equation 13–2 (the equation that describes airflow into or out of the lungs), as it will be essential to distinguish these equations from each other (**Figure 13.9**).

Transpulmonary pressure is the **transmural pressure** that governs the static properties of the lungs. *Transmural* means "across a wall" and, by convention, is represented by the pressure in the inside of the structure (P_{in}) minus the pressure outside the structure (P_{out}). Inflation of a balloonlike structure like the lungs requires an increase in the transmural pressure such that P_{in} increases relative to P_{out}.

Table 13.2 and Figure 13.9 show the major transmural pressures of the respiratory system. The transmural pressure acting on the lungs (P_{tp}) is $P_{alv} - P_{ip}$ and, on the chest wall, (P_{cw}) is $P_{ip} - P_{atm}$. The muscles of the chest wall contract and cause the chest wall to expand during inspiration; simultaneously, the diaphragm contracts downward, further enlarging the thoracic cavity. As the volume of the thoracic cavity expands, P_{ip} decreases. P_{tp} becomes more positive as a result and the lungs expand. As this occurs, P_{alv} becomes more negative compared to P_{atm} (due to Boyle's law), and air flows inward (inspiration, equation 13–2). Therefore, the transmural pressure across the lungs (P_{tp}) is increased to fill them with air by actively decreasing the pressure surrounding the lungs (P_{ip}) relative to the pressure inside the lungs (P_{alv}). When the respiratory muscles relax, elastic recoil of the lungs drives passive expiration back to the starting point.

How Is a Stable Balance Achieved Between Breaths?

Figure 13.10 illustrates the transmural pressures of the respiratory system at rest—that is, at the end of an unforced expiration when the respiratory muscles are relaxed and there is no airflow. By definition, if there is no airflow, P_{alv} must equal P_{atm} (see equation 13–2). Because the lungs always have air in them, the transmural pressure of the lungs (P_{tp}) must always be positive; therefore, $P_{alv} > P_{ip}$. At rest, when there is no airflow and $P_{alv} = 0$, P_{ip} must be negative, providing the force that keeps the lungs open and the chest wall in.

What are the forces that cause P_{ip} to be negative? The first, the **elastic recoil** of the lungs, is defined as the tendency of an elastic structure to oppose stretching or distortion. Even

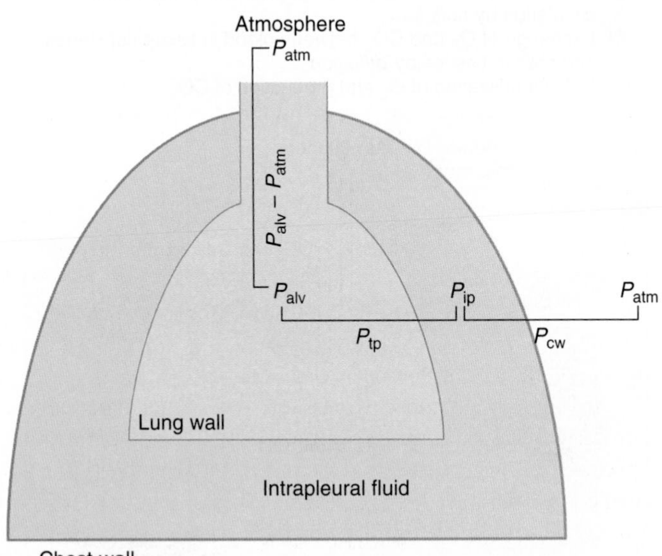

Figure 13.9 APIR Pressure differences involved in ventilation. Transpulmonary pressure ($P_{tp} = P_{alv} - P_{ip}$) is a determinant of lung size. Intrapleural pressure (P_{ip}) at rest is a balance between the tendency of the lung to collapse and the tendency of the chest wall to expand. P_{cw} represents the transmural pressure across the chest wall ($P_{ip} - P_{atm}$). $P_{alv} - P_{atm}$ is the driving pressure gradient for airflow into and out of the lungs. (The volume of intrapleural fluid is greatly exaggerated for visual clarity.)

TABLE 13.2 Two Important Transmural Pressures of the Respiratory System			
Transmural Pressure	**$P_{in} - P_{out}$***	**Value at Rest**	**Explanatory Notes**
Transpulmonary (P_{tp})	$P_{alv} - P_{ip}$	$0 - [-4] = 4$ mmHg	Pressure difference holding lungs open (opposes inward elastic recoil of the lung)
Chest wall (P_{cw})	$P_{ip} - P_{atm}$	$-4 - 0 = -4$ mmHg	Pressure difference holding chest wall in (opposes outward elastic recoil of the chest wall)

*P_{in} is pressure inside the structure, and P_{out} is pressure surrounding the structure.

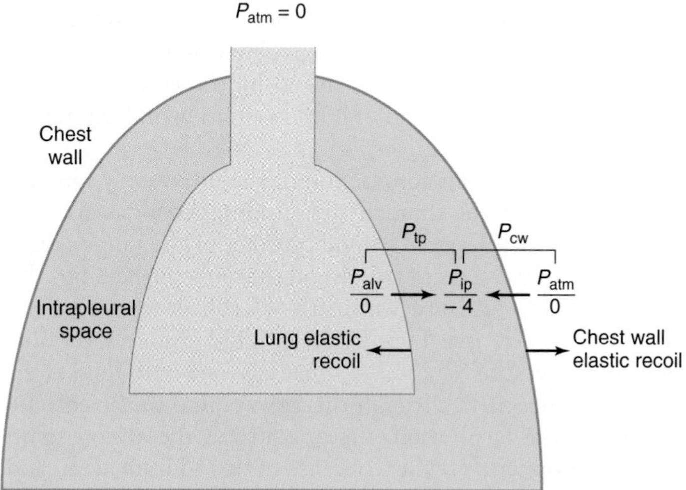

Figure 13.10 AP|R Alveolar (P_{alv}), intrapleural (P_{ip}), transpulmonary (P_{tp}), and trans-chest-wall (P_{cw}) pressures (mmHg) at the end of an unforced expiration—that is, between breaths when there is no airflow. The transpulmonary pressure ($P_{alv} - P_{ip}$) exactly opposes the elastic recoil of the lung, and the lung volume remains stable. Similarly, trans-chest-wall pressure ($P_{ip} - P_{atm}$) is balanced by the outward elastic recoil of the chest wall. Notice that the transmural pressure is the pressure inside the wall minus the pressure outside the wall. (The volume of intrapleural fluid is greatly exaggerated for clarity.)

at rest, the lungs contain air, and their natural tendency is to collapse because of elastic recoil. The lungs are held open by the positive P_{tp}, which, at rest, exactly opposes elastic recoil. The chest wall also has elastic recoil, and, at rest, its natural tendency is to expand.

At rest, all of these transmural pressures balance each other out. It is clear that the subatmospheric (negative) intrapleural pressure (P_{ip}) is the essential factor keeping the lungs partially expanded between breaths. An extremely important question is, "What is the reason for a subatmospheric ('negative') P_{ip}?"

As the lungs tend to collapse and the thoracic wall tends to expand, they move ever so slightly away from each other. This causes an infinitesimal enlargement of the fluid-filled intrapleural space between them. But fluid cannot expand the way air can, so even this tiny enlargement of the intrapleural space—so small that the pleural surfaces still remain in contact with each other—decreases the intrapleural pressure to below atmospheric pressure. In this way, the elastic recoil of both the lungs and chest wall creates the subatmospheric intrapleural pressure that keeps them from moving apart more than a very tiny amount. Again, imagine trying to pull apart two glass slides that have a drop of water between them. The fluid pressure generated between the slides will be lower than atmospheric pressure.

The importance of the transpulmonary pressure in achieving this stable balance can be seen when, during surgery or trauma, the chest wall is pierced without damaging the lung. Atmospheric air enters the intrapleural space through the wound, a phenomenon called ***pneumothorax,*** and the intrapleural pressure increases from −4 mmHg to 0 mmHg. That is, P_{ip} increases from 4 mmHg lower than P_{atm} to a P_{ip} value equal to P_{atm}. The transpulmonary pressure acting to hold the lung open is thus eliminated, and the lung collapses (**Figure 13.11**).

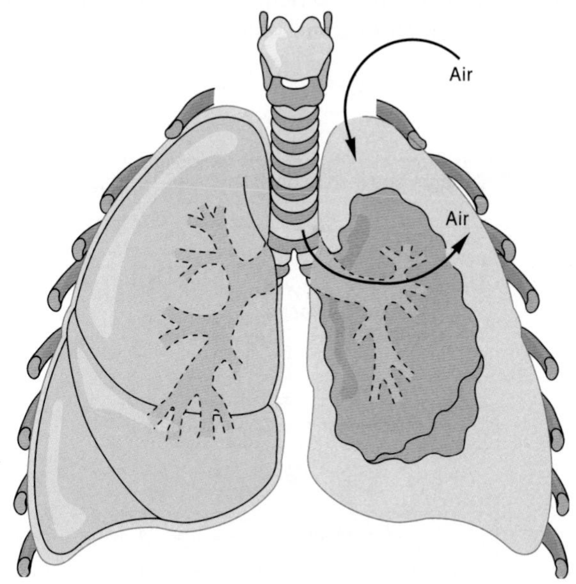

Figure 13.11 Pneumothorax. The lung collapses as air enters from the pleural cavity either from inside the lung or from the atmosphere through the thoracic wall. The combination of lung elastic recoil and surface tension causes collapse of the lung when pleural and airway pressures equalize.

PHYSIOLOGICAL INQUIRY

- How can a collapsed lung be re-expanded in a patient with a pneumothorax? (*Hint:* What changes in P_{ip} and P_{tp} would be needed to re-expand the lung?)

Answer can be found at end of chapter.

At the same time, the chest wall moves outward because its elastic recoil is also no longer opposed. Also notice in Figure 13.11 that a pneumothorax can result when a hole is made in the lung such that a significant amount of air leaks from inside the lung to the pleural space. This can occur, for example, when high airway pressure is applied during artificial ventilation of a premature infant whose lung surface tension is high and whose lungs are fragile. The thoracic cavity is divided into right and left sides by the mediastinum—the central part of the thorax containing the heart, trachea, esophagus and other structures—so a pneumothorax is often unilateral.

Inspiration

Figure 13.12 and **Figure 13.13** summarize the events that occur during normal inspiration at rest. Inspiration is initiated by the neurally induced contraction of the diaphragm and the external intercostal muscles located between the ribs (**Figure 13.14**). The diaphragm is the most important inspiratory muscle that acts during normal quiet breathing. When activation of the motor neurons within the **phrenic nerves** innervating the diaphragm causes it to contract, its dome moves downward into the abdomen, enlarging the thorax (see Figure 13.14). Simultaneously, activation of the motor neurons in the intercostal nerves to the inspiratory intercostal muscles causes them to contract, leading to an upward and outward movement of the ribs and a further increase in thoracic size. Also notice in Figure 13.14 that there are several other sets of muscles that participate in the expansion of the thoracic cavity, which become important during a maximal inspiration.

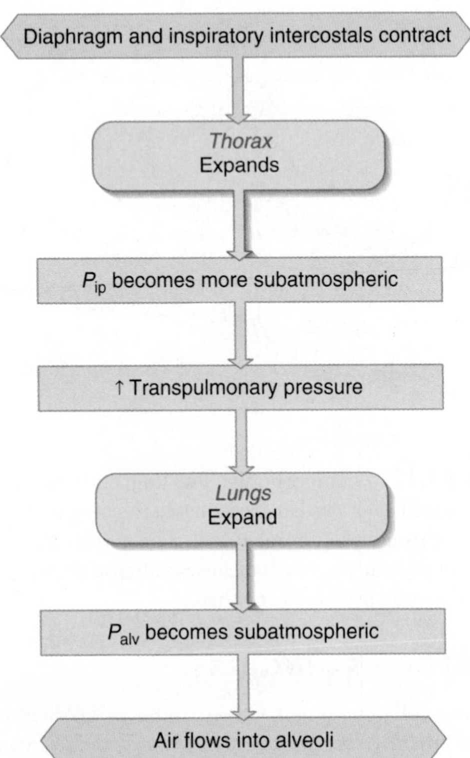
Diaphragm and inspiratory intercostals contract
Thorax
Expands
P_{ip} becomes more subatmospheric
↑ Transpulmonary pressure
Lungs
Expand
P_{alv} becomes subatmospheric
Air flows into alveoli

Figure 13.12 **AP|R** Sequence of events during inspiration. Figure 13.13 illustrates these events quantitatively.

The crucial point is that contraction of the inspiratory muscles, by *actively* increasing the size of the thorax, upsets the stability set up by purely elastic forces between breaths. As the thorax enlarges, the thoracic wall moves ever so slightly farther away from the lung surface. The intrapleural fluid pressure therefore becomes even more subatmospheric than it was between breaths. This decrease in intrapleural pressure *increases* the transpulmonary pressure. Therefore, the force acting to expand the lungs—the transpulmonary pressure—is now greater than the elastic recoil exerted by the lungs at this moment, and so the lungs expand further. Note in Figure 13.13 that, by the end of inspiration, equilibrium *across the lungs* is once again established because the more inflated lungs exert a greater elastic recoil, which equals the increased transpulmonary pressure. In other words, lung volume is stable whenever transpulmonary pressure is balanced by the elastic recoil of the lungs (that is, at the end of both inspiration and expiration when there is no airflow).

Therefore, when contraction of the inspiratory muscles actively increases the thoracic dimensions, the lungs are passively forced to enlarge. The enlargement of the lungs causes an increase in the sizes of the alveoli throughout the lungs. By Boyle's law, the pressure within the alveoli decreases to less than atmospheric (see Figure 13.13). This produces the difference in pressure ($P_{alv} < P_{atm}$) that causes a bulk flow of air from the atmosphere through the airways into the alveoli. By the end of the inspiration, the pressure in the alveoli again equals atmospheric pressure because of this additional air, and airflow ceases.

Expiration

Figure 13.13 and **Figure 13.15** summarize the sequence of events that occur during expiration. At the end of inspiration, the motor neurons to the diaphragm and inspiratory intercostal muscles decrease their firing and so these muscles relax. The diaphragm and chest wall are no longer actively pulled outward by the muscle contractions, and so they start to recoil inward to their original smaller dimensions that existed between breaths. This immediately makes the intrapleural pressure less subatmospheric, thereby *decreasing* the transpulmonary pressure. Therefore, the transpulmonary pressure acting to expand the lungs is now smaller than the elastic recoil exerted by the more expanded lungs and the lungs passively recoil to their original dimension.

As the lungs become smaller, air in the alveoli becomes temporarily compressed so that, by Boyle's law, alveolar pressure exceeds atmospheric pressure (see Figure 13.13). Therefore, air flows from the alveoli through the airways out into the atmosphere. Thus, expiration at rest is passive, depending only upon the relaxation of the inspiratory muscles and the elastic recoil of the stretched lungs.

Under certain conditions, such as during exercise, expiration of larger volumes is achieved by contraction of a different set of intercostal muscles and the abdominal muscles, which *actively* decrease thoracic dimensions (see Figure 13.14). The internal intercostal muscles insert on the ribs in such a way that their contraction pulls the chest wall downward and inward, thereby decreasing thoracic volume. Contraction of

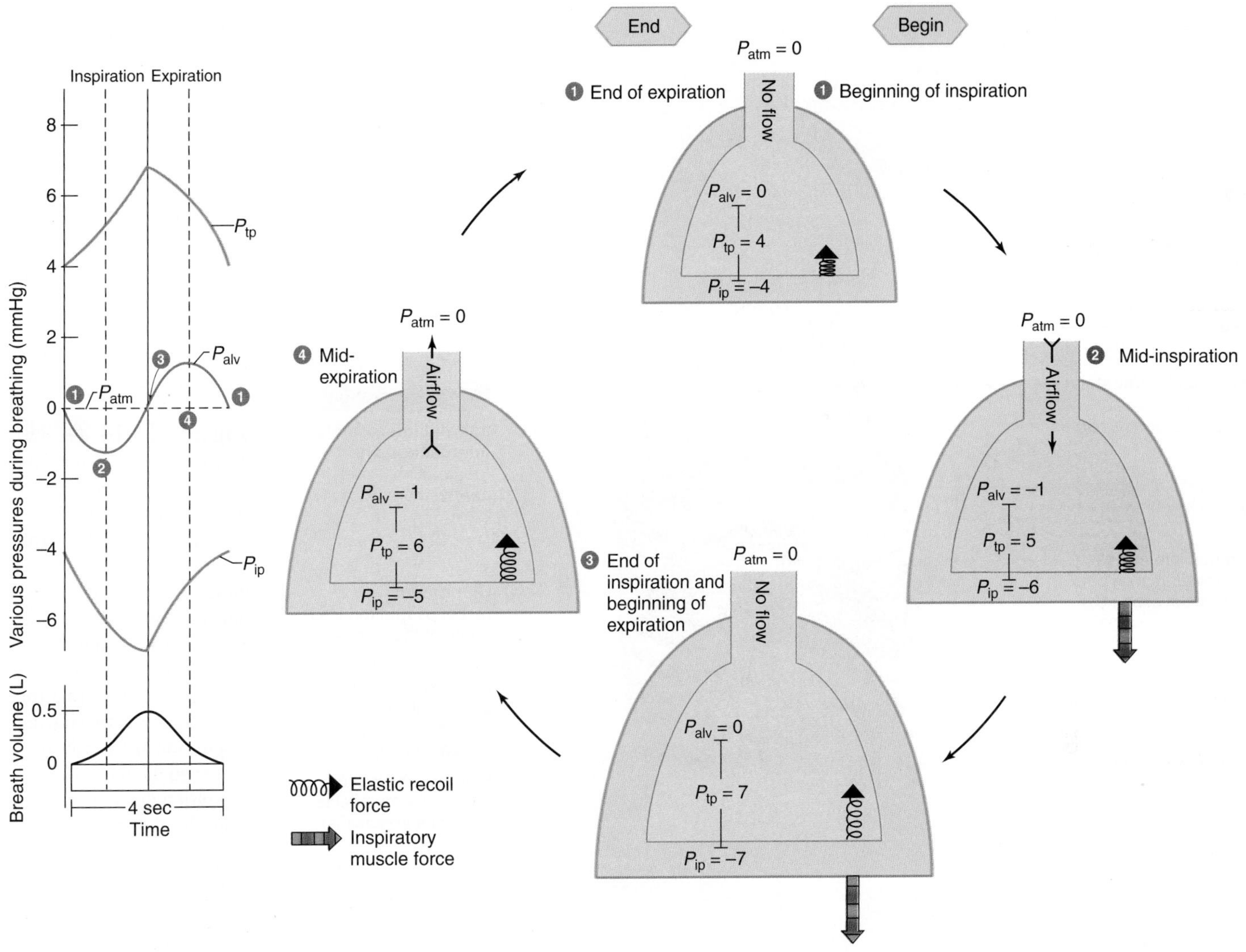

Figure 13.13 APIR Summary of alveolar (P_{alv}), intrapleural (P_{ip}), and transpulmonary (P_{tp}) pressure changes and airflow during a typical respiratory cycle. At the end of expiration ❶, P_{alv} is equal to P_{atm} and there is no airflow. At mid-inspiration ❷, the chest wall is expanding, lowering P_{ip} and making P_{tp} more positive. This expands the lung, making P_{alv} negative and results in an inward airflow. At end of inspiration ❸, the chest wall is no longer expanding but has yet to start passive recoil. Because lung size is not changing and the glottis is open to the atmosphere, P_{alv} is equal to P_{atm} and there is no airflow. As the respiratory muscles relax, the lungs and chest wall start to passively collapse due to elastic recoil. At mid-expiration ❹, the lung is collapsing, thus compressing alveolar gas. As a result, P_{alv} is positive relative to P_{atm} and airflow is outward. The cycle starts over again at the end of expiration. Notice that throughout a typical respiratory cycle with a normal tidal volume, P_{ip} is negative relative to P_{atm}. In the graph on the left, the difference between P_{alv} and P_{ip} ($P_{alv} - P_{ip}$) at any point along the curves is equivalent to P_{tp}. For clarity, the chest-wall elastic recoil (as in Figure 13.10) is not shown.

PHYSIOLOGICAL INQUIRY

- How do the changes in P_{tp} between each step (❶–❹) explain whether the volume of the lung is increasing or decreasing?

Answer can be found at end of chapter.

the abdominal muscles increases intra-abdominal pressure and forces the relaxed diaphragm up into the thorax.

Lung Compliance

To repeat, the degree of lung expansion at any instant is proportional to the transpulmonary pressure, $P_{alv} - P_{ip}$. But just how much any given change in transpulmonary pressure expands the lungs depends upon the stretchability, or compliance, of the lungs. **Lung compliance (C_L)** is defined as the magnitude of the change in lung volume (ΔV_L) produced by a given change in the transpulmonary pressure:

$$C_L = \Delta V_L / \Delta P_{tp} \qquad (13\text{–}4)$$

Thus, the greater the lung compliance, the easier it is to expand the lungs at any given change in transpulmonary pressure (**Figure 13.16**). Compliance can be considered the inverse of stiffness. A low lung compliance means

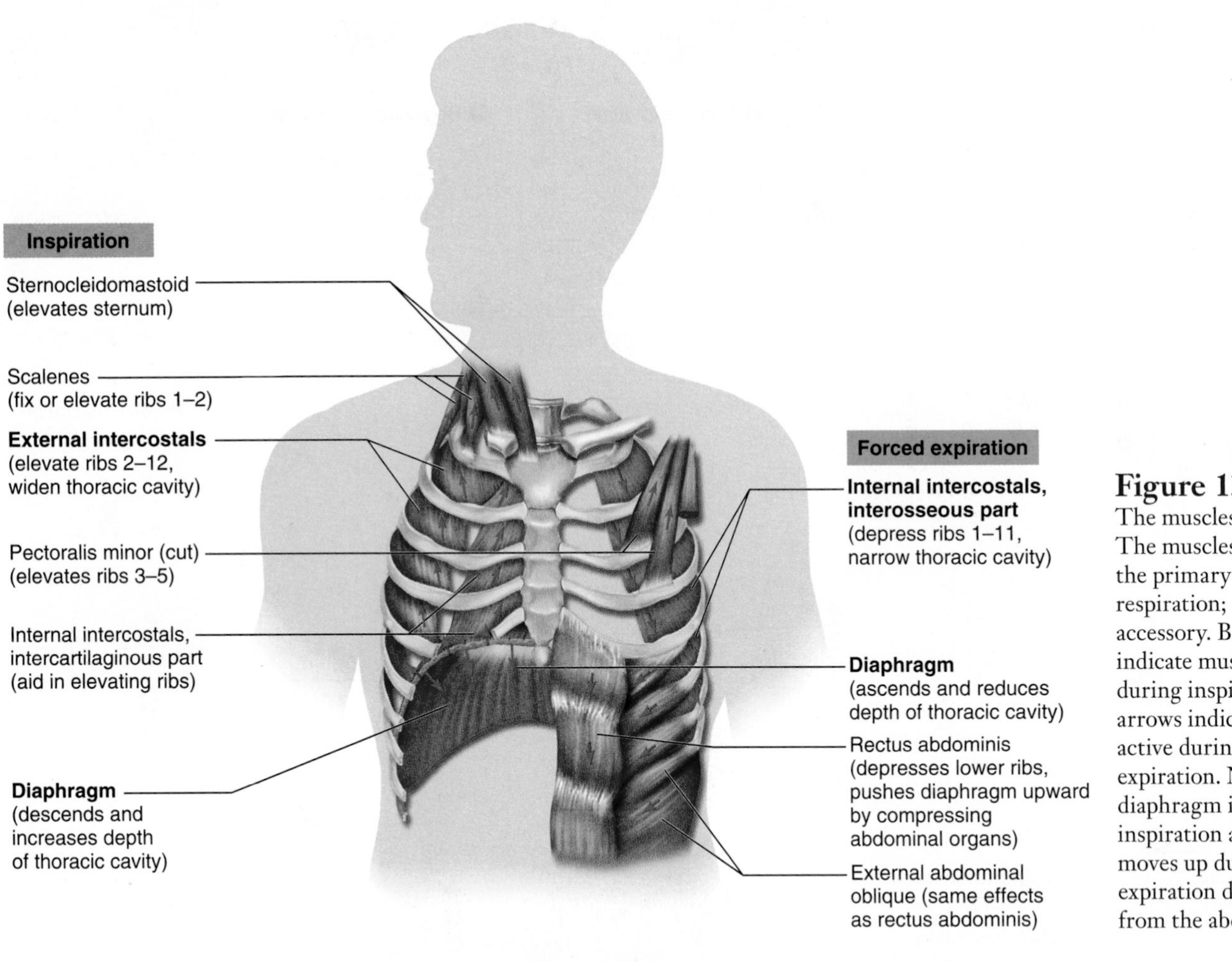

Figure 13.14 AP|R The muscles of respiration. The muscles in bold are the primary muscles of respiration; the others are accessory. Blue arrows indicate muscles active during inspiration; green arrows indicate muscles active during forced expiration. Notice that the diaphragm is active during inspiration and passively moves up during a forced expiration due to pressure from the abdomen.

that a greater-than-normal transpulmonary pressure must be developed across the lung to produce a given amount of lung expansion. In other words, when lung compliance is abnormally low (increased stiffness), intrapleural pressure must be made more subatmospheric than usual during inspiration to achieve lung expansion. This requires more vigorous contractions of the diaphragm and inspiratory intercostal muscles. Thus, the less compliant the lung, the more energy is required to produce a given amount of expansion. Persons with low lung compliance due to disease tend to breathe shallowly and at a higher frequency to inspire an adequate volume of air.

Determinants of Lung Compliance

There are two major determinants of lung compliance. One is the stretchability of the lung tissues, particularly their elastic connective tissues. Thus, a thickening of the lung tissues decreases lung compliance. However, an equally if not more important determinant of lung compliance is not the elasticity of the lung tissues but the surface tension at the air–water interfaces within the alveoli.

The surface of the alveolar cells is moist, so the alveoli can be pictured as air-filled sacs lined with water. At an air–water interface, the attractive forces between the water molecules, known as **surface tension,** make the water lining like a stretched balloon that constantly tends to shrink and resists further stretching. Thus, expansion of the lung requires energy not only to stretch the connective tissue of the lung but also to overcome the surface tension of the water layer lining the alveoli.

Indeed, the surface tension of pure water is so great that were the alveoli lined with pure water, lung expansion would require exhausting muscular effort and the lungs would tend to collapse. It is extremely important, therefore, that the type II alveolar cells secrete the detergent-like substance mentioned earlier, known as **surfactant,** which markedly reduces the cohesive forces between water molecules on the alveolar surface. Therefore, surfactant lowers the surface tension, which increases lung compliance and makes it easier to expand the lungs.

Surfactant is a mixture of both lipids and proteins, but its major component is a phospholipid that inserts its hydrophilic end into the water layer lining the alveoli; its hydrophobic ends form a monomolecular layer between the air and water at the alveolar surface. The amount of surfactant tends to decrease when breaths are small and constant. A deep breath, which people normally intersperse frequently in their breathing pattern, stretches the type II cells, which stimulates the secretion of surfactant. This is why patients who have had thoracic or abdominal surgery

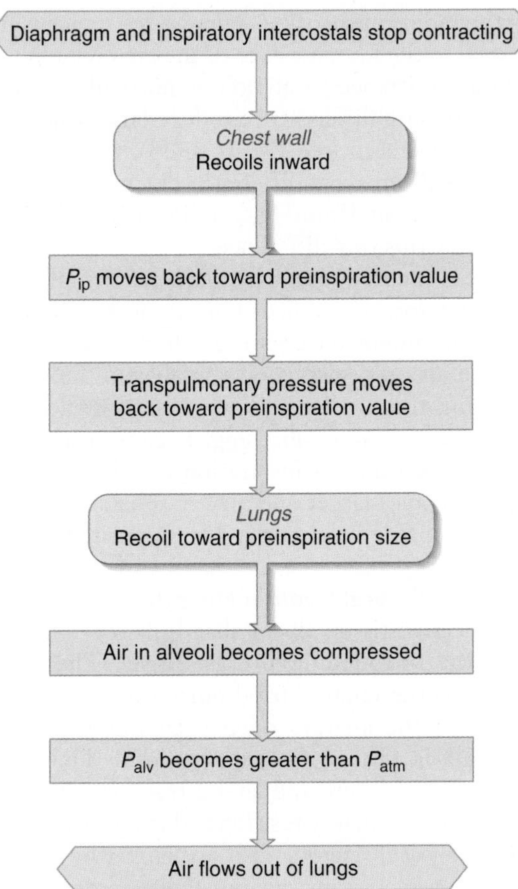

Figure 13.15 APR Sequence of events during expiration. Figure 13.13 illustrates these events quantitatively.

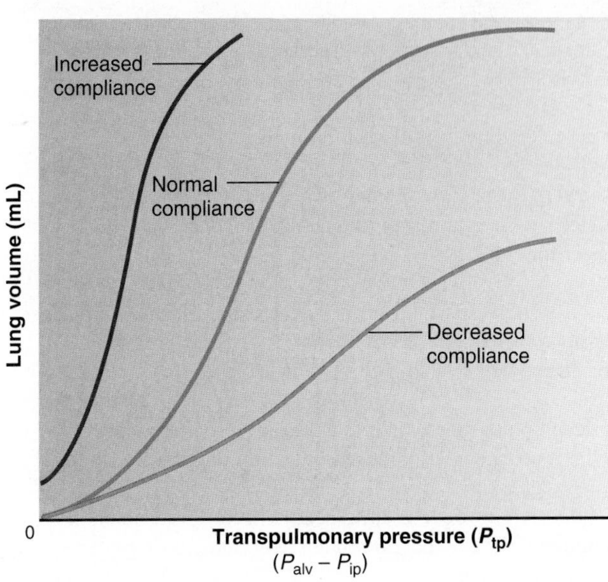

Figure 13.16 A graphic representation of lung compliance. Changes in lung volume and transpulmonary pressure are measured as a subject takes progressively larger breaths. When compliance is lower than normal (the lung is stiffer), there is a lesser increase in lung volume for any given increase in transpulmonary pressure. When compliance is increased, as in emphysema, small decreases in P_{tp} allow the lung to collapse.

PHYSIOLOGICAL INQUIRY

- Premature infants with inadequate surfactant have decreased lung compliance (respiratory distress syndrome of the newborn). If surfactant is not available to administer for therapy, what can be done to inflate the lung?

Answer can be found at end of chapter.

and are breathing shallowly because of the pain must be urged to take occasional deep breaths.

The **Law of Laplace** describes the relationship between pressure (P), surface tension (T), and the radius (r) of an alveolus, shown in **Figure 13.17**:

$$P = 2T/r \qquad (13\text{–}5)$$

As the radius inside the alveolus decreases, the pressure increases. Now imagine two alveoli next to each other sharing an alveolar duct (see Figure 13.17). The radius of alveolus a (r_a) is greater than the radius of alveolus b (r_b). If surface tension (T) were equivalent between these two alveoli, alveolus b would have a higher pressure than alveolus a by the Law of Laplace. If P_b is higher than P_a, air would flow from alveolus b into alveolus a, and alveolus b would collapse. Therefore, small alveoli would be unstable and would collapse into large alveoli. Another important property of surfactant is that it stabilizes alveoli of different sizes by altering surface tension, depending on the surface area of the alveolus. As an alveolus gets smaller, the

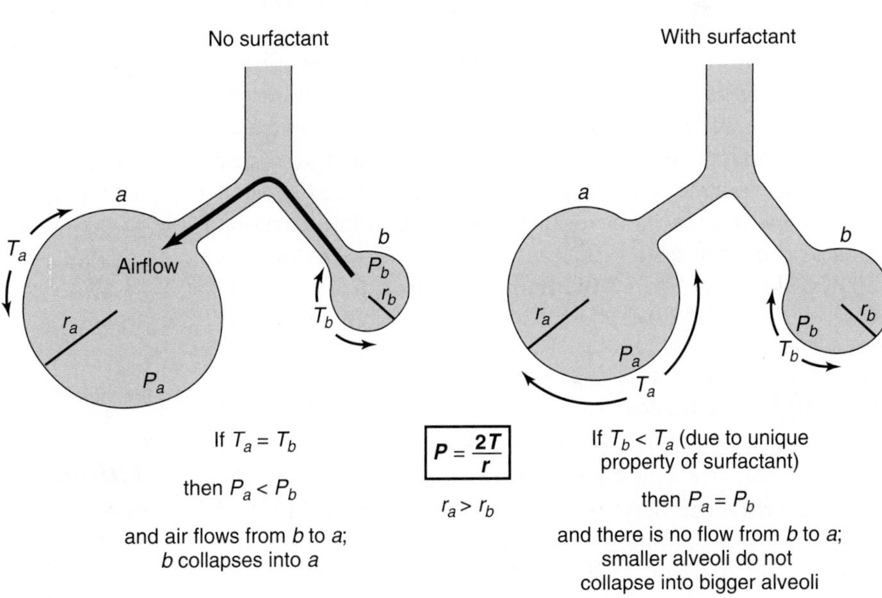

Figure 13.17 Stabilizing effect of surfactant. P is pressure inside the alveoli, T is a surface tension, and r is the radius of the alveolus. The Law of Laplace is described by the equation in the box.

TABLE 13.3	Some Important Facts About Pulmonary Surfactant
Pulmonary surfactant is a mixture of phospholipids and protein.	
It is secreted by type II alveolar cells.	
It lowers the surface tension of the water layer at the alveolar surface, which increases lung compliance, thereby making it easier for the lungs to expand.	
Its effect is greater in smaller alveoli, thus reducing the surface tension of small alveoli below that of larger alveoli. This stabilizes the alveoli.	
A deep breath increases its secretion by stretching the type II cells. Its concentration decreases when breaths are small.	
Production in the fetal lung occurs in late gestation and is stimulated by the increase in cortisol (glucocorticoid) secretion that occurs then.	

molecules of surfactant on its inside surface are less spread out, thus reducing surface tension. The reduction in surface tension helps to maintain a pressure in smaller alveoli equal to that in larger ones. This gives stability to alveoli of different sizes. **Table 13.3** summarizes some of the important aspects of pulmonary surfactant.

A striking example of what occurs when surfactant is deficient is the disease known as ***respiratory distress syndrome of the newborn.*** This is a leading cause of death in premature infants, in whom the surfactant-synthesizing cells may be too immature to function adequately. Respiratory movements in the fetus do not require surfactant because the lungs are filled with amniotic fluid, and the fetus receives oxygen from the maternal blood. Because of low lung compliance, the affected infant can inspire only by the most strenuous efforts, which may ultimately cause complete exhaustion, inability to breathe, lung collapse, and death. Before the development of newer treatments over the past 30 years, almost half of infants with this condition died. Current therapy includes assisted breathing with a mechanical ventilator and the administration of natural or synthetic surfactant given through the infant's trachea. These improved methods of treatment have markedly reduced mortality, and most infants treated adequately now survive.

Airway Resistance

As previously stated, the volume of air that flows into or out of the alveoli per unit time is directly proportional to the pressure difference between the atmosphere and alveoli and is inversely proportional to the resistance to flow of the airways (see equation 13–2). The factors that determine airway resistance are analogous to those determining vascular resistance in the circulatory system: tube length, tube radius, and interactions between moving molecules (gas molecules, in this case). As in the circulatory system, the most important factor by far is the radius of the tube—airway resistance is inversely proportional to the fourth power of the airway radii.

Airway resistance to airflow is normally so small that very small pressure differences produce large volumes of airflow. As we have seen (see Figure 13.13), the average atmosphere-to-alveoli pressure difference during a normal breath when at rest is about 1 mmHg; yet approximately 500 mL of air is moved by this tiny difference.

Physical, neural, and chemical factors affect airway radii and therefore resistance. One important physical factor is the transpulmonary pressure, which exerts a distending force on the airways, just as on the alveoli. This is a major factor keeping the smaller airways—those without cartilage to support them—from collapsing. Because transpulmonary pressure increases during inspiration (see Figure 13.13), airway radius becomes larger and airway resistance lower as the lungs expand during inspiration. The opposite occurs during expiration.

A second physical factor holding the airways open is the elastic connective-tissue fibers that link the outside of the airways to the surrounding alveolar tissue. These fibers are pulled upon as the lungs expand during inspiration; in turn, they help pull the airways open even more than between breaths. This is termed **lateral traction.** Thus, both the transpulmonary pressure and lateral traction act in the same direction, reducing airway resistance during inspiration.

Such physical factors also explain why the airways become narrower and airway resistance increases during a forced expiration. The increase in intrapleural pressure compresses the small conducting airways and decreases their radii. Therefore, because of increased airway resistance, there is a limit to how much one can increase the airflow rate during a forced expiration no matter how intense the effort. The harder one pushes, the greater the compression of the airways, further limiting expiratory airflow.

In addition to these physical factors, a variety of neuroendocrine and paracrine factors can influence airway smooth muscle and thereby airway resistance. For example, the hormone epinephrine relaxes airway smooth muscle by an effect on beta-adrenergic receptors, whereas the leukotrienes, members of the eicosanoid family produced in the lungs during inflammation, contract the muscle.

Why are we concerned with all the physical and chemical factors that *can* influence airway resistance when airway resistance is normally so low that it poses no impediment to airflow? The reason is that, under abnormal circumstances, changes in these factors may cause significant increases in airway resistance. Asthma and chronic obstructive pulmonary disease provide important examples, as we see next.

Asthma

Asthma is a disease characterized by intermittent episodes in which airway smooth muscle contracts strongly, markedly increasing airway resistance. The basic defect in asthma is chronic inflammation of the airways, the causes of which vary from person to person and include, among others, allergy, viral infections, and sensitivity to environmental factors. The underlying inflammation makes the airway smooth muscles hyperresponsive and causes them to contract strongly in response to such things as exercise (especially in cold, dry air), cigarette smoke, environmental pollutants, viruses, allergens, normally released bronchoconstrictor chemicals, and a variety of other potential triggers. In fact, the incidence of asthma is increasing in the United States, possibly due in part to environmental pollution.

The first aim of therapy for asthma is to reduce the chronic inflammation and airway hyperresponsiveness with ***anti-inflammatory drugs,*** particularly leukotriene inhibitors and inhaled glucocorticoids. The second aim is to overcome acute excessive airway smooth muscle contraction with ***bronchodilator drugs,*** which relax the airways. The latter drugs work on the airways either by relaxing airway smooth muscle or by blocking the actions of bronchoconstrictors. For example, one class of bronchodilator drugs mimics the normal action of epinephrine on beta-2 (β_2) adrenergic receptors. Another class of inhaled drugs blocks muscarinic cholinergic receptors, which have been implicated in bronchoconstriction.

Chronic Obstructive Pulmonary Disease

The term ***chronic obstructive pulmonary disease (COPD)*** refers to emphysema, chronic bronchitis, or a combination of the two. These diseases, which cause severe difficulties not only in ventilation but in oxygenation of the blood, are among the major causes of disability and death in the United States. In contrast to asthma, increased smooth muscle contraction is *not* the cause of the airway obstruction in these diseases.

Emphysema is discussed later in this chapter; suffice it to say here that the cause of obstruction in this disease is destruction and collapse of the smaller airways.

Chronic bronchitis is characterized by excessive mucus production in the bronchi and chronic inflammatory changes in the small airways. The cause of obstruction is an accumulation of mucus in the airways and thickening of the inflamed airways. The same agents that cause emphysema—smoking, for example—also cause chronic bronchitis, which is why the two diseases frequently coexist. Bronchitis may also be acute—for example, in response to viral infections such as those that cause upper respiratory infections. In such cases, the coughing and excess sputum and phlegm production associated with acute bronchitis typically resolve within 2 to 3 weeks.

Lung Volumes and Capacities

Normally, the volume of air entering the lungs during a single inspiration—the **tidal volume** (V_t)—is approximately equal to the volume leaving on the subsequent expiration. The tidal volume during normal quiet breathing—the resting tidal volume—is approximately 500 mL depending on body size. As illustrated in **Figure 13.18,** the maximal amount of air that can be increased above this value during deepest inspiration—the **inspiratory reserve volume (IRV)**—is about 3000 mL—that is, six times greater than resting tidal volume.

After expiration of a resting tidal volume, the lungs still contain a large volume of air. As described earlier, this is the resting position of the lungs and chest wall when there is no contraction of the respiratory muscles; this amount of air—the **functional residual capacity (FRC)**—averages about 2400 mL. Thus, the 500 mL of air inspired with each resting breath adds to and mixes with the much larger volume of air already in the lungs; then 500 mL of the total is expired. Through maximal active contraction of the expiratory muscles, it is possible to expire much more of the air remaining after the resting tidal volume has been expired. This additional expired volume—the **expiratory reserve volume (ERV)**—is about 1200 mL. Even after a maximal active expiration, approximately 1200 mL of air still remains in the lungs—the **residual volume (RV)**. Thus, the lungs are never completely emptied of air.

The **vital capacity (VC)** is the maximal volume of air a person can expire after a maximal inspiration. Under these conditions, the person is expiring both the resting tidal volume and the inspiratory reserve volume just inspired, plus the expiratory reserve volume (see Figure 13.18). In other words, the vital capacity is the sum of these three volumes and is an important measurement when assessing pulmonary function.

A variant on this measurement is the ***forced expiratory volume in 1 sec*** (***FEV_1***), in which the person takes a maximal inspiration and then exhales maximally as fast as possible. The important value is the fraction of the total "forced" vital capacity expired in 1 sec. Healthy individuals can expire approximately 80% of the vital capacity in 1 sec.

Measurement of vital capacity and FEV_1 are useful diagnostically and are known as ***pulmonary function tests.*** For example, people with ***obstructive lung diseases*** (increased airway resistance as in asthma) typically have an FEV_1 that is less than 80% of the vital capacity because it is difficult for them to expire air rapidly through the narrowed airways. In contrast to obstructive lung diseases, ***restrictive lung diseases*** are characterized by normal airway resistance but impaired respiratory movements because of abnormalities in the lung tissue, the pleura, the chest wall, or the neuromuscular machinery. Restrictive lung diseases are typically characterized by a reduced vital capacity but a normal ratio of FEV_1 to vital capacity.

Alveolar Ventilation

The total ventilation per minute—the **minute ventilation** ($\dot{V}_E$)—is equal to the tidal volume multiplied by the respiratory rate:

$$\underset{(\text{mL/min})}{\text{Minute ventilation}} = \underset{(\text{mL/breath})}{\text{Tidal volume}} \times \underset{(\text{breaths/min})}{\text{Respiratory rate}}$$

$$\dot{V}_E = V_t \cdot f \qquad (13\text{–}6)$$

For example, at rest, a typical healthy adult moves approximately 500 mL of air in and out of the lungs with each breath and takes 12 breaths each minute. The minute ventilation is therefore 500 mL/breath × 12 breaths/minute = 6000 mL of air per minute. However, because of dead space, not all this air is available for exchange with the blood, as we see next.

Dead Space

The conducting airways have a volume of about 150 mL. Exchanges of gases with the blood occur only in the alveoli and not in this 150 mL of the airways. Picture, then, what occurs during expiration of a tidal volume of 500 mL. The

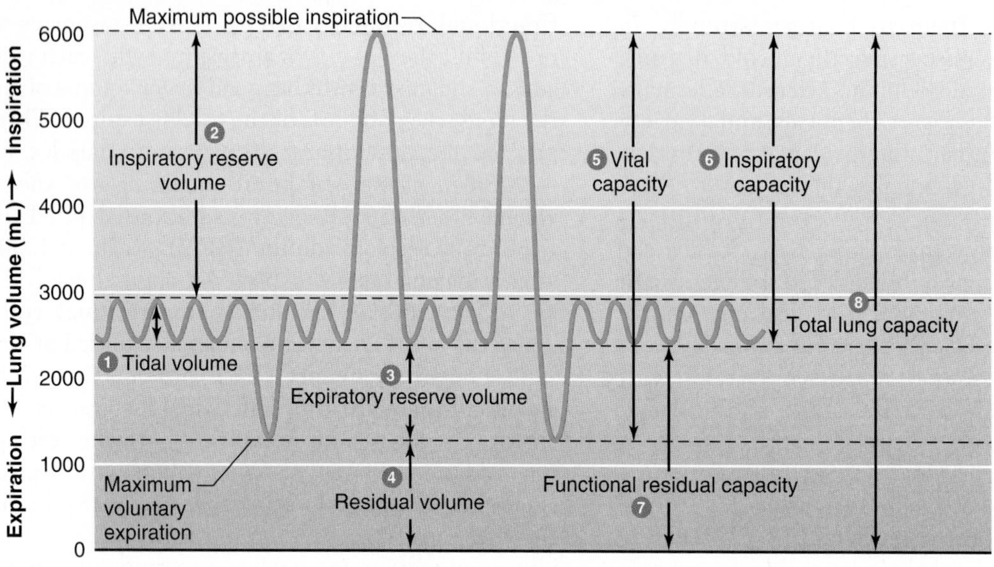

Respiratory Volumes and Capacities for an Average Young Adult Male		
Measurement	Typical Value*	Definition
Respiratory Volumes		
1 Tidal volume (TV)	500 mL	Amount of air inhaled or exhaled in one breath
2 Inspiratory reserve volume (IRV)	3000 mL	Amount of air in excess of tidal inspiration that can be inhaled with maximum effort
3 Expiratory reserve volume (ERV)	1200 mL	Amount of air in excess of tidal expiration that can be exhaled with maximum effort
4 Residual volume (RV)	1200 mL	Amount of air remaining in the lungs after maximum expiration; keeps alveoli inflated between breaths and mixes with fresh air on next inspiration
Respiratory Capacities		
5 Vital capacity (VC)	4700 mL	Amount of air that can be exhaled with maximum effort after maximum inspiration (ERV + TV + IRV); used to assess strength of thoracic muscles as well as pulmonary function
6 Inspiratory capacity (IC)	3500 mL	Maximum amount of air that can be inhaled after a normal tidal expiration (TV + IRV)
7 Functional residual capacity (FRC)	2400 mL	Amount of air remaining in the lungs after a normal tidal expiration (RV + ERV)
8 Total lung capacity (TLC)	5900 mL	Maximum amount of air the lungs can contain (RV + VC)
*Typical value at rest		

Figure 13.18 Lung volumes and capacities recorded on a spirometer, an apparatus for measuring inspired and expired volumes. When the subject inspires, the pen moves up; with expiration, it moves down. The capacities are the sums of two or more lung volumes. The lung volumes are the four distinct components of total lung capacity. Note that residual volume, total lung capacity, and functional residual capacity cannot be measured with a spirometer.

500 mL of air is forced out of the alveoli and through the airways. Approximately 350 mL of this alveolar air is exhaled at the nose or mouth, but approximately 150 mL remains in the airways at the end of expiration. During the next inspiration (**Figure 13.19**), 500 mL of air flows into the alveoli, but the first 150 mL entering the alveoli is not atmospheric air but the 150 mL left behind in the airways from the last breath. Thus, only 350 mL of new atmospheric air enters the alveoli during the inspiration. The end result is that 150 mL of the 500 mL of atmospheric air entering the respiratory system during each inspiration never reaches the alveoli but is merely moved in and out of the airways. Because these airways do not permit gas exchange with the blood, the space within them is called the **anatomical dead space** (**V_D**).

Thus, the volume of *fresh* air entering the alveoli during each inspiration equals the tidal volume *minus* the volume of air in the anatomical dead space. For the previous example,

Tidal volume (V_t) = 500 mL

Anatomical dead space (V_D) = 150 mL

Fresh air entering alveoli in one inspiration (V_A) = 500 mL − 150 mL = 350 mL

The total volume of fresh air entering the alveoli per minute is called the **alveolar ventilation** (**$\dot{V}_A$**):

$$\begin{array}{c}\text{Alveolar ventilation (mL/min)} = \left(\text{Tidal volume (mL/breath)} - \text{Dead space (mL/breath)}\right) \times \text{Respiratory rate (breaths/min)}\end{array}$$

$$\dot{V}_A = (V_t - V_D) \cdot f \qquad (13\text{–}7)$$

Alveolar ventilation, rather than minute ventilation, is the more important factor in the effectiveness of gas exchange.

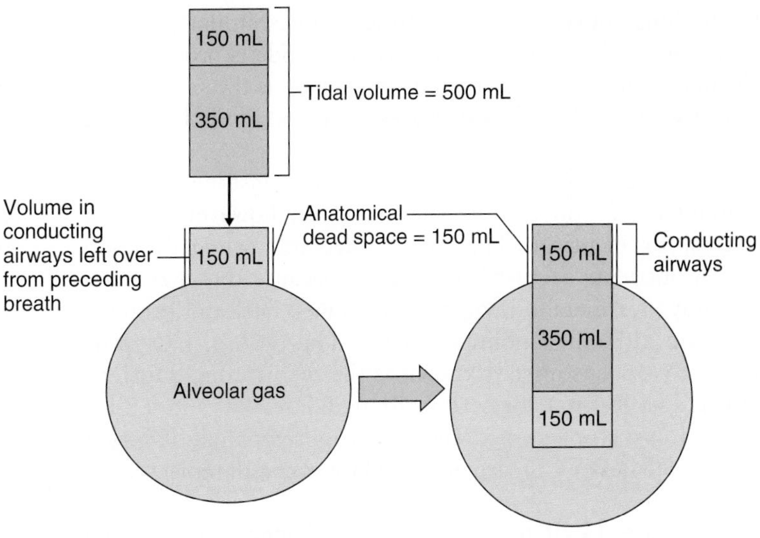

Figure 13.19 Effects of anatomical dead space on alveolar ventilation. Anatomical dead space is the volume of the conducting airways. Of a 500 mL tidal volume breath, 350 mL enters the airway involved in gas exchange. The remaining 150 mL remains in the conducting airways and does not participate in gas exchange.

PHYSIOLOGICAL INQUIRY

- What would be the effect of breathing through a plastic tube with a length of 20 cm and diameter of 4 cm? (*Hint:* Use the formula for the volume of a perfect cylinder.)

Answer can be found at end of chapter.

This generalization is demonstrated readily by the data in **Table 13.4**. In this experiment, subject A breathes rapidly and shallowly, B normally, and C slowly and deeply. Each subject has exactly the same minute ventilation; that is, each is moving the same amount of air in and out of the lungs per minute. Yet, when we subtract the anatomical-dead-space ventilation from the minute ventilation, we find marked differences in alveolar ventilation. Subject A has no alveolar ventilation and would become unconscious in several minutes, whereas C has a considerably greater alveolar ventilation than B, who is breathing normally.

Another important generalization drawn from this example is that increased *depth* of breathing is far more effective in increasing alveolar ventilation than an equivalent increase in breathing *rate*. Conversely, a decrease in depth can lead to a critical reduction in alveolar ventilation. This is because a fixed volume of each tidal volume goes to the dead space. If the tidal volume decreases, the fraction of the tidal volume going to the dead space increases until, as in subject A, it may represent the entire tidal volume. On the other hand, any increase in tidal volume goes entirely toward increasing alveolar ventilation. These concepts have important physiological implications. Most situations that produce an increase in ventilation, such as exercise, reflexively call forth a relatively greater increase in breathing depth than in breathing rate.

The anatomical dead space is not the only type of dead space. Some fresh inspired air is not used for gas exchange with the blood even though it reaches the alveoli because some alveoli may, for various reasons, have little or no blood supply. This volume of air is known as **alveolar dead space.** It is quite small in healthy persons but may be very large in persons with several kinds of lung disease. As we shall see, local mechanisms that match air and blood flows minimize the alveolar dead space. The sum of the anatomical and alveolar dead spaces is known as the **physiological dead space.** This is also known as wasted ventilation because it is air that is inspired but does not participate in gas exchange with blood flowing through the lungs.

13.3 Exchange of Gases in Alveoli and Tissues

We have now completed the discussion of the lung mechanics that produce alveolar ventilation, but this is only the first step in the respiratory process. Oxygen must move across the alveolar membranes into the pulmonary capillaries, be transported by the blood to the tissues, leave the tissue capillaries and enter the extracellular fluid, and finally cross plasma membranes to gain entry into cells. Carbon dioxide must follow a similar path, but in reverse.

In the steady state, the volume of oxygen that leaves the tissue capillaries and is consumed by the body cells per unit time is equal to the volume of oxygen added to the blood

TABLE 13.4 Effect of Breathing Patterns on Alveolar Ventilation

Subject	Tidal Volume (mL/breath)	×	Frequency (breaths/min)	=	Minute Ventilation (mL/min)	Anatomical-Dead-Space Ventilation (mL/min)	Alveolar Ventilation (mL/min)
A	150		40		6000	150 × 40 = 6000	0
B	500		12		6000	150 × 12 = 1800	4200
C	1000		6		6000	150 × 6 = 900	5100

in the lungs during the same time period. Similarly, in the steady state, the rate at which carbon dioxide is produced by the body cells and enters the systemic blood is the same as the rate at which carbon dioxide leaves the blood in the lungs and is expired.

The amount of oxygen the cells consume and the amount of carbon dioxide they produce, however, are not necessarily identical. The balance depends primarily upon which nutrients are used for energy, because the enzymatic pathways for metabolizing carbohydrates, fats, and proteins generate different amounts of CO_2. The ratio of CO_2 produced to O_2 consumed is known as the **respiratory quotient (RQ)**. The RQ is 1 for carbohydrate, 0.7 for fat, and 0.8 for protein. On a mixed diet, the RQ is approximately 0.8; that is, 8 molecules of CO_2 are produced for every 10 molecules of O_2 consumed.

Figure 13.20 presents typical exchange values during 1 min for a person at rest with an RQ of 0.8, assuming a cellular oxygen consumption of 250 mL/min, a carbon dioxide production of 200 mL/min, an alveolar ventilation of 4000 mL/min (4 L/min), and a cardiac output of 5000 mL/min (5 L/min).

Because only 21% of the atmospheric air is oxygen, the total oxygen entering the alveoli per min in our illustration is 21% of 4000 mL, or 840 mL/min. Of this inspired oxygen, 250 mL crosses the alveoli into the pulmonary capillaries, and the rest is subsequently exhaled. Note that blood entering the lungs already contains a large quantity of oxygen, to which the new 250 mL is added. The blood then flows from the lungs to the left side of the heart and is pumped by the left ventricle through the aorta, arteries, and arterioles into the tissue capillaries, where 250 mL of oxygen leaves the blood per minute for cells to take up and utilize. Thus, the quantities of oxygen added to the blood in the lungs and removed in the tissues are the same.

The story reads in reverse for carbon dioxide. A significant amount of carbon dioxide already exists in systemic arterial blood; to this is added an additional 200 mL per minute, the amount the cells produce, as blood flows through tissue capillaries. This 200 mL leaves the blood each minute as blood flows through the lungs and is expired.

Blood pumped by the heart carries oxygen and carbon dioxide between the lungs and tissues by bulk flow, but diffusion is responsible for the net movement of these molecules between the alveoli and blood, and between the blood and the cells of the body. Understanding the mechanisms involved in these diffusional exchanges depends upon some basic chemical and physical properties of gases, which we will now discuss.

Partial Pressures of Gases

Gas molecules undergo continuous random motion. These rapidly moving molecules collide and exert a pressure, the magnitude of which is increased by anything that increases the rate of movement. The pressure a gas exerts is proportional to temperature (because heat increases the speed at which molecules move) and the concentration of the gas—that is, the number of molecules per unit volume.

As **Dalton's law** states, in a mixture of gases, the pressure each gas exerts is independent of the pressure the others exert. This is because gas molecules are normally so far apart that they do not affect each other. Each gas in a mixture behaves as

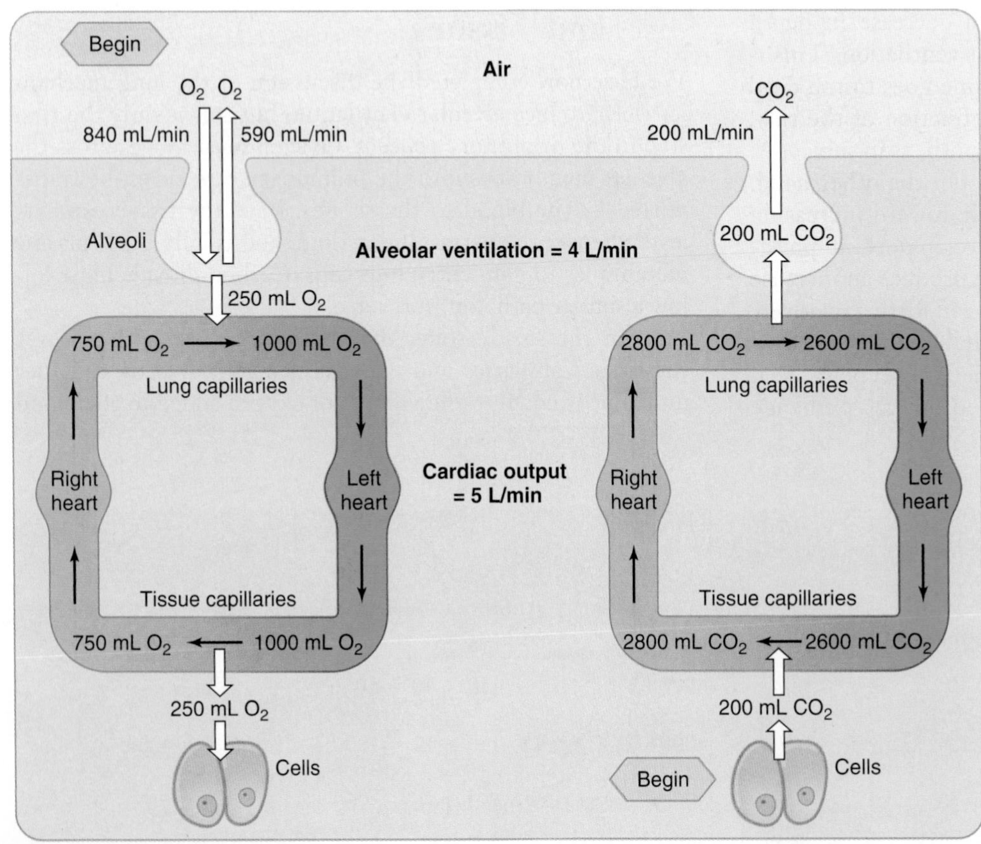

Figure 13.20 Summary of typical oxygen and carbon dioxide exchanges between atmosphere, lungs, blood, and tissues *during 1 min* in a resting individual. Note that the values in this figure for oxygen and carbon dioxide in blood are *not* the values per liter of blood but, rather, the amounts transported *per minute* in the cardiac output (5 L in this example). The volume of oxygen in 1 L of arterial blood is 200 mL O_2/L of blood—that is, 1000 mL O_2/5 L of blood.

though no other gases are present, so the total pressure of the mixture is simply the sum of the individual pressures. These individual pressures, termed **partial pressures,** are denoted by a *P* in front of the symbol for the gas. For example, the partial pressure of oxygen is expressed as P_{O_2}. The partial pressure of a gas is directly proportional to its concentration. Net diffusion of a gas will occur from a region where its partial pressure is high to a region where it is low. An appreciation of the importance of Dalton's law is another example of the general principle that physiological processes are dictated by the laws of chemistry and physics.

Atmospheric air consists of approximately 79% nitrogen and approximately 21% oxygen, with very small quantities of water vapor, carbon dioxide, and inert gases. The sum of the partial pressures of all these gases is called atmospheric pressure, or barometric pressure. It varies in different parts of the world as a result of local weather conditions and gravitational differences due to altitude; at sea level, it is 760 mmHg. Because the partial pressure of any gas in a mixture is the fractional concentration of that gas times the total pressure of all the gases, the P_{O_2} of atmospheric air at sea level is 0.21×760 mmHg $=$ 160 mmHg at sea level.

Diffusion of Gases in Liquids

When a liquid is exposed to air containing a particular gas, molecules of the gas will enter the liquid and dissolve in it. Another physical law, called **Henry's law,** states that the amount of gas dissolved will be directly proportional to the partial pressure of the gas with which the liquid is in equilibrium. A corollary is that, at equilibrium, the partial pressures of the gas molecules in the liquid and gaseous phases must be identical. Suppose, for example, that a closed container contains both water and gaseous oxygen. Oxygen molecules from the gas phase constantly bombard the surface of the water, some entering the water and dissolving. The number of molecules striking the surface is directly proportional to the P_{O_2} of the gas phase, so the number of molecules entering the water and dissolving in it is also directly proportional to the P_{O_2} As long as the P_{O_2} in the gas phase is higher than the P_{O_2} in the liquid, there will be a net diffusion of oxygen into the liquid. Diffusion equilibrium will be reached only when the P_{O_2} in the liquid is equal to the P_{O_2} in the gas phase, and there will then be no further net diffusion between the two phases.

Conversely, if a liquid containing a dissolved gas at high partial pressure is exposed to a lower partial pressure of that same gas in a gas phase, a net diffusion of gas molecules will occur out of the liquid into the gas phase until the partial pressures in the two phases become equal.

The exchanges *between* gas and liquid phases described in the preceding two paragraphs are precisely the phenomena occurring in the lungs between alveolar air and pulmonary capillary blood. In addition, *within* a liquid, dissolved gas molecules also diffuse from a region of higher partial pressure to a region of lower partial pressure, an effect that underlies the exchange of gases between cells, extracellular fluid, and capillary blood throughout the body.

Why must the diffusion of gases into or within liquids be presented in terms of partial pressures rather than "concentrations," the values used to deal with the diffusion of all other solutes? The reason is that the concentration of a gas in a liquid is proportional not only to the partial pressure of the gas but also to the solubility of the gas in the liquid. The more soluble the gas, the greater its concentration will be at any given partial pressure. Thus, if a liquid is exposed to two different gases having the same partial pressures, at equilibrium the *partial pressures* of the two gases will be identical in the liquid, but the *concentrations* of the gases in the liquid will differ, depending upon their solubilities in that liquid.

With these basic gas properties as the foundation, we can now discuss the diffusion of oxygen and carbon dioxide across alveolar and capillary walls and plasma membranes. The partial pressures of these gases in air and in various sites of the body for a resting person at sea level appear in **Figure 13.21**. We start our discussion with the alveolar gas pressures because their values set those of systemic arterial blood. This fact cannot be emphasized too strongly: The alveolar P_{O_2} and P_{CO_2}

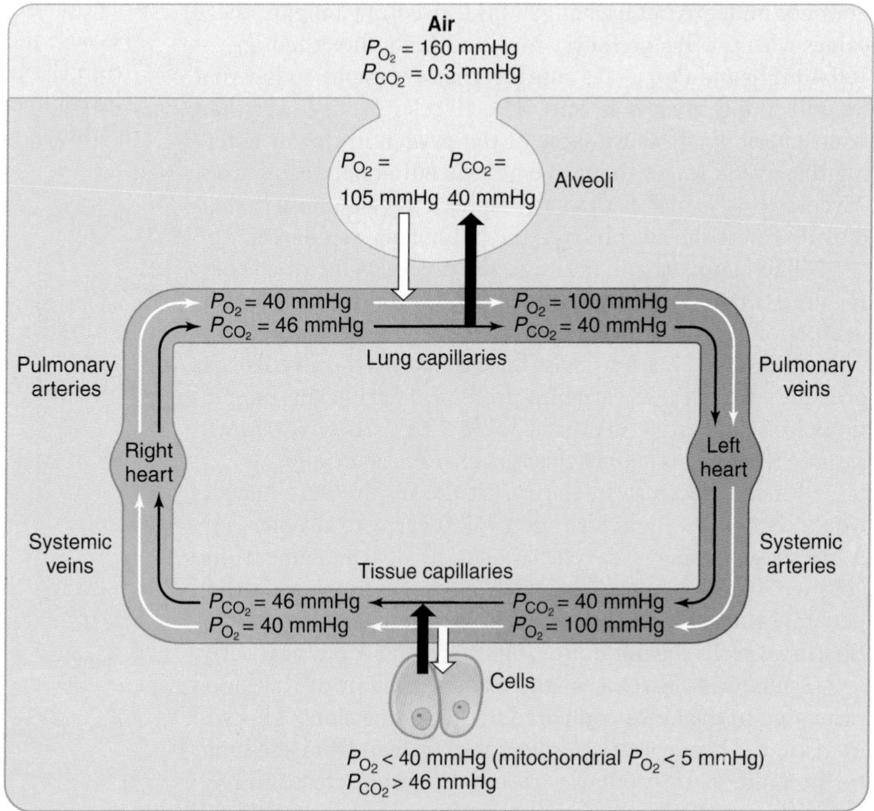

Figure 13.21 APIR Partial pressures of carbon dioxide and oxygen in inspired air at sea level and in various places in the body. The reason that the alveolar P_{O_2} and pulmonary vein P_{O_2} are not exactly the same is described later in the text. Note also that the P_{O_2} in the systemic arteries is shown as identical to that in the pulmonary veins; for reasons involving the anatomy of the blood flow through the lungs, the systemic arterial value is actually slightly less, but we have ignored this for the sake of clarity.

TABLE 13.5 Effects of Various Conditions on Alveolar Gas Pressures		
Condition	**Alveolar P_{O_2}**	**Alveolar P_{CO_2}**
Breathing air with low P_{O_2}	Decreases	No change*
↑ Alveolar ventilation and unchanged metabolism	Increases	Decreases
↓ Alveolar ventilation and unchanged metabolism	Decreases	Increases
↑ Metabolism and unchanged alveolar ventilation	Decreases	Increases
↓ Metabolism and unchanged alveolar ventilation	Increases	Decreases
Proportional increases in metabolism and alveolar ventilation	No change	No change

*Breathing air with low P_{O_2} has no direct effect on alveolar P_{CO_2}. However, as described later in the text, people in this situation will reflexively increase their ventilation, and that will lower P_{CO_2}.

determine the systemic arterial P_{O_2} and P_{CO_2}. So, what determines alveolar gas pressures?

Alveolar Gas Pressures

Typical alveolar gas pressures are P_{O_2} = 105 mmHg and P_{CO_2} = 40 mmHg. (*Note:* We do not deal with nitrogen, even though it is the most abundant gas in the alveoli, because nitrogen is biologically inert under normal conditions and does not undergo net exchange in the alveoli.) Compare these values with the gas pressures in the air being breathed: P_{O_2} = 160 mmHg and P_{CO_2} = 0.3 mmHg, the latter value so low that we will simply treat it as zero. The alveolar P_{O_2} is lower than atmospheric P_{O_2} because some of the oxygen in the air entering the alveoli leaves them to enter the pulmonary capillaries. Alveolar P_{CO_2} is higher than atmospheric P_{CO_2} because carbon dioxide enters the alveoli from the pulmonary capillaries.

The factors that determine the precise value of alveolar P_{O_2} are (1) the P_{O_2} of atmospheric air, (2) the rate of alveolar ventilation, and (3) the rate of total-body oxygen consumption. Although equations exist for calculating the alveolar gas pressures from these variables, we will describe the interactions in a qualitative manner (**Table 13.5**). To start, we will assume that only one of the factors changes at a time.

First, a decrease in the P_{O_2} of the inspired air, such as would occur at high altitude, will decrease alveolar P_{O_2}. A decrease in alveolar ventilation will do the same thing (**Figure 13.22**) because less fresh air is entering the alveoli per unit time. Finally, an increase in the oxygen consumption in the cells during, for example, strenuous physical activity, results in a decrease in the oxygen content of the blood returning to the lungs compared to the resting state. This will increase the concentration gradient of oxygen from the lungs to the pulmonary capillaries resulting in an increase in oxygen diffusion. If alveolar ventilation does not change, this will lower alveolar P_{O_2} because a larger fraction of the oxygen in the entering fresh air will leave the alveoli to enter the blood for use by the tissues. (Recall that in the steady state, the volume of oxygen entering the blood in the lungs per unit time is always equal to the volume utilized by the tissues.) This discussion has been in terms of factors that lower alveolar P_{O_2}; just reverse the direction of change of the three factors to see how to increase alveolar P_{O_2}.

The situation for alveolar P_{CO_2} is analogous, again assuming that only one factor changes at a time. There is normally essentially no carbon dioxide in inspired air and so we can ignore that factor. A decreased alveolar ventilation will decrease the amount of carbon dioxide exhaled, thereby increasing the alveolar P_{CO_2} (see Figure 13.22). Increased production of carbon dioxide will also increase the alveolar P_{CO_2} because more carbon dioxide will be diffusing into the alveoli from the blood per unit time. Recall that in the steady state, the volume of carbon dioxide entering the alveoli per unit time is always equal to the volume produced by the tissues. Just

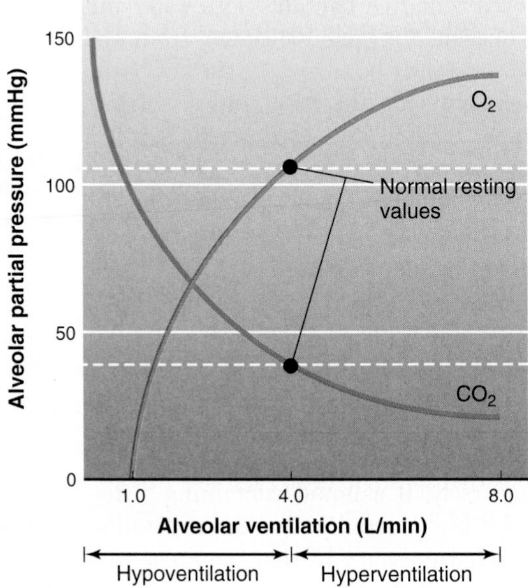

Figure 13.22 Effects of increasing or decreasing alveolar ventilation on alveolar partial pressures in a person having a constant metabolic rate (cellular oxygen consumption and carbon dioxide production). Note that alveolar P_{O_2} approaches zero when alveolar ventilation is about 1 L/min. At this point, all the oxygen entering the alveoli crosses into the blood, leaving virtually no oxygen in the alveoli.

TABLE 13.6 Normal Gas Pressure

	Venous Blood	Arterial Blood	Alveoli	Atmosphere
P_{O_2}	40 mmHg	100 mmHg*	105 mmHg*	160 mmHg
P_{CO_2}	46 mmHg	40 mmHg	40 mmHg	0.3 mmHg

*The reason that the arterial P_{O_2} and alveolar P_{O_2} are not exactly the same is described later in this chapter.

reverse the direction of the changes to see how to decrease alveolar P_{CO_2}.

For simplicity, we assumed only one factor would change at a time, but if more than one factor changes, the effects will either add to or subtract from each other. For example, if oxygen consumption and alveolar ventilation both increase at the same time, their opposing effects on alveolar P_{O_2} will tend to cancel each other out, and alveolar P_{O_2} will not change.

This last example emphasizes that, at any particular atmospheric P_{O_2}, it is the *ratio* of oxygen consumption to alveolar ventilation that determines alveolar P_{O_2}—the higher the ratio, the lower the alveolar P_{O_2}. Similarly, alveolar P_{CO_2} is determined by the ratio of carbon dioxide production to alveolar ventilation—the higher the ratio, the higher the alveolar P_{CO_2}.

We can now define two terms that denote the adequacy of ventilation—that is, the relationship between metabolism and alveolar ventilation. These definitions are stated in terms of carbon dioxide rather than oxygen. ***Hypoventilation*** exists when there is an increase in the ratio of carbon dioxide production to alveolar ventilation. In other words, a person is hypoventilating if the alveolar ventilation cannot keep pace with the carbon dioxide production. The result is that alveolar P_{CO_2} increases above the normal value. ***Hyperventilation*** exists when there is a decrease in the ratio of carbon dioxide production to alveolar ventilation, that is, when alveolar ventilation is actually too great for the amount of carbon dioxide being produced. The result is that alveolar P_{CO_2} decreases below the normal value.

Note that "hyperventilation" is not synonymous with "increased ventilation." Hyperventilation represents increased ventilation *relative to metabolism*. Thus, for example, the increased ventilation that occurs during moderate exercise is not hyperventilation because, as we will see, the increase in production of carbon dioxide in this situation is proportional to the increased ventilation.

Gas Exchange Between Alveoli and Blood

The blood that enters the pulmonary capillaries is systemic venous blood pumped to the lungs through the pulmonary arteries. Having come from the tissues, it has a relatively high P_{CO_2} (46 mmHg in a healthy person at rest) and a relatively low P_{O_2} (40 mmHg) (see Figure 13.21 and **Table 13.6**). The differences in the partial pressures of oxygen and carbon dioxide on the two sides of the alveolar-capillary membrane result in the net diffusion of oxygen from alveoli to blood and of carbon dioxide from blood to alveoli. (For simplicity, we are ignoring the small diffusion barrier provided by the interstitial space.) As this diffusion occurs, the P_{O_2} in the pulmonary capillary blood increases and the P_{CO_2} decreases. The net diffusion of these gases ceases when the capillary partial pressures become equal to those in the alveoli.

In a healthy person, the rates at which oxygen and carbon dioxide diffuse are high enough and the blood flow through the capillaries slow enough that complete equilibrium is reached well before the blood reaches the end of the capillaries (**Figure 13.23**).

Thus, the blood that leaves the pulmonary capillaries to return to the heart and be pumped into the systemic arteries has essentially the same P_{O_2} and P_{CO_2} as alveolar air. (They are not exactly the same, for reasons given later.) Accordingly, the factors described in the previous section—atmospheric P_{O_2}, cellular oxygen consumption and carbon dioxide production, and alveolar ventilation—determine the alveolar gas pressures, which then determine the systemic arterial gas pressures.

Given that diffusion between alveoli and pulmonary capillaries normally achieves complete equilibration, the more capillaries that participate in this process, the more total

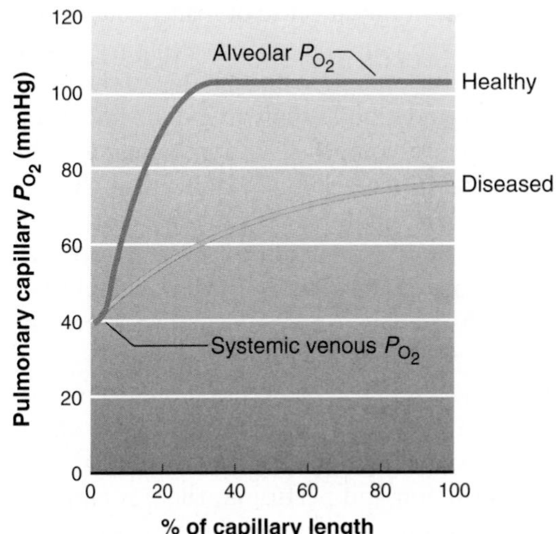

Figure 13.23 AP|R Equilibration of blood P_{O_2} with an alveolus with a P_{O_2} of 105 mmHg along the length of a pulmonary capillary. Note that in an abnormal alveolar-diffusion barrier (diseased), the blood is not fully oxygenated.

PHYSIOLOGICAL INQUIRY

- What is the effect of exercise on P_{O_2} at the end of a capillary in a normal region of the lung? In a region of the lung with diffusion limitation due to disease?

Answers can be found at end of chapter.

oxygen and carbon dioxide are exchanged. Many of the pulmonary capillaries at the apex (top) of each lung are normally closed at rest. During exercise, these capillaries open and receive blood, thereby enhancing gas exchange. The mechanism by which this occurs is a simple physical one; the pulmonary circulation at rest is at such a low blood pressure that the pressure in these apical capillaries is inadequate to keep them open, but the increased cardiac output of exercise increases pulmonary vascular pressures, which opens these capillaries.

The diffusion of gases between alveoli and capillaries may be impaired in a number of ways (see Figure 13.23), resulting in inadequate oxygen diffusion into the blood. For one thing, the total surface area of all of the alveoli in contact with pulmonary capillaries may be decreased. In ***pulmonary edema***, some of the alveoli may become filled with fluid. (As described in Section C of Chapter 12, edema is the accumulation of fluid in tissues; in the alveoli, this increases the diffusion barrier for gases.) Diffusion may also be impaired if the alveolar walls become severely thickened with connective tissue (fibrotic), as, for example, in the disease called ***diffuse interstitial fibrosis.*** In this disease, fibrosis may arise from infection, autoimmune disease, hypersensitivity to inspired substances, exposure to toxic airborne chemicals, and many other causes. Typical symptoms of these types of diffusion diseases are shortness of breath and poor oxygenation of blood. Pure diffusion problems of these types are restricted to oxygen and usually do not affect the elimination of carbon dioxide, which diffuses more rapidly than oxygen.

Matching of Ventilation and Blood Flow in Alveoli

The major disease-induced cause of inadequate oxygen movement between alveoli and pulmonary capillary blood is not a problem with diffusion but, instead, is due to the mismatching of the air supply and blood supply in individual alveoli.

The lungs are composed of approximately 300 million alveoli, each capable of receiving carbon dioxide from, and supplying oxygen to, the pulmonary capillary blood. To be most efficient, the correct proportion of alveolar airflow (ventilation) and capillary blood flow (perfusion) should be available to *each* alveolus. Any mismatching is termed ***ventilation–perfusion inequality.***

The major effect of ventilation–perfusion inequality is to decrease the P_{O_2} of systemic arterial blood. Indeed, largely because of gravitational effects on ventilation and perfusion, there is enough ventilation–perfusion inequality in healthy people to decrease the arterial P_{O_2} about 5 mmHg. One effect of upright posture is to increase the filling of blood vessels at the bottom of the lung due to gravity, which contributes to a difference in blood-flow distribution in the lung. This is the major explanation of the fact, given earlier, that the P_{O_2} of blood in the pulmonary veins and systemic arteries is normally about 5 mmHg less than that of average alveolar air (see Table 13.6).

In disease states, regional changes in lung compliance, airway resistance, and vascular resistance can cause marked ventilation–perfusion inequalities. The extremes of this phenomenon are easy to visualize: (1) There may be ventilated alveoli with no blood supply at all (dead space or wasted ventilation) due to a blood clot, for example; or (2) there may be blood flowing through areas of lung that have no ventilation (this is termed a ***shunt***) due to collapsed alveoli, for example. However, the inequality need not be all-or-none to be significant.

Carbon dioxide elimination is also impaired by ventilation–perfusion inequality but not nearly to the same degree as oxygen uptake. Although the reasons for this are complex, small increases in arterial P_{CO_2} lead to increases in alveolar ventilation, which usually prevent further increases in arterial P_{CO_2}. Nevertheless, severe ventilation–perfusion inequalities in disease states can lead to an increase in arterial P_{CO_2}.

There are several local homeostatic responses within the lungs that minimize the mismatching of ventilation and blood flow and thereby maximize the efficiency of gas exchange (**Figure 13.24**). Probably the most important of these is a direct effect of low oxygen on pulmonary blood vessels. A decrease in ventilation within a group of alveoli—which might occur, for example, from a mucous plug blocking the small airways—leads to a decrease in alveolar P_{O_2} and the area around it, including the blood vessels. A decrease in P_{O_2} in these alveoli and nearby blood vessels leads to vasoconstriction, diverting blood flow away from the poorly ventilated area. This local adaptive effect, unique to the pulmonary arterial blood vessels, ensures that blood flow is directed away from diseased areas of the lung toward areas that are well ventilated. Another factor to improve the match between ventilation and perfusion can occur if there is a local decrease in blood flow within a lung region due to, for example, a small blood clot in a pulmonary arteriole. A local decrease in blood flow brings less systemic CO_2 to that area, resulting in a local decrease in P_{CO_2}. This causes local bronchoconstriction, which diverts airflow away to areas of the lung with better perfusion.

The net adaptive effects of vasoconstriction and bronchoconstriction are to (1) supply less blood flow to poorly ventilated areas, thus diverting blood flow to well-ventilated areas;

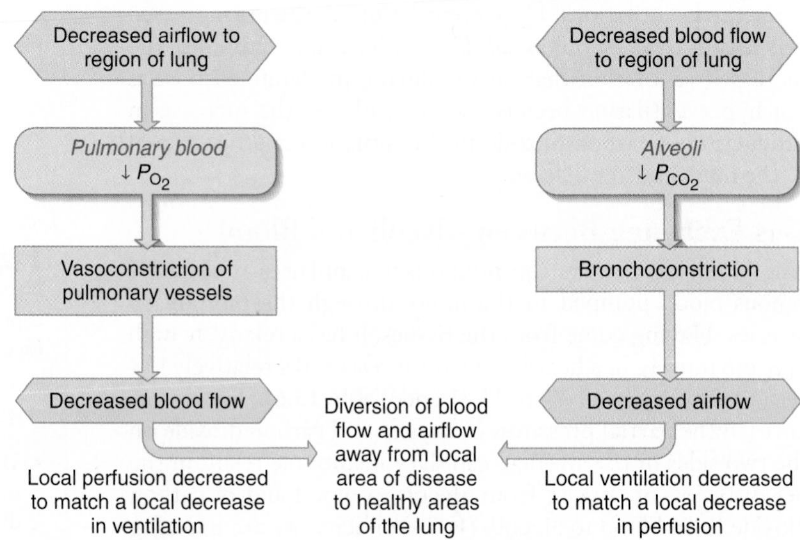

Figure 13.24 Local control of ventilation–perfusion matching.

and (2) redirect air away from diseased or damaged alveoli and toward healthy alveoli. These factors greatly improve the efficiency of pulmonary gas exchange, but they are not perfect even in the healthy lung. There is always a small mismatch of ventilation and perfusion, which, as just described, leads to the normal alveolar-arterial O_2 gradient of about 5 mmHg.

Gas Exchange Between Tissues and Blood

As the systemic arterial blood enters capillaries throughout the body, it is separated from the interstitial fluid by only the thin capillary wall, which is highly permeable to both oxygen and carbon dioxide. The interstitial fluid, in turn, is separated from the intracellular fluid by the plasma membranes of the cells, which are also quite permeable to oxygen and carbon dioxide. Metabolic reactions occurring within cells are constantly consuming oxygen and producing carbon dioxide. Therefore, as shown in Figure 13.21, intracellular P_{O_2} is lower and P_{CO_2} higher than in arterial blood. The lowest P_{O_2} of all—less than 5 mmHg—is in the mitochondria, the site of oxygen utilization. As a result, a net diffusion of oxygen occurs from blood into cells and, within the cells, into the mitochondria, and a net diffusion of carbon dioxide occurs from cells into blood. In this manner, as blood flows through systemic capillaries, its P_{O_2} decreases and its P_{CO_2} increases. This accounts for the systemic venous blood values shown in Figure 13.21 and Table 13.6.

In summary, the supply of new oxygen to the alveoli and the consumption of oxygen in the cells create P_{O_2} gradients that produce net diffusion of oxygen from alveoli to blood in the lungs and from blood to cells in the rest of the body. Conversely, the production of carbon dioxide by cells and its elimination from the alveoli via expiration create P_{CO_2} gradients that produce net diffusion of carbon dioxide from cells to blood in the rest of the body and from blood to alveoli in the lungs.

13.4 Transport of Oxygen in Blood

Table 13.7 summarizes the oxygen content of systemic arterial blood, referred to simply as arterial blood. Each liter normally contains the number of oxygen molecules equivalent to 200 mL of pure gaseous oxygen at atmospheric pressure. The oxygen is present in two forms: (1) dissolved in the plasma and erythrocyte cytosol and (2) reversibly combined with hemoglobin molecules in the erythrocytes.

TABLE 13.7 Oxygen Content of Systemic Arterial Blood at Sea Level

1 liter (L) arterial blood contains		
	3 mL	O_2 physically dissolved (1.5%)
	197 mL	O_2 bound to hemoglobin (98.5%)
Total:	200 mL	O_2
Cardiac output = 5 L/min		
O_2 carried to tissues/min = 5 L/min × 200 mL O_2/L		
= 1000 mL O_2/min		

As predicted by Henry's law, the amount of oxygen dissolved in blood is directly proportional to the P_{O_2} of the blood. Because the solubility of oxygen in water is relatively low, only 3 mL can be dissolved in 1 L of blood at the normal arterial P_{O_2} of 100 mmHg. The other 197 mL of oxygen in a liter of arterial blood—more than 98% of the oxygen content in the liter—is transported in the erythrocytes, reversibly combined with hemoglobin.

Each **hemoglobin** molecule is a protein made up of four subunits bound together. Each subunit consists of a molecular group known as **heme** and a polypeptide attached to the heme. The four polypeptides of a hemoglobin molecule are collectively called **globin.** Each of the four heme groups in a hemoglobin molecule (**Figure 13.25**) contains one atom of iron (Fe^{2+}), to which molecular oxygen binds. Because each iron atom can bind one molecule of oxygen, a single hemoglobin molecule can bind four oxygen molecules (see Figure 2.19). However, for simplicity, the equation for the reaction between oxygen and hemoglobin is usually written in terms of a single polypeptide–heme subunit of a hemoglobin molecule:

$$O_2 + Hb \rightleftharpoons HbO_2 \qquad (13\text{–}8)$$

Therefore, hemoglobin can exist in one of two forms—**deoxyhemoglobin (Hb)** and **oxyhemoglobin (HbO_2).** In a blood sample containing many hemoglobin molecules, the fraction of all the hemoglobin in the form of oxyhemoglobin is expressed as the **percent hemoglobin saturation:**

$$\text{Percent Hb saturation} = \frac{O_2 \text{ bound to Hb}}{\text{Maximal capacity of Hb to bind } O_2} \times 100 \qquad (13\text{–}9)$$

For example, if the amount of oxygen bound to hemoglobin is 40% of the maximal capacity, the sample is said to

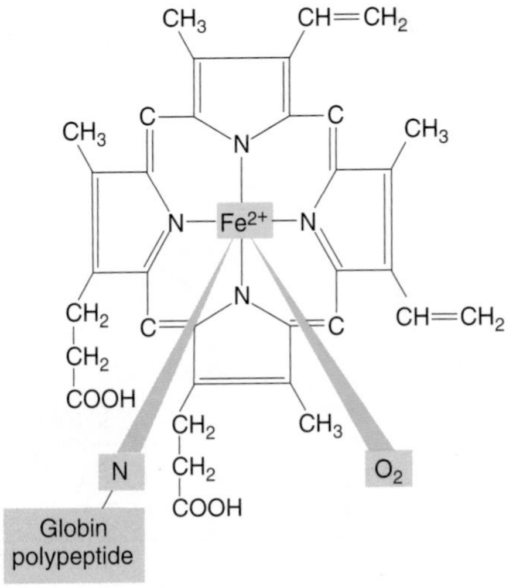

Figure 13.25 Heme in two dimensions. Oxygen binds to the iron atom (Fe^{2+}). Heme attaches to a polypeptide chain by a nitrogen atom to form one subunit of hemoglobin. Four of these subunits bind to each other to make a single hemoglobin molecule. See Figure 2.19, which shows the arrangements of polypeptide chains that make up the hemoglobin molecule.

be 40% saturated. The denominator in this equation is also termed the **oxygen-carrying capacity** of the blood.

What factors determine the percent hemoglobin saturation? By far the most important is the blood P_{O_2}. Before turning to this subject, however, it must be stressed that the *total amount* of oxygen carried by hemoglobin in the blood depends not only on the percent saturation of hemoglobin but also on how much hemoglobin is in each liter of blood. A significant decrease in hemoglobin in the blood is called ***anemia***. For example, if a person's blood contained only half as much hemoglobin per liter as normal, then at any given percent saturation, the oxygen content of the blood would be only half as much. The most common way in which the hemoglobin content of blood is decreased is due to a low hematocrit, for example, due to chronic blood loss and to certain dietary deficiencies resulting in inadequate production of erythrocytes in the bone marrow.

What Is the Effect of P_{O_2} on Hemoglobin Saturation?

Based on equation 13–8 and the law of mass action (see Chapter 3), it is evident that increasing the blood P_{O_2} should increase the combination of oxygen with hemoglobin. The quantitative relationship between these variables is shown in **Figure 13.26,** which is called an **oxygen–hemoglobin dissociation curve.** (The term *dissociate* means "to separate," in this case, oxygen from hemoglobin; it could just as well have been called an "oxygen–hemoglobin association" curve.) The curve is sigmoid because, as stated earlier, each hemoglobin molecule contains four subunits. Each subunit can combine with one molecule of oxygen, and the reactions of the four subunits occur sequentially, with each combination facilitating the next one.

This combination of oxygen with hemoglobin is an example of cooperativity, as described in Chapter 3, and is a classic example of the general principle of physiology that understanding the laws of chemistry and physics is vital to understanding function. The explanation in this case is as follows. The globin

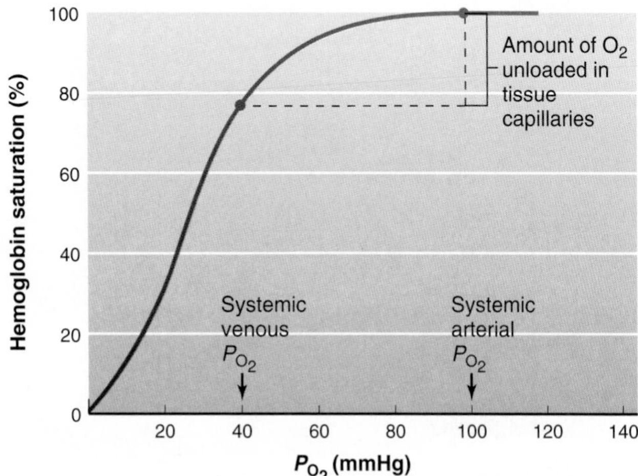

Figure 13.26 Oxygen–hemoglobin dissociation curve. This curve applies to blood at 37°C and a normal arterial H^+ concentration. At any given blood hemoglobin concentration, the *y*-axis could also have plotted oxygen content in milliliters of oxygen. At 100% saturation, the amount of hemoglobin in normal blood carries 200 mL of oxygen.

units of deoxyhemoglobin are tightly held by electrostatic bonds in a conformation with a relatively low affinity for oxygen. The binding of oxygen to a heme molecule breaks some of these bonds between the globin subunits, leading to a conformation change that leaves the remaining oxygen-binding sites more exposed. Thus, the binding of one oxygen molecule to deoxyhemoglobin increases the affinity of the remaining sites on the same hemoglobin molecule, and so on.

The shape of the oxygen–hemoglobin dissociation curve is extremely important in understanding oxygen exchange. The curve has a steep slope between 10 and 60 mmHg P_{O_2} and a relatively flat portion (or plateau) between 70 and 100 mmHg P_{O_2}. Thus, the extent to which oxygen combines with hemoglobin increases very rapidly as the P_{O_2} increases from 10 to 60 mmHg, so that at a P_{O_2} of 60 mmHg, approximately 90% of the total hemoglobin is combined with oxygen. From this point on, a further increase in P_{O_2} produces only a small increase in oxygen binding.

This plateau at higher P_{O_2} values has a number of important implications. In many situations, including at high altitude and with pulmonary disease, a moderate reduction occurs in alveolar and therefore arterial P_{O_2}. Even if the P_{O_2} decreased from the normal value of 100 to 60 mmHg, the total quantity of oxygen carried by hemoglobin would decrease by only 10% because hemoglobin saturation is still close to 90% at a P_{O_2} of 60 mmHg. The plateau provides an excellent safety factor so that even a significant limitation of lung function still allows almost normal oxygen saturation of hemoglobin.

The plateau also explains why, in a healthy person at sea level, increasing the alveolar (and therefore the arterial) P_{O_2} either by hyperventilating or by breathing 100% oxygen does not appreciably increase the total content of oxygen in the blood. A small additional amount dissolves; but because hemoglobin is already almost completely saturated with oxygen at the normal arterial P_{O_2} of 100 mmHg, it simply cannot pick up any more oxygen when the P_{O_2} is increased beyond this point. This applies only to healthy people at sea level. If a person initially has a low arterial P_{O_2} because of lung disease or high altitude, then there would be a great deal of deoxyhemoglobin initially present in the arterial blood. Therefore, increasing the alveolar and thereby the arterial P_{O_2} would result in significantly more oxygen transport.

The steep portion of the curve from 60 mmHg down to 20 mmHg is ideal for unloading oxygen in the tissues. That is, for a small decrease in P_{O_2} due to diffusion of oxygen from the blood to the cells, a large quantity of oxygen can be unloaded in the peripheral tissue capillary.

We now retrace our steps and reconsider the movement of oxygen across the various membranes, this time including hemoglobin in our analysis. It is essential to recognize that the oxygen bound to hemoglobin does *not* contribute directly to the P_{O_2} of the blood; only dissolved oxygen does so. Therefore, oxygen diffusion is governed only by the dissolved portion, a fact that permitted us to ignore hemoglobin in discussing transmembrane partial pressure gradients. However, the presence of hemoglobin plays a critical role in determining the *total amount* of oxygen that will diffuse, as illustrated by a simple example (**Figure 13.27**). Two solutions separated by a semipermeable membrane contain equal quantities of oxygen. The gas pressures in both solutions are equal, and no net diffusion

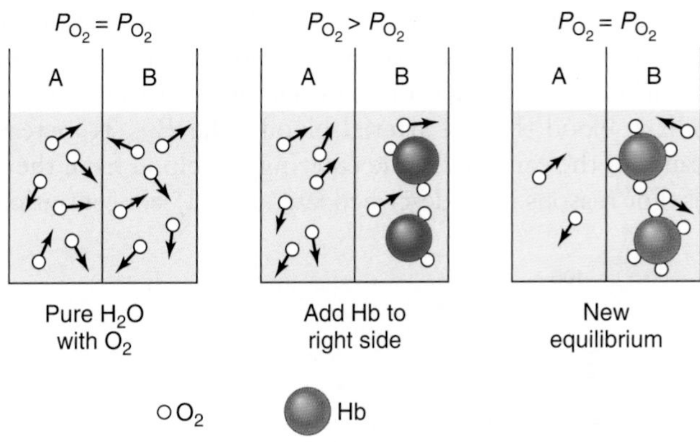

Figure 13.27 Effect of added hemoglobin on oxygen distribution between two compartments containing a fixed number of oxygen molecules and separated by a semipermeable membrane. At the new equilibrium, the P_{O_2} values are again equal to each other but lower than before the hemoglobin was added. However, the total oxygen—in other words, the oxygen dissolved plus that combined with hemoglobin—is now much higher on the right side of the membrane. Adapted from Comroe.

of oxygen occurs. Addition of hemoglobin to compartment B disturbs this equilibrium because much of the oxygen combines with hemoglobin. Despite the fact that the total *quantity* of oxygen in compartment B is still the same, the number of *dissolved* oxygen molecules has decreased. Therefore, the P_{O_2} of compartment B is less than that of A, and so there is a net diffusion of oxygen from A to B. At the new equilibrium, the oxygen pressures are once again equal, but almost all the oxygen is in compartment B and has combined with hemoglobin.

Let us now apply this analysis to capillaries of the lungs and tissues (**Figure 13.28**). The plasma and erythrocytes entering the lungs have a P_{O_2} of 40 mmHg. As we can see from Figure 13.26, hemoglobin saturation at this P_{O_2} is 75%. The alveolar P_{O_2}—105 mmHg—is higher than the blood P_{O_2} and so oxygen diffuses from the alveoli into the plasma. This increases plasma P_{O_2} and induces diffusion of oxygen into the erythrocytes, elevating erythrocyte P_{O_2} and causing increased combination of oxygen and hemoglobin. Most of the oxygen diffusing into the blood from the alveoli does not remain dissolved but combines with hemoglobin. Therefore, the blood P_{O_2} normally remains less than the alveolar P_{O_2} until hemoglobin is virtually 100% saturated. Thus, the diffusion gradient favoring oxygen movement into the blood is maintained despite the very large transfer of oxygen.

In the tissue capillaries, the process is reversed. Because the mitochondria of the cells all over the body are utilizing oxygen, the cellular P_{O_2} is less than the P_{O_2} of the surrounding interstitial fluid. Therefore, oxygen is continuously diffusing into the cells. This causes the interstitial fluid P_{O_2} to always be less than the P_{O_2} of the blood flowing through the tissue capillaries, so net diffusion of oxygen occurs from the plasma within the capillary into the interstitial fluid. As a result, plasma P_{O_2} becomes lower than erythrocyte P_{O_2}, and oxygen diffuses out of the erythrocyte into the plasma. The decrease in erythrocyte P_{O_2} causes the dissociation of oxygen from hemoglobin, thereby liberating oxygen, which then diffuses out of the erythrocyte. The net result is a transfer, purely by diffusion, of large quantities of oxygen from hemoglobin to plasma to interstitial fluid to the mitochondria of tissue cells.

In most tissues under resting conditions, hemoglobin is still 75% saturated as the blood leaves the tissue capillaries. This fact underlies an important local mechanism by which cells can obtain more oxygen whenever they increase their activity. For example, an exercising muscle consumes more oxygen, thereby lowering its tissue P_{O_2}. This increases the blood-to-tissue P_{O_2} gradient. As a result, the rate of oxygen

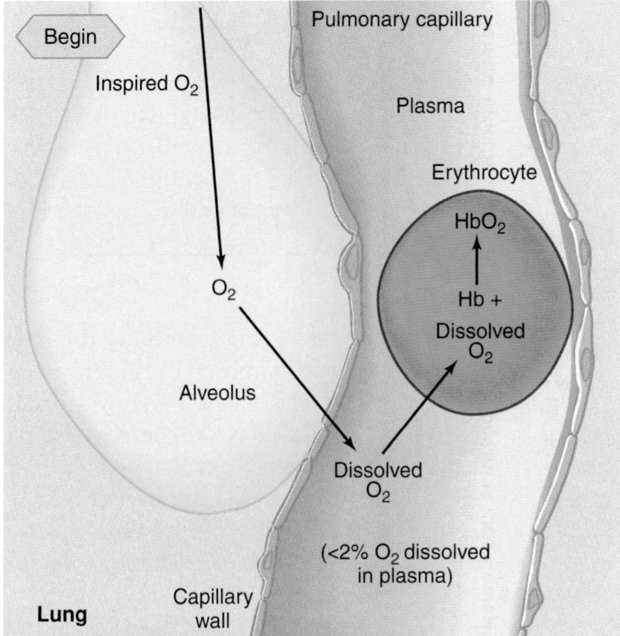

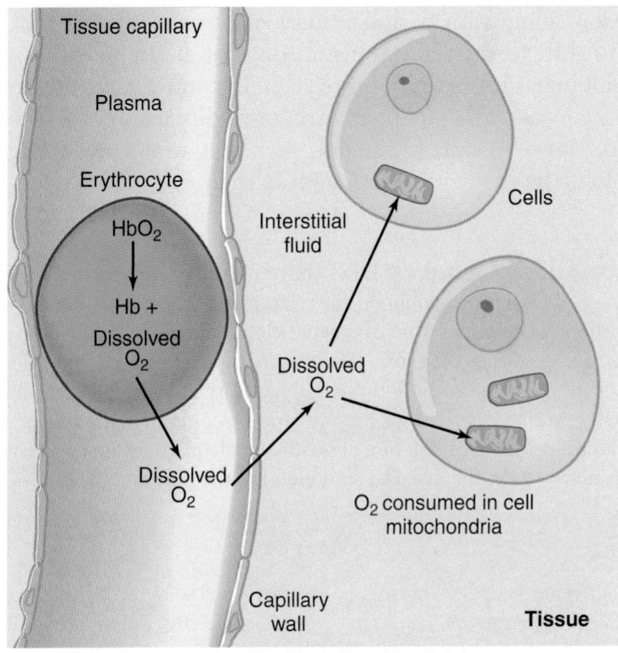

Figure 13.28 APIR Oxygen movement in the lungs and tissues. Movement of inspired air into the alveoli is by bulk flow; all movements across membranes are by diffusion.

diffusion from blood to cells increases. In turn, the resulting reduction in erythrocyte P_{O_2} causes additional dissociation of hemoglobin and oxygen. In this manner, the extraction of oxygen from blood in an exercising muscle is much greater than the usual 25%. In addition, an increased blood flow to the muscles, called active hyperemia (Chapter 12), also contributes greatly to the increased oxygen supply.

Effect of Carbon Monoxide on Oxygen Binding to Hemoglobin

Carbon monoxide is a colorless, odorless gas that is a product of the incomplete combustion of hydrocarbons, such as gasoline. It is one of the more common causes of sickness and death due to poisoning, both intentional and accidental. Its most striking pathophysiological characteristic is its extremely high affinity—210 times that of oxygen—for the oxygen-binding sites in hemoglobin. For this reason, it reduces the amount of oxygen that combines with hemoglobin in pulmonary capillaries by competing for these sites. It also exerts a second deleterious effect: It alters the hemoglobin molecule so as to shift the oxygen–hemoglobin dissociation curve to the left, thus decreasing the unloading of oxygen from hemoglobin in the tissues. As we will see later, the situation is worsened by the fact that persons suffering from carbon monoxide poisoning do not show any reflex increase in their ventilation.

Effects of CO_2 and Other Factors in the Blood and Different Isoforms on Hemoglobin Saturation

At any given P_{O_2}, a variety of other factors influence the degree of hemoglobin saturation. These include blood P_{CO_2}, H^+ concentration, temperature, the concentration of a substance produced by erythrocytes called **2,3-diphosphoglycerate** (**DPG**) (also known as bisphosphoglycerate [BPG]), and the presence of a special kind of hemoglobin usually only found in the fetal blood. As illustrated in **Figure 13.29**, an increase in DPG concentration, temperature, and acidity causes the dissociation curve to shift to the right. This means that at any given P_{O_2}, hemoglobin has less affinity for oxygen. In contrast, a decrease in DPG concentration, temperature, or acidity causes the dissociation curve to shift to the left, such that at any given P_{O_2}, hemoglobin has a greater affinity for oxygen.

The effects of increased P_{CO_2}, H^+ concentration, and temperature are continuously exerted on the blood in tissue capillaries, because each of these factors is greater in tissue capillary blood than in arterial blood. The P_{CO_2} is increased because of the carbon dioxide entering the blood from the tissues. For reasons to be described later, the H^+ concentration is

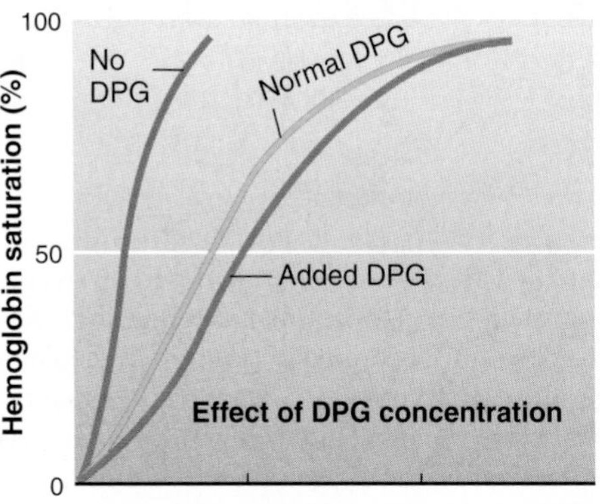

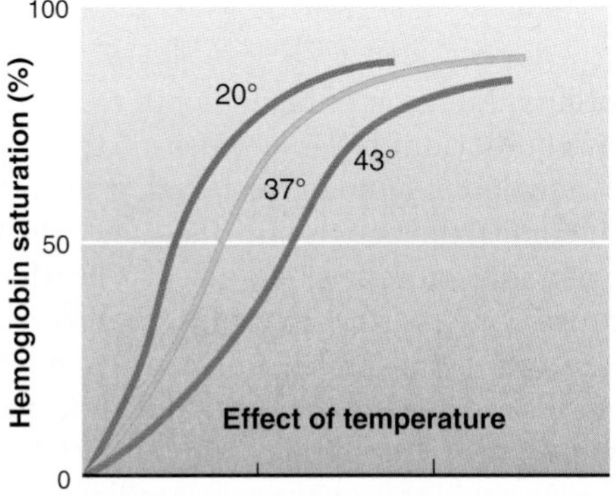

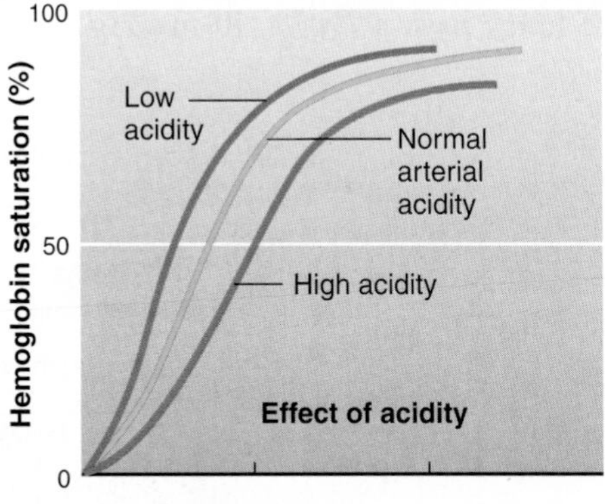

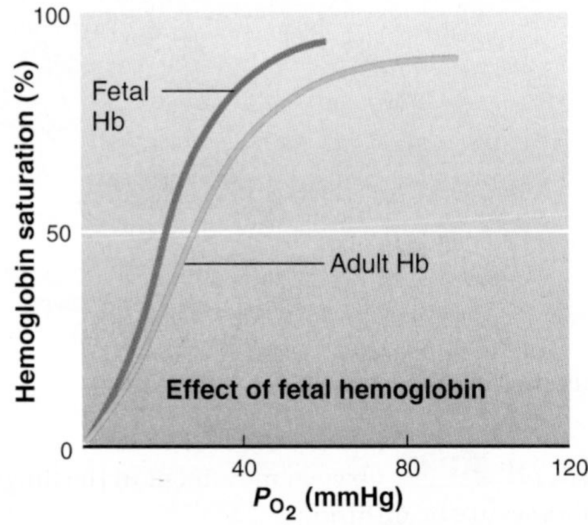

Figure 13.29 Effects of DPG concentration, temperature, acidity, and the presence of fetal hemoglobin on the relationship between P_{O_2} and hemoglobin saturation. The temperature of normal blood, of course, never diverges from 37°C as much as shown in the figure, but the principle is still the same when the changes are within the physiological range. High acidity and low acidity can be caused by high P_{CO_2} and low P_{CO_2}, respectively. Fetal hemoglobin has a higher affinity for oxygen than adult hemoglobin, allowing an adequate oxygen content from oxygen diffusion from the maternal to fetal blood in the placenta. Adapted from Comroe.

PHYSIOLOGICAL INQUIRY

- Researchers are developing blood substitutes to meet the demand for emergency transfusions. What would be the effect of artificial blood in which binding of O_2 is not altered by acidity?

Answer can be found at end of chapter.

increased because of the elevated P_{CO_2} and the release of metabolically produced acids such as lactic acid. The temperature is increased because of the heat produced by tissue metabolism. Hemoglobin exposed to this elevated blood P_{CO_2}, H^+ concentration, and temperature as it passes through the tissue capillaries has a decreased affinity for oxygen. Thus, hemoglobin gives up even more oxygen than it would have if the decreased tissue capillary P_{O_2} had been the only operating factor.

The more metabolically active a tissue is, the greater its P_{CO_2}, H^+ concentration, and temperature will be. At any given P_{O_2}, this causes hemoglobin to release more oxygen during passage through the tissue's capillaries and provides the more active cells with additional oxygen. Here, then, is another local mechanism that increases oxygen delivery to tissues with increased metabolic activity.

What is the mechanism by which these factors influence the affinity of hemoglobin for oxygen? Carbon dioxide and H^+ do so by combining with the globin portion of hemoglobin and altering the conformation of the hemoglobin molecule. Therefore, these effects are a form of allosteric modulation (Chapter 3). An elevated temperature also decreases hemoglobin's affinity for oxygen by altering its conformation.

DPG, which is produced during glycolysis, reversibly binds with hemoglobin, allosterically causing it to have a lower affinity for oxygen (see Figure 13.29). Erythrocytes have no mitochondria and, therefore, rely exclusively upon glycolysis. Consequently, erythrocytes contain large quantities of DPG, which is present in only trace amounts in cells with mitochondria. The net result is that whenever DPG levels increase, there is enhanced unloading of oxygen from hemoglobin as blood flows through the tissues. Such an increase in DPG concentration is triggered by a variety of conditions associated with inadequate oxygen supply to the tissues and helps to maintain oxygen delivery. For example, the increase in DPG is important during exposure to high altitude when the P_{O_2} of the blood is decreased because DPG increases the unloading of oxygen in the tissue capillaries.

Finally, the fetus has a unique form of hemoglobin called **fetal hemoglobin** (see Figure 13.29). Fetal hemoglobin contains subunits that are coded for by different genes than those that are expressed postnatally. These subunits alter the shape of the final protein and result in a hemoglobin molecule that has a higher affinity for oxygen than adult hemoglobin. That is, fetal hemoglobin binds considerably more oxygen than adult hemoglobin at any given P_{O_2}. This allows an increase in oxygen uptake across the placental diffusion barrier. Therefore, although fetal arterial P_{O_2} is much lower than that in the air-breathing newborn, fetal hemoglobin allows adequate oxygen uptake in the placenta to supply the developing fetus.

13.5 Transport of Carbon Dioxide in Blood

Remember that CO_2 is a waste product that has toxicity in part because it generates H^+. Large changes in H^+ concentration, if not buffered, would lead to significant changes in pH, thus altering the tertiary structure of proteins, including enzymes. In a resting person, metabolism generates about 200 mL of carbon dioxide per minute. When arterial blood flows through tissue capillaries, this volume of carbon dioxide diffuses from the tissues into the blood (**Figure 13.30a**).

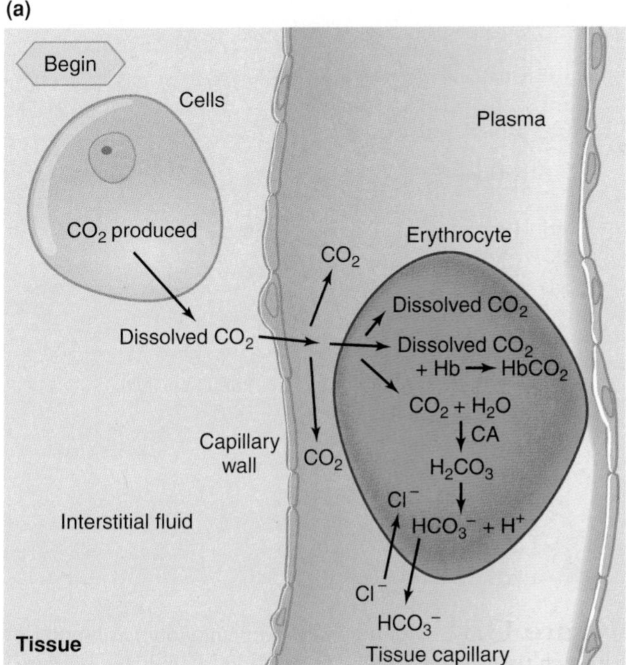

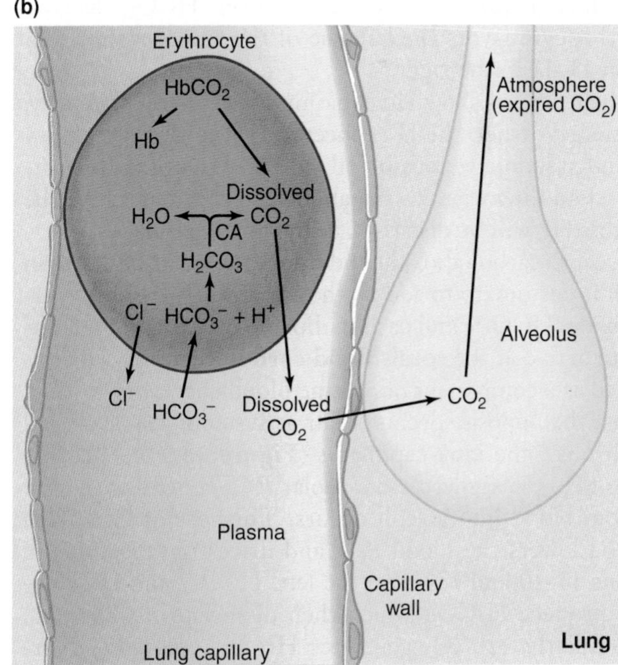

Figure 13.30 APIR Summary of CO_2 movement. Expiration of CO_2 is by bulk flow, whereas all movements of CO_2 across membranes are by diffusion. Arrows reflect relative proportions of the fates of the CO_2. About two-thirds of the CO_2 entering the blood in the tissues ultimately is converted to HCO_3^- in the erythrocytes because carbonic anhydrase (CA) is located there, but most of the HCO_3^- then moves out of the erythrocytes into the plasma in exchange for Cl^- (the "chloride shift"). See Figure 13.31 for the fate of the H^+ generated in the erythrocytes.

Carbon dioxide is much more soluble in water than is oxygen, so blood carries more dissolved carbon dioxide than dissolved oxygen. Even so, only about 10% of the carbon dioxide entering the blood dissolves in the plasma and erythrocytes. In order to transport all of the CO_2 produced in the tissues to the lung, CO_2 in the blood must be carried in other forms.

Another 25% to 30% of the carbon dioxide molecules entering the blood react reversibly with the amino groups of hemoglobin to form **carbaminohemoglobin.** For simplicity, this reaction with hemoglobin is written as

$$CO_2 + Hb \rightleftharpoons HbCO_2 \tag{13–10}$$

This reaction is aided by the fact that deoxyhemoglobin, formed as blood flows through the tissue capillaries, has a greater affinity for carbon dioxide than does oxyhemoglobin.

The remaining 60% to 65% of the carbon dioxide molecules entering the blood in the tissues is converted to HCO_3^-:

$$CO_2 + H_2O \underset{}{\overset{\text{carbonic anhydrase}}{\rightleftharpoons}} \underset{\text{carbonic acid}}{H_2CO_3} \rightleftharpoons \underset{\text{bicarbonate}}{HCO_3^-} + H^+ \tag{13–11}$$

The first reaction in equation 13–11 is rate limiting and is very slow unless catalyzed in both directions by the enzyme **carbonic anhydrase.** This enzyme is present in the erythrocytes but not in the plasma; therefore, this reaction occurs mainly in the erythrocytes. In contrast, carbonic acid dissociates very rapidly into HCO_3^- and H^+ without any enzyme assistance. Once formed, most of the HCO_3^- moves out of the erythrocytes into the plasma via a transporter that exchanges one HCO_3^- for one chloride ion (this is called the "chloride shift," which maintains electroneutrality). HCO_3^- leaving the erythrocyte favors the balance of the reaction shown in equation 13–11 to the right.

The reactions shown in equation 13–11 also explain why, as mentioned earlier, the H^+ concentration in tissue capillary blood and systemic venous blood is higher than that in arterial blood and increases as metabolic activity increases. The fate of this H^+ will be discussed in the next section.

Because carbon dioxide undergoes these various fates in blood, it is customary to add up the amounts of dissolved carbon dioxide, HCO_3^-, and carbon dioxide in carbaminohemoglobin to arrive at the **total-blood carbon dioxide,** which is measured as a component of routine blood chemistry testing.

Just the opposite events occur as systemic venous blood flows through the lung capillaries (**Figure 13.30b**). Because the blood P_{CO_2} is higher than alveolar P_{CO_2}, a net diffusion of CO_2 from blood into alveoli occurs. This loss of CO_2 from the blood lowers the blood P_{CO_2} and drives the reactions in equations 13–10 and 13–11 to the left. HCO_3^- and H^+ combine to produce H_2CO_3, which then dissociates to CO_2 and H_2O. Similarly, $HbCO_2$ generates Hb and free CO_2. Normally, as fast as CO_2 is generated from HCO_3^- and H^+ and from $HbCO_2$, it diffuses into the alveoli. In this manner, the CO_2 that was delivered into the blood in the tissues is now delivered into the alveoli, from where it is eliminated during expiration.

13.6 Transport of Hydrogen Ion Between Tissues and Lungs

As blood flows through the tissues, a fraction of oxyhemoglobin loses its oxygen to become deoxyhemoglobin, while simultaneously a large quantity of carbon dioxide enters the blood and undergoes the reactions that generate HCO_3^- and H^+. What happens to this H^+?

Deoxyhemoglobin has a much greater affinity for H^+ than does oxyhemoglobin, so it binds (buffers) most of the H^+ (**Figure 13.31**). Indeed, deoxyhemoglobin can be abbreviated HbH rather than Hb to denote its binding of H^+. In effect, the reaction is

$$HbO_2 + H^+ \rightleftharpoons HbH + O_2$$

In this manner, only a small amount of the H^+ generated in the blood remains free. This explains why venous blood (pH = 7.36) is only slightly more acidic than arterial blood (pH = 7.40).

As the venous blood passes through the lungs, this reaction is reversed. Deoxyhemoglobin becomes converted to oxyhemoglobin and, in the process, releases the H^+ it picked up in the tissues. The H^+ reacts with HCO_3^- to produce carbonic acid, which, under the influence of carbonic anhydrase, dissociates to form carbon dioxide and water. The carbon dioxide diffuses into the alveoli to be expired. Normally, all the H^+ that is generated in the tissue capillaries from the reaction of carbon dioxide and water recombines with HCO_3^- to form carbon

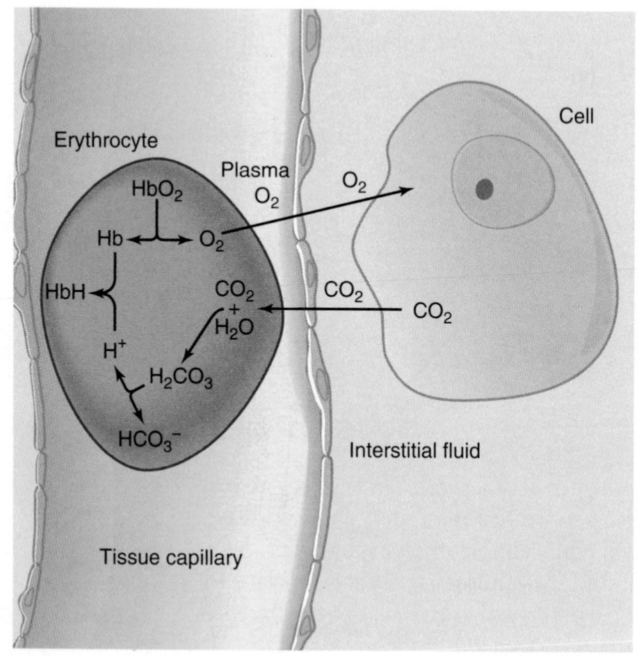

Figure 13.31 Binding of H^+ by hemoglobin as blood flows through tissue capillaries. This reaction is facilitated because deoxyhemoglobin, formed as oxygen dissociates from hemoglobin, has a greater affinity for H^+ than does oxyhemoglobin. For this reason, "Hb" and "HbH" are both abbreviations for deoxyhemoglobin. For simplicity, not shown is that H^+ binding to HbO_2 increases oxygen unloading.

TABLE 13.8	Effects of Various Factors on Hemoglobin
The affinity of hemoglobin for oxygen is decreased by • Increased H^+ concentration • Increased P_{CO_2} • Increased temperature • Increased DPG concentration	
The affinity of hemoglobin for both H^+ and CO_2 is decreased by increased P_{O_2}; that is, deoxyhemoglobin has a greater affinity for H^+ and CO_2 than does oxyhemoglobin.	

dioxide and water in the pulmonary capillaries. Therefore, none of this H^+ appears in the *arterial* blood.

What happens when a person is hypoventilating or has a lung disease that prevents normal elimination of carbon dioxide? Not only would arterial P_{CO_2} increase as a result, but so would arterial H^+ concentration. Increased arterial H^+ concentration due to carbon dioxide retention is termed ***respiratory acidosis.*** Conversely, hyperventilation would decrease arterial P_{CO_2} and H^+ concentration, producing ***respiratory alkalosis.***

The factors that influence the binding of CO_2 and O_2 by hemoglobin are summarized in **Table 13.8**.

Another aspect of the remarkable hemoglobin molecule is its ability to bind and transport **nitric oxide.** A present hypothesis is that as blood passes through the lungs, hemoglobin picks up and binds not only oxygen but also nitric oxide that is synthesized there, carries it to the peripheral tissues, and releases it along with oxygen. Simultaneously, via a different binding site, when nitric oxide production is increased in peripheral tissue (see Chapter 12), hemoglobin can pick up and catabolize nitric oxide. Theoretically, this cycle could play an important role in determining the peripheral concentration of nitric oxide and, thereby, the overall effect of this vasodilator agent. For example, by supplying net nitric oxide to the periphery, the process could cause additional vasodilation by systemic blood vessels. This would have effects on both local blood flow and systemic arterial blood pressure.

13.7 Control of Respiration

The control of breathing at rest, altitude, and during and after exercise has intrigued physiologists for centuries. It is a wonderful example of several general principles of physiology, including how homeostasis is essential for health and survival, and how physiological functions are controlled by multiple regulatory systems, often working in opposition.

Neural Generation of Rhythmic Breathing

The diaphragm and intercostal muscles are skeletal muscles and therefore do not contract unless motor neurons stimulate them to do so. Thus, breathing depends entirely upon cyclical respiratory muscle excitation of the diaphragm and the intercostal muscles by their motor neurons. Destruction of these neurons or a disconnection between their origin in the brain stem and the respiratory muscles results in paralysis of the respiratory muscles and death, unless some form of artificial respiration can be instituted.

Inspiration is initiated by a burst of action potentials in the spinal motor neurons to inspiratory muscles like the diaphragm. Then the action potentials cease, the inspiratory muscles relax, and expiration occurs as the elastic lungs recoil. In situations such as exercise when the contraction of expiratory muscles facilitates expiration, the neurons to these muscles, which were not active during inspiration, begin firing during expiration.

By what mechanism are impulses in the neurons innervating the respiratory muscles alternately increased and decreased? Control of this neural activity resides primarily in neurons in the medulla oblongata, the same area of the brain that contains the major cardiovascular control centers. (For the rest of this chapter, we will refer to the medulla oblongata simply as the medulla.) There are two main anatomical components of the **medullary respiratory center** (**Figure 13.32**). The neurons of the **dorsal respiratory group** (**DRG**) primarily fire during inspiration and have input to the spinal motor neurons that activate respiratory muscles involved in inspiration—the diaphragm and inspiratory intercostal muscles. The primary inspiratory muscle at rest is the diaphragm, which is innervated by the phrenic nerves. The **ventral respiratory group** (**VRG**) is the other main complex of neurons in the medullary respiratory center. The **respiratory rhythm generator** is located in the **pre-Bötzinger complex** of neurons in the upper part of the VRG. This rhythm generator appears to be composed of pacemaker cells and a complex neural network that, acting together, set the basal respiratory rate.

The VRG contains expiratory neurons that appear to be most important when large increases in ventilation are required (for example, during strenuous physical activity). During active expiration, motor neurons activated by the expiratory output from the VRG cause the expiratory muscles to contract. This helps to move air out of the lungs rather than depending only on the passive expiration that occurs during quiet breathing.

During quiet breathing, the respiratory rhythm generator activates inspiratory neurons in the VRG that depolarize the inspiratory spinal motor neurons, causing the inspiratory muscles to contract. When the inspiratory motor neurons stop firing, the inspiratory muscles relax, allowing passive expiration. During increases in breathing, the inspiratory and expiratory motor neurons and muscles are not activated at the same time but, rather, alternate in function.

The medullary inspiratory neurons receive a rich synaptic input from neurons in various areas of the pons, the part of the brainstem just above the medulla. This input fine-tunes the output of the medullary inspiratory neurons and may help terminate inspiration by inhibiting them. It is likely that an area of the lower pons called the **apneustic center** is the major source of this output, whereas an area of the upper pons called the **pneumotaxic center** modulates the activity of the apneustic center (see Figure 13.32). The pneumotaxic center, also known as the **pontine respiratory group,** helps to smooth the transition between inspiration and expiration.

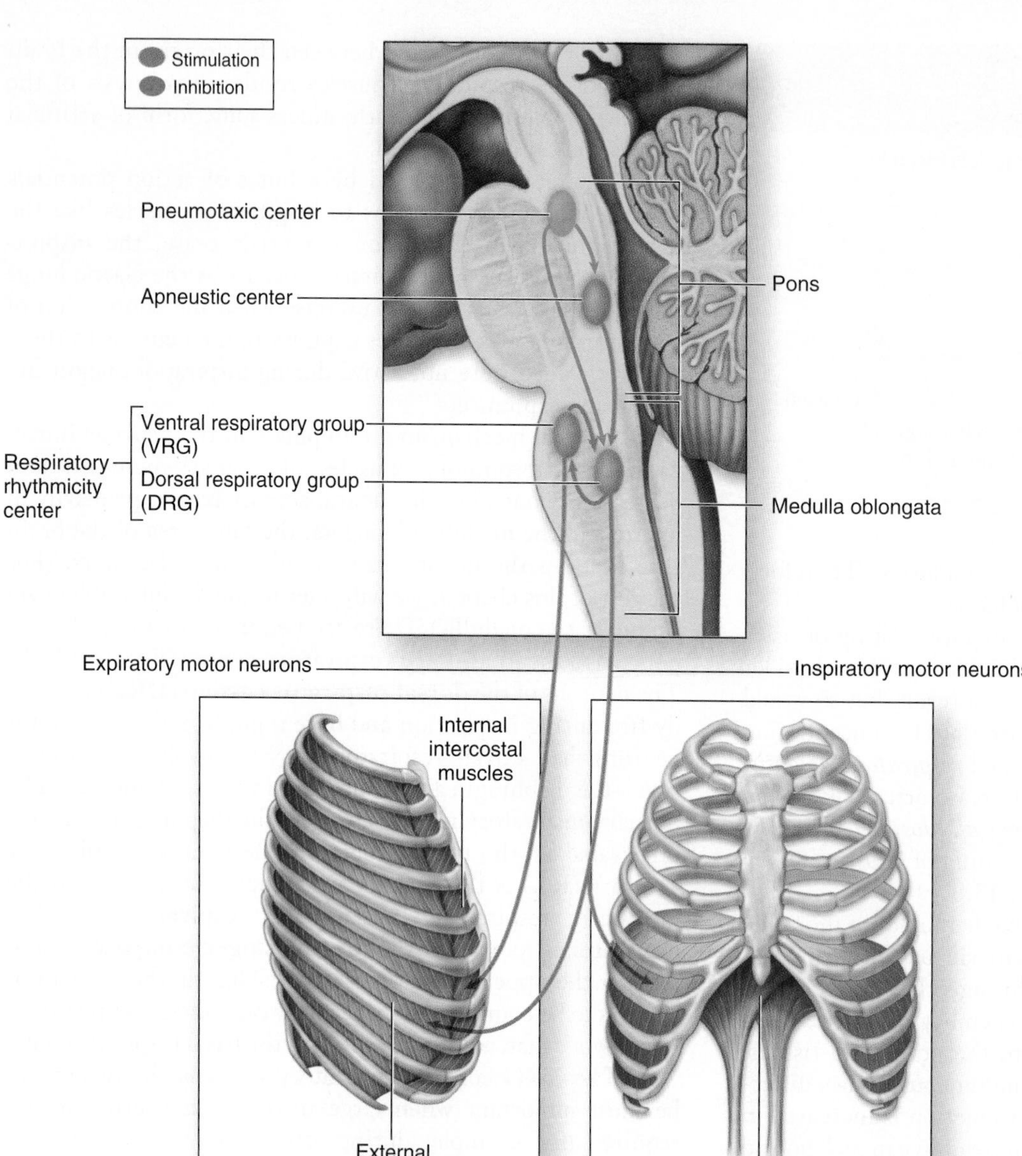

Figure 13.32 AP|R A simplified depiction of the brainstem centers that control respiratory rate and depth. Inspiratory motor neurons are driven primarily by the DRG while expiratory motor neurons (active mostly during forced expiration and strenuous exercise) are driven primarily by the VRG. Note that DRG and VRG innervate each other allowing phasic inspiration and expiration. The centers in the upper pons are primarily responsible for fine-tuning respiratory control.

The respiratory nerves in the medulla and pons also receive synaptic input from higher centers of the brain such that the pattern of respiration is controlled voluntarily during speaking, diving, and even with emotions and pain.

Another cutoff signal for inspiration comes from **pulmonary stretch receptors,** which lie in the airway smooth muscle layer and are activated by a large lung inflation. Action potentials in the afferent nerve fibers from the stretch receptors travel to the brain and inhibit the activity of the medullary inspiratory neurons. This is called the **Hering–Breuer reflex.** Thus, feedback from the lungs helps to terminate inspiration by inhibiting inspiratory nerves in the DRG. However, this reflex plays a role in setting respiratory rhythm only under conditions of very large tidal volumes, as in strenuous exercise. The arterial chemoreceptors described next also have important input to the respiratory control centers such that the rate and depth of respiration can be increased when the levels of arterial oxygen decrease, or when arterial carbon dioxide or H^+ concentration increases.

A final point about the medullary inspiratory neurons is that they are quite sensitive to inhibition by drugs such as barbiturates and morphine. Death from an overdose of these drugs is often due directly to a cessation of breathing.

Control of Ventilation by P_{O_2}, P_{CO_2}, and H^+ Concentration

Respiratory rate and tidal volume are not fixed but can be increased or decreased over a wide range. For simplicity, we will describe the control of ventilation without discussing whether rate or depth makes the greater contribution to the change.

There are many inputs to the medullary inspiratory neurons, but the most important for the automatic control of ventilation at rest come from peripheral (arterial) chemoreceptors and central chemoreceptors.

The **peripheral chemoreceptors,** located high in the neck at the bifurcation of the common carotid arteries and in the thorax on the arch of the aorta (**Figure 13.33**) are called

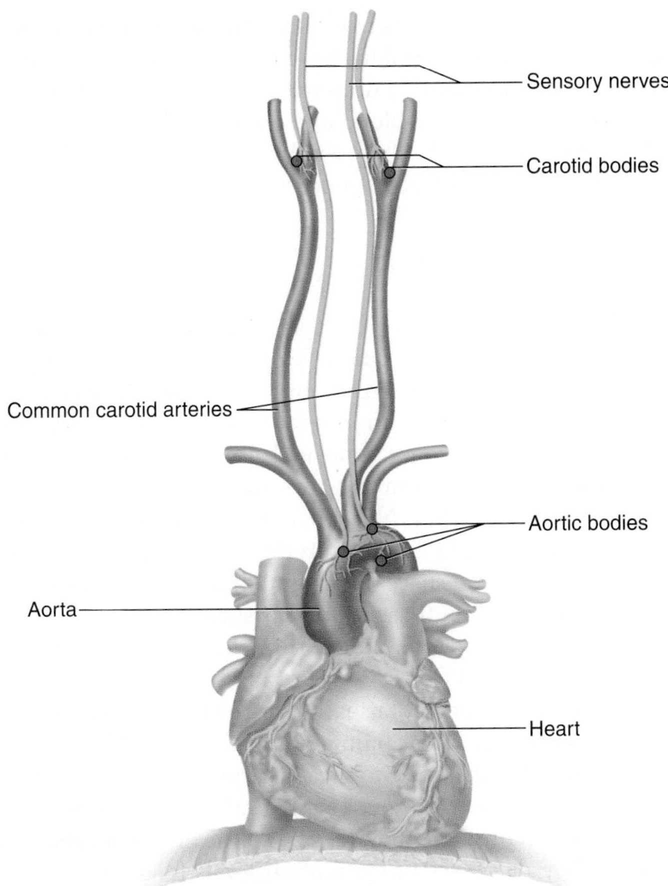

Figure 13.33 AP|R Location of the carotid and aortic bodies. Note that each carotid body is quite close to a carotid sinus, the major arterial baroreceptor (see Figure 12.53). Both right and left common carotid bifurcations contain a carotid sinus and a carotid body.

PHYSIOLOGICAL INQUIRY

- Several decades ago, removal of the carotid bodies was tried as a treatment for asthma. It was thought that it would reduce shortness of breath and airway hyperreactivity. What would be the effect of bilateral carotid body removal on someone taking a trip to the top of a mountain (an altitude of 3000 meters)? (*Hint:* Look ahead to Table 13.10.)

Answer can be found at end of chapter.

the **carotid bodies** and **aortic bodies,** respectively. In both locations, they are quite close to, but distinct from, the arterial baroreceptors and are in intimate contact with the arterial blood. The carotid bodies, in particular, are strategically located to monitor oxygen supply to the brain. The peripheral chemoreceptors are composed of specialized receptor cells stimulated mainly by a decrease in the arterial P_{O_2} and an increase in the arterial H^+ concentration (**Table 13.9**). These cells communicate synaptically with neuron terminals from which afferent nerve fibers pass to the brainstem. There they provide excitatory synaptic input to the medullary inspiratory neurons. The carotid body input is the predominant peripheral chemoreceptor involved in the control of respiration.

TABLE 13.9	Major Stimuli for the Central and Peripheral Chemoreceptors
Peripheral chemoreceptors—carotid bodies and aortic bodies—respond to changes in the arterial blood. They are stimulated by • Significantly decreased P_{O_2} (hypoxia) • Increased H^+ concentration (metabolic acidosis) • Increased P_{CO_2} (respiratory acidosis)	
Central chemoreceptors—located in the medulla oblongata—respond to changes in the *brain extracellular fluid.* They are stimulated by increased P_{CO_2} via associated changes in H^+ concentration (see equation 13–11).	

The **central chemoreceptors** are located in the medulla and, like the peripheral chemoreceptors, provide excitatory synaptic input to the medullary inspiratory neurons. They are stimulated by an increase in the H^+ concentration of the brain's extracellular fluid. As we will see later, such changes result mainly from changes in blood P_{CO_2}.

Control by P_{O_2}

Figure 13.34 illustrates an experiment in which healthy subjects breathe low-P_{O_2} gas mixtures for several minutes. The experiment is performed in a way that keeps arterial P_{CO_2} constant so that the pure effects of changing only P_{O_2} can be studied. Little increase in ventilation is observed until the oxygen concentration of the inspired air is reduced enough to lower arterial P_{O_2} to 60 mmHg. Beyond this point, any further reduction in arterial P_{O_2} causes a marked reflex increase in ventilation.

This reflex is mediated by the peripheral chemoreceptors (**Figure 13.35**). The low arterial P_{O_2} increases the rate at which the receptors discharge, resulting in an increased number of action potentials traveling up the afferent nerve fibers and stimulating the medullary inspiratory neurons. The resulting increase in ventilation provides more oxygen to the

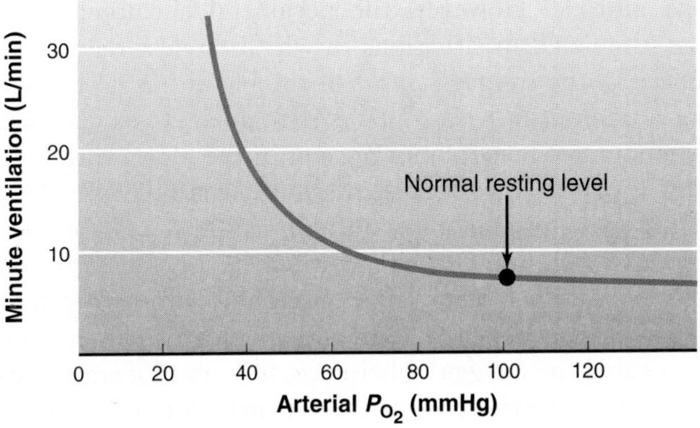

Figure 13.34 The effect on ventilation of breathing different oxygen mixtures. The arterial P_{CO_2} was maintained at 40 mmHg throughout the experiment.

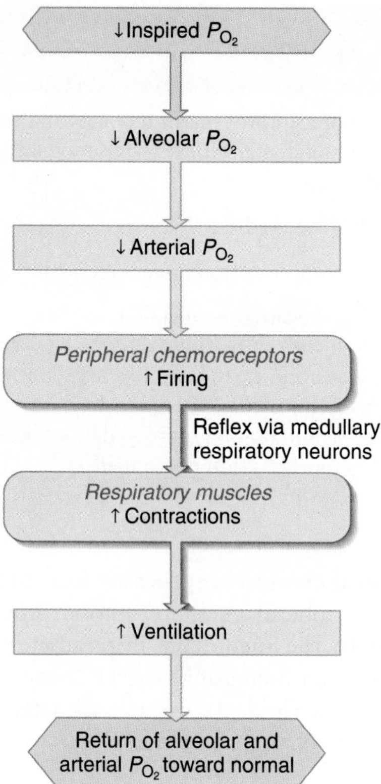

Figure 13.35 Sequence of events by which a low arterial P_{O_2} causes hyperventilation, which maintains alveolar (and, hence, arterial) P_{O_2} at a value higher than would exist if the ventilation had remained unchanged.

alveoli and minimizes the decrease in alveolar and arterial P_{O_2} produced by the low-P_{O_2} gas mixture.

It may seem surprising that we are insensitive to smaller reductions of arterial P_{O_2} but look again at the oxygen–hemoglobin dissociation curve (see Figure 13.26). Total oxygen transport by the blood is not really reduced very much until the arterial P_{O_2} falls below about 60 mmHg. Therefore, increased ventilation would not result in much more oxygen being added to the blood until that point is reached.

To reiterate, the peripheral chemoreceptors respond to decreases in arterial P_{O_2}, as occurs in lung disease or exposure to high altitude. However, the peripheral chemoreceptors are *not* stimulated in situations in which modest reductions take place in the oxygen *content* of the blood but no change occurs in arterial P_{O_2}. As stated earlier, anemia is a decrease in the amount of hemoglobin present in the blood without a decrease in arterial P_{O_2}, because the concentration of dissolved oxygen in the arterial blood is normal; that is, the P_{O_2} of arterial blood is determined primarily by the oxygen-diffusion capacity of the lung, whereas the total amount of oxygen in the blood is also dependent on the amount of hemoglobin there to carry the oxygen. Therefore, mild to moderate anemia, in which arterial P_{O_2} is usually normal, does not activate peripheral chemoreceptors and does not stimulate increased ventilation.

This same analysis holds true when oxygen content is reduced moderately by the presence of carbon monoxide, which, as described earlier, reduces the amount of oxygen combined with hemoglobin by competing for these sites. Because carbon monoxide does not affect the amount of oxygen that can dissolve in blood and does not alter the oxygen-diffusion capacity of the lung, the arterial P_{O_2} is unaltered, and no increase in peripheral chemoreceptor output or ventilation occurs.

Control by P_{CO_2}

Figure 13.36 illustrates an experiment in which subjects breathe air with variable quantities of carbon dioxide added. The presence of carbon dioxide in the inspired air causes an increase in alveolar P_{CO_2}, and therefore the diffusion gradient for CO_2 is reversed from the normal situation. This results in a net uptake of CO_2 from the alveolar air and, therefore, an increase in arterial P_{CO_2}. Note that even a very small increase in arterial P_{CO_2} causes a marked reflex increase in ventilation. Experiments like this have documented that the reflex mechanisms controlling ventilation prevent small increases in arterial P_{CO_2} to a much greater degree than they prevent equivalent decreases in arterial P_{O_2}.

Of course, we do not usually breathe bags of gas containing carbon dioxide. Some pulmonary diseases, such as emphysema, can cause the body to retain carbon dioxide, resulting in an increase in arterial P_{CO_2} that stimulates ventilation. This promotes the elimination of the carbon dioxide. Conversely, if arterial P_{CO_2} decreases below normal levels for whatever reason, this removes some of the stimulus for ventilation. This reduces ventilation and allows metabolically produced carbon dioxide to accumulate, thereby returning the P_{CO_2} to normal. In this manner, the arterial P_{CO_2} is stabilized near the normal value of 40 mmHg.

The ability of changes in arterial P_{CO_2} to control ventilation reflexively is largely due to associated changes in H^+ concentration (see equation 13–11). As summarized in

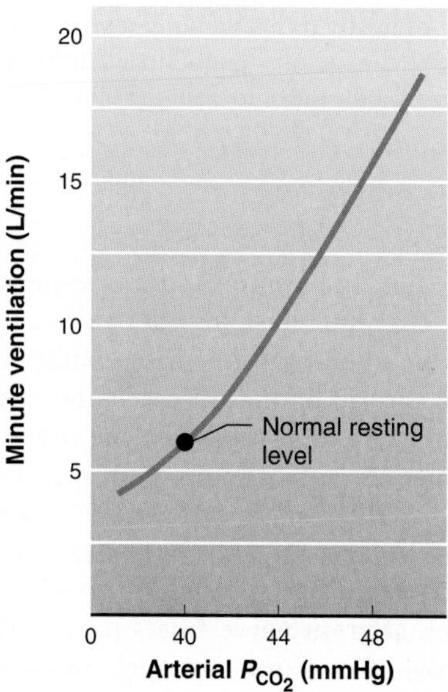

Figure 13.36 Effects on respiration of increasing arterial P_{CO_2} achieved by adding CO_2 to inspired air.

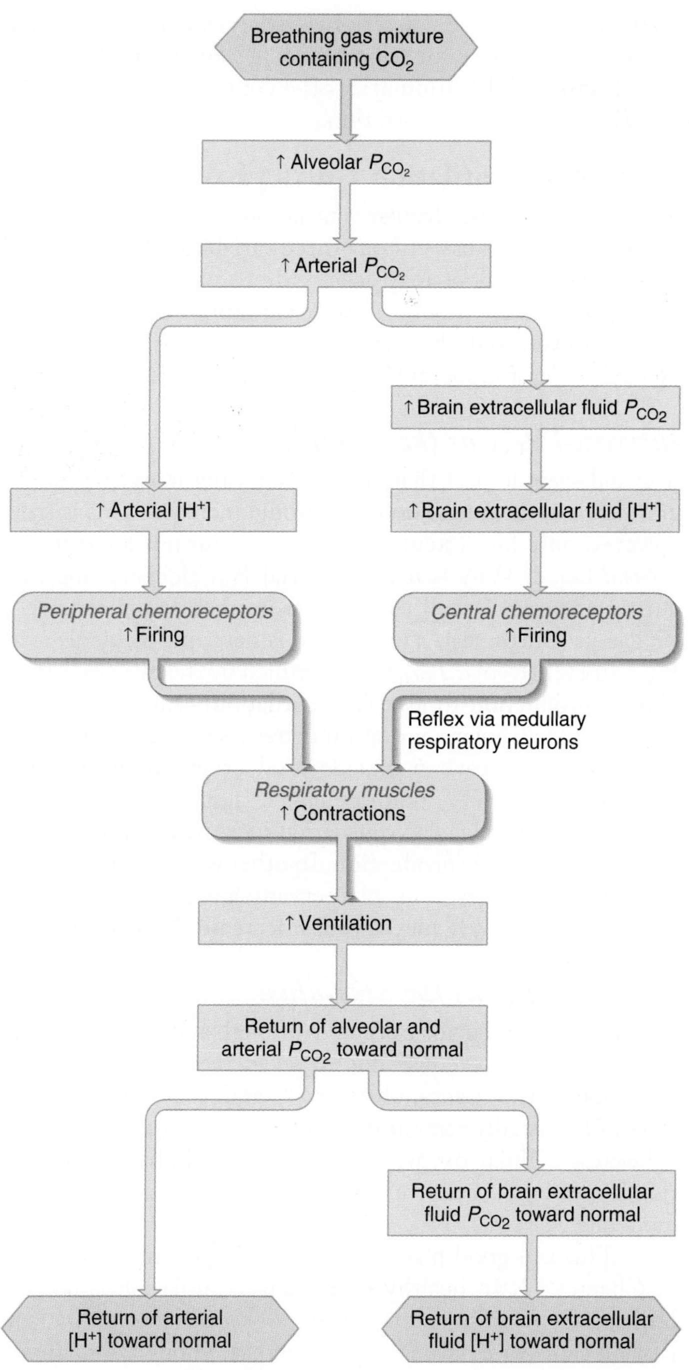

Figure 13.37 Pathways by which increased arterial P_{CO_2} stimulates ventilation. Note that the peripheral chemoreceptors are stimulated by an *increase* in H^+ concentration, whereas they are also stimulated by a *decrease* in P_{O_2} (see Figure 13.35).

Figure 13.37, both the peripheral and central chemoreceptors initiate the pathways that mediate these reflexes. The peripheral chemoreceptors are stimulated by the increased arterial H^+ concentration resulting from the increased P_{CO_2}. At the same time, because carbon dioxide diffuses rapidly across the membranes separating capillary blood and brain tissue, the increase in arterial P_{CO_2} causes a rapid increase in brain extracellular fluid P_{CO_2}. This increased P_{CO_2} increases *brain extracellular fluid* H^+ concentration, which stimulates the central chemoreceptors. Inputs from both the peripheral and central chemoreceptors stimulate the medullary inspiratory neurons to increase ventilation. The end result is a return of arterial and brain extracellular fluid P_{CO_2} and H^+ concentration toward normal. Of the two sets of receptors involved in this reflex response to elevated P_{CO_2}, the central chemoreceptors are the more important, accounting for about 70% of the increased ventilation.

It should also be noted that the effects of increased P_{CO_2} and decreased P_{O_2} not only exist as independent inputs to the medulla but potentiate each other's effects. The acute ventilatory response to combined low P_{O_2} and high P_{CO_2} is considerably greater than the sum of the individual responses.

Throughout this section, we have described the stimulatory effects of carbon dioxide on ventilation via reflex input to the medulla, but very high levels of carbon dioxide actually *inhibit* ventilation and may be lethal. This is because such concentrations of carbon dioxide act directly on the medulla to inhibit the respiratory neurons by an anesthesia-like effect, another example of a harmful effect of excess carbon dioxide. Other symptoms caused by very high blood P_{CO_2} include severe headaches, restlessness, and dulling or loss of consciousness.

Control by Changes in Arterial H^+ Concentration That Are Not Due to Changes in Carbon Dioxide

We have seen that retention or excessive elimination of carbon dioxide causes respiratory acidosis and respiratory alkalosis, respectively. There are, however, many normal and pathological situations in which a change in arterial H^+ concentration is due to some cause other than a primary change in P_{CO_2}. This is termed ***metabolic acidosis*** when H^+ concentration is increased and ***metabolic alkalosis*** when it is decreased. In such cases, the peripheral chemoreceptors play the major role in altering ventilation.

For example, the addition of lactic acid to the blood, as in strenuous exercise, causes hyperventilation almost entirely by stimulation of the peripheral chemoreceptors (**Figure 13.38** and **Figure 13.39**). The central chemoreceptors are only

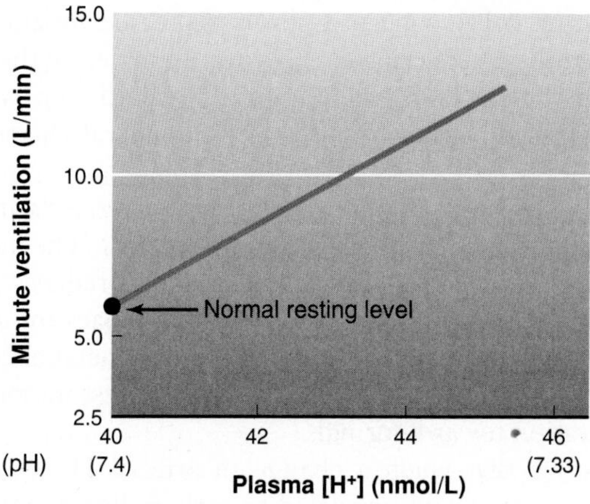

Figure 13.38 Changes in ventilation in response to an elevation of plasma H^+ concentration produced by the administration of lactic acid. Adapted from Lambertsen.

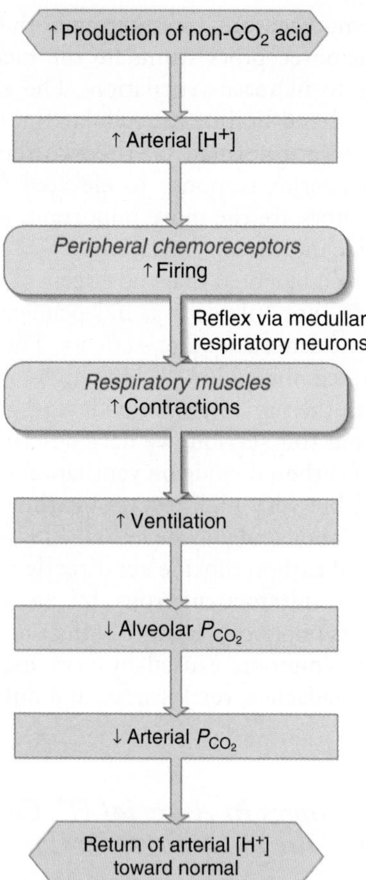

Figure 13.39 Reflexively induced hyperventilation minimizes the change in arterial H^+ concentration when acids are produced in excess in the body. Note that under such conditions, arterial P_{CO_2} is reflexively reduced below its normal value.

minimally stimulated in this case because brain H^+ concentration is increased to only a small extent, at least early on, by the H^+ generated from the lactic acid. This is because H^+ penetrates the blood–brain barrier very slowly. In contrast, as described earlier, carbon dioxide penetrates the blood–brain barrier easily and changes brain H^+ concentration.

The converse of the previous situation is also true: When arterial H^+ concentration is decreased by any means other than by a reduction in P_{CO_2} (for example, by the loss of H^+ from the stomach when vomiting), ventilation is reflexively depressed because of decreased peripheral chemoreceptor output.

The adaptive value such reflexes have in regulating arterial H^+ concentration is shown in Figure 13.39. The increased ventilation induced by a metabolic acidosis reduces arterial P_{CO_2}, which lowers arterial H^+ concentration back toward normal. Similarly, hypoventilation induced by a metabolic alkalosis results in an elevated arterial P_{CO_2} and a restoration of H^+ concentration toward normal.

Notice that when a change in arterial H^+ concentration due to some acid unrelated to carbon dioxide influences ventilation via the peripheral chemoreceptors, P_{CO_2} is displaced from normal. This is a reflex that regulates arterial H^+ concentration at the expense of changes in arterial P_{CO_2}. Maintenance of normal arterial H^+ is necessary because most enzymes of the body function best at physiological pH.

Figure 13.40 summarizes the control of ventilation by P_{O_2}, P_{CO_2}, and H^+ concentration.

Control of Ventilation During Exercise

During exercise, the alveolar ventilation may increase as much as 20-fold. On the basis of our three variables—P_{O_2}, P_{CO_2}, and H^+ concentration—it may seem easy to explain the mechanism that induces this increased ventilation. This is not the case, however, and the major stimuli to ventilation during exercise, at least moderate exercise, remain unclear.

Increased P_{CO_2} as the Stimulus?

It would seem logical that, as the exercising muscles produce more carbon dioxide, blood P_{CO_2} would increase. This is true, however, only for systemic *venous* blood but not for systemic *arterial* blood. Why is it that arterial P_{CO_2} does not increase during exercise? Recall two facts from the section on alveolar gas pressures: (1) Arterial P_{CO_2} is determined by alveolar P_{CO_2}, and (2) alveolar P_{CO_2} is determined by the ratio of carbon dioxide production to alveolar ventilation. During moderate exercise, the alveolar ventilation increases in exact proportion to the increased carbon dioxide production, so alveolar and therefore arterial P_{CO_2} do not change. In fact, in very strenuous exercise, the alveolar ventilation increases relatively more than carbon dioxide production. In other words, during strenuous exercise, a person may hyperventilate; thus, alveolar and systemic arterial P_{CO_2} may actually decrease (**Figure 13.41**)!

Decreased P_{O_2} as the Stimulus?

The story is similar for oxygen. Although systemic *venous* P_{O_2} decreases during exercise due to an increase in oxygen consumption in the tissues, alveolar P_{O_2} and, therefore, systemic *arterial* P_{O_2} usually remain unchanged (see Figure 13.41). This is because cellular oxygen consumption and alveolar ventilation increase in exact proportion to each other, at least during moderate exercise.

This is a good place to recall an important point made in Chapter 12. In healthy individuals, ventilation is not the limiting factor in strenuous exercise—cardiac output is. Ventilation can, as we have just seen, increase enough to maintain arterial P_{O_2}.

Increased H^+ Concentration as the Stimulus?

Because the arterial P_{CO_2} does not change during moderate exercise and decreases during strenuous exercise, there is no accumulation of excess H^+ resulting from carbon dioxide accumulation. However, during strenuous exercise, there *is* an increase in arterial H^+ concentration (see Figure 13.41) due to the generation and release of lactic acid into the blood. This change in H^+ concentration is responsible, in part, for stimulating the hyperventilation accompanying strenuous exercise.

Other Factors

A variety of other factors play some role in stimulating ventilation during exercise. These include (1) reflex input from mechanoreceptors in joints and muscles, (2) an increase in

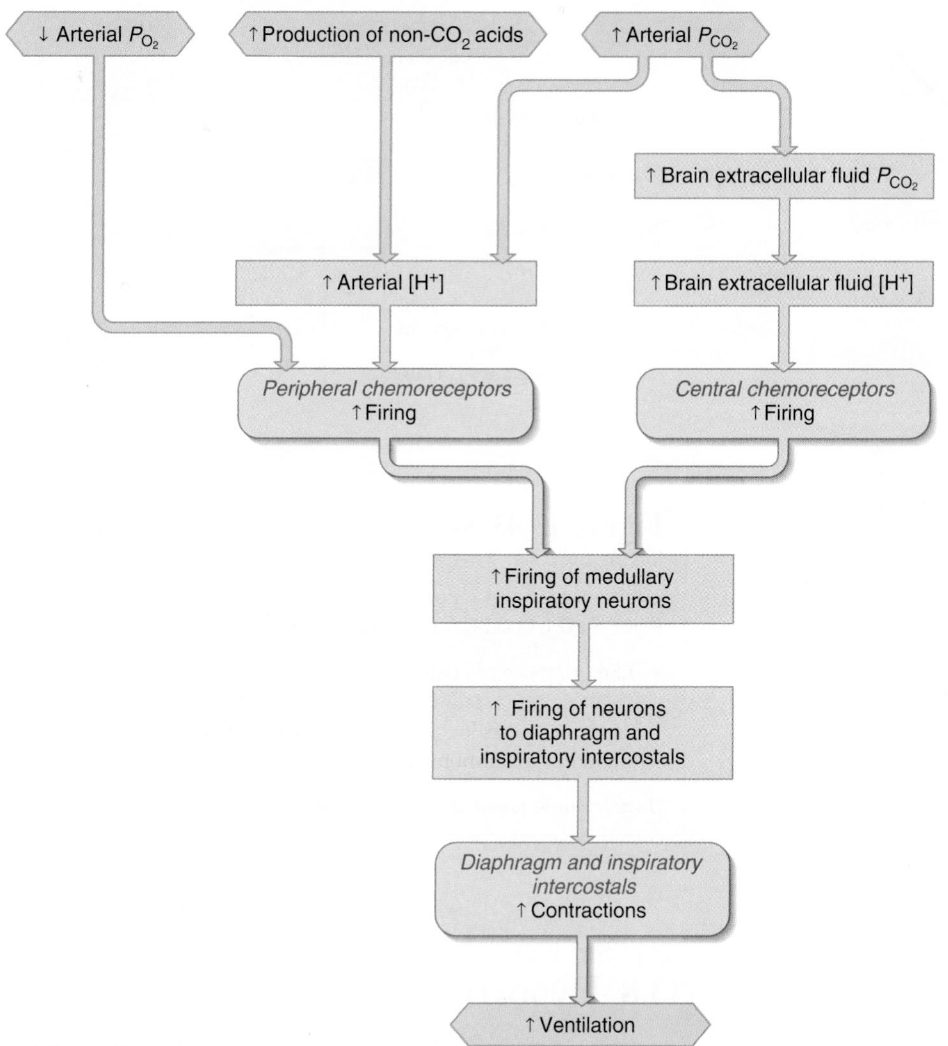

Figure 13.40 Summary of the major chemical inputs that stimulate ventilation. This is a combination of Figures 13.35, 13.37, and 13.39. When arterial P_{O_2} increases or when P_{CO_2} or H^+ concentration decreases, ventilation is reflexively decreased.

body temperature, (3) inputs to the respiratory neurons via branches from axons descending from the brain to motor neurons supplying the exercising muscles (central command), (4) an increase in the plasma epinephrine concentration, (5) an increase in the plasma potassium concentration due to movement of potassium out of the exercising muscles, and (6) a conditioned (learned) response mediated by neural input to the respiratory centers. The operation of factors (1) and (3) are most likely and can be seen in **Figure 13.42**. There is an abrupt increase—within seconds—in ventilation at the onset of exercise and an equally abrupt decrease at the end; these changes occur too rapidly to be explained by alteration of chemical constituents of the blood or by altered body temperature.

Figure 13.43 summarizes various factors that influence ventilation during exercise. The possibility that oscillatory changes in arterial P_{O_2}, P_{CO_2}, or H^+ concentration occur—despite unchanged average levels of these variables—and play some role has been proposed, but this remains unproven.

Other Ventilatory Responses

Protective Reflexes

A group of responses protect the respiratory system from irritant materials. Most familiar are the cough and the sneeze reflexes, which originate in sensory receptors located between airway epithelial cells. The receptors for the sneeze reflex are in the nose or pharynx; those for cough are in the larynx, trachea, and bronchi. When the receptors initiating a cough are stimulated, the medullary respiratory neurons reflexively cause a deep inspiration and a violent expiration. In this manner, particles and secretions are moved from smaller to larger airways and aspiration of materials into the lungs is also prevented.

Alcohol inhibits the cough reflex, which may partially explain the susceptibility of alcoholics to choking and pneumonia.

Another example of a protective reflex is the immediate cessation of respiration that is often triggered when noxious agents are inhaled. Chronic smoking may cause a loss of this reflex.

Voluntary Control of Breathing

Although we have discussed in detail the involuntary nature of most respiratory reflexes, the voluntary control of respiratory movements is important. Voluntary control is accomplished by descending pathways from the cerebral cortex to the motor neurons of the respiratory muscles. This voluntary control of respiration cannot be maintained when the involuntary stimuli, such as an elevated P_{CO_2} or H^+ concentration, become intense. An example is the inability to hold your breath for very long.

The opposite of breath holding—deliberate hyperventilation—lowers alveolar and arterial P_{CO_2} and increases P_{O_2}. Unfortunately, swimmers sometimes voluntarily hyperventilate immediately before underwater swimming to be able to hold their breath longer. We say "unfortunately" because the low P_{CO_2} may still permit breath holding at a time when the exertion is decreasing the arterial P_{O_2} to levels that can cause unconsciousness and lead to drowning.

Besides the obvious forms of voluntary control, respiration must also be controlled during such complex actions as speaking, singing, and swallowing.

Reflexes from J Receptors

In the lungs, either in the capillary walls or the interstitium, are a group of sensory receptors called **J receptors.** They are normally dormant but are stimulated by an increase in lung

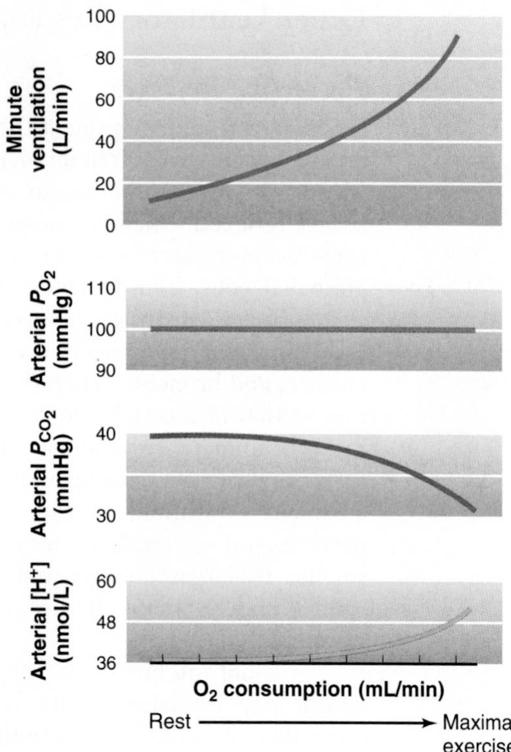

Figure 13.41 The effect of exercise on ventilation, arterial gas pressures, and H^+ concentration. All these variables remain constant during moderate exercise; any change occurs only during strenuous exercise, when the person is actually hyperventilating (decrease in P_{CO_2}). Adapted from Comroe.

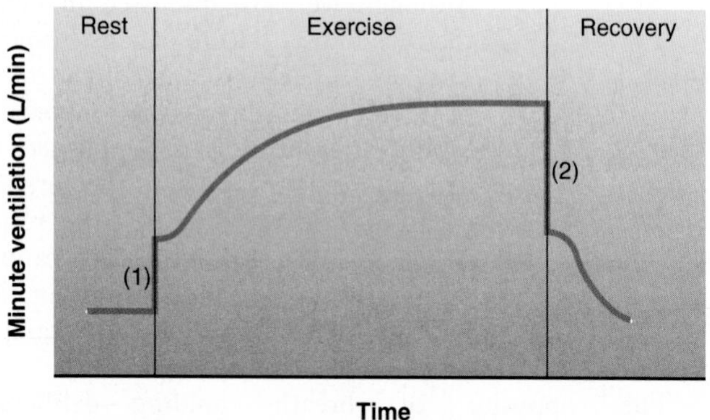

Figure 13.42 Ventilation changes during exercise. Note (1) the abrupt increase at the onset of exercise and (2) the equally abrupt but larger decrease at the end of exercise.

interstitial pressure caused by the collection of fluid in the interstitium. Such an increase occurs during the vascular congestion caused by either occlusion of a pulmonary vessel (called a ***pulmonary embolism***) or left ventricular heart failure (Chapter 12), as well as by strenuous exercise in healthy people. The main reflex effects are rapid breathing (tachypnea) and a dry cough. In addition, neural input from J receptors gives rise to sensations of pressure in the chest and ***dyspnea***—the feeling that breathing is labored or difficult.

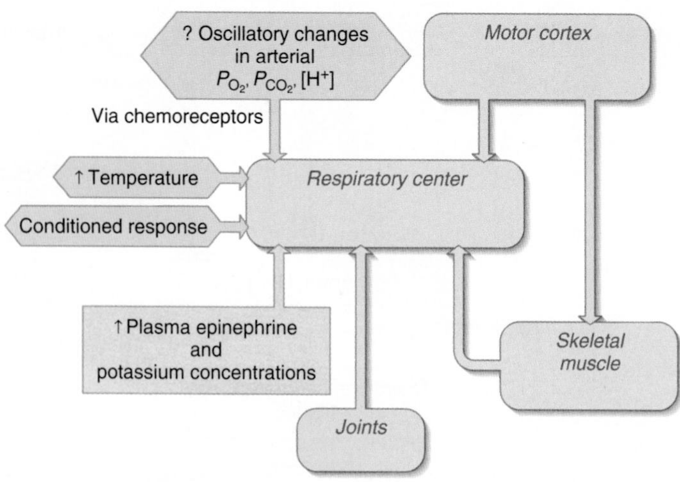

Figure 13.43 Summary of factors that stimulate ventilation during exercise. *Note:* "?" indicates a theoretical input.

PHYSIOLOGICAL INQUIRY

- The existence of chemoreceptors in the pulmonary artery has been suggested. Hypothesize a function for peripheral chemoreceptors located on and sensing the P_{O_2} and P_{CO_2} of the blood in the pulmonary artery.

Answer can be found at end of chapter.

13.8 Hypoxia

Hypoxia is defined as a deficiency of oxygen at the tissue level. There are many potential causes of hypoxia, but they can be classified into four general categories: (1) ***hypoxic hypoxia*** (also termed ***hypoxemia***), in which the arterial P_{O_2} is reduced; (2) ***anemic hypoxia*** or ***carbon monoxide hypoxia,*** in which the arterial P_{O_2} is normal but the total oxygen *content* of the blood is reduced because of inadequate numbers of erythrocytes, deficient or abnormal hemoglobin, or competition for the hemoglobin molecule by carbon monoxide; (3) ***ischemic hypoxia*** (also called *hypoperfusion hypoxia*), in which blood flow to the tissues is too low; and (4) ***histotoxic hypoxia,*** in which the quantity of oxygen reaching the tissues is normal but the cell is unable to utilize the oxygen because a toxic agent—cyanide, for example—has interfered with the cell's metabolic machinery.

Hypoxic hypoxia is a common cause of hypoxia. The primary causes of hypoxic hypoxia in disease are listed in **Table 13.10**. Exposure to the reduced P_{O_2} of high altitude also causes hypoxic hypoxia but is, of course, not a disease. The brief summaries in Table 13.10 provide a review of many of the key aspects of respiratory physiology and pathophysiology described in this chapter.

This table also emphasizes that some of the diseases that produce hypoxia also produce carbon dioxide retention and an increased arterial P_{CO_2} (***hypercapnia***). In such cases, treating only the oxygen deficit by administering oxygen may be inadequate because it does nothing about the hypercapnia. Indeed,

TABLE 13.10	Causes of a Decreased Arterial P_{O_2} (Hypoxic Hypoxia) in Disease

I. ***Hypoventilation*** may be caused by
   A. A defect anywhere along the respiratory control pathway, from the medulla through the respiratory muscles
   B. Severe thoracic cage abnormalities
   C. Major obstruction of the upper airway

The hypoxemia of hypoventilation is always accompanied by an increased arterial P_{CO_2}.

II. ***Diffusion impairment*** results from thickening of the alveolar membranes or a decrease in their surface area. In turn, it causes blood P_{O_2} and alveolar P_{O_2} to fail to equilibrate. Often, it is apparent only during exercise. Arterial P_{CO_2} is either normal because carbon dioxide diffuses more readily than oxygen or reduced if the hypoxemia reflexively stimulates ventilation.

III. A ***shunt*** is
   A. An anatomical abnormality of the cardiovascular system that causes mixed venous blood to bypass ventilated alveoli in passing from the right side of the heart to the left side
   B. An intrapulmonary defect in which mixed venous blood perfuses unventilated alveoli. Arterial P_{CO_2} generally does not increase because the effect of the shunt on arterial P_{CO_2} is counterbalanced by the increased ventilation reflexively stimulated by the hypoxemia.

IV. ***Ventilation–perfusion inequality*** is by far the most common cause of hypoxemia. It occurs in chronic obstructive lung diseases and many other lung diseases. Arterial P_{CO_2} may be normal or increased, depending upon how much ventilation is reflexively stimulated.

such therapy may be dangerous. The primary respiratory drive in such patients is the hypoxia, because for several reasons the reflex ventilatory response to an increased P_{CO_2} may be lost in chronic situations. The administration of pure oxygen may cause such patients to stop breathing; consequently, such individuals are typically treated with a mixture of air and oxygen rather than 100% oxygen.

Why Do Ventilation–Perfusion Abnormalities Affect O_2 More Than CO_2?

As described in Table 13.10, ventilation–perfusion inequalities often cause hypoxemia without associated increases in P_{CO_2}. The explanation for this resides in the fundamental difference between the transport of O_2 and the transport of CO_2 in the blood. Recall that the shape of the oxygen–hemoglobin dissociation curve is sigmoidal (see Figure 13.26). An increase in P_{O_2} above 100 mmHg does not add much oxygen to hemoglobin that is already almost 100% saturated. If poorly ventilated, diseased alveoli are perfused with blood and they will contribute blood with low oxygen to the pulmonary vein and, thus, to the general circulation. If increases in ventilation ensue in order to compensate for this, the increase in P_{O_2} in the healthy part of the lung does not add much oxygen to the blood from that region because of the minimal increase in oxygen saturation. As blood from these different areas of the lung mix in the pulmonary vein, the net result is still deoxygenated blood (hypoxemia).

The situation for CO_2, however, is very different. The CO_2 content curve is relatively linear because CO_2 is transported in the blood mainly as highly soluble HCO_3^-, which does not reach saturating levels at physiological concentrations. Therefore, although poorly ventilated areas of the lungs do cause increases in the CO_2 content of the blood entering the pulmonary vein (because CO_2 accumulates in the alveoli in those areas), a compensatory increase in ventilation *lowers* CO_2 content below normal in the blood from the well-ventilated areas of the lung. The net result, as blood mixes in the pulmonary vein in this case, is essentially normal arterial CO_2 content and P_{CO_2}. Thus, clinically significant ventilation–perfusion mismatching can lead to low arterial P_{O_2} with normal P_{CO_2}.

Emphysema

The pathophysiology of emphysema, a major cause of hypoxia, offers an instructive review of many basic principles of respiratory physiology. ***Emphysema*** is characterized by a loss of elastic tissue and the destruction of the alveolar walls leading to an increase in compliance. Furthermore, atrophy and collapse of the lower airways—those from the terminal bronchioles on down—can occur. The lungs actually self-destruct, attacked by proteolytic enzymes secreted by leukocytes in response to a variety of factors. Cigarette smoking is by far the most important of these factors; it stimulates the release of the proteolytic enzymes and destroys other enzymes that normally protect the lung against them.

As a result of alveolar-wall loss, adjacent alveoli fuse to form fewer but larger alveoli, and there is a loss of the pulmonary capillaries that were originally in the walls. The merging of alveoli, often into huge balloonlike structures, reduces the *total* surface area available for diffusion, and this impairs gas exchange. Moreover, because the destructive changes are not uniform throughout the lungs, some areas may receive large amounts of air and little blood, whereas others show just the opposite pattern. The result is marked ventilation–perfusion inequality.

In addition to problems in gas exchange, emphysema is associated with a large increase in airway resistance, which greatly increases the work of breathing and, if severe enough, may cause hypoventilation. This is why emphysema is classified, as noted earlier in this chapter, as a "chronic *obstructive* pulmonary disease." The airway obstruction in emphysema is caused by the collapse of the lower airways, particularly during expiration. To understand this, recall that two physical factors passively holding the airways open are the transpulmonary pressure and the lateral traction of connective-tissue fibers attached to the airway exteriors. Both of these factors are diminished in emphysema because of the destruction of the lung elastic tissues, so the airways collapse.

In summary, patients with emphysema suffer from decreased elastic recoil of the lungs, increased airway resistance, decreased total area available for diffusion, and ventilation–perfusion inequality. The result, particularly of the ventilation–perfusion inequality, is always some degree of hypoxia. As already explained, an increase in arterial P_{CO_2} will not occur until the disease becomes extensive and prevents increases in alveolar ventilation.

Acclimatization to High Altitude

Atmospheric pressure progressively decreases as altitude increases. Thus, at the top of Mt. Everest (approximately 29,029 ft or 8848 m), the atmospheric pressure is 253 mmHg, compared to 760 mmHg at sea level. The air is still 21% oxygen, which means that the inspired P_{O_2} is 53 mmHg (0.21 × 253 mmHg). Therefore, the alveolar and arterial P_{O_2} must decrease as persons ascend unless they breathe pure oxygen. The highest villages permanently inhabited by people are in the Andes at approximately 18,000 ft (5486 m).

The effects of oxygen deprivation vary from one individual to another, but most people who ascend rapidly to altitudes above 10,000 ft experience some degree of ***mountain sickness*** (***altitude sickness***). This disorder consists of breathlessness, headache, nausea, vomiting, insomnia, fatigue, and impairment of mental processes. Much more serious is the appearance, in some individuals, of life-threatening pulmonary edema, which is the leakage of fluid from the pulmonary capillaries into the alveolar walls and eventually the airspaces themselves. This occurs because of the development of pulmonary hypertension, as pulmonary arterioles reflexively constrict in the presence of low oxygen, as described earlier. Brain edema can also occur. Supplemental oxygen and diuretic therapy are used to treat mountain sickness; diuretics help reduce blood pressure, including in the pulmonary circulation, by promoting water loss in the urine. This reduces the amount of fluid leaving the capillaries in the lungs and brain.

Over the course of several days, the symptoms of mountain sickness usually disappear, although maximal physical capacity remains reduced. Acclimatization to high altitude is achieved by the compensatory mechanisms listed in **Table 13.11**.

TABLE 13.11 Acclimatization to the Hypoxia of High Altitude
The peripheral chemoreceptors stimulate ventilation.
Erythropoietin, a hormone secreted primarily by the kidneys, stimulates erythrocyte synthesis—resulting in increased erythrocyte and hemoglobin concentration in blood—and the oxygen-carrying capacity of blood.
DPG increases and shifts the oxygen–hemoglobin dissociation curve to the right, facilitating oxygen unloading in the tissues. However, this DPG change is not always adaptive and may be maladaptive. For example, at very high altitudes, a right shift in the curve impairs oxygen *loading* in the lungs, an effect that outweighs any benefit from facilitation of *unloading* in the tissues.
Increases in skeletal muscle capillary density (due to hypoxia-induced expression of the genes that code for angiogenic factors), number of mitochondria, and muscle myoglobin occur, all of which increase oxygen transfer.
Plasma volume can be decreased, resulting in an increased concentration of the erythrocytes and hemoglobin in the blood.

Finally, note that the responses to high altitude are essentially the same as the responses to hypoxia from any other cause. Thus, a person with severe hypoxia from lung disease may show many of the same changes—increased hematocrit, for example—as a high-altitude sojourner.

13.9 Nonrespiratory Functions of the Lungs

The lungs perform a variety of functions in addition to their roles in gas exchange and regulation of H^+ concentration. Most notable are the influences they have on the arterial concentrations of a large number of biologically active substances. Many substances (neurotransmitters and paracrine agents, for example) released locally into interstitial fluid may diffuse into capillaries and thus make their way into the systemic venous system. The lungs partially or completely remove some of these substances from the blood and thereby prevent them from reaching other locations in the body via the arteries. The cells that perform this function are the endothelial cells lining the pulmonary capillaries.

In contrast, the lungs may also produce new substances and add them to the blood. Some of these substances play local regulatory roles within the lungs, but if produced in large enough quantity, they may diffuse into the pulmonary capillaries and be carried to the rest of the body. For example, inflammatory responses (see Chapter 18) in the lung may lead, via excessive release of potent chemicals such as histamine, to alterations of systemic blood pressure or flow. In at least one case, the lungs contribute to the production of a hormone, angiotensin II, which is produced by the action of an enzyme located on endothelial cells throughout much of the body (see Chapter 14).

Finally, the lungs also act as a sieve that traps small blood clots generated in the systemic circulation, thereby preventing them from reaching the systemic arterial blood where they could occlude blood vessels in other organs.

Table 13.12 summarizes the functions of the respiratory system.

TABLE 13.12 Functions of the Respiratory System
Provides oxygen
Eliminates carbon dioxide
Regulates the blood's hydrogen ion concentration (pH) in coordination with the kidneys
Forms speech sounds (phonation)
Defends against microbes
Influences arterial concentrations of chemical messengers by removing some from pulmonary capillary blood and producing and adding others to this blood
Traps and dissolves blood clots arising from systemic veins such as those in the legs

SUMMARY

Organization of the Respiratory System

I. The respiratory system comprises the lungs, the airways leading to them, and the chest structures responsible for moving air into and out of them.
   a. The conducting zone of the airways consists of the trachea, bronchi, and terminal bronchioles.
   b. The respiratory zone of the airways consists of the alveoli, which are the sites of gas exchange, and those airways to which alveoli are attached.
   c. The alveoli are lined by type I cells and some type II cells, which produce surfactant.
   d. The lungs and interior of the thorax are covered by pleura; between the two pleural layers is an extremely thin layer of intrapleural fluid.

II. The lungs are elastic structures whose volume depends upon the pressure difference across the lungs—the transpulmonary pressure—and how stretchable the lungs are.

III. The steps involved in respiration are summarized in Figure 13.6. In the steady state, the net volumes of oxygen and carbon dioxide exchanged in the lungs per unit time are equal to the net volumes exchanged in the tissues.

Ventilation and Lung Mechanics

I. Bulk flow of air between the atmosphere and alveoli is proportional to the difference between the alveolar and atmospheric pressures and inversely proportional to the airway resistance: $F = (P_{alv} - P_{atm})/R$.

II. Between breaths at the end of an unforced expiration, $P_{atm} = P_{alv}$, no air is flowing, and the dimensions of the lungs and thoracic cage are stable as the result of opposing elastic forces. The lungs are stretched and are attempting to recoil, whereas the chest wall is compressed and attempting to move outward. This creates a subatmospheric intrapleural pressure and hence a transpulmonary pressure that opposes the forces of elastic recoil.

III. During inspiration, the contractions of the diaphragm and inspiratory intercostal muscles increase the volume of the thoracic cage.
   a. This makes intrapleural pressure more subatmospheric, increases transpulmonary pressure, and causes the lungs to expand to a greater degree than they do between breaths.
   b. This expansion initially makes alveolar pressure subatmospheric, which creates the pressure difference between the atmosphere and alveoli to drive airflow into the lungs.

IV. During expiration, the inspiratory muscles cease contracting, allowing the elastic recoil of the lungs to return them to their original between-breaths size.
   a. This initially compresses the alveolar air, raising alveolar pressure above atmospheric pressure and driving air out of the lungs.
   b. In forced expirations, the contraction of expiratory intercostal muscles and abdominal muscles actively decreases chest dimensions.

V. Lung compliance is determined by the elastic connective tissues of the lungs and the surface tension of the fluid lining the alveoli. The latter is greatly reduced—and compliance increased—by surfactant, produced by the type II cells of the alveoli. Surfactant also stabilizes alveoli by decreasing surface tension in smaller alveoli.

VI. Airway resistance determines how much air flows into the lungs at any given pressure difference between atmosphere and alveoli. The major determinants of airway resistance are the radii of the airways.

VII. The vital capacity is the sum of resting tidal volume, inspiratory reserve volume, and expiratory reserve volume. The volume expired during the first second of a forced vital capacity measurement is the FEV_1 and normally averages 80% of forced vital capacity.

VIII. Minute ventilation is the product of tidal volume and respiratory rate. Alveolar ventilation = (Tidal volume − Anatomical dead space) × Respiratory rate.

Exchange of Gases in Alveoli and Tissues

I. Exchange of gases in lungs and tissues is by diffusion as a result of differences in partial pressures. Gases diffuse from a region of higher partial pressure to one of lower partial pressure. At rest and at a respiratory quotient (RQ) of 0.8, oxygen consumption is approximately 250 mL per minute, whereas carbon dioxide production is approximately 200 mL per minute.

II. Normal alveolar gas pressure for oxygen is 105 mmHg and for carbon dioxide is 40 mmHg.
   a. At any given inspired P_{O_2}, the ratio of oxygen consumption to alveolar ventilation determines alveolar P_{O_2}—the higher the ratio, the lower the alveolar P_{O_2}.
   b. The higher the ratio of carbon dioxide production to alveolar ventilation, the higher the alveolar P_{CO_2}.

III. The average value at rest for systemic venous P_{O_2} is 40 mmHg and for P_{CO_2} is 46 mmHg.

IV. As systemic venous blood flows through the pulmonary capillaries, there is net diffusion of oxygen from alveoli to blood and of carbon dioxide from blood to alveoli. By the end of each pulmonary capillary, the blood gas pressures have become equal to those in the alveoli.

V. Inadequate gas exchange between alveoli and pulmonary capillaries may occur when the alveolar-capillary surface area is decreased, when the alveolar walls thicken, or when there are ventilation–perfusion inequalities.

VI. Significant ventilation–perfusion inequalities cause the systemic arterial P_{O_2} to be reduced. An important mechanism for opposing mismatching is that a low local P_{O_2} causes local vasoconstriction, diverting blood away from poorly ventilated areas.

VII. In the tissues, net diffusion of oxygen occurs from blood to cells and net diffusion of carbon dioxide from cells to blood.

Transport of Oxygen in Blood

I. Each liter of systemic arterial blood normally contains 200 mL of oxygen, more than 98% bound to hemoglobin and the rest dissolved.

II. The major determinant of the degree to which hemoglobin is saturated with oxygen is blood P_{O_2}.
   a. Hemoglobin is almost 100% saturated at the normal systemic arterial P_{O_2} of 100 mmHg. The fact that saturation is already more than 90% at a P_{O_2} of 60 mmHg permits relatively normal uptake of oxygen by the blood even when alveolar P_{O_2} is moderately reduced.
   b. Hemoglobin is 75% saturated at the normal systemic mixed venous P_{O_2} of 40 mmHg. Thus, only 25% of the oxygen has dissociated from hemoglobin and diffused into the tissues.

III. The affinity of hemoglobin for oxygen is decreased by an increase in P_{CO_2}, H^+ concentration, and temperature. All these conditions exist in the tissues and facilitate the dissociation of oxygen from hemoglobin.

IV. The affinity of hemoglobin for oxygen is also decreased by binding DPG, which is synthesized by the erythrocytes. DPG increases in situations associated with inadequate oxygen supply and helps maintain oxygen release in the tissues.

Transport of Carbon Dioxide in Blood

I. When carbon dioxide molecules diffuse from the tissues into the blood, 10% remain dissolved in plasma and erythrocytes, 25% to 30% combine in the erythrocytes with deoxyhemoglobin to form carbamino compounds, and 60% to 65% combine in the erythrocytes with water to form carbonic acid, which then dissociates to yield HCO_3^- and H^+. Most of the HCO_3^- then moves out of the erythrocytes into the plasma in exchange for chloride ions.

II. As venous blood flows through lung capillaries, blood P_{CO_2} decreases because of the diffusion of carbon dioxide out of the blood into the alveoli, and the reactions are reversed.

Transport of Hydrogen Ion Between Tissues and Lungs

I. Most of the H^+ generated in the erythrocytes from carbonic acid during blood passage through tissue capillaries binds to deoxyhemoglobin because deoxyhemoglobin, formed as oxygen unloads from oxyhemoglobin, has a high affinity for H^+.

II. As the blood flows through the lung capillaries, H^+ bound to deoxyhemoglobin is released and combines with HCO_3^- to yield carbon dioxide and water.

Control of Respiration

I. Breathing depends upon cyclical inspiratory muscle excitation by the nerves to the diaphragm and intercostal muscles. This neural activity is triggered by the medullary inspiratory neurons.

II. The medullary respiratory center is composed of the dorsal respiratory group, which contains inspiratory neurons, and the ventral respiratory group, where the respiratory rhythm generator is located.

III. The most important inputs to the medullary inspiratory neurons for the involuntary control of ventilation are from the peripheral chemoreceptors—the carotid and aortic bodies—and the central chemoreceptors.

IV. Ventilation is reflexively stimulated via the peripheral chemoreceptors by a decrease in arterial P_{O_2} but only when the decrease is large.

V. Ventilation is reflexively stimulated via both the peripheral and central chemoreceptors when the arterial P_{CO_2} increases even a slight amount. The stimulus for this reflex is not the increased P_{CO_2} itself but the concomitant increased H^+ concentration in arterial blood and brain extracellular fluid.

VI. Ventilation is also stimulated, mainly via the peripheral chemoreceptors, by an increase in arterial H^+ concentration resulting from causes other than an increase in P_{CO_2}. The result of this reflex is to restore H^+ concentration toward normal by lowering P_{CO_2}.

VII. Ventilation is reflexively inhibited by an increase in arterial P_{O_2} and by a decrease in arterial P_{CO_2} or H^+ concentration.

VIII. During moderate exercise, ventilation increases in exact proportion to metabolism, but the signals causing this are not known. During very strenuous exercise, ventilation increases more than metabolism.

a. The proportional increases in ventilation and metabolism during moderate exercise cause the arterial P_{O_2}, P_{CO_2}, and H^+ concentration to remain unchanged.

b. Arterial H^+ concentration increases during very strenuous exercise because of increased lactic acid production. This accounts for some of the hyperventilation that occurs.

IX. Ventilation is also controlled by reflexes originating in airway receptors and by conscious intent.

Hypoxia

I. The causes of hypoxic hypoxia are listed in Table 13.10.

II. During exposure to hypoxia, as at high altitude, oxygen supply to the tissues is maintained by the five responses listed in Table 13.11.

Nonrespiratory Functions of the Lungs

I. The lungs influence arterial blood concentrations of biologically active substances by removing some from systemic venous blood and adding others to systemic arterial blood.

II. The lungs also act as sieves that trap and dissolve small clots formed in the systemic tissues.

REVIEW QUESTIONS

1. List the functions of the respiratory system.
2. At rest, how many liters of air flow in and out of the lungs and how many liters of blood flow through the lungs per minute?
3. Describe four functions of the conducting portion of the airways.
4. Which respiration steps occur by diffusion and which by bulk flow?
5. What are normal values for intrapleural pressure, alveolar pressure, and transpulmonary pressure at the end of an unforced expiration?
6. Between breaths at the end of an unforced expiration, in what directions do the lungs and chest wall tend to move? What prevents them from doing so?
7. State typical values for oxygen consumption, carbon dioxide production, and cardiac output at rest. How much oxygen (in milliliters per liter) is present in systemic venous and systemic arterial blood?
8. Write the equation relating airflow into or out of the lungs to alveolar pressure, atmospheric pressure, and airway resistance.
9. Describe the sequence of events that cause air to move into the lungs during inspiration and out of the lungs during expiration. Diagram the changes in intrapleural pressure and alveolar pressure.
10. What factors determine lung compliance? Which is most important?
11. How does surfactant increase lung compliance? How does surfactant stabilize alveoli by preventing small alveoli from emptying into large alveoli?
12. How is airway resistance influenced by airway radii?
13. List the physical factors that alter airway resistance.
14. Contrast the causes of increased airway resistance in asthma, emphysema, and chronic bronchitis.
15. What distinguishes lung capacities, as a group, from lung volumes?
16. State the formula relating minute ventilation, tidal volume, and respiratory rate. Give representative values for each in a normal person at rest.
17. State the formula for calculating alveolar ventilation. What is an average value for alveolar ventilation?

18. The partial pressure of a gas is dependent upon what two factors?
19. State the alveolar partial pressures for oxygen and carbon dioxide in a healthy person at rest.
20. What factors determine alveolar partial pressures?
21. What is the mechanism of gas exchange between alveoli and pulmonary capillaries? In a healthy person at rest, what are the gas pressures at the end of the pulmonary capillaries relative to those in the alveoli?
22. Why does thickening of alveolar membranes impair oxygen movement but has little effect on carbon dioxide exchange?
23. What is the major result of ventilation–perfusion inequalities throughout the lungs? Describe homeostatic responses that minimize mismatching.
24. What generates the diffusion gradients for oxygen and carbon dioxide in the tissues?
25. In what two forms is oxygen carried in the blood? What are the normal quantities (in milliliters per liter) for each form in arterial blood?
26. Describe the structure of hemoglobin.
27. Draw an oxygen–hemoglobin dissociation curve. Put in the points that represent systemic venous and systemic arterial blood (ignore the rightward shift of the curve in systemic venous blood). What is the adaptive importance of the plateau? Of the steep portion?
28. Would breathing pure oxygen cause a large increase in oxygen transport by the blood in a healthy person? In a person with a low alveolar P_{O_2}?
29. Describe the effects of increased P_{CO_2}, H^+ concentration, and temperature on the oxygen–hemoglobin dissociation curve. How are these effects adaptive for oxygen unloading in the tissues?
30. Describe the effects of increased DPG on the oxygen–hemoglobin dissociation curve. What is the adaptive importance of the effect of DPG on the curve?
31. Draw figures showing the reactions carbon dioxide undergoes entering the blood in the tissue capillaries and leaving the blood in the alveoli. What fractions are contributed by dissolved carbon dioxide, HCO_3^-, and carbaminohemoglobin?
32. What happens to most of the H^+ formed in the erythrocytes from carbonic acid? What happens to blood H^+ concentration as blood flows through tissue capillaries?
33. What are the effects of P_{O_2} on carbaminohemoglobin formation and H^+ binding by hemoglobin?
34. Describe the area of the brain in which automatic control of rhythmic respirations resides.
35. Describe the function of the pulmonary stretch receptors.
36. What changes stimulate the peripheral chemoreceptors? The central chemoreceptors?
37. Why is it that moderate anemia or carbon monoxide exposure does not stimulate the peripheral chemoreceptors?
38. Is respiratory control more sensitive to small changes in arterial P_{O_2} or in arterial P_{CO_2}?
39. Describe the pathways by which increased arterial P_{CO_2} stimulates ventilation. What pathway is more important?
40. Describe the pathway by which a change in arterial H^+ concentration independent of altered carbon dioxide influences ventilation. What is the adaptive value of this reflex?
41. What happens to arterial P_{O_2}, P_{CO_2}, and H^+ concentration during moderate and strenuous exercise? List other factors that may stimulate ventilation during exercise.
42. List four general causes of hypoxic hypoxia.
43. Explain how ventilation–perfusion mismatch due to regional lung disease can cause hypoxic hypoxia but not hypercapnia.
44. Describe two general ways in which the lungs can alter the concentrations of substances other than oxygen, carbon dioxide, and H^+ in the arterial blood.
45. List two types of sleep apnea. Why does nasal CPAP prevent obstructive sleep apnea?

KEY TERMS

CLINICAL TERMS

CHAPTER 13 Clinical Case Study: High Blood Pressure and Chronic Sleepiness in an Obese Man

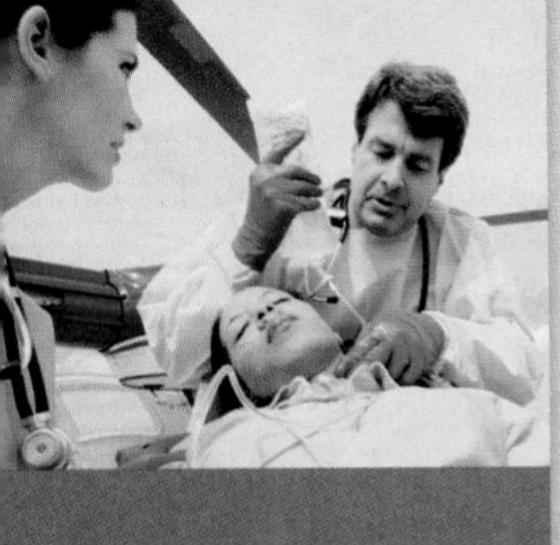

An obese man is discovered to have high blood pressure (hypertension) and is sleepy all of the time. His wife reports that he snores very loudly and often sounds like he stops breathing in his sleep. The doctor orders a sleep study, and the diagnosis of obstructive sleep apnea is made.

Sleep apnea is characterized by periodic cessation of breathing during sleep. This results in the combination of hypoxemia and hypercapnia (termed ***asphyxia***). In severe cases, this may occur more than 20 times an hour. During a sleep study, these frequent blood oxygen desaturations are documented. Sleep apnea has two general types. ***Central sleep apnea*** is primarily due to a decrease in neural output from the respiratory center in the medulla to the phrenic motor nerve to the diaphragm. ***Obstructive sleep apnea*** is caused by increased airway resistance because of narrowing or collapse of the upper airways (primarily the pharynx) during inspiration (Figure 13.44). Obstructive sleep apnea may occur in as much as 4% of the adult population with a greater frequency in elderly persons and in men. Significant snoring may be an early sign of the eventual development of obstructive sleep apnea. Obesity is clearly a contributing factor because the excess fat in the neck decreases the diameter of the upper airways. A decrease in the activity of the upper airway dilating muscles, particularly during REM sleep, also contributes to airway collapse. Finally, anatomical narrowing and increased compliance of the upper airways contributes to periodic inspiratory obstruction during sleep.

Untreated sleep apnea can have many serious consequences, including hypertension of the pulmonary arteries (pulmonary hypertension) and added strain on the right ventricle of the heart. This can lead to heart failure and abnormal heart rhythm, either of which can be fatal. The periodic arousal that occurs during these apneic episodes results in serious disruption of normal sleep patterns and can lead to sleepiness during the day (***daytime somnolence***). Increased catecholamine release during these frequent arousals can also contribute to the development of high blood pressure.

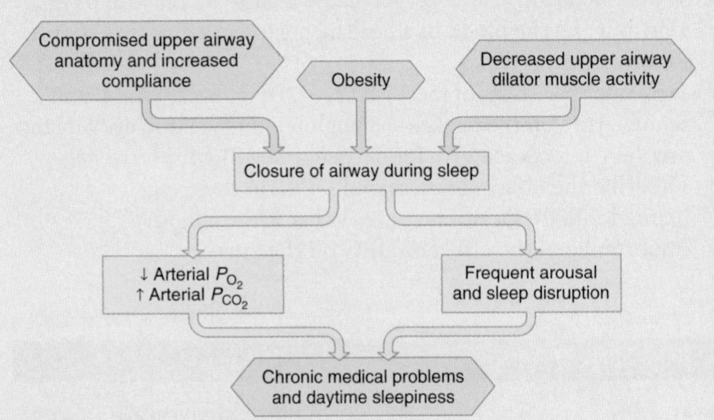

Figure 13.44 Pathogenesis of obstructive sleep apnea.

A variety of treatments exist for obstructive sleep apnea. Surgery such as laser-assisted widening of the soft palate and uvula can sometimes be of benefit. Weight loss is often quite helpful. However, the mainstay of therapy is ***continuous positive airway pressure*** (***CPAP***) (Figure 13.45). The patient wears a small mask over the nose during sleep, which is attached to a positive-pressure-generating device. By increasing airway pressure greater than P_{atm}, the collapse of the upper airways during inspiration is prevented. Although the CPAP nasal mask may seem obtrusive, many patients sleep much better with it, and many of the symptoms resolve with this treatment. Our patient was treated with CPAP during the night and also was able to lose a considerable amount of body weight. As a result, his daytime somnolence and hypertension improved over the next year.

(continued)

(continued)

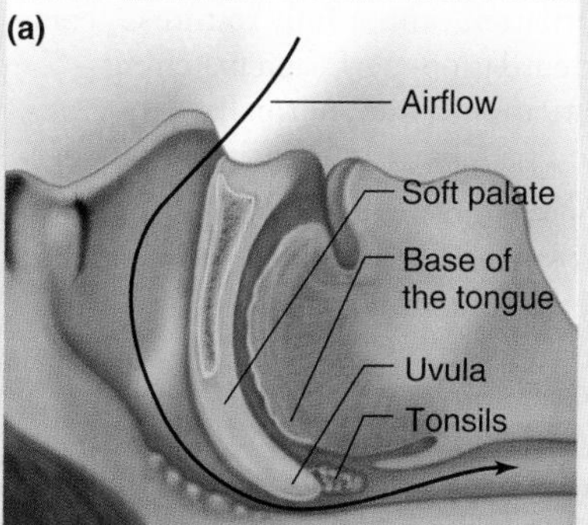

During normal sleep, air flows freely past the structures in the throat.

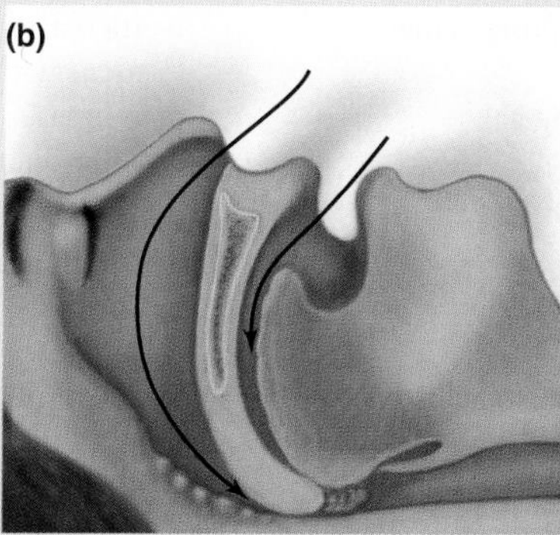

During sleep apnea, airflow is completely blocked.

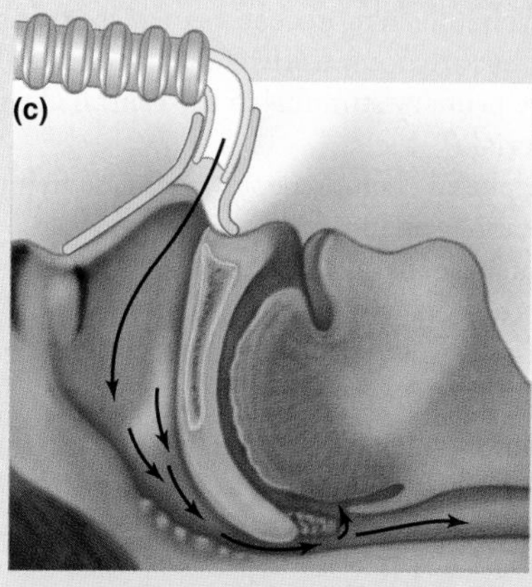

With CPAP, a mask over the nose gently directs air into the throat to keep the air passage open.

Figure 13.45 The pathophysiology and a standard treatment of obstructive sleep apnea. (a) Normal sleep with air flowing freely past the structures of the throat during an inspiration. (b) In obstructive sleep apnea (particularly with the patient sleeping in the supine position), the soft palate, uvula, and tongue occlude the airway, greatly increasing the resistance to airflow. (c) Continuous positive airway pressure (CPAP) is applied with a nasal mask, preventing airway collapse.

Clinical terms: asphyxia, central sleep apnea, continuous positive airway pressure (CPAP), daytime somnolence, obstructive sleep apnea, sleep apnea

See Chapter 19 for complete, integrative case studies.

CHAPTER 13 TEST QUESTIONS

Answers found in Appendix A.

1. If $P_{atm} = 0$ mmHg and $P_{alv} = -2$ mmHg, then
   a. transpulmonary pressure (P_{tp}) is 2 mmHg.
   b. it is the end of the normal inspiration and there is no airflow.
   c. it is at the end of the normal expiration and there is no airflow.
   d. transpulmonary pressure (P_{tp}) is -2 mmHg.
   e. air is flowing into the lung.
2. Transpulmonary pressure (P_{tp}) increases by 3 mmHg during a normal inspiration. In subject A, 500 mL of air is inspired. In subject B, 250 mL of air is inspired for the same change in P_{tp}. Which is *true?*
   a. The compliance of the lung of subject B is less than that of subject A.
   b. The airway resistance of subject A is greater than that of subject B.
   c. The surface tension in the lung of subject B is less than that in subject A.
   d. The lung of subject A is deficient in surfactant.
   e. The compliance cannot be estimated from the data provided.
3. If alveolar ventilation is 4200 mL/min, respiratory frequency is 12 breaths per minute, and tidal volume is 500 mL, what is the anatomical-dead-space ventilation?
   a. 1800 mL/min
   b. 6000 mL/min
   c. 350 mL/min
   d. 1200 mL/min
   e. It cannot be determined from the data provided.
4. Which of the following will increase alveolar P_{O_2}?
   a. increase in metabolism and no change in alveolar ventilation
   b. breathing air with 15% oxygen at sea level
   c. increase in alveolar ventilation matched by an increase in metabolism
   d. increased alveolar ventilation with no change in metabolism
   e. carbon monoxide poisoning
5. Which of the following will cause the largest increase in systemic arterial oxygen saturation in the blood?
   a. an increase in red cell concentration (hematocrit) of 20%
   b. breathing 100% O_2 in a healthy subject at sea level
   c. an increase in arterial P_{O_2} from 40 to 60 mmHg
   d. hyperventilation in a healthy subject at sea level
   e. breathing a gas with 5% CO_2, 21% O_2, and 74% N_2 at sea level
6. In arterial blood with a P_{O_2} of 60 mmHg, which of the following situations will result in the lowest blood oxygen saturation?
   a. decreased DPG with normal body temperature and blood pH
   b. elevated body temperature, acidosis, and increased DPG
   c. decreased body temperature, alkalosis, and increased DPG
   d. normal body temperature with alkalosis
   e. elevated body temperature with alkalosis
7. Which of the following is *not* true about asthma?
   a. The basic defect is chronic airway inflammation.
   b. It is always caused by an allergy.
   c. The airway smooth muscle is hyperresponsive.
   d. It can be treated with inhaled steroid therapy.
   e. It can be treated with bronchodilator therapy.

8. Which of the following is *true?*
   a. Peripheral chemoreceptors increase firing with low arterial P_{O_2} but are not sensitive to an increase in arterial P_{CO_2}.
   b. The primary stimulus to the central chemoreceptors is low arterial P_{O_2}.
   c. Peripheral chemoreceptors increase firing during a metabolic alkalosis.
   d. The increase in ventilation during exercise is due to a decrease in arterial P_{O_2}.
   e. Peripheral and central chemoreceptors both increase firing when arterial P_{CO_2} increases.
9. Ventilation–perfusion inequalities lead to hypoxemia because
   a. the relationship between P_{CO_2} and the content of CO_2 in blood is sigmoidal.
   b. a decrease in ventilation–perfusion matching in a lung region causes pulmonary arteriolar vasodilation in that region.
   c. increases in ventilation cannot fully restore O_2 content in areas with low ventilation–perfusion matching.
   d. increases in ventilation cannot normalize P_{CO_2}.
   e. pulmonary blood vessels are not sensitive to changes in P_{O_2}.
10. After the expiration of a normal tidal volume, a subject breathes in as much air as possible. The volume of air inspired is the
    a. inspiratory reserve volume.
    b. vital capacity.
    c. inspiratory capacity.
    d. total lung capacity.
    e. functional residual capacity.

CHAPTER 13 GENERAL PRINCIPLES ASSESSMENT

Answers found in Appendix A.

1. A general principle of physiology highlighted throughout this chapter is that *physiological processes are dictated by the laws of chemistry and physics.* What are some examples of how this applies to lung mechanics and the transport of oxygen and carbon dioxide in blood?
2. How is the anatomy of the alveoli and pulmonary capillaries an example of the principle that *structure is a determinant of—and has coevolved with—function?*
3. A general principle of physiology is that *most physiological functions are controlled by multiple regulatory systems, often working in opposition.* What are some examples of factors that have opposing regulatory effects on alveolar ventilation in humans?

CHAPTER 13 QUANTITATIVE AND THOUGHT QUESTIONS

Answers found in Appendix A.

1. At the end of a normal expiration, a person's lung volume is 2 L, his alveolar pressure is 0 mmHg, and his intrapleural pressure is −4 mmHg. He then inhales 800 mL of air. At the end of inspiration, the alveolar pressure is 0 mmHg and the intrapleural pressure is −8 mmHg. Calculate this person's lung compliance.
2. A patient is unable to produce surfactant. To inhale a normal tidal volume, will her intrapleural pressure have to be more or less subatmospheric during inspiration, relative to a healthy person?
3. A 70 kg adult patient is artificially ventilated by a machine during surgery at a rate of 20 breaths/min and a tidal volume of 250 mL/breath. Assuming a normal anatomical dead space of 150 mL, is this patient receiving an adequate alveolar ventilation?
4. Why must a person floating on the surface of the water and breathing through a snorkel increase his tidal volume and/or breathing frequency if alveolar ventilation is to remain normal?
5. A healthy person breathing room air voluntarily increases alveolar ventilation twofold and continues to do so until reaching new steady-state alveolar gas pressures for oxygen and carbon dioxide. Are the new values higher or lower than normal?
6. A person breathing room air has an alveolar P_{O_2} of 105 mmHg and an arterial P_{O_2} of 80 mmHg. Could hypoventilation due to, say, respiratory muscle weakness produce these values?
7. A person's alveolar membranes have become thickened enough to moderately decrease the rate at which gases diffuse across them at any given partial pressure differences. Will this person necessarily have a low arterial P_{O_2} at rest? During exercise?
8. A person is breathing 100% oxygen. How much will the oxygen content (in milliliters per liter of blood) of the arterial blood increase compared to when the person is breathing room air?
9. Which of the following have higher values in systemic venous blood than in systemic arterial blood: plasma P_{CO_2}, erythrocyte P_{CO_2}, plasma bicarbonate concentration, erythrocyte bicarbonate concentration, plasma hydrogen ion concentration, erythrocyte hydrogen ion concentration, erythrocyte carbamino concentration?
10. If the spinal cord were severed where it joins the brainstem, what would happen to respiration?
11. Which inspired gas mixture leads to the largest increase in minute ventilation?
    a. 10% O_2/5% CO_2
    b. 100% O_2/5% CO_2
    c. 21% O_2/5% CO_2
    d. 10% O_2/0% CO_2
    e. 0.1% CO/5% CO_2
12. Patients with severe uncontrolled type 1 diabetes mellitus produce large quantities of certain organic acids. Can you predict the ventilation pattern in these patients and whether their arterial P_{O_2} and P_{CO_2} would increase or decrease?
13. Why does an inspired O_2 of 100% increase arterial P_{O_2} much more in a patient with ventilation–perfusion mismatch than in a patient with pure anatomical shunt?

CHAPTER 13 ANSWERS TO PHYSIOLOGICAL INQUIRIES

Figure 13.4 The rate of diffusion of gases between the air and the capillaries may be decreased due to the increased resistance to diffusion (see Chapter 4 for discussion of forces affecting diffusion).

Figure 13.11 A tube is placed through the chest wall into the now enlarged pleural space. (The original hole causing the pneumothorax would need to be repaired first.) Suction is then applied to the chest tube. The negative pressure decreases P_{ip} below P_{atm} and thereby increases P_{tp}, which results in re-expansion of the lung.

Figure 13.13

	P_{alv}	P_{ip}	P_{tp} ($P_{alv} - P_{ip}$)	Change in Lung Volume
1	0	−4	4	
				> P_{tp} is increasing → lung volume↑
2	−1	−6	5	
				> P_{tp} is increasing → lung volume↑
3	0	−7	7	
				> P_{tp} is decreasing → lung volume↓
4	1	−5	6	
				> P_{tp} is decreasing → lung volume↓
1	0	−4	4	

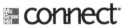

Note: The actual volume increase or decrease in mL is determined by the compliance of the lung (see Figure 13.16).

Figure 13.16 Anything that increases P_{tp} during inspiration will, theoretically, increase lung volume. This can be done with positive airway pressure generated by mechanical ventilation, which will increase P_{alv}. This approach can work but also increases the risk of pneumothorax by inducing air leaks from the lung into the intrapleural space.

Figure 13.19 The anatomical dead space would be increased by about 251 mL (or 251 cm^3). (The volume of the tube can be approximated as that of a perfect cylinder [$\pi r^2 h = 3.1416 \times 2^2 \times 20$].) This large increase in anatomical dead space would decrease alveolar ventilation (see Table 13.5), and tidal volume would have to be increased in compensation. (There would also be an increase in airway resistance, which is discussed later.)

Figure 13.23 The increase in cardiac output with exercise greatly increases pulmonary blood flow and decreases the amount of time erythrocytes are exposed to increased oxygen from the alveoli. In a normal region of the lung, there is a large safety factor such that a large increase in blood flow still allows normal oxygen uptake. However, even small increases in the rate of capillary blood flow in a diseased portion of the lung will decrease oxygen uptake due to a loss of this safety factor.

Figure 13.29 Less O_2 will be unloaded in peripheral tissue as the blood is exposed to increased P_{CO_2} and decreased pH because the oxygen–hemoglobin dissociation curve will not shift to the right as it does in real blood. Also, less O_2 will be loaded in the lungs as P_{CO_2} diffuses from blood into the alveoli because the oxygen–hemoglobin dissociation curve will not shift to the left as it normally would with removal of CO_2 and decreased acidity.

Figure 13.33 The ventilatory response to the hypoxia of altitude would be greatly diminished, and it is likely that the person would be extremely hypoxemic as a result. Carotid body removal did not help in the treatment of asthma, and this approach was abandoned.

Figure 13.43 These receptors may facilitate the increase in alveolar ventilation that occurs during exercise because pulmonary artery P_{O_2} will decrease and pulmonary artery P_{CO_2} will increase.

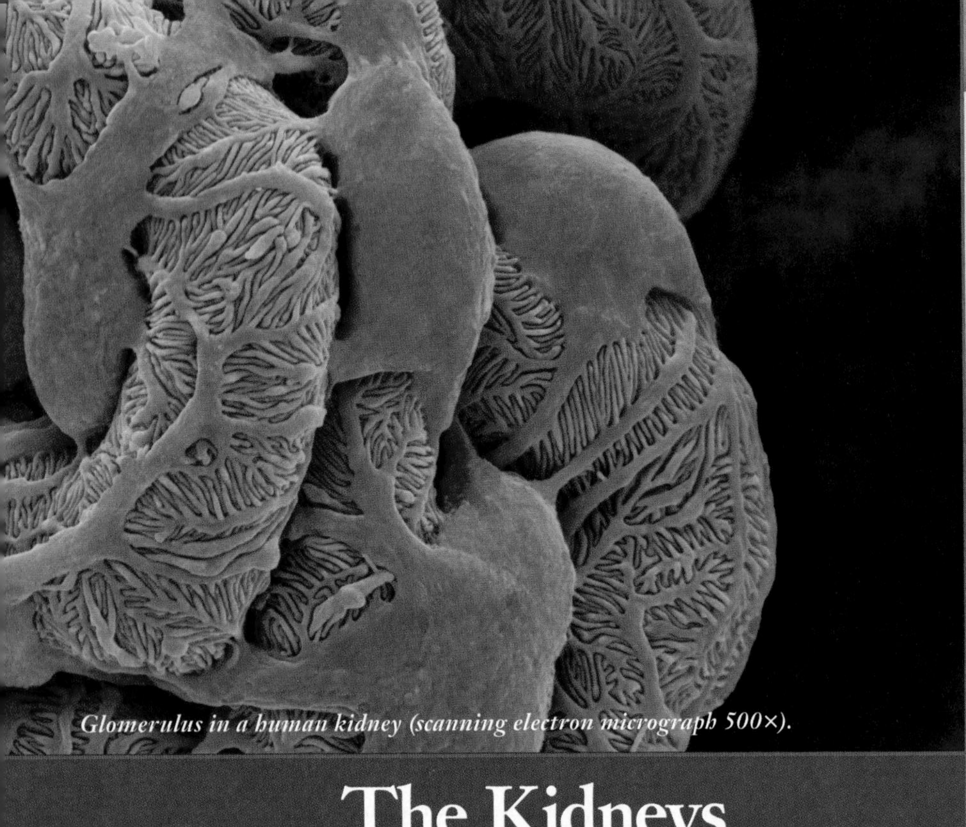

Glomerulus in a human kidney (scanning electron micrograph 500×).

14 The Kidneys and Regulation of Water and Inorganic Ions

The importance of normal electrolyte concentrations in the function of excitable tissue was explained in reference to neurons (Chapter 6) and muscle (Chapter 9) and in the homeostasis of bone in Chapter 11. You have also learned about how the maintenance of normal hydration is important in cardiovascular function in Chapter 12. Finally, Chapter 13 highlighted the importance of the respiratory system in the short-term control of acid–base balance. We now deal with the homeostatic regulation of body water volume and balance, and the inorganic ion composition of the internal environment. Furthermore, this chapter explains how the urinary system eliminates organic waste products of metabolism and, working with the respiratory system, is critical to the long-term control of acid–base balance. The kidneys play the central role in these processes.

Regulation of the total-body balance of any substance can be studied in terms of the balance concept described in Chapter 1. Theoretically, a substance can appear in the body either as a result of ingestion or synthesized as a product of metabolism. On the loss side of the balance, a substance can be excreted from the body or can be broken down by metabolism. Therefore, if the quantity of any substance in the body is to be maintained within a normal homeostatic range over a period of time, the total amounts ingested and produced must equal the total amounts excreted and broken down. Reflexes that alter excretion via the urine constitute the major mechanisms that regulate the body balances of water and many of the inorganic ions that determine the properties of the extracellular fluid. Typical values for the extracellular concentrations of these ions appeared in Table 4.1. We will first describe the general principles of kidney function, then apply this information to how the kidneys process specific substances like Na^+, H_2O, H^+, and K^+ and participate in reflexes that regulate these substances.

As you read about the structure, function, and control of the function of kidney, you will encounter numerous examples of the general principles of physiology that were outlined in Chapter 1. The homeostatic control of the excretion of metabolic wastes, as well as the ability of the kidneys to reclaim needed ions and organic molecules that would otherwise be lost in the process, is a hallmark of the general principle of physiology that homeostasis is essential for health and survival; failure of kidney function not only causes a buildup of toxic waste products in the body but can also lead to a loss of important ions and nutrients (such as glucose and amino acids) in the urine. Another general principle of physiology—that most physiological functions are controlled by multiple regulatory systems, often working in opposition—is apparent in the renal system. An example is the control of the filtration rate of the kidney. The general principle of physiology that controlled exchange of materials occurs between compartments and across cellular membranes is also integral to this chapter—as already mentioned, total-body balance of important nutrients and ions is precisely controlled by the healthy kidneys. Finally, the functional unit of the kidney—the nephron—and the blood vessels associated with it are elegant examples of the general principle of physiology that structure is a determinant of—and has coevolved with—function; form and function are inextricably intertwined.

SECTION A
Basic Principles of Renal Physiology

14.1 Renal Functions

The adjective **renal** means "pertaining to the kidneys." The kidneys process the plasma portion of blood by removing substances from it and, in a few cases, by adding substances to it. In so doing, they perform a variety of functions, as summarized in **Table 14.1**.

First, the kidneys play a central role in regulating the water concentration, inorganic ion composition, acid–base balance, and the fluid volume of the internal environment (e.g., blood volume). They do so by excreting just enough water and inorganic ions to keep the amounts of these substances in the body within a narrow homeostatic range. For example, if you increase your consumption of salt (sodium chloride), your kidneys will increase the amount of the salt excreted to match the intake. Alternatively, if there is not enough salt in the body, the kidneys will excrete very little salt.

Second, the kidneys excrete metabolic waste products into the urine as fast as they are produced. This keeps waste products, which can be toxic, from accumulating in the body. These metabolic wastes include **urea** from the catabolism of protein, **uric acid** from nucleic acids, **creatinine** from muscle creatine, the end products of hemoglobin breakdown (which give urine much of its color), and many others.

A third function of the kidneys is the urinary excretion of some foreign chemicals—such as drugs, pesticides, and food additives—and their metabolites.

TABLE 14.1	Functions of the Kidneys
I. Regulation of water, inorganic ion balance, and acid–base balance (in cooperation with the lungs; Chapter 13)	
II. Removal of metabolic waste products from the blood and their excretion in the urine	
III. Removal of foreign chemicals from the blood and their excretion in the urine	
IV. Gluconeogenesis	
V. Production of hormones/enzymes: A. Erythropoietin, which controls erythrocyte production (Chapter 12) B. Renin, an enzyme that controls the formation of angiotensin, which influences blood pressure and sodium balance (this chapter) C. Conversion of 25-hydroxyvitamin D to 1,25-dihydroxyvitamin D, which influences calcium balance (Chapter 11)	

A fourth function is gluconeogenesis. During prolonged fasting, the kidneys synthesize glucose from amino acids and other precursors and release it into the blood (see Figure 3.48).

Finally, the kidneys act as endocrine glands, releasing at least two hormones: erythropoietin (described in Chapter 12), and 1,25-dihydroxyvitamin D (described in Chapter 11). The kidneys also secrete an enzyme, renin (pronounced "REE-nin"), that is important in the control of blood pressure and sodium balance (described later in this chapter).

14.2 Structure of the Kidneys and Urinary System

The two kidneys lie in the back of the abdominal wall but not actually in the abdominal cavity. They are retroperitoneal, meaning they are just behind the peritoneum, the lining of this cavity. The urine flows from the kidneys through the **ureters** into the **bladder** and then is eliminated via the **urethra** (**Figure 14.1a**). The major structural components of the kidney are shown in cross section in **Figure 14.1b.** The indented surface of the kidney is called the **hilum,** through which courses the blood vessels perfusing (**renal artery**) and draining (**renal vein**) the kidneys. The nerves that innervate the kidney and the tube that drains urine from the kidney (the ureter) also pass through the hilum. The ureter is formed from the **calyces** (singular, **calyx**), which are funnel-shaped structures that drain urine into the ureter. Also notice that the kidney is surrounded by a protective **capsule** made of connective tissue. The kidney is divided into an outer **renal cortex** and inner **renal medulla,** described in more detail later. The connection between the tip of the medulla and the calyx is called the **papilla.**

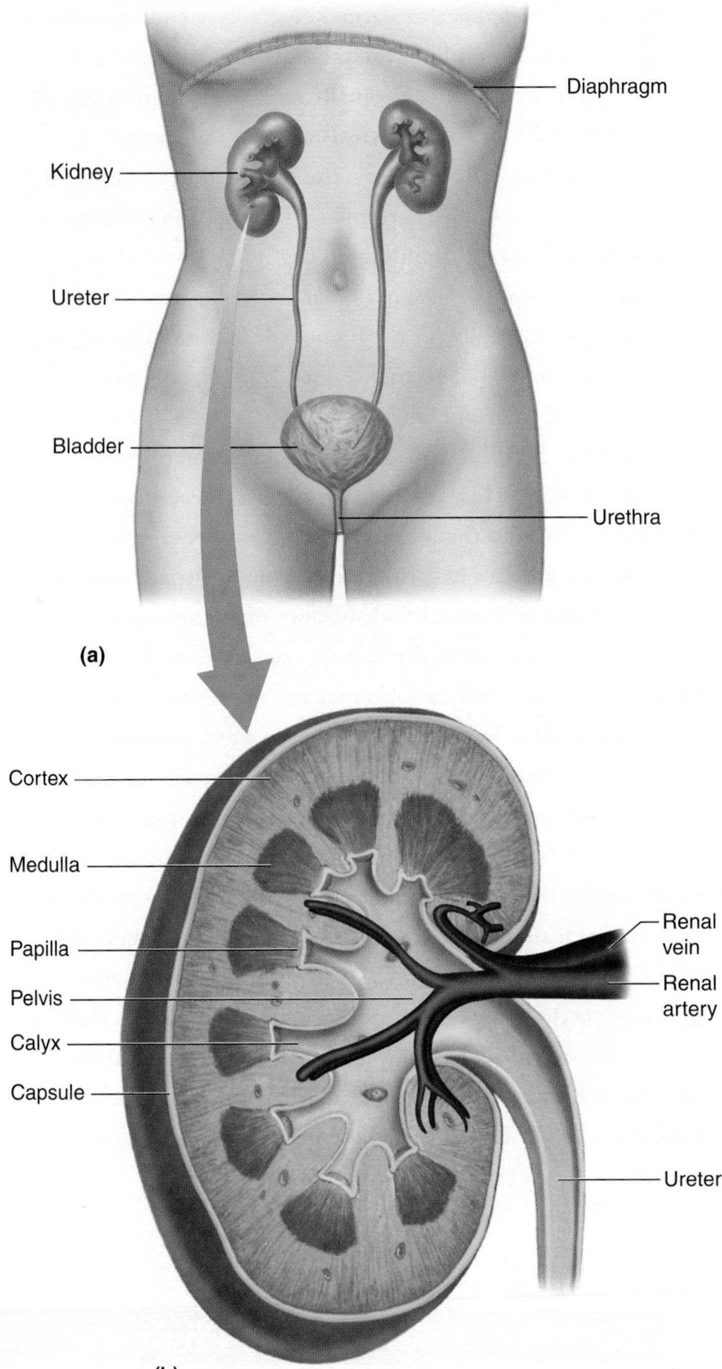

Figure 14.1 APIR (a) Urinary system in a woman. In the male, the urethra passes through the penis (Chapter 17). The diaphragm is shown for orientation. (b) Major structural components of the kidney. Kibble, 2009.

Each kidney contains approximately 1 million similar subunits called **nephrons.** Each nephron consists of (1) an initial filtering component called the **renal corpuscle** and (2) a **tubule** that extends from the renal corpuscle (**Figure 14.2a**). The renal tubule is a very narrow, hollow cylinder made up of a single layer of epithelial cells resting

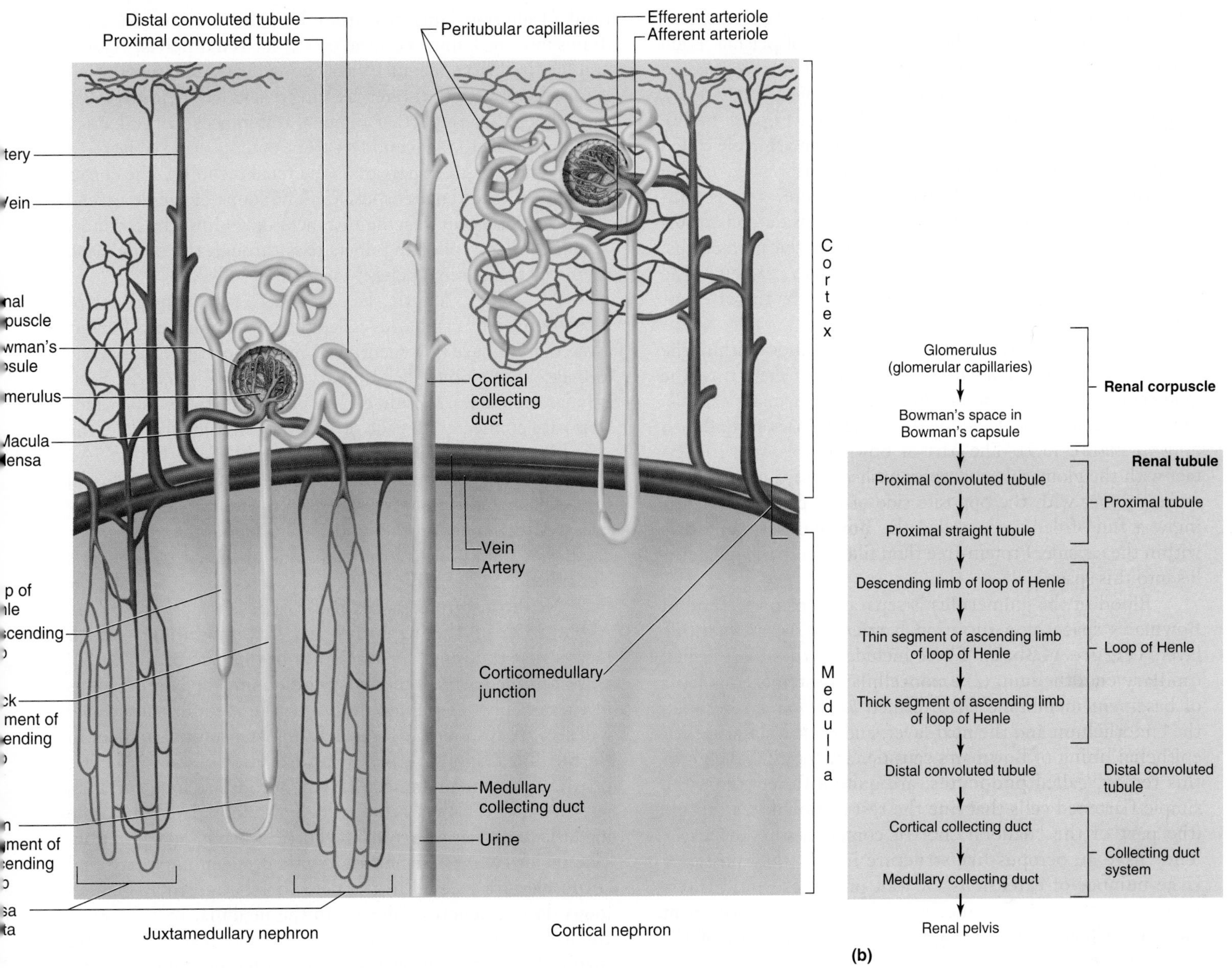

Figure 14.2 AP|R Basic structure of a nephron. (a) Anatomical organization. The macula densa is not a distinct segment but a plaque of cells in the ascending loop of Henle where the loop passes between the arterioles supplying its renal corpuscle of origin. The outer area of the kidney is called the cortex, and the inner is called the medulla. Two types of nephrons are shown—the juxtamedullary nephrons have long loops of Henle that penetrate deeply into the medulla, whereas the cortical nephrons have short (or no) loops of Henle. Note that the efferent arterioles of juxtamedullary nephrons give rise to long, looping vasa recta, whereas efferent arterioles of cortical nephrons give rise to peritubular capillaries. Not shown (for clarity) are the peritubular capillaries surrounding the portions of the juxtamedullary nephron's tubules located in the cortex. These peritubular capillaries arise primarily from other cortical nephrons. (b) Consecutive segments of the nephron. All segments in the yellow area are parts of the renal tubule; the terms to the right of the brackets are commonly used for several consecutive segments.

on a basement membrane. The epithelial cells differ in structure and function along the length of the tubule, and at least eight distinct segments are now recognized (**Figure 14.2b**). It is customary, however, to group two or more contiguous tubular segments when discussing function, and we will follow this practice.

The renal corpuscle forms a filtrate from blood that is free of cells, larger polypeptides, and proteins. This filtrate then leaves the renal corpuscle and enters the tubule. As it flows through the tubule, substances are added to or removed from it. Ultimately, the fluid remaining at the end of each nephron combines in the collecting ducts and exits the kidneys as urine.

Let us look first at the anatomy of the renal corpuscles—the filters. The renal corpuscle is a classic example of the general principle of physiology that structure is a determinant of function. Not only do the many capillaries in each corpuscle greatly increase the surface area for filtration of waste products from the plasma, but their structure creates an efficient sieve for the ultrafiltration of plasma. Each renal corpuscle contains a compact tuft of interconnected capillary loops called the **glomerulus** (plural, *glomeruli*), or **glomerular capillaries** (Figure 14.2 and **Figure 14.3a**). Each glomerulus is supplied with blood by an arteriole called an **afferent arteriole.** The glomerulus protrudes into a fluid-filled capsule called **Bowman's capsule.** The combination of a glomerulus and a Bowman's capsule constitutes a renal corpuscle. As blood flows through the glomerulus, about 20% of the plasma filters into Bowman's capsule. The remaining blood then leaves the glomerulus by the **efferent arteriole.**

One way of visualizing the relationships within the renal corpuscle is to imagine a loosely clenched fist—the glomerulus—punched into a balloon—the Bowman's capsule. (This is similar to the depiction of the pleural sacs around each lung in Figure 13.5). The part of Bowman's capsule in contact with the glomerulus becomes pushed inward but does not make contact with the opposite side of the capsule. Accordingly, a fluid-filled space called the **Bowman's space** exists within the capsule. Protein-free fluid filters from the glomerulus into this space.

Blood in the glomerulus is separated from the fluid in Bowman's space by a filtration barrier consisting of three layers (**Figure 14.3b, c**). These include (1) the single-celled capillary endothelium, (2) a noncellular proteinaceous layer of basement membrane (also termed *basal lamina*) between the endothelium and the next layer, and (3) the single-celled epithelial lining of Bowman's capsule. The epithelial cells in this region, called **podocytes,** are quite different from the simple flattened cells that line the rest of Bowman's capsule (the part of the "balloon" not in contact with the "fist"). They have an octopus-like structure in that they possess a large number of extensions, or foot processes. Fluid filters first across the endothelial cells, then through the basement membrane, and finally between the foot processes of the podocytes.

In addition to the capillary endothelial cells and the podocytes, **mesangial cells**—a third cell type—are modified smooth muscle cells that surround the glomerular capillary loops but are not part of the filtration pathway. Their function will be described later.

The segment of the tubule that drains Bowman's capsule is the **proximal tubule,** comprising the proximal convoluted tubule and the proximal straight tubule shown in Figure 14.2b. The next portion of the tubule is the **loop of Henle,** which is a sharp, hairpinlike loop consisting of a **descending limb** coming from the proximal tubule and an **ascending limb** leading to the next tubular segment, the **distal convoluted tubule.** Fluid flows from the distal convoluted tubule into the **collecting-duct system,** which is comprised of the **cortical collecting duct** and then the **medullary collecting duct.** The reasons for the terms *cortical* and *medullary* will be apparent shortly.

From Bowman's capsule to the collecting-duct system, each nephron is completely separate from the others. This separation ends when multiple cortical collecting ducts merge. The result of additional mergings from this point on is that the urine drains into the kidney's central cavity, the **renal pelvis,** via several hundred large medullary collecting ducts. The renal pelvis is continuous with the ureter draining that kidney (**Figure 14.4**).

There are important regional differences in the kidney (see Figures 14.1b, 14.2, and 14.4). The outer portion is the renal cortex, and the inner portion is the renal medulla. The cortex contains all the renal corpuscles. The loops of Henle extend from the cortex for varying distances down into the medulla. The medullary collecting ducts pass through the medulla on their way to the renal pelvis.

All along its length, the part of each tubule in the cortex is surrounded by capillaries called the **peritubular capillaries.** Note that we have now mentioned two sets of capillaries in the kidneys—the glomerular capillaries (glomeruli) and the peritubular capillaries. Within each nephron, the two sets of capillaries are connected to each other by an efferent arteriole, the vessel by which blood leaves the glomerulus (see Figure 14.2 and Figure 14.3a). Thus, the renal circulation is very unusual in that it includes *two* sets of arterioles and *two* sets of capillaries. After supplying the tubules with blood, the peritubular capillaries then join to form the veins by which blood leaves the kidney.

Nephrons are of two general types (see Figure 14.2a). About 15% of the nephrons are **juxtamedullary,** which means that the renal corpuscle lies in the part of the cortex closest to the cortical–medullary junction. The Henle's loops of these nephrons plunge deep into the medulla and, as we will see, are responsible for generating an osmotic gradient in the medulla responsible for the reabsorption of water. In close proximity to the juxtamedullary nephrons are long capillaries known as the **vasa recta,** which also loop deeply into the medulla and then return to the cortical–medullary junction. The majority of nephrons are **cortical,** meaning their renal corpuscles are located in the outer cortex and their Henle's loops do not penetrate deep into the medulla. In fact, some cortical nephrons do not have a Henle's loop at all; they are involved in reabsorption and secretion but do not contribute to the hypertonic medullary interstitium described later in the chapter.

One additional anatomical detail involving both the tubule and the arterioles is important. Near its end, the ascending limb of each loop of Henle passes between the afferent and efferent arterioles of that loop's own nephron (see Figure 14.2). At this point, there is a patch of cells in the wall of the ascending limb as it becomes the distal convoluted tubule called the **macula densa,** and the wall of the afferent arteriole contains secretory cells known as **juxtaglomerular (JG) cells.** The combination of macula densa and juxtaglomerular cells is known as the **juxtaglomerular apparatus (JGA)** (see Figure 14.3a and **Figure 14.5**). The juxtaglomerular cells secrete renin into the blood.

14.3 Basic Renal Processes

Urine formation begins with the filtration of plasma from the glomerular capillaries into Bowman's space. This process is termed **glomerular filtration,** and the filtrate is called

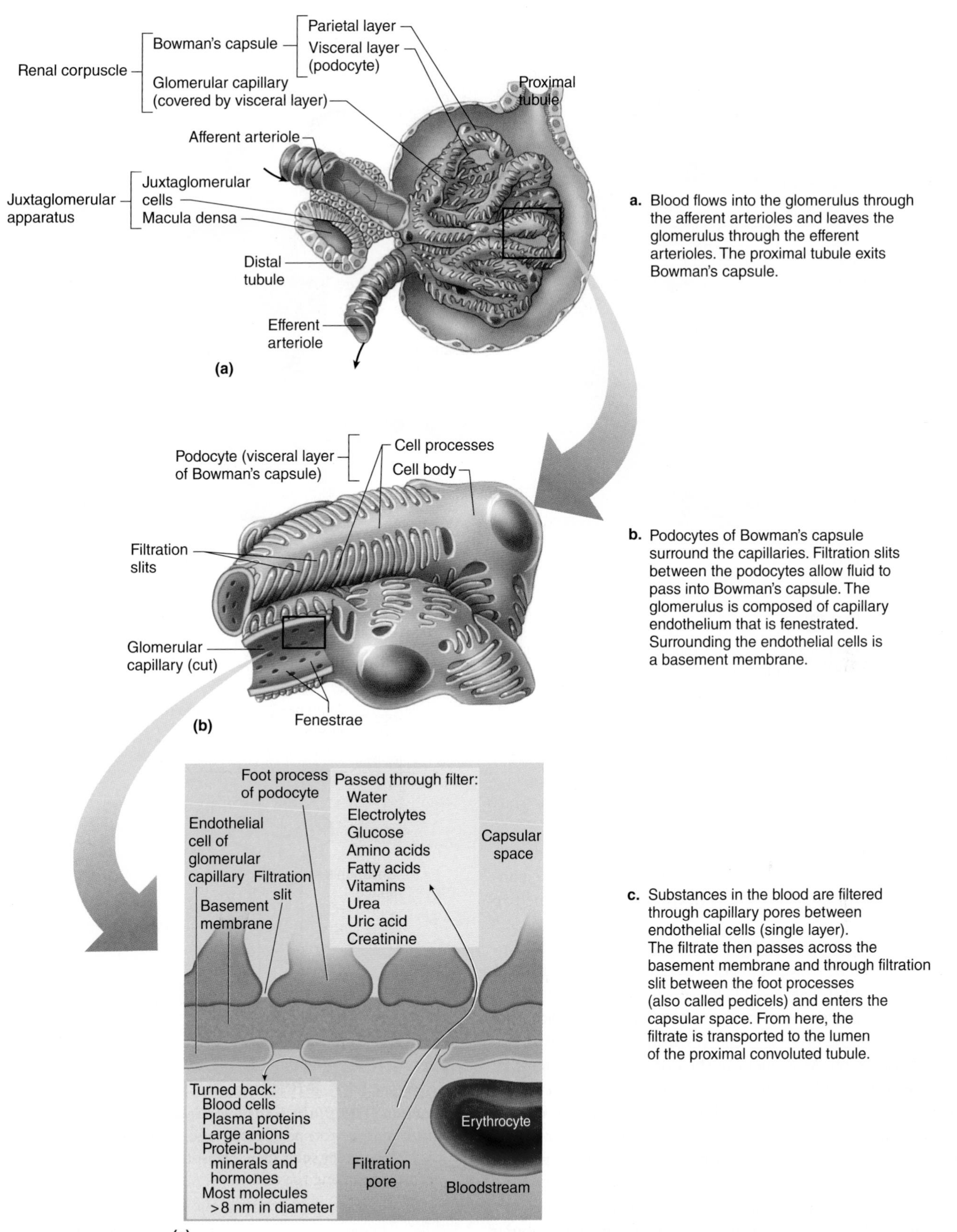

Figure 14.3 AP|R The renal corpuscle. (a) Anatomy of the renal corpuscle. (b) Inset view of podocytes and capillaries. (c) Glomerular filtration membrane.

PHYSIOLOGICAL INQUIRY

- What would happen if a significant number of glomerular capillaries were clogged, as can happen in someone with very high blood glucose concentrations for a long period of time (as can occur in untreated diabetes mellitus)?

Answer can be found at end of chapter.

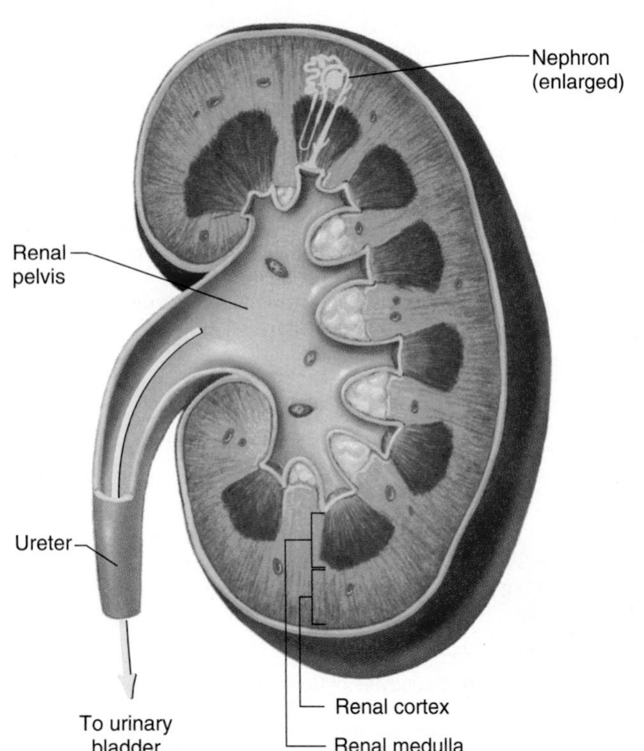

Figure 14.4 APIR Section of a human kidney. For clarity, the juxtamedullary nephron illustrated to show nephron orientation is not to scale—its outline would not be clearly visible without a microscope. The outer kidney, which contains all the renal corpuscles, is the cortex, and the inner kidney is the medulla. Note that in the medulla, the loops of Henle and the collecting ducts run parallel to each other. The medullary collecting ducts drain into the renal pelvis.

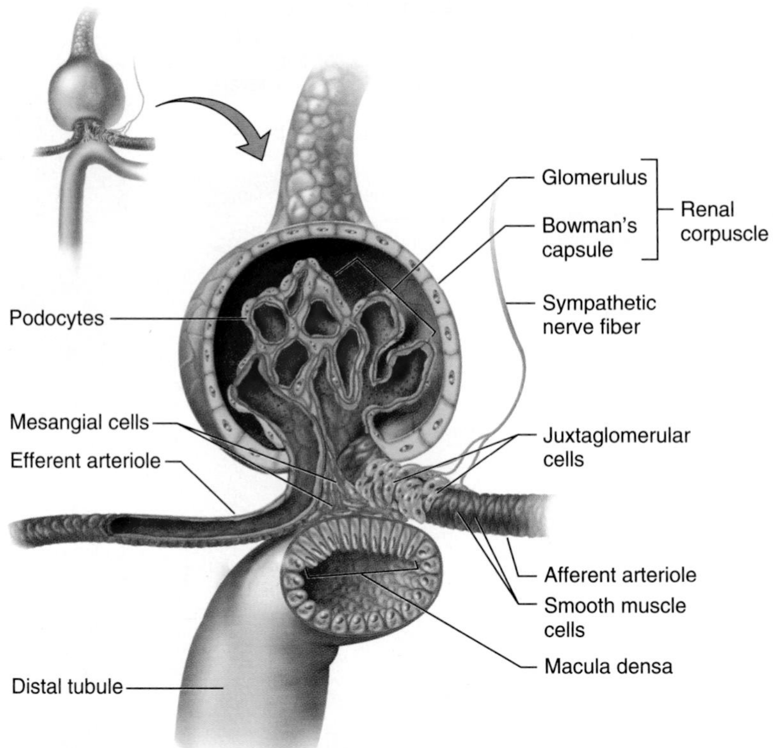

Figure 14.5 APIR The juxtaglomerular apparatus.

the **glomerular filtrate.** It is cell-free and, except for larger proteins, contains all the substances in virtually the same concentrations as in plasma. This type of filtrate is also termed an *ultrafiltrate.*

During its passage through the tubules, the filtrate's composition is altered by movements of substances from the tubules to the peritubular capillaries, and vice versa (**Figure 14.6**). When the direction of movement is from tubular lumen to peritubular capillary plasma, the process is called **tubular reabsorption** or, simply, reabsorption. Movement in the opposite direction—that is, from peritubular plasma to tubular lumen—is called **tubular secretion** or, simply, secretion. Tubular secretion is also used to denote the movement of a solute from the cell interior to the lumen in the cases in which the kidney tubular cells themselves generate the substance.

To summarize, a substance can gain entry to the tubule and be excreted in the urine by glomerular filtration or tubular secretion or both. Once in the tubule, however, the substance does not have to be excreted but can be completely reabsorbed. Thus, the amount of any substance excreted in the urine is equal to the amount filtered plus the amount secreted minus the amount reabsorbed.

$$\text{Amount excreted} = \text{Amount filtered} + \text{Amount secreted} - \text{Amount reabsorbed}$$

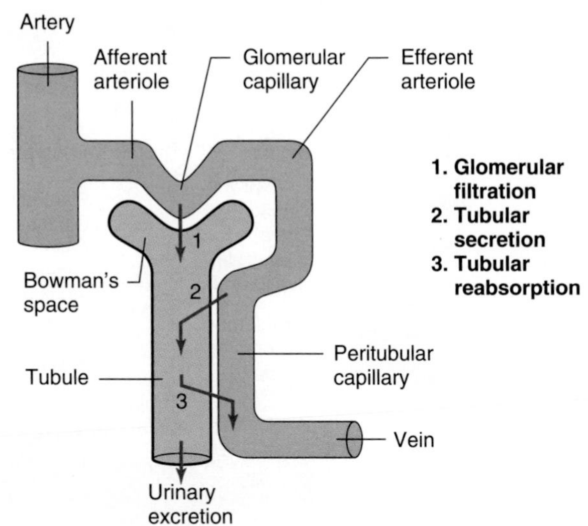

Figure 14.6 APIR The three basic components of renal function. This figure is to illustrate only the *directions* of reabsorption and secretion, not specific sites or order of occurrence. Depending on the particular substance, reabsorption and secretion can occur at various sites along the tubule.

It is important to stress that not all these processes—filtration, secretion, and reabsorption—apply to all substances. For example, important solutes like glucose are completely reabsorbed, whereas toxins are secreted and not reabsorbed.

To emphasize the general principles of renal function, **Figure 14.7** illustrates the renal handling of three hypothetical substances that might be found in blood. Approximately

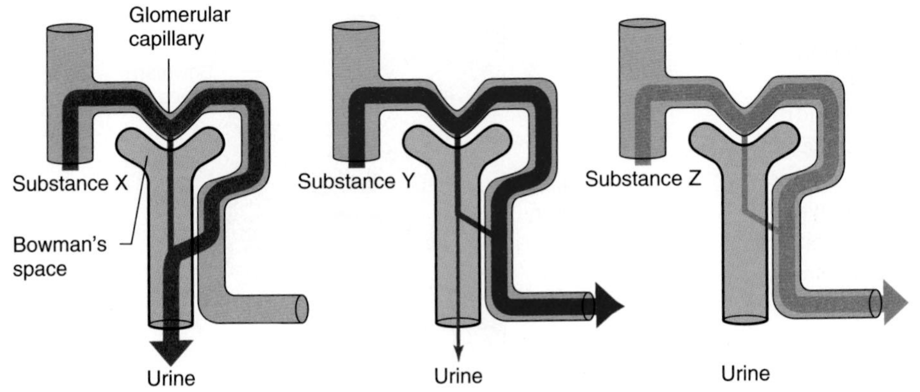

Figure 14.7 APIR Renal handling of three hypothetical filtered substances X, Y, and Z. X is filtered and secreted but not reabsorbed. Y is filtered, and a fraction is then reabsorbed. Z is filtered and completely reabsorbed. The thickness of each line in this hypothetical example suggests the magnitude of the process.

20% of the plasma that enters the glomerular capillaries is filtered into Bowman's space. This filtrate, which contains X, Y, and Z in the same concentrations as in the capillary plasma, enters the proximal tubule and begins to flow through the rest of the tubule. Simultaneously, the remaining 80% of the plasma, containing X, Y, and Z, leaves the glomerular capillaries via the efferent arteriole and enters the peritubular capillaries.

Assume that the tubule can secrete 100% of the peritubular capillary substance X into the tubular lumen but cannot reabsorb X. Therefore, by the combination of filtration and tubular secretion, the plasma that originally entered the renal artery is cleared of all of its substance X, which leaves the body via the urine. Logically, this tends to be the pattern for renal handling of foreign substances that are potentially harmful to the body.

By contrast, assume that the tubule can reabsorb but not secrete Y and Z. The amount of Y reabsorption is moderate so that some of the filtered material is not reabsorbed and escapes from the body. For Z, however, the reabsorptive mechanism is so powerful that all the filtered Z is reabsorbed back into the plasma. Therefore, no Z is lost from the body. Hence, for Z, the processes of filtration and reabsorption have canceled each other out and the net result is as though Z had never entered the kidney. Again, it is logical to assume that substance Y is important to retain but requires maintenance within a homeostatic range; substance Z is presumably very important for health and is therefore completely reabsorbed.

A specific combination of filtration, tubular reabsorption, and tubular secretion applies to each substance in the plasma. The critical point is that, for many substances, the rates at which the processes proceed are subject to physiological control. By triggering changes in the rates of filtration, reabsorption, or secretion whenever the amount of a substance in the body is higher or lower than the normal limits, homeostatic mechanisms can regulate the substance's bodily balance. For example, consider what happens when a normally hydrated person drinks more water than usual. Within 1 to 2 hours, all the excess water has been excreted in the urine, partly as a result of an increase in filtration but mainly as a result of decreased tubular reabsorption of water. In this example, the kidneys are the effector organs of a homeostatic process that maintains total-body water within very narrow limits.

Although glomerular filtration, tubular reabsorption, and tubular secretion are the three basic renal processes, a fourth process—metabolism by the tubular cells—is also important for some substances. In some cases, the renal tubular cells remove substances from blood or glomerular filtrate and metabolize them, resulting in their disappearance from the body. In other cases, the cells *produce* substances and add them either to the blood or tubular fluid; the most important of these, as we will see, are ammonium ion, hydrogen ion, and HCO_3^-.

In summary, one can evaluate the normal renal processing of any given substance by asking a series of questions:

1. To what degree is the substance filterable at the renal corpuscle?
2. Is the substance reabsorbed?
3. Is the substance secreted?
4. What factors regulate the quantities filtered, reabsorbed, or secreted?
5. What are the pathways for altering renal excretion of the substance to maintain stable body balance?

Glomerular Filtration

As stated previously, the glomerular filtrate—that is, the fluid in Bowman's space—normally contains no cells but contains all plasma substances except proteins in virtually the same concentrations as in plasma. This is because glomerular filtration is a bulk-flow process in which water and all low-molecular-weight substances (including smaller polypeptides) move together. Most plasma proteins—the albumins and globulins—are excluded almost entirely from the filtrate. One reason for their exclusion is that the renal corpuscles restrict the movement of such high-molecular-weight substances. A second reason is that the filtration pathways in the corpuscular membranes are negatively charged, so they oppose the movement of these plasma proteins, most of which are negatively charged.

The only exceptions to the generalization that all nonprotein plasma substances have the same concentrations in the glomerular filtrate as in the plasma are certain low-molecular-weight substances that would otherwise be filterable but are bound to plasma proteins and therefore not filtered. For example, half the plasma calcium and virtually all of the plasma fatty acids are bound to plasma protein and so are not filtered.

Forces Involved in Filtration

Once again we return to the general principle that physiological processes are dictated by the laws of chemistry and physics; the importance of physical forces is critical to understanding the fundamental processes of homeostasis. As was discussed in Chapter 12, filtration across capillaries is determined by opposing Starling forces. To review, Starling forces are (1) the hydrostatic pressure difference across the capillary wall that favors filtration and (2) the protein concentration difference across the wall that creates an osmotic force that opposes filtration.

This also applies to the glomerular capillaries, as summarized in **Figure 14.8.** The blood pressure in the glomerular capillaries—the glomerular capillary hydrostatic pressure (P_{GC})—is a force favoring filtration. The fluid in Bowman's space exerts a hydrostatic pressure (P_{BS}) that opposes this filtration. Another opposing force is the osmotic force (π_{GC}) that results from the presence of protein in the glomerular capillary plasma. Recall that there is usually no protein in the filtrate in Bowman's space because of the unique structure of the areas of filtration in the glomerulus, so the osmotic force in Bowman's space (π_{BS}) is zero. The unequal distribution of protein causes the water concentration of the plasma to be slightly less than that of the fluid in Bowman's space, and this difference in water concentration favors fluid movement by osmosis from Bowman's space into the glomerular capillaries—that is, it opposes glomerular filtration.

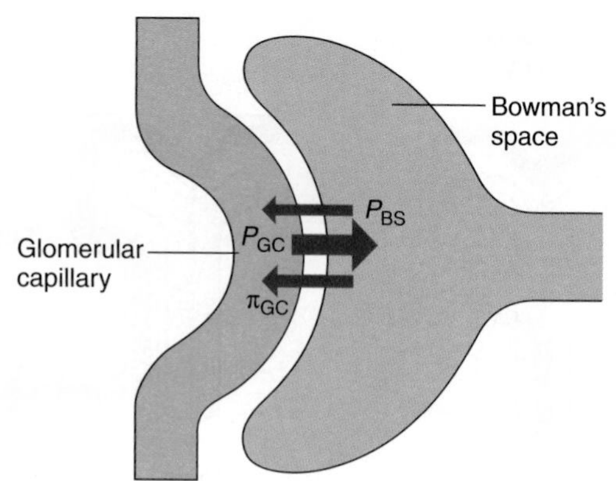

Forces	**mmHg**
Favoring filtration:	
Glomerular capillary blood pressure (P_{GC})	60
Opposing filtration:	
Fluid pressure in Bowman's space (P_{BS})	15
Osmotic force due to protein in plasma (π_{GC})	29
Net glomerular filtration pressure = $P_{GC} - P_{BS} - \pi_{GC}$	16

Figure 14.8 APIR Forces involved in glomerular filtration. The symbol π denotes the osmotic force due to the presence of protein in glomerular capillary plasma. (*Note:* The concentration of protein in Bowman's space is so low that π_{BS}, a force that would favor filtration, is considered zero.)

PHYSIOLOGICAL INQUIRY

- What would be the effect of an increase in plasma albumin (the most abundant plasma protein) on glomerular filtration rate (GFR)?

Answer can be found at end of chapter.

Note that, in Figure 14.8, the value given for this osmotic force—29 mmHg—is slightly larger than the value—28 mmHg—for the osmotic force given in Chapter 12 for plasma in all arteries and nonrenal capillaries. The reason is that, unlike the situation elsewhere in the body, enough water filters out of the glomerular capillaries that the protein left behind in the plasma becomes more concentrated than in arterial plasma. In other capillaries, in contrast, little water filters out and the capillary protein concentration remains essentially unchanged from its value in arterial plasma. In other words, unlike the situation in other capillaries, the plasma protein concentration and, therefore, the osmotic force increase from the beginning to the end of the glomerular capillaries. The value given in Figure 14.8 for the osmotic force is the average value along the length of the capillaries.

To summarize, the **net glomerular filtration pressure** is the sum of three relevant forces:

$$\text{Net glomerular filtration pressure} = P_{GC} - P_{BS} - \pi_{GC}$$

Normally, the net filtration pressure is always positive because the glomerular capillary hydrostatic pressure (P_{GC}) is larger than the sum of the hydrostatic pressure in Bowman's space (P_{BS}) and the osmotic force opposing filtration (π_{GC}). The net glomerular filtration pressure initiates urine formation by forcing an essentially protein-free filtrate of plasma out of the glomerulus and into Bowman's space and then down the tubule into the renal pelvis.

Rate of Glomerular Filtration

The volume of fluid filtered from the glomeruli into Bowman's space per unit time is known as the **glomerular filtration rate (GFR).** GFR is determined not only by the net filtration pressure but also by the permeability of the corpuscular membranes and the surface area available for filtration. In other words, at any given net filtration pressure, the GFR will be directly proportional to the membrane permeability and the surface area. The glomerular capillaries are much more permeable to fluid than most other capillaries. Therefore, the net glomerular filtration pressure causes massive filtration of fluid into Bowman's space. In a 70 kg person, the GFR averages 180 L/day (125 mL/min)! This is much higher than the combined net filtration of 4 L/day of fluid across all the other capillaries in the body, as described in Chapter 12.

When we recall that the total volume of plasma in the cardiovascular system is approximately 3 L, it follows that the kidneys filter the entire plasma volume about 60 times a day. This opportunity to process such huge volumes of plasma enables the kidneys to regulate the constituents of the internal environment rapidly and to excrete large quantities of waste products.

GFR is not a fixed value but is subject to physiological regulation. This is achieved mainly by neural and hormonal input to the afferent and efferent arterioles, which causes changes in net glomerular filtration pressure (**Figure 14.9**). The glomerular capillaries are unique in that they are situated between two sets of arterioles—the afferent and efferent arterioles. Constriction of the afferent arterioles decreases hydrostatic pressure in the glomerular capillaries (P_{GC}). This is similar to arteriolar constriction in other organs and is due to a greater loss of pressure between arteries and capillaries (**Figure 14.9a**).

In contrast, efferent arteriolar constriction alone has the opposite effect on P_{GC} in that it *increases* it (**Figure 14.9b**). This occurs because the efferent arteriole lies beyond the glomerulus, so that efferent arteriolar constriction tends to "dam back" the blood in the glomerular capillaries, raising P_{GC}. Dilation of the efferent arteriole (**Figure 14.9c**) decreases P_{GC} and thus GFR, whereas dilation of the afferent arteriole increases P_{GC} and thus GFR (**Figure 14.9d**). Finally, simultaneous constriction or dilation of both sets of arterioles tends to leave P_{GC} unchanged because of the opposing effects. The control of GFR is an example of the general principle of physiology that most physiological functions are controlled by multiple regulatory systems, often working in opposition.

In addition to the neural and endocrine input to the arterioles, there is also neural and humoral input to the mesangial cells that surround the glomerular capillaries. Contraction of these cells reduces the surface area of the capillaries, which causes a decrease in GFR at any given net filtration pressure.

It is possible to measure the total amount of any nonprotein or non-protein-bound substance filtered into Bowman's space by multiplying the GFR by the plasma concentration of the substance. This amount is called the **filtered load** of the substance. For example, if the GFR is 180 L/day and plasma glucose concentration is 1 g/L, then the filtered load of glucose is 180 L/day $\times$ 1 g/L = 180 g/day.

Once the filtered load of the substance is known, it can be compared to the amount of the substance excreted. This indicates whether the substance undergoes net tubular reabsorption or net secretion. Whenever the quantity of a substance excreted in the urine is less than the filtered load, tubular reabsorption must have occurred. Conversely, if the amount excreted in the urine is greater than the filtered load, tubular secretion must have occurred.

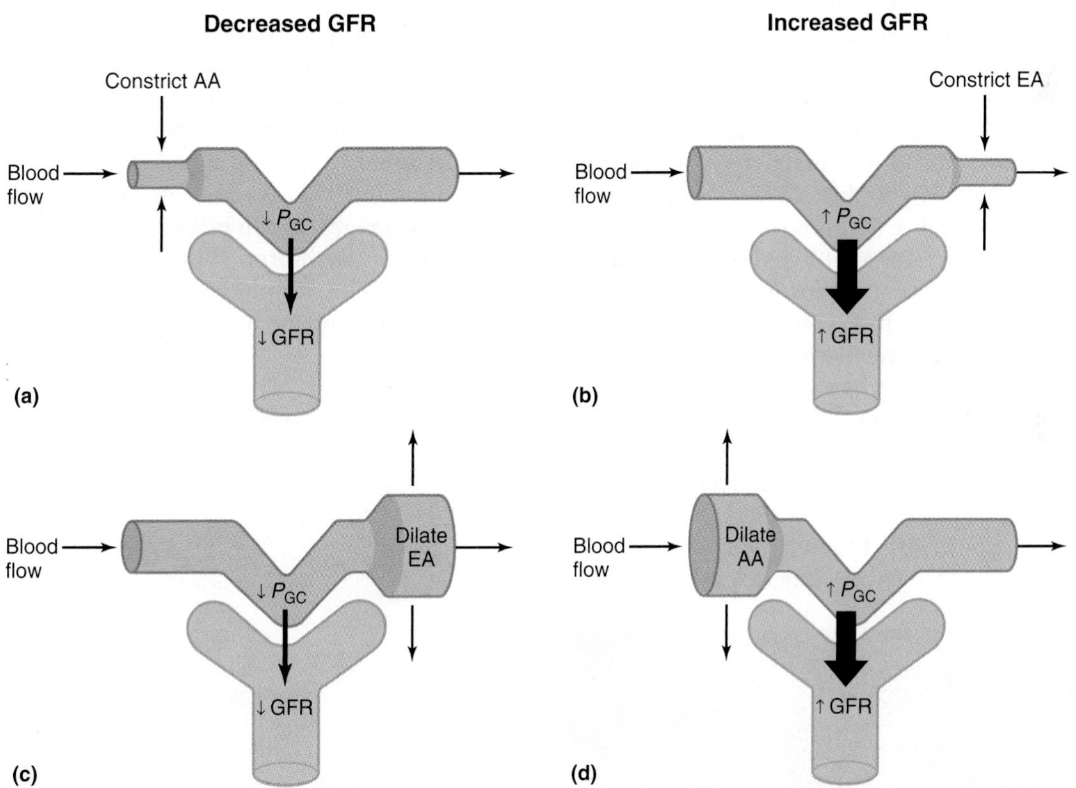

Figure 14.9 APIR Control of GFR by constriction or dilation of afferent arterioles (AA) or efferent arterioles (EA). (a) Constriction of the afferent arteriole or (c) dilation of the efferent arteriole reduces P_{GC}, thus decreasing GFR. (b) Constriction of the efferent arteriole or (d) dilation of the afferent arteriole increases P_{GC}, thus increasing GFR.

PHYSIOLOGICAL INQUIRY

- Describe the immediate consequences of a blood clot occluding the afferent arteriole or the efferent arteriole.

Answer can be found at end of chapter.

Tubular Reabsorption

Table 14.2 summarizes data for a few plasma components that undergo filtration and reabsorption. It gives an idea of the magnitude and importance of reabsorptive mechanisms. The values in this table are typical for a healthy person on an average diet. There are at least three important conclusions we can draw from this table: (1) The filtered loads are enormous, generally larger than the amounts of the substances in the body. For example, the body contains about 40 L of water, but the volume of water filtered each day is 180 L. (2) Reabsorption of waste products is relatively incomplete (as in the case of urea), so that large fractions of their filtered loads are excreted in the urine. (3) Reabsorption of most useful plasma components, such as water, inorganic ions, and organic nutrients, is relatively complete so that the amounts excreted in the urine are very small fractions of their filtered loads.

An important distinction should be made between reabsorptive processes that can be controlled physiologically and those that cannot. The reabsorption rates of most organic nutrients, such as glucose, are always very high and are not physiologically regulated. Thus, the filtered loads of these substances are normally completely reabsorbed, with none appearing in the urine. For these substances, like substance Z in Figure 14.7, it is as though the kidneys do not exist because the kidneys do not eliminate these substances from the body at all. Therefore, the kidneys do not regulate the plasma concentrations of these organic nutrients. Rather, the kidneys merely maintain whatever plasma concentrations already exist.

Recall that a major function of the kidneys is to eliminate soluble waste products. To do this, the blood is filtered in the glomeruli. One consequence of this is that substances necessary for normal body functions are filtered from the plasma into the tubular fluid. To prevent the loss of these important nonwaste products, the kidneys have powerful mechanisms to reclaim useful substances from tubular fluid while simultaneously allowing waste products to be excreted. The reabsorptive rates for water and many ions, although also very high, are under physiological control. For example, if water intake is decreased, the kidneys can increase water reabsorption to minimize water loss.

In contrast to glomerular filtration, the crucial steps in tubular reabsorption—those that achieve movement of a substance from tubular lumen to interstitial fluid—do *not* occur by bulk flow because there are inadequate pressure differences across the tubule and inadequate permeability of the tubular membranes. Instead, two other processes are involved. (1) The reabsorption of some substances from the tubular lumen is by diffusion, often across the tight junctions connecting the tubular epithelial cells (**Figure 14.10**). (2) The reabsorption of all other substances involves mediated transport, which requires the participation of transport proteins in the plasma membranes of tubular cells.

The final step in reabsorption is the movement of substances from the interstitial fluid into peritubular capillaries that occurs by a combination of diffusion and bulk flow. We will assume that this final process occurs automatically once the substance reaches the interstitial fluid.

TABLE 14.2 Average Values for Several Components That Undergo Filtration and Reabsorption

Substance	Amount Filtered per Day	Amount Excreted per Day	Percentage Reabsorbed
Water, L	180	1.8	99
Sodium, g	630	3.2	99.5
Glucose, g	180	0	100
Urea, g	54	30	44

Reabsorption by Diffusion

The reabsorption of urea by the proximal tubule provides an example of passive reabsorption by diffusion. An analysis of urea concentrations in the proximal tubule will help clarify the mechanism. Because the corpuscular membranes are freely filterable to urea, the urea concentration in the fluid within Bowman's space is the same as that in the peritubular capillary plasma and the interstitial fluid surrounding the tubule. Then, as the filtered fluid flows through the proximal tubule, water reabsorption occurs (by mechanisms to be described later). This removal of water increases the concentration of urea in the tubular fluid so it is higher than in the interstitial fluid and peritubular capillaries. Therefore, urea diffuses down this concentration gradient from tubular lumen to peritubular capillary. Urea reabsorption is thus dependent upon the reabsorption of water. Reabsorption by diffusion in this manner occurs for a variety of lipid-soluble organic substances, both naturally occurring and foreign (e.g., the pesticide DDT).

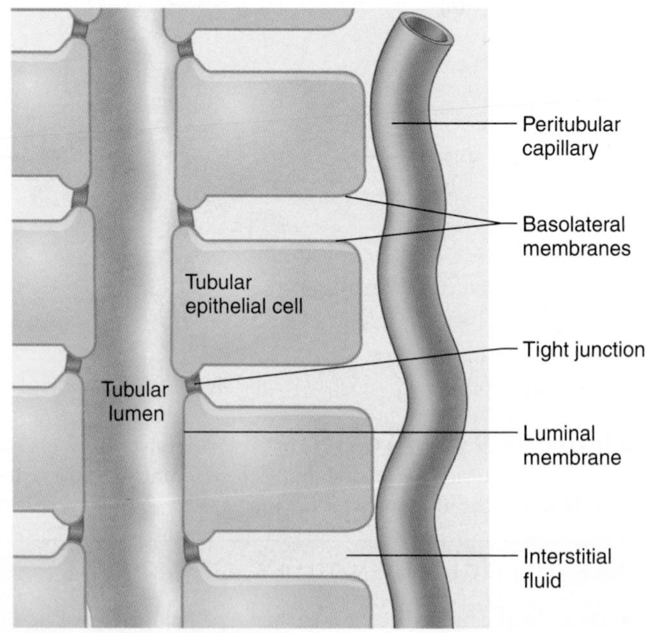

Figure 14.10 APIR Diagrammatic representation of tubular epithelium. The luminal membrane is also called the apical membrane.

Reabsorption by Mediated Transport

Figure 14.10 demonstrates that a substance reabsorbed by mediated transport must first cross the **luminal membrane** (also called the *apical membrane*) that separates the tubular lumen from the cell interior. Then, the substance diffuses through the cytosol of the cell and, finally, crosses the **basolateral membrane,** which begins at the tight junctions and constitutes the plasma membrane of the sides and base of the cell. The movement by this route is termed *transcellular* epithelial transport.

A substance does not need to be actively transported across *both* the luminal and basolateral membranes in order to be actively transported across the overall epithelium, thus moving from lumen to interstitial fluid against its electrochemical gradient. For example, Na^+ moves "downhill" (passively) into the cell across the luminal membrane either by diffusion or by facilitated diffusion and then is actively transported "uphill" out of the cell across the basolateral membrane via Na^+/K^+-ATPases in this membrane.

The reabsorption of many substances is coupled to the reabsorption of Na^+. The cotransported substance moves uphill into the cell via a secondary active cotransporter as Na^+ moves downhill into the cell via this same cotransporter. This is precisely how glucose, many amino acids, and other organic substances undergo tubular reabsorption. The reabsorption of several inorganic ions is also coupled in a variety of ways to the reabsorption of Na^+.

Many of the mediated-transport-reabsorptive systems in the renal tubule have a limit to the amounts of material they can transport per unit time known as the **transport maximum** (T_m). This is because the binding sites on the membrane transport proteins become saturated when the concentration of the transported substance increases to a certain level. An important example is the secondary active-transport proteins for glucose, located in the proximal tubule. As noted earlier, glucose does not usually appear in the urine because all of the filtered glucose is reabsorbed. This is illustrated in **Figure 14.11,** which shows the relationship between plasma glucose concentrations and the filtered load, reabsorption, and excretion of glucose. Plasma glucose concentration in a healthy person normally does not exceed 150 mg/100 mL even after the person eats a sugary meal. Notice that this level of plasma glucose is below the threshold at which glucose starts to appear in urine (***glucosuria***). Also notice that the T_m for the entire kidney is higher than the threshold for glucosuria. This is because the nephrons have a range of T_m values that, when averaged, give a T_m for the entire kidney, as shown in Figure 14.11. When plasma glucose concentration exceeds the transport maximum for a significant number of nephrons, glucose starts to appear in urine. In people with significant hyperglycemia (for example, in poorly controlled ***diabetes mellitus***), the plasma glucose concentration often exceeds the threshold value of 200 mg/100 mL, so that the filtered load exceeds the ability of the nephrons to reabsorb glucose. In other words, although the capacity of the kidneys to reabsorb glucose can be normal in diabetes mellitus, the tubules cannot reabsorb the large increase in the filtered load of glucose. As you will learn later in this chapter and in Chapter 16, the high filtered load of glucose can also lead to significant disruption of normal renal function (***diabetic nephropathy***).

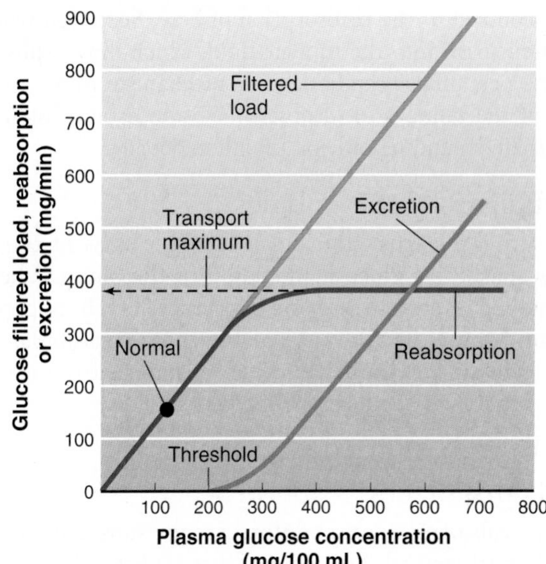

Figure 14.11 The relationship between plasma glucose concentration and the rate of glucose filtered (filtered load), reabsorbed, or excreted. The dotted line shows the transport maximum, which is the maximum rate at which glucose can be reabsorbed. Notice that as plasma glucose exceeds its threshold, glucose begins to appear in the urine.

PHYSIOLOGICAL INQUIRY

- How would you calculate the filtered load and excretion rate of glucose?

Answer can be found at end of chapter.

The pattern described for glucose is also true for a large number of other organic nutrients. For example, most amino acids and water-soluble vitamins are filtered in large amounts each day, but almost all of these filtered molecules are reabsorbed by the proximal tubule. If the plasma concentration becomes high enough, however, reabsorption of the filtered load will not be as complete and the substance will appear in larger amounts in the urine. Thus, people who ingest very large quantities of vitamin C have increased plasma concentrations of vitamin C. Eventually, the filtered load may exceed the tubular reabsorptive T_m for this substance, and any additional ingested vitamin C is excreted in the urine.

Tubular Secretion

Tubular secretion moves substances from peritubular capillaries into the tubular lumen. Like glomerular filtration, it constitutes a pathway from the blood into the tubule. Like reabsorption, secretion can occur by diffusion or by transcellular mediated transport. The most important substances secreted by the tubules are H^+ and K^+. However, a large number of normally occurring organic anions, such as choline and creatinine, are also secreted; so are many foreign chemicals such as penicillin. Active secretion of a substance requires active transport either from the blood side (the interstitial fluid) into the tubule cell (across the basolateral membrane) or out of the cell into the lumen (across the luminal membrane). As in reabsorption, tubular secretion is usually coupled to the reabsorption of Na^+. Secretion from the interstitial space into the tubular fluid, which draws substances from the peritubular capillaries, is a mechanism to increase the ability of the kidneys to dispose of substances at a higher rate rather than depending only on the filtered load.

Metabolism by the Tubules

We noted earlier that, during fasting, the cells of the renal tubules synthesize glucose and add it to the blood. They can also catabolize certain organic substances, such as peptides, taken up from either the tubular lumen or peritubular capillaries. Catabolism eliminates these substances from the body just as if they had been excreted into the urine.

Regulation of Membrane Channels and Transporters

Tubular reabsorption or secretion of many substances is under physiological control. For most of these substances, control is achieved by regulating the activity or concentrations of the membrane channel and transporter proteins involved in their transport. This regulation is achieved by hormones and paracrine or autocrine factors.

Understanding the structure, function, and regulation of renal, tubular-cell ion channels and transporters makes it possible to explain the underlying defects in some genetic diseases. For example, a genetic mutation can lead to an abnormality in the Na^+–glucose cotransporter that mediates reabsorption of glucose in the proximal tubule. This can lead to the appearance of glucose in the urine (***familial renal glucosuria***). Contrast this condition to diabetes mellitus, in which the ability to reabsorb glucose is usually normal but the filtered load of glucose exceeds the threshold for the tubules to reabsorb glucose (see Figure 14.11).

"Division of Labor" in the Tubules

To excrete waste products adequately, the GFR must be very large. This means that the filtered volume of water and the filtered loads of all the nonwaste plasma solutes are also very large. *The primary role of the proximal tubule is to reabsorb most of this filtered water and these solutes.* Furthermore, with K^+ as the one major exception, the proximal tubule is the major site of solute secretion. Henle's loop also reabsorbs relatively large quantities of the major ions and, to a lesser extent, water.

Extensive reabsorption by the proximal tubule and Henle's loop ensures that the masses of solutes and the volume of water entering the tubular segments beyond Henle's loop are relatively small. These distal segments then do the fine-tuning for most substances, determining the final amounts excreted in the urine by adjusting their rates of reabsorption and, in a few cases, secretion. It should not be surprising, therefore, that most homeostatic controls act upon the more distal segments of the tubule.

14.4 The Concept of Renal Clearance

A useful way of quantifying renal function is in terms of clearance. The renal **clearance** of any substance is the volume of plasma from which that substance is completely removed ("cleared") by the kidneys per unit time. Every substance has its own distinct clearance value, but the units are always in volume of plasma per unit of time. The basic clearance formula for any substance S is

$$\text{Clearance of } S = \frac{\text{Mass of } S \text{ excreted per unit time}}{\text{Plasma concentration of } S}$$

Thus, the clearance of a substance is a measure of the volume of plasma completely cleared of the substance per unit time. This accounts for the mass of the substance excreted in the urine.

Because the mass of S excreted per unit time is equal to the urine concentration of S multiplied by the urine volume during that time, the formula for the clearance of S becomes

$$C_S = \frac{U_S V}{P_S}$$

where

C_S = Clearance of S
U_S = Urine concentration of S
V = Urine volume per unit time
P_S = Plasma concentration of S

Let us examine some particularly interesting examples of clearance. What would be the clearance of glucose, for example, under normal conditions? Recall from Figure 14.11 that all of the glucose filtered from the plasma into the glomeruli is normally reabsorbed by the epithelial cells of the proximal tubules. Therefore, the clearance of glucose (C_{gl}) can be written as the following equation:

$$C_{gl} = \frac{(U_{gl})(V)}{(P_{gl})}$$

where the subscript "gl" indicates glucose. Because glucose is usually completely reabsorbed, its urinary concentration under normal conditions is zero (see Table 14.2). Therefore, this equation reduces to

$$C_{gl} = \frac{(0)(V)}{(P_{gl})} \text{ or } C_{gl} = 0$$

The clearance of glucose is normally zero because all of the glucose that is filtered from the plasma into the glomeruli is reabsorbed back into the blood. As shown in Figure 14.11, only when the T_m for glucose is exceeded would the clearance become a positive value, which, as described earlier, would suggest the possibility of renal disease or very high blood glucose such as in untreated diabetes mellitus.

Now imagine a substance that is freely filtered but neither reabsorbed nor secreted. In other words, such a substance is not physiologically important like glucose—nor toxic like certain compounds that are secreted—and is, therefore, "ignored" by the kidneys. The human body does not produce such compounds that perfectly fit these characteristics, but there are examples found in nature. One such compound is the polysaccharide called **inulin** (not insulin), which is present in some of the vegetables and fruits that we eat. If inulin were infused intravenously in a person, what would happen? The amount of inulin entering the nephrons from the plasma—that is, the filtered load—would be equal to the amount of inulin excreted in the urine, and none of it would be reabsorbed or secreted. Recall that the filtered load of a substance is the glomerular filtration rate (GFR) multiplied by the plasma concentration of the substance. The excreted amount of the substance is *UV*, as just described. Therefore, for the special case of inulin (subscript "in"),

$$(GFR)(P_{in}) = (U_{in})(V)$$

By rearranging this equation, we get an equation that looks like the general equation for clearance shown earlier:

$$GFR = \frac{(U_{in})(V)}{(P_{in})}$$

In other words, the GFR of a person is equal to the clearance of inulin (*UV*/*P*)! If it were necessary to determine the GFR of a person, for example, someone suspected of having kidney disease, a physician would only need to determine the clearance of inulin. **Figure 14.12** shows a mathematical example of the renal handling of inulin. Notice that the GFR is 7.5 L/h, which is 125 mL/min, as described earlier in this section.

The clearance of any substance handled by the kidneys in the same way as inulin—filtered, but not reabsorbed, secreted, or metabolized—would equal the GFR. Unfortunately, there are no substances normally present in the plasma that perfectly meet these criteria, and for technical reasons it is not practical to perform an inulin clearance test in clinical situations. For clinical purposes, the **creatinine clearance** (**C_{Cr}**) is commonly used to approximate the GFR as follows. Creatinine is a waste product released by muscle; it is filtered at the renal corpuscle but does not undergo reabsorption. It does undergo a small amount of secretion, however, so that some peritubular plasma is cleared of its creatinine by secretion. Therefore, C_{Cr} slightly overestimates the GFR but is close enough to be highly useful in most clinical situations.

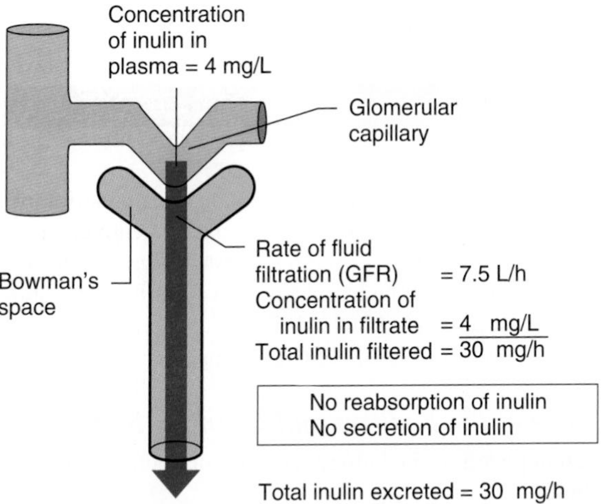

Figure 14.12 Example of renal handling of inulin, a substance that is filtered by the renal corpuscles but is neither reabsorbed nor secreted by the tubule. Therefore, the mass of inulin excreted per unit time is equal to the mass filtered during the same time period. As explained in the text, the clearance of inulin is equal to the glomerular filtration rate.

Usually, the concentration of creatinine in the blood is the only measurement necessary because it is assumed that creatinine production by the body is constant and similar between individuals. Therefore, an increase in creatinine concentration in the blood usually indicates a decrease in GFR, one of the hallmarks of kidney disease.

This leads to an important generalization. When the clearance of any substance is greater than the GFR, that substance must undergo tubular secretion. Look back at our hypothetical substance X (see Figure 14.7): X is filtered, and all the X that escapes filtration is secreted; no X is reabsorbed. Consequently, all the plasma that enters the kidney per unit time is cleared of its X. Therefore, the clearance of X is a measure of **renal plasma flow.** A substance that is handled like X is the organic anion para-aminohippurate (PAH), which is used for this purpose experimentally. (Like inulin, it must be administered intravenously.)

A similar logic leads to another important generalization. When the clearance of a filterable substance is less than the GFR, that substance must undergo some reabsorption. Performing calculations such as these provides important information about the way in which the kidneys handle a given solute. Suppose a newly developed drug is being tested for its safety and effectiveness. The dose of drug required to achieve a safe and therapeutic effect will depend at least in part on how rapidly it is cleared by the kidneys. Assume that we measure the clearance of the drug and find that it is greater than the GFR as determined by creatinine clearance. This means that the drug is secreted into the nephron tubules and a higher dose of drug than otherwise predicted may be needed to reach an optimal concentration in the blood.

14.5 Micturition

Urine flow through the ureters to the bladder is propelled by contractions of the ureter wall smooth muscle. The urine is stored in the bladder and intermittently ejected during urination, or **micturition.**

The bladder is a balloonlike chamber with walls of smooth muscle collectively termed the **detrusor muscle.** The contraction of the detrusor muscle squeezes on the urine in the bladder lumen to produce urination. That part of the detrusor muscle at the base (or "neck") of the bladder where the urethra begins functions as the **internal urethral sphincter.** Just below the internal urethral sphincter, a ring of skeletal muscle surrounds the urethra. This is the **external urethral sphincter,** the contraction of which can prevent urination even when the detrusor muscle contracts strongly.

The neural controls that influence bladder structures during the phases of filling and micturition are shown in **Figure 14.13.** While the bladder is filling, the parasympathetic input to the detrusor muscle is minimal, and, as a result, the muscle is relaxed. Because of the arrangement of the smooth muscle fibers, when the detrusor muscle is relaxed, the internal urethral sphincter is passively closed. Additionally, there is strong sympathetic input to the internal urethral sphincter and strong input by the somatic motor neurons to the external urethral sphincter. Therefore, the detrusor muscle is relaxed and both the internal and external sphincters are closed during the filling phase.

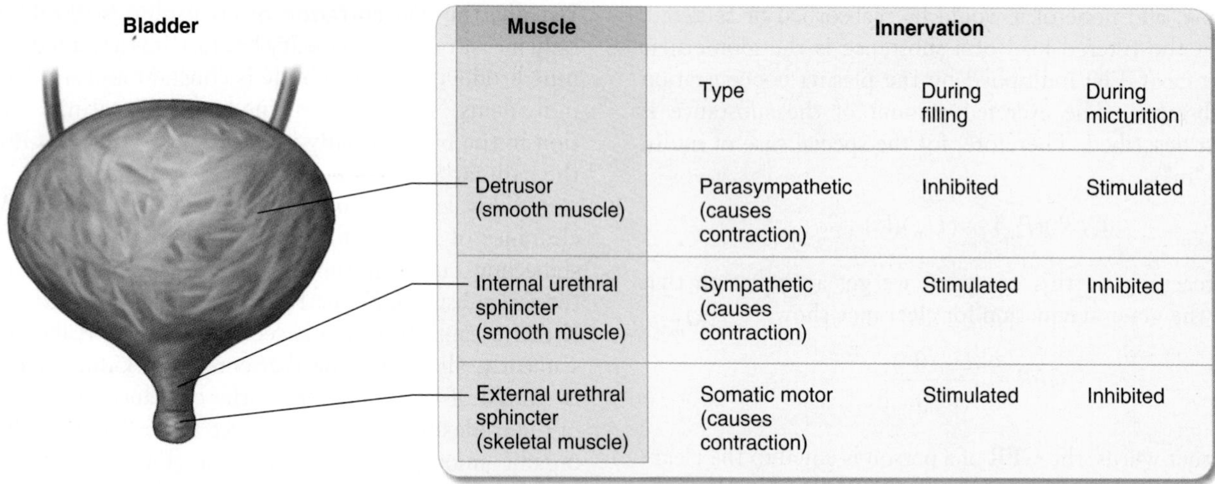

Muscle	Innervation		
	Type	During filling	During micturition
Detrusor (smooth muscle)	Parasympathetic (causes contraction)	Inhibited	Stimulated
Internal urethral sphincter (smooth muscle)	Sympathetic (causes contraction)	Stimulated	Inhibited
External urethral sphincter (skeletal muscle)	Somatic motor (causes contraction)	Stimulated	Inhibited

Figure 14.13 AP|R Control of the bladder.

What happens during micturition? As the bladder fills with urine, the pressure within it increases, which stimulates stretch receptors in the bladder wall. The afferent neurons from these receptors enter the spinal cord and stimulate the parasympathetic neurons, which then cause the detrusor muscle to contract. When the detrusor muscle contracts, the change in shape of the bladder pulls open the internal urethral sphincter. Simultaneously, the afferent input from the stretch receptors reflexively inhibits the sympathetic neurons to the internal urethral sphincter, which further contributes to its opening. In addition, the afferent input also reflexively inhibits the somatic motor neurons to the external urethral sphincter, causing it to relax. Both sphincters are now open, and the contraction of the detrusor muscle can produce urination.

We have thus far described micturition as a local spinal reflex, but descending pathways from the brain can also profoundly influence this reflex, determining the ability to prevent or initiate micturition voluntarily. Loss of these descending pathways as a result of spinal cord damage eliminates the ability to voluntarily control micturition. As the bladder distends, the input from the bladder stretch receptors causes, via ascending pathways to the brain, a sense of bladder fullness and the urge to urinate. But in response to this, urination can be voluntarily prevented by activating descending pathways that stimulate both the sympathetic nerves to the internal urethral sphincter and the somatic motor nerves to the external urethral sphincter. In contrast, urination can be voluntarily initiated via the descending pathways to the appropriate neurons. Complex interactions in different areas in the brain control micturition. Briefly, there are areas in the brainstem that can both facilitate and inhibit voiding. Furthermore, an area of the midbrain can inhibit voiding, and an area of the posterior hypothalamus can facilitate voiding. Finally, strong inhibitory input from the cerebral cortex, learned during toilet training in early childhood, prevents involuntary urination.

Incontinence

Incontinence is the involuntary release of urine, which can be a disturbing problem both socially and hygienically. The most common types are ***stress incontinence*** (due to sneezing, coughing, or exercise) and ***urge incontinence*** (associated with the desire to urinate). Incontinence is more common in women and may occur one to two times per week in more than 25% of women older than 60. It is very common in older women in nursing homes and assisted-living facilities. In women, stress incontinence is usually due to a loss of urethral support provided by the anterior vagina (see Figure 17.17a). Medications (such as estrogen-replacement therapy to improve vaginal tone) can often relieve stress incontinence. Severe cases may require surgery to improve vaginal support of the bladder and urethra. The cause of urge incontinence is often unknown in individual patients. However, any irritation to the bladder or urethra (e.g., with a bacterial infection) can cause urge incontinence. Urge incontinence can be treated with drugs such as tolterodine or oxybutynin, which antagonize the effects of the parasympathetic nerves on the detrusor muscle. Because these drugs are anticholinergic, they can have side effects such as blurred vision, constipation, and increased heart rate.

SECTION A SUMMARY

Renal Functions

I. The kidneys regulate the water and ionic composition of the body, excrete waste products, excrete foreign chemicals, produce glucose during prolonged fasting, and release factors and hormones into the blood (renin, 1,25-dihydroxyvitamin D, and erythropoietin). The first three functions are accomplished by continuous processing of the plasma.

Structure of the Kidneys and Urinary System

I. Each nephron in the kidneys consists of a renal corpuscle and a tubule.
   a. Each renal corpuscle comprises a capillary tuft, termed a glomerulus, and a Bowman's capsule that the tuft protrudes into.
   b. The tubule extends from Bowman's capsule and is subdivided into the proximal tubule, loop of Henle, distal convoluted tubule, and collecting-duct system. At the level of the collecting ducts, multiple tubules join and empty into

the renal pelvis, from which urine flows through the ureters to the bladder.

c. Each glomerulus is supplied by an afferent arteriole, and an efferent arteriole leaves the glomerulus to branch into peritubular capillaries, which supply the tubule.

Basic Renal Processes

I. The three basic renal processes are glomerular filtration, tubular reabsorption, and tubular secretion. In addition, the kidneys synthesize and/or catabolize certain substances. The excretion of a substance is equal to the amount filtered plus the amount secreted minus the amount reabsorbed.

II. Urine formation begins with glomerular filtration—approximately 180 L/day—of essentially protein-free plasma into Bowman's space.

a. Glomerular filtrate contains all plasma substances other than proteins (and substances bound to proteins) in virtually the same concentrations as in plasma.

b. Glomerular filtration is driven by the hydrostatic pressure in the glomerular capillaries and is opposed by both the hydrostatic pressure in Bowman's space and the osmotic force due to the proteins in the glomerular capillary plasma.

III. As the filtrate moves through the tubules, certain substances are reabsorbed either by diffusion or by mediated transport.

a. Substances to which the tubular epithelium is permeable are reabsorbed by diffusion because water reabsorption creates tubule-interstitium-concentration gradients for them.

b. Active reabsorption of a substance requires the participation of transporters in the luminal or basolateral membrane.

c. Tubular reabsorption rates are very high for nutrients, ions, and water, but they are lower for waste products.

d. Many of the mediated-transport systems exhibit transport maximums. When the filtered load of a substance exceeds the transport maximum, large amounts may appear in the urine.

IV. Tubular secretion, like glomerular filtration, is a pathway for the entrance of a substance into the tubule.

The Concept of Renal Clearance

I. The clearance of any substance can be calculated by dividing the mass of the substance excreted per unit time by the plasma concentration of the substance.

II. GFR can be measured by means of the inulin clearance and estimated by means of the creatinine clearance.

Micturition

I. In the basic micturition reflex, bladder distension stimulates stretch receptors that trigger spinal reflexes; these reflexes lead to contraction of the detrusor muscle, mediated by parasympathetic neurons, and relaxation of both the internal and the external urethral sphincters, mediated by inhibition of the neurons to these muscles.

II. Voluntary control is exerted via descending pathways to the parasympathetic nerves supplying the detrusor muscle, the sympathetic nerves supplying the internal urethral sphincter, and the motor nerves supplying the external urethral sphincter.

III. Incontinence is the involuntary release of urine that occurs most commonly in elderly people (particularly women).

SECTION A REVIEW QUESTIONS

1. What are the functions of the kidneys?
2. What three hormones/factors do the kidneys secrete into the blood?
3. Fluid flows in sequence through what structures from the glomerulus to the bladder? Blood flows through what structures from the renal artery to the renal vein?
4. What are the three basic renal processes that lead to the formation of urine?
5. How does the composition of the glomerular filtrate compare with that of plasma?
6. Describe the forces that determine the magnitude of the GFR. What is a normal value of GFR?
7. Contrast the mechanisms of reabsorption for glucose and urea. Which one shows a T_m?
8. Diagram the sequence of events leading to micturition.

SECTION A KEY TERMS

SECTION A CLINICAL TERMS

SECTION **B**

Regulation of Ion and Water Balance

14.6 Total-Body Balance of Sodium and Water

Chapter 1 explained that water composes about 55% to 60% of the normal body weight, and that water is distributed throughout different compartments of the body (Figure 1.3). Since water is of such obvious importance to homeostasis, the regulation of total-body-water balance is critical to survival. This highlights two important general principles of physiology: (1) Homeostasis is essential for health and survival; and (2) controlled exchange of materials—in this case, water—occurs between compartments and across cellular membranes. **Table 14.3** summarizes total-body-water balance. These are average values that are subject to considerable normal variation. There are two sources of body water gain: (1) water produced from the oxidation of organic nutrients, and (2) water ingested in liquids and food (a rare steak is approximately 70% water). Four sites lose water to the external environment: skin, respiratory airways, gastrointestinal tract, and urinary tract. Menstrual flow constitutes a fifth potential source of water loss in women.

The loss of water by evaporation from the skin and the lining of the respiratory passageways is a continuous process. It is called **insensible water loss** because the person is unaware of its occurrence. Additional water can be made available for evaporation from the skin by the production of sweat. Normal gastrointestinal loss of water in feces is generally quite small, but it can be significant with diarrhea and vomiting.

Table 14.4 is a summary of total-body balance for sodium chloride. The excretion of Na^+ and Cl^- via the skin and gastrointestinal tract is normally small but increases markedly during severe sweating, vomiting, or diarrhea. Hemorrhage can also result in the loss of large quantities of both salt and water.

Under normal conditions, as Tables 14.3 and 14.4 show, salt and water losses equal salt and water gains, and no net change in body salt and water occurs. This matching of losses and gains is primarily the result of the regulation of urinary loss, which can be varied over an extremely wide range. For example, urinary water excretion can vary from approximately 0.4 L/day to 25 L/day, depending upon whether one is lost in the desert or drinking too much water. Similarly, some individuals ingest 20 to 25 g of sodium chloride per day, whereas a person on a low-salt diet may ingest only 0.05 g. Healthy kidneys can readily alter the excretion of salt over this range to balance loss with gain.

TABLE 14.3	Average Daily Water Gain and Loss in Adults
Intake	
In liquids	1400 mL
In food	1100 mL
Metabolically produced	350 mL
Total	**2850 mL**
Output	
Insensible loss (skin and lungs)	900 mL
Sweat	50 mL
In feces	100 mL
Urine	1800 mL
Total	**2850 mL**

14.7 Basic Renal Processes for Sodium and Water

Both Na^+ and water freely filter from the glomerular capillaries into Bowman's space because they have low molecular weights and circulate in the plasma in the free form (unbound to protein). They both undergo considerable reabsorption—normally more than 99% (see Table 14.2)—but no secretion. Most renal energy utilization is used in this enormous reabsorptive task. The bulk of Na^+ and water reabsorption (about two-thirds) occurs in the proximal tubule, but the major hormonal control of reabsorption is exerted on the distal convoluted tubules and collecting ducts.

The mechanisms of Na^+ and water reabsorption can be summarized in two generalizations: (1) Na^+ reabsorption is an active process occurring in all tubular segments except the descending limb of the loop of Henle; and (2) water reabsorption is by osmosis and is dependent upon Na^+ reabsorption.

Primary Active Na^+ Reabsorption

The essential feature underlying Na^+ reabsorption throughout the tubule is the primary active transport of Na^+ out of the cells and into the interstitial fluid, as illustrated for the proximal tubule and cortical collecting duct in **Figure 14.14.** This transport is achieved by Na^+/K^+-ATPase pumps in the basolateral membrane of the cells. The active transport of Na^+ out of the cell keeps the intracellular concentration of Na^+ low compared to the tubular lumen, so Na^+ moves "downhill" out of the tubular lumen into the tubular epithelial cells.

The mechanism of the downhill Na^+ movement across the luminal membrane into the cell varies from segment to

TABLE 14.4	Daily Sodium Chloride Intake and Loss
Intake	
Food	**8.50 g**
Output	
Sweat	0.25 g
Feces	0.25 g
Urine	8.00 g
Total	**8.50 g**

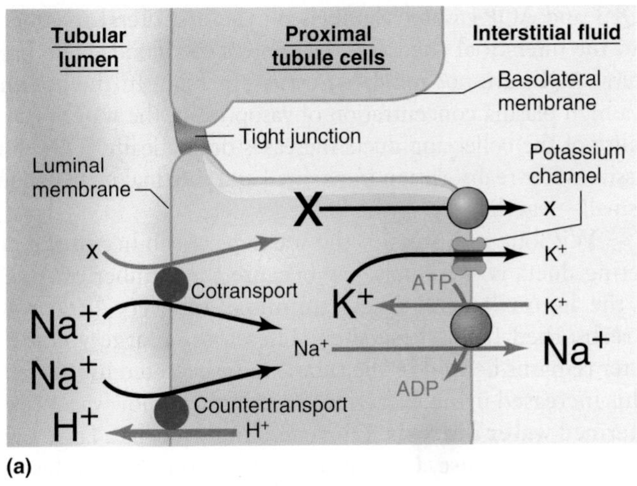

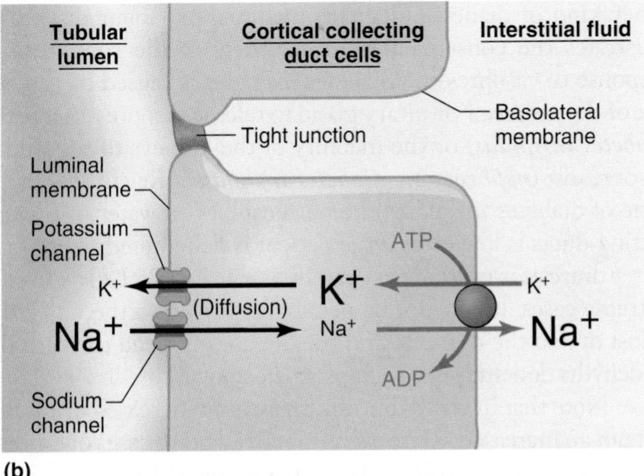

Figure 14.14 AP|R Mechanism of Na^+ reabsorption in the (a) proximal tubule and (b) cortical collecting duct. (Figure 14.15 shows the movement of the reabsorbed Na^+ from the interstitial fluid into the peritubular capillaries.) The sizes of the letters denote high and low concentrations. "X" represents organic molecules such as glucose and amino acids that are cotransported with Na^+. The fate of the K^+ that the Na^+/K^+-ATPase pumps transport is discussed in the later section dealing with renal K^+ handling.

PHYSIOLOGICAL INQUIRY

- Referring to part (b), what would be the effect of a drug that blocks the Na^+ channels in the cortical collecting duct?

Answer can be found at end of chapter.

segment of the tubule depending on which channels and/or transport proteins are present in their luminal membranes. For example, the luminal entry step in the proximal tubule cell occurs by cotransport with a variety of organic molecules, such as glucose, or by countertransport with H^+. In the latter case, H^+ moves out of the cell to the lumen as Na^+ moves into the cell (**Figure 14.14a**). Thus, in the proximal tubule, Na^+ reabsorption drives the reabsorption of the cotransported substances and secretion of H^+. In actuality, the luminal membrane of the proximal tubular cell has a brush border composed of numerous microvilli (for clarity, not shown in Figure 14.14a). This greatly increases the surface area for reabsorption. The luminal entry step for Na^+ in the cortical collecting duct occurs primarily by diffusion through Na^+ channels (**Figure 14.14b**).

The movement of Na^+ downhill from lumen into cell across the *luminal membrane* varies from one segment of the tubule to another. By contrast, the *basolateral membrane* step is the same in all Na^+-reabsorbing tubular segments—the primary active transport of Na^+ out of the cell is via Na^+/K^+-ATPase pumps in this membrane. It is this transport process that decreases intracellular Na^+ concentration and so makes possible the downhill luminal entry step.

Coupling of Water Reabsorption to Na^+ Reabsorption

As Na^+, Cl^-, and other ions are reabsorbed, water follows passively by osmosis (see Chapter 4). **Figure 14.15** summarizes this coupling of solute and water reabsorption. (1) Na^+ is transported from the tubular lumen to the interstitial fluid across the epithelial cells. Other solutes, such as glucose, amino acids, and HCO_3^-, whose reabsorption depends on Na^+ transport, also contribute to osmosis. (2) The removal of solutes from the tubular lumen decreases the local osmolarity of the tubular fluid adjacent to the cell (i.e., the local water concentration increases). At the same time, the appearance of solute in the interstitial fluid just outside the cell increases the local osmolarity (i.e., the local water concentration decreases). (3) The difference in water concentration between lumen and interstitial fluid causes net diffusion of water from the lumen across the tubular cells' plasma membranes and/or tight junctions into the interstitial fluid. (4) From there, water, Na^+, and everything else dissolved in the interstitial fluid move together by bulk flow into peritubular capillaries as the final step in reabsorption.

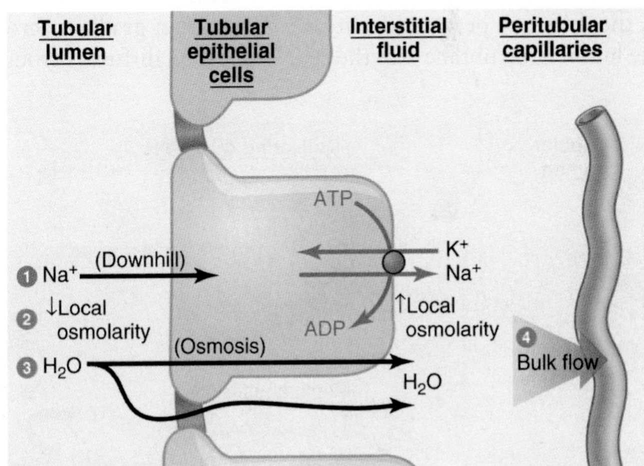

Figure 14.15 AP|R Coupling of water and Na^+ reabsorption. See text for explanation of circled numbers. The reabsorption of solutes other than Na^+—for example, glucose, amino acids, and HCO_3^-—also contributes to the difference in osmolarity between lumen and interstitial fluid, but the reabsorption of all these substances ultimately depends on direct or indirect cotransport and countertransport with Na^+ (see Figure 14.14a). Therefore, they are not shown in this figure.

Water movement across the tubular epithelium can only occur if the epithelium is permeable to water. No matter how large its concentration gradient, water cannot cross an epithelium impermeable to it. Water permeability varies from tubular segment to segment and depends largely on the presence of water channels, called **aquaporins,** in the plasma membranes. The water permeability of the proximal tubule is always very high, so this segment reabsorbs water molecules almost as rapidly as Na^+. As a result, the proximal tubule reabsorbs large amounts of Na^+ and water in the same proportions.

We will describe the water permeability of the next tubular segments—the loop of Henle and distal convoluted tubule—later. Now for the really crucial point—the water permeability of the last portions of the tubules, the cortical and medullary collecting ducts, can vary greatly due to physiological control. These are the only tubular segments in which water permeability is under such control.

The major determinant of this controlled permeability and, therefore, of passive water reabsorption in the collecting ducts is a peptide hormone secreted by the posterior pituitary gland and known as **vasopressin,** or **antidiuretic hormone** (**ADH**; see Chapter 11). Vasopressin stimulates the insertion into the luminal membrane of a particular group of aquaporin water channels made by the collecting-duct cells. More than 10 different aquaporins have been identified throughout the body, and they are identified as AQP1, AQP2, and so on. **Figure 14.16** shows the function of the aquaporin water channels in the cells of the collecting ducts of the kidney. When vasopressin from the blood enters the interstitial fluid and binds to its receptor on the basolateral membrane, the intracellular production of the second-messenger cAMP is increased. This activates the enzyme cAMP-dependent protein kinase (also called protein kinase A, or PKA), which, in turn, phosphorylates proteins that increase the rate of fusion of vesicles containing AQP2 with the luminal membrane. This leads to an increase in the number of AQP2s inserted into the luminal membrane from vesicles in the cytosol. This allows an increase in the diffusion of water down its concentration gradient across the luminal membrane into the cell. Water then diffuses through AQP3 and AQP4 water channels on the basolateral membrane into the interstitial fluid and then enters the blood. (The basolateral AQPs are not regulated by vasopressin.) In the presence of a high plasma concentration of vasopressin, the water permeability of the collecting ducts increases dramatically. Therefore, passive water reabsorption is maximal and the final urine volume is small—less than 1% of the filtered water.

Without vasopressin, the water permeability of the collecting ducts is extremely low because the number of AQP2s in the luminal membrane is minimal and very little water is reabsorbed from these sites. Therefore, a large volume of water remains behind in the tubule to be excreted in the urine. This increased urine excretion resulting from low vasopressin is termed **water diuresis. Diuresis** simply means a large urine flow from any cause. In a subsequent section, we will describe the control of vasopressin secretion.

The disease ***diabetes insipidus,*** which is distinct from the other kind of diabetes (diabetes mellitus, or "sugar diabetes"), illustrates the consequences of disorders of the control of or response to vasopressin. Diabetes insipidus is caused by the failure of the posterior pituitary gland to release vasopressin (***central diabetes insipidus***) or the inability of the kidneys to respond to vasopressin (***nephrogenic diabetes insipidus***). Regardless of the type of diabetes insipidus, the permeability to water of the collecting ducts is low even if the patient is dehydrated. A constant water diuresis is present that can be as much as 25 L/day; in such extreme cases, it may not be possible to replenish the water that is lost due to the diuresis, and the disease may lead to death due to dehydration and very high plasma osmolarity.

Note that in water diuresis, there is an increased urine flow but not an increased solute excretion. In all other cases of diuresis, termed **osmotic diuresis,** the increased urine flow is the result of a primary increase in solute excretion. For example, failure of normal Na^+ reabsorption causes both increased Na^+ excretion and increased water excretion, because, as we have seen, water reabsorption is dependent on solute reabsorption. Another example of osmotic diuresis occurs in people with uncontrolled diabetes mellitus; in this case, the glucose that escapes reabsorption

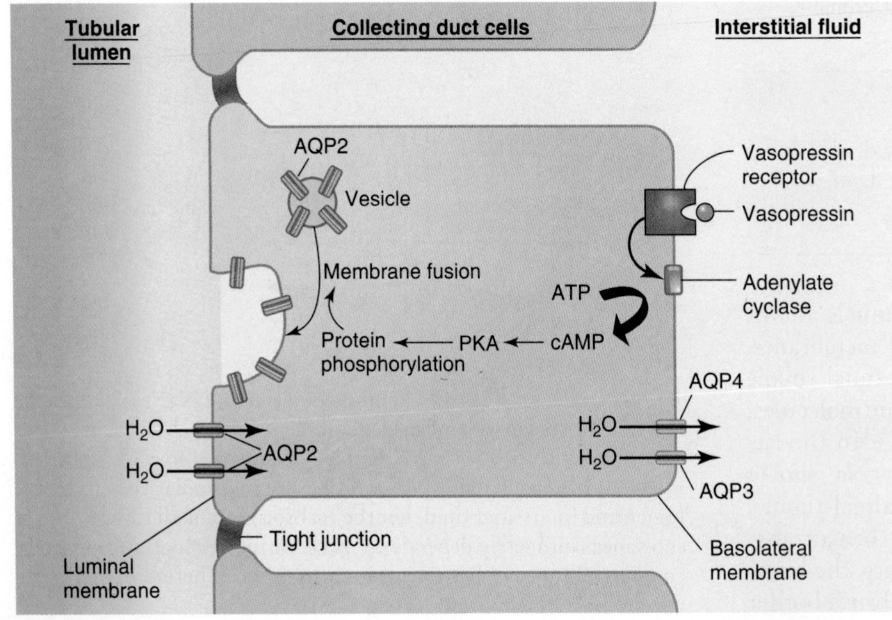

Figure 14.16 APIR The regulation and function of aquaporins (AQPs) in the medullary-collecting-duct cells to increase water reabsorption. Vasopressin binding to its receptor increases intracellular cAMP via activation of a Gs protein (not shown) and subsequent activation of adenylate cyclase. cAMP increases the activity of the enzyme protein kinase A (PKA). PKA increases the phosphorylation of specific proteins that increase the rate of the fusion of vesicles (containing AQP2) with the luminal membrane. This leads to an increase in the number of AQP2 channels in the luminal membrane. This allows increased passive diffusion of water into the cell. Water exits the cell through AQP3 and AQP4, which are not vasopressin sensitive.

because of the huge filtered load retains water in the lumen, causing it to be excreted along with the glucose.

To summarize, any loss of solute in the urine must be accompanied by water loss (osmotic diuresis), but the reverse is not true. That is, water diuresis is not necessarily accompanied by equivalent solute loss.

Urine Concentration: The Countercurrent Multiplier System

Before reading this section, you should review, by looking up in the glossary, several terms presented in Chapter 4—**hypoosmotic, isoosmotic,** and **hyperosmotic.**

In the section just concluded, we described how the kidneys produce a small volume of urine when the plasma concentration of vasopressin is high. Under these conditions, the urine is concentrated (hyperosmotic) relative to plasma. This section describes the mechanisms by which this hyperosmolarity is achieved.

The ability of the kidneys to produce hyperosmotic urine is a major determinant of the ability to survive with limited water intake. The human kidney can produce a maximal urinary concentration of 1400 mOsmol/L, almost five times the osmolarity of plasma, which is typically in the range of 285 to 300 mOsmol/L (rounded off to 300 mOsmol/L for convenience). The typical daily excretion of urea, sulfate, phosphate, other waste products, and ions amounts to approximately 600 mOsmol. Therefore, the minimal volume of urine water in which this mass of solute can be dissolved equals

$$\frac{600 \text{ mOsmol/day}}{1400 \text{ mOsmol/L}} = 0.444 \text{ L/day}$$

This volume of urine is known as the **obligatory water loss.** The loss of this minimal volume of urine contributes to dehydration when water intake is zero.

Urinary concentration takes place as tubular fluid flows through the *medullary* collecting ducts. The interstitial fluid surrounding these ducts is very hyperosmotic. In the presence of vasopressin, water diffuses out of the ducts into the interstitial fluid of the medulla and then enters the blood vessels of the medulla to be carried away.

The key question is, How does the medullary interstitial fluid become hyperosmotic? The answer involves several interrelated factors: (1) the countercurrent anatomy of the loop of Henle of juxtamedullary nephrons, (2) reabsorption of NaCl in the ascending limbs of those loops of Henle, (3) impermeability to water of those ascending limbs, (4) trapping of urea in the medulla, and (5) hairpin loops of vasa recta to minimize washout of the hyperosmotic medulla. Recall that Henle's loop forms a hairpinlike loop between the proximal tubule and the distal convoluted tubule (see Figure 14.2). The fluid entering the loop from the proximal tubule flows down the descending limb, turns the corner, and then flows up the ascending limb. The opposing flows in the two limbs are called countercurrent flows, and the entire loop functions as a **countercurrent multiplier system** to create a hyperosmotic medullary interstitial fluid.

Because the proximal tubule always reabsorbs Na^+ and water in the same proportions, the fluid entering the descending limb of the loop from the proximal tubule has the same osmolarity as plasma—300 mOsmol/L. For the moment, let us skip the descending limb because the events in it can only be understood in the context of what the *ascending* limb is doing. Along the entire length of the ascending limb, Na^+ and Cl^- are reabsorbed from the lumen into the medullary interstitial fluid (**Figure 14.17a**). In the upper (thick) portion of the ascending limb, this reabsorption is achieved by transporters that actively cotransport Na^+ and Cl^-. Such transporters are not present in the lower (thin) portion of the ascending limb, so the reabsorption there is by simple diffusion. For simplicity in the explanation of the countercurrent multiplier, we shall treat the entire ascending limb as a homogeneous structure that actively reabsorbs Na^+ and Cl^-.

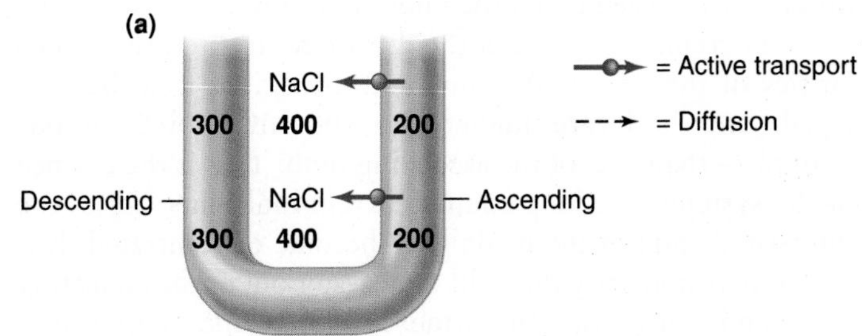

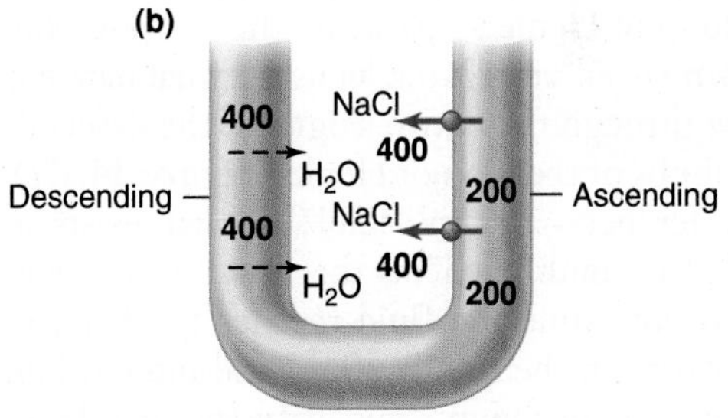

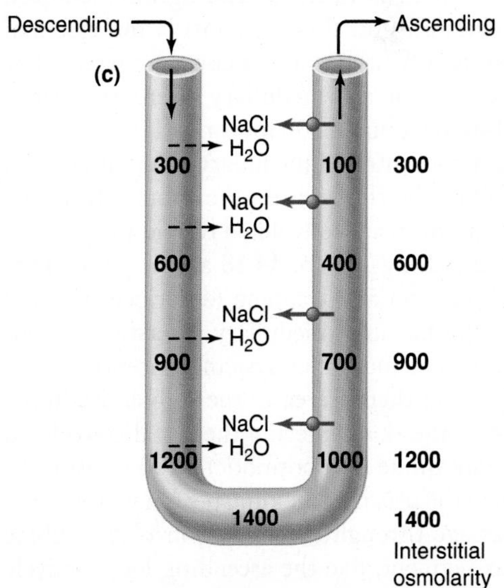

Figure 14.17 APIR Generating a hyperosmolar medullary renal interstitium. (a) NaCl active transport in ascending limbs (impermeable to H_2O). (b) Passive reabsorption of H_2O in descending limb. (c) Multiplication of osmolarity occurs with fluid flow through the tubular lumen.

Very importantly, *the ascending limb is relatively impermeable to water*, so little water follows the salt. The net result is that the interstitial fluid of the medulla becomes hyperosmotic compared to the fluid in the ascending limb because solute is reabsorbed without water.

We now return to the descending limb. This segment, in contrast to the ascending limb, does not reabsorb sodium chloride and is highly permeable to water (**Figure 14.17b**). Therefore, a net diffusion of water occurs out of the descending limb into the more concentrated interstitial fluid until the osmolarities inside this limb and in the interstitial fluid are again equal. The interstitial hyperosmolarity is maintained during this equilibration because the ascending limb continues to pump sodium chloride to maintain the concentration difference between it and the interstitial fluid.

Therefore, because of the diffusion of water, the osmolarities of the descending limb and interstitial fluid become equal, and both are higher—by 200 mOsmol/L in our example—than that of the ascending limb. This is the essence of the system: The loop countercurrent multiplier causes the interstitial fluid of the medulla to become concentrated. It is this hyperosmolarity that will draw water out of the collecting ducts and concentrate the urine. However, one more crucial feature—the "multiplication"—must be considered.

So far, we have been analyzing this system as though the flow through the loop of Henle stops while the ion pumping and water diffusion are occurring. Now, let us see what happens when we allow flow through the entire length of the descending and ascending limbs of the loop of Henle (**Figure 14.17c**). The osmolarity difference—200 mOsmol/L—that exists at each horizontal level is "multiplied" as the fluid goes deeper into the medulla. By the time the fluid reaches the bend in the loop, the osmolarity of the tubular fluid and interstitium has been multiplied to a very high osmolarity that can be as high as 1400 mOsmol/L. Keep in mind that the active sodium chloride transport mechanism in the ascending limb (coupled with low water permeability in this segment) is the essential component of the system. Without it, the countercurrent flow would have no effect on loop and medullary interstitial osmolarity, which would simply remain 300 mOsmol/L throughout.

Now we have a concentrated medullary interstitial fluid, but we must still follow the fluid within the tubules from the loop of Henle through the distal convoluted tubule and into the collecting-duct system, using **Figure 14.18** as our guide. Furthermore, urea reabsorption and trapping (described in detail later) contribute to the maximal medullary interstitial osmolarity. The countercurrent multiplier system concentrates the descending-loop fluid but then decreases the osmolarity in the ascending loop so that the fluid entering the distal convoluted tubule is actually more dilute (hypoosmotic)—100 mOsmol/L in Figure 14.18—than the plasma. The fluid becomes even more dilute during its passage through the distal convoluted tubule because this tubular segment, like the ascending loop, actively transports Na^+ and Cl^- out of the tubule but is relatively impermeable to water. This hypoosmotic fluid then enters the cortical collecting duct. Because of the significant volume reabsorption, the flow of fluid at the end of the ascending limb is much less than the flow that entered the descending limb.

As noted earlier, vasopressin increases tubular permeability to water in both the cortical and medullary collecting ducts. In contrast, vasopressin does not directly influence water reabsorption in the parts of the tubule prior to the collecting ducts. Thus, regardless of the plasma concentration of this hormone, the fluid entering the cortical collecting duct is hypoosmotic. From there on, however, vasopressin is crucial. In the presence of high concentrations of vasopressin, water reabsorption occurs by diffusion from the hypoosmotic fluid in the cortical collecting duct until the fluid in this segment becomes isoosmotic to the interstitial fluid and peritubular plasma of the cortex—that is, until it is once again at 300 mOsmol/L.

The isoosmotic tubular fluid then enters and flows through the *medullary* collecting ducts. In the presence of high plasma concentrations of vasopressin, water diffuses out of the ducts into the medullary interstitial fluid as a result of

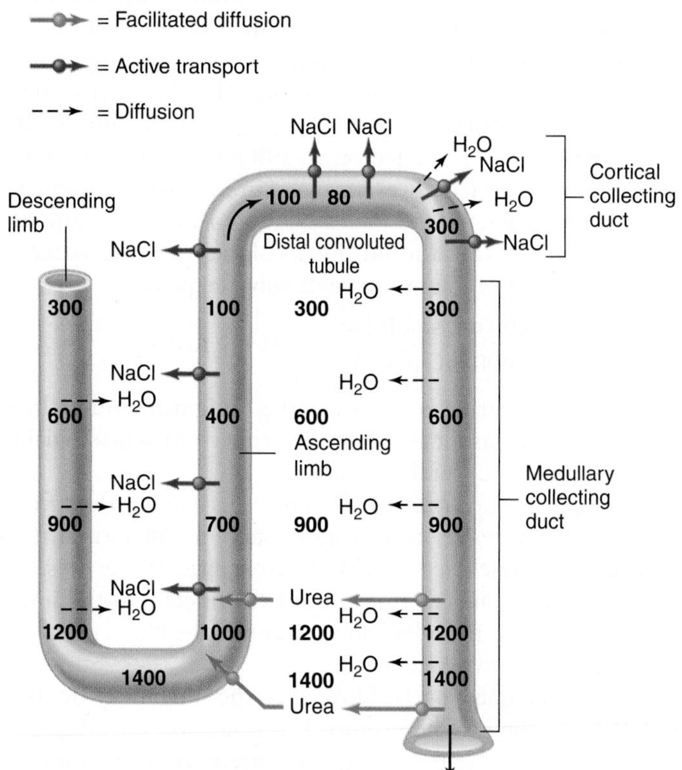

Figure 14.18 APIR Simplified depiction of the generation of an interstitial fluid osmolarity gradient by the renal countercurrent multiplier system and its role in the formation of hyperosmotic urine in the presence of vasopressin. Notice that the hyperosmotic medulla depends on NaCl reabsorption and urea trapping (described in Figure 14.20).

PHYSIOLOGICAL INQUIRY

- Certain types of lung tumors secrete one or more hormones. What would happen to plasma and urine osmolarity and urine volume in a patient with a lung tumor that secretes vasopressin?

Answer can be found at end of chapter.

the high osmolarity that the loop countercurrent multiplier system and urea trapping establish there. This water then enters the medullary capillaries and is carried out of the kidneys by the venous blood. Water reabsorption occurs all along the lengths of the medullary collecting ducts so that, in the presence of vasopressin, the fluid at the end of these ducts has essentially the same osmolarity as the interstitial fluid surrounding the bend in the loops—that is, at the bottom of the medulla. By this means, the final urine is hyperosmotic. By retaining as much water as possible, the kidneys minimize the rate at which dehydration occurs during water deprivation.

In contrast, when plasma vasopressin concentration is low, both the cortical and medullary collecting ducts are relatively impermeable to water. As a result, a large volume of hypoosmotic urine is excreted, thereby eliminating an excess of water in the body.

The Medullary Circulation

A major question arises with the countercurrent system as described previously: "Why doesn't the blood flowing through medullary capillaries eliminate the countercurrent gradient set up by the loops of Henle?" One would think that as plasma with the usual osmolarity of 300 mOsm/L enters the highly concentrated environment of the medulla, there would be massive net diffusion of Na^+ and Cl^- into the capillaries and water out of them and, thus, the interstitial gradient would be "washed away." However, the blood vessels in the medulla (vasa recta) form hairpin loops that run parallel to the loops of Henle and medullary collecting ducts. As shown in **Figure 14.19**, blood enters the top of the vessel loop at an osmolarity of 300 mOsm/L, and as the blood flows down the loop deeper and deeper into the medulla, Na^+ and Cl^- do indeed diffuse into—and water out of—the vessel. However, after the bend in the loop is reached, the blood then flows up the ascending vessel loop, where the process is almost completely reversed. Thus, the hairpin-loop structure of the vasa recta minimizes excessive loss of solute from the interstitium by *diffusion*. At the same time, both the salt and water being reabsorbed from the loops of Henle and collecting ducts are carried away in equivalent amounts by *bulk flow*, as determined by the usual capillary Starling forces. This maintains the steady-state countercurrent gradient set up by the loops of Henle. Because of NaCl and water reabsorbed from the loop of Henle and collecting ducts, the amount of blood flow leaving the vasa recta is at least twofold higher than the blood flow entering the vasa recta. Finally, the total blood flow going through all of the vasa recta is a small percentage of the total renal blood flow. This helps to minimize the washout of the hypertonic interstitium of the medulla.

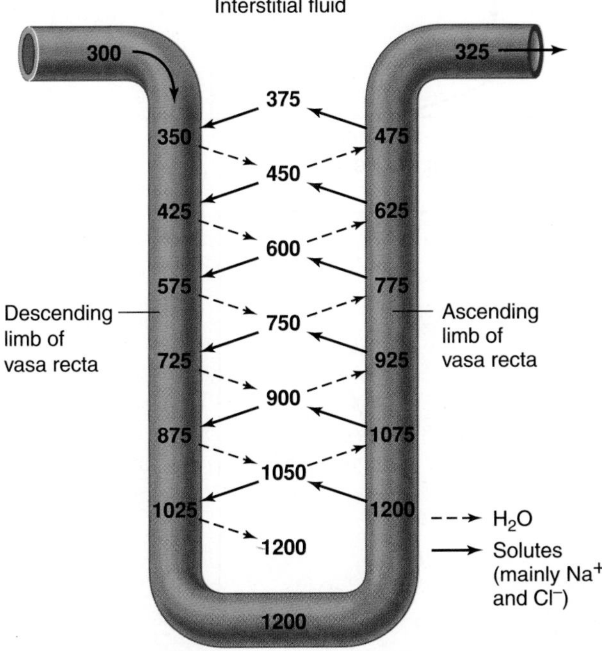

Figure 14.19 APIR Function of the vasa recta to maintain the hypertonic interstitial renal medulla. All movements of water and solutes are by diffusion. Not shown is the simultaneously occurring uptake of interstitial fluid by bulk flow.

The Recycling of Urea Helps to Establish a Hypertonic Medullary Interstitium

As was just described, the countercurrent multiplier establishes a hypertonic medullary interstitium that the vasa recta help to preserve. We already learned how the reabsorption of water in the proximal tubule mediates the reabsorption of urea by diffusion. As urea passes through the remainder of the nephron, it is reabsorbed, secreted into the tubule, and then reabsorbed again (**Figure 14.20**). This traps urea, an osmotically active molecule, in the medullary interstitium, thus increasing its osmolarity. In fact, as shown in Figure 14.18, urea contributes to the total osmolarity of the renal medulla.

Urea is freely filtered in the glomerulus. Approximately 50% of the filtered urea is reabsorbed in the proximal tubule, and the remaining 50% enters the loop of Henle. In the

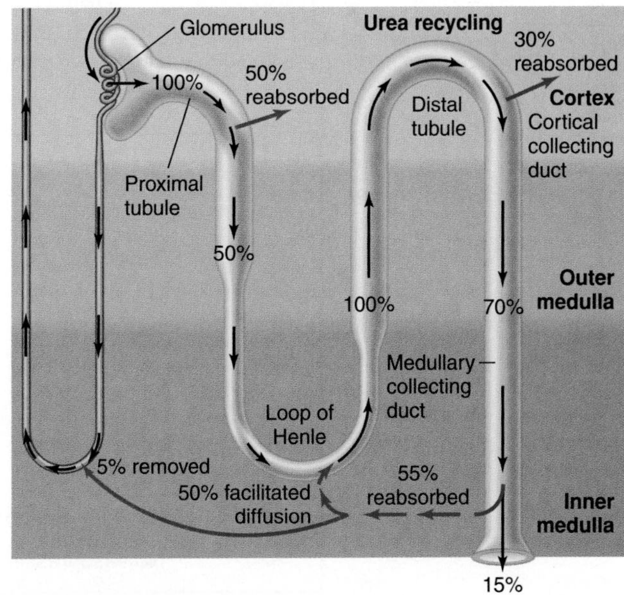

Figure 14.20 APIR Urea recycling. The recycling of urea "traps" urea in the inner medulla, which increases osmolarity and helps to establish and maintain hypertonicity.

thin descending and ascending limbs of the loop of Henle, urea that has accumulated in the medullary interstitium is secreted back into the tubular lumen by facilitated diffusion. Therefore, virtually all of the urea that was originally filtered in the glomerulus is present in the fluid that enters the distal tubule. Some of the original urea is reabsorbed from the distal tubule and cortical collecting duct. Thereafter, about half of the urea is reabsorbed from the *medullary* collecting duct, whereas only 5% diffuses into the vasa recta. The remaining amount is secreted back into the loop of Henle. Fifteen percent of the urea originally filtered remains in the collecting duct and is excreted in the urine. This recycling of urea through the medullary interstitium and minimal uptake by the vasa recta trap urea there and contribute to the high osmolarity shown in Figure 14.18. Of note is that medullary interstitial urea concentration is increased in antidiuretic states and contributes to water reabsorption. This occurs due to vasopressin, which, in addition to its effects on water permeability, also increases the permeability of the inner medullary collecting ducts to urea.

Summary of Vasopressin Control of Urine Volume and Osmolarity

This is a good place to review the reabsorption of water and the role of vasopressin in the generation of a concentrated or dilute urine. **Figure 14.21** is a convenient way to do this. First, notice that almost 75% of the volume reabsorbed in the juxtamedullary nephron is not controlled by vasopressin and occurs isosmotically in the proximal tubule. The direct effect of vasopressin in the collecting ducts participates in the development of increased osmolarity in the renal medullary interstitium. As a result, there is increased water reabsorption from the lumen in the thin descending loop of Henle with a resultant increase in tubular fluid osmolarity even though vasopressin does not have a direct effect on the loop. Note that the tubular fluid osmolarity decreases in the latter half of the loop of Henle under both conditions while there is no change in tubular fluid volume; this reflects the selective reabsorption of solutes from the tubular fluid in these water-impermeable segments of the nephron. Therefore, the ultimate determinant of the volume of urine excreted and the concentration of urine under any set of conditions is vasopressin. In the

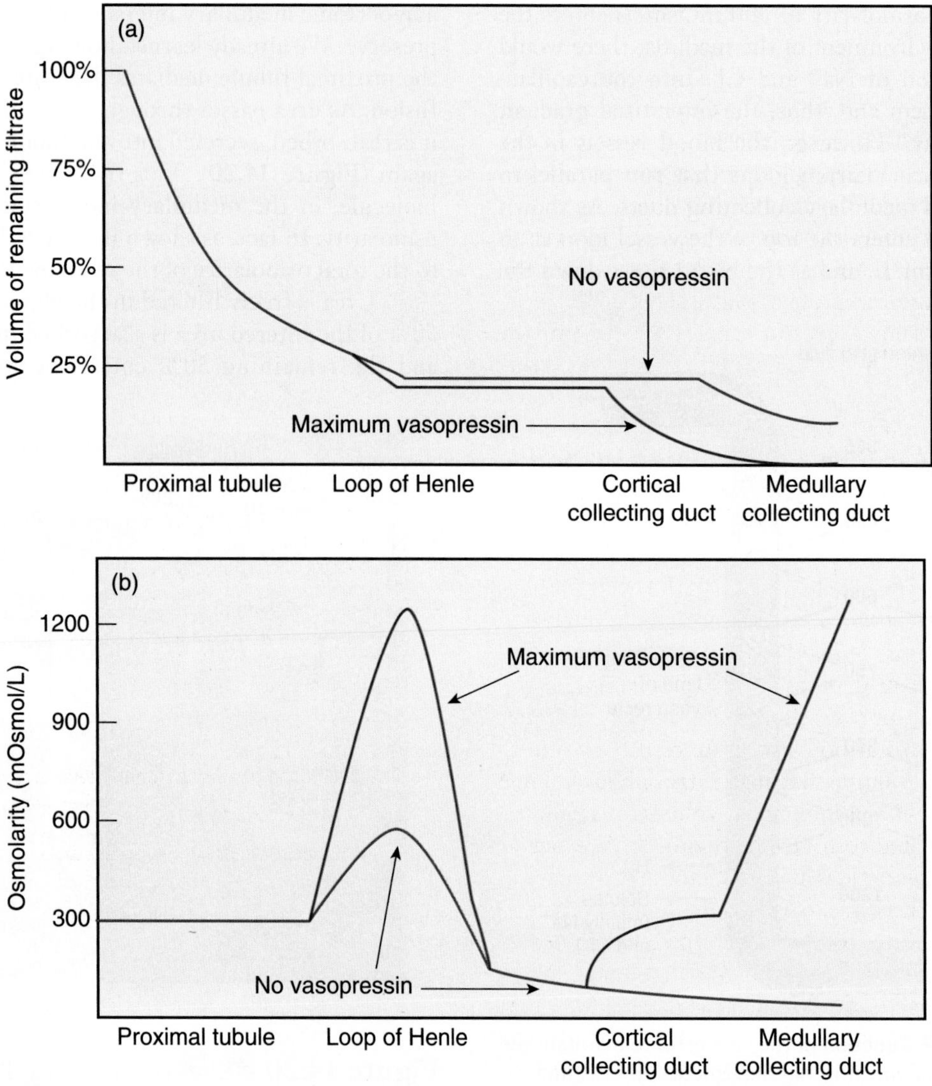

Figure 14.21 The effect of no vasopressin and maximum vasopressin concentration in the blood on (a) the volume remaining in the filtrate in the nephron as well as (b) the osmolarity of the tubular fluid along the length of the nephron.

absence of vasopressin, there is minimal water reabsorption in the collecting ducts so there is little decrease in the volume of the filtrate; this results in a diuresis and hypoosmotic urine. In the presence of maximum vasopressin during, for example, severe water restriction, most of the water is reabsorbed in the collecting ducts leading to a very small urine volume (antidiuresis) and hypertonic urine. In reality, most humans with access to water have an intermediate vasopressin concentration in the blood.

14.8 Renal Sodium Regulation

In healthy individuals, urinary Na^+ excretion increases when there is an excess of sodium in the body and decreases when there is a sodium deficit. These homeostatic responses are so precise that total-body sodium normally varies by only a few percentage points despite a wide range of sodium intakes and the occasional occurrence of large losses via the skin and gastrointestinal tract.

As we have seen, Na^+ is freely filterable from the glomerular capillaries into Bowman's space and is actively reabsorbed but not secreted. Therefore,

$$Na^+ \text{ excreted} = Na^+ \text{ filtered} - Na^+ \text{ reabsorbed}$$

The body can adjust Na^+ excretion by changing both processes on the right side of the equation. For example, when total-body sodium decreases for any reason, Na^+ excretion decreases below normal levels because Na^+ reabsorption increases.

The first issue in understanding the responses controlling Na^+ reabsorption is to determine what inputs initiate them; that is, what variables are receptors actually sensing? Surprisingly, there are no important receptors capable of detecting the total amount of sodium in the body. Rather, the responses that regulate urinary Na^+ excretion are initiated mainly by various cardiovascular baroreceptors, such as the carotid sinus, and by sensors in the kidneys that monitor the filtered load of Na^+.

As described in Chapter 12, baroreceptors respond to pressure changes within the cardiovascular system and initiate reflexes that rapidly regulate these pressures by acting on the heart, arterioles, and veins. The new information in this chapter is that *regulation of cardiovascular pressures by baroreceptors also simultaneously achieves regulation of total-body sodium.*

Na^+ is the major extracellular solute constituting, along with associated anions, approximately 90% of these solutes. Therefore, changes in total-body sodium result in similar changes in extracellular volume. Because extracellular volume comprises plasma volume and interstitial volume, plasma volume is also directly related to total-body sodium. We saw in Chapter 12 that plasma volume is an important determinant of the blood pressures in the veins, cardiac chambers, and arteries. Thus, the chain linking total-body sodium to cardiovascular pressures is completed: Low total-body sodium leads to low plasma volume, which leads to a decrease in cardiovascular pressures. These lower pressures, via baroreceptors, initiate reflexes that influence the renal arterioles and tubules so as to decrease GFR and increase Na^+ reabsorption. These latter events decrease Na^+ excretion, thereby retaining Na^+ in the body and preventing further decreases in plasma volume and cardiovascular pressures. Increases in total-body sodium have the reverse reflex effects.

To summarize, the amount of Na^+ in the body determines the extracellular fluid volume, the plasma volume component of which helps determine cardiovascular pressures, which initiate the responses that control Na^+ excretion.

Control of GFR

Figure 14.22 summarizes the major mechanisms by which an example of increased Na^+ loss elicits a decrease in GFR. The main direct cause of the reduced GFR is a reduced net glomerular filtration pressure. This occurs both as a consequence of a decreased arterial pressure in the kidneys and, more importantly,

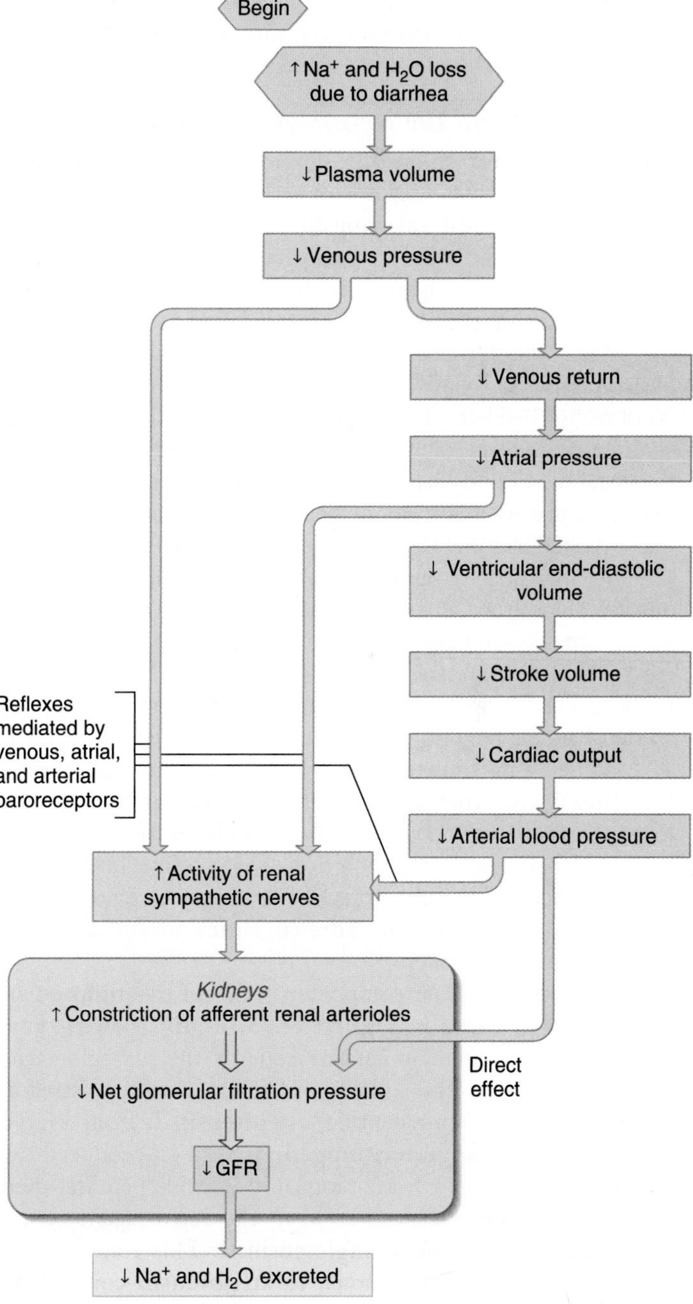

Figure 14.22 Direct and neurally mediated reflex pathways by which the GFR and, thus, Na^+ and water excretion decrease when plasma volume decreases.

as a result of reflexes acting on the renal arterioles. Note that these reflexes are the basic baroreceptor reflexes described in Chapter 12—a decrease in cardiovascular pressures causes neurally mediated reflex vasoconstriction in many areas of the body. As we will see later, the hormones angiotensin II and vasopressin also participate in this renal vasoconstrictor response.

Conversely, an increase in GFR is usually elicited by neuroendocrine inputs when an increased total-body-sodium level increases plasma volume. This increased GFR contributes to the increased renal Na^+ loss that returns extracellular volume to normal.

Control of Na^+ Reabsorption

For the long-term regulation of Na^+ excretion, the control of Na^+ reabsorption is more important than the control of GFR. The major factor determining the rate of tubular Na^+ reabsorption is the hormone aldosterone.

Aldosterone and the Renin–Angiotensin System

The adrenal cortex produces a steroid hormone, **aldosterone,** which stimulates Na^+ reabsorption by the distal convoluted tubule and the cortical collecting ducts. An action affecting these late portions of the tubule is just what one would expect for a fine-tuning input because most of the filtered Na^+ has been reabsorbed by the time the filtrate reaches the distal parts of the nephron. When aldosterone is completely absent, approximately 2% of the filtered Na^+ (equivalent to 35 g of sodium chloride per day) is not reabsorbed but excreted. In contrast, when the plasma concentration of aldosterone is high, essentially all the Na^+ reaching the distal tubule and cortical collecting ducts is reabsorbed. Normally, the plasma concentration of aldosterone and the amount of Na^+ excreted lie somewhere between these extremes.

As opposed to vasopressin, which is a peptide and acts quickly, aldosterone is a steroid and acts more slowly because it induces changes in gene expression and protein synthesis. In the case of the nephron, the proteins participate in Na^+ transport. Look again at Figure 14.14b. Aldosterone induces the synthesis of all the channels and pumps shown in the cortical collecting duct.

When a person eats a diet high in sodium, aldosterone secretion is low, whereas it is high when the person ingests a low-sodium diet or becomes sodium-depleted for some other reason. What controls the secretion of aldosterone under these circumstances? The answer is the hormone angiotensin II, which acts directly on the adrenal cortex to stimulate the secretion of aldosterone.

Angiotensin II is a component of the **renin–angiotensin system,** summarized in **Figure 14.23. Renin** is an enzyme secreted by the juxtaglomerular cells of the juxtaglomerular apparatuses in the kidneys. Once in the bloodstream, renin splits a small polypeptide, **angiotensin I,** from a large plasma protein, **angiotensinogen,** which is produced by the liver. Angiotensin I, a biologically inactive peptide, then undergoes further cleavage to form the active agent of the renin–angiotensin system, angiotensin II. This conversion is mediated by an enzyme known as **angiotensin-converting enzyme** (**ACE**), which is found in very high concentration on the luminal surface of capillary endothelial cells. Angiotensin II exerts many effects, but the most important are the stimulation of the secretion of aldosterone and the constriction of arterioles (described in Chapter 12). Plasma angiotensin II is high during salt depletion and low when salt intake is high. It is this change in angiotensin II that brings about the changes in aldosterone secretion.

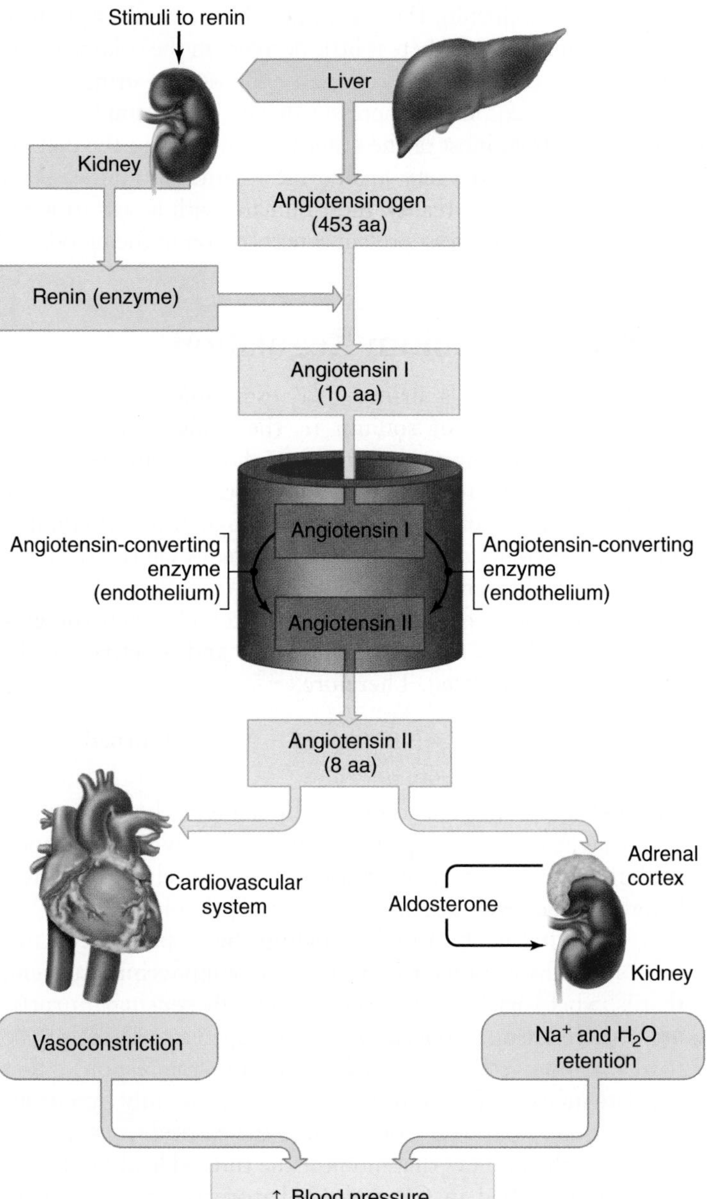

Figure 14.23 Summary of the renin–angiotensin system and the stimulation of aldosterone secretion by angiotensin II. Angiotensin-converting enzyme (ACE) is located on the surface of capillary endothelial cells. The plasma concentration of renin is the rate-limiting factor in the renin–angiotensin system; that is, it is the major determinant of the plasma concentration of angiotensin II. (aa = Amino acids)

PHYSIOLOGICAL INQUIRY

- What effect would an ACE inhibitor have on renin secretion and angiotensin II production? What effect would an angiotensin II receptor blocker (ARB) have on renin secretion and angiotensin II production? (*Hint:* Also look ahead to Figure 14.24.)

Answers can be found at end of chapter.

What causes the changes in plasma angiotensin II concentration with changes in salt balance? Angiotensinogen and angiotensin-converting enzyme are usually present in excess, so the rate-limiting factor in angiotensin II formation is the plasma renin concentration. Thus, the chain of events in salt depletion is increased renin secretion → increased plasma renin concentration → increased plasma angiotensin I concentration → increased plasma angiotensin II concentration → increased aldosterone release → increased plasma aldosterone concentration.

What are the mechanisms by which sodium depletion causes an increase in renin secretion (**Figure 14.24**)? There are at least three distinct inputs to the juxtaglomerular cells: (1) the renal sympathetic nerves, (2) intrarenal baroreceptors, and (3) the macula densa. This is an excellent example of the general principle of physiology that most physiological functions (like renin secretion) are controlled by multiple regulatory systems, often working in opposition.

The renal sympathetic nerves directly innervate the juxtaglomerular cells, and an increase in the activity of these nerves stimulates renin secretion. This makes sense because these nerves are reflexively activated via baroreceptors whenever a reduction in body sodium (and, therefore, plasma volume) decreases cardiovascular pressures (see Figure 14.22).

The other two inputs for controlling renin release—intrarenal baroreceptors and the macula densa—are contained within the kidneys and require no external neuroendocrine input (although such input can influence them). As noted earlier, the juxtaglomerular cells are located in the walls of the afferent arterioles. They are sensitive to the pressure within these arterioles and, therefore, function as **intrarenal baroreceptors.** When blood pressure in the kidneys decreases, as occurs when plasma volume is decreased, these cells are stretched less and, therefore, secrete more renin (see Figure 14.24). Thus, the juxtaglomerular cells respond simultaneously to the combined effects of sympathetic input, triggered by baroreceptors external to the kidneys, and to their own pressure sensitivity.

The other internal input to the juxtaglomerular cells is via the macula densa, which, as noted earlier, is located near the ends of the ascending loops of Henle (see Figure 14.2). The macula densa senses the amount of Na^+ in the tubular fluid flowing past it. A decreased salt delivery causes the release of paracrine factors that diffuse from the macula densa to the nearby JG cells, thereby activating them and causing the release of renin. Therefore, in an indirect way, this mechanism is sensitive to changes in sodium intake. If salt intake is low, less Na^+ is filtered and less appears at the macula densa. Conversely, a high salt intake will cause a very low rate of release of renin. If blood pressure is significantly decreased, glomerular filtration rate can decrease. This will decrease the tubular flow rate such that less Na^+ is presented to the macula densa. This input also results in increased renin release at the same time that the sympathetic nerves and intrarenal baroreceptors are doing so (see Figure 14.24).

The importance of this system is highlighted by the considerable redundancy in the control of renin secretion. Furthermore, as illustrated in Figure 14.24, the various mechanisms can all be participating at the same time.

By helping to regulate sodium balance and thereby plasma volume, the renin–angiotensin system contributes to the control of arterial blood pressure. However, this is not the only way in which it influences arterial pressure. Recall from Chapter 12 that angiotensin II is a potent constrictor of arterioles in many parts of the body and that this effect on peripheral resistance increases arterial pressure.

Drugs have been developed to manipulate the angiotensin II and aldosterone components of the system. ACE inhibitors, such as ***lisinopril***, reduce angiotensin II production from angiotensin I by inhibiting angiotensin-converting enzyme. Angiotensin II receptor blockers, such as ***losartan***, prevent angiotensin II from binding to its receptor on target tissue (e.g., vascular smooth muscle and the adrenal cortex). Finally, drugs such as ***eplerenone*** block the binding of aldosterone to its receptor in the kidney. Although

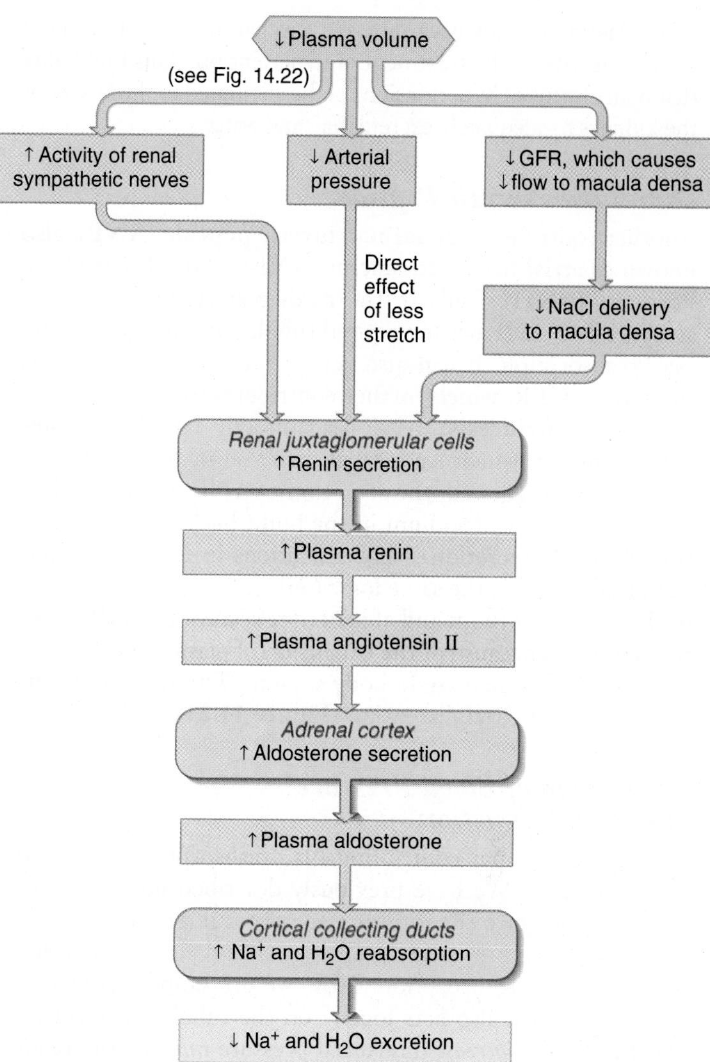

Figure 14.24 Pathways by which decreased plasma volume leads, via the renin–angiotensin system and aldosterone, to increased Na^+ reabsorption by the cortical collecting ducts and hence to decreased Na^+ excretion.

PHYSIOLOGICAL INQUIRY

- What would be the effect of denervation (removal of sympathetic neural input) of the kidneys on Na^+ and water excretion?

Answer can be found at end of chapter.

these classes of drugs have different mechanisms of action, they are all effective in the treatment of hypertension. This highlights that many forms of hypertension can be attributed to the failure of the kidneys to adequately excrete Na^+ and water.

Atrial Natriuretic Peptide

Another controller is **atrial natriuretic peptide (ANP)**, also known as atrial natriuretic factor (ANF) or atrial natriuretic hormone (ANH). Cells in the cardiac atria synthesize and secrete ANP. ANP acts on several tubular segments to inhibit Na^+ reabsorption. It can also act on the renal blood vessels to increase GFR, which further contributes to increased Na^+ excretion (**natriuresis**). ANP also directly inhibits aldosterone secretion, which leads to an increase in Na^+ excretion. As would be predicted, the secretion of ANP increases when there is an excess of sodium in the body, but the stimulus for this increased secretion is not alterations in Na^+ concentration. Rather, using the same logic (only in reverse) that applies to the control of renin and aldosterone secretion, ANP secretion increases because of the expansion of plasma volume that accompanies an increase in body sodium. The specific stimulus is increased atrial distension (**Figure 14.25**).

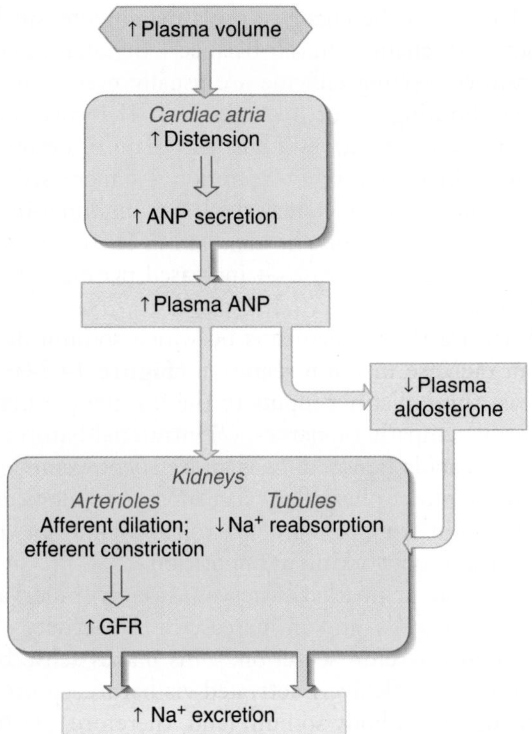

Figure 14.25 Atrial natriuretic peptide (ANP) increases Na^+ excretion.

Interaction of Blood Pressure and Renal Function

An important input controlling Na^+ reabsorption is arterial blood pressure. We have previously described how the arterial blood pressure constitutes a signal for important reflexes (involving the renin–angiotensin system and aldosterone) that influence Na^+ reabsorption. Now we are emphasizing that arterial pressure also acts locally on the tubules themselves. Specifically, an *increase* in arterial pressure *inhibits* Na^+ reabsorption and thereby increases Na^+ excretion in a process termed **pressure natriuresis.** The actual transduction mechanism of this direct effect is unknown.

Thus, an increased blood pressure reduces Na^+ reabsorption by two mechanisms: (1) It reduces the activity of the renin-angiotensin-aldosterone system, and (2) it also acts locally on the tubules. Conversely, a decreased blood pressure decreases Na^+ excretion by both stimulating the renin-angiotensin-aldosterone system and acting on the tubules to enhance Na^+ reabsorption.

Now is a good time to look back at Figure 12.57, which describes the strong, causal, reciprocal relationship between arterial blood pressure and blood volume, the result of which is that blood volume is perhaps the major long-term determinant of blood pressure. The direct effect of blood pressure on Na^+ excretion is, as Figure 12.57 shows, one of the major links in these relationships. An important hypothesis is that most people who develop hypertension do so because their kidneys, for some reason, do not excrete enough Na^+ in response to a normal arterial pressure. Consequently, at this normal pressure, some dietary sodium is retained, which causes the pressure to increase enough to produce adequate Na^+ excretion to balance sodium intake, although at an increased body sodium content. The integrated control of sodium balance is a useful example of the general principles of physiology that the functions of organ systems are coordinated with each other and that controlled exchange of materials occurs between compartments and across cellular membranes.

14.9 Renal Water Regulation

Water excretion is the difference between the volume of water filtered (the GFR) and the volume reabsorbed. Thus, the changes in GFR initiated by baroreceptor afferent input described in the previous section tend to have the same effects on water excretion as on Na^+ excretion. As is true for Na^+, however, the rate of water reabsorption is the most important factor for determining how much water is excreted. As we have seen, this is determined by vasopressin; therefore, total-body water is regulated mainly by reflexes that alter the secretion of this hormone.

As described in Chapter 11, vasopressin is produced by a discrete group of hypothalamic neurons whose axons terminate in the posterior pituitary gland, which releases vasopressin into the blood. The most important of the inputs to these neurons come from osmoreceptors and baroreceptors.

Osmoreceptor Control of Vasopressin Secretion

We have seen how changes in extracellular volume simultaneously elicit reflex changes in the excretion of *both* Na^+ and water. This is adaptive because the situations causing extracellular volume alterations are very often associated with loss or gain of both Na^+ and water in proportional amounts. In contrast, changes in total-body water with no corresponding change in total-body sodium are compensated for by altering water excretion *without altering* Na^+ *excretion.*

A crucial point in understanding how such reflexes are initiated is realizing that changes in water alone, in contrast to Na^+, have relatively little effect on extracellular volume. The reason is that water, unlike Na^+, distributes throughout all the body fluid compartments, with about two-thirds entering the intracellular compartment rather than simply staying in the extracellular compartment, as Na^+ does. Therefore, cardiovascular pressures and baroreceptors are only slightly affected by pure water gains or losses. In contrast, the major effect of water loss or gain out of proportion to Na^+ loss or gain is a change in the osmolarity of the body fluids. This is a key point because, under conditions due predominantly to water gain or loss, the sensory receptors that initiate the reflexes controlling vasopressin secretion are **osmoreceptors** in the hypothalamus. These receptors are responsive to changes in osmolarity.

As an example, imagine that you drink 2 L of water. The excess water decreases the body fluid osmolarity, which results in an inhibition of vasopressin secretion via the hypothalamic osmoreceptors (**Figure 14.26**). As a result, the water permeability of the collecting ducts decreases dramatically, water reabsorption of these segments is greatly reduced, and a large volume of hypoosmotic urine is excreted. In this manner, the excess water is eliminated and body fluid osmolarity is normalized.

At the other end of the spectrum, when the osmolarity of the body fluids increases because of water deprivation, vasopressin secretion is reflexively increased via the osmoreceptors, water reabsorption by the collecting ducts increases, and a very small volume of highly concentrated urine is excreted. By retaining relatively more water than solute, the kidneys help reduce the body fluid osmolarity back toward normal.

To summarize, regulation of body fluid osmolarity requires separation of water excretion from Na^+ excretion. That is, it requires the kidneys to excrete a urine that, relative to plasma, either contains more water than Na^+ and other solutes (water diuresis) or less water than solute (concentrated urine). This is made possible by two physiological factors: (1) osmoreceptors and (2) vasopressin-dependent water reabsorption without Na^+ reabsorption in the collecting ducts.

Baroreceptor Control of Vasopressin Secretion

The minute-to-minute control of plasma osmolarity is primarily by the osmoreceptor-mediated vasopressin secretion already described. There are, however, other important controllers of vasopressin secretion. The best understood of these is baroreceptor input to vasopressinergic neurons in the hypothalamus.

A decreased extracellular fluid volume due, for example, to diarrhea or hemorrhage, elicits an increase in aldosterone release via activation of the renin–angiotensin system. However, the decreased extracellular volume also triggers an increase in vasopressin secretion. This increased vasopressin increases the water permeability of the collecting ducts. More water is passively reabsorbed and less is excreted, so water is retained to help stabilize the extracellular volume.

This reflex is initiated by several baroreceptors in the cardiovascular system (**Figure 14.27**). The baroreceptors decrease their rate of firing when cardiovascular pressures

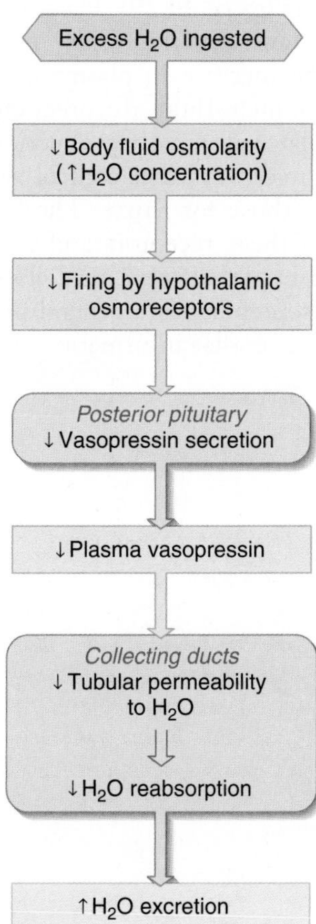

Figure 14.26 Osmoreceptor pathway that decreases vasopressin secretion and increases water excretion when excess water is ingested. The opposite events (an increase in vasopressin secretion) occur when osmolarity increases, as during water deprivation.

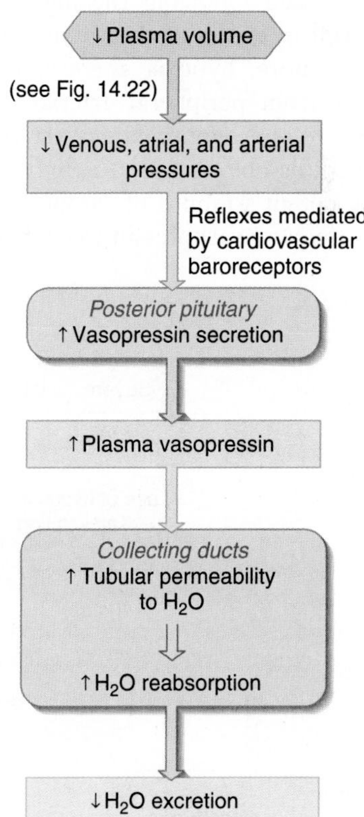

Figure 14.27 Baroreceptor pathway by which vasopressin secretion increases when plasma volume decreases. The opposite events (culminating in a decrease in vasopressin secretion) occur when plasma volume increases.

decrease, as occurs when blood volume decreases. Therefore, the baroreceptors transmit fewer impulses via afferent neurons and ascending pathways to the hypothalamus, and the result is increased vasopressin secretion. Conversely, increased cardiovascular pressures cause more firing by the baroreceptors, resulting in a decrease in vasopressin secretion. The mechanism of this inverse relationship is an inhibitory neurotransmitter released by neurons in the afferent pathway.

In addition to its effect on water excretion, vasopressin, like angiotensin II, causes widespread arteriolar constriction. This helps restore arterial blood pressure toward normal (Chapter 12).

The baroreceptor reflex for vasopressin, as just described, has a relatively high threshold—that is, there must be a sizable reduction in cardiovascular pressures to trigger it. Therefore, this reflex, compared to the osmoreceptor reflex described earlier, generally plays a lesser role under most physiological circumstances, but it can become very important in pathological states, such as hemorrhage.

Other Stimuli to Vasopressin Secretion

We have now described two afferent pathways controlling the vasopressin-secreting hypothalamic cells, one from osmoreceptors and the other from baroreceptors. To add to the complexity, the hypothalamic cells receive synaptic input from many other brain areas, so that vasopressin secretion—and, therefore, urine volume and concentration—can be altered by pain, fear, and a variety of drugs. For example, ethanol inhibits vasopressin release, and this may account for the increased urine volume produced following the ingestion of alcohol, a urine volume well in excess of the volume of the beverage consumed. Furthermore, hypoxia alters vasopressin release via afferent input from peripheral arterial chemoreceptors (see Figure 13.33) to the hypothalamus via ascending pathways from the medulla oblongata to the hypothalamus. Nausea is also a very potent stimulus of vasopressin release. The vasoconstrictor effects of vasopressin (see Chapter 12) acting on the blood vessels that perfuse the small intestines help to shift blood flow away from the gastrointestinal tract, thereby decreasing the absorption of ingested toxic substances.

14.10 A Summary Example: The Response to Sweating

Figure 14.28 shows the factors that control renal Na^+ and water excretion in response to severe sweating. You may notice the salty taste of sweat on your upper lip when you exercise. Sweat does contain Na^+ and Cl^-, in addition to water, but is actually hypoosmotic compared to the body fluids from which it is derived. Therefore, sweating causes both a decrease in extracellular volume and an increase in body fluid osmolarity. The renal retention of water and Na^+ minimizes the deviations from normal caused by the loss of water and salt in the sweat.

14.11 Thirst and Salt Appetite

Deficits of salt and water must eventually be compensated for by ingestion of these substances, because the kidneys cannot create new Na^+ or water. The kidneys can only minimize their excretion until ingestion replaces the losses.

The subjective feeling of thirst is stimulated by an increase in plasma osmolarity and by a decrease in extracellular fluid volume (**Figure 14.29**). Plasma osmolarity is the single most important stimulus under normal physiological conditions. The increase in plasma osmolarity and the decrease in extracellular fluid are precisely the same two changes that stimulate vasopressin production, and the osmoreceptors and baroreceptors that control vasopressin secretion are similar to those for thirst. The brain centers that receive input from these receptors and that mediate thirst are located in the hypothalamus, very close to those areas that synthesize vasopressin. The general principle of physiology this highlights is that information flow—in this case,

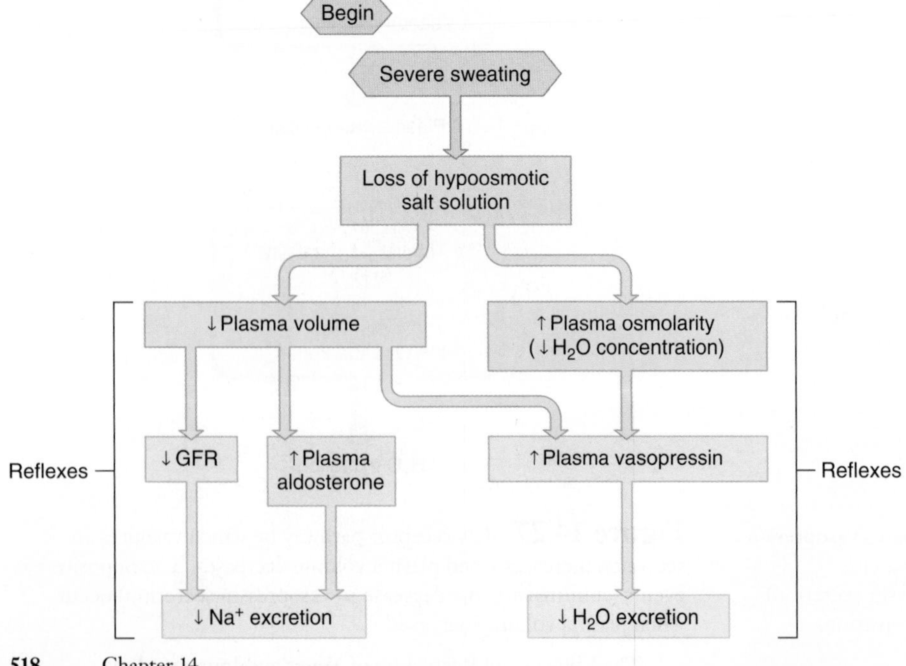

Figure 14.28 Pathways by which Na^+ and water excretion decrease in response to severe sweating. This figure is an amalgamation of Figures 14.22, 14.24, 14.27, and the reverse of Figure 14.26.

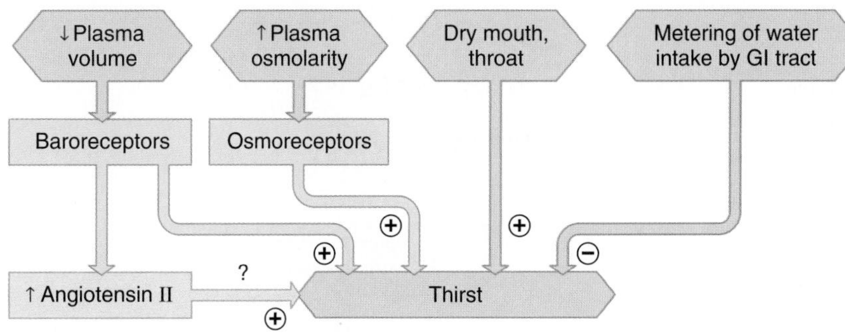

Figure 14.29 Inputs controlling thirst. The osmoreceptor input is the single most important stimulus under most physiological conditions. Psychological factors and conditioned responses are not shown. The question mark (?) indicates that evidence for the effects of angiotensin II on thirst comes primarily from experimental animals.

from the osmoreceptors to the release of vasopressin and the stimulation of thirst—is an essential feature of homeostasis and allows for the integration of physiological processes—in this case, to maintain water balance by increasing intake and minimizing loss.

There are still other pathways controlling thirst. For example, dryness of the mouth and throat causes thirst, which is relieved by merely moistening them. Some kind of "metering" of water intake by other parts of the gastrointestinal tract also occurs. For example, a thirsty person given access to water stops drinking after replacing the lost water. This occurs well before most of the water has been absorbed from the gastrointestinal tract and has a chance to eliminate the stimulatory inputs to the systemic baroreceptors and osmoreceptors. This is probably mediated by afferent sensory nerves from the mouth, throat, and gastrointestinal tract and prevents overhydration.

Salt appetite is an important part of sodium homeostasis and consists of two components, "hedonistic" appetite and "regulatory" appetite. Most mammals "like" salt and eat it whenever they can, regardless of whether they are salt-deficient. Human beings have a strong hedonistic appetite for salt, as manifested by almost universally large intakes of salt whenever it is cheap and readily available. For example, the average American consumes 10–15 g/day despite the fact that human beings can survive quite normally on less than 0.5 g/day. However, humans have relatively little regulatory salt appetite, at least until a bodily salt deficit becomes extremely large.

14.12 Potassium Regulation

K^+ is the most abundant intracellular ion. Although only 2% of total-body potassium is in the extracellular fluid, the K^+ concentration in this fluid is extremely important for the function of excitable tissues, notably, nerve and muscle. Recall from Chapter 6 that the resting membrane potentials of these tissues are directly related to the relative intracellular and extracellular K^+ concentrations. Consequently, either increases (***hyperkalemia***) or decreases (***hypokalemia***) in extracellular K^+ concentration can cause abnormal rhythms of the heart (***arrhythmias***) and abnormalities of skeletal muscle contraction and neuronal action potential conduction.

A healthy person remains in potassium balance in the steady state by daily excreting an amount of potassium in the urine equal to the amount ingested minus the amounts eliminated in feces and sweat. Like Na^+ losses, K^+ losses via sweat and the gastrointestinal tract are normally quite small, although vomiting or diarrhea can cause large quantities to be lost. The control of urinary K^+ excretion is the major mechanism regulating body potassium.

Renal Regulation of K^+

K^+ is freely filterable in the glomerulus. Normally, the tubules reabsorb most of this filtered K^+ so that very little of the filtered K^+ appears in the urine. However, the cortical collecting ducts can secrete K^+ and changes in K^+ excretion are due mainly to changes in K^+ secretion by this tubular segment (**Figure 14.30**).

During potassium depletion, when the homeostatic response is to minimize potassium loss, there is no K^+ secretion by the cortical collecting ducts. Only the small amount of filtered K^+ that escapes tubular reabsorption is excreted. With normal fluctuations in potassium intake, a variable amount of K^+ is added to the small amount filtered and not reabsorbed. This maintains total-body potassium balance.

Figure 14.14b illustrated the mechanism of K^+ secretion by the cortical collecting ducts. In this tubular segment, the K^+ pumped into the cell across the basolateral membrane by Na^+/K^+-ATPases diffuses into the tubular lumen through K^+ channels in the luminal membrane. Thus, the secretion of K^+ by the cortical collecting duct is associated with the reabsorption of Na^+ by this tubular segment. K^+ secretion does not occur in other Na^+-reabsorbing tubular segments because there are few K^+ channels in the luminal membranes of their cells. Rather, in these segments, the K^+ pumped into the cell by Na^+/K^+-ATPase simply diffuses back across the basolateral membrane through K^+ channels located there (see Figure 14.14a).

What factors influence K^+ secretion by the cortical collecting ducts to achieve homeostasis of bodily potassium?

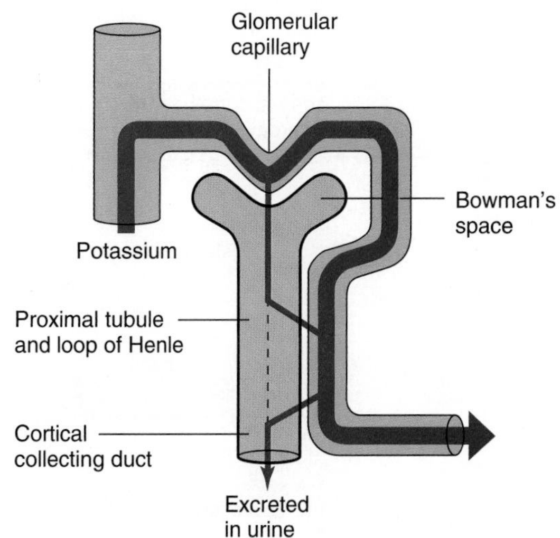

Figure 14.30 APIR Simplified model of the basic renal processing of potassium.

The single most important factor is as follows. When a high-potassium diet is ingested (**Figure 14.31**), plasma K^+ concentration increases, though very slightly, and this drives enhanced basolateral uptake via the Na^+/K^+-ATPase pumps. Thus, there is an enhanced K^+ secretion. Conversely, a low-potassium diet or a negative potassium balance, such as results from diarrhea, decreases basolateral K^+ uptake. This reduces K^+ secretion and excretion, thereby helping to reestablish potassium balance.

A second important factor linking K^+ secretion to potassium balance is the hormone aldosterone (see Figure 14.31). Besides stimulating tubular Na^+ reabsorption by the cortical collecting ducts, aldosterone simultaneously enhances K^+ secretion by this tubular segment.

The homeostatic mechanism by which an excess or deficit of potassium controls aldosterone production (see Figure 14.31) is different from the mechanism described earlier involving the renin–angiotensin system. The aldosterone-secreting cells of the adrenal cortex are sensitive to the K^+ concentration of the extracellular fluid. Thus, an increased intake of potassium leads to an increased extracellular K^+ concentration, which in turn directly stimulates the adrenal cortex to produce aldosterone. The increased plasma aldosterone concentration increases K^+ secretion and thereby eliminates the excess potassium from the body.

Conversely, a decreased extracellular K^+ concentration decreases aldosterone production and thereby reduces K^+ secretion. Less K^+ than usual is excreted in the urine, thereby helping to restore the normal extracellular concentration.

Figure 14.32 summarizes the control and major renal tubular effects of aldosterone. The fact that a single hormone regulates both Na^+ and K^+ excretion raises the question of potential conflicts between homeostasis of the two ions. For example, if a person was sodium-deficient and therefore secreting large amounts of aldosterone, the K^+-secreting effects of this hormone would tend to cause some K^+ loss even though potassium balance was normal to start with. Usually, such conflicts cause only minor imbalances because there are a variety of other counteracting controls of Na^+ and K^+ excretion.

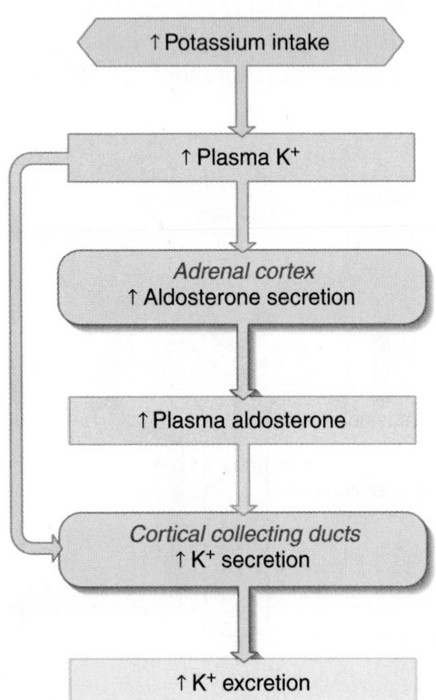

Figure 14.31 Pathways by which an increased potassium intake induces greater K^+ excretion.

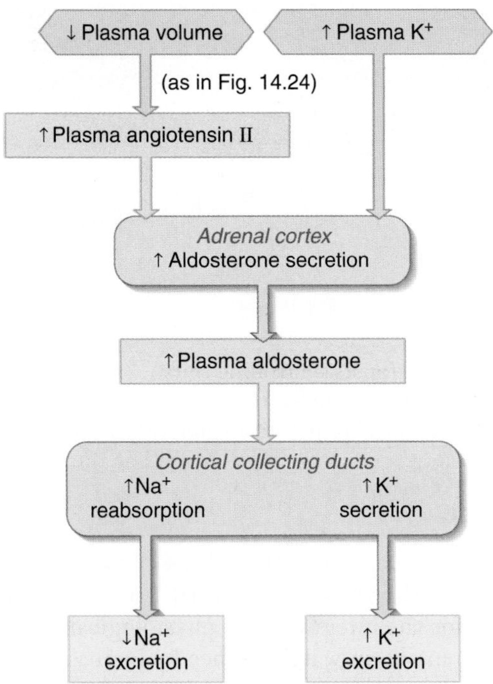

Figure 14.32 Summary of the control of aldosterone and its effects on Na^+ reabsorption and K^+ secretion.

14.13 Renal Regulation of Calcium and Phosphate Ion

Calcium and phosphate balance are controlled primarily by parathyroid hormone and $1,25(OH)_2D$, as described in detail in Chapter 11. Approximately 60% of plasma calcium is available for filtration in the kidney. The remaining plasma calcium is protein-bound or complexed with anions. Because calcium is so important in the function of every cell in the body, the kidneys have powerful mechanisms to reabsorb calcium ion from the tubular fluid. More than 60% of calcium ion reabsorption is not under hormonal control and occurs in the proximal tubule. The hormonal control of calcium ion reabsorption occurs mainly in the distal convoluted tubule and early in the cortical collecting duct. When plasma calcium is low, the secretion of parathyroid hormone (PTH) from the parathyroid glands increases. PTH stimulates the opening of calcium channels in these parts of the nephron, thereby increasing calcium ion reabsorption. As discussed in Chapter 11, another important action of PTH in the kidneys is to increase the activity of the 1-hydroxylase enzyme, thus activating 25(OH)-D to $1,25(OH)_2D$, which then goes on to increase calcium and phosphate ion absorption in the gastrointestinal tract.

About half of the plasma phosphate is ionized and is filterable. Like calcium, most of the phosphate ion that is filtered is reabsorbed in the proximal tubule. Unlike calcium ion, phosphate ion reabsorption is decreased by PTH, thereby increasing the excretion of phosphate ion. Thus, when plasma calcium is low, and PTH and calcium ion reabsorption are increased as a result, phosphate ion excretion is increased.

14.14 Summary—Division of Labor

Table 14.5 summarizes the division of labor of renal function along the renal tubule. So far, we have discussed all of these processes except the transport of acids and bases, which Section C of this chapter will cover.

14.15 Diuretics

Drugs used clinically to increase the volume of urine excreted are known as ***diuretics.*** Most act on the tubules to inhibit the reabsorption of Na^+, along with Cl^- and/or HCO_3^-, resulting in increased excretion of these ions. Because water reabsorption is dependent upon solute (particularly Na^+) reabsorption, water reabsorption is also reduced, resulting in increased water excretion.

A large variety of clinically useful diuretics are available and are classified according to the specific mechanisms by which they inhibit Na^+ reabsorption. For example, ***loop diuretics,*** such as ***furosemide,*** act on the ascending limb of the loop of Henle to inhibit the first step in Na^+ reabsorption in this segment—cotransport of Na^+ and Cl^- across the luminal membrane into the cell.

Except for one category of diuretics, called ***potassium-sparing diuretics,*** all diuretics not only increase Na^+ excretion but also cause increased K^+ excretion, which is often an unwanted side effect. The potassium-sparing diuretics inhibit Na^+ reabsorption in the cortical collecting duct, without increasing K^+ secretion there. Potassium-sparing diuretics either block the action of aldosterone (e.g., ***spironolactone*** or *eplerenone*) or block the epithelial Na^+ channel in the cortical collecting duct (e.g., ***triamterene*** or ***amiloride***). This explains why they do not cause increased K^+ excretion. ***Osmotic diuretics*** such as ***mannitol*** are filtered but not reabsorbed, thus retaining water in the urine. This is the same reason that uncontrolled diabetes mellitus and its associated glucosuria can cause excessive water loss and dehydration (see Figure 16.21).

Diuretics are among the most commonly used medications. For one thing, they are used to treat diseases characterized by renal retention of salt and water. As emphasized earlier in this chapter, the regulation of blood pressure normally produces stability of total-body-sodium mass and extracellular volume because of the close correlation between these variables. In contrast, in several types of disease, this correlation is disrupted and the reflexes that maintain blood pressure can cause renal retention of Na^+. Na^+ excretion may decrease to almost nothing despite continued sodium ingestion, leading to abnormal expansion of the extracellular fluid (***edema***). Diuretics are used to prevent or reverse this renal retention of Na^+ and water.

The most common example of this phenomenon is ***congestive heart failure*** (Chapter 12). A person with a failing heart manifests a decreased GFR and increased aldosterone secretion, both of which contribute to the virtual absence of Na^+ in the urine. The net result is extracellular volume expansion and edema. The Na^+-retaining responses are triggered by the lower cardiac output (a result of cardiac failure) and the

TABLE 14.5 Summary of "Division of Labor" in the Renal Tubules

Tubular Segment	Major Functions	Controlling Factors
Glomerulus/Bowman's capsule	Forms ultrafiltrate of plasma	Starling forces (P_{GC}, P_{BS}, π_{GC})
Proximal tubule	Bulk reabsorption of solutes and water Secretion of solutes (except K^+) and organic acids and bases	Active transport of solutes with passive water reabsorption Parathyroid hormone inhibits phosphate ion reabsorption
Loop of Henle	Establishes medullary osmotic gradient (juxtamedullary nephrons) Secretion of urea	
Descending limb	Bulk reabsorption of water	Passive water reabsorption
Ascending limb	Reabsorption of NaCl	Active transport
Distal tubule and cortical collecting ducts	Fine-tuning of the reabsorption/secretion of small quantity of solute remaining	Aldosterone stimulates Na^+ reabsorption and K^+ secretion Parathyroid hormone stimulates calcium ion reabsorption
Cortical and medullary collecting ducts	Fine-tuning of water reabsorption Reabsorption of urea	Vasopressin increases passive reabsorption of water

decrease in arterial blood pressure that results directly from this decrease in cardiac output.

Another disease in which diuretics are often used is hypertension (Chapter 12). The decrease in body sodium and water resulting from the diuretic-induced excretion of these substances brings about arteriolar dilation and a lowering of the blood pressure. The precise mechanism by which decreased body sodium causes arteriolar dilation is not known.

SECTION B SUMMARY

Total-Body Balance of Sodium and Water

I. The body gains water via ingestion and internal production, and it loses water via urine, the gastrointestinal tract, and evaporation from the skin and respiratory tract (as insensible loss and sweat).

II. The body gains Na^+ and Cl^- by ingestion and loses them via the skin (in sweat), the gastrointestinal tract, and urine.

III. For both water and Na^+, the major homeostatic control point for maintaining stable balance is renal excretion.

Basic Renal Processes for Sodium and Water

I. Na^+ is freely filterable at the glomerulus, and its reabsorption is a primary active process dependent upon Na^+/K^+-ATPase pumps in the basolateral membranes of the tubular epithelium. Na^+ is not secreted.

II. Na^+ entry into the cell from the tubular lumen is always passive. Depending on the tubular segment, it is either through channels or by cotransport or countertransport with other substances.

III. Na^+ reabsorption creates an osmotic difference across the tubule, which drives water reabsorption, largely through water channels (aquaporins).

IV. Water reabsorption is independent of the posterior pituitary gland hormone vasopressin until it reaches the collecting-duct system, where vasopressin increases water permeability. A large volume of dilute urine is produced when plasma vasopressin concentration and, hence, water reabsorption by the collecting ducts are low.

V. A small volume of concentrated urine is produced by the renal countercurrent multiplier system when plasma vasopressin concentration is high.
   a. The active transport of sodium chloride by the ascending loop of Henle causes increased osmolarity of the interstitial fluid of the medulla but a dilution of the luminal fluid.
   b. Vasopressin increases the permeability to water of the cortical collecting ducts by increasing the number of AQP2 water channels inserted into the luminal membrane. Water is reabsorbed by this segment until the luminal fluid is isoosmotic to plasma in the cortical peritubular capillaries.
   c. The luminal fluid then enters and flows through the medullary collecting ducts, and the concentrated medullary interstitium causes water to move out of these ducts, made highly permeable to water by vasopressin. The result is concentration of the collecting-duct fluid and the urine.
   d. The hairpin-loop structure of the vasa recta prevents the countercurrent gradient from being washed away.

Renal Sodium Regulation

I. Na^+ excretion is the difference between the amount of Na^+ filtered and the amount reabsorbed.

II. GFR and, hence, the filtered load of Na^+ are controlled by baroreceptor reflexes. Decreased vascular pressures cause decreased baroreceptor firing and, hence, increased sympathetic outflow to the renal arterioles, resulting in vasoconstriction and decreased GFR. These changes are generally relatively small under most physiological conditions.

III. The major control of tubular Na^+ reabsorption is the adrenal cortical hormone aldosterone, which stimulates Na^+ reabsorption in the cortical collecting ducts.

IV. The renin–angiotensin system is one of the two major controllers of aldosterone secretion. When extracellular volume decreases, renin secretion is stimulated by three inputs:
   a. Stimulation of the renal sympathetic nerves to the juxtaglomerular cells by extrarenal baroreceptor reflexes;
   b. Pressure decreases sensed by the juxtaglomerular cells, themselves acting as intrarenal baroreceptors; and
   c. A signal generated by low Na^+ or Cl^- concentration in the lumen of the macula densa.

V. Many other factors influence Na^+ reabsorption. One of these, atrial natriuretic peptide, is secreted by cells in the atria in response to atrial distension; it inhibits Na^+ reabsorption, and it also increases GFR.

VI. Arterial pressure acts locally on the renal tubules to influence Na^+ reabsorption; an increased pressure causes decreased reabsorption and, hence, increased excretion.

Renal Water Regulation

I. Water excretion is the difference between the amount of water filtered and the amount reabsorbed.

II. GFR regulation via the baroreceptor reflexes plays some role in regulating water excretion, but the major control is via vasopressin-mediated control of water reabsorption.

III. Vasopressin secretion by the posterior pituitary gland is controlled by osmoreceptors and by non-osmotic sensors such as cardiovascular baroreceptors in the hypothalamus.
   a. Via the osmoreceptors, a high body fluid osmolarity stimulates vasopressin secretion and a low osmolarity inhibits it.
   b. A low extracellular volume stimulates vasopressin secretion via the baroreceptor reflexes, and a high extracellular volume inhibits it.

A Summary Example: The Response to Sweating

I. Severe sweating can lead to a decrease in plasma volume and an increase in plasma osmolarity.

II. This will result in a decrease in GFR and an increase in aldosterone, which together decrease Na^+ excretion, and an increase in vasopressin, which decreases H_2O excretion.

III. The net result of the renal retention of Na^+ and H_2O is to minimize hypovolemia and maintain plasma osmolarity.

Thirst and Salt Appetite

I. Thirst is stimulated by a variety of inputs, including baroreceptors, osmoreceptors, and possibly angiotensin II.

II. Salt appetite is not of major regulatory importance in human beings.

Potassium Regulation

I. A person remains in potassium balance by excreting an amount of potassium in the urine equal to the amount ingested minus the amounts lost in feces and sweat.

II. K^+ is freely filterable at the renal corpuscle and undergoes both reabsorption and secretion, the latter occurring in the cortical collecting ducts and serving as the major controlled variable determining K^+ excretion.
III. When body potassium increases, extracellular potassium concentration also increases. This increase acts directly on the cortical collecting ducts to increase K^+ secretion and also stimulates aldosterone secretion. The increased plasma aldosterone then also stimulates K^+ secretion.
IV. The most common cause of hyperaldosteronism (too much aldosterone in the blood) is a noncancerous adrenal tumor (adenoma) that secretes aldosterone in the absence of stimulation from angiotensin II. Primary aldosteronism is sometimes called Conn's syndrome. The excess aldosterone causes increased renal Na^+ reabsorption and fluid retention and is a common cause of endocrine hypertension.

Renal Regulation of Calcium and Phosphate Ion

I. About half of the plasma calcium and phosphate is ionized and filterable.
II. Most calcium and phosphate ion reabsorption occurs in the proximal tubule.
III. PTH increases calcium ion absorption in the distal convoluted tubule and early cortical collecting duct. PTH decreases phosphate ion reabsorption in the proximal tubule.

Summary—Division of Labor

I. Each segment of the nephron is responsible for a different function.
II. The proximal tubule is responsible for the bulk reabsorption of solute and water.
III. The loop of Henle generates the medullary osmotic gradient that allows for the passive reabsorption of water in the collecting ducts.
IV. The distal tubules and collecting ducts are the site of most regulation (fine-tuning) of the excretion of solutes and water.

Diuretics

I. Most diuretics inhibit reabsorption of Na^+ and water, thereby enhancing the excretion of these substances. Different diuretics act on different nephron segments.

SECTION B REVIEW QUESTIONS

1. What are the sources of water gain and loss in the body? What are the sources of Na^+ gain and loss?
2. Describe the distribution of water and Na^+ between the intracellular and extracellular fluids.
3. What is the relationship between body sodium and extracellular fluid volume?
4. What is the mechanism of Na^+ reabsorption, and how is the reabsorption of other solutes coupled to it?
5. What is the mechanism of water reabsorption, and how is it coupled to Na^+ reabsorption?
6. What is the effect of vasopressin on the renal tubules, and what are the sites affected?
7. Describe the characteristics of the two limbs of the loop of Henle with regard to their transport of Na^+, Cl^-, and water.
8. Diagram the osmolarities in the two limbs of the loop of Henle, distal convoluted tubule, cortical collecting duct, cortical interstitium, medullary collecting duct, and medullary interstitium in the presence of vasopressin. What happens to the cortical and medullary collecting-duct values in the absence of vasopressin?
9. What two processes determine how much Na^+ is excreted per unit time?
10. Diagram the sequence of events in which a decrease in blood pressure leads to a decreased GFR.
11. List the sequence of events leading from increased renin secretion to increased aldosterone secretion.
12. What are the three inputs controlling renin secretion?
13. Diagram the sequence of events leading from decreased cardiovascular pressures or from an increased plasma osmolarity to an increased secretion of vasopressin.
14. What are the stimuli for thirst?
15. Which of the basic renal processes apply to potassium? Which of them is the controlled process, and which tubular segment performs it?
16. Diagram the steps leading from increased plasma potassium to increased K^+ excretion.
17. What are the two major controls of aldosterone secretion, and what are this hormone's major actions?
18. Contrast the control of calcium and phosphate ion excretion by PTH.
19. List the different types of diuretics and briefly summarize their mechanisms of action.
20. List several diseases that diuretics can be used to treat.

SECTION B KEY TERMS

aldosterone 514
angiotensin I 514
angiotensin II 514
angiotensin-converting enzyme (ACE) 514
angiotensinogen 514
antidiuretic hormone (ADH) 508
aquaporin 508
atrial natriuretic peptide (ANP) 516
countercurrent multiplier system 509
diuresis 508
hyperosmotic 509
hypoosmotic 509
insensible water loss 506
intrarenal baroreceptors 515
isoosmotic 509
natriuresis 516
obligatory water loss 509
osmoreceptor 517
osmotic diuresis 508
pressure natriuresis 516
renin 514
renin–angiotensin system 514
salt appetite 519
vasopressin 508
water diuresis 508

SECTION B CLINICAL TERMS

amiloride 521
arrhythmia 519
central diabetes insipidus 508
congestive heart failure 521
diabetes insipidus 508
diuretics 521
edema 521
eplerenone 515
furosemide 521
hyperkalemia 519
hypokalemia 519
lisinopril 515
loop diuretic 521
losartan 515
mannitol 521
nephrogenic diabetes insipidus 508
osmotic diuretics 521
potassium-sparing diuretic 521
spironolactone 521
triamterene 521

SECTION C

Hydrogen Ion Regulation

The understanding of the regulation of acid–base balance requires appreciation of a general principle of physiology that physiological processes are dictated by the laws of chemistry and physics. Metabolic reactions are highly sensitive to the H^+ concentration of the fluid in which they occur. This sensitivity is due to the influence that H^+ has on the shapes of proteins, such as enzymes, such that their function can be altered. Not surprisingly, then, the H^+ concentration of the extracellular fluid is tightly regulated. At this point, the reader might want to review the section on H^+, acidity, and pH in Chapter 2.

This regulation can be viewed in the same way as the balance of any other ion—that is, as matching gains and losses. When loss exceeds gain, the arterial plasma hydrogen ion concentration decreases and pH exceeds 7.4. This is termed ***alkalosis.*** When gain exceeds loss, the arterial plasma hydrogen ion concentration increases and the pH is less than 7.4. This is termed ***acidosis.***

14.16 Sources of Hydrogen Ion Gain or Loss

Table 14.6 summarizes the major routes for gains and losses of H^+. As described in Chapter 13, a huge quantity of CO_2—about 20,000 mmol—is generated daily as the result of oxidative metabolism. These CO_2 molecules participate in the generation of H^+ during the passage of blood through peripheral tissues via the following reactions:

$$CO_2 + H_2O \xrightleftharpoons{\text{carbonic anhydrase}} H_2CO_3 \rightleftharpoons HCO_3^- + H^+ \quad (14\text{–}1)$$

This source does not normally constitute a net gain of H^+. This is because the H^+ generated via these reactions is reincorporated into water when the reactions are reversed during the passage of blood through the lungs (see Chapter 13). Net retention of CO_2 does occur in hypoventilation or respiratory disease and in such cases causes a net gain of H^+. Conversely, net loss of CO_2 occurs in hyperventilation, and this causes net elimination of H^+.

The body also produces both organic and inorganic acids from sources other than CO_2. These are collectively termed **nonvolatile acids.** They include phosphoric acid and sulfuric acid, generated mainly by the catabolism of proteins, as well as lactic acid and several other organic acids. Dissociation of all of these acids yields anions and H^+. Simultaneously, however, the metabolism of a variety of organic anions utilizes H^+ and produces HCO_3^-. Thus, the metabolism of "nonvolatile" solutes both generates and utilizes H^+. With the high-protein diet typical in the United States, the generation of nonvolatile acids predominates in most people, with an average net production of 40 to 80 mmol of H^+ per day.

A third potential source of the net gain or loss of H^+ in the body occurs when gastrointestinal secretions leave the body. Vomitus contains a high concentration of H^+ and so constitutes a source of net loss. In contrast, the other gastrointestinal secretions are alkaline. They contain very little H^+, but their concentration of HCO_3^- is higher than in plasma. Loss of these fluids, as in diarrhea, in essence constitutes a *gain* of H^+. Given the mass-action relationship shown in equation 14–1, *when HCO_3^- is lost from the body, it is the same as if the body had gained hydrogen ion.* This is because loss of the HCO_3^- causes the reactions shown in equation 14–1 to be driven to the right, thereby generating hydrogen ion within the body. Similarly, when the body gains HCO_3^-, it is the same as if the body had lost hydrogen ion, as the reactions of equation 14–1 are driven to the left.

Finally, the kidneys constitute the fourth source of net hydrogen ion gain or loss. That is, the kidneys can either remove H^+ from the plasma or add it.

TABLE 14.6 Sources of Hydrogen Ion Gain or Loss

Gain

- Generation of H^+ from CO_2
- Production of nonvolatile acids from the metabolism of proteins and other organic molecules
- Gain of H^+ due to loss of HCO_3^- in diarrhea or other nongastric GI fluids
- Gain of H^+ due to loss of HCO_3^- in the urine

Loss

- Utilization of H^+ in the metabolism of various organic anions
- Loss of H^+ in vomitus
- Loss of H^+ in the urine
- Hyperventilation

14.17 Buffering of Hydrogen Ion in the Body

Any substance that can reversibly bind H^+ is called a **buffer.** Most H^+ is bound by extracellular and intracellular buffers. The normal extracellular fluid pH of 7.4 corresponds to a hydrogen ion concentration of only 0.00004 mmol/L (40 nmol/L). Without buffering, the daily turnover of the 40 to 80 mmol of H^+ produced from nonvolatile acids generated in the body from metabolism would cause huge changes in body fluid hydrogen ion concentration.

The general form of buffering reactions is

$$\text{Buffer} + H^+ \rightleftharpoons \text{HBuffer} \quad (14\text{–}2)$$

Recall the law of mass action described in Chapter 3, which governs the net direction of the reaction in equation 14–2. HBuffer is a weak acid in that it can dissociate to buffer H^+ or it can exist as the undissociated molecule (HBuffer). When H^+ concentration increases for any reason, the reaction is forced to the right and more H^+ is bound by buffer to form HBuffer. For example, when H^+ concentration is increased because of increased production of lactic acid, some of the H^+ combines with the body's buffers, so the hydrogen ion concentration does not increase as much as it otherwise would have. Conversely, when H^+ concentration decreases because of the loss of H^+ or the addition of alkali, equation 14–2 proceeds to the left and H^+ is released from HBuffer. In this manner, buffers stabilize H^+ concentration against changes in either direction.

The major extracellular buffer is the CO_2/HCO_3^- system summarized in equation 14–1. This system also plays some role in buffering within cells, but the major intracellular buffers are phosphates and proteins. An example of an intracellular protein buffer is hemoglobin, as described in Chapter 13.

This buffering does not eliminate H^+ from the body or add it to the body; it only keeps the H^+ "locked up" until balance can be restored. How balance is achieved is the subject of the rest of our description of hydrogen ion regulation.

14.18 Integration of Homeostatic Controls

The kidneys are ultimately responsible for balancing hydrogen ion gains and losses so as to maintain plasma hydrogen ion concentration within a narrow range. Thus, the kidneys normally excrete the excess H^+ from nonvolatile acids generated from metabolism—that is, all acids other than carbonic acid. An additional net gain of H^+ can occur with increased production of these nonvolatile acids, with hypoventilation or respiratory malfunction, or with the loss of alkaline gastrointestinal secretions. When this occurs, the kidneys increase the elimination of H^+ from the body to restore balance. Alternatively, if there is a net loss of H^+ from the body due to hyperventilation or vomiting, the kidneys replenish this H^+.

Although the kidneys are the ultimate hydrogen ion balancers, the respiratory system also plays a very important homeostatic role. We have pointed out that hypoventilation, respiratory malfunction, and hyperventilation can cause a hydrogen ion imbalance. Now we emphasize that when a hydrogen ion imbalance is due to a nonrespiratory cause, then ventilation is reflexively altered so as to help compensate for the imbalance. We described this phenomenon in Chapter 13 (see Figure 13.38). An increased arterial hydrogen ion concentration stimulates ventilation, which lowers arterial P_{CO_2} that, by mass action, reduces hydrogen ion concentration. Alternatively, a decreased plasma hydrogen ion concentration inhibits ventilation, thereby increasing arterial P_{CO_2} and the hydrogen ion concentration.

In this way, the respiratory system and kidneys work together. The respiratory response to altered plasma hydrogen ion concentration is very rapid (minutes) and keeps this concentration from changing too much until the more slowly responding kidneys (hours to days) can actually eliminate the imbalance. If the respiratory system is the actual cause of the hydrogen ion imbalance, then the kidneys are the sole homeostatic responder. Conversely, malfunctioning kidneys can create a hydrogen ion imbalance by eliminating too little or too much hydrogen ion from the body, and then the respiratory response is the only one in control. As you can see, therefore, the control of acid–base balance requires that the functions of organ systems be coordinated with each other—another general principle of physiology highlighted in this book.

14.19 Renal Mechanisms

The kidneys eliminate or replenish H^+ from the body by altering plasma bicarbonate concentration. The key to understanding how altering plasma bicarbonate concentration eliminates or replenishes H^+ was stated earlier. That is, the excretion of HCO_3^- in the urine increases the plasma hydrogen ion concentration just as if a hydrogen ion had been added to the plasma. Similarly, the addition of HCO_3^- to the plasma decreases the plasma hydrogen ion concentration just as if a hydrogen ion had been removed from the plasma.

Thus, when the plasma hydrogen ion concentration decreases (alkalosis) for whatever reason, the kidneys' homeostatic response is to excrete large quantities of HCO_3^-. This increases plasma hydrogen ion concentration toward normal. In contrast, when plasma hydrogen ion concentration increases (acidosis), the kidneys do not excrete HCO_3^- in the urine. Rather, kidney tubular cells produce *new* HCO_3^- and add it to the plasma. This decreases the plasma hydrogen ion concentration toward normal.

HCO_3^- Handling

HCO_3^- is completely filterable at the renal corpuscles and undergoes significant tubular reabsorption in the proximal tubule, ascending loop of Henle, and cortical collecting ducts. It can also be secreted in the collecting ducts. Therefore,

$$HCO_3^- \text{ excretion} = HCO_3^- \text{ filtered} + HCO_3^- \text{ secreted} - HCO_3^- \text{ reabsorbed}$$

For simplicity, we will ignore the secretion of HCO_3^- because it is always much less than tubular reabsorption, and we will treat HCO_3^- excretion as the difference between filtration and reabsorption.

HCO_3^- reabsorption is an active process, but it is not accomplished in the conventional manner of simply having an active pump for HCO_3^- at the luminal or basolateral membrane of the tubular cells. Instead, HCO_3^- reabsorption depends on the tubular secretion of H^+, which combines in the lumen with filtered HCO_3^-.

Figure 14.33 illustrates the sequence of events. Begin this figure inside the cell with the combination of CO_2 and H_2O to form H_2CO_3, a reaction catalyzed by the enzyme carbonic anhydrase. The H_2CO_3 immediately dissociates to yield H^+ and HCO_3^-. The HCO_3^- moves down its concentration gradient via facilitated diffusion across the basolateral membrane into interstitial fluid and then into the blood. Simultaneously, the H^+ is secreted into the lumen. Depending on the tubular segment, this secretion is achieved by some combination of primary H^+-ATPase pumps, primary H^+/K^+-ATPase pumps, and Na^+/H^+ countertransporters.

The secreted H^+, however, is not excreted. Instead, it combines in the lumen with a filtered HCO_3^- and generates CO_2 and H_2O, both of which can diffuse into the cell and be available for another cycle of hydrogen ion generation. The overall result is that the HCO_3^- filtered from the plasma at the renal corpuscle has disappeared, but its place in the plasma has been taken by the HCO_3^- that was produced inside the cell. In this manner, no net change in plasma bicarbonate concentration has occurred. It may seem inaccurate to refer to this process as

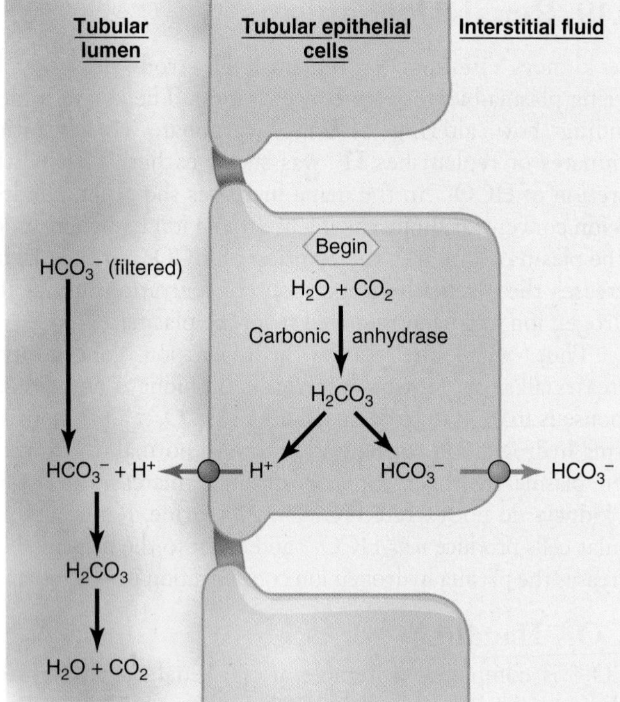

Figure 14.33 General model of the reabsorption of HCO_3^- in the proximal tubule and cortical collecting duct. Begin looking at this figure inside the cell, with the combination of CO_2 and H_2O to form H_2CO_3. As shown in the figure, active H^+-ATPase pumps are involved in the movement of H^+ out of the cell across the luminal membrane; in several tubular segments, this transport step is also mediated by Na^+/H^+ countertransporters and/or H^+/K^+-ATPase pumps.

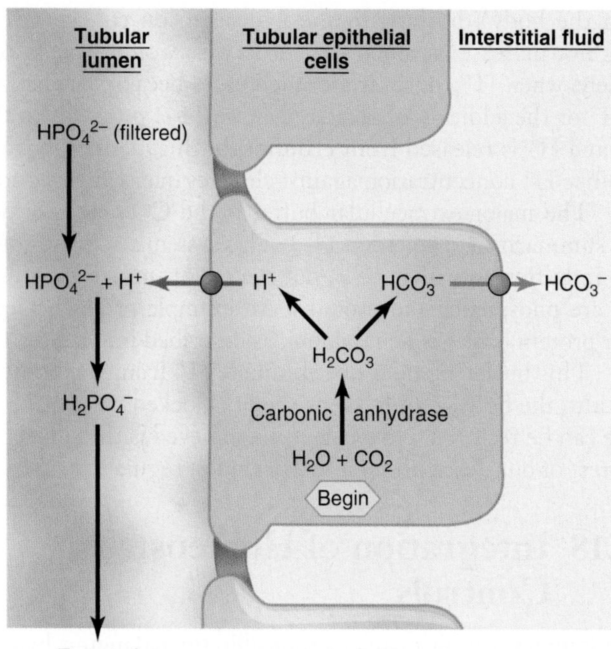

Figure 14.34 Renal contribution of new HCO_3^- to the plasma as achieved by tubular secretion of H^+. The process of intracellular H^+ and HCO_3^- generation, with H^+ moving into the lumen and HCO_3^- into the plasma, is identical to that shown in Figure 14.33. Once in the lumen of the proximal tubule, however, the H^+ combines with filtered phosphate ion ($H_2PO_4^{2-}$) rather than filtered HCO_3^- and is excreted as $H_2PO_4^-$. As described in the legend for Figure 14.33, the transport of H^+ into the lumen is accomplished not only by H^+-ATPase pumps but, in several tubular segments, by Na^+/H^+ countertransporters and/or H^+/K^+-ATPase pumps as well.

HCO_3^- "reabsorption" because the HCO_3^- that appears in the peritubular plasma is not the same HCO_3^- that was filtered. Yet, the overall result is the same as if the filtered HCO_3^- had been reabsorbed in the conventional manner like Na^+ or K^+.

Except in response to alkalosis, discussed in the next section, the kidneys normally reabsorb all filtered HCO_3^-, thereby preventing the loss of HCO_3^- in the urine.

Addition of New HCO_3^- to the Plasma

An essential concept shown in Figure 14.32 is that as long as there are still significant amounts of filtered HCO_3^- in the lumen, almost all secreted H^+ will combine with it. But what happens to any secreted H^+ once almost all the HCO_3^- has been reabsorbed and is no longer available in the lumen to combine with the H^+?

The answer, illustrated in **Figure 14.34,** is that the extra secreted H^+ combines in the lumen with a filtered nonbicarbonate buffer, the most important of which is HPO_4^{2-}. The hydrogen ion is then excreted in the urine as part of the HPO_4^{2-} ion. Now for the critical point: Note in Figure 14.34 that, under these conditions, the HCO_3^- generated within the tubular cell by the carbonic anhydrase reaction and entering the plasma constitutes a *net gain* of HCO_3^- by the plasma, not merely a replacement for filtered HCO_3^-. Therefore, when secreted hydrogen ion combines in the lumen with a buffer other than HCO_3^-, the overall effect is not merely one of HCO_3^- conservation, as in Figure 14.33, but, rather, of addition to the plasma of *new* HCO_3^-. This increases the HCO_3^- concentration of the plasma and alkalinizes it.

To repeat, significant amounts of H^+ combine with filtered nonbicarbonate buffers like HPO_4^{2-} only after the filtered HCO_3^- has virtually all been reabsorbed. The main reason is that there is such a large load of filtered HCO_3^-—25 times more than the load of filtered nonbicarbonate buffers—competing for the secreted H^+.

There is a second mechanism by which the tubules contribute new HCO_3^- to the plasma that involves not hydrogen ion secretion but, rather, the renal production and secretion of ammonium ion (NH_4^+) (**Figure 14.35**). Tubular cells, mainly those of the proximal tubule, take up glutamine from both the glomerular filtrate and peritubular plasma and metabolize it. In the process, both NH_4^+ and HCO_3^- are formed inside the cells. The NH_4^+ is actively secreted via Na^+/NH_4^+ countertransport into the lumen and excreted, while the HCO_3^- moves into the peritubular capillaries and constitutes new plasma bicarbonate.

A comparison of Figures 14.34 and 14.35 demonstrates that the overall result—renal contribution of new HCO_3^- to the plasma—is the same regardless of whether it is achieved by (1) H^+ secretion and excretion on nonbicarbonate buffers such as phosphate (see Figure 14.34) or (2) by glutamine metabolism with excretion (see Figure 14.35). It is convenient, therefore, to view the latter as representing H^+ excretion "bound" to NH_3, just as the former case constitutes H^+ excretion bound to nonbicarbonate buffers. Thus, the amount of H^+ excreted in the urine in these two forms is a measure of the amount of new HCO_3^- added to the plasma by the kidneys. Indeed, "urinary

TABLE 14.7 Renal Responses to Acidosis and Alkalosis

Responses to acidosis

- Sufficient H^+ is secreted to reabsorb all the filtered HCO_3^-.
- Still more H^+ is secreted, and this contributes new HCO_3^- to the plasma as the H^+ is excreted bound to nonbicarbonate urinary buffers such as HPO_4^{2-}.
- Tubular glutamine metabolism and ammonium excretion are enhanced, which also contributes new HCO_3^- to the plasma.

Net result: More new HCO_3^- ion than usual is added to the blood, and plasma bicarbonate is increased, thereby compensating for the acidosis. The urine is highly acidic (lowest attainable pH = 4.4).

Responses to alkalosis

- Rate of hydrogen ion secretion is inadequate to reabsorb all the filtered HCO_3^-, so significant amounts of HCO_3^- are excreted in the urine, and there is little or no excretion of H^+ on nonbicarbonate urinary buffers.
- Tubular glutamine metabolism and ammonium excretion are decreased so that little or no new HCO_3^- is contributed to the plasma from this source.

Net result: Plasma bicarbonate concentration is decreased, thereby compensating for the alkalosis. The urine is alkaline (pH > 7.4).

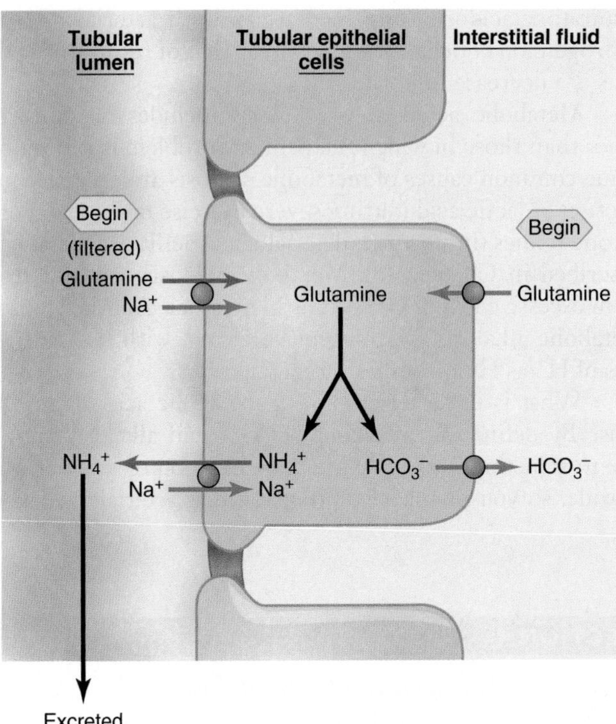

Figure 14.35 Renal contribution of new HCO_3^- to the plasma as achieved by renal metabolism of glutamine and excretion of ammonium (NH_4^+). Compare this figure to Figure 14.34. This process occurs mainly in the proximal tubule.

H^+ excretion" and "renal contribution of new HCO_3^- to the plasma" are really two sides of the same coin.

The kidneys normally contribute enough new HCO_3^- to the blood by excreting H^+ to compensate for the H^+ from nonvolatile acids generated in the body.

14.20 Classification of Acidosis and Alkalosis

The renal responses to the presence of acidosis or alkalosis are summarized in **Table 14.7.** To repeat, acidosis refers to any situation in which the hydrogen ion concentration of arterial plasma is increased above normal whereas alkalosis denotes a decrease. All such situations fit into two distinct categories (**Table 14.8**): (1) ***respiratory acidosis*** or ***alkalosis*** and (2) ***metabolic acidosis*** or ***alkalosis.***

As its name implies, respiratory acidosis results from altered alveolar ventilation. Respiratory acidosis occurs when the respiratory system fails to eliminate carbon dioxide as fast as it is produced. Respiratory alkalosis occurs when the respiratory system eliminates carbon dioxide faster than it is produced. As described earlier, the imbalance of arterial hydrogen ion concentrations in such cases is completely explainable in terms of mass action. Thus, the hallmark of

TABLE 14.8 Changes in the Arterial Concentrations of H^+, HCO_3^-, and Carbon Dioxide in Acid–Base Disorders

Primary Disorder	H^+	HCO_3^-	CO_2	Cause of HCO_3^- Change	Cause of CO_2 Change
Respiratory acidosis	↑	↑	↑	Renal compensation	Primary abnormality
Respiratory alkalosis	↓	↓	↓		
Metabolic acidosis	↑	↓	↓	Primary abnormality	Reflex ventilatory compensation
Metabolic alkalosis	↓	↑	↑		

PHYSIOLOGICAL INQUIRY

- A patient has an arterial P_{O_2} of 50 mmHg, an arterial P_{CO_2} of 60 mmHg, and an arterial pH of 7.36. Classify the acid–base disturbance and hypothesize a cause.

Answer can be found at end of chapter.

respiratory acidosis is an increase in both arterial P_{CO_2} and hydrogen ion concentration, whereas that of respiratory alkalosis is a decrease in both.

Metabolic acidosis or alkalosis includes all situations other than those in which the primary problem is respiratory. Some common causes of metabolic acidosis are excessive production of lactic acid (during severe exercise or hypoxia) or of ketone bodies (in uncontrolled diabetes mellitus or fasting, as described in Chapter 16). Metabolic acidosis can also result from excessive loss of HCO_3^-, as in diarrhea. Another cause of metabolic alkalosis is persistent vomiting, with its associated loss of H^+ as HCl from the stomach.

What is the arterial P_{CO_2} in metabolic acidosis or alkalosis? By definition, metabolic acidosis and alkalosis must be due to something other than excess retention or loss of carbon dioxide, so you might have predicted that arterial P_{CO_2} would be unchanged, but this is not the case. As emphasized earlier in this chapter, the increased hydrogen ion concentration associated with metabolic acidosis *reflexively* stimulates ventilation and decreases arterial P_{CO_2}. By mass action, this helps restore the hydrogen ion concentration toward normal. Conversely, a person with metabolic alkalosis will reflexively have ventilation inhibited. The result is an increase in arterial P_{CO_2} and, by mass action, an associated restoration of hydrogen ion concentration toward normal.

To reiterate, the plasma P_{CO_2} changes in metabolic acidosis and alkalosis are not the *cause* of the acidosis or alkalosis but the *result* of compensatory reflexive responses to nonrespiratory abnormalities. Thus, in metabolic as opposed to respiratory conditions, the arterial plasma P_{CO_2} and hydrogen ion concentration move in opposite directions, as summarized in Table 14.8.

SECTION C SUMMARY

Sources of Hydrogen Ion Gain or Loss

I. Total-body balance of H^+ is the result of both metabolic production of these ions and of net gains or losses via the respiratory system, gastrointestinal tract, and urine (Table 14.6).

II. A stable balance is achieved by regulation of urinary losses.

Buffering of Hydrogen Ion in the Body

I. Buffering is a means of minimizing changes in hydrogen ion concentration by combining these ions reversibly with anions such as HCO_3^- and intracellular proteins.

II. The major extracellular buffering system is the CO_2/HCO_3^- system, and the major intracellular buffers are proteins and phosphates.

Integration of Homeostatic Controls

I. The kidneys and the respiratory system are the homeostatic regulators of plasma hydrogen ion concentration.

II. The kidneys are the organs that achieve body hydrogen ion balance.

III. A decrease in arterial plasma hydrogen ion concentration causes reflex hypoventilation, which increases arterial and, hence, increases plasma hydrogen ion concentration toward normal. An increase in plasma hydrogen ion concentration causes reflexive hyperventilation, which decreases arterial and, hence, decreases hydrogen ion concentration toward normal.

Renal Mechanisms

I. The kidneys maintain a stable plasma hydrogen ion concentration by regulating plasma bicarbonate concentration. They can either excrete HCO_3^- or contribute new HCO_3^- to the blood.

II. HCO_3^- is reabsorbed when H^+, generated in the tubular cells by a process catalyzed by carbonic anhydrase, is secreted into the lumen and combine with filtered HCO_3^-. The secreted H^+ is not excreted in this situation.

III. In contrast, when the secreted H^+ combines in the lumen with filtered phosphate ion or other nonbicarbonate buffer, it is excreted, and the kidneys have contributed new HCO_3^- to the blood.

IV. The kidneys also contribute new HCO_3^- to the blood when they produce and excrete ammonium.

Classification of Acidosis and Alkalosis

I. Acid–base disorders are categorized as respiratory or metabolic.
   a. Respiratory acidosis is due to retention of carbon dioxide, and respiratory alkalosis is due to excessive elimination of carbon dioxide.
   b. All other causes of acidosis or alkalosis are termed ***metabolic*** and reflect gain or loss, respectively, of H^+ from a source other than carbon dioxide.

SECTION C REVIEW QUESTIONS

1. What are the sources of gain and loss of H^+ in the body?
2. List the body's major buffer systems.
3. Describe the role of the respiratory system in the regulation of hydrogen ion concentration.
4. How does the tubular secretion of H^+ occur, and how does it achieve HCO_3^- reabsorption?
5. How does hydrogen ion secretion contribute to the renal addition of new HCO_3^- to the blood? What determines whether secreted hydrogen ion will achieve these results or will instead cause HCO_3^- reabsorption?
6. How does the metabolism of glutamine by the tubular cells contribute new HCO_3^- to the blood and ammonium to the urine?
7. What two quantities make up "hydrogen ion excretion"? Why can this term be equated with "contribution of new HCO_3^- to the plasma"?
8. How do the kidneys respond to the presence of acidosis or alkalosis?
9. Classify the four types of acid–base disorders according to plasma hydrogen ion concentration, HCO_3^- concentration, and P_{CO_2}.
10. Explain how overuse of certain diuretics can lead to metabolic alkalosis.

SECTION C KEY TERMS

buffer 524
nonvolatile acid 524

SECTION C CLINICAL TERMS

acidosis 524
alkalosis 524
metabolic acidosis 527
metabolic alkalosis 527
respiratory acidosis 527
respiratory alkalosis 527

CHAPTER 14

Clinical Case Study: Severe Kidney Disease in a Woman with Diabetes Mellitus

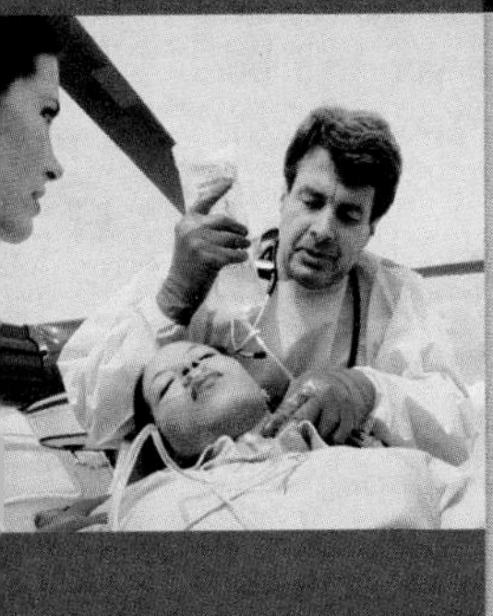

A patient with poorly controlled, long-standing type 2 diabetes mellitus has been feeling progressively weaker over the past few months. She has also been feeling generally ill and has been gaining weight although she has not changed her eating habits. During a routine visit to her family doctor, some standard blood and urine tests are ordered as an initial evaluation. In addition, her previously diagnosed mild high blood pressure has gotten significantly worse. The physician is concerned when the testing shows an increase in creatinine in her blood and a significant amount of protein in her urine. The patient is referred to a nephrologist (kidney-disease expert) who makes the diagnosis of diabetic kidney disease (diabetic nephropathy).

Many diseases affect the kidneys. Potential causes of kidney damage include congenital and inherited defects, metabolic disorders, infection, inflammation, trauma, vascular problems, and certain forms of cancer. Obstruction of the urethra or a ureter may cause injury from the buildup of pressure and may predispose the kidneys to bacterial infection. A common cause of renal failure is poorly controlled diabetes mellitus. The increase in blood glucose interferes with normal renal filtration and tubular function (see Section 14.13 of this chapter and Chapter 16), and high blood pressure common to patients with type 2 diabetes mellitus causes vascular damage in the kidney.

One of the earliest signs of a decrease in kidney function is an increase in creatinine in the blood, which was found to be the case in our patient. As described in Section 14.3 of this chapter, creatinine is a waste product of muscle metabolism that is filtered in the glomerulus and not reabsorbed. Although a small amount of creatinine is secreted in the renal tubule, creatinine clearance is a good estimate of glomerular filtration rate (GFR). Because a decrease in GFR occurs early in kidney disease, and because creatinine production is fairly constant, an increase in creatinine in the blood is a useful warning sign that creatinine clearance is decreasing and that kidney failure is occurring. Another frequent sign of kidney disease, which was also observed in our patient, is the appearance of protein in the urine. In normal kidneys, there is a tiny amount of protein in the glomerular filtrate because the filtration barrier membranes are not completely impermeable to proteins, particularly those with lower molecular weights. However, the cells of the proximal tubule completely remove this filtered protein from the tubular lumen and no protein appears in the final urine. In contrast, in diabetic nephropathy, the filtration barrier may become much more permeable to protein, and diseased proximal tubules may lose their ability to remove filtered protein from the tubular lumen. The result is that protein appears in the urine. The loss of protein in the urine leads to a decrease in the amount of protein in the blood. This results in a decrease in the osmotic force retaining fluid in the blood and subsequently the formation of edema throughout the body (see Chapter 12). In our patient, this resulted in an increase in body weight.

Although many diseases of the kidneys are self-limited and produce no permanent damage, others worsen if untreated. The symptoms of profound renal malfunction are relatively independent of the damaging agent and are collectively known as ***uremia,*** literally, "urea in the blood."

The severity of uremia depends upon how well the impaired kidneys can preserve the constancy of the internal environment. Assuming that the person continues to ingest a normal diet containing the usual quantities of nutrients and electrolytes, what problems arise? The key fact to keep in mind is that the kidney destruction markedly reduces the number of functioning nephrons. Accordingly, the many substances, particularly potentially toxic waste products that gain entry to the tubule by filtration, build up in the blood. In addition, the excretion of K^+ is impaired because there are too few nephrons capable of normal tubular secretion of this ion. The person may also develop acidosis because the reduced number of nephrons fails to add enough new HCO_3^- to the blood to compensate for the daily metabolic production of nonvolatile acids.

The remarkable fact is how large the safety factor is in renal function. In general, the kidneys are still able to perform their regulatory function quite well as long as 10% to 30% of the nephrons are functioning. This is because these remaining nephrons undergo alterations in function—filtration, reabsorption, and secretion—to compensate for the missing nephrons. For example, each remaining nephron increases its rate of K^+ secretion, so that the total amount of K^+ the kidneys excrete is maintained at normal levels. The limits of regulation are restricted, however. To use K^+ as our example again, if someone with severe renal disease were to go on a diet high in potassium, the remaining nephrons might not be able to secrete enough K^+ to prevent potassium retention.

Other problems arise in uremia because of abnormal secretion of the hormones the kidneys produce. Thus, decreased secretion of erythropoietin results in anemia (see Chapter 12). Decreased ability to form 1,25-$(OH)_2$D results in deficient absorption of calcium ion from the gastrointestinal tract, with a resulting decrease in plasma calcium, increase in PTH, and inadequate bone calcification (secondary hyperparathyroidism). Erythropoietin and 1,25-$(OH)_2$D (calcitriol) can be administered to patients with uremia to improve hematocrit and calcium balance.

In the case of the secreted enzyme renin, there is rarely too little secretion; rather, there is too much secretion by the juxtaglomerular cells of the damaged kidneys. The main reason for the increase in renin is decreased perfusion of affected nephrons (intrarenal baroreceptor). The result is increased plasma angiotensin II concentration and the development of ***renal hypertension.*** ACE inhibitors and angiotensin II receptor blockers can be used to decrease blood pressure and improve sodium and water balance. Our patient was counseled to more carefully and aggressively control her blood glucose and blood pressure with diet, exercise, and medications. She was also started on an ACE inhibitor. Unfortunately, her blood creatinine and proteinuria continued to worsen to the point of end-stage renal disease requiring hemodialysis.

Hemodialysis, Peritoneal Dialysis, and Transplantation

Failing kidneys may reach a point when they can no longer excrete water and ions at rates that maintain body balances of these substances, nor can they excrete waste products as fast as they

(continued)

(continued)

are produced. Dietary alterations can help minimize but not eliminate these problems. For example, decreasing potassium intake reduces the amount of K^+ to be excreted. The clinical techniques used to perform the kidneys' excretory functions are hemodialysis and peritoneal dialysis. The general term ***dialysis*** means to separate substances using a permeable membrane.

The artificial kidney is an apparatus that utilizes a process termed ***hemodialysis*** to remove wastes and excess substances from the blood (**Figure 14.36**). During hemodialysis, blood is pumped from one of the patient's arteries through tubing that is surrounded by special dialysis fluid. The tubing then conducts the blood back into the patient by way of a vein. The dialysis tubing is generally made of cellophane that is highly permeable to most solutes but relatively impermeable to protein and completely impermeable to blood cells—characteristics quite similar to those of capillaries. The dialysis fluid is a salt solution with ionic concentrations similar to or lower than those in normal plasma, and it contains no creatinine, urea, or other substances to be completely removed from the plasma. As blood flows through the tubing, the concentrations of nonprotein plasma solutes tend to reach diffusion equilibrium with those of the solutes in the bath fluid. For example, if the plasma K^+ concentration of the patient is above normal, K^+ diffuses out of the blood across the cellophane tubing and into the dialysis fluid. Similarly, waste products and excesses of other substances also diffuse into the dialysis fluid and thus are eliminated from the body.

Patients with acute reversible renal failure may require hemodialysis for only days or weeks. Patients like the woman in our case with chronic irreversible renal failure require treatment for the rest of their lives, however, unless they receive a kidney transplant. Such patients undergo hemodialysis several times a week.

Another way of removing excess substances from the blood is ***peritoneal dialysis,*** which uses the lining of the patient's own abdominal cavity (peritoneum) as a dialysis membrane. Fluid is injected via an indwelling plastic tube inserted through the abdominal wall into this cavity and allowed to remain there for hours, during which solutes diffuse into the fluid from the person's blood. The dialysis fluid is then removed and replaced with new fluid. This procedure can be performed several times daily by a patient who is simultaneously doing normal activities.

The long-term treatment of choice for most patients with permanent renal failure is kidney transplantation. Rejection of the transplanted kidney by the recipient's body is a potential problem, but great strides have been made in reducing the frequency of rejection (see Chapter 18). Many people who could benefit from a transplant, however, do not receive one. Currently, the major source of kidneys for transplantation is recently deceased persons. Recently, donation from a living, related donor has become more common. Because of the large safety factor, the donor can function quite normally with one kidney. In 2009, approximately 84,000 people in the United States were waiting for a kidney transplant.

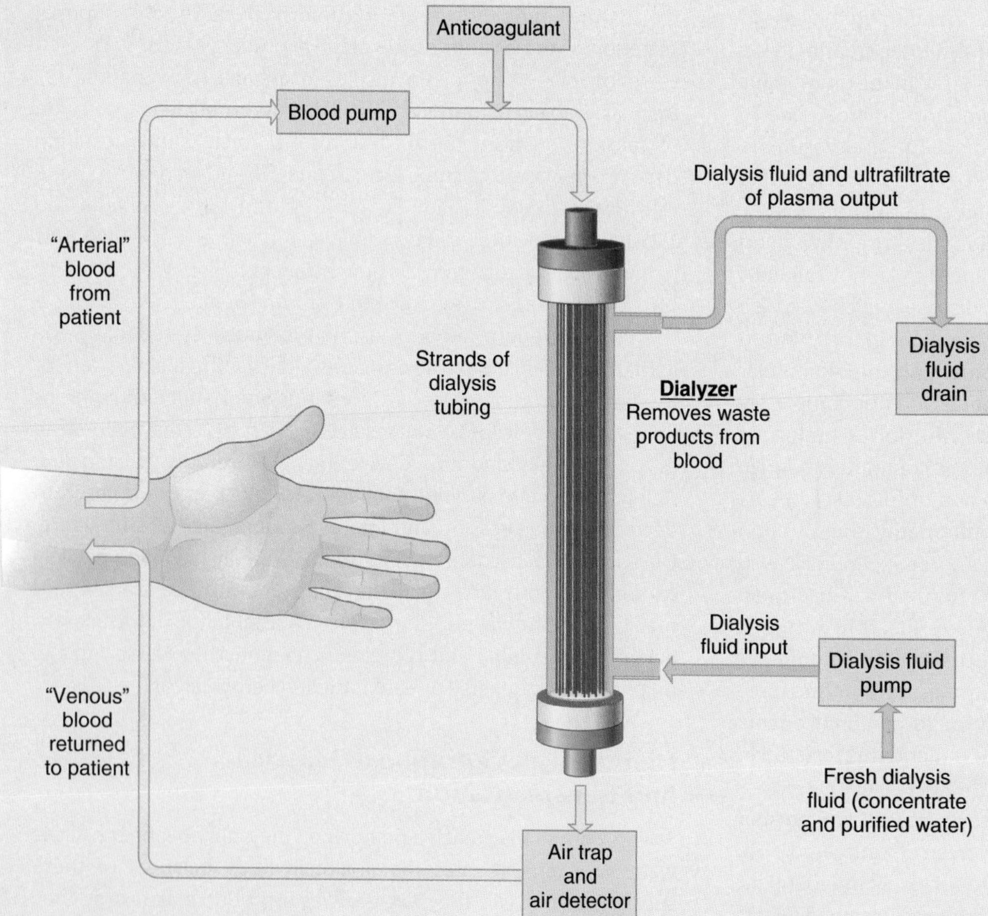

Figure 14.36 Simplified diagram of hemodialysis. Note that blood and dialysis fluid flow in opposite directions through the dialyzer (countercurrent). The blood flow can be 400 mL/min, and the dialysis fluid flow rate can be 1000 mL/min! During a 3 to 4 h dialysis session, approximately 72 to 96 L of blood and 3000 to 4000 L of dialysis fluid pass through the dialyzer. The dialyzer is composed of many strands of very thin dialysis tubing. Blood flows inside each tube, and dialysis fluid bathes the outside of the dialysis tubing. This provides a large surface area for diffusion of waste products out of the blood and into the dialysis fluid.

(continued)

(continued)

There were approximately 11,000 deceased donor and 6000 living donor kidney transplants in 2009, highlighting the shortage of transplantable kidneys. It is hoped that improved public understanding will lead to many more individuals giving permission in advance to have their kidneys and other organs used following their death. Our patient continued on hemodialysis three times a week for several years waiting for a kidney transplant. It was determined that her older brother was a compatible organ match, and he donated his kidney to our patient, allowing her to stop hemodialysis treatments. She continues to aggressively control her blood glucose and blood pressure.

Clinical terms: dialysis, hemodialysis, peritoneal dialysis, renal hypertension, uremia

See Chapter 19 for complete, integrative case studies.

CHAPTER 14 TEST QUESTIONS

Answers found in Appendix A.

1. Which of the following will lead to an increase in glomerular fluid filtration in the kidneys?
   a. an increase in the protein concentration in the plasma
   b. an increase in the fluid pressure in Bowman's space
   c. an increase in the glomerular capillary blood pressure
   d. a decrease in the glomerular capillary blood pressure
   e. constriction of the afferent arteriole
2. Which of the following is true about renal clearance?
   a. It is the amount of a substance excreted per unit time.
   b. A substance with clearance > GFR undergoes only filtration.
   c. A substance with clearance > GFR undergoes filtration and secretion.
   d. It can be calculated knowing only the filtered load of a substance and the rate of urine production.
   e. Creatinine clearance approximates renal plasma flow.
3. Which of the following will *not* lead to a diuresis?
   a. excessive sweating
   b. central diabetes insipidus
   c. nephrogenic diabetes insipidus
   d. excessive water intake
   e. uncontrolled diabetes mellitus
4. Which of the following contributes directly to the generation of a hypertonic medullary interstitium in the kidney?
   a. active Na^+ transport in the descending limb of Henle's loop
   b. active water reabsorption in the ascending limb of Henle's loop
   c. active Na^+ reabsorption in the distal convoluted tubule
   d. water reabsorption in the cortical collecting duct
   e. secretion of urea into Henle's loop
5. An increase in renin is caused by
   a. a decrease in sodium intake.
   b. a decrease in renal sympathetic nerve activity.
   c. an increase in blood pressure in the renal artery.
   d. an aldosterone-secreting adrenal tumor.
   e. essential hypertension.
6. An increase in parathyroid hormone will
   a. increase plasma 25(OH) D.
   b. decrease plasma 1,25-$(OH)_2$D.
   c. decrease calcium ion excretion.
   d. increase phosphate ion reabsorption.
   e. increase calcium ion reabsorption in the proximal tubule.
7. Which of the following is a component of the renal response to metabolic acidosis?
   a. reabsorption of H^+
   b. secretion of HCO_3^- into the tubular lumen
   c. secretion of ammonium into the tubular lumen
   d. secretion of glutamine into the interstitial fluid
   e. carbonic anhydrase-mediated production of HPO_4^{2-}
8. Which of the following is consistent with respiratory alkalosis?
   a. an increase in alveolar ventilation during mild exercise
   b. hyperventilation
   c. an increase in plasma HCO_3^-
   d. an increase in arterial CO_2
   e. urine pH < 5.0
9. Which is *true* about the difference between cortical and juxtamedullary nephrons?
   a. Most nephrons are juxtamedullary.
   b. The efferent arterioles of cortical nephrons give rise to most of the vasa recta.
   c. The afferent arterioles of the juxtamedullary nephrons give rise to most of the vasa recta.
   d. All cortical nephrons have a loop of Henle.
   e. Juxtamedullary nephrons generate a hyperosmotic medullary interstitium.
10. Which of the following is consistent with untreated chronic renal failure?
    a. proteinuria
    b. hypokalemia
    c. increased plasma 1,25-$(OH)_2$D
    d. increased plasma erythropoietin
    e. increased plasma HCO_3^-

CHAPTER 14 GENERAL PRINCIPLES ASSESSMENT

Answers found in Appendix A.

1. A general principle of physiology is that *structure is a determinant of—and has coevolved with—function.* How does the anatomy of the renal corpuscle and associated structures determine function?
2. *Physiological processes are dictated by the laws of chemistry and physics.* Give one example each of how a law of chemistry and a law of physics are important in understanding the regulation of renal function.
3. How does the control of vasopressin secretion highlight the general principle of physiology that *most physiological functions are controlled by multiple regulatory systems, often working in opposition?*

CHAPTER 14 QUANTITATIVE AND THOUGHT QUESTIONS

Answers found in Appendix A.

1. Substance T is present in the urine. Does this prove that it is filterable at the glomerulus?
2. Substance V is not normally present in the urine. Does this prove that it is neither filtered nor secreted?
3. The concentration of glucose in plasma is 100 mg/100 mL, and the GFR is 125 mL/min. How much glucose is filtered per minute?
4. A person is excreting abnormally large amounts of a particular amino acid. Just from the theoretical description of T_m-limited reabsorptive mechanisms in the text, list several possible causes.
5. The concentration of urea in urine is always much higher than the concentration in plasma. Does this mean that urea is secreted?
6. If a person takes a drug that blocks the reabsorption of Na^+, what will happen to the reabsorption of water, urea, Cl^-, glucose, and amino acids and to the secretion of H^+?
7. Compare the changes in GFR and renin secretion occurring in response to a moderate hemorrhage in two individuals—one taking a drug that blocks the sympathetic nerves to the kidneys and the other not taking such a drug.
8. If a person is taking a drug that completely inhibits angiotensin-converting enzyme, what will happen to aldosterone secretion when the person goes on a low-sodium diet?
9. In the steady state, what is the amount of sodium chloride excreted daily in the urine of a normal person ingesting 12 g of sodium chloride per day: (a) 12 g/day, or (b) less than 12 g/day? Explain.
10. A young woman who has suffered a head injury seems to have recovered but is thirsty all the time. What do you think might be the cause?
11. A patient has a tumor in the adrenal cortex that continuously secretes large amounts of aldosterone. What is this condition called, and what effects does this have on the total amount of sodium and potassium in her body?
12. A person is taking a drug that inhibits the tubular secretion of H^+. What effect does this drug have on the body's balance of sodium, water, and H^+?
13. How can the overuse of diuretics lead to metabolic alkalosis?

CHAPTER 14 ANSWERS TO PHYSIOLOGICAL INQUIRIES

Figure 14.3 The glomerular filtration rate would be greatly decreased. This would result in a decrease in the removal of toxic substances from the blood. As you will learn, kidney disease is a common and troubling consequence of long-term untreated diabetes mellitus.

Figure 14.8 GFR will decrease because the increase in plasma osmotic force from albumin will oppose filtration.

Figure 14.9 A blood clot occluding the afferent arteriole would decrease blood flow to that glomerulus and greatly decrease GFR in that individual glomerulus. A blood clot in the efferent arteriole would increase P_{GC} and, therefore, GFR. If this only occurred in a few glomeruli, it would not have a significant effect on renal function because of the large number of total glomeruli in the two kidneys providing a safety factor.

Figure 14.11 Filtered load = GFR × Plasma glucose concentration. Excretion rate = Urine glucose concentration × Urine flow rate.

Figure 14.14 It would decrease sodium reabsorption from the tubular fluid. This will result in an increase in urinary sodium excretion. The osmotic force of sodium will carry water with it, thus increasing urine output. Examples of such diuretics are triamterene and amiloride.

Figure 14.18 The increased vasopressin would cause maximal water reabsorption. Urine volume would be low (antidiuresis) and urine osmolarity would remain high. The continuous water reabsorption would cause a decrease in plasma sodium concentration (hyponatremia) due to dilution of sodium. Consequently, the plasma would have very low osmolarity. The decreased plasma osmolarity would not inhibit vasopressin secretion from the tumor because it is not controlled by the hypothalamic osmoreceptors. This is called the *syndrome of inappropriate antidiuretic hormone* (*SIADH*) and is one of several possible causes of hyponatremia in humans.

Figure 14.23 An ACE inhibitor will decrease angiotensin II production. The resultant increase in Na^+ and water excretion would decrease blood pressure, leading to a reflexive increase in renin secretion. An ARB would also decrease blood pressure and therefore increase renin secretion. However, with an ARB, angiotensin II would increase because angiotensin-converting-enzyme activity would be normal.

Figure 14.24 Under normal conditions, the redundant control of renin release, as indicated in this figure, as well as the participation of vasopressin (see Figure 14.27), would allow the maintenance of normal sodium and water balance even with denervated kidneys. However, during severe decreases in plasma volume, like in dehydration, the denervated kidney may not produce sufficient renin to maximally decrease Na^+ excretion.

Table 14.8 The patient has respiratory acidosis with renal compensation (hypercapnia with a normalization of arterial pH). The patient is hypoxic, which, with normal lung function, usually leads to hyperventilation and respiratory alkalosis. Therefore, the patient is likely to have chronic lung disease resulting in hypoxemia and retention of carbon dioxide (hypercapnia). We know it is chronic because the kidneys have had time to compensate for the acidosis by increasing the HCO_3^- added to the blood, thus restoring arterial pH almost to normal (see Figures 14.33 to 14.35).

Visit this book's website at **www.mhhe.com/widmaier13** for chapter quizzes, interactive learning exercises, and other study tools.

HUMAN PHYSIOLOGY

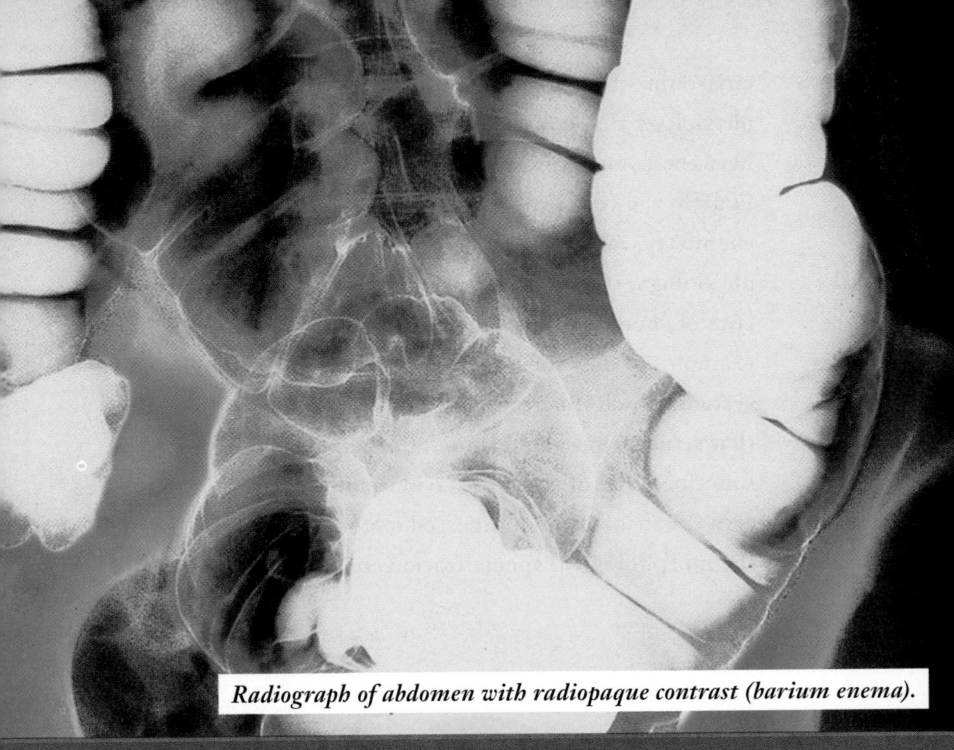
Radiograph of abdomen with radiopaque contrast (barium enema).

15 The Digestion and Absorption of Food

The digestive system is responsible for the absorption of ingested nutrients, water, minerals, and other essential factors and is central to the regulation and integration of metabolic processes throughout the body. Normal function of the digestive system is necessary for long-term whole-body homeostasis as well as normal functioning of individual organ systems. In Chapter 1, you were introduced to the concept of total-body balance where the gain of a substance in the body equals loss of that substance from the body (Figure 1.11). You will now learn several specific examples of total-body balance as they apply to the digestive system. You will also learn how the enteric nervous system, first introduced in Chapter 6, interacts with other parts of the nervous system to provide information to and from the brain, and regulates the local control of gastrointestinal function. In Chapter 14, you learned how water and electrolyte balance are achieved through the regulation of their excretion (output) by the kidneys. You will now learn about the mechanisms and integrated regulation of the absorption (input) of water, electrolytes, vitamins, and nutrients into the body.

This chapter has many examples demonstrating the general principles of physiology introduced in Chapter 1. First, the control of gastrointestinal function illustrates the general principle of physiology that information flow between cells, tissues, and organs is an essential feature of homeostasis and allows for integration of physiological processes; this is highlighted by the intimate relationship between the absorptive capacity of the gastrointestinal tract and the circulatory and lymphatic systems as pathways to deliver these nutrients to the tissues. Second, many of the functions of the gastrointestinal tract illustrate the general principle of physiology that most physiological functions are controlled by multiple regulatory systems, often working in opposition. For example, the acidity of the contents of the stomach is increased or decreased by the influence of hormones released from the gastrointestinal tract as well as paracrine factors and neuronal inputs. Third, the digestive tract regulates the transfer of materials from and to the environment, which exemplifies the general principle of physiology that controlled exchange of materials occurs between compartments and across cellular membranes. Fourth, the very process of digestion depends on basic chemistry, reflecting yet another general principle of physiology, that physiological processes are dictated by the laws of chemistry and physics. Finally, this chapter has many examples of how form follows the function of the digestive system, which illustrates the general principle of physiology that structure is a determinant of—and has coevolved with—function. One of the most vivid examples is the large surface area for absorption of ingested materials made possible by the morphological specializations of the small intestine.

15.1 Overview of the Digestive System

The **digestive system** (**Figure 15.1**) includes the **gastrointestinal (GI) tract,** consisting of the mouth, pharynx, esophagus, stomach, small intestine, and large intestine; and the accessory organs and tissues, consisting of the salivary glands, liver, gallbladder, and exocrine pancreas. The accessory organs are not part of the tract but secrete substances into it via connecting ducts. The GI tract is also known as the **alimentary canal.** The overall function of the digestive system is to process ingested foods into molecular forms that are then transferred, along with salts and water, to the body's internal environment, where the circulatory system can distribute them to cells. The digestive system is under the local neural control of the enteric nervous system and also of the central nervous system.

The adult gastrointestinal tract is a tube approximately 9 m (30 feet) in length, running through the body from mouth to **anus.** The lumen of the tract is continuous with the external environment, which means that its contents are technically outside the body. This fact is relevant to understanding some of the tract's properties. For example, the large intestine is colonized by billions of bacteria, most of which are harmless and even beneficial in this location. However, if the same bacteria enter the internal environment, as may happen, for example, if a portion of the large intestine is perforated, they may cause a severe infection (see Chapter 19).

Most food enters the gastrointestinal tract as large particles containing macromolecules, such as proteins and polysaccharides, which are unable to cross the intestinal epithelium. Before ingested food can be absorbed, therefore, it must be dissolved and broken down into small molecules. (Small nutrients such as vitamins and minerals do not need to be broken down and can cross the epithelium intact.) This dissolving and breaking-down process is called **digestion** and is accomplished by the action of hydrochloric acid in the stomach, bile from the liver, and a variety of digestive enzymes released by the system's exocrine glands. Each of these substances is released into the lumen of the GI tract through the process of **secretion.** In addition, some digestive enzymes are located on the luminal

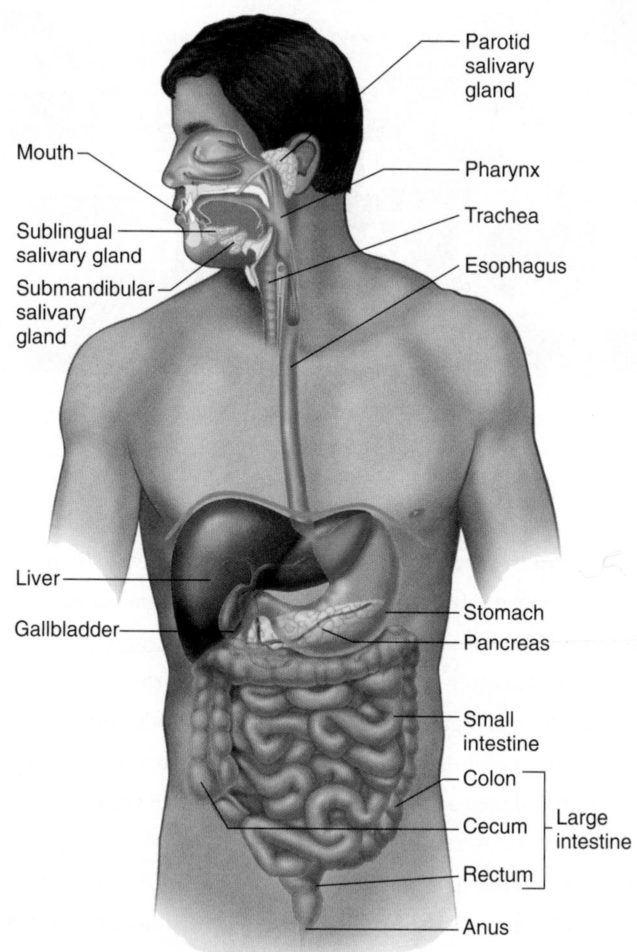

Figure 15.1 APR Anatomy of the digestive system. The liver overlies the gallbladder and a portion of the stomach, and the stomach overlies part of the pancreas. See Table 15.1 for the functions of the organs of the digestive system.

membranes of the intestinal epithelium. The molecules produced by digestion, along with water and small nutrients that do not require digestion, then move from the lumen of the gastrointestinal tract across a layer of epithelial cells and enter the blood or lymph. This process is called **absorption.**

While digestion, secretion, and absorption are taking place, contractions of smooth muscles in the gastrointestinal tract wall serve two functions: They mix the luminal contents with the various secretions, and they move the contents through the tract from mouth to anus. These contractions are referred to as the **motility** of the gastrointestinal tract. In some cases, muscular movements travel in a wave-like fashion in one direction along the length of a part of the tract, a process called **peristalsis.** The functions of the digestive system can be described in terms of these four major processes—digestion, secretion, absorption, and motility (**Figure 15.2**)—and the mechanisms controlling them.

Within fairly wide limits, the digestive system will absorb as much of any particular substance that is ingested, with a few important exceptions (to be described later). Therefore, the digestive system does not regulate the total amount of nutrients absorbed or their concentrations in the internal environment. The plasma concentration and distribution of the absorbed nutrients throughout the body are primarily controlled by hormones from a number of endocrine glands (see Chapters 11 and 16) and by the kidneys (see Chapter 14).

Small amounts of certain metabolic end products are excreted via the gastrointestinal tract, primarily by way of the bile. This represents a minor function of the GI tract in healthy individuals—**elimination.** In fact, the lungs and kidneys are usually responsible for the elimination of most of the body's waste products. The material known as **feces** leaves the system at the end of the gastrointestinal tract. Feces consist almost entirely of bacteria and ingested material that was neither digested nor absorbed, that is, material that was never actually absorbed into the internal environment.

15.2 Structure of the Gastrointestinal Tract Wall

From the mid-esophagus to the anus, the wall of the gastrointestinal tract has the general structure illustrated in **Figure 15.3**. Most of the luminal (inside) surface is highly convoluted, a feature that greatly increases the surface area available for absorption. From the stomach on, this surface is covered by a single layer of epithelial cells linked together along the edges of their luminal surfaces by tight junctions. Included in this epithelial layer are exocrine cells that secrete mucus into the lumen of the tract and endocrine cells that release hormones into the blood. Invaginations of the epithelium into the underlying tissue form exocrine glands that secrete acid, enzymes, water, ions, and mucus into the lumen.

Just below the epithelium is the **lamina propria,** which is a layer of loose connective tissue through which pass small blood vessels, nerve fibers, and lymphatic vessels. (Some of these structures do not appear in Figure 15.3 but are in Figure 15.4.) The lamina propria is separated from underlying tissues by the **muscularis mucosa,** which is a thin layer of smooth muscle that may be involved in the movement of villi, described subsequently. The combination of these three layers—the epithelium, lamina propria, and muscularis mucosa—is called the **mucosa** (see Figure 15.3).

Beneath the mucosa is the **submucosa,** which is a second connective-tissue layer. This layer also contains a network of neurons, the **submucosal plexus,** and blood and lymphatic vessels whose branches penetrate into both the overlying mucosa and the underlying layers of smooth muscle called the **muscularis externa.** Contractions of these muscles provide the forces for moving and mixing the gastrointestinal contents. Except for the stomach, which has three layers, the

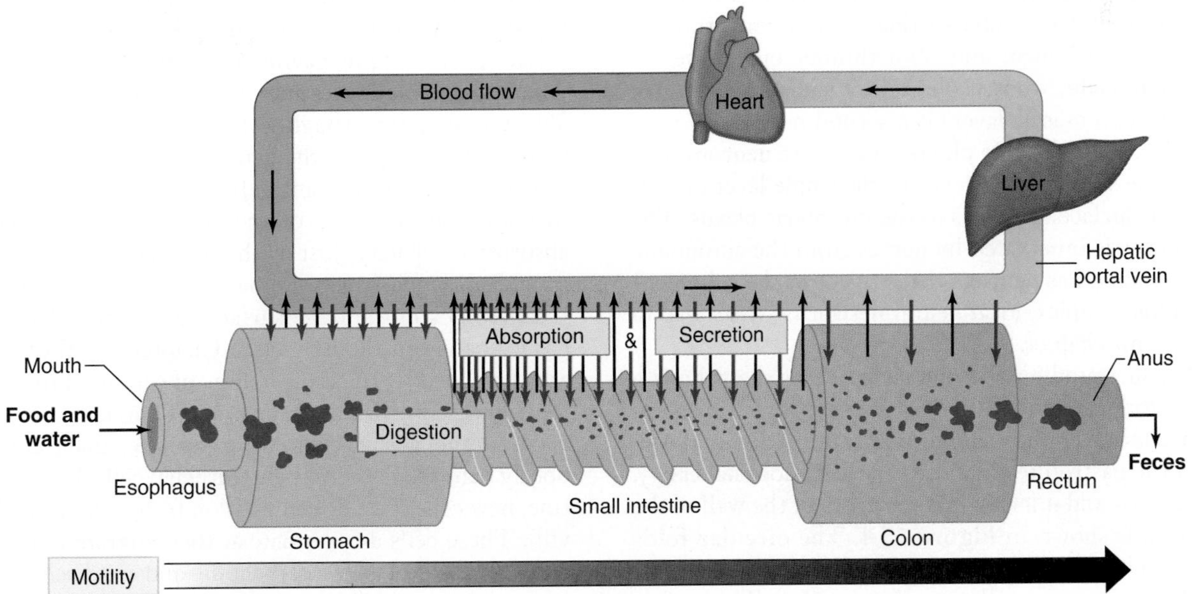

Figure 15.2 APR Four major processes the gastrointestinal tract carries out: digestion, secretion, absorption, and motility. Outward-pointing (black) arrows indicate absorption of the products of digestion, water, minerals, and vitamins into the blood. Inward-pointing (red) arrows represent the secretion of ions, enzymes, and bile salts into the GI tract. The length and density of the arrows indicate the relative importance of each segment of the tract; the small intestine is where most absorption and secretion occurs. The feces represent a fifth function of the GI tract: elimination. The wavy configuration of the small intestine represents muscular contractions (motility) throughout the tract.

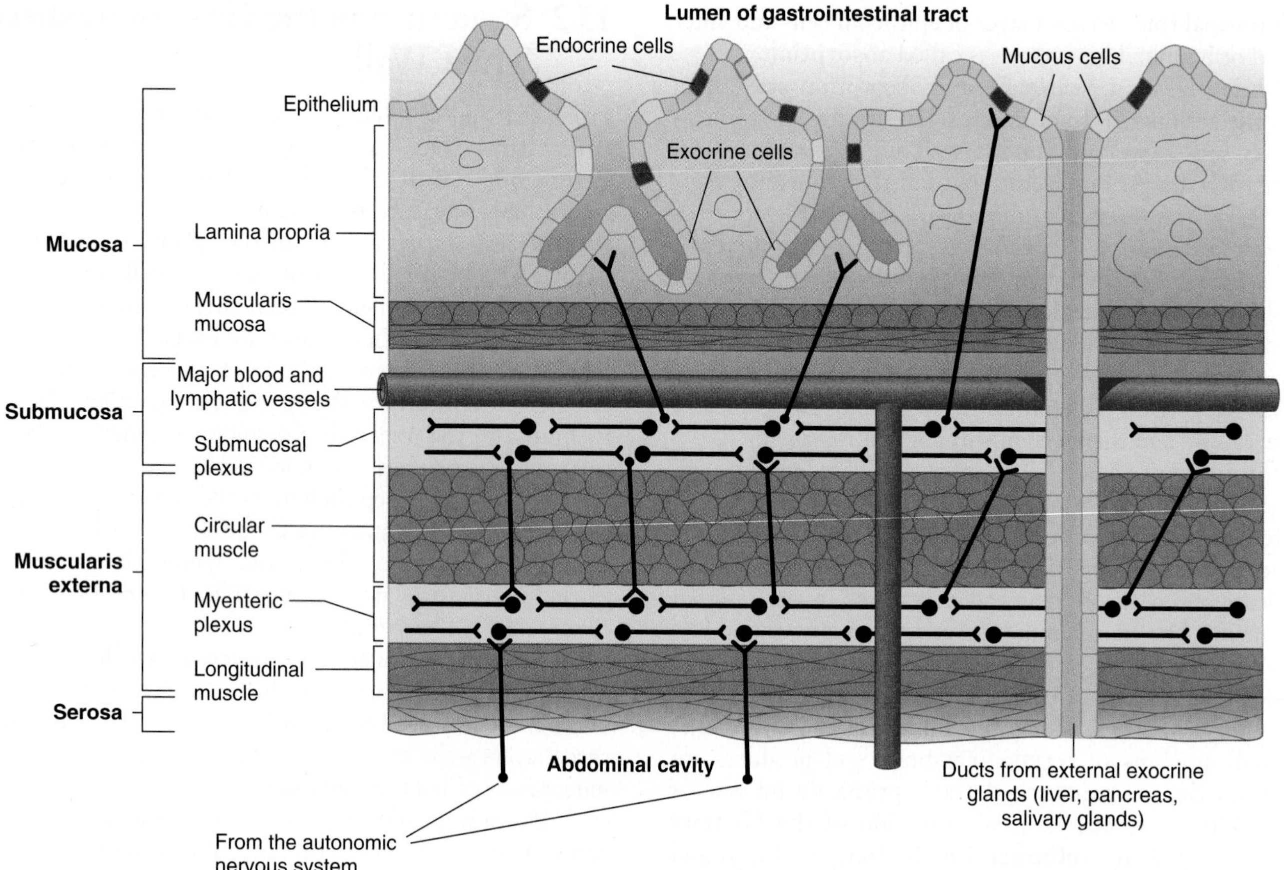

Figure 15.3 APIR Structure of the gastrointestinal wall in longitudinal section. Not shown are the smaller blood vessels and lymphatics and neural terminations on muscles.

muscularis externa has two layers: (1) a relatively thick inner layer of **circular muscle,** whose fibers are oriented in a circular pattern around the tube so that contraction produces a narrowing of the lumen; and (2) a thinner outer layer of **longitudinal muscle,** whose contraction shortens the tube. Between these two muscle layers is a second network of neurons known as the **myenteric plexus.** There are neurons projecting from the submucosal plexus to the single layer of cells on the luminal surface as well as to the myenteric plexus. The myenteric plexus is innervated by nerves from the autonomic nervous system and has neurons that project to the submucosal plexus. This complex, local neural network is described in detail later in this chapter.

Finally, surrounding the outer surface of the tube is a thin layer of connective tissue called the **serosa.** Thin sheets of connective tissue connect the serosa to the abdominal wall and support the gastrointestinal tract in the abdominal cavity.

The macro- and microscopic structure of the wall of the small intestine is shown in **Figure 15.4**. The **circular folds** (mucosa and submucosa) are covered with fingerlike projections called **villi** (singular, **villus;** see Figure 15.4). The surface of each villus is covered with a layer of epithelial cells whose surface membranes form small projections called **microvilli** (singular, **microvillus;** also known collectively as the **brush border**) (**Figure 15.5**). Interspersed between these absorptive epithelial cells with microvilli are **goblet cells** that secrete mucus that lubricates the wall of the small intestine. The combination of circular folds, villi, and microvilli increases the small intestine's surface area about 600-fold over that of a flat-surfaced tube having the same length and diameter. The human small intestine's total surface area is about 250 to 300 square meters, roughly the area of a tennis court. This is a dramatic example of the general principle of physiology that structure is a determinant of function; in this case, the greatly increased surface area of the small intestine maximizes its absorptive capacity. Just as the folding of the cerebral cortex provides a much larger number of neurons in the cranium (see Chapter 6) and the large surface area of the alveoli enhances gas exchange in the lungs (see Chapter 13), the large surface area provided by the morphology of the small intestine allows for the highly efficient absorption of nutrients.

Epithelial surfaces in the gastrointestinal tract are continuously being replaced by new epithelial cells. In the small intestine, new cells arise by cell division from cells at the base of the villi. These cells differentiate as they migrate to the top of the villus, replacing older cells that die and are discharged into the intestinal lumen. These dead cells release their intracellular enzymes into the lumen, which then contribute to the digestive process. About 17 billion epithelial cells are replaced each day, and the entire epithelium of the small intestine is replaced approximately every 5 days. It is because of this rapid cell turnover that the lining of the intestinal tract is so susceptible to

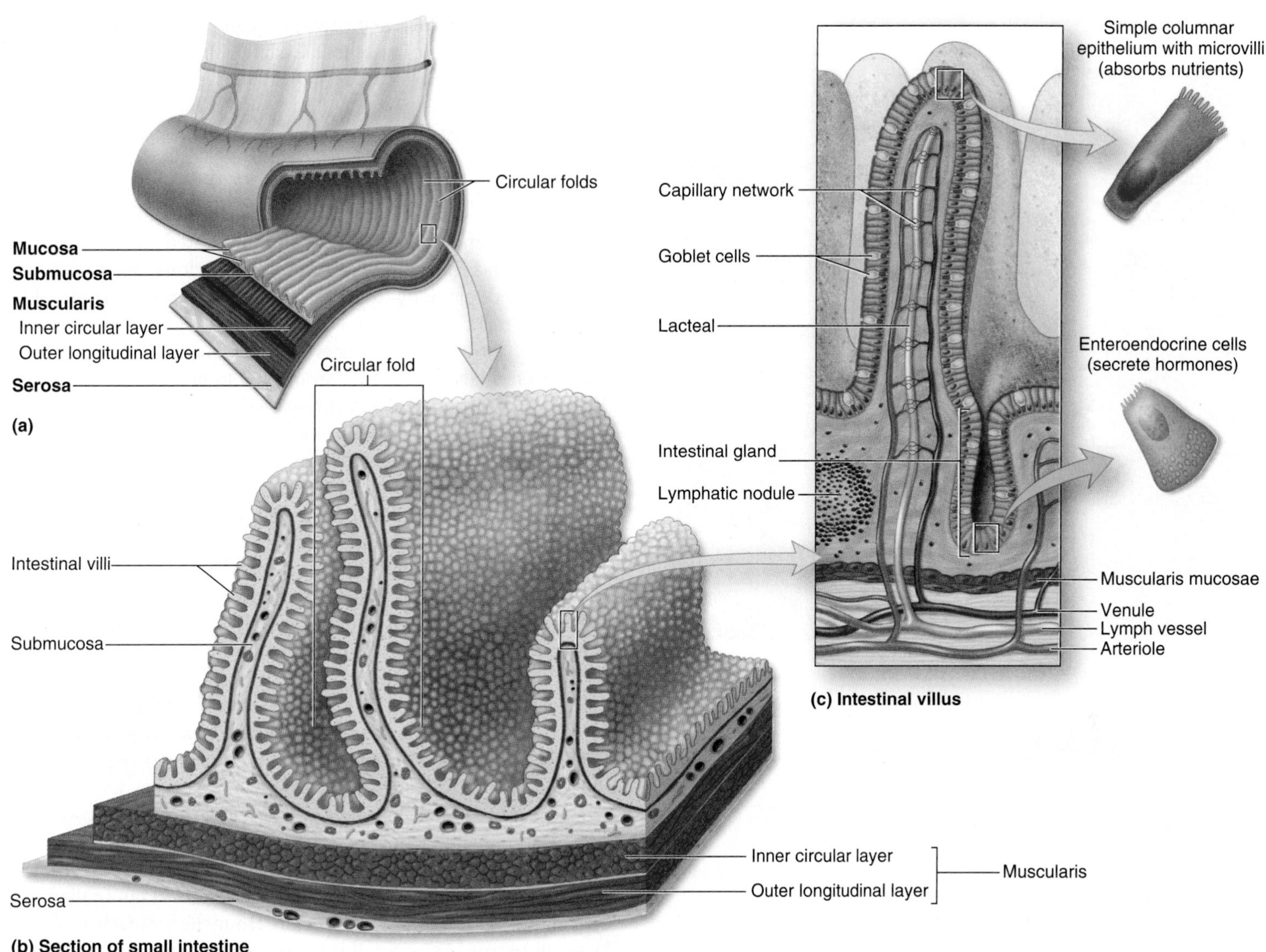

Figure 15.4 APIR Microscopic structure of the small-intestine wall demonstrates increased surface area. (a) Circular folds formed from the mucosa and submucosa increase surface area. (b) Surface area further increased by villi formed from mucosa. (c) Structure of the villus—epithelial microvilli further increase surface area.

damage by treatments that inhibit cell division, such as anticancer drugs and radiation therapy. Also at the base of the villi are **enteroendocrine cells** that secrete hormones that, as you will learn, control a wide variety of gastrointestinal functions, including motility and exocrine pancreatic secretions.

The center of each intestinal villus is occupied by both a single, blind-ended lymphatic vessel—a **lacteal**—and a capillary network (see Figure 15.4). As we will see, most of the fat absorbed in the small intestine enters the lacteals. Material absorbed by the lacteals reaches the general circulation by eventually emptying from the lymphatic system into large veins through a structure called the **thoracic duct.**

Other absorbed nutrients enter the blood capillaries. The venous drainage from the small intestine—as well as from the large intestine, pancreas, and portions of the stomach—does not empty directly into the vena cava but passes first, via the **hepatic portal vein,** to the liver. (The term **hepatic** refers to the liver.) There it flows through a second capillary network before leaving the liver to return to the heart. Because of this portal circulation, material that is absorbed into the intestinal capillaries, in contrast to the lacteals, can be processed by the liver before entering the general circulation. This is important because the liver contains enzymes that can metabolize (detoxify) harmful compounds that may have been ingested, thereby preventing them from entering the circulation. The relationship between the lymphatic system, the circulatory system, and the absorptive surface of the GI tract shown in Figures 15.3 and 15.4 emphasizes the general principle of physiology that there is coordination between the function of different organ systems. One must understand the distribution of blood flow to the GI tract and lymphatic drainage from the GI tract to appreciate its huge absorptive and secretory capacity.

The gastrointestinal tract also has a variety of immune functions, allowing it to produce antibodies and fight

Figure 15.5 APIR Microvilli on the surface of intestinal epithelial cells.

PHYSIOLOGICAL INQUIRY

- Do you recall learning about a brush border in any other body structure? (*Hint:* Refer back to Chapter 14.)

Answer can be found at end of chapter.

infectious organisms that are not destroyed by the acidity of the stomach. For example, the small intestine has regions of immune tissue called **Peyer's patches** that contain immune cells; these cells secrete factors (e.g., cytokines; see Chapter 18) that alter intestinal motility and kill microorganisms.

15.3 General Functions of the Gastrointestinal and Accessory Organs

Using **Table 15.1** as a guide, this section briefly surveys the gastrointestinal functions that will be described in detail later in this chapter. Digestion begins with chewing in the **mouth** where large pieces of food are broken up into smaller particles that we can swallow. **Saliva,** secreted by three pairs of exocrine **salivary glands** located in the head (see Figure 15.1), drains into the mouth through a series of short ducts. Saliva, which contains mucus, moistens and lubricates the food particles before swallowing. It also contains the enzyme **amylase,** which partially digests polysaccharides (complex sugars) described later. A third function of saliva is to dissolve some of the food molecules. Only in the dissolved state can these molecules react with chemoreceptors in the mouth, giving rise to the sensation of taste (see Chapter 7). Finally, saliva has antibacterial properties. See **Table 15.2** for the major functions of saliva.

The next segments of the tract, the **pharynx** and **esophagus,** do not contribute to digestion but provide the pathway for ingested materials to reach the stomach. The muscles in the walls of these segments control swallowing.

The **stomach** is a saclike organ located between the esophagus and the small intestine. Its functions are to store, dissolve, and partially digest the macromolecules in food and to regulate the rate at which the contents of the stomach empty into the small intestine. The acidic environment in the **gastric** (adjective for "stomach") lumen alters the ionization of polar molecules, leading to denaturation of protein (see Chapter 2). This exposes more sites for digestive enzymes to break down the proteins, and disrupts the extracellular network of connective-tissue proteins that form the structural framework of the tissues in food. Polysaccharides and fat are major food components that are not dissolved to a significant extent by acid. The low pH also kills most of the bacteria that enter along with food. This process is not completely effective, and some bacteria survive to colonize and multiply in the gastrointestinal tract, particularly the large intestine.

The digestive actions of the stomach reduce food particles to a solution known as **chyme,** which contains molecular fragments of proteins and polysaccharides; droplets of fat; and salt, water, and various other small molecules ingested in the food. Virtually none of these molecules, except water, can cross the epithelium of the gastric wall, and thus little absorption of organic nutrients occurs in the stomach.

Most absorption and digestion occur in the next section of the tract, the **small intestine,** a tube about 2.4 cm in diameter and 3 m in length, which leads from the stomach to the **large intestine.** (The small intestine is almost twice as long if removed from the abdomen because the muscular wall loses its tone.) Hydrolytic enzymes in the small intestine break down molecules of intact or partially digested carbohydrates, fats, proteins, and nucleic acids into monosaccharides, fatty acids, amino acids, and nucleotides. Some of these enzymes are on the luminal surface of the intestinal lining cells, whereas others are secreted by the pancreas and enter the intestinal lumen. The products of digestion are absorbed across the epithelial cells and enter the blood and/or lymph. Vitamins, minerals, and water, which do not require enzymatic digestion, are also absorbed in the small intestine.

The small intestine is divided into three segments: An initial short segment, the **duodenum,** is followed by the **jejunum** and then by the longest segment, the **ileum.** Normally, most of the chyme entering from the stomach is digested and absorbed in the first quarter of the small intestine in the duodenum and jejunum. Therefore, the small intestine has a very large reserve for the absorption of most nutrients; removal of portions of the small intestine as a treatment for disease does not necessarily result in nutritional deficiencies, depending on which part of the intestine is removed.

Two major organs—the pancreas and liver—secrete substances that flow via ducts into the duodenum. The **pancreas,** an elongated gland located behind the stomach, has both

TABLE 15.1 Functions of the Gastrointestinal Organs

Organ	Exocrine Secretions	Functions Related to Digestion and Absorption
Mouth and pharynx		Chewing begins; initiation of swallowing reflex
Salivary glands	Salt and water	Moisten and dissolve food
	Mucus	Lubrication
	Amylase	Polysaccharide-digesting enzyme
Esophagus		Move food to stomach by peristaltic waves
	Mucus	Lubrication
Stomach		Store, mix, dissolve, and continue digestion of food; regulate emptying of dissolved food into small intestine
	HCl	Solubilization of food particles; kill microbes; activation of pepsinogen to pepsin
	Pepsin	Begin the process of protein digestion in the stomach
	Mucus	Lubricate and protect epithelial surface
Pancreas		Secretion of enzymes and bicarbonate; also has nondigestive endocrine functions
	Enzymes	Digest carbohydrates, fats, proteins, and nucleic acids
	Bicarbonate	Neutralize HCl entering small intestine from stomach
Liver		Secretion of bile
	Bile salts	Solubilize water-insoluble fats
	Bicarbonate	Neutralize HCl entering small intestine from stomach
	Organic waste products and trace metals	Elimination in feces
Gallbladder		Store and concentrate bile between meals
Small intestine		Digestion and absorption of most substances; mixing and propulsion of contents
	Enzymes	Digestion of macromolecules
	Salt and water	Maintain fluidity of luminal contents
	Mucus	Lubrication and protection
Large intestine		Storage and concentration of undigested matter; absorption of salt and water; mixing and propulsion of contents; defecation
	Mucus	Lubrication

endocrine (see Chapter 16) and exocrine functions, but only the latter are directly involved in gastrointestinal function and are described in this chapter. The exocrine portion of the pancreas secretes digestive enzymes and a fluid rich in HCO_3^-. The high acidity of the chyme coming from the stomach would inactivate the pancreatic enzymes in the small intestine if the acid were not neutralized by the HCO_3^- in the pancreatic fluid.

TABLE 15.2 Major Functions of Saliva

Moistens and lubricates food
Initiates small amount of digestion of polysaccharides by amylase (described in detail later)
Dissolves a small amount of food (which facilitates taste)
Kills bacteria

The **liver,** a large organ located in the upper-right portion of the abdomen, has a variety of functions, which are described in various chapters. We will be concerned in this chapter primarily with the liver's exocrine functions that are directly related to the secretion of **bile.**

Bile contains HCO_3^-, cholesterol, phospholipids, bile pigments, a number of organic wastes, and—most important—a group of substances collectively termed **bile salts.** The HCO_3^-, like that from the pancreas, helps neutralize acid from the stomach, whereas the bile salts, as we shall see, solubilize dietary fat. These fats would otherwise be insoluble in water, and their solubilization increases the rates at which they are digested and absorbed.

Bile is secreted by the liver into small ducts that join to form the common hepatic duct. Between meals, secreted bile is stored in the **gallbladder,** a small sac underneath the liver that branches from the common hepatic duct. The gallbladder concentrates the organic molecules in bile by absorbing some salts and water. During a meal, the smooth muscles in the gallbladder wall contract, causing a concentrated bile solution to be injected into the duodenum via the **common bile duct** (**Figure 15.6**), an extension of the common hepatic duct.

In the small intestine, monosaccharides and amino acids are absorbed by specific transporter-mediated processes in the plasma membranes of the intestinal epithelial cells, whereas fatty acids enter these cells primarily by diffusion. Most mineral ions are actively absorbed by transporters, and water diffuses passively down osmotic gradients.

The motility of the small intestine, brought about by the smooth muscles in its walls, (1) mixes the luminal contents with the various secretions, (2) brings the contents into contact with the epithelial surface where absorption takes place, and (3) slowly advances the luminal material toward the large intestine, the next segment of the alimentary canal. Because most substances are absorbed in the small intestine, only a small amount of water, salts, and undigested material passes on to the large intestine. The large intestine temporarily stores the undigested material (some of which is metabolized by bacteria) and concentrates it by absorbing salts and water. Contractions of the **rectum,** the final segment of the large intestine, and relaxation of associated sphincter muscles expel the feces in a process called **defecation.**

The average American adult consumes about 500–800 g of food and 1200 mL of water per day, but this is only a fraction of the material entering the lumen of the gastrointestinal tract. An additional 7000 mL of fluid from salivary glands, gastric glands, pancreas, liver, and intestinal glands is secreted into the tract each day (**Figure 15.7**). Of the approximately 8 L of fluid entering the tract, 99% is absorbed; only about 100 mL is normally lost in the feces. This small amount of fluid loss represents only 4% of the total fluids lost from the body each day. Most fluid loss is via the kidneys and respiratory system. Almost all the salts in the secreted fluids are also reabsorbed into the blood. Moreover, the secreted digestive enzymes are themselves digested, and the resulting amino acids are absorbed into the blood.

Finally, a critical component in the control of gastrointestinal functions is the role of the central nervous system. The CNS receives information from the GI tract (afferent input) and has a vital influence on GI function (efferent output).

This completes our brief overview of some of the general functions of the organs of the digestive system. Because its major tasks are digestion and absorption, we begin our more detailed description with these processes. Subsequent sections of the chapter will then describe, organ by organ, regulation of the secretions and motility that produce the optimal conditions for digestion and absorption.

15.4 Digestion and Absorption

This section describes how ingested nutrients are broken down (digested) and taken up (absorbed) in the GI tract. The process of absorption illustrates the general principle of physiology that controlled exchange of materials occurs between compartments (in this case, from the lumen of the GI tract to the blood and lymph) and across cellular membranes (of the cells lining the GI tract).

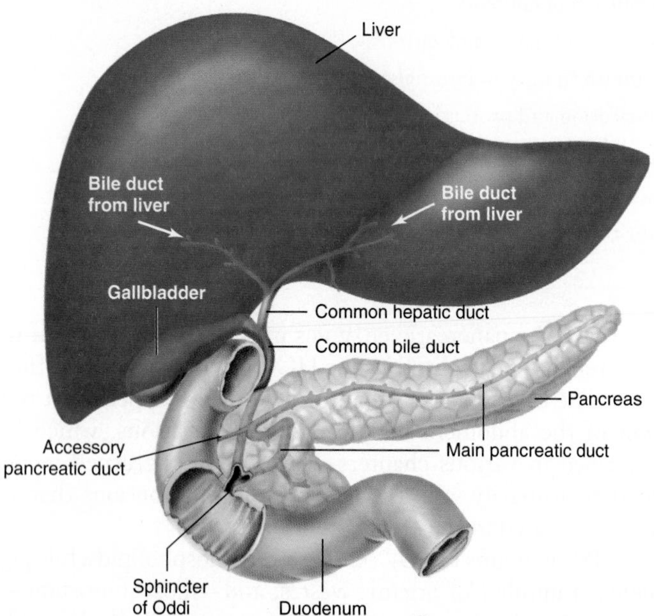

Figure 15.6 APIR Bile ducts from the liver converge to form the common hepatic duct, from which branches the duct leading to the gallbladder. Beyond this branch, the common hepatic duct becomes the common bile duct. The common bile duct and the main pancreatic duct converge and empty their contents into the duodenum at the sphincter of Oddi. Some people have an accessory pancreatic duct.

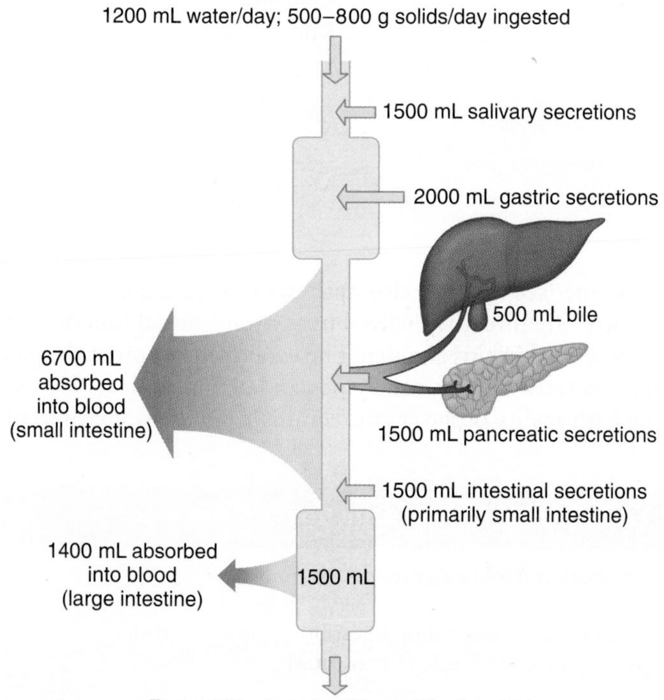

Figure 15.7 Average amounts of solids and fluid ingested, secreted, absorbed, and excreted from the gastrointestinal tract daily.

Carbohydrate

The average daily intake of carbohydrates is about 250 to 300 g per day in a typical American diet. This represents about half the average daily intake of calories. About two-thirds of this carbohydrate is the plant polysaccharide starch, and most of the remainder consists of the disaccharides sucrose (table sugar) and lactose (milk sugar) (**Table 15.3**). Only small amounts of monosaccharides are normally present in the diet. Cellulose and certain other complex polysaccharides found in vegetable matter—referred to as **fiber**—are not broken down by the enzymes in the small intestine and pass on to the large intestine, where they are partially metabolized by bacteria.

The digestion of starch by salivary amylase begins in the mouth but accounts for only a small fraction of total starch digestion. It continues very briefly in the upper part of the stomach before gastric acid inactivates the amylase. Most (~95% or more) starch digestion is completed in the small intestine by pancreatic amylase (**Figure 15.8**). The products of both salivary and pancreatic amylase are the disaccharide maltose and a mixture of short, branched chains of glucose molecules. These products, along with ingested sucrose and lactose, are broken down into monosaccharides—glucose, galactose, and fructose—by enzymes located on the luminal membranes of the small-intestine epithelial cells (brush border). These monosaccharides are then transported across the intestinal epithelium into the blood. Fructose enters the epithelial cells by facilitated diffusion via a glucose transporter (GLUT), whereas glucose and galactose undergo secondary active transport coupled to Na^+ via the sodium–glucose cotransporter (SGLT). These monosaccharides then leave the epithelial cells and enter the interstitial fluid by way of facilitated diffusion via GLUT proteins in the basolateral membranes of the epithelial cells. From there, the monosaccharides diffuse into the blood through capillary pores. Most ingested carbohydrates are digested and absorbed within the first 20% of the small intestine.

TABLE 15.3 Carbohydrates in Food

Class	Examples	Composed Of:
Polysaccharides	Starch	Glucose
	Cellulose	Glucose
	Glycogen	Glucose
Disaccharides	Sucrose	Glucose–fructose
	Lactose	Glucose–galactose
	Maltose	Glucose–glucose
Monosaccharides	Glucose	
	Fructose	
	Galactose	

Protein

A healthy adult requires only 40 to 50 g of protein per day to supply essential amino acids and replace the nitrogen contained in amino acids that are converted to urea. A typical American diet contains about 60 to 90 g of protein per day. This represents about one-sixth of the average daily caloric intake. In addition, a large amount of protein, in the form of enzymes and mucus, is secreted into the gastrointestinal tract or enters it via the disintegration of epithelial cells. Regardless of the source, most of the protein in the lumen is broken down into dipeptides, tripeptides, and amino acids, all of which are absorbed by the small intestine.

Proteins are first partially broken down to peptide fragments in the stomach by **pepsin** that, as you will learn, is produced from a precursor **pepsinogen.** Further breakdown is completed in the small intestine by **trypsin** and **chymotrypsin,** the major proteases secreted by the pancreas. These fragments can be absorbed or are further digested to free amino acids by **carboxypeptidases** from the pancreas and **aminopeptidases,** located on the luminal membranes of the small-intestine

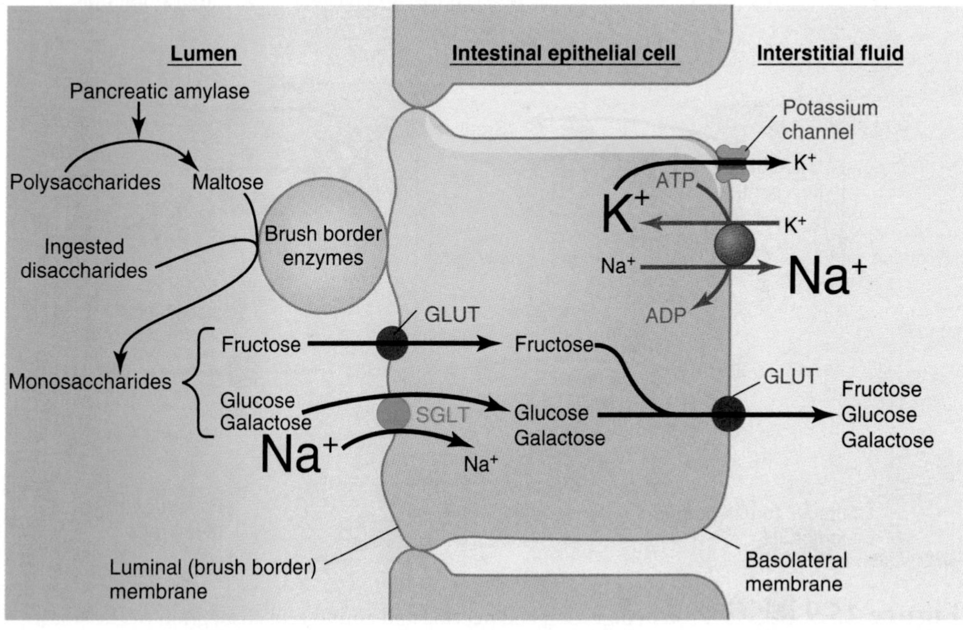

Figure 15.8 APIR Carbohydrate digestion and sugar absorption in the small intestine. Starches (polysaccharides) and ingested small sugars (disaccharides) are metabolized to simple sugars (monosaccharides) by enzymes from the pancreas and on the luminal membrane (brush border). Fructose is absorbed into the cell by facilitated diffusion via a glucose transporter (GLUT). Glucose and galactose are absorbed into the cell by cotransport with Na^+ via sodium–glucose cotransporters (SGLTs). Sugars are then absorbed across the basolateral membrane into the interstitial fluid by facilitated diffusion (GLUTs) and diffuse into the blood. The energy required for absorption is provided primarily by Na^+/K^+-ATPase pumps on the basolateral membrane. Also, remember that carbohydrate digestion begins in the mouth by salivary amylase. The wavy shape of the luminal membrane represents the brush border shown in Figure 15.5.

epithelial cells (**Figure 15.9**). These last two enzymes split off amino acids from the carboxyl and amino ends of peptide chains, respectively. At least 20 different peptidases are located on the luminal membrane of the epithelial cells, with various specificities for the peptide bonds they attack.

Most of the products of protein digestion are absorbed as short chains of two or three amino acids by a secondary active transport coupled to the H^+ gradient (see Figure 15.9). The absorption of small peptides contrasts with carbohydrate absorption, in which molecules larger than monosaccharides are not absorbed. Free amino acids, by contrast, enter the epithelial cells by secondary active transport coupled to Na^+. There are many different amino acid transporters that are specific for the different amino acids, but only one transporter is shown in Figure 15.9 for simplicity. Within the cytosol of the epithelial cell, the dipeptides and tripeptides are hydrolyzed to amino acids; these, along with free amino acids that entered the cells, then leave the cell and enter the interstitial fluid through facilitated-diffusion transporters in the basolateral membranes. As with carbohydrates, protein digestion and absorption are largely completed in the upper portion of the small intestine.

Very small amounts of intact proteins are able to cross the intestinal epithelium and gain access to the interstitial fluid. They do so by a combination of endocytosis and exocytosis. The absorptive capacity for intact proteins is much greater in infants than in adults, and antibodies (proteins involved in the immunologic defense system of the body) secreted into the mother's milk can be absorbed by the infant, providing some immunity until the infant begins to produce his or her own antibodies.

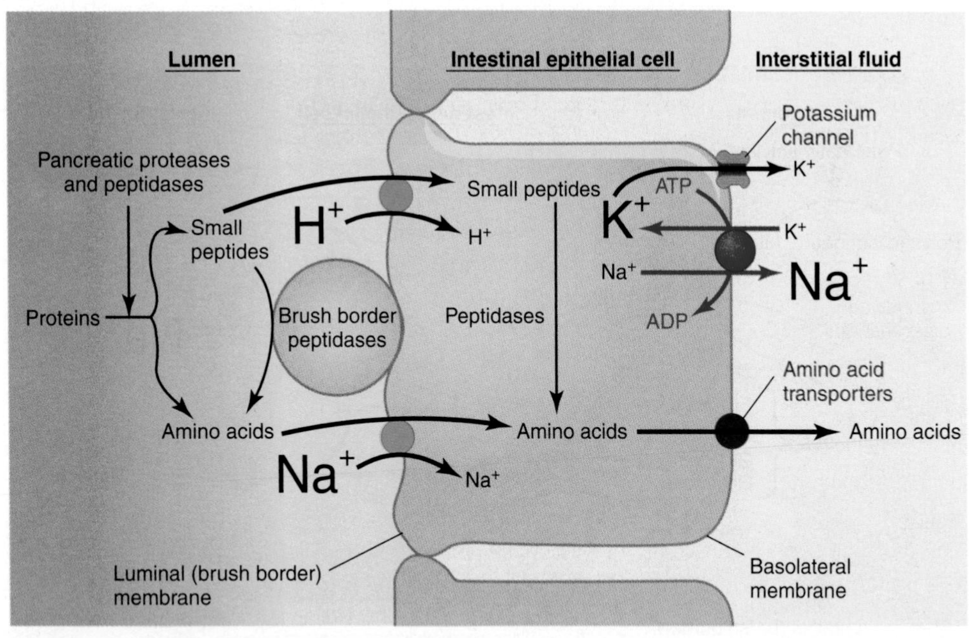

Figure 15.9 APIR Protein digestion and peptide and amino acid absorption in the small intestine. Proteins and peptides are digested in the lumen of the intestine to small peptides and amino acids. Small peptides can be absorbed by cotransport with H^+ into the cytosol where they are catabolized to amino acids by peptidases. Small peptides in the lumen are also catabolized to amino acids by peptidases located on the luminal (brush border) membrane. Amino acids are absorbed into the cytosol by cotransport with Na^+. Amino acids then cross the basolateral membrane by facilitated diffusion via many different specific amino acid transporters (only one is shown in the figure for clarity). Amino acids then diffuse into the blood from the interstitial fluid through capillary pores. The energy for these processes is provided primarily by Na^+/K^+-ATPase pumps on the basolateral membrane. Also remember that protein digestion begins in the acidic environment of the stomach. The wavy shape of the luminal membrane represents the brush border shown in Figure 15.5.

Fat

The average daily intake of lipids is 70 to 100 g per day in a typical American diet, most of this in the form of fat (triglycerides). This represents about one-third of the average daily caloric intake. Triglyceride digestion occurs to a limited extent in the mouth and stomach, but it predominantly occurs in the small intestine. The major digestive enzyme in this process is pancreatic **lipase,** which catalyzes the splitting of bonds linking fatty acids to the first and third carbon atoms of glycerol, producing two free fatty acids and a monoglyceride as products:

$$\text{Triglyceride} \xrightarrow{\text{lipase}} \text{Monoglyceride} + 2 \text{ Fatty acids}$$

The lipids in the ingested foods are insoluble in water and aggregate into large lipid droplets in the upper portion of the stomach. This is like a mixture of oil and vinegar after shaking. Because pancreatic lipase is a water-soluble enzyme, its digestive action in the small intestine can take place only at the *surface* of a lipid droplet. Therefore, if most of the ingested fat remained in large lipid droplets, the rate of triglyceride digestion would be very slow because of the small surface-area-to-volume ratio of these big fat droplets. The rate of digestion is, however, substantially increased by division of the large lipid droplets into many very small droplets, each about 1 mm in diameter, thereby increasing their surface area and accessibility to lipase action. This process is known as **emulsification,** and the resulting suspension of small lipid droplets is an emulsion.

The emulsification of fat requires (1) mechanical disruption of the large lipid droplets into smaller droplets, and (2) an emulsifying agent, which acts to prevent the smaller droplets from reaggregating back into large droplets. The mechanical disruption is provided by the motility of the gastrointestinal tract, occurring in the lower portion of the stomach and in the small intestine, which grinds and mixes the luminal contents. Phospholipids in food, along with phospholipids and bile salts secreted in the bile, provide the emulsifying agents. Phospholipids are amphipathic molecules (see Chapter 2) consisting of two nonpolar fatty acid chains attached to glycerol, with a charged phosphate group located on glycerol's third carbon. Bile salts are formed from cholesterol in the liver and are also amphipathic (**Figure 15.10**). The nonpolar portions of the phospholipids and bile salts associate with the nonpolar interior of the lipid droplets, leaving the polar portions exposed at the water surface. There, they repel other lipid droplets that are similarly coated with these emulsifying agents, thereby preventing their reaggregation into larger fat droplets (**Figure 15.11**).

The coating of the lipid droplets with these emulsifying agents, however, impairs the accessibility of the water-soluble lipase to its lipid substrate. To overcome this problem, the pancreas secretes a protein known as **colipase,** which is amphipathic and lodges on the lipid droplet surface. Colipase binds the lipase enzyme, holding it on the surface of the lipid droplet.

Although emulsification speeds up digestion, absorption of the water-insoluble products of the lipase reaction would still be very slow if it were not for a second action of the bile salts, the formation of **micelles,** which are similar in structure to emulsion droplets but much smaller—4 to 7 nm in diameter. Micelles consist of bile salts, fatty acids, monoglycerides, and phospholipids all clustered together with the polar ends of each molecule oriented toward the micelle's surface and the nonpolar portions forming the micelle's core (**Figure 15.12**). Also included in the core of the micelle are small amounts of fat-soluble vitamins and cholesterol.

How do micelles increase absorption? Although fatty acids and monoglycerides have an extremely low solubility in water, a few molecules do exist in solution and are free to diffuse across the lipid portion of the luminal plasma membranes of the epithelial cells lining the small intestine. Micelles, containing the products of fat digestion, are in equilibrium with the small concentration of fat-digestion products that are free

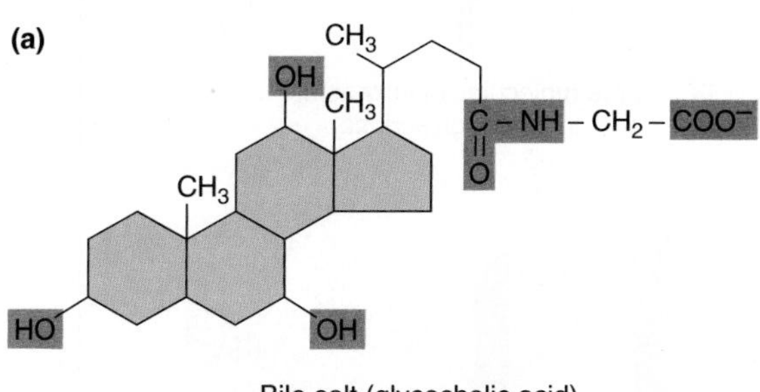

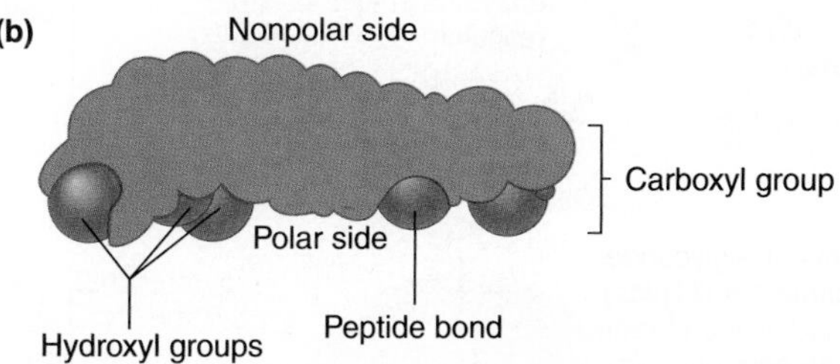

Figure 15.10 Structure of bile salts. (a) Chemical formula of glycocholic acid, one of several bile salts secreted by the liver (polar groups in color). Note the similarity to the structure of steroids (see Figure 11.4). (b) Three-dimensional structure of a bile salt, showing its polar and nonpolar surfaces.

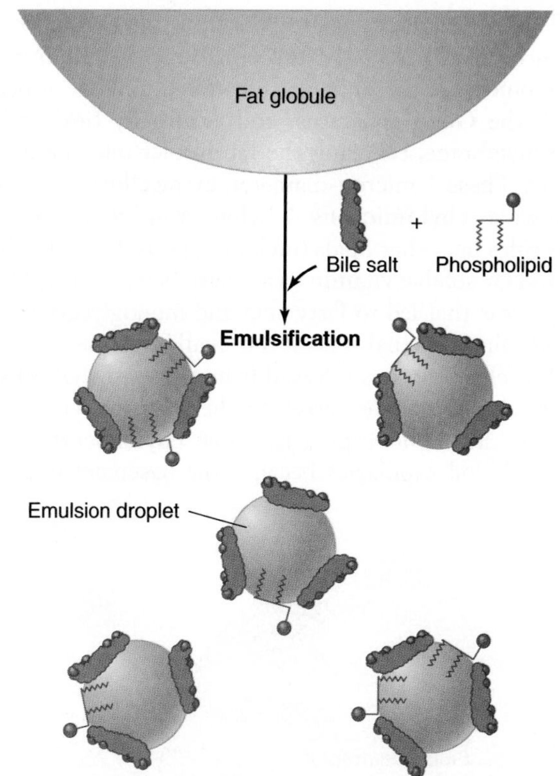

Figure 15.11 Emulsification of fat by bile salts and phospholipids. Note that the nonpolar sides (green) of bile salts and phospholipids are oriented toward fat, whereas the polar sides (red) of these compounds are oriented outward.

in solution. Thus, micelles are continuously breaking down and reforming. As the concentrations of free lipids decrease because of their diffusion into epithelial cells, more lipids are released into the free phase from micelles as they begin to break down (see Figure 15.12). Meanwhile, the process of digestion, which is still ongoing, provides additional small lipids that replenish the micelles. Micelles, therefore, provide a means of keeping most of the insoluble fat-digestion products in small, soluble aggregates, while at the same time replenishing the small amount of products in solution that are free to diffuse into the intestinal epithelium. Note that it is not the micelle that is absorbed but, rather, the individual lipid molecules released from the micelle. You can think of micelles as a "holding station" for small, nonsoluble lipids, releasing their contents slowly to prevent the lipids from coming out of solution while permitting digestion to continue unabated.

Although fatty acids and monoglycerides enter epithelial cells from the intestinal lumen, triglycerides are released on the other side of the cell into the interstitial fluid. In other words, during their passage through the epithelial cells, fatty acids and monoglycerides are resynthesized into triglycerides. This occurs in the smooth endoplasmic reticulum, where the enzymes for triglyceride synthesis are located. This process decreases the concentration of cytosolic free fatty acids and monoglycerides and thereby maintains a diffusion gradient for these molecules into the cell from the intestinal lumen. The resynthesized fat aggregates into small droplets coated with amphipathic proteins that perform an emulsifying function similar to that of bile salts.

The exit of these fat droplets from the cell follows the same pathway as a secreted protein. Vesicles containing the droplet pinch off the endoplasmic reticulum, are processed through the Golgi apparatus, and eventually fuse with the plasma membrane, releasing the fat droplet into the interstitial fluid. These 1-micron-diameter, extracellular fat droplets are known as **chylomicrons.** Chylomicrons contain not only triglycerides but other lipids (including phospholipids, cholesterol, and fat-soluble vitamins) that have been absorbed by the same process that led to fatty acid and monoglyceride movement into the epithelial cells of the small intestine.

The chylomicrons released from the epithelial cells pass into lacteals—lymphatic vessels in the intestinal villi—rather than into the blood capillaries. The chylomicrons cannot enter the blood capillaries because the basement membrane (an extracellular glycoprotein layer) at the outer surface of the capillary provides a barrier to the diffusion of large chylomicrons. In contrast, the lacteals have large pores between their endothelial cells that allow the chylomicrons to pass into the lymph. The lymph from the small intestine, as from everywhere else in the body, eventually empties into systemic veins. In Chapter 16, we describe how the lipids in the circulating blood chylomicrons are made available to the cells of the body.

Figure 15.13 summarizes the pathway fat takes in moving from the intestinal lumen into the lymphatic system.

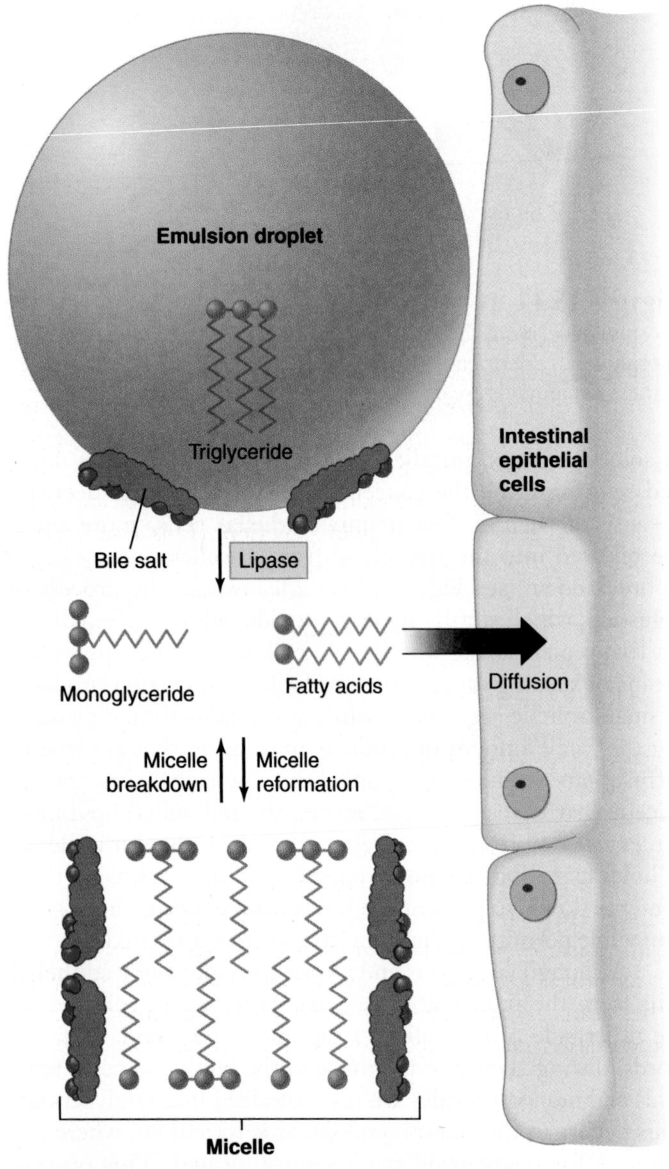

Vitamins

The fat-soluble vitamins—A, D, E, and K—follow the pathway for fat absorption described in the previous section. They are solubilized in micelles; thus, any interference with the secretion of bile or the action of bile salts in the intestine decreases the absorption of the fat-soluble vitamins, a pathological condition called ***malabsorption.*** Malabsorption syndromes can lead

Figure 15.12 The products of fat digestion by lipase are held in solution in the micellar state, combined with bile salts and phospholipids. For simplicity, the phospholipids and colipase (see text) are not shown and the size of the micelle is greatly exaggerated. Note that micelles and free fatty acids are in equilibrium so that as fatty acids are absorbed, more can be released from the micelles.

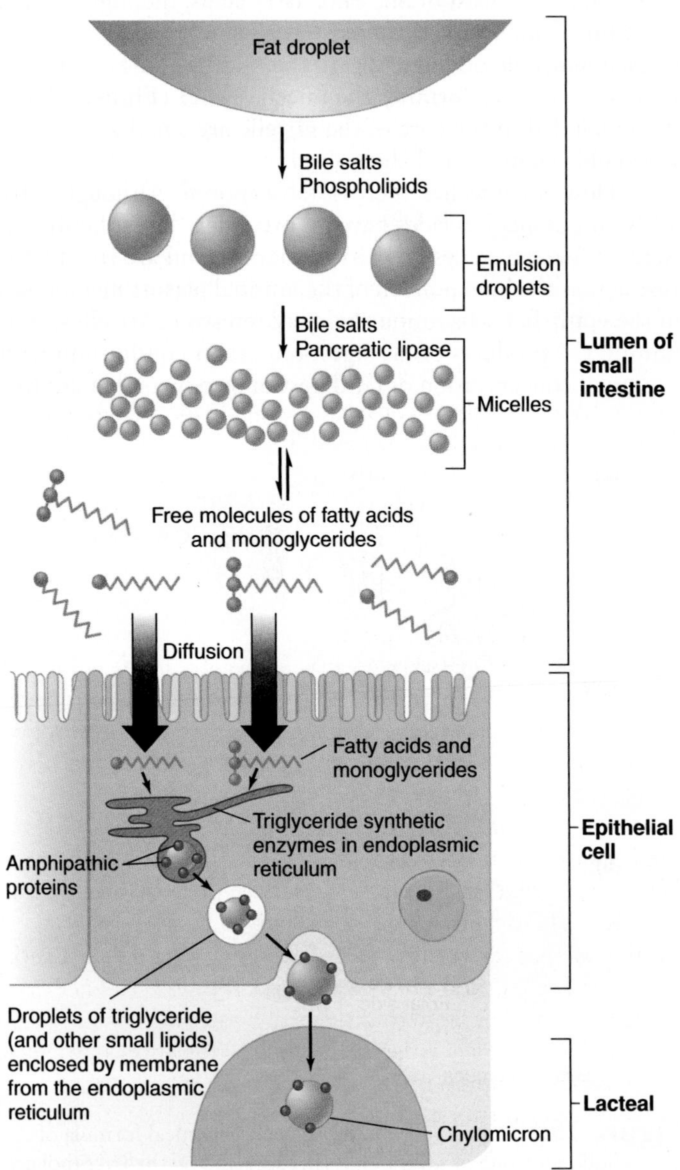

Figure 15.13 Summary of fat absorption across the epithelial cells of the small intestine.

to deficiency of fat-soluble vitamins. For example, ***nontropical sprue***, also known as ***celiac disease*** or ***gluten-sensitive enteropathy***, is due to an autoimmune-mediated loss of intestinal surface area due to sensitivity to the wheat proteins collectively known as **gluten.** The loss of intestinal brush border surface area can lead to decreased absorption of many nutrients, which in turn may result in a variety of health consequences. For example, it is often associated with vitamin D malabsorption, which ultimately results in a decrease in calcium ion absorption in the GI tract (see Chapter 11).

With one exception, water-soluble vitamins are absorbed by diffusion or mediated transport. The exception, vitamin B_{12} (cyanocobalamin), is a very large, charged molecule. To be absorbed, vitamin B_{12} must first bind to a protein known as **intrinsic factor,** which is secreted by the acid-secreting cells in the stomach. Intrinsic factor with bound vitamin B_{12} then binds to specific sites on the epithelial cells in the lower portion of the ileum, where vitamin B_{12} is absorbed by endocytosis. As described in Chapter 12, vitamin B_{12} is required for erythrocyte formation, and deficiencies result in ***pernicious anemia.*** This form of anemia may occur when the stomach either has been removed (for example, to treat ulcers or gastric cancer) or fails to secrete intrinsic factor (often due to autoimmune destruction of acid-producing cells). Because the absorption of vitamin B_{12} occurs in the lower part of the ileum, removal or dysfunction of this segment due to disease can also result in pernicious anemia. Although healthy individuals can absorb oral vitamin B_{12}, it is not very effective in patients with pernicious anemia because of the absence of intrinsic factor. Therefore, the treatment of pernicious anemia usually requires injections of vitamin B_{12}.

Water and Minerals

Water is the most abundant substance in chyme. Approximately 8000 mL of ingested and secreted water enters the small intestine each day, but only 1500 mL passes on to the large intestine because 80% of the fluid is absorbed in the small intestine. Small amounts of water are absorbed in the stomach, but the stomach has a much smaller surface area available for diffusion and lacks the solute-absorbing mechanisms that create the osmotic gradients necessary for net water absorption. The epithelial membranes of the small intestine are very permeable to water, and net water diffusion occurs across the epithelium whenever a water concentration difference is established by the active absorption of solutes. The mechanisms coupling solute and water absorption by epithelial cells were described in Chapter 4.

Na^+ accounts for much of the actively transported solute because it constitutes the most abundant solute in chyme. Na^+ absorption is a primary active process—using the Na^+/K^+-ATPase pumps as described in Chapter 4—and is similar to that for renal tubular Na^+ and water reabsorption (Chapter 14). Cl^- and HCO_3^- are absorbed with the Na^+ and contribute another large fraction of the absorbed solute.

Other minerals present in smaller concentrations, such as potassium, magnesium, and calcium ions, are also absorbed, as are trace elements such as iron, zinc, and iodide. Consideration of the transport processes associated with each of these is beyond the scope of this book, and we shall briefly consider as an example the absorption of only one—iron. Calcium ion absorption and its regulation were described in Chapter 11.

Iron

Iron is necessary for normal health because it is the O_2-binding component of hemoglobin, and it is also a key component of many enzymes. Only about 10% of ingested iron is absorbed into the blood each day. Iron ions are actively transported into intestinal epithelial cells, where most of them are incorporated into **ferritin,** the protein–iron complex that functions as an intracellular iron store (see Chapter 12). The absorbed iron that does not bind to ferritin is released on the blood side, where it circulates throughout the body bound to the plasma protein transferrin. Most of the iron bound to ferritin in the epithelial cells is released back into the intestinal lumen when the cells at the tips of the villi disintegrate, and the iron is then excreted in the feces.

Iron absorption depends on the body's iron content. When body stores are ample, the increased concentration of free iron in the plasma and intestinal epithelial cells leads to an increased transcription of the gene encoding the ferritin protein and, as a consequence, an increased synthesis of ferritin. This results in the increased binding of iron in the intestinal epithelial cells and a reduction in the amount of iron released into the blood. When body stores of iron decrease (for example, after a loss of blood), the production of intestinal ferritin decreases. This leads to a decrease in the amount of iron bound to ferritin, thereby increasing the unbound iron released into the blood.

Once iron has entered the blood, the body has very little means of excreting it, so it accumulates in tissues. Although the control mechanisms for iron absorption tend to maintain the iron content of the body at a fairly constant level, a very large ingestion of iron can overwhelm them, leading to an increased deposition of iron in tissues and producing toxic effects such as changes in skin pigmentation, diabetes mellitus, liver and heart failure, and decreased testicular function. This condition is termed ***hemochromatosis***. Some people have genetically defective control mechanisms and therefore develop hemochromatosis even when iron ingestion is normal. They can be treated with frequent blood withdrawal (***phlebotomy***), which removes iron contained in red blood cells (hemoglobin) from the body.

Iron absorption also depends on the types of food ingested because it binds to many negatively charged ions in food, which can retard its absorption. For example, iron in ingested liver is much more absorbable than iron in egg yolk because the latter contains phosphates that bind the iron to form an insoluble and unabsorbable complex.

The absorption of iron is typical of that of most trace metals in several respects: (1) Cellular storage proteins and plasma carrier proteins are involved; and (2) the control of absorption, rather than urinary excretion, is the major mechanism for the homeostatic control of the body's content of the trace metal.

15.5 How Are Gastrointestinal Processes Regulated?

Unlike control systems that regulate variables in the internal environment, the control mechanisms of the gastrointestinal system regulate conditions in the lumen of the tract. With few exceptions, like those just discussed for iron and other trace metals, these control mechanisms are governed by the volume and composition of the luminal contents rather than by the nutritional state of the body.

Basic Principles

Gastrointestinal reflexes are initiated by a relatively small number of luminal stimuli: (1) distension of the wall by the volume of the luminal contents; (2) chyme osmolarity (total solute concentration); (3) chyme acidity; and (4) chyme concentrations of specific digestion products like monosaccharides, fatty acids, peptides, and amino acids. These stimuli act on mechanoreceptors, osmoreceptors, and chemoreceptors located in the wall of the tract and trigger reflexes that influence the effectors—the muscle layers in the wall of the tract and the exocrine glands that secrete substances into its lumen.

Neural Regulation

The gastrointestinal tract has its own local nervous system, a division of the autonomic nervous system known as the **enteric nervous system.** The cells in this system form two networks or plexuses of neurons, the myenteric plexus and the submucosal plexus (see Figure 15.3). These neurons either synapse with other neurons within a given plexus or end near smooth muscles, glands, and epithelial cells. Many axons leave the myenteric plexus and synapse with neurons in the submucosal plexus, and vice versa, so that neural activity in one plexus influences the activity in the other. Moreover, stimulation at one point in the plexus can lead to impulses that are conducted both up and down the tract. For example, stimuli in the upper part of the small intestine may affect smooth muscle and gland activity in the stomach as well as in the lower part of the intestinal tract. In general, the myenteric plexus influences smooth muscle activity whereas the submucosal plexus influences secretory activity.

The enteric nervous system contains adrenergic and cholinergic neurons as well as neurons that release other neurotransmitters, such as nitric oxide, several neuropeptides, and ATP.

The effectors mentioned earlier—muscle cells and exocrine glands—are supplied by neurons that are part of the enteric nervous system. This permits neural reflexes that are completely within the tract—that is, independent of the CNS. In addition, nerve fibers from both the sympathetic and parasympathetic branches of the autonomic nervous system enter the intestinal tract and synapse with neurons in both plexuses. Via these pathways, the CNS can influence the motility and secretory activity of the gastrointestinal tract.

Thus, two types of neural-reflex arcs exist (**Figure 15.14**): (1) **short reflexes** from receptors through the nerve plexuses to effector cells; and (2) **long reflexes** from receptors in the tract to the CNS by way of afferent nerves, and back to the nerve plexuses and effector cells by way of autonomic nerve fibers.

Finally, it should be noted that not all neural reflexes are initiated by signals *within* the tract. Hunger, the sight or smell of food, and the emotional state of an individual can have significant effects on the gastrointestinal tract, effects that are mediated by the CNS via autonomic neurons.

Hormonal Regulation

The hormones that control the gastrointestinal system are secreted mainly by endocrine cells scattered throughout the epithelium of the stomach and small intestine. That is, these cells

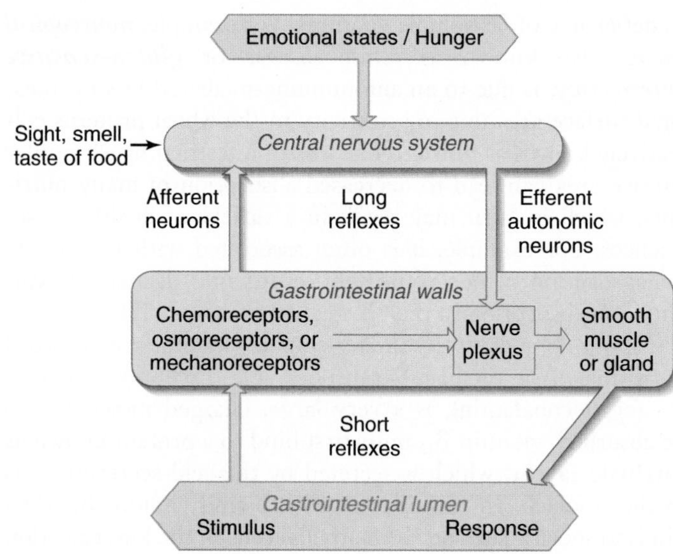

Figure 15.14 APR Long and short neural-reflex pathways activated by stimuli in the gastrointestinal tract. The long reflexes utilize neurons that link the central nervous system to the gastrointestinal tract. Chemoreceptors are stimulated by chemicals, osmoreceptors are sensitive to changes in osmolarity (salt concentration), and mechanoreceptors respond to distension of the gastrointestinal wall.

are not clustered into discrete organs like the thyroid or adrenal glands. One surface of each endocrine cell is exposed to the lumen of the gastrointestinal tract. At this surface, various chemical substances in the chyme stimulate the cell to release its hormones from the opposite side of the cell into the blood. The gastrointestinal hormones reach their target cells via the circulation.

The four best-understood gastrointestinal hormones are **secretin, cholecystokinin (CCK), gastrin,** and **glucose-dependent insulinotropic peptide (GIP). Table 15.4** summarizes the characteristics of these GI hormones and not only serves as a reference for future discussions but also illustrates the following generalizations: (1) Each hormone participates in a feedback control system that regulates some aspect of the GI luminal environment, and (2) most GI hormones affect more than one type of target cell.

These two generalizations can be illustrated by CCK. The presence of fatty acids and amino acids in the small intestine triggers CCK secretion from cells in the small intestine into the blood. Circulating CCK then stimulates the pancreas to increase the secretion of digestive enzymes and causes the sphincter of Oddi to relax. CCK also causes the gallbladder to contract, delivering to the intestine the bile salts required for micelle formation. As fatty acids and amino acids are absorbed, their concentrations in the lumen decrease, removing the signal for CCK release.

In many cases, a single effector cell contains receptors for more than one hormone, as well as receptors for neurotransmitters and paracrine agents. The result is a variety of inputs that can affect the cell's response. One such event is the phenomenon known as **potentiation,** which is exemplified by the interaction between secretin and CCK. Secretin strongly stimulates pancreatic HCO_3^- secretion, whereas CCK is a weak stimulus of HCO_3^- secretion. Both hormones together, however, stimulate pancreatic HCO_3^- secretion more strongly

TABLE 15.4 Properties of Gastrointestinal Hormones

	Gastrin	CCK	Secretin	GIP
Chemical class	Peptide	Peptide	Peptide	Peptide
Site of production	Antrum of stomach	Small intestine	Small intestine	Small intestine
Stimuli for hormone release	Amino acids, peptides in stomach; parasympathetic nerves	Amino acids, fatty acids in small intestine	Acid in small intestine	Glucose, fat in small intestine
Factors inhibiting hormone release	Acid in stomach; somatostatin			
		Target Organ Responses		
Stomach				
Acid secretion	Stimulates	Inhibits	Inhibits	
Motility	Stimulates	Inhibits	Inhibits	
Pancreas				
HCO_3^- secretion		Potentiates secretin's actions	Stimulates	
Enzyme secretion		Stimulates	Potentiates CCK's actions	
Insulin secretion				Stimulates
Liver (bile ducts)				
HCO_3^- secretion		Potentiates secretin's actions	Stimulates	
Gallbladder				
Contraction		Stimulates		
Sphincter of Oddi		Relaxes		
Small intestine				
Motility	Stimulates ileum			
Large intestine	Stimulates mass movement			

PHYSIOLOGICAL INQUIRY

- Gastrinomas are tumors of the GI tract that secrete gastrin, leading to very high plasma concentrations. What might be some of the effects of a gastrinoma?

Answer can be found at end of chapter.

than would be predicted by the sum of their individual stimulatory effects. This is because CCK amplifies the response to secretin. One of the consequences of potentiation is that small changes in the plasma concentration of one gastrointestinal hormone can have large effects on the actions of other gastrointestinal hormones. In addition to their stimulation (or, in some cases, inhibition) of effector cell functions, the gastrointestinal hormones also have trophic (growth-promoting) effects on various tissues, including the gastric and intestinal mucosa and the exocrine portions of the pancreas. Finally, many additional GI hormones have been described, some of which are involved in the control of blood glucose by serving as a feedforward signal from the GI tract to the endocrine pancreas (see Chapter 16).

Phases of Gastrointestinal Control

The neural and hormonal control of the gastrointestinal system is, in large part, divisible into three phases—cephalic, gastric, and intestinal—according to where the stimulus is perceived.

The **cephalic** (from a Greek word for "head") **phase** is initiated when sensory receptors in the head are stimulated by sight, smell, taste, and chewing. Various emotional states can also initiate this phase. The efferent pathways for these reflexes are primarily mediated by parasympathetic fibers carried in the vagus nerves. These fibers activate neurons in the gastrointestinal nerve plexuses, which in turn affect secretory and contractile activity.

Four stimuli in the stomach initiate the reflexes that constitute the **gastric phase** of regulation: distension, acidity, amino acids, and peptides formed during the digestion of ingested protein. The responses to these stimuli are mediated by short and long neural reflexes and by release of the hormone gastrin.

Finally, the **intestinal phase** is initiated by stimuli in the intestinal tract: distension, acidity, osmolarity, and various digestive products. The intestinal phase is mediated by both short and long neural reflexes and by the gastrointestinal hormones secretin, CCK, and GIP, all of which are secreted by endocrine cells in the small intestine.

We reemphasize that each of these phases is named for the site at which the various stimuli initiate the reflex and not for the sites of effector activity. Each phase is characterized by efferent output to virtually all organs in the gastrointestinal tract. Also, these phases do not occur in temporal sequence except at the very beginning of a meal. Rather, during ingestion and the much longer absorptive period, reflexes characteristic of all three phases may be occurring simultaneously.

Keeping in mind the neural and hormonal mechanisms available for regulating gastrointestinal activity, we can now examine the specific contractile and secretory processes that occur in each segment of the gastrointestinal system.

Mouth, Pharynx, and Esophagus

Chewing

Chewing is controlled by the somatic nerves to the skeletal muscles of the mouth and jaw. In addition to the voluntary control of these muscles, rhythmic chewing motions are reflexively activated by the pressure of food against the gums, hard palate at the roof of the mouth, and tongue. Activation of these mechanoreceptors leads to reflexive inhibition of the muscles holding the jaw closed. The resulting relaxation of the jaw reduces the pressure on the various mechanoreceptors, leading to a new cycle of contraction and relaxation.

Chewing prolongs the subjective pleasure of taste. Chewing also breaks up food particles, creating a bolus that is easier to swallow and, possibly, digest. Attempting to swallow a large particle of food can lead to choking if the particle lodges over the trachea, blocking the entry of air into the lungs.

Saliva

There are three pairs of salivary glands—the parotid, sublingual, and submandibular glands (see Figure 15.1). The secretion of saliva is controlled by both sympathetic and parasympathetic neurons. Unlike their antagonistic activity in most organs, both systems stimulate salivary secretion, with the parasympathetic neurons producing the greater response. There is no hormonal regulation of salivary secretion. In the absence of ingested material, a low rate of salivary secretion keeps the mouth moist. The smell or sight of food induces a cephalic phase of salivary secretion. This reflex can be conditioned to other cues, a phenomenon made famous by Pavlov. Salivary secretion can increase markedly in response to a meal. This reflex response is initiated by chemoreceptors (acidic fruit juices are particularly strong stimuli) and pressure receptors in the walls of the mouth and on the tongue.

Increased saliva secretion is accomplished by a large increase in blood flow to the salivary glands, which is mediated primarily by an increase in parasympathetic neural activity. The volume of saliva secreted per gram of tissue is the largest secretion of any of the body's exocrine glands.

Sjögren's syndrome is a fascinating immune disorder in which many different exocrine glands are rendered nonfunctional by the infiltration of white blood cells and immune complexes. The loss of salivary gland function, which frequently occurs, can be treated by taking frequent sips of water and with oral fluoride treatment to prevent tooth decay. In addition, these patients—mostly women—can have an impaired sense of taste, difficulty chewing, and even ulcers (holes) in the mucosa of the mouth.

Swallowing

Swallowing is a complex reflex initiated when pressure receptors in the walls of the pharynx are stimulated by food or drink forced into the rear of the mouth by the tongue (**Figure 15.15a**). These receptors send afferent impulses to the **swallowing center** in the medulla oblongata of the brainstem. This center then elicits swallowing via efferent fibers to the muscles in the pharynx and esophagus as well as to the respiratory muscles.

As the ingested material moves into the pharynx, the soft palate elevates and lodges against the back wall of the pharynx, preventing food from entering the nasal cavity (**Figure 15.15b**). Impulses from the swallowing center inhibit respiration, raise the larynx, and close the **glottis** (the area around the vocal cords and the space between them), keeping food from moving into the trachea. As the tongue forces the food farther back into the pharynx, the food tilts a flap of tissue, the **epiglottis,** backward to cover the closed glottis (**Figure 15.15c**). This prevents **aspiration** of food, a potentially dangerous situation in which food travels down the trachea and can cause choking, or regurgitated stomach contents are allowed into the lungs causing damage.

The next stage of swallowing occurs in the esophagus (**Figure 15.15d**), the tube that passes through the thoracic cavity, penetrates the diaphragm (which separates the thoracic cavity from the abdominal cavity), and joins the stomach a few centimeters below the diaphragm. Skeletal muscle surrounds the upper third of the esophagus, and smooth muscle surrounds the lower two-thirds.

As described in Chapter 13, the pressure in the thoracic cavity is negative relative to atmospheric pressure, and this subatmospheric pressure is transmitted across the thin wall of the intrathoracic portion of the esophagus to the lumen. In contrast, the luminal pressure in the pharynx at the opening to the esophagus is equal to atmospheric pressure, and the pressure at the opposite end of the esophagus in the stomach is slightly greater than atmospheric pressure. Therefore, pressure differences could tend to force both air (from above) and gastric contents (from below) into the esophagus. This does not occur, however, because both ends of the esophagus are normally closed by the contraction of **sphincter** muscles. A ring of skeletal muscle surrounds the esophagus just below the pharynx and forms the **upper esophageal sphincter** (see Figure 15.15), whereas the smooth muscle in the last portion of the esophagus forms the **lower esophageal sphincter** (**Figure 15.16**).

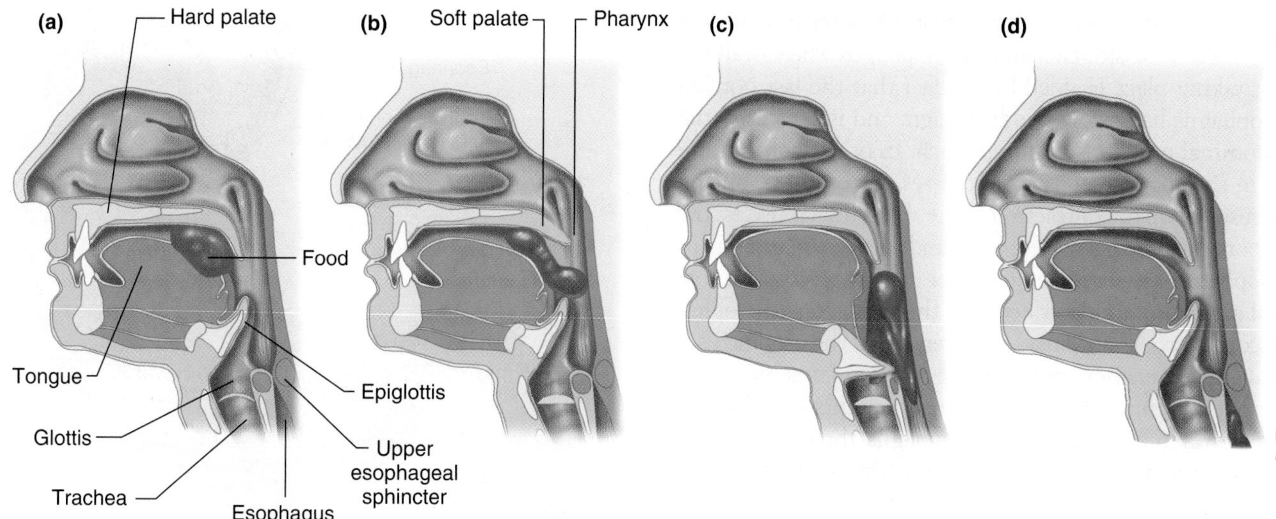

Figure 15.15 APIR Movements of food through the pharynx and upper esophagus during swallowing. (a) The tongue pushes the food bolus to the back of the pharynx. (b) The soft palate elevates to prevent food from entering the nasal passages. (c) The epiglottis covers the glottis to prevent food or liquid from entering the trachea (aspiration), and the upper esophageal sphincter relaxes. (d) Food descends into the esophagus.

PHYSIOLOGICAL INQUIRY

- Referring to parts (b) and (c), what are some of the consequences of aspiration?

Answer can be found at end of chapter.

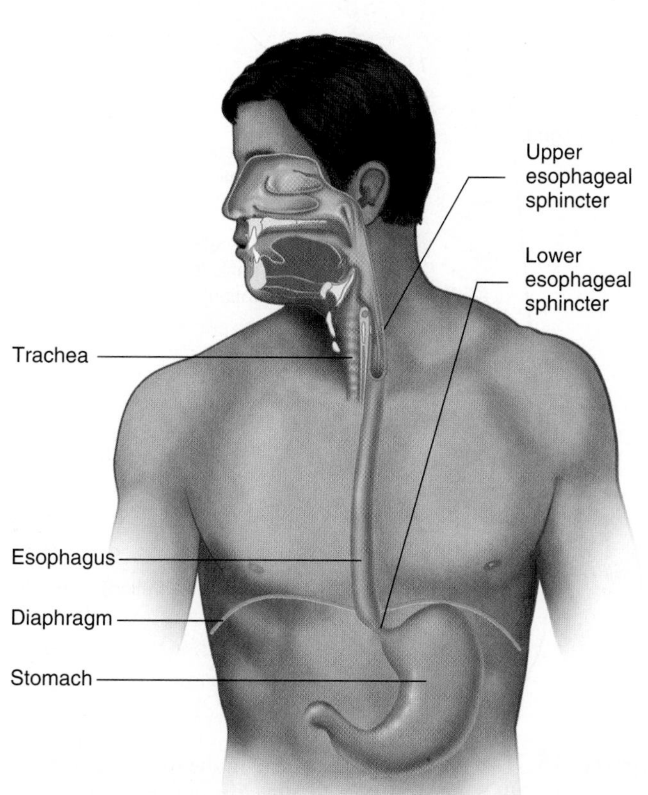

Figure 15.16 APIR Location of upper and lower esophageal sphincters.

The esophageal phase of swallowing begins with relaxation of the upper esophageal sphincter. Immediately after the food has passed, the sphincter closes, the glottis opens, and breathing resumes. Once in the esophagus, the food moves toward the stomach by a progressive wave of muscle contractions that proceeds along the esophagus, compressing the lumen and forcing the food ahead. Such waves of contraction in the muscle layers surrounding a tube are known as **peristaltic waves.** One esophageal peristaltic wave takes about 9 seconds to reach the stomach. Swallowing can occur even when a person is upside down or in zero gravity (outer space) because it is not primarily gravity but the peristaltic wave that moves the food to the stomach.

The lower esophageal sphincter opens and remains relaxed throughout the period of swallowing, allowing the arriving food to enter the stomach. After the food passes, the sphincter closes, resealing the junction between the esophagus and the stomach.

The act of swallowing is a neural and muscular reflex coordinated by a group of brainstem nuclei collectively called the swallowing center. Both skeletal and smooth muscles are involved, so the swallowing center must direct efferent activity in both somatic nerves (to skeletal muscle) and autonomic nerves (to smooth muscle). Simultaneously, afferent fibers from receptors in the esophageal wall send information to the swallowing center; this can alter the efferent activity. For example, if a large food bolus does not reach the stomach during the initial peristaltic wave, the maintained distension of the esophagus by the bolus activates receptors that initiate reflexes, causing repeated waves of peristaltic activity (**secondary peristalsis**).

The ability of the lower esophageal sphincter to maintain a barrier between the stomach and the esophagus when swallowing is not taking place is aided by the fact that the last portion of the esophagus lies below the diaphragm and is subject to the same abdominal pressures as the stomach. In other words, if the pressure in the abdominal cavity increases, for example, during cycles of respiration or contraction of the abdominal muscles, the pressures on both the gastric contents and the terminal segment of the esophagus are increased together. This prevents the formation of a pressure gradient between the stomach and esophagus that could force the stomach's contents into the esophagus.

During pregnancy, the growth of the fetus not only increases the pressure on the abdominal contents but also can push the terminal segment of the esophagus through the diaphragm into the thoracic cavity. The sphincter is therefore no longer assisted by changes in abdominal pressure. Consequently, during the last half of pregnancy, increased abdominal pressure tends to force some of the gastric contents up into the esophagus (***gastroesophageal reflux***). The **hydrochloric acid** from the stomach irritates the esophageal walls, producing pain known as ***heartburn*** (because the pain appears to be located in the area of the heart). Heartburn often subsides in the last weeks of pregnancy prior to delivery, as the uterus descends lower into the pelvis, decreasing the pressure on the stomach.

Gastroesophageal reflux and the pain of heartburn also occur in the absence of pregnancy. Some people have less efficient lower esophageal sphincters, resulting in repeated episodes of gastric contents refluxing into the esophagus. In extreme cases, ulceration, scarring, obstruction, or perforations (holes) of the lower esophagus may occur. Gastroesophageal reflux can also occur after a large meal, which can sufficiently increase the pressure in the stomach to force acid into the esophagus. It can also cause coughing and irritation of the larynx in the absence of any esophageal symptoms, and it has even been implicated in the onset of asthmatic symptoms in susceptible individuals.

The lower esophageal sphincter undergoes brief periods of relaxation not only during a swallow but also in the absence of a swallow. During these periods of relaxation, small amounts of the acid contents from the stomach normally reflux into the esophagus. The acid in the esophagus triggers a secondary peristaltic wave and also stimulates increased salivary secretion, which helps to neutralize the acid and clear it from the esophagus.

Stomach

The epithelial layer lining the stomach invaginates into the mucosa, forming many tubular glands. Glands in the thin-walled upper portions of the **body** of the stomach (**Figure 15.17**) secrete mucus, hydrochloric acid, and the enzyme precursor pepsinogen. The uppermost part of the body of the stomach is called the **fundus** and is functionally part of the body. The lower portion of the stomach, the **antrum,** has a much thicker layer of smooth muscle and is responsible for mixing and grinding the stomach contents. The glands in this region secrete little acid but contain the endocrine cells that secrete the hormone gastrin.

The cells at the opening of the glands secrete mucus (**Figure 15.18**). Lining the walls of the glands are **parietal cells** (also known as oxyntic cells), which secrete acid and intrinsic

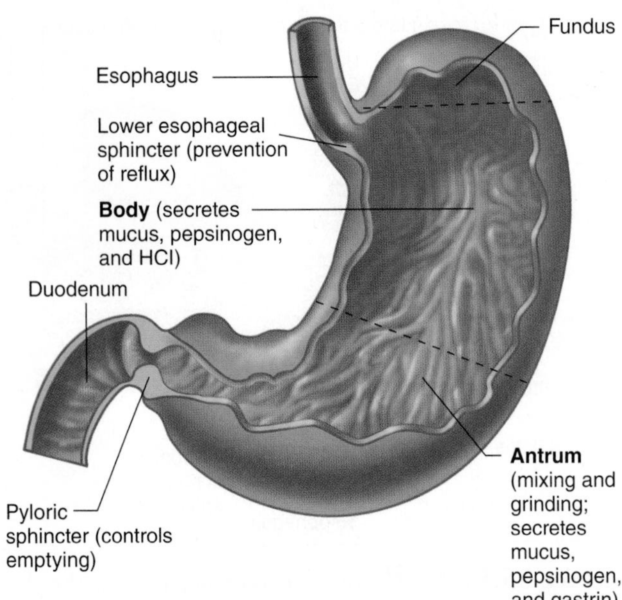

Figure 15.17 APIR The two regions of the stomach: body and antrum. The fundus is the uppermost portion of the body of the stomach and is functionally considered part of the body.

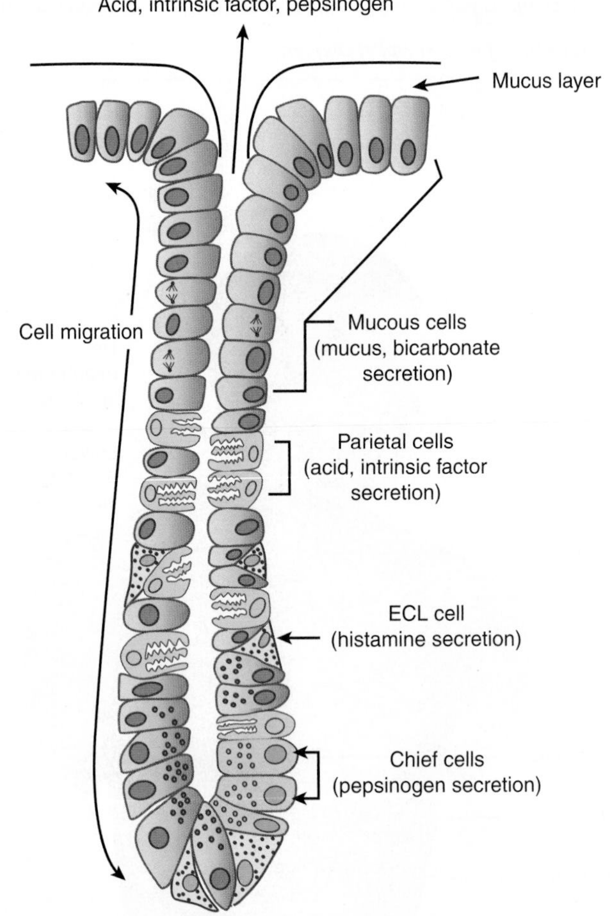

Figure 15.18 APIR A gastric gland in the stomach. Not shown are D cells, which release somatostatin and are located primarily in and around the glands in the antral region. The unique invaginations of the luminal membranes of parietal cells are called canaliculi and greatly increase the surface area for secretion.

factor, and **chief cells,** which secrete pepsinogen. The unique invaginations of the luminal membrane of parietal cells shown in Figure 15.18 are called **canaliculi** (singular, **canaliculus**); these increase the surface area of the parietal cells thereby maximizing secretion into the lumen of the stomach. This again illustrates the general principle of physiology that structure (increased surface area) is a determinant of function (efficient secretion). Thus, each of the three major exocrine secretions of the stomach—mucus, acid, and pepsinogen—is secreted by a different cell type. The gastric glands in the antrum also contain enteroendocrine cells, which secrete gastrin. In addition, **enterochromaffin-like (ECL) cells,** which release the paracrine agent histamine, and endocrine cells called D cells, which secrete the peptide **somatostatin,** are scattered throughout the tubular glands or in surrounding tissue; both of these substances play roles in regulating acid secretion by the stomach.

HCl Production and Secretion

The stomach secretes about 2 L of hydrochloric acid per day. The concentration of H^+ in the lumen of the stomach may reach >150 mM, which is 1 to 3 million times greater than the concentration in the blood. This requires an efficient production mechanism to generate large numbers of hydrogen ions. The origin of the hydrogen ions is CO_2 in the parietal cell. Recall from Chapter 13 that the enzyme carbonic anhydrase catalyzes the reaction between CO_2 with water to produce carbonic acid, which dissociates to H^+ and HCO_3^-. Primary H^+/K^+-ATPases in the luminal membrane of the parietal cells pump these hydrogen ions into the lumen of the stomach (**Figure 15.19**). This primary active transporter also pumps K^+ into the cell, which then leaks back into the lumen through K^+ channels. As H^+ is secreted into the lumen, HCO_3^- is secreted on the opposite side of the cell into the blood in exchange for Cl^-. Removal of the end products of this reaction enhance the forward rate of the reaction by the law of mass action (see Chapter 3). In this way, production and secretion of H^+ are coupled.

Increased acid secretion, stimulated by factors described in the next paragraph, results from the transfer of H^+/K^+-ATPase proteins from the membranes of intracellular vesicles to the plasma membrane by fusion of these vesicles with the membrane, thereby increasing the number of pump proteins in the plasma membrane. This process is analogous to that described in Chapter 14 for the transfer of water channels (aquaporins) to the plasma membrane of kidney collecting-duct cells in response to ADH.

Four chemical messengers regulate the insertion of H^+/K^+-ATPases into the plasma membrane and therefore acid secretion: gastrin (a gastric hormone), acetylcholine (ACh, a neurotransmitter), histamine, and somatostatin (two paracrine agents). Parietal cell membranes contain receptors for all four of these molecules (**Figure 15.20**). Somatostatin inhibits acid secretion, whereas the other three stimulate secretion. This illustrates the general principle of physiology that most physiological functions—in this case, the secretion of H^+ into the stomach lumen—are controlled by multiple regulatory systems, often working in opposition.

These chemical messengers not only act directly on the parietal cells but also influence each other's secretion. For example, histamine markedly potentiates the response to the other two stimuli, gastrin and ACh. As we will discuss later

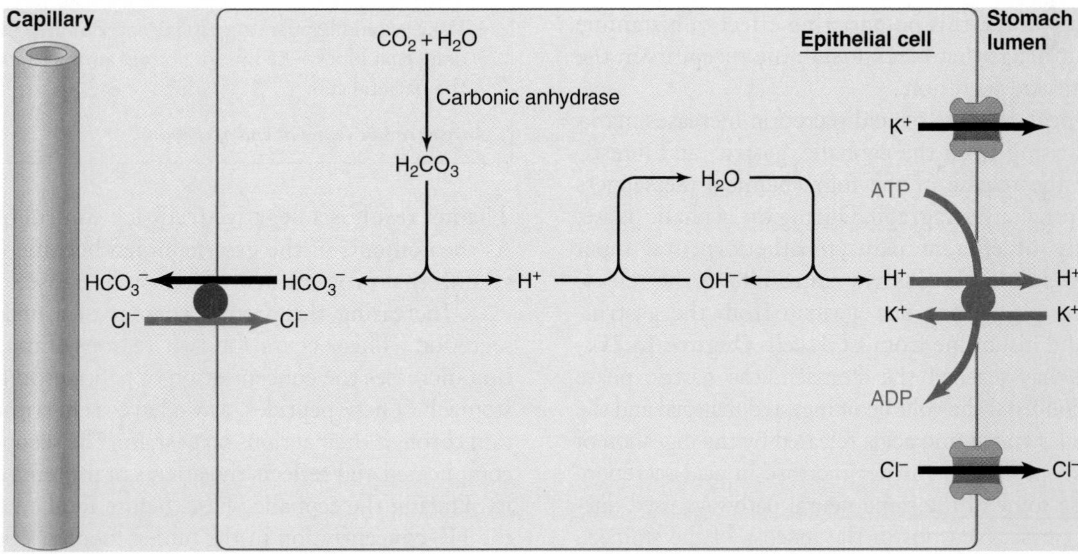

Figure 15.19 APR Secretion of hydrochloric acid by parietal cells. The H^+ secreted into the lumen by primary active transport is derived from the breakdown of water molecules, leaving hydroxyl ion (OH^-) behind. This OH^- is neutralized by combination with other H^+ generated by the reaction between carbon dioxide and water, a reaction catalyzed by the enzyme carbonic anhydrase, which is present in high concentrations in parietal cells. The HCO_3^- formed by this reaction is transported out of the parietal cell on the blood side in exchange for Cl^-.

PHYSIOLOGICAL INQUIRY

- Why doesn't the high concentration of H^+ in the stomach lumen destroy the lining of the stomach wall?

Answer can be found at end of chapter.

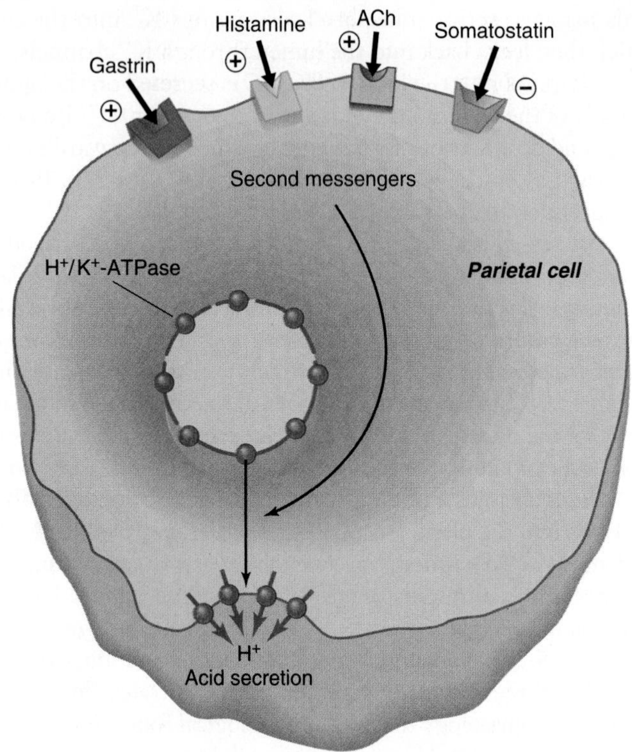

Figure 15.20 APIR The four neurohumoral inputs to parietal cells that regulate acid secretion by generating second messengers. These second messengers control the transfer of the H^+/K^+-ATPase pumps in cytoplasmic vesicle membranes to the plasma membrane. Not shown are the effects of peptides and amino acids on acid secretion.

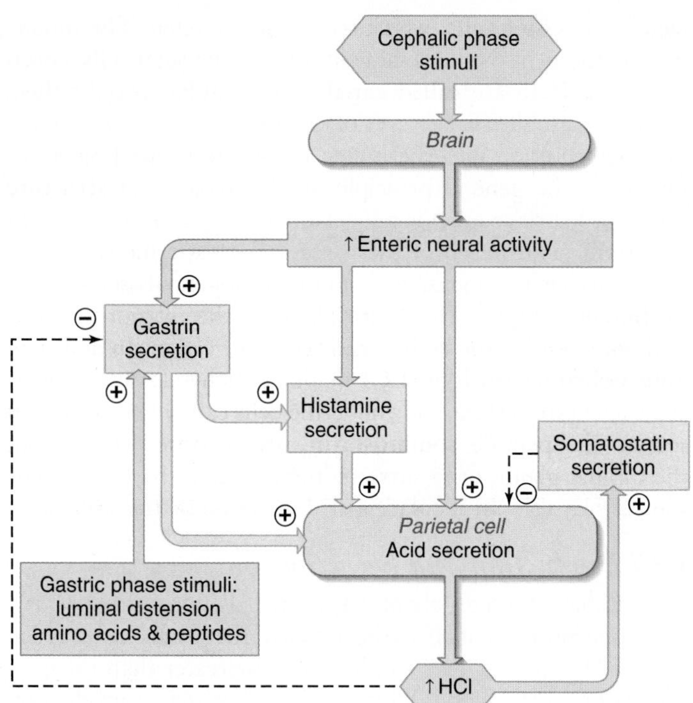

Figure 15.21 APIR Cephalic and gastric phases controlling acid secretion by the stomach. The dashed line and ⊖ indicate that an increase in acidity inhibits the secretion of gastrin and that somatostatin inhibits the release of HCl. HCl inhibition of gastrin and somatostatin inhibition of HCl are negative feedback loops limiting overproduction of HCl.

PHYSIOLOGICAL INQUIRY

- What would happen to gastrin secretion in a patient taking a drug that blocks the binding of histamine to its receptor on the parietal cell?

Answer can be found at end of chapter.

when considering ulcers, this potentiating effect of histamine is the reason that drugs that block histamine receptors in the stomach suppress acid secretion.

During a meal, the rate of acid secretion increases markedly as stimuli arising from the cephalic, gastric, and intestinal phases alter the release of the four chemical messengers described in the previous paragraph. During the cephalic phase, increased activity of efferent parasympathetic neural input to the stomach's enteric nervous system results in the release of ACh from the plexus neurons, gastrin from the gastrin-releasing cells, and histamine from ECL cells (**Figure 15.21**).

Once food has reached the stomach, the gastric phase stimuli—distension from the volume of ingested material and the presence of peptides and amino acids released by the digestion of luminal proteins—produce a further increase in acid secretion. These stimuli use some of the same neural pathways used during the cephalic phase. Neurons in the mucosa of the stomach respond to these luminal stimuli and send action potentials to the cells of the enteric nervous system, which in turn can relay signals to the gastrin-releasing cells, histamine-releasing cells, and parietal cells. In addition, peptides and amino acids can act directly on the gastrin-releasing endocrine cells to promote gastrin secretion.

The concentration of acid in the gastric lumen is itself an important determinant of the rate of acid secretion because H^+ (acid) directly inhibits gastrin secretion. It also stimulates the release of somatostatin from endocrine cells in the gastric wall. Somatostatin then acts on the parietal cells to inhibit acid secretion; it also inhibits the release of gastrin and histamine. The net result is a negative feedback control of acid secretion. As the contents of the gastric lumen become more acidic, the stimuli that promote acid secretion decrease.

Increasing the protein content of a meal increases acid secretion. This occurs for two reasons. First, protein ingestion increases the concentration of peptides in the lumen of the stomach. These peptides, as we have seen, stimulate acid secretion through their actions on gastrin. The second reason is more complicated and reflects the effects of proteins on luminal acidity. During the cephalic phase, before food enters the stomach, the H^+ concentration in the lumen increases because there are few buffers present to bind any secreted H^+. Thereafter, the rate of acid secretion soon decreases because high acidity reflexively inhibits acid secretion (see Figure 15.21). The protein in food is an excellent buffer, however, so as it enters the stomach, the H^+ concentration decreases as H^+ binds to proteins and begins to denature them. This decrease in acidity removes the inhibition of acid secretion. The more protein in a meal, the greater the buffering of acid and the more acid secreted.

We now come to the intestinal phase that controls acid secretion—the phase in which stimuli in the early portion of the small intestine influence acid secretion by the stomach.

High acidity in the duodenum triggers reflexes that inhibit gastric acid secretion. This inhibition is beneficial because the digestive activity of enzymes and bile salts in the small intestine is strongly inhibited by acidic solutions. This reflex limits gastric acid production when the H^+ concentration in the duodenum increases due to the entry of chyme from the stomach.

Acid, distension, hypertonic solutions, solutions containing amino acids, and fatty acids in the small intestine reflexively inhibit gastric acid secretion. The extent to which acid secretion is inhibited during the intestinal phase varies, depending upon the amounts of these substances in the intestine; the net result is the same, however—balancing the secretory activity of the stomach with the digestive and absorptive capacities of the small intestine.

The inhibition of gastric acid secretion during the intestinal phase is mediated by short and long neural reflexes and by hormones that inhibit acid secretion by influencing the four signals that directly control acid secretion: ACh, gastrin, histamine, and somatostatin. The hormones released by the intestinal tract that reflexively inhibit gastric activity are collectively called **enterogastrones** and include secretin and CCK.

Table 15.5 summarizes the control of acid secretion.

Pepsin Secretion

Pepsin is secreted by chief cells in the form of an inactive precursor called pepsinogen (**Figure 15.22**). Exposure to low pH in the lumen of the stomach activates a very rapid, autocatalytic process in which pepsin is produced from pepsinogen.

The synthesis and secretion of pepsinogen, followed by its intraluminal activation to pepsin, provide an example of a process that occurs with many other secreted proteolytic enzymes in the gastrointestinal tract. These enzymes are synthesized and stored intracellularly in inactive forms, collectively referred to as **zymogens.** Consequently, zymogens do not act on proteins inside the cells that produce them; this protects the cell from proteolytic damage.

Pepsin is active only in the presence of a high H^+ concentration (low pH). It is irreversibly inactivated when it enters the small intestine, where the HCO_3^- secreted into the small intestine neutralizes the H^+. The primary pathway for stimulating pepsinogen secretion is input to the chief cells from the enteric nervous system. During the cephalic, gastric, and intestinal phases, most of the factors that stimulate or inhibit acid secretion exert the same effect on pepsinogen secretion. Thus, pepsinogen secretion parallels acid secretion.

Pepsin is not essential for protein digestion because in its absence, as occurs in some pathological conditions, protein can

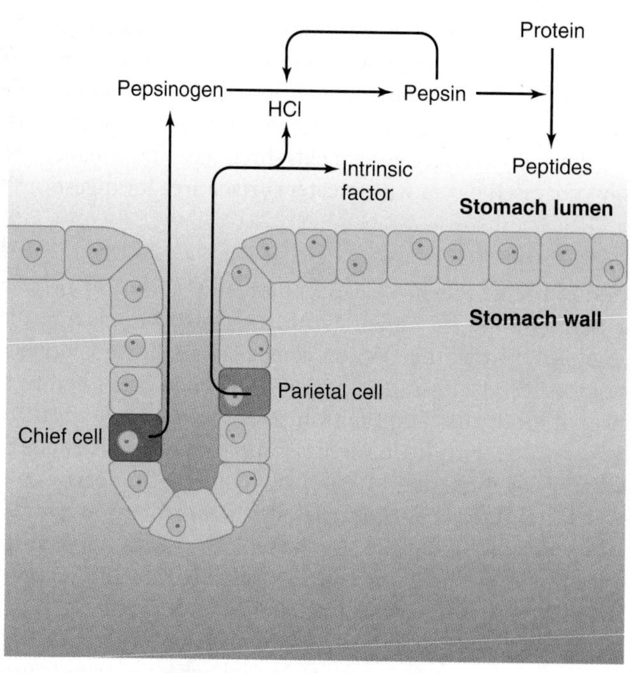

Figure 15.22 APIR Conversion of pepsinogen to pepsin in the lumen of the stomach. An increase in HCl acidifies the stomach contents. High acidity (low pH) maximizes pepsin cleavage from pepsinogen. The pepsin thus formed also catalyzes its own production by acting on additional molecules of pepsinogen. The parietal cells also secrete intrinsic factor, which is needed to absorb vitamin B_{12} in the small intestine.

TABLE 15.5 Control of HCl Secretion During a Meal

Stimuli	Pathways	Result
Cephalic phase Sight Smell Taste Chewing	Parasympathetic nerves to enteric nervous system	↑HCl secretion
Gastric contents (gastric phase) Distension ↑Peptides ↓H^+ concentration	Long and short neural reflexes and direct stimulation of gastrin secretion	↑HCl secretion
Intestinal contents (intestinal phase) Distension ↑H^+ concentration ↑Osmolarity ↑Nutrient concentrations	Long and short neural reflexes; secretin, CCK, and other duodenal hormones	↓HCl secretion

be completely digested by enzymes in the small intestine. However, pepsin accelerates protein digestion and normally accounts for about 20% of total protein digestion. It is also important in the digestion of collagen contained in the connective-tissue matrix of meat. This is useful because it helps shred meat into smaller, more easily processed pieces with greater surface area for digestion.

Gastric Motility

An empty stomach has a volume of only about 50 mL, and the diameter of its lumen is only slightly larger than that of the small intestine. When a meal is swallowed, however, the smooth muscles in the fundus and body relax before the arrival of food, allowing the stomach's volume to increase to as much as 1.5 L with little increase in pressure. This **receptive relaxation** is mediated by the parasympathetic nerves to the stomach's enteric nerve plexuses, with coordination provided by afferent input from the stomach via the vagus nerve and by the swallowing center in the brain. Nitric oxide and serotonin released by enteric neurons mediate this relaxation.

As in the esophagus, the stomach produces peristaltic waves in response to the arriving food. Each wave begins in the body of the stomach and produces only a ripple as it proceeds toward the antrum; this contraction is too weak to produce much mixing of the luminal contents with acid and pepsin. As the wave approaches the larger mass of wall muscle surrounding the antrum, however, it produces a more powerful contraction, which both mixes the luminal contents and *closes* the **pyloric sphincter,** a ring of smooth muscle and connective tissue between the antrum and the duodenum (**Figure 15.23**). The pyloric sphincter muscles contract upon arrival of a peristaltic wave. As a consequence of the sphincter closing, only a small amount of chyme is expelled into the duodenum with each wave. Most of the antral contents are forced backward toward the body of the stomach. This backward motion of chyme, called **retropulsion,** generates strong shear forces that helps to disperse the food particles and improve mixing of the chyme. Recall that the lower esophageal sphincter prevents this retrograde movement of stomach contents from entering the esophagus.

What is responsible for producing gastric peristaltic waves? Their rhythm (three per minute) is generated by pacemaker cells in the longitudinal smooth muscle layer. These smooth muscle cells undergo spontaneous depolarization–repolarization cycles (slow waves) known as the **basic electrical rhythm** of the stomach. These slow waves are conducted through gap junctions along the stomach's longitudinal muscle layer and also induce similar slow waves in the overlying circular muscle layer. In the absence of neural or hormonal input, however, these depolarizations are too small to cause significant contractions. Excitatory neurotransmitters and hormones act upon the smooth muscle to further depolarize the membrane, thereby bringing it closer to threshold. Action potentials may be generated at the peak of the slow-wave cycle if threshold is reached (**Figure 15.24**), causing larger contractions. The number of spikes fired with each wave determines the strength of the muscle contraction. Therefore, whereas the frequency of contraction is determined by the intrinsic basic electrical rhythm and remains essentially constant, the force of contraction—and, consequently, the amount of

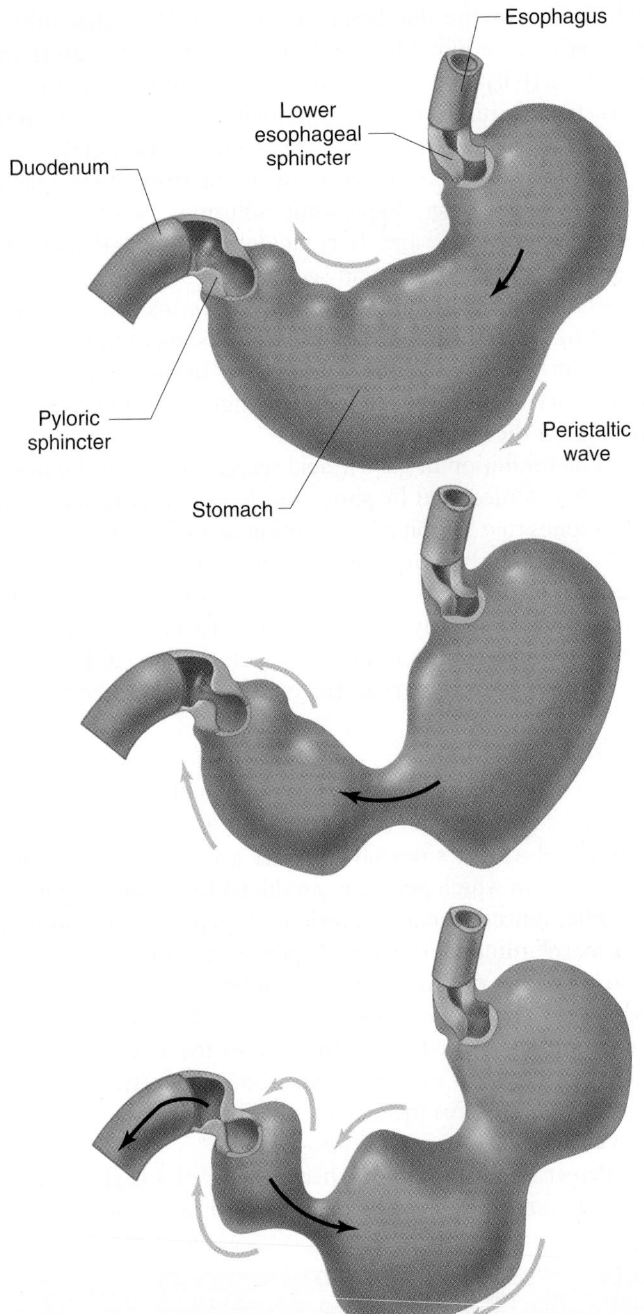

Figure 15.23 AP|R Peristaltic waves passing over the stomach force a small amount of luminal material into the duodenum. Black arrows indicate movement of luminal material; purple arrows indicate movement of the peristaltic wave in the stomach wall.

gastric emptying per contraction—is determined reflexively by neural and hormonal input to the antral smooth muscle.

The initiation of these reflexes depends upon the contents of both the stomach and small intestine. All the factors previously discussed that regulate acid secretion (see Table 15.5) can also alter gastric motility. For example, gastrin in sufficiently high concentrations increases the force of antral smooth muscle contractions. Distension of the stomach also increases the force of antral contractions through long and short reflexes triggered by mechanoreceptors in the stomach wall. Therefore, after a

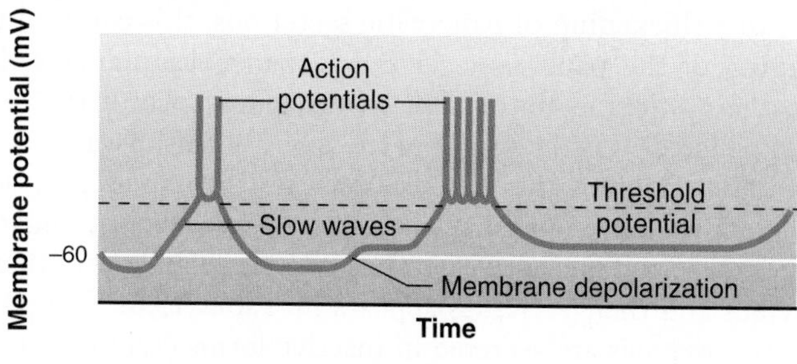

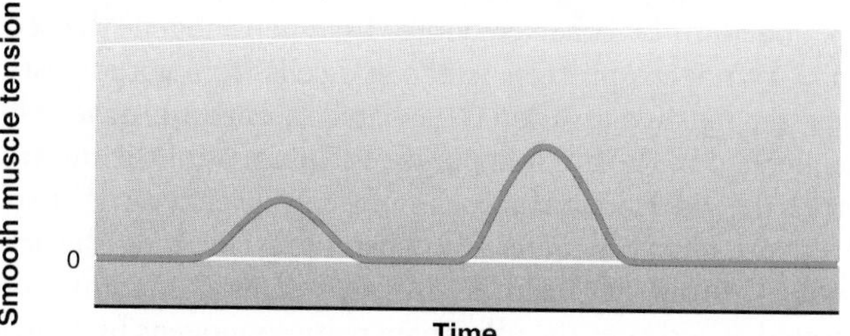

Figure 15.24 Slow-wave oscillations in the membrane potential of gastric smooth muscle fibers trigger bursts of action potentials when threshold potential is reached at the wave peak. Membrane depolarization brings the slow wave closer to threshold, increasing the action potential frequency and thus the force of smooth muscle contraction.

large meal, the force of initial stomach contractions is greater, which results in a greater emptying per contraction.

In contrast, gastric emptying is inhibited by distension of the duodenum or the presence of fat, high acidity (low pH), or hypertonic solutions in the lumen of the duodenum (**Figure 15.25**). These are the same factors that inhibit acid and pepsin secretion in the stomach. Fat is the most potent of these chemical stimuli. This prevents overfilling of the duodenum. The rate of gastric emptying has significant clinical implications particularly when considering what food type is eaten with oral medications. A meal rich in fat content tends to slow oral drug absorption due to a delay of the drug entering the small intestine through the pyloric sphincter.

Autonomic nerve fibers to the stomach can be activated by the CNS independently of the reflexes originating in the stomach and duodenum and can influence gastric motility. An increase in parasympathetic activity increases gastric motility, whereas an increase in sympathetic activity decreases motility. Via these pathways, pain and emotions can alter motility; however, different people show different gastrointestinal responses to apparently similar emotional states. As we have seen, a hypertonic solution in the duodenum is one of the stimuli inhibiting gastric emptying. This reflex prevents the fluid in the duodenum from becoming too hypertonic. It does so by slowing the rate of entry of chyme and thereby the delivery of large molecules that can rapidly be broken down into many small molecules by enzymes in the small intestine.

Once the contents of the stomach have emptied over a period of several hours, the peristaltic waves cease and the empty stomach is mostly quiescent. During this time, however, there are brief intervals of peristaltic activity that we will describe along with the events controlling intestinal motility.

Pancreatic Secretions

The exocrine portion of the pancreas secretes HCO_3^- and a number of digestive enzymes into ducts that converge into the pancreatic duct, which joins the common bile duct from the liver just before it enters the duodenum (see Figure 15.6). The enzymes are secreted by gland cells at the pancreatic end of the duct system, whereas HCO_3^- is secreted by the epithelial cells lining the ducts (**Figure 15.26**).

The pancreatic duct cells secrete HCO_3^- (produced from CO_2 and water) into the duct lumen via an apical membrane Cl^-/HCO_3^- exchanger, while the H^+ produced is exchanged for extracellular Na^+ on the basolateral side of the cell (**Figure 15.27**). The H^+ enters the pancreatic capillaries to eventually meet up in portal vein blood with the HCO_3^- produced by the stomach during the generation of luminal H^+ (see Figure 15.19). As with most transport systems, the energy for secretion of HCO_3^- is ultimately provided by Na^+/K^+-ATPase pumps on the basolateral membrane. Cl^- normally does not accumulate within the cell because these ions are recycled into the lumen through the **cystic fibrosis transmembrane conductance regulator (CFTR)** that you learned about in

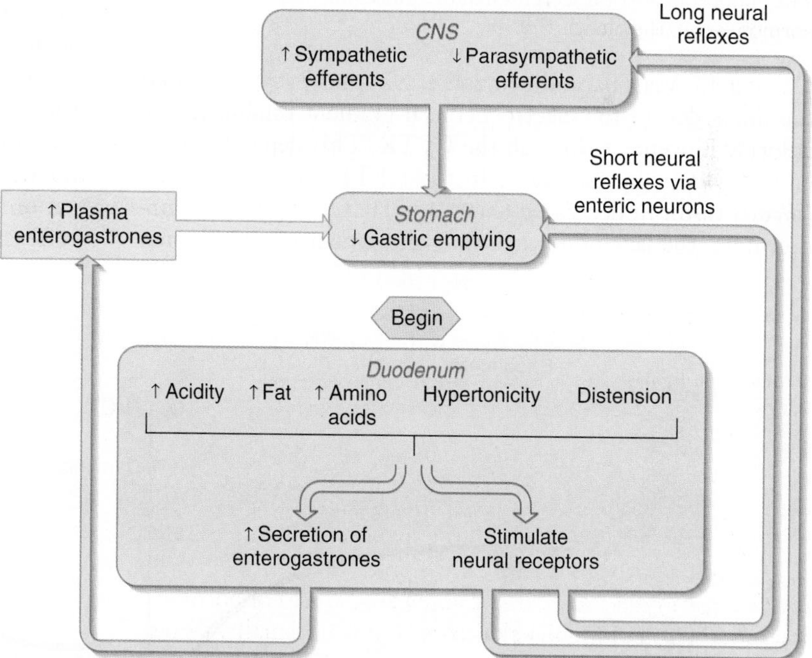

Figure 15.25 APIR Intestinal phase pathways inhibiting gastric emptying.

PHYSIOLOGICAL INQUIRY

- What might occur if a patient whose stomach has been removed eats a large meal?

Answer can be found at end of chapter.

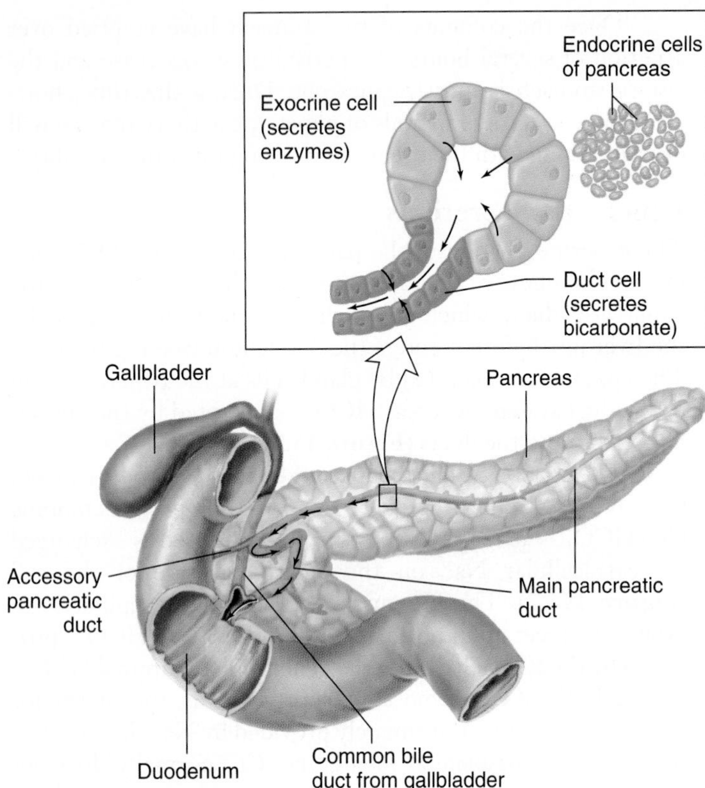

Figure 15.26 APIR Structure of the pancreas. The exocrine portion secretes enzymes and HCO_3^- into the pancreatic ducts. The endocrine portion secretes insulin, glucagon, and other hormones into the blood.

Chapter 13. Via a paracellular route, Na^+ and water move into the ducts due to the electrochemical gradient established by chloride movement through the CFTR. This dependence on Cl^- explains why mutations in the CFTR that cause ***cystic fibrosis*** result in decreased pancreatic HCO_3^- secretion. Furthermore, the lack of normal water movement into the lumen leads to a thickening of pancreatic secretions; this can lead to clogging of the pancreatic ducts and pancreatic damage. In fact, the cystic and fibrotic (scarring) appearance of the diseased pancreas was the origin of the name of this disease.

The enzymes the pancreas secretes digest fat, polysaccharides, proteins, and nucleic acids to fatty acids, sugars, amino acids, and nucleotides, respectively. A partial list of these enzymes and their activities appears in **Table 15.6.** The proteolytic enzymes are secreted in inactive forms (zymogens), as described for pepsinogen in the stomach, and then activated in the duodenum by other enzymes. Like pepsinogen, the secretion of zymogens protects pancreatic cells from autodigestion. A key step in this activation is mediated by **enterokinase,** which is embedded in the luminal plasma membranes of the intestinal epithelial cells. Enterokinase is a proteolytic enzyme that splits off a peptide from pancreatic **trypsinogen,** forming the active enzyme trypsin. Trypsin is also a proteolytic enzyme; once activated, it activates the other pancreatic zymogens by splitting off peptide fragments (**Figure 15.28**). This activating function is in addition to the role of trypsin in digesting ingested protein. The nonproteolytic enzymes secreted by the pancreas (e.g., amylase and lipase) are released in fully active form.

Pancreatic secretion increases during a meal, mainly as a result of stimulation by the hormones secretin and CCK (see Table 15.4). Secretin is the primary stimulant for HCO_3^- secretion, whereas CCK mainly stimulates enzyme secretion.

Because the function of pancreatic HCO_3^- is to neutralize acid entering the duodenum from the stomach, it is appropriate that the major stimulus for secretin release is increased acidity in the duodenum (**Figure 15.29**). In analogous fashion, CCK stimulates the secretion of digestive enzymes, including those for fat and protein digestion, so it is appropriate that the stimuli for its release are fatty acids and amino acids in the duodenum (**Figure 15.30**). Luminal acid and fatty acids also act on afferent nerve endings in the intestinal wall, initiating reflexes that act on the pancreas to increase both enzyme and

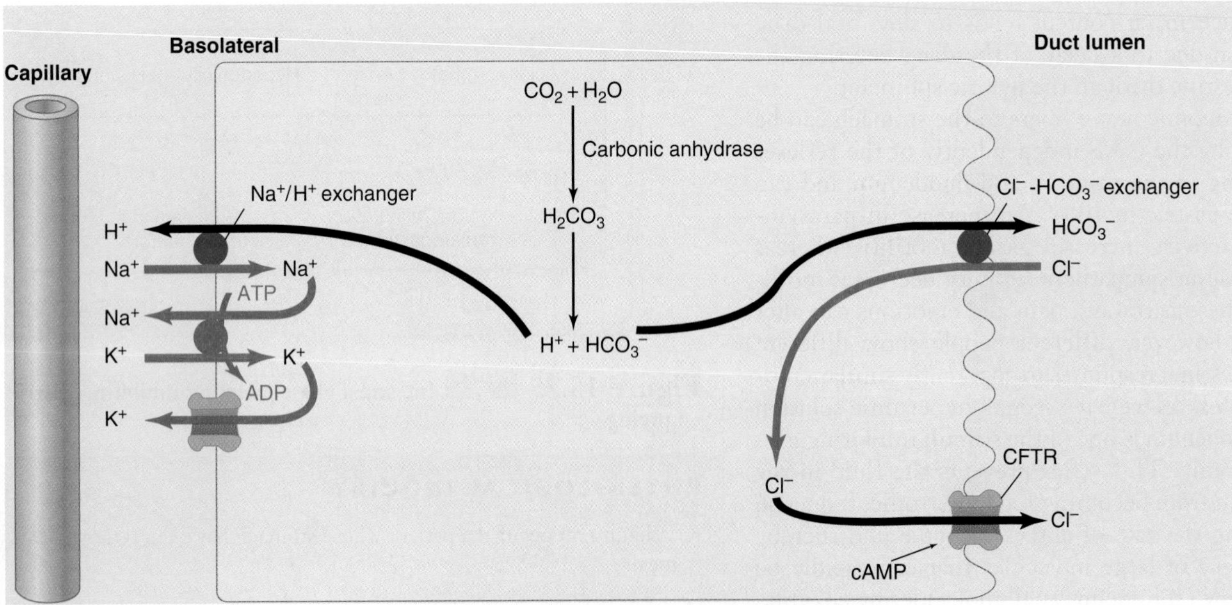

Figure 15.27 Ion-transport pathways in pancreatic duct cells. (CFTR = Cystic fibrosis transmembrane conductance regulator)

TABLE 15.6 Pancreatic Enzymes		
Enzyme	**Substrate**	**Action**
Trypsin, chymotrypsin, elastase	Proteins	Break peptide bonds in proteins to form peptide fragments
Carboxypeptidase	Proteins	Splits off terminal amino acid from carboxyl end of protein
Lipase	Fats	Splits off two fatty acids from triglycerides, forming free fatty acids and monoglycerides
Amylase	Polysaccharides	Splits polysaccharides into glucose and maltose
Ribonuclease, deoxyribonuclease	Nucleic acids	Split nucleic acids into free mononucleotides

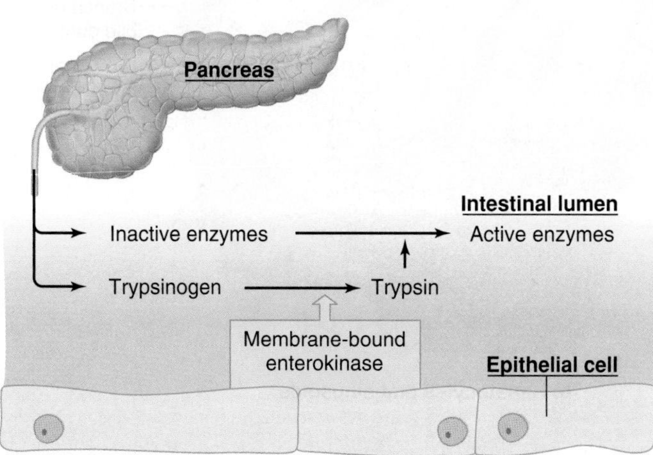

Figure 15.28 Activation of pancreatic enzyme precursors in the small intestine.

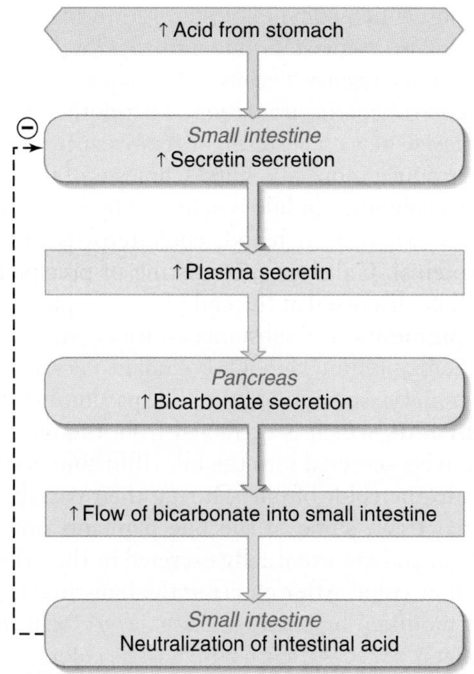

Figure 15.29 Hormonal regulation of pancreatic HCO_3^- secretion. Dashed line and ⊖ indicate that neutralization of intestinal acid (↑pH) turns off secretin secretion (negative feedback).

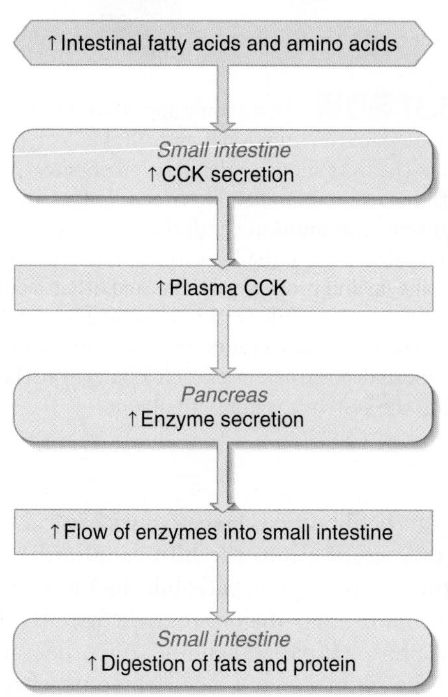

Figure 15.30 Hormonal regulation of pancreatic enzyme secretion.

HCO_3^- secretion. In these ways, the organic nutrients in the small intestine initiate neural and endocrine reflexes that control the secretions involved in their own digestion.

Although most of the pancreatic exocrine secretions are controlled by stimuli arising from the intestinal phase of digestion, cephalic and gastric stimuli also play a role by way of the parasympathetic nerves to the pancreas. Thus, the taste of food or the distension of the stomach by food will lead to increased pancreatic secretion.

Bile Secretion

The functional unit of the liver is the **hepatic lobule** (**Figure 15.31**). Within the lobule, the **portal triad** is composed of branches of the bile duct, the hepatic and portal veins, and the hepatic artery (which brings oxygenated blood to the liver). Substances absorbed from the small intestine wind up in the hepatic sinusoid either to reach the vena cava via the central vein or are taken up by the **hepatocytes** (liver cells) in

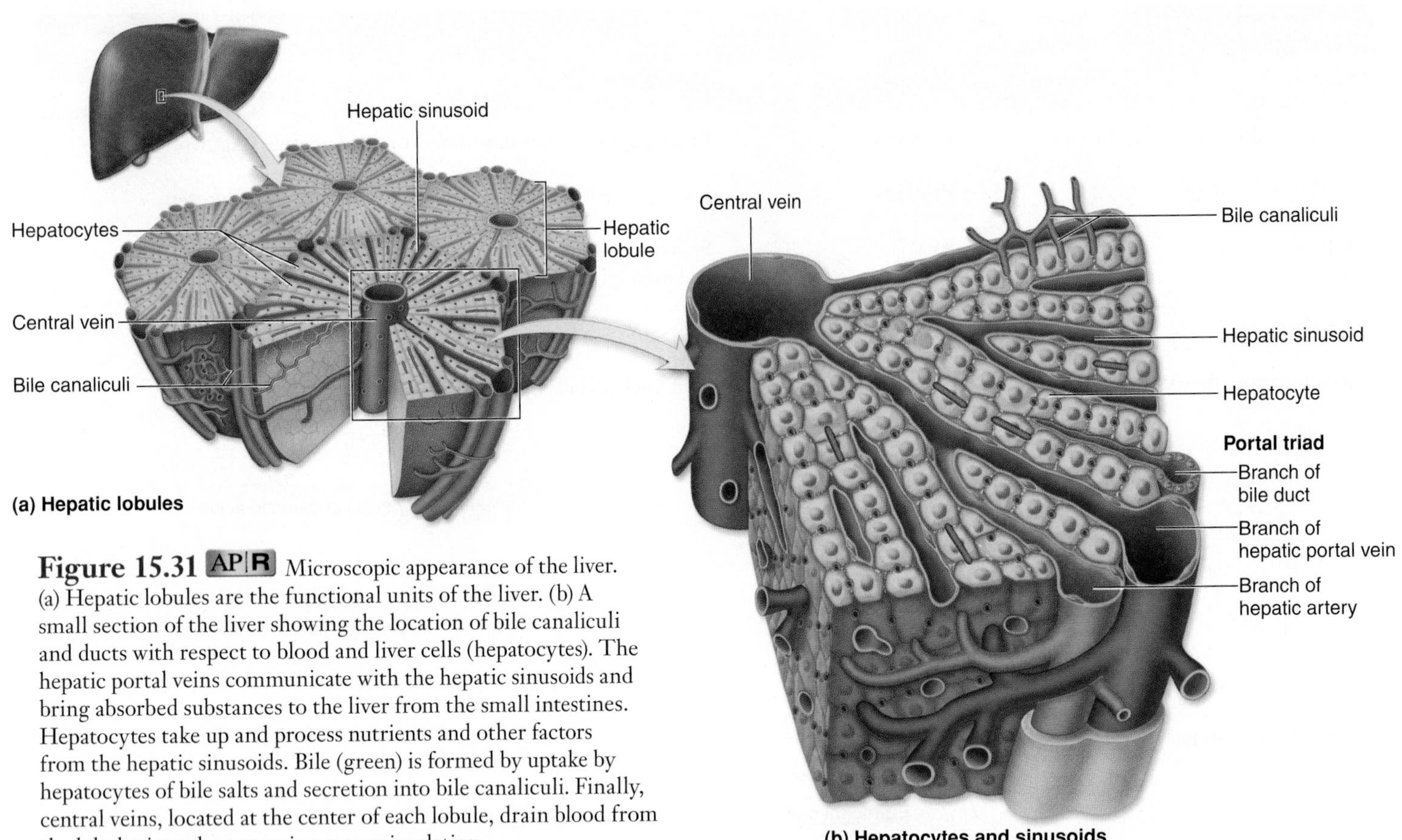

Figure 15.31 APR Microscopic appearance of the liver. (a) Hepatic lobules are the functional units of the liver. (b) A small section of the liver showing the location of bile canaliculi and ducts with respect to blood and liver cells (hepatocytes). The hepatic portal veins communicate with the hepatic sinusoids and bring absorbed substances to the liver from the small intestines. Hepatocytes take up and process nutrients and other factors from the hepatic sinusoids. Bile (green) is formed by uptake by hepatocytes of bile salts and secretion into bile canaliculi. Finally, central veins, located at the center of each lobule, drain blood from the lobules into the systemic venous circulation.

which they can be modified. Hepatocytes can rid the body of substances by secretion into the **bile canaliculi,** which converge to form the common hepatic bile duct (see Figure 15.6).

Bile contains six major ingredients: (1) bile salts, (2) lecithin (a phospholipid), (3) HCO_3^- and other salts, (4) cholesterol, (5) bile pigments and small amounts of other metabolic end products, and (6) trace metals. Bile salts and lecithin are synthesized in the liver and, as we have seen, help solubilize fat in the small intestine. HCO_3^- neutralizes acid in the duodenum, and the last three ingredients represent substances extracted from the blood by the liver and excreted via the bile.

The most important digestive components of bile are the bile salts. During the digestion of a fatty meal, most of the bile salts entering the intestinal tract via the bile are absorbed by specific Na^+-coupled transporters in the ileum (the last segment of the small intestine). The absorbed bile salts are returned via the portal vein to the liver, where they are once again secreted into the bile. Uptake of bile salts from portal blood into hepatocytes is driven by secondary active transport coupled to Na^+. This recycling pathway from the liver to the intestine and back to the liver is known as the **enterohepatic circulation (Figure 15.32).** A small amount (5%) of the bile salts escapes this recycling and is lost in the feces, but the liver synthesizes new bile salts from cholesterol to replace it. During the digestion of a meal, the entire bile salt content of the body may be recycled several times via the enterohepatic circulation.

In addition to synthesizing bile salts from cholesterol, the liver also secretes cholesterol extracted from the blood into the bile. Bile secretion, followed by excretion of cholesterol in the feces, is one of the mechanisms for maintaining cholesterol homeostasis in the blood (see Chapter 16) and is also the process by which some cholesterol-lowering drugs work. Dietary fiber also sequesters bile and thereby lowers plasma cholesterol. This occurs because the sequestered bile salts escape the enterohepatic circulation. Therefore, the liver must either synthesize new cholesterol, or remove it from the blood, or both to produce more bile salts. Cholesterol is insoluble in water, and its solubility in bile is achieved by its incorporation into micelles (whereas in blood, cholesterol is incorporated into lipoproteins). Gallstones, consisting of precipitated cholesterol, will be discussed at the end of this chapter.

Bile pigments are substances formed from the heme portion of hemoglobin when old or damaged erythrocytes are broken down in the spleen and liver. The predominant bile pigment is **bilirubin,** which is extracted from the blood by liver cells and actively secreted into the bile. Bilirubin is yellow and contributes to the color of bile. During their passage through the intestinal tract, some of the bile pigments are absorbed into the blood and are eventually excreted in the urine, giving urine its yellow color. After entering the intestinal tract, some bilirubin is modified by bacterial enzymes to form the brown pigments that give feces their characteristic color.

The components of bile are secreted by two different cell types. The bile salts, cholesterol, lecithin, and bile pigments are secreted by hepatocytes, whereas most of the HCO_3^--rich solution is secreted by the epithelial cells lining the bile ducts.

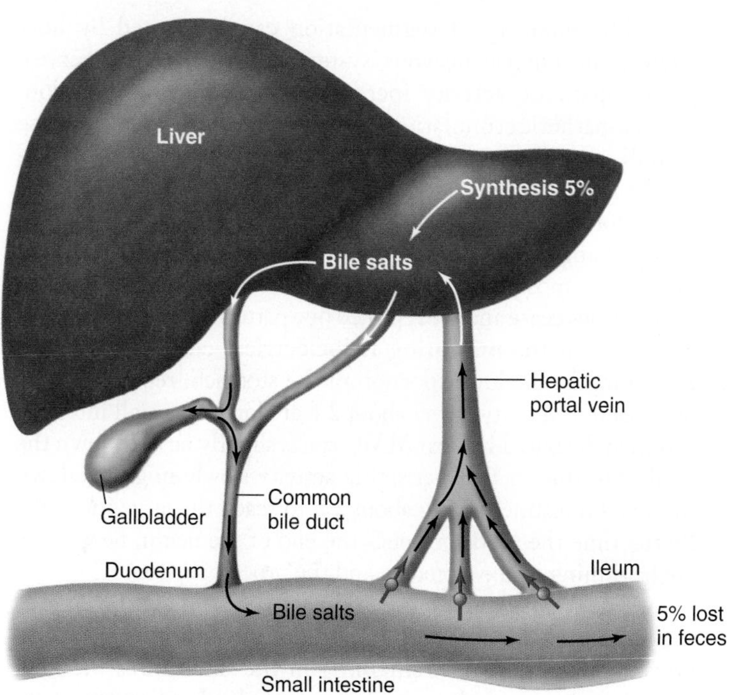

Figure 15.32 APIR Enterohepatic circulation of bile salts. Bile salts are secreted into bile (green) and enter the duodenum through the common bile duct. Bile salts are reabsorbed from the intestinal lumen into hepatic portal blood (red arrows). The liver (hepatocytes) reclaims bile salts from hepatic portal blood. The hepatic portal vein drains blood from the entire intestine, not just the ileum as shown here for simplicity.

PHYSIOLOGICAL INQUIRY

- In addition to the hepatic portal vein, can you name another portal-vein system and explain the meaning of the term *portal?*

Answer can be found at end of chapter.

Secretion of the HCO_3^--rich solution by the bile ducts, just like the secretion by the pancreas, is stimulated by secretin in response to the presence of acid in the duodenum.

Although bile secretion is greatest during and just after a meal, the liver is always secreting some bile. Surrounding the common bile duct at the point where it enters the duodenum is a ring of smooth muscle known as the **sphincter of Oddi.** When this sphincter is closed, the dilute bile secreted by the liver is shunted into the gallbladder. Here, the organic components of bile become concentrated as some NaCl and water are absorbed into the blood.

Shortly after the beginning of a fatty meal, the sphincter of Oddi relaxes and the gallbladder contracts, discharging concentrated bile into the duodenum. The signal for gallbladder contraction and sphincter relaxation is the intestinal hormone CCK—appropriately so, because, as we have seen, the presence of fat in the duodenum is a major stimulus for this hormone's release. It is from this ability to cause contraction of the gallbladder that cholecystokinin received its name: *chole,* "bile"; *cysto,* "bladder"; and *kinin,* "to move." **Figure 15.33** summarizes the factors controlling the entry of bile into the small intestine.

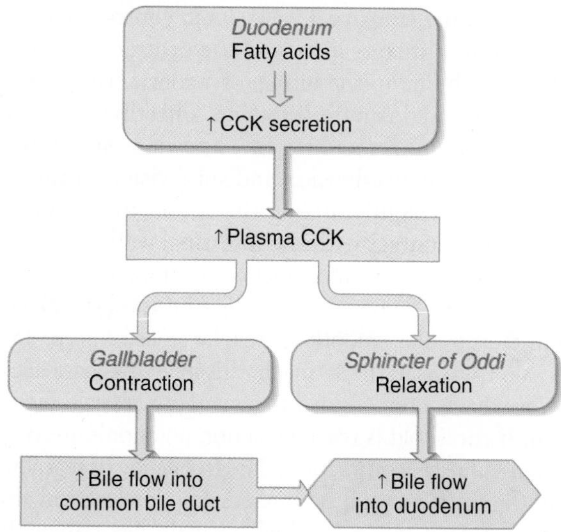

Figure 15.33 Regulation of bile entry into the small intestine.

Small Intestine

Secretion

Approximately 1500 mL of fluid is secreted by the walls of the small intestine from the blood into the lumen each day. One of the causes of water movement (secretion) into the lumen is that the intestinal epithelium at the base of the villi secretes a number of mineral ions—notably, Na^+, Cl^-, and HCO_3^-—into the lumen, and water follows by osmosis. These secretions, along with mucus, lubricate the surface of the intestinal tract and help protect the epithelial cells from excessive damage by the digestive enzymes in the lumen. Some damage to these cells still occurs, however, and the intestinal epithelium has one of the highest cell-renewal rates of any tissue in the body.

As stated earlier, water movement into the lumen also occurs when the chyme entering the small intestine from the stomach is hypertonic because of a high concentration of solutes in the meal and because digestion breaks down large molecules into many more small molecules. This hypertonicity causes the osmotic movement of water from the isotonic plasma into the intestinal lumen.

Absorption

Normally, virtually all of the fluid secreted by the small intestine is absorbed back into the blood. In addition, a much larger volume of fluid, which includes salivary, gastric, hepatic, and pancreatic secretions, as well as ingested water, is simultaneously absorbed from the intestinal lumen into the blood. Thus, overall there is a large net absorption of water from the small intestine. Absorption is achieved by the transport of ions, primarily via Na^+ and nutrient cotransport (see Figures 15.8 and 15.9) from the intestinal lumen into the blood, with water following by osmosis.

Motility

In contrast to the peristaltic waves that sweep over the stomach, the most common motion in the small intestine during digestion of a meal is a stationary contraction and relaxation of intestinal segments, with little apparent net movement toward the large intestine (**Figure 15.34**). Each contracting segment is only a few centimeters long, and the contraction lasts a few seconds. The chyme in the lumen of a contracting segment is forced both up and down the intestine. This rhythmic contraction and relaxation of the intestine, known as **segmentation,** produces a continuous division and subdivision of the intestinal contents, thoroughly mixing the chyme in the lumen and bringing it into contact with the intestinal wall.

These segmenting movements are initiated by electrical activity generated by pacemaker cells (the **interstitial cells of Cajal**) in the circular smooth muscle layer (see Figure 15.4). As with the slow waves in the stomach, this intestinal basic electrical rhythm produces oscillations in the smooth muscle membrane potential. If threshold is reached, action potentials are triggered that increase muscle contraction. The frequency of segmentation is set by the frequency of the intestinal basic electrical rhythm; unlike the stomach, however, which normally has a single rhythm (three per minute), the intestinal rhythm varies along the length of the intestine, each successive region having a slightly lower frequency than the one above. For example, segmentation in the duodenum occurs at a frequency of about 12 contractions/min, whereas in the last portion of the ileum the rate is only 9 contractions/min. Segmentation produces, therefore, a slow migration of the intestinal contents toward the large intestine because more chyme is forced downward, on average, than upward.

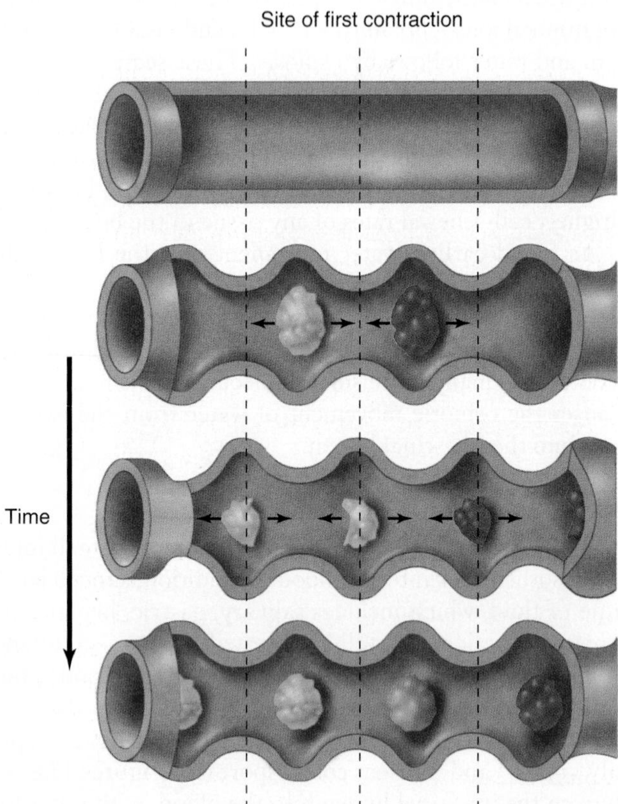

Figure 15.34 Segmentation contractions in a portion of the small intestine in which segments of the intestines contract and relax in a rhythmic pattern but do *not* undergo peristalsis. This is the rhythm encountered during a meal. Dotted lines are reference points to show the site of the first contraction in time (starting at the top). As contractions occur at the next site, the chyme is divided and pushed back and forth, mixing the luminal contents.

The intensity of segmentation can be altered by hormones, the enteric nervous system, and autonomic nerves; parasympathetic activity increases the force of contraction, and sympathetic stimulation decreases it. Thus, cephalic phase stimuli, as well as emotional states, can alter intestinal motility. As is true for the stomach, these inputs produce changes in the force of smooth muscle contraction but do not significantly change the frequencies of the basic electrical rhythms.

After most of a meal has been absorbed, the segmenting contractions cease and are replaced by a pattern of peristaltic activity known as the **migrating myoelectrical complex (MMC)**. Beginning in the lower portion of the stomach, repeated waves of peristaltic activity travel about 2 feet along the small intestine and then die out. The next MMC starts slightly farther down the small intestine so that peristaltic activity slowly migrates down the small intestine, taking about 2 h to reach the large intestine. By the time the MMC reaches the end of the ileum, new waves are beginning in the stomach, and the process repeats.

The MMC moves any undigested material still remaining in the small intestine into the large intestine and also prevents bacteria from remaining in the small intestine long enough to grow and multiply excessively. In diseases characterized by an aberrant MMC, bacterial overgrowth in the small intestine can become a major problem. Upon the arrival of a meal in the stomach, the MMC rapidly ceases in the intestine and is replaced by segmentation.

An increase in the plasma concentration of the intestinal hormone **motilin** is thought to initiate the MMC. Feeding inhibits the release of motilin; motilin stimulates MMCs via both the enteric and autonomic nervous systems.

The contractile activity in various regions of the small intestine can be altered by reflexes initiated at different points along the gastrointestinal tract. For example, segmentation intensity in the ileum increases during periods of gastric emptying; this is known as the **gastroileal reflex.** Large distensions of the intestine, injury to the intestinal wall, and various bacterial infections in the intestine lead to a complete cessation of motility, the **intestino-intestinal reflex.**

As much as 500 mL of air may be swallowed during a meal. Most of this air travels no farther than the esophagus, from which it is eventually expelled by belching. Some of the air reaches the stomach, however, and is passed on to the intestines, where its percolation through the chyme as the intestinal contents mix produces gurgling sounds that can be quite loud.

Large Intestine

Anatomy and Function

The large intestine is a tube about 6.5 cm (2.5 inches) in diameter and about 1.5 m (5 feet) long. Although the large intestine has a greater diameter than the small intestine, its epithelial surface area is far smaller because the large intestine is shorter than the small intestine, its surface is not convoluted, and its mucosa lacks villi found in the small intestine (see Figure 15.4). The first portion of the large intestine is the **cecum.** A sphincter between the ileum and the cecum is called the **ileocecal valve** (or **sphincter**) and is composed primarily of circular smooth muscle innervated by sympathetic nerves. The circular muscle contracts with distension of the colon and limits the movement of colonic contents backward into the ileum. This prevents bacteria from the large intestine from colonizing the final part of the small intestine. The **appendix** is a small, fingerlike projection that extends from the cecum and may participate in immune function but is not essential (**Figure 15.35**). The **colon** consists of three relatively straight segments—the ascending, transverse, and descending portions. The terminal portion of the descending colon is S-shaped, forming the sigmoid colon, which empties into a relatively straight segment of the large intestine, the rectum, which ends at the anus.

The primary function of the large intestine is to store and concentrate fecal material before defecation. The secretions of the large intestine are scanty, lack digestive enzymes, and consist mostly of mucus and fluid containing HCO_3^- and K^+.

About 1500 mL of chyme enters the large intestine from the small intestine each day. This material is derived largely from the secretions of the lower small intestine because most of the ingested food is absorbed before reaching the large intestine. Fluid absorption by the large intestine normally accounts for only a small fraction of the fluid absorbed by the gastrointestinal tract each day.

The primary absorptive process in the large intestine is the active transport of Na^+ from lumen to extracellular fluid, with the accompanying osmotic absorption of water. If fecal material remains in the large intestine for a long time, almost all the water is absorbed, leaving behind hard fecal pellets. There is normally a net movement of K^+ from blood into the large intestine lumen. Severe depletion of total-body potassium can result when large volumes of fluid are excreted in the feces. There is also a net movement of HCO_3^- into the lumen coupled to Cl^- absorption from the lumen, and loss of this HCO_3^- (a base) in patients with prolonged diarrhea can cause metabolic acidosis (see Chapter 14).

The large intestine also absorbs some of the products formed by the bacteria colonizing this region. It is now recognized that the colonic bacteria make a vital metabolic contribution to health. Undigested polysaccharides (fiber) are converted

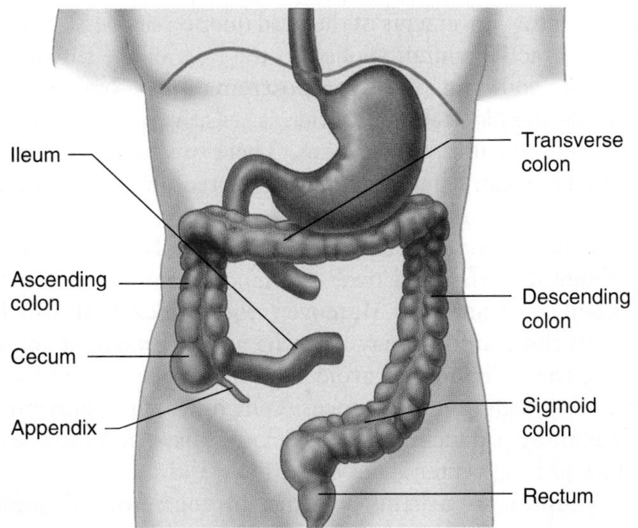

Figure 15.35 APIR The segments of the large intestine. (A portion of the ileum is shown to indicate where the large intestine connects with the small intestine.)

to short-chain fatty acids by bacteria in the large intestine and absorbed by passive diffusion as well as actively via specific short-chain fatty acid transporters. This route of absorption can represent a significant source of ingested calories and can be even more in obesity. The HCO_3^- secreted by the large intestine helps to neutralize the increased acidity resulting from the formation of these fatty acids. These bacteria also produce small amounts of vitamins, especially vitamin K, for absorption into the blood. Although this source of vitamins generally provides only a small part of the normal daily requirement, it may make a significant contribution when dietary vitamin intake is low. An individual who depends on absorption of nutrients and vitamins formed by bacteria in the large intestine can have adverse health consequences if treated with antibiotics that inhibit other species of bacteria in addition to the disease-causing bacteria.

Other bacterial products include gas (**flatus**), which is a mixture of nitrogen and carbon dioxide, with small amounts of the gases hydrogen, methane, and hydrogen sulfide. Bacterial fermentation of undigested polysaccharides produces these gases in the colon (except for nitrogen, which is derived from swallowed air) at the rate of about 400 to 700 mL/day. Certain foods (beans, for example) contain large amounts of carbohydrates that cannot be digested by intestinal enzymes but are readily metabolized by bacteria in the large intestine, producing large amounts of gas.

Motility and Defecation

Contractions of the circular smooth muscle in the large intestine produce a segmentation motion with a rhythm considerably slower (one every 30 min) than that in the small intestine. Because of the slow propulsion of the large-intestine contents, material entering the large intestine from the small intestine remains for about 18 to 24 h. This provides time for bacteria to grow and multiply. Three to four times a day, generally following a meal, a wave of intense contraction known as a **mass movement** spreads rapidly over the transverse segment of the large intestine toward the rectum. The large intestine is innervated by parasympathetic and sympathetic nerves. Parasympathetic input increases segmental contractions, whereas sympathetic input decreases colonic contractions.

The anus, the exit from the rectum, is normally closed by the **internal anal sphincter,** composed of smooth muscle, and the **external anal sphincter,** composed of skeletal muscle under voluntary control. The sudden distension of the walls of the rectum produced by the mass movement of fecal material into it initiates the neurally mediated **defecation reflex.** The conscious urge to defecate, mediated by mechanoreceptors, accompanies distension of the rectum. The reflex response consists of a contraction of the rectum and relaxation of the internal anal sphincter but *contraction* of the external anal sphincter (initially) and increased motility in the sigmoid colon. Eventually, a pressure is reached in the rectum that triggers reflex *relaxation* of the external anal sphincter, allowing the feces to be expelled.

Via descending pathways to somatic nerves to the external anal sphincter, however, brain centers can override the reflex signals that eventually would relax the sphincter, thereby keeping the external sphincter closed and allowing a person to delay defecation. In this case, the prolonged distension of the rectum initiates a reverse movement, driving the rectal contents back into the sigmoid colon. The urge to defecate then subsides until the next mass movement again propels more feces into the rectum, increasing its volume and again initiating the defecation reflex. Voluntary control of the external anal sphincter is learned during childhood. Spinal cord damage can lead to a loss of voluntary control over defecation.

Defecation is normally assisted by a deep breath, followed by closure of the glottis and contraction of the abdominal and thoracic muscles, producing an increase in abdominal pressure that is transmitted to the contents of the large intestine and rectum. This maneuver (termed the Valsalva maneuver) also causes an increase in intrathoracic pressure, which leads to a transient increase in blood pressure followed by a decrease in pressure as the venous return to the heart is decreased. The cardiovascular changes resulting from excessive strain during defecation may in rare instances precipitate a stroke or heart attack, especially in constipated elderly people with cardiovascular disease.

15.6 Pathophysiology of the Gastrointestinal Tract

Because the end result of gastrointestinal function is the absorption of nutrients, salts, and water, most malfunctions of this organ system affect either the nutritional state of the body or its salt and water content. The following are a few common examples of disordered gastrointestinal function.

Ulcers

Considering the high concentration of acid and pepsin secreted by the stomach, it is natural to wonder why the stomach does not digest itself. Several factors protect the walls of the stomach from being digested. (1) The surface of the mucosa is lined with cells that secrete slightly alkaline mucus that forms a thin layer over the luminal surface. Both the protein content of mucus and its alkalinity neutralize H^+ in the immediate area of the epithelium. In this way, mucus forms a chemical barrier between the highly acidic contents of the lumen and the cell surface. (2) The tight junctions between the epithelial cells lining the stomach restrict the diffusion of H^+ into the underlying tissues. (3) Damaged epithelial cells are replaced every few days by new cells arising by the division of cells within the gastric pits.

At times, these protective mechanisms can prove inadequate, and erosion (***ulcers***) of the gastric surface can develop. Ulcers can occur not only in the stomach but also in the lower part of the esophagus and in the duodenum. Indeed, duodenal ulcers are about 10 times more frequent than gastric ulcers, affecting about 10% of the U.S. population. Damage to blood vessels in the tissues underlying the ulcer may cause bleeding into the gastrointestinal lumen (**Figure 15.36**). On occasion, the ulcer may penetrate the entire wall, resulting in leakage of the luminal contents into the abdominal cavity. A device used to diagnose gastric and duodenal ulcers is the ***endoscope*** (see Figure 15.36). This uses either fiber-optic or video technology to directly visualize the gastric and duodenal mucosa. Furthermore, the endoscopist can apply local treatments and take samples of tissue (***biopsy***) during upper endoscopy. Similar devices can be used to visualize the colon (flexible ***sigmoidoscopy*** or ***colonoscopy***).

Ulcer formation involves breaking the mucosal barrier and exposing the underlying tissue to the corrosive action of acid and pepsin, but it is not always clear what produces the initial damage to the barrier. Although acid is essential for ulcer formation, it is not necessarily the primary factor; many patients with ulcers have normal or even subnormal rates of acid secretion.

Many factors, including genetic susceptibility, drugs, alcohol, bile salts, and an excessive secretion of acid and pepsin, may contribute to ulcer formation. The major factor, however, is the presence of a bacterium, *Helicobacter pylori*, that is present in the stomachs of a majority of patients with ulcers or ***gastritis*** (inflammation of the stomach walls). Suppression of these bacteria with antibiotics usually helps heal the damaged mucosa.

Once an ulcer has formed, the inhibition of acid secretion can remove the constant irritation and allow the ulcer to heal. Two classes of drugs are potent inhibitors of acid secretion. One class of inhibitors acts by blocking a specific class of histamine receptors (H_2) found on parietal cells, which stimulate acid secretion. An example of an H_2 receptor antagonist is ***cimetidine***. The second class of drugs directly inhibits the H^+/K^+-ATPase pump in parietal cells. Examples of these so-called proton-pump inhibitors are ***omeprazole*** and ***lansoprazole***. Although both classes of drugs are effective in healing ulcers, the ulcers tend to recur if the *Helicobacter pylori* bacteria are not removed.

Despite popular notions, the role of stress in producing ulcers remains unclear. Once the ulcer has been formed, however, emotional stress can aggravate it by increasing acid secretion and also decreasing appetite and food intake.

Vomiting

Vomiting is the forceful expulsion of the contents of the stomach and upper intestinal tract through the mouth. Like swallowing, vomiting is a complex reflex coordinated by a region in the brainstem medulla oblongata, in this case known as the **vomiting center.** Neural input to this center from receptors in many different regions of the body can initiate the vomiting reflex. For example, excessive distension of the stomach or small intestine, various substances acting upon chemoreceptors in the intestinal wall or in the brain, increased pressure within the skull, rotating movements of the head (motion sickness), intense pain, and tactile stimuli applied to the back of the throat can all initiate vomiting. The **area postrema** in the brain, which is outside the blood–brain barrier, is sensitive to toxins in the blood and can initiate vomiting. There are many chemicals (***emetics***) that can stimulate vomiting via receptors in the stomach, duodenum, or brain.

What is the adaptive value of this reflex? Obviously, the removal of ingested toxic substances before they can be absorbed is beneficial. Moreover, the nausea that usually accompanies vomiting may have the adaptive value of conditioning the individual to avoid the future ingestion of foods containing such toxic substances. Why other types of stimuli, such as those producing motion sickness, have become linked to the vomiting center is not clear.

Vomiting is usually preceded by increased salivation, sweating, increased heart rate, pallor, and nausea. The events leading to vomiting begin with a deep breath, closure of the glottis, and elevation of the soft palate. The abdominal muscles then contract, thereby increasing the abdominal pressure,

Endoscope

From power source

To video monitor

Trachea

Upper esophageal sphincter

Diaphragm

Lower esophageal sphincter

Duodenum

Stomach

Endoscope

Pyloric sphincter

(a)

Stomach

Duodenal ulcer

Gastric ulcers

Duodenum

Mucosa

Submucosa

Muscularis

Serosa

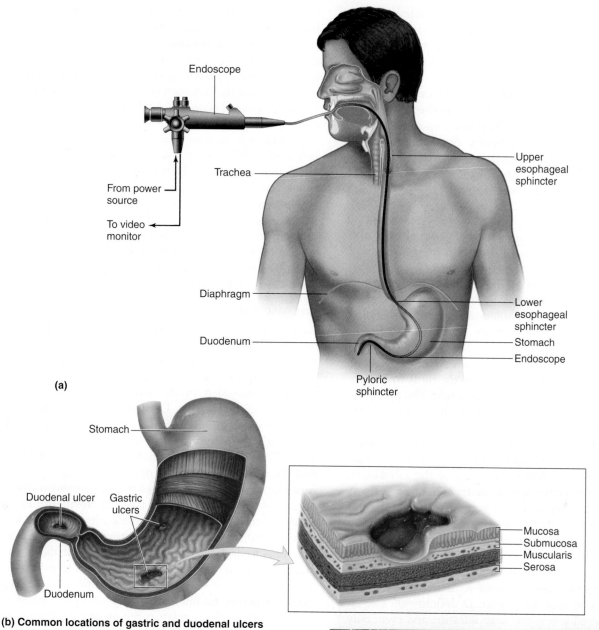

(b) Common locations of gastric and duodenal ulcers

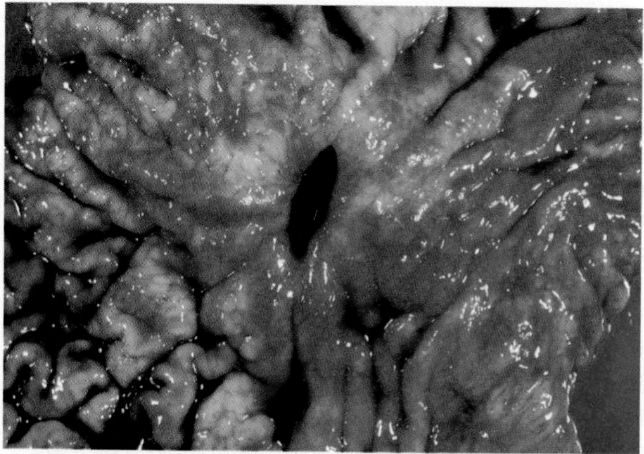

(c) Perforated gastric ulcer

Figure 15.36 APIR (a) Video endoscopy of the upper GI tract. The physician passes the endoscope through the mouth (or nose) down the esophagus, through the stomach, and into the duodenum. A light source at the tip of the endoscope illuminates the mucosa. The tip also has a miniature video chip, which transmits images up the endoscope to a video recorder. Local treatments can be applied and small tissue samples (biopsies) can be taken with the endoscope. Earlier versions of this device used fiber-optic technology. (b) and (c) Illustration and photo of the typical location and appearance of gastric and duodenal ulcers.

which is transmitted to the stomach's contents. The lower esophageal sphincter relaxes, and the high abdominal pressure forces the contents of the stomach into the esophagus. This initial sequence of events, which can occur repeatedly without expulsion via the mouth, is known as ***retching.*** Vomiting occurs when the abdominal contractions become so strong that the increased intrathoracic pressure forces the contents of the esophagus through the upper esophageal sphincter.

Vomiting is also accompanied by strong contractions in the upper portion of the small intestine—contractions that tend to force some of the intestinal contents back into the stomach for expulsion. Thus, some bile may be present in the vomitus.

Excessive vomiting can lead to large losses of the water and salts that normally would be absorbed in the small intestine. This can result in severe dehydration, upset the body's salt balance, and produce circulatory problems due to a decrease in plasma volume. The loss of acid from vomiting results in metabolic alkalosis (see Chapter 14). A variety of antiemetic drugs can suppress vomiting.

Gallstones

As described earlier, bile contains not only bile salts but also cholesterol and phospholipids, which are water-insoluble and are maintained in soluble form in the bile as micelles. When the concentration of cholesterol in the bile becomes high in relation to the concentrations of phospholipid and bile salts, cholesterol crystallizes out of solution, forming ***gallstones.*** This can occur if the liver secretes excessive amounts of cholesterol or if the cholesterol becomes overly concentrated in the gallbladder as a result of salt and water absorption. Although cholesterol gallstones are the most frequently encountered gallstones in the Western world, the precipitation of bile pigments can also occasionally be responsible for gallstone formation.

If a gallstone is small, it may pass through the common bile duct into the intestine with no complications. A larger stone may become lodged in the opening of the gallbladder, causing painful contractile spasms of the smooth muscle. A more serious complication arises when a gallstone lodges in the common bile duct, thereby preventing bile from entering the intestine. A large decrease in bile can decrease fat digestion and absorption. Furthermore, impaired absorption of the fat-soluble vitamins A, D, K, and E can occur, leading to, for example, clotting problems (vitamin K deficiency) and calcium malabsorption (due to vitamin D deficiency). The fat that is not absorbed enters the large intestine and eventually appears in the feces (a condition known as ***steatorrhea***). Furthermore, bacteria in the large intestine convert some of this fat into fatty acid derivatives that alter salt and water movements, leading to a net flow of fluid into the large intestine. The results are diarrhea and fluid and nutrient loss.

Because the duct from the pancreas joins the common bile duct just before it enters the duodenum, a gallstone that becomes lodged at this point prevents both bile and pancreatic secretions from entering the intestine. This results in failure to both neutralize acid and adequately digest most organic nutrients, not just fat. The end results are severe nutritional deficiencies.

The buildup of very high pressure in a blocked common bile duct is transmitted back to the liver and interferes with the further secretion of bile. As a result, bilirubin, which is normally secreted into the bile by uptake from the blood in the liver, accumulates in the blood and diffuses into tissues, producing a yellowish coloration of the skin and eyes known as ***jaundice.***

At birth, the liver's capacity to secrete bilirubin is not fully developed. During the first few days of life, this may result in ***hemolytic jaundice of the newborn,*** which normally clears spontaneously. Excessive accumulation of bilirubin during the neonatal period, as occurs, for example, with hemolytic disease of the newborn (see Chapter 18), carries a risk of bilirubin-induced neurological damage during a critical phase in the development of the nervous system.

Although surgery may be necessary to remove an inflamed gallbladder (***cholecystectomy***) or stones from an obstructed duct, newer techniques use drugs to dissolve gallstones. Patients who have had a cholecystectomy still make bile and transport it to the small intestine via the bile duct. Therefore, fat digestion and absorption can be maintained, but bile secretion and fat intake in the diet are no longer coupled. Thus, large, fatty meals are difficult to digest because of the absence of a large pool of bile normally released from the gallbladder in response to CCK. A diet low in fat content is usually advisable.

Lactose Intolerance

Lactose is the major carbohydrate in milk. It cannot be absorbed directly but must first be digested into its components, glucose and galactose, which are readily absorbed by active transport. Lactose is digested by the enzyme **lactase,** which is embedded in the luminal plasma membranes of intestinal epithelial cells. Lactase is usually present at birth and allows the nursing infant to digest the lactose in breast milk. Because the only dietary source of lactose is from milk and milk products, all mammals—including most humans—lose the ability to digest this disaccharide around the time of weaning. With the exception of people descended from a few regions of the world—notably, those of Northern Europe and parts of central Africa, the vast majority of people undergo a decline in lactase production beginning at about 2 years of age. This leads to ***lactose intolerance***—the inability to completely digest lactose such that its concentration increases in the small intestine. Current hypotheses for why certain populations of people retained the ability to express lactase relate to a mutation in the regulatory region of the lactase gene that occurred around the time certain groups of neolithic humans domesticated cattle as a food source.

Because the absorption of water requires prior absorption of solute to provide an osmotic gradient, the unabsorbed lactose in persons with lactose intolerance prevents some of the water from being absorbed. This lactose-containing fluid is passed on to the large intestine, where bacteria digest the lactose. They then metabolize the released monosaccharides, producing large quantities of gas (which distends the colon, producing pain) and short-chain fatty acids, which cause fluid movement into the lumen of the large intestine, producing diarrhea. The response to ingestion of milk or dairy products by adults whose lactase levels have diminished varies from mild discomfort to severely dehydrating diarrhea, according to the volume of milk and dairy products ingested and the amount of lactase present in the intestine. The person can avoid these symptoms by either drinking milk in which the lactose has been predigested with added lactase enzyme or taking pills containing lactase along with the milk.

Constipation and Diarrhea

Many people have a mistaken belief that, unless they have a bowel movement every day, the absorption of "toxic" substances from fecal material in the large intestine will somehow poison them. Attempts to identify such toxic agents in the blood following prolonged periods of fecal retention have been unsuccessful, and there appears to be no physiological necessity for having bowel movements at frequent intervals. This reinforces a point made earlier in this chapter that the contribution of the GI tract to the elimination of waste products is usually small compared to the lungs and kidneys. Whatever maintains a person in a comfortable state is physiologically adequate, whether this means a bowel movement after every meal, once a day, or only once a week.

On the other hand, some symptoms—headache, loss of appetite, nausea, and abdominal distension—may arise when defecation has not occurred for several days or even weeks, depending on the individual. These *symptoms* of ***constipation*** are caused not by toxins but by distension of the rectum. The longer that fecal material remains in the large intestine, the more water is absorbed and the harder and drier the feces become, making defecation more difficult and sometimes painful.

Decreased motility of the large intestine is the primary factor causing constipation. This often occurs in elderly people, or it may result from damage to the colon's enteric nervous system or from emotional stress.

One of the factors increasing motility in the large intestine—and thus opposing the development of constipation—is distension. As noted earlier, dietary fiber (cellulose and other complex polysaccharides) is not digested by the enzymes in the small intestine and is passed on to the large intestine, where its bulk produces distension and thereby increases motility. Bran, most fruits, and vegetables are examples of foods that have a relatively high fiber content.

Laxatives, agents that increase the frequency or ease of defecation, act through a variety of mechanisms. Fiber provides a natural laxative. Some laxatives, such as mineral oil, simply lubricate the feces, making defecation easier and less painful. Others contain magnesium and aluminum salts, which are poorly absorbed and therefore lead to water retention in the intestinal tract. Still others, such as castor oil, stimulate the motility of the colon and inhibit ion transport across the wall, resulting in decreased water absorption.

Excessive use of laxatives in an attempt to maintain a preconceived notion of regularity leads to a decreased responsiveness of the large intestine to normal defecation-promoting signals. In such cases, a long period without defecation may occur following cessation of laxative intake, appearing to confirm the necessity of taking laxatives to promote regularity.

Diarrhea is characterized by large, frequent, watery stools. Diarrhea can result from decreased fluid absorption, increased fluid secretion, or both. The increased motility that accompanies diarrhea probably does not cause most cases of diarrhea (by decreasing the time available for fluid absorption) but, rather, results from the distension produced by increased luminal fluid.

A number of bacterial, protozoan, and viral diseases of the intestinal tract cause secretory diarrhea. ***Cholera,*** which is endemic in many parts of the world, is caused by a bacterium that releases a toxin that stimulates the production of cyclic AMP in the secretory cells at the base of the intestinal villi. This leads to an increased frequency in the opening of the Cl^- channels in the luminal membrane and, hence, increased secretion of Cl^-. An accompanying osmotic flow of water into the intestinal lumen occurs, resulting in massive diarrhea that can be life threatening due to dehydration and decreased blood volume that leads to circulatory shock. The salt and water lost by this severe form of diarrhea can be balanced by ingesting a simple solution containing salt and glucose. The active absorption of these solutes is accompanied by absorption of water, which replaces the fluid lost by diarrhea. ***Traveler's diarrhea,*** produced by several species of bacteria, produces a secretory diarrhea by the same mechanism as the cholera bacterium but is usually less severe.

In addition to decreased blood volume due to salt and water loss, other consequences of severe diarrhea are potassium depletion and metabolic acidosis (see Chapter 14) resulting from the excessive fecal loss of K^+ and HCO_3^-, respectively.

SUMMARY

Overview of the Digestive System

I. The digestive system transfers digested organic nutrients, minerals, and water from the external environment to the internal environment. The four major processes used to accomplish this function are digestion, secretion, absorption, and motility.
   a. The system functions to maximize the absorption of most nutrients, not to regulate the amount absorbed.
   b. The system does not play a major role in the removal of waste products from the internal environment; therefore, elimination is usually not listed as a major function compared to the lungs and kidneys.

Structure of the Gastrointestinal Tract Wall

I. Figure 15.3 diagrams the structure of the wall of the gastrointestinal tract.
   a. The area available for absorption in the small intestine is greatly increased by the folding of the intestinal wall and by the presence of villi and microvilli on the surface of the epithelial cells.
   b. The epithelial cells lining the intestinal tract are continuously replaced by new cells arising from cell division at the base of the villi.
   c. The venous blood from the small intestine, containing absorbed nutrients other than fat, passes to the liver via the hepatic portal vein before returning to the heart. Fat is absorbed into the lymphatic vessels (lacteals) in each villus.

General Functions of the Gastrointestinal and Accessory Organs

I. Table 15.1 summarizes the names and functions of the gastrointestinal organs.

II. Each day, the gastrointestinal tract secretes about six times more fluid into the lumen than is ingested. Only 1% of this fluid is excreted in the feces.

Digestion and Absorption

I. Starch is digested by amylases secreted by the salivary glands and pancreas. The resulting products, as well as ingested disaccharides, are digested to monosaccharides by enzymes in the luminal membranes of epithelial cells in the small intestine.
   a. Most monosaccharides are then absorbed by secondary active transport.
   b. Some polysaccharides, such as cellulose, cannot be digested and pass to the large intestine, where bacteria metabolize them.

II. Proteins are broken down into small peptides and amino acids, which are absorbed by secondary active transport in the small intestine.
   a. The breakdown of proteins to peptides is catalyzed by pepsin in the stomach and by the pancreatic enzymes trypsin and chymotrypsin in the small intestine.
   b. Peptides are broken down into amino acids by pancreatic carboxypeptidase and intestinal aminopeptidase.
   c. Small peptides consisting of two to three amino acids can be actively absorbed into epithelial cells and then broken down to amino acids, which are released into the blood.

III. The digestion and absorption of fat by the small intestine require mechanisms that solubilize the fat and its digestion products.
   a. Large fat globules leaving the stomach are emulsified in the small intestine by bile salts and phospholipids secreted by the liver.
   b. Lipase from the pancreas digests fat at the surface of the emulsion droplets, forming fatty acids and monoglycerides.
   c. These water-insoluble products of lipase action, when combined with bile salts, form micelles, which are in equilibrium with the free molecules.
   d. Free fatty acids and monoglycerides diffuse across the luminal membranes of epithelial cells, where they are enzymatically recombined to form triglycerides, which are released as chylomicrons from the blood side of the cell by exocytosis.
   e. The released chylomicrons enter lacteals in the intestinal villi and pass by way of the lymphatic system and the thoracic duct to the venous blood returning to the heart.

IV. Fat-soluble vitamins are absorbed by the same pathway used for fat absorption. Most water-soluble vitamins are absorbed in the small intestine by diffusion or mediated transport. Vitamin B_{12} is absorbed in the ileum by endocytosis after combining with intrinsic factor secreted into the lumen by parietal cells in the stomach.

V. Water is absorbed from the small intestine by osmosis following the active absorption of solutes, primarily sodium chloride.

How Are Gastrointestinal Processes Regulated?

I. Most gastrointestinal reflexes are initiated by luminal stimuli: distension, osmolarity, acidity, and digestion products.
   a. Neural reflexes are mediated by short reflexes in the enteric nervous system and by long reflexes involving afferent and efferent neurons to and from the CNS.
   b. Endocrine cells scattered throughout the epithelium of the stomach secrete gastrin; and cells in the small intestine secrete secretin, CCK, and GIP. Table 15.4 lists the properties of these hormones.
   c. The three phases of gastrointestinal regulation—cephalic, gastric, and intestinal—are each named for the location of the stimulus that initiates the response.

II. Chewing breaks up food into particles suitable for swallowing, but it is not essential for the eventual digestion and absorption of food.

III. Salivary secretion is stimulated by food in the mouth acting reflexively via chemoreceptors and pressure receptors and by sensory stimuli (e.g., sight or smell of food). Both sympathetic stimulation and parasympathetic stimulation increase salivary secretion.

IV. Food moved into the pharynx by the tongue initiates swallowing, which is coordinated by the swallowing center in the brainstem medulla oblongata.
   a. Food is prevented from entering the trachea by inhibition of respiration and by closure of the glottis.
   b. The upper esophageal sphincter relaxes as food is moved into the esophagus, and then the sphincter closes.
   c. Food is moved through the esophagus toward the stomach by peristaltic waves. The lower esophageal sphincter remains open throughout swallowing.
   d. If food does not reach the stomach with the first peristaltic wave, distension of the esophagus initiates secondary peristalsis.

V. Table 15.5 summarizes the factors controlling acid secretion by parietal cells in the stomach.

VI. Pepsinogen, secreted by the gastric chief cells in response to most of the same reflexes that control acid secretion, is converted to the active proteolytic enzyme pepsin in the stomach's lumen, primarily by acid.

VII. Peristaltic waves sweeping over the stomach become stronger in the antrum, where most mixing occurs. With each wave, only a small portion of the stomach's contents is expelled into the small intestine through the pyloric sphincter.
   a. Cycles of membrane depolarization, the basic electrical rhythm generated by gastric smooth muscle, determine gastric peristaltic wave frequency. Contraction strength can be altered by neural and hormonal changes in membrane potential, which is imposed on the basic electrical rhythm.
   b. Distension of the stomach increases the force of contractions and the rate of emptying. Distension of the small intestine and fat, acid, or hypertonic solutions in the intestinal lumen inhibit gastric contractions.

VIII. The exocrine portion of the pancreas secretes digestive enzymes and HCO_3^-, all of which reach the duodenum through the pancreatic duct.
   a. The HCO_3^- neutralizes acid entering the small intestine from the stomach.
   b. Most of the proteolytic enzymes, including trypsin, are secreted by the pancreas in inactive forms. Trypsin is activated by enterokinase located on the membranes of the small-intestine cells; trypsin then activates other inactive pancreatic enzymes.
   c. The hormone secretin, released from the small intestine in response to increased luminal acidity, stimulates pancreatic HCO_3^- secretion. The small intestine releases CCK in response to the products of fat and protein digestion. CCK then stimulates pancreatic enzyme secretion.
   d. Parasympathetic stimulation increases pancreatic secretion.

IX. The liver secretes bile, the major ingredients of which are bile salts, cholesterol, lecithin, HCO_3^-, bile pigments, and trace metals.
   a. Bile salts undergo continuous enterohepatic recirculation during a meal. The liver synthesizes new bile salts to replace those lost in the feces.
   b. The greater the bile salt concentration in the hepatic portal blood, the greater the rate of bile secretion.
   c. Bilirubin, the major bile pigment, is a breakdown product of hemoglobin and is absorbed from the blood by the liver and secreted into the bile.
   d. Secretin stimulates HCO_3^- secretion by the cells lining the bile ducts in the liver.
   e. Bile is concentrated in the gallbladder by the absorption of NaCl and water.
   f. Following a meal, the release of CCK from the small intestine causes the gallbladder to contract and the sphincter of Oddi to relax, thereby injecting concentrated bile into the intestine.

X. In the small intestine, the digestion of polysaccharides and proteins increases the osmolarity of the luminal contents, producing water flow into the lumen.

XI. Na^+, Cl^-, HCO_3^-, and water are secreted by the small intestine. However, most of these secreted substances, as well as those entering the small intestine from other sources, are absorbed back into the blood.

XII. Intestinal motility is coordinated by the enteric nervous system and modified by long and short reflexes and hormones.
   a. During and shortly after a meal, the intestinal contents are mixed by segmenting movements of the intestinal wall.
   b. After most of the food has been digested and absorbed, the migrating myoelectrical complex (MMC), which moves the undigested material into the large intestine by a migrating segment of peristaltic waves, replaces segmentation.

XIII. The primary function of the large intestine is to store and concentrate fecal matter before defecation.
   a. Water is absorbed from the large intestine secondary to the active absorption of Na^+, leading to the concentration of fecal matter.
   b. Flatus is produced by bacterial fermentation of undigested polysaccharides.
   c. Three to four times a day, mass movements in the colon move its contents into the rectum.
   d. Distension of the rectum initiates defecation, which is assisted by a forced expiration against a closed glottis.
   e. Defecation can be voluntarily controlled through somatic nerves to the skeletal muscles of the external anal sphincter.

Pathophysiology of the Gastrointestinal Tract

I. The factors that normally prevent breakdown of the mucosal barrier and formation of ulcers are secretion of an alkaline mucus, tight junctions between epithelial cells, and rapid replacement of epithelial cells.
   a. The bacterium *Helicobacter pylori* is a major cause of damage to the mucosal barrier, leading to ulcers.
   b. Drugs that block histamine receptors or inhibit the H^+/K^+-ATPase pump inhibit acid secretion and promote ulcer healing.

II. Vomiting is coordinated by the vomiting center in the brainstem medulla oblongata. Contractions of abdominal muscles force the contents of the stomach into the esophagus (retching); if the contractions are strong enough, they force the contents of the esophagus through the upper esophageal sphincter into the mouth (vomiting).

III. Precipitation of cholesterol or, less often, bile pigments in the gallbladder forms gallstones, which can block the exit of the gallbladder or common bile duct. In the latter case, the failure of bile salts to reach the intestine causes decreased fat digestion and absorption; the accumulation of bile pigments in the blood and tissues causes jaundice.

IV. Lactase activity, which is present at birth, undergoes a genetically determined decrease during childhood in many individuals. In the absence of lactase, lactose cannot be digested, and its presence in the small intestine can cause diarrhea and increased flatus production when milk products are ingested.

V. Constipation is primarily the result of decreased colonic motility. The symptoms of constipation are produced by overdistension of the rectum, not by the absorption of toxic bacterial products.

VI. Diarrhea can be caused by decreased fluid absorption, increased fluid secretion, or both.

REVIEW QUESTIONS

1. List the four processes that accomplish the functions of the digestive system.
2. List the primary functions performed by each of the organs in the digestive system.
3. Approximately how much fluid is secreted into the gastrointestinal tract each day compared with the amount of food and drink ingested? How much of this appears in the feces?
4. What structures are responsible for the large surface area of the small intestine?
5. Where does the venous blood go after leaving the small intestine?
6. Identify the enzymes involved in carbohydrate digestion and the mechanism of carbohydrate absorption in the small intestine.
7. List three ways in which proteins or their digestion products can be absorbed from the small intestine.
8. Describe the process of fat emulsification.
9. What is the role of micelles in fat absorption?
10. Describe the movement of fat-digestion products from the intestinal lumen to a lacteal.
11. How does the absorption of fat-soluble vitamins differ from that of water-soluble vitamins?
12. Specify two conditions that may lead to failure to absorb vitamin B_{12}.
13. How are salts and water absorbed in the small intestine?
14. Describe the role of ferritin in the absorption of iron.
15. List the four types of stimuli that initiate most gastrointestinal reflexes.
16. Describe the location of the enteric nervous system and its role in both short and long reflexes.
17. Name the four best-understood gastrointestinal hormones and state their major functions.
18. Describe the neural reflexes leading to increased salivary secretion.
19. Describe the sequence of events that occur during swallowing.
20. List the cephalic, gastric, and intestinal phase stimuli that stimulate or inhibit acid secretion by the stomach.
21. Describe the function of gastrin and the factors controlling its secretion.

22. By what mechanism is pepsinogen converted to pepsin in the stomach?
23. Describe the factors that control gastric emptying.
24. Describe the mechanisms controlling pancreatic secretion of HCO_3^- and enzymes.
25. How are pancreatic proteolytic enzymes activated in the small intestine?
26. List the major constituents of bile.
27. Describe the recycling of bile salts by the enterohepatic circulation.
28. What determines the rate of bile secretion by the liver?
29. Describe the effects of secretin and CCK on the bile ducts and gallbladder.
30. What causes water to move from the blood to the lumen of the duodenum following gastric emptying?
31. Describe the type of intestinal motility found during and shortly after a meal and the type found several hours after a meal.
32. Describe the production of flatus by the large intestine.
33. Describe the factors that initiate and control defecation.
34. Why is the stomach's wall normally not digested by the acid and digestive enzymes in the lumen?
35. Describe the process of vomiting.
36. What are the consequences of blocking the common bile duct with a gallstone?
37. What are the consequences of the failure to digest lactose in the small intestine?
38. Contrast the factors that cause constipation with those that produce diarrhea.
39. Describe the two main types of inflammatory bowel disease.

KEY TERMS

absorption 535
alimentary canal 534
aminopeptidase 541
amylase 538
antrum 550
anus 534
appendix 561
area postrema 562
aspiration 548
basic electrical rhythm 554
bile 539
bile canaliculi 558
bile pigment 558
bile salt 539
bilirubin 558
body (of stomach) 550
brush border 536
canaliculus (parietal cell) 551
carboxypeptidase 541
cecum 560
cephalic phase 547
chief cell 551
cholecystokinin (CCK) 546
chylomicron 544
chyme 538
chymotrypsin 541
circular fold 536
circular muscle 536
colipase 543
colon 561
common bile duct 540
cystic fibrosis transmembrane conductance regulator (CFTR) 555
defecation 540
defecation reflex 561
digestion 534
digestive system 534
duodenum 538
elimination 535
emulsification 542
enteric nervous system 546
enterochromaffin-like (ECL) cell 551
enteroendocrine cell 537
enterogastrone 553
enterohepatic circulation 558
enterokinase 556
epiglottis 548
esophagus 538
external anal sphincter 561
feces 535
ferritin 545
fiber 541
flatus 561
fundus 550
gallbladder 540
gastric 538
gastric phase 548
gastrin 546
gastroileal reflex 560
gastrointestinal (GI) tract 534
glottis 548
glucose-dependent insulinotropic peptide (GIP) 546
gluten 545
goblet cells 536
hepatic 537
hepatic lobules 557
hepatic portal vein 537
hepatocyte 557
hydrochloric acid 550
ileocecal valve (sphincter) 560
ileum 538
internal anal sphincter 561
interstitial cells of Cajal 560
intestinal phase 548
intestino-intestinal reflex 560
intrinsic factor 545
jejunum 538
lactase 564
lacteal 537
lamina propria 535
large intestine 538
lipase 542
liver 539
longitudinal muscle 536
long reflex 546
lower esophageal sphincter 548
mass movement 561
micelle 543
microvilli 536
migrating myoelectrical complex (MMC) 560
motilin 560
motility 535
mouth 538
mucosa 535
muscularis externa 535
muscularis mucosa 535
myenteric plexus 536
pancreas 538
parietal cell 550
pepsin 541
pepsinogen 541
peristalsis 535
peristaltic waves 549
Peyer's patches 538
pharynx 538
portal triad 557
potentiation 546
pyloric sphincter 554
receptive relaxation 554
rectum 540
retropulsion 554
saliva 538
salivary gland 538
secondary peristalsis 549
secretin 546
secretion 534
segmentation 560
serosa 536
short reflex 546
small intestine 538
somatostatin 551
sphincter 548
sphincter of Oddi 559
stomach 538
submucosa 535
submucosal plexus 535
swallowing center 548
thoracic duct 537
trypsin 541
trypsinogen 556
upper esophageal sphincter 548
villi 536
vomiting center 562
zymogen 553

CLINICAL TERMS

biopsy 562
cholecystectomy 564
cholera 565
cimetidine 562
colonoscopy 562
constipation 565
cystic fibrosis 556
diarrhea 565
emetics 562
endoscope 562
gallstones 564
gastritis 562
gastroesophageal reflux 550
heartburn 550
hemochromatosis 545
hemolytic jaundice of the newborn 564
jaundice 564
lactose intolerance 564
lansoprazole 562
laxatives 565
malabsorption 544
nontropical sprue (celiac disease; gluten-sensitive enteropathy) 545
omeprazole 562
pernicious anemia 545
phlebotomy 545
retching 563
sigmoidoscopy 562
Sjögren's syndrome 548
steatorrhea 564
traveler's diarrhea 565
ulcers 562

Clinical Case Study: A College Student with Weight Loss, Cramps, Diarrhea, and Chills

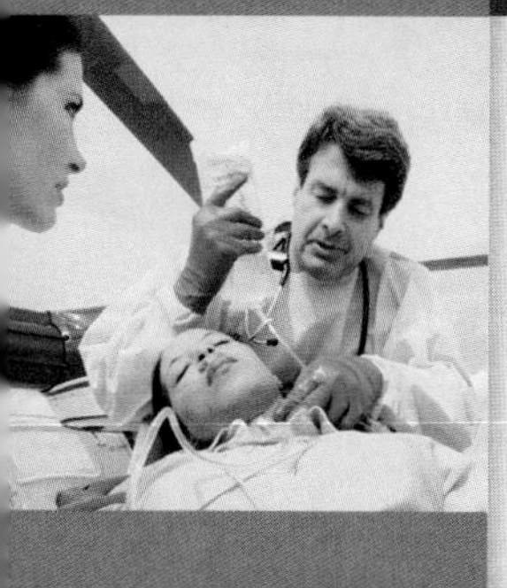

A 19-year-old college student has noticed some lower-right-quadrant abdominal cramping followed by diarrhea, particularly a few hours after eating popcorn, salads with a lot of lettuce, and uncooked vegetables. Over the semester, the cramps and diarrhea have gotten progressively worse and he has started to have fevers and chills. Despite eating a normal caloric intake, he has noticed some weight loss. He finally goes to the student health clinic, and the nurse practitioner refers him to a gastroenterologist (a physician specializing in diseases of the digestive system). After ruling out acute appendicitis, the physician orders a radiological test called a GI series with small-bowel follow-through. In these tests, the patient drinks a liquid containing barium (which is radiopaque) and then x-ray images are taken of the small and large intestine as the barium moves through the gastrointestinal tract (**Figure 15.37**). ***Strictures*** (narrowing) and other abnormalities of the intestines due to inflammation of the mucosa are readily observed with this test and were visible in the terminal ileum of our patient. Based on his symptoms and the result of the barium test, a diagnosis of inflammatory bowel disease (IBD)—specifically, Crohn's disease—was made.

The general term ***inflammatory bowel disease*** comprises two related diseases—***Crohn's disease*** and ***ulcerative colitis***. Both diseases involve chronic inflammation of the bowel. Crohn's disease can occur anywhere along the GI tract from the mouth to the anus, although it is most common near the end of the ileum, as in our patient. Colitis is confined to the colon. The incidence of IBD in the United States is 7 to 11 per 100,000 people and is most common in Caucasian people, particularly those of Ashkenazi Jewish descent. The most common ages of onset for IBD are in the late teens to early 20s and then again in people older than 60.

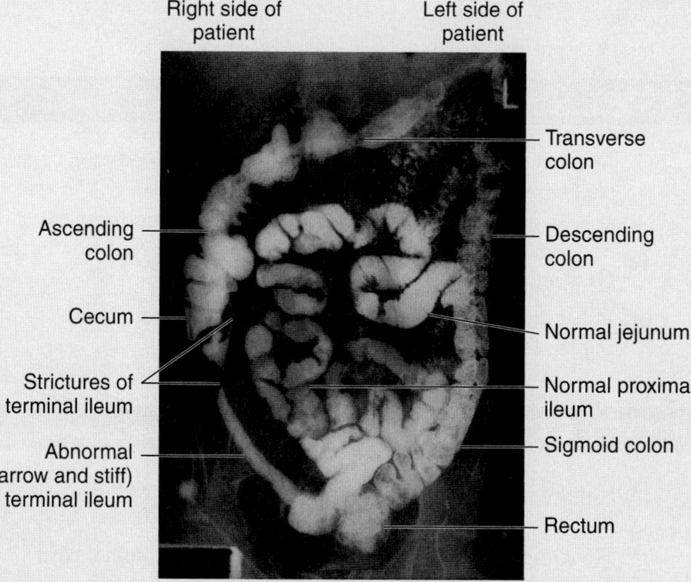

Figure 15.37 Radiograph (x-ray image) of the abdomen with barium contrast in the lumen of the small and large intestine. Notice the severe narrowing (strictures) of the terminal ileum in the lower-right quadrant of the patient, which is characteristic of Crohn's disease. This narrowing of the lumen is due to the inflammation and swelling of the mucosa. A segment of ileum below the strictures is also abnormal—it lacks the normal convolutions of the small intestine because of the inflammation of the mucosa. Figure courtesy of David Olson, M.D., Aurora St. Luke's Medical Center.

Although the precise cause or causes of IBD are not certain, it seems that it occurs as a combination of environmental and genetic factors. There appears to be a genetic predisposition for an abnormal response of the bowel mucosa to infection and the presence of normal luminal bacteria. Therefore, IBD appears to result from inappropriate immune and tissue-repair responses to essentially normal microorganisms in the intestinal lumen.

Active Crohn's disease shows inflammation and thickening of the bowel wall such that the lumen can become narrowed to the point at which it may even become blocked or obstructed, which can be very painful. The abdominal pain is often aggravated by eating meals rich in fiber (like uncooked vegetables and popcorn)—this roughage physically irritates the inflamed bowel. The part of the small intestine at the end of the ileum is the most common site of Crohn's disease, so the first symptoms experienced by patients with this disease are often pain in the lower-right abdomen and diarrhea. Because the disease is often accompanied by fever due to the immune response and pain in the lower-right quadrant of the abdomen, the initial symptoms can be mistaken for acute appendicitis (see Chapter 19). Because of its obstructive nature due to luminal narrowing, the abdominal pain in Crohn's disease can be temporarily relieved by defecation.

Ulcerative colitis is caused by disruption of the normal mucosa with the presence of bleeding, edema, and ulcerations (losses of tissue due to inflammation). When ulcerative colitis is most extreme, the bowel wall can get so thin and the loss of tissue so great that perforations all the way through the bowel wall can occur. The main symptoms of ulcerative colitis are diarrhea, rectal bleeding, and abdominal cramps.

The current initial treatment of IBD is the use of 5-aminosalicylate drugs, such as ***sulfasalazine,*** which appear to have both antibacterial and anti-inflammatory effects, and this is what our patient was treated with. However, he was advised by his physician that if the symptoms became more severe, additional drug therapy might be required. He was also advised to alter his diet to decrease the amount of roughage. Often, in more severe cases, the use of glucocorticoids as anti-inflammatory drugs can be very useful, although their overuse has significant risks such as loss of bone mass. It is often helpful to make adjustments in the diet to allow the inflamed bowel time to heal. Finally, new drug therapy using immunosuppressive medicines such as ***tacrolimus*** and ***cyclosporine*** show promise. When IBD becomes sufficiently severe and not responsive to drug therapy, surgery is sometimes necessary to remove the diseased bowel.

Clinical terms: Crohn's disease, cyclosporine, inflammatory bowel disease, stricture, sulfasalazine, tacrolimus, ulcerative colitis

See Chapter 19 for complete, integrative case studies

CHAPTER 15 TEST QUESTIONS

Answers found in Appendix A.

1–4: Match the gastrointestinal hormone (a–d) with its description (1–4).

Hormone:

a. gastrin
b. CCK
c. secretin
d. GIP

Description:

1. It is stimulated by the presence of acid in the small intestine and stimulates HCO_3^- release from the pancreas and bile ducts.
2. It is stimulated by glucose and fat in the small intestine and increases insulin and amplifies the insulin responses to glucose.
3. It is inhibited by acid in the stomach and stimulates acid secretion from the stomach.
4. It is stimulated by amino acids and fatty acids in the small intestine and stimulates pancreatic enzyme secretion.
5. Which of the following is *true* about pepsin?
   a. Most pepsin is released directly from chief cells.
   b. Pepsin is most active at high pH.
   c. Pepsin is essential for protein digestion.
   d. Pepsin accelerates protein digestion.
   e. Pepsin accelerates fat digestion.
6. Micelles increase the absorption of fat by
   a. binding the lipase enzyme and holding it on the surface of the lipid emulsion droplet.
   b. keeping the insoluble products of fat digestion in small aggregates.
   c. promoting direct absorption across the intestinal epithelium.
   d. metabolizing triglyceride to monoglyceride.
   e. facilitating absorption into the lacteals.
7. Which of the following inhibit/inhibits gastric HCl secretion during a meal?
   a. stimulation of the parasympathetic nerves to the enteric nervous system
   b. the sight and smell of food
   c. distension of the duodenum
   d. presence of peptides in the stomach
   e. distension of the stomach
8. Which component/components of bile is/are not primarily secreted by hepatocytes?
   a. HCO_3^-
   b. bile salts
   c. cholesterol
   d. lecithin
   e. bilirubin
9. Which of the following is *true* about segmentation in the small intestine?
   a. It is a type of peristalsis.
   b. It moves chyme only from the duodenum to the ileum.
   c. Its frequency is the same in each intestinal segment.
   d. It is unaffected by cephalic phase stimuli.
   e. It produces a slow migration of chyme to the large intestine.
10. Which of the following is the primary absorptive process in the large intestine?
    a. active transport of Na^+ from the lumen to the blood
    b. absorption of water
    c. active transport of potassium from the lumen to the blood
    d. active absorption of HCO_3^- into the blood
    e. active secretion of Cl^- from the blood

CHAPTER 15 GENERAL PRINCIPLES ASSESSMENT

Answers found in Appendix A.

1. A general principle of physiology is that *structure is a determinant of—and has coevolved with—function.* One example highlighted in this chapter is the large surface area provided by the villous and microvillous structure of the cells lining the small intestine (Figures 15.4 and 15.5). How does the anatomy of the hepatic lobule shown in Figure 15.31 provide another example of increased surface area to maximize function?
2. Another general principle of physiology states that *physiological processes are dictated by the laws of chemistry and physics.* Give at least two examples of how this principle is important in understanding the processes of absorption and secretion in the GI tract.
3. What general principle of physiology is demonstrated by Figure 15.14?

CHAPTER 15 QUANTITATIVE AND THOUGHT QUESTIONS

Answers found in Appendix A.

1. If the salivary glands were unable to secrete amylase, what effect would this have on starch digestion?
2. Whole milk or a fatty snack consumed before the ingestion of alcohol decreases the rate of intoxication. By what mechanism may fat be acting to produce this effect?
3. A patient brought to a hospital after a period of prolonged vomiting has an elevated heart rate, decreased blood pressure, and below-normal blood K^+ and acidity. Explain these symptoms in terms of the consequences of excessive vomiting.
4. Can fat be digested and absorbed in the absence of bile salts? Explain.
5. How might damage to the lower portion of the spinal cord affect defecation?
6. One of the older but no longer used procedures in the treatment of ulcers is abdominal vagotomy, surgical cutting of the vagus (parasympathetic) nerves to the stomach. By what mechanism might this procedure help ulcers to heal and decrease the incidence of new ulcers?

CHAPTER 15 ANSWERS TO PHYSIOLOGICAL INQUIRIES

Figure 15.5 A brush border is also found along the luminal surface of the proximal tubules of the renal nephrons. Like the intestinal brush border, that of the proximal tubules is an adaptation that increases surface area and allows for increased transport of solutes across the epithelium.

Table 15.4 The most common finding is an abnormally high production of gastric (hydrochloric) acid due to gastrin stimulation of the parietal cell of the stomach (see Figure 15.21). This high acidity can cause injury to the duodenum because the pancreas cannot produce sufficient quantities of HCO_3^- to neutralize it (see Figure 15.29). The low pH in the duodenum can also inactivate pancreatic enzymes (see Figure 15.30), which can ultimately lead to diarrhea due to unabsorbed nutrients and increased fat in the stool. The spectrum of findings in a patient with a gastrinoma is called the Zollinger–Ellison syndrome.

Figure 15.15 Aspiration of food during swallowing can lead to occlusion (blockage) of the airways, which can result in a disruption of oxygen delivery and carbon dioxide removal from the pulmonary system. Aspiration of stomach contents can lead to severe lung damage primarily due to the low pH of the material.

Figure 15.19 Mucus secreted by the cells in the gastric gland (see Figure 15.18) creates a protective coating and traps HCO_3^-. This gastric mucosal barrier protects the stomach from the luminal acidity.

Figure 15.21 A decrease in histamine action would result in a decrease in acid secretion and an increase in the pH of the material in the lumen of the stomach. This would decrease the H^+-induced inhibition of gastrin secretion; consequently, gastrin secretion would increase. Because a large part of the effect of gastrin on acid secretion is by stimulating histamine release, as shown in Figure 15.21, the parietal cell acid secretion would still be decreased. This is why histamine-receptor blockers (called H2 blockers) are effective in increasing stomach pH and alleviating the symptoms of gastroesophageal reflux (heartburn) described earlier in this chapter.

Figure 15.25. A person whose stomach has been removed because of disease (e.g., cancer) must eat more frequent small meals instead of the usual three large meals per day. A large meal in the absence of the controlled emptying by the stomach could rapidly enter the intestine, producing a hypertonic solution. This hypertonic solution could cause enough water to flow (by osmosis) into the intestine from the blood to lower the blood volume and produce circulatory complications. The large distension of the intestine by the entering fluid can also trigger vomiting in such individuals. All of these symptoms produced by the rapid entry of large quantities of ingested material into the small intestine are known as the dumping syndrome. You already learned earlier in this chapter that the lack of intrinsic factor from parietal cells can lead to pernicious anemia.

Figure 15.32 A portal vein carries blood from one capillary bed to another capillary bed (rather than from capillaries to venules as described in Chapter 12). The hypothalamo–pituitary portal veins carry hypophysiotropic hormones from the capillaries of the median eminence to the anterior pituitary gland where they stimulate or inhibit the release of pituitary gland hormones (see Chapter 11).

Genetically obese mouse and normal mouse.

16 Regulation of Organic Metabolism and Energy Balance

Chapter 3 introduced the concepts of energy and organic metabolism at the level of the cell. This chapter deals with two topics that are concerned in one way or another with those same concepts—but for the entire body. First, this chapter describes how the metabolic pathways for carbohydrate, fat, and protein are integrated and controlled so as to provide continuous sources of energy to the various tissues and organs, even during periods of fasting. Next, the factors that determine total-body energy balance and the regulation of body temperature are described.

In Section A, you will learn how the control of metabolism is a good example of the general principle of physiology that most physiological functions are controlled by multiple regulatory systems, often working in opposition. This will be particularly evident by the opposing effects of the primary regulatory hormone insulin and the counterregulatory hormones cortisol, growth hormone, glucagon, and epinephrine on the balance of glucose and other energy sources in the blood. The control of metabolism and energy balance also illustrates the general principles of physiology that homeostasis is essential for health and survival and that physiological processes require the transfer and balance of matter and energy. In Section B, energy balance and homeostasis are again general themes. This section will also illustrate how physiological processes are dictated by the laws of chemistry and physics, particularly in relation to heat transfer between the body and the environment.

SECTION A

Control and Integration of Carbohydrate, Protein, and Fat Metabolism

16.1 Events of the Absorptive and Postabsorptive States

The regular availability of food is a very recent event in the history of humankind and, indeed, is still not universal. It is not surprising, therefore, that mechanisms have evolved for survival during alternating periods of food availability and fasting. The two functional states or periods the body undergoes in providing energy for cellular activities are the **absorptive state,** during which ingested nutrients enter the blood from the gastrointestinal tract, and the **postabsorptive state,** during which the gastrointestinal tract is empty of nutrients and the body's own stores must supply energy. Because an average meal requires approximately 4 h for complete absorption, our usual three-meal-a-day pattern places us in the postabsorptive state during the late morning, again in the late afternoon, and during most of the night. We will refer to more than 24 h without eating as fasting.

During the absorptive state, some of the ingested nutrients provide the energy requirements of the body and the remainder is added to the body's energy stores to be called upon during the next postabsorptive state. Total-body energy stores are adequate for the average person to withstand a fast of many weeks, provided water is available.

Absorptive State

The events of the absorptive state are summarized in **Figure 16.1.** A typical meal contains all three of the major energy-supplying food groups—carbohydrates, fats, and proteins—with carbohydrates constituting most of a typical meal's energy content (calories). Recall from Chapter 15 that carbohydrates and proteins are absorbed primarily as monosaccharides and amino acids, respectively, into the blood leaving the gastrointestinal tract. The blood then drains directly into the liver by way of the hepatic portal vein. This allows the liver to alter the nutrient composition of the blood before it returns to the heart to be pumped to the rest of the body. This mechanism likely evolved as a means of inactivating toxins that were inadvertently ingested with a meal; liver cells express numerous enzymes capable of chemically altering and rendering harmless a wide range of potentially toxic compounds. In contrast to monosaccharides and amino acids, fat is absorbed into the *lymph* in chylomicrons, which are too large to enter capillaries. The lymph then drains into the

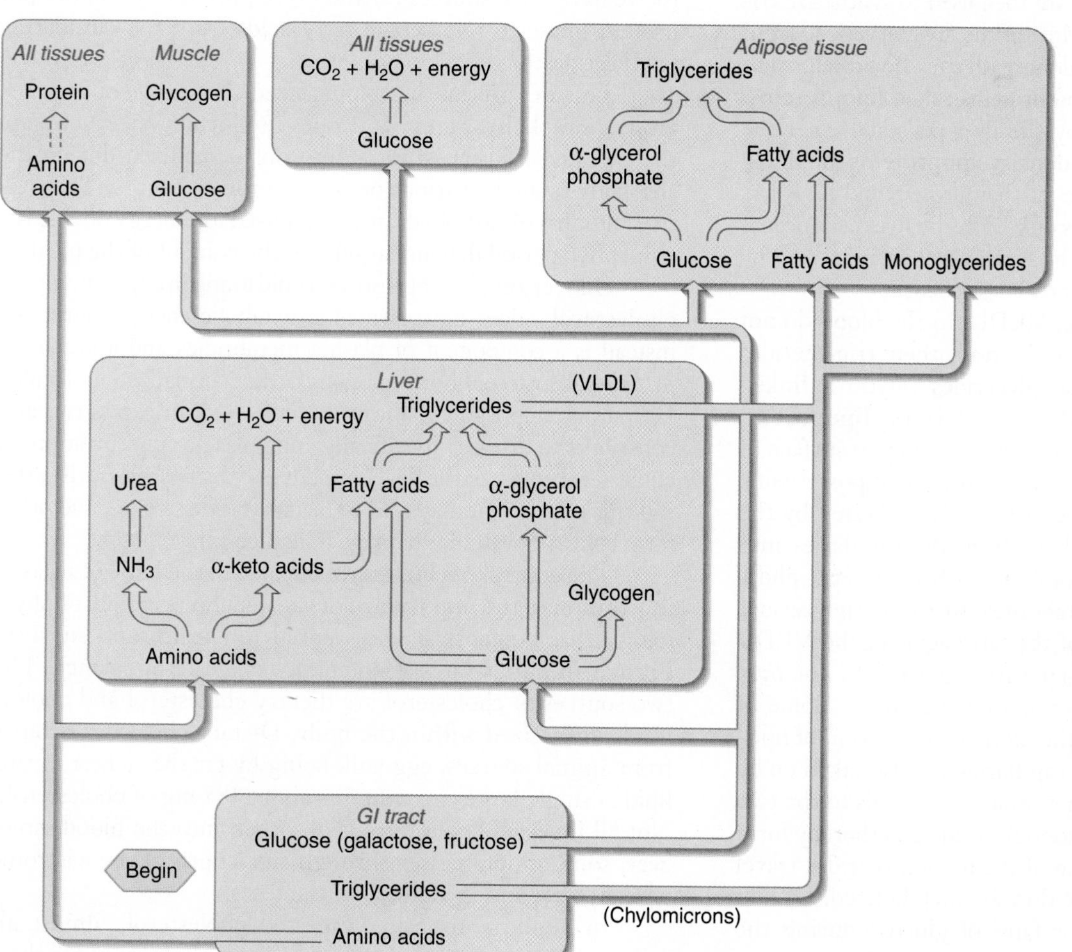

Figure 16.1 Major metabolic pathways of the absorptive state. The arrow from amino acids to protein is dashed to denote the fact that excess amino acids are not stored as protein (see text). All arrows between boxes denote transport of the substance via the blood (VLDL = very-low-density lipoproteins; Energy = ATP).

PHYSIOLOGICAL INQUIRY

- Would eating a diet that is low in fat content ensure that a person could not gain fat mass?

Answer can be found at end of chapter.

systemic venous system. Consequently, the liver cannot first modify absorbed fat before it reaches other tissues.

Absorbed Carbohydrate

Some of the carbohydrate absorbed from the gastrointestinal tract is galactose and fructose. Because these sugars are either converted to glucose by the liver or enter essentially the same metabolic pathways as glucose, we will for simplicity refer to absorbed carbohydrates as glucose.

Glucose is the body's major energy source during the absorptive state. Much of the absorbed glucose enters cells and is catabolized to carbon dioxide and water, in the process releasing energy that is used for ATP formation (as described in Chapter 3). Skeletal muscle makes up the majority of body mass, so it is the major consumer of glucose, even at rest. Skeletal muscle not only catabolizes glucose during the absorptive phase but also converts some of the glucose to the polysaccharide glycogen, which is then stored in the muscle for future use.

Adipose-tissue cells (adipocytes) also catabolize glucose for energy, but the most important fate of glucose in adipocytes during the absorptive phase is its transformation to fat (triglycerides). Glucose is the precursor of both α-glycerol phosphate and fatty acids, and these molecules are then linked together to form triglycerides, which are stored in the cell.

Another large fraction of the absorbed glucose enters liver cells. This is a very important point: During the absorptive period, there is net *uptake* of glucose by the liver. It is either stored as glycogen, as in skeletal muscle, or transformed to α-glycerol phosphate and fatty acids, which are then used to synthesize triglycerides, as in adipose tissue. Most of the fat synthesized from glucose in the liver is packaged along with specific proteins into molecular aggregates of lipids and proteins called **lipoproteins.** These aggregates are secreted by the liver cells and enter the blood. They are called **very-low-density lipoproteins (VLDLs)** because they contain much more fat than protein and fat is less dense than protein. The synthesis of VLDLs by liver cells occurs by processes similar to those for the synthesis of chylomicrons by intestinal mucosal cells, as Chapter 15 described.

Because of their large size, VLDLs in the blood do not readily penetrate capillary walls. Instead, their triglycerides are hydrolyzed mainly to monoglycerides (glycerol linked to one fatty acid) and fatty acids by the enzyme **lipoprotein lipase.** This enzyme is located on the blood-facing surface of capillary endothelial cells, especially those in adipose tissue. In adipose-tissue capillaries, the fatty acids generated by the action of lipoprotein lipase diffuse from the capillaries into the adipocytes. There, they combine with α-glycerol phosphate, supplied by glucose metabolites, to form triglycerides once again. As a result, most of the fatty acids in the VLDL triglycerides originally synthesized from glucose by the *liver* end up being stored in triglyceride in *adipose tissue.* Some of the monoglycerides formed in the blood by the action of lipoprotein lipase in adipose-tissue capillaries are also taken up by adipocytes, where enzymes can reattach fatty acids to the two available carbon atoms of the monoglyceride and thereby form a triglyceride. In addition, some of the monoglycerides travel via the blood to the liver, where they are metabolized.

To summarize, the major fates of glucose during the absorptive phase are (1) utilization for energy, (2) storage as glycogen in liver and skeletal muscle, and (3) storage as fat in adipose tissue.

Absorbed Lipids

As described in Chapter 15, many of the absorbed lipids are packaged into chylomicrons that enter the lymph and, from there, the circulation. The processing of the triglycerides in chylomicrons in plasma is similar to that just described for VLDLs produced by the liver. The fatty acids of plasma chylomicrons are released, mainly within adipose-tissue capillaries, by the action of endothelial lipoprotein lipase. The released fatty acids then diffuse into adipocytes and combine with α-glycerol phosphate, synthesized in the adipocytes from glucose metabolites, to form triglycerides.

The importance of glucose for triglyceride synthesis in adipocytes cannot be overemphasized. Adipocytes do not have the enzyme required for phosphorylation of glycerol, so α-glycerol phosphate can be formed in these cells only from glucose metabolites (refer back to Figure 3.41 to see how these metabolites are produced) and not from glycerol or any other fat metabolites.

In contrast to α-glycerol phosphate, there are three major sources of the fatty acids found in adipose-tissue triglyceride: (1) glucose that enters adipose tissue and is broken down to provide building blocks for the synthesis of fatty acids; (2) glucose that is used in the liver to form VLDL triglycerides, which are transported in the blood and taken up by the adipose tissue; and (3) ingested triglycerides transported in the blood in chylomicrons and taken up by adipose tissue. As we have seen, sources (2) and (3) require the action of lipoprotein lipase to release the fatty acids from the circulating triglycerides.

This description has emphasized the *storage* of ingested fat. For simplicity, Figure 16.1 does not include the fraction of the ingested fat that is not stored but is oxidized during the absorptive state by various organs to provide energy. The relative amounts of carbohydrate and fat used for energy during the absorptive period depend largely on the content of the meal.

One very important absorbed lipid found in chylomicrons—**cholesterol**—does not serve as a metabolic energy source but instead is a component of plasma membranes and a precursor for bile salts, steroid hormones, and other specialized molecules. Despite its importance, however, cholesterol in excess can also contribute to disease. Specifically, high plasma concentrations of cholesterol enhance the development of ***atherosclerosis,*** the arterial thickening that may lead to heart attacks, strokes, and other forms of cardiovascular damage (Chapter 12).

The control of cholesterol balance in the body is a classic illustration of the importance of the general principle of physiology that homeostasis is essential for health and survival. **Figure 16.2** illustrates a schema for cholesterol balance. The two sources of cholesterol are dietary cholesterol and cholesterol synthesized within the body. Dietary cholesterol comes from animal sources, egg yolk being by far the richest in this lipid (a single large egg contains about 185 mg of cholesterol). Not all ingested cholesterol is absorbed into the blood, however; some simply passes through the length of the gastrointestinal tract and is excreted in the feces.

In addition to using ingested cholesterol, almost all cells can synthesize some of the cholesterol required for their

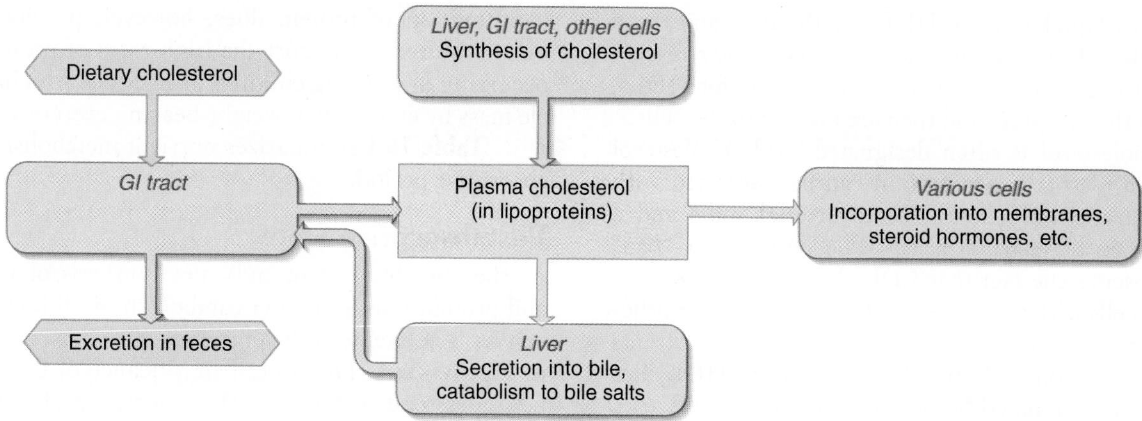

Figure 16.2 Cholesterol balance. Most of the cholesterol that is converted to bile salts, stored in the gallbladder, and secreted into the intestine gets recycled back to the liver. Changes in dietary cholesterol can modify plasma cholesterol concentration, but not usually dramatically. Cholesterol synthesis by the liver is up-regulated when dietary cholesterol is decreased, and vice versa.

own plasma membranes, but most cannot do so in adequate amounts and depend upon receiving cholesterol from the blood. This is also true of the endocrine cells that produce steroid hormones from cholesterol. Consequently, most cells *remove* cholesterol from the blood. In contrast, the liver and small intestine can produce large amounts of cholesterol, most of which *enters* the blood.

Now we look at the other side of cholesterol balance—the pathways, all involving the liver, for net cholesterol loss from the body. First, some plasma cholesterol is taken up by liver cells and secreted into the bile, which carries it to the gallbladder and from there to the lumen of the small intestine. Here, it is treated much like ingested cholesterol, some being absorbed back into the blood and the remainder excreted in the feces. Second, much of the cholesterol taken up by the liver cells is metabolized into bile salts (Chapter 15). After their production by the liver, these bile salts, like secreted cholesterol, eventually flow through the bile duct into the small intestine. (As described in Chapter 15, many of these bile salts are then reclaimed by absorption back into the blood across the epithelium of the distal small intestine.)

The liver is clearly the major organ that controls cholesterol homeostasis, for the liver can add newly synthesized cholesterol to the blood and it can remove cholesterol from the blood, secreting it into the bile or metabolizing it to bile salts. The homeostatic control mechanisms that keep plasma cholesterol concentrations within a normal range operate on all of these hepatic processes, but the single most important response involves cholesterol synthesis. The liver's synthesis of cholesterol is inhibited whenever dietary—and, therefore, plasma—cholesterol is increased. This is because cholesterol inhibits the enzyme HMG-CoA reductase, which is critical for cholesterol synthesis by the liver.

Thus, as soon as the plasma cholesterol concentration increases because of cholesterol ingestion, hepatic synthesis of cholesterol is inhibited and the plasma concentration of cholesterol remains close to its original value. Conversely, when dietary cholesterol is reduced and plasma cholesterol decreases, hepatic synthesis is stimulated (released from inhibition). This increased synthesis opposes any further decrease in plasma cholesterol. The sensitivity of this negative feedback control of cholesterol synthesis differs greatly from person to person, but it is the major reason why, for most people, it is difficult to decrease plasma cholesterol concentration very much by altering only dietary cholesterol.

So far, the maintenance of plasma cholesterol concentration within a homeostatic range has been emphasized. However, environmental and physiological factors can significantly alter plasma cholesterol concentrations. Perhaps the most important of these factors are the quantity and type of dietary fatty acids. Ingesting saturated fatty acids, which are the dominant fatty acids of animal fat (particularly high in red meats, most cheeses, and whole milk), increases plasma cholesterol. In contrast, eating either polyunsaturated fatty acids (the predominant plant fatty acids) or monounsaturated fatty acids, such as those in olive or peanut oil, decreases plasma cholesterol. The various fatty acids exert their effects on plasma cholesterol concentration by altering cholesterol synthesis, excretion, and metabolism to bile salts.

A variety of drugs now in common use are also capable of decreasing plasma cholesterol by influencing one or more of the metabolic pathways for cholesterol—for example, inhibiting HMG-CoA reductase—or by interfering with intestinal absorption of bile salts.

The story is more complicated than this, however, because not all plasma cholesterol has the same function or significance for disease. Like most other lipids, cholesterol circulates in the plasma as part of various lipoprotein complexes. These include chylomicrons, VLDLs, **low-density lipoproteins (LDLs)**, and **high-density lipoproteins (HDLs)**, each distinguished by their ratio of fat to protein. LDLs are the main cholesterol carriers, and they *deliver* cholesterol to cells throughout the body. LDLs bind to plasma membrane receptors specific for a protein component of the LDLs and are then taken up by the cells by endocytosis. In contrast to LDLs, HDLs *remove* excess cholesterol from blood and tissue, including the cholesterol-loaded cells of atherosclerotic plaques. They then deliver this cholesterol to the liver, which secretes it into the bile or converts it to bile salts. Along with LDLs, HDLs also deliver cholesterol to steroid-producing endocrine cells. Uptake of the HDLs by the liver and these endocrine cells is facilitated by the presence in their plasma membranes of large numbers of receptors specific for HDLs, which bind to the receptors and then are taken into the cells.

LDL cholesterol is often designated "bad" cholesterol because a high plasma concentration can be associated with increased deposition of cholesterol in arterial walls and a higher incidence of heart attacks. (The designation "bad" should not obscure the fact that LDL cholesterol is essential for supplying cells with the cholesterol they require to synthesize cell membranes and, in the case of the gonads and adrenal glands, steroid hormones.) Using the same criteria, HDL cholesterol has been designated "good" cholesterol.

The best single indicator of the likelihood of developing atherosclerotic disease is not necessarily total plasma cholesterol concentration but rather the ratio of plasma LDL cholesterol to plasma HDL cholesterol—the lower the ratio, the lower the risk. Cigarette smoking, a known risk factor for heart attacks, decreases plasma HDL, whereas weight reduction (in overweight persons) and regular exercise usually increase it. Estrogen not only decreases LDL but increases HDL, which explains, in part, why the incidence of coronary artery disease in premenopausal women is lower than in men. After menopause, the cholesterol values and coronary artery disease rates in women not on estrogen-replacement therapy become similar to those in men.

Finally, a variety of disorders of cholesterol metabolism have been identified. In ***familial hypercholesterolemia***, for example, LDL receptors are decreased in number or are nonfunctional. Consequently, LDL accumulates in the blood to very high concentrations. If untreated, this disease may result in atherosclerosis and heart disease at unusually young ages.

Absorbed Amino Acids

Some amino acids are absorbed into liver cells and used to synthesize a variety of proteins, including liver enzymes and plasma proteins, or they are converted to carbohydrate-like intermediates known as **α-keto acids** by removal of the amino group. This process is called deamination. The amino groups are used to synthesize urea in the liver, which enters the blood and is excreted by the kidneys. The α-keto acids can enter the Krebs (tricarboxylic acid) cycle (see Chapter 3, Figure 3.44) and be catabolized to provide energy for the liver cells. They can also be converted to fatty acids, thereby participating in fat synthesis by the liver.

Most ingested amino acids are not taken up by the liver cells but instead enter other cells (see Figure 16.1), where they may be used to synthesize proteins. All cells require a constant supply of amino acids for protein synthesis and participate in protein metabolism.

Protein synthesis is represented by a dashed arrow in Figure 16.1 to call attention to an important fact: There is a net synthesis of protein during the absorptive period, but this basically just replaces the proteins catabolized during the postabsorptive state. In other words, excess amino acids are not stored as protein in the sense that glucose is stored as glycogen or that both glucose and fat are stored as fat. Rather, ingested amino acids in excess of those required to maintain a stable rate of protein turnover are converted to carbohydrate or fat. Therefore, eating large amounts of protein does not in itself cause increases in total-body protein. Increased daily consumption of protein does, however, provide the amino acids required to support the high rates of protein synthesis occurring in growing children or in adults who increase muscle mass by engaging in weight-bearing exercises.

Table 16.1 summarizes nutrient metabolism during the absorptive period.

Postabsorptive State

As the absorptive state ends, net synthesis of glycogen, fat, and protein ceases and net catabolism of all these substances begins. The events of the postabsorptive state are summarized in **Figure 16.3**. The overall significance of these events can be understood in terms of the essential problem during the postabsorptive state: No glucose is being absorbed from the gastrointestinal tract, yet the plasma glucose concentration must be maintained because the central nervous system normally utilizes only glucose for energy. If the plasma glucose concentration decreases too much, alterations of neural activity occur, ranging from subtle impairment of mental function to seizures, coma, and even death.

Like cholesterol, the control of glucose balance is another classic example of the general principle of physiology that homeostasis is essential for health and survival. The events that maintain plasma glucose concentration fall into two categories: (1) reactions that provide sources of blood glucose; and (2) cellular utilization of fat for energy, thereby "sparing" glucose.

Sources of Blood Glucose

The sources of blood glucose during the postabsorptive state are as follows (see Figure 16.3):

1. **Glycogenolysis**, the hydrolysis of glycogen stores to monomers of glucose 6-phosphate, occurs in the liver and skeletal muscle. In the liver, glucose 6-phosphate is enzymatically converted to glucose, which then enters the blood. Hepatic glycogenolysis begins within seconds of an appropriate stimulus, such as sympathetic nervous system activation. As a result, it is the first line of defense in maintaining the plasma glucose concentration within a homeostatic range. The amount of glucose available from this source, however, can supply the body's requirements for only several hours before hepatic glycogen is nearly depleted.

TABLE 16.1 Summary of Nutrient Metabolism During the Absorptive State
Energy is provided primarily by absorbed carbohydrate in a typical meal.
There is net uptake of glucose by the liver.
Some carbohydrate is stored as glycogen in liver and muscle, but most carbohydrates and fats in excess of that used for energy are stored as fat in adipose tissue.
There is some synthesis of body proteins, but some of the amino acids in dietary protein are used for energy or converted to fat.

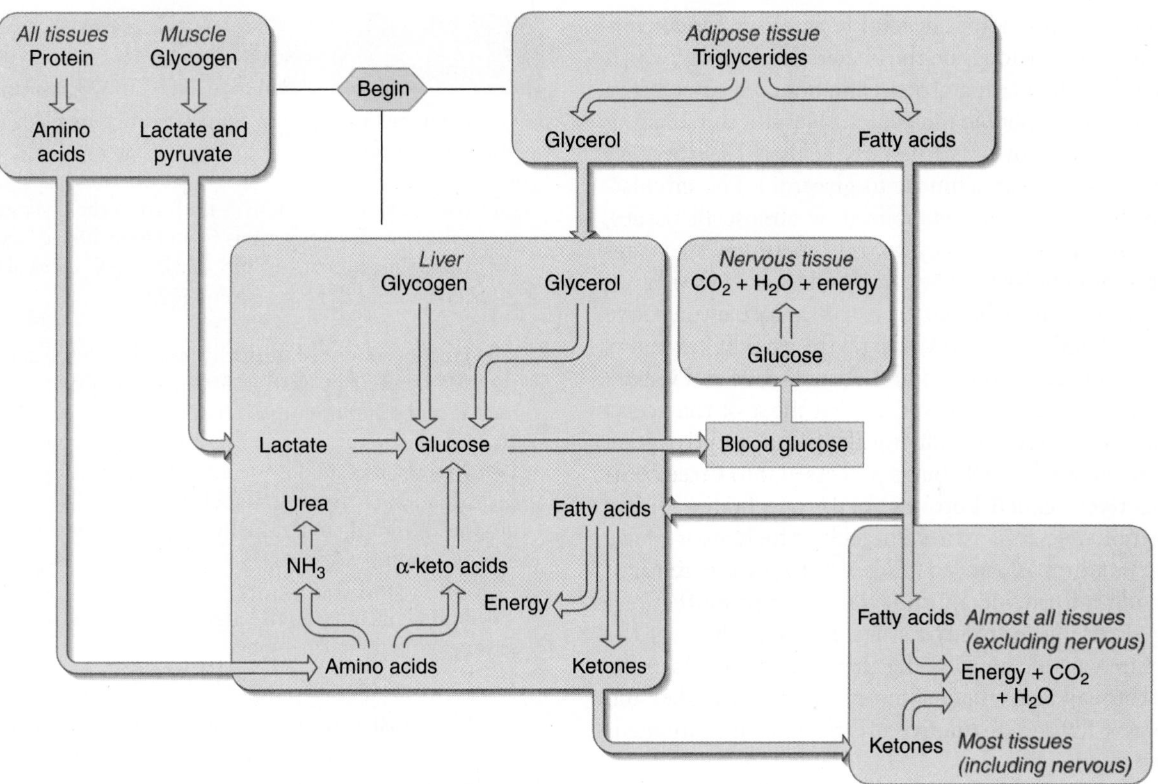

Figure 16.3 Major metabolic pathways of the postabsorptive state. The central focus is regulation of the blood glucose concentration. All arrows between boxes denote transport of the substance via the blood.

Glycogenolysis also occurs in skeletal muscle, which contains approximately the same amount of glycogen as the liver. Unlike the liver, however, muscle cells lack the enzyme necessary to form glucose from the glucose 6-phosphate formed during glycogenolysis; therefore, muscle glycogen is not a source of blood glucose. Instead, the glucose 6-phosphate undergoes glycolysis within muscle to yield ATP, pyruvate, and lactate. The ATP and pyruvate are used directly by the muscle cell. Some of the lactate, however, enters the blood, circulates to the liver, and is converted into glucose, which can then leave the liver cells to enter the blood. Thus, muscle glycogen contributes to the blood glucose indirectly via the liver's processing of lactate.

2. The catabolism of triglycerides in adipose tissue yields glycerol and fatty acids, a process termed **lipolysis.** The glycerol and fatty acids then enter the blood by diffusion. The glycerol reaching the liver is enzymatically converted through a series of steps to glucose. Thus, an important source of glucose during the postabsorptive state is the glycerol released when adipose-tissue triglyceride is broken down.
3. A few hours into the postabsorptive state, protein becomes another source of blood glucose. Large quantities of protein in muscle and other tissues can be catabolized without serious cellular malfunction. There are, of course, limits to this process, and continued protein loss during a prolonged fast ultimately means disruption of cell function, sickness, and death. Before this point is reached, however, protein breakdown can supply large quantities of amino acids. These amino acids enter the blood and are taken up by the liver, where some can be converted via the α-keto acid pathway to glucose. This glucose is then released into the blood.

Synthesis of glucose from such precursors as amino acids and glycerol is known as **gluconeogenesis**—that is, "creation of new glucose." During a 24 h fast, gluconeogenesis provides approximately 180 g of glucose. Although historically this process was considered to be almost entirely carried out by the liver with a small contribution by the kidneys, recent evidence strongly suggests that the kidneys contribute much more substantially to gluconeogenesis than previously believed.

Glucose Sparing (Fat Utilization)

The approximately 180 g of glucose per day produced by gluconeogenesis in the liver (and kidneys) during fasting supplies 720 kcal of energy. As described later in this chapter, typical total energy expenditure for an average adult is 1500 to 3000 kcal/day. Therefore, gluconeogenesis cannot supply all the energy demands of the body. An adjustment must therefore take place during the transition from the absorptive to the postabsorptive state. Most organs and tissues, other than those of the nervous system, significantly decrease their glucose catabolism and increase their fat utilization, the latter becoming the major energy source. This metabolic adjustment, known as **glucose sparing,** "spares" the glucose produced by the liver for use by the nervous system.

The essential step in this adjustment is lipolysis, the catabolism of adipose-tissue triglyceride, which liberates glycerol and fatty acids into the blood. We described lipolysis earlier in terms of its importance in providing glycerol to the liver for conversion to glucose. Now, we focus on the liberated fatty acids, which circulate bound to the plasma protein albumin, which acts as a carrier for these hydrophobic molecules. (Despite this binding to protein, they are known as free fatty acids [FFAs] because they are "free" of their attachment to glycerol.) The circulating FFAs are taken up and metabolized by almost all tissues, *excluding the nervous system.* They provide energy in two ways (see Chapter 3 for details): (1) They first undergo beta oxidation to yield hydrogen atoms (that go on to participate in oxidative phosphorylation) and acetyl CoA, and (2) the acetyl CoA enters the Krebs cycle and is catabolized to carbon dioxide and water.

The liver is unique, however, in that most of the acetyl CoA it forms from fatty acids during the postabsorptive state does not enter the Krebs cycle but is processed into three compounds collectively called **ketones,** or ketone bodies. (*Note:* Ketones are not the same as α-keto acids, which, as we have seen, are metabolites of amino acids.) Ketones are released into the blood and provide an important energy source during prolonged fasting for many tissues, *including* those of the nervous system, capable of oxidizing them via the Krebs cycle. One of the ketones is acetone, some of which is exhaled and accounts in part for the distinctive breath odor of individuals undergoing prolonged fasting.

The net result of fatty acid and ketone utilization during fasting is the provision of energy for the body while at the same time sparing glucose for the brain and nervous system. Moreover, as just emphasized, the brain can use ketones for an energy source, and it does so increasingly as ketones build up in the blood during the first few days of a fast. The survival value of this phenomenon is significant; when the brain decreases its glucose requirement by utilizing ketones, much less protein breakdown is required to supply amino acids for gluconeogenesis. Consequently, the ability to withstand a long fast without serious tissue damage is enhanced.

Table 16.2 summarizes the events of the postabsorptive state. The combined effects of glycogenolysis, gluconeogenesis, and the switch to fat utilization are so efficient that, after several days of complete fasting, the plasma glucose concentration is decreased by only a few percentage points. After 1 month, it is decreased by only 25% (although in very thin persons, this happens much sooner).

16.2 Endocrine and Neural Control of the Absorptive and Postabsorptive States

We now turn to the endocrine and neural factors that control and integrate these metabolic pathways. We will focus primarily on the following questions, summarized in **Figure 16.4**: (1) What controls net anabolism of protein, glycogen, and triglyceride in the absorptive phase, and net catabolism in the postabsorptive phase? (2) What induces the cells to utilize primarily glucose for energy during the absorptive phase but fat during the postabsorptive phase? (3) What stimulates net glucose uptake by the liver during the absorptive phase but gluconeogenesis and glucose release during the postabsorptive phase?

TABLE 16.2 Summary of Nutrient Metabolism During the Postabsorptive State
Glycogen, fat, and protein syntheses are curtailed, and net breakdown occurs.
Glucose is formed in the liver both from the glycogen stored there and by gluconeogenesis from blood-borne lactate, pyruvate, glycerol, and amino acids. The kidneys also perform gluconeogenesis during a prolonged fast.
The glucose produced in the liver (and kidneys) is released into the blood, but its utilization for energy is greatly decreased in muscle and other nonneural tissues.
Lipolysis releases adipose-tissue fatty acids into the blood, and the oxidation of these fatty acids by most cells and of ketones produced from them by the liver provides most of the body's energy supply.
The brain continues to use glucose but also starts using ketones as they build up in the blood.

The most important controls of these transitions from feasting to fasting, and vice versa, are two pancreatic hormones—**insulin** and **glucagon.** Also playing a role are the hormones epinephrine and cortisol from the adrenal glands, growth hormone from the anterior pituitary gland, and the sympathetic nerves to the liver and adipose tissue.

Insulin and glucagon are peptide hormones secreted by the **islets of Langerhans** (or, simply, pancreatic islets), clusters of endocrine cells in the pancreas. There are several distinct types of islet cells, each of which secretes a different hormone. The **beta cells** (or B cells) are the source of insulin, and the **alpha cells** (or A cells) are the source of glucagon. There are other molecules secreted by still other islet cells, but the functions of these other molecules in humans are less well established.

Insulin

Insulin is the most important controller of organic metabolism. Its secretion—and, therefore, its plasma concentration—is increased during the absorptive state and decreased during the postabsorptive state.

The metabolic effects of insulin are exerted mainly on muscle cells (both cardiac and skeletal), adipocytes, and hepatocytes. **Figure 16.5** summarizes the most important responses of these target cells. Compare the top portion of this figure to Figure 16.1 and to the left panel of Figure 16.4, and you will see that the responses to an increase in insulin are the same as the events of the absorptive-state pattern. Conversely, the effects of a decrease in plasma insulin are the same as the events of the postabsorptive pattern in Figure 16.3 and the right panel of Figure 16.4. The reason for these correspondences is that an increased plasma concentration of insulin is the major cause of the absorptive-state events, and a decreased plasma concentration of insulin is the major cause of the postabsorptive events.

Like all peptide hormones, insulin induces its effects by binding to specific receptors on the plasma membranes of its

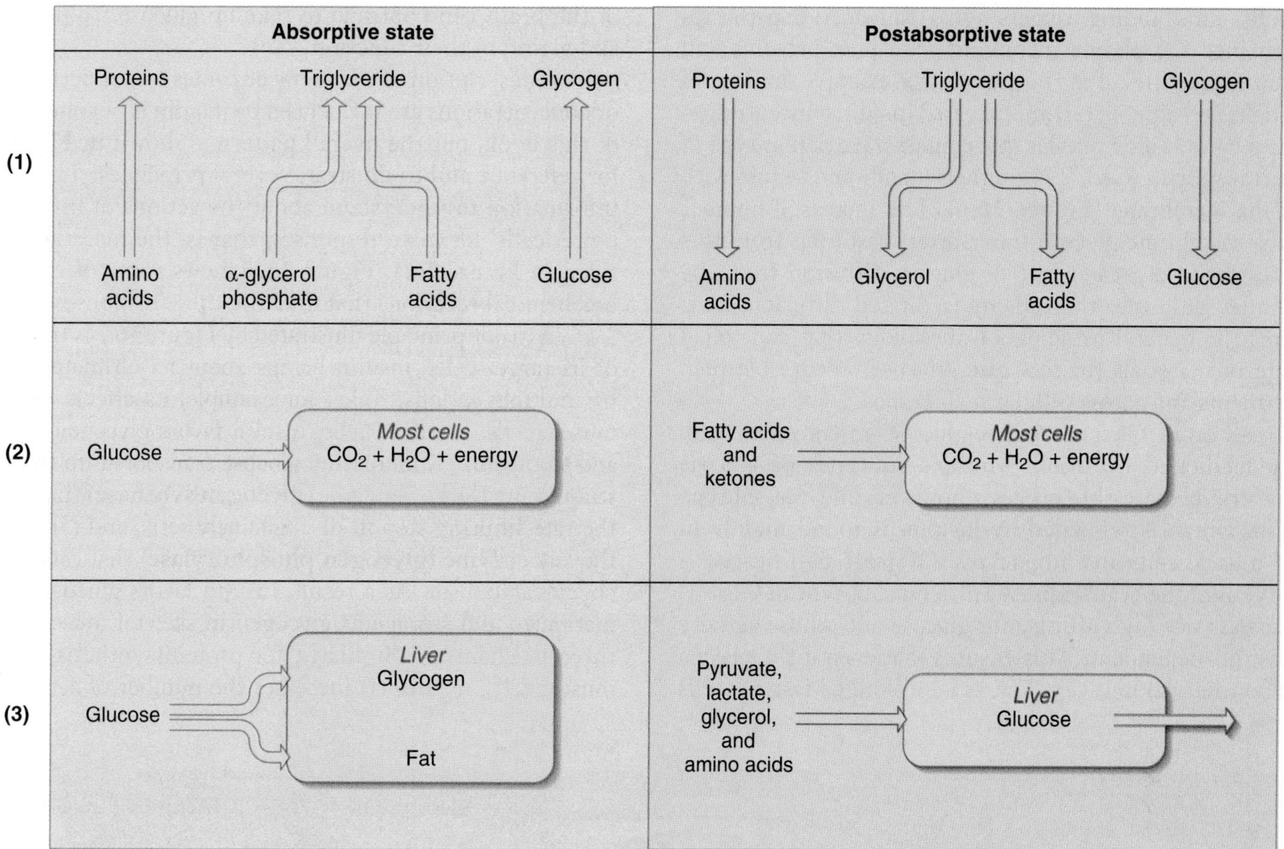

Figure 16.4 Summary of critical points in transition from the absorptive state to the postabsorptive state. The term *absorptive state* could be replaced with *actions of insulin*, and the term *postabsorptive state* with *results of decreased insulin*. The numbers at the left margin refer to discussion questions in the text.

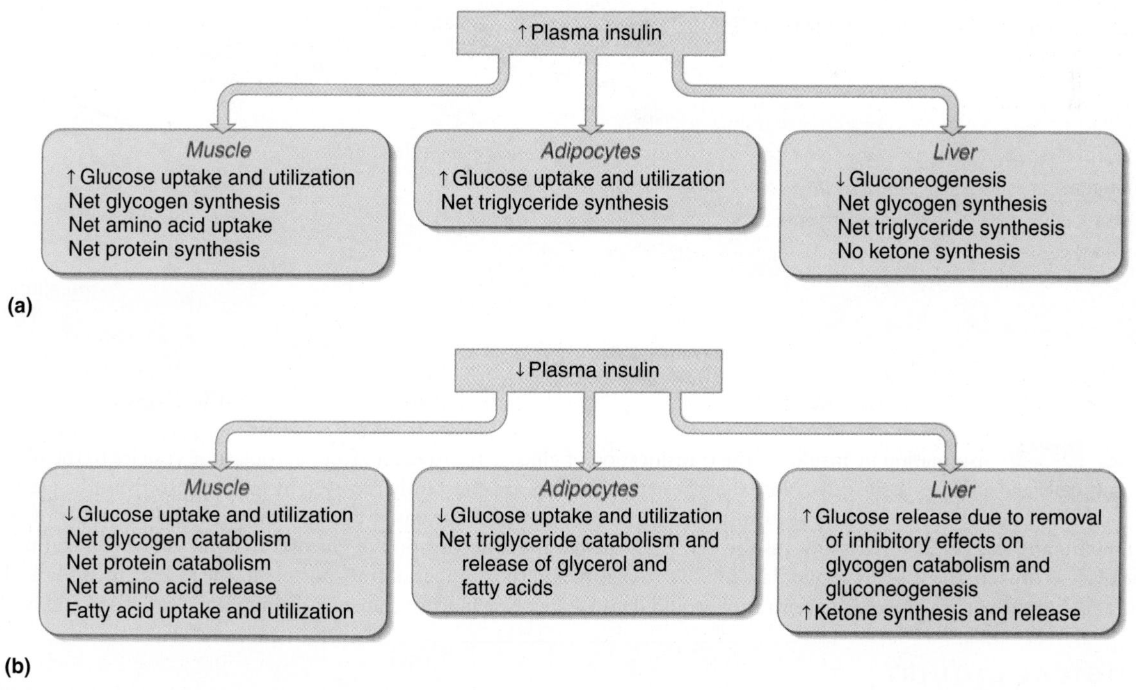

Figure 16.5 Summary of overall target-cell responses to (a) an increase or (b) a decrease in the plasma concentration of insulin. The responses in (a) are virtually identical to the absorptive-state events of Figure 16.1 and the left panel of Figure 16.4; the responses in (b) are virtually identical to the postabsorptive-state events of Figure 16.3 and the right panel of Figure 16.4.

target cells. This binding triggers signal transduction pathways that influence the plasma membrane transport proteins and intracellular enzymes of the target cell. For example, in skeletal muscle cells and adipocytes, an increased insulin concentration stimulates cytoplasmic vesicles that contain a particular type of glucose transporter (GLUT-4) in their membrane to fuse with the plasma membrane (**Figure 16.6**). The increased number of plasma membrane glucose transporters resulting from this fusion results in a greater rate of glucose diffusion from the extracellular fluid into the cells by facilitated diffusion. This illustrates the general principle of physiology that controlled exchange of materials (in this case, glucose) occurs between compartments and across cellular membranes.

Recall from Chapter 4 that glucose enters most body cells by facilitated diffusion. Multiple subtypes of glucose transporters mediate this process, however, and the subtype GLUT-4, which is regulated by insulin, is found mainly in skeletal muscle cells and adipocytes. Of great significance is that the cells of the brain express a different subtype of GLUT, one that has very high affinity for glucose and whose activity is *not* insulin-dependent. This ensures that even if the plasma insulin concentration is very low, as in prolonged fasting, cells of the brain can continue to take up glucose from the blood and maintain their function.

A description of the many enzymes whose activities and/or concentrations are influenced by insulin is beyond the scope of this book, but the overall pattern is shown in **Figure 16.7** for reference and to illustrate several principles. The essential information to understand about the actions of insulin is the target cells' ultimate responses, that is, the material summarized in Figure 16.5. Figure 16.7 shows some of the specific biochemical reactions that underlie these responses.

A major principle illustrated by Figure 16.7 is that, in each of its target cells, insulin brings about its ultimate responses by multiple actions. Take, for example, its effects on skeletal muscle cells. In these cells, insulin favors glycogen formation and storage by (1) increasing glucose transport into the cell, (2) stimulating the key enzyme (**glycogen synthase**) that catalyzes the rate-limiting step in glycogen synthesis, and (3) inhibiting the key enzyme (**glycogen phosphorylase**) that catalyzes glycogen catabolism. As a result, insulin favors glucose transformation to and storage as glycogen in skeletal muscle through three mechanisms. Similarly, for protein synthesis in skeletal muscle cells, insulin (1) increases the number of active plasma

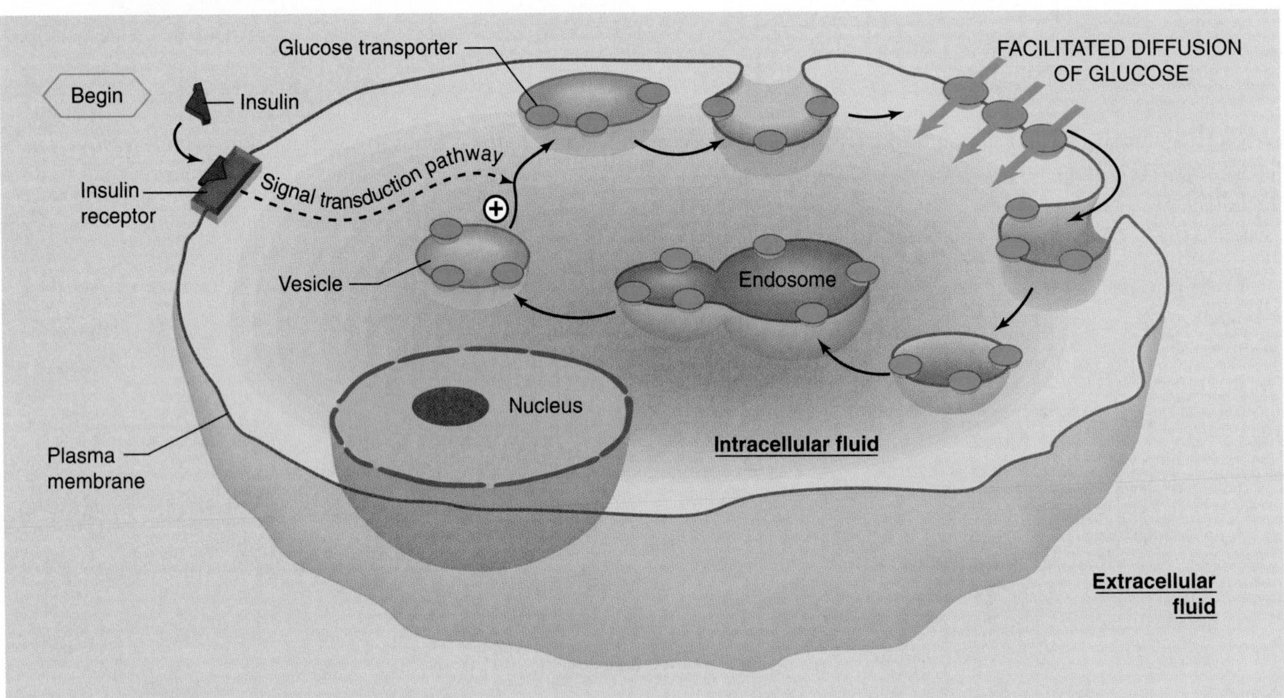

Figure 16.6 AP|R Stimulation by insulin of the translocation of glucose transporters from cytoplasmic vesicles to the plasma membrane in skeletal muscle cells and adipose-tissue cells. Note that these transporters are constantly recycled by endocytosis from the plasma membrane back through endosomes into vesicles. As long as insulin concentration is elevated, the entire cycle continues and the number of transporters in the plasma membrane stays high. This is how insulin decreases the plasma concentration of glucose. In contrast, when insulin concentration decreases, the cycle is broken, the vesicles accumulate in the cytoplasm, and the number of transporters in the plasma membrane decreases. Thus, without insulin, the plasma glucose concentration would increase, because glucose transport from plasma to cells would be decreased.

PHYSIOLOGICAL INQUIRY

- What advantage is there to having insulin-dependent glucose transporters already synthesized and prepackaged in a cell, even before it is stimulated by insulin?

Answer can be found at end of chapter.

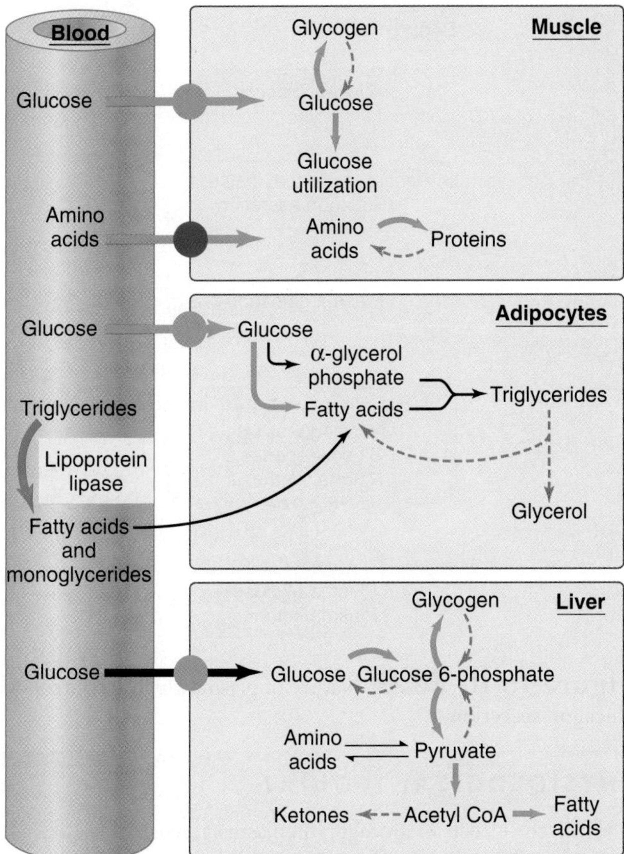

Figure 16.7 Illustration of the key biochemical events that underlie the responses of target cells to insulin as summarized in Figure 16.5. Each green arrow denotes a process stimulated by insulin, whereas a dashed red arrow denotes inhibition by insulin. Except for the effects on the transport proteins for glucose and amino acids, all other effects are exerted on insulin-sensitive enzymes. The bowed arrows denote pathways whose reversibility is mediated by different enzymes; such enzymes are commonly the ones influenced by insulin and other hormones. The black arrows are processes that are not *directly* affected by insulin but are enhanced in the presence of increased insulin as the result of mass action.

membrane transporters for amino acids, thereby increasing amino acid transport into the cells; (2) stimulates the ribosomal enzymes that mediate the synthesis of protein from these amino acids; and (3) inhibits the enzymes that mediate protein catabolism.

Control of Insulin Secretion

The major controlling factor for insulin secretion is the plasma glucose concentration. An increase in plasma glucose concentration, as occurs after a meal, acts on the beta cells of the islets of Langerhans to stimulate insulin secretion, whereas a decrease in plasma glucose removes the stimulus for insulin secretion. The feedback nature of this system is shown in **Figure 16.8**; following a meal, the increase in plasma glucose concentration stimulates insulin secretion. The insulin stimulates the entry of glucose into muscle and adipose tissue, as well as net uptake rather than net output of glucose by the liver. These effects eventually decrease the blood concentration of glucose to its premeal level, thereby removing the stimulus for insulin secretion and causing it to return to its previous level. This is a classic example of a homeostatic process regulated by negative feedback.

In addition to plasma glucose concentration, several other factors control insulin secretion (**Figure 16.9**). For example, increased amino acid concentrations stimulate insulin secretion. This is another negative feedback control; amino acid concentrations increase in the blood after ingestion of a protein-containing meal, and the increased plasma insulin stimulates the uptake of these amino acids by muscle and other cells, thereby lowering their concentrations.

There are also important hormonal controls over insulin secretion. For example, a family of hormones known as **incretins**—secreted by endocrine cells in the gastrointestinal tract in response to eating—amplifies the insulin response to glucose. The major incretins include glucagon-like peptide 1 (GLP-1) and glucose-dependent insulinotropic peptide (GIP). The actions of incretins provide a feedforward component to glucose regulation during the ingestion of a meal. Consequently, insulin secretion increases more than it would if plasma glucose were the only controller, thereby minimizing the absorptive peak in plasma glucose concentration. This mechanism minimizes the likelihood of large increases in plasma glucose after a meal, which among other things could

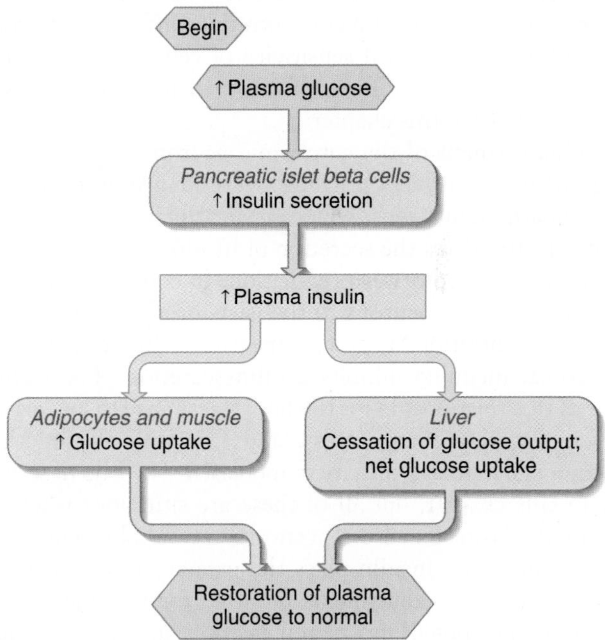

Figure 16.8 APIR Nature of plasma glucose control over insulin secretion. As glucose concentration increases in plasma (e.g., after a meal containing carbohydrate), insulin secretion is rapidly stimulated. The increase in insulin stimulates glucose transport from extracellular fluid into cells, thus decreasing plasma glucose concentrations. Insulin also acts to inhibit hepatic glucose output.

PHYSIOLOGICAL INQUIRY

- Notice that the brain is not listed as being insulin-sensitive. Why is that advantageous?

Answer can be found at end of chapter.

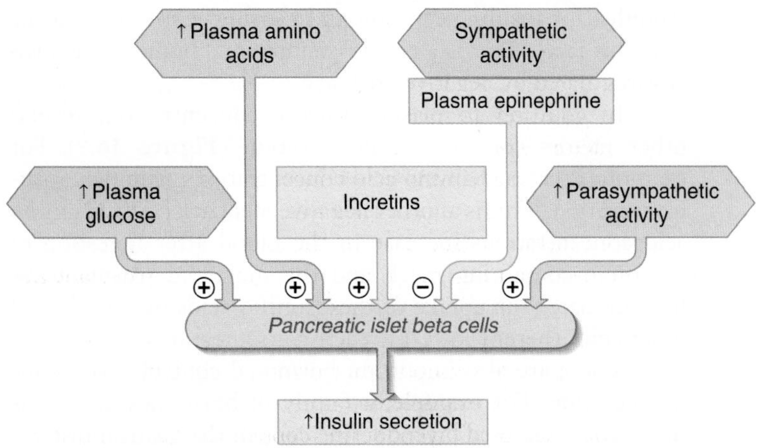

Figure 16.9 APIR Major controls of insulin secretion. The ⊕ and ⊖ symbols represent stimulatory and inhibitory actions, respectively. Incretins are gastrointestinal hormones that act as feedforward signals to the pancreas.

exceed the capacity of the kidneys to completely reabsorb all of the glucose that appears in the filtrate in the renal nephrons. An analog of GLP-1 is currently used for the treatment of type 2 diabetes mellitus, in which the pancreas often produces insufficient insulin and the body's cells are less responsive to insulin. Injection of this analog before a meal may increase a person's circulating insulin concentration sufficiently to compensate for the decreased sensitivity of cells to insulin. The clinical features of the different forms of diabetes mellitus will be covered later in this chapter.

Finally, input of the autonomic neurons to the islets of Langerhans also influences insulin secretion. Activation of the parasympathetic neurons, which occurs during the ingestion of a meal, stimulates the secretion of insulin and constitutes a second type of feedforward regulation. In contrast, activation of the sympathetic neurons to the islets or an increase in the plasma concentration of epinephrine (the hormone secreted by the adrenal medulla) inhibits insulin secretion. The significance of this relationship for the body's response to low plasma glucose (hypoglycemia), stress, and exercise—all situations in which sympathetic activity is increased—will be described later in this chapter, but all of these are situations where an increase in plasma glucose concentration would be beneficial.

In summary, insulin plays the primary role in controlling the metabolic adjustments required for feasting or fasting. Other hormonal and neural factors, however, also play significant roles. They all oppose the action of insulin in one way or another and are known as **glucose-counterregulatory controls.** As described next, the most important of these are glucagon, epinephrine, sympathetic nerves, cortisol, and growth hormone.

Glucagon

As mentioned earlier, glucagon is the peptide hormone produced by the alpha cells of the pancreatic islets. The major physiological effects of glucagon occur within the liver and oppose those of insulin (**Figure 16.10**). Thus, glucagon (1) stimulates glycogenolysis, (2) stimulates gluconeogenesis, and (3) stimulates the synthesis of ketones. The overall results are to increase the plasma concentrations of glucose and ketones, which are important for the postabsorptive state, and to prevent hypoglycemia. The effects, if any, of glucagon on adipocyte function in humans are still unresolved.

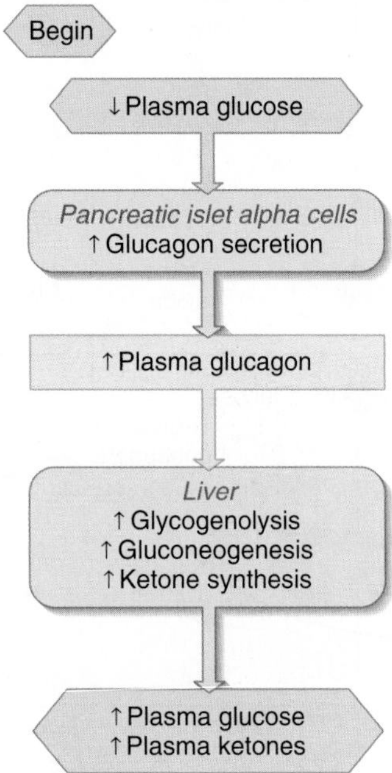

Figure 16.10 APIR Nature of plasma glucose control over glucagon secretion.

PHYSIOLOGICAL INQUIRY

- Given the effects of glucagon on plasma glucose concentrations, what effect do you think fight-or-flight (stress) reactions would have on the circulating level of glucagon?

Answer can be found at end of chapter.

The major stimulus for glucagon secretion is a decrease in the circulating concentration of glucose (which in turn causes a decrease in plasma insulin). The adaptive value of such a reflex is clear; a decreased plasma glucose concentration induces an increase in the secretion of glucagon into the blood, which, by its effects on metabolism, serves to restore normal blood glucose concentration by glycogenolysis and gluconeogenesis. At the same time, glucagon supplies ketones for utilization by the brain. Conversely, an increased plasma glucose concentration inhibits the secretion of glucagon, thereby helping to return the plasma glucose concentration toward normal. As a result, during the postabsorptive state, there is an increase in the glucagon/insulin ratio in the plasma, and this accounts almost entirely for the transition from the absorptive to the postabsorptive state.

The secretion of glucagon, like that of insulin, is controlled not only by the plasma concentration of glucose and other nutrients but also by neural and hormonal inputs to the islets. For example, the sympathetic nerves to the islets stimulate glucagon secretion—just the opposite of their effect on insulin secretion. The dual and opposite actions of glucagon and insulin on glucose homeostasis clearly illustrate the general principle of physiology that most physiological functions are controlled by multiple regulatory systems, often working in opposition.

Epinephrine and Sympathetic Nerves to Liver and Adipose Tissue

As noted earlier, epinephrine and the sympathetic nerves to the pancreatic islets inhibit insulin secretion and stimulate glucagon secretion. In addition, epinephrine also affects nutrient metabolism directly (**Figure 16.11**). Its major direct effects include stimulation of (1) glycogenolysis in both the liver and skeletal muscle, (2) gluconeogenesis in the liver, and (3) lipolysis in adipocytes. Activation of the sympathetic nerves to the liver and adipose tissue elicits the same responses from these organs as does circulating epinephrine.

In adipocytes, epinephrine stimulates the activity of an enzyme called **hormone-sensitive lipase (HSL)**. Once activated, HSL works along with other enzymes to catalyze the breakdown of triglycerides to free fatty acids and glycerol. Both are then released into the blood, where they serve directly as an energy source (fatty acids) or as a gluconeogenic precursor (glycerol). Not surprisingly, insulin inhibits the activity of HSL during the absorptive state, because it would not be beneficial to break down stored fat when the blood is receiving nutrients from ingested food. Thus, enhanced sympathetic nervous system activity exerts effects on organic metabolism—specifically, increased plasma concentrations of glucose, glycerol, and fatty acids—that are opposite those of insulin.

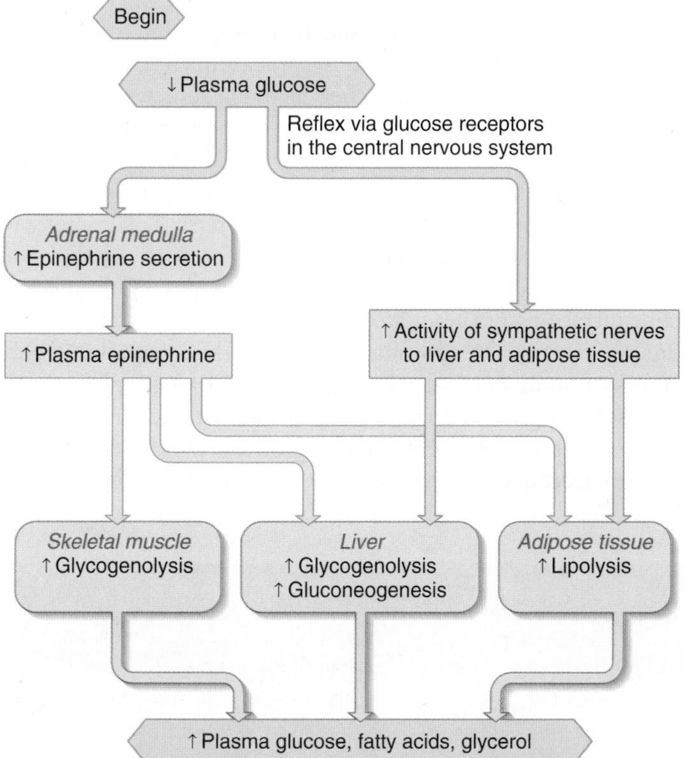

Figure 16.11 AP|R Participation of the sympathetic nervous system in the response to a low plasma glucose concentration (hypoglycemia). Glycogenolysis in skeletal muscle contributes to restoring plasma glucose by releasing lactate, which is converted to glucose in the liver and released into the blood. Recall also from Figure 16.9 and the text that the sympathetic nervous system inhibits insulin and stimulates glucagon secretion, which further contributes to the increased plasma energy sources.

As might be predicted from these effects, low blood sugar leads to increases in both epinephrine secretion and sympathetic nerve activity to the liver and adipose tissue. This is the same stimulus that leads to increased glucagon secretion, although the receptors and pathways are totally different. When the plasma glucose concentration decreases, glucose-sensitive cells in the central nervous system (and, possibly, the liver) initiate the reflexes that lead to increased activity in the sympathetic pathways to the adrenal medulla, liver, and adipose tissue. The adaptive value of the response is the same as that for the glucagon response to hypoglycemia; blood glucose returns toward normal, and fatty acids are supplied for cell utilization.

Cortisol

Cortisol, the major glucocorticoid produced by the adrenal cortex, plays an essential permissive role in the adjustments to fasting. We have described how fasting is associated with the stimulation of both gluconeogenesis and lipolysis; however, neither of these critical metabolic transformations occurs to the usual degree in a person deficient in cortisol. In other words, the plasma cortisol level does not need to increase much during fasting, but the presence of cortisol in the blood maintains the concentrations of the key liver and adipose-tissue enzymes required for gluconeogenesis and lipolysis—for example, HSL. Therefore, in response to fasting, people with a cortisol deficiency can develop hypoglycemia significant enough to interfere with cellular function. Moreover, cortisol can play more than a permissive role when its plasma concentration does increase, as it does during stress. At high concentrations, cortisol elicits many metabolic events ordinarily associated with fasting (**Table 16.3**). In fact, cortisol actually decreases the sensitivity of muscle and adipose cells to insulin, which helps to maintain plasma glucose concentration during fasting, thereby providing a regular source of energy for the brain. Clearly, here is another hormone that, in addition to glucagon and epinephrine, can exert actions opposite those of insulin. Indeed, people with pathologically high plasma concentrations of cortisol or who are given synthetic glucocorticoids for medical reasons can develop symptoms similar to those seen in individuals, such as those with type 2 diabetes mellitus, whose cells do not respond adequately to insulin.

TABLE 16.3	Effects of Cortisol on Organic Metabolism

I. Basal concentrations are permissive for stimulation of gluconeogenesis and lipolysis in the postabsorptive state.

II. Increased plasma concentrations cause
   A. Increased protein catabolism
   B. Increased gluconeogenesis
   C. Decreased glucose uptake by muscle cells and adipose-tissue cells
   D. Increased triglyceride breakdown

Net result: Increased plasma concentrations of amino acids, glucose, and free fatty acids

Growth Hormone

The primary physiological effects of growth hormone are to stimulate both growth and protein synthesis (by means of its effects on insulin-like growth factor 1; see Chapter 11). Compared to these effects, those it exerts on carbohydrate and lipid metabolism are less significant. Nonetheless, as is true for cortisol, either deficiency or excess of growth hormone does produce significant abnormalities in lipid and carbohydrate metabolism. Growth hormone's effects on these nutrients, in contrast to those on protein metabolism, are similar to those of cortisol and opposite those of insulin. Growth hormone (1) increases the responsiveness of adipocytes to lipolytic stimuli, (2) stimulates gluconeogenesis by the liver, and (3) reduces the ability of insulin to stimulate glucose uptake by muscle and adipose tissue. These three effects are often termed growth hormone's "anti-insulin effects." Because of these effects, some of the symptoms observed in people with acromegaly (excess growth hormone production; see the Chapter 11 Clinical Case Study) are similar to those observed in people with insulin resistance due to type 2 diabetes mellitus.

A summary of the hormonal control of metabolism is given in **Table 16.4**.

Hypoglycemia

Hypoglycemia is broadly defined as an abnormally low plasma glucose concentration. The plasma glucose concentration can decrease to very low values, usually during the postabsorptive state, in persons with several types of disorders. ***Fasting hypoglycemia*** and the relatively uncommon disorders responsible for it can be understood in terms of the regulation of blood glucose concentration. They include (1) an excess of insulin due to an insulin-producing tumor, drugs that stimulate insulin secretion, or taking too much insulin (if the person is diabetic); and (2) a defect in one or more glucose-counterregulatory controls, for example, inadequate glycogenolysis and/or gluconeogenesis due to liver disease or cortisol deficiency.

Fasting hypoglycemia causes many symptoms. Some—increased heart rate, trembling, nervousness, sweating, and anxiety—are accounted for by activation of the sympathetic nervous system caused reflexively by the hypoglycemia. Other symptoms, such as headache, confusion, dizziness, loss of coordination, and slurred speech, are direct consequences of too little glucose reaching the brain. More serious brain effects, including convulsions and coma, can occur if the plasma glucose concentration decreases sufficiently.

16.3 Energy Homeostasis in Exercise and Stress

During exercise, large quantities of fuels must be mobilized to provide the energy required for muscle contraction. These include plasma glucose and fatty acids as well as the muscle's own glycogen.

The additional plasma glucose used during exercise is supplied by the liver, both by breakdown of its glycogen stores and by gluconeogenesis. Glycerol is made available to the liver by a large increase in adipose-tissue lipolysis due to activation of HSL, with a resultant release of glycerol and fatty acids into the blood; the fatty acids serve as an additional energy source for the exercising muscle.

What happens to plasma glucose concentration during exercise? It changes very little in short-term, mild-to-moderate exercise and may even increase slightly with strenuous, short-term activity due to the counterregulatory actions of hormones. However, during prolonged exercise (**Figure 16.12**)—more than about 90 min—plasma glucose concentration does decrease but usually by less than 25%. Clearly, glucose output by the liver increases approximately in proportion to increased glucose utilization during exercise, at least until the later stages of prolonged exercise when it begins to lag somewhat.

The metabolic profile of an exercising person—increases in hepatic glucose production, triglyceride breakdown, and fatty acid utilization—is similar to a fasting person, and the endocrine controls are also the same. Exercise is characterized by a decrease in insulin secretion and an increase in glucagon secretion (see Figure 16.12), and the changes in the plasma concentrations of these two hormones are the major controls during exercise. In addition, activity of the sympathetic nervous system increases (including secretion of epinephrine) and cortisol and growth hormone secretion both increase as well.

What triggers increased glucagon secretion and decreased insulin secretion during exercise? One signal, at least during

TABLE 16.4 Summary of Glucose-Counterregulatory Controls*

	Glucagon	Epinephrine	Cortisol	Growth Hormone
Glycogenolysis	✓	✓		
Gluconeogenesis	✓	✓	✓	✓
Lipolysis		✓	✓	✓
Inhibition of glucose uptake by muscle cells and adipose tissue cells			✓	✓

*A ✓ indicates that the hormone stimulates the process; no ✓ indicates that the hormone has no major physiological effect on the process. Epinephrine stimulates glycogenolysis in both liver and skeletal muscle, whereas glucagon does so only in liver.

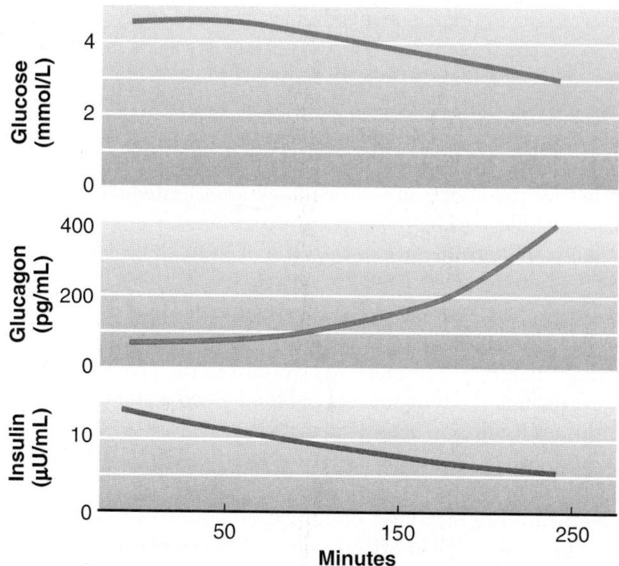

Figure 16.12 Plasma concentrations of glucose, glucagon, and insulin during prolonged (240 min) moderate exercise at a fixed intensity (pg/mL = Picograms per milliliter; μU/mL = Microunits per milliliter). Adapted from Felig and Wahren.

prolonged exercise, is the modest decrease in plasma glucose that occurs (see Figure 16.12). This is the same signal that controls the secretion of these hormones in fasting. Other inputs at all intensities of exercise include increased circulating epinephrine and increased activity of the sympathetic neurons supplying the pancreatic islets. Thus, the increased sympathetic nervous system activity characteristic of exercise not only contributes directly to energy mobilization by acting on the liver and adipose tissue but contributes indirectly by inhibiting the secretion of insulin and stimulating that of glucagon. This sympathetic output is not triggered by changes in plasma glucose concentration but is mediated by the central nervous system as part of the neural response to exercise.

One component of the response to exercise is quite different from the response to fasting; in exercise, glucose uptake and utilization by the muscles are increased, whereas during fasting they are markedly decreased. How is it that, during exercise, the movement of glucose via facilitated diffusion into skeletal muscle can remain high in the presence of decreased plasma insulin and increased plasma concentrations of cortisol and growth hormone, all of which decrease glucose uptake by skeletal muscle? By an as-yet-unidentified mechanism, muscle contraction causes migration of an intracellular store of glucose transporters to the plasma membrane and an increase in synthesis of the transporters. For this reason, even though exercising muscles require more glucose than do muscles at rest, less insulin is required to induce glucose transport into muscle cells.

Exercise and the postabsorptive state are not the only situations characterized by the endocrine profile of decreased insulin and increased glucagon, sympathetic activity, cortisol, and growth hormone. This profile also occurs in response to a variety of nonspecific stresses, both physical and emotional. The adaptive value of these endocrine responses to stress is that the resulting metabolic shifts prepare the body for exercise ("fight or flight") in the face of real or threatened injury. In addition, the amino acids liberated by the catabolism of body protein stores because of decreased insulin and increased cortisol not only provide energy via gluconeogenesis but also constitute a potential source of amino acids for tissue repair should injury occur.

Chronic, intense exercise can also be stressful for the human body. In such cases, certain nonessential functions shut down so that nutrients can be directed primarily to muscle. One of these nonessential functions is reproduction. Consequently, adolescents engaged in rigorous daily training regimens, such as Olympic-caliber gymnasts, may show delayed puberty. Similarly, women who perform chronic, intense exercise may become temporarily infertile, a condition known as ***exercise-induced amenorrhea*** (the lack of regular menstrual cycles—see Chapter 17). This condition occurs in a variety of occupations that combine weight loss and strenuous exercise, such as may occur in professional ballerinas. Whether exercise-induced infertility occurs in men is uncertain, but most evidence suggests it does not.

SECTION A SUMMARY

Events of the Absorptive and Postabsorptive States

I. During absorption, energy is provided primarily by absorbed carbohydrate. Net synthesis of glycogen, triglyceride, and protein occurs.
   a. Some absorbed carbohydrate not used for energy is converted to glycogen, mainly in the liver and skeletal muscle, but most is converted in liver and adipocytes to α-glycerol phosphate and fatty acids, which then combine to form triglycerides. The liver releases its triglycerides in very-low-density lipoproteins, the fatty acids of which are picked up by adipocytes.
   b. The fatty acids of some absorbed triglycerides are used for energy, but most are rebuilt into fat in adipose tissue.
   c. Plasma cholesterol is a precursor for the synthesis of plasma membranes, bile salts, and steroid hormones.
   d. Cholesterol synthesis by the liver is controlled so as to homeostatically regulate plasma cholesterol concentration; it varies inversely with ingested cholesterol.
   e. The liver also secretes cholesterol into the bile and converts it to bile salts.
   f. Plasma cholesterol is carried mainly by low-density lipoproteins, which deliver it to cells; high-density lipoproteins carry cholesterol from cells to the liver and steroid-producing cells. The LDL/HDL ratio correlates with the incidence of coronary heart disease.
   g. Some absorbed amino acids are converted to proteins, but excess amino acids are converted to carbohydrate and fat.
   h. There is a net uptake of glucose by the liver.

II. In the postabsorptive state, blood glucose level is maintained by a combination of glucose production by the liver and a switch from glucose utilization to fatty acid and ketone utilization by most tissues.
   a. Synthesis of glycogen, fat, and protein is curtailed, and net breakdown of these molecules occurs.
   b. The liver forms glucose by glycogenolysis of its own glycogen and by gluconeogenesis from lactate and pyruvate (from the breakdown of muscle glycogen), glycerol (from adipose-tissue lipolysis), and amino acids (from protein catabolism).

c. Glycolysis is decreased, and most of the body's energy supply comes from the oxidation of fatty acids released by adipose-tissue lipolysis and of ketones produced from fatty acids by the liver.
d. The brain continues to use glucose but also starts using ketones as they build up in the blood.

Endocrine and Neural Control of the Absorptive and Postabsorptive States

I. The major hormones secreted by the pancreatic islets of Langerhans are insulin by the beta cells and glucagon by the alpha cells.

II. Insulin is the most important hormone controlling metabolism.
  a. In muscle, it stimulates glucose uptake, glycolysis, and net synthesis of glycogen and protein. In adipose tissue, it stimulates glucose uptake and net synthesis of triglyceride. In liver, it inhibits gluconeogenesis and glucose release and stimulates the net synthesis of glycogen and triglycerides.
  b. The major stimulus for insulin secretion is an increased plasma glucose concentration, but secretion is also influenced by many other factors, which are summarized in Figure 16.9.

III. Glucagon, epinephrine, cortisol, and growth hormone all exert effects on carbohydrate and lipid metabolism that are opposite, in one way or another, to those of insulin. They increase plasma concentrations of glucose, glycerol, and fatty acids.
  a. Glucagon's physiological actions are on the liver, where glucagon stimulates glycogenolysis, gluconeogenesis, and ketone synthesis.
  b. The major stimulus for glucagon secretion is hypoglycemia, but secretion is also stimulated by other inputs, including the sympathetic nerves to the islets.
  c. Epinephrine released from the adrenal medulla in response to hypoglycemia stimulates glycogenolysis in the liver and muscle, gluconeogenesis in the liver, and lipolysis in adipocytes. The sympathetic nerves to liver and adipose tissue exert effects similar to those of epinephrine.
  d. Cortisol is permissive for gluconeogenesis and lipolysis; in higher concentrations, it stimulates gluconeogenesis and blocks glucose uptake. These last two effects are also exerted by growth hormone.

IV. Hypoglycemia is defined as an abnormally low glucose concentration in the blood. Symptoms of hypoglycemia are similar to those of sympathetic nervous system activation. However, severe hypoglycemia can lead to brain dysfunction and even death if untreated.

Energy Homeostasis in Exercise and Stress

I. During exercise, the muscles use as their energy sources plasma glucose, plasma fatty acids, and their own glycogen.
  a. Glucose is provided by the liver, and fatty acids are provided by adipose-tissue lipolysis.
  b. The changes in plasma insulin, glucagon, and epinephrine are similar to those that occur during the postabsorptive state and are mediated mainly by the sympathetic nervous system.

II. Stress causes hormonal changes similar to those caused by exercise.

SECTION A REVIEW QUESTIONS

1. Using a diagram, summarize the events of the absorptive period.
2. In what two organs does major glycogen storage occur?
3. How do the liver and adipose tissue metabolize glucose during the absorptive period?
4. How does adipose tissue metabolize absorbed triglyceride, and what are the three major sources of the fatty acids in adipose-tissue triglyceride?
5. Using a diagram, describe the sources of cholesterol gain and loss. Include the roles the liver plays in cholesterol metabolism, and describe the controls over these processes.
6. What are the effects of saturated and unsaturated fatty acids on plasma cholesterol?
7. What is the significance of the ratio of LDL cholesterol to HDL cholesterol?
8. What happens to most of the absorbed amino acids when a high-protein meal is ingested?
9. Using a diagram, summarize the events of the postabsorptive state; include the four sources of blood glucose and the pathways leading to ketone formation.
10. Distinguish between the roles of glycerol and free fatty acids during fasting.
11. List the overall responses of muscle, adipose tissue, and liver to insulin. What effects occur when the plasma insulin concentration decreases?
12. Describe several inputs controlling insulin secretion and the physiological significance of each.
13. List the effects of glucagon on the liver and their consequences.
14. Discuss two inputs controlling glucagon secretion and the physiological significance of each.
15. List the metabolic effects of epinephrine and the sympathetic nerves to the liver and adipose tissue, and state the net results of each.
16. Describe the permissive effects of cortisol and the effects that occur when plasma cortisol concentration increases.
17. List the effects of growth hormone on carbohydrate and lipid metabolism.
18. Which hormones stimulate gluconeogenesis? Glycogenolysis in the liver? Lipolysis in adipose tissue? Which hormone or hormones inhibit glucose uptake into cells?
19. Describe how plasma glucose, insulin, glucagon, and epinephrine concentrations change during exercise and stress. What causes the changes in the concentrations of the hormones?

SECTION A KEY TERMS

absorptive state 573
alpha cell 578
α-keto acid 576
beta cell 578
cholesterol 574
glucagon 578
gluconeogenesis 577
glucose-counterregulatory control 582
glucose sparing 577
glycogenolysis 576
glycogen phosphorylase 580
glycogen synthase 580
high-density lipoprotein (HDL) 575
hormone-sensitive lipase (HSL) 583
hypoglycemia 584
incretins 581
insulin 578
islets of Langerhans 578
ketone 578
lipolysis 577
lipoprotein 574
lipoprotein lipase 574
low-density lipoprotein (LDL) 575
postabsorptive state 573
very-low-density lipoprotein (VLDL) 574

SECTION A CLINICAL TERMS

atherosclerosis 574
exercise-induced amenorrhea 585
familial hypercholesterolemia 576
fasting hypoglycemia 584

SECTION **B**

Regulation of Total-Body Energy Balance and Temperature

16.4 General Principles of Energy Expenditure

The breakdown of organic molecules liberates the energy locked in their chemical bonds. Cells use this energy to perform the various forms of biological work, such as muscle contraction, active transport, and molecular synthesis. These processes illustrate the general principle of physiology that physiological processes are dictated by the laws of chemistry and physics. The first law of thermodynamics states that energy can be neither created nor destroyed but can be converted from one form to another. Therefore, internal energy liberated (ΔE) during breakdown of an organic molecule can either appear as heat (H) or be used to perform work (W).

$$\Delta E = H + W$$

During metabolism, about 60% of the energy released from organic molecules appears immediately as heat, and the rest is used for work. The energy used for work must first be incorporated into molecules of ATP. The subsequent breakdown of ATP serves as the immediate energy source for the work. The body is incapable of converting heat to work, but the heat released in its chemical reactions helps to maintain body temperature.

Biological work can be divided into two general categories: (1) **external work**—the movement of external objects by contracting skeletal muscles; and (2) **internal work**—all other forms of work, including skeletal muscle activity not used in moving external objects. As just stated, much of the energy liberated from nutrient catabolism appears immediately as heat. What may not be obvious is that internal work, too, is ultimately transformed to heat except during periods of growth. For example, internal work is performed during cardiac contraction, but this energy appears ultimately as heat generated by the friction of blood flow through the blood vessels.

Thus, the total energy liberated when cells catabolize organic nutrients may be transformed into body heat, can be used to do external work, or can be stored in the body in the form of organic molecules. The **total energy expenditure** of the body is therefore given by the equation

$$\text{Total energy expenditure} = \text{Internal heat produced} + \text{External work performed} + \text{Energy stored}$$

Metabolic Rate

The basic metric unit of energy is the joule. When quantifying the energy of metabolism, however, another unit is used, called the **calorie** (equal to 4.184 joules). One calorie is the amount of heat required to raise the temperature of one gram of water from 14.5°C to 15.5°C. Because the amount of energy stored in food is quite high relative to a calorie, a more convenient expression of energy in this context is the **kilocalorie (kcal),** which is equal to 1000 calories. (In the field of nutrition, the terms "Calorie" with a capital *C* and "kilocalorie" are synonyms; they are both 1000 "calories," with a small *c*.) Total energy expenditure per unit time is called the **metabolic rate.**

Because many factors cause the metabolic rate to vary (**Table 16.5**), the most common method for evaluating it specifies certain standardized conditions and measures what is known as the **basal metabolic rate** (**BMR**). In the basal condition, the subject is at rest in a room at a comfortable temperature and has not eaten for at least 12 h (i.e., is in the postabsorptive state). These conditions are arbitrarily designated "basal," even though the metabolic rate during sleep may be lower than the

TABLE 16.5 Some Factors Affecting the Metabolic Rate

Sleep (↓ during sleep)	
Age (↓ with increasing age)	
Gender (women less than men at any given size)	
Fasting (BMR decreases, which conserves energy stores)	
Height, weight, and body surface area	The presence of, or an increase in, any of these factors causes an increase in metabolic rate
Growth	
Pregnancy, menstruation, lactation	
Infection or other disease	
Body temperature	
Recent ingestion of food	
Muscular activity	
Emotional stress	
Environmental temperature	
Circulating concentrations of various hormones, especially epinephrine, thyroid hormone, and leptin	

BMR. The BMR is sometimes called the "metabolic cost of living," and most of the energy involved is expended by the heart, muscle, liver, kidneys, and brain. For the following discussion, the term *BMR* can be applied to metabolic rate only when the specified conditions are met. The next sections describe several of the important determinants of BMR and metabolic rate.

Thyroid Hormones

The thyroid hormones (T_3 and T_4) are the single most important determinant of BMR regardless of body size, age, or gender. T_3 and T_4 increase the oxygen consumption and heat production of most body tissues, a notable exception being the brain. This ability to increase BMR is known as a **calorigenic effect.**

Long-term excessive T_3 and T_4, as in people with hyperthyroidism (see Chapter 11 and the first case study in Chapter 19), induce a host of effects secondary to the calorigenic effect. For example, the increased metabolic demands markedly increase hunger and food intake. The greater intake often remains inadequate to meet metabolic demands. The resulting net catabolism of protein and fat stores leads to loss of body weight. Of importance is the fact that the more metabolically active a particular cell is, the greater are its requirements for vitamins, which serve as cofactors for many enzymes and for ATP production. Therefore, even with increased dietary intake, the onset of hyperthyroidism may result in symptoms of vitamin deficiency. Also, the greater heat production activates heat-dissipating mechanisms, such as skin vasodilation and sweating, and the person feels intolerant to warm environments. In contrast, the hypothyroid person may experience cold intolerance.

Epinephrine

Epinephrine is another hormone that exerts a calorigenic effect. This effect may be related to its stimulation of glycogen and triglyceride catabolism, as ATP hydrolysis and energy liberation occur during both the breakdown and subsequent resynthesis of these molecules. As a result, when epinephrine secretion by the adrenal medulla is stimulated, the metabolic rate increases.

Diet-Induced Thermogenesis

The ingestion of food increases the metabolic rate by 10% to 20% for a few hours after eating. This effect is known as **diet-induced thermogenesis.** Ingested protein produces the greatest effect, and carbohydrate and fat produce less. Most of the increased heat production is caused by the processing of the absorbed nutrients by the liver, the energy expended by the gastrointestinal tract in digestion and absorption, and the storage of energy in adipose and other tissue. Because of the contribution of diet-induced thermogenesis, a BMR measurement would have to be performed in the postabsorptive state. As we will see, *prolonged* alterations in food intake (either increased or decreased total calories) also have significant effects on metabolic rate.

Muscle Activity

The factor that can increase metabolic rate the most is altered skeletal muscle activity. Even minimal increases in muscle contraction significantly increase metabolic rate, and strenuous exercise may increase energy expenditure several-fold (**Figure 16.13**). Therefore, depending on the degree of physical activity, total energy expenditure may vary for a healthy young adult from a value of approximately 1500 kcal/24 h (for a sedentary individual) to more than 7000 kcal/24 h (for someone who is extremely active). Changes in muscle activity also account in part for the changes in metabolic rate that occur during sleep (decreased muscle contraction) and during exposure to a low environmental temperature (increased muscle contraction due to shivering).

Approximate Energy Expenditure During Different Types of Activity for a 70 kg (154 lb) Person

Form of Activity	Energy kcal/h
Sitting at rest	100
Walking on level ground at 4.3 km/h (2.6 mi/h)	200
Walking on 3% grade at 4.3 km/h (2.6 mi/h)	360
Weight lifting *(light workout)*	220
Bicycling on level ground at 9 km/h (5.3 mi/h)	300
Shoveling snow	480
Jogging at 9 km/h (5.3 mi/h)	570
Rowing at 20 strokes/ min	830

Figure 16.13 Rates of energy expenditure for a variety of common activities.

16.5 Regulation of Total-Body Energy Stores

Under normal conditions, for body weight to remain stable, the total energy expenditure (metabolic rate) of the body must equal the total energy intake. We have already identified the ultimate forms of energy expenditure: internal heat production, external work, and net molecular synthesis (energy storage). The source of input is the energy contained in ingested food. Therefore,

$$\text{Energy from food intake} = \text{Internal heat produced} + \text{External work} + \text{Energy stored}$$

This equation includes no term for loss of energy from the body via excretion of nutrients because normally only negligible losses occur via the urine, feces, and sloughed hair and skin. In certain diseases, however, the most important being diabetes mellitus, urinary losses of organic molecules may be quite large and would have to be included in the equation.

Rearranging the equation to focus on energy storage gives

$$\text{Energy stored} = \text{Energy from food intake} - (\text{Internal heat produced} + \text{External work})$$

Consequently, whenever energy intake differs from the sum of internal heat produced and external work, changes in energy storage occur; that is, the total-body energy content increases or decreases. Normally, energy storage is mainly in the form of fat in adipose tissue.

It is worth emphasizing at this point that "body weight" and "total-body energy content" are not synonymous. Body weight is determined not only by the amount of fat, carbohydrate, and protein in the body but also by the amounts of water, bone, and other minerals. For example, an individual can lose body weight quickly as the result of sweating or an excessive increase in urinary output. It is also possible to gain large amounts of weight as a result of water retention, as occurs, for example, during heart failure. Moreover, even focusing only on the nutrients, a constant body weight does not mean that total-body energy content is constant. The reason is that 1 g of fat contains 9 kcal, whereas 1 g of either carbohydrate or protein contains 4 kcal. Aging, for example, is usually associated with a gain of fat and a loss of protein; the result is that even though the person's body weight may stay constant, the total-body energy content has increased. Apart from these qualifications, however, in the remainder of this chapter, changes in body weight are equated with changes in total-body energy content and, more specifically, changes in body fat stores.

Body weight in adults is usually regulated around a stable set point. Theoretically, this regulation can be achieved by reflexively adjusting caloric intake and/or energy expenditure in response to changes in body weight. It was once assumed that regulation of caloric intake was the only important adjustment, and the next section will describe this process. However, it is now clear that energy expenditure can also be adjusted in response to changes in body weight.

A typical demonstration of this process in human beings follows. Total daily energy expenditure was measured in nonobese subjects at their usual body weight and again after they either lost 10% of their body weight by underfeeding or gained 10% by overfeeding. At their new body weight, the overfed subjects manifested a large (15%) increase in both resting and nonresting energy expenditure, and the underfed subjects showed a similar decrease. These changes in energy expenditure were much greater than could be accounted for simply by the altered metabolic mass of the body or having to move a larger or smaller body.

The generalization that emerges is that a dietary-induced change in total-body energy stores triggers, in negative feedback fashion, an alteration in energy expenditure that opposes the gain or loss of energy stores. This phenomenon helps explain why some dieters lose about 5 to 10 pounds fairly easily and then become stuck at a plateau.

Control of Food Intake

The control of food intake can be analyzed in the same way as any other biological control system. As the previous section emphasized, the variable being maintained in this system is total-body energy content or, more specifically, total fat stores. An essential component of such a control system is the peptide hormone **leptin,** synthesized by adipocytes and released from the cells in proportion to the amount of fat they contain. This hormone acts on the hypothalamus to cause a decrease in food intake, in part by inhibiting the release of **neuropeptide Y,** a hypothalamic neurotransmitter that stimulates appetite. Leptin also increases BMR and, therefore, plays an important role in the changes in energy expenditure that occur in response to overfeeding or underfeeding, as described in the previous section. Thus, as illustrated in **Figure 16.14**, leptin functions in a negative feedback system to maintain a stable total-body energy content by signaling to the brain how much fat is stored.

It should be emphasized that leptin is important for *long-term* matching of caloric intake to energy expenditure. In addition, it is thought that various other signals act on the hypothalamus (and other brain areas) over short periods of time to regulate individual meal length and frequency (**Figure 16.15**). These **satiety signals** (factors that decrease appetite) cause the person to cease feeling hungry and set the time period before hunger returns. For example, the rate of insulin-dependent glucose utilization by certain areas of the hypothalamus increases during eating, and this probably constitutes a satiety signal. Insulin, which increases during food absorption, also acts as a direct satiety signal. Diet-induced thermogenesis tends to increase body temperature slightly, which acts as yet another satiety signal. Finally, some satiety signals are initiated by the presence of food within the gastrointestinal tract. These include neural signals triggered by stimulation of both stretch receptors and chemoreceptors in the stomach and duodenum, as well as by certain of the hormones (cholecystokinin, for example) released from the stomach and duodenum during eating.

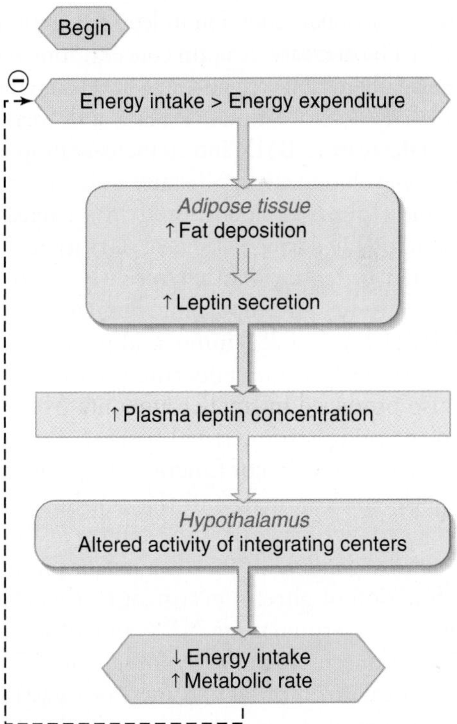

Figure 16.14 Postulated role of leptin in the control of total-body energy stores. Note that the direction of the arrows within the boxes would be reversed if energy (food) intake were less than energy expenditure.

PHYSIOLOGICAL INQUIRY

- Under what circumstances might the appetite-suppressing action of leptin be counterproductive?

Answer can be found at end of chapter.

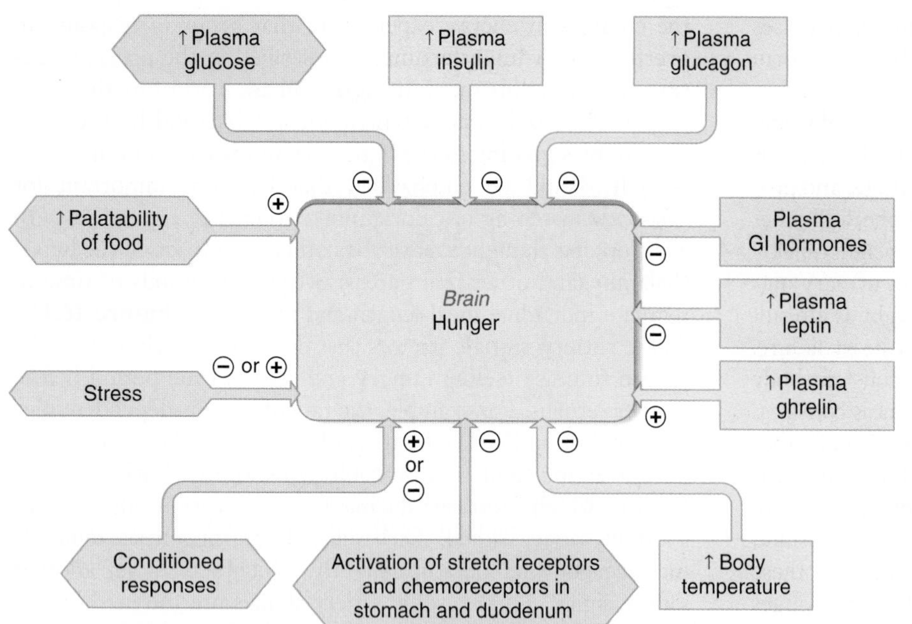

Figure 16.15 Short-term inputs controlling appetite and, consequently, food intake. The ⊖ symbols denote hunger suppression, and the ⊕ symbols denote hunger stimulation.

PHYSIOLOGICAL INQUIRY

- As shown, stretch receptors in the gut after a meal can suppress hunger. Would drinking a large glass of water before a meal be an effective means of dieting?

Answer can be found at end of chapter.

Although we have focused on leptin and other factors as satiety signals, it is important to realize that a primary function of leptin is to increase metabolic rate. If a person is subjected to starvation, his or her adipocytes begin to shrink, as catabolic hormones mobilize triglycerides from adipocytes. This decrease in size causes a proportional reduction in leptin secretion from the shrinking cells. The decrease in leptin concentration removes the signal that normally inhibits appetite and speeds up metabolism. The result is that a loss of fat mass leads to a decrease in leptin and, thereby, a decrease in BMR and an increase in appetite. This may be the true evolutionary significance of leptin, namely that its disappearance from the blood results in a decreased BMR, thereby prolonging life during periods of starvation.

In addition to leptin, another recently discovered hormone appears to be an important regulator of appetite. **Ghrelin** (GREH-lin) is a 28-amino-acid peptide synthesized and released primarily from endocrine cells in the stomach. Ghrelin is also produced in smaller amounts from other gastrointestinal and nongastrointestinal tissues.

Ghrelin has several major functions that have been identified in experimental animals and that appear to be true in humans. One is to increase growth *h*ormone *rel*ease—the derivation of the word *ghrelin*—from the anterior pituitary gland. The major function of ghrelin pertinent to this chapter is to increase hunger by stimulating NPY and other neuropeptides in the feeding centers in the hypothalamus. Ghrelin also decreases the breakdown of fat and increases gastric motility and acid production. It makes sense, then, that the major stimuli to ghrelin are fasting and a low-calorie diet.

Ghrelin, therefore, participates in several feedback loops. Fasting or a low-calorie diet leads to an increase in ghrelin. This stimulates hunger and, if food is available, food intake. The food intake subsequently decreases ghrelin, possibly through stomach distention, caloric absorption, or some other mechanism.

Overweight and Obesity

The clinical definition of ***overweight*** is a functional one, a state in which an increased amount of fat in the body results in a significant impairment of health from a variety of diseases or disorders—notably, hypertension, atherosclerosis, heart disease, diabetes, and sleep apnea. ***Obesity*** denotes a particularly large accumulation of fat—that is, extreme overweight. The difficulty has been establishing at what point fat accumulation begins to constitute a health risk. This is evaluated by epidemiologic studies that correlate disease rates with some measure of the amount of fat in the body. Currently, the preferred simple method for assessing the latter is not the body weight but the **body mass index (BMI)**, which is calculated by dividing the weight (in kilograms) by the square of the height (in meters). For example, a 70 kg person with a height of 180 cm would have a BMI of 21.6 kg/m^2 (70/1.8^2).

Current National Institutes of Health guidelines categorize BMIs of greater than 25 kg/m^2 as overweight (i.e., as having some increased health risk because of excess fat) and those greater than 30 kg/m^2 as obese, with a significantly increased health risk. According to these criteria, more than half of U.S. women and men age 20 and older are now considered to be overweight and one-quarter or more to be clinically obese! Even more troubling is that the incidence of childhood overweight and obesity is increasing in the United States and other countries. These guidelines, however, are controversial. First, the epidemiologic studies do not always agree as to where along the continuum of BMIs between 25 and 30 kg/m^2 health risks begin to significantly increase. Second, even granting increased risk above a BMI of 25 kg/m^2, the studies do not always account for confounding factors associated with being overweight or even obese, particularly a sedentary lifestyle. Instead, the increased health risk may be at least partly due to lack of physical activity, not body fat, per se.

To add to the complexity, there is growing evidence that not just total fat but where the fat is located has important consequences. Specifically, people with mostly abdominal fat are at greater risk for developing serious conditions such as diabetes and cardiovascular diseases than people whose fat is mainly in the lower body on the buttocks and thighs. There is currently no agreement as to the explanation of this phenomenon, but there are important differences in the physiology of adipose-tissue cells in these regions. For example, adipose-tissue cells in the abdomen are much more adept at breaking down fat stores and releasing the products into the blood.

What is known about the underlying causes of obesity? Identical twins who have been separated soon after birth and raised in different households manifest strikingly similar body weights and incidences of obesity as adults. Twin studies, therefore, indicate that genetic factors play an important role in obesity. It has been postulated that natural selection favored the evolution in our ancestors of so-called **thrifty genes,** which boosted the ability to store fat from each feast in order to sustain people through the next fast. Given today's relative abundance of high-fat foods in many countries, such an adaptation is now a liability. Despite the importance of genetic factors, psychological, cultural, and social factors can also play a significant role. For example, the increasing incidence of obesity in the United States and other industrialized nations during the past 40 years cannot be explained by changes in our genes.

Much recent research has focused on possible abnormalities in the leptin system as a cause of obesity. In one strain of mice (shown in the chapter-opening photo), the gene that codes for leptin is mutated so that adipose-tissue cells produce an abnormal, inactive leptin, resulting in hereditary obesity. The same is *not* true, however, for the vast majority of obese people. The leptin secreted by these people is normal, and leptin concentrations in the blood are increased, not decreased. This observation indicates that leptin secretion is not at fault in these people. Consequently, such people are leptin-resistant in much the same way that people with type 2 diabetes mellitus are insulin-resistant. Moreover, there are multiple genes that interact with one another and with environmental factors to influence a person's susceptibility to weight gain.

The methods and goals of treating obesity are now undergoing extensive rethinking. An increase in body fat must be due to an excess of energy intake over energy expenditure, and low-calorie diets have long been the mainstay of therapy. However, it is now clear that such diets alone have limited effectiveness in obese people; over 90% regain all or most of the lost weight within 5 years. Another important reason for the ineffectiveness of such diets is that, as described earlier, the person's metabolic rate decreases as leptin concentration decreases, sometimes decreasing low enough to prevent further weight loss on as little as 1000 calories a day. Because of this, many obese people continue to gain weight or remain in stable energy balance on a caloric intake equal to or less than the amount consumed by people of normal weight. These persons must either have less physical activity than normal or have lower basal metabolic rates. Finally, at least half of obese people—those who are more than 20% overweight—who try to diet down to desirable weights suffer medically, physically, and psychologically. This is what would be expected if the body were "trying" to maintain body weight (more specifically, fat stores) at the higher set point.

Such studies, taken together, indicate that crash diets are not an effective long-term method for controlling weight. Instead, caloric intake should be set at a level that can be maintained for the rest of one's life. Such an intake in an overweight person should lead to a slow, steady weight loss of no more than 1 pound per week until the body weight stabilizes at a new, lower level. The most important precept is that any program of weight loss should include increased physical activity. The exercise itself uses calories, but more importantly, it partially offsets the tendency, described earlier, for the metabolic rate to decrease during long-term caloric restriction and weight loss. Also, the combination of exercise and caloric restriction may cause the person to lose more fat and less protein than with caloric restriction alone, although some recent studies suggest this may not always be true.

Let us calculate how rapidly a person can expect to lose weight on a reducing diet (assuming, for simplicity, no change in energy expenditure). Suppose a person whose steady-state metabolic rate per 24 h is 2000 kcal goes on a 1000 kcal/day diet. How much of the person's own body fat will be required to supply this additional 1000 kcal/day? Because fat contains 9 kcal/g,

$$\frac{1000 \text{ kcal/day}}{9 \text{ kcal/g}} = 111 \text{ g/day, or } 777 \text{ g/week}$$

Approximately another 77 g of water is lost from the adipose tissue along with this fat (adipose tissue is 10% water), so that the grand total for 1 week's loss equals 854 g, or 1.8 pounds. Therefore, even on this severe diet, the person can reasonably expect to lose approximately this amount of weight per week, assuming no decrease in metabolic rate occurs.

Eating Disorders: Anorexia Nervosa and Bulimia Nervosa

Two of the major eating disorders are found primarily in adolescent girls and young women. The typical person with ***anorexia nervosa*** becomes pathologically obsessed with her weight and body image. She may decrease her food intake so severely that she may die of starvation. There are many other abnormalities associated with anorexia nervosa—cessation of menstrual periods, low blood pressure, low body temperature, and altered secretion of many hormones, including increased concentrations of ghrelin. It is likely that these are simply the results of starvation, although it is possible that some represent signs, along with the eating disturbances, of primary hypothalamic malfunction.

Bulimia nervosa, usually called simply *bulimia,* is a disorder characterized by recurrent episodes of binge eating. It is usually associated with regular self-induced vomiting and use of laxatives or diuretics, as well as strict dieting, fasting, or vigorous exercise to lose weight or to prevent weight gain. Like individuals with anorexia nervosa, those with bulimia manifest a persistent heightened concern with body weight, although they generally remain within 10% of their ideal weight. This disorder too, is accompanied by a variety of physiological abnormalities, but it is unknown in some cases whether they are causal or secondary.

In addition to anorexia and bulimia, rare lesions or tumors within the hypothalamic centers that normally regulate appetite can result in overfeeding or underfeeding.

What Should We Eat?

In recent years, more and more dietary factors have been associated with the cause or prevention of many diseases or disorders, including not only coronary artery disease but hypertension, cancer, birth defects, osteoporosis, and others. These associations come mainly from animal studies, epidemiologic studies on people, and basic research concerning potential mechanisms. Some of these findings may be difficult to interpret or may be conflicting. One of the most commonly used sets of dietary recommendations, issued by the National Research Council, is presented in **Table 16.6**.

TABLE 16.6 Summary of National Research Council Dietary Recommendations

Reduce fat intake to 30% or less of total calories; most fat consumed should be mono- or polyunsaturated fats. Reduce saturated fatty acid intake to less than 10% of calories and intake of cholesterol to less than 300 mg daily.
Every day eat five or more servings of a combination of vegetables and fruits, especially green and yellow vegetables and citrus fruits. Also, increase complex carbohydrates by eating six or more daily servings of a combination of whole-grain breads, cereals, and legumes.
Maintain protein intake at moderate levels (approximately 0.8 g/kg body mass).
Balance food intake and physical activity to maintain appropriate body weight.
Alcohol consumption is not recommended. For those who drink alcoholic beverages, limit consumption to the equivalent of 1 ounce of pure alcohol in a single day.
Limit total daily intake of sodium to 2.3 g or less.
Maintain adequate calcium intake.
Avoid taking dietary supplements in excess of the RDA (Recommended Dietary Allowance) in any one day.
Maintain an optimal intake of fluoride, particularly during the years of primary and secondary tooth formation and growth. Most bottled water does not contain fluoride.

16.6 Regulation of Body Temperature

In the preceding discussion, it was emphasized that energy expenditure is linked to our ability to maintain a stable, homeostatic body temperature. In this section, we discuss the mechanisms by which the body gains or loses heat in a variety of healthy or pathological settings.

Humans are **endotherms,** meaning that they generate their own internal body heat and do not rely on the energy of sunlight to warm the body. Moreover, humans maintain their body temperatures within very narrow limits despite wide fluctuations in ambient temperature and are, therefore, also known as **homeotherms.** The relatively stable body temperature frees biochemical reactions from fluctuating with the external temperature. However, the maintenance of a warm body temperature (approximately 37°C in healthy persons) imposes a requirement for precise regulatory mechanisms because large elevations of temperature cause nerve malfunction and protein denaturation. Some people suffer convulsions at a body temperature of 41°C (106°F), and 43°C is considered to be the absolute limit for survival.

A few important generalizations about normal human body temperature should be stressed at the outset. (1) Oral temperature averages about 0.5°C less than rectal, which is generally used as an estimate of internal temperature (also known as **core body temperature**). Not all regions of the body, therefore, have the same temperature. (2) Internal temperature is not constant; although it does not vary much, it does change slightly in response to activity patterns and changes in external temperature. Moreover, there is a characteristic circadian fluctuation of about 1°C (**Figure 16.16**), with temperature being lowest during the night and highest during the day. (3) An added variation in women is a higher temperature during the second half of the menstrual cycle due to the effects of the hormone progesterone.

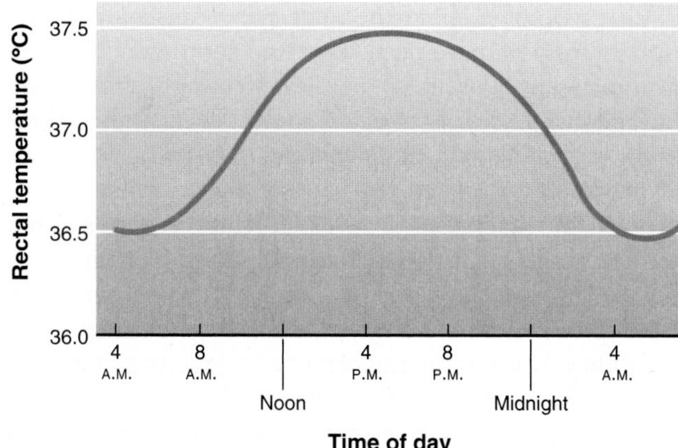

Figure 16.16 Circadian changes in core (measured as rectal) body temperature in a typical person. This figure does not take into account daily minor swings in temperature due to such things as exercise, eating, and menstrual cycle; nor are the absolute values on the *y*-axis representative of all individuals. Adapted from Scales et al.

Temperature regulation can be studied by our usual balance methods. The total heat content gained or lost by the body is determined by the net difference between heat gain (from the environment and produced in the body) and heat loss. Maintaining a stable body temperature means that, in the steady state, heat gain must equal heat loss.

Mechanisms of Heat Loss or Gain

The surface of the body can lose heat to the external environment by radiation, conduction, convection, and the evaporation of water (**Figure 16.17**). Before defining each of these processes, however, it must be emphasized that radiation, conduction, and convection can, under certain circumstances, lead to heat *gain* instead of loss.

Radiation is the process by which the surfaces of all objects constantly emit heat in the form of electromagnetic waves. It is a principle of physics that the rate of heat emission is determined by the temperature of the radiating surface. As a result, if the body surface is warmer than the various surfaces in the environment, net heat is lost from the body, the rate being directly dependent upon the temperature difference between the surfaces. Conversely, the body gains heat by absorbing electromagnetic energy emitted by the sun.

Conduction is the loss or gain of heat by transfer of thermal energy during collisions between adjacent molecules. In essence, heat is "conducted" from molecule to molecule. The body surface loses or gains heat by conduction through direct contact with cooler or warmer substances, including the air or water. Not all substances, however, conduct heat equally. Water is a better conductor of heat than is air; therefore, more heat is lost from the body in water than in air of similar temperature.

Convection is the process whereby conductive heat loss or gain is aided by movement of the air or water next to the body. For example, air next to the body is heated by conduction.

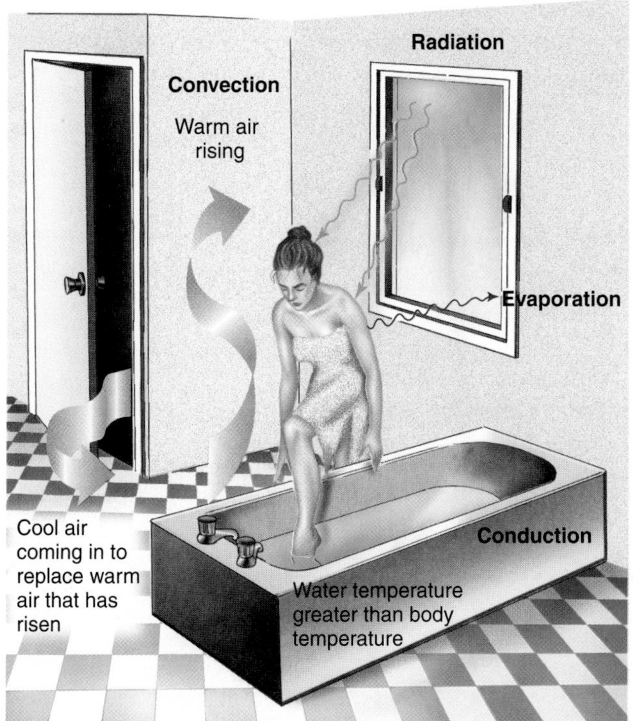

Figure 16.17 Mechanisms of heat transfer.

PHYSIOLOGICAL INQUIRY

- Evaporation is an important mechanism for eliminating heat, particularly on a hot day or when exercising. What are some of the negative consequences of this mechanism of heat loss?

Answer can be found at end of chapter.

Because warm air is less dense than cool air, the heated air around the body surface rises, thereby carrying away the heat just taken from the body. The air that moves away is replaced by cooler air, which in turn follows the same pattern. Convection is always occurring because warm air is less dense and therefore rises, but it can be greatly facilitated by external forces such as wind or fans. Consequently, convection aids conductive heat exchange by continuously maintaining a supply of cool air. Therefore, in the rest of this chapter, the term *conduction* will also imply convection.

Evaporation of water from the skin and membranes lining the respiratory tract is the other major process causing loss of body heat. A very large amount of energy—600 kcal/L—is required to transform water from the liquid to the gaseous state. As a result, whenever water vaporizes from the body's surface, the heat required to drive the process is conducted from the surface, thereby cooling it.

Temperature-Regulating Reflexes

Temperature regulation offers a classic example of a homeostatic control system, as described in Chapter 1. The balance between heat production (gain) and heat loss is continuously being disturbed, either by changes in metabolic rate (exercise being the most powerful influence) or by changes in the external environment such as air temperature. The resulting changes in body temperature are detected by thermoreceptors. These receptors initiate reflexes that change the output of various effectors so that heat production and/or loss are modified and body temperature is restored toward normal.

Figure 16.18 summarizes the components of these reflexes. There are two locations of thermoreceptors, one in the skin (**peripheral thermoreceptors**) and the other (**central thermoreceptors**) in deep body structures, including abdominal organs and thermoreceptive neurons in the hypothalamus. Because it is the core body temperature—not the skin temperature—that is maintained in a narrow homeostatic range, the central thermoreceptors provide the essential negative feedback component of the reflexes. The peripheral thermoreceptors provide feedforward information, as described in Chapter 1, and also account for the ability to identify a hot or cold area of the skin.

The hypothalamus serves as the primary overall integrator of the reflexes, but other brain centers also exert some control over specific components of the reflexes. Output from the hypothalamus and the other brain areas to the effectors is via (1) sympathetic nerves to the sweat glands, skin arterioles, and the adrenal medulla; and (2) motor neurons to the skeletal muscles.

Control of Heat Production

Changes in muscle activity constitute the major control of heat production for temperature regulation. The first muscle change in response to a decrease in core body temperature is a gradual and general increase in skeletal muscle contraction. This may lead to shivering, which consists of oscillating, rhythmic muscle contractions and relaxations occurring at a rapid rate. During shivering, the efferent motor nerves to the skeletal muscles are influenced by descending pathways under the primary control of the hypothalamus. Because almost no external work is performed by shivering, most of the energy liberated by the metabolic machinery appears as internal heat, a process known as **shivering thermogenesis.** People also use their muscles for voluntary heat-producing activities such as foot stamping and hand rubbing.

The opposite muscle reactions occur in response to heat. Basal muscle contraction is reflexively decreased, and voluntary movement is also diminished. These attempts to decrease heat production are limited, however, because basal muscle contraction is quite low to start with and because any increased core temperature produced by the heat acts *directly* on cells to increase metabolic rate. In other words, an increase in cellular temperature directly accelerates the rate at which all of its chemical reactions occur. This is due to the increased thermal motion of dissolved molecules, making it more likely that they will encounter each other. The result is that ATP is expended at a higher rate because ATP participates in many of a cell's chemical reactions. This, in turn, results in a compensatory increase in ATP production from cellular energy stores, which also generates heat as a by-product of metabolism. Thus, increasing cellular temperature can itself result in the production of additional heat through increased metabolism.

Muscle contraction is not the only process controlled in temperature-regulating reflexes. In many experimental mammals, chronic cold exposure induces an increase in metabolic rate (and therefore heat production) that is not due to increased muscle activity and is termed **nonshivering thermogenesis.** Its causes are an increased adrenal secretion of epinephrine, increased thyroid hormone secretion, and increased sympathetic activity to

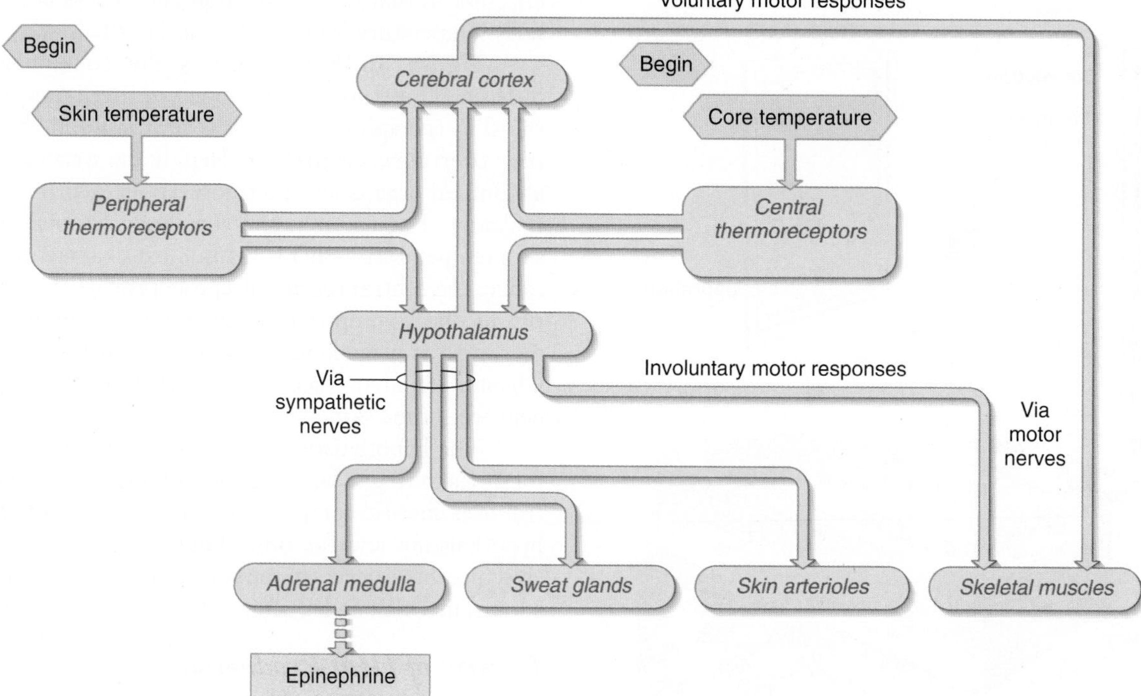

Figure 16.18 Summary of temperature-regulating mechanisms beginning with peripheral thermoreceptors and central thermoreceptors. The dashed arrow from the adrenal medulla indicates that this hormonal pathway is of minor importance in adult human beings. The solid arrows denote neural pathways. The hypothalamus influences sympathetic nerves via descending pathways.

a special type of adipose tissue called brown fat, or **brown adipose tissue.** This type of adipose tissue is stimulated by thyroid hormone, epinephrine, and the sympathetic nervous system; it contains large amounts of a class of proteins called uncoupling proteins. These proteins uncouple oxidation from phosphorylation (Chapter 3) and, in effect, make metabolism less efficient (less ATP is generated). The major product of this inefficient metabolism is heat, which then contributes to maintaining body temperature. Brown adipose tissue is present in infant humans. Nonshivering thermogenesis does occur in infants, therefore, whose shivering mechanism is not yet fully developed.

Control of Heat Loss by Radiation and Conduction

For purposes of temperature control, the body may be thought of as a central core surrounded by a shell consisting of skin and subcutaneous tissue. The temperature of the central core is regulated at approximately 37°C, but the temperature of the outer surface of the skin changes considerably.

If the skin and its underlying tissue were a perfect insulator, no heat would ever be lost from the core. The temperature of the outer skin surface would equal the environmental temperature, and net conduction would be zero. The skin is not a perfect insulator, however, so the temperature of its outer surface generally is somewhere between that of the external environment and that of the core. Instead of acting as an insulator, the skin functions as a variable regulator of heat exchange. Its effectiveness in this capacity is subject to physiological control by a change in blood flow. The more blood reaching the skin from the core, the more closely the skin's temperature approaches that of the core. In effect, the blood vessels can carry heat to the skin surface to be lost to the external environment. These vessels are controlled largely by vasoconstrictor sympathetic nerves, which are reflexively stimulated in response to cold and inhibited in response to heat. There is also a population of sympathetic neurons to the skin whose neurotransmitters cause active vasodilation. Certain areas of skin participate much more than others in all these vasomotor responses, and so skin temperatures vary with location.

Finally, the three *behavioral* mechanisms for altering heat loss by radiation and conduction are changes in surface area, changes in clothing, and choice of surroundings. Curling up into a ball, hunching the shoulders, and similar maneuvers in response to cold reduce the surface area exposed to the environment, thereby decreasing heat loss by radiation and conduction. In human beings, clothing is also an important component of temperature regulation, substituting for the insulating effects of feathers in birds and fur in other mammals. The outer surface of the clothes forms the true "exterior" of the body surface. The skin loses heat directly to the air space trapped by the clothes, which in turn pick up heat from the inner air layer and transfer it to the external environment. The insulating ability of clothing is determined primarily by the thickness of the trapped air layer. The third behavioral mechanism for altering heat loss is to seek out warmer or colder surroundings, for example, by moving from a shady spot into the sunlight.

Control of Heat Loss by Evaporation

Even in the absence of sweating, there is loss of water by diffusion through the skin, which is not completely waterproof. A similar amount is lost from the respiratory lining during expiration. These two losses are known as **insensible water loss** and amount to approximately 600 mL/day in human beings. Evaporation of this water can account for a significant fraction of total heat loss. In contrast to this passive water loss, sweating requires the active secretion of fluid by **sweat glands** and its extrusion into ducts that carry it to the skin surface.

Production of sweat is stimulated by sympathetic nerves to the glands. Sweat is a dilute solution containing sodium chloride as its major solute. Sweating rates of over 4 L/h have been reported; the evaporation of 4 L of water would eliminate almost 2400 kcal of heat from the body!

Sweat must evaporate in order to exert its cooling effect. The most important factor determining evaporation rate is the water vapor concentration of the air—that is, the relative humidity. The discomfort suffered on humid days is due to the failure of evaporation; the sweat glands continue to secrete, but the sweat simply remains on the skin or drips off.

Integration of Effector Mechanisms

By altering heat loss, changes in skin blood flow alone can regulate body temperature over a range of environmental temperatures known as the **thermoneutral zone.** In humans, the thermoneutral zone is approximately 25°C to 30°C or 75°F to 86°F for a nude individual. At temperatures lower than this, even maximal vasoconstriction of blood vessels in the skin cannot prevent heat loss from exceeding heat gain and the body must increase its heat production to maintain temperature. At environmental temperatures above the thermoneutral zone, even maximal vasodilation cannot eliminate heat as fast as it is produced, and another heat-loss mechanism—sweating—therefore comes strongly into play. At environmental temperatures above that of the body, heat is actually added to the body by radiation and conduction. Under such conditions, evaporation is the sole mechanism for heat loss. A person's ability to tolerate such temperatures is determined by the humidity and by his or her maximal sweating rate. For example, when the air is completely dry, a person can tolerate an environmental temperature of 130°C (225°F) for 20 min or longer, whereas very humid air at 46°C (115°F) is bearable for only a few minutes.

Temperature Acclimatization

Changes in the onset, volume, and composition of sweat determine the ability to adapt to chronic high temperatures. A person newly arrived in a hot environment has poor ability to do work; body temperature increases, and severe weakness may occur. After several days, there is a great improvement in work tolerance, with much less increase in body temperature, and the person is said to have acclimatized to the heat. Body temperature does not increase as much because sweating begins sooner and the volume of sweat produced is greater.

There is also an important change in the composition of the sweat, namely, a significant reduction in its salt concentration. This adaptation, which minimizes the loss of sodium ions from the body via sweat, is due to increased secretion of the adrenal cortex hormone aldosterone. The sweat-gland secretory cells produce a solution with a sodium ion concentration similar to that of plasma, but some of the sodium ions are absorbed back into the blood as the secretion flows along the sweat-gland ducts toward the skin surface. Aldosterone stimulates this absorption in a manner identical to its stimulation of sodium ion reabsorption in the renal tubules.

Cold acclimatization has been much less studied than heat acclimatization because of the difficulty of subjecting people to total-body cold stress over long enough periods to produce acclimatization. Moreover, people who live in cold climates generally dress very warmly and so would not develop acclimatization to the cold.

16.7 Fever and Hyperthermia

Fever is an increase in body temperature due to a resetting of the "thermostat" in the hypothalamus. A person with a fever still regulates body temperature in response to heat or cold but at a higher set point. The most common cause of fever is infection, but physical trauma and tissue damage can also induce fever.

The onset of fever during infection is often gradual, but it is most striking when it occurs rapidly in the form of a chill. In such cases, the temperature setting of the brain thermostat is suddenly increased. Because of this, the person feels cold, even though his or her actual body temperature may be normal. As a result, the typical actions that are used to increase body temperature, such as vasoconstriction and shivering, occur. The person may also curl up and put on blankets. This combination of decreased heat loss and increased heat production serves to drive body temperature up to the new set point, where it stabilizes. It will continue to be regulated at this new value until the thermostat is reset to normal and the fever "breaks." The person then feels hot, throws off the covers, and manifests profound vasodilation and sweating.

What is the basis for the thermostat resetting? Chemical messengers collectively termed **endogenous pyrogen (EP)** are released from macrophages (as well as other cell types) in the presence of infection or other fever-producing stimuli. The next steps vary depending on the precise stimulus for the release of EP. As illustrated in **Figure 16.19**, in some cases, EP probably circulates in the blood to act upon the thermoreceptors in the hypothalamus (and perhaps other brain areas), altering their input to the integrating centers. In other cases, EP may be produced by macrophage-like cells in the liver and stimulate neural receptors there that give rise to afferent neural input to the hypothalamic thermoreceptors. In both cases, the immediate cause of the resetting is a local synthesis and release of prostaglandins within the hypothalamus. ***Aspirin*** reduces fever by inhibiting this prostaglandin synthesis.

The term *EP* was coined at a time when the identity of the chemical messenger(s) was not known. At least three peptides, interleukin 1-beta (IL-1β), interleukin 6 (IL-6), and tumor necrosis factor-alpha (TNFα), are now known to function as EPs. In addition to their effects on temperature, these peptides have many other effects (described in Chapter 18) that enhance resistance to infection and promote the healing of damaged tissue.

One would expect fever, which is such a consistent feature of infection, to play some important protective role. Most evidence suggests that this is the case. For example, increased body temperature stimulates a large number of the body's defensive responses to infection, including the proliferation and activity of pathogen-fighting white blood cells. The likelihood that fever is a beneficial response raises important questions about the use of aspirin and other drugs to suppress fever during infection. It must be emphasized that these questions apply to the usual modest fevers. There is no question that an extremely high fever can be harmful—particularly in its effects on the central nervous system—and must be vigorously opposed with drugs and other forms of therapy.

Fever, then, is an increased body temperature caused by an elevation of the thermal set point. When body temperature is

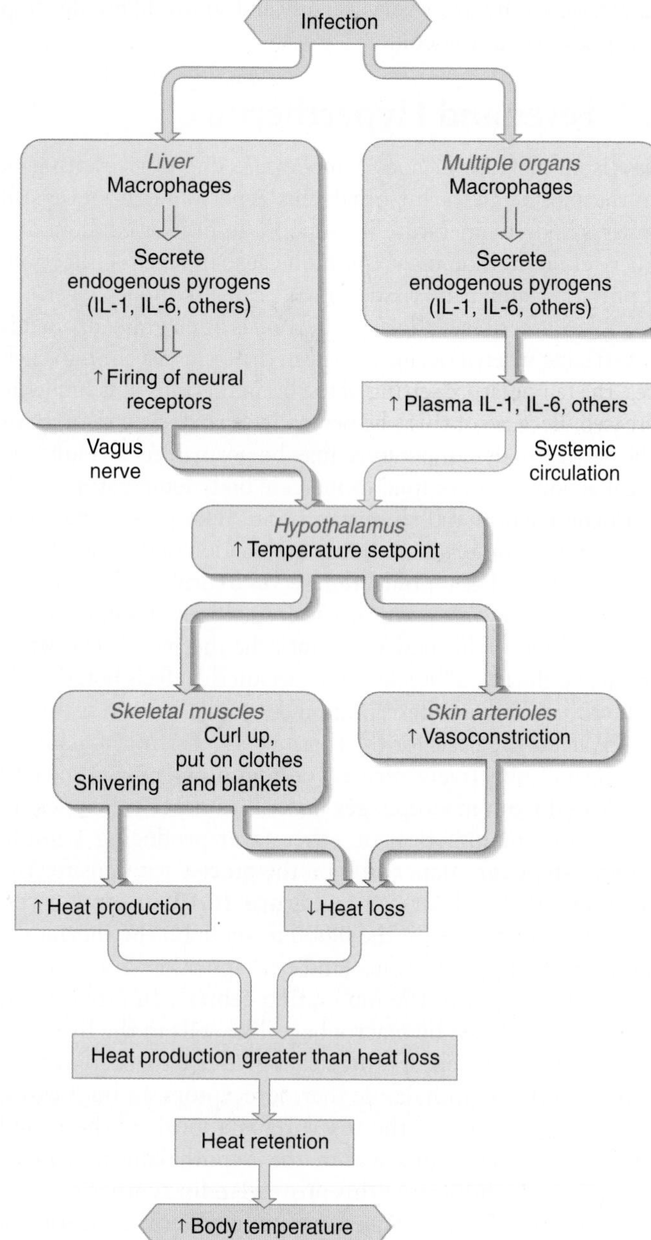

Figure 16.19 Pathway by which infection causes fever (IL-1 = Interleukin 1; IL-6 = Interleukin 6). The effector responses serve to *increase* body temperature during an infection.

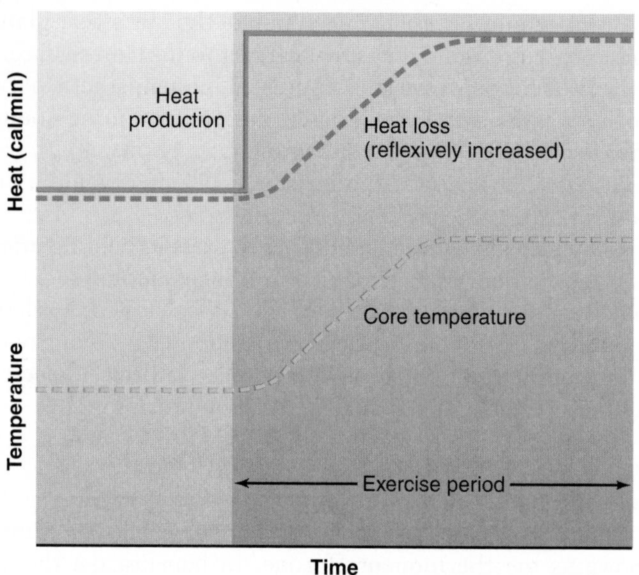

Figure 16.20 Thermal changes during exercise. Heat loss is reflexively increased. When heat loss once again equals heat production, core temperature stabilizes.

elevated for any other reason beyond a narrow normal range but without a change in the temperature set point, it is termed ***hyperthermia.*** The most common cause of hyperthermia in a typical person is exercise; the increase in body temperature above set point is due to the internal heat generated by the exercising muscles.

As shown in **Figure 16.20**, heat production increases immediately during the initial stage of exercise and exceeds heat loss, causing heat storage in the body and an increase in the core temperature. This increase in core temperature triggers reflexes, via the central thermoreceptors, that cause increased heat loss. As skin blood flow and sweating increase, the discrepancy between heat production and heat loss starts to diminish but does not disappear. Therefore, core temperature continues to increase. Ultimately, core temperature will be high enough to drive (via the central thermoreceptors) the heat-loss reflexes at a rate such that heat loss once again equals heat production. At this point, core temperature stabilizes at this elevated value despite continued exercise. In some situations, hyperthermia may lead to life-threatening consequences.

Heat exhaustion is a state of collapse, often taking the form of fainting, due to hypotension brought on by depletion of plasma volume secondary to sweating and extreme dilation of skin blood vessels. Recall from Chapter 12 that blood pressure, cardiac output, and total peripheral resistance are related according to the equation $MAP = CO \times TPR$. Thus, decreases in both cardiac output (due to the decreased plasma volume) and peripheral resistance (due to the vasodilation) contribute to the hypotension. Heat exhaustion occurs as a direct consequence of the activity of heat-loss mechanisms. Because these mechanisms have been so active, the body temperature is only modestly elevated. In a sense, heat exhaustion is a safety valve that, by forcing a cessation of work in a hot environment when heat-loss mechanisms are overtaxed, prevents the larger increase in body temperature that would cause the far more serious condition of heatstroke.

In contrast to heat exhaustion, ***heatstroke*** represents a complete breakdown in heat-regulating systems so that body temperature keeps increasing. It is an extremely dangerous situation characterized by collapse, delirium, seizures, or prolonged unconsciousness—all due to greatly increased body temperature. It almost always occurs in association with exposure to or overexertion in hot and humid environments. In some individuals, particularly elderly persons, heatstroke may appear with no apparent prior period of severe sweating (refer back to the Chapter 1 Clinical Case Study for an example), but in most cases, it comes on as the end stage of prolonged untreated heat exhaustion. Exactly what triggers the transition to heatstroke is not clear, although impaired circulation to the brain due to dehydration is one factor. The striking finding, however, is that even in the face of a rapidly increasing body temperature, the person fails to sweat. Heatstroke is a positive feedback situation in which the increasing body temperature directly stimulates metabolism, that is, heat production, which further increases body temperature. For both heat exhaustion and heatstroke, the remedy is external cooling, fluid replacement, and cessation of activity.

SECTION B SUMMARY

General Principles of Energy Expenditure

I. The energy liberated during a chemical reaction appears either as heat or work.

II. Total energy expenditure = Heat produced + External work done + Energy stored

III. Metabolic rate is influenced by the many factors summarized in Table 16.5.

IV. Metabolic rate is increased by the thyroid hormones and epinephrine.

Regulation of Total-Body Energy Stores

I. Energy storage as fat can be positive when the metabolic rate is less than, or negative when the metabolic rate is greater than, the energy content of ingested food.
   a. Energy storage is regulated mainly by reflexive adjustment of food intake.
   b. In addition, the metabolic rate increases or decreases to some extent when food intake is chronically increased or decreased, respectively.

II. Food intake is controlled by leptin, which is secreted by adipose-tissue cells, and a variety of satiety factors, as summarized in Figures 16.14 and 16.15.

III. Being overweight or obese, the result of an imbalance between food intake and metabolic rate, increases the risk of many diseases.

Regulation of Body Temperature

I. Core body temperature shows a circadian rhythm, with temperature highest during the day and lowest at night.

II. The body exchanges heat with the external environment by radiation, conduction, convection, and evaporation of water from the body surface.

III. The hypothalamus and other brain areas contain the integrating centers for temperature-regulating reflexes, and both peripheral and central thermoreceptors participate in these reflexes.

IV. Body temperature is regulated by altering heat production and/or heat loss so as to change total-body heat content.
   a. Heat production is altered by increasing muscle tone, shivering, and voluntary activity.
   b. Heat loss by radiation, conduction, and convection depends on the temperature difference between the skin surface and the environment.
   c. In response to cold, skin temperature is decreased by decreasing skin blood flow through reflexive stimulation of the sympathetic nerves to the skin. In response to heat, skin temperature is increased by inhibiting these nerves.
   d. Behavioral responses, such as putting on more clothes, also influence heat loss.
   e. Evaporation of water occurs all the time as insensible loss from the skin and respiratory lining. Additional water for evaporation is supplied by sweat, stimulated by the sympathetic nerves to the sweat glands.
   f. Increased heat production is essential for temperature regulation at environmental temperatures below the thermoneutral zone, and sweating is essential at temperatures above this zone.

V. Temperature acclimatization to heat is achieved by an earlier onset of sweating, an increased volume of sweat, and a decreased salt concentration of the sweat.

Fever and Hyperthermia

I. Fever is due to a resetting of the temperature set point so that heat production is increased and heat loss is decreased in order to increase body temperature to the new set point and keep it there. The stimulus is endogenous pyrogen, in the form of interleukin 1 and other peptides.

II. The hyperthermia of exercise is due to the increased heat produced by the muscles, and it is partially offset by skin vasodilation.

III. Extreme increases in body temperature can result in heat exhaustion or heatstroke. In heat exhaustion, blood pressure decreases due to vasodilation. In heatstroke, the normal thermoregulatory mechanisms fail; thus, heatstroke can be fatal.

SECTION B REVIEW QUESTIONS

1. State the formula relating total energy expenditure, heat produced, external work, and energy storage.
2. What two hormones alter the basal metabolic rate?
3. State the equation for total-body energy balance. Describe the three possible states of balance with regard to energy storage.
4. What happens to the basal metabolic rate after a person has either lost or gained weight?
5. List several satiety signals; where do satiety signals act?
6. List three beneficial effects of exercise in a weight-loss program.
7. Compare and contrast the four mechanisms for heat loss.
8. Describe the control of skin blood vessels during exposure to cold or heat.
9. With a diagram, summarize the reflexive responses to heat or cold. What are the dominant mechanisms for temperature regulation in the thermoneutral zone and in temperatures below and above this range?
10. What changes are exhibited by a heat-acclimatized person?
11. Summarize the sequence of events leading to a fever; contrast this to the sequence leading to hyperthermia during exercise.

SECTION B KEY TERMS

basal metabolic rate (BMR) 587
body mass index (BMI) 590
brown adipose tissue 594
calorie 587
calorigenic effect 588
central thermoreceptor 593
conduction 592
convection 592
core body temperature 592
endogenous pyrogen (EP) 595
endotherm 592
evaporation 593
external work 587
diet-induced thermogenesis 588
ghrelin 590
homeotherm 592
insensible water loss 594
internal work 587
kilocalorie (kcal) 587
leptin 589
metabolic rate 587
neuropeptide Y 589
nonshivering thermogenesis 593
peripheral thermoreceptor 593
radiation 592
satiety signal 589
shivering thermogenesis 593
sweat gland 595
thermoneutral zone 595
thrifty gene 591
total energy expenditure 587

SECTION B CLINICAL TERMS

anorexia nervosa 591
aspirin 595
bulimia nervosa 591
fever 595
heat exhaustion 596
heatstroke 596
hyperthermia 596
obesity 590
overweight 590

Clinical Case Study: An Overweight Man with Tingling, Thirst, and Blurred Vision

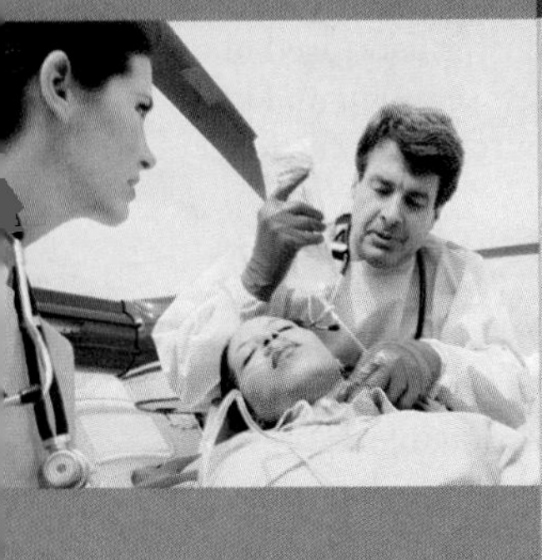

A 46-year-old man visited an ophthalmologist because of recent episodes of blurry vision. In addition to examining the man's eyes, the ophthalmologist took a medical history and assessed the patient's overall health. The patient was 6 feet tall and weighed 265 pounds (BMI equal to 36 kg/m^2). He had recently been experiencing "tingling" sensations in his hands and feet and was sleeping poorly because he was waking up several times during the night with a full bladder. He had also taken to carrying bottled water with him wherever he went, because he often felt very thirsty. He reported that he worked as a taxicab driver and rarely if ever had occasion to engage in much physical activity or exercise. The patient attributed the tingling sensations to "sitting in one position all day" and was convinced that his eye problems were the natural result of aging. Examination of the eyes, however, revealed a greatly weakened accommodation reflex in both eyes (see Chapter 7). These signs and symptoms suggested to the ophthalmologist that the patient might have ***diabetes mellitus,*** and he therefore referred the patient to a physician at the diabetes unit of his local hospital.

The physician at the hospital performed a series of tests to confirm the diagnosis of diabetes mellitus. First, the fasting plasma glucose concentration was determined on two separate days. After an overnight fast, blood was drawn and the concentration of glucose in the plasma was determined. Normal values are generally below 100 mg/dL, but the two values determined for this patient were 156 and 144 mg/dL. Consequently, a second test called an *oral glucose tolerance test* was performed. In this test, the patient fasts overnight and then drinks a solution of 75 grams of glucose dissolved in water. Two hours later, blood is drawn and again the plasma glucose concentration is determined. In healthy individuals, the plasma glucose concentration will be below 140 mg/dL by this time, because their circulating insulin will have responded to the increase in glucose and will be in the process of restoring glucose to normal. In two separate tests, however, the glucose concentrations were 215 and 236 mg/dL; these results suggested that the patient's pancreas failed to secrete sufficient insulin in response to the glucose challenge, or that the sensitivity of his cells to insulin was decreased, or both. Finally, a third test was performed to determine what percentage of the patient's hemoglobin was glycosylated. Hemoglobin is found in red blood cells, which have a lifetime of 2 to 4 months. When glucose concentrations are above normal, certain proteins including hemoglobin become bound to glucose (that is, they become glycosylated); once bound, the glucose molecules remain on hemoglobin for the lifetime of the cell. The longer the duration of the elevation in plasma glucose, the greater the percentage of glycosylated hemoglobin, abbreviated HbA1c. Therefore, this test is a measure of the average glucose values in the blood over the previous few months. Normal values are between 4% and 6%, but in our patient, HbA1c was 6.9%. Together, these tests confirmed the diagnosis of diabetes mellitus.

Diabetes mellitus can be due to a deficiency of insulin and/or to a decreased responsiveness to insulin. Diabetes mellitus is therefore classified into two distinct diseases depending on the cause. In ***type 1 diabetes mellitus*** (***T1DM***), formerly called *insulin-dependent diabetes mellitus* or *juvenile diabetes,* insulin is completely or almost completely absent from the islets of Langerhans and the plasma. Therefore, therapy with insulin is essential. In ***type 2 diabetes mellitus*** (***T2DM***), formerly called *non-insulin-dependent diabetes mellitus* or *adult-onset diabetes mellitus,* insulin is present in plasma but cellular sensitivity to insulin is less than normal (***insulin resistance***). In many patients with T2DM, the response of the pancreatic beta cells to glucose is also impaired. Therefore, therapy may involve some combination of drugs that increase cellular sensitivity to insulin, increase insulin secretion from beta cells, or decrease hepatic glucose production; or the therapy may involve insulin administration itself.

T1DM is less common, affecting approximately 5% of diabetic patients in the United States. T1DM is due to the total or near-total autoimmune destruction of the pancreatic beta cells by the body's white blood cells. As you will learn in Chapter 18, an autoimmune disease is one in which the body's immune cells attack and destroy normal, healthy tissue. The triggering events for this autoimmune response are not yet fully established. Treatment of T1DM involves the administration of insulin by injection, because insulin administered orally would be destroyed by gastrointestinal enzymes.

Because of insulin deficiency, *untreated* patients with T1DM always have increased glucose concentrations in their blood. The increase in plasma glucose occurs because (1) glucose fails to enter insulin's target cells normally, and (2) the liver continuously makes glucose by glycogenolysis and gluconeogenesis and secretes the glucose into the blood. Recall also that insulin normally suppresses lipolysis and ketone formation. Consequently, another result of the insulin deficiency is pronounced lipolysis with subsequent elevation of plasma glycerol and fatty acids. Many of the fatty acids are then converted by the liver into ketones, which are released into the blood.

If extreme, these metabolic changes culminate in the acute life-threatening emergency called ***diabetic ketoacidosis*** (**Figure 16.21**). Some of the problems are due to the effects that extremely elevated plasma glucose concentration produces on renal function. Chapter 14 pointed out that a typical person does not excrete glucose because all glucose filtered at the renal glomeruli is reabsorbed by the tubules. However, the elevated plasma glucose of diabetes mellitus increases the filtered load of glucose beyond the maximum tubular reabsorptive capacity and, therefore, large amounts of glucose are excreted. For the same reasons, large amounts of ketones may also appear in the urine. These urinary losses deplete the body of nutrients and lead to weight loss. Far worse, however, is the fact that these unreabsorbed solutes cause an osmotic diuresis—increased urinary excretion of sodium ions and water, which can lead, by the sequence of events shown in Figure 16.21, to hypotension, brain damage, and death. It should be noted, however, that apart from this extreme example, diabetics are more often prone to hypertension, not hypotension (due to several causes, including vascular and kidney damage).

The other serious abnormality in diabetic ketoacidosis is the increased plasma hydrogen ion concentration caused by the accumulation of ketones. As described in Chapter 3, ketones are four-carbon breakdown products of fatty acids. Two ketones,

(continued)

(continued)

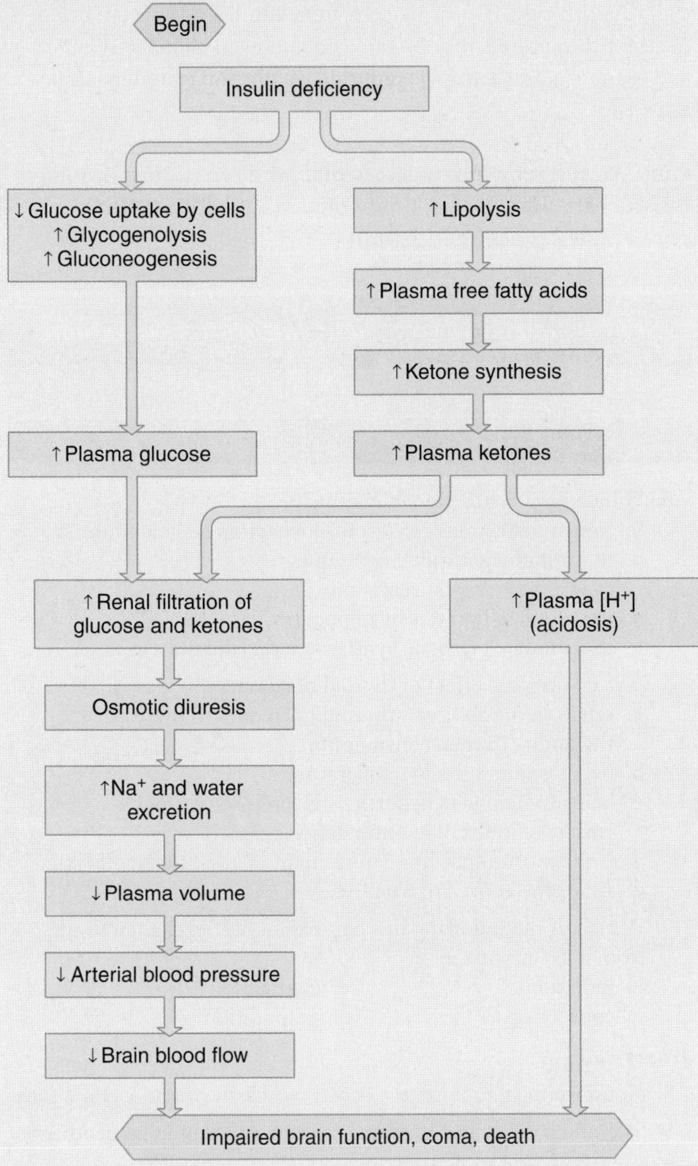

Figure 16.21 Diabetic ketoacidosis. Events caused by severe untreated insulin deficiency in type 1 diabetes mellitus.

known as hydroxybutyric acid and acetoacetic acid, are acidic at the pH of blood. This increased hydrogen ion concentration causes brain dysfunction that can contribute to coma and death.

Diabetic ketoacidosis occurs primarily in patients with *untreated* T1DM, that is, those with almost total inability to secrete insulin. However, more than 90% of diabetic patients are in the T2DM category and usually do not develop metabolic derangements severe enough to develop diabetic ketoacidosis. T2DM is a syndrome mainly of overweight adults, typically starting in middle life. However, T2DM is *not* an age-dependent syndrome. As the incidence of childhood obesity has soared in the United States, so too has the incidence of T2DM in children and adolescents. Given the earlier mention of progressive weight loss in T1DM as a symptom of diabetes, why is it that most people with T2DM are overweight? One reason is that people with T2DM, in contrast to those with T1DM, do not excrete enough glucose in the urine to cause weight loss. Moreover, in T2DM, it is the excessive weight gain that is the *cause* of the diabetes.

Several factors combine to cause T2DM. One major problem is target-cell hyporesponsiveness to insulin, termed insulin resistance. Obesity accounts for much of the insulin resistance in T2DM, although a minority of people develop T2DM without obesity for reasons that are unknown. Obesity in any person—diabetic or not—usually induces some degree of insulin resistance, particularly in muscle and adipose-tissue cells. One hypothesis is that the excess adipose tissue overproduces messengers—perhaps inflammatory cytokines—that cause downregulation of insulin-responsive glucose transporters or in some other way blocks insulin's actions. Another hypothesis is that excess fat deposition in non-adipose tissue (for example, in muscle) causes a decrease in insulin sensitivity.

As stated earlier, many people with T2DM not only have insulin resistance but also have a defect in the ability of their beta cells to secrete insulin adequately in response to an increase in the concentration of plasma glucose. In other words, although insulin resistance is the primary factor inducing hyperglycemia in T2DM, an as-yet-unidentified defect in beta-cell function prevents these cells from responding maximally to the hyperglycemia. It is currently thought that the mediators of decreased insulin sensitivity described earlier may also interfere with a normal insulin secretory response to hyperglycemia.

The most effective therapy for obese persons with T2DM is weight reduction. An exercise program is also very important because insulin sensitivity is increased by frequent endurance-type exercise, independent of changes in body weight. This occurs, at least in part, because exercise causes a substantial increase in the total number of plasma membrane glucose transporters in skeletal muscle cells. Because a program of weight reduction, exercise, and dietary modification typically requires some time before it becomes effective, T2DM patients are usually also given orally active drugs that lower plasma glucose concentration by a variety of mechanisms. A recently approved synthetic incretin and another class of drugs called ***sulfonylureas*** lower plasma glucose concentration by acting on the beta cells to stimulate insulin secretion. Other drugs increase cellular sensitivity to insulin or decrease hepatic gluconeogenesis. Finally, in some cases, the use of high doses of insulin itself is warranted in T2DM.

Unfortunately, people with either form of diabetes mellitus tend to develop a variety of chronic abnormalities, including atherosclerosis, hypertension, kidney failure, blood vessel and nerve disease, susceptibility to infection, and blindness. Chronically increased plasma glucose concentration contributes to most of these abnormalities either by causing the intracellular accumulation of certain glucose metabolites that exert harmful effects on cells when present in high concentrations or by linking glucose to proteins, thereby altering their function. In our subject, the high glucose concentrations led to an accumulation of glucose metabolites in the lenses, causing them to swell due to osmosis; this, in turn, reduced the ability of his eyes to accurately focus light on the retina. He also had signs of nerve damage evidenced by the tingling sensations in his hands and feet. In many cases, symptoms such as his diminish or even disappear within days to months of receiving therapy. Nonetheless, over the long term, the aforementioned problems may still arise.

(continued)

(continued)

Our patient was counseled to begin a program of brisk walking for 30 minutes a day, at least five times a week, with the goal of increasing the duration and intensity of the exercise over the course of several months. He was also referred to a nutritionist, who advised him on a weight-loss program that involved a reduction in total daily saturated fat and calorie intake and increased consumption of fruits and vegetables. In addition, he was started immediately on two drugs, one that increases secretion of insulin from the pancreas and one that suppresses production of glucose from the liver. With time, the need for these drugs may be reduced and even eliminated if diet and exercise are successful in reducing weight and restoring insulin sensitivity.

Clinical terms: diabetes mellitus, diabetic ketoacidosis, insulin resistance, sulfonylureas, type 1 diabetes mellitus (T1DM), type 2 diabetes mellitus (T2DM)

See Chapter 19 for complete, integrative case studies.

CHAPTER 16 TEST QUESTIONS

Answers found in Appendix A.

1. Which is *incorrect?*
   a. Fatty acids can be converted into glucose in the liver.
   b. Glucose can be converted into fatty acids in adipose cells.
   c. Certain amino acids can be converted into glucose by the liver.
   d. Triglycerides are absorbed from the GI tract in the form of chylomicrons.
   e. The absorptive state is characterized by ingested nutrients entering the blood from the GI tract.
2. During the postabsorptive state, epinephrine stimulates breakdown of adipose triglycerides by
   a. inhibiting lipoprotein lipase.
   b. stimulating hormone-sensitive lipase.
   c. increasing production of glycogen.
   d. inhibiting hormone-sensitive lipase.
   e. promoting increased adipose ketone production.
3. Which is true of strenuous, prolonged exercise?
   a. It results in an increase in plasma glucagon concentration.
   b. It results in an increase in plasma insulin concentration.
   c. Plasma glucose concentration does not change.
   d. Skeletal muscle uptake of glucose is inhibited.
   e. Plasma concentrations of cortisol and growth hormone both decrease.
4. Untreated type 1 diabetes mellitus is characterized by
   a. decreased sensitivity of adipose and skeletal muscle cells to insulin.
   b. higher-than-normal plasma insulin concentration.
   c. loss of body fluid due to increased urine production.
   d. age-dependent onset (only occurs in adults).
   e. obesity.
5. Which is *not* a function of insulin?
   a. to stimulate amino acid transport across cell membranes
   b. to inhibit hepatic glucose output
   c. to inhibit glucagon secretion
   d. to stimulate lipolysis in adipocytes
   e. to stimulate glycogen synthase in skeletal muscle
6. The calorigenic effect of thyroid hormones
   a. refers to the ability of thyroid hormones to increase the body's oxygen consumption.
   b. helps maintain body temperature.
   c. helps explain why hyperthyroidism is sometimes associated with symptoms of vitamin deficiencies.
   d. is the most important determinant of basal metabolic rate.
   e. All of the above are true.
7. Which of the following mechanisms of heat exchange results from local air currents?
   a. radiation
   b. convection
   c. conduction
   d. evaporation

True or False

8. Nonshivering thermogenesis occurs outside the thermoneutral zone.
9. Skin and core temperature are both kept constant in homeotherms.
10. Leptin inhibits and ghrelin stimulates appetite.
11. Actively contracting skeletal muscles require more insulin than they do at rest.
12. Body mass index is calculated as height in meters divided by weight in kilograms.
13. In conduction, heat moves from a surface of higher temperature to one of lower temperature.
14. Skin blood vessels constrict in response to elevated core body temperature.
15. Evaporative cooling is most efficient in dry weather.

CHAPTER 16 GENERAL PRINCIPLES ASSESSMENT

Answers found in Appendix A.

1. A general principle of physiology is that *most physiological functions are controlled by multiple regulatory systems, often working in opposition.* How is this principle illustrated by the pancreatic control of glucose homeostasis? (*Note:* Compare Figures 16.5, 16.8, and 16.10 for help.)
2. This same principle also applies to the control of appetite. Give at least five examples of factors that regulate appetite in humans, including some that stimulate and some that inhibit appetite.
3. Body temperature homeostasis is critical for maintenance of healthy cells, tissues, and organs. Using Figure 16.17 as your guide, explain how the control of body temperature reflects the general principle of physiology that *physiological processes are dictated by the laws of chemistry and physics.*

CHAPTER 16 QUANTITATIVE AND THOUGHT QUESTIONS

Answers found in Appendix A.

1. What happens to the triglyceride concentrations in the plasma and in adipose tissue after administration of a drug that blocks the action of lipoprotein lipase?
2. A person has a defect in the ability of her small intestine to reabsorb bile salts. What effect will this have on her plasma cholesterol concentration?
3. A well-trained athlete is found to have a moderately elevated plasma total cholesterol concentration. What additional measurements would you advise this person to have taken in order to gain a better understanding of the importance of the elevated cholesterol?
4. A resting, unstressed person has increased plasma concentrations of free fatty acids, glycerol, amino acids, and ketones. What situations might be responsible and what additional plasma measurement would distinguish among them?
5. A healthy volunteer is given an injection of insulin. The plasma concentrations of which hormones increase as a result?
6. If the sympathetic preganglionic fibers to the adrenal medulla were cut in an animal, would this eliminate the sympathetically mediated component of increased gluconeogenesis and lipolysis during exercise? Explain.
7. What are the sources of heat loss for a person immersed up to the neck in a 40°C bath?
8. Lizards regulate their body temperatures primarily through behavioral means. Can you predict what they do when they are infected with bacteria?

CHAPTER 16 ANSWERS TO PHYSIOLOGICAL INQUIRIES

Figure 16.1 Eating a diet that is low in fat content does not mean that a person cannot gain additional adipose mass, because as shown in this figure, glucose and amino acids can be converted into fat in the liver. From there, the fat is transported and deposited in adipose tissue. A diet that is low in fat but rich in sugar, for example, could still result in an increase in fat mass in the body.

Figure 16.6 Having the transporters already synthesized and packaged into intracellular vesicle membranes means that glucose transport can be tightly and quickly coupled with changes in glucose concentrations in the blood. This protects the body against the harmful effects of excess blood glucose concentrations and also prevents urinary loss of glucose by keeping the rate of glucose filtration below the maximum rate at which the kidney can reabsorb it. This tight coupling could not occur if the transporters were required to be synthesized each time a cell was stimulated by insulin.

Figure 16.8 The brain is absolutely necessary for immediate survival and can maintain glucose uptake from the plasma in the fasted state when insulin concentrations are very low.

Figure 16.10 Fight-or-flight reactions result in an increase in sympathetic nerve activity. These neurons release norepinephrine from their axon terminals (see Chapter 6), which stimulates glucagon release from the pancreas. Glucagon then contributes to the increase in energy sources such as glucose in the blood, which facilitates fight-or-flight reactions.

Figure 16.14 The body's normal response to leptin is to decrease appetite and increase metabolic rate. This would not be adaptive during times when it is important to increase body energy (fat) stores. An example of such a situation is pregnancy, when gaining weight in the form of increased fat mass is important for providing energy to the growing fetus. In nature, another example is the requirement of hibernating animals to store large amounts of fat prior to hibernation. In these cases, the effects of leptin are decreased or ignored by the brain.

Figure 16.15 In the short term, drinking water before a meal may decrease appetite by stretching the stomach, and this may contribute to eating a smaller meal. However, as described in Chapter 15, water is quickly absorbed by the GI tract and provides no calories; thus, hunger will soon return once the meal is over.

Figure 16.17 The amount of fluid in the body decreases as water evaporates from the surface of the skin. This fluid must be replaced by drinking or the body will become dehydrated. In addition, sweat is salty (as you may have noticed by the salt residue remaining on hats or clothing once the sweat has dried). This means that the body's salt content also needs to be restored. This is a good example of how maintaining homeostasis for one variable (body temperature) may result in disruption of homeostasis for other variables (water and salt).

Scanning electron micrograph of a single sperm cell on the surface of an egg.

17 Reproduction

Reproduction is the process by which a species is perpetuated. As opposed to most of the physiological processes you have learned about in this book, reproduction is one of the few that is not necessary for the survival of an individual. However, normal reproductive function is essential for the production of healthy offspring and, therefore, for *survival of the species.* Sexual reproduction and the merging of parental chromosomes provide the biological variation of individuals that is necessary for adaptation of the species to our changing environment.

Reproduction includes the processes by which the male gamete (the sperm) and the female gamete (the ovum) develop, grow, and unite to produce a new and unique combination of genes in a new organism. This new entity, the zygote, develops into an embryo and then a fetus within the maternal uterus. The gametes are produced by gonads—the testes in the male and the ovaries in the female. Reproduction also includes the process by which a fetus is born. Over the course of a lifetime, reproductive functions also include sexual maturation (puberty), as well as pregnancy and lactation in women.

The gonads produce hormones that influence development of the offspring into male or female phenotypes. The gonadal hormones are controlled by and influence the secretion of hormones from the hypothalamus and the anterior pituitary gland. Together with the nervous system, these hormones regulate the cyclical activities of female reproduction, including the menstrual cycle, and provide a striking example of the general principle of physiology that most physiological processes are controlled by multiple regulatory systems, often working in opposition. The process of gamete maturation requires communication and feedback between the gonads, anterior pituitary gland, and brain, demonstrating the importance of two related general principles of physiology, namely, that information flow between cells, tissues, and organs is an essential feature of homeostasis and allows for integration of physiological processes; and that the functions of organ systems are coordinated with each other.

SECTION **A**

Gametogenesis, Sex Determination, and Sex Differentiation; General Principles of Reproductive Endocrinology

The primary reproductive organs are known as the **gonads:** the **testes** (singular, **testis**) in the male and the **ovaries** (singular, **ovary**) in the female. In both sexes, the gonads serve dual functions. The first of these is **gametogenesis,** which is the production of the reproductive cells, or **gametes.** These are **spermatozoa** (singular, **spermatozoan,** usually shortened to **sperm**) in males and **ova** (singular, **ovum**) in females. Secondly, the gonads secrete steroid hormones, often termed **sex hormones** or **gonadal steroids.** The major sex hormones are **androgens** (including **testosterone** and **dihydrotestosterone [DHT]**), **estrogens** (primarily **estradiol**), and **progesterone.** Both sexes have each of these hormones, but androgens predominate in males and estrogens and progesterone predominate in females.

17.1 Gametogenesis

The process of gametogenesis is depicted in **Figure 17.1.** At any point in gametogenesis, the developing gametes are called **germ cells.** The first stage in gametogenesis is proliferation of the primordial (undifferentiated) germ cells by mitosis. With the exception of the gametes, the DNA of each nucleated human cell is contained in 23 pairs of chromosomes, giving a total of 46. The two corresponding chromosomes in each pair are said to be homologous to each other, with one coming from each parent. In **mitosis,** the 46 chromosomes of the dividing cell are replicated. The cell then divides into two new cells called daughter cells. Each of the two daughter cells resulting from the division receives a full set of 46 chromosomes identical to those of the original cell. Thus, each daughter cell receives identical genetic information during mitosis.

In this manner, mitosis of primordial germ cells, each containing 46 chromosomes, provides a supply of identical germ cells for the next stages. The timing of mitosis in germ cells differs greatly in females and males. In the male, some mitosis occurs in the embryonic testes to generate the population of **primary spermatocytes** present at birth, but mitosis really begins in earnest in the male at puberty and usually continues throughout life. In the female, mitosis of germ cells in the ovary occurs primarily during fetal development, generating **primary oocytes.** The second stage of gametogenesis is **meiosis,** in which each resulting gamete receives only 23 chromosomes from a 46-chromosome germ cell, one chromosome from each homologous pair. Meiosis consists of two cell divisions in succession (see Figure 17.1). The events preceding the first meiotic division are identical to those preceding a *mitotic*

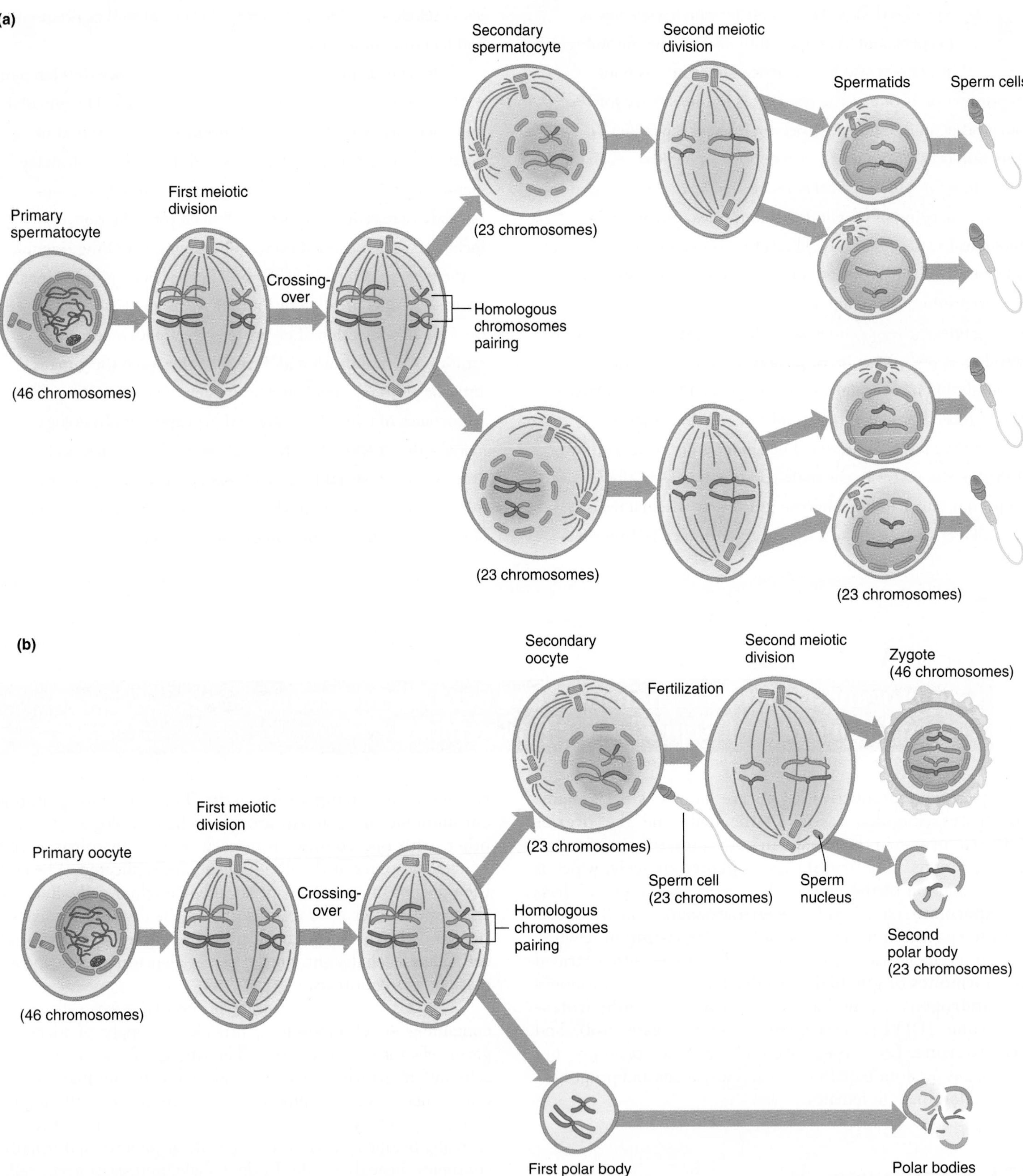

Figure 17.1 APIR An overview of gametogenesis in (a) the testes and (b) the ovary. Only four chromosomes (two sets) are shown for clarity instead of the normal 46 in humans. Chromosomes from one parent are purple, and those from the other parent are blue. The size of the cells can vary quite dramatically in ova development.

division. During the interphase period, which precedes a mitotic division, chromosomal DNA is replicated. Thus, after DNA replication, an interphase cell has 46 chromosomes, but each chromosome consists of two identical strands of DNA, called sister chromatids, which are joined together by a centromere.

As the first meiotic division begins, homologous chromosomes, each consisting of two identical sister chromatids, come together and line up adjacent to each other. Thus, 23 pairs of homologous chromosomes (called **bivalents**) are formed. The sister chromatids of each chromosome condense into thick, rodlike structures. Then within each homologous pair, corresponding segments of homologous chromosomes align closely. This allows two nonsister chromatids to undergo an exchange of sites of breakage in a process called **crossing-over** (see Figure 17.1). Thus, crossing-over results in the recombination of genes on homologous chromosomes. Recombination is one of the most significant features of sexual reproduction that creates genetic diversity.

Following crossing-over, the homologous chromosomes line up in the center of the cell. The orientation of each pair on the equator is random, meaning that sometimes the maternal portion points to a particular pole of the cell and sometimes the paternal portion does so. The cell then divides (the first meiotic division), with the maternal chromatids of any particular pair going to one of the two cells resulting from the division and the paternal chromatids going to the other. The results of the first meiotic division are the **secondary spermatocytes** in males and the **secondary oocyte** in females. Note in Figure 17.1 that, in females, one of the two cells arising from the first meiotic division is the **first polar body** that has no function. Because of the random orientation of the homologous pairs at the equator, it is extremely unlikely that all 23 maternal chromatids will end up in one cell and all 23 paternal chromatids in the other. Over 8 million (2^{23}) different combinations of maternal and paternal chromosomes can result during this first meiotic division.

The second meiotic division occurs without any further replication of DNA. The sister chromatids—both of which were originally either maternal or paternal—of each chromosome separate and move apart into the new daughter cells. The daughter cells resulting from the second meiotic division, therefore, contain 23 one-chromatid chromosomes. Although the concept is the same, the timing of the second meiotic division is different in males and females. In males, this occurs continuously after puberty with the production of **spermatids** and ultimately mature sperm cells described in detail in the next section. In females, the second meiotic division does not occur until after fertilization of a secondary oocyte by a sperm. This results in production of the **zygote,** which contains 46 chromosomes—23 from the oocyte (maternal) and 23 from the sperm (paternal)—and the **second polar body,** which, like the first polar body, has no function.

To summarize, gametogenesis produces daughter cells having only 23 chromosomes, and two events during the first meiotic division contribute to the enormous genetic variability of the daughter cells: (1) crossing-over and (2) the random distribution of maternal and paternal chromatid pairs between the two daughter cells.

17.2 Sex Determination

The complete genetic composition of an individual is known as the **genotype.** Genetic inheritance sets the gender of the individual, or **sex determination,** which is established at the moment of fertilization. Gender is determined by genetic inheritance of two chromosomes called the **sex chromosomes.** The larger of the sex chromosomes is called the **X chromosome** and the smaller, the **Y chromosome.** Males possess one X and one Y, whereas females have two X chromosomes. Therefore, the key difference in genotype between males and females arises from this difference in one chromosome. As you will learn in the next section, the presence of the Y chromosome leads to the development of the male gonads—the testes; the absence of the Y chromosome leads to the development the female gonads—the ovaries.

The ovum can contribute only an X chromosome, whereas half of the sperm produced during meiosis are X and half are Y. When the sperm and the egg join, 50% should have XX and 50% XY. Interestingly, however, sex ratios at birth are not exactly 1:1; rather, there tends to be a slight preponderance of male births, possibly due to functional differences in sperm carrying the X versus Y chromosome.

An easy method exists for determining whether a person's cells contain two X chromosomes, the typical female pattern. When two X chromosomes are present, only one is functional; the nonfunctional X chromosome condenses to form a nuclear mass called the **sex chromatin,** or **Barr body,** which is readily observable with a light microscope. Scrapings from the cheek mucosa or white blood cells are convenient sources of cells to be examined. The single X chromosome in male cells rarely condenses to form sex chromatin.

A more exacting technique for determining sex chromosome composition employs tissue culture visualization of all the chromosomes—a **karyotype.** This technique can be used to identify a group of genetic sex abnormalities characterized by such unusual chromosomal combinations such as XXX, XXY, and XO (the O denotes the absence of a second sex chromosome). The end result of such combinations is usually the failure of normal anatomical and functional sexual development. The karyotype is also used to evaluate many other chromosomal abnormalities such as the characteristic trisomy 21 of Down syndrome described later in this chapter.

17.3 Sex Differentiation

The multiple processes involved in the development of the reproductive system in the fetus are collectively called **sex differentiation.** It is not surprising that people with atypical chromosomal combinations can manifest atypical sex differentiation. However, careful study has also revealed individuals with normal chromosomal combinations but abnormal sexual appearance and function (**phenotype**). In these people, sex differentiation has been atypical, and their gender phenotype may not correspond with the presence of XX or XY chromosomes.

It will be important to bear in mind during the following description one essential generalization: The genes directly determine only whether the individual will have testes or ovaries. The rest of sex differentiation depends upon the presence or absence of substances produced by the genetically determined gonads, in particular, the testes.

Differentiation of the Gonads

The male and female gonads derive embryologically from the same site—an area called the urogenital (or gonadal) ridge. Until the sixth week of uterine life, primordial gonads are undifferentiated (see Figure 17.2). In the genetic male, the testes begin to develop during the seventh week. A gene on the Y chromosome (the ***SRY* gene,** for *s*ex-determining *r*egion of the *Y* chromosome) is expressed at this time in the urogenital ridge cells and triggers this development. In the absence of a Y chromosome and, consequently, the *SRY* gene, testes do not develop. Instead, ovaries begin to develop in the same area.

By what mechanism does the *SRY* gene induce the formation of the testes? This gene codes for a protein, SRY, which sets into motion a sequence of gene activations ultimately leading to the formation of testes from the various embryonic cells in the urogenital ridge.

Differentiation of Internal and External Genitalia

The internal duct system and external genitalia of the fetus are capable of developing into either sexual phenotype (**Figure 17.2** and **Figure 17.3**). Before the functioning of the fetal gonads, the undifferentiated reproductive tract includes a double genital duct system, comprised of the **Wolffian ducts** and **Müllerian ducts,** and a common opening to the outside for the genital ducts and urinary system. Usually, most of the reproductive tract develops from only one of these duct systems. In the male, the Wolffian ducts persist and the Müllerian ducts regress, whereas in the female, the opposite happens. The external genitalia in the two genders and the outer part of the vagina do not develop from these duct systems, however, but from other structures at the body surface.

Which of the two duct systems and types of external genitalia develops depends on the presence or absence of fetal testes. These testes secrete testosterone and a protein hormone called **Müllerian-inhibiting substance** (**MIS**) (see Figure 17.2). SRY protein induces the expression of the gene for MIS; MIS then causes the degeneration of the Müllerian duct system. Simultaneously, testosterone causes the Wolffian ducts to differentiate into the epididymis, vas deferens, ejaculatory duct, and seminal vesicles. Externally and somewhat later, under the influence primarily of dihydrotestosterone (DHT) produced from testosterone in target tissue, a penis forms and the tissue near it fuses to form the scrotum (see Figure 17.3). The testes will ultimately descend into the scrotum, stimulated to do so by testosterone. Failure of the testes to descend is called ***cryptorchidism*** and is common in infants with decreased androgen secretion. Because sperm production requires about 2°C lower temperature than normal core body temperature, sperm production is usually decreased in cryptorchidism. Treatments include hormone therapy and surgical approaches to move the testes into the scrotum.

In contrast, the female fetus, not having testes (because of the absence of the *SRY* gene), does not secrete testosterone and MIS. In the absence of MIS, the Müllerian system does not degenerate but rather develops into fallopian tubes and a uterus (see Figure 17.2). In the absence of testosterone, the Wolffian ducts degenerate and a vagina and female external genitalia develop from the structures at the body surface (see Figure 17.3). Ovaries, though present in the female fetus, do not play a role in these developmental processes. In other words, female fetal development will occur automatically unless stopped from doing so by the presence of factors released from functioning testes. The events in sex determination and sex differentiation in males and females are summarized in **Figure 17.4**.

There are various conditions in which normal sex differentiation does not occur. For example, in ***androgen insensitivity syndrome*** (also called ***testicular feminization***), the genotype is XY and testes are present but the phenotype (external genitalia and vagina) is female. It is caused by a mutation in the androgen-receptor gene that renders the receptor incapable of normal binding to testosterone. Under the influence of SRY protein, the fetal testes differentiate as usual and they secrete both MIS and testosterone. MIS causes the Müllerian ducts to regress, but the inability of the Wolffian ducts to respond to testosterone also causes them to regress, and so no duct system develops. The tissues that develop into external genitalia are also unresponsive to androgen, so female external genitalia and a vagina develop. The testes do not descend, and they are usually removed when the diagnosis is made. The syndrome is usually not detected until menstrual cycles fail to begin at puberty.

Whereas androgen insensitivity syndrome is caused by a failure of the developing fetus to respond to fetal androgens, ***congenital adrenal hyperplasia*** is caused by the production of too much androgen in the fetus. Rather than the androgen coming from the fetal testes, it is caused by adrenal androgen overproduction due to a partial defect in the ability of the fetal adrenal gland to synthesize cortisol. This is almost always due to a mutation in the gene for an enzyme in the cortisol synthetic pathway (**Figure 17.5**) leading to a partial decrease in the activity of the enzyme. The resultant decrease in cortisol in the fetal blood leads to an increase in the secretion of ACTH from the fetal pituitary gland due to a loss of glucocorticoid negative feedback. The increase in fetal plasma ACTH stimulates the fetal adrenal cortex to try to make more cortisol to overcome the partial enzyme dysfunction. Remember, however, that the adrenal cortex can synthesize androgens from the same precursor as cortisol (see Figure 11.5). ACTH stimulation results in an increase in androgen production because the precursors cannot be efficiently converted to cortisol. This increase in fetal androgen production results in ***virilization*** of an XX fetus (masculinized external genitalia). If untreated in the fetus, the XX baby is usually born with ***ambiguous genitalia***—it is not obvious whether the baby is a phenotypic boy or girl. These babies require treatment with cortisol replacement.

Sexual Differentiation of the Brain

With regard to sexual behavior, differences in the brain may form during fetal and neonatal development. For example, genetic female monkeys treated with testosterone during their late fetal life manifest evidence of masculine sex behavior as adults, such as mounting. In this regard, a potentially important difference in human brain anatomy has been reported; the size of a particular nucleus (neuronal cluster) in the hypothalamus is

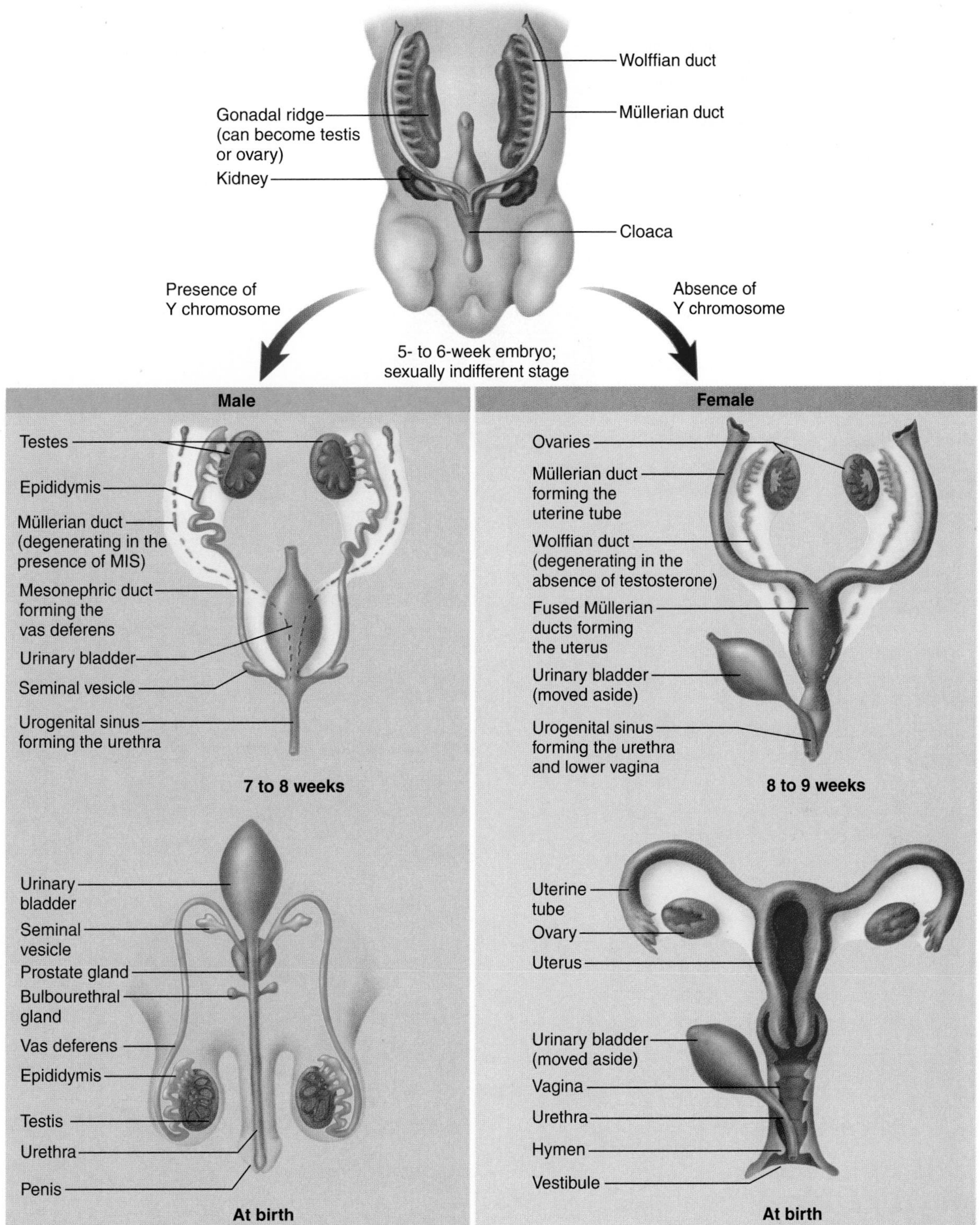

Figure 17.2 Embryonic sex differentiation of the male and female internal reproductive tracts. The testes develop in the presence of the Y chromosome (due to the expression of SRY protein), whereas the ovaries develop in the absence of the Y chromosome (due to the absence of SRY protein). In males, the testes secrete testosterone, which stimulates the maturation of the Wolffian duct into the vas deferens and associated structures, and Müllerian-inhibiting substance (MIS), which induces the degeneration of the Müllerian ducts and associated structures. At birth, the testes have descended into the scrotum. In the female, the absence of testosterone allows the Wolffian ducts to degenerate and the absence of MIS allows the Müllerian ducts to develop into the uterine (fallopian) tubes and the uterus.

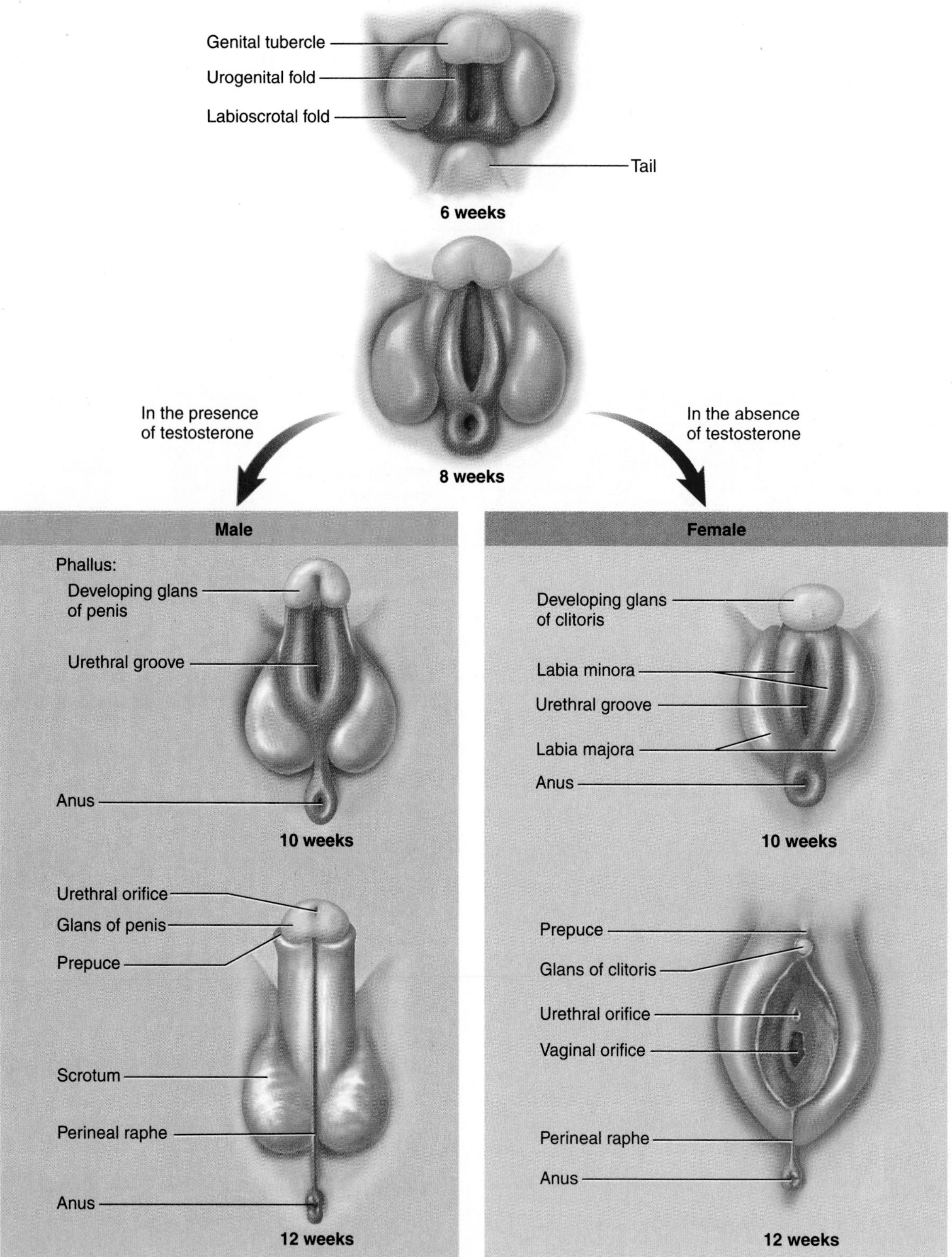

Figure 17.3 Development of the external genitalia in males and females. The major signal for sex differentiation of the external genitalia is the presence of testosterone in the male (produced by the testes shown in Figure 17.2) and its local conversion to dihydrotestosterone (DHT) in target tissue. By about 6 weeks of development, the three primordial structures of the embryo that will become the male or female external genitalia are the genital tubercle, the urogenital fold, and the labioscrotal fold. Sexual differentiation becomes apparent at 10 weeks of fetal life and is unmistakable by 12 weeks of fetal life. The female phenotype develops in the absence of testosterone and DHT. Matching colors identify homologous structures in the male and female.

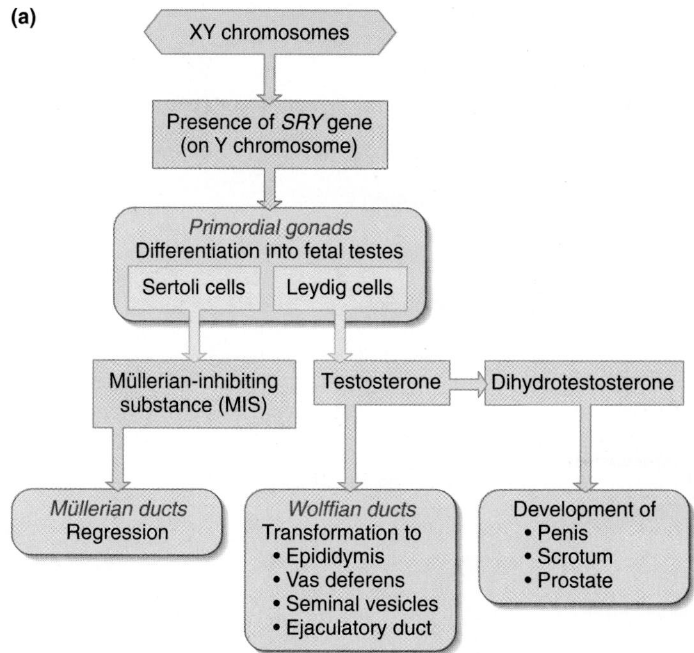

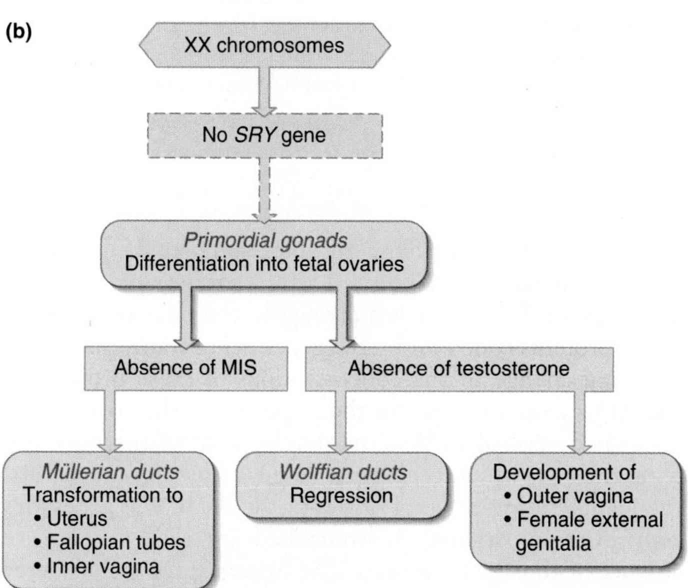

Figure 17.4 Summary of sex differentiation. (a) Male. (b) Female. The *SRY* gene codes for the SRY protein. Conversion of testosterone to dihydrotestosterone occurs primarily in target tissue. The Sertoli and Leydig cells in the testes will be described in Section C.

PHYSIOLOGICAL INQUIRY

- Referring to part (a), 5-α-reductase inhibitors, which block the conversion of testosterone to dihydrotestosterone (DHT) in target tissue, are used to treat some men with benign swelling of their prostate glands. (The prostate gland cells contain 5-α-reductase and are target tissues of locally produced DHT.) Examples of these drugs are finasteride and dutasteride. Why are pregnant women instructed not to take or even handle these drugs? (*Hint:* Some drugs can cross the placenta and enter the circulatory system of the fetus.)

Answer can be found at end of chapter.

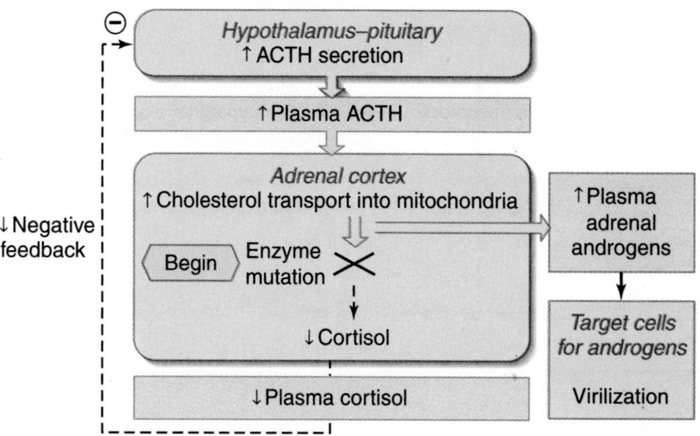

Figure 17.5 Mechanism of virilization in female fetuses with congenital adrenal hyperplasia. An enzyme defect (usually partial) in the steroidogenic pathway leads to decreased production of cortisol and a shift of precursors into the adrenal androgen pathway. Because cortisol negative feedback is decreased, ACTH release from the fetal pituitary gland increases. Although cortisol can eventually be normalized, it is at the expense of ACTH-stimulated adrenal hypertrophy and excess fetal adrenal androgen production.

significantly larger in men. There is also an increase in gonadal steroid secretion in the first year of postnatal life that contributes to the sexual differentiation of the brain. Sex-linked differences in appearance or form within a species are called **sexual dimorphisms.**

17.4 General Principles of Reproductive Endocrinology

This is a good place to review the synthesis of gonadal steroid hormones introduced in Chapter 11 (**Figure 17.6**). These steroidogenic pathways are excellent examples of how the understanding of physiological control is aided by an appreciation of fundamental chemical principles. Each step in this synthetic pathway is catalyzed by enzymes encoded by specific genes. Mutations in these enzymes can lead to atypical gonadal steroid synthesis and secretion and can have profound consequences on sexual development and function. As in the adrenal gland, steroid synthesis starts with cholesterol (see Figures 11.5 and 11.7). Testosterone belongs to a group of steroid hormones that have similar masculinizing actions and are collectively called androgens. In the male, most of the circulating testosterone is synthesized in the testes. Other circulating androgens are produced by the adrenal cortex, but they are much less potent than testosterone and are unable to maintain male reproductive function if testosterone secretion is inadequate. Furthermore, these adrenal androgens are also secreted by women. Some adrenal androgens, like dehydroepiandrosterone (DHEA) and androstenedione, are sold as dietary supplements and touted as miracle drugs with limited data showing effectiveness. Finally, some testosterone is converted to the more potent androgen dihydrotestosterone in target tissue by the action of the enzyme **5-α-reductase.**

Estrogens are a class of steroid hormones secreted in large amounts by the ovaries and placenta. There are three

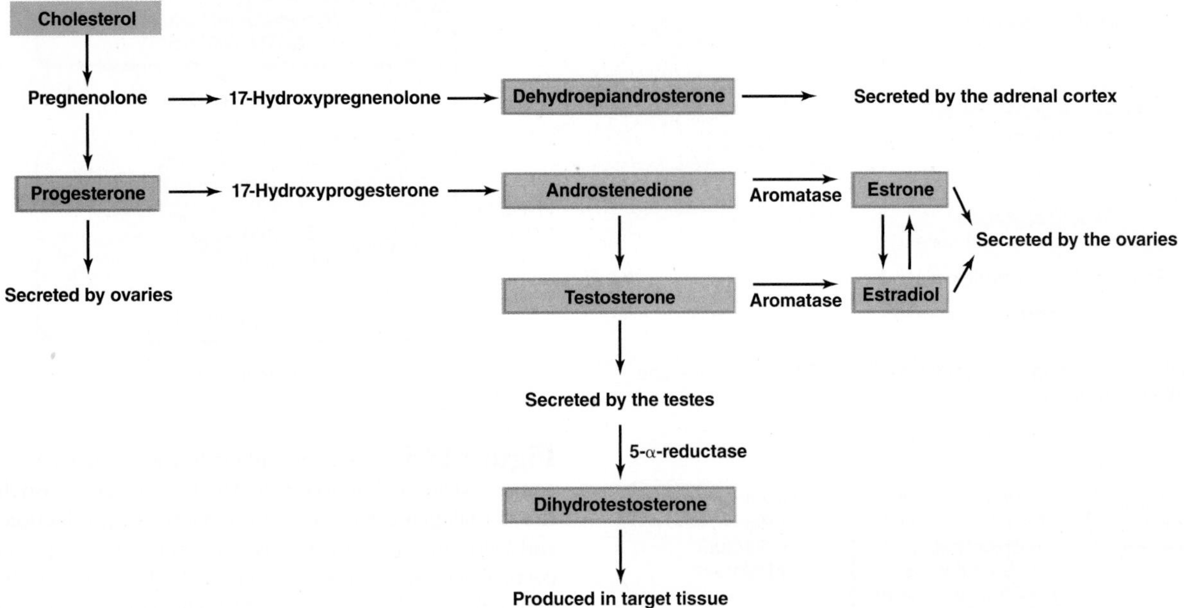

Figure 17.6 Synthesis of androgens in the testes and adrenal gland, and progesterone and estrogens in the ovaries. As in the adrenal cortex (see Figure 11.5), cholesterol is the precursor of steroid hormone synthesis. Progesterone and the estrogens (estrone and estradiol) are the main secretory products of the ovaries depending on the time in the menstrual cycle (see Figure 17.22). The adrenal cortex produces weak androgens in men and women. The primary gonadal steroid produced by the testes is testosterone, which can be activated to the more potent dihydrotestosterone (DHT) in target tissue. *Note:* Men can also produce some estrogen from testosterone by peripheral conversion due to the action of aromatase in some target tissue (particular adipocytes). For the basic chemical structure of some of these steroid hormones, see Figure 11.4.

major estrogens in humans. As noted earlier, estradiol is the predominant estrogen in the plasma. It is produced by the ovary and placenta and is often used synonymously with the generic term estrogen. **Estrone** is also produced by the ovary and placenta. **Estriol** is found primarily in pregnant women in whom it is produced by the placenta. In all cases, estrogens are produced from androgens by the enzyme **aromatase** (see Figure 17.6). Because plasma concentrations of the different estrogens vary widely depending on the circumstances, and because they have similar actions in the female, we will refer to them throughout this chapter as *estrogen.*

As mentioned earlier, estrogens are not unique to females, nor are androgens to males. Estrogen in the blood in males is derived from the release of small amounts by the testes and from the conversion of androgens to estrogen by the aromatase enzyme in some nongonadal tissues (notably, adipose tissue). Conversely, in females, small amounts of androgens are secreted by the ovaries and larger amounts by the adrenal cortex. Some of these androgens are then converted to estrogen in nongonadal tissues, just as in men, and released into the blood.

Progesterone in females is a major secretory product of the ovary at specific times of the menstrual cycle, as well as of the placenta during pregnancy (see Figure 17.6). Progesterone is also an intermediate in the synthetic pathways for adrenal steroids, estrogens, and androgens.

As described in Chapters 5 and 11, all steroid hormones act in the same general way. They bind to intracellular receptors, and the hormone–receptor complex then binds to DNA in the nucleus to alter the rate of formation of particular mRNAs. The result is a change in the rates of synthesis of the proteins coded for by the genes being transcribed. The resulting change in the concentrations of these proteins in the target cells accounts for the responses to the hormone.

As described earlier, the development of the duct systems through which the sperm or eggs are transported and the glands lining or emptying into the ducts (the **accessory reproductive organs**) is controlled by the presence or absence of gonadal hormones. The breasts are also considered accessory reproductive organs; their development is under the influence of ovarian hormones. The development of the **secondary sexual characteristics,** comprising the many external differences between males and females, is also under the influence of gonadal steroids. Examples are hair distribution, body shape, and average adult height. The secondary sexual characteristics are not directly involved in reproduction.

Reproductive function is largely controlled by a chain of hormones (**Figure 17.7**). The first hormone in the chain is **gonadotropin-releasing hormone** (**GnRH**). As described in Chapter 11, GnRH is one of the hypophysiotropic hormones involved in the control of anterior pituitary gland function. It is secreted by neuroendocrine cells in the hypothalamus, and it reaches the anterior pituitary gland via the hypothalamo–pituitary portal blood vessels. In the anterior pituitary gland, GnRH stimulates the release of the pituitary **gonadotropins—follicle-stimulating hormone**

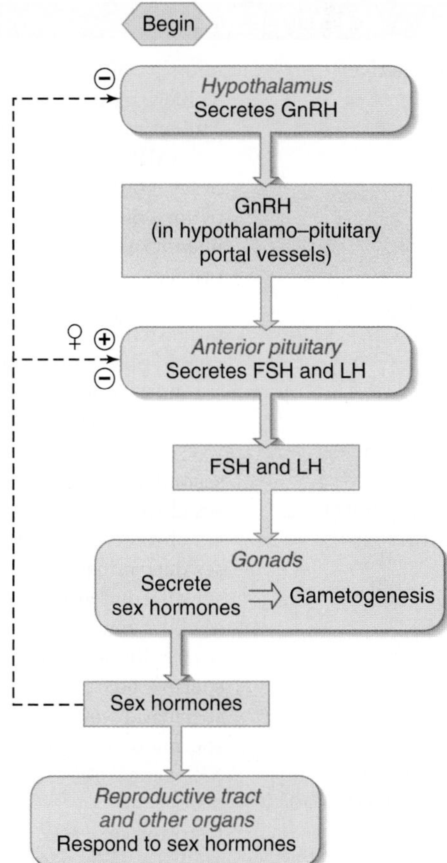

Figure 17.7 APIR General pattern of reproduction control in both males and females. GnRH, like all hypothalamic–hypophysiotropic hormones, reaches the anterior pituitary gland via the hypothalamo–hypophyseal portal vessels. The arrow within the box marked "gonads" denotes the fact that the sex hormones act locally as paracrine agents to influence the gametes. ⊖ indicates negative feedback inhibition. ♀⊕ indicates estrogen stimulation of FSH and LH in the middle of the menstrual cycle in women (positive feedback).

PHYSIOLOGICAL INQUIRY

- What would be the short- and long-term effects of removal of one of the two gonads in an adult?

Answer can be found at end of chapter.

(**FSH**) and **luteinizing hormone** (**LH**), which in turn stimulate gonadal function. The brain is, therefore, the primary regulator of reproduction.

The cell bodies of the GnRH neurons receive input from throughout the brain as well as from hormones in the blood. This is why certain stressors, emotions, and trauma to the central nervous system can inhibit reproductive function. It has recently been discovered that neurons in discrete areas of the hypothalamus synapse on GnRH neurons and release a peptide called **kisspeptin** that is intimately involved in the activation of GnRH neurons. Secretion of GnRH is triggered by action potentials in GnRH-producing hypothalamic neuroendocrine cells. These action potentials occur periodically in brief bursts, with virtually no secretion in between. The pulsatile pattern of GnRH secretion is important because the cells of the anterior pituitary gland that secrete the gonadotropins lose sensitivity to GnRH if the concentration of this hormone remains constantly elevated. This phenomenon is exploited by the administration of synthetic analogs of GnRH to men with androgen-sensitive prostate cancer and to women with estrogen-sensitive breast cancer. Although one may think that administration of a GnRH analog would stimulate FSH and LH, the constant nonpulsatile overstimulation actually decreases FSH and LH and results in a decrease in gonadal steroid secretion.

LH and FSH were named for their effects in the female, but their molecular structures are the same in both sexes. The two hormones act upon the gonads, the result being (1) the maturation of sperm or ova and (2) stimulation of sex hormone secretion. In turn, the sex hormones exert many effects on all portions of the reproductive system, including the gonads from which they come and other parts of the body as well. In addition, the gonadal steroids exert feedback effects on the secretion of GnRH, FSH, and LH. It is currently thought that gonadal steroids exert negative feedback effects on GnRH both directly and through inhibition of kisspeptin neuron cell bodies in the hypothalamus that have input to the GnRH neurons. Gonadal protein hormones such as **inhibin** also exert feedback effects on the anterior pituitary gland.

Each link in this hormonal chain is essential. A decrease in function of the hypothalamus or the anterior pituitary gland can result in failure of gonadal steroid secretion and gametogenesis just as if the gonads themselves were diseased.

As a result of changes in the amount and pattern of hormone secretions, reproductive function changes markedly during a person's lifetime and may be divided into the stages summarized in **Table 17.1**.

TABLE 17.1 Stages in the Control of Reproductive Function
During the initial stage, which begins during fetal life and ends in the first year of life (infancy), GnRH, the gonadotropins, and gonadal sex hormones are secreted at relatively high levels.
From infancy to puberty, the secretion rates of these hormones are very low and reproductive function is quiescent.
Beginning at puberty, hormonal secretion rates increase markedly, showing large cyclical variations in women during the menstrual cycle. This ushers in the period of active reproduction.
Finally, reproductive function diminishes later in life, largely because the gonads become less responsive to the gonadotropins. The ability to reproduce ceases entirely in women.

SECTION A SUMMARY

Gametogenesis

I. The first stage of gametogenesis is mitosis of primordial germ cells.

II. This is followed by meiosis, which is a sequence of two cell divisions resulting in each gamete receiving 23 chromosomes.

III. Crossing-over and random distribution of maternal and paternal chromatids to the daughter cells during meiosis cause genetic variability in the gametes.

Sex Determination

I. Gender is determined by the two sex chromosomes; males are XY, and females are XX.

Sex Differentiation

I. A gene on the Y chromosome is responsible for the development of testes. In the absence of a Y chromosome, testes do not develop and ovaries do instead.

II. When functioning male gonads are present, they secrete testosterone and MIS, so a male reproductive tract and external genitalia develop. In the absence of testes, the female system develops.

III. A sexually dimorphic brain region exists in humans and certain experimental animals that may be linked with male-type or female-type sexual behavior.

General Principles of Reproductive Endocrinology

I. The gonads have a dual function—gametogenesis and secretion of sex hormones.

II. The male gonads are the testes, which produce sperm and secrete the steroid hormone testosterone.

III. The female gonads are the ovaries, which produce ova and secrete the steroid hormones estrogen and progesterone.

IV. Gonadal function is controlled by the gonadotropins (FSH and LH) from the pituitary gland whose release is controlled by gonadotropin-releasing hormone (GnRH) from the hypothalamus.

SECTION A REVIEW QUESTIONS

1. Describe the stages of gametogenesis and how meiosis results in genetic variability.
2. State the genetic difference between males and females and a method for identifying genetic sex.
3. Describe the sequence of events, the timing, and the control of the development of the gonads and the internal and external genitalia.
4. Explain how administration of glucocorticoids to a pregnant woman would treat congenital adrenal hyperplasia in her fetus.

SECTION A KEY TERMS

accessory reproductive organ 610
androgen 603
aromatase 610
Barr body 605
bivalent 605
crossing-over 605
dihydrotestosterone (DHT) 603
estradiol 603
estriol 610
estrogen 605
estrone 610
first polar body 605
5-α-reductase 609
follicle-stimulating hormone (FSH) 610
gamete 603
gametogenesis 603
genotype 605
germ cell 603
gonad 603
gonadal steroid 603
gonadotropin 610
gonadotropin-releasing hormone (GnRH) 610
inhibin 611
karyotype 605
kisspeptin 611
luteinizing hormone (LH) 611
meiosis 603
mitosis 603
Müllerian duct 606
Müllerian-inhibiting substance (MIS) 606
ovary 603
ovum 603
phenotype 605
primary oocyte 603
primary spermatocyte 603
progesterone 603
second polar body 605
secondary oocyte 605
secondary sexual characteristic 610
secondary spermatocyte 605
sex chromatin 605
sex chromosome 605
sex determination 605
sex differentiation 605
sex hormone 603
sexual dimorphism 609
sperm 603
spermatid 605
spermatozoan 603
SRY gene 606
testis 603
testosterone 603
Wolffian duct 606
X chromosome 605
Y chromosome 605
zygote 605

SECTION A CLINICAL TERMS

ambiguous genitalia 606
androgen insensitivity syndrome 606
congenital adrenal hyperplasia 606
cryptorchidism 606
testicular feminization 606
virilization 606

SECTION B
Male Reproductive Physiology

17.5 Anatomy

The male reproductive system includes the two testes, the system of ducts that store and transport sperm to the exterior, the glands that empty into these ducts, and the penis. The duct system, glands, and penis constitute the male accessory reproductive organs.

The testes are suspended outside the abdomen in the **scrotum,** which is an outpouching of the abdominal wall and is divided internally into two sacs, one for each testis. During early fetal development, the testes are located in the abdomen; but during later **gestation** (usually in the seventh month of pregnancy), they usually descend into the scrotum (see Figure 17.2). This descent is essential for normal sperm

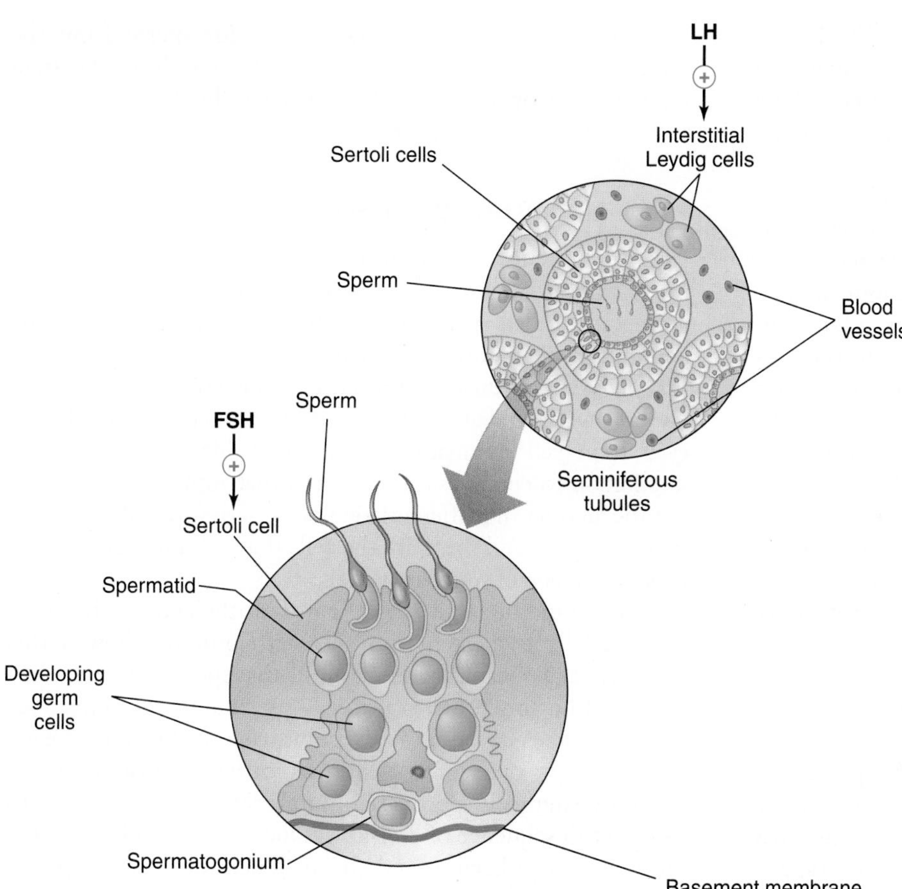

Figure 17.8 APIR Cross section of an area of testis. The Sertoli cells (stimulated by FSH to increase spermatogenesis and produce inhibin) are in the seminiferous tubules, the sites of sperm production. The tubules are separated from each other by interstitial space (colored light blue) that contains Leydig cells (stimulated by LH to produce testosterone) and blood vessels.

production during adulthood, because sperm formation requires a temperature approximately 2°C lower than normal internal body temperature. Cooling is achieved by air circulating around the scrotum and by a heat-exchange mechanism in the blood vessels supplying the testes. In contrast to spermatogenesis, testosterone secretion can usually occur normally at internal body temperature, so failure of testes descent usually does not impair testosterone secretion.

The sites of **spermatogenesis** (sperm formation) in the testes are the many tiny, convoluted **seminiferous tubules** (**Figure 17.8**). The combined length of these tubes is 250 m (the length of over 2.5 football fields). Each seminiferous tubule is bounded by a basement membrane. In the center of each tubule is a fluid-filled lumen containing the mature sperm cells, called spermatozoa. The tubular wall is composed of developing germ cells and their supporting cells called **Sertoli cells.**

The **Leydig cells,** or interstitial cells, which lie in small, connective-tissue spaces between the tubules, are the cells that synthesize and release testosterone. Thus, the sperm-producing and testosterone-producing functions of the testes are carried out by different structures—the seminiferous tubules and Leydig cells, respectively.

The seminiferous tubules from different areas of a testis converge to form a network of interconnected tubes, the **rete testis** (**Figure 17.9**). Small ducts called efferent ductules leave the rete testis, pierce the fibrous covering of the testis, and empty into a single duct within a structure called the **epididymis** (plural, *epididymides*). The epididymis is loosely attached to the outside of the testis. The duct of the epididymis is so convoluted that, when straightened out at dissection, it measures 6 m. The epididymis draining each testis leads to a **vas deferens** (plural, *vasa deferentia*), a large, thick-walled tube

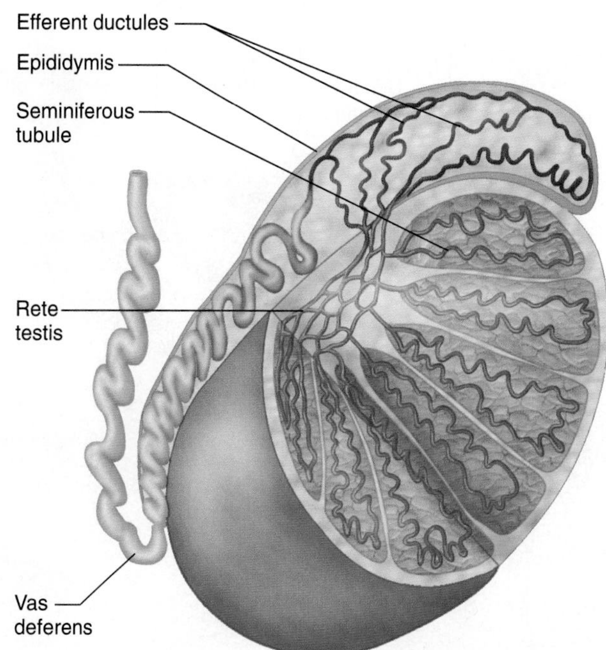

Figure 17.9 APIR Section of a testis. The upper portion of the testis has been removed to show its interior.

lined with smooth muscle. Not shown in Figure 17.9 is that the vas deferens and the blood vessels and nerves supplying the testis are bound together in the **spermatic cord,** which passes to the testis through a slitlike passage, the inguinal canal, in the abdominal wall.

After entering the abdomen, the two vasa deferentia—one from each testis—continue to behind the urinary bladder base (**Figure 17.10**). The ducts from two large glands, the **seminal vesicles,** which lie behind the bladder, join the two vasa deferentia to form the two **ejaculatory ducts.** The ejaculatory ducts then enter the **prostate gland** and join the urethra, coming from the bladder. The prostate gland is a single walnut-sized structure below the bladder and surrounding the upper part of the urethra, into which it secretes fluid through hundreds of tiny openings in the side of the urethra. The urethra emerges from the prostate gland and enters the penis. The paired **bulbourethral glands,** lying below the prostate, drain into the urethra just after it leaves the prostate.

The prostate gland and seminal vesicles secrete most of the fluid in which ejaculated sperm are suspended. This fluid plus the sperm cells constitute **semen,** the sperm contributing a small percentage of the total volume. The glandular secretions contain a large number of different chemical substances, including (1) nutrients, (2) buffers for protecting the sperm against the acidic vaginal secretions and residual acidic urine in the male urethra, (3) chemicals (particularly from the seminal vesicles) that increase sperm motility, and (4) prostaglandins. The function of the prostaglandins, which are produced by the seminal vesicles, is still not clear. The bulbourethral glands contribute a small volume of lubricating mucoid secretions.

In addition to providing a route for sperm from the seminiferous tubules to the exterior, several of the duct system segments perform additional functions to be described in the section on sperm transport.

17.6 Spermatogenesis

The various stages of spermatogenesis were introduced in Figure 17.1 and are summarized in **Figure 17.11**. The undifferentiated germ cells, called spermatogonia (singular, **spermatogonium**), begin to divide mitotically at puberty. The daughter cells of this first division then divide again and again for a specified number of division cycles so that a clone of spermatogonia is produced from each stem cell spermatogonium. Some differentiation occurs in addition to cell division. The cells that result from the final mitotic division and differentiation in the series are called primary spermatocytes, and these are the cells that will undergo the first meiotic division of spermatogenesis.

It should be emphasized that if all the cells in the clone produced by each stem cell spermatogonium followed this pathway, the spermatogonia would disappear—that is, they would all be converted to primary spermatocytes. This does not occur because, at an early point, one of the cells of each clone "drops out" of the mitosis–differentiation cycle to remain a stem cell spermatogonium that will later enter into its own full sequence of divisions. One cell of the clone it produces will do likewise, and so on. Therefore, the supply of undifferentiated spermatogonia does not decrease.

Each primary spermatocyte increases markedly in size and undergoes the first meiotic division (see Figure 17.11) to form two secondary spermatocytes, each of which contains

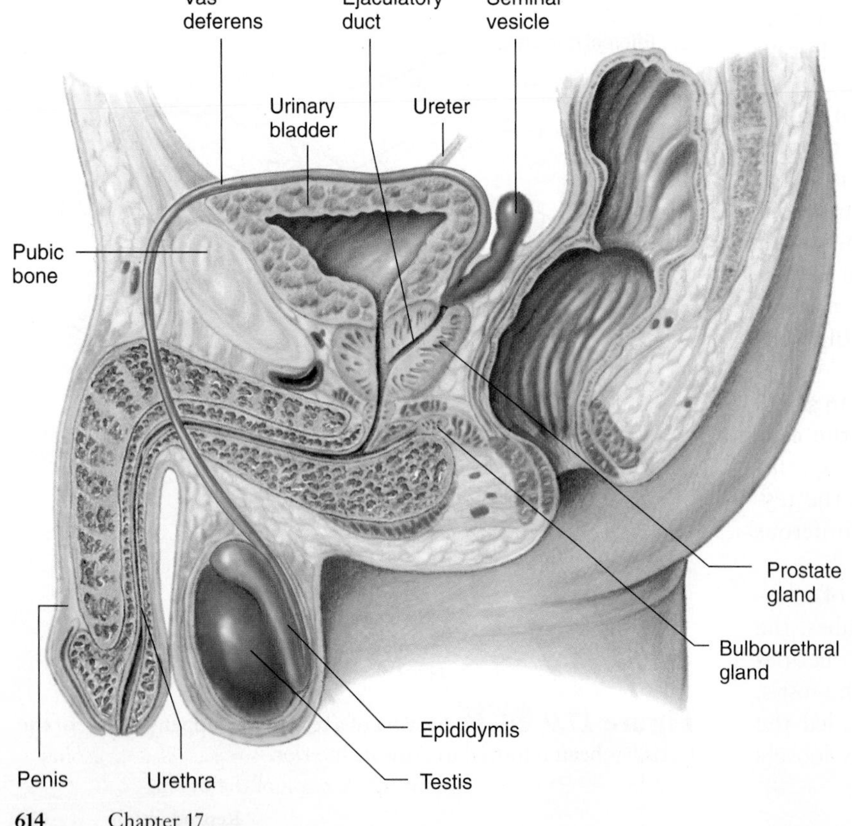

Figure 17.10 APIR Anatomical organization of the male reproductive tract. This figure shows the testis, epididymis, vas deferens, ejaculatory duct, seminal vesicle, and bulbourethral gland on only one side of the body, but they are all paired structures. The urinary bladder and a ureter are shown for orientation but are not part of the reproductive tract. Once the ejaculatory ducts join the urethra in the prostate, the urinary and reproductive tracts have merged.

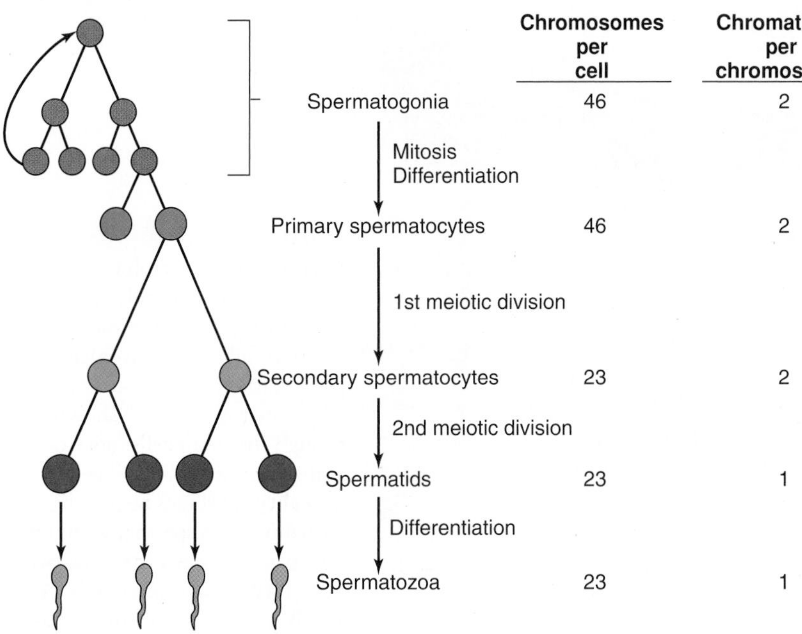

Figure 17.11 APIR Summary of spermatogenesis, which begins at puberty. Each spermatogonium yields, by mitosis, a clone of spermatogonia; for simplicity, the figure shows only two such cycles, with a third mitotic cycle generating two primary spermatocytes. The arrow from one of the spermatogonia back to a stem cell spermatogonium denotes the fact that one cell of the clone does not go on to generate primary spermatocytes but reverts to an undifferentiated spermatogonium that gives rise to a new clone. Each primary spermatocyte produces four spermatozoa.

23 two-chromatid chromosomes. Each secondary spermatocyte undergoes the second meiotic division (see Figure 17.1) to form spermatids. Thus, each primary spermatocyte, containing 46 two-chromatid chromosomes, produces four spermatids, each containing 23 one-chromatid chromosomes.

The final phase of spermatogenesis is the differentiation of the spermatids into spermatozoa (sperm). This process involves extensive cell remodeling, including elongation, but no further cell divisions. The head of a sperm cell (**Figure 17.12**) consists almost entirely of the nucleus, which contains the genetic information (DNA). The tip of the nucleus is covered by the **acrosome,** a protein-filled vesicle containing several enzymes that play an important role in fertilization. Most of the tail is a flagellum—a group of contractile filaments that produce whiplike movements capable of propelling the sperm at a velocity of 1 to 4 mm per min. Mitochondria form the midpiece of the sperm and provide the energy for movement.

The entire process of spermatogenesis, from primary spermatocyte to sperm, takes approximately 64 days. The typical human male manufactures approximately 30 million sperm per day.

Thus far, spermatogenesis has been described without regard to its orientation within the seminiferous tubules or the participation of Sertoli cells, the second type of cell in the seminiferous tubules, with which the developing germ cells are closely associated. Each seminiferous tubule is bounded by a basement membrane. Each Sertoli cell extends from the basement membrane all the way to the lumen in the center of the tubule and is joined to adjacent Sertoli cells by means of tight junctions (**Figure 17.13**). Thus, the Sertoli cells form an unbroken ring around the outer circumference of the seminiferous tubule. The tight junctions divide the tubule into two compartments—a basal compartment, between the basement membrane and the tight junctions, and a central compartment, beginning at the tight junctions and including the lumen.

The ring of interconnected Sertoli cells forms the **Sertoli cell barrier** (blood–testes barrier), which prevents the movement of many chemicals from the blood into the lumen of the seminiferous tubule and helps retain luminal fluid. This ensures proper conditions for germ cell development and differentiation in the tubules. The arrangement of Sertoli cells also permits different stages of spermatogenesis to take place in different compartments and, therefore, in different environments.

Mitotic cell divisions and differentiation of spermatogonia to yield primary spermatocytes take place entirely in the basal compartment. The primary spermatocytes then move through the tight junctions of the Sertoli cells (which open in front of them while at the same time forming new tight junctions behind them) to gain entry into the central compartment. In this central compartment, the meiotic divisions of spermatogenesis occur, and the spermatids differentiate into sperm while contained in recesses formed by invaginations of the Sertoli cell plasma membranes. When sperm formation is

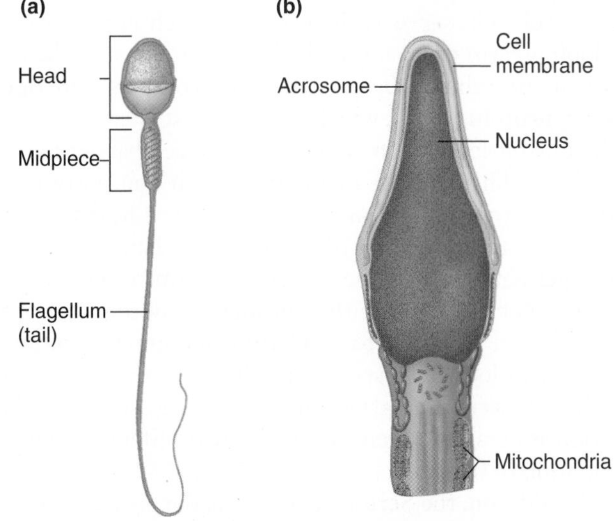

Figure 17.12 APIR (a) Diagram of a human mature sperm. (b) A close-up of the head drawn from a different angle. The acrosome contains enzymes required for fertilization of the ovum.

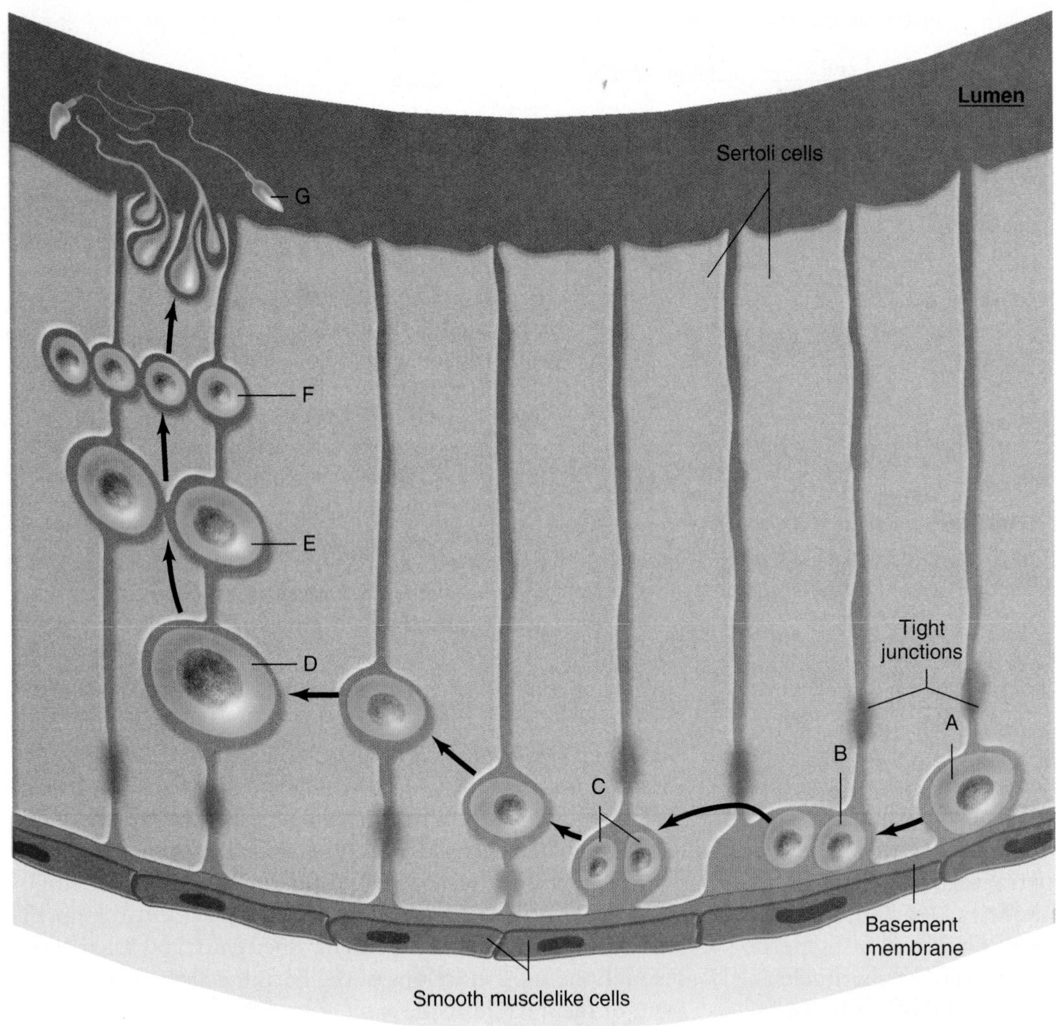

Figure 17.13 APIR Relation of the Sertoli cells and germ cells. The Sertoli cells form a ring (barrier) around the entire tubule. For convenience of presentation, the various stages of spermatogenesis are shown as though the germ cells move down a line of adjacent Sertoli cells; in reality, all stages beginning with any given spermatogonium take place between the same two Sertoli cells. Spermatogonia (A and B) are found only in the basal compartment (between the tight junctions of the Sertoli cells and the basement membrane of the tubule). After several mitotic cycles (A to B), the spermatogonia (B) give rise to primary spermatocytes (C). Each of the latter crosses a tight junction, enlarges (D), and divides into two secondary spermatocytes (E), which divide into spermatids (F), which in turn differentiate into spermatozoa (G). This last step involves loss of cytoplasm by the spermatids. Adapted from Tung.

complete, the cytoplasm of the Sertoli cell around the sperm retracts and the sperm are released into the lumen to be bathed by the luminal fluid.

Sertoli cells serve as the route by which nutrients reach developing germ cells, and they also secrete most of the fluid found in the tubule lumen. This fluid contains **androgen-binding protein (ABP)**, which binds the testosterone secreted by the Leydig cells and crosses the Sertoli cell barrier to enter the tubule. This protein maintains a high concentration of total testosterone in the lumen of the tubule. The dissociation of free testosterone from ABP continuously bathes the developing spermatocytes and Sertoli cells in testosterone.

Sertoli cells do more than influence environment of the germ cells. In response to FSH from the anterior pituitary gland and to local testosterone produced in the Leydig cell, Sertoli cells secrete a variety of chemical messengers. These function as paracrine agents to stimulate proliferation and differentiation of the germ cells.

In addition, the Sertoli cells secrete the protein hormone inhibin, which acts as a negative feedback controller of FSH, and paracrine agents that affect Leydig cell function. The many functions of Sertoli cells, several of which remain to be described later in this chapter, are summarized in **Table 17.2**.

TABLE 17.2 Functions of Sertoli Cells
Provide Sertoli cell barrier to chemicals in the plasma
Nourish developing sperm
Secrete luminal fluid, including androgen-binding protein
Respond to stimulation by testosterone and FSH to secrete paracrine agents that stimulate sperm proliferation and differentiation
Secrete the protein hormone inhibin, which inhibits FSH secretion from the pituitary gland
Secrete paracrine agents that influence the function of Leydig cells
Phagocytize defective sperm
Secrete Müllerian-inhibiting substance (MIS), which causes the primordial female duct system to regress during embryonic life

17.7 Transport of Sperm

From the seminiferous tubules, the sperm pass through the rete testis and efferent ducts into the epididymis and from there to the vas deferens. The vas deferens and the portion of the epididymis closest to it serve as a storage reservoir for sperm until **ejaculation,** the discharge of semen from the penis.

Movement of the sperm as far as the epididymis results from the pressure that the Sertoli cells create by continuously secreting fluid into the seminiferous tubules. The sperm themselves are normally nonmotile at this time.

During passage through the epididymis, the concentration of the sperm increases dramatically due to fluid absorption from the lumen of the epididymis. Therefore, as the sperm pass from the end of the epididymis into the vas deferens, they are a densely packed mass whose transport is no longer facilitated by fluid movement. Instead, peristaltic contractions of the smooth muscle in the epididymis and vas deferens cause the sperm to move.

The absence of a large quantity of fluid accounts for the fact that ***vasectomy,*** the surgical tying off and removal of a segment of each vas deferens as a method of male contraception, does not cause the accumulation of much fluid behind the tie-off point. The sperm, which are still produced after vasectomy, do build up, however, and eventually break down, with their chemical components absorbed into the bloodstream. Vasectomy does not affect testosterone secretion because it does not alter the function of the Leydig cells. The next step in sperm transport is ejaculation.

Erection

The penis consists almost entirely of three cylindrical, vascular compartments running its entire length. Normally, the small arteries supplying the vascular compartments are constricted so that the compartments contain little blood and the penis is flaccid. During sexual excitation, the small arteries dilate, blood flow increases, the three vascular compartments become engorged with blood at high pressure, and the penis becomes rigid (**erection**). The vascular dilation is initiated by neural input to the small arteries of the penis. As the vascular compartments expand, the veins emptying them are passively compressed, further increasing the local pressure, thus contributing to the engorgement while blood flow remains elevated. This entire process occurs rapidly with complete erection sometimes taking only 5 to 10 seconds.

What are the neural inputs to the small arteries of the penis? At rest, the dominant input is from sympathetic neurons that release norepinephrine, which causes the arterial smooth muscle to contract. During erection, this sympathetic input is inhibited. Much more important is the activation of nonadrenergic, noncholinergic autonomic neurons to the arteries (**Figure 17.14**). These neurons and associated endothelial cells release **nitric oxide,** which relaxes the arterial smooth muscle.

Which receptors and afferent pathways initiate these reflexes? The primary stimulus comes from mechanoreceptors in the genital region, particularly in the head of the penis. The afferent fibers carrying the impulses synapse in the lower spinal cord on interneurons that control the efferent outflow.

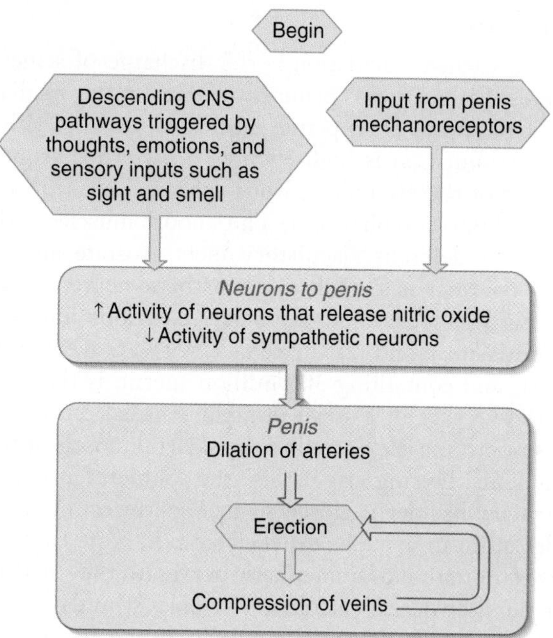

Figure 17.14 Reflex pathways for erection. Nitric oxide, a vasodilator, is the most important neurotransmitter to the arteries in this reflex.

It must be stressed, however, that higher brain centers, via descending pathways, may also exert profound stimulatory or inhibitory effects upon the autonomic neurons to the small arteries of the penis. Thus, mechanical stimuli from areas other than the penis, as well as thoughts, emotions, sights, and odors, can induce erection in the complete absence of penile stimulation (or prevent erection even though stimulation is present).

Erectile dysfunction (also called *impotence*) is the consistent inability to achieve or sustain an erection of sufficient rigidity for sexual intercourse and is a common problem. Although it can be mild to moderate in degree, complete erectile dysfunction is present in as many as 10% of adult American males between the ages of 40 and 70. During this period of life, its rate almost doubles. The organic causes are multiple and include damage to or malfunction of the efferent nerves or descending pathways, endocrine disorders, various therapeutic and "recreational" drugs (e.g., alcohol), and certain diseases, particularly diabetes mellitus. Erectile dysfunction can also be due to psychological factors (such as depression), which are mediated by the brain and the descending pathways.

There are now a group of orally active ***cGMP-phosphodiesterase type 5*** (PDE5) ***inhibitors*** including sildenafil (*Viagra*), vardenafil (*Levitra*), and tadalafil (*Cialis*) that greatly improve the ability of many men with erectile dysfunction to achieve and maintain an erection. The most important event leading to erection is the dilation of penile arteries by nitric oxide, released from autonomic neurons. Nitric oxide stimulates the enzyme guanylyl cyclase, which catalyzes the formation of cyclic GMP (cGMP), as described in Chapter 5. This second messenger then continues the signal transduction pathway leading to the relaxation of the arterial smooth muscle. The sequence of events is terminated by an enzyme-dependent breakdown of cGMP. PDE5 inhibitors block the action of this enzyme and thereby permit a higher concentration of cGMP to exist.

Ejaculation

As stated earlier, ejaculation is the discharge of semen from the penis. Ejaculation is primarily a spinal reflex mediated by afferent pathways from penile mechanoreceptors. When the level of stimulation is high enough, a patterned sequence of discharge of the efferent neurons ensues. This sequence can be divided into two phases: (1) The smooth muscles of the epididymis, vas deferens, ejaculatory ducts, prostate, and seminal vesicles contract as a result of sympathetic nerve stimulation, emptying the sperm and glandular secretions into the urethra (**emission**); and (2) the semen, with an average volume of 3 mL and containing 300 million sperm, is then expelled from the urethra by a series of rapid contractions of the urethral smooth muscle as well as the skeletal muscle at the base of the penis. During ejaculation, the sphincter at the base of the urinary bladder is closed so that sperm cannot enter the bladder, nor can urine be expelled from it. Note that erection involves inhibition of sympathetic nerves (to the small arteries of the penis), whereas ejaculation involves stimulation of sympathetic nerves (to the smooth muscles of the duct system).

The rhythmic muscular contractions that occur during ejaculation are associated with intense pleasure and many systemic physiological changes, collectively termed an **orgasm.** Marked skeletal muscle contractions occur throughout the body, and there is a transient increase in heart rate and blood pressure.

Once ejaculation has occurred, there is a latent period during which a second erection is not possible. The latent period is quite variable but may last from minutes to hours.

17.8 Hormonal Control of Male Reproductive Functions

Control of the Testes

Figure 17.15 summarizes the control of the testes. In a normal adult man, the GnRH-secreting neuroendocrine cells in the hypothalamus fire a brief burst of action potentials approximately every 90 min, secreting GnRH at these times. The GnRH reaching the anterior pituitary gland via the hypothalamo–hypophyseal portal vessels during each periodic pulse triggers the release of both LH and FSH from the same cell type, although not necessarily in equal amounts. Thus, plasma concentrations of FSH and LH also show pulsatility—rapid increases followed by slow decreases over the next 90 min or so as the hormones are slowly removed from the plasma.

There is a clear separation of the actions of FSH and LH within the testes (see Figure 17.15). FSH acts primarily on the Sertoli cells to stimulate the secretion of paracrine agents required for spermatogenesis. LH, by contrast, acts primarily on the Leydig cells to stimulate testosterone secretion. In addition to its many important systemic effects as a hormone, the testosterone secreted by the Leydig cells also acts locally, in a paracrine manner, by diffusing from the interstitial spaces into the seminiferous tubules. Testosterone enters Sertoli cells, where it facilitates spermatogenesis. Thus, despite the absence of a *direct* effect on cells in the seminiferous tubules, LH exerts an essential *indirect* effect because the testosterone secretion stimulated by LH is required for spermatogenesis.

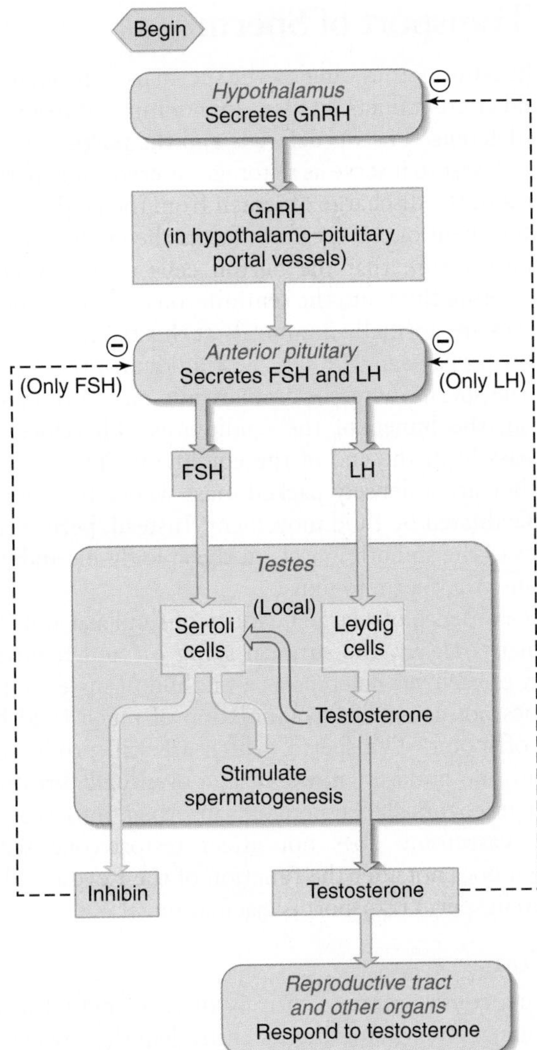

Figure 17.15 APIR Summary of hormonal control of male reproductive function. Note that FSH acts only on the Sertoli cells, whereas LH acts primarily on the Leydig cells. The secretion of FSH is inhibited mainly by inhibin, a protein hormone secreted by the Sertoli cells, and the secretion of LH is inhibited mainly by testosterone, the steroid hormone secreted by the Leydig cells. Testosterone, acting locally on Sertoli cells, stimulates spermatogenesis, whereas FSH stimulates inhibin release from Sertoli cells.

PHYSIOLOGICAL INQUIRY

- Men with decreased anterior pituitary gland function often have decreased sperm production as well as low testosterone concentrations. Would you expect the administration of testosterone alone to restore sperm production to normal?

Answer can be found at end of chapter.

The last components of the hypothalamo–hypophyseal control of male reproduction that remain to be discussed are the negative feedback effects exerted by testicular hormones. Even though FSH and LH are produced by the same cell type, their secretion rates can be altered to different degrees by negative feedback inputs.

Testosterone inhibits LH secretion in two ways (see Figure 17.15): (1) It acts on the hypothalamus to decrease the amplitude of GnRH bursts, which results in a decrease in the secretion of gonadotropins; and (2) it acts directly on the anterior pituitary gland to decrease the LH response to any given amount of GnRH.

How do the testes reduce FSH secretion? The major inhibitory signal, exerted directly on the anterior pituitary gland, is the protein hormone inhibin secreted by the Sertoli cells (see Figure 17.15). This is a logical completion of a negative feedback loop such that FSH stimulates Sertoli cells to increase both spermatogenesis and inhibin production, and inhibin decreases FSH release.

Despite all these complexities, the total amounts of GnRH, LH, FSH, testosterone, and inhibin secreted and of sperm produced do not change dramatically from day to day in the adult male. This is completely different from the large cyclical variations of activity so characteristic of female reproductive processes.

Testosterone

In addition to its essential paracrine action within the testes on spermatogenesis and its negative feedback effects on the hypothalamus and anterior pituitary gland, testosterone exerts many other effects, as summarized in **Table 17.3**.

In Chapter 11, we mentioned that some hormones undergo transformation in their target cells in order to be more effective. This is true of testosterone in many (but not all) of its target cells. In some cells, like in the adult prostate, after its entry into the cytoplasm, testosterone is converted to dihydrotestosterone (DHT), which is more potent than testosterone (see Figure 17.6). This conversion is catalyzed by the enzyme 5-α-reductase, which is expressed in several androgen target tissues. In certain other target cells (e.g., the brain), testosterone is transformed not to dihydrotestosterone but to estradiol, which is the active hormone in these cells. The enzyme aromatase catalyzes this conversion. In the latter case, the "male" sex hormone is converted to the "female" sex hormone to be active in the male. The fact that, depending on the target cells, testosterone may act as testosterone, or be converted to dihydrotestosterone or estradiol, has important pathophysiological implications because some men lack 5-α-reductase or aromatase in some tissues. Therefore, they will exhibit certain signs of testosterone deficiency but not others. For example, an XY fetus with 5-α-reductase deficiency will have normal differentiation of male reproductive duct structures (an effect of testosterone, per se) but will not have normal development of external male genitalia, which requires DHT.

Therapy for ***prostate cancer*** makes use of these facts: Prostate cancer cells are stimulated by dihydrotestosterone, so the cancer can be treated with inhibitors of 5-α-reductase. Furthermore, ***male pattern baldness*** may also be treated with 5-α-reductase inhibitors because DHT tends to promote hair loss from the scalp.

TABLE 17.3 Effects of Testosterone in the Male
Required for initiation and maintenance of spermatogenesis (acts via Sertoli cells)
Decreases GnRH secretion via an action on the hypothalamus
Inhibits LH secretion via a direct action on the anterior pituitary gland
Induces differentiation of male accessory reproductive organs and maintains their function
Induces male secondary sex characteristics; opposes action of estrogen on breast growth
Stimulates protein anabolism, bone growth, and cessation of bone growth
Required for sex drive and may enhance aggressive behavior
Stimulates erythropoietin secretion by the kidneys

Accessory Reproductive Organs

The fetal differentiation and later growth and function of the entire male duct system, glands, and penis all depend upon testosterone (see Figures 17.2 and 17.3). Following the loss of testicular function and decrease in testosterone production, the accessory reproductive organs decrease in size, the glands significantly reduce their secretion rates, and the smooth muscle activity of the ducts is diminished. Sex drive (**libido**), erection, and ejaculation are usually impaired. These defects lessen with the administration of testosterone. This would also occur with ***castration*** (removal of the gonads), which may be done to treat testicular cancer, for example.

17.9 Puberty

Puberty is the period during which the reproductive organs mature and reproduction becomes possible. In males, this usually occurs between 12 and 16 years of age. Some of the first signs of puberty are due not to gonadal steroids but to increased secretion of adrenal androgens, probably under the stimulation of adrenocorticotropic hormone (ACTH). These androgens cause the very early development of pubic and axillary (armpit) hair, as well as the early stages of the pubertal growth spurt in concert with growth hormone and insulin-like growth factor I (see Chapter 11). All other developments in puberty, however, reflect increased activity of the hypothalamo–pituitary–gonadal axis.

The amplitude and pulse frequency of GnRH secretion increase at puberty, probably stimulated by input from kisspeptin neurons in the hypothalamus. This causes increased secretion of pituitary gonadotropins, which stimulate the seminiferous tubules and testosterone secretion. Testosterone, in addition to its critical role in spermatogenesis, induces the pubertal changes that occur in the accessory reproductive organs, secondary sex characteristics, and sex drive. The mechanism of the brain change that results in increased GnRH secretion at puberty remains unknown. One important event is that the brain becomes less sensitive to the negative feedback effects of gonadal hormones at the time of puberty.

Secondary Sex Characteristics and Growth

Virtually all the male secondary sex characteristics are dependent on testosterone and its metabolite, DHT. For example, a male lacking normal testicular secretion of testosterone before puberty has minimal facial, axillary, or pubic hair. Other androgen-dependent secondary sexual characteristics are deepening of the voice resulting from the growth of the larynx, thick secretion of the skin oil glands (often causing acne), and the masculine pattern of fat distribution. Androgens also stimulate bone growth, mostly through the stimulation of growth hormone secretion. Ultimately, however, androgens terminate bone growth by causing closure of the bones' epiphyseal plates. Androgens are "anabolic steroids" in that they exert a direct stimulatory effect on protein synthesis in muscle. Finally, androgens stimulate the secretion of the hormone erythropoietin by the kidneys; this is a major reason why men have a higher hematocrit than women.

Behavior

Androgens are essential in males for the development of sex drive at puberty, and they play an important role in maintaining sex drive (libido) in the adult male. Whether androgens influence other human behaviors in addition to sexual behavior is not certain. However, there is no doubt that androgen-dependent behavioral differences based on gender do exist in other mammals. For example, aggression is clearly greater in males and is androgen-dependent.

Anabolic Steroid Use

The abuse of synthetic androgens (anabolic steroids) is a major public health problem, particularly in younger athletes. Although there are positive effects on muscle mass and athletic performance, the negative effects—such as overstimulation of prostate tissue and increase in aggressiveness—are of significant concern. Ironically, the increase in muscle mass and other masculine characteristics in men belies the fact that negative feedback has decreased LH. This results in a decrease in endogenous testosterone and FSH secretion, reducing the stimulation of spermatogenesis in Sertoli cells. This actually induces a decrease in testicular size and low sperm count (infertility) as described in the next section. In fact, administration of low doses of anabolic steroids is being tested as a potential male birth control pill.

17.10 Hypogonadism

A decrease in testosterone release from the testes—***hypogonadism***—can be caused by a wide variety of disorders. In general, they can be classified into testicular failure (primary hypogonadism) or a failure to supply the testes with appropriate gonadotrophic stimulus (secondary hypogonadism). The loss of normal testicular androgen production before puberty can lead to a failure to develop secondary sex characteristics such as deepening of the voice, pubic and axillary hair, and increased libido, as well as a failure to develop normal sperm production.

A relatively common genetic cause of primary hypogonadism is ***Klinefelter's syndrome.*** The most common cause of this disorder, occurring in 1 in 500 male births, is an extra X chromosome (XXY) caused by meiotic nondisjunction. Nondisjunction is the failure of a pair of chromosomes to separate during meiosis, such that two chromosome pairs go to one daughter cell and the other daughter cell fails to receive either chromosome. The classic form of Klinefelter's syndrome is caused by the failure of the two sex chromosomes to separate during the first meiotic division in gametogenesis (see Figure 17.1). The extra X chromosome can come from either the egg or the sperm. That is, if nondisjunction occurs in the ovary leading to an XX ovum, an XXY genotype will result if fertilized by a Y sperm. If nondisjunction occurs in the testis leading to an XY sperm, an XXY genotype will result if that sperm fertilizes a normal (single X) ovum.

Male children with the XXY genotype appear normal before puberty. However, after puberty, the testes remain small and poorly developed, with insufficient Leydig and Sertoli cell function. The abnormal Leydig cell function results in decreased concentrations of plasma and testicular testosterone; this, in turn, leads to abnormal development of the seminiferous tubules and therefore decreased sperm production. Normal secondary sex characteristics do not appear, and breast size increases (***gynecomastia***) (**Figure 17.16**). Men with this set of characteristics have relatively high gonadotropin concentrations (LH and FSH) due to loss of androgen and inhibin negative feedback. Men with Klinefelter's syndrome can be treated with androgen-replacement therapy to increase libido and decrease breast size.

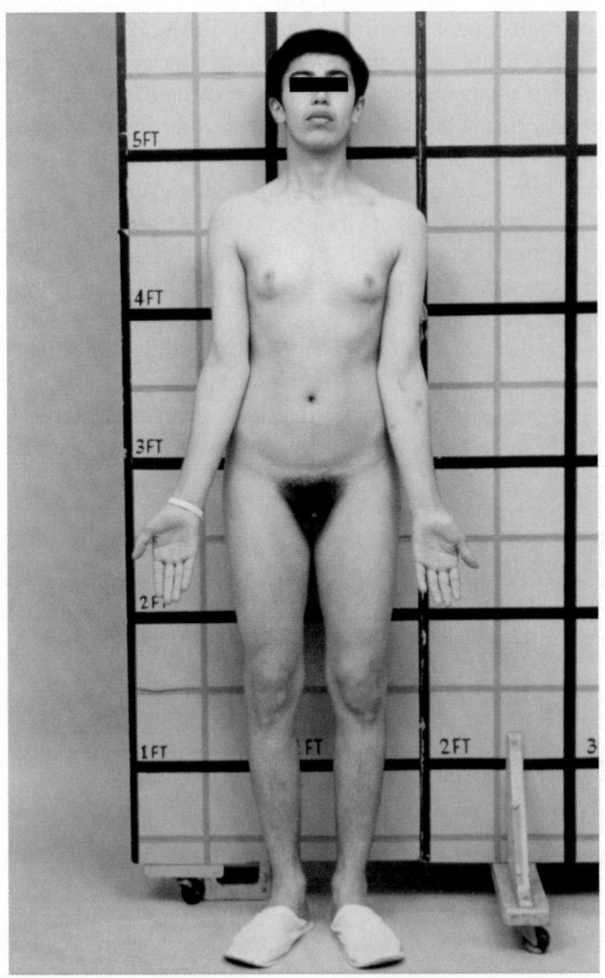

Figure 17.16 Klinefelter's syndrome in a 20-year-old man. Note relatively increased lower/upper body segment ratio, gynecomastia, small penis, and sparse body hair with a female pubic hair pattern. Courtesy of Glenn D. Braunstein, M.D.

Hypogonadism in men can also be caused by a decrease in LH and FSH secretion (secondary hypogonadism). Although there are many causes of the loss of function of pituitary gland cells that secrete LH and FSH, ***hyperprolactinemia*** (increased prolactin in the blood) is one of the most common. Although prolactin probably has only minor effects in men under normal conditions, the pituitary gland still has cells (lactotrophs) that secrete prolactin. Pituitary gland tumors arising from prolactin-secreting cells can develop and secrete too much prolactin. One of the effects of increased prolactin concentrations in the blood is to inhibit LH and FSH secretion from the anterior pituitary gland. (This occurs in men and women.) Hyperprolactinemia is discussed in more detail at the end of this chapter. Another cause of secondary hypogonadism is the total loss of anterior pituitary gland function, called ***hypopituitarism*** or panhypopituitarism. There are many causes of hypopituitarism, including head trauma, infection, and inflammation of the pituitary gland. When all anterior pituitary gland function is decreased or absent, male patients need to be treated with testosterone. In addition, male and female patients are treated with cortisol because of low ACTH, and with thyroid hormone because of low TSH. Children and some adults are also treated with growth hormone injections. In most circumstances, posterior pituitary gland function remains intact so that vasopressin does not need to be administered to avoid diabetes insipidus (see Chapter 14, Section B).

17.11 Andropause

Changes in the male reproductive system with aging are less drastic than those in women (described later in this chapter). Once testosterone and pituitary gland gonadotropin secretions are initiated at puberty, they continue, at least to some extent, throughout adult life. There is a steady decrease, however, in testosterone secretion, beginning at about 40 years of age, which apparently reflects slow deterioration of testicular function and failure of the gonads to respond to the pituitary gland gonadotropins. Along with the decreasing testosterone concentrations in the blood, libido decreases and sperm become less motile. Despite these events, many elderly men continue to be fertile. With aging, some men manifest increased emotional problems, such as depression, and this is sometimes referred to as the ***andropause*** (***male climacteric***). It is not clear, however, what role hormonal changes play in this phenomenon.

SECTION B SUMMARY

Anatomy

I. The male gonads, the testes, produce sperm in the seminiferous tubules and secrete testosterone from the Leydig cells.

Spermatogenesis

I. The meiotic divisions of spermatogenesis result in sperm containing 23 chromosomes, compared to the original 46 of the spermatogonia.

II. The developing germ cells are intimately associated with the Sertoli cells, which perform many functions, as summarized in Table 17.2.

Transport of Sperm

I. From the seminiferous tubules, the sperm pass into the epididymis, where they are concentrated and become mature.

II. The epididymis and vas deferens store the sperm, and the seminal vesicles and prostate secrete most of the semen.

III. Erection of the penis occurs because of vascular engorgement accomplished by relaxation of the small arteries and passive occlusion of the veins.

IV. Ejaculation includes emission—emptying of semen into the urethra—followed by expulsion of the semen from the urethra.

Hormonal Control of Male Reproductive Functions

I. Pulses of hypothalamic GnRH stimulate the anterior pituitary gland to secrete FSH and LH, which then act on the testes: FSH on the Sertoli cells to stimulate spermatogenesis and inhibin secretion, and LH on the Leydig cells to stimulate testosterone secretion.

II. Testosterone, acting locally on the Sertoli cells, is essential for maintaining spermatogenesis.

III. Testosterone exerts a negative feedback inhibition on both the hypothalamus and the anterior pituitary gland to reduce mainly LH secretion. Inhibin exerts a negative feedback inhibition on FSH secretion.

IV. Testosterone maintains the accessory reproductive organs and male secondary sex characteristics and stimulates the growth of muscle and bone. In many of its target cells, it must first undergo transformation to dihydrotestosterone or to estrogen.

Puberty

I. A change in brain function at the onset of puberty results in increases in the hypothalamo–pituitary–gonadal axis (because of increases in GnRH).

II. The first sign of puberty is the appearance of pubic and axillary hair.

Hypogonadism

I. Male hypogonadism is a decrease in testicular function. Klinefelter's syndrome (usually XXY genotype) is a common cause of male hypogonadism.

II. Hypogonadism can be caused by testicular failure (primary hypogonadism) or a loss of gonadotrophic stimuli to the testes (secondary hypogonadism).

Andropause

I. The andropause is a decrease in testosterone with aging (but usually not a complete cessation of androgen production).

SECTION B REVIEW QUESTIONS

1. Describe the sequence of events leading from spermatogonia to sperm.
2. List the functions of the Sertoli cells.
3. Describe the path sperm take from the seminiferous tubules to the urethra.
4. Describe the roles of the prostate gland, seminal vesicles, and bulbourethral glands in the formation of semen.
5. Describe the neural control of erection and ejaculation.
6. Diagram the hormonal chain controlling the testes. Contrast the effects of FSH and LH.

7. What are the feedback controls from the testes to the hypothalamus and pituitary gland?
8. Define *puberty* in the male. When does it usually occur?
9. List the effects of androgens on accessory reproductive organs, secondary sex characteristics, growth, protein metabolism, and behavior.
10. Describe the conversion of testosterone to DHT and estrogen.
11. How does hyperprolactinemia cause hypogonadism?

nitric oxide 617
orgasm 618
prostate gland 614
puberty 619
rete testis 613
scrotum 612
semen 614
seminal vesicle 614
seminiferous tubule 613
Sertoli cell 613
Sertoli cell barrier 615
spermatic cord 614
spermatogenesis 613
spermatogonium 614
vas deferens 613

SECTION B KEY TERMS

acrosome 615
androgen-binding protein (ABP) 616
bulbourethral gland 614
ejaculation 617
ejaculatory duct 614
emission 618
epididymis 613
erection 617
gestation 612
Leydig cell 613
libido 619

SECTION B CLINICAL TERMS

andropause (male climacteric) 621
castration 619
cGMP-phosphodiesterase type 5 inhibitor 617
erectile dysfunction 617
gynecomastia 620
hyperprolactinemia 621
hypogonadism 620
hypopituitarism 621
Klinefelter's syndrome 620
male pattern baldness 619
prostate cancer 619
vasectomy 617

SECTION C Female Reproductive Physiology

Unlike the continuous sperm production of the male, the maturation of the female gamete (the ovum) followed by its release from the ovary—**ovulation**—is cyclical. The female germ cells, like those of the male, have different names at different stages of development. However, the term **egg** is often used to refer to the female germ cells at any stage, and we will follow that convention unless otherwise noted. The structure and function of certain components of the female reproductive system (e.g., the uterus) are synchronized with these ovarian cycles. In human beings, these cycles are called **menstrual cycles.** The length of a menstrual cycle varies considerably from woman to woman, and even in any particular woman, but averages about 28 days. The first day of menstrual flow (**menstruation**) is designated as day 1.

Menstruation is the result of events occurring in the uterus. However, the uterine events of the menstrual cycle are due to cyclical changes in hormone secretion by the ovaries. The ovaries are also the sites for the maturation of gametes. One oocyte usually becomes fully mature and is ovulated around the middle of each menstrual cycle.

The interactions among the ovaries, hypothalamus, and anterior pituitary gland produce the cyclical changes in the ovaries that result in (1) maturation of a gamete each cycle and (2) hormone secretions that cause cyclical changes in all of the female reproductive organs (particularly the uterus). The interaction of these different structures in the adult female reproductive cycle is an excellent example of the general principle of physiology that the functions of organ systems are coordinated with each other. These changes prepare the uterus to receive and nourish the developing embryo; only when there is no pregnancy does menstruation occur.

17.12 Anatomy

The female reproductive system includes the two ovaries and the female reproductive tract—two **fallopian tubes** (or oviducts), the uterus, the cervix, and the vagina. These structures are termed the **female internal genitalia** (**Figure 17.17**). Unlike in the male, the urinary and reproductive duct systems of the female are entirely separate from each other. Before proceeding with this section, the reader should review Figures 17.2 and 17.3 concerning the development of the internal and external female genitalia.

The ovaries are almond-sized organs in the upper pelvic cavity, one on each side of the uterus. The ends of the fallopian tubes are not directly attached to the ovaries but open into the abdominal cavity close to them. The opening of each fallopian tube is funnel-shaped and surrounded by long, fingerlike projections (the **fimbriae**) lined with ciliated epithelium. The other ends of the fallopian tubes are attached to the uterus and empty directly into its cavity. The **uterus** is a hollow, thick-walled, muscular organ lying between the urinary bladder and rectum. The uterus is the source of menstrual flow and is where the fetus develops during pregnancy. The lower portion of the uterus is the **cervix.** A small opening in the cervix leads to the **vagina,** the canal leading from the uterus to the outside.

The **female external genitalia** (**Figure 17.18**) include the mons pubis, labia majora, labia minora, clitoris, vestibule of the vagina, and vestibular glands. The term **vulva** is another name for all these structures. The mons pubis is the rounded fatty prominence over the junction of the pubic bones. The labia majora, the female homologue of the scrotum, are two prominent skin folds that form the outer lips of the vulva. (The terms *homologous* and *analogous* mean that the two structures are derived embryologically from the same source [see Figures 17.2 and 17.3] and/or have similar functions.) The labia minora are

(a)

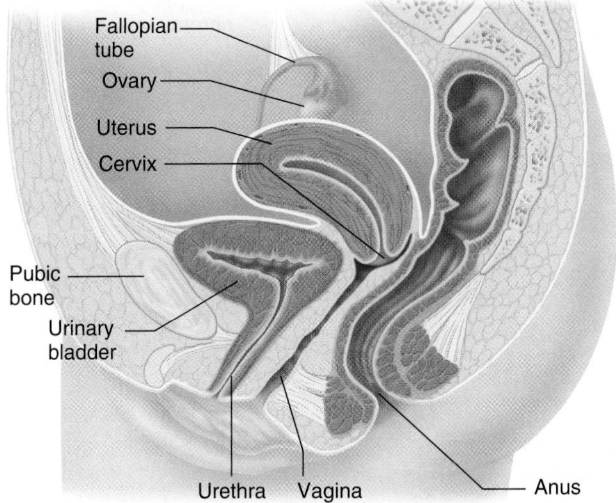

(b)

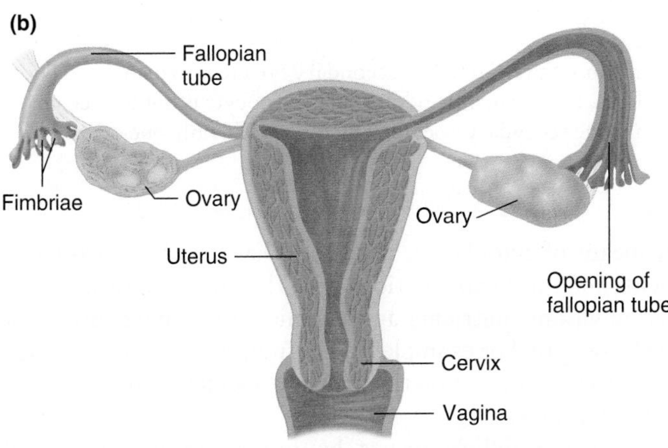

Figure 17.17 APIR Female reproductive system. (a) Side view of a section through a female pelvis. (b) Frontal view cut away on the right (left side of the body) to show the continuity between the organs of the reproductive duct system—fallopian tubes, uterus, and vagina.

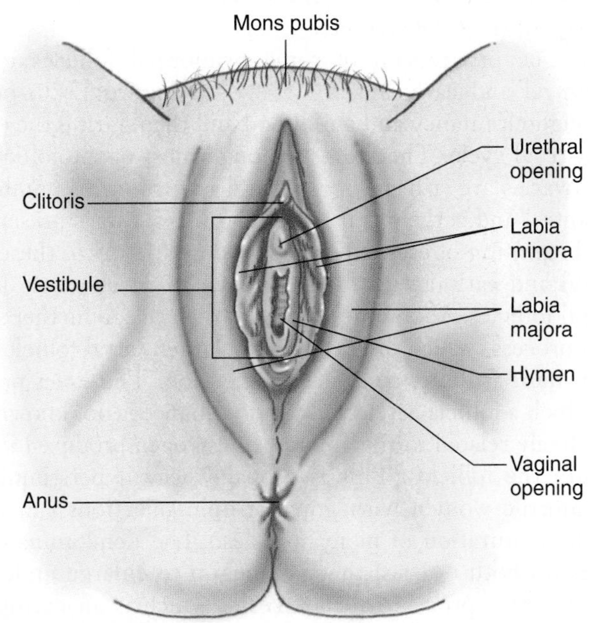

Figure 17.18 APIR Female external genitalia.

small skin folds lying between the labia majora. They surround the urethral and vaginal openings, and the area thus enclosed is the vestibule, into which secretory glands empty. The vaginal opening lies behind the opening of the urethra. Partially overlying the vaginal opening is a thin fold of mucous membrane, the **hymen.** The **clitoris,** the female homologue of the penis, is an erectile structure located at the top of the vulva.

17.13 Ovarian Functions

As noted at the beginning of this chapter, the ovary, like the testis, serves several functions: (1) **oogenesis,** the production of gametes during the fetal period; (2) maturation of the oocyte; (3) expulsion of the mature oocyte (ovulation); and (4) secretion of the female sex steroid hormones (estrogen and progesterone), as well as the peptide hormone inhibin. Before ovulation, the maturation of the oocyte and endocrine functions of the ovaries take place in a single structure, the follicle. After ovulation, the follicle, now without an egg, differentiates into a corpus luteum, which only has an endocrine function. For comparison, recall that in the testes, the production of gametes and the secretion of sex steroids take place in different compartments—in the seminiferous tubules and in the Leydig cells, respectively.

Oogenesis

At birth, the ovaries contain an estimated total of 2 to 4 million eggs, and no new ones appear after birth. Thus, in marked contrast to the male, the newborn female already has all the germ cells she will ever have. Only a few, perhaps 400, will be ovulated during a woman's lifetime. All the others degenerate at some point in their development so that few, if any, remain by the time a woman reaches approximately 50 years of age. One result of this developmental pattern is that the eggs ovulated near age 50 are 35 to 40 years older than those ovulated just after puberty. It is possible that certain chromosomal defects more common among children born to older women are the result of aging changes in the egg.

During early fetal development, the primitive germ cells, or **oogonia** (singular, **oogonium**) undergo numerous mitotic divisions (**Figure 17.19**). Oogonia are analogous to spermatogonia in the male (see Figure 17.1). Around the seventh month of gestation, the fetal oogonia cease dividing. Current thinking is that from this point on, no new germ cells are generated.

During fetal life, all the oogonia develop into primary oocytes (analogous to primary spermatocytes), which then begin a first meiotic division by replicating their DNA. They do not, however, complete the division in the fetus. Accordingly, all the eggs present at birth are primary oocytes containing 46 chromosomes, each with two sister chromatids. The cells are said to be in a state of **meiotic arrest.**

This state continues until puberty and the onset of renewed activity in the ovaries. Indeed, only those primary oocytes destined for ovulation will ever complete the first meiotic division, for it occurs just before the egg is ovulated. This division is analogous to the division of the primary spermatocyte, and each daughter cell receives 23 chromosomes, each with two chromatids. In this division, however, one of the two daughter cells, the secondary oocyte, retains virtually all the

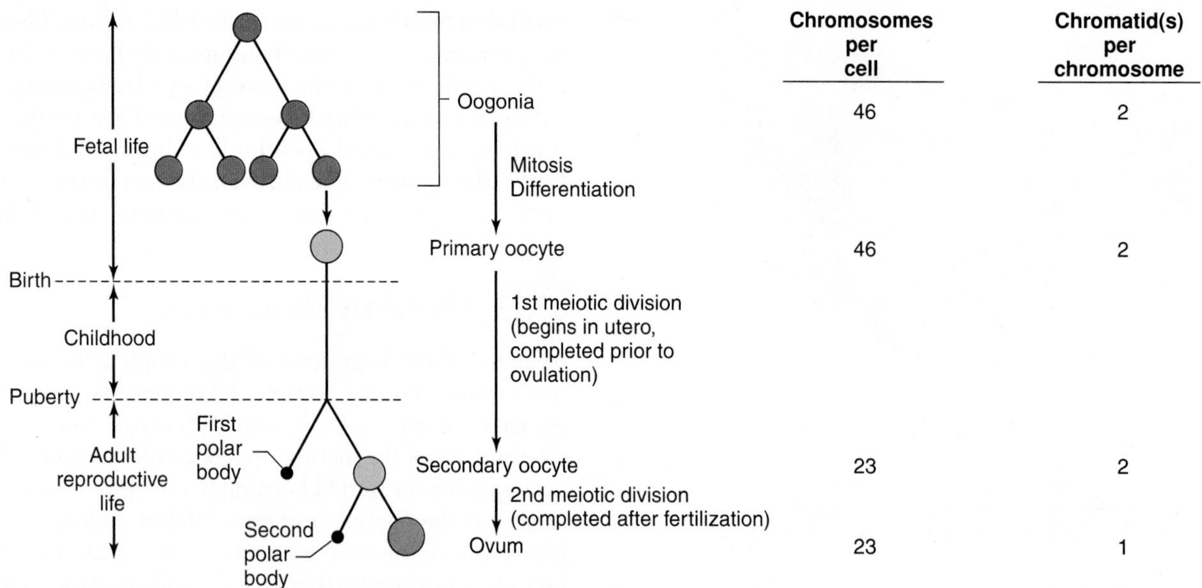

Figure 17.19 APIR Summary of oogenesis. Compare with the male pattern in Figure 17.11. The secondary oocyte is ovulated and does not complete its meiotic division unless it is penetrated (fertilized) by a sperm. Thus, it is a semantic oddity that the oocyte is not termed an *egg* or *ovum* until after fertilization occurs. Note that each primary oocyte yields only one secondary oocyte, which can yield only one ovum.

cytoplasm. The other, the first polar body, is very small and nonfunctional. Thus, the primary oocyte, which is already as large as the egg will be, passes on to the secondary oocyte just half of its chromosomes but almost all of its nutrient-rich cytoplasm.

The second meiotic division occurs in a fallopian tube *after ovulation,* but only if the secondary oocyte is fertilized—that is, penetrated by a sperm (see Figure 17.1). As a result of this second meiotic division, the daughter cells each receive 23 chromosomes, each with a single chromatid. Once again, one daughter cell, now called an ovum, retains nearly all the cytoplasm. The other daughter cell, the second polar body, is very small and nonfunctional. The net result of oogenesis is that each primary oocyte can produce only one ovum (see Figure 17.19). In contrast, each primary spermatocyte produces four viable spermatozoa.

Follicle Growth

Throughout their life in the ovaries, the eggs exist in structures known as **follicles.** Follicles begin as **primordial follicles,** which consist of one primary oocyte surrounded by a single layer of cells called **granulosa cells.** The granulosa cells secrete estrogen, small amounts of progesterone just before ovulation, and the peptide hormone inhibin. Further development from the primordial follicle stage (**Figure 17.20**) is characterized by an increase in the size of the oocyte; a proliferation of the granulosa cells into multiple layers; and the separation of the oocyte from the inner granulosa cells by a thick layer of material, the **zona pellucida,** secreted by the surrounding follicular cells. The zona pellucida contains glycoproteins that play a role in the binding of a sperm cell to the surface of an egg after ovulation.

Despite the presence of a zona pellucida, the inner layer of granulosa cells remains closely associated with the oocyte by means of cytoplasmic processes that traverse the zona pellucida and form gap junctions with the oocyte. Through these gap junctions, nutrients and chemical messengers are passed to the oocyte. For example, the granulosa cells produce one or more factors that act on the primary oocytes to maintain them in meiotic arrest.

As the follicle grows by mitosis of granulosa cells, connective-tissue cells surrounding the granulosa cells differentiate and form layers of cells known as the **theca,** which function together with the granulosa cells in the synthesis of estrogen. Shortly after this, the primary oocyte reaches full size (~115μm in diameter), and a fluid-filled space, the **antrum,** begins to form in the midst of the granulosa cells as a result of fluid they secrete.

The progression of some primordial follicles to the preantral and early antral stages (see Figure 17.20) occurs throughout infancy and childhood and then during the entire menstrual cycle. Therefore, although most of the follicles in the ovaries are still primordial, a nearly constant number of preantral and early antral follicles are also always present. At the beginning of each menstrual cycle, 10 to 25 of these preantral and early antral follicles begin to develop into larger antral follicles. About one week into the cycle, a further selection process occurs: only one of the larger antral follicles, the **dominant follicle,** continues to develop. The exact process by which a follicle is selected for dominance is not known, but it is likely related to the amount of estrogen produced locally within the follicle. (This is probably why hyperstimulation of infertile women with gonadotropin injections can result in the maturation of many follicles.) The nondominant follicles (in both ovaries) that had begun to enlarge undergo a degenerative process called **atresia,** which is an example of programmed cell death, or apoptosis. The eggs in the degenerating follicles also die.

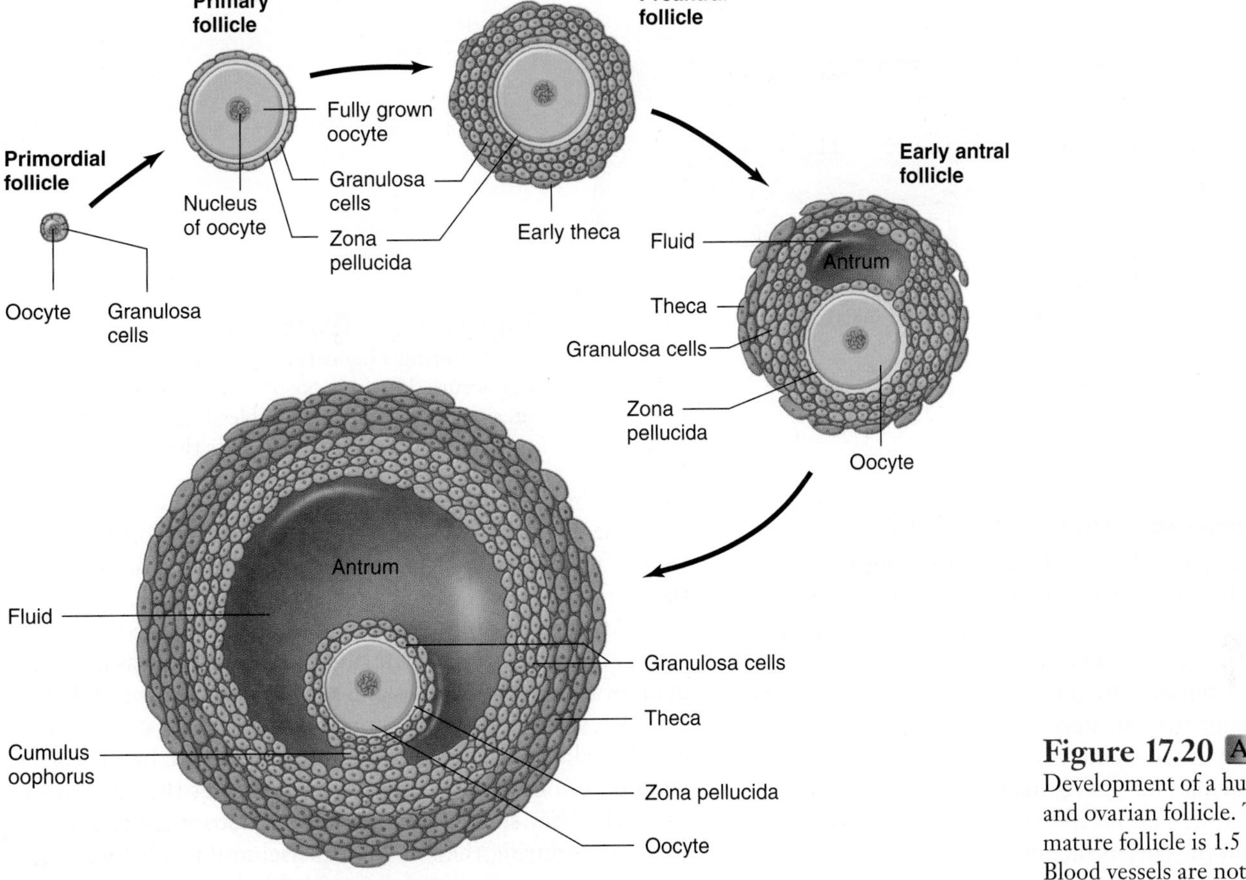

Figure 17.20 AP|R Development of a human oocyte and ovarian follicle. The fully mature follicle is 1.5 cm in diameter. Blood vessels are not shown. Adapted from Erickson et al.

Atresia is not limited to just antral follicles, however, for follicles can undergo atresia at any stage of development. Indeed, this process is already occurring in the female fetus, so that the 2 to 4 million follicles and eggs present at birth represent only a small fraction of those present earlier in gestation. Atresia then continues all through prepubertal life so that only 200,000 to 400,000 follicles remain when active reproductive life begins. Of these, all but about 400 will undergo atresia during a woman's reproductive life. Therefore, 99.99% of the ovarian follicles present at birth will undergo atresia.

The dominant follicle enlarges as a result of an increase in fluid, causing the antrum to expand. As this occurs, the granulosa cell layers surrounding the egg form a mound that projects into the antrum and is called the **cumulus oophorus** (see Figure 17.20). As the time of ovulation approaches, the egg (a primary oocyte) emerges from meiotic arrest and completes its first meiotic division to become a secondary oocyte. The cumulus separates from the follicle wall so that it and the oocyte float free in the antral fluid. The mature follicle (also called a **graafian follicle**) becomes so large (diameter about 1.5 cm) that it balloons out on the surface of the ovary.

Ovulation occurs when the thin walls of the follicle and ovary rupture at the site where they are joined because of enzymatic digestion. The secondary oocyte, surrounded by its tightly adhering zona pellucida and granulosa cells, as well as the cumulus, is carried out of the ovary and onto the ovarian surface by the antral fluid. All this happens on approximately day 14 of the menstrual cycle.

Occasionally, two or more follicles reach maturity, and more than one egg may be ovulated. This is the most common cause of multiple births. In such cases, the siblings are **fraternal (dizygotic) twins,** not identical, because the eggs carry different sets of genes and are fertilized by different sperm. We will describe later how identical twins form.

Formation of the Corpus Luteum

After the mature follicle discharges its antral fluid and egg, it collapses around the antrum and undergoes a rapid transformation. The granulosa cells enlarge greatly, and the entire glandlike structure formed is called the **corpus luteum,** which secretes estrogen, progesterone, and inhibin. If the discharged egg, now in a fallopian tube, is not fertilized by fusing with a sperm cell, the corpus luteum reaches its maximum development within approximately 10 days. It then rapidly degenerates by apoptosis. As we will see, it is the loss of corpus luteum function that leads to menstruation and the beginning of a new menstrual cycle.

In terms of ovarian function, therefore, the menstrual cycle may be divided into two phases approximately equal in length and separated by ovulation (**Figure 17.21**): (1) the **follicular phase,** during which a mature follicle and secondary oocyte develop; and (2) the **luteal phase,** beginning after ovulation and lasting until the death of the corpus luteum. As you will see, these ovarian phases correlate with and control the changes in the appearance of the uterine lining (to be described subsequently).

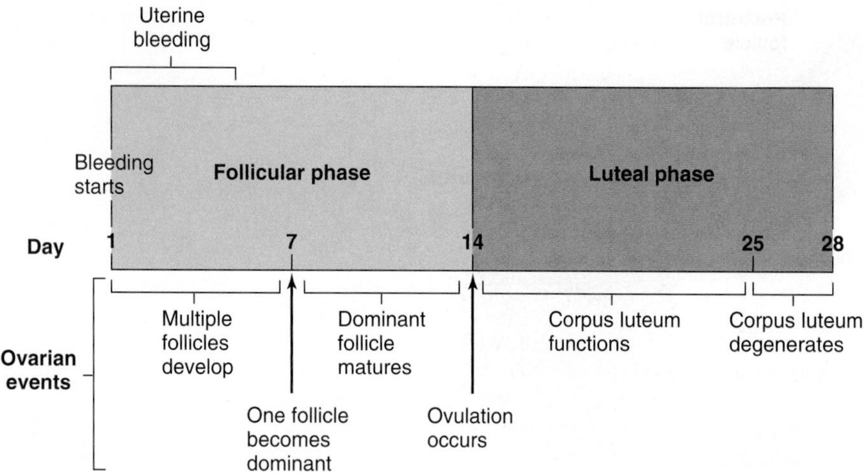

Figure 17.21 APIR Summary of ovarian events during a menstrual cycle (if fertilization does not occur). The first day of the cycle is named for a uterine event—the onset of bleeding—even though ovarian events are used to denote the cycle phases.

Sites of Synthesis of Ovarian Hormones

The synthesis of gonadal steroids was introduced in Figure 17.6 and can be summarized as follows. Estrogen is synthesized and released into the blood during the follicular phase mainly by the granulosa cells. After ovulation, estrogen is synthesized and released by the corpus luteum. Progesterone, the other major ovarian steroid hormone, is synthesized and released in very small amounts by the granulosa and theca cells just before ovulation, but its major source is the corpus luteum. Inhibin, a peptide hormone, is secreted by both the granulosa cells and the corpus luteum.

17.14 Control of Ovarian Function

The major factors controlling ovarian function are analogous to the controls described for testicular function. They constitute a hormonal system made up of GnRH, the anterior pituitary gland gonadotropins FSH and LH, and gonadal sex hormones—estrogen and progesterone.

As in the male, the entire sequence of controls depends upon the pulsatile secretion of GnRH from hypothalamic neuroendocrine cells. In the female, however, the frequency and amplitude of these pulses during a 24-hour period change over the course of the menstrual cycle. Also, the responsiveness both of the anterior pituitary gland to GnRH and of the ovaries to FSH and LH changes during the cycle.

Let us look first at the patterns of hormone concentrations in systemic plasma during a normal menstrual cycle (**Figure 17.22**). (Plasma GnRH is not shown because it does not reflect GnRH secretion from the hypothalamus into the hypothalamo–hypophyseal portal blood vessels.) In Figure 17.22, the lines are plots of average daily concentrations; that is, the increases and decreases during a single day stemming from episodic secretion have been averaged. For now, ignore both the legend and circled numbers in this figure because we are concerned here only with hormonal patterns and not the explanations of these patterns.

FSH increases in the early part of the follicular phase and then steadily decreases throughout the remainder of the cycle except for a small midcycle peak. LH is constant during most of the follicular phase but then shows a very large midcycle increase—the **LH surge**—peaking approximately 18 h *before* ovulation. This is followed by a rapid decrease and then a further slow decline during the luteal phase.

After remaining fairly low and stable for the first week, estrogen increases rapidly during the second week as the dominant ovarian follicle grows and secretes more estrogen. Estrogen then starts decreasing shortly before LH has peaked. This is followed by a second increase due to secretion by the corpus luteum and, finally, a rapid decrease during the last days of the cycle. Very small amounts of progesterone are released by the ovaries during the follicular phase until just before ovulation. Very soon after ovulation, the developing corpus luteum begins to release large amounts of progesterone; from this point, the progesterone pattern is similar to that for estrogen.

Not shown in Figure 17.22 is the plasma concentration of inhibin. Its pattern is similar to that of estrogen: It increases during the late follicular phase, remains high during the luteal phase, and then decreases as the corpus luteum degenerates.

The following discussion will explain how these hormonal changes are interrelated to produce a self-cycling pattern. The numbers in Figure 17.22 are keyed to the text. The feedback effects of the ovarian hormones to be described in the text are summarized for reference in **Table 17.4**.

Follicle Development and Estrogen Synthesis During the Early and Middle Follicular Phases

Before reading this section, the reader should review Figure 17.20 to appreciate the structure of the developing follicles. There are always a number of preantral and early antral follicles in the ovary between puberty and menopause. Further development of the follicle beyond these stages requires stimulation by FSH. Prior to puberty, the plasma concentration of FSH is too low to induce such development. This changes during puberty, and menstrual cycles commence. The increase in FSH secretion that occurs as one cycle ends and the next begins (numbers ⑯ to ① in Figure 17.22) provides this stimulation, and a group of preantral and early antral follicles enlarge ②. The increase in FSH at the end of the cycle (⑯ to ①) is due to decreased progesterone, estrogen, and inhibin (removal of negative feedback).

During the next week or so, there is a division of labor between the actions of FSH and LH on the follicles: FSH acts

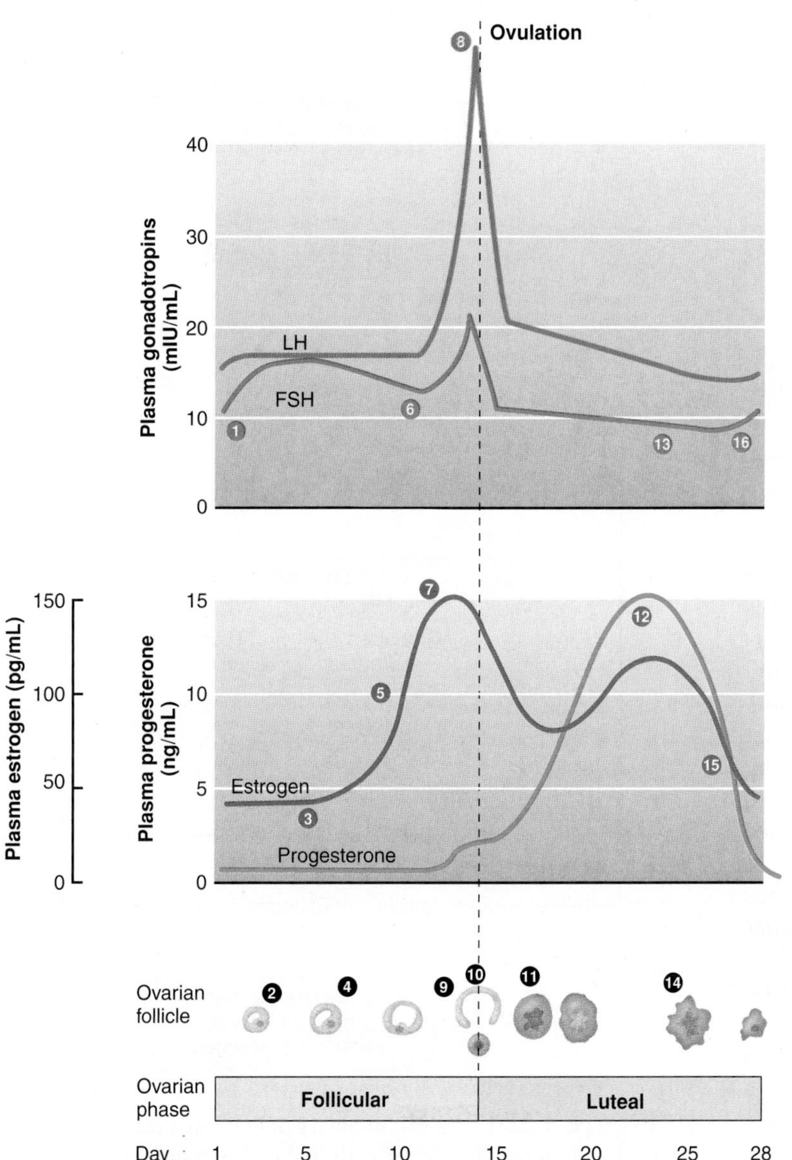

Figure 17.22 APR Summary of systemic plasma hormone concentrations and ovarian events during the menstrual cycle. The events marked by the circled numbers are described later in the text and are listed here to provide a summary. The arrows in this legend denote causality. ➊ FSH and LH secretion increase (because plasma estrogen concentration is low and exerting little negative feedback). → ➋ Multiple antral follicles begin to enlarge and secrete estrogen. → ➌ Plasma estrogen concentration begins to rise. ➍ One follicle becomes dominant and secretes very large amounts of estrogen. → ➎ Plasma estrogen concentration increases markedly. → ➏ FSH secretion and plasma FSH concentration decrease, causing atresia of nondominant follicles, but then ➐ increasing plasma estrogen exerts a "positive" feedback on gonadotropin secretion. → ➑ An LH surge is triggered. → ➒ The egg completes its first meiotic division and cytoplasmic maturation while the follicle secretes less estrogen accompanied by some progesterone, ➓ ovulation occurs, and ⓫ the corpus luteum forms and begins to secrete large amounts of both estrogen and progesterone. → ⓬ Plasma estrogen and progesterone increase. → ⓭ FSH and LH secretion are inhibited and their plasma concentrations decrease. ⓮ The corpus luteum begins to degenerate (cause unknown) and decrease its hormone secretion. → ⓯ Plasma estrogen and progesterone concentrations decrease. → ⓰ FSH and LH secretions begin to increase, and a new cycle begins (back to ➊).

PHYSIOLOGICAL INQUIRY

- (1) Why do blood FSH concentrations increase at the end of the luteal phase? (2) What naturally occurring event could rescue the corpus luteum and prevent its degeneration starting in the middle of the luteal phase?

Answers can be found at end of chapter.

TABLE 17.4 Summary of Major Feedback Effects of Estrogen, Progesterone, and Inhibin

Estrogen, in low plasma concentrations, causes the anterior pituitary gland to secrete less FSH and LH in response to GnRH and also may inhibit the hypothalamic neurons that secrete GnRH. *Result:* Negative feedback inhibition of FSH and LH secretion during the early and middle follicular phase.
Inhibin acts on the pituitary gland to inhibit the secretion of FSH. *Result:* Negative feedback inhibition of FSH secretion.
Estrogen, when increasing dramatically, causes anterior pituitary gland cells to secrete more LH and FSH in response to GnRH. Estrogen can also stimulate the hypothalamic neurons that secrete GnRH. *Result:* Positive feedback stimulation of the LH surge, which triggers ovulation.
High plasma concentrations of progesterone, in the presence of estrogen, inhibit the hypothalamic neurons that secrete GnRH. *Result:* Negative feedback inhibition of FSH and LH secretion and prevention of LH surges during the luteal phase and pregnancy.

on the granulosa cells, and LH acts on the theca cells. The reasons are that, at this point in the cycle, granulosa cells have FSH receptors but no LH receptors and theca cells have just the reverse. FSH stimulates the granulosa cells to multiply and produce estrogen, and it also stimulates enlargement of the antrum. Some of the estrogen produced diffuses into the blood and maintains a relatively stable plasma concentration ➌. Estrogen also functions as a paracrine or autocrine agent within the follicle, where, along with FSH and growth factors, it stimulates the proliferation of granulosa cells, which further increases estrogen production.

The granulosa cells, however, require help to produce estrogen because they are deficient in the enzymes required to produce the androgen precursors of estrogen (see Chapter 11). The granulosa cells are aided by the theca cells. As shown in **Figure 17.23**, LH acts upon the theca cells, stimulating them not only to proliferate but also to synthesize androgens. The androgens diffuse into the granulosa cells and are converted to estrogen by aromatase. Thus, the secretion of estrogen by the granulosa cells requires the interplay of both types of follicle cells and both pituitary gland gonadotropins.

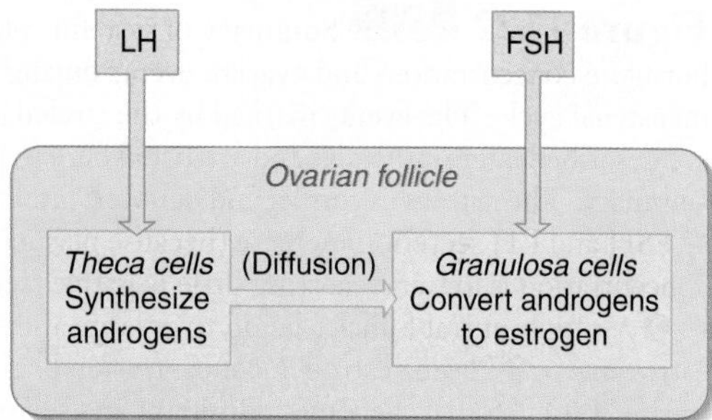

Figure 17.23 APIR Control of estrogen synthesis during the early and middle follicular phases. (The major androgen secreted by the theca cells is androstenedione.) Androgen diffusing from theca to granulosa cell passes through the basement membrane (not shown).

At this point, it is worthwhile to emphasize the similarities that the two types of follicle cells bear to cells of the testes during this period of the cycle. The granulosa cell is similar to the Sertoli cell in that it controls the microenvironment in which the germ cell develops and matures, and it is stimulated by both FSH and the major gonadal sex hormone. The theca cell is similar to the Leydig cell in that it produces mainly androgens and is stimulated to do so by LH. This makes sense when one considers that the testes and ovaries arise from the same embryonic structure (see Figure 17.2).

By the beginning of the second week, one follicle has become dominant (number ❹ in Figure 17.22) and the other developing follicles degenerate. The reason for this is that, as shown in Figure 17.22, the plasma concentration of FSH, a crucial factor necessary for the survival of the follicle cells, begins to decrease and there is no longer enough FSH to prevent atresia. Although it is not known precisely how a specific follicle is selected to become dominant, there are several reasons why this follicle, having gained a head start, is able to continue maturation. First, its granulosa cells have achieved a greater sensitivity to FSH because of increased numbers of FSH receptors. Second, its granulosa cells now begin to be stimulated not only by FSH but by LH as well. We emphasized in the previous section that, during the first week or so of the follicular phase, LH acts only on the theca cells. As the dominant follicle matures, this situation changes, and LH receptors, induced by FSH, also begin to appear in large numbers on the granulosa cells. The increase in local estrogen within the follicle results from these factors.

The dominant follicle now starts to secrete enough estrogen that the plasma concentration of this steroid begins to increase ❺. We can now also explain why plasma FSH starts to decrease at this time. Estrogen, at these still relatively low concentrations, is exerting a *negative feedback* inhibition on the secretion of gonadotropins (Table 17.4 and **Figure 17.24**). A major site of estrogen action is the anterior pituitary gland, where it reduces the amount of FSH and LH secreted in response to any given amount of GnRH. Estrogen probably also acts on the hypothalamus to decrease the amplitude of GnRH pulses and, therefore, the total amount of GnRH secreted over any time period.

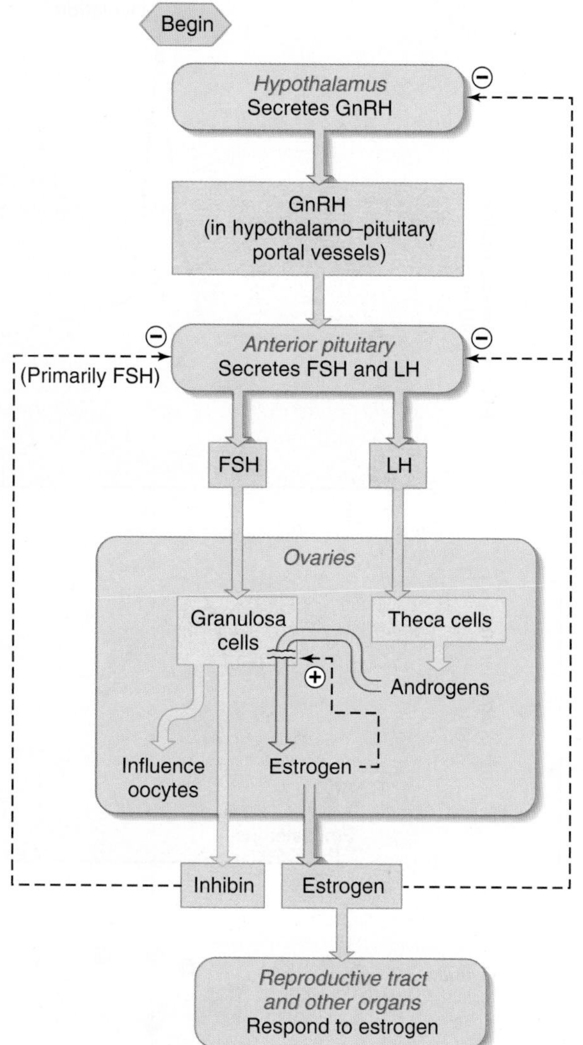

Figure 17.24 APIR Summary of hormonal control of ovarian function during the early and middle follicular phases. Compare with the analogous pattern of the male (see Figure 17.15). Inhibin is a protein hormone that inhibits FSH secretion. The wavy broken lines in the granulosa cells denote the conversion of androgens to estrogen in these cells, as shown in Figure 17.23. The dashed line with an arrow within the ovaries indicates that estrogen increases granulosa cell function (local positive feedback).

PHYSIOLOGICAL INQUIRY

- A 30-year-old woman has failed to have menstrual cycles for the past few months; her pregnancy test is negative. Her plasma FSH and LH concentrations are increased, whereas her plasma estrogen concentrations are low. What is the likely cause of her failure to menstruate?

Answer can be found at end of chapter.

Therefore, as expected from this negative feedback, the plasma concentration of FSH (and LH, to a lesser extent) begins to decrease as a result of the increasing concentration of estrogen as the follicular phase continues (❻ in Figure 17.22). One reason that FSH decreases more than LH is that the granulosa cells also secrete inhibin, which, as in the male, inhibits mainly the secretion of FSH (see Figure 17.24).

LH Surge and Ovulation

The inhibitory effect of estrogen on gonadotropin secretion occurs when plasma estrogen concentration is relatively low, as during the early and middle follicular phases. In contrast, increasing plasma concentrations of estrogen for 1 to 2 days, as occurs during the estrogen peak of the late follicular phase (❼ in Figure 17.22), act upon the anterior pituitary gland to enhance the sensitivity of LH-releasing cells to GnRH (Table 17.4 and **Figure 17.25**) and may also stimulate GnRH release from the hypothalamus. The estrogen-induced increase in GnRH release may be mediated by activation of kisspeptin neurons in the hypothalamus described earlier in this chapter. The stimulation of gonadotropin release by estrogen is a particularly important example of *positive feedback* in physiological control systems, and normal menstrual cycles and ovulation would not occur without it.

The net result is that rapidly increasing estrogen leads to the LH surge (❽ in Figure 17.22). As shown in Figure 17.22 ❾, an increase in FSH and progesterone also occurs at the time of the LH surge.

The midcycle surge of LH is the primary event that induces ovulation. The high plasma concentration of LH acts upon the granulosa cells to cause the events, presented in **Table 17.5**, that culminate in ovulation ❿, as indicated by the dashed vertical line in Figure 17.22.

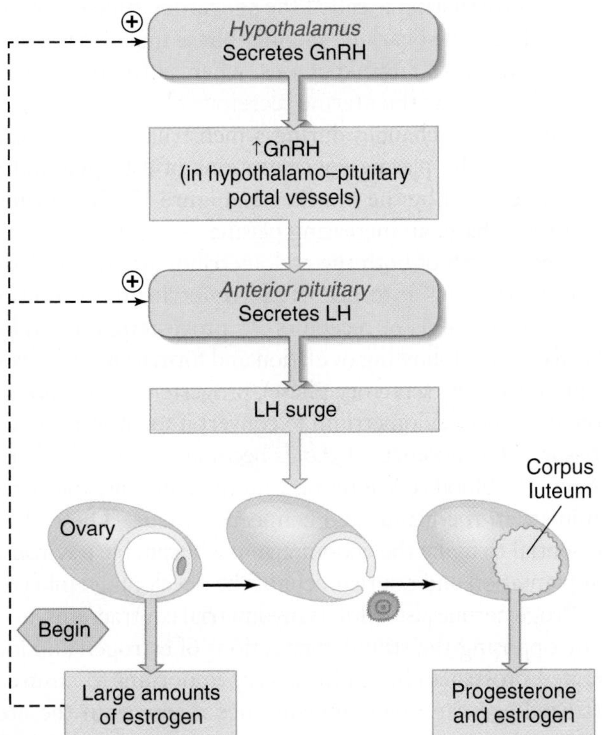

Figure 17.25 APIR In the late follicular phase, the dominant follicle secretes large amounts of estrogen, which act on the anterior pituitary gland and, possibly, the hypothalamus to cause an LH surge. The increased plasma LH then triggers both ovulation and formation of the corpus luteum. These actions of LH are mediated via the granulosa cells.

The function of the granulosa cells in mediating the effects of the LH surge is the last in the series of these cells' functions described in this chapter. They are all summarized in **Table 17.6**. The LH surge peaks and starts to decline just as ovulation occurs. Although the precise signal to terminate the LH surge is not known, it may be due to negative feedback from the small increase in progesterone described earlier (see Figure 17.22) as well as down-regulation of LH receptors in the ovary reducing estrogen-induced positive feedback.

The Luteal Phase

The LH surge not only induces ovulation by the mature follicle but also stimulates the reactions that transform the remaining granulosa and theca cells of that follicle into a

TABLE 17.5 Effects of the LH Surge on Ovarian Function
The primary oocyte completes its first meiotic division and undergoes cytoplasmic changes that prepare the ovum for implantation should fertilization occur. These LH effects on the oocyte are mediated by messengers released from the granulosa cells in response to LH.
Antrum size (fluid volume) and blood flow to the follicle increase markedly.
The granulosa cells begin releasing progesterone and decreasing the release of estrogen, which accounts for the midcycle decrease in plasma estrogen concentration and the small rise in plasma progesterone concentration just before ovulation.
Enzymes and prostaglandins, synthesized by the granulosa cells, break down the follicular–ovarian membranes. These weakened membranes rupture, allowing the oocyte and its surrounding granulosa cells to be carried out onto the surface of the ovary.
The remaining granulosa cells of the ruptured follicle (along with the theca cells of that follicle) are transformed into the corpus luteum, which begins to release progesterone and estrogen.

TABLE 17.6 Functions of Granulosa Cells
Nourish oocyte
Secrete chemical messengers that influence the oocyte and the theca cells
Secrete antral fluid
The site of action for estrogen and FSH in the control of follicle development during early and middle follicular phases
Express aromatase, which converts androgen (from theca cells) to estrogen
Secrete inhibin, which inhibits FSH secretion via an action on the pituitary gland
The site of action for LH induction of changes in the oocyte and follicle culminating in ovulation and formation of the corpus luteum

corpus luteum (⓫ in Figure 17.22). A low but adequate LH concentration maintains the function of the corpus luteum for about 14 days.

During its short life in the nonpregnant woman, the corpus luteum secretes large quantities of progesterone and estrogen ⓬, as well as inhibin. In the presence of estrogen, the high plasma concentration of progesterone causes a decrease in the secretion of the gonadotropins by the pituitary gland. It probably does this by acting on the hypothalamus to *suppress* the pulsatile secretion of GnRH. (The progesterone also prevents any LH surges during the first half of the luteal phase despite the high concentrations of estrogen at this time.) The increase in plasma inhibin concentration in the luteal phase also contributes to the suppression of FSH secretion. Consequently, during the luteal phase of the cycle, plasma concentrations of the gonadotropins are very low ⓭. The feedback suppression of gonadotropins in the luteal phase is summarized in **Figure 17.26**.

The corpus luteum has a finite life in the absence of an increase in gonadotropin secretion. If pregnancy does not occur, the corpus luteum degrades within 2 weeks ⓮.

With degeneration of the corpus luteum, plasma progesterone and estrogen concentrations decrease ⓯. The secretion of FSH and LH (and probably GnRH, as well) increases (⓰ and ❶) as a result of being freed from the inhibiting effects of high concentrations of ovarian hormones. The cycle then begins anew.

This completes the description of the control of ovarian function during a typical menstrual cycle. It should be emphasized that, although the hypothalamus and anterior pituitary gland are essential controllers, events within the *ovary* are the real sources of timing for the cycle. When the ovary secretes enough estrogen, the LH surge is induced, which in turn causes ovulation. When the corpus luteum degenerates, the decrease in hormone secretion allows the gonadotropin concentrations to increase enough to promote the growth of another group of follicles. Thus, ovarian events, via hormonal feedback, control the hypothalamus and anterior pituitary gland.

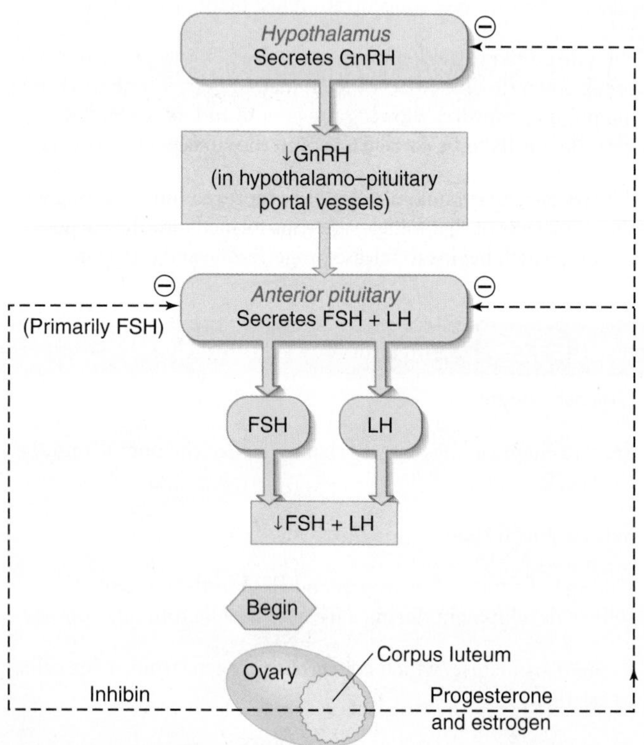

Figure 17.26 APR Suppression of FSH and LH during luteal phase. If implantation of a developing conceptus does not occur and hCG does not appear in the blood, the corpus luteum dies, progesterone and estrogen decrease, menstruation occurs, and the next menstrual cycle begins.

17.15 Uterine Changes in the Menstrual Cycle

The phases of the menstrual cycle can also be described in terms of uterine events (**Figure 17.27**). Day 1 is, as noted earlier, the first day of menstrual flow, and the entire duration of menstruation is known as the **menstrual phase** (generally about 3 to 5 days in a typical 28-day cycle). During this time, the epithelial lining of the uterus—the **endometrium**—degenerates, resulting in the menstrual flow. The menstrual flow then ceases, and the endometrium begins to thicken as it regenerates under the influence of estrogen. This period of growth, the **proliferative phase,** lasts for the 10 days or so between cessation of menstruation and the occurrence of ovulation. Soon after ovulation, under the influence of progesterone and estrogen, the endometrium begins to secrete glycogen in the glandular epithelium, followed by glycoproteins and mucopolysaccharides. Thus, the part of the menstrual cycle between ovulation and the onset of the next menstruation is called the **secretory phase.** As shown in Figure 17.27, the ovarian follicular phase includes the uterine menstrual and proliferative phases, whereas the ovarian luteal phase is the same as the uterine secretory phase.

The uterine changes during a menstrual cycle are caused by changes in the plasma concentrations of estrogen and progesterone secreted by the ovaries (see Figure 17.22). During the proliferative phase, an increasing plasma estrogen concentration stimulates growth of both the endometrium and the underlying uterine smooth muscle (called the **myometrium**). In addition, it induces the synthesis of receptors for progesterone in endometrial cells. Then, following ovulation and formation of the corpus luteum (during the secretory phase), progesterone acts upon this estrogen-primed endometrium to convert it to an actively secreting tissue. The endometrial glands become coiled and filled with glycogen, the blood vessels become more numerous, and enzymes accumulate in the glands and connective tissue. These changes are essential to make the endometrium a hospitable environment for implantation and nourishment of the developing embryo.

Progesterone also inhibits myometrial contractions, in large part by opposing the stimulatory actions of estrogen and locally generated prostaglandins. This is very important to ensure that a fertilized egg can safely implant once it arrives in the uterus. Uterine quiescence is maintained by progesterone throughout pregnancy and is essential to prevent premature delivery.

Estrogen and progesterone also have important effects on the secretion of mucus by the cervix. Under the influence of estrogen alone, this mucus is abundant, clear, and watery. All of these characteristics are most pronounced at the time of ovulation and allow sperm deposited in the vagina to move easily

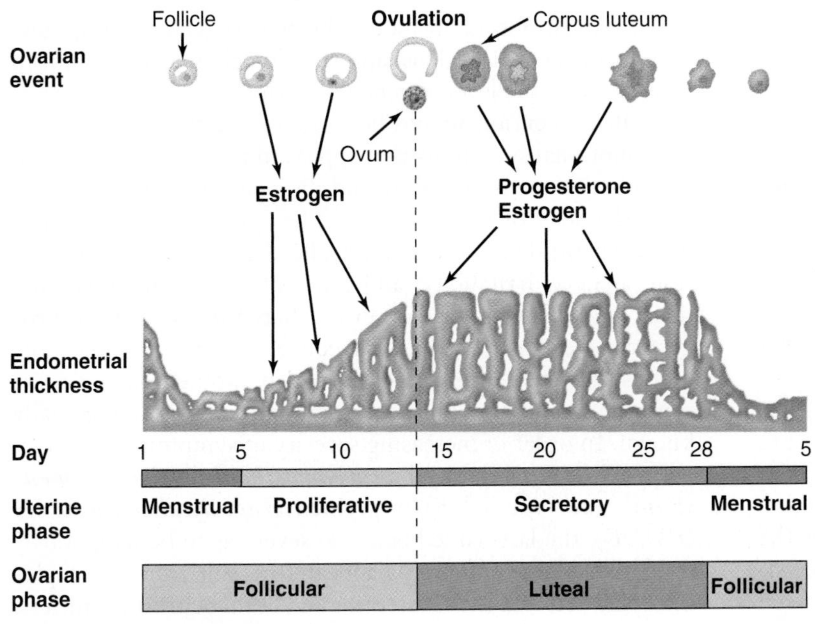

Figure 17.27 APIR Relationships between ovarian and uterine changes during the menstrual cycle. Refer to Figure 17.22 for specific hormonal changes.

through the mucus on their way to the uterus and fallopian tubes. In contrast, progesterone, present in significant concentrations only after ovulation, causes the mucus to become thick and sticky—in essence, a "plug" that prevents bacteria from entering the uterus from the vagina. The antibacterial blockage protects the uterus and the embryo if fertilization has occurred.

The decrease in plasma progesterone and estrogen concentrations that results from degeneration of the corpus luteum deprives the highly developed endometrium of its hormonal support and causes menstruation. The first event is profound constriction of the uterine blood vessels, which leads to a diminished supply of oxygen and nutrients to the endometrial cells. Disintegration starts in the entire lining, except for a thin, underlying layer that will regenerate the endometrium in the next cycle. Also, the uterine smooth muscle begins to undergo rhythmic contractions.

Both the vasoconstriction and uterine contractions are mediated by prostaglandins produced by the endometrium in response to the decrease in plasma estrogen and progesterone concentrations. The major cause of menstrual cramps, ***dysmenorrhea***, is overproduction of these prostaglandins, leading to excessive uterine contractions. The prostaglandins also affect smooth muscle elsewhere in the body, which accounts for some of the systemic symptoms that sometimes accompany the cramps, such as nausea, vomiting, and headache.

After the initial period of vascular constriction, the endometrial arterioles dilate, resulting in hemorrhage through the weakened capillary walls. The menstrual flow consists of this blood mixed with endometrial debris. Typical blood loss per menstrual period is about 50 to 150 mL.

The major events of the menstrual cycle are summarized in **Table 17.7**. This table, in essence, combines the information in Figures 17.22 and 17.27.

TABLE 17.7 Summary of the Menstrual Cycle

Day(s)	Major Events
1–5	Estrogen and progesterone are low because the previous corpus luteum is regressing. *Therefore:* a. Endometrial lining sloughs. b. Secretion of FSH and LH is released from inhibition, and their plasma concentrations increase. *Therefore:* Several growing follicles are stimulated to mature.
7	A single follicle (usually) becomes dominant.
7–12	Plasma estrogen increases because of secretion by the dominant follicle. *Therefore:* Endometrium is stimulated to proliferate.
7–12	LH and FSH decrease due to estrogen and inhibin negative feedback. *Therefore:* Degeneration (atresia) of nondominant follicles occurs.
12–13	LH surge is induced by increasing plasma estrogen. *Therefore:* a. Oocyte is induced to complete its first meiotic division and undergo cytoplasmic maturation. b. Follicle is stimulated to secrete digestive enzymes and prostaglandins.
14	Ovulation is mediated by follicular enzymes and prostaglandins.
15–25	Corpus luteum forms and, under the influence of low but adequate levels of LH, secretes estrogen and progesterone, increasing plasma concentrations of these hormones. *Therefore:* a. Secretory endometrium develops. b. Secretion of FSH and LH from the anterior pituitary gland is inhibited, lowering their plasma concentrations. *Therefore:* No new follicles develop.
25–28	Corpus luteum degenerates (if implantation of the conceptus does not occur). *Therefore:* Plasma estrogen and progesterone concentrations decrease. *Therefore:* Endometrium begins to slough at conclusion of day 28, and a new cycle begins.

17.16 Additional Effects of Gonadal Steroids

Estrogen has other effects in addition to its paracrine function within the ovaries, its effects on the anterior pituitary gland and the hypothalamus, and its uterine actions. They are summarized in **Table 17.8**.

Progesterone also exerts a variety of effects (also shown Table 17.8). Because plasma progesterone concentration is markedly increased only after ovulation has occurred, several of these effects can be used to indicate whether ovulation has taken place. First, progesterone inhibits proliferation of the cells lining the vagina. Second, there is a small increase (approximately 0.5°C) in body temperature that usually occurs after ovulation and persists throughout the luteal phase; this change is probably due to an action of progesterone on temperature regulatory centers in the brain. This is an example of the general principle of physiology that the functions of organ systems are coordinated with each other.

Note that in its myometrial and vaginal effects, as well as several others listed in Table 17.8, progesterone exerts an "antiestrogen effect," probably by decreasing the number of estrogen receptors. In contrast, the synthesis of progesterone receptors is stimulated by estrogen in many tissues (for example, the endometrium), and so responsiveness to progesterone usually requires the presence of estrogen (**estrogen priming**).

Like all steroid hormones, both estrogen and progesterone act in the cell nucleus, and their biochemical mechanism of action is at the level of gene transcription.

Brief mention should be made of the transient physical and emotional symptoms that appear in many women prior to the onset of menstrual flow and disappear within a few days after the start of menstruation. The symptoms—which may include painful or swollen breasts; headache; backache; depression; anxiety; irritability; and other physical, emotional, and behavioral changes—are often attributed to estrogen or progesterone excess. The plasma concentrations of these hormones, however, are usually normal in women having these symptoms, and the cause of the symptoms is not actually known. In order of increasing severity of symptoms, the overall problem is categorized as ***premenstrual tension, premenstrual syndrome*** (*PMS*), or ***premenstrual dysphoric disorder*** (*PMDD*), the last-named being so severe as to be temporarily disabling. These symptoms appear to result from a complex interplay between the sex steroids and brain neurotransmitters.

Androgens are present in the blood of women as a result of production by the adrenal glands and ovaries (see Figure 17.6). These androgens play several important roles in the female, including stimulation of the growth of pubic hair, axillary hair, and, possibly, skeletal muscle, and maintenance of sex drive. Excess androgens may cause ***virilization:*** The female fat distribution lessens, a beard appears along with the male body hair distribution, the voice lowers in pitch, the skeletal muscle mass increases, the clitoris enlarges, and the breasts diminish in size.

TABLE 17.8 Some Effects of Female Sex Steroids

I. Estrogen
- A. Stimulates growth of ovary and follicles (local effects).
- B. Stimulates growth of smooth muscle and proliferation of epithelial linings of reproductive tract. In addition:
  1. Fallopian tubes: Increases contractions and ciliary activity.
  2. Uterus: Increases myometrial contractions and responsiveness to oxytocin. Stimulates secretion of abundant, watery cervical mucus. Prepares endometrium for progesterone's actions by inducing progesterone receptors.
  3. Vagina: Increases layering of epithelial cells.
- C. Stimulates external genitalia growth, particularly during puberty.
- D. Stimulates breast growth, particularly ducts and fat deposition during puberty.
- E. Stimulates female body configuration development during puberty: narrow shoulders, broad hips, female fat distribution (deposition on hips and breasts).
- F. Stimulates fluid secretion from lipid (sebum)-producing skin glands (sebaceous glands). (This "anti-acne" effect opposes the acne-producing effects of androgen.)
- G. Stimulates bone growth and ultimate cessation of bone growth (closure of epiphyseal plates); protects against osteoporosis; does not have an anabolic effect on skeletal muscle.
- H. Vascular effects (deficiency produces "hot flashes").
- I. Has feedback effects on hypothalamus and anterior pituitary gland (see Table 17.4).
- J. Stimulates prolactin secretion but inhibits prolactin's milk-inducing action on the breasts.
- K. Protects against atherosclerosis by effects on plasma cholesterol (Chapter 16), blood vessels, and blood clotting (Chapter 12).

II. Progesterone
- A. Converts the estrogen-primed endometrium to an actively secreting tissue suitable for implantation of an embryo.
- B. Induces thick, sticky cervical mucus.
- C. Decreases contractions of fallopian tubes and myometrium.
- D. Decreases proliferation of vaginal epithelial cells.
- E. Stimulates breast growth, particularly glandular tissue.
- F. Inhibits milk-inducing effects of prolactin.
- G. Has feedback effects on hypothalamus and anterior pituitary gland (see Table 17.4).
- H. Increases body temperature.

17.17 Puberty

Puberty in females is a process similar to that in males (described earlier in this chapter). It usually starts earlier in girls (10 to 12 years old) than in boys. In the female, GnRH, the pituitary gland gonadotropins, and estrogen are all secreted at very low concentrations during childhood. For this reason, there is no follicle maturation beyond the early antral stage and menstrual cycles do not occur. The female accessory sex organs remain small and nonfunctional, and there are minimal secondary sex characteristics. The onset of puberty is caused, in large part, by an alteration in brain function that increases the secretion of GnRH. It is currently thought that activation of kisspeptin neurons in the hypothalamus is involved in the increase in GnRH that occurs early in puberty. GnRH in turn stimulates the secretion of pituitary gland gonadotropins, which stimulate follicle development and estrogen secretion. Estrogen, in addition to its critical role in follicle development, induces the changes in the accessory sex organs and secondary sex characteristics associated with puberty. **Menarche,** the first menstruation, is a late event of puberty (averaging about 12.5 years of age in the United States).

As in males, the mechanism of the brain change that results in increased GnRH secretion in girls at puberty remains unknown. The brain may become less sensitive to the negative feedback effects of gonadal hormones at the time of puberty. Also, the adipose-tissue hormone leptin (see Chapter 16) is known to stimulate the secretion of GnRH and may play a role in puberty. This may explain why the onset of puberty tends to correlate with the attainment of a certain level of energy stores (fat) in the girl's body. The failure to have menstrual flow (menses) is called ***amenorrhea.*** Primary amenorrhea is the failure to initial normal menstrual cycles at puberty (menarche), whereas secondary amenorrhea is defined as the loss of previously normal menstrual cycles. As we will see, the most common causes of secondary amenorrhea are pregnancy and menopause. Excessive exercise and ***anorexia nervosa*** (self-imposed starvation) can cause primary or secondary amenorrhea. There are a variety of theories for why this is so. One unifying theory is that the brain can sense a loss of body fat, possibly via decreased concentrations of the hormone leptin, and that this leads the hypothalamus to cease GnRH pulses. From a teleological view, this makes sense because pregnant women must supply a large caloric input to the developing fetus and a lack of body fat would indicate inadequate energy stores. The prepubertal appearance of female gymnasts who have minimal body fat may indicate hypogonadism and probably amenorrhea, which can persist for many years after menarche would normally take place.

The onset of puberty in both sexes is not abrupt but develops over several years, as evidenced by slowly increasing plasma concentrations of the gonadotropins and testosterone or estrogen. The age of the normal onset of puberty is controversial, although it is generally thought that pubertal onset before the age of 6 to 7 in girls and 8 to 9 in boys warrants clinical investigation. ***Precocious puberty*** is defined as the very premature appearance of secondary sex characteristics and is usually caused by an early increase in gonadal steroid production. This leads to an early onset of the puberty growth spurt, maturation of the skeleton, breast development (in girls), and enlargement of the genitalia (in boys). Therefore, these children are usually taller at an early age. However, because gonadal steroids also stop the pubertal growth spurt by inducing epiphyseal closure, final adult height is usually less than predicted. Although there are a variety of causes for the premature increase in gonadal steroids, *true* (or complete) precocious puberty is caused by the premature activation of GnRH and LH and FSH secretion. This is often caused by tumors or infections in the area of the central nervous system that controls GnRH release. Treatments that decrease LH and FSH release are important to allow normal development.

17.18 Female Sexual Response

The female response to sexual intercourse is characterized by marked increases in blood flow and muscular contraction in many areas of the body. For example, increasing sexual excitement is associated with vascular engorgement of the breasts and erection of the nipples, resulting from contraction of smooth muscle fibers in them. The clitoris, which has a rich supply of sensory nerve endings, increases in diameter and length as a result of increased blood flow. During intercourse, the blood flow to the vagina increases and the vaginal epithelium is lubricated by mucus.

Orgasm in the female, as in the male, is accompanied by pleasurable feelings and many physical events. There is a sudden increase in skeletal muscle activity involving almost all parts of the body; the heart rate and blood pressure increase, and there is a transient rhythmic contraction of the vagina and uterus. Orgasm seems to play a minimal role in ensuring fertilization because fertilization can occur in the absence of an orgasm.

Sexual desire in women is probably more dependent upon androgens, secreted by the adrenal glands and ovaries, than estrogen. Sex drive is also maintained beyond menopause, a time when estrogen concentrations become very low. New studies have suggested that low-dose androgen therapy may be useful for the treatment of decreased libido in women. These effects are mediated by a direct effect of androgen and by conversion of androgens to estrogen by aromatase in the brain.

17.19 Pregnancy

For pregnancy to occur, the introduction of sperm must occur between 5 days before and 1 day after ovulation. This is because the sperm, following their ejaculation into the vagina, remain capable of fertilizing an egg for up to 4 to 6 days, and the ovulated egg remains viable for only 24 to 48 h.

Egg Transport

At ovulation, the egg is extruded onto the surface of the ovary. Recall that the fimbriae at the ends of the fallopian tubes are lined with ciliated epithelium. At ovulation, the smooth muscle of the fimbriae causes them to pass over the ovary while the cilia beat in waves toward the interior of the duct. These ciliary motions sweep the egg into the fallopian tube as it emerges onto the ovarian surface.

Within the fallopian tube, egg movement, driven almost entirely by fallopian-tube cilia, is so slow that the egg takes about 4 days to reach the uterus. Thus, if fertilization is to occur, it must do so in the fallopian tube because of the short viability of the unfertilized egg.

Intercourse, Sperm Transport, and Capacitation

Ejaculation, described earlier in this chapter, results in deposition of semen into the vagina during intercourse. The act of intercourse itself provides some impetus for the transport of sperm out of the vagina to the cervix because of the fluid pressure of the ejaculate. Passage into the cervical mucus by the swimming sperm is dependent on the estrogen-induced changes in consistency of the mucus described earlier. Sperm can enter the uterus within minutes of ejaculation. Furthermore, the sperm can usually survive for up to a day or two within the cervical mucus, from which they can be released to enter the uterus. Transport of the sperm through the length of the uterus and into the fallopian tubes occurs via the sperm's own propulsions and uterine contractions.

The mortality rate of sperm during the trip is huge. One reason for this is that the vaginal environment is acidic, a protection against yeast and bacterial infections. Another is the length and energy requirements of the trip. Of the several hundred million sperm deposited in the vagina in an ejaculation, only about 100 to 200 reach the fallopian tube. This is the major reason there must be so many sperm in the ejaculate for fertilization to occur.

Sperm are not able to fertilize the egg until they have resided in the female tract for several hours and been acted upon by secretions of the tract. This process, called **capacitation,** causes (1) the previously regular wavelike beats of the sperm's tail to be replaced by a more whiplike action that propels the sperm forward in strong surges and (2) the sperm's plasma membrane to become altered so that it will be capable of fusing with the surface membrane of the egg.

Fertilization

Fertilization begins with the fusion of a sperm and egg, usually within a few hours after ovulation. The egg usually must be fertilized within 24 to 48 hours of ovulation. Many sperm, after moving between the granulosa cells of the corona radiata still surrounding the egg, bind to the zona pellucida (**Figure 17.28**). The zona pellucida glycoproteins function

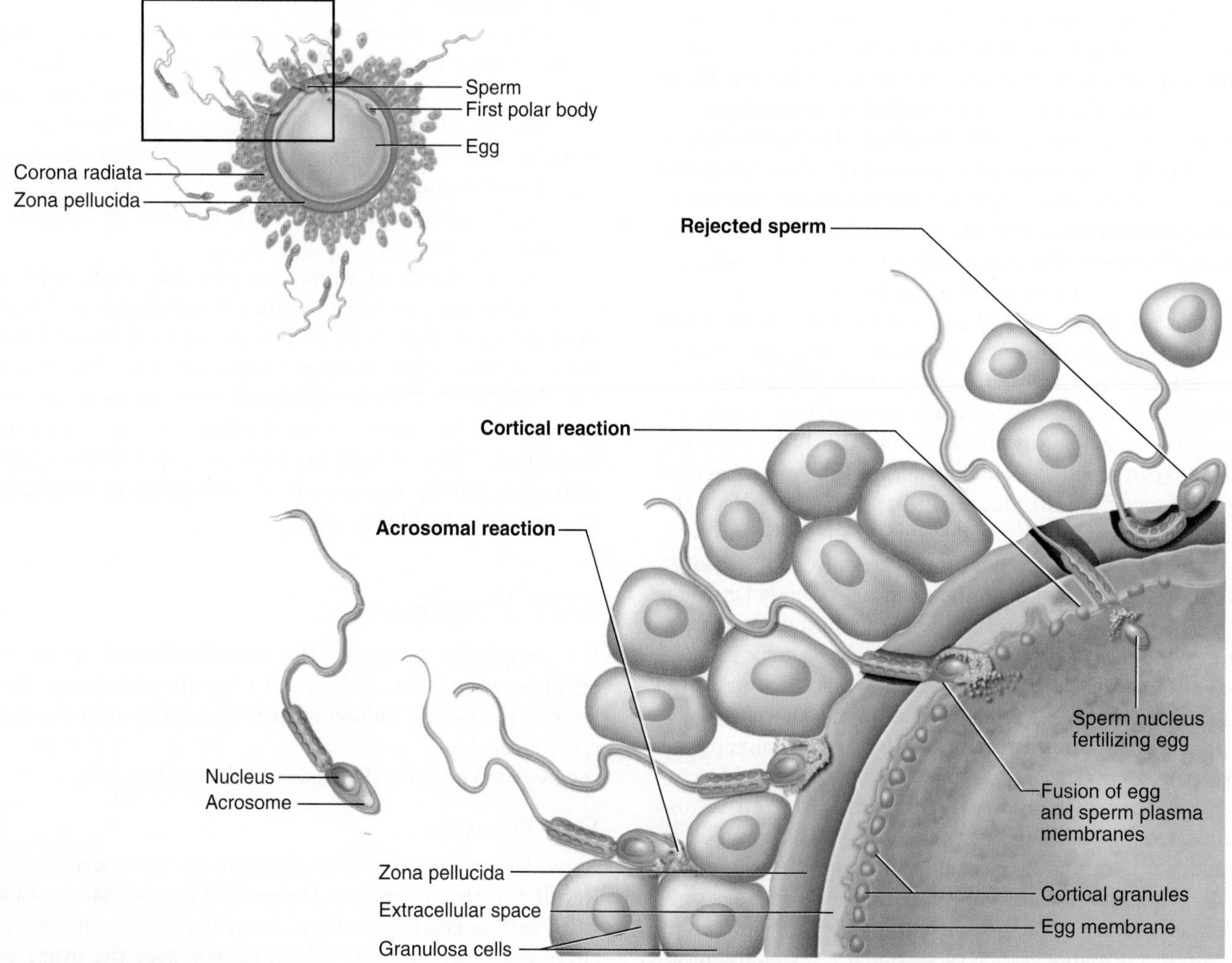

Figure 17.28 APIR Fertilization and the block to polyspermy. Rectangle on top image indicates area of enlargement below. The size of the sperm is exaggerated for clarity. The photograph on the first page of this chapter shows the actual size relationship between the sperm and the egg.

as receptors for sperm surface proteins. The sperm head has many of these proteins and so becomes bound simultaneously to many sperm receptors on the zona pellucida.

This binding triggers what is termed the **acrosome reaction** in the bound sperm: The plasma membrane of the sperm head is altered so that the underlying membrane-bound acrosomal enzymes are now exposed to the outside—that is, to the zona pellucida. The enzymes digest a path through the zona pellucida as the sperm, using its tail, advances through this coating. The first sperm to penetrate the entire zona pellucida and reach the egg's plasma membrane fuses with this membrane. The head of the sperm then slowly passes into the cytosol of the egg.

Viability of the newly fertilized egg, now called a zygote, depends upon preventing the entry of additional sperm. A specific mechanism mediates this **block to polyspermy.** The initial fusion of the sperm and egg plasma membranes triggers a reaction that changes membrane potential, preventing additional sperm from binding. Subsequently, during the **cortical reaction,** cytosolic secretory vesicles located around the egg's periphery release their contents, by exocytosis, into the narrow space between the egg plasma membrane and the zona pellucida. Some of these molecules are enzymes that enter the zona pellucida and cause both inactivation of its sperm-binding sites and hardening of the entire zona pellucida. This prevents additional sperm from binding to the zona pellucida and those sperm already advancing through it from continuing.

The fertilized egg completes its second meiotic division over the next few hours, and the one daughter cell with practically no cytoplasm—the second polar body—is extruded and disintegrates. The two sets of chromosomes—23 from the egg and 23 from the sperm, which are surrounded by distinct membranes and are known as pronuclei—migrate to the center of the cell. During this period of a few hours, the DNA of the chromosomes in both pronuclei is replicated, the pronuclear membranes break down, the cell is ready to undergo a mitotic division, and fertilization is complete. Fertilization also triggers activation of the egg enzymes required for the ensuing cell divisions and embryogenesis. The major events of fertilization are summarized in **Figure 17.29**. If fertilization had not occurred, the egg would have slowly disintegrated and been phagocytized by cells lining the uterus.

Rarely, a fertilized egg remains in a fallopian tube and embeds itself in the tube wall. Even more rarely, a fertilized egg may move backward out of the fallopian tube into the abdominal cavity, where implantation can occur. Both kinds of ***ectopic pregnancies*** cannot succeed, and surgery is necessary to end the pregnancy (unless there is a spontaneous abortion) because of the risk of maternal hemorrhage.

Early Development, Implantation, and Placentation

The previously described events from ovulation and fertilization to implantation of the blastocyst are summarized in **Figure 17.30**. The **conceptus**—a collective term for everything ultimately derived from the original zygote (fertilized egg) throughout the pregnancy—remains in the fallopian tube for 3 to 4 days. The major reason is that estrogen maintains the contraction of the smooth muscle near where the fallopian tube enters the wall of the uterus. As plasma progesterone concentrations increase, this smooth muscle relaxes and

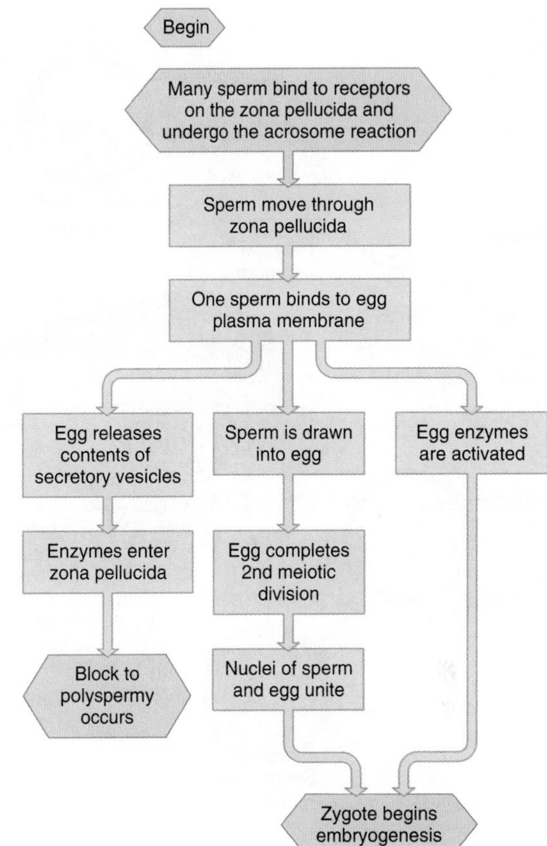

Figure 17.29 Events leading to fertilization, block to polyspermy, and the beginning of embryogenesis.

allows the conceptus to pass. During its stay in the fallopian tube, the conceptus undergoes a number of mitotic cell divisions, a process known as **cleavage.** These divisions, however, are unusual in that no cell growth occurs before each division. Thus, the 16- to 32-cell conceptus that reaches the uterus is essentially the same size as the original fertilized egg.

Each of these cells is **totipotent**—that is, they are **stem cells** that have the capacity to develop into an entire individual. Therefore, identical (monozygotic) twins result when, at some point during cleavage, the dividing cells become completely separated into two independently growing cell masses. In contrast, as described earlier, dizygotic twins result when two eggs are ovulated and fertilized.

After reaching the uterus, the conceptus floats free in the intrauterine fluid, from which it receives nutrients, for approximately 3 days, all the while undergoing further cell divisions to approximately 100 cells. Soon the conceptus reaches the stage known as a **blastocyst,** by which point the cells have lost their totipotentiality and have begun to differentiate. The blastocyst consists of an outer layer of cells called the **trophoblast,** an **inner cell mass,** and a central fluid-filled cavity (**Figure 17.31**). During subsequent development, the inner cell mass will give rise to the developing human—called an **embryo** during the first 2 months and a **fetus** after that—and some of the membranes associated with it. The trophoblast will surround the embryo and fetus throughout development and be involved in its nutrition as well as in the secretion of several important hormones.

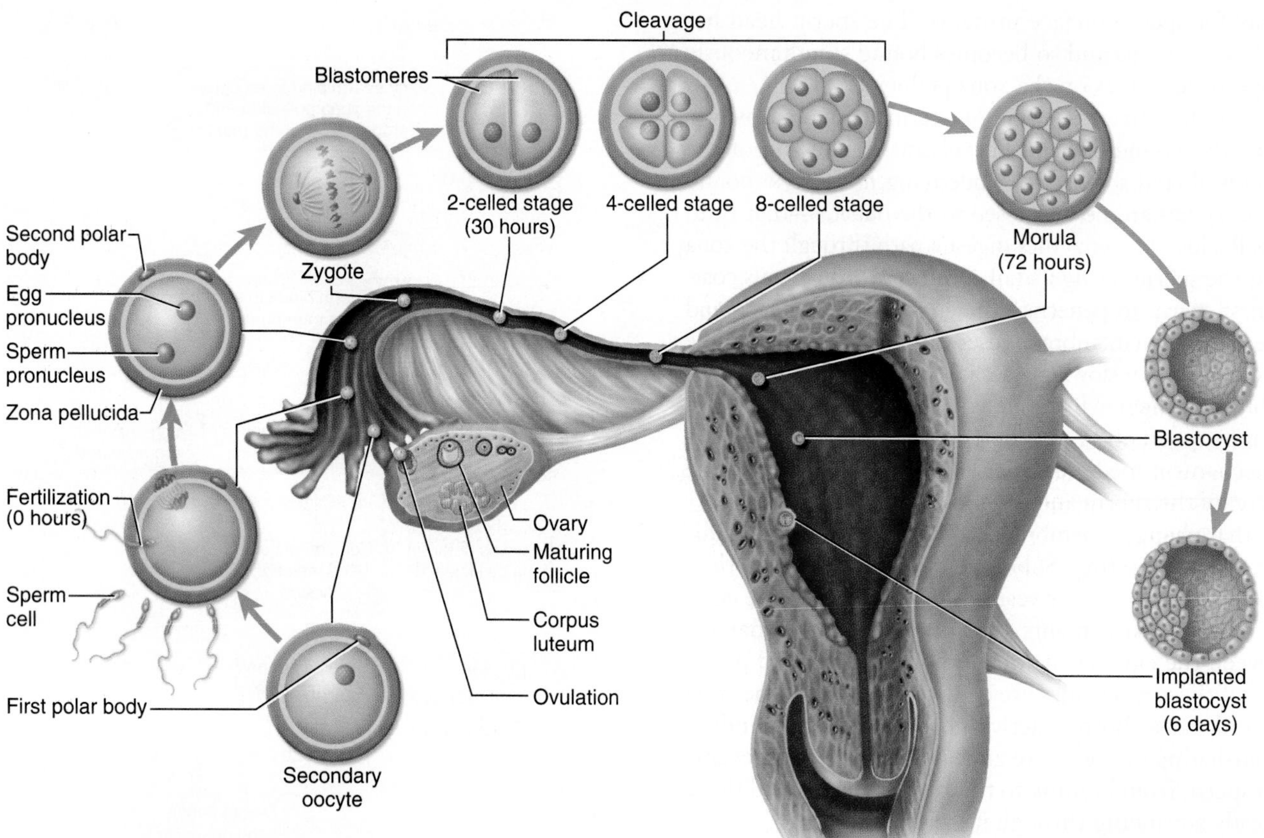

Figure 17.30 APIR Events from ovulation to implantation. Only one ovary and one fallopian tube are shown (right side of patient).

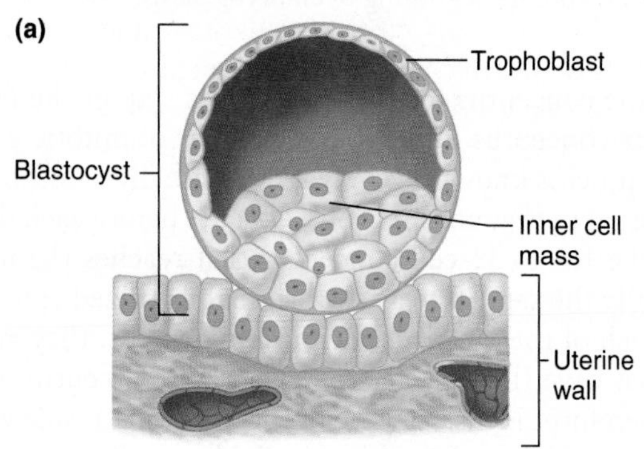

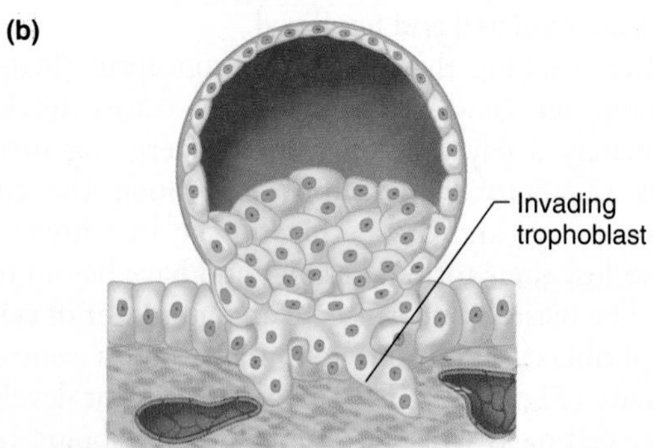

Figure 17.31 APIR (a) Contact and (b) implantation of the blastocyst into the uterine wall at about 6–7 days after the previous LH peak. The trophoblast cells secrete hCG into the maternal circulation, which rescues the corpus luteum and maintains pregnancy. The trophoblast eventually develops into a component of the placenta.

The period during which the zygote develops into a blastocyst corresponds with days 14 to 21 of the typical menstrual cycle. During this period, the uterine lining is being prepared by progesterone (secreted by the corpus luteum) to receive the blastocyst. By approximately the twenty-first day of the cycle (that is, 7 days after ovulation), **implantation**—the embedding of the blastocyst into the endometrium—begins (see Figure 17.31). The trophoblast cells are quite sticky, particularly in the region overlying the inner cell mass, and it is this portion of the blastocyst that adheres to the endometrium and initiates implantation.

The initial contact between blastocyst and endometrium induces rapid proliferation of the trophoblast, the cells of which penetrate between endometrial cells. Proteolytic enzymes secreted by the trophoblast allow the blastocyst to bury itself in the endometrial layer. The endometrium, too, is undergoing changes at the site of contact. Implantation requires communication—via several paracrine signals—between the blastocyst and the cells of the endometrium. Implantation is soon completed, and the nutrient-rich endometrial cells provide the metabolic fuel and raw materials required for early growth of the embryo.

This simple nutritive system, however, is only adequate to provide for the embryo during the first few weeks, when it is very small. The structure that takes over this function is the **placenta,** a combination of interlocking fetal and maternal tissues, which serves as the organ of exchange between mother and fetus for the remainder of the pregnancy.

The embryonic portion of the placenta is supplied by the outermost layers of trophoblast cells, the **chorion,** and the maternal portion by the endometrium underlying the chorion. Fingerlike projections of the trophoblast cells, called

chorionic villi, extend from the chorion into the endometrium (**Figure 17.32**). The villi contain a rich network of capillaries that are part of the embryo's circulatory system. The endometrium around the villi is altered by enzymes and other paracrine molecules secreted from the cells of the invading villi so that each villus becomes completely surrounded by a pool, or **sinus,** of maternal blood supplied by maternal arterioles.

The maternal blood enters these placental sinuses via the uterine artery; the blood flows through the sinuses and then exits via the uterine veins. Simultaneously, blood flows from the fetus into the capillaries of the chorionic villi via the **umbilical arteries** and out of the capillaries back to the fetus via the **umbilical vein.** All of these umbilical vessels are contained in the **umbilical cord,** a long, ropelike structure that connects the fetus to the placenta.

Five weeks after implantation, the placenta has become well established; the fetal heart has begun to pump blood; the entire mechanism for nutrition of the embryo and, subsequently, fetus and the excretion of waste products is in operation. A layer of epithelial cells in the villi and of endothelial cells in the fetal capillaries separates the maternal and fetal blood. Waste products move from blood in the fetal capillaries across these layers into the maternal blood; nutrients, hormones, and growth factors move in the opposite direction. Some substances, such as oxygen and carbon dioxide, move by diffusion. Others, such as glucose, use transport proteins in the plasma membranes of the epithelial cells. Still other substances (e.g., several amino acids and hormones) are produced by the trophoblast layers of the placenta itself and added to the fetal and maternal blood. Note that there is an exchange of materials between the two bloodstreams but no actual mixing of the fetal and maternal blood. Umbilical veins carry oxygen and nutrient-rich blood from the placenta to the fetus, whereas umbilical arteries carry blood with waste products and a low oxygen content to the placenta.

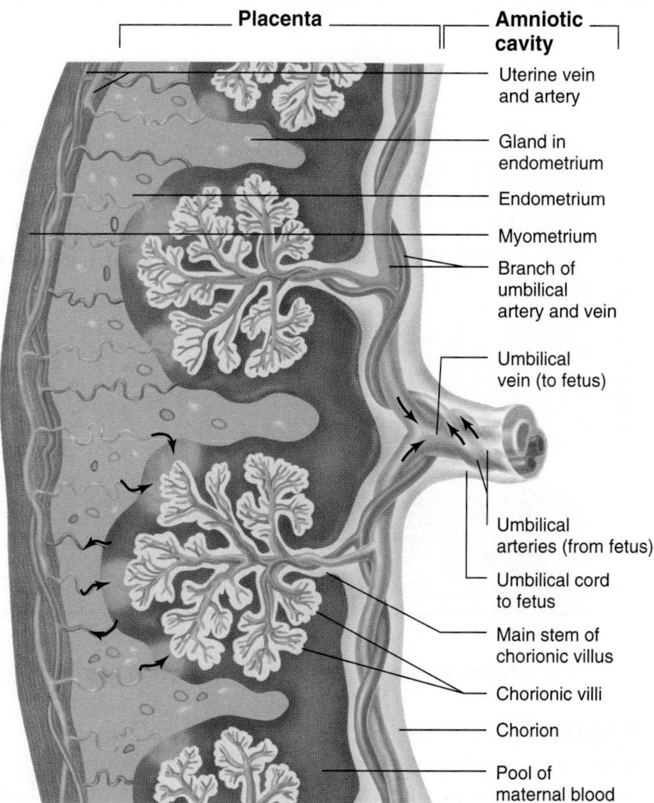

Figure 17.32 Interrelations of fetal and maternal tissues in the formation of the placenta. See Figure 17.33 for the orientation of the placenta. From B. M. Carlson, *Patten's Foundations of Embryology*, 5th ed., McGraw-Hill, New York.

PHYSIOLOGICAL INQUIRY

- How can you determine if a significant amount of fetal blood is leaking into the maternal circulatory system?

Answer can be found at end of chapter.

Meanwhile, a space called the **amniotic cavity** has formed between the inner cell mass and the chorion (**Figure 17.33**). The epithelial layer lining the cavity is derived from the inner cell mass and is called the **amnion,** or **amniotic sac.** It eventually fuses with the inner surface of the chorion so that only a single combined membrane surrounds the fetus. The fluid in the amniotic cavity, the **amniotic fluid,** resembles the fetal extracellular fluid, and it buffers mechanical disturbances and temperature variations. The fetus, floating in the amniotic cavity and attached by the umbilical cord to the placenta, develops into a viable infant during the next 8 months.

Amniotic fluid can be sampled by ***amniocentesis*** as early as the sixteenth week of pregnancy. This is done by inserting a needle into the amniotic cavity. Some genetic diseases can be diagnosed by the finding of certain chemicals either in the fluid or in sloughed fetal cells suspended in the fluid. The chromosomes of these fetal cells can also be examined for diagnosis of certain disorders as well as to determine the sex of the fetus. Another technique for fetal diagnosis is ***chorionic villus sampling.*** This technique, which can be performed as early as 9 to 12 weeks of pregnancy, involves obtaining tissue from a chorionic villus of the placenta. This technique, however, carries a higher risk of inducing the loss of the fetus (***miscarriage***) than does amniocentesis. A third technique for fetal diagnosis is ultrasound, which provides a "picture" of the fetus without the use of x-rays. A fourth technique for screening for fetal abnormalities involves obtaining only *maternal* blood and analyzing it for several normally occurring substances whose concentrations change in the presence of these abnormalities. For example, particular changes in the concentrations of two hormones produced during pregnancy—human chorionic gonadotropin and estriol—and alpha-fetoprotein (a major fetal plasma protein that crosses the placenta into the maternal blood) can identify many cases of ***Down syndrome,*** a genetic form of intellectual and developmental disability associated with distinct facial and body features.

Maternal nutrition is crucial for the fetus. Malnutrition early in pregnancy can cause specific abnormalities that are **congenital,** that is, existing at birth. Malnutrition retards fetal growth and results in infants with higher-than-normal death rates, reduced growth after birth, and an increased incidence of learning disabilities and other medical problems. Specific nutrients, not just total calories, are also very important. For example, there is an increased incidence of neural defects in the offspring of mothers who are deficient in the

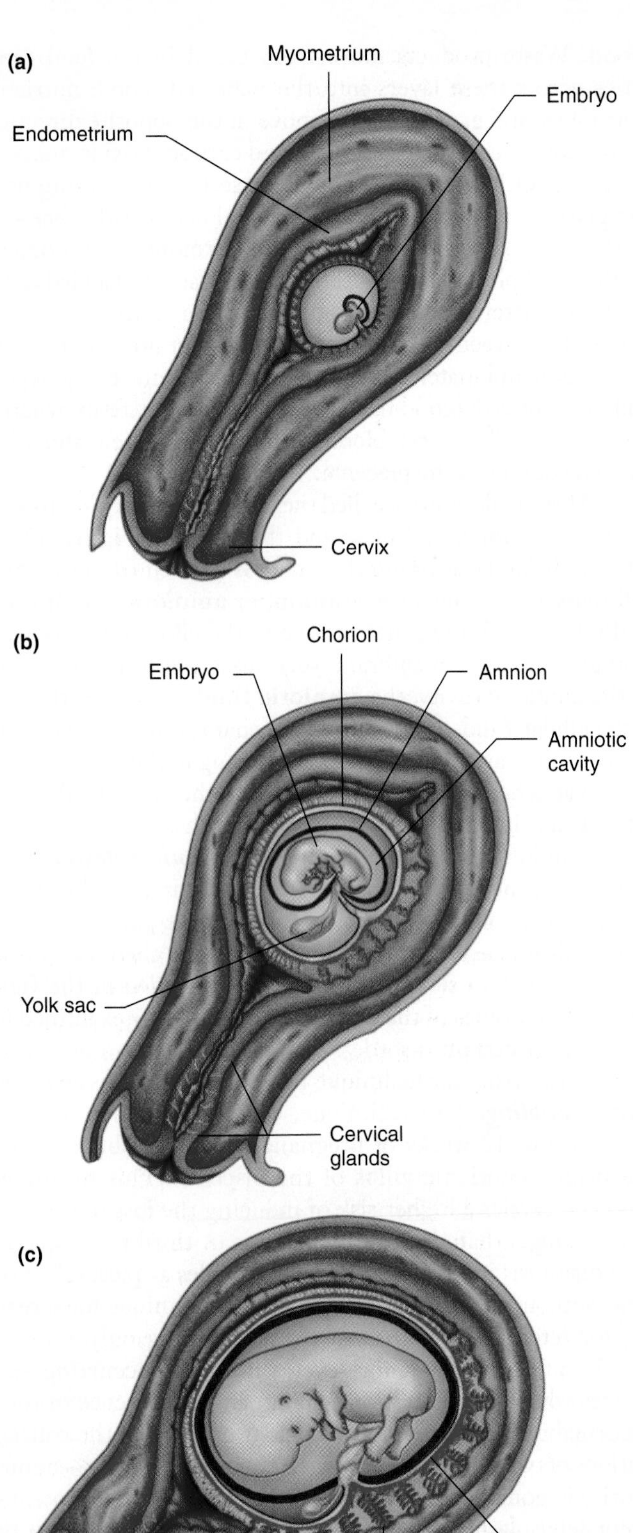

Figure 17.33 The uterus at (a) 3, (b) 5, and (c) 8 weeks after fertilization. Embryos and their membranes are drawn to actual size. Uterus is within actual size range. The yolk sac is formed from the trophoblast. It has no nutritional function in humans but is important in embryonic development. From B. M. Carlson, *Patten's Foundations of Embryology*, 5th ed., McGraw-Hill, New York.

B-vitamin folate (also called folic acid and folacin). Recall from Chapter 11 that normal maternal and fetal thyroid hormone concentrations are necessary for normal fetal development.

The developing embryo and fetus are also subject to considerable influences by a host of nonnutrient factors, such as noise, radiation, chemicals, and viruses, to which the mother may be exposed. For example, drugs taken by the mother can reach the fetus via transport across the placenta and can impair fetal growth and development. In this regard, it must be emphasized that aspirin, alcohol, and the chemicals in cigarette smoke are very potent agents, as are illicit drugs such as cocaine. Any agent that can cause birth defects in the fetus is known as a ***teratogen.***

Because half of the fetal genes—those from the father—differ from those of the mother, the fetus is in essence a foreign transplant in the mother. The integrity of the fetal–maternal blood barrier also protects the fetus from immunologic attack by the mother.

Hormonal and Other Changes During Pregnancy

Throughout pregnancy, plasma concentrations of estrogen and progesterone continually increase (**Figure 17.34**). Estrogen stimulates the growth of the uterine muscle mass,

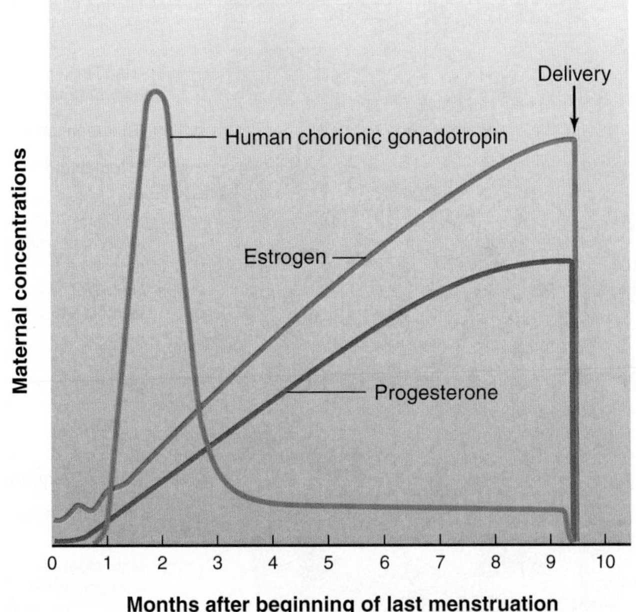

Figure 17.34 Maternal concentrations of estrogen, progesterone, and human chorionic gonadotropin during pregnancy. Curves depicting hormone concentrations are not drawn to scale. Note that the concentrations of estrogen and progesterone achieved in the maternal blood during pregnancy are much higher than during a typical menstrual cycle shown in Figure 17.22.

PHYSIOLOGICAL INQUIRY

- Why do progesterone and estrogen concentrations continue to increase during pregnancy even though human chorionic gonadotropin (hCG) concentration decreases?

Answer can be found at end of chapter.

which will eventually supply the contractile force needed to deliver the fetus. Progesterone inhibits uterine contractility so that the fetus is not expelled prematurely. During approximately the first 2 months of pregnancy, almost all the estrogen and progesterone are supplied by the corpus luteum.

Recall that if pregnancy had not occurred, the corpus luteum would have degenerated within 2 weeks after its formation. The persistence of the corpus luteum during pregnancy is due to a hormone called **human chorionic gonadotropin (hCG)**, which the trophoblast cells start to secrete around the time they start their endometrial invasion. Human chorionic gonadotropin gains entry to the maternal circulation, and the detection of this hormone in the mother's plasma and/or urine is used as a test for pregnancy. This glycoprotein is very similar to LH, and it not only prevents the corpus luteum from degenerating but strongly stimulates its steroid secretion. Thus, the signal that preserves the corpus luteum comes from the conceptus, not the mother's tissues. The rescue of the corpus luteum by hCG is an example of the general principle of physiology that information flow between organs allows for integration of physiological processes. That is, hCG secreted into maternal blood from the developing trophoblasts of embryonic origin stimulates the maternal ovaries to continue to secrete gonadal steroids. This, via negative feedback on maternal gonadotropin secretion, prevents additional menstrual cycles that would otherwise result in the loss of the implanted embryo.

The secretion of hCG reaches a peak 60 to 80 days after the last menstruation (see Figure 17.34). It then decreases just as rapidly, so that by the end of the third month it has reached a low concentration that changes little for the duration of the pregnancy. Associated with this decrease in hCG secretion, the placenta begins to secrete large quantities of estrogen and progesterone. The very marked increases in plasma concentrations of estrogen and progesterone during the last 6 months of pregnancy are due entirely to their secretion by the trophoblast cells of the placenta, and the corpus luteum regresses after 3 months.

An important aspect of placental steroid secretion is that the placenta has the enzymes required for the synthesis of progesterone but not those required for the formation of androgens, which are the precursors of estrogen. The placenta is supplied with androgens via the maternal ovaries and adrenal glands and by the *fetal* adrenal glands. The placenta converts the androgens into estrogen by expressing the enzyme aromatase.

The secretion of GnRH and, therefore, of LH and FSH is powerfully inhibited by high concentrations of progesterone in the presence of estrogen. Both of these gonadal steroids are secreted in high concentrations by the corpus luteum and then by the placenta throughout pregnancy, so the secretion of the pituitary gland gonadotropins remains extremely low. As a consequence, there are no ovarian or menstrual cycles during pregnancy.

The trophoblast cells of the placenta produce not only hCG and steroids but also inhibin and many other hormones that can influence the mother. One unique hormone that is secreted in very large amounts has effects similar to those of both prolactin and growth hormone. This protein hormone, **human placental lactogen,** mobilizes fats from maternal adipose tissue and stimulates glucose production in the liver (growth-hormone-like) in the mother. It also stimulates breast development (prolactin-like) in preparation for lactation. Some of the many other physiological changes, hormonal and nonhormonal, in the mother during pregnancy are summarized in **Table 17.9**.

Approximately 5% to 10% of pregnant women retain too much fluid (edema) and have protein in the urine and hypertension. These are the symptoms of ***preeclampsia;*** when convulsions also occur, the condition is termed ***eclampsia.*** These two syndromes are collectively called ***toxemia of pregnancy.*** This can result in decreased growth rate and death of the fetus. The factors responsible for eclampsia are unknown, but the evidence strongly implicates abnormal vasoconstriction of the maternal blood vessels and inadequate invasion of the endometrium by trophoblast cells, resulting in poor blood perfusion of the placenta.

Pregnancy Sickness

Some women suffer from ***pregnancy sickness*** (popularly called morning sickness), which is characterized by nausea and vomiting during the first 3 months (first trimester) of pregnancy. The exact cause is unknown, but high concentrations of estrogen and other substances may be responsible. It may also be linked with increased sensitivity to odors, such as those of certain foods. Whether or not pregnancy sickness has adaptive value is currently being debated. It has been speculated, for example, that pregnancy sickness may prevent ingestion of certain foods that may contain toxic alkaloid compounds or that carry parasites or other infectious organisms that could harm the developing fetus.

Parturition

A normal human pregnancy lasts approximately 40 weeks, counting from the first day of the last menstrual cycle, or approximately 38 weeks from the day of ovulation and conception. Survival of premature infants is now possible from about the twenty-fourth week of pregnancy. Treatment of these infants often requires heroic efforts, often with significant deficits in the infant.

During the last few weeks of pregnancy, a variety of events occur in the uterus and the fetus, culminating in the birth (delivery) of the infant, followed by the placenta. All of these events, including delivery, are collectively called **parturition.** Throughout most of pregnancy, the smooth muscle cells of the myometrium are relatively disconnected from each other and the uterus is sealed at its outlet by the firm, inflexible collagen fibers that constitute the cervix. These features are maintained mainly by progesterone. During the last few weeks of pregnancy, as a result of ever-increasing concentrations of estrogen, the smooth muscle cells synthesize *connexins*, proteins that form gap junctions between the cells, which allow the myometrium to undergo coordinated contractions. Simultaneously, the cervix becomes soft and flexible due to an enzymatically mediated breakdown of its collagen fibers. The synthesis of the enzymes is

TABLE 17.9	Maternal Responses to Pregnancy
Placenta	Secretion of estrogen, progesterone, human chorionic gonadotropin, inhibin, human placental lactogen, and other hormones
Anterior pituitary gland	Increased secretion of prolactin Secretes very little FSH and LH
Adrenal cortex	Increased secretion of aldosterone and cortisol
Posterior pituitary gland	Increased secretion of vasopressin
Parathyroids	Increased secretion of parathyroid hormone
Kidneys	Increased secretion of renin, erythropoietin, and 1,25-dihydroxyvitamin D Retention of salt and water *Cause:* Increased aldosterone, vasopressin, and estrogen
Breasts	Enlarge and develop mature glandular structure *Cause:* Estrogen, progesterone, prolactin, and human placental lactogen
Blood volume	Increased *Cause:* Total erythrocyte number increased by erythropoietin, and plasma volume by salt and water retention; however, plasma volume usually increases more than red cells, thereby leading to small decreases in hematocrit
Bone turnover	Increased *Cause:* Increased parathyroid hormone and 1,25-dihydroxyvitamin D
Body weight	Increased by average of 12.5 kg, 60% of which is water
Circulation	Cardiac output increases, total peripheral resistance decreases (vasodilation in uterus, skin, breasts, GI tract, and kidneys), and mean arterial pressure stays constant
Respiration	Hyperventilation occurs (arterial P_{CO_2} decreases) due to the effects of increased progesterone
Organic metabolism	Metabolic rate increases Plasma glucose, gluconeogenesis, and fatty acid mobilization all increase *Cause:* Hyporesponsiveness to insulin due to insulin antagonism by human placental lactogen and cortisol
Appetite and thirst	Increased (particularly after the first trimester)
Nutritional RDAs*	Increased

*RDA—Recommended daily allowance

mediated by a variety of messengers, including estrogen and placental prostaglandins, the synthesis of which is stimulated by estrogen. The peptide hormone **relaxin** is secreted by the ovaries, placenta, and uterus and softens cartilaginous joints in the pelvis. Estrogen has yet another important effect on the myometrium during this period: It induces the synthesis of receptors for the posterior pituitary hormone oxytocin, which is a powerful stimulator of uterine smooth muscle contraction.

Delivery is produced by strong rhythmic contractions of the myometrium. Actually, weak and infrequent uterine contractions begin at approximately 30 weeks and gradually increase in both strength and frequency. During the last month, the entire uterine contents shift downward so that the near-term fetus is brought into contact with the cervix. In over 90% of births, the baby's head is downward and acts as the wedge to dilate the cervical canal when labor begins (**Figure 17.35**). Occasionally, a baby is oriented with some other part of the body downward (***breech presentation***). This can require the surgical delivery of the fetus and placenta through an abdominal and uterine incision (***cesarean section***).

At the onset of labor and delivery or before, the amniotic sac ruptures, and the amniotic fluid flows through the vagina. When labor begins in earnest, the uterine contractions become strong and occur at approximately 10 to 15 min intervals. The contractions begin in the upper portion of the uterus and sweep downward.

As the contractions increase in intensity and frequency, the cervix is gradually forced open (dilation) to a maximum

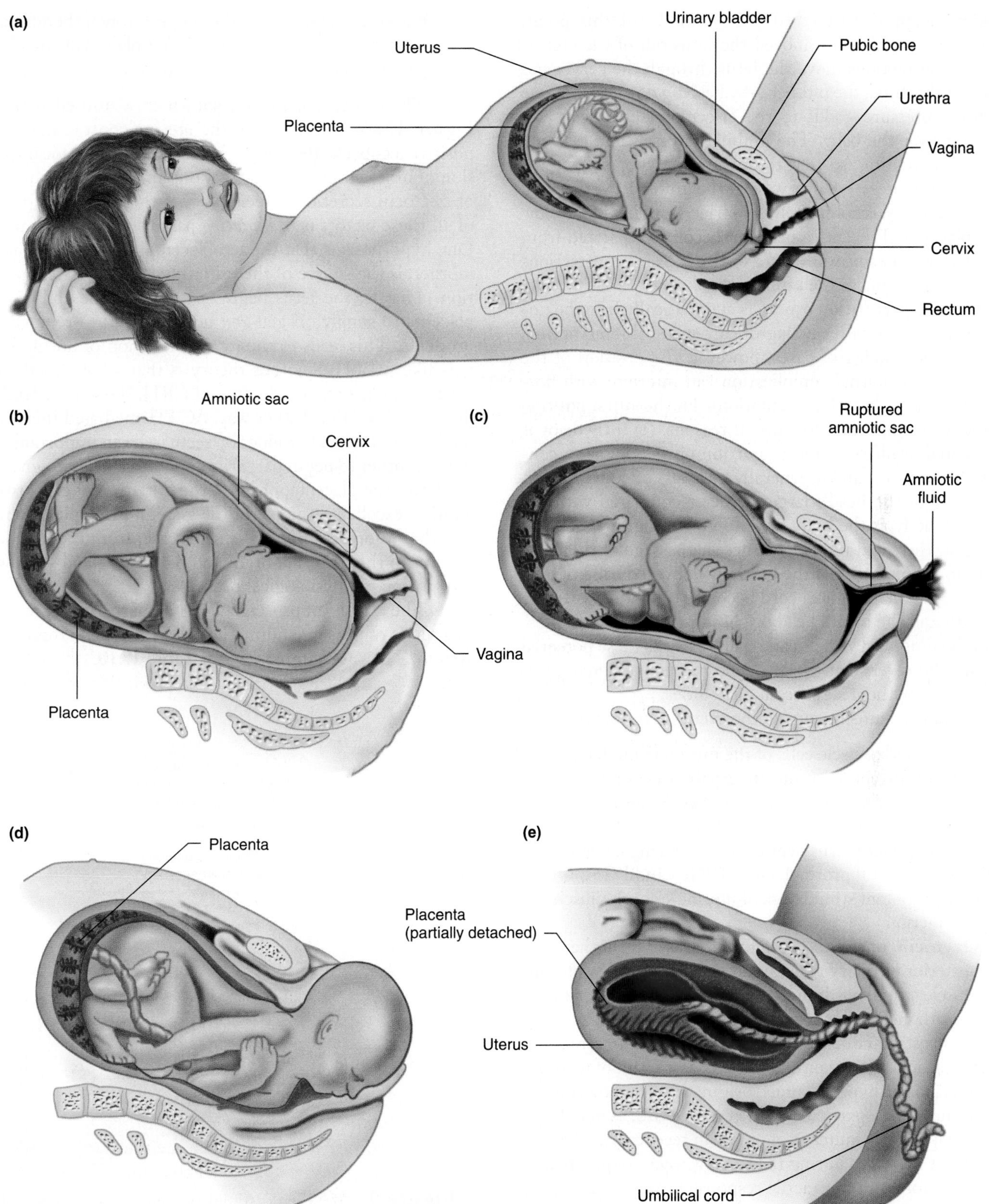

Figure 17.35 Stages of parturition. (a) Parturition has not yet begun. (b) The cervix is dilating. (c) The cervix is completely dilated, and the fetus's head is entering the cervical canal; the amniotic sac has ruptured and the amniotic fluid escapes. (d) The fetus is moving through the vagina. (e) The placenta is coming loose from the uterine wall in preparation for its expulsion.

diameter of approximately 10 cm (4 in). Until this point, the contractions have not moved the fetus out of the uterus. Now the contractions move the fetus through the cervix and vagina. At this time, the mother—by bearing down to increase abdominal pressure—adds to the effect of uterine contractions to deliver the baby. The umbilical vessels and placenta are still functioning, so that the baby is not yet on its own; but within minutes of delivery, both the umbilical vessels and the placental vessels completely constrict, stopping blood flow to the placenta. The entire placenta becomes separated from the underlying uterine wall, and a wave of uterine contractions delivers the placenta as the **afterbirth.**

Usually, parturition proceeds automatically from beginning to end and requires no significant medical intervention. In a small percentage of cases, however, the position of the baby or some maternal complication can interfere with normal delivery (e.g., breech presentation). The headfirst position of the fetus is important for several reasons. (1) If the baby is not oriented headfirst, another portion of its body is in contact with the cervix and is generally a far less effective wedge. (2) Because of the head's large diameter compared with the rest of the body, if the body were to go through the cervical canal first, the canal might obstruct the passage of the head, leading to problems when the partially delivered baby tries to breathe. (3) If the umbilical cord becomes caught between the canal wall and the baby's head or chest, mechanical compression of the umbilical vessels can result. Despite these potential problems, however, many babies who are not oriented headfirst are born without significant difficulties.

What mechanisms control the events of parturition?

1. The smooth muscle cells of the myometrium have inherent rhythmicity and are capable of autonomous contractions, which are facilitated as the muscle is stretched by the growing fetus.
2. The pregnant uterus near term and during labor secretes several prostaglandins (PGE_2 and $PGF_{2\alpha}$) that are potent stimulators of uterine smooth muscle contraction.
3. **Oxytocin,** one of the hormones released from the posterior pituitary gland, is an extremely potent uterine muscle stimulant. It not only acts directly on uterine smooth muscle but also stimulates it to synthesize the prostaglandins. Oxytocin is reflexively secreted from the posterior pituitary gland as a result of neural input to the hypothalamus, originating from receptors in the uterus, particularly the cervix. Also, as noted previously, the number of oxytocin receptors in the uterus increases during the last few weeks of pregnancy. Therefore, the contractile response to any given plasma concentration of oxytocin is greatly increased at parturition.
4. Throughout pregnancy, progesterone exerts an essential powerful inhibitory effect upon uterine contractions by decreasing the sensitivity of the myometrium to estrogen, oxytocin, and prostaglandins. Unlike the situation in many other species, however, the rate of progesterone secretion does not decrease before or during parturition in women (until after delivery of the placenta, the source of the progesterone); therefore, progesterone withdrawal does not play a role in parturition.

These mechanisms are shown in a unified pattern in **Figure 17.36**. Once started, the uterine contractions exert a positive feedback effect upon themselves via both local facilitation of inherent uterine contractions and reflexive stimulation of oxytocin secretion. Precisely what the relative importance of all these factors is in *initiating* parturition remains unclear. One hypothesis is that the fetoplacental unit, rather than the mother, is the source of the initiating signals to start parturition. That is, the fetus begins to outstrip the ability of the placenta to supply oxygen and nutrients and to remove waste products. This leads to the fetal production of hormonal signals like ACTH. Another theory is that a "placental clock," acting via placental production of CRH, signals the fetal production of ACTH. Either way, ACTH-mediated increases in fetal adrenal steroid production seem to be an important signal to the mother to begin parturition. Whether it is a signal from the fetus, the placenta, or both, the initiation of parturition is another excellent example of the general principle of physiology that information flow—in this case, from the fetoplacental unit to the maternal brain and pituitary gland—allows for integration of physiological processes.

The actions of prostaglandins on parturition are the last in a series of prostaglandin effects on the female reproductive system. They are summarized in **Table 17.10**.

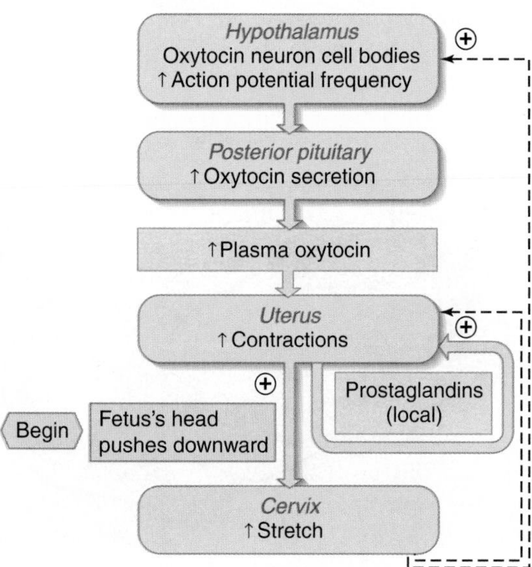

Figure 17.36 Factors stimulating uterine contractions during parturition. Note the positive feedback nature of several of the inputs.

PHYSIOLOGICAL INQUIRY

- If a full-term fetus is oriented feet-first in the uterus, parturition may not proceed in a timely manner. Why?

Answer can be found at end of chapter.

TABLE 17.10	Some Effects of Prostaglandins* on the Female Reproductive System	
Site of Production	**Action of Prostaglandins**	**Result**
Late antral follicle	Stimulate production of digestive enzymes	Rupture of follicle
Corpus luteum	May interfere with hormone secretion and function	Death of corpus luteum
Uterus	Constrict blood vessels in endometrium	Onset of menstruation
	Cause changes in endometrial blood vessels and cells early in pregnancy	Facilitates implantation
	Increase contraction of myometrium	Helps to initiate both menstruation and parturition
	Cause cervical ripening	Facilitates cervical dilation during parturition

*The term *prostaglandins* is used loosely here, as is customary in reproductive physiology, to include all the eicosanoids.

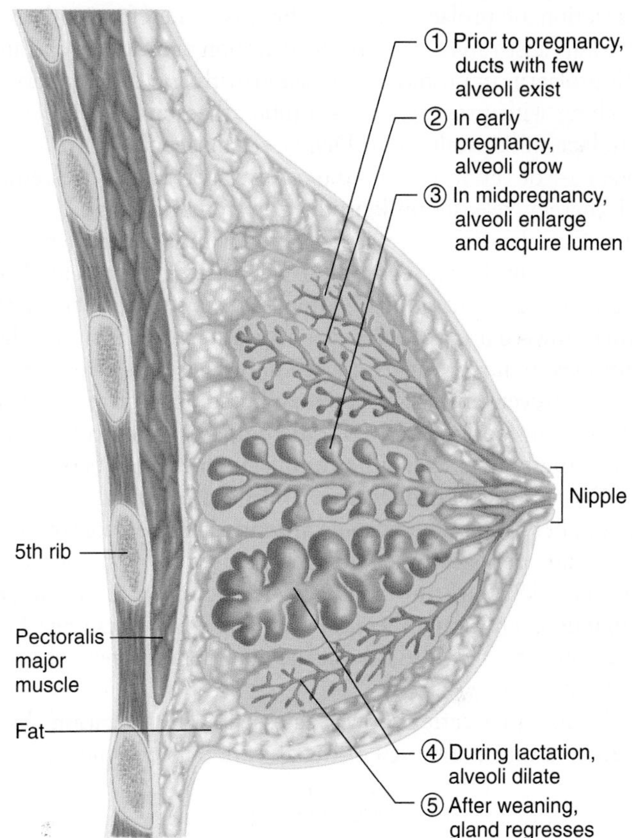

① Prior to pregnancy, ducts with few alveoli exist
② In early pregnancy, alveoli grow
③ In midpregnancy, alveoli enlarge and acquire lumen
Nipple
5th rib
Pectoralis major muscle
Fat
④ During lactation, alveoli dilate
⑤ After weaning, gland regresses

Figure 17.37 APIR Anatomy of the breast. The numbers refer to the sequential changes that occur over time. Adapted from Elias et al.

Lactation

The production and secretion of milk by the **mammary glands,** which are located within the breasts, is called **lactogenesis.** The mammary glands undergo an increase in size and cell number during late pregnancy. After birth of the baby, milk is produced and secreted; this process is also known as **lactation** (or nursing). Each breast contains numerous mammary glands, each with ducts that branch all through the tissue and converge at the nipples (**Figure 17.37**). These ducts start in saclike structures called **alveoli** (the same term is used to denote the lung air sacs). The breast alveoli, which are the sites of milk secretion, look like bunches of grapes with stems terminating in the ducts. The alveoli and the ducts immediately adjacent to them are surrounded by specialized contractile cells called **myoepithelial cells.**

Before puberty, the breasts are small with little internal glandular structure. With the onset of puberty in females, the increased estrogen concentration stimulates duct growth and branching but relatively little development of the alveoli; much of the breast enlargement at this time is due to fat deposition. Progesterone secretion also commences at puberty during the luteal phase of each cycle, and this hormone contributes to breast growth by stimulating the growth of alveoli.

During each menstrual cycle, the breasts undergo fluctuations in association with the changing blood concentrations of estrogen and progesterone. These changes are small compared with the breast enlargement that occurs during pregnancy as a result of the stimulatory effects of high plasma concentrations of estrogen, progesterone, prolactin, and human placental lactogen. Except for prolactin, which is secreted by the maternal anterior pituitary gland, these hormones are secreted by the placenta. Under the influence of these hormones, both the ductal and the alveolar structures become fully developed.

As described in Chapter 11, other factors influence the anterior pituitary gland cells that secrete prolactin. They are inhibited by **dopamine,** which is secreted by the hypothalamus. They are probably stimulated by at least one **prolactin-releasing factor** (**PRF**), also secreted by the hypothalamus (the chemical identity of PRF in humans is still uncertain). The dopamine and PRF secreted by the hypothalamus are hypophysiotropic hormones that reach the anterior pituitary gland by way of the hypothalamo–hypophyseal portal vessels. This positive and negative hypophysiotropic control of the secretion of prolactin is reminiscent of the dual hypophysiotropic control of growth hormone described in Figure 11.28 and is an example of the general principle of physiology that functions are controlled by multiple regulatory systems, often acting in opposition.

Under the dominant inhibitory influence of dopamine, prolactin secretion is low before puberty. It then increases considerably at puberty in girls but not in boys, stimulated by the increased plasma estrogen concentration that occurs at this time. During pregnancy, there is a further large increase in prolactin secretion due to stimulation by estrogen.

Prolactin is the major hormone stimulating the production of milk. However, despite the fact that prolactin concentrations are increased and the breasts are considerably enlarged and fully developed as pregnancy progresses, there is usually no secretion of milk. This is because estrogen and progesterone, in large concentrations, prevent milk production by inhibiting this action of prolactin on the breasts. Therefore, although estrogen causes an increase in the secretion of prolactin and acts with prolactin in promoting breast growth and differentiation, it—along with progesterone—inhibits the ability of prolactin to induce milk production. Delivery removes the source—the placenta—of the large amounts of estrogen and progesterone and, thereby, releases milk production from inhibition.

The decrease in estrogen following parturition also causes *basal* prolactin secretion to decrease from its peak, late-pregnancy concentrations. After several months, prolactin returns toward prepregnancy concentrations even if the mother continues to nurse. Superimposed upon these basal concentrations, however, are large secretory bursts of prolactin during each nursing period. The episodic pulses of prolactin are signals to the breasts to maintain milk production. These pulses usually cease several days after the mother completely stops nursing her infant but continue as long as nursing continues.

The reflexes mediating the surges of prolactin (**Figure 17.38**) are initiated by afferent input to the hypothalamus from nipple receptors stimulated by suckling. This input's major effect is to inhibit the hypothalamic neurons that release dopamine.

One other reflex process is essential for lactation. Milk is secreted into the lumen of the alveoli, but the infant cannot suck the milk out of the breast. It must first be moved into the ducts, from which it can be suckled. This movement is called the **milk ejection reflex** (also called milk letdown) and is accomplished by contraction of the myoepithelial cells surrounding the alveoli. The contraction is under the control of oxytocin, which is reflexively released from posterior pituitary gland neurons in response to suckling (see Figure 17.38). Higher brain centers can also exert an important influence over oxytocin release; a nursing mother may actually leak milk when she hears her baby cry or even thinks about nursing.

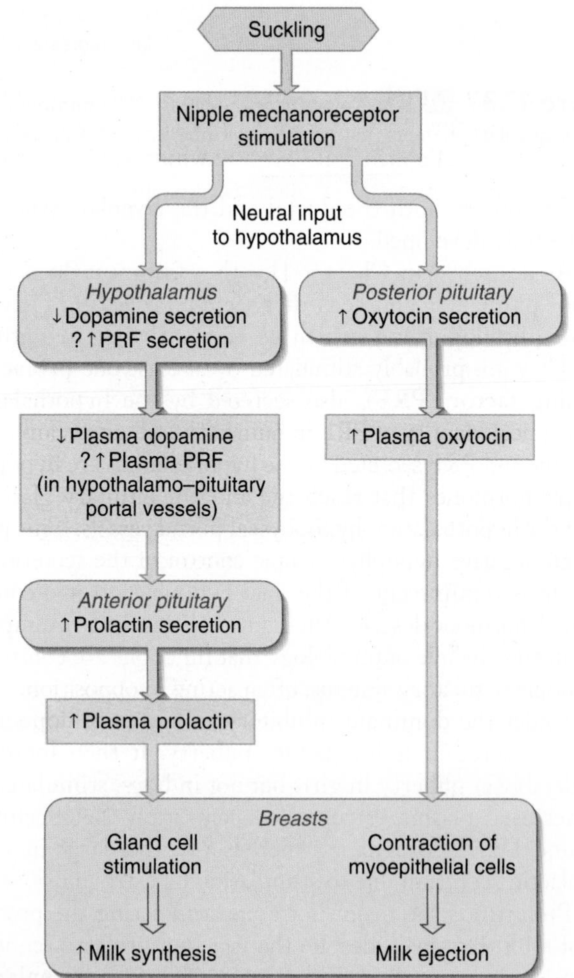

Figure 17.38 Major controls of the secretion of prolactin and oxytocin during nursing. The importance of PRF (prolactin-releasing factors) in humans is not known (indicated by ?).

Suckling also inhibits the hypothalamo–hypophyseal–ovarian axis at a variety of steps, with a resultant block of ovulation. This is probably due to increased prolactin, which directly inhibits gonadotropin secretion, and direct effects on the hypothalamic GnRH neurons. If suckling is continued at high frequency, ovulation can be delayed for months to years. This "natural" birth control may help to space out pregnancies. When supplements are added to the baby's diet and the frequency of suckling is decreased, however, most women will resume ovulation even though they continue to nurse. However, ovulation may resume even without a decrease in nursing. Failure to use adequate birth control may result in an unplanned pregnancy in nursing women.

After delivery, the breasts initially secrete a watery, protein-rich fluid called **colostrum.** After about 24 to 48 hours, the secretion of milk itself begins. Milk contains six major nutrients: water, proteins, lipids, the carbohydrate lactose (milk sugar), minerals, and vitamins.

Colostrum and milk also contain antibodies, leukocytes, and other messengers of the immune system, all of which are important for the protection of the newborn, as well as for longer-term activation of the child's own immune system. Milk also contains many growth factors and hormones thought to help in tissue development and maturation, as well as a large number of neuropeptides and endogenous opioids that may subtly shape the infant's brain and behavior. Some of these substances are synthesized by the breasts themselves, not just transported from blood to milk. The reasons the milk proteins can gain entry to the newborn's blood are that (1) the low gastric acidity of the newborn does not denature them, and (2) the newborn's intestinal epithelium is more permeable to proteins than is the adult epithelium.

Unfortunately, infectious agents, including the virus that causes AIDS, can also be transmitted through breast milk, as can some drugs. For example, the concentration of alcohol in breast milk is approximately the same as in maternal plasma.

Breast-feeding for at least the first 6 to 12 months is strongly advocated by health care professionals. In less-developed countries, where alternative formulas are often either contaminated or nutritionally inadequate because of improper dilution or inadequate refrigeration, breast-feeding significantly reduces infant sickness and mortality. In the United States, effects on infant survival are not usually apparent, but breast-feeding reduces the severity of gastrointestinal infections, has positive effects on mother–infant interaction, is economical, and has long-term health benefits. Cow's milk has many but not all of the constituents of mother's milk—and often in very different concentrations, and it is difficult to duplicate mother's milk in a commercial formula.

Contraception

Physiologically, pregnancy is said to begin not at fertilization but after implantation is complete, approximately one week *after* fertilization. Birth control methods that work prior to implantation are called ***contraceptives*** (**Table 17.11**). Procedures that cause the death of the embryo or fetus after implantation are called ***abortions;*** chemical substances used to induce abortions are called ***abortifacients.***

Some forms of contraception, such as vasectomy, tubal ligation, vaginal diaphragms, vaginal caps, spermicides, and condoms, prevent sperm from reaching the egg. In addition, condoms significantly reduce the risk of ***sexually transmitted diseases*** (***STDs***) such as AIDS, syphilis, gonorrhea, chlamydia, and herpes.

Oral contraceptives are based on the fact that estrogen and progesterone can inhibit pituitary gland gonadotropin release, thereby preventing ovulation. One type of oral contraceptive is a combination of a synthetic estrogen and a progesterone-like substance (a progestogen or progestin). Another type is the so-called minipill, which contains only the progesterone-like substance. In actuality, the oral contraceptives, particularly the minipill, do not always prevent ovulation, but they are still effective because they have other contraceptive effects. For example, progestogens affect the composition of the cervical mucus, reducing the ability of the sperm to pass through the cervix, and they also inhibit the estrogen-induced proliferation of the endometrium, making it inhospitable for implantation. There are now many different other types of oral contraceptive pills that utilize different timing, combinations, and doses of hormones. An extensive discussion of these is beyond the depth of this chapter—more details can be found at www.fda.gov.

Another method of delivering a contraceptive progestogen is via tiny capsules that are implanted beneath the skin and last for 5 years. Yet another method is the intramuscular injection of a different progestogen substance (e.g., ***Depo-Provera*** or ***Lunelle***) every 1 to 3 months. Alternate methods of providing highly efficacious hormonal contraception include skin patches and vaginal rings.

The ***intrauterine device*** (***IUD***) works beyond the point of fertilization but before implantation has begun or is complete. The presence of one of these small objects in the uterus somehow interferes with the endometrial preparation for acceptance of the blastocyst.

In addition to the methods used before intercourse (precoital contraception), there are a variety of drugs used within 72 h *after* intercourse (postcoital or emergency contraception). These most commonly interfere with ovulation, transport of the conceptus to the uterus, or implantation. One approach is a high dose of estrogen, or two large doses (12 h apart) of a combined estrogen–progestin oral contraceptive. Another approach has used the drug ***RU 486*** (***mifepristone***), which has antiprogesterone activity because it binds competitively to progesterone receptors in the uterus but does not activate them. Antagonism of progesterone's effects causes the endometrium to erode and the contractions of the fallopian tubes and myometrium to increase. RU 486 can also be used later in pregnancy as an abortifacient.

The ***rhythm method*** uses abstention from sexual intercourse near the time of ovulation. Unfortunately, it is difficult to time ovulation precisely, even with laboratory techniques. For example, the small increase in body temperature or change in vaginal epithelium, both of which are indicators of ovulation, occur only *after* ovulation. This, combined with the

TABLE 17.11 Some Forms of Contraception

Method	First-Year Failure Rate*	Physiological Mechanism of Effectiveness
Barrier methods	12%–23%	Prevent sperm from entering uterus
Condoms (♂ and ♀)		
Diaphragm/cervical cap (♀)		
Spermicides (♀)	20%–50%	Kill sperm in the vagina (after insemination)
Sterilization	<0.5%	
Vasectomy (♂)		Prevents sperm from becoming part of seminal fluid
Tubal ligation (♀)		Prevents sperm from reaching egg
Intrauterine device (IUD) (♀)	<3%	Prevents implantation of blastocyst
Estrogens and/or progestins		Prevent ovulation by suppressing LH surge (negative feedback); thicken cervical mucus (prevents sperm from entering uterus); alter endometrium to prevent implantation of blastocyst
Oral contraceptive pill (♀)	3%	
Emergency oral contraception (♀)	1%	
Injectable or implantable progestins (♀)	<0.5%	
Transdermal (skin patch) (♀)	1%–2%	
Vaginal ring (♀)	1%–2%	

*From Hall, J. E., Infertility and Fertility Control, *Harrison's Principles of Internal Medicine*, McGraw-Hill, 2004; Rosen, M., and Cedars, M. I., Female Reproductive Endocrinology and Infertility, *Basic and Clinical Endocrinology*, 7th ed., McGraw-Hill, 2004; ACOG Practice Bulletin, Emergency Contraception, *Obstet. Gynecol.* 2005, 106:1443–52. See also www.fda.gov. Failure rate assumes proper and consistent use.

Notes:

Spermicides are often used in combination with diaphragm/cervical cap and condoms.

Only condoms are effective in preventing sexually transmitted diseases.

The cervical sponge was made available again in 2009.

Rhythm method (abstinence around time of ovulation) and coitus interruptus (withdrawal) are not listed because they are not reliable.

Only total abstinence is 100% effective in preventing pregnancy.

marked variability of the time of ovulation in many women—from day 5 to day 15 of the cycle, explains why the rhythm method has a high failure rate.

There are still no effective chemical agents for male contraception. One potential approach is to decrease gonadotropin concentrations, which would decrease spermatogenesis. Testosterone would then have to be given to maintain libido.

Infertility

Approximately 12% of men and women of reproductive age in the United States are infertile. The numbers of infertile men and women are approximately equal until about age 30, after which infertility becomes more prevalent in women. In many cases, infertility can be successfully treated with drugs, artificial insemination, or corrective surgery.

When the cause of infertility cannot be treated, it can sometimes be circumvented in women by the technique of ***in vitro fertilization.*** First, the woman is injected with drugs that stimulate multiple egg production. Immediately before ovulation, at least one egg is then removed from the ovary via a needle inserted into the ovary through the top of the vagina or the lower abdominal wall. The egg is placed in a dish for several days with sperm. After the fertilized egg has developed into a cluster of two to eight cells, it is then transferred to the woman's uterus. The success rate of this procedure, when one egg is transferred, is only about 15% to 20%.

17.20 Menopause

When a woman is around the age of 50, on average, menstrual cycles become less regular. Ultimately, they cease entirely in all women; this cessation is known as **menopause,** which is a natural and normal event. The phase of life during which menstrual irregularity begins is termed **perimenopause.** It involves many physical and emotional changes accompanying the cessation of reproductive function.

Menopause and the irregular function leading to it are caused primarily by ovarian failure. The ovaries lose their ability to respond to the gonadotropins, mainly because most, if not all, ovarian follicles and eggs have disappeared by this time through atresia. The hypothalamus and anterior pituitary gland continue to function relatively normally as demonstrated by the fact that the gonadotropins are secreted in greater amounts. The main reason for this is that the decreased plasma estrogen and inhibin do not exert as much negative feedback on gonadotropin secretion.

A small amount of estrogen usually persists in plasma beyond menopause, mainly from the peripheral conversion of adrenal androgens to estrogen by aromatase, but the concentration is inadequate to maintain estrogen-dependent tissues. The breasts and genital organs gradually atrophy to a large degree. Thinning and dryness of the vaginal epithelium can cause sexual intercourse to be painful. Because estrogen is a potent bone-protective hormone, significant decreases in bone mass may occur (***osteoporosis***). This results in an increased risk of bone fractures in postmenopausal women. The ***hot flashes*** so typical of menopause are periodic sudden feelings of warmth, dilation of the skin arterioles, and marked sweating. In addition, the incidence of cardiovascular disease increases after menopause. Women have much less coronary artery disease than men until after menopause, when the incidence becomes similar in both sexes, a pattern that is due to the protective effects of estrogen; estrogen exerts beneficial actions on plasma cholesterol and also exerts multiple direct protective actions on vessel walls. Recent studies, however, have questioned the long-term protective effects of estrogen in the prevention of heart disease.

Many of the symptoms associated with menopause, as well as the development of osteoporosis, can be reduced by the administration of estrogen. Recent studies also indicate that estrogen use may reduce the risk of developing Alzheimer disease and may also be useful in the treatment of this disease.

The desirability of administering estrogen to postmenopausal women is controversial, however, because estrogen administration increases the risk of developing uterine endometrial cancer and breast cancer. The increased risk of endometrial cancer can be reduced by the administration of a progestogen along with estrogen, but the progestogen does not influence the risk of breast cancer. The progestogen only slightly lessens estrogen's protective effect against coronary artery disease.

Relevant to the question of hormone-replacement therapy (as well as to the hormonal treatment of breast and uterine cancer) is the development of drugs, such as ***tamoxifen,*** that exert some proestrogenic and some antiestrogenic effects. These drugs are collectively termed ***selective estrogen receptor modulators*** (***SERMs***) because they activate estrogen receptors in certain tissues but not in others; moreover, in these latter tissues, SERMs act as estrogen antagonists. Obviously, the ideal would be to have a SERM that has the proestrogenic effect of protecting against osteoporosis, heart attacks, and Alzheimer disease but opposes the development of breast and uterine cancers. What makes this type of SERM possible? One important contributor is that there are two distinct forms of estrogen receptors, which are affected differentially by different SERMs.

SECTION C SUMMARY

Anatomy

I. The female internal genitalia are the ovaries, fallopian tubes, uterus, cervix, and vagina.
II. The female external genitalia include the mons pubis, labia, clitoris, and vestibule of the vagina. These are also called the vulva.

Ovarian Functions

I. The female gonads, the ovaries, produce eggs and secrete estrogen, progesterone, and inhibin.
II. The two meiotic divisions of oogenesis result in each ovum having 23 chromosomes, in contrast to the 46 of the original oogonia.
III. The follicle consists of the egg, inner layers of granulosa cells surrounding the egg, and outer layers of theca cells.
IV. At the beginning of each menstrual cycle, a group of preantral and early antral follicles continues to develop, but soon only the dominant follicle continues its development to full maturity and ovulation.
V. Following ovulation, the remaining cells of that follicle differentiate into the corpus luteum, which lasts about 10 to 14 days if pregnancy does not occur.
VI. The menstrual cycle can be divided, according to ovarian events, into a follicular phase and a luteal phase, which each lasts approximately 14 days; they are separated by ovulation.

Control of Ovarian Function

I. The menstrual cycle results from a finely tuned interplay of hormones secreted by the ovaries, the anterior pituitary gland, and the hypothalamus.

II. During the early and middle follicular phases, FSH stimulates the granulosa cells to proliferate and secrete estrogen, and LH stimulates the theca cells to proliferate and produce the androgens that the granulosa cells use to make estrogen.
   a. During this time, estrogen exerts negative feedback on the anterior pituitary gland to inhibit the secretion of the gonadotropins. It probably also inhibits the secretion of GnRH by the hypothalamus.
   b. Inhibin preferentially inhibits FSH secretion.

III. During the late follicular phase, plasma estrogen increases to elicit a surge of LH, which then causes, via the granulosa cells, completion of the egg's first meiotic division and cytoplasmic maturation, ovulation, and formation of the corpus luteum.

IV. During the luteal phase, under the influence of small amounts of LH, the corpus luteum secretes progesterone and estrogen. Regression of the corpus luteum results in a cessation of the secretion of these hormones.

V. Secretion of GnRH and the gonadotropins is inhibited during the luteal phase by the combination of progesterone, estrogen, and inhibin.

Uterine Changes in the Menstrual Cycle

I. The ovarian follicular phase is equivalent to the uterine menstrual and proliferative phases, the first day of menstruation being the first day of the cycle. The ovarian luteal phase is equivalent to the uterine secretory phase.
   a. Menstruation occurs when the plasma estrogen and progesterone concentrations decrease as a result of regression of the corpus luteum.
   b. During the proliferative phase, estrogen stimulates growth of the endometrium and myometrium and causes the cervical mucus to be readily penetrable by sperm.
   c. During the secretory phase, progesterone converts the estrogen-primed endometrium to a secretory tissue and makes the cervical mucus relatively impenetrable to sperm. It also inhibits uterine contractions.

Additional Effects of Gonadal Steroids

I. The many effects of estrogen and progesterone are summarized in Table 17.8.

II. Androgens are produced in women and have several functions including growth of pubic and axillary hair.

III. Excess androgen can cause virilization.

Puberty

I. At puberty, the hypothalamo–pituitary–gonadal axis becomes active as a result of a change in brain function that permits increased secretion of GnRH.

II. The first sign of puberty is the appearance of pubic and axillary hair.

Female Sexual Response

I. Sexual intercourse results in increases in blood flow and muscular contractions throughout the body.

II. Androgens appear to be important in libido in women.

Pregnancy

I. After ovulation, the egg is swept into the fallopian tube, where a sperm, having undergone capacitation and the acrosome reaction, fertilizes it.

II. Following fertilization, the egg undergoes its second meiotic division and the nuclei of the egg and sperm fuse. Reactions in the ovum block penetration by other sperm and trigger cell division and embryogenesis.

III. The conceptus undergoes cleavage, eventually becoming a blastocyst, which implants in the endometrium on approximately day 7 after ovulation.
   a. The trophoblast gives rise to the fetal part of the placenta, whereas the inner cell mass develops into the embryo proper.
   b. Although they do not mix, fetal blood and maternal blood both flow through the placenta, exchanging gases, nutrients, hormones, waste products, and other substances.
   c. The fetus is surrounded by amniotic fluid in the amniotic sac.

IV. The progesterone and estrogen required to maintain the uterus during pregnancy come from the corpus luteum for the first 2 months of pregnancy, their secretion stimulated by human chorionic gonadotropin produced by the trophoblast.

V. During the last 7 months of pregnancy, the corpus luteum regresses and the placenta itself produces large amounts of progesterone and estrogen.

VI. The high concentrations of progesterone, in the presence of estrogen, inhibit the secretion of GnRH and thereby that of the gonadotropins, so that menstrual cycles do not occur.

VII. Delivery occurs by rhythmic contractions of the uterus, which first dilate the cervix and then move the infant, followed by the placenta, through the vagina. The contractions are stimulated in part by oxytocin, released from the posterior pituitary gland in a reflex triggered by uterine mechanoreceptors, and by uterine prostaglandins.

VIII. The breasts develop markedly during pregnancy as a result of the combined influences of estrogen, progesterone, prolactin, and human placental lactogen.
   a. Prolactin secretion is stimulated during pregnancy by estrogen acting on the anterior pituitary gland, but milk is not synthesized because high concentrations of estrogen and progesterone inhibit the milk-producing action of prolactin on the breasts.
   b. As a result of the suckling reflex, large bursts of prolactin and oxytocin are released during nursing. The prolactin stimulates milk production and the oxytocin causes milk ejection.

Menopause

I. When a woman is around the age of 50, her menstrual cycles become less regular and ultimately disappear—menopause.
   a. The cause of menopause is a decrease in the number of ovarian follicles and their hyporesponsiveness to the gonadotropins.
   b. The symptoms of menopause are largely due to the marked decrease in plasma estrogen concentration.

SECTION C REVIEW QUESTIONS

1. Draw the female reproductive tract.
2. Describe the various stages from oogonium to mature ovum.
3. Describe the progression from a primordial follicle to a dominant follicle.
4. Name three hormones produced by the ovaries and name the cells that produce them.
5. Diagram the changes in plasma concentrations of estrogen, progesterone, LH, and FSH during the menstrual cycle.

6. What are the analogies between the granulosa cells and the Sertoli cells and between the theca cells and the Leydig cells?
7. List the effects of FSH and LH on the follicle.
8. Describe the effects of estrogen and inhibin on gonadotropin secretion during the early, middle, and late follicular phases.
9. List the effects of the LH surge on the egg and the follicle.
10. What are the effects of the sex steroids and inhibin on gonadotropin secretion during the luteal phase?
11. Describe the hormonal control of the corpus luteum and the changes that occur in the corpus luteum in a nonpregnant cycle and in a cycle when pregnancy occurs.
12. What happens to the sex steroids and the gonadotropins as the corpus luteum degenerates?
13. Compare the phases of the menstrual cycle according to uterine and ovarian events.
14. Describe the effects of estrogen and progesterone on the endometrium, cervical mucus, and myometrium.
15. Describe the uterine events associated with menstruation.
16. List the effects of estrogen on the accessory sex organs and secondary sex characteristics.
17. List the effects of progesterone on the breasts, cervical mucus, vaginal epithelium, and body temperature.
18. What are the sources and effects of androgens in women?
19. How does the egg get from the ovary to a fallopian tube?
20. Where does fertilization normally occur?
21. Describe the events that occur during fertilization.
22. How many days after ovulation does implantation occur, and in what stage is the conceptus at that time?
23. Describe the structure of the placenta and the pathways for exchange between maternal and fetal blood.
24. State the sources of estrogen and progesterone during different stages of pregnancy. What is the dominant estrogen of pregnancy, and how is it produced?
25. What is the state of gonadotropin secretion during pregnancy, and what is the cause?
26. What anatomical feature permits coordinated contractions of the myometrium?
27. Describe the mechanisms and messengers that contribute to parturition.
28. List the effects of prostaglandins on the female reproductive system.
29. Describe the development of the breasts after puberty and during pregnancy, and list the major hormones responsible.
30. Describe the effects of estrogen on the secretion and actions of prolactin during pregnancy.
31. Diagram the suckling reflex for prolactin release.
32. Diagram the milk ejection reflex.
33. List two main types of amenorrhea and give examples of each.
34. What is the state of estrogen and gonadotropin secretion before puberty and after menopause?
35. List the hormonal and anatomical changes that occur after menopause.

SECTION C KEY TERMS

acrosome reaction 635
afterbirth 642
alveoli 643
amnion 637
amniotic cavity 637
amniotic fluid 637
amniotic sac 637
antrum 624
atresia 624
blastocyst 635
block to polyspermy 635
capacitation 634
cervix 622
chorion 636
chorionic villi 637
cleavage 635
clitoris 623
colostrum 644
conceptus 635
congenital 637
corpus luteum 625
cortical reaction 635
cumulus oophorus 625
dominant follicle 624
dopamine 643
egg 622
embryo 635
endometrium 630
estrogen priming 632
fallopian tube 622
female external genitalia 622
female internal genitalia 622
fertilization 634
fetus 635
fimbria 622
follicle 624
follicular phase 625
fraternal (dizygotic) twins 625
graafian follicle 625
granulosa cell 624
human chorionic gonadotropin (hCG) 639
human placental lactogen 639
hymen 623
implantation 636
inner cell mass 635
lactation 643
lactogenesis 643
LH surge 626
luteal phase 625
mammary gland 643
meiotic arrest 623
menarche 633
menopause 646
menstrual cycle 622
menstrual phase 630
menstruation 622
milk ejection reflex 644
myoepithelial cell 643
myometrium 630
oogenesis 623
oogonium 623
ovulation 622
oxytocin 642
parturition 639
perimenopause 646
placenta 636
primordial follicle 624
prolactin-releasing factor (PRF) 643
proliferative phase 630
relaxin 640
secretory phase 630
sinus 637
stem cells 635
theca 624
totipotent 635
trophoblast 635
umbilical artery 637
umbilical cord 637
umbilical vein 637
uterus 622
vagina 622
vulva 622
zona pellucida 624

SECTION C CLINICAL TERMS

abortifacient 645
abortion 645
amenorrhea 633
amniocentesis 637
anorexia nervosa 633
breech presentation 640
cesarean section 640
chorionic villus sampling 637
contraceptive 645
Depo-Provera 645
Down syndrome 637
dysmenorrhea 631
eclampsia 639
ectopic pregnancy 635
hot flash 646
intrauterine device (IUD) 645
in vitro fertilization 646
Lunelle 645
miscarriage 637
oral contraceptive 645
osteoporosis 646
precocious puberty 633
preeclampsia 639
pregnancy sickness 639
premenstrual dysphoric disorder (PMDD) 632
premenstrual syndrome (PMS) 632
premenstrual tension 632
rhythm method 645
RU 486 (mifepristone) 645
selective estrogen receptor modulators (SERMs) 646
sexually transmitted disease (STD) 645
tamoxifen 646
teratogen 638
toxemia of pregnancy 639
virilization 632

Clinical Case Study: Cessation of Menstrual Cycles in a 21-Year-Old College Student

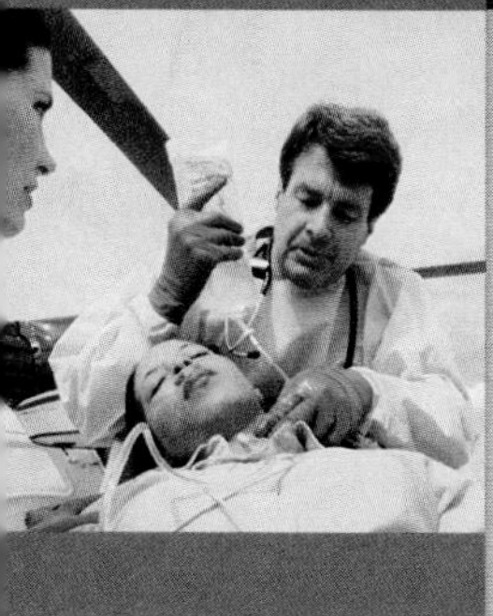

A 21-year-old female college student underwent menarche at 13 years of age. After 5 years of normal menses, her menstrual periods became less frequent and finally stopped (***secondary amenorrhea***). She does not use oral contraception nor is she sexually active, and a urine pregnancy test is negative. She also complains of headaches in the front of her head. During a physical examination by her family practitioner, a milky discharge can be expressed from both nipples. The clinician also finds that the patient has loss of temporal (peripheral) vision in both eyes. A pituitary gland tumor secreting prolactin is suspected. A magnetic resonance image (MRI) reveals the presence of a pituitary gland tumor, and when a blood test for prolactin concentration comes back very high, the diagnosis of *hyperprolactinemia* (excess prolactin in the blood) is confirmed.

Tumors of the lactotrophs of the anterior pituitary gland can hypersecrete prolactin, which in turn suppresses LH and FSH secretion. Thus, menstrual cycles cannot continue because gonadotropin concentrations are low. This is often accompanied by ***galactorrhea***—inappropriate milk production—because prolactin stimulates the mammary gland. Prolactin-secreting tumors (***prolactinomas***) are the most common of the functioning pituitary gland tumors. (Recall from Chapter 11 that pituitary gland tumors arising from different pituitary gland cell types can secrete other pituitary gland hormones—such as growth hormone, causing gigantism and acromegaly, and ACTH, causing Cushing's disease.) If the tumor becomes large enough, it can cause headaches due to stretching of the dura mater near the pituitary gland. The mechanism of the loss of vision in our patient is shown in **Figure 17.39.** The pituitary gland is located just below the optic chiasm. As the tumor grows, it can press on the optic chiasm, interrupting afferent nerve transmission. Because the nerves from the medial parts of the retina cross just above the pituitary gland, they are usually most affected by compression from pituitary gland tumors. As illustrated in the figure, the loss of afferent input from the medial parts of the retina leads to a loss of lateral vision in both eyes. Hyperprolactinemia is usually treated with dopamine agonists such as bromocriptine or

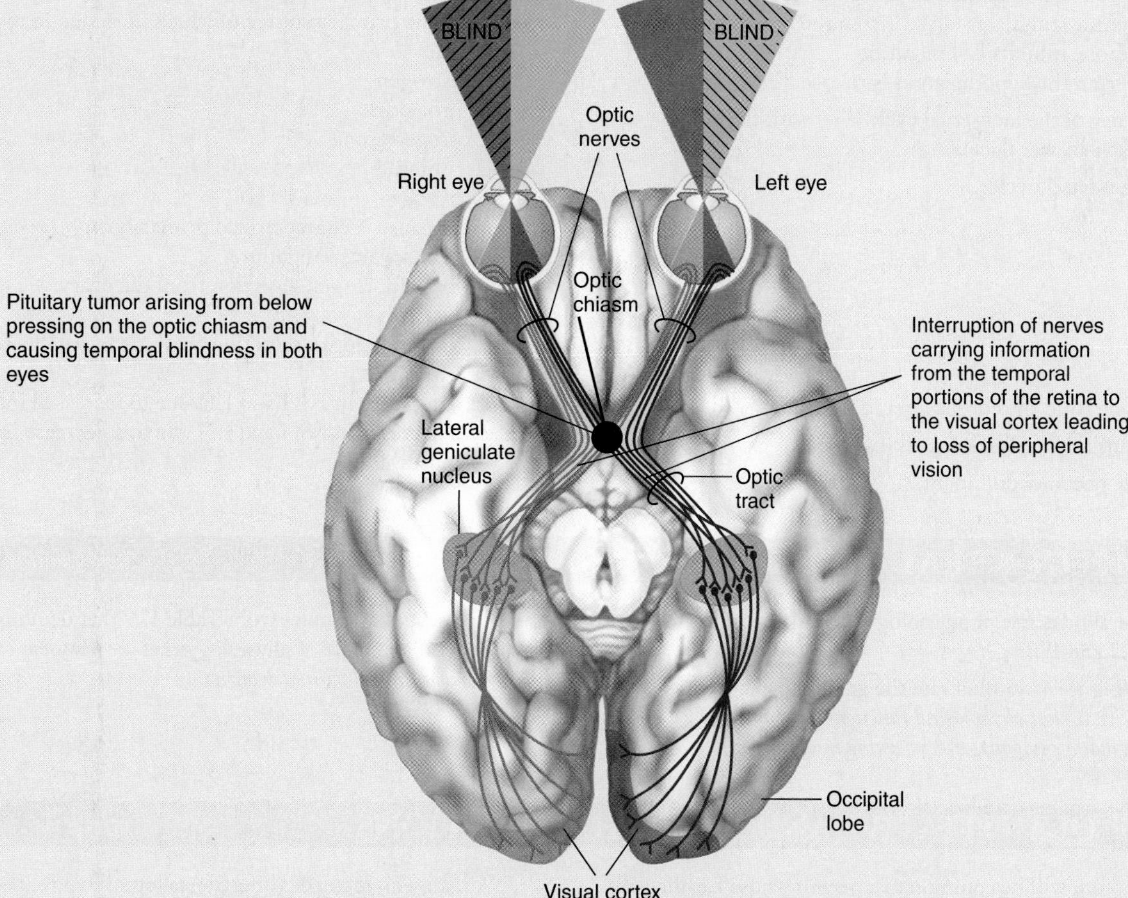

Figure 17.39 Mechanism of loss of lateral visual fields due to a large pituitary gland tumor pressing up from below on the optic chiasm. Refer back to Figure 7.31 for details about the optic tracts and chiasm. This view is from below the brain.

(continued)

(continued)

cabergoline, because prolactin is primarily under the inhibitory control of hypothalamic dopamine. Not only do dopamine agonists decrease the concentrations of prolactin in the blood, but they often lead to a shrinking of the pituitary gland tumor, thus relieving the compression of the optic chiasm with the accompanying restoration of vision. If the pituitary gland tumor is very large or if it does not shrink adequately with medical therapy, pituitary gland surgery may be necessary to remove as much of the tumor as possible. Our patient was treated with cabergoline; fortunately, the tumor gradually got smaller over several months, her visual fields improved, her blood prolactin concentrations normalized, and her menstrual periods returned to normal. Her physician measures her plasma prolactin concentrations every 6 months to monitor for a recurrence of tumor growth.

Clinical terms: galactorrhea, prolactinoma, secondary amenorrhea

See Chapter 19 for complete, integrative case studies.

CHAPTER 17 TEST QUESTIONS

Answers found in Appendix A.

1. Development of normal female internal and external genitalia requires
   a. Müllerian-inhibiting substance.
   b. expression of the *SRY* gene.
   c. insensitivity to circulating testosterone.
   d. complete absence of testosterone.
   e. absence of a Y chromosome.
2. Which is *not* characteristic of a normal postpubertal male?
   a. Inhibin from the Sertoli cells decreases FSH secretion.
   b. Testosterone has paracrine effects on the Sertoli cells.
   c. Testosterone stimulates GnRH from the hypothalamus.
   d. Testosterone inhibits LH secretion.
   e. GnRH from the hypothalamus is released in pulses.

3–7. Match the day of the menstrual cycle (a–e) with the event (3–7; use each answer once).

Day of menstrual cycle:
a. day 1
b. day 7
c. day 13
d. day 23
e. day 26

Event:

3. Progesterone from the corpus luteum peaks.
4. Estrogen positive feedback is peaking.
5. One follicle becomes dominant.
6. Estrogen and progesterone are both decreasing.
7. Increase in FSH stimulates antral follicles to begin to secrete estrogen.
8. The Leydig cell is primarily characterized by
   a. aromatization of testosterone.
   b. secretion of inhibin.
   c. secretion of testosterone.
   d. expression of receptors only to FSH.
   e. transformation into the corpus luteum.
9. During the third trimester of pregnancy, the placenta is *not* the primary source of which hormone in maternal blood?
   a. estrogen
   b. prolactin
   c. progesterone
   d. inhibin
   e. hCG
10. Menopause is characterized primarily by
    a. primary ovarian failure.
    b. loss of estrogen secretion from the ovary due to a decrease in LH.
    c. loss of estrogen secretion from the ovary due to a decrease in FSH.
    d. a decrease in FSH and LH due to increased inhibin.
    e. a decrease in FSH and LH due to a decrease in GnRH pulses.

CHAPTER 17 GENERAL PRINCIPLES ASSESSMENT

Answers found in Appendix A.

1. What general principle of physiology is illustrated in Figures 17.2 and 17.3?
2. How does Figure 17.15 illustrate the general principle of physiology that *most physiological functions are controlled by multiple regulatory systems, often working in opposition?*
3. List several examples from Table 17.9 that demonstrate the general principle of physiology that *the functions of organ systems are coordinated with each other.*

CHAPTER 17 QUANTITATIVE AND THOUGHT QUESTIONS

Answers found in Appendix A.

1. What symptom will be common to a person whose Leydig cells have been destroyed and to a person whose Sertoli cells have been destroyed? What symptom will not be common?
2. A male athlete taking large amounts of an androgenic steroid becomes sterile (unable to produce sperm capable of causing fertilization). Explain.
3. A man who is sterile (infertile) is found to have the following: no evidence of demasculinization, an increased blood concentration of FSH, and a normal plasma concentration of LH. What is the most likely basis of his infertility?
4. If you were a scientist trying to develop a male contraceptive acting on the anterior pituitary gland, would you try to

block the secretion of FSH or LH? Explain the reason for your choice.

5. A 30-year-old man has very small muscles, a sparse beard, and a high-pitched voice. His plasma concentration of LH is elevated. Explain the likely cause of all these findings.
6. There are disorders of the adrenal cortex in which excessive amounts of androgens are produced. If any of these occur in a woman, what will happen to her menstrual cycles?
7. Women with inadequate secretion of GnRH are often treated for their infertility with drugs that mimic the action of this hormone. Can you suggest a possible reason that such treatment is often associated with multiple births?
8. Which of the following would be a signal that ovulation is soon to occur: the cervical mucus becoming thick and sticky, an increase in body temperature, or a marked rise in plasma LH?
9. The absence of what phenomenon would interfere with the ability of sperm obtained by masturbation to fertilize an egg in a test tube?
10. If a woman 7 months pregnant is found to have a marked decrease in plasma estrogen but a normal plasma progesterone for that time of pregnancy, what would you conclude?
11. What types of drugs might you work on if you were trying to develop one to stop premature labor?
12. If a genetic male failed to produce MIS during fetal life, what would the result be?
13. Could the symptoms of menopause be treated by injections of FSH and LH?

CHAPTER 17 ANSWERS TO PHYSIOLOGICAL INQUIRIES

Figure 17.4 These drugs would be absorbed by the pregnant woman and cross the placenta to enter the fetal circulation. These drugs would block production of dihydrotestosterone in target tissues with 5-α-reductase activity, thereby interfering with the development of normal sexual differentiation of the penis, scrotum, and prostate in the male fetus.

Figure 17.7 In the short term, there would be a decrease in sex hormone secretion that, because of a reduction in negative feedback, would result in an increase in GnRH secretion from the hypothalamus and LH and FSH from the anterior pituitary gland. Because of the trophic effects of LH and FSH, in the long term, this would eventually increase the size and function of the remaining gonad. This results in a restoration of sex hormone concentrations in the blood to normal. (See Chapter 11 for a general description of the effects of tropic/trophic anterior pituitary gland hormones.)

Figure 17.15 Testosterone alone usually does not restore spermatogenesis to normal. FSH is necessary to stimulate spermatogenesis from the Sertoli cell independently of local testosterone production. Furthermore, giving testosterone as a drug is usually not sufficient to replace the local production of testosterone in the testes necessary to maintain spermatogenesis. Therefore, gonadotropins with a mixture of activity for receptors to LH (to stimulate local testosterone production) and FSH (to stimulate the Sertoli cells) usually must be given to restore spermatogenesis.

Figure 17.22 (1) FSH increases because the corpus luteum is degenerating. The loss of the negative feedback by progesterone and estrogen from the corpus luteum relieves the pituitary gland of this inhibitory effect and allows FSH to increase, thus stimulating a group of follicles for the next menstrual cycle. (2) If conception occurs and the developing blastocyst implants (pregnancy), the trophoblast cells of the implanted blastocyst release a gonadotropin—human chorionic gonadotropin (hCG)—into the maternal blood, thus rescuing the corpus luteum in very early pregnancy. Production of progesterone from the corpus luteum of pregnancy prevents menses and the loss of the implanted embryo. The measurement of hCG in maternal blood or urine is the basis of the pregnancy test.

Figure 17.24 The increased pituitary gland gonadotropins suggest a lack of estrogen and inhibin negative feedback, pointing to premature ovarian failure as a diagnosis. One cause of premature ovarian failure is autoimmune ovarian destruction. Like Graves' disease and Addison's disease (see Chapters 11 and 19), premature ovarian failure is a form of endocrine autoimmunity.

Figure 17.32 Measurement of a protein specific to fetal blood in a maternal blood sample, such as fetal hemoglobin, would be evidence that fetal blood is leaking into the maternal circulation.

Figure 17.34 hCG stimulates progesterone and estrogen from the corpus luteum early in pregnancy. The placenta takes over this function during the second trimester of pregnancy such that most of the maternal estrogen and progesterone later in pregnancy is from the placenta. Placental production of these steroids does not require gonadotropin stimulation.

Figure 17.36 The feet may not provide sufficient cervical stretch to maintain the positive feedback stimulation of oxytocin and uterine contraction.

Visit this book's website at **www.mhhe.com/widmaier13** for chapter quizzes, interactive learning exercises, and other study tools.

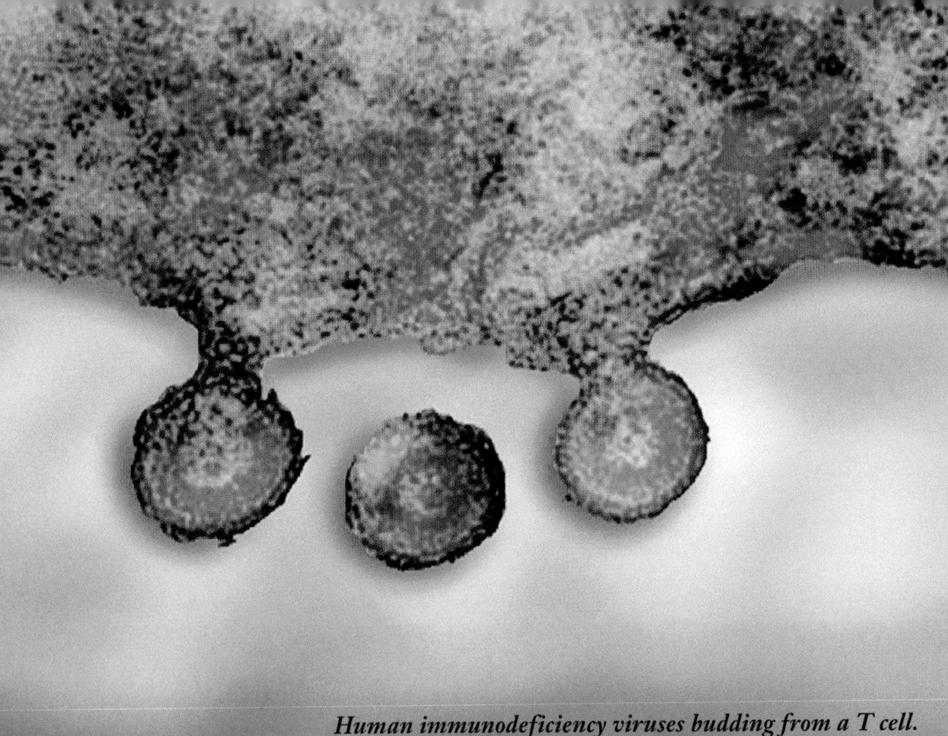

Human immunodeficiency viruses budding from a T cell.

18 The Immune System

You have learned about numerous organ systems in previous chapters, some of which, such as the digestive system, consist of anatomically connected organs. By contrast, the immune system consists of a diverse collection of disease-fighting cells found in the blood and lymph and in tissues and organs throughout the body. **Immunology** is the study of the physiological defenses by which the body (the host) recognizes itself from nonself (foreign matter). In the process, foreign matter, both living and nonliving, is destroyed or rendered harmless. In distinguishing self from nonself, immune defenses (1) protect against infection by **pathogens**—viruses, and **microbes** including bacteria, fungi, and eukaryotic parasites; (2) isolate or remove foreign substances; and (3) destroy cancer cells that arise in the body, a function known as **immune surveillance**.

Immune defenses, or immunity, can be classified into two categories, innate and adaptive, which interact with each other. **Innate immune responses** defend against foreign substances or cells without having to recognize their specific identities. The mechanisms of protection used by these defenses are not unique to the particular foreign substance or cell. For this reason, innate immune responses are also known as nonspecific immune responses. **Adaptive immune responses** depend upon specific recognition by lymphocytes of the substance or cell to be attacked. For this reason, adaptive immune responses are also called specific immune responses. Innate and adaptive immune responses function together. For example, components of innate immunity provide instructions that activate the cells that carry out adaptive responses.

The pathogens with which we will be most concerned in this chapter are bacteria and viruses. These are the dominant infectious agents in the United States and other industrialized nations. On a global basis, however, infections with parasitic eukaryotic organisms are responsible for a huge amount of illness and death. For example, several hundred million people now have malaria, a disease caused by infection with protists of the *Plasmodium* genus.

Bacteria are unicellular organisms that have an outer coating (the cell wall) in addition to a plasma membrane but no intracellular membrane-bound organelles. Bacteria can damage tissues at the sites of bacterial replication, or they can release toxins that enter the blood and disrupt physiological functions in other parts of the body.

Viruses are essentially nucleic acids surrounded by a protein coat. Unlike bacteria, viruses lack the enzyme machinery for metabolism and the ribosomes essential for protein synthesis. Consequently, they cannot multiply by themselves but must exist inside other cells and use the molecular apparatuses of those cells. The viral nucleic acid directs the host cell to synthesize the proteins required for viral replication, with the required nucleotides and energy sources also supplied by the host cell. The effect of viral habitation and replication within a cell depends on the type of virus. After entering a cell, some viruses (the common cold virus, for example) multiply rapidly, kill the cell, and then move on to other cells. Other viruses, such as the one that causes genital herpes, can lie dormant in infected cells before suddenly undergoing the rapid replication that causes cell damage. Finally, certain viruses can transform their host cells into cancer cells.

Of the general principles of physiology described in Chapter 1, one that is fundamental to the immune system is the principle that homeostasis is essential for health and survival. Indeed, illness can often be thought of as a disruption in one or more homeostatic processes. A key way in which the immune system regulates homeostasis is via cell-to-cell signaling. As you read this chapter, therefore, consider also how this general principle of physiology applies: Information flow between cells, tissues, and organs is an essential feature of homeostasis and allows for integration of physiological processes.

18.1 Cells and Secretions Mediating Immune Defenses

We begin our survey of the human immune system with an overview of some of the key cells and cellular secretions that make up the innate and adaptive immune responses. The appearance, production, and blood concentrations of immune cells were introduced in Section F of Chapter 12 and should be reviewed at this time.

Immune Cells

The cells of the immune system are the various types of white blood cells collectively known as **leukocytes;** representative histological appearances of some of these can be seen in the human blood smear in **Figure 18.1** (also refer back to Figure 12.67). Unlike erythrocytes, leukocytes can leave the circulatory system to enter the tissues where they function. Leukocytes can be classified into two groups: myeloid cells and lymphoid cells. The myeloid cells include the **neutrophils, basophils, eosinophils,** and **monocytes,** all of whose functions will be described later. Lymphoid cells include several types of **lymphocytes,** including **B lymphocytes** (**B cells**), **T lymphocytes** (**T cells**), **natural killer** (**NK**) **cells,** and **plasma cells.** Plasma cells are not really a distinct cell type but differentiate from B lymphocytes during immune responses. The major functions of plasma cells are to synthesize and secrete antibodies. The functions of the other lymphocytes will be described shortly.

Other immune cells include **macrophages;** these are found in virtually all organs and tissues, their structures varying somewhat from location to location. They are derived from monocytes that pass through the walls of blood vessels to enter the tissues and transform into macrophages. In keeping with one of their major functions, the engulfing of particles and pathogens by **phagocytosis** (the form of endocytosis whereby a cell engulfs and usually destroys particulate matter), macrophages are strategically placed where they will encounter their targets. For example, they are found in large numbers in the various epithelia in contact with the external environment, such as the skin and internal surfaces of respiratory and digestive system tubes. In several organs, they line the vessels through which blood or lymph flows.

There are also cell populations that are not macrophages but exert certain macrophage-like functions such as phagocytosis. These are termed **dendritic cells** because of the characteristic extensions from their plasma membranes at certain stages of their life cycle (not to be confused with the dendrites found on neurons). They are highly motile and are found

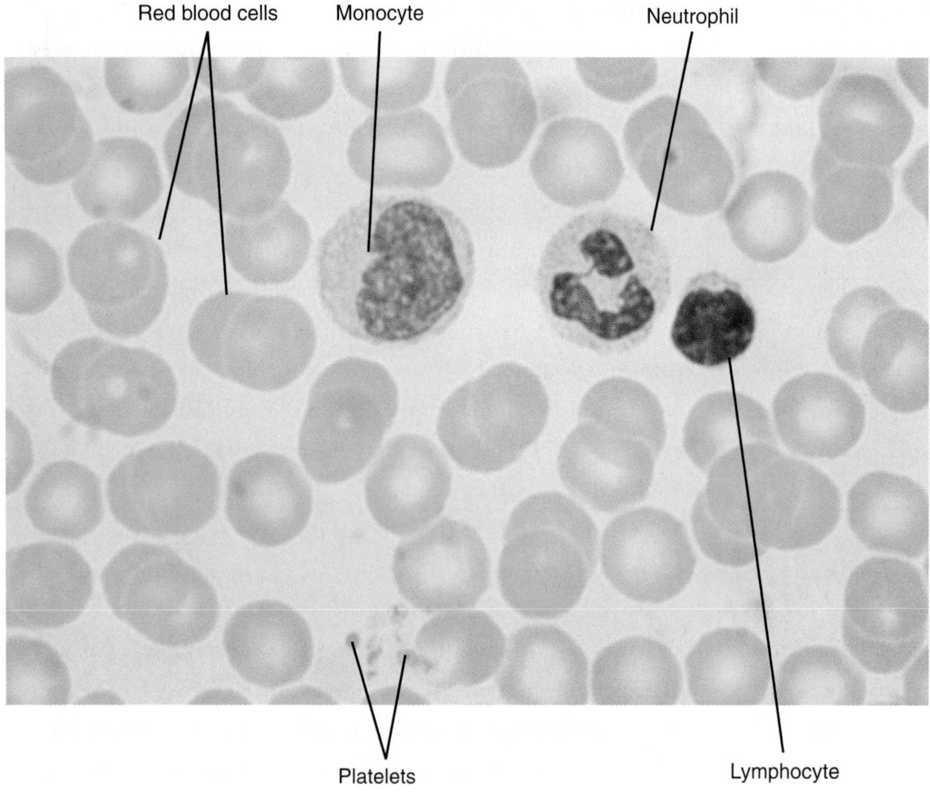

Figure 18.1 AP|R A light micrograph of a human blood smear showing the histological appearance of a few types of leukocytes along with numerous red blood cells and platelets.

scattered in almost all tissues, but particularly at sites where the internal and external environments meet, such as the digestive tract. Upon activation, dendritic cells process phagocytosed pathogens and migrate through the lymphatic vessels to secondary lymphoid organs where they activate T cells.

Mast cells are found throughout connective tissues, particularly beneath the epithelial surfaces of the body. They are derived from the differentiation of a unique set of bone marrow cells that have entered the blood and then left the blood vessels to enter connective tissue, where they differentiate and undergo cell division. Consequently, mature mast cells—unlike basophils, with which they share many characteristics—are not normally found in the blood. The most striking anatomical feature of mast cells is their very large number of cytosolic vesicles, which secrete locally acting chemical messengers such as histamine.

The sites of production and functions of all these cells are briefly listed in **Table 18.1** for reference and will be described in subsequent sections. For now, we emphasize two points. First, lymphocytes serve as recognition cells in adaptive immune responses and are essential for all aspects of these responses. Second, neutrophils, monocytes, macrophages, and dendritic cells have a variety of activities, but particularly important is their ability to secrete inflammatory mediators and to function as **phagocytes.** A phagocyte denotes any cell capable of phagocytosis.

Cytokines

The cells of the immune system secrete a multitude of protein messengers that regulate host cell division (mitosis) and function in both innate and adaptive immune responses. "**Cytokines**" is the collective term for these messengers, each of which has its own unique name. Cytokines are produced not by distinct specialized glands but rather by a variety of individual cells. The great majority of their actions occur at the site at which they are secreted, the cytokine acting as an autocrine or paracrine substance. In some cases, however, the cytokine circulates in the blood to exert hormonal effects on distant organs and tissues involved in host defenses.

Cytokines link the components of the immune system together. They are the chemical communication network that allows different immune system cells to "talk" to one another. This is called *cross talk*, and it is essential for the precise timing of the functions of the immune system. Most cytokines are secreted by more than one type of immune system cell and by nonimmune cells as well (for example, by endothelial cells and fibroblasts). This often produces cascades of cytokine secretion, in which one cytokine stimulates the release of another, and so on. Any given cytokine may exert actions on an extremely broad range of target cells. For example, the cytokine interleukin 2 influences the function of most cells of the immune system. There is great redundancy in cytokine action; that is, different cytokines can have very similar effects. Cytokines are also involved in many nonimmunologic processes, such as bone formation and uterine function.

This chapter will be limited to a discussion of a few of the important cytokines and their most important functions, which are summarized in **Table 18.2**.

18.2 Innate Immune Responses

Innate immune responses defend against foreign cells or matter without having to recognize specific identities. These defenses recognize some *general* molecular property marking the invader as foreign. The most common such identity tags are often found in particular classes of carbohydrates or lipids that are in microbial cell walls. Plasma membrane receptors on certain immune cells, as well as a variety of circulating proteins (particularly a family of proteins called complement), can bind to these carbohydrates and lipids at crucial steps in innate responses. This use of a system based on carbohydrate and lipid for detecting the presence of foreign cells is a key feature that distinguishes innate responses from adaptive ones, which recognize foreign cells mainly by specific proteins the foreign cells produce.

The innate immune responses include defenses at the body surfaces, the response to injury or infection known as *inflammation*, and a family of antiviral proteins called interferons.

TABLE 18.1 Cells Mediating Immune Responses

Name	Site Produced	Functions
Leukocytes (white blood cells)		
Neutrophils	Bone marrow	1. Phagocytosis 2. Release chemicals involved in inflammation (vasodilators, chemotaxins, etc.)
Basophils	Bone marrow	Carry out functions in blood similar to those of mast cells in tissues (see below)
Eosinophils	Bone marrow	1. Destroy multicellular parasites 2. Participate in immediate hypersensitivity reactions
Monocytes	Bone marrow	1. Carry out functions in blood similar to those of macrophages in tissues (see below) 2. Enter tissues and transform into macrophages
Lymphocytes	Mature in bone marrow (B cells and NK cells) and thymus (T cells); activated in peripheral lymphoid organs	Serve as recognition cells in specific immune responses and are essential for all aspects of these responses
B cells		1. Initiate antibody-mediated immune responses by binding specific antigens to the B cell's plasma membrane receptors, which are immunoglobulins 2. Upon activation, are transformed into plasma cells, which secrete antibodies 3. Present antigen to helper T cells
Cytotoxic T cells (CD8 cells)		Bind to antigens on plasma membrane of target cells (virus-infected cells, cancer cells, and tissue transplants) and directly destroy the cells
Helper T cells (CD4 cells)		Secrete cytokines that help to activate B cells, cytotoxic T cells, NK cells, and macrophages
NK cells		1. Bind directly and nonspecifically to virus-infected cells and cancer cells and kill them 2. Function as killer cells in antibody-dependent cellular cytotoxicity (ADCC)
Plasma cells	Peripheral lymphoid organs; differentiate from B cells during immune responses	Secrete antibodies
Macrophages	Bone marrow; reside in almost all tissues and organs; differentiate from monocytes	1. Phagocytosis 2. Extracellular killing via secretion of toxic chemicals 3. Process and present antigens to helper T cells 4. Secrete cytokines involved in inflammation, activation and differentiation of helper T cells, and systemic responses to infection or injury (the acute phase response)
Dendritic cells	Almost all tissues and organs; microglia in the central nervous system	Phagocytosis, antigen presentation
Mast cells	Bone marrow; reside in almost all tissues and organs; differentiate from bone marrow cells	Release histamine and other chemicals involved in inflammation

TABLE 18.2 Features of Selected* Cytokines

Cytokine	Source	Target Cells	Major Functions
Interleukin 1, tumor necrosis factor-alpha, and interleukin 6	Antigen-presenting cells such as macrophages	Helper T cells; certain brain cells; numerous systemic cells	Stimulate IL-2 receptor expression; induce fever; stimulate systemic responses to inflammation, infection, and injury
Interleukin 2	Most immune cells	Helper T cells; cytotoxic T cells; NK cells; B cells	Stimulate proliferation Promote conversion to plasma cells
Interferons (type I)	Most cell types	Most cell types	Stimulate cells to produce antiviral proteins (innate response)
Interferons (type II)	NK cells and activated helper T cells	NK cells and macrophages	Stimulate proliferation and secretion of cytotoxic compounds
Chemokines	Damaged cells, including endothelial cells	Neutrophils and other leukocytes	Facilitate accumulation of leukocytes at sites of injury and inflammation
Colony-stimulating factors	Macrophages	Bone marrow	Stimulate proliferation of neutrophils and monocytes

**Note:* This list is not meant to be exhaustive. There are >100 known cytokines.

Defenses at Body Surfaces

Though not immune *responses*, the first lines of defense against pathogens are the barriers offered by surfaces exposed to the external environment, because very few pathogens can penetrate the intact skin. Other specialized surface defenses are the hairs at the entrance to the nose and the cough and sneeze reflexes. The various skin glands, salivary glands, and lacrimal (tear) glands play a more active role in immunity by secreting antimicrobial chemicals. These may include antibodies; enzymes such as lysozyme, which destroys bacterial cell walls; and an iron-binding protein called lactoferrin, which prevents bacteria from obtaining the iron they require to function properly.

The mucus secreted by the epithelial linings of the respiratory and upper gastrointestinal tracts also contains antimicrobial chemicals; more importantly, however, mucus is sticky. Particles that adhere to it are prevented from entering the blood. They are either swept by ciliary action up into the pharynx and then swallowed, as occurs in the upper respiratory tract, or are phagocytosed by macrophages in the various linings. Finally, the acid secretion of the stomach can also kill pathogens, although some bacteria can survive to colonize the large intestine where they provide beneficial gastrointestinal functions.

Inflammation

Inflammation is the local response to infection or injury. The functions of inflammation are to destroy or inactivate foreign invaders and to set the stage for tissue repair. The key mediators are the cells that function as phagocytes. As noted earlier, the most important phagocytes are neutrophils, macrophages, and dendritic cells.

In this section, inflammation is described as it occurs in the innate responses induced by the invasion of pathogens. Most of the same responses can be elicited by a variety of other injuries—cold, heat, and trauma, for example. Moreover, we will see later that inflammation accompanies many *adaptive* immune responses in which the inflammation becomes amplified.

The sequence of local events in a typical innate inflammatory response to a bacterial infection—one caused, for example, by a cut with a bacteria-covered splinter—is summarized in **Figure 18.2**. The familiar signs of tissue injury and inflammation are local redness, swelling, heat, and pain.

The events of inflammation that underlie these signs are induced and regulated by a large number of chemical mediators, some of which are summarized for reference in **Table 18.3** (not all of these will be described in this chapter). Note in this table that some of these mediators are cytokines. Any given event of inflammation, such as vasodilation, may be induced by multiple mediators. Moreover, any given mediator may induce more than one event. Based on their origins, the mediators fall into two general categories: (1) peptides (kinins, for example) generated in the infected area by enzymatic actions on proteins that circulate in the plasma and (2) substances secreted into the extracellular fluid from cells that either already exist in the infected area (injured cells or mast cells, for example) or enter it during inflammation (neutrophils, for example).

Let us now go step by step through the process summarized in Figure 18.2, assuming that the bacterial infection in our example is localized to the tissue just beneath the skin. If the invading bacteria enter the blood or lymph, then similar inflammatory responses would take place in any other tissue or organ the blood-borne or lymph-borne microorganisms reach.

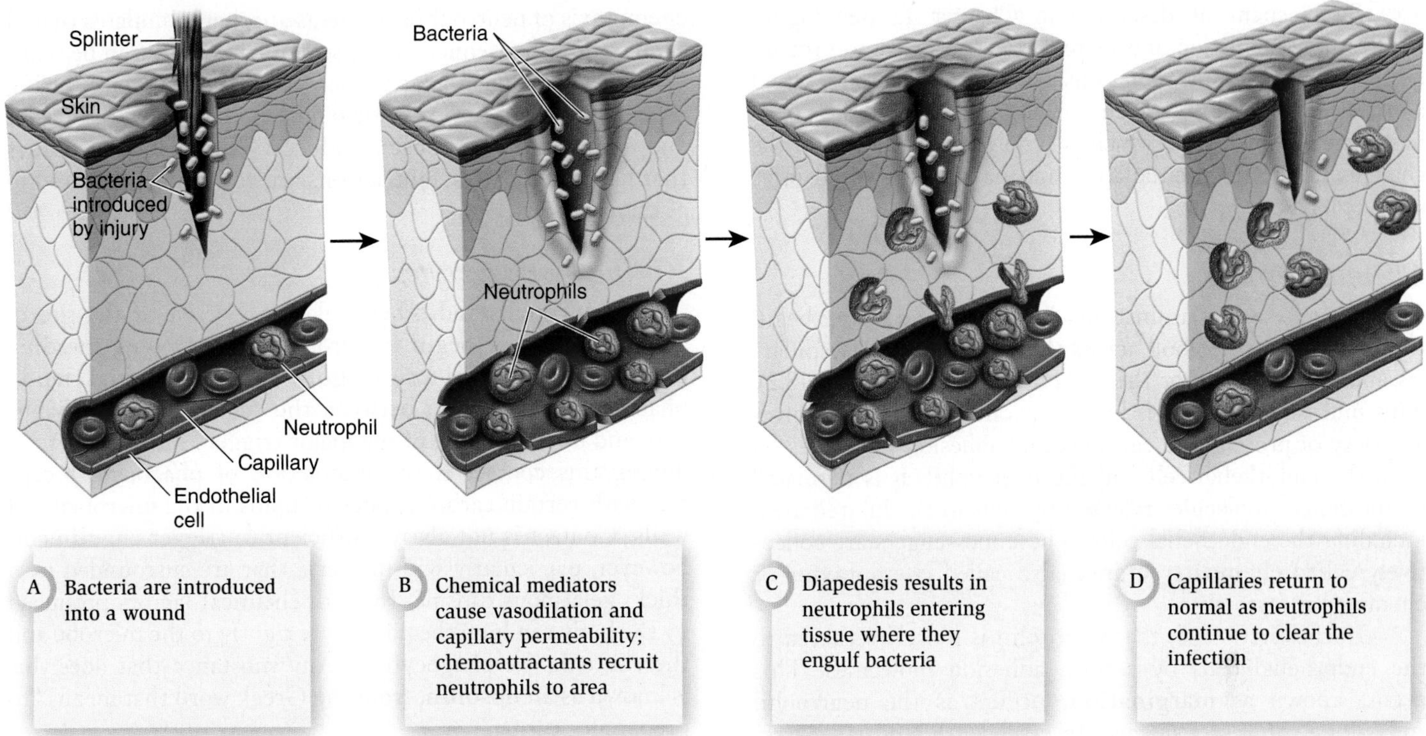
Splinter
Skin
Bacteria introduced by injury
Neutrophil
Capillary
Endothelial cell
Bacteria
Neutrophils
A Bacteria are introduced into a wound
B Chemical mediators cause vasodilation and capillary permeability; chemoattractants recruit neutrophils to area
C Diapedesis results in neutrophils entering tissue where they engulf bacteria
D Capillaries return to normal as neutrophils continue to clear the infection

Figure 18.2 APIR The local inflammatory events occurring in response to a wound.

TABLE 18.3 Some Important Local Inflammatory Mediators

Mediator	Source
Kinins	Generated from enzymatic action on plasma proteins
Complement	Generated from enzymatic action on plasma proteins
Products of blood clotting	Generated from enzymatic action on plasma proteins
Histamine	Secreted by mast cells and injured cells
Eicosanoids	Secreted by many cell types including myeloid cells
Platelet-activating factor	Secreted by many cell types including myeloid cells, endothelial cells, platelets, damaged tissue cells
Cytokines, including chemokines	Secreted by activated immune cells, monocytes, macrophages, neutrophils, lymphocytes, and several nonimmune cell types, including endothelial cells and fibroblasts
Lysosomal enzymes, nitric oxide, and other oxygen-derived substances	Secreted by injured cells, neutrophils, and macrophages

Vasodilation and Increased Permeability to Protein

A variety of chemical mediators dilate most of the microcirculation vessels in an infected and/or damaged area. The mediators also cause the local capillaries and venules to become permeable to proteins by inducing their endothelial cells to contract, opening spaces between them through which the proteins can move.

The adaptive value of these vascular changes is twofold: (1) The increased blood flow to the inflamed area (which accounts for the redness and warmth) increases the delivery of proteins and leukocytes; and (2) the increased permeability to protein ensures that the plasma proteins that participate in inflammation—many of which are normally restrained by the intact endothelium—can gain entry to the interstitial fluid.

By mechanisms described in Chapter 12 (see Figure 12.42), the vasodilation and increased permeability to protein, however, cause net filtration of plasma into the interstitial fluid and the development of edema. This accounts for the swelling in an inflamed area, which is simply a consequence of the changes in the microcirculation and has no known adaptive value of its own.

Chemotaxis

With the onset of inflammation, circulating neutrophils begin to move out of the blood across the endothelium of capillaries and venules to enter the inflamed area (see Figure 18.2). This multistage process is known as **chemotaxis.** It involves a variety of protein and carbohydrate adhesion molecules on both the endothelial cell and the neutrophil. It is regulated by messenger molecules released by cells in the injured area, including the endothelial cells. These messengers are collectively called **chemoattractants** (also called **chemotaxins** or chemotactic factors).

In the first stage, the neutrophil is loosely tethered to the endothelial cells by certain adhesion molecules. This event, known as **margination,** occurs as the neutrophil rolls along the vessel surface. In essence, this initial reversible event exposes the neutrophil to chemoattractants being released in the injured area. These chemoattractants act on the neutrophil to induce the rapid appearance of another class of adhesion molecules in its plasma membrane—molecules that bind tightly to their matching molecules on the surface of endothelial cells. As a result, the neutrophils collect along the site of injury rather than being washed away with the flowing blood.

In the next stage, known as **diapedesis,** a narrow projection of the neutrophil is inserted into the space between two endothelial cells, and the entire neutrophil squeezes through the endothelial wall and into the interstitial fluid. In this way, huge numbers of neutrophils migrate into the inflamed area. Once in the interstitial fluid, neutrophils follow a chemotactic gradient and migrate toward the site of tissue damage (chemotaxis). This occurs because pathogen-stimulated innate immune cells release chemoattractants. As a result, neutrophils tend to move toward the pathogens that entered into an injured area.

Movement of leukocytes from the blood into the damaged area is not limited to neutrophils. Monocytes follow later; once in the tissue, they undergo anatomical and functional changes that transform them to macrophages. As we will see later, lymphocytes undergo chemotaxis in adaptive immune responses, as do basophils and eosinophils under certain conditions.

An important aspect of the multistep chemotaxis process is that it provides selectivity and flexibility for the migration of the various leukocyte types. Multiple adhesion molecules that are relatively distinct for the different leukocytes are controlled by different sets of chemoattractants. Particularly important in this regard are those cytokines that function as chemoattractants for distinct subsets of leukocytes. For example, one type of cytokine stimulates the chemotaxis of neutrophils, whereas another stimulates that of eosinophils. Consequently, subsets of leukocytes can be stimulated to enter particular tissues at designated times during an inflammatory response, depending on the type of invader and the cytokine response it induces. The various cytokines that have chemoattractant actions are collectively referred to as **chemokines.**

Killing by Phagocytes

Once neutrophils and other leukocytes arrive at the site of an infection, they begin the process of destroying invading pathogens by phagocytosis (**Figure 18.3**). The initial step in phagocytosis is contact between the surfaces of the phagocyte and microbe. One of the major triggers for phagocytosis during this contact is the interaction of phagocyte receptors with certain carbohydrates or lipids in the microbial cell walls. Contact is not always sufficient to trigger engulfment, however, particularly with bacteria that are surrounded by a thick, gelatinous capsule. Instead, chemical factors produced by the body can bind the phagocyte tightly to the microbe and thereby enhance phagocytosis. Any substance that does this is known as an **opsonin,** from the Greek word that means "to prepare for eating."

As the phagocyte engulfs the microbe (**Figure 18.4**), the internal, microbe-containing sac formed in this step is called a **phagosome.** A layer of plasma membrane separates the microbe from the cytosol of the phagocyte. The phagosome membrane then makes contact with one of the phagocyte's lysosomes, which is filled with a variety of hydrolytic enzymes. The membranes of the phagosome and lysosome fuse, and the combined vesicles are now called a **phagolysosome.** Inside the phagolysosome, the lysosomal enzymes break down the microbe's macromolecules. In addition, other enzymes in the phagolysosome membrane produce **nitric oxide** as well as **hydrogen peroxide** and other oxygen derivatives, all of which are extremely destructive to the microbe's macromolecules.

Such intracellular destruction is not the only way phagocytes can kill pathogens. The phagocytes also release antimicrobial substances into the extracellular fluid, where these chemicals can destroy the pathogens without prior phagocytosis. Some of these substances (for example, nitric oxide) secreted into the extracellular fluid (**Figure 18.5**) also function as inflammatory mediators. Thus, when phagocytes enter the area and encounter pathogens, positive feedback mechanisms cause inflammatory mediators, including chemokines, to be released that bring in more phagocytes.

Complement

The family of plasma proteins known as **complement** provides another means for extracellular killing of pathogens without prior phagocytosis. Certain complement proteins are always circulating in the blood in an inactive state. Upon activation of a complement protein in response to infection or damage, a cascade occurs so that this active protein activates a second complement protein, which activates a third, and so on. In this

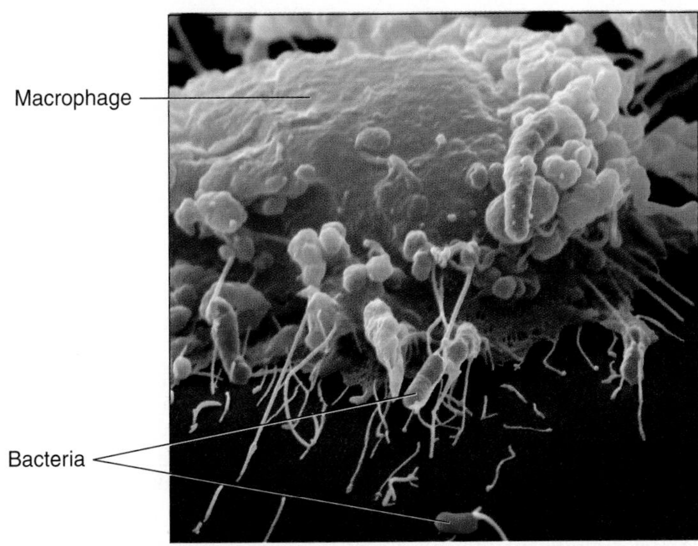

Figure 18.3 AP|R Macrophage contacting bacteria and preparing to engulf them.

way, multiple active complement proteins are generated in the extracellular fluid of the infected area from inactive complement molecules that have entered from the blood. Because this system consists of at least 30 distinct proteins, it is extremely complex, and we will identify the roles of only a few of the individual complement proteins.

The central protein in the complement cascade is C3. Activation of C3 initiates a series of events. The first is the deposition of **C3b,** a component of C3, on the microbial surface. C3b acts as an opsonin that is recognized by phagocytes targeting the pathogen for destruction, as shown for a bacterium in **Figure 18.6**. C3b is also part of a proteolytic enzyme that amplifies the complement cascade and leads to the downstream development of a multiunit protein called the **membrane attack complex** (**MAC**). The MAC embeds itself in the bacterial plasma membrane and forms porelike channels in the membrane, making it leaky. Water, ions, and small molecules enter the microbe, which disrupts the intracellular environment and kills the microbe.

In addition to supplying a means for direct killing of pathogens, the complement system serves other important functions in inflammation (**Figure 18.7**). Some of the activated complement molecules along the cascade cause, either directly or indirectly (by stimulating the release of other inflammatory mediators), vasodilation, increased microvessel permeability to protein, and chemotaxis.

As we will see later, antibodies, a class of proteins secreted by certain lymphocytes, are required to activate the very first complement protein (C1) in the full sequence known as the **classical complement pathway.** However, lymphocytes are not involved in *nonspecific* inflammation, our present topic. How, then, is the complement sequence initiated during nonspecific inflammation? The answer is that there is an **alternative complement pathway,** one that is not antibody dependent and that bypasses C1. The alternative pathway is initiated as the result of interactions between carbohydrates on the surface of the microbes and inactive complement molecules beyond C1. These

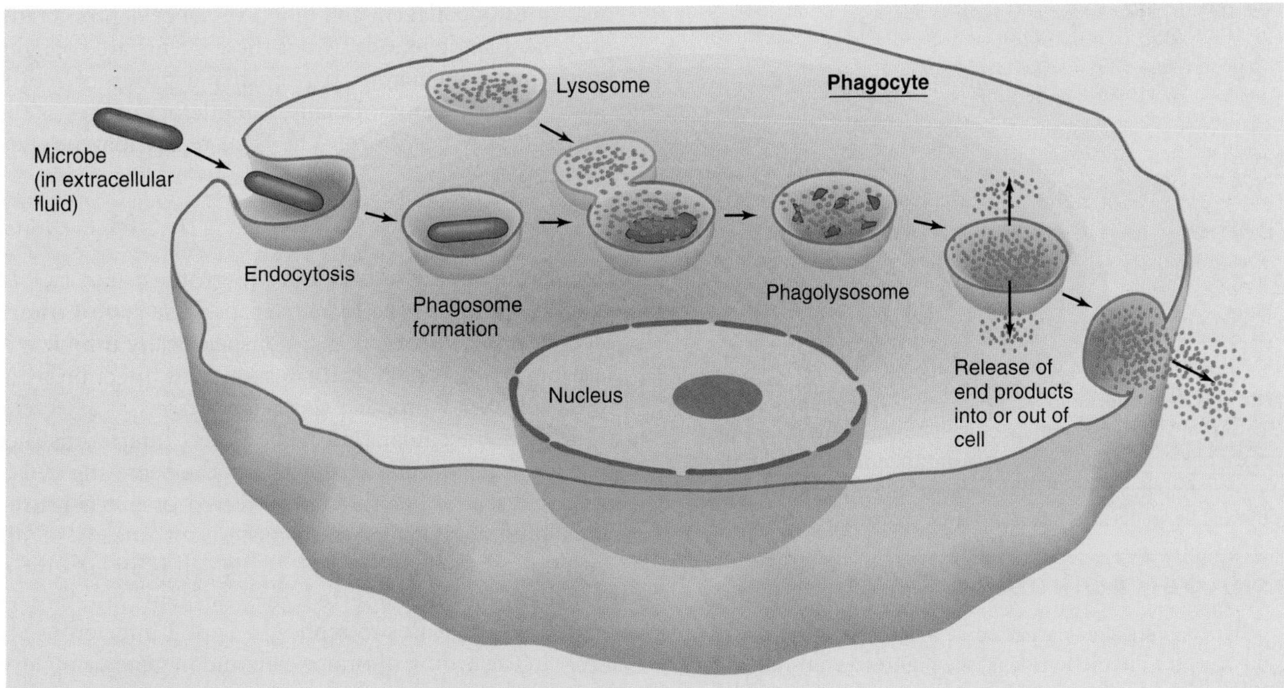

Figure 18.4 AP|R Phagocytosis and intracellular destruction of a microbe. After destruction has taken place in the phagolysosome, the end products are released to the outside of the cell by exocytosis or used by the cell for its own metabolism.

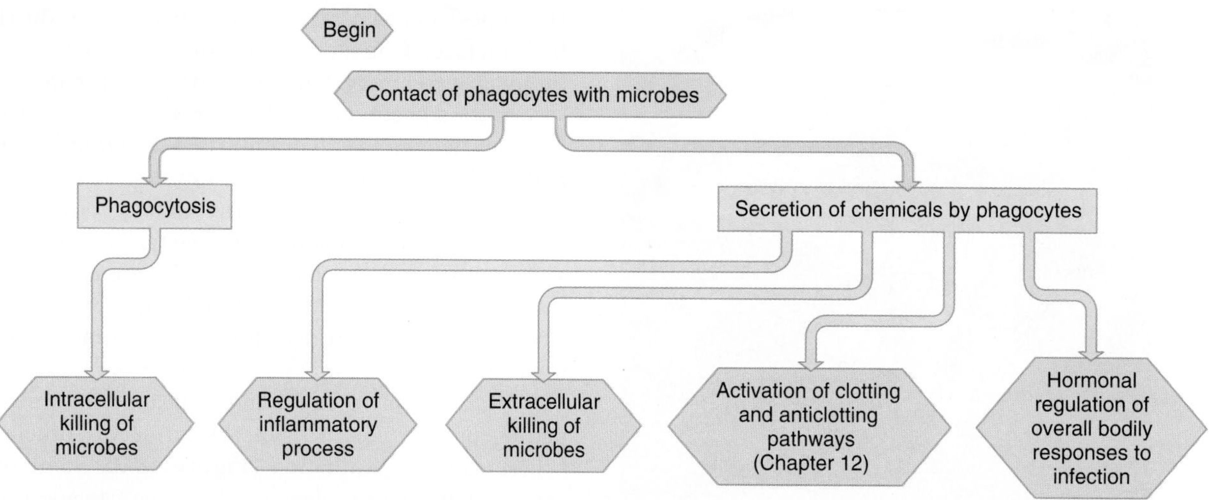

Figure 18.5 APIR Role of phagocytes in innate immune responses. Hormonal regulation of overall bodily responses to infection, partly addressed in Chapter 11, will also be discussed later in this chapter.

interactions lead to the formation of active C3b, the opsonin described in the previous paragraph, and the activation of the subsequent complement molecules in the pathway. However, not all microbes have a surface conducive to initiating the alternative pathway.

Other Opsonins in Innate Responses

In addition to complement C3b, other plasma proteins can bind nonspecifically to carbohydrates or lipids in the cell wall of microbes and facilitate opsonization. Many of these—for example, **C-reactive protein**—are produced by the liver and are always found at some concentration in the plasma. Their production and plasma concentrations, however, are greatly increased during inflammation.

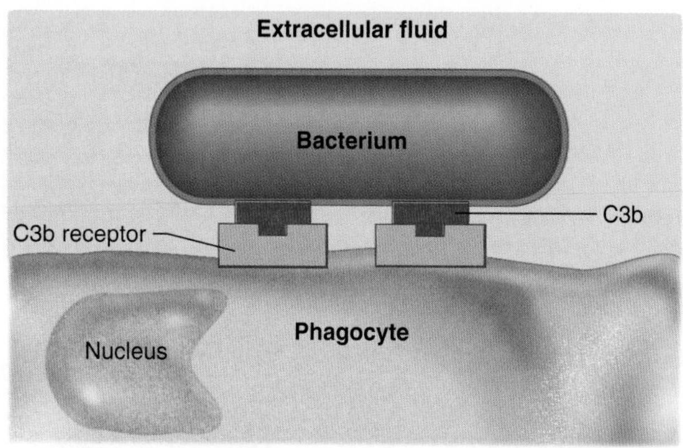

Figure 18.6 Function of complement C3b as an opsonin. One portion of C3b binds nonspecifically to carbohydrates on the surface of the bacterium, whereas another portion binds to specific receptor sites for C3b on the plasma membrane of the phagocyte. The structures are not drawn to scale.

PHYSIOLOGICAL INQUIRY

- In earlier chapters, you learned some of the characteristics of ligand-receptor interactions (e.g., see Figures 3.26 through 3.31). What general features of the C3b receptor may make it suitable for binding C3b and not other ligands?

Answer can be found at end of chapter.

Tissue Repair

The final stage of inflammation is tissue repair. Depending upon the tissue involved, multiplication of organ-specific cells by cell division may or may not occur during this stage. For example, liver cells multiply but skeletal muscle cells do not. In any case, fibroblasts (a type of connective-tissue cell) that reside in the area divide rapidly and begin to secrete large quantities of collagen, and blood vessel cells proliferate in the process of angiogenesis. All of these events are brought about by chemical mediators, particularly a group of locally produced growth factors. Finally, remodeling occurs as the healing process winds down. The final repair may be imperfect, leaving a scar.

Interferons

Interferons are cytokines and are grouped into two families called type I and type II interferons. The **type I interferons** include several proteins that nonspecifically inhibit viral replication inside host cells. In response to infection by a virus, most cell types produce these interferons and secrete them into the extracellular fluid. The type I interferons then bind to plasma membrane receptors on the secreting cell and on other cells, whether they are infected or not (**Figure 18.8**). This binding triggers the synthesis of dozens of different antiviral proteins by the cell. If the cell is already infected or eventually becomes infected, these proteins interfere with the ability of the viruses to replicate. Type I interferons also play a role in the killing of tumor cells and in generating fever during an infection.

The actions of type I interferons just described are not specific. Many kinds of viruses induce interferon synthesis, and interferons in turn can inhibit the multiplication of

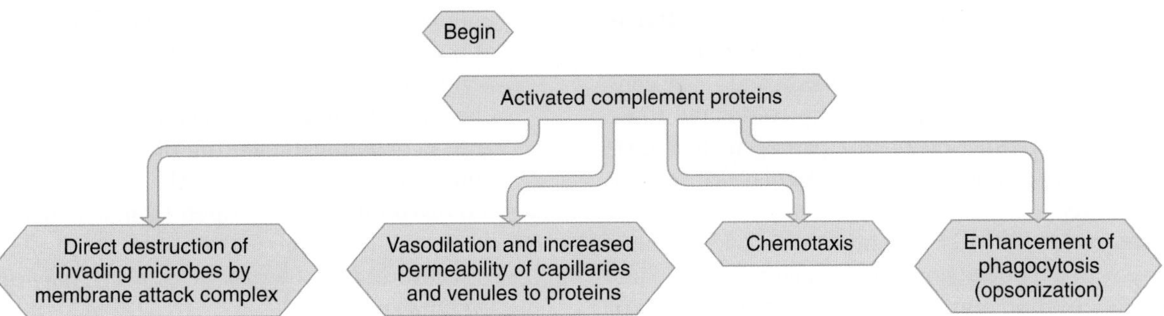

Figure 18.7 Functions of complement proteins. The effects on blood vessels and chemotaxis are exerted both directly by complement molecules and indirectly via other inflammatory mediators (for example, histamine) that are released by the complement molecules.

many kinds of viruses. Recent research, however, has revealed that type I interferons also influence the nature of certain aspects of the adaptive immune response.

The one member of the **type II interferons**—called **interferon-gamma**—is produced by immune cells. This interferon potentiates some of the actions of type I interferons, enhances the bacteria-killing activity of macrophages, and acts as a chemokine in the inflammatory process.

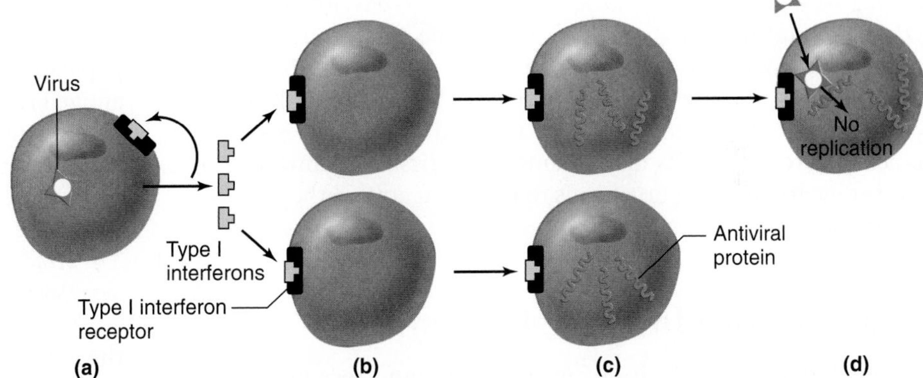

Figure 18.8 Role of type I interferon in preventing viral replication. (a) Most cell types, when infected with viruses, secrete type I interferons, which enter the interstitial fluid and (b) bind to type I interferon receptors on the secreting cells themselves (autocrine function) and adjacent cells (paracrine function). In addition, some type I interferons enter the blood and bind to type I interferon receptors on far-removed cells (endocrine function). (c) The binding of type I interferons to their receptors induces the synthesis of proteins that (d) inhibit viral replication should viruses enter the cell.

PHYSIOLOGICAL INQUIRY

- Are there other examples besides immune secretions in which a single substance may act as both an endocrine and paracrine substance? (*Hint:* Refer back to Chapters 11, 15, and 17 for help if necessary.)

Answer can be found at end of chapter.

Toll-Like Receptors

At the beginning of this section, we mentioned that innate immunity often depends upon an immune cell recognizing some general molecular feature common to many types of pathogens. These features are called **pathogen-associated molecular patterns (PAMPs)**. We now ask, How is that recognition accomplished? In 1985, researchers interested in how embryonic animals differentiate into mature organisms discovered a protein they named Toll (now called Toll-1) that was required for the proper dorsoventral orientation of fruit flies. In 1996, however, it was discovered that Toll-1 also conferred upon *adult* fruit flies the ability to fight off fungal infections, a discovery that was recognized in 2011 with the awarding of the Nobel Prize in Physiology or Medicine. Since that time, a family of Toll proteins has been discovered in animals from nematodes to mammals, including humans, expressed in the plasma and endosomal membranes of macrophages and dendritic cells, among others. One function of these proteins is to recognize and bind to highly conserved molecular features associated with pathogens (that is, PAMPs); these include lipopolysaccharide and other lipids and carbohydrates, viral and bacteria nucleic acids, and a protein found in the flagellum of many bacteria. When binding of one of these ligands occurs on the plasma membrane, second messengers are generated within the immune cell, which leads to secretion of inflammatory mediators such as IL-1, IL-12, and TNF-α. These in turn stimulate the activity of immune cells involved in the innate immune response. Some of these signals also activate cells involved in the adaptive immune response. Because many of the Toll proteins are plasma-membrane-bound, bind to extracellular ligands, and induce second-messenger formation, they are referred to as *receptors;* the family of proteins is known as **Toll-like receptors (TLRs)**. Despite this, not all TLRs generate intracellular signals when bound to a ligand; some TLRs induce attachment of a microbe to a macrophage, for example, and thereby its phagocytosis and subsequent destruction.

TLRs belong to a family of proteins called **pattern-recognition receptors (PRRs)**, all of which recognize and bind to a variety of pathogen ligands. These ligands have conserved molecular features that are generally considered to be vital to the survival or function of that pathogen. It is estimated that as many as a thousand such molecular features are recognized by PRRs.

The importance of TLRs in mammals has been demonstrated in mice with a mutated form of one member of the family called Toll-4. These mice are hypersensitive to the effects of injections with lipopolysaccharide (to mimic a bacterial infection) and are less able to ward off bacterial infection. In humans, recent studies suggest that certain naturally occurring variants in a specific TLR are associated with increased risk of certain diseases.

TLRs are currently an active area of investigation among biologists because of their importance as developmental factors in invertebrates and their immune significance in some adult invertebrates and possibly all vertebrates. Certain domains of these receptors have even been identified in plants, where they seem also to be involved in disease resistance. Therefore, TLRs may be among the first mechanisms to ever evolve in living organisms to protect against pathogen infection.

18.3 Adaptive Immune Responses

Because of the complexity of adaptive immune responses, the following is presented as a brief orientation before more detail is given regarding the various components of the response.

Overview

Lymphocytes are the essential cells in adaptive immune responses. Unlike innate response mechanisms, lymphocytes must recognize the specific foreign material to be attacked. Any molecule that can trigger an adaptive immune response against itself or the cell bearing it is called an **antigen.** (Immunologists prefer the more technically correct term *immunogen.*) Most antigens are either proteins or very large polysaccharides. The term *antigen* is a functional term; that is, any molecule, regardless of its location or function, that can induce a specific immune response against itself is by definition an antigen. Therefore, an antigen is any molecule that the host does not recognize as self. Antigens include the protein coats of viruses, specific proteins on foreign cells, some cancer cells, transplanted cells, and toxins. The ability of lymphocytes to distinguish one antigen from another confers specificity upon the immune responses in which they participate.

A typical adaptive immune response can be divided into three stages:

1. *The encounter and recognition of an antigen by lymphocytes.* During its development, each lymphocyte synthesizes and inserts into its plasma membrane multiple copies of a single type of receptor that can bind to a specific antigen. If, at a later time, the lymphocyte ever encounters that antigen, the antigen becomes bound to the receptors. This binding is the physicochemical meaning of the word *recognize* in immunology. As a result, the ability of lymphocytes to distinguish one antigen from another is determined by the nature of their plasma membrane receptors. *Each lymphocyte is specific for just one type of antigen.*
2. *Lymphocyte activation.* The binding of an antigen to a receptor must occur for **lymphocyte activation.** Upon binding to an antigen, the lymphocyte becomes activated and undergoes multiple rounds of cell division. As a result, many daughter lymphocytes develop from a single progenitor that are identical in their ability to recognize a specific antigen; this is called **clonal expansion.** It is estimated that in a typical person the lymphocyte population expresses more than 100 million distinct antigen receptors. After activation, some lymphocytes will function as effector lymphocytes to carry out the attack response. Others will be set aside as **memory cells,** poised to recognize the antigen if it returns in the future.
3. *The attack launched by the activated lymphocytes and their secretions.* The activated effector lymphocytes launch an attack against the antigens that are recognized by the antigen-specific receptor. Activated B cells, which comprise one group of lymphocytes, differentiate into plasma cells that secrete antibodies into the blood. These antibodies opsonize pathogens or foreign substances and target them for attack by innate immune cells. Activated cytotoxic T cells, another type of lymphocyte, directly attack and kill the cells bearing the antigens. Once the attack is successfully completed, the great majority of the B cells, plasma cells, and T cells that participated in it die by apoptosis. The timely death of these effector cells is a homeostatic response that prevents the immune response from becoming excessive and possibly destroying its own tissues. However, memory cells persist even after the immune response has been successfully completed.

Lymphoid Organs and Lymphocyte Origins

Our first task is to describe the organs and tissues in which lymphocytes originate and come to reside. Then the various types of lymphocytes alluded to in the overview and summarized in Table 18.1 will be described.

Lymphoid Organs

Like all leukocytes, lymphocytes circulate in the blood. At any moment, the great majority of lymphocytes are not actually in the blood, however, but in a group of organs and tissues collectively called the **lymphoid organs.** These are subdivided into primary and secondary lymphoid organs.

The **primary lymphoid organs** are the bone marrow and thymus. These organs are the initial sites of lymphocyte development. They supply the body with mature but naive lymphocytes—that is, lymphocytes that have not yet been activated by specific antigen. The bone marrow and thymus are not normally sites in which naive lymphocytes undergo activation during an immune response.

The **secondary lymphoid organs** include the lymph nodes, spleen, tonsils, and lymphocyte accumulations in the linings of the intestinal, respiratory, genital, and urinary tracts. It is in the secondary lymphoid organs that naive lymphocytes are activated to participate in adaptive immune responses.

We have stated that the bone marrow and thymus supply mature lymphocytes to the secondary lymphoid organs. Most of the lymphocytes in the secondary organs are not, however, the same cells that originated in the primary lymphoid organs. The explanation of this seeming paradox is that, once in the secondary organ, a mature lymphocyte coming from the bone marrow or thymus can undergo cell division to produce additional identical lymphocytes, which in turn undergo cell division, and so on. In other words, all lymphocytes are *descended* from ancestors that matured in the bone marrow or thymus but may not themselves have arisen in those organs. All the progeny cells derived by cell division from a single lymphocyte constitute a lymphocyte **clone.**

There are no anatomical links, other than via the cardiovascular system, between the various lymphoid organs. Let us look briefly at these organs—with the exception of the bone marrow, which was described in Section F of Chapter 12.

The **thymus** lies in the upper part of the chest. Its size varies with age, being relatively large at birth and continuing to grow until puberty, when it gradually atrophies and is replaced by fatty tissue. Before its atrophy, the thymus consists mainly of immature lymphocytes that will develop into mature T cells that will eventually migrate via the blood to the secondary lymphoid organs.

Recall from Chapter 12 that the fluid flowing in the lymphatic vessels is called *lymph*, which is interstitial fluid that has entered the lymphatic capillaries and is routed to the large lymphatic vessels that drain into systemic veins. During this trip, the lymph flows through **lymph nodes** scattered along the vessels. Lymph, therefore, is the route by which lymphocytes in the lymph nodes encounter the antigens that activate them. Each node is a honeycomb of lymph-filled sinuses (**Figure 18.9**) with large clusters of lymphocytes (the lymphatic nodules) between the sinuses. The lymph nodes also contain many macrophages and dendritic cells.

The **spleen** is the largest of the secondary lymphoid organs and lies in the left part of the abdominal cavity between the stomach and the diaphragm. The spleen is to the circulating blood what the lymph nodes are to the lymph. Blood percolates through the vascular meshwork of the spleen's interior, where large collections of lymphocytes, macrophages, and dendritic cells are found. The macrophages of the spleen, in addition to interacting with lymphocytes, also phagocytose aging or dead erythrocytes.

The **tonsils** and **adenoids** are a group of small, rounded lymphoid organs in the pharynx. They are filled with lymphocytes, macrophages, and dendritic cells, and they have openings called crypts to the surface of the pharynx. Their lymphocytes respond to microbes that arrive by way of ingested food as well as through inspired air.

At any moment in time, some lymphocytes are on their way from the bone marrow or thymus to the secondary lymphoid organs. The vast majority, though, are cells that are participating in lymphocyte traffic *between* the secondary lymphoid organs, blood, lymph, and all the tissues of the body. Lymphocytes from all the secondary lymphoid organs constantly enter the lymphatic vessels that drain them (all lymphoid organs, not just lymph nodes, are drained by lymphatic vessels) and are carried to the blood. Simultaneously, some blood lymphocytes are pushing through the endothelium of venules all over the body to enter the interstitial fluid. From there, they move into lymphatic capillaries and along the lymphatic vessels to lymph nodes. They may then leave the lymphatic vessels to take up residence in the node.

This recirculation is going on all the time, not just during an infection, although the migration of lymphocytes into an inflamed area is greatly increased by the chemotaxis process (see Figure 18.2). Lymphocyte trafficking greatly increases the likelihood that any given lymphocyte will encounter the antigen it is specifically programmed to recognize. (In contrast to the lymphocytes, polymorphonuclear granulocytes and monocytes do not recirculate; once they leave the bloodstream and enter a tissue, they remain there or die.)

Lymphocyte Origins

The multiple populations and subpopulations of lymphocytes are summarized in Table 18.1. *B lymphocytes* (*B cells*) mature in the bone marrow and then are carried by the blood to the secondary lymphoid organs (**Figure 18.10**). This process of maturation and migration continues throughout a person's life. All generations of lymphocytes that subsequently arise from these cells by cell division in the secondary lymphoid organs will be identical to the parent cells; that is, they will be B-cell clones.

In contrast to the B cells, other lymphocytes leave the bone marrow in an immature state during fetal and early neonatal life. They are carried to the thymus and mature there before moving to the secondary lymphoid organs. These cells are called *T lymphocytes* (or *T cells*). Like B cells, T cells also undergo cell division in secondary lymphoid organs, the progeny being identical to the original T cells and thereby part of that T-cell clone.

In addition to the B and T cells, there is another distinct population of lymphocytes called *natural killer* (*NK*) *cells.* These cells arise in the bone marrow, but their precursors and life history are still unclear. As we will see, NK cells, unlike B and T cells, are not specific to a given antigen.

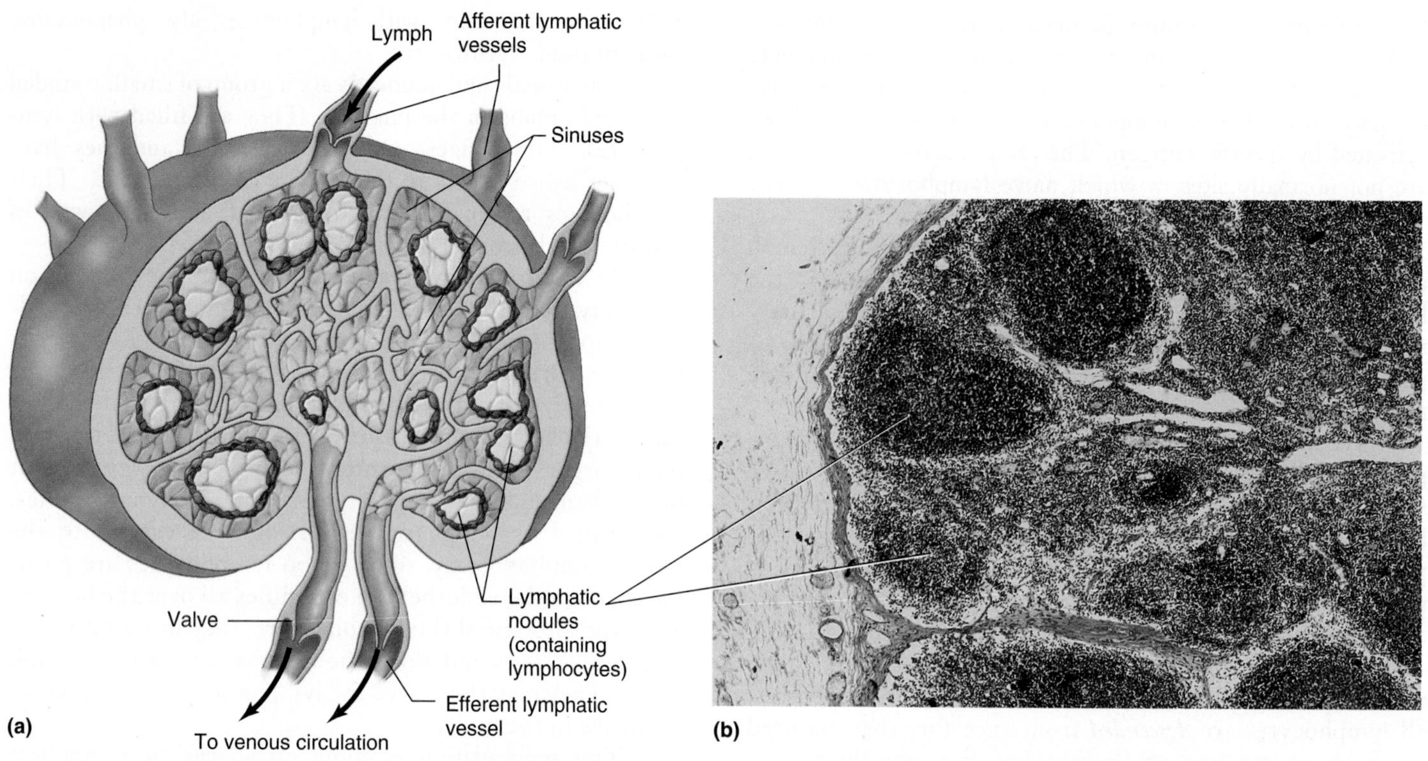

Figure 18.9 AP|R Anatomy of a lymph node as seen in (a) a sketch and in (b) a section viewed by light microscopy.

PHYSIOLOGICAL INQUIRY

- The innate immune response includes vasodilation of the microcirculation and an increase in protein permeability of the capillaries (see Figure 18.2). How might these changes enhance the adaptive immune response during an infection? (*Hint:* What effect would these circulatory changes have on the volume of fluid in the interstitial space and, therefore, lymph flow?)

Answer can be found at end of chapter.

Functions of B Cells and T Cells

Upon activation, B cells differentiate into plasma cells, which secrete **antibodies**, proteins that travel all over the body to reach antigens identical to those that stimulated their production. In the body fluids outside of cells, the antibodies combine with these antigens and guide an attack that eliminates the antigens or the cells bearing them.

Antibody-mediated responses are also called *humoral* responses, the adjective *humoral* denoting communication "by way of soluble chemical messengers" (in this case, antibodies in the blood). Antibody-mediated responses have an extremely wide diversity of targets and are the major defense against bacteria, viruses, and other pathogens in the extracellular fluid and against toxic molecules (toxins).

In contrast to humoral responses, T-cell responses are *cell-mediated* responses. T cells constitute a family that has at least two major functional subsets, **cytotoxic T cells** and **helper T cells.** Recently, it has become clear that a third subset—called suppressor or **regulatory T cells**—inhibits the function of both B cells and cytotoxic T cells.

Another way to categorize T cells is not by function but rather by the presence of certain proteins, called CD4 and CD8, in their plasma membranes. Cytotoxic T cells have CD8 and so are also commonly called CD8+ cells; helper T cells and regulatory T cells express CD4 and so are also commonly called CD4+ cells.

Cytotoxic T cells are "attack" cells. Following activation, they travel to the location of their target, bind to them via antigen on these targets, and directly kill their targets via secreted chemicals. Responses mediated by cytotoxic T cells are directed against the body's own cells that have become cancerous or infected with viruses (or certain bacteria and parasites that, like viruses, take up residence inside host cells).

It is worth emphasizing the important geographic difference in antibody-mediated responses and responses mediated by cytotoxic T cells. The B cells (and plasma cells derived from them) remain in whatever location the recognition and activation steps occurred. The plasma cells send their antibodies forth via the blood to seek out antigens identical to those that triggered the response. Cytotoxic T cells must enter the blood and seek out the targets.

We have now assigned general roles to the B cells and cytotoxic T cells. What role is performed by the helper T cells? As their name implies, these cells do not themselves

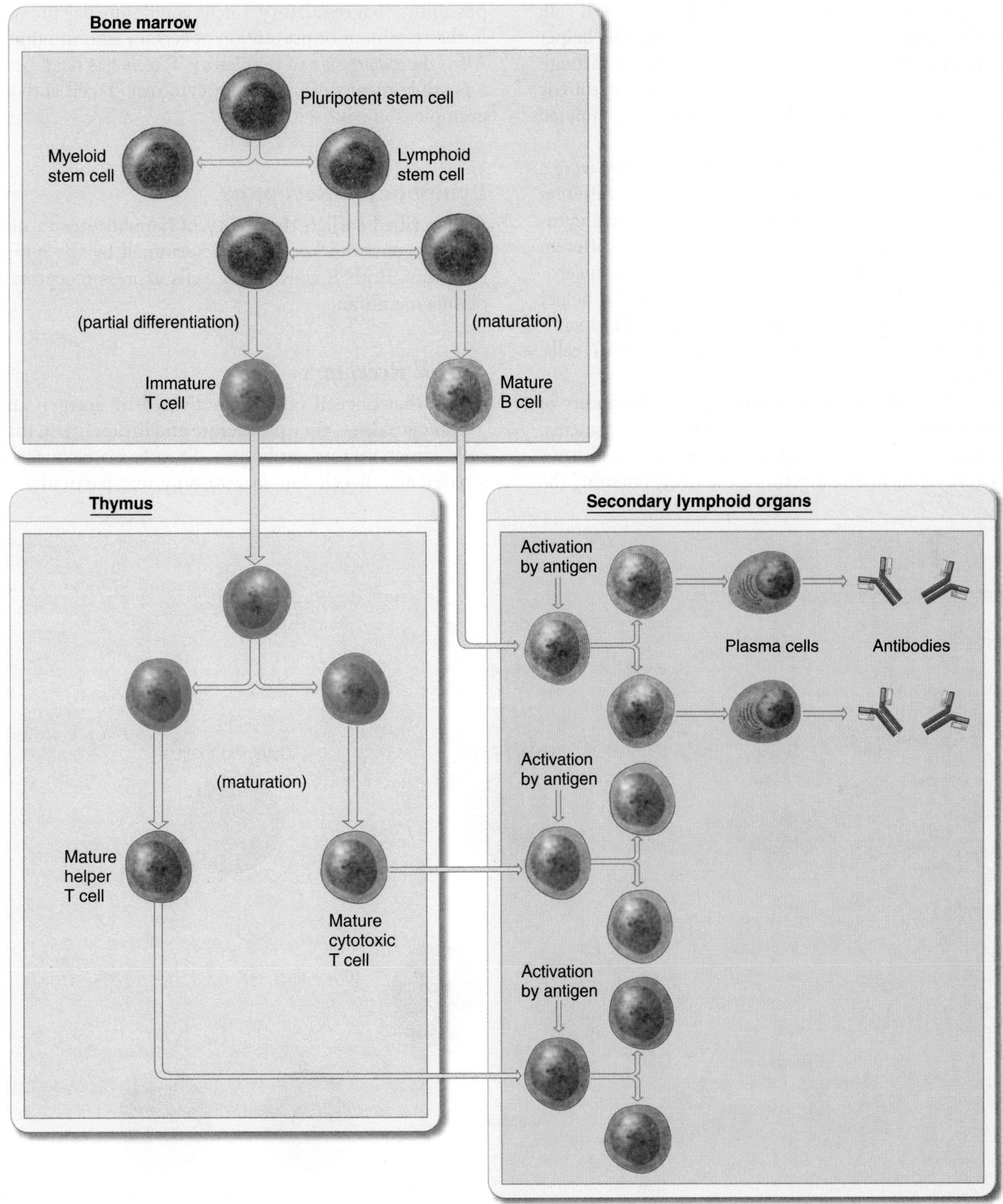

Figure 18.10 APIR Derivation of B cells and T cells. NK cells are not shown because their transformations, if any, after leaving the bone marrow are still not clear.

function as attack cells but, rather, assist in the activation and function of B cells, macrophages, and cytotoxic T cells. Helper T cells go through the usual first two stages of the immune response. First, they combine with antigen and then undergo activation. Once activated, they migrate to the site of B-cell activation. B cells that have bound antigen present it to activated helper cells. Antigen-specific helper T cells make direct contact with the B cell, and the communication given by surface receptors—along with the secretion of cytokines—induces B-cell activation. The role of helper T cells in cytotoxic T-cell activation is more complex. To activate cytotoxic T cells, activated helper T cells help other cells, most likely dendritic cells, to activate cytotoxic T cells. Unlike the B cell, which directly interacts with the helper T cell, the helper T cell assists cytotoxic T-cell activation indirectly through other cells. With only a few exceptions, B cells and cytotoxic T cells cannot function adequately unless they are stimulated by cytokines from helper T cells.

Helper T cells will be considered as though they were a homogeneous cell population, but in fact, there are different subtypes of helper T cells, distinguished by the different cytokines they secrete when activated. By means of these different cytokines, they help different sets of lymphocytes, macrophages, and NK cells. Some of the cytokines secreted by helper T cells also act as inflammatory mediators. **Figure 18.11** summarizes the basic interactions among B cells, cytotoxic T cells, and helper T cells.

Regulatory T cells are believed to suppress the ability of certain B and cytotoxic T cells to attack a person's own proteins, which can occur in diseases known as autoimmune diseases (described later). As such, investigators are actively pursuing the possibility that regulatory T cells could someday prove effective in the treatment or prevention of certain autoimmune diseases. Also, the *suppression* of regulatory T cells has been proposed as a possible means of increasing cytotoxic T-cell activity in, for example, someone with cancer.

Lymphocyte Receptors

As described earlier, the ability of lymphocytes to distinguish one antigen from another is determined by the lymphocytes' receptors. Both B cells and T cells express receptors on their plasma membrane.

B-Cell Receptors

Recall that once B cells are activated by antigen and helper T-cell cytokines, they proliferate and differentiate into plasma cells, which secrete antibodies. The plasma cells derived from a particular B cell can secrete only one particular antibody.

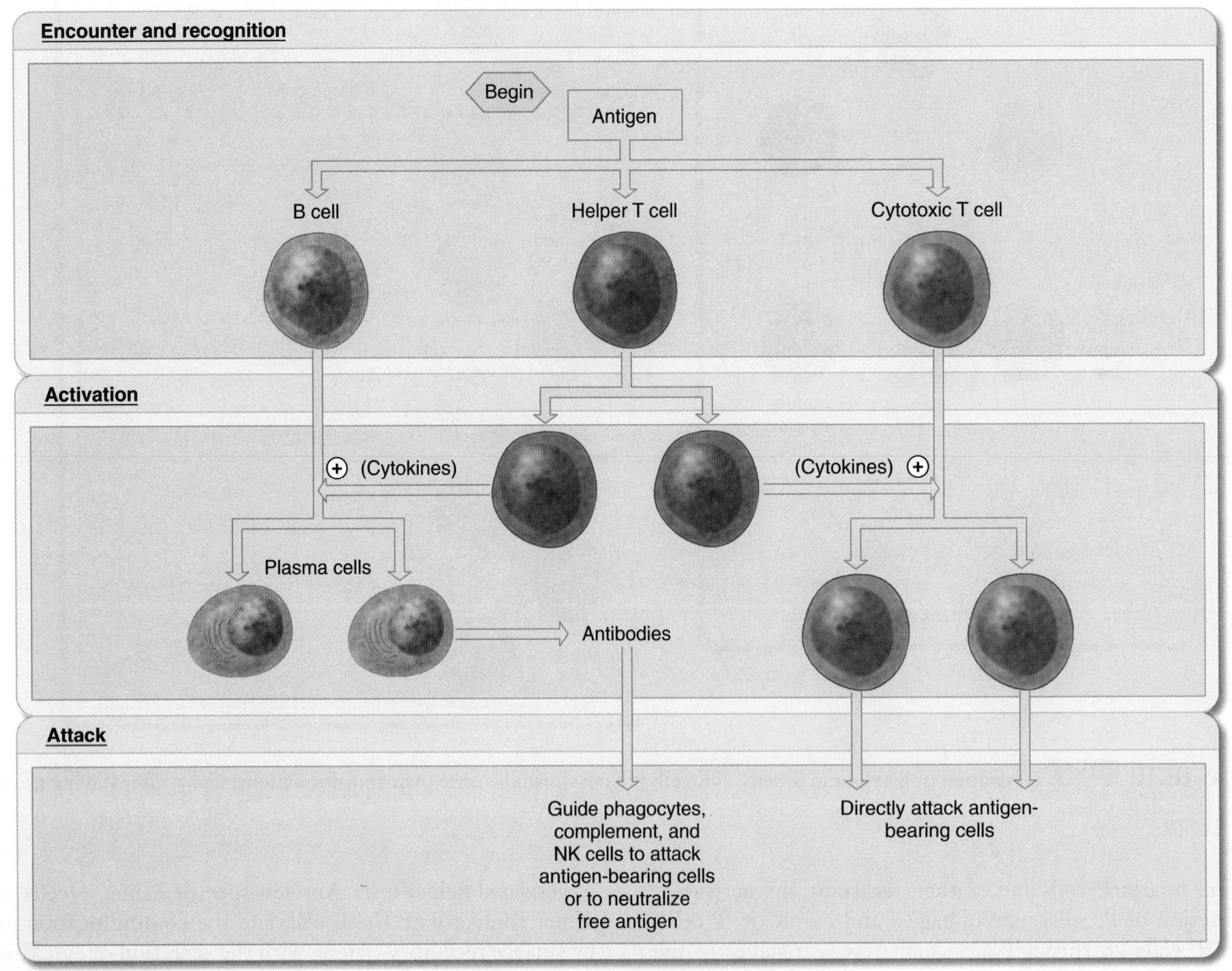

Figure 18.11 APR Summary of the roles of B, cytotoxic T, and helper T cells in immune responses. Events of the attack phase are described in later sections. The ⊕ symbol denotes a stimulatory effect (activation) of cytokines.

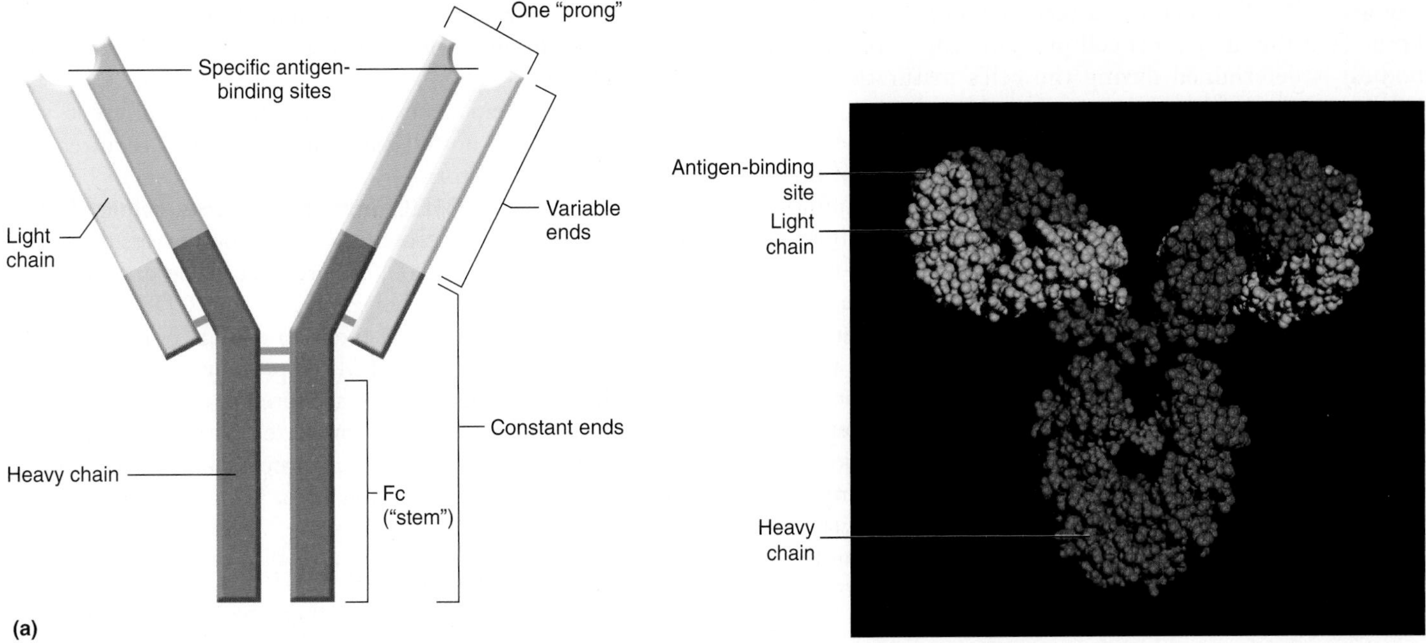

Figure 18.12 APIR Immunoglobulin structure. (a) The Fc portions and an extended region of the heavy chains are the same for all immunoglobulins of a particular class. A small portion of the light chains are also the same for a given immunoglobulin class. Collectively, these portions of the heavy and light chains are called "constant ends." Each "prong" contains a variable amino acid sequence, which represents the single antigen-binding site. The links between chains represent disulfide bonds. (b) Three-dimensional simulation of an immunoglobulin showing antigen-binding sites and the light and heavy chains. The purple region represents associated carbohydrate, the function of which is uncertain but may be related to binding of immunoglobulins to substrates.

Each B cell always displays on its plasma membrane copies of the particular antibody its plasma cell progeny can produce. This surface protein (glycoprotein, to be more accurate) acts as the receptor for the antigen specific to it.

B-cell receptors and plasma cell antibodies constitute the family of proteins known as **immunoglobulins.** The receptors themselves, even though they are identical to the antibodies to be secreted by the plasma cell derived from the activated B cell, are technically not antibodies because only *secreted* immunoglobulins are called antibodies. Each immunoglobulin molecule is composed of four interlinked polypeptide chains (**Figure 18.12**). The two long chains are called heavy chains, and the two short ones, light chains. There are five major classes of immunoglobulins, determined by the amino acid sequences in the heavy chains and a portion of the light chains. The classes are designated by the letters A, D, E, G, and M following the symbol Ig for immunoglobulin; thus, we have IgA, IgD, and so on.

As illustrated in Figure 18.12, immunoglobulins have a "stem" called the **Fc** portion and comprising the lower half of the two heavy chains. The upper part of each heavy chain and its associated light chain form an **antigen-binding site**—the amino acid sequences that bind antigen. The amino acid sequences of the Fc portion plus an additional portion of the heavy chains and part of the light chains are identical for all immunoglobulins of a single class (IgA, IgD, and so on). In contrast to the identical (or "constant") regions of the heavy and light chains, the amino acid sequences of the antigen-binding sites vary from immunoglobulin to immunoglobulin in a given class and are therefore known as variable ends. Each of the five classes of antibodies, therefore, could contain up to millions of unique immunoglobulins, each capable of combining with only one specific antigen (or, in some cases, several antigens whose structures are very similar). The interaction between an antigen-binding site of an immunoglobulin and an antigen is analogous to the lock-and-key interactions that apply generally to the binding of ligands by proteins.

One more point should be mentioned: B-cell receptors can bind antigen whether the antigen is a molecule dissolved in the extracellular fluid or is present on the surface of a foreign cell, such as a microbe, floating free in the fluids. In the latter case, the B cell becomes linked to the foreign cell via the bonds between the B-cell receptor and the surface antigen.

To summarize so far, any given B cell or clone of identical B cells possesses unique immunoglobulin receptors—that is, receptors with unique antigen-binding sites. Consequently, the body arms itself with millions of clones of different B cells to ensure that specific receptors exist for the vast number of different antigens the organism *might* encounter during its lifetime. The particular immunoglobulin that any given B cell displays as a receptor on its plasma membrane (and that its plasma cell progeny will secrete as antibodies) is determined during the cell's maturation in the bone marrow.

This raises a very interesting question. In the human genome, there are only about 200 genes that code for immunoglobulins. How, then, can the body produce immunoglobulins having millions of different antigen-binding sites, given that each immunoglobulin requires coding by a distinct gene? This diversity arises as the result of a genetic process unique to developing lymphocytes because only these cells express the enzymes required to catalyze the process. The DNA in each of the genes that code for immunoglobulin antigen-binding sites is cut into small segments, randomly rearranged along the gene, and then rejoined to form new DNA molecules. This cutting and rejoining varies from B cell to B cell, thereby resulting in great diversity of the genes coding for the immunoglobulins of all the B cells taken together.

T-Cell Receptors

T-cell receptors for antigens are two-chained proteins that, like immunoglobulins, have specific regions that differ from one T-cell clone to another. However, T-cell receptors remain embedded in the T-cell membrane and are not secreted like antibodies. As in B-cell development, multiple DNA rearrangements occur during T-cell maturation, leading to millions of distinct T-cell clones—distinct in that the cells of any given clone possess receptors of a single specificity. For T cells, this maturation occurs during their residence in the thymus.

In addition to their general structural differences, the B-cell and T-cell receptors differ in a much more important way: *The T-cell receptor cannot combine with antigen unless the antigen is first complexed with certain of the body's own plasma membrane proteins.* The T-cell receptor then combines with the entire complex of antigen and body (self) protein.

The self plasma membrane proteins that must be complexed with the antigen in order for T-cell recognition to occur constitute a group of proteins coded for by genes found on a single chromosome (chromosome 6) and known collectively as the **major histocompatibility complex (MHC)**. The proteins are therefore called **MHC proteins** (in humans, also known as the human leukocyte antigens, or HLAs). Because no two persons other than identical twins have the same sets of MHC genes, no two individuals have the same MHC proteins on the plasma membranes of their cells. MHC proteins are, in essence, cellular "identity tags"—that is, genetic markers of biological self.

The MHC proteins are often called "restriction elements" because the ability of a T cell's receptor to recognize an antigen is restricted to situations in which the antigen is first complexed with an MHC protein. There are two classes of MHC proteins: I and II. **Class I MHC proteins** are found on the surface of virtually all cells of the body except erythrocytes. **Class II MHC proteins** are found mainly on the surface of macrophages, B cells, and dendritic cells. Under certain conditions, other cell types are induced to express class II MHC.

Another important point is that the different subsets of T cells do not all have the same MHC requirements (**Table 18.4**). Cytotoxic T cells require antigen to be associated with class I MHC proteins, whereas helper T cells require class II MHC proteins. One reason for this difference in requirements stems from the presence, as described earlier, of CD4 proteins on the helper T cells and CD8 proteins on the cytotoxic T cells; CD4 binds to class II MHC proteins, whereas CD8 binds to class I MHC proteins.

How do antigens, which are foreign, end up on the surface of the body's own cells complexed with MHC proteins? The answer is provided by the process known as **antigen presentation,** to which we now turn.

Antigen Presentation to T Cells

T cells can bind antigen only when the antigen appears on the plasma membrane of a host cell complexed with the cell's MHC proteins. Cells bearing these complexes, therefore, function as **antigen-presenting cells (APCs)**.

Presentation to Helper T Cells

Helper T cells require class II MHC proteins to function. Only macrophages, B cells, and dendritic cells express class II MHC proteins and therefore can function as APCs for helper T cells.

The function of the macrophage or dendritic cell as an APC for helper T cells is depicted in **Figure 18.13**, which shows that the cells form a link between innate and adaptive immune responses. After a microbe or noncellular antigen has been phagocytosed by a macrophage or dendritic cell in a *nonspecific* response, it is partially broken down into smaller peptide fragments by the cell's proteolytic enzymes. The resulting digested fragments then bind (within endosomes) to class II MHC proteins synthesized by the cell. This entire complex is then transported to the cell surface, where it is displayed in the plasma membrane. It is to this complex on the cell surface of the macrophage or dendritic cell that a specific helper T cell binds.

TABLE 18.4 MHC Restriction of the Lymphocyte Receptors

Cell Type	MHC Restriction
B	Do not interact with MHC proteins
Helper T	Class II, found only on macrophages, dendritic cells, and B cells
Cytotoxic T	Class I, found on all nucleated cells of the body
NK	Interaction with MHC proteins not required for activation

Note that it is not the intact antigen but rather the peptide fragments, called antigenic determinants or **epitopes**, of the antigen that are complexed to the MHC proteins and presented to the T cell. Despite this, it is customary to refer to "antigen" presentation rather than "epitope" presentation.

How B cells process antigen and present it to helper T cells is essentially the same as just described for dendritic cells and macrophages (**Figure 18.13b**). The ability of B cells to present antigen to helper T cells is a *second* function of B cells in response to antigenic stimulation, the other being the differentiation of the B cells into antibody-secreting plasma cells.

The binding between a helper T-cell receptor and an antigen bound to class II MHC proteins on an APC is the essential *antigen-specific* event in helper T-cell activation. However, this binding by itself will not result in T-cell activation. In addition, interactions occur between other (nonantigenic) pairs of proteins on the surfaces of the attached helper T cell and APC, and these provide a necessary **costimulus** for T-cell activation (**Figure 18.14**).

Finally, the antigenic binding of the APC to the T cell—along with the costimulus—causes the APC to secrete large amounts of the cytokines **interleukin 1 (IL-1)** and **tumor necrosis factor-alpha (TNF-α)**, which act as paracrine substances on the attached helper T cell to provide yet another important stimulus for activation.

Thus, the APC participates in the activation of a helper T cell in three ways: (1) antigen presentation; (2) provision of a costimulus in the form of a matching nonantigenic plasma membrane protein; and (3) secretion of IL-1, TNF-α, and other cytokines (see Figure 18.14).

The activated helper T cell itself now secretes various cytokines that have both autocrine effects on the helper T cell and paracrine effects on adjacent B cells and any nearby

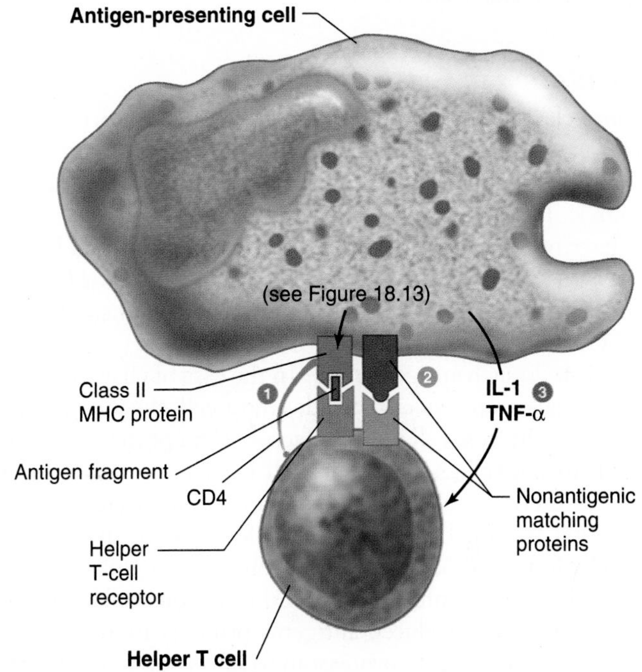

Figure 18.14 APIR Three events are required for the activation of helper T cells: (1) presentation of the antigen bound to a class II MHC protein on antigen-presenting cell (APC); (2) the binding of matching nonantigenic proteins in the plasma membranes of the APC and the helper T cell (costimulus); and (3) secretion by the APC of the cytokines interleukin 1 (IL-1), tumor necrosis factor-alpha (TNF-α), and other cytokines, which act on the helper T cell.

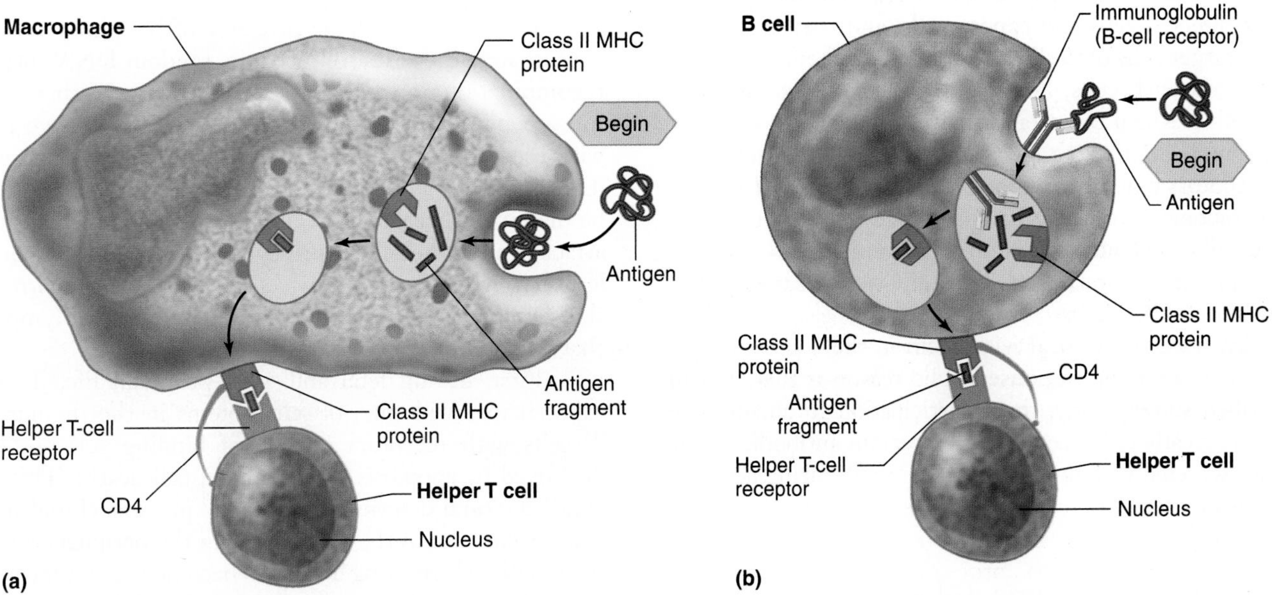

Figure 18.13 APIR Sequence of events by which antigen is processed and presented to a helper T cell by (a) a macrophage or (b) a B cell. In both cases, begin the figure with the antigen in the extracellular fluid.

cytotoxic T cells, NK cells, and still other cell types. Recent evidence suggests that helper T cells may program dendritic cells to activate CD8+ T cells. These processes will be described in later sections.

Presentation to Cytotoxic T Cells

Because class I MHC proteins are synthesized by virtually all nucleated cells, any such cell can act as an APC for a cytotoxic T cell. This distinction helps explain the major function of cytotoxic T cells—destruction of *any* of the body's own cells that have become cancerous or infected with viruses. The key point is that the antigens that complex with class I MHC proteins arise *within* body cells. They are endogenous antigens, synthesized by a body cell.

How do such antigens arise? In the case of viruses, once a virus has taken up residence inside a host cell, the viral nucleic acid causes the host cell to manufacture viral proteins that are foreign to the cell. A cancerous cell has had one or more of its genes altered by chemicals, radiation, or other factors. The altered genes, called ***oncogenes,*** code for proteins that are not normally found in the body. Such proteins act as antigens.

In both virus-infected cells and cancerous cells, some of the endogenously produced antigenic proteins are hydrolyzed by cytosolic enzymes (in proteasomes) into peptide fragments, which are transported into the endoplasmic reticulum. There, they are complexed with the host cell's class I MHC proteins and then shuttled by exocytosis to the plasma membrane surface, where a cytotoxic T cell specific for the complex can bind to it (**Figure 18.15**).

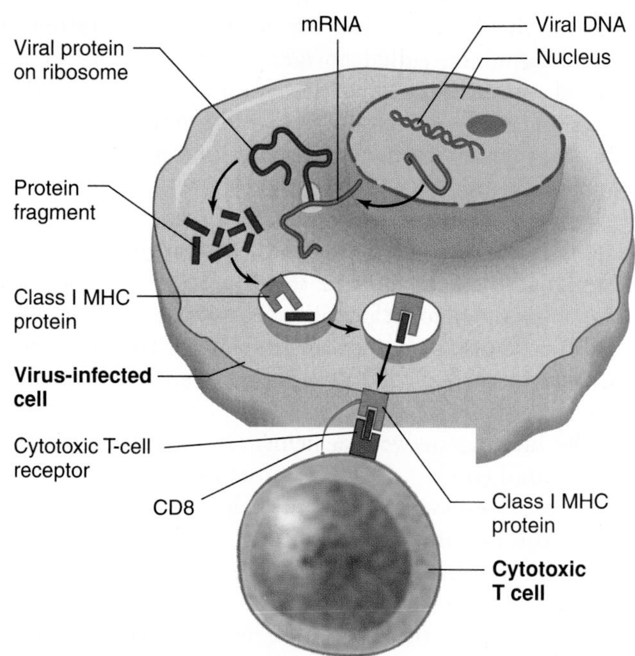

Figure 18.15 APIR Processing and presentation of viral antigen to a cytotoxic T cell by an infected cell. Begin this figure with the viral DNA in the cell's nucleus. The viral DNA induces the infected cell to produce viral protein, which is then hydrolyzed (by proteasomes). The fragments are complexed to the cell's class I MHC proteins in the endoplasmic reticulum, and these complexes are then shuttled to the plasma membrane.

NK Cells

As noted earlier, NK (natural killer) cells constitute a distinct class of lymphocytes. They have several functional similarities to those of cytotoxic T cells. For example, their major targets are virus-infected cells and cancer cells, and they attack and kill these target cells directly after binding to them. However, unlike cytotoxic T cells, NK cells are not antigen-specific; that is, each NK cell can attack virus-infected cells or cancer cells without recognizing a specific antigen. They have neither T-cell receptors nor the immunoglobulin receptors of B cells, and the exact nature of the NK-cell surface receptors that permits the cells to identify their targets is unknown (except in one case presented later). MHC proteins are not involved in the activation of NK cells.

Why, then, do we deal with them in the context of *specific* (adaptive) immune responses? The reason is that, as will be described subsequently, their participation in an immune response is greatly enhanced either by certain antibodies or by cytokines secreted by helper T cells activated during adaptive immune responses.

Development of Immune Tolerance

Our basic framework for understanding adaptive immune responses requires consideration of one more crucial question. How does the body develop what is called **immune tolerance**—lack of immune responsiveness to self? This may seem a strange question given the definition of an antigen as a foreign molecule that can generate an immune response. How is it, though, that the body "knows" that its own molecules, particularly proteins, are not foreign but are self molecules?

Recall that the huge diversity of lymphocyte receptors is ultimately the result of multiple, random DNA cutting and recombination processes. It is virtually certain, therefore, that in each person, clones of lymphocytes would have emerged with receptors that could bind to that person's own proteins. The existence and functioning of such lymphocytes would be disastrous because such binding would launch an immune attack against the cells expressing these proteins. There are at least two mechanisms—*clonal deletion* and *clonal inactivation*—that explain why normally there are no active lymphocytes that respond to self components.

First, during fetal and early postnatal life, T cells are exposed to a wide mix of self proteins in the thymus. Those T cells with receptors capable of binding self proteins are destroyed by apoptosis (programmed cell death). This process is called **clonal deletion.** The second process, **clonal inactivation**, occurs not in the thymus but in the periphery and causes potentially self-reacting T cells to become nonresponsive.

What are the mechanisms of clonal deletion and inactivation during fetal and early postnatal life? Recall that full activation of a helper T cell requires not only an antigen-specific stimulus but a nonspecific costimulus (interaction between complementary nonantigenic proteins on the APC and the T cell). If this costimulus is *not* provided, the helper T cell not only fails to become activated by antigen but dies or becomes inactivated forever. This is the case during early life. The induction of costimulatory molecules requires activated, antigen-presenting cells. Signaling through TLRs and secretion of inflammatory cytokines are two mechanisms of activating antigen-presenting cells to express costimulatory molecules that provide costimulus for T-cell activation.

This completes the framework for understanding adaptive immune responses. The next two sections utilize this framework in presenting typical responses from beginning to end, highlighting the interactions between lymphocytes and describing the attack mechanisms used by the various pathways.

Antibody-Mediated Immune Responses: Defenses Against Bacteria, Extracellular Viruses, and Toxins

A classical antibody-mediated response is one that results in the destruction of bacteria. The sequence of events, which is quite similar to the response to a virus in the extracellular fluid, is summarized in **Table 18.5** and **Figure 18.16**.

Antigen Recognition and B-Cell Activation

This process starts the same way as for nonspecific responses, with the bacteria penetrating one of the body's linings and entering the interstitial fluid. The bacteria then enter the lymphatic system and/or the bloodstream and are taken up by the lymph nodes and/or the spleen, respectively. There, a B cell, using its immunoglobulin receptor, recognizes the bacterial surface antigen and binds the bacterium.

In a few cases (notably, bacteria with cell-wall polysaccharide capsules), this binding is all that is needed to trigger B-cell activation. For the great majority of antigens, however, antigen binding is not enough, and signals in the form of cytokines released into the interstitial fluid by helper T cells near the antigen-bound B cells are also required.

For helper T cells to react against bacteria by secreting cytokines, they must bind to a complex of antigen and class II MHC protein on an APC. Let us assume that in this case the APC is a macrophage that has phagocytosed one of the bacteria, hydrolyzed its proteins into peptide fragments, complexed them with class II MHC proteins, and displayed the complexes on its surface. A helper T cell specific for the complex then binds to it, beginning the activation of the helper T cell. Moreover, the macrophage helps this activation process in two other ways: (1) It provides a costimulus via nonantigenic plasma membrane proteins, and (2) it secretes IL-1 and TNF-α.

The costimulus activates the helper T cell to secrete another cytokine named **interleukin-2** (**IL-2**). Among other functions, IL-1 and TNF-α stimulate the helper T cell to express more receptors for IL-2. IL-2, acting in an autocrine manner, then provides a proliferative stimulus to the activated helper T cell (see Figure 18.16). The cell divides, beginning the mitotic cycles that lead to the formation of a clone of activated helper T cells; these cells then release not only IL-2 but other cytokines as well.

Once activated, helper T cells migrate to lymph nodes where they interact with antigen-presenting B cells. The helper T cell stimulates B-cell activation by direct contact and cytokine release. Other cytokines—notably, IL-4 possibly produced by basophils—are also important in this step. Once activated, the B cell differentiates into a plasma cell that secretes antibodies that recognize the specific antigen. Thus, as shown in Figure 18.16, a series of protein messengers interconnects the various cell types, the helper T cells serving as the central coordinators.

As stated earlier, however, some of the B-cell progeny differentiate not into plasma cells but instead into memory cells, whose characteristics permit them to respond more

TABLE 18.5 Summary of Events in Antibody-Mediated Immunity Against Bacteria

I. In secondary lymphoid organs, bacterial antigen binds to specific receptors on the plasma membranes of B cells.
II. Antigen-presenting cells (APCs)—most likely the dendritic cells but macrophages and B cells— A. Present to helper T cells' processed antigen complexed to class II MHC proteins on the APCs; B. Provide a costimulus in the form of another membrane protein; and C. Secrete IL-1, TNF-α, and other cytokines, which act on the helper T cells.
III. In response, the helper T cells secrete IL-2, which stimulates the helper T cells themselves to proliferate and secrete IL-2 and other cytokines. These activate antigen-bound B cells to proliferate and differentiate into plasma cells. Some of the B cells differentiate into memory cells rather than plasma cells.
IV. The plasma cells secrete antibodies specific for the antigen that initiated the response, and the antibodies circulate all over the body via the blood.
V. These antibodies combine with antigen on the surface of the bacteria anywhere in the body.
VI. Presence of antibody bound to antigen facilitates phagocytosis of the bacteria by neutrophils and macrophages. It also activates the complement system, which further enhances phagocytosis and can directly kill the bacteria by the membrane attack complex. It may also induce antibody-dependent cellular cytotoxicity mediated by NK cells that bind to the antibody's Fc portion.

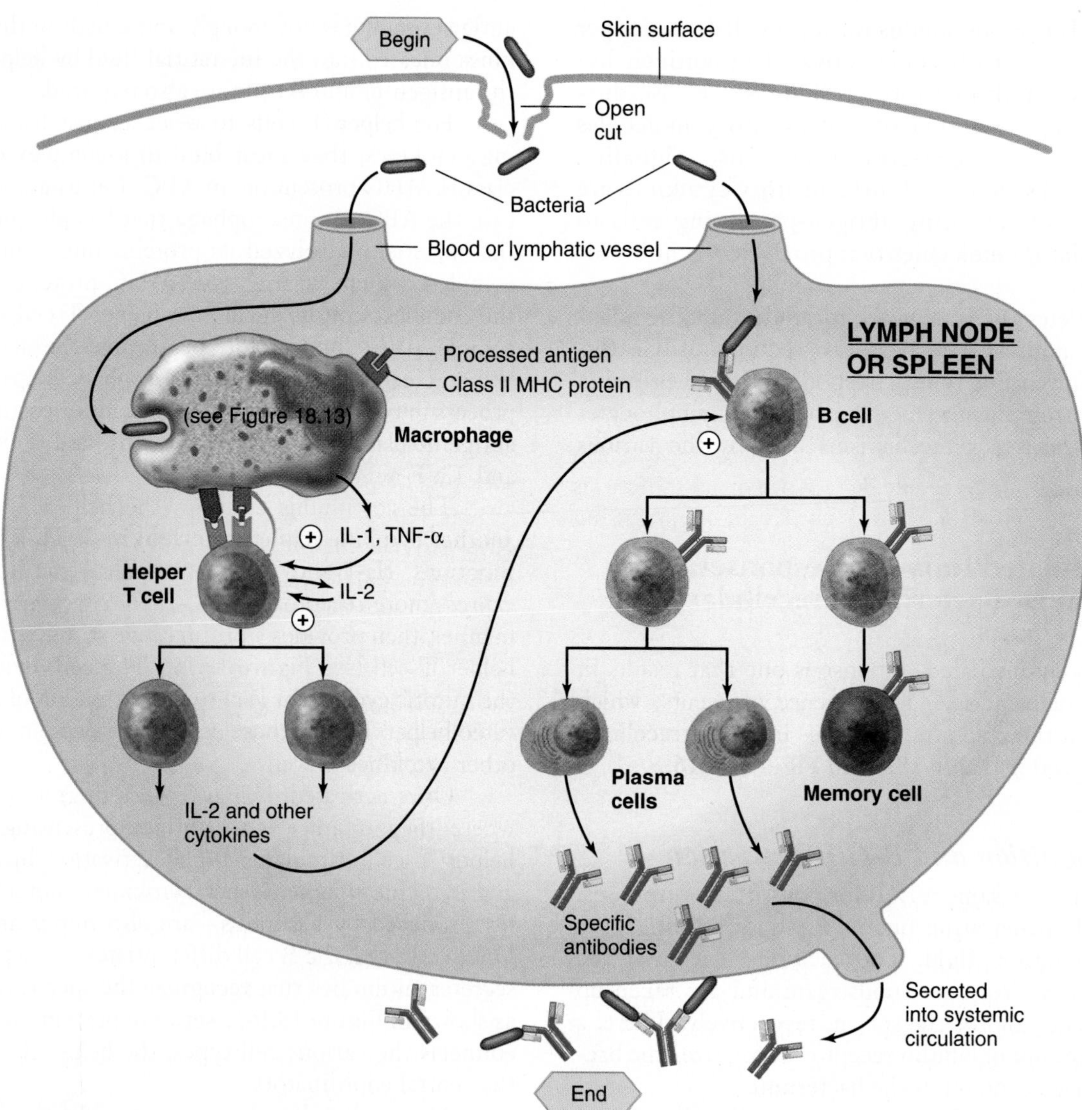

Figure 18.16 APIR Summary of events by which a bacterial infection leads to antibody synthesis in secondary lymphoid organs. Refer back to Figure 18.13 for additional details about intracellular processing of antigen. The secreted antibodies travel by the blood to the site of infection, where they bind to bacteria of the type that induced the response. The attack triggered by antibodies' binding to bacteria is described in the text.

rapidly and vigorously should the antigen reappear at a future time (see Figure 18.16).

The example we have been using employed a macrophage as the APC to helper T cells, but B cells can also serve in this role (see Figure 18.13). The binding of the helper T cell to the antigen-bound B cell ensures maximal stimulation of the B cell by the cytokines secreted by that helper T cell and any of its progeny that remain nearby.

Antibody Secretion

After their differentiation from B cells, plasma cells produce thousands of antibody molecules per second before they die in a day or so. We mentioned earlier that there are five major classes of antibodies. The most abundant are the **IgG** antibodies, commonly called **gamma globulin,** and **IgM** antibodies. These two groups together provide the bulk of specific immunity against bacteria and viruses in the extracellular fluid. **IgE** antibodies participate in defenses against multicellular parasites and also mediate allergic responses. **IgA** antibodies are secreted by plasma cells in the linings of the gastrointestinal, respiratory, and genitourinary tracts; these antibodies generally act locally in the linings or on their surfaces. They are also secreted by the mammary glands and, therefore, are the major antibodies in milk. The functions of **IgD** are still unclear.

In the kind of infection described in this chapter, the B cells and plasma cells, sitting on the nodes near the infected tissues, recognize antigen and are activated to make antibodies. The antibodies (mostly IgG and IgM) circulate through the lymph and blood to return to the infected site. At sites of infection, the antibodies leave the blood (recall that nonspecific inflammation has already made capillaries and venules leaky at these sites) and combine with the type of bacterial surface antigen that initiated the immune response (see Figure 18.16). These antibodies then direct the attack (see following discussion) against the bacteria to which they are now bound.

Consequently, immunoglobulins play two distinct roles in immune responses during the initial recognition step: (1) Those on the surface of B cells bind to antigen brought to them; and (2) those secreted by the plasma cells (antibodies) bind to bacteria bearing the same antigens, "marking" them as the targets to be attacked.

The Attack: Effects of Antibodies

The antibodies bound to antigen on the microbial surface do not directly kill the microbe but instead link up the microbe physically to the actual killing mechanisms—phagocytes (neutrophils and macrophages), complement, or NK cells. This linkage not only triggers the attack mechanism but ensures that the killing effects are restricted to the microbe. Linkage to specific antibodies helps protect adjacent normal structures from the toxic effects of the chemicals employed by the killing mechanisms.

Direct Enhancement of Phagocytosis Antibodies can act directly as opsonins. The mechanism is analogous to that for complement C3b (see Figure 18.6) in that the antibody links the phagocyte to the antigen. As shown in **Figure 18.17**, the phagocyte has membrane receptors that bind to the Fc portion of an antibody. This linkage promotes attachment of the antigen to the phagocyte and the triggering of phagocytosis of the bacterium.

Activation of the Complement System As described earlier in this chapter, the plasma complement system is activated in *nonspecific* (innate) inflammatory responses via the alternative complement pathway. In contrast, in *adaptive* immune responses, the presence of antibody of the IgG or IgM class bound to antigen activates the *classical complement pathway.* The first molecule in this pathway, C1, binds to the Fc portion of an antibody that has combined with antigen (**Figure 18.18**). This results in activation of the enzymatic portions of C1, thereby initiating the entire classical pathway. The end product of this cascade, the membrane attack complex (MAC), can kill the cells the antibody is bound to by making their membranes leaky. In addition, as we saw in Figure 18.6, another activated complement molecule (C3b) functions as an opsonin to enhance phagocytosis of the microbe by neutrophils and macrophages (see Figure 18.18). As a result, antibodies enhance phagocytosis both directly (see Figure 18.17) and via activation of complement C3b.

It is important to note that C1 binds not to the unique antigen-binding sites in the antibody's prongs but rather to complement-binding sites in the Fc portion. Because the latter are the same in virtually all antibodies of the IgG and IgM classes, the complement molecule will bind to *any* antigen-bound antibodies belonging to these classes. In other words, there is only one set of complement molecules and, once activated, they do essentially the same thing regardless of the specific identity of the invader.

Antibody-Dependent Cellular Cytotoxicity We have seen that both a particular complement molecule (C1) and a phagocyte can bind nonspecifically to the Fc portion of an antibody bound to antigen. NK cells can also do this (just substitute an NK cell for the phagocyte in Figure 18.17). Thus, antibodies can link target cells to NK cells, which then kill the targets directly by secreting toxic chemicals. This is called **antibody-dependent cellular cytotoxicity** (**ADCC**), because killing (cytotoxicity) is carried out by cells (NK cells) but the process depends upon the presence of antibody. Note that the antibodies confer specificity upon ADCC, just as they do on antibody-dependent phagocytosis and complement activation. This mechanism for bringing NK cells into play is the one exception, mentioned earlier, to the generalization that the mechanism by which NK cells identify their targets is unclear.

Direct Neutralization of Bacterial Toxins and Viruses Toxins secreted by bacteria into the extracellular fluid can act as antigens to induce antibody production. The antibodies then combine with the free toxins, thereby preventing interaction of the toxins with susceptible cells. Because each antibody has two binding sites for antigen, clumplike chains of antibody–antigen complexes form, and these clumps are then phagocytosed.

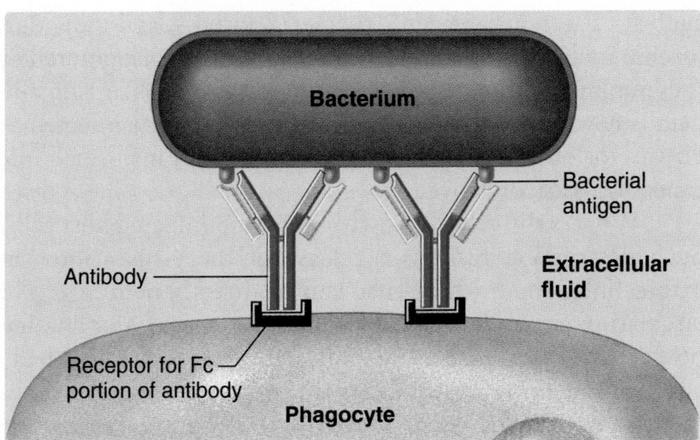

Figure 18.17 APIR Direct enhancement of phagocytosis by antibody. The antibody links the phagocyte to the bacterium. Compare this mechanism of opsonization to that mediated by complement C3b (see Figure 18.6).

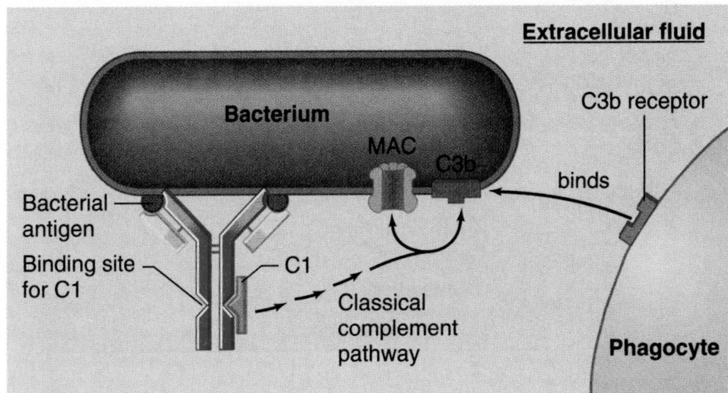

Figure 18.18 Activation of classical complement pathway by binding of antibody to bacterial antigen. C1 is activated by its binding to the Fc portion of the antibody. The membrane attack complex (MAC) is then generated, along with C3b, which acts as an opsonin by binding the bacteria to a phagocyte. C3b also plays a role in initiating the MAC (not shown here).

A similar binding process occurs as part of the major antibody-mediated mechanism for eliminating viruses in the extracellular fluid. Certain of the viral surface proteins serve as antigens, and the antibodies produced against them combine with them, preventing attachment of the virus to plasma membranes of potential host cells. This prevents the virus from entering a cell. As with bacterial toxins, chains of antibody–virus complexes are formed and can be phagocytosed.

Active and Passive Humoral Immunity

The response of the antibody-producing machinery to invasion by a foreign antigen varies enormously, depending upon whether the machinery has previously been exposed to that antigen. Antibody production occurs slowly over several weeks following the first contact with an antigen, but any subsequent infection by the same invader elicits an immediate and considerable outpouring of additional specific antibodies (**Figure 18.19**). This response, which is mediated by the memory B cells described earlier, is one of the key features that distinguishes innate and adaptive immunity. It confers a greatly enhanced resistance toward subsequent infection with that particular microorganism. Resistance built up as a result of the body's contact with microorganisms and their toxins or other antigenic components is known as **active immunity.**

Until the twentieth century, the only way to develop active immunity was to suffer an infection, but now the injection of microbial derivatives in vaccines is used. A ***vaccine*** may consist of small quantities of living or dead pathogens, small quantities of toxins, or harmless antigenic molecules derived from the microorganism or its toxin. The general principle is always the same: Exposure of the body to the antigenic substance results in an active immune response along with the induction of the memory cells required for rapid, effective response to possible future infection by that particular organism.

A second kind of immunity, known as **passive immunity**, is simply the direct transfer of antibodies from one person to another, the recipient thereby receiving preformed antibodies. Such transfers occur between mother and fetus because IgG can

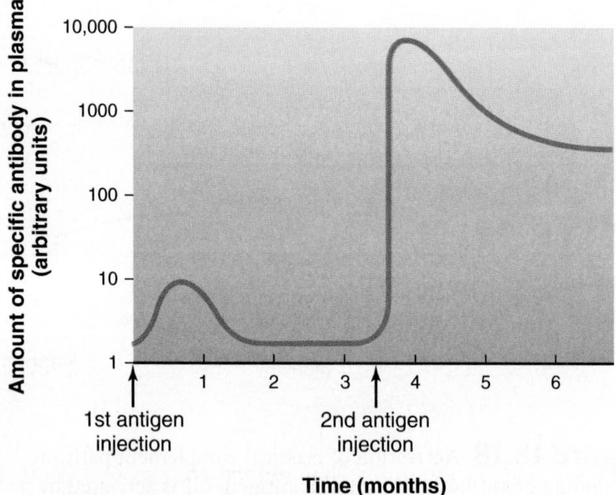

Figure 18.19 Rate of antibody production following initial exposure to an antigen and subsequent exposure to the same antigen. Note that the *y*-axis is a log scale.

move across the placenta. Also, a breast-fed child receives IgA antibodies in the mother's milk; the intestinal mucosa is permeable to IgA antibodies during early life. These are important sources of protection for the infant during the first months of life, when the antibody-synthesizing capacity is relatively poor.

The same principle is used clinically when specific antibodies (produced by genetic engineering) or pooled gamma globulin injections are given to patients exposed to or suffering from certain infections such as hepatitis. Because antibodies are proteins with a limited life span, the protection afforded by this transfer of antibodies is relatively short-lived, usually lasting only a few weeks or months.

Summary

It is now possible to summarize the interplay between innate and adaptive immune responses in resisting a bacterial infection. When a particular bacterium is encountered for the first time, *innate* defense mechanisms resist its entry and, if entry is gained, attempt to eliminate it by phagocytosis and nonphagocytic killing in the inflammatory process. Simultaneously, bacterial antigens induce the relevant specific B-cell clones to differentiate into plasma cells capable of antibody production. If the innate defenses are rapidly successful, these slowly developing *specific* immune responses may never play an important role. If the innate responses are only partly successful, the infection may persist long enough for significant amounts of antibody to be produced. The presence of antibody leads to both enhanced phagocytosis and direct destruction of the foreign cells, as well as to neutralization of any toxins the bacteria secrete. All subsequent encounters with that type of bacterium will activate the specific responses much sooner and with greater intensity. That is, the person may have active immunity against those bacteria.

The defenses against viruses in the extracellular fluid are similar, resulting in destruction or neutralization of the virus.

Defenses Against Virus-Infected Cells and Cancer Cells

The previous section described how antibody-mediated immune responses constitute the major long-term defense against exogenous antigens—bacteria, viruses, and individual foreign molecules that enter the body and are encountered by the immune system in the extracellular fluid. This section now details how the body's own cells that have become infected by viruses (or other intracellular pathogens) or transformed into cancer cells are destroyed.

What is the value of destroying virus-infected host cells? Such destruction results in release of the viruses into the extracellular fluid, where they can be directly neutralized by circulating antibody, as just described. Generally, only a few host cells are sacrificed in this way, but once viruses have had a chance to replicate and spread from cell to cell, so many virus-infected host cells may be killed by the body's own defenses that organ malfunction may occur.

Role of Cytotoxic T Cells

Figure 18.20 summarizes a typical cytotoxic T-cell response triggered by viral infection of body cells. The response

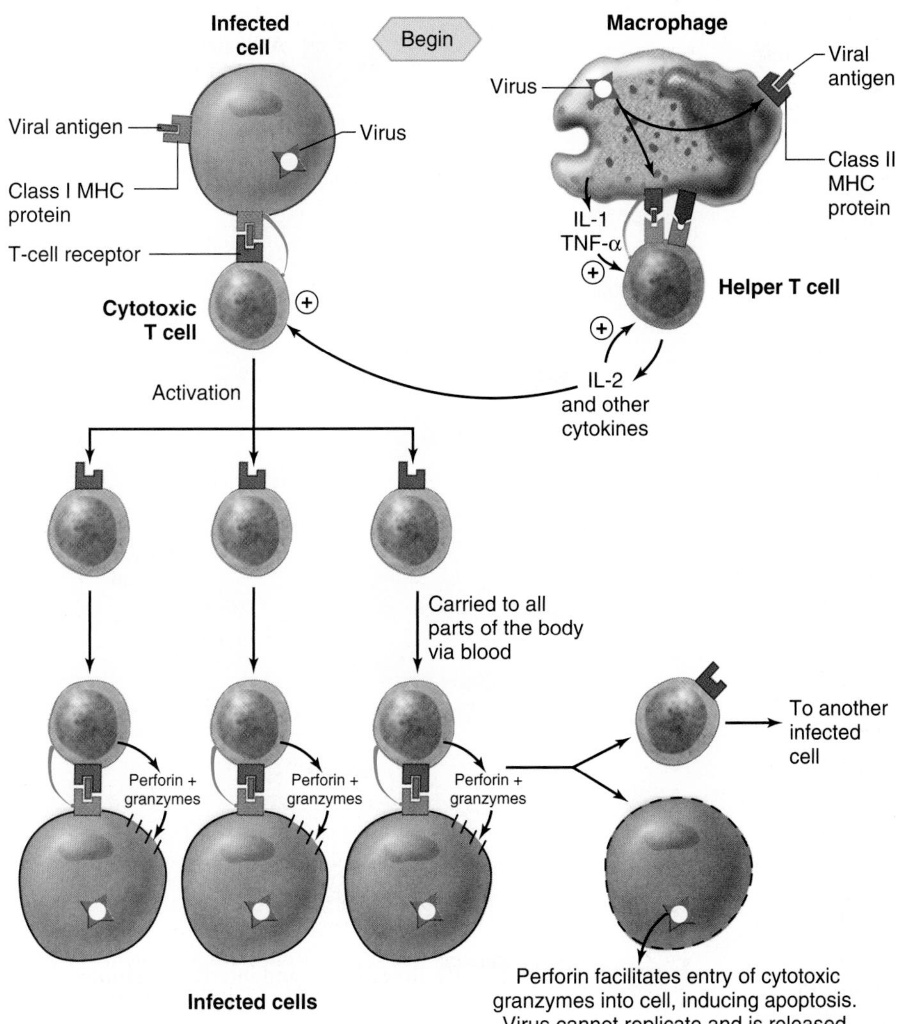

Figure 18.20 APIR Summary of events in the killing of virus-infected cells by cytotoxic T cells. The released viruses can then be phagocytosed. The precise mechanism of action of perforin is uncertain. The sequence would be similar if the inducing cell were a cancer cell rather than a virus-infected cell.

triggered by a cancer cell would be similar. As described earlier, a virus-infected or cancer cell produces foreign proteins, "endogenous antigens," which are processed and presented on the plasma membrane of the cell complexed with class I MHC proteins. Cytotoxic T cells specific for the particular antigen can bind to the complex; just as with B cells, however, binding to antigen alone does not cause activation of the cytotoxic T cell. Cytokines from adjacent activated helper T cells are also required.

What role do the helper T cells play in these cases? Figure 18.20 illustrates the most likely mechanism. Macrophages phagocytose free extracellular viruses (or, in the case of cancer, antigens released from the surface of the cancerous cells) and then process and present antigen, in association with class II MHC proteins, to the helper T cells. In addition, the macrophages provide a costimulus and also secrete IL-1 and TNF-α. The activated helper T cell releases IL-2 and other cytokines. IL-2 then acts as an autocrine substance to stimulate proliferation of the helper T cell.

The IL-2 also acts as a paracrine substance on the cytotoxic T cell bound to the surface of the virus-infected or cancer cell, stimulating this attack cell to proliferate. Other cytokines secreted by the activated helper T cell perform the same functions. Why is proliferation important if a cytotoxic T cell has already found and bound to its target? The answer is that there is rarely just one virus-infected cell or one cancer cell. By expanding the clone of cytotoxic T cells capable of recognizing the particular antigen, proliferating attack cells increase the likelihood that other virus-infected or cancer cells will be encountered by the specific type of cytotoxic T cell.

There are several mechanisms of target-cell killing by activated cytotoxic T cells, but one of the most important is as follows (see Figure 18.20). The cytotoxic T cell releases, by exocytosis, the contents of its secretory vesicles into the extracellular space between itself and the target cell to which it is bound. These vesicles contain a protein, **perforin,** which is similar in structure to the proteins of the complement system's membrane attack complex. Exactly how perforin acts is currently uncertain. However, it is believed that at least one mechanism by which perforin acts is to facilitate the transport of cytotoxic enzymes called granzymes, released by the cytotoxic T cells, into the infected cell. These enzymes then activate intracellular enzymes that induce apoptosis, killing the cell. The fact that perforin is released directly into the space between the tightly attached cytotoxic T cell and the target ensures that uninfected host bystander cells will not be killed, because perforin is not at all specific.

Some cytotoxic T cells generated during proliferation following an initial antigenic stimulation do not complete their full activation at this time but remain as memory cells. Thus, active immunity exists for cytotoxic T cells just as for B cells.

Role of NK Cells and Activated Macrophages

Although cytotoxic T cells are very important attack cells against virus-infected and cancer cells, they are not the only ones. NK cells and activated macrophages also destroy such cells by secreting toxic chemicals.

In the section on antibody-dependent cellular cytotoxicity (ADCC), we pointed out that NK cells can be linked to target cells by antibodies; this constitutes one potential method of bringing them into play against virus-infected or cancer cells. In most cases, however, strong antibody responses are not triggered by virus-infected or cancer cells, and the NK cell must bind *directly* to its target, without the help of antibodies. As noted earlier, NK cells do not have antigen specificity; rather, they nonspecifically bind to any virus-infected or cancer cell.

The major signals for NK cells to proliferate and secrete their toxic chemicals are IL-2 and interferon-gamma, secreted by the helper T cells that have been activated specifically by the targets (**Figure 18.21**). (Whereas essentially all body cells can produce the type I interferons, as described earlier, only activated helper T cells and NK cells can produce interferon-gamma.)

Thus, the attack by the NK cells is nonspecific, but a specific immune response on the part of the helper T cells is required to bring the NK cells into play. Moreover, there is a positive feedback mechanism at work here because activated NK cells can themselves secrete interferon-gamma (see Figure 18.21).

IL-2 and interferon-gamma act not only on NK cells but on macrophages in the vicinity to enhance their ability to kill cancer cells and cells infected with viruses and other pathogens. Macrophages stimulated by IL-2 and interferon-gamma are called **activated macrophages** (see Figure 18.21). In addition to phagocytosis, they secrete large amounts of many chemicals that are capable of killing cells by a variety of mechanisms. As long as there is a pathogen at the site of infection, activated macrophages will continue to present antigens to T cells that will maintain the ensuing immune response. Once cleared of infection, tissue repair will continue and the immune response will wane as T cells are no longer being activated against the pathogen.

Table 18.6 summarizes the multiple defenses against viruses described in this chapter.

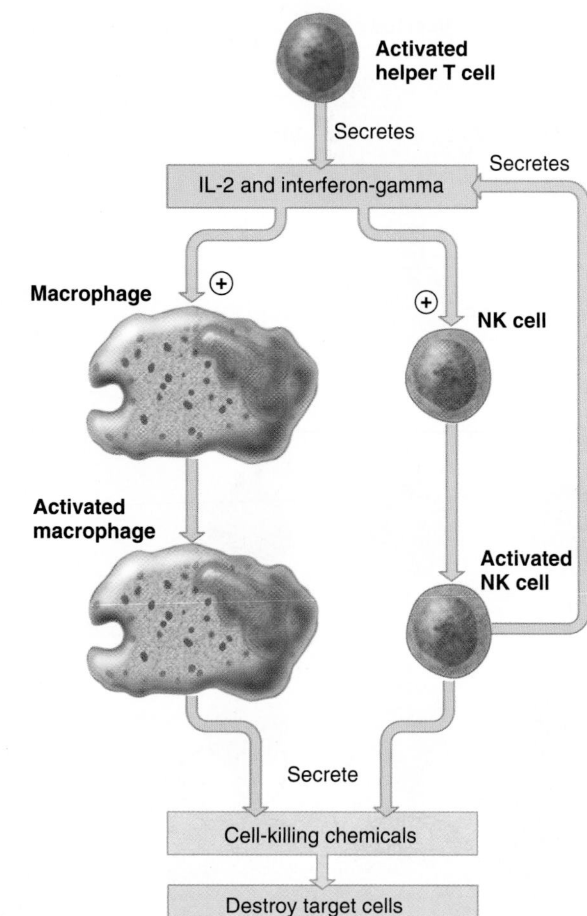

Figure 18.21 APIR Role of IL-2 and interferon-gamma, secreted by activated helper T cells, in stimulating the killing ability of NK cells and macrophages.

18.4 Systemic Manifestations of Infection

There are many *systemic* responses to infection, that is, responses of organs and tissues distant from the site of infection or immune response. These systemic responses are collectively known as the **acute phase response** (**Figure 18.22**). It is natural to think of these responses as part of the disease, but the fact is that most of them actually represent the body's own adaptive responses to the infection.

The single most common and striking systemic sign of infection is fever, the mechanism of which is described in Chapter 16. Present evidence suggests that moderate fever can be beneficial because an increase in body temperature enhances many of the protective responses described in this chapter.

Decreases in the plasma concentrations of iron and zinc occur in response to infection and are due to changes in the uptake and/or release of these elements by liver, spleen, and other tissues. The decrease in plasma iron concentration has adaptive value because bacteria require a high concentration of iron to multiply. The role of the decrease in zinc is not known.

Another adaptive response to infection is the secretion by the liver of a group of proteins known collectively as **acute phase proteins.** These proteins exert many effects on the inflammatory process that serve to minimize the extent of local tissue damage. In addition, they are important for tissue repair and for clearance of cell debris and the toxins released from microbes. An example of an acute phase protein is C-reactive protein, which functions as a nonspecific opsonin to enhance phagocytosis.

Another response to infection, increased production and release of neutrophils and monocytes by the bone marrow, is of obvious value. Also occurring is a release of amino acids from muscle; the amino acids provide the building blocks for the

TABLE 18.6 Summary of Host Responses to Viruses

	Main Cells Involved	Comment on Action
Innate responses		
Anatomical barriers	Body surface linings	Provide physical barrier; antiviral chemicals
Inflammation	Tissue macrophages	Provide phagocytosis of extracellular virus
Interferon (type I)	Most cell types after viruses enter them	Type I interferon nonspecifically prevents viral replication inside host cells
Adaptive responses		
Antibody-mediated	Plasma cells (derived from B cells) that secrete antibodies	Antibodies neutralize virus and thus prevent viral entry into cell Antibodies activate complement, which leads to enhanced phagocytosis of extracellular virus Antibodies recruit NK cells via antibody-mediated cellular cytotoxicity
Helper	Helper T cells	Secrete interleukins; keep NK cells, macrophages, cytotoxic T cells, and helper T cells active; also help convert B cells to plasma cells
Direct cell killing	Cytotoxic T cells, NK cells, and activated macrophages	Destroy host cell via secreted chemicals and thus induce release of virus into extracellular fluid where it can be phagocytosed Activity stimulated by IL-2 and interferon-gamma

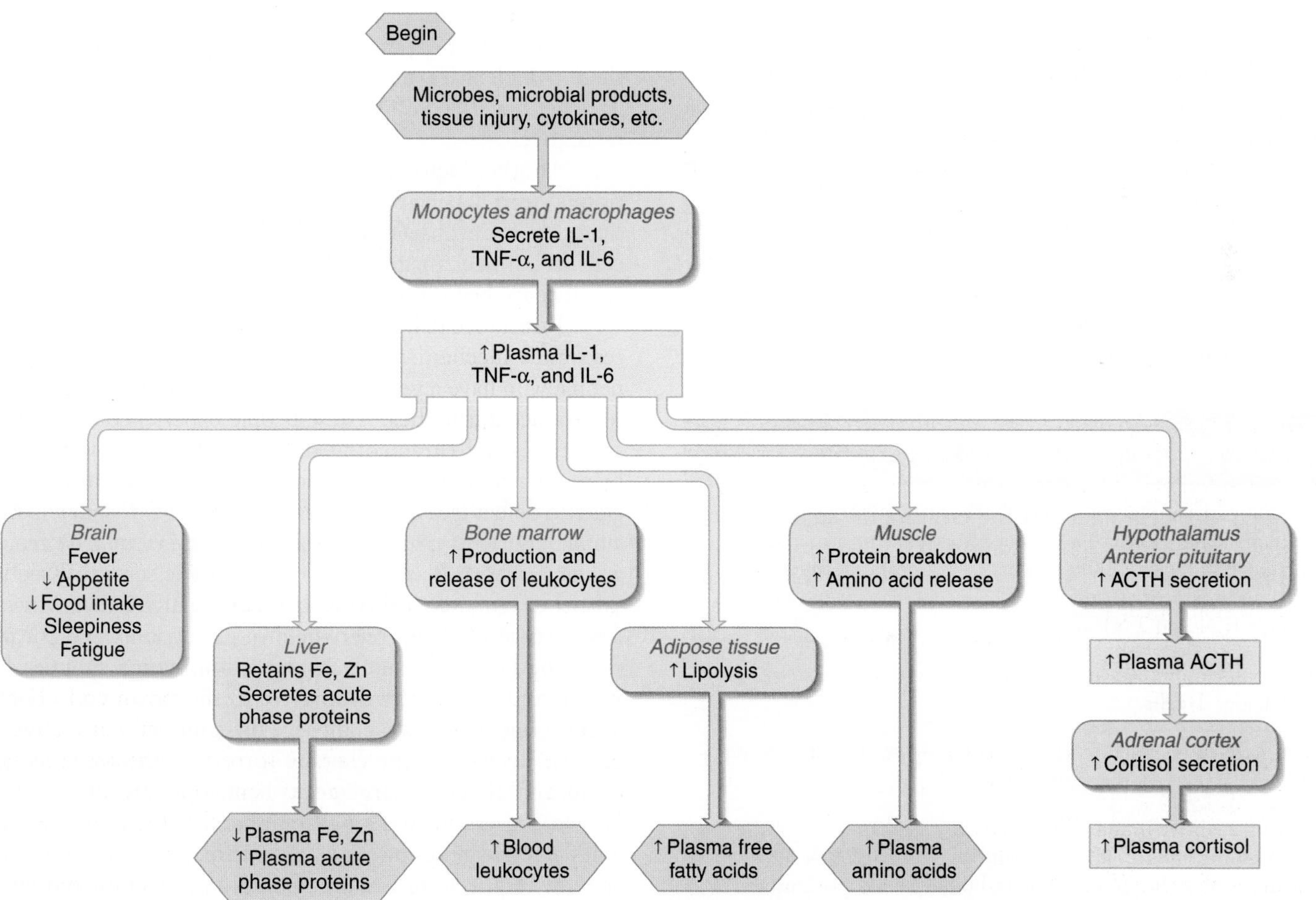

Figure 18.22 Systemic responses to infection or injury (the acute phase response). Other cytokines probably also participate. This figure does not include all the components of the acute phase response; for example, IL-1 and several other cytokines also stimulate the secretion of insulin and glucagon. The effect of cortisol on the immune response is inhibitory; cortisol provides a negative feedback action to prevent excessive immune activity (see Chapter 11 for the control mechanisms and basic functions of cortisol).

synthesis of proteins required to fight the infection and for tissue repair. Increased release of fatty acids from adipose tissue also occurs, providing a source of energy. The secretion of many hormones—notably, cortisol—is increased in the acute phase response, exerting negative feedback actions on immune function.

All of these systemic responses to infection and many others are elicited by one or more of the cytokines released from activated macrophages and other cells (see Figure 18.22). In particular, IL-1, TNF-α, and another cytokine—**interleukin 6 (IL-6)**, all of which serve local roles in immune responses, also serve as hormones to elicit distant responses such as fever.

Several other cytokines are also known to participate in the acute phase response. For example, colony-stimulating factors, which are secreted by macrophages, lymphocytes, endothelial cells, and fibroblasts, provide a major stimulus to the bone marrow to produce more neutrophils and monocytes.

The participation of macrophages in the acute phase response completes our discussion of these cells, the various functions of which are summarized in **Table 18.7**.

18.5 Factors That Alter the Resistance to Infection

Many factors determine the capacity to resist infection; a few important examples are presented here. Protein–calorie malnutrition is, worldwide, the single greatest contributor to decreased resistance to infection. Because inadequate amino acids are available to synthesize essential proteins, immune function is impaired. Deficits of specific nutrients other than protein can also lower resistance to infection.

A preexisting disease, infectious or noninfectious, can also predispose the body to infection. People with diabetes mellitus, for example, are more likely to develop infections, at least partially explainable on the basis of defective leukocyte function. Moreover, any injury to a tissue lowers its resistance,

TABLE 18.7	Role of Macrophages in Immune Responses
In innate inflammation, macrophages phagocytose particulate matter, including microbes. They also secrete antimicrobial chemicals and protein messengers (cytokines) that function as local inflammatory mediators. The inflammatory cytokines include IL-1 and TNF-α.	
Macrophages process and present antigen to cytotoxic T cells and helper T cells.	
The secreted IL-1 and TNF-α stimulate helper T cells to secrete IL-2 and to express the receptor for IL-2.	
During adaptive immune responses, macrophages perform the same killing and inflammation-inducing functions as above but are more efficient because antibodies act as opsonins and because the cells are transformed into activated macrophages by IL-2 and interferon-gamma, both secreted by helper T cells.	
The secreted IL-1, TNF-α, and IL-6 mediate many of the systemic responses to infection or injury.	

perhaps by altering the chemical environment or interfering with the blood supply.

Both stress and a person's state of mind can either enhance or reduce resistance to infection (and cancer). There are multiple mechanisms that constitute the links in these "mind–body" interactions. For example, lymphoid tissue is innervated, and the cells that mediate immune defenses have receptors for many neurotransmitters and hormones. Conversely, as we have seen, some of the cytokines the immune cells release have important effects on the brain and endocrine system. Moreover, lymphocytes secrete several of the same hormones produced by endocrine glands. Thus, the immune system can alter neural and endocrine function; in turn, neural and endocrine activity can modify immune function. For example, it has been shown in mice and rats that the production of antibodies can be altered by psychological conditioning. If this proves to be the case in humans, it could someday partially replace the requirement for medications to control the immune activity of persons with autoimmune disease.

The influence of physical exercise on the body's resistance to infection and cancer has been debated for decades. Present evidence indicates that the intensity, duration, chronicity, and psychological stress of the exercise all have important influences, both negative and positive, on a host of immune functions (for example, the number of circulating NK cells). Most experts in the field believe that, despite all these complexities, modest exercise and physical conditioning have net beneficial effects on the immune system and on host resistance.

Another factor associated with decreased immune function is sleep deprivation. For example, loss of a single night's sleep has been observed to reduce the activity of blood NK cells. The mechanism of this response is uncertain, but the results have been replicated by numerous investigators.

Resistance to infection will be impaired if one of the basic resistance mechanisms itself is deficient, as, for example, in people who have a genetic deficiency that impairs their ability to produce antibodies. These people experience frequent and sometimes life-threatening infections that can be prevented by regular replacement injections of gamma globulin. Another genetic defect is ***severe combined immunodeficiency (SCID)***, which is actually a group of related diseases that arise from an absence of both B and T cells and, in some cases, NK cells. If untreated, infants with this disorder usually die within their first year of life from overwhelming infections. SCID can be cured by bone marrow transplantation, which supplies both B cells and cells that will migrate to the thymus and become T cells, but these transplants are difficult and not always successful. Recently, gene therapy to restore the defective gene using a viral vector targeted to hematopoietic stem cells has proven successful in a small number of SCID patients. Several defective genes have been identified, including one for an enzyme required for immunoglobulin production and one for an enzyme that protects immature lymphocytes against toxic by-products of purine metabolism.

An environmentally induced decrease in the production of leukocytes is also an important cause of lowered resistance. This can occur, for example, in patients given drugs to inhibit the rejection of tissue or organ transplants (see the section on graft rejection that follows).

In terms of the numbers of people involved, the most important example of the lack of a basic resistance mechanism is the disease called *acquired immune deficiency syndrome* (*AIDS*).

Acquired Immune Deficiency Syndrome (AIDS)

Acquired immune deficiency syndrome (***AIDS***) is caused by the ***human immunodeficiency virus*** (***HIV***), which incapacitates the immune system. HIV belongs to the retrovirus family, whose nucleic acid core is RNA rather than DNA. Retroviruses possess an enzyme called reverse transcriptase, which, once the virus is inside a host cell, transcribes the virus's RNA into DNA, which is then integrated into the host cell's chromosomes. Replication of the virus inside the cell causes the death of the cell.

The cells that HIV preferentially (but not exclusively) enters are helper T cells. HIV infects these cells because the CD4 protein on the plasma membrane of helper T cells acts as a receptor for one of the HIV's surface proteins called gp120. As a result, the helper T cell binds the virus, making it possible for the virus to enter the cell. Very importantly, this binding of the HIV gp120 protein to CD4 is not sufficient to grant the HIV entry into the helper T cell. In addition, another surface protein on the helper T cell, one that serves normally as a receptor for certain chemokines, must serve as a coreceptor for the gp120. It has been found that persons who have a mutation in this chemokine receptor are highly resistant to infection with HIV. Much research is now focused on the possible therapeutic use of chemicals that can interact with and block this coreceptor.

Once in the helper T cell, the replicating HIV can directly kill the helper T cell but also indirectly causes its death via the body's usual immune attack. The attack is mediated in this case mainly by cytotoxic T cells attacking the virus-infected cells. In addition, by still poorly understood mechanisms, HIV causes the death of many *uninfected* helper T cells by apoptosis. Without adequate numbers of helper T cells, neither B cells nor cytotoxic T cells can function normally. As a result, the AIDS patient dies from infections and cancers that the immune system would ordinarily readily handle.

AIDS was first described in 1981, and it has since reached epidemic proportions worldwide. The great majority of persons now infected with HIV have no symptoms of AIDS. It is important to distinguish between the presence of the symptomatic disease—AIDS—and asymptomatic infection with HIV. The latter is diagnosed by the presence of anti-HIV antibodies or HIV RNA in the blood. It is thought, however, that most infected persons will eventually develop AIDS, although at highly varying rates.

The path from HIV infection to AIDS commonly takes about 10 years in untreated persons. Typically, during the first 5 years, the rapidly replicating viruses continually kill large numbers of helper T cells in lymphoid tissues, but these are replaced by new cells. Therefore, the number of helper T cells stays relatively normal (about 1000 cells/mm^3 of blood) and the person is asymptomatic. During the next 5 years, this balance is lost; the number of helper T cells, as measured in blood, decreases to about half the normal level but many people still remain asymptomatic. As the helper T-cell count continues to decrease, however, the symptoms of AIDS begin—infections with bacteria, viruses, fungi, and parasites. These are accompanied by systemic symptoms of weight loss, lethargy, and fever—all caused by high concentrations of the cytokines that induce the acute phase response. Certain unusual cancers (such as ***Kaposi's sarcoma***) also occur with relatively high frequency. In untreated persons, death usually ensues within 2 years after the onset of AIDS symptoms.

The major routes of transmission of HIV are through (1) transfer of contaminated blood or blood products from one person to another, (2) unprotected sexual intercourse with an infected partner, (3) transmission from an infected mother to her fetus across the placenta during pregnancy and delivery, or (4) transfer via breast milk during nursing.

Two components to the therapeutic management of HIV-infected persons include one directed against the virus itself to delay progression of the disease and one to prevent or treat the opportunistic infections and cancers that ultimately cause death. The present recommended treatment for HIV infection itself is a simultaneous battery of at least four drugs. Two of these inhibit the action of the HIV enzyme (reverse transcriptase) that converts the viral RNA into the host cell's DNA; a third drug inhibits the HIV enzyme (α-protease) that cleaves a large protein into smaller units required for the assembly of new HIV; and a fourth drug blocks fusion of the virus with the T cell. The use of this complex and expensive regimen (called ***HAART,*** for *highly active anti-retroviral therapy*) greatly reduces the replication of HIV in the body and ideally should be introduced very early in the course of HIV infection, not just after the appearance of AIDS.

The ultimate hope for prevention of AIDS is the development of a vaccine. For a variety of reasons related to the nature of the virus (it generates large numbers of distinct subspecies) and the fact that it infects helper T cells, which are crucial for immune responses, vaccine development is not an easy task.

Antibiotics

The most important of the drugs employed in helping the body to resist microbes, mainly bacteria, are antibiotics. An ***antibiotic*** is any molecule or substance that kills bacteria. Antibiotics may be produced by one strain of bacteria to defend against other strains. Since the mid-twentieth century, commercial manufacture of antibiotics such as ***penicillin*** has revolutionized our ability to treat disease.

Antibiotics inhibit a wide variety of processes, including bacterial cell-wall synthesis, protein synthesis, and DNA replication. Fortunately, a number of the reactions involved in the synthesis of protein by bacteria and the proteins themselves are sufficiently different from those in human cells that certain antibiotics can inhibit them without interfering with the body's own protein synthesis. For example, the antibiotic ***erythromycin*** blocks the movement of ribosomes along bacterial messenger RNA.

Antibiotics, however, must not be used indiscriminately. They may exert allergic reactions, and they may exert toxic effects on the body's cells. Another reason for judicious use is the escalating and very serious problem of drug resistance. Most large bacterial populations contain a few mutants that are resistant to the drug, and these few may be capable of multiplying into large populations resistant to the effects of that particular antibiotic. Alternatively, the antibiotic can induce the expression of a latent gene that confers resistance. Finally, resistance can be transferred from one resistant microbe directly to another previously nonresistant microbe by means of DNA passed between them. (One example of how drug resistance can spread by these phenomena is that many bacterial strains that were once highly susceptible to penicillin now produce an enzyme that cleaves the penicillin molecule.) Yet another reason for the judicious use of antibiotics is that these substances may actually contribute to a new infection by eliminating certain species of relatively harmless bacteria that ordinarily prevent the growth of more dangerous ones. One site in which this may occur is the large intestine, where the loss of harmless bacteria may account for the symptoms of cramps and diarrhea that occur in some individuals taking certain types of antibiotics.

18.6 Harmful Immune Responses

Until now, we have focused on the mechanisms of immune responses and their protective effects. The following section discusses how immune responses can sometimes actually be harmful or unwanted.

Graft Rejection

The major obstacle to successful transplantation of tissues and organs is that the immune system recognizes the transplants, called grafts, as foreign and launches an attack against them. This is called ***graft rejection.*** Although B cells and macrophages play some role, cytotoxic T cells and helper T cells are mainly responsible for graft rejection.

Except in the case of identical twins, the class I MHC proteins on the cells of a graft differ from the recipient's as do the class II molecules present on the macrophages in the graft (recall that virtually all organs and tissues have macrophages). Consequently, the MHC proteins of both classes are recognized as foreign by the recipient's T cells, and the cells bearing these proteins are destroyed by the recipient's cytotoxic T cells with the aid of helper T cells.

Some of the tools aimed at reducing graft rejection are radiation and drugs that kill actively dividing lymphocytes and thereby decrease the recipient's T-cell population. A very effective drug, however, is ***cyclosporin,*** which does not kill lymphocytes but rather blocks the production of IL-2 and other cytokines by helper T cells. This eliminates a critical signal for proliferation of both the helper T cells themselves and the cytotoxic T cells. Synthetic adrenal corticosteroids are also used to reduce the rejection.

Problems with the use of drugs like cyclosporin and potent synthetic adrenal corticosteroids include the following: (1) Immunosuppression with them is nonspecific, so patients taking them are at increased risk for infections and cancer; (2) they exert other toxic side effects; and (3) they must be used continuously to inhibit rejection. An important new kind of therapy, one that may be able to avoid these problems, is under study. Recall that immune tolerance for self proteins is achieved by clonal deletion and/or inactivation and that the mechanism for this is absence of a nonantigenic costimulus at the time the antigen is first encountered. The hope is that, at the time of graft surgery, treatment with drugs that block the complementary proteins constituting the costimulus may induce a permanent state of immune tolerance toward the graft.

The Fetus as a Graft

During pregnancy, the fetal trophoblast cells of the placenta lie in direct contact with maternal immune cells. Because half of the fetal genes are paternal, all proteins coded for by these genes are foreign to the mother. Why does the mother's immune system refrain from attacking the trophoblast cells, which express such proteins, and thereby fail to reject the placenta? This issue is far from solved, but one critical mechanism (there are certainly others) is as follows. Trophoblast cells, unlike virtually all other nucleated cells, do not express the usual class I MHC proteins. Instead, they express a unique class I MHC protein that maternal immune cells do not recognize as foreign.

Transfusion Reactions

Transfusion reaction, the illness caused when erythrocytes are destroyed during blood transfusion, is a special example of tissue rejection, one that illustrates the fact that antibodies rather than cytotoxic T cells can sometimes be the major factor in rejection. Erythrocytes do not have MHC proteins, but they do have plasma membrane proteins and carbohydrates (the latter linked to the membrane by lipids) that can function as antigens when exposed to another person's blood. There are more than 400 erythrocyte antigens, but the ABO system of carbohydrates is the most important for transfusion reactions.

Some people have the gene that results in synthesis of the A antigen, some have the gene for the B antigen, some have both genes, and some have neither gene. (Genes cannot code for the carbohydrates that function as antigens; rather, they code for the particular enzymes that catalyze the formation of the carbohydrates.) The erythrocytes of those with neither gene are said to have O-type erythrocytes. Consequently, the possible blood types are A, B, AB, and O (**Table 18.8**).

Type A individuals always have anti-B antibodies in their plasma. Similarly, type B individuals have plasma anti-A antibodies. Type AB individuals have neither anti-A nor anti-B antibody, and type O individuals have both. These antierythrocyte antibodies are called natural antibodies. How they arise naturally—that is, without exposure to the appropriate antigen-bearing erythrocytes—is not clear.

With this information as background, we can predict what happens if a type A person is given type B blood. There are two incompatibilities: (1) The recipient's anti-B antibodies cause the transfused cells to be attacked; and (2) the anti-A antibodies in the transfused plasma cause the recipient's cells to be attacked. The latter is generally of little consequence, however, because the transfused antibodies become so diluted in the recipient's plasma that they are ineffective in inducing a response. It is the destruction of the transfused cells by the recipient's antibodies that produces the problem.

TABLE 18.8 Human ABO Blood Groups

Blood Group	Percentage*	Antigen on RBC	Genetic Possibilities: Homozygous	Genetic Possibilities: Heterozygous	Antibody in Blood
A	42	A	AA	AO	Anti-B
B	10	B	BB	BO	Anti-A
AB	3	A and B	—	AB	Neither anti-A nor anti-B
O	45	Neither A nor B	OO	—	Both anti-A and anti-B

*In the United States.

Similar analyses show that the following situations would result in an attack on the transfused erythrocytes: a type B person given either A or AB blood; a type A person given either B or AB blood; a type O person given A, B, or AB blood. Type O people are, therefore, sometimes called universal donors, whereas type AB people are universal recipients. These terms are misleading, however, because besides antigens of the ABO system, many other erythrocyte antigens and plasma antibodies exist. Therefore, except in a dire emergency, the blood of the donor and recipient must be tested for incompatibilities directly by the procedure called ***cross-matching.*** The recipient's serum is combined on a glass slide with the prospective donor's erythrocytes (a "major" cross-match), and the mixture is observed for rupture (hemolysis) or clumping (agglutination) of the erythrocytes, either of which indicates a mismatch. In addition, the recipient's erythrocytes can be combined with the prospective donor's serum (a "minor" cross-match), looking again for mismatches.

Another group of erythrocyte membrane antigens of medical importance is the Rh system of proteins. There are more than 40 such antigens, but the one most likely to cause a problem is called Rh_o, known commonly as the **Rh factor** because it was first studied in rhesus monkeys. Human erythrocytes either have the antigen (Rh-positive) or lack it (Rh-negative). About 85% of the U.S. population are Rh-positive.

Antibodies in the Rh system, unlike the "natural antibodies" of the ABO system, follow the classical immunity pattern in that no one has anti-Rh antibodies unless exposed to Rh-positive cells from another person. This can occur if an Rh-negative person is subjected to multiple transfusions with Rh-positive blood, but its major occurrence involves the mother–fetus relationship. During pregnancy, some of the fetal erythrocytes may cross the placental barriers into the maternal circulation. If the mother is Rh-negative and the fetus is Rh-positive, this can induce the mother to synthesize anti-Rh antibodies. This occurs mainly during separation of the placenta at delivery. Consequently, a first Rh-positive pregnancy rarely offers any danger to the fetus because delivery occurs before the mother makes the antibodies. In future pregnancies, however, these antibodies will already be present in the mother and can cross the placenta to attack and hemolyze the erythrocytes of an Rh-positive fetus. This condition, which can cause an anemia severe enough to cause the death of the fetus in utero or of the newborn, is called ***hemolytic disease of the newborn.*** The risk increases with each Rh-positive pregnancy as the mother becomes more and more sensitized.

Fortunately, this disease can be prevented by giving an Rh-negative mother human gamma globulin against Rh-positive erythrocytes within 72 h after she has delivered an Rh-positive infant. These antibodies bind to the antigenic sites on any Rh-positive erythrocytes that might have entered the mother's blood during delivery and prevent them from inducing antibody synthesis by the mother. The administered antibodies are eventually metabolized.

You may be wondering whether ABO incompatibilities are also a cause of hemolytic disease of the newborn. For example, a woman with type O blood has antibodies to both the A and B antigens. If her fetus is type A or B, this theoretically should cause a problem. Fortunately, it usually does not, partly because the A and B antigens are not strongly expressed in fetal erythrocytes and partly because the antibodies, unlike the anti-Rh antibodies, are of the IgM type, which do not readily cross the placenta.

Allergy (Hypersensitivity)

Allergy (***hypersensitivity***) refers to diseases in which immune responses to environmental antigens cause inflammation and damage to the body itself. Antigens that cause allergy are called ***allergens;*** common examples include those in ragweed pollen and poison ivy. Most allergens themselves are relatively or completely harmless—the immune responses to them cause the damage. In essence, then, allergy is immunity gone wrong, for the response is inappropriate to the stimulus.

A word about terminology is useful here. There are four major types of hypersensitivity, as categorized by the different immunologic effector pathways involved in the inflammatory response. The term *allergy* is sometimes used popularly to denote only one of these types, that mediated by IgE antibodies. We will follow the common practice, however, of using the term *allergy* in its broader sense as synonymous with *hypersensitivity.*

To develop a particular allergy, a genetically predisposed person must first be exposed to the allergen. This initial exposure causes "sensitization." The subsequent exposures elicit the damaging immune responses that we recognize as the disease. The diversity of allergic responses reflects the different immunologic effector pathways elicited. The classification of allergic diseases is based on these mechanisms (**Table 18.9**).

TABLE 18.9 Major Types of Hypersensitivity
I. Delayed hypersensitivity A. Mediated by helper T cells and macrophages B. Independent of antibodies
II. Immune-complex hypersensitivity A. Mediated by antigen–antibody complexes deposited in tissue
III. Cytotoxic hypersensitivity A. Mediated by antibodies that lead to damage or destruction of cells, as in hemolytic disease of the newborn
IV. Immediate hypersensitivity A. Mediated by IgE antibodies, mast cells, and eosinophils

In one type of allergy, the inflammatory response is independent of antibodies. It is due to pronounced secretion of cytokines by helper T cells activated by antigen in the area. These cytokines themselves act as inflammatory mediators and also activate macrophages to secrete their potent mediators. Because it takes several days to develop, this type of allergy is known as ***delayed hypersensitivity.*** The tuberculin skin test is an example.

In contrast to this are the various types of antibody-mediated allergic responses. One important type is called ***immune-complex hypersensitivity.*** It occurs when so many antibodies (of either the IgG or IgM types) combine with free antigens that large numbers of antigen–antibody complexes precipitate out on the surface of endothelial cells or are trapped in capillary walls, particularly those of the renal corpuscles. These immune complexes activate complement, which then induces an inflammatory response that damages the tissues immediately surrounding the complexes.

A third type of hypersensitivity or ***cytotoxic hypersensitivity*** occurs when antibodies bind to cell-surface-associated antigens that lead to tissue injury or altered receptor function. An example of this type of hypersensitivity, just discussed, is hemolytic disease of the newborn.

Immediate Hypersensitivity

The more common type of antibody-mediated allergic response is called ***immediate hypersensitivity,*** because the response is usually very rapid in onset. It is also called ***IgE-mediated hypersensitivity*** because it involves IgE antibodies. In immediate hypersensitivity, initial exposure to the antigen leads to some antibody synthesis and, more important, to the production of memory B cells that mediate active immunity. Upon reexposure, the antigen elicits a more powerful antibody response. So far, none of this is unusual; the difference is that the particular antigens that elicit immediate hypersensitivity reactions stimulate, in genetically susceptible persons, the production of type IgE antibodies. Production of IgE requires the participation of a particular subset of helper T cells that are activated by the allergens presented by B cells. These activated helper T cells then release cytokines that preferentially stimulate differentiation of the B cells into IgE-producing plasma cells.

Upon their release from plasma cells, IgE antibodies circulate throughout the body and become attached via binding sites on their Fc portions to connective-tissue mast cells (**Figure 18.23**). When the same antigen type subsequently enters the body and combines with the IgE bound to the mast

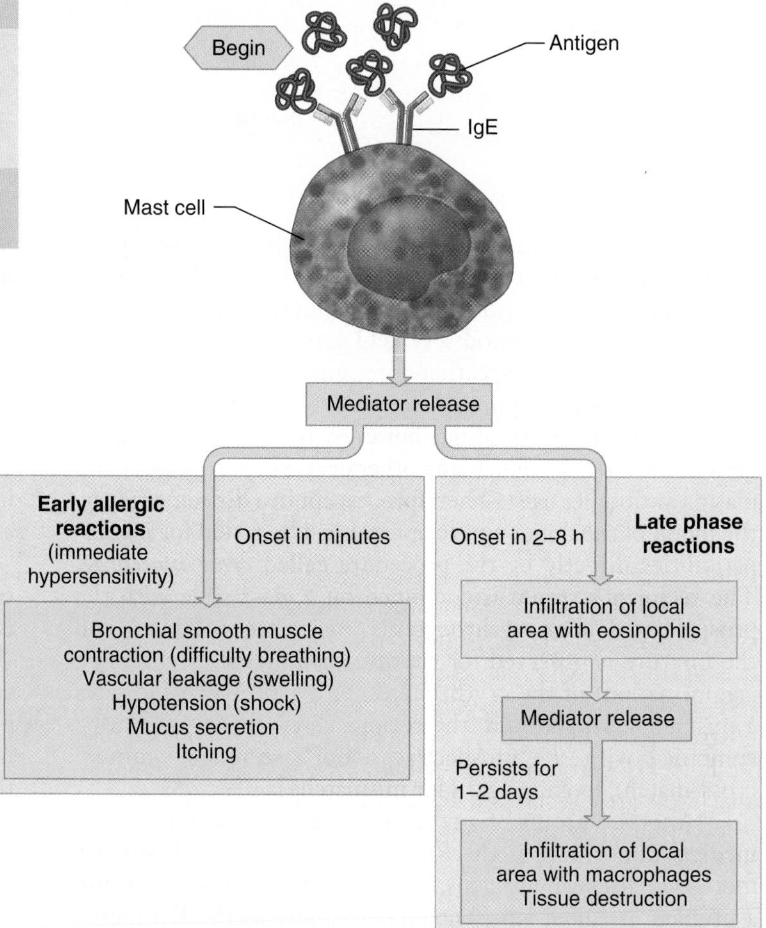

Figure 18.23 APIR Immediate hypersensitivity allergic response. (a) Sequence of events. (b) Colorized electron micrograph of a mast cell, showing numerous secretory vesicles.

cell, this triggers the mast cell to secrete many inflammatory mediators, including **histamine,** various eicosanoids, and chemokines. All of these mediators then initiate a local inflammatory response. (The entire sequence of events just described for mast cells can also occur with basophils in the circulation.)

Consequently, the symptoms of IgE-mediated allergy reflect the various effects of these inflammatory mediators and the body site in which the antigen–IgE–mast cell combination occurs. For example, when a previously sensitized person inhales ragweed pollen, the antigen combines with IgE on mast cells in the respiratory passages. The mediators released cause increased secretion of mucus, increased blood flow, swelling of the epithelial lining, and contraction of the smooth muscle surrounding the airways. As a result, the symptoms that characterize hay fever follow—congestion, runny nose, sneezing, and difficulty breathing. Immediate hypersensitivities to penicillin and insect venoms sometimes occur, and these are usually correlated with IgE production.

Allergic symptoms are usually localized to the site of antigen entry. If very large amounts of the chemicals released by the mast cells (or blood basophils) enter the circulation, however, systemic symptoms may result and cause severe hypotension and bronchiolar constriction. This sequence of events, called ***anaphylaxis,*** can cause death due to circulatory and respiratory failure; it can be elicited in some sensitized people by the antigen in a single bee sting.

The very rapid components of immediate hypersensitivity often proceed to a ***late phase reaction*** lasting many hours or days, during which large numbers of leukocytes, particularly eosinophils, migrate into the inflamed area. The chemoattractants involved are cytokines released by mast cells and helper T cells activated by the allergen. The eosinophils, once in the area, secrete mediators that prolong the inflammation and sensitize the tissues so that less allergen is required the next time to evoke a response.

Given the inappropriateness of most immediate hypersensitivity responses, how did such a system evolve? The normal physiological function of the IgE–mast cell–eosinophil pathways is to repel invasion by multicellular parasites that cannot be phagocytosed. The mediators released by the mast cells stimulate the inflammatory response against the parasites, and the eosinophils serve as the major killer cells against them by secreting several toxins. How this system also came to be inducible by harmless substances is not clear.

Autoimmune Disease

Whereas allergy is due to an inappropriate response to an environmental antigen, ***autoimmune disease*** is due to an inappropriate immune attack triggered by the body's own proteins acting as antigens. The immune attack, mediated by autoantibodies and self-reactive T cells, is directed specifically against the body's own cells that contain these proteins.

We explained earlier how the body is normally in a state of immune tolerance toward its own cells. Unfortunately, there are situations in which this tolerance breaks down and the body does in fact launch antibody-mediated or killer cell–mediated attacks against its own cells and tissues. A growing number of human diseases are being recognized as autoimmune in origin, some of which have been described elsewhere in this textbook. Examples are ***multiple sclerosis,*** in which myelin is attacked (see Chapter 6); ***myasthenia gravis,*** in which the nicotinic receptors for acetylcholine on skeletal muscle cells are the target (see Chapter 9); ***rheumatoid arthritis,*** in which connective tissues in joints are damaged; and ***type 1 diabetes mellitus,*** in which the insulin-producing cells of the pancreas are destroyed (see Chapter 16). Some possible causes for the body's failure to recognize its own cells are summarized in **Table 18.10**.

Excessive Inflammatory Responses

Recall that complement, other inflammatory mediators, and the toxic chemicals secreted by neutrophils and macrophages are not specific with regard to their targets. Consequently, during an inflammatory response directed against pathogens, there can be so much generation or release of these substances that adjacent normal tissues may be damaged. These substances can also cause potentially lethal systemic responses. For example, macrophages release very large amounts of IL-1 and TNF-α, both of which are powerful inflammatory mediators (in addition to their other effects) in response to an infection with certain types of bacteria. These cytokines can cause profound vasodilation throughout the body, precipitating a type of hypotension called ***septic shock.*** This is often accompanied by dangerously high fevers. In other words, the cytokines released in response to the bacteria, not the bacteria themselves, cause septic shock.

Another important example of damage produced by excessive inflammation in response to pathogens is the dementia that occurs in AIDS. HIV does not itself attack neurons, but it does infect microglia. Such invasion causes the microglia, which function as macrophage-like cells, to produce very high concentrations of inflammatory cytokines and other

TABLE 18.10 Some Possible Causes of Autoimmune Attack
There may be failure of clonal deletion in the thymus or of clonal inactivation in the periphery. This is particularly true for "sequestered antigens," such as certain proteins that are unavailable to the immune system during critical early-life periods.
Normal body proteins may be altered by combination with drugs or environmental chemicals. This leads to an attack on the cells bearing the now "foreign" protein.
In immune attacks on virus-infected bodily cells, so many cells may be destroyed that disease results.
Genetic mutations in the body's cells may yield new proteins that serve as antigens.
The body may encounter pathogens whose antigens are so close in structure to certain of the body's own proteins that the antibodies or cytotoxic T cells produced against these microbial antigens also attack cells bearing the self proteins.
Proteins normally never encountered by lymphocytes may become exposed as a result of some other disease.

molecules that are toxic to neurons. (Microglia are also implicated in noninfectious brain disorders, like ***Alzheimer disease,*** that are characterized by inflammation.)

Excessive chronic inflammation can also occur in the absence of pathogen infection. Thus, various major diseases, including ***asthma,*** rheumatoid arthritis, and ***inflammatory bowel disease,*** are categorized as ***chronic inflammatory diseases.*** The causes of these diseases and the interplay between genetic and environmental factors are still poorly understood (see Chapters 13 and 15 for additional details on the nature of asthma and inflammatory bowel disease, respectively). Some, like rheumatoid arthritis, are mainly autoimmune in nature, but all appear to be associated with positive feedback increases in the production of cytokines and other inflammatory mediators.

Yet another example of excessive inflammation in a noninfectious state is the development of atherosclerotic plaques in blood vessels (see Figure 12.66). It is likely that, in response to endothelial cell dysfunction, the vessel wall releases inflammatory cytokines (IL-1, for example) that promote all stages of atherosclerosis—excessive clotting, chemotaxis of various leukocytes (as well as smooth muscle cells), and so on. The endothelial-cell dysfunction is caused by initially subtle vessel-wall injury by lipoproteins and other factors, including elevated blood pressure and homocysteine (see Chapter 12).

In summary, the various mediators of inflammation and immunity are a double-edged sword. In usual amounts, they are essential for normal resistance; in excessive amounts, however, they can cause illness.

This completes the section on immunology. **Table 18.11** presents a summary of immune mechanisms in the form of a mini-glossary of cells and chemical mediators involved in immune responses. All of the material in this table has been covered in this chapter.

TABLE 18.11 A Mini-Glossary of Chemical Mediators and Cells Involved in Immune Functions

Chemical Mediators

Acute phase proteins Group of proteins secreted by the liver during systemic response to injury or infection; stimuli for their secretion are IL-1, IL-6, and other cytokines.

Antibodies Immunoglobulins secreted by plasma cells; combine with the type of antigen that stimulated their production and direct an attack against the antigen or a cell bearing it.

C1 The first protein in the classical complement pathway.

Chemoattractants A general name given to any chemical mediator that stimulates chemotaxis of neutrophils or other leukocytes.

Chemokines Any cytokine that functions as a chemoattractant.

Chemotaxin A synonym for chemoattractant.

Complement A group of plasma proteins that, upon activation, kill pathogens directly and facilitate the various steps of the inflammatory process, including phagocytosis; the classical complement pathway is triggered by antigen–antibody complexes, whereas the alternative pathway can operate independently of antibody.

C-reactive protein One of several proteins that function as nonspecific opsonins; production by the liver is increased during the acute phase response.

Cytokines General term for protein messengers that regulate immune responses; secreted by macrophages, monocytes, lymphocytes, neutrophils, and several nonimmune cell types; function both locally and as hormones.

Eicosanoids General term for products of arachidonic acid metabolism (prostaglandins, thromboxanes, leukotrienes); function as important inflammatory mediators.

Histamine An inflammatory mediator secreted mainly by mast cells; acts on microcirculation to cause vasodilation and increased permeability to protein.

IgA The class of antibodies secreted by cells lining the GI, respiratory, and genitourinary tracts.

IgD A class of antibodies whose function is unknown.

IgE The class of antibodies that mediates immediate hypersensitivity and resistance to parasites.

IgG The most abundant class of plasma antibodies.

IgM A class of antibodies that is produced first in all immune responses. Along with IgG, it provides the bulk of specific humoral immunity against bacteria and viruses.

Immunoglobulin (Ig) Proteins that function as B-cell receptors and antibodies; the five major classes are IgA, IgD, IgE, IgG, and IgM.

Interferons (type I) Group of cytokines that nonspecifically inhibit viral replication.

TABLE 18.11 A Mini-Glossary of Chemical Mediators and Cells Involved in Immune Functions *(continued)*

Chemical Mediators

Interferon (type II) Also called interferon-gamma, it stimulates the killing ability of NK cells and macrophages.

Interleukin 1 (IL-1) Cytokine secreted by macrophages (and other cells) that activates helper T cells, exerts many inflammatory effects, and mediates many of the systemic acute phase responses, including fever.

Interleukin 2 (IL-2) Cytokine secreted by activated helper T cells that causes helper T cells, cytotoxic T cells, and NK cells to proliferate, and causes activation of macrophages.

Interleukin 6 (IL-6) Cytokine secreted by macrophages (and other cells) that exerts multiple effects on immune system cells, inflammation, fever, and the acute phase response.

Kinins Peptides that split from kininogens in inflamed areas and facilitate the vascular changes associated with inflammation; they also activate neuronal pain receptors.

Membrane attack complex (MAC) Group of complement proteins that forms channels in the surface of a microbe, making it leaky and killing it.

Natural antibodies Antibodies to the erythrocyte antigens (of the A or B type).

Opsonin General name given to any chemical mediator that promotes phagocytosis.

Perforin Protein secreted by cytotoxic T cells and NK cells that forms channels in the plasma membrane of the target cell, making it leaky and killing it; its structure and function are similar to that of the MAC in the complement system.

Tumor necrosis factor-alpha (TNF-α) Cytokine secreted by macrophages (and other cells) that has many of the same actions as IL-1.

Cells

Activated macrophages Macrophages whose killing ability has been enhanced by cytokines, particularly IL-2 and interferon-gamma.

Antigen-presenting cell (APC) Cell that presents antigen, complexed with MHC proteins, on its surface to T cells.

B cells Lymphocytes that, upon activation, proliferate and differentiate into antibody-secreting plasma cells; provide major defense against bacteria, viruses in the extracellular fluid, and toxins; and can function as antigen-presenting cells to helper T cells.

Cytotoxic T cells The class of T lymphocytes that, upon activation by specific antigen, directly attack the cells bearing that type of antigen; are major killers of virus-infected cells and cancer cells; and bind antigen associated with class I MHC proteins.

Dendritic cells Cells that carry out phagocytosis and serve as antigen-presenting cells.

Eosinophils Leukocytes involved in destruction of parasites and in immediate hypersensitivity responses.

Helper T cells The class of T cells that, via secreted cytokines, play a stimulatory role in the activation of B cells and cytotoxic T cells; also can activate NK cells and macrophages; and bind antigen associated with class II MHC proteins.

Lymphocytes The type of leukocyte responsible for adaptive immune responses; categorized mainly as B cells, T cells, and NK cells.

Macrophages Cell type that (1) functions as a phagocyte, (2) processes and presents antigen to helper T cells, and (3) secretes cytokines involved in inflammation, activation of lymphocytes, and the systemic acute phase response to infection or injury.

Mast cells Tissue cells that bind IgE and release inflammatory mediators in response to parasites and immediate hypersensitivity reactions.

Memory cells B cells and cytotoxic T cells that differentiate during an initial immune response and respond rapidly during a subsequent exposure to the same antigen.

Monocytes A type of leukocyte; leaves the bloodstream and is transformed into a macrophage.

Natural killer (NK) cells Class of lymphocytes that bind to cells bearing foreign antigens without specific recognition and kill them directly; major targets are virus-infected cells and cancer cells; participate in antibody-dependent cellular cytotoxicity (ADCC).

Neutrophils Leukocytes that function as phagocytes and also release chemicals involved in inflammation.

Plasma cells Cells that differentiate from activated B lymphocytes and secrete antibodies.

T cells Lymphocytes derived from precursors that differentiated in the thymus; see *Cytotoxic T cells* and *Helper T cells.*

SUMMARY

Cells and Secretions Mediating Immune Defenses

I. Immune defenses may be nonspecific, so that the identity of the target is not recognized, or they may be specific, so that it is recognized.

II. The cells of the immune system are leukocytes (neutrophils, eosinophils, basophils, monocytes, and lymphocytes), plasma cells, macrophages, dendritic cells, and mast cells. The leukocytes use the blood for transportation but function mainly in the tissues.

III. Cells of the immune system (as well as some other cells) secrete protein messengers that regulate immune responses and are collectively called cytokines.

Innate Immune Responses

I. External barriers to infection are the skin; the linings of the respiratory, gastrointestinal, and genitourinary tracts; the cilia of these linings; and antimicrobial chemicals in glandular secretions.

II. Inflammation, the local response to infection, includes vasodilation, increased vascular permeability to protein, phagocyte chemotaxis, destruction of the invader via phagocytosis or extracellular killing, and tissue repair.
   a. The mediators controlling these processes, summarized in Table 18.3, are either released from cells in the area or generated extracellularly from plasma proteins.
   b. The main cells that function as phagocytes are the neutrophils, monocytes, macrophages, and dendritic cells. These cells also secrete many inflammatory mediators.
   c. One group of inflammatory mediators—the complement family of plasma proteins activated during nonspecific inflammation by the alternative complement pathway—not only stimulates many of the steps of inflammation but mediates extracellular killing via the membrane at tack complex.
   d. The final response to infection or tissue damage is tissue repair.

III. Interferons stimulate the production of intracellular proteins that nonspecifically inhibit viral replication.

IV. Toll-like receptors are evolutionarily ancient proteins that recognize pathogen-associated molecular patterns that are highly conserved features of pathogens. TLRs belong to a family of proteins called pattern-recognition receptors and may be among the first molecules to have evolved in eukaryotic organisms to combat microbial diseases.

Adaptive Immune Responses

I. Lymphocytes mediate adaptive immune responses.

II. Adaptive immune responses occur in three stages.
   a. A lymphocyte programmed to recognize a specific antigen encounters it and binds to it via plasma membrane receptors specific for the antigen.
   b. The lymphocyte undergoes activation—a cycle of cell divisions and differentiation.
   c. The multiple active lymphocytes produced in this manner launch an attack all over the body against the specific antigens that stimulated their production.

III. The lymphoid organs are categorized as primary (bone marrow and thymus) or secondary (lymph nodes, spleen, tonsils, and lymphocyte collections in the linings of the body's tracts).
   a. The primary lymphoid organs are the sites of maturation of lymphocytes that will then be carried to the secondary lymphoid organs, which are the major sites of lymphocyte cell division and adaptive immune responses.
   b. Lymphocytes undergo a continuous recirculation among the secondary lymphoid organs, lymph, blood, and all the body's organs and tissues.

IV. The three broad populations of lymphocytes are B, T, and NK cells.
   a. B cells mature in the bone marrow and are carried to the secondary lymphoid organs, where additional B cells arise by cell division.
   b. T-cell precursors leave the bone marrow, migrate to the thymus, and undergo maturation there. These cells then circulate between the blood and secondary lymphoid organs. Stimulation with antigen and costimulatory molecules lead to T cells' expansion by cell division.
   c. NK cells originate in the bone marrow.

V. B cells and T cells have different functions.
   a. B cells, upon activation, differentiate into plasma cells, which secrete antibodies. Antibody-mediated responses constitute the major defense against bacteria, viruses, and toxins in the extracellular fluid.
   b. Cytotoxic T cells directly attack and kill virus-infected cells and cancer cells, without the participation of antibodies.
   c. Helper T cells stimulate B cells and cytotoxic T cells via the cytokines they secrete. With few exceptions, this help is essential for activation of the B cells and cytotoxic T cells.

VI. B-cell plasma membrane receptors are copies of the specific antibody (immunoglobulin) that the cell is capable of producing.
   a. Any given B cell or clone of B cells produces antibodies that have a unique antigen-binding site.
   b. Antibodies are composed of four interlocking polypeptide chains; the variable regions of the antibodies are the sites that bind antigen.

VII. T-cell surface plasma membrane receptors are not immunoglobulins, but they do have specific antigen-binding sites that differ from one T-cell clone to another.
   a. The T-cell receptor binds antigen only when the antigen is complexed to one of the body's own plasma membrane MHC proteins.
   b. Class I MHC proteins are found on all nucleated cells of the body, whereas class II MHC proteins are found only on macrophages, B cells, and dendritic cells. Cytotoxic T cells require antigen to be complexed to class I proteins, whereas helper T cells require class II proteins.

VIII. Antigen presentation is required for T-cell activation.
   a. Only macrophages, B cells, and dendritic cells function as antigen-presenting cells (APCs) for helper T cells. The antigen is internalized by the APC and hydrolyzed to peptide fragments, which are complexed with class II MHC proteins. This complex is then shuttled to the plasma membrane of the APC, which also delivers a nonspecific costimulus to the T cell and secretes interleukin 1 (IL-1) and tumor necrosis factor-alpha (TNF-α).

b. A virus-infected cell or cancer cell can function as an APC for cytotoxic T cells. The viral antigen or cancer-associated antigen is synthesized by the cell itself and hydrolyzed to peptide fragments, which are complexed to class I MHC proteins. The complex is then shuttled to the plasma membrane of the cell.

IX. NK cells have the same targets as cytotoxic T cells, but they are not antigen-specific; most of their mechanisms of target identification are not understood.

X. Immune tolerance is the result of clonal deletion and clonal inactivation.

XI. In antibody-mediated responses, the membrane receptors of a B cell bind antigen, and at the same time a helper T cell also binds antigen in association with a class II MHC protein on a macrophage or other APC.

a. The helper T cell, activated by the antigen, by a nonantigenic protein costimulus, and by IL-1 and TNF-α secreted by the APC, secretes IL-2, which then causes the helper T cell to proliferate into a clone of cells that secrete additional cytokines.

b. These cytokines then stimulate the antigen-bound B cell to proliferate and differentiate into plasma cells, which secrete antibodies. Some of the activated B cells become memory cells, which are responsible for active immunity.

c. There are five major classes of secreted antibodies: IgG, IgM, IgA, IgD, and IgE. The first two are the major antibodies against bacterial and viral infection.

d. The secreted antibodies are carried throughout the body by the blood and combine with antigen. The antigen–antibody complex enhances the inflammatory response, in large part by activating the complement system. Complement proteins mediate many steps of inflammation, act as opsonins, and directly kill antibody-bound cells via the membrane attack complex.

e. Antibodies of the IgG class also act directly as opsonins and link target cells to NK cells, which directly kill the target cells.

f. Antibodies also neutralize toxins and extracellular viruses.

XII. Virus-infected cells and cancer cells are killed by cytotoxic T cells, NK cells, and activated macrophages.

a. A cytotoxic T cell binds via its membrane receptor to cells bearing a viral antigen or cancer-associated antigen in association with a class I MHC protein.

b. Activation of the cytotoxic T cell also requires cytokines secreted by helper T cells, themselves activated by antigen presented by a macrophage. The cytotoxic T cell then releases perforin, which kills the attached target cell by making it leaky.

c. NK cells and macrophages are also stimulated by helper T-cell cytokines, particularly IL-2 and interferon-gamma, to attack and kill virus-infected or cancer cells.

Systemic Manifestations of Infection

I. The acute phase response is summarized in Figure 18.22.

II. The major mediators of this response are IL-1, TNF-α, and IL-6.

Factors That Alter the Resistance to Infection

I. The body's capacity to resist infection is influenced by nutritional status, the presence of other diseases, psychological factors, and the intactness of the immune system.

II. AIDS is caused by a retrovirus that destroys helper T cells and therefore reduces the body's ability to resist infection and cancer.

III. Antibiotics interfere with the synthesis of macromolecules by bacteria.

Harmful Immune Responses

I. Rejection of tissue transplants is initiated by MHC proteins on the transplanted cells and is mediated mainly by cytotoxic T cells.

II. Transfusion reactions are mediated by antibodies.

a. Transfused erythrocytes will be destroyed if the recipient has natural antibodies against the antigens (type A or type B) on the cells.

b. Antibodies against Rh-positive erythrocytes can be produced following the exposure of an Rh-negative person to such cells.

III. Allergies (hypersensitivity reactions) caused by allergens are of several types.

a. In delayed hypersensitivity, the inflammation is due to the interplay of helper T-cell cytokines and macrophages. Immune-complex hypersensitivity is due to complement activation by antigen–antibody complexes.

b. In immediate hypersensitivity, antigen binds to IgE antibodies, which are themselves bound to mast cells. The mast cells then release inflammatory mediators, such as histamine, that produce the symptoms of allergy. The late phase of immediate hypersensitivity is mediated by eosinophils.

IV. Autoimmune attacks are directed against the body's own proteins acting as antigens. Reasons for the failure of immune tolerance are summarized in Table 18.10.

V. Normal tissues can be damaged by excessive inflammatory responses to pathogens.

REVIEW QUESTIONS

1. What are the major cells of the immune system and their general functions?
2. Describe the major anatomical and biochemical barriers to infection.
3. Name the three cell types that function as phagocytes.
4. List the sequence of events in an inflammatory response and describe each step.
5. Name the sources of the major inflammatory mediators.
6. What triggers the alternative pathway for complement activation? What roles does complement play in inflammation and cell killing?
7. Describe the antiviral role of type I interferon.
8. Name the lymphoid organs. Contrast the functions of the bone marrow and thymus with those of the secondary lymphoid organs.
9. Name the various populations and subpopulations of lymphocytes and discuss their roles in adaptive immune responses.
10. Contrast the major targets of antibody-mediated responses and responses mediated by cytotoxic T cells and NK cells.
11. How do the Fc and variable regions of antibodies differ?
12. What are the differences between B-cell receptors and T-cell receptors? Between cytotoxic T-cell receptors and helper T-cell receptors?

13. Compare and contrast antigen presentation to helper T cells and cytotoxic T cells.
14. Compare and contrast cytotoxic T cells and NK cells.
15. What two processes contribute to immune tolerance?
16. Diagram the sequence of events in an antibody-mediated response, including the role of helper T cells, interleukin 1, and interleukin 2.
17. Contrast the general functions of the different antibody classes.
18. How is complement activation triggered in the classical complement pathway, and how does complement "know" what cells to attack?
19. Name two ways in which the presence of antibodies enhances phagocytosis.
20. How do NK cells recognize which cells to attack in ADCC?
21. Diagram the sequence of events by which a virus-infected cell is attacked and destroyed by cytotoxic T cells. Include the roles of cytotoxic T cells, helper T cells, interleukin 1, and interleukin 2.
22. Contrast the extracellular and intracellular phases of immune responses to viruses, discussing the role of interferons.
23. List the systemic responses to infection or injury and the mediators responsible for them.
24. What factors influence the body's resistance to infection?
25. What is the major defect in AIDS, and what causes it?
26. What is the major cell type involved in graft rejection?
27. Diagram the sequences of events in immediate hypersensitivity.

KEY TERMS

activated macrophage 676
active immunity 674
acute phase protein 676
acute phase response 676
adaptive immune response 652
adenoid 663
alternative complement pathway 659
antibody 664
antibody-dependent cellular cytotoxicity (ADCC) 673
antibody-mediated response 664
antigen 662
antigen-binding site 667
antigen presentation 668
antigen-presenting cell (APC) 668
basophil 653
B lymphocyte (B cell) 653
chemoattractant 658
chemokine 658
chemotaxin 658
chemotaxis 658
classical complement pathway 659
class I MHC protein 668
class II MHC protein 668
clonal deletion 670
clonal expansion 662
clonal inactivation 670
clone 663
complement 658
costimulus 669
C3b 659
C-reactive protein 660
cytokine 654
cytotoxic T cell 664
dendritic cell 653
diapedesis 658
eosinophil 653
epitope 669
Fc 667
gamma globulin 672
helper T cell 664
histamine 683
hydrogen peroxide 658
IgA 672
IgD 672
IgE 672
IgG 672
IgM 672
immune surveillance 652
immune system 652
immune tolerance 670
immunoglobulin 667
immunology 652
inflammation 656
innate immune response 652
interleukin 1 (IL-1) 669
interleukin 2 (IL-2) 671
interleukin 6 (IL-6) 678
leukocyte 653
lymph node 663
lymphocyte 653
lymphocyte activation 662
lymphoid organ 662
macrophage 653
major histocompatibility complex (MHC) 668
margination 658
mast cell 654
membrane attack complex (MAC) 659
memory cell 662
MHC proteins 668
microbes 652
monocyte 653
natural killer (NK) cell 653
neutrophil 653
nitric oxide 658
opsonin 658
passive immunity 674
pathogen-associated molecular patterns (PAMPs) 661
pathogens 652
pattern-recognition receptors (PRRs) 662
perforin 675
phagocyte 654
phagocytosis 653
phagolysosome 658
phagosome 658
plasma cell 653
primary lymphoid organ 663
regulatory T cell 664
Rh factor 681
secondary lymphoid organ 663
spleen 663
T lymphocyte (T cell) 653
thymus 663
Toll-like receptors (TLRs) 661
tonsil 663
tumor necrosis factor-alpha (TNF-α) 669
type I interferon 660
type II interferon (interferon-gamma) 661

CLINICAL TERMS

Because of the subject matter of this chapter, it is difficult to distinguish between physiological key terms and "clinical" terms. This list is limited largely to specific diseases, their causes, symptoms and signs, and treatments.

acquired immune deficiency syndrome (AIDS) 679
allergen 681
allergy (hypersensitivity) 681
Alzheimer disease 684
anaphylaxis 683
antibiotic 679
asthma 684
autoimmune disease 683
bacteria 653
chronic inflammatory disease 684
cross-matching 681
cyclosporin 680
cytotoxic hypersensitivity 682
delayed hypersensitivity 682
erythromycin 679
graft rejection 680
HAART 679
hemolytic disease of the newborn 681
human immunodeficiency virus (HIV) 679
IgE-mediated hypersensitivity 682
immediate hypersensitivity 682
immune-complex hypersensitivity 682
inflammatory bowel disease 684
Kaposi's sarcoma 679
late phase reaction 683
multiple sclerosis 683
myasthenia gravis 683
oncogene 670
penicillin 679
rheumatoid arthritis 683
septic shock 683
severe combined immunodeficiency (SCID) 678
transfusion reaction 680
type 1 diabetes mellitus 683
vaccine 674
virus 653

Clinical Case Study: A Teenage Girl with Widespread Pain and Severe Facial Rash

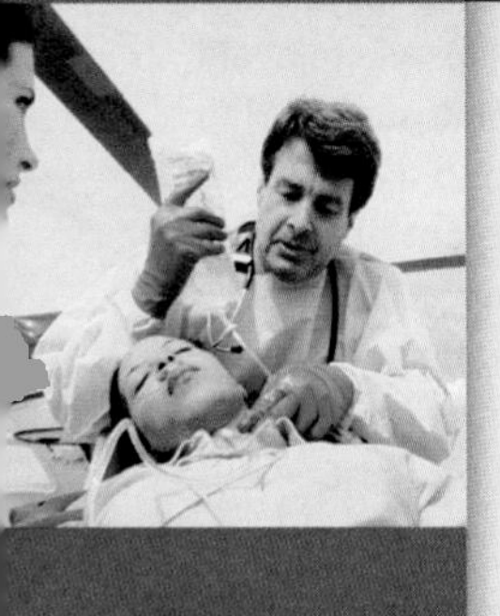

A 17-year-old Caucasian girl returned from a long day at the beach one sunny, late-summer day complaining of a sunburn and fatigue. Over the next few days, the "sunburn" took on the form of a rash across her cheeks and the bridge of her nose, and the girl began to feel sick, tired, and "achy all over." She assumed her symptoms were from severe sunburn. After a few days, the rash subsided a bit, but over the next several weeks she regularly felt pain and stiffness in her knees, wrists, and fingers. She did not alert her parents of this, however, thinking it was of no importance and would eventually subside. During this time, she spent considerable time outdoors in after-school activities and on weekends, being exposed to the sun. One day, while sitting at the computer, her fingers became so stiff that she had to stop typing. She could see that her fingers were swollen. She also felt nauseated, and upon standing, her knees felt stiff and very painful. At this point, she told her parents she was feeling very ill, and a visit was scheduled to see her physician.

The physician noted that the girl had an unremarkable medical history with no chronic illnesses, had until recently been very fit and active, and had no history of major allergies or disease; upon examination, however, she did appear extremely fatigued and weak. The joints in her fingers, wrists, knees, and toes were slightly swollen and had restricted movement. The rash had also reappeared on her face. At the time of her visit, the girl had a slightly elevated body temperature of 37.6°C (99.7°F). Also, the girl indicated that recently it "hurt to breathe" and that she felt "winded" all the time, which the physician took to mean that the girl was experiencing ***dyspnea*** (shortness of breath). The physician listened to her heart and chest sounds through a stethoscope and detected sounds that suggested inflammation. A chest radiograph revealed fluid buildup in the pleural membranes around the lungs and in the pericardium around the heart. Blood tests indicated an increased concentration of liver enzymes, suggesting that some liver cells were damaged and had released their contents into the blood. The concentration of albumin, the major protein in blood, was lower than normal. Because albumin is made in the liver, this was another sign that the liver was not functioning normally. The tests also revealed that the concentration of creatinine in the blood was slightly elevated (see Chapter 14), and a urinalysis revealed trace amounts of protein and blood in the urine. This suggested that the girl's kidneys were not functioning properly. Finally, the girl's hematocrit was 34.1%, which is below normal (see Chapter 12). Taken together, these test results were sufficiently serious that the physician admitted the girl to the hospital so that her condition could be carefully monitored and treated and additional tests could be performed.

The physician concluded that the girl may have an autoimmune disease known as ***systemic lupus erythematosus*** (***SLE***). Although a relatively uncommon disease (about 1.5 million total cases in the United States), all of the signs in this girl were consistent with a diagnosis of SLE. As with most autoimmune diseases, the majority (>90%) of SLE sufferers are female. The disease can occur at any age, but it most commonly appears in women of childbearing age and its onset can be quite sudden.

The two major immune dysfunctions in SLE are hyperactivity of T and B cells, with overexpression of "self" antibodies, and decreased negative regulation of the immune response. In some other autoimmune diseases, one or a small number of antigens appear to be the target of the immune attack, and these are often localized to one or a few organs. In SLE, however, the reaction is much more widespread. The most common antigens are proteins and double-stranded DNA in the nuclei of all nucleated cells. Because all nucleated cells share most of the same DNA and nuclear proteins, few—if any—parts of the body are not susceptible to immune attack in SLE. A subsequent blood test in this patient was positive for the presence of circulating antibodies that recognize cell nuclear material, confirming the diagnosis of SLE.

Exactly what initiates the immune response in SLE is unclear. However, it is known that most people with this disease are photosensitive—that is, their skin cells are readily damaged by ultraviolet light from the sun. When these cells die, their nuclear contents become exposed to phagocytes and other components of the immune system. It is also believed that UV light induces intact skin cells to express certain proteins that are antigenic in SLE. As a result, symptoms of SLE tend to flare up when a person with the disease is exposed to excessive sunlight. This is what happened to our patient after a day at the beach without sunscreen and as she continued to spend considerable time outdoors thereafter.

SLE has a strong genetic component, as evidenced by the fact that approximately 40% to 50% of identical twins share the disease when one is afflicted. Moreover, there is an increased frequency of five specific class II MHC variants in people with SLE, as well as deficient or abnormal complement proteins. Still, environmental triggers almost certainly elicit the disease in genetically susceptible people (because, as stated, in half the cases in which one twin has SLE, the other does not). There is no conclusive evidence that infections due to viral invasion are a trigger for the development of SLE. In addition to sunlight, other triggers associated with the appearance of SLE are certain chemicals and foods, such as alfalfa sprouts.

SLE can be mild or severe, intermittent or chronic. In most cases, though, the effects are widespread. Typically, connective-tissue involvement is extensive, with repeated episodes of inflammation in joints and skin. The outer covering of the heart (pericardium) and the pleural membranes of the lungs may become inflamed. Gastrointestinal function may be affected, resulting in nausea or diarrhea, and retinal damage is sometimes observed. Even the brain is not spared, as cognitive dysfunction and even seizures may arise in severe cases. The skin often develops inflamed patches, notably on the face along the cheeks and bridge of the nose, forming the so-called ***butterfly*** (***malar***) ***rash*** seen in some patients with SLE (**Figure 18.24**). One of the most serious manifestations of SLE occurs when immune complexes and immunoglobulins accumulate in the glomeruli of the nephrons of the kidney (see Chapter 14 for description of nephrons). This often leads to ***nephritis*** (inflammation of the nephrons) and results in damaged, leaky glomeruli. The appearance of protein or blood in the urine, therefore, is a clinical finding often associated with SLE.

(continued)

(continued)

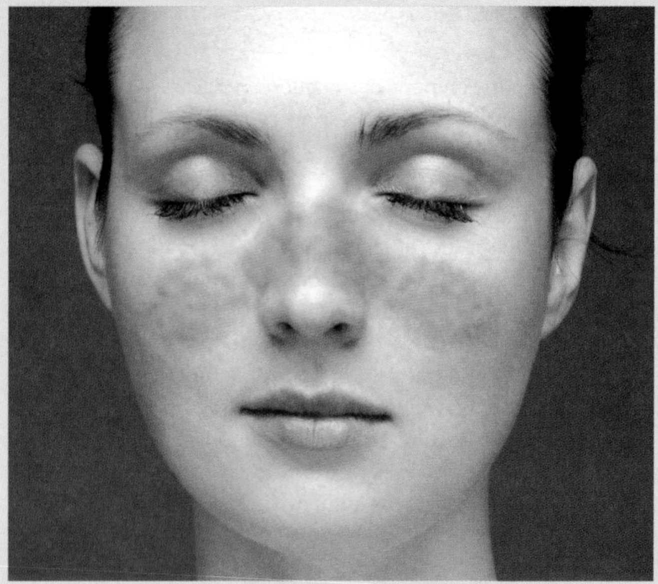

Figure 18.24 Characteristic butterfly or malar rash in a patient with systemic lupus erythematosus.

Finally, certain proteins on the plasma membranes of red blood cells and platelets may also become antigenic in SLE. When the immune system attacks these structures, the results are lysis of red blood cells and destruction and loss of platelets (***thrombocytopenia***). Loss of red blood cells in this manner contributes to the condition known as ***hemolytic anemia,*** a common manifestation of SLE. Our patient demonstrated widespread organ malfunction, evidenced by blood tests assessing liver and kidney function, radiograph results, and urinalysis. She also had mild hemolytic anemia. Considering the extent to which her disease affected her skin and other organs, it is not surprising that she felt ill and "achy all over."

In addition to the production of self antibodies in large numbers, there also appears to be a failure of the immune system to regulate itself in SLE. Consequently, the immune attacks, once begun, do not stop after a few days but instead continue. Some investigators believe this may be related to a deficiency or inactivity of regulatory T cells, but this has not been proven. It is clear, however, that the circulating concentrations of numerous cytokines—notably, IL-10, IL-12, and TNF-α—are abnormal in persons with SLE.

The treatments for SLE depend on its severity and the overall physical condition of the patient. In mild flare-ups, nonsteroidal anti-inflammatory drugs (NSAIDs) may be sufficient to control pain and inflammation, together with changes in lifestyle to avoid potential triggers. In more advanced cases, immunosuppression with high doses of synthetic adrenal corticosteroids (such as prednisone) or other potent immunosuppressant drugs is employed. Our patient was started on prednisone at an initially high dosage to control the widespread inflammation and immune attacks. The dose was tapered off once her blood tests were restored to nearly normal, because chronic high dosages of prednisone can have severe side effects (see Section D of Chapter 11 for a discussion of the effects of high concentrations of glucocorticoids). She was additionally started on ***hydroxychloroquine,*** an antimalarial drug commonly used in treatment of SLE due to its immunomodulatory effects. She was advised to immediately begin taking ibuprofen (an NSAID) whenever her symptoms worsened in the future and to use hydrocortisone skin cream if she developed rashes again. She was counseled on lifestyle changes that she would need to follow for the rest of her life. These included eating a healthy diet and exercising to promote cardiovascular health, to avoid smoking (which is a major risk factor for blood vessel disease and hypertension), and most significantly to avoid exposure to the sun when possible. This meant using sunscreen and a wide-brimmed hat at all times when outdoors, not just when at the beach, and even indoors because fluorescent and halogen lights emit sufficient UV light to trigger symptoms in some SLE patients. As she was of reproductive age, she was counseled about the possible effects of SLE on pregnancy and was advised against the use of estrogen-containing oral contraceptives, as estrogen has been reported to trigger or worsen flare-ups of SLE. After several days, a follow-up urinalysis indicated an absence of protein; therefore, kidney damage was minimal. Additional blood tests were near normal for liver and kidney function, and a chest radiograph was normal. She was released from the hospital but returned 2 weeks later for follow-up tests, which were all nearly or completely normal. One month after beginning treatment, she was able to resume normal activities and most of the stiffness in her joints had disappeared. Her steroid dosage was reduced to a very low dose every other day and then stopped. She was advised to call her physician if and when symptoms flared so that a new course of therapy could be initiated quickly.

Clinical terms: butterfly (malar) rash, dyspnea, hemolytic anemia, hydroxychloroquine, nephritis, systemic lupus erythematosus (SLE), thrombocytopenia,

See Chapter 19 for complete, integrative case studies.

CHAPTER 18 TEST QUESTIONS

Answers found in Appendix A.

1. Which of the following is an opsonin?
   a. IL-2
   b. C1 protein
   c. C3b protein
   d. C-reactive protein
   e. membrane attack complex

2. Which is/are important in innate immune responses?
   a. interferons
   b. clonal inactivation
   c. lymphocyte activation
   d. secretion of antibodies from plasma cells
   e. class 1 MHC proteins

3. A second exposure to a given foreign antigen elicits a rapid and pronounced immune response because
   a. passive immunity occurs after the first exposure.
   b. some B cells differentiate into memory B cells after the first exposure.
   c. a greater number of antigen-presenting cells are available due to the earlier exposure.
   d. the array of class II MHC proteins expressed by antigen-presenting cells is permanently altered by the first exposure.
   e. Both a and b are correct.
4. Which statement is incorrect?
   a. The most abundant immunoglobulins in serum are IgG and IgM antibodies.
   b. IgG antibodies are involved in adaptive immune responses against bacteria and viruses in the extracellular fluid.
   c. IgM antibodies are primarily involved in immune defense mechanisms found in the surface or lining of the gastrointestinal, respiratory, and genitourinary tracts.
   d. All antibodies of a given class have an Fc portion that is identical in amino acid sequence.
   e. Antibodies can exist at the surface of a B cell or be circulating freely in the blood.

True or False

5. Antibiotics are useful for treating illnesses caused by viruses.
6. Chronic inflammatory diseases may occur even in the absence of any infection.
7. All T cells are lymphocytes, but not all lymphocytes are T cells.
8. Edema (swelling), which occurs during inflammation, has important adaptive value in helping defend against infection or injury.
9. Bone marrow and the thymus are examples of secondary lymphoid organs.

CHAPTER 18 GENERAL PRINCIPLES ASSESSMENT

Answer found in Appendix A.

1. *Homeostasis is essential for health and survival.* Using Figure 18.22 as your guide, describe several ways in which infection may result in a disruption of homeostasis.

CHAPTER 18 QUANTITATIVE AND THOUGHT QUESTIONS

Answers found in Appendix A.

1. If an individual failed to develop a thymus because of a genetic defect, what would happen to the immune responses mediated by antibodies and those mediated by cytotoxic T cells?
2. What abnormalities would a person with a neutrophil deficiency display? A person with a monocyte deficiency?
3. An experimental animal is given a drug that blocks phagocytosis. Will this drug prevent the animal's immune system from killing foreign cells via the complement system?
4. If the Fc portion of a patient's antibodies is abnormal, what effects could this have on antibody-mediated responses?
5. Would you predict that patients with AIDS would develop fever in response to an infection? Explain.

CHAPTER 18 ANSWERS TO PHYSIOLOGICAL INQUIRIES

Figure 18.6. The C3b receptor should have a ligand-binding site that is *specific* for C3b and that binds C3b with high *affinity.*

Figure 18.8 Many molecules in the body act this way. For example, somatostatin acts locally in the stomach to control acid production (paracrine) and is secreted into the hypothalamo–pituitary portal veins to control growth hormone secretion (endocrine). Testosterone acts locally within the testes (paracrine) and reaches other targets through the blood (endocrine).

Figure 18.9 Vasodilation and increased protein permeability of the microcirculation both contribute to an increase in the rate of filtration of fluid from the plasma into the interstitial space. Because lymph vessels are the main route by which fluid and protein are returned from the interstitial space to the circulatory system (see Figure 12.47), these changes will lead to increased flow of lymph. As that fluid flows through the lymph nodes, lymphocytes are exposed to antigens from the invading pathogen, thus activating the adaptive immune response.

Visit this book's website at **www.mhhe.com/widmaier13** for chapter quizzes, interactive learning exercises, and other study tools.

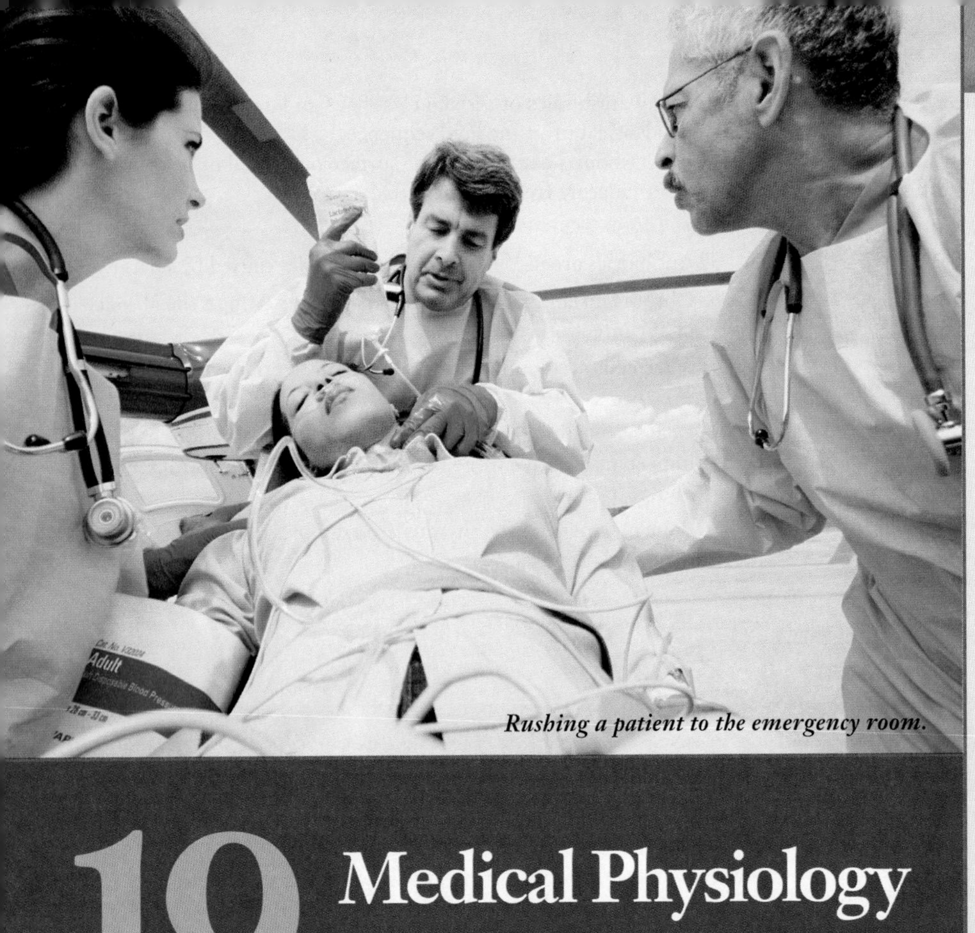

Rushing a patient to the emergency room.

19 Medical Physiology

INTEGRATION USING CLINICAL CASES

Physiology is one of the pillars of the health-related professions, including nursing, occupational health, physical therapy, dentistry, and medicine. In fact, the term *pathophysiology*—the changes in function associated with disease—highlights the intertwining of physiology and medicine. You need a thorough understanding of the general principles of physiology to properly diagnose and treat diseases and disorders. We are aware that many users of this textbook may not be planning a career in the health professions. However, teachers of physiology can attest to the use of clinical examples as an effective approach to highlight and reinforce the understanding of the functions and interactions of the organ systems of the body.

This chapter uses clinical cases to allow you to continue to explore the material you learned from this book and, at the same time, review some of the general principles of physiology that were first introduced in Chapter 1. You have been introduced to the educational power of clinical cases at the end of each chapter of this book. This chapter continues this theme with more extensive cases. More importantly, this chapter illustrates the concept of *integrative physiology*. In real life, complicated clinical cases involve multiple organ systems. The true art of medicine is the ability of clinicians to recall these basic principles and put them together in the evaluation of the patient. Each case in this chapter has a section called "Physiological Integration" to highlight this fact. As you read these sections, you should consider the relationships among disease, integrative physiology, and homeostasis, the last of which has been a theme throughout this textbook.

Some of the conditions and physiological interactions described in this chapter are not explicitly described in the book and may be new to you. Interspersed at key points in the chapter are several places where you will be asked to "Reflect and Review." In some cases, specific answers to these questions are not provided in the case itself. We encourage you to answer these questions as the case unfolds by, if necessary, referring back to the appropriate section of the book. Furthermore, we have annotated each case with figure and table numbers to facilitate review of material covered in previous chapters. In some cases, the figures and tables from previous chapters do not specifically answer the question but provide an opportunity to review the control system in question to allow the student to propose potential answers.

We hope that the cases in this chapter will motivate you to synthesize and integrate information from throughout the book and perhaps even go beyond what you have learned. In fact, you may enjoy consulting other sources to answer some of the more challenging questions or learn more about specific aspects of each case that interests you.

We hope you enjoy this chapter and encourage you as readers of the book to send us comments and suggestions for additional cases.

CASE A
Woman with Palpitations and Heat Intolerance

19.A1 Case Presentation

A 23-year-old woman visits her family physician with complaints of a 12-month history of increasing nervousness, irritability, and ***palpitations*** (a noticeable increase in the force of her heartbeat). Furthermore, she feels very warm in a room when everyone else feels comfortable. Her skin is unusually warm and moist to the touch. She has lost 30 pounds of body weight over this period despite having a voracious appetite and increased food intake.

Reflect and Review #1

- Describe the general principles of the control of body temperature (see Figures 16.16 through 16.18). What may have caused her skin to feel warm and moist?

Two years ago, she was jogging about 20 miles per week. However, she had not done any running for the past year because she "didn't feel up to it" and complained of general muscle weakness. She said she often felt irritable and had mood swings. Her menstrual periods have been less frequent over the past year. Her previous medical history was normal for a person her age. She states that she has double vision when looking to the side but does not have any loss of vision when using only one eye or the other.

Reflect and Review #2

- Which hypothalamic, anterior pituitary gland, and ovarian hormones control the menstrual cycle? (See Figure 17.22 and Table 17.7.)
- What anterior pituitary gland disorder can cause a decrease in menstrual cycle frequency and loss of vision? (See Figure 17.39.)

19.A2 Physical Examination

The patient is a 5' 7" (170 cm), 110-pound (50 kg) woman. Her systolic/diastolic blood pressure is 140/60 mmHg (normal for a young, healthy woman is about 110/70 mmHg). Her resting pulse rate is 100 beats per minute. Before she became ill, her resting heart rate was about 60–70 beats per minute. Her respiratory rate is 17 breaths per minute (normal for her was approximately 12–14 breaths per minute). Her skin is warm and moist. Her eyes are bulging out (***proptosis*** or ***exophthalmos***) (**Figure 19.1a**). Finally, when she is asked to gaze to the far right, her right eye does not move as far as does her left eye and she says she has double vision (***diplopia***).

Reflect and Review #3

- Briefly describe the control of systemic blood pressure, heart rate, and respiratory rate (see Figures 12.23 and 12.51 and Figure 13.32). What might be causing her hypertension, ***tachycardia*** (increased heart rate), and ***tachypnea*** (increased respiratory rate)?
- Describe the muscles that control eye movement (see Figure 7.35).

Upon further examination, the physician notes an enlargement of a structure in the front, lower part of her neck (**Figure 19.1b**). It is smooth (no bumps or nodules felt) and painless. When the patient swallows, this enlarged structure moves up and down. When a stethoscope is placed over this structure, the physician can hear a swishing sound (called a ***bruit*** [BREW-ee]) with each heartbeat.

Reflect and Review #4

- What structure might be responsible for the swelling in the patient's lower neck? (See Figures 11.20a and 15.16.) What are the major functions of this structure?

Her patellar tendon (knee-jerk) reflexes are hyperactive. When she holds her hands out straight, she exhibits fine tremors (shaking).

Reflect and Review #5

- What are the neural pathways involved in the knee-jerk reflex? (See Figure 10.6.) Could the enlarged structure in her neck account for the abnormal reflexes observed?

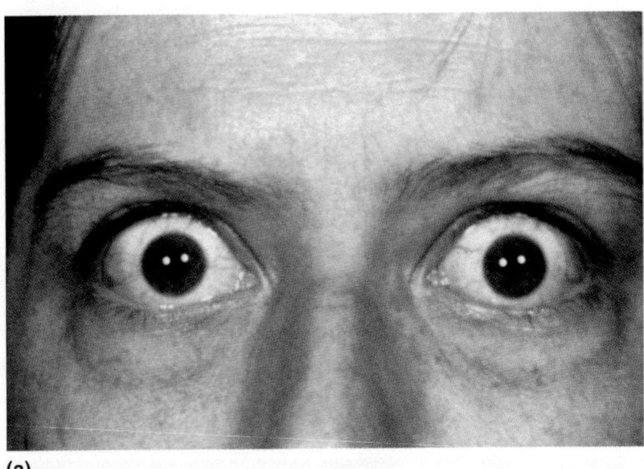

(a)

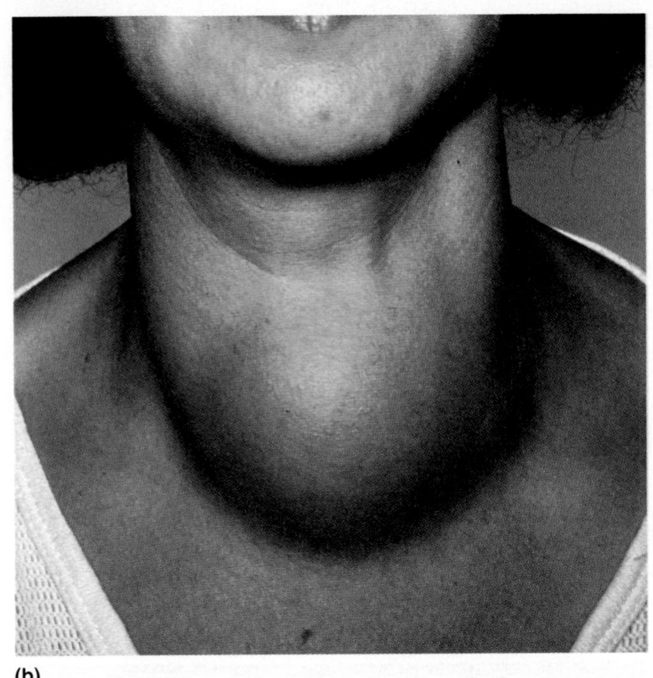

(b)

Figure 19.1 (a) Proptosis and (b) goiter.

19.A3 Laboratory Tests

The family physician considers the history and physical exam and decides to order some blood tests. The results are shown in **Table 19.1**.

Reflect and Review #6

- Describe the feedback control loops of the hormones whose values were abnormal (see Figure 11.22 and Figure 17.24). Which, if any, of these hormones might account for the symptoms in this patient? What might have contributed to the woman's feelings of excessive warmth?
- Why is the serum glucose sample obtained in the fasted state? (See Figure 16.8.) Does the serum glucose concentration rule out diabetes mellitus as a factor in this patient's illness?

TABLE 19.1 Laboratory Results for Patient

Blood Measurements*	Result	Normal Range
Sodium	136 mmol/L	135–146 mmol/L
Potassium	5.0 mmol/L	3.8–5.0 mmol/L
Chloride	102 mmol/L	97–110 mmol/L
pH	7.39	7.38–7.45
Calcium (total)	9.6 mg/dL	9.0–10.5 mg/dL
Parathyroid hormone	15 pg/mL	10–75 pg/mL
Glucose (fasting)	80 mg/dL	70–110 mg/dL
Prolactin	10.4 ng/mL	1.4–24.2 ng/mL
Estrogen (midcycle)	100 pg/mL	150–750 pg/mL
Total T_4†	20 μg/dL	5–11 μg/dL
Free T_4	2.8 ng/dL	0.8–1.6 ng/dL
Thyroid-stimulating hormone (TSH)	0.01 μU/mL	0.3–4.0 μU/mL

*In actuality, these measurements are performed in blood serum or plasma.

†T_4, thyroxine

19.A4 Diagnosis

The most likely explanation for the findings is an increase in thyroid hormone in the patient's blood. When increased thyroid hormone causes significant symptoms, it is part of a condition called ***hyperthyroidism*** or ***thyrotoxicosis.*** The enlarged organ in the neck is likely the thyroid gland, although large thyroid glands (***goiters***) also occur in hypothyroidism (see Figure 11.23 for an extreme example). In order to interpret the thyroid function tests shown in Table 19.1, first review the control of thyroid hormone synthesis and release (see Figures 11.20 through 11.22).

There are two circulating thyroid hormones—thyroxine (T_4) and triiodothyronine (T_3). Whereas T_4 is the main secretory product of the thyroid gland, T_3 is actually more potent and is actively produced in target tissues by the removal of one iodine molecule from T_4. Nonetheless, for practical reasons, T_4 is the form of thyroid hormone that is routinely measured in clinical situations. The release of T_4 by the thyroid gland is normally controlled by thyroid-stimulating hormone (TSH) secreted by the anterior pituitary gland. Binding of TSH to its G-protein-coupled plasma membrane receptor activates adenylyl cyclase and cAMP formation, which then stimulates cAMP-dependent protein kinase (see Figure 5.6). Like most anterior pituitary gland tropic/trophic hormones, TSH not only stimulates the activity of the thyroid gland but also stimulates its growth. As with most other pituitary gland–target hormone systems, the target-gland hormone (T_4) inhibits the release of the anterior pituitary gland hormone controlling it (in this case, TSH) via negative feedback (see Figure 11.22).

There are several reasons why the thyroid gland in this patient could be producing too much thyroid hormone, leading to thyrotoxicosis. The most common condition to focus on here is called ***Graves' disease.*** In this condition, the thyroid gland is stimulated by antibodies that activate the receptor for TSH on the follicular cell of the thyroid (**Figure 19.2**). Therefore, these TSH receptor-stimulating antibodies mimic the action of TSH but are distinct from authentic TSH from the anterior pituitary gland. These ***thyroid-stimulating immunoglobulins*** (***TSIs***) are characteristic of an autoimmune disorder in which the patient makes antibodies that bind to one or more proteins expressed in his or her own tissues (see Table 18.10). The exact cause of an increase in TSIs in individual patients is usually not known. TSIs are produced by B lymphocytes that, in addition to residing in lymph nodes, can actually infiltrate the thyroid gland in Graves' disease. In Chapter 9, you learned about a disease called myasthenia gravis, in which autoantibodies bind to and destroy the nicotinic acetylcholine receptor in the neuromuscular junction. This is typical of antibody–antigen reactions, in which antigens are removed from the body (see Chapter 18). In Graves' disease, however, the autoantibodies are highly unusual in that they not only recognize and bind to the TSH receptor on thyroid follicular cells but this binding *stimulates* rather than destroys the receptor. Therefore, TSIs stimulate the thyroid gland to synthesize and secrete excess T_4 independently of TSH. The increase in T_4 would be predicted to suppress the secretion of TSH from the anterior pituitary gland by negative feedback, which is consistent with the low serum TSH concentration measured in the patient's blood. The increased serum T_4 probably also suppressed the synthesis and release of thyrotropin-releasing hormone (TRH) from the hypothalamus via negative feedback. (Serum TRH concentrations are not determined in such situations because TRH is secreted directly into the hypothalamo–pituitary portal circulation. The actual amount of TRH from the hypothalamus that reaches the systemic circulation is too small for its measurement in a blood sample from a peripheral vein to be useful.)

The total and free (not bound to plasma proteins) T_4 concentrations in the blood of this patient are increased, confirming the diagnosis of hyperthyroidism. Measurement of free T_4 is helpful because most of the circulating thyroid hormone in the blood is bound to plasma proteins, so measuring the serum T_4 that is not bound to plasma proteins proves that

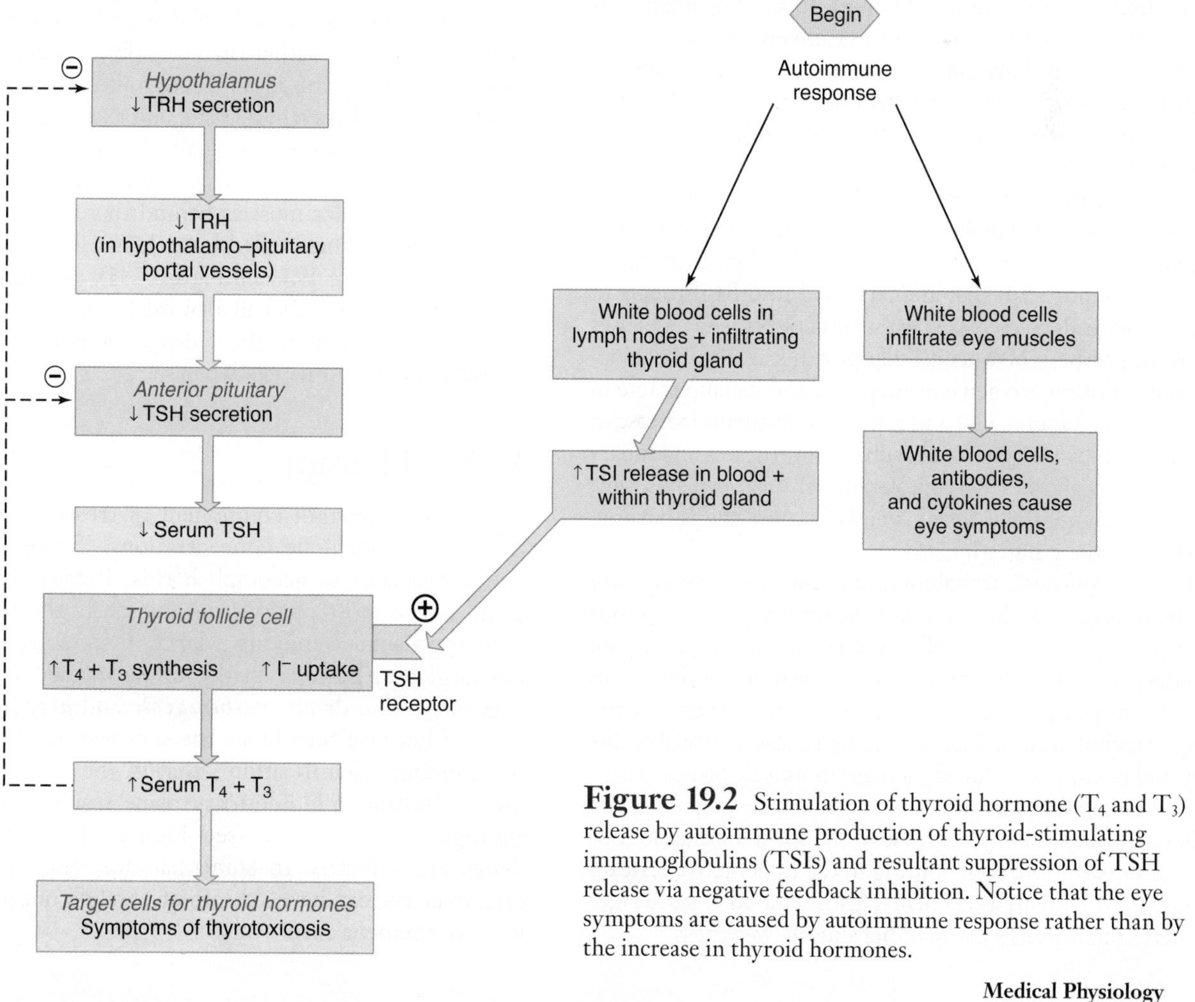

Figure 19.2 Stimulation of thyroid hormone (T_4 and T_3) release by autoimmune production of thyroid-stimulating immunoglobulins (TSIs) and resultant suppression of TSH release via negative feedback inhibition. Notice that the eye symptoms are caused by autoimmune response rather than by the increase in thyroid hormones.

there is an increase in the amount of biologically active T_4. The suppressed TSH confirms that the T_4 is increased independently of stimulation from the anterior pituitary gland. This suppression of serum TSH, as in our patient, is one of the hallmarks of Graves' disease. The measurement of serum TSH concentration is used as a screening test for many disorders of the thyroid gland. Although TSI concentrations can be measured in the serum in some patients, it is often not necessary because the diagnosis of Graves' disease is the most likely, considering that it causes the majority of cases of hyperthyroidism. It was not necessary to measure TSIs in our patient.

Although Graves' disease was by far the most likely diagnosis, the physician ordered some additional tests to rule out other possible causes of the symptoms. Serum electrolytes were measured because they are important in the generation and maintenance of membrane potentials (Chapter 6) and their abnormalities can lead to weakness and palpitations. Serum calcium and parathyroid hormone were measured because weakness is a common finding in primary hyperparathyroidism (Chapter 11). A normal fasting serum glucose and pH indicated that diabetes mellitus was probably not the cause of the patient's weakness and fatigue. A normal prolactin concentration indicated that she does not have hyperprolactinemia, which can cause abnormalities in the menstrual cycle and visual disturbances (see Chapter 17 Clinical Case Study).

19.A5 Physiological Integration

Thyroid diseases are common. Up to 10% of women will develop hyperthyroidism or hypothyroidism by the age of 60 to 65. Thyroid hormone has a wide range of effects throughout the body; therefore, an understanding of all the organ systems is extremely useful in understanding the symptoms of thyroid disease.

One of the main effects of thyroid hormone is calorigenic—it increases the basal metabolic rate (BMR). This increase in metabolic rate is caused by activation of intracellular thyroid hormone receptors (see Figure 5.4) that are expressed in cells throughout the body. This leads to increased expression of Na^+/K^+-ATPases as well as the synthesis of other cellular proteins involved in oxidative phosphorylation, oxygen consumption, and metabolic rate in many tissues (see Figures 3.44 and 3.45). The resultant increase in heat production by our patient explains the warmness and moistness of her skin and her heat intolerance. It also explains why, despite eating more, she is losing weight because she is burning more fuel than she is ingesting.

The nervousness, irritability, and emotional swings are likely due to effects of thyroid hormone on the central nervous system, although the exact cellular mechanism of this is not well understood. The symptoms also appear to be due to an increased sensitivity within the central nervous system to circulating catecholamines. The muscle weakness is probably due to a thyroid hormone–induced increase in muscle protein turnover, local metabolic changes, and loss of muscle mass. Despite this, there appears to be an increase in the speed of muscle contraction and relaxation, contributing to the hyperactive reflexes observed in our patient. The normal fasting blood glucose rules out diabetes mellitus as a cause of her muscle weakness.

Her thyroid gland is enlarged because TSIs are mimicking the actions of TSH to stimulate the thyroid gland to grow. The enlarged thyroid with increased metabolic activity explains why a bruit was heard over the thyroid gland. The thyroid gland has a high blood flow per gram of tissue even in healthy individuals. The increase in thyroid function in Graves' disease leads to a large increase in blood flow to the thyroid—so much so that it is audible with a stethoscope during systole in some patients.

Her increased systolic blood pressure and heart rate can be explained in several ways. First, there are direct effects of thyroid hormones on the heart, such as an increase in transcription of the myosin genes. Second, as described in Chapter 11, Section C, thyroid hormone has permissive effects to potentiate the effects of catecholamines on the cardiovascular system. Finally, the small decrease in diastolic pressure may result from arteriolar vasodilation and reduced total peripheral resistance in response to increased tissue temperature and metabolite concentrations (see Figure 12.51).

Increased thyroid hormone can directly inhibit the release of the pituitary gland gonadotropins FSH and LH, particularly in the middle of the menstrual cycle when the LH and FSH surge that stimulates ovulation occurs. This can lead to a decrease in release of gonadal steroids from the ovaries, an irregular pattern or complete loss of menstrual periods, and a lack of ovulation. This also explains the lower serum estrogen concentrations at the middle of the menstrual cycle in our patient.

The eye findings are among the most striking in many patients with Graves' disease (see Figure 19.1). The proptosis (bulging out of the eye) is likely due to the autoimmune component of the disease, rather than to a direct effect of thyroid hormone. Supporting this idea is that proptosis can occur before the development of hyperthyroidism, and excessive thyroid hormone therapy for hypothyroidism usually does not cause proptosis. Furthermore, proptosis is caused by infiltration of white blood cells into the extraocular muscles behind the eye, rather than being caused by TSIs. These cells release chemicals that result in inflammation (see Figure 19.1 and Figure 7.35), causing the muscles to swell and forcing the eyeball forward. Sometimes, particular muscles of the eye are more affected than others, which explains the double vision of our patient when she gazes to one side.

19.A6 Therapy

The most important component of treatment is to decrease the thyroid hormone concentrations. There are three general approaches to accomplish this. Removal of the thyroid gland is the most obvious but currently the least frequently used approach. Removing a large, hyperactive thyroid gland has surgical risk and is usually not performed unless absolutely necessary. The drugs ***methimazole*** and ***propylthiouracil*** can be used because they block the synthesis of thyroid hormone by reducing organification—that is, the oxidation and subsequent binding of iodide to tyrosine residues in the colloidal thyroglobulin molecule (see Figure 11.21). Although these drugs are effective in some patients, they sometimes lose effectiveness, can have side effects, and do not provide a definitive, permanent cure.

In the United States, a common approach is a more permanent, nonsurgical treatment. This involves the partial destruction of the thyroid gland with a high dose of orally administered ***radioactive iodine.*** Remember that iodide (the active anion of iodine) is a critical component of thyroid hormone (see Figure 11.21) and the thyroid gland has a mechanism to trap iodide by secondary active transport from the blood into the follicular cell. Radioactive iodide is trapped by the thyroid; the local emission of radioactive decay destroys most of the thyroid gland over time. However, the procedure does not work equally well in all people. In fact, sometimes patients have so much of their thyroid gland destroyed that they develop permanent hypothyroidism. Such people must take T_4 pills for the rest of their lives to maintain thyroid hormones in the normal range.

In the short term, while waiting for the treatments to take effect, patients benefit from treatment with beta-adrenergic receptor blockers (see Table 12.9) to reduce the effects of increased sensitivity to circulating catecholamines. This often helps control the palpitations and increased heart rate, as well as some of the other symptoms such as nervousness and tremors. Because proptosis is not caused by the increase in T_4, its treatment can be accomplished, if necessary, with anti-inflammatory drugs, such as glucocorticoids, or surgery or radiation therapy of the eye muscles.

With adequate treatment, patients generally get better over time with most, if not all, of the symptoms resolving. Our patient was treated with radioactive iodide, and her symptoms slowly resolved over several months.

CASE B

Man with Chest Pain After a Long Airplane Flight

19.B1 Case Presentation

A 50-year-old, obese man has just returned from vacationing in Hawaii. He took an 8 h flight during which he sat by the window and did not leave his seat. In the taxi on the way home from the airport, he starts to feel chest pain and has shortness of breath, increased respiratory rate, and nausea. Thinking he is having a heart attack (***myocardial infarction***), he asks the taxi driver to take him to the nearest hospital.

19.B2 Physical Examination

An examination of the patient at the hospital emergency room indicates that he has dull, aching chest pain and is clearly upset and anxious, short of breath, and overweight. He is 68 in (173 cm) tall and weighs 300 pounds (136 kg). The emergency room nurse practitioner performs an electrocardiogram (ECG), primarily to rule out a heart attack. The ECG shows an increased heart rate (105 beats per min) but does not show changes consistent with a heart attack or with left heart failure.

Reflect and Review #7

- What are the main factors that control heart rate? (See Figure 12.23.) Might any of them explain the increased heart rate in our patient?
- How might damage to the heart be detected in an ECG? (See Figures 12.15 and 12.16 for a general discussion of ECG.)

A chest x-ray is performed in an attempt to determine the cause of the patient's chest pain and shortness of breath. The results indicate no abnormalities such as pneumonia or collapse of lung lobes (***atelectasis***).

19.B3 Laboratory Tests

Based on the patient's history and symptoms, the physician obtains a sample of the patient's arterial blood in order to measure the levels of oxygen, carbon dioxide, bicarbonate, hydrogen ions (pH), and hemoglobin. The findings are shown in **Table 19.2**.

TABLE 19.2 Blood Gas, Bicarbonate, and Hemoglobin Results While Patient Breathes Room Air

Blood Measurement	Result	Normal Range
Arterial P_{O_2}	60 mmHg	80–100 mmHg
Arterial P_{CO_2}	30 mmHg	35–45 mmHg
Arterial pH	7.50	7.38–7.45
Bicarbonate	22 mmol/L	23–27 mmol/L
Hemoglobin	15 g/dL	12–16 g/dL

Reflect and Review #8

- What is the cause of the change in arterial pH in our patient? (See Table 14.8.)

The results of these tests reveal that the patient has hypoxic hypoxia (hypoxemia), as indicated by the low arterial P_{O_2}, and is hyperventilating, leading to respiratory alkalosis (see Figure 13.22), as indicated by the low arterial P_{CO_2} and bicarbonate, and high arterial pH. The normal hemoglobin concentration indicates that the patient is not anemic.

Reflect and Review #9

- What are some possible causes of hypoxemia? (See Table 13.10.)
- What are the two main types of alkalosis? (See Table 14.8.)
- How do we know the alkalosis in our patient was acute (of recent, short-term origin)? (See Table 14.8.)

The patient is given 100% oxygen to breathe through a mask over his mouth and nose. This results in an increase in arterial P_{O_2} to 205 mmHg, a small increase in arterial P_{CO_2} to 32 mmHg, and a small decrease in arterial pH to 7.48. The normal response to breathing 100% oxygen in a healthy person is an increase in arterial P_{O_2} to greater than 600 mmHg, with no change in arterial P_{CO_2} or pH.

Reflect and Review #10

- Explain why increasing arterial P_{O_2} with supplemental oxygen caused the observed changes in arterial P_{CO_2} and pH (see Figures 13.35 and 13.40).

19.B4 Diagnosis

Because a heart attack has been ruled out, the physician suspects that the patient has at least one ***pulmonary embolism.*** An ***embolism*** (plural, *emboli*) is a blockage of blood flow through a blood vessel produced by an obstruction. It is often caused by a blood clot—or ***thrombus***—in the pulmonary arteries/arterioles. These clots usually arise from larger clots in leg veins.

To confirm his diagnosis, the physician orders a ***ventilation–perfusion scan,*** which is actually the combination of two different scans. In the ventilation scan, the patient inhales a small amount of radioactive gas. Special imaging devices are then used to detect the inhaled radioactive molecules and visualize which parts of the lung are adequately ventilated. Poorly ventilated areas of the lung will contain less radioactive gas. In the perfusion scan, a small amount of albumin, a naturally occurring plasma protein, tagged with a radioactive tracer, is injected into a vein. As the radioactive protein enters the pulmonary circulation, its distribution can be monitored using the same imaging device as just described. This procedure allows the physician to determine if parts of the lungs are receiving less than their normal share of blood flow because poorly perfused areas of the lungs will contain less radioactive albumin. The ventilation scan was normal, but the perfusion scan showed abnormalities. **Figure 19.3** shows the results of the perfusion scan, demonstrating dramatic decreases in perfusion in specific regions of the lung. These results supported the physician's diagnosis of several pulmonary emboli.

A variety of materials can occlude pulmonary arterial blood vessels, including air, fat, foreign bodies, parasite eggs, and tumor cells. The most common embolus is a thrombus that can theoretically come from any large vein but usually comes from the deep veins of the muscles in the calves (***deep vein thrombosis***). The fact that our patient sat on an 8 h flight without moving around greatly increased the chances for the formation of a deep vein thrombosis in the leg. This is because without skeletal muscle contractions, blood is not adequately pushed back toward the heart (see Figure 12.45). This allows blood to pool in the leg veins, which increases the chance for the formation of clots. After the abnormal lung perfusion scan, an ultrasound examination of the legs was performed to confirm whether clots were present in the leg veins. The results showed a large clot in the femoral and popliteal veins in the right leg.

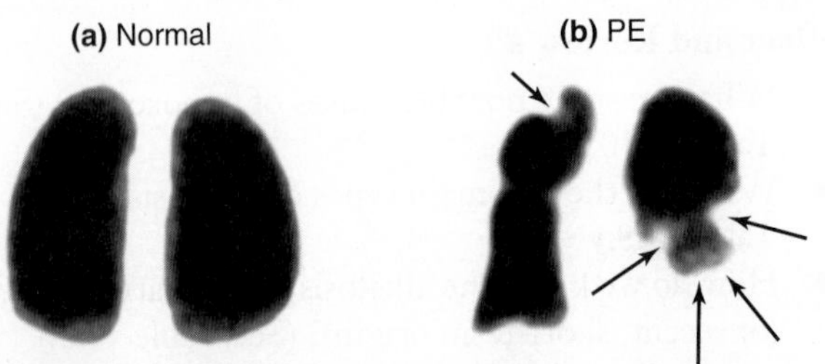

Figure 19.3 Pulmonary embolism (PE) from a deep vein thrombosis shown on a lung perfusion scan (posterior) with radiolabeled albumin. (a) A normal perfusion scan. (b) Multiple perfusion defects are shown (arrows).

Pulmonary embolism is a common and potentially fatal result of deep vein thrombosis. In fact, pulmonary embolism and deep vein thrombosis can be considered part of one syndrome. It may cause as many as 200,000 deaths each year in the United States. Most cases are not diagnosed until after death (on postmortem examination) either because the symptoms are initially mild or because the syndrome is misdiagnosed. Most small clots that form in small veins in the calves of the lower legs remain fixed in place, associated with the lining of the vein, and do not cause symptoms. However, if a clot enlarges and migrates into larger veins such as the femoral and popliteal veins, as in our patient, it can break off and migrate up the vena cava, through the right atrium and right ventricle, and into the pulmonary arterial circulation, where it can become lodged (see Figure 12.2 for an overview of the circulatory system). When this happens, blood flow is reduced or cut off to one or more large segments of the lung.

Reflect and Review #11

- Why will regional decreases in pulmonary blood flow lead to hypoxemia? (See Figure 13.24 and Table 13.10.)

Fortunately, these clots are too large to pass through the pulmonary circulation into the systemic circulation. When clots do form in the systemic circulation, they can occlude arteries and arterioles, thereby depriving vital organs of oxygen and nutrients and preventing the removal of toxic waste products. If this occurs in the cerebral arterial circulation, it can lead to a stroke. If this occurs in the coronary arteries, it can lead to a heart attack (see Chapter 12, Section E).

19.B5 Physiological Integration

The presence of hypoxemia and hyperventilation (the cause of the acute respiratory alkalosis), the history, and symptoms suggest that the patient is suffering from an acute decrease in pulmonary blood flow to some parts of the lung. Remember that hyperventilation is defined as a decrease in the ratio of CO_2 production to alveolar ventilation (see Figure 13.22). That is, if whole-body CO_2 production stays the same and alveolar ventilation increases as in our patient, arterial P_{CO_2} will decrease resulting in an increase in arterial pH. The acute decrease in pulmonary blood flow in some regions of the lung results in a clinically significant ventilation–perfusion inequality (see Table 13.10). The hyperventilation is only partly due to the mild hypoxemia, because the arterial P_{O_2} of 60 mmHg in our patient, although low, is just at the threshold oxygen level that stimulates the peripheral chemoreceptors (see Figures 13.33 and 13.34). Other causes of hyperventilation may be anxiety and pain, which may also explain the increased heart rate observed in the patient at the emergency room.

The ventilation–perfusion inequality means that the patient is ventilating areas of the lung to which blood is not flowing, leading to increased alveolar dead space (see Figure 13.19). The extra blood flows to other nearby lung regions leading to a local decrease in the ratio of ventilation to perfusion (physiological shunt). This results in some blood leaving the lung without adequate oxygenation. Remember that disruption of the delicate balance between regional ventilation and perfusion throughout the lung results in a failure to fully oxygenate the blood leaving the lung. In addition, hypoxia within the pulmonary circulation leads to vasoconstriction of the arterioles in the lungs and an increase in pulmonary artery pressure (see Figure 13.24).

We know that the hyperventilation was acute and not a long-standing problem because the arterial pH was still alkaline from the decrease in P_{CO_2}. This indicates that the kidneys did not have time to respond to the change in pH by increasing bicarbonate excretion in the urine (see Table 14.7). When the kidney has time to compensate, the condition is called respiratory alkalosis with metabolic compensation.

Why did the pulmonary embolism cause a decrease in arterial P_{O_2} but did not increase and, in fact, decreased arterial P_{CO_2}? Remember from Chapter 13 that the relationship between partial pressure and content is sigmoidal for oxygen but relatively linear for CO_2. Because of the plateau of O_2 content as P_{O_2} increases above 60 mmHg (see Figure 13.26), increasing alveolar O_2 in over-ventilated regions of the lung does not significantly increase O_2 content of the blood leaving that region. Therefore, although hyperventilation does increase O_2 in some alveoli, it does not compensate for the significant decrease in O_2 content in some pulmonary capillaries due to ventilation–perfusion inequalities. Increasing ventilation can decrease the CO_2 content of blood due to the linearity of the relationship between P_{CO_2} and CO_2 content of the blood. The overall net effect is acute respiratory alkalosis due to decreased arterial P_{CO_2}. Interestingly, the hypoxemia can be partially overcome if the patient breathes gas that is enriched in oxygen because, although ventilation and perfusion are not well matched, there is not complete shunting of blood in the lungs. Thus, increasing alveolar P_{O_2} can still increase oxygenation of some areas of the lung with ventilation–perfusion mismatching, at least somewhat. The arterial P_{CO_2} may have increased a little and pH decreased a little on supplemental O_2 because the improved arterial P_{O_2} decreased peripheral chemoreceptor stimulation and the degree of hyperventilation lessened (see Figure 13.34).

Our patient's initial complaint was chest pain, which made him think he was having a heart attack. He was actually fortunate to have chest pain because it caused him to go to the emergency room, which may have saved his life. Although the exact reasons for chest pain in pulmonary embolism are uncertain, one possibility is that the clots result in an acute increase in pulmonary artery pressure, which can result in pain.

Why did this man have a pulmonary embolism? Several risk factors for the development of deep vein thrombosis can result in pulmonary embolism. Prolonged sitting often causes a stagnant pooling of blood in the lower legs (see Figures 12.45 and 12.60). That is why it is highly recommended to avoid sitting for extended periods of time. Even sitting at a computer for just a few hours is discouraged. Contraction of the leg skeletal muscles compresses the leg veins. This results in intermittent emptying of the veins, decreasing the chances for clot formation. Obesity also increased the risk of deep vein thrombosis in our patient by further increasing the pooling of blood in the leg veins (due to obstruction of venous outflow and weakening of venous valves), increasing the amount of certain clotting factors in the blood, and changing platelet function.

A number of gene defects can also lead to an increased tendency to form clots, a condition called inherited ***hypercoagulability.*** The most common is resistance to activated protein C (see Figure 12.78), which can occur in up to 3% of healthy adults in the United States. In fact, our patient was tested and found to have resistance to activated protein C. Therefore, the combination of obesity, sitting for a prolonged period of time, and hypercoagulability is the likely cause of deep vein thrombosis and pulmonary embolism in our patient.

19.B6 Therapy

As soon as the diagnosis of pulmonary embolism was made, our patient was immediately started on intravenous heparin and ***recombinant tissue plasminogen activator*** (***rec-tPA***). Heparin is an anticlotting factor that counteracts the hypercoagulability. Rec-tPA is a synthetic form of a naturally occurring molecule that helps dissolve clots. The ventilation–perfusion scan was repeated a few days later and lung blood flow was almost normal. Supplemental oxygen was reduced over this time and then stopped when blood gases normalized.

Considering that this patient has an inherited cause of hypercoagulability, he has an increased probability to have another deep vein thrombosis and even pulmonary embolism in the near future. It is also possible that some of his family members have the same defect, for which they should be tested and adequately counseled. Our patient was sent home and continued to receive oral anticoagulants for 6 months (see description of anticlotting drugs in Chapter 12, Section F) and was actively followed by his primary care physician. He was encouraged to lose weight because obesity increases the risk of a deep vein thrombosis occurring again. Some physicians even advocate lifelong anticoagulation therapy for a patient such as ours.

CASE C

Man with Abdominal Pain, Fever, and Circulatory Failure

19.C1 Case Presentation

A 21-year-old healthy college student and his friends were canoeing deep in the Alaskan wilderness when he felt the first twinge of abdominal pain. Thinking that he either ate some undercooked fish or strained a muscle while paddling, he stopped to rest for a day, but the pain steadily intensified. He began to shiver and felt extremely cold even though it was a warm day. These symptoms worsened during the 36 hours it took to paddle to the outpost camp and be airlifted to the nearest medical center.

Reflect and Review #12

- Based on your knowledge of the homeostatic control of body temperature, why might this young man feel cold despite the signs that his body temperature is increased? (See Figures 16.17 through 16.19.)
- What might be the cause of the abdominal pain?

19.C2 Physical Examination

On arrival at the hospital emergency room, the young man is confused and lapsing into and out of consciousness. His temperature is 39.2°C (normal range ~36.5°C–37.5°C), heart rate is 140 beats per min (normal range 65–85), respiration rate is 34 breaths per min (normal ~12), and blood pressure is 84/44 mmHg (normal for a young man ~120/80). He is taking deep breaths, but his lungs are clear when listened to with a stethoscope. His abdomen is rigid and extremely tender when gently pressed on, especially in the lower-right quadrant. Upon questioning, his friends state that he has not urinated in over 24 hours. Therefore, a hollow tube called a ***catheter*** is inserted through the urethra into the urinary bladder to collect his urine. However, an abnormally small amount of urine (10 mL) is collected (see Figures 14.22 through 14.28 for a review of the control of urine output).

Reflect and Review #13

- What mechanisms link low systemic blood pressure in this patient to the low urine output? (See Figure 14.22.)
- What organs are located in the lower-right quadrant of the abdominal cavity? (See Figures 15.1 and 15.35.)

19.C3 Laboratory Tests

Additional measurements are then performed, and the results are shown in **Table 19.3**.

TABLE 19.3 Initial Laboratory Results with the Patient Breathing Room Air

Blood Measurement*	Result	Normal Range
White blood cells	$25.0 \times 10^3/mm^3$	$4.3–10.8 \times 10^3/mm^3$
Arterial P_{O_2}	90 mmHg	80–100 mmHg
Arterial P_{CO_2}	28 mmHg	35–45 mmHg
Arterial pH	7.25	7.38–7.45
Arterial bicarbonate	13 mmol/L	23–27 mmol/L
Lactate	8 mmol/L	0.5–2.2 mmol/L
Glucose	90 mg/dL	70–110 mg/dL
Creatinine	2.2 mg/dL	0.8–1.4 mg/dL

*In actuality, these measurements are done in whole blood or blood serum.

Reflect and Review #14

- Explain the relationship between arterial P_{CO_2} and pH values. Why is his arterial bicarbonate so low? (See Table 14.8.)
- What functions do white blood cells serve? What might be the cause of their abnormal values in this patient? (See Figure 12.67 and Table 18.1.)
- What metabolic processes produce lactate (lactic acid)? Under what circumstances would lactate production be increased above normal? (See Figures 3.41 and 3.42.)
- What effect does an increase in lactate have on alveolar ventilation? (See Figure 13.38.)
- Why did creatinine concentration in the blood increase? (See the discussion of Figure 14.12.)

19.C4 Diagnosis

A catheter is placed into an arm vein so that an intravenous infusion of isotonic saline (NaCl) can be started. Antibiotics are added to the saline to fight the apparent infection. A ***computed tomography*** (***CT***) scan of the abdomen is performed, which reveals an inflamed appendix (**Figure 19.4**). The patient is admitted to the intensive care unit (ICU) for continued intravenous fluid replacement, physiological monitoring, and the insertion of additional catheters that can be used for the measurement of arterial and right atrial blood pressures.

The patient is then taken to the operating room for abdominal exploration. Surgeons remove an inflamed appendix that is found to have a small hole (***perforation***) and shows signs of ***necrosis*** (dying or dead tissue).

Reflect and Review #15

- Where is the appendix located? (See Figure 15.35.)

A bacterial infection of the membranes surrounding the abdominal organs is found. This type of infection, called ***peritonitis***, results in ***pus*** (yellow liquid made up of white blood cells, bacteria, and cellular debris) being produced. The pus is removed, the abdominal organs are thoroughly washed with saline and antibiotics, and the patient is returned to the ICU where arterial and central venous blood pressures and urine output are monitored.

Reflect and Review #16

- What is the purpose of monitoring right atrial blood pressure? (See Figure 12.46.) Suggest other variables to monitor in this patient.

In the hours after surgery, the patient is maintained on mechanical ventilation. Gurgling breath sounds and decreasing arterial oxygen partial pressure indicate the presence of fluid in his lungs. Supplemental oxygen is provided to minimize the decrease in arterial oxygen by having the patient breathe a mixture of air enriched in oxygen. Widespread swelling of body tissues indicates that interstitial fluid volume is increasing, and his blood pressure and urine output remain dangerously below normal. In addition to providing continued intravenous fluids and antibiotic therapy, the ICU staff infuses norepinephrine and vasopressin (vasoconstrictors), and methylprednisolone (a synthetic glucocorticoid given at pharmacological doses).

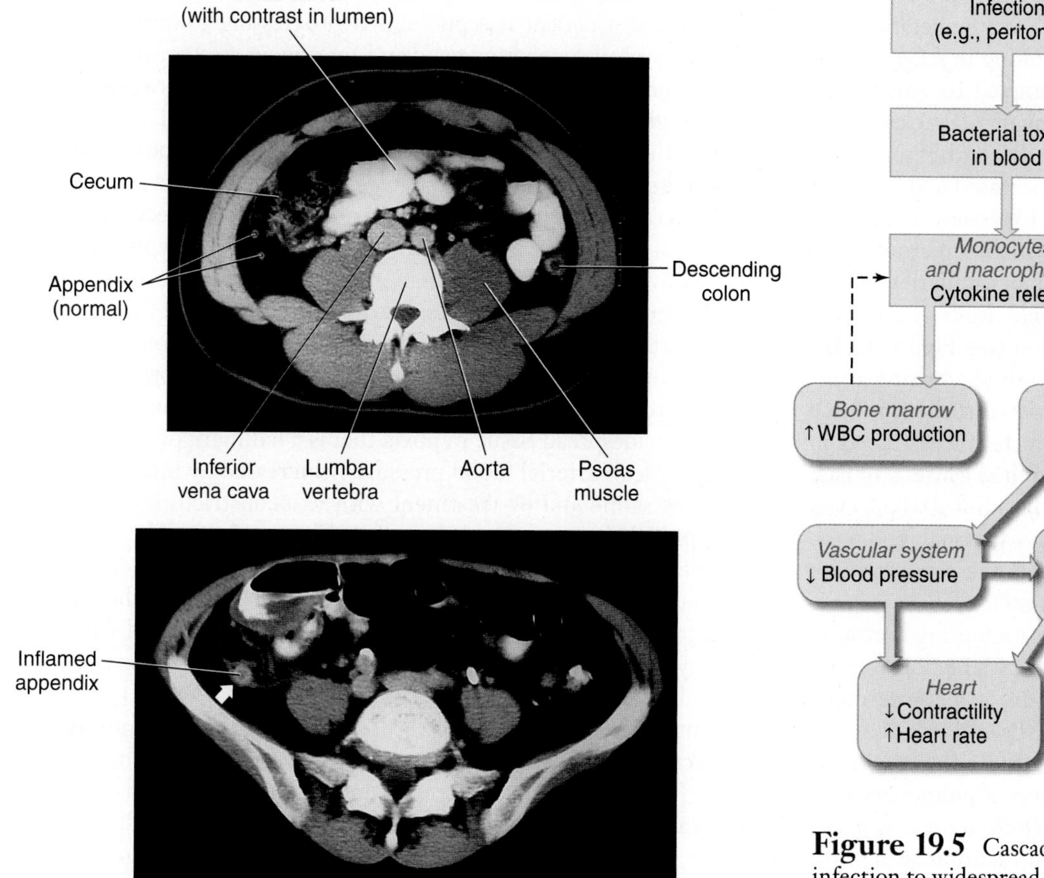

Figure 19.4 Normal abdominal CT scan (top) identifying major structures. CT scan on the bottom shows an inflamed appendix (arrow).

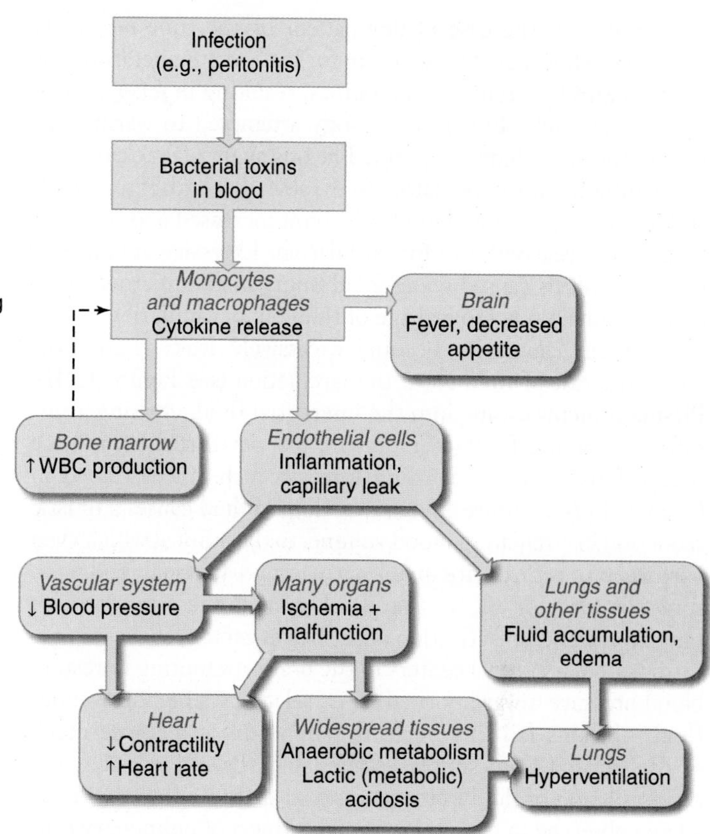

Figure 19.5 Cascade of some of the events from a serious infection to widespread organ failure in septic shock.

For the next several days, the patient is critically ill while his condition is continuously monitored. Appropriate treatment adjustments are implemented as needed to attempt to normalize his blood volume, blood pressure, serum lactate, blood pH, and gas partial pressures in his blood.

This patient's condition began as acute ***appendicitis,*** but the delay in treatment allowed it to progress to the potentially lethal condition known as ***septic shock.*** Although *Escherichia coli* and other bacterial species are normally present in the large intestine and its associated appendix, blockage of the lumen of the appendix or the blood supply to the appendix can allow those normally harmless bacteria to multiply out of control. When this happens, the appendix becomes distended and the pressure inside the appendix increases significantly due to inflammation. Eventually, these factors can lead to ulceration of the mucosa of the appendix, followed by perforation and ultimately rupture of the organ. This releases bacteria into the peritoneal cavity. The bacteria then release toxins that diffuse into the blood vessels in the abdomen, leading to a dramatic cascade of events (**Figure 19.5**). When a bacterial infection is accompanied by a ***systemic inflammatory response*** (defined by symptoms such as increases in body temperature, pulse rate, respiratory rate, and white blood cell count), the condition is referred to as ***sepsis.*** The most common sites of bacterial infections leading to sepsis are the lungs, abdomen (as in our patient), urinary tract, and sites where catheters penetrate the skin or blood vessels. If sepsis progresses to septic shock, patients also develop a significant decrease in blood pressure (a decrease in systolic pressure of greater than 40 mmHg or a mean arterial pressure less than 65 mmHg) that is not reversible by intravenous infusion of large volumes of isotonic saline solution. This type of circulatory failure is an example of ***low-resistance shock,*** defined as a decrease in total peripheral resistance and blood pressure due to an excessive release of vasodilatory substances (see Chapter 12, Section E).

19.C5 Physiological Integration

Bacterial infections stimulate the body to mount a rapid and widespread defense reaction (see Figures 18.16 through 18.19 and 18.22). Monocytes and macrophages (two types of white blood cells) secrete a variety of signaling molecules known generally as cytokines (see Table 18.2), which include substances such as interleukins and tumor necrosis factor. Target tissues for cytokines include (1) the brain, where they mediate the onset of fever, a decrease in appetite, fatigue, and an increase in ACTH secretion; (2) the bone marrow, where they stimulate an increase in the rate of white blood cell production; and (3) endothelial cells throughout the vasculature, where they stimulate processes leading to inflammation and increased capillary leakiness. Many species of bacteria release toxins, which greatly accelerate and exaggerate cytokine release and effects, often resulting in a maladaptive or life-threatening overreaction. The systemic inflammatory response has far-reaching effects on all body systems.

Such was the case of our patient by the time he finally reached the hospital. The set point for his body temperature was reset upward by circulating cytokines, resulting in ***fever***, and he shivered and felt chilled as his body attempted to warm itself toward the new, higher set point. The onslaught of cytokines and other inflammatory mediators (see Table 18.3 and Figure 18.2) accelerated as his white blood cell count increased and bacterial toxins were released into his circulation. Excessive amounts of those chemicals caused widespread injury to the microvascular endothelium and led to leakage of fluid out of capillaries.

When capillaries become excessively leaky, bulk flow favors the exit of fluid from the circulation (see Figure 12.41). Plasma proteins escape into the interstitial fluid, creating a significant osmotic force that draws fluid out through capillary pores. This is due to Starling forces, which are described in Chapter 12 (see Figure 12.42). This loss of fluid causes a drastic reduction in circulating blood volume, to the point at which even baroreceptor reflexes are unable to maintain arterial blood pressure (see Chapter 12, Section D). Dramatic increases in heart rate are evidence of activation of the baroreceptor reflexes via the cardiovascular control centers in the brain attempting to restore blood pressure toward normal. Even relatively large intravenous fluid infusions fail to reverse this hypotension because much of the infused fluid simply escapes into the interstitial space. Accumulation of fluid in the interstitial space leads to the tissue edema observed in our patient, and leakiness of pulmonary capillaries eventually led to fluid in his lungs (***pulmonary edema***).

Decreased systemic arterial blood pressure makes it difficult to produce adequate blood flow through the tissues. When blood flow is inadequate to meet demands for oxygen and nutrients (***ischemia***), tissues, organs, and organ systems malfunction. For example, our patient's inability to form urine resulted from low blood flow through his kidneys (see Figure 14.22). The increase in serum creatinine concentration was evidence that glomerular filtration rate was decreased (see discussion of Figure 14.12).

A more general consequence of reduced oxygen availability is that cells must resort to anaerobic pathways to manufacture ATP, and lactic acid (lactate) is produced as a by-product (see Figure 3.41 and Figure 9.22). This led to the marked metabolic acidosis seen in our patient. His hyperventilation was driven by the peripheral chemoreceptors (primarily the carotid bodies), in an attempt to compensate by removing CO_2-derived acid from the plasma (see Figure 13.37). Another mechanism designed to combat acidosis is the addition of new bicarbonate to the plasma and the excretion of H^+ via the kidney (Chapter 14, Section C), but the decrease in renal blood flow and glomerular filtration rate rendered this mechanism ineffective. His oxygen delivery to tissues was further compromised by the fluid buildup in his lungs. The added barrier to oxygen diffusion from lung alveoli into pulmonary capillaries (see Figure 13.28) reduced the oxygen partial pressure of his systemic arterial blood.

19.C6 Therapy

Septic shock is an extremely challenging condition to treat, with mortality rates of 40% to 60%. One of the most important factors in determining patient survival is early recognition of the condition and onset of treatment. As soon as it has been determined that a patient is septic and is progressing toward septic shock, survival depends on rapid and continuous assessment of his or her physiological condition and timely therapeutic responses to changing conditions. Among the variables monitored, in addition to those listed in Table 19.3, are body temperature, heart rate, blood pressure, arterial and venous oxygen saturation, mean arterial and right atrial blood pressures, urine output, and specific biochemical plasma indicators of the function of other organs, such as the liver. Using this information, clinicians can take steps to improve cardiovascular and respiratory function while at the same time battling the infection that is the root cause of the condition.

Immediate interventions in the treatment of septic shock are aimed at restoring systemic oxygen delivery and thus relieving the widespread tissue hypoxia that is a hallmark of the condition. Mean arterial blood pressure is increased by infusion of isotonic saline and by treatment with vasoconstrictors such as norepinephrine and vasopressin (see Figure 12.51). The extra circulating fluid volume increases cardiac output by increasing venous pressure and cardiac filling (see Figure 12.46), whereas norepinephrine (the neurotransmitter normally released from postsynaptic sympathetic nerve endings) increases cardiac contractility and arteriolar vasoconstriction (see Figure 12.51). Maintaining mean arterial pressure between 65 and 90 mmHg is necessary to ensure adequate flow of blood through the tissues. Right atrial pressure is monitored because it is a good index of venous return and the volume of fluid within the cardiovascular system (see Figure 12.57). The oxygen content of the blood is maintained by ventilating the lungs with supplemental oxygen to make sure that hemoglobin is saturated with oxygen (see Figure 13.26). It is also helpful to reduce the patient's demand for oxygen by paralyzing the respiratory muscles with drugs and providing mechanical ventilation, usually through a tube placed in the trachea attached to a positive-pressure pump. Otherwise, the increase in rate and depth of breathing that is typical of a patient in septic shock causes a marked increase in oxygen use by the respiratory muscles and directs blood flow away from other organs already suffering from lack of oxygen.

The infection must be treated while also restoring cardiovascular function. Antibiotics that act on a wide variety of types of bacteria are administered as soon as possible after sepsis is diagnosed. The source of the infection is then located, accumulated pus and dead tissue are removed, and the surrounding tissue is thoroughly cleaned. Ideally, samples of blood and/or pus from the site of infection can be grown in culture, and within 48 hours the specific bacterial species involved in the infection can be identified. The intravenous antibiotic therapy can then be altered to use drugs known to specifically target the invading species.

Recent clinical studies have suggested other therapeutic measures that can increase the survival rate of patients with septic shock. Pharmacological doses of glucocorticoid injections have also shown promise in some patients with septic shock. These hormones activate mechanisms throughout many tissues of the body that help the body cope with stress (see Table 11.3). Important among those effects are the inhibition of the inflammatory response and the enhancement of the sensitivity of vascular smooth muscle to adrenergic agents like norepinephrine.

Over a 6-day period, the condition of our patient gradually improved. His blood pressure increased and stabilized, and the intravenous fluid and norepinephrine infusions were gradually reduced and then stopped. The edema in his lungs and tissues slowly subsided, he regained consciousness, and he was eventually able to maintain oxygen saturation in his arterial blood without mechanical ventilation. During his 2-week hospital stay, the brain, liver, and kidney function returned to normal, and he had no apparent long-term organ damage from his ordeal. He has been extremely fortunate; approximately 500,000 cases of severe septic shock occur in the United States each year, and less than half of those patients survive. His youth and relatively good initial physical condition were most likely instrumental in helping him beat the odds.

CASE **D**

College Student with Nausea, Flushing, and Sweating

19.D1 Case Presentation

A 21-year-old female Caucasian college student visits the student health clinic because of several episodes of nausea (without vomiting), flushing (redness and warmth in the face), and sweating. Although she admits to some binge drinking in the past, her recent episodes of nausea do not correlate with those events and occur without any identifiable trigger. Following the onset of her symptoms, she also notices mild tingling ("pins and needles") and rhythmic jerking beginning in the left side of her face and progressively marching down her body to include the left arm and left leg. These symptoms persist for about 3–4 minutes and then completely go away. The student health service physician assistant asks the patient if she has had any recent head injuries that could account for her symptoms. The patient reports that no such injuries have occurred. During the physical exam, the patient becomes nauseated, visibly flushed in the face, and sweaty. After a few seconds, twitching of the left side of her face occurs, with progressive involvement of the left arm, followed by the left leg. After a minute or so, the student loses consciousness and starts to have rhythmic ***convulsions*** (violent spasms) of both arms and legs that look like an ***epileptic seizure*** (see Figure 8.2). A seizure is a storm of uncontrolled electrical activity in the brain that in some cases can become rhythmic. In addition, her back becomes arched and stiff, and her eyes roll back into their sockets. The physician assistant applies a ***transcutaneous*** (through the skin) ***oxygen monitor***, which is placed on the patient's finger. The patient's oxygen saturation is found to be low at 83% (normal is 95%). The convulsions stop after about 2–3 min, but the patient does not regain consciousness and soaks her pants with urine. The physician assistant immediately calls an ambulance, and the student is rushed to a nearby hospital emergency room.

Reflect and Review #17

- What can cause a sudden decrease in oxygen saturation? (See Figure 13.26 and Table 13.10.)
- What could be causing the flushing and sweating? (See Table 6.11 and Figures 16.17 and 16.18.)
- What controls micturition (urination)? (See Figure 14.13.)

19.D2 Physical Examination

The emergency room physician assesses the vital signs of the patient. Her blood pressure is increased at 159/83 mmHg, her heart rate is increased at 114 beats per minute, and her body temperature is normal at 98.8°F (37.1°C). A thin tube called a catheter is placed in the antecubital vein in one of her arms; a blood sample is drawn for the measurement of hematocrit, white blood cell count, electrolytes, glucose, and creatinine (**Table 19.4**). A slow infusion of 0.9% normal saline containing 150 mmol/L of sodium and 150 mmol/L of chloride (300 mOsm/L) is then started. A cursory neurological exam shows that the patient can be aroused but does not follow commands consistently and seems somewhat dazed. The pupils are similar in size and constrict symmetrically when a light is shone in either eye, which is normal. The patient does not seem to be moving the left arm and leg as much as the extremities on the right side. When the physician taps on the elbows and knees with a reflex hammer, the reflexes at the joints on the left side are more active, or brisker, than those of the right side. Based on this neurological exam, the physician orders an MRI scan of the head.

Reflect and Review #18

- What could cause her increase in heart rate? (See Figures 12.23, 12.27, and 12.51.)
- What does hematocrit measure? (See Figure 12.1.)

TABLE 19.4 Laboratory Tests in the Emergency Room

Blood Measurement*	Result	Normal Range
Hematocrit	47%	37%–48%
White blood cell count	$5.8 \times 10^3/mm^3$	$4.3–10.8 \times 10^3/mm^3$
Sodium	140 mmol/L	135–146 mmol/L
Potassium	4.0 mmol/L	3.5–5.0 mmol/L
Chloride	101 mmol/L	97–110 mmol/L
Calcium (total)	9.5 mg/dL	9.0–10.5 mg/dL
Glucose	130 mg/dL	70–110 mg/dL
Creatinine	0.9 mg/dL	0.8–1.4 mg/dL

*In actuality, sodium, potassium, chloride, calcium, glucose, and creatinine are measured in blood serum or plasma.

- Why was blood glucose measured? (See Figure 16.11 and the description of hypoglycemia in Chapter 16.)
- Why was blood creatinine concentration measured? (See section on renal clearance in Chapter 14.)
- Why was 0.9% normal saline infused? (See Table 4.1.)
- What is the significance of the increased reflexes in the left arm and leg? (See Figures 10.3 and 10.6.)

19.D3 Laboratory Tests

Magnetic resonance imaging (***MRI***) uses a powerful magnet to create a strong magnetic field around a patient's body (**Figure 19.6**). This field acts on the spin—or resonance—of the nuclei (protons) of hydrogen atoms in the body, aligning them in the same direction. The part of the body being examined—in this case, the brain—is then subjected to a pulse of radio waves. The atoms of the brain absorb the energy of the waves and the resonance of their nuclei changes, thus altering their alignment with the magnetic field. The realignment of the hydrogen nuclei within the magnetic field is dependent on the type of tissue and is detected as a change in the characteristics of an electrical current passing through the radio frequency coils. Protons in different tissues like brain, adipose, and muscle behave differently, because their behavior is dependent upon the local environment such as the content of fat and water. Therefore, the different behavior of protons in different tissues can be analyzed by a computer to generate an image of the internal structures of the brain and many abnormalities and disease states.

19.D4 Diagnosis

The MRI shows a lesion in the right temporal lobe of the brain. (See Figure 6.38 and **Figure 19.7** for the location of the temporal lobe.) There are at least two possible explanations for this lesion. First, an infection may have led to the formation of an ***abscess,*** which is an inflammation characterized by a collection of neutrophils, bacteria, and fluid. Second, the lesion may be a ***neoplasm,*** which means "new growth," or tumor. Some neoplasms are malignant, that is, they are cancerous and may spread to other parts of the brain. Many CNS tumors are benign or noncancerous. Benign tumors are generally less dangerous because they usually do not grow as rapidly or spread to other organs, but they can still cause problems due to local growth. The only way to determine the tissue diagnosis is by surgical removal of the abnormal tissue via a ***craniotomy,*** in which a part of the skull is removed to give access to underlying brain tissue. This is performed on the patient and a histological diagnosis of a tumor of astrocytes (***astrocytoma***) is made (see Figure 6.6). Specifically, the pathologist examining the stained histological sections of this tumor under a microscope determines that the patient has a ***glioblastoma multiforme.*** These tumors get their name because they arise from glia cells (in this case, astrocytes) that are not fully differentiated; such cells are known as blast cells. The tumors are "multiforme" because they can attain varied appearances depending on their age, location, and the extent of surrounding damage to the brain. Unfortunately, glioblastoma multiforme is a cancerous form of tumor.

Reflect and Review #19

- What is the significance of the anatomical location of this lesion? (See Figure 7.13.)
- What might possibly explain the appearance of the lesion found in the MRI?

19.D5 Physiological Integration

Glioblastoma multiforme is a fast-growing and potentially lethal form of brain cancer. Of the approximately 13,000 new cases of brain tumors in the United States each year, about

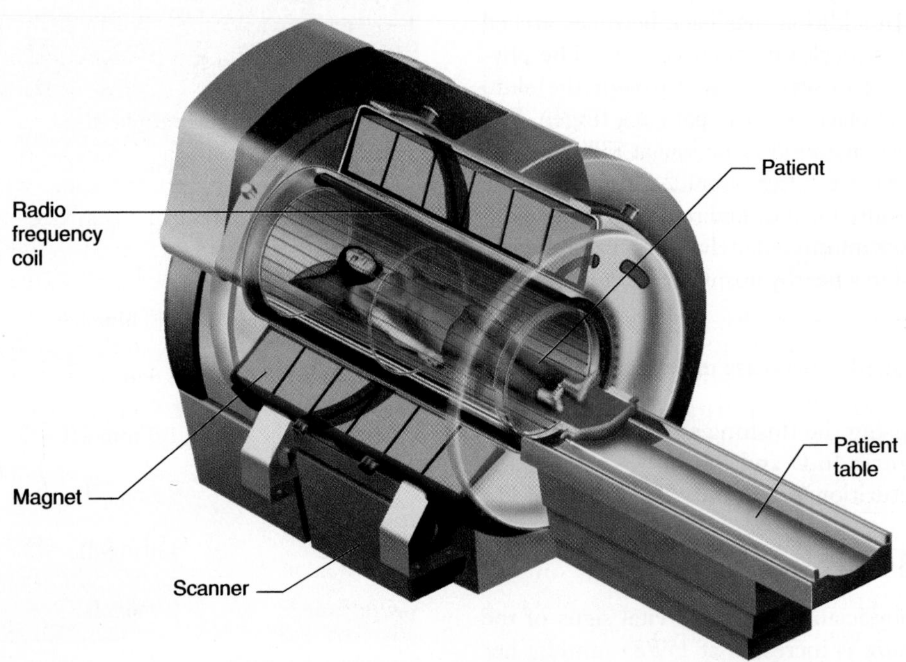

Figure 19.6 Cutaway diagram of an MRI scanner. Figure 19.6 was modified from an image on the following website: www.magnet.fsu.edu.

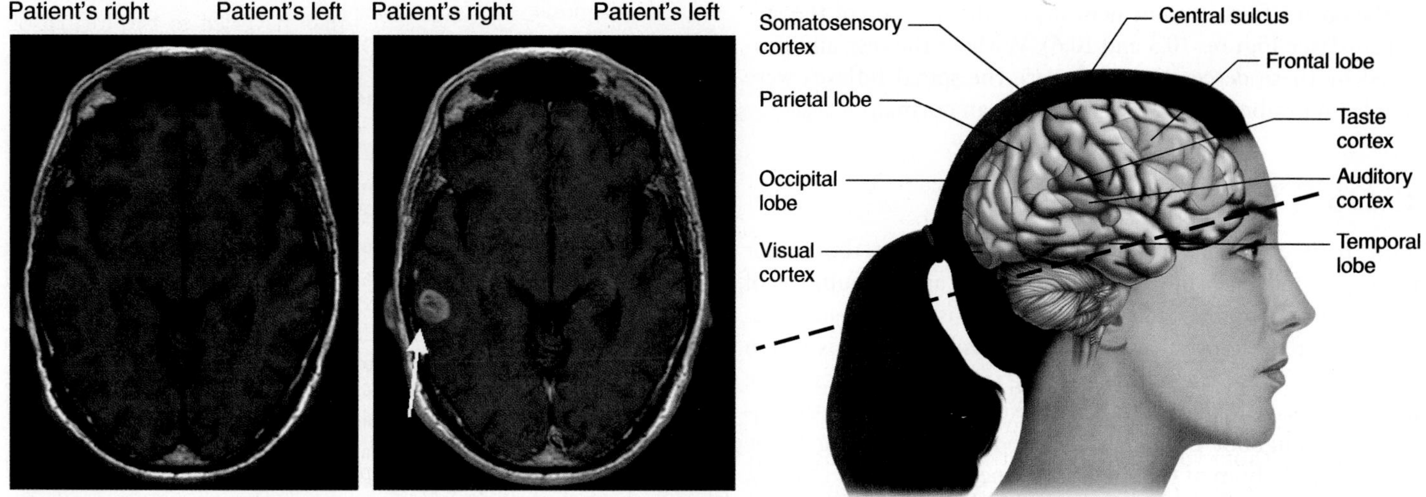

Figure 19.7 In these images, the settings on the MRI scanner are first set so that the brain tissue looks homogeneously gray, the fat surrounding the brain is lighter, and the water within the cerebral ventricles is dark (left scan). By convention, the MRI images are reversed so that the right side of the brain appears on the left side of the image. A contrast agent containing the element gadolinium is then infused intravenously into the patient and a repeat scan is taken (right scan). Gadolinium has paramagnetic properties, which are magnetic properties that only arise in the presence of an externally applied magnetic field. When infused intravenously, the contrast agent can enter the brain in regions where the blood–brain barrier (see Figure 6.6) is absent or damaged, as is sometimes the case in sites of brain injury or disease. Once inside the brain, the association of gadolinium with water and fat changes the local environment and causes an area of higher intensity. This MRI scan demonstrates an area of signal abnormality in the right temporal lobe of the brain that measures about 2 cm in diameter (white arrow). The dashed line on the right image shows the plane of the MRI image. MRI images courtesy of Douglas Woo, M.D., Medical College of Wisconsin.

65% are of glial origin and are known collectively as gliomas. These tumors arise from astrocytes and invade normal brain tissue. As they grow, these tumors can infiltrate, compress, and destroy the healthy brain tissue surrounding the tumor. In addition, these invading tumor cells can irritate the brain, causing seizures. In fact, like our patient, approximately 20–30% of patients with brain neoplasms experience epileptic-like seizures (see Figure 8.2). During seizures, there is often a large increase in sympathetic nerve activity that was, at least in part, the cause of the nausea, facial flushing, sweatiness, and increase in blood pressure and heart rate that occurred in our patient. The decrease in oxygen saturation was due to a rigid and prolonged contraction of the respiratory muscles during the seizure leading to hypoventilation (see Table 13.10). The patient urinated after the seizure because, when the increased sympathetic activity from the seizure subsided, the remaining parasympathetic tone resulted in micturition (see Figure 14.13).

Until the brain MRI was done, the physicians did not know the cause of the seizures. A variety of metabolic disturbances can cause seizures. Abnormalities in blood electrolytes such as Na^+, K^+, and Ca^{2+} can interfere with normal neuronal resting membrane and action potentials (see Section B of Chapter 6). This could not explain the patient's seizures, however, as blood electrolytes were normal (see Table 19.4). The patient was given an infusion of 0.9% normal saline because its osmolarity is very similar to that of plasma. This fluid infusion helps to maintain blood volume and also ensures that the intravenous line stays open in case drugs need to be infused. Renal failure can also cause metabolic and fluid-balance abnormalities leading to abnormal brain activity. Because the concentration of creatinine in the blood is a good estimate for glomerular filtration rate in the kidney, we know that this patient had normal renal function (see Table 19.4). Severe hypoglycemia can decrease the amount of glucose available for brain metabolism, which can cause seizures. This did not occur in our patient (see Table 19.4). In fact, she had a small increase in blood glucose concentration that was probably due to an increase in the blood concentrations of stress hormones such as cortisol and epinephrine (see Section D of Chapter 11, Figure 16.11, and Table 16.3).

Another problem with intracranial lesions is that they may interfere with the drainage of cerebrospinal fluid from the lateral and third ventricles. If this were to happen, it could result in an increase in pressure within the cerebral ventricles. This leads to an enlargement of the ventricles that results in compression of the brain within the cranium. This is called ***hydrocephalus*** (from the Greek words for "water" and "head"; see Figure 6.47). It can cause many functional abnormalities including the convulsions that occurred in our patient. The MRI scan of our patient, however, did not show signs of hydrocephalus such as increases in the size of the cerebral ventricles.

A revealing aspect of this patient's condition was that most of the neurological symptoms were localized to one side of her body—in this case, the left. This included tingling, rhythmic jerking, and loss of motion. Just as sensory afferent information crosses from one side of the body to the other side of the brain (see Figure 7.19), motor control by descending pathways from the cerebral cortex to skeletal muscles also crosses from one side of the body to the other (see Figure 10.12). Therefore, the lesion on the right side of the temporal lobe caused seizures primarily on the right side of the brain leading to increased rhythmic motor activity on the left side of the body. Furthermore, the increase in reflexes on the left side was due to a loss of descending inhibition of spinal reflexes from the right side of the cortex to the motor neurons on the left side of the spinal cord (see Figures 10.3 and 10.6). Without the restraint provided by these descending pathways, the spinal reflexes were free from inhibition and were brisker than normal.

19.D6 Therapy

This patient underwent brain surgery to have the tumor removed, followed by radiation therapy and a number of courses of chemotherapy. Chemotherapy is usually administered by an oncologist and typically involves administration of drugs that are toxic to fast-growing tumors. However, these drugs also have toxicity to normal tissue in which growth continues throughout life, such as blood cell–producing tissue and the epithelium of the small intestine. In radiation therapy, a beam of radiation is directed onto the tumor site to kill the tumor cells. In addition to these treatments, the patient was given an antiepileptic drug to prevent more seizures. One such drug is ***phenytoin*** (***Dilantin***), which acts by blocking voltage-gated Na^+ channels (see Figure 6.18), particularly in neurons that are very active and firing with a high frequency. The patient was also treated with high doses of potent synthetic glucocorticoids because of their anti-inflammatory and anti-edema properties; these hormones, therefore, were given to reduce the swelling in the region of the patient's brain that was affected by the tumor.

After removal of the tumor and a small part of the surrounding right temporal lobe, our patient's right auditory cortex was damaged (see Figure 7.13) and she had trouble recognizing familiar musical melodies. Discrimination of melody (as opposed to rhythm) is a function that has been localized by researchers to the right temporal lobe of the human brain. Our patient remained stable for 16 months after her diagnosis but subsequently had a recurrence of the tumor that could not be surgically removed because of its position and size. She underwent further rounds of chemotherapy and radiation therapy. Sadly, however, only about 25% of patients survive more than 2 years from the time of diagnosis of glioblastoma multiforme.

SUMMARY

Case A: Woman with Palpitations and Heat Intolerance

I. Case Presentation
   a. Her symptoms are nervousness, palpitations, feelings of warmth in a cool room, and significant weight loss despite eating a lot.

II. Physical Examination
   a. Her systolic blood pressure is increased, and her diastolic pressure is decreased. Her resting heart rate is 100 beats per minute.
   b. She has an enlarged thyroid gland (goiter) and her eyes bulge out (proptosis).
   c. She has hyperactive knee-jerk reflexes and her hands are shaking.

III. Laboratory Tests
   a. She has increased thyroid hormone and decreased thyroid-stimulating hormone in the blood.

IV. Diagnosis
   a. She is diagnosed with hyperthyroidism (excess thyroid hormone activity).
   b. Hyperthyroidism is usually caused by Graves' disease—an autoimmune disease.

V. Physiological Integration
   a. Autoimmune production of thyroid-stimulating immunoglobulins (TSIs) stimulates the thyroid gland to produce too much thyroid hormone and to enlarge. The excess thyroid hormone suppresses the release of thyroid-stimulating hormone from the anterior pituitary gland.
   b. Infiltration of the muscles controlling eye movement by white blood cells leads to inflammation and proptosis.
   c. Increased thyroid hormone in the blood leads to an increase in sensitivity to catecholamines, resulting in an increase in systolic blood pressure and heart rate.
   d. Increased thyroid hormone leads to increased metabolic rate in a variety of tissues. This causes heat intolerance, hyperactive reflexes, and a small decrease in diastolic pressure.

VI. Therapy
   a. Three possible therapies include radioactive iodide administration to destroy much of the thyroid gland, drugs that block the synthesis of thyroid hormone, or surgical removal of the thyroid gland.

Case B: Man with Chest Pain After a Long Airplane Flight

I. Case Presentation
   a. A man has chest pain and shortness of breath after an 8 h flight.

II. Physical Examination
   a. He has an increased heart rate, but his ECG does not show evidence of a heart attack.
   b. His chest x-ray is essentially normal.

III. Laboratory Tests
   a. He is hypoxemic and has an acute respiratory alkalosis.

IV. Diagnosis
   a. His ventilation–perfusion scan shows evidence of a pulmonary embolism (blockage of pulmonary blood flow).
   b. An ultrasound of his legs shows a deep vein thrombosis.
   c. A clot formed in his leg veins because he sat for a long period of time. In addition, there is evidence that he has a genetic disorder of coagulation. The clot migrated to the lung, causing a pulmonary embolus.

V. Physiological Integration
   a. Hypoxemia is caused by a dramatic disruption of the regional balance between ventilation and perfusion throughout the lung.
   b. Hyperventilation due to anxiety and pain, as well as hypoxemia, caused an acute respiratory alkalosis.

VI. Therapy
   a. Treatment focuses on anticoagulation with heparin (to prevent clotting) and recombinant tissue plasminogen activator (to dissolve the clots).
   b. Long-term anticoagulation therapy is recommended.

Case C: Man with Abdominal Pain, Fever, and Circulatory Failure

I. Case Presentation
   a. A young man has increasing abdominal pain over 3 days.

II. Physical Examination
   a. He has a fever, increased heart and respiratory rates, and low blood pressure.

b. He has pain and rigidity localized to the lower-right quadrant of his abdomen.
c. His urine output is low.

III. Laboratory Tests
a. His white blood cell count is increased, suggesting an infection.
b. He has a metabolic (lactic) acidosis with a respiratory compensation (low arterial P_{CO_2}).
c. His blood creatinine concentration is increased, which indicates a decrease in glomerular filtration rate.

IV. Diagnosis
a. A computed tomography (CT) scan shows an inflamed appendix, suggesting a diagnosis of appendicitis. The low blood pressure suggests septic shock due to peritonitis (caused by a ruptured appendix).
b. The diagnosis is confirmed in an abdominal exploration during which a perforated appendix is removed. The membranes near it are infected, proving peritonitis.

V. Physiological Integration
a. Toxins from the bacteria have caused the low blood pressure because of vasodilation.
b. The decreased glomerular filtration rate is due to low blood pressure and decreased renal perfusion.

VI. Therapy
a. Therapy consists of intravenous fluids before and after surgery to support cardiac output and blood pressure and vasoconstrictor drugs to maintain blood pressure.
b. Antibiotic therapy is given to fight the peritoneal infection.

Case D: College Student with Nausea, Flushing, and Sweating

I. Case Presentation
a. A 21-year-old woman has several episodes of nausea, flushing, and sweating.
b. She also has tingling and jerking on the left side of her face, which progresses to the left arm and leg. This is followed by a loss of consciousness and convulsions.

II. Physical Examination
a. She has a decrease in motion on her left side.
b. She has an increase in her reflexes in the left arm and leg.

III. Laboratory Tests
a. Her blood tests are essentially normal except for a small increase in blood glucose.
b. An MRI of the brain is administered with gadolinium contrast injected intravenously.

IV. Diagnosis
a. The MRI of the brain reveals a bright 2-cm-diameter lesion in the right temporal lobe.
b. A craniotomy is performed to obtain a tissue sample of the lesion, which the pathologist identifies as a glioblastoma multiforme, a malignant brain tumor arising from astrocytes.

V. Physiological Integration
a. The tumor in the right temporal lobe causes seizures on the left side of the body because descending motor pathways cross from one side of the brain to the other side of the body.
b. Increased reflexes on the left side are due to a loss of descending inhibition from the right side of the brain to the spinal motor nerves on the left.

VI. Therapy
a. After as much of the tumor as possible is removed, the patient is treated with radiation and chemotherapy.
b. In addition, antiepileptic medicine and glucocorticoid therapy to decrease swelling and edema are administered.

CLINICAL TERMS

abscess 704
appendicitis 701
astrocytoma 704
atelectasis 697
bruit 693
catheter 700
computed tomography (CT) 700
convulsions 703
craniotomy 704
deep vein thrombosis 698
diplopia 693
embolism 698
epileptic seizure 703
exophthalmos 693
fever 702
glioblastoma multiforme 704
goiter 694
Graves' disease 695
hydrocephalus 705
hypercoagulability 699
hyperthyroidism 694
ischemia 702
low-resistance shock 701
magnetic resonance imaging (MRI) 704
methimazole 696
myocardial infarction 697
necrosis 700
neoplasm 704
palpitation 693
perforation 700
peritonitis 700
phenytoin (Dilantin) 706
proptosis 693
propylthiouracil 696
pulmonary edema 702
pulmonary embolism 698
pus 700
radioactive iodine 697
recombinant tissue plasminogen activator (rec-tPA) 699
sepsis 701
septic shock 701
systemic inflammatory response 701
tachycardia 693
tachypnea 693
thrombus 698
thyroid-stimulating immunoglobulin (TSI) 695
thyrotoxicosis 694
transcutaneous oxygen monitor 703
ventilation–perfusion scan 698

Visit this book's website at **www.mhhe.com/widmaier13** for chapter quizzes, interactive learning exercises, and other study tools.

Appendix A ANSWERS TO TEST QUESTIONS, QUANTITATIVE AND THOUGHT QUESTIONS, AND GENERAL PRINCIPLES ASSESSMENTS

CHAPTER 1

Test Questions

1.1 b The four basic cell types are epithelial, muscle, nervous, and connective.

1.2 a Steady state requires energy input, but equilibrium does not.

1.3 c Muscles carry out the response (removing the hand from the stove).

1.4 c Circadian rhythms are typically entrained by the light–dark cycle, but in the absence of such cues, the rhythms "free-run" with their own endogenous cycle length.

1.5 b Intracellular fluid volume is greater than the sum of plasma and interstitial fluid.

Quantitative and Thought Questions

1.1 No. There may in fact be a genetic difference, but there is another possibility: The altered skin blood flow in the cold could represent an *acclimatization* undergone by each Inuit during his or her lifetime as a result of performing such work repeatedly.

1.2 This could occur in many ways. For example, suppose that an individual were to become dehydrated. What would happen to his or her plasma Na^+ *concentration?* Initially, the loss of fluid would result in an increased Na^+ concentration, even though the absolute amount of sodium may not have changed much. The increase in Na^+ concentration would trigger endocrine and renal responses that return the Na^+ concentration to normal. Another example occurs during mountain climbing. At high altitude, a person who is not acclimatized to low oxygen pressures will greatly increase the rate and depth of breathing to get more oxygen into his or her blood. One consequence of this, though, is that more of the carbon dioxide in the body is exhaled. Carbon dioxide tends to produce hydrogen ions in the blood (Chapters 13 and 14). Thus, ascent to high altitude leads to alkaline blood, which must then be compensated for by renal, endocrine, and other responses.

CHAPTER 2

Test Questions

2.1 e The continued creation of new free radicals is a chain reaction and contributes to the potentially damaging effects of a given free radical.

2.2 d

2.3 b This is a dehydration reaction. The reverse reaction would be hydrolysis.

2.4 b Uracil is found in RNA; thymine is found in DNA.

2.5 b

2.6 Sucrose (b); Glucose (a); Glycogen (c); Fructose (a); Starch (c)

2.7 c The other reactions in which larger molecules are formed occur via dehydration reactions.

Quantitative and Thought Questions

2.1 0.79 mol/L. The molecular weight of fructose can be calculated by adding up the weights of the individual atoms. However, since it is an isomer of glucose, you know that it must have the same molecular weight—180 daltons—as glucose. Thus, $[100g/0.7L] \times [1mole/180g] = 0.79$ mol/L.

2.2 Using a calculator, simply enter –1.5 and select the inverse log function. The answer is approximately 0.03 mol/L or 3×10^{-2} M.

2.3 Recall that atomic mass is the sum of the protons and neutrons in a nucleus. Regardless of its ionization state, potassium has (39 – 19) or 20 neutrons. The number of electrons is equal to the number of protons in a nonionized atom; therefore, K has 19 electrons. When ionized, K^+ has a single positive charge; it still has 19 protons and 20 neutrons, but it now has only 18 electrons.

General Principles Assessment

2.1 The chemical and physical properties of atoms, such as the number of electrons in their outer shells or their solubility in water, determine their reactivity with other atoms and molecules. For example, proteins are made by the linkage of amino acids through peptide bonds, which depend on the reactivity between amino and carboxyl groups. Further chemical and physical interactions, such as electrostatic attraction or repulsion, and hydrophobicity of amino acid side groups, bend and twist the protein into its final three-dimensional shape. Some of these same forces may in certain cases create a larger protein from several subunits. Without the correct chemical and physical properties, proteins would not assume a proper shape; this is extremely important in physiology because the shape of a protein is critically linked with its function.

CHAPTER 3

Test Questions

3.1 a

3.2 b Transcription refers to the conversion of a gene's DNA into RNA; translation is the conversion of mRNA into protein.

3.3 a Allosteric modulation occurs at a site separate from the ligand-binding site. The resulting change in three-dimensional structure of the protein may enhance or reduce the ability of the protein to bind its ligand.

3.4 b

3.5 c

3.6 d Catabolism refers to the breakdown of fatty acids into usable forms for the production of ATP.

Quantitative and Thought Questions

3.1 Nucleotide bases in DNA pair A to T and G to C. Given the base sequence of one DNA strand as

A—G—T—G—C—A—A—G—T—C—T

a. The complementary strand of DNA would be

T—C—A—C—G—T—T—C—A—G—A

b. The sequence in RNA transcribed from the first strand would be

U—C—A—C—G—U—U—C—A—G—A

Recall that uracil (U) replaces thymine (T) in RNA.

3.2 The triplet code G—T—A in DNA will be transcribed into mRNA as C—A—U, and the anticodon in tRNA corresponding to C—A—U is G—U—A.

3.3 If the gene were only composed of the triplet exon code words, the gene would be 300 nucleotides in length because a triplet of three nucleotides codes for one amino acid. However, because of the presence of intron segments in most genes, which account for 75% to 90% of the nucleotides in a gene, the gene would be between 1200 and 3000 nucleotides long; moreover, it would also contain termination codons. Thus, the exact size of a gene cannot be determined by knowing the number of amino acids in the protein for which the gene codes.

3.4 A drug could decrease acid secretion by (a) binding to the membrane sites that normally inhibit acid secretion, which would produce the same effect as the body's natural messengers that inhibit acid secretion; (b) binding to a membrane protein that normally stimulates acid secretion but not itself triggering acid secretion, thereby preventing the body's natural messengers from binding (competition); or (c) having an allosteric effect on the binding sites, which would increase the affinity of the sites that normally bind inhibitor messengers or decrease the affinity of those sites that normally bind stimulatory messengers.

3.5 The reason for a lack of insulin effect could be either a decrease in the number of available binding sites insulin can bind to or a decrease in the affinity of the binding sites for insulin so that less insulin is bound. A third possibility, which does not involve insulin binding, would be a defect in the way the binding site triggers a cell response once it has bound insulin.

3.6 (a) Acid secretion could be increased to 40 mmol/h by (1) increasing the concentration of compound X from 2 pM to 8 pM, thereby increasing the number of binding sites occupied; or (2) increasing the affinity of the binding sites for compound X, thereby increasing the amount bound without changing the concentration of compound X. (b) Increasing the concentration of compound X from 20 pM to 28 pM will not increase acid secretion because, at 20 pM, all the binding sites are occupied (the system is saturated) and there are no further binding sites available.

3.7 The maximum rate at which the end product E can be formed is 5 molecules per second, the rate of the slowest (rate-limiting) reaction in the pathway.

3.8 Under normal conditions, the concentration of oxygen at the level of the mitochondria in cells, including muscle at rest, is sufficient to saturate the enzyme that combines oxygen with hydrogen to form water. The rate-limiting reactions in the electron-transport chain depend on the available concentrations of ADP and P_i, which are combined to form ATP.

Thus, increasing the oxygen concentration above normal will not increase ATP production. If a muscle is contracting, it will break down ATP into ADP and P_i, which become the major rate-limiting substrates for increasing ATP production. With intense muscle activity, the level of oxygen may fall below saturating levels, limiting the rate of ATP production, and intensely active muscles must then use anaerobic glycolysis to provide additional ATP. Under these circumstances, increasing the oxygen concentration in the blood will increase the rate of ATP production. As discussed in Chapter 12, it is not the concentration of oxygen in the blood that is increased during exercise but the rate of blood flow to a muscle, resulting in greater quantities of oxygen delivery to the tissue.

3.9 During starvation, in the absence of ingested glucose, the body's stores of glycogen are rapidly depleted. Glucose, which is the major fuel used by the brain, must now be synthesized from other types of molecules. Most of this newly formed glucose comes from the breakdown of proteins to amino acids and their conversion to glucose. To a lesser extent, the glycerol portion of fat is converted to glucose. The fatty acid portion of fat cannot be converted to glucose.

3.10 Ammonia is formed in most cells during the oxidative deamination of amino acids and then travels to the liver via the blood. The liver detoxifies the ammonia by converting it to the nontoxic compound urea. Because the liver is the site in which ammonia is converted to urea, diseases that damage the liver can lead to an accumulation of ammonia in the blood, which is especially toxic to neurons. Note that it is not the liver that produces the ammonia.

General Principles Assessments

3.1 The extensive folding of the inner mitochondrial membrane increases the total surface area of the membrane. As shown in Figure 3.45, this is where the enzymes are located that are required for the generation of ATP. Thus, the structure of this membrane increases the ability of mitochondria to carry out their major function. The general principle that *structure is a determinant of—and has coevolved with—function* is also evident at the molecular (protein) level. In Figure 3.28, for example, it is clear that a protein's structure determines its function—in this case, its ability to bind particular ligands. Figure 3.32b shows how a protein's function is altered due to allosteric changes in its structure.

3.2 Proteins and ligands interact due to a variety of forces and molecular features, including complementary shapes. In addition, however, chemical or physical properties of molecules often strongly influence their ability to interact or bind with each other. In Figure 3.27, you can see how the structure of the protein results in an arrangement of certain charged amino acids. The fundamental property of physics that opposite charges attract one another means that a ligand with the correct electrical charges will be more likely to bind to this protein than another ligand without those charges.

3.3 Figure 3.53 summarizes how nutrients such as amino acids, glucose, and small lipids can be metabolized by a variety of mechanisms leading to the production of smaller molecules, which in turn can be used to eventually generate ATP. It is ATP that provides the energy required for the events that mediate all homeostatic processes, such as muscle contraction, neuron signaling, and so on. Recall from Chapter 1 (see Figure 1.6) that the generation of ATP is under negative feedback control, such that cells generate more ATP when required, and less when not required. Negative feedback is an essential component of homeostasis.

CHAPTER 4

Test Questions

4.1 c Channels are proteins that span the membrane and are opened by ligands, voltage, or mechanical stimuli.

4.2 d Facilitated diffusion does not require ATP. Recall that secondary active transport *indirectly* requires ATP because ion pumps were required to establish the electrochemical gradient for a particular ion (such as Na^+).

4.3 b After the initial movement of water out of the cells due to osmosis, the urea concentration quickly equilibrates across each cell's plasma membrane, removing any osmotic stimulus.

4.4 e Segregation of function on different surfaces of the cell, and the ability to secrete chemicals (e.g., from the pancreas), are two of the most important features of epithelial cells.

4.5 a Diffusion is slowed by the resistance of a membrane.

4.6 e Because ions are charged, both the chemical and the electrical gradients determine their rate and direction of diffusion.

Quantitative and Thought Questions

4.1 (a) During diffusion, the net flux always occurs from high to low concentration. Therefore, it will be from 2 to 1 in A and from 1 to 2 in B. (b) At equilibrium, the concentrations of solute in the two compartments will be equal: 4 mM in case A and 31 mM in case B. (c) Both will reach diffusion equilibrium at the same rate because the absolute difference in concentration across the membrane is the same in each case, 2 mM [$(3 - 5) = -2$, and $(32 - 30) = 2$]. The two one-way fluxes will be much larger in B than in A, but the net flux has the same magnitude in both cases, although it is oriented in opposite directions.

4.2 The ability of one amino acid to decrease the flux of a second amino acid across a cell membrane is an example of the competition of two molecules for the same binding site, as explained in Chapter 3. The binding site for alanine on the transport protein can also bind leucine. The higher the concentration of alanine, the greater the number of binding sites that it occupies and the fewer available for binding leucine. Consequently, less leucine will move into the cell.

4.3 The net transport will be out of the cell in the direction from the higher-affinity site on the intracellular surface to the lower-affinity site on the extracellular surface. More molecules will be bound to the transporter on the higher-affinity side of the membrane, and therefore more will move out of the cell than into it, until the concentration in the extracellular fluid becomes great enough that the number of molecules bound to transporters at the extracellular surface is equal to the number bound at the intracellular surface.

4.4 Although ATP is not used directly in secondary active transport, it is necessary for the primary active transport of Na^+ out of cells. Because it is the Na^+ concentration gradient across the plasma membrane that provides the energy for most secondary active transport systems, a decrease in ATP production will decrease primary active Na^+ transport, leading to a decrease in the sodium ion concentration gradient and therefore to a decrease in secondary active transport.

4.5 The solution with the greatest osmolarity will have the lowest water concentration. Recall that NaCl forms two ions in solution and $CaCl_2$ forms three. Thus, the osmolarities are

A. $20 + 30 + (2 \times 150) + (3 \times 10) = 380$ mOsm
B. $10 + 100 + (2 \times 20) + (3 \times 50) = 300$ mOsm
C. $100 + 200 + (2 \times 10) + (3 \times 20) = 380$ mOsm
D. $30 + 10 + (2 \times 60) + (3 \times 100) = 460$ mOsm

Solution D has the lowest water concentration. Solution B is isoosmotic because it has the same osmolarity as intracellular fluid. Solutions A and C have the same osmolarity.

4.6 Initially, the osmolarity of compartment 1 is $(2 \times 200) + 100 = 500$ mOsm and that of 2 is $(2 \times 100) + 300 = 500$ mOsm. The two solutions therefore have the same osmolarity, and there is no difference in water concentration across the membrane. Because the membrane is permeable to urea, this substance will undergo net diffusion until it reaches the same concentration (200 mM) on the two sides of the membrane. In other words, in the steady state, it will not affect the volumes of the compartments. In contrast, the higher initial NaCl concentration in compartment 1 than in compartment 2 will cause, by osmosis, the movement of water from compartment 2 to compartment 1 until the concentration of NaCl in both is 150 mM. Note that the same volume change would have occurred if there were no urea present in either compartment. It is only the concentration of nonpenetrating solutes (NaCl in this case) that determines the volume change, regardless of the concentration of any penetrating solutes that are present.

4.7 The osmolarities and nonpenetrating solute concentrations are

Solution	Osmolarity (mOsm)	Nonpenetrating Solute Concentration (mOsm)
A	$(2 \times 150) + 100 = 400$	$2 \times 150 = 300$
B	$(2 \times 100) + 150 = 350$	$2 \times 100 = 200$
C	$(2 \times 200) + 100 = 500$	$2 \times 200 = 400$
D	$(2 \times 100) + 50 = 250$	$2 \times 100 = 200$

Only the concentration of nonpenetrating solutes (NaCl in this case) will determine the change in cell volume. The intracellular concentration of nonpenetrating solute is typically about 300 mOsm, so solution A will produce no change in cell volume. Solutions B and D will cause cells to swell because they have a lower concentration of nonpenetrating solute (higher water concentration) than the intracellular fluid. Solution C will cause cells to shrink because it has a higher concentration of nonpenetrating solute than the intracellular fluid.

4.8 Solution A is isotonic because it has the same concentration of nonpenetrating solutes as intracellular fluid (300 mOsm). Solution A is also hyperosmotic because its total osmolarity is greater than 300 mOsm, as is also true for solutions B and C. Solution B is hypotonic because its concentration of nonpenetrating solutes is less than 300 mOsm. Solution C is hypertonic because its concentration of nonpenetrating solutes is greater than 300 mOsm. Solution D is hypotonic (less than 300 mOsm of nonpenetrating solutes) and also hypoosmotic (having a total osmolarity of less than 300 mOsm).

4.9 Exocytosis is triggered by an increase in cytosolic Ca^{2+} concentration. Calcium ions are actively transported out of cells, in part by secondary countertransport coupled to the downhill entry of sodium ions on the same transporter (see Figure 4.15). If the intracellular concentration of sodium ions were increased, the sodium ion concentration gradient across the membrane would be decreased, and this would decrease the secondary active transport of Ca^{2+} out of the cell. This would lead to an increase in cytosolic Ca^{2+} concentration, which would trigger increased exocytosis.

General Principles Assessments

4.1 One example of the general principle that *homeostasis is essential for health and survival* illustrated in Figures 4.8–4.10 is mediated transport across plasma membranes. For example, the controlled movement of glucose transporters (GLUTs) to plasma membranes in response to the hormone insulin helps maintain homeostatic concentrations of glucose in the extra- and intracellular fluids. This is important because glucose is the major source of energy for cells. Also, the regulated changes in aquaporin numbers in the epithelial cells of the kidneys help maintain water homeostasis by controlling the rate at which water is lost in the urine; this is particularly important in situations such as dehydration. A third example is osmosis, which regulates water flux across membranes (see Figure 4.17); this, in turn, helps maintain proper cell shape and size and the ability of cells to perform signaling functions.

4.2 The general principle that *controlled exchange of materials occurs between compartments and across cellular membranes* is apparent from the many diverse types of mechanisms by which solutes may cross plasma membranes. The control arises from such mechanisms as gates in ion channels that may open or close depending on cell requirements, and the just-mentioned glucose transporters and aquaporins, the concentrations of which can increase or decrease in plasma membranes under different conditions.

4.3 The general principle that *physiological processes are dictated by the laws of chemistry and physics* is evident from the relationship between the chemical nature (e.g., degree of hydrophobicity) of solutes and the ease with which they can diffuse through a lipid bilayer. The greater a molecule's hydrophobicity, the more likely it is to dissolve in the lipid bilayer of membranes and thus diffuse across cells. Electrochemical gradients aid in the diffusion of charged molecules (ions) through membrane channels because of the basic physical principle that like charges repel and opposite charges attract each other. Finally, molecular movement (and therefore potential interactions between molecules) is directly related to heat energy; solutes move through solution at faster rates at higher temperatures.

CHAPTER 5

Test Questions

5.1 b
5.2 a
5.3 e

5.4 a Calmodulin is a calcium-binding protein that is inactive in the absence of Ca^{2+}.

5.5 d Lipid-soluble messengers cross the plasma membrane and act primarily on cytosolic and nuclear receptors.

5.6 b

5.7 d

5.8 a

5.9 e Neurotransmitters and hormones are just two of many types of ligands that act as signaling molecules and first messengers, via their binding to a receptor.

5.10 b

Quantitative and Thought Questions

5.1 Patient A's drug very likely acts to block phospholipase A_2, whereas patient B's drug blocks lipoxygenase (see Figure 5.12).

5.2 The chronic loss of exposure of the heart's receptors to norepinephrine causes an up-regulation of this receptor type (i.e., more receptors in the heart for norepinephrine). The drug, being an agonist of norepinephrine (i.e., able to bind to norepinephrine's receptors and activate them) is now more effective because there are more receptors for it to combine with.

5.3 None. You are told that all six responses are mediated by the cAMP system; consequently, blockage of any of the steps listed in the question would eliminate all six of the responses. This is because the cascade for all six responses is identical from the receptor through the formation of cAMP and activation of cAMP-dependent protein kinase. Therefore, the drug must be acting at a point beyond this kinase (e.g., at the level of the phosphorylated protein mediating this response).

5.4 Not in most cells, because there are other physiological mechanisms by which signals impinging on the cell can increase cytosolic Ca^{2+} concentration. These include (a) second-messenger-induced release of Ca^{2+} from the endoplasmic reticulum and (b) voltage-sensitive Ca^{2+} channels.

5.5 Intracellular second messengers do not disappear immediately upon removal of a first messenger. Instead, some second messengers (such as cAMP) may linger inside the cell for seconds, minutes, or even longer after the first messenger is gone.

General Principles Assessments

5.1 Figures 5.5a and 5.9 illustrate ways in which movement of ions, for example, is controlled by first and second messengers. These messengers may open ion channels or activate or induce production of ion transporters in plasma membranes. In this way, ions may move between fluid compartments in the body—for example, from interstitial fluid to intracellular fluid.

5.2 Certain forms of cell signaling require a supply of ATP to form cAMP, a major second messenger, and to phosphorylate proteins. Without a homeostatic balance of cellular energy stored in the terminal bond of ATP molecules, most cell signaling pathways would be deficient or impossible.

CHAPTER 6

Test Questions

6.1 b Afferent neurons have peripheral axon terminals associated with sensory receptors, cell bodies in the dorsal root ganglion of the spinal cord, and central axon terminals that project into the spinal cord.

6.2 c Oligodendrocytes form myelin sheaths in the central nervous system.

6.3 d Insert the given chloride ion concentrations into the Nernst equation; remember to use -1 as the valence (Z).

6.4 d A, B, and C all are correct. Using the Nernst equation to calculate the Na^+ equilibrium potential gives values of +31, +36, and +40 mV for A, B, and C. If the membrane potential was +42 mV, the outward electrical force on Na^+ would be greater than the inward concentration gradient, so Na^+ would move out of the cell in each of these cases.

6.5 e Neither Na^+ nor K^+ is in equilibrium at the resting membrane potential, but the action of the Na^+/K^+-ATPase pump prevents the small but steady leak of both ions from dissipating the concentration gradients.

6.6 a Because Na^+ is farther away from its electrochemical equilibrium than is K^+, there would be more Na^+ entry than K^+ exit, causing local depolarization and local current flow that would decrease with distance from the site of the stimulus.

6.7 c Due to the persistent open state of the voltage-gated K^+ channels, for a brief time at the end of an action potential the membrane is hyperpolarized. When the voltage-gated K^+ channels eventually close, the K^+ leak channels once again determine the resting membrane potential.

6.8 d The IPSP caused by neuron B would summate with (subtract from) the amplitude of the EPSP caused by neuron A's firing.

6.9 a Dopamine, like norepinephrine and epinephrine, is a catecholamine neurotransmitter manufactured by enzymatic modification of the amino acid tyrosine.

6.10 b Norepinephrine is the neurotransmitter released by postganglionic neurons onto smooth muscle cells.

Quantitative and Thought Questions

6.1 Little change in the resting membrane potential would occur when the pump first stops because the pump's *direct* contribution to charge separation is very small. With time, however, the membrane potential would depolarize progressively toward zero because the Na^+ and K^+ concentration gradients, which depend on the Na^+/K^+-ATPase pumps and which give rise to the membrane potential, run down.

6.2 The resting potential would decrease (i.e., become less negative) because the concentration gradient causing net diffusion of this positively charged ion out of the cell would be smaller. The action potential would fire more easily (i.e., with smaller stimuli) because the resting potential would be closer to threshold. It would repolarize more slowly because repolarization depends on net K^+ diffusion from the cell, and the concentration gradient driving this diffusion is lower. Also, the after hyperpolarization would be smaller.

6.3 The hypothalamus was probably damaged. It plays a critical role in appetite, thirst, and sexual capacity.

6.4 The drug probably blocks cholinergic muscarinic receptors. These receptors on effector cells mediate the actions of parasympathetic nerves. Therefore, the drug would remove the slowing effect of these nerves on the heart, allowing the heart to speed up. Blocking their effect on the salivary glands would cause the dry mouth. We know that the drug is not blocking cholinergic nicotinic receptors because the skeletal muscles are not affected.

6.5 Because the membrane potential of the cells in question depolarizes (i.e., becomes less negative) when Cl^- channels are blocked, we can assume there was net Cl^- diffusion into the cells through these channels prior to treatment with the drug. Therefore, we can also predict that this passive inward movement was being exactly balanced by active transport of Cl^- out of the cells.

6.6 Without acetylcholinesterase, more acetylcholine would remain bound to the receptors, and all the actions normally caused by acetylcholine would be accentuated. Consequently, there would be significant narrowing of the pupils, airway constriction, stomach cramping and diarrhea, sweating, salivation, slowing of the heart, and decrease in blood pressure. On the other hand, in skeletal muscles, which must repolarize after excitation in order to be excited again, there would be weakness, fatigue, and finally inability to contract. In fact, lethal poisoning by high doses of cholinesterase inhibitors occurs because of paralysis of the muscles involved in respiration. Low doses of these compounds are used therapeutically.

6.7 These K^+ channels, which open after a short delay following the initiation of an action potential, increase K^+ diffusion out of the cell, hastening repolarization. They also account for the increased K^+ permeability that causes the after hyperpolarization. Therefore, the action potential would be broader (that is, longer in duration) and would return to resting level more slowly, and the after hyperpolarization would be absent.

General Principles Assessments

6.1 The autonomic nervous system controls many physiological functions through its sympathetic and parasympathetic subdivisions. The most common structural pattern is dual innervation—organs receive signals along neurons from both the sympathetic and parasympathetic division—and typically the effects of those signals are opposite. For example, action potentials along parasympathetic neurons increase secretions and contractions of the gastrointestinal tract, while action potentials along sympathetic pathways tend to decrease them. By having such dual regulatory control, more precise regulation of organ function is made possible. Other examples of dual sympathetic/parasympathetic regulatory control can be found in Figure 6.44.

6.2 The establishment of neuronal resting membrane potential clearly demonstrates at least two general principles of physiology: *Controlled exchange of materials occurs between compartments and across cellular membranes*, and *Physiological processes are dictated by the laws of chemistry and physics*. The concentration and movement of Na^+ and K^+ ions across the plasma membrane are carefully controlled as a result of the hydrophobic properties of the phospholipid bilayer, the action of Na^+/K^+ ATPase pumps, and the gating of ion-specific channels. Given the establishment of concentration gradients for these ions (and associated anions) across the membrane, Fick's diffusion equation (Chapter 4) and the electrical repulsion and attraction between charged ions then enable the storage of energy (electrical potential) across the membrane. The potential energy stored in this gradient is the basis of a substantial amount of cellular activity in nerve, skeletal muscle, cardiac muscle, and many other tissues.

6.3 As discussed in Section A, 6.1, some neurons have a large number of dendrites—as many as 400,000—that vastly increase the surface area over which the cell can receive inputs from other neurons. Additionally, the human cerebral cortex is elaborately folded into sulci and gyri, which vastly increases the surface area. As Figure 6.39 shows, the majority of the cells of the cerebral hemispheres lie within a few millimeters of the surface. The tortuous folding of the cortex allows far more cells to fit within the confines of the cranium, and along with a greater number of cells comes a greater potential for neural processing power. This accounts in part for the advanced cognitive capabilities and complex behaviors of humans as compared to animals with less complex folding of the cerebral cortex.

CHAPTER 7

Test Questions

7.1 a For example, photons of light are the adequate stimulus for photoreceptors of the eye, and sound is the adequate stimulus for hair cells of the ear.

7.2 b Receptor potentials generate only local currents in the receptor membrane that transduces the stimulus, but when they reach the first node of Ranvier, they depolarize the membrane to threshold, and there the voltage-gated Na^+ channels first initiate action potentials. Beyond that point, the receptor potential decreases with distance, whereas action potentials propagate all the way to the central axon terminals.

7.3 d Lateral inhibition increases the contrast between the region at the center of a stimulus and regions at the edges of the stimulus, which increases the acuity of stimulus localization.

7.4 a The occipital lobe of the cortex is the initial site of visual processing. (Review Figure 7.13.)

7.5 e Somatic sensations include those from the skin, muscles, bones, tendons, and joints, but not encoding of sound by cochlear hair cells.

7.6 b A myopic (nearsighted) person has an eyeball that is too long. When the ciliary muscles are relaxed and the lens is as flat as possible, parallel light rays from distant objects focus in front of the retina, whereas diverging rays from near objects are able to focus on the retina. (Recall that with normal vision, it takes ciliary muscle contraction and a rounded lens to focus on near objects.)

7.7 d When the right optic tract is destroyed, perception of images formed on the right half of the retina in both eyes is lost, so nothing is visible at the left side of a person's field of view. (Review Figure 7.31.)

7.8 a Pressure waves traveling down the cochlea make the cochlear duct vibrate, moving the basilar membrane against the stationary tectorial membrane and bending the hair cells that bridge the gap between the two.

7.9 c With the sudden head rotation from left to right, inertia of the endolymph causes it to rotate from right to left with respect to the semicircular canal that lies in the horizontal plane. This fluid flow bends the cupula and embedded hair cells within the ampulla, which influences the firing of action potentials along the vestibular nerve.

7.10 d "Umami" is derived from the Japanese word meaning "delicious" or "savory"; the stimulation of these taste receptors by glutamate produces the perception of a rich, meaty flavor.

Quantitative and Thought Questions

7.1 (a) Use drugs to block transmission in the pathways that convey information about pain to the brain. For example, if substance P is the neurotransmitter at the central endings of the nociceptor afferent fibers, give a drug that blocks the substance P receptors. (b) Cut the dorsal root at the level of entry of the nociceptor fibers to prevent transmission of their action potentials into the central nervous system. (c) Give a drug that activates receptors in the descending pathways that block transmission of the incoming or ascending pain information. (d) Stimulate the neurons in these same descending pathways to increase their blocking activity (stimulation-produced analgesia or, possibly, acupuncture). (e) Cut the ascending pathways that transmit information from the nociceptor afferents. (f) Deal with emotions, attitudes, memories, and so on to decrease sensitivity to the pain. (g) Stimulate nonpain, low-threshold afferent fibers to block transmission through the pain pathways (TENS). (h) Block transmission in the afferent nerve with a local anesthetic such as Novocaine or Lidocaine.

7.2 Information regarding temperature is carried via the anterolateral system to the brain. Fibers of this system cross to the opposite side of the body in the spinal cord at the level of entry of the afferent fibers (see Figure 7.19a). Damage to the left side of the spinal cord or any part of the left side of the brain that contains fibers of the pathways for temperature would interfere with awareness of a heat stimulus on the right. Thus, damage to the somatosensory cortex of the left cerebral hemisphere (i.e., opposite the stimulus) would interfere with awareness of the stimulus. Injury to the spinal cord at the point at which fibers of the anterolateral system from the two halves of the spinal cord cross to the opposite side would interfere with the awareness of heat applied to either side of the body, as would the unlikely event that damage occurred to relevant areas of both sides of the brain.

7.3 Vision would be restricted to the rods; therefore, it would be normal at very low levels of illumination (when the cones would not be stimulated anyway). At higher levels of illumination, however, clear vision of fine details would be lost, and everything would appear in shades of gray, with no color vision. In very bright light, there would be no vision because of bleaching of the rods' rhodopsin.

7.4 (a) The individual lacks a functioning primary visual cortex. (b) The individual lacks a functioning visual association cortex.

7.5 Because it is common for somatic receptors in visceral organs to converge onto ascending pathways for receptors in the skin, muscles, and joints (see Figure 7.17), physicians must be aware that complaints about pain in superficial structures may indicate a deeper problem. For example, a person having a heart attack may complain of pain in the left arm, a patient with stomach cancer may experience pain in the middle of the back, and a patient with kidney stones may complain of an ache in the upper thigh or hip. Review Figure 7.18 for a map of surface regions of the body where referred pain from deeper organs can be perceived.

General Principles Assessments

7.1 Nociceptors detect stimuli indicating potential or actual damage to tissues, which could threaten homeostasis. By allowing us to perceive those stimuli, nociceptors not only help us to learn to avoid them but also let us respond quickly to minimize damage when they occur (like quickly removing your hand from a hot stove burner). In these ways, we can avoid injuries like burns or cuts that may threaten homeostasis by causing fluid loss from the body. As another example, pain stops us temporarily from overusing injured limbs, giving them time to heal so that our ability to move and obtain food or avoid life-threatening situations is not permanently impaired.

7.2 A good example of the importance of controlled exchange between extracellular compartments in the vestibular and auditory systems is the endolymph found within the cochlear duct and vestibular apparatus. The unusually high K^+ concentration allows current to flow into the cells when tip links are stretched, generating a receptor potential that leads to neurotransmitter release from the hair cells. This, in turn, generates action potentials in the afferent neuron (review Figure 7.41). In addition, like in all neurons and excitable cells, the maintenance of Na^+ and K^+ concentration gradients between the intracellular and extracellular fluid compartments by Na^+/K^+-ATPase pumps is essential for the transmission of action potentials in the auditory and vestibular afferent neurons (review Chapter 6, Section B).

7.3 An excellent example of a body structure that has maximized surface area to maximize function is a photoreceptor cell. Repeated foldings of the membranous discs in rods and cones greatly increases the surface area available for the retinal-containing photopigments, making the eye exquisitely sensitive to light.

CHAPTER 8

Test Questions

8.1 d

8.2 c

8.3 a

8.4 b

8.5 e See Figures 8.6 and 8.7.

8.6 b If by experience you discover that a persistent stimulus like the noise from a fan does not have relevance, there is a reduction in conscious attention directed toward that stimulus. This is an example of "habituation."

8.7 c The mesolimbic dopamine pathway mediates the perception of reward that is associated with adaptive behaviors, including goal-directed behaviors related to preserving homeostasis, like eating and drinking.

8.8 d Serotonin-specific reuptake inhibitors (SSRIs), also called selective serotonin reuptake inhibitors, are the most widely used antidepressant drugs, although other types of antidepressants additionally enhance signaling by norepinephrine.

8.9 a Short-term, or "working" memories are transferred into new long-term memories in the process of consolidation, which requires a functional hippocampus. When the hippocampus is destroyed, previously formed long-term memories remain intact, but the ability to form new memories is lost.

8.10 c Broca's area is located near the region of the left frontal lobe motor cortex that controls the face; when it is damaged, individuals have "expressive aphasia." This means that they comprehend language but are unable to articulate their own thoughts into words.

Quantitative and Thought Questions

8.1 Dopamine is depleted in the basal ganglia of people with Parkinson disease, and they are therapeutically given dopamine agonists, usually L-dopa. This treatment raises dopamine concentrations in other parts of the brain, however, where the dopamine concentrations were previously normal. Schizophrenia is associated with increased brain dopamine concentrations, and symptoms of this disease appear when dopamine concentrations are high. The converse therapeutic problem can occur during the treatment of schizophrenics with dopamine-lowering drugs, which sometimes cause the symptoms of Parkinson disease to appear.

8.2 Experiments on anesthetized animals often involve either stimulating a brain part to observe the effects of increased neuronal activity, or damaging ("lesioning") an area to observe resulting deficits. Such experiments on animals, which lack the complex language mechanisms humans have, cannot help with language studies. Diseases sometimes mimic these two experimental situations, and behavioral studies of the resulting language deficits in people with aphasia, coupled with study of their brains after death, have provided a wealth of information.

General Principles Assessments

8.1 A general principle of physiology demonstrated very well by Figure 8.7 states that *most physiological functions are controlled by multiple regulatory systems, often working in opposition.* The orexin and monoaminergic RAS neurons compete with the sleep center in regulating the state of consciousness. When the orexin/RAS neurons are active, not only do they arouse the cortex and cause wakefulness, but they also inhibit the sleep center. When the sleep center neurons become active, the exact opposite occurs.

8.2 There seems to be a homeostatic set point for the amount of sleep we need. In addition to a daily increase in activity of the SCN that wakes us up, inputs related to energy homeostasis also prevent sleep from being prolonged (see Figure 8.7). On the other hand, sleep deprivation impairs the immune system, causes cognitive and memory defects, can result in decreased growth hormone secretion and growth velocity in children, and if prolonged can lead to psychosis and even death. When sleep is disrupted or postponed for even one day, we respond with bouts of "make-up" sleep, as though some chemical or factor has gone too far from its homeostatic set point and needs to be restored toward normal. Adenosine has been proposed to be a homeostatic sleep regulator.

CHAPTER 9

Test Questions

9.1 a A single skeletal muscle fiber, or cell, is composed of many myofibrils.

9.2 e The dark stripe in a striated muscle that constitutes the A band results from the aligned thick filaments within myofibrils, so thick filament length is equal to A-band width.

9.3 b As filaments slide during a shortening contraction, the I band becomes narrower, so the distance between the Z line and the thick filaments (at the end of the A band) must decrease.

9.4 d DHP receptors act as voltage sensors in the T-tubule membrane and are physically linked to ryanodine receptors in the sarcoplasmic reticulum membrane. When an action potential depolarizes the T-tubule membrane, DHP receptors change conformation and trigger the opening of the ryanodine receptors. This allows Ca^{2+} to diffuse from the interior of the sarcoplasmic reticulum into the cytosol.

9.5 c In an isometric twitch, tension begins to rise as soon as excitation–contraction is complete and the first cross-bridges begin to attach. In an isotonic twitch, excitation–contraction coupling takes the same amount of time, but the fiber is delayed from shortening until after enough cross-bridges have attached to move the load.

9.6 b In the first few seconds of exercise, mass action favors transfer of the high-energy phosphate from creatine phosphate to ADP by the enzyme creatine kinase.

9.7 d Fast-oxidative-glycolytic fibers are an intermediate type that are designed to contract rapidly but to resist fatigue. They utilize both aerobic and anaerobic energy systems; thus, they are red fibers with high myoglobin (which facilitates production of ATP by oxidative phosphorylation), but they also have a moderate ability to generate ATP through glycolytic pathways. (Refer to Table 9.3.)

9.8 c In smooth muscle cells, dense bodies serve the same functional role as Z lines do in striated muscle cells—they serve as the anchoring point for the *thin* filaments.

9.9 b When myosin-light-chain kinase transfers a phosphate group from ATP to the myosin light chains of the cross-bridges, binding and cycling of cross-bridges are activated.

9.10 d Stretching a sheet of single-unit smooth muscle cells opens mechanically gated ion channels, which causes a depolarization that propagates through gap junctions, followed by Ca^{2+} entry and contraction. This does not occur in multiunit smooth muscle.

9.11 e The amount of Ca^{2+} released during a typical resting heart beat exposes less than half of the thin filament cross-bridge binding sites. Autonomic neurotransmitters and hormones can increase or decrease the amount of Ca^{2+} released to the cytosol during EC coupling.

Quantitative and Thought Questions

9.1 Under resting conditions, the myosin has already bound and hydrolyzed a molecule of ATP, resulting in an energized molecule of myosin (M · ADP · P_i). Because ATP is necessary to detach the myosin cross-bridge from actin at the end of cross-bridge movement, the absence of ATP will result in rigor mortis, in which case the cross-bridges become bound to actin but do not detach, leaving myosin bound to actin (A · M).

9.2 The distance from the elbow joint to the hand (30 cm) is 10 times greater than the distance from the elbow joint to the biceps insertion (3 cm), so her hand will move 20 m/sec when her biceps contracts at 2 m/sec (see Figure 9.30).

9.3 The length–tension relationship states that the maximum tension developed by a muscle decreases at lengths below L_0. During normal shortening, as the sarcomere length becomes shorter than the optimal length, the maximum tension that can be generated decreases. With a light load, the muscle will continue to shorten until its maximal tension just equals the load. No further shortening is possible because at shorter sarcomere lengths the tension would be less than the load. The heavier the load, the less the distance shortened before reaching the isometric state.

9.4 Maximum tension is produced when the fiber is (a) stimulated by an action potential frequency that is high enough to produce a maximal tetanic tension and (b) at its optimum length L_0, where the thick and thin filaments have overlap sufficient to provide the greatest number of cross-bridges for tension production.

9.5 Moderate tension—for example, 50% of maximal tension—is accomplished by recruiting sufficient numbers of motor units to produce this degree of tension. If activity is maintained at this level for prolonged periods, some of the active fibers will begin to fatigue and their contribution to the total tension will decrease. The same level of total tension can be maintained, however, by recruiting new motor units as some of the original ones fatigue. At this point, for example, one may have 50% of the fibers active, 25% fatigued, and 25% still unrecruited. Eventually, when all the fibers have fatigued and there are no additional motor units to recruit, the whole muscle will fatigue.

9.6 The oxidative motor units, both fast and slow, will be affected first by a decrease in blood flow because they depend on blood flow to provide both the fuel—glucose and fatty acids—and the oxygen required to metabolize the fuel. The fast-glycolytic motor units will be affected more slowly because they rely predominantly on internal stores of glycogen, which is anaerobically metabolized by glycolysis.

9.7 Two factors lead to the recovery of muscle force. (a) Some new fibers can be formed by the fusion and development of undifferentiated satellite cells. This will replace some, but not all, of the fibers that were damaged. (b) Some of the restored force results from hypertrophy of the surviving fibers. Because of the loss of fibers in the accident, the remaining fibers must produce more force to move a given load. The remaining fibers undergo increased synthesis of actin and myosin, resulting in increases in fiber diameter and, consequently, their force of contraction.

9.8 In the absence of extracellular Ca^{2+}, skeletal muscle contracts normally in response to an action potential generated in its plasma membrane because the Ca^{2+} required to trigger contraction comes entirely from the sarcoplasmic reticulum within the muscle fibers. If the motor neuron to the muscle is stimulated in a Ca^{2+}-free medium, however, the muscle will not contract because the influx of Ca^{2+} from the extracellular fluid into the motor nerve terminal is necessary to trigger the release of acetylcholine that in turn triggers an action potential in the muscle.

In a Ca^{2+}-free solution, smooth muscles would not respond either to stimulation of the nerve or to the plasma membrane. Stimulating the nerve would have no effect because Ca^{2+} entry into presynaptic terminals is necessary for neurotransmitter release. Stimulating the smooth muscle cell membrane would also not cause a response in the absence of Ca^{2+} because in all of the various types of smooth muscle, Ca^{2+} must enter from outside the cell to trigger contraction. In some cases, the external Ca^{2+} directly initiates contraction, and in others it triggers the release of Ca^{2+} from the sarcoplasmic reticulum (Ca^{2+}-induced Ca^{2+} release).

9.9 The simplest model to explain the experimental observations is as follows. Upon parasympathetic nerve stimulation, a neurotransmitter is released that binds to receptors on the membranes of smooth muscle cells and triggers contraction. The substance released, however, is not acetylcholine (ACh) for the following reason.

Action potentials in the parasympathetic nerves are essential for initiating nerve-induced contraction. When the nerves were prevented from generating action potentials by blockage of their voltage-gated Na^+ channels, there was no response to nerve stimulation. ACh is the neurotransmitter released from most, but not all, parasympathetic endings. When the muscarinic receptors for ACh were blocked, however, stimulation of the parasympathetic nerves still produced a contraction, providing evidence that some substance other than ACh is being released by the neurons and producing contraction.

9.10 Elevation of extracellular fluid Ca^{2+} concentration would increase the amount of Ca^{2+} entering the cytosol through L-type Ca^{2+} channels. This would result in a greater depolarization of cardiac muscle cell membranes during action potentials. The strength of cardiac muscle contractions would also be increased because this larger Ca^{2+} entry would trigger more Ca^{2+} release through ryanodine receptor channels, and consequently there would be a greater activation of cross-bridge cycling.

9.11 In order for unfused tetanus to occur, action potentials must occur more closely in time than the duration of a twitch cycle. Frequency is the inverse of cycle duration, so to produce unfused tetanus, action potentials must occur at a frequency greater than 1/0.04 seconds, or 25 action potentials per second.

General Principles Assessments

9.1 The control of cardiac muscle pacemaker cell activity by sympathetic and parasympathetic neurotransmitters is an excellent example of the general principle that *most physiological functions are controlled by multiple regulatory systems, often working in opposition.*

9.2 The forward motion of cross-bridges during the cross-bridge cycle (power stroke) is associated with a chemical reaction in which ADP and P_i are released as products (see step 2 in Figure 9.15). During high-frequency stimulation of muscles when cross-bridges cycle repeatedly, the concentrations of ADP and P_i build up in the muscle cytosol. Due to the law of mass action, the buildup of these products inhibits the rate of the chemical reaction and, thus, the power stroke of the cross-bridge cycle. This contributes to the reduction of contraction speed and force that occurs when muscles are fatigued.

9.3 The general principle that *controlled exchange of materials occurs between compartments and across cellular membranes* is demonstrated by the movements of Ca^{2+} and other ions involved in the skeletal muscle excitation–contraction coupling mechanism (see Figure 9.40). Controlled movement of Na^+, K^+ and Ca^{2+} across muscle cell plasma membranes maintains the resting membrane potential and allows the generation and propagation of action potentials. Sequestering Ca^{2+} in the sarcoplasmic reticulum allows the resting state of muscle to be maintained until controlled release of Ca^{2+} into the cytosol activates cross-bridge cycling and muscle contraction. The termination of muscle contraction requires the return of Ca^{2+} into the sarcoplasmic reticulum and extracellular fluid.

CHAPTER 10

Test Questions

10.1 b The basal nuclei, sensorimotor cortex, thalamus, brainstem, and cerebellum are all middle-level structures that create a motor program based on the intention to carry out a voluntary movement.

10.2 c When a given muscle is stretched, muscle-spindle stretch receptors send action potentials along afferent fibers that synapse directly on alpha motor neurons to extrafusal fibers to that muscle, causing it to contract back toward the prestretched length.

10.3 a Afferent action potentials from pain receptors in the injured left foot would stimulate the withdrawal reflex of the left leg (activation of flexor muscles and inhibition of extensors) and the opposite pattern in the right leg (the crossed-extensor reflex).

10.4 d Activating the gamma motor neurons would cause contraction of the ends of intrafusal muscle fibers, stretching the muscle-spindle receptors, and the resulting action potentials would monosynaptically excite the alpha motor neurons innervating the extrafusal fibers of the stretch receptors.

10.5 c See Figure 10.10.

10.6 T Most descending corticospinal pathways cross the midline of the body in the medulla oblongata.

10.7 F Upper motor neuron disorders are typically characterized by hypertonia and spasticity.

10.8 F The reverse is actually true.

10.9 F In Parkinson disease, a deficit of dopamine from neurons of the substantia nigra results in "resting tremors."

10.10 T *Clostridium tetani* toxin specifically blocks the release of neurotransmitter from neurons that normally inhibit motor neurons. The resulting imbalance of excitatory and inhibitory inputs causes spastic contractions of muscles.

Quantitative and Thought Questions

10.1 None. The gamma motor neurons are important in preventing the muscle-spindle stretch receptors from going slack, but when this reflex is tested, the intrafusal fibers are not flaccid. The test is performed with a bent knee, which stretches the extensor muscles in the thigh (and the intrafusal fibers within the stretch receptors). The stretch receptors are therefore responsive.

10.2 The efferent pathway of the reflex arc (the alpha motor neurons) would not be activated, the effector cells (the extrafusal muscle fibers) would not be activated, and there would be no reflexive response.

10.3 The drawing must have excitatory synapses on the motor neurons of both ipsilateral extensor and ipsilateral flexor muscles.

10.4 A toxin that interferes with the inhibitory synapses on motor neurons would leave unbalanced the normal excitatory input to these neurons. Thus, the otherwise normal motor neurons would fire excessively, which would result in increased muscle contraction. This is exactly what happens in lockjaw as a result of the toxin produced by the tetanus bacillus.

10.5 In mild cases of tetanus, agonists (stimulators) of the inhibitory interneuron neurotransmitter gamma-aminobutyric acid (GABA) can shift the balance back toward the inhibition of alpha motor neurons. In more severe cases, paralysis can be induced by administering long-lasting drugs that block the nicotinic acetylcholine receptors at the neuromuscular junction.

10.6 Having a person pull the arms apart during the performance of the knee-jerk test is called the Jendrassik maneuver (named for a Hungarian physician who first described it). The exact mechanism by which the reflex increases is unknown. It is most commonly thought that performing a task with the arms simply distracts the person so that there is less descending inhibition of the motor neurons to the leg muscles. In other words, a person may be more able to truly relax the leg muscles (thus allowing the reflex to more fully occur) when her attention is not focused on the legs or anticipating the strike of the reflex hammer. Another possible explanation is that voluntarily flexing arm muscles produces a general activation and increase in excitability of interneurons in the spinal cord that integrate synchronized arm and leg movements; those inputs add to those from the stretch receptors to enhance activation of the motor neurons to leg extensors.

General Principles Assessments

10.1 Unlike smooth and cardiac muscle cells, which are regulated directly by both excitatory and inhibitory inputs, skeletal muscle fibers only have excitatory inputs, so must be inhibited indirectly. They are inhibited from contracting when there are no action potentials arriving along their associated alpha motor neurons, so inhibition must occur at the level of the alpha motor neurons. The dendrites and cell bodies of alpha motor neurons found in the brainstem and spinal cord receive both excitatory and inhibitory inputs from interneurons, sensory neurons, and neurons in descending pathways. When the inhibitory inputs predominate, the alpha motor neuron does not generate action potentials and the muscle fibers it innervates remain relaxed.

10.2 One way that the withdrawal reflex contributes to homeostasis is by minimizing the extent of tissue injury that could potentially result from prolongation of a painful stimulus. Rapidly withdrawing a limb from a position where it is being cut, burned, or crushed helps to minimize the loss of blood, tissue fluid, and tissue function that could compromise homeostasis.

CHAPTER 11

Test Questions

11.1 c

11.2 a

11.3 e

11.4 b

11.5 d

11.6 a At any given concentration of hormone, more A is bound to receptor than B.

11.7 d Goiter results from dysfunction of the thyroid gland.

11.8 e Recall that thyroid hormone potentiates the effects of epinephrine and the sympathetic nervous system.

11.9 b

11.10 e Recall that there exists a large store of iodinated thyroglobulin in thyroid follicles.

11.11 c Low plasma Ca^{2+} decreases the filtered load of Ca^{2+}. It also stimulates parathyroid hormone, which increases Ca^{2+} reabsorption from the distal tubule. This helps to prevent the further loss of Ca^{2+} in the urine.

11.12 d Parathyroid hormone is a potent stimulator of Ca^{2+} resorption from bone.

11.13 T T_4 is the chief circulating form, but T_3 is more active.

11.14 F Acromegaly is associated with hyperglycemia and hypertension.

11.15 T

Quantitative and Thought Questions

11.1 Epinephrine decreases to very low concentrations during rest and fails to increase during stress. The sympathetic preganglionics provide the only major control of the adrenal medulla.

11.2 The increased concentration of binding protein causes more T_3 and T_4 to be bound, thereby lowering the plasma concentration of *free* T_3 and T_4. This causes less negative feedback inhibition of TSH secretion by the anterior pituitary gland, and the increased TSH causes the thyroid to secrete more T_3 and T_4 until the free concentration has returned to normal. The end result is an increased *total* plasma T_3 and T_4—most bound to the protein—but a normal free T_3 and T_4. There is no hyperthyroidism because it is only the free concentration that exerts effects on T_3 and T_4 target cells.

11.3 Destruction of the anterior pituitary gland or hypothalamus. These symptoms reflect the absence of, in order, growth hormone, the gonadotropins, and ACTH (the symptom is due to the resulting decrease in cortisol secretion). The problem is either primary hyposecretion of anterior pituitary gland hormones or secondary hyposecretion because the hypothalamus is not secreting hypophysiotropic hormones normally.

11.4 Vasopressin and oxytocin (the posterior pituitary gland hormones) secretion would decrease. The anterior pituitary gland hormones would not be affected because the influence of the hypothalamus on these hormones is exerted not by connecting nerves but via the hypophysiotropic hormones in the portal vascular system.

11.5 The secretion of GH increases. Somatostatin, coming from the hypothalamus, normally exerts an inhibitory effect on the secretion of this hormone.

11.6 Norepinephrine and many other neurotransmitters are released by neurons that terminate on the hypothalamic neurons that secrete the hypophysiotropic hormones. Therefore, manipulation of these neurotransmitters will alter secretion of the hypophysiotropic hormones and thereby the anterior pituitary gland hormones.

11.7 The high dose of the cortisol-like substance inhibits the secretion of ACTH by feedback inhibition of (1) hypothalamic corticotropin releasing hormone and (2) the response of the anterior pituitary gland to this hypophysiotropic hormone. The lack of ACTH causes the adrenal to atrophy and decrease its secretion of cortisol.

11.8 The hypothalamus. The low basal TSH indicates either that the pituitary gland is defective or that it is receiving inadequate stimulation (TRH) from the hypothalamus. If the thyroid itself were defective, basal TSH would be elevated because of less negative feedback inhibition by T_3 and T_4. The TSH increase in response to TRH shows that the pituitary gland is capable of responding to a stimulus and so is unlikely to be defective. Therefore, the problem is that the hypothalamus is secreting too little TRH (in reality, this is very rare).

11.9 In utero malnutrition. Neither growth hormone nor the thyroid hormones influence in utero growth.

11.10 Androgens stimulate growth but also cause the ultimate cessation of growth by closing the epiphyseal plates. Therefore, there might be a rapid growth spurt in response to the androgens but a subsequent premature cessation of growth. Estrogens exert similar effects.

General Principles Assessments

11.1 Despite having many different actions, epinephrine, cortisol, and growth hormone all act on adipocytes and the liver to regulate energy balance. They do this by stimulating the production and/or release of glucose from liver cells, and the breakdown in adipocytes of triglycerides into usable substrates for energy that can enter the bloodstream. It should not be surprising that a function as critical as energy homeostasis would be regulated by multiple factors; indeed, these three hormones are only one part of a larger control mechanism that regulates energy balance (see Chapter 16).

11.2 The structure of the thyroid gland differs from most other endocrine glands in that it consists of colloid-filled follicles that contain hormone precursors. These precursors can be metabolized to produce thyroid hormones as required. This structure most likely evolved as an adaptation to the relative rarity of iodine in animal diets, including our own. Because iodine is required for the synthesis of thyroid hormones, having a large store of iodinated precursors available in the thyroid gland ensures that even with prolonged absences of dietary intake of the element, thyroid hormones can still be produced.

11.3 Parathyroid hormone is a key part of the mechanism that regulates calcium ion homeostasis. The absence of PTH would have devastating health consequences, because it would result in decreased Ca^{2+} concentrations in the blood; Ca^{2+} is vitally important for proper functioning of all types of muscle tissue, including the heart, and also regulates neuronal function, among other actions. Antidiuretic hormone (vasopressin) contributes to the control of blood pressure and to water balance, because of its actions on kidney tubules. In its absence, blood pressure would be difficult to maintain, and the body would lose considerable volumes of water in the urine. That, in turn, would further compromise blood pressure and would also alter solute concentrations in the extracellular fluid. T_3 (thyroid hormone), through its calorigenic actions, is a major part of the mechanism by which body temperature homeostasis is maintained. In the absence of T_3, most people generally develop cold intolerance.

CHAPTER 12

Test Questions

12.1 c Blood in the right ventricle is relatively deoxygenated after returning from the tissues.

12.2 e Resistance decreases as the fourth power of an increase in radius, and in direct proportion to a decrease in vessel length.

12.3 d See Figure 12.19.

12.4 d The large total cross-sectional area of capillaries results in very slow blood velocity.

12.5 a Increasing colloid osmotic pressure would decrease filtration of fluid from capillaries into the tissues.

12.6 d Pressures are higher in the systemic circuit, but because the cardiovascular system is a closed loop, the flow must be the same in both.

12.7 b The AV node is the only conduction point between atria and ventricles, and the slow propagation through it delays the beginning of ventricular contraction.

12.8 c The diastolic pressure in this example is 85; adding 1/3 of the pulse pressure gives a *MAP* of 101.7 mmHg.

12.9 d Reduced firing to arterioles would reduce total peripheral resistance and thereby reduce mean arterial pressure toward normal.

12.10 e Ventricular muscle cells do not have a pacemaker potential, and the L-type Ca^{2+} channel is not open during this phase of the action potential even in autorhythmic cells.

12.11 c

12.12 a Increased sympathetic nerve firing and norepinephrine release during exercise constrict vascular beds in the kidneys, GI tract, and other tissues to compensate for the large dilation of muscle vascular beds.

12.13 b Reduced oxygen delivery to the kidneys increases the secretion of erythropoietin, which stimulates bone marrow to increase production of erythrocytes.

12.14 c

12.15 e t-PA is part of the fibrinolytic system that dissolves clots.

Quantitative and Thought Questions

12.1 No. Decreased erythrocyte volume is certainly one possible explanation, but there is a second: The person may have a normal erythrocyte volume but an abnormally increased plasma volume. Convince yourself of this by writing the hematocrit equation as

Erythrocyte volume/(Erythrocyte volume + Plasma volume)

12.2 A halving of tube radius. Resistance is directly proportional to blood viscosity but inversely proportional to the *fourth power* of tube radius.

12.3 The plateau of the action potential and the contraction would be absent. You may think that contraction would persist because most Ca^{2+} in excitation–contraction coupling in the heart comes from the sarcoplasmic reticulum. However, the signal for the release of this Ca^{2+} is the Ca^{2+} entering across the plasma membrane.

12.4 The SA node is not functioning, and the ventricles are being driven by a pacemaker in the AV node or the bundle of His.

12.5 The person has a narrowed aortic valve. Normally, the resistance across the aortic valve is so small that there is only a tiny pressure difference between the left ventricle and the aorta during ventricular ejection. In the example given here, the large pressure difference indicates that resistance across the valve must be very high.

12.6 This question is analogous to question 12.5 in that the large pressure difference across a valve while the valve is open indicates an abnormally narrowed valve—in this case, the left AV valve.

12.7 Decreased heart rate and contractility. These are effects mediated by the sympathetic nerves on beta-adrenergic receptors in the heart.

12.8 120 mmHg. $MAP = DP + 1/3\ (SP - DP)$.

12.9 The drug must have caused the arterioles in the kidneys to dilate enough to reduce their resistance by 50%. Blood flow to an organ is determined by mean arterial pressure and the organ's resistance to flow. Another important point can be deduced here: If mean arterial pressure has not changed even though renal resistance has dropped 50%, then either the resistance of some other organ or actual cardiac output has gone up.

12.10 The experiment suggests that acetylcholine causes vasodilation by releasing nitric oxide or some other vasodilator from endothelial cells.

12.11 A low plasma protein concentration. Capillary pressure is, if anything, lower than normal and so cannot be causing the edema. Another possibility is that capillary permeability to plasma proteins has increased, as occurs in burns.

12.12 20 mmHg/L per minute. $TPR = MAP/CO$.

12.13 Nothing. Cardiac output and *TPR* have remained unchanged, so their product, *MAP*, also remains unchanged. This question emphasizes that *MAP* depends on cardiac output but not on the combination of heart rate and stroke volume that produces the cardiac output.

12.14 It increases. There are a certain number of impulses traveling up the nerves from the arterial baroreceptors. When these nerves are cut, the number of impulses reaching the medullary cardiovascular center goes to zero, just as it would physiologically if the mean arterial pressure were to decrease markedly. Accordingly, the medullary cardiovascular center responds to the absent impulses by reflexively increasing arterial pressure.

12.15 It decreases. The hemorrhage causes no immediate change in hematocrit because erythrocytes and plasma are lost in the same proportion. As interstitial fluid starts entering the capillaries, however, it expands the plasma volume and decreases hematocrit. (This is too soon for any new erythrocytes to be synthesized.)

12.16 Using the following equation, $MAP = DP + 1/3(SP - DP)$, inserting 85 for *MAP* and 105 for *SP*, solving for *DP* gives a value of 75 mmHg. Pulse pressure $= SP - DP$, or in this case, $105 - 75 = 30$ mmHg.

12.17 Transplant recipients can increase cardiac output during exercise in two ways. When exercise begins, epinephrine is released from the adrenal medulla and stimulates β-adrenergic receptors on the heart. This increases heart rate and contractility just like would happen in response to norepinephrine released directly from sympathetic neurons; only the response will be delayed in onset. Also, when the individual starts to exercise and venous return to the heart is increased, end-diastolic volume is increased. This initiates the Frank–Starling mechanism, increasing stroke volume and contributing to an increased cardiac output.

12.18 In lead aVR, the electrical poles of the leads are oriented nearly the opposite of lead 1: Lead 1 is a vector oriented from the right side of the body toward a positive pole on the left arm, while lead aVR is a vector oriented from the left side of the body toward a positive pole on the right arm. Thus, if the sweep of depolarization toward the positive pole in lead 1 generates an upright P wave, you can expect that same sweep of depolarization away from the positive pole in lead aVR to produce a downward P wave.

12.19 The stroke volume can be determined by inserting cardiac output and heart rate into the equation $CO = HR \times SV$: 5400 mL/min = 75 beats/min $\times$ *SV*; so $SV = 72$ mL. Next, the end-diastolic volume (*EDV*) can be determined using the equation $SV = EDV - ESV$: 72 mL $= EDV - 60$; so $EDV = 132$ mL. Finally, the ejection fraction (*EF*) is $EF = SV/EDV$, so $EF = 72$ mL/132 mL = 54.5%.

12.20 A small blood clot (thrombus) that results in a blockage of blood flow (embolism) is more dangerous if it forms in the pulmonary veins, because after returning to the heart and being pumped into the systemic arteries, it could lodge in a coronary artery, leading to a heart attack, or in a brain artery, causing a stroke; it could also cause ischemic damage to other organs. A small clot that formed in the systemic circuit will be trapped in the lungs, where the blockage of a small pulmonary artery will do little harm, because blood can flow through alternate branches to pick up fresh O_2 and eliminate CO_2. Small clots trapped in the lungs are eventually dissolved by the fibrinolytic mechanisms without causing much harm. See Chapter 19 for a case study discussion of the dangers of large clots forming in systemic veins.

General Principles Assessments

12.1 Hormones of the endocrine system represent vital information that integrates the function of cells and organs that are widely distributed in the body. The circulatory system delivers blood and any hormones it may contain rapidly and efficiently to all cells throughout the body. Without this information-delivery system, the endocrine system could not function in the regulation of homeostasis.

12.2 Although it is possible that the difference in valve leaflet number is simply a random quirk of how the heart develops, a clear difference in the functional demands on the two AV valves is the amount of pressure they must withstand. At the peak of systole, the typical pressure gradient across the right AV valve is approximately 25 mmHg (pulmonary systolic pressure), while across the left AV valve it is approximately 120 mmHg (systemic systolic pressure). Having one less valve leaflet, the left AV valve has a smaller area where the edges of valve leaflets must seal. It seems likely that this structure makes it less susceptible to failure despite the greater pressure it encounters.

12.3 The liver produces plasma proteins at a rate that keeps their concentration in the plasma within a narrow range. Plasma proteins do not freely exchange across capillary walls, and their concentration determines the value of π_C, the main force that opposes bulk flow of fluid from the plasma to the interstitial fluid (see Figure 12.42). Maintaining balance in the bulk flow forces is essential for controlling the movement of fluid between the interstitial and plasma compartments. The failure of the liver to maintain plasma protein concentration in individuals who are protein starved (kwashiorkor) results in excessive filtration of fluid from the plasma and tissue edema.

CHAPTER 13

Test Questions

13.1 e If alveolar pressure (P_{alv}) is negative with respect to atmospheric pressure (P_{atm}), the driving force for airflow is inward (from the atmosphere into the lung).

13.2 a For the same change in transpulmonary pressure, a less compliant (i.e., stiffer) lung will have a smaller change in lung volume.

13.3 a Total minute ventilation is comprised of dead space plus alveolar ventilation. Minute ventilation is respiratory frequency (12 breaths per minute) multiplied by tidal volume (500 mL/breath) = 6000 mL/min. Subtract from that alveolar ventilation (4200 mL/min) and one gets 1800 mL/min.

13.4 d An increase in alveolar P_{O_2} results from an increase in alveolar ventilation (supply of oxygen) relative to metabolic rate (consumption of oxygen).

13.5 c The relationship between arterial P_{O_2} and arterial oxygen saturation is described by the oxygen–hemoglobin dissociation curve. The greatest increase in oxygen saturation for the same change in P_{O_2} occurs at the steepest part of the curve—a P_{O_2} of between 40 and 60 mmHg.

13.6 b Increases in blood temperature, decreases in blood pH, and increases in DPG shift the oxygen–hemoglobin curve downward, leading to a lower oxygen saturation at the same P_{O_2}.

13.7 b There are forms of asthma that are not primarily due to the presence of allergens. Examples are exercise-induced or cold-air-induced asthma.

13.8 e Respiratory acidosis (increase in blood P_{CO_2} and decrease in pH) is a major stimulus to ventilation—this is mediated both by afferents from the peripheral chemoreceptors and by an increase in central chemoreceptor activity.

13.9 c Because of the shape of the oxygen–hemoglobin dissociation curve, small increases in P_{O_2} due to increases in ventilation cannot fully saturate hemoglobin. When the desaturated blood mixes with saturated blood, the average is still hypoxemic.

13.10 c Remember that a lung capacity is the sum of at least two volumes. Inspiratory capacity is the sum of tidal volume and inspiratory reserve volume.

Quantitative and Thought Questions

13.1 200 mL/mmHg.

$$\text{Lung compliance} = \Delta \text{ lung volume}/\Delta (P_{alv} - P_{ip})$$
$$= 800 \text{ mL}/[0 - (-8)] \text{ mmHg} - [0 - (-4)] \text{ mmHg}$$
$$= 800 \text{ mL}/4 \text{ mmHg} = 200 \text{ mL/mmHg}$$

13.2 More subatmospheric than normal. A decreased surfactant level causes the lungs to be less compliant (i.e., more difficult to expand). Therefore, a greater transpulmonary pressure ($P_{alv} - P_{ip}$) is required to expand them a given amount.

13.3 No.

$$\text{Alveolar ventilation} = (\text{Tidal volume} - \text{Dead space}) \times \text{Breathing rate}$$
$$= (250 \text{ mL} - 150 \text{ mL})/\text{breath} \times 20 \text{ breaths/min}$$
$$= 2000 \text{ mL/min}$$

Normal alveolar ventilation is approximately 4000 mL/min in a 70 kg adult.

13.4 The volume of the snorkel constitutes an additional dead space, so total pulmonary ventilation must be increased if alveolar ventilation is to remain constant.

13.5 The alveolar P_{O_2} will be higher than normal, and the alveolar P_{CO_2} will be lower. To better understand why, review the factors that determine the alveolar gas pressures (see Table 13.5).

13.6 No. Hypoventilation reduces arterial P_{O_2} but only because it reduces alveolar P_{O_2}. That is, in hypoventilation, *both* alveolar and arterial P_{O_2} are decreased to essentially the same degree. In this problem, alveolar P_{O_2} is normal, and so the person is not hypoventilating. The low arterial P_{O_2} must therefore represent a defect that causes a discrepancy between alveolar P_{O_2} and arterial P_{O_2}. Possibilities include impaired diffusion, a shunting of blood from the right side of the heart to the left through a hole in the heart wall, and a mismatch between airflow and blood flow in the alveoli.

13.7 Not at rest, if the defect is not too severe. Recall that equilibration of alveolar air and pulmonary capillary blood is normally so rapid that it occurs well before the end of the capillaries. Therefore, even though diffusion may be slowed as in this problem, there may still be enough time for equilibration to be reached. In contrast, the time for equilibration is decreased during exercise, and failure to equilibrate is much more likely to occur, resulting in a lowered arterial P_{O_2}.

13.8 Only a few percent (specifically, from approximately 200 mL O_2/L blood to approximately 215 mL O_2/L blood). The reason the increase is so small is that almost all the oxygen in blood is carried bound to hemoglobin, and hemoglobin is almost 100% saturated at the arterial P_{O_2} achieved by breathing room air. The high arterial P_{O_2} achieved by breathing 100% oxygen does cause a directly proportional increase in the amount of oxygen *dissolved* in the blood (the additional 15 mL), but this still remains a small fraction of the total oxygen in the blood. Review the numbers given in the chapter.

13.9 All. Venous blood contains products of metabolism released by cells, such as carbon dioxide.

13.10 It would cease. Respiration depends on descending input from the medulla to the nerves supplying the diaphragm and the inspiratory intercostal muscles.

13.11 (a) The combination of hypercapnia (increased P_{CO_2} due to increased inspired CO_2) and hypoxia (due to decreased inspired O_2) greatly augments ventilation by stimulating central and peripheral chemoreceptors. Although CO decreases O_2 content, chemoreceptors are not stimulated and ventilation does not increase.

13.12 These patients have profound hyperventilation, with large increases in both the depth and rate of ventilation. The stimulus, mainly via the peripheral chemoreceptors, is the large increase in their arterial hydrogen ion concentration due to the acids produced. The hyperventilation causes an increase in their arterial P_{O_2} and a decrease in their arterial P_{CO_2}.

13.13 In pure anatomical shunt, blood passes through the lung without exposure to any alveolar air. Therefore, increases in alveolar P_{O_2} caused by increased inspired O_2 will not affect the P_{O_2} of the shunt blood. By contrast, there is still some blood flowing through a region of the lung with a ventilation–perfusion mismatch. Therefore, an increase in P_{O_2} in the alveoli can increase the P_{O_2} in this blood, which, when mixing with blood leaving other areas of the lung, can increase the blood in the pulmonary vein and hence the arterial circulation.

General Principles Assessments

13.1 Boyle's law (see Figure 13.8) explains that the pressure exerted by a constant number of gas molecules (at constant temperature) is inversely proportional to the volume of a container. Therefore, when the volume of the lung increases during negative pressure breathing, the resultant decrease in pressure draws air into the lungs (inspiration). Conversely, when the lung deflates, the pressure in it increases pushing air out of the lung (expiration). The Law of Laplace (Figure 13.17) demonstrates that the larger the radius of a sphere (e.g., an alveolus), the lower the surface tension. This explains the need for pulmonary surfactant, which lowers the surface tension of smaller alveoli, thereby preventing smaller alveoli from collapsing. Dalton's law states that, in a mixture of gases, the pressure each gas exerts is independent of the pressure the others exert and is proportional to the percentage of that gas in the mixture. This explains, therefore, why the partial pressure of oxygen in air at sea level is equal to 0.21×760 mmHg, or 160 mmHg. Henry's law states that the amount of gas dissolved in a liquid will be directly proportional to the partial pressure of the gas with which the liquid is in equilibrium. This is extremely important in understanding the transfer of oxygen from the alveolar gas to the blood. Finally, the unique allosteric properties of hemoglobin shown in Figures 13.26 and 13.29 allow the appropriate delivery of oxygen from the lungs to the tissues. As the CO_2 diffuses out of the pulmonary capillaries, the decrease in CO_2 in the blood shifts the oxygen dissociation curve to the left allowing more oxygen uptake. Conversely, as the blood enters the tissue, CO_2 diffuses into the blood and shifts the oxygen dissociation curve to the right allowing a greater unloading of oxygen to the tissues.

13.2 The thinness of the alveolar wall minimizes the barrier for oxygen and carbon dioxide diffusion allowing an efficient transfer of gases to and from the blood (Figure 13.4). The multiple branching of the airways into respiratory bronchioles and alveoli and the branching of the pulmonary artery into the pulmonary arterioles and capillaries greatly increase the surface area for gas exchange (Figure 13.3).

13.3 Some of the factors that influence alveolar ventilation are summarized in Figure 13.40. The three major stimulatory factors in the blood are a decrease in P_{O_2}, an increase in nonvolatile acids, and an increase in P_{CO_2}. Conversely, a decrease in acids and P_{CO_2} in the blood inhibit ventilation. These factors often work in opposition during the adaptation to hypoxia due, for example, to high altitude. In this case, P_{O_2} decreases due to a decrease in barometric pressure. The resulting increase in alveolar ventilation (Figure 13.35) leads to a decrease in P_{CO_2} (hyperventilation). This respiratory alkalosis attenuates the increase in alveolar ventilation that would have otherwise occurred with arterial hypoxia.

CHAPTER 14

Test Questions

14.1 c The main driving force favoring fluid filtration from the glomerular capillary to Bowman's space is glomerular capillary blood pressure (P_{GC}).

14.2 c In order for a substance to appear in the urine at a faster rate than its filtration rate, it must also be actively secreted into the tubular fluid.

14.3 a Excessive sweating will decrease blood volume. This will lead to compensatory mechanisms to preserve total-body water, including a decrease in urine production (antidiuresis).

14.4 e Urea is trapped in the medullary interstitium and is an osmotically active solute. The resultant increase in tonicity helps to maintain the gradient for medullary passive water reabsorption.

14.5 a A decrease in sodium intake stimulates renin because of the decrease in Na^+ delivery to the macula densa. This is detected and results in an increase in renin release from the juxtaglomerular cells.

14.6 c Parathyroid hormone stimulates Ca^{2+} reabsorption in the distal tubules of the nephron, thereby decreasing Ca^{2+} excretion. Because parathyroid hormone is increased in hypocalcemic states, the resulting decrease in Ca^{2+} excretion helps to restore blood Ca^{2+} to normal.

14.7 c Secretion of ammonium into the renal tubule is one way to rid the body of excess hydrogen ion (metabolic acidosis).

14.8 b Increases in ventilation greater than metabolic rate "blow off" CO_2 and result in a decrease in arterial P_{CO_2}. Because of the buffering of bicarbonate ions, this increases arterial pH (respiratory alkalosis).

14.9 e Cortical nephrons either have short or absent loops of Henle. Only juxtamedullary nephrons have long loops of Henle, which plunge into the renal medulla and create a hyperosmotic interstitium via countercurrent multiplication.

14.10 a When the renal corpuscles become diseased, they greatly increase their permeability to protein. Furthermore, diseased proximal tubules cannot remove the filtered protein from the tubular lumen. This results in increased protein in the urine (proteinuria).

Quantitative and Thought Questions

14.1 No. This is a possible answer, but there is another. Substance T may be secreted by the tubules.

14.2 No. It is a possibility, but there is another. Substance V may be filtered and/or secreted, but the substance V entering the lumen via these routes may be completely reabsorbed.

14.3 125 mg/min. The amount of any substance filtered per unit time is given by the product of the *GFR* and the filterable plasma concentration of the substance—in this case, 125 mL/min $\times$ 100 mg/100 mL = 125 mg/min.

14.4 The plasma concentration may be so high that the T_m for the amino acid is exceeded, so all the filtered amino acid is not reabsorbed. A second possibility is that there is a specific defect in the tubular transport for this amino acid. A third possibility is that some other amino acid is present in the plasma in high concentration and is competing for reabsorption.

14.5 No. Urea is filtered and then partially reabsorbed. The reason its concentration in the tubule is higher than in the plasma is that relatively more water is reabsorbed than urea. Therefore, the urea in the tubule becomes concentrated. Despite the fact that urea *concentration* in the urine is greater than in the plasma, the *amount excreted* is less than the filtered load (that is, net reabsorption has occurred).

14.6 They would all be decreased. The transport of all these substances is coupled, in one way or another, to that of Na^+.

14.7 *GFR* would not decrease as much, and renin secretion would not increase as much as in a person not receiving the drug. The sympathetic nerves are a major pathway for both responses during hemorrhage.

14.8 There would be little if any increase in aldosterone secretion. The major stimulus for increased aldosterone secretion is angiotensin II, but this substance is formed from angiotensin I by the action of angiotensin-converting enzyme, and so blockade of this enzyme would block the pathway.

14.9 (b) Urinary excretion in the steady state must be less than ingested sodium chloride by an amount equal to that lost in the sweat and feces. This is normally quite small, less than 1 g/day, so that urine excretion in this case equals approximately 11 g/day.

14.10 If the hypothalamus had been damaged, there may be inadequate secretion of ADH. This would cause loss of a large volume of urine, which would tend to dehydrate the person and make her thirsty. Of course, the area of the brain involved in thirst might have suffered damage.

14.11 This is primary hyperaldosteronism or Conn's syndrome. Because aldosterone stimulates Na^+ reabsorption and K^+ secretion, there will be total-body retention of Na^+ and loss of K^+. Interestingly, the person in this situation actually retains very little Na^+ because urinary Na^+ excretion returns to normal after a few days despite the continued presence of the high aldosterone. One explanation for this is that *GFR* and atrial natriuretic factor both increase as a result of the initial Na^+ retention.

14.12 Sodium and water balance would become negative because of increased excretion of these substances in the urine. The person would also develop a decreased plasma bicarbonate ion concentration and metabolic acidosis because of increased bicarbonate ion excretion. The effects on acid–base status are explained by the fact that hydrogen ion secretion—blocked by the drug—is required both for HCO_3^- reabsorption and for the excretion of hydrogen ion (contribution of new HCO_3^- to the blood). The increased Na^+ excretion reflects the fact that much Na^+ reabsorption by the proximal tubule is achieved by Na^+/H^+ countertransport. By blocking hydrogen ion secretion, therefore, the drug also partially blocks Na^+ reabsorption. The increased water excretion occurs because the failure to reabsorb Na^+ and HCO_3^- decreases water reabsorption (remember that water reabsorption is secondary to solute reabsorption), resulting in an osmotic diuresis.

14.13 The overuse of diuretics can lead to significant hypovolemia, which leads to an increase in the release of renin from the kidney (see Figure 14.24). The resultant increase in angiotensin II and therefore aldosterone increases the distal tubular secretion of hydrogen ions (mostly in the form of NH_4^+), because of its exchange with sodium (see Figure 14.35). As you learned in Section B, 14.15, most diuretics not only increase sodium excretion (the desired effect) but increase potassium excretion. The resultant potassium depletion can weakly stimulate tubular hydrogen ion secretion. These two factors—increased aldosterone and potassium depletion—lead to an increase in the reabsorption of all the filtered bicarbonate as well as the generation of new bicarbonate from glutamine (see Figure 14.35). This can generate a marked metabolic alkalosis that can have profound effects on multiple organ systems.

General Principles Assessments

14.1 The anatomy of the renal corpuscle is ideally suited to filter the plasma. As you learned in Figure 14.3, the fenestrated capillaries of the glomerulus allow the filtration of plasma but prevent the loss of larger molecules (like albumin). The juxtaglomerular apparatus is ideally located to sense the amount of sodium in the distal tubule such that renin secretion can be appropriately regulated. The anatomical placement of the afferent and efferent arterioles allows the precise regulation of the blood pressure within the glomerulus, thus regulating glomerular filtration rate.

14.2 The appreciation of the physical forces—such as hydrostatic pressure—that determine net movement of plasma out of capillaries (Starling's forces; Figure 14.8) is vital to understand the ultimate glomerular filtration rate. The expression of the enzyme carbonic anhydrase in the tubular epithelial cells catalyzes the conversion of H_2O and CO_2 to H_2CO_3, which then breaks down to provide H^+ for secretion into the tubular lumen and HCO_3^- for reabsorption into the interstitial fluid. The equilibrium of this reaction obeys the chemical law known as mass action (see Chapter 3).

14.3 There are a variety of stimulatory and inhibitory inputs involved in the control of vasopressin (Figures 14.26, 14.27, and 14.28). For example, an increase in the osmolarity of the blood increases vasopressin by stimulation of the central osmoreceptor, whereas an increase in plasma volume decreases vasopressin by stimulation of the low-pressure baroreceptors in the heart. So, a person with an increased plasma osmolarity and plasma volume due to, for example, an extremely high salt intake, would demonstrate a smaller increase in vasopressin than a person with increased osmolarity but decreased plasma volume that may occur during dehydration.

CHAPTER 15

Test Questions

15.1 c When the stomach contents, which are very acidic, move into the small intestine, it stimulates the release of secretin, which circulates to the pancreas and stimulates the release of HCO_3^- into the small intestine. This neutralizes the acid and protects the small intestine.

15.2 d GIP release is a feedforward mechanism to signal the islet cells in the pancreas that the products of food digestion are on their way to the blood. This results in an augmented insulin response to a meal.

15.3 a Gastrin is a major controller of acid secretion by the stomach. When the stomach becomes very acidic, gastrin release is inhibited, preventing continued acid production.

15.4 b Cholecystokinin is the primary signal from the small intestine to the pancreas to increase digestive enzyme release into the small intestine.

15.5 d The enzyme pepsin is produced from pepsinogen in the presence of acid. This zymogen accelerates protein digestion.

15.6 b Because fat is insoluble in an aqueous environment, micelles keep fat droplets from re-aggregating and small enough to be absorbed.

15.7 c Distention of the duodenum signals the stomach that the meal has moved on and continued acid secretion in the stomach is not necessary until the next meal.

15.8 a HCO_3^- in the bile is secreted by the epithelial cells lining the bile ducts.

15.9 e Although the primary movement of chyme in segmentation is back and forth, the overall, net movement of chyme is from the small intestine to the large intestine.

15.10 a The active transport of Na^+ in the large intestine is the driving force for the osmotic absorption of water.

Quantitative and Thought Questions

15.1 If the salivary glands fail to secrete amylase, the undigested starch that reaches the small intestine will still be digested by the amylase the pancreas secretes. Thus, starch digestion is not significantly affected by the absence of salivary amylase.

15.2 Alcohol can be absorbed across the stomach wall, but absorption is much more rapid from the small intestine with its larger surface area. Ingestion of foods containing fat releases enterogastrones from the small intestine, and these hormones inhibit gastric emptying and thereby prolong the time alcohol spends in the stomach before reaching the small intestine. Milk, contrary to popular belief, does not "protect" the lining of the stomach from alcohol by coating it with a fatty layer. Rather, the fat content of milk decreases the rate of absorption of alcohol by decreasing the rate of gastric emptying.

15.3 Vomiting results in the loss of fluid and acid from the body. The fluid comes from the luminal contents of the stomach and duodenum, most of which was secreted by the gastric glands, pancreas, and liver and thus is derived from the blood. The cardiovascular symptoms of this patient are the result of the decrease in blood volume that accompanies vomiting.

The secretion of acid by the stomach produces an equal number of bicarbonate ions, which are released into the blood. Normally, these bicarbonate ions are neutralized by hydrogen ions released into the blood by the pancreas when this organ secretes bicarbonate ions. Because gastric acid is lost during vomiting, the pancreas is not stimulated to secrete HCO_3^- by the usual high-acidity signal from the duodenum, and no corresponding hydrogen ions are formed to neutralize the

HCO_3^- released into the blood by the stomach. As a result, the acidity of the blood decreases. Loss of K^+ from the loss of stomach contents can also lead to hypokalemia.

15.4 Fat can be digested and absorbed in the absence of bile salts, but in greatly decreased amounts. Without adequate emulsification of fat by bile salts and phospholipids, only the fat at the surface of large lipid droplets is available to pancreatic lipase, and the rate of fat digestion is very slow. Without the formation of micelles with the aid of bile salts, the products of fat digestion become dissolved in the large lipid droplets, where they are not readily available for diffusion into the epithelial cells. In the absence of bile salts, only about 50% of the ingested fat is digested and absorbed. The undigested fat is passed on to the large intestine, where bacteria produce compounds that increase colonic motility and promote the secretion of fluid into the lumen of the large intestine, leading to diarrhea.

15.5 Damage to the lower portion of the spinal cord produces a loss of voluntary control over defecation due to disruption of the somatic nerves to the skeletal muscle of the external anal sphincter. Damage to the somatic nerves leaves the external sphincter in a continuously relaxed state. Under these conditions, defecation occurs whenever the rectum becomes distended and the defecation reflex is initiated.

15.6 Vagotomy decreases the secretion of acid by the stomach. Impulses in the parasympathetic nerves directly stimulate acid secretion by the parietal cells and also cause the release of gastrin, which in turn stimulates acid secretion. Impulses in the vagus nerves are increased during both the cephalic and gastric phases of digestion. Vagotomy, by decreasing the amount of acid secreted, decreases irritation of existing ulcers, which promotes healing and decreases the probability of acid contributing to the production of new ulcers.

General Principles Assessments

15.1 The liver is ideally situated to process materials absorbed from the lumen of the small intestine that end up in the hepatic portal vein (Figure 15.32). One very important example of this is the detoxification of harmful substances that are ingested and absorbed. Notice in Figure 15.31 that the hepatocytes (liver cells) form sheets, thereby maximizing their contact with blood in the hepatic sinusoids. This ensures that most, if not all, of the toxic substances absorbed in the small intestine can be taken up from the blood in the branches of the portal vein and rendered harmless in the hepatocytes. Furthermore, contact with the bile canaliculi ensures the ability of the hepatocytes to rid the body of toxic metabolites by secretion into the bile.

15.2 (1) Figures 15.10, 15.11, 15.12, and 15.13 demonstrate the chemical property of polarity. That is, steroids are nonpolar rendering them relatively insoluble in water. Chemical additions to the basic structure of the steroid molecule (for example, hydroxyl groups) result in polar portions exposed on the surface of the molecule that are water soluble. This results in a molecule that is amphipathic enabling it to bind to lipids on the nonpolar regions and also to dissolve in water on the polar region, thereby emulsifying lipids for absorption. Interestingly, chemical emulsifiers are often added to salad dressing to allow the oil and the water portions to stay mixed after shaking. (2) Figure 15.19 demonstrates the ability of an enzyme—carbonic anhydrase—to catalyze the conversion of CO_2 and H_2O to H_2CO_3 which then breaks down to HCO_3^- and H^+; the secretion of the latter in the lumen of the stomach results in a very acidic environment ideal for the initial digestion of proteins as well as a way to kill most ingested bacteria. (3) Another interesting example of chemistry is shown in Figure 15.22 in which an inactive enzyme precursor (pepsinogen) is activated in the acidic environment of the gastric lumen to the active enzyme pepsin that catalyzes the breakdown of proteins to peptides. (Figure 15.28 gives another example of this concept for pancreatic enzymes.) In both cases, the secretion of an inactive form of the enzyme prevents self-destruction of the cells responsible for producing the enzyme.

15.3 Figure 15.14 illustrates in several ways the general principle that *information flow between cells, tissues, and organs is an essential feature of homeostasis and allows for integration of physiological processes.* How do you perceive the sensation of "fullness" when you have ingested a large meal? Afferent nerves from the upper GI tract "tell" the brain that you are full. How do emotions influence gastrointestinal motility? Efferent autonomic input to the GI tract can alter the activity of the enteric nervous system, thus altering smooth muscle activity in the GI tract.

CHAPTER 16

Test Questions

16.1 a Glucose can be converted to fat, but fatty acids cannot be converted to glucose.

16.2 b HSL is an intracellular enzyme that acts on triglycerides.

16.3 a Glucagon acts to prevent hypoglycemia from occurring.

16.4 c If untreated, type 1 DM causes an osmotic diuresis when the transport maximum for glucose is exceeded in the kidneys.

16.5 d Insulin stimulates lipogenesis, not lipolysis.

16.6 e Recall that vitamin deficiencies can occur even with normal dietary intake of vitamins, because the metabolic rate is increased in hyperthyroidism.

16.7 b

16.8 T

16.9 F Core temperature is generally kept fairly constant, but skin temperature can vary.

16.10 T

16.11 F As muscles begin contracting during exercise, they become partially insulin-independent.

16.12 F BMI equals body mass in kg divided by (height in meters)^2.

16.13 T

16.14 F Skin vessels dilate in such conditions in order to help dissipate heat by bringing warm blood close to the skin surface.

16.15 T

Quantitative and Thought Questions

16.1 The concentration in plasma would increase, and the amount stored in adipose tissue would decrease. Lipoprotein lipase cleaves plasma triglycerides, so its blockade would decrease the rate at which these molecules were cleared from plasma and would decrease the availability of the fatty acids in them for the synthesis of intracellular triglycerides. However, this would only reduce but not eliminate such synthesis, because the adipose-tissue cells could still synthesize their own fatty acids from glucose.

16.2 It will lower plasma cholesterol concentration. Bile salts are formed from cholesterol, and losses of these bile salts in the feces will be replaced by the synthesis of new ones from cholesterol. Chapter 15 describes how bile salts are normally absorbed from the small intestine so that very few of those secreted into the bile are normally lost from the body.

16.3 Plasma concentrations of HDL and LDL. It is the ratio of LDL cholesterol to HDL cholesterol that best correlates with the development of atherosclerosis (HDL cholesterol is "good" cholesterol). The answer to this question would have been the same regardless of whether the person was an athlete, but the question was phrased this way to emphasize that people who exercise generally have increased HDL cholesterol.

16.4 The person may have type 1 diabetes mellitus and require insulin, or may be a healthy fasting person; plasma glucose would be increased in the first case but decreased in the second. Plasma insulin concentration would be useful because it would be decreased in both cases. The fact that the person was resting and unstressed was specified because severe stress or strenuous exercise could also produce the plasma changes mentioned. Plasma glucose would increase during stress and decrease during strenuous exercise.

16.5 Glucagon, epinephrine, cortisol, and growth hormone. The insulin will produce hypoglycemia, which then induces reflexive increases in the secretion of all these hormones.

16.6 It may reduce it but not eliminate it. The sympathetic effects on organic metabolism during exercise are mediated not only by circulating epinephrine but also by sympathetic nerves to the liver (glycogenolysis and gluconeogenesis), to adipose tissue (lipolysis), and to the pancreatic islets (inhibition of insulin secretion and stimulation of glucagon secretion).

16.7 Heat loss from the head, mainly via convection and sweating, is the major route for loss under these conditions. The rest of the body is *gaining* heat by conduction, and sweating is of no value in the rest of the body because the water cannot evaporate. Heat is also lost via the expired air (insensible loss), and some people actually begin to pant under such conditions. The rapid, shallow breathing increases airflow and heat loss without causing hyperventilation.

16.8 They seek out warmer places, if available, so that their body temperature increases. That is, they use behavior to develop a fever.

General Principles Assessments

16.1 Insulin and glucagon are both secreted by the endocrine pancreas; they have opposite effects on plasma concentrations of glucose. They achieve these effects in part through opposite actions on key metabolic organs such as the liver. In the liver, insulin stimulates glycogen synthesis and inhibits gluconeogenesis, whereas glucagon stimulates glycogen breakdown and gluconeogenesis. Insulin and glucagon are always present in plasma; it is the ratio of the two hormones that determines the net effect that will be to either decrease (insulin) or increase (glucagon) the concentration of plasma glucose.

16.2 The factors that control hunger (appetite) are summarized in Figure 16.15. Neural and endocrine signals arising from the gastrointestinal tract and adipocytes appear to be very important regulators of appetite. Other factors, such as plasma glucose and insulin concentrations, body temperature, and behavioral mechanisms also play a role.

16.3 As described in the chapter, the first law of thermodynamics states that energy can neither be created nor destroyed but can be transformed from one type to another. This is demonstrated by the production of heat within cells during the breakdown of organic molecules such as glucose. Some of the energy from the chemical bonds in organic molecules is transferred to ATP, and some is released as heat. This heat contributes to body temperature. Maintaining body temperature in a homeostatic range also depends upon the properties of heat; for example, heat flows from a region of higher temperature to one of lower temperature. In Figure 16.17, for example, heat is shown entering the body by radiation from the sun and conduction from the hot water.

CHAPTER 17

Test Questions

17.1 e Without the presence of the Y chromosome in the testes and the local production of SRY protein, the undifferentiated gonads are programmed to differentiate into ovaries.

17.2 c Only females exhibit gonadal steroid (estrogen) positive feedback on GnRH release.

17.3 d The luteal phase of the ovary, when progesterone production is maximal, occurs after ovulation but before the end of the menstrual cycle.

17.4 c Estrogen stimulates LH release (positive feedback) just before the LH surge and ovulation (usually on day 14).

17.5 b One follicle becomes dominant early in the menstrual cycle.

17.6 e The death of the corpus luteum (in the absence of pregnancy and hCG) results in a dramatic decrease in ovarian progesterone and estrogen production.

17.7 a The loss of ovarian steroid production with the death of the corpus luteum releases the pituitary gland from negative feedback and allows FSH to increase. This stimulates the maturation of a small number of follicles for the next menstrual cycle.

17.8 c The primary function of the Leydig cell is the production of testosterone in response to stimulation with LH.

17.9 b Prolactin is produced by the maternal pituitary gland. It is homologous to but not the same peptide as human placental lactogen, which is produced by the placenta.

17.10 a The primary event in menopause is the loss of ovarian function. The decrease in estrogen leads to an increase in pituitary gland gonadotropin release (loss of negative feedback).

Quantitative and Thought Questions

17.1 Sterility due to lack of spermatogenesis would be the common finding. The Sertoli cells are essential for spermatogenesis, and so is testosterone produced by the Leydig cells. The person with Leydig cell destruction, but not the person with Sertoli cell destruction, would also have other symptoms of testosterone deficiency.

17.2 The androgens act on the hypothalamus and anterior pituitary gland to inhibit the secretion of the gonadotropins. Therefore, spermatogenesis is inhibited. Importantly, even if this man were given FSH, the sterility would probably remain because the lack of LH would cause deficient testosterone secretion, and *locally* produced testosterone is required for spermatogenesis (i.e., the exogenous androgen cannot do this job).

17.3 Impaired function of the seminiferous tubules, notably of the Sertoli cells. The increased plasma FSH concentration is due to the lack of negative feedback inhibition of FSH secretion by inhibin, itself secreted by the Sertoli cells. The Leydig cells seem to be functioning normally in this person because the lack of demasculinization and the normal plasma LH indicate normal testosterone secretion.

17.4 FSH secretion. FSH acts on the Sertoli cells and LH acts on the Leydig cells, so sterility would result in either case, but the loss of LH would also cause undesirable elimination of testosterone and its effects.

17.5 These findings are all due to testosterone deficiency. You would also expect to find that the testes and penis were small if the deficiency occurred before puberty.

17.6 They will be eliminated or become very irregular. The androgens act on the hypothalamus to inhibit the secretion of GnRH and on the pituitary gland to inhibit the response to GnRH. The result is inadequate secretion of gonadotropins and therefore inadequate stimulation of the ovaries. In addition to the loss of regular menstrual cycles, the woman may suffer some degree of masculinization of the secondary sex characteristics because of the combined effects of androgen excess and estrogen deficiency.

17.7 Such treatment may cause so much secretion of FSH that multiple follicles become dominant and have their eggs ovulated during the LH surge.

17.8 An increased plasma LH. The other two are due to increased plasma progesterone and so do not occur until *after* ovulation and formation of the corpus luteum.

17.9 The absence of sperm capacitation. When test-tube fertilization is performed, special techniques are used to induce capacitation.

17.10 The fetus is in difficulty. The placenta produces progesterone entirely on its own, whereas estriol secretion requires participation of the fetus, specifically, the fetal adrenal cortex.

17.11 Prostaglandin antagonists, oxytocin antagonists, and drugs that lower cytosolic Ca^{2+} concentration. You might not have thought of the last category because Ca^{2+} is not mentioned in this context in the chapter, but as in all muscle, Ca^{2+} is the immediate cause of contraction in the myometrium.

17.12 This person would have normal male external genitals and testes, although the testes might not have descended fully, but would also have some degree of development of uterine tubes, a uterus, and a vagina. These internal female structures would tend to develop because no MIS was present to cause degeneration of the Müllerian duct system.

17.13 No. These two hormones are already increased in menopause, and the problem is that the ovaries are unable to respond to them with estrogen secretion. Thus, the treatment must be with estrogen itself.

General Principles Assessments

17.1 Although several answers are possible, differentiation of the internal and external genitalia is a wonderful example of the general principle that *structure is a determinant of—and has coevolved with—function.* The male and female genitalia arise from the same primordial cluster of cells in the embryo. The reproductive structures diverge in early embryonic development to form organs suited for their function. For the male, it is the production of sperm and the development of a penis that evolved to fit into the vagina of the female. In the female, it is to produce ova and to receive sperm to allow fertilization of the ova. So even though they started the same, through differentiation, the male and female tracts develop into complementary structures ideally suited for their functions.

17.2 The amount of FSH and LH secreted from the gonadotrophs of the anterior pituitary at any one time in the male is determined by two opposing inputs. Stimulatory input is from GnRH released from hypophysiotropic nerves into the hypophyseal portal blood, and inhibitory negative feedback input is from the two different hormones released by the testes—inhibin and testosterone—that reach the anterior pituitary from the systemic circulation. The effect of inhibin at the anterior pituitary primarily reduces the release of FSH, whereas testosterone primarily reduces the release of LH.

17.3 The adaptation to pregnancy is one of the best examples of integration of multiple organ systems. Here are some examples that are listed in Table 17.9:

- Increase in maternal bone turnover to supply calcium and phosphorus to the placenta necessary for normal fetal bone development.
- Increase in maternal blood volume and red blood cell production. This allows the increase in cardiac output and perfusion of the rapidly growing placenta as well as increase in blood flow to, for example, the maternal kidneys to enable the excretion of the additional waste products produced by the fetus.
- Increase in maternal alveolar ventilation enables the mother to rid the body of the extra carbon dioxide produced by the fetus.
- Mobilization of maternal glucose meets the metabolic needs of the developing fetus.

As a test of your knowledge, you should be able to explain the mechanism of these and other adaptations to pregnancy listed in Table 17.9.

CHAPTER 18

Test Questions

18.1 c

18.2 a

18.3 b This is known as active immunity.

18.4 c IgA antibodies act in this way.

18.5 F Antibiotics are bactericidal. They are sometimes given in viral diseases to eliminate or prevent secondary infections caused by bacteria, however.

18.6 T For example, rheumatoid arthritis and inflammatory bowel disease are not associated with infection.

18.7 T Some lymphocytes are B cells.

18.8 F Edema is a consequence of inflammation and has no known adaptive value.

18.9 F These are the primary lymphoid organs. An example of a secondary organ is a lymph node.

Quantitative and Thought Questions

18.1 Both would be impaired because T cells would not differentiate. The absence of cytotoxic T cells would eliminate responses mediated by these cells. The absence of helper T cells would impair antibody-mediated responses because most B cells require cytokines from helper T cells to become activated.

18.2 Neutrophil deficiency would impair nonspecific (innate) inflammatory responses to bacteria. Monocyte deficiency, by causing macrophage deficiency, would impair both innate inflammation and adaptive immune responses.

18.3 The drug may reduce but would not eliminate the action of complement, because this system destroys cells directly (via the membrane attack complex) as well as by facilitating phagocytosis.

18.4 Antibodies would bind normally to antigen but may not be able to activate complement, act as opsonins, or recruit NK cells in ADCC. The reason for these defects is that the sites to which complement C1, phagocytes, and NK cells bind are all located in the Fc portion of antibodies.

18.5 They do develop fever, although often not to the same degree as normal. They can do so because IL-1 and other cytokines secreted by macrophages cause fever, whereas the defect in AIDS is failure of helper T-cell function.

General Principles Assessments

18.1 As shown in Figure 18.22, a wide range of changes occur in physiological variables following infection, including changes in plasma concentrations of minerals (iron, zinc), energy sources (fatty acids, amino acids), and hormones (cortisol). In each case, the respective variable is decreased or increased beyond its usual homeostatic range. Although these changes are adaptive to fight infection, they may come with a cost, as does any challenge to homeostasis. For example, elevated concentrations of cortisol may temporarily result in hyperglycemia, water retention, and potentiated actions of catecholamines on cardiovascular function. Other responses to infection, such as fever, accelerate the rate of chemical reactions in all cells (increase metabolism) and, if fever is sufficiently high, may damage neuronal function.

Appendix B INDEX OF CLINICAL TERMS

DISEASES AND DISORDERS

INFECTIOUS OR CAUSATIVE AGENTS

SIGNS AND SYMPTOMS

TREATMENTS, DIAGNOSTICS, AND THERAPEUTIC DRUGS

Glossary

A

A band one of the transverse bands making up repeated striations of cardiac and skeletal muscle; region of aligned myosin-containing thick filaments

abortion spontaneous or clinically-induced death of an embryo or fetus after implantation

absolute refractory period time during which an excitable membrane cannot generate an action potential in response to any stimulus

absorption movement of materials across an epithelial layer from body cavity or compartment toward the blood

absorptive state period during which nutrients enter bloodstream from gastrointestinal tract

accessory reproductive organ duct through which sperm or egg is transported, or a gland emptying into such a duct (in the female, the breasts are usually included)

acclimatization (ah-climb-ah-tih-ZAY-shun) environmentally induced improvement in functioning of a physiological system with no change in genetic endowment

accommodation adjustment of eye for viewing various distances by changing shape of lens

acetylcholine (ACh) (ass-ih-teel-KOH-leen) a neurotransmitter released by pre- and postganglionic parasympathetic neurons, preganglionic sympathetic neurons, somatic neurons, and some CNS neurons

acetylcholinesterase (ass-ih-teel-koh-lin-ES-ter-ase) enzyme that breaks down acetylcholine into acetic acid and choline

acetyl coenzyme A (acetyl CoA) (ASS-ih-teel koh-EN-zime A) metabolic intermediate that transfers acetyl groups to Krebs cycle and various synthetic pathways

acid molecule capable of releasing a hydrogen ion; solution having an H^+ concentration greater than that of pure water (that is, pH less than 7); *see also* strong acid, weak acid

acidic solution any solution with a pH less than 7.0

acidity concentration of free, unbound hydrogen ion in a solution; the higher the H^+ concentration, the greater the acidity

acquired reflex behaviors that appear to be stereotypical and automatic but that in fact result from considerable conscious effort to be learned; also called *learned reflex*

acrosome (AK-roh-sohm) cytoplasmic vesicle containing digestive enzymes and located at head of a sperm

acrosome reaction process that occurs in the sperm after it binds to the zona pellucida of the egg, exposing acrosomal enzymes

actin filaments polymers of G-actin that form part of the cell cytoskeleton and are part of the contractile apparatus of muscle cells; also called *microfilaments*

action potential electrical signal propagated by neurons and muscle cells; an all-or-none depolarization of membrane polarity; has a threshold and refractory period and is conducted without decrement

action potential propagation the movement of an action potential along an axon; in myelinated axons, it occurs via saltatory conduction

activated macrophage macrophage whose killing ability has been enhanced by cytokines, particularly IL-2 and interferon-gamma

activation energy energy necessary to disrupt existing chemical bonds during a chemical reaction

active hyperemia (hy-per-EE-me-ah) increased blood flow through a tissue associated with increased metabolic activity

active immunity resistance to reinfection acquired by contact with microorganisms, their toxins, or other antigenic material; *compare* passive immunity

active site region of enzyme to which substrate binds

active transport energy-requiring system that uses transporters to move ions or molecules across a membrane against an electrochemical difference; *see also* primary active transport, secondary active transport

active zone region within an axon terminal where neurotransmitter vesicles are clustered prior to secretion

acuity sharpness or keenness of perception

acute phase protein group of proteins secreted by liver during systemic response to injury or infection

acute phase response responses of tissues and organs distant from site of infection or immune response

adaptation (evolution) a biological characteristic that favors survival in a particular environment; (neural) decrease in action potential frequency in a neuron despite constant stimulus

adaptive immune response the specific response of the cells of the immune system to a particular pathogen; subsequent responses to the same pathogen are amplified

adenine one of the four bases making up DNA; also a breakdown product of ATP used as a neurotransmitter

adenoid lymphoid tissue; also known as *pharyngeal tonsil*

adenosine a nucleoside composed of adenine bound to a ribose sugar; building block for ATP; neurotransmitter in CNS

adenosine diphosphate (ADP) (ah-DEN-oh-seen dye-FOS-fate) two-phosphate product of ATP breakdown

adenosine triphosphate (ATP) nucleotide that transfers energy from metabolism to cell functions during its breakdown to ADP and release of P_i

adenylyl cyclase (ad-DEN-ah-lil SYE-klase) enzyme that catalyzes transformation of ATP to cyclic AMP

adequate stimulus the modality of stimulus to which a particular sensory receptor is most sensitive

adipocyte (ad-DIP-oh-site) cell specialized for triglyceride synthesis and storage; fat cell

adipose tissue (AD-ah-poze) tissue composed largely of fat-storing cells

adrenal cortex (ah-DREE-nal KORE-tex) endocrine gland that forms outer shell of each adrenal gland; secretes steroid hormones—mainly cortisol, aldosterone, and androgens; *compare* adrenal medulla

adrenal gland one of a pair of endocrine glands above each kidney; each gland consists of outer *adrenal cortex* and inner *adrenal medulla*

adrenal medulla (meh-DUL-ah or meh-DOOL-ah) endocrine gland that forms inner core of each adrenal gland; secretes amine hormones, mainly epinephrine; *compare* adrenal cortex

adrenergic (ad-ren-ER-jik) pertaining to norepinephrine or epinephrine; compound that acts like norepinephrine or epinephrine

adrenocorticotropic hormone (ACTH) (ad-ren-oh-kor-tih-koh-TROH-pik) polypeptide hormone secreted by anterior pituitary gland; stimulates adrenal cortex to secrete cortisol; also called *corticotropin*

aerobic (air-OH-bik) in presence of oxygen

afferent arteriole vessel in kidney that carries blood from artery to renal corpuscle

afferent division (of the peripheral nervous system) neurons in the peripheral nervous system that project to the central nervous system

afferent neuron neuron that carries information from sensory receptors at its peripheral endings to CNS; cell body lies outside CNS

afferent pathway component of reflex arc that transmits information from receptor to integrating center

affinity strength with which ligand binds to its binding site

afterbirth placenta and associated membranes expelled from uterus after delivery of infant

afterhyperpolarization decrease in membrane potential in neurons at the end of the action potential due to opened voltage-gated K^+ channels

afterload the work the heart does while ejecting blood; a function of the arterial blood pressure, as well as the diameter and thickness of the ventricles

agonist (AG-ah-nist) chemical messenger that binds to receptor and triggers cell's response; often refers to drug that mimics action of chemical normally in the body

airway tubes through which air flows between external environment and lung alveoli

albumin (al-BU-min or AL-bu-min) most abundant plasma protein

aldosterone (al-doh-STEER-own or al-DOS-stir-own) mineralocorticoid steroid hormone secreted by adrenal cortex; regulates electrolyte balance

alkaline solution any solution having H^+ concentration lower than that of pure water (that is, having a pH greater than 7)

all-or-none pertaining to event that occurs maximally or not at all

allosteric protein (al-low-STAIR-ik or al-low-STEER-ik) protein whose binding site characteristics are subject to allosteric modulation in which modulator molecules that bind to regions of the protein other than the binding site alter the protein's ligand-binding capacity

alpha-adrenergic receptor one type of plasma membrane receptor for epinephrine and norepinephrine; also called *alpha adrenoceptor; compare* beta-adrenergic receptor

alpha cell glucagon-secreting cell of pancreatic islets of Langerhans

alpha–gamma coactivation simultaneous firing of action potentials along alpha motor neurons to extrafusal fibers of a muscle and along gamma motor neurons to the contractile ends of intrafusal fibers within that muscle

α-glycerol phosphate three-carbon molecule that combines with fatty acids to form triglyceride; also called *glycerol 3-phosphate*

alpha helix coiled regions of proteins or DNA formed by hydrogen bonds

α-ketoacid (AL-fuh KEY-toh) molecule formed from amino acid metabolism and containing carbonyl (—CO—) and carboxyl (—COOH) groups

alpha motor neuron motor neuron that innervates extrafusal skeletal muscle fibers

alpha rhythm prominent 8 to 13 Hz oscillation on the electroencephalograms of awake, relaxed adults with their eyes closed

alternative complement pathway sequence for complement activation that bypasses first steps in classical pathway and is not antibody dependent

alveolar dead space (al-VEE-oh-lar) volume of fresh inspired air that reaches alveoli but does not undergo gas exchange with blood

alveolar pressure (P_{alv}) air pressure in pulmonary alveoli

alveolar ventilation ($\dot{V}_A$) volume of atmospheric air entering alveoli each minute

alveolus (al-VEE-oh-lus or al-vee-OH-lus) (lungs) thin-walled, air-filled "outpocketing" from terminal air passageways in lungs; (glands) cell cluster at end of duct in secretory gland

amacrine cell (AM-ah-krin) a specialized type of neuron found in the retina of the eye that integrates information between local photoreceptor cells

amine hormone (ah-MEEN) hormone derived from amino acid tyrosine; includes thyroid hormones, epinephrine, norepinephrine, and dopamine

amino acid (ah-MEEN-oh) molecule containing amino group, carboxyl group, and side chain attached to a carbon atom; molecular subunit of protein

amino acid side chain the variable portions of amino acids; may contain acidic or basic charged regions, or may be hydrophobic

amino group —NH_2; ionizes to —NH_3^+

aminopeptidase (ah-meen-oh-PEP-tih-dase) one of a family of enzymes located in the intestinal epithelial membrane; breaks peptide bond at amino end of polypeptide

amnion another term for amniotic sac

amniotic cavity (am-nee-AHT-ik) fluid-filled space surrounding the developing fetus enclosed by amniotic sac

amniotic fluid liquid within amniotic cavity that has a composition similar to extracellular fluid

amniotic sac membrane surrounding fetus in utero

AMPA receptor receptor protein found in the membrane of some brain neurons, named for its binding to alpha-amino-3 hydroxy-5 methyl-4 isoxazole proprionic acid

amphipathic (am-fuh-PATH-ik) a molecule containing polar or ionized groups at one end and nonpolar groups at the other

ampulla structure in the wall of the semicircular canals containing hair cells that respond to head movement

amylase (AM-ih-lase) enzyme that partially breaks down polysaccharides

anabolism (an-AB-oh-lizm) cellular synthesis of organic molecules

anaerobic (an-ih-ROH-bik) in the absence of oxygen

anatomical dead space (V_D) space in respiratory tract airways where gas exchange does not occur with blood

androgen (AN-dro-jen) any hormone with testosterone-like actions

androgen-binding protein (ABP) synthesized and secreted by Sertoli cell of the testes—binds to and increases local testosterone concentration in fluid in the seminiferous tubule

anemia (ah-NEE-me-ah) reduction in total blood hemoglobin

anemic hypoxia decrease in oxygen content of the blood due to a reduction in the amount of hemoglobin (usually due to a reduction in the number of erythrocytes)

angiogenesis (an-gee-oh-JEN-ah-sis) the development and growth of capillaries; stimulated by angiogenic factors

angiogenic factor chemical signal that induces the development and growth of blood vessels

angiotensin I small polypeptide generated in plasma by the action of the enzyme renin on angiotensinogen; inactive precursor of angiotensin II

angiotensin II hormone formed by action of angiotensin-converting enzyme on angiotensin I; stimulates aldosterone secretion from adrenal cortex, vascular smooth muscle contraction, and possibly thirst

angiotensin-converting enzyme (ACE) enzyme on capillary endothelial cells that catalyzes removal of two amino acids from angiotensin I to form angiotensin II

angiotensinogen (an-gee-oh-ten-SIN-oh-gen) plasma protein precursor of angiotensin I; produced by liver

anion (AN-eye-on) negatively charged ion; *compare* cation

antagonist (muscle) muscle whose action opposes intended movement; (drug) molecule that competes with another for a receptor and binds to the receptor but does not trigger the cell's response

anterior pituitary gland anterior portion of pituitary gland; synthesizes, stores, and releases ACTH, GH, TSH, PRL, FSH, and LH

anterograde (AN-ter-oh-grayd) movement of a substance or action potential in the forward direction from a neuron's dendrites and/or cell body toward the axon terminal

anterolateral pathway ascending neural pathway running in the anterolateral column of the spinal cord white matter; conveys information about pain and temperature

antibody (AN-tih-bah-dee) immunoglobulin secreted by plasma cell; combines with type of antigen that stimulated its production; directs attack against antigen or cell bearing it

antibody-dependent cellular cytotoxicity (ADCC) killing of target cells by toxic chemicals secreted by NK cells; the target cells are linked to the NK cells by antibodies

antibody-mediated response humoral immune response mediated by circulating antibodies; major defense against microbes and toxins in the extracellular fluid

anticodon (an-tie-KOH-don) three-nucleotide sequence in tRNA able to base-pair with complementary codon in mRNA during protein synthesis

antidiuretic hormone (ADH) (an-tye-dye-yoor-ET-ik or an-tee-dye-yoor-ET-ik) *see* vasopressin

antigen (AN-tih-jen) any molecule that stimulates a specific immune response

antigen-binding site one of the two variable "prongs" on an immunoglobulin capable of binding to a specific antigen

antigen presentation process by which an antigen-presenting cell, such as a macrophage, combines proteolytic fragments of a foreign antigen with host cell class II MHC proteins, which are transported to the host cell's surface

antigen-presenting cell (APC) cell that presents antigen, complexed with MHC proteins on its surface, to T cells

antithrombin III a plasma protein activated by heparin that limits clot formation by inactivating thrombin and other clotting factors

antrum (AN-trum) (gastric) lower portion of stomach (that is, region closest to pyloric sphincter); (ovarian) fluid-filled cavity in maturing ovarian follicle

anus lowest opening of the digestive tract through which fecal matter is extruded

aorta (a-OR-tah) largest artery in body; carries blood from left ventricle of heart to thorax and abdomen

aortic arch baroreceptor (a-OR-tik) *see* arterial baroreceptor

aortic body chemoreceptor located near aortic arch; sensitive to arterial blood O_2 content and H^+ concentration

aortic valve valve between left ventricle of heart and aorta

apical membrane the surface of an epithelial cell that faces a lumen, such as that of the intestines

apneustic center (ap-NOOS-tik) area in the lower pons in the brain with input to the medullary inspiratory neurons; helps to terminate inspiration

apoptosis (ay-pop-TOE-sis) programmed cell death that typically occurs during differentiation and development

appendix small fingerlike projection from cecum of large intestine

aprosodia (ay-proh-SO-dee-ah) neurological disorder involving the loss of ability to understand the emotional content of language

aquaporin (ah-qua-PORE-in) protein membrane channel through which water can diffuse

aqueous humor fluid filling the anterior chamber of the eye

arachidonic acid (ah-rak-ah-DON-ik) polyunsaturated fatty acid precursor of eicosanoids

arachnoid mater (ah-RAK-noid) the middle of three membranes (meninges) covering the brain

area postrema a circumventricular organ outside the blood–brain barrier

aromatase enzyme that converts androgens to estrogens; located predominantly in the ovaries, the placenta, the brain, and adipose tissue

arterial baroreceptor neuronal endings sensitive to stretch or distortion produced by arterial blood pressure changes; located in carotid sinus or aortic arch; also called *carotid sinus* and *aortic arch baroreceptor*

arteriole (ahr-TEER-ee-ole) blood vessel between artery and capillary, surrounded by smooth muscle; primary site of vascular resistance

arteriosclerosis (ahr-TEER-ee-oh-sklare-OH-sis) "hardening" of arterial walls that can have different causes, including deposition of collagenous fibers that occurs with aging

artery (AHR-ter-ee) thick-walled elastic vessel that carries blood away from heart to arterioles

ascending limb portion of Henle's loop of renal tubule leading to distal convoluted tubule

ascending pathway neural pathway that goes to the brain; also called *sensory pathway*

aspartate (ah-SPAR-tate) an excitatory neurotransmitter in CNS; ionized form of the amino acid aspartic acid

aspiration inhalation of liquid or a foreign body into the airways

astrocyte a form of glial cell that regulates composition of extracellular fluid around neurons and forms part of the blood–brain barrier

atmospheric pressure (P_{atm}) air pressure surrounding the body (760 mmHg at sea level); also called *barometric pressure*

atom smallest unit of matter that has unique chemical characteristics; has no net charge; combines with other atoms to form chemical substances

atomic mass (also called *atomic weight*) value that indicates an atom's mass relative to mass of other types of atoms based on the assignment of a value of 12 to carbon atom

atomic nucleus dense region, consisting of protons and neutrons, at center of atom

atomic number number of protons in nucleus of atom

ATP *see* adenosine triphosphate

ATP synthase the enzyme complex present in mitochondria responsible for the synthesis of ATP using the energy of an electrochemical gradient for hydrogen ions

atresia degeneration of nondominant follicles in the ovary

atrial natriuretic peptide (ANP) (nay-tree-yor-ET-ik) peptide hormone secreted by cardiac atrial cells in response to atrial distension; causes increased renal sodium excretion

atrioventricular (AV) node (ay-tree-oh-ven-TRIK-you-lar) region at base of right atrium near interventricular septum, containing specialized cardiac muscle cells through which electrical activity must pass to go from atria to ventricles

atrioventricular (AV) valve valve between atrium and ventricle of heart; AV valve on right side of heart is the *tricuspid valve*, and that on left side is the *mitral valve*

atrium (AY-tree-um) chamber of heart that receives blood from veins and passes it on to ventricle on same side of heart

atropine (AT-roh-peen) a drug that specifically blocks the binding of acetylcholine to muscarinic acetylcholine receptors

audition (aw-DIH-shun) sense of hearing

auditory cortex region of cerebral cortex that receives nerve fibers from auditory (hearing) pathways

autocrine substance (AW-toh-crin) chemical messenger secreted into extracellular fluid that acts upon the cell that secreted it; *compare* paracrine substance

automaticity (aw-toh-mah-TISS-ih-tee) capable of spontaneous, rhythmic self-excitation

autonomic ganglion group of neuron cell bodies in the peripheral nervous system

autonomic nervous system (aw-toh-NAHM-ik) component of efferent division of peripheral nervous system that consists of sympathetic and parasympathetic subdivisions; innervates cardiac muscle, smooth muscle, and glands; *compare* somatic nervous system

autoreceptor a receptor on a cell affected by a chemical messenger released from the same cell

autotransfusion shift of fluid from the interstitial space to the blood following a decrease in blood pressure

axo–axonic synapse presynaptic synapse where an axon stimulates the presynaptic terminal of another axon

axon (AX-ahn) extension from neuron cell body; propagates action potentials away from cell body; also called a *nerve fiber*

axon hillock part of the axon nearest the cell body where the action potential begins

axon terminal end of axon; forms synaptic or neuroeffector junction with postjunctional cell

axonal transport process involving intracellular filaments by which materials are moved from one end of axon to other

B

baroreceptor receptor sensitive to pressure and to rate of change in pressure; *see also* arterial baroreceptor, intrarenal baroreceptor

Barr body sex chromatin nuclear mass formed by the nonfunctional X chromosome in female cell nuclei

basal cell cell found within taste buds that can divide and differentiate to replace worn-out taste receptor cells

basal ganglia *see* basal nuclei

basal metabolic rate (BMR) metabolic rate when a person is at mental and physical rest but not sleeping, at comfortable temperature, and has fasted at least 12 h; also called *metabolic cost of living*

basal nuclei nuclei deep in cerebral hemispheres that code and relay information associated with control of body movements; specifically, caudate nucleus, globus pallidus, and putamen; also called *basal ganglia*

base (acid–base) any molecule that can combine with H^+; (nucleotide) molecular ring of carbon and nitrogen that, with a phosphate group and a sugar, constitutes a nucleotide

basement membrane thin layer of extracellular proteinaceous material upon which epithelial and endothelial cells sit

basic electrical rhythm spontaneous depolarization–repolarization cycles of pacemaker cells in longitudinal smooth muscle layer of stomach and intestines; coordinates repetitive muscular activity of GI tract

basilar membrane (BAS-ih-lar) membrane that separates cochlear duct and scala tympani in inner ear; supports organ of Corti

basolateral membrane (bay-zo-LAH-ter-al) sides of epithelial cell other than luminal surface; also called *serosal* or *blood side* of cell

basophil (BAY-zo-fill) polymorphonuclear granulocytic leukocyte whose granules stain with basic dyes; enters tissues and becomes mast cell

B cell (immune system) *see* B lymphocyte; (endocrine cell) *see* beta cell

beta-adrenergic receptor (BAY-ta ad-ren-ER-jik) a type of plasma membrane receptor for epinephrine and norepinephrine; *compare* alpha-adrenergic receptor; also called *beta adrenoceptor*

beta cell insulin-secreting cell in pancreatic islets of Langerhans; also called *B cell*

beta-endorphin putative hormone released from the anterior pituitary gland, believed to play a role in adaptation to stress and pain relief; also acts as a neurotransmitter

beta-lipotropin a protein formed from the proopiomelanocortin precursor in the anterior pituitary gland; further processing results in the putative hormone beta-endorphin

beta oxidation (ox-ih-DAY-shun) series of reactions that generate hydrogen atoms (for oxidative phosphorylation) from breakdown of fatty acids to acetyl CoA

beta pleated sheet a form of secondary protein structure determined by the relative hydrophobicity of amino acid side chains

beta rhythm low, fast EEG oscillations in alert, awake adults who are paying attention to (or thinking hard about) something

bicuspid valve another term for the left atrioventricular valve, also called the *mitral valve*

bile fluid secreted by liver into bile canaliculi; contains bicarbonate, bile salts, cholesterol, lecithin, bile pigments, metabolic end products, and certain trace metals

bile canaliculi (kan-al-IK-you-lee) small ducts adjacent to liver cells into which bile is secreted

bile pigment colored substance, derived from breakdown of heme group of hemoglobin, secreted in bile

bile salt one of a family of steroid molecules produced from cholesterol and secreted in bile by the liver; promotes solubilization and digestion of fat in small intestine

bilirubin (bil-eh-RUE-bin) yellow substance resulting from heme breakdown; excreted in bile as a bile pigment

binding site region of protein to which a specific ligand binds

binocular vision visual perception of overlapping fields from the two eyes

biogenic amine (by-oh-JEN-ik ah-MEEN) one of family of neurotransmitters having basic formula R—NH_2; includes dopamine, norepinephrine, epinephrine, serotonin, and histamine

bipolar cell type of neuron that has one input branch and one output branch

bivalent paired homologous chromosomes, each with two sister chromatids, that are produced during meiosis

bladder urinary bladder; thick-walled sac composed of smooth muscle; stores urine prior to urination

blastocyst (BLAS-toh-cyst) particular early embryonic stage consisting of ball of developing cells surrounding central cavity

block to polyspermy process that prevents more than one sperm cell from fertilizing an ovum

blood pressurized contents of the cardiovascular system composed of a liquid phase (plasma) and cellular phase (red and white blood cells, platelets)

blood–brain barrier group of anatomical barriers and transport systems in brain capillary endothelium that controls kinds of substances entering brain extracellular space from blood and their rates of entry

blood coagulation (koh-ag-you-LAY-shun) blood clotting

blood vessel tubular structures of various sizes that transport blood throughout the body

B lymphocyte lymphocyte that, upon activation, proliferates and differentiates into antibody-secreting plasma cell; also called *B cell*

body (of stomach) middle portion of the stomach; secretes mucus, pepsinogen, and hydrochloric acid

body mass index (BMI) method for assessing degree of obesity; calculated as weight in kilograms divided by square of height in meters

bone age an x-ray determination of the degree of bone development; often used in assessing reasons for unusual stature in children

bone marrow highly vascular, cellular substance in central cavity of some bones; site of erythrocyte, leukocyte, and platelet synthesis

Bowman's capsule blind sac at beginning of tubular component of kidney nephron

Bowman's space fluid-filled space within Bowman's capsule into which protein-free fluid filters from the glomerulus

Boyle's law pressure of a fixed amount of gas in a container is inversely proportional to container's volume

bradykinin (braid-ee-KYE-nin) protein formed by action of the enzyme kallikrein on precursor

brain self-stimulation phenomenon in which animals will press a bar to get electrical stimulation of certain parts of their brains

brainstem brain subdivision consisting of medulla oblongata, pons, and midbrain and located between spinal cord and forebrain

brainstem pathway descending motor pathway whose cells of origin are in the brainstem

Broca's area (BRO-kahz) region of left frontal lobe associated with speech production

bronchiole (BRON-key-ole) small airway distal to bronchus

bronchus (BRON-kus) large-diameter air passage that enters lung; located between trachea and bronchioles

brown adipose tissue type of adipose (fat) tissue found in newborns and in many mammals, with a higher heat-producing capacity than ordinary white fat; may be important in regulating body temperature in extreme conditions

brush border small projections (microvilli) of epithelial cells covering the villi of the small intestine; major absorptive surface of the small intestine

buffer weak acid or base that can exist in undissociated (H buffer) or dissociated (H^+ + buffer) form

bulbourethral gland (bul-bo-you-REETH-ral) one of paired glands in male that secretes fluid components of semen into the urethra

bulk flow movement of fluids or gases from region of higher pressure to one of lower pressure

bundle branches (right and left) pathway composed of cells that rapidly conduct electrical signals down the right and left sides of the interventricular septum; these pathways connect the bundle of His to the Purkinje network

bundle of His (HISS) nervelike structure composed of modified heart cells that carries electrical impulses from the atrioventricular node down the interventricular septum

C

cadherin protein that extends from a cell surface and links up with cadherins from other cells; important in the formation of tissues

calcitonin hormone from the thyroid gland that inhibits bone resorption, although physiological role in humans is minimal

caldesmon (kal-DEZ-mun) protein involved in regulating contraction in some smooth muscles and non-muscle tissue

calmodulin (kal-MADJ-you-lin) intracellular calcium-binding protein that mediates many of calcium's second-messenger functions

calmodulin-dependent protein kinase an intracellular enzyme that, when activated by calcium and the protein calmodulin, phosphorylates many protein substrates within cells; it is a component of many intracellular signaling mechanisms

calorie (cal) unit of heat–energy measurement; amount of heat needed to raise temperature of 1 g of water 1° C; *compare* kilocalorie

calorigenic effect (kah-lor-ih-JEN-ik) increase in metabolic rate caused by epinephrine or thyroid hormones

calyx (KAY-licks) funnel-shaped structure that drains urine into the ureter

cAMP-dependent protein kinase (KYE-nase) *see* cyclic AMP-dependent protein kinase

cAMP phosphodiesterase an enzyme in all cells that converts cAMP into an inactive molecule of AMP

canaliculus (parietal cell) thin canal formed by invagination of the cell membrane

capacitation process by which sperm in female reproductive tract gains ability to fertilize egg; also called *sperm capacitation*

capillary one of the smallest blood vessels across which most exchange of nutrients and wastes occurs with interstitial fluid

capillary filtration coefficient a measure of fluid flow across a capillary wall at a given hydrostatic pressure gradient; determined by porosity of the barrier

capsaicin (kap-SAY-sin) the molecule in chili peppers that causes sensations of heat and pain in the mouth and throat

capsule connective tissue surrounding an organ, such as the kidneys or adrenal glands

carbaminohemoglobin (kar-bah-MEEN-oh-HEE-ma-gloh-bin) compound resulting from combination of carbon dioxide and amino groups in hemoglobin

carbohydrate organic substance composed of carbon, hydrogen, and oxygen; includes mono-, di-, and polysaccharides

carbonic anhydrase (an-HYE-drase) enzyme that catalyzes the reaction $CO_2 + H_2O \leftrightarrow H_2CO_3$

carbon monoxide CO; gas that binds to hemoglobin; decreases blood oxygen-carrying capacity and shifts oxygen–hemoglobin dissociation curve to the left; also acts as an intracellular messenger in neurons

carboxyl group (kar-BOX-il) —COOH; ionizes to carboxyl ion (—COO^-)

carboxypeptidase (kar-box-ee-PEP-tih-dase) enzyme secreted into small intestine by exocrine pancreas as precursor, procarboxypeptidase; breaks peptide bond at carboxyl end of protein

cardiac cycle one contraction–relaxation sequence of heart

cardiac muscle heart muscle

cardiac output (CO) blood volume pumped by each ventricle per minute (not total output pumped by both ventricles)

cardiovascular system heart, blood, and blood vessels

carotid body chemoreceptor near main branching of carotid artery; sensitive to blood O_2 and CO_2 content and H^+ concentration

carotid sinus region of internal carotid artery just above main carotid branching; location of carotid baroreceptors

catabolism (kuh-TAB-oh-lizm) cellular breakdown of organic molecules

catalyst (KAT-ah-list) substance that accelerates chemical reactions but does not itself undergo any net chemical change during the reaction

catch-up growth a period of rapid growth during which a child attains his or her predicted height for a given age after a temporary period of slow growth due to illness or malnourishment

catecholamine (kat-eh-COLE-ah-meen) dopamine, epinephrine, or norepinephrine, all of which have similar chemical structures

cation (KAT-eye-on) ion having net positive charge; *compare* anion

caveolus (kav-ee-OH-lus) small invagination of the plasma membrane that pinches off and forms endocytotic vesicles that deliver their contents directly to the cytosol

cecum (SEE-come) dilated pouch at beginning of large intestine into which the ileum, colon, and appendix open

cell the functional unit of living organisms; four broad classes included epithelial, connective, nervous, and muscle

cell body in cells with long extensions, the part that contains the nucleus

cell differentiation process by which unspecialized cells acquire specialized structural and functional properties

cell organelle (or-guh-NEL) membrane-bound compartment, nonmembranous particle, or filament that performs specialized functions in cell

central chemoreceptor receptor in brainstem medulla oblongata that responds to changes in H^+ concentration of brain extracellular fluid

central command fatigue muscle fatigue due to failure of appropriate regions of cerebral cortex to excite motor neurons

central nervous system (CNS) brain and spinal cord

central sulcus a deep infolding on each half of the brain that separates the parietal and central lobes

central thermoreceptor temperature receptor in hypothalamus, spinal cord, abdominal organ, or other internal location

centriole (SEN-tree-ole) small cytoplasmic body having nine fused sets of microtubules; participates in nuclear and cell division

centrosome region of cell cytoplasm in which microtubule formation and elongation occur, particularly during cell division

cephalic phase (seh-FAL-ik) (of gastrointestinal control) initiation of the neural and hormonal reflexes regulating gastrointestinal functions by stimulation of receptors in head, that is, cephalic receptors—sight, smell, taste, and chewing—as well as by emotional states

cerebellum (ser-ah-BEL-um) brain subdivision lying behind forebrain and above brainstem; plays important role in skeletal muscle movement control

cerebral cortex (SER-ah-brul or sah-REE-brul) cellular layer covering the cerebrum

cerebral hemisphere either left or right half of the cerebral cortex

cerebral ventricle one of four interconnected spaces in the brain; filled with cerebrospinal fluid

cerebrospinal fluid (CSF) (sah-ree-broh-SPY-nal) fluid that fills cerebral ventricles and the subarachnoid space surrounding brain and spinal cord

cerebrum (SER-ah-brum or sah-REE-brum) part of the brain that, with diencephalon, forms the forebrain

cervix (SIR-vix) lower portion of uterus; cervical opening connects uterine and vaginal lumens

cGMP-dependent protein kinase (KYE-nase) enzyme that is activated by cyclic GMP and then phosphorylates specific proteins, thereby altering their activity

cGMP phosphodiesterase an enzyme in cells that converts cGMP into GMP

channel gating process of opening and closing ion channels

chemical element specific type of atom

chemical equilibrium state when rates of forward and reverse components of a chemical reaction are equal, and no net change in reactant or product concentration occurs

chemical specificity *see* specificity

chemical synapse (SIN-aps) synapse at which neurotransmitters released by one neuron diffuse across an extracellular gap to influence a second neuron's activity

chemiosmosis the mechanism by which ATP is formed during oxidative phosphorylation; the movement of protons across mitochondrial inner membranes is coupled with ATP production

chemoattractant any mediator that causes chemotaxis; also called *chemotaxin*

chemokine any cytokine that functions as a chemoattractant

chemoreceptor afferent neuron ending (or cell associated with it) sensitive to concentrations of certain chemicals

chemotaxin (kee-moh-TAX-in) *see* chemoattractant

chemotaxis (kee-moh-TAX-iss) movement of cells, particularly phagocytes, in a specific direction in response to a chemical stimulus

chief cell gastric gland cell that secretes pepsinogen, precursor of pepsin

cholecystokinin (CCK) (koh-lee-sis-toh-KYE-nin) peptide hormone secreted by duodenum that regulates gastric motility and secretion, gallbladder contraction, and pancreatic enzyme secretion; possible satiety signal

cholesterol particular steroid molecule; precursor of steroid hormones and bile salts and a component of plasma membranes

cholinergic (koh-lin-ER-jik) pertaining to acetylcholine; a compound that acts like acetylcholine or a neuron that contains acetylcholine

chondrocyte (KON-droh-site) cell types that form new cartilage

chordae tendineae (KORE-day TEN-den-ay) strong, fibrous cords that connect papillary muscles to the edges of atrioventricular valves; they prevent backward flow of blood during ventricular systole

chorion outermost fetal membrane derived from trophoblast cells; becomes part of the placenta

chorionic villi fingerlike projections of the trophoblast cells extending from the chorion into the endometrium of the uterus

choroid (KORE-oyd) pigmented layer of eye that lies next to retina

choroid plexus highly vascular epithelial structure lining portions of cerebral ventricles; responsible for much of cerebrospinal fluid formation

chromatin (KROM-ih-tin) combination of DNA and nuclear proteins; principal component of chromosomes

chromophore retinal light-sensitive component of a photopigment

chromosome highly coiled, condensed form of chromatin formed in cell nucleus during mitosis and meiosis

chylomicron (kye-loh-MYE-kron) small droplet consisting of lipids and protein released from intestinal epithelial cells into the lacteals during fat absorption

chyme (kyme) solution of partially digested food in stomach and intestinal lumens

chymotrypsin enzyme secreted by exocrine pancreas; breaks certain peptide bonds in proteins and polypeptides

cilia (SIL-ee-ah) hairlike projections from specialized epithelial cells that sweep back and forth in a synchronized way to propel material along epithelial surface

ciliary muscle involved in movement and shape of the lens during accommodation

circadian rhythm (sir-KAY-dee-an) occurring in an approximately 24 h cycle

circular muscle smooth muscle layer in stomach and intestinal walls that has muscle fibers circumferentially oriented around these organs

circulatory system (SIRK-you-la-tor-ee) the heart and system of vessels that deliver blood to all parts of the body

citric acid cycle *see* Krebs cycle

classical complement pathway antibody-dependent system for activating complement; begins with complement molecule Cl

class I MHC proteins form complexes with antigens on all cells except erythrocytes; required for T-cell recognition

class II MHC proteins form complexes with antigens on surface of macrophages, B lymphocytes, and dendritic cells; required for T-cell recognition

clathrin a cytosolic protein that binds to regions of the plasma membrane and helps initiate receptor-mediated endocytosis

clathrin-coated pits aggregations of ligand-bound receptors on a cell membrane that pinches off and is internalized into the cell

clearance volume of plasma from which a particular substance has been completely removed in a given time

cleavage mitotic cell division

clitoris (KLIT-or-iss) small body of erectile tissue in female external genitalia; homologous to penis

clonal deletion destruction by apoptosis in the thymus of those T cells that have receptors capable of binding to self proteins

clonal expansion lymphocyte cell divisions initiated by binding of an antigen to a lymphocyte cell membrane receptor

clonal inactivation process occurring in the periphery (that is, not in the thymus) that causes potentially self-reacting T cells to become nonresponsive

clone one of a set of genetically identical molecules, cells, or organisms

clot solid phase of blood, formed from platelets, trapped blood cells, and a polymer of the protein fibrin

clotting phase transition of blood from a liquid cell suspension into a solid, gel-like mass

cochlea (KOK-lee-ah) inner ear; fluid-filled spiral-shaped compartment that contains cochlear duct

cochlear duct (KOK-lee-er) fluid-filled membranous tube that extends length of inner ear, dividing it into compartments; contains organ of Corti

coding process by which neural signals from sensory receptors are converted into action potentials in the CNS

codon (KOH-don) three-base sequence in mRNA that determines the position of a specific amino acid during protein synthesis or that designates the end of the coded sequence of a protein

coenzyme (koh-EN-zime) organic cofactor; generally serves as a carrier that transfers atoms or small molecular fragments from one reaction to another; is not consumed in the reaction and can be reused

cofactor organic or inorganic substance that binds to a specific region of an enzyme and is necessary for the enzyme's activity

colipase protein secreted by pancreas that binds lipase, bringing it in contact with lipid droplets in the small intestine

collagen fiber (KOLL-ah-jen) strong, fibrous protein that functions as extracellular structural element in connective tissue

collateral branch of a neuron axon

collecting-duct system portion of renal tubules between distal convoluted tubules and renal pelvis; comprises *cortical collecting duct* and *medullary collecting duct*

colloid (KOLL-oid) large molecule, mainly protein, to which capillaries are relatively impermeable; also, part of the inner structure of the thyroid gland

colon (KOH-lun) a portion of the large intestine, specifically the part extending from cecum to rectum

colostrum watery, protein-rich liquid secreted by mother's breasts for first 24 to 48 hours after delivery of baby

commissure (KOM-ih-shur) bundle of nerve fibers linking right and left halves of the brain

common bile duct carries bile from gallbladder to small intestine

competition ability of similar molecules to combine with the same binding site or receptor

complement (KOM-plih-ment) one of a group of plasma proteins that, upon activation, kills microbes directly and facilitates the inflammatory process, including phagocytosis

compliance stretchability; *see also* lung compliance

concentration amount of solute per unit volume of solution

concentric contraction muscle activity that involves shortening of muscle length

conceptus collective term for the fertilized egg and everything derived from it

conducting system network of cardiac muscle fibers specialized to conduct electrical activity between different areas of heart

conducting zone air passages that extend from top of trachea to beginning of respiratory bronchioles and have walls too thick for gas exchange between air and blood

conduction (heat) transfer of thermal energy during collisions of adjacent molecules

cone one of two retinal receptor types for photic energy; gives rise to color vision

conformation three-dimensional shape of a molecule

congenital existing at birth; usually referring to a birth defect

connective tissue one of the four major categories of tissues in the body; major component of extracellular matrices, cartilage, and bone

connective-tissue cell cell specialized to form extracellular elements that connect, anchor, and support body structures

conscious experience things of which a person is aware; thoughts, feelings, perceptions, ideas, and reasoning during any state of consciousness

consolidation process by which short-term memories are converted into long-term memories

contractility (kon-trak-TIL-ity) force of heart contraction that is independent of sarcomere length

contraction operation of the force-generating process in a muscle

contraction time time between beginning of force development and peak twitch tension by the muscle

contralateral on the opposite side of the body

convection (kon-VEK-shun) process by which a fluid or gas next to a warm body is heated by conduction, moves away, and is replaced by colder fluid or gas that in turn follows the same cycle

convergence (neuronal) many presynaptic neurons synapsing upon one postsynaptic neuron; (of eyes) turning of eyes inward (that is, toward nose) to view near objects

cooperativity interaction between functional binding sites in a multimeric protein

core body temperature temperature of inner body

cornea (KOR-nee-ah) transparent structure covering front of eye; forms part of eye's optical system and helps focus an object's image on retina

coronary artery vessel delivering oxygenated blood to the muscular walls of the heart

coronary blood flow blood flow to heart muscle

corpus callosum (KOR-pus kal-LOH-sum) wide band of nerve fibers connecting the two cerebral hemispheres; a brain commissure

corpus luteum (KOR-pus LOO-tee-um) ovarian structure formed from the follicle after ovulation; secretes estrogen and progesterone

cortical association area region of cerebral cortex that receives input from various sensory types, memory stores, and so on, and performs further perceptual processing

cortical collecting duct primary site of sodium ion reabsorption at the distal end of a nephron

cortical (nephron) functional unit of the kidney contained in the renal cortex and with a small (or no) loop of Henle

cortical reaction release of factors by the ovum that hardens the zona pellucida

corticobulbar pathway (kor-tih-koh-BUL-bar) descending pathway having its neuron cell bodies in cerebral cortex; its axons pass without synapsing to region of brainstem motor neurons

corticospinal pathway descending pathway having its neuron cell bodies in cerebral cortex; its axons pass without synapsing to region of spinal motor neurons; also called the *pyramidal tract; compare* brainstem pathway, corticobulbar pathway

corticotropin-releasing hormone (CRH) (kor-tih-koh-TROH-pin) hypophysiotropic peptide hormone that stimulates ACTH (corticotropin) secretion by anterior pituitary gland

cortisol (KOR-tih-sol) main glucocorticoid steroid hormone secreted by adrenal cortex; regulates various aspects of organic metabolism

costameres clusters of structural proteins linking Z disks of sarcomeres to the sarcolemma of striated muscle cells

costimulus nonspecific interactions between proteins on the surface of antigen-presenting cells and helper T cells; required for T-cell activation

cotransmitter chemical messenger released with a neurotransmitter from synapse or neuroeffector junction

cotransport form of secondary active transport in which net movement of actively transported substance and "downhill" movement of molecule supplying the energy are in the same direction

countercurrent multiplier system mechanism associated with loops of Henle that creates a region having high interstitial fluid osmolarity in renal medulla

countertransport form of secondary active transport in which net movement of actively transported molecule is in direction opposite "downhill" movement of molecule supplying the energy

covalent bond (koh-VAY-lent) chemical bond between two atoms in which each atom shares one of its electrons with the other

covalent modulation alteration of a protein's shape, and therefore its function, by the covalent binding of various chemical groups to it

cranial nerve one of 24 peripheral nerves (12 pairs) that join brainstem or forebrain with structures outside CNS

C-reactive protein an acute phase protein that functions as a nonspecific opsonin

creatine phosphate (CP) (KREE-ah-tin) molecule that transfers phosphate and energy to ADP to generate ATP

creatinine (kree-AT-ih-nin) waste product derived from muscle creatine

creatinine clearance (C_{Cr}) plasma volume from which creatinine is removed by the kidneys per unit time; approximates glomerular filtration rate

cristae (mitochondrial) the inner membrane of mitochondria, which may assume sheetlike or tubular appearances; site containing cytochrome P450 enzymes involved in steroid hormone production

cross-bridge in muscle, myosin projection extending from thick filament and capable of exerting force on thin filament, causing the filaments to slide past each other

cross-bridge cycle sequence of events between binding of a cross-bridge to actin, its release, and reattachment during muscle contraction

crossed-extensor reflex increased activation of extensor muscles contralateral to limb flexion

crossing-over process in which segments of maternal and paternal chromosomes exchange with each other during chromosomal pairing in meiosis

crystalloid low-molecular-weight solute in plasma

C3b a complement molecule that attaches phagocytes to microbes; also amplifies complement cascade

cumulus oophorous layers of granulosa cells that surround the egg within the dominant follicle

cupula a gelatinous mass within the semicircular canals that contains stereocilia and responds to head movement

current movement of electrical charge; in biological systems, this is achieved by ion movement

cusp a flap or "leaflet" of a heart valve

cyclic AMP (cAMP) cyclic 3′,5′-adenosine monophosphate; cyclic nucleotide that serves as a second messenger for many "first" chemical messengers

cyclic AMP-dependent protein kinase (KYE-nase) enzyme that is activated by cyclic AMP and then phosphorylates specific proteins, thereby altering their activity; also called *protein kinase A*

cyclic endoperoxide eicosanoid formed from arachidonic acid by cyclooxygenase

cyclic GMP (cGMP) cyclic 3′,5′-guanosine monophosphate; cyclic nucleotide that acts as second messenger in some cells

cyclooxygenase (COX) (sye-klo-OX-ah-jen-ase) enzyme that acts on arachidonic acid and initiates production of cyclic endoperoxides, prostaglandins, and thromboxanes

cystic fibrosis transmembrane conductance regulator (CFTR) epithelial chloride channel; mutations in the *CFTR* gene can cause cystic fibrosis

cytochrome (SYE-toe-krom) one of a series of enzymes that couples energy to ATP formation during oxidative phosphorylation

cytokine (SYE-toh-kine) general term for protein extracellular messengers that regulate immune responses; secreted by macrophages, monocytes, lymphocytes, neutrophils, and several nonimmune cell types

cytoplasm (SYE-toh-plasm) region of cell interior outside the nucleus

cytosine (C) (SYE-toh-seen) pyrimidine base in DNA and RNA

cytoskeleton cytoplasmic filamentous network associated with cell shape and movement

cytosol (SYE-toh-sol) intracellular fluid that surrounds cell organelles and nucleus

cytotoxic T cell (SYE-toh-TOX-ik) T lymphocyte that, upon activation by specific antigen, directly attacks a cell bearing that type of antigen and destroys it; major killer of virus-infected and cancer cells

D

Dalton's law pressure exerted by each gas in a mixture of gases is independent of the pressure exerted by the other gases

dark adaptation process by which photoreceptors in the retina adjust to darkness

declarative memory memories of facts and events

decremental decreasing in amplitude

decussation (dek-uh-SAY-shun) crossover of neuronal pathways from one side of the body to the other

defecation (def-ih-KAY-shun) expulsion of feces from rectum

defecation reflex urge to extrude feces caused by sudden distension of the walls of the rectum

defensins (dee-FENS-ins) small peptides released by immune cells involved in destroying bacteria, fungi, and some viruses

dehydration type of chemical reaction in which two smaller molecules, such as amino acids, are joined to form a larger molecule; a single molecule of water is lost in the process

delta rhythm slow-wave, high-amplitude EEG waves associated with the deepest stages of slow-wave sleep

dendrite (DEN-drite) highly branched extension of neuron cell body; receives synaptic input from other neurons

dendritic cell a type of immune cell with phagocytic and antigen-presenting properties

dendritic spine a small protrusion from a dendrite that receives a synapse from an axon

dense body cytoplasmic structure to which thin filaments of a smooth muscle fiber are anchored

deoxyhemoglobin (Hb) (dee-ox-see-HEE-moh-gloh-bin) hemoglobin not combined with oxygen; reduced hemoglobin

deoxyribonucleic acid (DNA) (dee-ox-see-rye-boh-noo-KLAY-ik) nucleic acid that stores and transmits genetic information; consists of double strand of nucleotide subunits that contain deoxyribose

deoxyribose a ribose molecule with a single hydroxyl group removed; a component of DNA

depolarize to change membrane potential value toward zero so that cell interior becomes less negative than resting level

descending limb (of Henle's loop) segment of renal tubule into which proximal tubule drains

descending pathway neural pathways that go from the brain down to the spinal cord

desmosome (DEZ-moh-some) junction that holds two cells together; consists of plasma membranes of adjacent cells linked by fibers, yet separated by a 20 nm extracellular space filled with a cementing substance

detrusor muscle (duh-TRUSS-or) the smooth muscle that forms the wall of the urinary bladder

diacylglycerol (DAG) (dye-ace-ul-GLIS-er-ol) second messenger that activates protein kinase C, which then phosphorylates a large number of other proteins

diapedesis (dye-app-uh-DEE-suhs) passage of leukocytes out of the blood and into the surrounding tissue

diaphragm (DYE-ah-fram) dome-shaped skeletal muscle sheet that separates the abdominal and thoracic cavities; principal muscle of respiration

diastole (dye-ASS-toh-lee) period of cardiac cycle when ventricles are relaxing

diastolic pressure (DP) (dye-ah-STAL-ik) minimum blood pressure during cardiac cycle

dicrotic notch deflection of the arterial pressure wave associated with closing of the semilunar valve

diencephalon (dye-en-SEF-ah-lon) core of anterior part of brain; lies beneath cerebral hemispheres and contains *thalamus* and *hypothalamus*

diet-induced thermogenesis the creation of heat within the body following a meal, particularly one rich in protein; at least part of the heat is generated secondarily to the increased activity of the gastrointestinal tract

diffusion (dif-FU-shun) movement of molecules from one location to another because of random thermal molecular motion; net diffusion always occurs from a region of higher concentration to a region of lower concentration; *see* simple diffusion, facilitated diffusion

diffusion equilibrium state during which diffusion fluxes in opposite directions are equal; that is, the net flux equals zero

digestion process of breaking down large particles and high-molecular-weight substances into small molecules

digestive system the gastrointestinal tract and its accessory organs

dihydropyridine (DHP) receptor (dye-hydro-PEER-a-deen) nonconducting calcium channels in the T-tubule membranes of skeletal muscle cells, which act as voltage sensors in excitation–contraction coupling

dihydrotestosterone (DHT) (dye-hy-droh-tes-TOS-ter-own) steroid formed by enzyme-mediated alteration of testosterone; active form of testosterone in certain of its target cells

1,25-dihydroxyvitamin D [1,25-$(OH)_2$D] (1-25-dye-hy-DROX-ee-vy-tah-min DEE) hormone that is formed by kidneys and is the active form of vitamin D

diiodotyrosine (DIT) a doubly iodinated tyrosine molecule that is an intermediate in the formation of thyroid hormones

2,3-diphosphoglycerate (DPG) (2-3-dye-fos-foh-GLISS-er-ate) substance produced by erythrocytes during glycolysis; binds reversibly to hemoglobin, causing it to release oxygen

disaccharide (dye-SAK-er-ide) carbohydrate molecule composed of two monosaccharides

disc layer of membranes in outer segment of photoreceptor; contains photopigments

distal convoluted tubule portion of kidney tubule between loop of Henle and collecting-duct system

disulfide bond R—S—S—R bonds in a protein

diuresis (dye-uh-REE-sis) increased urine excretion

diuretic (dye-uh-RET-ik) substance that inhibits fluid reabsorption in renal tubule, thereby increasing urine excretion

divergence (dye-VER-gence) (neuronal) one presynaptic neuron synapsing upon many postsynaptic neurons; (of eyes) turning of eyes outward to view distant objects

dominant follicle most mature developing follicle in the ovary from which the mature egg is ovulated

dopamine (DA) (DOPE-ah-meen) biogenic amine (catecholamine) neurotransmitter and hormone; precursor of epinephrine and norepinephrine

dorsal column pathway ascending pathway for somatosensory information; runs through dorsal area of spinal white matter

dorsal horn region of gray matter in the spinal cord that receives sensory input and connects with motor neurons in ventral horn

dorsal respiratory group (DRG) neurons in the medullary respiratory center that fire during inspiration

dorsal root group of afferent nerve fibers that enters dorsal region of spinal cord

dorsal root ganglion group of sensory neuron cell bodies that have axons projecting to the dorsal horn of the spinal cord

down-regulation decrease in number of target-cell receptors for a given messenger in response to a chronic high concentration of that messenger; *compare* up-regulation

dual innervation (in-ner-VAY-shun) innervation of an organ or gland by both sympathetic and parasympathetic nerve fibers

duodenum (doo-oh-DEE-num or doo-ODD-en-um) first portion of small intestine (between stomach and jejunum)

dura mater thick, outermost membrane (meninges) covering the brain

dynamic constancy a way of describing homeostasis that includes the idea that a variable such as blood glucose may vary in the short term but is stable and predictable when averaged over the long term

dynein (DYE-neen) motor protein that uses the energy from ATP to transport attached cellular cargo molecules along microtubules

dynorphin (dye-NOR-fin) one of a group of endogenous opioid peptides that act as neuromodulators in the brain

dystrophin protein in muscle cells that links actin to proteins embedded in sarcolemma; stabilizes muscle cells during contractions

E

eccentric contraction muscle activity that is accompanied by lengthening of the muscle generally by an external load that exceeds muscle force

ECG lead combination of a reference electrode (designated negative) and a recording electrode (designated positive); this combination is placed on the surface of the body and provides a "view" of the electrical activity of the heart

edema (ed-DEE-mah) accumulation of excess fluid in interstitial space

EEG arousal transformation of EEG pattern from alpha to beta rhythm during increased levels of attention

effector (ee-FECK-tor) cell or cell collection whose change in activity constitutes the response in a control system

efferent arteriole renal vessel that conveys blood from glomerulus to peritubular capillaries

efferent division (of the peripheral nervous system) neurons in the peripheral nervous system that project out of the central nervous system

efferent neuron neuron that carries information away from CNS

efferent pathway component of reflex arc that transmits information from integrating center to effector

egg female germ cell at any of its stages of development

eicosanoid (eye-KOH-sah-noid) general term for modified fatty acids that are products of arachidonic acid metabolism (cyclic endoperoxides, prostaglandins, thromboxanes, and leukotrienes); function as paracrine or autocrine substances

ejaculation (ee-jak-you-LAY-shun) discharge of semen from penis

ejaculatory duct (ee-JAK-you-lah-tory) continuation of vas deferens after it is joined by seminal vesicle duct; joins urethra in prostate gland

ejection fraction (EF) the ratio of stroke volume to end-diastolic volume; EF = SV/EDV

elastic recoil tendency of an elastic structure to oppose stretching or distortion

elastin fiber a protein with elastic or springlike properties; found in large arteries and in the airways

electrical potential (*E*) (or electrical potential difference) *see* potential

electrical synapse (SIN-aps) synapse at which local currents resulting from electrical activity flow between two neurons through gap junctions joining them

electrocardiogram (ECG, *also abbreviated* EKG) (ee-lek-troh-KARD-ee-oh-gram) recording at skin surface of the electrical currents generated by cardiac muscle action potentials

electrochemical gradient the driving force across a plasma membrane that dictates whether an ion will move into or out of a cell; established by both the concentration difference and the electrical charge difference between the cytosolic and extracellular surfaces of the membrane

electroencephalogram (EEG) (eh-lek-troh-en-SEF-ah-loh-gram) recording of brain electrical activity from scalp

electrogenic pump (elec-troh-JEN-ik) active-transport system that directly separates electrical charge, thereby producing a potential difference

electrolyte (ee-LEK-troh-lite) substance that dissociates into ions when in aqueous solution

electron (ee-LEK-tron) subatomic particle that carries one unit of negative charge

electron-transport chain a series of metal-containing proteins within mitochondria that participate in the flow of electrons from proteins to molecular oxygen; they are key components of the energy-producing processes in all cells

electronegativity measure of an atom's ability to attract electrons in a covalent bond

embryo (EM-bree-oh) organism during early stages of development; in human beings, the first 2 months of intrauterine life

emission (ee-MISH-un) movement of male genital duct contents into urethra prior to ejaculation

emotional behavior outward expression and display of inner emotions

emulsification (eh-mul-suh-fah-KAY-shun) division of large lipid droplets into very small droplets that are prevented from coalescing through the action of amphipathic substances

end-diastolic volume (EDV) (dye-ah-STAH-lik) amount of blood in ventricle just prior to systole

endocrine gland (EN-doh-krin) group of epithelial cells that secrete into the extracellular space hormones that then diffuse into bloodstream; also called a *ductless gland*

endocrine system all the body's hormone-secreting glands

endocytosis (en-doh-sye-TOH-sis) process in which plasma membrane folds into the cell, forming small pockets that pinch off to produce intracellular, membrane-bound vesicles; *see also* phagocytosis

endogenous opioid (en-DAHJ-en-us OH-pee-oid) an example of certain neuropeptides—endorphin, dynorphin, or enkephalin

endogenous pyrogen (EP) (en-DAHJ-en-us PY-roh-jen) any of the cytokines (including interleukin 1 and interleukin 6) that act physiologically in the brain to cause fever

endolymph extracellular fluid found in the cochlea and vestibular apparatus

endometrium (en-doh-MEE-tree-um) glandular epithelium lining uterine cavity

endoplasmic reticulum (en-doh-PLAS-mik reh-TIK-you-lum) cell organelle that consists of interconnected network of membrane-bound branched tubules and flattened sacs; two types are distinguished: *rough*, with ribosomes attached, and *smooth*, which is smooth-surfaced (does not contain ribosomes)

endorphins (en-DOR-fins) endogenous opioid peptide neurotransmitters released during exercise and other active neurological states; involved in inhibition of pain pathways and creation of positive mood

endosome (EN-doh-some) intracellular vesicles and tubular elements between Golgi apparatus and plasma membrane; sorts and distributes vesicles during endocytosis and exocytosis

endothelial cell *see* endothelium

endothelin-1 (ET-1) (en-doh-THEE-lin) one member of a family of peptides secreted by many tissues that can act as a paracrine or hormonal signal; one major action is vasoconstriction

endothelium (en-doh-THEE-lee-um) thin layer of cells that lines heart cavities and blood vessels

endothelium-derived relaxing factor (EDRF) nitric oxide and possibly other substances; secreted by vascular endothelium, it relaxes vascular smooth muscle and causes arteriolar dilation

endotherm an animal that generates its own internal body heat without having to rely on the environment

end-plate potential (EPP) depolarization of motor end plate of skeletal muscle fiber in response to acetylcholine; initiates action potential in muscle plasma membrane

end-product inhibition inhibition of a metabolic pathway by final product's action upon allosteric site on an enzyme (usually the rate-limiting enzyme) in the pathway

end-systolic volume (ESV) (sis-TAH-lik) amount of blood remaining in ventricle after ejection

enkephalin (en-KEF-ah-lin) peptide neurotransmitter at some synapses activated by opiate drugs; an endogenous opioid

enteric nervous system (en-TAIR-ik) neural network residing in and innervating walls of gastrointestinal tract

enterochromaffin-like (ECL) cell histamine-secreting cell of the stomach

enteroendocrine cell cell located in the gastric gland in the stomach; secretes gastrin

enterogastrones (en-ter-oh-GAS-trones) collective term for hormones released by intestinal tract; inhibit stomach activity

enterohepatic circulation (en-ter-oh-hih-PAT-ik) reabsorption of bile salts (and other substances) from intestines, passage to liver (via hepatic portal vein), and secretion back to intestines (via bile)

enterokinase (en-ter-oh-KYE-nase) enzyme in luminal plasma membrane of intestinal epithelial cells; converts pancreatic trypsinogen to trypsin

entrainment (en-TRAIN-ment) adjusting biological rhythm to environmental cues

enzyme (EN-zime) protein catalyst that accelerates specific chemical reactions but does not itself undergo net chemical change during the reaction

enzyme activity rate at which enzyme converts reactant to product; may be measure of the properties of enzyme's active site as altered by allosteric or covalent modulation; affects rate of enzyme-mediated reaction

eosinophil (ee-oh-SIN-oh-fil) polymorphonuclear granulocytic leukocyte whose granules take up red dye eosin; involved in parasite destruction and allergic responses

ependymal cell (ep-END-ih-mel) type of glial cell that lines internal cavities of the brain and produces cerebrospinal fluid

epicardium (epp-ee-KAR-dee-um) layer of connective tissue closely affixed to outer surface of the heart

epididymis (ep-ih-DID-ih-mus) portion of male reproductive duct system located between seminiferous tubules and vas deferens

epiglottis (ep-ih-GLOT-iss) thin cartilage flap that folds down, covering trachea, during swallowing

epinephrine (ep-ih-NEF-rin) amine hormone secreted by adrenal medulla and involved in regulation of organic metabolism; a biogenic amine (catecholamine) neurotransmitter; also called *adrenaline*

epiphyseal closure (ep-ih-FIZ-ee-al) conversion of epiphyseal growth plate to bone

epiphyseal growth plate actively proliferating cartilage near bone ends; region of bone growth

epiphysis (eh-PIF-ih-sis) end of long bone

epithalamus a small portion of the dorsal posterior diencephalon containing the pineal gland

epithelial cell (ep-ih-THEE-lee-al) cell at surface of body or hollow organ; specialized to secrete or absorb ions and organic molecules; with other epithelial cells, forms an *epithelium*

epithelial tissue one of the four major tissue types in the body, comprised of aggregates of epithelial cells

epithelium (ep-ih-THEE-lee-um) tissue that covers all body surfaces, lines all body cavities, and forms most glands

epitope (EP-ih-tope) antigenic portion of a molecule complexed to the MHC protein and presented to the T cell; also called an *antigenic determinant*

equilibrium (ee-quah-LIB-ree-um) no net change occurs in a system; requires no energy

equilibrium potential voltage gradient across a membrane that is equal in force but opposite in direction to concentration force affecting a given ion species

erection penis or clitoris becoming stiff due to vascular congestion

erythrocyte (eh-RITH-roh-site) red blood cell

erythropoiesis (eh-rith-roh-poy-EE-sis) erythrocyte production

erythropoietin (eh-rith-roh-POY-ih-tin) peptide hormone secreted mainly by kidney cells; stimulates red blood cell production; one of the hematopoietic growth factors

esophagus (eh-SOF-uh-gus) portion of digestive tract that connects throat (pharynx) and stomach

essential amino acid amino acid that cannot be formed by the body at all (or at a rate adequate to meet metabolic requirements) and so must be obtained from diet

essential nutrient substance required for normal or optimal body function but synthesized by the body either not at all or in amounts inadequate to prevent disease

estradiol (es-tra-DYE-ol) steroid hormone of estrogen family; major female sex hormone

estriol (ES-tree-ol) estrogen present in pregnancy; produced primarily by the placenta

estrogen (ES-troh-jen) group of steroid hormones that have effects similar to estradiol on female reproductive tract

estrogen priming increase in responsiveness to progesterone caused by prior exposure to estrogen (e.g., in the uterus)

estrone estrogen that is less prominent than estradiol

eukaryotic cell cell containing a membrane-enclosed nucleus with genetic material; plant and animal cells

eustachian tube (yoo-STAY-shee-an) duct connecting the middle ear with the nasopharynx

evaporation the loss of body water by perspiration, resulting in cooling

excitability ability to produce electrical signals

excitable membrane membrane capable of producing action potentials

excitation–contraction coupling in muscle fibers, mechanism linking plasma membrane stimulation with cross-bridge force generation

excitatory amino acid amino acid that acts as an excitatory (depolarizing) neurotransmitter in the nervous system

excitatory postsynaptic potential (EPSP) (post-sin-NAP-tic) depolarizing graded potential in postsynaptic neuron in response to activation of excitatory synapse

excitatory synapse (SIN-aps) synapse that, when activated, increases likelihood that postsynaptic neuron will undergo action potentials or increases frequency of existing action potentials

excitotoxicity (eggs-SYE-toe-tocks-ih-city) spreading damage to brain cells due to release of glutamate from ruptured neurons

exocrine gland (EX-oh-krin) cluster of epithelial cells specialized for secretion and having ducts that lead to an epithelial surface

exocytosis (ex-oh-sye-TOE-sis) process in which intracellular vesicle fuses with plasma membrane, the vesicle opens, and its contents are liberated into the extracellular fluid

exon (EX-on) DNA gene region containing code words for a part of the amino acid sequence of a protein

expiration (ex-pur-AY-shun) movement of air out of lungs

expiratory reserve volume (ERV) (ex-PYE-ruh-tor-ee) volume of air that can be exhaled by maximal contraction of expiratory muscles after normal resting expiration

extension straightening a joint

external anal sphincter ring of skeletal muscle around lower end of rectum

external auditory canal outer canal of the ear between the pinna and the tympanic membrane

external environment environment surrounding external surface of an organism

external urethral sphincter ring of skeletal muscle that surrounds the urethra at base of bladder

external work movement of external objects by skeletal muscle contraction

extracellular fluid fluid outside cell; interstitial fluid and plasma

extracellular matrix (MAY-trix) a complex consisting of a mixture of proteins (and, in some cases, minerals) interspersed with extracellular fluid

extrafusal fiber primary muscle fiber in skeletal muscle, as opposed to modified (intrafusal) fiber in muscle spindle

extrapyramidal system *see* brainstem pathway

extrinsic pathway formation of fibrin clots by pathway using tissue factor on cells in interstitium; once activated, it also recruits the intrinsic clotting pathway beyond factor XII

F

facilitated diffusion (fah-SIL-ih-tay-ted) system using a transporter to move molecules from high to low concentration across a membrane; energy not required

F-actin the polymerized form of actin found in actin filaments

FAD flavin adenine dinucleotide, a coenzyme derived from the B-vitamin riboflavin that participates in transfer of hydrogen atoms during metabolism

fallopian tube one of two tubes that carries egg from ovary to uterus

fast fiber skeletal muscle fiber that contains myosin having high ATPase activity

fast-glycolytic fiber type of skeletal muscle fiber that has high intrinsic contraction speed and abundant capacity for production of ATP by anaerobic glycolysis

fast-oxidative-glycolytic fiber type of skeletal muscle fiber that has high intrinsic contraction speed and abundant capacity for production of ATP by aerobic oxidative phosphorylation

fat-soluble vitamin *see* vitamin

fatty acid carbon chain with carboxyl group at one end through which chain can be linked to glycerol to form triglyceride; *see also* polyunsaturated fatty acid, saturated fatty acid, unsaturated fatty acid

Fc "stem" part of antibody

feces (FEE-sees) material expelled from large intestine during defecation

feedforward aspect of some control systems that allows system to anticipate changes in a regulated variable

female external genitalia mons pubis, labia majora, labia minora, clitoris, outer vagina, and its glands

female internal genitalia (jen-ih-TALE-ee-ah) ovaries, uterine tubes, uterus, and vagina

ferritin (FERR-ih-tin) iron-binding protein that stores iron in body

fertilization union of sperm and egg

fetal hemoglobin oxygen-carrying molecule with high oxygen affinity

fetus (FEE-tus) human being from third month of intrauterine life until birth

fiber *see* muscle fiber, nerve fiber

fibrin (FYE-brin) protein polymer resulting from enzymatic cleavage of fibrinogen; can turn blood into gel (clot)

fibrinogen (fye-BRIN-oh-jen) plasma protein precursor of fibrin

fibrinolytic system (fye-brin-oh-LIT-ik) cascade of plasma enzymes that breaks down clots; also called *thrombolytic system*

fight-or-flight response activation of sympathetic nervous system during stress

filtered load amount of any substance filtered from renal glomerular capillaries into Bowman's capsule

fimbria (FIM-bree-ah) opening of the fallopian tube; it has fingerlike projections lined with ciliated epithelium through which the ovulated egg passes into the fallopian tube

first messenger extracellular chemical messenger such as a hormone

first polar body non-functional structure containing one of the two nuclei resulting from the first meiotic division of a primary oocyte in the ovary

5-α-reductase intracellular enzyme that converts testosterone to dihydrotestosterone

flatus (FLAY-tus) intestinal gas expelled through anus

flexion (FLEK-shun) bending a joint

flow autoregulation ability of individual arterioles to alter their resistance in response to changing blood pressure so that relatively constant blood flow is maintained

fluid endocytosis invagination of a plasma membrane by which a cell can engulf extracellular fluid

fluid-mosaic model (moh-ZAY-ik) cell membrane structure consists of proteins embedded in bimolecular lipid that has the physical properties of a fluid, allowing membrane proteins to move laterally within it

flux amount of a substance crossing a surface in a unit of time; *see also* net flux

folic acid (FOH-lik) vitamin of B-complex group; essential for formation of nucleotide thiamine

follicle (FOL-ih-kel) egg and its encasing follicular, granulosa, and theca cells at all stages prior to ovulation; also called *ovarian follicle*

follicle-stimulating hormone (FSH) protein hormone secreted by anterior pituitary gland in males and females that acts on gonads; a gonadotropin

follicular phase (fuh-LIK-you-lar) that portion of menstrual cycle during which follicle and egg develop to maturity prior to ovulation

foot process large extension of sarcoplasmic reticulum calcium channels (ryanodine receptors), which connect them to the T-tubule membrane and mediate excitation–contraction coupling in skeletal muscle; also known as *junctional feet*

forebrain large, anterior brain subdivision consisting of right and left cerebral hemispheres (the cerebrum) and diencephalon

formed element solid phase of blood, including cells (erythrocytes and leukocytes) and cell fragments (platelets)

fovea centralis (FOH-vee-ah) area near center of retina where cones are most concentrated; gives rise to most acute vision

Frank–Starling mechanism the relationship between stroke volume and end-diastolic volume such that stroke volume increases as end-diastolic volume increases; also called *Starling's law of the heart*

fraternal twins dizygotic twins that occur when two eggs are fertilized

free radical atom that has an unpaired electron in its outermost orbital; molecule containing such an atom

free-running rhythm cyclical activity driven by biological clock in absence of environmental cues

frequency number of times an event occurs per unit time

frontal lobe region of anterior cerebral cortex where motor areas, Broca's speech center, and some association cortex are located

F-type channel the "funny" sodium-conducting channel mainly responsible for the inward flow of positive current in autorhythmic cardiac cells

functional residual capacity lung volume after relaxed expiration

functional site binding site on allosteric protein that, when activated, carries out protein's physiological function; also called *active site*

functional unit one of a number of small structures within an organ that act similarly to carry out an organ's function; for example, nephrons are the functional units of the kidneys

fundus upper portion of the stomach; secretes mucus, pepsinogen, and hydrochloric acid

fused tetanus (TET-ah-nuss) skeletal muscle activation in which action potential frequency is sufficiently high to cause a smooth, sustained, maximal strength contraction

fused-vesicle channel endocytotic or exocytotic vesicles that have fused to form a continuous water-filled channel through capillary endothelial cell

G

GABA (gamma-aminobutyric acid) an amino acid neurotransmitter commonly occurring at inhibitory synapses in the central nervous system

G-actin a monomer of actin that polymerizes to form F-actin, that makes up actin filaments

gallbladder small sac under the liver; concentrates bile and stores it between meals; contraction of gallbladder ejects bile, which eventually flows into small intestine

gamete (GAM-eet) germ cell or reproductive cell; sperm in male and egg in female

gametogenesis (gah-mee-toh-JEN-ih-sis) gamete production

gamma globulin immunoglobulin G (IgG), most abundant class of plasma antibodies

gamma motor neuron small motor neuron that controls intrafusal muscle fibers in muscle spindles

gamma rhythm high-frequency (30–100 Hz) pattern detected on electroencephalogram associated with processing sensory inputs and other specific cognitive tasks

ganglion (GANG-lee-on) (plural, *ganglia*) generally reserved for cluster of neuron cell bodies outside CNS

ganglion cell retinal neuron that is postsynaptic to bipolar cells; axons of ganglion cells form optic nerves

gap junction protein channels linking cytosol of adjacent cells; allows ions and small molecules to flow between cytosols of the connected cells

gastric (GAS-trik) pertaining to the stomach

gastric phase (of gastrointestinal control) initiation of neural and hormonal gastrointestinal reflexes by stimulation of stomach wall

gastrin (GAS-trin) peptide hormone secreted by antral region of stomach; stimulates gastric acid secretion

gastroileal reflex (gas-troh-IL-ee-al) increase in contractions of ileum during gastric emptying

gastrointestinal (GI) tract mouth, pharynx, esophagus, stomach, small and large intestines, and anus

gene unit of hereditary information; portion of DNA containing information required to determine a protein's amino acid sequence

genome complete set of an organism's genes

genotype the set of alleles present in an individual; determines genetic sex (XX, female; XY, male)

germ cell cell that gives rise to male or female gametes (sperm and eggs)

gestation (jess-TAY-shun) length of time of intrauterine fetal development (usually about 9 months in humans)

ghrelin (GREH-lin) hormone released from cells of the stomach; stimulates hunger

glial cell (GLEE-al) nonneuronal cell in CNS; helps regulate extracellular environment of CNS; also called *neuroglia*

globin (GLOH-bin) collective term for the four polypeptide chains of the hemoglobin molecule

globulin (GLOB-you-lin) one of a family of proteins found in blood plasma

glomerular capillary very small blood vessel within the glomerulus of the kidney through which plasma is filtered

glomerular filtrate ultrafiltrate of plasma produced in the glomerulus that is usually free of cells and large proteins

glomerular filtration process by which components of plasma in the glomerular capillary are passed to the Bowman's space of the glomerulus; process is governed by net glomerular filtration pressure

glomerular filtration rate (GFR) volume of fluid filtered from renal glomerular capillaries into Bowman's capsule per unit time

glomerulus (gloh-MER-you-lus) tufts of glomerular capillaries at beginning of kidney nephron

glottis opening between vocal cords through which air passes, and surrounding area

glucagon (GLOO-kah-gahn) peptide hormone secreted by alpha cells of pancreatic islets of Langerhans; leads to rise in plasma glucose

glucagon-like peptide 1 (GLP-1) an incretin hormone secreted by cells of the small intestine following a meal; enhances the insulin response to glucose

glucocorticoid (gloo-koh-KOR-tih-koid) steroid hormone produced by adrenal cortex and having major effects on nutrient metabolism and the body's response to stress

gluconeogenesis (gloo-koh-nee-oh-JEN-ih-sis) formation of glucose by the liver or kidneys from pyruvate, lactate, glycerol, or amino acids

glucose major monosaccharide in the body; a six-carbon sugar, $C_6H_{12}O_6$; also called *blood sugar*

glucose-counterregulatory control neural or hormonal factors that oppose insulin's actions; includes glucagon, epinephrine, sympathetic nerves to liver and adipose tissue, cortisol, and growth hormone

glucose-dependent insulinotropic peptide (GIP) intestinal hormone; stimulates insulin secretion in response to glucose and fat in small intestine

glucose sparing switch from glucose to fat utilization by most cells during postabsorptive state

glutamate (GLU-tah-mate) anion formed from the amino acid glutamic acid; a major excitatory CNS neurotransmitter

gluten a collective term for several proteins found in wheat and other foods; some individuals develop autoimmunity to these proteins

glycerol (GLISS-er-ol) three-carbon carbohydrate; forms backbone of triglyceride

glycine (GLYE-seen) an amino acid; a neurotransmitter at some inhibitory synapses in CNS

glycocalyx (glye-koh-KAY-lix) fuzzy coating on extracellular surface of plasma membrane; consists of short, branched carbohydrate chains

glycogen (GLYE-koh-jen) highly branched polysaccharide composed of glucose subunits; major carbohydrate storage form in body

glycogenolysis (glye-koh-jen-NOL-ih-sis) glycogen breakdown to glucose

glycogen phosphorylase intracellular enzyme required to begin the process of breaking down glycogen into glucose; inhibited by insulin

glycogen synthase intracellular enzyme required to synthesize glycogen; stimulated by insulin

glycolysis (glye-KOL-ih-sis) metabolic pathway that breaks down glucose to two molecules of pyruvate (aerobically) or two molecules of lactate (anaerobically)

glycolytic fiber skeletal muscle fiber that has a high concentration of glycolytic enzymes and large glycogen stores; white muscle fiber

glycoprotein protein containing covalently linked carbohydrates

Goldman-Hodgkin-Katz (GHK) equation calculation for electrochemical equilibrium when a membrane is permeable to more than one ion

Golgi apparatus (GOAL-gee) cell organelle consisting of flattened membranous sacs; usually near nucleus; processes newly synthesized proteins for secretion or distribution to other organelles

Golgi tendon organ tension-sensitive mechanoreceptor ending of afferent nerve fiber; wrapped around collagen bundles in tendon

gonad (GOH-nad) gamete-producing reproductive organ—testes in male and ovaries in female

gonadal steroid hormone synthesized in the testes (testosterone) and ovaries (estrogen and progesterone)

gonadotropic hormone *see gonadotropin*

gonadotropin glycoprotein hormone secreted by anterior pituitary gland (LH, FSH) and placenta (hCG) that influence gonadal function

gonadotropin-releasing hormone (GnRH) hypophysiotropic hormone that stimulates LH and FSH secretion by anterior pituitary gland in males and females

G protein one protein from a family of regulatory proteins that reversibly bind guanosine nucleotides; plasma membrane G proteins interact with membrane ion channels or enzymes

G-protein-coupled receptor a cell membrane protein that binds an extracellular signal and then activates an associated G protein, leading to activation of another protein such as adenylyl cyclase

graafian follicle (GRAF-ee-un) mature follicle just before ovulation

graded potential membrane potential change of variable amplitude and duration that is conducted decrementally; has no threshold or refractory period

gram atomic mass amount of element in grams equal to the numerical value of its atomic weight

granulosa cell (gran-you-LOH-sah) cell that contributes to the layers surrounding egg and antrum in ovarian follicle; secretes estrogen, inhibin, and other messengers that influence the egg

gray matter area of brain and spinal cord that appears gray in unstained specimens and consists mainly of cell bodies and unmyelinated portions of nerve fibers

growth cone tip of developing axon

growth factor one of a group of peptides that is highly effective in stimulating cell division and/or differentiation of certain cell types

growth hormone (GH) peptide hormone secreted by anterior pituitary gland; stimulates insulin-like growth factor 1 release; enhances body growth by stimulating protein synthesis

growth hormone–releasing hormone (GHRH) hypothalamic peptide hormone that stimulates growth hormone secretion by anterior pituitary gland

guanine (G) (GWAH-neen) purine base in DNA and RNA

guanylyl cyclase (GUAN-ah-lil) enzyme that catalyzes transformation of GTP to cyclic GMP

gustation (gus-TAY-shun) the sense of taste

gustatory cortex (GUS-ta-toree) region of cerebral cortex receiving primary sensory inputs from the taste buds

gyrus (JYE-rus) sinuous raised ridges on the outer surface of the cerebral cortex

H

habituation (hab-bit-you-A-shun) reversible decrease in response strength upon repeatedly administered stimulation

hair cell mechanoreceptor cell in organ of Corti and vestibular apparatus characterized by stereocilia on cell surface

heart muscular pump that generates blood pressure and flow in the cardiovascular system

heart rate number of heart contractions per minute

heart sound noise that results from vibrations due to closure of atrioventricular valves (first heart sound) or pulmonary and aortic valves (second heart sound)

heavy chain pair of large, coiled polypeptides that makes up the rod and globular head of a myosin molecule

helicotrema outer point in the cochlea where the scala vestibuli and scala tympani meet

helper T cell T cell that, via secreted cytokines, enhances the activation of B cells and cytotoxic T cells

hematocrit (heh-MAT-oh-krit) percentage of total blood volume occupied by red blood cells

hematopoietic growth factor (HGF) (heh-MAT-oh-poi-ET-ik) group of protein hormones and paracrine agents that stimulate proliferation and differentiation of various types of blood cells

heme (heem) iron-containing organic complex bound to each of the four polypeptide chains of hemoglobin or to cytochromes

hemodynamics the factors describing what determines the movement of blood, in particular, pressure, flow, and resistance

hemoglobin (HEE-ma-gloh-bin) protein composed of four polypeptide chains, each attached to a heme; located in erythrocytes and transports most blood oxygen

hemostasis (hee-moh-STAY-sis) stopping blood loss from a damaged vessel

Henry's law amount of gas dissolved in a liquid is proportional to the partial pressure of gas with which the liquid is in equilibrium

heparin (HEP-ah-rin) anticlotting agent found on endothelial cell surfaces; binds antithrombin III to tissues; used as an anticoagulant drug

hepatic (hih-PAT-ik) pertaining to the liver

hepatic lobule functional unit of the liver

hepatic portal vein vein that conveys blood from capillaries in the intestines and portions of the stomach and pancreas to capillaries in the liver

hepatocyte parenchymal cell of the liver

Hering–Breuer reflex inflation of the lung stimulates afferent nerves, which inhibit the inspiratory nerves in the medulla and thereby help to terminate inspiration

hertz (Hz) (hurts) cycles per second; measure used for wave frequencies

hexose a six-carbon sugar, such as glucose

high-density lipoprotein (HDL) lipid-protein aggregate having low proportion of lipid; promotes removal of cholesterol from cells

hilum (HIGH-lum) indented surface of the kidney through which blood vessels enter and leave

hippocampus (hip-oh-KAM-pus) portion of limbic system associated with learning and emotions

histamine (HISS-tah-meen) inflammatory chemical messenger secreted mainly by mast cells; monoamine neurotransmitter

histone class of proteins that participate in the packaging of DNA within the nucleus; strands of DNA form coils around the histones

homeostasis (home-ee-oh-STAY-sis) relatively stable condition of internal environment that results from regulatory system actions

homeostatic control system (home-ee-oh-STAT-ik) collection of interconnected components that keeps a physical or chemical variable of internal environment within a predetermined normal range of values

homeotherm an animal that maintains a relatively narrow range of body temperature despite changes in ambient temperature

horizontal cell a specialized type of neuron found in the retina of the eye that integrates information from local photoreceptor cells

hormone chemical messenger synthesized by specific endocrine cells in response to certain stimuli and secreted into the blood, which carries it to target cells

hormone-sensitive lipase (HSL) an enzyme present in adipose tissue that acts to break down triglycerides into glycerol and fatty acids, which then enter the circulation; it is inhibited by insulin and stimulated by catecholamines

human chorionic gonadotropin (hCG) (kor-ee-ON-ik go-NAD-oh-troh-pin) glycoprotein hormone secreted by trophoblastic cells of embryo; maintains secretory activity of corpus luteum during first 3 months of pregnancy

human placental lactogen (plah-SEN-tal LAK-toh-jen) hormone produced by placenta that has effects similar to those of growth hormone and prolactin

hydrochloric acid (hy-droh-KLOR-ik) HCl; strong acid secreted into stomach lumen by parietal cells

hydrogen bond weak chemical bond between two molecules or parts of the same molecule in which negative region of one polarized substance is electrostatically attracted to a positively charged region of polarized hydrogen atom in the other

hydrogen peroxide H_2O_2; chemical produced by phagosome and highly destructive to macromolecules and pathogens

hydrogen sulfide a type of gas that sometimes functions as a neurotransmitter

hydrolysis (hye-DRAHL-ih-sis) breaking of chemical bond with addition of elements of water (—H and —OH) to the products formed; also called *hydrolytic reaction*

hydrophilic (hye-droh-FIL-ik) attracted to, and easily dissolved in, water

hydrophobic (hye-droh-FOH-bik) not attracted to, and insoluble in, water

hydrostatic pressure (hye-droh-STAT-ik) pressure exerted by fluid

hydroxyapatite crystals composed primarily of calcium and phosphate deposited in bone matrix (mineralization)

hydroxyl group (hye-DROX-il) —OH

hymen membrane that partially covers the opening to the vagina

hypercalcemia increased plasma calcium

hyperemia (hye-per-EE-me-ah) increased blood flow; *see also* active hyperemia

hyperosmotic (hye-per-oz-MAH-tik) having total solute concentration greater than normal extracellular fluid

hyperpolarize to change membrane potential so cell interior becomes more negative than its resting state

hypertension chronically increased arterial blood pressure

hypertonic (hye-per-TAH-nik) solutions containing a higher concentration of effectively membrane-impermeable solute particles than normal (isotonic) extracellular fluid

hypertrophy (hye-PER-troh-fee) enlargement of a tissue or organ due to increased cell size rather than increased cell number

hypnic jerk (HIP-nik) brief muscle twitches sometimes occurring at the beginning of sleep

hypocalcemia the condition of low blood (and interstitial) calcium concentration

hypocretins (high-poe-CREE-tins) *see* orexin

hypoglycemia (hye-poh-gly-SEE-me-ah) low blood glucose (sugar) concentration

hypoosmotic (hye-poh-oz-MAH-tik) having total solute concentration less than that of normal extracellular fluid

hypophysiotropic hormone (hye-poh-fiz-ee-oh-TROH-pik) any hormone secreted by hypothalamus that controls secretion of an anterior pituitary gland hormone

hypotension low blood pressure

hypothalamo–pituitary portal vessels small veins that link the capillaries of the median eminence at the base of the hypothalamus to capillaries that bathe the cells of the anterior pituitary gland; neurohormones are secreted from the hypothalamus into these vessels

hypothalamus (hye-poh-THAL-ah-mus) brain region below thalamus; responsible for integration of many basic neural, endocrine, and behavioral functions, especially those concerned with regulation of internal environment

hypotonic (hye-poh-TAH-nik) solutions containing a lower concentration of effectively nonpenetrating solute particles than normal (isotonic) extracellular fluid

H zone one of transverse bands making up striated pattern of cardiac and skeletal muscle; light region that bisects A band

I

I band one of transverse bands making up repeating striations of cardiac and skeletal muscle; located between A bands of adjacent sarcomeres and bisected by Z line

IgA class of antibodies secreted by, and acting locally in, lining of gastrointestinal, respiratory, and genitourinary tracts

IgD class of antibodies whose function is unknown

IgE class of antibodies that mediate immediate hypersensitivity and resistance to parasites

IgG gamma globulin; most abundant class of antibodies

IgM class of antibodies that, along with IgG, provide major specific humoral immunity against bacteria and viruses

ileocecal sphincter (il-ee-oh-SEE-kal) ring of smooth muscle separating small and large intestines (that is, ileum and cecum)

ileum (IL-ee-um) final, longest segment of small intestine; site of bile salt reabsorption

immune surveillance (sir-VAY-lence) recognition and destruction of cancer cells that arise in body

immune system widely dispersed cells and tissues that participate in the elimination of foreign cells, microbes, and toxins from the body

immune tolerance the lack of immune responses to self components

immunoglobulin (Ig) (im-mune-oh-GLOB-you-lin) proteins that are antibodies and antibody-like receptors on B cells (five classes are IgG, IgA, IgD, IgM, and IgE)

immunology the study of the defenses by which the body destroys or neutralizes foreign cells, microbes, and toxins

implantation (im-plan-TAY-shun) event during which fertilized egg becomes embedded in uterine wall

inactivation gate portion of the voltage-gated sodium or potassium channel that closes the channel

incretins gut hormones such as GLP-1 and GIP that amplify the insulin response to glucose

incus one of three bones in the inner ear that transmit movements of the tympanic membrane to the inner ear

inferior vena cava (VEE-nah KAY-vah) large vein that carries blood from lower parts of body to right atrium of heart

inflammation (in-flah-MAY-shun) local response to injury or infection characterized by swelling, pain, heat, and redness

infundibulum (in-fun-DIBB-yoo-lum) the stalk of tissue connecting the median eminence at the base of the hypothalamus with the pituitary gland

inhibin (in-HIB-in) protein hormone secreted by seminiferous-tubule Sertoli cells and ovarian granulosa cells; inhibits FSH secretion

inhibitory postsynaptic potential (IPSP) hyperpolarizing graded potential that arises in postsynaptic neuron in response to activation of inhibitory synaptic endings upon it

inhibitory synapse (SIN-aps) synapse that, when activated, decreases likelihood that postsynaptic neuron will fire an action potential (or decreases frequency of existing action potentials)

initial segment first portion of axon plus the part of the cell body where axon arises

initiation factor a protein required for ribosomal assembly and the establishment of an initiation complex that allows new protein synthesis to begin

innate immune response the nonspecific immune response to conserved molecular features of pathogens; response that nonselectively protects against foreign material without having to recognize its specific identity

inner cell mass portion of the blastocyst that becomes the embryo

inner ear cochlea; contains organ of Corti

inner emotion emotional feelings that are entirely within a person

inner hair cells cells of the cochlea with stereocilia that transduce pressure waves into electrical signals

inner segment portion of photoreceptor that contains cell organelles; synapses with bipolar cells of retina

inositol trisphosphate (IP_3) (in-OS-ih-tol-tris-FOS-fate) second messenger that causes release of calcium from endoplasmic reticulum into cytosol

insensible water loss water loss of which a person is unaware—that is, loss by evaporation from skin (excluding sweat) and respiratory passage lining

inspiration air movement from atmosphere into lungs

inspiratory reserve volume (IRV) maximal air volume that can be inspired above resting tidal volume

insulin (IN-suh-lin) peptide hormone secreted by beta cells of pancreatic islets of Langerhans; has metabolic and growth-promoting effects; stimulates glucose and amino acid uptake by most cells and stimulates protein, fat, and glycogen synthesis

insulin-like growth factor 1 (IGF-1) insulin-like growth factor that mediates mitosis-stimulating effect of growth hormone on bone and other tissues and has feedback effect on anterior pituitary gland

insulin-like growth factor 2 (IGF-2) mitogenic hormone active during fetal life; postnatal role, if any, is unknown

integral membrane protein protein embedded in membrane lipid layer; may span entire membrane or be located at only one side

integrating center *see* integrator

integrator brain region that compares the actual value of a variable such as body temperature to a set point

integrin (in-TEH-grin or IN-teh-grin) transmembrane protein in plasma membrane; binds to specific proteins in extracellular matrix and on adjacent cells to help organize cells into tissues

intercalated disk (in-TER-kuh-lay-tid) structure connecting adjacent cardiac myocytes, having components for tensile strength (desmosomes) and low-resistance electrical pathways (gap junctions)

intercellular cleft a narrow, water-filled space between capillary endothelial cells

intercostal muscle (in-ter-KOS-tal) skeletal muscle that lies between ribs and whose contraction causes rib cage movement during breathing

interferon (type I) (in-ter-FEER-on) family of proteins that nonspecifically inhibit viral replication inside host cells

interferon-gamma (type II interferon) stimulates the killing ability of macrophages and NK cells

interleukin 1 (IL-1) cytokine secreted by macrophages and other cells that activates helper T cells; exerts many inflammatory effects; mediates many of the systemic, acute phase responses, including fever

interleukin 2 (IL-2) cytokine secreted by activated helper T cells that causes antigen-activated helper T, cytotoxic T, and NK cells to proliferate; also causes activation of macrophages

interleukin 6 (IL-6) cytokine secreted by macrophages and other cells that exerts multiple effects on immune system cells, inflammation, and the acute phase response

intermediate filament actin-containing filament associated with desmosomes

internal anal sphincter smooth muscle ring around lower end of rectum

internal environment extracellular fluid (interstitial fluid and plasma)

internalization down-regulation of plasma membrane receptors by receptor-mediated endocytosis

internal urethral sphincter (you-REE-thrul) part of smooth muscle of urinary bladder wall that opens and closes the bladder outlet

internal work energy-requiring activities in body; *compare* external work

interneuron neuron whose cell body and axon lie entirely in CNS

internodal pathway (in-ter-NO-dal) low-resistance conducting-cell pathway connecting the sinoatrial and atrioventricular nodes of the heart

interstitial fluid extracellular fluid surrounding tissue cells; excludes plasma

interstitium (in-ter-STISH-um) interstitial space; fluid-filled space between tissue cells

interventricular septum the muscular wall separating the right and left ventricles of the heart

intestinal phase (of gastrointestinal control) initiation of neural and hormonal gastrointestinal reflexes by simulation of intestinal tract walls

intestino-intestinal reflex cessation of contractile activity in intestines in response to various stimuli in intestine

intracellular fluid fluid in cells; cytosol plus fluid in cell organelles, including nucleus

intrafusal fiber modified skeletal muscle fiber in muscle spindle

intrapleural fluid (in-trah-PLUR-al) thin fluid film in thoracic cavity between pleura lining the inner wall of thoracic cage and pleura covering lungs

intrapleural pressure (P_{ip}) pressure in pleural space; also called *intrathoracic pressure*

intrarenal baroreceptor pressure-sensitive juxtaglomerular cells of afferent arterioles, which respond to decreased renal arterial pressure by secreting more renin

intrinsic factor glycoprotein secreted by stomach epithelium and necessary for absorption of vitamin B_{12} in the ileum

intrinsic pathway intravascular sequence of fibrin clot formation initiated by factor XII or, more usually, by the initial thrombin generated by the extrinsic clotting pathway

intrinsic tone spontaneous low-level contraction of smooth muscle, independent of neural, hormonal, or paracrine input

intron (IN-trahn) regions of noncoding nucleotides in a gene

inulin polysaccharide that is filtered but not reabsorbed, secreted, or metabolized in the renal tubules; can be used to measure glomerular filtration rate

iodide trapping active transport of iodide from extracellular fluid across the thyroid follicular cell membrane, followed by diffusion of iodide into the colloid of the follicle

iodine chemical found in certain foods and as an additive to table salt; concentrated by the thyroid gland, where it is incorporated into the structure of thyroid hormone

ion (EYE-on) atom or small molecule containing unequal number of electrons and protons and therefore carrying a net positive or negative electrical charge

ion channel small passage in plasma membrane formed by integral membrane proteins and through which certain small-diameter molecules and ions can diffuse; *see also* ligand-gated channel, mechanically gated channel, voltage-gated channel

ionic bond (eye-ON-ik) strong electrical attraction between two oppositely charged ions

ionotropic receptor (eye-ohn-uh-TROPE-ik) membrane protein through which ionic current is controlled by the binding of extracellular signaling molecules

ipsilateral (ip-sih-LAT-er-al) on the same side of the body

iris ringlike structure surrounding and determining the diameter of the pupil of eye

iron an element that forms part of each subunit of hemoglobin and binds molecular oxygen

irreversible reaction chemical reaction that releases large quantities of energy and results in almost all the reactant molecules being converted to product; *compare* reversible reaction

ischemia (iss-KEE-me-ah) reduced blood supply to a region of the body

islet of Langerhans (EYE-let of LAN-ger-hans) cluster of pancreatic endocrine cells; distinct islet cells secrete insulin, glucagon, somatostatin, and pancreatic polypeptide

isometric contraction (eye-soh-MET-rik) contraction of muscle under conditions in which it develops tension but does not change length

isoosmotic (eye-soh-oz-MAH-tik) having the same total solute concentration as extracellular fluid

isotonic (eye-soh-TAH-nik) containing the same number of effectively nonpenetrating solute particles as normal extracellular fluid; *see also* isotonic contraction

isotonic contraction contraction of muscle under conditions in which load on the muscle remains constant but muscle changes length

isotope an atom consisting of one or more additional neutrons than protons in its nucleus

isovolumetric ventricular contraction (eye-soh-vol-you-MET-rik) early phase of systole when atrioventricular and aortic valves are closed and ventricular size remains constant

isovolumetric ventricular relaxation early phase of diastole when atrioventricular and aortic valves are closed and ventricular size remains constant

J

janus kinase (JAK) cytoplasmic kinase bound to a receptor but not intrinsic to it

jejunum (jeh-JU-num) middle segment of small intestine

J receptor receptor in the lung capillary walls or interstitium that responds to increased lung interstitial pressure

junctional feet *see* foot process

juxtaglomerular apparatus (JGA) (jux-tah-gloh-MER-you-lar) renal structure consisting of macula densa and juxtaglomerular cells; site of renin secretion and sensors for renin secretion and control of glomerular filtration rate

juxtaglomerular (JG) cell renin-secreting cells in the afferent arterioles of the renal nephron in contact with the macula densa

juxtamedullary (nephron) functional unit of the kidney with glomeruli in the deep cortex and a long loop of Henle, which plunges into the medulla

K

kallikrein (KAL-ih-cryn) an enzyme produced by gland cells that catalyzes the conversion of the circulating protein kininogen into the signaling molecule bradykinin

karyotype chromosome characteristics of a cell, usually visualized with a microscope

K complex large-amplitude waveform seen in the electroencephalogram during stage 2 sleep

keto acid a class of breakdown products formed from the deamination of amino acids

ketone (KEE-tone) product of fatty acid metabolism that accumulates in blood during starvation and in severe untreated diabetes mellitus; acetoacetic acid, acetone, or B-hydroxybutyric acid; also called *ketone body*

kilocalorie (kcal) (KIL-oh-kal-ah-ree) amount of heat energy required to raise the temperature of 1 kg water by 1°C; also called *Calorie* (capital *C*)

kinesin (kye-NEE-sin) motor protein that uses the energy from ATP to transport attached cellular cargo along microtubules

kinesthesia (kin-ess-THEE-zee-ah) sense of movement derived from movement at a joint

kininogen (kye-NIN-oh-jen) plasma protein from which kinins are generated in an inflamed area

kisspeptin peptide produced in neurons in the hypothalamus involved in the control of GnRH secretion

knee jerk reflex often used in clinical assessment of nerve and muscle function; striking the tendon just below the kneecap causes reflex contraction of anterior thigh muscles, which extends the knee

Korotkoff's sounds (Kor-OTT-koff) sounds caused by turbulent blood flow during determination of blood pressure with a pressurized cuff

Krebs cycle mitochondrial metabolic pathway that utilizes fragments derived from carbohydrate, protein, and fat breakdown and produces carbon dioxide, hydrogen (for oxidative phosphorylation), and small amounts of ATP; also called *tricarboxylic acid cycle* or *citric acid cycle*

L

labeled lines principle describing the idea that a unique anatomical pathway of neurons connects a given sensory receptor directly to the CNS neurons responsible for processing that modality and location on the body

labyrinth complicated bony structure that houses the cochlea and vestibular apparatus

lactase (LAK-tase) small intestine enzyme that breaks down lactose (milk sugar) into glucose and galactose

lactate ionized form of lactic acid, a three-carbon molecule formed by glycolytic pathway; production is increased in absence of oxygen

lactation (lak-TAY-shun) production and secretion of milk by mammary glands

lacteal (lak-TEEL) blind-ended lymph vessel in center of each intestinal villus

lactogenesis the synthesis of milk by the mammary glands

lamina propria layer of connective tissue under an epithelium

laminar flow (LAM-ih-ner) when a fluid (e.g., blood) flows smoothly through a tube in concentric layers, without any turbulence

large intestine part of the gastrointestinal tract between the small intestine and rectum; absorbs salts and water

larynx (LAR-inks) part of air passageway between pharynx and trachea; contains the vocal cords

latch state contractile state of some smooth muscles in which force can be maintained for prolonged periods with very little energy use; cross-bridge cycling slows to the point where thick and thin filaments are effectively "latched" together

latent period (LAY-tent) period lasting several milliseconds between action potential initiation in a muscle fiber and beginning of mechanical activity

lateral inhibition method of refining sensory information in afferent neurons and ascending pathways whereby fibers inhibit each other, the most active fibers causing the greatest inhibition of adjacent fibers

lateral sac (*see* terminal cisternae)

lateral traction force (in the lung) holding small airways open; exerted by elastic connective tissue linked to surrounding alveolar tissue

Law of Laplace (lah-PLAHS) transmural pressure difference $= 2 \times$ surface tension divided by the radius of a hollow ball (e.g., an alveolus)

law of mass action maxim that an increase in reactant concentration causes a chemical reaction to proceed in direction of product formation; the opposite occurs with decreased reactant concentration

L-dopa L-dihydroxyphenylalanine; precursor to dopamine formation; also called *levodopa*

leak K^+ channels potassium channels that are open when a membrane is at rest

learned reflex *see* acquired reflex

learning acquisition and storage of information as a result of experience

lengthening contraction contraction as an external force pulls a muscle to a longer length despite opposing forces generated by the active cross-bridges

lens adjustable part of eye's optical system, which helps focus object's image on retina

leptin adipose-derived hormone that acts within the brain to decrease appetite and increase metabolism

leukocyte (LOO-koh-site) white blood cell

leukotrienes (loo-koh-TRYE-eenz) type of eicosanoid that is generated by lipoxygenase pathway and functions as inflammatory mediator

Leydig cell (LYE-dig or LAY-dig) testosterone-secreting endocrine cell that lies between seminiferous tubules of testes; also called *interstitial cell*

LH surge large rise in luteinizing hormone secretion by anterior pituitary gland about day 14 of menstrual cycle

libido (luh-BEE-doh) sex drive

ligand (LYE-gand) any molecule or ion that binds to protein surface by noncovalent bonds

ligand-gated channel membrane channel operated by the binding of specific molecules to channel proteins

light adaptation process by which photoreceptors in the retina adjust to sudden bright light

light chain pair of small polypeptides bound to each globular head of a myosin molecule; function is to *modulate* contraction

limbic system (LIM-bik) interconnected brain structures in cerebrum; involved with emotions and learning

lingual papillae taste buds located on the tongue

lipase (LYE-pase) enzyme that hydrolyzes triglyceride to monoglyceride and fatty acids; *see also* lipoprotein lipase

lipid (LIP-id) molecule composed primarily of carbon and hydrogen and characterized by insolubility in water

lipid raft cholesterol-rich regions of reduced membrane fluidity that are believed to serve as organizing centers for the generation of complex intracellular signals

lipolysis (lye-POL-ih-sis) triglyceride breakdown

lipoprotein (lip-oh-PROH-teen or LYE-poh-proh-teen) lipid aggregate partially coated by protein; involved in lipid transport in blood

lipoprotein lipase capillary endothelial enzyme that hydrolyzes triglyceride in lipoprotein to monoglyceride and fatty acids

lipoxygenase (lye-POX-ih-jen-ase) enzyme that acts on arachidonic acid and leads to leukotriene formation

liver large organ located in the upper right portion of the abdomen with exocrine, endocrine, and metabolic functions

load external force acting on muscle

local control mechanism existing within tissues that modulates activity independent of neural or hormonal input (e.g., blood flow into a local vascular bed)

local homeostatic response (home-ee-oh-STAT-ik) response acting in immediate vicinity of a stimulus, without nerves or hormones, and having net effect of counteracting stimulus

longitudinal muscle thin outer layer of the intestine; contraction shortens the length of the tube

long-loop negative feedback inhibition of anterior pituitary gland and/or hypothalamus by hormone secreted by third endocrine gland in a sequence

long reflex neural loop from afferents in the gastrointestinal tract to the central nervous system and back to nerve plexuses and effector cells via the autonomic nervous system; involved in the control of motility and secretory activity

long-term depression condition in which nerves show reduced responses to stimuli after an earlier stimulation

long-term memory information stored in the brain for prolonged periods

long-term potentiation (LTP) process by which certain synapses undergo long-lasting increase in effectiveness when heavily used

loop of Henle (HEN-lee) hairpinlike segment of kidney nephron with *descending* and *ascending limbs;* situated between proximal and distal tubules

low-density lipoprotein (LDL) (lip-oh-PROH-teen) protein–lipid aggregate that is major carrier of plasma cholesterol to cells

lower esophageal sphincter smooth muscle of last portion of esophagus; can close off esophageal opening into the stomach

lower motor neurons neurons that synapse directly onto muscle cells and stimulate their contraction

L-type Ca^{2+} channel voltage-gated channel permitting calcium entry into heart cells during the action potential; L denotes the long-lasting open time that characterizes these channels

luminal membrane *see* apical membrane

lung compliance (C_L) (come-PLYE-ance) change in lung volume caused by a given change in transpulmonary pressure; the greater the lung compliance, the more readily the lungs are expanded

luteal phase (LOO-tee-al) last half of menstrual cycle following ovulation; corpus luteum is active ovarian structure

luteinizing hormone (LH) (LOO-tee-en-ize-ing) peptide gonadotropic hormone secreted by anterior pituitary gland; rapid increase in females at midmenstrual cycle initiates ovulation; stimulates Leydig cells in males

lymph (limf) fluid in lymphatic vessels

lymphatic capillary (lim-FAT-ik) smallest-diameter vessel type of the lymphatic system; site of entry of excess extracellular fluid

lymphatic system network of vessels that conveys lymph from tissues to blood and to lymph nodes along these vessels

lymphatic vessel any vessel of the lymphatic system in which excess interstitial fluid is transported and returned to the circulation; along the way, the fluid (lymph) passes through lymph nodes

lymph node small organ containing lymphocytes, located along lymph vessel; a site of lymphocyte cell division and initiation of adaptive immune responses

lymphocyte (LIMF-oh-site) type of leukocyte responsible for adaptive immune defenses; B cells, T cells, and NK cells

lymphocyte activation cell division and differentiation of lymphocytes following antigen binding

lymphoid organ (LIMF-oid) bone marrow, lymph node, spleen, thymus, tonsil, or aggregate of lymphoid follicles; *see also* primary lymphoid organ, secondary lymphoid organ

lysosome (LYE-soh-some) membrane-bound cell organelle containing digestive enzymes in a highly acid solution that break down bacteria, large molecules that have entered the cell, and damaged components of the cell

M

macromolecule large organic molecule composed of up to thousands of atoms, such as a protein or polysaccharide

macrophage (MAK-roh-fahje or MAK-roh-fayj) cell that phagocytizes foreign matter, processes it, presents antigen to lymphocytes, and secretes cytokines (monokines) involved in inflammation, activation of lymphocytes, and systemic acute phase response to infection or injury; *see also* activated macrophage

macula densa (MAK-you-lah DEN-sah) specialized sensor cells of renal tubule at end of loop of Henle; component of juxtaglomerular apparatus

macula lutea a region at the center of the retina that is relatively free of blood vessels and that is specialized for highly acute vision

major histocompatibility complex (MHC) group of genes that code for major histocompatibility complex proteins, which are important for specific immune function

malleus one of three bones in the inner ear that transmit movements of the tympanic membrane to the inner ear

mammary gland milk-secreting gland in breast

margination initial step in leukocyte action in inflamed tissues, in which leukocytes adhere to the endothelial cell

mass movement contraction of large segments of colon; propels fecal matter into rectum

mast cell tissue cell that releases histamine and other chemicals involved in inflammation

matrix (mitochondrial) the innermost mitochondrial compartment

maximal oxygen consumption ($\dot{V}_{O_2}$ max) peak rate of oxygen use as physical exertion is increased; increments in workload above this point must be fueled by anaerobic metabolism

mean arterial pressure (MAP) average blood pressure during cardiac cycle; approximately diastolic pressure plus one-third pulse pressure

mechanically gated channel membrane ion channel that is opened or closed by deformation or stretch of the plasma membrane

mechanoreceptor (meh-KAN-oh-ree-sep-tor or MEK-an-oh-ree-sep-tor) sensory neuron specialized to respond to mechanical stimuli such as touch receptors in the skin and stretch receptors in muscle

median eminence (EM-ih-nence) region at base of hypothalamus containing capillary tufts into which hypophysiotropic hormones are secreted

mediated transport movement of molecules across membrane by binding to protein transporter; characterized by specificity, competition, and saturation; includes facilitated diffusion and active transport

medulla oblongata (ob-long-GOT-ah) part of the brainstem closest to the spinal cord; controls many vegetative functions such as breathing, heart rate and others

medullary cardiovascular center neuron cluster in medulla oblongata that serves as major integrating center for reflexes affecting heart and blood vessels

medullary collecting duct terminal component of the nephron in which vasopressin-sensitive passive water reabsorption occurs

medullary respiratory center part of the medulla oblongata involved in the neural control of rhythmic breathing

megakaryocyte (meg-ah-KAR-ee-oh-site) large bone marrow cell that gives rise to platelets

meiosis (my-OH-sis) process of cell division leading to gamete (sperm or egg) formation; daughter cells receive only half the chromosomes present in original cell

meiotic arrest state of primary oocytes from fetal development until puberty, after which meiosis is completed

melatonin an amine derived from tryptophan produced in the pineal gland and that plays a role in circadian rhythms

membrane attack complex (MAC) group of complement proteins that form channels in microbe surface and destroy microbe

membrane potential voltage difference between inside and outside of cell

memory *see* declarative memory, procedural memory, working memory

memory cell B cell or T cell that differentiates during an initial infection and responds rapidly during subsequent exposure to same antigen

memory encoding processes by which an experience is transformed to a memory of that experience

menarche (MEN-ark-ee) onset, at puberty, of menstrual cycling in women

meninges (men-IN-jees) protective membranes that cover brain and spinal cord

menopause (MEN-ah-paws) cessation of menstrual cycling in middle age

menstrual cycle (MEN-stroo-al) cyclical rise and fall in female reproductive hormones and processes, beginning with menstruation

menstrual phase time during menstrual cycle in which menstrual blood is present

menstruation (men-stroo-AY-shun) flow of menstrual fluid from uterus; also called *menstrual period*

menthol an alcohol derived from mint oil that activates ion channels found in temperature receptors that sense cool temperatures

mesangial cell modified smooth muscle cell that surrounds renal glomerular capillary loops; they help to control glomerular filtration rate

mesolimbic dopamine pathway neural pathway through the limbic system that uses dopamine as its neurotransmitter and is involved in reward

messenger RNA (mRNA) ribonucleic acid that transfers genetic information for a protein's amino acid sequence from DNA to ribosome

metabolic pathway sequence of enzyme-mediated chemical reactions by which molecules are synthesized and broken down in cells

metabolic rate total-body energy expenditure per unit time

metabolism (meh-TAB-uhl-izm) chemical reactions that occur in a living organism

metabotropic receptor (meh-tab-oh-TRO-pik) membrane receptor in neurons that initiates formation of second messengers when bound with ligand

metarteriole (MET-are-teer-ee-ole) blood vessel that directly connects arteriole and venule

MHC protein (class I and class II) plasma membrane protein coded for by a major histocompatibility complex; restricts T-cell receptor's ability to combine with antigen on cell

micelle (MY-sell) soluble cluster of amphipathic molecules in which molecules' polar regions line surface and nonpolar regions orient toward center; formed from fatty acids, monoglycerides, and bile salts during fat digestion in small intestine

microcirculation blood circulation in arterioles, capillaries, and venules

microglia a type of glial cell that acts as a macrophage

microtubule tubular cytoplasmic filament composed of the protein tubulin; provides internal support for cells and allows change in cell shape and organelle movement in cell

microvillus (my-kroh-VIL-us) small fingerlike projection from epithelial-cell surface; microvilli greatly increase surface area of cell; characteristic of epithelium lining small intestine and kidney nephrons

micturition (mik-chur-RISH-un) urination

midbrain the most rostral section of the brainstem

middle ear air-filled space in temporal bone; contains three ear bones that conduct sound waves from tympanic membrane to cochlea

migrating myoelectrical complex (MMC) pattern of peristaltic waves that pass over small segments of intestine after absorption of meal

milk ejection reflex process by which milk is moved from mammary gland alveoli into ducts, from which it can be sucked; due to oxytocin

mineralization the process of calcifying bone collagen to form lamellar bone

mineralocorticoid (min-er-al-oh-KORT-ih-koid) steroid hormone produced by adrenal cortex; has major effect on sodium and potassium balance; major mineralocorticoid is aldosterone

minute ventilation ($\dot{V}_E$) total ventilation per minute; equals tidal volume times respiratory rate

mitochondrion (my-toh-KON-dree-un) rod-shaped or oval cytoplasmic organelle that produces most of cell's ATP; site of Krebs cycle and oxidative-phosphorylation enzymes

mitogen (MY-tuh-jen) chemical that stimulates cell division

mitosis (my-TOH-sis) process in cell division in which DNA is duplicated and copies of each chromosome are passed to daughter cells as the nucleus divides

mitral valve (MY-tral) valve between left atrium and left ventricle of heart

M line transverse stripe occurring at the center of the A band in cardiac and skeletal muscle; location of energy-generating enzymes and proteins connecting adjacent thick filaments

modality (moh-DAL-ih-tee) type of sensory stimulus

modulator molecule ligand that, by acting at an allosteric regulatory site, alters properties of other binding sites on a protein and thus regulates its functional activity

molecular weight sum of atomic weights of all atoms in molecule

molecule chemical substance formed by linking atoms together

monoamine oxidase (MAO) enzyme that breaks down catecholamines in axon terminal and synapse

monocular vision visual perception by a single eye

monocyte (MAH-noh-site) type of leukocyte; leaves bloodstream and is transformed into a macrophage

monoiodotyrosine (MIT) a singly iodinated tyrosine molecule that is an intermediate in the synthesis of thyroid hormones

monosaccharide (mah-noh-SAK-er-ide) carbohydrate consisting of one sugar molecule, which generally contains five or six carbon atoms

monosynaptic reflex (mah-noh-sih-NAP-tik) reflex in which the afferent neuron directly activates motor neurons

monounsaturated fatty acid a fatty acid, such as oleic acid, in which one carbon–carbon double bond is formed within the hydrocarbon chain due to the removal of two hydrogen atoms

mood a long-term inner emotion that affects how individuals perceive their environment

motilin (moh-TIL-in) intestinal hormone thought to initiate the migrating myoelectrical complex in the GI tract

motility movement of the gastrointestinal tract mediated by muscular contractions

motivation *see* primary motivated behavior

motor having to do with muscles and movement

motor cortex strip of cerebral cortex along posterior border of frontal lobe; gives rise to many axons descending in corticospinal and multineuronal pathways; also called *primary motor cortex*

motor end plate specialized region of muscle cell plasma membrane that lies directly under axon terminal of a motor neuron

motor neuron somatic efferent neuron, which innervates skeletal muscle

motor neuron pool all the motor neurons for a given muscle

motor program pattern of neural activity required to perform a certain movement

motor unit motor neuron plus the muscle fibers it innervates

mouth general term for the expanded uppermost portion of the digestive tract

mucosa (mew-KOH-sah) three layers of gastrointestinal tract wall nearest lumen—that is, *epithelium*, *lamina propria*, and *muscularis mucosa*

Müller cells (Myoo-ler) funnel-shaped glial cells that aid light transmission through the retina

Müllerian duct (mul-AIR-ee-an) part of embryo that, in a female, develops into reproductive system ducts, but in a male, degenerates

Müllerian-inhibiting substance (MIS) protein secreted by fetal testes that causes Müllerian ducts to degenerate

multimeric protein a protein in which two or more proteins are associated via hydrogen bonds, hydrophobic attractions, and other forces, to yield a single, larger protein

multiunit smooth muscle smooth muscle that exhibits little, if any, propagation of electrical activity from fiber to fiber and whose contractile activity is closely coupled to its neural input

muscarinic receptor (muss-kur-IN-ik) acetylcholine receptor that responds to the mushroom poison muscarine; located on smooth muscle, cardiac muscle, some CNS neurons, and glands

muscle number of muscle fibers bound together by connective tissue

muscle cell specialized cell containing actin and myosin filaments and capable of generating force and movement

muscle fatigue decrease in muscle tension with prolonged activity

muscle fiber muscle cell

muscle spindle a receptor organ, made up of specialized muscle fibers, that detects stretch of skeletal muscles

muscle-spindle stretch receptor capsule-enclosed arrangement of afferent nerve fiber endings around specialized skeletal muscle fibers; sensitive to stretch

muscle tissue one of the four major tissue types in the body, comprising smooth, cardiac, and skeletal muscle; can be under voluntary or involuntary control

muscle tone degree of resistance of muscle to passive stretch due to ongoing contractile activity; *see also* smooth muscle tone

muscularis externa two layers of muscle in the gastrointestinal tract consisting of circular and longitudinal muscle

muscularis mucosa layer of muscular tissue beneath the lamina propria of the gut

mutagen (MUTE-uh-jen) factor in the environment that increases mutation rate

mutation (mew-TAY-shun) any change in base sequence of DNA that changes genetic information

myelin (MYE-uh-lin) insulating material covering axons of many neurons; consists of layers of myelin-forming cell plasma membrane wrapped around axon

myenteric plexus (mye-en-TER-ik PLEX-us) nerve cell network between circular and longitudinal muscle layers in esophagus, stomach, and intestinal walls

myoblast (MYE-oh-blast) embryological cell that gives rise to muscle fibers

myocardium (mye-oh-KARD-ee-um) cardiac muscle, which forms heart walls

myoepithelial cell (mye-oh-ep-ih-THEE-lee-al) specialized contractile cell in certain exocrine glands; contraction forces gland's secretion through ducts

myofibril (mye-oh-FY-bril) bundle of thick and thin contractile filaments in cytoplasm of striated muscle; myofibrils exhibit a repeating sarcomere pattern along longitudinal axis of muscle

myogenic response (mye-oh-JEN-ik) response originating in muscle

myoglobin (mye-oh-GLOH-bin) muscle fiber protein that binds oxygen

myometrium (mye-oh-MEE-tree-um) uterine smooth muscle

myosin (MYE-oh-sin) contractile protein that forms thick filaments in muscle fibers

myosin ATPase enzymatic site on globular head of myosin that catalyzes ATP breakdown to ADP and P_i, releasing the chemical energy used to produce force of muscle contraction

myosin light-chain kinase smooth muscle protein kinase; when activated by Ca^{2+}–calmodulin, phosphorylates myosin light chain

myosin light-chain phosphatase enzyme that removes high-energy phosphate from myosin; important in the relaxation of smooth muscle cells

myostatin (my-oh-STAT-in) a protein secreted from skeletal muscle cells as a negative regulator of muscle growth

N

NAD^+ nicotinamide adenine dinucleotide; formed from the B-vitamin niacin and involved in transfer of hydrogens during metabolism

Na^+/K^+-ATPase pump primary active-transport protein that hydrolyzes ATP and releases energy used to transport sodium ions out of cell and potassium ions in

natriuresis significant increase in sodium excretion in the urine, which secondarily causes water loss

natural killer (NK) cell type of lymphocyte that binds to virus-infected and cancer cells without specific recognition and kills them directly; participates in antibody-dependent cellular cytotoxicity

natural selection the process whereby mutations in a gene lead to traits that favor survival of an organism

negative balance loss of substance from body exceeds gain, and total amount in body decreases; also used for physical parameters such as body temperature and energy; *compare* positive balance

negative feedback characteristic of control systems in which system's response opposes the original change in the system; *compare* positive feedback

nephron (NEF-ron) functional unit of kidney; has vascular and tubular components

Nernst equation calculation for electrochemical equilibrium across a membrane for any single ion

nerve group of many nerve fibers traveling together in peripheral nervous system

nerve fiber axon of a neuron

nervous tissue one of the four major tissue types in the body, responsible for coordinated control of muscle activity, reflexes, and conscious thought

net filtration pressure (NFP) algebraic sum of inward- and outward-directed forces that determine the direction and magnitude of fluid flow across a capillary wall

net flux difference between two one-way fluxes

net glomerular filtration pressure sum of the relevant forces resulting in glomerular filtration; it is the hydrostatic pressure within the glomerular capillary (P_{GC}) minus the hydrostatic pressure in Bowman's space (P_{BS}) and minus the osmotic force in the glomerular capillary (π_{GC})

neuromodulator chemical messenger that acts on neurons, usually by a second-messenger system, to alter response to a neurotransmitter

neuromuscular junction synapselike junction between an axon terminal of an efferent nerve fiber and a skeletal muscle fiber

neuron (NUR-ahn) cell in nervous system specialized to initiate, integrate, and conduct electrical signals

neuropeptide family of more than 50 neurotransmitters composed of 2 or more amino acids; often also functions as chemical messenger in nonneural tissues

neuropeptide Y a peptide found in the brain whose actions include control of reproduction, appetite, and metabolism

neurotransmitter chemical messenger used by neurons to communicate with each other or with effectors

neurotrophic factor (neur-oh-TRO-fic) protein that stimulates growth and differentiation of some neurons

neutral solution a solution that is neither basic nor acidic (pH 7.0)

neutron noncharged component of the nucleus of an atom

neutrophil (NOO-troh-fil) polymorphonuclear granulocytic leukocyte whose granules show preference for neither eosin nor basic dyes; functions as phagocyte and releases chemicals involved in inflammation

nicotinic receptor (nik-oh-TIN-ik) acetylcholine receptor that responds to nicotine; primarily, receptors at motor end plate and on postganglionic autonomic neurons

nitric oxide a gas that functions as intercellular messenger, including neurotransmitters; is endothelium-derived relaxing factor; destroys intracellular microbes

NMDA receptor (*N*-methyl-D-aspartate receptor) ionotropic glutamate receptor involved in learning and memory

nociceptor (NOH-sih-sep-tor) sensory receptor whose stimulation causes pain

node of Ranvier (RAHN-vee-ay) space between adjacent myelin-forming cells along myelinated axon where axonal plasma membrane is exposed to extracellular fluid; also called *neurofibril node*

nonpenetrating solute dissolved substance that does not passively diffuse across a plasma membrane

nonpolar covalent bond a bond between two atoms of similar electronegativities

nonpolar molecule any molecule with characteristics that favor solubility in oil and decreased solubility in water

nonshivering thermogenesis the creation of bodily heat by processes other than shivering; for example, certain hormones can stimulate metabolism in brown adipose tissue, resulting in heat production in infants (but this does not occur to any significant extent in adults)

nonspecific ascending pathway chain of synaptically connected neurons in CNS that are activated by sensory units of several different types; signals general information; *compare* specific ascending pathway

nonvolatile acid organic (e.g., lactic) or inorganic (e.g., phosphoric and sulfuric) acid not derived directly from carbon dioxide

norepinephrine (NE) (nor-ep-ih-NEF-rin) biogenic amine (catecholamine) neurotransmitter released at most sympathetic postganglionic endings, from adrenal medulla, and in many CNS regions

NREM sleep sleep state associated with large, slow EEG waves and considerable postural muscle tone but not dreaming; also called *slow-wave sleep*

nuclear bag fiber specialized stretch receptor in skeletal muscle spindles that responds to both the magnitude of muscle stretch and the speed at which it is stretched

nuclear chain fiber specialized stretch receptor in skeletal muscle spindles that responds in direct proportion to the length of a muscle

nuclear envelope double membrane surrounding cell nucleus

nuclear pore opening in nuclear envelope through which molecular messengers pass between nucleus and cytoplasm

nucleic acid (noo-KLAY-ik) nucleotide polymer in which phosphate of one nucleotide is linked to the sugar of the adjacent one; stores and transmits genetic information; includes DNA and RNA

nucleolus (noo-KLEE-oh-lus or noo-klee-OH-lus) densely staining nuclear region containing portions of DNA that code for ribosomal proteins

nucleosome (NOO-clee-oh-some) nuclear complexes of several histones and their associated coils of DNA

nucleotide (NOO-klee-oh-tide) molecular subunit of nucleic acid; purine or pyrimidine base, sugar, and phosphate

nucleus (NOO-klee-us) (plural, *nuclei*) (cell) large membrane-bound organelle that contains cell's DNA; (neural) cluster of neuron cell bodies in CNS

O

obligatory water loss minimal amount of water required to excrete waste products

occipital lobe (ok-SIP-ih-tul) posterior region of cerebral cortex where primary visual cortex is located

odorant molecule received by the olfactory system that induces a sensation of smell

Ohm's law current (I) is directly proportional to voltage (V) and inversely proportional to resistance (R) such that $I = V/R$

olfaction (ol-FAK-shun) sense of smell

olfactory bulb (ol-FAK-tor-ee) anterior protuberance of the brain containing cells that process odor inputs

olfactory cortex region on the inferior and medial surface of the frontal lobe of the cerebral cortex where information about the sense of smell is processed

olfactory epithelium mucous membrane in upper part of nasal cavity containing receptors for sense of smell

oligodendrocyte (oh-lih-goh-DEN-droh-site) type of glial cell; responsible for myelin formation in CNS

oogenesis (oh-oh-JEN-ih-sis) gamete production in female

oogonium (oh-oh-GOH-nee-um) primitive germ cell that gives rise to primary oocyte

opponent color cell ganglion cells in the retina that are inhibited by input from one type of cone photoreceptor but activated by another type of cone photoreceptor

opsin (OP-sin) protein component of photopigment

opsonin (op-SOH-nin or OP-soh-nin) any substance that binds a microbe to a phagocyte and promotes phagocytosis

optic chiasm (KYE-azm) place at base of brain at which optic nerves meet; some neurons cross here to other side of brain

optic disc region of the retina where neurons to the brain exit the eye; lack of photoreceptors here results in a "blind spot"

optic nerve bundle of neurons connecting the eye to the optic chiasm

optic tract bundle of neurons connecting the optic chiasm to the lateral geniculate nucleus of the thalamus

optimal length (L_0) sarcomere length at which muscle fiber develops maximal isometric tension

orexins (oh-REK-sins) peptide neurotransmitters involved in the regulation of wakefulness, food intake, and energy expenditure; also known as *hypocretins*

organ collection of tissues joined in structural unit to serve common function

organ of Corti (KOR-tee) structure in inner ear capable of transducing sound wave energy into action potentials

organ system organs that together serve an overall function

orgasm (OR-gazm) inner emotions and systemic physiological changes that mark apex of sexual intercourse, usually accompanied in the male by ejaculation

orienting response behavior in response to a novel stimulus; that is, the person stops what he or she is doing, looks around, listens intently, and turns toward stimulus

osmol (OZ-mole) 1 mole of solute ions and molecules

osmolarity (oz-moh-LAR-ih-tee) total solute concentration of a solution; measure of water concentration in that the higher the solution osmolarity, the lower the water concentration

osmoreceptor (OZ-moh-ree-sep-tor) receptor that responds to changes in osmolarity of surrounding fluid

osmosis (oz-MOH-sis) net diffusion of water across a selective barrier from region of higher water concentration (lower solute concentration) to region of lower water concentration (higher solute concentration)

osmotic diuresis increase in urine flow resulting from increased solute excretion (e.g., glucose in uncontrolled diabetes mellitus)

osmotic pressure (oz-MAH-tik) pressure that must be applied to a solution on one side of a membrane to prevent osmotic flow of water across the membrane from a compartment of pure water; a measure of the solution's osmolarity

osteoblast (OS-tee-oh-blast) cell type responsible for laying down protein matrix of bone; called osteocyte after calcified matrix has been set down

osteoclast (OS-tee-oh-clast) cell that breaks down previously formed bone

osteocyte cell transformed from osteoblast when surrounded by mineralized bone matrix

osteoid collagen matrix in bone that becomes mineralized

otolith (OH-toe-lith) calcium carbonate crystal embedded in the mucous covering of the auditory hair cell

outer hair cells cells of the cochlea with stereocilia that sharpen frequency tuning by modulating the movement of the tectorial membrane

outer segment light-sensitive portion of the photoreceptor containing photopigments

oval window membrane-covered opening between middle ear cavity and scala vestibuli of inner ear

ovary (OH-vah-ree) gonad in female

overshoot part of the action potential in which the membrane potential goes above zero

ovulation (ov-you-LAY-shun) release of egg, surrounded by its zona pellucida and granulosa cells, from ovary

ovum (plural, *ova*) gamete of female; egg

oxidative deamination (dee-am-ih-NAY-shun) reaction in which an amino group (—NH_2) from an amino acid is replaced by oxygen to form a keto acid

oxidative fiber muscle fiber that has numerous mitochondria and therefore a high capacity for oxidative phosphorylation; red muscle fiber

oxidative phosphorylation (fos-for-ih-LAY-shun) process by which energy derived from reaction between hydrogen and oxygen to form water is transferred to ATP during its formation

oxygen-carrying capacity maximum amount of oxygen the blood can carry; in general, proportional to the amount of hemoglobin per unit volume of blood

oxygen debt decrease in energy reserves during exercise that results in an increase in oxygen consumption and an increased production of ATP by oxidative phosphorylation following the exercise

oxygen–hemoglobin dissociation curve *S*-shaped (sigmoid) relationship between the gas pressure of oxygen (partial pressure of O_2) and amount of oxygen bound to hemoglobin per unit blood (hemoglobin saturation)

oxyhemoglobin (HbO_2) (ox-see-HEE-moh-gloh-bin) hemoglobin combined with oxygen

oxytocin (ox-see-TOE-sin) peptide hormone synthesized in hypothalamus and released from posterior pituitary; stimulates mammary glands to release milk and uterus to contract

P

pacemaker neurons that set rhythm of biological clocks independent of external cues; any neuron or muscle cell that has an inherent autorhythmicity and determines activity pattern of other cells

pacemaker potential spontaneous gradual depolarization to threshold of some neurons and muscle cells' plasma membrane

pancreas elongated gland behind the stomach with both exocrine (secretes digestive enzymes into the gastrointestinal tract) and endocrine (secretes insulin into the blood) functions

papilla (puh-PIL-ah) connection between the tip of the medulla and the calyx in the kidney

papillary muscle (PAP-ih-lair-ee) muscular projections from interior of ventricular chambers that connect to atrioventricular valves and prevent backward flow of blood during ventricular contraction

paracellular pathway the space between adjacent cells of an epithelium through which some molecules diffuse as they cross the epithelium

paracrine substance (PAR-ah-krin) chemical messenger that exerts its effects on cells near its secretion site; by convention, excludes neurotransmitters; *compare* autocrine substance

paradoxical sleep *see* REM sleep

parasympathetic division (of the autonomic nervous system) (par-ah-sim-pah-THET-ik) portion of autonomic nervous system whose preganglionic fibers leave CNS from brainstem and sacral portion of spinal cord; most of its postganglionic fibers release acetylcholine; *compare* sympathetic division

parathyroid gland one of four parathyroid-hormone-secreting glands on thyroid gland surface

parathyroid hormone (PTH) peptide hormone secreted by parathyroid glands; regulates calcium and phosphate concentrations of extracellular fluid

parietal cell (pah-RYE-ih-tal) gastric gland cell that secretes hydrochloric acid and intrinsic factor

parietal lobe region of cerebral cortex containing sensory cortex and some association cortex

parietal-lobe association cortex region of cerebrum involved in integrating inputs from primary sensory cortices, as well as higher-order cognitive processing and motor control

parietal pleura (pah-RYE-it-al ploor-ah) serous membranes covering the inside of the chest wall, the diaphragm, and the mediastinum

partial pressure that part of total gas pressure due to molecules of one gas species; measure of concentration of a gas in a gas mixture

parturition events leading to and including delivery of infant

passive immunity resistance to infection resulting from direct transfer of antibodies or sensitized T cells from one person (or animal) to another; *compare* active immunity

pathogen virus or microbe that elicits an immune response in the body, and which may cause disease

pathogen-associated molecular patterns (PAMPs) conserved molecular features common to many types of pathogens; they are recognized by cells mediating the innate immune response

pathophysiology the study of disease states

pathway series of connected neurons that move a particular type of information from one part of the brain to another part

pattern-recognition receptors (PRRs) a family of proteins that bind to ligands found in many types of pathogens; include the Toll-like receptors found on dendritic cells

pentose any five-carbon monosaccharide

pepsin (PEP-sin) family of several protein-digesting enzymes formed in the stomach; breaks protein down to peptide fragments

pepsinogen (pep-SIN-ah-jen) inactive precursor of pepsin; secreted by chief cells of gastric mucosa

peptide (PEP-tide) short polypeptide chain; by convention, having fewer than about 50 amino acids

peptide bond polar covalent chemical bond joining the amino and carboxyl groups of two amino acids; forms protein backbone

peptide hormone any of a family of hormones, like insulin, composed of approximately two to 50 amino acids; generally soluble in acid, unlike larger protein hormones, which are insoluble

peptidergic neuron that releases peptides

percent hemoglobin saturation the percentage of available hemoglobin subunits bound to molecular oxygen at any given time

perception understanding of objects and events of external world that we acquire from neural processing of sensory information

perforin protein secreted by cytotoxic T cells; may form channels in plasma membrane of target cell, which destroys it

pericardium (per-ee-KAR-dee-um) connective-tissue sac surrounding heart

perilymph fluid that fills the cochlear duct of the inner ear

perimenopause beginning period leading to cessation of menstruation

peripheral chemoreceptor carotid or aortic body; responds to changes in arterial blood P_{O_2} and H^+ concentration

peripheral membrane protein hydrophilic proteins associated with cytoplasmic surface of cell membrane

peripheral nervous system nerve fibers extending from CNS

peripheral thermoreceptor cold or warm receptor in skin or certain mucous membranes

peripheral vein blood vessel outside the chest cavity that returns blood from capillaries toward the heart

peristaltic wave (per-ih-STAL-tik) progressive wave of smooth muscle contraction and relaxation that proceeds along wall of a tube, compressing the tube and causing its contents to move

peritubular capillary capillary closely associated with renal tubule

permeability coefficient *P* number that defines the proportionality between a flux and a concentration gradient and depends on the properties of the membrane and the diffusing molecule

permissiveness the facilitation of the action of one hormone by another; for example, the effects of epinephrine are exacerbated by thyroid hormone and by cortisol

peroxisome (per-OX-ih-some) cell organelle that destroys certain toxic products by oxidative reactions

Peyer's patches lymphatic tissue located in the lamina propria of the ileum of the small intestine

pH expression of a solution's acidity; negative logarithm to base 10 of H^+ concentration; pH decreases as acidity increases

phagocyte (FA-go-site) any cell capable of phagocytosis

phagocytosis (fag-oh-sye-TOH-sis) engulfment of particles by a cell

phagolysosome an intracellular vesicle formed when a lysosome and a phagosome combine; the contents of the lysosome begin the process of destroying the contents of the phagosome

phagosome plasma-membrane-bound, intracellular sac formed when a phagocyte engulfs a microbe

pharynx (FA-rinks) throat; passage common to routes taken by food and air

phase-shift a resetting of the circadian clock due to altered environmental cues

phenotype (FEE-noh-type) gender based on physical appearance

phospholipase A_2 (fos-foh-LY-pase A-two) enzyme that splits arachidonic acid from plasma membrane phospholipid

phospholipase C receptor-controlled plasma membrane enzyme that catalyzes phosphatidylinositol bisphosphate breakdown to inositol trisphosphate and diacylglycerol

phospholipid (fos-foh-LIP-id) lipid subclass similar to triglyceride except that a phosphate group (—PO_4^{2-}) and small nitrogen-containing molecule are attached to third hydroxyl group of glycerol; major component of cell membranes

phosphoprotein phosphatase (FOS-fah-tase) enzyme that removes phosphate from protein

phosphorylation (fos-for-ah-LAY-shun) addition of phosphate group to an organic molecule

photopigment light-sensitive molecule altered by absorption of photic energy of certain wavelengths; consists of opsin bound to a chromophore

photoreceptor sensory cell specialized to respond to light; contains pigments that make it sensitive to different light wavelengths

phrenic nerves main motor nerves innervating the diaphragm and providing the impulses to inspire

physiological dead space sum of the anatomical and alveolar dead spaces; it is the part of the respiratory tree in which gas exchange with blood does not occur

physiology (fiz-ee-OL-uh-jee) branch of biology dealing with the mechanisms by which living organisms function

pia mater (PEE-ah MAH-ter) innermost of three membranes (meninges) covering the brain

pigment epithelium dark, innermost layer of the retina; absorbs light that bypasses photopigments

pineal gland part of the epithalamus of the brain; produces melatonin involved in circadian rhythms

pinocytosis (pin-oh-sye-TOH-sis or PYE-no-sye-toh-sis) endocytosis when the vesicle encloses extracellular fluid or specific molecules in the extracellular fluid that have bound to proteins on the extracellular surface of the plasma membrane

pituitary gland (pih-TOO-ih-tar-ee) endocrine gland that lies in bony pocket below hypothalamus; constitutes anterior pituitary gland and posterior pituitary gland

placenta (plah-SEN-tah) interlocking fetal and maternal tissues that serve as organ of molecular exchange between fetal and maternal circulations

plasma (PLAS-muh) liquid portion of blood; component of extracellular fluid

plasma cell cell that differentiates from activated B lymphocytes and secretes antibodies

plasma membrane membrane that forms outer surface of cell and separates cell's contents from extracellular fluid

plasma protein most are albumins, globulins, or fibrinogen

plasmin (PLAZ-min) proteolytic enzyme able to decompose fibrin and thereby to dissolve blood clots

plasminogen (plaz-MIN-oh-jen) inactive precursor of plasmin

plasminogen activator any plasma protein that activates proenzyme plasminogen

plasticity (plas-TISS-ih-tee) ability of neural tissue to change its responsiveness to stimulation because of its past history of activation

platelet (PLATE-let) cell fragment present in blood; plays several roles in blood clotting

platelet activation changes in the metabolism, shape, and surface proteins of platelets that begin the clotting process

platelet aggregation positive feedback process resulting in platelets sticking together

platelet factor (PF) phospholipid exposed in membranes of aggregated platelets; important in activation of several plasma factors in clot formation

platelet plug blockage of a vessel by activated, adherent platelets

pleura (PLOOR-ah) thin cellular sheet attached to thoracic cage interior (*parietal pleura*) and, folding back upon itself, attached to lung surface (*visceral pleura*); forms two enclosed *pleural sacs* in thoracic cage

pleural sac membrane enclosing each lung

pluripotent hematopoietic stem cells (plur-ih-POH-tent) single population of bone marrow cells from which all blood cells are descended

pneumotaxic center (noo-moh-TAK-sik) area of the upper pons in the brain that modulates activity of the apneustic center

podocyte epithelial cells lining Bowman's capsule, whose foot processes form filtration slits

polar covalent bond covalent chemical bond in which two electrons are shared unequally between two atoms of different electronegativities; atom to which the electrons are drawn becomes slightly negative, while other atom becomes slightly positive; also called *polar bond*

polar molecule pertaining to molecule or region of molecule containing polar covalent bonds or ionized groups; part of molecule to which electrons are drawn becomes slightly negative, and region from which electrons are drawn becomes slightly positive; molecule is soluble in water

polymer (POL-ih-mer) large molecule formed by linking together smaller similar subunits

polymodal neuron sensory neuron that responds to more than one type of stimulus

polymorphonuclear granulocyte (pol-ee-morf-oh-NUKE-lee-er GRAN-you-loh-site) subclass of leukocytes consisting of eosinophils, basophils, and neutrophils

polypeptide (pol-ee-PEP-tide) polymer consisting of amino acid subunits joined by peptide bonds

polysaccharide (pol-ee-SAK-er-ide) large carbohydrate formed by linking monosaccharide subunits together

polysynaptic a neuronal pathway such as occurs in some reflexes in which two or more synapses are present

polyunsaturated fatty acid fatty acid that contains more than one double bond

pons large area of the brainstem containing many neuron axons

pontine respiratory group neurons in the pons that modulate respiratory rhythms

pool the readily available quantity of a substance in the body; often equals amounts in extracellular fluid

portal system a type of circulation characterized by two capillary beds connected by veins called portal veins

portal triad structure in the liver composed of branches of the hepatic artery, the hepatic portal vein, and the bile duct

positive balance gain of substance exceeds loss, and amount of that substance in body increases; *compare* negative balance

positive feedback characteristic of control systems in which an initial disturbance sets off train of events that increases the disturbance even further; *compare* negative feedback

positive nitrogen balance a period in which there is net gain of nitrogen (amino acids) in the body

postabsorptive state period during which nutrients are not being absorbed by gastrointestinal tract and energy must be supplied by body's endogenous stores

posterior pituitary portion of pituitary gland from which oxytocin and vasopressin are released

postganglionic neuron (post-gang-glee-ON-ik) autonomic-nervous-system neuron or nerve fiber whose cell body lies in a ganglion; conducts impulses away from ganglion toward periphery; *compare* preganglionic neuron

postsynaptic density area in the postsynaptic cell membrane that contains neurotransmitter receptors and structural proteins important for synapse function

postsynaptic neuron (post-sin-NAP-tik) neuron that conducts information away from a synapse

postural reflex reflex that maintains or restores upright, stable posture

potential (or potential difference) voltage difference between two points; *see also* action potential, graded potential

potential difference a difference in charge between two points

potentiation (poh-ten-she-AY-shun) presence of one agent enhances response to a second such that final response is greater than sum of the two individual responses

potocytosis (poh-toe-si-toe-sis) a type of receptor-mediated endocytosis in which vesicle contents are delivered directly to the cytosol

power stroke the step of a cross-bridge cycle involving physical rotation of the globular head

preattentive processing neural processes that occur to direct our attention to a particular aspect of the environment

pre-Botzinger complex neurons of the ventral respiratory group in the medulla that are the respiratory rhythm generator

precapillary sphincter (SFINK-ter) smooth muscle ring around capillary where it exits from thoroughfare channel or arteriole

preganglionic neuron autonomic-nervous-system neuron or nerve fiber whose cell body lies in CNS and whose axon terminals lie in a ganglion; conducts action potentials from CNS to ganglion; *compare* postganglionic neuron

preinitiation complex a group of transcription factors and accessory proteins that associate with promoter regions of specific genes; the complex is required for gene transcription to commence

preload the amount of filling of ventricles just prior to contraction; the end-diastolic volume

premotor area region of the cerebral cortex found on the lateral sides of the brain in front of the primary motor cortex; involved in planning and enacting complex muscle movements

pre-mRNA *see* primary RNA transcript

pressure natriuresis increase in sodium excretion induced by a local action within the renal tubules due to an increase in the arterial pressure within the kidney

presynaptic facilitation (pre-sin-NAP-tik) excitatory input to neurons through synapses at the nerve terminal

presynaptic inhibition inhibitory input to neurons through synapses at the axon terminal

presynaptic neuron neuron that conducts action potentials toward a synapse

primary active transport active transport in which chemical energy is transferred directly from ATP to transporter protein

primary lymphoid organs organs that supply secondary lymphoid organs with mature lymphocytes; bone marrow and thymus

primary motivated behavior behavior related directly to achieving homeostasis

primary motor cortex *see* motor cortex

primary oocyte (OH-oh-site) female germ cell that undergoes first meiotic division to form secondary oocyte and polar body

primary RNA transcript an RNA molecule transcribed from a gene before intron removal and splicing

primary spermatocyte (sper-MAT-uh-site) male germ cell derived from spermatogonia; undergoes meiotic division to form two secondary spermatocytes

primary structure the amino acid sequence of a protein

primordial follicle (FAH-lik-el) an immature oocyte encased in a single layer of granulosa cells

procedural memory the memory of how to do things

process long extension from neuron cell body

progesterone (proh-JES-ter-own) steroid hormone secreted by corpus luteum and placenta; stimulates uterine gland secretion, inhibits uterine smooth muscle contraction, and stimulates breast growth

prohormone peptide precursor from which are cleaved one or more active peptide hormones

prokaryotic cell cell such as a bacterium that does not contain its genetic information within a membrane-enclosed nucleus

prolactin (pro-LAK-tin) peptide hormone secreted by anterior pituitary gland; stimulates milk synthesis by mammary glands

prolactin-releasing factor (PRF) putative hypothalamic factor that stimulates prolactin release

proliferative phase (pro-LIFF-er-ah-tive) stage of menstrual cycle between menstruation and ovulation during which endometrium repairs itself and grows

promoter specific nucleotide sequence at beginning of gene that controls the initiation of gene transcription; determines which of the paired strands of DNA is transcribed into RNA

proprioception (PROH-pree-oh-sep-shun) sense of posture and position; sensory information dealing with the position of the body in space and its parts relative to one another

prosody (PRO-so-dee) attributes of human speech that include rhythm, emphasis, and intonation

prostacyclin eicosanoid that inhibits platelet aggregation in blood clotting; also called *prostaglandin* I_2 *(*PGI_2*)*

prostaglandin (pross-tah-GLAN-din) one class of a group of modified unsaturated fatty acids (eicosanoids) that function mainly as paracrine or autocrine factors

prostaglandin I_2 **(**PGI_2**)** *see* prostacyclin

prostate gland (PROSS-tate) large gland encircling urethra in the male; secretes seminal fluid into urethra

protease (PROH-tee-ase) an enzyme capable of breaking peptide bonds in a protein

proteasome a complex of proteins capable of denaturing (unfolding) other proteins and assisting in protein degradation

protein large polymer consisting of one or more sequences of amino acid subunits joined by peptide bonds to form a functional molecule with multiple levels of structure

protein binding site *see* binding site

protein C plasma protein that inhibits clotting

protein kinase (KYE-nase) any enzyme that phosphorylates other proteins by transferring to them a phosphate group from ATP

protein kinase C enzyme that phosphorylates certain intracellular proteins when activated by diacylglycerol

proteolysis the process whereby peptides and proteins are cleaved into smaller molecules, by the actions of specific enzymes (proteases)

proteome all of the proteins expressed by a particular cell at a given time

prothrombin (proh-THROM-bin) inactive precursor of thrombin; produced by liver and normally present in plasma

proton (PROH-tahn) positively charged subatomic particle

proximal tubule first tubular component of a nephron after Bowman's capsule; comprises *convoluted* and *straight segments*

puberty attainment of sexual maturity when conception becomes possible; as commonly used, refers to 3 to 5 years of sexual development that culminates in sexual maturity

pulmonary (PUL-mah-nar-ee) pertaining to lungs

pulmonary artery large, branching vessel carrying oxygen-poor blood away from the heart toward the lungs

pulmonary circulation circulation through lungs; portion of cardiovascular system between pulmonary trunk, as it leaves the right ventricle, and pulmonary veins, as they enter the left atrium

pulmonary stretch receptor afferent neuron ending located in airway smooth muscle and activated by lung inflation

pulmonary trunk large artery that splits into the pulmonary arteries that carry blood from right ventricle of heart to lungs

pulmonary valve valve between right ventricle of heart and pulmonary trunk

pulmonary vein large, converging vessel that returns oxygen-rich blood toward the heart from the lungs

pulse pressure difference between systolic and diastolic arterial blood pressures

pupil opening in iris of eye through which light passes to reach retina

purine (PURE-ene) double-ring, nitrogen-containing subunit of nucleotide; adenine or guanine

Purkinje fiber (purr-KIN-jee) specialized myocardial cell that constitutes part of conducting system of heart; conveys excitation from bundle branches to ventricular muscle

P wave component of electrocardiogram reflecting atrial depolarization

pyloric sphincter (py-LOR-ik) ring of smooth muscle between stomach and small intestine

pyramidal cell large neuron with characteristic pyramid-shaped cell body and apical dendrite

pyramidal system descending nervous system pathways that originate in the cerebral cortex, cross over the midline in the medulla, and control fine movements of the distal extremities

pyramidal tract *see* corticospinal pathway

pyrimidine (pi-RIM-ih-deen) single-ring, nitrogen-containing subunit of nucleotide; cytosine, thymine, or uracil

pyrogen *see* endogenous pyrogen

pyruvate (PYE-roo-vayt or pye-ROO-vayt) anion formed when pyruvic acid loses a hydrogen ion

pyruvic acid (pye-ROO-vik) three-carbon intermediate in glycolysis that, in absence of oxygen, forms lactic acid or, in presence of oxygen, enters Krebs cycle

Q

QRS complex component of electrocardiogram corresponding to ventricular depolarization

quaternary structure formed when two or more proteins associate with each other by hydrogen bonds and other forces; the individual proteins are then termed *subunits*

R

radiation emission of heat from the surface of an object

rapid eye movement sleep *see* REM sleep

rapidly adapting receptor sensory receptor that fires for a brief period at the onset and/or offset of a stimulus

rate-limiting reaction slowest reaction in metabolic pathway; catalyzed by rate-limiting enzyme

reactive hyperemia (hye-per-EE-me-ah) transient increase in blood flow following release of occlusion of blood supply

receptive field (of neuron) area of body that, if stimulated, results in activity in that neuron

receptive relaxation relaxation of the smooth muscles of the stomach (fundus and body) when food is swallowed; mediated by parasympathetic nerves in the enteric nerve plexuses

receptor (for messengers) protein either on cell surface, in the cytosol, or in the nucleus that binds a chemical messenger such as a hormone or neurotransmitter and mediates its actions; (in sensory system) specialized peripheral ending of afferent neuron, or separate cell intimately associated with it, that detects changes in some aspect of environment

receptor activation change in receptor conformation caused by combination of messenger with receptor

receptor desensitization temporary inability of a receptor to respond to its ligand due to prior ligand binding

receptor-mediated endocytosis the specific uptake of ligands in the extracellular fluid by regions of the plasma membrane that invaginate and form intracellular vesicles

receptor potential graded potential that arises in afferent neuron ending, or a specialized cell intimately associated with it, in response to stimulation

receptor tyrosine kinase the major type of receptor protein that is itself an enzyme; these receptors are on plasma membranes and respond to many different water-soluble chemical messengers

reciprocal innervation inhibition of motor neurons activating muscles whose contraction would oppose an intended movement

recognition binding of antigen to receptor specific for that antigen on lymphocyte surface

recruitment activation of additional cells in response to increased stimulus strength; increasing the number of active motor units in a muscle

rectum short segment of large intestine between sigmoid colon and anus

red muscle fiber muscle fiber having high oxidative capacity and large amount of myoglobin

reflex (REE-flex) biological control system linking stimulus with response and mediated by a reflex arc

reflex arc neural or hormonal components that mediate a reflex; usually includes receptor, afferent pathway, integrating center, efferent pathway, and effector

refraction bending of light rays when passing between compartments of different density, as from air into the cornea of the eyes

refractory period (of cardiac muscle) (reh-FRAK-tor-ee) time during which an excitable membrane does not respond to a stimulus that normally causes response; *see also* absolute refractory period, relative refractory period

regulatory site site on protein that interacts with modulator molecule; alters functional site properties

regulatory T cell a type of immune (T) cell that is believed to suppress immune function and may minimize the likelihood of autoimmunity

relative refractory period time during which excitable membrane will produce action potential but only to a stimulus of greater strength than the usual threshold strength

relaxation return of muscle to a low force-generating state, caused by detachment of cross-bridges

relaxin hormone secreted by the ovary before parturition

REM sleep (rem) sleep state associated with small, rapid EEG oscillations, complete loss of tone in postural muscles, and dreaming; also called *rapid eye movement sleep, paradoxical sleep*

renal (REE-nal) pertaining to kidneys

renal artery high pressure vessel bringing blood to the kidney

renal corpuscle combination of glomerulus and Bowman's capsule

renal cortex outer portion of the kidney

renal medulla inner portion of the kidney

renal pelvis cavity at base of each kidney; receives urine from collecting-duct system and empties it into ureter

renal plasma flow the total amount of plasma (blood minus red cell volume) that passes through both kidneys per unit time

renal vein low pressure vessel draining blood from the kidney

renin (REE-nin) enzyme secreted by kidneys that catalyzes splitting off of angiotensin I from angiotensinogen in plasma

renin–angiotensin system hormonal system consisting of renin-stimulated angiotensin I production followed by conversion to angiotensin II by angiotensin-converting enzyme

repolarize return transmembrane potential to its resting level

residual volume (RV) air volume remaining in lungs after maximal expiration

resistance (R) hindrance to movement through a particular substance, tube, or opening

respiration (1) utilization of oxygen and production of carbon dioxide at the cellular level (i.e., cellular respiration); (2) exchange of oxygen and carbon dioxide between the organism and the environment via the lungs

respiratory bronchiole largest branch of the respiratory tree in which the units of gas exchange (alveoli) appear

respiratory cycle changes in the lung volumes from the beginning of an inspiration, including the expiration, to the beginning of the next inspiration

respiratory physiology the study of the respiratory system, including its structures and functions and regulation

respiratory pump mechanism whereby reductions in intrathoracic pressure during the breathing cycle tend to favor the return of blood to the heart from peripheral veins

respiratory quotient (RQ) ratio of carbon dioxide produced to oxygen consumed during metabolism

respiratory rate number of breaths per minute

respiratory rhythm generator neural network in the brainstem that generates output to the phrenic nerve

respiratory system the anatomical pathway of air from the atmosphere to the alveoli

respiratory zone portion of airways from beginning of respiratory bronchioles to alveoli; contains alveoli across which gas exchange occurs

resting membrane potential voltage difference between inside and outside of cell in absence of excitatory or inhibitory stimulation; also called *resting potential*

rest-or-digest state homeostatic state characteristic of parasympathetic nervous system activation

rete testes (REE-tee TES-teez) network of canals at the ends of the seminiferous tubules in the testes

reticular activating system (RAS) extensive neuron network extending through brainstem core; receives and integrates information from many afferent pathways and from other CNS regions; also called *reticular formation*

reticulocyte (ruh-TIK-you-low-site) name given to immature red blood cells that have a weblike pattern in the cytosol due to the persistence of ribosomes

retina thin layer of neural tissue lining back of eyeball; contains receptors for vision

retinal (ret-in-AL) form of vitamin A that forms chromophore component of photopigment

retrograde movement of a substance or action potential backward along a neuron, from axon terminals toward the cell body and dendrites

reuptake active process that recaptures excess secreted neurotransmitter back into the presynaptic cell; can be inhibited with drugs

reversible reaction chemical reaction in which energy release is small enough for reverse reaction to occur readily; *compare* irreversible reaction

Rh factor group of erythrocyte plasma membrane antigens that may (Rh^+) or may not (Rh^-) be present

rhodopsin (roh-DOP-sin) photopigment in rods

ribonucleic acid (RNA) (rye-boh-noo-KLAY-ik) single-stranded nucleic acid involved in transcription of genetic information and translation of that information into protein structure; contains the sugar ribose; *see also* messenger RNA, ribosomal RNA, transfer RNA

ribose the sugar backbone of RNA

ribosomal RNA (rRNA) (rye-boh-SOME-al) type of RNA used in ribosome assembly; becomes part of ribosome

ribosome (RYE-boh-some) cytoplasmic particle that mediates linking together of amino acids to form proteins; attached to endoplasmic reticulum as bound ribosome, or suspended in cytoplasm as free ribosome

rigor mortis (rig-or MOR-tiss) stiffness of skeletal muscles after death due to failure of cross-bridges to dissociate from actin because of the loss of ATP

RNA polymerase (poh-LIM-uh-rase) enzyme that forms RNA by joining together appropriate nucleotides after they have base-paired to DNA

rod one of two receptor types for photic energy; contains the photopigment rhodopsin

round window membrane-covered opening in the cochlea that responds to fluid movement in the scala tympani

ryanodine receptor calcium-release channel found in the lateral sacs of the sarcoplasmic reticulum in skeletal muscle cells

S

saccade (sah-KAAD) short, jerking eyeball movement

saccule structure in the semicircular canals that responds to changes in linear movement of the head by mechanical forces on otoliths located on its surface

saliva watery solution of salts and proteins, including mucins and amylase, secreted by salivary glands

salivary gland one of three pairs of exocrine glands around the mouth that produce saliva

salt appetite desire for salt, consisting of hedonistic and regulatory components

saltatory conduction propagation of action potentials along a myelinated axon such that the action potentials jump from one node of Ranvier in the myelin sheath to the next

sarcomere (SAR-kuh-meer) repeating structural unit of myofibril; composed of thick and thin filaments; extends between two adjacent Z lines

sarcolemma (sar-ko-LEM-uh) the plasma membrane surrounding muscle cells

sarcoplasmic reticulum (sar-koh-PLAZ-mik reh-TIK-you-lum) endoplasmic reticulum in muscle fiber; site of storage and release of calcium ions

satellite cell undifferentiated cell found within skeletal muscle tissue that can fuse and develop into new muscle fiber following muscle injury

satiety signal (sah-TYE-ih-tee) input to appetite-control centers that causes hunger to cease and sets time period before hunger returns

saturated fatty acid fatty acid whose carbon atoms are all linked by single covalent bonds

saturation occupation of all available binding sites by their ligand

scala tympani (SCALE-ah TIM-pah-nee) fluid-filled inner-ear compartment that receives sound waves from basilar membrane and transmits them to round window

scala vestibuli (ves-TIB-you-lee) fluid-filled inner-ear compartment that receives sound waves from oval window and transmits them to basilar membrane and cochlear duct

Schwann cell nonneural cell that forms myelin sheath in peripheral nervous system

sclera (SKLAIR-ah) the tough, outermost tissue layer of the eyeball

scrotum (SKROH-tum) sac that contains testes and epididymides

second polar body nonfunctional structure containing one of two nuclei resulting from the second meiotic division in the ovary

secondary active transport active transport in which energy released during transmembrane movement of one substance from higher to lower concentration is transferred to the simultaneous movement of another substance from lower to higher concentration

secondary lymphoid organ lymph node, spleen, tonsil, or lymphocyte accumulation in gastrointestinal, respiratory, urinary, or reproductive tract; site of stimulation of lymphocyte response

secondary oocyte daughter cell (23 chromosomes) retaining most cytoplasm resulting from first meiotic division in the ovary

secondary peristalsis (per-ih-STAL-sis) esophageal peristaltic waves not immediately preceded by pharyngeal phase of swallow

secondary sexual characteristic external difference between male and female not directly involved in reproduction

secondary spermatocyte a 23-chromosome cell resulting from the first meiotic division of the primary spermatocyte in the testes

secondary structure the alpha-helical and beta pleated sheet structures of a protein

second messenger intracellular substance that serves as relay from plasma membrane to intracellular biochemical machinery, where it alters some aspect of cell's function

secretin (SEEK-reh-tin) peptide hormone secreted by upper small intestine; stimulates pancreas to secrete bicarbonate into small intestine

secretion (sih-KREE-shun) elaboration and release of organic molecules, ions, and water by cells in response to specific stimuli

secretory phase (SEEK-rih-tor-ee) stage of menstrual cycle following ovulation during which secretory type of endometrium develops

secretory vesicle membrane-bound vesicle produced by Golgi apparatus; contains protein to be secreted by cell

segmentation (seg-men-TAY-shun) series of stationary rhythmic contractions and relaxations of rings of intestinal smooth muscle; mixes intestinal contents

selective attention paying attention to or focusing on a particular stimulus or event while ignoring other ongoing sources of information

semen (SEE-men) sperm-containing fluid of male ejaculate

semicircular canal passage in temporal bone; contains sense organs for equilibrium and movement

seminal vesicle exocrine glands (in males) that secrete fluid into vas deferens

seminiferous tubule (sem-ih-NIF-er-ous) tubule in testis in which sperm production occurs; lined with Sertoli cells

semipermeable membrane (sem-ee-PER-me-ah-bul) membrane permeable to some substances (usually water) but not to others (some solutes)

sensation the mental perception of a stimulus

sensorimotor cortex (sen-sor-ee-MOH-tor) all areas of cerebral cortex that play a role in skeletal muscle control

sensory information information that originates in stimulated sensory receptors

sensory pathway a group of neuron chains, each chain consisting of three or more neurons connected end to end by synapses; carries action potentials to those parts of the brain involved in conscious recognition of sensory information

sensory receptor a cell or portion of a cell that contains structures or chemical molecules sensitive to changes in an energy form in the outside world or internal environment; in response to activation by this energy, the sensory receptor initiates action potentials in that cell or an adjacent one

sensory system part of nervous system that receives, conducts, or processes information that leads to perception of a stimulus

sensory transduction neural process of changing a sensory stimulus into a change in neuronal function

sensory unit afferent neuron plus receptors it innervates

serosa (sir-OH-sah) connective-tissue layer surrounding outer surface of stomach and intestines

serotonin (sair-oh-TONE-in) biogenic amine neurotransmitter; paracrine agent in blood platelets and digestive tract; also called *5-hydroxytryptamine* or *5-HT*

Sertoli cell (sir-TOH-lee) cell intimately associated with developing germ cells in seminiferous tubule; creates blood–testis barrier, secretes fluid into seminiferous tubule, and mediates hormonal effects on tubule

Sertoli cell barrier barrier to the movement of chemicals from the blood into the lumen of the seminiferous tubules in the testes

serum (SEER-um) blood plasma from which fibrinogen and other clotting proteins have been removed as result of clotting

set point steady-state value maintained by homeostatic control system

sex chromatin (CHROM-ah-tin) nuclear mass not usually found in cells of males; condensed X chromosome

sex chromosome X or Y chromosome

sex determination genetic basis of individual's sex, XY determining male, and XX, female

sex differentiation development of male or female reproductive organs

sex hormone estrogen, progesterone, testosterone, or related hormones

sexual dimorphism sex-linked differences in appearance or form

shaft portion of bone between epiphyseal plates

shear stress force exerted perpendicular to a surface (e.g., force exerted on the walls of a vessel by fluid flowing past)

shivering thermogenesis neurally induced cycles of contraction and relaxation of skeletal muscle in response to decreased body temperature; little or no external work is performed, and thus the increased metabolism of muscle leads primarily to heat production

short-loop negative feedback influence of hypothalamus by an anterior pituitary gland hormone

short reflex local neural loop from gastrointestinal receptors to nerve plexuses

short-term memory storage of incoming neural information for seconds to minutes; may be converted into long-term memory

signal sequence initial portion of newly synthesized protein (if protein is destined for secretion)

signal transduction pathway sequence of mechanisms that relay information from plasma membrane receptor to cell's response mechanism

simple diffusion movement of solutes down a concentration gradient without a transporter or ATP hydrolysis

single-unit smooth muscle smooth muscle that responds to stimulation as single unit because gap junctions join muscle fibers, allowing electrical activity to pass from cell to cell

sinoatrial (SA) node (sye-noh-AY-tree-al) region in right atrium of heart containing specialized cardiac muscle cells that depolarize spontaneously faster than other cells in the conducting system; determines heart rate

sinus vascular channel for the passage of blood or lymph

skeletal muscle striated muscle attached to bone or skin and responsible for skeletal movements and facial expression; controlled by somatic nervous system

skeletal muscle pump pumping effect of contracting skeletal muscles on blood flow through underlying vessels

sleep spindles high-frequency waveforms seen in the electroencephalogram during stage 2 sleep

sliding-filament mechanism process of muscle contraction in which shortening occurs by thick and thin filaments sliding past each other

slow fiber muscle fiber whose myosin has low ATPase activity

slowly adapting receptor sensory receptor that fires repeatedly as long as a stimulus is ongoing

slow-oxidative fiber type of skeletal muscle fiber that has slow intrinsic contraction speed but fatigues very slowly due to abundant capacity for production of ATP by aerobic oxidative phosphorylation

slow wave slow, rhythmic oscillation of smooth muscle membrane potentials toward and away from threshold, due to regular fluctuations in ionic permeability

small intestine longest portion of the gastrointestinal tract; between the stomach and large intestine

smooth muscle nonstriated muscle that surrounds hollow organs and tubes; *see also* multiunit smooth muscle, single-unit smooth muscle

smooth muscle tone smooth muscle tension due to low-level cross-bridge activity in absence of external stimuli

SNARE protein soluble *N*-ethylmaleimide-sensitive fusion protein attachment protein receptor

solute (SOL-yoot) substances dissolved in a liquid

solution liquid (solvent) containing dissolved substances (solutes)

solvent liquid in which substances are dissolved

soma cell body of neuron

somatic nervous system component of efferent division of peripheral nervous system; innervates skeletal muscle; *compare* autonomic nervous system

somatic receptor neural receptor in the framework or outer wall of the body that responds to mechanical stimulation of skin or hairs and underlying tissues, rotation or bending of joints, temperature changes, or painful stimuli

somatic sensation feelings/perceptions coming from muscle, skin, and bones

somatosensory cortex (suh-mat-uh-SEN-suh-ree) strip of cerebral cortex in parietal lobe in which nerve fibers transmitting somatic sensory information synapse

somatostatin (SS) (suh-mat-uh-STAT-in) hypophysiotropic hormone that inhibits growth hormone secretion by anterior pituitary gland; possible neurotransmitter; also found in stomach and pancreatic islets

somatotopic map a representation of the different regions of the body formed by neurons of the cerebral cortex

spatial summation adding together effects of simultaneous inputs to different places on a neuron to produce potential change greater than that caused by single input

specific ascending pathway chain of synaptically connected neurons in CNS, all activated by sensory units of same type

specificity selectivity; ability of binding site to react with only one, or a limited number of, types of molecules

sperm *see* spermatozoan

spermatic cord structure including the vas deferens and blood vessels and nerves supplying the testes

spermatid (SPER-mah-tid) immature sperm

spermatogenesis (sper-mah-toh-JEN-ih-sis) sperm formation

spermatogonium (sper-mah-toh-GOH-nee-um) undifferentiated germ cell that gives rise to primary spermatocyte

spermatozoan (sper-ma-toh-ZOH-in) male gamete; also called *sperm*

sphincter (SFINK-ter) smooth muscle ring that surrounds a tube, closing tube as muscle contracts

sphincter of Oddi (OH-dye) smooth muscle ring surrounding common bile duct at its entrance into duodenum

spinal nerve one of 86 peripheral nerves (43 pairs) that join spinal cord

spleen largest lymphoid organ; located between stomach and diaphragm

spliceosome protein and nuclear RNA complex that removes introns and links exons together during gene transcription

***SRY* gene** gene on the Y chromosome that determines development of testes in genetic male

stable balance net loss of substance from body equals net gain, and amount of substance in body neither increases nor decreases; *compare* negative balance, positive balance

stapedius (stah-PEE-dee-us) skeletal muscle that attaches to the stapes and protects the auditory apparatus by dampening the movement of the ear ossicles during persistent, loud sounds

stapes one of three bones in the inner ear that transmit movements of the tympanic membrane to the inner ear

Starling force factor that determines direction and magnitude of fluid movement across capillary wall

state of consciousness degree of mental alertness—that is, whether awake, drowsy, asleep, and so on

steady state no net change; continual energy input to system is required, however, to prevent net change; *compare* equilibrium

stem cell undifferentiated cell that divides and forms supply of cells for differentiation into mature cells

stereocilia (ster-ee-oh-SIL-ee-ah) nonmotile cilia containing actin filaments

steroid (STER-oid) lipid subclass; molecule consists of four interconnected carbon rings to which polar groups may be attached

steroid hormone any of a family of hormones, like progesterone, whose structure is derived from cholesterol

steroid-hormone-receptor superfamily class of intracellular receptor proteins that bind steroid hormones and other lipophilic molecules and induce changes in gene transcription

stimulus detectable change in internal or external environment

stomach expandable, saclike structure in the gastrointestinal tract between the esophagus and small intestine; site of initial digestion of proteins

stop signal three-nucleotide sequence in mRNA that signifies end of protein-coding sequence

stress environmental change that must be adapted to if health and life are to be maintained; event that elicits increased cortisol secretion

stretch reflex monosynaptic reflex, mediated by muscle-spindle stretch receptor, in which muscle stretch causes contraction of that muscle

striated muscle (STRY-ay-ted) muscle having transverse banding pattern due to repeating sarcomere structure; *see also* cardiac muscle, skeletal muscle

stroke volume (SV) blood volume ejected by a ventricle during one heartbeat

strong acid acid that ionizes completely to form hydrogen ions and corresponding anions when dissolved in water; *compare* weak acid

strychnine an alkaloid nervous system poison that blocks the action of the inhibitory neurotransmitter, glycine

subarachnoid space space between the arachnoid and pia mater meninges containing cerebrospinal fluid

subcortical nuclei groups of cells in brain below the cerebral cortex

submucosa layer of tissue beneath the gastrointestinal mucosa

submucosal plexus (sub-mu-KOH-zal PLEX-us) neuronal network in submucosa of esophageal, stomach, and intestinal walls

substance P neuropeptide neurotransmitter released by afferent neurons in pain pathway as well as other sites

substantia nigra (sub-STAN-sha NIE-gra) a subcortical nucleus containing dark-staining neurons that release dopamine and are important for suppressing extraneous muscle activity

substrate (SUB-strate) reactant in enzyme-mediated reaction

substrate-level phosphorylation (fos-for-ih-LAY-shun) direct transfer of phosphate group from metabolic intermediate to ADP to form ATP

subthreshold potential depolarization less than threshold potential

subthreshold stimulus stimulus capable of depolarizing membrane but not by enough to reach threshold

sucrose (SOO-krose) disaccharide composed of glucose and fructose; also called *table sugar*

sulcus (plural, *sulci*) a deep groove between gyri on the surface of the cerebral cortex

summation (sum-MAY-shun) increase in muscle tension or shortening in response to rapid, repetitive stimulation relative to single twitch

superior vena cava (VEE-nah KAY-vah) large vein that carries blood from upper half of body to right atrium of heart

supplementary motor cortex region of the cerebral cortex found on the medial side of brain hemispheres in front of the primary motor cortex; involved in planning and enacting complex muscle movements

suprachiasmatic nucleus group of cells in the hypothalamus involved in production of circadian rhythms

surface tension attractive forces between water molecules at an air–water interface resulting in net force that acts to reduce surface area

surfactant (sir-FAK-tent) detergent-like phospholipid–protein mixture produced by pulmonary type II alveolar cells; reduces surface tension of fluid film lining alveoli

swallowing center area of the medulla oblongata in the central nervous system that receives afferent neural input from the mouth and sends efferent output to the muscles of the pharynx, esophagus, and respiratory system, coordinating swallowing

sweat gland gland beneath the skin that is capable of secreting a salty fluid through ducts to the surface of the skin in response to heat-induced neural signals from the autonomic nervous system

Sylvian fissure a large sulcus in both brain hemispheres that divides the temporal lobes from the frontal and parietal lobes

sympathetic division (of the autonomic nervous system) portion of autonomic nervous system whose preganglionic fibers leave CNS at thoracic and lumbar portions of spinal cord; *compare* parasympathetic division

sympathetic trunk one of paired chains of interconnected sympathetic ganglia that lie on either side of vertebral column

synapse (SIN-aps) anatomically specialized junction between two neurons where electrical activity in one neuron influences excitability of second; *see also* chemical synapse, electrical synapse, excitatory synapse, inhibitory synapse

synaptic cleft narrow extracellular space separating pre- and postsynaptic neurons at chemical synapse

synaptic delay length of time it takes for neurotransmitters to diffuse from the presynaptic to the postsynaptic membrane and initiate electrical changes in postsynaptic cell

synaptic vesicle cellular structure that holds and releases neurotransmitter at the synapse

synaptotagmin (sin-ap-toh-TAG-min) protein present in wall of synaptic vesicle that binds calcium and helps stimulate the process of exocytosis

synergistic muscle (sin-er-JIS-tik) muscle that exerts force to aid intended motion

systemic circulation (sis-TEM-ik) circulation from left ventricle through all organs except lungs and back to heart

systole (SIS-toh-lee) period of ventricular contraction

systolic pressure (SP) (sis-TAHL-ik) maximum arterial blood pressure during cardiac cycle

T

target cell cell influenced by a certain hormone

taste bud sense organ that contains chemoreceptors for taste

T cell *see* T lymphocyte

tectorial membrane (tek-TOR-ee-al) structure in organ of Corti in contact with receptor cell hairs

template strand the DNA strand with the correct orientation relative to a promoter to bind RNA polymerase

temporal lobe region of cerebral cortex where primary auditory cortex and Wernicke's speech center are located

temporal summation membrane potential produced as two or more inputs, occurring at different times, are added together; potential change is greater than that caused by single input

tendon (TEN-don) collagen fiber bundle that connects skeletal muscle to bone and transmits muscle contraction force to the bone

tension in muscle physiology, the force exerted by a contracting muscle on object

tensor tympani muscle skeletal muscle that attaches to the ear drum and protects the auditory apparatus from loud sounds by dampening the movement of the tympanum

terminal cisternae (ter-mih-null sys-TER-nay) expanded regions of sarcoplasmic reticulum, associated with T-tubules and involved in the storage and release of Ca^{2+} in skeletal muscle cells; also known as *lateral sacs*

tertiary structure the three-dimensional folded structure of a protein formed by hydrogen bonds, hydrophobic attractions, electrostatic interactions, and cysteine cross-bridges

testis (TES-tiss) (plural, *testes*) gonad in male

testosterone (test-TOS-ter-own) steroid hormone produced in interstitial cells of testes; major male sex hormone

tetanus (TET-ah-nus) maintained mechanical response of muscle to high-frequency stimulation; also the disease lockjaw

thalamus (THAL-ah-mus) subdivision of diencephalon; integrating center for sensory input on its way to cerebral cortex; also contains motor nuclei

theca (THEE-kah) cell layer that surrounds ovarian-follicle granulosa cells

thermoneutral zone temperature range over which changes in skin blood flow can regulate body temperature

thermoreceptor sensory receptor for temperature and temperature changes, particularly in low (cold receptor) or high (warm receptor) range

theta rhythm slow-frequency, high-amplitude waves of the EEG associated with early stages of slow-wave sleep

thick filament myosin filament in muscle cell

thin filament actin filament in muscle cell

thorax (THOR-aks) closed body cavity between neck and diaphragm; contains lung, heart, thymus, large vessels, and esophagus; also called the *chest*

threshold potential membrane potential above which an excitable cell fires an action potential

threshold stimulus stimulus capable of depolarizing membrane just to threshold

thrifty gene gene postulated to have evolved in order to increase the body's ability to store fat

thrombin (THROM-bin) enzyme that catalyzes conversion of fibrinogen to fibrin; has multiple other actions in blood clotting

thrombomodulin an endothelial receptor to which thrombin can bind, thereby eliminating thrombin's clot-producing effects and causing it to bind and activate protein C

thromboxane an eicosanoid derived from arachidonic acid by the action of cyclooxygenase; among other functions, thromboxanes are involved in platelet aggregation

thromboxane A_2 an eicosanoid formed in platelets that stimulates platelet aggregation and secretion of clotting factors

thrombus (THROM-bus) blood clot

thymine (T) (THIGH-meen) pyrimidine base in DNA but not RNA

thymus (THIGH-mus) lymphoid organ in upper part of chest; site of T-lymphocyte differentiation

thyroglobulin (thigh-roh-GLOB-you-lin) large protein precursor of thyroid hormones in colloid of follicles in thyroid gland; storage form of thyroid hormones

thyroid hormone collective term for amine hormones released from thyroid gland—that is, thyroxine (T_4) and triiodothyronine (T_3)

thyroid peroxidase enzyme within the thyroid gland that mediates many of the steps of thyroid hormone synthesis

thyroid-stimulating hormone (TSH) glycoprotein hormone secreted by anterior pituitary gland; induces secretion of thyroid hormone; also called *thyrotropin*

thyrotropin-releasing hormone (TRH) hypophysiotropic hormone that stimulates thyrotropin and prolactin secretion by anterior pituitary gland

thyroxine (T_4) (thigh-ROCKS-in) tetraiodothyronine; iodine-containing amine hormone secreted by thyroid gland

tidal volume (V_t) air volume entering or leaving lungs with single breath during any state of respiratory activity

tight junction cell junction in which extracellular surfaces of the plasma membrane of two adjacent cells are joined together; extends around epithelial cell and restricts molecule diffusion through space between cells

tip link small, extracellular fiber connecting adjacent stereocilia that activates ion channels when the cilia are bent

tissue aggregate of single type of specialized cell; also denotes general cellular fabric of a given organ

tissue factor protein involved in initiation of clotting via the extrinsic pathway; located on plasma membrane of subendothelial cells

tissue factor pathway inhibitor (TFPI) a plasma protein secreted by endothelial cells; one of several mechanisms for protecting against excessive blood coagulation

tissue plasminogen activator (t-PA) plasma protein produced by endothelial cells; after binding to fibrinogen, activates the proenzyme plasminogen

titin protein that extends from the Z line to the thick filaments and M line of skeletal muscle sarcomere

T lymphocyte (T cell) lymphocyte derived from precursor that differentiated in thymus; *see also* cytotoxic T cell, helper T cell

Toll-like receptors (TLRs) members of the pattern-recognition-receptor family that bind to ligands commonly found on many types of pathogens

tonsil one of several small lymphoid organs in pharynx

total-blood carbon dioxide sum total of dissolved carbon dioxide, bicarbonate, and carbamino-CO_2

total energy expenditure sum of external work done plus heat produced plus energy stored by body

total peripheral resistance (TPR) total resistance to flow in systemic blood vessels from beginning of aorta to ends of venae cavae

totipotent cells of the conceptus that have the capacity to develop into a normal, mature fetus

trace element mineral present in body in extremely small quantities

trachea (TRAY-kee-ah) single airway connecting larynx with bronchi; windpipe

tract large, myelinated nerve fiber bundle in CNS

transamination (trans-am-in-NAY-shun) reaction in which an amino acid amino group (—NH_2) is transferred to a keto acid, the keto acid thus becoming an amino acid

transcellular pathway crossing an epithelium by movement into an epithelial cell, diffusion through the cytosol of that cell, and exit across the opposite membrane

transcription formation of RNA containing, in linear sequence of its nucleotides, the genetic information of a specific gene; first stage of protein synthesis

transcription factor one of a class of proteins that act as gene switches, regulating the transcription of a particular gene by activating or repressing the initiation process

transducin (trans-DOO-sin) G protein in disc membranes of photoreceptor; initiates inactivation of cGMP

trans fatty acid an unsaturated fatty acid in which the hydrogen atoms around a carbon:carbon double bond are distributed in a trans orientation (on the same side); implicated in a variety of negative health consequences

transferrin (trans-FERR-in) iron-binding protein that carries iron in plasma

transfer RNA (tRNA) type of RNA; different tRNAs combine with different amino acids and with codon on mRNA specific for that amino acid, thus arranging amino acids in sequence to form specific protein

transient receptor potential (TRP) proteins family of ion channel proteins involved in sensing temperature

translation during protein synthesis, assembly of amino acids in correct order according to genetic instructions in mRNA; occurs on ribosomes

transmembrane protein a protein that spans the plasma membrane and contains both hydrophilic and hydrophobic regions; often acts as a receptor or an ion channel

transmural pressure pressure difference exerted on the two sides of a wall

transporter integral membrane protein that mediates passage of molecule through membrane; also called *carrier*

transport maximum (T_m) upper limit to amount of material that carrier-mediated transport can move across the renal tubule

transpulmonary pressure (P_{tp}) difference in pressure between the inside and outside of the lung (alveolar pressure minus the intrapleural pressure)

transverse tubule (T-tubule) tubule extending from striated muscle plasma membrane into the fiber, passing between opposed sarcoplasmic reticulum segments; conducts muscle action potential into muscle fiber

tricarboxylic acid cycle *see* Krebs cycle

tricuspid valve (try-CUSS-pid) valve between right atrium and right ventricle of heart

triglyceride subclass of lipids composed of glycerol and three fatty acids

triiodothyronine (T_3) (try-eye-oh-doh-THIGH-roh-neen) iodine-containing amine hormone secreted by thyroid gland

trophoblast (TROH-foh-blast) outer layer of blastocyst; gives rise to fetal portion of placental tissue

tropic hormone hormone that stimulates the secretion of another hormone

tropomyosin (troh-poh-MY-oh-sin) regulatory protein capable of reversibly converting binding sites on actin; associated with muscle thin filaments

troponin (troh-POH-nin) regulatory protein bound to actin and tropomyosin of striated muscle thin filaments; site of calcium binding that initiates contractile activity

trypsin (TRIP-sin) enzyme secreted into small intestine by exocrine pancreas as precursor trypsinogen; breaks certain peptide bonds in proteins and polypeptides

trypsinogen (trip-SIN-oh-jen) inactive precursor of trypsin; secreted by exocrine pancreas

T-type Ca^{2+} channel channel that carries inward calcium current that briefly supports diastolic depolarization of cardiac pacemaker cells (T: "transient")

tubular reabsorption transfer of materials from kidney tubule lumen to peritubular capillaries

tubular secretion transfer of materials from peritubular capillaries to kidney tubule lumen

tubule a hollow structure lined by epithelial cells, often involved in transport processes such as those in the kidney nephrons

tubulin (TOOB-you-lin) the major protein component of microtubules

tumor necrosis factor-alpha (TNF-α) (neh-KROH-sis) cytokine secreted by macrophages (and other cells); has many of the same functions as IL-1

T wave component of electrocardiogram corresponding to ventricular repolarization

twitch mechanical response of muscle to single action potential

tympanic membrane (tim-PAN-ik) membrane stretched across end of ear canal; also called *eardrum*

type I alveolar cell a flat epithelial cell that with others forms a continuous layer lining the air-facing surface of the pulmonary alveoli

type II alveolar cell pulmonary cell that produces surfactant

U

ubiquitin (you-BIK-wit-in) small intracellular peptide that attaches to proteins and directs them to proteasomes

ultrafiltrate (ul-tra-FIL-trate) protein-free fluid formed from plasma as it is forced through capillary walls by pressure gradient

umami (oo-MOM-ee) unique taste sensation roughly equivalent to "flavorfulness"

umbilical artery artery transporting blood from the fetus into the capillaries of the chorionic villi

umbilical cord (um-BIL-ih-kul) long, ropelike structure that connects the fetus to the placenta and contains umbilical arteries and vein

umbilical vein vein transporting blood from the chorionic villi capillaries back to the fetus

unfused tetanus stimulation of skeletal muscle at a low-to-moderate action potential frequency that results in oscillating, submaximal force

unsaturated fatty acid fatty acid containing one or more double bonds

upper airway part of the respiratory tree consisting of the nose, mouth, pharynx, and larynx

upper esophageal sphincter (ih-soff-ih-JEE-al SFINK-ter) skeletal muscle ring surrounding esophagus just below pharynx that, when contracted, closes entrance to esophagus

upper motor neuron neuron of the motor cortex and descending pathways involved in motor control; they are not technically "motor neurons" because they synapse on neurons, not muscle cells

up-regulation increase in number of target-cell receptors for given messenger in response to chronic low extracellular concentration of that messenger; *compare* down-regulation

uracil (U) (YOOR-ah-sil) pyrimidine base; present in RNA but not DNA

urea (you-REE-ah) major nitrogenous waste product of protein breakdown and amino acid catabolism

ureter (YOOR-ih-ter) tube that connects kidney to bladder

urethra (you-REE-thrah) tube that connects bladder to outside of body

uric acid (YOOR-ik) waste product derived from nucleic acid catabolism

uterus (YOU-ter-us) hollow organ in pelvic region of females; houses fetus during pregnancy; also called *womb*

utricle structure in the semicircular canals that responds to changes in linear movement of the head by mechanical forces on otoliths located on its surface

V

vagina (vah-JY-nah) canal leading from uterus to outside of body

vagus nerve (VAY-gus) cranial nerve X; major parasympathetic nerve

van der Waals forces (walls) weak forces between atoms and molecules due to transient electrical forces generated by the orbits of electrons in the outer energy shells of atoms

varicosity (vair-ih-KOS-ih-tee) swollen region of axon; contains neurotransmitter-filled vesicles; analogous to presynaptic ending

vasa recta (VAY-zuh REK-tah) blood vessels that form loops parallel to the loops of Henle in the renal medulla

vascular system closed system of blood vessels that includes all arteries, arterioles, capillaries, venules, and veins

vas deferens (vas DEF-er-enz) one of paired male reproductive ducts that connect epididymis of testis to urethra; also called *ductus deferens*

vasoconstriction (vayz-oh-kon-STRIK-shun) decrease in blood vessel diameter due to vascular smooth muscle contraction

vasodilation (vayz-oh-dy-LAY-shun) increase in blood vessel diameter due to vascular smooth muscle relaxation

vasopressin (vayz-oh-PRES-sin) peptide hormone synthesized in hypothalamus and released from posterior pituitary gland; increases water permeability of kidneys' collecting ducts and causes vasoconstriction; also called *antidiuretic hormone (ADH)*

vault recently discovered cytoplasmic structures composed of protein and RNA; their function is uncertain but may involve cytoplasmic-nuclear transport and modulation of a cell's sensitivity to certain drugs

vein any vessel that returns blood to heart

venous return (VR) blood volume flowing *to* heart per unit time

ventilation air exchange between atmosphere and alveoli; alveolar airflow

ventral horn the ventral gray matter of the spinal cord that contains cell bodies of motor neurons

ventral respiratory group (VRG) region of the brainstem containing expiratory neurons important during exercise

ventral root one of two groups of efferent fibers that leave ventral side of spinal cord

ventricle (VEN-trih-kul) cavity, as in cerebral ventricle or heart ventricle; lower chamber of heart

ventricular ejection phase of the cardiac pump cycle during ventricle contraction when blood exits through the semilunar valves

ventricular filling phase of the cardiac pump cycle during which the ventricles are resting and blood enters through the atrioventricular valves

ventricular-function curve relation of the increase in stroke volume as end-diastolic volume increases, all other factors being equal

venule (VEEN-ule) small vessel that carries blood from capillary network to vein

very-low-density lipoprotein (VLDL) (lip-oh-PROH-teen) lipid–protein aggregate having high proportion of fat

vestibular apparatus sense organ in temporal bone of skull; consists of three semicircular canals, a utricle, and a saccule; also called *sense organ of balance, vestibular system*

vestibulocochlear nerve (ves-tibb-yoo-loh-KOKE-lee-ar) eighth cranial nerve; transmits sensory information about sound and motion from the inner ear to the brain

villus (VIL-us) fingerlike projection from highly folded surface of small intestine; covered with single-layered epithelium

visceral pleura (VISS-er-al PLOO-rah) serous membranes covering the surface of the lung

viscosity (viss-KOS-ih-tee) measure of friction between adjacent layers of a flowing liquid; property of fluid that makes it resist flow

visible spectrum wavelengths of electromagnetic radiation capable of stimulating photoreceptors of the eye

vital capacity (VC) maximal amount of air that can be expired, regardless of time required, following maximal inspiration

vitamin organic molecule required in trace amounts for normal health and growth; usually not manufactured in the body and must be supplied by diet; classified as water-soluble (vitamins C and the B complex) and fat-soluble (vitamins A, D, E, and K)

vitamin B_{12} an essential vitamin found in animal products that plays an important role in the production of red blood cells

vitamin D secosteroid absorbed in the diet or released from the skin under UV light; there are two forms: D_2 is from plants and D_3 is from animals

vitamin D_2 (ergocalciferol) plant vitamin D

vitamin D_3 (cholecalciferol) animal vitamin D

vitamin K a lipid-soluble substance absorbed from the diet and manufactured by bacteria of the large intestine; required for production of numerous factors involved in blood clotting

vitreous humor jellylike fluid filling the posterior chamber of the eye

vocal cord one of two elastic-tissue bands stretched across laryngeal opening and caused to vibrate when air moves past them, producing sounds

volt (V) unit of measurement of electrical potential between two points

voltage measure of potential of separated electrical charges to do work; measure of electrical force between two points

voltage-gated channel cell membrane ion channel opened or closed by changes in membrane potential

voluntary movement consciously carried-out motions mediated by the somatic nervous system and skeletal muscle contraction

vomiting center neurons in brainstem medulla oblongata that coordinate vomiting reflex

von Willebrand factor (vWF) (von-VILL-ih-brant) plasma protein secreted by endothelial cells; facilitates adherence of platelets to damaged vessel wall

vulva (VUL-vah) female external genitalia; mons pubis, labia majora and minora, clitoris, vestibule of vagina, and vestibular glands

W

water diuresis increase in urine flow due to increased fluid output (usually due to decreased secretion or action of vasopressin)

water-soluble vitamin *see* vitamin

wavelength distance between two successive wave peaks in oscillating medium

weak acid acid whose molecules do not completely ionize to form hydrogen ions when dissolved in water; *compare* strong acid

Wernicke's area brain area involved in language comprehension

white matter portion of CNS that appears white in unstained specimens and contains primarily myelinated nerve fibers

white muscle fiber muscle fiber lacking appreciable amounts of myoglobin

withdrawal reflex bending of those joints that withdraw an injured part away from a painful stimulus

Wolffian duct (WOLF-ee-an) part of embryonic duct system that, in male, remains and develops into reproductive system ducts, but in female, degenerates

working memory short-term memory storage process serving as initial depository of information

X

X chromosome one of the two sex chromosomes; found in females and males

Y

Y chromosome one of the two sex chromosomes; found only in males

Z

Z line structure running across myofibril at each end of striated muscle sarcomere; anchors one end of thin filaments and titin

zona pellucida (ZOH-nah peh-LOO-sih-dah) thick, clear layer separating egg from surrounding granulosa cells

zonular fiber connecting the ciliary muscles with the lens of the eye

zygote (ZYE-goat) a newly fertilized egg

zymogen (ZYE-moh-jen) enzyme precursor requiring some change to become active

Photo Credits

Chapter 1

Opener: © Photodisc Red/Getty Images.

Chapter 2

Opener: © Drs. Ali Yazdani& Daniel J. Hornbaker/Photo Researchers, Inc.;2.2: © Living Art Enterprises/Photo Researchers, Inc.

Chapter 3

Opener: © Professors P. Motta & T. Naguro/ Science Photo Library/Photo Researchers, Inc.;3.2: © Don W. Fawcett/Photo Researchers, Inc.;3.5a: From "Unit Membranes" J. D. Robertson in Michael Locke (ed.), "Cell Membranes in Development," © 1964 by Academic Press;3.9c: Reproduced from The Journal of Cell Biology, 1963, 17:375-412 by copyright permission of The Rockefeller University Press;3.10 (left): Courtesy of the Keith Porter Endowment Fund for Cell Biology;3.11: Electron micrograph from D. W. Fawcett, The Cell, An Atlas of Fine Structure, W. B. Saunders Company, Philadelphia, 1966;3.12 (left): © Dr. Dennis Kunkel/Visuals Unlimited;3.13 (left): Courtesy of the Keith Porter Endowment Fund for Cell Biology;3.14: Courtesy of Hans Hoppeler.

Chapter 4

Opener: © VVG/Science Photo Library/Photo Researchers, Inc.

Chapter 5

Opener: © Pr. Lavery, Laboratory of Biochemical Theory/Eurelios/Phototake.

Chapter 6

Opener: © Su-Chun Zhang, MD, PhD;6.2c: © C. Raines/Science VU/Visuals Unlimited.

Chapter 7

Opener: © Getty Images/Brand X;7.22c: © Lisa Klancher;7.27: Courtesy of Beckman Vision Center at UCSF School of Medicine/D. Copenhagen, S. Mittman and M. Maglio;7.41a: From C.M. Hackney and D.N. Furness (1995) "Mechanotransduction in vertebrate hair cells: the structure and function of the stereocillary bundle" in American Journal Physiology, 268: (Cell Physiol. 37): CA-C13. Micrograph by C.M. Hackney and D. N. Furness.;7.47c: © Ed Reschke.

Chapter 8

Opener: © Richard T. Nowitz/Photo Researchers, Inc.;8.12, 8.16: Courtesy Marcus E. Raichle, MD, Washington University School of Medicine;8.17 (both): © Shaywitz, et al., 1995 NMR Research/ Yale Medical School;8.18: Courtesy of Lee Faucher, MD, University of Wisconsin SMPH.

Chapter 9

Opener: © Steve Gschmeissner/Photo Researchers, Inc.;9.1a, 9.1b: © Ed Reschke;9.1c: © McGraw-Hill Higher Education;9.4a: © Marion L. Greaser, University of Wisconsin;9.5a: From H.E. Huxley, Journal of Molecular Biology, 37:507-520, 1968;9.8a: © Don W. Fawcett/Photo Researchers, Inc.;9.24: © Dr. Gladden Willis/ Visuals Unlimited;9.32, 9.39a: © Ed Reschke.

Chapter 10

Opener: © USA-Stock Inc/Alamy;10.14 (both): © Kevin Strang.

Chapter 11

Opener: © ISM/Phototake;11.20b: © Biophoto Assoicates/Photo Researchers, Inc.;11.23: © CNRI/Phototake;11.25 (both): Source: From H.G. Turney of London, "Discussion on Disease of the Pituitary Body" in Proceedings of the Royal Society of Medicine, 1913.;11.33: © Marcelo Sayao/epa/Corbis.

Chapter 12

Opener: © Lunagrafix, Inc./Photo Researchers, Inc.;12.28: © Carolina Biological Supply/ Phototake;12.37b: © Michael Noel Hart, M.D., Dept. of Pathology, University of Wisconsin, Madison;12.48: © R. UmeshChandran, TDR, WHO/SPL/Photo Researchers, Inc.;12.66 (all): © Matthew R. Wolff, M.D., University of Wisconsin, Madison;12.68: © Dr. Dennis Kunkel/ Visuals Unlimited;12.71: © Dr. Stanley Flegler/ Visuals Unlimited/Corbis;12.75: © Science Photo Library RF/Getty Images.

Chapter 13

Opener: © SPL/Photo Researchers, Inc.

Chapter 14

Opener: © Dennis Kunkel Microscopy, Inc./ Visuals Unlimited.

Chapter 15

Opener: © SPL/Photo Researchers, Inc.;15.5: © Science Photo Library RF/Getty Images;15.36c: Courtesy Fernando Carballo, M.D.;15.37: Courtesy of Dr. David Olson.

Chapter 16

Opener: AP Photo/The Rockefeller University.

Chapter 17

Opener: © David M. Phillips/Photo Researchers, Inc.;17.16: © Glenn D. Braunstein, M.D., Cedars-Sinai Medical Center, Los Angeles, CA.

Chapter 18

Opener: © Superstock;18.1: © Biophoto Associates/Photo Researchers, Inc.;18.3: © Eye of Science/Photo Researchers, Inc.;18.9b: © Dr. GopalMurti/SPL/Photo Researchers, Inc.;18.12b: Courtesy of Mike Clark, Cambridge University;18.23b: © Dr. Fred Hossler/Visuals Unlimited;18.24: © agencyby/iStockphoto.

Chapter 19

Opener: © Comstock/Jupiter Images;19.1 (both): © Custom Medical Stock;19.3 (both): From Lawrence M. Tierney, Current Medical Diagnosis and Treatment, 2006;19.4 (both): © Dr. David Schwartz, New York University School of Medicine from Schwartz DT, Reisdorff EJ Emergency Radiology, McGraw-Hill 2000;19.7 (both): Courtesy of Dr. Douglas Woo/Medical College of Wisconsin;Clinical Case Studies Boxes: © Comstock/Jupiter Images.

Index

Page numbers followed by f or t indicate figures or tables respectively.

Concentration Ranges of Commonly Measured Variables in Blood

	Traditional units	SI units
Blood gases		
P_{O_2} (arterial)	80–100 mmHg	11–13 kPa (kilopascals)
(*Note:* P_{O_2} declines with age, being close to 100 mmHg in childhood, and decreasing to 80 and even lower in old age.)		
P_{CO_2} (arterial)	35–45 mmHg	4.7–5.9 kPa
Electrolytes		
Ca^{2+}		
Total	9.0–10.5 mg/dL	2.2–2.6 mmol/L
Ionized	4.5–5.6 mg/dL	1.1–1.4 mmol/L
Cl^-		97–110 mmol/L
K^+		3.5–5.0 mmol/L
Na^+		135–146 mmol/L
Hormones		
Aldosterone	30–100 pg/ml	83–277 pmol/L
Cortisol		
8:00 A.M.	5–25 μg/dL	140–690 nmol/L
4:00 P.M.	1.5–12.0 μg/dL	40–330 nmol/L
Estradiol		
Women (early follicular phase)	20–100 pg/ml	73–367 pmol/L
Women (midcycle peak)	150–750 pg/ml	551–2753 pmol/L
Men	10–50 pg/ml	37–184 pmol/L
Insulin (fasting)	6–26 μU/ml	43–186 pmol/L
	(0.2–1.1 ng/ml)	
Insulin-like growth hormone-1 (IGF-1)		
16–24 years old	182–780 ng/ml	182–780 μg/L
25–50 years old	114–492 ng/ml	114–492 μg/L
Parathyroid hormone	10–75 pg/ml	10–75 ng/L
Progesterone		
Women (luteal phase)	2–27 ng/ml	6–81 nmol/L
Women (pregnancy)	5–255 ng/ml	15–770 nmol/L
Men	0.2–1.4 ng/ml	0.6–4.3 nmol/L
Testosterone		
Women	<1ng/ml	<3.5 nmol/L
Men	2.5–10.0 ng/ml	9–35 nmol/L
Thyroid-stimulating hormone (TSH)	0.3–4.0 μU/ml	0.3–4.0 mU/L
Thyroxine (T_4) (adults)	5–11 μg/dL	64–140 nmol/L